Metric Handbook CD

Planning and Design Data

David Adler BSc DIC CEng MICE
Civil Engineering Consultant

This CD

- is an invaluable time-saving tool for architects and designers

- has over 1700 symbols dealing with all the principal building types

- gives you additional search, select and insert facilities

- shows you space requirements between furniture as well as standard sizing specifications

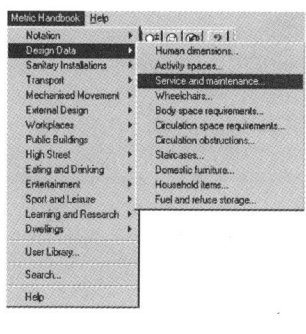

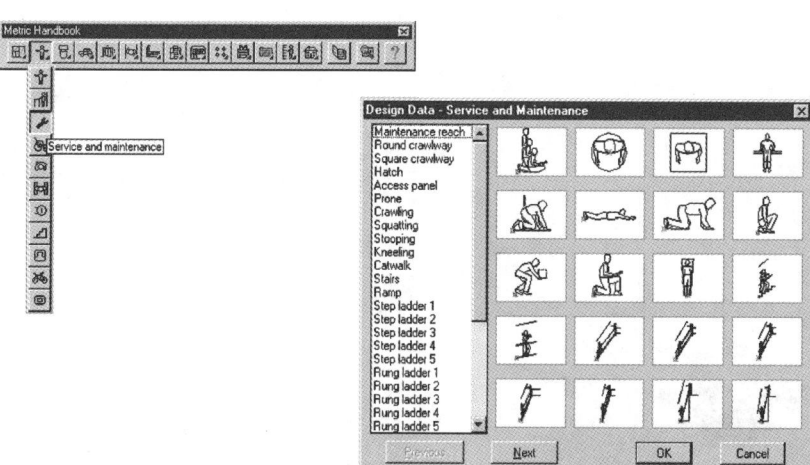

The drawings can be used with AutoCAD R12, R13, R14 and AutoCAD LT also with MicroStation SE, MicroStation 95 and MicroStation TriForma and IntelliCAD 98.

CONTENTS: Notation; Design Data; Sanitary Installations; Transport; Mechanised Movement; External Design; Workplaces; Public Buildings; High Street; Eating and Drinking; Entertainment; Sport and Leisure; Learning and Research; Dwellings

0 7506 3293 3   CD-Rom   1999   £150.00 + VAT

ORDER YOUR COPY TODAY
Fax: +44 (0) 1865 314572   Credit Card Hot Line Tel: +44 (0) 1865 888 180
E-mail: bhuk.orders@repp.co.uk

Please add p&p at £3 for UK, £6 for Europe and £10 for Rest of World, and supply full delivery address & phone number with your order.

METRIC HANDBOOK
Planning and Design Data

EDITED BY

David Adler

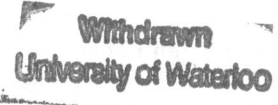

Architectural Press

OXFORD   AUCKLAND   BOSTON   JOHANNESBURG   MELBOURNE   NEW DELHI

Architectural Press
An imprint of Butterworth-Heinemann
Linacre House, Jordan Hill, Oxford OX2 8DP
225 Wildwood Avenue, Woburn, MA 01801-2041
A division of Reed Educational and Professional Publishing Ltd

℞ A member of the Reed Elsevier plc group

First published as *AJ Metric Handbook* by The Architectural Press 1968
Second edition 1969
Third edition 1970
First published as *New Metric Handbook* 1979
Revised reprint 1981
Reprinted 1984, 1985, 1988, 1992, 1993, 1994, 1995, 1996, 1997, 1998
Second edition (as *Metric Handbook*) 1999
Reprinted 1999

British Library Cataloguing in Publication Data
Metric handbook. – 2nd ed.
   1. Architecture – Handbooks, manuals, etc.
   2. Architecture – Standards – Handbooks, manuals, etc.
   I. Adler, David
   721'.028

ISBN 0 7506 0899 4

Composition by Genesis Typesetting, Laser Quay, Rochester, Kent
Printed and bound in Great Britain

Contents

Preface

Seventeen years have passed since the last main revision of the *Metric Handbook*. While the changeover from the Imperial system of measurement to metric in the building industry has passed into the mists of time (it started over thirty years ago), we are still in the throes of an almost equally traumatic change. This is the change from our British system of standards and codes of practice to ones that will eventually be common over most of Europe, and even in some cases over the whole world.

This radical revision of our standards is still in process. While the information in this new edition is as up to date as possible, further changes occur almost daily. While the basic concepts of design are constant so the information should be adequate for initial design purposes, the latest and fullest information should be consulted before finalisation. The bibliographies at the end of most of the chapters should assist in this.

In a handbook covering such a wide field as this, it is inevitable that not everything can be as detailed as one would prefer. Statements are made that may require qualification. When frequently repeated, it becomes tedious to continually read terms such as generally, normally, in many cases. The actual use of such terms has been restricted, but the reader should treat all statements made in the book as covered by a general proviso. Each situation is unique, and its problems may demand solutions that break rules found in sources such as this.

Very many people have assisted me in the preparation of this new edition, and I have built upon the many others who were responsible for material in earlier editions, going back to the three special editions of the *Architects' Journal* in 1970 that started it off. I thank all of those that I remember in the *Acknowledgements* which follow, and apologise to those whom I fail to mention. Fuller details of major contributors than can be included in the chapter headings will be found in Appendix C at the end of the book.

This new edition marks the honoured passing of the doyen of architectural reference books. I refer to *Planning, The Architect's Handbook* which is now not to be republished since the recent death of its distinguished last editor, Derek Mills CBE. *Planning* evolved in the 1930s from weekly notes in the Architect and Building News, and was a vade-mecum for generations of architects – I myself found it invaluable as an engineering student in the fifties. I have incorporated some of its material in this new edition of the *Metric Handbook*, and I hope that this, while something of a johnny-come-lately, will be regarded a worthy successor.

A project of this scale is bound to contain errors, and I would be grateful to be informed of any that are found. However, neither I, the contributors nor the publishers can accept responsibility for loss or damage resulting from inaccuracies or omissions.

David Adler
November 1998

Acknowledgements

Organizations who have contributed and/or helped are: the British Standards Institution, Department of Environment, Transport and the Regions, Health and Safety Executive, Institution of Structural Engineers, Steel Construction Institute, the late lamented Greater London Council, County Councils of Cheshire, Devon, Essex and Lancashire, and the Cyclists' Touring Club.

Individuals who have made substantial contributions to the book are generally named in the chapter headings. In addition, the editor has received help from a large number of other people over the years for this and for previous editions. He wishes to express his sincere thanks to all of these. Some of those in the list below are unfortunately no longer with us, but deserve to be remembered. If anyone is omitted from the list (which is in alphabetical order), my apologies – it will be due to a fallible memory!

Peter Ackroyd
Don Adie
Tanya Bocking
Brian Barclay
Brian Brookes
Geoff Burt
Ruth Cannock
John Carter
Mike Cash
Richard Chisnell
Mike Chrimes

Renata Corbani
Susan Cunningham
Betsy Dinesen
Francis Duffy
Peter Forbes
Brenda Goddard
Selwyn Goldsmith
Godfrey Golzen
John Gridley
Simon Inglis
Geraint John

John Jordan
John Keenan
Alexander Kira
David Knipe
Leslie Knopp
Sarah Kors
Mary Langshaw
David Lush
Jim McCluskey
Tony McKendry
Jay McMahan
Bruce Martin
Colin Moore
John Nelson
Anthony Noakes
George Noble
John Noble

Paul Noble
Julian Oseley
Oliver Palmer
Tim Pharoah
Esmond Reid
David Schreiber
Steve Scrivens
Jan Sliwa
Peter Stubbs
Patricia Tutt
Maritz Vandenberg
Neil Warnock-Smith
John Weller
Jeremy Wilson
David Wolchover
Zoë Youd

A special acknowledgement to my wife Jill Adler, who took on the mammoth task of proof-reading.

Extracts from British Standards are reproduced with the permission of BSI under licence number PD/19990450. Complete copies can be obtained by post from BSI Customer Services, 389 Chiswick High Road, London, W4 4AL.

1 Notation, drawing office practice and dimensional coordination

CI/SfB (1976 revised) (A3t) and (F43)
UDC: 744 and 69.032

KEY POINT:

● *For clear understanding the conventions must be followed.*

Contents
1 Notation
2 Paper sizes
3 Ordnance survey maps
4 Drawings
5 Measuring instruments
6 Dimensional coordination
7 Planning
8 References

1 NOTATION

1.01 Decimal marker

The decimal marker (full stop) on the baseline is the standard decimal point in the UK; but the marker at the halfway position is also acceptable. It should be noted that Continental practice is to use the comma on the baseline.

When the value to be expressed is less than unity it should be preceded by zero (e.g. 0.6 not .6). Whole numbers may be expressed without a decimal marker. The appropriate number of decimal places should be chosen depending on the circumstances in which the resulting value is to be used.

Thousand marker

To avoid confusion with the Continental decimal marker, no thousand marker should be used. Where legibility needs to be improved a space can be left in large groups of digits at every thousand point. Where there are only four digits, a space between the first digit and the others is not desirable (e.g. 15 000, 1500). (However, the comma is used in currency, e.g. £115,000.)

1.02 Symbols

1 The main symbols should be used as shown in Table I. The same symbol, i.e. m, mm, kg, should be used for singular and plural values (1 kg, 10 kg), and no full stops or other punctuation marks should be used after the symbol unless it occurs at the end of a sentence. Use a 'solidus' or sloping line as a separator between numerator and denominator, i.e. 3 kg/m^3 or 3 kg/cu m (three kilograms per cubic metre).

2 A single space should separate figures from symbols: 10 m, not 10m.

3 The unit should be written in full if there is any doubt about the symbol. For example, the recognised unit symbol l for the unit litre can be confused with the number 1 and it is less confusing to write litre in full. Also, the unit symbol t for tonne may in some circumstances be confused with the imperial ton, and the unit tonne should then be written in full.

4 When symbols are raised to various powers, it is only the symbol which is involved and not the number attached to it. Thus 3 m^3 equals 3 (m)^3 and not $3 \text{ m} \times 3 \text{ m} \times 3 \text{ m}$ (i.e. the answer is 3 cubic metres and not 27 cubic metres).

5 Difficulty may be experienced when reproducing the squaring and cubing indices m^2 or mm^2, and m^3 or mm^3. In such cases, units may be written with the indices on the line instead of as superscripts (m2, m3). Alternatively, particularly when the

Table I Summary of symbols and notation

Quantity	Description	Correct unit symbol	Acceptable alternatives	Incorrect use	Notes
Numerical values		0.1 0.01 0.001		.1 .01 .001	When the value is *less* than unity, the decimal point should be *preceded* by zero
Length	metre millimetre	m mm		m. M meter m.m. mm. MM M.M. milli-metre	
Area	square metre	m^2	sq m	m.sq sm sq.m sq m.	
Volume	cubic metre cubic millimetre	m^3 mm^3.	cu m cu mm	cu.m m.cu. cu.mm. mm.cub. mm.cu.	
	litre (liquid volume)	l, ltr		l. lit.	Preferably write *litre* in full to avoid 'l' being taken for figure 'one'
Mass (weight)	tonne	t		ton	Preferably write *tonne* in full to avoid being mistaken for imperial ton
	kilogram	kg		Kg kG kg. kilogramme	
	gram	g		g. G.	
Force	newton	N		N. n	Note that when used in written text, the unit of newton is spelled out in full and begins with a lower-case letter 'n'. When used as unit symbol, in calculation or in a formula it is then expressed as capital letter 'N'

general public is involved, the abbreviations 'sq' and 'cu' may be used (sq m, cu m).

6 Units should not be hyphenated (milli-metres).

1.03 Notation

1 As a rule the sizes of components should be expressed in consistent and not mixed units, e.g. 1500 mm $\times$ 600 mm $\times$ 25 mm thick and not 1.5 m $\times$ 600 mm $\times$ 25 mm thick. However, for long thin components such as timbers, it is preferable to mix the units, e.g. 100 mm $\times$ 75 mm $\times$ 10 m long.

2 It is important to distinguish clearly between the metric tonne and the imperial ton. The tonne is equivalent to 2204.6 lb while the ton is equal to 2240 lb – a difference of 1.6 per cent.

3 The interval of temperature should be referred to as degree Celsius (°C) and not as centigrade. The word centigrade is used by the Continental metric countries as a measure of plane angle and equals 1/10 000th part of a right angle.

Examples

Correct use	Incorrect use
33 m	3 cm 3 mm
10.100 m	10 m 100 mm*
50.750 kg	50 kg 750 g

*Note. Some metric values are expressed differently in certain countries. The value of 10.100 m, for example, could mean ten thousand one hundred metres and not ten metres one hundred millimetres, as in the UK.

2 PAPER SIZES

The International A-series of paper sizes is used for all drawings and written material.

2.01 Sizes in the A-series

The A range is derived from a rectangle A0, **1.1**, of area 1 m^2 with sides x and y such that x:y = 1:$\sqrt{2}$ (i.e. x = 841 mm; y = 1189 mm). The other sizes in the series are derived downwards by progressively halving the size above across its larger dimension. The proportions of the sizes remain constant, **1.2**.

2.02 Trimmed sizes and tolerances

The A formats are trimmed sizes and therefore exact; stubs of tear-off books, index tabs, etc. are always additional to the A dimensions. Printers purchase their paper in sizes allowing for the following tolerances of the trimmed sizes:

● For dimensions up to and including 150 mm, +1.5 mm
● For dimensions greater than 150 mm up to and including 600 mm, +2 mm
● For dimensions greater than 600 mm, +3 mm. Recommended methods of folding the larger A-sized prints are given in **1.3**.

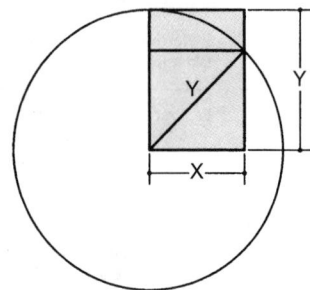

1.1 *Derivation of the rectangle A0, which has a surface area of 1 m²*

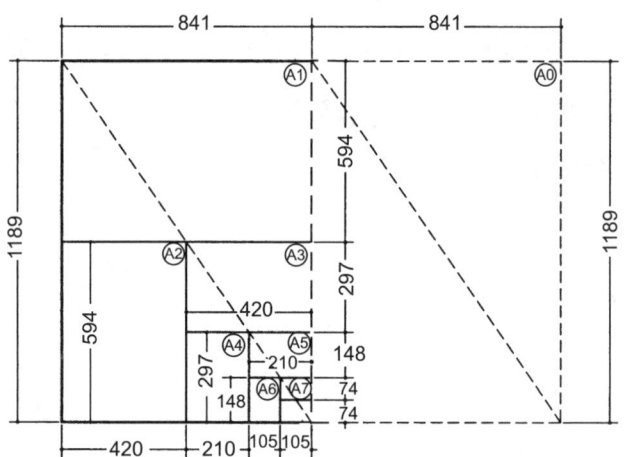

1.2 *A-sizes retain the same proportion (1 : √2), each size being half the size above*

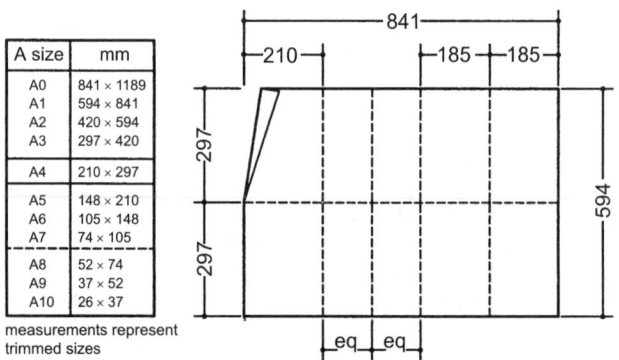

A size	mm
A0	841 × 1189
A1	594 × 841
A2	420 × 594
A3	297 × 420
A4	210 × 297
A5	148 × 210
A6	105 × 148
A7	74 × 105
A8	52 × 74
A9	37 × 52
A10	26 × 37

measurements represent trimmed sizes

folding A1 size

1.3 *A-series of paper sizes*

2.03 Pre-metric paper sizes

Old drawings will frequently be found in the sizes common prior to the changeover to metric. These sizes are given in Table II.

2.04 Drawing boards

Drawing boards are currently manufactured to fit A-size paper, while vertical and horizontal filing cabinets and chests have internal dimensions approximately corresponding to the board sizes listed in Table III. Boards, cabinets and chests designed for the pre-metric paper sizes are still in use.

3 ORDNANCE SURVEY MAPS

3.01

Ordnance Survey maps are now based completely on metric measurements and are immediately available to the following scales:

1:50 000, 1:25 000, 1:10 000, 1:25 000 and 1:1250.

However, new computer methods of storage and retrieval mean that maps can be supplied to any desired scale.

Table II Pre-metric paper and drawing board sizes

Name	Paper size	Board size
Half imperial	559 × 381	594 × 405
Imperial	762 × 559	813 × 584
Double elephant	1016 × 679	1092 × 737
Antiquarian	1346 × 787	1372 × 813

Table III Nominal sizes of drawing boards for use with parallel motion or drafting machines attached

Type of board	Size	Width (mm)	Length (mm)
Parallel motion unit only or parallelogram type drafting machine	A2	470	650
	A1	730	920
	A0	920	1270
	2A0	1250	1750
Track or trolley type drafting machine requiring additional 'parking' area to one side	A1 extended	650	1100
	A0 extended	920	1500
Parallel motion unit with drafting head requiring additional 'parking' area at bottom of board	A1 deep	730	920
	A0 deep	1000	1270

Architects and surveyors inevitably need to refer back to old maps and plans from time to time. These may have been drawn to almost any scale, but the common scales to which OS maps were drawn were as follows:

1 inch to the mile (1:63 360)
6 inches to the mile (1:10 560)
88 feet to the inch (1:1056)

Where these are stored on microfiche, etc., they can be reproduced to a scale more suited to modern use.

3.02 Bench marks and levels

Points used for measuring and marking levels are known as *bench marks*. On a particular site a temporary bench mark (TBM) may be established, to which all other levels on that site are referred. The level value allocated to the TBM may be to Ordnance Datum; more commonly it is given an arbitrary value. This value should be large enough not to require any negative levels (including levels of drains, etc.), as these can lead to errors. All levels in and around buildings are recommended to be given to three decimal places, although BS 1192 permits two decimal places for landscape work.

The heights of Ordnance Survey bench marks are given in Bench Mark Lists obtainable from Ordnance Survey Headquarters, Romsey Road, Maybush, Southampton SO9 4DH. Modern OS maps to the larger scales include Ordnance Bench Marks related to Newlyn Datum. Older maps may have levels to Liverpool Datum; levels on maps other than of Great Britain will be related to other datums. Where known, the datum and date of levelling should be stated.

OS maps include contours. On the 1:10 000 series the contour interval is 10 metres in the more mountainous areas and 5 metres in the remainder of the country.

4 DRAWINGS

4.01 Centimetres or millimetres

Continental building practice uses metres or centimetres depending on the particular application. In the UK, since the change to metric dictated the practice, the millimetre is used instead of the centimetre, although this does lead to a mistaken perception of the degree of accuracy.

On a drawing, either metres or millimetres should be used: these units should not be mixed. If this rule is followed, ambiguity is avoided – it is not possible to confuse which units are intended. Dimensions in metres should include either the decimal marker or the letter m: 2.0 or 2 m.

Avoid using capital M for metres. M is used to indicate the number of *modules*: e.g. where a module of 100 mm is adopted 5M means 500 mm.

4.02 Specifying both imperial and metric sizes

If work is being done on an old building that was built to imperial dimensions, and it is desired to show these on new drawings, show them in feet, inches and fractions of an inch to an accuracy of 1/16th inch, followed by the metric equivalent in brackets to the nearest millimetre. The reverse should never be required.

Imperial dimensions may be indicated by the abbreviations *ft* and *in*: 4ft-6in, or using single and double inverted commas: 4'-6". The hyphen is used as the separator.

4.03 Levels on plan

It is important to differentiate on site layout drawings between existing levels and intended levels, thus:

Existing level: × 58.210

Intended level: 60.255

The exact position to which the level applies should be indicated by 'x'. Finished floor levels should be indicated by the letters FFL followed by the figures of the level, thus: FFL *12.335*.

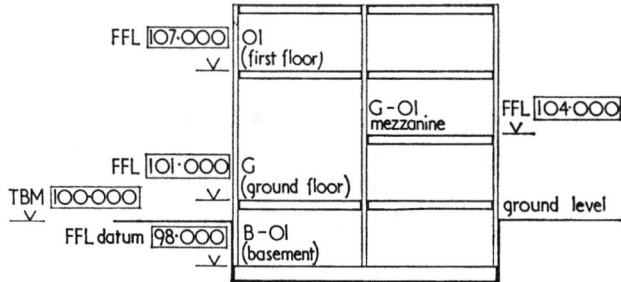

1.4 *Method of indicating levels on sections and elevations*

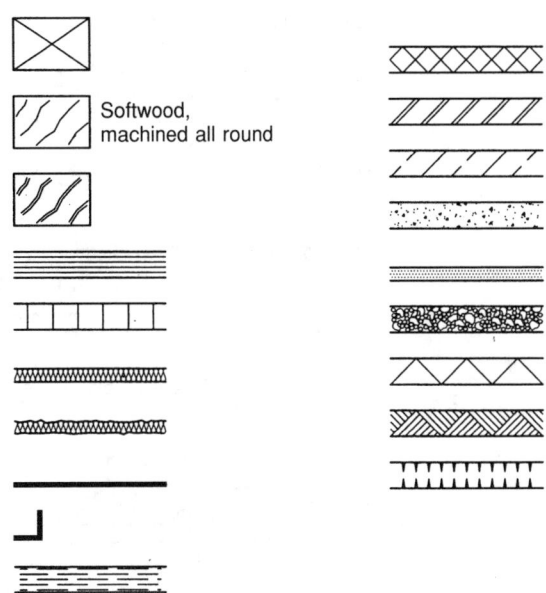

1.5 *Conventional shadings for various materials in section*

4.04 Levels on section and elevation
The same method should be used as for levels on plan except that the level should be projected beyond the drawing with an arrowhead indicating the appropriate line, as in **1.4**.

4.05 Conventional symbols
BS 1153 specifies certain standard symbols for use on drawings. A selection of these are given in **1.5**.

4.06 Scales
The internationally agreed and recommended range of scales for use in the construction industry is given in Table IV. The scale or scales used should be stated on each drawing; drawings that are to read by the non-specialist (e.g. sketch drawings) or that are to be microfilmed or published should have a drawn scale in addition. Where two or more scales are used on the same sheet, these should be clearly indicated. **1.6** shows some dimensions to various scales.

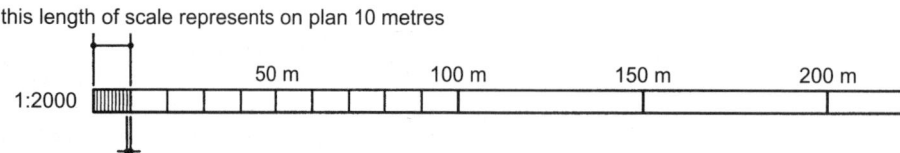

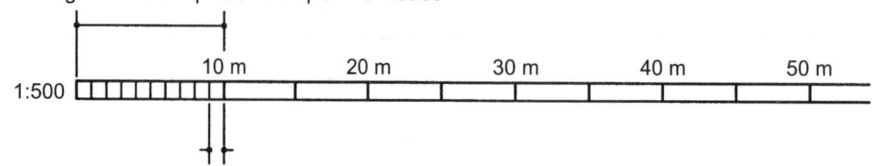

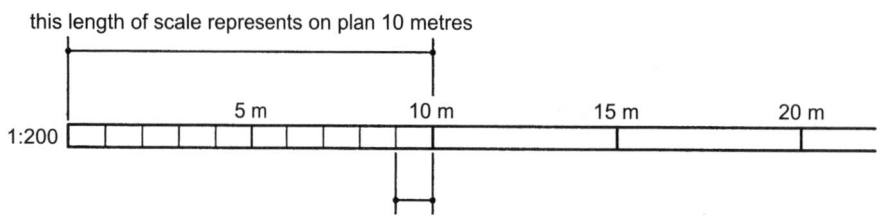

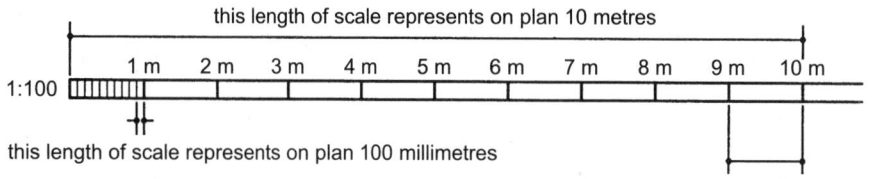

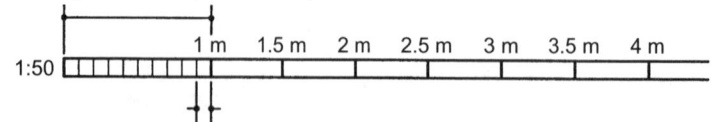

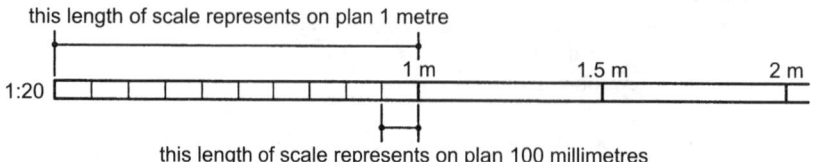

1.6 *Representations of lengths to scale. This drawing may be used to check the correct interpretation of a scale*

Table IV preferred scales

Use	Scale
Maps	1:1 000 000
	1:500 000
	1:200 000
	1:100 000
Town surveys	1:50 000
	1:20 000
	1:10 000
	1:5000
	1:2500
	1:2000
Block plan	1:2500
	1:2000
	1:1250
	1:1000
Location drawings	
Site plan	1:500
	1:200
General location	1:200
	1:100
	1:50
Ranges	1:100
	1:50
	1:20
Component drawings	
Assembly	1:20
	1:10
	1:5
Details	1:10
	1:5
	1:1

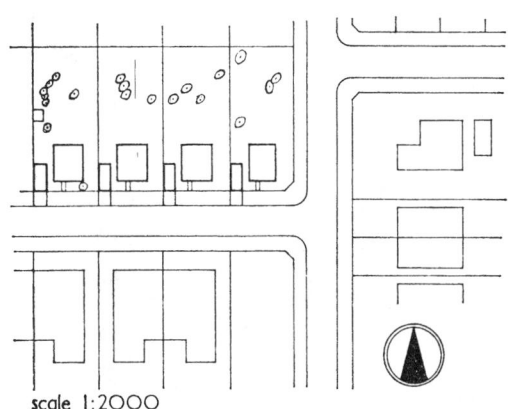

scale 1:2000

1.7 *Layout plan (note that the Ordnance Survey continue to use the 1:2500 scale)*

4.07 Types of drawings

Types of drawings done to the most suitable scales are shown in **1.7** to **1.13**. Note that in **1.10** and **1.11** alternative dimensional units are shown for comparison. The method of expressing dimensions as shown in the shaded drawings is not recommended.

5 MEASURING INSTRUMENTS

The following notes are based on BS 4484.

5.01 Folding rules and rods, laths, and pocket tape rules

Lengths of instruments are as follows:

(a) Folding rules: 1 m
(b) Laths: 1 m, 1.5 m or 2 m
(c) Folding and multi-purpose rods: 2 m
(d) Pocket tape rules: 1 m, 2 m, 3 m, or 5 m.

The forms of graduation are shown in **1.14**. The instruments are graduated in millimetres along one edge with 5 m and 10 m graduation marks. Along the other edge the millimetre graduations are omitted.

5.02 Steel and synthetic tapes

Lengths are 10 m, 20 m, or 30 m long. Etched steel bands are available in 30 m and 50 m lengths.

Tapes are graduated at intervals of 100 mm, 10 mm (with the 50 mm centre graduation mark 'arrowed') and 5 mm. The first and last metre of the tape are further subdivided into minor graduation marks at 1 mm intervals (see **1.15**). Note that synthetic material tapes, however, are not subdivided into millimetres over the first and last metre.

5.03 Chains

Studded steel band chains are in lengths of 20 metres, divided by brass studs at every 200 mm position and figured at every 5 metres. The first and last metre are further divided into 10 mm intervals by

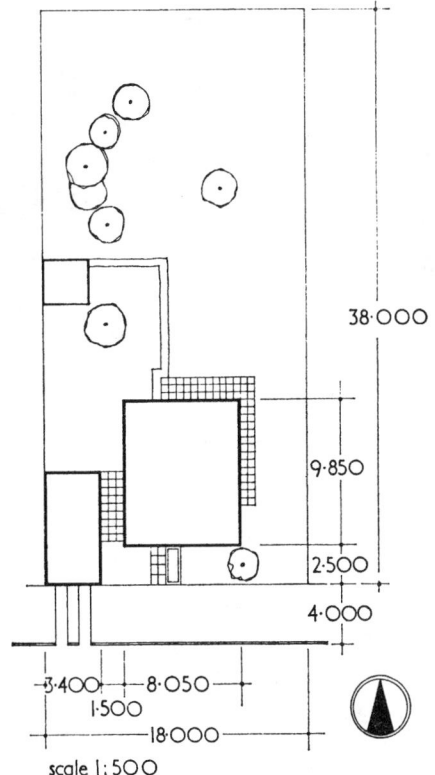

scale 1:500

1.8 *Site plan*

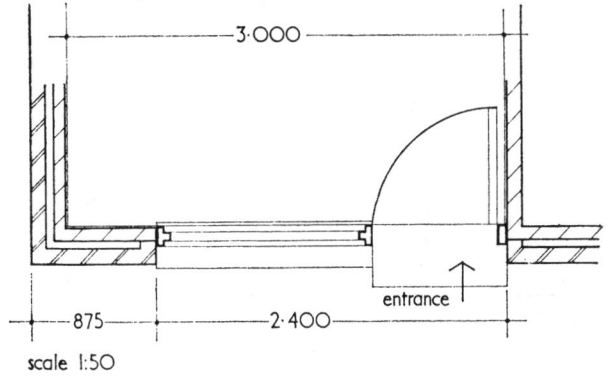

scale 1:50

1.9 *Location drawing*

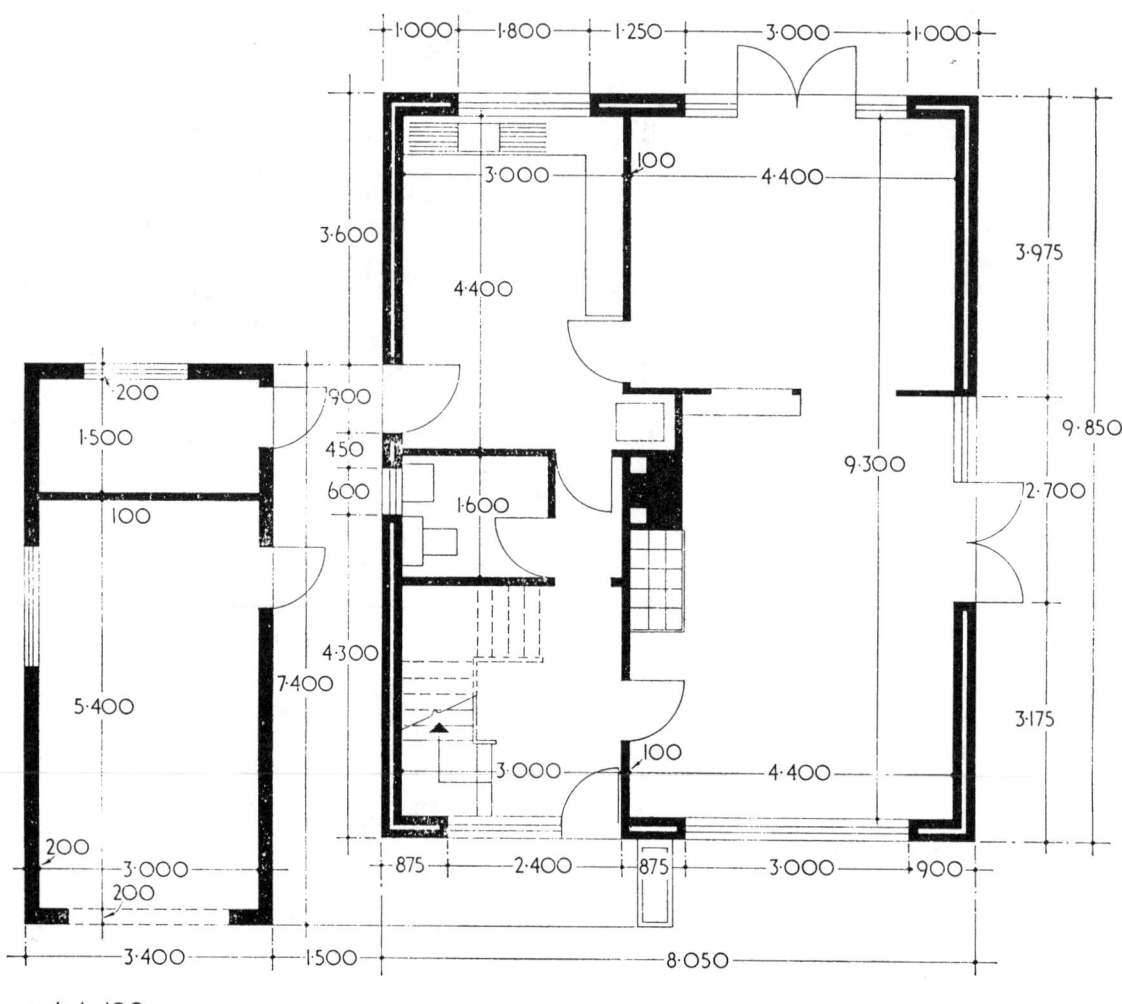

scale 1 : 100

1.10 *Location drawing (sketch plan)*

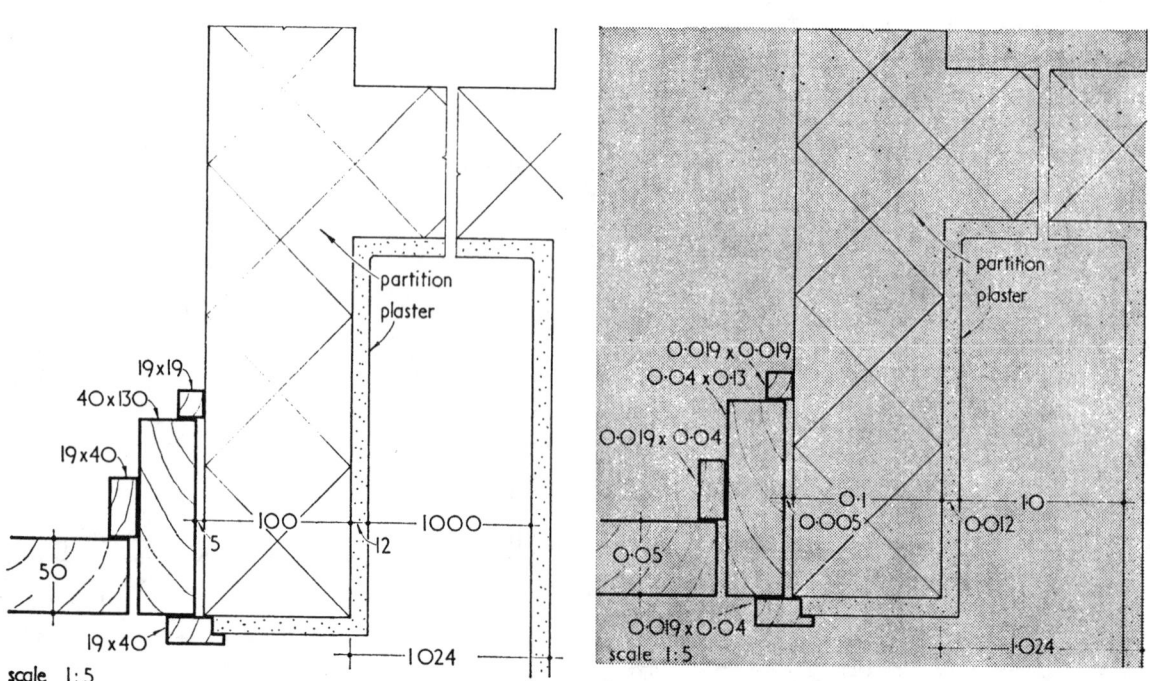

1.11 *Assembly detail drawing (shaded version not recommended)*

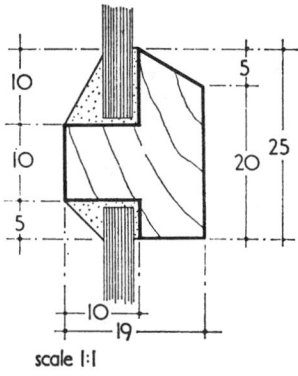

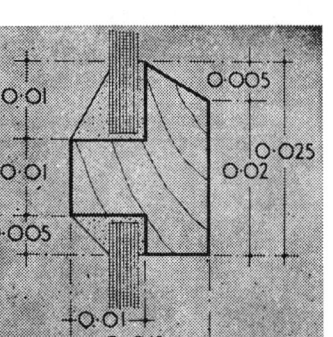

1.12 *Full size detail (shaded version not recommended)*

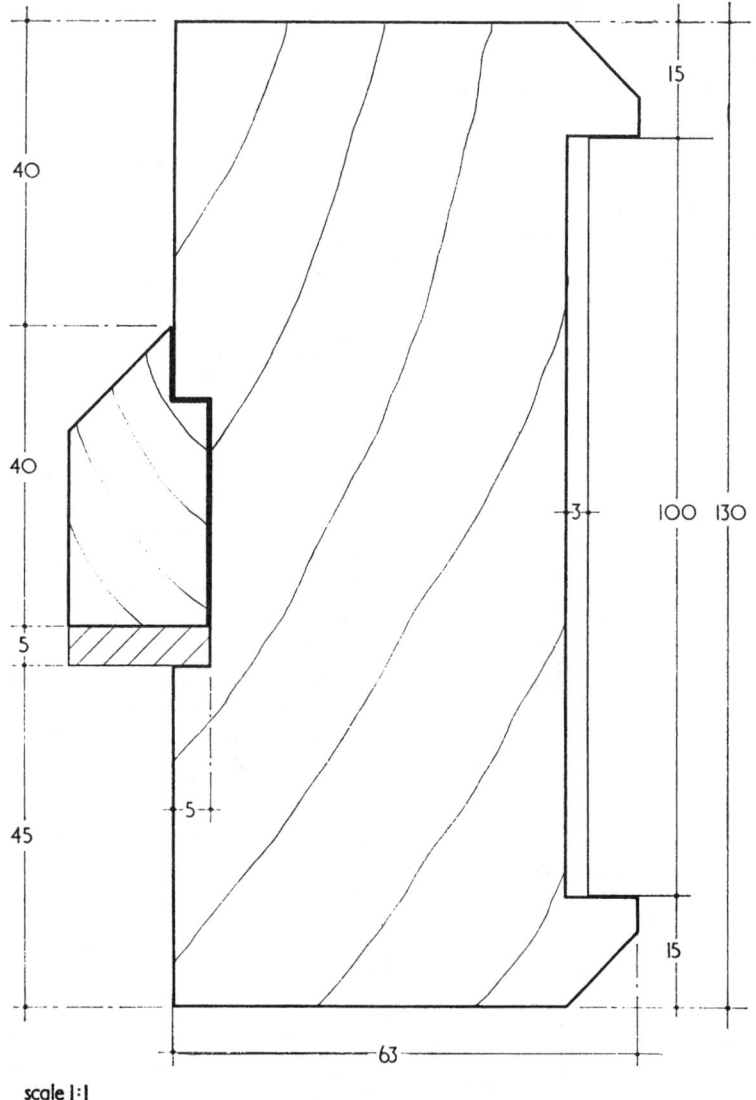

scale 1:1

1.13 *Full size detail*

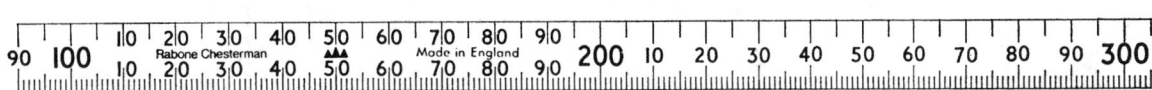

1.14 *Graduation markings for folding rules and rods, laths and pocket tape rules*

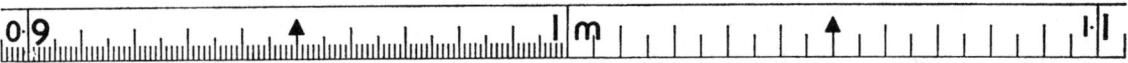

1.15 *Graduation markings for steel tapes*

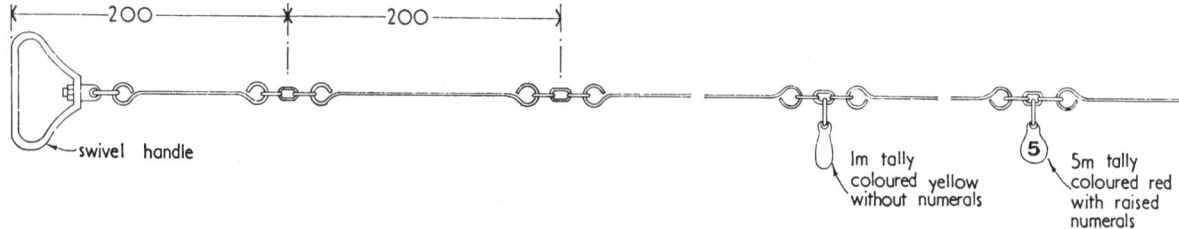

1.16 *Land chain markings*

smaller brass studs with a small washer or other identification at half-metre intervals. The markings appear on both sides of the band.

Land chains are also in lengths of 20 metres, made up of links, which from centre to centre of each middle connecting link measure 200 mm. Tally markers are attached to the middle connecting ring at every whole-metre position. Red markers are used for 5 m positions, with raised numerals; yellow markers of a different shape and with no markings are used for the rest, **1.16**.

5.04 Levelling staffs

Lengths are 3 m, 4 m or 5 m long with a reading face not less than 38 mm wide. Graduation marks are 10 mm deep, spaced at 10 mm intervals. At every 100 mm the graduation marks offset to the left and right of centre, **1.17**. The outside edges of the lower three graduation marks join together to form an 'E' shape. Different colours distinguish graduation marks in alternate metres. Staffs are figured at every 100 mm interval with metre numbers (small numerals) followed by the decimal point and first decimal part of the metre (large numerals).

5.05 Ranging rods

Lengths are 2 m, 2.5 m or 3 m painted in either 200 mm or 500 mm bands alternating red and white. A rod of 2 m length painted in 200 mm bands is shown in **1.18**.

6 DIMENSIONAL COORDINATION

6.01

Current building practice involves the assembly of many factory-made components: in some cases (called *industrialised building*) the whole project consists of such components slotted together like a child's construction kit. Dimensional coordination (DC) is essential to ensure the success of the system, and consists of a range of dimensions relating to the sizing of building components and assemblies, and to the buildings incorporating them. DC enables the coordination of the many parts that go to make up the total construction which are supplied from widely separated sources. At an international level, 100 mm is accepted as the basic module (often referred to by the letter 'M').

Dimensional coordination relies on establishment of rectangular three-dimensional grids of basic modules into which components can be introduced in an interrelated pattern of sizes, **1.19**. The modular grid network delineates the space into which each component fits. The most important factor of dimensional coordination is that the component must always be undersized in relation to the space grid into which it has to fit (but not to too great an extent).

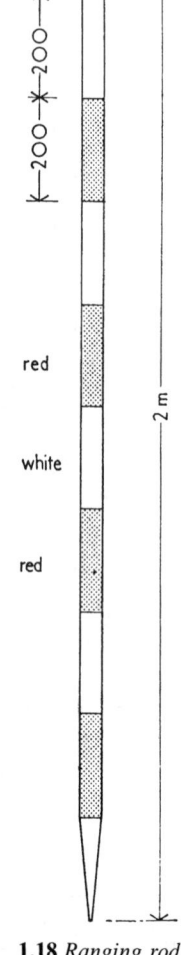

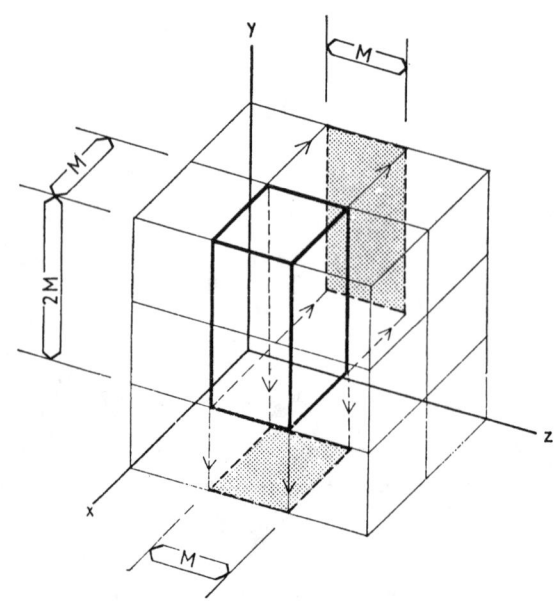

1.17 *Levelling staff marked in 10 mm increments*

1.18 *Ranging rod*

1.19 *Three-dimensional grid of basic modules*

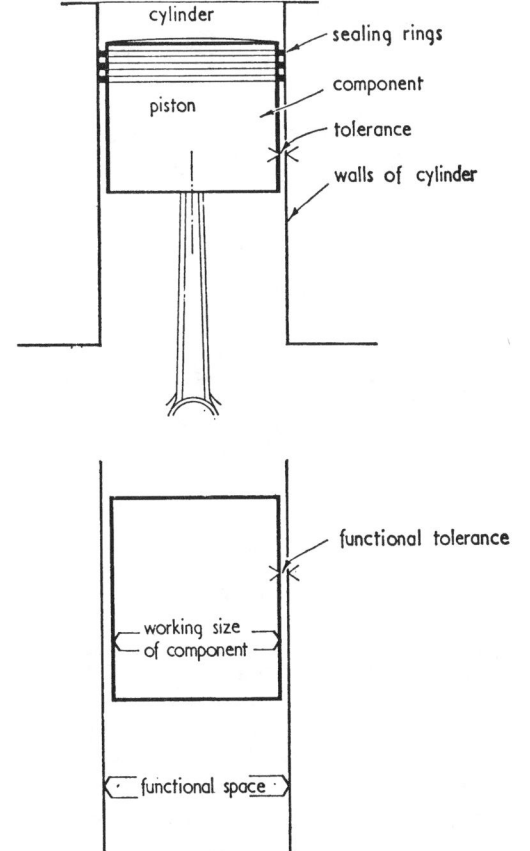

1.20 *The piston and cylinder principle*

In the engineering world the piston and cylinder principle establishes the size relationship between dimensional space grid and component, **1.20**. The size of the cylinder must allow for the right degree of accuracy and tolerance to enable the piston to move up and down.

The degree of inaccuracy to be allowed for in the building process is related to the economics of jointing. Adequate space must be allowed for size of component plus joint. Transgressing the rules of locating components within the allotted space

contained by grid lines will cause considerable difficulty in site assembly.

The basic arrangement of components within the grid layout shows them fitting into the spaces allocated to them: dimensionally they are coordinated, thus allowing the designer maximum use of standard components, **1.21**.

6.02

The basic aims of DC (as was defined in BS 4011:1966) were:

- To obtain maximum economy in the production of components
- To reduce the manufacture of non-standard units
- To avoid wasteful cutting on-site.

Advantages to designers may include:

- Reduction in design labour
- Reduced production of working drawings by the use of standard details
- Choice of interrelated standard components at the various price levels.

Potential advantages to manufacturers include:

- More effective use of labour in producing standard lines
- Reduction in the stocking, invoicing and other operations connected with numerous differently sized products. There should also be advantages to contractors, not only through better design of components for fit but also through increasing familiarity with standard components.

BS 4011 has now been superseded by BS 6750:1986.

6.03 Basic elements of DC

Preference for size
The preferred increments are:

- First preference (multimodule) multiples of 300 mm
- Second preference (basic module) multiples of 100 mm
- Third preference (submodule) multiples of 50 mm up to 300 mm
- Fourth preference (submodule) multiples of 25 mm up to 300 mm.

Reference system
Grid and line
The DC reference system identifies controlling dimensions by the use of a grid on plans and a series of horizontal lines on elevations and sections.
The terminology is precise:

- Controlling dimensions lie between key reference planes (e.g. floor-to-floor height). They provide a framework within which to design and to which components and assemblies may be related.
- Key reference planes define the boundaries of controlling zones or structural axes.
- Controlling lines on a drawing represent a key reference plane.
- Axial controlling lines are shown on drawings by a chain dotted line with a circle at the end, in which the grid reference is given.
- Face controlling lines are shown by a continuous line with a circle at the end in which the grid reference is given.
- Zones between vertical or horizontal reference planes provide spaces for one or more components which do not necessarily fill the space. Provided that use of associated components is not inhibited, a building component (or group of components) may extend beyond the zone boundary, as may trims and finishes.

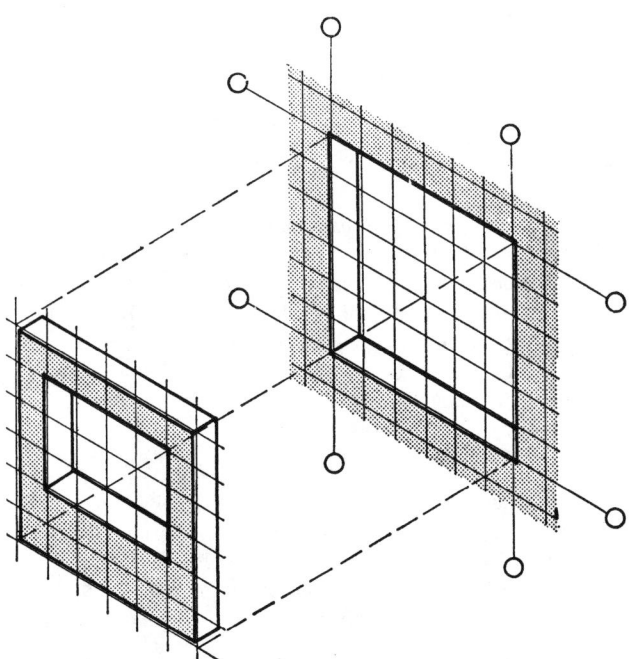

1.21 *Fitting a component into a dimensionally coordinated grid*

6.04 Drawings

A typical project will require three series of drawings:

1 *General location drawings* showing controlling lines with identifiers
2 *Assembly drawings* showing the relationships between the components and the controlling lines
3 *Component drawings*, where required.

Specialists such as structural and service engineers provide assembly and component drawings in their own disciplines to fit in with this system.

The representation of the dimensional coordination framework should be consistent on all drawings. On general location drawings a grid representing 300 mm (or a multiple of 300 mm) may be used. Assembly details may use grids of 300 or 100 mm.

Reference lines
Reference lines or grids should be thin, to distinguish them from other, particularly constructional, lines.

Gridded paper and scales
Table V gives the recommended range of scales for each type of drawing related to appropriate paper grid sizes. Scale and the increment represented by the grid should be indicated on all gridded sheets.

Dimension lines
Different types of dimensions should be distinguished by the type of arrowhead, **1.22**.

Running dimensions should be set off from a datum, **1.23**.

Assembly details
Assembly details should show components in their context, i.e. in relation to the adjoining element, with details of the joint.

Table V Choice of scales and grids

Type of drawing	Scale	Paper grid size (mm)	Increment represented (mm)
Block plan	1:2000	Not applicable	
	1:1000		
Site plan	1:500	Not applicable	
	1:200		
Sketch	1:200	6	1200
	1:100	3*	300
General location	1:100	6	600
		3*	300
	1:50	6	300
		2*	100
Component ranges	1:100	6	600
		3*	300
	1:50	6	300
		2*	100
	1:20	15	300
		5	100
Component details	1:10	10	100
		5	50
	1:5	20	100
		10	50
		5	25
	1:1	100	100
		50	50
		25	25
Assembly	1:20	15	300
		5	100
	1:10	10	100
		5	50
	1:5	20	100
		10	50
		5	25

* These sizes are below the limits for hand-drawn grids.

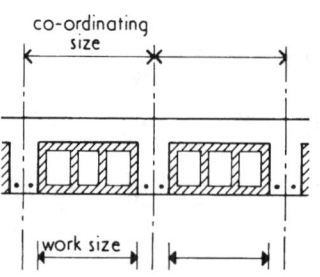

1.22 *Coordinating and work sizes*

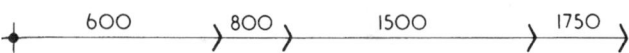

1.23 *Running dimensions. The symbol at the datum should be as shown. An arrowhead is sometimes used, but is not the preferred alternative*

6.05 Locating components by grid

Types of grid
The structural grid of axial controlling lines, **1.24**, is established physically by the contractor on-site; it serves as the main reference in construction. It is subject to setting-out deviations which affect the spaces required for assemblies of components; but this should have been allowed for in the design stage. A planning grid of face controlling lines, **1.25**, locates non-structural elements.

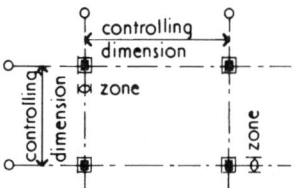

1.24 *Axial control*

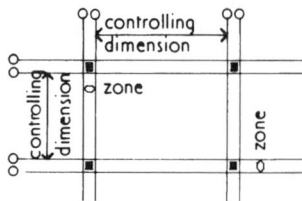

1.25 *Facial control*

Relation between structural and planning grids
Structural and planning grids may coincide but do not necessarily do so. The controlling dimensions for spacing structural elements on plan on axial lines are in multiples of 300 mm (Table VI). If a 300 mm square grid is used then axial controlling lines will coincide with the grid, **1.26**, but if the grid is a multiple of 300 mm then the controlling lines will be offset from the axial grid by 300 mm or by a multiple of 300 mm, **1.27**.

Relating zones to a 300 mm grid
If widths of structural zones are multiples of 300 mm, the grid is continuous, **1.28**. If the zone is not a multiple of 300 mm, however, the grid is interrupted by the dimension of that zone, **1.29**. This is referred to as a neutral zone.

● A neutral zone is a zone that does not conform to the recommended dimensions given in Table VI.

Table VI Sizing of zones and heights

Range (mm)	Multiples of size (mm)
Horizontal controlling dimensions	
Widths of zones for columns and loadbearing walls	
100 to 600	300 (first preference)
	100 (second preference)
Spacing of zones for columns and loadbearing walls	
From 900[1]	300
Vertical controlling dimensions	
Floor to ceiling heights	
2300[2] to 3000	100
3000 to 6600	300
over 6600	600
Heights of zones for floors and roofs	
100 to 600[3]	100
over 600	300
Floor to floor (and roof) heights	
2700[4] to 8400	300
over 8400	600
Changes in level	
300 to 2400	300
above 2400	600

1 Housing may use 800
2 Farm buildings may use 1500 and 1800
   Domestic garages may use 2100
   Housing may use 2350
3 Housing may use 250
4 Housing may use 2600

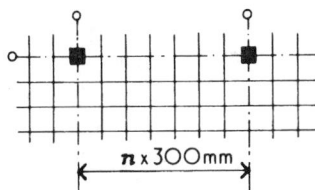

1.26 *Uninterrupted grid*

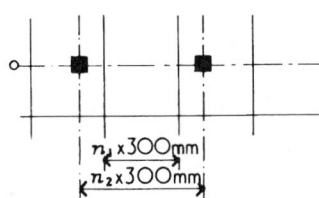

1.27 *Controlling lines offset from grid*

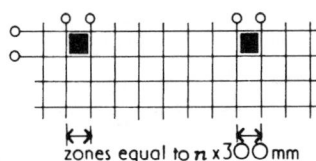

1.28 *Continuous grid*

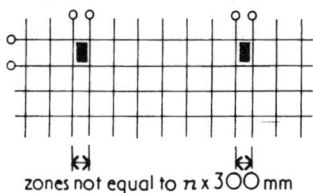

1.29 *Interrupted grid and neutral zones (tartan)*

Key reference planes
Key reference planes, **1.30**, should generally occur at:

- Finished floor level
- Finished suspended ceiling level
- Finished wall surface.

Sizes of zones indicated by key reference planes should be selected from Table VI. Where controlling or reference lines bound floor or roof soffits, deflection should be allowed for in the zone.

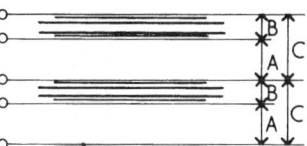

1.30 *Vertical control: A being floor-to-ceiling height controlling dimension; B floor and roof zone; C floor-to-floor and floor-to-roof controlling dimension*

6.06 Size of components

Coordinating and work sizes
Controlling dimensions are coordinating sizes:

- Coordinating sizes, **1.22**, make allowance for fitting and jointing. They represent the overlaid grid which does not usually coincide with actual junction lines on the face of the building. They are indicated by open arrowheads.
- Work sizes are the specified manufactured sizes (within permissible deviations). They are indicated by closed arrowheads.

Tolerance and fit
Joint sizes are critical. There are graphical aids (see References) to help reconcile all the factors affecting tolerance, such as

- Expansion and contraction
- Variability in manufactured size
- Satisfactory joint clearance range
- Variations in setting out dimensions, adjacent components, etc.
- Number of components in an assembly
- Variations in interpretation of work size from a given coordinating size.

Degree of accuracy
Designers should identify where fit is critical and where not, or they must assess:

- Where standard sizes are appropriate and readily available
- If some components can be made to order without a significant cost penalty
- Whether cutting is acceptable (and the effect on performance)
- The likely order of assembly.

6.07 Boundary conditions
Some assembly and support conditions may necessitate variations in elements to allow for:

- An extended floor slab beyond the clear span to gain a bearing on a wall
- Reduction in size to permit the application of a finish
- An increased height of positioning to allow for building directly off the floor slab or extending through a suspended ceiling to reach the soffit of the floor slab.

These allowances (termed 'boundary conditions') should be in multiples of 25 mm. They may be uneconomic to produce, limiting the applications of the product to which they apply.

Table VII Planning use classes under the Town and Country Planning (use Classes) Order 1987 as amended 1991 and twice in 1992

Class	Used for the main or primary purpose
A1 Shops open to the public	(a) Selling goods retail other than hot food (b) Post office (c) Ticket or travel agency (d) Take-away selling sandwiches or other cold food (e) Hairdresser (f) Funeral director (g) Displaying goods for sale (h) Hiring out domestic or personal goods or articles (i) Washing or cleaning clothes or fabrics (j) Receiving goods to be washed, cleaned or repaired
A2 Financial and professional services where provided mainly to visiting members of the public	(a) Financial services (b) Professional services (other than health or medical services) (c) Any other services (including use as a betting office) appropriate to provide in a shopping area
A3 Food and drink	The sale of food or drink for consumption on the premises or of hot food for consumption off the premises
B1 Business, providing the use can exist in a residential area without detriment because of noise, vibration, smell, fumes, smoke, soot, ash, dust or grit	(a) An office other than a use within class A2 (b) Research and development or products or processes (c) Any industrial process
B2 General industrial	Carrying on an industrial process other than one in class B1 or B4 to B7
B3	Deleted class
B4 Special Industrial Group B, except where the process is carried out in association with and adjacent to a quarry or mine	(a) Smelting, calcining, sintering or reducing ores, minerals, concentrates or mattes (b) Converting, refining, reheating, annealing, hardening, melting, carburising, forging or casting metals or alloys other than pressure die-casting (c) Recovering metal from scrap or drosses or ashes (e) Pickling or treating metal in acid (f) Chromium plating
B5 Special Industrial Group C, except where the process is carried out in association with and adjacent to a quarry or mine	(a) Burning bricks or pipes (b) Burning lime or dolomite (c) Producing zinc oxide, cement or alumina (d) Foaming, crushing, screening or heating minerals or slag (e) Processing pulverised fuel ash by heat (f) Producing carbonate of lime or hydrated lime (g) Producing inorganic pigments by calcining, roasting or grinding
B6 Special Industrial Group D	(a) Distilling, refining or blending oils (other than petroleum or petroleum products) (b) Producing or using cellulose or using other pressure sprayed metal finishes (other than in vehicle repair workshops in connection with minor repairs, or the application of plastic powder by the use of fluidised bed and electrostatic spray techniques) (c) Boiling linseed oil or running gum (d) Processes involving the use of hot pitch or bitumen (except the use of bitumen in the manufacture of roofing felt at temperatures not exceeding 220°C and also the manufacture of coated roadstone) (e) Stoving enamelled ware (f) Producing aliphatic esters of the lower fatty acids, butyric acid, caramel, hexamine, iodioform, napthols, resin products (excluding plastic moulding or extrusion operations and producing plastic sheets, rods, tubes, filaments, fibres or optical components produced by casting, calendering, moulding, shaping or extrusion), salicylic acid or sulphonated organic compounds (g) Producing rubber from scrap (h) Chemical processes in which chlorphenols or chlorcresols are used as intermediates (i) Manufacturing acetylene from calcium carbide (j) Manufacturing, recovering or using pyridine or picolines, any methyl or ethyl amine or acrylates
B7 Special Industrial Group E	Boiling blood, chitterlings, nettlings or soap Boiling, burning, grinding or steaming bones Boiling or cleaning tripe Breeding maggots from putrescible animal matter Cleaning, adapting or treating animal hair Curing fish Dealing in rags and bones (including receiving, storing, sorting or manipulating rags in, or likely to become in, an offensive condition, or any bones, rabbit skins, fat or putrescible animal products of a similar nature) Dressing or scraping fish skins Drying skins Making manure from bones, fish, offal, blood, spent hops, beans or other putrescible animal or vegetable matter Making or scraping guts Manufacturing animal charcoal, blood albumen, candles, catgut, glue, fish oil, size or feeding stuff for animals or poultry from meat, fish, blood, bone, feathers, fat or animal offal either in an offensive condition or subjected to any process causing noxious or injurious effluvia Melting, refining or extracting fat or tallow Preparing skins for working

Table VII Continued

Class	Used for the main or primary purpose
B8 Storage or distribution	Storage or as a distribution centre
C1 Hotels and hostels	Hotel, boarding or guest house or a hostel where, in each case, no significant element of care is provided
C2 Residential institutions	Residential accommodation and care for people (other than a use within class C3) Hospital or nursing home Residential school, college, training centre
C3 Dwelling houses whether or not sole or main residences	(a) For a single person or by people living together as a family, or (b) By not more than 6 residents living together as a single household (including a household where care is provided for residents)
D1 Non-residential institutions	(a) For any medical or health services except when attached to the residence of the consultant or practitioner (b) Crèche, day nursery, day centre (c) For education (d) For the display of works of art (otherwise than for sale or hire) (e) Museum (f) Public library, public reading room (g) Public hall, exhibition hall (h) Public worship, religious instruction
D2 Assembly and leisure	(a) Cinema (b) Concert hall (c) Bingo hall or casino (d) Dance hall (e) Swimming bath, skating rink, gymnasium, area for other indoor or outdoor sports or recreations, not involving motorised vehicles or firearms
UNCLASSED	(a) Theatre (b) Amusement arcade or centre, funfair (c) Laundrette (d) Petrol station (e) Motor vehicle showroom (f) Taxi or motor hire office (g) Scrapyard, yard for the storage or distribution of minerals or car-breaking (h) For any work registerable under the Alkali, etc. Works Regulation Act 1906

6.08 Dimensionally co-ordinated products

Section 5 of DD 51 lists British Standards where products are dimensionally coordinated. Many appear in Chapter 46 of this handbook.

7 PLANNING

7.01

In most countries of the world some permit or permission is required for building to take place. In Britain, this involves seeking planning permission from the local authority in whose area the development is proposed. There are a number of circumstances under which permission is not required, and the local authority will, if asked, provide a certificate to that effect in each particular case. Generally, permission will be required for:

● A building, engineering or mining operation on land,
● The material change of *use* of a building or land.

Building operations which affect only the interior of a building or which do not materially affect the external appearance of a building do not generally require planning permission. The exception to this is where works on *Listed Buildings* are involved. In this instance *Listed Building Consent* is required for both internal and external works, and always where demolition is involved, whether in part or whole.

7.02 Change of use

The more common uses of buildings are classified by statute into classes which are detailed in Table VII. Planning permission is required for any change of use from one class to another; for example, from a funeral directors (A1f) to a solicitor's office (A2b). However, some changes from one class to another can be made without permission, e.g. from A3 to A1 or A2 but not the other way round. Changes permitted in this way are ones which would generally constitute an environmental improvement.

7.03 Conservation areas

Certain areas, such as the centres of historic towns or areas of particular environmental quality, are designated *Conservation Areas*. The controls in these areas are generally similar to those elsewhere, except with regard to demolition and permitted development rights. Furthermore, where permission is required, there is a duty that development must not harm the character or appearance of the Conservation Area (i.e. undermine the reasons why the Conservation Areas was designated). Demolition of buildings or parts of buildings in a Conservation Area requires *Conservation Area Consent*.

7.04 Permitted development

Some categories of development enjoy permitted development rights. This means that some development can take place *without* permission from the local authority. The removal of some or all of these rights can be undertaken by the local authority through the issuing of an *Article 4 direction*. Article 4 directions are generally made where some environmental harm would be caused if these rights were exercised (e.g. in Conservation Areas). Consult the appropriate planning authority in each case to discover the local controls. Most permitted development rights apply only to single-family dwelling houses, and relate to such matters as garden walls, porches, changes to windows, etc.

8 REFERENCES

British Standards Institution

BS 1192: Part 1: 1984 Construction drawing practice, recommendations for general principles

BS 1192: Part 2: 1987 Construction drawing practice, recommendations for architectural and engineering drawings

BS 1192: Part 3: 1987(1993) Construction drawing practice, recommendations for symbols and other graphic conventions

BS 1192: Part 4: 1984 Construction drawing practice, recommendations for landscape drawings

BS 4484: Part 1: 1969 Measuring instruments for constructional works. Metric graduation and figuring of instruments for linear measurement

BS 5606: 1990 Guide to accuracy in building

BS 6750: 1986 Modular co-ordination in building

International Organisation For Standardisation

ISO 1791: 1973 Modular co-ordination – vocabulary

ISO 1006: 1973 Modular co-ordination – basic module

ISO 2848: 1974 Modular co-ordination – principles and rules

ISO 1040: 1973 Modular co-ordination – multimodules for horizontal co-ordinating dimensions

ISO R 1790: 1970 Modular co-ordination – reference lines of horizontal controlling coordinating dimensions

ISO 1789: 1973 Modular co-ordination – storey heights and room heights for residential buildings

ISO 2776: 1974 Modular co-ordination – co-ordinating sizes for door-sets – external and internal

General

Graphical aids for tolerances and fits: handbook for manufacturers, designers and builders, Building Research Establishment Report, London, HMSO, 1974

2 Basic design data

David Adler

KEY POINTS:
- *Certain dimensions are crucial to individual use and health*
- *Satisfying the average situation is unlikely to help the majority*
- *Each case must be carefully considered with all classes of users, particularly people with different disabilities, in mind*

Contents

1 INTRODUCTION

In this chapter will be found basic data which are needed for the design of most types of buildings. However, some basic matters are dealt with in later chapters, principally the following:

- Sanitary provision and activity spaces in Chapter 3
- Requirements for vehicles in Chapter 4
- External and landscape design in Chapter 6
- Eating and drinking in other than domestic situations in Chapter 18.

2 ANTHROPOMETRICS

2.01

Anthropometrics is the science concerned with the measurement of humankind. Inevitably it is bound up with statistics, as people vary considerably in most dimensions. Anthropometrics is of crucial importance to architects as the ultimate basis of the design of most buildings must be the size of the people using them. Average dimensions for British adults are given in **2.1** and **2.2**, but in most cases the use of an average dimension will not produce satisfaction for the majority of users.

2.02 Normal distribution

When surveys are taken of adult males, for example, they show a 'normal distribution' curve: the traditional statistical bell shape,

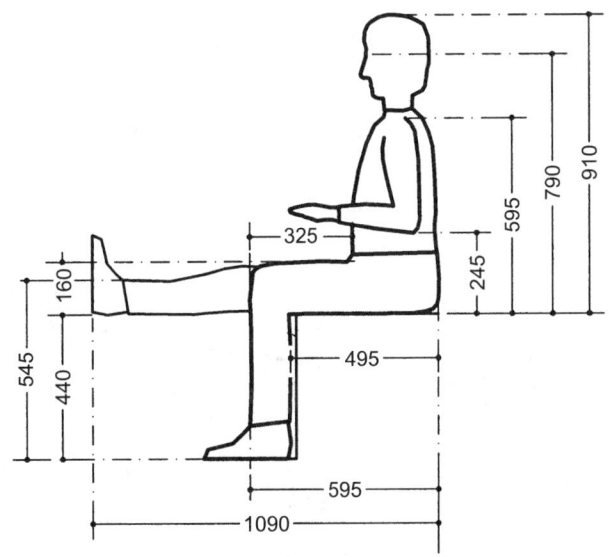

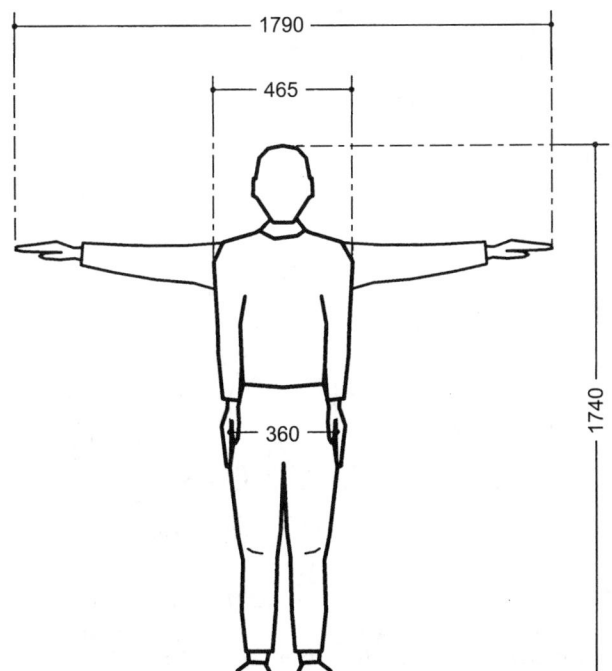

2.1 *Mean average (50th percentile) dimensions of adult British males*

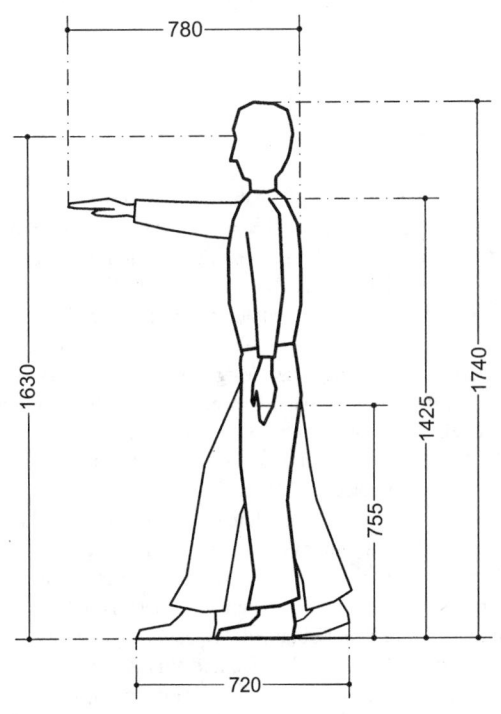

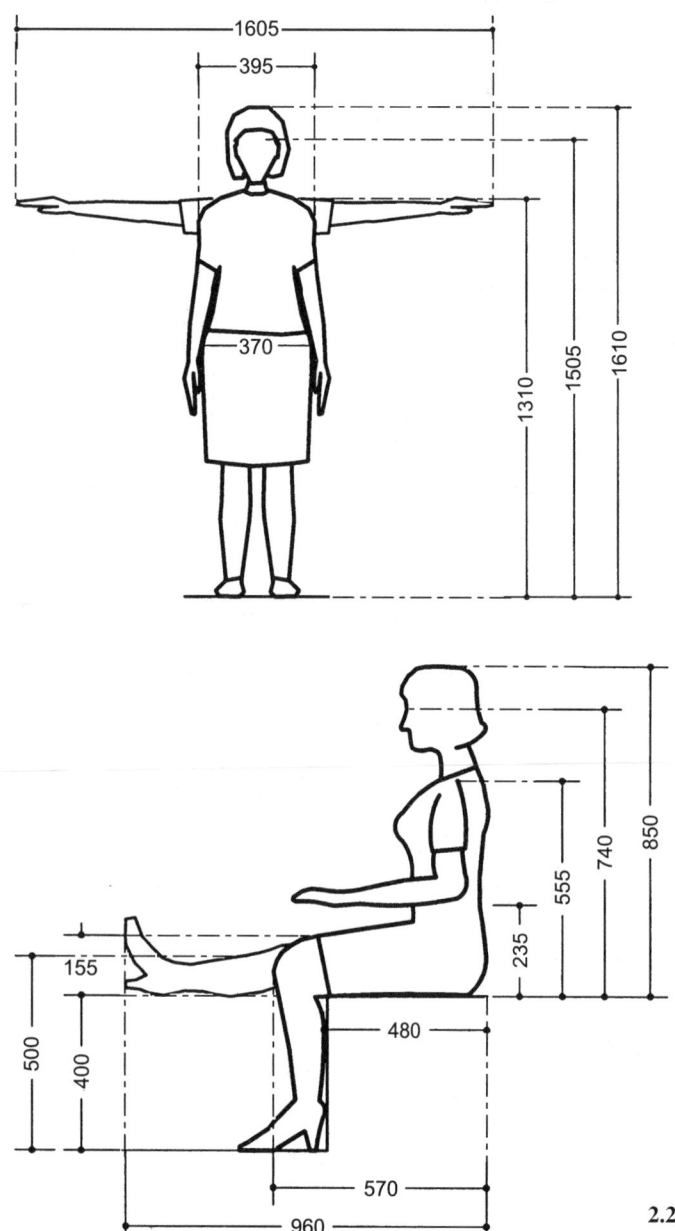

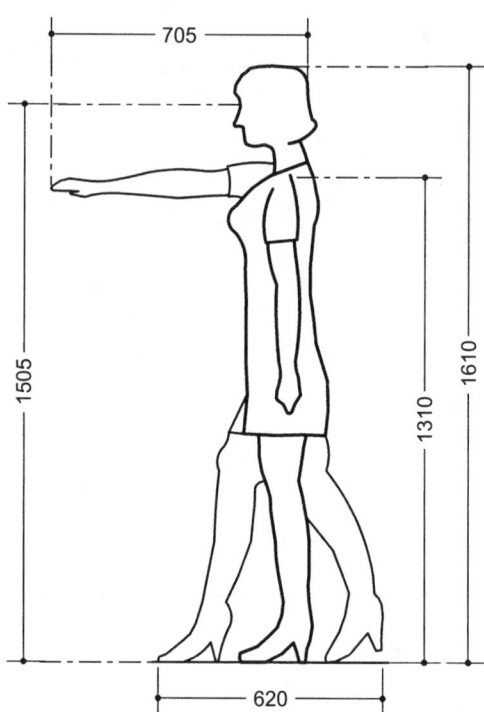

2.2 *Mean average (50th percentile) dimensions of adult British females*

2.3. This shape is totally definable by the two parameters, mean and standard deviation (SD). The mean (in this case) is the average already discussed. For the purposes of the architect, the standard deviation can be taken as the difference from the mean within which 84 per cent of the population are included. The percentage included is called the 'percentile', and it has become accepted (with certain exceptions) that designers generally seek to accommodate those within the band between the 5th and 95th percentile – that is, they do not attempt to satisfy the last 10 per cent of the people. In each case it is the job of the architect to decide whether in fact this will be acceptable.

Table II gives the principal dimensions as shown in **2.4** for men and women, for the 5th, 50th and 95th percentiles.

When a survey of a non-cohesive group (such as of mixed-age adolescents, or men and women together) is taken, a normal distribution curve is not obtained. We cannot predict the percentile dimensions for these populations, and this is why the tables here and elsewhere segregate populations into groups. Within these groups the dimensions are calculable given the mean and the SD, using the formula:

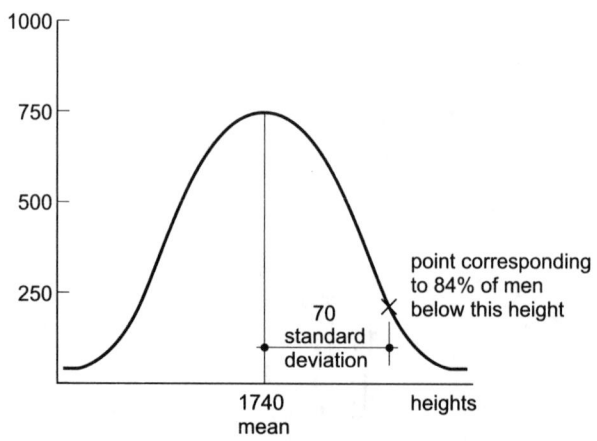

2.3 *Normal distribution 'bell' curve. The y-axis plots the numbers of men (in this example) in a group who are the height given on the x-axis (within certain limits). In a normal distribution the average, the mean and the median are all equal*

$$X_{(p)} = \text{mean} + \text{SD} \times z$$

where: $X_{(p)}$ is the value of the dimension for
the pth percentile
z is a factor from Table I

In the tables the standard deviation is not directly given, but may itself be calculated from the values of the 50th (or mean) and 95th percentiles: e.g.

$$X_{(95)} - \text{mean} = \text{SD} \times 1.64 \text{ (the value of } z \text{ for } p = 95)$$

Example: A doorway is to be designed to accommodate 99.9 per cent of British men. We see from Table II that the mean stature is 1740 mm and the SD is $(1855 - 1740) \div 1.64 = 70$. The height that will fulfil the 99.9 per cent criterion is thus $1740 + (70 \times 3.09) = 1956$ mm, a considerable increase on the value of 1855 mm which accommodates the 95th percentile. In both cases the addition of a further 25 mm would be necessary to allow for footwear (see Table III).

2.03 Clothing
The tables are all consistent in giving the dimensions of the unclothed body. Increases due to clothing vary considerably but Table III gives the normally acceptable values.

2.04 Other nationalities
Dimensional surveys taken elsewhere show considerable variations. Table IV gives the range of stature found in various countries. For most purposes other dimensions can be approximately derived by proportionality with Table II, but more accurate figures can be obtained from the References at the end of this chapter.

2.05 Children and adolescents
Statures (or equivalents) for various ages in Britain are given in Table V. Here proportionality may not give sufficient accuracy, and reference should be made to one of the references for other dimensions.

Table I Selected p and z values for the normal distribution curve

p	z
0.001	−4.26
0.01	−3.72
0.1	−3.09
0.5	−2.58
1	−2.33
2	−2.05
2.5	−1.96
3	−1.88
4	−1.75
5	−1.64
10	−1.28
20	−0.84
25	−0.67
30	−0.52
40	−0.25
50	0
60	0.25
70	0.52
75	0.67
80	0.84
90	1.28
95	1.64
96	1.75
97	1.88
97.5	1.96
98	2.05
99	2.33
99.5	2.58
99.9	3.09
99.99	3.72
99.999	4.26

2.06 Elderly people
People tend to shrink slightly with age. More significantly, the body tends to be less flexible in regard to adapting to dimensionally unfavourable situations. It is therefore more important that design allows for elderly people where that is appropriate, accepting that younger people may be slightly disadvantaged. Table VI gives dimensions for people between the ages of 65 and 80.

Table II Dimensions of British adults

	Men Percentiles			Women Percentiles			
	5th	50th	95th	5th	50th	95th	
Standing							
1 Stature	1625	1740	1855	1505	1610	1710	95th: minimum floor to roof clearance; allow for shoes and headgear in appropriate situations
2 Eye height	1515	1630	1745	1405	1505	1610	50th: height of visual devices, notices, etc.
3 Shoulder height	1315	1425	1535	1215	1310	1405	5th: height for maximum forward reach controls worktop height (see para. 302)
4 Elbow height	1005	1090	1180	930	1005	1085	controls worktop height (see para. 302)
5 Hand (knuckle) height	690	755	825	660	720	780	95th: maximum height of grasp points for lifting
6 Reach upwards	1925	2060	2190	1790	1905	2020	5th: maximum height of controls; subtract 40 mm to allow for full grasp
Sitting							
7 Height above seat level	850	910	965	795	850	910	95th: minimum seat to roof clearance; may need to allow for headgear
8 Eye height above seat level	735	790	845	685	740	795	50th: height of visual devices above seat level
9 Shoulder height above seat level	540	595	645	505	555	610	50th: height above seat level for maximum forward reach
10 Length from elbow to fingertip	440	475	510	400	430	460	50th: easy reach forward at table height
11 Elbow above seat level	195	245	295	185	235	280	50th: height above seat of armrests or desk tops
12 Thigh clearance	135	160	185	125	155	180	95th: space under tables
13 Top of knees, height above floor	490	545	595	455	500	540	95th: clearance under tables above floor or footrest
14 Popliteal height	395	440	490	355	400	445	50th: height of seat above floor or footrest
15 Front of abdomen to front of knees	253	325	395	245	315	385	95th: minimum forward clearance at thigh level from front of body or from obstruction, e.g. desktop
16 Buttock – popliteal length	440	495	550	435	480	530	5th: length of seat surface from backrest to front edge
17 Rear of buttocks to front of knees	540	595	645	520	570	620	95th: minimum forward clearance from seat back at height for highest seating posture
18 Extended leg length	985	1070	1160	875	965	1055	5th (less than): maximum distance of foot controls, footrest, etc. from seat back
19 Seat width	310	360	405	310	370	435	95th: width of seats, minimum distance between armrests
Sitting and standing							
20 Forward grip reach	720	780	835	650	705	755	5th: maximum comfortable forward reach at shoulder level
21 Fingertip span	1655	1790	1925	1490	1605	1725	5th: limits of lateral fingertip reach, subtract 130 mm to allow for full grasp
22 Width over elbows akimbo	865	945	1020	780	850	920	95th: lateral clearance in workspace
23 Shoulder width	420	465	510	355	395	435	95th: minimum lateral clearance in workspace above waist
24 Chest or bust depth	215	250	285	210	250	295	
25 Abdominal depth	220	270	320	205	255	305	

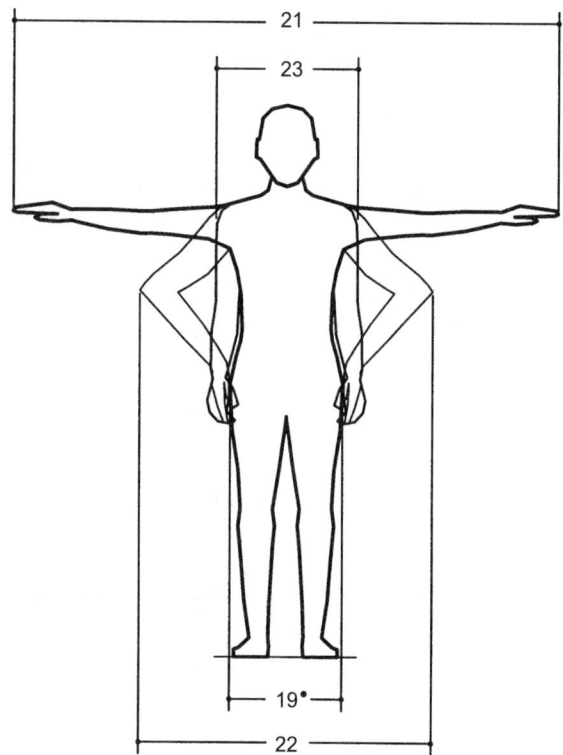

2.4 *Key dimensions listed in Table II. These figures are based on surveys of unclothed volunteers, and in using them allowances should be made for the wearing of clothes and shoes (see Table III). Dimension references marked • are most commonly used*

Table III Allowance for clothing

	Men	Women
Shoe height	25 mm	45 mm
Hat height	75 mm	100 mm

Table IV Statures of the adults of various nationalities

	Men Percentiles			Women Percentiles		
	5th	50th	95th	5th	50th	95th
British	1625	1740	1855	1505	1610	1710
US	1640	1755	1870	1520	1625	1730
French	1600	1715	1830	1500	1600	1700
German	1645	1745	1845	1520	1635	1750
Swedish	1630	1740	1850	1540	1640	1740
Swiss	1535	1690	1845	1415	1590	1765
Polish	1595	1695	1795	1480	1575	1670
Japanese	1560	1655	1750	1450	1530	1610
Hong Kong Chinese	1585	1680	1775	1455	1555	1655
Indian	1535	1640	1745	1415	1515	1615

Table V Statures (or equivalents) for Britons in various age groups

	Percentiles		
	5th	50th	95th
New-born infants	465	500	535
Infants less than 6 months old	510	600	690
Infants 6 months to 1 year old	655	715	775
Infants 1 year to 18 months	690	745	800
Infants 18 months to 2 years	780	840	900

	Boys/men Percentiles			Girls/women Percentiles		
	5th	50th	95th	5th	50th	95th
Children, 2 years old	850	930	1010	825	890	955
Children, 3 years old	910	990	1070	895	970	1045
Children, 4 years old	975	1050	1125	965	1050	1135
Children, 5 years old	1025	1110	1195	1015	1100	1185
Children, 6 years old	1070	1170	1270	1070	1160	1250
Children, 7 years old	1140	1230	1320	1125	1220	1315
Children, 8 years old	1180	1280	1380	1185	1280	1375
Children, 9 years old	1225	1330	1435	1220	1330	1440
Children, 10 years old	1290	1390	1490	1270	1390	1510
Children, 11 years old	1325	1430	1535	1310	1440	1570
Children, 12 years old	1360	1490	1620	1370	1500	1630
Children, 13 years old	1400	1550	1700	1430	1550	1670
Children, 14 years old	1480	1630	1780	1480	1590	1700
15 years old	1555	1690	1825	1510	1610	1710
16 years old	1620	1730	1840	1520	1620	1720
17 years old	1640	1750	1860	1520	1620	1720
18 years old	1660	1760	1860	1530	1620	1710
Aged 19–25	1640	1760	1880	1520	1620	1720
Aged 19–45	1635	1745	1860	1515	1615	1715
Aged 19–65	1625	1740	1855	1505	1610	1710
Aged 45–65	1610	1720	1830	1495	1595	1695
Aged 65–85	1575	1685	1790	1475	1570	1670
Elderly people	1515	1640	1765	1400	1515	1630

3 ERGONOMICS

3.01

This is the discipline that deals with the dimensions of people at work, including activities not directly connected with earning a living. Such matters as the space required by people using motorcars, flying aeroplanes and operating machinery come under this heading. Many of the dimensions required for this will be found in Table II.

Table VI Dimensions for British people aged 65 to 80

	Men Percentiles			Women Percentiles		
	5th	50th	95th	5th	50th	95th
Standing						
1 Stature	1575	1685	1790	1475	1570	1670
2 Eye height	1470	1575	1685	1375	1475	1570
3 Shoulder height	1280	1380	1480	1190	1280	1375
4 Elbow height	975	895	975	740	810	875
5 Hand (knuckle) height	670	730	795	645	705	760
6 Reach upwards	1840	1965	2090	1725	1835	1950
Sitting						
7 Height above seat level	815	875	930	750	815	885
8 Eye height above seat level	705	760	815	645	710	770
9 Shoulder height above seat level	520	570	625	475	535	590
10 Length from elbow to fingertip	425	460	490	390	420	450
11 Elbow above seat level	175	220	270	165	210	260
12 Thigh clearance	125	150	175	115	145	170
13 Top of knees, height above floor	480	525	575	455	500	540
14 Popliteal height	385	425	470	355	395	440
15 Front of abdomen to front of knees	210	280	350	325	295	365
16 Buttock – popliteal length	430	485	535	430	480	525
17 Rear of buttocks to front of knees	530	580	625	520	565	615
19 Seat width	305	350	395	310	370	430
Sitting and standing						
20 Forward grip reach	700	755	805	640	685	735
21 Fingertip span	1605	1735	1860	1460	1570	1685
23 Shoulder width	400	445	485	345	385	380

3.02 Worktop heights

The most common ailment after the common cold is probably the 'bad back'. Many believe that this can be caused by working on a surface that is too low, causing stooping. Both when standing and sitting to work, it is important that the worktop should be as follows:

- For manipulative tasks involving moderate degrees of both force and precision: between 50 and 100 mm below elbow height of the person concerned
- For delicate tasks: between 50 and 100 mm above elbow height
- For heavy tasks, particularly those involving downward pressure on the workpiece: between 100 and 300 mm below elbow height.

3.02 Standing worktops

Worktops at which people stand are found in factories and in the home kitchen. Since women are generally shorter in stature than men, the heights of these respective surfaces have tended to reinforce the traditional roles of the sexes: factory worktops at 1050 mm being seen as too high for many women and kitchen worktops at 900 mm (or lower) being too low for men. It is possible in factories to provide small moveable platforms to assist women workers, but this type of solution is not available where the worktop is too low for the user.

In **2.5** the percentage comfortable at each worktop height is plotted assuming that the users are wearing shoes and comfort is achieved with tops between 50 mm above elbow height and 100 mm lower. It can be seen that the standard kitchen worktop height of 900 mm actually seems to suit no-one. 850 mm would be a good height where only elderly women are likely to use it. The surprising thing is that 900 mm is uncomfortable for 84 per cent of all women! 1000 mm is ideal for most women, but only for 40 per cent of men. The traditional men's height of 1050 mm appears to satisfy both 76 per cent of men and 84 per cent of women.

3.03 Sink heights

One of the most common domestic chores is washing up. It is customary for sinks to be set into worktops, or fitted with their rims level with them. Since the effective working surface in this case is the base of the sink, usually about 100 mm lower than the rim, this

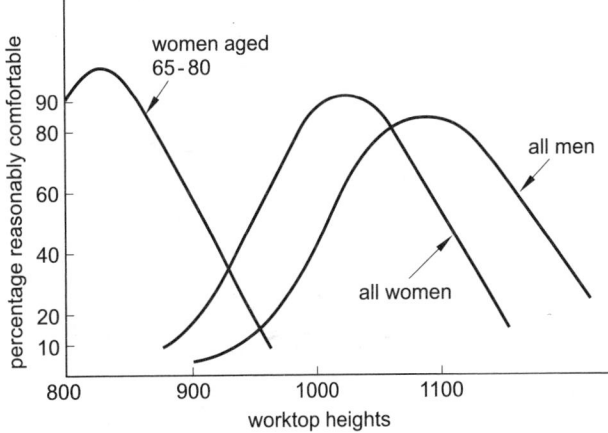

2.5 *Graphs of percentages comfortable at each worktop height. These assume that the worktop is between 50 mm above and 100 mm below elbow height, and that shoes are worn*

further worsens the situation. It is recommended that sink surrounds should be fitted at least 75 mm above normal worktop height.

3.04 Serveries

A particular type of standing worktop is a counter, **2.6**. This can be in a shop, restaurant or public house, or be a reception counter in an office or a hotel. There is often no good reason why the same height is needed on each side, and it is common for the non-public side to be higher than the other. Details of such can be found in the appropriate specialist chapters.

3.04 Sitting worktops

Traditionally, writing desks are standard in height at 710 mm, **2.7**. Desks for typewriters and word processors (where the working

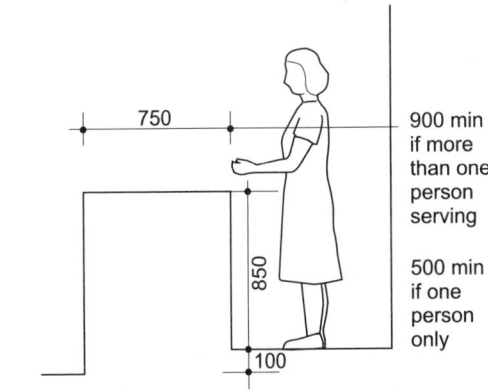

2.6 *Serving counter*

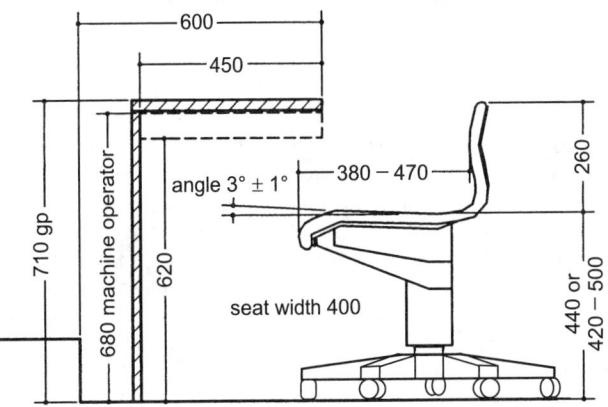

2.7 *Sitting worktop*

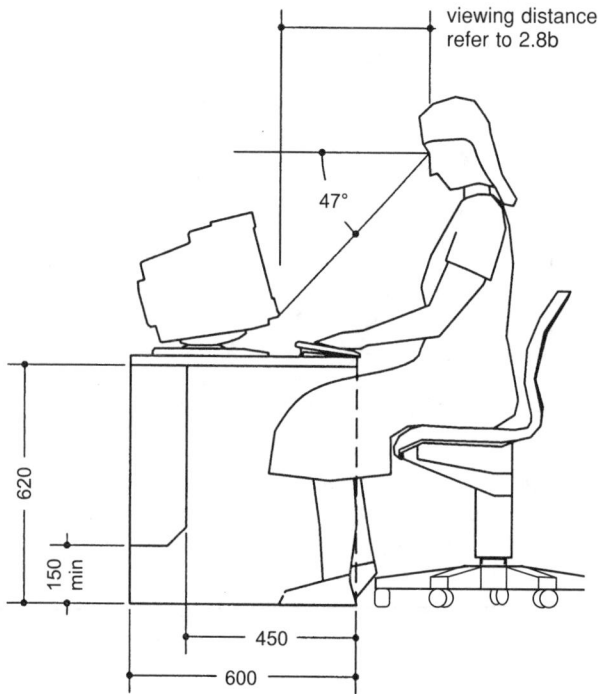

2.8 a Computer workstation

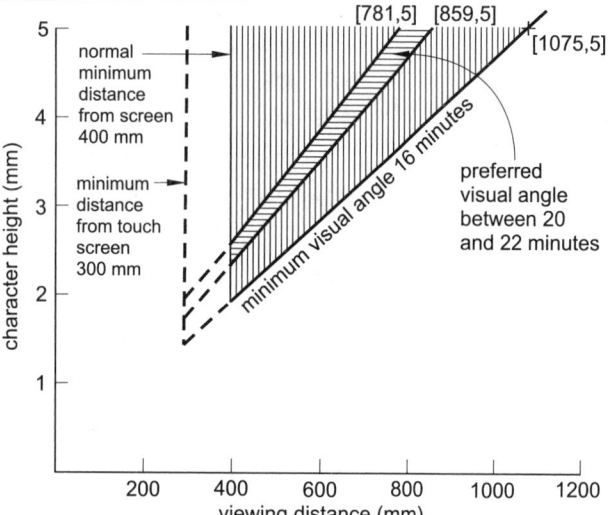

b Viewing distance

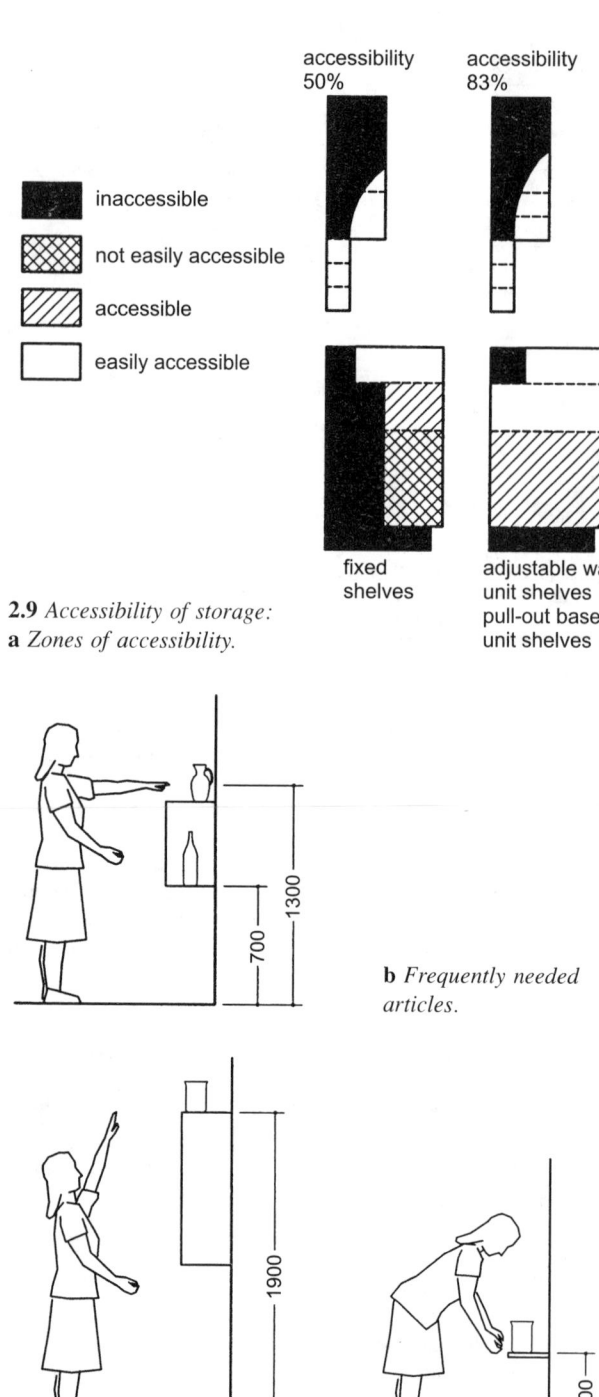

2.9 *Accessibility of storage:*
a *Zones of accessibility.*

b *Frequently needed articles.*

c *Less frequently needed articles higher*

d *Less frequently needed articles lower*

surface is the top of the keyboard) are available 30 mm lower. Chairs for sitting workers are now by legislation required to provide for vertical adjustment so that each individual can find the right relationship with the worktop. However, it is important that the feet remain in contact with the ground, and where this is not possible, footrests should be provided.

3.05 Computer work stations

Many office workers now work with visual display units (VDUs), and these introduce further requirements for comfortable and healthy working. People often find working at a screen tiring to the eyes. **2.8** gives the recommended dimensions for minimising fatigue; some people may need special spectacles. Most VDUs are placed at or above eye level so that normal bifocals do not help. Opticians are now used to supplying 'intermediate' spectacles with the normal bifocal facility for viewing the keyboard and material on the desk, with the upper part allowing focus on the near distance. This permits the VDU to be placed between 900 to 1000 mm distant from the user.

3.06 Storage

Two of the commonest operations at work and in the home is the stowage and retrieval of items into and from storage. **2.9** shows the recommended heights for various storage areas for general use; **2.10** gives particular requirements where elderly people are concerned.

3.07 Maintenance

Buildings and the services and plant therein need constant maintenance. Something frequently forgotten is the need for easy access to certain areas. It is reasonable to assume that people employed on maintenance work will be sufficiently agile and not greatly above average size. The dimensions shown in **2.11** to **2.18** are therefore less than would be required for use by the general public.

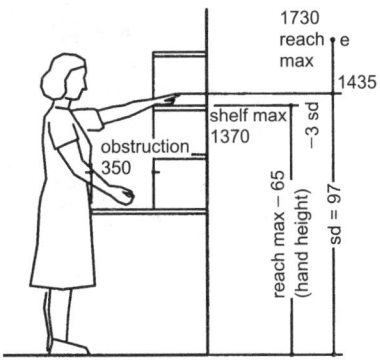

2.10 *Accessibility of storage used by elderly people:*
a *Maximum reach over worktop.*

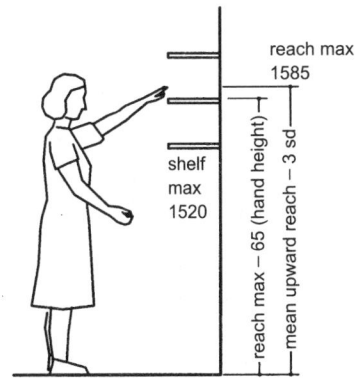

b *Maximum reach to unobstructed wall-mounted cupboard*

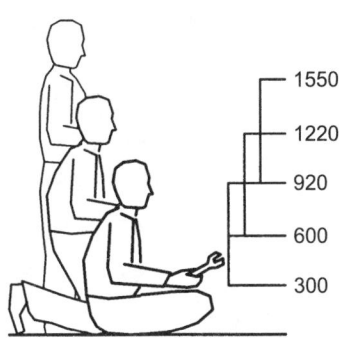

2.11 *Body clearance: maintenance reach levels*

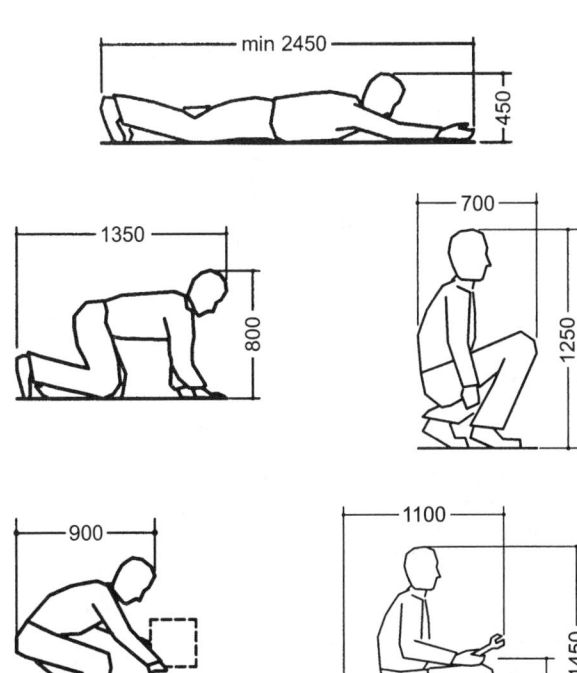

2.13 *Body clearances*

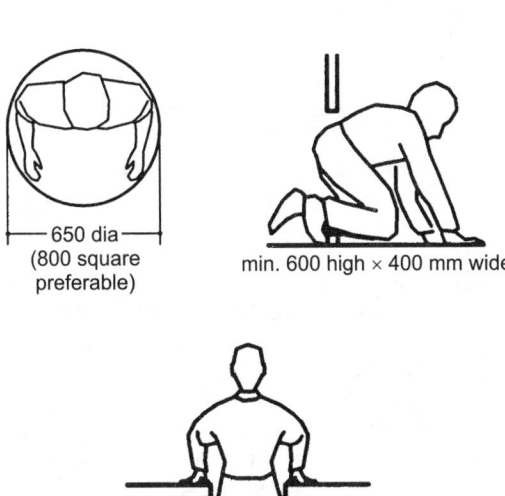

2.12 *Service accesses*

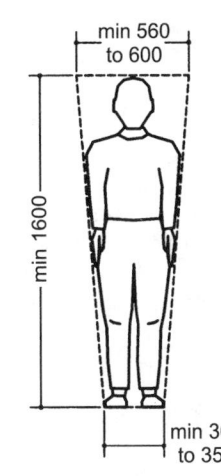

2.14 *Service access: catwalk*

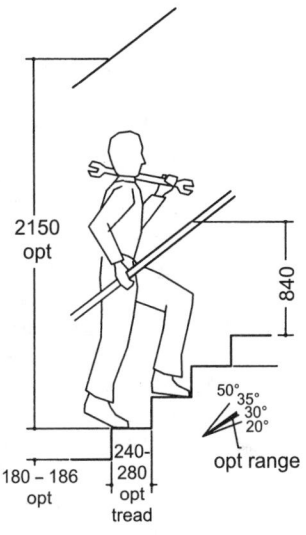

2.15 *Service access: stairs*

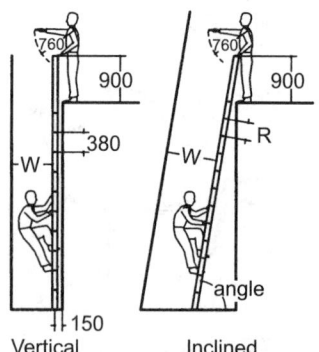

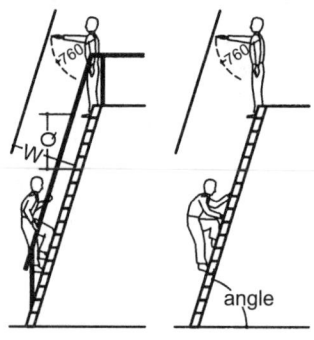

2.16 *Service access: ramps*

2.17 *Service access: step ladders*

recommended for angles 50° to 75°
handrails are required on both sides if risers are not
left open or if there are no side walls
widths: 500 mm to 600 mm with handrails
            600 mm min between side walls

angle	W(mm)	Q(mm)
50°−55°	1620°−1570°	880
57°−60°	1500°−1450°	900
63°−66°	1370°−1320°	910
69°−72°	1270°−1200°	920
74°−77°	1150°−1050°	950

recommended riser 180 mm to 250 mm
                 tread 75 mm to 150 mm
45 mm diam max for handrail

generally suitable for vertical movements
from 75° to 90° ladder frame should
extend 900 mm above platform
widths: 380 mm min, 450 mm desirable
            600 mm min between side walls
150 mm toe space

angle	R(mm)	W(mm)
75.0°	330	1150
78.0°	335	1050
80.5°	340	1000
83.0°	350	950
85.0°	360	900
87.5°	370	850
90.0°	380 max 300 min	800

provide back guard over 6000 mm high

2.18 *Service access: rung ladders*

4 DISABLED PEOPLE

4.01

At any one time about 8 per cent of people in Britain are in one way or another disabled. The principal disabilities of concern to the architect are those that mean the person has to use a wheelchair for most or all of the time. That person is handicapped by this in two significant ways: first, the eyes and arms are permanently at sitting rather than standing level, and second, the wheelchair itself takes up to five times the space needed by an ambulant person. While people in wheelchairs constitute only about one quarter of one per cent of the population, society has rightly decided that the design of most buildings should take their needs into account.

There are other forms of disability that are of importance to the building designer. People on crutches can be disadvantaged by ramps provided for wheelchairs, and all ramps should normally be paralleled by steps. Provision for blind people needs to be made in the design of signs, raised letters being preferable to Braille, particularly in lifts. Lifts should ideally provide audible as well as visual indication of floor level.

4.02 People in wheelchairs

Wheelchairs are of three main types:

- Manually self-propelled
- Propelled by motor
- Propelled by attendant

It is the manually self-propelled chair that is used by most active disabled people, and needs to be routinely catered for in buildings. **2.19** gives the dimensions relevant to this type of chair, and **2.20** and **2.21** has dimensions of men and women in such a chair.

4.03 Ramps

The most common provision made for wheelchairs is a ramp. However, most such ramps are difficult to use, both in mounting and in descending. Except for very short ramps (less than 0.5 m) they should be no steeper than 8 per cent (preferably 6 per cent) and unbroken lengths of ramp no longer than 10 m. For a rise of only 650 mm, therefore, a good ramp would take up a considerable area, **2.22**. The use of a chair lift or of ordinary lifts is therefore often preferable to a ramp, although these suffer from the need for adequate maintenance, and problems arise when they break down. Details of lifts designed for use by elderly and disabled people are given in Chapter 5.

4.04 Width of corridors

The other necessity for wheelchair users is adequate width and design of corridors and doorways. The width of a corridor should not be less than 900 mm for a self-propelled wheelchair, or 1.8 m if two wheelchairs are likely to want to pass each other, **2.23** to **2.26**.

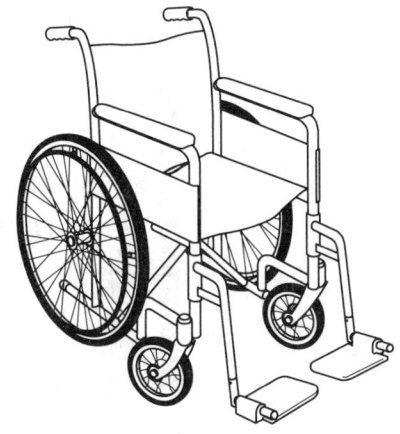

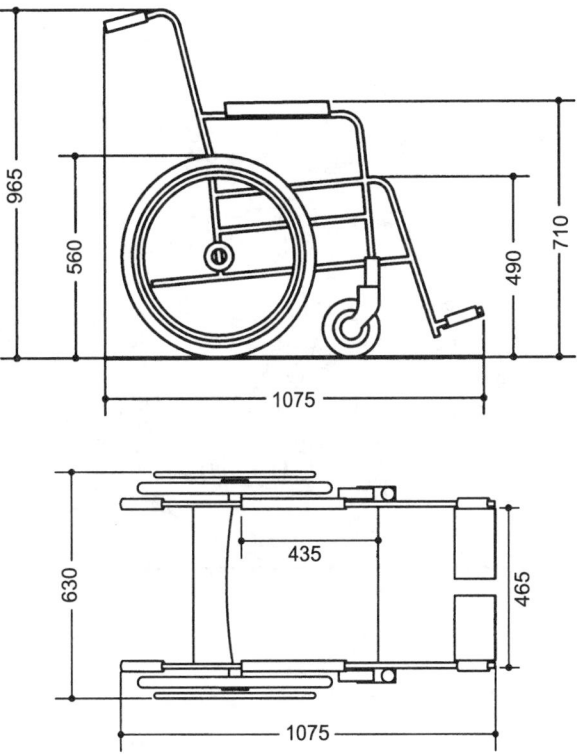

2.19 *DSS model 8G wheelchair, a common type*

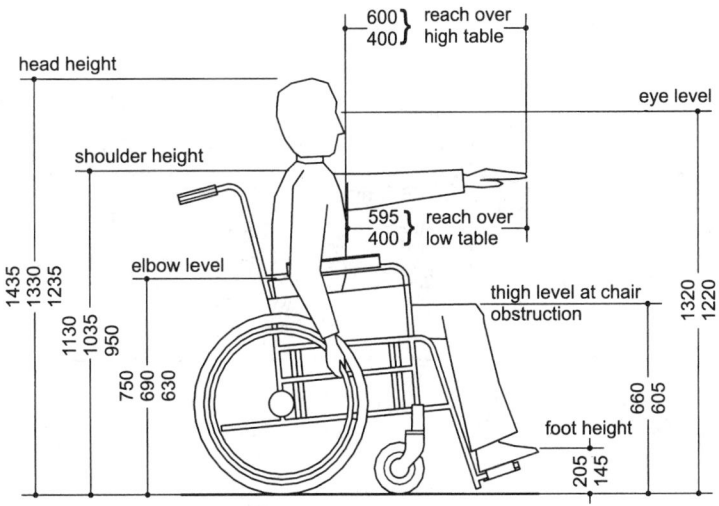

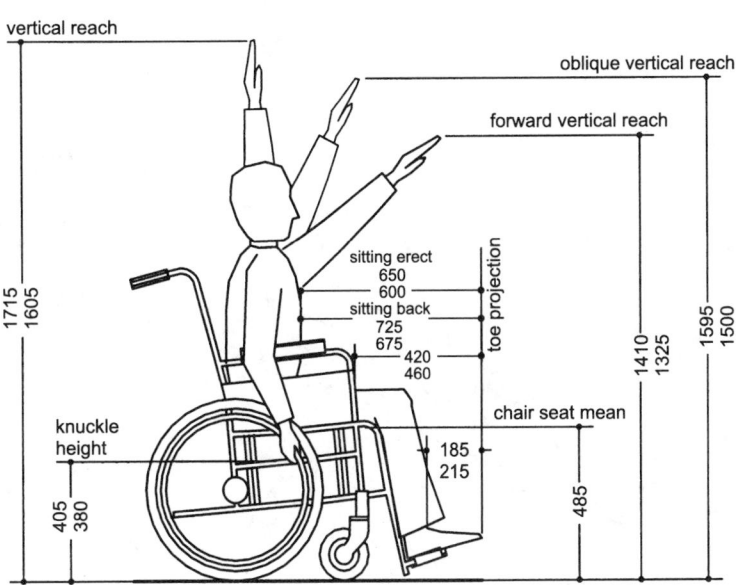

2.20 *Dimensions of different percentiles of adult male wheelchair users. These dimensions and those in* **2.21** *relate to people who use standard wheelchairs and have no major impairment of upper limbs. Figures are given for 95th, 50th and 5th percentiles or two of these*

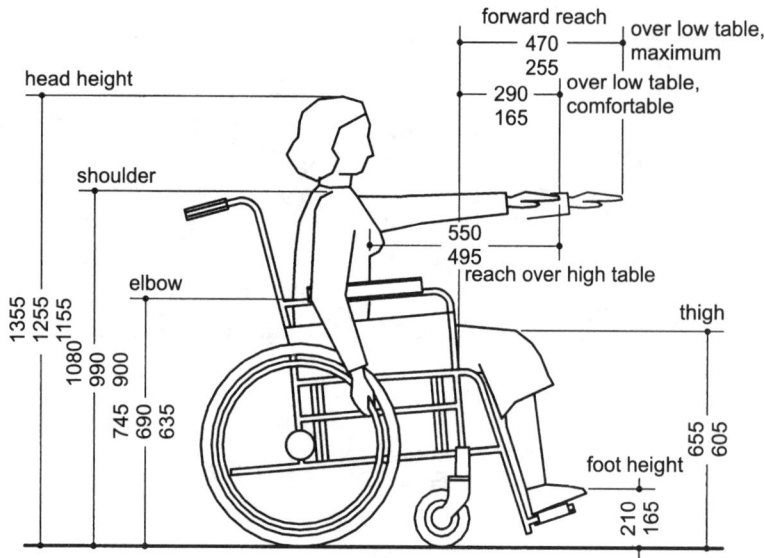

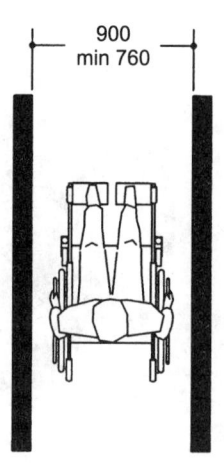

2.23 *Forward movement for self-propelled wheelchair*

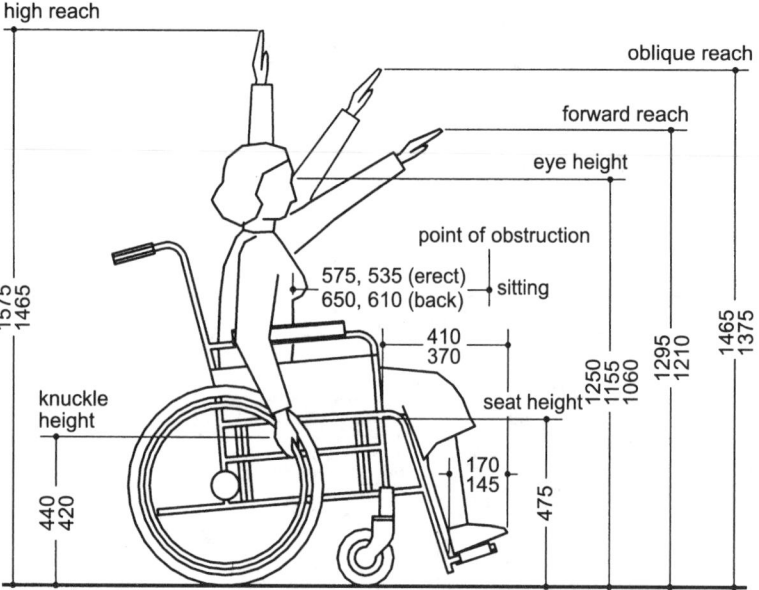

2.21 *Dimensions of adult female wheelchair users. Figures are given for 95th, 50th and 5th percentiles or two of these*

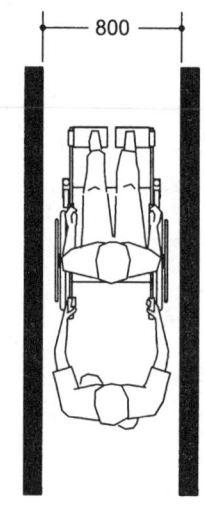

2.24 *Forward movement for wheelchair with attendant*

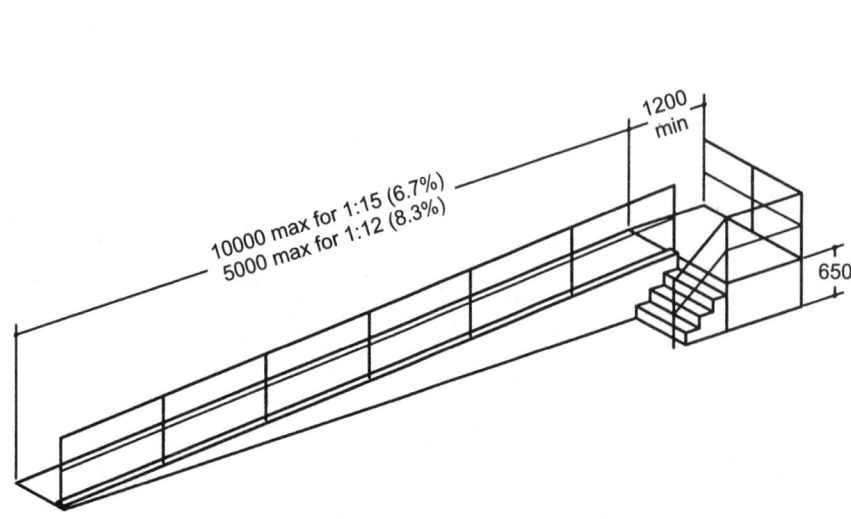

2.22 *Wheelchair ramp of rise 650 mm*

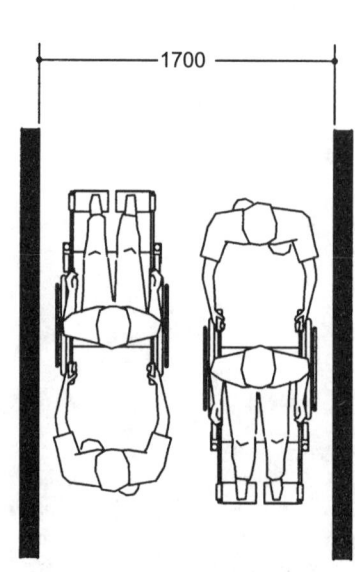

2.25 *Passing place for two wheelchairs with attendants*

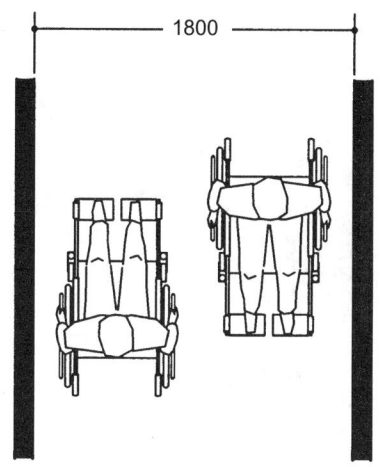

2.26 *Passing place for two self-propelled wheelchairs*

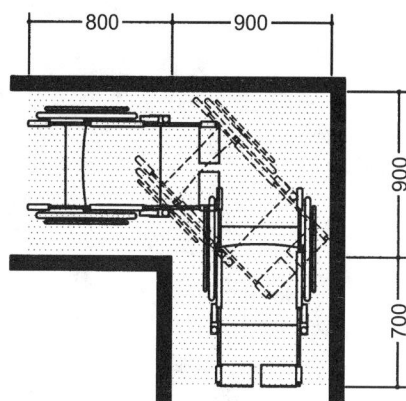

2.28 *Wheelchair forward turn through 90°*

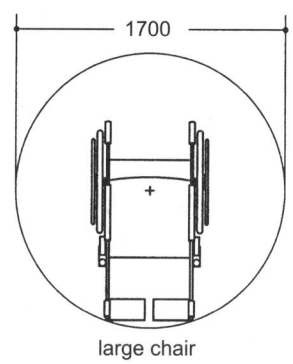

large chair

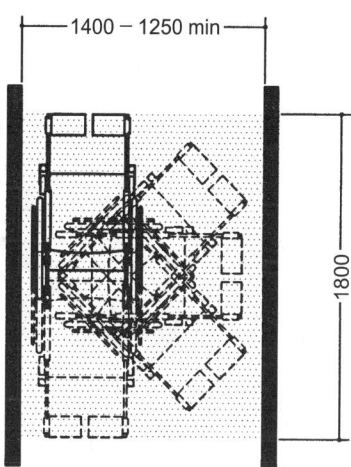

2.29 *Wheelchair turn through 180°*

4.05 Turning space

Most wheelchairs require a space 1.4 m square to turn around. This determines the minimum size of lift cars and circulation spaces in rooms.

Turning circles for manœuvering in various ways are shown in **2.27** to **2.29**.

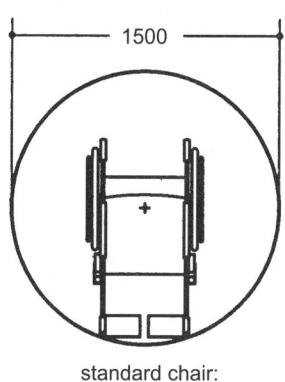

standard chair:
front propelling
wheels

4.06 Doorways

Since the minimum clear opening required is 750 mm, the standard 800 mm (coordinating size) doorset is not wide enough (clear opening 670 mm); a minimum 900 mm set should be used in most buildings. External doors should preferably be 1000 mm, although the 900 mm size has a clear opening just wide enough for most chairs. **2.30** illustrates wheelchairs using doorways.

Where a door opens off a corridor, it may be difficult for a wheelchair to turn sufficiently to go through a minimum width doorway unless the corridor is wide enough. **2.31** indicates preferred widths of opening for various corridor widths.

Where double or single swing doors are used these can be difficult for wheelchair users to open. In certain circumstances, sliding doors can be easiest and are often fitted in housing converted or specially built for wheelchair users.

In blocks of flats, offices, etc. the entrance doors are frequently heavy with strong springs to combat the effects of wind. These are not only difficult for wheelchair users, but often also for elderly, ambulant disabled and even people with prams. Consideration should be given to fitting such doors with mechanical opening and closing systems.

Other doors often give problems to people in wheelchairs and elderly people with limited strength. The doors to lavatories designed for disabled people can be particularly difficult. As a rule,

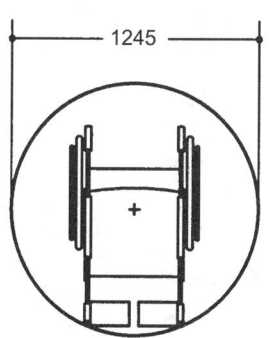

indoor chair: model 1
front propelling wheels

2.27 *Wheelchair turning circles*

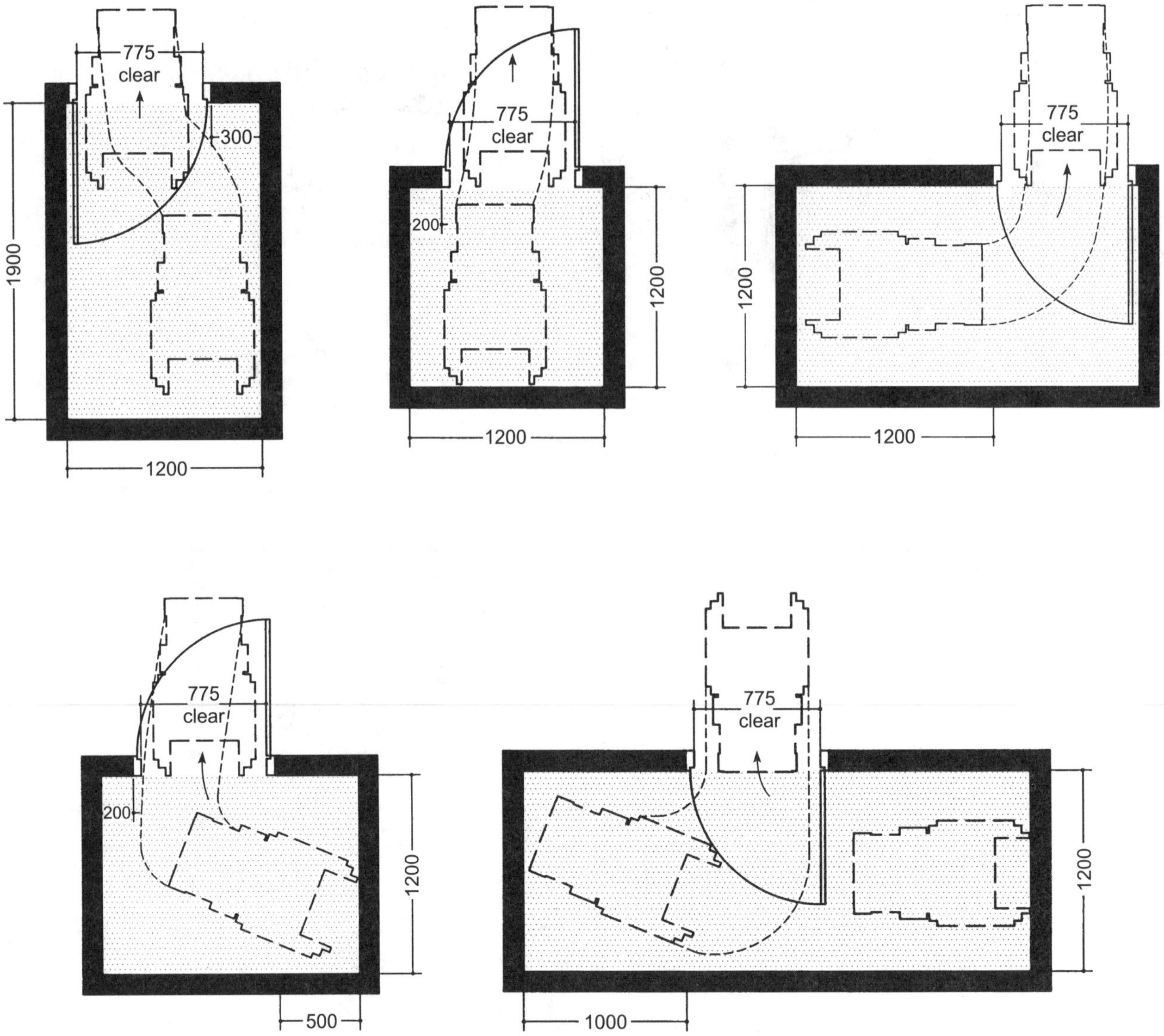

2.30 Wheelchairs negotiating various doorways

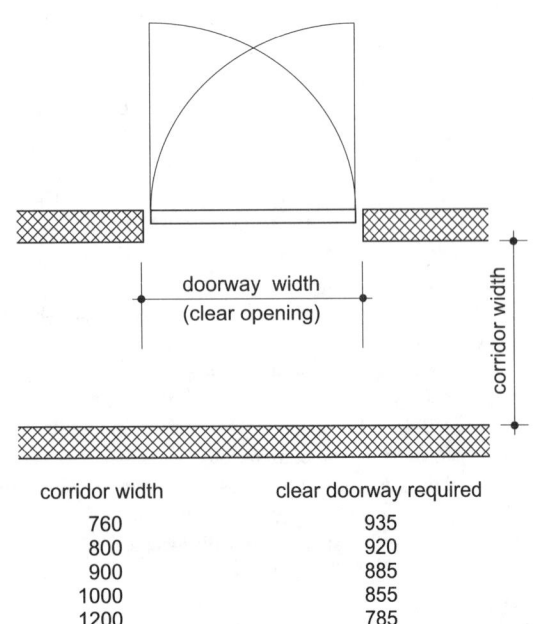

corridor width

doorway width
(clear opening)

corridor width	clear doorway required
760	935
800	920
900	885
1000	855
1200	785

2.31 Width of doorways opening off narrow corridors

the force required to open such a door should not exceed 35 N (based on a French standard).

4.07 People on crutches
2.32 gives generally accepted dimensions for a person using crutches. However, such people vary greatly. Most people use them for a short time following an accident, and will be inexpert in their use. Users fall into two broad groups: those who have some use of both legs and feet, and those who have use of only one leg. The former can usually negotiate most obstacles such as steps and staircases. However, those who can use only one leg require a handhold wherever there are steps, even a single step at a building threshold. There is little need for this to be provided for them on both sides as two good arms are needed to use crutches. However, elderly people may also need handholds, and many of these are only able to use one of their hands.

Crutch users often find ramps more of a problem than steps. Ideally, all wheelchair ramps should be adjacent to supplementary steps as in **2.22**.

4.08 People with other mobility impairments
Dimensions of people using walking sticks and walking frames are given in **2.33** and **2.34**.

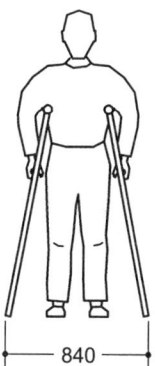

2.32 *Crutch user*

2.33 *Stick user*

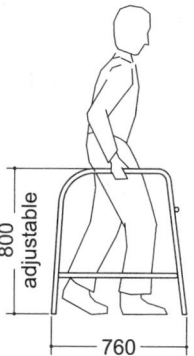

2.34 *Person using walking frame*

4.09 Large people

Pregnant women are not usually greatly disadvantaged except that stairs can be very tiring. There are a very small number of people who are so large that it is difficult to pass through a narrow doorway. A single door other than a cupboard should not be narrower than a 800 mm doorset with a clear opening width of 670 mm. In certain buildings such as football stadia, deliberately narrow doorways are used to ensure control over entry. In these cases, and also where turnstiles are used, additional provision for large people should be made.

Problems may also arise where there is fixed seating as, for example, in a theatre. A very small number of oversize seats or benches could be provided, or a loose seat of appropriate size could be used in a position normally occupied by a wheelchair.

5 CIRCULATION SPACES

5.01

Many aspects of internal circulation derive from regulations concerned with fire safety. These are covered in Chapter 42. Increasingly, others relate to the needs of disabled people.

For lifts and escalators see Chapter 5.

As a guide to assessing space allowances, the areas listed in Table VII may be used: these include requirements for both the activity and the associated circulation. Waiting areas are given in Table VIII and the flow capacities of corridors and staircases in Table IX.

5.02 Corridors

The properties of various corridor widths are shown in **2.35**. Some examples of space allowances from Germany are given in **2.36** to **2.39**. In **2.40** to **2.48** a variety of other corridor users are shown, and **2.49** details a number of obstructions commonly found in corridors, and for which additional width may need to be allowed for.

5.02 Internal stairs

Definitions of terms used in relation to staircases are shown in **2.50**. The preferred form and dimensions of steps for ambulant disabled and elderly people are shown in **2.51**. The formula for most staircases of twice the rise plus the going lies between 600 and 630 mm will give a suitable relationship. The rise should not exceed 190 mm, and the going should not be less than 250 mm.

Table VII Minimum areas per person in various types of buildings

Occupancy	Area per person (m²)
Assembly halls (closely seated)	0.46 m² (based on movable seats, usually armless, 450 mm centre to centre; with fixed seating at 500 mm centre to centre will increase to about 0.6 m²)
Dance halls	0.55 m² to 0.9 m²
Restaurants (dining areas)	0.9 m² to 1.1 m²
Retail shops and showrooms	4.6 m² to 7.0 m² (including upper floors of department stores except special sales areas)
Department stores, bazaars or bargain sales areas	0.9 m² (including counters, etc.) 0.46 m² (gangway areas only)
Offices	9.3 m² (excluding stairs and lavatories)
Factories	7 m²

Table VIII Area per person to be allowed in various circulation areas

Occupancy	Area per person (m²)
Overall allowance for public areas in public-handling buildings	2.3 to 2.8
Waiting areas, allowing 50 per cent seating, 50 per cent standing without baggage, allowing cross-flows (e.g. airport lounge)	1.1 to 1.4
Waiting areas, 25 per cent seating, 75 per cent standing, without serious cross-flows (e.g. waiting rooms, single access)	0.65 to 0.9
Waiting areas, 100 per cent standing, no cross-flows (e.g. lift lobby)	0.5 to 0.65
Circulating people in corridors, reduced to halt by obstruction	0.2
Standing people under very crowded conditions – acceptable temporary densities	Lift car capacities: 0.2 m² (four-person car); 0.3 m² (33-person car)

Table IX Flow capacities of corridors and staircases

General design purposes	0.8 m² per person
People moving at good walking pace (1.3 m/s)	3.7 m² per person
People moving at a shuffle (0.4 to 0.9 m/s)	0.27–0.37 m² per person
People at a standstill due to obstruction	0.2 m² per person

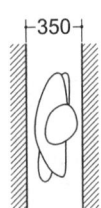

2.35 *Corridor widths.* **a** *Edging width: suitable for short distances or occasional use.*

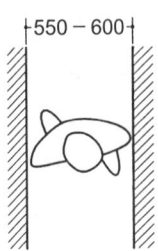

b *One person width (750 clearance would give comfort for various postures).*

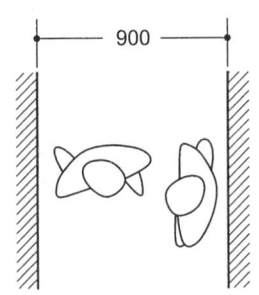

c *Normally used by one person, but occasional passing required.*

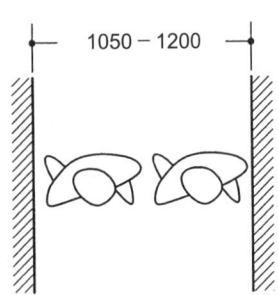

d *Two-person use in same direction.*

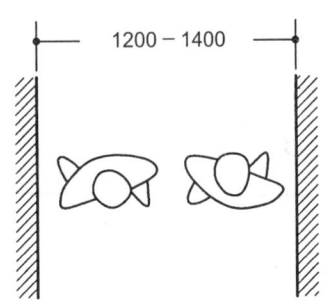

e *Two people passing*

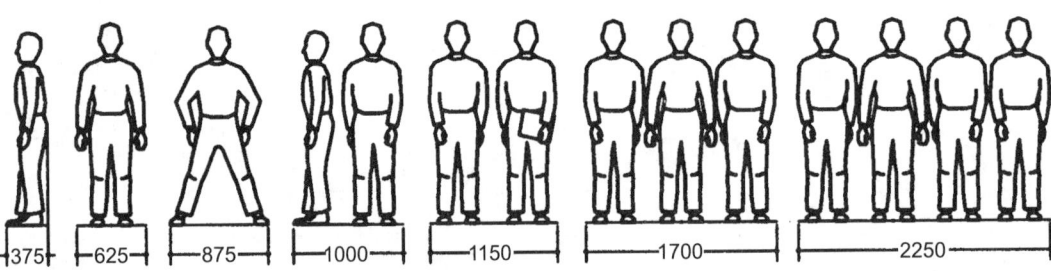

2.36 *Space requirements between walls allowing 10 per cent for easy movement*

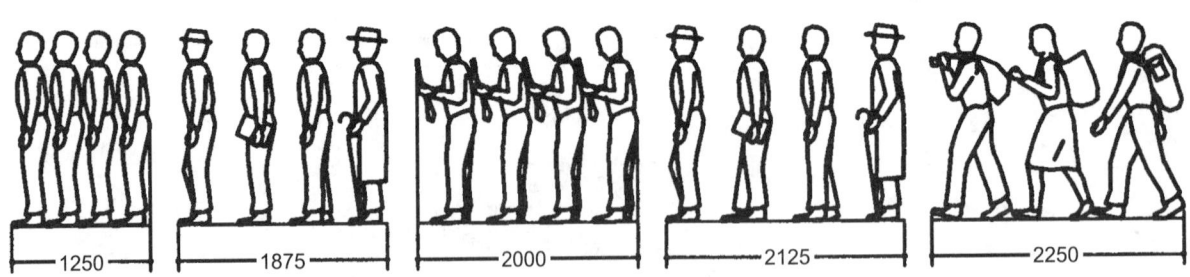

2.37 *Space requirements for closely spaced groups*

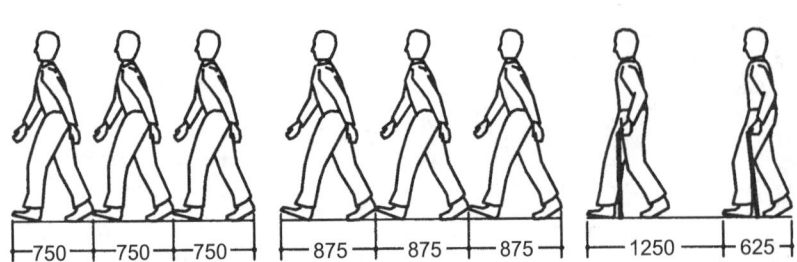

2.38 *Pace measurements*

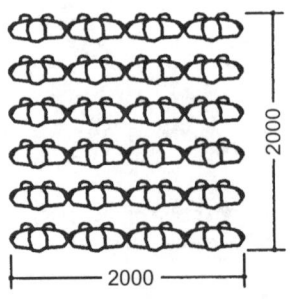

2.39 *Greatest density possible 6 people per m²*

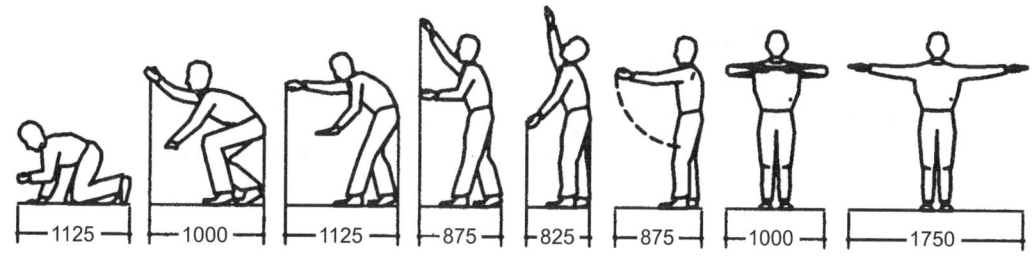

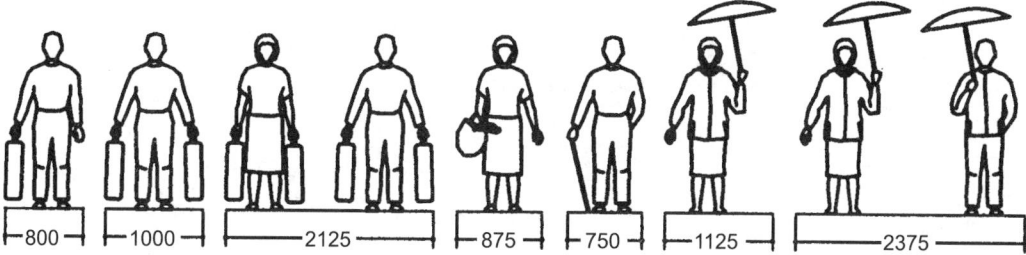

2.40 *Space for various body positions*

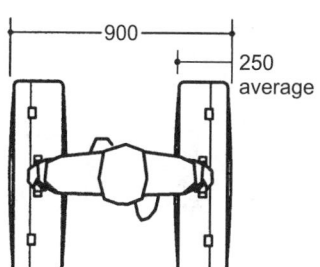

2.41 *Person with baggage*

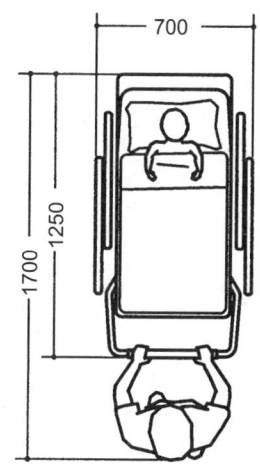

2.44 *Person with pram*

Type	L	W
Food (small)	600	450
Railway	1850	1100
Baggage (airport, hotel, etc.)	2500	800

2.46 *Person with trolley*

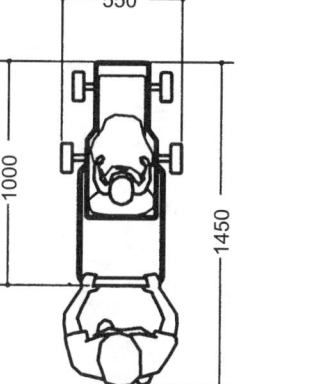

2.42 *Person with tray*

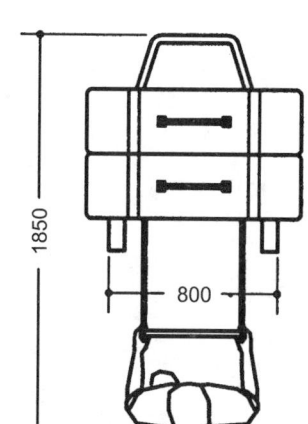

2.47 *Person with luggage trolley*

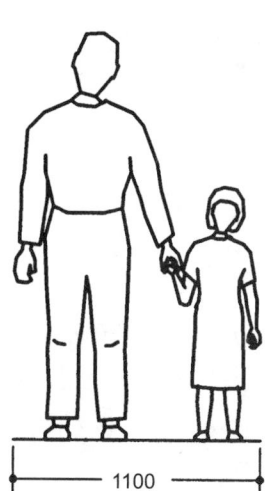

2.43 *Person with small child*

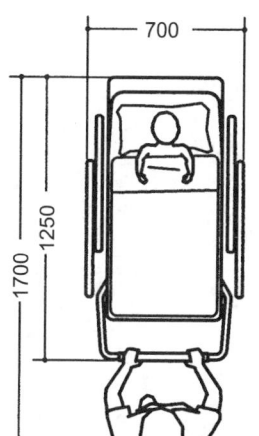

2.45 *Person with pushchair*

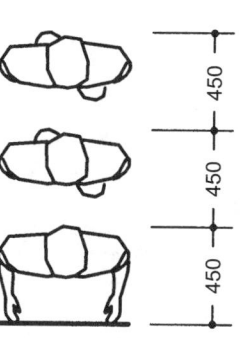

2.48 *Single queue no baggage*

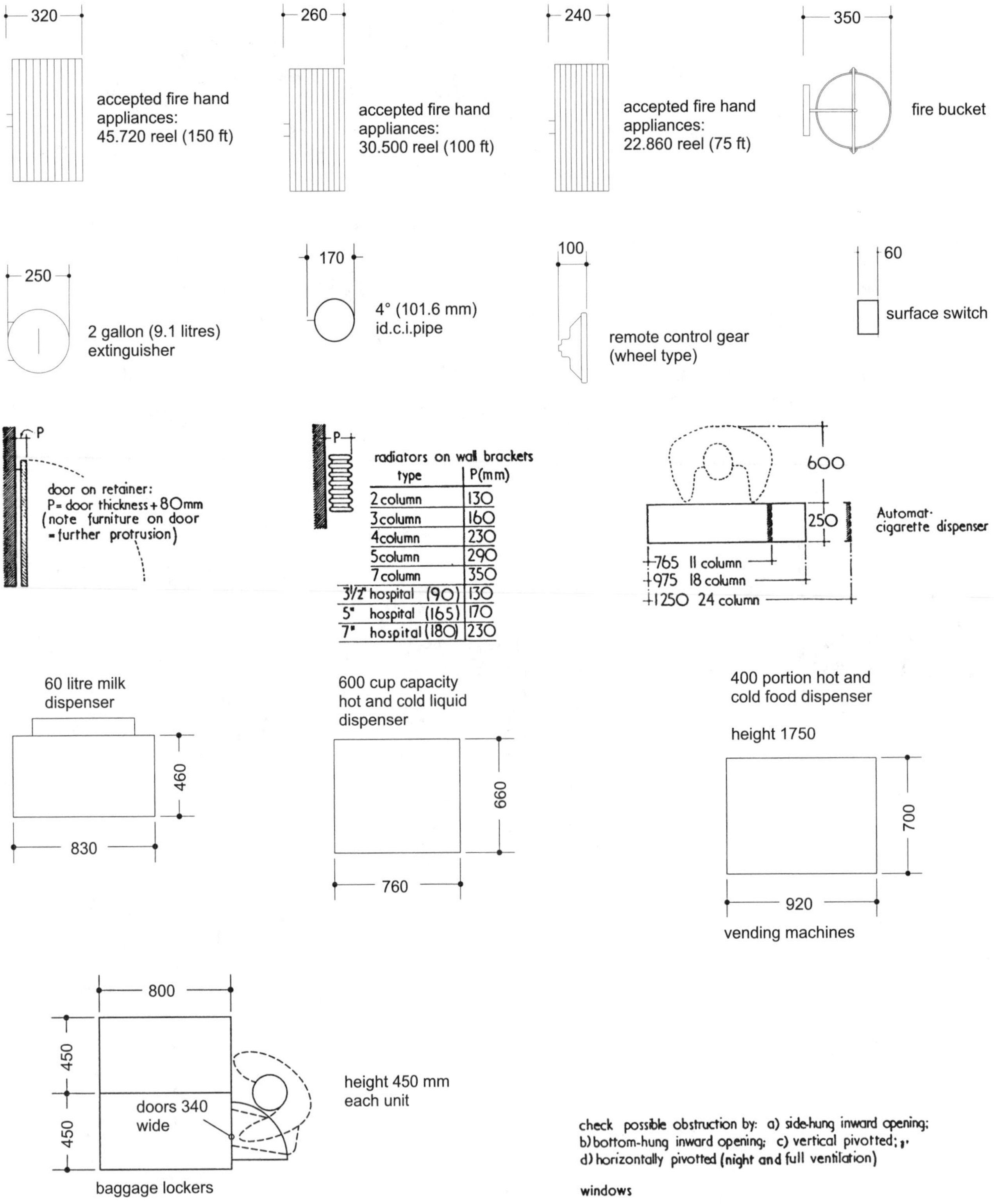

├── 320 ──┤

accepted fire hand
appliances:
45.720 reel (150 ft)

├── 260 ──┤

accepted fire hand
appliances:
30.500 reel (100 ft)

├── 240 ──┤

accepted fire hand
appliances:
22.860 reel (75 ft)

├── 350 ──┤

fire bucket

├── 250 ──┤

2 gallon (9.1 litres)
extinguisher

├ 170 ┤

4° (101.6 mm)
id.c.i.pipe

├ 100 ┤

remote control gear
(wheel type)

┤ 60 ├

surface switch

P

door on retainer:
P= door thickness + 80mm
(note furniture on door
= further protrusion)

radiators on wall brackets

type	P(mm)
2 column	130
3 column	160
4 column	230
5 column	290
7 column	350
3½" hospital (90)	130
5" hospital (165)	170
7" hospital (180)	230

600

250

Automat-
cigarette dispenser

765   11 column
975   18 column
1250 24 column

60 litre milk
dispenser

460

830

600 cup capacity
hot and cold liquid
dispenser

660

760

400 portion hot and
cold food dispenser

height 1750

700

920

vending machines

├── 800 ──┤

450

doors 340
wide

450

height 450 mm
each unit

baggage lockers

check possible obstruction by: a) side-hung inward opening;
b) bottom-hung inward opening; c) vertical pivotted; ,
d) horizontally pivotted (night and full ventilation)

windows

2.49 *Obstructions in corridors*

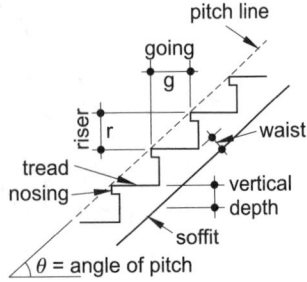

pitch line

going

g

riser r

waist

tread

nosing

vertical
depth

soffit

θ = angle of pitch

2.50 *Definitions of staircase terms*

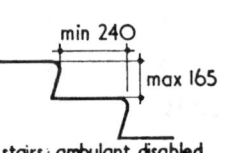

min 240

max 165

stairs: ambulant disabled

2.51 *Preferred form and dimensions of steps for elderly and
ambulant disabled people*

Table X Regulations for internal steps and staircases

Building Regulation		Maximum pitch	Minimum rise (mm)	Maximum rise (mm)	Minimum going (mm)	Maximum going (mm)	Minimum clear width (mm)	Maximum rise per flight
K1.3	Private stair	42°	155	220	220	260		
			165	200	223	300		
K1.3 B3.15	Institutional or assembly building with floor area less than 100 m²	35.7°	135	180	250	340	800 for 50 people 900 for 100 people	16 risers
K1.3 B3.15	Institutional and assembly stair	32.7°	135	180	280	340	1100 for 220 people plus 5 mm per person more than 220	
M2.21	Buildings in which provision for disabled people is mandatory	34.2°		170	250		1000	1800 mm
B2.30	Common stair	37.2°	150	190	250	320	1000*	
B2.30	Common stair also a firefighting stair	37.2°	150	190	250	320	1100*	
K1.3	Other	37.2°	150	190	250	320		

* Width in these cases may be encroached by stringers up to 30 mm and handrails up to 100 mm.

Table XI Design of staircases

This table is constructed on the following bases: Rise r is between 75 mm minimum and 220 mm maximum. Going g is greater than 220 mm minimum. In each box the figures represent: Twice the rise plus the going (2r + g) between 600 and 660 mm.
The angle of pitch (tan⁻¹ r/g) less than 40° and more than 30°. Shaded boxes indicate pitch angles greater than 35° which are less suitable for elderly and disabled people

Floor-to-floor	No of risers	rise r	Going g 220	230	240	250	260	270	280	290	300
2500	13	192.3		615 40.0°	625 38.7°	635 37.6°	645 36.5°	655 35.5°			
	14	178.6				607 35.5°	617 34.5°	627 33.5°	637 32.5°	647 31.6°	657 30.8°
	15	166.7						603 31.7°	613 30.8°	623 29.9°	
2600	13	200.0			640 39.8°	650 38.7°	660 37.6°				
	14	185.7		601 38.9°	611 37.7°	621 36.6°	631 35.5°	641 34.5°	651 33.6°	661 32.6°	
	15	173.3				597 34.7°	607 33.7°	617 32.7°	627 31.8°	637 30.9°	647 30.0°
	16	162.5							605 30.1°		
2700	14	192.9		616 40.0°	626 38.8°	636 37.7°	646 36.5°	656 35.5°			
	15	180.0			600 36.9°	610 35.8°	620 34.7°	630 33.7°	640 32.7°	650 31.8°	660 31.0°
	16	168.8					598 33.0°	608 32.0°	618 31.1°	628 30.2°	
	17	158.8							598 29.6°		
2800	14	200.0			640 39.8°	650 38.7°	660 37.6°				
	15	186.7		603 39.1°	613 37.9°	623 36.8°	633 35.7°	643 34.7°	653 33.7°		
	16	175.0				600 35.0°	610 33.9°	620 32.9°	630 32.0°	640 31.1°	650 30.3°
	17	164.7						599 31.4°	609 30.5°	619 29.6°	
2900	15	193.3		617 40.0°	627 38.8°	637 37.7°	647 36.6°	657 35.6°			
	16	181.2			602 37.1°	612 35.9°	622 34.9°	632 33.9°	642 32.9°	652 32.0°	
	17	170.6					601 33.3°	611 32.3°	621 31.4°	631 30.5°	
	18	161.1							602 29.2°		
3000	15	200.0			640 39.8°	650 38.7°	660 37.6°				
	16	187.5		605 39.2°	615 38.0°	625 36.9°	635 35.8°	645 34.8°	655 33.8°		
	17	176.5				603 35.2°	613 34.2°	623 33.2°	633 32.2°	643 31.3°	653 30.5°
	18	166.7						603 31.7°	613 30.8°	623 29.9°	

Building Regulations allow that twice the rise plus the going may be between 550 and 700 mm, and permits rises of up to 220 mm and goings of minimum 220 mm in private stairs. One Continental source recommends that twice the rise plus the going should lie between 630 and 660 mm.

Table X summarises the various statutory requirements for internal staircases. Table XI covers the design of common types of staircases. External stairs and steps should not be designed to internal standards, as they will often appear to be precipitous. See Chapter 6 for these.

2.52 to **2.57** show examples of different types of staircases, and **2.58** illustrates the moving of a wardrobe up a typical stair.

5.03 Handrails and balustrades

All staircases and steps should have handrails. If the staircase is less than 1 m wide they are not mandatory on both sides, but should if possible be so provided to allow for arthritic hands. The top of the handrail should be between 900 and 1000 mm above the pitch line,

and of a design to facilitate proper gripping. It is important, particularly for users of crutches, that they should extend at least one tread depth beyond the last riser at both top and bottom of each flight. In a multi-flight staircase, the handrails should be as continuous as possible to assist blind people; they will deduce that a break in the rail indicates a doorway or other way off the stairs.

Where there are likely to be small children, an additional handrail at about 425 mm high may be provided. Care should be taken to avoid designs that facilitate climbing over balustrades.

Open wells should be protected by walls or balustrades at least 900 mm high.

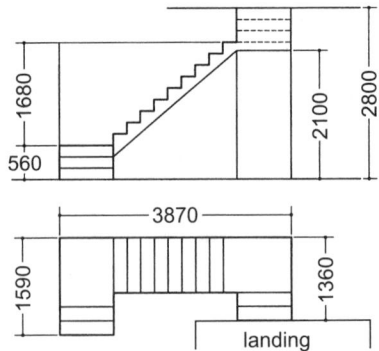

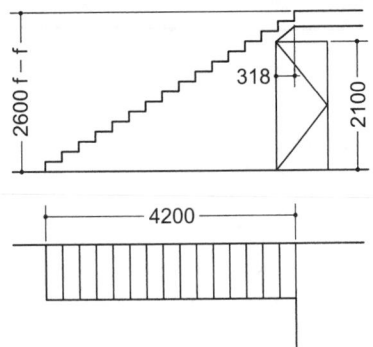

2.52 *Straight flight staircase*

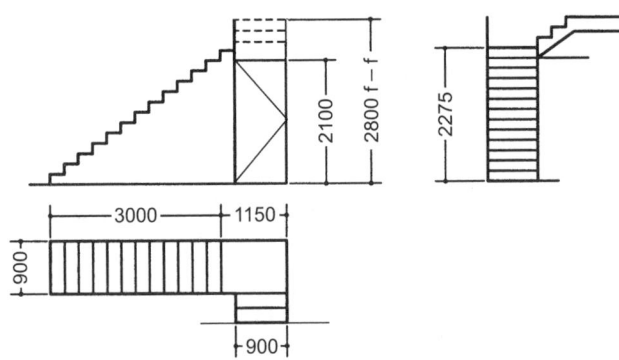

2.53 *Staircase with a short L at the top*

2.55 *Staircase with short Ls at top and bottom*

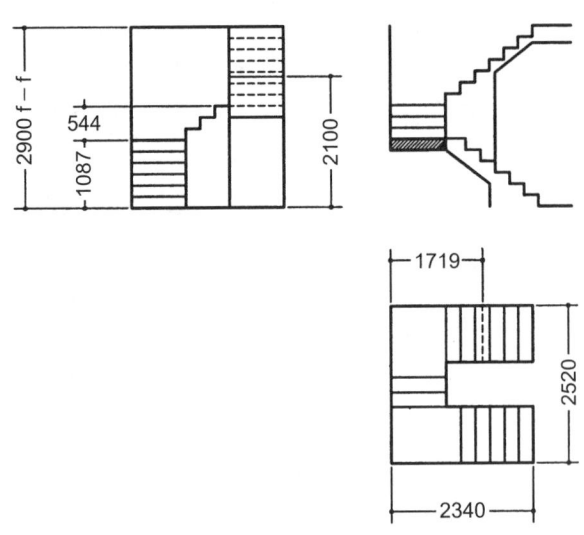

2.56 *Staircase around a square well*

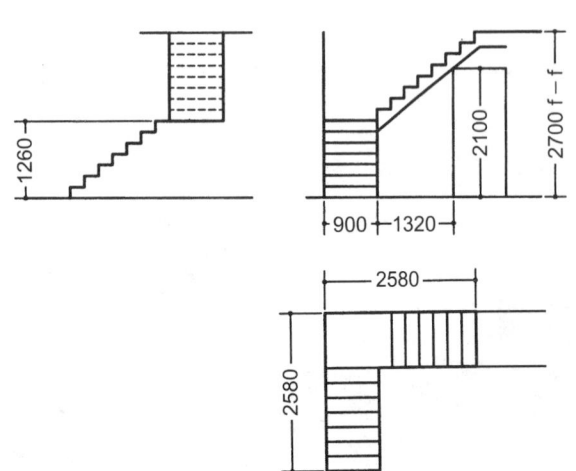

2.54 *Staircase with with 90° turn at half-height*

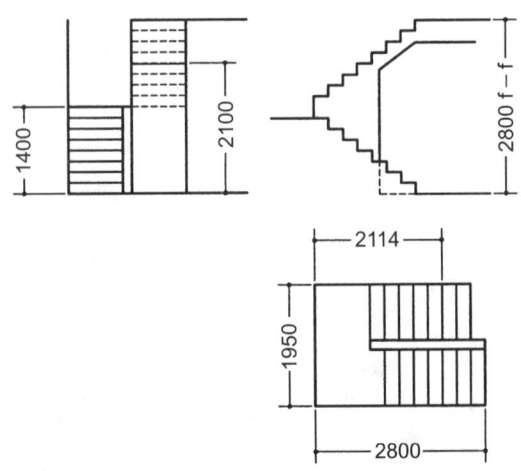

2.57 *Dog-leg staircase*

6 ACTIVITIES

2.59 to **2.71** illustrate the space requirements of a number of domestic activities; these are derived from data in *Activities and spaces* by John Noble.

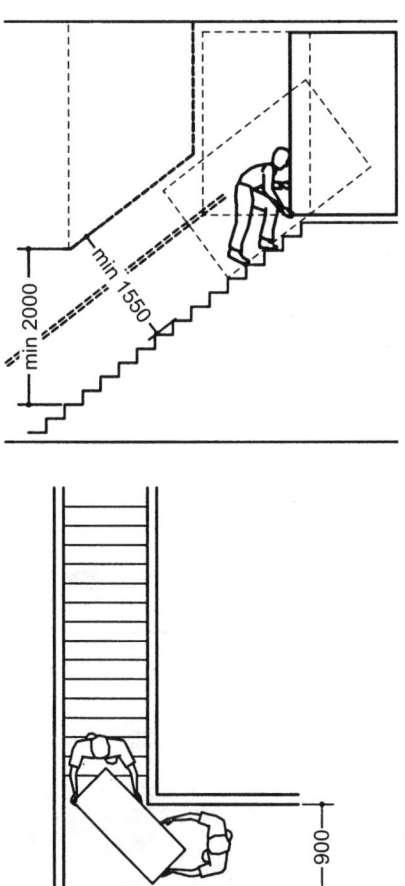

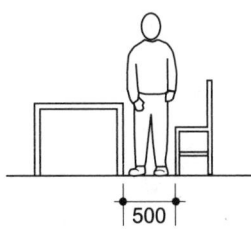

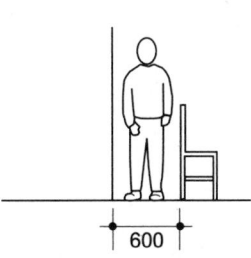

2.58 *Moving a double wardrobe up a staircase, showing minimum headroom, clearance, handrail height. Going 215 mm, rise 190 mm*

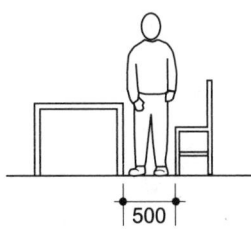

2.59 *Passing between two items of furniture, each table height or lower*

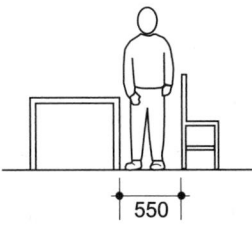

2.60 *Passing between two items of furniture, one table height or lower, the other higher on the wall*

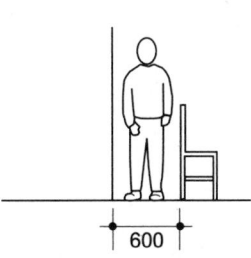

2.61 *Passing between the wall and tall furniture*

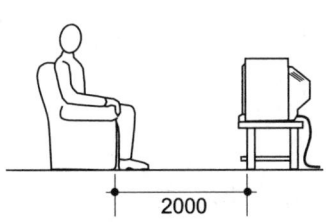

2.62 *Watching television. Most people prefer to sit a distance of more than eight times the height of the picture*

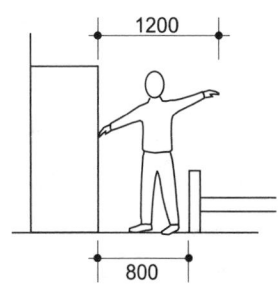

2.63 *Dressing in front of wardrobe*

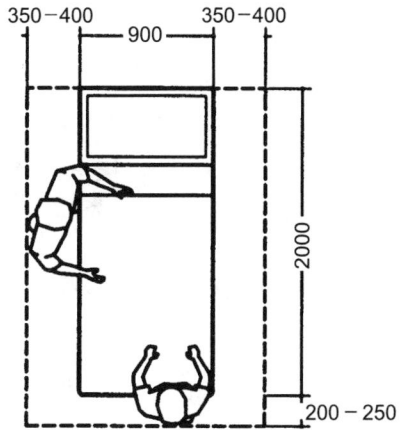

2.64 *Making single bed*

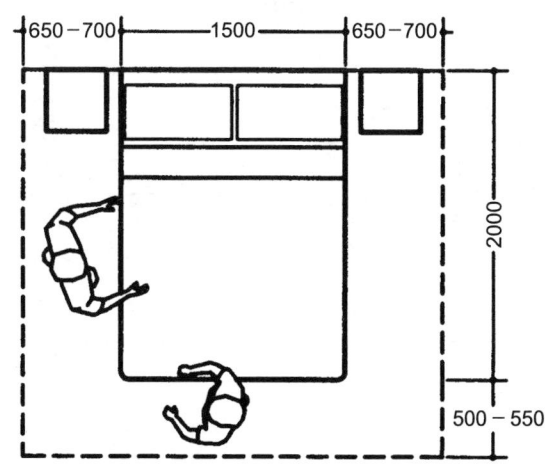

2.65 *Making double bed*

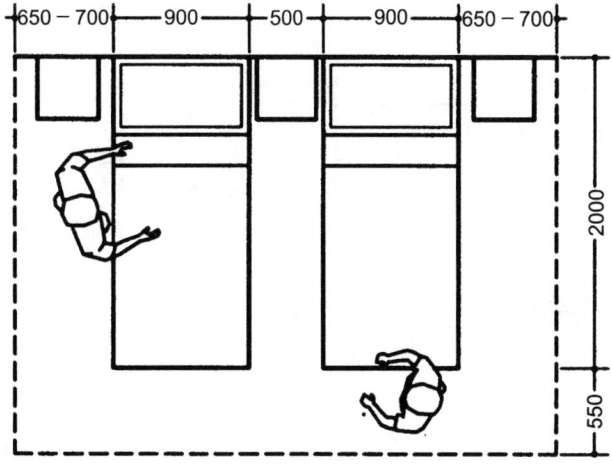

2.66 *Circulation around twin beds*

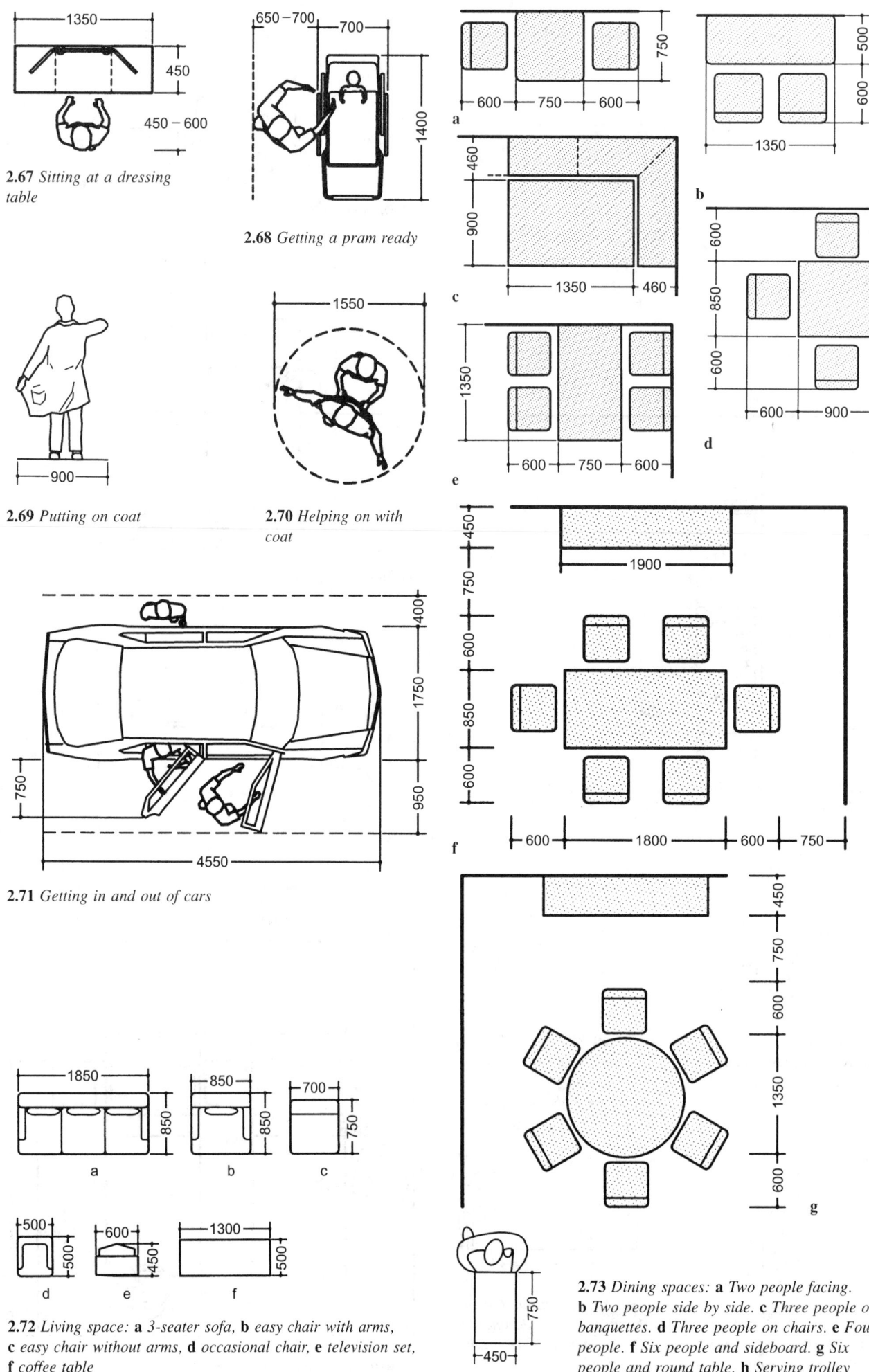

2.67 *Sitting at a dressing table*

2.68 *Getting a pram ready*

2.69 *Putting on coat*

2.70 *Helping on with coat*

2.71 *Getting in and out of cars*

2.72 *Living space: a 3-seater sofa, b easy chair with arms, c easy chair without arms, d occasional chair, e television set, f coffee table*

2.73 *Dining spaces: a Two people facing. b Two people side by side. c Three people on banquettes. d Three people on chairs. e Four people. f Six people and sideboard. g Six people and round table. h Serving trolley*

7 FURNITURE

The sizes of a number of common items of living room furniture are given in **2.72**. A number of different dining room arrangements are shown in **2.73**. Items of bedroom and kitchen furniture are covered in **2.74** and **2.75** respectively.

8 STORAGE

The spaces required to store domestic items and materials are shown in **2.76** to **2.88**. Various fuel storage facilities are covered in **2.89** to **2.91**, and refuse containers are shown in **2.92**.

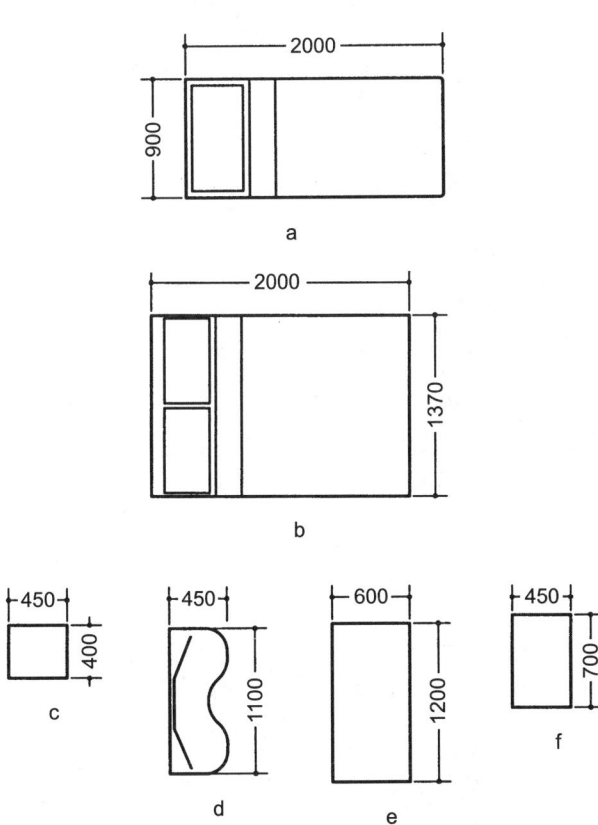

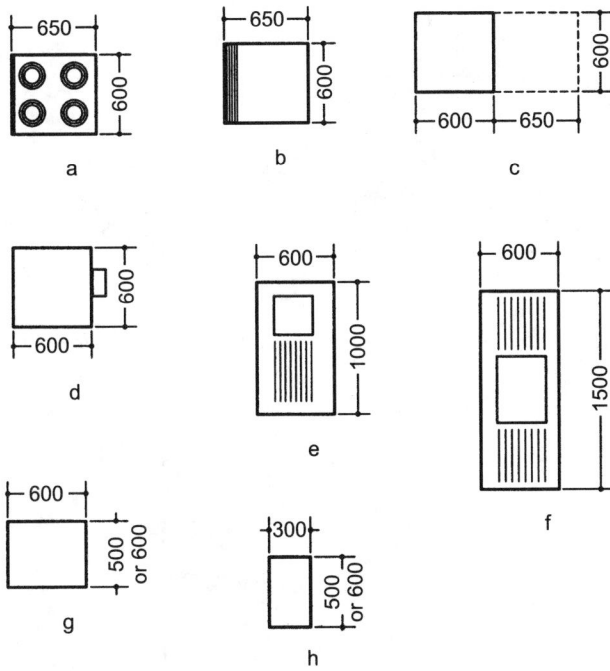

2.74 *Bedroom furniture:* **a** *single bed,* **b** *double bed,* **c** *bedside table,* **d** *dressing table,* **e** *wardrobe,* **f** *chest of drawers*

2.75 *Kitchen:* **a** *cooker,* **b** *fridge-freezer,* **c** *dishwasher,* **d** *washing machine,* **e** *sink with single drainer,* **f** *sink with double drainer,* **g** *large storage cupboard,* **h** *wall-hung storage cupboard*

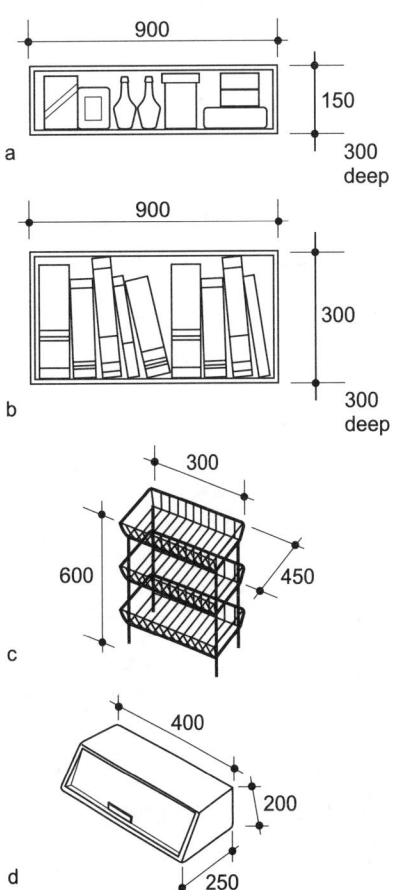

2.76 *Food storage:* **a** *tins and jars,* **b** *packets,* **c** *vegetable rack,* **d** *bread bin*

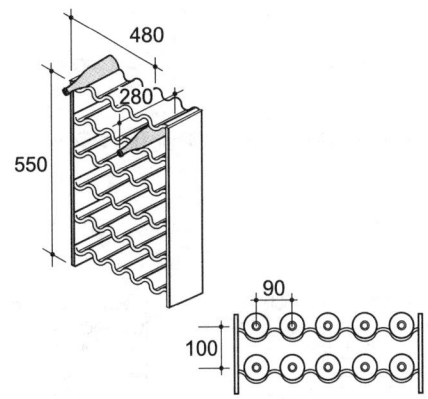

2.77 *Wine storage: a metal rack for 75 bottles*

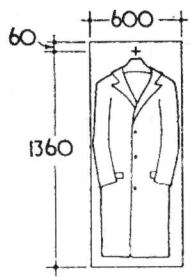

2.78 *Wardrobe for long coats and dresses*

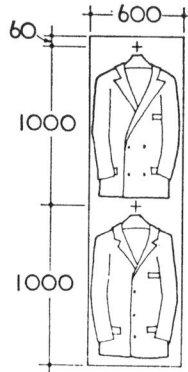

2.79 *Half-height hanging for jackets etc.*

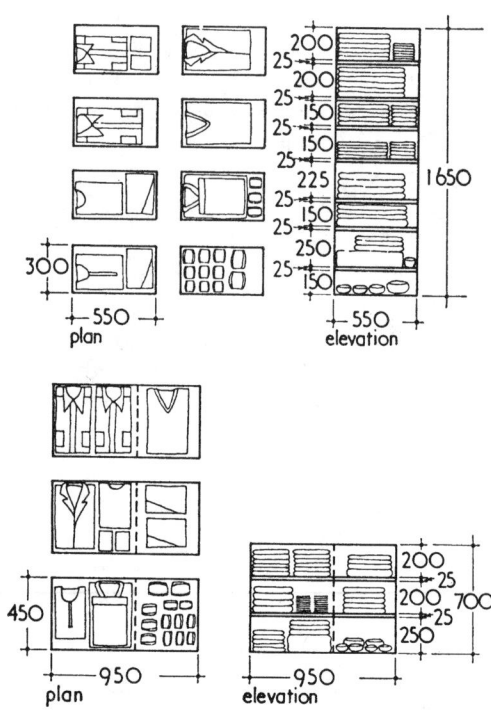

2.81 *Alternative storage arrangements for mens's clothing*

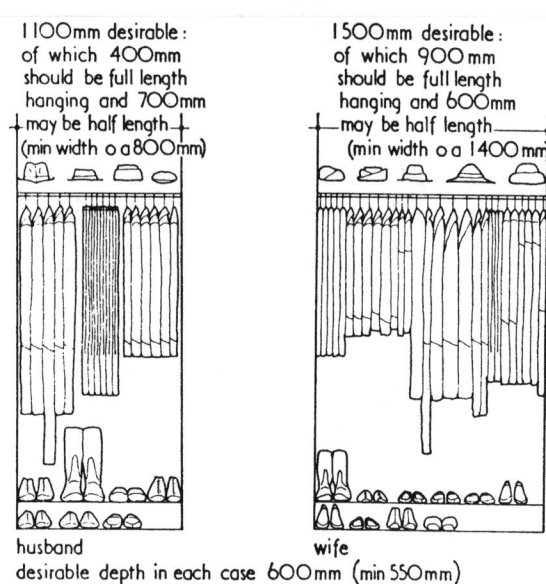

1100mm desirable:
of which 400mm
should be full length
hanging and 700mm
may be half length
(min width o a 800mm)

1500mm desirable:
of which 900mm
should be full length
hanging and 600mm
may be half length
(min width o a 1400mm)

husband

wife

desirable depth in each case 600mm (min 550mm)

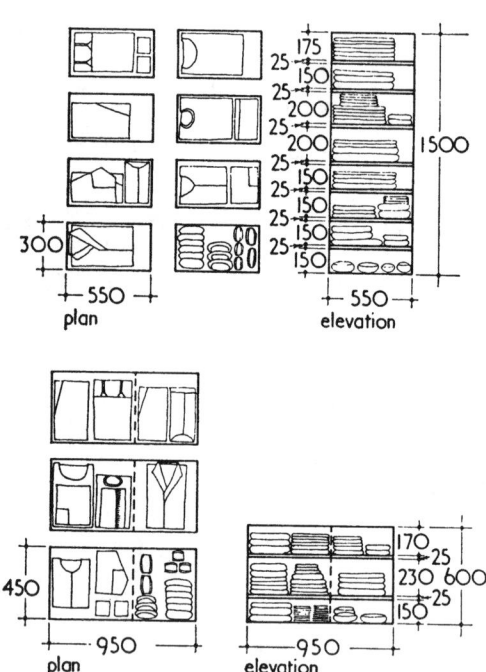

2.82 *Alternative storage arrangements for women's clothing*

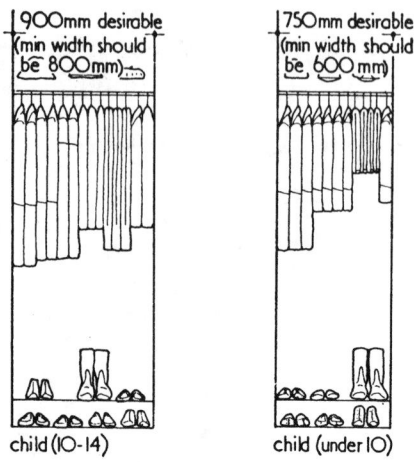

900mm desirable
(min width should
be 800mm)

750mm desirable
(min width should
be 600mm)

child (10-14)

child (under 10)

2.80 *Optimum hanging space for a family of four*

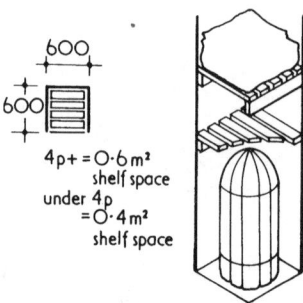

4p+ = 0·6 m²
shelf space
under 4p
= 0·4 m²
shelf space

2.83 *Airing cupboard for linen including hot water sotrage cylinder (not heavily lagged)*

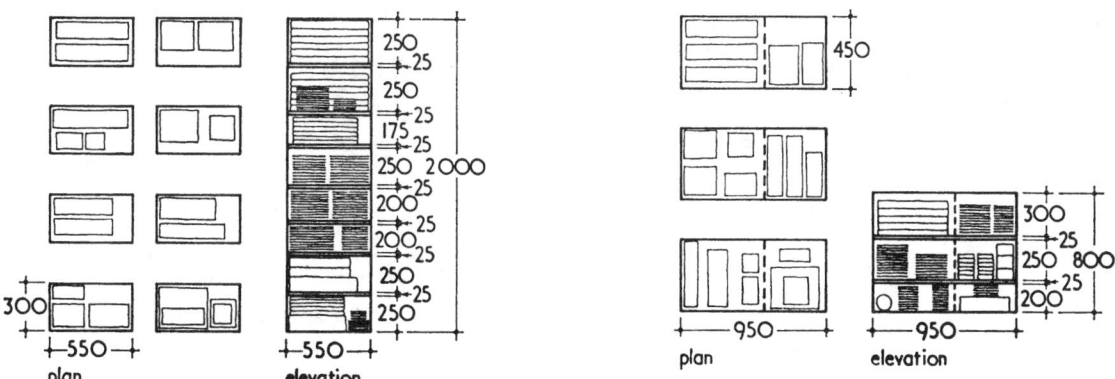

2.84 *Alternative storage arrangements for household linen for a five-person family*

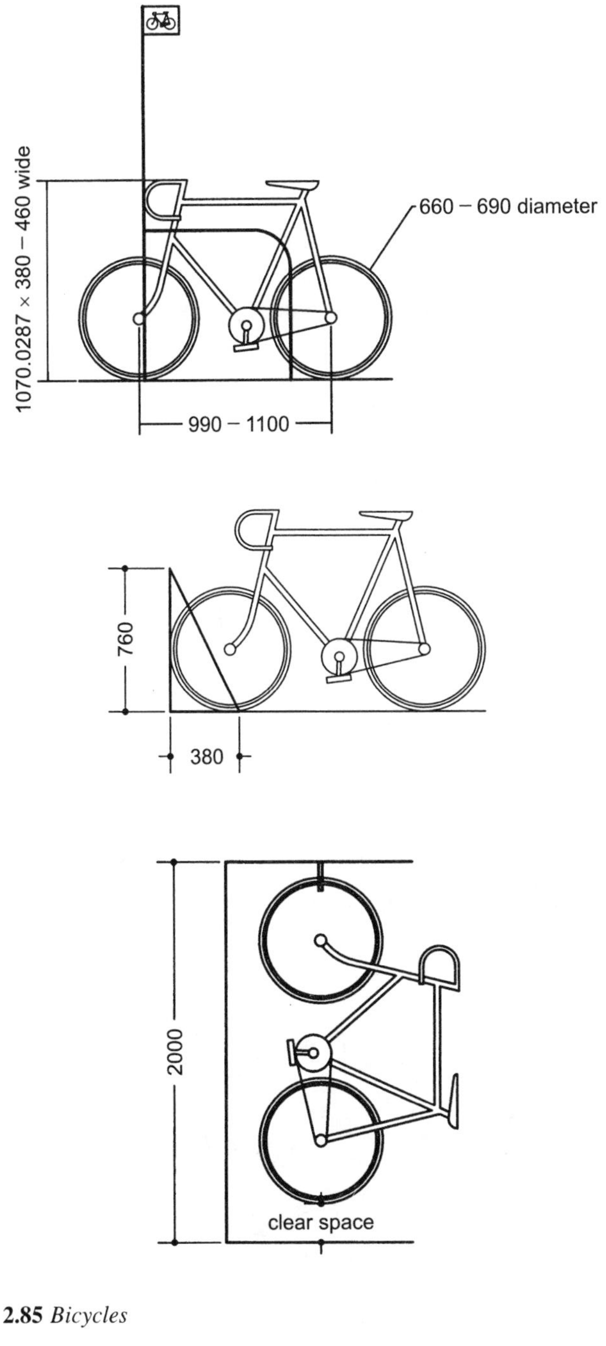

250
25
250
25
175
25
250 2000
25
200
25
200
25
250
25
250

300

550
plan

550
elevation

450

300
25
250 800
25
200

950
plan

950
elevation

1070.0287 × 380 − 460 wide

660 − 690 diameter

990 − 1100

760

380

2000

clear space

2.85 *Bicycles*

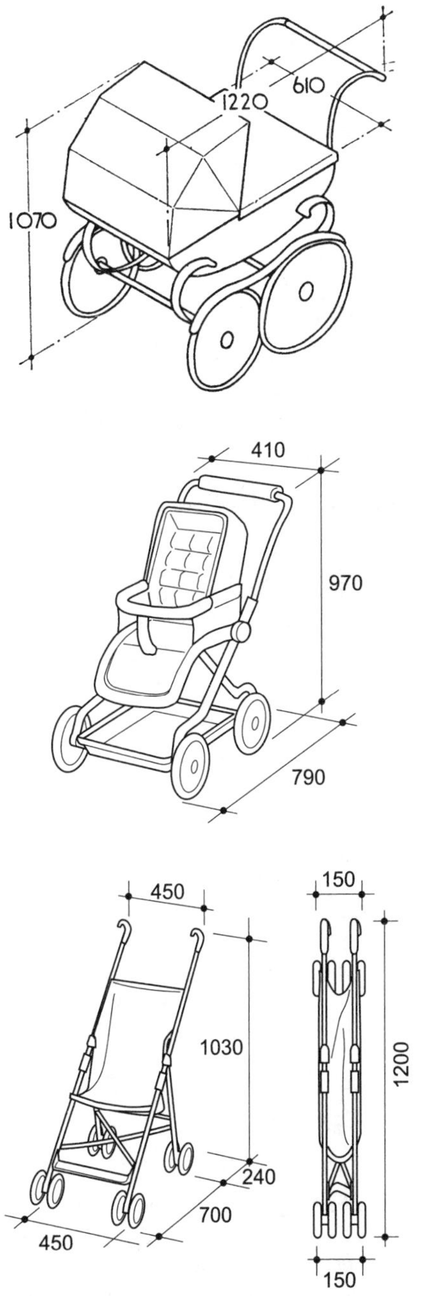

1220   610

1070

410

970

790

450

1030

240

700

450

150

1200

150

2.86 *Prams*

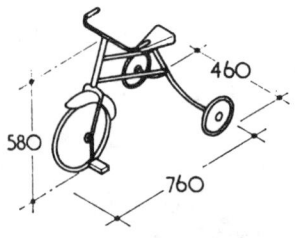
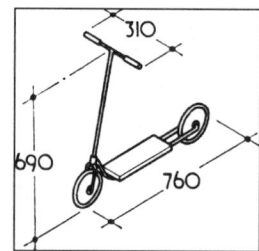

2.87 *Large toys*

capacity: 800 kg of coal and 450 kg of coke

2.91 *Solid fuel storage*

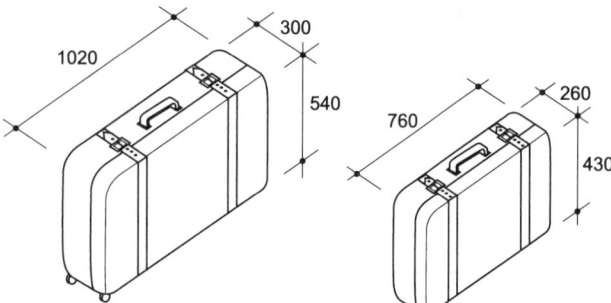

2.88 *Luggage*

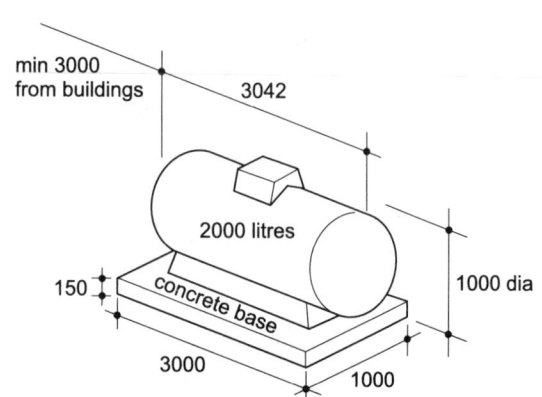

2.89 *Domestic gas storage for rural area (propane gas).*
Cylinders may now be buried if desired

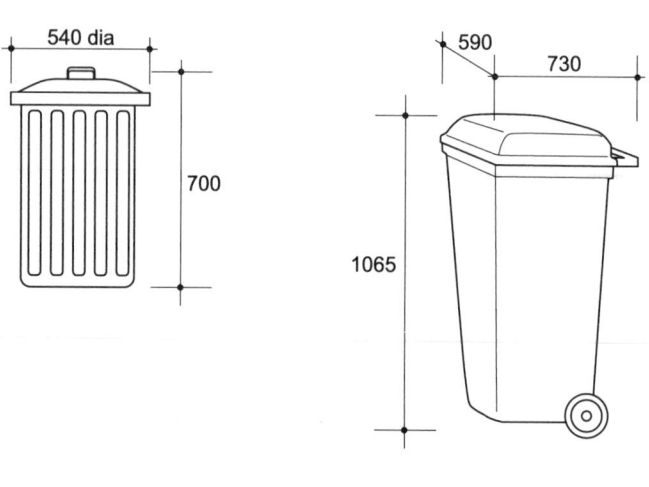

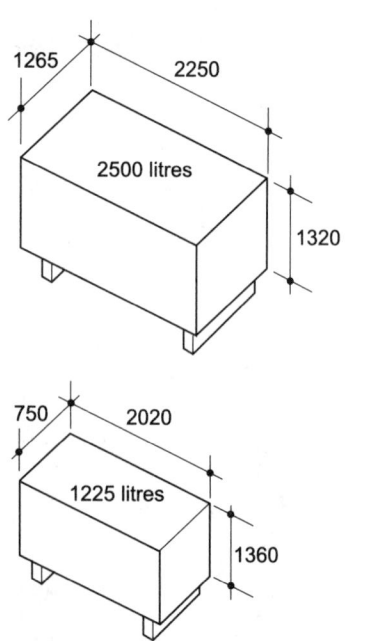

2.90 *Domestic oil storage tank. This may need a bund in certain*
circumstances. The oil flows to the boiler by gravity so the tank
bottom needs to be sufficiently elevated. If this is not possible
the fuel can be pumped, but the boiler must then be a pressure
jet type

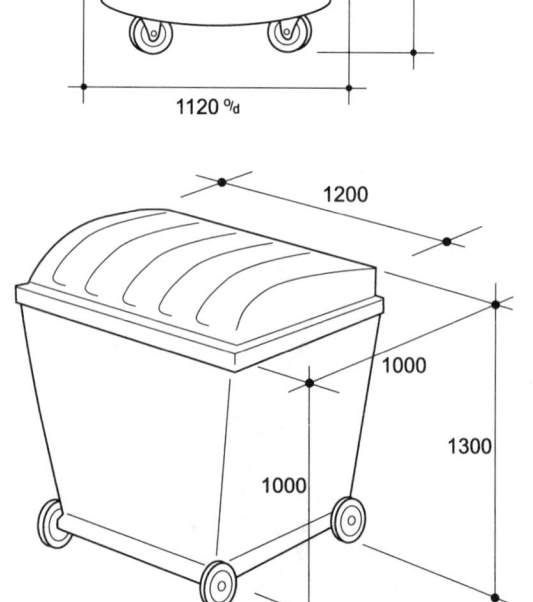

2.92 *Refuse storage:* **a** *dustbin,* **b** *wheely bin,* **c** *paladin bin,*
d *large bin*

9 REFERENCES

Official publications

The Building Regulations 1991, *approved document B, fire safety*, HMSO, 1992

The Building Regulations 1991, *approved document K, stairs, ramps and guards*, HMSO, 1992

The Building Regulations 1991, *approved document M, access and facilities for disabled people*, HMSO, 1992

British Standards

BS 4467:1991 *Guide to dimensions in designing for elderly people*, BSI, 1991

BS 5459 *Specification for performance requirements and tests for office furniture:*

   Part 1:1977 Desks and tables, BSI, 1977

   Part 2:1990 Office seating, BSI, 1990

BS 5619:1978 *Code of practice for design of housing for the convenience of disabled people*, BSI, 1978

BS 5810:1979 *Code of practice for access for the disabled to buildings*, BSI, 1979

BS 6180:1995 *Code of practice for barriers in and about buildings*, BSI, 1995

BS 7179:Part 5:1990 *Ergonomics of design and use of visual display terminals in offices, specifications for VDT workstation*, BSI, 1990

Other publications

PD 6523:1989 *Information on access to and movement within and around buildings and on certain facilities for disabled people*, London, BSI, 1989

Jane Randolph Cary, *How to Create Interiors for the Disabled*, New York, Pantheon Books, 1978

Niels Diffrient, Alvin R. Tilley and Joan C. Bardagjy, *Humanscale 1/2/3, a portfolio of information*, Cambridge Massachusetts, MIT Press, 1974

Henry Dreyfuss, *The Measure of Man, Human Factors in Design*, 2nd edn, New York, Whitney Library of Design, 1967

Selwyn Goldsmith, *Designing for the Disabled*, 3rd edn, London, RIBA, 1976

Ernest J. McCormick and Mark S. Sanders, *Human Factors in Engineering and Design*, 5th edn, New York, McGraw-Hill, 1982

John Noble, *Activities and Spaces, Dimensional Data for Housing Design*, London, The Architectural Press, 1983

Julius Panero and Martin Zelnik, *Human Dimension and Interior Space, A Source Book of Design Reference Standards*, New York, Whitney Library of Design, 1979

Stephen Pheasant, *Bodyspace, Anthropometry, Ergonomics and Design*, London, Taylor and Francis, 1986

Stephen Pheasant, *Ergonomics, standards and guidelines for designers*, London, BSI, 1987

Peter Tregenza, *The Design of Interior Circulation, People and Buildings*, London, Crosby Lockwood Staples, 1976

3 Sanitary installations and cloakrooms

Alan Tye Design Ltd

CI/Sfb: 94
UDC: 696.1

Alan Tye Design Ltd is a practice specialising in product design and architectural components

KEY POINTS:
- *women now demand parity with men: this means twice as many appliances for them*
- *unisex facilities providing for babies and small children are essential*
- *results of research into facilities for disabled people will cause further changes*

Contents

1 INTRODUCTION

1.01 Installation standards

Most sanitary installations are unsatisfactory. Professor Kira has emphasised two key factors:

- At the production end, there are no installation manufacturers, only material and appliance producers. Companies make dissimilar products such as dinner plates and WCs because they are ceramic, others make taps because they are metal and no one can conceive of an integrated entirety.
- Prefabricated or pre-assembled bathrooms can achieve far superior results than on-site work and is the best current method; but far more work is needed in the design of products and cleaning equipment.
- At the user end, the public are unaware of what to demand. Manufacturers do not know what the user needs as they sell through builders' merchants who somewhat arbitrarily decide and control what is to be sold.

Strong words, but in essence undeniably correct and one of the reasons why sanitary installations are so inadequate. Architects need to be much more critical and demanding about what manufacturers supply.

Public and semi-public conveniences are places where one is obliged to perform the most private functions in public with strangers of the same sex.

Quite different gangways are needed on a Tube train where to brush closely against Mr X is acceptable, as opposed to between two urinal rows where to brush against the same Mr X is almost criminal. Apart from the football club type of situation where camaraderie permits closeness or the traditional factory where closeness is born of economic necessity and lack of care, the fundamental point of planning spacing in public installations is that psychological not just physical clearances and spacing are required.

The purely physical and unacceptably tight spacing of proprietary sanitary wall systems naturally encourage users not to care about installations which are not really designed for them.

Certainly more design work is needed on this subject; for at the moment we generally both design and accept degrading and crude installations.

1.02 Types of installation

Installations can be:

1 Public conveniences, provided by municipalities, transport undertakings (including motorway service stations), shopping centres etc. Use of these facilities are generally open to any member of the public
2 Semi-public conveniences: theatres, stadia, refreshment houses, etc. where use is restricted to patrons of the provider
3 Private multi-use installations for staff in offices, factories, etc. and in hostels and old persons' homes
4 Domestic facilities.

All these will be covered in this chapter, although types 1 and 2 tend to differ only in superficial ways such as the standard and type of finishes.

1.03 Activity spaces

A number of different spaces are shown in the diagrams: space occupied by the appliance itself, additional space required by the user (the activity space), and further space required for luggage or circulation. In many cases these latter spaces may overlap on occasion. Common sense will dictate when this is appropriate, and when it is not.

2 NUMBERS OF APPLIANCES REQUIRED

The recommendations given in Tables I to XIII are derived principally from BS 6465: Part 1:1994, and are the minimum requirements.

In all situations, attention is drawn to the necessity to provide facilities for the disabled, baby changing and also for the disposal of sanitary towels and continence aids.

A common mistake is inadequate numbers of WCs for females, leading to long queues. Always err on the generous side.

Table XIV gives figures for various building types of the numbers of appliances to be provided for a total of 100 people evenly divided between the sexes. Toilets for wheelchair users are not included.

3 EARLY PLANNING

3.01 Guide to planning areas

In the previous edition of this book, if you wished to establish an overall sanitary installation area you could obtain the approximate size of an installation for any number of persons from a graph. This has not been included here, because:

- The numbers of items of equipment required in various building types has been significantly altered in the new edition of BS 6465, and, in particular

Table I Staff toilets in offices, shops, factories and other non-domestic premises used as place of work

Sanitary appliances for any group of staff		
Number of persons at work	Number of WCs	Number of washing stations
1 to 5	1	1
6 to 25	2	2
26 to 50	3	3
51 to 75	4	4
76 to 100	5	5
Above 100	One additional WC and washing station for every unit or fraction of a unit of 25 persons	

Alternative scale of provision of sanitary appliances for use by male staff only		
Number of men at work	Number of WCs	Number of urinals
1 to 15	1	1
16 to 30	2	1
31 to 45	2	2
46 to 60	3	2
61 to 75	3	3
76 to 90	4	3
91 to 100	4	4
Above 100	One additional WC for every unit or fraction of a unit 50 men provided at least an equal number of additional urinals are provided	

If public also use staff toilets, add 1 to each number of conveniences above

If work involves heavy soiling of hands and forearms	
Number of persons at work	Number of washing stations
1 to 50	1 per 10
more than 50	1 additional per 20 or part of 20

Table II Sanitary facilities for customers in shops and shopping malls having a net sales area more than 1000 m² and assuming equal numbers of male and female customers

Sales area of shop	Appliances	Male	Female
1000 m² to 2000 m²	WC	1	2
	Urinal	1	Nil
	Wash basin	1	2
	Toilet for disabled people	1 unisex	
	Baby-changing facilities	1 unisex *not* in disabled toilet	
2001 m² to 4000 m²	WC	1	4
	Urinal	2	Nil
	Wash basin	2	4
	Toilet for disabled people	1 unisex	
	Baby-changing facilities	2 unisex	
Greater than 4000 m²	In proportion to the size of the net sales area		

Table III Sanitary provision in restaurants, cafés, canteens and fast food outlets assuming equal numbers of male and female customers

Appliances	For male customers	For female customers
WC	1 per 100 up to 400 males. For over 400 males, add at the rate of 1 per 250 males of part thereof	2 per 50 up to 200 females. For over 200, add at the rate of 1 per 100 females or part thereof
Urinal	1 per 50 males	–
Wash basin	1 per WC and in addition 1 per 5 urinals or part thereof	1 per WC
Toilet for disabled people	1 unisex compartment should be reasonably close by but may be shared by other facilities (such as shops)	
Bucket/cleaners' sink	Adequate provision should be made for cleaning facilities including at least one cleaners' sink	

Table IV Sanitary provision in public houses and licensed bars
Assume 4 persons per 3 m² of EDA (effective drinking area) and 75%/25% male/female in public houses without public music and singing licences, 50%/50% elsewhere.

Appliances	For male customers	For female customers
WC	1 for up to 150 males plus 1 for every additional 150 males or part thereof	1 for up to 12 females plus 1 for 13 to 30 females plus 1 for every additional 25 females or part thereof
Urinal	2 for up to 75 males plus 1 for every additional 75 males or part thereof	
Wash basin	1 per WC and in addition 1 per 5 urinals or part thereof	1 per 2 WCs
Toilets for disabled persons	1 unisex	
Bucket/cleaners' sink	Adequate provision should be made for cleaning facilities including at least one bucket/cleaners' sink	

Table V Sanitary provision in buildings used for public entertainment
Assume, unless otherwise indicated, equal numbers of male and female customers. In cinema, multiplexes etc. where use is spread over all the time the building is open, assume 75% of total capacity, otherwise use 100%.

Appliances	Males	Females
WC	In single-screen cinemas, theatres, concert halls and similar premises without licensed bars: 1 for up to 250 males plus 1 for every additional 500 males or part thereof	For single-screen cinemas, theatres, concert halls and similar premises without licensed bars: 2 for up to 40 females 3 for 41 to 70 females 4 for 71 to 100 females plus 1 for every additional 40 females or part thereof
Urinal	In single-screen cinemas, theatres, concert halls and similar premises without licensed bars: 2 for up to 100 males plus 1 for every additional 80 males or part thereof	
Wash basins	1 per WC and in addition 1 per 5 urinals or part thereof	1, plus 1 per 2 WCs or part thereof
Toilets for disabled people	1 unisex minimum	
Bucket/cleaner's sink	Adequate provision should be made for cleaning facilities including at least one cleaner's sink	

If premises include a licensed bar, additional provision as Table IV will be needed.

Table VI Sanitary provision in swimming pools
Assume 50% male and 50% female users.

Appliances	For bathers	
	Male	Female
WC	2 for up to 100 males plus 1 for every additional 100 males or part thereof	1 per 5 females for up to 50 females plus 1 for every additional 10 females or part thereof
Urinal	1 per 20 males	
Wash basin	1 per WC and in addition 1 per 5 urinals or part thereof	1, plus 1 per 2 WCs or part thereof
Shower	1 per 10 males	1 per 10 females
Toilets for disabled people	1 unisex minimum	

Toilets for spectators should be provided as Table V and for staff as Table I.

Table VII Sanitary provision in Stadia

	Urinals	WCs	Wash hand basins
Male	1 per 70 males	1 for every 600 males, but minimum of 2 per toilet area	1 per 300 males, but minimum of 2 per toilet area
Female		1 for every 35 females, but minimum of 2 per toilet area	1 per 70 females, but minimum of 2 per toilet area
For disabled people	Where there is provision for more than 10 spectators with disabilities, provide at least 2 suitable unisex compartments within 40 m travel distance. Generally 1 unisex special WC per 12–15 disabled spectators		

Table VIII Minimum sanitary provision in stadia for different male:female ratios

Capacity of stand/ area	Type of provision	Male:female ratio			
		90/10	85/15	80/20	75/25
500		450:50	425:75	400:100	375:125
	Male urinals	7	7	6	6
	Male WCs	2	2	2	2
	Male whbs	2	2	2	2
	Female WCs	2	3	3	4
	Female whbs	2	2	2	2
1000		900:100	850:150	800:200	750:250
	Male urinals	13	13	12	11
	Male WCs	2	2	2	2
	Male whbs	3	3	3	3
	Female WCs	3	5	6	8
	Female whbs	2	3	3	4
2000		1800:200	1700:300	1600:400	1500:500
	Male urinals	26	25	23	22
	Male WCs	3	3	3	3
	Male whbs	6	6	6	5
	Female WCs	6	9	12	15
	Female whbs	3	5	6	8
3000		2700:300	2550:450	2400:600	2250:750
	Male urinals	39	37	35	33
	Male WCs	5	5	4	4
	Male whbs	9	9	8	8
	Female WCs	9	13	18	22
	Female whbs	5	7	9	11
5000		4500:500	4250:750	4000:1000	3750:1250
	Male urinals	65	61	58	54
	Male WCs	8	8	7	7
	Male whbs	15	15	14	13
	Female WCs	15	22	29	36
	Female whbs	8	11	15	18

- The ratio of provision for women as against provision for men, plus the greater space required by them, means that in many cases the area of female installations needs to exceed considerably that for male installations, which tends to reverse what has been the case until now.
- BS 6465: Part 2 has recently been issued. This gives design sizes of appliances (which may not correspond exactly with sizes available from manufacturers), and also recommends activity and circulation dimensions.

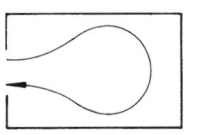 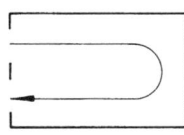 

3.1 *Circulation through sanitary installation*

These changes mean that there is no body of experience until a number of installations conforming to the new BS 6465 have been designed and built.

3.02 Planning the space
The planning of installations of types 1, 2 and 3 in **1.03** above requires sensitivity to the requirements of privacy and discretion. It is desirable that circulation of people through the sanitary area space is essentially one way, **3.1**. Single entry/exit plans can, however, work satisfactorily provided that the paths of users do not cross each other and the entry is wide enough. Placing the appliances in order of use simplifies circulation and reduces the distance walked. Hygiene should be encouraged by placing washing and drying facilities between the WC and/or urinal and the exit.

Vision is traditionally seriously considered in the planning of lavatories, although sound and odour are sources of considerable concern for many people and should also be considered, particularly in larger installations.

3.03 Vision
In larger installations, vision should be obstructed by the configuration of the entrance and in principle, entrance doors should be avoided, **3.2**. In smaller installations doors should open inwards and be hung so as to screen the appliances and the user as far as possible when opened. The doors to adjacent male and female rooms should not be close to each other as this is psychologically disturbing and aggravates vision problems. Consideration should also be given to positioning of mirrors and to the

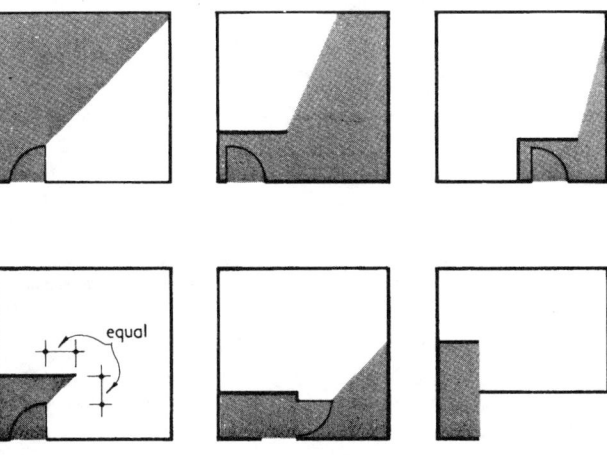

3.2 *Various screening arrangements for small installations, showing the area visible from outside in each case*

gap created by the hinges. Doors should be self-closing wherever possible.

3.04 Noise
It is difficult and costly to satisfactorily insulate lavatories acoustically and this problem should be tackled by planning isolation if possible.

3.05 Odour
Except in extremely well-naturally ventilated installations, some form of forced ventilation or air conditioning is desirable, particularly so in confined areas. Manually switched fans which continue to run for a set period after being switched off are useful in domestic situations.

3.06 Vandalism
No unsupervised installation can resist vandals. Even with the most vandal-resistant equipment (which would have to exclude all

Table IX Sanitary provision in schools

Type of school	Appliances	Number recommended	Remarks
Special	Fittings	1/10 of the number of pupils rounded up to the next nearest whole number	
	WC only	Girls: all fittings	
	Urinal and WC	Boys: not more than 2/3 of fittings should be urinals	
	Wash basin	As for secondary school	
	Shower	Although not required by statute, it is suggested that sufficient showers should be provided for physical education	
	Toilet for disabled person	At least 1 unisex depending on nature of special school	
	Bucket/cleaner's sink/slop hopper	At least one per floor	
Primary	Fittings	Aggregate of 1/10 of the number of pupils under 5 years old and 1/20 of the number of others. Not less than 4. Rounded up to the nearest whole number	
	WC only	Girls: all fittings	
	Urinal and WC	Boys: not more than 2/3 of fittings should be urinals	
	Wash basin	As for secondary school	
	Shower	Although not required by statute, it is suggested that sufficient showers should be provided for physical education	
	Toilet for disabled person	At least 1 unisex unless number of disabled pupils exceeds 10. Then provide 1 per 20 disabled pupils or part of 20	
	Bucket/cleaner's sink/slop hopper	At least one per floor	
Secondary	Fittings	1/20 of the number of pupils. Not less than 4. Rounded up to the nearest whole number	
	WC only	Girls: all fittings	
	Wash basin	1 in each washroom. At least 2 basins per 3 fittings	See clause 7
	Shower	As for primary school	
	Toilet for disabled person	As for primary school	
Nursery and play	WC	1 per 10 pupils (not less than 4)	
	Washbasins	1 per WC	See clause 7
	Sink	1 per 40 pupils	
Boarding	WC	1 per 5 boarding pupils	Where sanitary accommodation for day pupils is accessible to, and suitable for the needs of boarders, these requirements may be reduced to such an extent as may be approved in each case. See clause 7
	Wash basin	1 per 3 pupils for the first 60 boarding pupils; 1 per 4 pupils for the next 40 boarding pupils; 1 for every additional 5 boarding pupils;	
	Bath	1 per 10 boarding pupils	
	Shower	May be provided as alternative to not more than 3/4 of the minimum number of baths	
	Toilet for disabled person	As for primary school	

Table X Sanitary provision in dwellings

Type of dwellings	Appliances	Number per dwelling	Remarks
Dwellings on one level, e.g. bungalows and flats	WC	1 for up to 5 persons 2 for 6 or more	Except for single person's accommodation, where 1 WC is provided, the WC should be in a separate compartment. Where 2 WCs are provided 1 may be in the bathroom
	Bath/shower	1	
	Wash basin	1	
	Sink	1	
Dwellings on one or more levels e.g. houses and maisonettes	WC	1 for up to 4 persons 2 for 5 or more	Except for single person's accommodation, where 1 WC is provided, the WC should be in a separate compartment. Where 2 WCs are provided 1 may be in the bathroom
	Bath/shower	1	
	Wash basin	1	
	Sink	1	

For provision for disabled visitors see para. 4.06

Table XI Sanitary provision in accommodation for elderly people and sheltered housing

Type of accommodation	Appliances	Number per dwelling	Remarks
Self-contained for 1 or 2 elderly persons, or grouped apartments for 2 less-active elderly persons	WC	1	An additional WC may be provided in the bathroom.
	Bath/shower	1	Bathroom within apartment
	Wash basin	1	
	Sink	1	
Grouped apartments for less-active elderly persons	WC	1	
	Wash basin	1	
	Sink	1	
	Bath/shower	Not less than 1 per 4 apartments	Some may be Sitz baths or level access showers.
Additional provisions for communal facilities Common room for self-contained or grouped apartments	WC	1	Minimum number required. Should be available for use by visitors
	Wash basin	1	
The pantry or kitchen for self-contained or grouped apartments	Sink	1	Adjacent to common room
Laundry room for grouped apartment schemes	Sink	1	
	Washing machine	1	
	Tumble drier	1	
Cleaner's room	Bucket/cleaner's sink		1 in each cleaner's room

Table XII Sanitary provision in residential homes and nursing homes

Type of accommodation	Appliances	Number recommended	Remarks
Residents	WC	1 per 4 persons	An adjacent wash basin is also required
	Bath	1 per 10 persons	
	Wash basin	1 to each bedsitting room	
Staff	WC	At least 2 for non-residential staff	
	Wash basin	1	In WC compartment
Visitors	WC	1	
	Wash basin	1	In WC compartment
Kitchen	Sink	As appropriate	
Toilets for disabled people		A minimum of 1 depending on the number of disabled persons	
Cleaner's room	Bucket/cleaner's sink	1	In each cleaner's room
Other	Bed pan cleaning/disposal	As appropriate	Service area
	Wash basin	1	In each medical room, hairdressing, chiropodist, non-residential staff toilets and kitchen areas

Where en-suite facilities are provided, toilets for visitors and staff should also be provided.

Table XIII Sanitary provision in hotels

Type of accommodation	Appliances/facilities	Number required	Remarks
Hotel with en-suite accommodation	En-suite	1 per residential guest bedroom	Containing bath/shower, WC and wash basin
	Staff bathroom	1 per 9 residential staff	
	Bucket/cleaner's sink	1 per 30 bedrooms	At least 1 on every floor
Hotels and guest houses without en-suite accommodation	WC	1 per 9 guests	
	Wash basin	1 per bedroom	
	Bathroom	1 per 9 guests	Containing: bath/shower, wash basin and additional WC
	Bucket/cleaners' sink	1 per floor	
Tourist hostels	WC	1 per 9 guests	
	Wash basin	1 per bedroom or 1 for every 9 guests in a dormitory	
	Bathroom	1 per 9 guests	Containing: bath/shower, wash basin and additional WC
	Bucket/cleaners' sink	1 per floor	
All hotels	Toilet for disabled person	All hotels should provide at least 1 unisex compartment for disabled people	

Hotels incorporating other uses such as conference entertainment facilities, bars and restaurants may need additional provision as previous tables.

Table XIV Comparison of requirements in different buildings types for 100 people evenly divided between the sexes

	For men			For women	
	Urinals	WCs	WHBs	WCs	WHBs
Workplaces	2	3	3	3	3
Workplaces where more dirty conditions are met	2	3	5	3	5
Shop customers:					
1000–2000 m²	1	1	1	2	2
2000–4000 m²	2	1	2	4	4
Restaurants etc	1	1	2	2	2
Pubs etc.	2	1	2	3	2
Entertainment buildings	2	1	2	3	3
Swimming pools	3	2	3	10	6
Stadia	1	2	2	2	2
Schools:					
Special	3	2	2	5	2
Primary and secondary	1	1	2	2	2
Nursery	10 WCs and 10 WHBs for all				
Boarding	20 WCs and 30 WHBs for all				

ceramics) an unsupervised facility will inevitably become sub-standard. In such situations the use of an attendant will result in a high standard being maintained, possibly with reduced costs. A well-designed installation, easily kept clean, with an open layout, a high level of general lighting and robust equipment securely fixed will reduce the problem. Where vandal-resistant appliances are thought necessary, stainless steel is considerably less prone to damage than ceramics, but all designs should allow for individual items to be replaced. Pipework, traps, cisterns, electrical supplies, etc. should all be fully concealed and this is, of course, also highly desirable for hygiene and appearance. The modular plastic panel is not desirable in areas likely to be vandalised.

3.07 Ducts

As it is equally unacceptable to have pipes inside a room or outside it, ducts are an inevitable detail of sanitary installations. Although pipes are frequently buried into wall structures, notably in Germany where appropriate pipework fittings exist, the UK situation is that we consider access is needed to critical points such as traps and cisterns. To achieve this access, ducts may be walk-in or have access from one or other sides. For hygiene, cleaning maintenance, structural soundness and planning flexibility, plan **3.3** is superior to **3.4**.

Although if the appliance could be part of the wall, plan **3.4** would be very useful, in practice this plan usually results in the adoption of a standard ceramic appliance on a sheet plastic panel with its attendant impractical problems, details and module (which, in addition, seldom correctly relate to required activity spaces or correct operational heights).

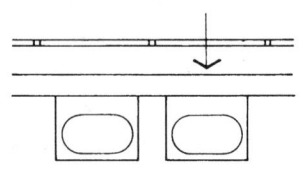

3.3 *Service duct, access from rear*

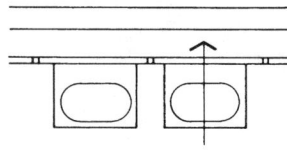

3.4 *Service duct, access from front*

On the other hand, **3.3** demands more detailed work from the architect and it is not always possible to utilise adjacent room areas for access.

Once the duct is provided it is logical and more hygienic to bring the water supplies directly through the duct wall to wall-mounted valves, rather than the pipework passing through the wall, sanitaryware, then on to deck-mounted valves.

It is similarly illogical to have traps hanging from appliances in the room if there is space in the duct for them, although some sanitaryware makes this unavoidable. Ducts should avoid maintenance problems and not have ferrous metal in their construction.

3.08 Tiles and modules

As UK manufacturers have never accepted the 100 mm modular tile (except as a special) and as UK manufacturers will not make sanitaryware modular, it is difficult to find a reason for choosing one module or another for the sanitary installation. It is, however, obvious, in view of the quite differing requirements of the various appliances and the individual situation, that any module should be as small as practicable. The best module is probably that used in Alvar Aalto's office of 1 mm!

4 DETAILED CONSIDERATIONS OF APPLIANCES

4.01 WCs

The principal appliance in any installation is the water closet or WC. This may be free-standing within a bathroom, or placed in a compartment or cubicle by itself, or with a hand-rinse basin.

A WC compartment is totally enclosed by walls that reach down to the floor and up to the ceiling, and has its own lighting and ventilation system. A cubicle is enclosed by light partitions that do not reach floor or ceiling. It shares the lighting and ventilation of the larger space of which it is a part.

3.5a shows the appliance, complete with cistern, and its normal activity space. If the cistern is at high level, or situated within a

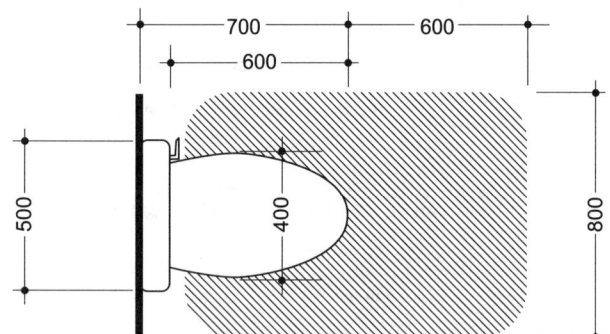

3.5a *WC and activity space. A duct mounted or high-level cistern would allow the WC pan to be placd closer to the wall*

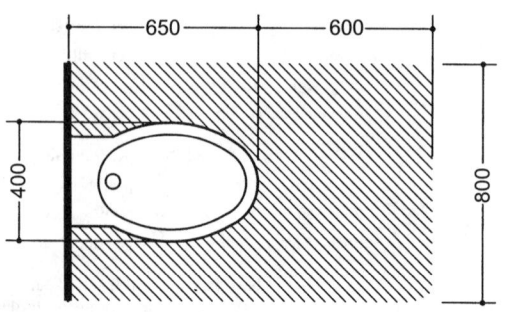

3.5b *Bidet and activity space*

duct, the space for the appliance is correspondingly reduced. However, it may then be found difficult to accommodate a sanitary bin in a place acceptable to the user. **3.5b** shows a bidet and its activity space.

In the UK it is normal for a WC cubicle door to open inwards (see **4.03**). This causes difficulties in entering some cubicles because there is nowhere to stand clear of the door swing. There is also a danger of clothes soiling by contact with the edge of the WC pan. BS 6465 now asks for a cylindrical volume 450 mm in diameter clear of all obstructions such as WC pan, door swing or toilet paper holder.

There are three basic types of WC compartment and cubicle (excluding those also containing a hand-rinse basin):

- A compartment in a house or flat where the user will be in indoor clothing and without impedimenta
- A cubicle in an office or factory, where the user is likely also to be in light clothing with no impedimenta
- A cubicle or compartment in a public place, such as a shopping centre or an airport, where the user may be in a coat and have heavy luggage, shopping or even a baby carrier that cannot, for security, be left outside.

3.6 shows a 'standard' WC cubicle with inward-opening door, the leaf of which is 700 mm wide. It is seen that with a normal pan central in the cubicle width, the cubicle is 1640 mm in depth. **3.7** shows an alternative where the pan is offset towards the door hinge side to provide space for a sanitary bin. In this case the depth is reduced to 1550 mm. These two designs are suitable for the first two situations above.

3.8 to **3.10** show designs appropriate where there is likely to be luggage etc.

It is seen that the width of a 'standard' cubicle is 800 mm. This width is also preferred by ambulant disabled people (see **4.05**).

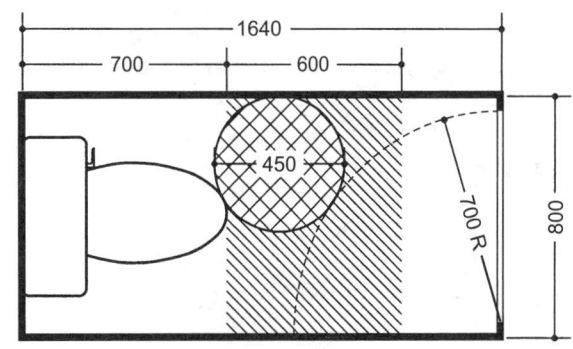

3.6 *WC cubicle, inward-opening door, no sanitary bin zone*

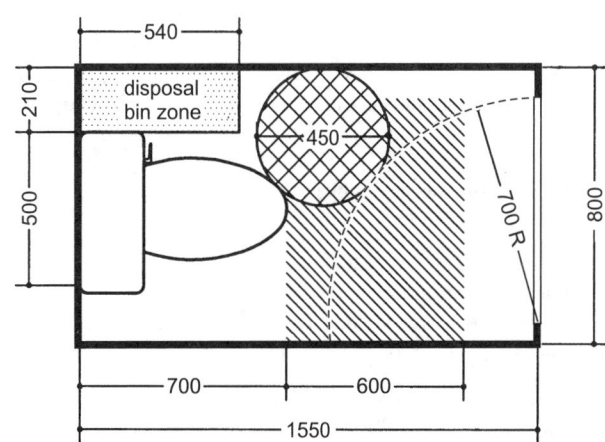

3.7 *WC cubicle, inward-opening door, sanitary bin zone*

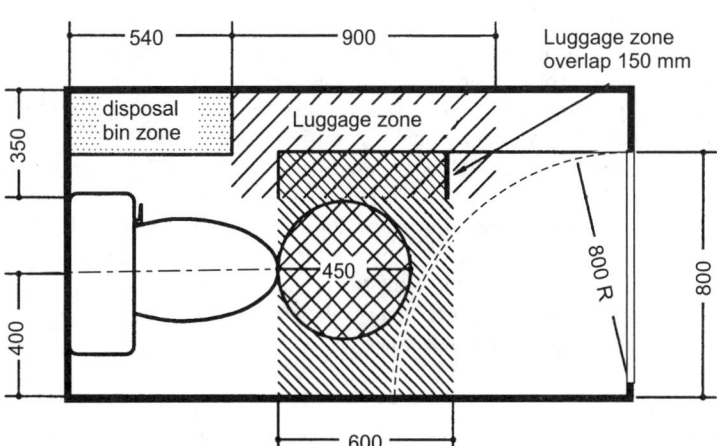

3.8 *Public WC cubicle, inward-opening door*

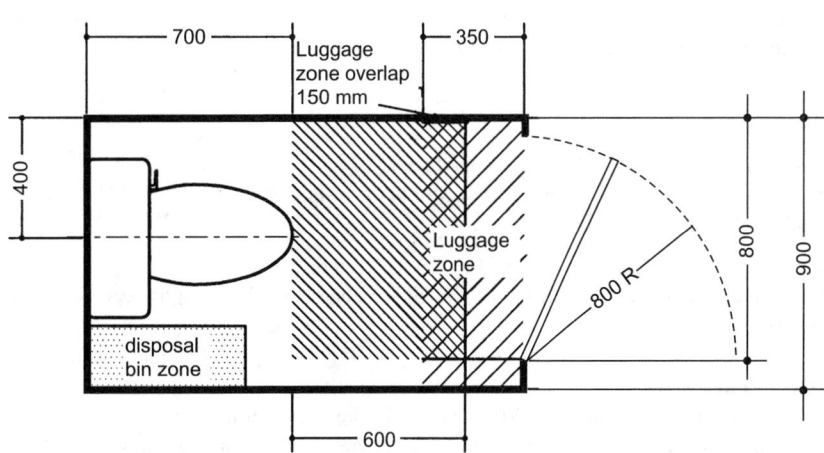

3.9 *Public WC cubicle, outward-opening door*

3.10 *Alternative public WC cubicle, inward-opening door, no sanitary bin*

However, many women find this width too narrow for them, and prefer a width of 900 mm as minimum, with a door opening 800 mm. A wider cubicle may also be needed for people who are oversize.

WC compartments and cubicles may also have to accommodate the following:

● Hand-rinse basin (see **4.03**)
● Large toilet roll holder and dispenser
● Bin for the disposal of sanitary dressings or continence aids
● Dispenser for disposable toilet seat covers
● Brush
● Shelf
● Clothes hooks

4.02 Height of WCs

There is no standard height of pan, but most are around 400 mm to the top of the pan, allow a further 25 mm for the seat. There was a vogue for pans as low as 250 mm at one time, because of medical advice that more of a squatting attitude was beneficial. However, there now seems to be little movement towards the 'health closet', as it is hampered by Western tradition, the difficulty of the elderly or infirm to use a low-level WC and the uselessness of a low WC as a seat or urinal which are common functions in domestic bathrooms.

A pan of height 355 mm is available for use in junior schools. Slightly higher pans are recommended for WCs for disabled people, and these are 450 mm to the top of the seat. People who find a WC seat too low can use removeable seat raisers which are available in a number of different heights.

4.03 Doors

Traditionally in the UK doors to WC compartments and cubicles open inwards. The advantages claimed for this are:

● Privacy, particularly when the door lock is missing or broken
● Elimination of hazard to those outside the cubicle
● The doors are hung so that empty cubicles have open doors and are easily found.

The disadvantages are:

● Restriction of space within the compartment
● Difficulty of reaching anyone taken ill within (a not-uncommon situation).

Inward-opening doors can be designed so that they can be lifted off their hinges should access be necessary when someone has fallen against one.

4.04 Squatting WCs

Some people prefer a squatting WC, **3.11**. These are common in continental public conveniences, and also where there is a

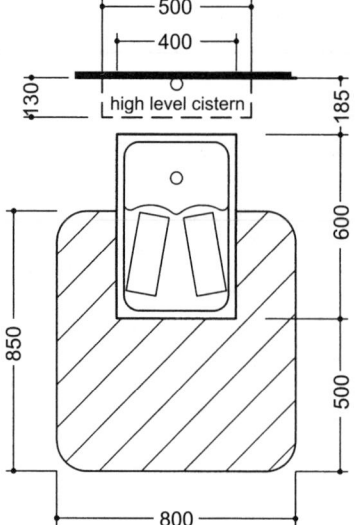

3.11 *Squatting WC and activity space*

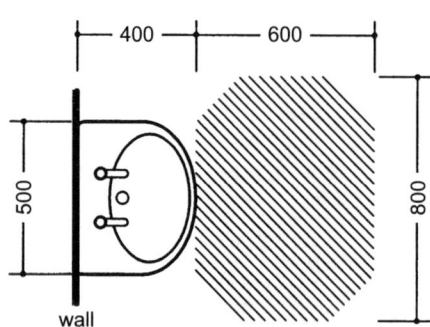

3.12 *Hand-rinse basin and activity space*

substantial Asian population. They can be accommodated in a 'standard' cubicle, although there should be grip handles fixed to the side walls. When intended for use by Muslims the compartment should not face or back in the direction of Mecca, and a low level cold water tap should be provided in addition to the flushing cistern.

4.05 WC compartments with hand-rinse basins

It is often desirable, and may be mandatory, for a compartment or cubicle to incorporate hand-rinsing facilities. **3.12** shows such an appliance with its activity space – which may overlap that of the WC. Where space is tight, a very small inset design may be used as shown in **3.13**.

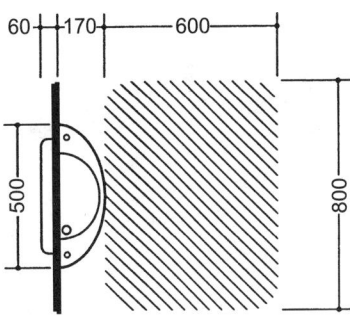

3.13 *Recessed hand-rinse basin and activity space*

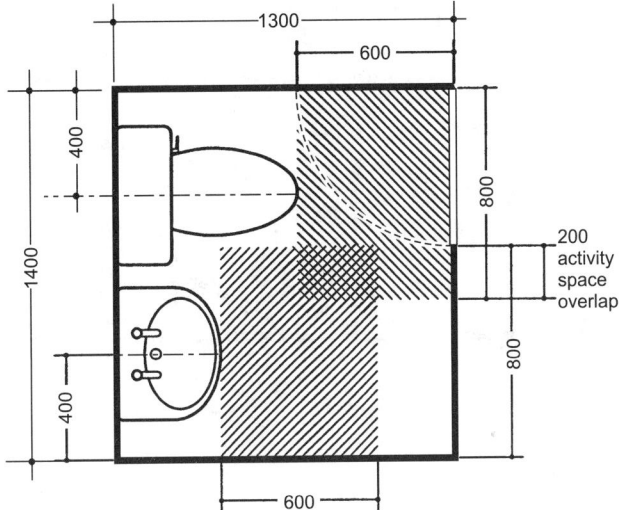

3.14 *WC and washbasin compartment, appliances on same wall*

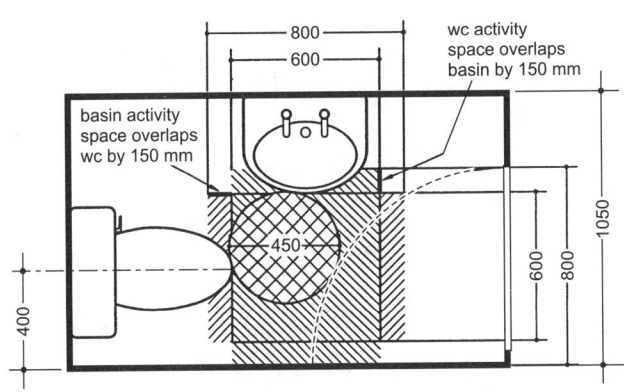

3.15 *WC and washbasin compartment, inward-opening door, appliances on adjacent walls*

3.14 to **3.18** show alternative designs of compartments with standard hand-rinse basins.

4.06 WC compartments for wheelchair users

Disabled people are remarkably adaptable and often of necessity extremely determined to manage for themselves in buildings designed primarily for able-bodied people. For many ambulant disabled people the difficulties are surmountable, but for wheelchair users the problems are more serious. If an area is not negotiable by a wheelchair the user is forbidden entry; this is intolerable, and may be illegal, in any new building.

Therefore proper consideration should be given to the provision of WC and washing facilities for disabled people. Selwyn Goldsmith's book *Designing for the disabled* is the most comprehensive study available. There is hardly any ergonomic

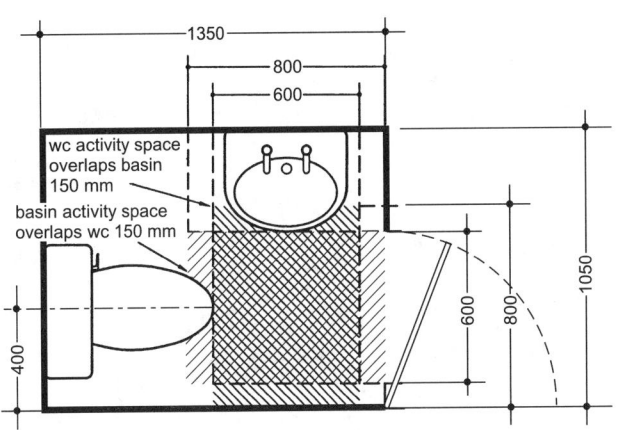

3.16 *WC and washbasin cubicle, outward-opening door, appliances on adjacent walls*

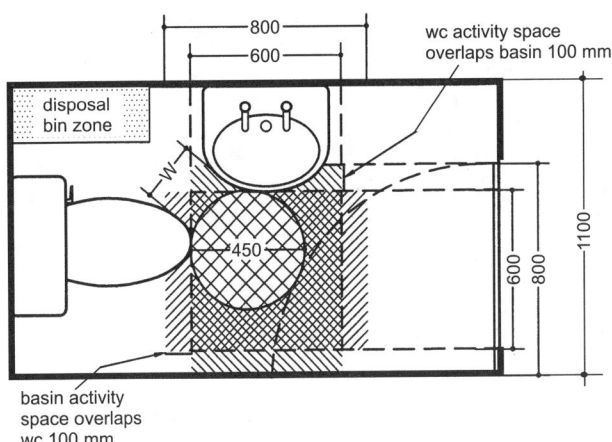

3.17 *WC and washbasin cubicle, sanitary bin zone, appliances on adjacent walls*

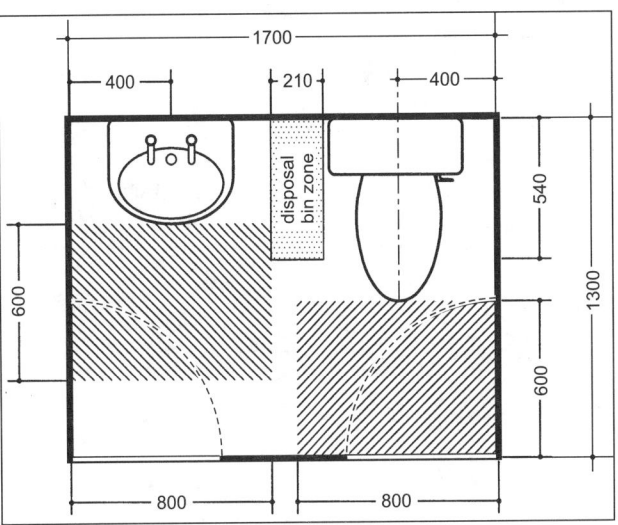

3.18 *WC and washbasin cubicle, sanitary bin zone, appliances on same wall*

evidence on this subject and the standard plans shauld be regarded as principles rather than unalterable working drawings.

WC compartments for disabled people are usually unisex; situated outside male and female multi-user facilities; this has several advantages:

● Husbands and wives can assist each other which is not possible in single-sex compartments

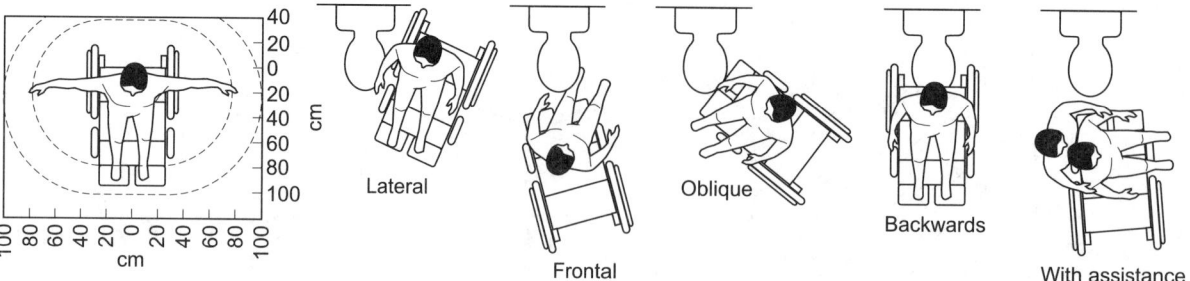

3.19 *A disabled person can transfer from a wheelchair to a sanitary appliance in a variety of ways. Toilets and bathrooms likely to be used by them should allow for a wheelchair turning circle of 1500 mm*

- They avoid the cost of duplicated facilities; one decent unisex facility is more economic than two inadequate single-sex units
- They simplify signposting and access for disabled people.

A WC compartment for general use by disabled people should allow for frontal or lateral transfer from the wheelchair, with space for an attendant to assist. **3.19** shows the various means of transfer that a wheelchair user might have to employ.

In WCs for wheelchair users a hand-rinse basin should be installed where it can be conveniently reached by a person seated on the WC. However, it is desirable that the basin is also usable from the wheelchair. These opposing criteria together with the requirements for handrails and supports present a difficult problem often resulting in a poor or even unworkable compromise.

Part M of the Building Regulations gives a standard design of compartment for a wheelchair user, **3.20**. Such standardisation is recommended because of use by visually impaired people. The handed version is permissible.

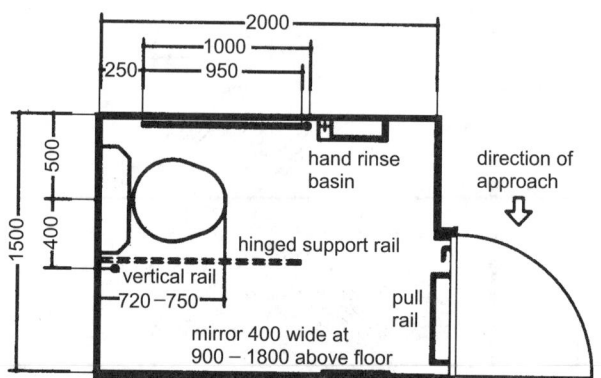

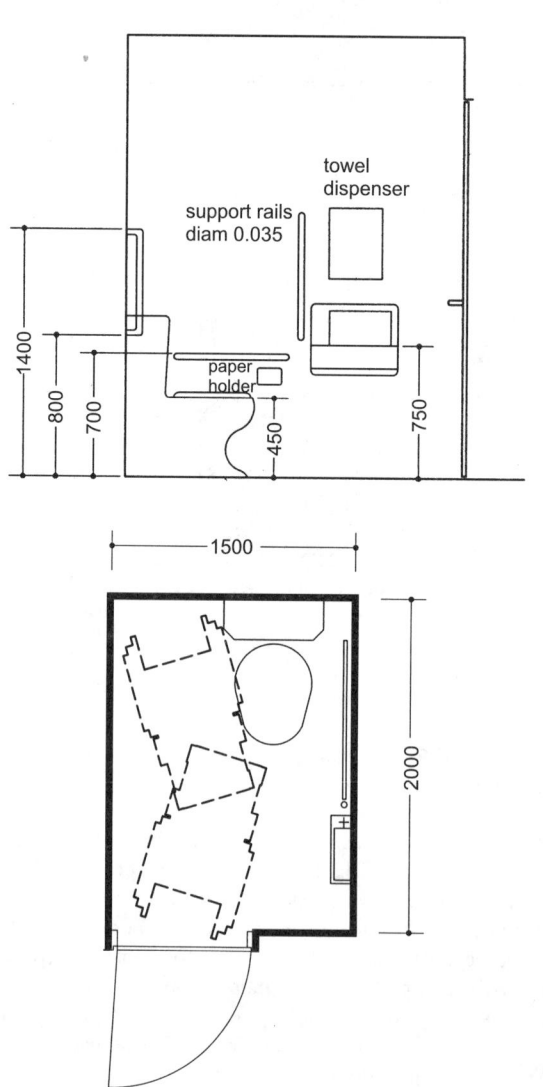

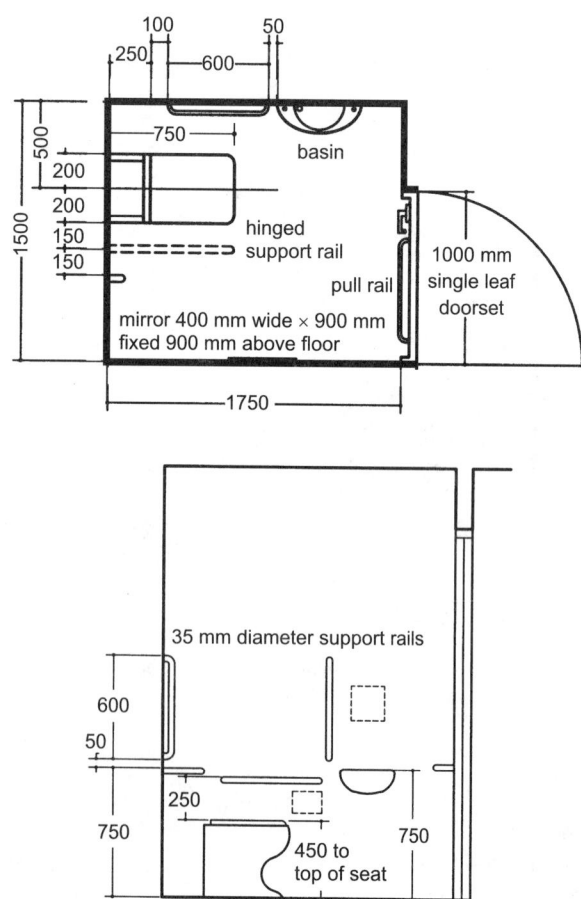

3.20 *Wheelchair-accessible WC compartment from Approved Document B*

3.21 *WC cubicles for the wheelchair user (from* Designing for the disabled*)*

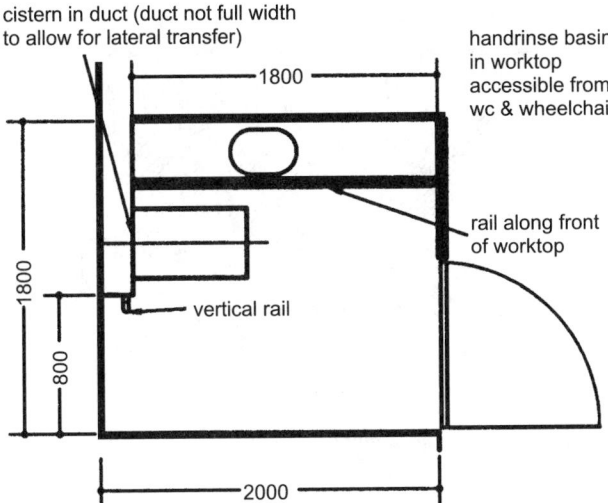

3.22 *An alternative facility (by Alan Tye Design)*

Selwyn Goldsmith's recommended WC compartment for chair-bound users, **3.21**, may be compared to an alternative plan by Alan Tye Design, **3.22**, embodying the principles of Selwyn Goldsmith's recommendations in a neat and pleasant facility.

There is controversy over the use of wheelchair-accessible WCs by other people such as the ambulant disabled and pregnant women. In some cases access to the WC is restricted to registered disabled people with a RADAR key. Since many people are temporarily disabled at some time in their lives, and are therefore not eligible for registration, this should only apply where constant abuse makes it essential. On the other hand, the combination of wheelchair accessible toilet and baby-changing facility should be deplored.

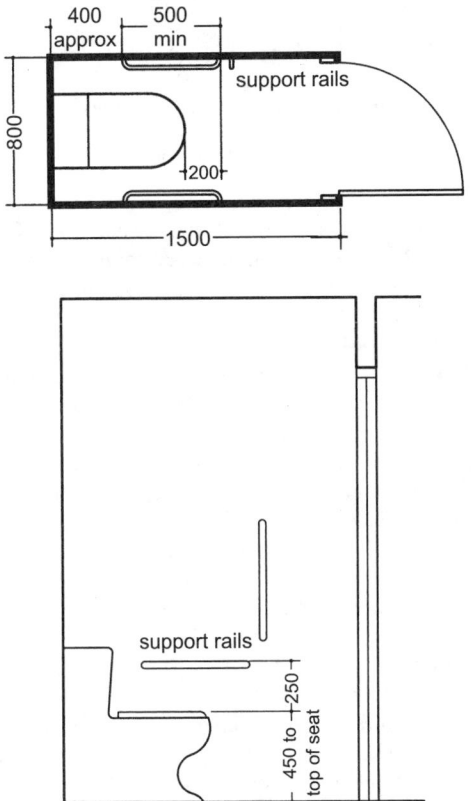

3.23 *WC compartment for ambulant disabled person from Approved Document M. the outward-opening door is preferred for people using crutches, but an inward-opening door can be used if the compartment is at least 200 mm deeper*

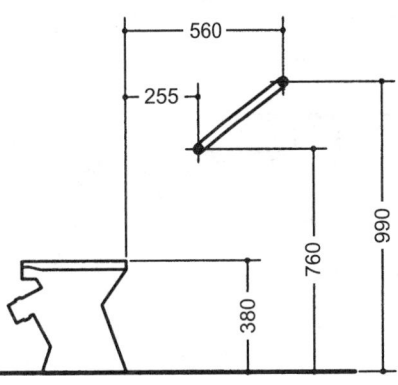

3.24 *Inclined rails mounted on walls of WC*

4.07 WC compartments for ambulant disabled

The standard facility for ambulant disabled people as given in Building Regulation Approved Document M (1992) is shown in **3.23**. The difference from a standard facility is principally in the provision of support and grab rails. People with visual impairment appreciate a standardised layout.

The narrow width is desirable as it allows the user to use the support rails on both sides of the compartment to raise themselves. In large public or semi-public conveniences, at least one cubicle should provide for ambulant disabled people.

Alexander Kira points out that grab rails, **3.24**, for able-bodied people, the elderly and children would virtually obviate the need for special provision for the disabled.

4.08 WC provision in domestic property

It is becoming clear that many people wish to stay in their own homes as long as possible when increasing disability or age occurs. Also, wheelchair users would like to make visits to their friends. This has led the Access Committee for England to recommend that all new houses and flats should be wheelchair accessible if possible, and that they should have WCs at entrance level which can be used by a wheelchair user, although the chair itself may not be able to be fully accommodated inside the WC compartment with the door shut. **3.25** and **3.26** show three ways of achieving this.

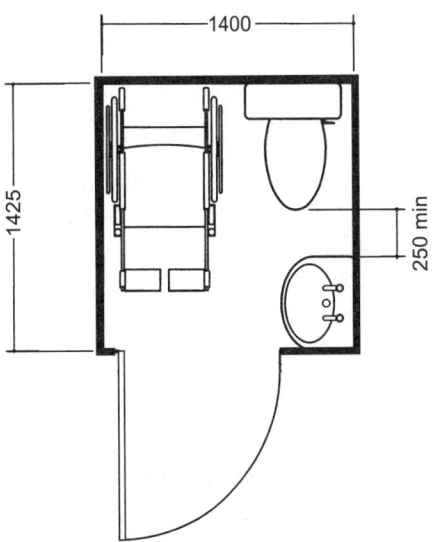

3.25 *Small wheelchair-accessible WC compartment at entrance level in a family house*

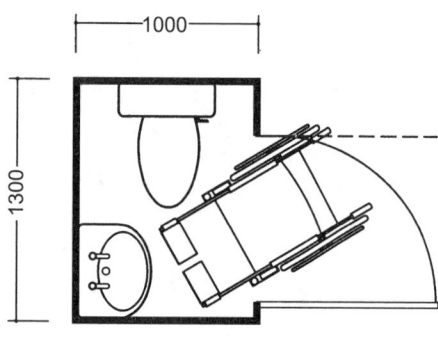

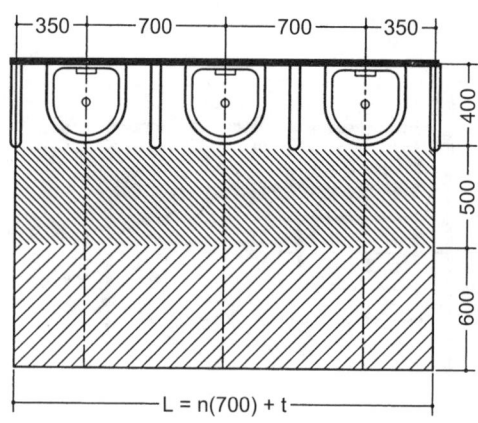

3.28 *Range of urinals, activity and circulation spaces*

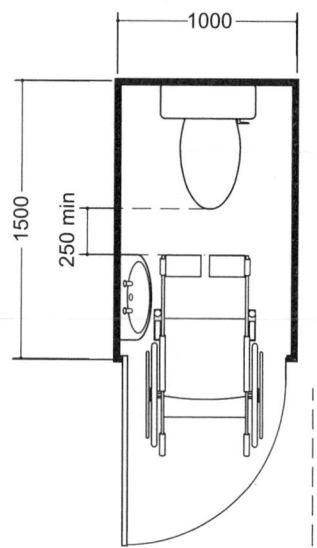

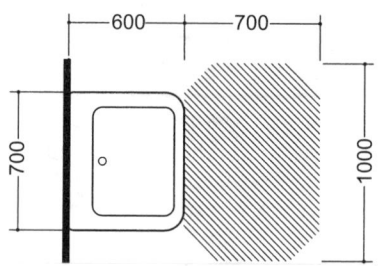

3.29 *Domestic washbasin and activity spaces*

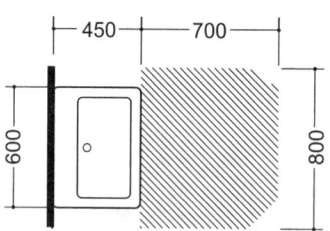

3.26 *Even smaller WCs for entrance level WCs in family houses. In these, transfer cannot be achieved with the door shut*

3.30 *Non-domestic washbasin and activity space*

4.09 Urinals

Although a number of female urinal designs have been produced, none have been successful. However, they are ubiquitous in public and semi-public facilities for men, and research shows that there is often over-provision of WCs for men.

Urinals are of two types: slab and bowl. Slabs are rarely used these days because they are more difficult to service and repair than bowls. A bowl and its activity area are shown in **3.27**.

Urinals are usually provided in ranges. In the past a centre-to-centre dimension of 600 mm was common, but it is now accepted that this is too close. It is also desirable to have small modesty screens between bowls. **3.28** shows a range of urinals with activity and circulation spaces.

Urinal bowls are usually fixed with their forward rims 610 mm above floor level. One in each range should be lower at 510 mm for use by small boys.

4.10 Washbasins

Washbasins come in a variety of sizes. The standard domestic washbasin, **3.29** is for washing the face and the upper part of the body and for wet shaving as well as hand-rinsing. A slightly smaller washbasin, **3.30**, is common in non-domestic situations such as factories, offices and schools where they are often used in ranges **3.31**. Sometimes washbasins are set into a flat top forming a vanitory unit, and the dimensions of these do not vary significantly from the standard.

Hand-rinse basins have already been mentioned in connection with WC compartments. When they are used in a range the dimensions in **3.32** should be followed.

The traditional fixing height of basins is 785 or 800 mm to the rim. For adults this height requires considerable bending as one is actually washing one's hands below the rim height. Alexander Kira suggests a height of 865 to 915 mm, but for normal use by a wide range of users 850 mm is preferred. The Department of Health recommends 760 mm in hospitals.

In any case, these heights would be unsatisfactory for small children, who need to be encouraged to wash their hands. A washbasin fitted at 700 mm could be provided for them, and **3.33** shows a family bathroom provided with a second basin for the children. A common alternative to provide a small step-up for children to use the standard basin. This would not be appropriate in a public convenience, where a lower washbasin should be provided unless a dedicated children's facility such as described in

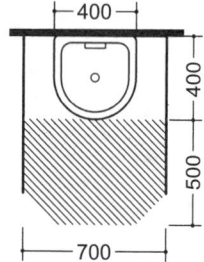

3.27 *Single urinal and activity space*

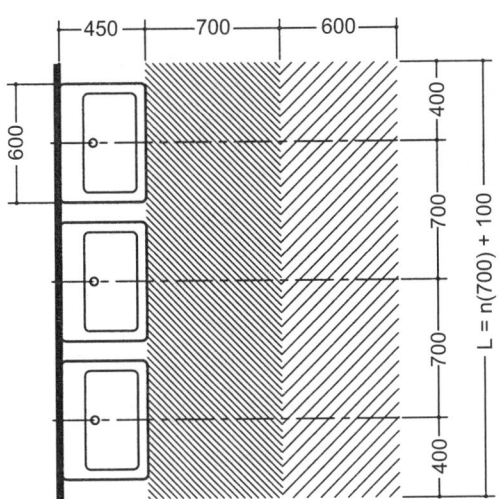

3.31 *Range of non-domestic washbasins, activity and circulation spaces*

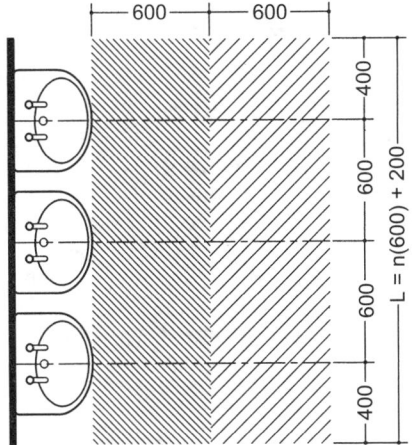

3.32 *Range of hand-rinse basins (non-recessed), activity and circulation spaces*

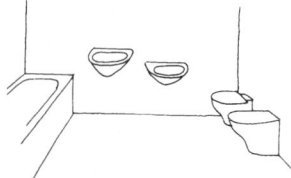

3.33 *Family bathroom incorporating second washbasin for children's use*

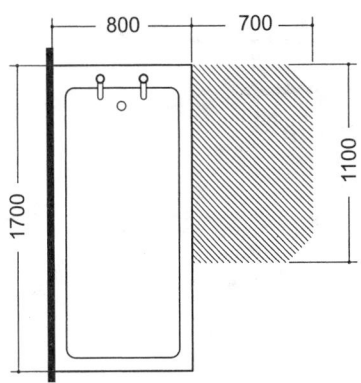

3.34 *Bathtub and activity space*

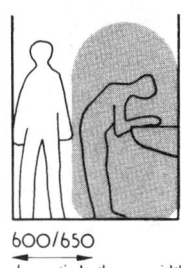

3.35 *Minimum width in domestic bathroom*

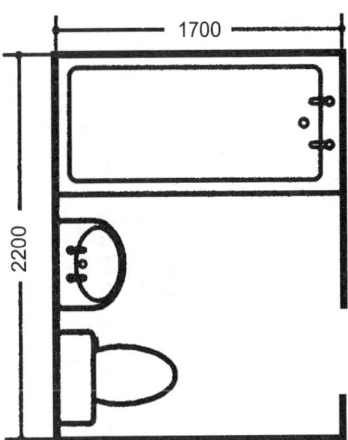

3.36 *Minimum bathroom including WC*

4.15 is nearby. Children also deserve and appreciate consideration in the placement of dryers, towels, coat hooks and mirrors, etc.

As already shown, basins specifically for wheelchair users have rims 750 mm high. Plumbing, etc. underneath such basins should be arranged not to obstruct the knees of the user in the chair.

4.11 Baths and bathrooms

Baths are also available in many sizes, shapes and types; but the standard one and its activity area are shown in **3.34**. Baths are now rarely found outside bathrooms; and bathrooms normally also include at least a washbasin. The minimum width of a domestic bathroom is illustrated in **3.35**. All bathrooms should ideally be large enough for undressing and dressing, and for someone to lend a hand. Three domestic bathroom arrangements are shown in **3.36** to **3.38** and variations on these are also appropriate in non-

domestic situations such as hotels, schools etc. A matrix of virtually all possible arrangements will be found in BS 6465: Part 2.

Baths can be provided for disabled people which have rims at 380 mm above the floor instead of the normal 500 mm. Alternatively, the bath may be set with the trap below floor level. It should have as flat a bottom as possible and should not be longer than 1.5 m; lying down is not encouraged.

Other special baths tip up or have openable sides. However, a standard bath with a mobility aid is usually more practical, particularly in the home. Lifting and lowering devices are available that can be fixed to a floor, wall or ceiling – or can even be simply sat on the floor. As suggested above, all bathrooms should ideally provide for handrails; a pole is invaluable for anyone less than fully agile **3.39**. Adaptation of the standard bath

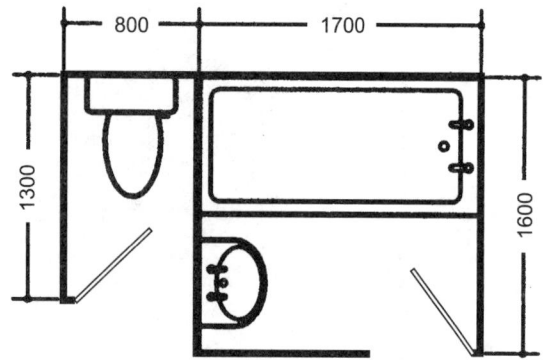

3.37 *WC in separate compartment adjacent to bathroom*

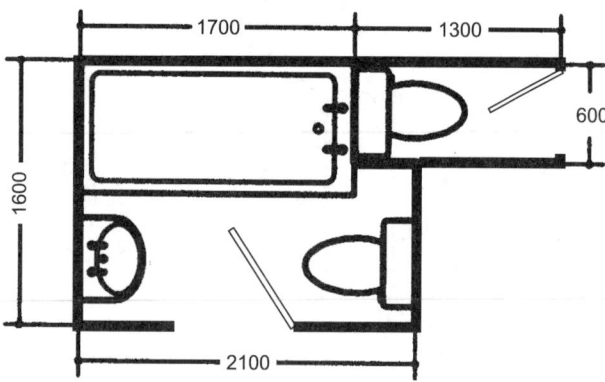

3.38 *WC in separate compartment adjacent to bathroom also containing WC*

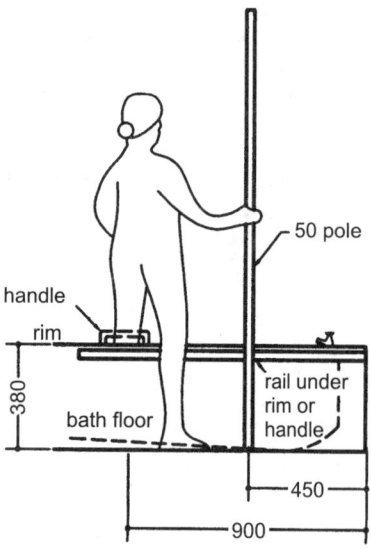

3.39 *Aids for getting in and out of the bath: pole, handle and rim. Maximum height of rim from floor 380 mm*

rim to make it easier to grasp is shown in **3.40**. A seat at rim height is useful for sitting on to wash legs and feet.

Bathroom and lavatory doors should preferably open out, with locks operable from the outside in emergencies.

4.12 Taps

Choose taps that can be manipulated by small and arthritic fingers. Surgeons' taps are not recommended, however, as in extreme cases ordinary taps can be modified to provide similar facility. Under a European standard it is now obligatory in new installations for the

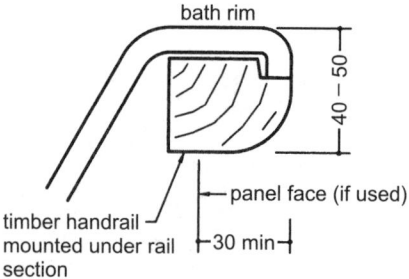

3.40 *Bath rim adapted for easy gripping*

cold tap to be on the right and the hot on the left, unless there are compelling reasons otherwise: this is in order to assist visually impaired people. Tops should be boldly colour coded, additional tactile identification is currently under discussion.

4.13 Showers

It is becoming common to install showers which are more economical in water and energy use than bathtubs. Disabled people in particular often find it easier to shower than to get in and out of a tub.

Showers come with and without trays and enclosures, **3.41** to **3.43**. Trays are not altogether suitable for disabled people unless they can be installed with the rim level with the floor and provided with a duckboard. Continental practice of an impervious non-slip bathroom floor laid to fall to a gulley has not been traditionally followed in the UK, although this can be ideal for a wheelchair user. A shower installation specifically designed for an elderly or disabled person is shown in **3.44**. The compartment should be well heated, with a fold-away seat and with pegs for clothes on the dry side, divided from the wet with a shower curtain. The water supply should be automatically controlled to supply only between 35°C

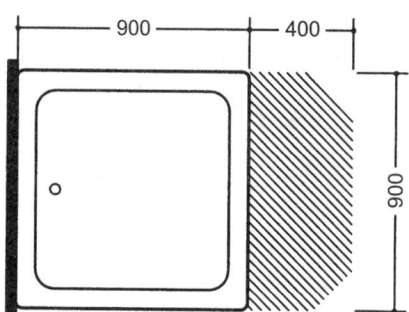

3.41 *Unenclosed shower with tray, and activity space. This is for access from one side of the tray, and to facilitate initial drying within the shower. A nearby area of 1100 × 900 will be needed for final drying and dressing*

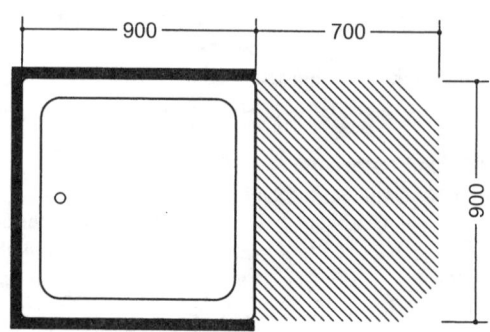

3.42 *Enclosed shower with tray, and activity space adequate for drying. A nearby dressing space is presumed*

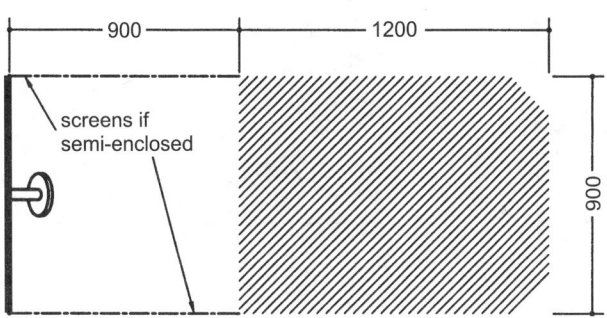

3.43 *Unenclosed shower without tray, and activity space for drying and dressing*

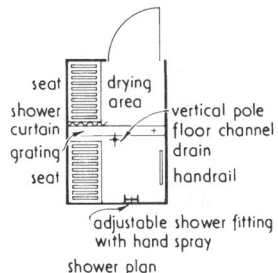

3.44 *Plan of shower room for elderly or disabled person, showing seats and aids*

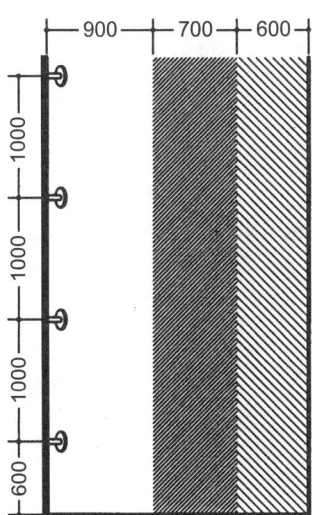

3.45 *Range of unenclosed showers, activity and circulation spaces*

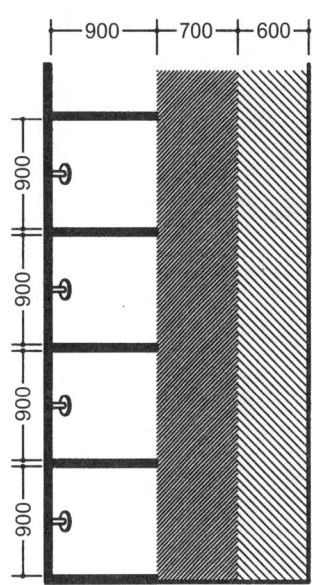

3.46 *Range of semi-enclosed showers, activity and circulation spaces*

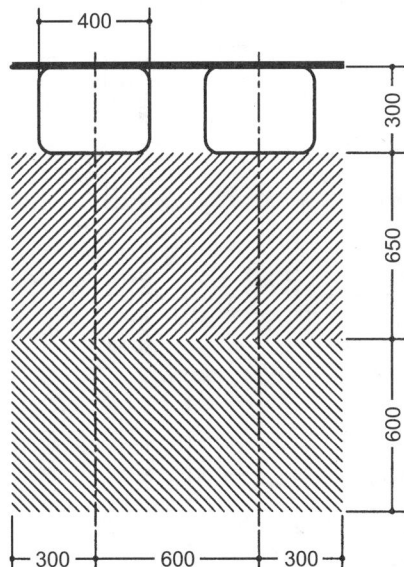

3.47 *Range of hand dryers, activity and circulation spaces*

and 49°C. The shower head should be on the end of a flexible hose, with a variety of positions available for clipping it on.

In sports centres and swimming pools showers are provided in ranges as **3.45** or **3.46**.

BS 6465: Part 2 recommends 900 mm square as the minimum size for a shower enclosure, but most of the shower trays and enclosures manufactured are between 700 mm and 800 mm square.

4.14 Public conveniences

In addition to the appliances covered above, public installations also include drying facilities **3.47** which could be electric hand dryers or roller towels. Occasionally disposal for sanitary towels and continence aids is provided outside cubicles, **3.48**, although this is not recommended practice.

The factors affecting the widths of public conveniences are covered in **3.49** to **3.51**. Appliances should be arranged so that the

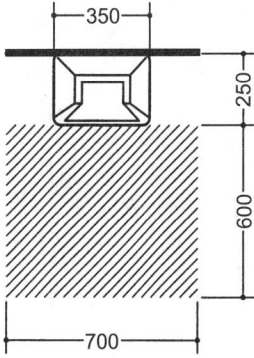

3.48 *Sanitary towel or continence aid disposal apliance not in a cubicle and activity space*

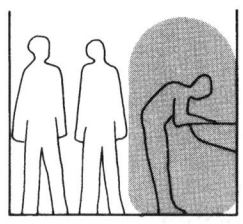

1200/1400
minimum public installation width

3.49 *Minimum width in a public in a public installation with appliances on one side*

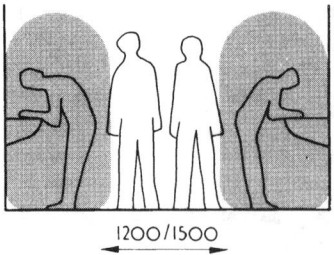

1200/1500

3.50 *Minimum width in a public in a public installation with appliances on both sides*

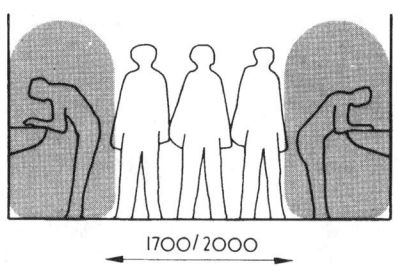

1700/2000

3.51 *Width of a larger public installation*

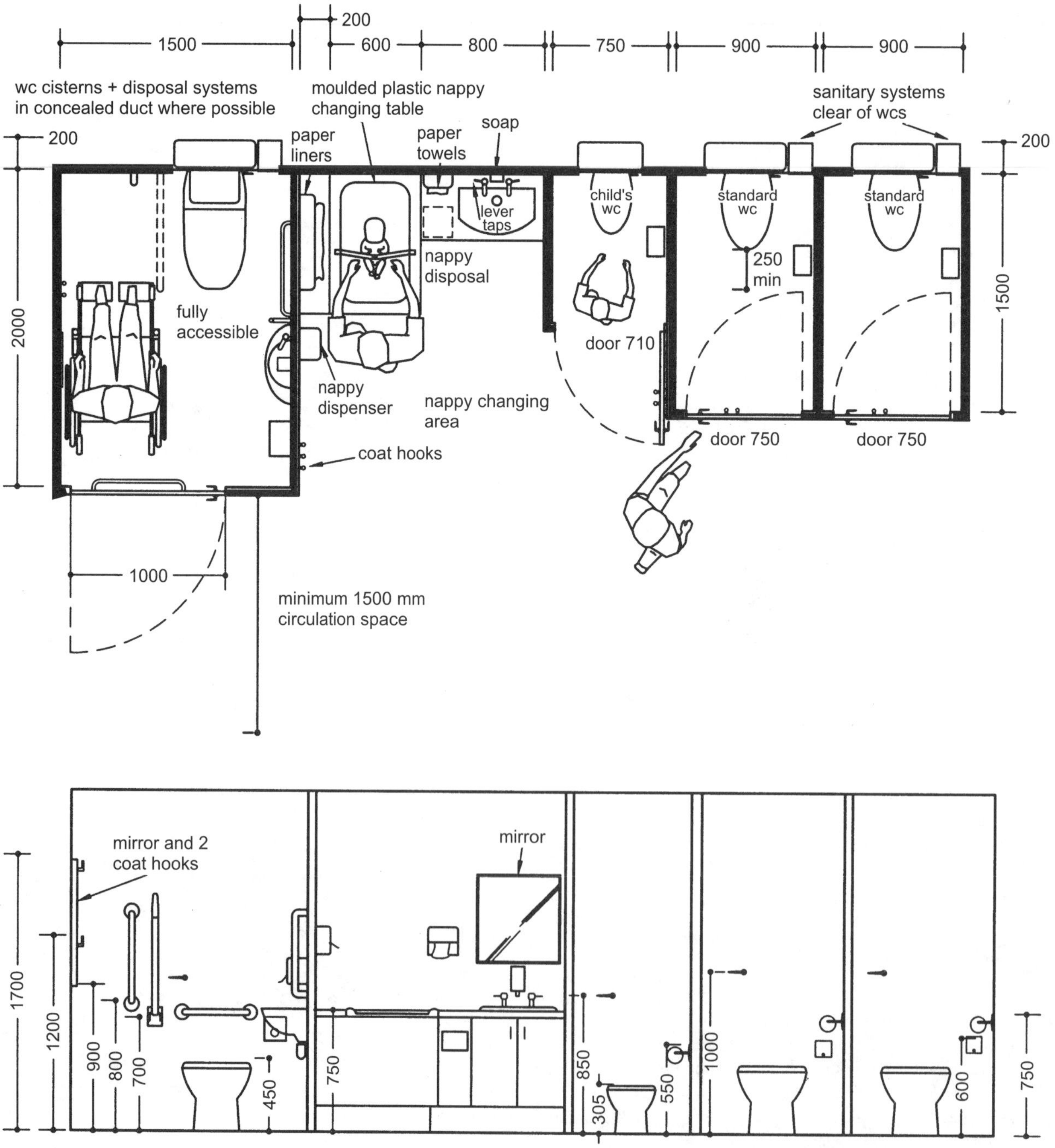

wc cisterns + disposal systems in concealed duct where possible

moulded plastic nappy changing table

paper liners

paper towels

soap

lever taps

nappy disposal

nappy dispenser

nappy changing area

coat hooks

fully accessible

child's wc

door 710

standard wc

250 min

standard wc

sanitary systems clear of wcs

door 750

door 750

minimum 1500 mm circulation space

1500   200   600   800   750   900   900

200   2000   1000   1500   200

3.52 *Layout for a public convenience including wheelchair access compartment, child's WC and nappy-changing facility. This design is suitable for a ladies' facility, although nappy changing, child's WC and wheelchair access would be ideally unisex*

mirror and 2 coat hooks

mirror

1700   1200   900   800   700   450   750   850   305   550   1000   600   750

space is concentrated into larger areas, as it is psychologically and practically preferable to be able to see the whole of the room on entering. Narrow dead ends and corridors should be avoided and the circulation pattern planned to ensure that washing facilities are provided between WC/urinals and the exit to encourage hand washing.

Circulation areas must be considered as being around both appliance and activity spaces rather than merely around appliances, although some encroachment of the circulation area into the appliance/activity space will normally be acceptable depending on the likelihood of full use of appliances.

4.15 Baby changing
A full public installation should include a baby-changing facility and a child's WC. An arrangement recommended by The Continence Foundation and All Mod Cons, and designed by the Women's Design Service is shown in **3.52**.

4.16 Miscellaneous sanitary appliances
Some other water-using appliances and their activity spaces are shown in **3.53** to **3.56**.

4.17 Cleaning manual/mechanical
Cleanliness can either be visual or bacteriologically sterile or both. Most people are happy with visual cleanliness and would be unhappy with a dirty-looking though sterile installation. Good design and detailing therefore plays a vital part in sanitary accommodation cleanliness.

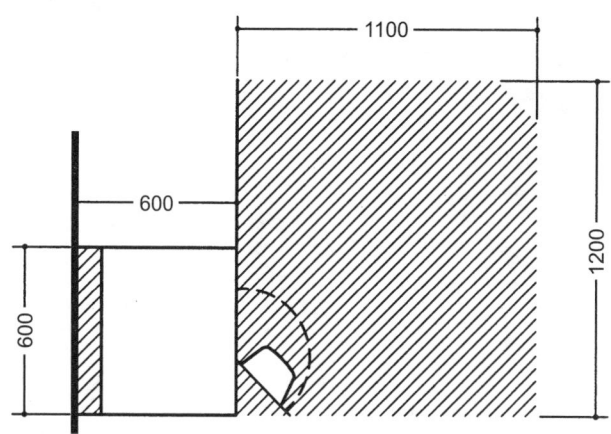

3.53 *Clothes washing machine and activity space*

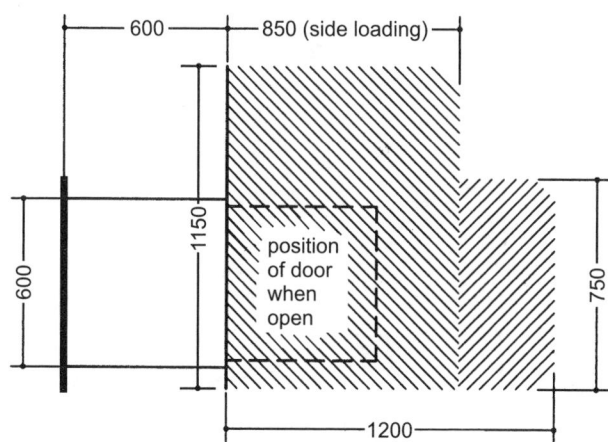

3.54 *Dishwasher and activity space*

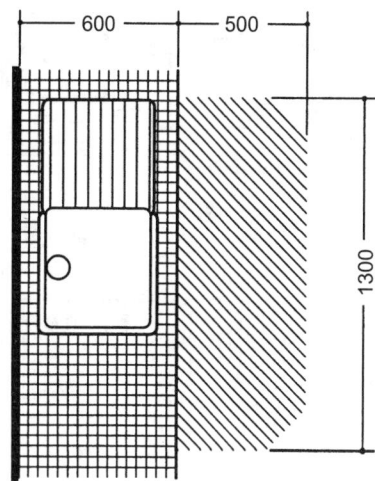

3.55 *Kitchen sink and activity space*

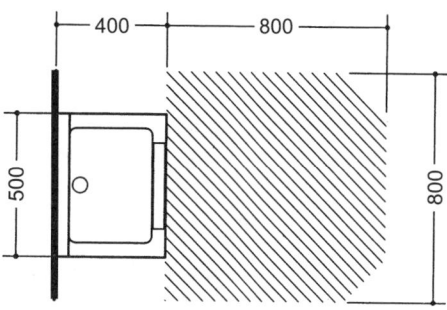

3.56 *Bucket/cleaners sink and activity space*

Cleaning is rarely considered very seriously in sanitary areas, for most proprietary appliances are badly designed and uncleanable, producing dark shadows around down-to-floor appliances, cubicle feet, etc. and too often one sees pipes and cistern exposed.

Consider carefully the cleaning method to be employed, and be critical of what manufacturers supply; for besides hygienic and aesthetic factors, dirty installations encourage sloppy use and vandalism. One should ensure that all surfaces are capable of thorough cleansing; floor details should be coved wherever possible and all possible interruptions of the floor, such as legs, pedestals and pipes, avoided.

Wall-mounted appliances are preferred, although many wall-mounted WCs leave so little floor clearance as actually to aggravate the cleaning problem. Appliances designed to eliminate uncleanable areas should be chosen; they should be cleanable not only in the appliance itself but also at its junction with the structural surfaces. Generally, the appliance is cleaned but the wall is not, so all appliances need upstands. Appliances should not be placed so close together that cleaning between them is hampered. Wall-mounted valves over washbasins promote better cleaning than deck-mounted ones.

5 SAUNAS

5.01 Origin of the sauna
The sauna, **3.57**, is essentially Finnish and in its original form is a one-room hut built of logs, with a rudimentary furnace or stove, over which rocks are piled, in one corner. Steps lead up to a slatted wooden platform along one side of the room where naked bathers

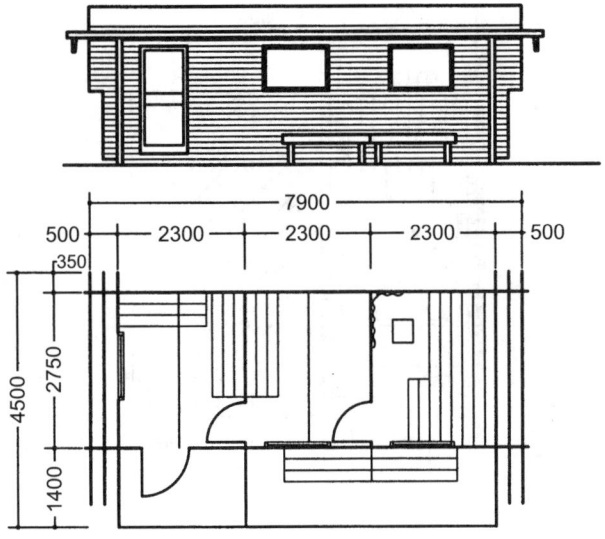

3.57 *Outdoor sauna with verandah, changing room, washing room and sauna room*

7 PUBLIC CLOAKROOMS

7.01 Calculating cloakroom areas

In the early planning stages, if you merely wish to establish an overall cloakroom area, you can obtain the size of a cloakroom to suit any number of coats from the graph, **3.58** (courtesy of G. & S. Allgood Ltd).

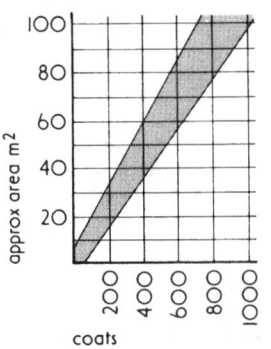

3.58 *Approximate guide to areas of cloakroom accommodation for use in early planning stage*

sit or lie in the hot air under the roof. The stove heats the room by convection and the rocks reach a high temperature. After sitting in the dry heat for some minutes, the bather produces steam from time to time by throwing small quantities of water onto the hot rocks.

The temperature varies from 88°C to 110°C and, provided that the moisture is properly absorbed by the wooden walls of the room, the air will not become saturated. Because the human body can stand a higher degree of dry heat than wet heat, the temperature is higher in a sauna than in a Turkish bath. After perspiration, bathers beat themselves with leafy birch twigs, wash and plunge into a nearby lake or take a cold shower. The cycle is repeated a few times until finally there is a period of rest while the body cools down completely. The time taken for the complete operation varies from 90 to 120 minutes.

5.02 Dimensions

The sauna room should be between 2.3 and 2.6 m high and have a minimum floor area of 1.8 × 2.1 m. Benches should be 600 to 760 mm wide and the platform at least 460 mm wide. The stove will take up 0.560 to 0.650 m² of floor area and will stand about 1.070 m high. Outside the sauna room, showers are required and if possible a cold 4–10°C plunge bath. Space for dressing and resting should be provided. Cubicles will strictly limit the maximum number of bathers, and an open layout is more flexible. Provision should be made for clothes lockers and a few dressing cubicles, and the rest of the area is occupied by resting couches/chairs and small tables.

Of the total number of bathers in an establishment at any time, 20–25 per cent are likely to be in the sauna room, an equal number in the shower/washing room and the remainder in the dressing/resting areas.

6 HYDRO-THERAPY SPA BATHS

This healthy new development in bathroom equipment is an alternative to the sauna. Spa baths or 'swirlpools' are small hydro-therapy pools that provide turbulent hot water as massage for the relief of aches, tensions and fatigue or simply for pleasure. These pools are usually of one-piece glass-fibre construction, available in a variety of sizes and shapes which are relatively easy and low-cost to install and are used indoors or out.

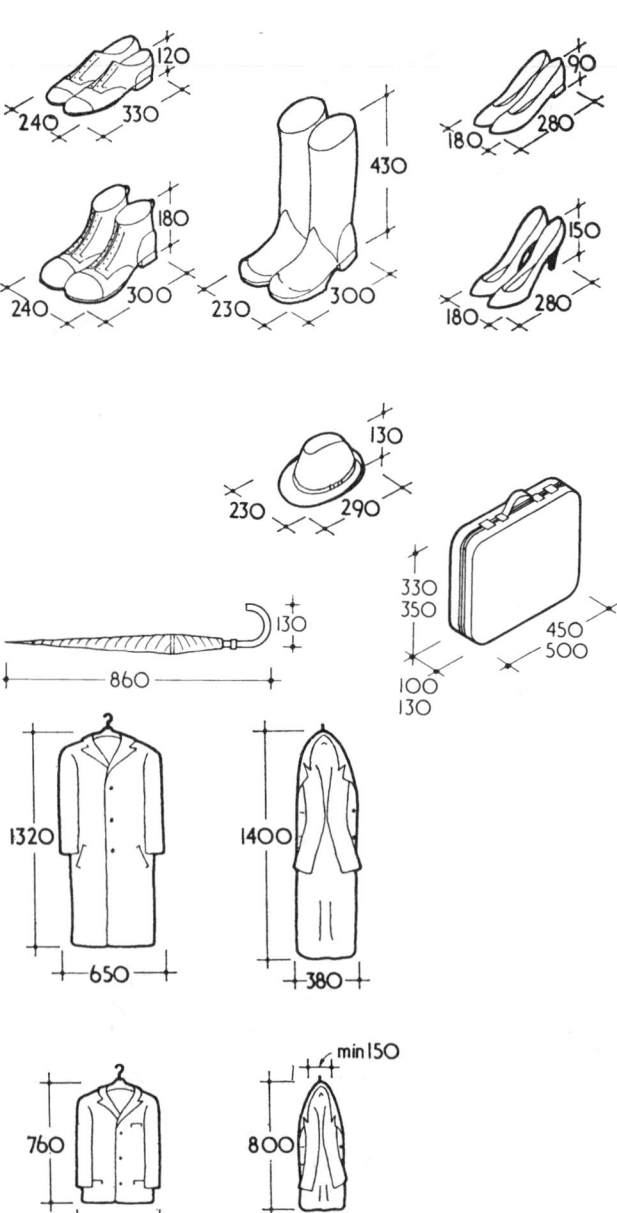

3.59 *Sizes of items commonly stored in cloakrooms*

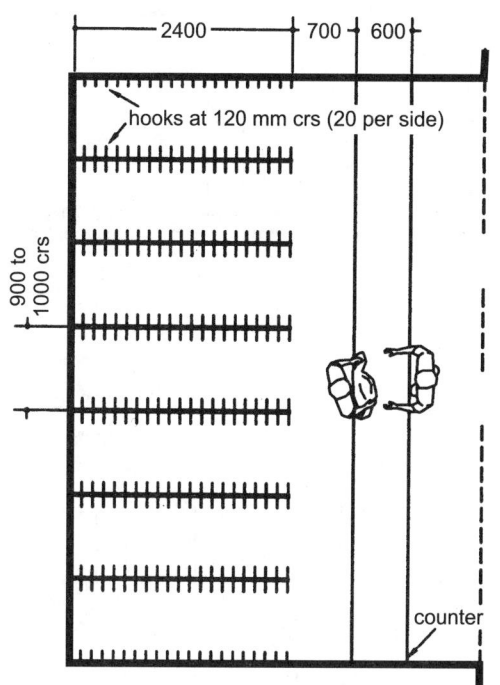

3.60 *Fixed rows of hooks. 0.08 m² per user including counter, 0.1 m² including 1200 mm on public side*

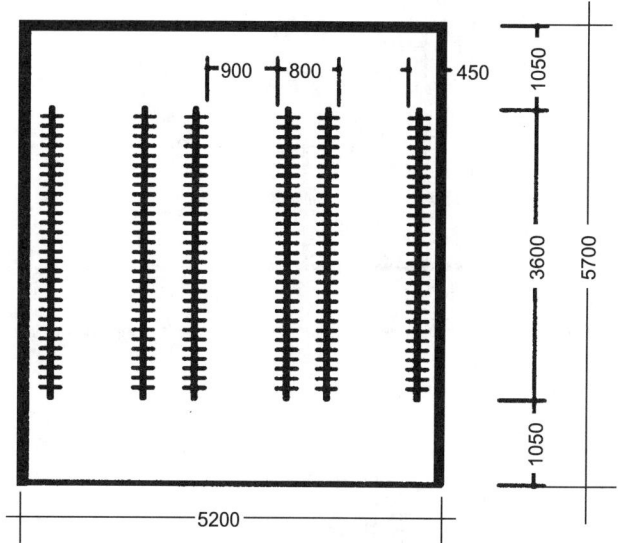

3.62 *Method of calculating space required by each user: 6 rows each 3600 mm long of double tier hangers at 150 mm centres = 300 hangers area of room = 5.7 × 5.2= 29.6 m² Hewnce space allowance 0.098 m² per user*

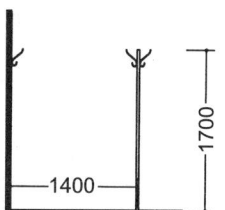

3.63 *Hooks in line: 0.16 m² per user including circulation*

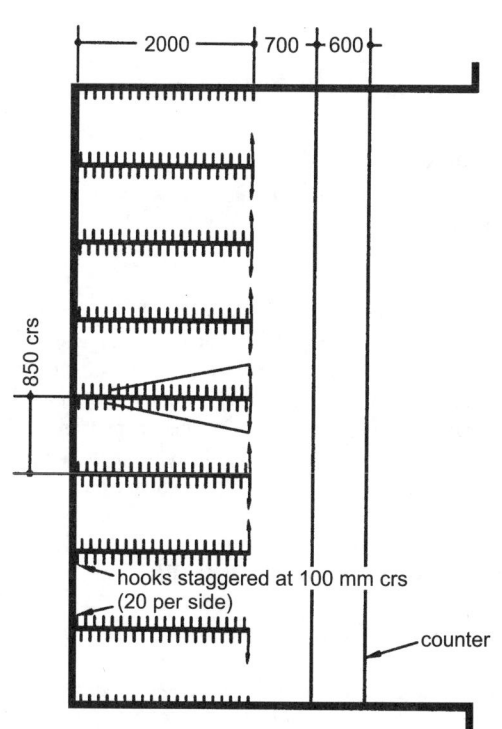

3.61 *Hinged rows of hooks, 0.007 m² per user incuding counter, 0.09 m² including 1200 mm on public side*

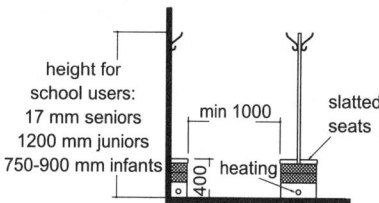

3.64 *Hooks with seating: 0.02 m² per user including circulation*

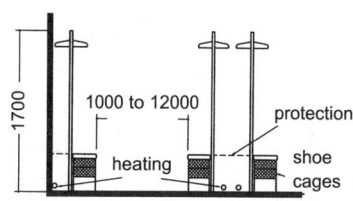

3.65 *Hooks with seating: 0.26 m² per user including circulation*

7.02 Items commonly stored

Typical sizes of items stored are given in **3.59**.

7.03 Attended storage

Typical arrangements and space requirements per user are shown in **3.60** and **3.61**.

7.04 Unattended storage

The space allowances per user in **3.62** to **3.66** are based upon hangers or hooks at 150 mm in rows 3600 mm long with 1050 mm clear circulation space at ends of rows.

The proprietary system given in **3.67** provides unattended locked storage for coats and umbrellas.

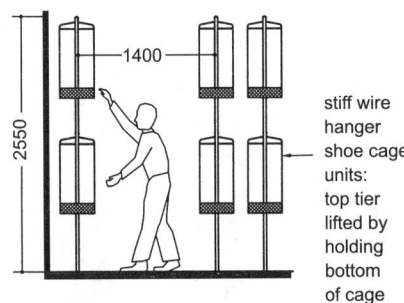

3.66 *Double tier hangers: 0.13 m² per user including circulation*

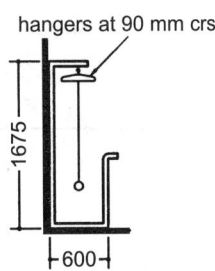

3.67 *Proprietry system affording security: 0.16 m² per user including circulation*

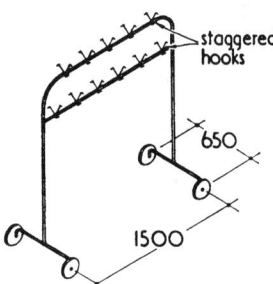

3.68 *Mobile coat rack*

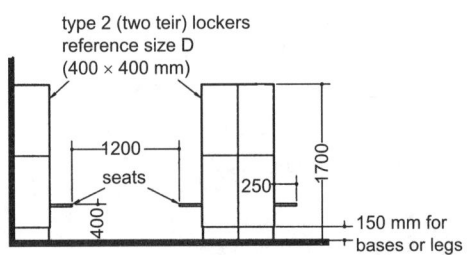

3.70 *Cross-section of lockers with seats*

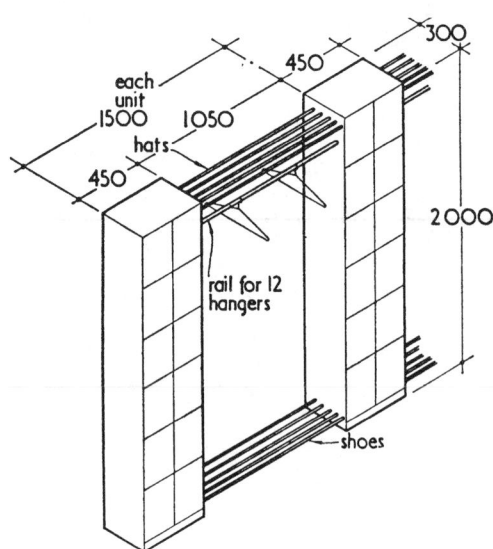

3.71 *Lockers with coat rail, hat and shoe racks*

7.05 Mobile storage

These are proprietary units and the measurements shown in **3.68** are approximate.

7.06 Lockers

Lockers may be full height with a hat shelf and space to hang a coat and store shoes or parcels; or half height to take a jacket; or quarter height to take either parcels or folded clothes, **3.69** and **3.70**. Combination units such as **3.71** are also available.

Note: Many of the units shown in this chapter are proprietary systems and metric measurements are only approximate. Manufacturers should be consulted after preliminary planning stages.

8 REFERENCES AND BIBLIOGRAPHY

Official publications

The Building Regulations 1991 *Approved document G, Hygiene,* HMSO, 1992

The Building Regulations 1991 *Approved document M, Access and facilities for disabled people,* HMSO, 1992

Department of the Environment, *Spaces in the home, bathroom and Wcs,* HMSO 1972

Department of the Environment, *Sanitary provision for people with special needs, volume 1,* DoE, 1992

British Standards

BS 5810:1979 *Code of practice for access for the disabled to buildings,* BSI, 1979

BS 6465:Part 1:1994 *Sanitary Installations Part 1 Code of practice for scale of practice for scale of provision, selection and installation of sanitary appliances,* BSI, 1994

BS 6465:Part 2:1996 *Sanitary Installations Part 2 Code of practice for space requirements for sanitary appliances,* BSI, 1996

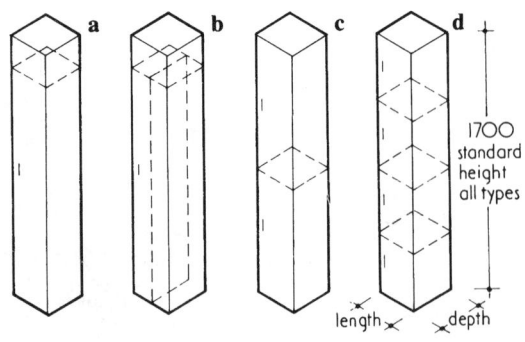

reference size (mm)					
	A	B	C	D	E	F
length	300	300	300	400	400	500
depth	300	400	500	400	500	500

3.69 *Lockers: **a** type 1a with hat shelf; **b** type 1b with hat shelf and vertical divider. Not available in A, B or C **c** type 2, two tier; **d** type 3, three, four, five or six tier*

Other publications

Access Committee for England, *Building Homes for Successive Generations*, ACE, 1992

A. Arstila, *The Finnish Sauna*, Weilin + Göös, 1983

S. Cavanagh and V. Ware, *At Women's Convenience, A Handbook on the Design of Women's Public Toilets*, Womens Design Service, 1990

S. Cunningham and C. Norton, *Public In-Conveniences, Suggestions for Improvements (2nd ed)*, All Mod Cons and The Continence Foundation, 1995

S. Goldsmith, *Designing for the Disabled (3rd ed)*, RIBA, 1976

The Football Trust, *Toilet Facilities at Stadia*, The Sports Council, 1993

J. Penton, *Tourism for all – Providing Accessible Accommodation*, English Tourist Board

Prof. A. Kira, *The Bathroom (rev ed)*, Bantam Books, New York, 1974

Dr C. Llewelyn *Toilet Issues: a survey of the provision and adequacy of public toilets in eighteen towns and cities*, Welsh Consumer Council, 1996

T. Palfreyman, *Designing for Accessibility – An Introductory Guide* Centre for Accessible Environments 1996

I. Woolley, *Sanitation Details* (rev. ed) International Business Publishing, 1990

4 Design for the vehicle

David Adler

CI/SFb 12
UDC 656.1

The section on bikeways was written by Michael Littlewood, and that on service stations is based on the chapter in the previous edition written by the late John Carter

KEY POINTS:
- *Commercial vehicles are getting larger and heavier*
- *More separate provision for bicyles is being made*
- *More consideration is being given to the needs of pedestrians*
- *Better facilities for disabled people including wheelchair users and people with visual impairment are becoming essential*

Contents

1 VEHICLES

1.01 Scope
This section deals with data on:

- Cycles
- Motor-cycles and scooters
- Automobiles: cars and small vans up to 2½ tonnes unladen weight
- Commercial vehicles up to 10 tonnes unladen weight
- Public Service Vehicles (PSVs): buses and coaches
- 'Juggernauts', large commercial vehicles maximum 40 t. This class includes those with draw-bar trailers (see **4.1**).

4.1 *Dimensions, weights and turning circoles of typical road vehicles:*

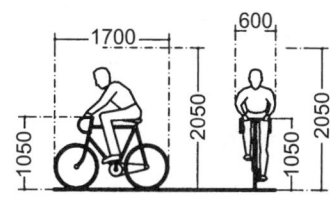

bicycle

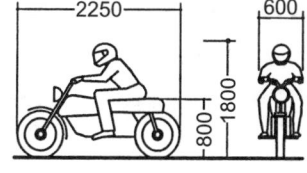

motor bicycle

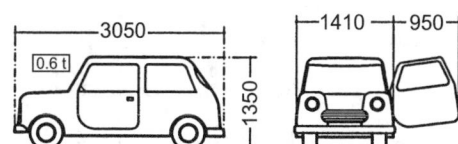

small car (Mini)

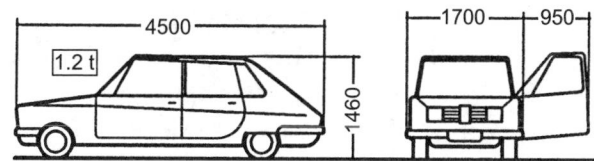

family saloon

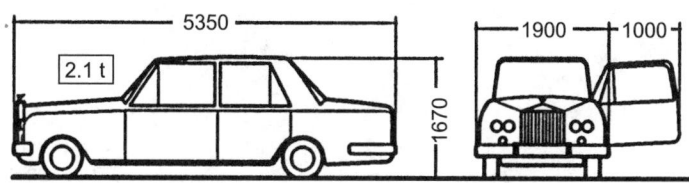

large car (Rolls Royce)

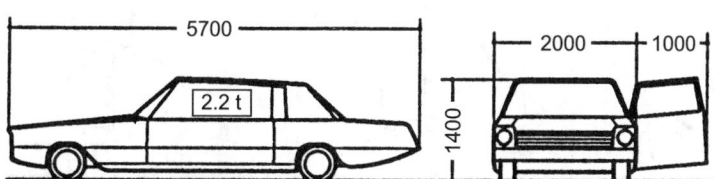

large American car

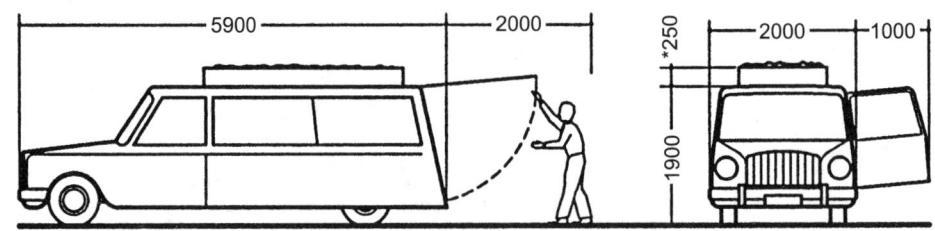

typical British hearse (Daimler, Mercedes)
in London area, Cockney funerals sometimes have elaborate floral arrangements up to 900 mm high

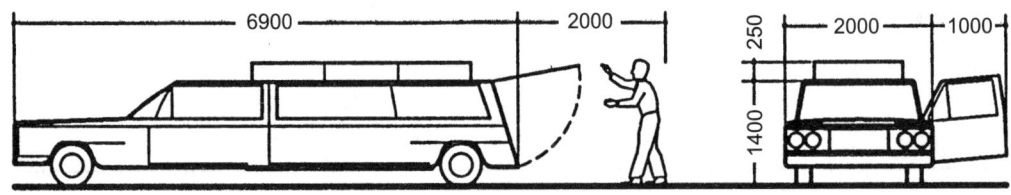

American hearse (Cadillac)

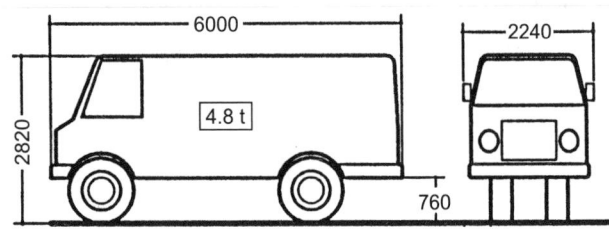

2 tonne van (long wheelbase for laundry etc)

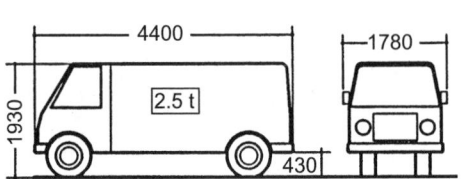

1 tonne van, rear engine (smaller vans as cars)

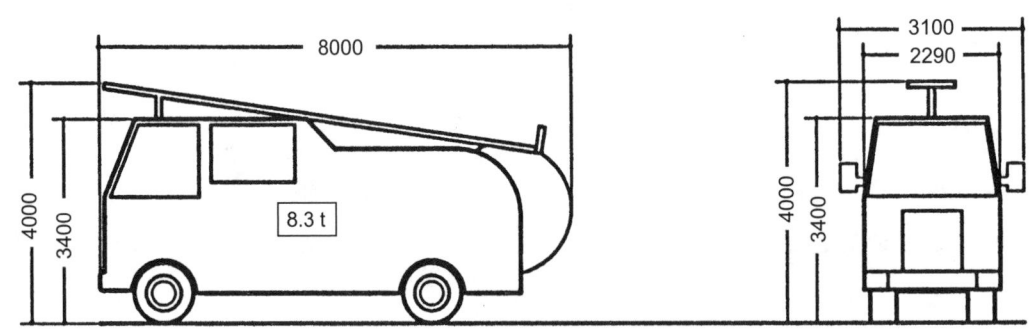

fire appliance, medium size

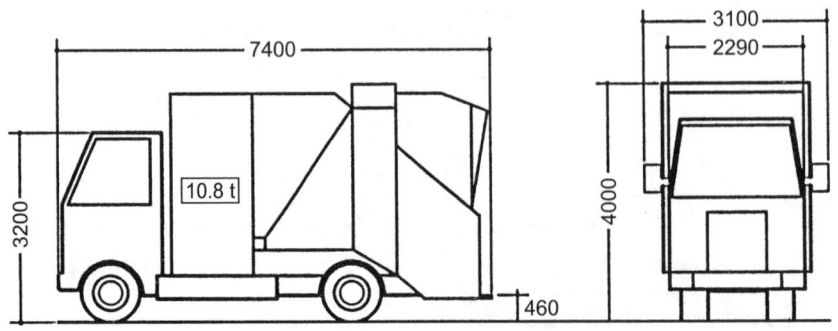

dustcart, medium capacity

three-axle tipper or skip lorry; if under 5.64 m outer axle spread, 20.1 t

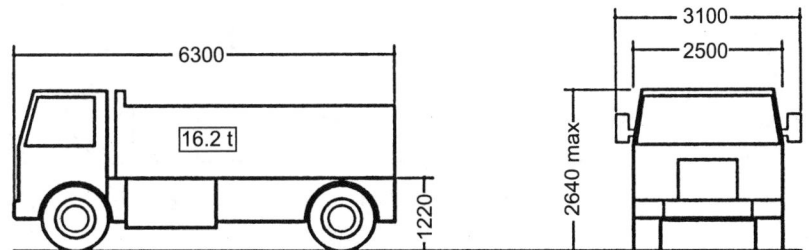

tipper, same size for two-axle skip lorries and truck mixers

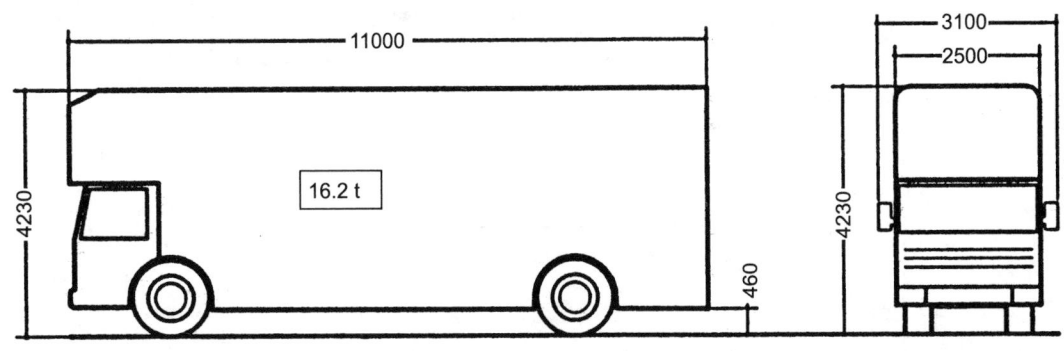

pantechnicon

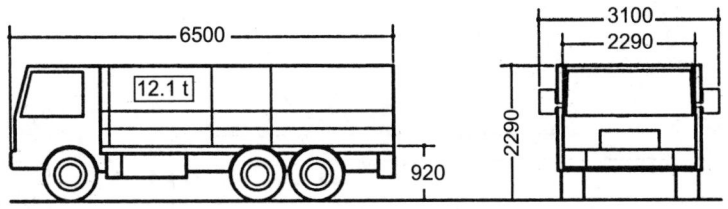

brewer's dray (three axle, 400 mm wheels for low height loading)

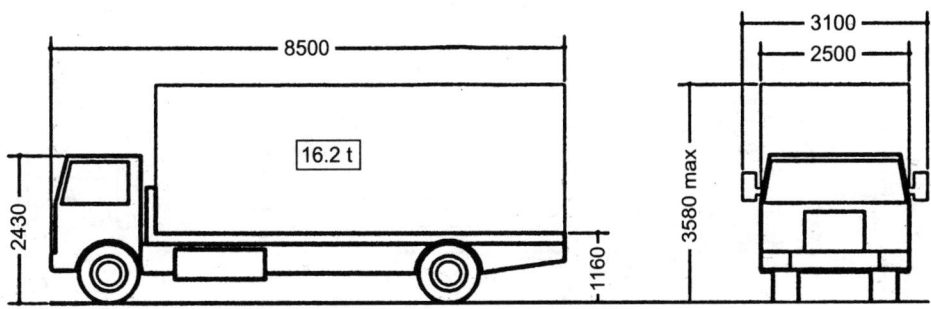

16 tonne rigid

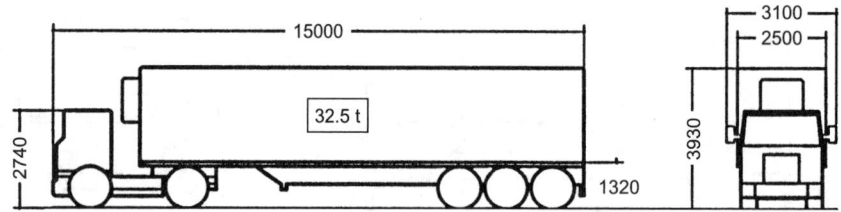

five axle articulated with refrigerated body

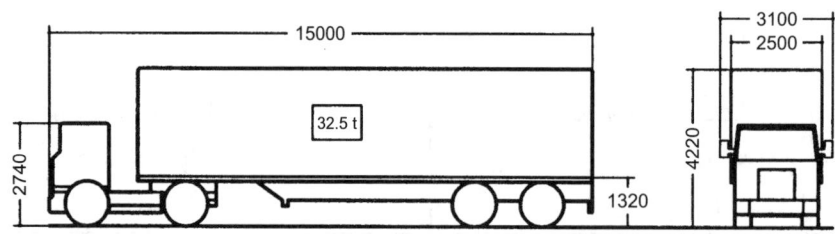

four axle articulated with wide spread trailer axles

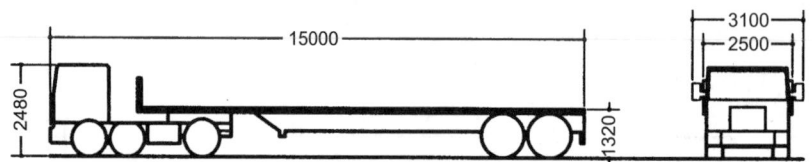

tractor with twin steer front bogie

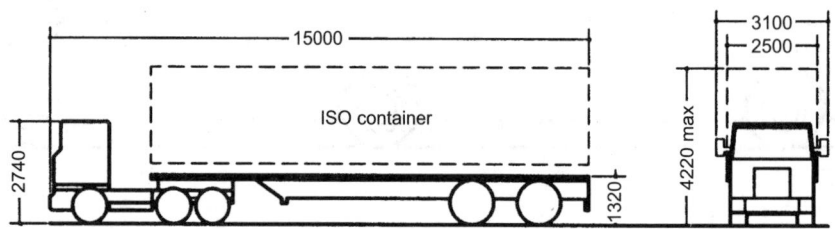

three axle tractor; second steered axle as part of rear bogie with wide spread trailer axles, suitable for unevenly laden containers

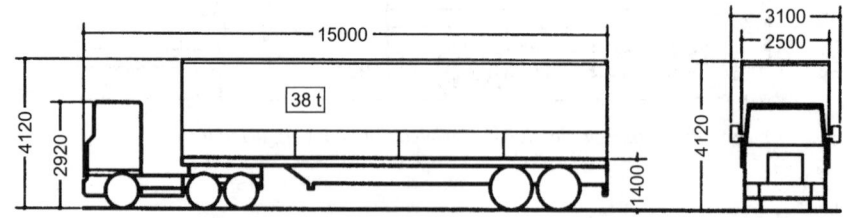

three axle tractor, typical TIR continental outfit

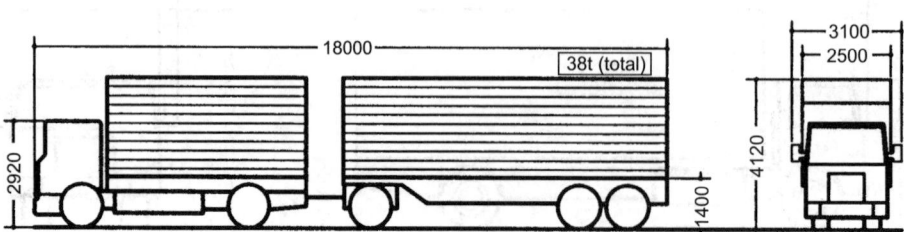

two axle truck, three axle drawbar trailer, typical European vehicle

1.02 Dimensions

The dimensions of some examples of each class are given in **4.1**. In any specific case, the manufacturer's data should be consulted.

1.03 Unit construction

In the field of the larger commercial vehicles, unit construction is now almost universally employed. In this system a given chassis can be fitted with a variety of body shells for specific purposes and loads, mainly of standard dimensions. The body can be changed at will, permitting one body to be loaded while the chassis is on the road with another body delivering goods elsewhere.

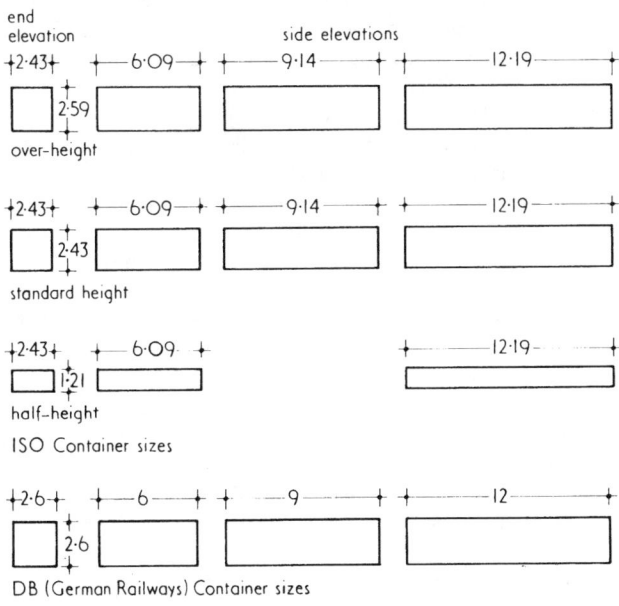

4.2 *Dimensions of standard containers*

A particular example is the standard container, which is used on lorries, ships, railways or even as a storage unit in the open, **4.2**. As this system was first developed in the USA, the standard dimensions are imperial, but the German railways developed a parallel version.

1.04 Turning circles

Apart from the physical dimensions, it is necessary to know the critical characteristics of the vehicle in motion, particularly when manoeuvring while parking or preparing to load. These characteristics are complicated, and usually the manufacturer will quote solely the diameter of the turning circle, either between kerbs or between walls.

Manoeuvring diagrams have been published for various vehicles for the following operations:

- Turning through 90°
- Causing the vehicle to face in the opposite direction by means of a 360° turn in forward gear
- Ditto in reverse gear
- Causing the vehicle to face in the opposite direction by means of both the forward and reverse gears (three-point turn), in T-form
- Ditto in Y-form
- Ditto in a forward side turn
- Ditto in a reverse side turn.

4.3 shows the 90° turns for some of the common vehicles. The other diagrams will be needed for the design of turn-rounds in cul-de-sacs, etc. The use of the published turning circle sizes is not sufficient for the following additional factors:

- The distance required for the driver to turn the steering wheel from straight ahead to full lock depends on the speed, which for the purposes of **4.3** is between 8 and 16 km/h.
- The radius of turn differs between a right-hand and a left-hand turn.

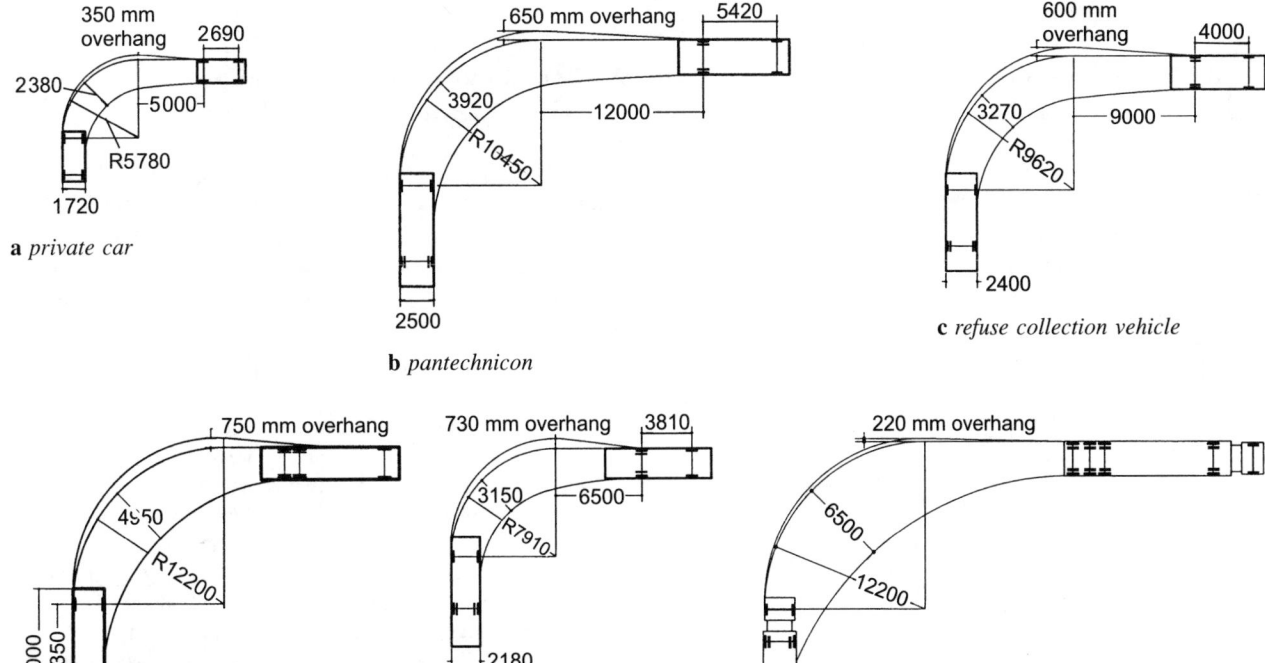

a *private car*

b *pantechnicon*

c *refuse collection vehicle*

d *medium commercialvehicle*

e *fire appliance*

f *largest commercial vehicles*

4.3 *Geometric characteristics of typical vehicles turning through 90°*

● The path traversed by the rear wheels is different from that by the front wheels. In a commercial vehicle travelling at slow speed, the rear wheels follow a smaller arc to the front wheels, the amount depending largely on the distance between the axles. The divergence between the arcs of the wheels on the same side of the vehicle is termed the 'cut in', and value of this determines the total track width of the turning vehicle, always greater than when on the straight.

● While few vehicles have a measurable side overhang of the body beyond the wheel track, many have considerable overhang at front and rear. This is important at the front: the extra width beyond the wheel tracks described by the body is known as 'cut-out'. Allowance should be made for front and rear overhang when designing turn-rounds, etc. by having no vertical obstructions within 1.2 m of the carriageway edge.

2   ROADS IN GENERAL

2.01   Hierarchy
The broad hierarchy of roads is:

● Motorways and trunk roads
● Distributors (primary, district and local)
● Access roads.

Table I Recommended carriageway widths

Road type	Recommended carriageway width (m) between kerbs or edge lines	
Primary distributor	One-way, four lanes	14.6
	Overall width for divided carriageway, two lanes each way with central refuges	14.6
	Two-way, four lanes total, no refuges	13.5
	One-way, three lanes	11
	Two-way, three lanes (recommended only for tidal flow)	9
	One-way, two lanes	7.3
District distributor	One-way, two lanes	7.3
	One-way, two lanes if the proportion of heavy commercial traffic is fairly low	6.75
	Two-way, two lanes	7.3
Local distributor and access road in industrial district	Two-way, two lanes	7.3
Local distributor and access road in commercial district	Two-way, two lanes	6.75
	Minimum two-way, two lane back service road used occasionally by heavy vehicles	5
Local distributor in residential district	Two-way, two lanes used by heavy vehicles minimum	6
Access road in residential district	see text and **4.5**	
	Where all vehicles are required to be able to pass each other	5.5
	Where a wide car can pass a pantechnicon	4.8
	Where two wide cars can pass each other, but a pantechnicon can only pass a cyclist	4.1
	Where a single track only is provided, as for a one-way system, or where passing places are used	
	for all vehicles	3
	for cars only (drives)	2.75
Rural roads	One-way, four lanes	14.6
	One-way, three lanes	11
	Two-way, three lanes	10
	One-way, two lanes	7.3
	Two-way, two lanes	7.3
	Motorway slip road	6
	Minimum for two-way, two lanes	5.5
	Minimum at junctions	4.5
	Single-track between passing places	3.5
	Overall at passing place	6

2.02
This chapter will generally deal only with roads and facilities within development sites, such as industrial parks and housing estates. Public roads are not normally the concern of the architect, but Table I gives the recommended carriageway widths for most road types.

2.03   Definitions
Carriageway: the area of road surface dedicated to vehicles
Carriageway width: the distance between the kerbs forming the carriageway edges
Dual carriageway: a road with a central reservation, each separate carriageway carrying traffic in the reverse direction
lane: a width of carriageway capable of carrying a single line of vehicles, usually delineated with white-painted dashed lines on the carriageway surface
Lane width: since the maximum vehicle width permitted is 2.5 m, and the minimum clearance between parallel vehicles is 0.5 m, the minimum lane width is 3 m. However, vehicles travelling at speed require greater clearance and large vehicles need greater widths on curves, so faster roads have wider lanes
Cycle track or cycle path: a completely separated right-of-way primarily for the use of bicycles
Cycle lane: a portion of a roadway which has been designated by striping, signing, and pavement markings for preferential or exclusive use by cyclists
Shared roadway: a right-of-way designated by signs or permanent markings as a bicycle route, but which is also shared with pedestrians and motorists
Footway: an area of road devoted solely for the use of pedestrians, including those in wheelchairs or with prams, and running alongside the vehicular carriageway. In Britain the footway is also called the 'pavement', in the USA the 'sidewalk'
Footpath: a facility for pedestrians not forming part of a road.

Footway and footpath recomendations will be found in Chapter 6.

3   ROADS IN RESIDENTIAL AREAS

3.01   Environmental areas
This section focuses mainly on roads in residential areas and in housing estates. However, the principles are the same in industrial and business areas, only the details will differ.

An 'environmental area' is surrounded by distributor roads from which access to the properties within is gained solely via the access roads within it. The access road network is designed with the following in mind:

● Road access to within 25 m (or 15 m in certain cases) of each house
● Road access to all private garages, whether within curtilages or in garage courts; and to all parking areas
● Through traffic from one distributor road to another, or to another part of the same road (avoiding a traffic blockage) is either impossible, or severly discouraged
● Necessary tradesmen, e.g. 'milk-rounds', calling at all or most properties in sequence, are not unreasonably diverted
● In general, traffic is not allowed to proceed too fast, but visibility at all times is at least the stopping distance for the possible (not the legal) speed limit.

4.4 illustrates typical access road layouts.

3.02   Types of access road
Access roads in residential areas are of three types:

● *Major access roads (or transitional)*. These are short lengths of road connecting a distributor road with the minor access road

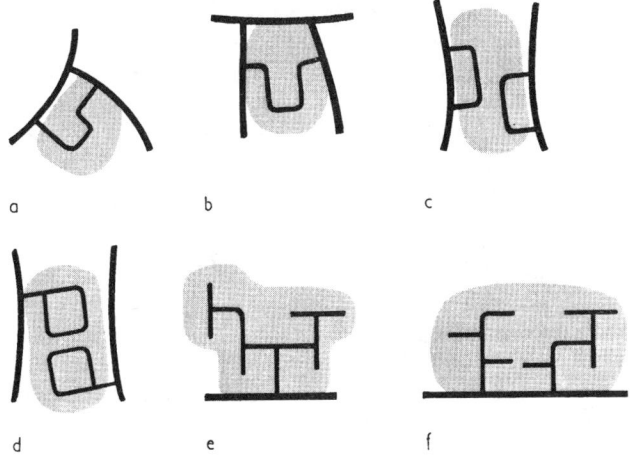

a   b   c

d   e   f

4.4 a *and* **b** *are through roads, so tortuous as to discourage through traffic;* **c** *and* **d** *are non-through systems, but avoid the need for hammer-head turnrounds;* **e** *is a cul-de-sac system, but will have substantial traffic at the entrance;* **f** *is to be preferred on this count, although both systems post problems for the 'milk round'*

network, the latter at a T-junction. They are normally 6 m wide, have no direct access to property along their length, and serve from 200 to 400 dwellings.

● *Minor access or collector roads.* These form the backbone of the network, will serve up to 200 dwellings and be 5.5 m wide

with only one footway. Occasionally a single track 'car way' 2.75 m wide is used for access to about 50 dwellings, in conjunction with a separate footpath system.

● *Shared private drives, mews courts, garage courts and housing squares.* Generally these facilities serve up to 20 dwellings, and are designed for joint pedestrian/vehicle use with hard surfaces, no upstand kerbs and no footways. Access to them from the collector roads is marked by some device such as a short ramp or rough surface material, with the purpose of slowing down the traffic.

3.03 Designed controls

Conventionally roads were designed so that cars could be parked on both sides, and two cars could still pass. This encouraged use by vehicles trying to avoid congestion on main roads, with excessive speed and consequent nuisance and danger to the inhabitants. **4.5** shows the characteristics of the various carriageway widths.

While legal penalties can apply to misuse of these roads, these require enforcement resources which are rarely available. It is therefore the designer's responsibility to build-in the discouragement required. Closures, narrowing and speed humps are now used in existing roads; but these have unwanted side-effects such as complications for ambulances, fire engines and even local buses. In new developments it should be possible to avoid these measures and still provide sufficient restraints.

4.6 to **4.8** show typical arrangements of humps. The slowing effect of various ramps is detailed in **4.9**. **4.10** and **4.11** give the Department of Transport requirements for hump dimensions.

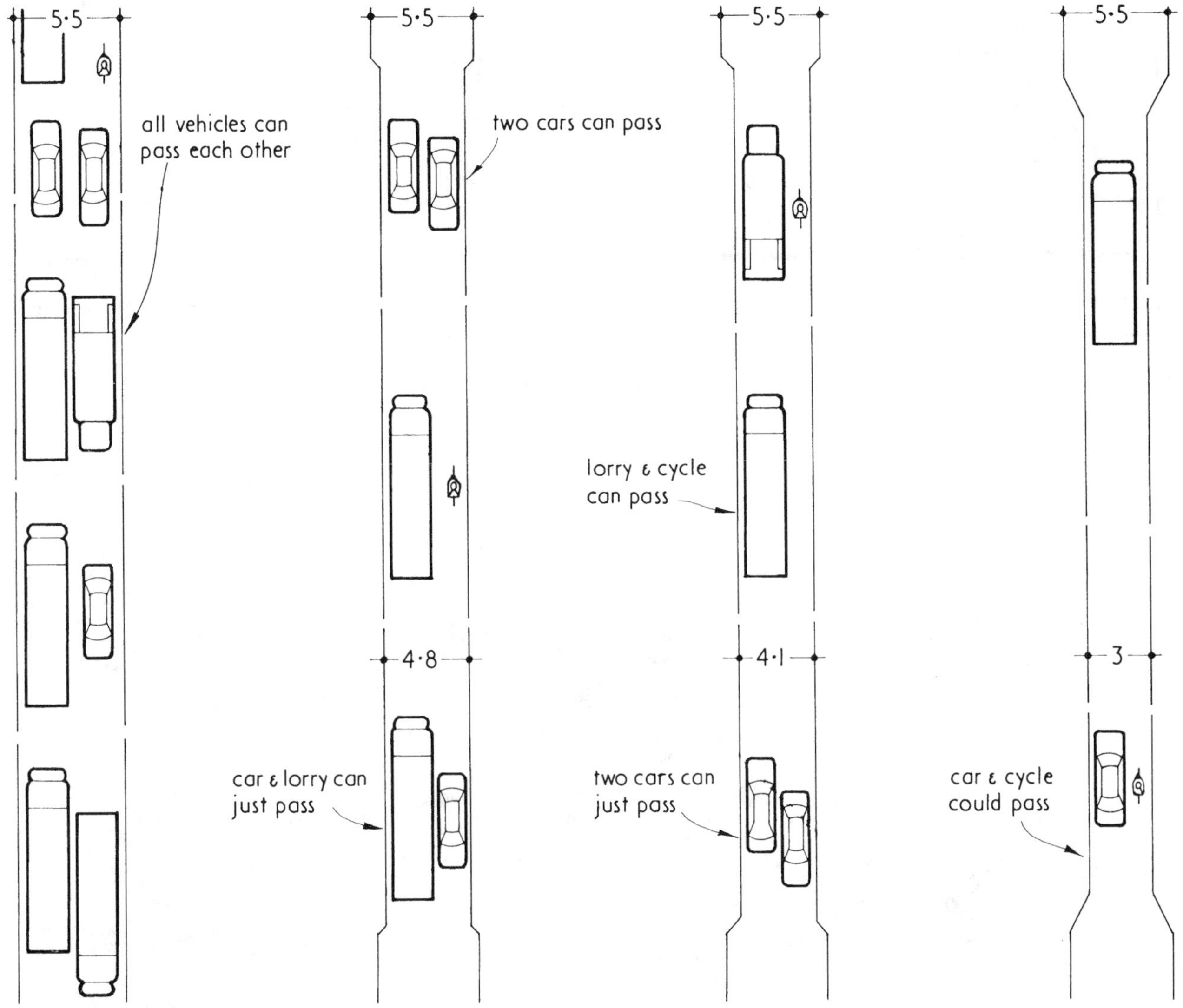

├─ 5·5 ─┤   ├─ 5·5 ─┤   ├─ 5·5 ─┤   ├─ 5·5 ─┤

all vehicles can pass each other

two cars can pass

lorry & cycle can pass

├─ 4·8 ─┤   ├─ 4·1 ─┤   ├─ 3 ─┤

car & lorry can just pass

two cars can just pass

car & cycle could pass

4.5 *Characteristics of various carriageway widths on two-way roads*

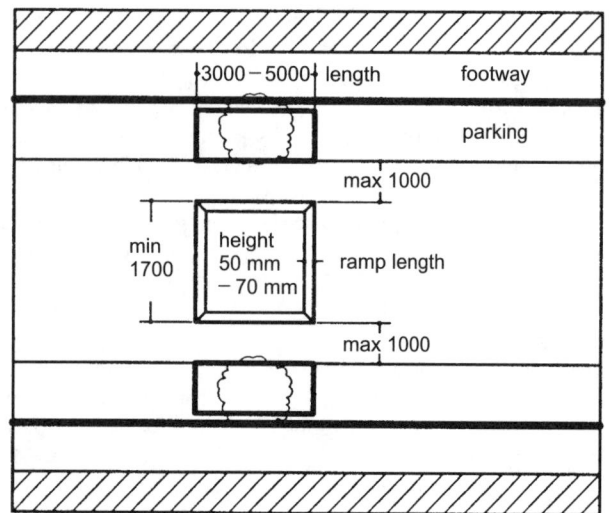

4.6 *Cushion hump*

There are considerable disadvantages to the use of humps. Vehicles, such as delivery vans, that are continuously using roads with humps find that maintenance costs on tyres, wheels and suspensions are significantly increased. Buses and ambulances find that their passengers experience discomfort and even danger. An alternative slowing device to the hump is the 'chicane', examples of which are shown in **4.12**.

Once garages and visitors' parking spaces are provided, kerbside parking may be discouraged by constructing one-way roads with minimum carriageway widths. However, occasional access by large furniture vans (and, unfortunately, fire appliances) will be necessary; and regular visits by refuse collection vehicles have to be as trouble-free as possible. For example, local authorities dislike cul-de-sacs with end turning areas permanently obstructed by parked cars, and may well insist on residents bringing their refuse to the entrance of the road.

Refuse vehicles and delivery vans blocking narrow roads cause annoyance to other residents trying to pass; consider having at least two routes of access/egress for most parts of the area.

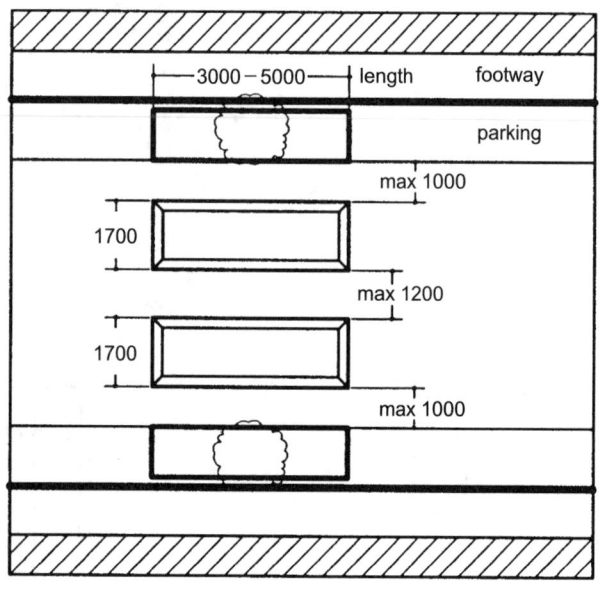

4.7 *Double cushion humps*

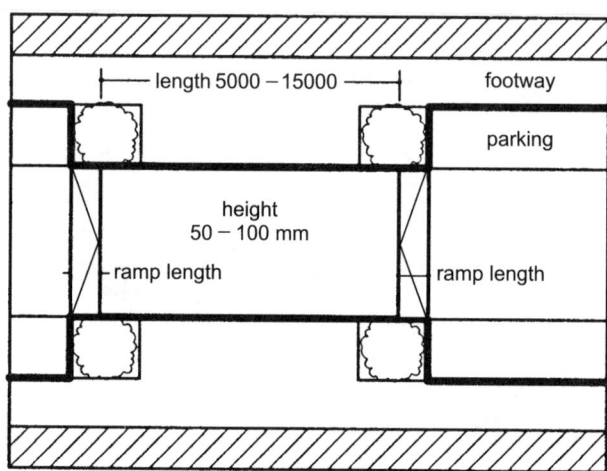

4.8 *Flat top hump used as a pedestrian crossing*

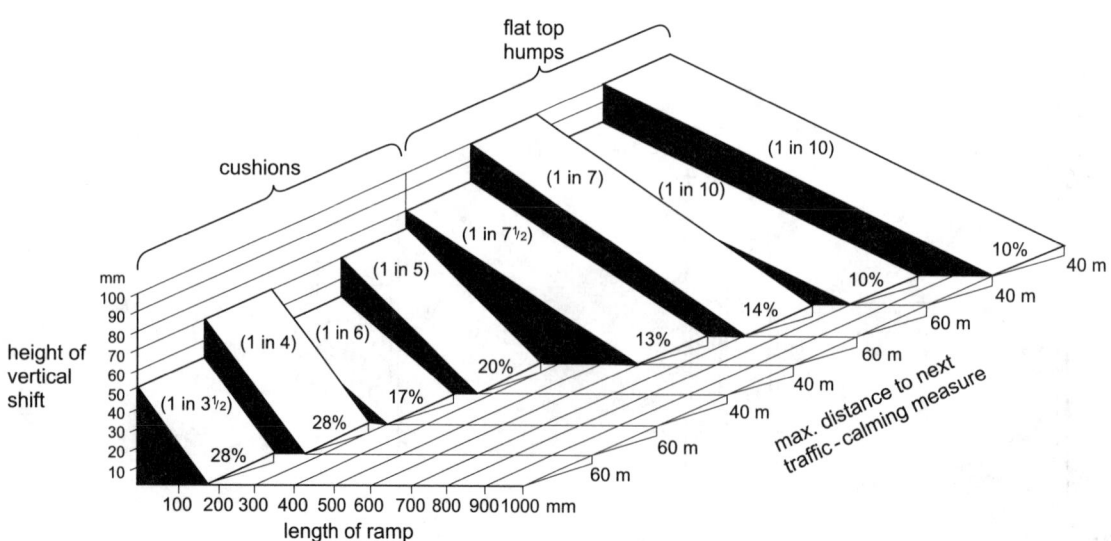

4.9 *Results of research into ramp dimensions for 85 percentile speed of 32 kph (20 mph)*

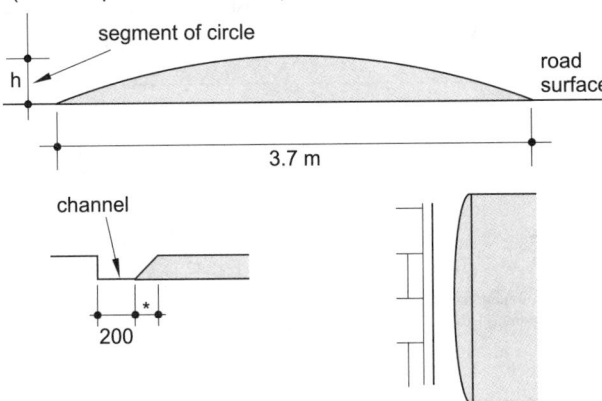

4.10 *Dimensions of round top road hump from the Highways (Road Hump) Regulations 1990*

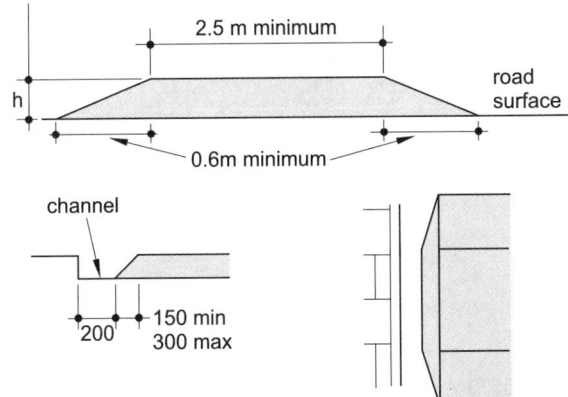

4.11 *Dimensions of flat-top hump from the same source*

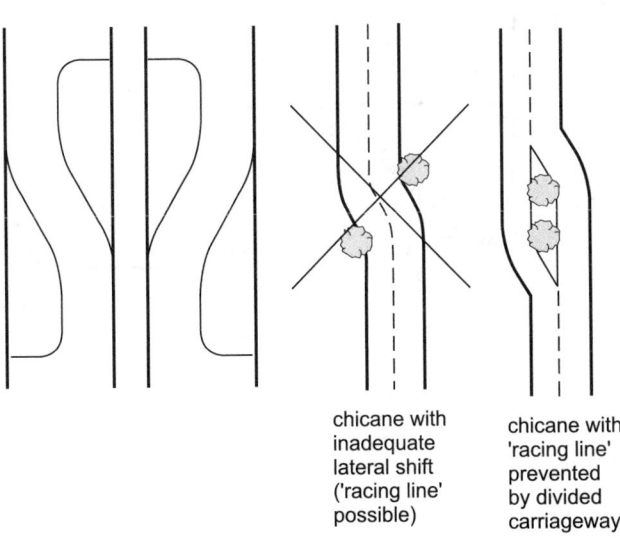

4.12 *Chicane types of traffic slowing device*

4 ROADS IN INDUSTRIAL PARKS

These must provide for use by the largest vehicles, but otherwise pose the same problems as roads in housing estates. Layout should discourage traffic using the roads as a cut-through, and should also ensure that the speed of the legitimate traffic is kept low. This is not a simple matter, as corner radii cannot be too sharp when heavy vehicles constitute a substantial proportion of the traffic.

5 ROAD DESIGN DETAILS

5.01 Visibility and stopping distance

It is an axiom of road design that the driver should be able to see a distance at least as far as the distance he or she needs to stop in. If the object seen is also a moving vehicle, the sight distance must allow both vehicles to stop before colliding.

4.13 gives the design stopping distances for speeds up to 110 km/h (approx 70 mph). These distances are about $2\frac{1}{4}$ times the stopping distances given in the *Highway Code* for vehicles with good brakes in ideal conditions. This is to allow for reduced brake performance, poor weather conditions and impaired visibility.

When emerging from a side road onto a through road the driver must be able to see a vehicle on the through road a distance of that vehicle's stopping distance. When crossing a footway the driver should be able to see 2.4 m along it. Where small children are to be expected this visibility should be to within 600 mm of the ground; but where there are no small children (such as in industrial areas) 1050 mm will be sufficient. **4.14** and **4.15** indicate the areas that must be free of obstruction, and Table II gives some recommended standards in residential areas.

5.02 Curves

As mentioned in Section **1.04**, when a vehicle travels round a curve the road width it occupies is greater than the track width on the straight. Table III combined with **4.16** indicates the magnitude of this – the width of carriageway should be increased on curves to compensate.

4.14 *Required heights for unobstructed visibility*

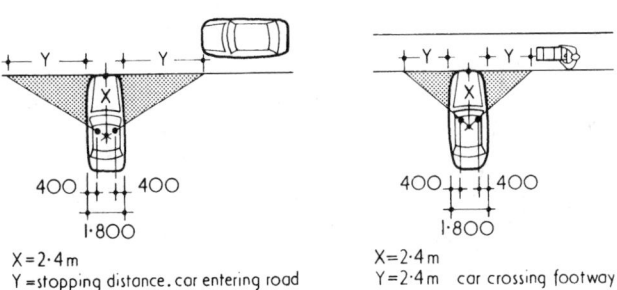

4.15 *Required distances for unobstructed visibility*

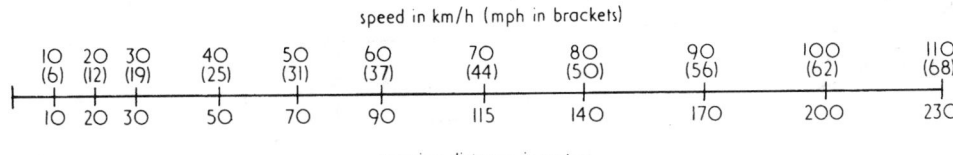

4.13 *Design stopping distances*

Table II Recommended standards in junction design

Junction type		Radius (m) R	Minimum junction spacing (m) adjacent	Opposite	Sightlines (m)	
Road A	Road B				X	Y
Local distributor	Any other road	10	80	40	5	60 in 30 mph zone 80 in 40 mph zone 100 in 50 mph zone
Minor access road	Major access road	6			2.4	40
Minor access road	Minor access road	6	25	8	2.4	40
Minor access road	entrance to mews or garage court	4.2	25	8	2.4	40
Single track road	entrance to mews or garage court	8 & 5 Offset	25	8	Junctions must be intervisible	
Mews or garage court	entrance to mews or garage court	4.2			2.4	10

Table III Outside turning radius of front axle (m)

Minimum radius			15		30		45		60		75–400		400+		
R	X	Y	X	Y	X	Y	X	Y	X	Y	X	Y	X	Y	
10.45	3.92	4.57	3.44	3.89	2.96	3.19	2.80	2.95	2.73	2.84	2.68	2.77	2.53	2.54	Pantechnicon
9.62	3.27	3.87	2.94	3.33	2.66	2.85	2.58	2.71	2.53	2.63	2.50	2.58	2.42	2.43	Refuse vehicle
7.91	3.15	3.88	2.67	3.06	2.42	2.61	2.34	2.47	2.30	2.40	2.27	2.35	2.19	2.20	Fire appliance
5.78	2.38	2.73	1.96	2.10	1.84	1.91	1.80	1.85	1.78	1.81	1.76	1.78	1.73	1.74	Private car

X = Maximum width of wheel path
Y = Maximum width of wheel path plus overhang

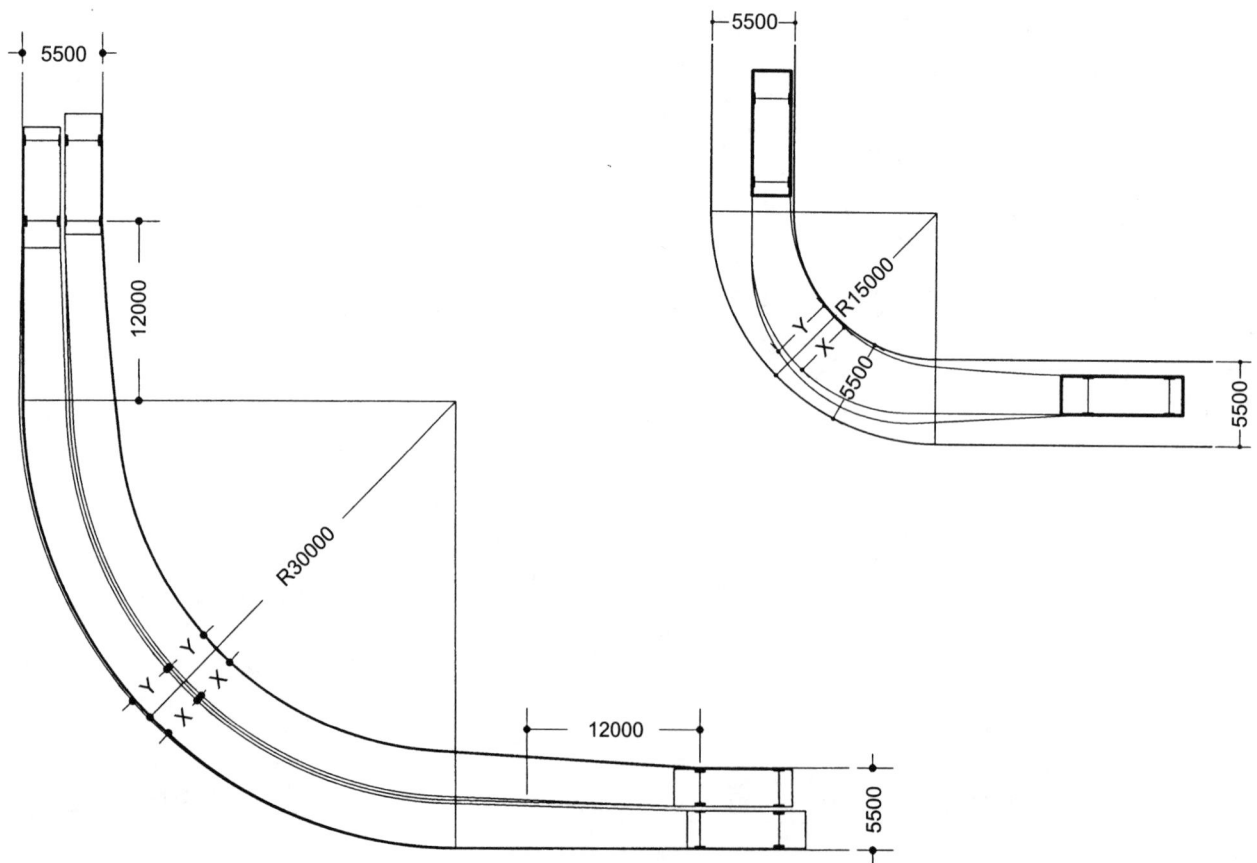

4.16 *Widening on bends; dimensions X and Y are given in Table III*

5.03 Corners

Since the internal radius of turn of a large commercial vehicle is about 8 m, it will be seen that a kerb radius of 10 m will be needed for such vehicles to maintain a constant distance from the kerb while turning the corner, also allowing some spare for the distance covered while turning the steering wheel. A kerb radius of 10 m in all cases would mean large areas of carriageway at junctions, and would be inappropriate in scale in many places, particularly in residential areas. Where traffic volumes are low there is no reason why the occasional large vehicle should not encroach on the opposite side of the road, provided that clear visibility is maintained so that vehicles affected by the manoeuvre can take avoiding action in time. **4.17** illustrates the effects of using radii of 10, 6 and 4 m.

5.04 Turn-round areas

Where conventional arrangements are used in turn-round areas in mews courts and housing squares, the minimum standards in **4.18** can be employed. Some local authorities require more generous minimum standards for their refuse collection and fire-fighting vehicles. In cases of doubt, use the specimen vehicle track diagrams in **4.3**.

5.05 Gradients

Acceptable gradients are hard to define. What would be quite normal in the Peak district would be considered horrendous in Lincolnshire. Consider the likelihood of snow and icy conditions

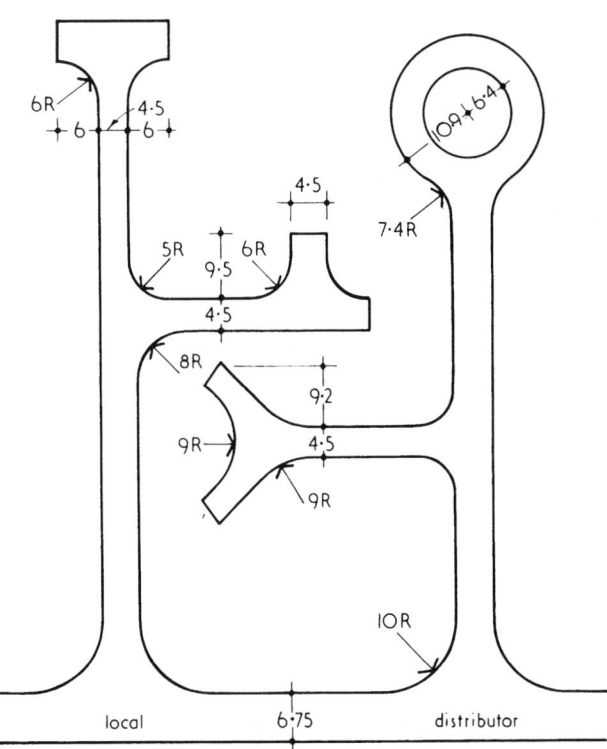

4.18 *Typical recommended dimensions for use in urban areas*

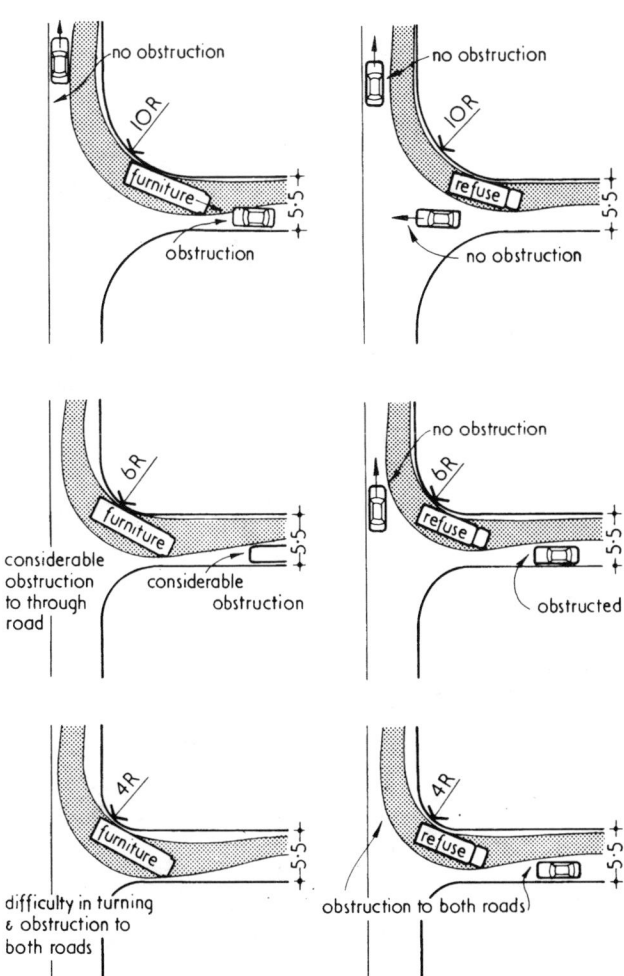

4.17 *Junction design; the effect of kerb radius on traffic vlow at the T-junction of two 5.5 m wide roads*

in winter, when anything greater than about 12 per cent becomes impassable without snow tyres or chains. Most general-purpose roads are now constructed to 7 per cent or less. Ramps to lorry loading bays and car parking garages are limited to 10 per cent. Some car parks in basements or multi-storey have gradients up to 15 per cent (and occasionally beyond). These steep gradients require vertical transition curves at each end to avoid damage to vehicles. Also, steep gradients either up or down should be avoided close to the back of pavement line or road edge, as it is difficult to see clearly, or to take preventative action if needed.

5.06 Verges

Where there is no footway, a soft verge of 1 m width should be provided for the accommodation of services (water, gas, electricity, communications, etc.) and to allow for vehicular overhang.

6 BIKEWAYS AND CYCLE PARKING

6.01

For definitions see Section **2.02**.

6.02 Gradients

Cyclists will avoid steep gradients. Studies show that if gradients exceed 5 per cent there will be a sharp drop in the length of uphill grade that cyclists will tolerate. **4.19** illustrates commonly accepted maximum uphill grades based on length of grade; downhill gradients of 6.5 per cent are acceptable.

6.03 Width

Factors to consider when determining widths for bikeways must include:

● The dimensions of the cyclist and the bicycle
● Manoeuvring space required for balancing
● Additional clearance required to avoid obstacles.

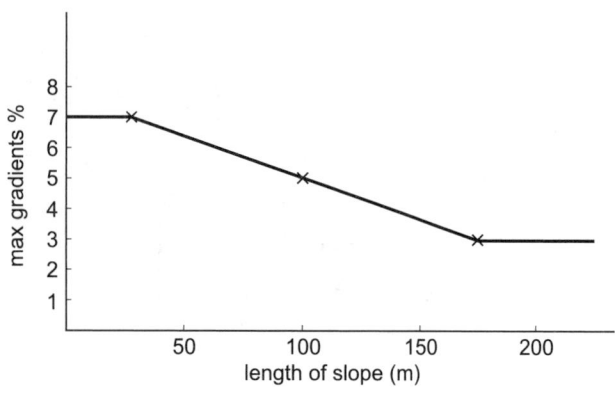

4.19 *Acceptable gradients for bikeways*

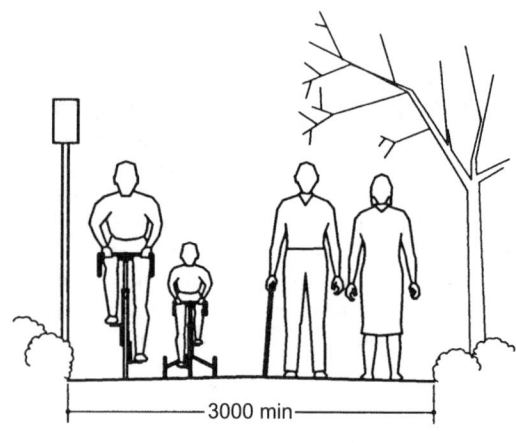

4.22 *Cycle path shared with pedestrians*

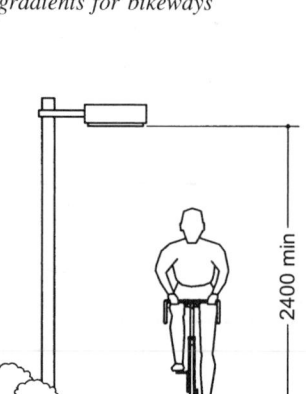

4.20 *Single-track cycle path*

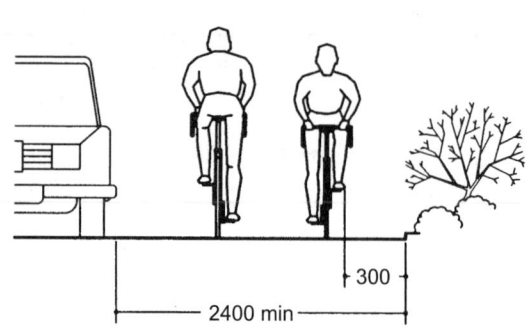

4.23 *Cycle lane on all-purpose roadway*

A width of 2.75 m is recommended for single-track bikeways, although 1.8 m, **4.20**, is acceptable. For two-way traffic 3.6 m is advisable. **4.21** shows a two-way right-of-way based on US practice. There should be no obstruction within 1.2 m of the edge of the riding surface, as this could be a danger. If the path is alongside a wall or fence, ensure that a line is painted on the surface at least 300 mm from it.

In almost all cases two-way travel will occur on cycle paths regardless of design intentions; appropriate widths should be provided. **4.22** illustrates a typical path where cycles share with pedestrians, and **4.23** a cycle lane on the near side of an all-purpose road.

6.04 Surfacings

A separate bikeway should have a smooth non-stick surface and have a thickness capable of supporting maintenance vehicles. Asphalt, concrete, gravel and stabilised earth are materials commonly used.

6.05 Drainage

Surfaces should have a crossfall of at least 2 per cent to provide positive drainage. Drainage grilles should have their slots diagonal to the route of the cyclist and be designed and located to minimise danger.

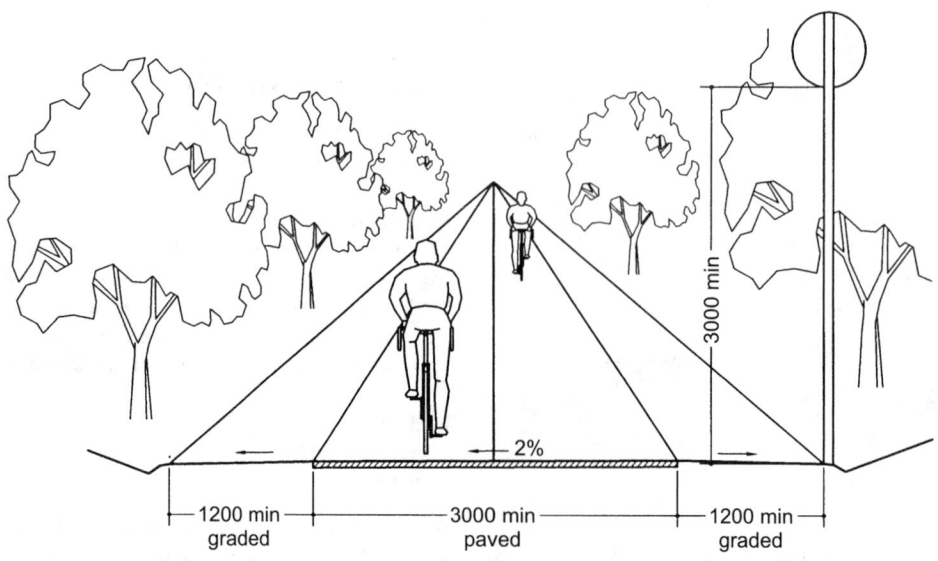

4.21 *Two-way bicyle path on separated right of way*

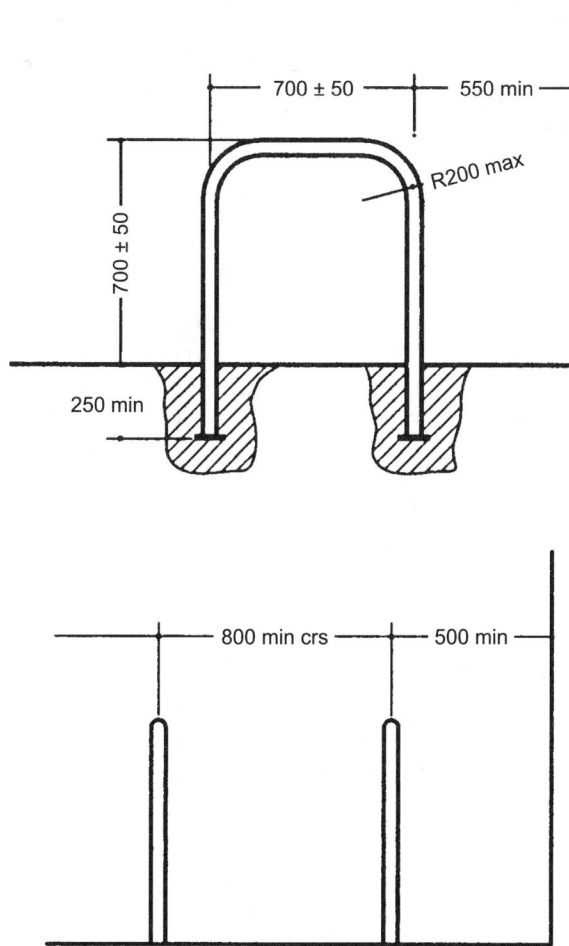

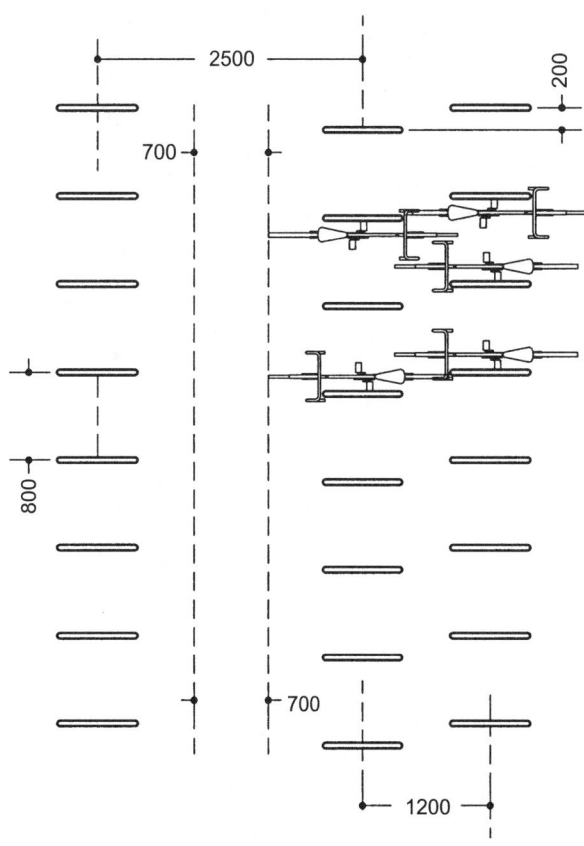

4.24 *Basic Sheffield parking stand*

4.26 *It is important that arrays of Sheffield stands make best use of space. Attempts at closer spacing than shown will not succeed due to blocking of some positions by carelessly parked cycles*

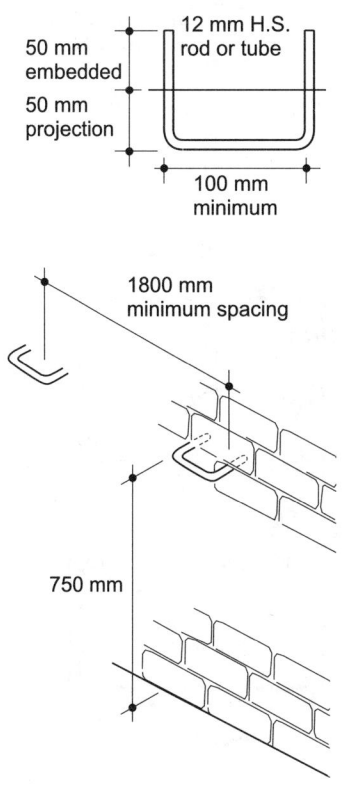

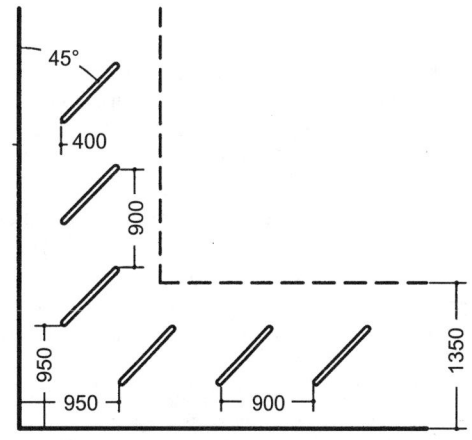

4.27 *An arrangement in an angle between two walls*

6.06 Cycle parking

This should be located as close to destinations as possible without interfering with pedestrian traffic; and where visual supervision, lighting and shelter from inclement weather can be achieved. It is essential to provide facilities for securely locking the bicycle frame and the front wheel wheel to something immoveable. The favourite is the Sheffield stand **4.24** or in certain situations, wall bars **4.25**. The groove in the concrete paving slab illustrated in the previous edition of this book is to be deplored: it provides no security, and can easily damage the wheel. In extreme cases, lockers large enough to contain a bicycle can be provided. **4.26** to **4.29**, show arrangements where larger numbers of cycles are expected. See Section 7 for suggested scale of cycle parking provision.

4.25 *Wall bar, suitable for smallparking spaces where short-term parking is required*

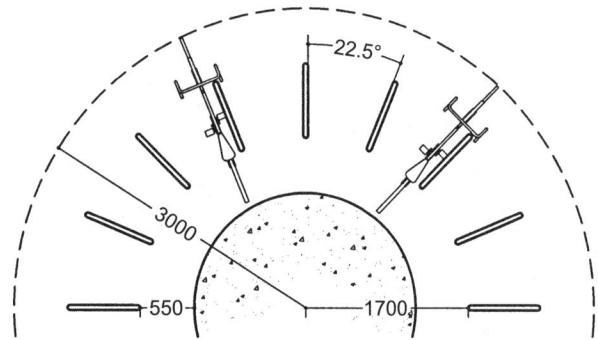

4.28 *Circular array with a capacity for 32 cycles*

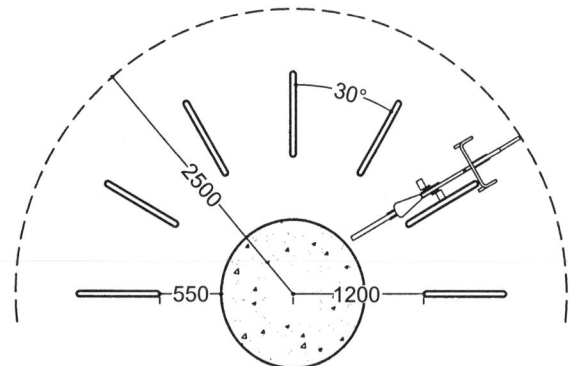

4.29 *Circular array with a capacity for 24 cycles*

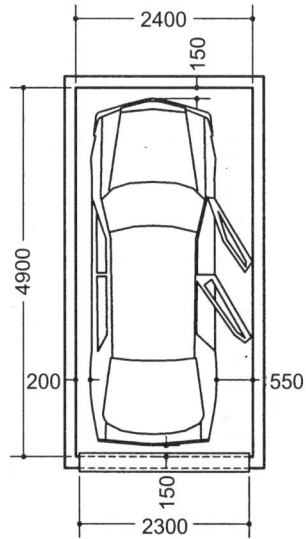

4.30 *A domestic garage of minimum dimensions*

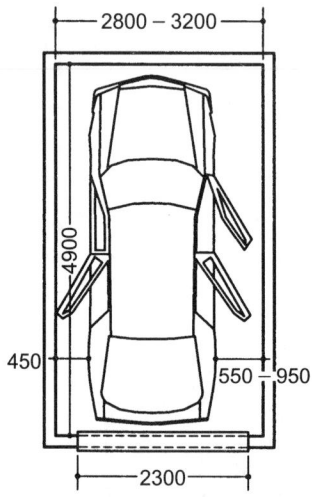

4.31 *A more generous garage permitting passenger access*

7 PARKING

7.01

A clear parking policy for each area is an essential. Many facilities now provide little or no parking in order to discourage the use of private transport. This is only effective if it is clearly impossible to park on the adjacent roads, and if there is adequate public transport available. Consider also the needs of disabled people.

There are no statutory requirements and few guidelines for the scale of parking provision. Table IV gives recommendations, but each specific case should be examined to determine expected requirements. Some planning authorities now restrict parking provision for cars in order to give a measure of restraint to traffic.

Table IV also includes recommendations for the scale of bicycle parking. These are quite generous so as to encourage greater use of bicycles. However, account should be taken of the local conditions – in places such as Cambridge where there are substantially more bicycles than average, greater provision should be made.

7.02 Domestic garages

The domestic garage is the basic provision for residential areas. This can be:

● Within the envelope of the house or block of flats
● A separate detached building or
● One of a number in a garage court.

4.30 to **4.36** show a number of typical arrangements.

7.03 Car parks

Once the scale of provision has been decided, the form will depend on the size and shape of the available area, and also on the type of

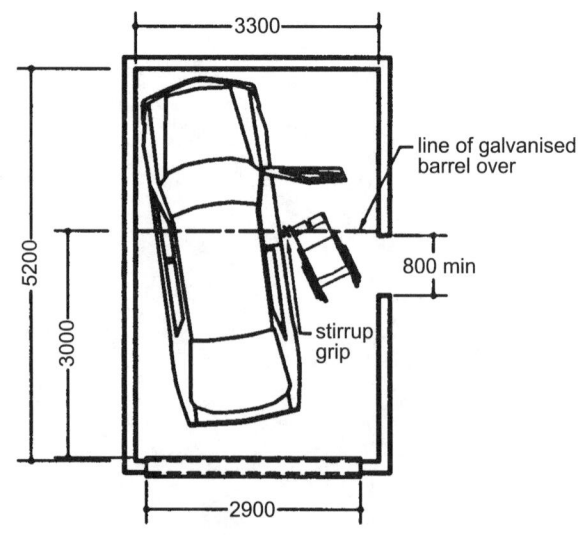

4.32 *Garage for a driver who is a wheelchair user (for an ambulant disabled driver, a width of 2.8 m is adequate)*

Table IV Parking and loading/unloading requirements

Type of building	Car parking provision	Loading/unloading provision		Cycle parking
Normal housing	Residents: one garage space for each occupancy, (preferably within the curtilage) Visitors: where houses are served directly from a road, driveways provide a minimum of one car space within curtilage of each Where visitors cannot park within curtilage, one off-street space per four dwellings	Refuse collection vehicle within 25 m of each disposal point (dustbin position). Some authorities require vehicle within 15 m. Where communal containers (paladins) are used, maximum distance 9 m Furniture removal vehicle as near as possible, not further than 25 m		
Minimum-cost housing	Space should be provided, if not laid out, to allow for one resident's or visitor's parking space per dwelling, provided public transport is available	As above		
Old people's housing	One garage space per two dwellings	As above		
Sheltered housing	Resident and non-resident staff: one car space per two members present at peak period Visitors: use empty staff places, but provide one additional place per five dwellings	As above, plus provision for special passenger vehicle with tail lift, etc Minimum provision for daily loading/unloading 50 m^2		
Shops	Staff: one car space (preferably in enclosed yard behind shop) for each 100 m^2 gross floor area or, if known, one space per managerial staff plus one for every four other staff Customers: one space for each 25 m^2 gross floor area. In superstores with gross floor area exceeding 2000 m^2 allow one space per 10 m^2. (Not appropriate when goods sold are obviously bulky, e.g. carpets, boats)	See diagrams of loading bays. General minima as follows: Gross floor space not exceeding: 500 m^2 1000 2000 each additional 1000 m^2	Minimum space required: 50 m^2 100 150 50 m^2	1 per 200 m^2 with minimum of 4
Banks	Staff: one space for each managerial or executive staff, plus one per four others Customers: one space per 10 m^2 of net public floor space in banking hall	Minimum 25 m^2		2
Offices	Staff: one space for each 25 m^2 of gross floor area, or one space for each managerial and executive staff, plus one space per four others Visitors: 10% of staff parking provision	General minima: Gross floor space not exceeding: 100 m^2 500 1000 each additional 1000 m^2	Minimum space required: 50 m^2 100 150 25 m^2	1 per 200 m^2 with minimum of 4
Production buildings (factories)	Staff: one car space per 50 m^2 of gross floor area Visitors: 10% of staff parking provision	See loading bay diagram. Provision to be commensurate with expected traffic General minima as follows: Gross floor space not exceeding: 100 m^2 250	Minimum space required: 70 m^2 140	1 per 500 m^2 with minimum of 4
Storage buildings (warehouses)	Staff: one space per each 200 m^2 of gross floor space	500 1000 2000 each additional 1000 m^2	170 200 300 50 m^2	1 per 1000 m^2 with minimum of 4
Hotels, motels and public houses	Resident staff: one space per household Non-resident staff: one space for each three staff members employed at peak period Resident guests: one space per bedroom Bar customers: one space for each 4 m^2 of net public space in bars Occasional diners: no additional provision required If conferences are held in the hotel, space required should be assessed separately at one space for each five seats	General minima as follows: Gross floor space not exceeding: 500 m^2 1000 2000 each additional 1000 m^2	Minimum space required: 140 m^2 170 200 25	1 per 10 beds with minimum of 4
Restaurants and cafés	Resident staff: one space per household Non-resident staff: one space per three members employed at peak period Diners: one space for each two seats in dining area (For transport cafés, the space should be a lorry space of 45 m^2, and the arrangement should be such that vehicles can enter and leave without reversing)	General minima as follows: Dining floor space not exceeding: 100 m^2 250 500	Minimum space required: 50 m^2 75 100	1 per 25 m^2 with minimum of 4
Licensed clubs	Resident staff: one space per household Non-resident staff: one space for each three members employed at peak period Performers: one space for each solo performer and/or group expected at peak Patrons: one space per two seats, or one space per 4 m^2 net public floor space	Minimum 50 m^2		1 per 25 m^2 with minimum of 4

Table IV (continued)

Type of building	Car parking provision	Loading/unloading provision	Cycle parking
Dance halls and discotheques	Staff: one space per three members at peak period Performers: three spaces Patrons: one space per 10 m² of net public floor space	Minimum 50 m²	1 per 25 m² with minimum of 4
Cinemas	Staff: one space per three members at peak period Patrons: one space per 5 seats	Minimum 50 m² Space required within site by main entrance for two cars to pick up and set down patrons	1 per 100 seats with minimum of 4
Theatres	Staff: one space per three members at peak period Performers: one space per 10 m² of gross dressing room accommodation Patrons: one space for each three seats	Minimum 100 m² Space required within site by main entrance for two cars to pick up and set down patrons	1 per 100 seats with minimum of 4
Swimming baths	Staff: one space for every two members normally present Patrons: one space per 10 m² pool area	Minimum 50m²	1 per 4 staff
Sports facilities and playing fields	Staff: one space per three members normally present Players: one space for each two players able to use the facility simultaneously, provided public transport is reasonably close. Otherwise two spaces for each three players Spectators: provide only if more than three times the number of players	Minimum 50 m²	1 per 4 staff
Marinas	Staff: one space per three members normally present Boat-users: two spaces for each three mooring-berths. (If other facilities are included, eg restaurant, shop etc, provide additional spaces at 50% normal provision for each additional facility)	Minimum 50 m²	1 per 4 staff
Community centres and assembly halls	Staff: one space for each three members normally present Patrons: one space for every five seats for which the building is licensed	Minimum 50 m²	1 per 4 staff
Places of worship	Worshippers: one space per ten seats in space for worship	Minimum 50 m² Space provided within site close to main entrance for two cars to set down and pick up worshippers	1 per 60 seats minimum 4
Museums and public art galleries	Staff: one space per two members normally on duty Visitors: one space per 30 m² of public display space	Minimum 50 m²	1 per 300 m² minimum 4
Public libraries	Staff: one space per three members normally on duty Borrowers: one space for each 500 adult ticket holders with a minimum of three spaces. If there are separate reference facilities, provide additional spaces at one for each ten seats	Minimum 50 m² If used as a base for a mobile library, provide another 50 m² to park this	1 per 300 m² minimum 4
Hospitals	Staff: one space for each doctor and surgeon, plus one space for each three others Outpatients and visitors: one space for each three beds	General minima as follows: Gross floor space not exceeding: / Minimum space required: 1000 m² — 200 m² 2000 — 300 4000 — 400 6000 — 500 every additional 2000 m² — 100 m²	1 per 12 beds
Health centres, surgeries, clinics	Staff: one space per doctor etc one space per two members of staff other than doctors etc employed at peak period Patients: two spaces per consulting room	Sufficient for requirements specified, including if necessary space for special vehicle for non-ambulant patients	4
Special schools, day-care centres and adult training centres	Staff: one space for each two members normally present Attenders: in many cases these will be transported to the centre. For certain centres for the physically handicapped, allow one space for special or adapted self-drive vehicle per four attenders	Minimum 30 m² Accommodation for special passenger vehicle Space provided within the site for cars and/or buses to set down and pick up	1 per 6 staff
Nursery and primary schools	Staff: one space per two members normally present Visitors: two spaces Hard surface play area used for parking on open days etc.	Minimum 30 m²	1 per 6 staff
Secondary schools	Staff: one space per two members normally present Visitors: schools with up to 1000 pupils – four spaces, larger schools – eight spaces. Hard surface play area used for parking on occasion	Minimum 50 m² Space provided within site for school buses to set down and pick up	1 per 6 staff 1 per 3 students

Table IV (continued)

Type of building	Car parking provision	Loading/unloading provision	Cycle parking
Sixth form colleges	Staff: one space per two members normally present Visitors: colleges with up to 1000 pupils – five spaces, larger schools – ten Hard surface play area used for parking on occasion	Minimum 50 m²	1 per 6 staff 1 per 3 students
Further education colleges and retraining centres	Staff: one space for each member normally present Students and visitors: one space for each three students normally present	Minimum 50 m²	1 per 6 staff 1 per 3 students

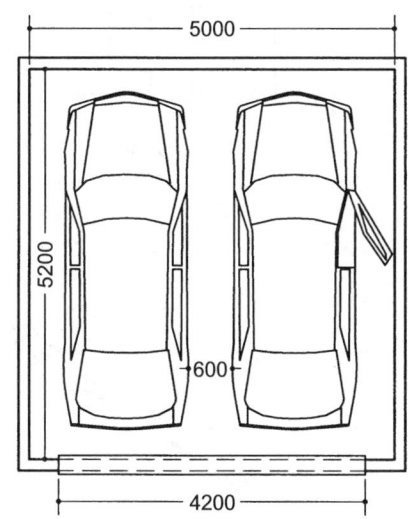

4.33 *A garage for two cars*

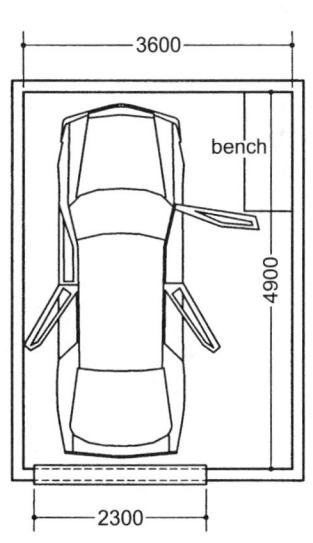

4.34 *A garage of minimum length but width sufficient for a workbench*

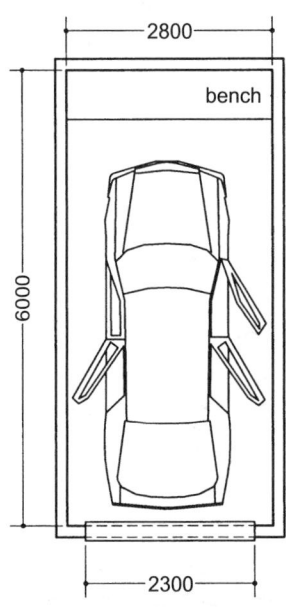

4.35 *A garage with a workbench at the end*

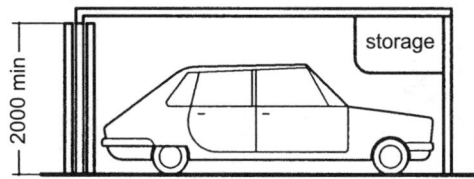

4.36 *Cross-section through a garage showing raised storage area*

4.37 *Basic parking dimensions. Standard European parking bay or stall 4.8 × 2.4, allow 24 m² per car, including half the clear zone but no access gangways*

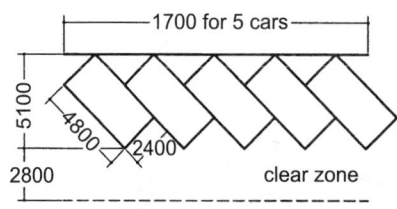

b *echelon parking at 45° (other angles can be used): 22.1 m² per car or 19.2 m² where interlocking in adjacent rows*

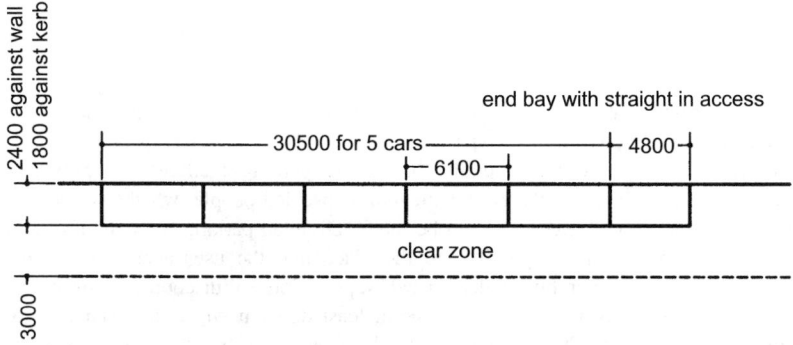

a *in-line parking 20.1 m² per car against kerb, 23.8 m² against wall*

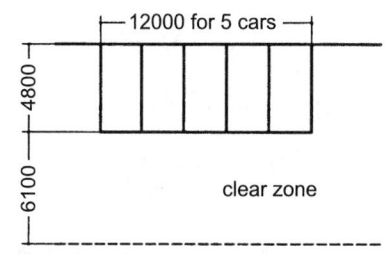

c *head-on parking, 18.8 m² per car*

4.38 *Basic parking dimensions. Large European parking or American bay or stall 5.8 × 2.8, allow 33 m² per car, including half the clear zone but no access gangways*

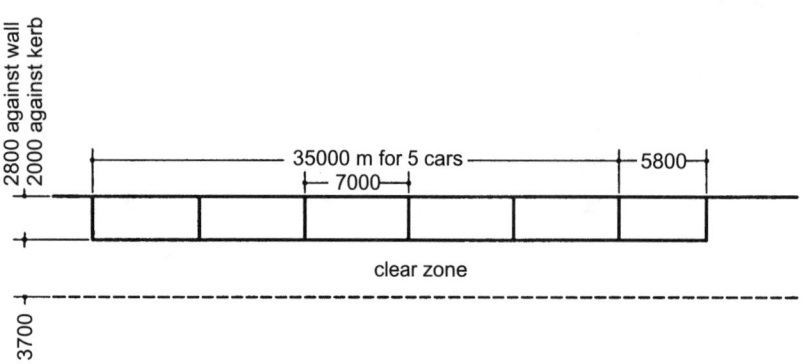

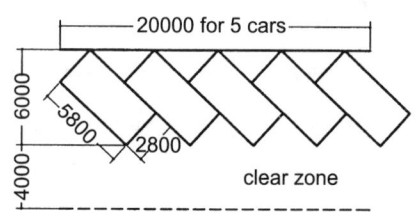

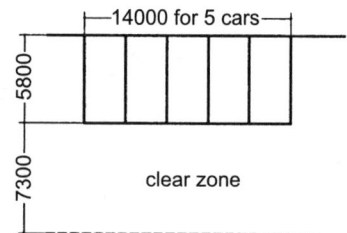

a *in-line parking 27.0 m² per car against kerb, 32.6 m² per car against wall*

b *echelon parking at 45° (other angles can be used): 32.0 m² per car or 28.0 m² where interlocking in adjacent rows*

c *head-on parking, 26.5 m² per car*

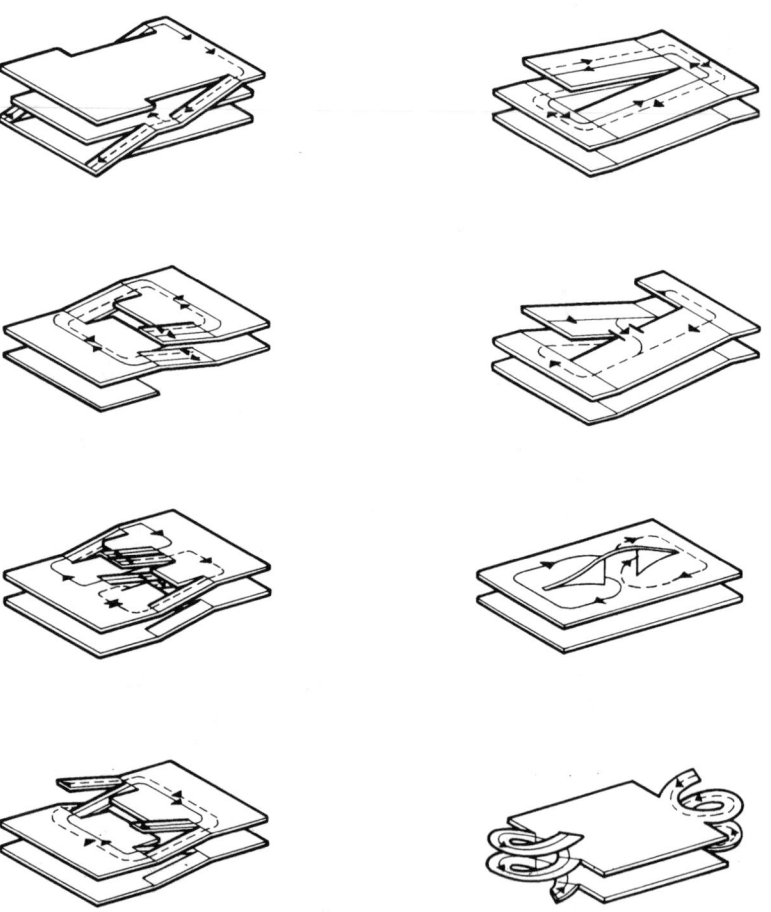

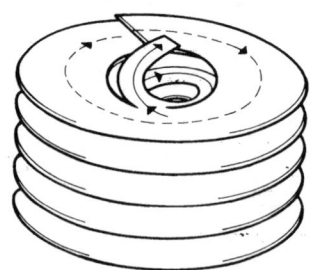

4.39 *Types of multi-storey car parks*

vehicle expected. **4.37** and **4.38** give examples of various arrangements, but again, these should be taken purely as a guide. This type of car park assumes that vehicles arrive and leave in a random fashion. In some situations, such as sporting events, a dense arrangement can be adopted which means that all vehicles have to leave approximately in the sequence in which they arrived.

4.39 shows various types of multi-storey garage. No dimensions are shown as these vary with the site. An additional type, not illustrated, incorporates a mechanical stacking system operated by attendants. In practice, this rarely shows any advantage over conventional types.

Wherever public or private parking facilities are provided, appropriate arrangements for disabled people, whether drivers or passengers, should be made. Disabled parking bays should be as close as possible to the place that the user needs to go, and preferably under visual supervision to discourage misuse by others. Bays should be at least 800 mm wider than standard, to permit manoevring of wheelchairs for transfer, and any kerbs should be ramped.

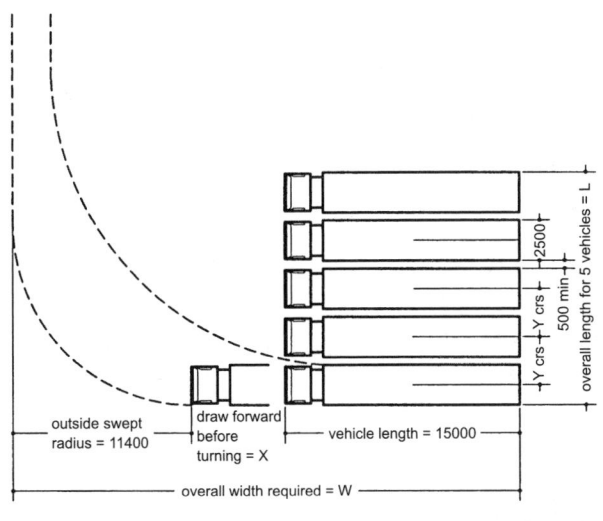

X draw forward	Y centres	W o/a width	L o/a length for 5	Area per vehicle (m²)
1	5.0	27.4	22.5	123
2	4.4	28.4	20.1	114
3	4.0	29.4	18.5	109
4	3.7	30.4	17.3	105
5	3.4	31.4	16.1	101
6	3.0	32.4	14.5	94

4.40 *Lorry parking and loading bays: head-on for the largest vehicles*

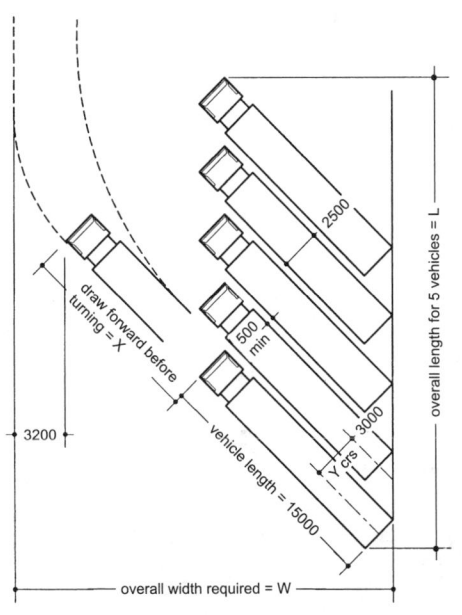

X draw forward	Y centres	W o/a width	L o/a length for 5	Area per vehicle (m²)	
				gross	net*
4	4.8	18.4	39.5	145	113
5	4.5	19.1	37.8	144	111
6	4.2	19.8	36.1	144	108
7	3.9	20.5	34.4	141	105
8	3.6	21.2	32.7	139	101
9	3.4	21.9	31.6	138	100
10	3.2	22.6	30.5	138	98
11	3.1	23.4	29.9	140	99
12	3.0	24.1	29.3	141	99

* Excluding the empty triangles at each end.

4.41 *Lorry parking and loading bays: diagonal (45°) for the largest vehicles*

8 LOADING AND UNLOADING

4.40 to **4.45** show requirements for loading, unloading and parking large vehicles.

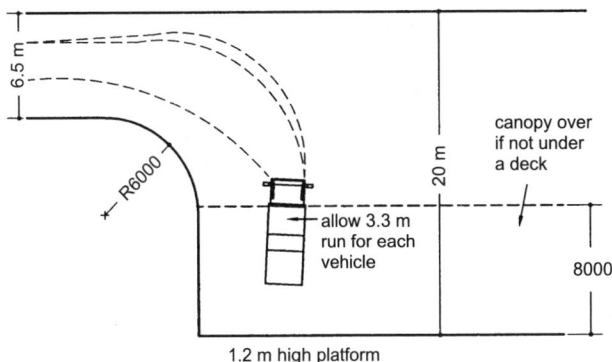

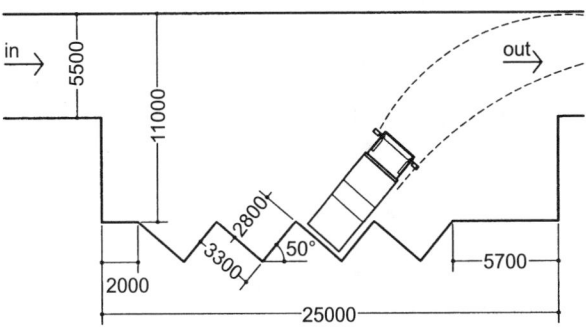

4.42 *Minimal loading docks appropriate for limited number of vehicles per day, extremely high land costs or other physical restraints*

9 SERVICE STATIONS

9.01 Types of service station
There are three main types:

- Petrol company owned and operated ('co-co'). There are only a few of these.
- Dealer-owned and operated. The petrol company may finance the construction, extension or improvement in their house style, in return for a agreement that only their petrol is sold. The dealer may be free to sell products such as lubricating oils from other companies. About 75 per cent of all service stations are of this type.
- Company owned but dealer operated.

The two company-owned types account for less than a quarter of all stations, but for nearly half of all petrol sales.

Petrol companies set great store by their visual image: motivation is totally commercial, and all design decisions are so influenced.

9.02 Petrol pumps
A pump is capable of dispensing up to 700 litres per hour to an unbroken queue of customers if it gives a choice of products. Single-product pumps have a slower output potential because customers have to manoeuvre to the pump they require. When calculating the number of pumps that will be required to service the expected trade, allow for pump down-time and maintenance averaging 10 per cent.

The range of available products has changed radically since the previous edition of this book. Of leaded petrol, only 4–star is now

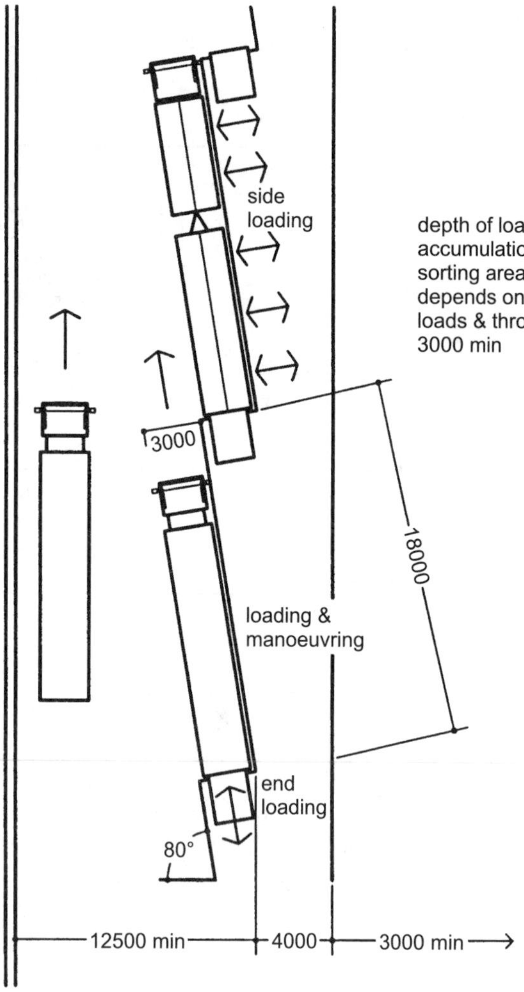

side
loading

depth of load
accumulation &
sorting area
depends on type of
loads & throughput
3000 min

3000

18000

loading &
manoeuvring

end
loading

80°

12500 min — 4000 — 3000 min →

4.43 *Finger dock, where manoeuvring depth is limited and side loading is required as well as end loading. Very fast turnround times are possible although capacity is small*

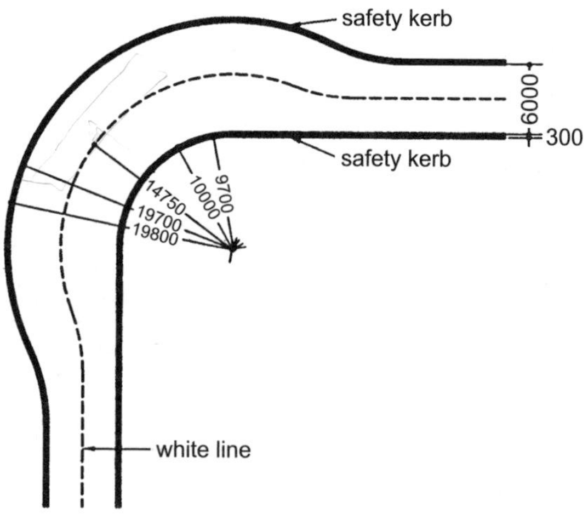

safety kerb

6000

300

safety kerb

14750
19700
19800
10000
9700

white line

4.44 *Ramp on a sharp curve, such as access to a shopping centre loading dock. Maximum gradients 10 per cent on straight, 7 per cent on inner kerb*

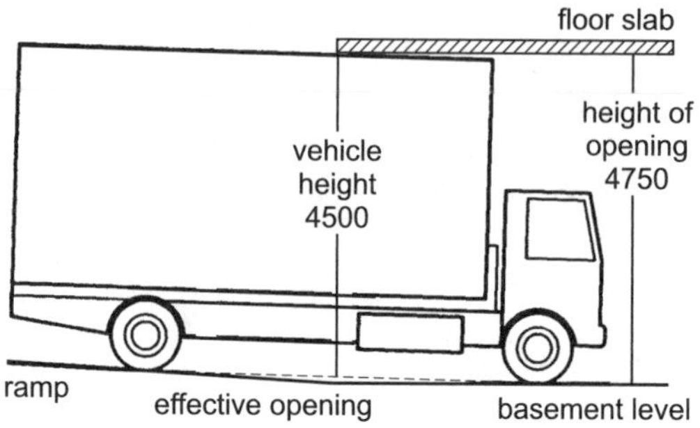

floor slab

vehicle
height
4500

height of
opening
4750

ramp

effective opening

basement level

4.45 *Headroom criteria for covered loading docks*

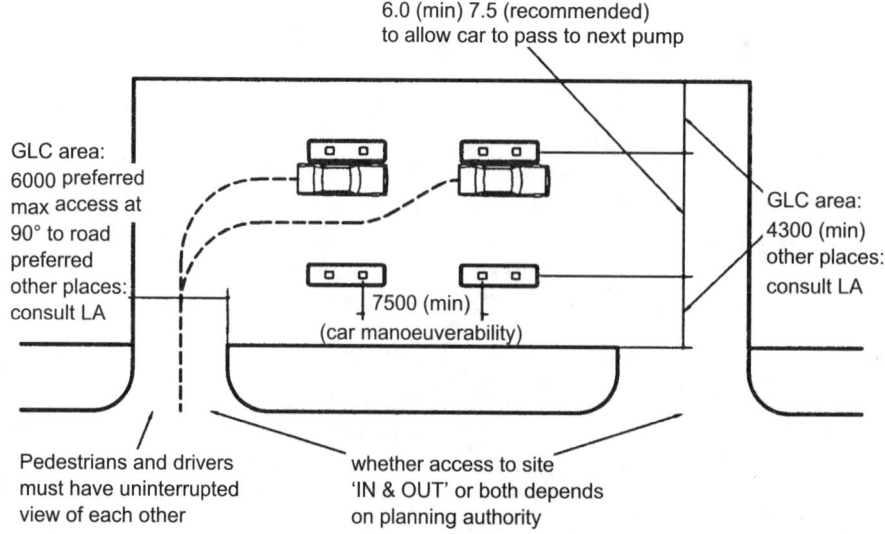

6.0 (min) 7.5 (recommended)
to allow car to pass to next pump

GLC area:
6000 preferred
max access at
90° to road
preferred
other places:
consult LA

GLC area:
4300 (min)
other places:
consult LA

7500 (min)
(car manoeuverability)

Pedestrians and drivers
must have uninterrupted
view of each other

whether access to site
'IN & OUT' or both depends
on planning authority

4.46 *Layout of petrol filling station. Petrol outlets such as service hoses, tank filler pipes, ventpipes, etc, have normally to be more than 4.3 m from the property boundary, 4.3 m from electrical equipment where sparking is possible, and 2 m from any flame or non-flameproof electrical appliance*

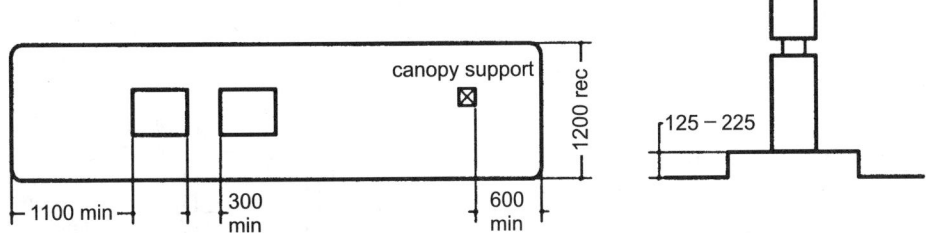

4.47 *Pump island. A kiosk is not advisable on the island unless electrical equipment such as heater and cash register can be more than 1.2 m from the pump*

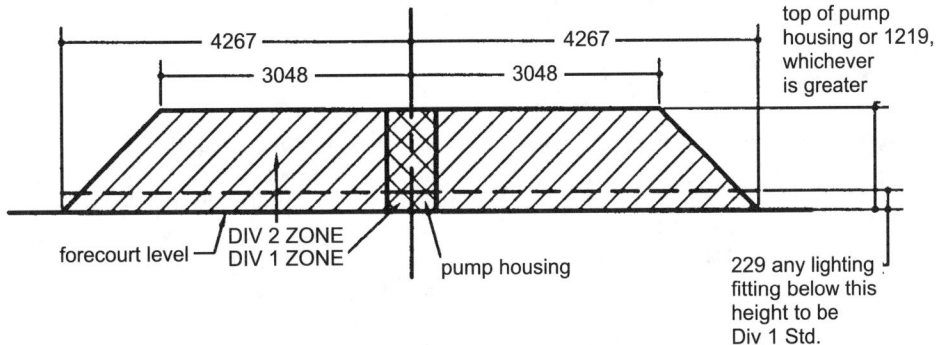

4.48 *Elevation of forecourt showing classification of areas: Division 1 – where a dangerous atmosphere is likely in normal conditions, and where only flameproof electrical fittings to CP1003 Part 1:1964 and BS 1259: 1958 can be used, Division 2 – where a dangerous atmosphere is likely only in very abnormal conditions, and where only non-sparking electrical fittings to CP1003 part 3: 1967 (sections 2 and 3) can be used*

Table V Approximate sizes of petrol storage tanks

Capacity (litres)	Diameter (mm)	Overall length (mm)
2 270	1 370	1 750
2 730	1 370	2 060
3 410	1 370	2 600
4 550	1 370	3 350
5 680	1 530	3 430
6 820	1 830	2 900
9 100	1 830	3 800
11 370	2 000	4 040
13 640	2 130	4 120
22 730	2 290	5 950

available, and there are now at least two types of lead-free petrol as well as diesel sold by most stations. There is reason to believe that further changes may be coming, so a flexible design approach is needed.

As much as 90 per cent of one day's sales may occur in the peak period hour, which will vary from station to station. To meet this factor, an efficient circulation pattern with no inbuilt delays or obstructions is essential, **4.46**. The lanes between the pump islands should be sufficiently wide (7.5 m) to allow waiting cars to move past cars being served. A pump island is shown in **4.47**.

The requirements of the Department of Transport's Model Code of Principles (see References and Bibliography) with regard to the safety zoning of forecourts are given in **4.48**.

Most service stations are now designed for both self- and attendant service. There are as yet few stations provided with automatic dispensing and charging, although the number is expected to increase.

9.03 Petrol storage

Tanks may be sited on or off the forecourt and vehicle manoeuvring space, but siting should allow for daily lifting of the inspection covers to check stocks by dipstick. Heavy-duty covers

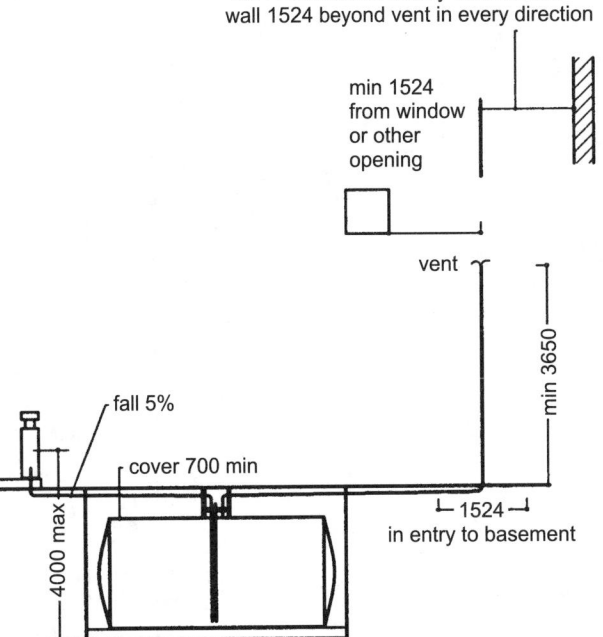

4.49 *Installation of petrol storage tank*

are required in vehicle areas. Common sizes of tanks are given in Table V. Tanks may be compartmented to hold the different products.

Choice of size is based on $4\frac{1}{2}$ days forecast of sales plus one road tanker load (25 000 litres), e.g. for a station selling 45 460 litres per week:

$4\frac{1}{2}$ days supply	29 500
Tanker load	25 000
Total	54 500 litres

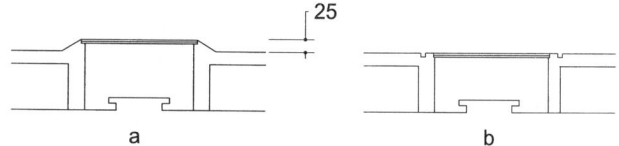

4.50 *Methods of installing inspection covers to prevent water ingress: 3a raising above general level* **b** *surrounding with a sunken channel*

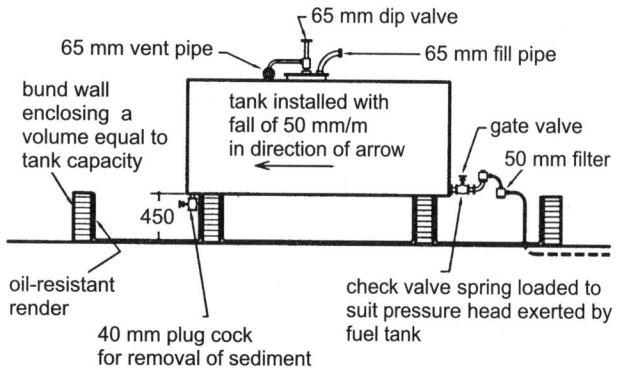

65 mm dip valve
65 mm vent pipe
65 mm fill pipe
bund wall enclosing a volume equal to tank capacity
tank installed with fall of 50 mm/m in direction of arrow
gate valve
50 mm filter
450
oil-resistant render
40 mm plug cock for removal of sediment
check valve spring loaded to suit pressure head exerted by fuel tank

4.51 *Installation of an above-ground tank for diesel oil, kerosene, etc*

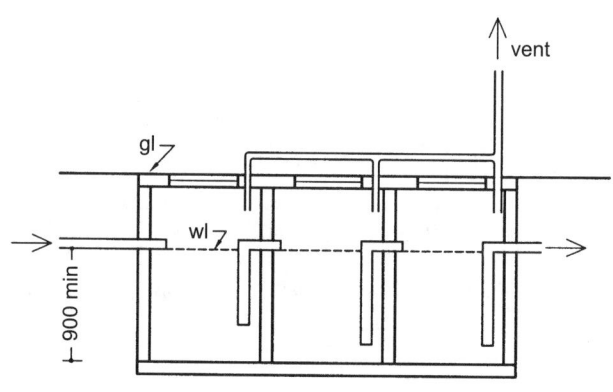

vent
gl
wl
900 min

4.52 *Petrol interceptor chamber*

Criteria affecting the installation of tanks are given in **4.49**. Note the interdependence of tank diameter, depth and distance of the pump. More details are given in the Model Code of Principles.

The 4.0 m maximum suction lift is to prevent gravitation and evaporation of the petrol. Petroleum regulations do not require encasement of the tank, but it is advisable, particularly beneath wheel loads (up to 11.5 tonnes) and to protect tanks against corrosive ground water. Encasement in sand in a brick pit is hardly less expensive than mass concrete, but the tank is easier to remove.

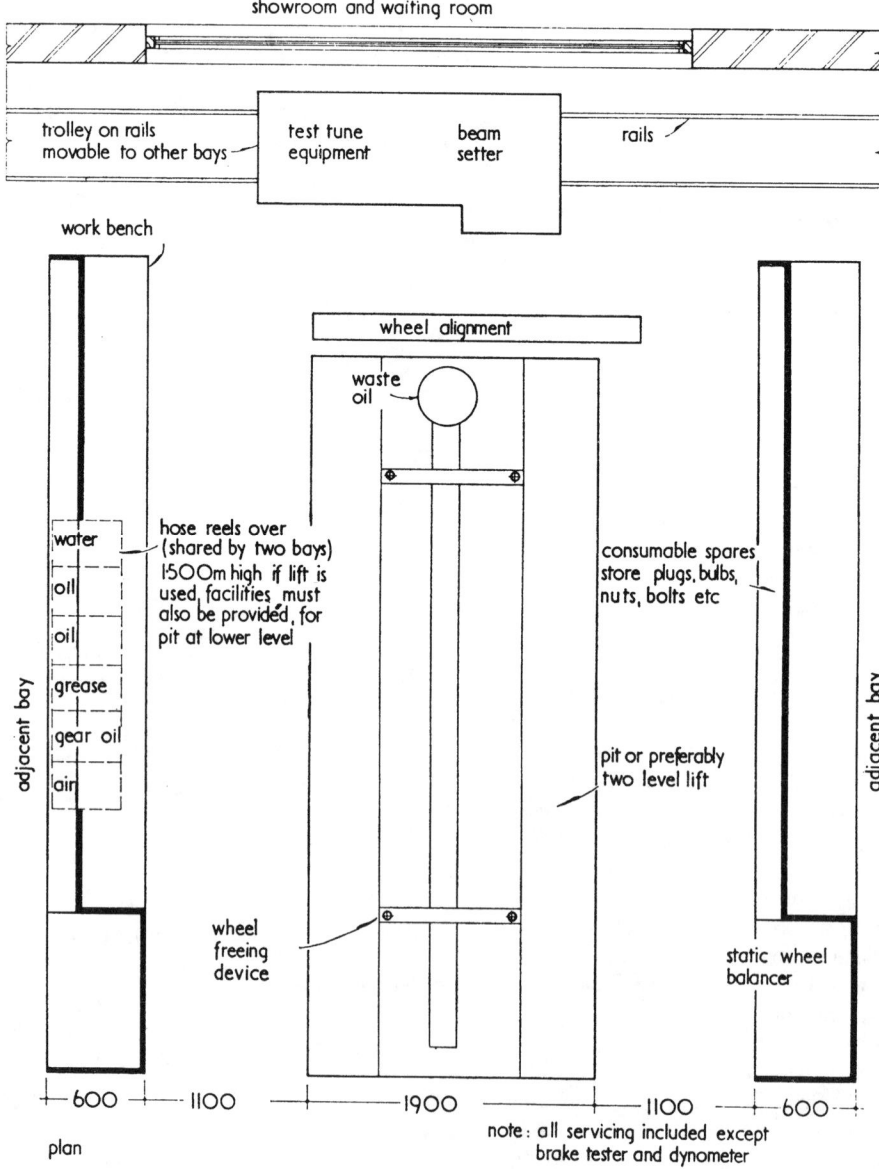

showroom and waiting room

trolley on rails movable to other bays
test tune equipment
beam setter
rails

work bench
wheel alignment
waste oil
water
oil
oil
grease
gear oil
air
hose reels over (shared by two bays) 1500m high if lift is used, facilities must also be provided, for pit at lower level
consumable spares store plugs, bulbs, nuts, bolts etc
pit or preferably two level lift
wheel freeing device
static wheel balancer
adjacent bay
adjacent bay

600   1100   1900   1100   600

plan

note: all servicing included except brake tester and dynometer

4.53 *'One-stop' service bay for lubrication and mechanical services*

4.54 *Service pits for private vehicles*

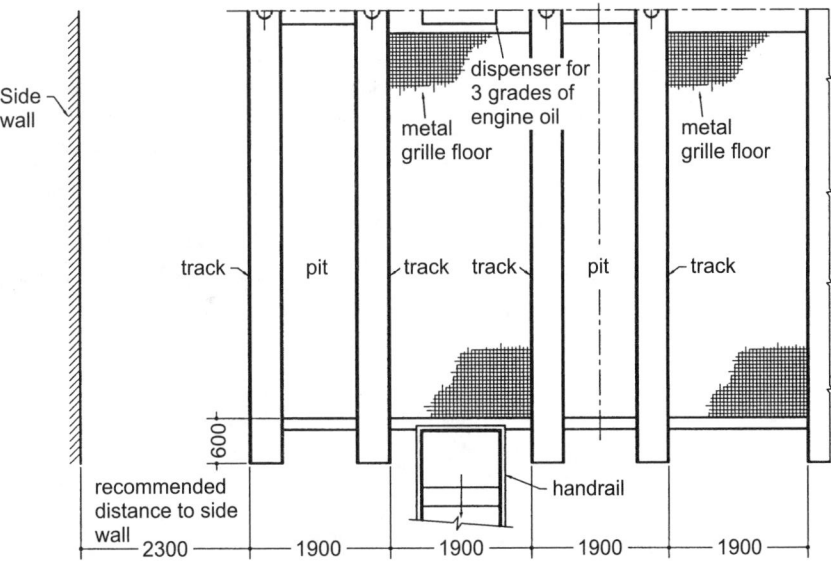

plan at ground level

4.54a

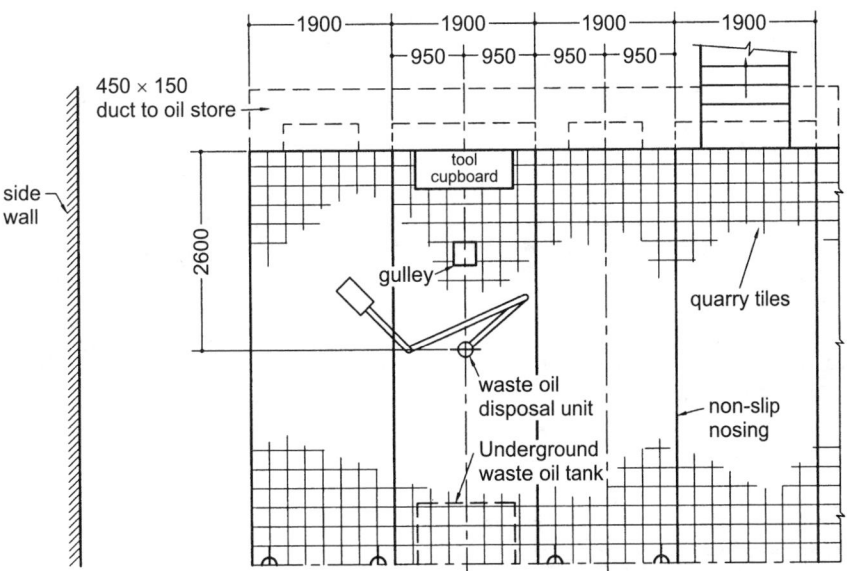

Plan below ground level

4.54b

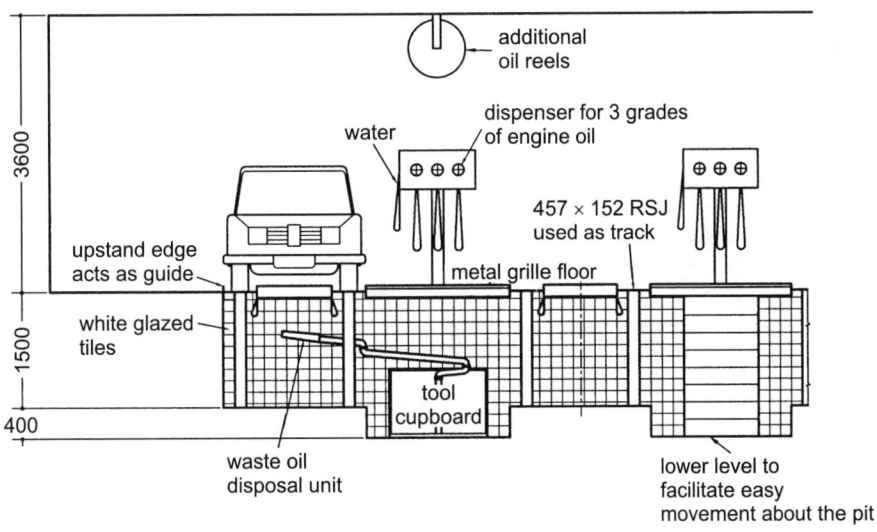

cross section

4.54c

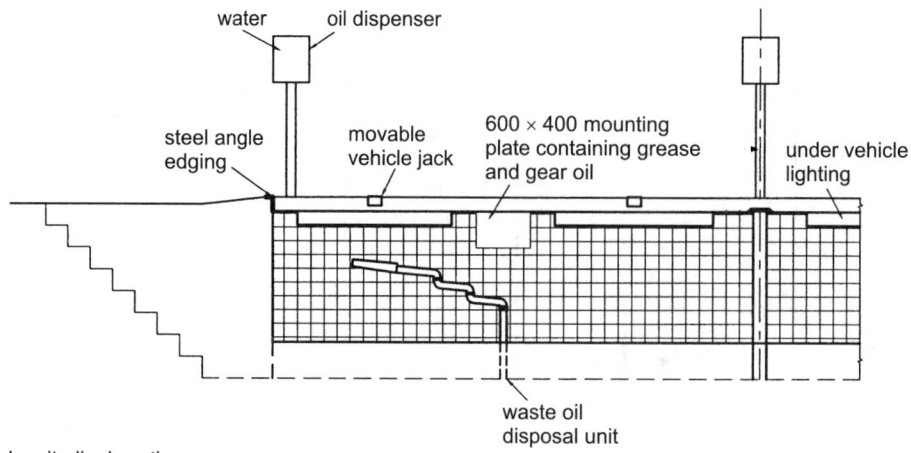

longitudinal section

4.54d

The tanks must be held down during concreting, preferably by strapping them down to the concrete base. They must be pressure tested by the controlling authority both before and after encasement.

Petrol must not escape from inspection chambers above or below ground, and rainwater should not percolate into them. The three alternatives are:

● Raising the cover above the general surface level, **4.50a**
● Surrounding the cover with a channel, **4.50b**
● Using a sealed cover.

Tanks may be required for various fuels other than petrol, particularly in rural areas. These are usually rectangular tanks above ground, **4.51**. The controlling authority may require a 'bund' wall around the tank to contain spillage of the entire contents in the event of a leak. The normal size of above-ground tanks is about 2700 litres,

Interceptor chambers are used to ensure that no petrol enters the main or rainwater drainage systems, **4.52**. Petrol is lighter than

water and will float to the top and evaporate through the exhaust manifold. The three chambers give it three channels in which to do this. The chamber is situated between the last surface water collecting inspection chamber and the sewer, and in a place where the local authority silt collection vehicle can reach it. Vents must be brought above ground before being connected to the manifold and main vent stack.

Local authorities usually require the chamber to have a 275-litre capacity, but some permit the use of smaller preformed plastic chambers. A brick chamber should not be internally rendered, as the render tends to fall off and block the pipes.

9.04 Vehicle servicing

The Conditions of Appointment of authorised examiners for the DoT test (under section 45 of the Road Traffic Act 1988) include appendices 'Requirements for premises and equipment'. These are very detailed, and the latest version should be consulted as the regulations are increasingly stringent with the aim of reducing the number of testing stations.

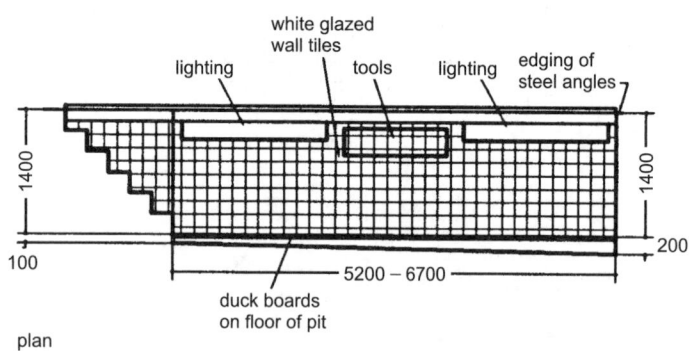

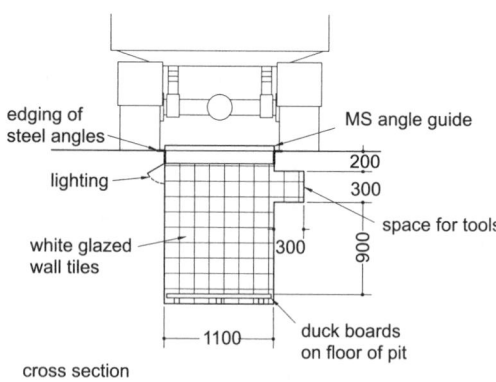

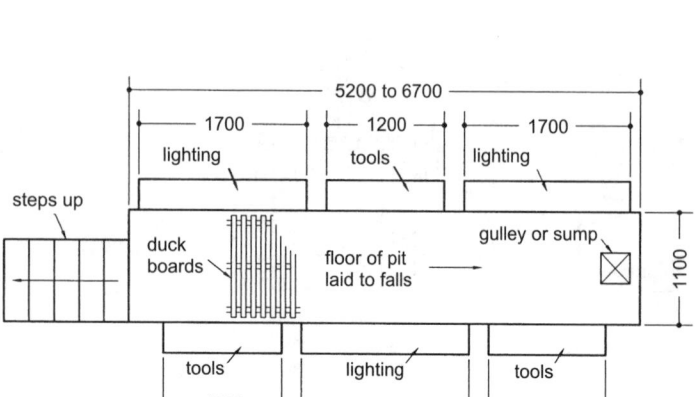

4.55 *Service pits for commercial vehicles*

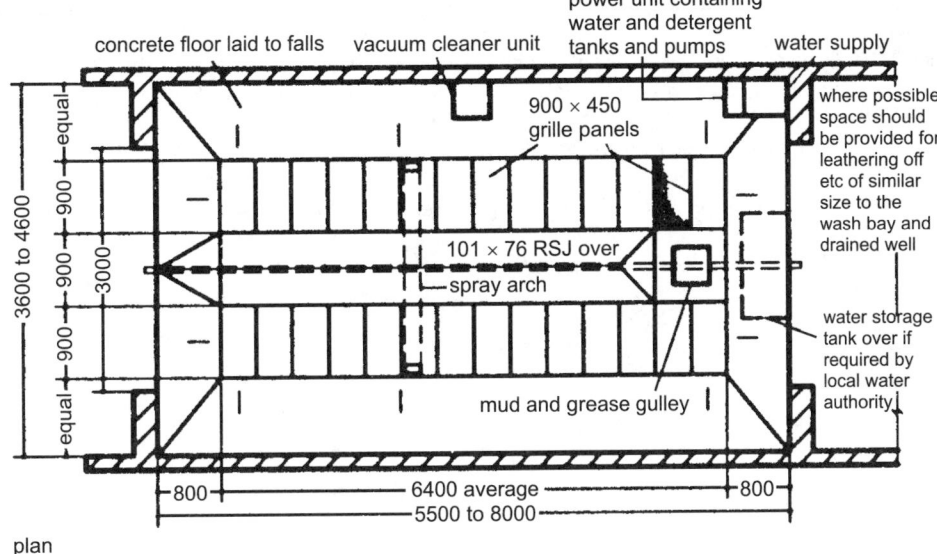

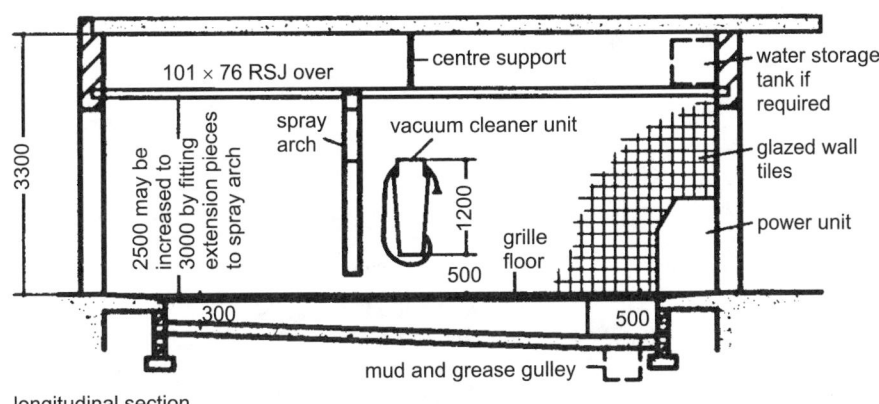

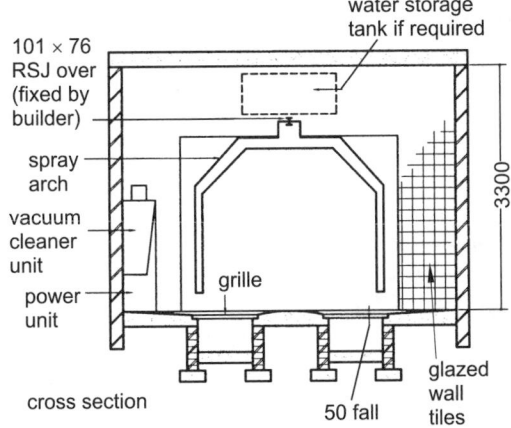

4.56 *Small washing bay with spray arch for automatic operation*

At least three servicing bays are needed to be economically viable, and they each require a space 9 m × 4 m, **4.53**.

Hoists are preferable to pits except for heavy commercial vehicles because of fire risk and drainage problems. They do require a minimum headroom of 4.8 m, whereas pits, **4.54** and **4.55**, only need 3.3 m.

An extract vent system in the servicing area may not draw air from less than 1.2 m above floor level, to avoid drawing petrol fumes into the system and through fan motors. All equipment should be approved non-sparking apparatus.

An automatic car wash layout is shown in **4.56**.

9.05 Other facilities

Depending on size and nature of business, a service station may need all or some of the following:

- *Office*, essential for most, to keep the safe for takings, DoT test certificate blanks, etc.
- *Toilets*, obligatory under the Workplace Directive. These may be shared with customers
- *Staff* rest room
- *Shop*, to sell motor accessories, confectionery, and possibly many other goods. Counters need space for self-service console and cash register. Shop should be at least 3 m wide, and at least 25 m² in area excluding goods storage
- *Security* design and detailing should ensure clear visibility from the road of any parts liable to forced entry.

10 REFERENCES AND BIBLIOGRAPHY

ASCE, *Bicycle transportation, a civil engineer's notebook for bicycle facilities*, 1980
Avon County Council, *Draft cycle parking standards*, 1991
Cheshire County Council, *Design aid, housing: roads*
CTC, *Technical note, cycle parking*
Department of Transport/Welsh Office, *Local Transport Note 1/89: Making way for cyclists, planning design and legal aspects of providing for cyclists, Annex A*, HMSO 1989
Department of Transport/Welsh Office, *Statutory Instrument 1990 No 703 The Highways (Road Hump) Regulations 1990*, HMSO 1990

Health and Safety Executive, *Petrol filling stations: construction and operation*, HMSO 1990

Vehicle Inspectorate, *MOT Testing scheme, conditions of appointment of authorised examiners and designated councils, class III and IV vehicles, rev Sept 1995*

M. Hudson, *The Bicycle Planning Book* Open Books/Friends of the Earth, 1978

J. McCluskey, *Road Form and Townscape*, Architectural Press, 1979

Sustrans, *Making Ways for the Bicycle, A Guide to Traffic-Free Path Construction*, Sustrans Ltd, 1994

Departments of the Environment and Transport, *Residential roads and footpaths: layout considerations. Design Bulletin 32, second edition.* HMSO April 1992.

Devon County Council, *Traffic calming guidelines*, December 1973

Essex County Council, *A design guide for residential areas*

Lancashire County Council, *Car parking standards,* 1976

York City Council, *Cycle parking standards,* 1989

5 Aids to pedestrian movement

David Adler, with acknowledgements to Frank Williams, contributor to the previous edition

CI/SfB: (66)
UDC: 621.876

KEY POINT:

● *The needs of wheelchair users increasingly predominate*

Contents

1 INTRODUCTION

1.01

This chapter covers a variety of transport systems ranging from domestic stairlifts to light railway systems. Motor vehicles, aircraft and heavy rail have been dealt with in Chapter 4.

1.02 Definitions

For the purpose of this general guide the following definitions apply:

● *Cable car*: a type of people mover consisting of cars suspended from cables supported at a height above ground.
● *Car*: the part of a lift installation designed to receive the people and/or loads to be transported.
● *Escalator*: a power-driven installation forming an endless moving stairway for the conveyance of passengers in the upward or downward direction.
● *Goods lift*: a lift intended primarily for carrying goods accompanied by personnel and having manually operated collapsible doors.
● *Group*: two to six passenger lifts with an integrated control system and common call buttons on the landings.
● *Light rail* (or *tramway*): a system consisting of single or articulated light cars running on rails for the purpose of transporting people between two or more places.
● *Passenger conveyor*: power-driven installation forming an endless moving walkway for conveyance of people either on the same level, or between different levels on a gentle incline.
● *Passenger lift*: a lift intended primarily for carrying people and having automatic sliding doors.
● *People mover*: an installation consisting of a series of cars linked together at wide intervals for conveying people between two or more places.
● *Pit*: the space below the lowest level served by the car.
● *Service lift*: a lift for transporting goods only (e.g. documents, food) and having a car not exceeding 1400 mm height and 1 20m² floor area.
● *Shaft* (or *well*): space in which the car and its counterweights move.
● *Stairlift*: an installation for transferring a seated person between two or more levels.
● *Wheelchair lift*: an installation for transferring a wheelchair and its occupant between two levels.

2 LIFTS

2.01 Traction systems

There are two common types of traction: electric and hydraulic.

2.02 Electric traction

In this system the car is supported by cables passing over a drum and balanced by counterweights, **5.1**. The drum is driven by an electric motor, which can be one of a variety of types depending on the use and standard of service. The whole is controlled by an elaborate system which is now almost completely electronic.

The machine room is normally placed on top of the shaft, and, as shown in the figures and tables, requires additional space. In cases where there are restrictions on the height of the building, the machine rooms can be situated adjacent to the shaft at any convenient level (such as in the basement, **5.2**), with the cables

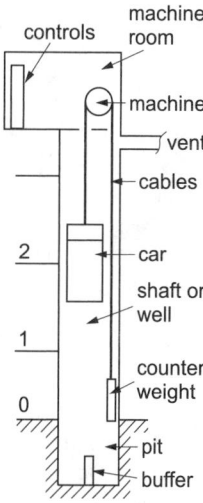

5.1 *Schematic diagram of a conventional electric traction lift with high-level machine room*

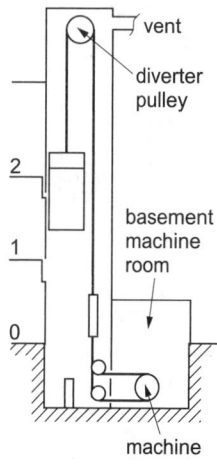

5.2 *Schematic diagram of an electric traction lift with semi-basement machine room*

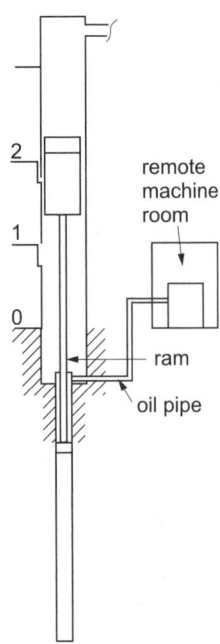

5.3 *Schematic diagram of a direct-acting hydraulic lift with remote machine room*

carried on diverter pulleys. The overrun height above the top level served is increased by the small amount needed for these pulleys. This type of system is best avoided if possible, as it will cost more and the cables, being much longer, will need to be adjusted for stretch at more frequent intervals.

2.03 Hydraulic traction

Despite its name, nowadays this is driven by oil-power. There are different types of installation, but the most common consists of a cylinder driven into the ground below the liftshaft to a depth slightly more than the height of the building. The car is directly attached to a ram raised in this cylinder by pumping oil into its base, **5.3**. The depth of the bore can be reduced by using a telescopic ram.

There are two major advantages to a hydraulic system:

● There are fewer moving parts, therefore, in theory a more reliable performance is given, and
● There is almost complete freedom in the placing of the machine room and its size is smaller than for traction machines.

2.04 General considerations

Below the lift shaft, a space used by people should be avoided wherever possible. Where there must be such a space, even a large duct, the necessary safety provisions will involve a wider or deeper well, additional structural support and/or additional lift equipment.

Lift shafts have to be vented at the top, directly or by duct to external air (not into machine rooms) for smoke-dispersal purposes. There should be safe and convenient access to the machine room for lift maintenance and for the handling of replacement assemblies. Access via a ladder and trapdoor should be avoided. No services installation or access route other than those provided for lift equipment and lift personnel should share or pass through the machine room or lift shaft.

3 PASSENGER LIFTS

3.01 Location

Passenger lifts should be within a reasonable walking distance from the furthest part of the floor areas served (say, 70 m maximum) and, where they are the only or main lifts, near an entrance but with the stairs nearer to the entrance. A shorter walking distance (say, 50 m maximum) is desirable in an office building where interfloor journeys are to be catered for. The location of goods and service lifts will depend on their function, but they should not open into passenger lift lobbies or public areas.

3.02 Single lift installations

Ideally, lifts should not be installed singly. No installation can be guaranteed to give service at all times, and in most buildings there are people who rely totally on using lifts. In addition, the life of a normal lift in constant use is about 20 years; major overhaul or replacement can take several months. In long blocks lifts can be spaced out to ensure that when all are working the 60 m limit is achieved, but another lift is usable at the cost of a longer walk. Alternatively, an additional shaft can be provided when the block is built into which a replacement lift can be installed when necessary, maintaining the original lift service until it is finished. Temporary floors and doors are often fitted in this shaft so that it can be used for storage until it is required.

3.03 Planning passenger lifts

Cul-de-sac or recessed lobbies, **5.4** and **5.5**, are essential to get the maximum performance from lift groups. Clearly, having called for lift service the waiting passengers should not have to walk further than necessary to the responding lift car, and should not be obstructed by passers-by. The lobbies for separate lifts or groups should be adequately separated in order to promote the channelling of their respective traffic and to discourage the duplication of calls on the landing buttons.

Within a group it is preferable for all the lifts to serve all levels in order to avoid a particularly annoying inconvenience to the users. If only one or some lifts of a group serve a basement car park, for example, a normal pushbutton system cannot ensure (at a higher floor) that the responding lift car will be one that is able to travel to the basement.

It used to be common practice for two lifts in tall social housing blocks each to serve alternate floors. This proved most unsatisfactory, and should not be used today.

In very tall buildings (such as Canary Wharf) it is normal to provide 'sky lobbies' near the halfway point. These are served by non-stop express lifts from entrance level, and passengers can then be carried on to upper floors; or more commonly change to a second bank of normal lifts.

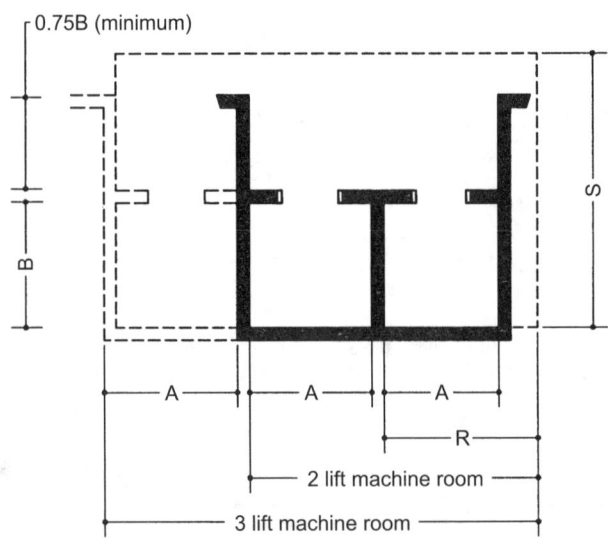

5.4 *Plan of recessed lobby and machine room for multi-lift installation*

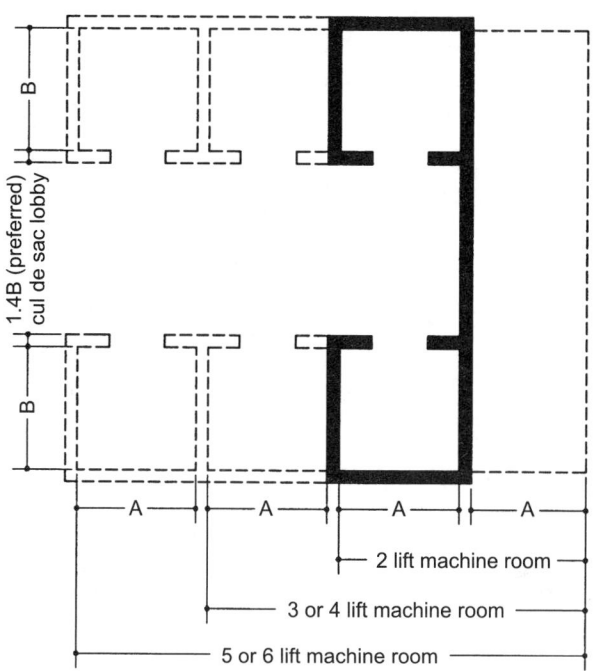

5.5 *Plan of cul-de-sac* lobby and machine room

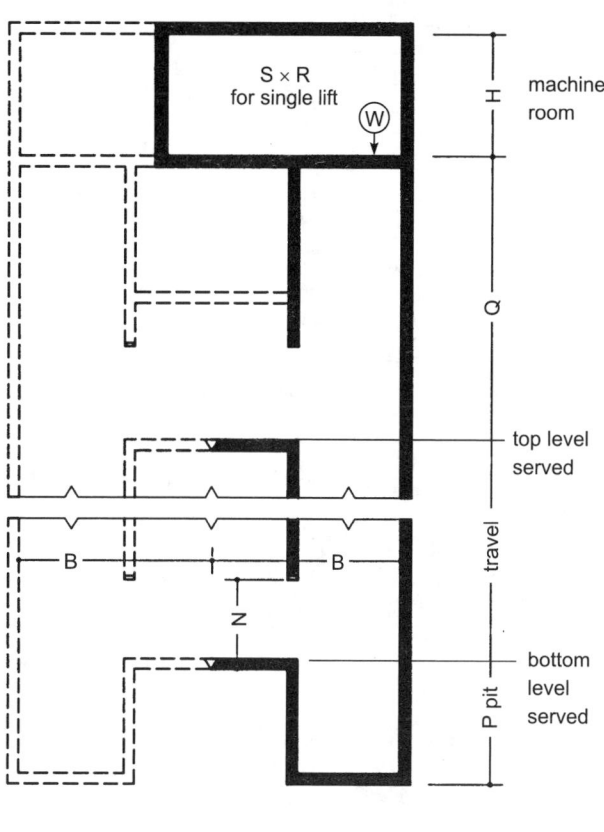

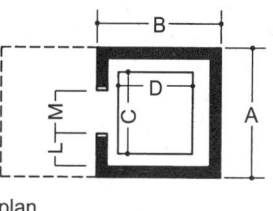

plan

5.6 *Passenger lifts, dimensions as in Table I. Prefer machine room floor on one level with lift-shaft capping. (Also see* **5.2** *and* **5.3***)*

3.04 Lift cars

A standard 8-person car is the minimum size normally acceptable as it is necessary to have sufficient door width to pass self-propelled wheelchairs. It is also the minimum suitable size for moving furniture.

Controls should be low enough to be operated from a wheelchair, and should be duplicated for those unable to stoop. Buttons should be clearly marked, and have raised figures (not necessarily Braille) to assist those with visual impairment. There should be both visual and audible notification of floor level (this facility is now generally available at small additional cost).

3.05 Selecting type, size, speed and number

The standard passenger lifts are shown in **5.6** and Table I. Types 1 to 5 are inappropriate to the main lift service of such as a large office building, especially in the single-speed motor form (speed 0.5 or 0.63 m/s), but their robust single-panel doors and associated specification package makes them particularly suitable for municipal housing and hostels. The doors of types 1 to 5 (which close relatively slowly from the side) are particularly suited to the infirm or for goods traffic. The quicker doors of types 6 to 8 maximise handling capacity and service quality, by minimising journey and waiting times.

The quality and quantity of the lift service needed by buildings other than offices is essentially a matter for individual assessment with the assistance of specialist advice and comparison with similar cases. However, for preliminary purposes it may be assumed that passenger lifts suited to an office building can be stretched (in terms of population and visitors served) up to 100 per cent for a hospital, hotel or shop. The passenger lift service (if any is required) for a two- or three-storey building, including offices but excluding hospitals and the like, will usually need to be only nominal, i.e. not related to the population figures.

3.04 Lifts in offices

For lift types 6 to 8 Table II gives the configurations for a good service when dealing with typical office building traffic. Table III gives single-lift schemes for situations where the previous table cannot be applied; as, for example, where only two lifts can be justified and have to be separated for functional reasons instead of being placed in the more efficient two-lift group.

The second column in Tables II and III gives the population per floor (averaged) for which the lift or group of lifts is suitable. For example, the second scheme in Table II is suitable for a population averaging over 60 per floor, and up to and including an average of 69 people per floor. The third column is an extension of the previous column, allowing 10 m² per person, and therefore gives some indication of the total net area for which the lift or group is suitable. Dividing the area figure by 10 will give an indication of the total population for which the lift or group is suitable.

The seventh column gives an indication of the likely costs, excluding builders' work, of the specific lift installation: based on 1 for a single 8-person, 1 m/s lift serving ground floor and three upper levels.

It is advisable to work within the tabulated population figures until any conditions that would reduce the suitability of the lifts can be assessed with specialist advice. These conditions include situations where:

- The floor-to-floor heights average more than 3.3 m
- There is more than one main floor, i.e. the lifts populate the building from the ground floor and another level or levels
- There are levels below the ground floor requiring normal service for passengers
- The distance from ground floor to first floor exceeds 3.3 m and/or the stairs are located so as to be unattractive to people entering the building

Table I Passenger lift dimensions

Type	Load capacity (persons/kg)	Speed (m/s)	Shaft size (nominal)		Car size (internal)			Doors		Pit	Machine room				Load
			A	B	C	D	E	M	N	P	Q	H	R	S	W
1 Light traffic electric traction	5/400	0.5 and 0.63 1.0	1800	1600	1100	950	2200	800	2000	1400 1500	3900 4000	2300	3200	2500	48
	8/630 ♿	0.5 and 0.63 1.0 1.6	1800	2100	1100	1400	2200	800	2000	1400 1700 1700	4000 4000 4200	2600	3700	2500	76
	10/800 ♿	0.5 and 0.63 1.0 1.6	1900	2300	1350	1400	2200	800	2000	1500 1700 1700	4000 4000 4200	2600	3700	2500	96
	13/1000 ♿	0.5 and 0.63 1.0 1.6	1800	2600	1100	2100	2200	800	2000	1500 1700 1700	4000 4000 4200	2600 2600 2700	4200	2500	120
2 Light traffic hydraulic	5/400	0.5 and 0.63 1.0	1800	1600	1100	950	2200	800	2000	1400 1500	3900 4000	2300	2000	1800	–
	8/630 ♿	0.5 and 0.63 1.0	1800	2100	1100	1400	2200	800	2000	1500 1700	4000	2300	2000	1800	–
	10/800 ♿	0.5 and 0.63 1.0	1900	2300	1350	1400	2200	800	2000	1500 1700	4000	2300	2000	1900	–
	13/1000 ♿	0.5 and 0.63 1.0	1800	2600	1100	2100	2200	800	2000	1500 1700	4000	2300	2000	1800	–
3 Residential electric traction	8/630 ♿	0.5 and 0.63 1.0	2000	1900	1100	1400	2200	800	2000	1400 1700	4000	2600	3700	2200	76
	13/1000 ♿	0.5 and 0.63 1.0	2000	2600	1100	2100	2200	800	2000	1500 1700	4000	2400	4200	2400	120
4 Occasional passenger electric traction	5/400	0.5 and 0.63	1600	1700	900	1250	2200	800	2000	1400	3900	2300	3200	2200	48
	8/630 ♿	0.5 and 0.63	1600	2100	1100	1400	2200	800	2000	1400	4000	2600	3700	2500	76
5 Occasional passenger hydraulic	5/40	0.63	1600	1700	900	1250	2200	800	2000	1400	3900	2300	2000	1600	–
	8/630 ♿	0.63	1600	2100	1100	1400	2200	800	2000	1400	4000	2300	2000	1600	–
6 General-purpose passenger traffic – electric traction	8/630 ♿	1.0 1.6	1800	2100	1100	1400	2200	800	2000	1700	4000 4200	2600	3700	2500	76
	10/800 ♿	1.0 1.6	1900	2300	1350	1400	2200	800	2000	1700	4000 4200	2600	3700	2500	96
	13/1000 ♿	1.0 1.6	2400	2300	1600	1400	2300	1100	2100	1800	4200	2700	4900	3200	120
	16/1250 ♿	1.0 1.6	2600	2300	1950	1400	2300	1100	2100	1900	4400	2700	4900	3200	150
	21/1600 ♿	1.0 1.6	2600	2600	1950	1750	2300	1100	2100	1900	4400	2800	5500	3200	192
7 Intensive passenger electric traction	13/1000 ♿	2.5 3.5	2400	2300	1600	1400	2300	1100	2100	2800 3400	9 400 10 400		4900	3200	120
	16/1250 ♿	2.5 3.5	2600	2300	1950	1400	2300	1100	2100	2800 3400	9 500 10 400		4900	3200	150
	21/1600 ♿	2.5 3.5	2600	2600	1950	1750	2300	1100	2100	2800 3400	9 700 10 600		5500	3200	192
8 Bed and passenger electric traction	21/1600 ♿	0.5 and 0.63 1.0 1.6 2.5	2400	3000	1400	2400	2300	1300	2100	1700 1700 1900 3200	4600	2800	5500	3200	192
	24/1800 ♿	0.5 and 0.63 1.0 1.6 2.5	2400	3000	1600	2400	2300	1300	2100	1700 1700 1900 3200	4600 4600 4600 9 700	2900 2900 2900	5800	3200	216
	26/2000 ♿	0.5 and 0.63 1.0 1.6 2.5	2400	3300	1500	2700	2300	1300	2100	1700 1700 1900 3200	4600 4600 4600 9 700	2900 2900 2900	5800	3200	240
	33/2500 ♿	0.5 and 0.63 1.0 1.6	2700	3300	1800	2700	2300	1300	2100	1800 1900 2100	4600	2900	5800	3500	300

Table II Selection table for a good passenger lift service
Based on the handling capacity of lift types (Table I) for typical office traffic

Table II (Continued)

Levels served	Population per floor	Net area served (m²)	No. of lifts in group	Load (persons)	Speed (m/s)	Cost level index
4	60	2 400	1	8	1.0	1.00
	69	2 760	1	10		1.07
	76	3 040	1	13		1.13
	147	5 880	2	8		2.00
	176	7 040	2	10		2.13
	202	8 080	2	13		2.27
5	33	1 650	1	8	1.0	1.07
	37	1 850	1	10		1.13
	88	4 400	2	8		2.13
	105	5 250	2	10		2.27
	147	7 350	2	10	1.6	2.67
	168	8 400	2	13		2.80
	199	9 950	2	16		2.93
6	51	3 060	2	8	1.0	2.27
	58	3 480	2	10		2.40
	63	3 780	2	13		2.53
	86	5 160	2	8	1.6	2.67
	100	6 000	2	10		2.80
	109	6 540	2	13		2.93
	121	7 260	2	16		3.07
	151	9 060	3	10		4.19
	168	10 080	3	13		4.40
	199	11 940	3	16		4.61
7	69	4 830	2	10	1.6	2.93
	75	5 250	2	13		3.07
	109	7 630	3	10		4.40
	122	8 540	3	13		4.61
	138	9 660	3	16		4.80
	152	10 640	3	21		5.08
	163	11 410	4	13		6.13
	184	12 880	4	16		6.40
	207	14 490	4	21		6.78
8	51	4 080	2	10	1.6	3.20
	84	6 720	3	10		4.80
	94	7 520	3	13		5.00
	109	8 720	3	16		5.20
	119	9 520	3	21		5.48
	125	10 000	4	13		6.67
	146	11 680	4	16		6.93
	165	13 200	4	21		7.31
	183	14 640	5	16		8.67
	206	16 480	5	21		9.14
9	75	6 750	3	13	1.6	5.20
	85	7 650	3	16		5.41
	92	8 280	3	21		5.68
	100	9 000	4	13		6.93
	116	10 440	4	16		7.20
	131	11 790	4	21		7.58
	146	13 140	5	16		9.00
	164	14 760	5	21		9.47
	175	15 750	6	16		10.80
	197	17 730	6	21		11.36
10	61	6 100	3	13	1.6	5.41
	68	6 800	3	16		5.60
	73	7 300	3	21		5.88
	82	8 200	4	13		7.20
	96	9 600	4	16		7.47
	107	10 700	4	21		7.84
	120	12 000	5	16		9.33
	134	13 400	5	21		9.80
	144	14 400	6	16		11.20
	161	16 100	6	21		11.76
11	51	5 610	3	13	1.6	5.6
	56	6 160	3	16		5.8
	61	6 710	3	13	2.5	7.4
	69	7 590	3	16		7.8
	73	8 030	3	21		8.8
	81	8 910	4	13		9.9
	93	10 230	4	16		10.4
	103	11 330	4	21		11.7
	112	12 320	4	24		12.0
	129	14 190	5	21		14.7
	140	15 400	5	24		15.0
	155	17 050	6	21		17.6
	168	18 480	6	24		18.0
12	53	6 360	3	13	2.5	7.6
	58	6 960	3	16		8.0
	61	7 320	3	21		9.0
	71	8 520	4	13		10.1
	80	9 600	4	16		10.7
	89	10 680	4	21		12.0
	96	11 520	4	24		12.3
	111	13 320	5	21		15.0
	120	14 400	5	24		15.3
	134	16 080	6	21		18.0
	144	17 280	6	24		18.4
13	46	5 980	3	13	2.5	7.8
	52	6 760	3	16		8.2
	61	7 930	4	13		10.4
	70	9 100	4	16		10.9
	77	10 010	4	21		12.3
	82	10 660	4	24		12.5
	97	12 610	5	21		15.3
	105	13 650	5	24		16.7
	116	15 080	6	21		18.4
	126	16 380	6	24		18.8
14	40	5 600	3	13	2.5	8.0
	54	7 560	4	13		10.7
	61	8 540	4	16		11.2
	68	9 520	4	21		12.5
	71	9 940	4	24		12.8
	77	10 780	5	16		14.0
	85	11 900	5	21		15.7
	92	12 880	5	24		16.0
	102	14 280	6	21		18.8
	110	15 400	6	24		19.2
15	48	7 200	4	13	2.5	10.9
	54	8 100	4	16		11.5
	60	9 000	4	21		12.8
	68	10 200	5	16		14.3
	76	11 400	5	21		16.0
	82	12 300	5	24		16.3
	91	13 650	6	21		19.2
	98	14 700	6	24		19.6
16	44	7 040	4	13	2.5	11.2
	50	8 000	4	16		11.7
	53	8 480	4	21		13.1
	62	9 920	5	16		14.7
	68	10 880	5	21		16.3
	74	11 840	5	24		16.7
	82	13 120	6	21		19.6
	89	14 240	6	24		20.0
17	40	6 800	4	13	2.5	11.5
	45	7 650	4	16		12.0
	47	7 990	4	21		13.3
	56	9 520	5	16		15.0
	62	10 540	5	21		16.7
	64	10 880	5	21	3.5	18.7
	77	13 090	6	21		22.4
18	42	7 560	4	16	3.5	13.8
	45	8 100	4	21		15.2
	53	9 540	5	16		17.3
	59	10 620	5	21		19.0
	71	12 780	6	21		22.8

● There is a canteen above the ground floor, especially where it is used by people not counted in the population served by the affected lift or group
● There are large numbers of visitors
● There is a significant amount of goods traffic or other 'requisitioning' which restricts availability for normal passenger traffic.

Firemen's lift service, where required (unusual under seven storeys), can usually be provided by the most suitably located passenger lift of at least 8-person capacity.

3.05 Lifts in social housing
Lift access is recommended for dwellings where there is a climb of more than two storeys to reach the front door **5.7**. The climb is measured from the ground, or from a main pedestrian deck. Where there are dwelling entrances on storeys up to the sixth storey

Table III Selection table for separated lifts
Based on estimated handling capacity of lift types 6 and 7 in Table I

Levels served	Population per floor	Net area served (m²)	Load (persons)	Speed (m/s)	Cost level index
5	64	3 200	8	1.60	1.27
	70	3 500	10		1.33
	77	3 850	13		1.40
6	40	2 400	8	1.60	1.33
	44	2 640	10		1.40
	47	2 820	13		1.47
7	29	2 030	10	1.60	1.47
	31	2 170	13		1.53

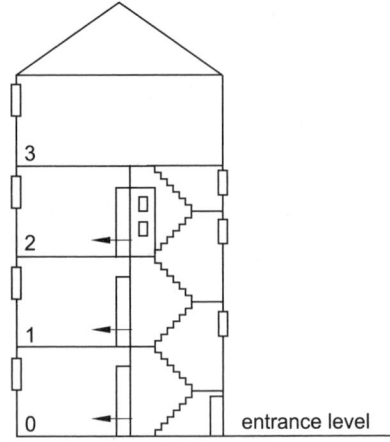

5.7 *A block of flats on four levels without lift service. The entrance door of any flat is no more than two levels from the entrance to the block.*

(counting the ground or pedestrian deck as the first) one lift is usually sufficient. Where there are dwelling entrances above the sixth storey, two lifts are provided to serve not less than 20 dwellings each, or more than 50. These numbers include the numbers of dwellings at ground or deck level.

In order to avoid the provision of lifts in three-storey blocks of flats, or four-storey maisonettes, it is frequent practice to have a further storey-height climb beyond the dwelling entrance.

Blocks in hilly areas (or with well-used pedestrian decks as principal access) can be provided with street access above the lowest habited level; in this case a maximum of two storeys below the street is acceptable without a lift. A lift-less block with six levels of flats is therefore possible, **5.8**. However, it is likely that regulations regarding accessibility to residential accommodation of all kinds for wheelchair users may eventually prohibit this practice.

There should be no direct lift access to enclosed underground or underdeck garage spaces for safety reasons. An open area should be provided between lift and garage. Stair access from the lift is acceptable unless there are parking spaces for the cars of wheelchair users in the garage.

For blocks not higher than 11 storeys including ground or deck level, the type of lift normally used is the 8-passenger (630 kg) lift

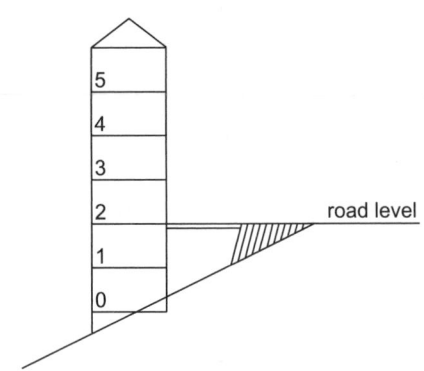

5.8 *A block of flats on six levels with no flat door more than two levels from the entrance*

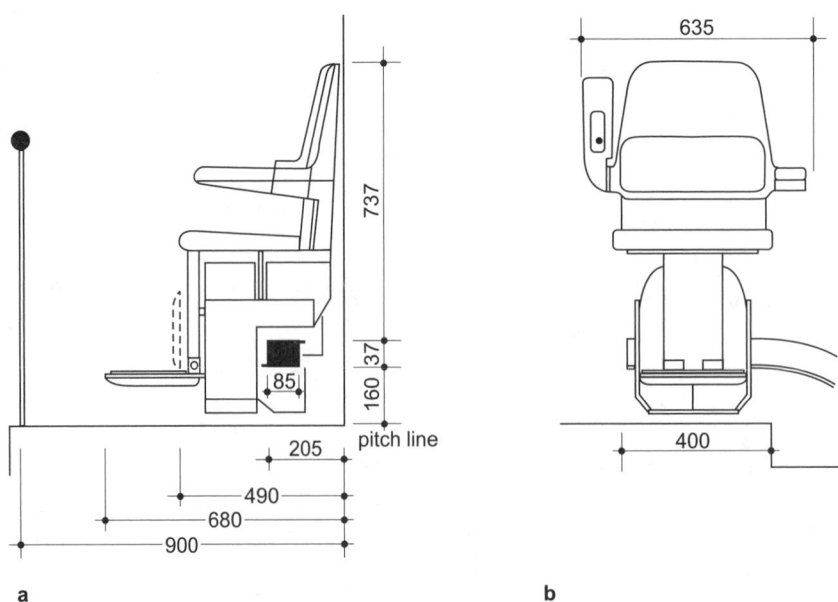

a   b

5.9 *A domestic stairlift. Such a device can usually be fitted to any domestic staircase. While normally used against a wall, it could alternatively be installed on the side of the banisters. This one has a fixed seat, but a swivelling seat is available for where there is insufficient space at the top or bottom of the flight for easy access to the seat. Note that the rail on which the lift travels projects into the staircase width by 205 mm. This may affect the ability of the staircase to pass larger furniture items. (Courtesy of* Stannah Stairlifts Limited. **a** *section,* **b** *elevation*

with standard speed 0.5 m/s (Table I). For higher blocks a faster speed may be necessary. For example, in a twenty-storey block, a person on the top floor calling the lift from the bottom and returning there, assuming four other 15-second stops en route, will take approximately 5 minutes at a speed of 0.5 m/s, 4½ minutes at 0.63 m/s and 3 minutes at 1 m/s. In large blocks the slow speed may well encourage overloading. If our passenger had just missed the lift, trip times will be increased by half as much again.

Lifts should be located in the block so that the walk to the dwelling entrance does not exceed 60 m. Habitable rooms, particularly bedrooms, should not abut liftshafts or machinery rooms as these often generate noise and vibration.

The standard lift car size is 1.1 × 1.4 × 2.2 m, and the door width is 0.8 m. It will be seen that this will accommodate a wheelchair and most items of furniture except the largest. It will not accommodate a stretcher or a coffin unless this can be stood on end. For this reason, in the past a stretcher recess was sometimes provided in one lift of a tall block. This projected into the shaft for only part of the car height, but usually for the full width. However, stretcher recesses were a problem where vandalism was concerned. They have mostly been taken out of use, and are never used in modern installations. Patients are now always strapped to stretchers, which can then be tipped. Coffins are very rarely taken into or out of flats; body shells are used whenever a corpse is removed.

3.06 Lifts in special housing for elderly and disabled people

It is now considered unsatisfactory to segregate people who are less able-bodied, and all housing schemes should take their requirements into account. However, where there is likely to be a preponderance of such people, or some with more severe disabilities, it may be necessary to provide accommodation specifically for them.

There is some difference of opinion on the desirable scale of provision in these cases. The Greater London Council did not accommodate these people above the fifth storey from the

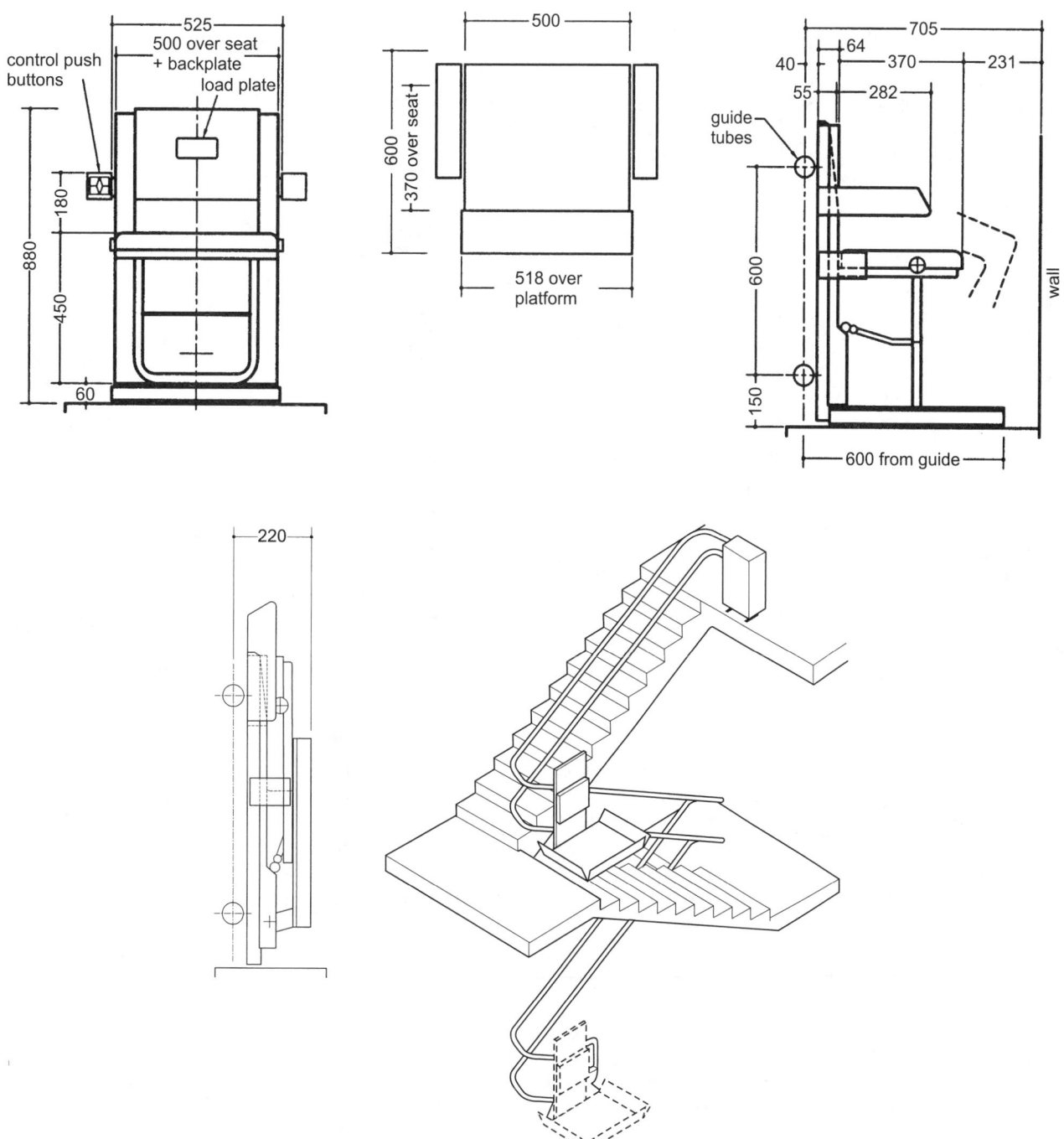

5.10 *Details of stair lift for wheelchair, or for seated passenger. (Courtesy of Gimson Stairlifts Ltd)*

normal pedestrian or vehicular level, whichever is the lower. However, the Department of the Environment permitted only one lift up to four storeys, and two lifts for five- and six-storey buildings only if there are at least 12 dwellings above fourth-storey level.

Where a reliable lift service is provided, high-rise accommodation is both suitable and appreciated by the elderly, as ground-floor flats can be subject to noise and security problems.

3.07 Private sector housing

The standards of lift accommodation in the private sector are not usually markedly more generous than in social housing. A faster speed might be provided, and the standard of finishing will probably be more luxurious and less vandal-resistant.

3.08 Hostels

Where students and nurses are accommodated it may be assumed that they are generally younger and fitter than the general population. It is therefore uncommon to install lifts unless more than four storey-heights have to be climbed. However, a goods hoist should be provided for linen, etc. over two storeys. For blocks higher than four storeys one lift will probably be sufficient. Provided no communal facilities are provided on upper floors there is no need at present for access by students in wheelchairs who are accommodated at ground level; in the future this may be found to be an unacceptable limitation.

3.09 Hotels

Provision in hotels should be based on the scale laid down for office buildings; although, depending on the facilities provided (such as conference suites) and the grading of the hotel the capacities may be adjusted upwards to a maximum of 100 per cent. Hotel bedrooms should not abut shafts or machinery rooms.

4 WHEELCHAIR AND STAIR LIFTS

4.01

Details of a simple stairlift to transport someone from ground to first floor in a common type of house are shown in **5.9**. Staircases in houses should be designed with the possible future need to install such a lift borne in mind, and legislation is likely to reinforce this. A more elaborate stairlift suitable for a public building is shown in **5.10**; this type will also take a wheelchair.

4.02

Wheelchair lifts are used in a variety of situations. They can be used in public and semi-public buildings to transfer a wheelchair between minor changes of level. In domestic property they can be installed where a stairlift is not possible, or appropriate for the user. They differ from standard lifts in that, moving relatively slowly, they commonly have no permanent enclosure, and require minimum pit depth. Motive power is often hydraulic.

5 GOODS LIFTS

Except for heavy industrial use (e.g. self-propelled trucks), standard goods lifts as in **5.11** and Table IV are usually satisfactory. The selected lift car size should allow for a person to accompany the largest item or batch of goods to be catered for in normal use (to operate the controls at the side of the car).

For over eight storeys, a requirement for a separate goods lift service is usually met by a lift of the passenger type having automatic side-opening doors, e.g. type 8 in Table I.

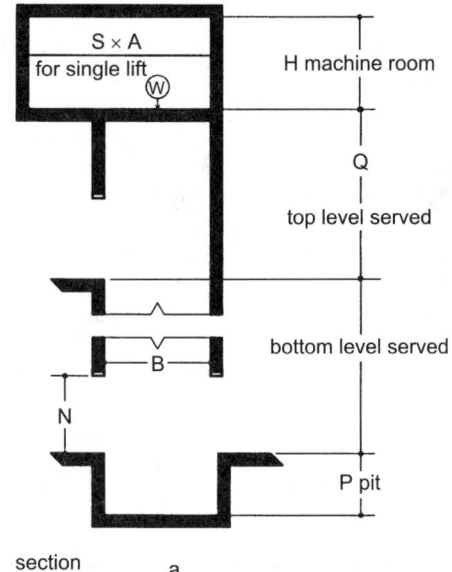

section   a

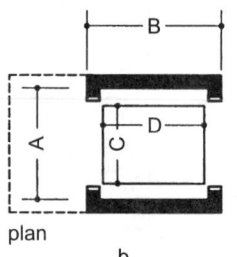

plan

b

5.11 *Goods lift, dimensions as in Table IV. Entrances can be front only or front and back. Prefer machine room floor on one level with lift shaft capping*

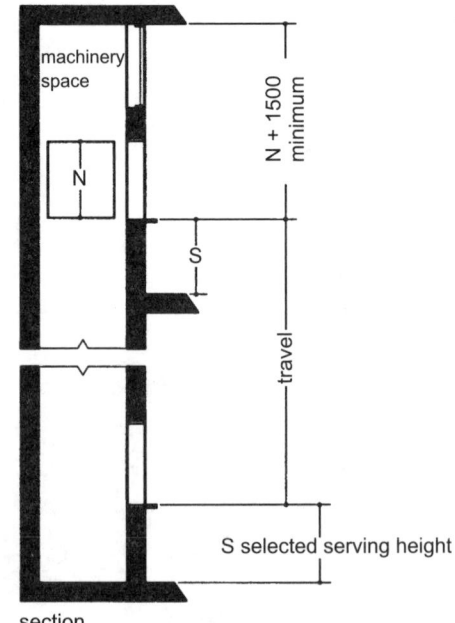

section

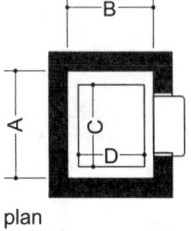

plan

5.12 *Medium-size service lift, dimensions as in Table V. Note: speed up to 0.5 m/s but prefer 0.38 m/s. Shaft size includes 25 mm allowance for out-of-plumb. Openings can be front and rear as required. Car can be fitted with shelves*

Table IV Goods lifts

Type	Load capacity (persons/kg)	Speed (m/s)	Shaft size (nominal)		Car size (internal)			Doors		Pit	Machine room				Load
			A	B	C	D	E	M	N	P	Q	H	R	S	W
9 General-purpose goods lifts, electric traction	500/6	0.5 0.63 and 1.0	1800	1500	1100	1200	2000	1100	2000	1400 1500	3800	2400	3700	2000	60
	1000/13	0.25 0.5 0.63 and 1.0	2100	2100	1400	1800	2000	1400	2000	1500	3800	2400	4300	2100	120
	1500/20	0.25 0.5 0.63 and 1.0	2500	2300	1700	2000	2300	1700	2300	1500 1700 1800	4000 4100 4200	2700	4500	2500	180
	2000/26	0.25 0.5 0.63 and 1.0	2500	2800	1700	2500	2300	1700	2300	1500 1700 1800	4100 4300 4500	2900	5100	2500	240
	2000/26	0.25 0.5 0.63 and 1.0	2800	2400	2000	2100	2300	2000	2300	1500 1700 1800	4100 4300 4500	2900	4700	2800	240
	3000/40	0.25 0.5 0.63	3000	3300	2000	3000	2300	2000	2300	1500 1700 1800	4200 4400 4500	2900	5600	3000	360
	3000/40	0.25 0.5 0.63	3500	2700	2500	2400	2300	2500	2300	1500 1700 1800	4200 4400 4500	2900	5000	3500	360
10 Heavy-duty goods electric traction	1500/20	0.25 0.5 0.63 and 1.0	2600	2400	1700	2000	2300	1700	2300	1500 1700 1800	4800	2700	4800	2600	180
	2000/26	0.25 0.5 0.63 and 1.0	2600	2900	1700	2000	2300	1700	2300	1500 1700 1800	4800	2900	5400	2600	240
	2000/26	0.25 0.5 0.63 and 1.0	2900	2500	2000	2100	2300	2000	2300	1500 1700 1800	4800	2900	5000	2900	240
	3000/40	0.25 0.5 0.63 and 1.0	3000	3400	2000	3000	2300	2000	2300	1500 1700 1800	4800	2900	5900	3000	360
	3000/40	0.25 0.5 0.63 and 1.0	3500	2800	2500	2400	2300	2500	2300	1500 1700 1800	4800	2900	5300	3500	360
	4000/53	0.25 0.5 0.63	3500	3400	2500	3000	2500	2500	2500	1500 1700 1800	5200	2900	6200	4000	480
	5000/66	0.25 0.5 0.63	3600	4000	2500	3600	2500	2500	2500	1500 1700 1800	5200	2900	6800	4000	600

6 SERVICE LIFTS AND HOISTS

There is no standard range from which to select service lifts, and makers' preferences on general arrangement, size and speed vary considerably; but most makers can provide lifts similar to those shown in **5.12** and **5.13**. Where there are other lifts in the building or associated buildings, a service lift by the same maker assists management and minimises maintenance costs.

A maker's own standard pre-assembled and clad unit might be advantageous for such as an existing building where minimum builder's work and quick delivery are overriding factors. These packages do have disadvantages for some applications, however, e.g. insufficient fire resistance of cladding, unsafe for location above a space used by people.

7 ESCALATORS AND PASSENGER CONVEYORS

Dimensions, speed and finishes vary but a 30° incline is available from all makers, **5.14**. For preliminary purposes or an approximate comparison with lifts' performance (Tables II and III), allow a handling capacity of 1600 people in 30 minutes per 600 mm of step width. In many buildings, of course, a lift or

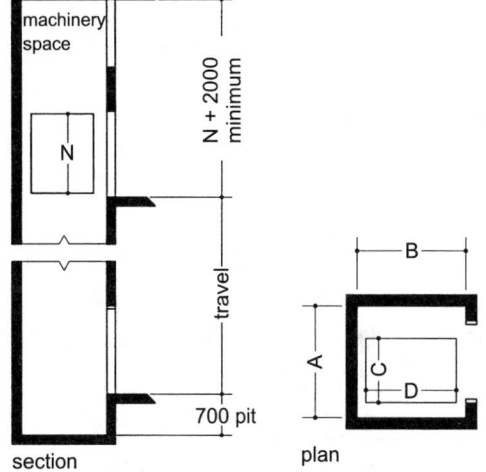

5.13 *Large service lift suitable for trolleys, dimensions as Table VI. Note: speed 0.25 or 0.38 m/s. Shaft size includes 25 mm allowance for out-of-plumb. Openings can be front and rear as required*

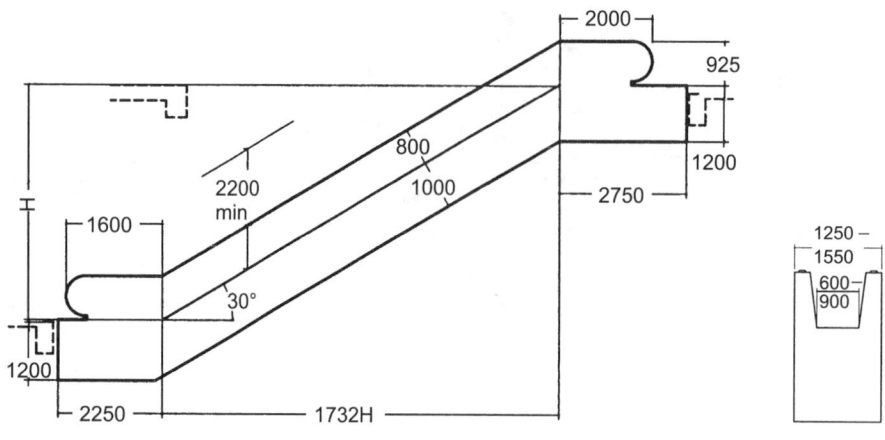

5.14 *Dimensions of 30° escalator, elevation and section*

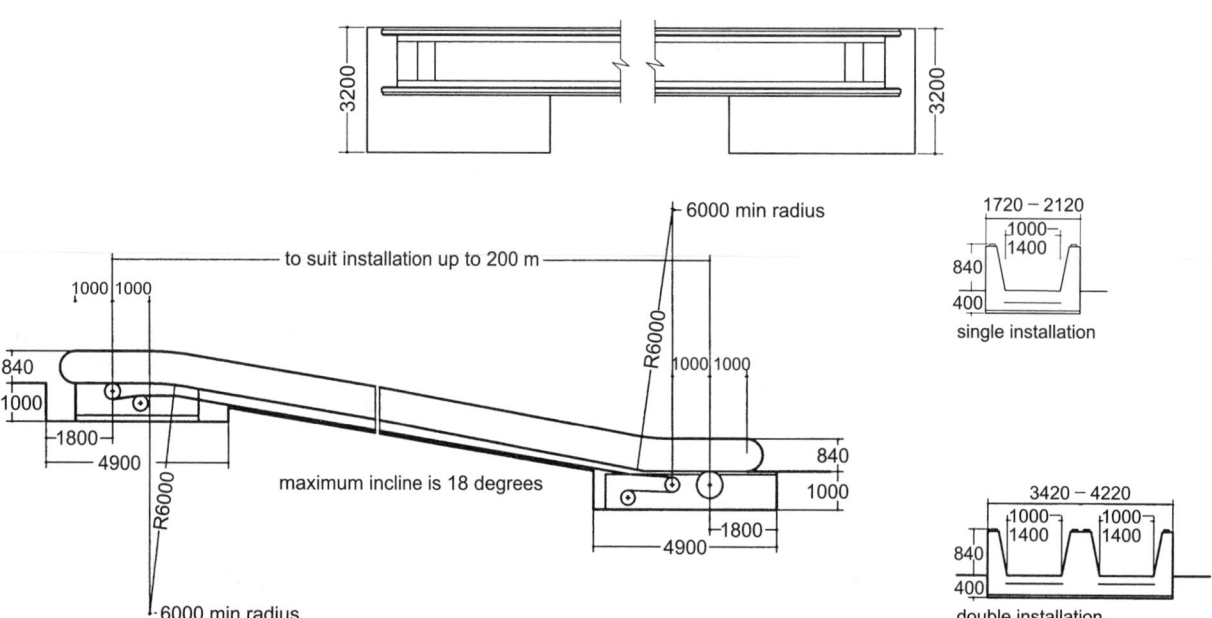

5.15 *A one-speed mechanised passenger conveyor system, may be flat, or up to 12° for prams, shopping trolleys, etc., or up to 15° for special installations. Other systems available permit 'valley' and 'hill' longitudinal profiles; also surface laying of conveyor on drive motor on existing floors. Capacity of system shown is 7200 persons per hour. Systems are available up to 8000 pph. Speed range is 0.45 to 0.6 m/s. Tread widths 1000 to 1400 mm*

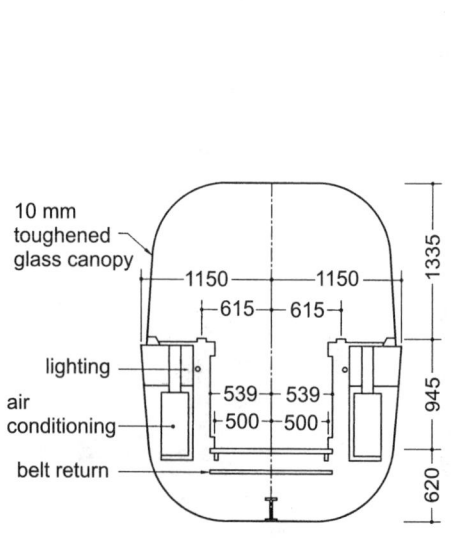

5.16 *Section through passenger conveyor at Charles de Gaulle Airport, Paris*

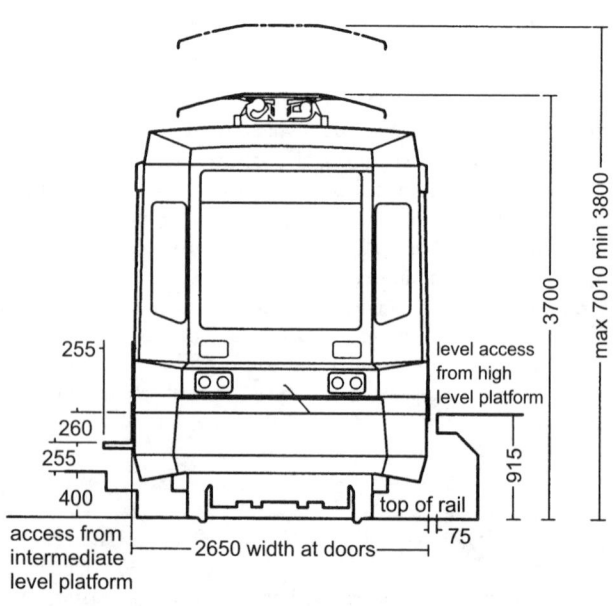

5.17 *Manchester Metrolink: a typical modern tramway system. Frontal view of a car, showing level access for wheelchairs from a high-level platform*

lifts will also be needed for the infirm, wheelchairs, prams and/or goods traffic.

If space permits a conveyor, **5.15** may be installed. This is able to take prams and suitably designed trolleys, and so is appropriate for supermarkets and air terminals etc. A more elaborate type is shown in **5.16**.

8 PEOPLE MOVERS AND LIGHT RAIL

There are a wide variety of these installations. **5.17** shows a typical light rail car designed to facilitate use by wheelchair users.

9 BIBLIOGRAPHY

Official publications

The European Parliament/The Council/European Union, *Directive 95/EC of the European Parliament and of the Council on the approximation of the laws of the member states relating to lifts (The Lifts Directive)*, 1995

British Standards

BS 2655: Part 8: 1971 Modernisation of lifts, escalators and paternosters, BS, 1971

BS 5655: Lifts and service lifts (published in 12 parts at different times covering different types of installation and specific components), BSI

Other publications

M. Barry, *Through the Cities, the Revolution in Light Rail*, The Frankfort Press, Dublin

E. Nömmik, (ed) *Elevators make life easier*, Swedish Council for Building Research, 1986

S. Thorpe, *Wheelchair Stairlifts and Platform Lifts*, Centre for Accessible Environments, 1993

6 Landscape design

Michael Littlewood

CI/Sfb 998
UDC 712

Michael Littlewood is a landscape architect and a consultant

KEY POINT:
- *The design of space between buildings is as important as that of the buildings themselves*

Contents

1 INTRODUCTION

1.01

The design of external spaces outside and between buildings, whether urban or rural, public or private, covers a wide variety of elements and requires considerable knowledge of the location, materials and construction. All too often parsimony results in schemes which are unsatisfactory both aesthetically and practically.

1.02 Basic human dimensions

The space requirements of people outside buildings are generally similar to those inside as illustrated in Chapter 2. A family group of six people on a lawn or terrace occupy a rough circle 4 m diameter; for ten people (the largest convenient simple group) the dimension becomes 6 m, which is the minimum useful size.

2 WALKWAYS

2.01

Full physical ability is a temporary condition. Most people become less than fully mobile at some time, perhaps carrying shopping or parcels; pregnancy; a sprained ankle; a dizzy spell; a broken high-heeled shoe; or just the normal course of ageing. Circulation routes should be planned bearing this in mind, integrating a design that is both functional and aesethetically pleasing, rather than adding on facilities for 'the disabled'.

2.02

Pedestrian routes should follow desire lines as directly as possible.

The details are of secondary importance if the connections are incomplete. Routes should be chosen by analysing and responding to the context of the site. One way of achieving this is not to provide paths in a newly created landscape scheme but to wait until the users make worn tracks and then to pave these. Routes should include loops rather than dead ends, incorporating places to stop and rest. There should be coordination between parking, paved and rest areas, building entries, etc. with adequate seating, lighting and signage.

2.03 Widths of pedestrian routes

These vary with the purpose of the route, the intensity of use and with the situation. As a general rule of thumb, provide 600 mm width for each pedestrian walking abreast: which suggests 2 m minimum for public walkways. The requirements of others than

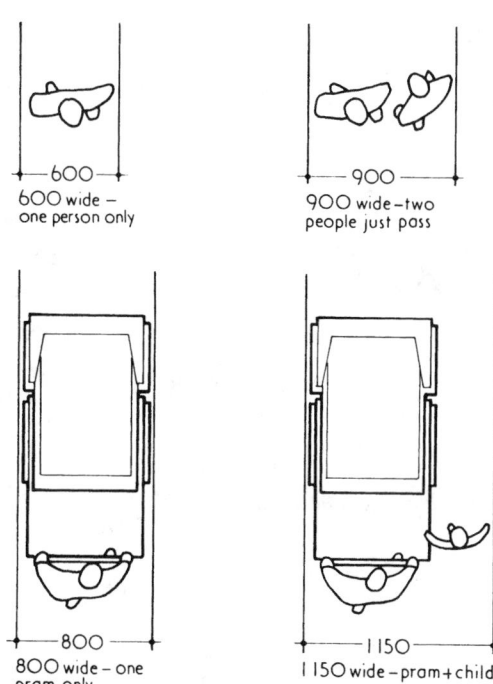

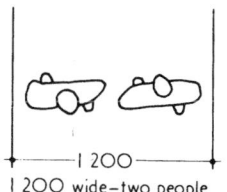

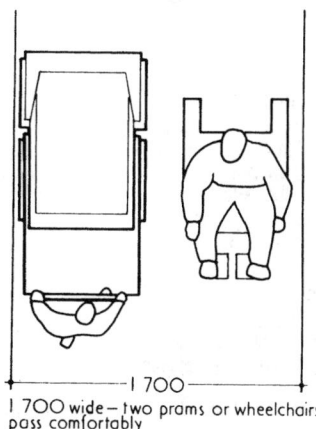

6.1 *Characteristics of various footway widths*

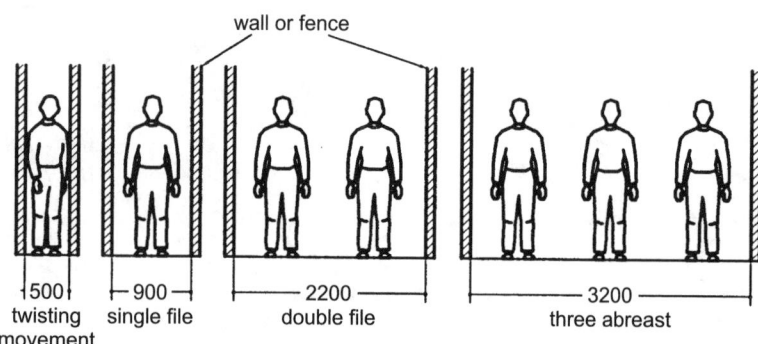

6.2 *Pedestrians between walls or fences, minimum dimensions. Add 25 per cent for free movement, prams, wheelchairs and bicycles*

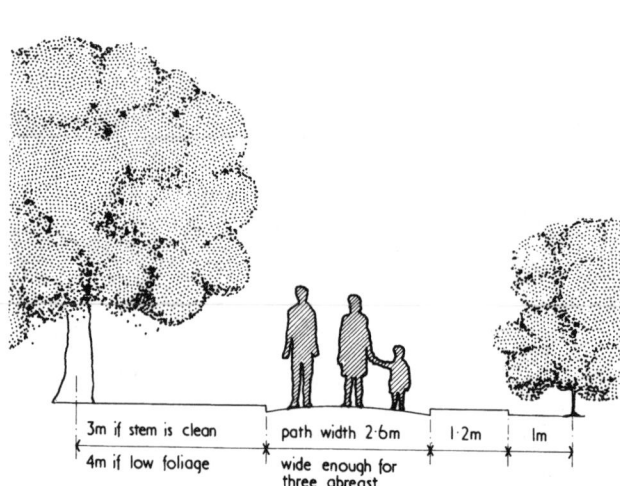

6.3 *Narrow path across open space*

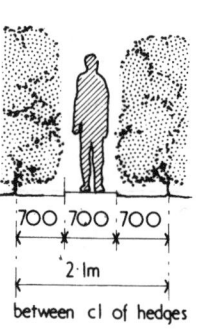

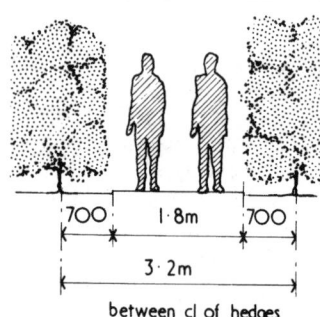

6.5 *Walking between clipped hedges with careful movement. Planting beds should be 400 mm wide for clipped hedges*

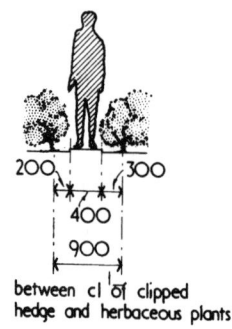

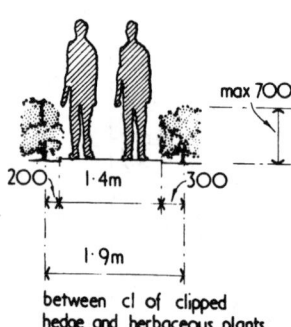

6.4 *Minimum path widths between low planting, but not suitable for prams. Planting beds should be 600 mm wide for herbaceous plants*

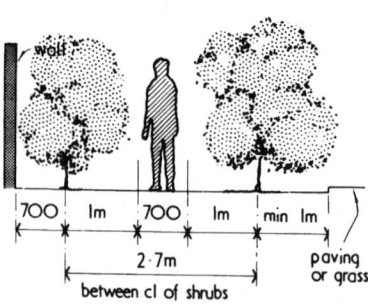

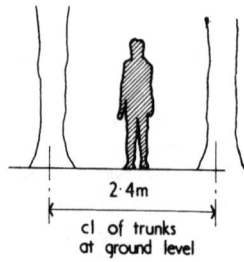

6.6 *Minimum dimensions for pedestrians between free-growing shrubs. Where there are prams allow 3 m between the centres of planting*

pedestrians that use these paths must also be considered, **6.1**. Minimum requirements between walls or fences are shown in **6.2**; **6.3** illustrates a path over open ground. Other situations are shown in **6.4** to **6.6**.

Pedestrians typically do not use the entire width of footpaths. The edge adjacent to a kerbed roadway about 75 m wide tends to be avoided, as is the 0.5 to 0.75 m width directly alongside a building, **6.7**. Only under conditions of congestion would these edges be used.

Street furniture such as trees, bollards, direction signs, parking meters, telephones, litter bins, fountains, sculpture and kiosks can also reduce footpath effective width. They should preferably be situated in the avoidance zones.

2.04 Slopes

6.8 and **6.9** provide longitudinal and cross-slope criteria for footpaths under various circumstances. Longitudinal slope criteria or gradients are based on user abilities and design objectives. Cross-slope criteria are based on the need for positive drainage (depending on paving material). Porous paving, for instance, does not require as much of a cross-slope for drainage as does a non-porous paving material.

2.05 Surfacing

The location of the footpath and its intensity of use will determine the surfacing material and its thickness. Some paths are also used for service vehicles and should be designed accordingly, particularly the edge details. Several factors influence the durability of paving materials; even high-quality materials can wear out or disintegrate if subjected to extremes of heavy traffic or inadequate maintenance. Surfacing irregularities should be minimized.

Some footpaths or walkways are required to have high traction ratings for safety use. Highly textured surfacings usually require steeper slopes for drainage (i.e. 2 per cent minimum) but every footpath must seek to achieve its design purpose in all weather conditions. A multitude of design patterns is now possible with the current wide range of unit pavers. Colour affects the degree to which heat and light are absorbed or reflected, and requires consideration.

The edges of a footpath play an extremely important part in both its appearance and function. Flexible materials such as macadam or sprayed chippings particularly need the support of an edging; so do unit paving blocks and bricks.

2.06 Tactile warning strips

These are used to give advance notice to people with impaired sight of abrupt grade changes, vehicular areas, dangerous exits, pools or water fountains, and the like **6.10**. They are recommended at the top and bottom of steps and in front of doors that lead to hazardous areas. However, such warnings should not be used at emergency exits, as they can inhibit their proper use.

Street furniture, including trees, should be located within a defined zone along the outer edge of walkways, leaving a clear path without obstruction. A linear tactile warning strip can define this zone. **6.11** shows a blind person using a white stick.

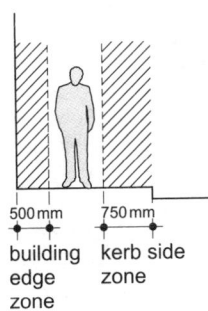

6.7 *Zones avoided by pedestrians*

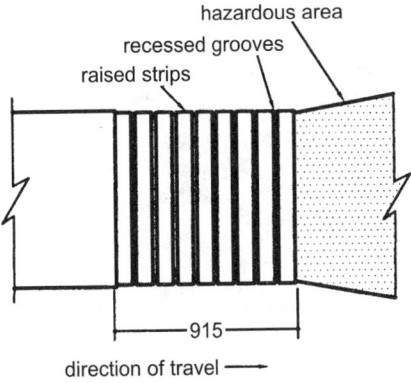

6.8 *Walking along a longitudinal slope: up to 3 per cent preferred, generally 5 per cent maximum, 5–10 per cent possible depending on climate. Between 5 per cent and 8 per cent slopes are considered to be ramps*

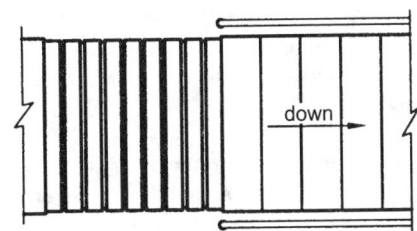

6.9 *Paths with cross-fall: 1 per cent minimum for drainage, depending on material of finish; 2 per cent is typical, 3 per cent maximum*

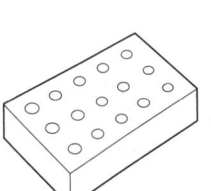

6.10 *Tactile warning pavings. These have value as devices to warn visually impaired people of hazards. They need to be in strips or areas large enough to be detectable*

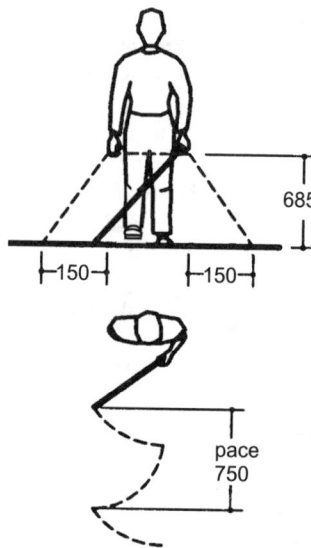

6.11 *Visually impaired person walking. The Typhlo cane is primarily used by those with limited vision. It will detect objects only within a specific range. Nothing should project into a pedestrian pathway above a height of 680 mm*

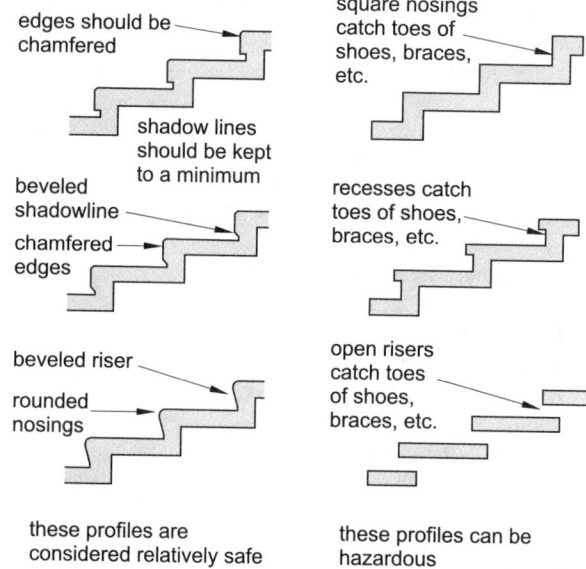

6.12 *Various tread profiles*

3 STEPS

3.01

Steps provide great opportunities for creating character and drama; good examples abound. They can be divided into three main types:

- Those steps which are sculptural as they have been literally carved out of the ground: earth or rock
- Those which are part of an element or structure; a retaining wall or a building – usually a plinth – eg the steps of St Paul's, London
- The cantilevered kind, sometimes no more than a ladder between levels.

3.02 Design

The design and materials of steps should aim to reinforce the character of their site. However, steps constitute a formidable barrier and safety hazard for those with visual or mobility impairment. Forty-four per cent of all accidents to visually impaired people occur at level changes. Locate any unexpected level changes out of the main line of pedestrian traffic.

Never have a single step in a walkway, except for kerbs. Preferably, use flights of at least three steps; their presence should be announced conspicuously, with visual and textural warnings at the top and bottom.

3.03 Nosing and shadow line profiles

Shadow lines are often included in steps for reasons of appearance. They can be hazardous if large enough to catch the toes of pedestrians. Nosings can also catch toes unless they are rounded.

6.12 shows various nosing and shadow line profiles some of which are hazardous, particularly to disabled people, and are therefore not recommended. The nose of each step should be easy to see, not obscured by confusing surfacing patterns. Treads should be visually distant from one another. Open treads and shadow line recesses can cause tripping and should be used with discretion.

3.04 Tread/riser

The steepness of a flight of steps has a crucial influence on its character. Outdoor scale makes it difficult to have a rule for the tread/riser ratio, although some guidance can be provided. Interior standards such as given in Chapter 2 should not be used externally; steps with those ratios become precipitous when descending. Also, people tend to move faster outdoors than they do indoors.

Inherent to a particular tread–riser ratio is the ease at which the steps can be used in relation to the person's natural pace and his or her sense of rhythm, **6.13**.

In dimensionally tight situations an appropriate tread–riser ratio has to be determined that will allow a given number of steps (includine landings if necessary) to fit the available space. Risers for outdoor stairways should be a minimum of 112 mm, a maximum of 175 mm.

Most examples show a more generous tread–riser than that achieved by formula. The steps to the Acropolis in Athens are 494 mm tread (going) × 173 mm rise; the Spanish Steps in Rome are 400 × 150 mm.

3.05 Surfacings

Textured materials are most suitable for treads as they provide a grip in wet and icy weather. It is also an advantage if they are in

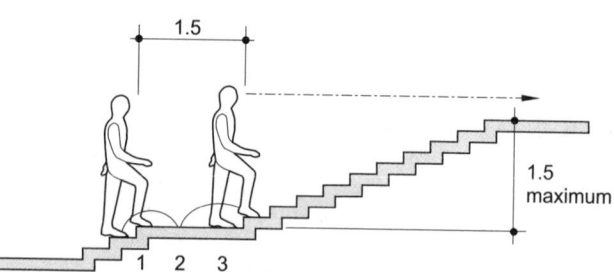

6.13 *Stair height and landing proportions: at least two, preferably three steps to be provided. Longer flights should preferably be in multiples of five treads to alternate the feet. Landings should be long enough to allow an easy cadence, at least three strides. Longer landings should be in multiples of 1.5 m. The rise between landings should not exceed 1.5 m so that the next landing is visible: greater heights are psychologically uninviting. If it unavoidable, provide a landing at least every 20 treads to minimise fatigue*

a lighter colour than the risers, as the nosings will contrast with their background.

3.06 Abutments

While many steps will have no abutments, others will have one or two. In some instances they may be retaining walls, especially where treads cannot fade away into adjoining ground. Where the flight projects out from the slope or bank, the construction below the treads should be carefully considered.

3.07 Landings

Long flights of steps are frightening and exhausting. Landings should be provided after twelve to fourteen steps to provide a pause or a change of direction. The height between stairway landings is an important factor for psychological reasons as well as for human endurance. The maximum should be 1.5 m for visual coherence and invitation between adjacent levels. Lower heights are preferred **6.14** and **6.15**.

3.08 Landing widths

Landings should allow for the convenient movement of people, especially for those who need assistance negotiating steps. Except in the case of very wide steps, such as those in front of imposing buildings, they should be at least as wide in both directions as the flights they serve, and may be wider.

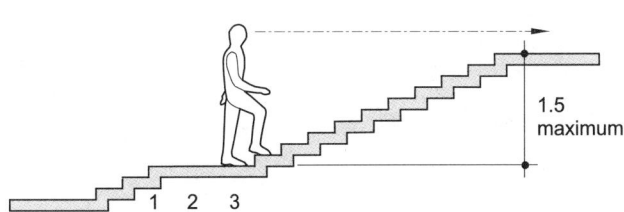

6.14 *Seeing over the landing from the bottom of the flight of steps*

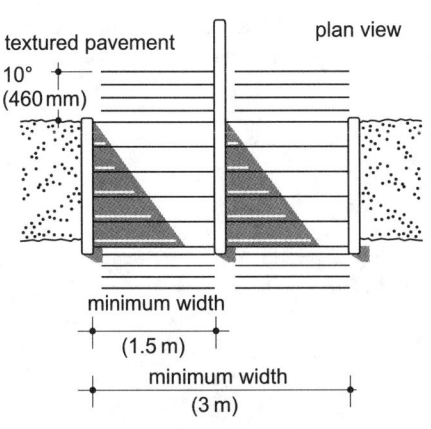

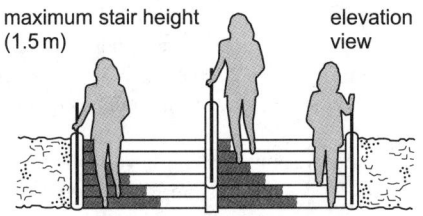

6.15 *Vertical height between landings should be minimised to accommodate people with limited stamina. Note that the minimum widths do not include the wall thicknesses*

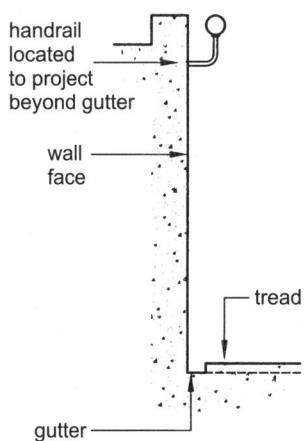

section through tread at wall

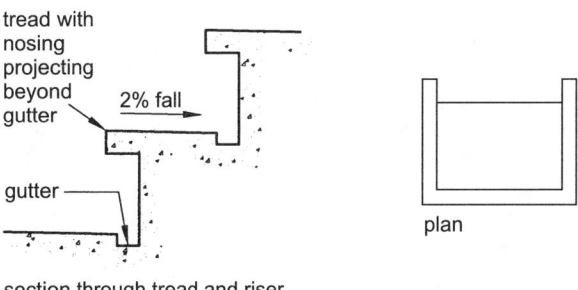

section through tread and riser

6.16 *In areas of heavy rainfall and/or hard frosts, the treads to a flight of steps might be given a slight backfall with tiny gutters which themselves fall to larger gutters at the flight edge*

3.09 Drainage

Surface water must be shed off steps as quickly as possible, especially in winter, and treads should fall by at least 2 per cent. In areas of heavy rainfall a detail such as shown in **6.16** could be used.

Landings are needed to moderate the flow of water down stair flights, and should incorporate gullies.

4 RAMPS

4.01 Pedestrian ramps

These are used to allow wheeled vehicles such as trolleys, wheelchairs and buggies to change levels. The important criteria is the angle of slope, the type of surfacing and the drainage of surface water.

Ramps are essential for those who use wheelchairs. The angle of slope may vary depending upon the location. A steep angle that is satisfactory for a short length will be unacceptable for a longer ramp. A zig-zag ramp which goes up a long bank needs to be almost level at its bends; otherwise the gradients on the insides of those bends will be very steep.

Ramps should have a landing at least every 9.0 m of length, **6.17**. Visual and textural indications should be provided at top and bottom.

4.02 Slopes

Outdoor ramps should generally be no steeper than 5 per cent; when enclosed and protected the maximum gradient is 8.5 per cent. Dropped kerbs are an exception, 12 per cent being acceptable if the running distance less than 1 m.

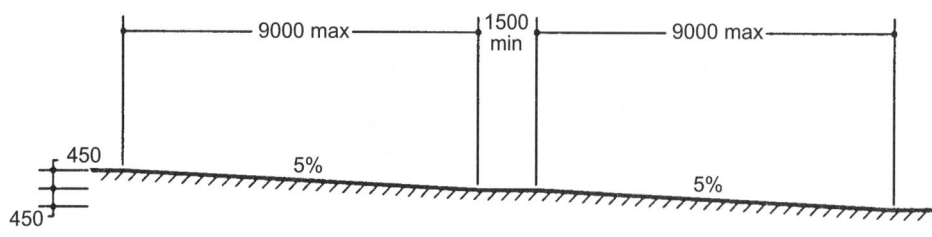

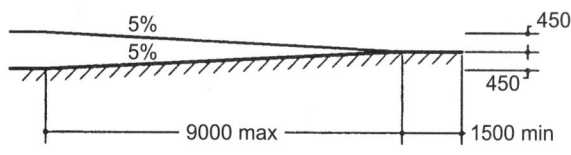

6.17 External ramps, straight and dog-leg

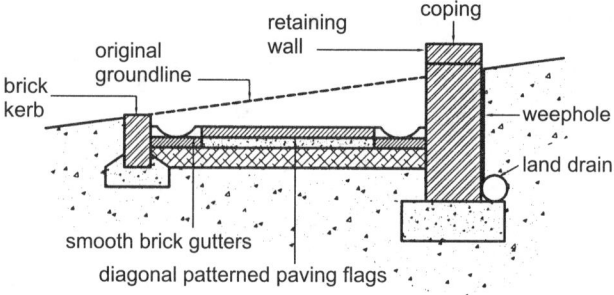

section

6.19 Diagonally rilled slabs can be used to pave a ramp surface. This provides grip, and rainwater drains to the side

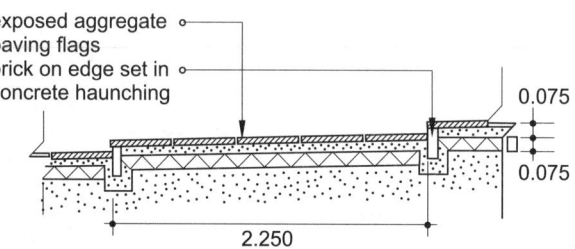

6.20 A perron, or stepped ramp. May be used where prams, pushchairs and trolleys are expected but not suitable for most wheelchair users

4.03 Widths

These are determined according to type and intensity of use. One-way travel requires a minimum width of 900 mm clear, whereas two-way travel needs 1500 mm, **6.18**. Where turns occur at landings adequate space for manoeuvring wheelchairs must be provided.

4.04 Edges

Usually one or both sides of a ramp will be higher or lower than adjacent ground. Where the side is lower than the ground, there will be a bank or a retaining wall. The base of a bank will need some form of kerbing.

Where the ramp is higher than adjacent ground, guarding will be necessary. See Section 5 of this chapter for details.

4.05 Surfacing

The surfacing of the ramp depends on its slope and location. A grassed ramp is suitable where the use is minimal and the slope is gentle as in a garden. In an urban situation with steep slopes a sealed surface of tarmac with chippings rolled in would be more appropriate. On extreme slopes bricks or blocks can be used, combined with drainage channels and gullies. A useful form of surface is shown in **6.19**.

Surfacings should have grip, with low kerbs (at least 50 mm high) along the edges of ramps and landings for detection by cane.

4.06 Drainage

Unless checked, rainwater will run rapidly down a ramp: landings are used to break the flow. Gullies should be placed where they will not cause problems to people or wheels. Linear drains are helpful at the bottom of a ramp.

4.07 Ramped steps or perrons

These can be useful for long hills where a ramp would be too steep. They are not suitable for wheelchairs. 50 mm risers can be negotiated by prams and buggies. Allowing three paces on each tread (2.2 m) an overall gradient of 7 per cent can be achieved, **6.20**.

5 HANDRAILS

5.01

Handrails should be provided to all stairways and ramps, and may also be installed along paths to assist less mobile people. They are important for safety, for support and for guidance of those with visual difficulties.

In recreational settings, ropes with periodic knots have been used as location devices enabling the visually impaired to enjoy areas and places which were previously inaccessible.

Handrails should not be an afterthought, or seen purely as a safety factor. It is preferable to provide handrails on both sides of a stairway or ramp because some people have one-sided strength. Extra-wide stairways should have centre railings no more than 6 m apart.

The ends of railings should extend beyond the top and bottom steps of stairways by 300 to 450 mm. They should be continuous across intermediate landings and should be capable of supporting 114 kg of mass. Handrails should be easy and comfortable to grip, **6.21**. There should be no sharp or protruding ends, edges or fixings. When fixed to walls they can obtrude or be inset, **6.22**.

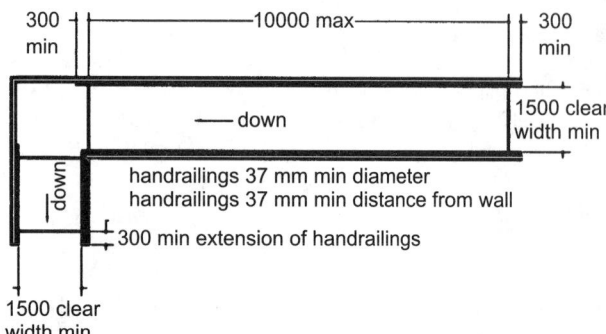

6.18 Dimensional criteria for a two-way ramp for wheelchairs. For one-way travel the minimum width is 900 mm

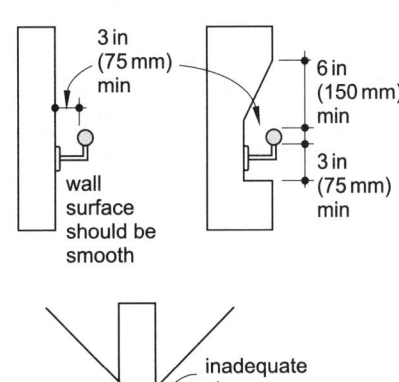

6.21 *Handrail profiles: preferred and deprecated. The preferred profiles allow a secure and comfortable natural grip*

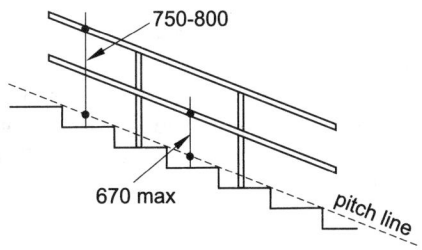

6.22 *Fixing handrails*

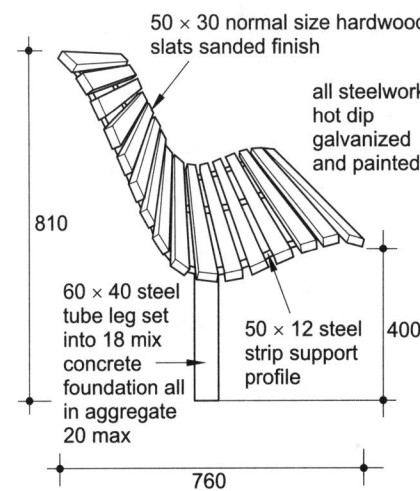

6.24 *A good park bench: from the GLC South Bank. Standard length modules 1 m, 1.5 m, 2 m, 2.5 m and 3 m. Longer lengths as special*

6.23 *Handrail heights*

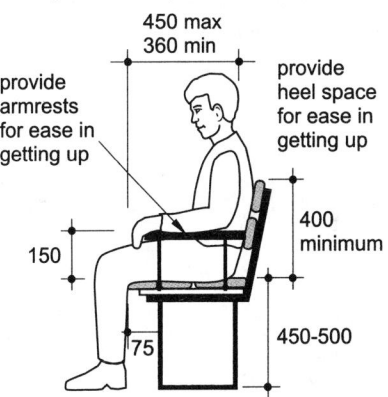

6.25 *Park bench seat, designed to suit people of limited strength. Armrests and heelspace are especially important*

5.02 Height

Handrailing heights for outdoor steps and ramps range from 750 to 850 mm, **6.23**. Below the top rail of handrailings there should be a second rail at a height of 670 mm or lower for children and for detection by cane users.

6 SEATING

6.01 Benches and other forms of outdoor seating

These are important. Reasons to sit vary widely, and many people find it essential to find a readily available place to rest.

The placing should be carefully considered. Avoid situations attractive to vagrants and alcoholics.

Benches should be designed for comfort. **6.24** illustrates preferred height and the seating angle for outdoor benches.

Consider the needs of elderly and disabled people. Some, for example, require armrests when getting into or out of a seated position. Heel space is necessary when rising from the seat, **6.25**.

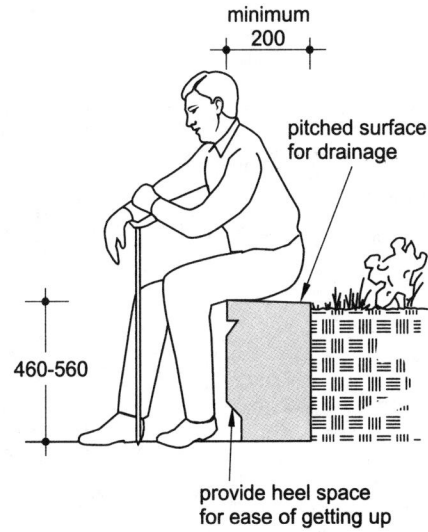

6.26 *Wall seating. Although wall heights can vary, they should be designed for a range of users*

Wheelchair users require places to stop and rest off the pedestrian flow, and somewhere to set packages. These should be adjacent to benches for their friends and carers.

Outdoor seating should be designed for easy maintenance and cleaning, and materials should resist vandalism. Surfaces should be pitched to shed water, but weep holes should not drain onto walking surfaces where wetness or ice may constitute a hazard.

6.02 Wall seating

Walls designed for sitting on are typically 400–450 mm wide, and between 350 and 550 mm in height, 400 mm being most common, **6.26**. For the elderly, a greater height is preferred.

7 STREET FURNITURE

7.01

Street furniture should be carefully organised for safety and easier negotiation for those with visual impairments. Elements should be easily detectable by cane, either in themselves or by way of a hazard strip. A linear textured surface can be used to separate a zone with furniture from clear walking space.

7.02 Litter bins

Provide types that are usable by disabled people, **6.27**. Open-top varieties are the easiest but allow snow and rain to collect. Semi-open tops prevent entry of snow and rain and are relatively easy to operate. Hinged-door varieties prevent entry of snow and rain, but many people find them difficult to use.

8 BARRIERS

8.01

The purposes of barriers are

- Privacy
- Safety
- Security
- Boundary definition
- Circulation control
- Environmental modification – climate, noise, etc
- Appearance

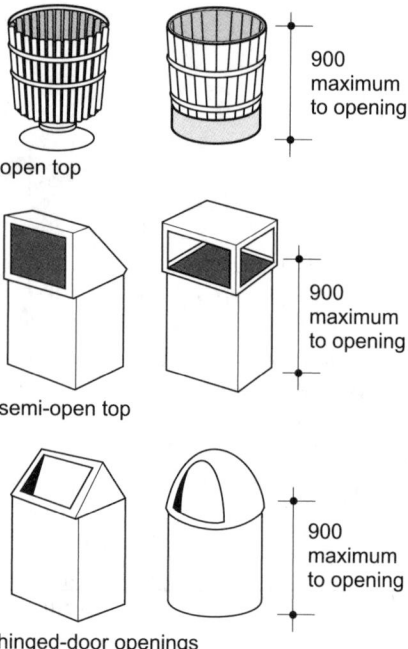

open top

semi-open top

hinged-door openings

900 maximum to opening

6.27 *Litter bins*

8.02

The type, size and the materials will largely be determined by the prime purpose (see Table I). The site and local character should influence the style, especially if it is not level. The design should also consider scale, proportion, rhythm, colour and texture. Practical matters, such as Building Regulations, accurate boundary surveys, easements, fire and safety access as well as economic factors, construction methods and maintenance, must not be overlooked.

8.03 Posts and bollards

These are mainly used to prevent vehicles encroaching on pedestrian areas. They should preferably not be placed in the main line of pedestrian travel and should allow free pedestrian movement, **6.28**.

Table I Choice of barrier related to function

Form of enclosure	Physical barrier (security)	Visual barrier (privacy)	Noise barrier	Windbreak	To define space	Durability	Climbable	Permanence	Remarks
Trees	✗	✓	✗	✓	✓	High	✗	High	
Walls: brick, stone, concrete	✓	✓	✓(i)	✓	✓	High	✗	High	(i) If properly placed and sized
Fences: timber	✓	✓	✓(i)	✓	✓	Low	✗(ii)	Low	(i) If properly placed and sized
Fences: precast concrete with timber panels	✓	✓	✓	✓	✓	Med	✗(i)	Med	(i) Depending on design
Fences: precast concrete with wires	✓	✗	✗	✗	✓	High	✓	Med	
Metal: wrought iron and mild steel	✓	✗	✗	✗	✓	High	✗(i)	High	(i) Depending on design
Chain link and woven wire fence	✓	✗(i)	✗	✗	✓	Med	✓(ii)	Med	(i) Woven wire can be a directional visual barrier, e.g. glare fences on motorway (ii) Chain link if large mesh
Strained wire fence	✓	✗	✗	✗	✓	Med	✓	Med	
Guard rails	✓(i)	✗	✗	✗	✗	Med	✓	Low	(i) Only for the law abiding
Hedge bank	✓	✗(i)	✗	✓(ii)	✓	Med	✓	Med	(i) Unless very high (ii) If high enough
Ha-ha	✓	✗	✗	✗	✗	High	✓	Low	
Cattle-grid	✓(i)	✗	✗	✗	✗	High	✗	High	(i) For animals
Hedges, shrubs	✓(i)	✓	✗	✓	✓	Med	✗	Med	(ii) If spiky, e.g. hawthorn, blackthorn
Bollards	✗	✗	✗	✗	✓	High	✓	Med	

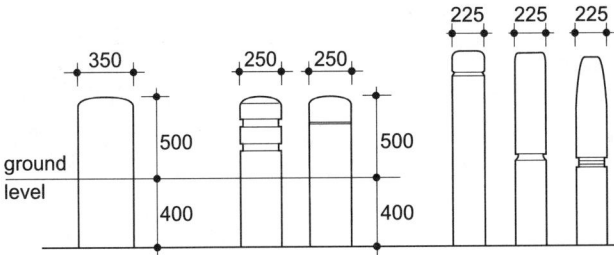

6.28 *Various styles of precast concrete bollards. Some of these can be supplied in alternatiove version with built-in lighting*

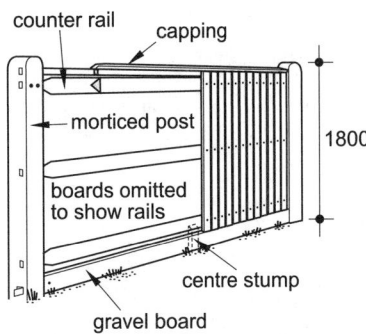

6.31 *Close boarded fence with capping and gravel board*

8.04 Chain barriers

These, especially when lower than 790 mm in height, are hazardous to pedestrians, cyclists, and motorcyclists since they are difficult to see, **6.29**. They are also difficult to detect by visually impaired cane users unless they are lower than 670 mm.

8.05 Guardrails

These can also be hazardous. They should be constructed high enough to be easily seen, but should also be designed for easy detection by those who are visually impaired, **6.30**.

8.06 Fences

The various types of fences are shown in Table II and **6.31** to **6.39**. They come in small, medium and tall heights (Table III), in closed, open, ornamental and security types, and in various styles. Higher fences should be designed with wind forces in mind – a plastic-coated wire chain link is 14 per cent solid.

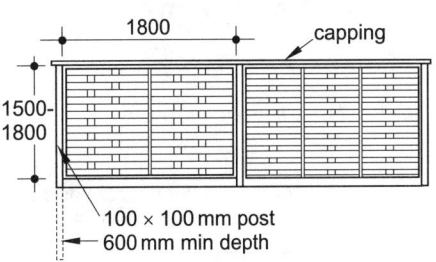

6.32 *Woven wood fence*

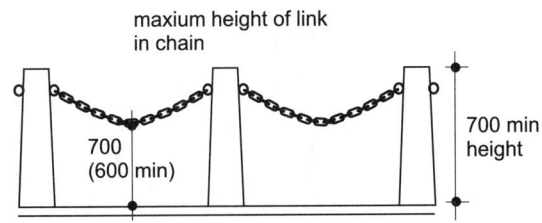

6.29 *Chain barrier*

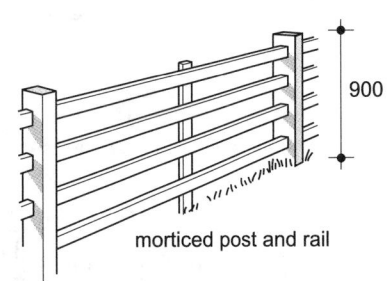

6.33 *Morticed post and rail fence*

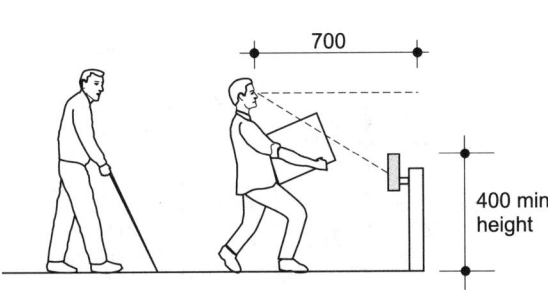

6.30 *Low barriers and the hazards they present*

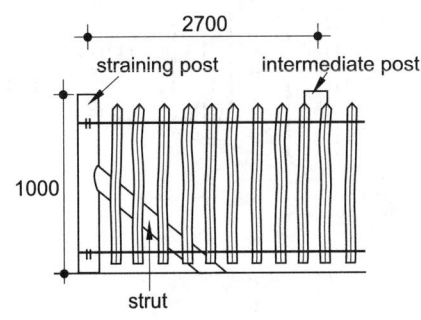

6.34 *Fence of chestnut palings supported on straining and intermediate posts*

Table II Fencing

Material Style	Timber		Metal		
	Closed	**Open**	**Ornamental**	**Security**	**Open**
	Close boarded **6.31** Woven panels **6.32**	Post and rail **6.33** Chestnut pale **6.34** Palisade/picket **6.35**	Steel bar railings **6.36**	Chain link **6.37** Steel palisade **6.38**	Post and wire **6.39**

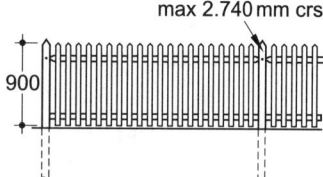

6.35 *Timber palisade fence*

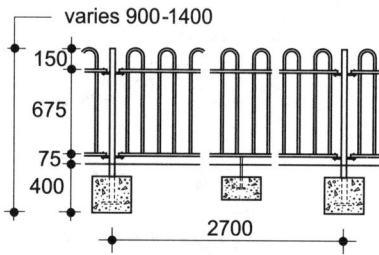

6.36 *Mild steel railings, hairpin top*

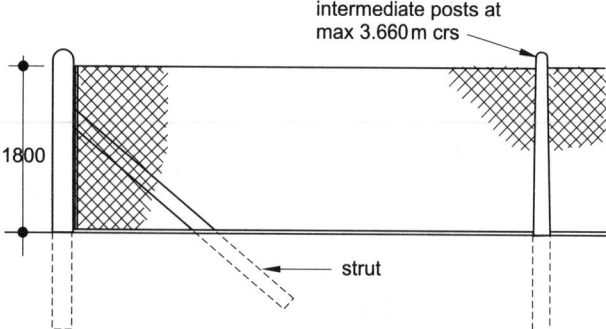

6.37 *Chain link fencing on precast concrete posts*

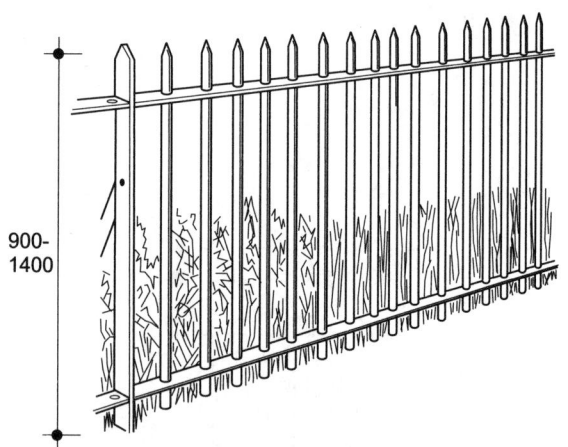

6.38 *Pointed top round bar fencing*

Table III Heights of fencing

Type	Height in (m)
House garden fronts and divisions	0.9
Minimum for children's playgrounds; general agricultural	1.2
House gardens; playing fields; recreation grounds; highways; railways	1.5–1.8
Commercial property	1.8
Industrial security fencing	2.1

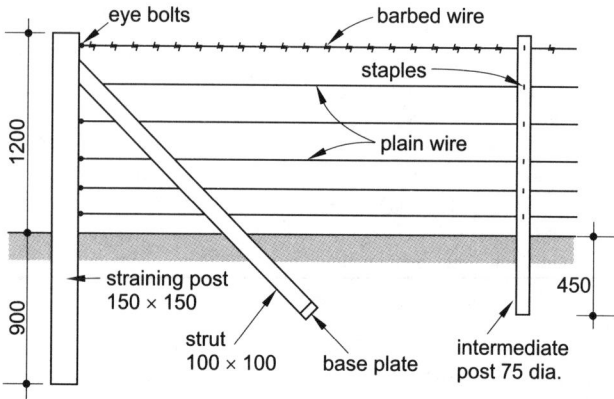

6.39 *Strained wire fence, end and corner posts braced*

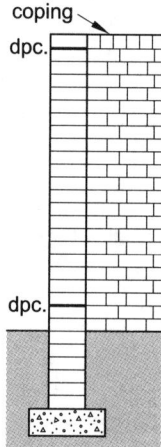

6.40 *Brick wall (showing various bonds and pointing details)*

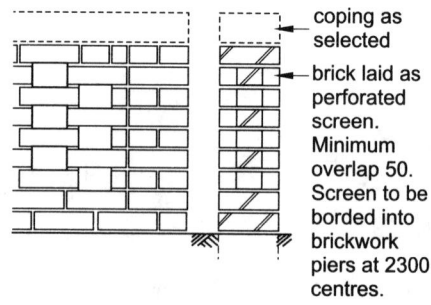

6.41 *Brick perforated screen wall*

8.07 Walls

Walls, whether free-standing, retaining or screen, can be built *in-situ* in concrete, concrete blocks, bricks, stone, timber and even metal, either on their own or in combination. Table IV and **6.40** to **6.48** list the main types.

Careful attention to detail is necessary for pleasing appearance, especially brick walls. Damp-proof courses and copings must be provided.

Heights should not exceed the safe limits given in Table V, based on the wind strength zones in **6.49**. Piers at intervals along a wall can increase its capacity to withstand wind, but staggering the wall as in **6.50** is more efficient. By this method a half-brick wall can be built up to 2.25 m high in Zone 1.

8.08 Open-screen walls

Scale, texture and pattern should decide the type of open-screen unit required. Since any large area would become boring, an open screen is usually more successful when used sparingly as a

Table IV Walls

Material	Solid	Screen
Brick	**6.40**	**6.41**
Stone	Drystone **6.42**	Not common
	Random rubble **6.43**	
	Ashlar **6.44**	
Concrete block	**6.45**	**6.46**
Composite	Stone hedge **6.47**	Ha-ha **6.48**

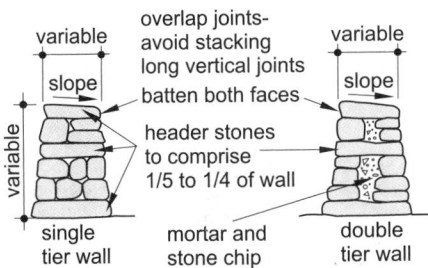

6.42 *Drystone wall*

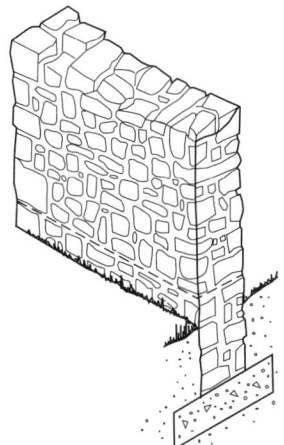

6.43 *Random rubble stone wall*

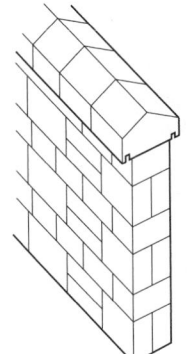

6.44 *Ashlar stone wall*

decorative element in a solid wall or in short lengths. These walls look their best when there is strong contrast of light and shade and especially when used with large foliage plants.

This type of walling is quite easy to erect and reinforcement is not usually necessary. Concrete blocks are available in several standard designs, but in general they are approximately 300 mm square, and 90 mm thick.

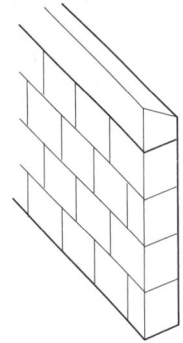

6.45 *Concrete block wall*

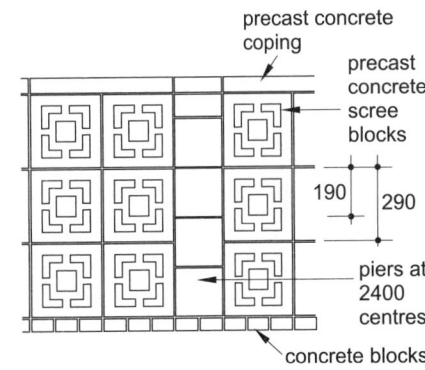

6.46 *Perforated concrete block screen wall*

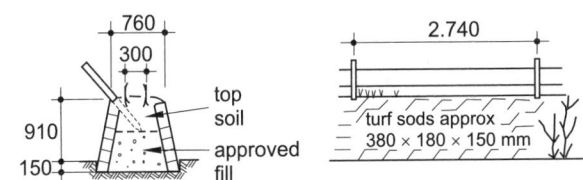

6.47 *Hedge bank, appropriate in a rural context*

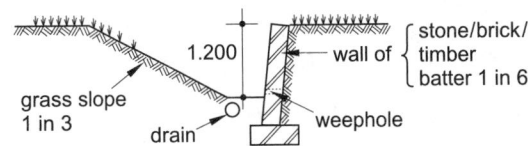

6.48 *Ha-ha*

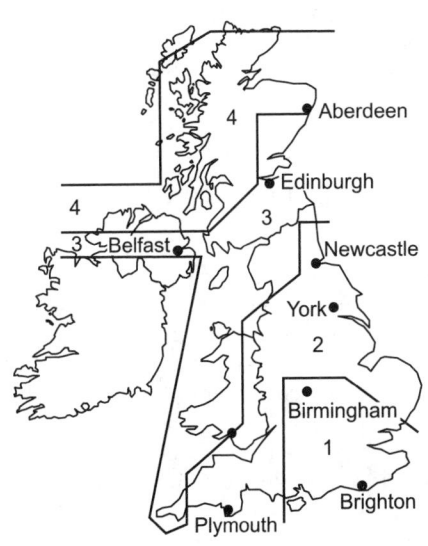

6.49 *Map of the United Kingdom showing zones for design of garden walls*

Table V Heights of masonry garden walls (from DoE leaflet *Your garden walls*)

Zone →				
Wall type and thickness ↓	Maximum height (mm)			
	1	2	3	4
Half brick (104 mm)	525	450	400	375
One brick (220 mm)	1450	1300	1175	1075
One and a half brick (330 mm)	2400	2175	2000	1825
100 mm block	450	400	350	325
200 mm block	1050	925	850	775
300 mm block	2000	1825	1650	1525

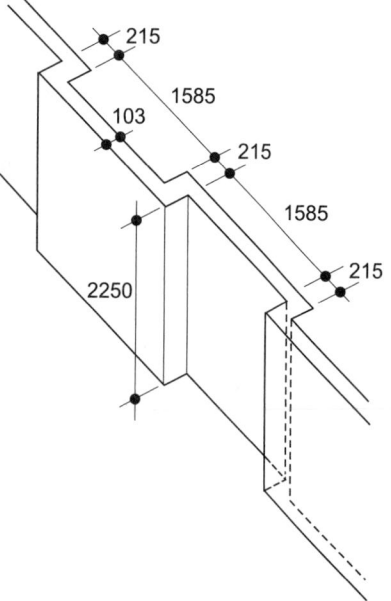

6.50 *Staggered brick wall*

8.09 Stone walls

The two basic methods of stone wall construction are dry wall and mortar-laid. Dry stone walls have no mortar, the stones are irregular in shape, and the stones are laid flat. Mortar-laid stone walls have continuous footings (and therefore are stronger and can be higher) and require fewer stones than dry walls.

Stonework patterns

Stonework can be random rubble or ashlar. The former has the stone as found, or cut by the mason in the field, while for the latter the stones are pre-cut and dressed before delivery to the site. Stones for a wall should be similar in size, or, if in a variety of shapes and sizes, should be evenly distributed to give a balanced appearance to the wall.

Styles

The British Isles is fortunate in having a variety of styles for stone walls based upon geographical regions. For new walls it is best to retain the local character.

8.10 Stone and hedge banks

Stone hedges are built with two faces of battered rubble stonework bedded on thin grass sods, with the centre filled with rammed earth. With time a stone hedge disappears behind naturalising vegetation. The construction of a hedge bank follows the same principle as a stone hedge but using turf instead of stone to form the faces. This limits height and so a simple post and wire fence is often incorporated when stock has to be contained.

8.11 Ha-has

These are useful devices for separating formal gardens from livestock without a visual barrier, using a retaining wall in stone, brick or timber with a link batter and the opposite ground graded to a 33 per cent slope.

9 RETAINING WALLS

9.01

These are used to make an abrupt change of level where there is insufficient room for a slope. Table V shows the principal types. In general they require careful structural design combined with an efficient drainage system.

9.02 Reinforced earth

This is a recent innovation consisting of a geotextile membrane tied back into the soil with anchors, **6.51**.

9.03 Masonry

Masonry structures for retaining ground can be constructed in many materials, both on their own or reinforced with steel bars:

- *In-situ* concrete, **6.52**
- Concrete blocks
- Precast concrete
- Brickwork
- Natural stone.

9.04 Concrete crib

This is constructed of precast reinforced concrete units laid in interlocking stretchers and headers to form vertical bins which are filled with crushed stone or other granular material, **6.53**. They are a particularly utilitarian solution for retaining fills in situations where excavation is not necessary. Reinforced projecting lugs on the headers are typically used to lock the headers and stretchers together.

9.03 Timber crib

Crib walls may be built of timber when a more natural appearance of wood is desired, **6.54**. All units should be pressure-treated with a preservative. Used railway sleepers were commonly used in

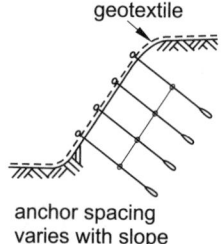

6.51 *Reinforced earth retaining structure*

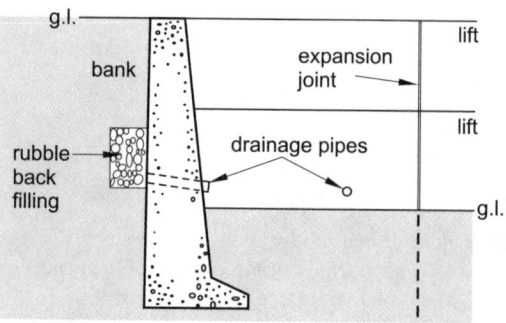

6.52 *Mass concrete retaining wall. Note rubble backfill and through pipes to facilitate drainage. Failure can occur if water pressure is allowed to build up behind the wall*

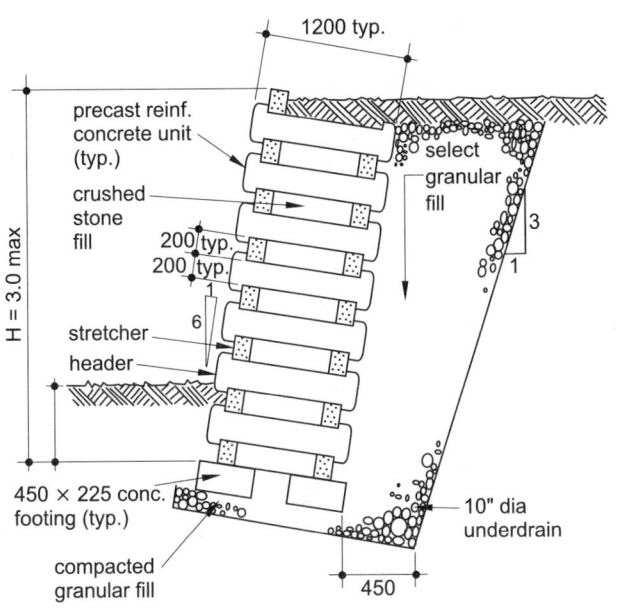

6.53 *Precast concrete crib wall*

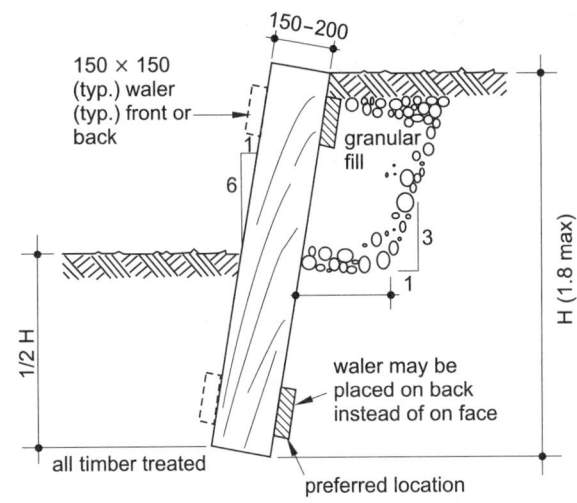

6.55 *Timber retaining walls of vertical railway sleepers*

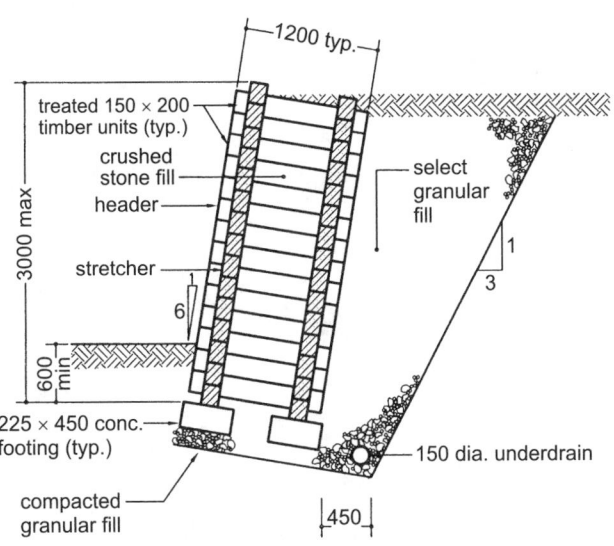

6.54 *Timber crib wall*

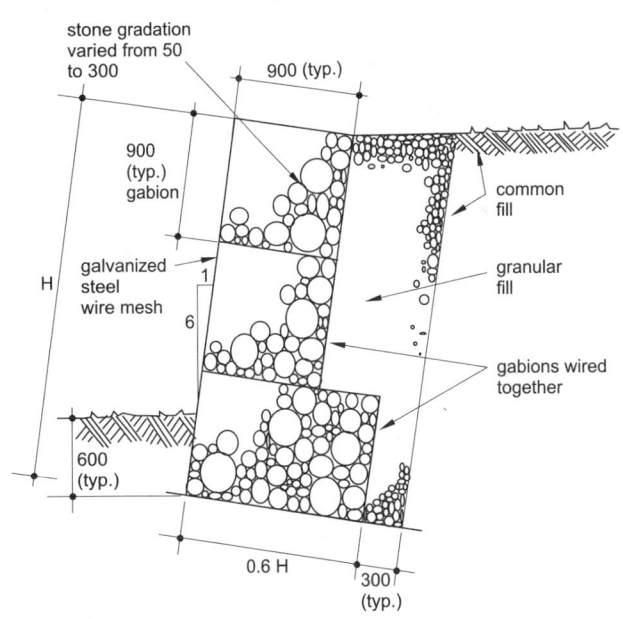

6.56 *Gabion wall*

early crib wall construction and continue to be employed for low walls. However, timber units cut to size and pressure-treated with copper salts or other non-bleeding preservatives are now widely available.

9.04 Timber

Retaining walls can be constructed using timbers driven into the ground, **6.55**. Since the wall's resistance to overturning depends upon one-half of its height being below finished level, it is often not economical or practical to use this type for retained heights greater than 1.5 m. The timber units in the horizontal wall can be of variable lengths over 1.5 m. The retained height should be less than 10 times the thickness of the timbers, and at least 50 per cent of their overall length should be buried below the lower ground level in average soil.

A structural engineer will need to be consulted.

9.06 Gabions

Gabions are rectangular baskets in standard sizes made of galvanised steel wire or polyvinyl-coated (PVC) wire hexagonal mesh which are filled with stone and tied together to form a wall. Each gabion has a lid and is sub-divided into 1 m cells. After being

filled with stone, the lid is closed and laced to the top edges of the gabion. Each gabion is then laced to the adjacent gabions, **6.56**.

Gabion walls, being flexible, can adapt to ground settlement. Their permeability allows water to drain through, making gabions especially suitable along stream and river banks where variations in water depths occur between flood and dry weather conditions. Volunteer vegetation establishes itself quickly in gabions, softening the structure's appearance in the landscape while also adding durability.

10 GATES AND DOORS

10.01

A gate must relate to the wall or fence in which it is placed, and state visually that there is an entrance or exit. Its construction and the supporting posts must be robust enough to withstand the effects of gravity and use, and it must be convenient to open and close.

10.02 Width

The appropriate width for a gate, or combination of gates, will be partially a matter of appearance and partially a matter of functional necessity: it must be wide enough for any vehicle needing to use it. A gate which, due to functional necessity, has to be large will

Table VI Widths of gates

Passing	Width (mm)
One person	600
Pram, pushchair, bicycle	800
Two people (just)	900
Wheelchair	1000
Pram or pushchair plus a walking child	1150
Two people (comfortably)	1200
Two wheelchairs or prams	1700
Small or medium car	2100
Large car, ambulance, medium van, small or medium tractor	2400
Car and bicycle, large tractor	3000
Fire engine, dustcart, lorry	3600
Two cars to pass (just)	4100
Combine harvester, two cars (comfortably), car and lorry (just)	4800
Any (normal) combination of two vehicles	5500

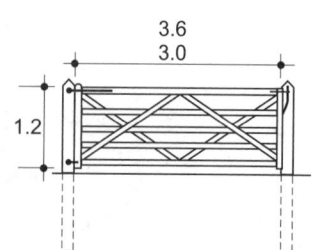

6.58 *Farm type gate*

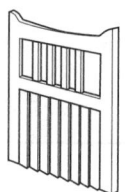

a *traditional*

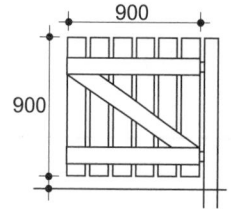

b *wood brace*

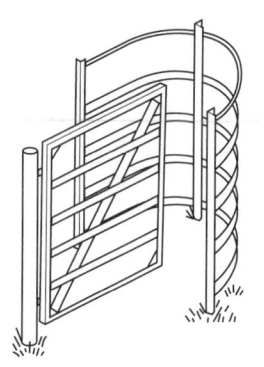

6.59 *Single and double farm gates*

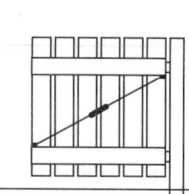

c *steel rod/wire with turnbuckle*

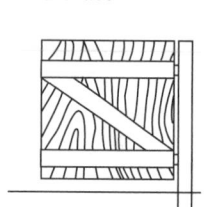

d *plywood panel*

6.57 *Single garden gates*

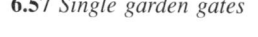

6.60 *Steel bow kissing gate*

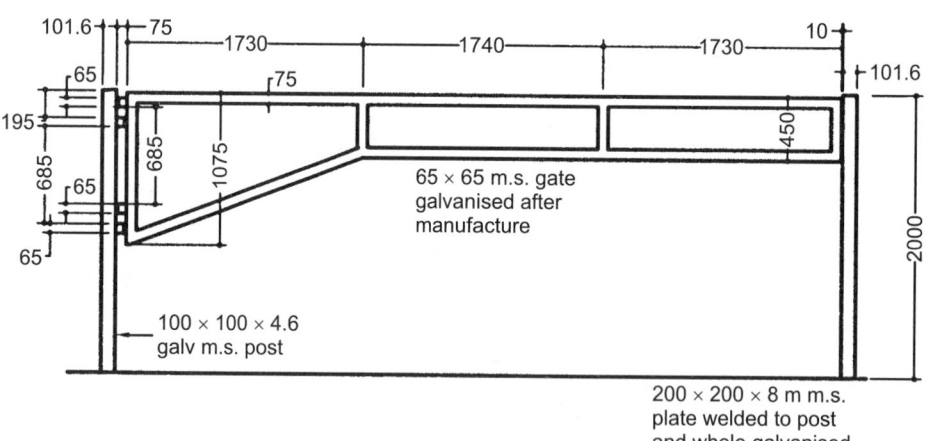

6.61 *Medium-duty car park barrier gate*

also have a degree of presence, even if that function is relatively humble.

Table VI gives some minimal dimensions for the passage of people and vehicles. These dimensions will allow people and vehicles to pass through a gate and each other. Clearance is not necessarily simply between gate posts – the open gate may, itself, occupy some of the available space. The dimensions assume straight travel but if a vehicle is also negotiating a bend, then widths will need to be greater.

6.57 to **6.62** show gate designs of different sizes and in various materials.

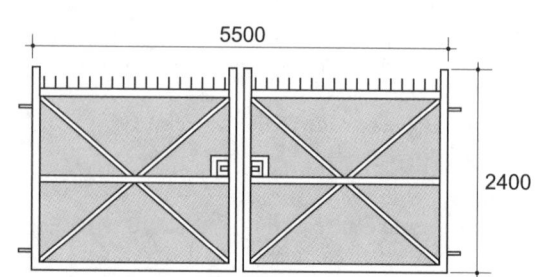

6.62 *Angle framed gates with spiked top*

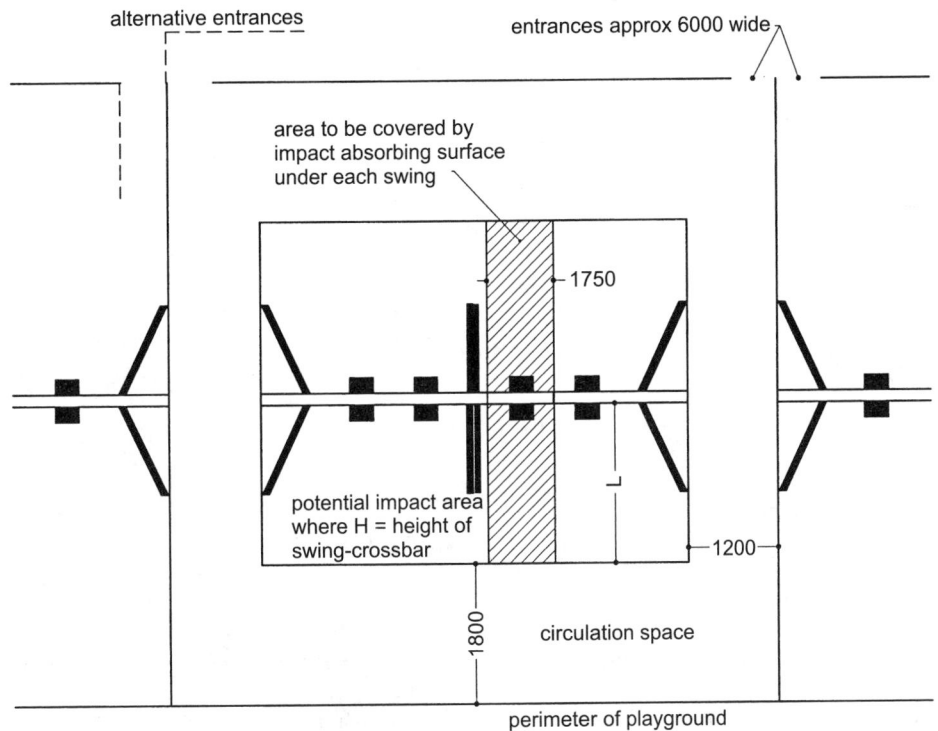

6.63 *Arrangement of barriers and impact absorbing surface for chldren's swings. L = (0.866 × distance from swing pivot to swing seat) + 1.75*

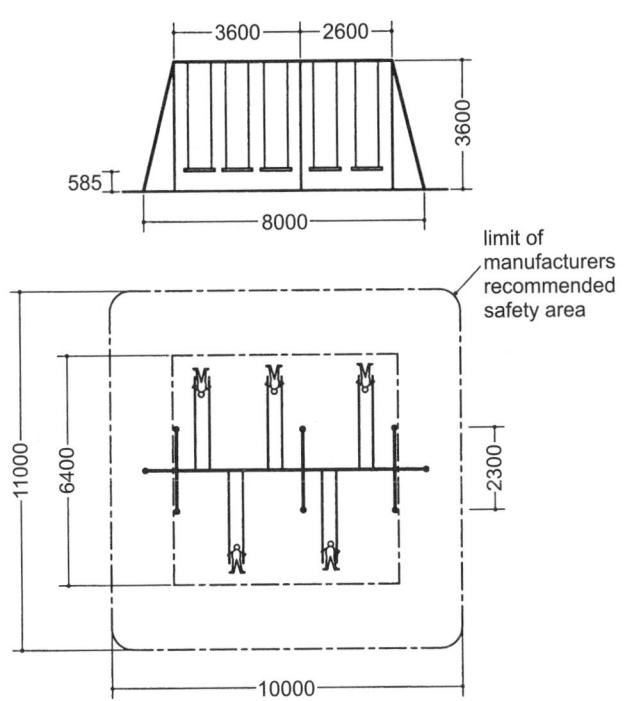

6.64 *Arrangement of full-size swing in a park. Smaller sizes are common*

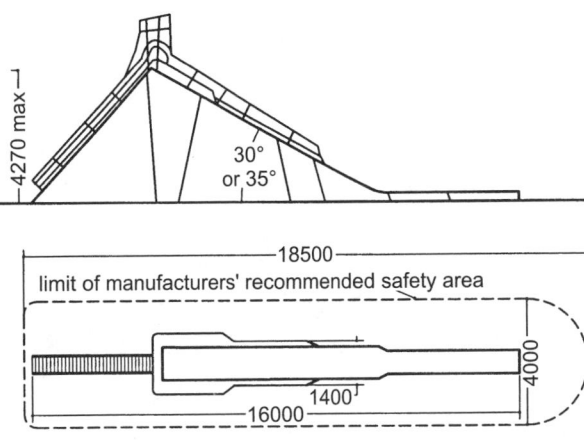

6.65 *Large slide for park. These are now normally installed on an earth mound to reduce the risk of falls*

11 CHILDREN'S PLAY EQUIPMENT

11.01

There are now many suppliers of play equipment whose design and appearance has changed dramatically over the last ten years. However, what has not changed is the need for the safety of children playing around the equipment.

6.63 to **6.67** show the distances required for safety around conventional equipment. All equipment should have impact-

6.66 *Roundabout*

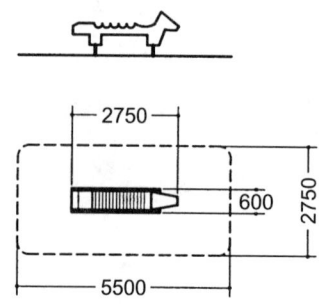

6.67 *Rocking horse. Only safe designs of this device may now be used*

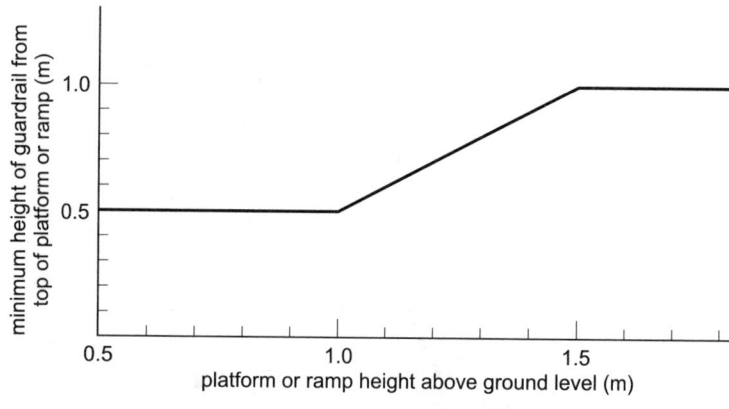

6.68 *Heights of guardrails for children's play equipment*

absorbing surfaces wherever a child can fall. To a small child, falling on its head a distance of no more than 150 mm can be fatal. There are a variety of impact-absorbing surfaces available, including loose materials, foam rubbers, etc., but each has disadvantages. Many are subject to damage by deliberate vandalism, some are prone to fouling.

Wherever possible, guardrails should be provided even where an impact-absorbing surface is used. **6.68** gives the recommended heights of such guardrails.

12 REFERENCES

Charles W. Harris and Nicholas T. Dines, *Time-saver Standards for Landscape Architecture*, McGraw-Hill, 1988

Michael Littlewood, *Landscape Detailing*, Butterworths, 1986

A. E. Weddle, *Landscape Techniques*, Van Nostrand Rheinhold, 1979

A. A. Pinder, *Beazley's Design and Detail of the Space between Buildings*, E. F. Spon, 1990

BTCV, *Dry and Stone Walling*, British Trust for Conservation Volunteers, 1986

TRADA, *Timber fencing*, 1978

Fencing by Goodman, M. L. Goodman & Son (Bristol) Ltd, 1980

7 Terminals and transport interchanges

Chris Blow

CI/SfB 114, 124, 144
UDC 725.3

Chris Blow is a partner in Scott, Brownrigg and Turner Ltd responsible for the design of many airport terminals

KEY POINTS:
- *This building type is subject to constant evolution and change*
- *Terminals are now more like shopping malls than Victorian railway stations*

Contents

1 INTRODUCTION

1.01
This chapter addresses the aspects of passenger requirements which are common to all terminals where passengers board aeroplanes, buses and coaches or railway trains or transfer between them. (Note that for practical purposes the consideration of baggage systems is limited to the airports section.)

1.02 Space standards
One person's congestion is another's profit: space standards are variable and subjective. The objective solution is to quote from the concept of Standard of Service. The application of this is common to all terminals and interchanges, and the differences arise, for example, from the amounts of baggage involved. Table I shows levels of service related to unit space standards in different types of space. For many passengers the criterion by which terminals such as airports are judged is the walking distance between one mode of transport and another. Although there is an inevitability about the length of a railway station platform or an airport pier, design can mitigate the strain of walking distance by providing passenger conveyors (see Chapter 5).

1.03 Security
In the case of air travel in particular but also in principle for long-distance rail and sea travel, the checking of passengers and their possessions requires the installation and manning of suitable equipment and the strategic location of the check point in order to both ensure that no passengers evade or avoid the checking procedure and that the procedure is carried out in the most efficient manner.

1.04 Border controls
Quite apart from security considerations, many terminals occur at national borders and therefore are the point of entry to or exit from sovereign areas. Accordingly, customs and immigration controls need to be conducted.

1.05 General legislation
Places of assembly of large numbers of people require special consideration of means of escape in case of fire as well as the normal controls on the standard of building construction.

1.06 Intermodal relationships
As the demand for efficient public transport systems returns after a phase when priority has been given to personal transport in the developed world, so the demand builds up for interchange between different modes. On the one hand, this can be for the reason of choice: allowing passengers to board Channel Tunnel trains in London or to drive on to them at Cheriton. Otherwise it can be for reasons of necessity: airports are located outside metropolitan areas and therefore need adjacent bus stations and railway stations, or even sea terminals in the case of Venice or Hong Kong.

1.07 Commercial opportunities
Wherever large numbers of people assemble and particularly wait, they need catering and business facilities. If they are by their very nature 'moneyed' there will be any number of shopping opportunities.

1.08 Terminal operator's requirements
The owner and/or the operator of the terminal will be out to make the maximum return on his or her investment and this will probably involve collecting revenue from the transport operator and the commercial concessionaire rather than the passengers or the public.

Table I Levels of service and space standards

Level of service		A	B	C	D	E	F
Criteria	Service level	Excellent	High	Good	Adequate	Unacceptable	Total breakdown
	Flow	Free	Stable	Stable	Unstable	Unstable	Congestion
	Delays	None		Acceptable	Some	Some	Unacceptable
	Subsystems	In balance	In balance	In balance		Not in balance	Total breakdown
	Routes	Direct					
	Comfort level	Excellent	High	Acceptable	Acceptable for short periods	Unacceptable	Unacceptable
Area with trolley per passenger (m²)	Check-in and baggage reclaim	1.6	1.4	1.2	1.0	0.8	–
	General waiting concourses	2.7	2.3	1.9	1.5	1.0	–
	Confined waiting	1.4	1.0	1.0	0.8	0.6	–

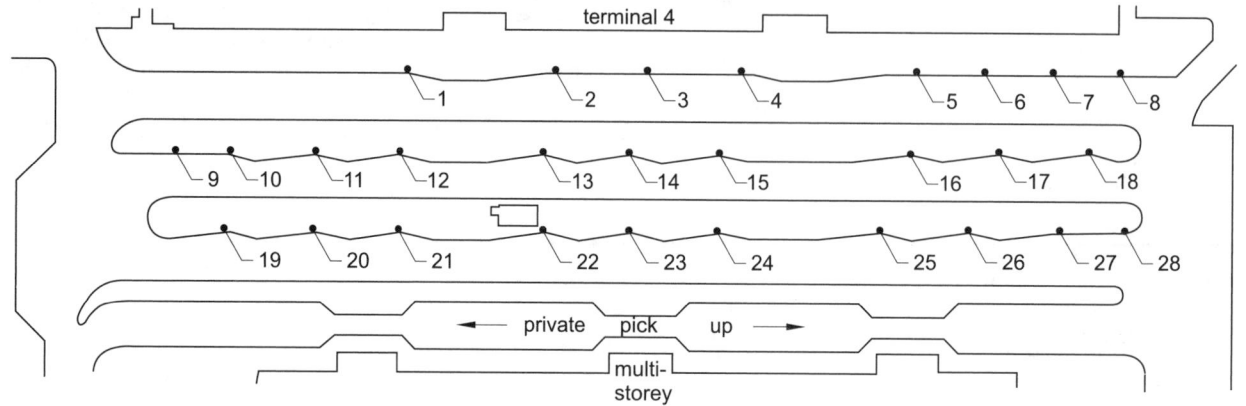

7.1 *Heathrow Terminal 4 cross section: Architects Scott Brownrigg & Turner, Guildford*

Key:

1 Multi-storey car park
2 Departures forecourt

3 Arrivals forecourt
4 Departures concourse
5 Arrivals concourse

6 Airside concourse
7 Arrivals corridor
8 London Underground station

7.2 *Heathrow Terminal 4 arrivals forecourt plan*

2–28 represent bus bays
Key:

1 Taxis
2 Railair/Rickards/Alder Valley
3 Long-term car park
4 Car rental concession
5 Transfer to Terminal 1
6 Transfer to T2 and T3
7 Alder Valley/Careline

8 Staff car park
9 Jetlink
10 National Express
11 City of Oxford
12 Speed link
13 Flightline
14 Flightline/Airbus
15 Airbus

16 Flightlink
17 National Express
18 Southend/Premier
19–24 Group travel
25 Green line
26 London Country
27 Local hotels
28 Off airport car parking/rental

1.09 Transport operator's requirements

On the other hand, the transport operator will want to get the passengers through the building as quickly as possible. Functional performance is paramount and related to speed, and the requirement for speed and efficiency is accentuated by the transfer facility. For example, the transfer time between connecting flights at airports is being increasingly reduced to provide a 'hub' and as different transport systems are integrated interchange times between, for example, train and plane need to be improved.

7.1 and **7.2** illustrate the interchange facilities at Heathrow Terminal 4 air/rail/bus.

2 AIRPORT PASSENGER TERMINALS

2.01

The airport terminal has been an established building type for only seventy years since London's airport was at Croydon, but many building forms have evolved. Each has been a response to the needs of the moment, but the speed of development of air travel has meant that buildings have rapidly become obsolete and needed either replacement or reconstruction.

2.02

A notable early example is the original terminal at Gatwick Airport, **7.3** which offered passengers in 1936 a direct and sheltered route from railway to terminal and from terminal to aeroplane. It was therefore an early true interchange facility.

2.03 Airport terminal planning

There are two major influences on airport and terminal size:

● Population demand, and
● Airline traffic scheduling.

Other factors and forms are listed and described in this section.

2.04

Worldwide each metropolis and major population centre has by now a giant airport in its vicinity. Most cities have airports appropriate to their needs. Either because the numbers of passengers, flights and choices of destination have increased to a certain level or because of its 'crossroads' location, a particular airport and its one or more terminals can take on a secondary growth pattern. Traffic attracts more traffic, since a wide range of airlines and destinations in turn attracts passengers from a larger area, possibly away from what would otherwise be their nearest airport, and also attracts airlines to feed connecting flights. Ultimately high volumes of traffic attract airlines to use their routes and facilities to the maximum by creating *hubs*, junctions for radiating routes with convenient transfer facilities for passengers. (See Section 2.15 for more about hub terminals.)

2.05 Airport terminal capacity and size

Passengers per year and passengers per hour are the key factors in terminal design. Large peak concentrations will produce a high hourly demand in relation to the annual traffic. A substantial constant traffic level will produce a high annual rate in relation to

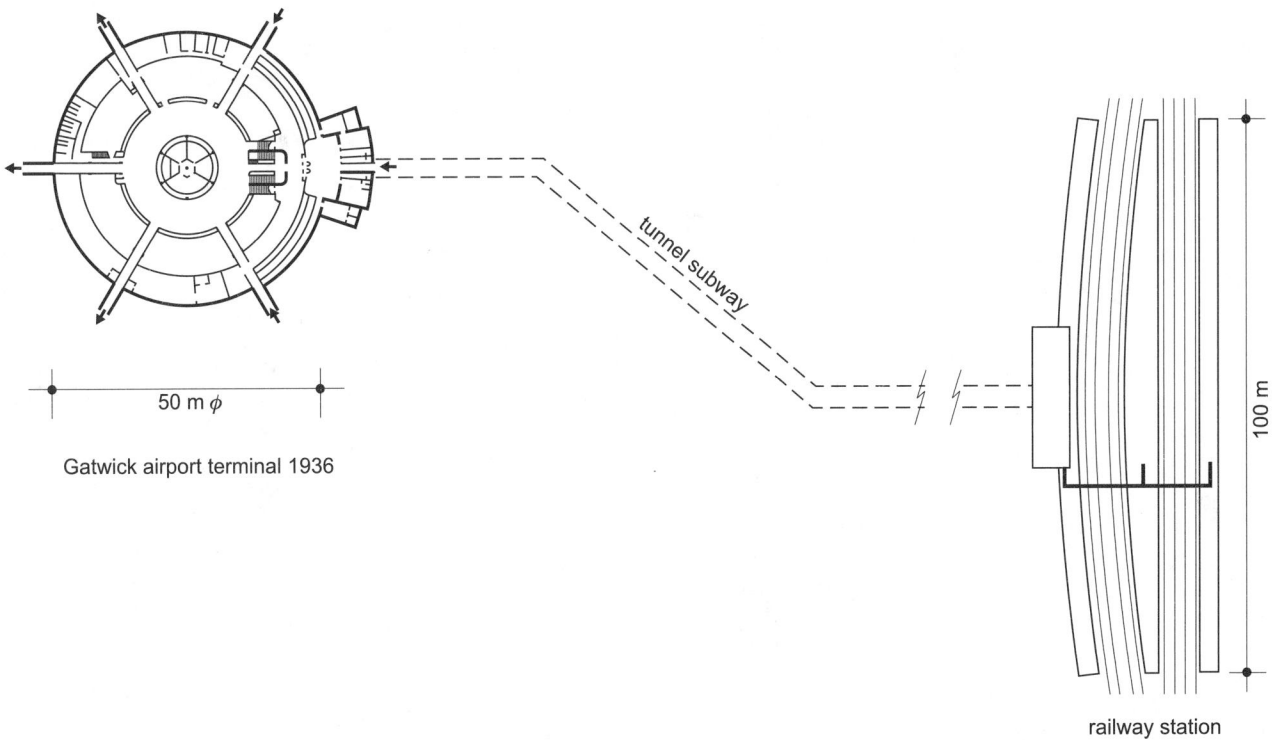

50 m φ

Gatwick airport terminal 1936

tunnel subway

100 m

railway station

7.3 *Gatwick Airport Terminal, 1936*

the hourly demand. Table II gives examples of predicted figures which determined the design of those terminals.

2.06
Sophisticated mathematical models can be used to represent the flow of passengers. Where appropriate, standards are applied to various future times; for example, five years on and a further prediction ten years ahead.

2.07
The term *standard busy rate* (*SBR*) is used in terminal design, and is the number of passengers predicted in the thirtieth busiest hour of scheduled use. This means that for 29 hours in the year the facilities will not match up to the requirement, but reasonable standards and economy are balanced.

2.08
Other factors to be considered are:

- *Aircraft movements*: number of arrivals and departures per hour, aircraft sizes, number of stands for each size or range of sizes, passenger load factors
- *Baggage quantities*: number of pieces per passenger, by class of travel and traffic (international/domestic)
- *Visitors*: number of accompanying visitors with departing and arriving passengers by class of traffic (international/domestic)

- *Employees*: number and proportion for airport, airline, concessionaire, control authorities, etc. and proportion of males and females
- *Landside transport*: number of passengers visitors and employees arriving by private vehicles (note ratio of owner-drivers), by public transport (note ratios by bus, coach, hire car, taxi, train, etc.)

2.09 Constraints on building form
In the 1930s multiple runways were common, but by the 1950s a pattern was emerging of single or twin runways. As traffic has grown so have the technical aids to support that growth. A single runway can now manage between 30 and 40 aircraft movements per hour, giving an airport capacity of about 25 million passengers per year.

A runway's capacity is affected by its independence from neighbouring runways, by the mix of aircraft and by the air traffic control system. Where a single runway is inadequate, a pair of parallel, and therefore independent, runways separated by at least 1600 metres is used. This allows the terminal buildings to be located between the runways, with minimal cross-runway aircraft movements.

Short runway airports or *STOLports* (short take-off and landing), limited to small aircraft, are appropriate for some locations.

Table II Annual and peak traffic at typical airport terminals

	Type	Passengers per year	Passengers per hour at peak
Manchester Terminal 2 Phase 1 Heathrow Terminal 4 Gatwick North Terminal (completed)	International terminals	6–9 million	1850–2500
Zurich Terminal B	Major city	6 million	3500
Hanover	Major city	4 million	2000

2.10

Clearances are laid down between taxiing aircraft and both parked aircraft and buildings: a series of imaginary surfaces are defined based on standards of instrumentation. These surfaces define the permissible height and position of buildings, and lines of sight from control towers and other key installations.

2.11 Ownership of terminal

- *Airport authority*: terminals are built and owned by the airport authority to ensure that the terminal is non-specific and therefore likely to be more able to cope with changing demands.
- *Airline*: terminals built by and for an airline tend to be designed to meet that airline's specific short- and medium-term requirements

2.12 Type of traffic

- *International*: international terminals involve customs and immigration procedures.
- *Domestic*: domestic terminals do not. They can therefore be simpler buildings. However, increasing need for passenger and baggage security has caused the grouping of facilities and channelling of passengers, and has reduced the distinction between the two types.
- *Combined international/domestic*, **7.4** is a flow diagram for such a terminal.

2.13 Level organisation

- *Side-by-side arrivals and departures on a single level*, **7.5a**. Suitable for the smaller-scale operations where first-floor movement of passengers from terminal to aircraft via telescopic loading bridges is not justified.
- *Side-by-side arrivals and departures on two levels*, **7.5b**. This avoids the need for elevated roads because all kerbside activity takes place at ground level. Escalators and lifts are provided to take departing passengers up to the boarding level.
- *Vertical stacking of arrivals and departures*, **7.5c**. Most larger terminals now adopt this configuration. Departures facilities are invariably at the high level with the baggage handling and arrivals facilities below. It is economic and convenient for both passenger and baggage movement: departing passengers arrive at an elevated forecourt and move either on the level or down a ramp to the aircraft loading point. Arriving passengers also move downwards to baggage reclaim and landside facilities.
- *Vertical segregation*. High passenger volumes, particularly with wide-bodied aircraft on long-haul routes, are best served by unidirectional circulation. Segregation could be either vertical or horizontal, but in practice the it has been found most feasible to have departing routes at high level with downwards circulation to the aircraft, and arriving passenger routes below.

2.14 Centralised or decentralised?

Most terminals are centralised, **7.6** to **7.9** with groups of functions, commercial, passenger and baggage processing, airline operations, etc. Centralisation gives economy of management if not passenger convenience. However, where control authorities are not needed as in domestic terminals, or where the prime concern is for passenger convenience, decentralisation has proved beneficial.

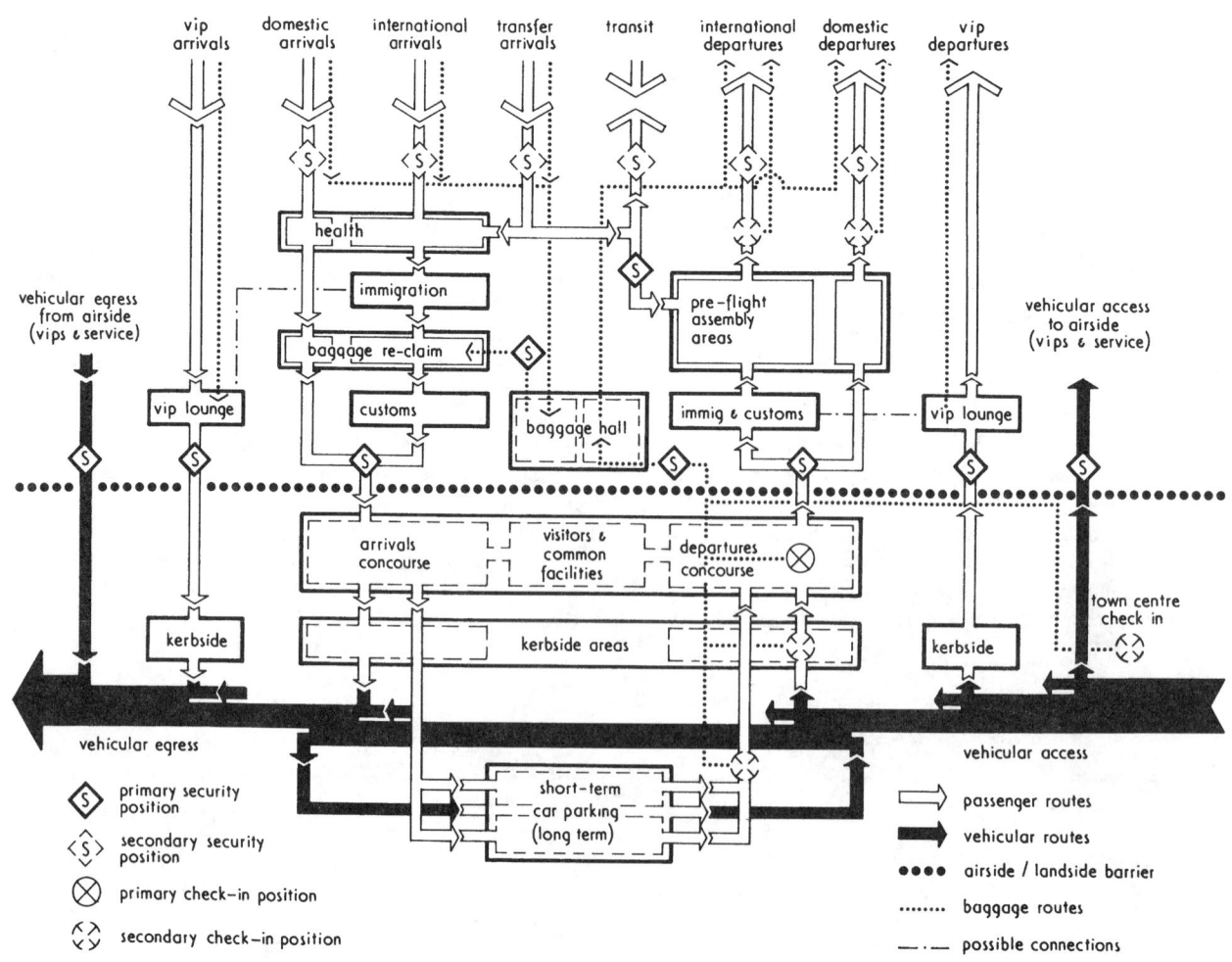

7.4 *Diagram showing both passenger and vehicular flow patterns for a international plus domestic airport terminal*

7.5 *Forms of typical terminals shown by cross-sections:*

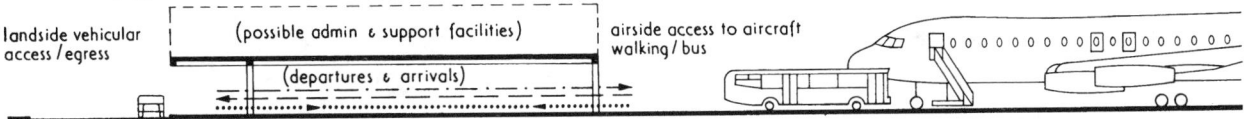

a *Single-level terminal, generally applicable to small or domestic terminals*
Arrival and departure routes split horizontally as flow plan diagram **7.4**

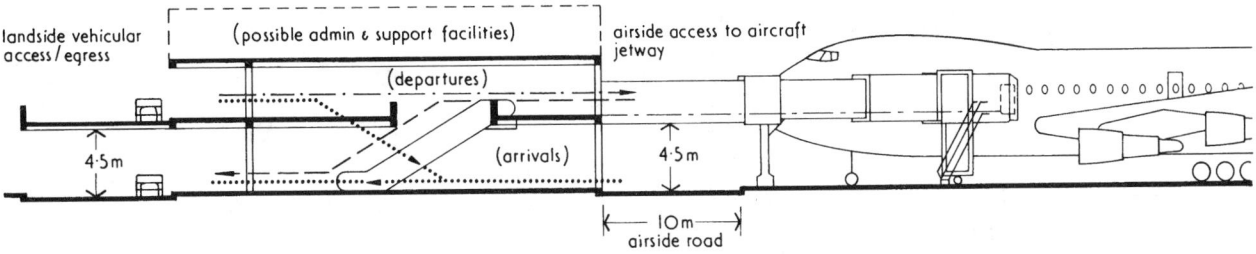

b *Two-level terminal – loading bridge type (horizontal split)*

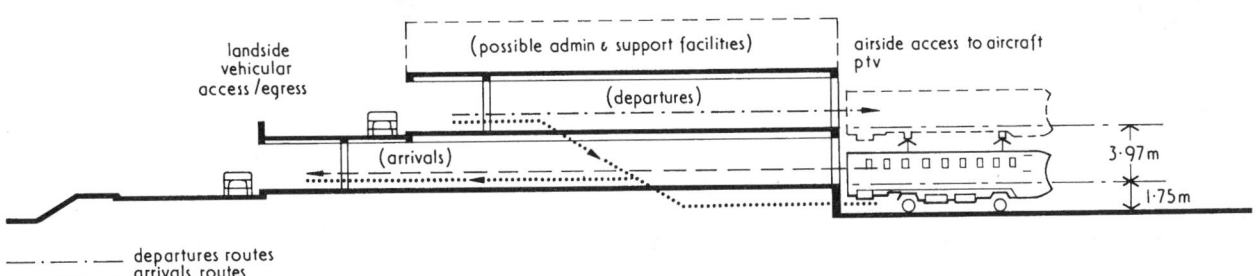

_ . _ . _ . _   departures routes
_ _ _ _ _   arrivals routes
....   baggage routes

c *Two-level terminal – loading bridge type (vertical segregation)*

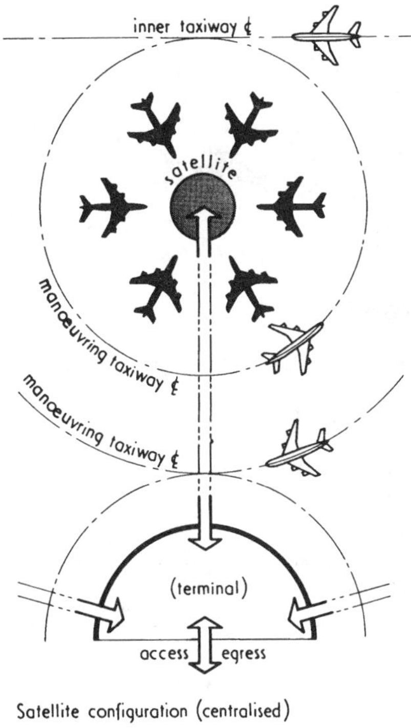

Satellite configuration (centralised)

Transporter configuration (centralised)

Pier configuration (centralised)

Linear configuration (de-centralised)

7.6 *Satellite configuration: Charles de Gaulle, Paris, France*

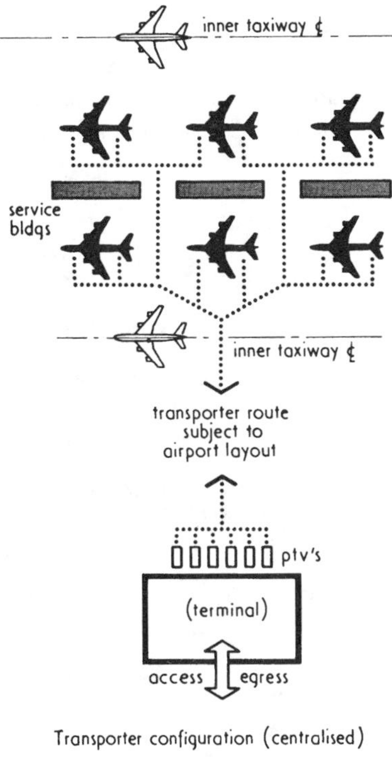

7.7 *Transporter configuration: Dulles, Washington, USA*

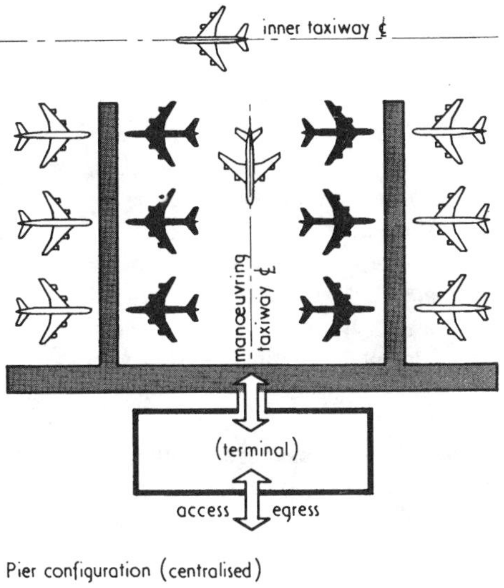

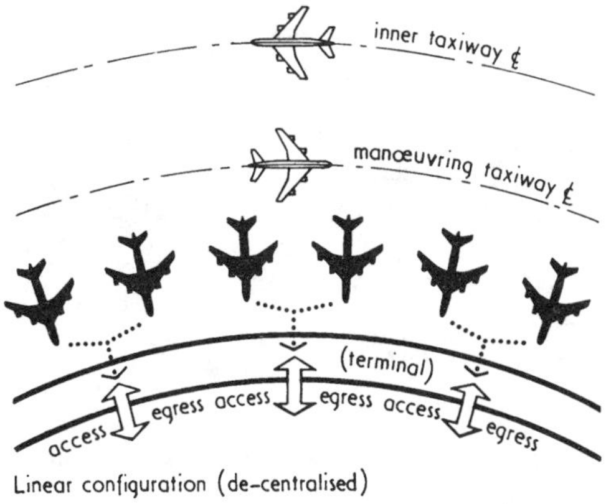

7.8 *Pier configuration: Heathrow, London, UK*

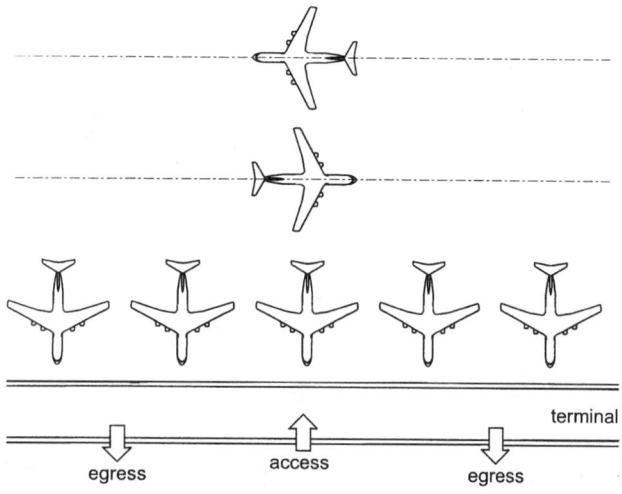

7.9 *Linear: New Munich Airport, Germany, opened 1992*

7.10 *Hub terminal forms from US examples*
a *Common landside with piers: Baltimore Washington International Airport*

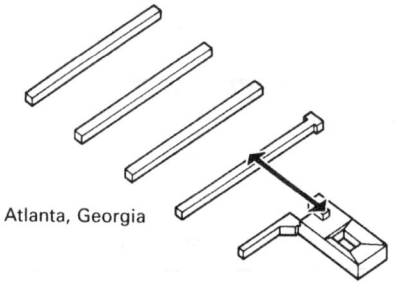

b *Common landside with satellite: Atanta Airport, Georgia*

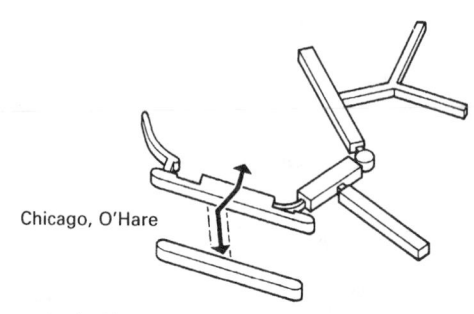

c *Unit terminal: O'Hare Airport, Chicago*

2.15 Hub terminals

A *hub terminal* is defined as one supporting a number of scheduled flights converging on an airport all within a short space of time in order to catch another series of onward flights also within a short space of time.

The flights are the spokes and the terminal is the hub. Short interchange periods can take place several times in one day.

The distinction needs to be drawn between transfer passengers who change planes and transit passengers who stop at the airport but do not change planes.

Most hub terminal experience worldwide is based on domestic traffic where the movement of passengers is not governed by frontiers with immigration and fiscal control. When and where airlines operate a mixture of international and domestic routes in a hub situation, passengers change from being international to domestic and vice versa.

As well as the full normal range of facilities for originating passengers, hub terminals need facilities for disembarkation and reboarding of aircraft for the transfer passengers. Normally when no flights have been delayed, transfer passengers move rapidly between flights. Most will have no hold baggage, being business travellers using frequent services on heavily trafficked routes between business centres. The rest with hold baggage may need to reclaim it for customs control. Especially for them, walking distances and queueing times must be kept short.

2.16 Hub terminal baggage handling

Successful terminals are said to depend on their baggage systems; hub terminals are no exception. Speed is even more vital in them; the transfer passenger is there only because the airline is unable to carry him or her directly from A to B. Transferring baggage from one aircraft to many others in a short time is very different from conventional manual or automatic sorting and make-up following check-in.

2.18 Hub terminal types

Rarely will the whole operation be hub-based, so the systems for interchange and for other passengers have to related. There are two fundamentally different principles:

- The hub terminal is part of a larger terminal, sharing kerbside, check-in, etc. with other airlines, or
- It is a unit terminal exclusive to the hub airline.

7.10 illustrates three forms as US examples applicable to Britain. 7.10c was the solution adopted for Birmingham.

2.19 Aircraft docking, terminal or remote

The number of aircraft parking places needed normally requires extended structures such as piers or satellites to provide sufficient frontage. Stands not thus connected physically to the terminal use coaches to carry passengers to and from it. Often these are superior types special to airport operation or mobile lounges which raise and lower to serve terminal and aircraft doors.

3 LANDSIDE FUNCTIONS

3.01 Arriving at or leaving the terminal by car or public transport

These are the factors to consider:

- *Security*: avoid vantage points useful to terrorists.
- *Commercial*: the whole forecourt or at least the private car section may be incorporated into the short-term or nearest car park. This will force motorists to pay for the privilege of parking close to the check-in area.
- *Baggage*: baggage trolleys should be available for passenger use. For heavy package tours traffic, with coaches setting down large pre-sorted amounts of baggage, a dedicated area and route to the baggage areas may be desirable.
- *Airline needs*: in large terminals shared by many airlines, signed sections of forecourt may be appropriate.
- *Predicted changes*: allow for predictable changes in traffic mix which may affect the modal split (the percentages of passengers arriving by car or bus).

3.02 Quantities to be assessed

- *Hourly passenger flows*: in the case of a combined departures and arrivals forecourt a planned two-way rate will be relevant.

- *Estimated dwell time*: an average of 1.5 minutes may be allowed for cars and taxis.
- *Modal split*: subject to local conditions, 50 per cent of passengers may use private cars and taxis. Many buses and coaches will call at the departures forecourt, but do not need dedicated set-down positions. To provide the shortest route for the greatest number of passengers, coach and bus bays should be nearest to the doors. However, in a single-level forecourt, designated pick-up and set-down bays for specific buses and coaches may be appropriate.

3.03

Typical space calculation based on 2000 originating passengers/hour:

- Number of passengers/hour at kerbside for cars + taxis: 1000
- Number of passengers per car or taxi: 1.7, say
- Number of cars and taxis: 1000/1.7 = 588 per hour
- Time spent at kerb by each vehicle: 1½ minutes, say
- Number of cars and taxis at one time: 588/40 = 16
- Length of kerb per vehicle: 6 m + 10 per cent
- Length of kerbside for cars and taxis: 105.6 m
- Overall rule of thumb: 1.0 m of total kerbside (including public transport) per 10 passengers/hour

3.04 Waiting in a landside public concourse
Policy decisions to be applied:

- Security: entry to the concourse can be controlled by a security comb, but this is unusual as it does involve searching passengers and visitors alike.
- *Commercial*: shopping and catering facilities will be appropriate here, together with bureau de change (international terminal only), flight insurance sales office (departures), hotel bookings, car hire desks (arrivals) and post office. Provision for spectators may be made as well as a car park pay station for the benefit of car drivers seeing passengers off and meeting passengers.
- *Baggage*: all circulation areas should make allowance for baggage trolleys.
- *Government controls*: access to airside for staff.
- *Airline needs*: airlines require ticket sales desks and offices.
- *Information systems*: public display of information on flights and information desk.
- *Predictable situations*: provision may be needed for exceptional conditions occasioned by delayed flights, with additional seating and extra catering space, which may also be usable as airside.

3.05 Quantity factors to be assessed

- Hourly passenger flows: two-way flow will be relevant where there is to be a combined departures and arrivals area.
- Visitor ratio: a common ratio in the West would be 0.5 to 0.2 visitors per passenger (with even lower ratios for certain domestic traffic) and in the East or Africa 2.5 to 6 or even higher.
- Estimated dwell time: a common time would be 20 minutes in departures or, in arrivals, 10 minutes for passengers and 30 minutes for meeters and greeters.

3.06 Typical space calculation based on 2000 originating passengers/hour

- Number of people per hour: 5000 (1.5 visitors/passenger)
- Number at one time (peaking factor, say 50 per cent in 20 minutes): 2500
- Space per person (level of service A): 2.7 m^2
- Area required: 6750 m^2. Some area may be in shops and catering spaces.

- Typical space calculation based on 2000 terminating passengers/hour:
- Number of people per hour: 5000 (1.5 visitors/passenger)
- Number at one time (2000/6 + 3000/2): 1833
- Space per person (level of service A): 2.7 m^2
- Area required: 4949 m^2. Some area may be in shops and catering spaces.

3.07 Checking-in, with or without baggage
Here passengers show their tickets, have seats allocated and if necessary have large items of baggage weighed (and possibly security screened) for registration and loading into the aircraft hold.

Policy decisions to be applied:

- *Security*: procedures are now being introduced whereby all baggage is searched by the airline's security staff at entry to their check-in area, or by the check-in and security staff at the desk by means of X-ray units at or near the desk. The constraint is that the owner of the bag must be at hand at the moment of search in the event of a problem arising.
- *Baggage*: one or more delivery points may be required for out-of-gauge baggage.
- *Government controls*: a customs check facility for certain heavy items of baggage may be provided in the check-in area.
- *Airline needs*: offices for airlines and handling agents will be needed with close relationship with the check-in desks and preferably with a visual link.
- *Information systems*: common user terminal equipment will make it possible to allocate desks to any airline at any time, thereby reducing the number of desks needed. Otherwise the number of desks required is the sum total of those required by each handling agent.
- *Predicted changes*: the biggest single change will arise from the predicted advent of automated ticketing and issuing of boarding passes. Information technology which links the manual (conventional check-in system with baggage registration) and automated system (where the passenger simply communicates with a small machine) will make it possible to reduce the number of check-in desks while retaining the necessary central control which check-in clerks have always had.

3.08 Quantities to be assessed

- *Hourly passenger flows*: if CUTE is in use the total hourly flow to all desks can be used to compute the number. Landside transfer passengers to be included.
- *Processing rate*: commonly about 1.5 minutes/passenger, with faster rates for domestic passengers.
- *Estimated dwell time*: this is dependent upon the number of staffed check-in desks for each flight, but all check-in layouts have to make provision for queueing. Assume a wait of 20 minutes is acceptable to passengers.
- *Percentage of passengers using gate check-in*: this is a new facility and trends have yet to be established. Ten per cent usage of gate-check-in would be a reasonable assumption where the facility is provided, although it may only be available there for certain flights.

3.09 Typical space calculation based on 2000 originating passengers/hour: central check-in:
This will be irrespective of the configuration of desks, **7.11**.

- *Number of passengers per hour*: 2000 excluding transfers and including gate check-in numbers
- *Equivalent number/hour* (peak factor, say 50 per cent in 20 minutes): 3000
- *Number of desks*: 3000/40 = 76
- *Queue depth* might be 20 passengers at 0.8 m per person with check-in desks at approximately 2.0 m centres (max.)

7.11 *Check-in installations without security control:*

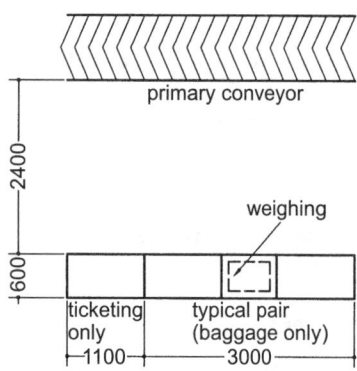

a *Linear, with manual handling*

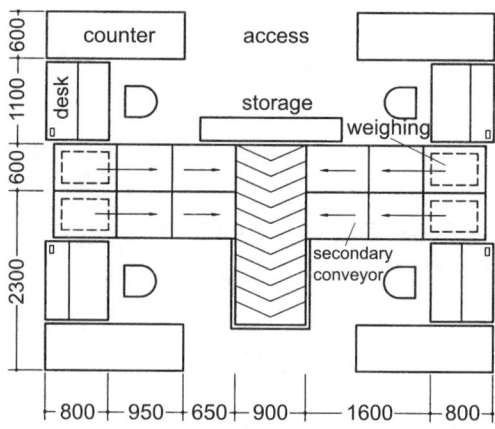

c *Island*

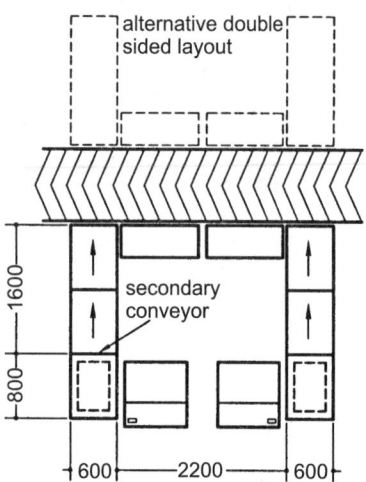

b *Linear, with power handling*

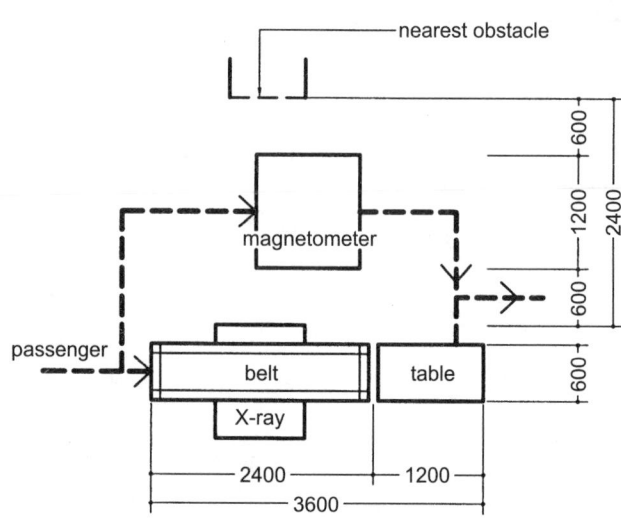

d *X-ray unit search of passengers and baggage*

- *Space per person* (level of service A): $1.6\,m^2$
- *Total queueing area*: $76 \times 2.0 \times 16 = 2432\,m^2$. Note that a discrete area is only applicable if there is a security-based separation between the landside public concourse and the check-in area.

3.10 Pre-departure security check

Factors to be considered:

- *Baggage*: in the case of central security, take account of baggage belonging to passengers using the gate check-in facility.
- *Government controls*: security control will be the responsibility either of the government or of the airport authority.
- *Airline needs*: some airlines conduct their own additional security checks.
- *Predictable changes*: as the demand for security increases changes can be expected.

3.11 Quantities to be assessed

- *Hourly passenger flows*: for central security and for gate security allow for transfer passengers.
- *Processing rate*: X-ray units handle 600 items per hour, with two X-ray units per metal detector archway.
- *Estimated dwell time*: this is not calculable, since a problem item or passenger can rapidly cause a queue to build up. The

security check should not unduly interrupt the flow of passengers. In reality staffing levels cannot totally eliminate queueing, and space for a long queue must be provided to avoid obstructing other functions.

3.12 Typical space calculation

This is based on 2000 originating passengers/hour at a central security check, **7.12**.

Assume two items of baggage or hand baggage per passenger

One set of equipment consisting of a personnel metal detector and two 2 X-ray units can handle 600 passengers per hour.

2000 passengers per hour, excluding transfers, require 4 sets.

4 AIRSIDE FUNCTIONS

4.01 Immigration check

Factors to be considered:

- *Security*: a central security control brings this area under surveillance.
- *Government controls*: national policy determines the allocation of separate channels for different passport holders. There may also be customs checks here for which offices and detention rooms will be required.
- *Predictable changes*: changes to border controls within the European Union are an example of the effect of international policy making.

7.12 *Immigration control desks, booths or open plan*

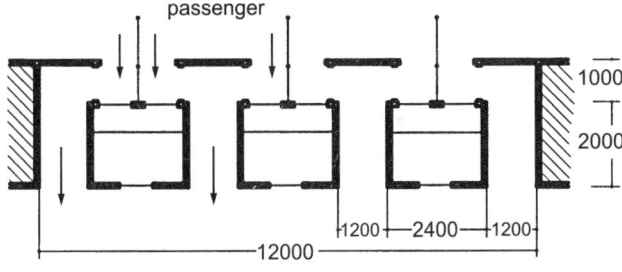

a *Frontal presentation*

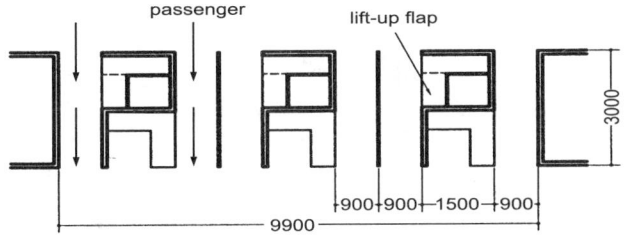

b *Side presentation*

4.02 Quantities to be assessed

- *Hourly passenger flows*: include landside transfers.
- *Processing rate*: commonly 10 seconds/passenger for departures, 30 seconds/international passenger and 6 seconds/domestic passenger for arrivals.

4.03 Typical space calculation based on 2000 originating passengers/hour

- *Number of passengers per hour*: 2000 excluding transfers
- *Number of desks required*: 5.5, say 6
- *Area required* at 25 m² per desk: 150 m², **7.12**.

4.04 Airside public concourse

Here passengers wait, shop, eat, drink and move sooner or later to their flight departure gate. That point may be the people-mover leading to a satellite or the coach station serving remote stands.

Factors to be considered:

- *Security:* no further security checks will be needed where there is comprehensive centralised security at entry to the airside. Otherwise checks may be made at each gate or entry to a lounge.
- *Commercial*: there will be shopping and catering facilities here, particularly duty-free.
- *Airline needs*: airlines will have specific requirements at the gates. They often have CIP (commercially important passengers) lounges for first-class and business-class passengers.
- *Information systems*: full information on flight numbers, departure times, delays and gate numbers must be provided, throughout but especially at the entries.

4.05 Quantities to be assessed

- *Hourly passenger flows*: include landside and airside transfers.
- *Estimated dwell time:* commonly about 30 minutes.

4.06 Typical space calculation based on 2000 originating passengers/hour

- *Passengers per hour*: 2000 excluding transfers.
- *Passengers at one time*: 1000
- *Space per person* (level of service A): 2.7 m²

- *Area required:* 2700 m². Some may be in shops and catering spaces.

4.07 Gate holding areas

These should be able to hold 80 per cent of the number of passengers boarding the largest aircraft which can dock here.

- *Space per person* (level of service A): 1.4 m².
- *Area for 400–seater aircraft*: 320 × 1.4 = 448 m².

4.08 Baggage reclaim

Here passengers await and reclaim their luggage which has been unloaded from the aircraft while they have been through the terminal and passing through the immigration control.

Factors to consider:

- *Baggage*: some means of delivering outsized luggage to the passengers is required. Also some passengers need to claim their baggage after they have passed through to the landside, either because they have forgotten it or because for some reason it has arrived on a different flight.
- *Information systems*: display the numbers of reclaim units against the arriving flight numbers, particularly where passengers enter the reclaim area.

4.09 Quantities to be assessed

- *Hourly passenger flows*: passengers transferring on the landside need to reclaim their baggage.
- *Processing rate*: there are several ways of calculating throughput in baggage reclaim, but the one used here is from the *IATA Airport Terminals Reference Manual*. Reclaim devices should have a length of 30–40 m for narrow-bodied aircraft, 50–65 m for wide-bodied. Average occupancy times are 20 and 45 minutes respectively.
- *Estimated dwell time*: Commonly about 30 minutes.
- *Number of checked-in bags per passenger:* average 1.0, depending on whether the flight is long haul or short haul, although the flow calculation method used does not depend upon this factor.

4.10 Typical space calculation based on 2000 terminating passengers/hour

- *Number of passengers per hour*: 2000 excluding transfers
- *Number of passengers at one time*: 1000
- *Space per person* (level of service A): 1.6 m²
- *Area required*: 1600 m² (a minimum inclusive of waiting area).

However, the important calculation is for the required number of reclaim units and the space round each for a flight load of passengers waiting:

Assume 50 per cent of passengers arrive by wide-bodied and 50 per cent by narrow-bodied aircraft.

- *Number of passengers* per narrow-bodied aircraft at 80 per cent load factor: 100
- *Number of passengers* per wide-bodied aircraft at 80 per cent load factor: 320
- *Number of narrow-bodied devices*: 1000 ÷ (3 × 100) = 3.3, say 4
- *Number of wide-bodied devices*: 1000 ÷ (1.33 × 320) = 2.35, say 3
- *Space per person* (level of service A): 1.6 m²
- *Waiting area* for narrow-bodied device: 160 m²
- *Waiting area* for wide-bodied device: 512 m²
- *Total waiting area*: 4 × 160 + 3 × 512 = 2176 m² (excluding central waiting space at entry to baggage reclaim area)

7.13 shows types of baggage reclaim installation.

7.13 *Four types of baggage reclaim installation*

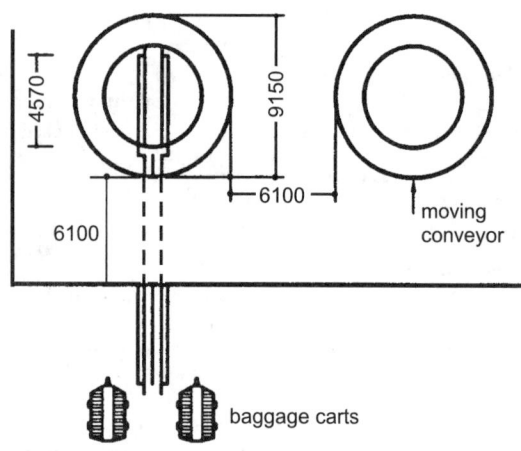

circular carousel

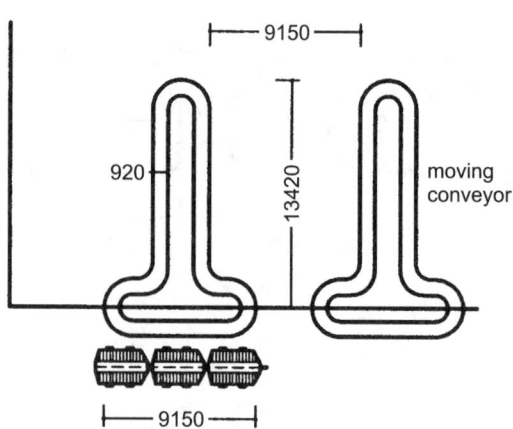

racetrack

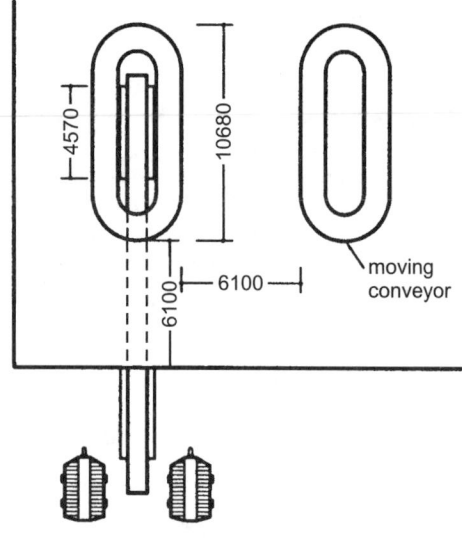

oval carousel

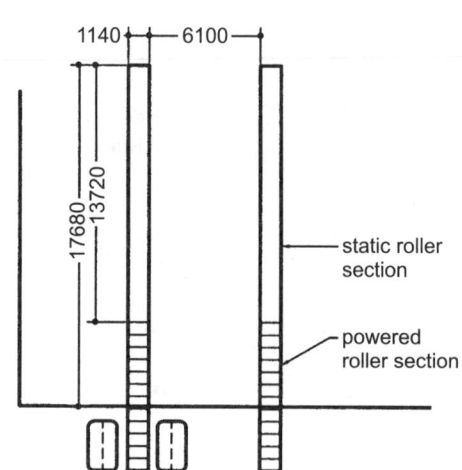

linear track

4.11 Inbound customs clearance

Factors for consideration:

- *Security*: customs officers are increasingly on the lookout for narcotics rather than contraband.
- *Government controls*: offices and search rooms will be required. Determine type of surveillance.
- *Predictable changes*: changes to border controls within the European Union post-1992, and the introduction of the blue channel for EU citizens moving freely between member states are an example of the effect of international policy making.

4.12 Quantities to be assessed

- *Hourly passenger flows*: include landside transfers.
- *Processing rate*: allow 2 minutes per passenger searched.

4.13 Space calculation based on 2000 terminating passengers/hour

- *Area required* if rule of thumb is 0.5 m² per passenger per hour: 1000 m².

5 AIRCRAFT AND APRON REQUIREMENTS

5.01 Baggage handling

7.14 shows a container and trailer used to assemble baggage. The manoeuvring of trains of these trailers determines the layout of baggage loading and unloading areas.

5.02 Loading bridges

7.15 shows three types of loading bridges, otherwise known as air-bridges, air-jetties or jetways, which connect terminal to aircraft.

5.03 Apron servicing

7.16 shows apron servicing arrangements with all necessary vehicles clustered around a parked aircraft. They determine the space requirement. Alternatively, fuel can be supplied by sub-apron hydrants and power by connection through the loading bridge.

5.04

Office, workshop, store and staff facilities will be required adjacent to the apron.

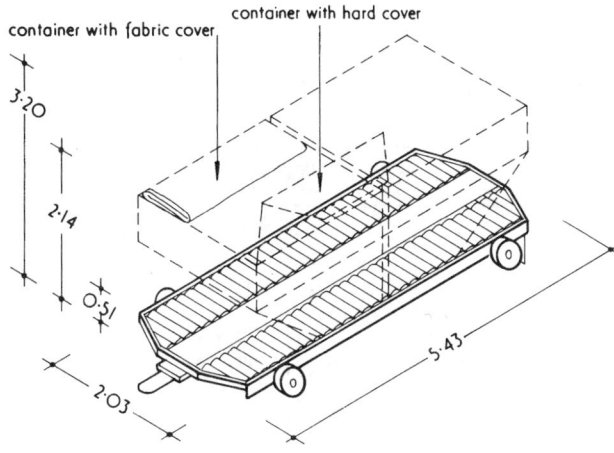

7.14 *Baggage handling transport: double container dolly*

6 BUS AND COACH STATIONS

6.01

A bus station is an area away from the general flow of road vehicles, which enables buses and coaches, to set down and pick up passengers in safety and comfort. The best locations are near shopping centres or other transport terminals. An airport terminal bus station is shown in **7.2**.

Two particular trends have affected urban bus and coach operations:

- One-driver buses for economy, and
- Deregulation with new companies with new operating methods and equipment such as minibuses.

6.02 Vehicles

A variety of bus and coach types are now used, **7.17** to **7.19**. Turning dimensions are shown in **7.20** to **7.22**. A kerbside bus stop in a layby is shown in **7.23**.

7.15 *Loading bridge types: plans and elevations*

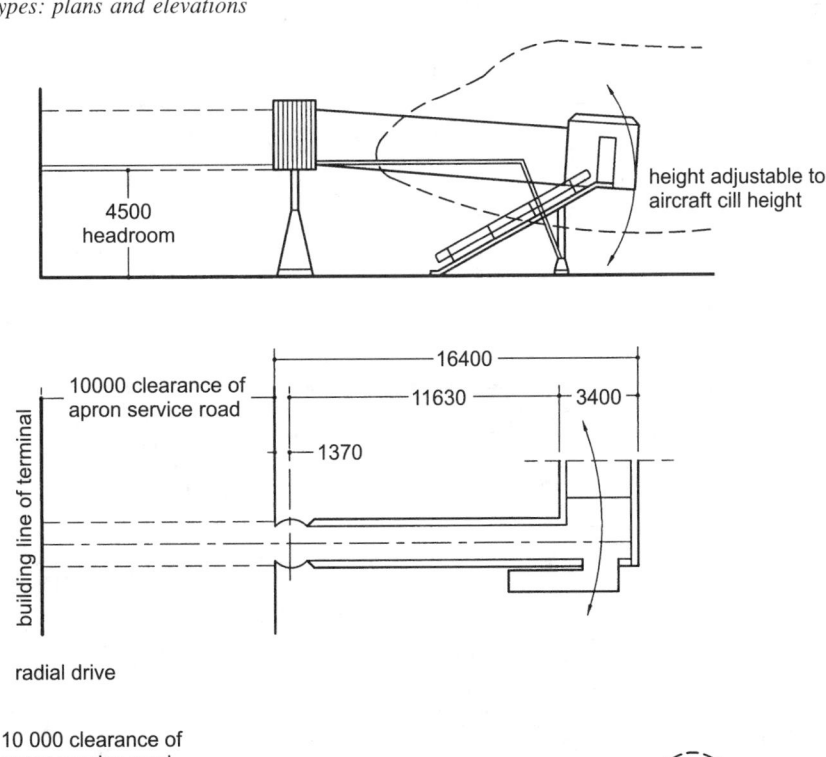

radial drive

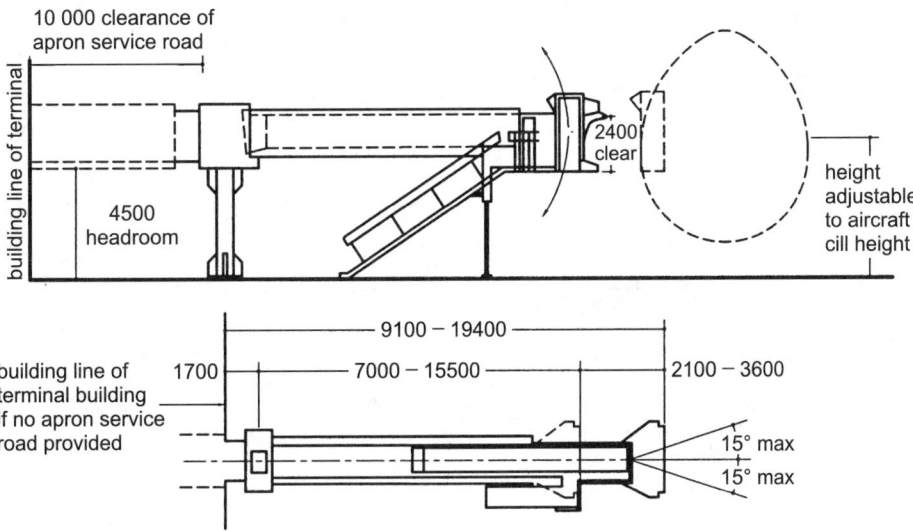

pedestal

7.15 *Continued. Loading bridge types: plans and elevations*

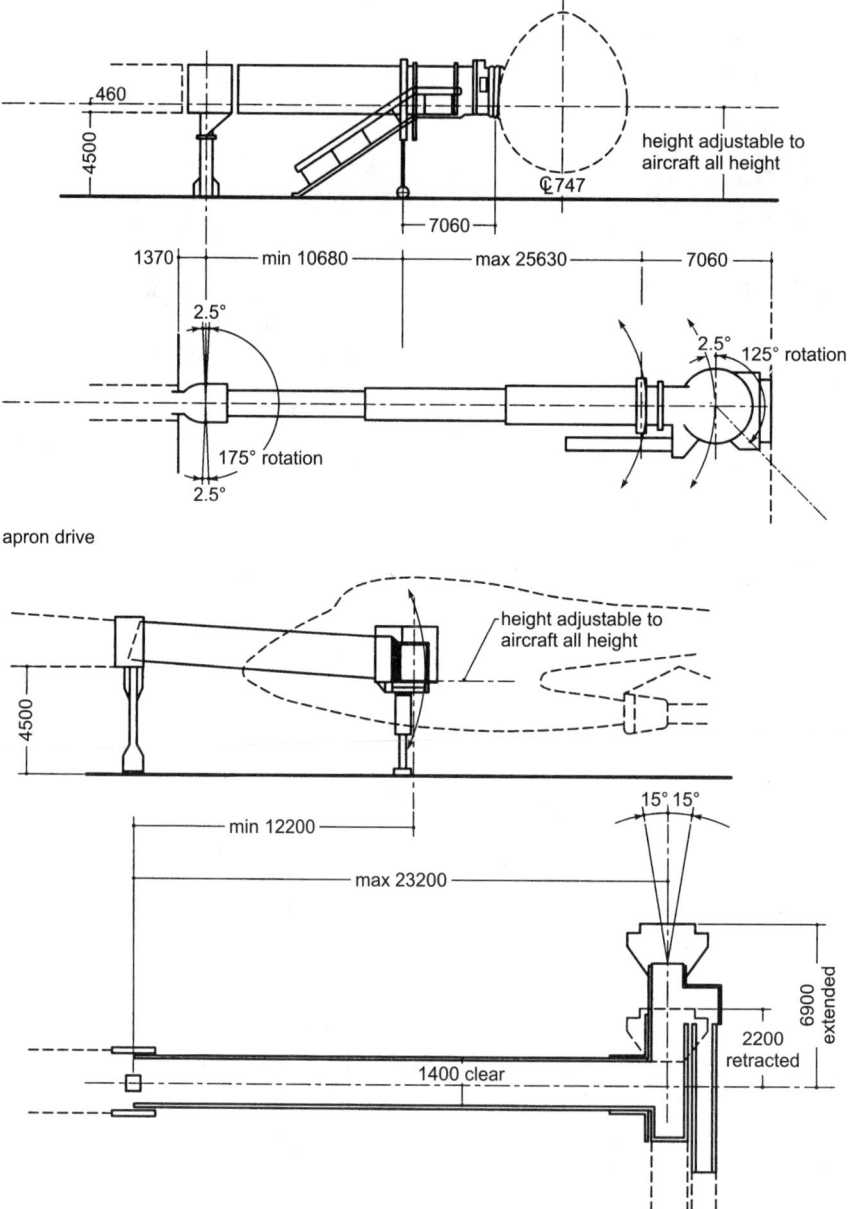

apron drive

elevating

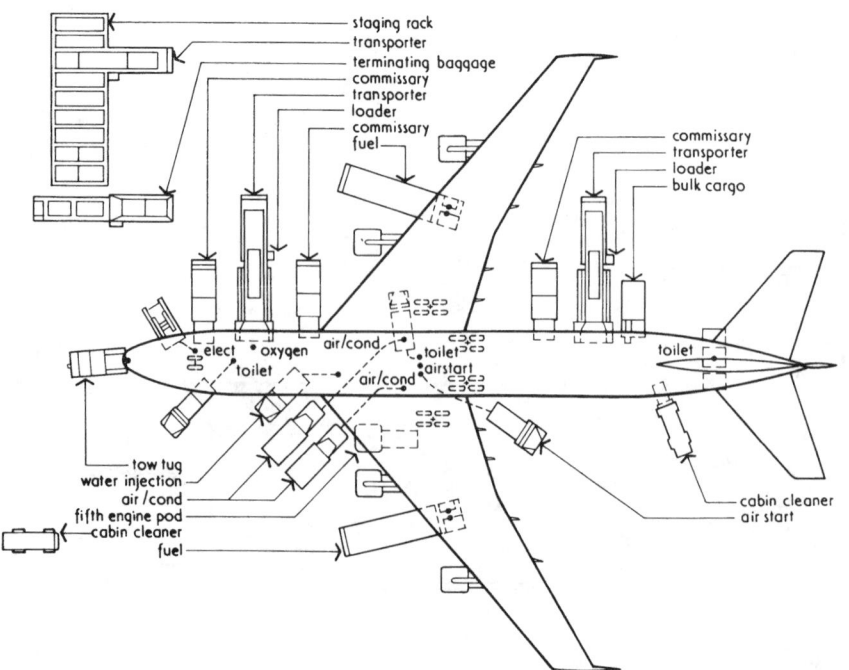

7.16 *Servicing arrangements for passenger model Boeing 747–100/200B + C. Under normal conditions external electric power, airstart and air conditioning are not required when the auxiliary power unit is used*

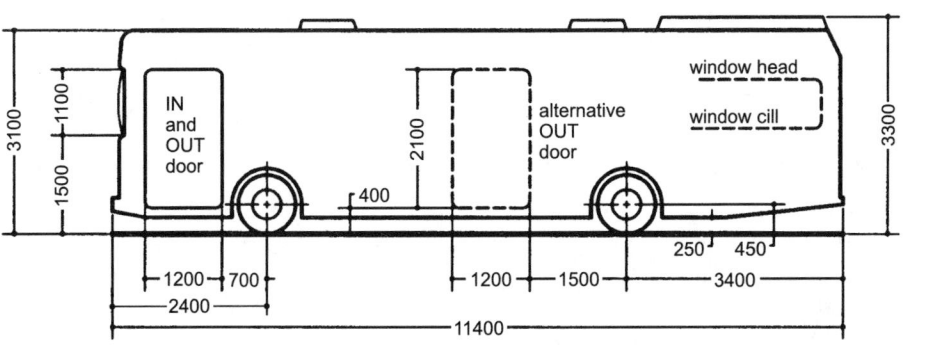
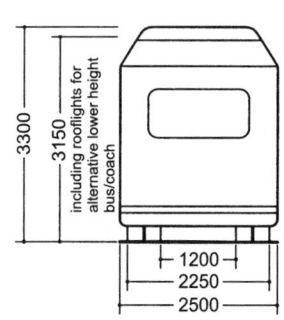

7.17 *Single-decker bus*

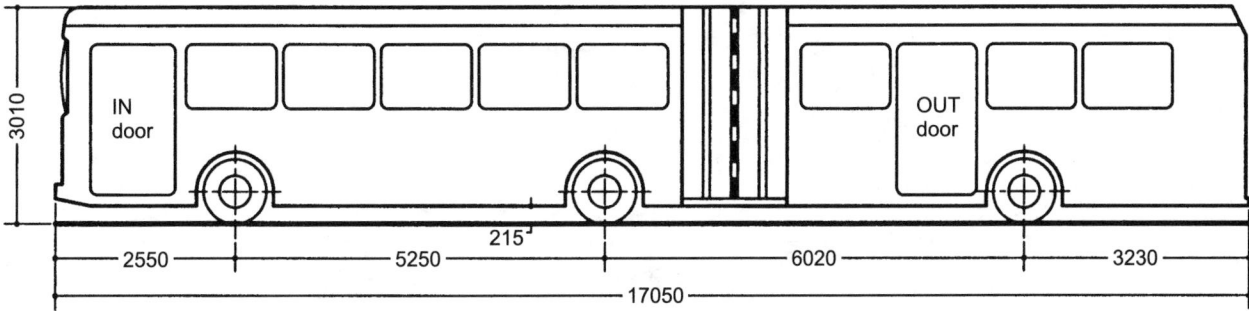

7.18 *Articulated bus*

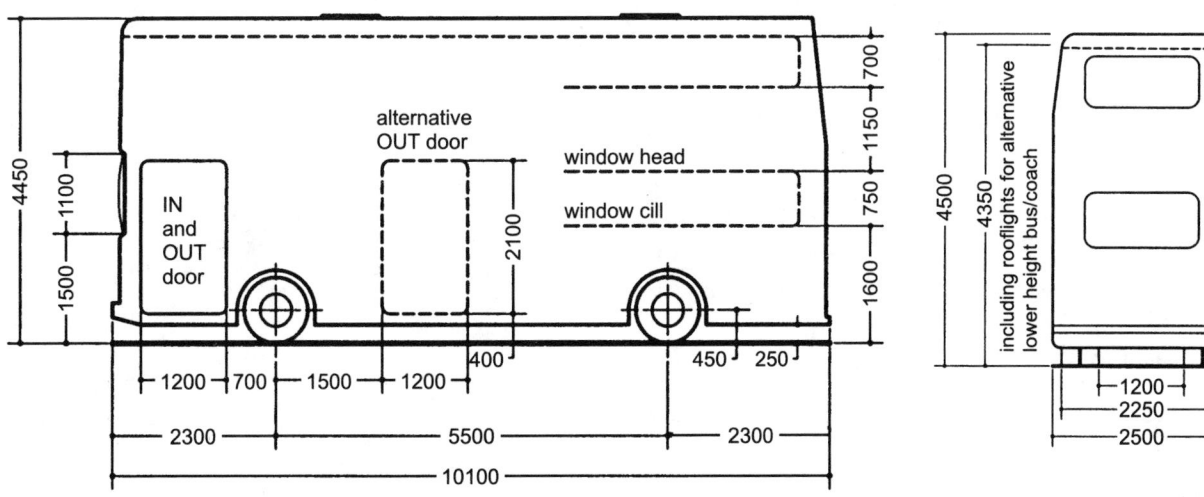

7.19 *Double-decker bus*

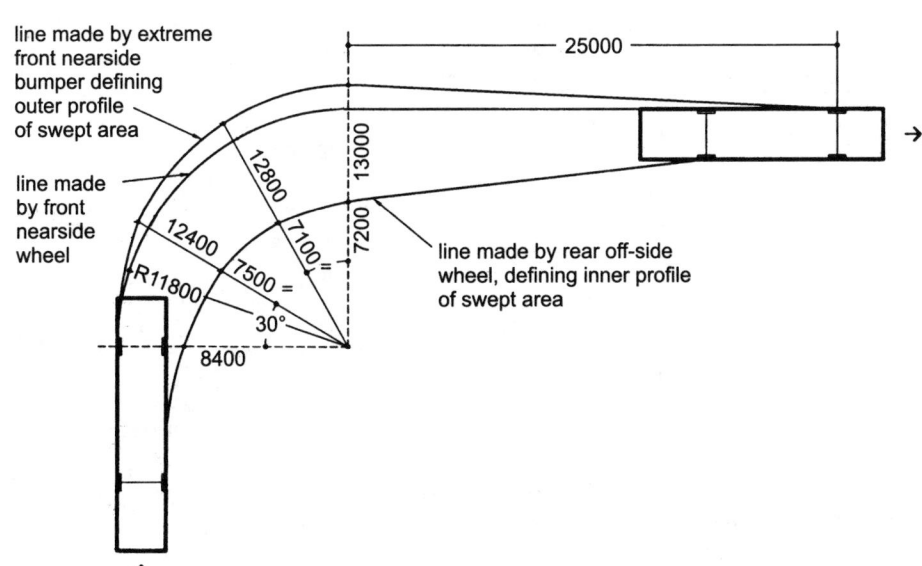

7.20 *Rigid 12 m vehicle turning through 90°*

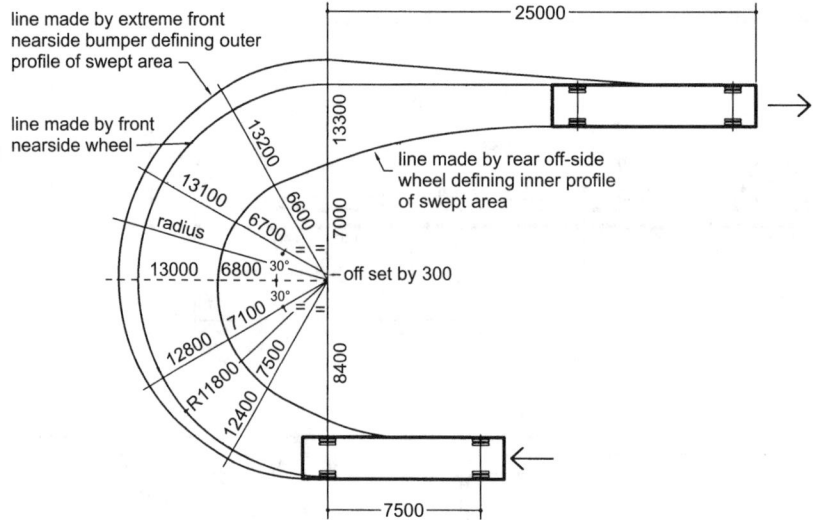

7.21 *Rigid 12 m vehicle turning through 180°*

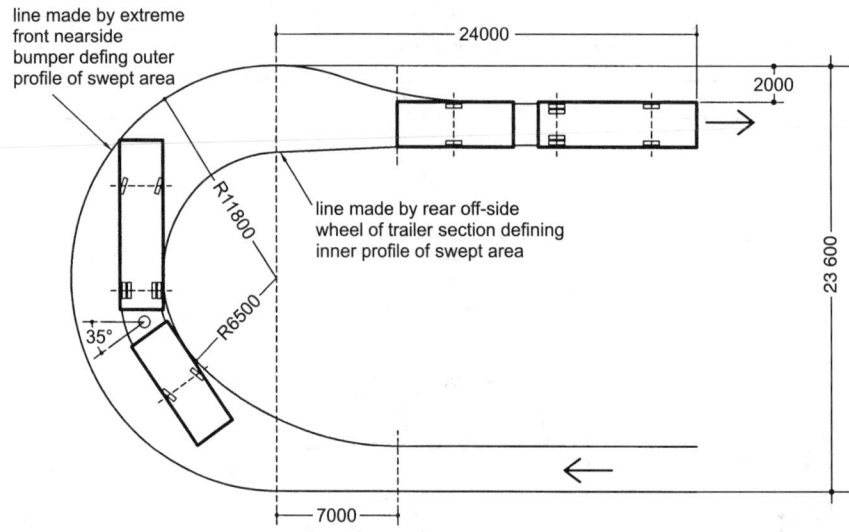

7.22 *17 m articulated vehicle turning through 180°*

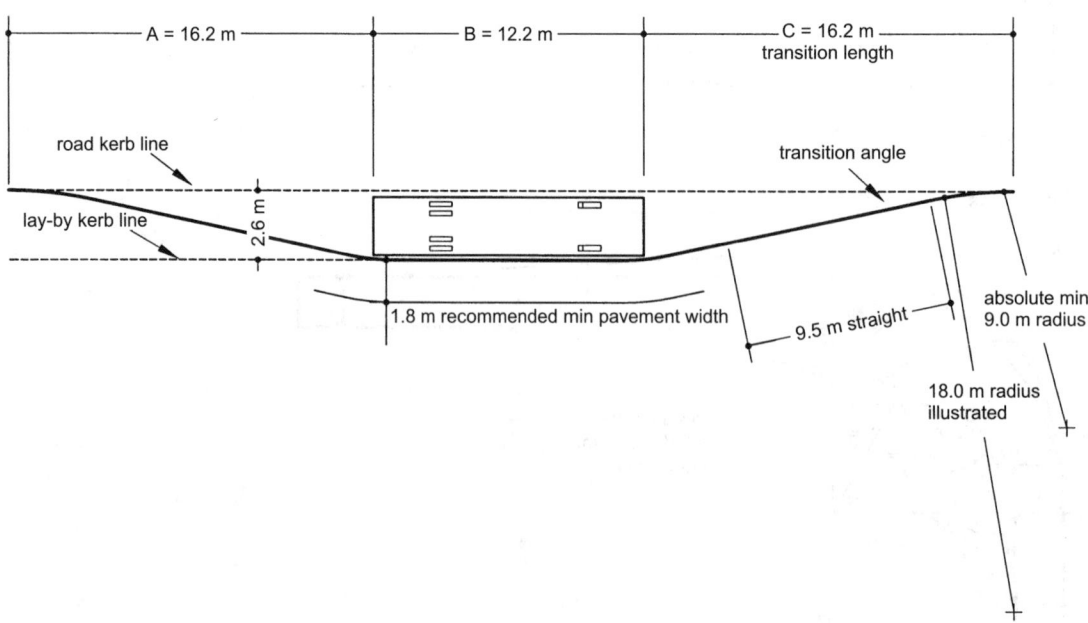

7.23 *A lay-by with one bus stop, assuming normal urban speed of approach. The transition length of 16.2 m is the minimum for a 12 m rigid vehicle. Three bus stops is the desirable maximum in a lay-by, the maximum comfortable distance for a passenger to walk.*

Overall length is $A + nB + C$, where n is the number of buses to be accommodated. So for one stop 44.6 m, two stops 56.8 m and three stops 69 m

6.03 Factors affecting size of station

Apart from the physical site constraints, station size is governed by the following:

- *Number of bays to be incorporated* (the term *bay* is used in bus stations instead of bus stop), determined by the number of services operated from the station; and by how practical it is, related to the timetable, to use each bay for a number of service routes.

- *Vehicle approaches to the bays.* Three types of manoeuvre are used, **7.24**. The 'saw-tooth' is further explored in **7.25** and **7.26**.

  The choice of manoeuvre will be influenced by the size and shape of the available site, the bus operators' present and anticipated needs, and in particular the preference of their staff. Some will accept the saw-tooth arrangement while others prefer the drive-through.

  The required area of the site is further increased by the need for *lay-over*. This is when vehicles are parked after setting down passengers, but which are not immediately required to collect more passengers. The layout for this should be as for parking,

7.27 and **7.28**, preferably so that no vehicle is boxed in or interferes with other bus movements.

Economy of space may be achieved, again dependent upon timetables, by using spare bays for lay-over purposes.

- *Facilities for passengers*: these will depend entirely upon anticipated intensity of use and existing amenities. If, for example, there are already public toilets, a bus and coach information centre and cafés nearby, then these will not be required on the station concourse. However, waiting room facilities may be required with someone on hand to give information and supervision. In more comprehensive schemes consider:

Waiting room
Buffet
Public toilets
Kiosks
Enquiry and booking
Left luggage
Lost property.

7.24 *Vehicle manoeuvres used in approaching parking bays:*

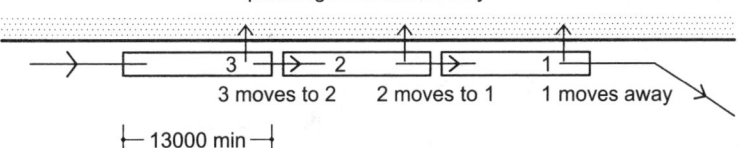

a *Shunting, where a vehicle only sets down passengers on the concourse before moving off to park or pick up more passengers. This avoids waiting to occupy a pre-determined bay, and reduces effective journey time*

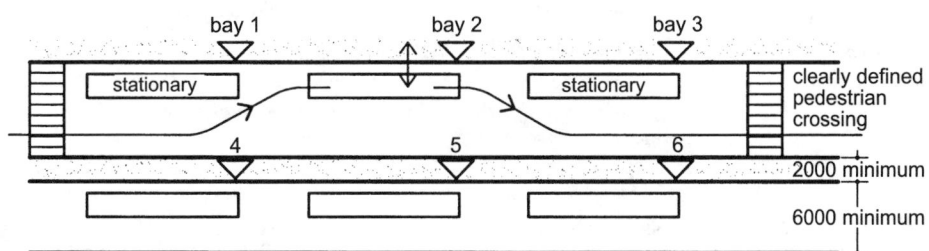

b *Drive-through bays are fixed positions for setting down and/or collecting passengers. They are in a line, so a vehicle often has to approach its bay between two stationary vehicles. In practice it is often necessary to to have isolated islands for additional bays, with the inevitable conflict between passenger and vehicle circulation*

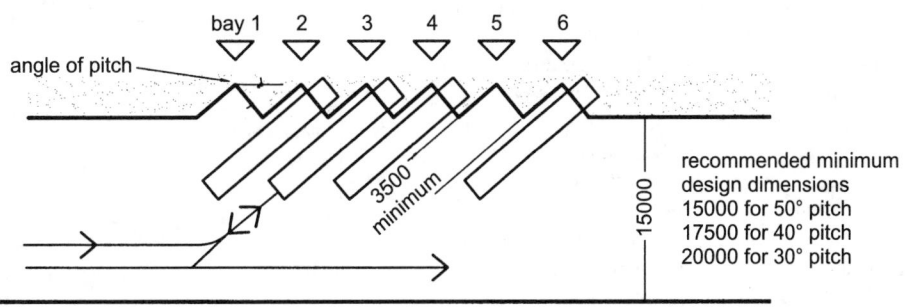

c *'Saw-tooth' layouts have fixed bay positions for setting down and/or collecting passengers with the profile of the concourse made into an echelon or saw-tooth pattern. In theory the angle of pitch between the vehicle front and the axis of the concourse can be anything from 1° to 90°; in practice it lies between 20° and 50°. The vehicle arrives coming forward, and leaves in reverse, thus reducing the conflicts between vehicle and passenger circulation, but demands extra care in reversing*

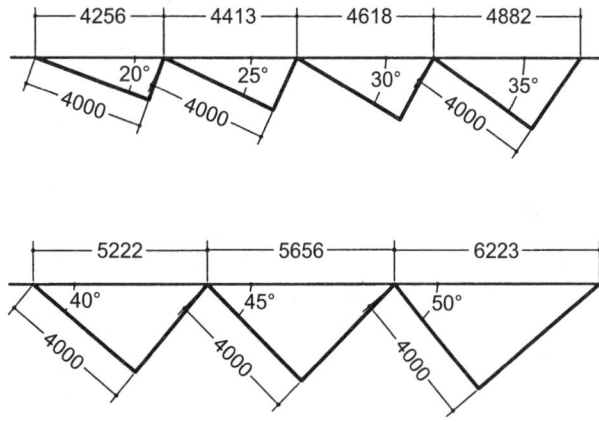

7.25 *As the angle of pitch in saw-tooth bays increases so does the distance between each bay*

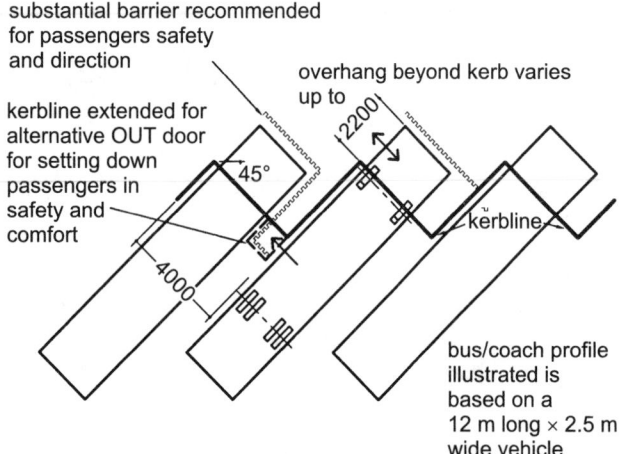

7.26 *Passenger safety and control are particularly important when detailing saw-tooth bays*

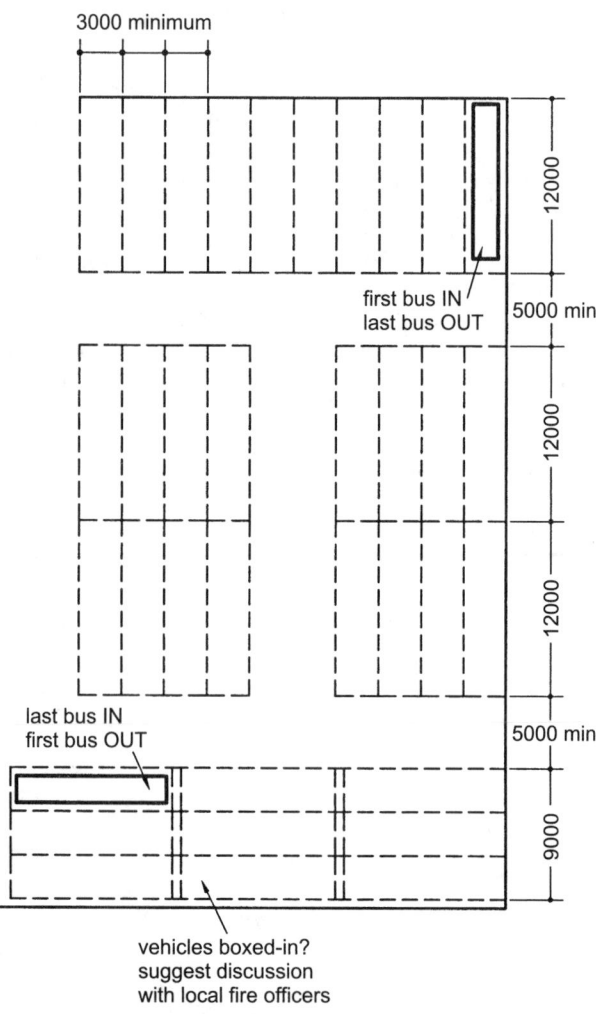

7.27 *Bus garaging layout for where the buses are parked in a pre-determined order to get the maximum number of buses in the available space, subject to the fire officer's limitations*

● *Facilities for staff*: there are invariably inspectors who, as well as assisting passengers, are primarily concerned with organising the movements of vehicles, and supervising their drivers and conductors. If there is a depot near the station then staff facilities will be provided there. If not, canteen and toilets facilities will be needed for staff on the station site, so that during breaks and between shifts they do not need to get back to the depot until they return their vehicle for long-term parking. Should the depot be even more remote, all facilities should be provided at the station and only basic amenities at the depot. In addition to those listed above these include a recreation area, locker rooms and a facility for paying in takings. This would be an office where drivers or conductors check, then hand over monies taken as fares, which in turn are checked and accounted for by clerical staff. Secure accommodation for any cash that cannot be immediately banked will be needed.

● *Facilities for vehicle maintenance*: the inspection, repair and servicing of buses and coaches is an integral part of an operator's responsibility. Normally such work would be carried out at a local depot, with a repair workshop together with fuelling, washing and garaging facilities. The provision of any such facility within a station complex is unusual, but not unique. For a new town bus station or one where it will be difficult and time consuming to drive to and from the station and depot because of traffic congestion, it would be advantageous to provide at least a workshop.

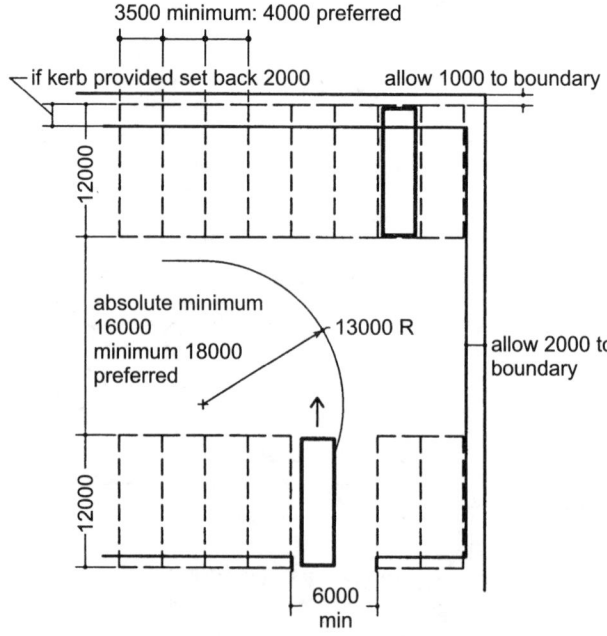

7.28 *Coach park for random arrival and departure of vehicles. The larger bay size (4 m) is necessary if coach parties enter and leave the coaches in the park*

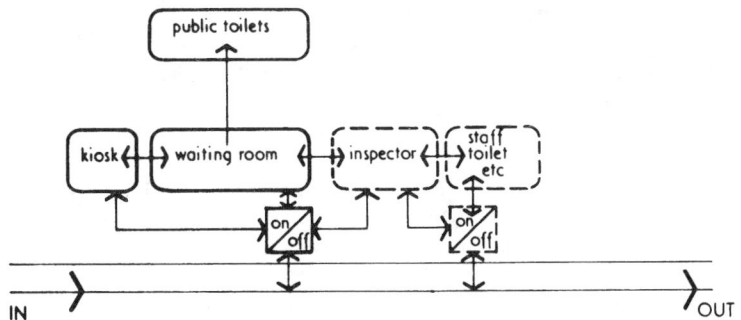

7.29 *Relationship diagram for different types of bus station:* **a** *In a small town where all services run through*

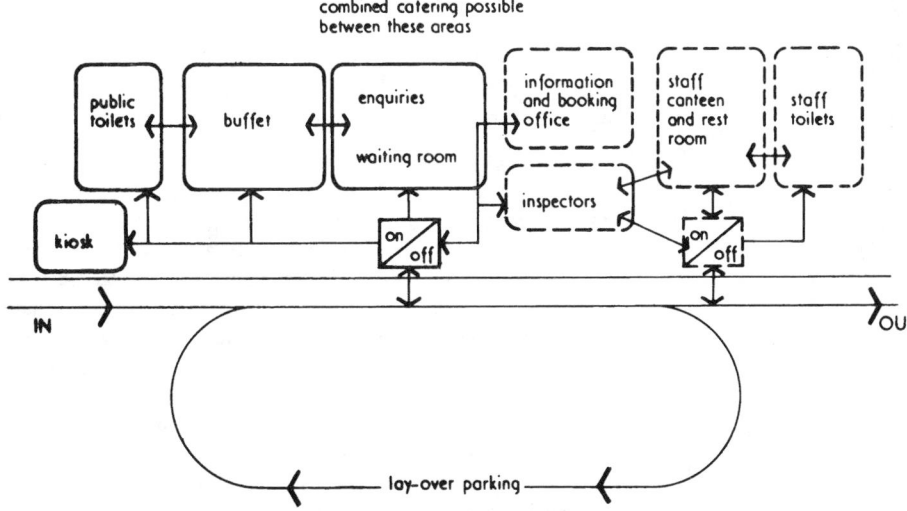

b *For a medium-sized town with both terminal and in-transit services.*

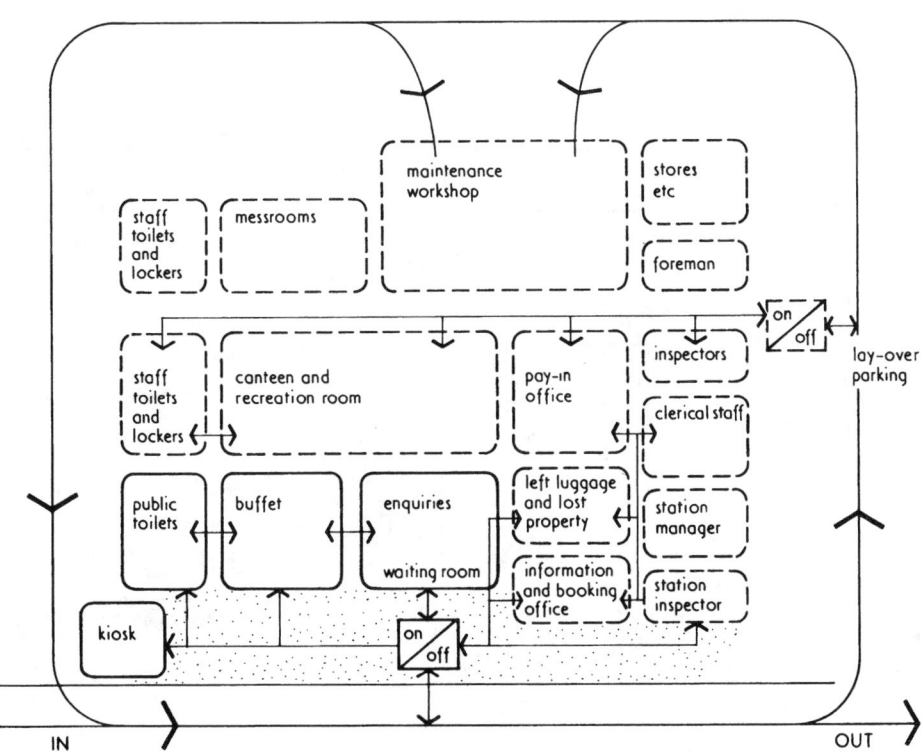

c *For a large new town*

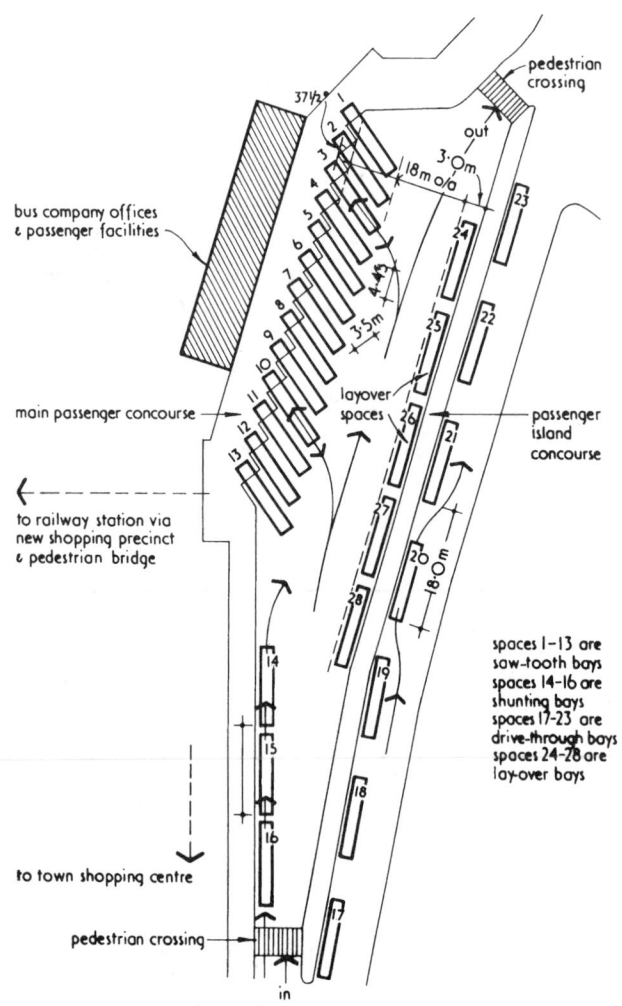

7.30 *Bus station accommodating two bus companies, each with different bay requirements.*

6.03
Whatever facilities are to be provided on the station site, the final arrangement must be carefully planned, **7.29**.

6.04 Joint company use
If two or more bus and coach companies operate from the same station, this can mean that different types of vehicle manoeuvre are used on one site. **7.30** is based on a proposal for a new station within a centre-town commercial development in the south-east of England, and illustrates this. The predominant company (which is a local one) favoured the saw-tooth layout, while the other preferred the drive-through arrangement. Full use has been made of a restricted site, and conflict between passenger and vehicular circulation has been minimised.

7 RAILWAY STATIONS

7.01
This section covers platform and related bridges only. In other respects railway stations have the common components of all passenger terminals: concourses, ticket offices, commercial outlets and catering and sanitary facilities.

7.02 Dimensional standards for railways
These have progressively converged in Europe ever since the days of 'the battle of the gauges'. However, the near-standardisation of the wheel gauge has not been matched by the loading gauge. Mainland Europe has built coaches and freight containers to larger cross-sections than in the UK. The advent of the Channel Tunnel in 1994 has highlighted the two principal standards for all-purpose stock while at the same time setting new and quite different standards for dedicated railway stock. The tunnel can accommodate 800-metre long trains of freight wagons 5.6 m high. but the passenger coaches in these trains are built to the British standard to fit under British, and therefore all bridge structures.

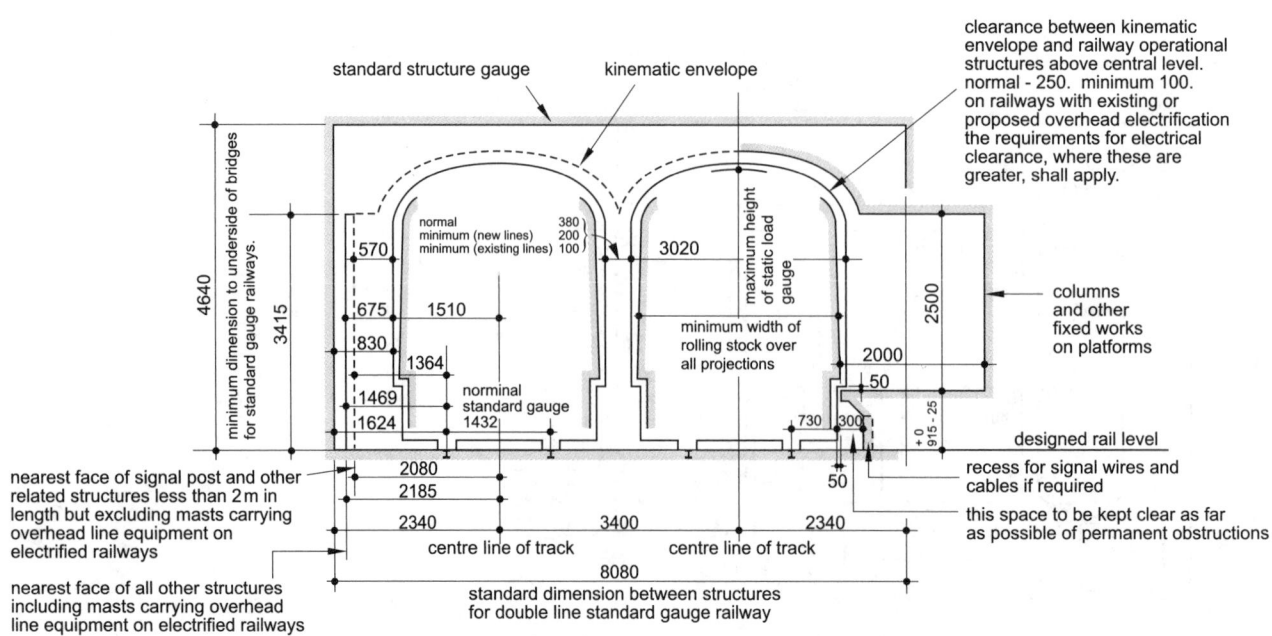

7.31 *Cross-section: controlling dimensions for railway structures, European (Berne gauge) standard*

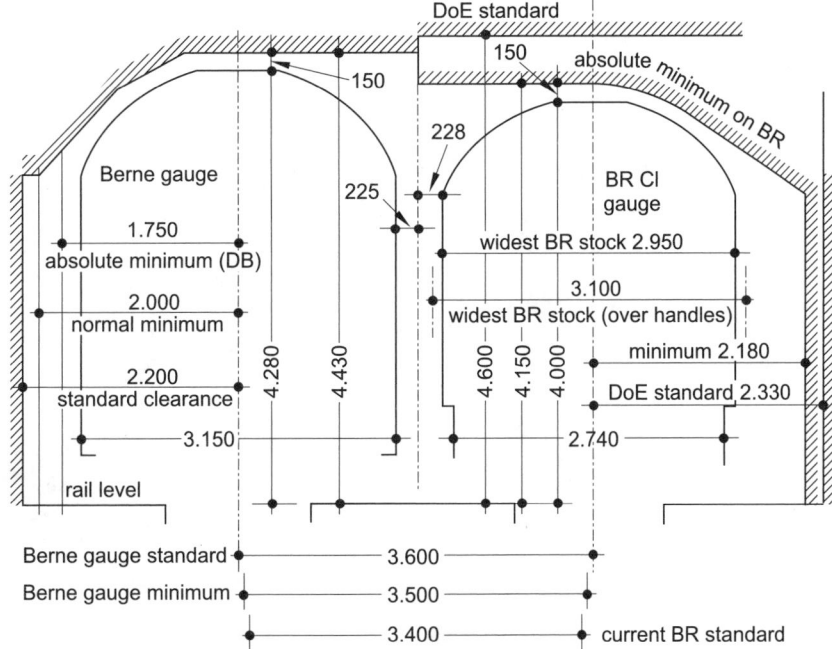

7.32 *Cross-section: controlling dimensions for railway structures, BR standard.*
Note that clearance dimensions are valid for straight and level track only. Due allowance must be made for the effects of horizontal and vertical curvature, including superelevation. Note that the DoT standard states that, to permit some flexibility in the design of overhead equipment, the minimum dimension between rail level and the underside of structures should be increased, preferably to 4780 mm, or more, if this can be achieved with reasonable economy

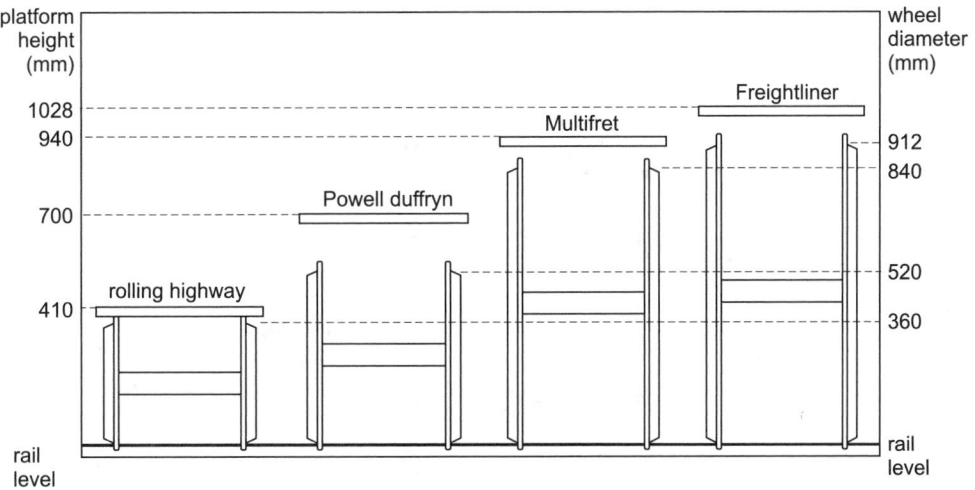

7.33 *Container waggon floors have different heights, and may also vary up to 100 mm in laden and unladen conditions*

7.31 and **7.32** show European and British platforms and bridge structures in section. Platform heights in freight terminals are shown in **7.33**. Platform lengths can vary, but 250 m is common for main-line stations. The Eurostar London–Paris and London–Brussels services exceptionally use trains 400 m long.

8 BIBLIOGRAPHY

8.01 Books and articles
N. J. Ashford, *Level of service design concept for airport passenger terminals – a European view*, Transportation Planning and Technology, 1987
Ashford Stanton and Moore, *Airport Operations*, Wiley Interscience, revised by Pitman, New York, 1991
Christopher J. Blow, *Airport Terminals*, Butterworth Architecture, 1991
Department of Transport, *Railway construction and operations requirements, structural and electrical clearances*, HMSO, 1977
W. Hart, *Airport Passenger Terminals*, Wiley, New York, 1986
Institution of Civil Engineers, *Proceedings of the World Airports Conferences; London, 1973, 1976, 1979, 1983, 1987, 1991*
International Air Transport Association, *Airport Terminals Reference Manual*, Montreal Canada, 1989. Supplemented by *Airport terminal capacity computer program*
International Civil Aviation Organisation publications

8.02 Specialist journals
Airport Forum
Airports International
Jane's Airport Review

8 Factories

Jolyon Drury

CI/SfB 282
UDC 725.4

The Jolyon Drury Consultancy advises on the design of production, distribution and storage systems and facilities

KEY POINTS:
- *Constant change is endemic*
- *Increasing demand for small units and starter accommodation*

Contents

1 INTRODUCTION

1.01 Functions of a factory
A factory is a complex network of functions, including materials storage, component manufacture, assembly, interprocess storage, packaging, despatch and transport interface all of which must work together, **8.1**.

1.02 History of factory development
The history of factory development has been one of continually changing requirements following improvements in production equipment, mechanical handling and motive power associated with shifts of philosophy from individual craftsmanship to soulless production line. The latest innovation is rapidly outdated, and the buildings designed to accommodate it are often obsolete before they are commissioned. The following will, in the future, probably be considered landmarks in factory development:

- Computer factory for IBM, Havant (1968), Arup Associates
- Diesel engine factory for Cummins, Darlington, Roche and Dinkeloo, **8.2**
- Cigarette factory for Players, Nottingham, Arup Associates
- Car assembly plant for Volvo, Kalmar, **8.3**

2 CLASSIFICATION OF PRODUCTION BUILDING TYPES
Factories can be classified as light, medium, heavy or bulk process industry.

2.01 Light industries
These include:

- High-precision work in laboratory-like conditions, **8.4**, **8.5** and **8.6**.
- Small-scale craft workshops as are now being encouraged in both urban and rural areas, **8.7**.

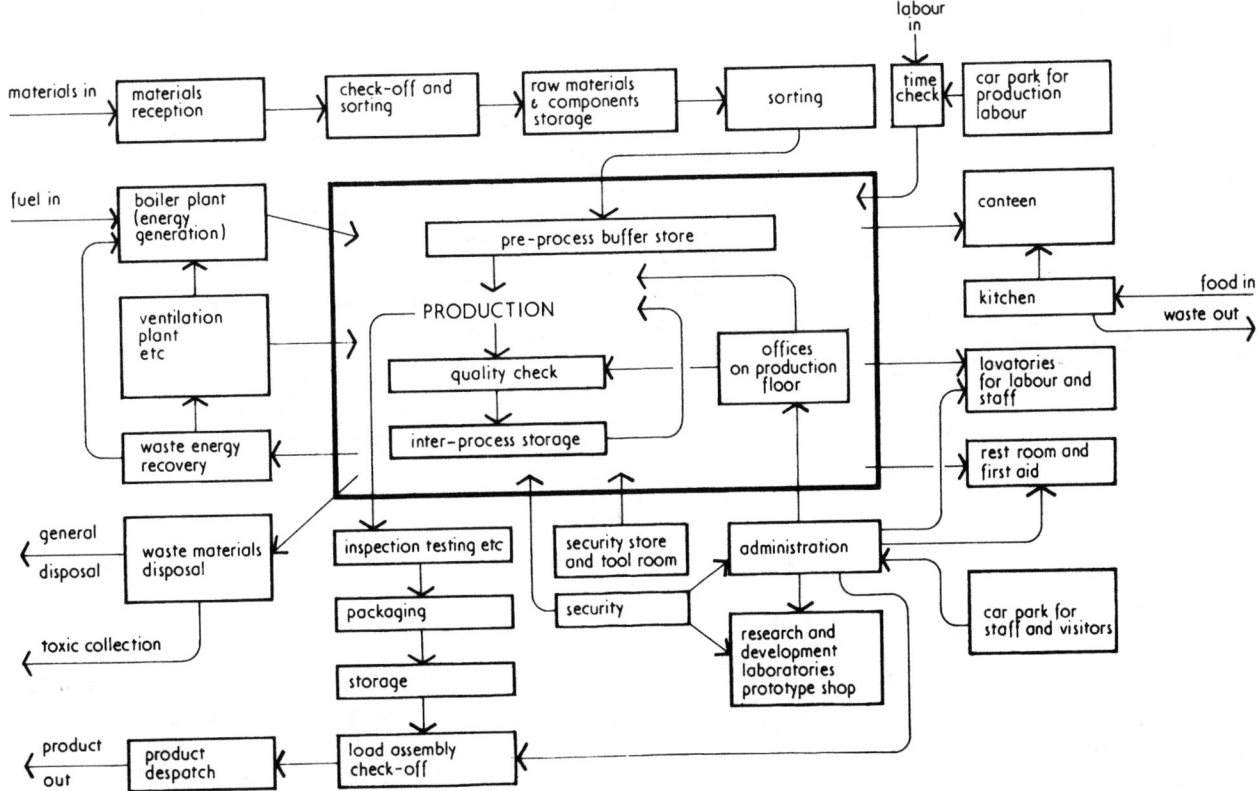

8.1 *Relationship diagram for a typical factory*

8.2 *Cummins' diesel engine factory at Darlington by Roche and Dinkeloo*

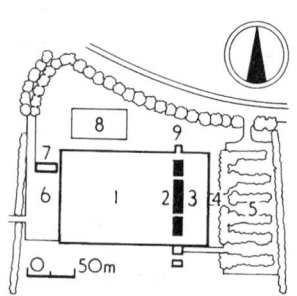

a *Site plan:*
1 factory area
2 brick-enclosed core
3 office area
4 main entrance
5 car parks
6 factory yard for incoming and
outgoing goods
7 stores building
8 pool
9 chimney

b *Factory building plan:*
1 entrance hall and reception
2 offices
3 canteen
4 kitchen
5 first-aid post
6 training room
7 lavatory
8 electric power plant
9 machinery
10 boiler room
11 calibration
12 metallurgical laboratory
13 chemical laboratory
14 servicing
15 stores room for assembly
components
16 assembly
17 tool stores
18 tools issue
19 main hall
20 raw materials
21 spares stores
22 stores of finished products
23 test cells
24 test stand
25 goods out
26 goods in
27 dynometer
28 inspection of incoming goods

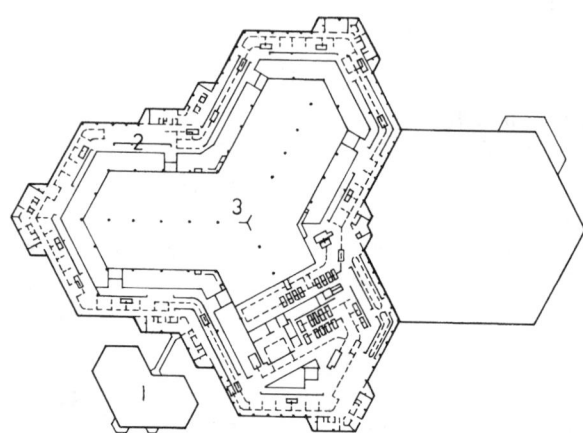

a *upper level*

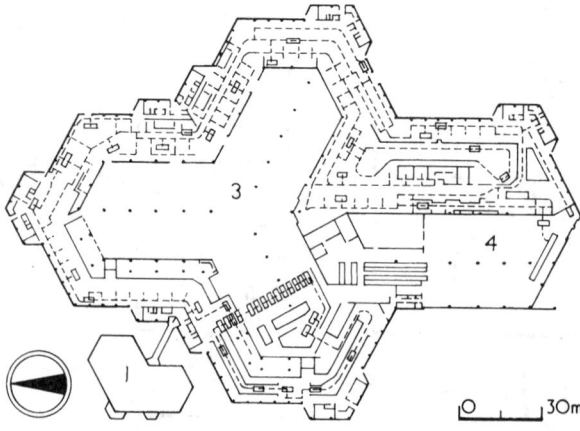

b *lower level*

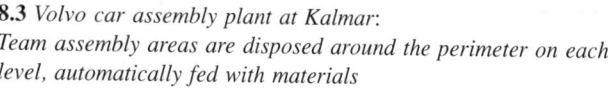

1 offices
2 assembly
3 parts storage
4 loading

8.3 *Volvo car assembly plant at Kalmar:*
Team assembly areas are disposed around the perimeter on each level, automatically fed with materials

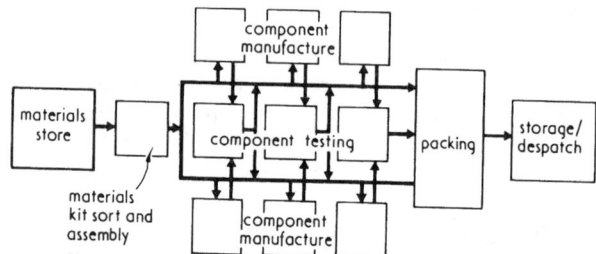

8.4 *Typical process flow diagram for light production and assembly such as small electronic components' manufacture, and similar high-technology processes. 'Kit sort' refers to the making up of kits of components for assemblers*

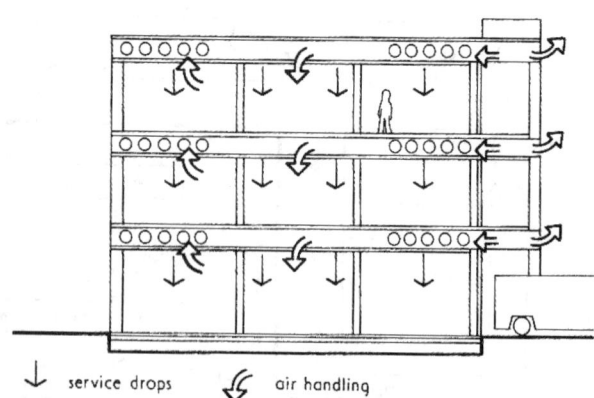

↓ service drops   ⤸ air handling

8.5 *Section through typical factories for light, high-technology production; multi-storey construction, as new or conversion of existing building: could be flatted units*

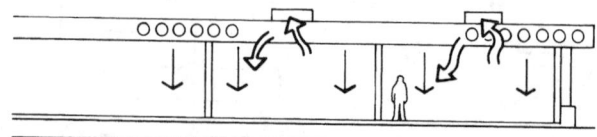

8.6 *Light production and assembly: single storey for small-scale and high-technology assembly. High degree of service freedom in roof zone*

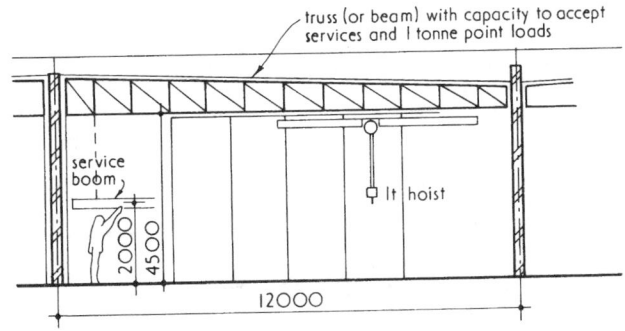

a *Section through unit*

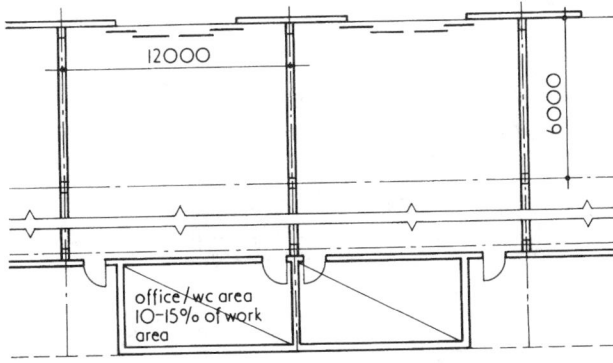

b *Part plan*

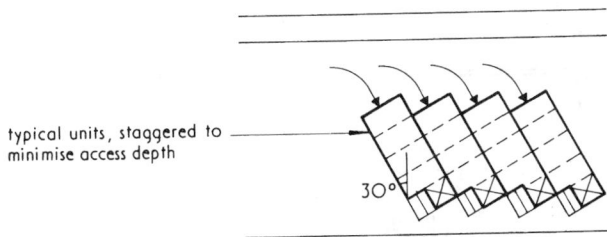

c *Units staggered in plan to reduce site depth required*

8.7 *Typical 'nursery' for light production and assembly, low technology, may be built speculatively*

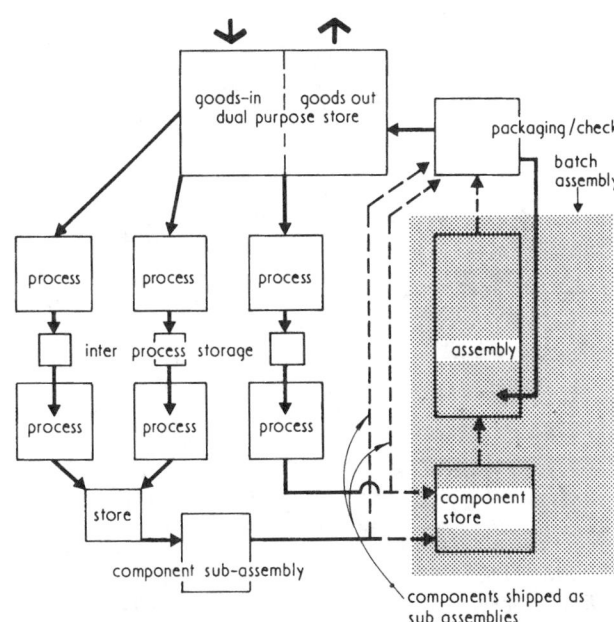

8.8 *Process flow diagram for batch production and assembly. Sometimes involves the assembly and shipping out of complete sub-assemblies, more commonly the production and despatch of batches of discrete components*

Design will depend on circumstances, but will tend to approximate to laboratory or office type design conforming to Planning B1 classification.

2.02 Medium industries
The greatest need for careful and thoughtful design is in this field. These industries can be subdivided into:

● light–medium small-scale engineering and assembly, clothing factories, paint shops, similar to **8.7**.
● General–medium batch production of components for other factories, medium-sized printing, **8.8** and **8.9**.
● Heavy–medium industries requiring intensive use of buildings and services as in mass production, **8.10** and **8.11**.

2.03 Heavy industries
Industries such as steel-making and ship-building require spaces (not necessarily enclosed) designed around the work or the

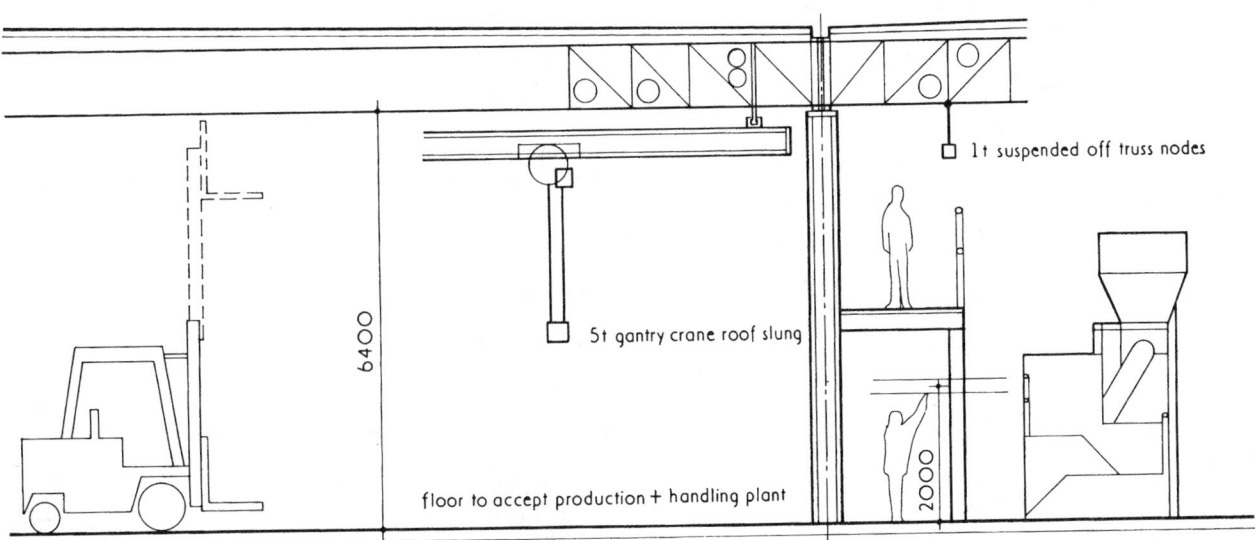

8.9 *Section through typical purpose-built batch production building. The spans, typically 18 × 12 m and trussed roof construction are selected for cheap and rapid adaptation to a variety of uses. Floor loading 25 kN/m²*

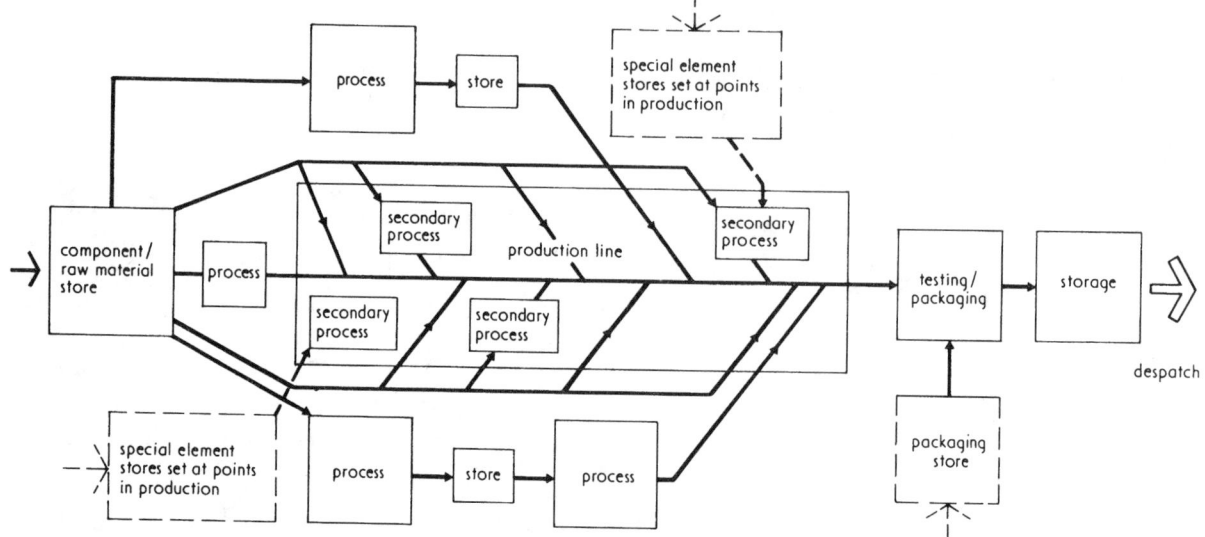

8.10 *Process flow diagram for mass production and assembly. This applies to high-volume line assembly as in the motor industry, with some components being built into sub-assemblies before final assembly on the main line*

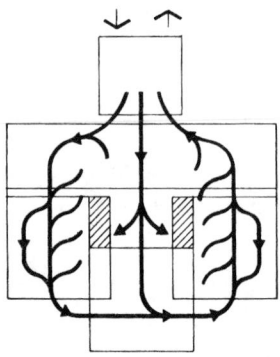

8.11 *Materials flow for mass production does not have to impose a predominantly linear building form. Group assembly 'cells' may feed onto a circulatory route, allowing personnel and services to be grouped into specifically equipped zones*

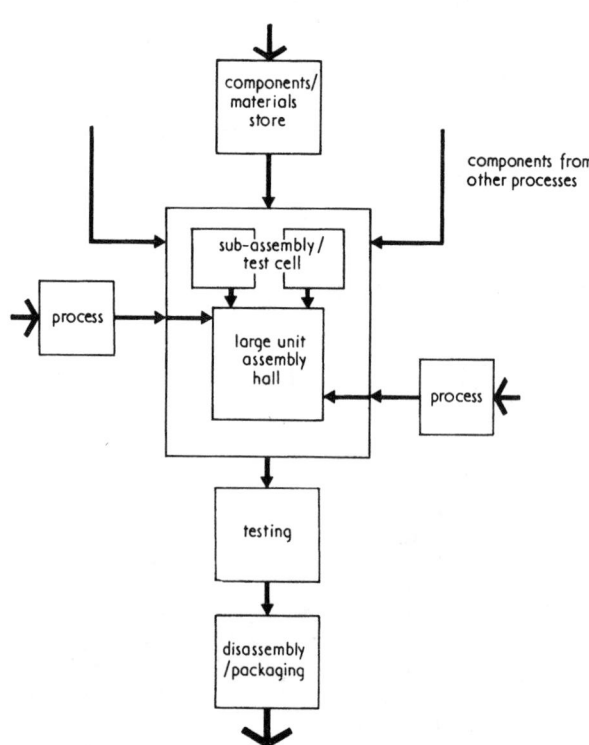

8.12 *Process flow diagram for typical heavy engineering. The workpiece is the centre to which sub-assemblies are routed. It is likely to be disassembled for shipment*

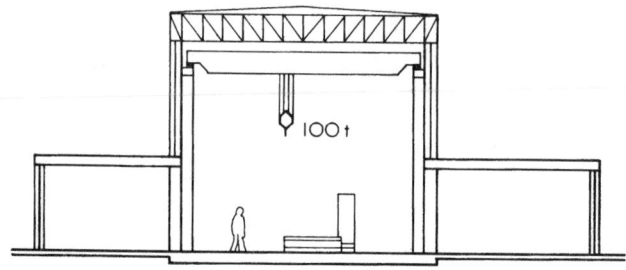

a *Section, and*

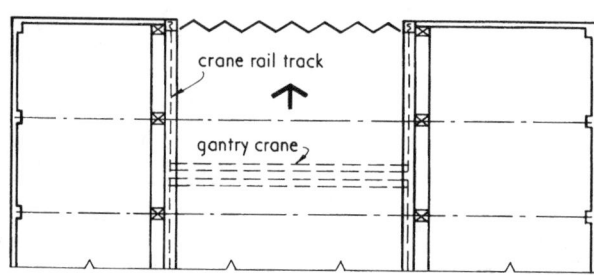

b *Part plan of traditional type. Heavy-duty gantry cranes move the workpiece to the appropriate machine tools and assembly areas*

8.13

mechanical plant, **8.12**. Traditionally it is difficult to build adaptable structures, **8.13**, but modern handling techniques enable 'loose fit' buildings to be designed **8.14**.

3 ADAPTABILITY

3.01 Design for change

The industrial building usually has to change all or part of its use several times during the payback period. Adaptability must therefore be built-in: a minimal first cost will soon be negated by the expense of fitting new processes or working methods into an inherently unsuitable building.

In the recent past, factories were either designed rigidly around a specific process or speculatively to a mean specification, resulting in buildings that are unsuitable for many of the modern processes.

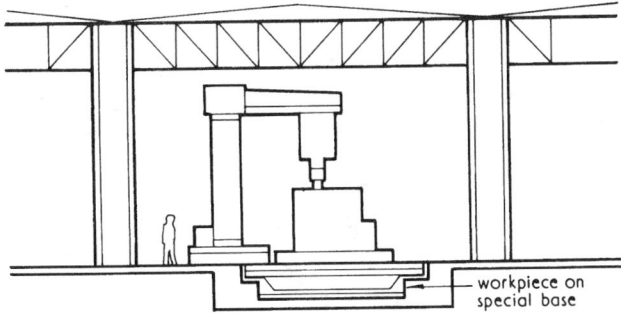

c *Section, and*

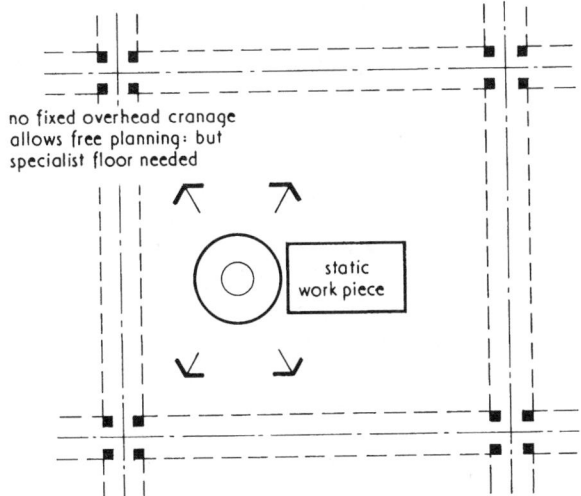

no fixed overhead cranage
allows free planning: but
specialist floor needed

static
work piece

d *Part plan of recently developed workshop where large
workpieces remain static, being built up on special bases
that are likely to be employed for transport and installation.
Machine tools and components are brought to the
workpiece, air-cushion techniques are widely used*

8.14

Adaptability must allow:

● Change of process to avoid obsolescence
● Change of process and product following change of
ownership.

Changes will normally only be within the broad groupings of
building types given in Section **2.02**.

3.02 Design for extension
Apart from alterations within the envelope, there may also be
requirements for extension; and the design should anticipate this,
8.15 and **8.16**.

4 WORKING METHODS

4.01 Alternative methods
The alternative methods of work organisation are:

● Linear assembly
● Team technology.

While the latter is a more recent introduction, there is no indication
that it will completely supplant the former. Consequently,
production buildings must be able to accommodate either or even
both in different areas, **8.17** and **8.18**.

4.02 Linear assembly
In this method, machines are arranged along work-travel routes. At
each station components are added, until the work has been

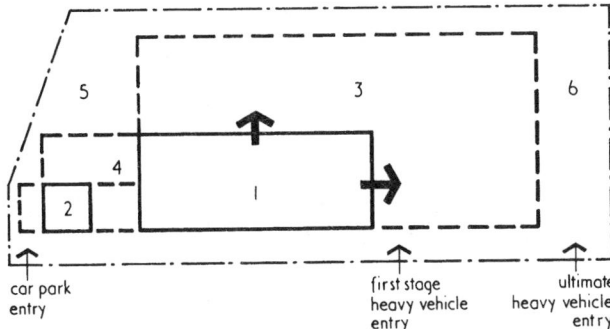

1 *first stage factory*   **4** *various options for office expansion*
2 *first stage office*   **5** *car park*
3 *factory expansion*   **6** *heavy vehicle area*

8.15 *Small or medium-size factory development, with a
free-standing office building. The uneven boundary increases the
possibility of conflict when the factory and offices expand
simultaneously, and restricts commensurate expansion of car
parking*

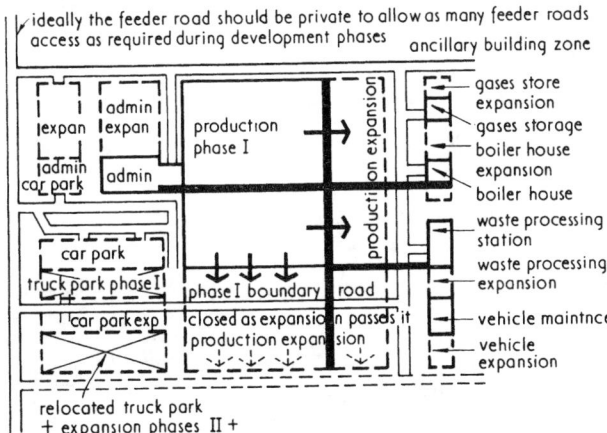

██████ *principal service road*

8.16 *A large plant with segregated development zones:*
● The factory and associated car and truck parking. When the
factory expands the truck park becomes the expanded car
park and a new truck park is constructed adjacent to despatch
● The administration block and associated car parking,
separated from manufacturing by landscaping
● The ancillary area, incorporating individual growth provision
for each element within the zone boundary

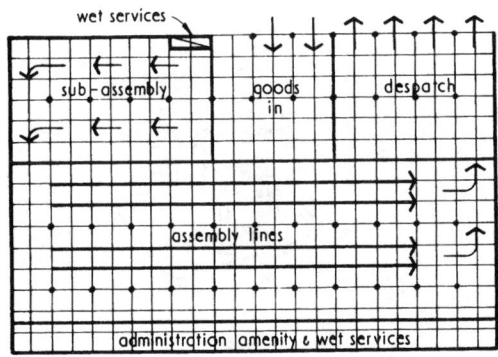

8.17 *Mass production buildings have to accept changes in
production technology. This plan shows a conventional line
assembly that may be adapted to the form in **8.18***

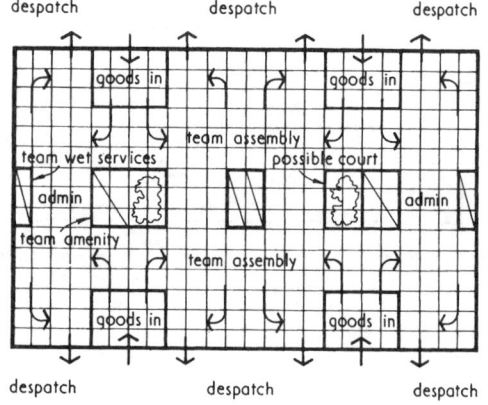

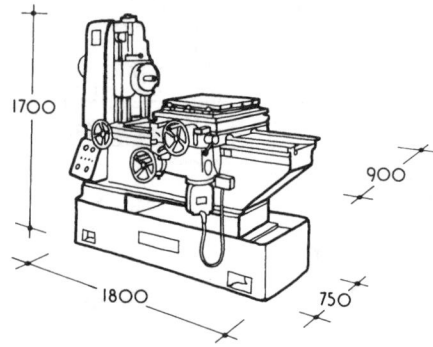

8.18 *The factory can change to team assembly due to new product. Note localisation of amenity and wet service areas to identify with teams. Chance of opening courts adjacent to amenity areas, though these may change position as production demands*

a *General purpose chuck lathe*

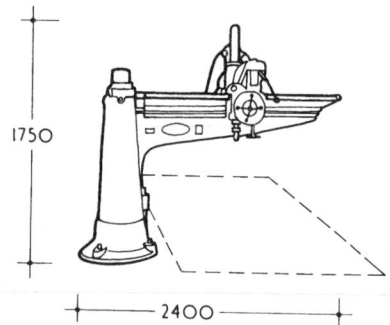

a *Plate drill*

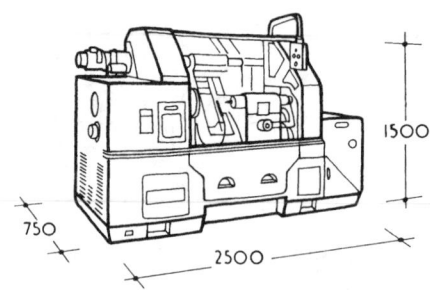

b *Hydraulic copying lathe*

8.20 *Lathes*

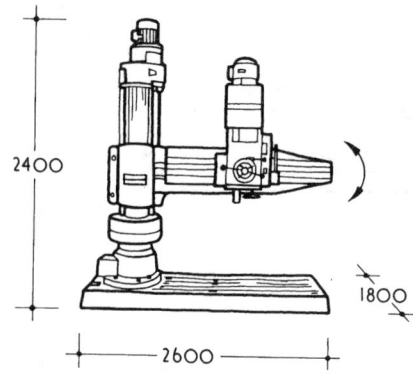

b *Radial drill*

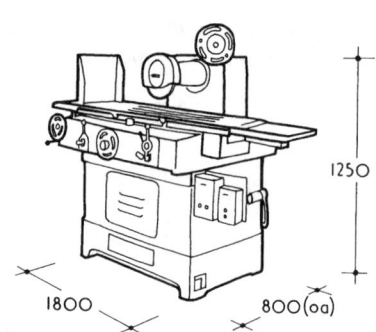

a *Surface grinder*

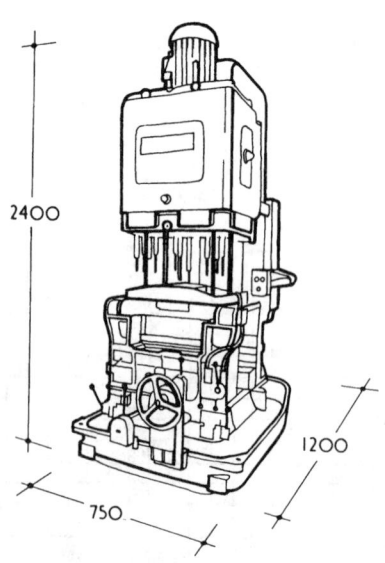

c *Adjustable multi-drill*

8.19 *Drilling machines*

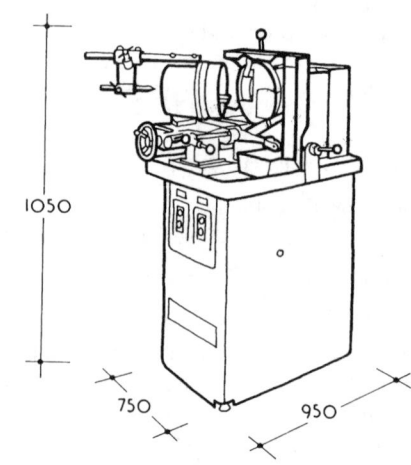

b *Twist drill grinding machine*

8.21 *Grinding machines*

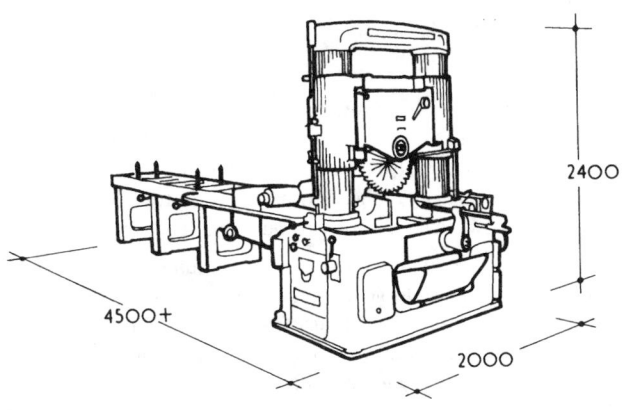

8.22 *Cold sawing machine*

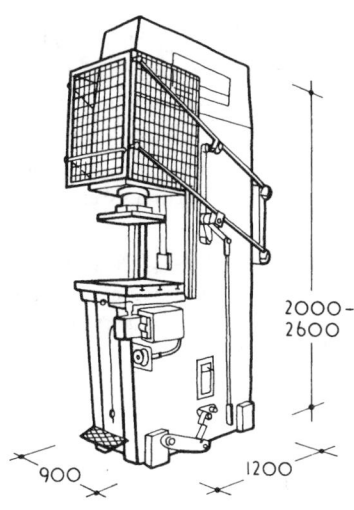

8.24 *Hydraulic pedal press*

8.19 to 8.24 *The majority of machine tools do not exceed 7.5 kN/m² in loading on the floor*

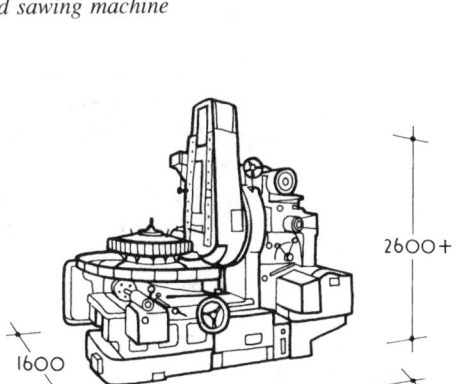

8.23 *Gear cutting machine*

completely assembled and finished. Supplies of components and materials are needed at each station; and waste must be removed.

4.03 Team technology
This appears to restore to the labour force a feeling of responsibility and achievement. The machines are arranged in groups, and all or a substantial part of the work is assembled within the group. There is a need for storage of materials and components. The main planning requirements are for unrestrictive space and strong floors to enable the machines to be relocated at will, with adaptable overhead services systems. Storage and assembly spaces should be interchangeable.

5 MACHINE SIZES
The sizes of typical machines for light and medium duty industries are shown in **8.19** to **8.24**.

---

6 OUTLINE SPECIFICATION OF A TYPICAL MULTI-STRATEGY FACTORY

Scope

Type of industries for which appropriate	Buildings of this type are suitable for most manufacturing functions, excluding 'light', 'heavy' and 'process' industries.
Size of project	Total area of production space can vary widely. Average size of all projects is 2500 m², so most are smaller. This specification is suitable for projects from about 1000 m² upwards.
Type of project	Forty per cent of industrial projects are adaptations and extensions of existing premises. This specification sets out the general requirements of those projects, or parts of projects, free from special restraints.

Criterion	Performance specification	Design notes

Requirements of the process

| Adaptability | Should be designed for general-purpose use and not around a particular process. General-purpose characteristics should be maintained wherever possible, e.g. in stores and production warehousing as well as in production space itself. | Building positioned on site leaving maximum possible room for extension, preferably in two directions.

Single-storey building designed as a large open space. Standardised, mainly dry construction, easily extended or modified. Framework able to carry a variety of alternative roof and wall claddings, services and handling equipment. Those external walls not on or near site boundaries designed for easy demolition. |

Criterion	Performance specification	Design notes
Requirements of the process (continued)		
Plan shape	Probably not critical except where linear flow-processes employed. Rectangular form maximises usable area, facilitates extension.	Rectangular plan form with ratio of long to short sides between 1:1 (minimises internal travel distances where no particular traffic routes are dictated by process) and say, 3:1 (average 2:1).
Physical environment	Process requirements will not usually be critical: workplace environment and energy efficiency very important.	See under 'Environmental requirements of labour force'. In general, the production process will not require special dust-free conditions, nor will it create a dusty or especially dirty atmosphere. If there are toxic or corrosive hazards within the general production space, these should be isolated by local compartmentation and extraction equipment. High standards of cleanliness (e.g. very exact avoidance of foreign matter) or hygiene (e.g. avoidance of bacterial contamination) for some high-technology factories.
Structural dimensions	Exact plan dimensions rarely critical, except where flow processes employed. Aim should be to optimise convenience for production layouts provided by open space, e.g. the convenience of stanchions for locating small equipment, switches, etc. balanced against the potential adaptability: freedom for service drops and the location of equipment against the cost of greater spans and the loss of overhead craneage.	Span 18 m; bay spacing 12 m or even 18 m (which would permit production line to be turned at right-angles if needed). These are proven dimensions in USA but they are greater than those found in many British factory buildings and (excluding 18 m square bays) are unlikely to increase costs significantly over smaller spans.
	Internal clear height probably most critical dimension, for once built can only be modified with difficulty. Height needed for high stacking, overhead equipment, possibly facility to install mezzanines (for works offices, lavatories, control gear, extension of production space, etc.), overhead conveyors, etc. Space for services needed above clear height level.	Internal clear height minimum 6 m. Main vehicle entrance doors (ground level loading) 5 m. For intensive manufacture, high stacking, overhead hoists or mezzanine floors a minimum height of 7.5 m is recommended.
Structural loadings	Within economic restraints, design for heaviest likely loads.	Ideally point loads of 36 kN, but 25 kN sufficient for general-purpose use for buildings less than 6 m high to eaves. For very dense storage, typically mini-load automated component stores, 30 kN/m^2 distributed loading.
Provision for services	Facility to take any production service (water, steam, gas, electrical power, etc.) to any point within production area with minimum disturbance to building, and therefore production.	Production and building services carried in roof space above level indicated by 'clear height', with vertical droppers as required to machine positions. This eliminates overhead craneage, but allows monorail hoists and conveyors. Roof structure designed appropriately. Drainage used to be below floor level, although alternative more costly but flexible arrangements are preferable. A permanent grid of drainage runs beneath the floor (a minimum of, say, one run in the middle of each 18 m span) will minimise disturbance.
Provision for movement of materials and equipment	It should be possible for the production engineer to use the type of material-handling equipment best suited to the product and production methods. Use of fork-lift trucks or similar wheeled materials-handling equipment will be general; overhead conveyors may be used. Cranes more usual in engineering than other industries. Heaviest floor loading is likely to result from wheels of fork-lift trucks (36 kN) and point loads from stacked storage cages and from pallet racking.	Separate foundations will be provided for any special or heavy equipment, especially that which vibrates. Wherever possible, the upper surface of such foundations will be at or below finished floor level. Much equipment is now 'stuck-down' to the floor. Conventionally, an RC floor slab with integral granolithic finish is used, although deterioration of the floor finish is a common problem in industrial buildings. Durable floors can be obtained, but they require a suitable base, good workmanship and close supervision. Particular finishes may be needed to resist attack from acids or oils used in certain processes.

Criterion	Performance specification	Design notes

Requirements of the process (continued)

Support for production loads

There are two opposed points of view about supports for such production loads as conveyors, local hoists and other overhead equipment. One is that since production loads cannot be predetermined, they should not be allowed to bear on the building structure, and should be loads carried either on the plant or on a separate structure, as and when this becomes necessary. This can lead to substructures inhibiting floor area and future flexibility. Although initially more expensive the preferred alternative is to design the roof structure to carry a general minimum of local loads, and to provide the facility to suspend conveyors, etc. at will.

Design assumptions might be that bottom boom of trusses (assumed spaced at 3 to 3.6 m centres) carry uniformly distributed load of 8 kN/m run, and a point load of 10 kN on any panel point at, say, 3 m centres. Structural supports for heavier loads are then provided on an *ad hoc* basis by the production engineer.

Environmental requirements of the labour force

Visual environment

Practically all visual tasks will be met by illumination levels within the range of 200 to 750 lux; illumination in the middle of the range will be most common. Limiting values of glare index (as IES Code) are likely to be within 22–28. Colour schemes should be designed both to assist the distribution of light and to minimise fatigue. Natural light design levels: warehouse, packing, large assembly, heavy forging, casting, saw mills, Daylight Factor 2% (say 10–15% floor area) 300–500 lux: Bench and machine work, fine casting, motor repair, general office work, average general purpose lighting, Daylight Factor 4–5% (say 12–15% floor area) 500 lux: Drawing work, medium assembly, weaving, small typesetting, Daylight Factor 6% (say, 15–20% floor area) 500–750 lux: Small inspection and assembly, small bench and machine work, 1000 lux + Daylight Factor 10%.

Either daylight or 'windowless' design. If daylight design, a monitor roof shape is a useful compromise between even light level and energy conservation. View windows in external walls. Fluorescent lighting installation arranged in regular pattern over whole production floor to give 300 to 500 lux consistent illumination level

$$\frac{E_{min}}{E_{max}} \text{ must be at least } 0.7$$

wired in three phases to reduce flicker, and in trunking for simple replacement. Point luminaires may be used in areas of higher headroom, or to provide a high and even intensity. Reflecting surfaces decorated with colours of high reflectivity (e.g. underside of roofs: Munsell value 9), but care that glare from surfaces does not disturb machine operators, e.g. fork-lift truck drivers.

For 10 per cent and over use PSALI (permanent supplementary artificial lighting installation).

For a general purpose building and for resale the design level should not be below a Daylight Factor of 5 per cent. The method of achieving this must be checked against insulation regulations.

Thermal environment

Optimum values of temperature, air movement, etc. will depend largely upon nature of work – whether, for example, it is sedentary or active. Main environmental problem will be to avoid uncomfortable heat in summer. Minimum temperatures: heavy work 10°, light work 13° C sedentary 16°C.

For most light industry plant should be able to provide air temperature of 18–21°C. Minimum value of thermal insulation for roof and walls $U = 0$–$7 \text{ W/m}^2 \text{°C}$

Mechanical ventilation, at least in factories of average or greater size. Air-change rate (fresh air supply) minimum 5 litres/second/person

Acoustic environment

Production processes highly variable in noise output. Control by encapsulating machinery and by using interspersed storage stacks.

Thermal insulation material can give a measure of acoustic control, particularly in providing absorption.

Fire protection

Some industries are regarded as having 'abnormal' fire risk because of the process or materials used; building design will be affected by requirements for additional compartmentation. Generally, fire hazard is classed as 'moderate' to 'low'. The general requirement of fire safety, of a maximum division of the production area into self-contained fire-resisting compartments, is at variance with the general production need for open space, and should be carefully considered.

Fire division walls may be required to obtain acceptable insurance rate. Areas will depend on process, etc. 'Fire curtains' in roof space. Fire vents in roof surface of total area not less than 1 per cent of floor area. Avoidance of combustible materials in sheeted claddings. Sprinklers are also being increasingly required by insurance companies, both over the process and in the roof depth to protect services.

Criterion	Performance specification	Design notes
Environmental requirements of the labour force (continued)		
Explosion hazard	Not normally considered critical, but can be accommodated with blow-out panels, or placing part of process outside the main building.	
Building economics	The cost of using a factory building is an important element in the long-term cost of manufacturing. Nevertheless, without adequate justification, few managements are prepared to pay more than the minimum to obtain their essential specification, one reason being that investment in plant, equipment, perhaps labour is likely to show a higher return than investment in buildings (see Sections **3.01**, **3.02**).	A 'basic' specification: concrete floor slab; exposed structural framework and services; simple finishes, such as painted steelwork, untreated concrete, fairfaced brickwork; self-finished insulating materials forming roof lining.

7 NON-PRODUCTION ACCOMMODATION

7.01 Offices
There is a tendency for administrative and production space to be interchangeable. Two types of offices will be required in close conjunction with the production space:

● Foreman's desk space in sight and proximity of work supervised. This is formed from easily demountable components to allow for rapid relocation. Sometimes to avoid floor obstructions this accommodation is raised to mezzanine levels where visibility is improved

● executive offices for the local administrative staff, or the company headquarters where these are not elsewhere. This type of accommodation is designed in accordance with Section 16, Offices, Shops and Railway Premises Act 1963, and will depend on the numbers to be accommodated. As a rough guide, allow 10–15 per cent of the production floor area, or $5\,m^2$ per person.

7.02 Lavatories
For sanitary accommodation see Chapter 3. A first aid facility is normally provided in conjunction with this.

7.03 Canteens
Staff are not allowed to eat in dirty or dusty surroundings. If the process demands a clean environment the reverse may apply, and the importation of food into the working area may need to be discouraged.

Canteens are therefore nearly always now provided. See Chapter 18 for details of design.

8 BIBLIOGRAPHY
J. Drury, *Architects' Journal Handbook of Factory Design*, Architectural Press, 1977–8
O. W. Grube, *Industrial Buildings and Factories*
Pemberton, *Plant Layout and Materials Handling*, Macmillan
Factories Act 1961
Offices, Shops and Railway Premises Act, 1963, HMSO
Insulation Act 1972
Health and Safety at Work Act 1974, HMSO
Health and Safety Booklets, HMSO
Workplace Directive, published as Workplace (Health, Safety and Welfare) Regulations, Approved Code of Practice, HMSO, 1992

9 Industrial storage buildings

Jolyon Drury

CI/SfB 284
UDC 725.35

KEY POINT:

● *Modern warehouses need the height to use mechanical aids at maximum efficiency*

Contents

1 INTRODUCTION

Few industrial storage buildings are designed to make a profit (steel stockholders and cash and carry stores are exceptions); the majority perform the function of a valve or pipeline, limiting the supply of a product to suit demand, to stabilise prices and allow steady and economic manufacture within fluctuating market conditions. Industrial storage is therefore a service at a cost that must be minimised.

The payback period most frequently chosen for such a building is 25 years. During that time, it is likely that the storage method will need to change at least three times, and that the type of goods handled will change even more frequently. Flexibility for expansion and manner of use are therefore important design considerations.

2 IDENTIFICATION OF WAREHOUSE AND STORAGE TYPES

The three main types are:

● Transit between manufacture and the market, **9.1**
● Distribution: similar to a transit unit, but accepts a wide variety of goods from a number of manufacturers, sorts them into orders and distributes them to a number of outlets, **9.2**. A components warehouse for a factory performs a similar function.
● Repository: a warehouse used for stockholding, either as a service (e.g. a furniture repository) or within a company (e.g. a cold store), **9.3**.

3 PRELIMINARY DECISIONS

The initial decision about what type of building is required will involve a choice between these three types, dependent on the client organisation's needs. Such a study is generally undertaken in cooperation with a specialist consultant. Other factors to be considered at the pre-design stage are:

1 The orientation of the loading bays and the heavy vehicle marshalling areas. Future expansion must be taken into account.

2 The orientation of the goods sorting and load accumulation areas which must be related to the disposition of the storage area, i.e. block stacks or racking and loading bays.
3 Will the required bulk of the building be acceptable in terms of planning consent?
4 Are the existing roads suitable to meet increased demand?
5 Is there public transport for operatives?
6 Are there night operating restrictions which will entail special features to muffle night noise?

Can this be catered for by any design measures/configurations?

4 HEIGHT, AREA AND TYPE OF HANDLING SYSTEM

The most economical way of gaining volume for storage is to use height, **9.4** and Table I; this affects the choice of the handling system to be employed. Consider:

● The type of unit load to be handled and the physical characteristic of the goods – crushability, durability, the type of unit loads that will be assembled after sorting (Table II)
● The speed of turnover. This will determine what storage method is the most efficient.

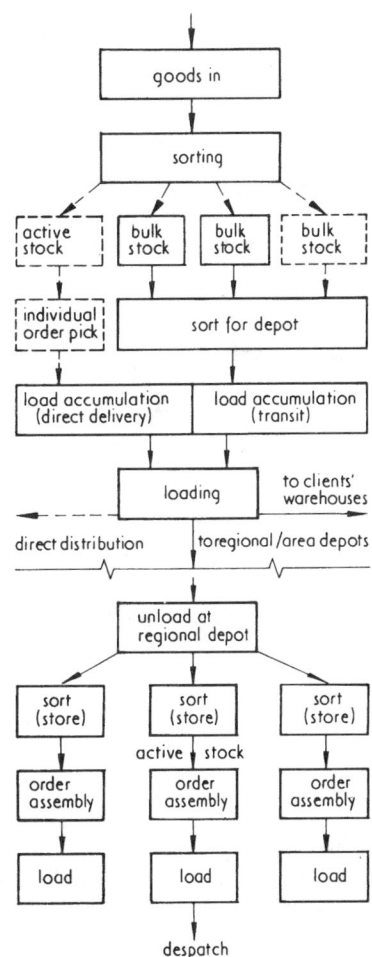

9.1 *Relationships in warehouse for transit between manufacturer and market*

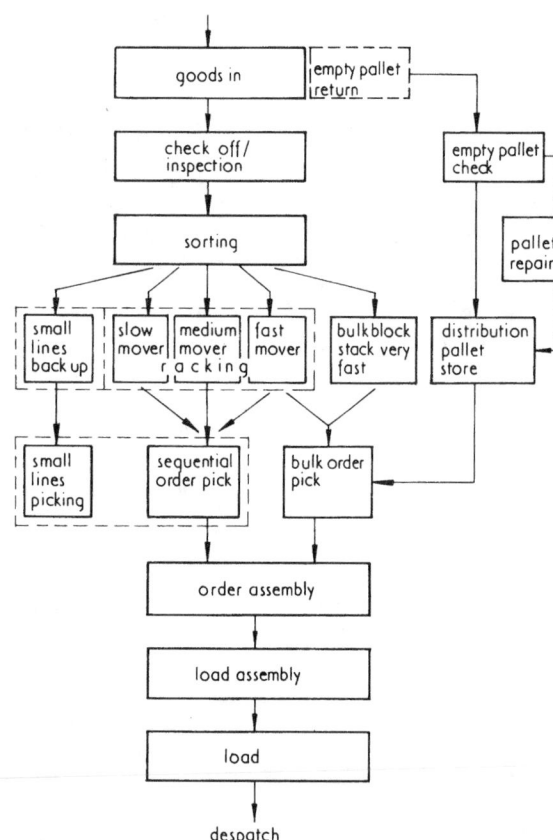

9.2 *Relationships in distribution warehouse*

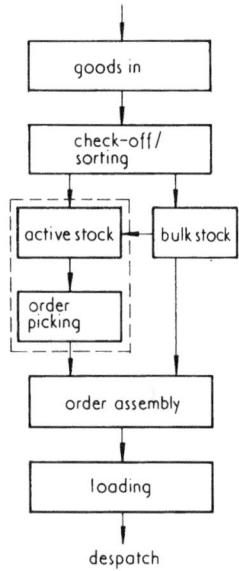

9.3 *Relationships in a stockholding warehouse. The bulk stock area is dominant*

5 STORAGE METHOD

Storage methods (see Tables III to V) include:

1 Very fast throughput involving a limited number of products: block stacking, **9.5**, rather than racking. First in, first out, or first in, last out configuration, depending on the shelf life of the goods

2 A wider variety of goods, but still with fast turnover: drive-in racking, **9.6**, or 'live' (roll-through) storage, **9.7**. Pallets are placed into racking up to four positions deep, with the pallets'

edges resting on runners attached to the rack's uprights. First in, last out. Live racking involves inclined storage lanes. For heavy pallets and shock-sensitive goods, braking and separating equipment can be incorporated.

3 Pallet racking, **9.8**, **9.9**. For a wide variety of goods, the speed of throughput decreases. Pallet racking is the solution with a large variety of products, brands or pack sizes. Each pallet is normally allotted a unique position in the racking.

Table I Typical internal clear heights for storage areas

Minimum clear internal height* (m)	Type of storage
5–5.5	Minimum-cost low-rise block stacking warehouse. Suitable for light industrial factory use
7.5	Minimum for any industrial storage building combining racking and block stacking
9+	When narrow-aisle trucks are used
15–30	Fully automatic, computer-controlled warehouses and stacker cranes are to be used

* Clearance for structural members, sprinklers, lighting must be added to obtain overall height of buildings

Table II Classification of materials for handling and storage as unit loads

Description	Examples	Storage method
Materials not strong enough to withstand crushing – not suitable as integral unit load	Automobile components, made-up textiles, electrical appliance components, manufacturing chemists' sundries, light engineering products, glassware	On pallet in rack
Materials strong enough to withstand crushing – suitable for unit loads	Casks and drums, sawn and machined timber, sheet materials	On pallet, or self-palletised and block stowed
Irregular-shaped materials, strong in themselves suitably packed into unit loads	Goods in cases, crates or cartons	On post pallets and stacked, on pallets in rack or self palletised
Bagged materials which form a flat surface under load	Grain, powder, and similar	On pallet and block stowed
Bagged materials which do not form a flat surface under load or will not take pressure	Forgings, moulded or machined parts, nuts and bolts	On pallet in rack
Large irregular loose materials	Moulded plastics; sheet metal pressings	On post pallets and stacked
Small irregular loose materials	Machined and moulded parts, pressings, forgings	In cage pallets and stacked
Materials hot from production process	Castings and forgings	On post pallets and stacked
Materials too long to be handled other than by side loader or boom	Steel sections, tubes, timber	Horizontally in tube or bar racks
Materials strong enough to withstand crushing but subject to damage	Partly machined automotive parts, painted finished materials, books	Steel box pallets with special partitions
Perishable goods	Frozen meat, vegetables, drink	Cartons, soft packs pallets, box pallets, etc.

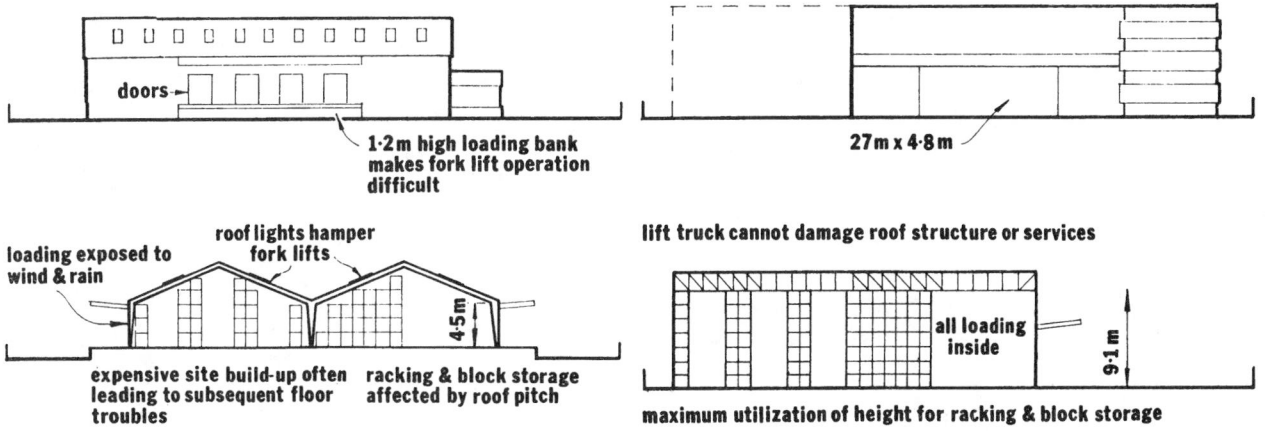

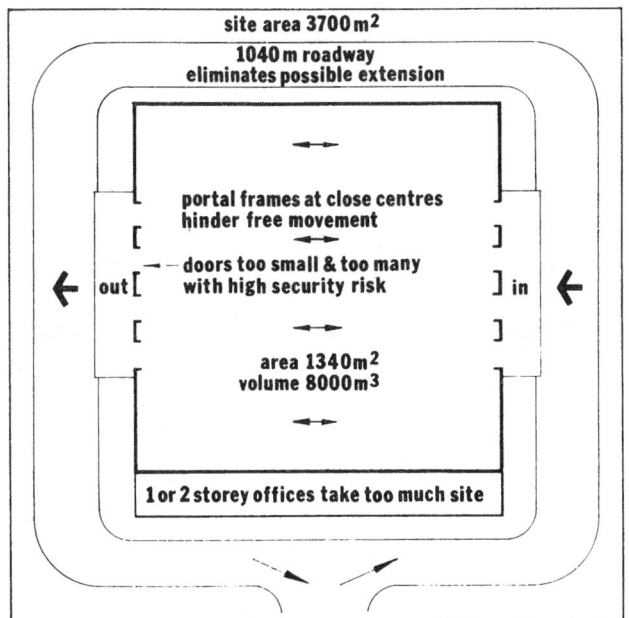

a *Traditional portal frame*

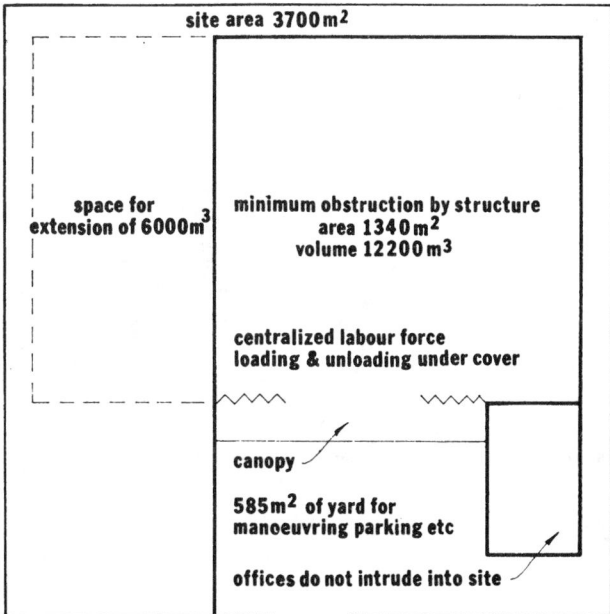

b *Modern 'big box'. This provides a much more flexible solution at lower cost when operating efficiency is assessed.*

9.4 *Comparison between typical alternative structures*

Table III Mechanical handling

	Block stacking	Post pallets	Drive-in racking	Beam pallet racking	Gravity live storage	Powered mobile racking
Cubic space utilisation (%)	100	90	65	35–50	80	80
Effective use of installation capacity (%)	75	75	75	100	70	100
Accessibility of unit loads (%)	10	10	30	100	30	100
Order picking (%)	Poor	30	30	100	30	100
Speed of throughput	Fastest	Good	Poor	Good	Good	Quite good
Load crushing	Bad	Nil	Nil	Nil	Some	Nil
Stability of load	Poor	Fair	Good	Good	Fair	Good
Ease of relocation	Not applicable	Not applicable	Fair	Good	Difficult	Difficult
Speed of installation	Not applicable	Not applicable	Good	Fastest	Fair	Slowest
Rotation of stock	Poor	Poor	Poor	Good	Excellent	Good

Table IV Manual handling

	Long-span shelving	Tiered shelving	Raised storage area	Cantilever shelving	Lightweight live storage	Fir tree racking
Cubic space utilisation (%)	45	45	80	50	65	25
Effective use in installation capacity (%)	95	95	50	100	70	70
Accessibility of goods	Good	Good	Poor	Good	Excellent	Good
Ease of relocation	Good	Fair	Difficult	Fair	Very difficult	Best
Load range (kN/m^2)	2–9.5	2–9.5	2.8–11	2–4.7	Up to 0.2 kN per m run of track	2.6–4.4 kN per arm
Speed of picking	Good	Fair	Poor	Good	Very good	Good
Speed of installation	Very good	Good	Fair	Fair	Slowest	Fastest
Rotation of stock	Very good	Good	Poor	Very good	Excellent	Very good

Table V Load mounting

Load mounting	Type of load								
	Heavy unstable load	Flat cards/sheets	Sacked/bagged loads	Small unit loads	Drums Reels Barrels	Coils	Casks	Bales	Textile Raw materials
Special cradle with/without pallet	*								
Standard pallet		*	*	*	*	*	*	*	
Flat board pallet + decking supports		*	*			*		*	
Direct mounting on timber panels		*	*	*		*	*	*	*
Drum supports					*				
Post pallets – cage/bin			*	*		*	*		*
Coil supports					*	*			
Skips/skeds with skids								*	

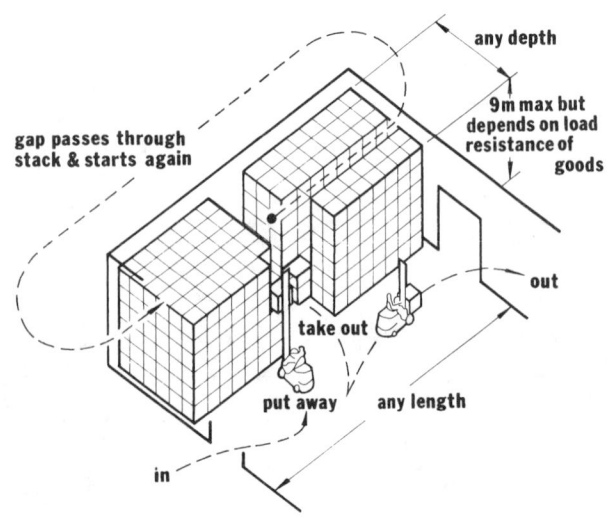

9.5 *Method of block stacking for stock rotation. Where cartons are being stacked on pallets, a height of three pallets is the normal maximum*

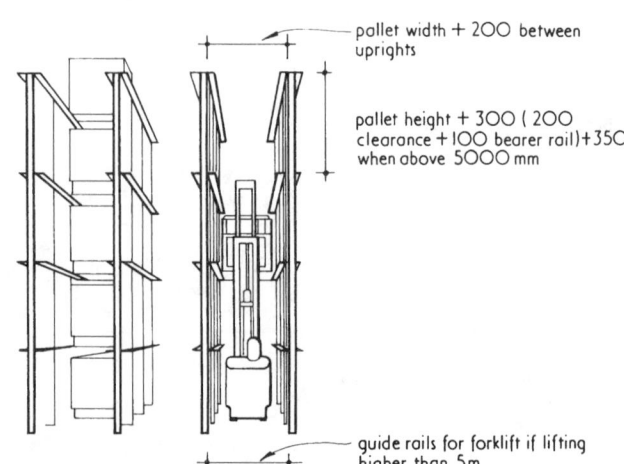

9.6 *Drive-in racking for fork-lift. A maximum depth of six pallets, with fluorescent lighting in the racking structure. Four-pallet depth is preferable*

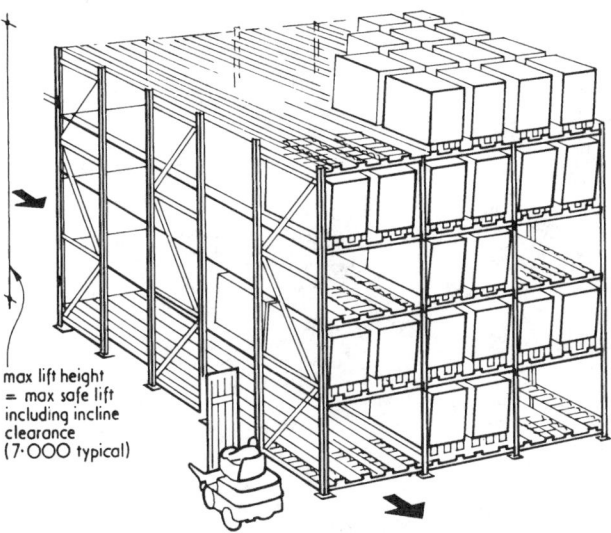

9.7 *Roll-through racking*

max lift height
= max safe lift
including incline
clearance
(7·000 typical)

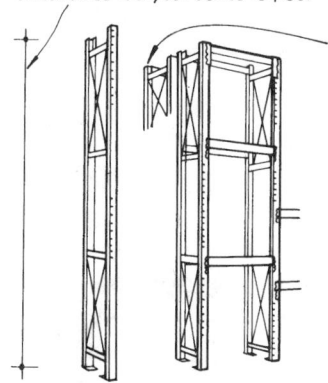

up to 6m high at 1·2t per pallet for single
unrestrained rack, but bolted to floor

can be used as double unit (back to
back) with spacers: up to 12m high,
bolted to floor

9.8 *Pallet racking*

6 DISPOSITION OF THE RACKING

There are two common alternatives:

● The rack is oriented at 90° to the order assembly areas, with the fast turnover stock in the bays nearest to it or
● One complete racking face is oriented along one side of the order assembly area and reserved for very fast-moving stock.

7 RELATIONSHIP OF STORAGE METHOD, MECHANICAL HANDLING EQUIPMENT AND BUILDING HEIGHT

The effect of handling equipment on warehouse section is shown in **9.10** to **9.13**. These factors depend on site conditions:

1 For very constricted sites where a large volume of goods needs to be held high-bay, automated warehouses can prove the most economical solution. Such warehouses have been built up to 30 m high, the racking being used as the roof and wall cladding supporting structure. Handling machines run on fixed tracks, **9.13**, **9.14**.
2 For medium- and large-scale installations where full automation is not justified, storage areas up to 12 m high allow free-standing racking (bolted to the floor) with aisle widths marginally wider than the largest pallet, **9.15**. 'Narrow-aisle trucks' used in this type of plant are free path machines based on fork-lift technology, **9.16**.
3 Where the cost of high-bay stacking and high-lift machinery is not justified, fork-lifts and reach trucks are used, **9.17**. Reach

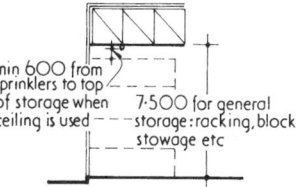

min 600 from
sprinklers to top
of storage when
ceiling is used

7·500 for general
storage: racking, block
stowage etc

9.10 *Section through small warehouse for fork-lift operation*

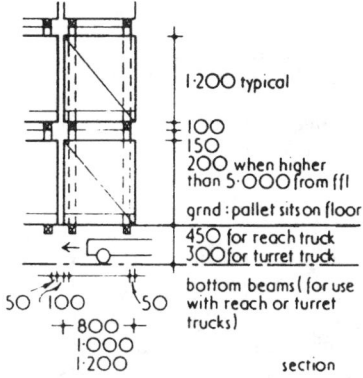

1·200 typical

100
150
200 when higher
than 5·000 from ffl

grnd: pallet sits on floor

450 for reach truck
300 for turret truck

bottom beams (for use
with reach or turret
trucks)

50 100   50
+ 800 +
1·000
1·200   section

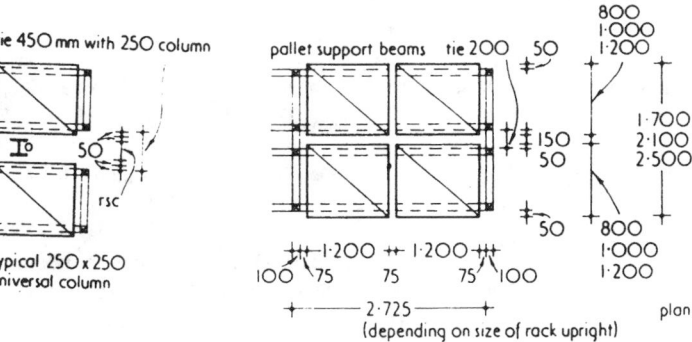

tie 450 mm with 250 column

typical 250 x 250
universal column

9.9 *Construction of
pallet racking*

pallet support beams   tie 200   50

800
1·000
1·200

150
50

1·700
2·100
2·500

50

800
1·000
1·200

100 75   75   75 100

1·200 ++ 1·200

2·725
(depending on size of rack upright)   plan

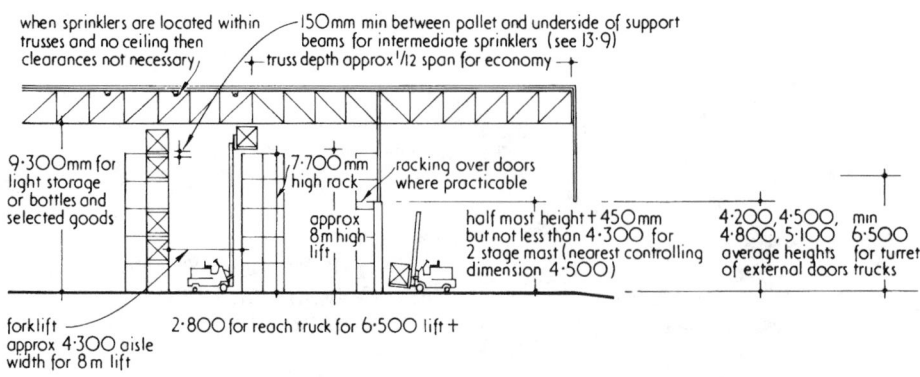

9.11 *Section through large warehouse for fork-lift or reach truck operation*

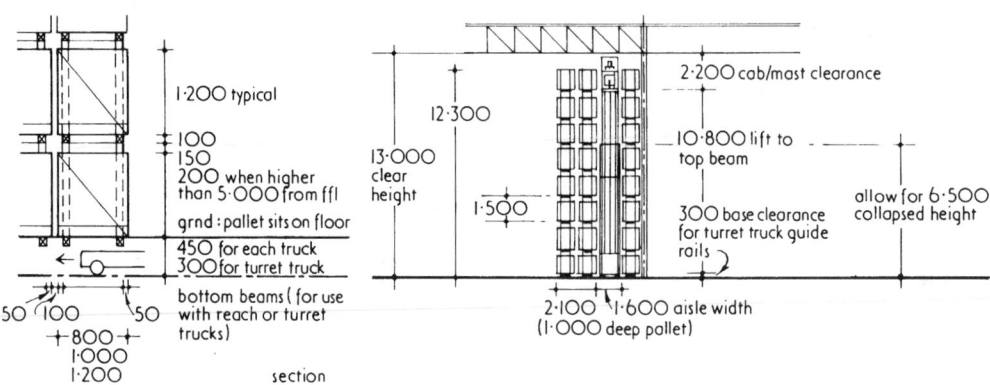

9.12 *Section through warehouse for narrow aisle truck operation. Floor tolerance ±3 mm in 3 m run*

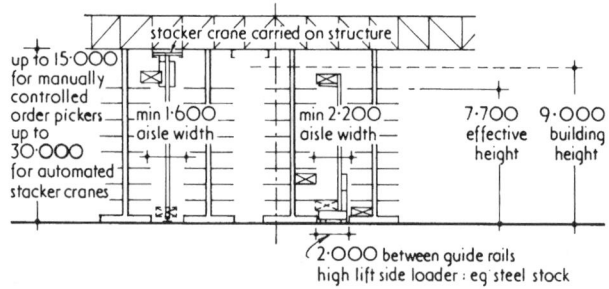

9.13 *Section through warehouse for stacker crane handling (left) and steel stockholding with side loader (right)*

trucks are suitable for conventional pallet weights (1 to 1.5 tonnes) over flat floors. They can lift to 9 m and operate in aisles of about 2.8 m. A fork-lift truck can carry heavier loads but requires aisles of 3.2 to 4 m width, **9.18**. Heavier trucks are required to lift greater heights and tend to require a greater aisle width.

4 Mobile racking where pallet racking is mounted on mobile bases and rests face to face may be suitable where storage is to be installed in an existing structure or where the site is limited in area and the turnover of products comparatively low. It is costly to install and the floor slab has to accept double the normal distributed load.

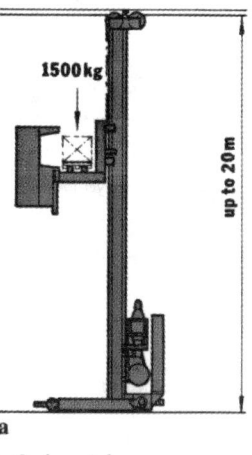

a *Order picker*

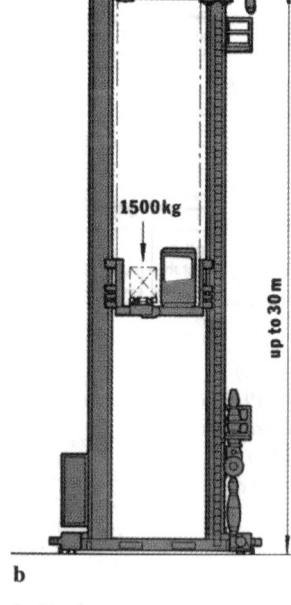

b

9.14 *Dimensions of:*   **b** *Stacker crane*

● The column pitch can be wide, **9.17** and **9.18**.
● They are more adaptable to a change of use or changes dictated by new processes
● They are more suitable for the installation of services such as cooled air.

8 OUTLINE SPECIFICATION

8.01 Storage area

Pitched roofs, though strong on first cost, waste storage volume and run the risk of being damaged by handling equipment: Three factors favour the flat or low pitch roof type:

8.02 Order picking and assembly

Space demanded will vary with the type of business involved and the method of order assembly, in turn generated by the method of despatch and transport For instance, a brewery warehouse may

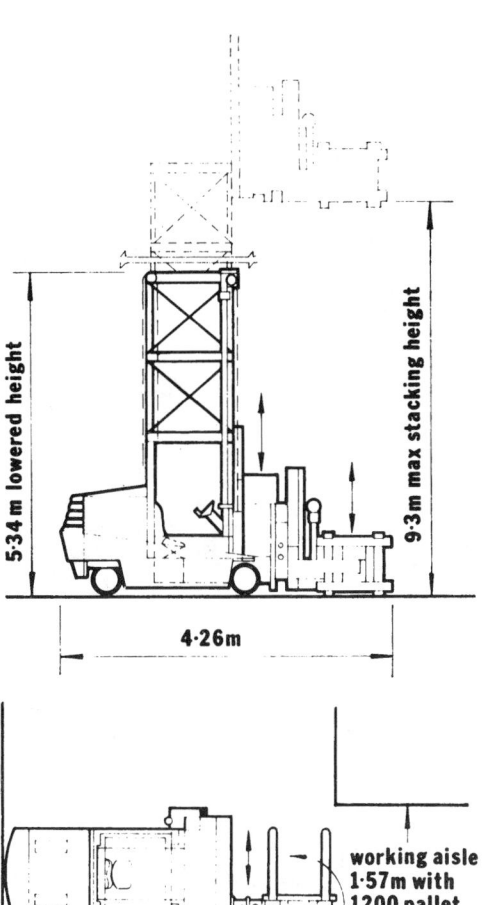

9.15 *Free path stacker/order picker with elevating cab, fixed mast and rotating fork. The four-post mast gives extra stability. Out of the aisle can also be used as a fork-lift truck. The free lift on the fork carriage also allows differential movement between the pallet and the picking platform. Minimum building height 2.2 m above top lifting level*

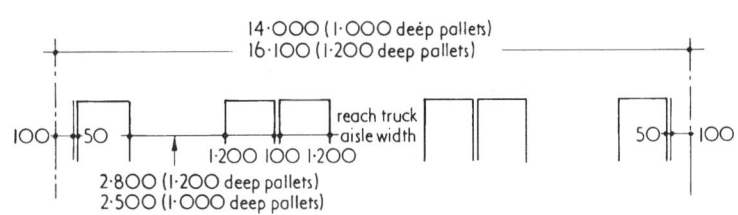

9.17 *Relationship to structure of reach truck aisles*

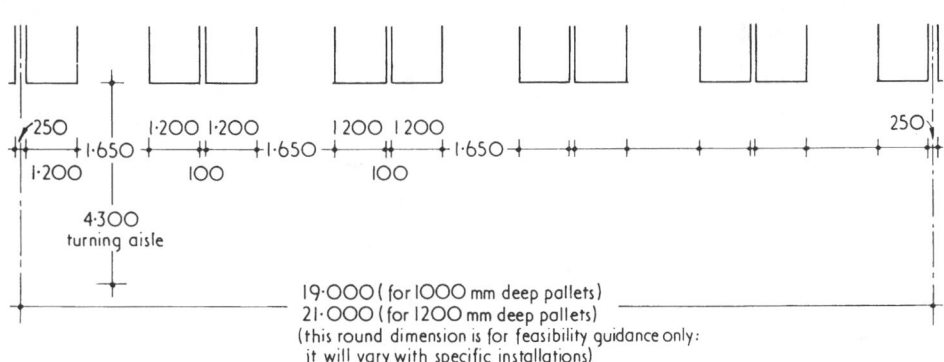

9.16 *Relationship to structure of narrow-aisle truck aisles*

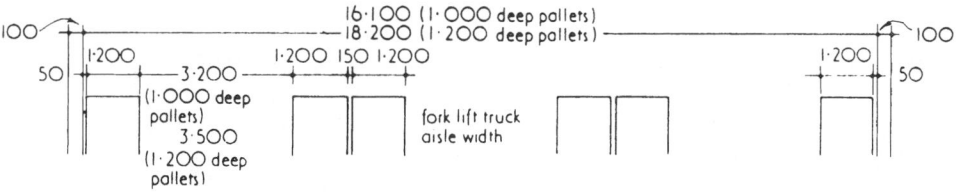

9.18 *Relationship to structure of fork-lift truck aisles. Note: 16 100 mm span is common to fork-lift and reach truck requirements*

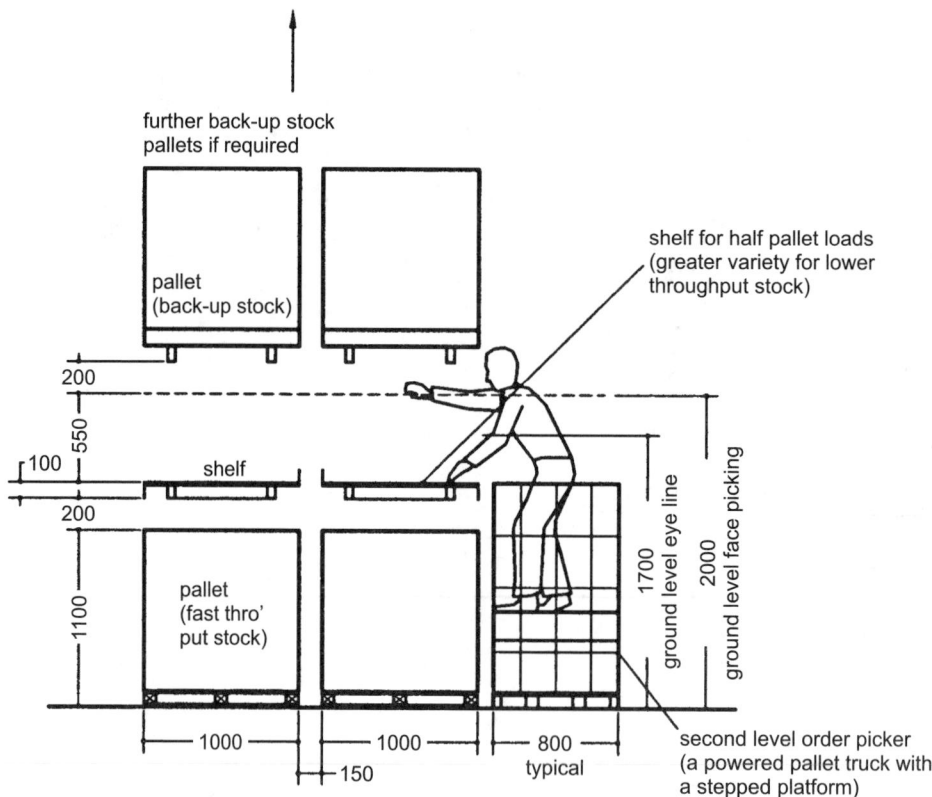

9.19 *Second level order picking, typically used for food distribution and supermarket replenishment. The operative fills a roll pallet or cage from the pallet on the floor and the shelf above it*

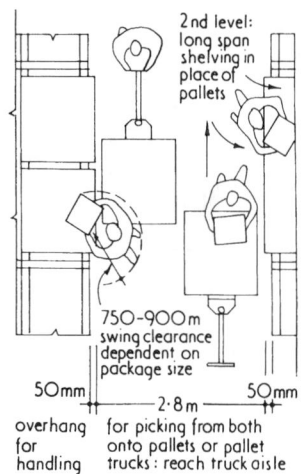

9.20 *Reach truck aisle for second-level order picking*

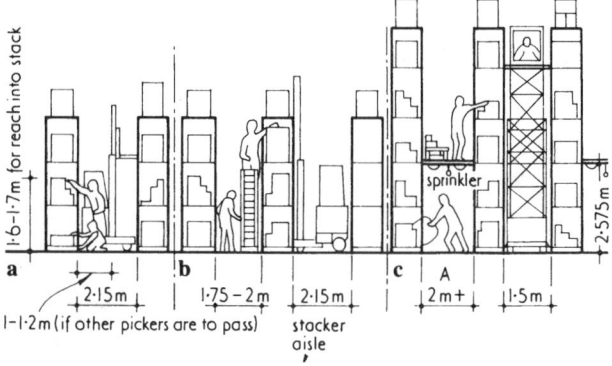

9.21 *Stacker aisles for order picking:*
a *Pulling from lower levels – replenished by stacker truck*
(9.25) b *Alternating pick-up and replenishment aisles* **c**
Multi-level alternative aisles, replenished by narrow aisle truck

despatch whole pallet loads **9.7**, but a pharmaceutical warehouse may handle and assemble a very large number of small items Therefore it may require a large area for order assembly, **9.19** to **9.21**.

8.03 Loading bay and load accumulation area
The loading bay is the critical link between the storage and distribution system (Table VI), **9.22**. It usually combines inward and despatch movements It must provide sufficient space for:

- Incoming goods to be checked off
- Empty unit load devices to be removed and
- Despatch loads to be accumulated (Table VII)

A full vehicle length (12 m) should be allowed as the zone behind the loading dock.

8.04 Office and amenity areas
Large warehouses can employ more than 100 order-picking staff (mainly female) each shift. Extensive washing and changing facilities will be required Also space for operatives to rest and smoke outside the storage area.

8.05 Equipment maintenance areas
Most mechanical handling equipment for internal use is battery-powered electric. The batteries need charging at night or after

9.22 *Combined arrival/despatch loading bays*

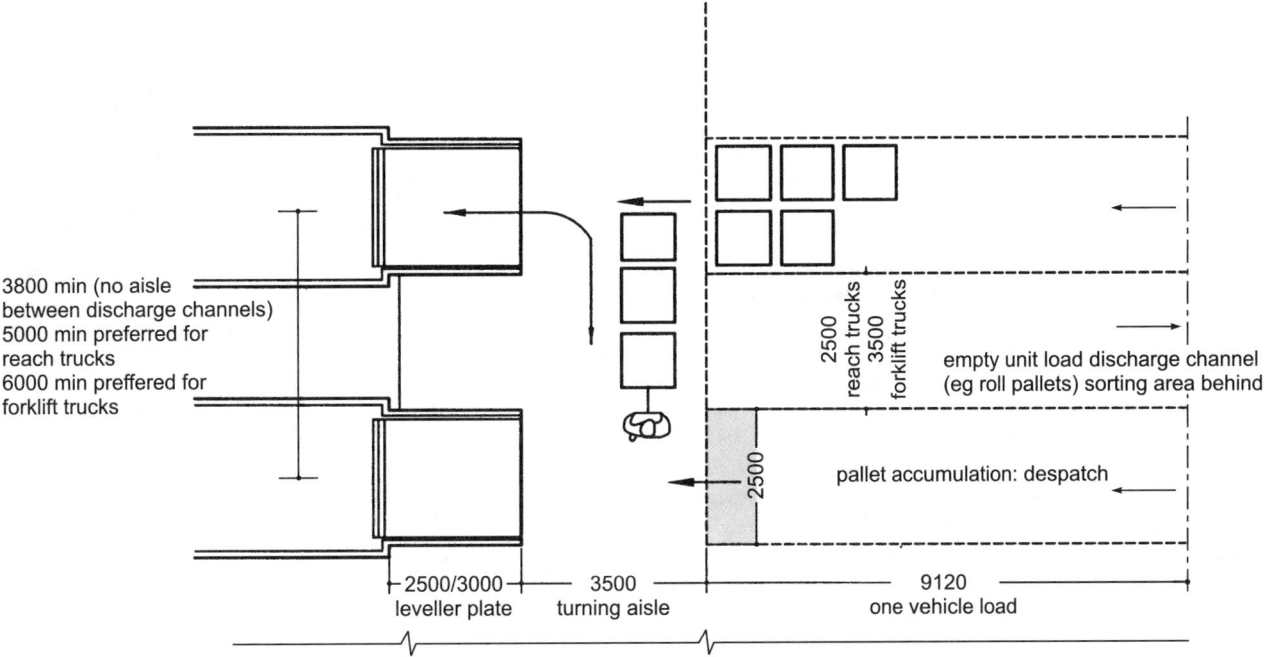

3800 min (no aisle
between discharge channels)
5000 min preferred for
reach trucks
6000 min preffered for
forklift trucks

2500 reach trucks
3500 forklift trucks

empty unit load discharge channel
(eg roll pallets) sorting area behind

2500

pallet accumulation: despatch

2500/3000
leveller plate

3500
turning aisle

9120
one vehicle load

a *Where available*

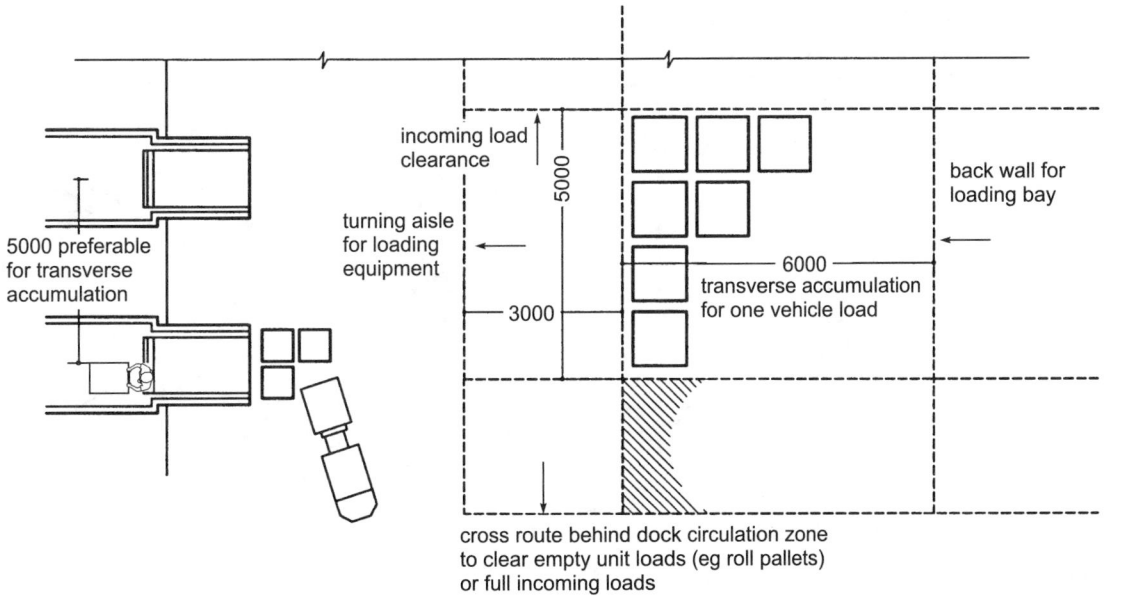

incoming load
clearance

5000

back wall for
loading bay

turning aisle
for loading
equipment

5000 preferable
for transverse
accumulation

6000
transverse accumulation
for one vehicle load

3000

cross route behind dock circulation zone
to clear empty unit loads (eg roll pallets)
or full incoming loads

b *Where depth is limited*

shifts of about 12 hours. Requirements for maintenance areas are:

- A distilled water supply
- 1 tonne hoisting tackle for removing batteries
- Fume extraction and
- Acid resistant floor.

Major services and repairs tend to be done off site.

9 SECURITY

Warehouses are, by definition, prone to theft. Most thefts are carried out during working hours This can be minimised by ensuring that:

- There is no direct access from loading bays to the warehouse, especially through the order-picking zone, without supervision
- Access from office accommodation to the warehouse should be visible from the office area
- The changing rooms, showers (necessary in cold stores) and WCs should not have direct access from the warehouse, and equally, should not be accessible from outside. Visiting drivers should have segregated WC facilities
- If small, valuable goods are involved, a search room may be required
- Operatives' parking should be well separated from heavy vehicles' parking and away from the loading area.

10 HANDLING EQUIPMENT

Some typical handling equipment is shown in **9.23** to **9.27**.

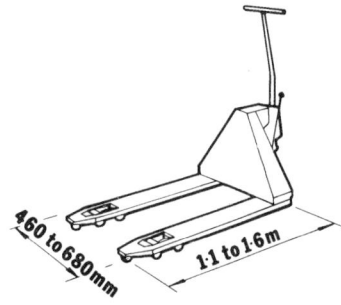

9.23 *Manual pallet truck. For use inside the warehouse building up orders, loading vehicles on raised docks or with tail-lifts, general pallet handling. Increasingly used in retail premises for handling bulk goods. Capacity up to 1500 kg generally and for short-distance travel (operatives soon tire when pushing heavy loads any distance). Forklengths available 0.8 to 1.6 m, widths from 460 to 680 mm. Heights: lowered 83 mm, raised 203 mm. Pallet width should be 150 mm over fork (typical length is 1.06 m for a 1.2 m pallet). Where gangways are narrow and stability is important, a heavy truck should be used with maximum width between forks. This device will turn in its own length but needs additional clearance for overhangs. Normally it requires level floors to operate satisfactorily, but large wheels in nylon or with solid rubber tyres plus articulating axles are available for use in older buildings; although instability may occur. Steel wheels are available but are less popular. Where loading ramps are used, pallet trucks with brakes should be used. Adaptors are available for use as a stillage truck*

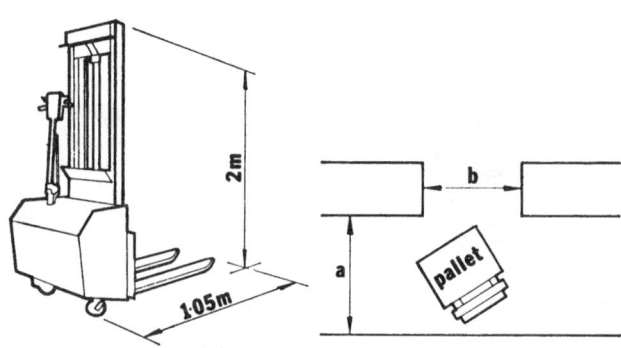

9.25 *Power travel and lift pedestrian-controlled stacker truck. When travelling the pallet rests on the stacker frame which has travel wheels. Power lifting is independent of the travel frame, and is directly into the rack. Only suitable for short travel distances. Lifting range up to 3.6 m. Can be supplied with attachments. Capacity up to 1500 kg at 600 mm centres, straddle width 0.86 to 1.3 m, travel speed up to 4.8 km/h laden. Will turn with full load on 2.1 m aisle*

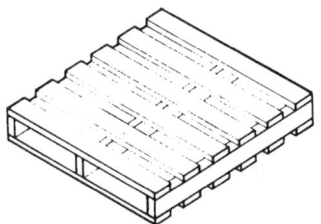

a *Two-way entry pallet*

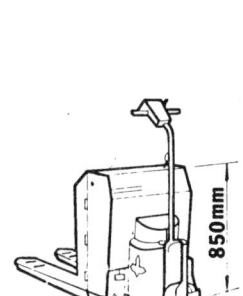 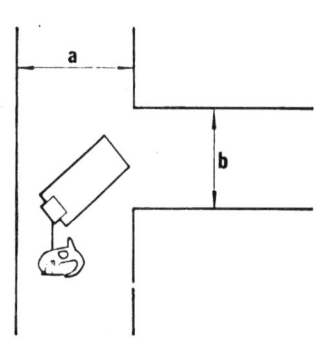

9.24 *Powered pallet truck. For internal transfer, loading vehicles on docks, order build-up, transporting roll pallets to load assembly position. For use with all types of pallet and cages. Capacity 1800 to 3000 kg, forklengths 0.75 to 1.8 m, speeds up to 3.6 km/h running light, widths up to 850 mm, usually 760 mm. Long forks available to carry three roll pallets at once. Special forks for drums and paper rolls. Will turn in its own length but needs additional clearance for overhangs. Some have 200° turn on the single power steering wheel. Aisle width depends on forklength:*
a *(90° stacking aisle) = 1840 mm (truck + 1 m pallet)*
b *(intersecting aisle) = 1570 mm*
Turning circle 1.78 m radius with 960 mm long forks. This device requires level floors and a three-phase charging point. It can manage ramps up to 10 per cent. Some larger-capacity units can also be ridden on, and can tow non-powered pallet trucks if long distances are involved

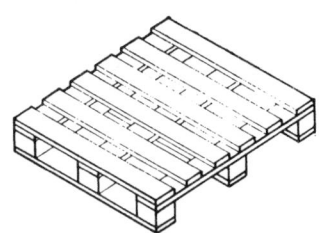

b *Four-way entry pallet*

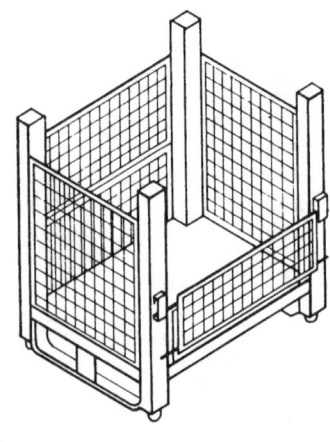

c *Post pallet*

9.26 *Types of pallet*

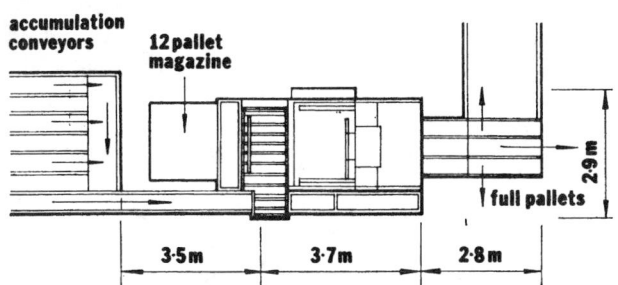

9.27 *Plan of typical palletising machine. Top right is buffer track required for slower shrink wrapper*

11 BIBLIOGRAPHY

Peter Falconer and Jolyon Drury, *Industrial Storage and Distribution* (AJ handbook of industrial storage), London, Architectural Press, 1975
Factories Act 1961, HMSO
Offices, Shops and Railway Premises Act 1963, HMSO
Insulation Act 1972
Health and Safety at Work, etc. Act 1974, HMSO
Fire Offices Committee, *Rules for automatic sprinkler installations*, 29th edition, revised 1973

10 Farm buildings

Based on information provided by John Weller and others

CI/SfB 26
UDC 728.94

John Weller is an architect specialising in rural work

KEY POINTS:
- *Farming is an industry subject to continual change*
- *Animal welfare and concern about pollution is leading to legislative constraints, both domestic and European*

Contents
1 Introduction
2 Farm animals
3 Farm machinery
4 Dairy cattle housing
5 Beef cattle and calf housing
6 Sheep housing
7 Pig housing
8 Poultry housing
9 Crop storage and effluent produced
10 Building legislation

1 INTRODUCTION

1.01 The agricultural economy
Agriculture in the UK and also in the rest of Europe (particularly in the west) is becoming big business. Small farms and small farmers are becoming increasingly rare; marginal land is coming out of production. Owners of hitherto agricultural land are seeking other revenue-earning uses such as golf courses.

1.02 Planning
Buildings, irrespective of the enterprise, should be planned in terms of their functions for storage, processing or production. Food, like other industrial processes, should be designed for materials handling and flowline production. Superimposing linear buildings within or over traditional courtyard forms is both a visual and a tactical problem.

Stock housing produces effluents. Farm waste management is an essential part of the building design and increasingly subject to statutory control. Wastes should normally be recycled, provided that this is done safely.

1.03 Building functions
Depending on managerial philosophy, building functions may be specialist, semi-specialist or flexible in their form. Farmers tend to equate flexibility with general-purpose layouts and with low capital investments; this can be a false equation. The loss of quality control, often difficult to evaluate, makes most 'cheap umbrellas' poor performers for specific end products.

The demand for flexibility reflects two factors – lack of confidence in politicians' ability to maintain stable markets, and the rapidity of technical change. UK food production is essentially in the hands of the EU (via CAP, the Common Agricultural Policy), which aims at market stability. Technical change is liable to continue, although expansion of power demand may become more selective.

1.04 Stock housing and storage requirements
In simple terms, most storage requirements are those of containers: cylinders, bins and bunkers. Wide-span portals are suitable for some layouts for cattle, bulk storage and implements. Compact and insulated 'boxes' of low profile are best for calves, pigs or poultry. They may include total or partial environmental control. In contrast, 'kennels' are cheaply framed, semi-open, mono-pitch structures suitable for some cattle and pig layouts.

1.05 Construction and procurement
Most buildings are partially or wholly prefabicated, or are purchased under package deals. Standard frames can be obtained 'off the shelf', and infilled by 'self-build'.

Performance specifications are rare. Overall costs are lower than for most buildings of similar type, partly due to lower standards being demanded (see BS 5502, Buildings and structures for agriculture, in its many parts).

1.06 Lifespan of buildings
Most pre-1960 buildings are inefficient for modern production and many traditional buildings are redundant. A few are suitable for casual storage, administration, isolation units, or spare boxes. The issue of redundancy is not easy to resolve. Some historic barns have been dismantled and relocated. Tourism, recreation and craft work are all encouraged in rural areas. A tenth of all farms have some tourist income. In upland areas, it may be the principal source of income. Farm planning should allow for alternative uses for buildings and land.

The normal economic life for farm buildings is ten years, though some are depreciated over five. This is a major design constraint. Some estates may permit a longer term of 20 to 60 years, especially for 'umbrella' enclosures. Grants are available for all except plastic, cheap tents and for factory farms (i.e. without supporting land). EU grants are more generous but require carefully prepared development proposals.

1.07 Appearance
Farm building appearance, especially since many are exempt from control and since most are cheap compared to other building types, is a contentious issue. Simple forms, good colour, defined planes, and coordinated fittings such as vent pipes and flues, combined with careful siting and landscaping, make buildings acceptable. However, large roof surfaces are likely to conflict with vernacular buildings and can, near rising land, become dominant. Component design is often poor and unrelated to the basic structure. Surrounds to buildings, including yards, tanks, fences, etc. are often more unsightly than the buildings.

1.08 Criteria
Farm management in relation to resources of land area and terrain, climate, soil, capital, etc., is such that every farm building problem is different, despite prefabrication, package deals and BS 5502. In many enterprises, it is difficult to establish a good design brief, but the basic layout, **10.1**, shows the relationships between the elements of the farm and the main service road. **10.2** shows a typical farm.

10-1

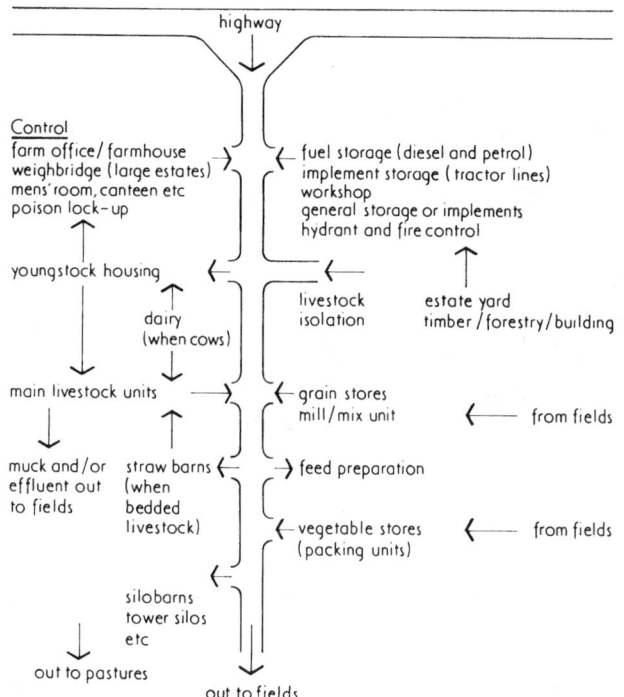

10.1 *Basic layout, mixed arable and stock farm. Although the arrangement shown has been stylised, in fact farms are usually linear to the main service road*

2 FARM ANIMALS

Average sizes and weights of animals are shown in **10.3**. Width of animal given is normal trough space allowed (i.e. about two-thirds of overall width). Length given is normal standing (not fully extended).

3 FARM MACHINERY

Average sizes and weights of tractors and other machinery are given in **10.4**.

4 DAIRY CATTLE HOUSING

Table I gives dimensions for cattle housing; examples suitable for a 120-cattle unit are shown in **10.5** and **10.6**. A typical cubicle house is 27 m wide × 55 m long plus 10 m turn area at one end plus a 4 m road. A 'kennel' has the same basic dimensions but the roof is lower and is held by the cubicle division and the passage is not completely roofed, as **10.7**. Various systems of milking parlour are shown in **10.8**. Rotary parlours are now considered obsolete, and the current favourite is the herringbone, **10.9**.

5 BEEF CATTLE AND CALF HOUSING

Strawed and slatted yards for beef cattle are shown in **10.10** and **10.11**. A calf house is illustrated in **10.12**, and **10.13** is a 'general-purpose' strawed yard for cattle (700 mm/head for manger for adults, 500 mm for yearlings).

10.2 *Typical farm: Wilcove:*

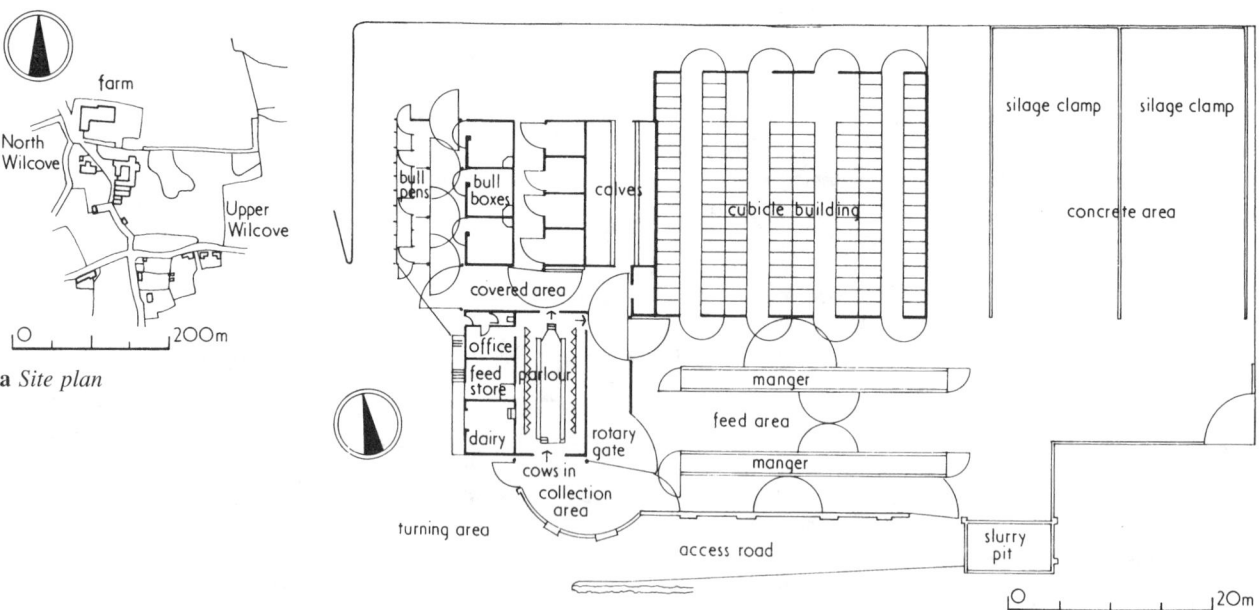

a *Site plan*

b *Plan*

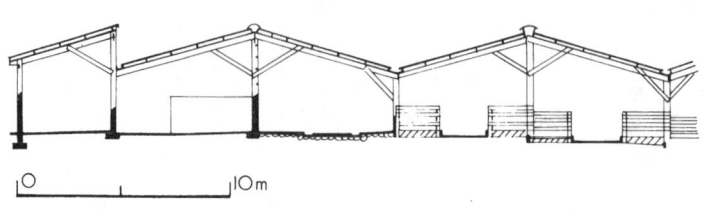

c *Part cross-section*

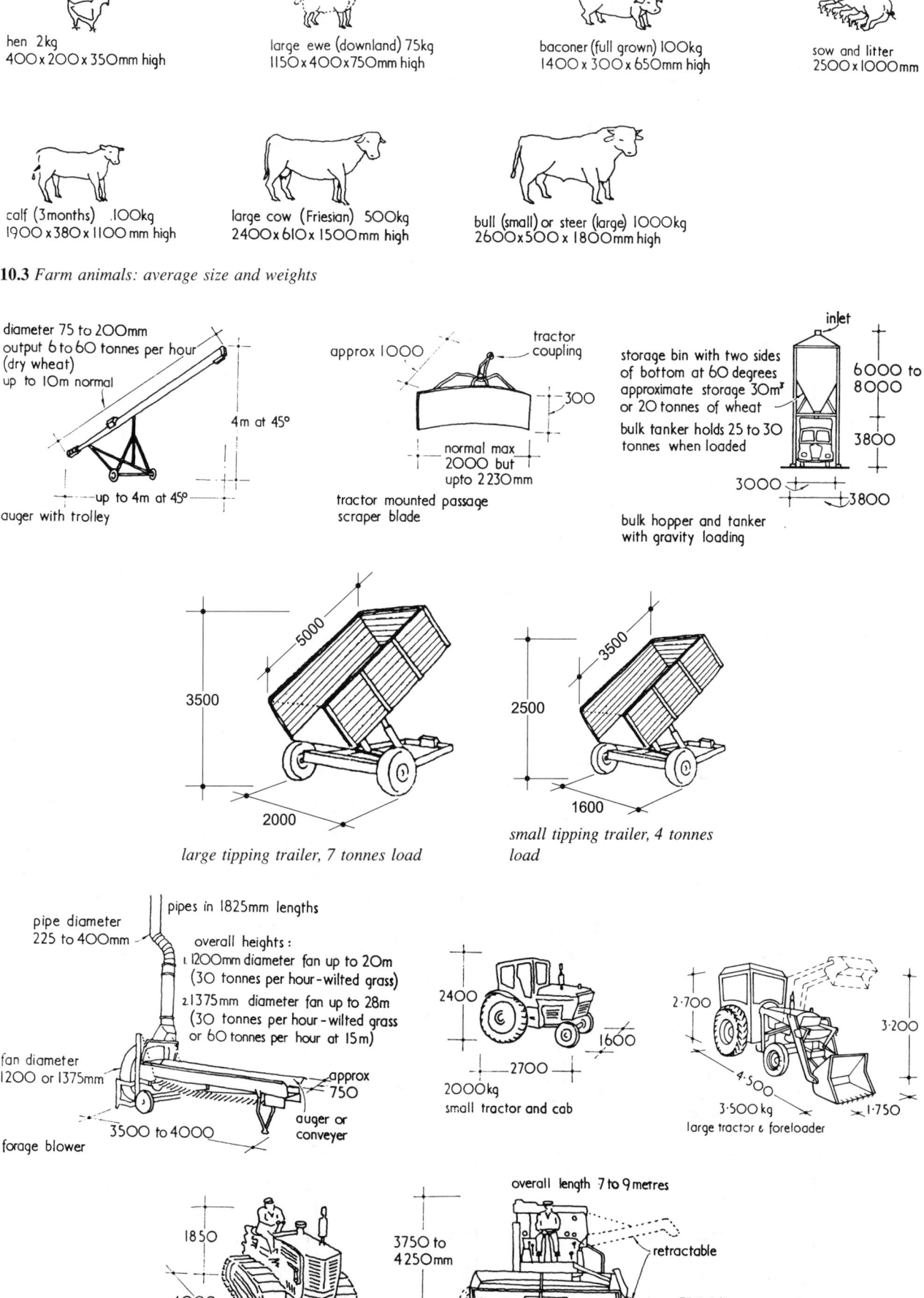

hen 2kg
400 x 200 x 350mm high

large ewe (downland) 75kg
1150 x 400 x 750mm high

baconer (full grown) 100kg
1400 x 300 x 650mm high

sow and litter
2500 x 1000mm

calf (3months) 100kg
1900 x 380 x 1100 mm high

large cow (Friesian) 500kg
2400 x 610 x 1500mm high

bull (small) or steer (large) 1000kg
2600 x 500 x 1800mm high

10.3 *Farm animals: average size and weights*

diameter 75 to 200mm
output 6 to 60 tonnes per hour
(dry wheat)
up to 10m normal

4m at 45°

up to 4m at 45°

auger with trolley

approx 1000

tractor coupling

300

normal max 2000 but upto 2230mm

tractor mounted passage scraper blade

inlet

storage bin with two sides of bottom at 60 degrees approximate storage 30m³ or 20 tonnes of wheat

bulk tanker holds 25 to 30 tonnes when loaded

6000 to 8000

3800

3000

3800

bulk hopper and tanker with gravity loading

5000

3500

2000

large tipping trailer, 7 tonnes load

3500

2500

1600

small tipping trailer, 4 tonnes load

pipes in 1825mm lengths

pipe diameter 225 to 400mm

overall heights:
1 1200mm diameter fan up to 20m (30 tonnes per hour - wilted grass)
2 1375mm diameter fan up to 28m (30 tonnes per hour - wilted grass or 60 tonnes per hour at 15m)

fan diameter 1200 or 1375mm

approx 750

auger or conveyer

3500 to 4000

forage blower

2400

1600

2700

2000kg
small tractor and cab

2·700

3·200

4·500

3·500 kg

1·750

large tractor & foreloader

1850

4000

5000kg

2400

large crawler

overall length 7 to 9 metres

3750 to 4250mm

retractable

3500 kg
(upto 5500kg loaded)

2500 to 4500mm
(cutter bar 3000mm normal)

combine harvester

10.4 *Farm machinery: average weights and sizes*

Table I Dimensions of cattle housing

Mass of cow (kg)	Dimensions of cubicles (m)			Dimensions of cowsheds (m)					
	Length including kerb	Length behind trough	Minimum clear width between partitions	Length of standing without trough	Length of standing behind 0.75 to 0.9 wide trough	Clear width between stall divisions of a two-cow standing	Gangway width	Minimum width of feed passage (if any)	Longitudinal fall along gangway and dung channel
350–500	2.00	1.45	1.00	2.00	1.45	2.00	single range: 2.0	0.9	1 per cent
500–600	2.15	1.60	1.10	2.15	1.60	2.15			
600–650	2.30	1.80	1.15	2.30	1.80	2.40	double range: 3.0		
650–700	2.30	1.80	1.15						
700–800	2.50	2.00	1.20						

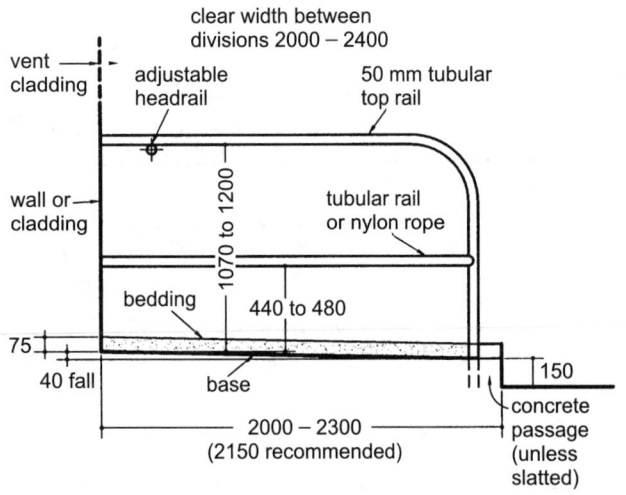

10.5 *Section showing cubicle division: dimensions for Friesian cows*

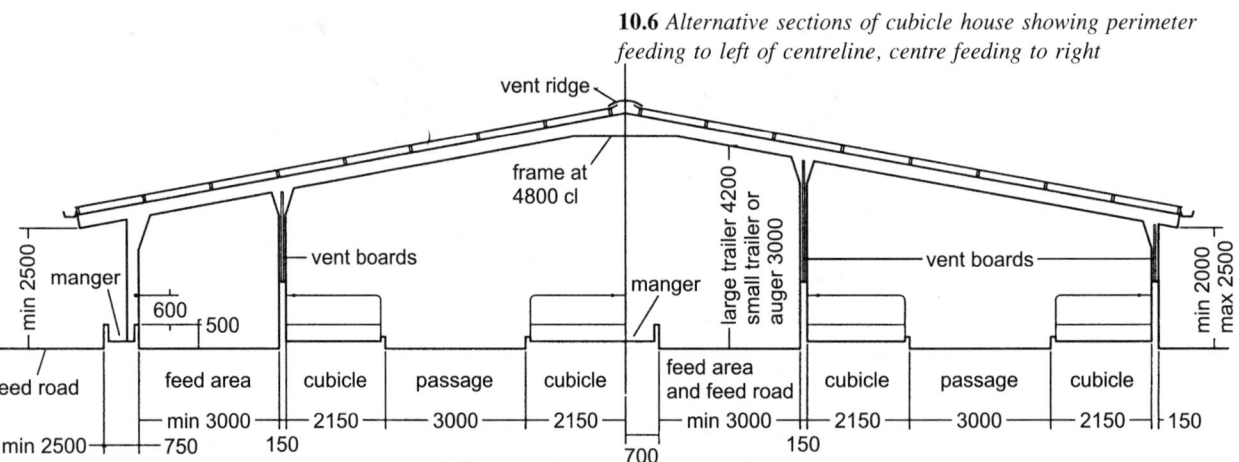

10.6 *Alternative sections of cubicle house showing perimeter feeding to left of centreline, centre feeding to right*

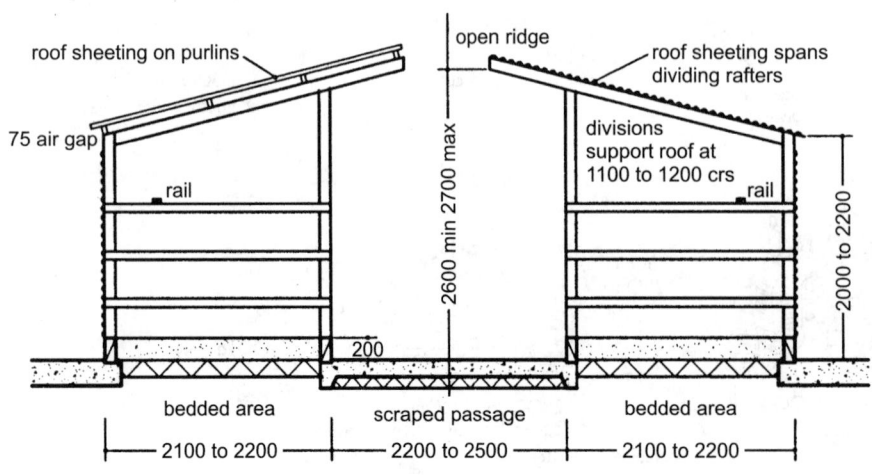

10.7 *Section through kennel for beef or dairy cattle*

10.8 *Milking parlour systems:*

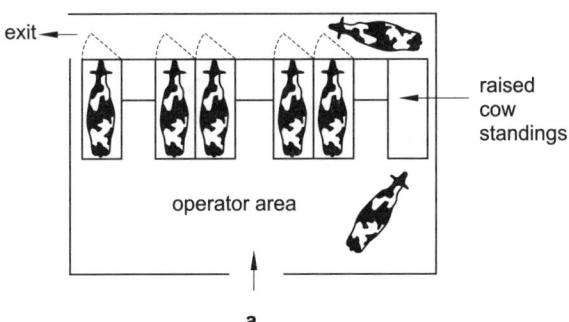

a *abreast*

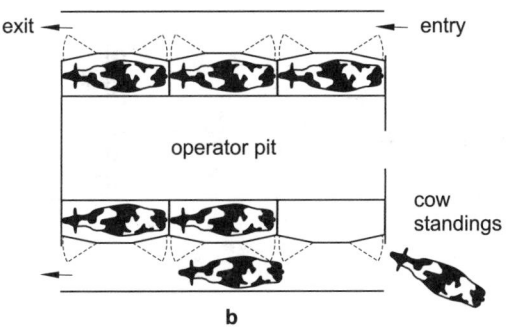

b *tandem*

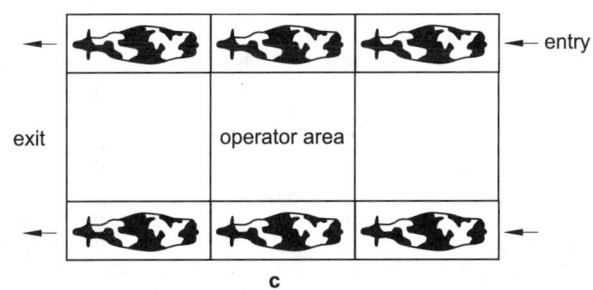

c *chute*

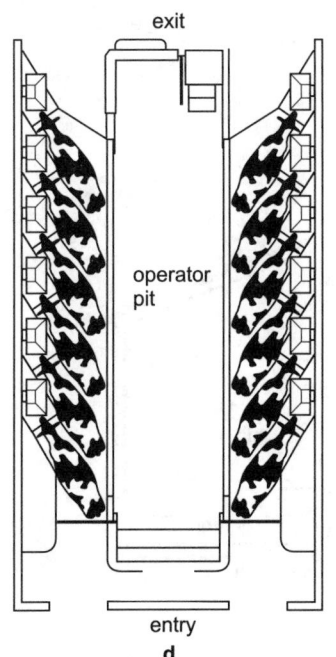

d *herringbone*

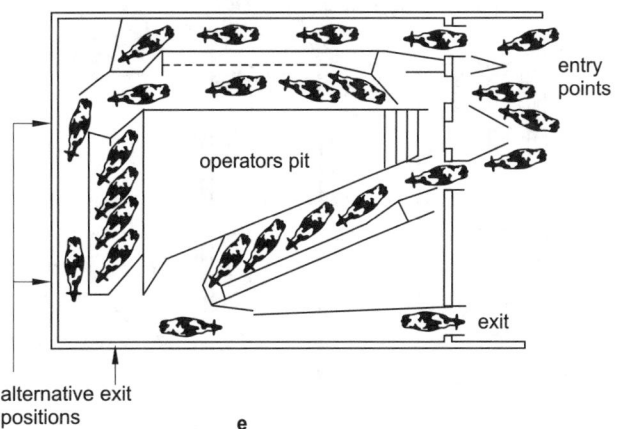

e *trigon*

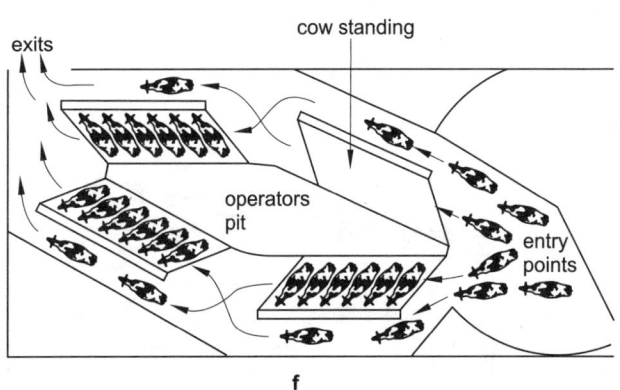

f *polygon*

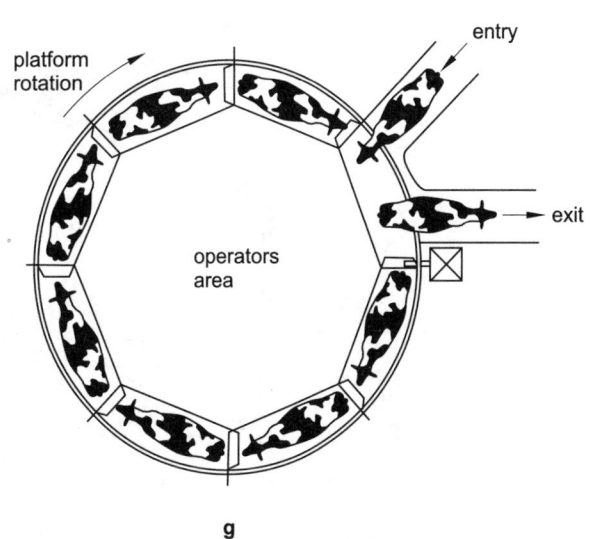

g *rotary*

10.9 *Herringbone system milking parlour:*

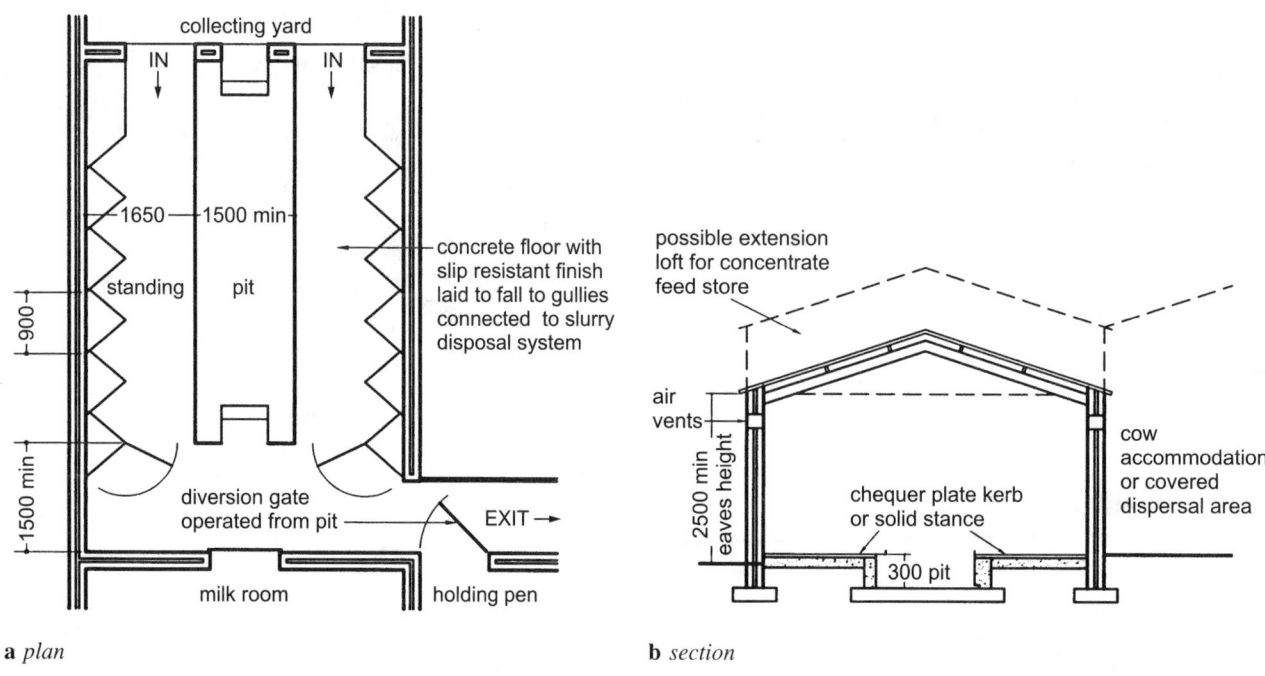

a *plan*   **b** *section*

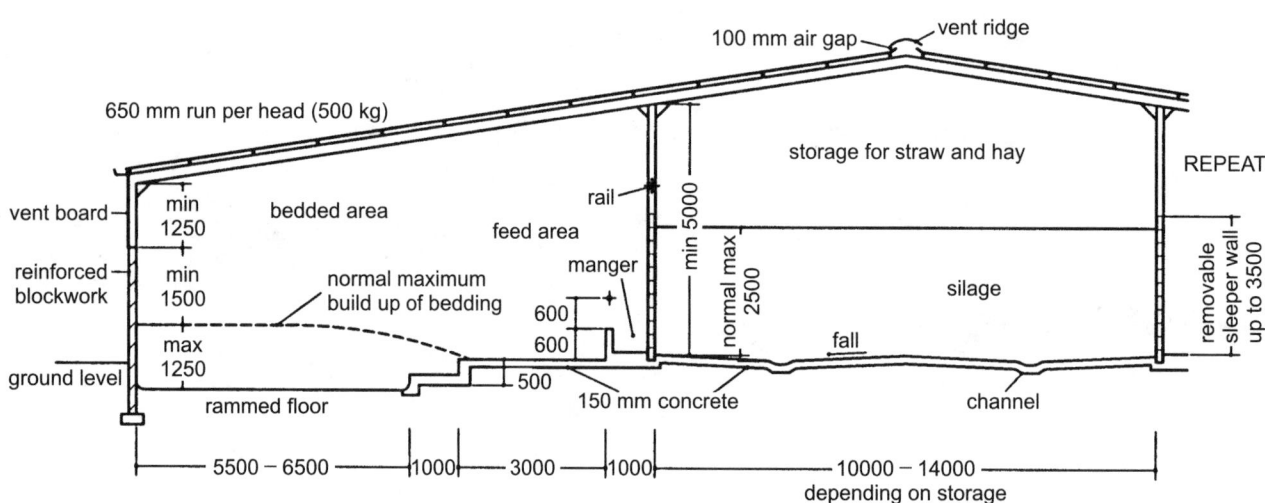

10.10 *Section through strawed yard for beef cattle with easy feeding*

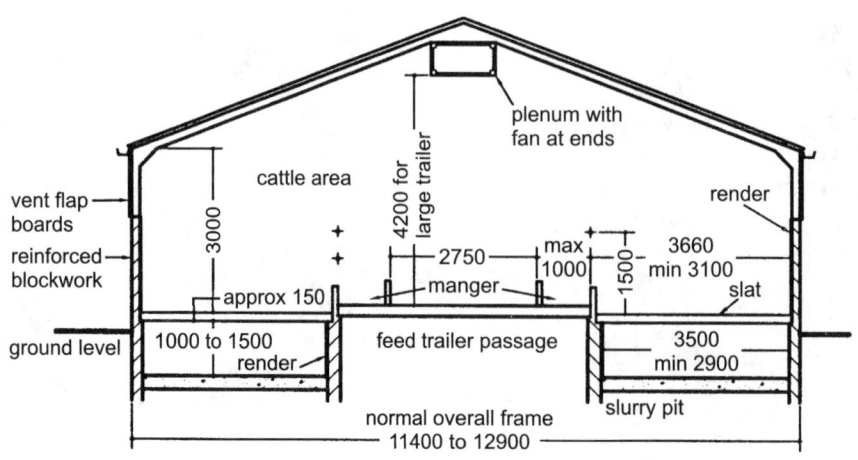

10.11 *Section through slatted yard for beef using self-unloading trailers. Note: fully slatted yards are not approved by Brambell Committee*

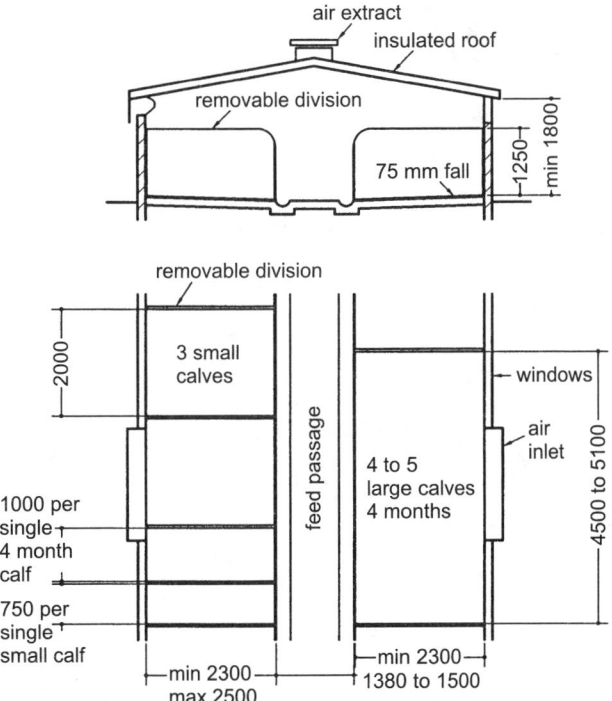

10.12 *Plan and section of calf house*

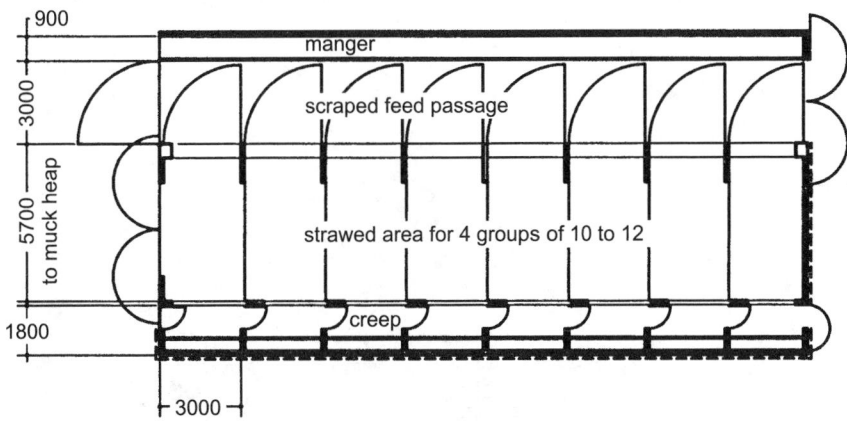

10.13 *Plan of general purpose strawed yard for cattle*

Table II Sheep housing

Type of sheep	Age or mass	Area per animal (m²)		Length of trough (mm) depending on feeding system		
		Perforated floor	Solid floor with straw	Compounds/ concentrates	Ad lib hay/silage	Big bale silage, self-feed
Pregnant ewes	45–60 kg	0.8	1.0	400	175	100
	60–75 kg	0.9	1.2	460	200	150
	75–90 kg	1.1	1.4	500	225	150
Ewes with lambs	Individually penned	–	2.2			
	Groups, 45 kg ewe	1.0	1.3	420	175	100
	Groups, 68 kg ewe	1.4	1.7	460	200	150
	Grouped, 90 kg ewe	1.7	1.8	500	225	150
Lambs	Individually penned	–	2.1			
	Group housed	–	1.5			
	Creep area at 2 weeks	–	0.15			
	Creep area at 4 weeks	–	0.4			
Hoggs	20–30 kg	0.5	0.7	300	125	100
	30–40 kg	0.6	0.8	350	150	100
	40–50 kg	0.8	0.9	400	175	100

6 SHEEP HOUSING

Required dimensions are given in Table II. A section through sheep housing is shown in 10.14. A dipping tank suitable for large breeds is shown in 10.15.

7 PIG HOUSING

Table III covers the dimensional requirements. Three types of fattening house are shown in 10.16 to 10.18, and two types of farrowing house in 10.19 and 10.20.

8 POULTRY HOUSING

Dimensions are given in Table IV. Rearing, fattening and egg houses are shown in 10.21 to 10.25 and a pole barn for fattening turkeys in 10.26.

9 CROP STORAGE AND EFFLUENT PRODUCED

Some typical feed and produce stores are shown in 10.27 to 10.34. Table V indicates the scope of manure likely to be produced.

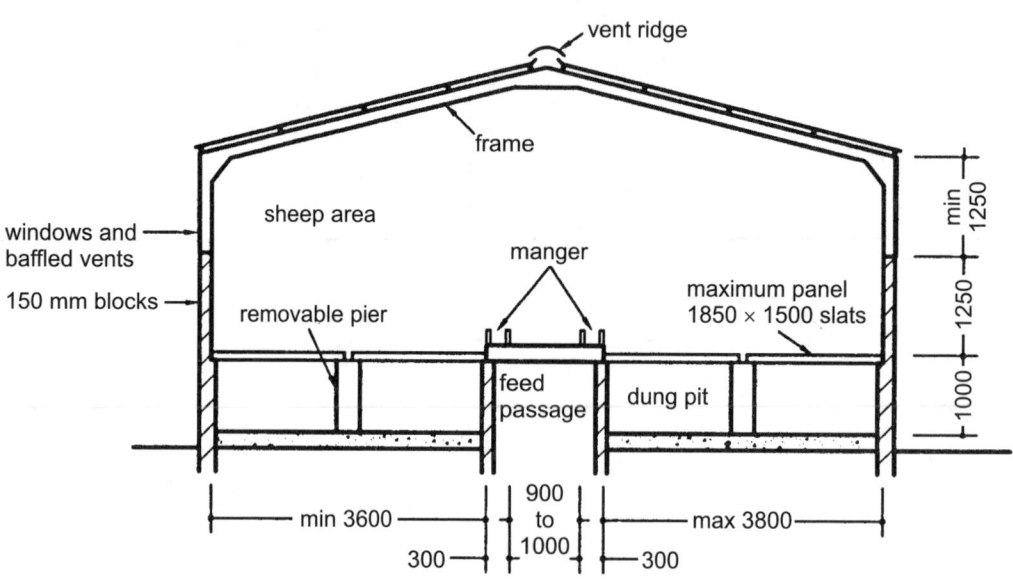

10.14 *Sheep housing, manger run per head:*
fattening lamb 300 mm
ewe and lamb 400 mm
yearling 500 mm

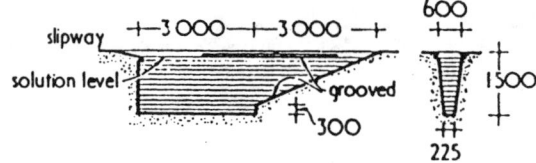

10.15 *Sections through dipping tank for large breed ewes.*
Allow 2.25 litres of solution per head

Table III Pig housing: dimensions required for ten animals

Typical age (days)	Mass (kg)	Type	Lying area (m²)	Min dung area (m²)	Total (m²)	Trough length (mm)	Lying pan depth (mm)
0	1.5	Piglets			1.3/litter	500	
20	5	Early weaners			1.75/litter	500	
35	9	Weaners	0.7	0.3	1.0	600	1170
65	20	Weaners	1.5	0.6	2.1	1750	860
115	50	Porkers	3.5	1.0	4.5	2250	1560
140	70	Cutters	4.6	1.6	6.2	2750	1280
160	85	Baconers	5.5	2.0	7.5	3000	1840
185	110	Heavy hogs	6.7	2.3	9.0	4000	1680
210	140	Overweight	8.5	3.0	11.5	5000	1700
–	–	Dry sows	15.0	5.0	20.0		3000
–	–	In-pig sows	15.0	5.0	20.0		3000
–	–	Boar			8.0/boar	500/boar	

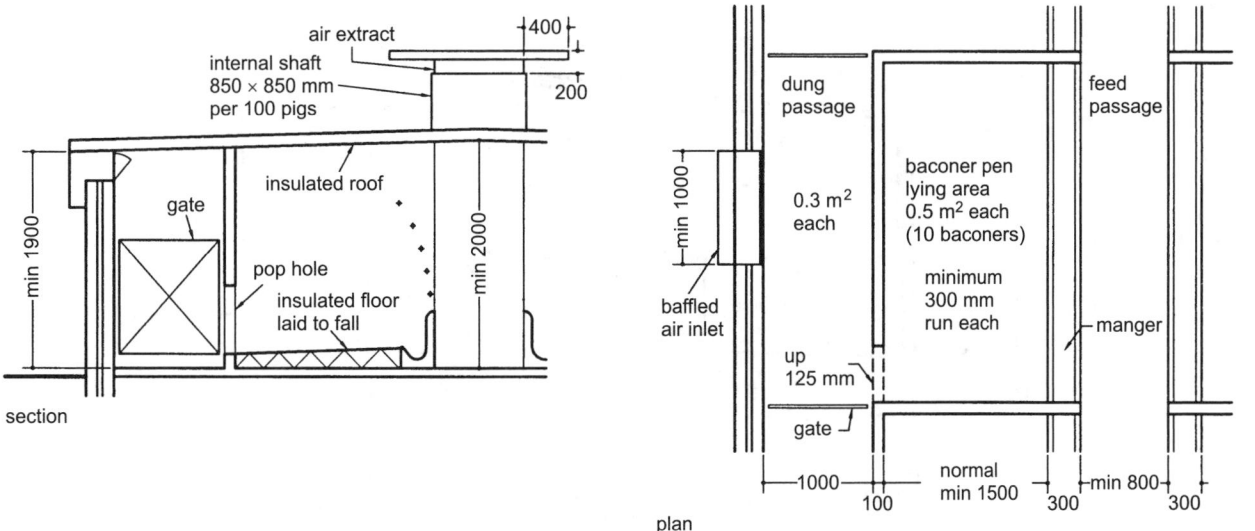

10.16 *Plan and section of fattening house with side dung passage*

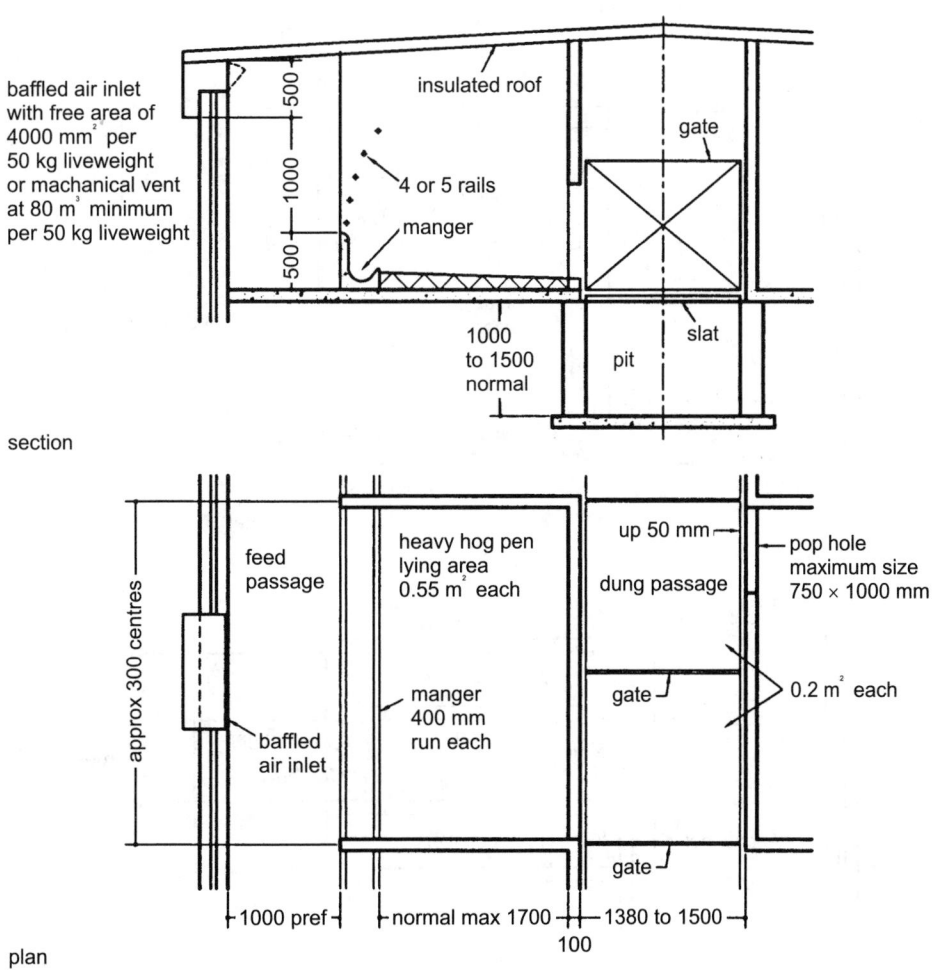

10.17 *Plan and section of fattening house with centre slatted dung passage*

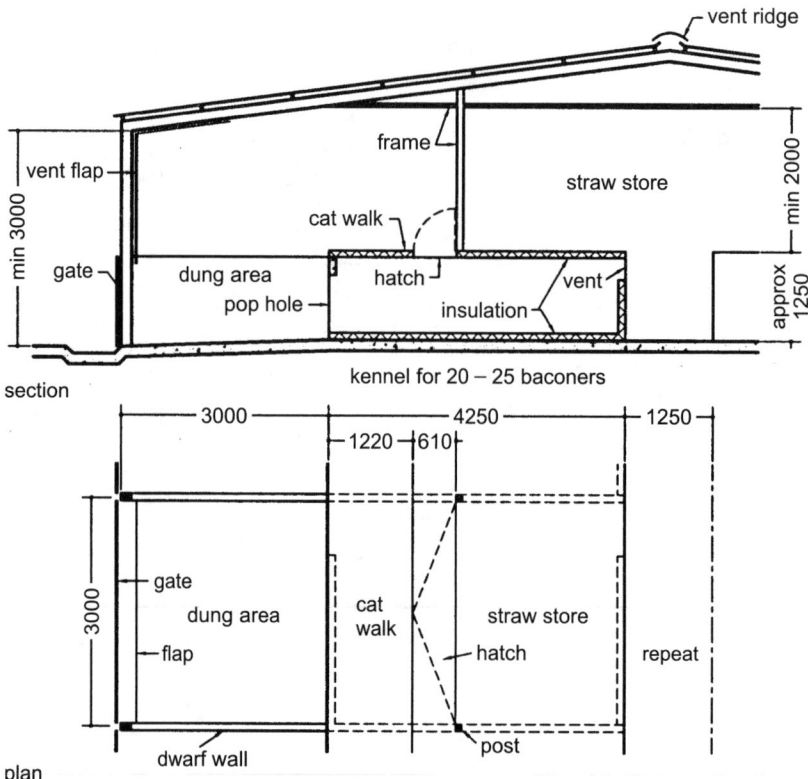

10.18 *Plan and section of fattening house with strawed system and floor feeding*

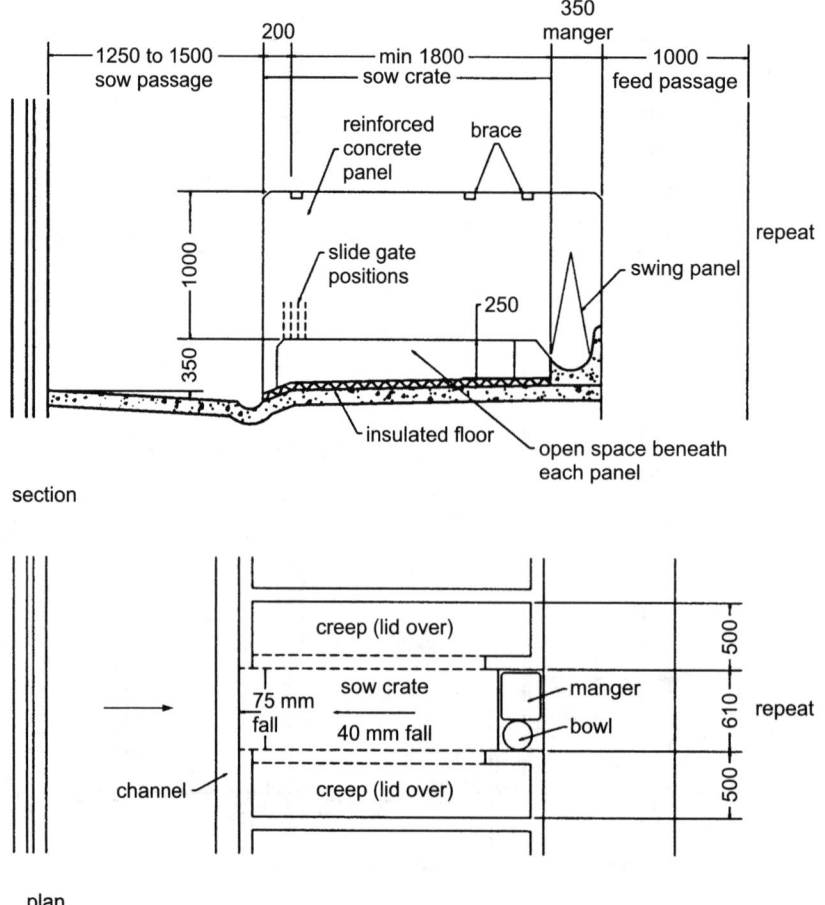

10.19 *Plan and section of permanent crate farrowing house*

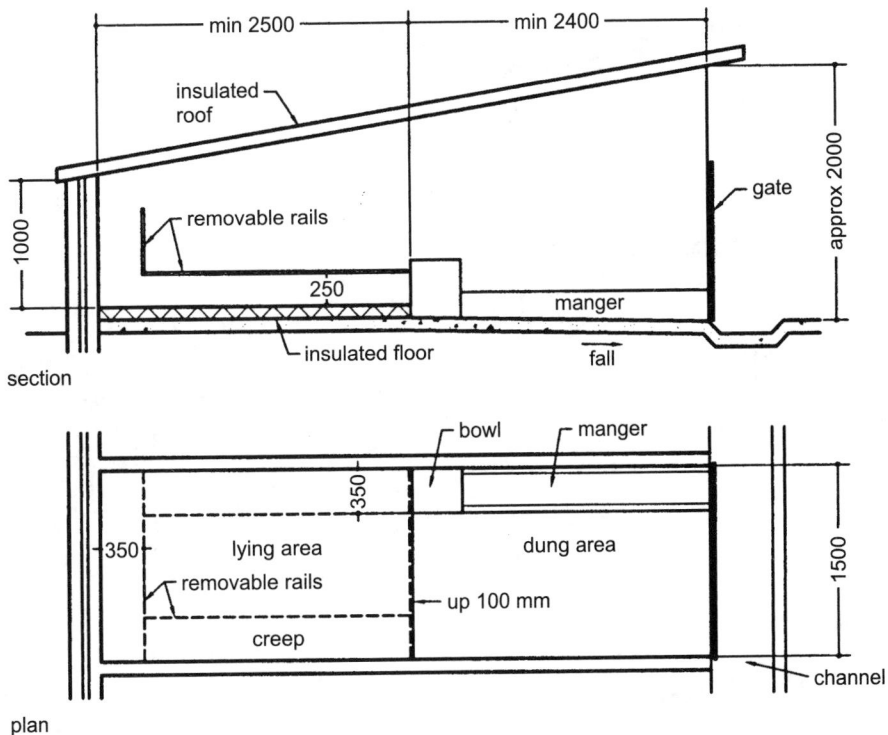

10.20 *Plan and section of Soleri open front farrowing house*

Table IV Poultry housing

System	Species/cage numbers	0–4 weeks	4–8 weeks	9–16 weeks
Battery or tier brooder and cooling cage	One hen in cage	0.1	0.1	0.1–0.43
	Two hens in cage	0.075	0.09	0.1–0.43
	Three hens in cage	0.055	0.09	0.1–0.43
	Four hens in cage	0.043	0.09	0.1–0.43
Floor rearing on litter	Layers	0.025	0.09	0.18–0.28
	Broilers		0.09	
	Turkeys	0.09	0.14	0.37–0.46
	Ducks	0.09	Free range	
Part wire or slatted floor rearing		0.015	0.09	0.09–0.14
Trough length (mm)	Birds in cages	100		
	Layers	30	40	60
	Broilers	30	50	75
	Turkeys	36	73	73
	Ducks	55	122	Free range

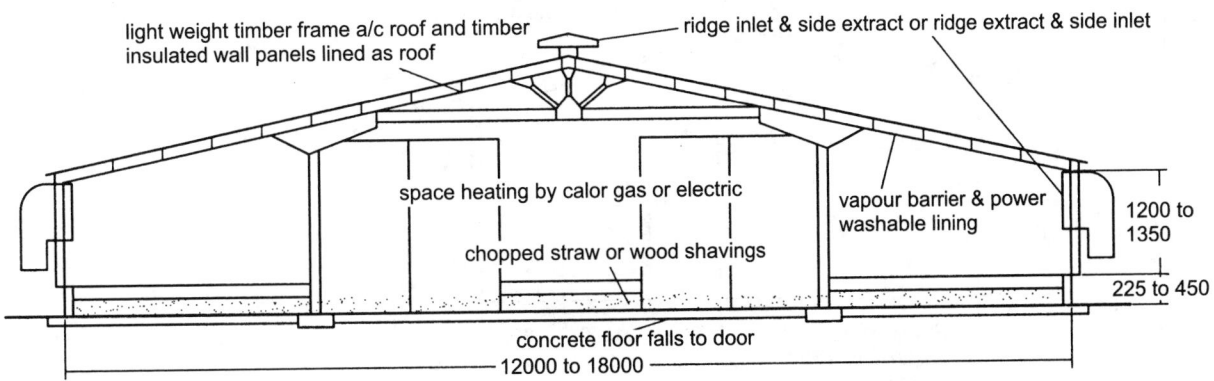

10.21 *Section through poultry broiler and rearing house. Roof insulated with minimum 25 mm rigid polyurethane or equivalent. Stocking density 10 birds/m², RH 60 per cent, temperature 30°C*

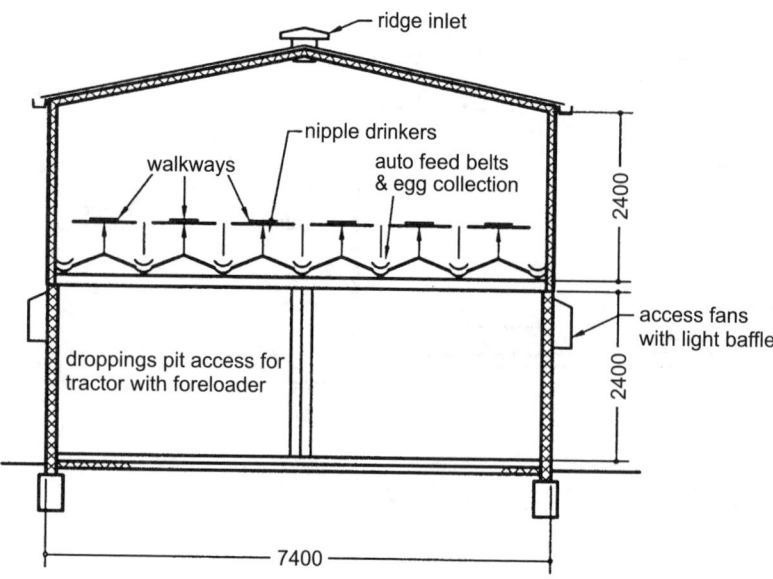

ridge inlet

nipple drinkers

walkways

auto feed belts & egg collection

access fans with light baffle

droppings pit access for tractor with foreloader

2400

2400

7400

10.22 *Section through flat deck deep pit battery house. Roof insulated with minimum 25 mm rigid polyurethane or equivalent. Stocking at 100 mm trough per bird in multibird cages for light hybrids, 125 mm for heavier birds. RH 60 per cent, temperature 20–25°C. If falls to 12° does not harm output but increases food conversion ratio*

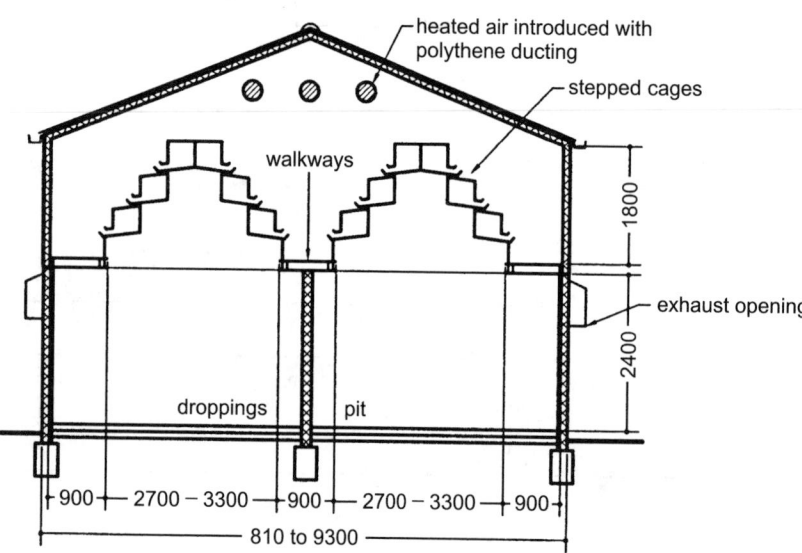

heated air introduced with polythene ducting

stepped cages

walkways

exhaust opening

droppings pit

1800

2400

900 — 2700 – 3300 — 900 — 2700 – 3300 — 900

810 to 9300

10.23 *Section through California cage deep pit battery house. Roof insulated with minimum 25 mm rigid polyurethane or equivalent*

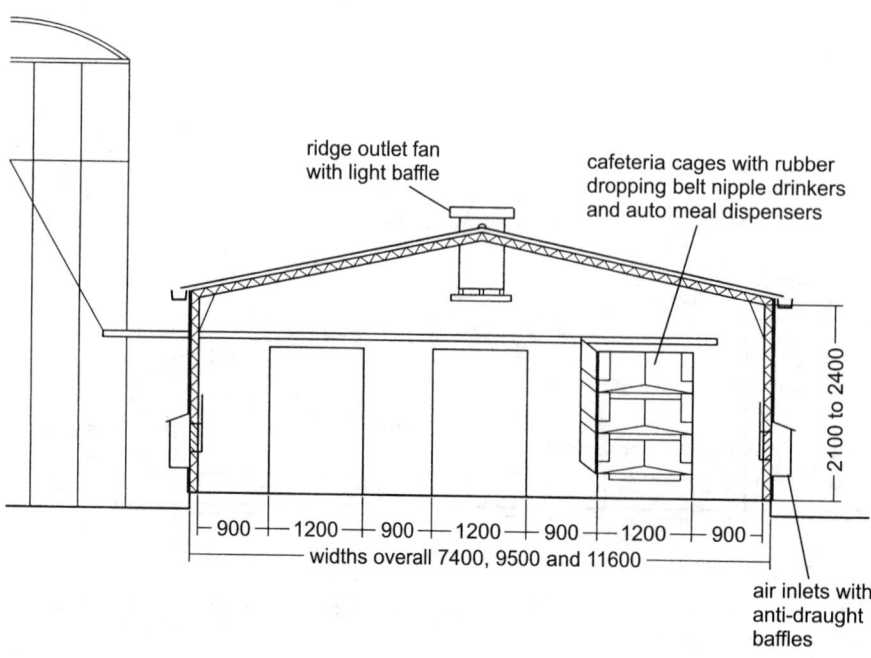

ridge outlet fan with light baffle

cafeteria cages with rubber dropping belt nipple drinkers and auto meal dispensers

2100 to 2400

900 — 1200 — 900 — 1200 — 900 — 1200 — 900

widths overall 7400, 9500 and 11600

air inlets with anti-draught baffles

10.24 *Section through cafeteria cage battery house*

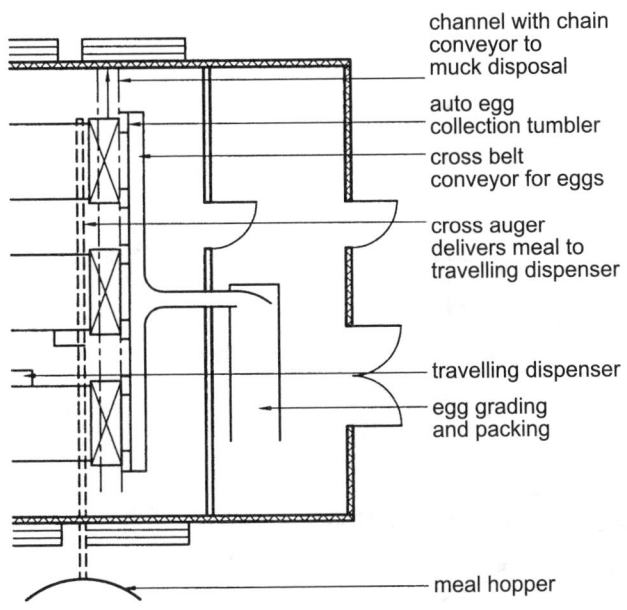

channel with chain conveyor to muck disposal

auto egg collection tumbler

cross belt conveyor for eggs

cross auger delivers meal to travelling dispenser

travelling dispenser

egg grading and packing

meal hopper

10.25 *Plan of end of cafeteria cage battery house showing gear*

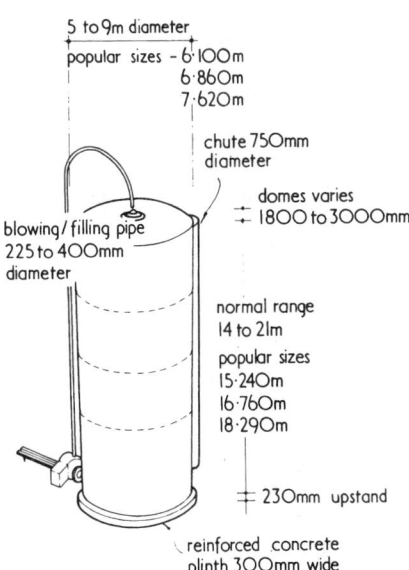

5 to 9m diameter
popular sizes - 6·100m
6·860m
7·620m

chute 750mm diameter

domes varies 1800 to 3000mm

blowing/filling pipe 225 to 400mm diameter

normal range 14 to 21m
popular sizes 15·240m
16·760m
18·290m

230mm upstand

reinforced concrete plinth 300mm wide

10.27 *Tower silo for wilted grass with 40–50 per cent dry matter. Wet grass is stored in towers of 6 m diameter × under 12 m height*

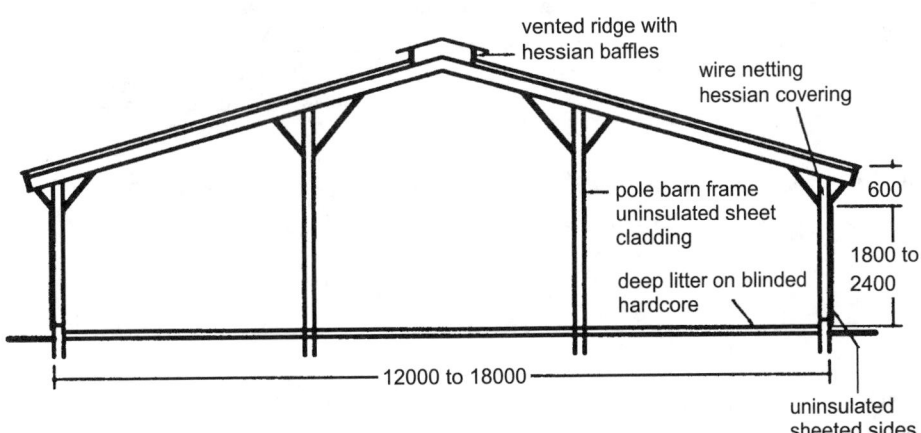

vented ridge with hessian baffles

wire netting hessian covering

pole barn frame uninsulated sheet cladding

deep litter on blinded hardcore

600

1800 to 2400

12000 to 18000

uninsulated sheeted sides

10.26 *Section through pole barn for fattening turkeys. Stocking density 30 kg/m²*

Table V Average production of effluent

		Production per head per week					
		Mass kg	Output litres	Volume m³	Total solids kg	BOD kg	BOD population equivalent
Man	Adult	75	10	0.01	0.57	0.41	1.0
Cow	Dairy	450	250	0.25	21.20	4.20	10.2
Cow	Large dairy	550	380	0.38	32.22	6.13	14.8
Calf	3-month	100	200	0.20	19.05	2.54	6.2
Pig	Porker	50	38	0.04	3.00	1.20	2.0
Pig	Baconer	95	51	0.05	3.50	1.40	3.4
Pig	Wet-fed	95	100	0.10	3.50	1.40	3.4
Pig	Farrow sow	110	75	0.08	3.60	1.45	3.6
Poultry	Adult layer	2.25	3.75	0.005	1.27	0.09	0.13
Sheep	Adult ewe	75	35	0.04	3.81	0.70	1.7
Silage	30% dry matter	tonne	3.20	0.001	–	–	–
Silage	20% dry matter	tonne	37.00	0.04	–	–	–

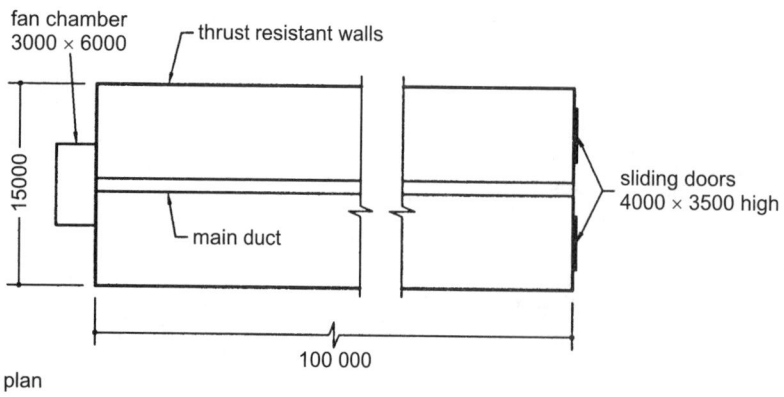

fan chamber
3000 × 6000

thrust resistant walls

15000

main duct

sliding doors
4000 × 3500 high

100 000

plan

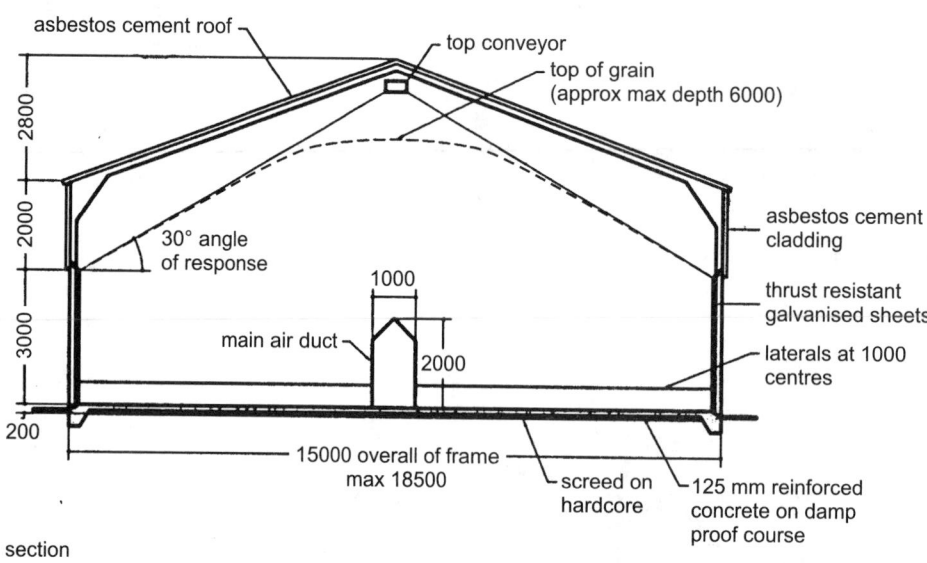

asbestos cement roof

top conveyor

top of grain
(approx max depth 6000)

2800

2000

3000

30° angle
of response

main air duct

1000

2000

asbestos cement
cladding

thrust resistant
galvanised sheets

laterals at 1000
centres

200

15000 overall of frame
max 18500

screed on
hardcore

125 mm reinforced
concrete on damp
proof course

section

10.28 *Plan and section of storage for food grain., showing lateral system for 1200 tonnes storage*

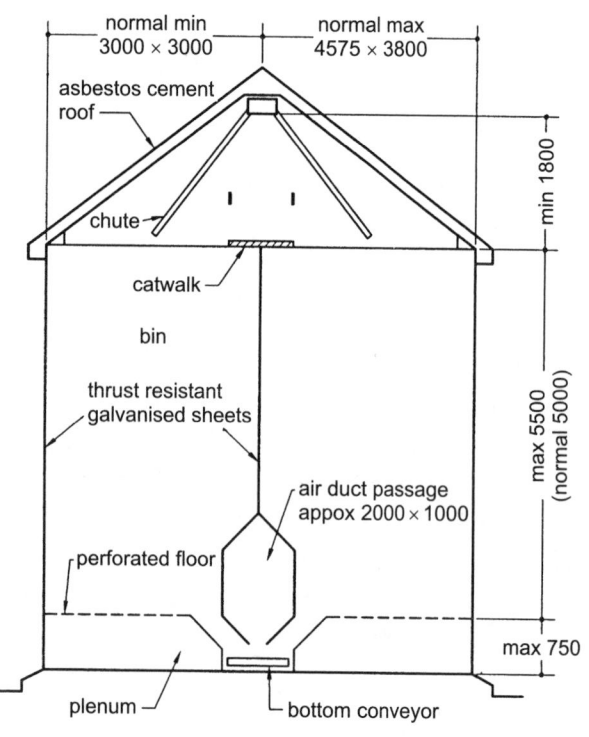

normal min
3000 × 3000

normal max
4575 × 3800

asbestos cement
roof

min 1800

chute

catwalk

bin

thrust resistant
galvanised sheets

air duct passage
appox 2000 × 1000

max 5500
(normal 5000)

perforated floor

max 750

plenum

bottom conveyor

10.29 *Grain drying and storage: section through a nest of bins (square or rectangular) with roof. A bin 4.575 × 3.8 × 5 m holds 60 tonnes of wheat*

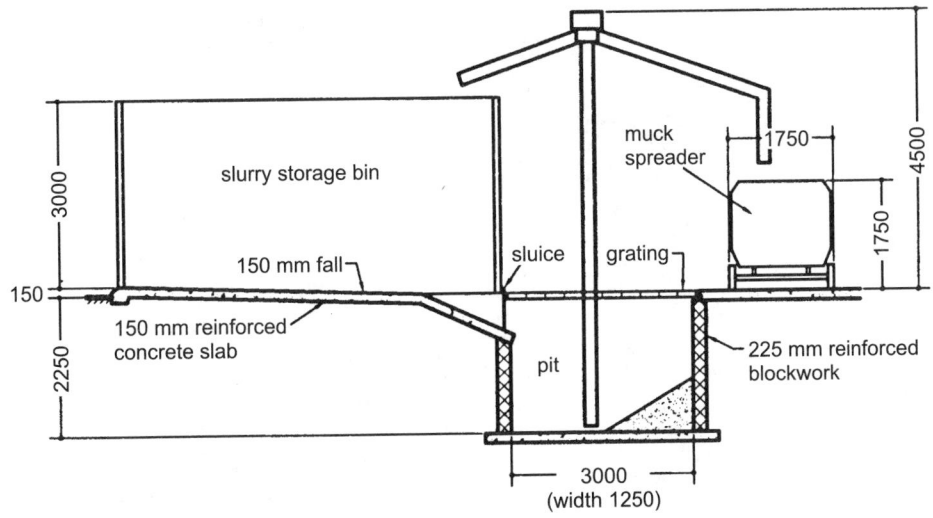

10.30 *Section through above-ground slurry storage.*
Capacities: 4575 mm diameter – 50 m³
                    6100 mm diameter – 88 m²
                    6860 mm diameter – 110 m³

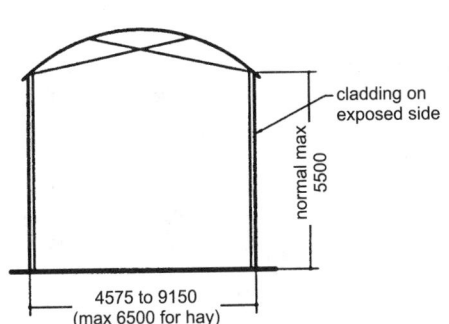

10.31 *Section through Dutch barn for bale storage. The capacities of a 4.575 m bay at 6.5 m span and 5.5 m high are:*
wheat straw – 12 tonnes
barley straw – 14 tonnes
hay – 27 tonnes

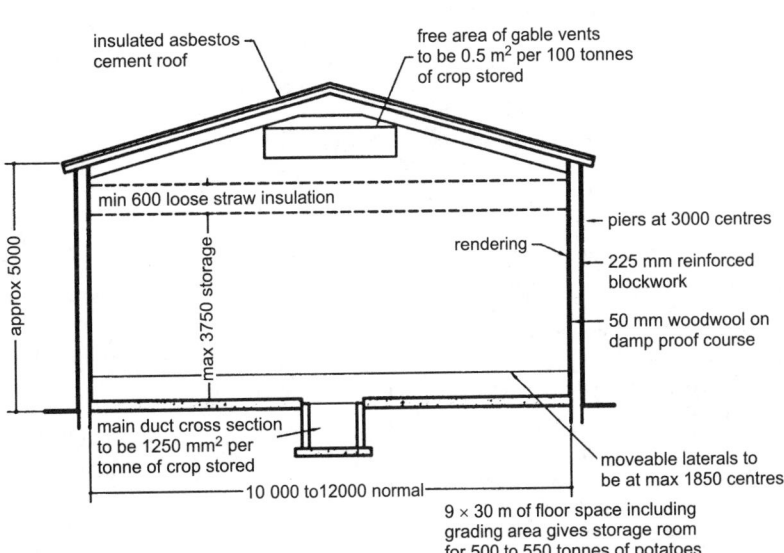

10.32 *Section through floor storage for potatoes. 9 × 30 m of floor space stores 500–550 tonnes. Movable laterals maximum 1.85 m centres. Free area of gable vents 0.5 m²/100 tonnes stored, main duct cross-section 1250 mm²/tonne*

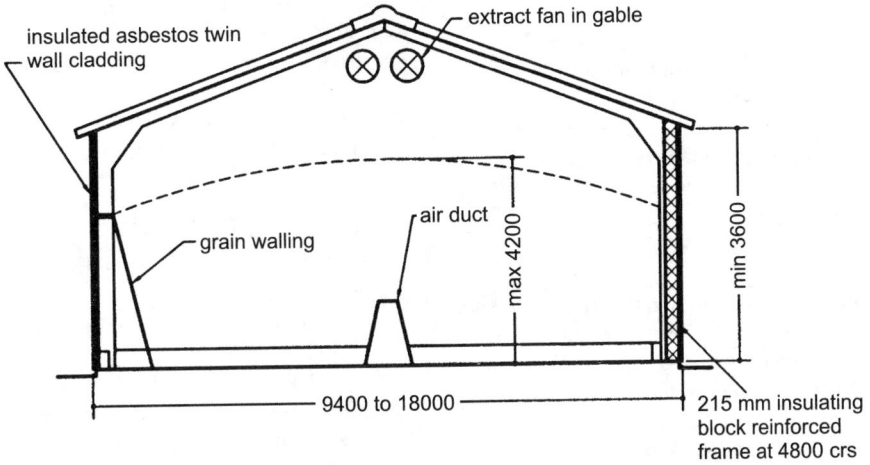

10.33 *Section through radial flow bins in a barn for grain drying and storage. The air duct delivers 400 m³/h.t to dry and 100 m³/h.t to store. Air temperature above 0°C, RH 75 per cent.*

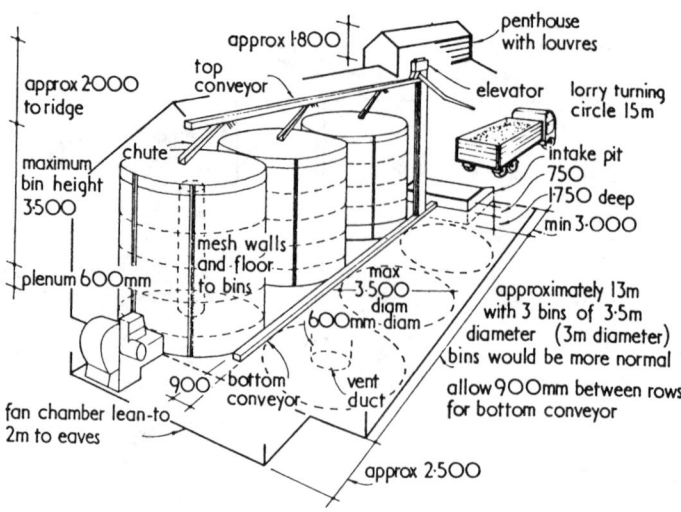

10.34 *Onion store*

10 BUILDING LEGISLATION

- *Town and Country Planning Act 1990*
  General Development Order 1988 amended and extended 1991

Many farm buildings and developments are no longer classed as Permitted Developments. Details of all schemes have to be sent to the local planning authority together with a fee. The authority will rule in each case whether further information needs to be submitted for formal planning approval before work can commence.

Particular developments normally requiring formal planning approval include:

- Buildings for non-agricultural purposes
- Dwelling houses
- Conversions of farm buildings to commercial or industrial or residential use
- Buildings not designed for agriculture, e.g. containers, lorry bodies, etc:
- Buildings exceeding 465 m² – in any 2-year period within 90 m – includes yards and slurry lagoons
- Buildings 12 m and over in height
- Buildings 3 m and over in height within 3 km of an airfield
- Buildings within 25 m from the metalled part of a classified road
- Livestock buildings within 400 m of a 'protected building'
- Caravan sites for which special rules apply
- Holiday cottages
- Recreational pursuits of a recurring nature, e.g.. adventure games, canoeing, hang gliding, windsurfing, water skiing, need consent if exceeding 28 days per year
- Farm shops: permission is needed for shops if produce is not derived from the farm involved and for new buildings to be used as shops. Particular care is required over access, parking and advertising signs.

The Building Regulations 1985
Many agricultural building are exempt from the Building Regulations 1985 – but not all. The following extract from the Regulations details the buildings that are exempt – all others are subject to Building Control and details must be submitted to the Local Authority before work commences.

Schedule 3 – Exempt Buildings and Works
Regulation 9 – Greenhouses and Agricultural Buildings

1. A building used as a greenhouse unless the main purpose is for retail packing or exhibiting.

2. (1) A building used for agriculture which is:
   (a) Sited at a distance not less than one and a half times its own height from any building containing sleeping accommodation, and
   (b) provided with an exit which may be used in the case of fire which is not more than 30 m from any point within the building (unless the main purpose for which the building is used is for retailing, packing and exhibiting).
   (2) In this paragraph 'agriculture' includes horticulture, fruit growing, seed growing, dairy farming, fish farming and the breeding and keeping of livestock (including any creature kept for the production of food, wool, skins or fur or for the purpose of farming the land).

Other relevant legislation
The Environmental Assessment Regulations 1988
Health and Safety at Work Act, etc. 1974
Control of Substances Hazardous to Health Regulations 1988 (COSHH)
Electricity at Work Regulation 1989
The Noise at Work Regulations 1989
The Food Safety Act 1990
The Food Hygiene (HQ) Regulation 1990
Code of Practice for the Control of Salmonella
The Environmental Protection Act 1990
The Code of Good Agricultural Practice for the Protection of Air.
Control of Pollution Act 1974 – Water Act 1989
The Control of Pollution (Silage, Slurry and Agricultural Fuel Oil) Regulations 1991
The Code of Good Agricultural Practice for the Protection of Water July 1991
The Welfare of Livestock Regulations
The Building Standards (Scotland) Regulations 1988

11 BIBLIOGRAPHY

BS 5502 Code of practice for the design of buildings and structures for agriculture.
Published in separate parts as follows:
Part 0: 1992 Introduction
Part 11: 1990 Guide to regulations and sources of information
Part 20: 1990 Code of practice for general design considerations
Part 21: 1990 Code of practice for the selection and use of construction materials
Part 22: 1993 Code of practice for design, construction and loading
Part 23: 1990 Code of practice for fire precautions

Part 25: 1991 Code of practice for design and installation of services and facilities

Part 30: 1992 Code of practice for control of infestation

Part 32: 1990 Guide to noise attenuation

Part 33: 1991 Guide to the control of odour pollution

Part 40: 1990 Code of practice for the design and construction of cattle buildings

Part 41: 1990 Code of practice for design and construction of sheep buildings and pens

Part 42: 1990 Code of practice for design and construction of pig buildings

Part 43: 1990 Code of practice for design and construction of poultry buildings

Part 49: 1990 Code of practice for design and construction of milking premises

Part 50: 1993 Code of practice for design, construction and use of storage tanks and reception pits for livestock slurry

Part 51: 1991 Code of practice for design and construction of slatted, perforated and mesh floors for livestock

Part 52: 1991 Code of practice for design of alarm systems and and emergency ventilation for livestock housing

Part 60: 1992 Code of practice for design and construction of buildings for mushrooms

Part 65: 1992 Code of practice for design and construction of crop processing buildings

Part 66: 1992 Code of practice for design and construction of chitting houses

Part 70: 1991 Code of practice for design and construction of ventilated on floor stores for combinable crops

Part 71: 1992 Code of practice for design and construction of ventilated stores for potatoes and onions

Part 72: 1992 Code of practice for design and construction of controlled environment stores for vegetables, fruit and flowers

Part 74: 1991 Code of practice for design and construction of bins and silos for combinable crops

Part 75: 1993 Code of practice for the design and construction of forage stores

Part 80: 1990 Code of practice for design and construction of workshops, maintenance and inspection facilities

Part 81: 1989 Code of practice for design and construction of chemical stores

Part 82: 1990 Code of practice for design of amenity buildings

11 Offices

DEGW

CI/SfB 32
UDC 725.25

*DEGW International Consultants are part of Twynstra Management Consultancy
and specialise in office planning and design*

KEY POINTS:
- *Changing expectations*
- *Occupants' demands*
- *Space standards*
- *Time sharing*
- *Atria, and their fire safety*
- *Floor loadings*
- *Building services*
- *Information technology*
- *Refurbishment*

Contents

NOTE

Some important aspects of design relevant to offices will be found
elsewhere in this handbook. In particular:

Sanitary accommodation in Chapter 3
Car parking in Chapter 4
Lifts and escalators in Chapter 5
External works in Chapter 6
Counters and cash offices in Chapter 14
Eating and drinking areas in Chapter 18
Thermal environment in Chapter 38
Lighting in Chapter 39
Acoustics in Chapter 40
Fire safety in Chapter 42
Security in Chapter 44
Access for cleaning Chapter 45
More on service distribution in Chapter 46

1 INTRODUCTION

1.01

Office design is at a turning point. For many decades, especially in
the developer-dominated Anglo-Saxon world, office users have
been passive. Vendors have concentrated on perfecting the
delivery of buildings at most profit, least risk and maximum
convenience for themselves. The buildings that result can satisfy
the relatively simple demands of highly routinised and unchanging
organisations. The key question is whether such office buildings
are capable, without substantial modification, of accommodating
the emerging requirements of organisations.

1.02

This is particularly relevant to the UK. British office buildings
were until the early 1980s a provincial variant of the North
American developer system, financed in much the same way but
much smaller, far less efficient in construction as well as plan
form, less serviced, and much more influenced by external
considerations forced upon the developers by the British town and
country planning system.

1.03

The contrast between the best new, North Americanised London
offices such as Broadgate or Canary Wharf with the best North
European offices such as SAS Frösundavik or Colonia – the sort of
buildings produced when the developer's influence on office
building design is relatively weak – is very striking.

1.04

User influence on recent office design in Scandinavia, Germany,
and the Netherlands has been direct and considerable, resulting in

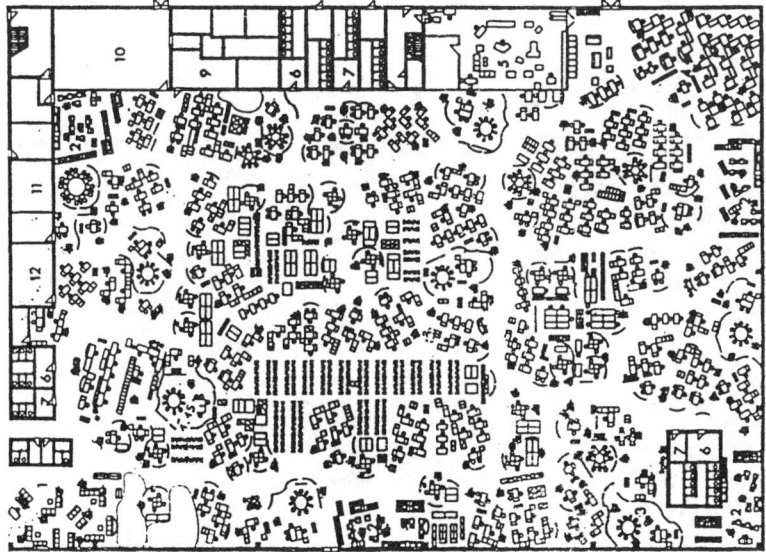

11.1 *The scientifically planned bürolandschaft
office (1950s)*

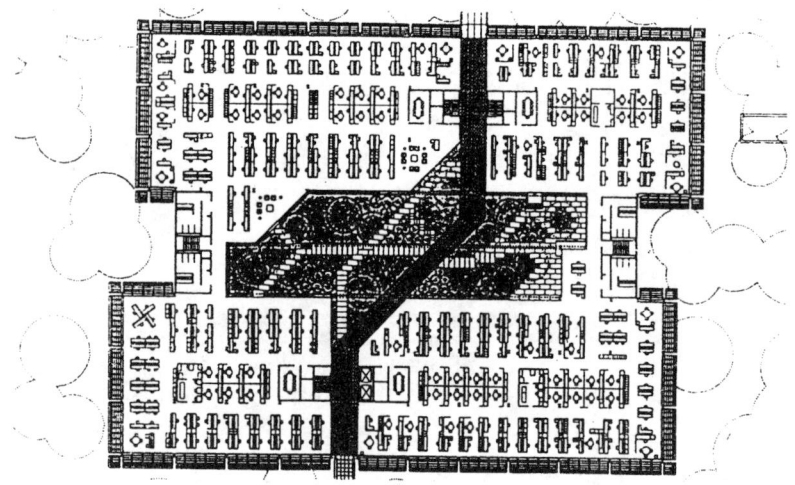

11.2 *The American influenced open plan with centralised space standards and single status workstations (1960s)*

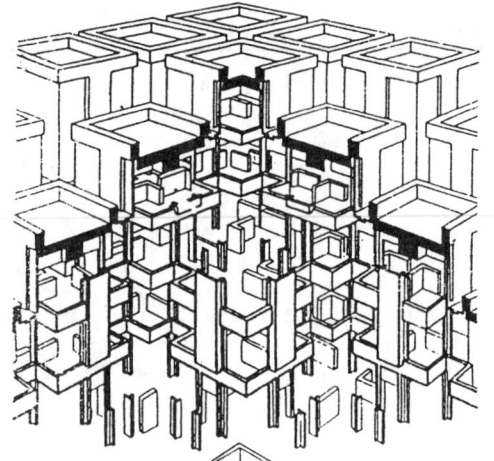

11.3 *Robust office shell designs, self-regulating structural grids (1970s)*

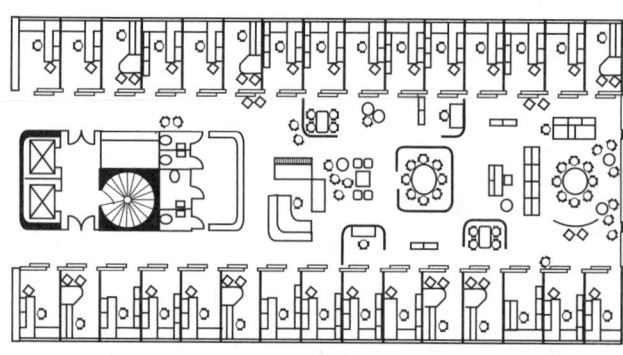

11.4 *The demand for higher standards, personal privacy – the 'combi-office'*

narrow and complex rather than deep plan forms, in very high degrees of cellularisation, and above all in extremely high standards of space, amenity and comfort for office workers. Buildings which have been shaped by direct user influence – through highly professional programming, through the competition system, and above all through Workers' Council negotiation – are sufficiently different from the supply-biased, developer-oriented offices of the USA and the UK to demonstrate that an

alternative kind of office is achievable, but at a cost, **11.1 to 11.4**. A comparison of the types is given in Table I.

1.05 The new office

Ten years ago offices suffered the effects of the first wave of distributed intelligence. Cable management, bigger heat gains, finer zoning of air conditioning were the symptoms; the major underlying problem was, and still is, how to accommodate

Table I Planning and design criteria for different types of office building

	Bürolandschaft	Traditional British speculative	New 'Broadgate' type of British speculative	Traditional North American speculative	New north European
No of storeys	5	10	10	80	5
Typical floor area (m²)	2000	1000	3000	3000	multiples of 200
Typical office depth (m)	40	13.5	18 and 12	18	10
Furthest distance from perimeter aspect (m)	20	7	9 to 12	18	5
Efficiency: net to gross		80%	85%	90%	70% (lots of public circulation)
Maximum cellularisation (% of usable)	20%	70%	40%	20%	80%
Type of core	Semi-dispersed	Semi-dispersed	Concentrated: extremely compact	Concentrated: extremely compact	Dispersed: stairs more prominent than lifts
Type of HVAC service	Centralised	Minimal	Floor by floor	Centralised	Decentralised: minimal use of HVAC

accelerating organisational change within long-term architecture. Today it is the indirect consequences of ubiquitous and addictive information technology that is reshaping organisations, changing their demography, and above all rescheduling their use of time. Whereas in the early 1980s what mattered was the obsolescence of particular office buildings, what matters now is the growing obsolescence of the nine-to-five office work – and of all the patterns of employment, location, and commuting that have shaped our cities for a hundred years.

1.06

Re-engineering (or changing the organisation of) office work is leading already to experiments in the intensification of space use – time sharing the office. This is hardly good news for developers whose enthusiasm in the late 1980s modernised the British office stock, but led also to overbuilding. While office users are intent on driving office space harder than ever before to succeed (or even to survive), developers are considering whether to offer more services to attract tenants (the intelligent building), to take secondary office space out of circulation (change of use), or to tailor-make offices to suit particular tenants.

1.07

Architects must get closer to the users, at both tactical facility management level and at a strategic level. Users are now where the real power lies – certainly no longer in the old, discredited, institution-dominated real estate market – and users' needs are changing faster and more spectacularly than ever before.

2 MATCHING SUPPLY AND DEMAND

2.01

The design of office buildings has suffered from oversimplified generalisations by architects, developers and clients, who have preferred to use a 'rule book' providing easy answers, rather than thinking the problems through. There is no such thing as the all-purpose building, a hard lesson for architects in the modern movement tradition of 'universal space'. Equally, speculative developers and funding institutions still have difficulty in coming to terms with the fact that the different sectors of the market have different requirements, and that those requirements are constantly changing.

2.02

We need to examine the frame of reference for designing office buildings. Those looking for premises have a choice between the new and the old. There are additional options – even for those seeking new, large, high-performance buildings which until recently did not exist. Buildings must be designed to reflect the requirements of the different sectors – horses suited to courses.

2.03

At one end of the spectrum are very large, rich and complex organisations which have spent considerable sums on computing and telecommunications. In recent years these firms have been able to move offices at short intervals to ensure that their accommodation kept pace with their growth and technological requirements.

2.04

The demand for space from professional firms with distinct usage and layout requirements puts them in the middle range. At the other end of the spectrum are the many small service firms which need only the simplest and cheapest accommodation. No one design can accommodate equally well such a wide spectrum of demand.

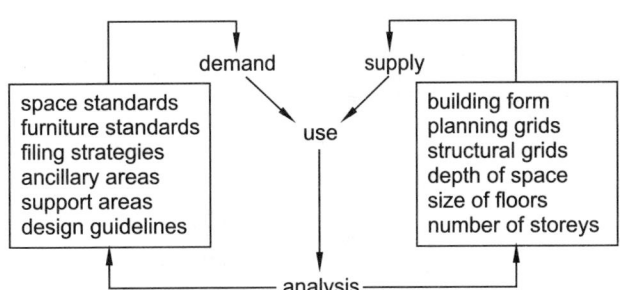

11.5 *Reconciling demand and supply*

2.05 Supply and demand

The essence of the design brief for office space is in the balance of the economic model of supply and demand, **11.5**. Producing a viable statement of requirements for a client is begun by investigating the demand for space. Depending on whether the project involves existing space or whether it is being built to suit, the final area requirement will be arrived at by reconciling space demands, such as workspace standards, furniture and filing strategies, with the supply issues of building form, planning and structural grids and depth of space. Table I covers planning and design criteria for various types of office.

2.06 Improving user satisfaction, health and comfort

A good building is an elusive thing, but it is one which satisfies organisational needs at reasonable cost and without unnecessary effort, and in which the inhabitants are happy to work. This brings us to a good brief, good design, and good management. There must be four key features:

- Adaptability to meet a range of space and servicing requirements. The building should not make it difficult for occupants to do what they want. For example, in addition to the current shell-and-core facilities, offices might accommodate a wider range of choice in internal environmental services, from natural ventilation and lighting upwards.
- Contact with the outside world. People like being near a window with clear glass. In Scandinavia and Germany this is now almost a right, and is having a major influence on office design, with deep open plans giving way to more diverse buildings with offices of a more domestic scale around a core or 'street' of common facilities. The degree to which similar views and solutions will prevail in the UK is not yet clear. Cultural and climatic differences make building types and their services difficult to export, however international they may feel, and new icons are just as likely to prove false gods as others have in the past.
- Better, healthier and more productive internal environmental quality. In all its aspects: heat, light, sound, colour, and air quality. This last is the most difficult as natural ventilation is more psychologically acceptable than any mechanical system, however poor the outside air. And, of course, delight: a building which both works and feels good to be in will be a much better investment in the long run than one which is functional but unloved.
- User control. Psychologists have observed that the human factor – for example, the openable window – is disproportionately significant to perceived wellbeing. The reasons may include social as much as design and health issues. For example, one writer observes that 'individuals measure their worth within an organisation as much by the control they possess over their environment (in the broadest sense) as by expenditure, however lavish, from an invisible and unfeeling corporate exchequer'. Not nearly enough is known about the behavioural aspects of both simple and advanced environmental control systems in buildings.

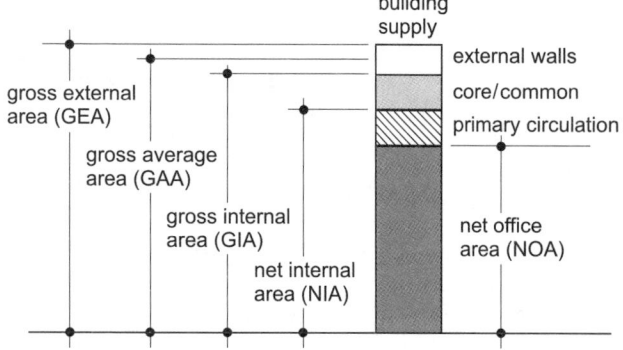

11.6 *The standard method of measurement in the Code of Measuring Practice published by the Royal Institution of Chartered Surveyors and the Incorporated Society of Valuers and Auctioneers*

3 STANDARD METHOD OF BUILDING MEASUREMENT

3.01

An understanding of the terms used by clients to specify floor areas, **11.6**, **11.7** and **11.8**, is essential:

Gross External Area (GEA): the floor area contained within the building measured to the external face of the external walls

Gross Internal Area (GIA): the floor area contained within the building measured to the internal face of the external walls

In all the above gross measures features such as atria are measured at the filled floor level; the clear voids are not included in the total area. Enclosed plant rooms on the roof are included in all gross measures.

Net Internal Area (NIA): is GIA less the floor areas taken up by:

- Common lobbies and foyers
- Enclosed plant on the roof
- Stairs and escalators

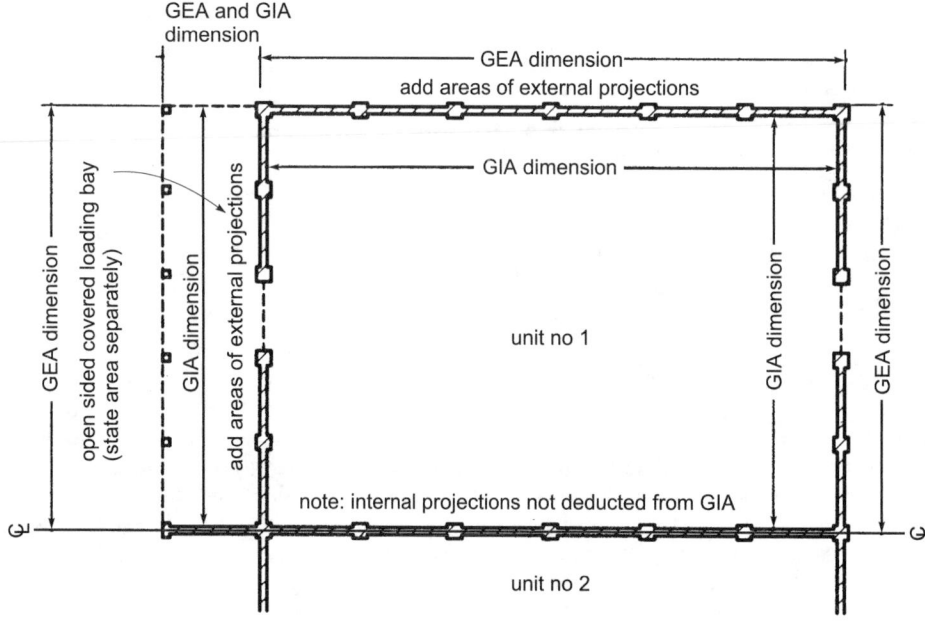

11.7 *An example of dimensions for GEA and GIA for an industrial/warehouse end terrace unit*

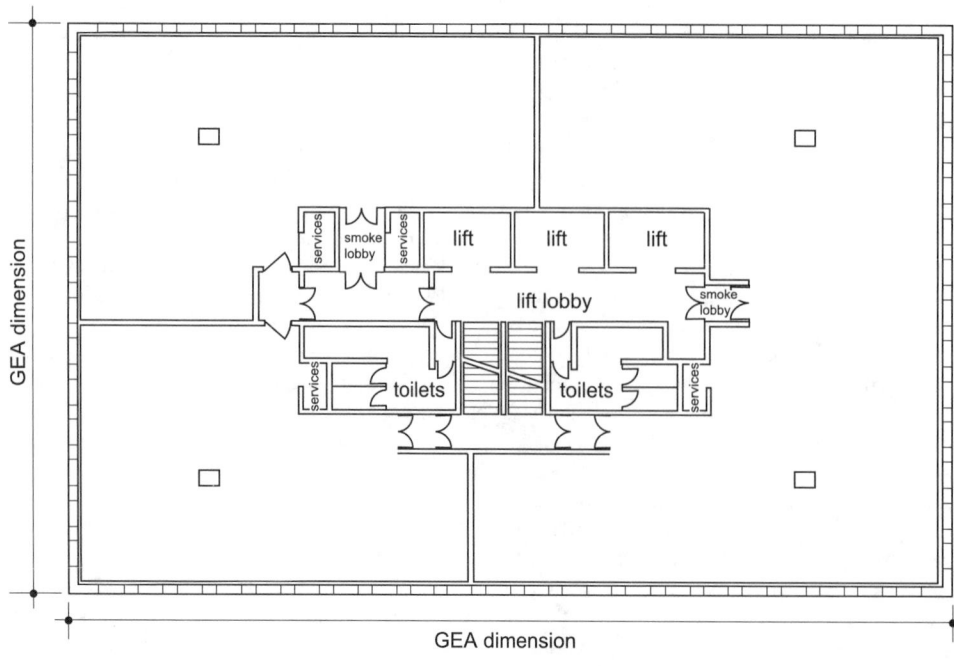

11.8 *An example of a multi-letting office floor showing NIAs*

- Mechanical and electrical services plant areas
- Lifts
  Internal structure, such as columns
- Toilet areas
- Functions within the core enclosure
- Ducts and risers
- Car parking which was included in gross area

These areas are often referred to as core and/or common areas.

3.02
An additional non-standard term encountered is *Net Office Area* (*NOA*). This is the NIA less the main corridors or primary circulation (as it is often called). These corridor routes are required to maintain life safety in emergency situations such as a fire, but do not include the routes used to access workstations off the main corridor (i.e. secondary circulation is included in NOA).

3.03 The space budget
The components of the space budget, **11.9** are as follows:

Workspace: the area given over to workstations and their immediate requirements, such as personal filing

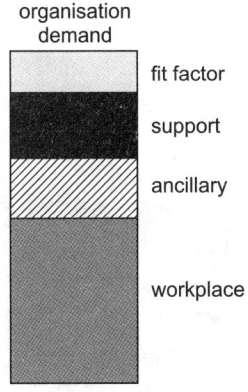

11.9 *The space budget represents the organisation's requirement for net usable area*

Ancillary: the area given over to functions that are managed by and support a section or working group, including local meeting places, project rooms, storage areas, shared terminals, refreshment and copy areas

Support: the area given over to functions that are centrally managed and support the whole organisation or building, including mail, reprographics, network rooms, switchboard rooms, library, conference, central meeting etc. The areas may be on separate floors or otherwise distant from individual departments or groups

Fit factor: buildings can rarely be 100 per cent efficient, for two prime reasons:

- Building configurations, grids and obstructions
- Departmental integrity.

4 THE TIME-BASED NATURE OF THE OFFICE ENVIRONMENT

4.01
Buildings are relatively permanent, while the organisations and activities within them are continuously changing. To allow for maximum flexibility, different time scales of building briefing and design can be distinguished into separate functions of:

- **The building shell** – the structure and enclosure of the building, **11.10**, lasting 50–75 years, while the functions within change many times over. The ability of the shell to allow for change is reflected in the depth of space, location of cores, floor-to-floor height to allow capacity for services, and the floorplate configuration.
- **Building services** – the heating, ventilation, and cabling infrastructure of a building, **11.11**, which have a life span of 15 years or less before the technology becomes obsolescent.
- **Scenery** – the fitting-out components of a building, such as ceilings, lighting, finishes, **11.12**, which adapt a building to a specific organisation's requirements. The life span of a fit-out is between 5 and 7 years.
- **Setting** – the day-to-day re-arrangement of the furniture and equipment, **11.13**, to meet changing needs.

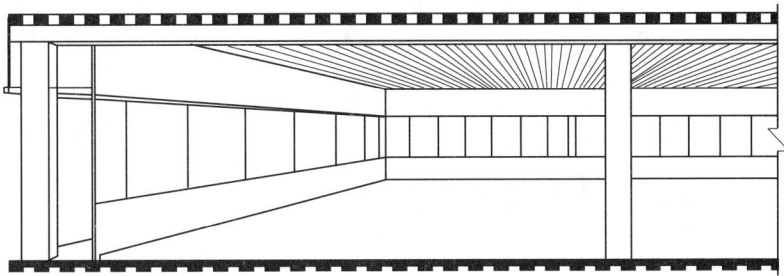

11.10 *The building shell, expected life 60 years*

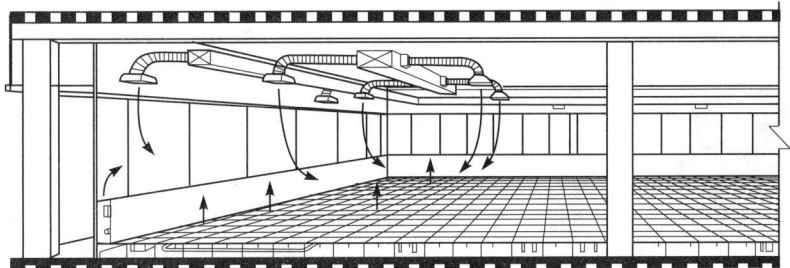

11.11 *Building services, expected life 15 years*

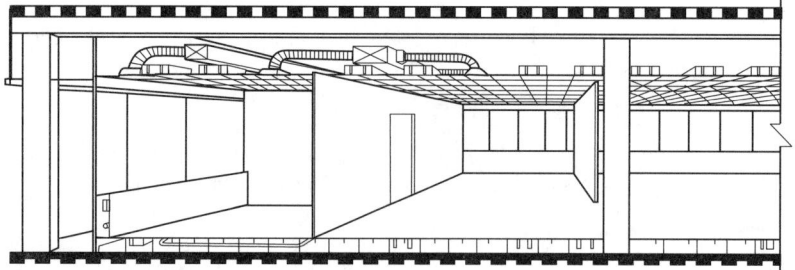

11.12 *Scenery, replaced after 7 years*

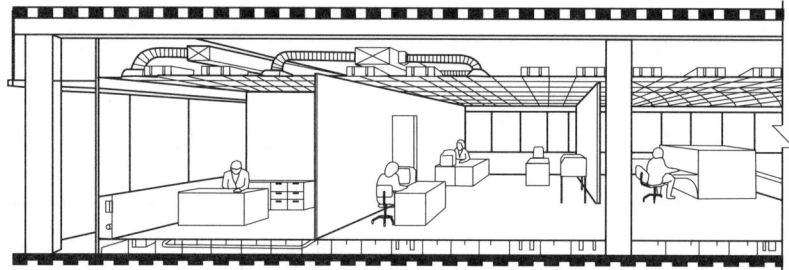

11.13 *Setting, changing from day to day*

4.02

The traditional role of the office building has been to accommodate people and their (largely paper) files. It has also provided a meeting place for customers, suppliers and consultants, as well as for the organisation's own staff. To this role, developments in technology have added the need to accommodate a wide variety of new equipment.

4.03

Information technology is changing the role of the office building. Computers make it possible for an increasing proportion of staff to work away from the office, which becomes a communications centre for the organisation. This has implications for the location and aesthetics of the building; and other implications, too. For instance, there is likely to be more travel outside rush hours. Office buildings should provide more meeting rooms, and a less ordinary desk space. Some of the office space will be allocated to staff on a temporary rather than a permanent basis.

4.04

Many organisations, particularly in the services sector, already find that up to 40 per cent of their staff are away from the building at any one time, **11.14**. It is not therefore appropriate to plan for 100 per cent occupancy by all employees. This leads to the concept of 'free addressing': an employee does not have a personally assigned desk, but uses any convenient free desk when he or she is in the office, and with mobile phones or new PABX technology they keep their own extension numbers.

5 THE OFFICE SHELL

5.01

Research into the requirements of building owners and facilities managers provides useful feedback into specification requirements which are high priority. These are:

● The ability to absorb change and minimise operating costs
● The freedom to address users' expectations for:
  – Opening windows
  – Environmentally friendly working spaces
● Local environmental control

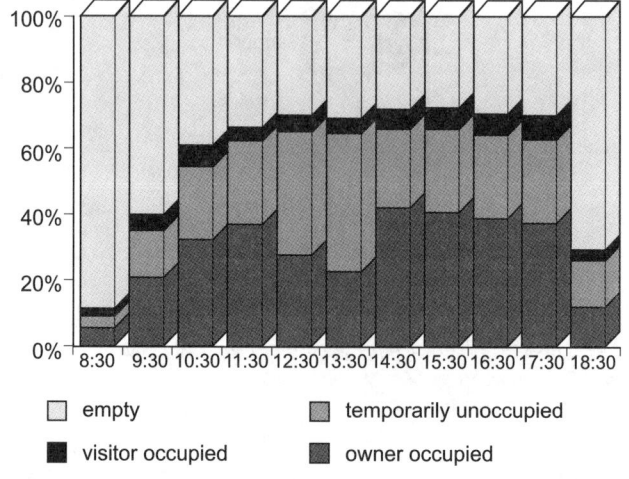

☐ empty   ▨ temporarily unoccupied
■ visitor occupied   ▨ owner occupied

11.14 *Time utilisation of traditional desks*

● Ease of maintenance
● Opportunity to participate fully in design decisions

5.02

The dimensions provided in this section are guidelines based on European case studies and good practice. In some circumstances, such as inner-city sites, a different approach may be necessary to stay within planning restrictions or to ensure financial viability.

5.03 Floor depth

This determines the quality and types of space available on each level. Aspect, natural ventilation and lighting, zoning of space, and support space should all be considered. Building depths are generally described as being predominantly 'glass to core' or 'glass to glass'.

● Glass-to-core depths of 9–12 m allow room for cellular office space or open plan plus storage.
● Glass-to-glass depths of 13.5–18 m allow two or three zones of office and support space.

5.04 Storey height (floor-to-floor height)

Related to floor depth and floor plate size, this has a major effect on air conditioning, cable distribution, ability to use natural ventilation and light, and on visual comfort.

- Floor-to-floor heights of 4–4.5 m provide maximum flexibility and good visual comfort.

5.05

Floor depth and storey height are interrelated and assuming glass-to-glass depths of 13.5–18 m should be thought of together. For example, narrower buildings do not require such generous storey heights because of the different servicing strategies that they use.

5.06 Floor size and configuration

These affect internal communications and circulation routes around the building. Small floors are inefficient in terms of the ratio between core space and usable floor area. Large departments have to be split over a number of floors, which is also inefficient. Very large floors, on the other hand, produce circulation routes with long distances between departments.

- Contiguous floor sizes between 500 m^2 and 2500 m^2 provide the most usable spaces. Landlord efficiency, expressed by the ratio of Net Internal Area to Gross Internal Area, should be 84–87 per cent if the building is mid- to high-rise, or 90 per cent + if low-rise. Tenant efficiency, expressed by the ratio of usable area to Net Internal Area, should be 85 per cent or above.

5.07 Floor loading

This determines the amount of equipment and storage that can be placed in the work area, and the overall stability of the structure. The tendency in the UK and certain other parts of Europe is to overspecify floor loading, which can add significantly to the construction costs of the building.

- A floor loading of 4 kN/m^2 is sufficient for general loading. If necessary, specific areas can be designed for higher loading to support heavy items.

5.08 Planning and partition grids

These determine how the organisation uses its space. The size of the planning grid is less important in a completely open-plan office. If part of the space is enclosed, however, the planning grid will determine the size of the office modules and the overall efficiency in the use of space.

- A 1.35 m grid allows 2.7 m wide offices; a 1.5 m grid will provide 3 m wide offices, and relates better to building components in 600 mm modules.

5.09 Building skin

The role is shifting from being a barrier to the environment to being an integral part of the servicing strategy. Natural ventilation is becoming increasingly important in Europe. See Section 6.

5.10 Communications infrastructure

Local- and wide-area communications are important, and the base building shell should be designed to accommodate them. Of particular significance are the entry points for external communications services including satellite services, and also the size and positioning of vertical risers.

- Risers for voice, data and other services, should not take up less than 2 per cent of Gross Floor Area (GFA), and there should be the capacity to knock through another 2 per cent easily if the need arises. The cores containing the risers should be widely distributed to avoid cable bottlenecks. A communications room measuring 2 × 1 m should serve each 500 m^2 of GFA.

- There should be space for dual-service entries into the building.
- Provide space on the roof, or nearby, with good sight-lines for satellite or microwave dishes.

5.11 Access for goods and materials

Ease of access for the entry of goods must be at least as good as for people to conflicts and bottlenecks. A clear strategy of entry supported by appropriate signage should keep people and goods separate. Typical materials which are regularly delivered are:

- Stationery and office supplies
- Office equipment, machinery and furniture
- Food and supplies to dining areas, vending machines, etc.
- Post and couriers
- Building maintenance supplies and equipment.

5.12

A summary of considerations in the design of shells is given in Table II.

Table II Summary of building shell considerations

Depth of building	• Flexibility of layout options • Amount of cellularisation • Need for mechanical ventilation • Spatial efficiency
Location of cores	• Ease of sub-letting • Security • Spatial efficiency
Floor-to-floor heights	• Method of cable distribution • Type of servicing
Floor size and shape	• Spatial efficiency • Planning flexibility • Size of working groups
Perimeter detail and planning grid	• Flexibility of sub-division • Efficient use of space • Solar gain/heat loss/condensation
Construction	• Ease of adaptation • Space for services • Image

6 BUILDING SERVICES

6.01 Natural ventilation or air conditioning?

It is usually a straight choice between natural ventilation and full air conditioning for both speculative and purpose-built offices. In the UK many organisations choose the latter, although they get twice the building services energy costs, and dearer maintenance and management. Not all these are directly related to the air conditioning system, but to the characteristics of the type of buildings which are air conditioned. Apart from improved comfort (not always realised), reasons for choosing air conditioning include:

- Prestige
- Standard requirements, particularly for many multinationals
- Deeper plans, partly for alleged organisational needs and partly to maximise usable area
- Flexibility to accommodate changing requirements, seldom achieved except at a high cost
- Higher rents giving a better rate of return for landlords
- Poor external environment, particularly traffic noise.

6.02

Recent trends in offices have moved from traditional climate-responsive forms, which were designed as coarse climate modifiers, to climate-rejecting, sealed designs where the internal environment is created largely or entirely artificially. This trend is now being questioned and some pointers to the future are:

- Communications systems question the need fo. large, deep spaces.
- Occupants are asking for environments to be more natural, with greater outside awareness, more daylight, natural ventilation, and better individual control, but often with mechanical and electrical systems available on demand for when the natural ones cannot cope. In essence, this includes opening windows and solar control linked to a computerised building management system. This system monitors the opening of windows so that heating, ventilating and air-conditioning systems are reconfigured accordingly.
- In difficult conditions it may not be possible to have opening windows, but some form of solar protection should be incorporated to minimise the cooling load.
- New materials, systems and design techniques permit closer integration of natural and mechanical systems with intelligent user-responsive controls, allowing buildings which are not fully air conditioned to provide a higher level of environmental control than hitherto.

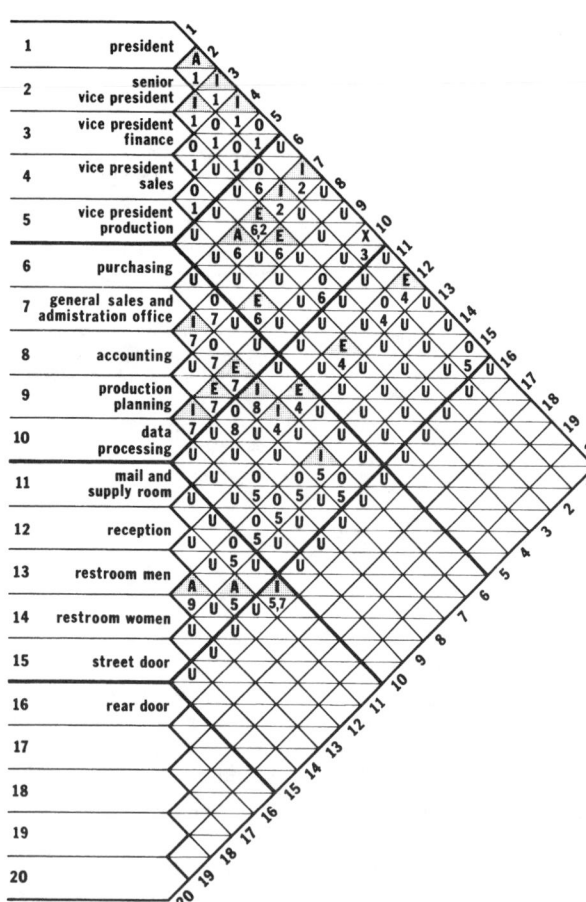

reason		importance	
code	reason	value	closeness
1	personal contacts	A	absolutely necessary
2	use of steno pool	E	especially important
3	noise	I	important
4	number of visitors	O	average satisfies
5	convenience	U	unimportant
6	supervisory control	X	undesirable
7	movement of paper		
8	use of supplies		
9	share same utilities		

reasons which govern closeness value

closeness rating

11.15 *Relationship chart for a small company*

- Concern for the global environment implies greater energy efficiency; ways of doing this are to use natural ventilation, light and solar heat where possible in place of mechanical and electrical systems.
- The energy consumption by desktop IT equipment will soon fall, reducing cooling loads in the general office though not necessarily in equipment rooms.

7 SCENERY AND SETTING OPTIONS

7.01

The arrangement used by an organisation depends on who needs to be close to whom, and what facilities are better at a distance from, for example, the directors' suite. **11.15** shows a relationship chart that is used to design the allocation of space.

7.01

The scenery and setting of the workplace need to be highly adaptive, **11.16** to **11.22**. They are also the least constrained area of procurement, and one with the fastest turnover. Furniture is a highly accessible tool which can add value to performance, of doing the most with the least.

7.03 Key features

- Less provision of workstations for full-time individuals
- Furniture and settings for groups, project teams, and space shared over time
- Furniture to support varied and intensive IT use
- Ability to support different users over time.

7.04

Layouts must balance the desire for cellularisation (common in Germany and Scandinavian offices) against the need to keep costs down and to add value with strongly interactive work patterns in open-plan settings. Open areas should be designed and managed to allow quiet and reflective work, and the flexible use of space at different times. Using IT to allow mobile working within the office suggests entirely new ways of planning space.

Managing the balance between:

Maximising communication and	Need for quiet and reflection
Need for group/team and /project work	Confidentiality and individual work
Provision of open areas for group work	Access to daylight, aspect, ventilation

7.05

11.23 to **11.38** give dimensions relevant to clerical-type workspaces. Standard dimensions for computer workspaces can be found in Chapter 2 (**2.8**). Drawing offices nowadays are nearly all run with computer aided design (CAD) workstations, but where drawing boards are still used **11.39** to **11.42** indicate the required dimensions.

7.06 Meeting rooms and spaces

These are key areas in any organisation. **11.43** to **11.45** cover a number of configurations. Some provision may be needed for televisual connection to remote sites.

7.07 Servicing strategy

Power and communication services can be taken to each workstation and meeting place in one of three ways:

- *In raised floors*, **11.46**

  This is a popular arrangement for developers, which is surprising as it is the most expensive method. Unless an unacceptably low ceiling is provided, it means that the floor-to-floor height is increased by the depth of the raised floor. Power and telecommunication outlets are in sunken boxes accessed

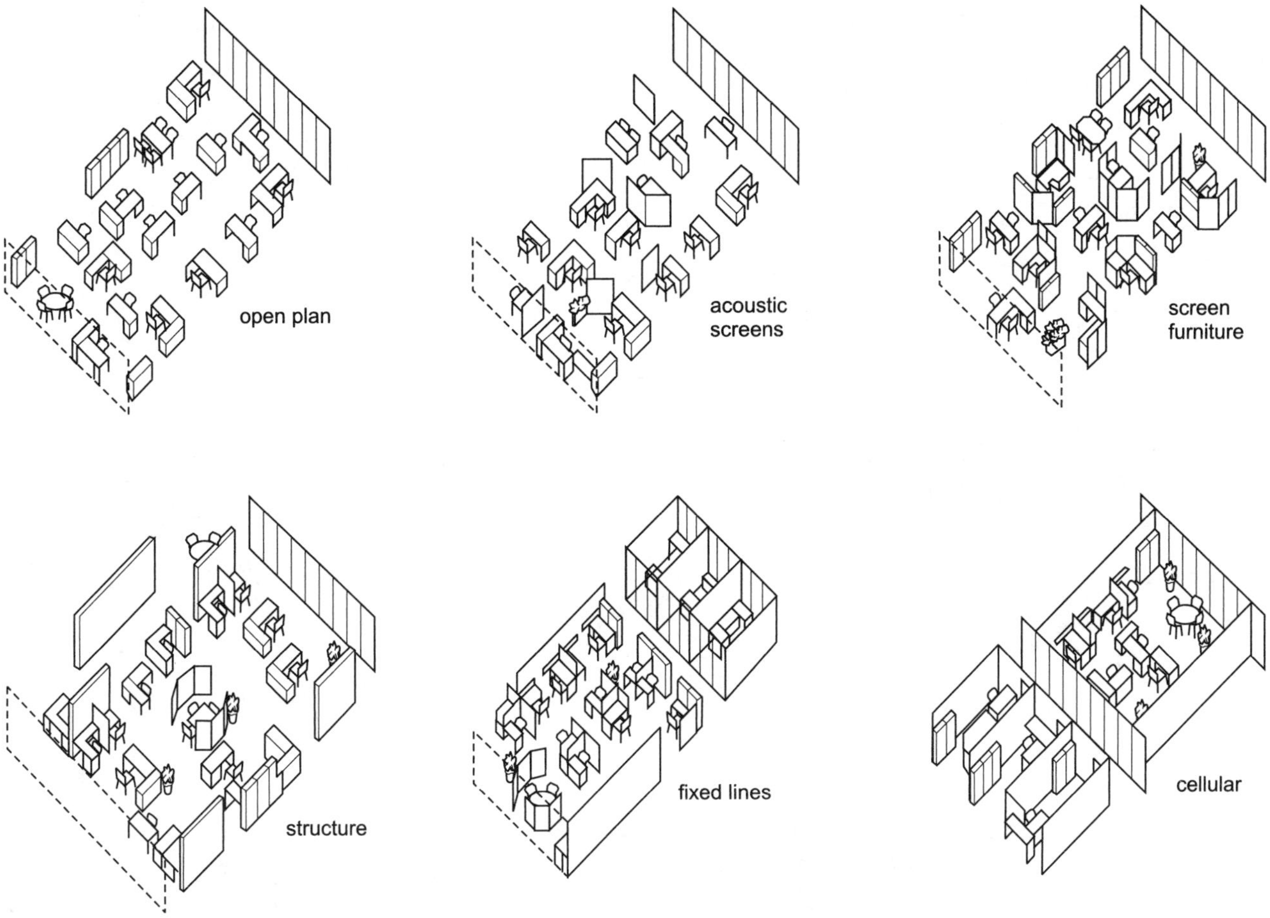

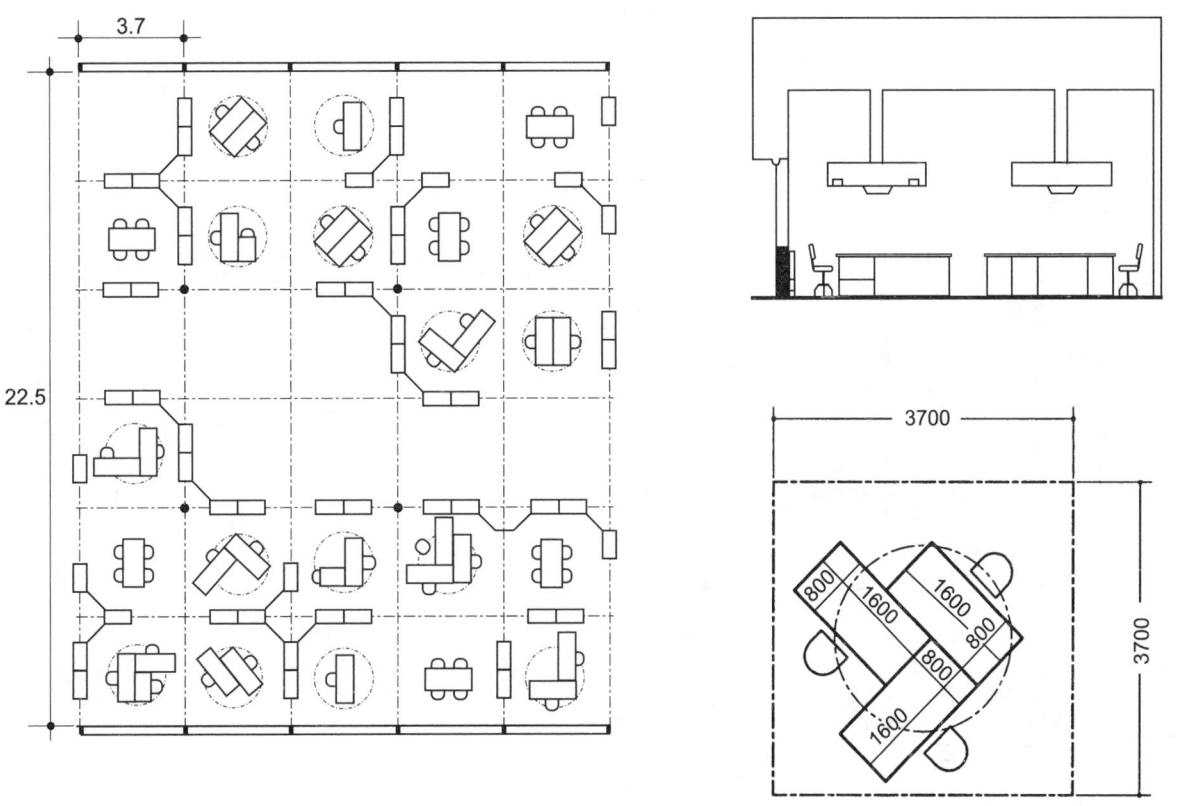

11.16 *Comparison of layout types. Layouts vary depending on: degree of enclosure, density of people, distribution of space*

open plan

acoustic
screens

screen
furniture

structure

fixed lines

cellular

3.7

22.5

3700

3700

800 1600 1600 800

800

1600

11.17 *Open plan*

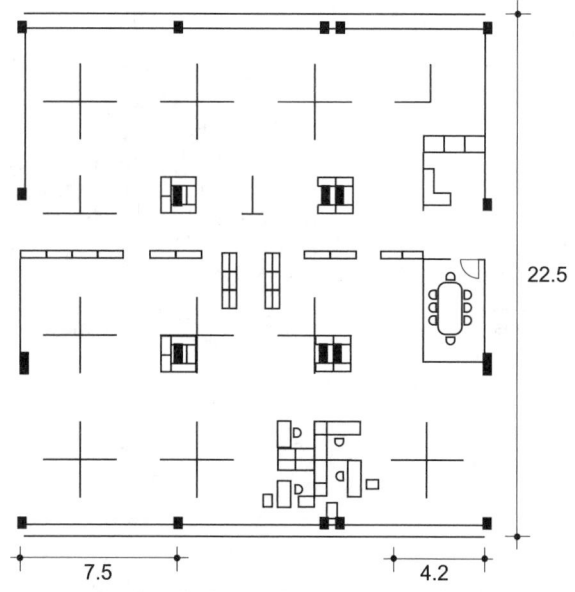

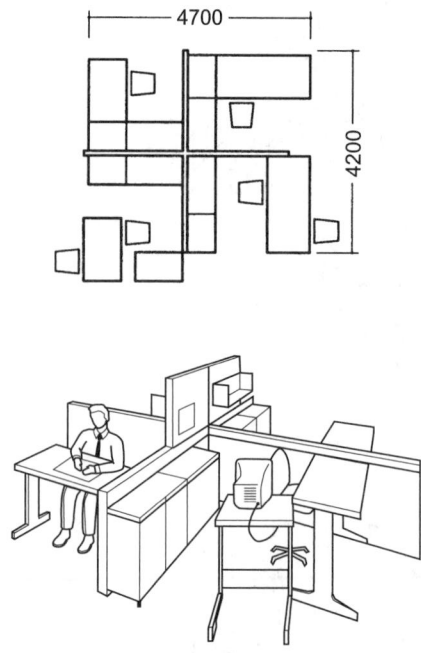

11.18 *Structured open plan*

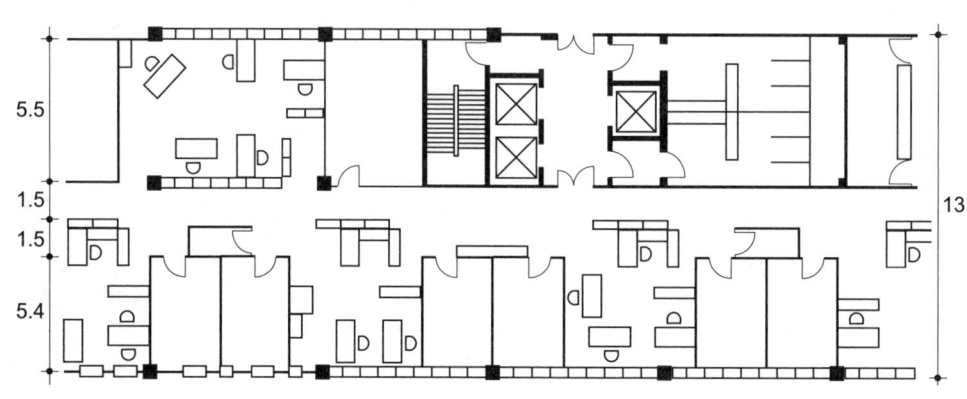

11.19 *Group space*

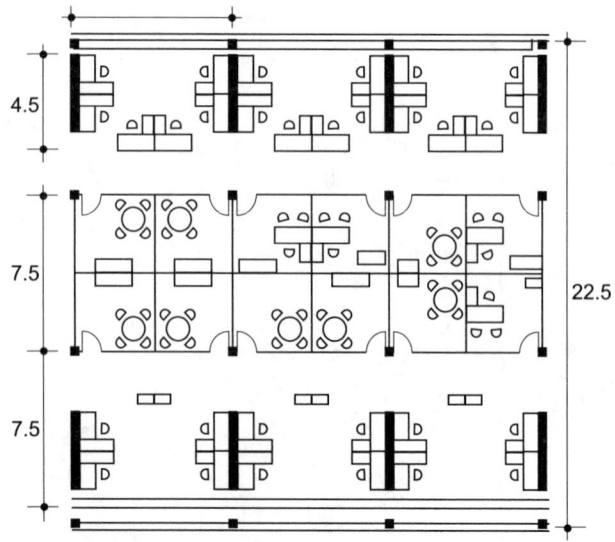

11.20 *Self-regulatory – mixed*

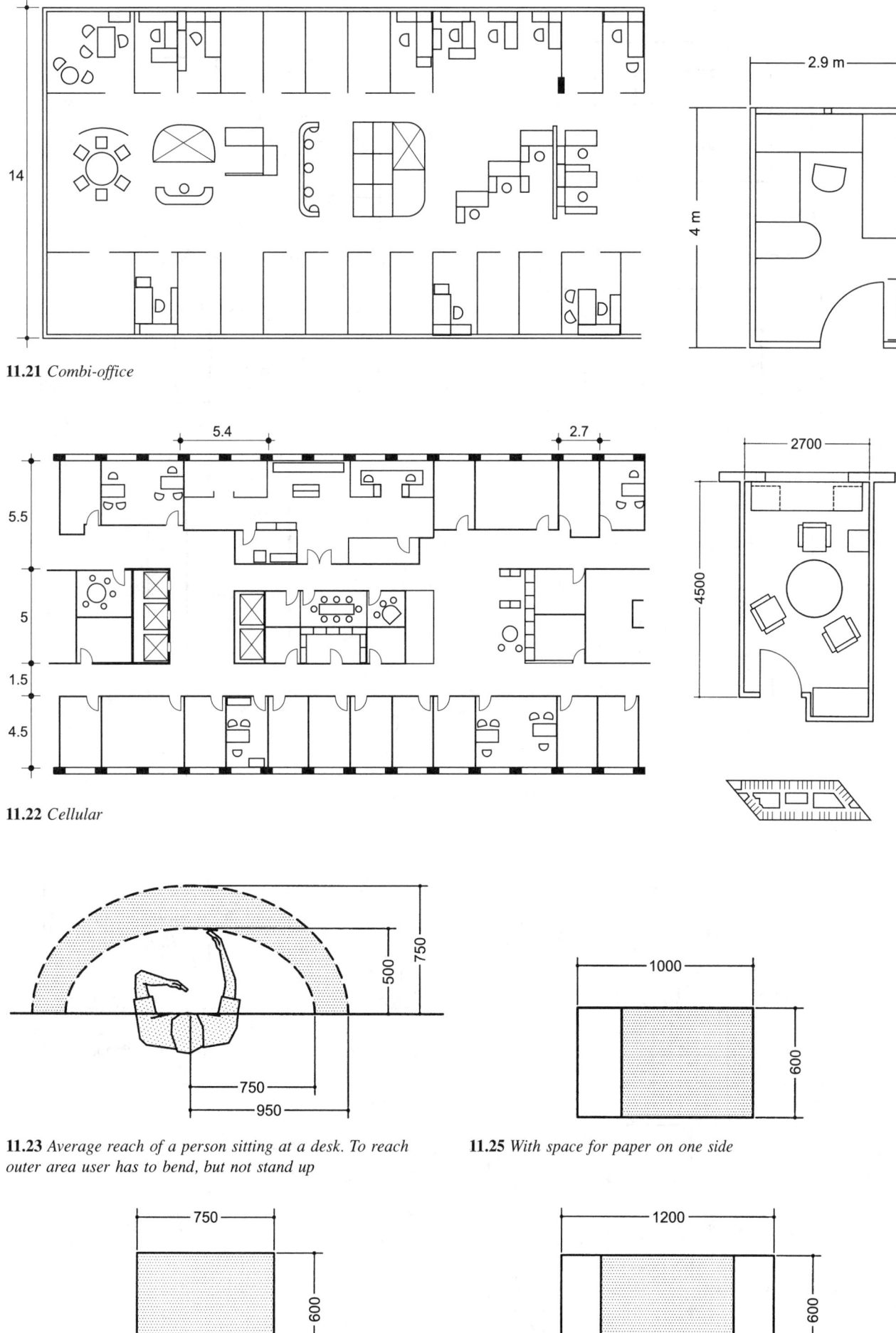

11.21 *Combi-office*

11.22 *Cellular*

11.23 *Average reach of a person sitting at a desk. To reach outer area user has to bend, but not stand up*

11.24 *Basic space for writing and typing*

11.25 *With space for paper on one side*

11.26 *With space for paper on both sides*

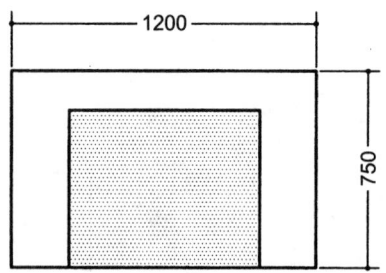

11.27 *Paper plus space for pens and telephones*

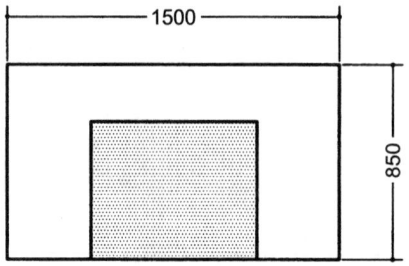

11.29 *Space for papers plus area for references*

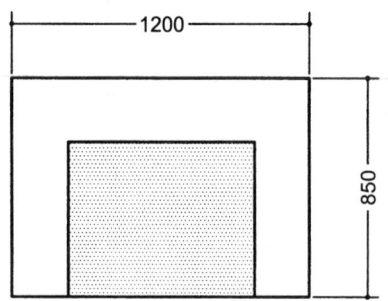

11.28 *Generous amount of space for paper*

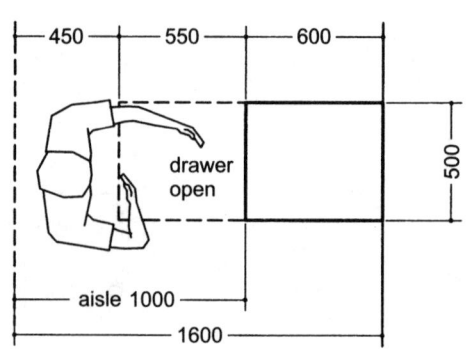

11.30 *Space requirements of drawer filing cabinet*

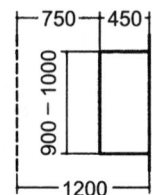

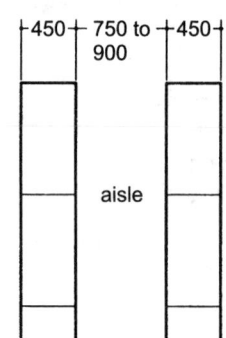

11.31 *Space requirements of lateral filing units*

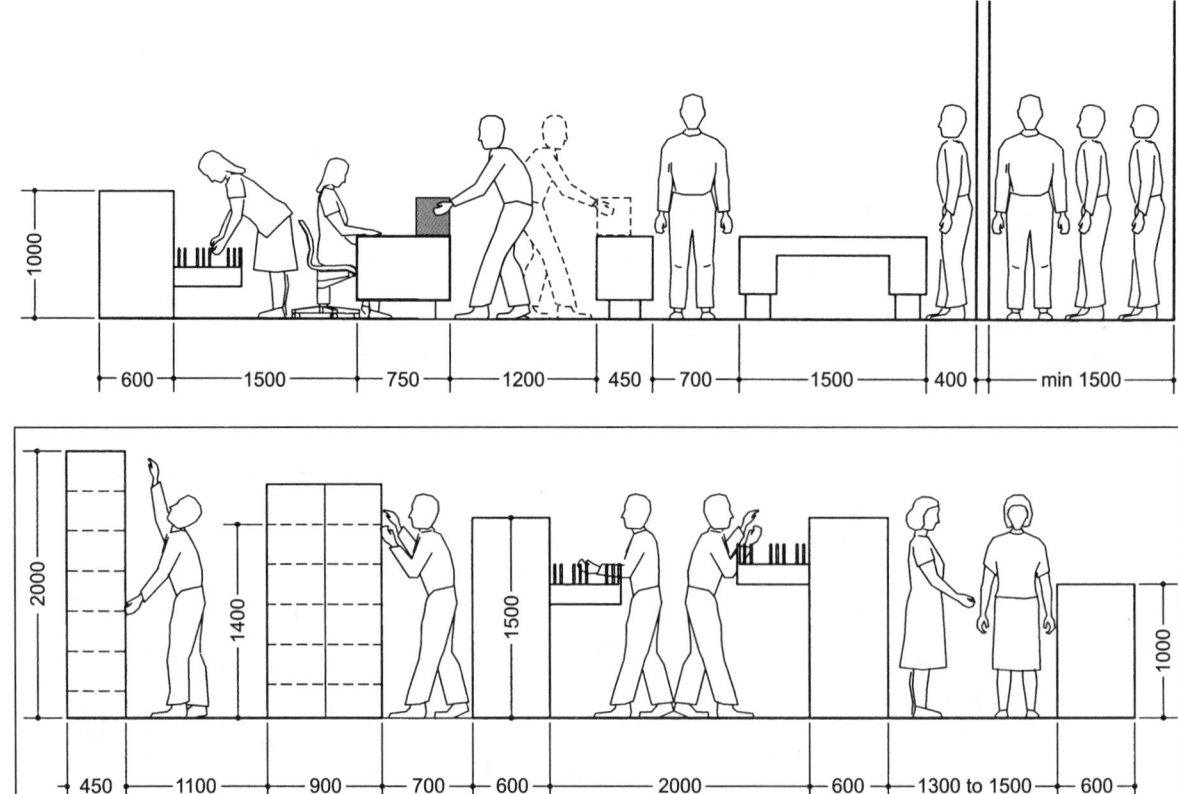

11.32 *Space and circulation requirements of filing and other office equipment*

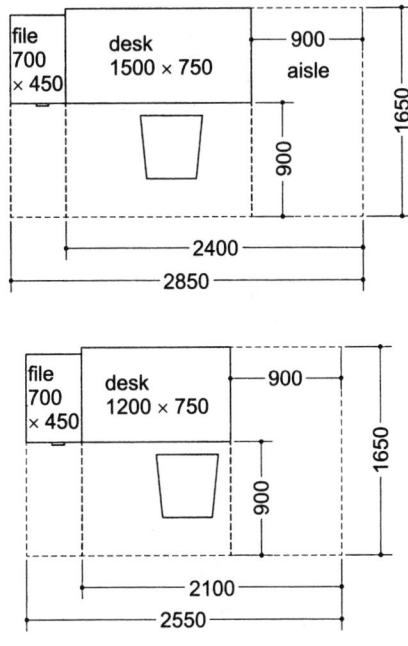

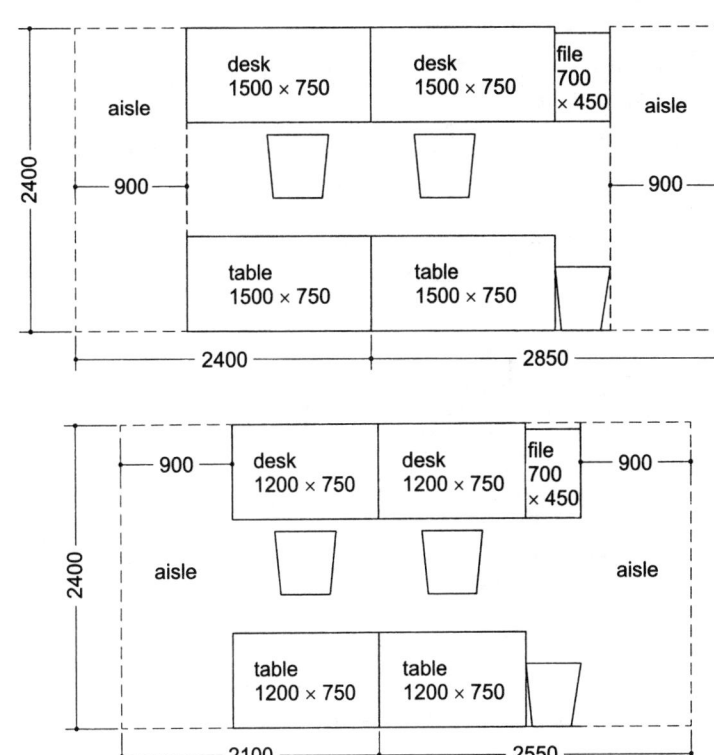

11.33 *Desk and file spacing and layout*

11.34 *Desk with tables, file and chair, spacing and layout*

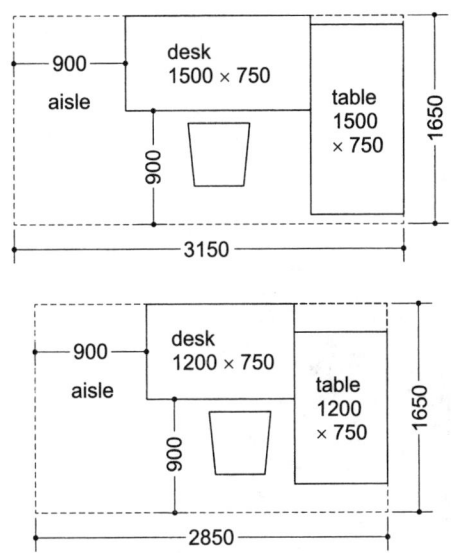

11.35 *Desk with adjacent table, spacing and layout*

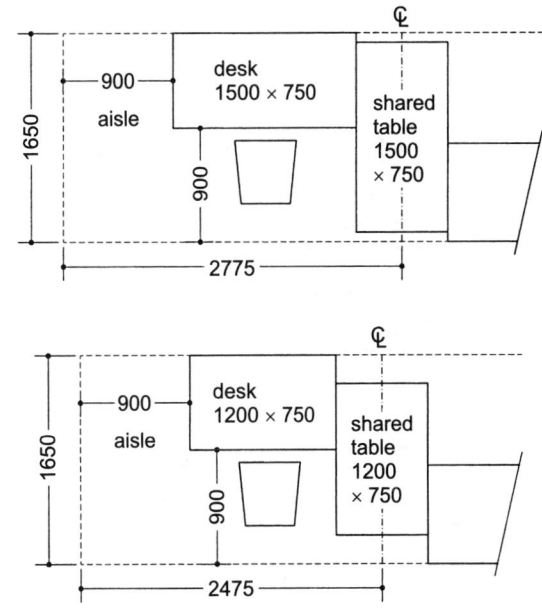

11.36 *Desk with shared table, spacing and layout*

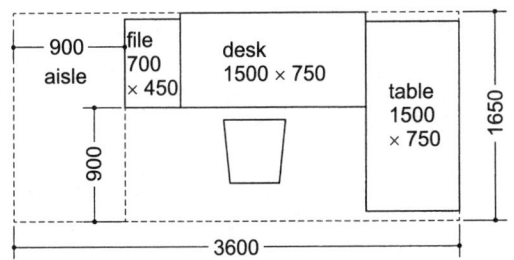

11.37 *Desk, table and file, spacing and layout*

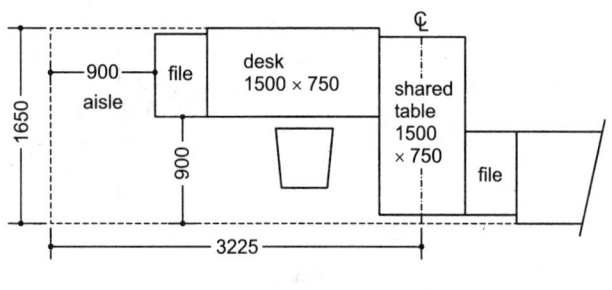

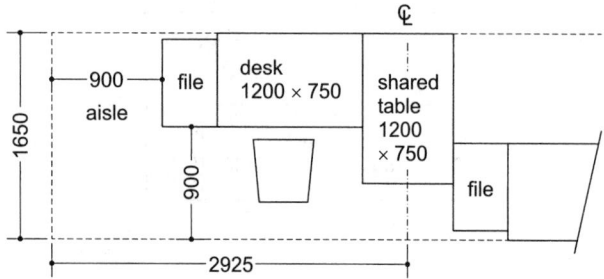

11.38 *Desk, shared table and file, spacing and layout*

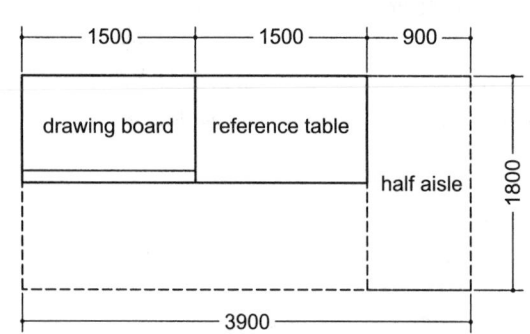

11.39 *Drawing board with front reference: area 7.0 m²*

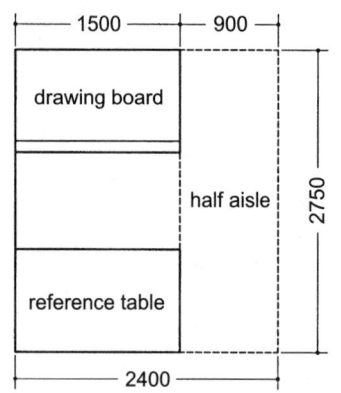

11.40 *Drawing board with back reference: area 6.6 m²*

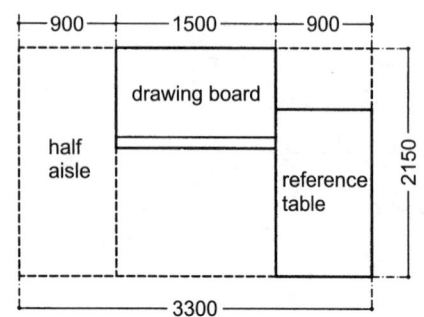

11.41 *Drawing board with side reference: area 7.1 m²*

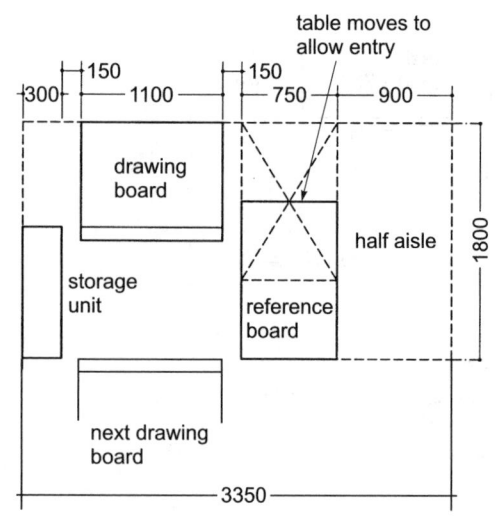

11.42 *Drawing board with mobile reference: area 6.0 m²*
(Building Design Partnership design)

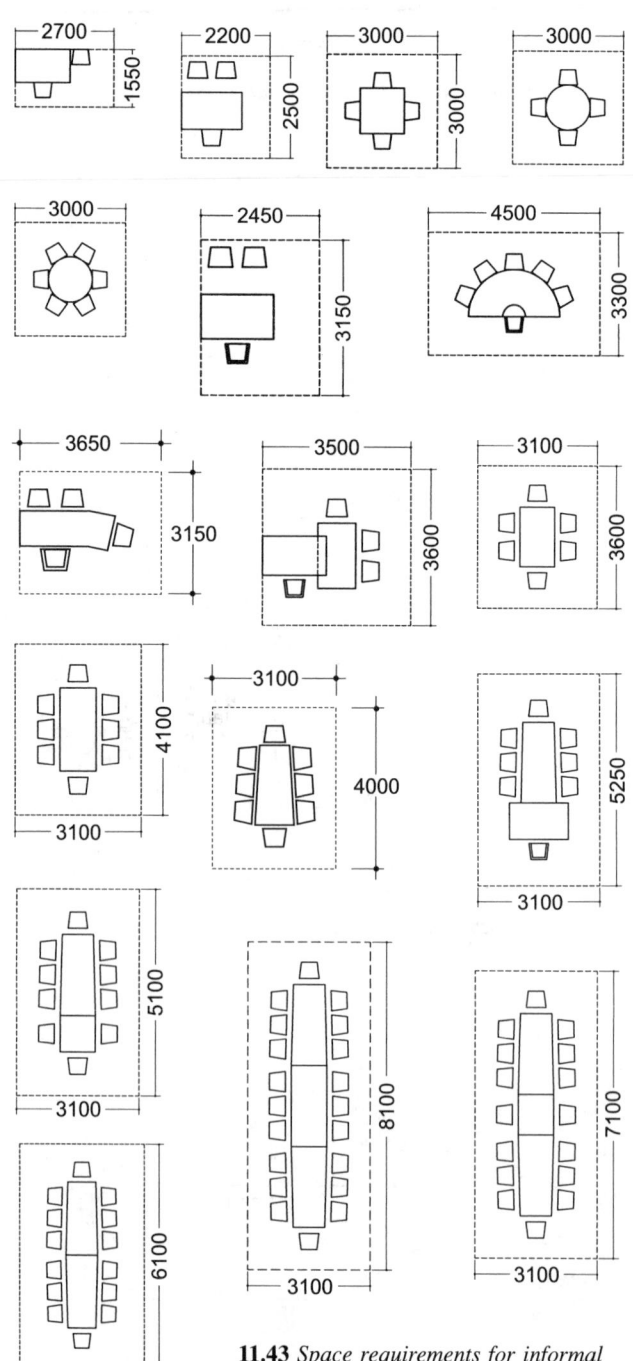

11.43 *Space requirements for informal meetings*

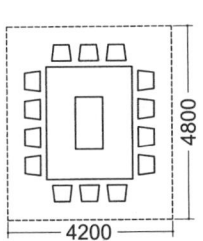
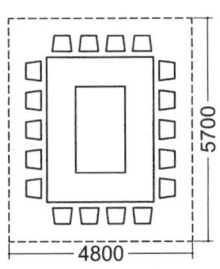
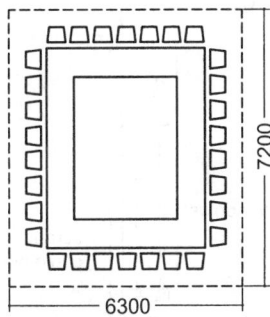

11.44 *Space requirements for formal meetings*

11.45 *Modular furniture designed to allow for alternative configurations*

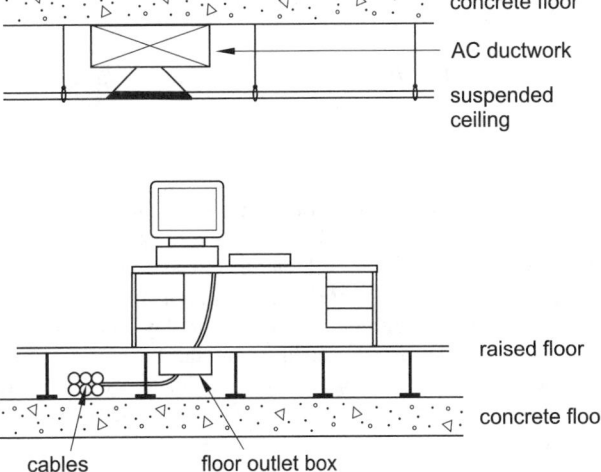

11.46 *Power and communication servicing through raised floor*

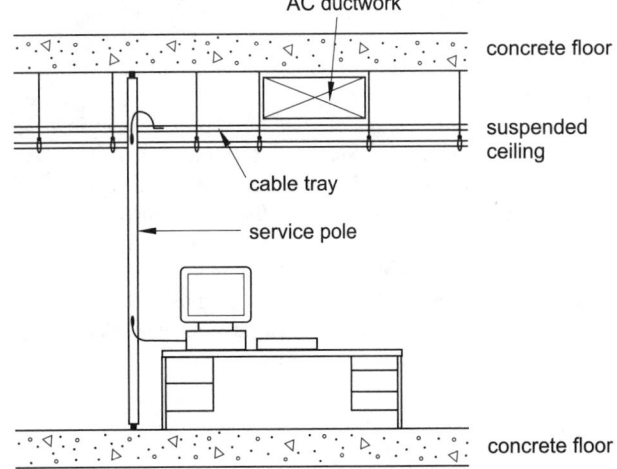

11.47 *Power and communication servicing through suspended ceiling*

through flaps with slots for the flexes. These boxes have a capacity limited by their size, and usually only have room for three power sockets and a double telephone socket. It is not that easy or cheap to provide more boxes, or to move the ones that are there, so that furniture and screen arrangements tend to be fixed in relation to them. Sometimes boxes find themselves within major traffic routes, where they cause a hazard.

● *In suspended ceilings*, **11.47**
Usually suspended ceilings are only half-full of air conditioning or ventilation ductwork, so the increase in depth to accommodate cabling is minimal. Power and telecommunication outlets can be accommodated in 'service poles'. These have

room for up to twenty miscellaneous outlets. They can be positioned virtually anywhere, and easily moved, as they are kept in place by simply being braced between the floor and the concrete soffit of the floor above. The disadvantage is that a multitude of service poles, apparently randomly placed, can appear unsightly.

● *In perimeter ducting connected to cable management systems within furniture and screens*, **11.48**
This is a system particularly suitable for naturally ventilated offices without suspended ceilings. It does make moving the furniture and screens difficult, and can inhibit easy movement between workspaces.

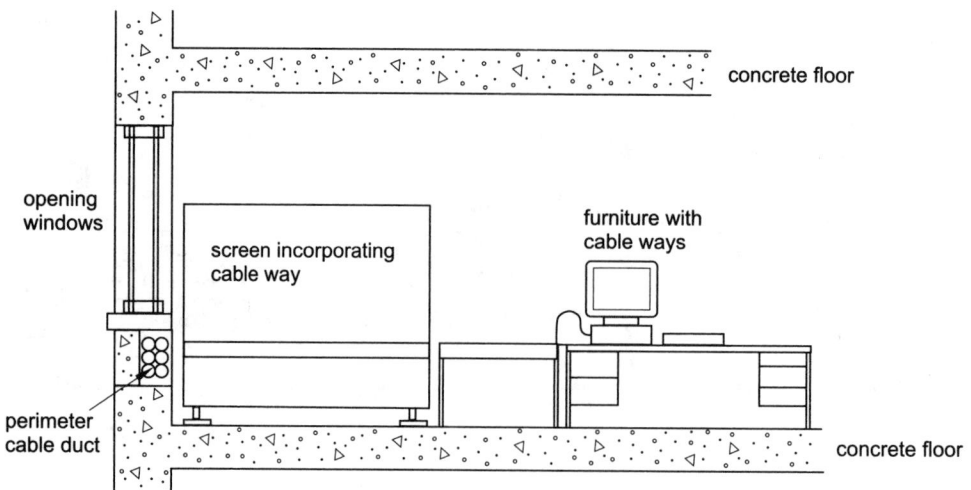

11.48 *Power and communication servicing through perimeter cable ducts, and cable management furniture*

Two other methods have been used in the past, but are no longer recommended. Ducts in the thickness of the floor screed require service outlets above floor level; and these can only be adjacent to the duct positions. These totally control the placing of furniture and pedestrian routes. An even worse system is to have the cables in the suspended ceiling below the floor in question. This means that when changes have to be made, work is done on a different floor which may be occupied by a totally different organisation!

8 BIBLIOGRAPHY

S. Bailey, *Offices*, Butterworth Architecture, 1990. A step-by-step guide through office briefing and design; a useful tool for early stages of project design.

F. Becker, *The Total Workplace: Facilities Management and the Elastic Organisation*, Van Nostrand Reinhold, 1990. The best text so far on organisational change and the workplace.

Building Research Establishment (ref BRE 183), *BREEAM 1/90: an environmental assessment for new office designs*, 1990 Environmental assessment for office buildings.

R. Crane and M. Dixon, *Office Spaces*, Architect's Data Sheets, ADT Press, 1991. An illustrative guide, if somewhat elementary, to office layouts and space standards.

CSC Index, *Intelligent Buildings: Designing and Managing the IT Infrastructure*, 1992. A detailed and up-to-date guide to the application of information technology in buildings.

S. Curwell, C. March and R. Venables (eds), *Buildings and Health: the Rosehaugh guide, RIBA Publications, 1990*. An excellent by-product of the great office boom. The basics of making healthy buildings.

F. Duffy, *The Changing Workplace*, Phaidon, 1992. An anthology of writings taken from the past 25 years. A history of the development of contemporary office design.

F. Duffy, A. Laing and V. Crisp, *The Responsible Workplace*, Butterworth Architecture, 1992. The results of a joint BRE/DEGW study into the trends in European office design. Contains a strategic approach to developing better office designs.

W. Kleeman, *Interior Design of the Electronic Office*, Van Nostrand Reinhold, 1991. This offers strategies to improve worker productivity, from technical issues to design psychology.

A. Konya and J. Worthington, *Fitting out the Workplace*, Architectural Press (out of print). A practical handbook for designers covering all elements of workplace design.

Anthony Speight, *The Architects' Legal Handbook*, 5th edn, Butterworth Architecture, 1990. Revised version updated to include changes in the law. An authoritative reference book.

J. Vischer, *Environmental Quality in Offices*, Van Nostrand Reinhold, 1988. Discusses building diagnosis and the systematic measurement of environmental quality in offices.

12 Law courts

Christopher Rainford

CI/Sfb: 317
UDC: 725.15

Christopher Rainford is the senior partner of Napper Architects, a practice considerably involved in the design of court buildings

KEYPOINTS:

- *the need for security against attacks from people both inside and outside the complex, while ensuring full access to those entitled makes design increasingly difficult.*

Contents
1 Introduction
2 The court system
3 The courtroom
4 The courtroom environment
5 Outside the courtroom

1 INTRODUCTION

1.01

The judicial system of England and Wales is in direct line of descent from that established by William I nearly a thousand years ago, subsequently modified by Magna Carta and many other reforms. Courthouses, therefore, are the visible manifestation of one of the most fundamental set of principles upon which our society is based.

How this is to be expressed in architectural terms is the particular challenge facing the designer of a courthouse. He or she will have to consider the contextual and environmental constraints that apply to any urban structure, especially those on prominent sites in town centres. Planning problems posed by the specific requirements for a courthouse must also be addressed, such as the four segregated circulation routes (for judge, jury, defendant in custody and public), the servicing of the many and varied spaces within a complex layout and the need for flexibility to accommodate future developments in information technology. Athough courtrooms built 200 years ago are still able to cope, the law is constantly evolving and both the courtrooms and the ancillaries need to be receptive to inevitable change.

2 THE COURT SYSTEM

2.01

The Court Service (formerly the Lord Chancellor's Department) has existed in various forms for over 900 years. It took on its present shape as a major government department with wide responsibilities for the administration of justice in England and Wales in 1972. Following the Courts Act 1971 it was given the task of running a new system covering all courts above the level of Magistrates' Courts. It is directly responsible for

- The Court of Appeal
- The Royal Courts of Justice
- The High Court
- The Crown Court
- The County Court.

The Crown Court is a national court which sits at different centres. Practically all its work is concerned with cases committed for trial or sentence from the Magistrates' Courts, or appeals against their decisions. Cases for trial are heard before a judge and jury. Centres are classified as first, second or third tier according to the nature and complexity of the court business.

3 THE COURTROOM

3.01

The Crown Court sits in a courtroom, the design of which will always be subject to the continuous adjustments dictated by changes in attitudes to child witnesses, the need to protect witnesses and jurors from possible intimidation and developments in technology.

3.02

The courtroom is the primary workspace and focal point in a courthouse, which is developed around it. It is the only place where all parties in a case are likely to meet. Of paramount importance is the need to segregate judge, jury, defendant and others in the courtroom and within the courthouse. Segregated circulation routes are provided so that the judge, jury and defendants (if in custody) make their way to the courtroom without meeting each other or any other users such as members of the public.

3.03

Dedicated entrances are provided for:

- Judge
- Jury
- Defendants in custody
- Public, witnesses and defendants on bail.

Some prosecution witnesses have to be protected from intimidation; a separate secure waiting room for them is often situated with its entrance off the vestibule provided between the public entrance and the courtroom itself. An alternative arrangement has a separate access from the secure waiting area into the courtroom adjacent to the witness box.

The public enter the court behind or to the side of the public seating at the rear of the courtroom; neither public nor witnesses pass areas dedicated to other participants (e.g. jury or defendants in custody) on entering or leaving the courtroom.

3.04 Relationships within the courtroom

Courtroom layout incorporates specific and well-defined relationships between the various participants by means of carefully arranged sight-lines, distances and levels. There are four main elements in Crown Court cases:

- Judge
- Jury
- Witness
- Counsel (barristers and solicitors).

Defendants do not take part except as witnesses. Each element must be closely related, and be able to see and hear each other clearly at all times without mechanical or electrical aids, and without excessive turning from side to side. The basic positioning of the occupants is shown in **12.1**. The theory behind these relationships can be summarised as follows:

12-1

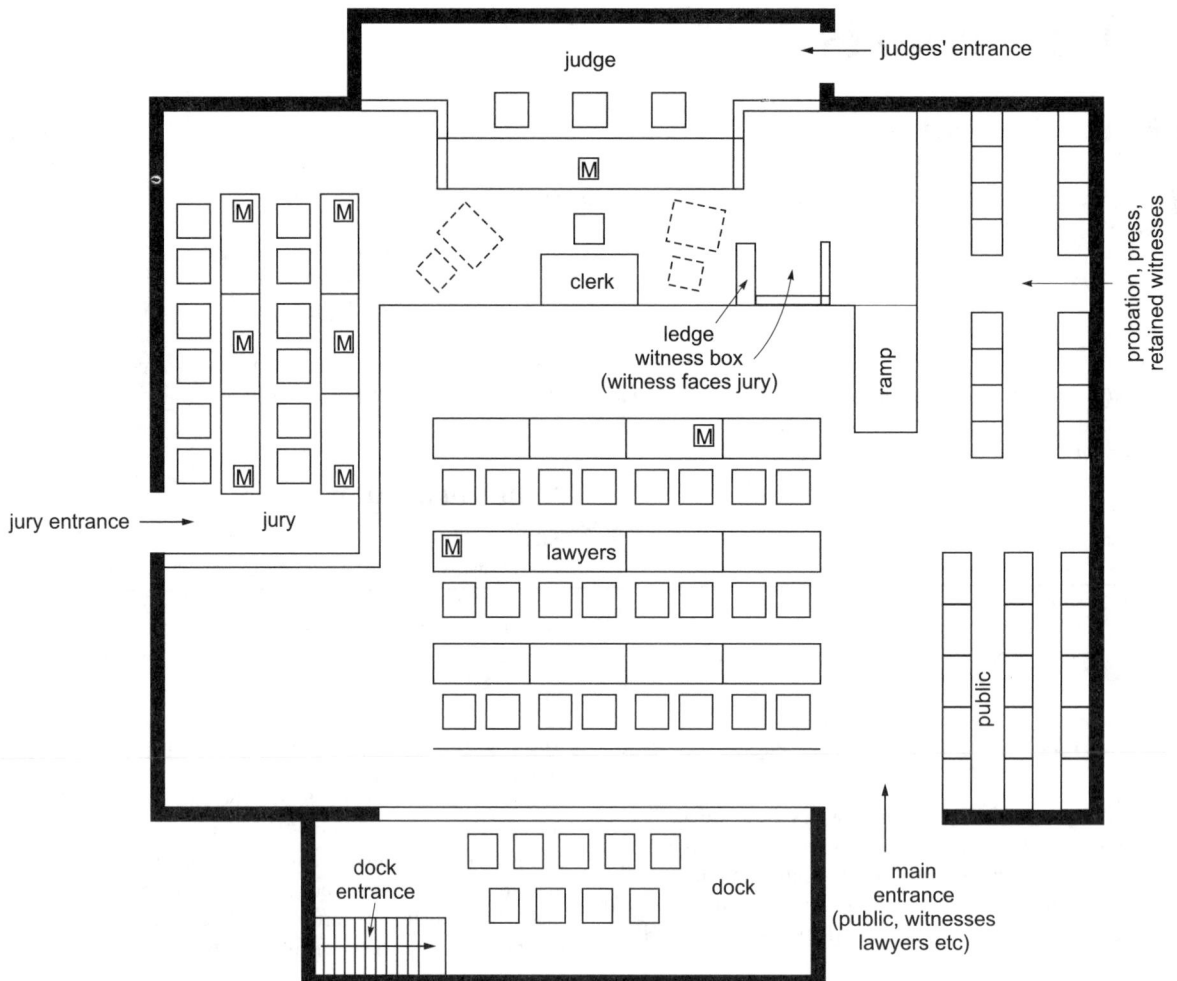

12.1 *Standard Crown Courtroom*

3.05 The judge
Presides over the courtroom, should be able to observe the whole of it, to see clearly the principal participants as well as the defendant in the dock and, when called, the antecedents and probation officers.

3.06 The court clerk
Administers the case and needs to keep a watching eye over the court. He or she often advises the judge and should be able to stand up and speak to the judge without being overheard.

3.07 The exhibit table
This is in front of the counsel benches for the display of exhibits put forward for evidence.

3.08 Counsel
These are barristers and solicitors who represent the defendant or prosecution. They need to be able to see the jury, judge and witness to whom they address their remarks. The barrister at each end of the front bench should be able to keep every jury member and the witness on the stand within about a 90° angle to obviate too much turning to ensure that the judge, the other main party, shall have at least a part face view. The counsel benches are wide enough to hold the large, and numerous, documents and books that are often in use.

3.09 The defendant
The defendant is assumed to be innocent until proved guilty and current practice is to reduce any prison-like appearance of the dock by lowering the barriers enclosing it as much as possible

compatible with security. Defendants sit in separate fixed seats and if they are thought to be a security risk a prison officer will sit on a seat immediately behind, or at each side of him. The dock is controlled by a dock officer and situated at the back of the courtroom.

3.10 The jury
This comprises twelve members of the public whose duty it is to reach a verdict based on the evidence presented. The jury sit opposite the witness stand and must be able to see the defendant in the dock, as well as the judge and counsel. They must have a writing surface and a place to put documents.

3.11 The witness
The witness waits outside the courtroom; and when called gives evidence from the witness stand near to the judge's bench. The stand faces the jury who must be able to observe the his or her face. The witness is questioned by the barristers and occasionally by the judge.

If the judge directs that a witness should be retained, he or she can wait seated within the courtroom.

3.12 The shorthand writer
This official keeps a transcript of the trial and consequently must be able to see and hear everyone who speaks.

3.13 Probation and antecedents officers
These give evidence from their seats after the jury have reached a verdict. This evidence is used to assist the judge in passing sentence.

3.14 The press

These are not party to the proceedings, but they should be able to see the participants.

3.15 The public

These are in court to see that 'justice is done'. They are placed at the near end of the courtroom and have a general view of the proceedings, but with the minimum possible direct eye contact with the jury to reduce the risk of intimidation. A public gallery over the jurors is the most effective method of eliminating possible intimidation; but access to such a gallery and the increase in height of the courtroom has to be considered. The glass screen between the public and the dock is partially obscured to prevent members of the public from seeing the defendants(s) (and vice versa) while seated.

4 THE COURTROOM ENVIRONMENT

4.01

The design of Crown courtrooms should seek perfection for their purpose. It should reflect the quiet dignity of the law rather than its power. A well-detailed, comfortable and quiet courtroom with efficient and simply managed ventilation, lighting and acoustics is the ideal.

4.02 Ventilation

Well-balanced environmental conditions within the courtroom are essential to the smooth running of the court. They keep the participants comfortable and interested, and avoid distractions. The current trend, supported by most users, is for natural ventilation with openable windows. This will subject the courtroom to wider temperature fluctuations; but this can be minimised by integrated automatic control systems.

4.03

Mechanical assistance (or in extreme cases full air conditioning) will be necessary where there would be unacceptable noise intrusion; or where the courtroom cannot have the height to induce

air flow by the natural stack effect. It is normally more economical and energy-efficient to have separate air handling units for each courtroom, managed by time switches and occupancy sensors.

4.04 Lighting

Daylight is provided if possible; but direct sunlight must be controlled and security risks avoided. The controlled use of daylight alone improves environmental comfort, but when it becomes for any reason insufficient, artificial lighting will be required. A combination of up-lighters and down-lighters reduces glare and contrast, and enhances the character of the courtroom. Lighting levels and colour should ensure correct colour rendering, and that all participants, exhibits and written evidence can be clearly seen without strain or dazzle.

4.05 Acoustics

The acoustics and noise levels should ensure that the proceedings can be heard in all parts of the courtroom; while avoiding distraction and annoyance from movement by the public, press or others. There may be a need for reflective or absorbent surface treatment to walls and ceilings.

5 OUTSIDE THE COURTROOM

5.01 Functional relationships

Courthouse accommodation is divided into areas, each with its own self-contained circulation. Movement between areas is limited and restricted. Even those who need to move freely can only enter certain restricted areas by passing through manned control points or other secure doors. The relationship and pattern of movement between the elements is shown in the functional relationship diagram 12.2.

5.02 Judiciary

The judiciary (judges, recorders, etc.) arrive at the court building and enter through a manned or otherwise restricted entry directly into their own secure area of the building. This contains the Judges' Retiring Rooms and all areas devoted to judicial use.

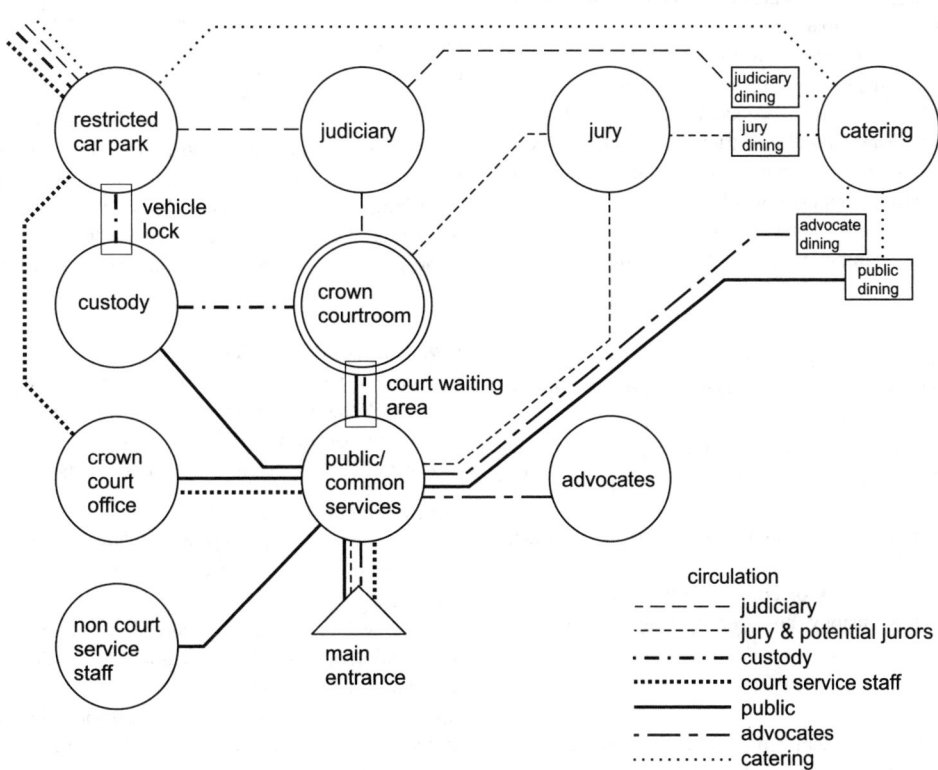

12.2 *Functional relationship diagram for a Courthouse*

The only other users of this area in 'working hours' are the staff, i.e. ushers, court clerks, security staff and invitees, i.e. legal representatives, guests and some members of the public invited to a Judge's Room. Invitees will always be escorted, and access for all will be either via the Judges' entrance into court or through staff areas. Each entrance will be via a self-locking, secure door.

5.03 Jurors

Persons, the number depending on the number and size of trials programmed, are summoned to the court building. They enter through the main public areas until they reach the reception area to the Jury Assembly Suite where they are booked in.

They then wait in the lounge or dining area where refreshments are available until called upon to form a jury panel. The period of waiting is variable and can be all day. Highest usage is before courts sit, and during lunch periods.

Egress from the Assembly Area, other than back past reception, is into jury-restricted circulation, which leads to Court and Jury Retiring Rooms. These should be adjacent or close to related Court Rooms, and all capable of supervision by one jury bailiff.

Once jurors have entered the Jury Assembly Suite they remain there, in court, or the Jury Retiring Room until sent home at the end of the day, or on dismissal.

5.04 Defendants

The Custody area is a self-contained compartment within the court building designated for the temporary use of prison governors in the discharge of their duties to the court to produce and retain prisoners in custody. It consists of the following principal parts, each separate from its neighbour and all non-custody uses:

- The custody core
- The vehicle entrance
- The visitors' entrance
- The courtroom entrance
- Three independent secure connecting routes:
  - custody core to vehicle dock
  - custody core to courtroom entrance
  - custody core to visitors' entrance.

While courts are sitting, the custody area is staffed and administered by prison officers. A principal or senior officer is in charge, supported by number of officers according to the number of courts and the level of risk. Some officers have fixed duties, for instance dock officer, cells officer; but the remainder are on escort duties.

Custody areas are designed and constructed to contain defendants, and to produce them to the court. Containment requires the meticulous and consistent application of passive security measures. Confinement and attendance at court for defendants is stressful, and this is compounded by natural frustration and anxiety.

The designer must:

- Give careful attention to all aspects of the design from the overall plan and its approaches, down to fixtures, fittings, fixings, finishes, alarms and communications
- Devise a layout that will achieve maximum control, make the best use of staff resources and maintain an acceptable level of safety and security
- Use the building fabric and the facilities within it to provide a secure envelope
- Deny the public direct view or contact with defendants while they are inside the custody area, except during authorised visits.

5.05 Public

The public areas with their associated circulation form the central core or axis from which most non- judicial functions of the court building radiate.

Except for the judiciary and specified car park users, all users enter the building by the main entrance door where space and facilities for security checks are provided. The arrival concourse contains the Information/Enquiry Point and the Cause List Display, both of which should be clearly seen on entering.

Public circulation then leads to Court Waiting Areas. These may be combined with associated circulation to form concourses off which are located the courtrooms and consultation/waiting rooms. Waiting areas should be visually interesting, preferably with external views.

Public circulation also gives access to private and semi-private accommodation occupied by Court Service (CS) staff, non-CS staff, the Probation Service, Custody Visits and to refreshment facilities. Access must also be available to the Crown Court Office counters. Direct access from the arrivals concourse to the Jury Assembly Area is desirable.

5.06 Advocates

Advocates enter the court building by the Main Entrance, reaching their suite via the public circulation. This is the area reserved for solicitors and barristers preparing for court, combining Lounge/ Study/Retiring Room for relaxation and quiet study in comfortable conditions, and for assembly, discussion, robing, etc. Lounge and Robing Room should if possible be contiguous otherwise direct access should be provided.

The suite has easy access to courtrooms via the public concourse where advocates meet clients, and to the Advocates' Dining Room. The Advocates' Clerks' room is closely related and shares the same private 'Advocates' circulation.

5.07 Crown Court Office

The Crown Court Office is occupied by executive and administrative staff engaged in the general administration of Crown Court business.

The General Office counter must be conveniently located to allow easy access for the public and for the legal profession; payment of expenses to jurors and witnesses may be made here.

There should be separate circulation to other staff areas and for direct access to the judges restricted circulation by ushers. Within the Crown Court offices, accommodation is provided for some more specialised groups:

- Court Clerks who are responsible for business in specific courtrooms and who spend part of their day in court
- Ushers who spend part of their time in court and also attending to judge and/or jury but will also do minor clerical work
- Listing Staff who are responsible for the planning and programming of the court timetable (lists of cases).

5.08 Non-courts Service Users

Non-courts Service Users includes Police, Crown Prosecution Service, Probation Service and Shorthand Writers, concerned with the running of the Court.

The Police area consists of two sections:

The Police Liaison Unit. This is the suite of offices for police staff attached to the courts and providing antecedents, etc. Included is a room where police witnesses can assemble and change if necessary.

The Police Law and Order Unit. This suite of offices is for police who maintain security or 'Law and Order' in the building (currently under review).

The Crown Prosecuting Service is responsible for the prosecution of defendants in court. It needs an office for law clerks to perform casework arising during the progress of the case, and to consult with members of the legal profession and witnesses.

The Probation Service, as attached to a Crown Court, will be active where persons have been made subjects of probation orders or inquiry reports at Court, although they may do some paperwork on other cases. The Probation Suite is a separate individual unit and where Night Reporting Facilities are required, must be able to operate in isolation while full security to the remainder of the court Building is maintained.

Shorthand writers are usually hired directly or via a service firm to take notes and transcribe Court proceedings.

5.09 Catering

Catering within Crown Courts involves self-service facilities for advocates, jurors, public and court staff, together with waitress service from a sideboard or servery for the Judiciary. The catering area should be sited on one floor with easy access for all court users, maximising usage and minimising operating costs. Multi-level catering areas should be avoided as less convenient and more expensive to operate.

13 Retail trading

Fred Lawson

CI/SfB(1976): 34
UDC: 725.21 & 725.26

Dr Fred Lawson is Visiting Professor, Department of Service Industries, University of Bournemouth. He is an international consultant and author of several books on planning and design

KEY POINTS:
- *Major changes have taken place in recent years*
- *More change can be expected*

Contents

1 INTRODUCTION

1.01

Retail premises consist of buildings or rooms where goods or services are sold to the public.

1.02 Scale and polarisation of business

Compared with other countries in Europe, the UK has a high ratio of retail outlets in relation to population. In 1991 there were over 240 000 retail businesses with 350 000 permanent outlets having a turnover approaching £124 billion and employing 2.5 million people.

13.1 and **13.2** indicate the magnitude of the retail sector for the last year of figures at present available.

Polarisation of business has had dramatic impacts on shop numbers: in 1960 there were 140 000 grocery shops with multiples commanding about 20 per cent of total sales; by 1980 grocery shops had reduced to 60 000 and by 1990 to around 50 000. In 1991 the five top multiple companies, with only 5 per cent of grocery outlets, commanded over 61 per cent of total grocery turnover. A similar concentration has occurred in the home improvement business.

1.03 Changes in space

Total shopfloor space grew from 76 million m^2 in 1971 to 93 million m^2 in 1992; almost $1.7 m^2$ retail space per head of population. About half of this growth was in the 1980s, mostly in shopping centres, retail warehouse parks and stand-alone superstores/retail warehouses.

2 TERMINOLOGY

2.01 Shopping activities

Shopping activities vary with different needs and may be described as essential, convenience, comparison, purposive (specific), leisure or remote (mail order, teleshopping).

2.02 Selling methods

Personal service: individual service, usually over counters or desks by staff in attendance. (Examples: high-value goods, technical equipment, specialist boutiques and salons, delicatessen shops, financial and travel agency services.)

Self-selection: by customers who handle, compare and select goods prior to taking them to cash points for payment and wrapping. (Examples: department stores, variety stores.)

Self-service: of prepackaged groceries and durables collected in baskets or trolleys and taken to checkout points for cashing and packing. (Examples: supermarkets, superstores, discount stores.)

Assisted service: self-selection by customers combined with despatch of similar goods from stockroom to collection point or home delivery. (Examples: hypermarket, warehouse stores, furniture stores.)

2.03 Stock

Forward or displayed stock: held in sales area.

Support or reserve stock: in stockrooms ready for replenishing sales. The method of replacing displayed stock is a critical consideration in planning and organisation.

Amounts of stock in reserve are related to the stock-turn (average time held prior to sale), weekly turnover, delivery frequency and stock control. Electronic point of sale (EPOS) monitoring is used to predict sales patterns, reduce reserve stock and coordinate distribution and manufacture.

2.04 Areas

Gross leasable area (GLA): total enclosed floor area occupied by a retailer. This is the total rented space and includes stockrooms, staff facilities, staircases, preparation and support areas. It is usually measured to outside of external walls and centre line between premises.

Net sales area (NSA): internal floor space of a retail unit used for selling and displaying goods and services. It includes areas accessible to the public, e.g. counter space, checkout space and window and display space. Net areas are used to calculate the density of trading turnover (sales per m^2 or ft^2).

The ratio of sales to ancillary space ranges from about 45:55 in small shops and departmental stores to 60:40 in supermarkets.

2.05 Rents

Rents are based on gross floor area measured in ft^2 or m^2 ($1 ft^2 = 0.0929 m^2$). Three main types of rental agreement are used:

Guaranteed rent: with minimum annual rent guaranteed by the tenant irrespective of sales

Percentage rent: based on a stated percentage of the gross sales of the tenant

Turnover lease: the rent being related to the actual gross turnover achieved by the tenant, based on the total trading receipts less stated allowable deductions.

Rents are normally subject to review every four or five years.

Leases usually include the right to assign after an initial period (five years) and may provide a landlord's option to buy back. Premiums may be charged when leases are sold for premises in good trading positions with favourable lease and rent review conditions.

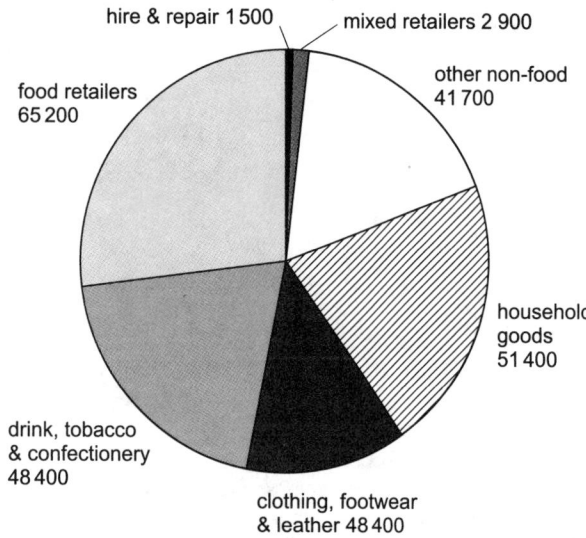

a *Numbers of businesses, total 241 700*

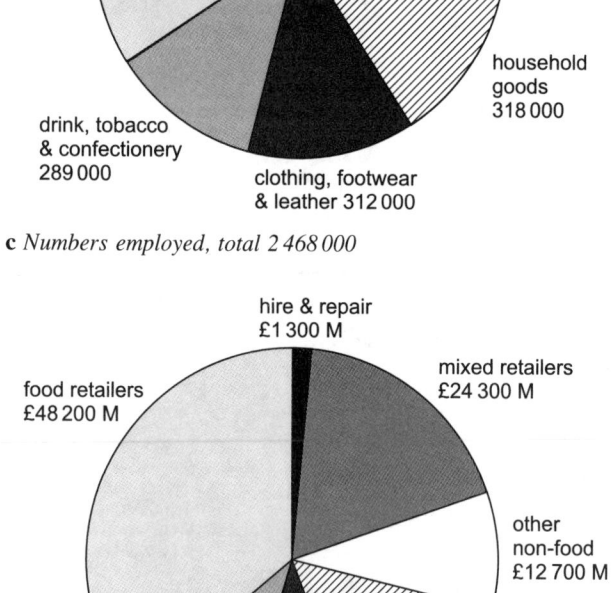

c *Numbers employed, total 2 468 000*

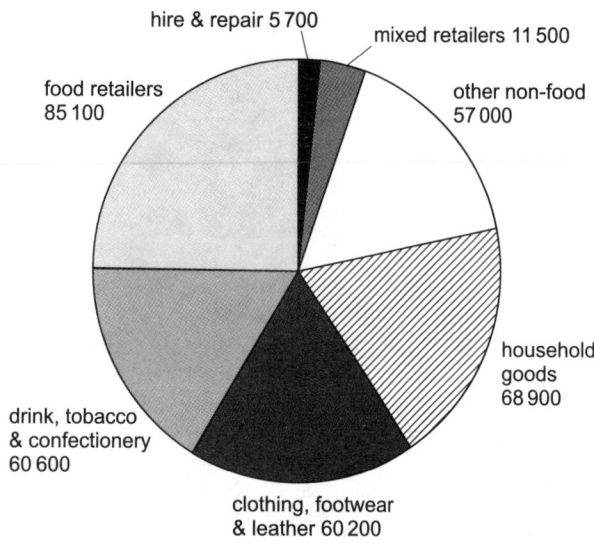

b *Numbers of outlets, total 348 900*

d *Annual turnover, total £132 700 million*

13.1 *Analysis of the retail trade by sectors*
(source: The retail pocket book 1994, Nielsen/NTC Publications, Oxford, 1994)

2.06 Retail operations

Independent: Shops and stores operated by individual or sole trader with less than ten branches (usually one or two). May be affiliated to a collective marketing and purchasing association.

Multiple: Mainly joint stock companies, with ten or more branches operated as a chain of shops and stores including large space users. Goods may include own-branded products.

Cooperative societies: Development has polarised into large supermarkets/superstores and small convenience shops serving local communities. Goods may be sourced through the Co-operative Wholesale Society or competitive suppliers.

Concessions: Granted rights to use land or premises to carry on a business – which may involve selling or promotion. The agreement may be based on rent, fees or profit sharing. (Examples are department stores, concourses in shopping centres, and catering operations.)

Franchises: Contractual relationships between two parties for the distribution of goods and services in which the franchisee sells a product designed, supplied and controlled by and with the support of the franchisor. (In the UK franchising has been mainly used in fast-food brands, launderettes, car maintenance, bridal wear and some electrical trading.)

3 MARKETS

3.01

A market is a public area, open or covered, provided with stalls, where traders may sell their wares on recognised market days subject to payment of a statutory charge. This franchise confers sole and exclusive market rights over a distance of 10.73 km.

Markets make up less than one per cent of total retail sales in the UK, but attract potential customers to the town area. The character of markets relies on variety, mix of traders, simplicity and liveliness.

3.02 Open markets

Markets may be set up in streets, squares and open spaces, **13.3**. Stands comprise erected stalls and fitted-out vans and trailers set out in line along kerbs or back to back between aisles. Key considerations are:

● Vehicle parking and loading (near stalls)
● Traffic control
● Garbage storage and collection
● Washing facilities
● Protection of exposed food.

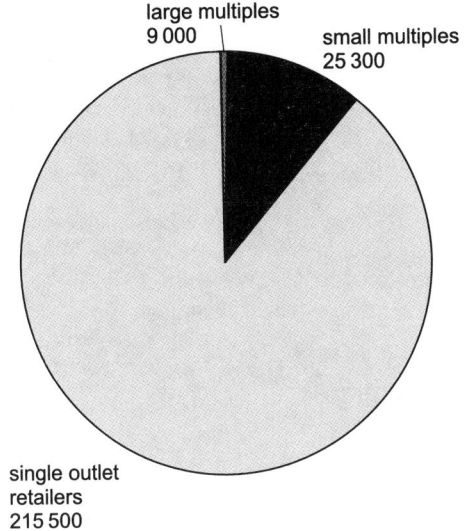

a *Numbers of businesses, total 241 700*

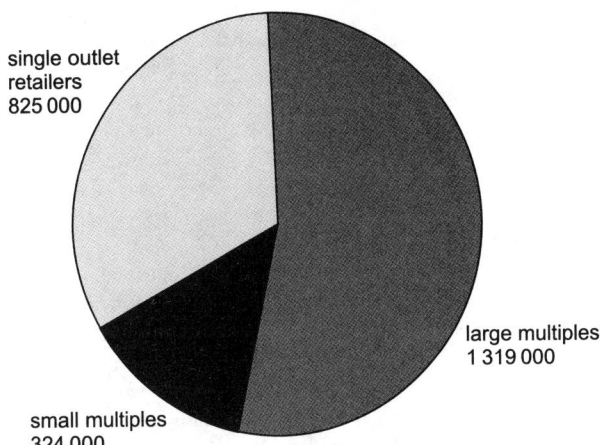

c *Numbers employed, total 2 468 000*

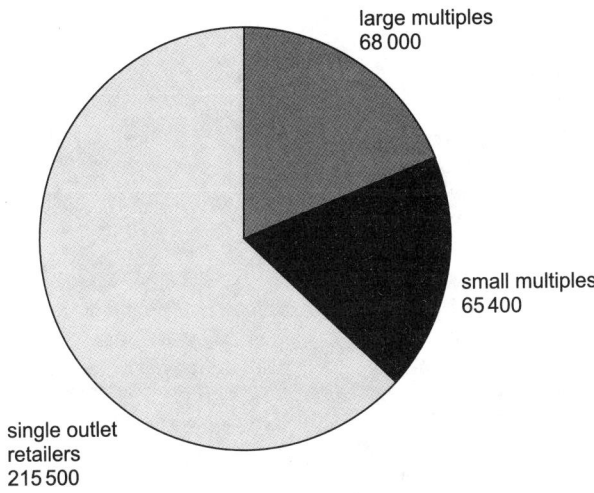

b *Numbers of outlets, total 348 900*

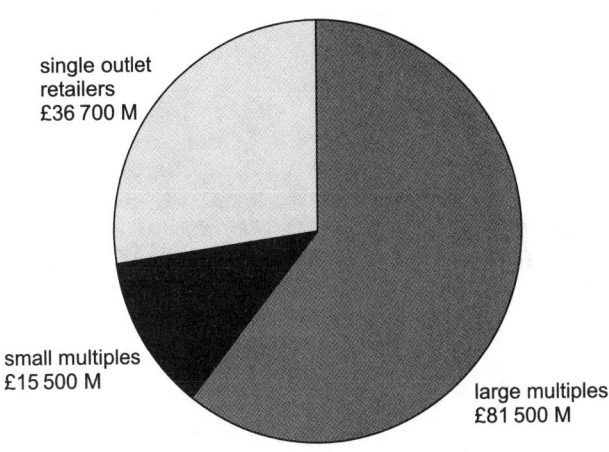

d *Annual turnover, total £133 700 million*

13.2 *Analysis of the retail trade by size of enterprise (source: Business Monitor, SDA 25, Central Statistical Office, London, 1994)*

13.3 *Markets*

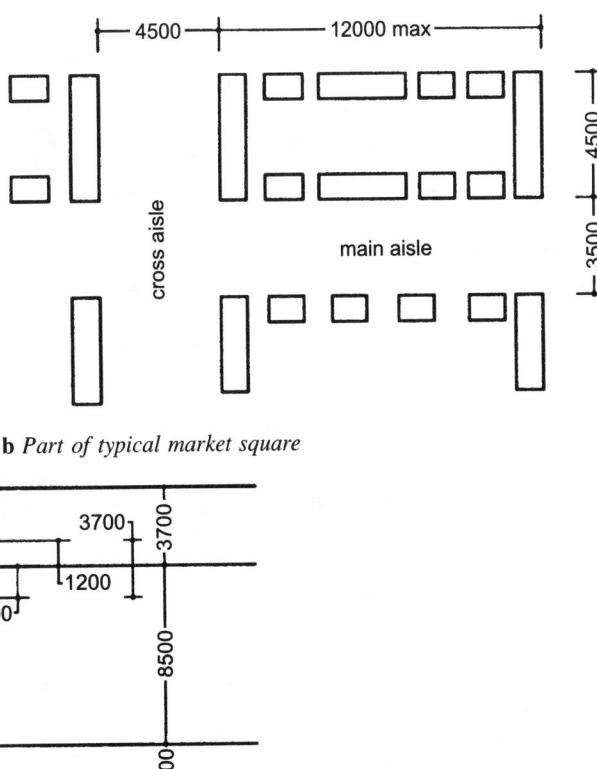

b *Part of typical market square*

a *Roadside, North End Road, Fulham*

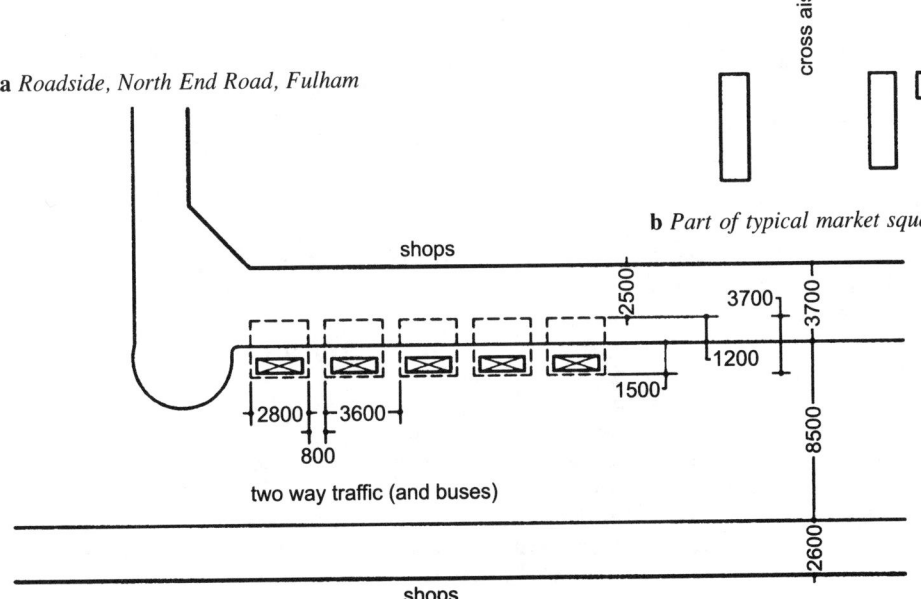

3.03 Covered markets

Permanent market stalls are sited in town centres and fringe areas (associated with auction rooms). New projects include craft markets (permanent or temporary) combined with workshops or forming part of shopping centres. Redevelopment of existing market halls often involves linkages with shopping centres and car parks.

3.04 Planning

Halls are usually designed to give a large-span open space having natural roof lighting, good ventilation and service connectlons. One-floor trading is preferred. Any upper floor is usually limited to a perimeter balcony served by escalators, stairs, goods and disabled lifts. Perimeter stalls and other grouped layouts have service corridors. Fish, meat and food stalls are sited in zoned areas with more sophisticated ventilation, drainage and services.

Key considerations: Access and linkage to car parks, shopping areas, goods delivery and parking bays. Mix of traders. Risk of fire (incombustible materials, fire-resistant construction smoke evacuation) and means of escape.

4 SHOPS AND STORES

4.01 Locations

Main locations for retail development in the UK are:

High street: inner cities and towns, including backland development of shopping centres, shopping malls and street frontages

Urban fringes: industrial wasteland, redevelopment areas (superstores, retail parks, discount stores)

Out-of-town: near motorway/main road junctions, easy access to large population catchment (retail complexes, regional centres, discount warehouses)

Neighbourhood: association with estate development, filling stations (convenience shops), nurseries (garden centres), tourist attractions (souvenir shops, cáfes)

Out-of-town retail developments generally allow much lower rents, easier access and parking, economical purpose-built 'shed' designs with flexible large-span spaces. Retail parks and complexes also generate mutual benefit from association of stores and services. Planning guidelines in the UK (1994) have stiffened resistance to development on greenfield sites with policies directed towards town-centre shopping and sensitive integration of new frontages.

4.02 Range of shops and stores

Retail outlets can be broadly divided into small shops (less than $280\,m^2$ sales area) and large space users. The latter include supermarkets and stores which may specialise in food or non-food lines or sell a wide variety of products (composite shops, variety shops, departmental stores).

Distinctions between stores tend to become blurred with:

- *Retail polarisation*: trends towards both larger (one-stop shopping) and smaller retailers (speciality and convenience shops, financial, etc. services, franchised units, workshop-craft outlets)
- *Competition*: innovation, market penetration and development of new merchandise and selling methods, creaming of popular lines
- *Acquisition*: merger of competing outlets, focusing of business and market positioning of company products, rationalisation of lines of goods and resources.
- *Image and service improvement*: extension of added value and high-profit value lines. Improved customer services and design environment.

4.03 Planning guidelines

Structural models	Width (m)	Notes
Small shops	5.3 to 6.0	Mostly 5.4 m
Large-space users	7.3 to 9.2	Depending on beam depth. Single-storey buildings – larger spans

Clear ceiling	Height(m)	To underside of beams
Small shops	3.3 to 3.8	Sales area
	3.2 to 3.6	Non-sales area
Large-space users	3.6 minimum	With floor: floor spacing 4 to 5 m

Typical floor loading	kN/m^2	
Shop sales area	5	
Shop storage	10	Increase in loading docks

Car parking	Car spaces per $100\,m^2$ gross retail area	
Supermarkets, superstores	10–12	
Shopping centres	4–5	

Goods and service docks	m	Notes
Typical provision for large-space user		
Two 15 m articulated lorries: width	10.7	Allowing 1.5 m each side
Minimum clearance height	4.7	Approach road – 5.00 m
Design load for service yard (See also Chapter 4)	$20\,kN/m^2$	

Deliveries may be controlled or random. Provision must be made for manoeuvring space and waiting bays, for separate refuse storage with compaction equipment, refrigerated garbage and collection skips.

Staff facilities (general guide only)
Staff numbers: net sales areas, 1: $50\,m^2$ to 1: $80\,m^2$

Additions to the net sales area

	Net areas	Gross areas
Staff facilities	10–15 per cent }	25–30 per cent
Offices	5–8 per cent }	

Staff facilities include: restaurant with kitchen and servery, coffee and recreation rooms, changing areas, toilets, personnel and training and reception/control area.

4.04 Shop fittings

Shop fittings may be individual bespoke designs, fabricated or modular units. While the range and style vary widely, fittings must satisfy functional needs (including ergonomics) and be compatible with the design, versatile, durable, stable and safe in use.

Display units can be broadly divided into wall-anchored fittings and free-standing units, the latter being designed for perimeter or central locations.

13.4 and **13.5** are examples of mobile display units, while **13.6** to **13.8** show units suitable for supermarkets.

Examples

Wall systems (slotted panels, frames, suspensions)
Fitted furniture (cupboards, wardrobes, trays)
Free-standing racks and garment rails
Gondolas and island displays
Cases (counters, showcases, wall cases)
Cabinets (front or top access)
Shelving systems (modular, adjustable)
Forms, mannequins, displays (counter or free-standing)
Bins, tables, risers
Counters (cash and wrap, checkout, service)

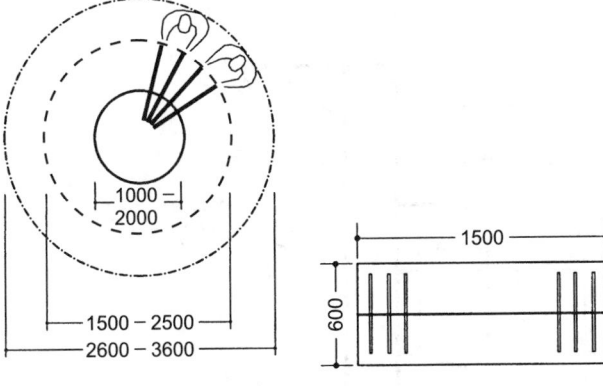

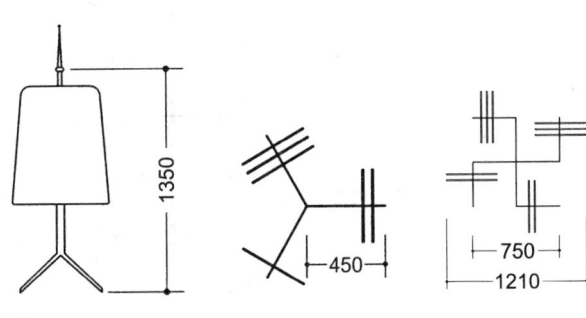

13.4 *Storage and display racks for clothing shops*

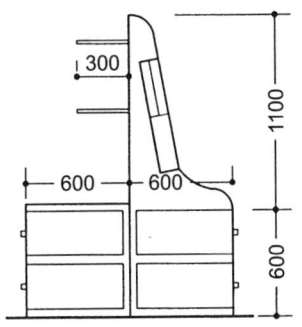

a *Greetings cards*

b *Paperback books*

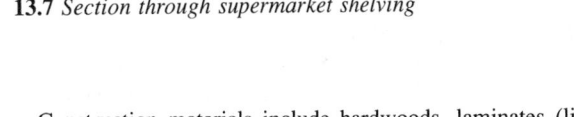

13.6 *Section through supermarket wall shelving*

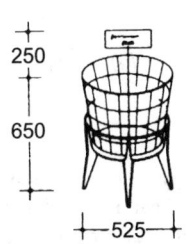

c *Bins, used everywhere*

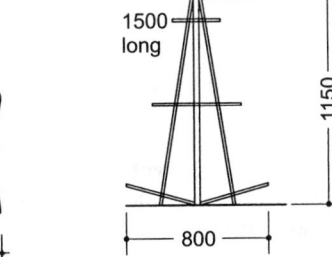

d *Island display of books*

13.7 *Section through supermarket shelving*

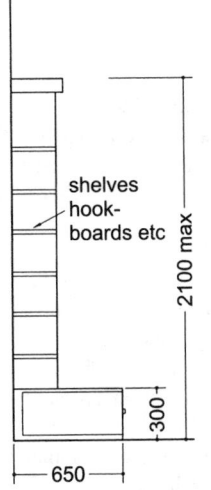

e *Wall units for stationery and books*

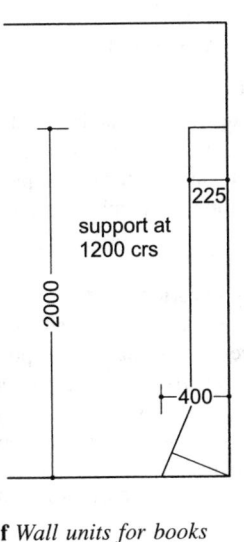

f *Wall units for books*

13.5 *Storage and display fittings for stationery and bookshops:*

Construction materials include hardwoods, laminates (lipped) acrylics, toughened glass, polycarbonate, UPVC, chrome-plated and stainless steel, anodised aluminum.

4.05 Environmental Standards

Lighting	Standard service illuminances (lux)	Notes
Conventional shops	500	Concentrated over displays
Supermarkets	500	Usually increased to 700–800 lux with three levels of control: 100 per cent – sales, 50 per cent – stacking, 30 per cent – security
Covered shopping centres	100–200	Malls, arcades, precincts
Lifts, main circulation	150	
Staffrooms	150	
External covered ways	30	

Luminaires include low-voltage units (displays), colour-balanced fluorescent (sales areas), metal halide (high intensities).

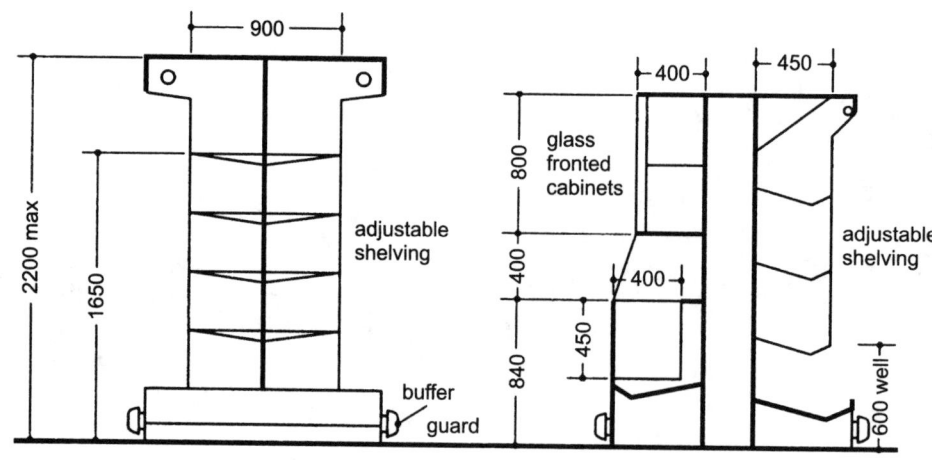

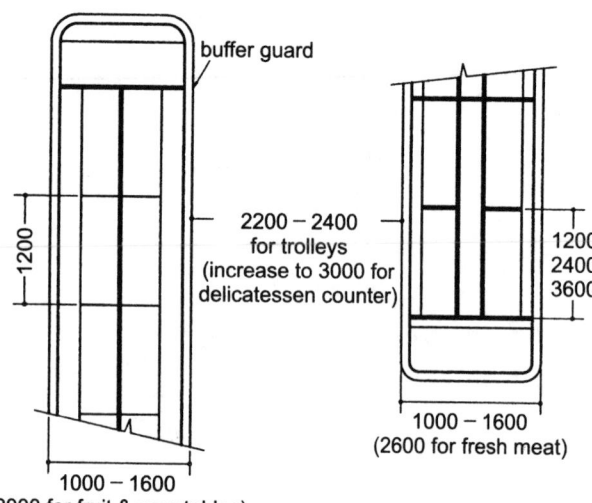

13.8 *Plan and section through supermarket display cabinets*

Temperatures: Design conditions

	Temperature (°C)	Air infiltration (Changes/ hour)	Ventilation allowance (W/m³°C)
Small shops	18	1	0.33
Large shops	18	½	0.17
Department stores	18	¼	0.08
Fitting rooms	21	1½	0.50
Store rooms	15	½	0.17

Recommended outdoor supply rates for airconditioning spaces

Recommended	*Minimum*
8 per person	5 per person, 3 per m² of floor area

Occupancies in large stores: average: 1 person per 5–6 m²; peak areas: 1 person per 1.8 m²

Air conditioning is usually designed for 18–21°C at 50 per cent ± 5 per cent RH (below-risk of static) pressurised to + 5 per cent actual air volumes

Fresh air regulated by CO_2 sensing.

In shed-type buildings design temperatures are 18°C with 10 per cent fresh air. Air cooling used 18–22°C and mechanical cooling above.

Display of food	*Cabinets* (°C)
Fresh products (chilled)	+8
Dairy products, cooked meats, ready meats	+3
Fresh meats, poultry, fish	0
Frozen foods	–18
(subject to EU regulations)	

4.06 Energy management

Most multiple and large stores use energy management systems. with remote station monitoring. Waste heat is recovered from refrigeration for hot water supplies and cool air recycled from refrigerated display areas. Refrigerants are changing to hcfc's (non-ozone reactive) with leakage-detection systems.

5 SMALL SHOPS

5.01

These are shops having a sales area less than 280 m² and not more than three stores, one of which may be a basement. Shops employing fewer than 20 people or 10 above the ground floor do not normally require a fire certificate.

5.02 Location

Convenience shops need to be near populated areas or stopping places (filling stations, airports, railway stations).

Speciality shops are best grouped with other shops and large space users to increase market exposure or in speciality areas associated with tourist attractions, etc.

Financial, etc. services: shop units usually combined with offices and ancillary rooms above (see Chapter 14).

5.03 Planning

Typical small shop plans are given in **13.9** to **13.12**.

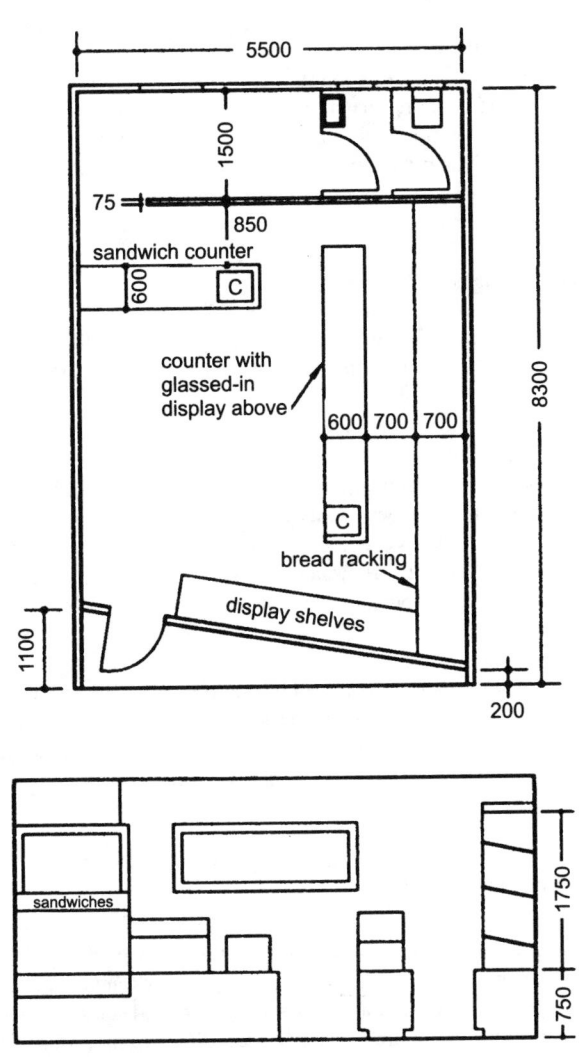

13.9 *Baker's shop, plan and section C cash register, W weighing machine*

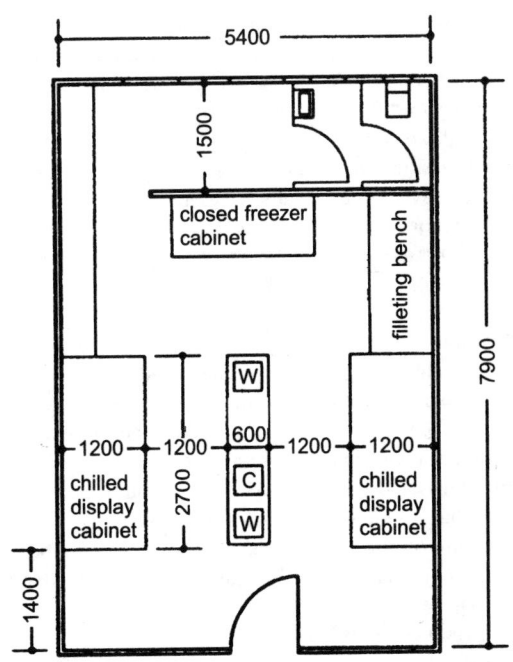

13.10 *Butcher's shop, plan and section*

	Typical	Minimum
Width of frontage	5.4 to 6.0 m	4.0 m
Depth	18.0 to 36.0 m	12.0 m
Height (depending on services)		3.0 m
Sales: ancillary areas	50:50	45:55
Staff facilities	1 wc plus 1 washbasin for each sex (minimum)	
	Changing area with individual lockers	
	Restroom with small food-preparation area	
Office	Files, safe, desk, terminals	

5.04 Servicing arrangements

- Stock replenishment and waste removal usually through a rear service road
- In a shopping complex this may be accessed through a service corridor and goods lift
- Some pedestrianised precincts allow vehicle access to front of shops outside restricted hours.

5.05 Design

The design of the shop frontage, graphics and window display is a major consideration. Multiple and franchised outlets usually reflect a uniform brand image. In environmentally sensitive areas, the scale and character of existing facades may need to be retained.

13.11 *Fishmonger's shop, plan*

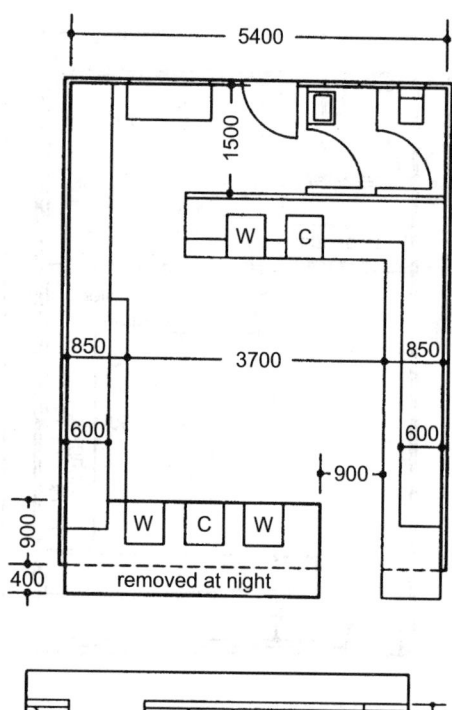

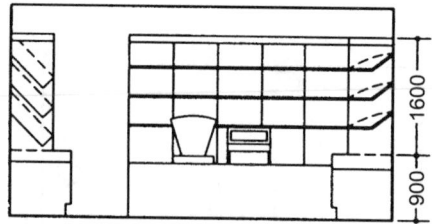

13.12 *Greengrocer's shop, plan and section*

Interior layouts, fittings and design features depend on the nature and volume of goods sold.

6 DEPARTMENT STORES

6.01

Department stores are large complex shops, invariably extending over several floor levels, selling a wide variety of goods, particularly clothes. Sales areas are grouped into departments corresponding to different categories of shops but are flexible in size and position. Departments may be operated directly by the store or let to other traders and franchisees.

Main high street stores usually have more than 20 000 m² sales areas but 'Junior' department stores in new shopping centres are less than 10 000 m² over two floors. Sales:gross area ratios are relatively low, 45:55.

6.02 Planning

A frontage to more than one street or mall is preferred for extended window displays, customer entrances and emergency exits. Separate staff entrances and goods delivery and despatch areas (with customer collection bay) are essential.

Internal areas must be planned for maximum clear space to allow for changes in seasonal sales and tenancy arrangements. Exceptions are food areas (food halls, food-preparation kitchens) which require permanently fitted equipment and special services.

6.03 Fire requirements

Compartmentation: most regulations permit up to 2000 m² and 7000 m³ or twice this size (4000 m²) with automatic sprinkler system.

Smoke evacuation: reservoir space with exhaust ventilation and controlled airflows.

Construction: fire-resisting structures and limitations on surface flame spread of lining materials.

Isolation: sprinklers, water curtains and physical separation of escalators, lift shafts and voids.

Means of escape: travel distances to protected staircases and adequate exits to street.

6.04 Locations

Locations for departments is rationalised by floor levels of related goods but influenced by turnover values and unit selling times. The ground floor is used for quick sales or small items to attract customer interest.

Restaurants, toilets and customer services are usually accessed through selling areas.

Subsidiary accommodation is needed to service departments on each floor but main stock rooms, staff facilities and administration are located in lower-value areas (rear, basement or upper floor).

Escalators and lifts are usually centrally positioned to create a focus and draw customers through departments.

6.05 Trends

Department stores have relative high staffing and operating costs. Life-cycle renovation may be used to remodel, divide and/or extend stores as shopping centres. Junior department stores are also sited in airports and regional shopping complexes.

7 VARIETY STORES

7.01

These are large-space users selling a wide range of non-food goods, mainly by self-selection in an open sales area. In some stores part of the area is used for self-service food sales. Includes independent and multiple chain stores (Woolworths, Marks & Spencer, Littlewood, etc.).

7.02 Size and location

Sales areas range from 500 to 15 000 m², most major stores being between 10 000 and 15 000 m² with sales:ancillary area ratios of 50:50.

Locations

- Prime high streets: serving sizeable catchment populations
- Shopping centres: multi-level links to upper and lower floors
- Regional shopping complexes and retail parks (space allowing introduction of wider ranges of goods).

Major stores require catchments of 80 000 to 100 000.

7.03 Planning

A rectangular plan with one-level trading is preferred with frontages on the high street and shopping mall. Sales floors in large stores are on two levels (sometimes three) with food areas having access to parking or collection points. Escalators, stairs and lifts for the disabled and goods distribution are kept to the perimeter to allow uninterrupted space for display and circulation planning.

7.04 Layout

Main aisles with distinctive flooring lead from entrances to assemblies of display fittings and cash and wrap points positioned for visibility and convenient access.

Displays include both perimeter and island fittings with related goods grouped together for easy location and comparison. Stores selling clothes and fashion goods must provide changing rooms and multiple mirror points. The self-service areas for food goods are planned on supermarket lines.

7.05 Facilities

Some stores provide a café or restaurant for customer use usually located on the upper floor to promote other impulse buying. Toilets and other customer services are in this vicinity.

Ancillary areas for staff and reserve stock are at the rear or on a higher floor, with separate staff entrance, reception and control leading to changing and associated facilities.

8 SUPERMARKETS

8.01

Supermarkets sell food and regular domestic necessities on self-service lines. The sales areas of large-space users range from 1000 to 2500 m² although many small grocers also use self-service.

8.02 Planning

Sales are invariably on one floor, planned to allow trolley circulation from car park through the store. Where required, upper floors are limited to non-food goods. A simple rectangular plan is preferred with 30 to 60 m frontage. (Minimum frontage (18 m) may require double-banked checkouts.)

The position and layout of the checkout points govern entrance, exit and circulation plans. Sales areas have large unobstructed spaces with structural grids of 9.0 m or more (to suit stand spacing) and 3.66 m clear ceiling heights.

8.03 Layout

A standard arrangement of parallel shelf racks and cabinets on each side of circulation aisles is invariably adopted. The main aisles are 2.2 to 2.5 m wide increasing to 2.8 to 3.2 m in front of delicatessen counters and fresh/frozen meat cabinets. 3.0 m across aisles are provided at the end of turns and a clear area 2.2 to 3.0 m deep on each side of the checkout line.

Displays are grouped into food, non-food and off-licence sections. Delicatessen, bakery and perishables prepared on the premises need to be adjacent to the preparation areas, with easy access to stores (refrigerated).

As a rule, refrigerated display cabinets are grouped together to facilitate service connections and airflow recovery.

Demand goods (vegetables, fruit) are usually placed near the entrance to initiate buying and promotional items displayed in bins and in racks at the end of rows and checkout stations.

Space has to be allocated for customers to collect and restore baskets and trolleys, **13.13** and **14**. Where virtually all customers arrive by car, trolley parks are normally situated within the car parking area, often in lightly covered kiosks; and few (if any) baskets are provided. In urban areas, substantial areas within the

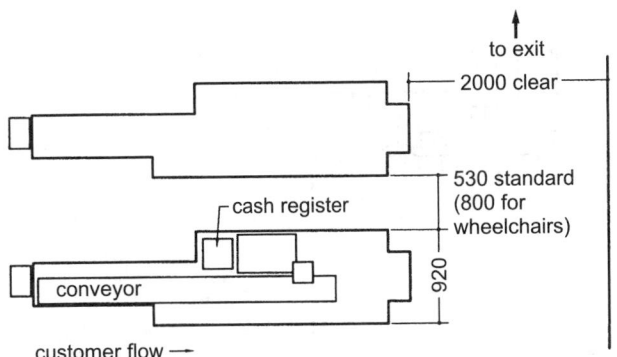

13.15 *Typical check-out*

store curtilage have to be provided, and many customers will use baskets.

In self-service shops, supermarkets and hypermarkets the customer pays for his or her purchases at a checkout. These vary greatly in design, depending on the type and quantities of merchandise, and the policies of the company concerned. Some contain automatic price-checking equipment and semi-automatic packing arrangements. **13.15** shows a fairly standard basic design.

Separate shop units (newsagents, florist, chemist, café) may be sited independently of the checkout and direct access is required to public toilets, public telephones and management offices.

8.04 Trends

The intensity of sales/m² is a critical consideration with trends towards increase of high added value (own-preparation bakery, butchery) and profit margins (delicatessen, wines, plant sales, made-up goods).

Technical equipment includes barcode scanning, EPOS monitoring and stock control, cheque printing and the introduction of liquid display shelf edge/labelling, robot packing and self-checkout facilities.

With opposition to out-of-town location, some multiples are developing convenience stores in town centres selling a limited range of goods.

9 HYPERMARKETS, SUPERSTORES, DISCOUNT STORES

9.01 Hypermarkets

These are very large stores on supermarket lines but with at least 2500 m² sales floor. Examples include Savacentres which provide 11 000 m² sales halls with 50 checkouts and gross floor areas of 20 000 m².

Compared with supermarkets the range of non-food lines is extended up to 50 per cent of the area. Hypermarkets tend to be built on derelict industrial land and urban fringes within large catchments, **13.16**.

Superstores are similar but tend to be larger with 5000 – 10 000 m² of selling space. Located out of town, they occupy large sites, with extensive parking, a petrol-filling station and an associated square or arcade of small shops, **13.17**. The overall development often combines out-of-town shopping with community facilities such as a village hall, public house, sports ground or/ and leisure centre.

Discount stores and warehouse clubs concentrate on lower costs by limiting the range of goods (e.g. 650 compared to a supermarket's 3500 brand lines) and using simpler warehouse-style buildings and fittings.

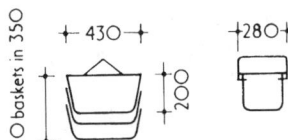

13.13 *Supermarket baskets*

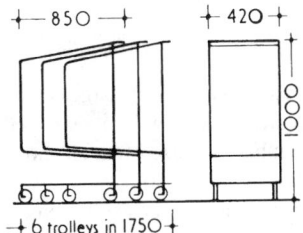

13.14 *Supermarket trolleys*

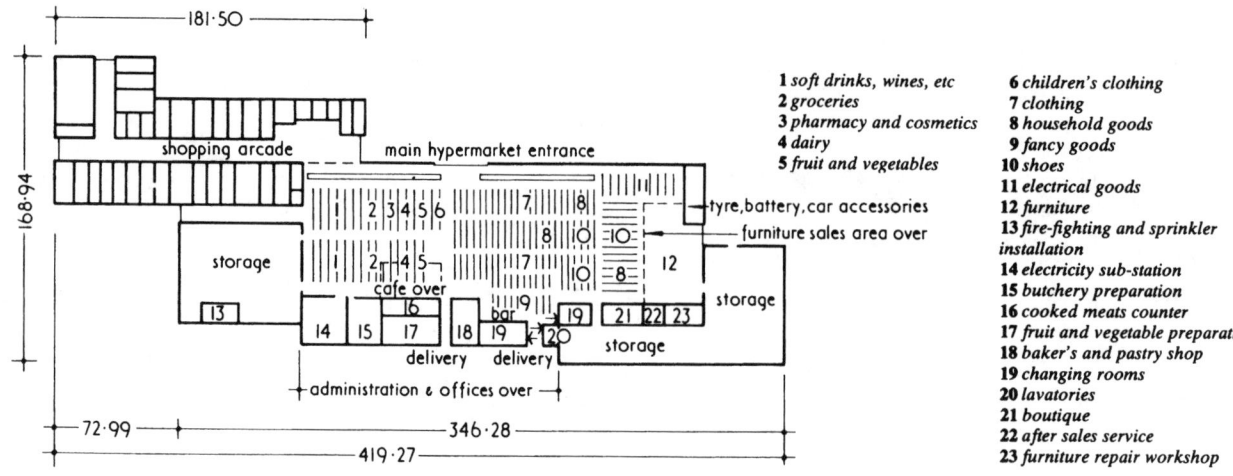

13.16 *General layout of a major hypermarket*

1 *soft drinks, wines, etc*
2 *groceries*
3 *pharmacy and cosmetics*
4 *dairy*
5 *fruit and vegetables*
6 *children's clothing*
7 *clothing*
8 *household goods*
9 *fancy goods*
10 *shoes*
11 *electrical goods*
12 *furniture*
13 *fire-fighting and sprinkler installation*
14 *electricity sub-station*
15 *butchery preparation*
16 *cooked meats counter*
17 *fruit and vegetable preparation*
18 *baker's and pastry shop*
19 *changing rooms*
20 *lavatories*
21 *boutique*
22 *after sales service*
23 *furniture repair workshop*

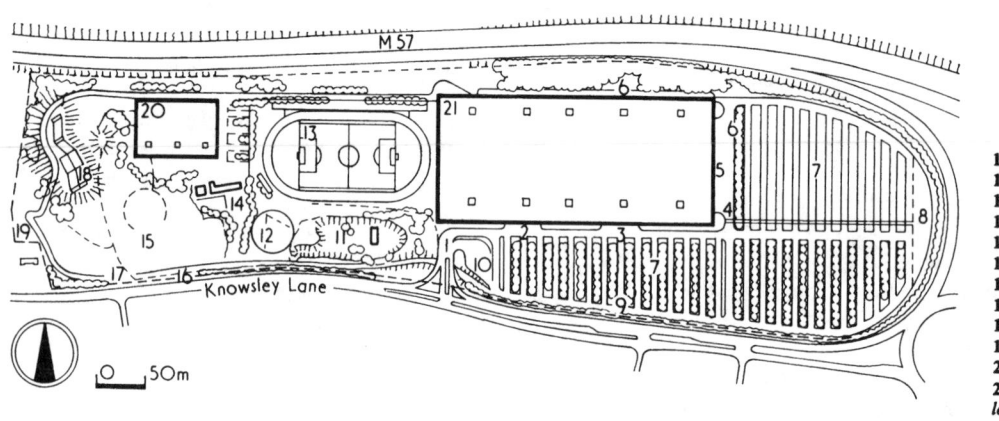

1 *site entrance*
2 *bus*
3 *taxi*
4 *service road*
5 *service bay*
6 *staff car park*
7 *car parking*
8 *coach parking*
9 *perimeter exit road*
10 *petrol service station*
11 *adventure playground*
12 *open play space*
13 *sports pitches and athletic track*
14 *horticultural centre*
15 *riding school field*
16 *bridle path*
17 *cycle training and racing track*
18 *dry ski and toboggan slopes*
19 *site boundary*
20 *riding school*
21 *pavilion containing superstore, leisure pool, sports hall, restaurants, library, cinema, exhibition gallery, etc*

13.17 *Superstore at Knowsley, Lancashire: site plan*
Architects: Foster Associates

9.02 Planning

Large stores are basically constructed as large rectangular boxes having large-span clearances to allow mainly one-level trading. If required, upper storeys are confined to part of the building and used for non-food sales, and ancillary services. The sales:ancillary ratio is high 60:40, with maximum goods on display and highly mechanised stock replenishment.

Compared with supermarkets, the stores use larger trolleys, wider and level circulation routes and easier transfer to car park areas (some with prepacking and mechanised conveyors).

10 SHOPPING CENTRES

10.01

These are planned shopping complex under one central management which has a high degree of overall control, leasing units to individual retailers.

Shopping centres may be:

- *Open*, in terraces, squares, piazzas or village-style groupings
- *Partially covered*, with canopies over frontages (3.6 m high for clearance) or setbacks creating arcades
- *Fully covered*, single-level or multi-level shopping malls, converted warehouses, etc.

10.02 Locations

New centres

- in new towns and expanding residential areas
- out-of-town regional shopping centres

Integrated centre

- in existing high street areas, to
- open up backland for commercial use
- provide linkages with other developments, carparks, etc.
- extend pedestrianised areas.

10.03 Planning

Centres should, where practicable, follow existing street patterns and be sensitively integrated into the existing street architecture.

Commercial and operational considerations

- Number, size and locations of large space users and other attractions (magnets) which will increase pedestrian flows
- Distribution, number and size of small shop units, numbers of shopping levels
- Servicing needs and access for goods vehicles
- Entrances and links with parking, public transport and other shopping areas

13.18 *L-shaped plan: Arndale Centre, Luton*

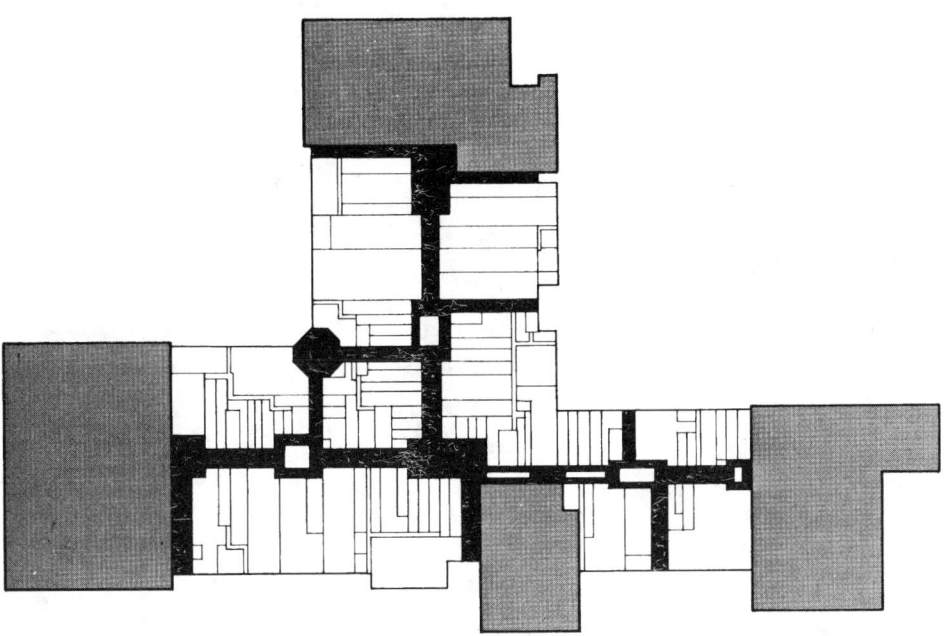

13.19 *T-shaped plan: Willowbrook Mall, New Jersey*

- Focuses and features to provide an identity and sense of place
- Environmental control in the mall and individual shops
- Fire regulations, safety and security requirements.

10.04 Plan forms

Shopping units are mainly one or two levels. Upper levels are usually required to join multi-storey variety and department stores and form galleries around a central square or atrium. Gross leasable areas vary, many infilling centres fall within 25 000 and 50 000 m² GLA providing 40 to 100 units. New regional centres may provide up to 100 000 m² GLA with 40 per cent allocated to large space users (magnets).

Magnets are sited near the ends of malls and branches to attract flows of shoppers past individual shops and have an effective range of 90 to 120 m. It is not practical to extend a mall more than 350 m and large developments calls for more than one level with concentrated plan forms. L, **13.18**, T, **13.19**, C and □ plans are common but out-of-town centres may use cruciform, **13.20**, pinwheel **13.21** and figure-of-eight, **13.22** layouts extending out from a central concourse.

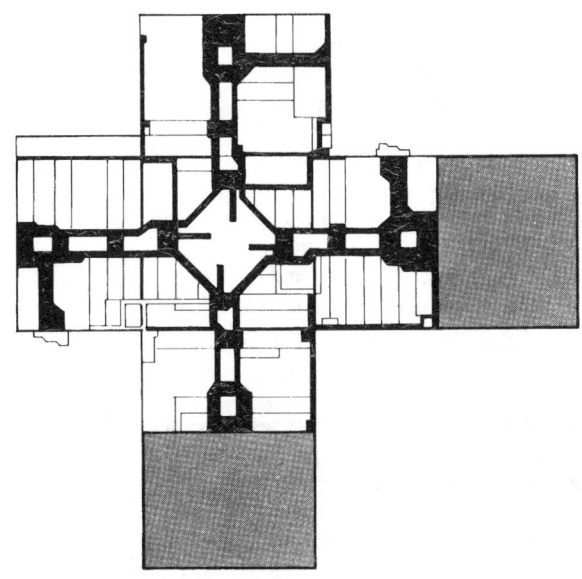

13.20 *Cruciform plan: La Puente, California*

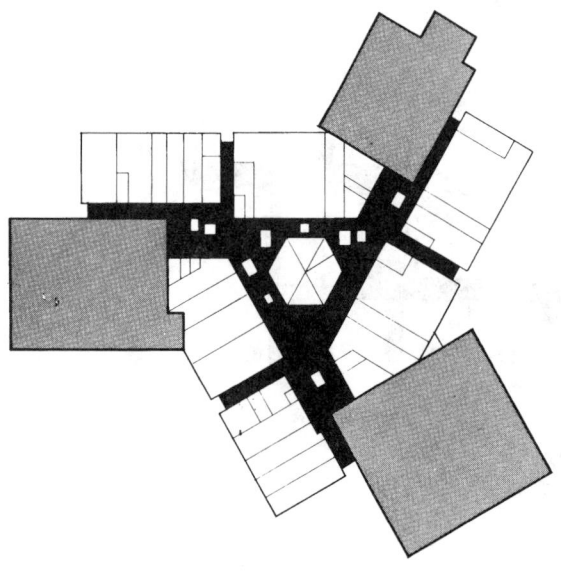

13.21 *Pinwheel plan: Randhurst, Illinois*

with incidental combustible material controlled, and have an automatic sprinkler system installed.

Specific requirements apply to adjoining or facing frontages of large space users (more than $2000\,m^2$).

Smoke control
Smoke reservoirs, **13.24**, are created by downstand beams on fascias at shop frontages and intervals along the mall. Smoke detectors activate exhaust fans in the reservoirs and lower fresh air supply fans to ensure clear escape routes. Further smoke ventilation and smoke control facilities are shown in **13.25** to **13.27**.

Escape routes
Maximum occupancy levels are estimated on the basis of:

- Shops, showrooms, supplementary areas – $7.0\,m^2$/person
- Supermarkets, department sales floors – $2.0\,m^2$/person

No more than 50 per cent of occupants should be assumed to escape through the rear of a shop, the rest using the mall. Escape routes from the mall must be provided at intervals with exits to open streets directly or via separated structures.

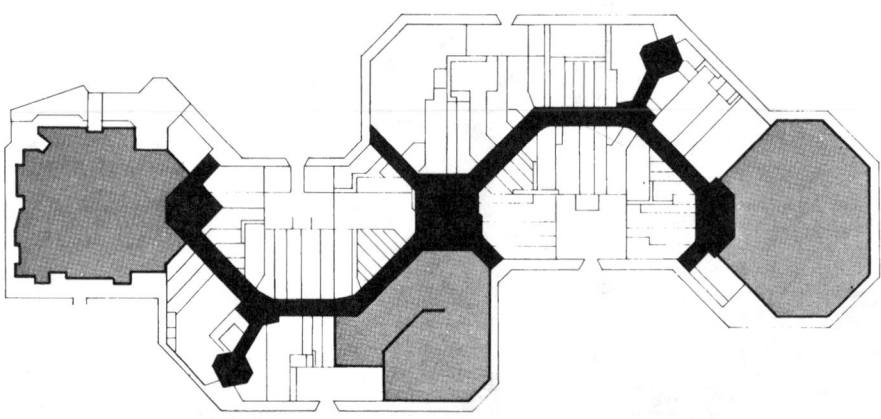

13.22 *Figure-of-eight plan: Sherway gardens, Toronto*

10.05 Details
In the UK mall widths have progressively increased from 5.4 m to 8 m or 9 m. The average French centre uses a 16 m mall while North American malls vary from 12 to 27 m. Galleries around central courts are often 4 m wide. The preferred frontage for small shops is 5.4 m to 7.3 m with a depth of 13 m to 39 m but smaller units (1.8 × 3.6 m) are often required for service outlets and specialised trades.

Glazed frontages are necessary when the mall remains open to the public at night but otherwise Continental (fully or partly open) frontages are more convenient with latticework shutters or fire barriers (if required) to secure the shop at night.

10.06 Food courts and focuses
Large atria and glazed courtyards provide activity spaces which are often landscaped and used as revenue-generating open restaurants or food courts. Features such as water fountains, kiosks, planted containers and children's play centres also create focuses for interest and direction.

10.07 Fire precautions
The design of shopping centres does not conform with conventional compartmentation arrangements and specific requirements will be stipulated by each fire authority.

Fire control
Fire separation walls are required between shops in different tenancies, **13.23**. Malls must be of non-combustible construction,

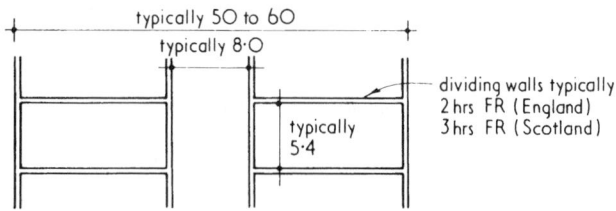

13.23 *Plan of a mall showing fire separation between shop units*

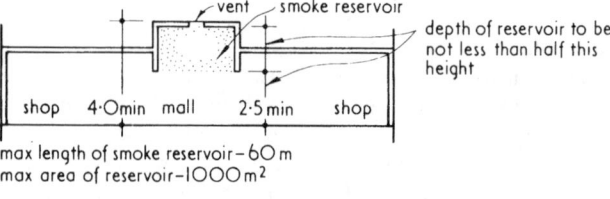

13.24 *Section showing smoke reservoir*

Controls
Automatic fire alarm and indication systems must be installed.

Access
Requirements of the fire authority for appliance access into the mall must be adopted together with positions for hydrants, hoses and extinguishers.

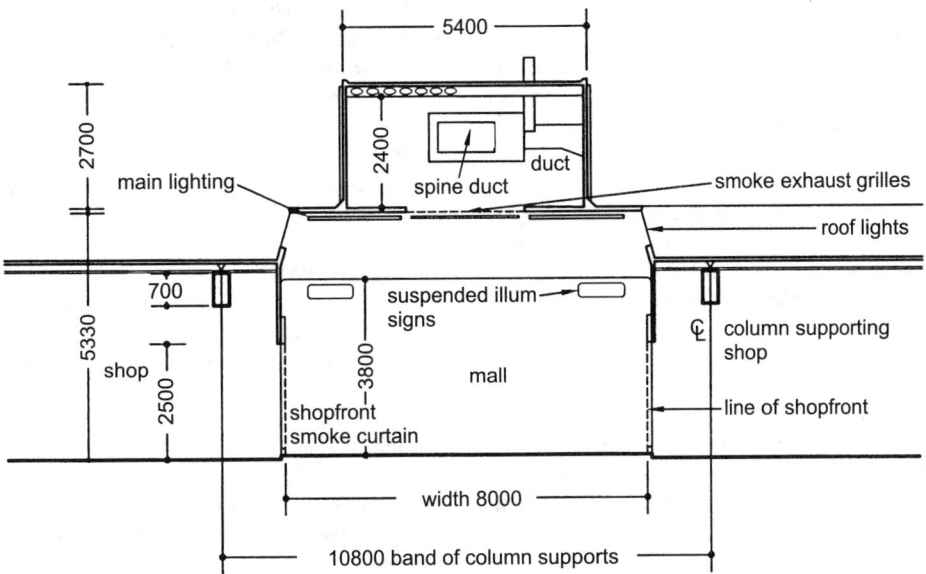

13.25 *Detail cross-section through a shopping mall*

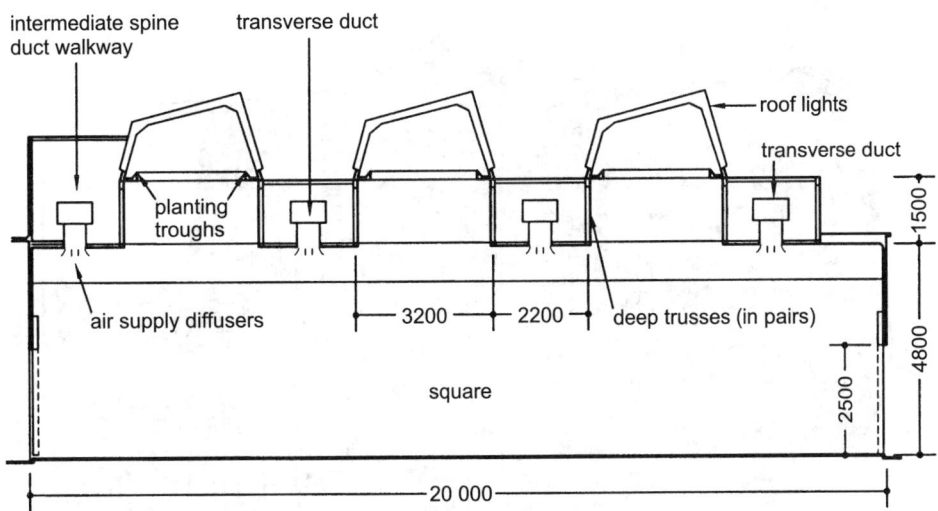

13.26 *Detail cross-section through central square*

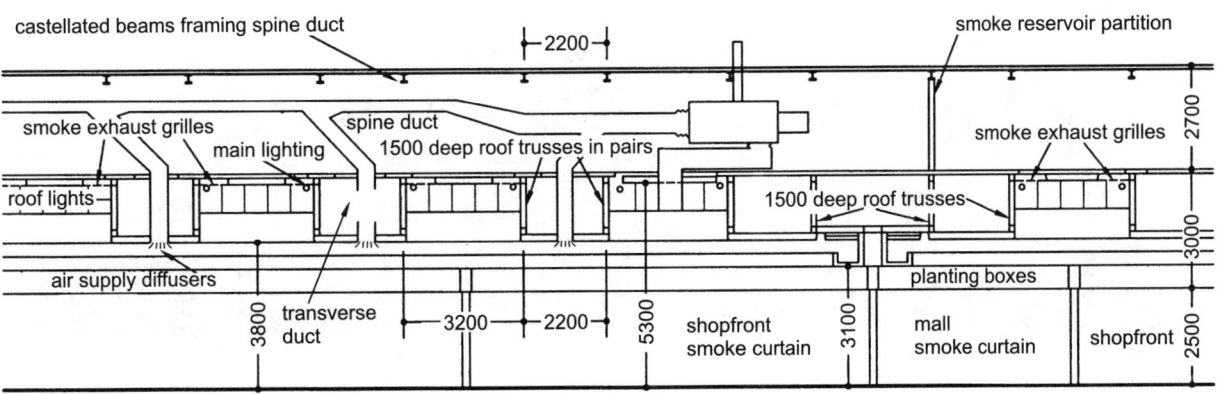

13.27 *Detail longitudinal section along mall*

10.08 Circulations

Vertical circulation between storeys requires escalators, featured lifts and stairs designed to stimulate interest. These are usually located in a spacious central concourse or atrium, at junctions or corners and within the large space users.

Servicing shops

Vehicular access is required to loading docks and waiting bays directly accessible to each of the larger stores, with service roads, goods lifts and tunnels extending to the rear of shops. Service entry is usually at basement and street level but may be at an upper level on sloping sites.

10.09 Engineering services

The landlord is normally responsible for installing mains and providing the communal services of the mall including comfort cooling and heating or air-conditioning, lighting, cleaning, fire control and security systems. As a rule, individual tenants instal their own services and equipment subject to agreement. Food-preparation areas, public toilets and plant areas require the installation of specific ventilation, drainage and electrical services.

Sections through a typical centre showing the complexity of structure and servicing are illustrated in 13.25 to 13.27.

10.10 Other facilities

Public toilets including facilities for the disabled are installed and maintained by the landlord. Access to a public car park is often a primary consideration in letting units.

10.11

Some recent town-centre shopping centres are shown in **13.28** to **13.30**.

11 RETAIL PARKS

These are centres of at least $4500\,m^2$ sited outside a town consisting of at least three single-storey units of $900\,m^2$. Retail parks cover non-food goods (DIY, furniture, furnishings, consumer durables, etc.). Buildings are generally of warehouse design and benefit from the combined attraction, shared infrastructure, parking and extra facilities (café/fast food outlets).

12 REGIONAL CENTRES

These are large multiple shopping complexes, located near major highway junctions to serve a wide catchment area.

Examples include the Metro Centre, Gateshead – 250 shops; Meadowhall, Sheffield – 230 shops (23 million visitors/year), **13.31**; Brent Cross, London, Lakeside, Thurrock. A range of leisure facilities, restaurants and amenities is provided for family attraction.

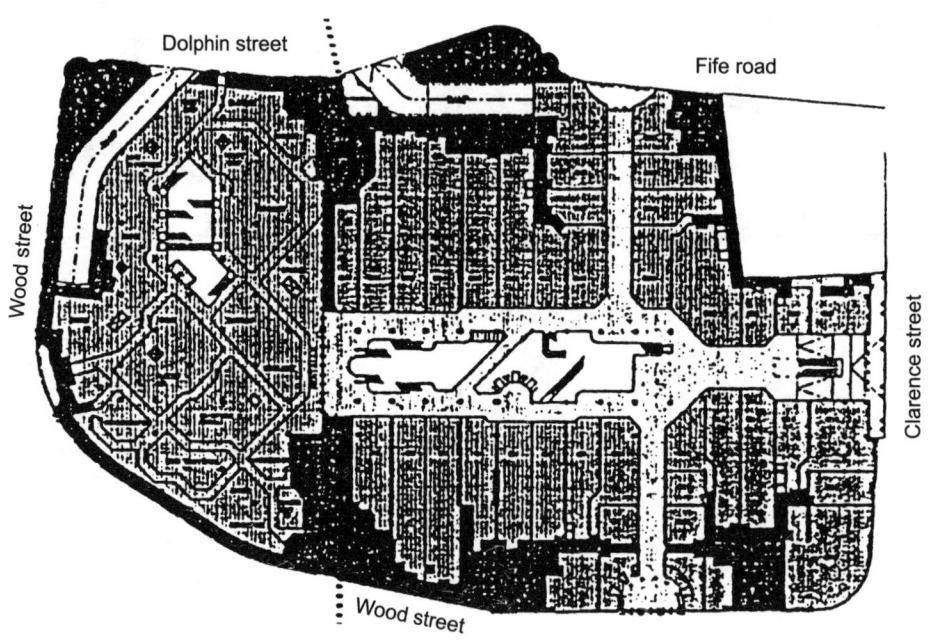

a *Ground-floor level*

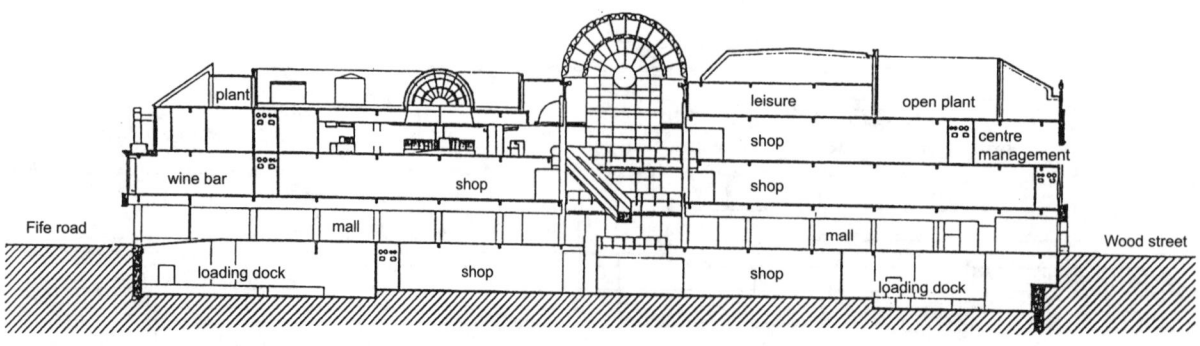

b *Mall cross-section*

13.28 *Bentall Centre, Kingston-on-Thames*

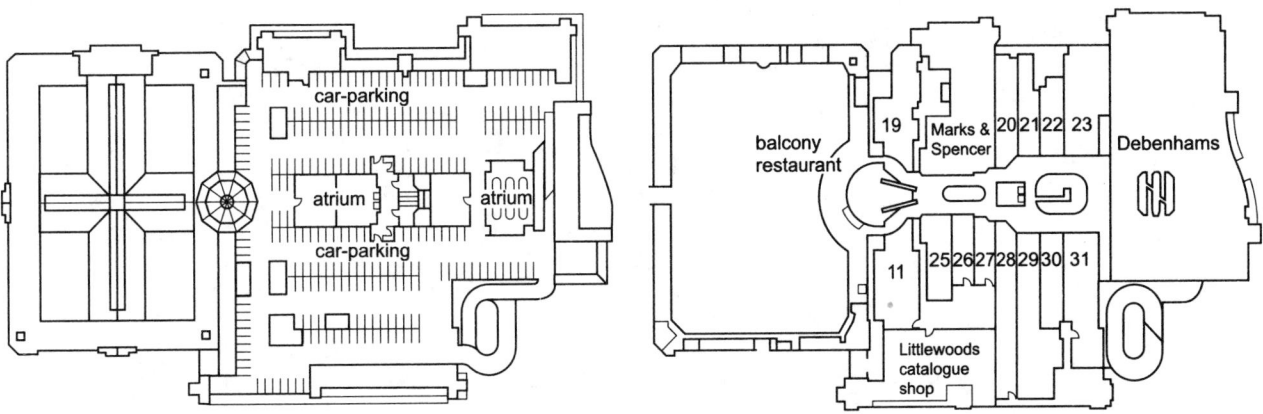

a *First-floor level*

b *Upper ground-floor level*

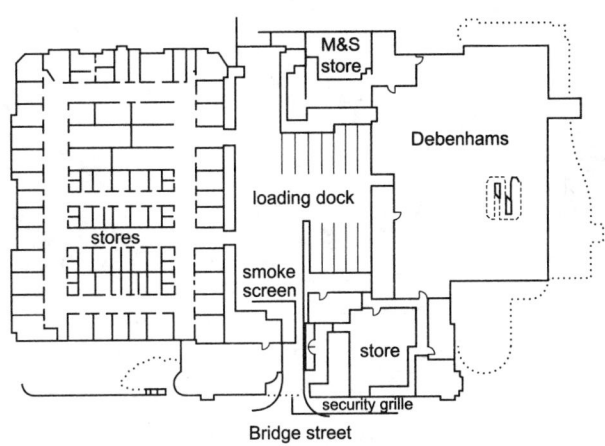

c *Ground-floor level*

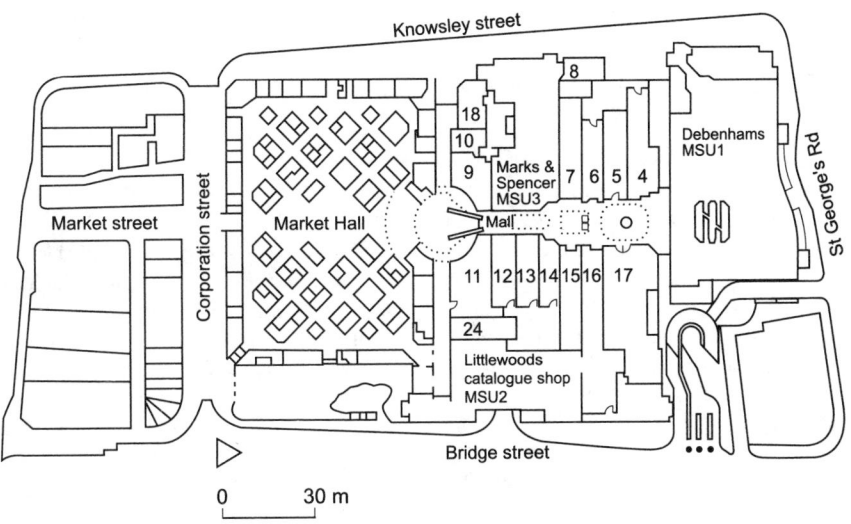

d *Lower ground-floor level*

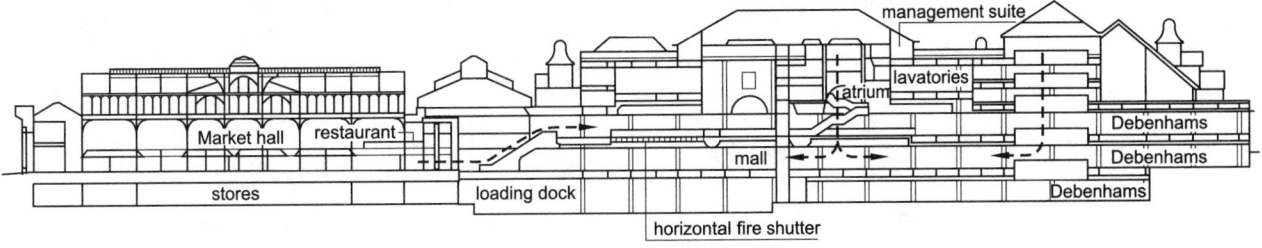

e *Section south–north*

13.29 *Bolton Market Place: a shopping centre on two levels linked to the refurbished existing Market Hall. Deliveries and storage are in the basement, and car parking on three upper floors. Total area is 49 796 m²*
Architects: Chapman Taylor & Partners

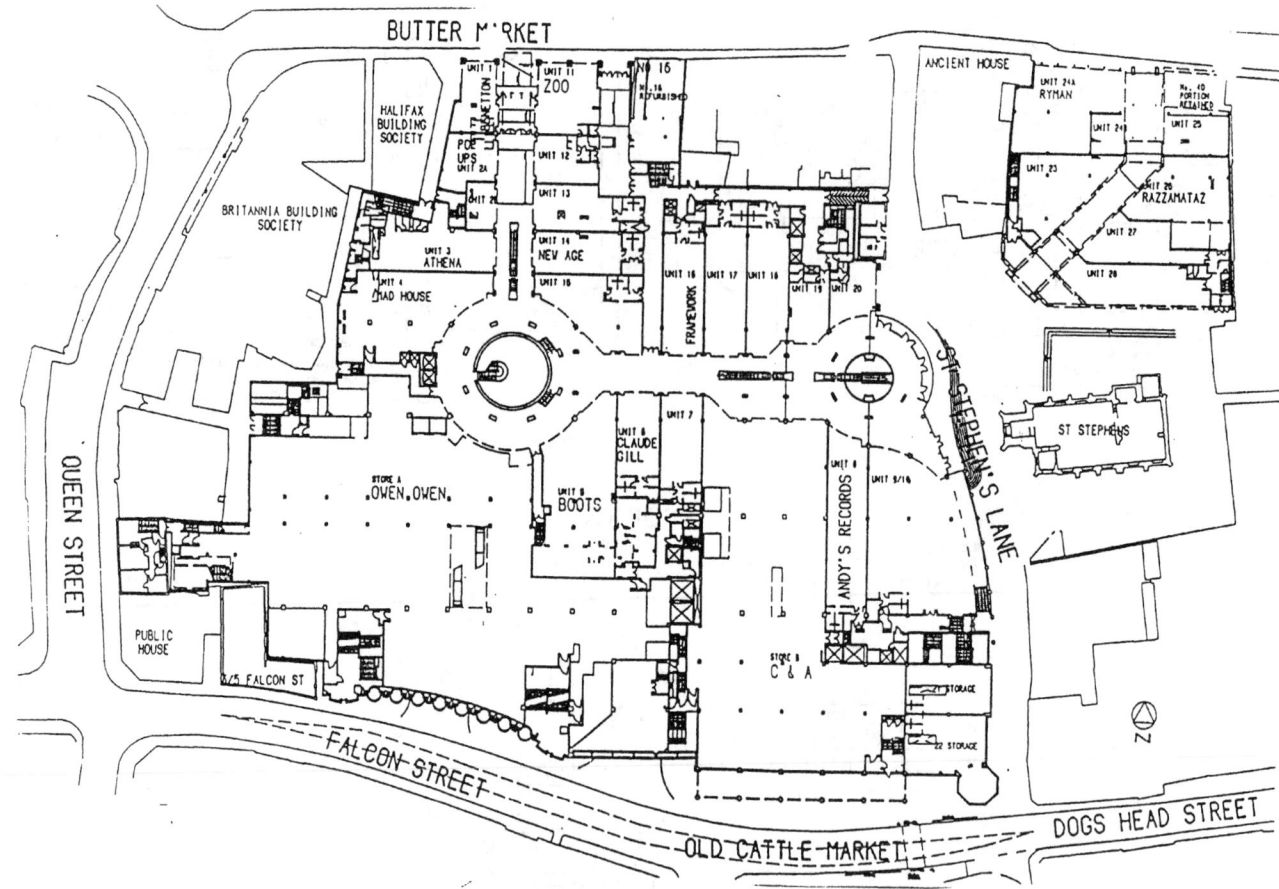

13.30 *Buttermarket, Ipswich. Development of a shopping centre in a sensitive historic area, incorporating a church restored as an amenity area, and two level basement parking. Completed in 1992 with 49 units. Built area 25 083 m², cost £37 million*
Ground-floor plan
Architects: Building Design Partnership

13 BIBLIOGRAPHY

N. Beddington (1991) *Shopping Centres*, 2nd ed, Butterworth Architecture, Oxford

N. Beddington (1985) 'Department stores, supermarkets and shops', in *Planning, The Architect's Handbook* (ed. E.D. Mills), Butterworths, London

R. Burn, 'Scots shop', *Building Services*, July 1990

N. Burns, 'The price is right', *Building Services*, October 1994

Chapman Taylor Partners, 'Trading architecture: the Bolton Market Place', *Architects' Journal*, 19 April 1989

Cox and Britain, *Retail Management*, MacDonald and Evans, 1993

G. Davies and J. Brooks, *Positioning Strategy in Retailing*, Paul Chapman, 1989

M. Field, 'Cathedrals of consumption', *Architects' Journal*, 2 December 1992

S. Gilchrist, 'Stores look for new ways to drive customers out of town', *The Times*, 29 March 1994

D. Gosling and B. Maitland, 'Retail trading', *New Metric Handbook*, (ed. P. Tutt and D. Adler) Butterworth Architecture, 1979

D. Harris and D. Walters, *Retail Operations Management*, Prentice Hall., 1992

J. Holyoak, 'Spending on a grand scale', *Architects' Journal* 21 November 1990

G. Johnson (ed.), *Business Strategy and Retailing*, Paul Chapman, 1989

P. McGoldrick, *Retail Marketing*, MacDonald and Evans, 1993

Nielson, *Retail Pocket Book*, MC Publications, 1993

G. Philpott (ed.), *Shop Spec: Shopfitting International*, Nexus Communications, 1994

G. Sivel and L. Dolon, 'Annual supermarkets shape up as food price fighters', *The Times*, 10 January 1995

R. Smith, 'Development economics, 3, Initial cost estimating', *Architects' Journal*, 1 June 1988

A. Tammes and D. Brennan, 'Architectural light: the retail show', *Architects' Journal*, 20 April 1988

Technical: Buildings Update: 'Superstores profiting by design', *Architects' Journal*, 7 June 1989

M. Teale, 'A look to the future', *Building Services*, May 1992

D. Walters, *Strategic Retailing Management*, Prentice Hall, 1989

PERIODICALS

International Review of Retail Distribution and Consumer Research, Routledge

International Journal of Retail and Distribution Management, MCB

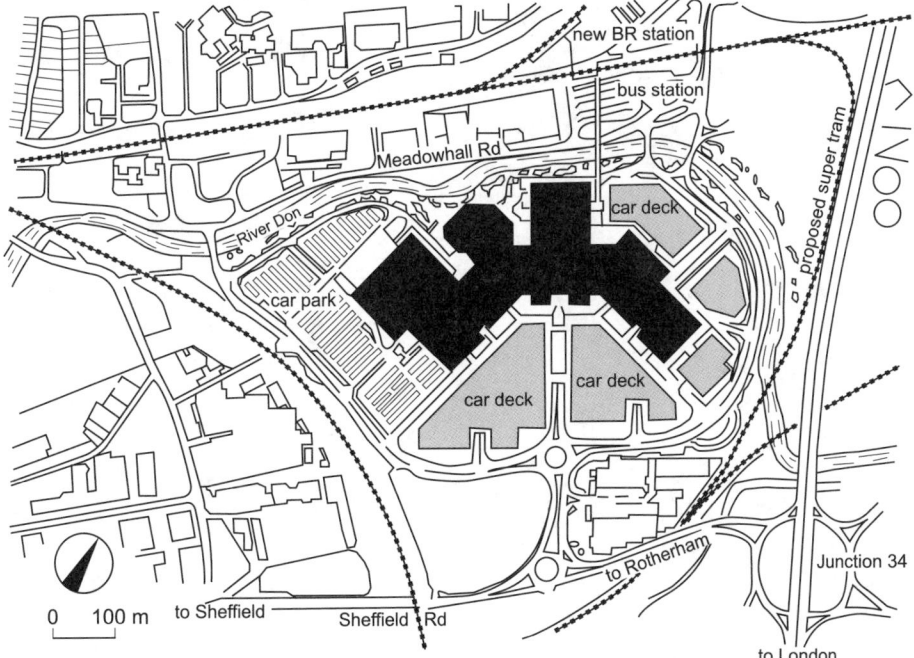

a *Site plan of the regional shopping centre*

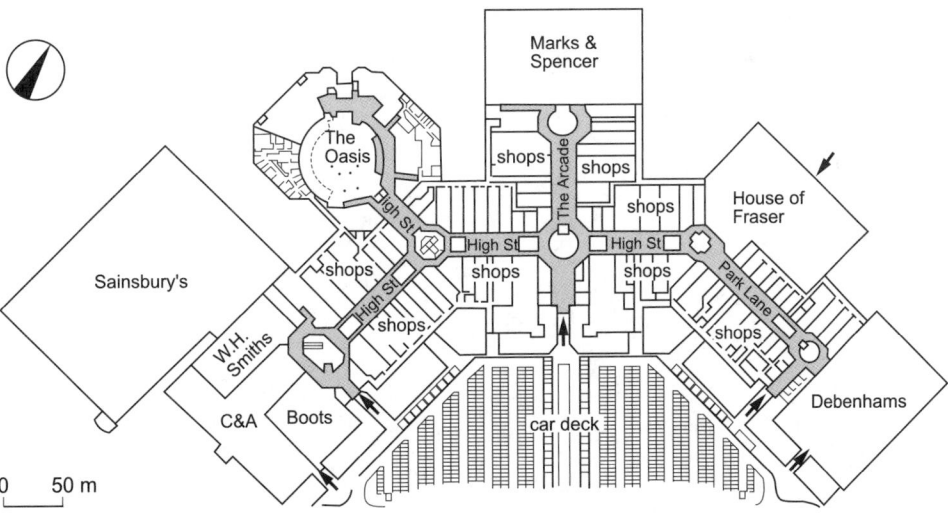

b *First-floor level of the dome's shopping mall with shops on two levels*

13.31 *Meadowhall Centre, Sheffield*

14 Payment and counselling offices

Derek Montefiore

CI/Sfb: 315, 336, 338
UDC: 725.12, 725.24

Derek Montefiore is a director of MHM Architects Ltd

KEY POINT:

● *These are all facilities where security is a major consideration*

Contents

1 INTRODUCTION

1.01

This chapter includes retail premises which do not involve the selling of actual goods to the public. They are generally characterised by the need for greater security for staff and premises than shops selling goods; either because of the attraction to the criminal of the money, etc. held in quantity, or (as in the case of Benefit Agency offices) because the customers may be sufficiently distressed to attack the staff.

1.02

In this general category are included:

● Banks
● Building societies
● Post offices
● Governmental and local governmental public access offices

The common factor between all these facilities is, as described above, the particular need for security for both staff and public. The methods of achieving such security vary both from time to time, and also between different organisations – even within the same sector.

1.03

While the need for additional security has affected all these facilities, so has a new attitude to the customer. It has now been accepted that he or she is not an interruption to the work of the organisation, but its very *raison d'être*. A more welcoming aspect is the common factor of current designs, with soft furnishings and floor coverings taking the place of intimidating and fortress-like interior designs.

Another change is the opening-up of the interiors to the street by large shop windows. This both aids security and contributes to the welcoming-in aspect. Supplementary customer facilities such as lavatories, catering and even TV are provided where waiting times are significant – mainly in government and local government offices.

1.04 Banks

The great change in the last ten years has been the universal adoption of the ATM, or automatic teller machine, commonly known as a cash dispenser (or colloquially as 'hole-in-the-wall'). This has reduced the need for counter service and has led to a shrinkage in both the number and size of bank branches. Further reductions may follow from similar automatic paying-in facilities such are already provided by some building societies.

Bank sizes fall into three categories of key branches, middle-range branches and sub-branches. Obviously staffing levels and customer requirements vary between these types. It should be noted that each bank company has a different opinion on priorities and layouts, and has its own laid-down design policy and manual. Consequently, the diagrams are indicative only.

1.05 Building societies

Building societies are becoming more like banks: some are even abandoning mutual status. Their operation has also been stream-lined by the provision of ATMs, and they also often have automatic facilities for paying in funds.

1.06 Post offices

Post offices differ from the other types of facility in this section by not having to provide any counselling facilities. However, they do need to be able to handle quite bulky parcels (often in both directions), and a special position is provided for passing these through the security screen. The Post Office is continually reassessing customer/staff relationships and is attempting to break down physical barriers by opening up serving positions and introducing more retail business.

Main post offices are usually sited in city and town centres as a normal retail outlet, and there are occasional sub-post offices in residential areas incorporated into shops. Some new main post offices are franchised inside supermarkets, stationery shops, etc. These are larger and more comprehensive than existing sub-post offices.

A rule of thumb to access the allocation of space within a main post office is 40 per cent customer area, 40 per cent staff area and 20 per cent welfare. Where a post shop is included, $45 \, m^2$ additional space is provided to the customer area. The sizes of offices vary in each location and an operational assessment is required to calculate the number of serving positions. Once this has been done a factor of $26 \, m^2$ is used per serving position. To this is added the additional space for the post shop if this is required.

1.07 Public offices

The principal types of governmental and local government public access offices are:

● Council housing offices
● Council rate and rent payment
● Department of Social Service (DSS) and Benefit Agency offices
● Law Centres
● Community Health Council (CHC) offices.

Rent and tax payment offices are very similar to banks and building societies in their requirements. Housing offices, Law Centres and CHC offices are similar in that they are concerned principally with counselling small numbers of people, and will be represented by CHC. DSS and Benefit Agency offices have to provide counselling for larger numbers and require somewhat different treatment.

1.08 CHC (and similar) offices

The main function of a CHC office is to give guidance and assistance to those members of the community who are finding it difficult or frustrating to comprehend or understand their National Health Service rights. Similar functions are provided in housing offices and Law Centres.

CHC offices are situated in town centres or shopping precincts, where access is easy.

The problem may result from language difficulties, frustration in being unable to comprehend a form to be filled in, or queries on access to or experiences of local health services. No money passes hands, but the staff do have to deal occasionally with very distressed individuals. In this respect a pleasing environmental atmosphere is important, and the security of the counsellors must be considered. Mothers and children are welcomed so that it is ideal to have a corner for toys and nappy-changing area in the toilet facilities, though it is emphasised that a crèche is not necessary.

1.09 Department of Social Security and Benefit Agency Offices

Branch Benefit Agency Offices have been reappraising their image; future designs are expected to be as user friendly as possible. More so than most other organisations, they have to deal on occasions with customers who become violent. Staff safety and security are paramount, so that screens are an unfortunate but necessary part of reception areas.

Both customer and staff areas are close carpeted; easily replaceable carpet tiles are used in customer areas. Customer surveys have identified that they give a high priority to personal privacy. This is reflected in the design of reception points and interview rooms.

Benefit Agency offices are situated in town centres or where lines of transport converge such as at bus or railway stations.

2 GENERAL AREAS

2.01 Banks

The general arrangement for banks is shown in **14.1**. The main area is the banking hall. This is an open space divided by a security screen into customer and staff areas.

There are two basically different arrangements used by banks:

● Open counters and/or desks within the customer area where no money is handled, plus a small number of cashiers' points behind the security screens

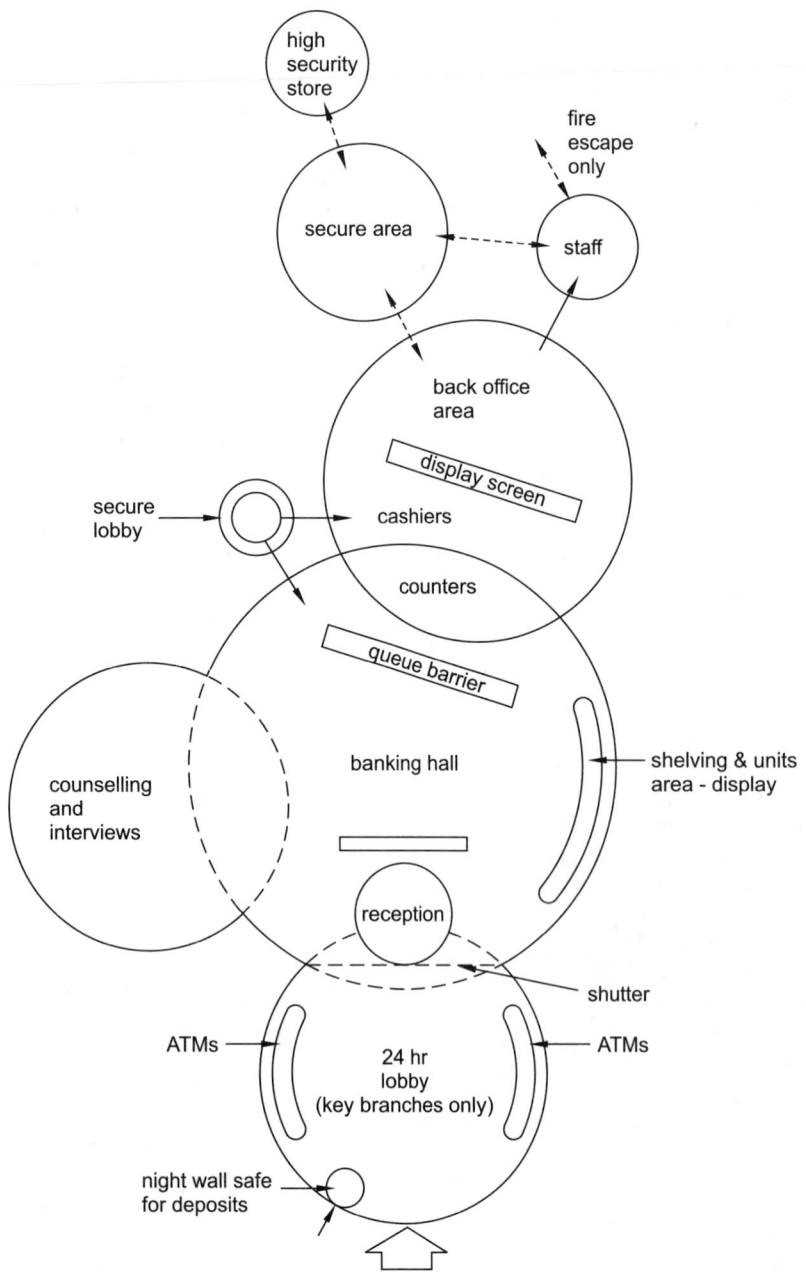

14.1 *Relationship and zoning diagram for a bank*

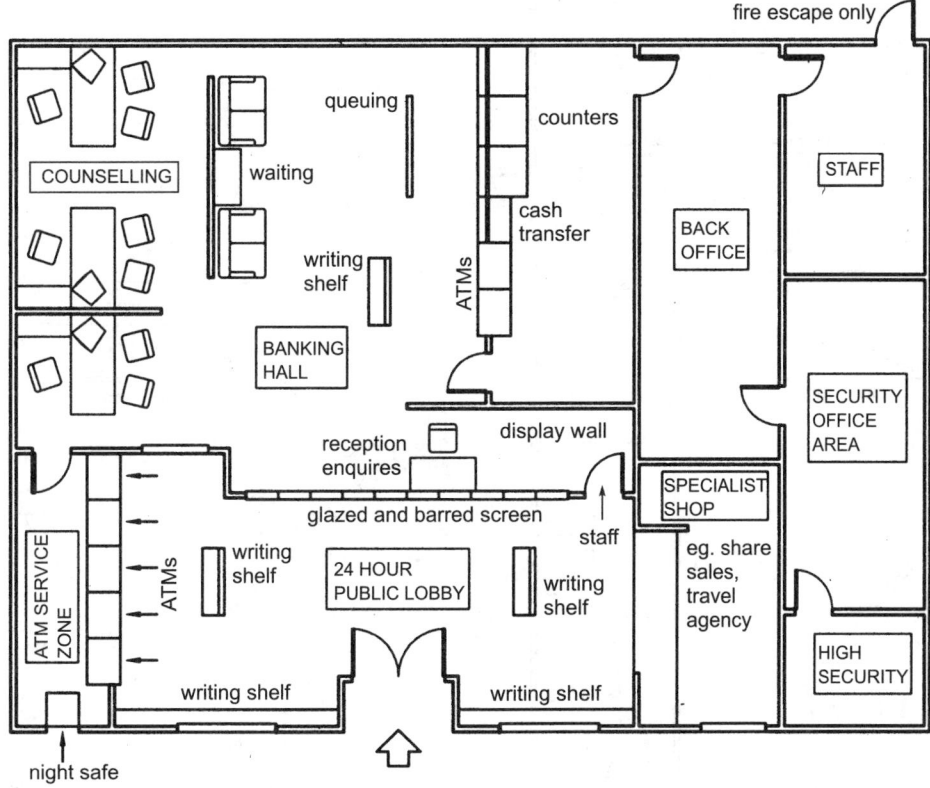

14.2 *Middle-range bank branch*

● All positions behind security screens, with flexibility as to whether they are used for handling money or for giving advice, etc.

Some banks install staffed reception/enquiry facilities in prominent positions adjacent to the entrance, or even outside within the 24-hour public lobby (see Section 3). In the customer area, there must be sufficient space for queueing, and positions for writing. As part of their more customer-related policies, bank managers and staff now come out from behind the security screen to meet and talk to them, and perhaps spend a considerable time helping them solve problems. The counselling areas and interview rooms should open directly off the banking hall and be closely connected to them.

The back-office area is often part of the banking hall, but is generally (but not always) screened from the customers. With the advent of computers there is less need for this space, which is becoming minimal.

Despite the growth of transactions on paper and 'plastic', the banks and other payment offices still have to deal with fairly large sums of money. To cope with these there must be a secure back-office area for staff and a high-security area (strong room or safes) off the back-office area where deliveries are made and cash is stored. The banks, for obvious reasons, are reticent about the details here, both of the planning and also of the arrangements, ensuring only authorised staff can gain access to the various areas. Architects are often asked to provide space only, the fitting-out being done by bank staff themselves after the main contract handover.

Staff facilities such as rest-rooms, toilets, etc. are also provided behind the back office. A fire escape from the area behind the security screen is essential, but this introduces a security risk. It is not usual to provide any entrance to bank premises other than through the front door. There is no reason why the security and staff areas could not be on different levels to the banking hall.

Plans of some actual banks (which cannot, of course, be identified) are given in **14.2**, **14.3** and **14.4**.

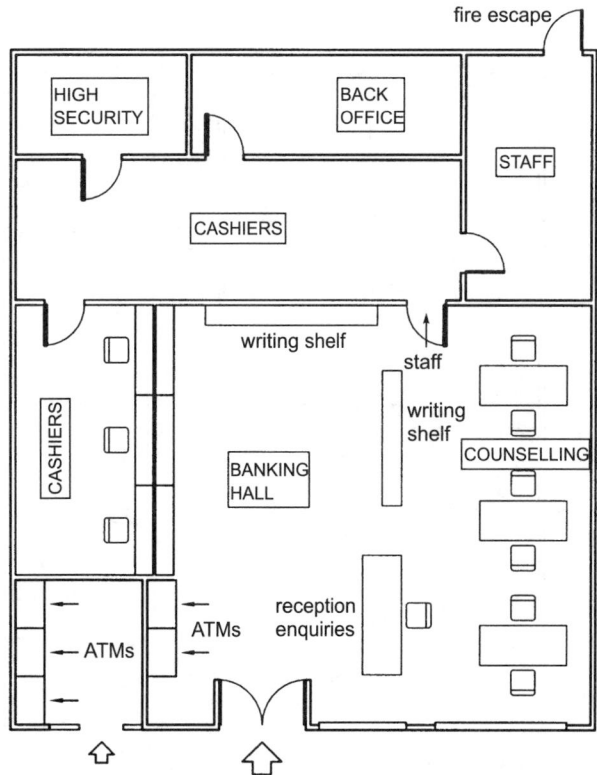

14.3 *Bank*

2.02 Building societies

The arrangement of building society offices is generally the same as for banks, although the smaller offices dispense with some of the areas. **14.5** is a plan of a building society office.

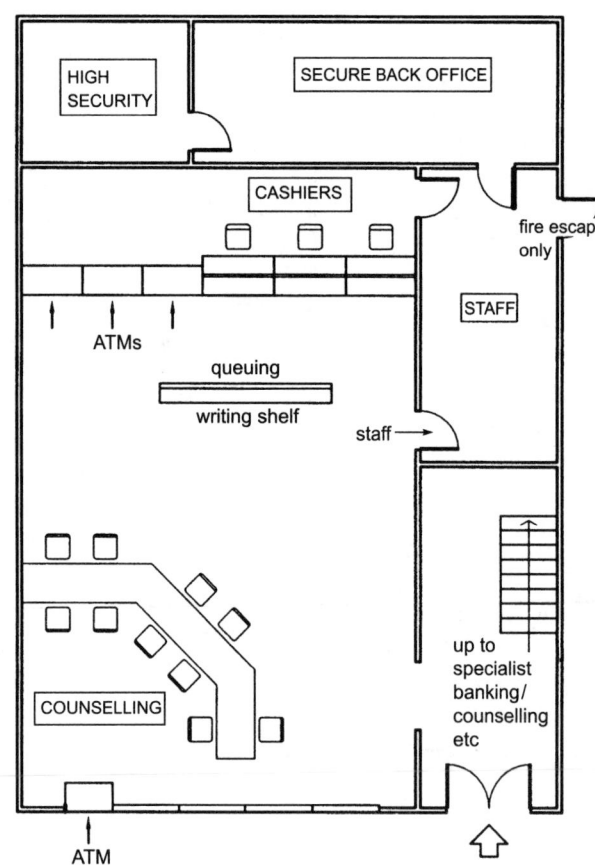

14.4 *Bank*

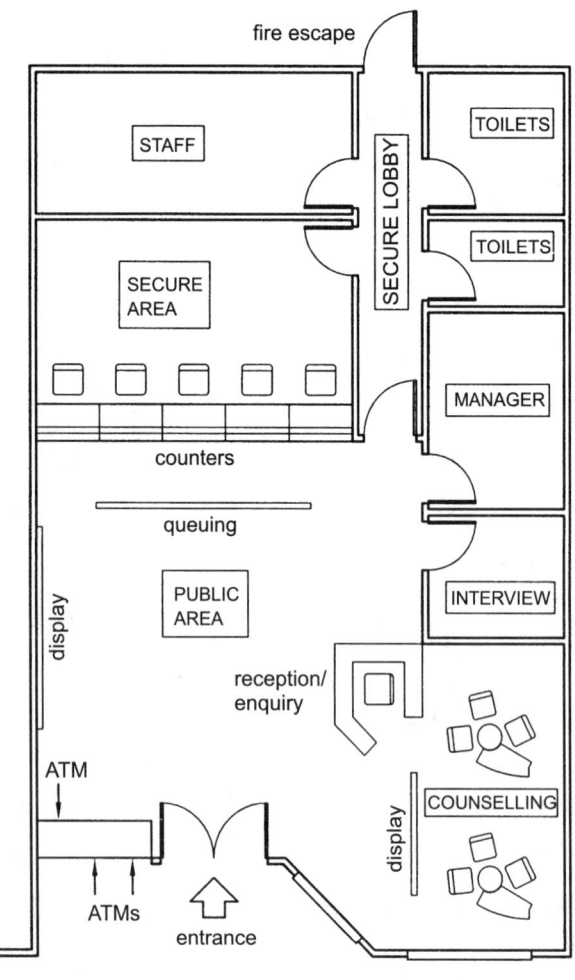

14.5 *Building society*

14.6 *Relationship and zoning diagram for a post office*

2.03 Post offices

The arrangement of a typical main post office is shown in **14.6**. The balancing area was where the counter staff periodically checked their book keeping and balance their day's takings. With the advent of universal computing systems much of this is no longer necessary. However, a small area screened from public view is usually provided. There are also safes or strong rooms as necessary – dependent on the size of the post office.

The syphon zones are secure areas and cannot be entered except by authorised personnel. The counter service consists of secure transactions such as cash for pensions, social security, etc. and non-secure transactions such as stamps, bill paying, vehicle licences and passports. Behind the counters there are racks for forms and each counter position has its own lockable facilities. **14.7** is a plan of a medium-size main post office.

There are proposals in hand which will radically change the way Post Office Counters operate, and therefore the design of their offices. Within the open customer area an operator will accept the customer's form and code it into a teller cash dispenser (TCD) similar to an ATM, which will supply the customer. This will reduce the number of fortress positions necessary, offer more flexibility to the layout and provide quicker and pleasanter service. Similarly, other transactions will be dealt with by automated dispensers, saving both queueing and staff time and numbers.

2.04 Community health council offices

14.8 is a zoning plan for a CHC office, and an actual office is shown in **14.9**. Near the entrance is an enquiry desk which also doubles for reception interviews or individual counselling. Adjacent to this is a reception/waiting area with display walls and brochure racks. There is also a private zone where further counselling takes place around a low table. The office accommodation can be adjacent or on another floor and is generally about the same area as the entrance waiting and consulting areas. This office area also deals with telephone enquiries.

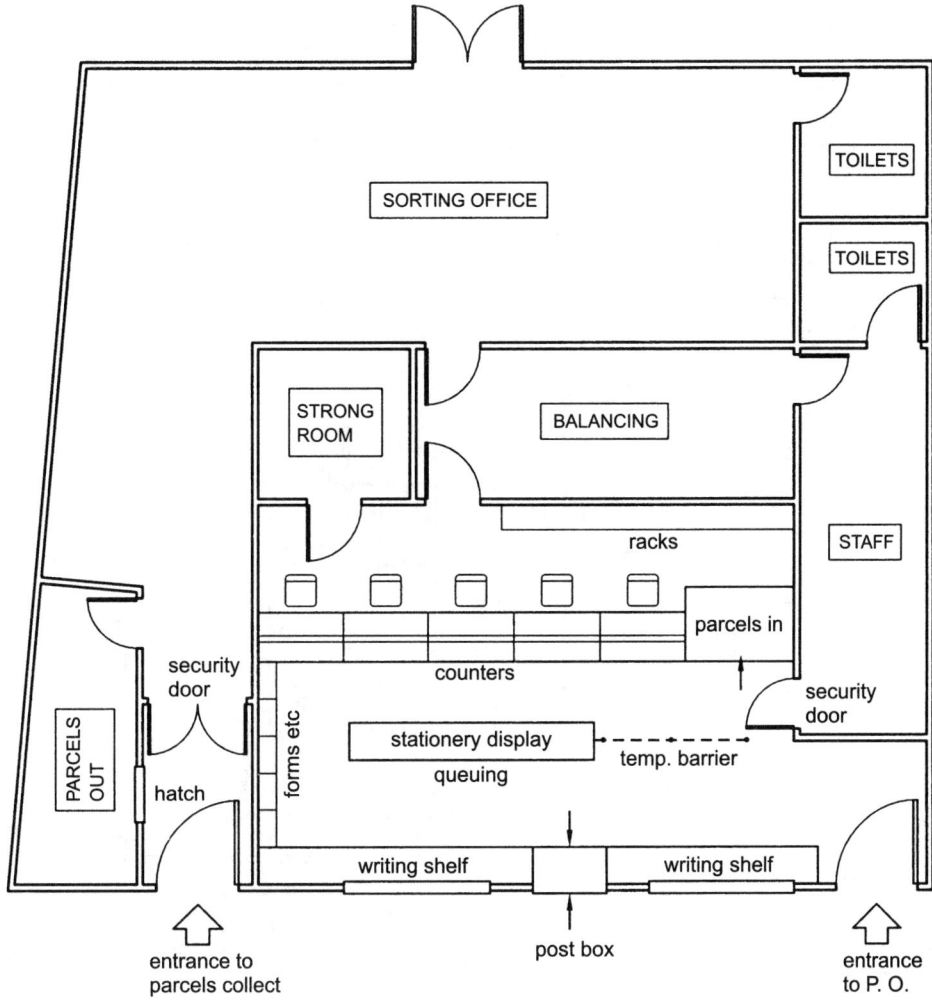

14.7 *A post office associated with a sorting office and a parcel-collect facility*

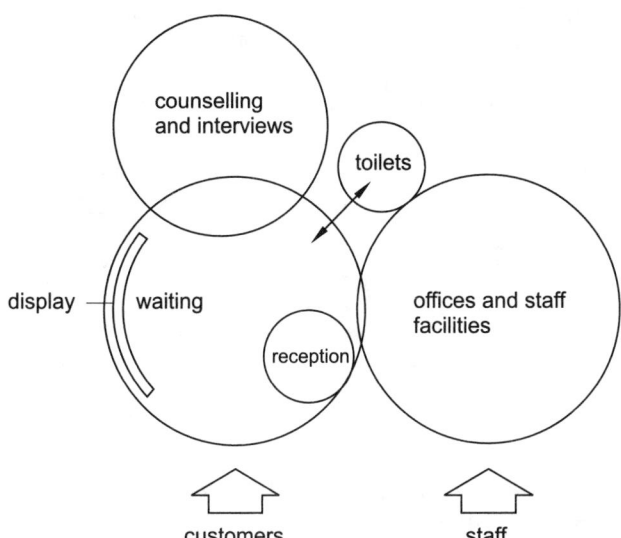

14.8 *Relationship and zoning diagram for a Community Health Council office*

2.05 Benefit Agency offices

14.10 is the zoning plan for a Benefit Agency office, while **14.11** illustrates one of these. The reception is the first port of call where customers are advised on whether they can be dealt with at a counter or make an appointment for interviewing. The counters deal with general queries, clerical matters and queries on form filling.

Customers requiring counter service stay in the waiting area until there is a position free. Queue control is by ticket, and waiting times can be considerable if the office is particularly busy. Toilet and baby-changing facilities for the customers are therefore essential.

A psychological approach has to be considered within the design to cope with extended waiting periods. It is helpful if seats are arranged to avoid eye contact and thus the likelihood of raising tension. They should also be spaced to avoid a rear seat occupier using the seat in front as a footrest. It has also been found that television helps to pass time and reduces tension. Smoking and intoxicant drinking are forbidden on the premises, and this has a marked effect on maintaining a cleaner and more pleasant atmosphere and ambience. Offices are generally equipped with machines vending soft drinks and snacks. A guard is provided with a position from which all the customer areas of the office are directly visible, or can be monitored by closed-circuit television.

More detailed interviews are dealt with in sessions on an appointment basis. There are four different organisations who all use the counters or interview rooms, although they may also visit customers' homes:

- Benefit advisers
- Contribution Agency
- Child Support Agency
- Fraud investigators

Depending on the depth of the interview taking place on the premises, a counter or a separate interview room will be used.

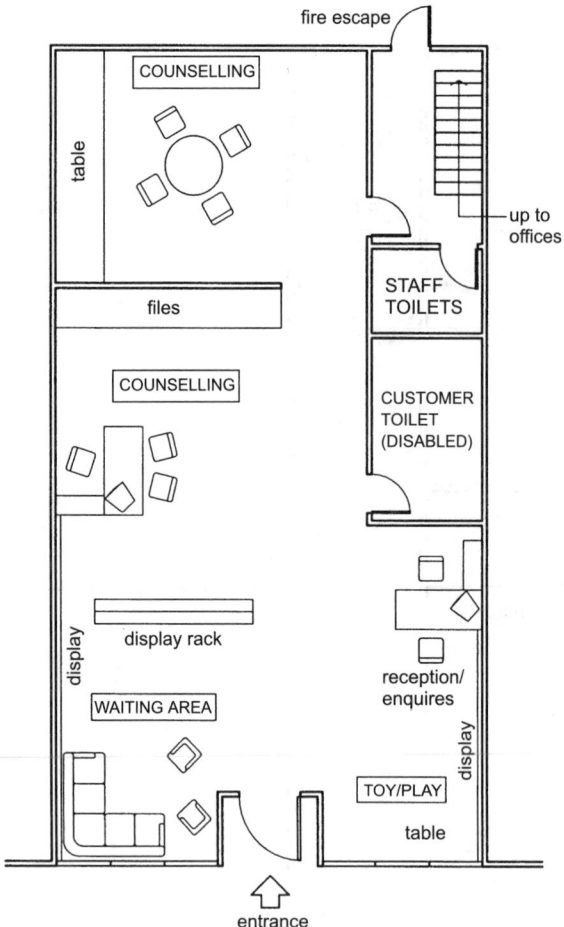

14.9 *Community Health Council counselling office*

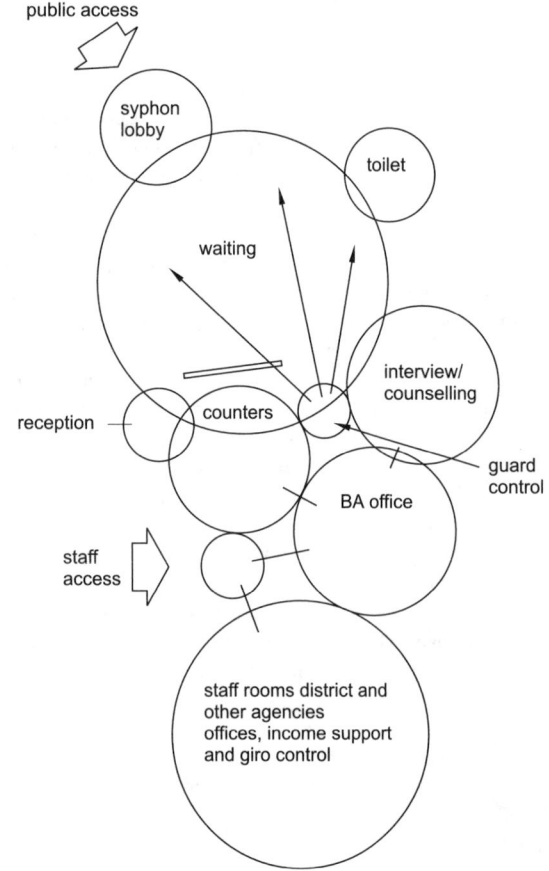

14.10 *Relationship and zoning diagram for a Benefits Agency office*

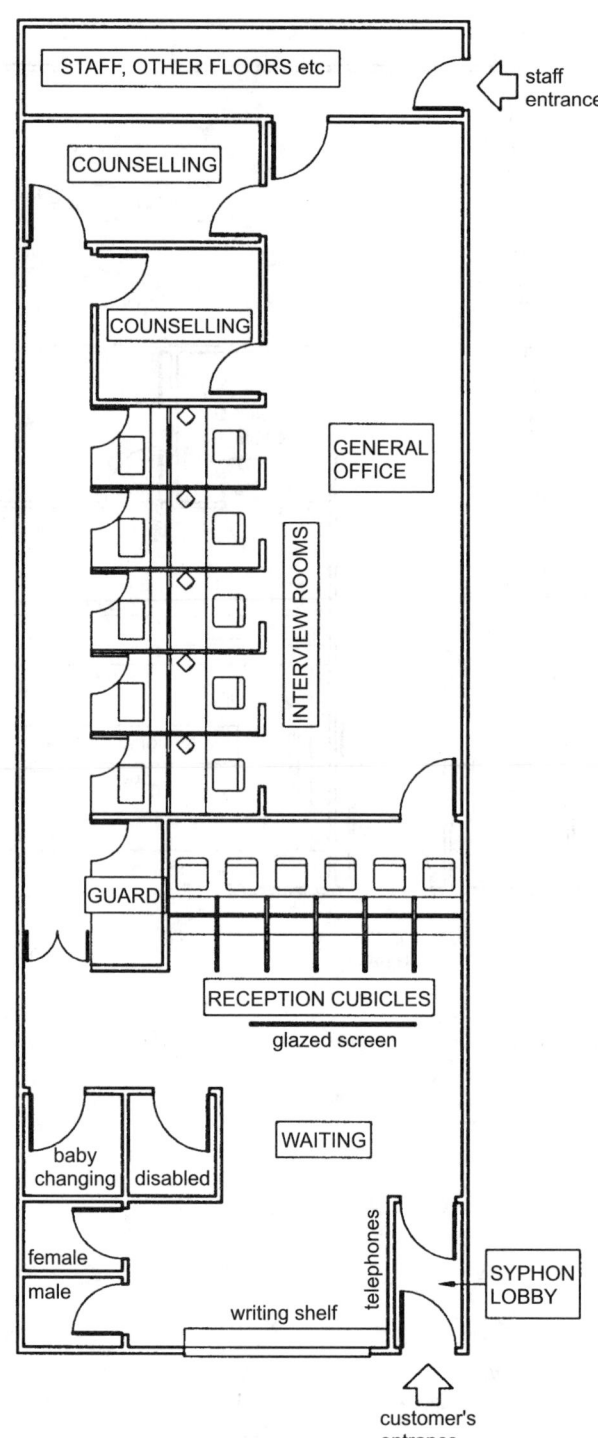

14.11 *A Benefits Agency office*

3 AUTOMATIC TELLER MACHINES (ATMS) AND 24 HOUR LOBBIES

3.01

14.12 shows a current design of ATM. ATMs are usually installed within the street frontage of the payment office, accessed by the public from the highway. This sometimes leads to obstruction by queues, and it is perhaps a matter of time before additional planning rules will be imposed.

3.02

However, it is becoming more common with banks for lobbies to be provided within the building, but generally accessible 24 hours a day. Sometimes these lobbies are fully open to the street, in other

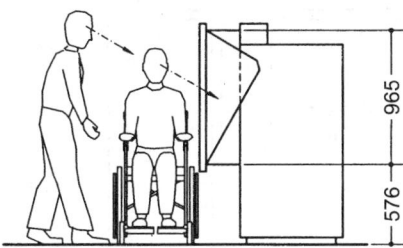

a *Section*

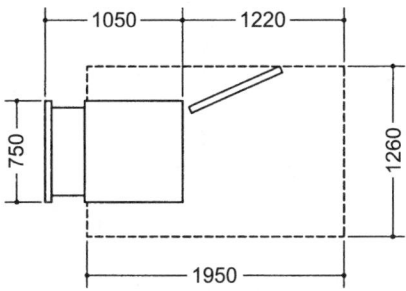

b *Plan*

14.12 *An ATM cash dispenser designed to be easy to use from a wheelchair*

cases access is obtained using a bank card, though this in itself can involve other problems: such as the area being used for student parties – this has yet to be overcome!

3.03
Only a few of the larger building society branches are using lobbies at present, but as they become more like banks it is certain that more will do so.

3.04
In the daytime the public lobby area is opened up to the banking or building society hall, with perhaps a reception and enquiry desk. Quick enquiries can be dealt with here, and behind the desk and in a position of major visibility will be an information screen giving latest marketing suggestions.

3.05
In 24-hour lobbies a number of machines both for drawing cash and for paying-in are usually provided. Continuous video surveillance and recording facilities are provided. Customers' access to bank night safes must be off the street – and not from within any 24–hour public lobby. ATMs have to be arranged so that the information projected can only be seen by the user, this is both a prudent security precaution and also a Data Protection Act requirement.

3.06
Banks which operate a 24–hour lobby normally use a glass screen between it and the banking hall. This permits vision into it, and folds completely away during normal banking hours. Access for staff and bullion and cash delivery to banks is always via the front access. A door is provided in the glass screen for when the bank itself is closed to the public.

3.07
ATMs require frequent filling with cash and also need occasional maintenance. These functions are preferably done from the rear, but for awkward situations (such as in **14.3**) designs serviceable from the front are available. Rear servicing can be from a service corridor as in **14.2**, or from one of the main bank or building society areas as in **14.4**.

3.4
As both banks and building societies seek to decrease their overhead costs by reducing staff and closing branches, it is likely that 24–hour lobbies will be installed in shopping areas with no staffed branches associated with them. The design of such lobbies need not vary significantly from the type in **14.2**.

4 COUNTERS

4.01
The major changes in recent years in the design of counters have been:

- The introduction of security screens
- The universal provision of computer terminals

Unfortunately, the perceived increase in lawnessness has extended the use of security counters even beyond banks and the like. Such facilities are now also provided in railway and bus stations. Significantly, British Rail ticket office positions are twice as long as those provided in banks, building societies and post offices, although there appears to be little functional reason for this.

4.02 Security screens
Bank counters used to be open and post office counters used to have wire grilles. Neither is now acceptable by staff as giving them sufficient protection. Screens of bulletproof glass are now ubiquitous. Communication is sometimes through protected apertures above or through the screen, often by means of microphone/speaker systems. Documents and cash are passed through trays, carefully designed not to compromise the security arrangements.

An alternative system which is available but appears to be rarely used is the rising shutter. This is a solid steel shutter contained within the counter. It is operated by a compressed-air mechanism, which when activated by a panic button, causes the shutter to shoot vertically upwards instantaneously.

4.03
Where there is little fear of firearms, but the possibility still exists of physical assault (such as in council housing offices), counters can be designed to be higher and deeper than normal, making it difficult for the enquirer to reach the staff. Staff can either stand or sit on low platforms behind the counter.

4.04
Counter positions for bank, building society and post office staff require much the same facilities:

- Cash storage tray
- Computer terminal
- Storage for forms, stamps, postal orders, cheques, etc.
- Personal storage (minimal)

In building societies where pass-books are used and cheques are issued for customers' use, space is also needed at the counter position for a printer linked to the computer. In banks printers are usually placed in the back area, and in some cases cashiers are not even provided with personal terminals.

4.05
Counter designs are of two basic types:

- Continuous counter, **14.13**. This is used where no computer terminal is required such as in some banks, or where the terminal requires minimal space, such as in a post office.
- L-shaped work position, **14.14**, providing additional space for terminal and printer. This design is appropriate for building societies.

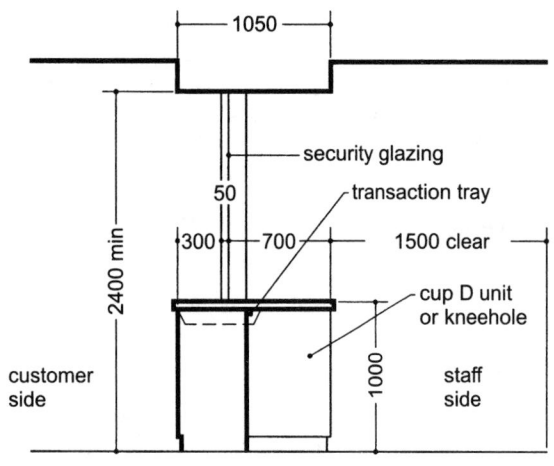

14.13 *Section through a counter of continuous type. Allow a length of 1400 mm per staff member*

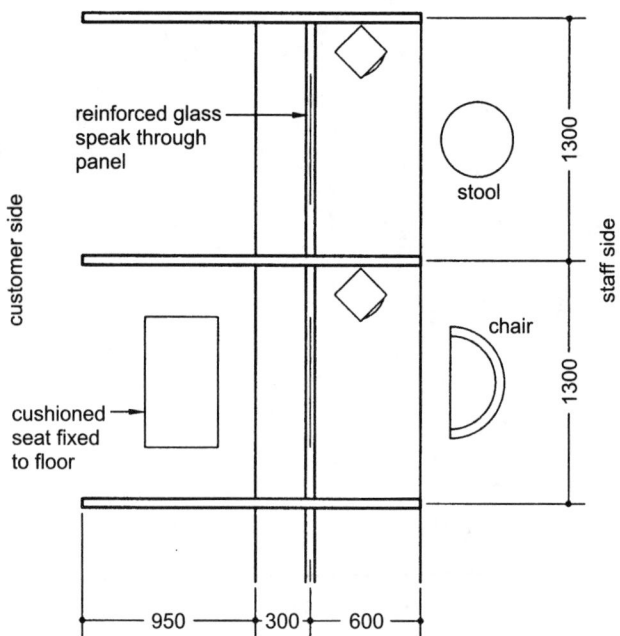

a *Plan*

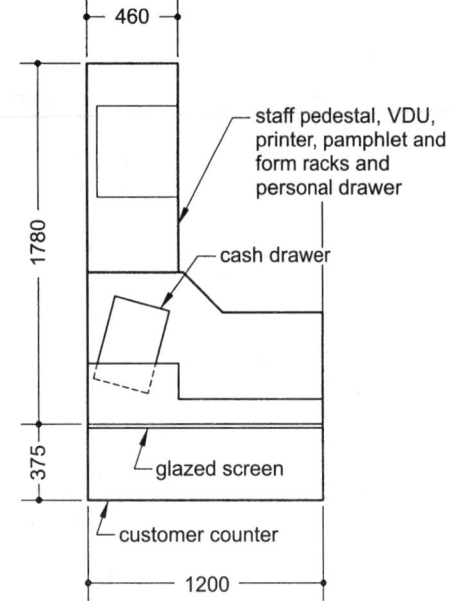

a *Section*

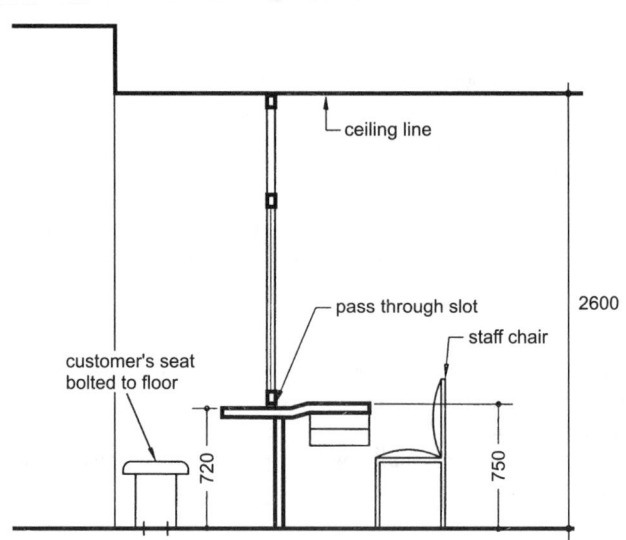

b *Section*

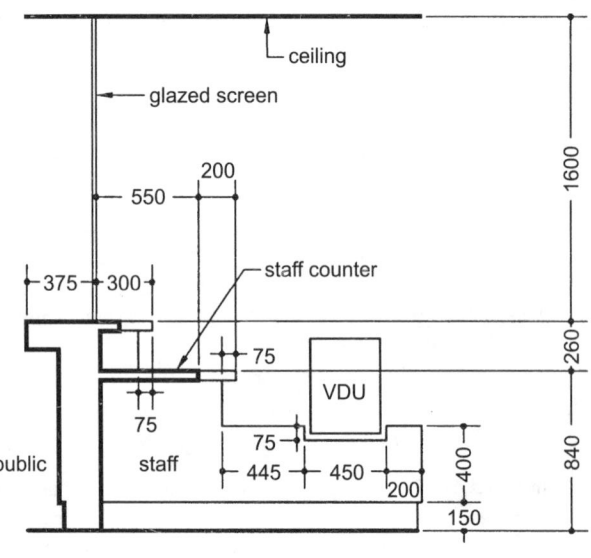

b *Plan*

14.14 *An L-shaped desk and counter*

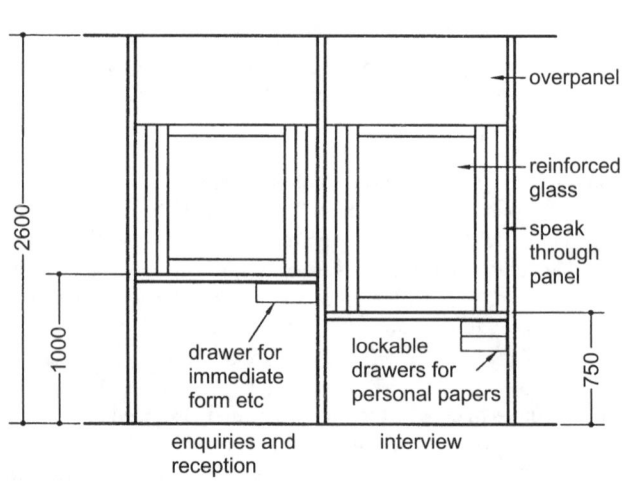

c *Elevation from the staff side*

14.15 *A counter in the Benefits Agency*

4.06

The two types of counter used in Benefit Agency offices are shown in **14.15**. The reception desks are for short-term enquiries and are, therefore, at standing height. General counters are at sitting height and the customers' bench is large enough to sit two people. All furniture is robust which allows for considerable wear and tear; all seats are fixed to the floor and all covers are removable for cleaning or replacing if damaged.

5 COUNSELLING

5.01

All these facilities except for post offices need provision for counselling. Banks and building societies advising their customers on their investments or loans are tending away from the 'two sides of a desk' system as in **14.16** (although in some circumstances this is still appropriate) and try to foster a more congenial atmosphere. The pod in **14.17** is one example.

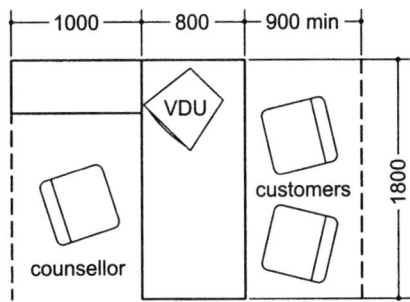

14.16 *At-desk counselling*

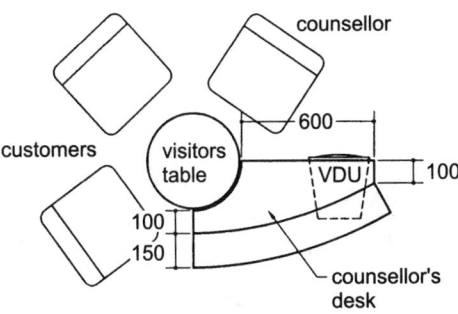

14.17 *Counselling pod*

In CHC offices counselling is often carried out in even more homely surroundings, sitting around low tables in easy chairs.

In Benefit Agency offices when the interview rooms with security screens are not used, interviewers still prefer to sit behind a desk rather than use a more informal method.

All these areas have to be private, so that no conversation can be overheard. Equally they should not be oppressive or secretive. Acoustic confidentiality is achieved by glazed screens, or by distance. However, some bank customers may not wish to be observed talking to their manager, so at least one of the counselling rooms should not have clear glass between it and the banking hall.

6 PROVISION FOR PEOPLE WITH DISABILITIES

6.01

All facilities are now very aware of the problems experienced by people with disabilities. It is now unusual for payment or counselling offices to be situated above ground-floor level, and level access to the counters and ATMs for people in wheelchairs is all but universal. ATMs and counters are at a height suitable for people in wheelchairs – so they are often uncomfortable for ambulant tall people to use!

6.02

However, ATMs are not at present suitable for people with severe visual impairment, and they need to use the services of a cashier. People with both hearing and seeing deprivation are not, unfortunately, at present well catered for in most payment offices. Sanitary facilities for the public are not provided in payment offices; they generally are in counselling offices where waiting times can be considerable. Where sanitary facilities are provided, disabled toilets and baby-changing facilties need to be included (the latter accessible to both men and women).

6.03

When planning banks or building society offices on more than one level, it should not be forgotten that there may be disabled people on the staff. All areas, including the high-security zone, should be accessible to wheelchairs.

NOTE:

No references or bibliography has been provided for this chapter as very little is available on the open market: most design manuals, etc. are confidential to the firms using them.

15 Public service buildings

Derek Montefiore

CI/SfB: 314, 372, 373, 374
UDC: 725.13, 725.191, 614.88, 725.188

KEY POINTS:
- *Many of these functions are tightly controlled by regulation*
- *Flexibility is needed to accommodate likely future change*
- *Value-for-money is a major design criterion*

Contents
1 Town halls
2 Fire stations
3 Ambulance stations
4 Police stations
5 References and bibliography

1 TOWN HALLS

1.01

Town halls have a variety of functions to fulfil, and many of their parts are covered in other chapters of this handbook. The principal constituents of a town hall are:

- A council chamber, with associated lobbies
- A civic suite, or mayor's parlour
- A number of committee rooms
- An assembly hall (see Chapter 20)
- Offices (see Chapter 11)
- A public reception and information desk
- A cash reception and disbursal facility (see Chapter 14)

1.02 Elected members' accommodation

The core of any town hall, county hall or city hall is the accommodation for those elected by the public. Apart from the council chamber itself, space is needed for the Mayor, the party leaders and for informal gatherings of the members. In addition, delegations of the public and visiting dignitaries of all kinds have to be received in suitable surroundings, **15.1**. **15.2** is by no means an over-elaborate arrangement; what cannot be seen from the drawing is the magnificence of the finishes!

1.02 Council chamber

Few local government bodies emulate the House of Commons in their council chambers. Their forms are mostly segmental or horseshoe, **15.3**, and the seating provides at least some accommodation for documentation, **15.4**. They are sized to seat every Councillor plus a number of Council officers, and incorporate speech-reinforcement systems. Some chambers are tiered to aid visibility, and have imposing seating for the Mayor; but others are flat-floored with moveable equipment – rather more like a large boardroom. Some provision for the general public is essential, preferably well separated as in a gallery.

It is usual to have one or more lobbies immediately outside the chamber for informal discussions. Voting is usually by a show of hands, or using voting machines; not by trooping through lobbies.

1.03 Civic suite

Some provision for entertaining important guests is essential, and this is often combined with the Mayor's office. This needs easy access to some form of catering facility.

1.04 Committee rooms

Local government business is conducted principally through numerous committees and sub-committees. Meeting rooms of various sizes are required; these (including the council chamber) are often available for letting by outside organisations, producing useful additional revenue for the Council. For this reason, if for no other, they should be well designed and fitted out.

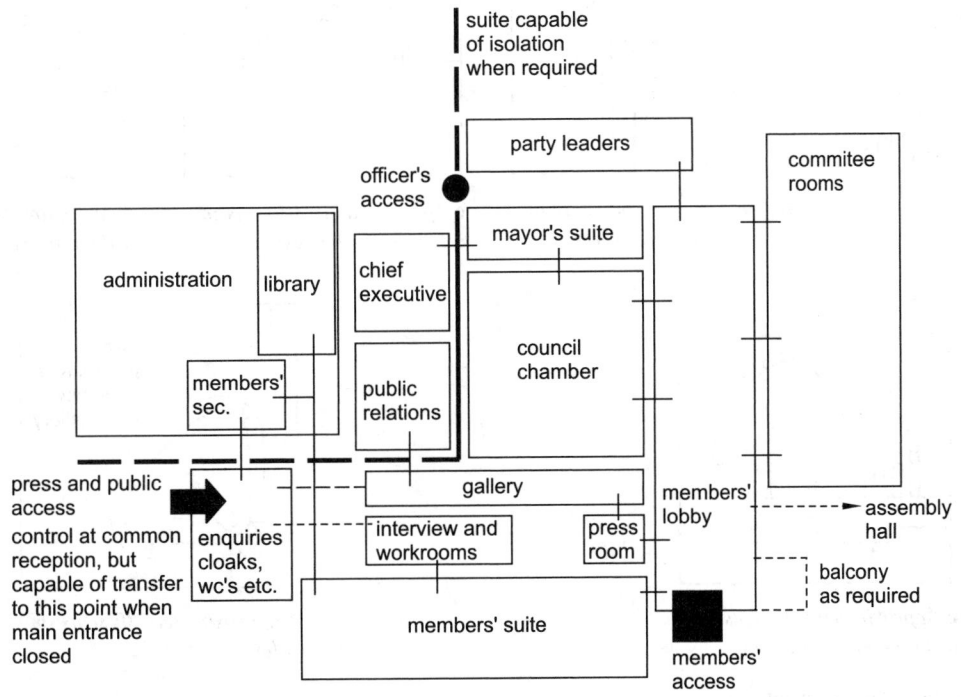

15.1 *Relationship diagram for the elected members' accommodation in town halls*

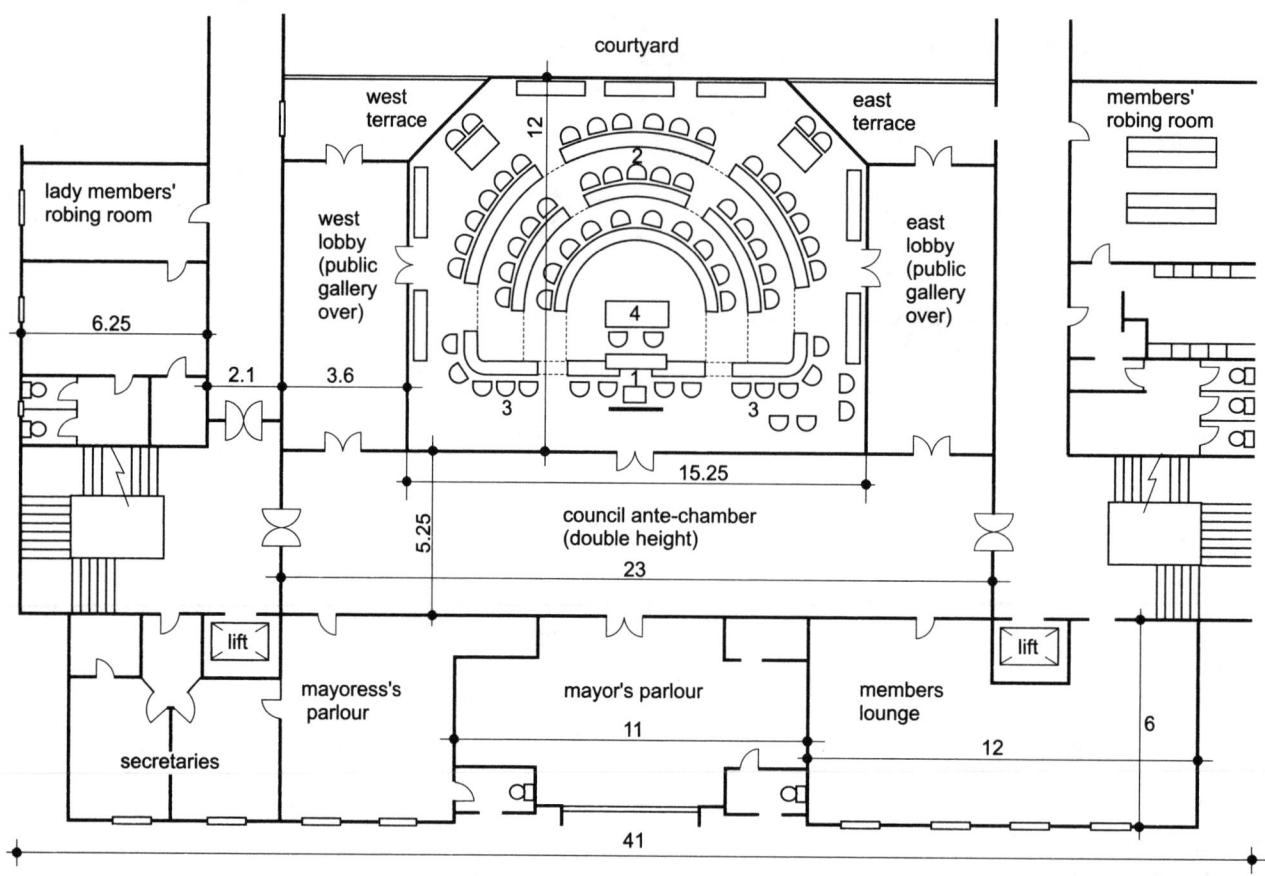

15.2 *Hammersmith Town Hall: Council Chamber suite*

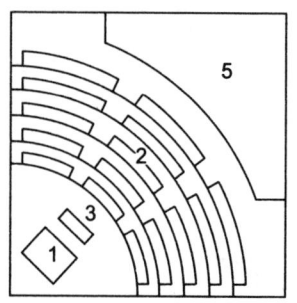

a *Approximately 300 seats in a five-tiered quadrant*

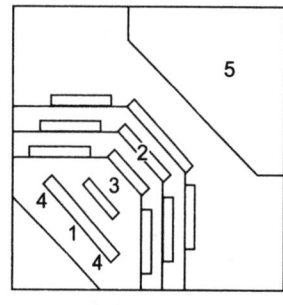

b *Approximately 60 seats in a three-tiered quadrant*

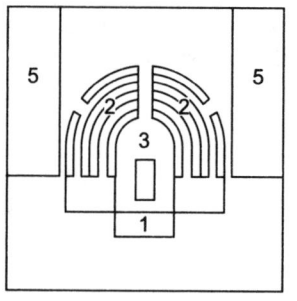

c *Approximately 30 seats in a two-tiered horseshoe*

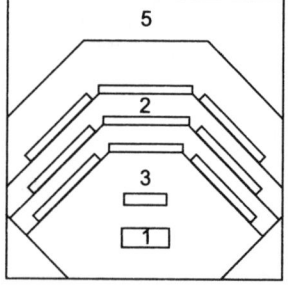

d *Approximately 100 seats in a three-tiered segment*

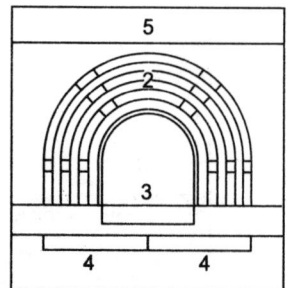

e *Approximately 60 seats in a three-tiered horseshoe*

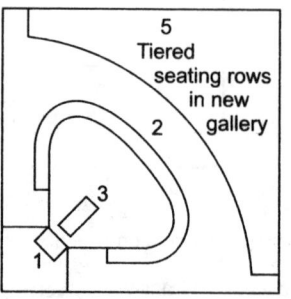

f *Approximately 30 seats on a level*

15.3 *Council chamber, various layout types:*
(1 = mayor, 2 = ordinary members, 3 = officers, 4 = committee clerks, 5 = press and public)

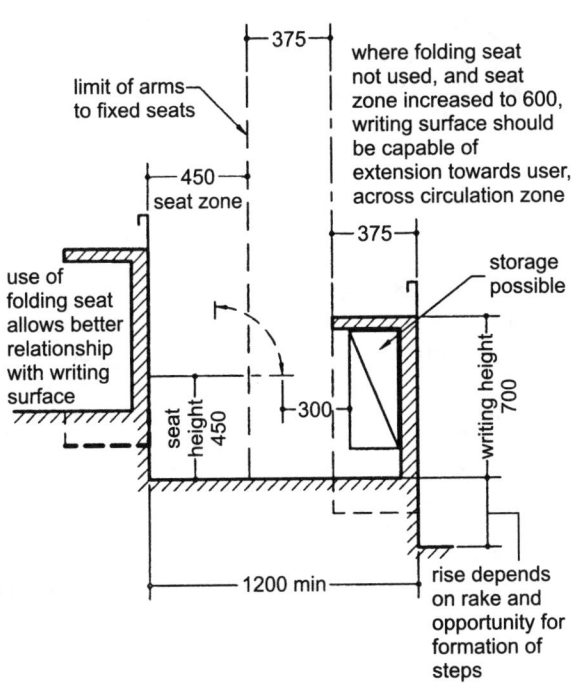

a *Section through fixed seating at 600 to 750 mm centres.*
Number of seats in a row limited to avoid disturbance

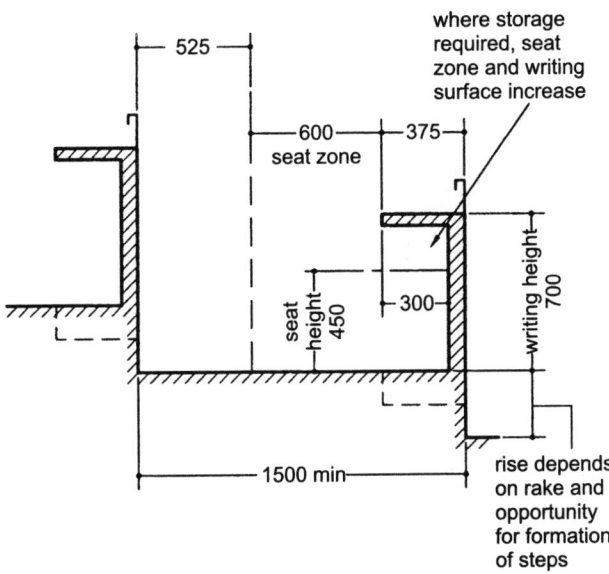

b *Section through moveable seating at 750 to 900 mm centres*

15.4 *Council chamber seating*

1.05 Assembly Hall

While not essential, this is a most valuable asset to a Town Hall; it brings in further income and also familiarises the public with the building and its occupants. It may be used for dances, exhibitions, concerts and recitals; and should have some associated accommodation for artistes, etc.

1.06 Offices

The major need is for office space for the Council's staff. They may be centralised in one building, or dispersed over many, some leased from the private sector. The principal requirement is for flexibility as, like most organisations, change is the only constant.

1.07 Public reception and information

The current philosophy is for a 'one-stop shop'. Particularly where the Council's staff are centralised, the idea is that advice on all matters (planning, building control, council tax, education, social services, leisure) should be available from one counter. Where a matter is more complex than the receptionist can deal with, other staff members come to the enquirer instead of the reverse. A few small interview rooms are available for such consultations adjacent to the counter.

Literature relating to the facilities of the area should be displayed in the reception area; some but not all of this will free. It could be set out rather like a small bookshop.

1.08 Cash facility

Some Council business is still transacted with cash, and a secure facility will be found necessary. Ideally this should be adjacent to the public reception and information to continue the 'one-stop shop' theme.

2 FIRE STATIONS

2.1

Fire stations are required to fulfil efficiently the functions laid down by the national, regional and metropolitan bodies that supervise their work. Each fire brigade has a detailed brief for the design of new fire stations with the aim of dealing with each incident as soon as possible after the emergency call is received in the control room, **15.5**, and this must be within the government's laid-down maximum response time.

Paramedics are now to be trained within the fire service; provision needs to be made for them in new stations. Fire Rescue Units may also need to be garaged.

Firefighters' operational activities are grouped into:

Wet/Dirty: mobilisation, call out
training and drill
cleaning and maintenance.
Clean/dry: administration
public interface
stand-down/recreation
arrival for duty.

A fire station may be built as part of a commercial development, but its long-term use must be assured, particularly in regard to ease of access and egress, radio communications reception and Fire Standards. Conversely, there must also be no interference with TV reception in adjacent properties.

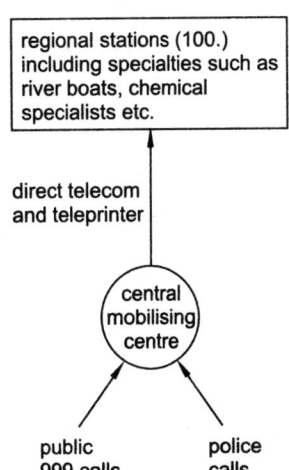

15.5 *Diagram of communications centre control operations*

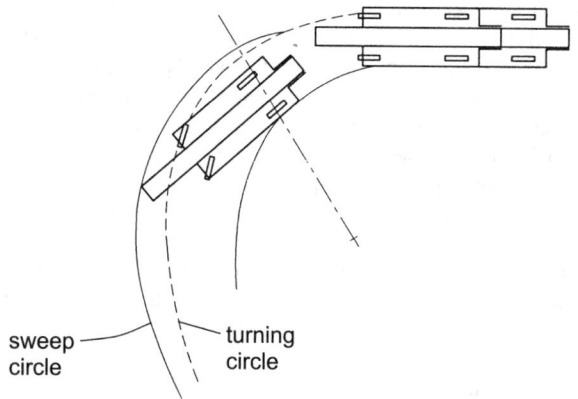

15.6 *Hydraulic platform (cherry-picker), turntable ladder and aerial ladder platform: appliance footprint (path):*
Roadway width 6 m, turning circle 22.5 m, sweep circle 25.2 m.
Max. length 11.3 m, max. height 3.77 m, max. width 2.5 m, max. width with jacks out 6.05 m
Laden weight 28.2 tonnes, max. loading weight on either front axle 6.5 tonnes, on either rear axle 10.5 tonnes, max. single pressure on one extended jack with boom extension at maximum 12.4 tonnes
Max. length wheelbase 5.6 m, track of rear wheels 2 m, minimum ground clearance 229 mm

2.2 Appliance areas

Most stations have two or three appliance bays. The usual appliances are pump ladder appliances and turntable ladders mounted on the basic chassis, and there are other appliances such as bulk foam pods or mobile training pods mounted onto the standard heavy-duty chassis. New stations must also be designed to accommodate aerial ladder platforms (ALPs), which are very large, **15.6**. ALPs are like large 'cherry-pickers' with hydraulically raised platforms but also incorporating ladders. Some will also accommodate special appliances outside the normal categories. The appliance area has a minimum headroom of 5 m. Appliances always face outwards and have a direct rear access to avoid reversing.

When a call is received the appliances need to get onto the road as quickly as possible. A separate route and maximum visibility are required for each appliance leaving the station. Appliances must be able to turn without crossing the crown of the road, **15.7** and **15.8**, which implies the need for a forecourt so that they can start to turn on exiting the bay doors. A forecourt 9 m deep permits appliances to pull clear of the automatic time-controlled doors. Returning appliances should also be able to drive easily from the return access to the covered washdown area, stopping on the centre line of its respective appliance bay.

All areas traversed by appliances must be capable of bearing the load of the heaviest appliance and the pressure of out-riggers; and also withstand close turning movements and braking stress.

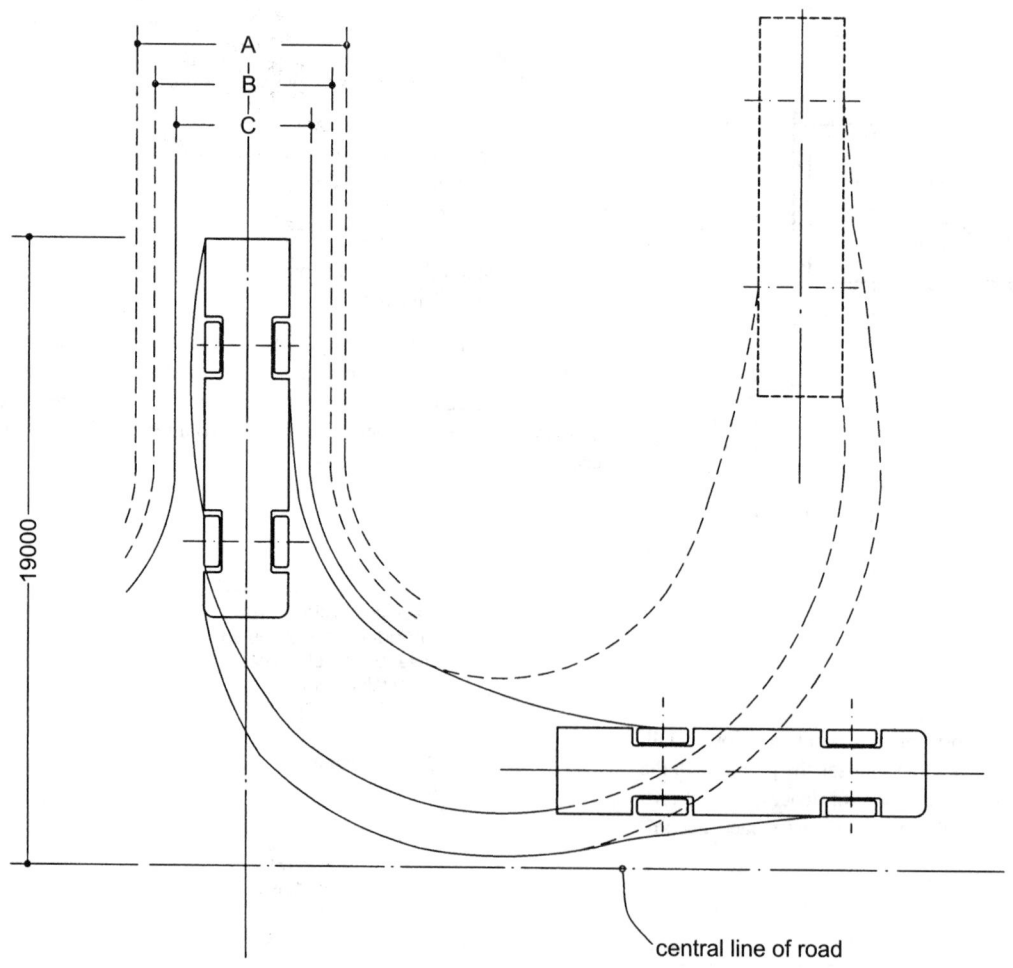

15.7 *Hydraulic platform (long chassis model) turning circle:*
Bay width with no forecourt 6.5 m
Bay width with forecourt 5.5 m
Minimum door width 4.2 m

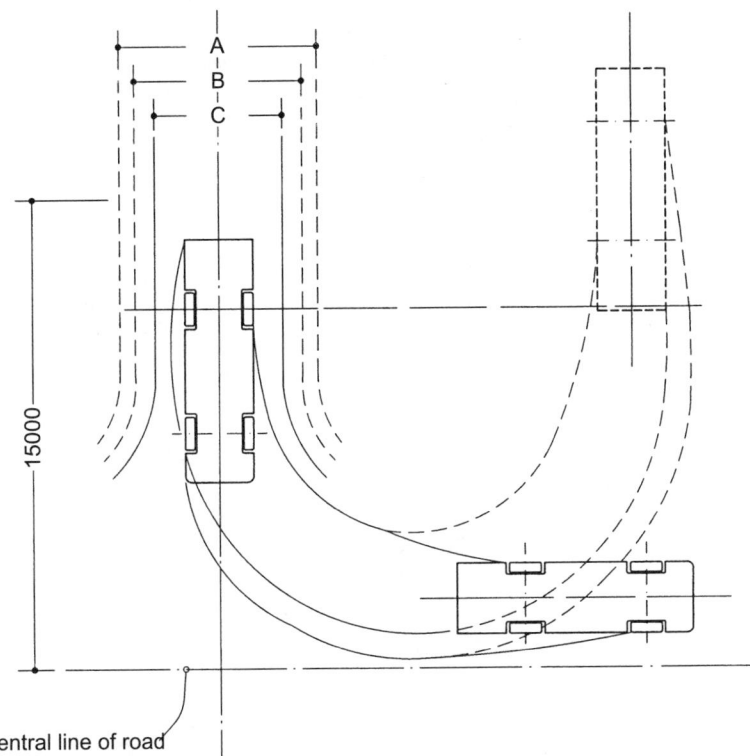

15.8 *Pump ladder turning circle:*
A=Bay width with no forecourt 6.5 m
B=Bay width with forecourt 5.5 m
C=Minimum door width 4.2 m

2.3 Station building

The public, particularly small boys, are not allowed into the fire station except when accompanied by a firefighter. While the appliances are out on a call the station is empty. All doors are automatically operated on electric controls with photo-electric cells and they close automatically after the appliances have left. This is important to avoid theft or damage to the building, particularly when paramedics are accommodated on the station as they need to store drugs for immediate use.

Everything in a fire station has to be very robust with the toughest finishes, easy to clean and maintenance free.

15.9 is a room relationship diagram for one type of fire station. Table I gives recommended areas for some of these spaces. **15.10** shows the necessary provisions to be made for rapid mobilisation,

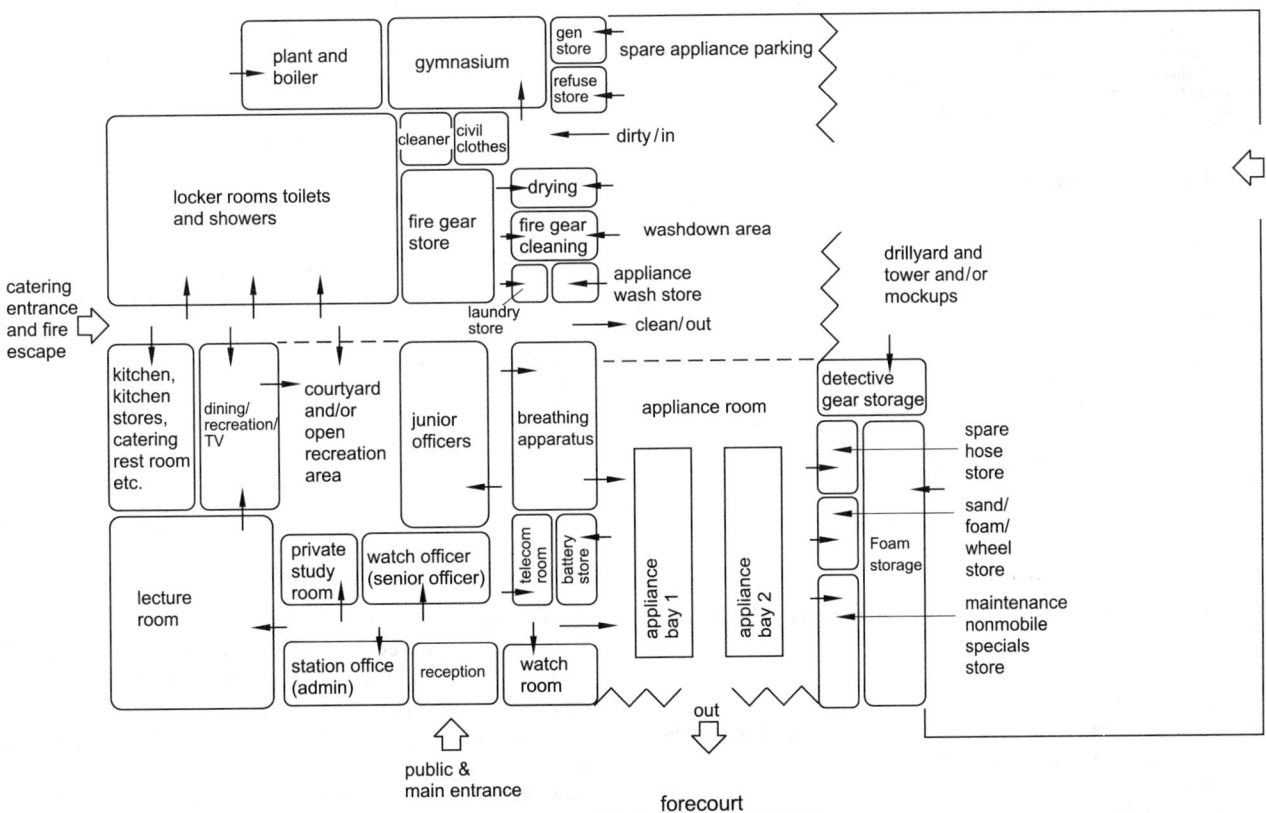

15.9 *Relationship diagram for a two-appliance fire station on one level*

Table I Fire station accommodation

	Above ground level?	Two-appliance	Three-appliance
OPERATIONAL			
Appliance Room	N	160	248
Slide poles		7	7
Fire gear (uniform) store	N	30	40
Operational equipment and general storage	N	27	27
Split into wet, dry and clean zones			
Operational equipment cleaning	N	8	8
Clothes drying room	N	10	10
The four spaces above need direct access to and from the appliances, and quick access from the rest areas. There may also be a small laundry in this area			
Breathing apparatus room	N	13	13
Storing, testing and overhauling equipment			
Fuel storage/pump	N		
Required so that the appliances can be refuelled in their station. Safety regulations are rigidly followed.			
Oil/paraffin/propane storage	N		
Sand/foam/wheel store	N		
Foam trailer garage	N		
Spare hose store	N		
Defective gear store	N		
Maintenance of non-mobile specials store	N		
CONTROL AND ADMINISTRATION			
Watchroom or Operations Centre	N	10	10
A critical room off the appliance bay. Must include teleprinter, radio controls, telephones, maps and route cards. Directly linked to Central Control.			
Station office	Y	17	17
Stationery store	Y		11
Waiting/reception	N	8	8
with entrance lobby for the public to visit the station and see exhibitions, etc. There should be a toilet here for wheelchair users			
Station Commander's office	Y	20	20
Watch Commander's room	Y	15	15
with wash area/toilet/shower and office with couch			
Commander's locker and washroom	Y	15	15
Fire safety office	Y	10	10
AMENITY			
Firefighters' lockers and changing room	Y	58	81
Ideally situated adjacent to the appliance room as the firefighters will change into uniform on arrival and after duty change back.			
Firefighters' toilets and washrooms	Y	32	41
Junior Officer study	Y	26	39
Junior Office toilet	4	4	
Lecture room	Y	45	75
Doubles as a rest area with fold-down beds for emergencies and extra standby shifts, video and TV, screens and whiteboards for teaching and debriefing. If a firefighter is killed or badly wounded a debriefing may involve several fire stations so that this room should be sufficiently large.			
Lecture Storage	Y	10	10
Gymnasium	Y	38	38
Needs direct or pole access to the appliance area			
Quiet/Study Room	Y	15	15
May double up as the Fire Prevention Office for public relations			
Kitchen	Y	25	25
Dining/TV viewing	Y	35	40
Needs direct or pole access to the appliance area			
Cleaner	Y	6	6
Consumables	Y	2	2
SERVICES			
Electrical Intake	N	3	3
Standby Generator	N	12	12
Boiler Room	N	15	15
Refuse Chamber	N	4	4
Gas Meter	N	1	1
Communications	Y	5	5
with BT/Mercury equipment linked to the Watchroom			
Water Meter	N		
Total		692	865
Total including 30% circulation (except to appliance room)		850	1050

and **15.11** the almost equally important arrangements for standing down.

Lockers and ablutions
Toilet and changing facilities must allow for the fact that there are now more women in the fire service.

Fire stations work on a four-watch duty system. Each watch consists of from 12 to 15 firefighters and a station commander. Each firefighter has their own locker and gear hanging space.

Taking into account junior officers and standby staff, at least 50 lockers should be allowed for; preferably a few more as there will be some staff on sick or general leave, retaining their individual lockers. Their temporary replacements will require their own lockers. The area required relates to the specific need of the particular station.

Under present policy men and women share locker rooms with changing cubicles, but have separate ablutions. This simplifies matters as the male/female ratio is never constant.

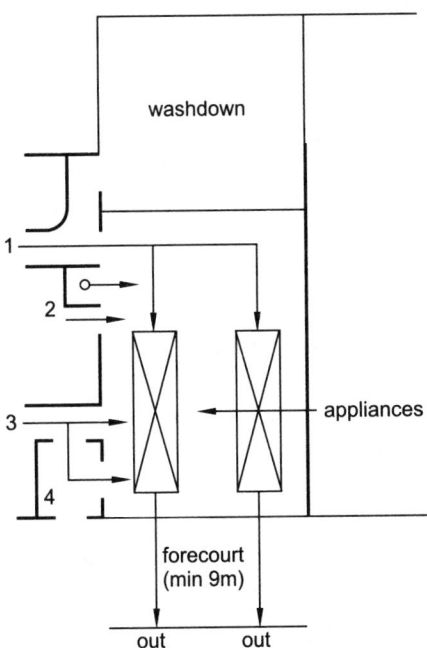

15.10 *Diagram of circulation routes for mobilisation:*
1 *Firefighters to appliances, rear access*
2 *Staircase or pole access when multi-storeyed*
3 *Firefighters to appliances, front access*
4 *Duty firefighters to watchrooms and appliances*

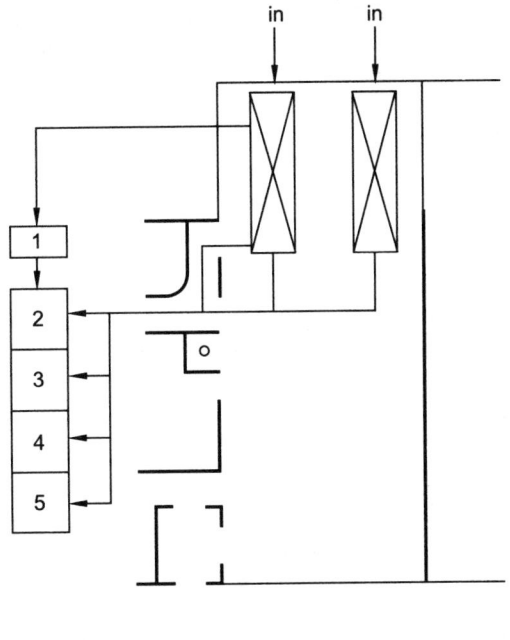

15.11 *Diagram of circulation routes on return to fire station:*
1 *External rear access*
2 *Operational equipment store*
3 *Operational equipment cleaning*
4 *Breathing apparatus room*
5 *Lockers and washroom*

On-site sleeping accommodation is no longer provided. This has eliminated much of the need for recreational facilities, as the firefighters are either on duty or away from the station with very few waiting or resting periods.

Recreation
A fully equipped gymnasium is required to facilitate firefighters achieving the level of physical fitness which their job demands. Television and darts are two other activities for which space is usually allocated within the dining/recreation area.

Station office
The administration in a fire station is covered by the station clerk who is sometimes non-uniformed. He or she deals with day-to-day routine and reports directly to the station commander.

Fire prevention office
The FPO relates to schools, scouts, etc. advises homes and businesses on dealing with the risk of fire. It will have leaflets on fire and smoke detectors, extinguishers, etc.

The function of the Fire Prevention Officer devolves on the fire station commander in some smaller stations.

2.4 Training facilities
Not all stations can sustain the full range of necessary training. Firefighting is now so hazardous, and includes many more dangers than straightforward fires, that firefighters tend to go on special courses to learn to deal with smoke, toxic fumes, ship fires, etc.

Static training for smoke and foam is required on each station. Many existing stations have very restricted external space, limiting the scope of on-station training to an unsatisfactory level. The minimum provision should not be reduced, even on a restricted site. The following three categories are a guide to what can be achieved, with approximate areas:

(a) *Two-appliance station with minimal training facilities*:

Site area approximately 945 m², the residual yard area approximately 400 m².

Facilities on such a site will be adequate for continuation training to be carried out at station level without the frequent need to go elsewhere:

● Training facility of three floors (which could form part of station accommodation), with the ability to test equipment (particularly ladders)
● Small yard with a single hydrant and as much space as possible for parking
● Gym and lecture facilities available nearby.

(b) *Two appliance station with basic training facilities*:

Site area approximately 1800 m², residual yard area approximately 700 m².

● Purpose-built training facility using a full range of standard ladders
● Separate gym and lecture room
● Drill yard with a single hydrant and pumping well, sufficiently large to enable the testing of ladders and the execution of drills using ladders and hose. When not required for training purposes it will provide car parking for station personnel.

(c) *Three appliance station with full training facilities*:

Where there is a demonstrable strategic area training need.
Site area approximately 3100 m², residual yard area approximately 1400 m².

● Training tower of four floors, incorporating a dry rising main and additional breathing apparatus training facilities
● Drill yard with two hydrants, pumping well and space for the partying out of comprehensive drills such as water relays. The

yard will be sufficiently large to accommodate the turning circle of the largest fire appliances, the testing of equipment and the execution of combined drills
● Roof ladder training facilities
● Separate lecture room equipped with audio-visual aids
● Gymnasium enlarged for the training of physical training instructors
● Derv pump and underground tank.

2.5 Drill yard

This area at the rear or side of the station serves several functions that cannot take place inside the appliance bays and ancillary accommodation:

● Vehicle return access to covered washdown area and appliance bays
● Drill/practice/instruction
● Fuel delivery
● Essential car parking.

The drill yard size and shape will be determined by the site constraints. Apart from routine training, it may also be used for special instruction incorporating a mock-up ship, factory or traffic situation to enable the trainees to gain experience of particular difficult and dangerous conditions.

The drill yard and tower must not cause nuisance to adjoining properties, and should not be overlooked by them. Firefighters under drill or training would not appreciate an audience, and the control of water jets in these situations is not always predictable.

Training involves the use of ALPs. The drill yard must be designed to take their heavy point loading as well as heavy vehicles. It should have a minimum fall of 1:50 to drain off the large quantities of water and foam to suitable gulleys.

2.6 Drill tower

Drill towers were previously used for drying hoses as well as training. Hoses are now made of plastic and do not require drying out. Thus towers are not always provided in new stations.

Where a tower is provided, it will include dry risers, firefighting lids, sprinkler systems, different types of windows and artificial smoke conduits for smoke exercises and use of breathing apparatus. There is less use of hose reels, now that Building Regulations have become so sophisticated.

A tower can be either part of the station building or free-standing. A number of features must be provided:

● Up to three working faces, each at least 3.2 m wide in one plane without copings or mouldings
● At least three drill platforms at heights approximately 3 m centres, each with at least 4.65 m² clear non-slip (even when wet), drainable working surface with a minimum width of 3.05 m across the face of the tower
● Orientation to avoid direct sunlight which could be dangerous during certain drills
● Clearance at the base of the working faces of at least 6 m free from hazards such as manholes, hydrant covers and bollards
● Ladders must continue through hatchways above drill platforms level to a point where the top rung is at least 1.5 m above the platform levels. The ladder apertures to be at least 840 × 840 mm, and access only by stepping sideways (never backwards). Ladders must comply with Health and Safety Standards as to rung spacings, wall distances and safety rails. Protected stepping off points to be provided at least 760 mm width
● Instead of ladders, a staircase could be used. In the case of a tower integrated into a station building, the staircase is acceptable as a secondary means of escape
● Cleats and anchor plates or points should be provided on each working face with shackle points of suspension fitted beyond

any sill projections capable of withstanding test loads of 1 tonne
● A section of roofing should also be available to train firefighters in ladder craft, roof drills and particularly safe transfer of personnel from vertical ladders to inclined roof ladders. Safety walkways and protective railings should, however, be included for the full width of the roof, and safety handrails fitted along two of the inclined edges. In integrated towers the main building roof can be utilised as a training roof.

3 AMBULANCE STATIONS

3.1

Ambulance stations are either control stations or their satellites. The control stations contain larger store areas and a divisional office, and may have dining, recreation and activity areas. On-site sleeping accommodation is no longer required. Satellite stations have from two to six ambulances and deal only with accident and emergency calls. They do not require dining or recreation facilities, as off-duty time is spent off the premises, but a rest room will be needed for waiting and relaxing between calls.

Because drugs may be stored on the premises all doors need to be lock controlled.

Like the police, more and more control equipment such as faxes, trackers and radios are in the ambulance, permitting greater use of these facilities with no need to return to base. However, to provide adequate hospital cover, ambulances are stationed there for half-hour periods.

3.2

Apart from accidents and emergencies, the larger stations also cover:

● Patient transfer
● Hospital to hospital
● Home to hospital for consultancy
● Taxi service

3.3

Regions are split into about four divisions with a central control. Each division normally consists of about six larger stations and twelve satellites, varying according to population density. All accident and emergency calls are received at central control.

3.4 Provision for vehicles

In small stations with less than seven ambulances, vehicles will be reversed onto their parking bays. The station will have an easy-to-open individual exit door to each bay, **15.12**. Larger stations use echelon parking with in-and-out access. There must be sufficient space behind the parked ambulance to permit easy removal of equipment.

Large stations require a fuel loading bay, but not the smaller stations. The current trend is towards using petrol rather than diesel, for smoother running and fewer fumes. A vehicle washdown is required for each station.

3.5 Vehicle workshops

Vehicle maintenance is carried out in separate workshop buildings, **15.13**, covering at least six stations. It does not need to be on the same site as an ambulance station.

A workshop normally caters for up to six vehicles at a time, so front access only is required. Larger workshops are designed for echelon parking with a through-access system. All workshops will be capable of carrying out day-to-day maintenance and repairs, including the equivalent of MOT testing, standard servicing and body repairs. They are not expected to replace engines or crankshafts or do heavy repairs. Finishes must be robust and durable and floor surfaces non-slip.

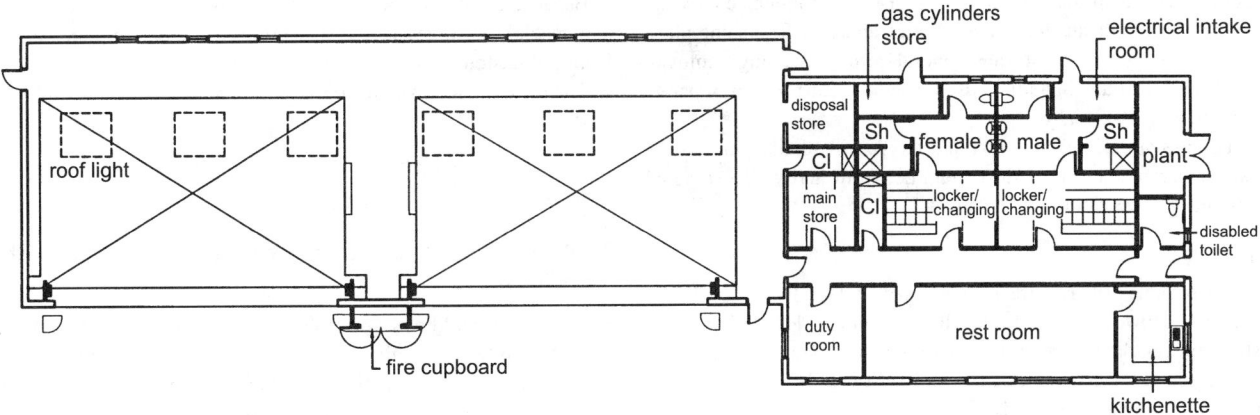

15.12 *Layout of an ambulance station with six vehicles*

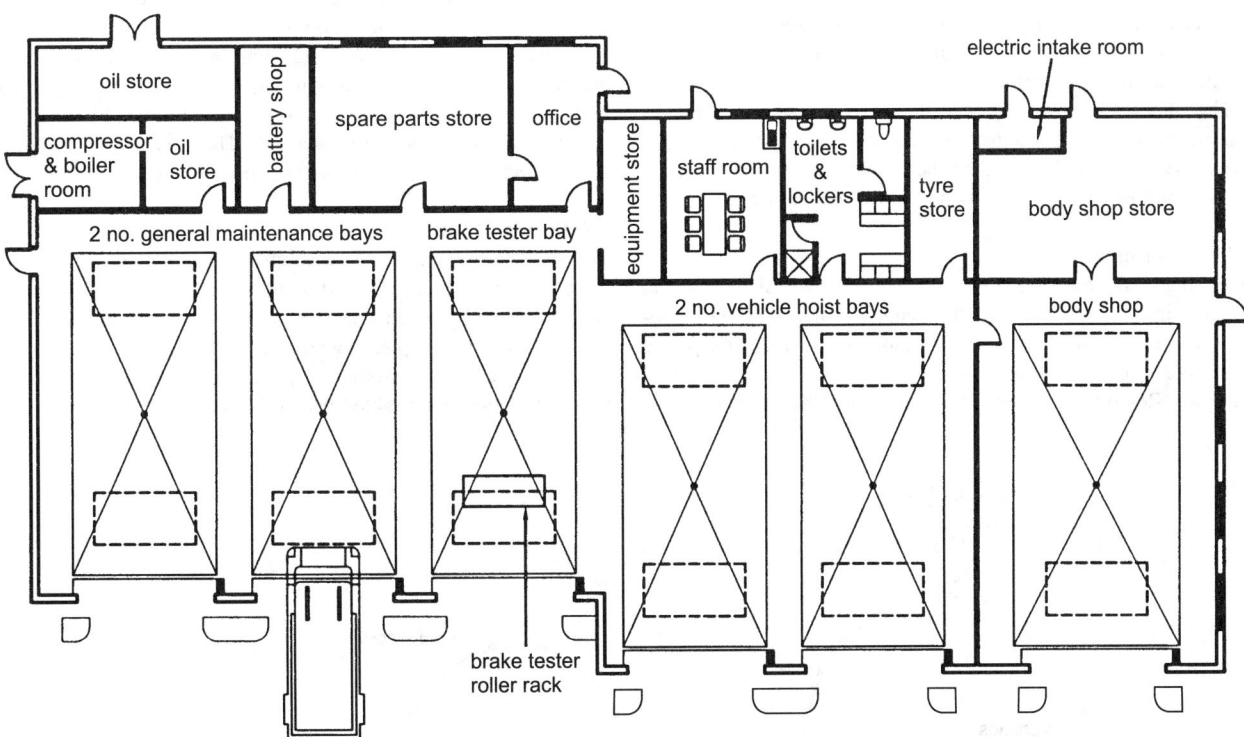

15.13 *Layout of a workshop for servicing ambulance vehicles*

3.6 Duty rooms

Duty rooms should be close to the garage, have adequate wall space for maps and natural lighting and ventilation. Staff in the rest room must be able to see what is happening in the duty room, so it should be adjacent with a glazed screen between.

3.7

Lockers and changing facilities are linked to showers and toilets. In the smaller stations unisex toilets and showers are acceptable. Elsewhere they should be designed to facilitate adjustment when the male/female ratio changes.

3.8

A toilet for wheelchair users and other disabled people is needed although the ambulance operatives themselves need to be fully able-bodied. This is because members of the public have come to expect such a facility to be provided at an ambulance station!

3.9 Stores

The main store needs to be a secure facility close to the garage. It will accommodate the following in a single area or in separate stores:

- Linen such as blankets, sheets, pillowcases and towels
- Medical supplies such as first-aid dressings, bandages and splints
- Paramedic equipment such as defibulators and resuscitators
- Spare items to replace equipment normally stored in the ambulance
- Trolleys, stretchers, etc. belonging to de-kitted vehicles
- Expendable items and documents, log books and files.

A separate store within the main store is required for drugs. This is separately lockable and alarmed to the duty room.

Blankets should be kept well ventilated and heated.

Dirty blankets, linen and contaminated clothes are temporarily kept in containers in a disposal store until they can be sent to a laundry. This disposal store should be near the ambulance parking, but away from clean stores and other clean areas. The same place can also be used for storing general refuse awaiting removal. Medical materials including used needles must be in separate containers for special disposal.

The gas store holds entonox and oxygen in small cylinders for use by paramedics. This store must be warm and well ventilated with easy access to the ambulances.

3.10

Some regions still require a small blanket laundry in the larger stations. However, due to health and safety legislation, with stringent regulations relating to temperature controls, cleanliness and hygiene, there is a strong move towards using contract cleaning companies instead.

4 POLICE STATIONS

4.1

The police aim to foster public goodwill; their buildings should be as pleasing and friendly to the visitor as possible compatible with essential security requirements.

The Home Office has produced most detailed and comprehensive guides covering legislative requirements, cost and design. New stations should be based on the *Home Office Building Guide 1994*, modified to suit the individual local requirements.

4.2 Organisation

Over the last few years there has been radical change in organisation. Some forces still maintain divisions and sub-divisions; others have gone over to regions and areas. Some police forces collaborate with others to provide support services for their joint use. Regional crime squads come under this heading.

Because so much of the work has become extremely technical and specialised, many of the specialities are accommodated away from the custody and public departments.

The different levels of the organisation require different building types:

1 Headquarters buildings with control extending over a force area,
2 Divisional HQs
3 sub-Divisional HQs, which may be located separately or may be combined.

Headquarters buildings and police stations are all based on the same principles, and only vary according to need. A facility like a custody suite or communications centre is located in the most suitable place regardless of the rank of the building.

4.3 Siting

Stations should be near public transport, readily available both to the local inhabitants and easily found by strangers. They no longer need to be near magistrates' courts. However, when they are, they should be totally separate with no shared facilities.

In busy shopping centres and high streets police posts with direct communications to their headquarters are proving popular with both police and public, who provide information there that might never be otherwise obtained. The authorities are even considering having police posts in supermarkets.

4.4 Design of the station

The zoning diagram, **15.14**, is a guide to circulation.

The public area must be designed with an awareness of the dangers posed by explosives and people with weapons. It should still try to maintain a pleasing and welcoming atmosphere. It must be easily accessible from the police area. Access and toilet accommodation for disabled people is essential.

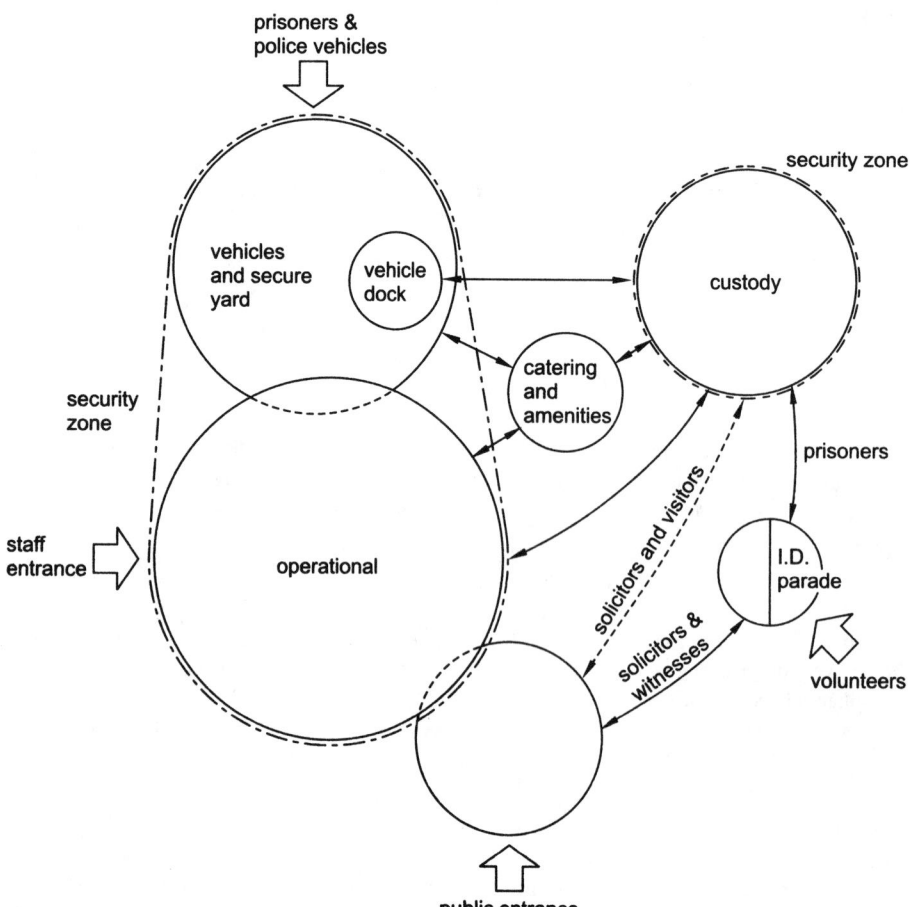

15.14 *Relationship and zoning diagram for a large police station*

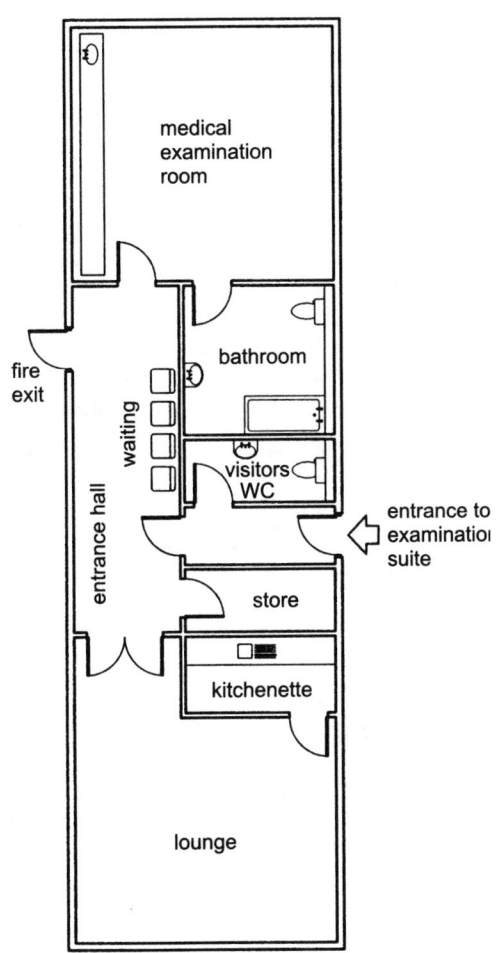

15.15 *Plan of a victim examination suite*

The reception counter should be located to permit officer-on-duty supervision of the building entrance. A security screen between counter area and waiting is desirable in some circumstances, so that only a limited number can enter at a time. This provides both privacy and security. Where there is no screen a privacy booth in or on the counter is desirable.

Waiting areas are provided with seating and notice boards for posters on road safety and crime prevention, etc.

The public interview area is entered off the waiting area. Interview rooms should be large enough to take several people at a time and are fitted with taping equipment.

The victim examination suite should be adjacent to the public entrance and is for interviewing and medical examination of assault, child molestation or rape victims. It must be pleasantly designed in order to reduce stress, **15.15**.

Found property

This is an area accessible only to the police for storing unclaimed stolen property and items handed in by the public or found by the police. No live animals are kept there, although some stations do have special facilities for animals.

People seeking lost property enquire for it at the reception counter, so this should have easy access to the found property store. Its size will depend on local requirements. Some forces use warehouses due to the very large quantities that are collected. Where no large store or warehouse is available, bulky items such as bicycles are usually stored in out-buildings.

Assembly room, lockers, changing and drying rooms

They should be located close to the police entrance. Showers and toilets should be adjacent to the lockers and to the drying areas which should be operational in summer as well as winter.

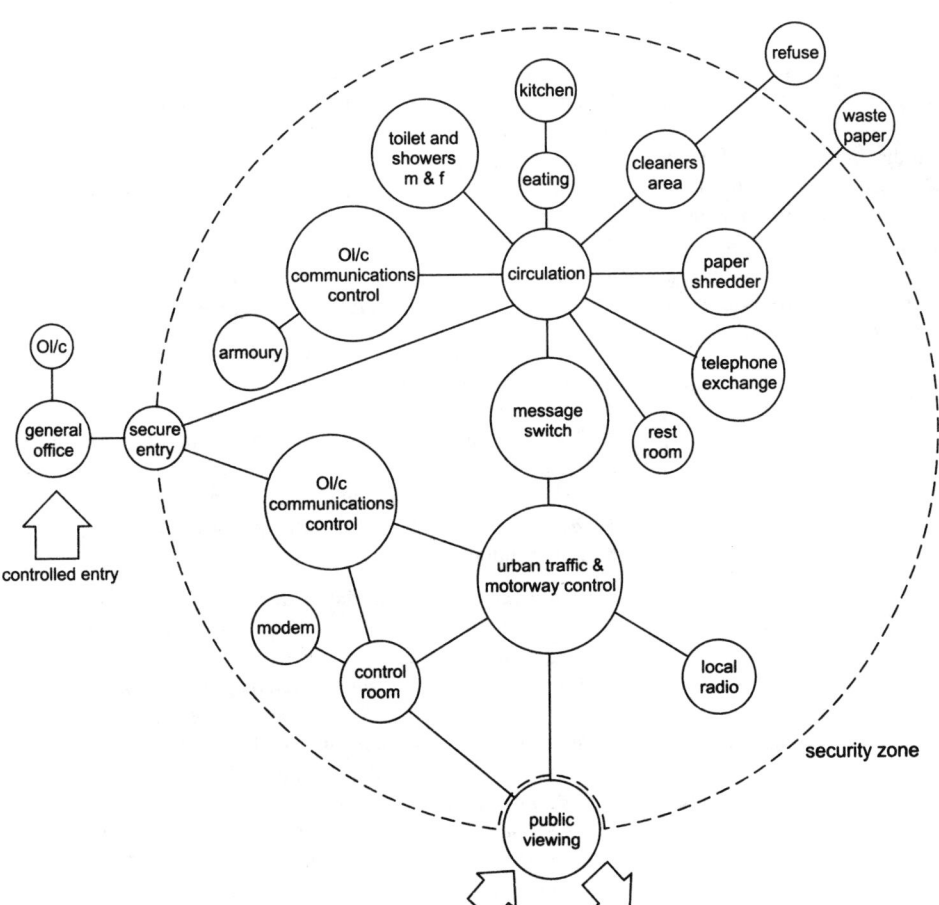

15.16 *Relationship diagram of a Control Room suite*

Report writing room
These should be adjacent to the assembly room. Booths and acoustic treatment are advisable.

Communications and control are central to the police function. Workload is extremely heavy and the working environment should be designed to mitigate stress, **15.16**. The control room deals with force or area-wide facilities including VHF radio, and has direct access to police resource information and criminal records. Communications rooms are principally used for message transfer and receipt of information.

The location and design of the central control room should be such as to frustrate any deliberate attempt to dislocate its vitally important functions by physical or electronic attack. Its vehicular access must ensure an uninterrupted road in an emergency; but no parking should be allowed within 15 m of its perimeter.

Major incident room
A force will on occasions need to work on serious crimes requiring extensive investigation, civil emergencies or major incidents. Accommodation with easy communication connections will be required for temporary use by CID, traffic or uniformed branches; when not so required, it will be designated for an alternative function such as a gymnasium.

Criminal justice office
This is for documentation of cases to be brought before the courts.

Criminal Investigation Department (CID)
In some cases CID would have their own unit separate from the police station.

Operational group provides office accommodation for

- Beat patrols
- Uniformed section
- Operational control
- General administration.

Administration covers general administration as opposed to operational dependent administration and activities.

Traffic includes accommodation for motor patrols, traffic wardens, garages and workshops.

Garages and workshops may be on the same site as the station, or be a separate unit with attached accommodation for motor patrols depending on the size of the area and the number of vehicles. It is preferable not to have this unit in a busy city centre where it would add to congestion, and also hinder police cars quickly reaching the scene of an incident. If the police area includes motorways the unit should be sited near an access point, or even within a motorway service area.

The police car is becoming more 'high tech', with built-in computers in addition to two-way radios. It is becoming an office in its own right, so that there is less need for the occupants to report in person to a police station.

Prisoners' vehicle dock
This must be provided away from the main police vehicle yard; totally secure and adjacent to the prisoners' entrance to the building, **15.17**. **15.18** gives data for the prisoner transport vehicle.

Identification parade facility
This has to be carefully sited outside the custody area but linked to it by a secure access route. Witnesses should be rigidly segregated from each other, and from all members of the parade before, during and after the parade; there must be no possibility of physical contact at any time, or visual contact except during the parade itself, **15.19**. Toilet facilities should be available for witnesses and volunteers.

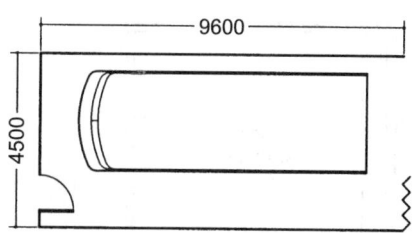

15.17 *Plan of a prisoner transport vehicle dock*

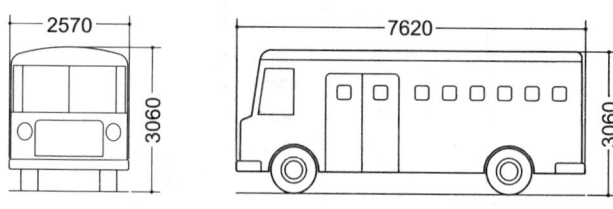

a *Dimensions*

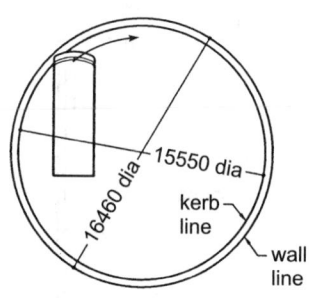

b *Turning circles*

15.18 *A vehicle for transporting prisoners*

Messing and recreation
Catering is usually provided by self-help appliances such as frozen packaged food with grills or microwave ovens and hot/cold drink dispensers. In large stations there may be a canteen, but 24–hour operation is easier to control through packaged meals.

Toilets
Lavatory accommodation is related to size of station and disposition of rooms. Separate provision is made for:

- Male sergeants, constables and civilian staff
- Female sergeants, constables and civilian staff
- Senior officers
- Chief constables and assistant chief constables have en-suite facilities
- Visitors, usually located at the public entrance
- Disabled people, also close to the public entrance
- Cell accommodation.

Blast proofing is now mandatory for all police stations; no car parking should be positioned within 15 m of the buildings, 10 m for operational vehicles.

Mechanical ventilation and cooling is provided for information and communications accommodation without natural ventilation.

Emergency electrical supply is essential throughout, not only for power failure but also in the event of fire. In large stations it will be necessary to ensure continuity of supply to the custody suite, radios, computers, teleprinters, and communication service equipment, and must have 'direct on-line automatic start'.

An uninterrupted power supply (UPS) will be required for computer areas.

4.5 Custody suite

This includes detention rooms, charge desk(s) and ancillary accommodation, **15.20** and **15.21**. The police have to be alert to the possibility of someone in custody attempting suicide. Care needs to be taken to avoid this eventuality particularly in the design of the cells (see Section **4.6** below).

The custody area should be securely separated from other parts of the building. It should be located on a single level to avoid moving prisoners up and down stairs which should be avoided at all costs. Where minor changes in level are unavoidable internally or externally, ramps should be used.

Corridors and cells for female prisoners should be segregated from those for male prisoners. Each should have separate access to the exercise yard. Detention rooms for juveniles should also be separate from adult areas.

Catering

Prisoners and police within the custody area need to be fed. However, a kitchenette within the custody area is undesirable as it would divert the custody officer from essential tasks and also be a fire risk. The self-catering facility in the amenity area is also unacceptable as it would take officers away from the custody area. There is little alternative, therefore, to a staffed kitchen imme-

diately outside the custody area preparing food in compliance with food hygiene regulations and providing the meals close to the users. If there is a canteen which is fully staffed for 24 hours, this may be used.

Provision for disabled people is not required for the custody suite which is exempt from the provisions of Part M of the Building Regulations.

Detention suite

This is a facility where the WC is outside the cell, **15.22**, where additional washing facilities can be securely provided.

WCs

The compartment should have a stable-type hinged door, not a sliding one, with an observation aperture. The cistern should be outside the compartment with secured access and a protected flushing pipe. The flushing device should be outside the reach of a prisoner attempting suicide by drowning, and should not be a chain or project from the wall. There should be no projecting toilet roll holder, exposed overflow pipe, bracket, service pipe or stopcock. Fittings should be not be able to be broken or extracted to make tools or weapons.

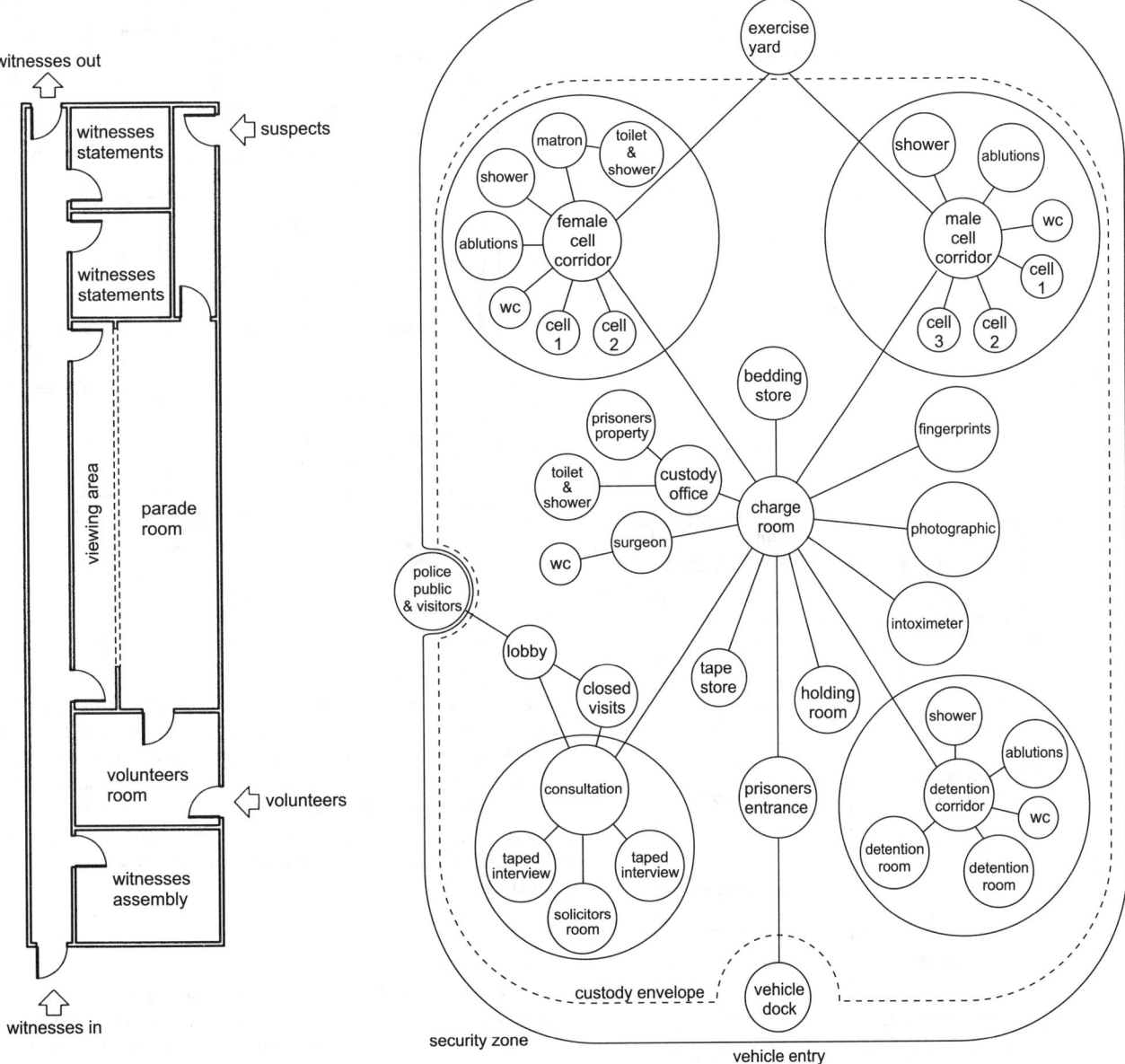

15.19 *Plan of an identity parade suite*

15.20 *Relationship and zoning diagram for a custody suite*

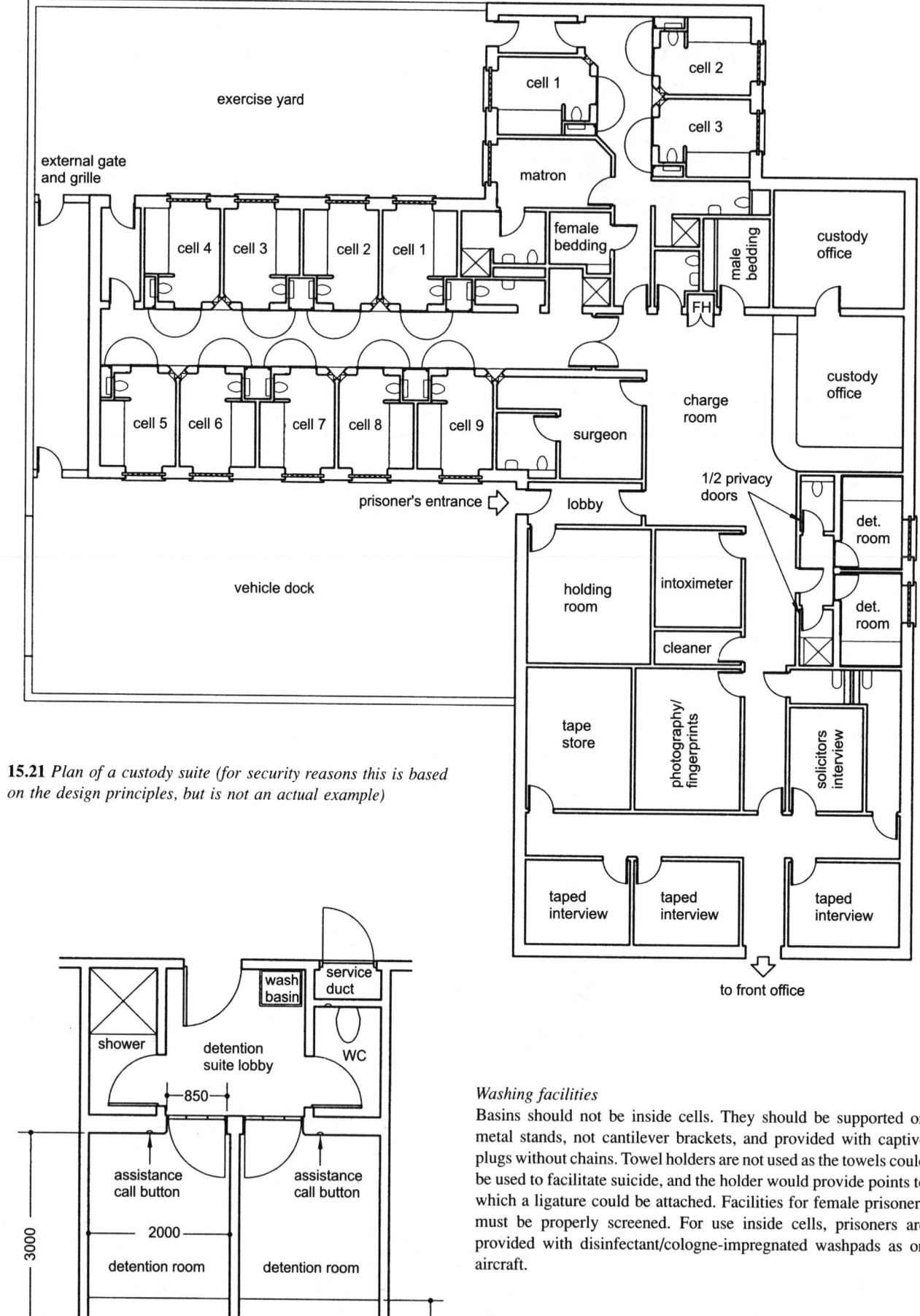

15.21 *Plan of a custody suite (for security reasons this is based on the design principles, but is not an actual example)*

15.22 *Plan of a detention suite*

Washing facilities

Basins should not be inside cells. They should be supported on metal stands, not cantilever brackets, and provided with captive plugs without chains. Towel holders are not used as the towels could be used to facilitate suicide, and the holder would provide points to which a ligature could be attached. Facilities for female prisoners must be properly screened. For use inside cells, prisoners are provided with disinfectant/cologne-impregnated washpads as on aircraft.

Cell corridor

The entrance should be fitted with an iron gate. The corridor should have alarm pushes for the custody officer's use if attacked. There should be no exposed pipes, valves, electric cables or conduit, and any thermometer should be outside the reach of a passing prisoner.

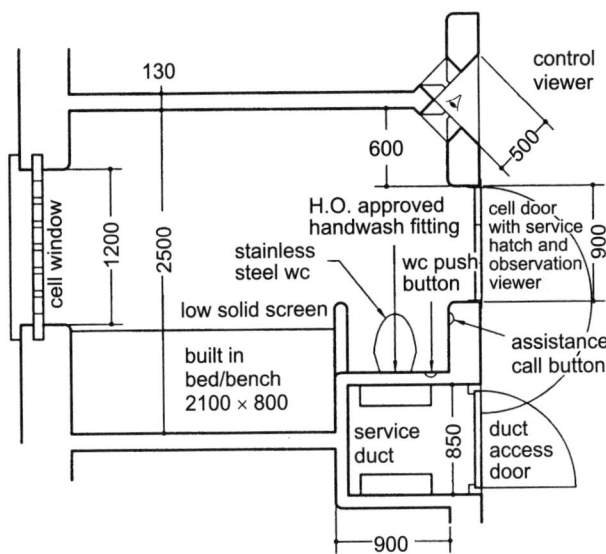

15.23 *Plan of a custody cell*

Exercise yard
The walls should be high enough to prevent a prisoner escaping, at least 3.6 m. There should be no ledges or other features which enable a prisoner to climb. However, where for any reason the height and detailing of the walls are deemed insufficient to prevent escape, a top cover may be used. There should be no doors or windows opening into the yard which might enable a prisoner to reach the top cover, nor any unlockable inspection chamber covers or gully gratings which could be lifted. Rainwater and soil pipes should be flaunched up in cement mortar to obviate handholds.

4.6 Cell design
The Police Design Guides are explicit in their requirements reflected in a typical design, **15.23**.

Windows
Cell windows which are unguarded and with openable panes should not overlook roads or other public areas. Windows overlooking exercise yards should be both guarded and screened to prevent observation. Windows to ancillary accommodation within the cell suite such as blanket store, property store, cell corridor, gaoler's room, toilets, etc. should all be guarded. The glazing should be of toughened opaque glass fitted flush to the wall with no protrusions to facilitate injury or suicide, or ledges facilitating escape and attacks on officers. The thickness of the glass increases with larger panes. Glass should not be replaced for ventilation purposes with, for example, perforated zinc.

Ceilings
Most suspended ceilings can be easily broken, giving access to other parts of the building and possibly providing improvised tools or weapons.

Doors
All doors should be prisoner-proof and flush.

Cell furniture
These should not be of timber or able to be prised loose to make a tool or a weapon.

Ventilation
Casings to trunking should be secure against breakage and use by prisoners to facilitate suicide. Grilles under cell benches should be securely fixed using non-withdrawable screws. High-level air vents with perforations should not be larger than 4.7 mm diameter, of a material that will break under load and fitted flush with the wall surface.

Lighting
Cell light fittings should be fitted flush with the ceiling with unwithdrawable screws. They should have twin lamp holders and plastic lenses. Electrical supplies should not be exposed and the switches should be outside the cell with cover plates that cannot be removed to gain access to live parts.

Heating
Electric radiant heaters with exposed wiring should not be used to heat cells, neither should exposed hot water radiators. There should be no protrusions of any kind to which a ligature could be attached.

Cell call system
This should comprise a press button within the cell fitted flush with the wall operating a bell and indicator light externally. It should be on a separate circuit from the lighting, and the indicator light board should be under constant observation by the officer-in-charge.

Maintenance
Damaged cells should be withdrawn from use.

5 REFERENCES AND BIBLIOGRAPHY
Home Office Building Guide 1994
NHS Estates, *Health Building Note 44*

16 Primary health care

Ann Noble

CI/Sfb: 423
UDC: 725.512

Ann Noble, after many years with the Medical Architecture Research Unit (MARU), is now a consulting architect in the all-important field of health facilities

KEY POINT:

- *We are in a period of major change, with more being provided at primary level rather than in hospitals*

Contents

1.0 INTRODUCTION

1.01

Until recently, primary health care has been delivered from one of four building types:

- Health centres
- General medical practicioners' (GPs') premises
- Clinics or
- Dental practitioner premises

located conveniently for the population served.

Now the distinctions between acute and primary health care services and between GP and health authority community services are becoming increasingly blurred; as are the distinctions between the different types of primary health care buildings.

1.2 Health Centres

A health centre was a building provided, equipped, maintained and staffed (with the exception of family doctors and dentists who were licensed tenants) by the local health authority. The purpose of the health centre was to draw together a combination of traditionally separate health services. Many health centres have been successful, some have been unpopular, some have become overcrowded as the activities and numbers of staff have expanded beyond the intended use, some have suffered from poor management and some from a lack of investment in building maintenance.

When in 1974 the responsibility for health centres was transferred from local to health authorities, it was anticipated that 80 per cent of GPs would be working from within them by 1980. The concept of primary health care teams gained acceptance but, as a result of changes in national policy, health authorities were subsequently discouraged from building more health centres, and by 1984, only 28 per cent of GPs were practising from them.

Family doctors and dentists have been licensed tenants in health centres; but after 1995 the NHS Trust owners will be looking to change the lease arrangements.

1.03 General practice premises

GP premises are provided by the practitioners for their own use as a surgery, and they are reimbursed by the NHS for providing these facilities for NHS patients.

As an alternative to NHS investment in health centres, GPs are encouraged to raise the capital to develop their own premises, and given financial incentives to do so by means of a 'cost rent reimbursement' scheme. The standards set for cost rent schemes represent substantial improvements over many existing premises: they require minimum space standards, facilities for a practice nurse, access for disabled patients and the possibility of offices for attached community nurses and health visitors. However, the range of services they can accommodate is far smaller than for a health centre.

1.04 Clinics

Clinics offer community health services such as ante-natal and baby clinics or chiropody and speech therapy where there is not a local health centre offering these. Many clinic buildings are of poor quality and under-used.

1.05 New directions

The primary health care needs of a local population have not changed significantly over the years: Finsbury Health Centre was built in 1932 and continues in use in the 1990s. However, recent trends are affecting the ways in which the services are organised and financed and, consequently, the buildings from which they are provided.

- There is an increasing emphasis on a wide range of primary health care and associated professionals working as teams and the advantages of their sharing accommodation.
- Changes in GP practice have led to many GPs offering an increased range of services, such as immunisation, child development, ante-natal care, family planning and minor surgery: activities which have been traditionally carried out in health centres and clinics, and for which many GP premises are not suitable. Some GPs work closely with other health care professionals such as acupuncturists and osteopaths, not normally associated with NHS primary health care, as well as with chiropodists, physiotherapists and dentists. These trends have been developing for many years, usually with the GP practice providing the accommodation.
- An increasing number of GP practices are designated as Fund Holders, enabling them to manage clinical budgets for their patients. This encourages them to provide diagnostic, therapeutic and out- patient consultants' services for their patients from their premises when this offers a more cost-effective way of doing so than purchasing them from elsewhere.
- There is increasing pressure to move consultant out-patient clinics, diagnostic and therapeutic activities out of acute hospitals into less costly, community settings.
- As with other health buildings, increasing emphasis is being placed on obtaining maximum and efficient use of all facilities, on the sharing of resources and on reducing running costs.
- Information technology, theoretically, if not yet operationally, makes information instantly available between primary, community, and acute health care locations, meaning that physical proximity to sources of information (such as test results, X-ray pictures, specialist opinion or medical records) is no longer a determinant of accessibility to the information.

● More education at all levels of most health care professionals is taking place in primary and community settings. In some cases, educational centres are integrated into health buildings.

2 NEW BUILDING TYPES

2.01

As a result of these new directions, wider ranges of services, activities and staff are being grouped together in different and larger configurations, often in buildings undertaken as joint ventures by different providers, with funding which reflects this. In addition to health centres and GP premises, terms such as *primary health care centres*, *medical centres*, *resource centres* and *polyclinics* are coming into use. There is no standard definition of services, staff, management, ownership or funding for any of these but the term *resource centre* implies some specialised facilities which are available for use by various practitioners and the term *polyclinic* implies a grouping of specialist consultant facilities with some diagnostic and treatment support.

2.02

Any of these building types could include general medical practitioners (GPs), dental, ophthalmic and pharmaceutical practitioners, community nursing services, specialist out-patient services, community services, such as chiropody, physiotherapy and speech therapy, non-acute beds, resource centres, educational facilities, out-of-hours services for GPs, 'drop-in treatment' and minor surgery facilities.

3 GP PREMISES

3.01

Notwithstanding the new building types, GP premises continue to comprise the largest number of primary health care buildings. GPs themselves may have limited experience and understanding of their current and future needs and may need guidance to achieve high standards of space and design. Without experienced financial advice they may limit themselves unnecessarily.

3.02

GPs are reimbursed for the use of their premises by the Family Health Services Authority (FHSA). This enables them either to raise capital to invest in premises themselves or to pay rent. It is imperative that the FHSA is involved in any development proposal, as its support is crucial. Some FHSAs offer better advice than others but the following points should be borne in mind:

● The space required for both the delivery of health care and for administrative support is frequently under-estimated by GPs.
● There is no limit to the size of premises for which an FHSA can reimburse GPs a current market rent (actual or as assessed by the District Valuer); provided the FHSA agrees that the space is both needed and used.
● The 'cost-rent scheme' was introduced in the 1960s as a basis for paying GP practices an enhanced reimbursement to encourage new purpose-built developments. The area on which the enhanced reimbursement can be made reflects the pattern of GP practice at that time and so does not include any allowance for facilities for minor surgery, for the increased role and numbers of practice nurses, for group activities such as baby clinics and relaxation classes, for bases for other primary health team members or for increased practice administration.
● The space standards included in the 'Statement of Fees and Allowances for GPs (known as the Red Book) set minimum standards for acceptability of premises under the rent and rates reimbursement schemes. These are not maximum or necessarily desirable standards of provision, and in some cases are misleading (in particular for consulting/examination rooms).

4 THE BRIEF

4.01

Decisions about which services are to be delivered from a particular building have to be made within the overall strategy for primary care provision for each locality, enabling the various facilities within the area to support and complement each other. For this reason, establishing a precise brief can be complicated, particularly when the building is seen as a means of enabling changes and developments in the delivery of services to take place.

4.02

The brief should be expressed in the following terms:

1 A list of services to be delivered (the functional content)
2 The scope and scale of the specific activities and the number of staff required for each of the services (e.g. the requirement for physiotherapy could range from a staff team and a fully equipped gymnasium to one physiotherapist using one treatment table for two sessions a week)
3 The number of staff to be based in the building
4 The number of staff working in the building on a sessional basis
5 The number of patients per session
6 Operational policies that affect the organisation and management of the whole building or individual services (e.g. having one shared or several separate reception points, or requiring to close some areas while others remain open).

4.03

This information enables schedules of accommodation to be developed and decisions about sharing or multi-use spaces to be made.

5 FUNCTIONAL CONTENT

5.01

Content will vary considerably including combinations of the following.

5.02 General practices

● General medical practice (varies between one and 30 GPs), in one or more practice partnerships
● General dental practice
● General pharmaceutical practice
● General ophthalmic practice
● Others such as osteopath, acupuncturist.

5.03 Community and school health and dental services

● Maternity and child welfare
● Ophthalmic services
● Child guidance
● Speech therapy
● Physiotherapy
● Community nursing services
● Community health visiting services
● Chiropody
● Health education
● Social services

5.04 Services traditionally hospital-based

● Hospital out-patient services
● Hospital diagnostic services
● X-ray services
● Minor surgical procedures
● Accident and emergency (A & E) facilities (uncommon)

- Drop-in treatment facilities
- Beds (uncommon)

5.05 Education

- Post-graduate education centres
- Teaching facilities for medical students or any of the allied professions

5.06 Space types

The activities generated by the range of services listed above do not all need different types of spaces. Their activities will require one or more of the following types of space:

- Entrance/waiting/reception/patient amenity
- Record storage/administration
- Consulting/examination rooms/interview rooms
- Treatment rooms (general and specialised)
- Diagnostic rooms (general and specialised)
- Large spaces with associated storage for group activities (baby clinics, health education, relaxation classes)
- Staff office bases
- Seminar rooms/meeting rooms/library
- Staff facilities
- Support facilities (clean and dirty utility rooms, storage, disposal, cleaners' rooms)
- Non-acute in-patient wards with support
- Plant rooms
- Car-parking/drop off points

5.07

To facilitate the multi-use of spaces, provide adequate and secure equipment storage; size rooms so that their function can be flexible. Where rooms are tailored too tightly to a specific function, it limits their flexibility.

6 DESIGN PRINCIPLES

6.01 Location

The location of the building in relation to the people it serves is crucial. If it serves a wider public than can walk to the building, it should be adequately served by public transport, and have appropriate facilities for those using private transport.

6.02 Circulation

The entrance to the building and the circulation within it should be designed with due consideration for wheelchair users, parents with small children, people with visual, audio or ambulatory disabilities, and the physically frail who constitute a large proportion of the users of primary care.

Everyone should be able to arrive at, move around and leave the building without unnecessary effort, anxiety or embarrassment. The pattern of circulation should be obvious to the visitor and should not rely on complicated signs. Staff also need to work efficiently, moving easily from one place and activity to another.

6.03 Zoning

To facilitate the translation of planning principles into the design, group activities within the building into the following three zones:

- Public zone: where callers are received and wait
- Clinical zone: where patients meet clinical staff
- Staff zone: where staff meet each other and work in private

Grouping spaces into these zones controls contact between staff and callers, ensures privacy, minimises unnecessary movement and increases security, **16.1**.

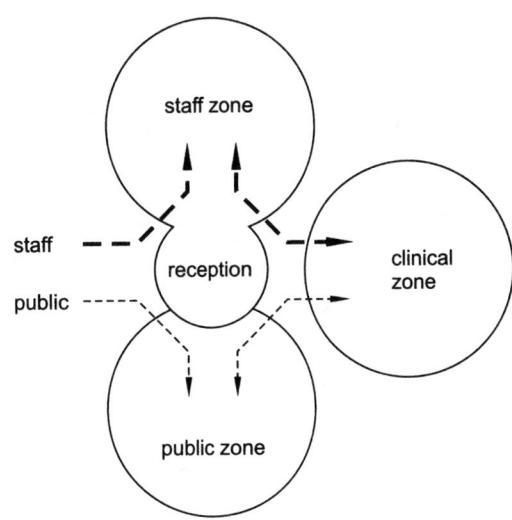

16.1 *Relationship and zoning diagram for a health centre*

6.04 Privacy

Privacy and confidentiality are important aspects of the relationship between a patient and staff members. Two places where these aspects suffer from poor design are:

- The reception desk, where one side of a telephone call can be overheard by people waiting, and
- Clinical rooms during consultations and treatments, where personal topics must be discussed freely and in confidence without fear of being seen or overheard; there should be no waiting outside doors.

6.05 Security and supervision

Movement of the public about the premises should be supervised by reception staff without disrupting their work. Supervision also promotes security within the building. Sub-waiting areas should be avoided unless they will be managed and supervised by staff.

Staff need security against personal assault; the equipment and facilities need security against theft and vandalism. The degree and types of security needed depends on the location and on the nature of the services being provided.

6.06 Environment

The building should be comfortable, welcoming, with good natural lighting and ventilation; and it should be easy to maintain and keep clean.

6.07 Running costs

Staff salaries are the largest component of the running costs so the design should facilitate efficient staffing. Energy-efficient, long-life and low-maintenance approaches should be adopted for the building.

6.08 Flexibility and growth

Designs should provide for the flexible use of some spaces from day to day; and for the inevitable changes in the demand for services and the pattern of delivery during the life of the building. Provision for extending it should be considered, as should the installation of hard standings and temporary building services connections for special, mobile diagnostic units.

7 SPACES

7.01 Car parking

Car parking needs to be provided for staff and patients. The number of places required will depend upon the functional content

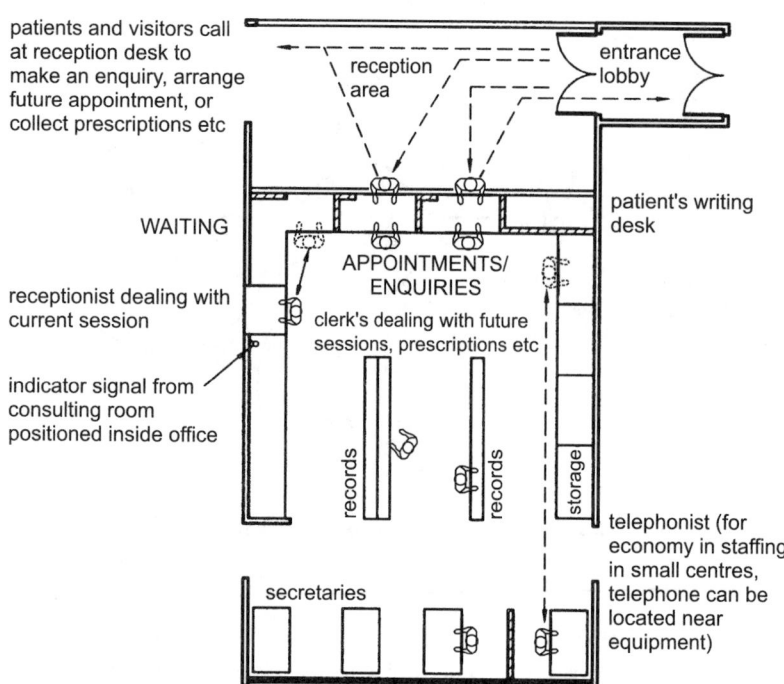

patients and visitors call at reception desk to make an enquiry, arrange future appointment, or collect prescriptions etc

reception area

entrance lobby

patient's writing desk

WAITING

APPOINTMENTS/ ENQUIRIES

receptionist dealing with current session

clerk's dealing with future sessions, prescriptions etc

indicator signal from consulting room positioned inside office

records

records

storage

telephonist (for economy in staffing in small centres, telephone can be located near equipment)

secretaries

16.2 *Plan of a reception area for a smaller health centre. Note the hatch overlooking the waiting area for calling patients to their appointments. All administrative functions are taking place behind the enquiry desk, and while visible and audible from it, tend also to be visible and audible from the reception and waiting areas*

of the building and on local circumstances. For traditional primary health care buildings, an approximate guide would be four parking spaces per consulting room (1.5 for staff, 2.5 for patients). Provision for disabled parking must be made adjacent to all buildings, and for patient transport by ambulance for some buildings.

7.02 Main entrance
The main entrance should be clearly visible, identifiable and easily accessible, preferably with a covered setting-down point from cars.

7.03 Reception
The reception area, **16.2** and **16.3**, should be visible from the main entrance. Receptionists need to oversee the waiting area and the main circulation routes. Allow 1.5 m counter length for each receptionist, and space in front of the counter for patients to stand without encroaching on circulation routes or waiting space. Counter design should be open but providing some protection for staff. Provision for people with disabilities should be incorporated, e.g. with a lower section for wheelchair users and incorporating aids to hearing.

7.04 Record storage
Record storage needs to be close to the reception area, but ideally not part of it. Records should be out of sight of patients and secure.

GP records will be kept centrally near reception. Other records may be held at reception or in staff offices. The space required can be extensive and needs to be calculated for the selected storage system (lateral shelving, filing cabinets, carousels).

7.05 Administration and office bases
Some clerical/administration is usually associated with the record storage. Offices are required for other administrative functions.

Some medical staff require offices for full-time use. Others, such as health visitors, district nurses and midwives, need to return to an office base once or twice a day. Consideration should be given to flexible arrangements which meet this requirement, eg

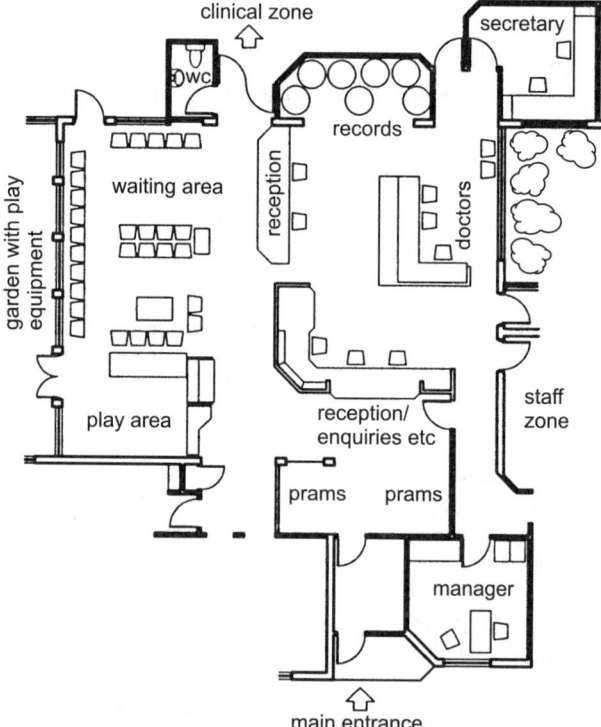

clinical zone

secretary

wc

garden with play equipment

waiting area

reception

records

doctors

play area

reception/ enquiries etc

staff zone

prams

prams

manager

main entrance

16.3 *Plan of a reception area in a larger centre. Ideally, the receptionists do not take phone calls that can be overheard by patients*

sometimes this is done by providing a run of work stations for use by anyone, with mobile personal storage units, rather than personal desks.

7.06 Waiting areas
Waiting areas should be visible from reception but sufficiently separated to provide some privacy for patients at the reception desk. Pram storage and WCs need to be near the reception and

waiting area. Part of the waiting area can be designed and furnished for children. Some seating suitable for the elderly should be provided.

Six seats should be allowed for each consulting room and treatment room, allowing $1.4\,m^2$ for each. This can be reduced for larger premises, particularly when appointment systems are operated. Arrangements can be made to screen off part of large areas to provide space for other activities at times when it is not all required for waiting.

Patients should not wait in corridors nor outside consulting or treatment room doors. Sub-waiting areas should usually be avoided.

7.07 Consulting/examination rooms

Consulting rooms are usually provided for each practitioner on a personal basis. Where this results in under-use, they can be scheduled for use by other staff or for other purposes. Combined consulting/examination rooms are more economical of space than having separate examination rooms but patterns of practice vary and separate rooms may be required.

If the desk is free-standing and access is provided to both sides of the couch, allow $17\,m^2$ as a general rule, **16.4**. If the desk is a built-in work surface and access is provided to the foot and one side of the couch only, allow $14-15\,m^2$, **16.5**.

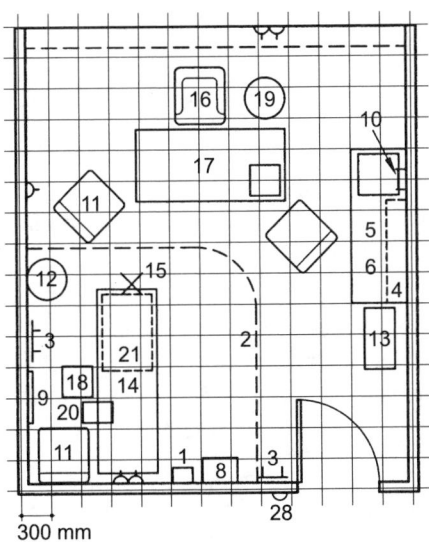

16.4 *Combined consulting/examination room, $17\,m^2$*

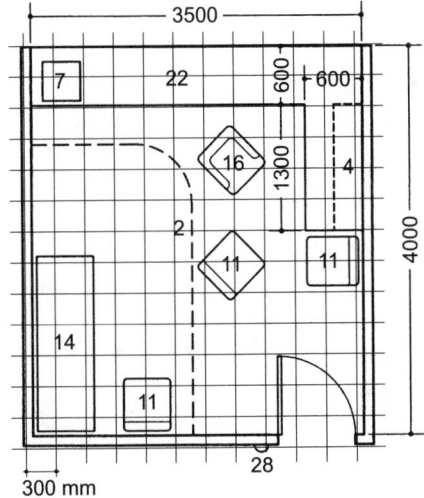

16.5 *Combined consulting/examination room, $14\,m^2$*

7.08 Treatment rooms

The increase in practice nurses, in addition to district and school nurses, has resulted in enhanced requirements for treatment facilities. Some GPs also use treatment rooms for some clinical procedures, e.g. fitting contraceptive coils. In addition, GPs now undertake minor surgery. As a result, the conventional provision of a treatment room of $17\,m^2$ for use by one nurse, **16.6**, is being replaced by treatment suites comprising several treatment rooms, with separate clean and dirty utility rooms, a specimen WC

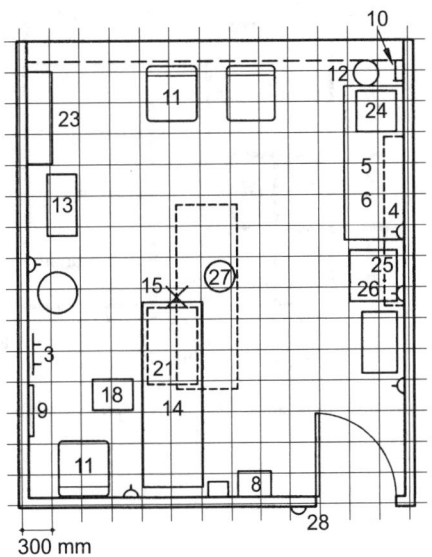

16.6 *Treatment room*

Key to 16.4, 16.5, 16.6 and 16.11
 1 *Bracket for sphygmomanometer*
 2 *Ceiling mounted curtain track*
 3 *Coat hooks*
 4 *High level storage*
 5 *Worktop*
 6 *Low level storage*
 7 *Wash hand basin*
 8 *Writing shelf*
 9 *Mirror*
 10 *Paper towel dispenser*
 11 *Chair*
 12 *Disposal bin*
 13 *Instrument/equipment trolley*
 14 *Examination couch*
 15 *Mobile examination lamp*
 16 *Swivel chair*
 17 *Desk*
 18 *Couch steps*
 19 *Waste paper bin*
 20 *Scales*
 21 *Couch cover dispenser*
 22 *Built-in work surface with storage under*
 23 *Shelving*
 24 *Sink and drainer*
 25 *DDA cupboard*
 26 *Refrigerator*
 27 *Stool*
 28 *Warning light*
 29 *Lockable cupboard for scheduled poisons*
 30 *Pedal waste bin*
 31 *Dental equipment cabinet*
 32 *Space for anæsthetic machine*
 33 *Dental chair*
 34 *Dental unit*

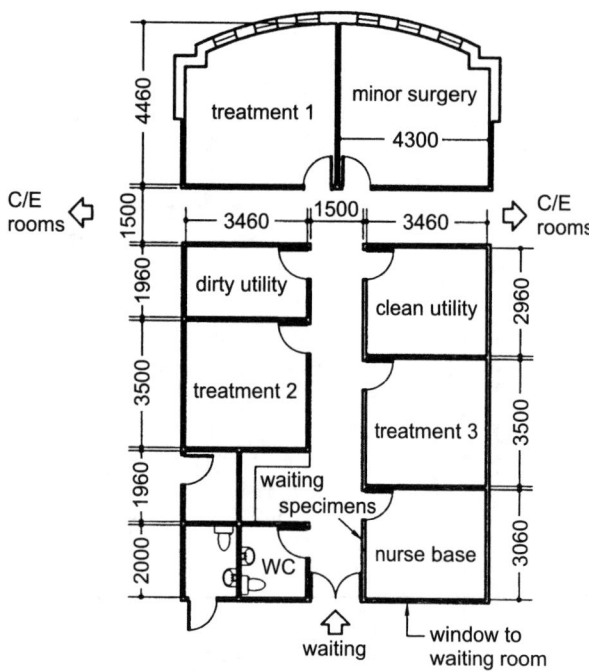

16.7 *Plan of a treatment suite in a converted building*

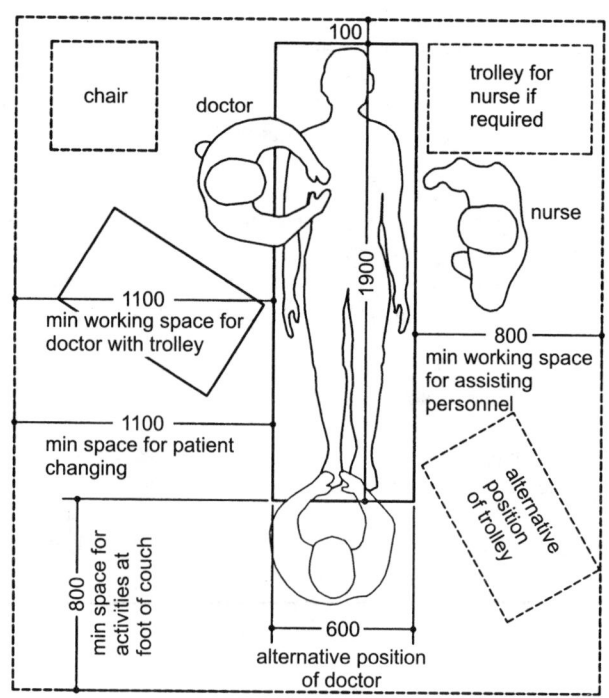

16.8 *Space requirements for treating a patient on a couch*

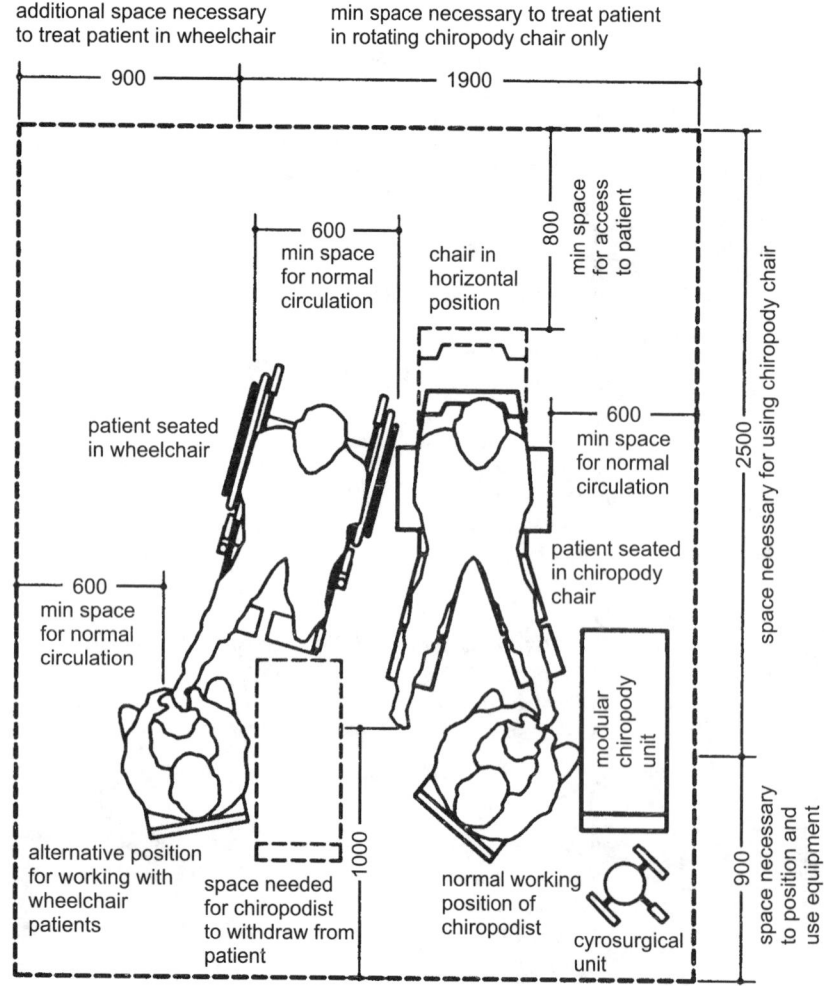

16.9 *Space requirements for chiropody*

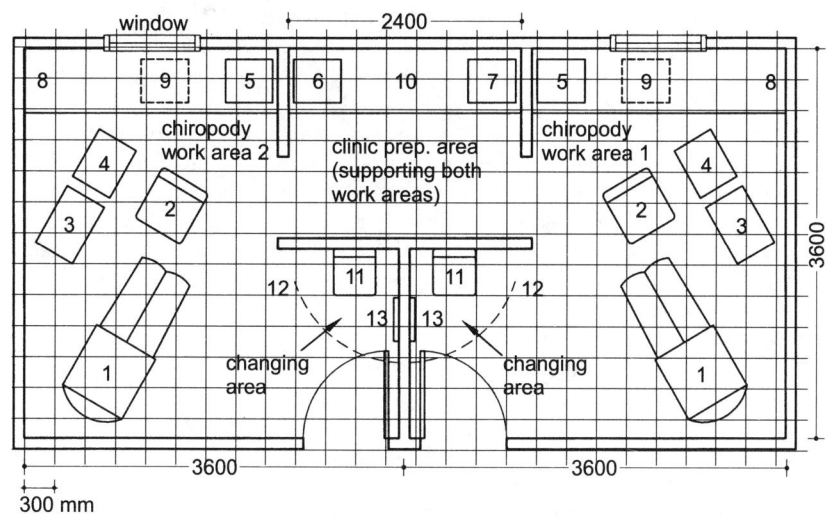

16.10 *Plan of a chiropody suite with two rooms*

1 *chiropody couch*
2 *operator's chair*
3 *unit with lamp and drill*
4 *instrument trolley*
5 *hand wash*
6 *instrument wash*
7 *auto clave*
8 *knee hole under*
9 *cupboard under mirror on wall*
10 *storage cupboards above and below worktop (including lockable pharmacy cupboard)*
11 *chair*
12 *curtain*
13 *grab rail*

(sometimes with a hatch to the dirty utility room) and a nurse base, **16.7**. A mix of treatment chairs and couches may be provided. Couches in treatment areas must be accessible from both sides and one end, **16.8**.

7.09 Minor surgery

Treatment spaces used for surgical procedures need to be equipped and finished to standards appropriate for the proposed procedures. There may be requirements for general anaesthetic (not for GPs), additional ventilation and a recovery space. Minor surgery facilities can be provided as separate suites with their own clean and dirty utility areas or as part of a larger treatment suite, sharing support spaces.

7.10 Chiropody treatment rooms

Allow 11 m² for a one-chair room plus changing facilities. Many chiropody patients will be in wheelchairs, **16.9** and **16.10**.

7.11 Speech therapy rooms

Requirements can range from rooms where individuals can be assessed and treated to larger spaces for groups of adults and children sometimes with viewing facilities. Noise levels need to be low, 40 dBA is recommended and must not exceed 45 dBA.

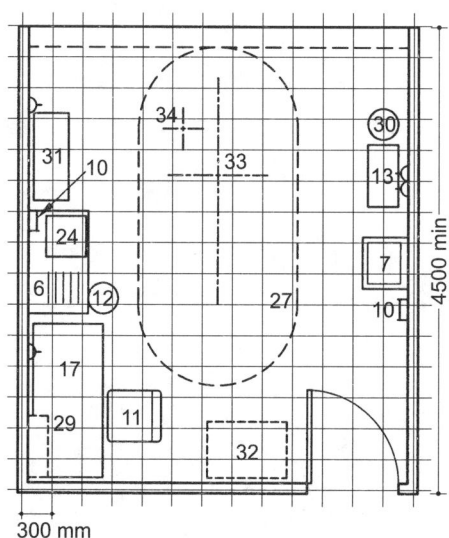

16.11 *Plan of a dental surgery*

7.12 Dental suites

Allow 16.5 m² for each surgery, **16.11**, and 28 m² for a laboratory if required. If the throughput of patients warrant it, separate waiting, reception and record storage may be required; but dental staff should not be isolated from other staff.

7.13 Multi-purpose rooms

Large rooms will be required for health education, baby clinics, relaxation classes, physiotherapy and other group activities. Associated storage is essential for chairs, relaxation mats, baby scales, etc. Hand-washing facilities are needed for some of the activities. Tea-making facilities are desirable. Ideally, this room should be accessible when the rest of the building is closed for evening activities. Allow 40 m² for eight relaxation mats.

7.14 Interview rooms

These are small rooms for two to four people to speak privately in a relaxed atmosphere.

7.15 WCs for patients

These must include at least one WC for wheelchair users; and facilities for baby changing. Patients may be required to produce urine specimens. A hatch can be provided between a WC and the dirty utility room (or treatment room if there is no separate dirty utility room). Patients should not be required to walk through public areas with specimens. The number and location of WCs required will depend on the design.

7.16 WCs for staff

These should be conveniently near working areas and common rooms.

7.17 Staff amenities

Kitchen and beverage facilities are usually provided. A shower is desirable. Lockers are needed for staff with no secure office base.

7.18 Out-patient consulting and diagnostic facilities

These should be to the same standards as in hospital out-patient departments (see Chapter 17).

7.19 Beds

Ward provision should usually be to community hospital standards with appropriate support facilities.

7.20 Educational facilities
Seminar and other teaching spaces should be to normal education standards. A student or students in a clinical area requires the room to be enlarged so that the clinical activity is not compromised.

7.21 Storage
Requirements for storage must be established and quantified for each of the services.

7.22 Building service requirements
Space requirements for heating, ventilation, electricity, telephone, security, computer, intercom and call systems will be determined by the operational policies.

7.23 Grouping of spaces
In grouping rooms within the building, consider the activities that spread across several spaces, e.g. a baby clinic may use the waiting/multi-purpose, consulting/examination and treatment rooms. Parts of the building may be in use when the rest is closed; for example, GP Saturday and evening surgeries, educational facilities, drop-in treatment facilities, health education or community groups in a multi-purpose room.

8 REFERENCES AND BIBLIOGRAPHY
R. Cammock, *Primary Health Care Buildings – Briefing and Design Guides for Architects and their Clients*, The Architectural Press, London, 1981

R. Cammock, *Health Centres Handbook*, MARU 1/73

Evaluating designs for GP premises (Information Sheet 2) MARU 5/89, Medical Architecture Research Unit, School of Architecture & Civil Engineering, Faculty of Environmental Studies, South Bank University, Borough Road, London SE1

HBN 36 (Draft), Health Centres, October, DHSS, HMSO, 1987

HBN 46, *General Medical Practice Premises*, HMSO, 1989

HBN, *Community Hospitals*, HMSO

HBN, *Out-patient Departments*, HMSO

NHS GMS, Statement of Fees and Allowances for Standards of Practice Accommodation and Procedural Requirements for GP cost-rent schemes and improvement grants (only available through GPs or FHSAs)

Scottish Out-patient Building Note

17 Hospitals

Rosemary Glanville and Anthony Howard

CI/SfB: 41
UDC: 725.51

*Rosemary Glanville is Director of the Medical Architecture Research Unit (MARU),
situated at South Bank University*

KEY POINTS:
- *Health services are trying to move closer to the patient*
- *More work is being undertaken in the primary sector*
- *Shorter stays in hospital are the norm*

Contents

1 INTRODUCTION

1.01 The hospital and the National Health Service

The National Health Service, founded in 1948, is still a universal and almost free service to users, organised under the Department of Health and through the NHS Management Executive in 15 Regional and about 200 District Health Authorities: general hospitals until recently were the direct responsibility of these Districts. The primary care sector (general practice, community nursing, etc.) is managed through Family Health Services Authorities (FHSAs). From April 1996, DHAs and FHSAs will be combined into Health Commissioning Agencies responsible for assessing need and purchasing services across the health spectrum.

However, in common with services abroad, the NHS is undergoing profound changes with the introduction of business methods and business ethics, dismantling of central planning organisations and the creation of 'purchaser' organisations (health authorities) who buy health services from 'provider' organisations (primarily hospitals with self-governing trust status).

The motivation is part political (introduction of the free market philosophy) and part economic. Economic problems derive from the rising costs of running a health service combined with the increasing health needs of an ageing population and with a reducing proportion of that population able to contribute to costs. Other dilemmas are emerging, such as that posed by medical advances which enable life to be prolonged, at a cost, in situations which would previously have been terminal.

1.02 The hospital and the community

In the search for ways of containing health service costs, health care delivery through the hierarchy of the organisation and the corresponding hierarchy of building types is also being reappraised. In general, health care is being devolved from the expensive acute sector out towards primary care organisations, community services and even into the home: the justification for delivering health care at a particular level, rather than in a simpler and cheaper environment, is being constantly questioned.

Similarly, the length of patient stay in hospital is being reduced; patients are being required earlier than before to recover at home, where they need additional community support; and many basic diagnostic and treatment procedures are being tested in the primary care setting. One consequence for the acute hospital is that patients who remain are, on average, more dependent and the procedures, on average, more sophisticated and complex.

Community Health Councils, representing patient interests, have to some extent had their teeth drawn and it can be argued that planning for clinical need – the *raison d'être* of the NHS – has been weakened by recent changes. Nevertheless, competition (and the requirements of the Patients' Charter) has focused the attention of providers on the nature of the patient's experience in hospital.

1.03 The hospital and the patient

Management concern for patients' response to the hospital service and environment encompasses such diverse issues as first impressions, signposting, waiting times in out-patient and accident departments and relationship with the ward nurse. It has recently been extended to reassessment of the basic relationships between treatment departments and the in-patient areas they serve. The idea of a hospital organised so as to ameliorate some of the more distressing aspects of patient stay – being shunted around the hospital, waiting in strange departments, disorientation and lack of a sense of place which is their own – has found expression in the 'patient-focused hospital'.

The principle can be implemented to various degrees but, at its most radical, involves partial decentralisation of diagnostic and treatment functions, embedding outposts of these departments within small ward groups. Most procedures can then be carried out within these mini-hospitals and patients may not need to be moved from their familiar environment.

The idea originated in the United States and, on the face of it, satisfies not only concern about the patient experience but also the principle of the cascade or devolution of care into the simplest appropriate environment. It has, however, not yet been properly evaluated – even in the American context – and certainly not tested in the particular UK environment of nurse skills, organisation and patient expectations.

1.04 Information technology

Technological developments in areas other than medical science will play a role in these changes, perhaps the most probable and significant being in IT (information technology) in which very large quantities of data are sent through optical fibres. High-definition images can now be cheaply transmitted between patient and specialist, between diagnostic service and GP, between GP and patient, and some procedures are increasingly being carried out remotely, calling in question the need for proximity between many elements of the service.

2 TYPES OF HEALTH BUILDING

2.01

It should now be clear that buildings which accommodate health care delivery can no longer be described as strictly defined types but rather as a spectrum: at one end we have the specialist, teaching and research institutions; at the other end the patient's home. As we move along the spectrum we move towards accommodation which is less specialist, less expensively equipped and staffed, and cheaper to build.

In addition, the interdependence of the four parts of the service – hospitals, primary care services, personal and community health services and local authority services – will be strengthened by initiatives such as the Community Care Act (which passed responsibility for care of the elderly and the mentally ill to local authorities) and pressures for joint working of health authorities, community trusts, family health services authorities (responsible for GP services) and local authorities.

Nevertheless, the building types which until recently defined the built environment for health care are still there and can be used as representative points to describe the whole. The designer should, however, be prepared to respond to client requirements which bridge individual definitions and call for new forms of facility.

2.02 General acute hospitals

The Ministry of Health Hospital Plan for England & Wales of 1962 initiated a building programme for a network of District General Hospitals (DGHs) serving a population of 100 000 to 150 000. These hospitals became identified with the Health Districts established under the reorganisation of the NHS in the mid-1970s and served by one or more DGHs.

Now that all general hospitals have been established as self-governing NHS Trusts, their services can in theory be sold to any purchaser (although this may be primarily a Health District) and the term DGH is not strictly applicable. In addition, the length of patient stay is shortening and ideas such as 'patient hotels' (with lower staffing levels and simpler clinical facilities) are being implemented on some hospital sites. General hospitals as a consequence are having to accommodate higher-dependency in-patients and this suggests the term 'acute' to distinguish such hospitals from community hospitals or other intermediate forms of care.

The other consequence of these changes is that the total number of required beds is dropping and smaller hospitals in particular are being closed.

The sizes of general hospitals can range from 300 to 1000 beds – mostly between 500 and 800 beds – and they provide 24-hour medical and nursing care of the sick and disabled. They also supply out-patient services and many now provide day-care facilities where patients are admitted for simple operations or diagnostic testing, to be returned home the same day. Selected hospitals will also incorporate an accident and emergency department.

These are the patient areas of the hospital (the in-patient wards taking up about half of the total floor area) which are supported, first, by diagnostic and treatment facilities such as operating theatres and radio-diagnostic departments and, second, by whole-hospital maintenance and support services, providing supplies, food and energy and maintaining the building fabric. **17.1** and **17.2** show contrasting hospitals.

2.03 Specialist hospitals

Although a small group of specialist hospitals, mainly in London, are among the leading centres of post-graduate teaching and research in their specialty, much more numerous are small maternity hospitals and those for a few other specialties such as children. These have been dwindling in number as the services are incorporated into general hospitals so as to provide better specialist back-up, better staff training and economies of scale. A recent school of thought, however, argues for the grouping of woman and child care in separate institutions.

Until recently, the greatest volume of specialty work was to be found in institutions for the mentally ill, the mentally handicapped and the elderly. As responsibility for their care devolved to Local Authorities, most of the larger institutions closed.

The 'hospice movement' is concerned with care of the dying and with teaching and research into pain control during terminal care. To provide for in-patient care there are at present about 120 hospices housing some 2300 beds and many of these will incorporate provision for day care and home support.

2.04 Community hospitals

All community hospitals, **17.3**, have the common purpose of providing a bridge between the community and the general acute hospital which, particularly in rural areas, may be remote from much of a dispersed population. They may, however, have different origins, house different functions, be of different sizes and be staffed in different ways.

The Ministry of Health Circular of 1974 – which, in response to the public outcry over the policy of closing all small hospitals, provided the only official recognition of this building type – defined the community hospital as providing medical and nursing care for out-patients, day patients and in-patients not needing specialised facilities but not able to be cared for at home or in residential accommodation.

The size was envisaged as lying between 50 and 150 beds, serving a population of 30 000 to 100 000. Only minor surgical procedures, dentistry and the simplest radiology were allowed for and maternity provision was restricted to out-patient clinics. They could receive terminal cases and patients for respite care. GPs would be responsible for all day-to-day care but consultants would also hold clinics. Health centres and group practice premises would be associated with the hospitals wherever possible.

However, those recognised for practical purposes as community hospitals by Regional Health Authorities are defined more broadly.

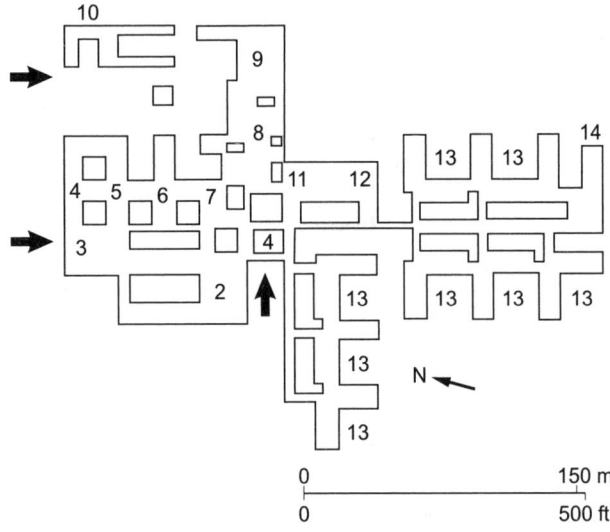

17.1 *Wexham Park Hospital. Planned almost entirely on one floor.*
Architects: Powell & Moya
Consultants: Llewelyn-Davies Weeks
  1 *Administration*
  2 *Outpatients*
  3 *Casualties*
  4 *Physiotherapy*
  5 *X-ray*
  6 *Pathology/mortuary*
  7 *Pharmacy*
  8 *Dining/kitchens*
  9 *Stores*
  10 *Boilers/workshop*
  11 *Central sterile supply department (CSSD)*
  12 *Operating*
  13 *General ward*
  14 *Children's ward*

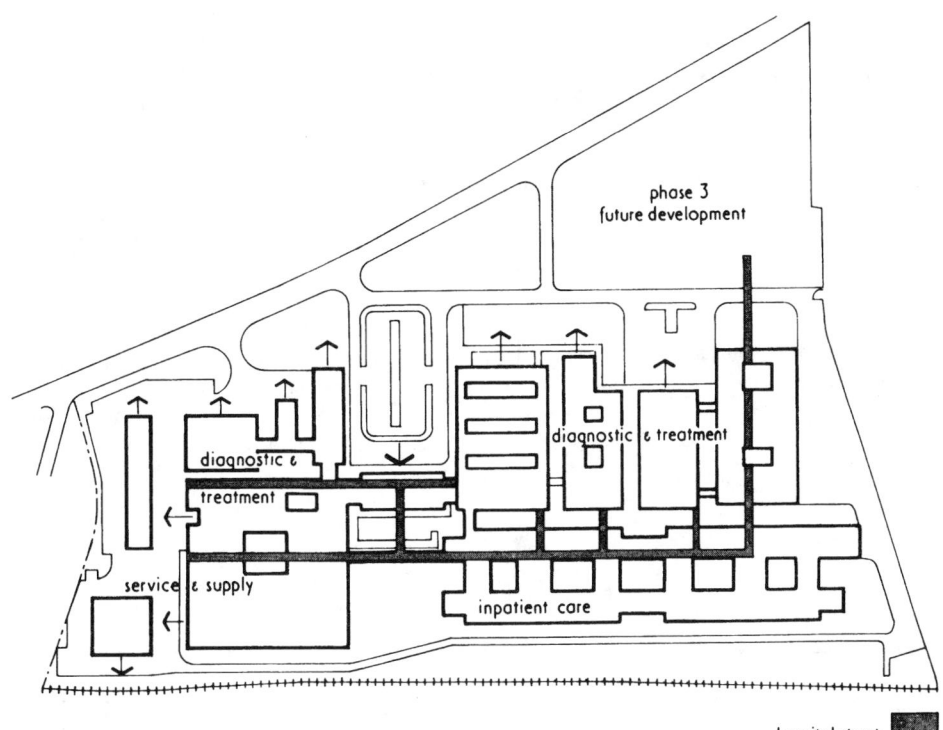

17.2 *York District Hospital site plan*
Architects: Llewelyn-Davies Weeks

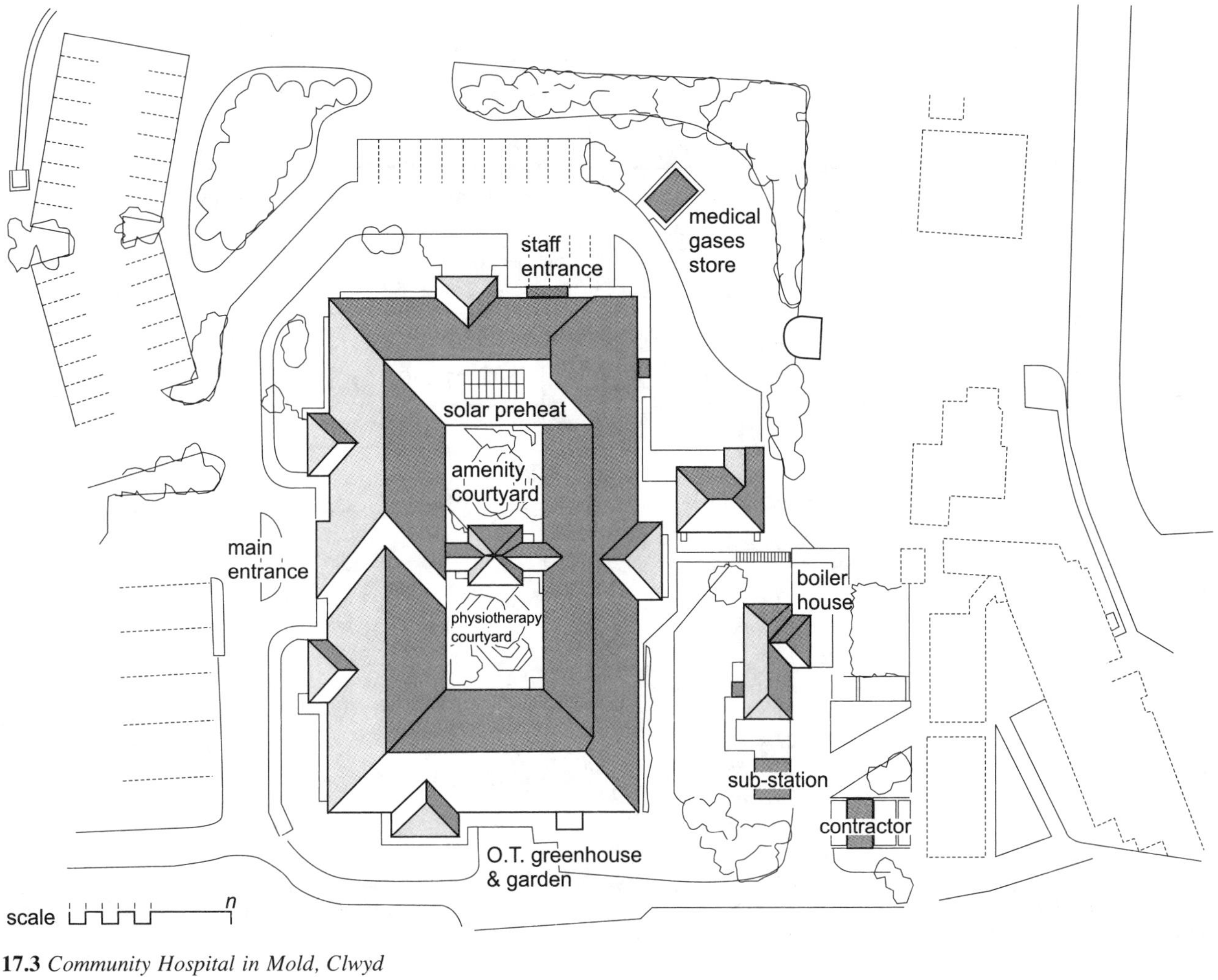

hospital street

17.3 *Community Hospital in Mold, Clwyd*
Architect: William H. Simpson, Chief Architect, WHCSA
a *Site plan*

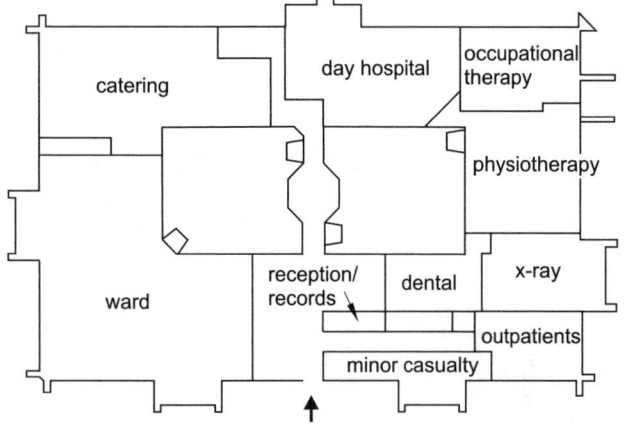

b *General areas*

They tend to be smaller, few have day hospitals and few have primary care facilities attached although over half have full operating facilities.

2.05 Intermediate care units
A recent development, not yet firmly established, is towards a level of care lying between primary and secondary, currently termed intermediate care. The distinction between intermediate care units and community hospitals is best drawn by reference to the type of patient for which each caters.

While the intermediate care unit, based on an acute hospital site, is designed for patients requiring acute care but simpler procedures, the community hospital provides for patients who are undergoing rehabilitation, are taken in to provide respite for home carers, are under the care of the GP or who otherwise are unlikely to need specialist services.

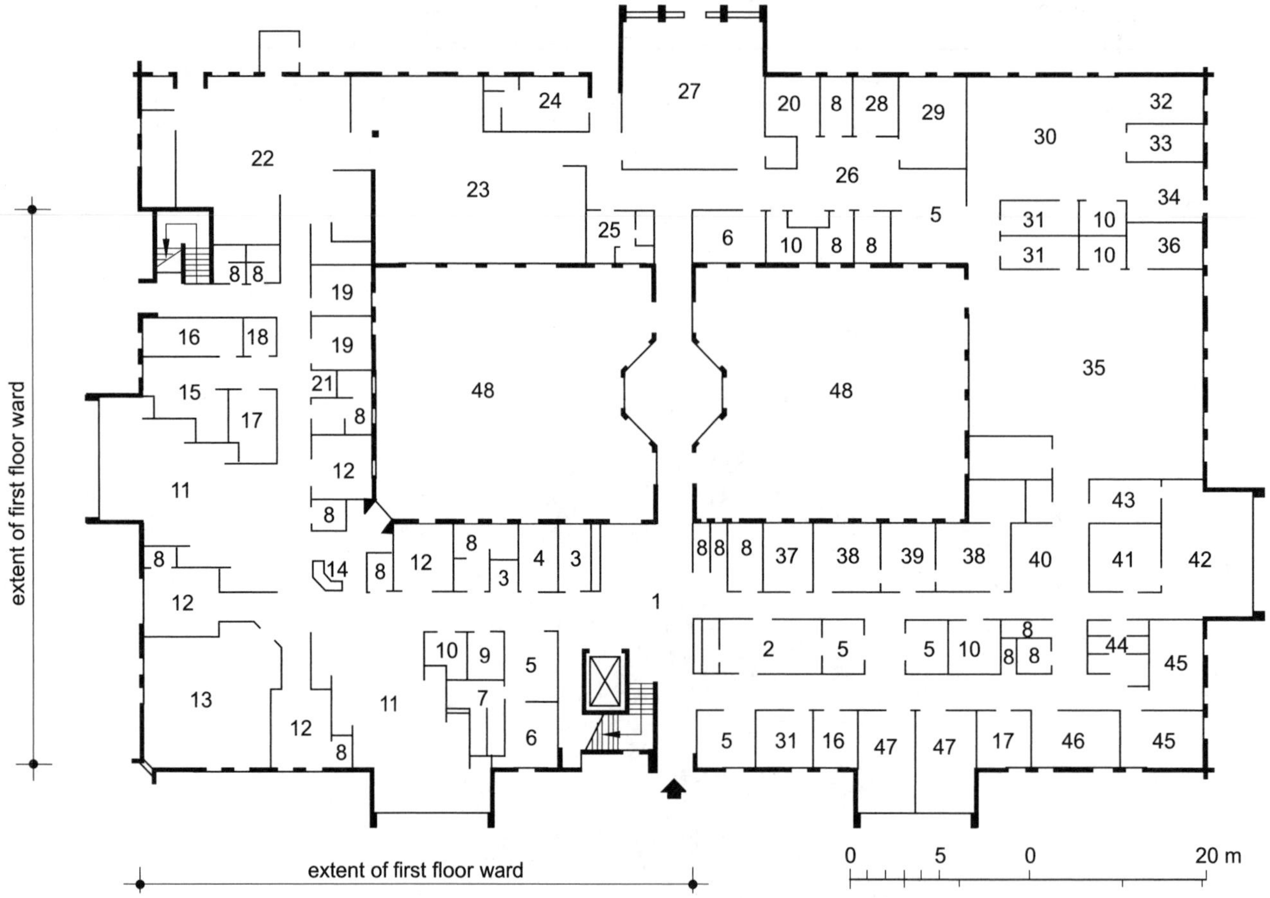

c *Detail plan:*

1 entrance foyer	**17** dirty utility	**33** bathroom
2 reception and records	**18** linen	**34** kitchen
3 beverages	**19** rest room	**35** physiotherapy
4 assisted shower	**20** assisted bath	**36** wax treatment
5 waiting	**21** wheelchair bay	**37** common room
6 sister	**22** kitchen	**38** dental surgery
7 staff cloaks	**23** staff dining and lounge	**39** dental recovery
8 toilet	**24** female staff cloaks	**40** X-ray waiting
9 cleaner	**25** male staff cloaks	**41** X-ray reception
10 store	**26** geriatric day hospital	**42** X-ray
11 eight-bed ward	**27** day dining room/chapel	**43** darkroom
12 single-bed ward	**28** dirty utility	**44** changing
13 dayroom	**29** clean utility and treatment	**45** consulting room
14 nurses' base	**30** occupational therapy	**46** consulting and minor treatment
15 treatment room	**31** office	**47** treatment room
16 clean utility	**32** ADL bedroom	**48** courtyard

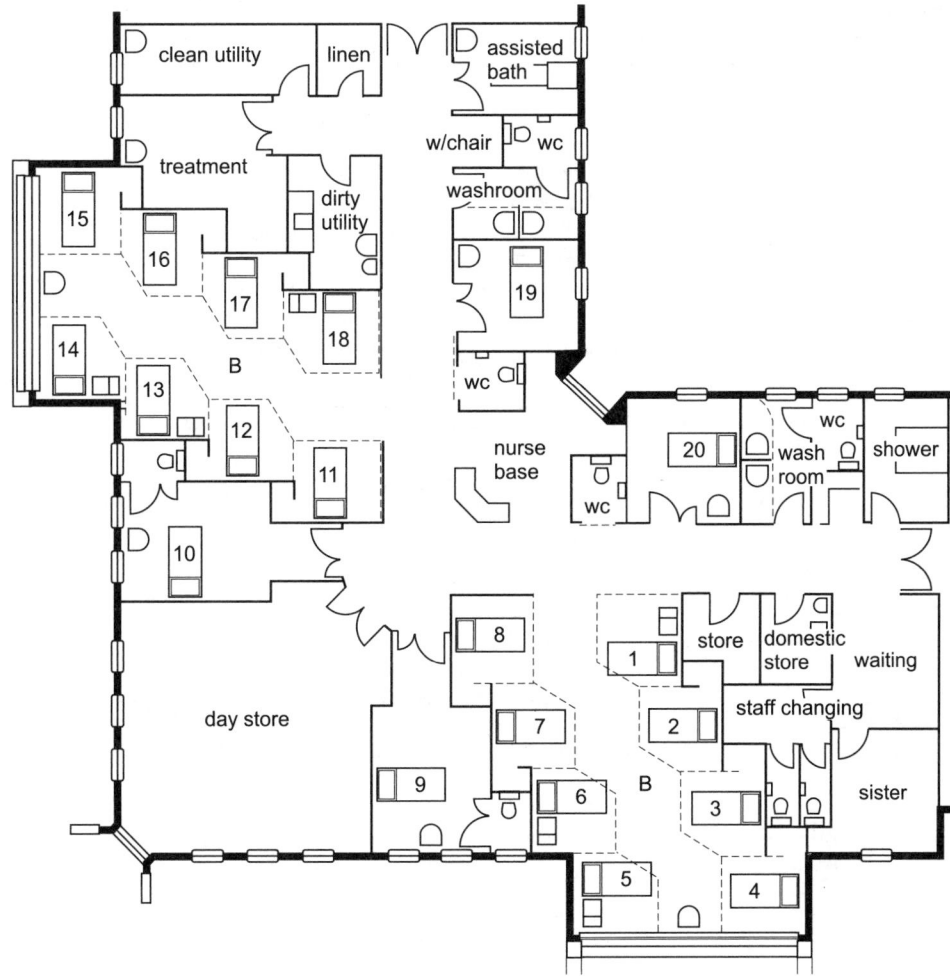

d *Plan of ward*

3 DETERMINANTS OF HOSPITAL FORM

3.01 General

The following discussion is presented particularly in the context of the general acute hospital but it is not difficult to extrapolate the arguments to the other smaller building types described above.

Although the NHS and its estate are in a period of radical change – and it is not easy to see when the position will stabilise – certain determinants of hospital form, external to the design process itself, are fundamental to the provision of the service.

3.02 Clinical need

For reasons outlined above we can no longer in health service planning talk easily of 'catchment populations' geographically defined, modified by cross-boundary flows. Discussion is rather in terms of purchasers, providers and markets for services (including the private sector). It is not entirely clear who now carries out the process known as 'health services planning' although health purchasing initiatives, as we saw in Section 1.01, are now the province of the new Health Commissioning Agencies. Whatever the mechanism, the health needs of the population determine the type and amount of services required.

This description of needs will determine, through a combination of planning and market forces, a pattern of health facilities as described in Section 2. For each health building a *functional content* can then be developed in terms of *functional units*, which are the units of measurement for each type of accommodation (Table I)

The size of a hospital is commonly indicated by numbers of beds and a rough idea of bed numbers of different types related to likely population need is given in Table II. However, the amount of accommodation required to support the bed areas varies considerably. The proportion of total area given over to wards ranges from 25 per cent in teaching hospitals to 50 per cent in general acute hospitals. These proportions are all changing further with the trends in provision described in Section 1.

3.03 Growth and change

The only predictable characteristic of a hospital's history is that it will grow and change in unpredictable ways. While this is true of all building types, it is particularly applicable to health buildings because they are subject to so many forces for change: political, demographic, operational, organisational, technological.

There are a three major ways in which hospitals can physically change:

- *Positive growth*, which can take place at departmental or whole hospital level, requiring space adjacent to growth points, provision for extension of services and plan arrangements which are not disrupted by extension of circulation routes;
- *Negative growth* requiring space to be taken over by other functions and
- *Rearrangement* requiring structures and service runs which do not get in the way and service feeds which can be extended or modified to serve additional fittings.

It was John Weeks who first clearly formulated principles of growth and change; he and others (in the UK, primarily the DHSS, Chief Architect Howard Goodman) developed a number of design

Table I Contents of a general acute hospital of 600 beds

Department	Size	Area (m²)	Access requirements	Location	Relationship	Notes
In-patient services						
1 Adult acute wards	400 beds	9500		Level not important	Surgical beds to theatres	
2 Children's wards	75 beds	2800	To outdoor play area	Preferably ground floor	Isolation unit; theatre	
					Includes parents overnight stay	
3 Geriatric wards	80 beds	2200		Preferably ground floor	Geriatric day hospital	
					Rehabilitation	
4 Intensive therapy unit	8 beds	500		Level not important	Accident dept; theatres	
5 Maternity dept					Ante-natal clinic in OPD	
5.1 Wards	75 beds	2200			Delivery suite	
5.2 Delivery suite		1700	Ambulance access may be required for dept as a whole	Level not important	Wards, theatres SCBU	Area includes dept. admin, etc.
5.3 Special care baby unit	20 cots	450			Delivery suite	
6 Psychiatric dept			External access	Self-contained units may need private internal access		
6.1 Wards	100 beds	2700				
6.2 Day hospital	120 places	2000				
7 Isolation ward	20 beds	800	Private external access for infectious cases	Level not important, but see 'access'	Children's dept	
Diagnosis and treatment						
8 Operating dept				Level not important	Surgical beds; accident dept	Special ventilation needs include refrigeration
9 X-ray dept				Usually ground floor	Accident dept; fracture clinic	Special ceiling heights and heavy equipment
10 Radiotherapy				Level not important	X-ray dept	
11 Pathology dept			External supply access may be required	Level not important but see 'access'	Radio isotopes, outpatient dept	Special attention to ventilation of noxious fumes
12 Mortuary and post-mortem			Private external access for undertakers' vehicles	Level not important, but see 'access'	Morbid anatomy / Section of pathology	Special attention to ventilation of post-mortem area
13 Rehabilitation			Ambulance access	Ground floor	Medical and geriatric beds	Includes physiotherapy gymnasium (extra height), hydrotherapy pool (special engineering requirements) and occupational therapy
14 Accident and emergency			Ambulance access for emergency cases	Usually ground floor – see 'access'	Direct access to X-ray dept, fracture clinic, main theatres, intensive therapy unit	Relationships assume no separate X-ray or theatres in accident department
15 Out-patient department including fracture clinic, ante-natal, dental, clinical measurement, ears, nose and throat, eyes, children's out-patients and comprehensive assessment			Pedestrian and ambulance access for large numbers, approx. 300–400 morning and afternoon	Main reception and waiting area usually ground floor but parts may be on other levels	Fracture clinic to accident dept, convenient access to pharmacy, good access to medical records dept – often adjacent	
16 Geriatric day hospital			Ambulance access, access to outdoor area	Usually ground floor – see 'access'	Geriatric wards, rehabilitation dept	
17 Adult day ward				Level not important	Theatres, X-ray, pathology	Includes additional space for 'sitting' cases
Support services						
18 Paramedical:						
18.1 Pharmacy		800	External supply, access may be required	Usually ground floor – see 'access'	OPD. hospital supply routes	
18.2 Sterile supply dept		500	External supply access	Usually ground floor – see 'access'	Hospital supply routes, operating dept	Special ventilation needs – wild heat problems
18.3 Medical illustration		150		Level not important		
18.4 Anaesthetics dept		200		Level not important	Theatres, intensive therapy	
19 Non-clinical:						
19.1 Kitchens	1500 meals	1200	External supply access	May be ground floor (for supply access) above ground (nearer to bed areas)	Hospital supply routes and bed areas served – dining room servery	
19.2 Dining room	770 meals	700		Level not important but see 'kitchens'	Access from kitchen to servery, good staff access from whole hospital	
19.3 Stores		700	Supplies vehicle	Usually in services area, ground door	Hospital supply routes	Special height may be needed for mechanical handling
19.4 Laundry		900	Supplies vehicle	Ground floor, service area	Hospital supply routes	
19.5 Boilerhouse – fuel storage		500	Fuel delivery vehicles	Usually ground floor in services area but may be elsewhere (e.g. rooftop) depending on choice of fuel	Work and transport dept	

Table I Continued

Department	Size	Area (m²)	Access requirements	Location	Relationship	Notes
19.6 Works – transport dept	650		Vehicle parking	Usually ground door in services area	Boiler house	
19.7 Administration	800			Level not important (tel. exchange ground floor)		Includes telephone exchange
19.8 Main entrance accommodation	200		External access for in-patients, visitors, perhaps out-patients and staff	Usually ground floor – see 'access'	In-patient reception area or medical records main hospital horizontal and vertical communication routes	Also includes facilities such as bank, shops, etc.
19.9 Medical records	700			Usually ground floor – see 'relationships'	Main entrance. OPD hospital communication routes	
20 Staff:						
20.1 Education centre	1800			Level not important		
20.2 Non-resident staff changing	800			On route between staff entrance and departments served, level not important	Hospital supply route for clean and dirty linen	
20.3 Occupational health service	200			Level not important		May be in OPD complex
21 Miscellaneous: This will include car parking, garages, medical gas installation, flammable stores, recreational buildings						

Note: Not every department listed above would appear on every DGH site since some (e.g. laundry, education centre) will usually serve a group of hospitals

techniques which allowed future change to take place without thwarting original planning intentions:

- *Open-endedness* allowing parts of the building to grow, **17.3**
- *Wide-span structures* in which columns do not obstruct rearrangements
- *Deep plan buildings* allowing more adjacency of departments and hence potential movement of department boundaries, **17.4a**
- *'Interstitial' service floors* providing freedom from vertical service ducts, **17.4b**
- *Adjacency of 'hard' and 'soft' areas* allowing the first (expensive, highly serviced) to expand into the second (simple, cheap) areas
- *Lattice circulation* arrangements providing efficient communication wherever the balance of future development lies, **17.5**
- *Loose fit* space standards which follow the duffle-coat principle of providing a small number of sizes to fit a large variety of occupants.

Various combinations of these techniques have been tried although not properly evaluated.

Table II Provision of beds

Service	No of beds per 1000 pop	Comments
Acute medical and surgical	2	Assumes increasing extent of domiciliary care in community
Maternity	0.3	Depending on birthrate and no. of beds for ante-natal care
Geriatrics	1 to 1.5	On basis of 10 beds per 1000 population over 65; areas with good housing and social services manage with less
Psychiatry	0.5	Numbers required for DGH-based service
Children	0.5	Provides for all children requiring acute or long-stay care

This table excludes provision for adults with severe learning difficulties.

3.04 Location

As with other building types, hospital form is subject to site density, plot ratio and other planning constraints. In some cases density may also be influenced by site value.

3.05 Means of escape

Crown buildings now have to comply with requirements for fire safety and means of escape: those for hospitals are set out in *Firecode* published by the Department of Health. Some of the requirements influence overall form and will be dealt with here; others affect internal organisation and will be dealt with in Section 5.06 below.

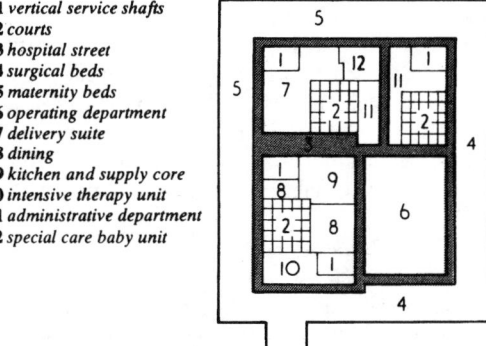

1 *vertical service shafts*
2 *courts*
3 *hospital street*
4 *surgical beds*
5 *maternity beds*
6 *operating department*
7 *delivery suite*
8 *dining*
9 *kitchen and supply core*
10 *intensive therapy unit*
11 *administrative department*
12 *special care baby unit*

a *Zoning plan of first floor*

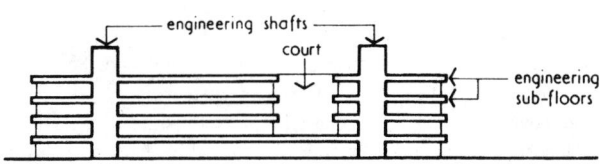

b *Section with exaggerated vertical scale*

17.4 *Greenwich District Hospital*

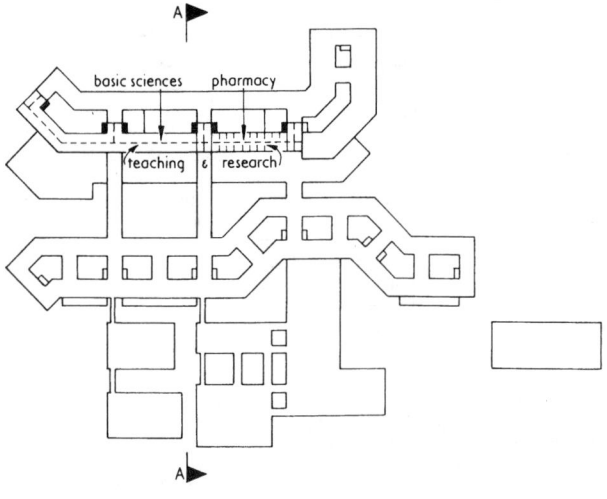

a *Plan*

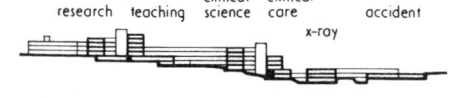

b *Section A-A*

17.5 *Leuven Hospital, Belgium*

Compartmentation

Compartmentation of a large building into areas of limited size, divided by fire-resisting partitions, allows escape away from the fire source into a nearby place of relative safety. In a hospital it is essential that this movement is horizontal. Lifts cannot generally be used in a fire and staircase evacuation of physically dependent patients takes far too long to be a practical means of escape in this first stage.

The compartments are limited to 2000 m² in area and a minimum of two for each floor are required to satisfy the above conditions. In general, the more compartments provided on each floor, the safer the hospital.

Travel distances and escape routes

There is a limitation on maximum travel distance within a compartment and to satisfy this requirement sub-compartments can be provided. There is also a limit on travel distance to a major escape route. The escape route is a protected, smoke-free path leading to an unenclosed space at ground level and the main hospital street is commonly designed to satisfy these criteria.

Relationship of departments by fire characteristics

The risk to human life is greatest in those areas where patients are confined to bed and especially where they would be incapable, in the event of a fire, of moving to a place of safety without assistance. Those areas are termed 'high life risk' departments and include wards, operating and rehabilitation departments. Elderly and psychiatric patients are particularly vulnerable.

Departments posing the fire threat are those such as supply zones, fuel stores and other materials stores containing large quantities of flammable materials ('high fire load') and those in which ignition is more likely such as kitchens, laundries, laboratories and boiler houses ('high fire risk'). The principle to be followed is that high *life* risk departments should not be placed above either high fire *load* or fire *risk* departments.

However, statistics show that laboratory fires are rarely serious because of the presence of trained staff while laundries, boiler houses and main supply areas tend to be zoned away from the main hospital building. The main kitchen constitutes the major problem because of its close relationship to patient areas. Either it can be

sited on an upper floor or a non-life risk department, such as education or management, can be placed above it.

3.06 Phasing

It is unusual for money to be available for a hospital to be built in a single contract: it then has to be built in a number of phases which presents particular difficulties. This is so even on a greenfield site, but more often a development will be on the site of an existing hospital which has to be kept running while construction work is under way. Phasing will influence the form of the development in a number of ways:

- *Prioritising of departments*: early phases will have to include those departments for which there is an urgent service need, which are having to be taken down to make way for the new buildings or which provide the essential nucleus for a new development. It may then be difficult to maintain ideal relationships between departments in the completed development
- *Location of departments on site*: site availability will constrain the location of early phases and, together with the prioritising of need mentioned above, may prevent location of departments in ideal positions relative to site entrance, parking or orientation.
- *Utilisation of departments*: a department provided in an early phase may not be fully used until completion of remaining phases: the choice then is to build the department in multiple phases or to temporarily use a part for some other purpose. Either method presents planning complications and additional capital (and possibly running) costs.

4 KEY CHOICES IN CONCEPTUAL DESIGN

4.01 Air conditioning and energy consumption

It is unusual in the UK for health buildings to be higher than three or four storeys so it is rare in this temperate climate for general air conditioning to be justified on grounds of environmental control. The other reason for providing it is to allow deep planning of spaces and, although there are difficulties in justifying the capital expenditure, this is one approach to provision for future change (see Section 3.03 and **17.4**).

Certain departments such as operating theatres and intensive care units require air conditioning for functional reasons, but there are cogent reasons for providing natural ventilation in the rest of the hospital – capital costs; revenue costs; patient and staff environment in which daylighting is generally preferred; and provision of local control.

4.02 Communication patterns

The dilemma in choice of communication pattern for a hospital is between compactness and provision for growth. The simple spine corridor, or street, advocated for example in Department of Health Nucleus developments, **17.6**, allows for unlimited growth at almost any point, either of the street itself or of individual departments. On the other hand, such streets can be up to 400 m long in a completed development. Despite the argument that a hospital is a series of villages (out-patient-/accident/radiography, surgical beds/operating department/ITU) it is difficult in this arrangement to avoid separation of some departments which should be more closely related. In addition, there is the daunting size of the institution as perceived by the users and the weakening of the sense of the institutional community.

The simplest way of reducing interdepartmental distances is by linking the ends of the street to form a ring, as in the 'Best Buy' developments, **17.7**. Growth can still be achieved outwards, but departments located in the core cannot grow without either displacing other departments or breaking through the corridor shell.

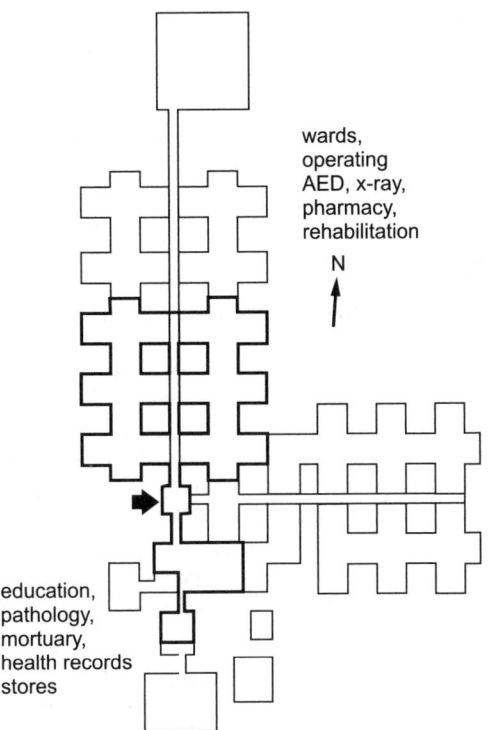

wards,
operating
AED, x-ray,
pharmacy,
rehabilitation

N

education,
pathology,
mortuary,
health records
stores

17.6 *Maidstone District Hospital, a two-storey Nucleus design.*
The heavy outline shows Stage 1, providing 300 beds
Architects: Powell, Moya and Partners

The principle is taken further in the lattice of horizontal and vertical communication routes, **17.5**, in which a number of route options are available.

Attempts have recently been made to create a focus for the hospital by means of a larger central space, such as an atrium, **17.2**, from which shorter circulation routes radiate. One problem with this arrangement is reconciling it with a preference for natural ventilation.

4.04 Differential fabric life and space standards

Equipment, mechanical services and internal layout will need to change many times before the structural fabric decays and should therefore be designed as far as possible for alteration and extension without jeopardising the integrity of the structure.

Disruption caused by changes to the hospital layout can be reduced by working to space standards which are not closely tailor-made to functional requirements: in other words, by providing spaces which are 'loose fit' for their present functions and hence capable of accommodating alternative activities. This, however, means persuading the client to invest against hypothetical future change.

5 DETERMINANTS OF INTERNAL ORGANISATION

5.01 Hospital entrances

Since expensive security provision is required at each entrance, the number of hospital entrances is usually restricted as far as possible.

The Accident and Emergency (A&E) Department will need its own entrance because it is open for 24 hours and because there are clinical and aesthetic reasons for not allowing accident traffic to mix with out-patients and visitors. Supply and catering departments will require heavy goods vehicle access with a loading bay. Fuel will have to be delivered to storage facilities, probably adjacent to the boiler house. The mortuary will need access for hearses.

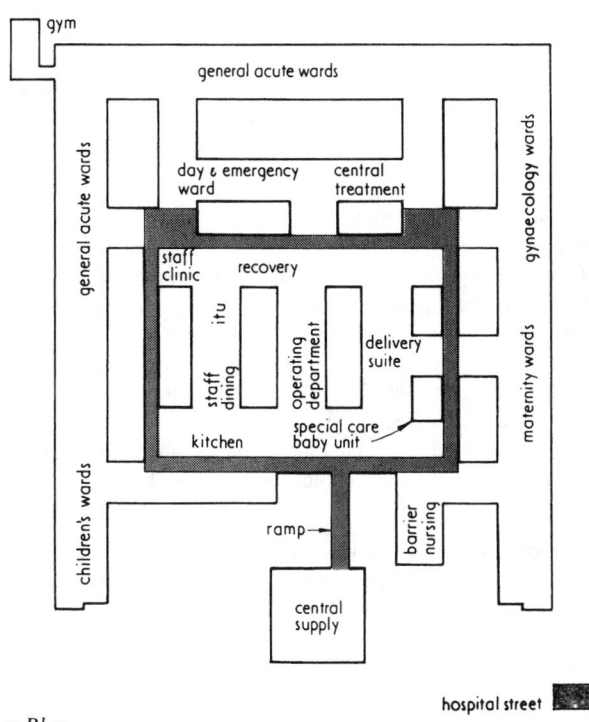

a *Plan*

hospital street

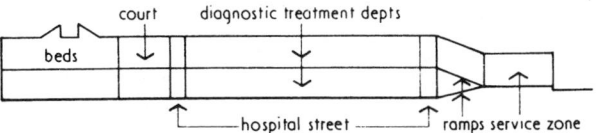

b *Section*

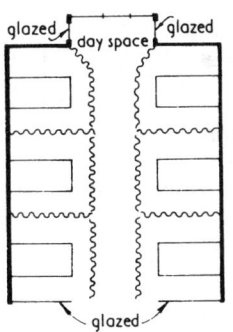

c *Six-bed bay with day space*

17.7 *West Suffolk Hospital (Bury St Edmunds), a Mark 1 'Best Buy' design*

In addition, certain departments such as day centres may have their own entrances, depending on the degree of autonomy they are given, and thought has to be given to patients who are brought in by ambulance for rehabilitation.

Otherwise, all traffic, including out-patients, 'cold' (pre-booked) admissions, staff and visitors should enter through a common main entrance which will become one of the hubs of hospital activity and may contain other facilities such as shops, bank and cafeteria.

These external access points have, in their location around the hospital street, to respect certain site features. The A&E Department requires easy access from the public highway and will need ambulance parking and some parking for cars. The main entrance, probably leading directly to the out-patient department, will have a similar requirement but will need more extensive adjacent car parking.

Loading bays for the supply centre could be placed more to the rear of the site as could access to the mortuary and boiler house fuel storage.

5.02 Whole hospital policies

Certain operational policies such as catering, supplies distribution, staff changing and theatre transportation are hospital-wide. Their direct effects are limited to minor differences in departmental accommodation, such as whether staff changing is provided locally, whether bed parks are needed in operating departments, what type of catering activities are allowed for in wards and what type of local linen storage is provided.

They do, however, have an influence on the amount and pattern of interdepartmental traffic and this is dealt with below.

5.03 Traffic between departments

Traffic between hospital departments consists of patients, staff of all kinds, visitors, beds, trollies with the materials they carry and smaller items such as specimens and reports. The smooth running of the hospital requires that this traffic be allowed to move as directly and conveniently as possible between origin and destination.

After the constraints of external access described above, internal traffic is the most important single determinant of department location within the hospital. Although studies have shown that a significant proportion of hospital traffic is unpredictable, its frequency can be largely derived from operational policies and, using weightings for urgency and bulk, values can be derived representing the relative importance of proximity between pairs of departments.

Despite this, no serious attempt has been made to provide traffic data which could be adapted to the conditions of a particular brief and used by the designer. The last official study was published by the DHSS in 1965 as Building Bulletin No. 5 but the data were provided in a form which can be used only with judgement. Table III shows approximate relative values of interdepartmental relationships, derived primarily from traffic loads and types.

One critical factor is hospital policy with regard to the movement of bed-bound patients. In some hospitals all such

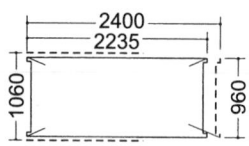

a *Plan*

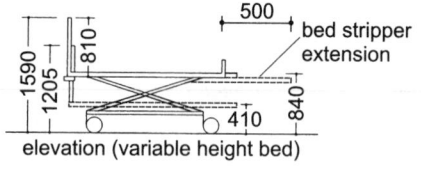

b *Elevation of the variable height bed*

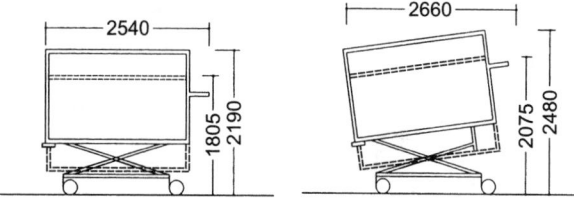

c *Elevations of the variable height bed with balkan beam*

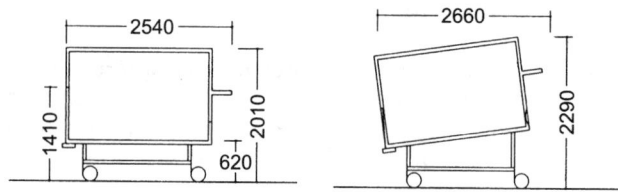

d *Elevations of fixed height bed with balkan beam*

17.8 *King's Fund bed; critical dimensions given. These are likely to occur frequently and/or importantly. They may be increased by the various accessories which are available*

Table III Interdepartmental relationships: relative importance in an AGH

		1	2	3	4	5	6	7	8	9	10	11	12	13	14	15	16	17
1	Wards and special depts	*	686	151	10	259	157	214	262	84	252	45	667	204	17	153	440	45
2	Operating theatre suites	*	*	30	7	63	51	7	110	22	7	15	20	16	3	23	2	13
3	Pharmacy	*	*	*	196	18	20	22	28	14	14	15	12	13	2	7	221	13
4	Out-patients	*	*	*	*	244	154	52	10	56	976	9	25	16	–	13	1950	14
5	Diagnostic X-ray	*	*	*	*	*	10	10	210	22	13	3	23	11	–	10	154	18
6	Pathology	*	*	*	*	*	*	10	34	10	10	9	23	11	40	10	120	15
7	Physical medicine	*	*	*	*	*	*	*	16	14	58	3	17	11	–	10	1510	16
8	Accident and emergency	*	*	*	*	*	*	*	*	25	58	9	16	14	10	13	1307	16
9	Administrative offices	*	*	*	*	*	*	*	*	*	29	8	42	23	–	31	52	36
10	Medical records	*	*	*	*	*	*	*	*	*	*	3	18	11	–	7	973	12
11	CSSD	*	*	*	*	*	*	*	*	*	*	*	11	9	–	15	3	10
12	Catering	*	*	*	*	*	*	*	*	*	*	*	*	50	1	38	42	37
13	Stores	*	*	*	*	*	*	*	*	*	*	*	*	*	–	15	161	10
14	Mortuary	*	*	*	*	*	*	*	*	*	*	*	*	*	*	–	81	1
15	Laundry	*	*	*	*	*	*	*	*	*	*	*	*	*	*	*	10	19
16	Outside the hospital	*	*	*	*	*	*	*	*	*	*	*	*	*	*	*	*	51
17	Maintenance services	*	*	*	*	*	*	*	*	*	*	*	*	*	*	*	*	*

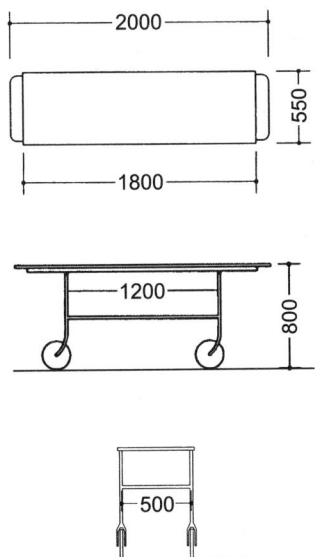

17.9 *Hospital trolley*

patients are moved from ward to ward, X-ray, theatre etc on their own beds. This means that corridors need to be wide enough, at least in places, for two beds to pass. **17.8** gives dimensions of the King's Fund bed, used in many hospitals.

In other hospitals patients are transferred onto trolleys, **17.9**. These trolleys being narrower than beds, even including for the ancillary equipment that they may need, do not require such wide corridors or doorways.

5.04 Clustering of departments

It has been argued that a study of traffic requirements suggests a hospital operating more like a number of villages than a single organism and Northwick Park Hospital was designed on this basis, **17.10**. Certainly there are clusters of departments which, once established, satisfy the major requirements of internal organisation.

Some of the major clusters are described below, but it is important that the architect establishes client intentions through the operational and planning policy statements since, for many crucial decisions affecting departmental relationships, there are a number of options.

THE OUT-PATIENT AND ACCIDENT AND EMERGENCY CLUSTER, 17.11

Because of the urgent nature of a high proportion of accident cases, the relationship with supporting departments is crucial. In particular there should be direct access – by separate entrance if necessary – to the X-ray Department for speedy diagnosis; alternatively separate X-ray facilities can be provided within A&E. Close proximity is also required to the Fracture Clinic because of the weight of traffic.

As direct access as possible should be provided from the A&E Department to the Operating Department although its location has to respect the overriding needs of surgical wards and the Intensive Therapy Unit (ITU).

We have already mentioned that out-patients should have access to the OPD directly through the Main Entrance. The OPD has the largest single daily requirement for provision of patients' records but whether this dictates a close relationship with Medical Records

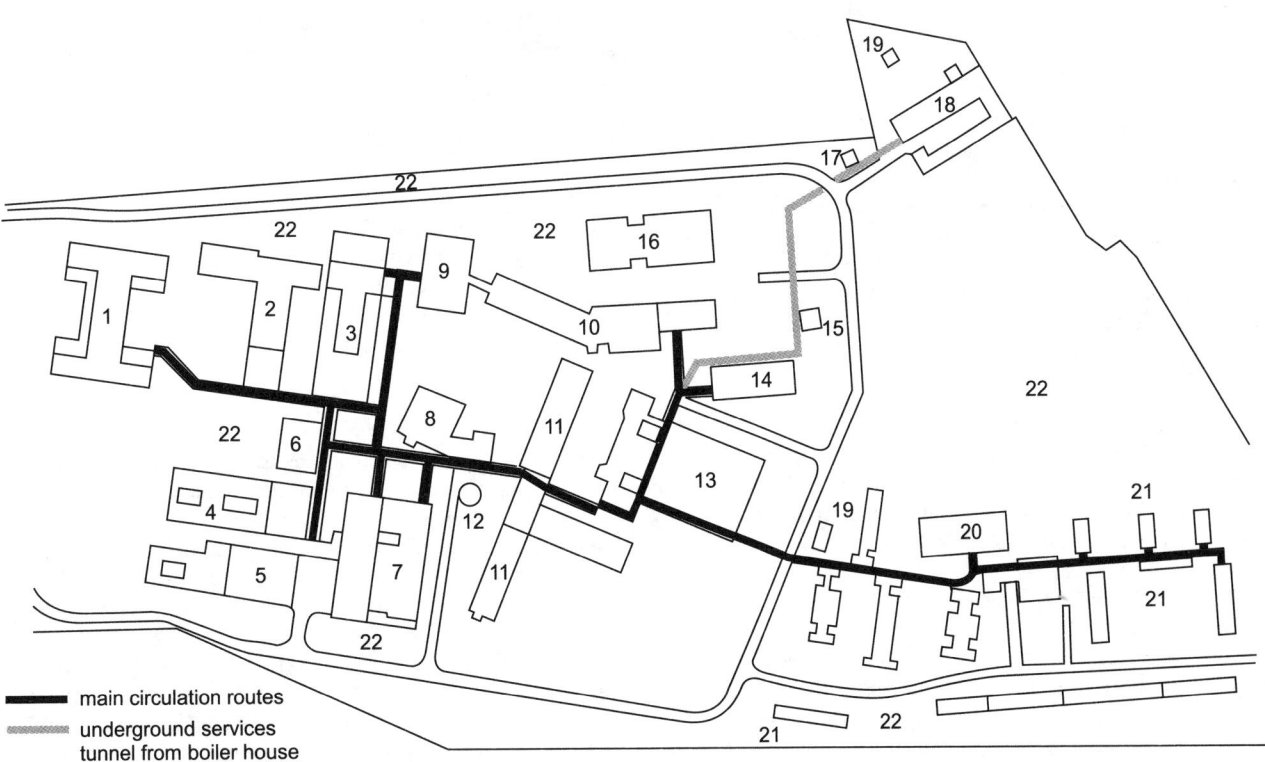

▬▬ main circulation routes

░░░ underground services
tunnel from boiler house

17.10 *Northwick Park Hospital*
Architects: Llewelyn-Davies Weeks

1 *maternity*
2 *psychological medicine*
3 *rehabilitation*
4 *outpatients*
5 *accidents and emergency*
6 *administration*
7 *diagnostic and central services*

8 *staff dining*
9 *institute library*
10 *clinical research institute*
11 *central wards*
12 *chapel*
13 *operating theatres*
14 *isolation unit*

15 *radio chemistry*
16 *animal house*
17 *oxygen*
18 *maintenance department*
19 *substations*
20 *school of nursing*
21 *residential*
22 *car parks*

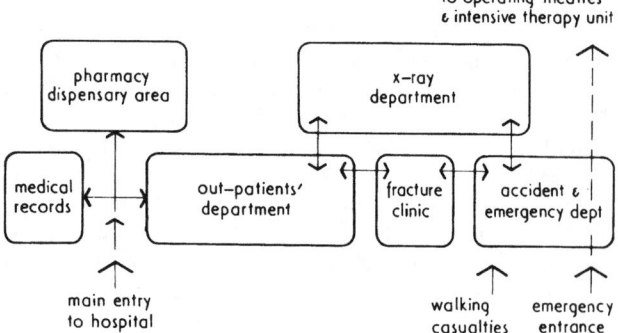

17.11 *Relationship diagram of out-patient and accident cluster*

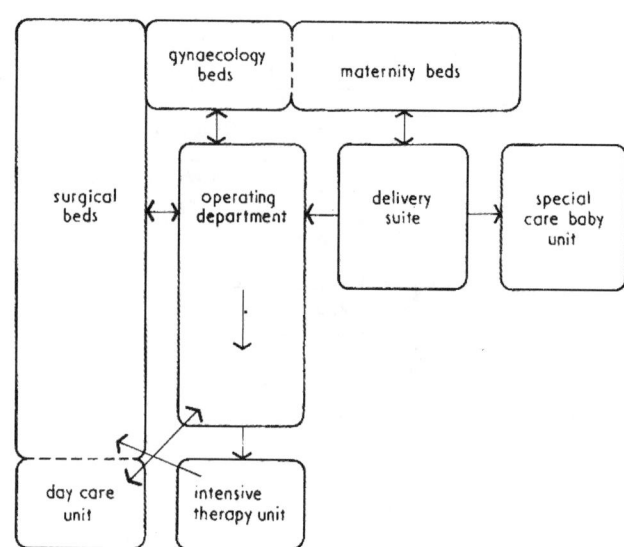

17.12 *Relationship diagram of operating and maternity clusters*

Department depends on the organisation and form of the records themselves.

There will be considerable traffic from the OPD to the X-ray Department and to the Fracture Clinic (which is usually shared with the A&E Department). Until recently, a large proportion of out-patients called in at the Pharmacy with their prescriptions but patients are now encouraged to use external community pharmacies and the location of the hospital department is not so critical, although it should be reasonably easy to find.

The operating cluster, **17.12**

The Operating Department has to be near both the departments it serves and the departments that support it. Primarily it serves the surgical wards and in the UK a horizontal relationship is preferred because of the amount of traffic and vulnerability of the patient during the return journey. However, with perhaps 40 per cent of beds in surgical wards, this arrangement is difficult to achieve entirely. Seriously ill patients may also be sent from the theatres to the ITU which should be adjacent.

A number of departments may be provided with their own theatres or may rely on the main Operating Department. Where day surgery is carried out, perhaps 40 operations a day may be performed and proximity of the Day Ward to the Department will then be more important than for a surgical ward. Again, a small but urgent amount of traffic would come from the A&E Department and from the Maternity Delivery Suite. While it is unlikely they could also be planned nearby, the route should be as direct as possible.

The maternity cluster, **17.12**

As discussed below, policy on maternity care can vary widely. At its most centralised, the maternity department can incorporate the ante-natal clinic for out-patients with its own entrance, maternity wards (ante-natal, post-natal or combined), delivery suite and special care baby unit.

However, the ante-natal clinic is more likely to be incorporated into the main OPD. Delivery facilities may be combined with the ward accommodation: wherever they are, they need convenient access to an operating theatre for caesarian sections. The clinical relationship between maternity and gynaecological wards, which in turn need access to the operating department, can draw the operating and maternity facilities into one cluster.

5.05 Decentralisation and patient-focused care

Decentralisation of some specialist functions is becoming possible to some extent because of increased (but far from total) acceptability of the multi-skilling of nursing staff, combined with simplification of operation of diagnostic equipment. This trend is epitomised in the idea of the 'patient-focused hospital' which has been touched on in Section 1.03 above.

In that one of the aims of this principle is to reduce patient travel to centralised diagnostic and treatment departments, many departmental relationships would be affected and the form of the hospital itself would need re-evaluating. It is, however, too early to speculate on the eventual success and level of application.

5.06 Fire safety

The influence of fire safety and means of escape on conceptual design was dealt with in Section 3.05 above. Clearly the fire characteristics of departments and the need to maintain major escape routes also affect the way in which departments are arranged around the main circulation routes.

5.07 IT and other technology

Fibre optics

The potential role of media such as fibre optics in changing the relationship between components of the health service has been mentioned in Section 1.04 above. This comment applies equally well within the hospital and this gives added force to the arguments for investing in provision for such changes (see Section 3.03 above).

Mechanical transportation systems

Pneumatic tube systems for carrying paper and specimens went out of favour some time ago after an evaluation by the Audit Commission but improved versions with greater reliability and more acceptable handling of specimens are now being installed. Recent changes in the health service have also generated more paperwork, for which they are particularly useful, and this trend will probably continue.

Apart from lifts and electric tugs (for moving trains of trollies on distribution and collection rounds) mechanisation of transport is not common in hospitals. Escalators were used at Greenwich, **17.4**, and paternoster lifts (continuously moving, step-on and step-off platforms) have found occasional application, but the investment is rarely considered justified, and on health and safety grounds their use is now frowned on.

5.08 Department sizes

The geometry of the hospital layout obviously depends partly on the size of component departments. Table I shows, for a typical 600–bed hospital, functional content and areas for each department. The table also gives location requirements, reflected in Table III.

6 IN-PATIENT SERVICE

6.01 The ward concept
Beds for in-patients in hospitals are grouped, for effective management, into wards of anything from 20 to 36 beds, under the charge of a sister or charge nurse who is supported by a team of qualified nurses, student nurses and aides. This team has to ensure that patients are monitored, fed, allowed to sleep and use toilet facilities, kept clean, treated if required and encouraged to move around.

Patients will be taken from the ward to other departments for more complex diagnostic testing and treatment. Doctors will visit ward patients at least daily and other staff will come to administer treatment such as physiotherapy.

The ward will be supplied with food, linen, pharmaceuticals and sterile goods and will hold equipment such as wheelchairs, drip stands and walking frames. Used returns and refuse in various categories will be collected on a regular basis.

With so much claim on ground-floor locations, wards tend to be on upper floors unless, like geriatric and children's wards, they have a particular need for access to outside space.

Wards occupy about half the total area of a hospital so it is not possible for all wards to be adjacent to the most relevant departments. For example, there will be about 10 surgical wards in a 600-bed general hospital, all needing to be as close as possible to the operating department. In the UK, location on the same floor is generally considered satisfactory on the grounds that horizontal travel is more reliable than vertical travel by lift.

Wards cater for many types of patient such as surgical, medical, paediatric (children), elderly, intensive therapy but it is important that a common general pattern be adopted as far as possible so that changes of use can be made without disruption.

6.02 Management of in-patient services: ward types

- *Adult acute wards* accommodate general medical or general surgical patients. Although a ward generally will accommodate either one or the other (for doctors' convenience and efficiency of location) there is no significant difference in their facility needs and the ward is standard in its area provision and layout. Between half and three quarters of a hospital's beds are to be found in these wards.
- *Children's wards* vary from adult acute wards in the greater areas devoted to day/play space and the need for access to an outside play area, the provision of education facilities and, of course, the specially designed fittings and furniture.
- *Wards for elderly people* again have more day space than adult acute wards because these patients spend longer in hospital and are ambulant for more of the time.
- *The intensive therapy unit* holds seriously ill patients, often transferred direct from the operating theatre. More space is required around the bed for monitoring and other equipment, no day space is required, and the bed areas are designed primarily

for efficient nursing. Because of the high staff/patient ratio, the size of the ward is usually limited to about 20 patients.

6.03 Admission policy options
While 'cold' (planned) admissions can be made during daylight hours, emergency admissions often have to be made at night when other patients might be disturbed. Such patients might be held until the next day in accident and emergency department observation beds; in a special admission ward (which, however, is difficult to preserve for this purpose when there is pressure on beds); or they may be admitted direct to the ward.

6.04 Patient dependency
It is useful to think of patients as belonging to a 'patient dependency' category, reflecting the amount of observation and nursing attention they need: thus a patient just returned from a major operation might be high dependency.

Wards used to be planned on the basis of 'progressive patient care' whereby high-dependency patients occupied beds nearest to the staff base while low-dependency patients were placed in more remote locations; however, the system required patients to be moved frequently. In addition, hospital stay is becoming shorter as other ways are developed of caring for recuperating patients in the community (see Sections 1.02 and 2.02): in this way expensive, highly staffed beds are not occupied unnecessarily. As a consequence, patients in the general hospital are, on average, of higher dependency.

6.05 Adult acute ward: function and organisation
17.13 shows the relationship between core ward functions and the following requirements, not necessarily in order of importance, need satisfying in the layout of an acute ward:

- *Observation* of as many bedheads as possible by nurses both in the course of their routine activities and from the nurses' station at night (this may or may not be at the staff base); at least one of the observed beds should be in a single room.
- *Proximity of sanitary facilities and day spaces to beds* so as to encourage early ambulation.
- *Reduction of nurse walking distances* by centralising rooms associated with the most frequent nursing functions such as provision and cleaning of bed pans, preparation and cleaning of dressings trollies, bathing dependent patients, feeding patients.
- *Observation of the ward entrance* by nurses during routine activities.
- *Facilities for carrying out dressings and other treatments:* the users' preference for location may be the bedside, a treatment room in each ward or a treatment room shared between two or more wards. Shared treatment rooms in practice have been found to cause problems of timetabling and, even where wards have a treatment room, the sister may prefer to use the bed

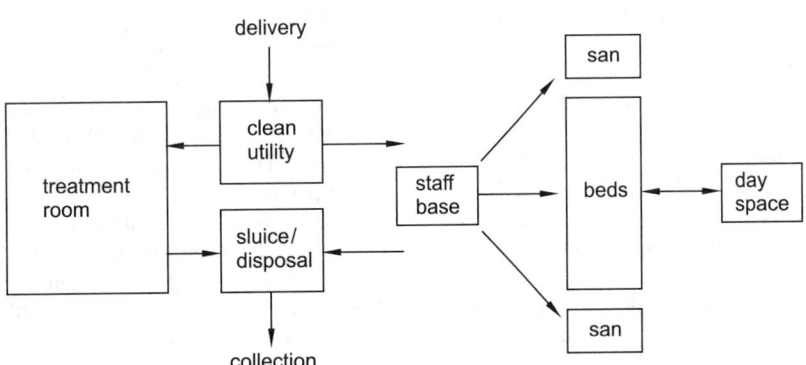

17.13 *Relationship diagram of core ward activities*

space, considering that moving the patient involves nurses' time and can upset the patient.

- *Privacy* for patients when required; this has to be balanced against their need for reassurance and stimulation through being in contact with nursing and general ward activity.
- A *restful and non-institutional atmosphere*, although too quiet an environment has been shown to have its own disadvantages such as oppressiveness and lack of aural privacy; a 'domestic' environment, although difficult to achieve, is a worthwhile objective.
- *Protection from infection from other patients* which is provided primarily by nursing discipline, general cleanliness, bed spacing and provision of appropriate mechanically ventilated accommodation (not necessarily on the ward) for infectious procedures.

6.06 Staff activities

Apart from nursing staff of various grades (see Section 6.01), the ward will be constantly visited by doctors, and patients will be attended by physiotherapists and laboratory staff. Cleaners will be either ward-based or hospital-based. Porters will deliver food and supplies. Routine staff activities will include the following:

- *Reporting and administration*: some discussions will be confidential.
- *Making the bed* and other activities at the bedside concerned with patient comfort; disposal of dirty linen.
- *Renewing dressings* and other treatments which can be carried out in a ward environment, using a dressings trolley laid up in the clean utility room, and disposing of waste afterwards in the dirty utility room.
- *Dispensing medicines*, mostly on a ward round twice daily.
- *Providing bed pans* (either disposable or with a disposable liner) from the dirty utility room, emptying and cleaning them afterwards in a bed pan washer.
- *Bathing dependent patients* in the assisted bathroom or shower.
- *Serving food* and helping some patients to eat; arranging for crockery return to the central kitchen.
- *Encouraging early ambulation* by helping patients walk to the toilet or the day space or carrying out other physiotherapy exercises.
- *Tending to flowers*, arranging and changing water.
- *Cleaning the ward*.

6.07 Design options

Although the Nightingale ward, **17.14**, provided excellent observation for nurses and some reassurance for patients, lack of privacy and disturbance to patients was felt to be compromised. Since the 1955 Nuffield Report, the UK has adopted four-, five- or six-bed bays or rooms as a basis for the general ward, **17.7c** and **17.15**. There is some use of this arrangement in other European countries but two- and three-bed rooms are more common. In the United States, insurance companies tend to require single or two-bed rooms and it is not clear to what extent current changes in the health service (discussed in Section 1) will eventually influence ward planning in the UK, **17.16**.

In the four-bed ward, each patient has a corner; in the five-bed, a local day space or WC cubicle can be provided. The deeper five- and six-bed arrangements contribute to a more compact ward although the innermost beds rely on supplementary artificial lighting for a large part of the time. The provision of a day space and WC to each bed bay is an obvious encouragement to early ambulation: the WC tends to block observation when on the corridor side, **17.17**.

In addition to the multi-bed rooms, about four single rooms are required for very ill patients, for patients liable to disturb others, for patients requiring quiet and possibly for patients liable to infect others or to need protection from infection.

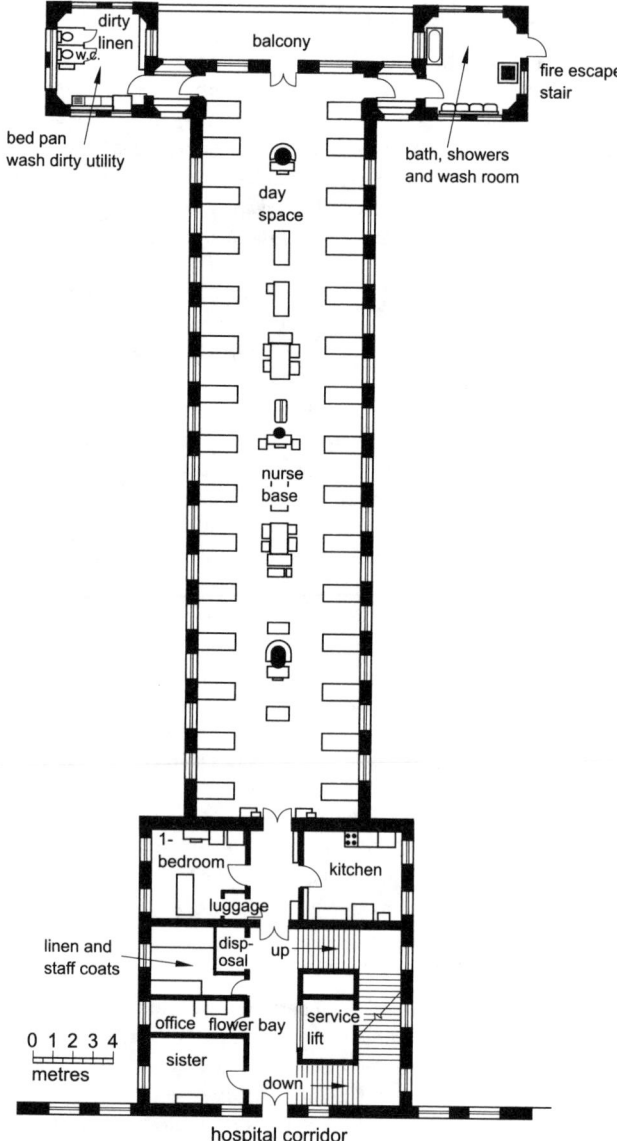

17.14 *Nightingale ward in St Thomas' Hospital*

The staff base (a term preferred to 'nurses' station' since nurses are not long stationary there except at night) is the organisational hub of the ward where the nurse-call system registers, paperwork is done and staff report at change of shift. It needs for these reasons to be centrally placed. Near to this hub are clean utility, dirty utility, assisted bathroom and at least one single bedroom with integral WC. Observation needs from the staff base were discussed above, **17.18** and **17.19**.

Two questions need to be resolved as part of the provision of day space provision: smoking and television. Where television is provided in the bed bay, earphone sockets at the bedhead should be provided; where it is not, one day room should be allocated for television. Some hospitals are moving towards a total ban on smoking but, where this is not the case, a separate day room is required. There is evidence that central dayrooms tend to be underused. Day rooms can be shared between two wards if the layout permits.

Where a WC is provided to each bed bay, at least one more is required for use when a patient's own WC is occupied. This could be a specimen-taking WC or in a bathroom. With higher-dependency and more elderly patients, there is an argument for all WCs to be designed for assistance by staff and some for wheelchair use. For the same reason, handrails along corridors used by patients are desirable.

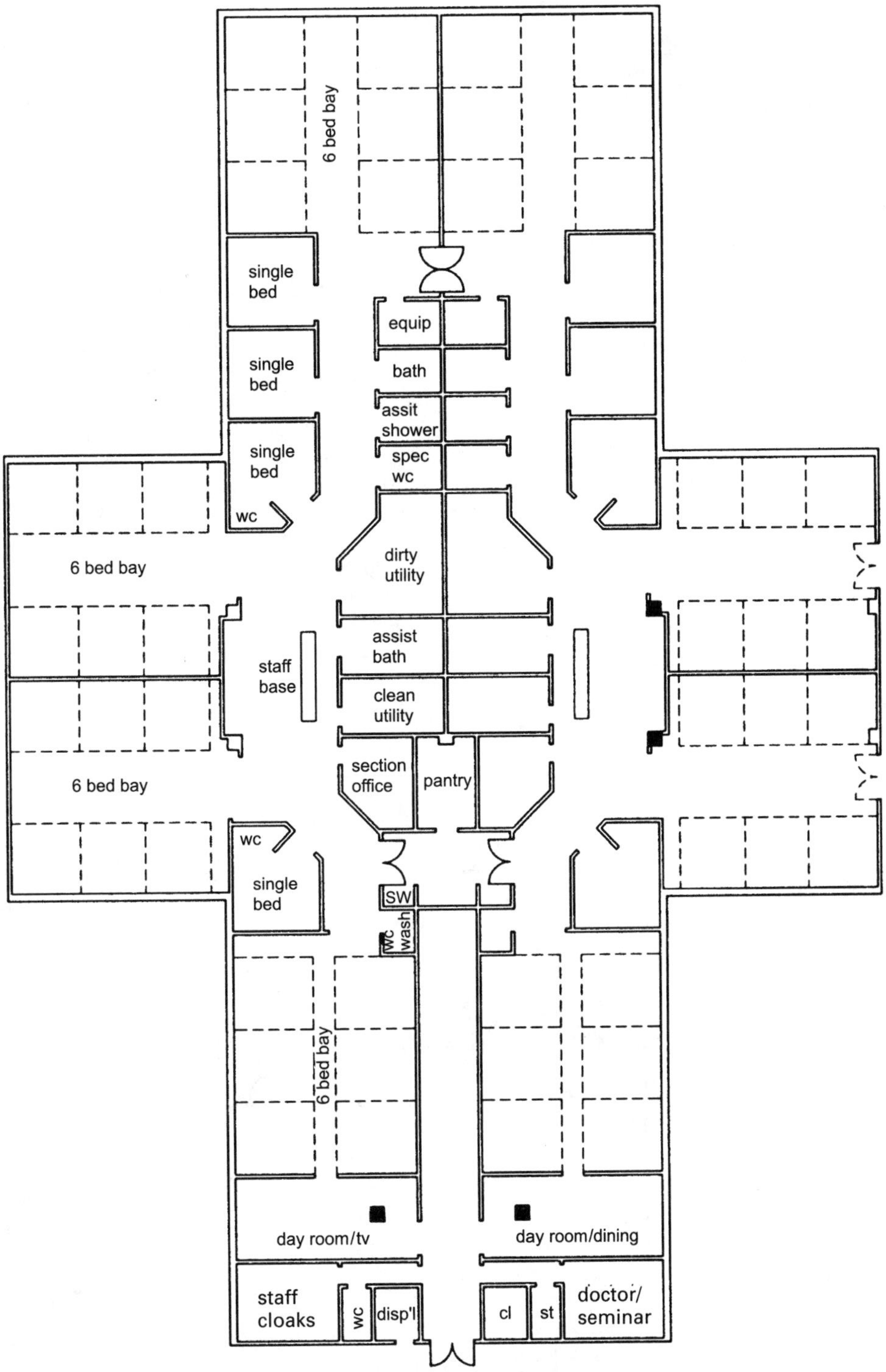

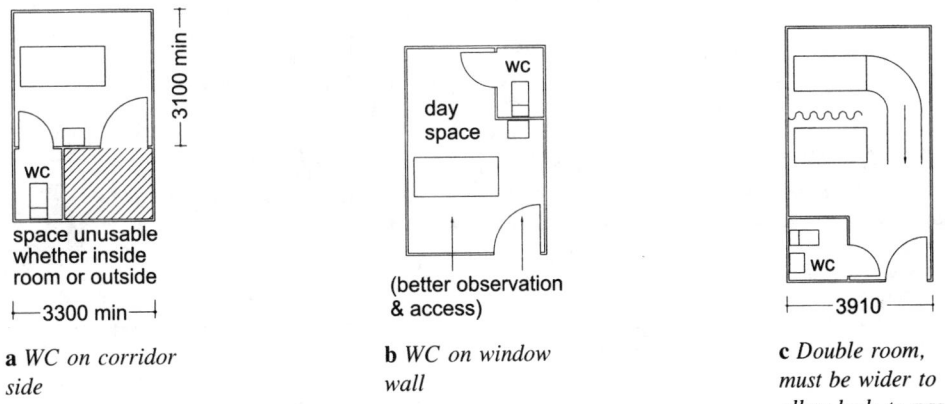

17.15 *Nucleus wards: pair of 28-bed wards* (Department of Health)

a *WC on corridor side*

space unusable whether inside room or outside

3100 min

3300 min

WC

single bed

b *WC on window wall*

day space

WC

(better observation & access)

c *Double room, must be wider to allow beds to pass*

WC

3910

17.16 *Single and double bedrooms:*

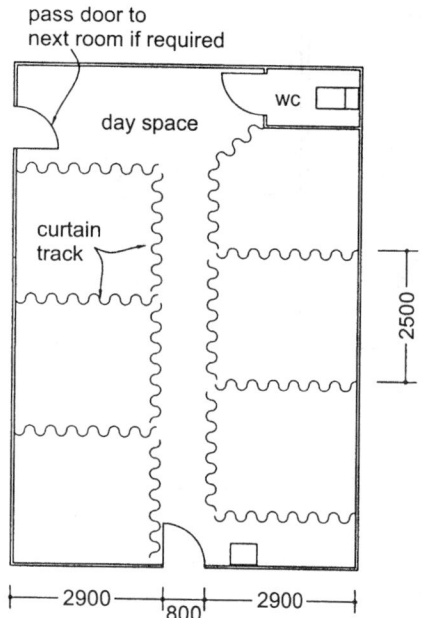

17.17 *Six-bed room with own WC and day space*

6.08 Intensive therapy unit and coronary care unit, 17.20

The ITU is for patients who need treatment involving much medical attention and complex equipment including life support systems (in the UK taken to be between 1 and 2 per cent of acute patients). Two single rooms are provided to cater for infectious and other patients requiring separation; the remainder are placed in one open room, for observation and swift attention, with as much as 3 metres between bed centres and a continuous bedhead service rail for monitoring. A staff room and relatives' room are required, with windows if possible and with a totally non-clinical decor to provide relief from the technological and stressful environment of the unit. There may be a separate CCU but, where integral, it should be planned in a separate zone. The Unit should be adjacent to the operating department and accessible from the A&E and in-patient areas.

6.09 Children's accommodation

The needs of children are best met by having them together in children's units, nursed by staff with the relevant qualifications. Accommodation is required for out-patient facilities; comprehensive assessment and care (for the investigation, treatment and diagnosis of children who fail to develop physically or mentally); in-patient facilities in twenty-bed wards; and a day care unit.

The out-patient unit and assessment accommodation should be on one floor, either at ground level or served by a convenient lift, near to public transport and car parking. The out-patient unit should be near the plaster room and fracture clinic and could adjoin the main OPD.

In the children's ward, the need for observation is greater than in an adult's, but the need for privacy is less and more partitions can be glazed. A number of bedrooms are needed in which a parent can stay with the child. Play space is required and space for teaching and physiotherapy, although these may double with other functions such as eating. Avoiding an institutional atmosphere in the design is important in adult wards but even more so in children's: a light and sunny atmosphere should be the aim.

The accommodation generally will need to provide for infants, toddlers, school-age children and adolescents: the design should as far as possible take account of their varying needs.

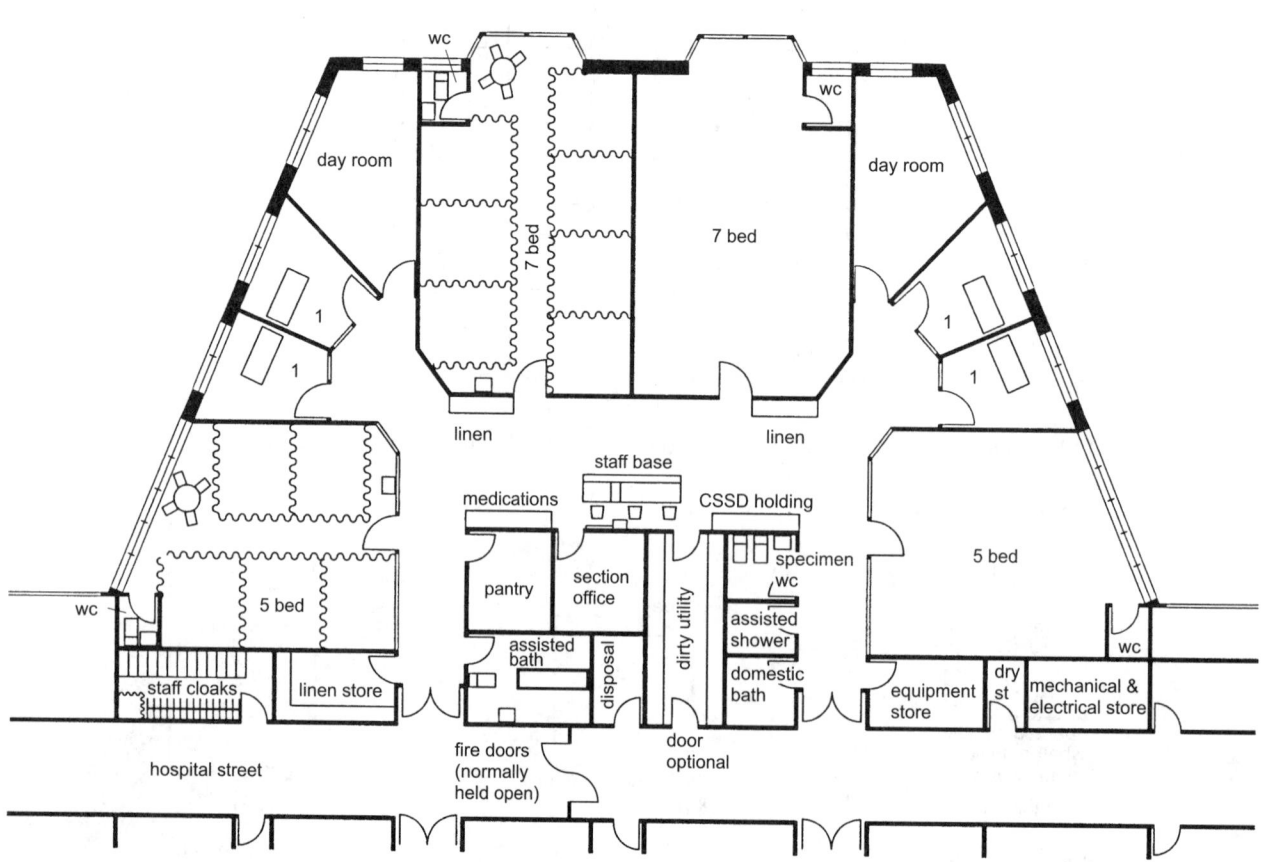

17.18 *28-bed ward designed for patient observation and compactness*
Architect: Tony Noakes

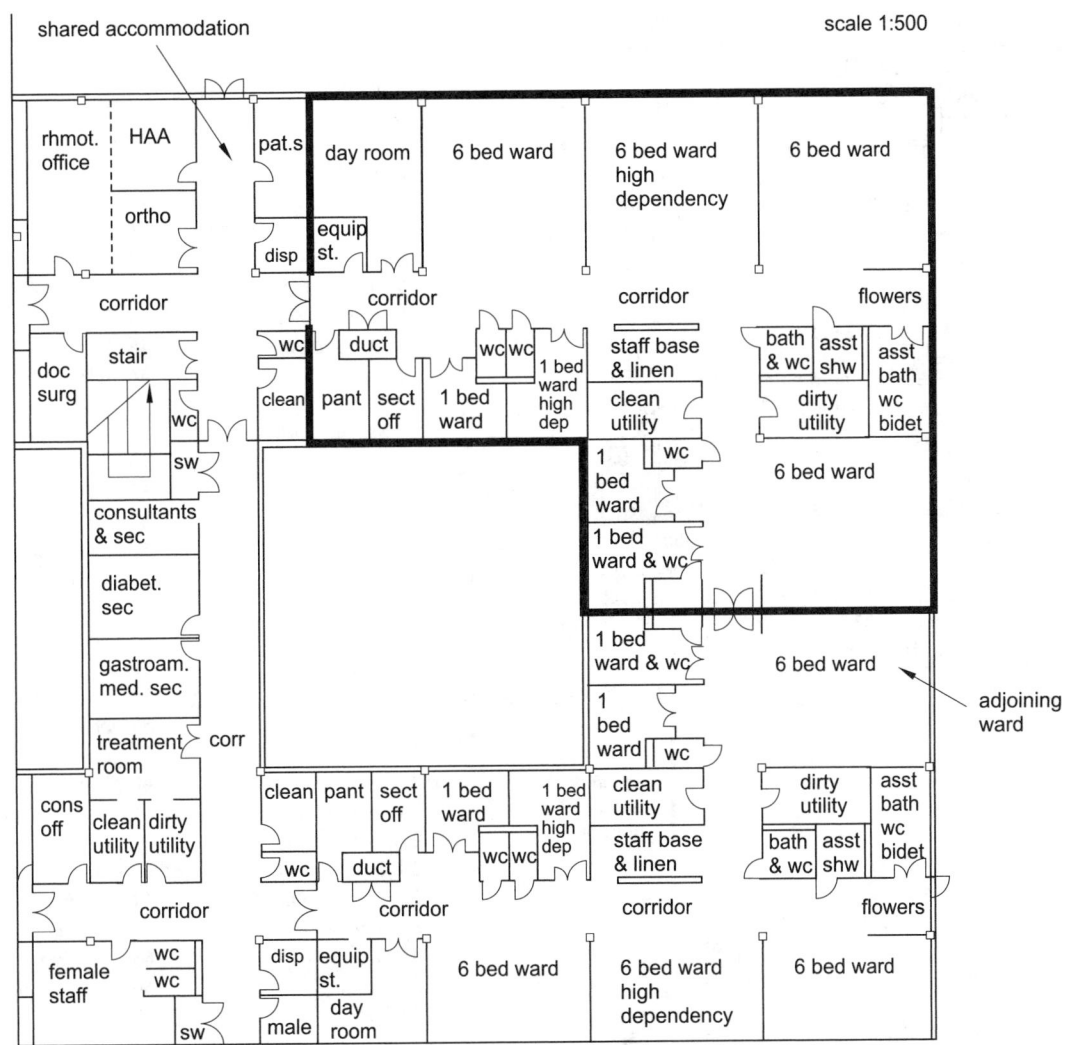

scale 1:500

17.19 *Homerton Hospital, 28-bed L-shaped ward*
Architects: YRM

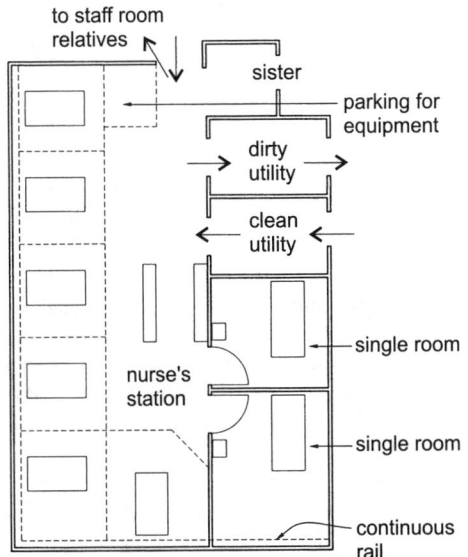

17.20 *Intensive therapy unit (ITU). Cubicle curtains are not used but movable screens may be. The location of the bed within the space varies with needs of patient, staff and equipment*

6.10 Accommodation for elderly people

More 'acute' elderly patients – those undergoing assessment or rehabilitation – are in most respects satisfied by the design for adult acute wards. Longer-stay elderly wards, including those for the mentally infirm, should be more like home than hospital and include a higher proportion of one- and two-bed rooms, with a bed-sitting room atmosphere, and more day space. More storage space is required for storing patients' belongings, including suitcases.

6.11 Maternity accommodation, 17.21

Policies concerning maternity care can vary widely and client policy towards the whole maternity process should be established at the outset. Nearly all births take place in hospital but current trends are towards increasing ante-natal testing and, on that basis, prioritising cases so that low-risk ones can be delivered in the community (at home or in a community hospital) while higher-risk cases are dealt with in the hospital where operating theatres and other back-up facilities are closer to hand.

A strengthened community care service, with midwives accommodated in community clinics or local health care resource centres, could deal with most of the ante-natal care process and minimise the need for visits to the hospital ante-natal clinic. Such buildings would incorporate spaces for ante-natal exercise classes and mother and baby clinics.

A number of philosophies concerning delivery may be encountered. Traditionally, the woman would be admitted direct to the delivery room or, if admitted early, to an ante-natal ward. During

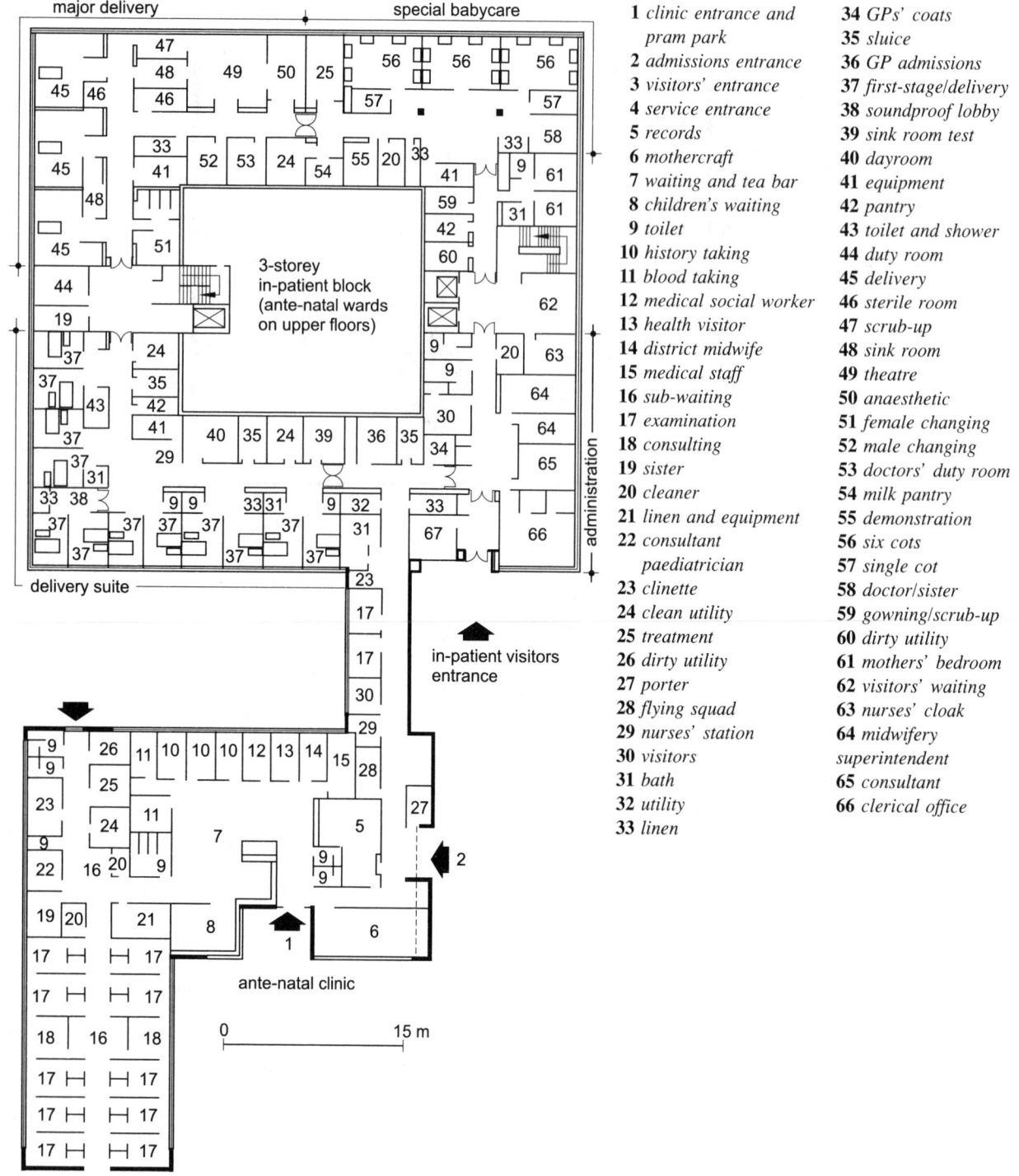

major delivery   special babycare

delivery suite

in-patient visitors entrance

ante-natal clinic

0   15 m

administration

3-storey
in-patient block
(ante-natal wards
on upper floors)

1 clinic entrance and pram park	34 GPs' coats
2 admissions entrance	35 sluice
3 visitors' entrance	36 GP admissions
4 service entrance	37 first-stage/delivery
5 records	38 soundproof lobby
6 mothercraft	39 sink room test
7 waiting and tea bar	40 dayroom
8 children's waiting	41 equipment
9 toilet	42 pantry
10 history taking	43 toilet and shower
11 blood taking	44 duty room
12 medical social worker	45 delivery
13 health visitor	46 sterile room
14 district midwife	47 scrub-up
15 medical staff	48 sink room
16 sub-waiting	49 theatre
17 examination	50 anaesthetic
18 consulting	51 female changing
19 sister	52 male changing
20 cleaner	53 doctors' duty room
21 linen and equipment	54 milk pantry
22 consultant paediatrician	55 demonstration
23 clinette	56 six cots
24 clean utility	57 single cot
25 treatment	58 doctor/sister
26 dirty utility	59 gowning/scrub-up
27 porter	60 dirty utility
28 flying squad	61 mothers' bedroom
29 nurses' station	62 visitors' waiting
30 visitors	63 nurses' cloak
31 bath	64 midwifery superintendent
32 utility	65 consultant
33 linen	66 clerical office

17.21 *Chase Farm Hospital, Enfield, maternity department*
Architects: Stillman and Eastwick-Field

labour she would move to a separate delivery room – perhaps in a suite, **17.21**, central to all the maternity wards and near to the neonatal unit for the nursing of small or ill babies – for delivery of the baby, then returned to a post-natal ward which would be designed to allow rest following birth and to allow the mother to get to know her baby.

One radical alternative is the 'complete stay room' (or LDRP room – labour, delivery, recovery and postpartum), **17.22**, in which the whole process is enacted and which may include accommodation for the mother's partner. The provision of a birthing pool is another option with planning implications.

Within this range there are many possible scenarios, each with its own implications for ward facilities (such as day rooms and sanitary provision) and for provision for abnormal delivery.

Occupancy of maternity wards is variable, throughout the year and with population changes. In principle they should therefore be planned for easy conversion to adult acute use, although this might be difficult with some options such as the complete stay room. In the post-natal ward, the baby will be nursed in a cot alongside the mother.

The out-patient suite will incorporate a suite of consulting/ examination rooms and supporting facilities; waiting areas which can double as space for classes and clinics; and a diagnostic ultrasound room with associated changing and waiting areas.

The design approach in all maternity accommodation should centre round the fact that the pregnant woman is not sick but undergoing a natural function: there is no strong reason for the environment to be particularly clinical in appearance.

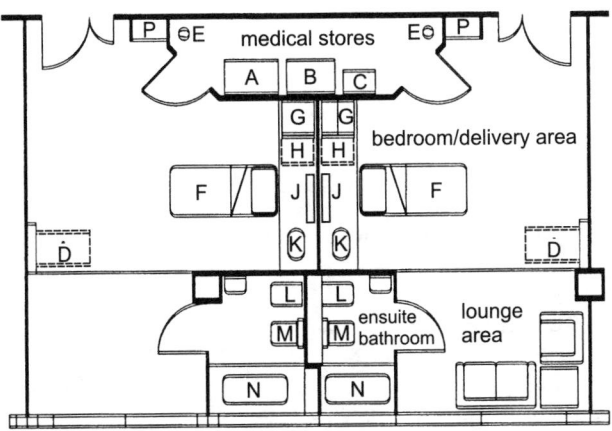

17.22 *Maternity 'complete stay' room*
A *resuscitation*
B *instrument trolley*
C *epidural trolley*
D *mobile foetal monitor*
E *kick bucket*
F *L/D/R bed*
G *wardrobe*
H *bedside cabinet*
J *medical gases panel*
K *clinical basin*
L *bidet*
M *WC*
N *bath/shower*
P *pass-through facility for clean and dirty linen*

6.12 Accommodation for mentally ill people
The scope of facilities for mentally ill people on the hospital site is subject to local initiative. It is, however, likely to include accommodation for the assessment and short-term treatment of adults, including the elderly, who are acutely mentally ill: this group of patients is most likely to need the support of diagnostic services and access to general acute facilities. They also gain from sharing catering, supply and disposal services.

The primary elements in the department will be the wards of up to thirty beds each and the day hospital which includes consulting, treatment and social areas together with occupational therapy. Very few adults will remain in the wards during the day but if ward and day hospital are intended to share day, dining, sitting and recreation facilities, experience has shown that full integration is required for this to work successfully.

The department should ideally be integrated into the hospital so as to facilitate communication but be independent enough to have its own (not too clinical) environment. Its configuration is unlikely to match that of other wards and evening activities may be disturbing to other in-patient departments. One solution is to plan it as a satellite with its own entrance, perhaps linked to the main hospital and possibly sharing some accommodation with an adjacent rehabilitation department.

Within wards, the current recommendation of Building Note 35 is for 30 per cent single rooms and this is based on two assumptions: that patient observation is easier in multi-bed rooms and that a measure of privacy can be provided in such rooms by arrangements of furniture: both have been subjects of discussion. The basis of the Building Note is that there is progressive patient care from single rooms through well-observed multi-bed rooms to a more hostel-like environment. Bed spacing in multi-bed wards can be closer (2.0 m to 2.2 m) than in acute wards. Clinical discussions and handover between shifts, because confidential, tend to take place in the sister's office which therefore needs to be larger.

Psychiatric out-patient clinics are generally held in the main OPD. Many patients never enter the psychiatric department but others may attend the day hospital from one to three days a week, undertaking various types of occupational therapy and group therapy. They are also given a mid-day meal in two sittings. These activities can be accommodated in a number of rooms with comfortable sitting space for 10 to 20 people. Electro-convulsive therapy (ECT) may need to be accommodated: it requires treatment and recovery rooms but they would only be in use for perhaps four hours a week and should be usable for other purposes.

Environmental design generally, particularly of the interior, is of even more importance in this department than elsewhere. Providing a non-institutional appearance, domestic scale and a 'sense of place' should be high priorities. Soft floor coverings are appropriate for all non-wet areas; divan beds and careful choice of soft furnishings are crucial in creating a suitable atmosphere. Sound attenuation is needed for all rooms used for confidential interviewing; noisy areas (e.g. music room, workshop) should be located to reduce nuisance.

7 DIAGNOSTIC AND TREATMENT DEPARTMENTS

7.01 Accident and emergency department, 17.11 and 17.23
The distinctive operational characteristic of the accident and emergency department (AED) is that patients arrive without appointment at any time of the day or night: it has therefore to be always open and always staffed by doctors and nurses. Patients may be seriously ill or injured and brought in by ambulance; or may be 'casual' attenders or other 'walking sick'.

Since ambulance cases are often urgent and may be in a condition distressing to other attenders, particularly children, a separate entrance is required with ambulance parking, screened from the walking entrance, with direct access to a fully equipped resuscitation area and with separate trolley waiting area.

The registration desk will overlook the main waiting area for walking patients which will in turn lead directly to the treatment area. However, on arrival the patients will first be 'triaged' (sorted to establish degree of urgency) in an adjacent cubicle.

The treatment area is an open space surrounded by cubicles. A number of the cubicles will be for ambulant patients who will sit for treatment, a roughly equal number will accommodate couches. Although the two types will be used mainly for walking and ambulance patients respectively, all should lead off a common central working area with a supplies base. Some of the cubicles will be for specialised purposes such as ENT, ophthalmic, paediatric and holding of drugs or alcoholic patients. Also off this area will be major treatment rooms (one of which might be a plaster room – possibly shared with the orthopaedic and fracture clinic – and one possibly of minor theatre standard), dirty utility and stores.

Some key issues need to be resolved with the client: whether X-ray facilities will be provided (this depends on the size of the AED and whether the main X-ray department can be accessed directly); and whether an observation/overnight stay/admission ward is provided and, if so, its exact function and how it relates to admission policy. With the blurring of the traditional boundaries between acute and primary care, the role of the GP in the AED is also currently open to discussion.

Also for discussion is whether a further separate entrance and waiting area is required for children, leading directly to their own treatment zone. This is difficult to achieve – creating a demand for three non-intersecting patient routes – but pressure is currently being applied to incorporate such provision.

Particular design issues are good signposting outside and in; swift reassurance and welcome at reception and security of staff.

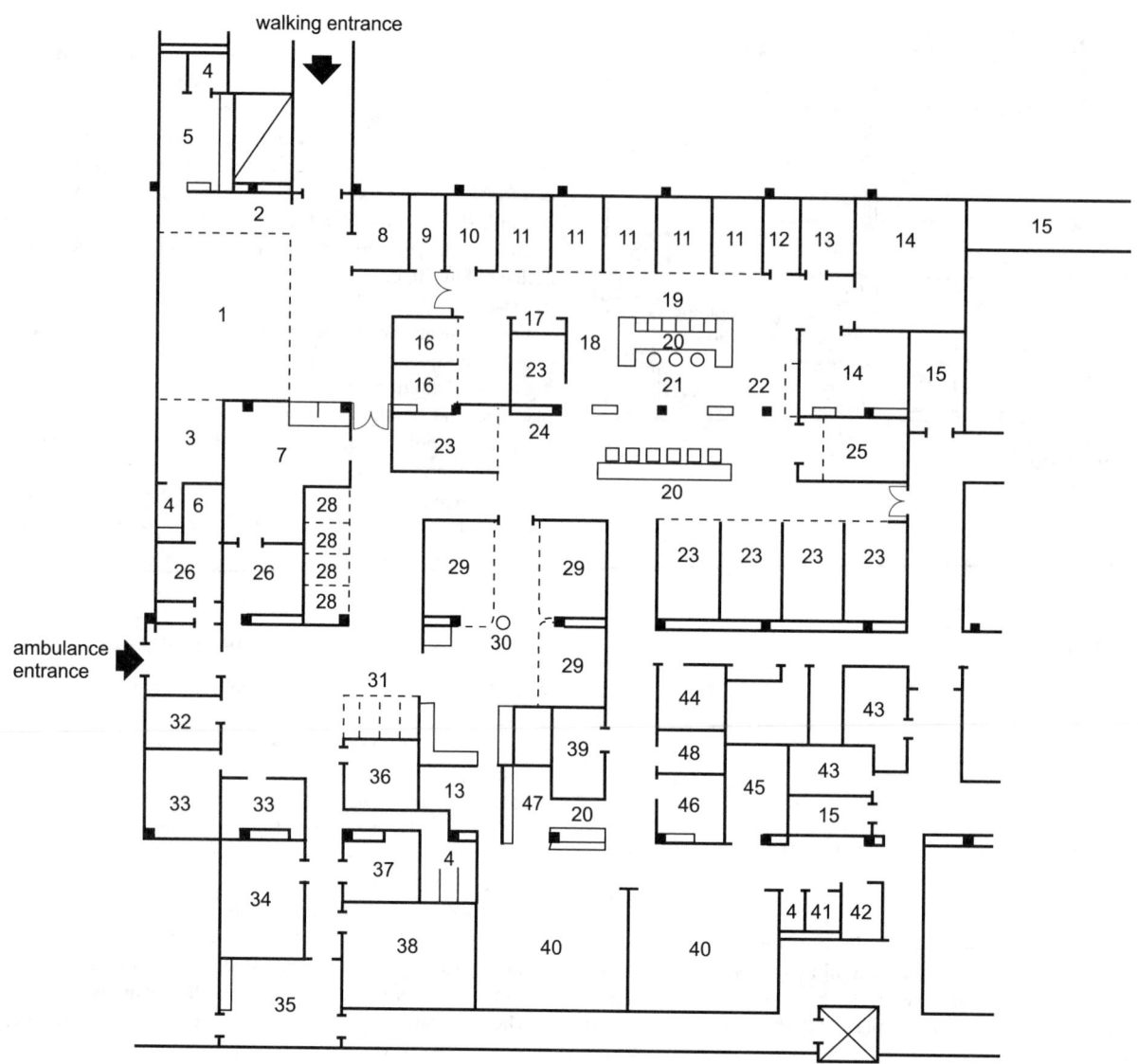

17.23 *Royal Free Hospital accident and emergency department*

1 *waiting*	**17** *splints*	**33** *consulting room*
2 *refreshments*	**18** *XR boxes*	**34** *staff restroom and lockers*
3 *children's play area*	**19** *sub-waiting*	**35** *MI store*
4 *WC*	**20** *staff base*	**36** *senior nursing manager*
5 *female toilets and nappy-changing*	**21** *supplies base*	**37** *sister*
6 *WC and shower*	**22** *linen*	**38** *teaching room*
7 *reception*	**23** *major injuries cubicle*	**39** *kitchen*
8 *triage*	**24** *whiteboard and notices*	**40** *four-bed ward bay*
9 *men's WC*	**25** *gynaecological room*	**41** *wheelchair-accessible WC*
10 *ophthalmic room*	**26** *patient cleanse and ID*	**42** *assisted bathroom*
11 *minor injuries cubicle*	**27** *secretaries (2)*	**43** *X-ray*
12 *specimen WC*	**28** *patient observation cubicle*	**44** *relatives*
13 *dirty utility*	**29** *resuscitation*	**45** *isolation bedroom*
14 *treatment room*	**30** *hosereel supply*	**46** *psychology interview room*
15 *notes store*	**31** *trolley park*	**47** *clean supplies*
16 *paediatric room*	**32** *doctor*	**48** *cleaner*

7.02 Out-patient department 17.11 and 17.24

The function of the OPD is to diagnose and treat home-based patients and if necessary admit them as in-patients. It is one of the largest departments in the hospital and is visited by the greatest number of patients daily. It is therefore best accessed directly from the main hospital entrance.

The patients' first point of contact is the main OP reception desk from which they are directed to the sub-waiting area serving the suite of consulting rooms in which their clinic is being held. The building block of the department is the consulting/examination suite which can be a number of combined C/E rooms ('Type A' in HBN 12) or some combination of consulting rooms and examination rooms ('Type B'), **17.25** to **17.31**.

In the Type A combined C/E room, the doctor will both consult with the patient and examine the patient on a couch; while the patient is dressing, the doctor may move to an adjoining C/E room

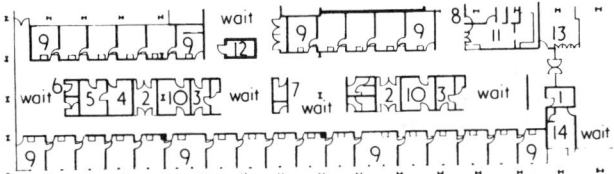

17.24 *Greenwich Hospital outpatients' department*

1 *sister*	**8** *clinical assistants*
2 *clean supply*	**9** *consulting/examination*
3 *dirty utility*	*rooms*
4 *electrocardiographic*	**10** *treatment*
technician	**11** *pathology out-station*
5 *electrocardiography*	**12** *audiometry*
6 *toys*	**13** *reception*
7 *cleaner*	**14** *porter*

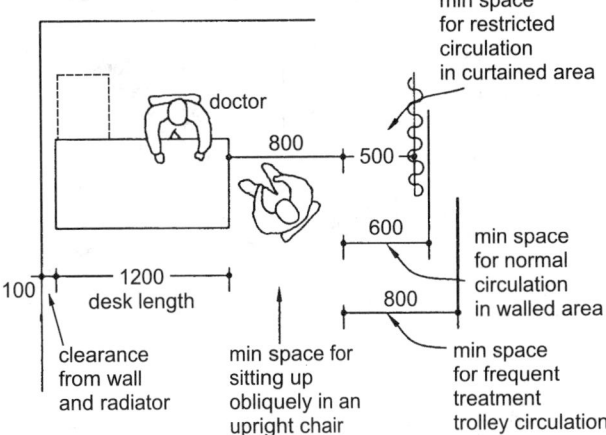

17.26 *Space requirement for room depth in consulting areas*

to deal with another patient and the rooms should therefore have interconnecting doors. In the Type B arrangement, the patient moves to the separate room, undresses and waits for the doctor. Because of the fixed ratio of consulting rooms to examination rooms in the Type B provision, Type A is generally considered more flexible and to have better utilisation. In a clinic where there is rapid throughput a consultant, registrar and house officer may occupy a string of six or seven combined C/E rooms; where the throughput is slower (e.g. psychiatry), each doctor will occupy one room only.

To provide such flexibility, strings of at least six rooms, and preferably twelve, are required. This can, however, make it difficult to provide an external view for the sub-waiting area, a provision valued more highly in Scottish guidance.

Orthopaedic and fracture clinics are often provided as part of the AED since many of their patients are receiving follow-up treatment resulting from injuries and some accommodation, like the plaster room, can be used in common.

Out-patient facilities for maternity patients, children, elderly and psychiatric patients are discussed under the appropriate service in Section 6.

7.03 Operating department, 17.12 and 17.32

An *operating department* consists of one or more operating suites together with common ancillary accommodation such as changing and rest rooms, reception, transfer and recovery areas. An *operating suite* includes the operating theatre with it own anaesthetic room, preparation room (for instrument trolleys), disposal room, scrub-up and gowning area and an exit area which may be part of the circulation space. An *operating theatre* is the room in which surgical operations and some diagnostic procedures are carried out.

Infection control is one of the key criteria in operating department design and this is one of the few departments requiring air conditioning. To assist infection control, four access zones are defined: *operative zone* (theatre and preparation room); *restricted*

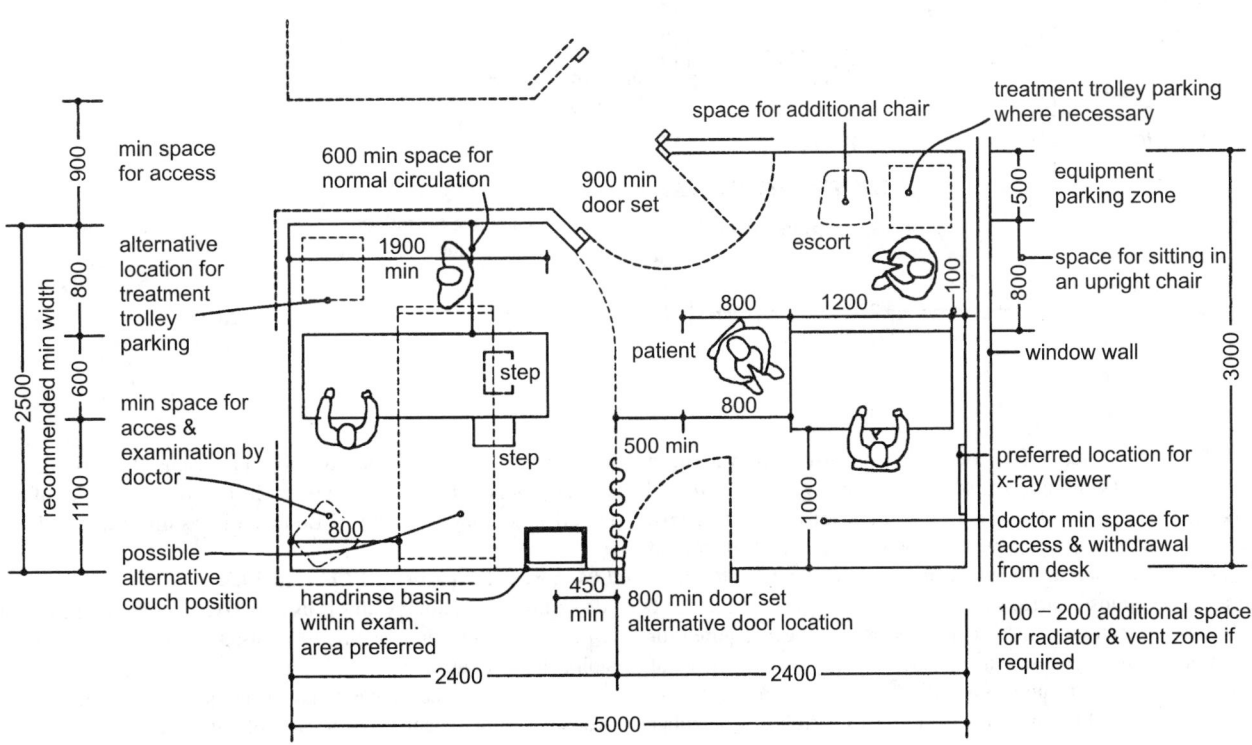

17.25 *Consulting/examination room layout*

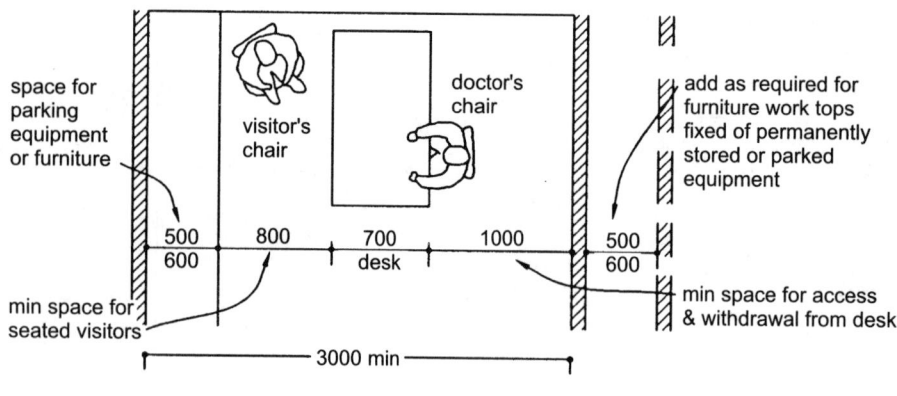

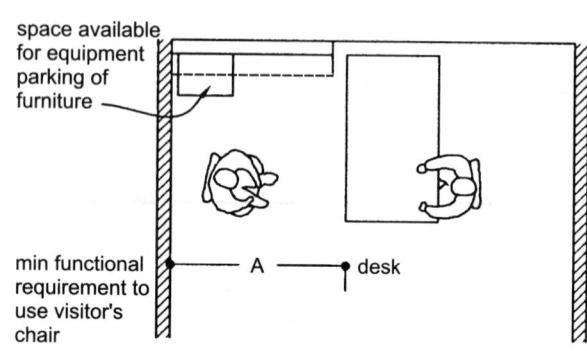

17.27 Space requirements for room width in consulting areas
Dimension A:

- *minimum 1200 mm, psychologically unsatisfactory. The space in front of the desk should be larger than that behind*
- *preferred minimum 1300 mm giving more flexibility in arrangement and use of the space in front of the desk, and psychologically more acceptable*
- *1400 mm is the minimum permitting movement past a seated visitor*
- *1500 mm will permit passage behind a seated visitor*

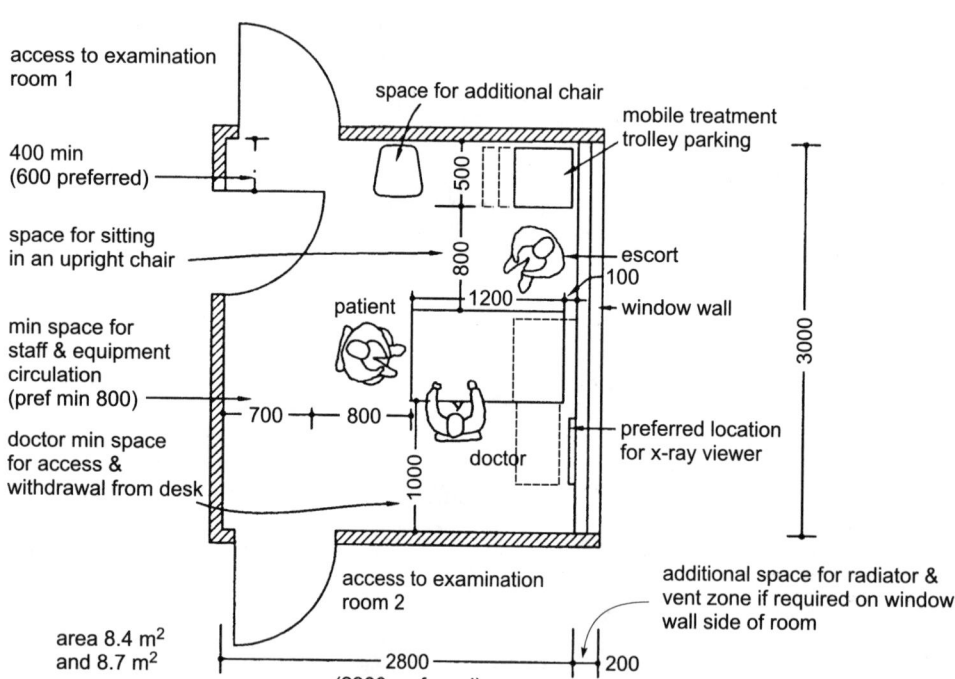

17.28 Separate consulting room

zone for those related to activities in the operative zone who need to be gowned (scrub-up, anaesthesia and utility rooms); *limited access zone* for those who need to enter areas adjacent to the above (recovery, mobile X-ray store, dark room, staff rest, cleaner); and *general access zone* to which anyone is admitted (staff changing, porters base, transfer area, stores).

Separate 'clean' and 'dirty' corridors are no longer required for infection control reasons, although the four major components of traffic (patients, staff, supplies and disposal) may be segregated, in a number of possible combinations, into two corridors – on either side of the theatre – for reasons of good workflow.

There are strong economic arguments for centralising operating

facilities in one department, located on the same floor as all – or as many as possible – of the surgical beds and in particular of the ITU. The journey from the AED should be as direct as possible.

7.04 X-ray department, 17.11 and 17.33
Also known as radiology, this is usually taken to refer to the use of X-rays for diagnostic imaging; when used for treatment, the term radiotherapy is used.

In addition to the conventional techniques for imaging bone structures, supplemented in the case of soft organs by the use of radio-opaque materials such as barium, an X-ray department will now sometimes accommodate a computerised tomography (CT)

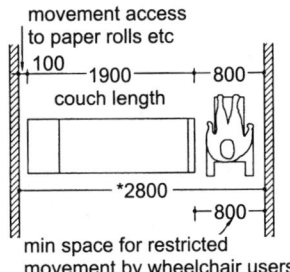

a *Access at foot end of couch for wheelchair movement.*
*2800 mm is also the preferred minimum dimension room length
when standing workspace at foot or head ends of couch is
required*

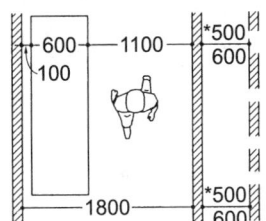

c *No access across foot end of couch*

17.29 *Space requirements for room lengths in examination areas*

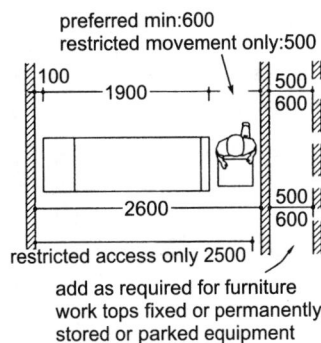

b *Where wheelchair movement at foot end not required*

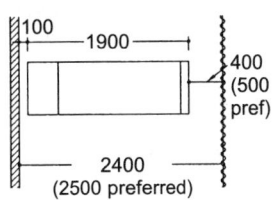

d *Minimum for restricted sideways access within curtained area*

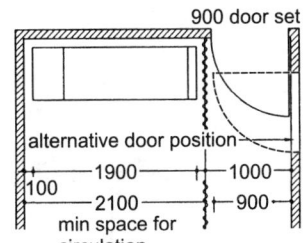

a *Access to one side of couch only. 1100 mm is the minimum
space for an ambulant patient changing*

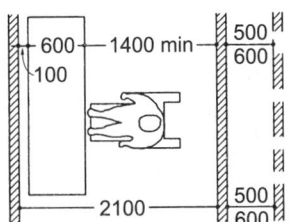

b *Access to one side of couch only. 1400 mm is the minimum
space for a wheelchair patient changing*

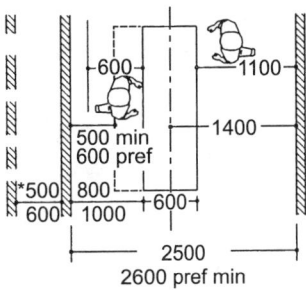

c *Access to both sides of couch*
*600 mm is the essential unobstructed space for access and
examination*
1100 mm is the space at the side of the couch for changing
*1400 mm is the space at the side of the couch for wheelchair
access*
*800 mm to 1000 mm is the clear workspace at the side of the
bed or couch for examination and treatment, preferred minimum
900 mm*
**add as required for furniture, workshop or equipment, which
may be fixed, permanently stored or parked.*

17.30 *Space requirements for room width in examination areas*

scanner which builds up three-dimensional images and, occasionally, a unit for magnetic resonance imaging (MRI). Of even greater impact in terms of throughput – and still growing – is imaging by ultrasound, which is simpler (not needing the protective measures demanded of X-rays), cheaper, faster and not requiring as much space.

Each of these services requires its own reception, waiting and changing areas. The X-ray services may in addition be grouped into, for example, specialised rooms, general-purpose rooms and barium rooms although the X-ray reception desk would probably be common to all.

The department should be located next to the AED and near the OPD with as direct an access as possible for in-patients. (Satellite departments in, for example, the AED are not generally cost-effective.) The layout should allow access to some diagnostic rooms outside working hours without opening the whole department.

7.05 Pathology department

This department carries out tests on patients and patient specimens; the test results are a crucial aid to diagnosis, patient management and population screening for clinicians in hospitals, in primary care and community care. Generally it incorporates four main functions:

● *Chemical pathology*: study of the chemistry of living tissue
● *Haematology*: study of the functions and disorders of the blood, including testing for compatibility in blood transfusions

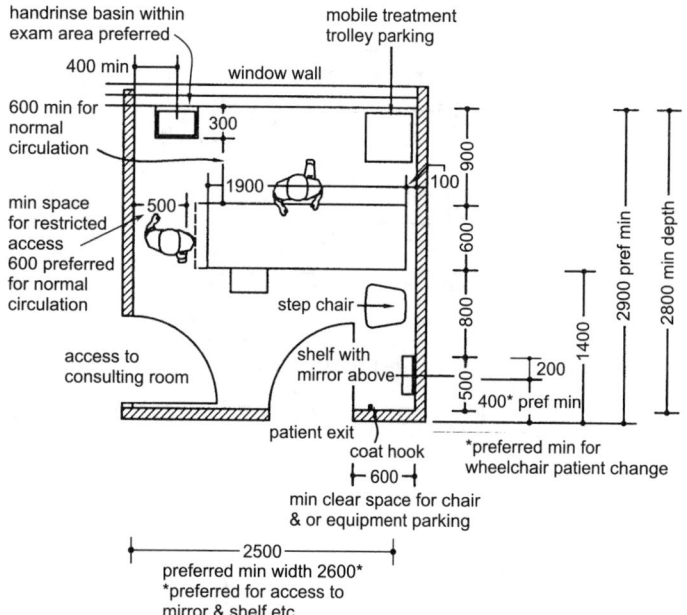

handrinse basin within exam area preferred

mobile treatment trolley parking

400 min

window wall

600 min for normal circulation

300

1900

100

900

600

800

500

min space for restricted access 600 preferred for normal circulation

500

step chair

access to consulting room

shelf with mirror above

patient exit

coat hook

├─ 600 ─┤

min clear space for chair & or equipment parking

200

1400

500

400* pref min

2900 pref min

2800 min depth

*preferred min for wheelchair patient change

├──────── 2500 ────────┤
preferred min width 2600*
*preferred for access to
mirror & shelf etc

17.31 *Separate examination room: area 7 m² and 7.6 m²*

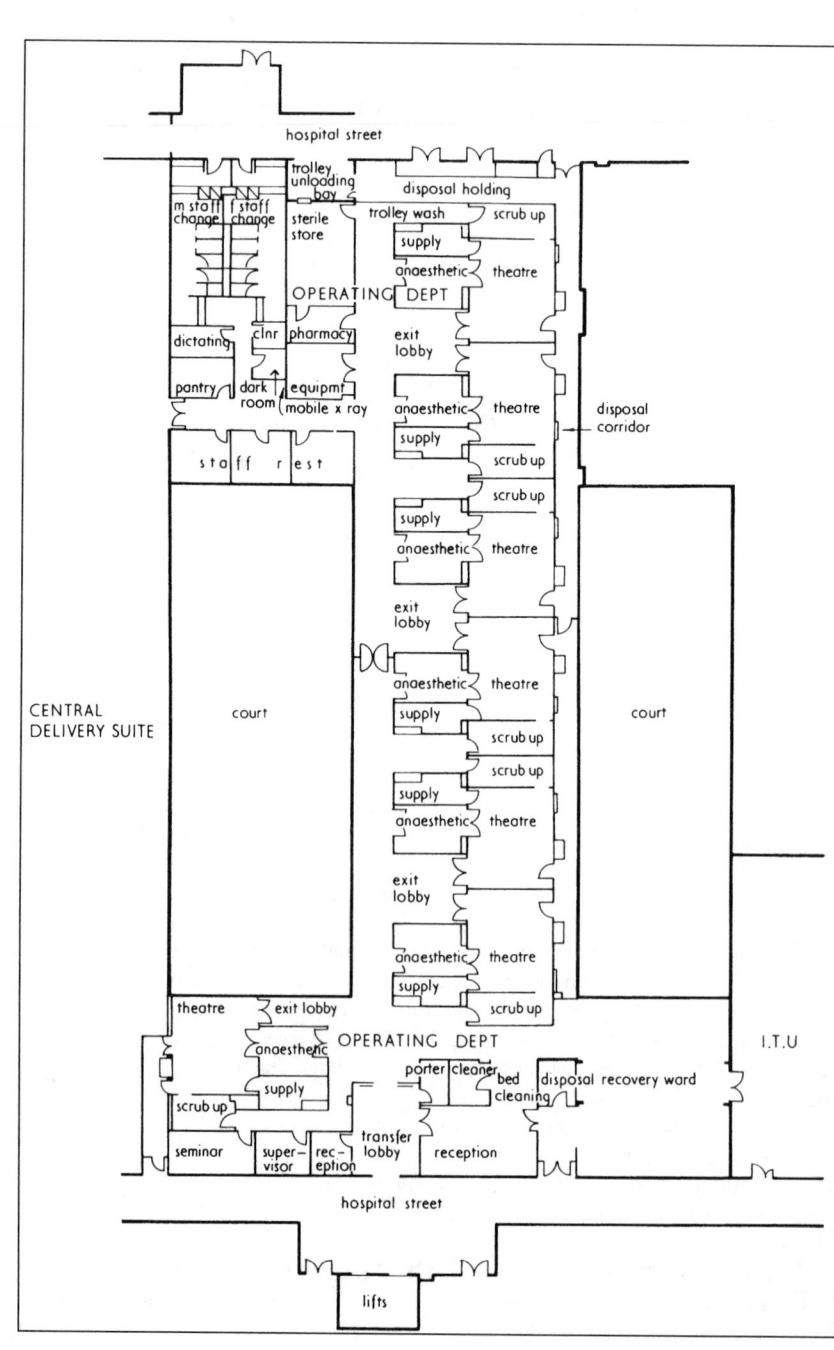

17.32 *Operating department with back disposal corridor at King's Lynn Hospital*

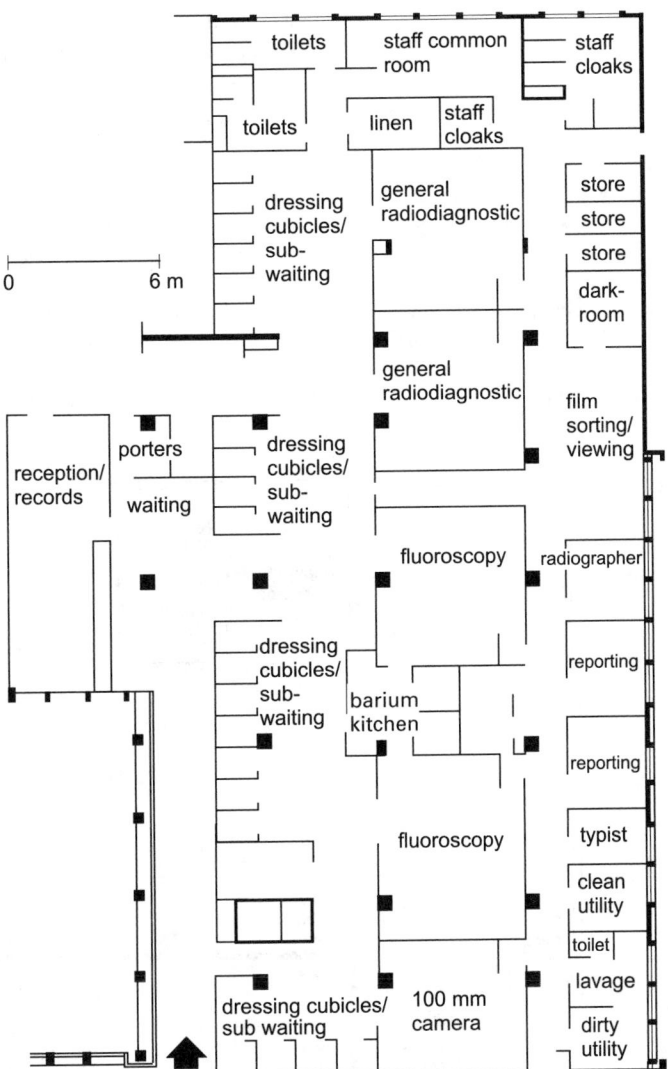

17.33 *X-ray department at King Edward Memorial Hospital, Ealing*

- *Histopathology*: the study of diseased tissue (surgical and post-mortem) and of cells (cytology)
- *Microbiology*: study of micro-organisms; including some aspects of parasitology, virology and mycology.

Both the balance and types of function in this department will probably change at an increasing rate with changing legislation (e.g. Health and Safety), medical and technological advances, changes in demand (particularly if the market-orientated health service survives) and in particular an increased demand from primary care clinicians as more services are devolved from the secondary sector. The size and composition of the pathology department may also be affected by potential needs outside the NHS if a Trust decides to market these services more widely.

The general planning criteria are not very different from those of other kinds of laboratories. To allow for flexibility (ability to change use without physical rearrangement) and adaptability (ability to rearrange the physical elements to accommodate different functions) the design should aim to incorporate modular laboratories with standard bench and service provision (rather than tailor-made for individual functions); a regular grid of service outlets; removable partitions; and moveable laboratory furniture.

The mortuary is the responsibility of the pathologist. An adjoining location is convenient but not essential: location to provide screened access for the hearse is more important.

7.06 Rehabilitation department

To encourage an integrated approach to patient treatment, the rehabilitation department encompasses a number of therapies:

- *Physiotherapy*: dealing with problems of mobility and function using natural approaches such as movement and manual therapy, supported by electrotherapy, cryotherapy and hydrotherapy.
- *Occupational therapy*: improving patients' function and minimising handicaps through the holistic use of selected activities, environment and equipment adaptation so they can achieve independence in daily living and regain competence in work and leisure.
- *Speech therapy*: dealing with communication problems, either individually or in groups, if necessary by introducing alternative methods of communication; family members may be involved and family counselling plays an important part.

In addition, accommodation is needed for consultant medical staff.

Patients may be disabled: the department may need its own entrance if it is remote from the main entrance and must be near to car parking. There are no strong internal relationships except between hydrotherapy and physiotherapy and between the central waiting space and all treatment areas.

8 SUPPORT SERVICES

8.01 Pharmacy, 17.34

In the hospital pharmacy, drugs are received, stored, dispensed to out-patients and issued to wards and other departments. If the hospital holds its own bulk stores, reception will be run by the pharmacist (and therefore reasonably accessible from the dispensary) and adjacent to unloading, checking and storage areas: these will be separated from other storage areas for security reasons. The pharmacy is unlikely to include its own manufacturing area, prepared drugs now being purchased from commercial sources. There is also a tendency to limit out-patient dispensing and to refer patients to community pharmacies ('chemists') but the dispensing counter needs to be near the OPD.

8.02 Sterile services

The purpose of this department is to supply sterilised instruments and packs for use in procedures in theatres and all clinical departments. The workload of the department will be affected not just by the needs of the hospital but also by the extent to which the hospital is supplying other users and using other suppliers.

The functions cover cleaning and disinfecting instruments, trays and other items; preparing, packaging and sterilising trays and packs; storing non-sterile materials and components; storing processed goods and purchasing sterilised goods; distributing processed goods to consumers. However, it is likely that packs for use in basic procedures, and some supplementary packs, will be purchased from a commercial source.

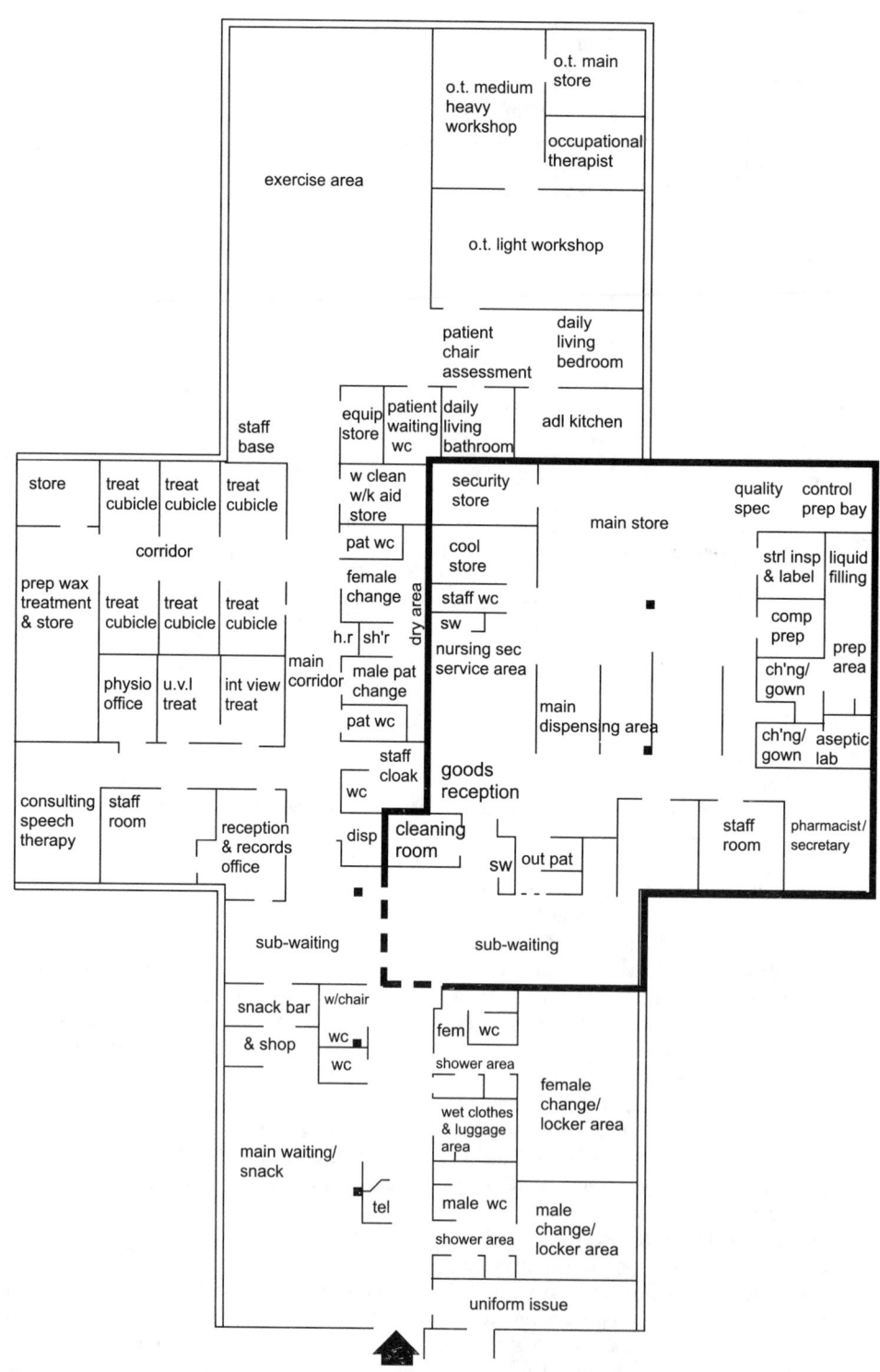

17.34 *Pharmacy department in Nucleus standard Department of Health*

Workflow is a progression from dirty to clean. Used items are sorted, washed, dried and passed to a packing room where trays and procedure packs are assembled under clean conditions (personnel pass through a gowning room). The packaged goods are moved through to the steriliser loading area and, after sterilisation, to the cooling room and stores.

8.03 Catering
This service covers the preparation and delivery of meals to patients and staff. In-patient meals will be delivered by trolley; staff will be provided with meals in an adjacent cafeteria with snack area and adjoining lounge, possibly supplemented by a call-order service and vending machines; a patient cafeteria may also be provided for out-patients, day patients and in-patients where there is, for example, a unit for the mentally ill.

The content of the kitchen will depend on the extent to which the hospital purchases prepared ingredients and prepared meals and whether it is contracted to supply other institutions. The basic flow is from general bulk stores to kitchen stores, preparation and cooking areas. Where a patients' tray service is provided, cooked food is plated on a tray conveyor and the trays loaded onto trolleys; the cooking area also serves the cafeteria servery. Day hospitals are more likely to be served from bulk food trolleys. All crockery is returned to the adjoining central wash-up.

The kitchen should be located on the same level as the staff dining room and, if possible, on the ground floor. As a high-fire risk area it should not be adjoining or under wards.

8.04 Supply and disposal services
Two principal factors will determine the content of the supplies department: the extent to which the hospital keeps its own stores (rather than receiving them from an area store) and the extent to which various processes such as laundry, sterilising, food preparation are carried out in the hospital rather than purchased commercially.

Distribution may be based on trains of trolleys pulled by a tug (when ramps may be used to change levels rather than lifts) or individual trolleys pushed by porters. The supply zone will probably be on the periphery of the hospital because of its different dimensional and construction requirements and the non-urgent nature of its distribution requirements.

8.05 Estate maintenance and works operations
Estate maintenance workshops need ground-floor vehicular access and access to hospital corridors but are likely to be noisy and best located in an industrial zone away from wards and clinical departments.

The department's responsibility now includes the workshop for maintenance of electronics and medical engineering (EME) equipment. This has different location requirements, with access to major user departments and remote from facilities which may cause electromagnetic interference such as sub-stations, welding workshops in the estate maintenance department and physiotherapy.

8.06 Office accommodation
Since the formation of Trusts and the establishment of purchaser and provider functions, it is not possible to generalise about the office accommodation that will be required within a hospital. The designer will have to establish with the client body what accommodation will be required for Trust and District Health Authority management purposes and for others such as community services and social work staff. Consultant medical staff will need office and support staff, shared where they are part-time, near to their main place of work (wards, clinical departments, specialist departments or management departments).

Offices should be grouped where possible to facilitate sharing of spaces for reception, waiting, conference, office machines, storage, utility and staff rooms.

8.07 Main entrance
The strategic questions concerning numbers of hospital entrances were dealt with in Section 5.01. The general implication was that, with certain exceptions, all staff, patients and visitors will use the main entrance. This should be a determining factor in planning parking space for cars and ambulances and public transport facilities such as bus stops. It also suggests that routes to departments, particularly wards, from the main entrance should be direct and, if possible, short. Other interdepartmental traffic should not cross the main entrance.

Since this department provides patients and visitors with their first experience of the hospital, environmental considerations, including decor, the use of natural light and courtyard views, are as important here as anywhere. As a traffic focus, the main entrance can provide the hospital with opportunities for income-generating facilities such as shops, vending machines, displays areas and stalls.

8.08 Health records
The health records department (HRD) encompasses the admissions office (which maintains waiting lists, arranges admissions and appointments and may be separately sited near the main entrance), the library (which handles filing, storage and retrieval of health records, both current and archived) and the office (which communicates with health professionals, sorts and maintains the notes and index). The content of the department will be affected by computerisation of patient administration systems, waiting lists and other functions.

Although there is considerable traffic to the HRD, particularly from the OPD, it is only necessary to ensure that routes to it are direct and that it is directly accessible from the main hospital street.

8.09 Education centre
Education for nurses and technicians developed historically from nurses' training schools, needing practical rooms and demonstration areas, incorporating key ward areas with beds and dummy patient. The education centre now includes facilities, in addition to those for basic training of nurses, for the post-basic training of all health professionals in an integrated manner. Education facilities may also be needed for post-graduate medical and dental education.

Educational requirements are constantly changing with increasing professionalisation of services, the changing nature of clinical and managerial roles, and increasing emphasis on financial management and other matters such as health and safety.

While facilities for nursing and midwife education, on the one hand (classrooms, demonstration rooms, discussion rooms, common rooms, staff rooms), and post-graduate medical and dental education, on the other (common room, dining room, servery, seminar room, offices), can be planned as separate zones within the centre, much of the accommodation should be shared. This includes the main entrance with refreshment facilities and display area, library, audio-visual department, lecture hall and other teaching accommodation.

9 ENVIRONMENT

9.01
While it is a truism that the designer needs to provide both a satisfactory working environment for staff who spend their working lives in the hospital and a pleasing, anxiety-reducing, perhaps healing environment for patients who are the real clients, it has to be recognised that these requirements have inherent conflicts. Typical examples are the different air temperatures required by the working nurse and the passive patient; ward lighting levels at night for the sleeping patient and the working

nurse. The resolution of such problems needs careful analysis and designer ingenuity.

9.02 Landscaping

Landscaping of areas close to the hospital building is to a large extent determined by functional requirements for car parking and access; privacy for ground-floor clinical rooms; sitting areas for children, the elderly and staff. The design of car parking so as to provide easy access to the main entrance while ameliorating the impression of the hospital floating in a sea of cars is one problem facing the designer. Service routes – particularly hearse access – should be screened. Courtyards are particularly useful for creating centres of visual interest as well as spaces for sitting out.

9.03 Interior design and lighting

Much has been done recently to encourage creation of internal environments in hospitals which reconcile functional and aesthetic needs, including preparation of a number of publications by the Department of Health and development of organisations such as Arts for Health, dedicated to encouraging expenditure of a modest amount of money on the arts. There is, however, little analytical (as opposed to illustrative) work dealing with the health building environment and nothing to match the authoritative US publication *Hospital Interior Architecture* by Jane Malkin.

There is strong preference for daylighting in most areas of the hospital but this is difficult to achieve where the building has upper storeys. The problem starts with the strategic layout where the designer has to decide the extent to which external walls, perhaps those adjoining courtyards, will be provided for main corridors (benefitting all users) at the expense of departmental spaces. Wards (and many other departments) tend to be deep and even the six-bed room needs supplementary artificial lighting.

10 BIBLIOGRAPHY

A. Cox, and P. Groves, *Hospitals and Health-care Facilities*, Butterworth Architecture, 1990

Department of Health, *Health Building Notes* (various), HMSO

P. James and W. Tatton-Brown, *Hospitals: design and development*, Architectural Press, 1986

J. Kelly *et al.*, *Building for Mental Health*, MARU, South Bank University, 1990

J. Malkin, *Hospital Interior Architecture*, Van Nostrand Reinhold, 1992

A. Noble and R. Dixon, *Ward Evaluation: St Thomas' Hospital*, MARU, South Bank University, 1977

Nuffield Provincial Hospitals Trust, *Studies in the Functions and Design of Hospitals*, Oxford University Press, 1955

J. D. Thompson and G. Goldin, *The Hospital: a social and architectural history*, Yale University Press, 1975

18 Eating and drinking

Fred Lawson, John Rawson and Frank Bradbeer

CI/SfB(1976): 51
UDC: 725.71

Fred Lawson is a consultant in the field of hotel and catering design, John Rawson and Frank Bradbeer are architects

Contents

1 INTRODUCTION

1.01
Spaces for eating and drinking have to be looked at from two points of view, that of the customer, and that of the proprietor.

- The customer will choose a particular establishment, not only because it sells food or drink but because it also sells:
  - somewhere to entertain a guest in peace: as in good restaurants
  - entertainment: as in nightspots, or dinner-dancing venues
  - fast service: as in cafés and fast-food outlets

- The proprietor is running a labour-intensive business for profit in a competitive environment. Efficiency of every part of the operation must be maximised. Skilful planning can have a big effect on labour requirements, and consequently on the cost of operating.

1.02 Types of facility
Eating and drinking establishments fall into a number of broad categories:

- Restaurants: commercial self-service and waiter service operations, possibly licensed for alcohol. Includes cafés and snack bars
- Canteens: semi- or non-commercial operations in educational, industrial, or government establishments
- Take-aways: fast-food outlets with or without customer seating space
- Transport catering: kitchens providing pre-packed meals in bulk, e.g. for airlines
- Public houses: alcohol sales with or without food service.

The differences between these operations lie in:

- Variety of food offered
- Method of service
- Space and facilities available to the customer
- Amount of food processed on site
- Emphasis on the sale of alcoholic drinks
- Decor and degree of sophistication
- Price level.

Boundaries between these factors can be blurred, and the whole field is constantly changing.

1.03 Location
Location will determine success or failure of a facility. Food service establishments should be located where people need to obtain food, such as:

- Motorway service areas
- Hotels
- City centres
- Tourist attractions
- Main railway stations
- Airports
- Department stores

These are best served by different types of outlets. For instance, chain fast-food outlets suit high street sites in city centres. Up-market restaurants are in less expensive locations in or near good hotels or major up-market residential areas.

A balance has to be found between:-

- The availability of customers
- Cost of the location
- Accessibility: customer parking and goods access

In a major location such as an airport or motorway service station a selection of outlets will be provided. The customers can choose between different types of meal depending on the time and money they have available. In a city centre there will be a number of different restaurants: fast-food, bistros, trattorias, ethnic, up-market, etc. also giving choice.

Self-advertising of the establishment may be vital: those hidden away in basements or on upper floors may not be able to catch much passing trade, and may also have extra costs in goods handling.

1.04 External planning
As in hotels, the external access is crucial. The entrances must be clearly defined, and separated. Customers, staff and goods must each be provided for. Parking must be available for customers and deliveries. External appearance is very important. The building should be self-advertising, and may need to be flood-lit at night.

2 BASIC PLANNING

2.01
Food supply and consumption can be thought of as three overlapping industrial processing circles: for cooking, dishes, and customers. Each circle rotates separately: the product (food) is transferred from circle to circle.

1 The cooking circle. This consists of:

- Goods inwards: food supplies
- Storage
- Processing
  - preparation
  - cooking
  - serving: food transferred to circle 2
  - equipment cleaned and prepared for re-use
- Goods outwards: disposal of waste

2 The servery circle. Crockery and cutlery, whether recyclable or disposable, has to be processed:

- Goods inwards; supplies purchased
- Storage
- Processing
  - servery: food added to dishes
  - moved to table; food moves to circle 3.
  - returned from table – dishwashing
  - storage for re-use
- Goods outwards: breakages and disposables.

One of the main decisions in a food system is whether the customers have access to the servery: In cheap establishments they do: it is self-service, though returns may be handled by staff. In higher-class ones, they do not: waiters carry plates from the servery to the table. Consequently, the servery will be placed either outside or inside the kitchen.

3 The customer circle. The customer is also processed:

- Customers inwards: parking, reception, cloakroom.
- Storage: bar, waiting area
- Processing
  - food transferred from circle 2
  - drinks provided
  - billing and payment
- Customers outwards, coats returned.

The space provided for the customer varies from very little in fast-food shops to considerable in the highest-class restaurants. The bill will vary too. Food is not the only thing being sold. Part of the charge will go towards space or entertainment.

3 PUBLIC AREAS

3.01

Detailed planning is complicated. Reference should be made to specialist publications such as *Restaurants, Clubs and Bars* by Fred Lawson (see Bibliography). Only the briefest outline can be given here.

3.02 Seating areas and table arrangements

There are significant differences in seating arrangements depending on:

- Types of customer: price level, expectations
- Type of establishment: self-service, waited service, counter seating
- Grouping: table sharing, flexibility of arrangement
- Room characteristics: shape, obstructions, windows.

Furniture falls into four categories:

- Fitted counters or bars
- Fixed tables, usually pedestal or cantilevered
- Movable tables, with legs or pedestals
- Stackable tables

Area required per diner for various table arrangements is given in Table I. Various layouts are given in **18.1**. Formal dinner and banquet arrangements are given in **18.2** and **18.3**. An area for a band platform is shown in **18.4**.

Minimum reasonable sizes for tables are given in Table II and **18.5**. Upmarket restaurants will need to be more generous. Table height is about 760 mm. Tables just for drinking can be smaller, **18.6** and **18.7**.

Arrangements of tables are shown in **18.8** and **18.9**. Table legs may inhibit the storage of chairs when not in full use, **18.10**. Sizes of chairs are given in **18.11**.

Table I Space allowances

Type of seating and service	Area per diner (m²)
Commercial restaurants	
Table service	
● Square tables in rows	
Parallel seating 2	1.7 to 2.0
Parallel seating 4	1.3 to 1.7
Diagonal seating 4*	1.0 to 1.2
● Rectangular tables in rows	
Seating 4	1.3 to 1.5
Seating 6	1.0 to 1.3
● Circular tables in rows	
Seating 4	0.9 to 1.4
Fixed banquette seating	
● In booths seating 4	
Waitress service	0.7 to 1.0
Including counter for self service	0.9 to 1.4
Counter seating	
Tunnel counters	1.4 to 1.6
Single counters	1.7 to 2.0
Single counters used with wall units	1.2 to 1.5
Banquet groupings	
Multiple rows	1.0 to 1.2
Single row	1.1 to 1.4
Self-service (trolley clearance)	
Rectangular tables in rows	
● Dining area only	
Seating 4	1.5 to 1.7
Seating 6	1.2 to 1.4
Seating 8	1.1 to 1.3
● Including counter area	
Seating 4	1.7 to 2.0
Seating 6	1.3 to 1.8
Seating 8	1.2 to 1.6
Self-service (self-clearance)	
Rectangular tables in rows	1.3 to 1.5
● Dining area only	1.0 to 1.2
Seating 4	1.3 to 1.5
Seating 6	1.0 to 1.2
Seating 8	0.9 to 1.1
● Including counter service	
Seating 4	1.5 to 1.9
Seating 6	1.2 to 1.6
Seating 8	1.1 to 1.5
Canteens (industrial and office)	
Cafeteria service, tables for 4 to 6	1.1 to 1.4
Cafeteria service, tables for 8 or over	0.74 to 0.9
School dining rooms	
Primary schools	
Counter service	0.74
Family service	0.83
Secondary schools generally	0.9
Colleges of further education	1.1

* Economy in space is obtained with tables at 45°

In self-service restaurants tables will need to be in orderly lines with wide aisles to allow easy circulation access with trolleys for collecting returns. In waited restaurants a more flexible layout is desirable, but circulation flows of staff and customers must not conflict. Typical table arrangements are shown in **18.12**; where banquettes are used in **18.13**. Service tables, trolley parks and cash desks must also be accommodated.

3.03 Snack bars

Where meals are eaten at a counter, dimensional requirements are shown in **18.14**. Large short-order facilities can be planned as **18.15**.

4 KITCHENS

4.01 Size and type

Kitchen sizes depend on the number of meals served at peak periods of the day: normally lunch, but in some cases dinner. A kitchen for a residential or commercial restaurant serving a varied menu over a long period will be larger than a school or factory kitchen serving a limited menu only at set times for the same

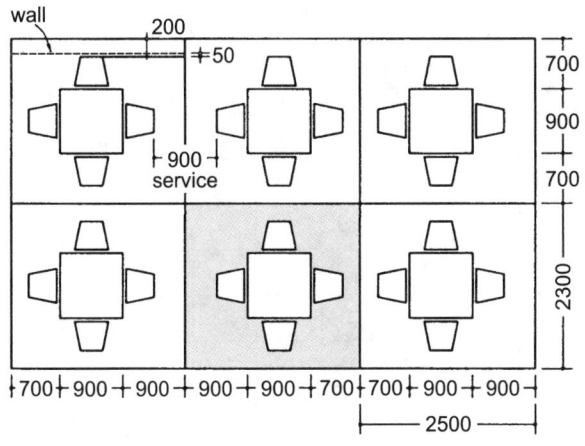

a *Square tables, square layout, local density 1.4 (in m² per diner)*

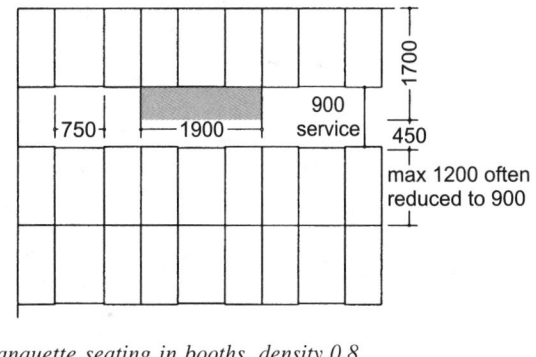

d *Banquette seating in booths, density 0.8*

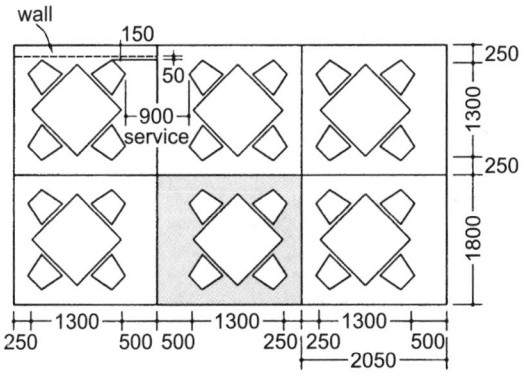

b *Square tables, diagonal layout, local density 0.92*

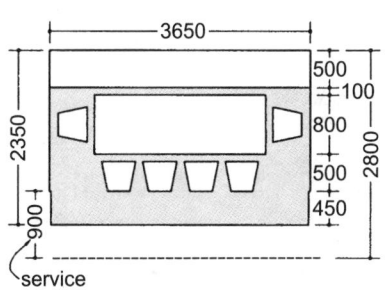

e *Large booth in recess, density 0.86 for 10 people, or 1.1 if only two people sit on bench seat*

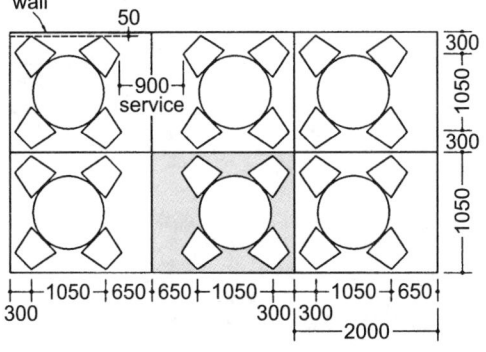

c *Circular tables, diagonal layout, density 0.82*

18.1 *Layouts for restaurant tables:*

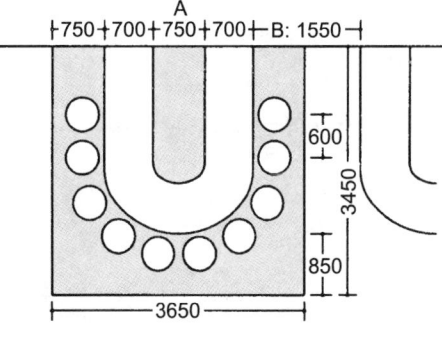

f *Counter service, density 1.26. (Dimensions A and B are increased where more than one waiter is employed)*

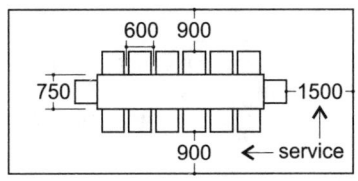

18.2 *Small formal dinner arrangement*

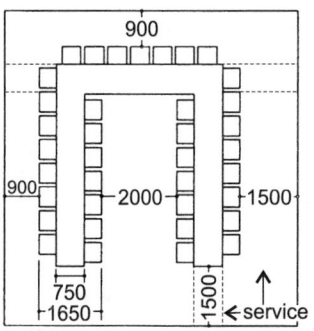

18.3 *Banquet layout. The U arrangement can be extended in both directions to the limits of the banqueting room*

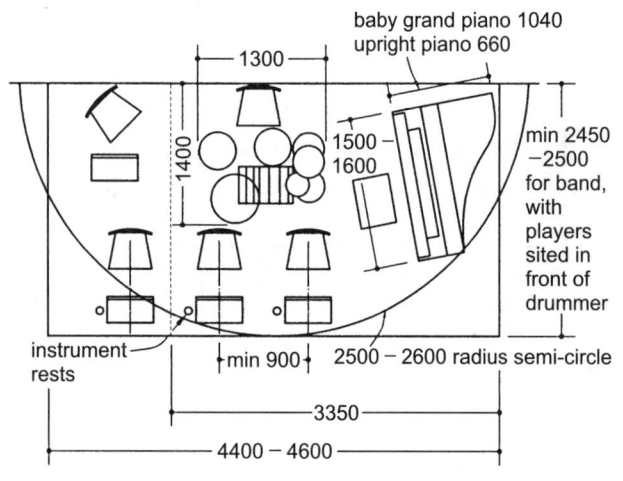

instrument rests

18.4 *A band platform*

baby grand piano 1040
upright piano 660

min 2450 −2500 for band, with players sited in front of drummer

2500 − 2600 radius semi-circle

	number of seats							
	1	2	3	4	5	6	7	8
A		⬚		⬚		⬚		⬚
B			⬚		⬚		⬚	
C				⬚		⬚		⬚
D	⬚	⬚	⬚					
E		⬚	⬚					
F			⬚					
G		⬚						
H	⬚							
I		⬚						
J								⬚
round	⬚	⬚	⬚	⬚	⬚	⬚	⬚	⬚

18.5 *Tables for various numbers of people (to be read together with Table II)*

Table II Table sizes for one to twelve diners (to be read in conjunction with 18.5)

Table type		Length of table in mm for widths of table in 50 mm increments													Round
No. of persons	Row	400	450	500	550	600	650	700	750	800	850	900	950	1000	1050	1100	Diam. (mm)
1	D	950	900	850	750	700	650										
	H				750	700	650										
	Round																750
2	A					950	900	850	800	750							
	E					950	900	850	800	750							
	D	1350	1250	1150	1100	1100	1100	1100									
	G				950	900	850	800	750								
	I	1300	1250	1050	950	900	850	800									
	Round																850
3	B								950	850							
	D	1800	1700	1700	1700	1700	1700	1700									
	E				1350	1350	1350	1350	1300	1100	1100	1100	1100	1100	1100	1100	
	F				1250	1200	1100	1050	950	900	850						
	Round																950
4	A								1150	1100	1100	1100	1100	1100	1100	1100	
	C								1100	1050	1000	950	900				
	Round																1050
5	B								1350	1350	1300	1300	1250	1200	1100	1100	
	Round																1100
6	A								1700	1700	1700	1700	1700	1700	1700	1700	
	C								1550	1550	1550	1450	1400	1250	1250	1200	
	Round																1200
7	B								1850	1800	1750	1750	1700	1700	1700	1700	
	Round																1300
8	A								2300	2300	2300	2300	2300	2300	2300	2300	
	C								1950	1900	1850	1750	1700	1700	1700	1700	
	J															1600	
	Round																1500
9	B								2400	2400	2350	2300	2300	2300	2300	2300	
10	A								2850	2850	2850	2850	2850	2850	2850	2850	
	C								2550	2500	2400	2350	2300	2300	2300	2300	
11	B								3000	2950	2950	2900	2850	2850	2850	2850	
12	A								3450	3450	3450	3450	3450	3450	3450	3450	
	C								3100	3050	3000	2900	2850	2850	2850	2850	

number of seats	table size: drinking mm	table size: eating mm
1	450 to 600	600 to 700
2	600 square	750 square
4	750 square	900 × 950
	–	1500 × 750
6	–	1400 × 950
	–	1700 × 750
8	–	1750 × 900
	–	2300 × 750

18.6 *Recommended rectangular table sizes relating to place numbers*

number of seats	table size: drinking mm	table size: eating mm
1	450 to 600	750
2	600	850
4	900	1050
6	1150	1200
8	1400	1500

18.7 *Recommended circular table sizes for various place numbers*

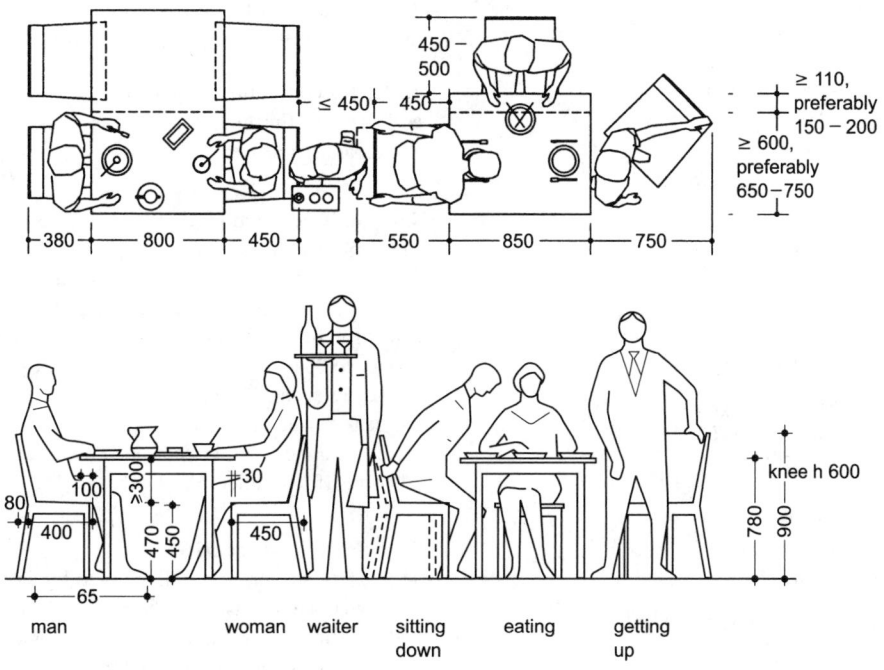

18.8 *Restaurant critical dimensions*

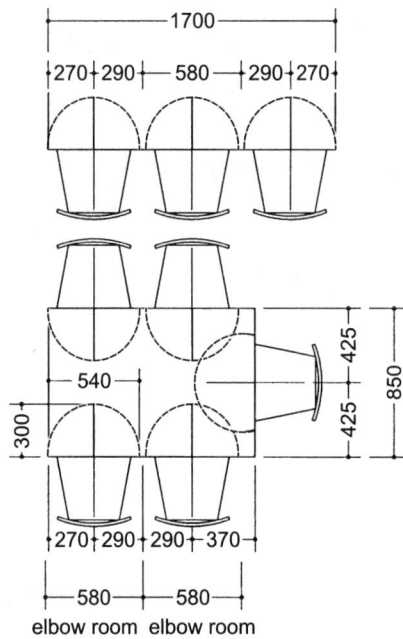

18.9 *Area required by an individual diner*

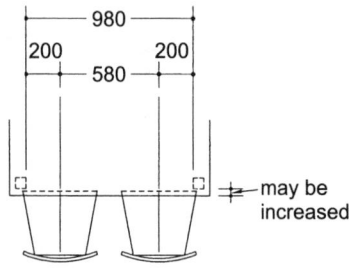

a *Allows comfort for diners, but chairs cannot be pushed under tables*

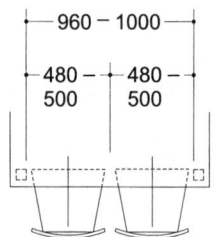

b *Allows stowage of chairs*

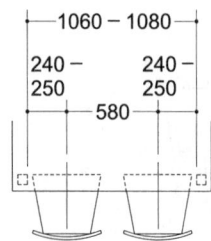

c *Chairs can be pushed inside table legs when diner comfortably seated*

18.10 *Obstruction by table legs:*

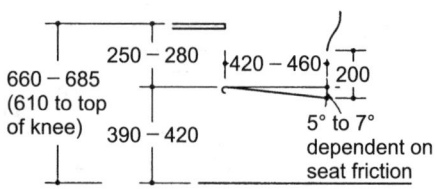

a *Dr Akerblom's recommendations*

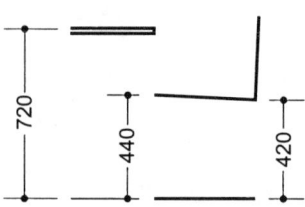

b *Chair without arms to Erik Berglund's recommendation*

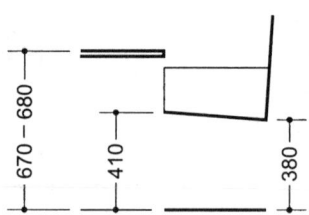

c *Chair with arms to Erik Berglund's recommendation*

18.11 *Heights of chairs and tables:*

number of people. As an approximate guide the ratio of dining to kitchen area will vary between:

- 3:1 where only one sitting
- 1:1 where two or three sittings per meal.

A 'finishing kitchen' for the cooking or heating up of 'convenience foods' will be smaller than the equivalent conventional kitchen, in which all the preparation and cooking processes are carried out. Typical requirements for a finishing kitchen are given in Table III. The ratio of total kitchen area to area required for servery, stores offices and staff facilities, **18.16**, will vary between:

- 2:1 for conventional kitchens
- 1.5:1 for finishing kitchens as finishing kitchens have less preparation space.

4.02 Staff accommodation
The employee ratios vary widely with the type of establishment. The average for commercial restaurants is 7.6 seats per employee. The number of meals sold per week per employee varies from 62 to 81 for full-menu table service to 151 for limited-menu table service to 234 for fast-food outlets. The peak number of employees may be relevant. The ratio of total employees to meals served over the peak period of is one employee to: 8 meals in full-menu table service, 20 meals in limited-menu table service and canteens, and 33 in fast-food outlets.

4.03 Safety and security
The Safety at Work Act will apply to kitchens. There will be risks to be guarded against from burns, scalds, cuts, bruises, breakages and electric shocks. All the usual fire protection will be necessary: self-closing smoke-control doors will be needed between the kitchen and dining room.

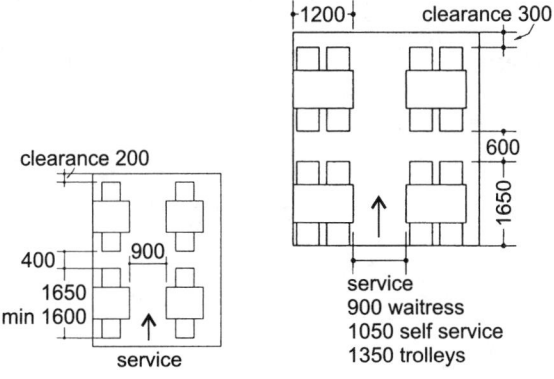

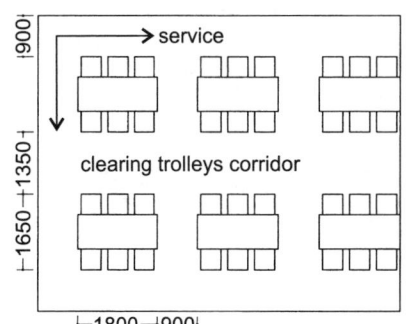

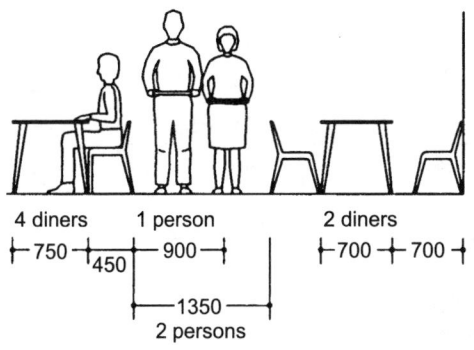

18.12 Minimum space between tables to allow for seating, access and circulation

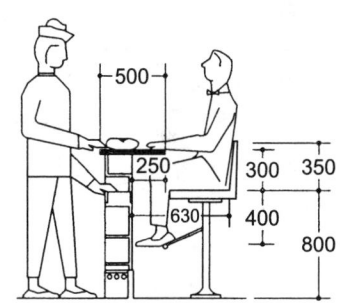

a High bar stool

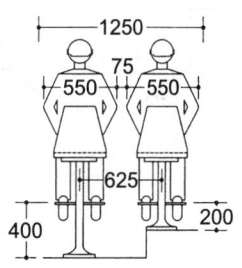

b Bar stool spacing

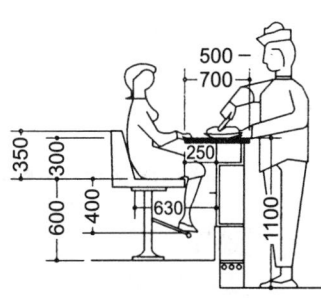

c Medium-height bar stool

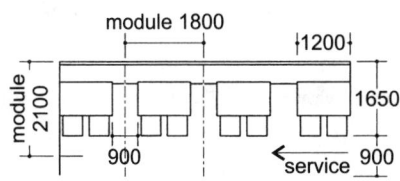

a Banquette seating along a wall

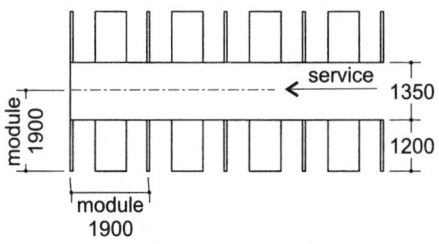

b Booth seating with banquettes

18.13

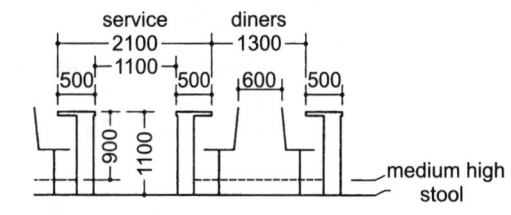

d High-density counter service

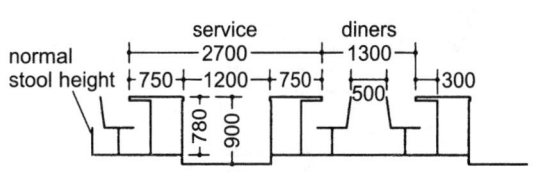

e Medium-density counter service

18.14 Counter-eating facilities:

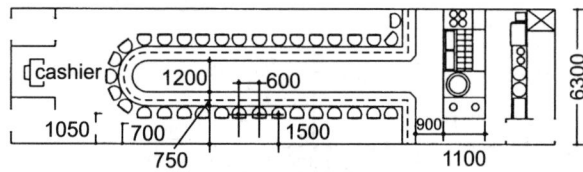

a *Long U-form counter*

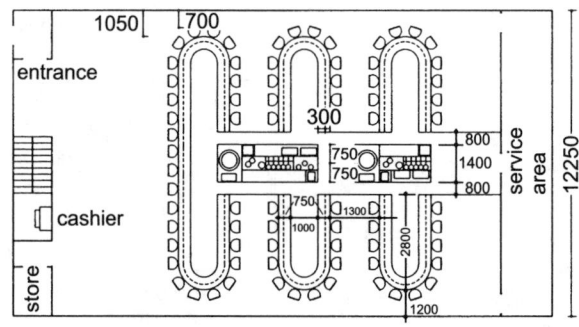

c *Paired U-form counters*

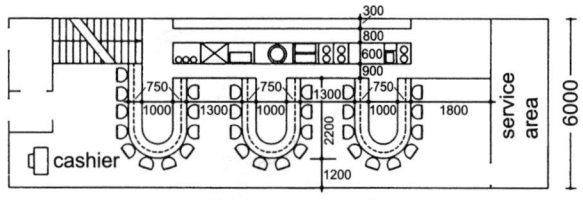

b *Multiple short U-forms counter*

18.15 *Counters for short-order restaurants*

Table III Finishing kitchens for pre-cooked frozen meals

Area	Equipment		Meals served per day – based on main meal period						
			50	100	200	400	600	800	1000
Goods entry	Scales capacity	kg	12.5	12.5	25.5	25.5	25.5	25.5	25.5
	Trolleys for frozen meal trays and general use		2	2	3	4	5	6	7
Cold stores	Deep freeze room (based on 7-day stock)	m³	1.3	2.5	5.0	10.0	15.0	20.0	22.0
	Normal cold room	m³	0.3	0.5	0.9	1.2	1.5	1.9	2.2
	(based on daily delivery of dairy produce, otherwise 3 deliveries per week)								
Dry stores	Shelving – width 450 mm length	m	6.1	9.1	15.2	21.3	27.4	33.5	39.6
	(for canned and dried items, 3 deliveries per week)								
Kitchen	Convection oven capacity	m³	0.09	0.18	0.37	1.02	1.10	1.47	1.84
	(based on reheating all frozen meals in 1 hour, ie 2 reheatings of average 30 minutes each)								
	Boiling tank or pressure steamer								
	(For 'boil-in-the-bag' food where this is to be used. Provision depends on type of equipment, e.g. rotating boiling tank 100 mm (40″) diameter produces a total of 120 bags/hour in 4 reheatings of approximately 15 minutes each)								
	Microwave oven 2 kilowatt units		1	1	1	1	2	2	3
	(Depends on number of snacks required and availability of alternative call-order equipment. Based on 30-second cycle of reheating with 4 snack items/loading)								
	Supplementary equipment Griller	m²	0.2	0.2	0.3	0.4	0.5	0.7	0.9
	(For call order grills and toast. Based on surface area)								
	Griddle	m²	0.2	0.3	0.4	0.5	0.7	0.8	1.0
	(for snack catering, particularly at breakfast)								
	Fryer	kg/hr	10	25	45	90	135	180	225
	(for 'flashing off' blanched frozen meals. Based on 15 minutes use before and 15 minutes during meal period)								
	Boiling rings	No	2	2	3	4	5	6	7
	(for reheating of canned vegetables, soups, etc)								
Wash-up (crockery, cutlery, etc.)	Wash-sterilising unit length for dishwashing	m	2.7	3.4	3.7				
	Capacity of machine	pieces/hr			1200	2400	3600	4800	6000
	Sink for serving dishes, etc (length)	mm	600	600	750	900	1050	1200	1200
	Burnishing machine		–	–	–	hand	hand	hand	hand
	Waste disposal units		1	1	1	1	2	2	2
	(based on 550 W machines assuming part refuse collection. For complete waste disposal 2230 W units employed)								

Source: Paper by D. J. Cottam given to Catering Teachers Association Annual Conference

Wolverhampton, October 1969. Based on equipment by Stotts of Oldham

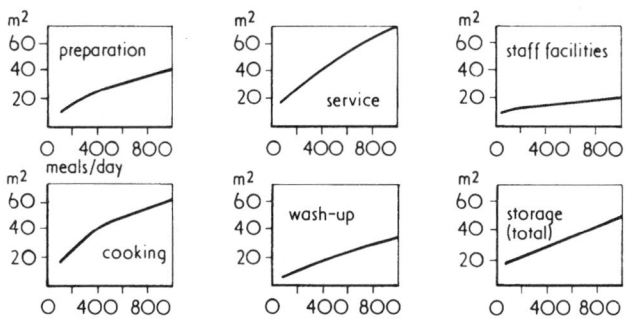

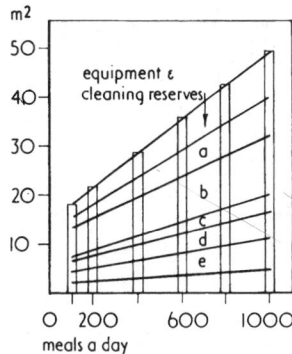

18.16 *Kitchen space requirements for various functions*
a *Preparation*
b *Service*
c *Staff facilities*
d *Cooking*
e *Washing up*
f *Storage* (*total*)

18.17 *Total storage requirements in conventional kitchens, segments are covered in detail in* **18.18**

Control of all accesses to the building will be advisable to reduce pilferage, owing to the value of the stocks. Substantial locks, doors and door-frames will be needed, and facilities for checking deliveries.

4.04 Goods access
For sizes of vehicles see Chapter 4. Typical delivery arrangements are:

- Dry goods: weekly or fortnightly
- Frozen food: weekly
- Vegetables: twice weekly
- Perishable foods: daily
- Refuse and waste removal: daily

Bulk refuse containers may be used instead of bins. These are 0.57–0.85 m³ capacity. Refuse may be sited in a refrigerated area to reduce nuisance from odour and flies, at a temperature of 2–5°C.

4.05 Storage area
Typical storage areas for conventional kitchens are given in **18.17** and in **18.18**. Racks for storage of containers should approximate to the heights and widths of the containers to be stored allowing about 50 mm between packages for easy access. The top shelf should not be higher than 1950 mm, **18.19**. Shelves and open bins must be kept at least 200 mm above the floor to allow a clear space for access and cleaning and to deter rodents. Shelves for frequently used or heavy items should be between 700 and 1500 mm high.

Containers may have to be returned to suppliers and space must be allowed for their storage and collection.

4.06 Preparation areas
Kitchen layout is determined by:

- The sizes of equipment and fittings
- Space for access and circulation.

Some typical dimensions are:

- Work top and sink top height: 900 mm (865 will do)
- Wall bench width: 600–750 mm
- Island bench or table width: 900–1050 mm
- Length of work area within convenient reach: 1200–1800 mm
- Length for two people working together: 2400–3000 mm.

There are usually four main areas of food preparation:

- Vegetables
- Meat and fish

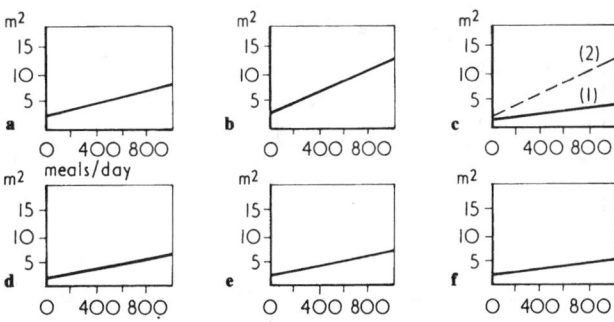

18.18 *Storage space requirements. These figures are based on the number of meals per day in a modern conventional kitchen using a proportion of frozen foods. Where mainly pre-cooked frozen meals are used, a separate vegetable store may not be needed; more deep freeze space should be provided*
a *Vegetable store for three deliveries per week*
b *Dry goods store, three days' supply*
c *Deep freeze, seven days' supply: (1) conventional use, (2) pre-cooked frozen meals*
d *Cold room, daily delivery of perishable food*
e *Goods entry area, including weighing and checking*
f *refuse store where bins are used*

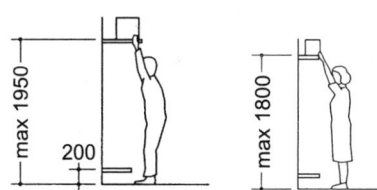

a *Limits for maximum reach for men and women*

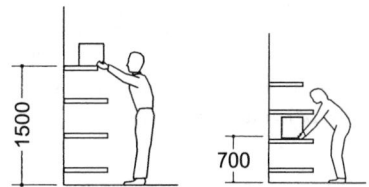

b *Convenient reach for heavy or frequently used items*

18.19 *Heights for storage shelving*

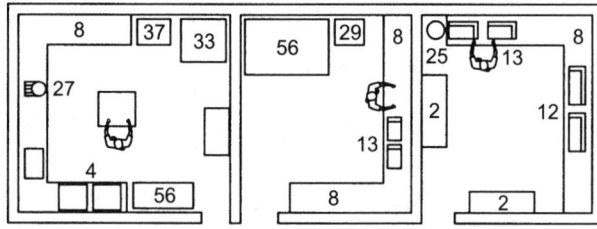

a *Separate rooms*

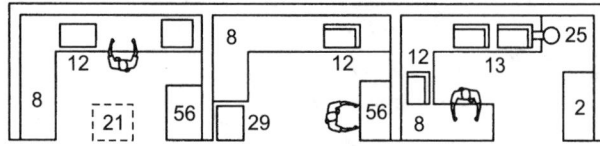

b *Bays*

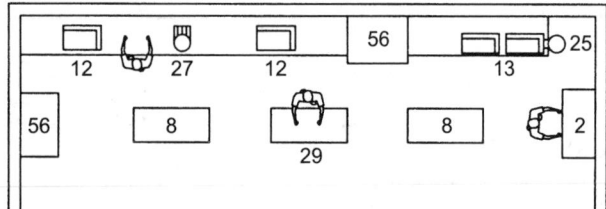

c *Open plan kitchen*

18.20 *Alternative preparation area arrangements (see **18.36** for key to numbers)*

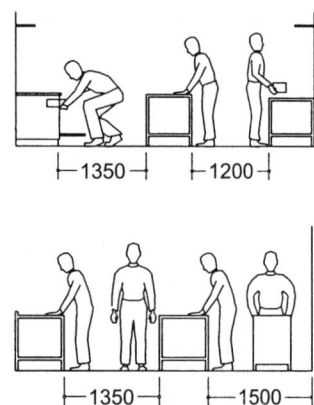

18.21 *Minimum space between equipment for working and circulation*

● Pastry
◑ General

Preparation areas may be segregated by:

● Separate rooms adjoining the main kitchen
● Low walls, approx 1200 mm high between these areas and main kitchen
● The arrangement of benches and fittings. Alternative arrangements for preparation areas are shown in **18.20**.

4.07 Cooking equipment

About 30 per cent of kitchen floor space is occupied by equipment, 10 per cent by worksurfaces and 60 per cent by circulation. Too little space will lead to obstruction and accidents. Too much will

18.22 *Kitchen equipment*

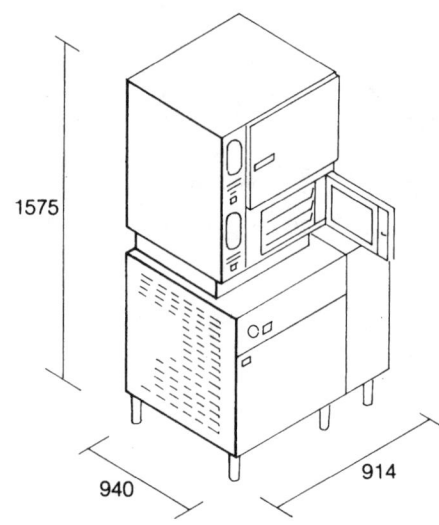

a *Convection steamer with two compartments*

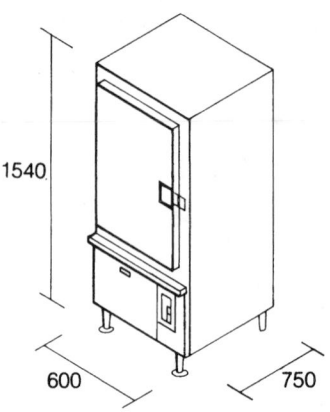

b *Atmospheric steaming oven with steam generator in base*

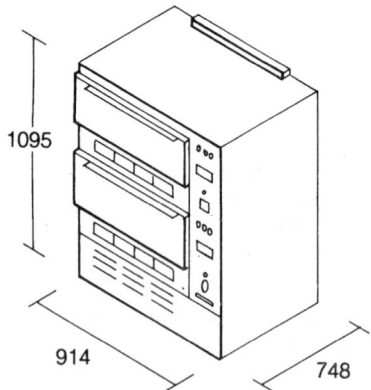

c *Tiered convection ovens, each 65 litres rated 8.8 kW*

lead to extended lines of circulation causing wasted time, and increased cleaning, lighting and maintenance costs. Recommended dimensions are shown in **18.21**.

Details of typical equipment are given in Tables IV and V. Some items are shown in **18.22**. A typical kitchen layout is given in **18.23**, with elevations of the equipment in **18.24**.

Placing equipment around the walls is common in smaller kitchens and leads to savings in engineering services. Island grouping will be necessary in larger kitchens: access for cleaning and maintenance is good, and the perimeter sites can be used for employees' workspaces. But island sites will need

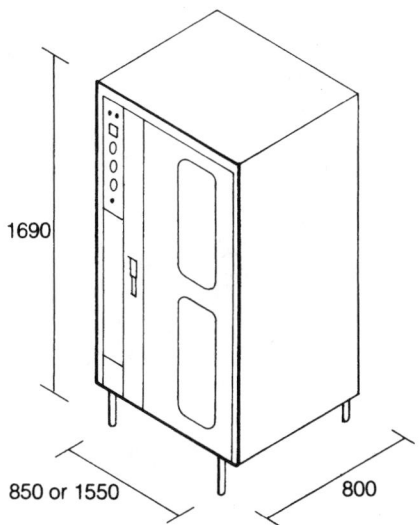

d *Autoreverse convection oven*

1690
850 or 1550
800

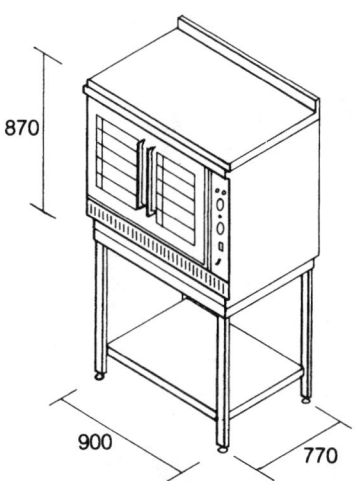

e *Forced convection oven on stand, 145 litres, 9.2 kW*

870
900
770

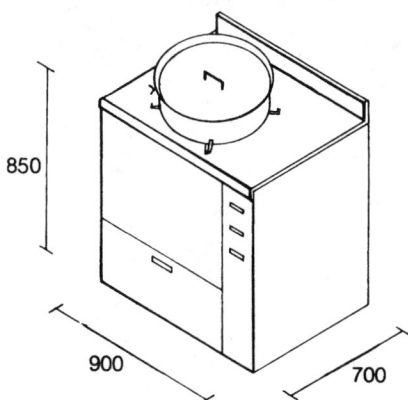

f *Dual-purpose boiling pan, 90 litres. Direct fired or steam jacketed*

850
900
700

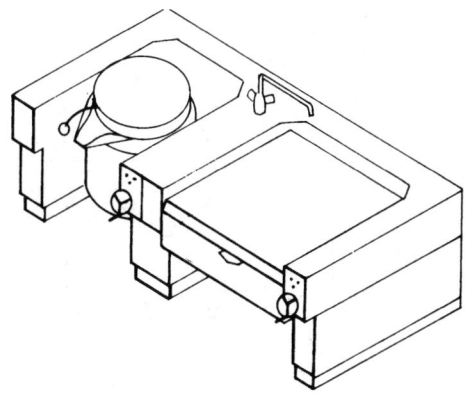

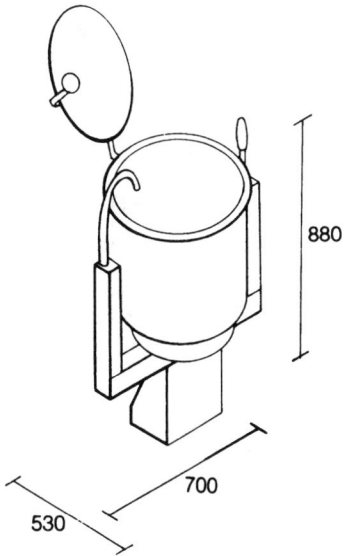

h *Tilting kettle with swivel cold water feed, 40 litres capacity, electric or steam heated*

880
700
530

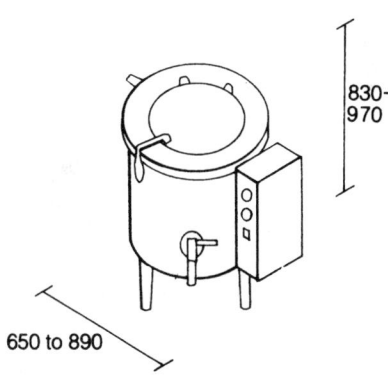

i *Vacuum boiling pan with electric or steam heated jacket, 20, 90 or 135 litres*

830-970
650 to 890

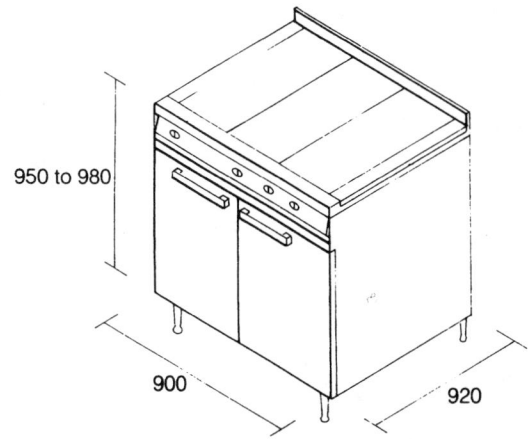

j *Heavy-duty oven range, 200 litres, 18 kW (electric), hob with three solid hotplates or griddle plate*

950 to 980
900
920

g *Tilting kettle and braising pan console:*

Unit width	Kettle Capacity	Rating	Bratt pan Capacity	Rating
1200 mm	*70 litres*	*15 kW*	*68 litres*	*9 kW*
1400 mm	*200 litres*	*27 kW*	*89 litres*	*12 kW*

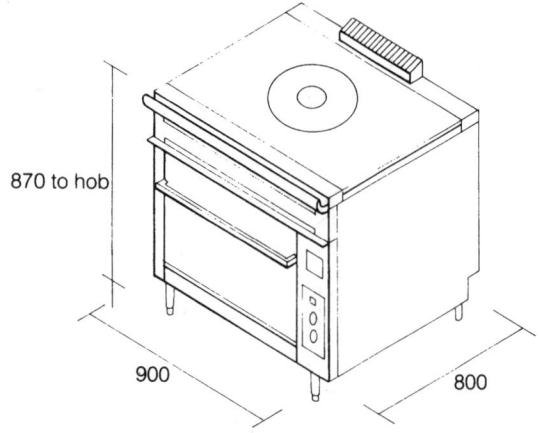

k *Heavy-duty oven range, 150 litres, 16.5 kW, with drop-down door and solid hob top with tapered heat*

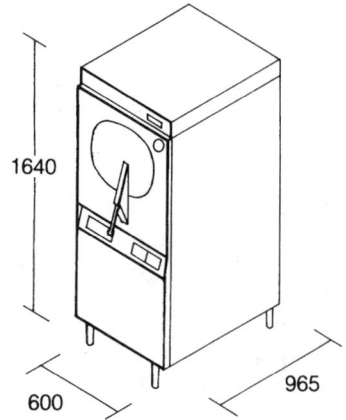

n *High-pressure steamer on stand, 12 kW rating*

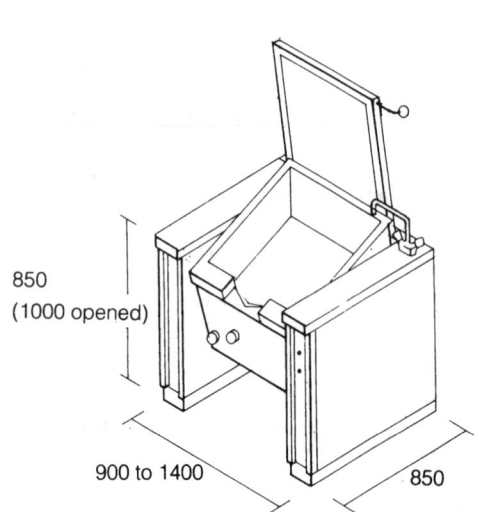

l *Bratt or braising pan with pillar support:*

Capacity	Width	Rating
40 litres	900 mm	6.4 kW
80	1200	11.8
100	1400	14.8

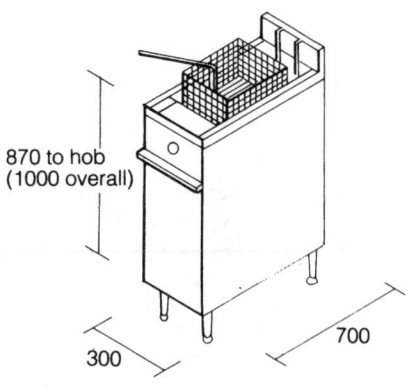

o *Deep fryer with one basket 16 litres oil capacity, 9 kW. Output 22.7 kg chips per hour*

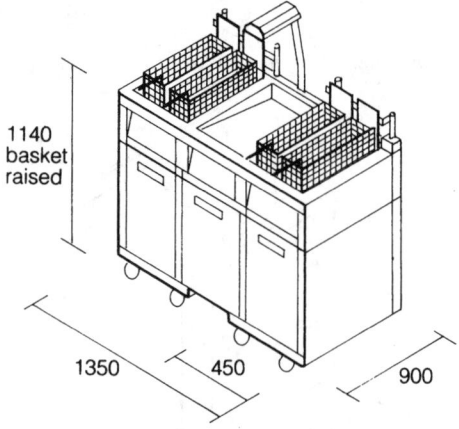

p *Combination fast food fryer with dual deep fryers and central chip dump. Each fryer 21.5 kW. Automatic basket lifting, integral oil filtration*

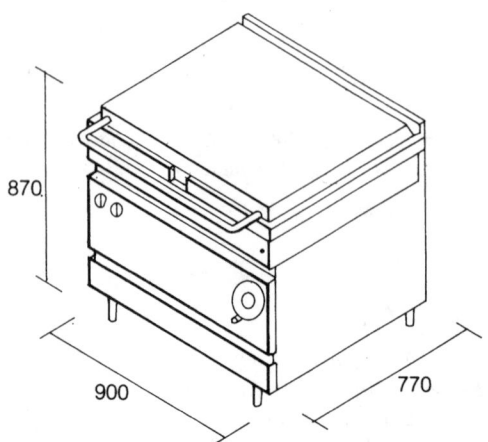

m *Tilting Bratt pan with operating wheel and trunion*

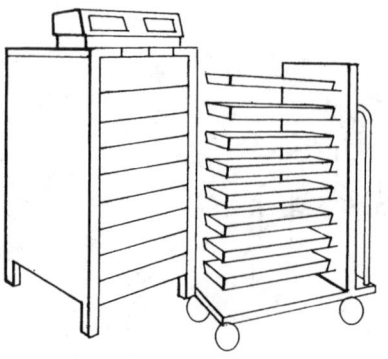

q *Infrared (regethermic) oven system, 4.7 to 5.0 kW*

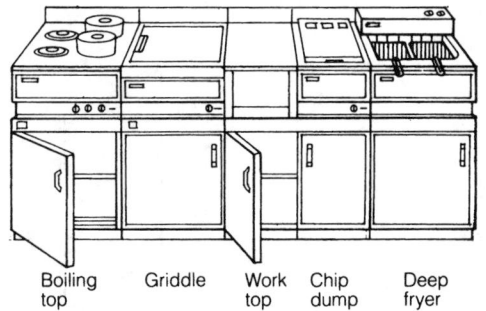

| Boiling top | Griddle | Work top | Chip dump | Deep fryer |

r *Example of combined units with under-counter cupboards*

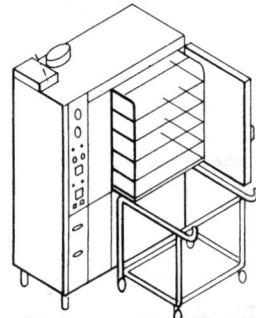

s *Bulk loading system with mobile transporter*

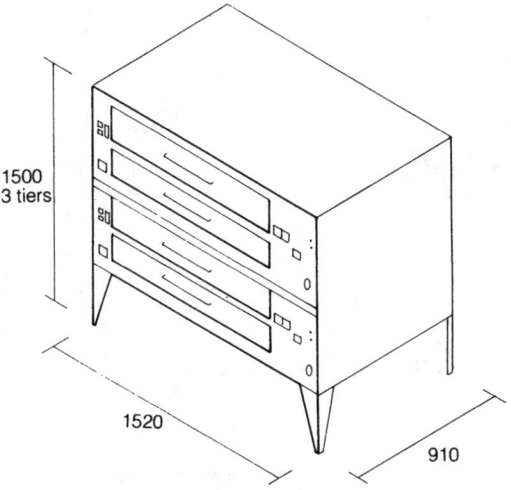

1500 3 tiers

1520 910

t *Tiered pastry or pizza oven*

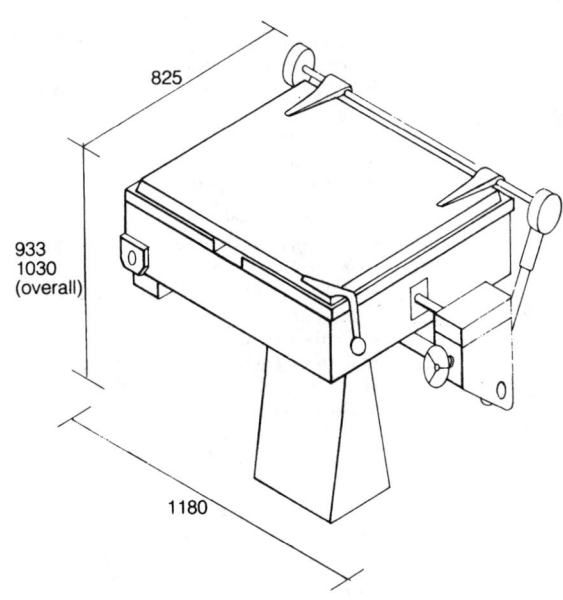

825

933 1030 (overall)

1180

u *Tilting bratt pan*

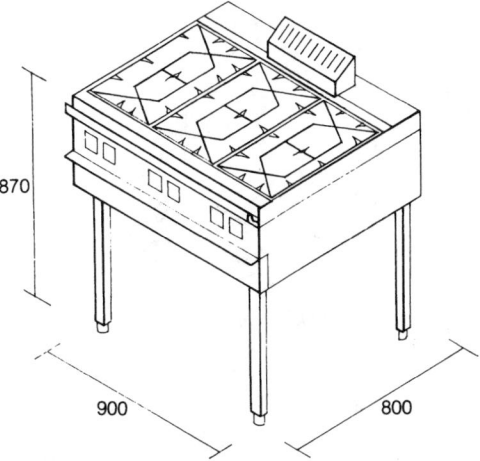

870

900 800

v *Heavy duty boiling table with open gas burners*

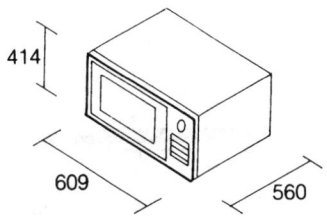

414

609 560

w *Microwave oven, 2.6 kW supply, 1300 W output rings, 8 kW rating*

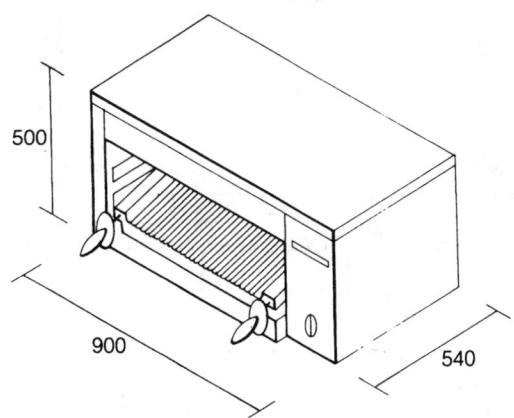

500

900 540

x *Salamander grill, wall or stand mounted, 7.5 kW rating*

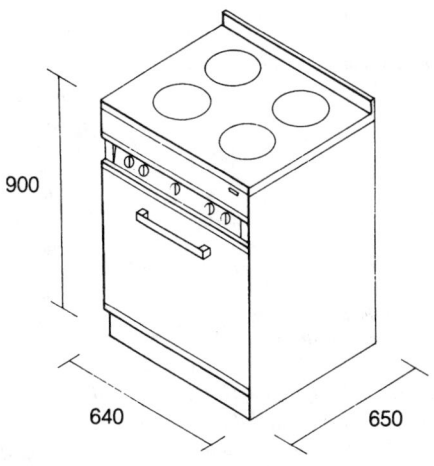

900

640 650

y *Medium-duty oven range, 84 litres with four radiant rings, 8 kW rating*

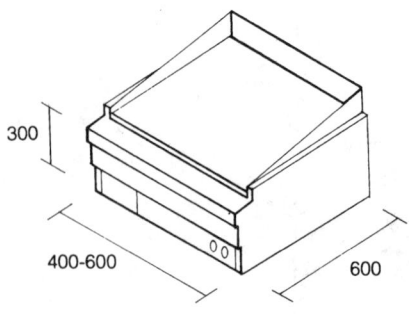

z *Griddle, counter or stand mounted, 8 kW rating*

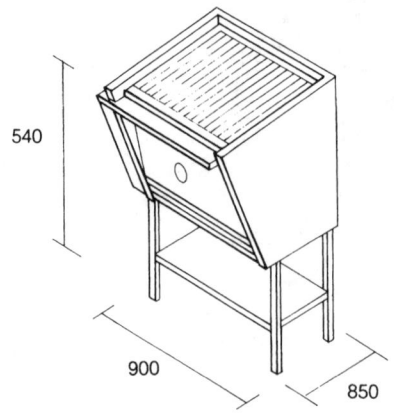

aa *Underfired grill, 37 kW*

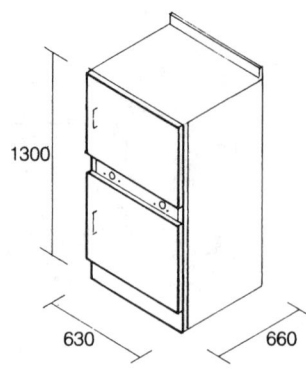

ab *Two-tier general purpose oven each 80 litres capacity*

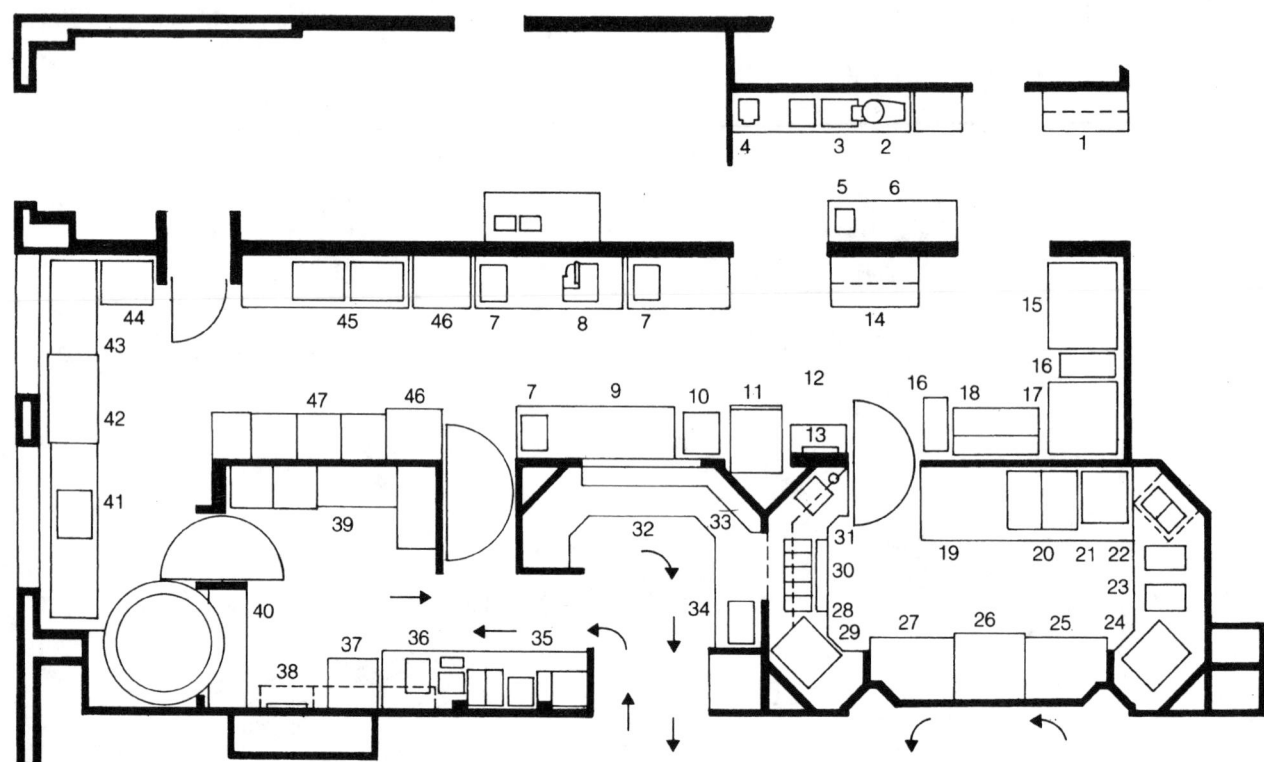

Vegetable preparation area
1 *Trolley*
2 *Potato peeler*
3 *Double sink*
4 *Cutter/chipper with knife rack*
5 *Vegetable mill, with blade rack*
6 *Mobile table*

General preparation area
7 *Workbench with sink and wall shelving*
8 *Meat slicer*
9 *Marble pastry slab with flour bins under bench*
10 *Food mixer*
11 *Refrigerator*
12 *Ultraviolet insect control (on wall)*
13 *Wash-hand basin*

Main kitchen, primary cooking area
14 *Mobile heated trolley*
15 *Mobile two-tier convection oven*
16 *Boiling unit*
17 *Two induction heaters*
18 *Mobile workbench with shelves over*

Display kitchen – finishing area and servery
19 *Tiled bench with access to time clocks and refrigerator valves*
20 *Two induction heaters over bench with chilled drawers*
21 *Boiling top*
22 *Grill/salamander mounted over tiled worktop with inset heated pans*
23 *Two fryers with chilled drawers under bench*
24 *Microwave convection oven on corner shelving*
25 *Tiled heated worktop over deep freeze cupboard*
26 *Gas broiler with shelving under*
27 *Tiled heated worktop*
28 *Tiled serving counter with shelf over*
29 *Microwave convection oven*
30 *Counter top with inset trays and cutting board*
31 *Inset sink and waste bin in corner recess*

Pantry and beverage area
32 *Fitted wall units*
33 *Two toasters*
34 *Large toaster over refrigerator*
35 *Beverage stand fitted with glass/cup racks and housing fruit juice dispenser, shake milk dispenser and two coffee machines*
36 *Water boiler stand with inset sink and drainer*
37 *Chest freezer*
38 *Wash-hand basin*
39 *Clean storage units*

Dishwashing area
40 *Carousel receiving unit with tray support shelf. Trolley bins under*
41 *Rack slide for soiled dishes with inset sink and basket shelves over*
42 *Conveyor dishwashing machine*
43 *Roller table for clean dishes*
44 *Mobile table*
45 *Double pot sink*
46 *Mobile pot racks*
47 *Mobile glass racks*

18.23 *Kitchens of Post House Hotel, Sevenoaks*
The plans of one of the latest Post House hotels illustrate the considerable advances made in food services equipment and planning in the 1980s. The facilities include separate main and display kitchens. Fortes, by far the largest hotel group in Great Britain, have also been a leading innovator in developing efficient systems of food production consistent with high quality.
Development: Trust House Forte Ltd. Plans prepared by Stangard Ltd

Table IV Kitchen equipment

Type	Main features	Typical size and rating		
Ovens	Transfer heat to food within an enclosure. May use hot air (circulated by natural or fan assisted convection), infrared or microwave emission	(s) – small units (m) – medium duty (h) – heavy duty		
General-purpose oven	Using hot air for baking, roasting or reheating. May be raised on stand or in tiers. Preloaded mobile racks used for speed and convenience. Working capacities: Trayed dishes 65–75 kg/m³ (4–5 lb/ft³) Poultry, meats 110–130 kg/m³ (7–8 lb/ft³)			
Oven range	Ovens combined with boiling hob top. Oven capacity based on shelf area. 0.015m² (24 in.²) per meal	(s) (m) (h)	80 l. 160 l. 200 l.	11 kw 14 kW 16 kW
Forced convection oven	Hot air circulated at high velocities up to 4.5 m/s (900 ft/min.) with directional flows to provide rapid heating, larger batch loadings, even temperatures. Normal cooking cycle: frozen food 25–35 min.	(s) (m) (m) (h)	50 l. 110 l. 200 l. 300 l.	2.6 kW 6 kW 9.3 kW 13.3 kW
Pastry oven	Tiered shallow ovens to give uniform heating for baking, pastry, pizza, etc. Capacity based on area: 0.004 m² (6 in.²) per meal			
Roasting cabinet	Special cabinets for roasting meat, or mechanised spit roasting (poultry, joints, kebabs)			
Rotary or reel ovens	Specialised equipment for large-scale bakeries and continuous-cooking ovens			
Low-temperature ovens	For slow cooking of meat, etc. at 107°C (225°F) to reduce moisture loss. Specialist applications			
Microwave ovens	High-frequency (2450 MHz alternating electromagnetic waves used to generate heat in dipolar molecules of food and water. Energy conversion factor high. Typical cooking cycle: 45–60 seconds (reducing with quantity)	(s) (m) (h)	20 l. 28 l. 28 l.	0.6 kW 1.3 kW 2 kW
Infra-red ovens	Interspaced rows of heating elements in quartz tubes emitting mainly radiant heat in waveband 1.5–5.0μm. Mainly used for reheating frozen food. Heating cycle 20–25 minutes			
Steam ovens	Free steam at or near atmospheric pressure: 3.5 kN/m² (1/2 lb/in.²). Used for large-scale catering	(m)	200 l.	9 kW
Pressure steamers	Pressure steam up to 103 kN/m² (15 lb/in.²) using jets for rapid heating of frozen food. May have option of free-vented steam	(m)		120 kW
Boiling and frying	May use loose pans and containers placed on or over external heat (gas burner, electric element, heated plate). Larger units incorporate heaters as part of design (with thermostatic control)			
Boiling tables	Usually provide four or six open burners or solid tops with tapered heat. Used as supplement or alternative to oven range	(s) (m)	2 ring solid	3.6 kW 11 kW
Halogen elements	Alternative to gas burners and electric radiant rings. Used in hobs to provide instantly adjustable heat output			
Induction heaters	Electromagnetic alternating currents of 25 kHz directed through ceramic hob. Used to induce eddying currents in steel pans producing indirect heating for boiling or frying	(s) (m) (h)	1 ring 2 ring 4 ring	3.6 kW 7 kW 14 kW
Boiling pans and kettles	Containers heated directly or indirectly (preferred). Emptied by tap or by tilting over drain. Output 45 litre pan: Root vegetables – 100–150 meals Soup – 150–200 meals	(m) (m) (h)	45 l. 90 l. 135 l.	7 kW 11.5 kW 14.5 kW
Bratt pans	Shallow tilting frying pans which are also used for stewing and braising. 150–350 mm (6–10 in.) deep. Mounted on trunnions for emptying	(m) (h)	0.28 m² 0.44 m²	6.4 kW 12 kW
Deep-fat fryers	Food immersed in heated oil. Frying temperatures typically 160–190°C (320–375°F). Fume extraction required. Cooking cycles: typically 6–7 minutes	(s) (m) (m) (h)	5 l. 7 l. 16 l. 20 l.	3 kW 5.8 kW 10 kW 20 kW
Pressure fat fryers	Fryer fitted with sealed lid. Operated at 63 kN/m² (9 lb/in.²), combining frying with pressure steaming of moisture. Output: 80–90 portions/hour			
Griddles	Shallow frying using surface contact with heated plate. Temperatures, 170–220°C (340–430°F)	(s) (m)	0.17 m² 0.4 m²	4 kW 7.5 kW
Grilling	Food exposed to elements emitting high intensity radiation in wave band 0.7–2.2 μm	(s) (m) (h)	0.1 m² 0.25 m² 0.27 m²	3 kW 5.7 kW 7.5 kW
Salamanders, broilers	Top heating over food on grating or branding plates			
Grills, char-grills, char-broilers	Bottom heating using red hot tiles, plates, or charcoal. Fume extraction required. May be featured in display cooking			
Water boilers, beverage-making equipment	Includes boilers operated by steam pressure or expansion of water. May be installed in kitchen, in vending units, under service counter or as café sets. Capacity: Per litre 4–5 cups Per gallon 18–20 cups	(s) (m) (h)	28 l./h 48 l./h 68 l./h	2.8 kW 5.3 kW 7.5 kW
Holding units	Used to keep food hot or cold until served. Mainly incorporated into service counters			
Bains-marie	Heated well-fitted with loose containers (standardised sizes). May be dry or water filled. Thermostatically controlled at about 74°C (165°F)	(s) (m)	2 units 4/6 units	0.5 kW 2 kW
Chilled shelves, wells and plates	For cold storage and display of salads, dairy products and prepared sweets. Usually incorporates under-counter refrigerator. Temperature about 3.5°C (37–41°F)			
Hot cupboards	Heated cabinets to keep plates and food warm prior to service. May be under-counter units, pass-through cabinets or mobile. Temperature kept at 76–88°C (170–190°F). Capacity: Standard 1,200 mm (4ft) counter unit holds about 300 plates	(m) (m)	1.2 m wide 1.8 m wide	3 kW 4.5 kW

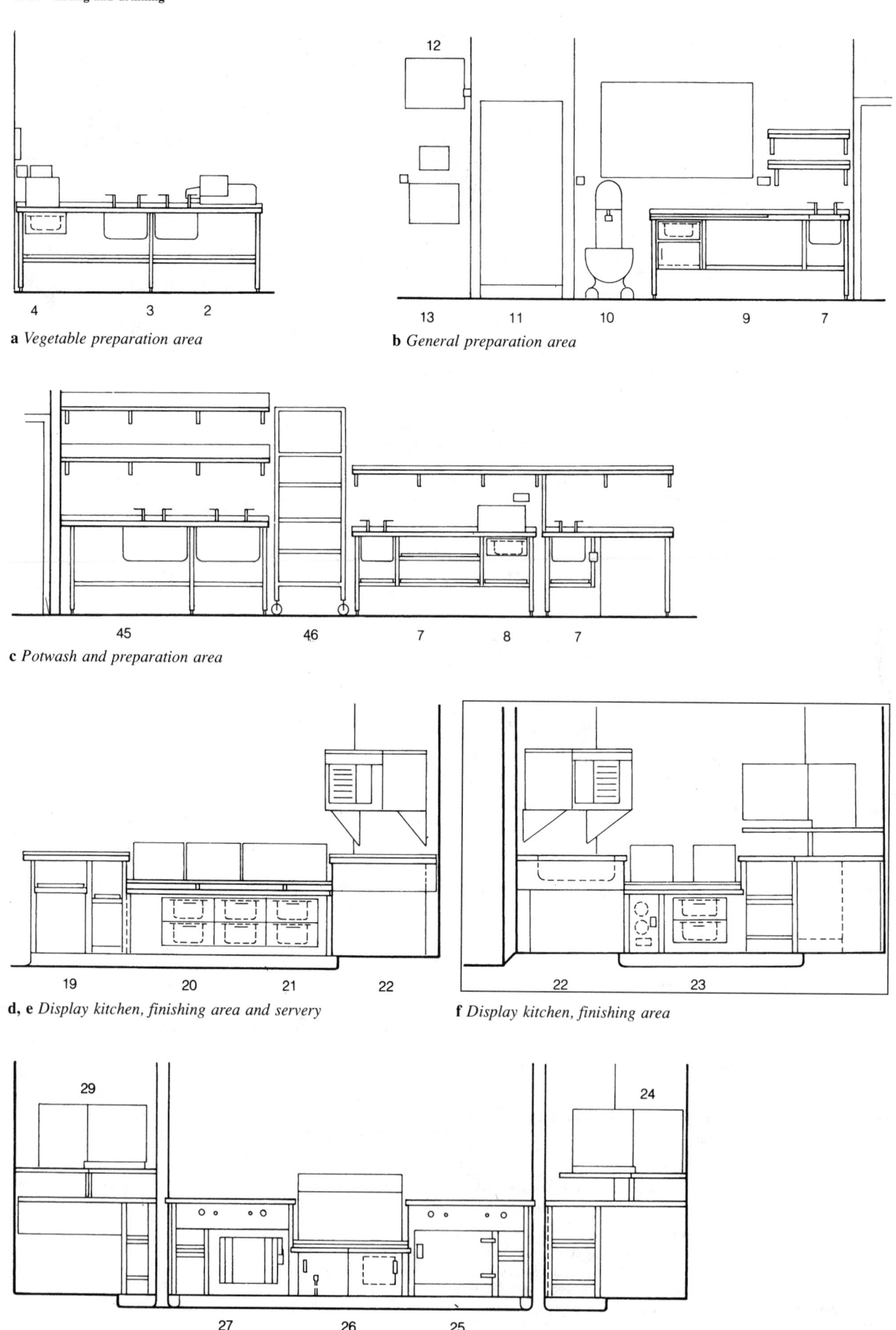

a Vegetable preparation area

b General preparation area

c Potwash and preparation area

d, e Display kitchen, finishing area and servery

f Display kitchen, finishing area

g Beverage counter

18.24 Elevations of installed kitchen equipment:

Table V Ovens and cooking equipment sizes and capacity

Oven type and capacity (m³)	Internal* size (mm)	External* size (mm)	Loading (kW)
Oven ranges			
0.113	530 × 460 × 460	760 × 810 × 870	11–14
0.142	600 × 600 × 400	910 × 870 × 870	12–15
Forced-air convection ovens			
0.113		810 × 810 × 870	8
0.198		1020 × 910 × 1370	10–12
0.283		1120 × 1170 × 1580	13–15
Pastry ovens			
1 deck	760 × 610 × 230	960 × 1090 × 1380	14.4
2 deck	760 × 910 × 230	1270 × 1090 × 1680	14.4
Roasting cabinets			
0.48	610 × 660 × 1220	1170 × 910 × 1600	8.5
0.85	840 × 760 × 1320	1400 × 1020 × 1680	12
Atmospheric type steaming oven			
0.17	450 × 530	770 × 840 × 1520	6
Boiling tables			
(Consult individual manufacturers		1220 × 760 × 860	12.4
for number of plates etc.)		1680 × 760 × 860	21.2
		2130 × 760 × 860	30.2
Gas-fired boiling pans			
45 litres		910 × 990 × 760	7
90 litres		1040 × 1120 × 840	11
135 litres		1190 × 1240 × 860	14.2
180 litres		1190 × 1300 × 910	16.5
Tilting kettle			
40 litres		760 × 510 × 860	7.5
Deep fat fryers			
Single unit		910 × 810 × 880	15.8
Double unit		1830 × 810 × 880	31.5
Shallow tilting frypan		1180 × 820 × 930	12
Grillers			
Grill area			
410 × 380 × 230		610 × 510 × 510	4
560 × 380 × 230		760 × 510 × 510	5
760 × 380 × 230		840 × 560 × 510	7

* Width × depth × height

Table VI Range and sizes of tableware in general use

Type	Range	Size (rounded)
Pots	Tea	430, 570, 850, 1140 ml
(related to cups and pint sizes)		
Jugs	Coffee, hot milk/water	280, 570, 850, 1140 ml
	Cream	30, 40, 70 ml
	Milk	140, 280, 430 ml
Cups	Tea	170, 200, 230 ml
	Coffee (demi-tasse)	110 ml
Saucers	Size related to cups but should be interchangeable	
Plates	Side	165, 180 mm
	Dessert	190, 205 mm
	Fish/dessert	215, 230 mm
	Meat	240, 255 mm
	Oval meat	240, 255 mm*
Bowls	Cereal/fruit	155, 165 mm
	Sugar	90 mm
	Soup	215, 230 mm

* Usually maximum size for a dishwashing machine

Table VII Allowances for dishwashing spaces (intermittent use)

Area/activity	Space (mm)
Collection area for unsorted table ware prior to sorting and scraping	600 length per 10 meals*
	Minimum 900
	Maximum 2400
Stacking area for tableware sorted and stacked for manual washing	300 length per 10 meals†
	Minimum 900
	Maximum 3600
Loading onto racks for machine washing	Depends on rack/basket size
	Minimum 1000
Draining and drying in racks or baskets after washing and sterilising	Manual process and brush type machines:
	Minimum 1200 Conveyor or spray type machines up to 3600
Unloading baskets and racks for clean crockery awaiting removal	100 length per 10 meals
	Minimum 600
	Maximum 2400
Spray-type machines with mechanised conveyor systems	Space occupied by machine conveyor system
Rotary conveyor type (600–1000 meals/hour)	Width: 1500 Length: 3900 to 4800
Flight-type escalator conveyor (over 1000 meals/hour)	Width: 750 to 1200 Length: 3900 to 7900

* Based on self-clearance. Smaller areas suitable where part stacking is provided
† Assumes some accumulation of dishes before washing up. The lengths relate to tabling 750 mm wide

canopies and mechanical ventilation, as well as all other services, which will lead to increased costs. The minimum aisle width is 1050 mm, but may need to be up to 1500 mm to accommodate cooker door swings or if trolleys are used.

4.08 Dishwashing

Dishwashing is expensive in terms of space, equipment, labour and energy. It is possible to use disposables, but there is an image problem, and the cost of the disposables may be high. Also the waste generated may require a compactor.

Methods of collection of used dishes include: self-removal, trolleys or table collection. This must be decided at the initial planning stage. Trolleys will require aisles minimum 1050 mm wide.

Manual dishwashing in a double sink can cope with a maximum of 50 meals per hour. Machines are of various sizes and can deal with 100 to 1000 meals per hour. Space is required for the loading and unloading of the racks that run through the machine, and for storing the crockery.

Typical sizes of tableware are given in Table VI. Allowances for dishwashing spaces are shown in Table VII. Dishwashing equipment is shown in **18.25**.

4.09

An elaborate kitchen designed for a variety of types of cuisine is shown in **18.26**, while a much simpler example is given in **18.27**.

5 SERVERIES

5.01

Some typical self-service counter arrangements are shown in **18.28**. The average rate is 6–9 person per minute. One cashier can serve 9 customers per minute, but the rate depends on:

- Variety of menu: simpler menu gives faster throughput
- Whether beverage service is separate from the rest
- Whether there are bypass facilities, counter length depends on menu and rate of service:
  - school canteen:: between 9 and 11 metres would be suitable for a menu offering two or three choices of main dish and serving about 80 to 90 customers in 10 minutes
  - public cafeteria: the same length would serve 60 to 70 in 10 minutes.

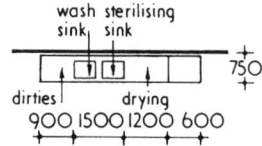

a *Manual washing up with wash and sterilising sinks*

b *Brush type dishwashing machine*

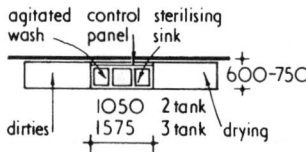

c *Agitated water type dishwasher*

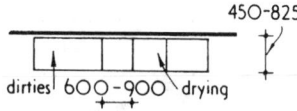

d *Small spray type dishwasher*

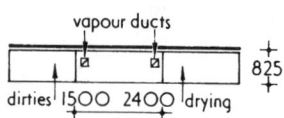

e *Medium-size automatic conveyor dishwasher*

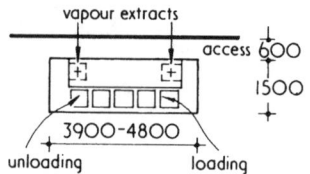

f *Rotary conveyor type dishwasher*

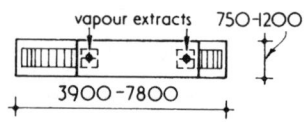

g *Large 'flight' type dishwashing machine with continuous escalator type conveyor*

18.25 *Alternative layouts for wash-up areas, with equipment dimensions:*

18.26 *Sheraton Muscat Hotel*
This is a recently built 350-room hotel in the Middle East, and illustrates the careful planning of food service facilities by the Sheraton Group. It offers a choice of Italian, French and Arabic restaurants in addition to banqueting for 250, a night club, various bars and room service. Food preparation is separated into specialised areas with common storage and dishwashing services. Development: Sheraton Corporation Food service consultants: David Humble Associates

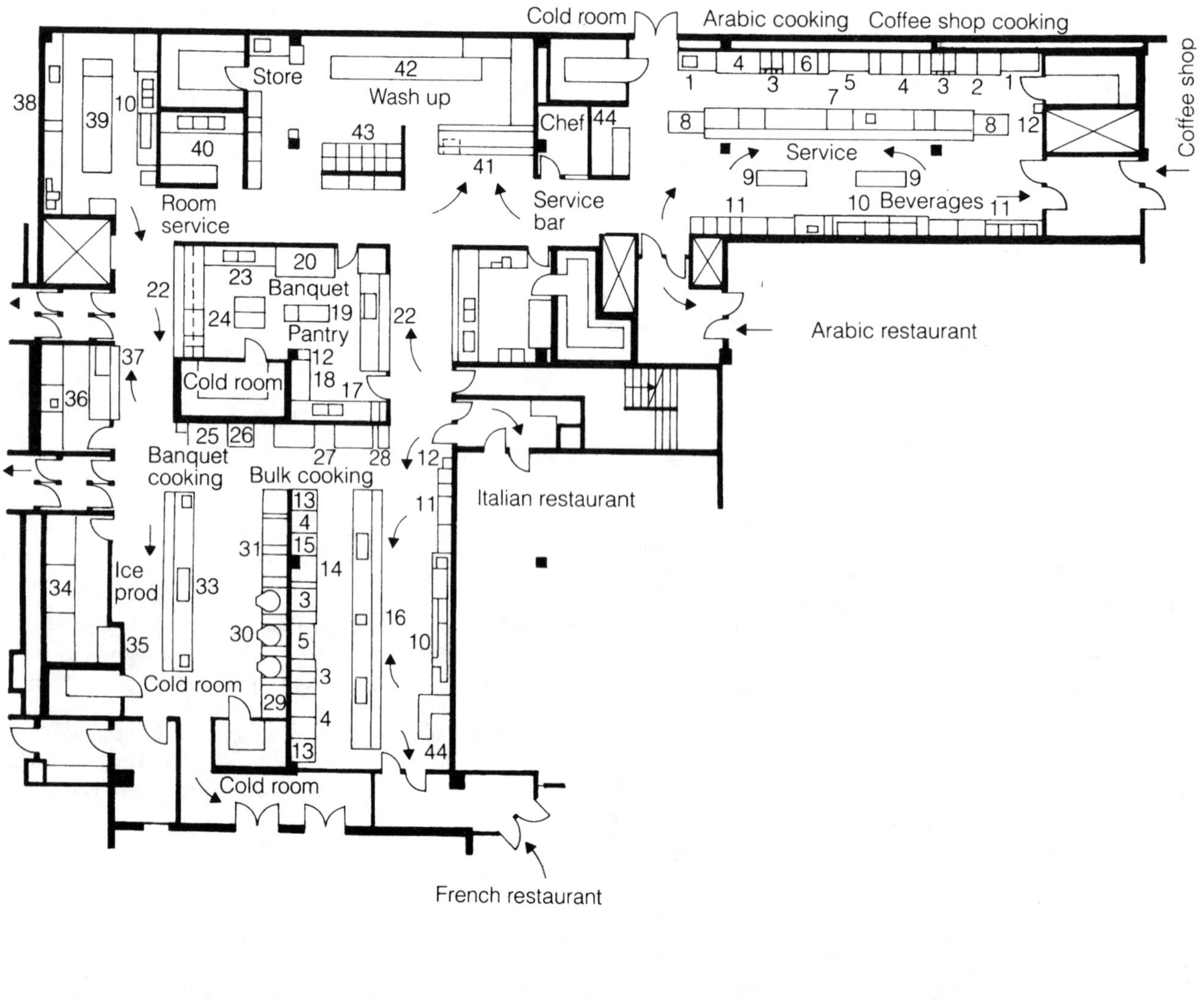

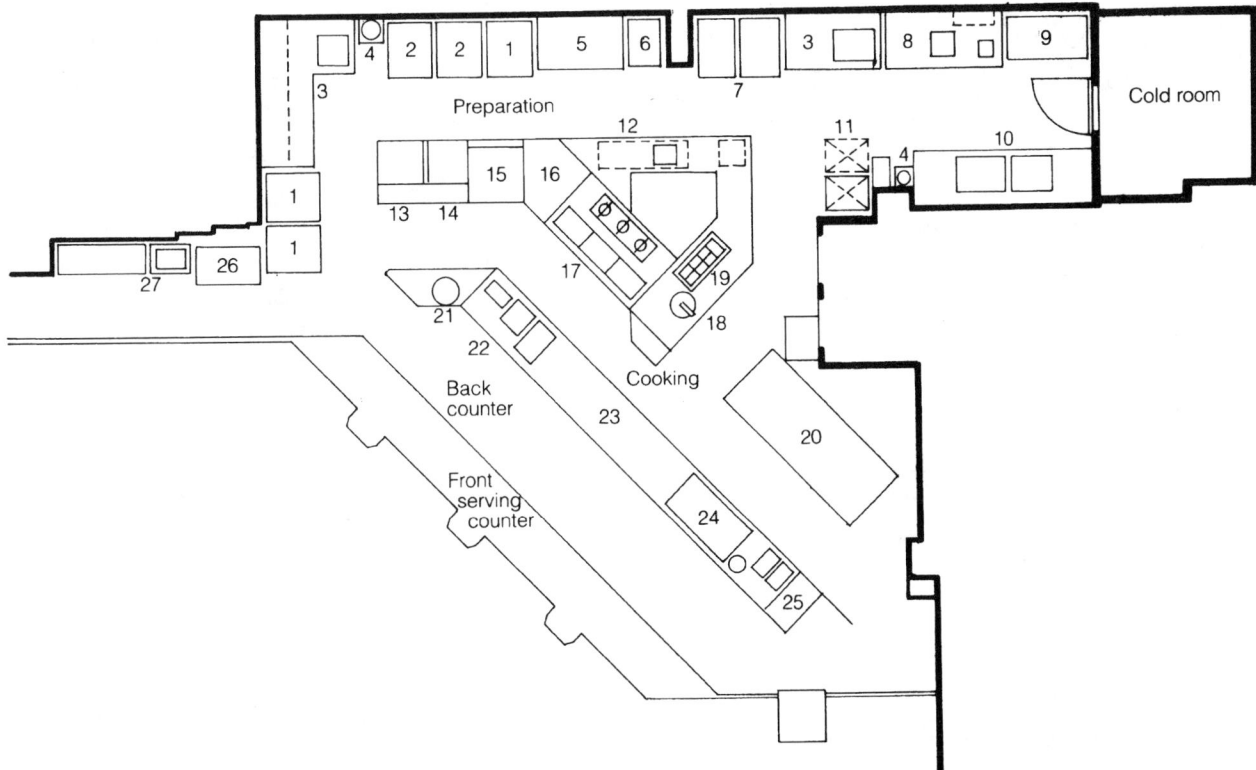

Preparation area

1 *Cabinet refrigerator*
2 *Workbench with sink and shelves*
3 *Wash-hand basin*
4 *Cabinet freezer*
5 *Mobile workbench*
6 *Mobile tray rack*
7 *Mobile proves*
8 *Workbench with sink*
9 *Workbench with cutter/slicer, can opener and cupboards*
10 *Five-tier mobile rack*

18.27 *Seasons pizzeria, London*

11 *Double sink*
12 *Trolley park*
13 *Pizza preparation bench with roller and tray racks*
Central cooking area
14 *Microwave convection oven*
15 *Steamer*
16 *Pasta cooker*
17 *Drainer*
18 *Heated bain-marie with infrared lamps over counter*
19 *Pizza-cutting machine*

20 *Chilled bain-marie with refrigerated cupboards under*
21 *Pizza oven*
Back counter to servery
22 *Post-mix, jet spray, ice well and drink dispenser cabinet*
23 *Heated pass-through chute*
24 *Beverage station with boiler, tea and coffee machines*
25 *Shake-machine*
26 *Ice maker*
27 *Cleaner's sink*

Key for **18.26**

1 *Sink with wall shelf*
2 *Griddles*
3 *Fryers with adjacent worktop*
4 *Hot top ranges (two) with overshelves*
5 *Refrigerator*
6 *Beverage and breakfast counter with automatic boiler, conveyor toaster, fruit juice and chocolate dispensers, espresso and coffee machines*
7 *Wash-hand basin*
8 *Radiant broiler*
9 *Cold food counter with overshelf and tray slide*
10 *Service racks and basket racks*
11 *Range-mounted broiler*
12 *Charcoal broiler*
13 *Hot and cold distribution counter with overshelf and tray slide*

14 *Pass-through refrigerators*
15 *Hot cupboards*
16 *Pasta cooker*
17 *Griddle*
18 *Hot food counter with overshelf and tray slide*
19 *Workbench with double sink and wall shelf. Conveyor toaster*
20 *Worktable with overshelf and trolley racks for Gastronorm containers*
21 *Worktable with refrigerator cupboard and slicing machine*
22 *Combined mixer*
23 *Ice cream conservator*
24 *Workbench with double sink and wall shelf*
25 *Worktables*
26 *Roasting oven*
27 *Pressure/pressureless steamer*
28 *Convection oven*

29 *Pasta machine*
30 *Worktable with weighing scales*
31 *Tilting kettles*
32 *Bratt pans*
33 *Hot food counter*
34 *Ice-making machines*
35 *Iceflaker*
36 *Cabinet refrigerators with adjacent sink and workbench*
37 *Beverage service counter*
38 *Sink and workbench with egg boiler and toaster*
39 *Trolley park*
40 *Pot wash area with triple sink and racking*
41 *Stripping shelves and rack slide with underbench waste containers*
42 *Flight dishwasher*
43 *Trolley park*
44 *Cashier desks*

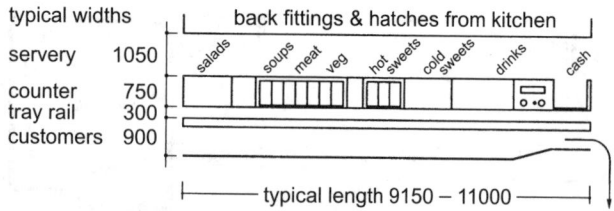

a *Single-line counter, 60–90 customers per minute*

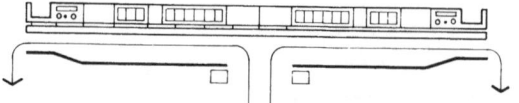

b *Divergent flow*

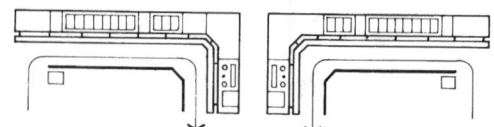

c *Convergent flow*

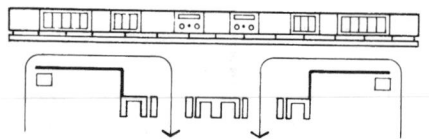

d *Multiple outlets*

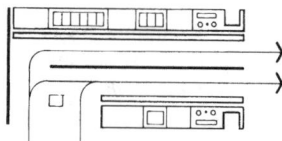

e *Parallel flow*

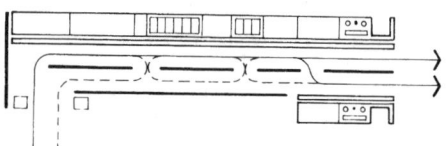

f *Bypassing*

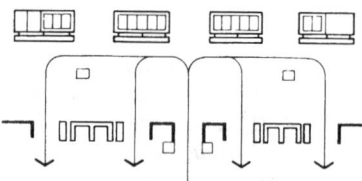

g *Free flow with counters in line*

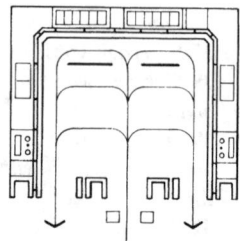

h *Free flow with counters in perimeter*

18.28 *Alternative arrangements for self-service counters*

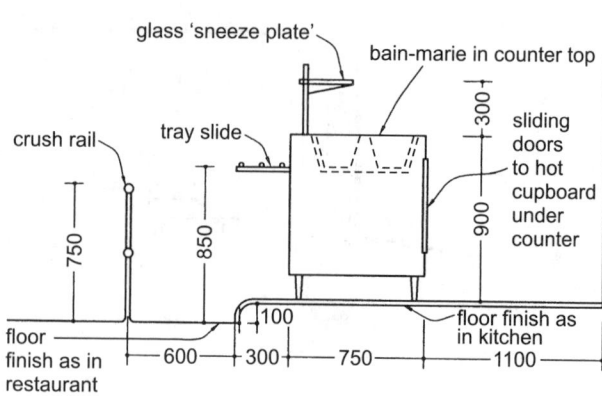

a *Section through counter for hot food*

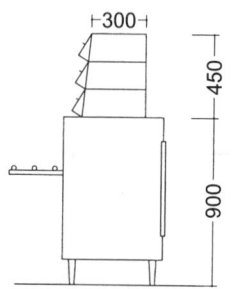

b *Section through cold food counter*

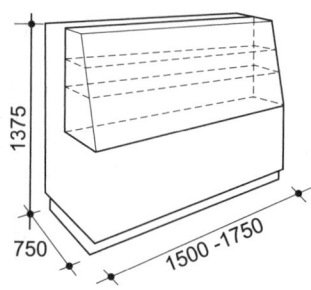

c *Refrigerated showcase*

18.29 *Servery equipment:*

5.02 Equipment requirements and sizes

Servery equipment requirements are given in Table VIII and shown in **18.29**. British Standards for equipment are given in the Bibliography. There are no universal standards for dimensions of equipment but the European Catering Equipment Manufacturers Association favours the Swiss 'Gastro-norm' system of dimensions, widely adopted on the Continent, **18.30**.

6 RESTAURANTS

6.01

Commercial restaurants are notoriously subject to fashion. They have a short life, not often over seven years. Money invested has to be recovered fast. The facilities provided for the customer, and the food available, may need to be frequently changed.

Full-service up-market restaurants are only 5 per cent of establishments. The mid-market range includes steak and seafood restaurants, grilles and rotisseries, and ethnic restaurants.

6.02 Ethnic restaurants

In Britain there are about 4000 Chinese restaurants and 2000 Indian/Pakistani. Design is often symbolic rather than authentic. Chinese cuisine is divided into: Canton, Peking, Szechuan and

Table VIII Equipment requirements for a self-service cafeteria

Equipment for servery		Meals served per day – based on main meal period								
		50	100	200	400	600	800		1000	
							1 (1–single line 2–double line)	2	1	2
Trays										
Tray storage length	m	0.45	0.45	0.60	1.35	0.60	1.35	2 × 0.6	1.35	2 × 0.6
Bread, rolls, butter, etc.*										
Unheated counter with self-service display above: length	m	0.45	0.45	0.75	1.20	1.65	1.80	2 × 1.2	2.30	2 × 1.5
Cold meats, salads, etc.*										
Refrigerated counter	m	0.45	0.75	0.90	1.20	1.80	2.30	2 × 1.2	2.60	2 × 1.5
with dole plate and glass display above, refrigerator under of capacity:	m³	0.06	0.06	0.08	0.08	0.11	0.11	2 × 0.08	0.14	2 × 0.11
Hot foods										
Hot cupboard with sectioned bain-marie and heated service shelf: length	m	0.9	1.5	2.4	3.6	4.9	6.1	2 × 3.6	7.3	2 × 4.3
Beverages – hot drinks†										
Counter length	m	0.9	1.1	1.2	1.4	1.5	1.8	2 × 1.2	2.1	2 × 1.5
Comprising water boiler capacity	litres/hr	55	115	170	225	340	455	2 × 225	570	2 × 285
Tea/coffee urns										
No. × capacity	litres	1 × 15	2 × 15	2 × 25	2 × 45	2 × 70	2 × 90	4 × 45	2 × 115	4 × 70
Storage racks under counter for cups/saucers:	capacity	50	100	150	200	250	350	2 × 200	450	2 × 250
Reserve cup and saucer storage behind counter:	capacity	–	–	50	200	350	450	2 × 200	550	2 × 250
Cold drinks, etc.†										
Counter length	m	0.6	0.9	1.2	1.8	2.1	2.4	2 × 1.8	2.7	2 × 2.1
Comprising refrigerator capacity	m³			0.06	0.08	0.08	0.11	2 × 0.08	0.11	2 × 0.08
Cold shelf length	m	0.45	0.6	0.6	0.9	1.2	1.2	2 × 0.9	1.5	2 × 1.2
Ice cream storage*	litres			4.5	9.0	13.5	18.0	2 × 9.0	22.5	2 × 13.5
Squash dispenser		1	1	1	1	1	1	2	1	2
Iced water point				1	1	1	1	2	1	2
Cutlery†										
Counter length	m	0.30	0.30	0.45	0.60	0.60	0.90	2 × 0.6	0.90	2 × 0.6
Cutlery boxes fitted in top-capacity pieces		250	300	400	600	900	1000	2 × 500	1700	2 × 650
Reserve cutlery under			200	600	1400	2200	3000	2 × 1400	3800	2 × 1850
Cashier counter-cut away for cash desk length	m	1.2	1.2	1.2	1.2	1.2	1.2	2 × 1.2	1.2	2 × 1.2
Standard cash desks		1	1	1	1	1	1	2	1	2
Automatic change machine						1	1		1	1

* Depends on type of meals and customer preferences
† May be located away from service counter
  Based on equipment by Stotts of Oldham

Shanghai. The kitchens need to provide the extensive menus required, which can be up to 300 items. Indian food is strongly spiced and much of it can be cooked by quite simple means such as boiling. Japanese food is subtle: preparation and service are seen as an art form. Greek restaurants are often designed as peasant-style tavernas. Seafood and cheap meat is much used. Greek music and dancing may be featured. Italian food is very popular and pizza has moved into the fast-food area. Pasta is the other national dish and comes in many forms including lasagne and ravioli. Spanish and Mexican restaurants are often also taverna-style. Mexican food is more spicy than Spanish. Scandinavian food relies on smoked food and cold meats.

6.03
A self service restaurant is shown in **18.31**. Details of a self-service counter are given in **18.32**. A drive-in restaurant is shown in **18.33**.

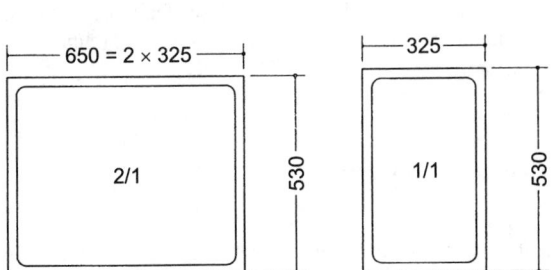
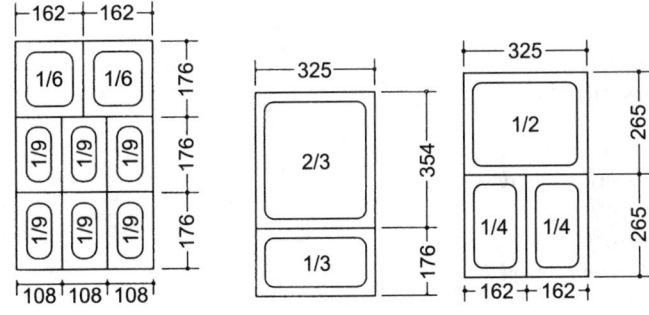

18.30 *Module sizes for Gastronorm containers*

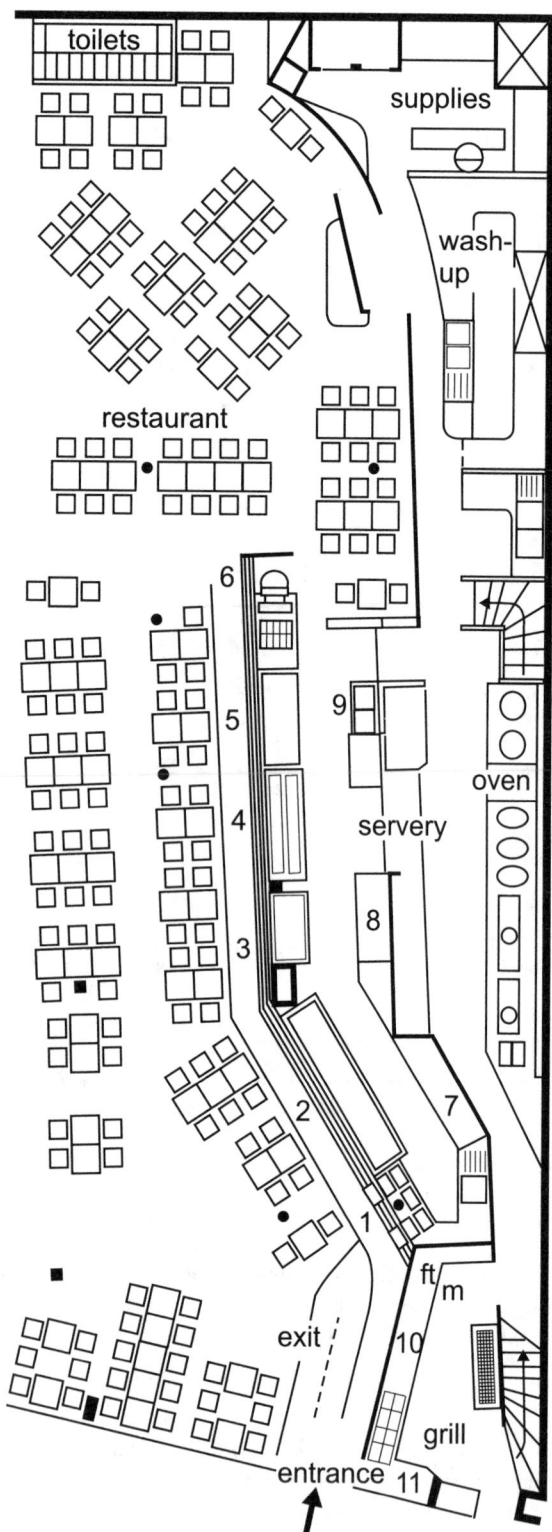

18.31 *Self-service restaurant in Paris*
Architect: Prunier

1 *Trays*
2 *Cold buffet*
3 *Beverages*
4 *Hot meals*
5 *Cheese and desserts*
6 *Cashier*
7 *Refrigerator*
8 *Beverages cupboard*
9 *Ice*
10 *Hot cupboard*
11 *Street sales counter*

7 CAFETERIAS

7.01

Cafeterias are self-service establishments, commonly run on a non-commercial basis as a service to staff and others such as students. They are characterised by:

- Scale of operation: usually fairly large, giving certain economies of scale
- Concentration of demand: a short service period demands a high rate of service. Above 600 meals a day, free-flow and multi-counter service is practical.
- Menus: balanced to meet nutritional standards. Degree of choice will determine counter layout and/or length.
- Operation: also used in high-demand commercial services (airports, stores, service stations)
- Space: counters add 0.2–$0.3\,\text{m}^2$ to area per seat in the dining room.

7.02

Two examples of cafeterias are shown in **18.34** and **18.35**. Both use the standard key **18.36**.

8 TAKE-AWAYS

8.01

Fast food is the fastest growing sector accounting for about one third of the market for meals outside the home. These outlets usually concentrate on popular products such as pizza, hamburgers, chicken or baked potatoes. They rely on high-volume sales and tight control of costs and margins to provide competitive prices.

If high street locations are used trading may have to be over a 15-hour day, seven days a week. Investment costs are high: sophisticated equipment is required so that untrained staff can use it, and wear and tear is heavy. Most operators aim for a door time, entering to leaving, of 3.5 minutes. The maximum queueing time is 2.5 minutes, allowing for 1 minute from placing the order to service.

8.02

Food will be delivered to the establishment ready-portioned and frozen or chilled. The entire procedure is closely controlled: unsold hot food is kept for only a fixed period before being discarded. Employees will be categorised as till operators, backers and crew. There is a move towards health-conscious markets, such as making orange juice, salads and low-fat products available.

8.03

Many medium-price restaurants will supply meals to take away in addition to in-house facilities. However, there are large numbers of dedicated take-aways (called carry-outs in Scotland) occupying standard shop units, most of which is taken up by storage and preparation areas. A small public area will contain a counter and little else; although some will provide a few seats, either for people waiting or even for a very few to eat. Local authorities encourage take-aways to provide and service refuse facilities in their immediate vicinity to reduce the nuisance caused by the litter they tend to generate.

9 TRANSPORT CATERING

9.01

Airport, station, ferry and cruise liner catering has much in common with other commercial and canteen outlets. Airline in-flight catering is provided by specialist sub-contractors who prepackage everything for restocking planes, which must not take

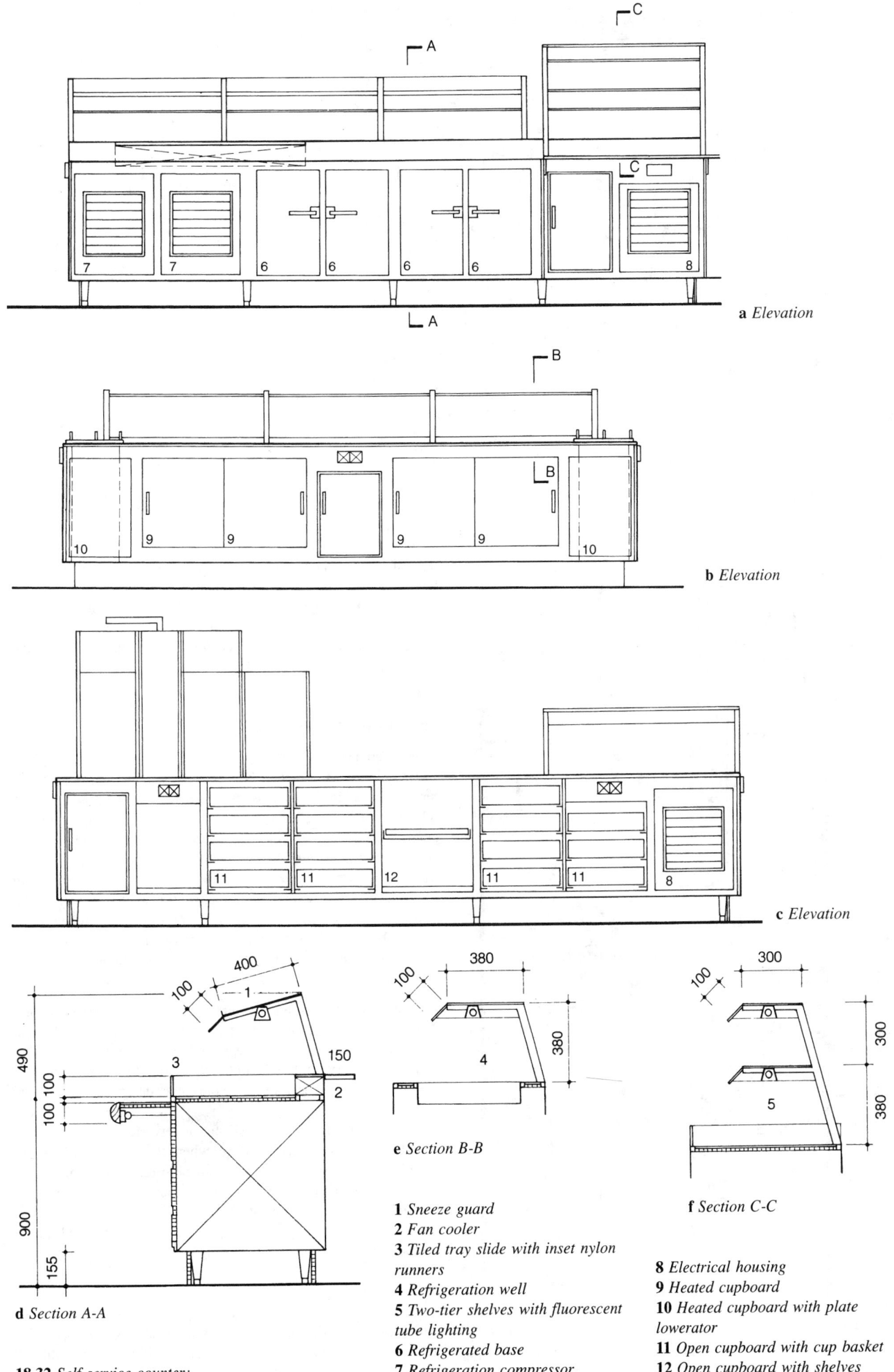

a *Elevation*

b *Elevation*

c *Elevation*

d *Section A-A*

e *Section B-B*

f *Section C-C*

18.32 *Self-service counter:*

1 *Sneeze guard*
2 *Fan cooler*
3 *Tiled tray slide with inset nylon runners*
4 *Refrigeration well*
5 *Two-tier shelves with fluorescent tube lighting*
6 *Refrigerated base*
7 *Refrigeration compressor*
8 *Electrical housing*
9 *Heated cupboard*
10 *Heated cupboard with plate lowerator*
11 *Open cupboard with cup basket*
12 *Open cupboard with shelves*

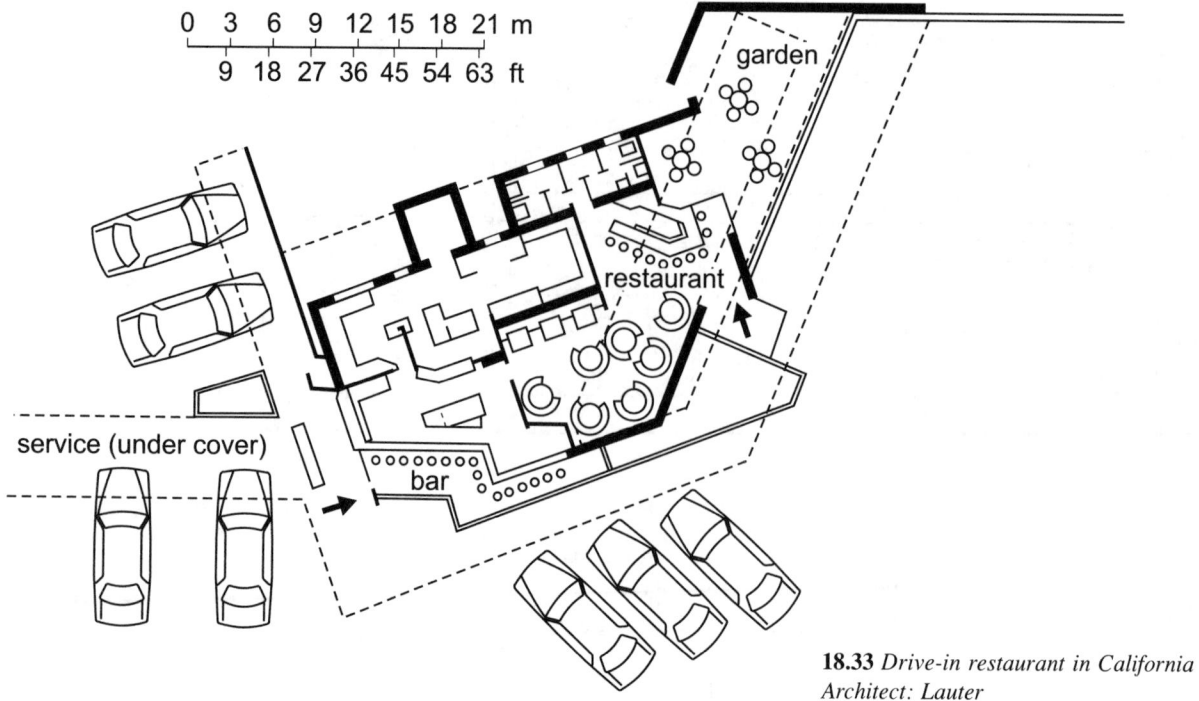

18.33 *Drive-in restaurant in California Architect: Lauter*

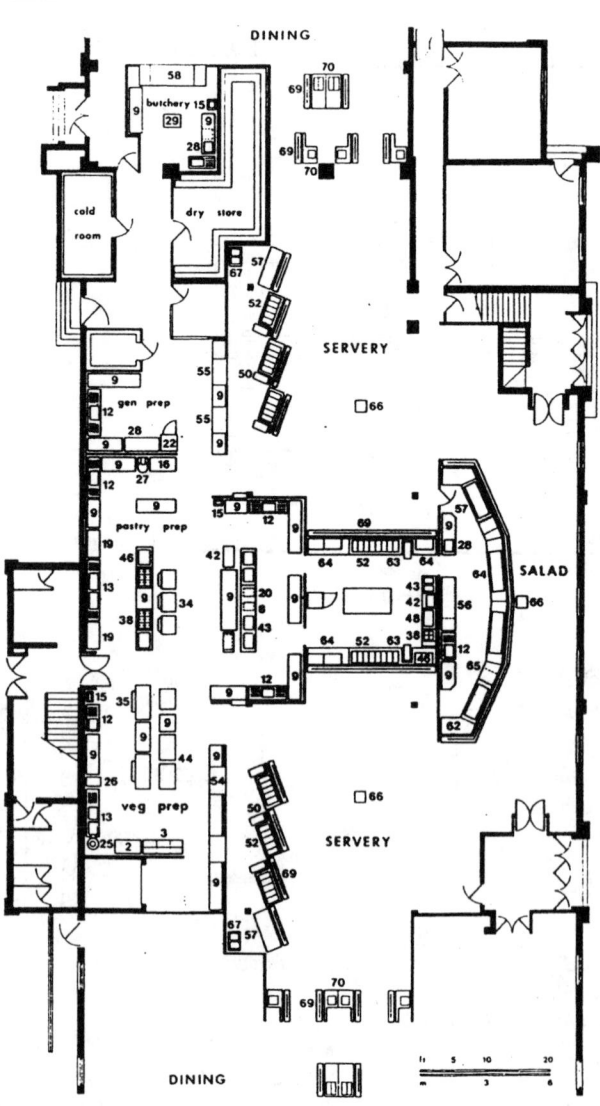

18.34 *Staff catering facilities, Plessey, Liverpool. Designed to provide up to 4000 meals within a period of 2½ hours. Equipment by Oliver Toms Ltd, standard key,* **18.36**

more than 20 minutes. The requirements are tight: food should not have strong flavours, it must be consumable in a small space, it must not be damaged by changes in temperature and pressure. Containers must be attractive, unbreakable and stackable, light and cheap. Production is done in specialised conveyorised kitchens to the exact demands of the airlines.

10 PUBLIC HOUSES

10.01 General
The requirements of public houses are different from other food-service outlets in that alcohol sales are the dominant rather than a subsidiary activity. Licences to sell alcoholic liquor will only be granted if the applicant and the premises are suitable for the purpose. The licensing justices will consider such things as safety, means of escape, sanitary facilities and separation of bars from other areas. Any structural alterations must also be approved by the justices, who can require changes before a licence is renewed.

Most building work on licensed premises is in the alteration of existing buildings. Few new pubs are built. Public houses consist of two parts:

- Public areas: bars and lavatories, where the customers are allowed. Often, particularly in older properties, the appeal to the customers can lie in the age and eccentricity, or even the inconvenience, of the layout. Optimum seating may not be possible, or even desirable, and the clever designer will turn this to advantage.
- Private areas: for staff, consisting of serveries, cellars, kitchen and staff accommodation. Here, where the staff do their work, and where the liquor is stored, specific dimensions and good planning assume great importance, and closely affect the efficient running of the establishment.

The relationships of the main spaces are shown in **18.37**. Some possible site layouts are shown in **18.38**.

10.02 Drink delivery
Vehicles deliver drink in bulk by tanker, in barrels or kegs, and in bottles in crates. For vehicle sizes see Chapter 4. The vehicular access must be convenient for the cellars, owing to the quantity of heavy goods handled. Empty containers will be returned.

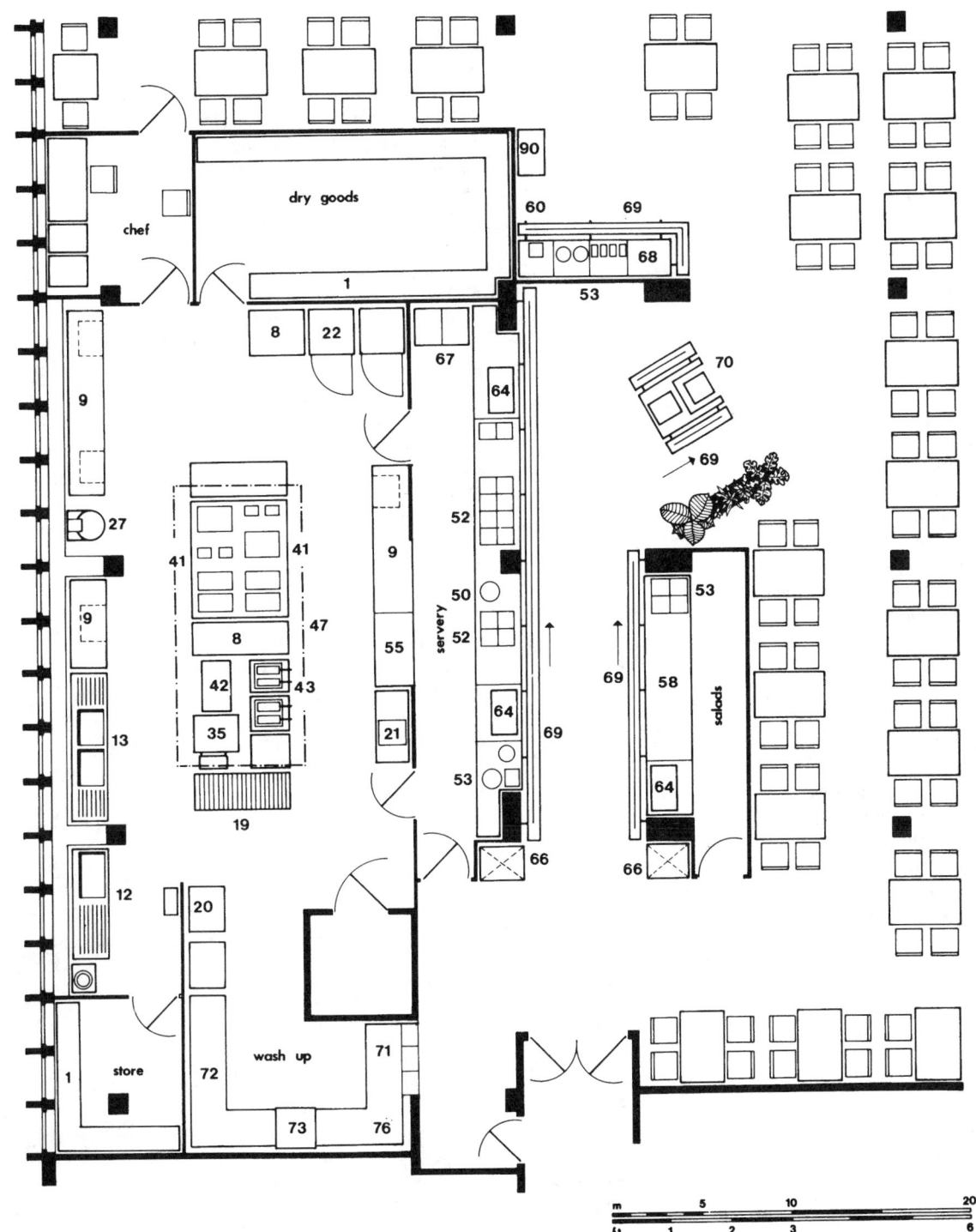

18.35 *British Relay Ltd, Crawley*
A self-service restaurant to serve 350 diners over a 1½-hour period. The island salad bar is designed to divide the flow and increase the speed of service. Standard key, **18.36**

10.03 Drink storage

Cellars may be below ground, at ground level, or in rare cases at an upper level. They must be planned to store the following economically:

- Kegs
- Bottles, usually in cases stacked on one another
- Wine and spirits, usually stacked on shelves in a separate store
- Bulk storage tanks
- CO₂ canisters

The size of the standard metal keg or of the case containing two dozen half-pint bottles is fairly standard. Wooden barrels on tilting stillages are now extremely rare, **18.39** to **18.46**.

Storage of empties is similar, except that it is easy to stack empty cases higher, so less space is required. For the purposes of design any beer other than bottles or cans, is referred to as 'draught'. Draught beer from the cellar is usually delivered under pressure. Beer travelling upwards one storey height is pumped electrically. Bottles travelling upwards one storey height are usually delivered by a case hoist, which is installed as a unit and

18.36 *Standard key for kitchen and restaurant layouts*

Storage areas
1 *Shelving*
2 *Vegetable racks*
3 *Vegetable bins*
4 *Storage bins*

Preparation areas
8 *Worktable or bench*
9 *Workbench with cupboards/drawers*
12 *Single sink with drainer*
13 *Double sink unit*
14 *Mobile sink*
15 *Wash-hand basin (with dryer)*
16 *Marble-topped bench*
19 *Pot rack*
20 *Trolley*
21 *Mobile trays*
22 *Refrigerator*
25 *Potato peeler*
26 *Chipping machine*
27 *Mixing machine*
28 *Slicing machine/vegetable mill*
29 *Chopping block*

Cooking area
34 *Forced-air convection oven*
35 *Steaming oven/pressure steamer*
36 *Microwave oven*
38 *Boiling top with oven top*
39 *Boiling top with solid top*
41 *Oven range with boiling top*
42 *Griller or salamander*
43 *Deep fat fryer*
46 *Open-well bain-marie*
47 *Extraction hood over equipment*

Serving area
50 *Plate lowerator or dispenser*
52 *Hot cupboard with bain-marie top*
53 *Bench type bain-marie unit*
54 *Pass-through unit – heated*
55 *Pass-through unit – cold*
56 *Refrigerator under-cupboard/drawer*
57 *Refrigerated cupboard with doleplate*
58 *Refrigerated display cabinet*
59 *Milk dispenser*
62 *Counter unit – unheated*
63 *Counter unit with infrared lamps above*
64 *Counter display cabinet*
65 *Compressor or boiler under counter*
66 *Tray stand*
67 *Ice cream conservator*
68 *Cutlery stand*
69 *Tray rail*
70 *Cashier's desk*

Wash-up area
71 *Receiving table for soiled dishes*
72 *Stacking table for clean dishes*
73 *Dishwashing machine – semi-automatic*
76 *Waste-disposal unit or scraping point*

Dining areas
90 *Beverage vending unit*
91 *Food vending unit*
92 *Waiter/waitress serving station*

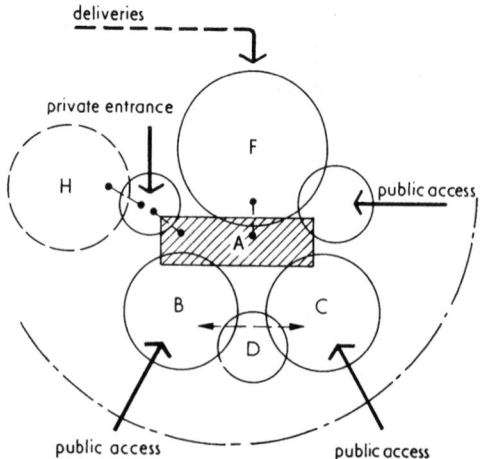

18.37 *Space relationship diagram for a public house*
A *Servery*
B, C *Drinking rooms*
D *Lavatories*
E *Off-sales*
F *Storage (cellars)*
G *Licensee's entrance*
H *Licensee's accommodation*

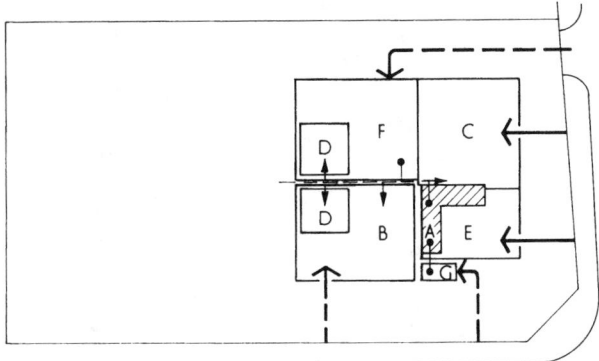

a *Corner site with building clear of all boundaries*

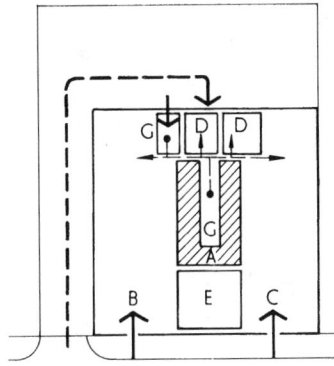

d *Straight site with delivery access at rear, and storage at lower level*

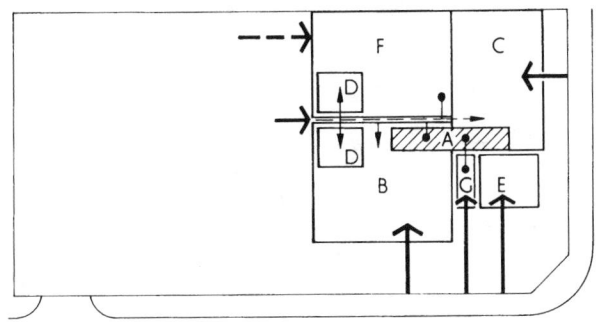

b *Corner site with building set against back boundary*

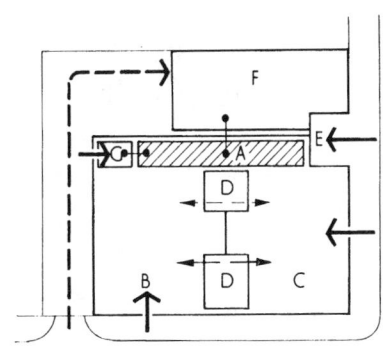

e *Restricted corner site*

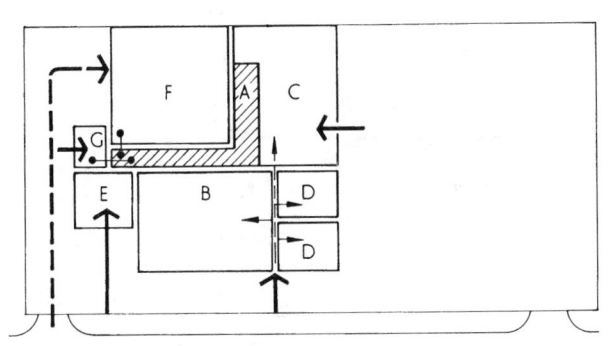

c *Straight site with delivery access at side*

18.38 *Planning public houses for different sites (key as for 18.37)*

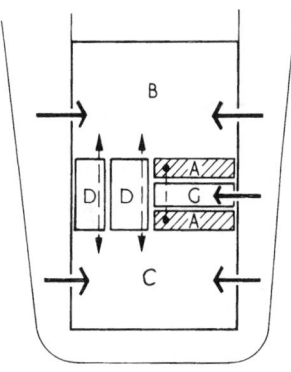

f *Island site with storage at lower level*

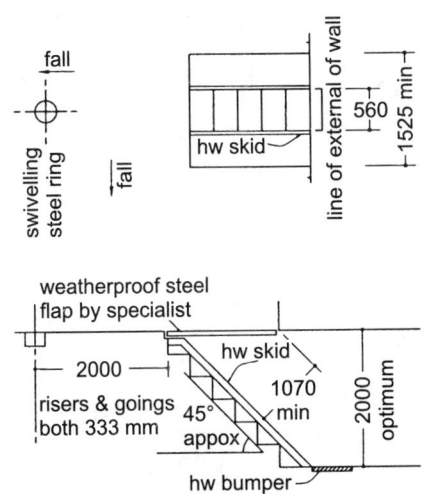

18.39 *Cellar flap and barrel chute for use with below-ground storage. Note: wooden barrels are no longer used, but kegs are also rolled in*

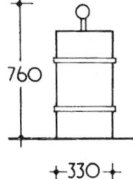

18.40 *Keg with valve attachment*

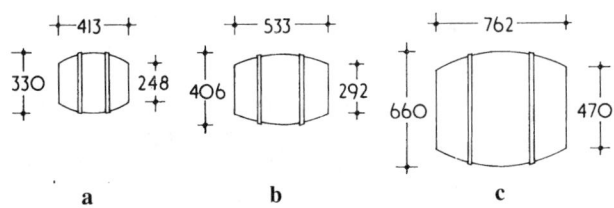

18.41 *Metal barrels or kegs:*
a *Pin, 4.5 gall/20.5 litres*
b *Firkin, 9 gall/40.9 litres*
c *Barrel, 36 gall/163.7 litres*

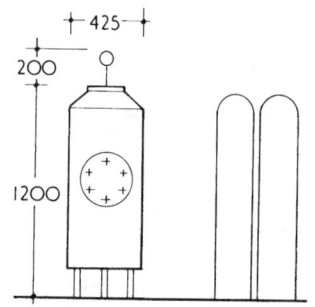

18.42 *Bulk storage in typical CO_2 canisters. Larger canisters also exist*

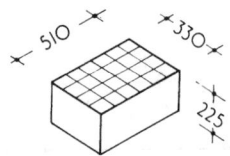

18.43 *Case storage, each case contains 24 half-pint bottles. Non-standard cases are normally smaller*

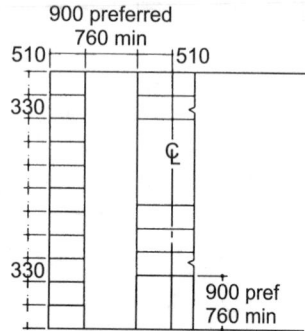

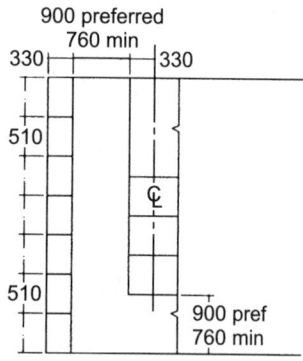

18.44 *Alternative plans of case storage*

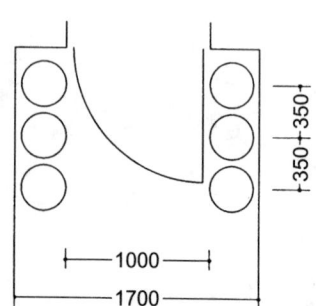

18.45 *Keg storage*

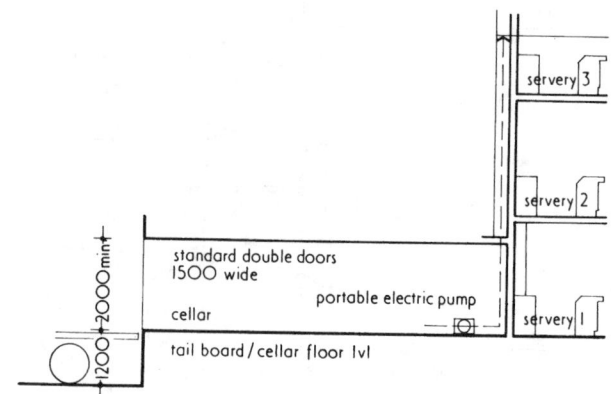

18.46 *Beer supplied through several storeys from ground-level cellar. A standard electric cellar pump will raise beer up to 9 m*

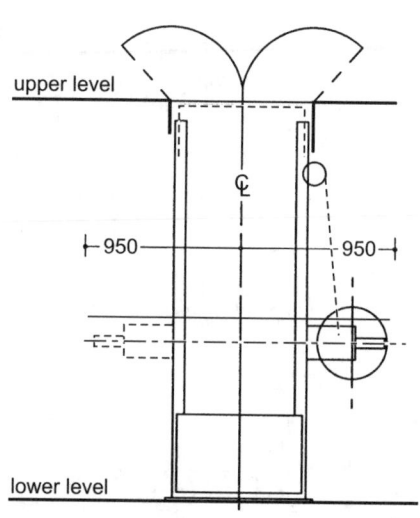

a *Front elevation*

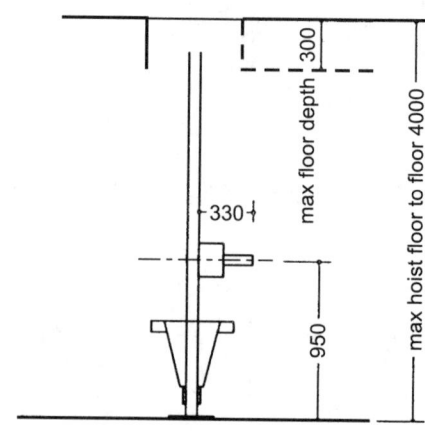

b *Side elevation*

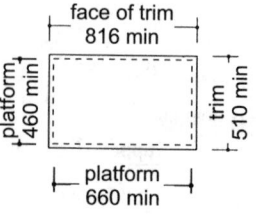

c *Plan at upper level*

18.47 *Small manual case hoist for two cases:*

can be manually or electrically operated. Manual operation is simpler and cheaper, **18.47**.

10.04 Drink dispensing

The servery consists of:

● The bar counter
● The back bar fitting
● The servery space between.

The length of the counter, **18.48**, will vary, but the height and width can be regarded as standard within narrow limits. The counter needs to incorporate at least one sink. Glasses may be stored in racks above the counter, and standard heights are important, **18.49** and **18.50**. The servery space is governed by ease of working and is usually of a standard width.

The backbar fitting will contain a sideboard top, often at the same height as the bar counter. Below this bottled beer will be stored often on cooled shelves. Above the sideboard top will be a

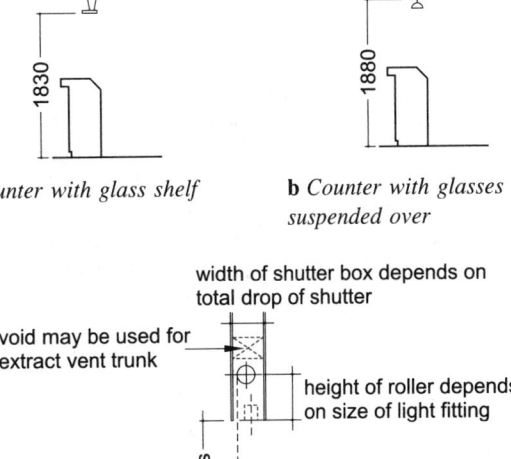

a *Counter with glass shelf over*

b *Counter with glasses suspended over*

c *Counter with roller shutter and flush lights. A lockable shutter of this kind is used when the counter is accessible from a room required for outside licensing hours, or when drink is not required*

18.50 *Above counter canopies:*

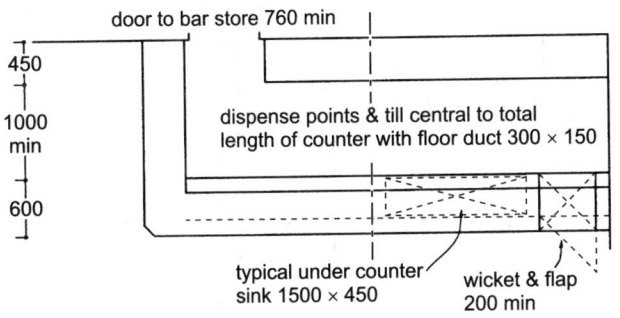

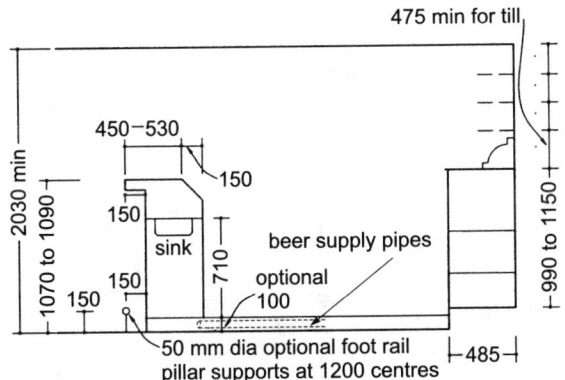

18.48 *Plan and section of a bar servery*

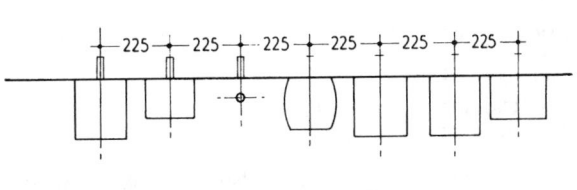

18.49 *Plan and elevation of a bar counter top, showing typical centres of dispenser points. Sizes and heights tend to vary with the brand*

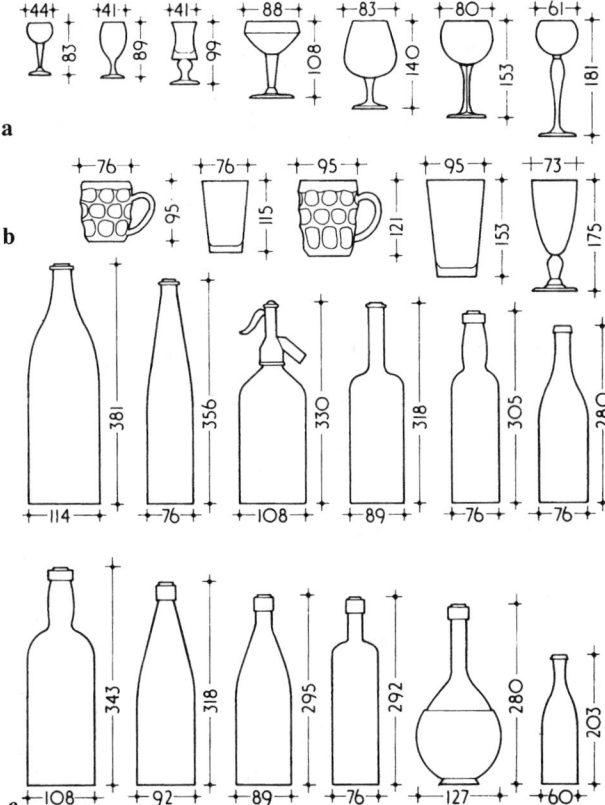

18.51 *Sizes of pub glassware:*
a *Wine and spirit glasses*
b *Beer and soft drink glasses*
c *Bottles*

display fitting holding spirits, often in 'optics', wine and glasses. Adjustable shelves are useful. The lowest shelf must be high enough to accommodate bottles, siphons, the till, etc. Sizes of bottles and glasses are shown in **18.51**.

The sizes of special equipment such as coolers, glass washers, etc. should be determined from consultation with the client as to preferred manufacturers. The sizes of ducts for the beer pipes, which are usually lagged, should be confirmed with the client.

10.05 Cooling

The temperature at which beer is kept and served is a critical factor. The two are not always the same. Recent fashion has tended towards colder dispensing, except for that of 'real ale'. This implies that two 'cellars' are needed: one naturally cool for the real ale, the other at ambient temperature for beers cooled in the pipeline or even at the bar. A 'remote cooler' is necessary for the latter processes; this should be installed where the heat generated from it does not unduly affect liquid stock. Requirements should be checked with the client and the supplier.

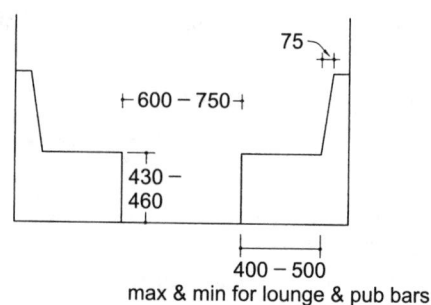

a *Section through booth*

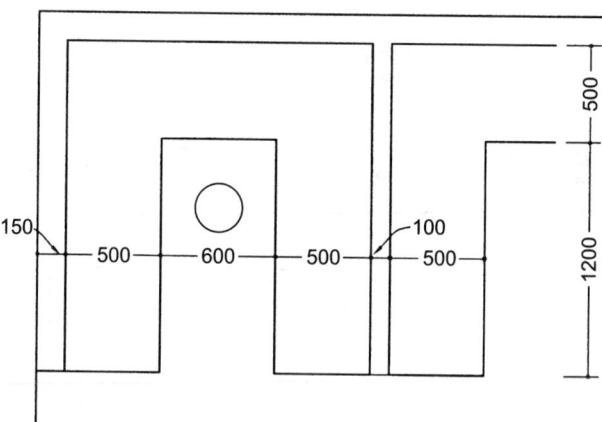

b *Plan of peninsular seating*

18.54 *Fixed seating of bench type:*

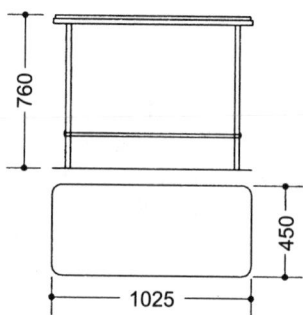

18.52 a *Rectangular cast iron base pub table*

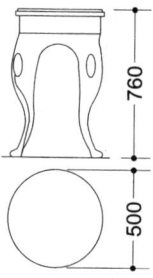

b *Round 'Britannia' cast iron base table*

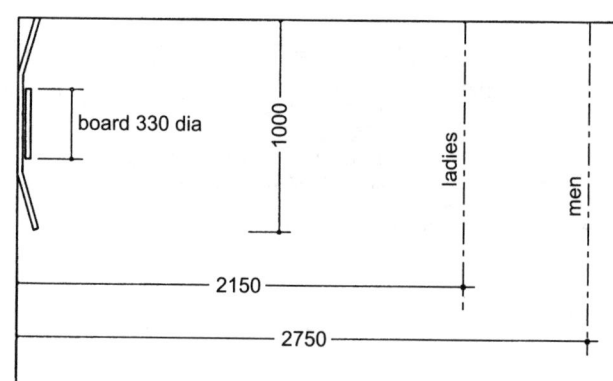

18.55 *Space required for darts*

10.06 Bars

Sizes of cast iron tables are fairly standard, but other types are very variable, **18.52**. Fixed seating can be from minimal to opulent, **18.53**. Stools are shown in **18.54**. Cill heights should be decided on with regard to fixed seating. Ceiling heights vary, and depend on the effect required.

Space may be needed for:

- Dartboard, **18.55**
- Fruit machine, **18.56**
- Pool table, **18.57**

These are becoming very popular. A larger size may be needed if championship matches are likely to be played.

- Bar billiards, **18.58**: this is becoming a rarity,
- Full-size billiards/snooker table, see Chapter 25
- Juke box – sizes vary considerably
- Piano or organ, **18.59**

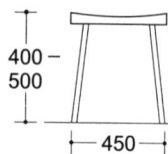

18.53 a *Low stool for use at a table*

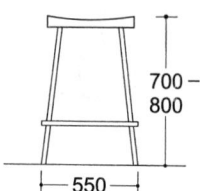

b *High stool for sitting at the bar*

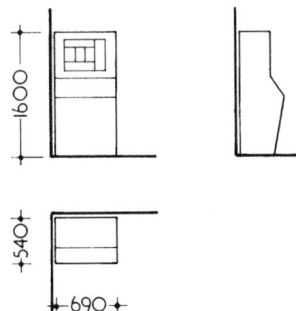

18.56 *Large fruit machine, requires an electrical supply*

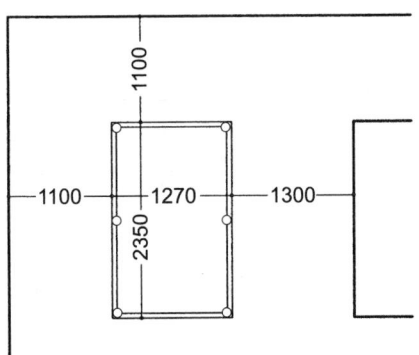

18.57 *Smallest size of pool table with cue space (for short cues) now common*

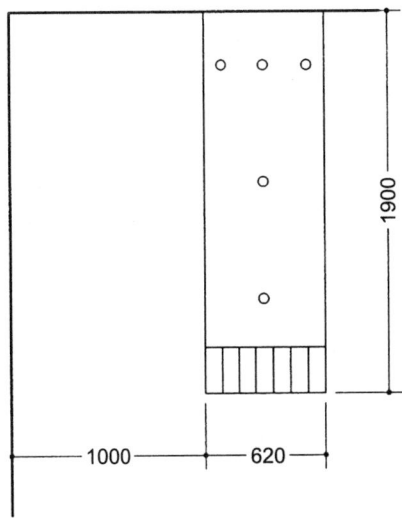

18.58 *Space required for bar billiards*

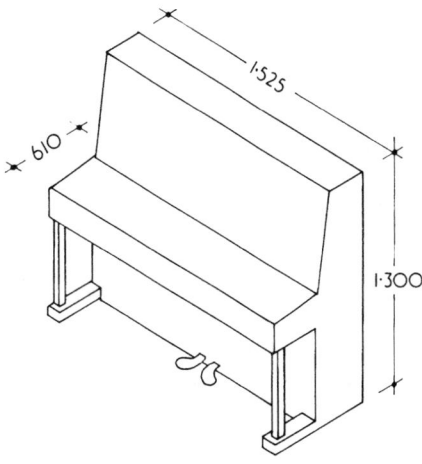

18.59 *Public house piano*

11 BIBLIOGRAPHY

S. Colgan, *Restaurant Design, Ninety-Five Spaces That Work*, Whitney Library of Design, New York, 1987

B. Davis, *The Traditional English Pub*, Architectural Press, 1981

F. Lawson, *Restaurants, Clubs and Bars*, Architectural Press, 1987

F. Lawson, *Principles of Catering Design* (2nd ed), Architectural Press, 1978

19 Studios for sound and vision

David Binns

David Binns is the senior partner of Sandy Brown Associates, architects and acoustic consultants

CI/SfB 528
Uniclass D527
UDC727.94

KEY POINTS:
- *Avoidance of extraneous sound is essential*
- *Production staff need both full observation and easy access to the studio floor*

Contents

1 INTRODUCTION

1.01 Scope

A TV studio is an area in which activities are performed specifically for observation. (Television cameras are also used outside studios for surveillance in stores, banks and so on.) A sound studio may be used for live broadcasts such as news bulletins, but is most likely to be required for making recordings.

1.02 Broadcasting studios

The greatest differences between studios will be in the ancillary areas rather than the studio *per se*. These differences reflect the nature and attitudes of the client: the BBC in the UK, for instance, is a public service organisation whereas the independent companies are not (although they must adhere to standards set by the Independent Broadcasting Authority).

1.03 Independent and educational studios

There are now many small independent studios, operating for private commercial use, for making programmes under contract, and for making educational and instructional videos. Some are attached to higher-education institutions.

2 STUDIO TYPES

2.01 Sound studios

Small sound studios may be used for such purposes as local broadcasting and for recording advertisements and jingles for commercial radio. **19.1** shows the scheme for such a facility. Where larger spaces are required, for example for recording orchestral music, studoios primarily designed for TV might well now be used. The principles behind both sound and TV studios are similar, although sound studios are more likely to have direct vision windows.

2.02 Multi-purpose TV production studios

Previously, TV studios differentiated between music and drama. Now, all are multi-purpose largely due to economic pressures. They have accepted acoustically 'dead' conditions, reverberation or presence being added electronically. Greater use of zoom lenses in preference to camera tracking means microphones are located

further from performers, necessitating low reverberation times and background noise levels. Camera tracking requires a floor laid to very precise tolerances (currently ±3 mm in 3 m). The floor is normally heavy duty linoleum sheet laid on an asphalt mastic screed; it requires a specialist floor laying contractor to achieve these fine tolerances.

Studio length-to-breadth ratio should be in the region of 1:1.5. The minimum practical floor area for a small commercial TV studio would be 60 m^2 with static cameras. TV station studios range between 200 and 400 m^2. The studio height is determined by the clear space required below the lighting grid (a function of the longest camera angle). The minimum height for a small studio is 4 m; in the larger studios 11 m to the grid with a clear height above of 2.5 m, making something over 13.5 m overall. In these studios an access gallery is required *at grid level approximately 4.5 m above studio floor level*. This is normally to avoid obstruction of access doors and observation window. Access to the galleries from studio floor level is mandatory and direct access to lighting grid level is desirable.

A cyclorama or backdrop cloth is suspended below lighting grid level. It should be at least 1.25 m away from the walls to allow a walkway around the studio and is on a sliding track with radiused corners to enable it to be stored.

2.03 Interview and announcers' studios

These studios range in size from 30 to 60 m^2 with a height of 4 to 6 m. Static cameras and a simple form of lighting grid combined with floor lighting stands are used.

2.04 Audience participation studios

Some productions require audience participation and fixed theatre-type seating on terraces is provided. In smaller studios this is demountable, so storage space has to be provided. Audiences place more stringent demands on the planning of a TV complex, as segregated access and emergency escape routes have to be provided (see Chapter 20, Auditoria).

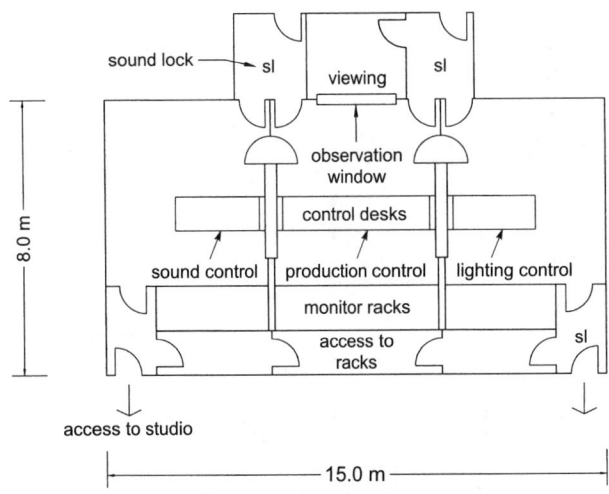

19.1 *Relationship diagram for sound recording studio suite*

3 PLANNING

3.01 Layout

A typical layout for a TV broadcasting studio complex is shown in **19.2**. Larger installations will have workshop facilities adjacent to the scene dock and if flats and backdrops are made on-site a paint frame will need to be the full height of the cyclorama curtain. Further details of such facilities will be found in Chapter 20.

Equipment areas
Ancillary equipment areas will include separate areas for VTR (video tape recording) and telecine (transference of filmed material to video). The machine operator should be able to hear sound track and cues above the noise of other machines in the room which are usually enclosed in open-fronted cubicles with heavily acoustically treated walls.

Master control room
Adjacent to these equipment areas will be the master control room, which is the last monitoring link in the video and audio chain before transmission. Here programme material, either recorded (VTR and telecine) or live from the studios, will be linked with continuity from the announcer's studio.

Dressing rooms
Artists' facilities adjoining the studio will include dressing rooms with associated wardrobe and laundry, rest and refreshment areas (see Chapter 20).

Rehearsal spaces
Separate rehearsal spaces are required as there is considerable pressure on studio floor time (much of which is used in setting and striking scenery, and setting up lighting and cameras for productions). These need not be the full studio size as several sets will occupy the studio floor and scenes are rehearsed individually, often in remote assembly halls.

Service spaces
In addition to the areas detailed in **19.2**, space will be required for a sub-station, emergency generator and tape stores. The small commercial and education studios which do not broadcast will have simpler planning arrangements.

3.02 Control suites

TV control rooms do not now overlook the studio they monitor for the following reasons:

- The cyclorama track and studio scenery are likely to interfere with the producer's view; production decisions are made off monitor screens.
- The chroma of glass in the observation windows must be adjusted to confirm colours reproduced by TV monitors. This is done using an applied tinted finish which requires frequent replacement.
- Windowless production suites do not need to be elevated, hence production staff have direct access to the studio floor. A typical control suite layout of this type is shown in **19.3**.

Minimum clear height in the control room, including a false ceiling for services, is 4 m.

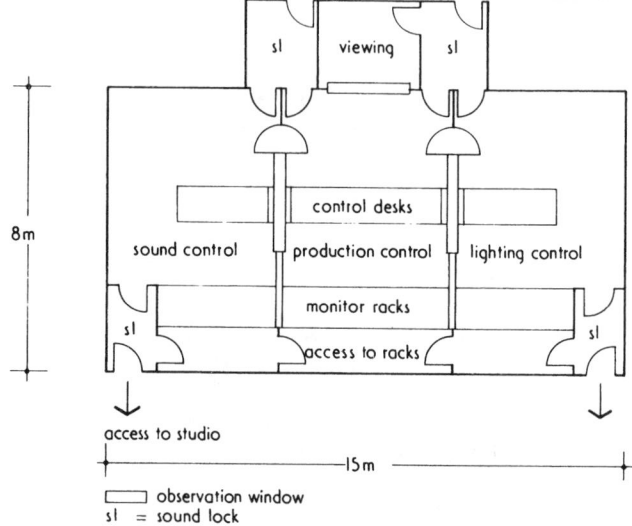

19.3 *Layout of a poduction control suite with no direct visual access to studio*

Separate control areas for production, lighting, and sound are required with 25 dB insulation between each and visual contact via observation windows. A viewing area for visitors separate from that for production staff is desirable.

The disadvantages of such a layout is that the producer has no direct visual contact with the floor manager or performers.

4 SERVICES

4.01 Lighting

Television studio lighting is highly specialised. The large production studio will have a remotely operated lighting grid, whereas the small studio will have a simple pre-set system.

Lamp support systems
There are three basic types of lamp support systems:

- The most elaborate is a grid of 'railway' tracks covering the whole studio. On these tracks run carriers which have a telescopic arm holding the lamp. The arm is motor driven

19.2 *TV studio complex; block planning diagram*

(either electrically or hydraulically) and lowers the lamp to studio floor level for setting and adjustment. Each lamp can be separately panned, tilted and dimmed remotely. An additional overhead rail at the perimeter of the grid will carry carts on to which the 'monopole telescopes' and lamps can be run off the grid to a lamp store. Where several studios exist this rail will interconnect them all via a central lamp store. The latest grids are equipped with an electronic memory to enable a whole production of lighting settings to be stored.

- A simpler form has lighting bars which can be raised or lowered electrically or manually fixed direct to the studio. The bars take several forms from the 'lazy scissors' principle to a simple bar on cables and pulleys.
- The third and simplest type is a fixed barrel grid. As in the second type no space is required above this grid for access as lamps are clamped direct to the bars and set from studio floor level.

Lighting to equipment and control areas needs to be carefully studied to avoid reflections and provide correct levels for viewing. Special fittings are often required.

4.02 Air conditioning
Air conditioning presents the designer with a number of unique problems: the large volume, the high heat loads generated by lamps, low background noise levels and the need to provide comfortable conditions in parts of the studio obscured in all but one plane by scenery. Low air speeds have to be used to achieve the noise levels. The most successful system has been the 'dump' system where cooled air is fed from a large plenum chamber above grid level and returns via natural convection of heat from the lamps to a similar exhaust plenum at an even higher level. Plant rooms, unless remote from the studios, require structural isolation to prevent vibration transmission (see para **5.03**); adequate space must be allowed for attenuation. Mechanical engineers are familiar with duct-borne noise problems, but do not normally investigate noise break-in through duct walls or the architectural acoustic problems. The architect should make certain that this forms part of the specialist consultant's brief.

4.03 Technical wiring
Extensive provision has to be made for power, audio and video wiring connecting the studio to control suites and equipment areas. Camera cables are approximately 50 mm in diameter and have a minimum bending radius of 0.5 m. Power wiring, which may include low-voltage power, has to be run in separate trunking from audio wiring to avoid interference. Trunking is often concealed within the acoustic finishes and all perforations of the studio enclosure have to be sealed airtight to avoid sound transmission.

4.04 Other services
Large production studios will require compressed air, gas, water (including drainage) and a smoke-detection system, in addition to electrical services.

5 ACOUSTICS

5.01 Identify standards
The standards to be achieved should be identified by the specialist consultant and agreed with the client at the outset. The two main sources are the BBC and the ISO (International Standards Organisation).

5.02 Airborne sound insulation
For every location a full one-third octave band, site noise level survey must be carried out to determine the design of the enclosing structures. Additionally, all internal transmission loss defined by

frequency should be established and can be extended to provide the mechanical engineer with the requirements for in-duct cross-talk attenuation. For this it will be necessary to establish the maximum permissible noise levels from all sources in each room.

5.03 Vibration isolation
The noise and vibration levels of all mechanical plant should be studied and the architect must identify who should be responsible for defining maximum permissible levels and designing to achieve them. Structure-borne sound transmission, particularly on the upper levels of framed buildings, may necessitate the 'floating' of plant rooms and noise-protected areas.

This involves isolating the walls, floor and roof from the surrounding structure. The walls are built off a secondary floor bearing on steel spring or rubber carpet mountings designed to a maximum natural frequency not exceeding 7 to 10 Hz. Footfall impact noise often requires floors to be carpeted with heavy underfelt or in extreme cases, the floating of studios.

5.04 Reverberation time
19.4 relates reverberation time to volume for television studios. Calculation will indicate the amount and type of absorption required. Details of a typical wide band modular absorber are shown in **19.5**. Approximately 200 mm should be added to the clear studio height and to each wall thickness to accommodate the acoustic treatment. Sound control rooms need to be similarly treated, with the other production control rooms and technical areas made as dead as possible.

5.05 Background noise levels
Maximum permissible background noise levels are shown in **19.6**. These should be related to the external ambient levels and to noise from air-conditioning plant. In certain situations where plant rooms are adjacent to noise-sensitive areas, maximum permissible noise levels at intake and extract louvres should be specified to limit this noise breaking back in through the external skin, particularly at windows.

5.06 Special details
Acoustic doors and sound lock
Typical details for an acoustic door and an observation window are shown in **19.7** and **19.8**. All noise-sensitive areas should be approached via a sound lock lobby consisting of acoustic doors, with either end of the lobby treated to be acoustically dead. The mean sound transmission loss of each door is 33 dB and sealing is affected by means of magnetic seals.

Scenery doors
The transfer of scenery into the studio requires an opening in the region of 5 m high by 5 m wide with a sound reduction index between 50–60 dB. This door will almost certainly be of steel

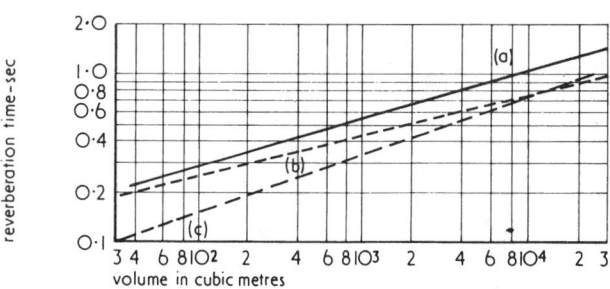

(a) highest acceptable reverberation time (b) optimum reverberation time
(c) lowest practicable reverberation time

19.4 *Reverbation times for TV studio*

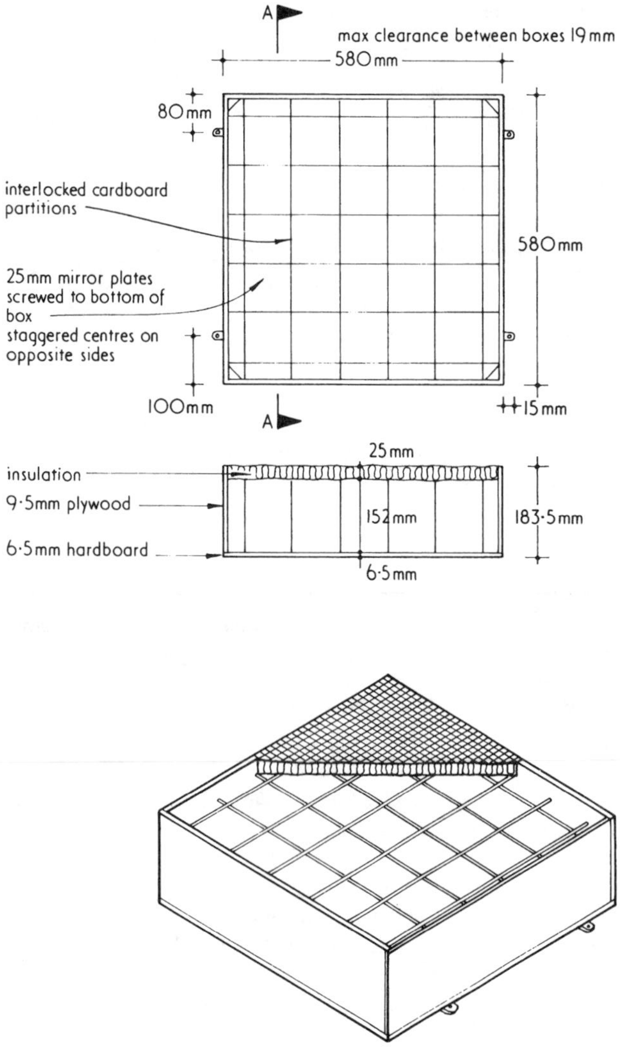

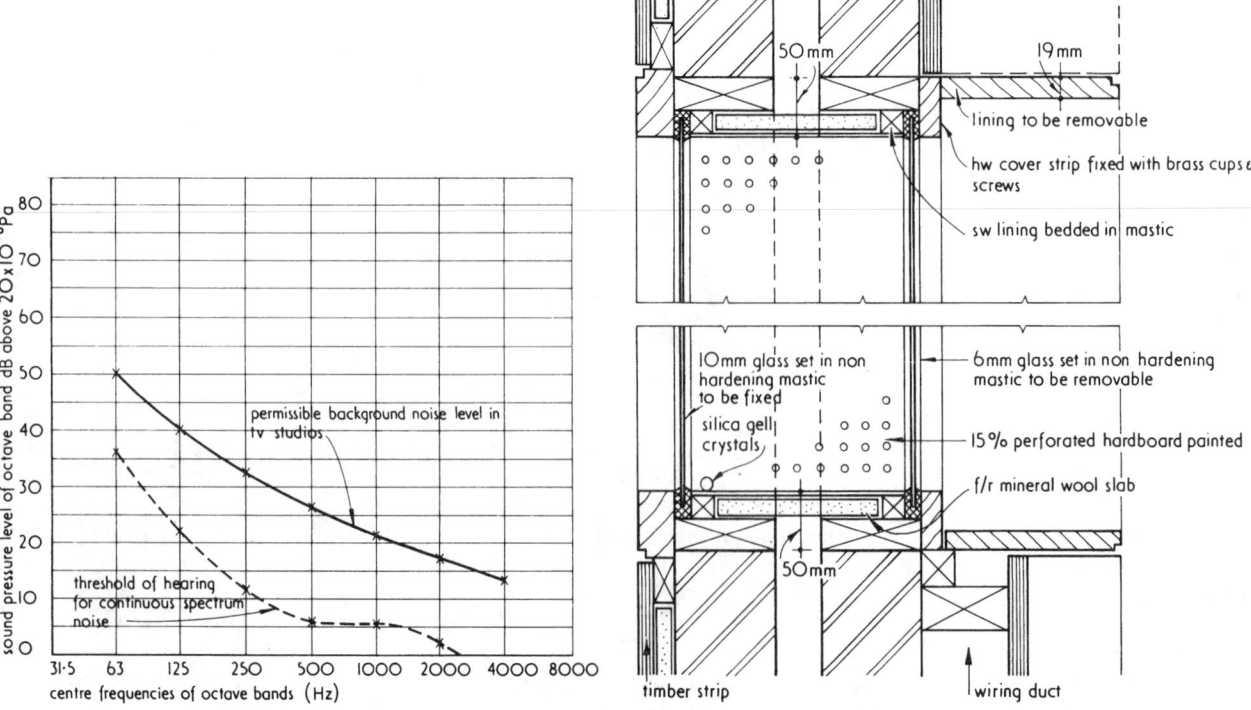

A

max clearance between boxes 19mm

580mm

80mm

interlocked cardboard
partitions

25mm mirror plates
screwed to bottom of
box
staggered centres on
opposite sides

100mm

15mm

580mm

A

insulation

9·5mm plywood

6·5mm hardboard

25mm

152mm

6·5mm

183·5mm

19.5 *Modular sound absorbing unit*

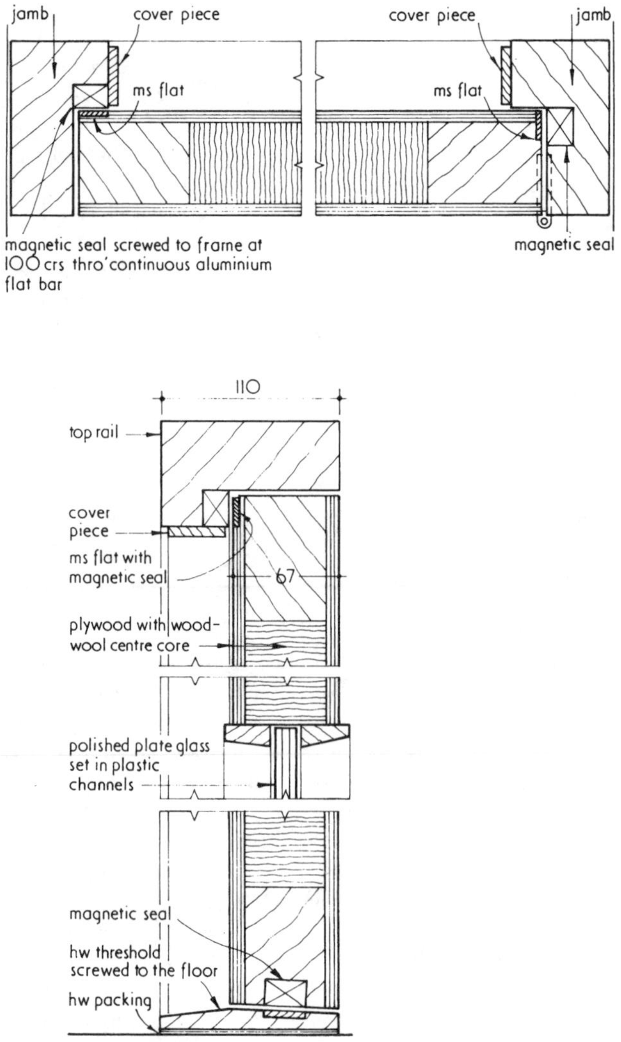

jamb   cover piece   cover piece   jamb

ms flat   ms flat

magnetic seal screwed to frame at
100 crs thro'continuous aluminium
flat bar

magnetic seal

110

top rail

cover
piece

ms flat with
magnetic seal

plywood with wood-
wool centre core

polished plate glass
set in plastic
channels

magnetic seal

hw threshold
screwed to the floor

hw packing

67

19.7 *Acoustic door construction*

19.6 *Background noise levels*

sound pressure level of octave band dB above 20×10⁻⁶Pa

80
70
60
50
40
30
20
10
0

permissible background noise level in
tv studios

threshold of hearing
for continuous spectrum
noise

31·5 63 125 250 500 1000 2000 4000 8000
centre frequencies of octave bands (Hz)

50mm

19mm

lining to be removable

hw cover strip fixed with brass cups &
screws

sw lining bedded in mastic

10mm glass set in non
hardening mastic
to be fixed

silica gell
crystals

50mm

6mm glass set in non hardening
mastic to be removable

15% perforated hardboard painted

f/r mineral wool slab

timber strip

wiring duct

19.8 *Observation window*

construction. Hinged doors have been used but the forces required to ensure that the edge seals close airtight produce operational difficulties. A 'lift and slide' door is more satisfactory. An electric or hydraulic drive opens and closes the door while radius arms lower it inwards and downward to compress the edge seals all round. This type of door does not require an upstanding threshold as does the hinged door, and this is a considerable operational advantage.

6 STATUTORY REQUIREMENTS

Careful examination should be given at the planning stage to means of escape and fire resistance. Statutory requirements vary considerably in all parts of the world, but the most stringent are those operated in the UK where Class O flame spread may be required for all finishes and up to a four-hour fire separation for the studio walls. This necessitates double steel roller shutters on all perforations through walls. Smoke vents are sometimes required and these must be designed to match the sound insulation of the roof.

7 BIBLIOGRAPHY

Data for the acoustic design of studios, BBC monograph no 64, Gilford, Burd and Spring

Christoper Gilford, *Acoustics for radio and television studios*, Stevenage, Peter Peregrinus Ltd, 1972

London Weekend television centre, buildings illustrated, *The Architects' Journal*, 6 February 1974

F. C. McLean, *The BBC television centre and its technical facilities*, Proceedings of the Institute of Electrical Engineers, vol. 109, part 13, no. 45, May 1962V.

S. Mankovsky, *Acoustics of studios and auditoria*, London, Focal Press, 1971

20 Auditoria

Ian Appleton
with additional material from Joe Aveline

Ian Appleton is a partner in The Appleton Partnership. Joe Aveline is a theatre consultant and lectures widely on the development of theatre and theatre equipment

CI/SfB 52
Uniclass D524, D525, D741
UDC 725.8

KEY POINTS:
- *Most auditoria are designed to fulfil a number of purposes*
- *The object is to ensure a near 100% of usage*
- *Every member of the audience should be able to see and hear the whole performance*

Contents

1 INTRODUCTION

The three-dimensional volume of an auditorium is conditioned by the need for all members of the audience to be able to see the whole of the platform or stage; and to hear the actor, singer, musician or speaker, **20.1**. Seating density, floor rake and seating layout are partly determined by this, partly to give the audience an appropriate level of comfort and essentially to ensure a means of escape in an emergency, such as a fire, within the time required by safety considerations and by legislation.

2 SEATING

2.01 Design of the auditorium seat
The aim is to provide an appropriate standard of comfort. The range of human body dimensions is wide; while in most auditoria a single size of seat is provided, **20.2** and Table I. Tolerance levels vary: young people can tolerate simple seating found less comfortable by older people. Those attending concerts of classical

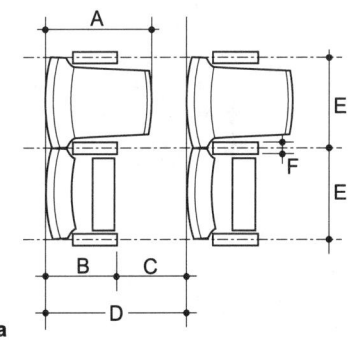

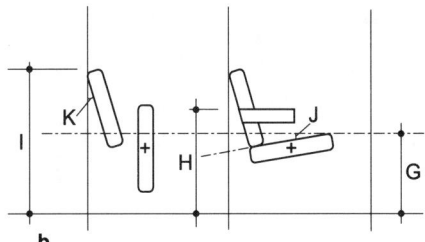

20.2 *Auditorium seating: definitions of terms and dimensional information (to be read in conjunction with Table I):* **a** *Plan.* **b** *Section*

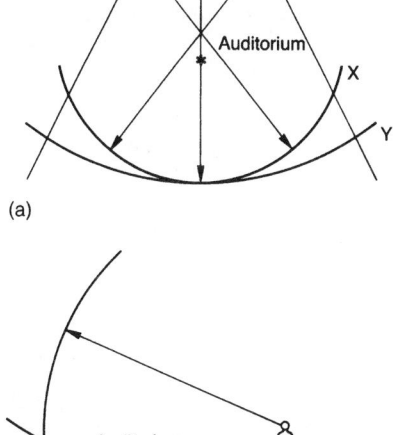

20.1 *Visual and aural limitations:* **a** *Plan: for a performer at centre stage B there is an arc Y beyond which visual and aural perceptions are impaired. However, for performers nearer the sides of the stage at A and C produce more restrictive curves X.* **b** *Section: Similarly, visual and aural limits in section also set an arc centred on the performer*

Table I Dimensions of auditorium seats

Dimension	Description	Minimum	Maximum	Drawn as
A	Overall seat depth	600 mm	720 mm	650 mm
B	Tipped seat depth (same as length of arm)	425	500	450
C	Seatway (unobstructed vertical space between rows)	305		400
D	Back-to-back seat spacing	760		850
E	Seat width for seats with arms	500	750	525
	Seat width for seats without arms	450		
F	Annrest width	50		50
G	Seat height	430	450	440
H	Armrest height	600		600
I	Seatback height	800	850	800
J	Seat inclination from horizontal	7°	9°	7°
K	Back inclination from vertical	15°	20°	15°

music seem to expect more comfort than those watching drama. Seats are generally designed for the average person expected to use it; this varies according to age and nationality. Minor variation is achieved by the upholstery and adjustment of the back and seat pan material when the seat is occupied: otherwise the seat selection is a common size within the whole, or part of, the auditorium layout. The best able to be achieved is in the order of 90% of the audience within an acceptable range of comfort.

2.02 Working dimensions

Seat width: the minimum dimension as stipulated by legislation is 500 mm with arms and 450 mm without. For seats with arms a width of 525 mm is the least for reasonable comfort.

Seat height: 430–450 mm.

Seat inclination: an angle to the horizontal of 7–9°.

Back height: 800–850 mm above floor level (may be increased for acoustic reasons).

Back inclination: angle to the vertical of 15–20°.

Seat depth: 600–720 mm for seat and back depth overall, reducing to 425–500 mm when the seat is tipped. The seat depth varies and depends on thickness of upholstery and backing and if the rear of the seat contains the air-conditioning. For a modest seat with arms, the dimensions can be as low as 520 mm deep, 340 mm when tipped. The ability of the seat to tip, activated silently by weight when not occupied, allows a clearway (which is a critical dimension) to pass along a row while limiting row to row distance. Where space is severely limited such as in studio theatres, an especially slim seat, **20.3** can be used.

Arm rests: 50 mm minimum width, with the length coinciding with the tipped seat to avoid obstructing the clearway; the height about 600 mm above floor level; the upper surface may be sloped or not.

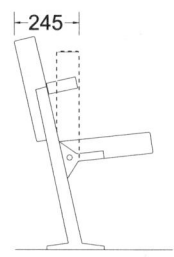

20.3 *A slim 'studio theatre' seat for use when space is limited*

2.03 Supports

The permanent fixing of a seat can be:

- Side supports shared by adjacent seats, **20.4**
- A pedestal or single vertical support, **20.5**
- Cantilevered brackets fixed to riser (if of sufficient height) and shared by adjacent seats, **20.6** or
- A bar supporting a group of seats with leg or bracket support, **20.7**

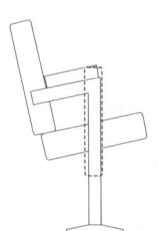

20.4 a *Tip-up seat.*

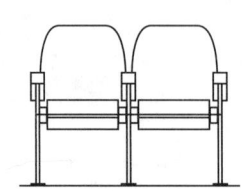

20.4 b *Fixed seating with side support off floor or tread*

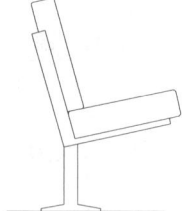

20.5 a *Fixed continuous upholstered bench seating.*

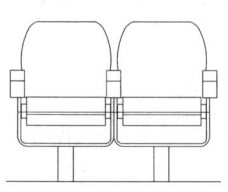

20.5 b *Fixed seating with pedestal support off floor or tread*

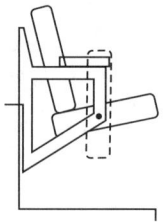

20.6 *Fixed seating with cantilevered support off high riser without overlap of riser*

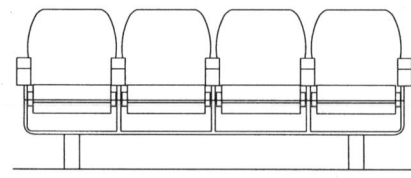

20.7 *Fixed seating with bar support off floor or tread*

2.04 Other factors

Acoustics: upholstery to satisfy the acoustic requirements, usually the level of absorbency when unoccupied, especially the case with music, **20.8**

Ventilation and heating: for air supply or extract under a seat, allow space in floor or riser to receive grille, **20.9**

Upholstery: thickness of padding should provide comfort and avoid fatigue, but not encourage excessive relaxation; material of padding and finish must satisfy fire regulations.

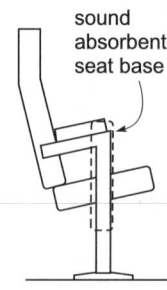

sound absorbent seat base

20.8 *Acoustic control seating (for when unoccupied)*

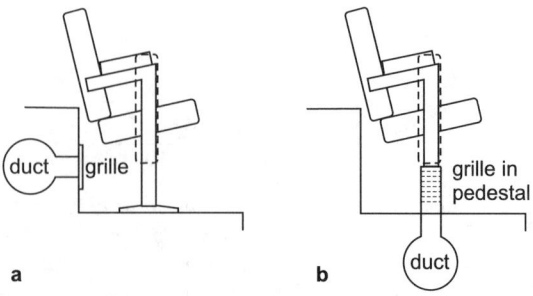

duct | grille

grille in pedestal

duct

a

b

20.9 a *Ventilation grille below seat in riser or floor.*
b *Ventilation grille incorporated into pedestal*

2.05 Writing surface

Conference use may require a writing surface for note-taking. The writing surface may be:

- A tablet fixed to each seat, **20.10**
- A removable tablet
- A tablet pivoted to slide away vertically, **20.11**
- A writing shelf on the back of the row in front, which can be fixed in position, hinged or retractable, **20.12**
- A fixed table with loose seat, or
- A fixed table with fixed pivoting or sliding seat, **20.13**.

Table seating has the advantage that delegates can pass behind the row of seats, and assistants can sit behind the delegates.

In a theatre or concert hall where there is occasional conference use every other row of seats can be used with temporary tables, **20.14**.

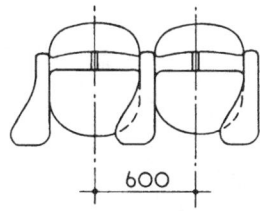

20.10 *Fixed tablet arm*

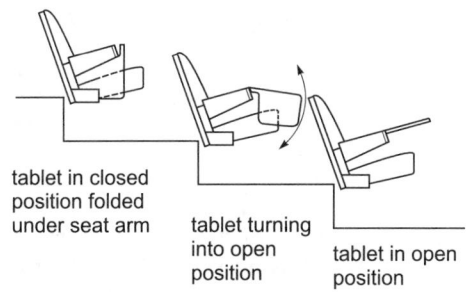

tablet in closed position folded under seat arm

tablet turning into open position

tablet in open position

20.11 *Folded writing tablet under seat arm*

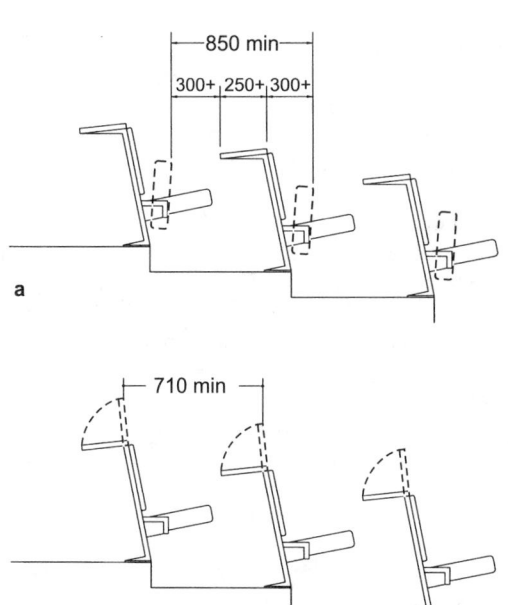

a

b

20.12 a *Fixed writing surface and tip-up seat.* **b** *Fixed seat and tip-up writing surface*

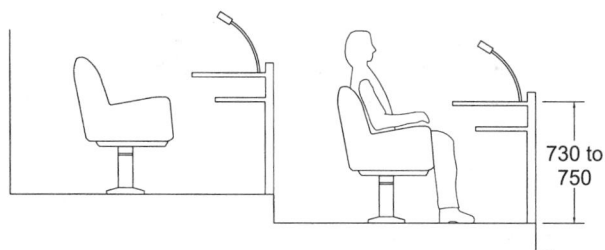

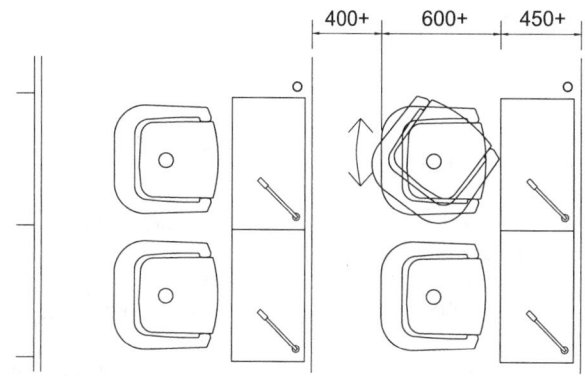

20.13 *Fixed writing surface, individual pivoting seats, section and plan*

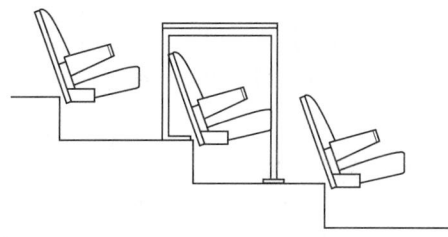

20.14 *Table added to every other row of fixed seating in theatre or concert hall for occasional conference use*

20.15 *Controls and microphone in seat arm*

2.06 Wired services

These may be required for conference use. They can be incorporated into the arm of the seat, **20.15** or into the rear of the seat or table in front. Further details will be found in para **7.04**.

For music, drama and cinema there may be provision for earphones for people with hearing impairment, or this facility may be provided by an induction loop.

3 AUDITORIUM DESIGN

3.01 Audience requirements

As stated above, every member of the audience should be able to see and hear clearly whatever is happening on every part of the stage or platform. This is an ideal rarely (if ever) totally attainable in practice. However, a clear view for everyone of the main part of the stage or platform is normally achievable in modern auditoria. Where an existing building is undergoing renovation, further compromises may well be necessary for some seats.

The greater the encirclement of the audience of platform or stage, more people can be accommodated within the aural and visual limitations up to 180° encirclement. With a full encirclement, the distance from platform or stage is restricted to six rows.

3.02 Visual limitations

Visual limitations determine the maximum distance from platform or stage at which the audience is able to appreciate the performance and for the performers or speaker to command an audience. This distance varies according to function type and the scale of the performance:

- For drama it is essential to discern facial expression, and the maximum distance should be 20 m measured from the setting line of a proscenium stage or geometric centre of an open stage.
- For opera and musicals discerning facial expressions is less critical and the distance can be 30 m.
- For dance the audience needs to appreciate the whole body of dancers and facial expression: the distance should not exceed 20 m.
- For full symphonic concerts acoustic conditions predominate.
- For chamber concerts acoustic conditions also predominate but visual definition assists achieving an intimate setting.
- For conference speaker and lecturer there are two scales: discerning facial expression, restricted by 20 m; larger scale where facial expression is not regarded as critical.
- For slide, video, television and overhead projection visual limitations are determined by their respective technologies.

3.03 Aural limitations

This refers to the distances across which speech, singing and music can be clearly heard without the need for amplification, and beyond which they cannot. For drama, opera and classical music amplification is deprecated; but it is acceptable for variety and pantomime and essential for rock music.

For amplified sound the auditorium requires a dead acoustic with no reflected sound from the platform or stage and limited or no reverberation; loudspeakers are positioned to provide full and even coverage of the audience.

The volume and quality of the unamplified sound is dependent on the volume, shape, size and internal finishes of the auditorium, and on its resultant reverberation time. It is therefore not possible to lay down limits as for visual appreciation. Even experts in acoustics find that their predictions are not always borne out in practice, although they should be consulted and their advice followed wherever possible. It has been found feasible to improve the acoustic of existing auditoria; for example, the famous 'flying saucers' in the hitherto notorious Royal Albert Hall.

3.04 Levels in the auditorium

With a single level only, the pitch of the rake requires particular attention to achieve a sense of enclosure. The Greek amphitheatre is the exemplar.

Seating capacity within aural and visual limitations can be increased by the addition of one or more balconies within the overall permissible volume of the auditorium. Similarly, boxes, side galleries and loges can be added to the side walls, especially in the case of the proscenium format.

3.05 Number of seats in a row

With traditional seating the maximum number is 22 if there are gangways at both ends of the row, and 11 for gangway at one end. Thus in all but the smallest auditorium the gangways divide the seating into blocks.

Rows with more than 22 seats are permitted if the audience is not thereby imperilled. The term 'continental seating' is used for rows of seats with an increased back-to-back dimension extending the width of the auditorium with exits at both ends. This arrangement is only appropriate to proscenium stages.

3.06 Row-to-row spacing

Spacing is controlled by the clearway between the leading edge of the seat (in an upright position, if tippable) and the rear of the back of the seat in front, 20.16. For traditional seating the minimum clearway for people to pass along the row is 300 mm and this dimension increases with the number of seats in a row. For continental seating the clearway is not less than 400 mm and not more than 500 mm. Legislation also dictates the minimum row-to-row dimension at 760 mm: this is usually not adequate and the minimum should be 850 mm for traditional seating.

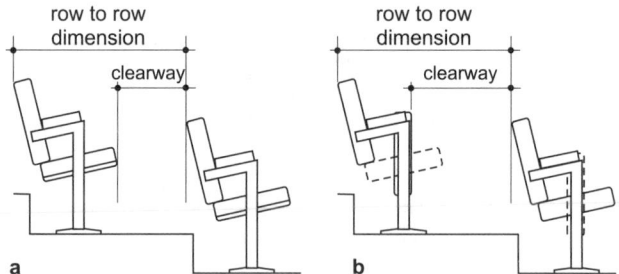

20.16 a *Row to row dimension and clearway with fixed seating.* **b** *Row to row dimension and clearway with tipped-up seating*

3.07 Gangways

As gangways are essential escape routes, their widths are determined by the number of seats served. The minimum is 1100 mm. They can be ramped up to 10%, but only 8.5% if likely to be used by people in wheelchairs. If the seating rake is steeper, gangways must have steps extending the full width and these must have consistent treads and risers in each run. This means that the row-to-row spacing and row rise should be compatible with a convenient gangway tread and riser; and this in turn means that the shallow curve produced by sightline calculations should be adjusted to a straight line.

3.08 Seating geometry

Seating is usually laid out in straight or curved rows focused towards the platform or stage. Further forms are the angled row, straight row with curved change of direction and straight rows within emphasised blocks of seats, 20.17 and 20.18.

3.09 Seating density

Seats with arms and tippable seat can occupy a space as small as 500 mm wide (less for seats without arms) with a row-to-row dimension of 760 mm; but can be as large as 750 mm wide by 1400 mm, 20.19. The area per seat therefore varies between 0.38 m² and 3.05 m². Increased dimensions reduces seating capacity. Minimum dimensions as laid down by legislation offer a low standard of comfort and should not be taken as a norm, but the social cohesion of the audience may be lost if the standards are too high.

In conference halls where writing space is required, lower densities are inevitable, 20.20.

3.10 Sightlines for a seated audience

For every member of the audience to have an uninterrupted view of the platform or stage over the heads in front and clear of overhangs the section and plan of the auditorium need to conform to certain limitations set by vertical and horizontal sightlines.

20.17 *Alternative auditorium seating arrangements:*

a *Straight rows on flat or sloping floor.*

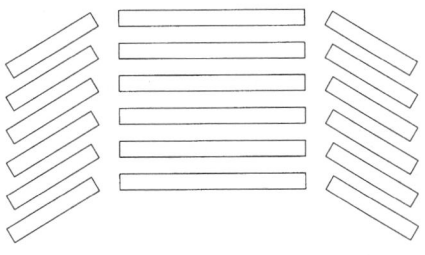

b *Straight rows with separate angled side blocks on flat or sloping floor.*

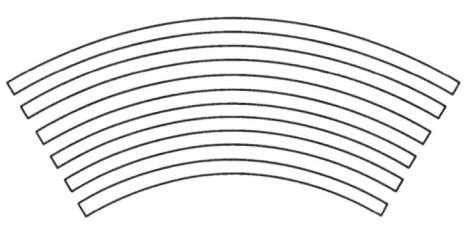

c *Curved rows on flat or sloping floor.*

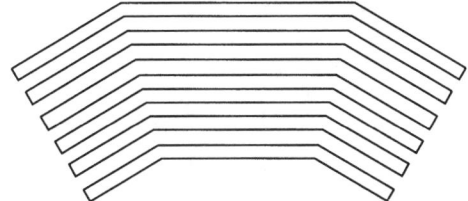

d *Straight and angled rows on flat or sloping floor.*

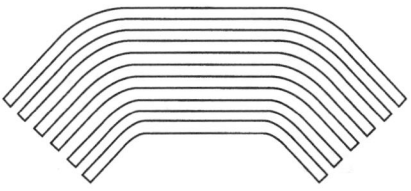

e *As d but with curves at change of angle.*

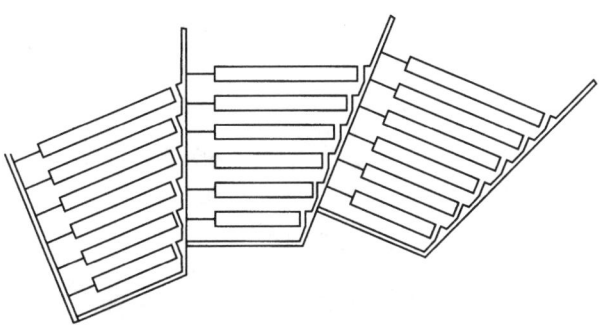

f *Separated stepped blocks focused on stage.*

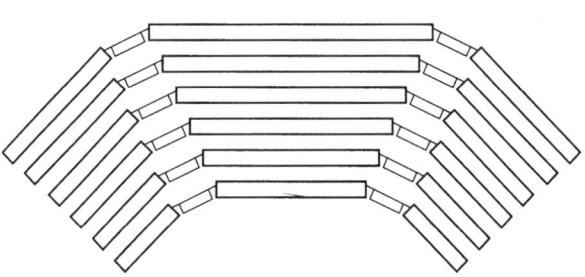

g *Straight stepped rows and separated angled side blocks*

20.18 *Setting-out of auditorium seating rows:*

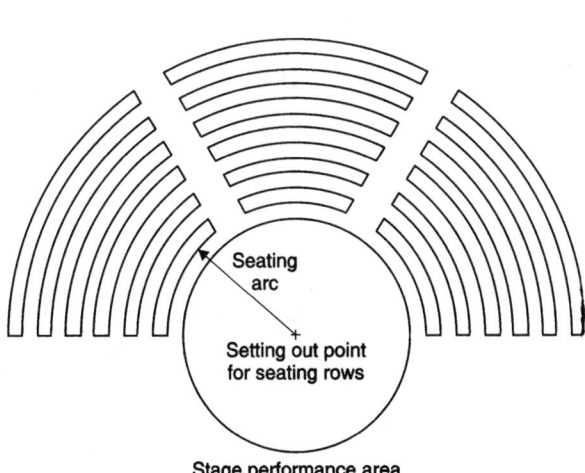

a *Open stage and theatre-in-the-round layouts.*

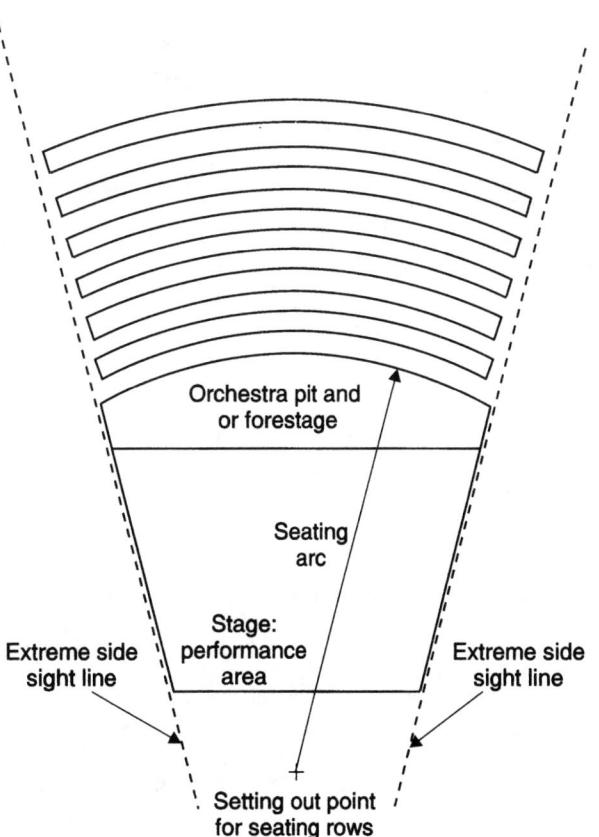

b *Proscenium layout.*

20.18 *continued*

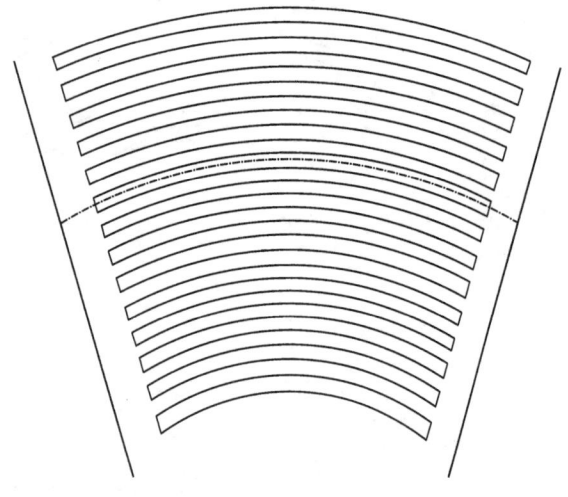

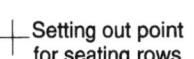

Setting out point
for seating rows

Stalls: lowest level of seating

c *Proscenium and end stage layout 1: stalls.*

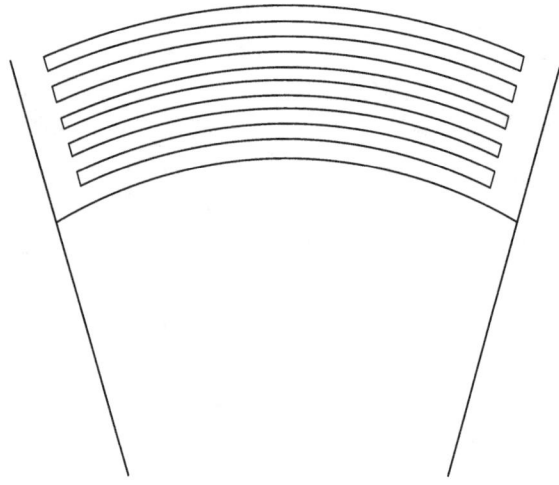

Setting out point
for seating rows

Balconies: upper seating levels

d *Proscenium and end stage layout 1: balcony.*

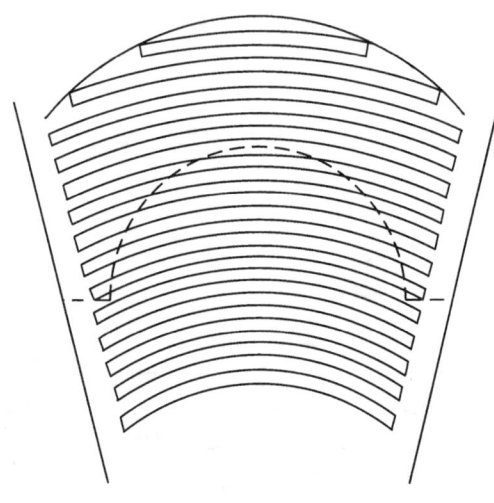

Setting out point
for seating rows

Stall: lowest level of seating

e *Proscenium and end stage layout 2: stalls.*

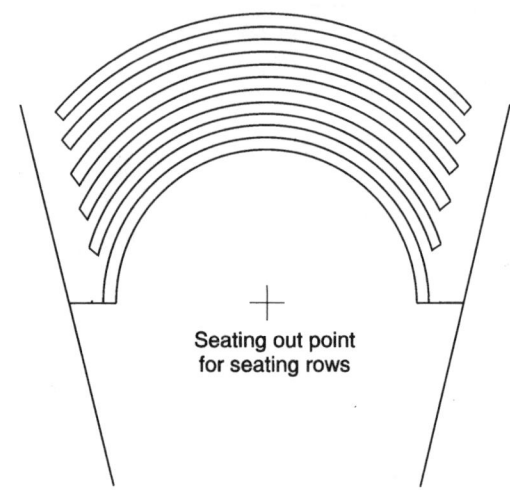

Seating out point
for seating rows

Balconies: upper seating levels

f *Proscenium and end stage layout 2: balcony*

Vertical sightlines, **20.21**, may be calculated by establishing:

P Lowest and nearest point of sight on the platform or stage for the audience to see clearly.

HD Horizontal distance between the eyes of the seated members of the audience, which relates to the row spacing and can vary from 760 mm to 1150 mm and more.

EH Average eye height at 1120 mm above the theoretical floor level: the actual eye point will depend on seat dimensions.

E Distance from the centre of the eye to the top of the head, taken as 100 mm as a minimum dimension for the calculations of sightlines. For assurance that there is a clear view over the heads of those in the row in front this dimension should be a least 125 mm.

D Front row of seats: the distance from point P to the edge of the average member of the audience in the front row. The relationship is shown in **20.21**.

The longitudinal section is a parabolic stepped floor as a theoretical rake produced by the sightline calculation. This gives every member of the audience similar viewing conditions. This may be reduced to a single angle or series of angles.

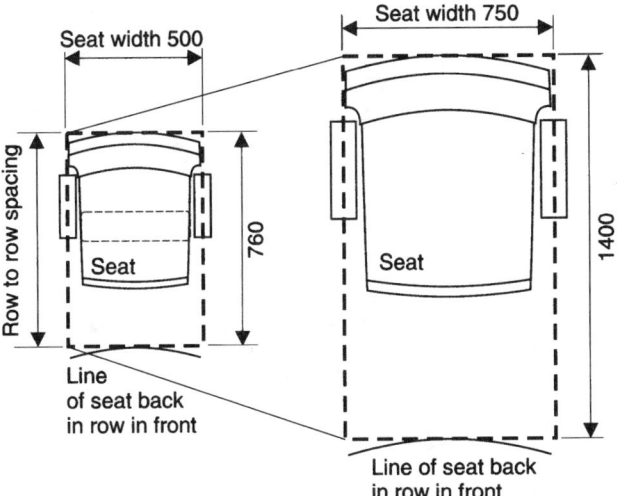

20.19 *Seating density, from 0.38 m² to 1.05 m² per person*

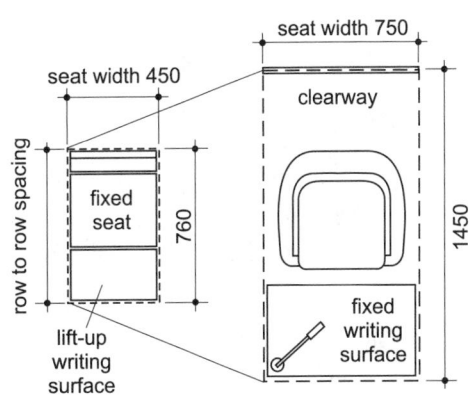

20.20 *Seating density in conference halls, from 0.34 m² to 1.09 m² per person*

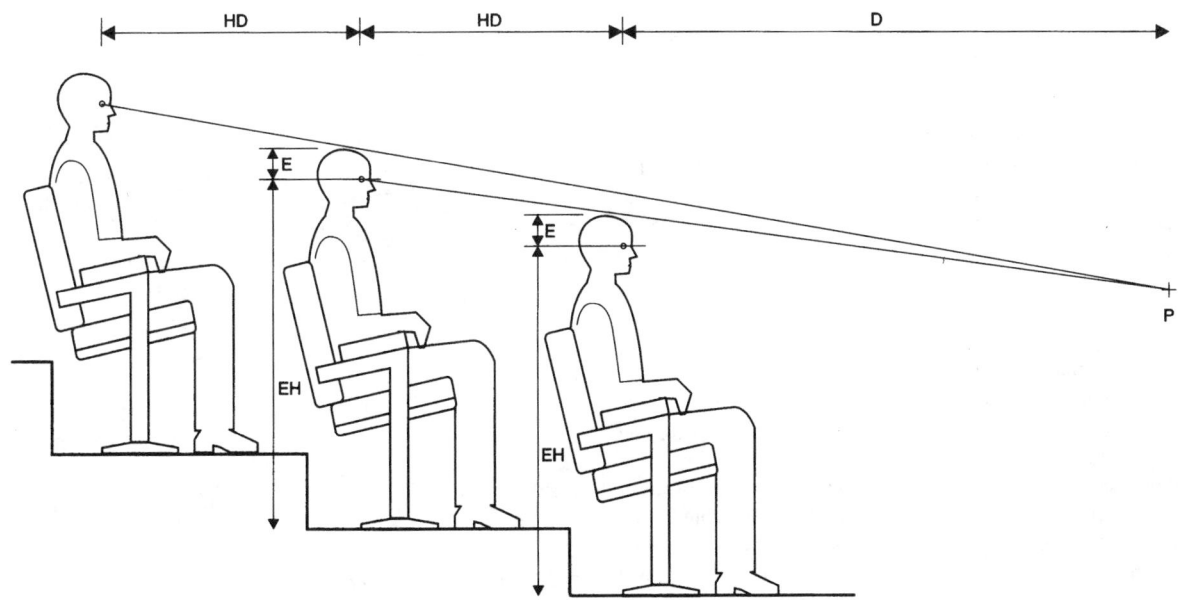

20.21 *Graphic representation of vertical sightlines, P lowest and nearest point on stage clearly visible by audience, HD horizontal distance between eyes in successive audience rows, EH average audience eye height above floor, E height between eye and top of head, D distance from eye of person in front row to P*

When applied as described the rake will also be steep. This is satisfactory for a single tier of seating with no balconies and is especially appropriate for open-stage formats. If a balcony or balconies are introduced, the rake of the lower bank of seats can be reduced, assuming vision to be every other row allowing for point P being seen between heads in the row in front. The vertical distance between point from eye to top of the head for calculation purposes can be reduced to 65 mm if seats are staggered. This is particularly applicable with the design of a large auditorium where, within the visual and aural limitations, the aim is to maximise the seating capacity. This implies a balance between sightlines, height of auditorium and seating capacity. Reducing the accumulative height of the lower level of seating allows more height for balconies.

With the smaller auditorium, especially with the audience partially or wholly surrounding the stage and a limited number of rows of seats, an increased height of the rake to the seating encourages a sense of enclosure of the stage, while providing good sightlines. **20.22** shows how the eye position relates to the seat and the stepped floor.

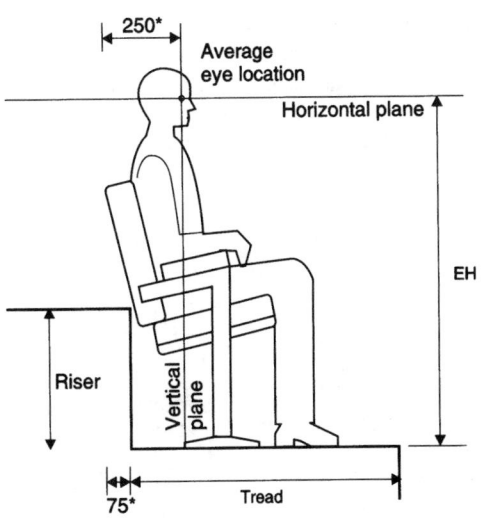

20.22 *Position of eye in relation to seat and stepped floor. Dimensions vary according to upholstery thickness, and inclinations of both seat and back. Working dimensions are starred* *

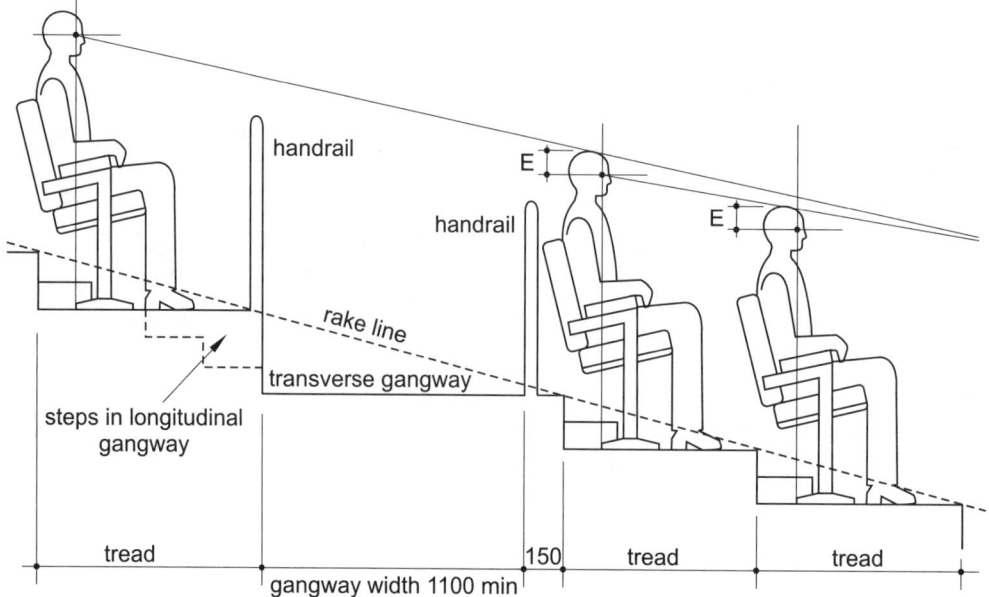

20.23 *Sightlines at transverse gangway; the angle of the rake line is constant*

Cross-gangways

With *cross-gangways* the line of the auditorium rake must continue so that the audience can see the performance area above the gangway as below. With stepped rows there requires a handrail to the upper side of the gangway and, if a steep rake, a handrail to the lower side. See **20.23**.

Horizontal sightlines

Given a particular size and shape of the platform or stage, horizontal sightlines limit the width of the seating area in the auditorium. This is more critical with the proscenium stage and with film, video and slide projection.

Without head movement, the arc to view the whole platform or stage on plan is 40° from the eye, **20.24**. Debatable is an acceptable head movement, where the seat is focused away from the platform or stage, such as with side galleries requiring the head to be turned by the member of the audience, **20.25**.

The horizontal sightline of the performer may also need consideration, **20.26**.

3.11 Wheelchair location

Regulations require a minimum of six places for wheelchair users, or 1/100th of the audience capacity, whichever if the greater. Their location as discrete areas can be at the rear, front, side or within the seating, **20.27**. Wheelchairs can be centrally positioned by forming a bay off a cross-gangway.

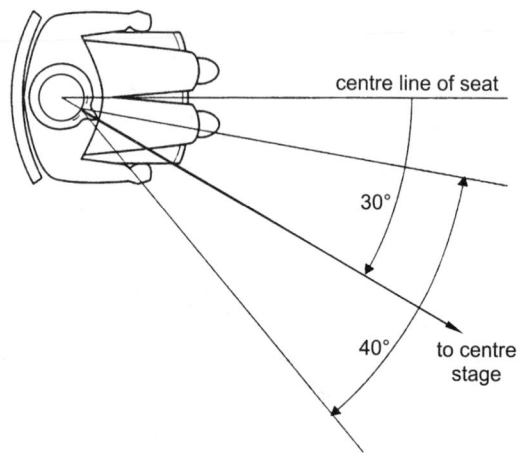

20.25 a *The maximum comfortable amount the head can be turned from the seat centreline is 30°.*

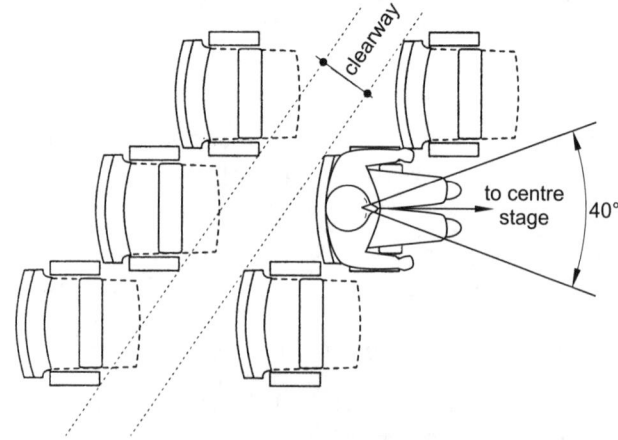

20.25 b *Where the head angle would exceed 30°, the seats may be angled within the row*

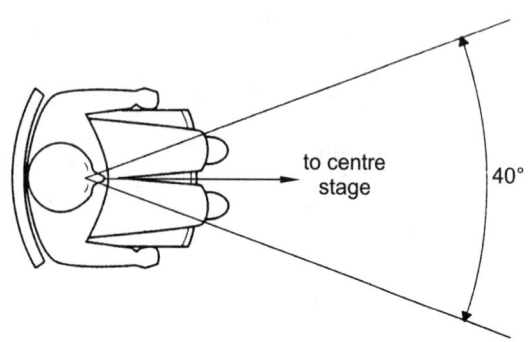

20.24 *The angle of horizontal vision for a stationary head is 40°*

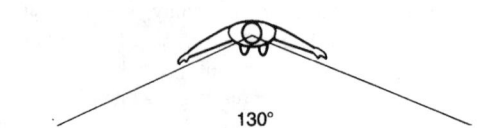

20.26 *Horizontal sightlines of the performer*

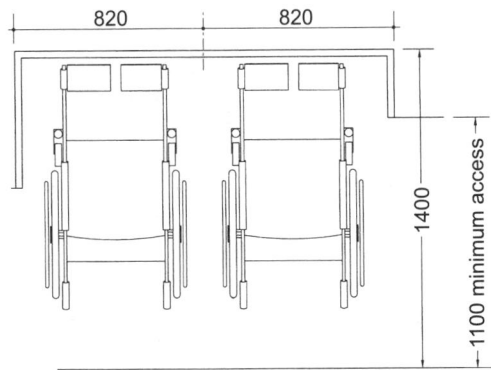

20.27 *Designated wheelchair area, required dimensions*

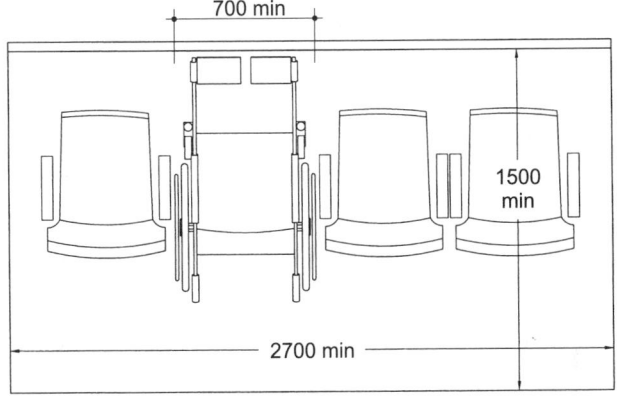

20.28 *Plan of a box designed for a wheelchair plus loose chairs*

A wheelchair user should be able to sit with a party of friends not in wheelchairs, **20.28**. Sightlines from the wheelchair should be checked, as should the sightlines of those audience members behind. Some wheelchair users can transfer into auditorium seats.

3.12 Means of escape

The aim is for all in the auditorium to be able to escape to a place of safety within a set period of time. The escape route is from the seat, along the clearway and gangway, and through exit doors immediately, or through an enclosed corridor, to the place of safety.

Travel distance

The maximum travel distance from seat to exit within the auditorium is determined by the need to evacuate from each level of the auditorium within 2½ minutes. For traditional seating the maximum travel distance is 18 m measured from the gangway, for continental seating 15 m from any seat.

Exits

From each level of the auditorium two separate exits must be provided for the first 500 seats with an additional exit for each further 250 seats. Table II gives the minimum total of exit widths required by legislation. Each exit from the auditorium must lead directly to a place of safety.

Table II Total exit widths required by legislation

Numbers of people	Minimum total exit width (m)
up to 200	2.2
201–300	2.4
301–400	2.8
401–500	3.2
501–750	4.8
751–1000	6.4
1001–2000	14.4
2001–3000	20.8

Exit routes

The route must be a consistent width the same as the exit. There must be no bottlenecks and all doors within the route must open in the direction of escape. Routes within the building should have fire-resistant enclosures. There are special requirements for all doors opening onto fire escape routes.

Stairs

Staircase flights should have at least two risers and not more than 16. All treads should be 275 mm and risers 180 mm.

Ramps

Wheelchair users should be provided with flat or ramped escape routes which may be separate from other routes. Ramps should not be longer than 4.5 m or steeper than 8.5%.

3.13 Circulation

While gangway lengths and widths are calculated as part of the fire escape route, they also provide the circulation through the auditorium, with possible additional gangways from the audience entry points to individual rows and seats.

3.14 Entry points

The audience can enter the auditorium from the foyer at the rear, at the sides of the seating or from vomitories within the seating banks, **20.29**; and the entry points need to connect directly with the

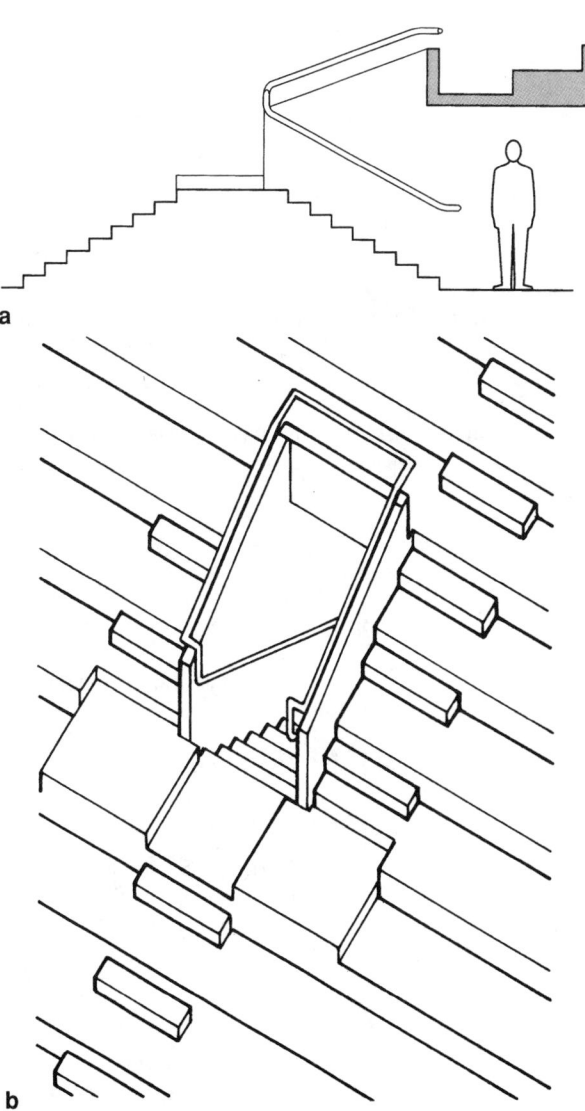

20.29 *Audience vomitory: a public entrance to and exit from the auditorium through a seating block as distinct from through the side or rear walls:* **a** *Section.* **b** *Axonometric view*

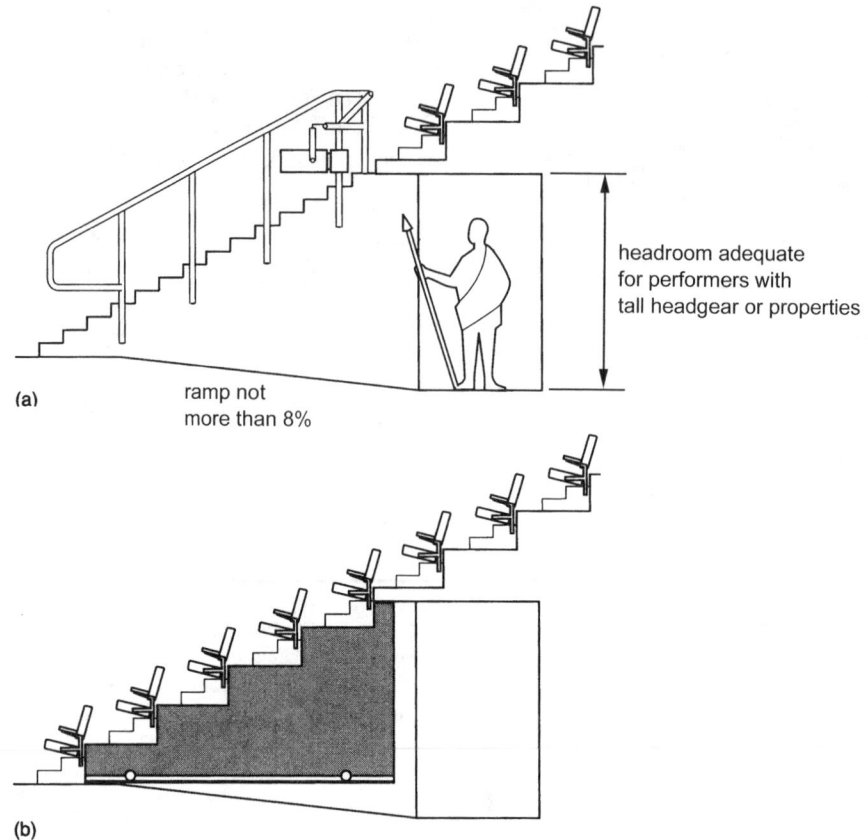

(a) ramp not more than 8%

headroom adequate for performers with tall headgear or properties

(b)

20.30 *Performers' vomitory: access to the stage through a block of seating, usually in an open stage or theatre-in-the round format.* **a** *Section.* **b** *Section showing removable seating in place when vomitory not required*

gangways. There should be a threshold space at the entry points for ticket check, programme sales and for members of the audience to orientate themselves.

Sometimes, particularly in theatre-in-the-round, performers make their entrances from within the audience area, **20.30**.

3.15 Handrails

Balcony handrails, **20.31**, are specified by legislation covering height, width and structure: they must also not interfere with sightlines.

Handrails will also be required to stepped gangways:

- Adjacent to enclosing wall, or
- If there is a drop at the side

They are also needed:

- At landings
- At the rear of rostra, and
- Where there is a drop of more than 600 mm.

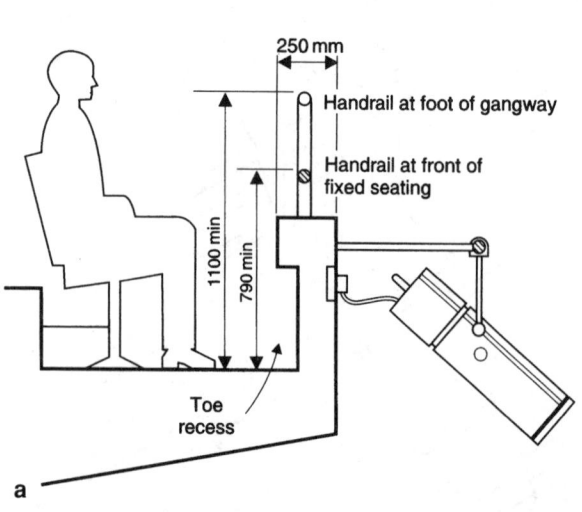

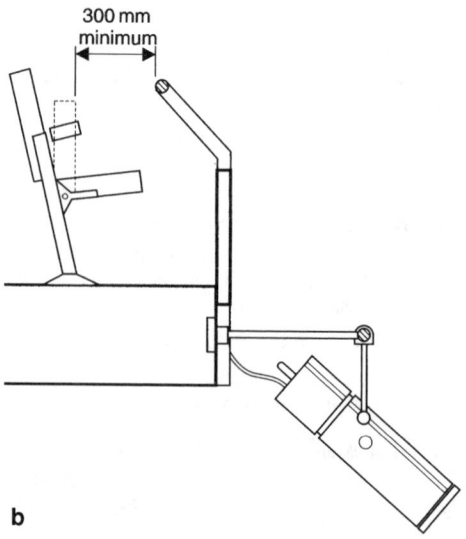

20.31 *The minimum balcony handrail height (BH) is set by legislation at 790 mm in front of fixed seating and 1100 mm at the ends of gangways. Balcony fronts are used to support performance lighting and need socket outlets connected to stage lighting controls:* **a** *Traditional balcony front incorporating shelf below handrail and adequate legroom.* **b** *Simpler front for side galleries with minimum clearway allowing the audience to lean on the handrail. This front is removable as part of a flexible auditorium*

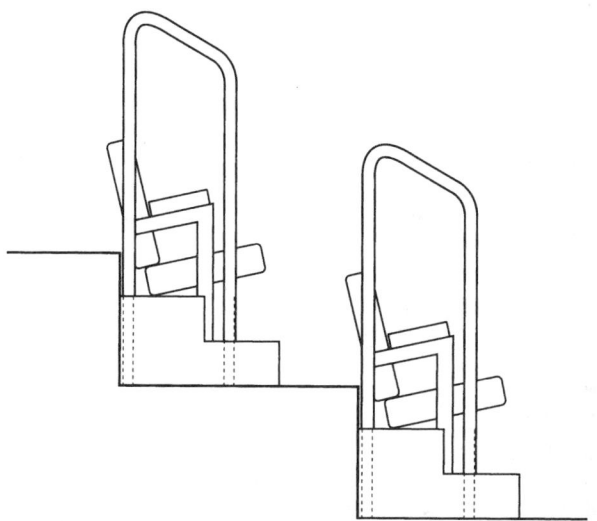

20.32 *Loop guardrail at the end of a row where the rake is steep*

Where the rake of a gangway is above 25° the ends of the rows should have a loop rail, **20.32**.

Rails are usually 900 mm above pitch line and 1200 mm above landings, with infill panels that are solid or have no gap greater than 100 mm.

3.16 Floors

The floor of the auditorium is an acoustic factor in the success of an auditorium. Some venues now dispense with carpets as plain wooden floorboards offer a better acoustic for orchestral music. Consideration should be given as to whether the auditorium floor should be flexible to account for acoustic variability.

3.17 Latecomers

A waiting area at the rear of the auditorium either within the auditorium or in a separate enclosed space with viewing panel and tannoyed sound, or elsewhere with a closed-circuit television facility.

3.18 Attendants

Legislation dictates a number of attendants present at public events, each requiring a seat in the auditorium.

3.19 Adaptation

In multi-purpose auditoria where different formats or uses are combined or part of the raked seating will require to be moved. This can be achieved by forming structure off a flat floor, and methods include:

- Bleacher seating, **20.33**: telescopic structure with tippable upholstered seating with backs, able to be retracted into the depth of a single and highest row; rows are straight and the extended structure is a simple rectangular block, which places a discipline on the seating layout.
- Rostra, **20.34**: complete raked units with either permanent or removable seats, on wheels or air palettes for ease of movement into storage areas when not in use.
- Sectional rostra, **20.35**: a set of boxes able to be built up to form raked units with removable seats; storage requirements less than complete rostra.
- Kit of parts, **20.36**: scaffolding or equivalent set of components able to form raked levels to receive seating; the most flexible system, efficient storage requirements, but labour intensive.
- Hydraulic lifts, **20.37**: mechanical method of raising sections of the flat floor to form a rake floor to receive seating.

Loose seats, **20.38**, secured in position when required for performances, can be used with functions requiring a flat floor.

Following a number of failures of such flexible spectator facilities, legislation has been tightened up and official inspections are often necessary whenever seating arrangements are changed. This means that it is not usually possible to stage a series of different events within a short space of time.

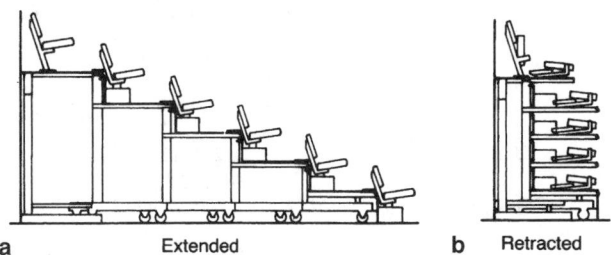

a Extended b Retracted

20.33 a *Bleacher seating: one of a number of proprietary systems of permanently installed retractable systems. The length of seating in a single unit is limited to 6 m. For tip-up seats with arms the minimum riser height is 250 mm.* **b** *Bleacher seating retracted*

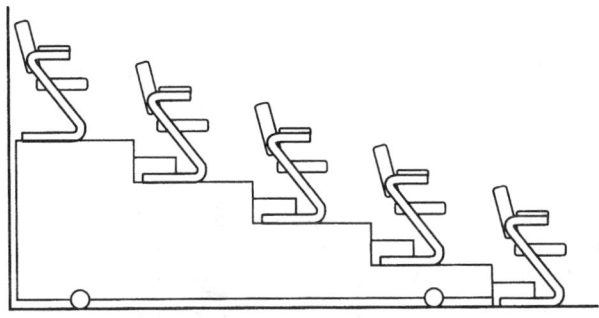

20.34 *Large units on brakable casters or air cushions*

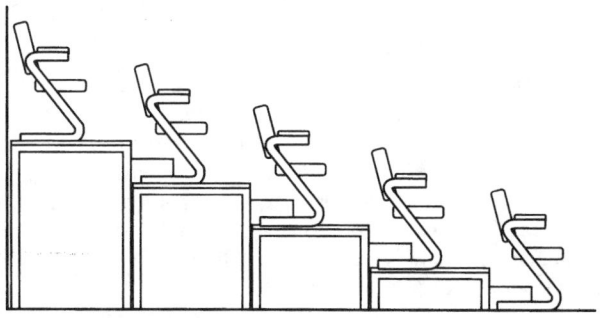

20.35 *Rostra: a set of metal or timber units built up to form a stepped floor on a flat base. Seats are secured onto floor or riser. Each rostrum unit collapsible for storage*

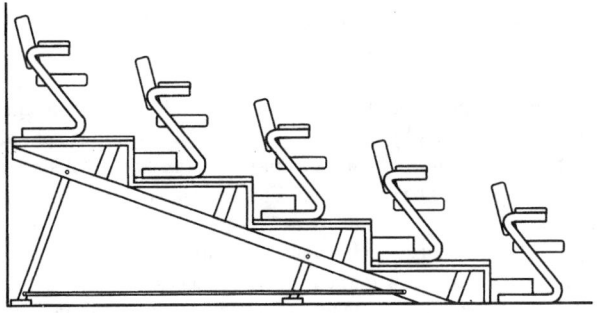

20.36 *Proprietary scaffolding-type system*

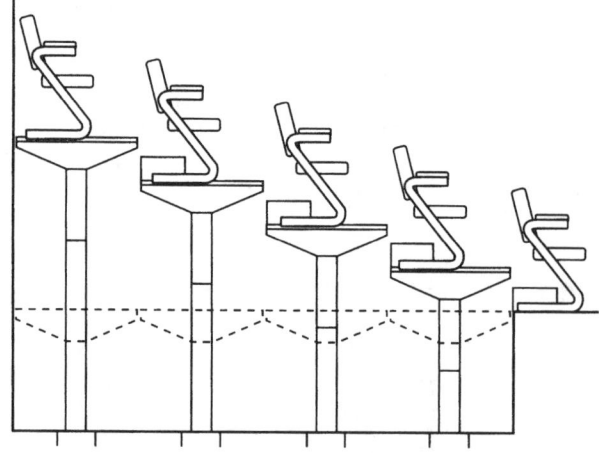

20.37 *Floor sections that can be raised and lowered hydraulically*

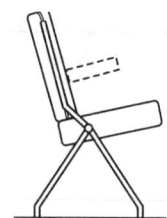

20.38 *Loose seating, capable of removal. May or may not have arms, and be stackable. Needs to be firmly fixed down when in public use*

3.20 Sound insulation from outside noise sources

The standards are expressed as Noise Rating (NR). To achieve the appropriate rating auditorium design may require:

- Isolation of the auditorium structurally
- Sound locks to all doors at point of entry
- Services acoustically sealed, and
- Noise reduction to air conditioning/heating/ventilation system.

3.21 Air conditioning, heating and ventilation

The design depends on the internal standards required in the auditorium, the thermal insulation of the enclosure and on the external climatic conditions. Ventilation needs to provide fresh air at a rate of change to achieve comfort conditions: rates are set down by legislation and include a proportion of recycled conditioned air which vary locally. A common condition is a minimum air supply per occupant of 8 litres per second, 75% of outside air and 25% recirculated.

Extract ductwork can be at ceiling level and under balconies with supply below the seating.

Plant should be remote from auditorium to avoid noise transmission.

3.22 Lighting

There are six different requirements for auditorium lighting.

Performance lighting

For theatre, opera and dance performance lighting is an integral part of the staging of productions, with lighting positions not only on the stage but also within the auditorium at ceiling level, on side and rear walls and balcony fronts. Further details are given in para **4.11** below.

For classical music and serious jazz sufficient lighting for the performers to see their music and the conductor (if any), and for them to be seen by the audience is usually all that is required. Similar lighting is required for the platform at conferences.

Pop music requires as complex lighting as for drama and opera – perhaps even exceeding that with elaborate effects.

House lighting before and after performance and during intervals

Illumination to enable the audience to move around, find their seats and read programmes; decorative lighting to emphasis architectural features. This form of lighting will also be required during conferences.

House lighting during performance

For cinema lighting is only for exit signs and escape routes. For the latter, small lights just above floor level have advantages in not obscuring the screen and being most effective in smoke-logged conditions.

For theatre a slightly higher level of illumination may be used, particularly if the performance demands a contrast with a time of almost total darkness. For classical music it is now usual to have sufficient lighting for near-normal vision and following scores.

Pop music may nowadays require house lighting as sophisticated as performance lighting, with strobe and laser facilities.

Certain lighting is required during performances to ensure safety in emergency, particularly the statutory exit signs. Other lighting may be required to come on automatically in emergency situations; this may work off a separate protected supply. Alternatively, each item can incorporate a battery and be programmed to come on when a failure in the mains supply is detected.

House lighting at other times

It should not be forgotten that the seating area will also require a working level of lighting for cleaning, maintenance and probably during rehearsals and auditions.

Front-of-house lighting

Escape routes have to be adequately lit at all times, during performances as well as before and after. Foyers, bars and ticket offices require careful lighting design to enhance their attraction.

Backstage lighting

Corridors are escape routes for the performers and service staff, and must be kept illuminated whenever the building is occupied. Dressing rooms and workshops will have normal lighting for such facilities, and may be fitted with proximity detectors to ensure that lights are not left on when the rooms are unoccupied.

3.23 Fire protection

Fire precautions should be discussed with the local fire authority and with fire insurers. Means of escape have already been covered in para **3.12**. However, it is important to consider four other factors:

Preventing fires occurring
- Non-combustibility of materials including finishes and seating
- Protection of electrical circuits
- Care with lighting, and
- Separation of hazardous processes such as scene-painting.

Detecting them early when they do occur
- Smoke and heat detectors backstage, in auditorium and all voids
- Alarms connected to the automatic detector system and central indicator panel, and possibly direct link to local fire station. These should be visual (flashing light) in auditorium and not audible.

Preventing them spreading
- Enclosing walls and floors to be fire-resistant
- Self-closing firedoors to openings
- Either a safety curtain to the stage area or special on-stage precautions.

Facilitating extinguishing

- Hose-reels
- Portable extinguishers
- Automatic sprinkler systems backstage (not allowed over seating areas).

3.24 Ceiling zone

Functional requirements cover:

- Acoustics: profiled reflector panels and possible adjustable diffusers. For non-amplified music, reflectors also over concert platform
- Lighting: bridges for access and support for auditorium lighting, working lights and emergency lighting as well as performance lighting
- Ventilation: air ducts and plenums, diffusers, noise attenuation and monitoring equipment, supporting hangers and means of access for servicing
- Production requirements: for operas, dance musicals and drama, a grid and pulley suspension for suspending scenery over forestage, including access by technicians
- Fire control: detection system in voids and fire dampers in ducts and
- Structure: support for roof, ducts, lighting bridges, etc.

4 THEATRE

4.01 Range

Theatre covers productions of drama, opera, ballet, musicals, variety and pantomime, **20.39**.

4.02 Types

Theatre structures are enormously varied and much alteration work is done in theatres during their working lives. This work usually includes upgrading or modernising the stage equipment, and improving the seating quality. The reasons are market driven: equipping to take larger or more complex productions, enabling more productions within a given time and labour-saving measures. Front-of-house improvements are made to attract greater attendance through increased facilities and comfort.

Theatres and studio spaces, which for these purposes also include 'fringe' venues formed out of existing buildings, also see themselves as fitting into a particular bracket, e.g. small, medium or large scale. These categories are determined by a sliding scale involving seating capacity, size of stage, backstage accommodation and even geographical location. The intended scale of use should be apparent in any brief, or should be clarified. It will need to be reflected in the design proposals.

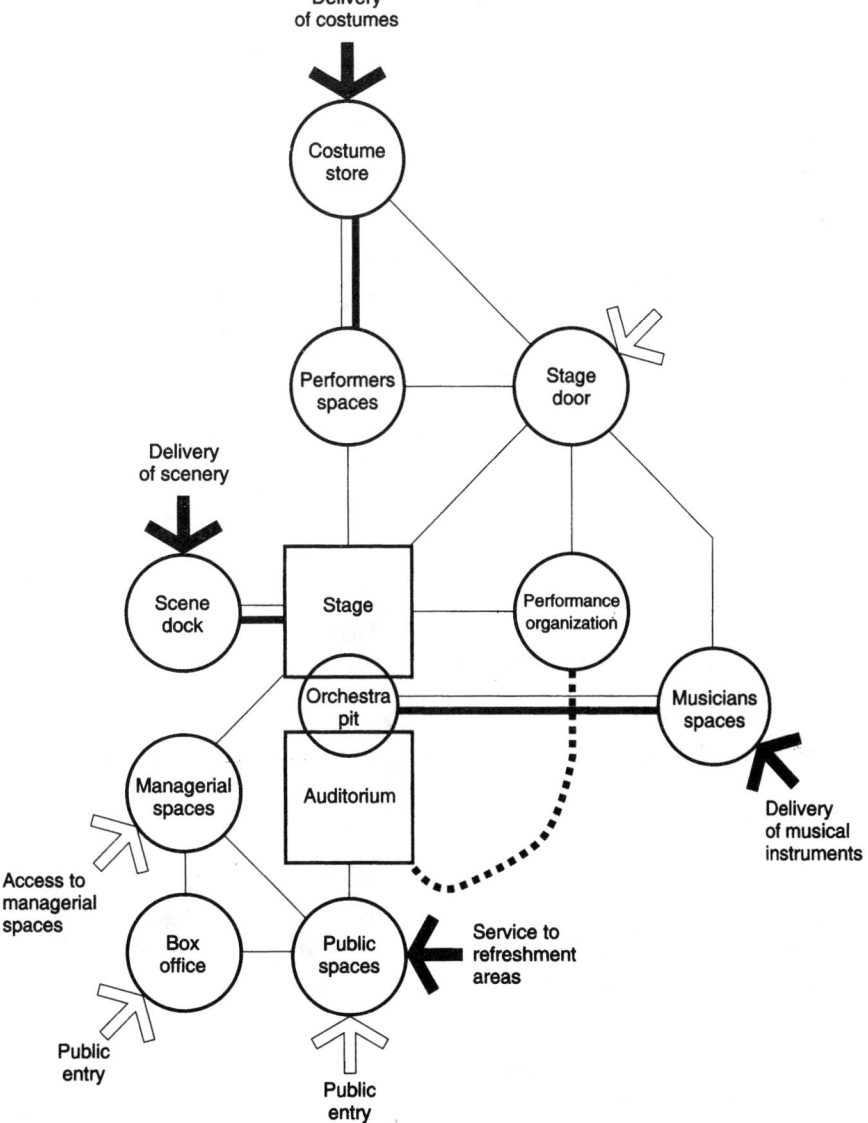

20.39 *Relationship diagrams for buildings for opera, musicals, dance and drama. If for drama only, the orchestra pit and musicians spaces may not be required:* **a** *Where the building serves only touring companies or with a resident company whose production facilities are elsewhere.*

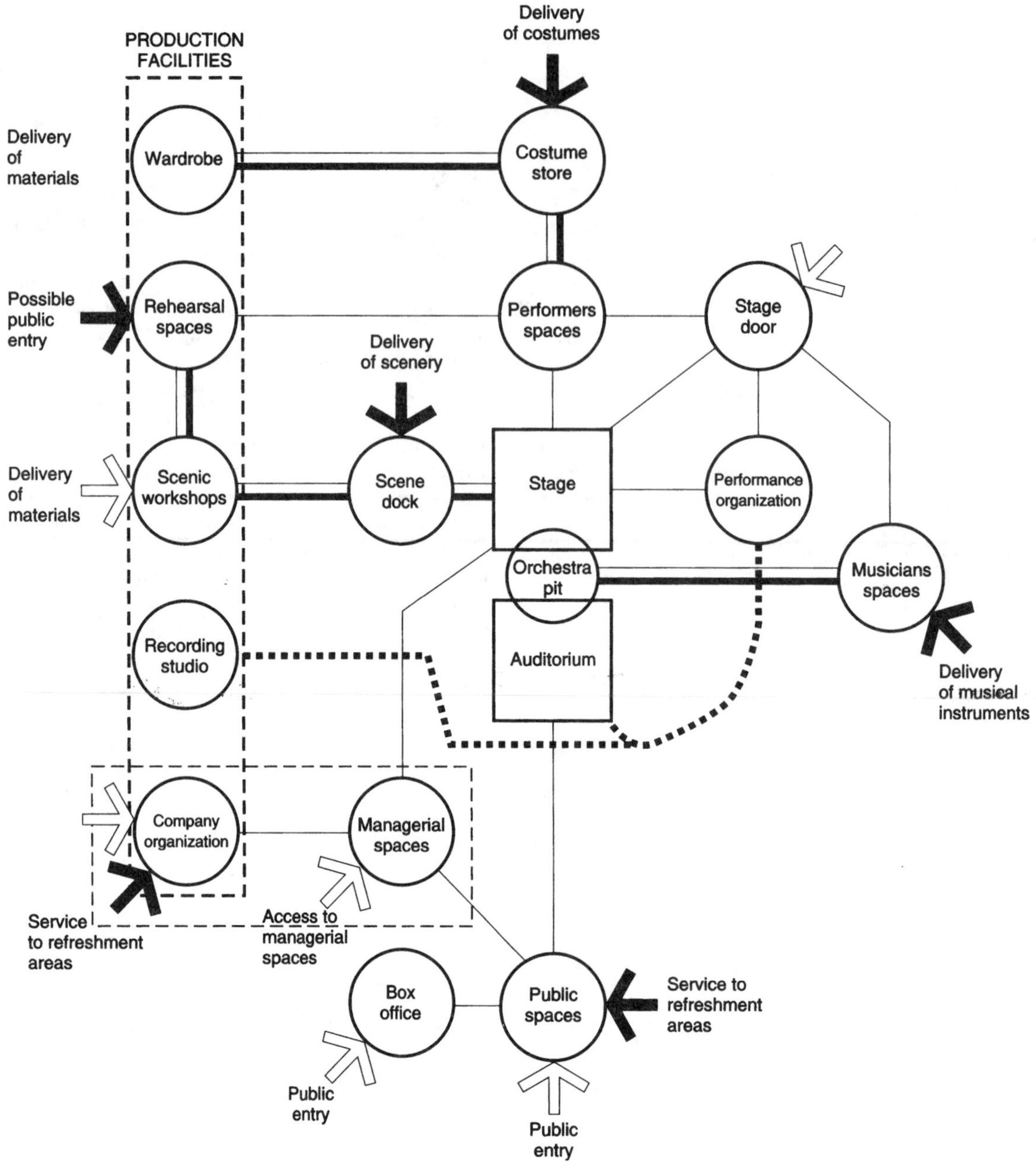

PRODUCTION FACILITIES

Delivery of costumes

Delivery of materials

Wardrobe

Costume store

Possible public entry

Rehearsal spaces

Performers spaces

Stage door

Delivery of scenery

Delivery of materials

Scenic workshops

Scene dock

Stage

Performance organization

Orchestra pit

Musicians spaces

Recording studio

Auditorium

Delivery of musical instruments

Company organization

Managerial spaces

Service to refreshment areas

Access to managerial spaces

Box office

Public spaces

Service to refreshment areas

Public entry

Public entry

20.39 b *Where production facilities are needed*

Medium-scale theatres would normally be considered as those with perhaps less than 1000-seat capacity, without a significant array of stage machinery, but provided with proper fly suspension systems and orchestra pit facilities suitable for taking smaller productions with cast not normally exceeding 20–25 individuals.

4.03 The proscenium

For most opera, dance and musicals, the formats are restricted to the proscenium and end stage. The proscenium form is a conventional arrangement placing the audience facing the stage, viewing the performance through an architectural opening. Scenery on the stage can be developed as a major design element. The traditional position is for the orchestra to be located in a pit between audience and stage, with the conductor in a pivotable location controlling orchestra and singers. The auditorium formats, **20.40**, include the horse-shoe, fan with or without balconies, and courtyard. The latter consists of shallow balconies of no more than three rows around three sides of the auditorium. The end stage is similar to the proscenium format but without the architectural

opening, placing audience and performance in the same space and suitable for small-scale productions.

For drama there is a wider range of formats: the initial distinction is between the proscenium format and open stage

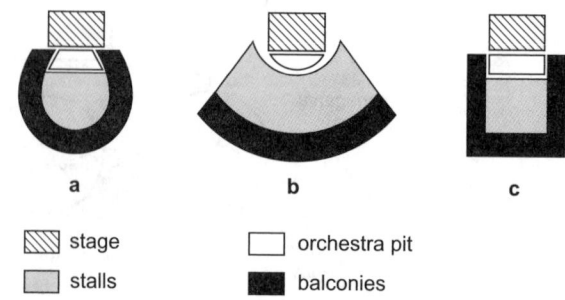

a	b	c

stage   orchestra pit

stalls   balconies

20.40 *Auditorium formats for opera, dance and musicals on proscenium stages:* **a** *Horse-shoe form, shallow rear and side balconies.* **b** *Fan shape with 90° arc, with or without rear balcony.* **c** *Shallow rear and side balconies*

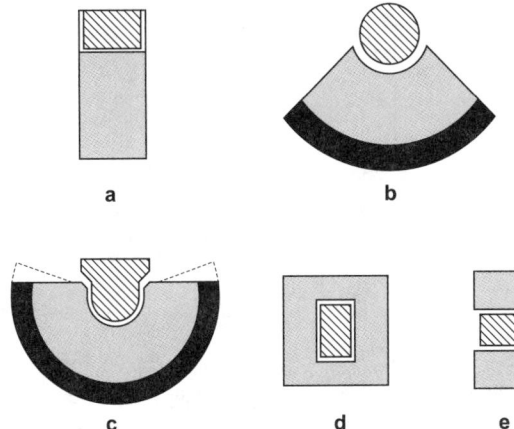

20.41 *Auditorium formats for drama on open stages:* **a** *End stage.* **b** *Fan shape, 90° arc with or without rear balcony.* **c** *Thrust stage, 180° + arc, with or without rear balcony.* **d** *Theatre-in-the-round.* **e** *Transverse: audience on sides of stage*

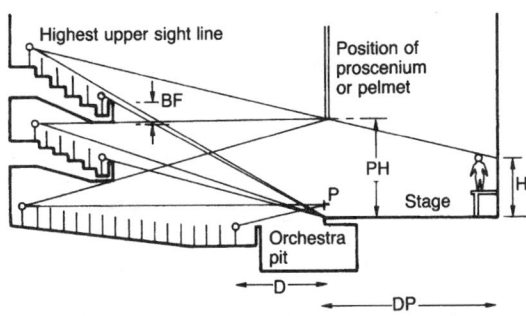

20.42 a *Vertical sightlines for proscenium stage.*

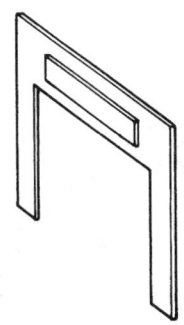

20.42 b *Subtitle panel over proscenium opening: needs to be visible to whole audience. These are increasingly essential for opera, and when drama is performed in a language foreign to most of the audience.*

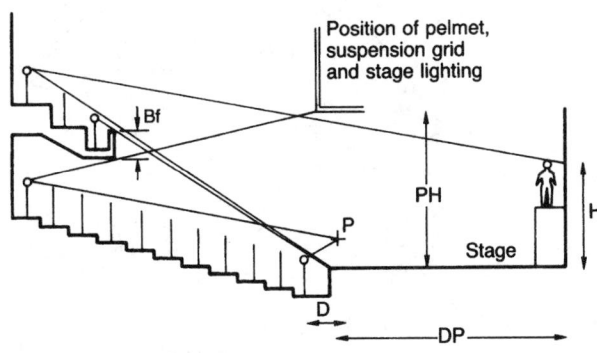

20.42 c *Vertical sightlines for open stage*

forms. The proscenium format is outlined above. There are five variations of open stage formats, **20.41**:

- End stage
- Fan-shaped
- Thrust stage
- Theatre-in-the-round
- Transverse stage.

The viewing criteria in the auditorium will depend on the performance volume on stage, **20.42**.

4.04 Stage

Stage refers to the main performance area and its associated flytower, side and rear stages and orchestra pit if these are provided. The stage floor is a vital part of the working system. It is essential that access can be made to the underside of the stage floor, and that it be constructed of such material that screws, nails etc can be used with relative ease.

4.05 Proscenium stage without flytower

For the smaller auditorium without a flytower, suspension of scenery, curtains, pelmets, borders and lighting barrels above the stage, **20.43**, is necessary. Lines can be fitted to pulleys hung on a grid, with flying from a side gallery above the stage, or from the stage level. Side stages are required for stacking spaces for flats, properties and rostra, as well as circulation routes within the stage.

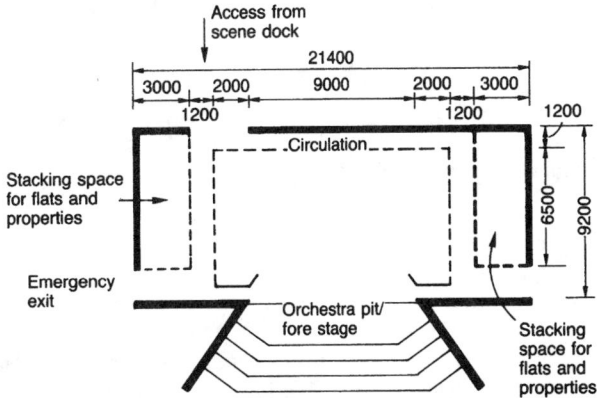

20.43 *Stage layout and dimensions for a medium-size theatre without flytower*

4.06 Proscenium stage with flytower

The dimensions and shape of the performance area are determined by the recommended proscenium opening as in Table III. A wider opening can be reduced by screens or curtains, so that an all-purpose stage should be sized for opera. Ideally, the depth of the performance area front to rear should be equal to the proscenium opening.

Table III Widths of proscenium opening in metres for various types of performance

	Small scale	Medium scale	Large scale
Drama	8	10	10
Opera	12	15	20
Dance	10	12	15
Musical	10	12	15
All-purpose	12	15	20

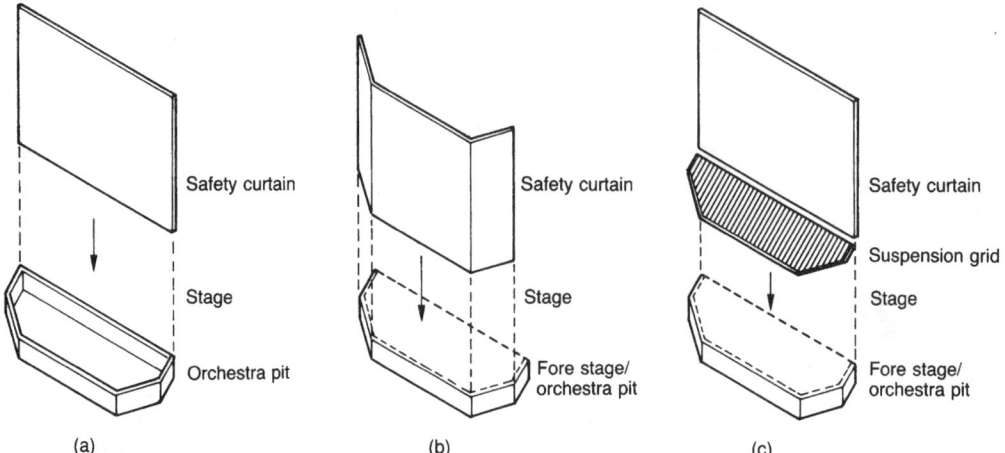

20.44 *Safety curtains, essential for a proscenium stage:* **a** *Simple flat design.* **b** *Cranked design for when orchestra pit is covered to make a forestage.* **c** *Flat design where scenery and properties on forestage are fully incombustible*

Raised stage

The height of the stage can be between 600 mm and 1100 mm with a straight, angled or curved front edge. The floor to the performance area, in part or total, may be a series of traps, that is modular sections usually 1200 mm square which can be removed selectively.

Side and rear stages

Sizes should relate to the size of the performance area. These areas may need to hold sets as on the performance area, with circulation all round. The clear height required to be the highest scenery plus 1 m.

Stage basement

The space under the stage should be fully accessible with a minimum headroom of 4.5 m.

Safety curtain

In the case of fire on the stage it must be separated from the auditorium, with the proscenium opening being closed off by a safety curtain. The normal form is a rigid curtain suspended immediately behind the proscenium opening and dropping on the stage from the flytower, **20.44**. The fire seal must continue below stage level.

Examples of existing fly-tower stages are shown in **20.45** to **20.48**.

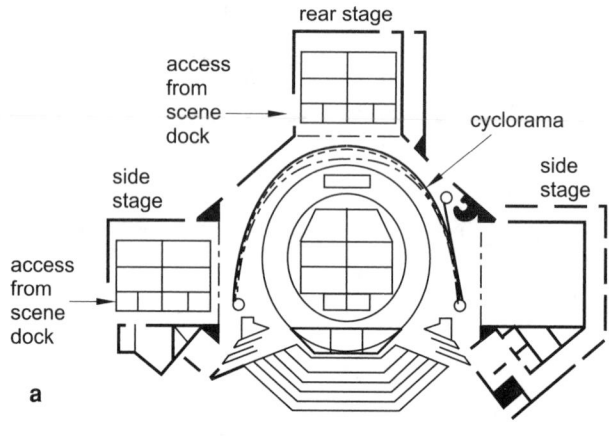

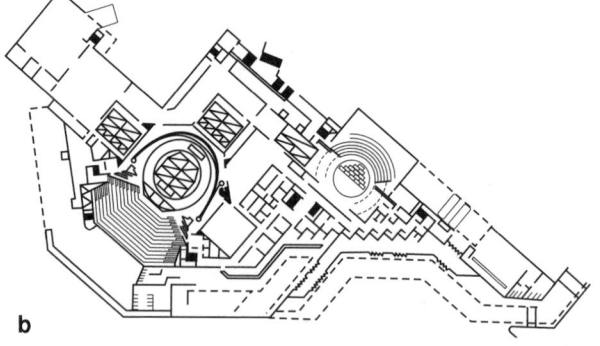

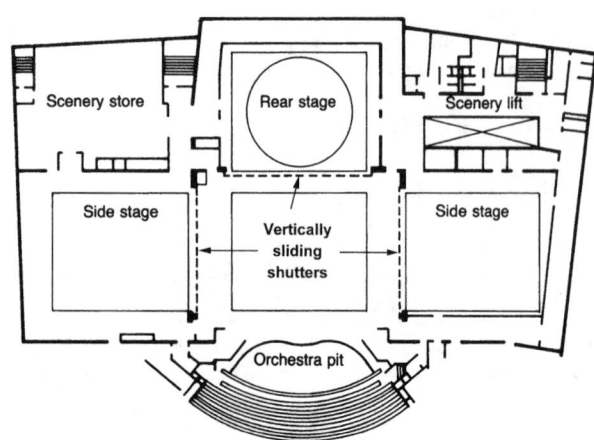

20.45 *Opera House, Essen: stage layout for a proscenium stage with a flytower for opera and dance*

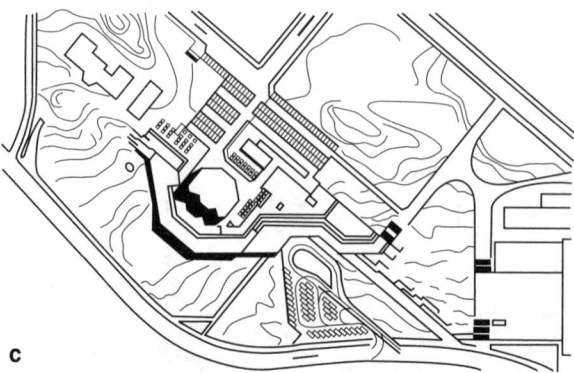

20.46 *Civic Theatre, Helsinki: a proscenium stage with flytower for drama and dance:* **a** *Stage layout.* **b** *Plan at entrance level.* **c** *Site plan*

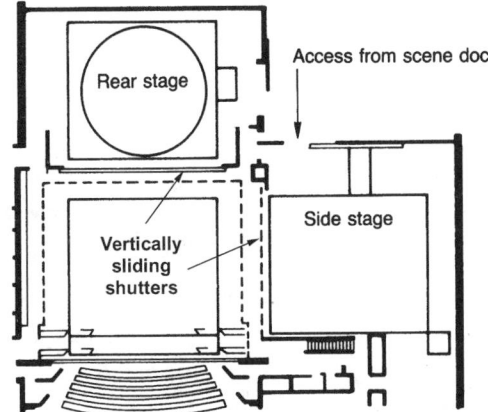

20.47 *Lyttleton Theatre, Royal National Theatre, London: proscenium stage with flytower for drama*

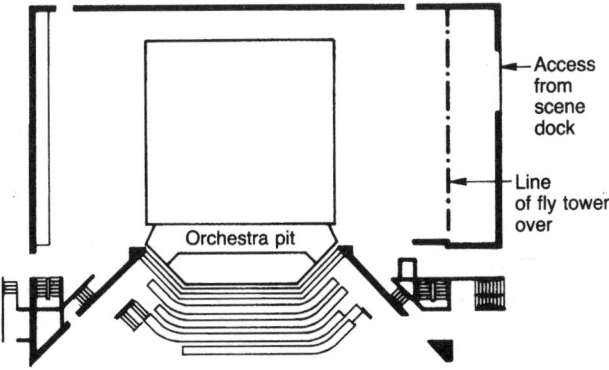

20.48 *Theatre Royal, Plymouth: stage for touring opera, dance, musicals, drama and concerts*

4.07 Stage machinery

Large dedicated buildings such as opera houses require an amount of stage machinery to be installed:

Bridges are long lifts which span the width of the proscenium opening, giving a rise and fall facility over the main acting area. They are driven by screw jacks, scissors, chain or hydraulic systems.

Revolving stages require to be set into the stage floor to provide a flush fit surface, but this can sometimes be organised to coincide with the system of lifts and bridges.

Wagon stages are large pallets capable of taking an entire set which may be moved into place behind the proscenium fully built, thereby saving labour during the performance period. If wagon stages are used, sound separation shuttering needs to be provided around the stage area to shut off the off-stage areas where work is going on to the wagon stages. Depending on the flying configuration, up to three wagon stage positions (left, right and upstage) may be involved in an immediate off stage situation. It is also possible to mount revolves in wagon stages. Much larger installations have in fact extended the wagon principle so that they are used as a system of gigantic palletised storage to store up to a dozen or more sets fully erected in large spaces below the stage, provision being made to have them lowered below the stage surface.

4.08 Flytower

Where there is a space dedicated for use as a stage, then it is essential to provide this with means of suspension overhead. This suspension to be used for both scenic and lighting instruments.

The grid above the stage from where the suspensions come should provide clear walking space above for personnel to move

about over the floor area. The received wisdom is to place the pulleys supporting the suspension bridge at the high point (see diagram) with the walking grid space below it. The key to overhead suspension is the load and the frequency of suspension points. Multi-use, intensively used venues will have bars suspended every 200 mm with load capacity up to 500 kgf per bar. Less intensively used installations may have bars 300 mm apart and, depending on the nature of the performance to be given, the load capacity may come down to 350 kgf per bar.

It is essential that the means of suspension can be lowered to the floor. Depending on the frequency of usage, this suspension system can either be winched, or in smaller installations be operated using rope hand lines. In the theatre, all items suspended overhead are 'flown'. The space above the stage is referred to as the 'flys'. The greater the height over the stage is usually considered the better, offering greater flexibility for designers both of scenic and lighting disciplines. Where the scenic suspension system is raised considerably above the stage it can then be described as a flytower.

Conventionally the clear height of the flytower was $2\frac{1}{2}$ times the proscenium height. Nowadays greater heights are usually demanded, with a minimum of $2\frac{1}{2}$ the proscenium height to the underside of the grid and a clear 2 m above the grid.

There are different means of suspension: the main ones are counterweight and hydraulic systems.

Counterweight systems

A 'cradle' laden with weights travels up and down special places vertically either side of the stage. There are two types:

- Single-purchase counterweights where the travel distance is equal to the height of the grid above the stage, **20.49**: a continuous vertical wall running higher than the grid is required for the guides.
- Double-purchase counterweights where the distance travelled by the counterweights is halved in relation to the distance of the suspension, **20.50**. This allows the operation to occur from a gallery above the stage level : an extra loading gallery is necessary between the flying gallery and grid.

Hydraulic systems

These obviate the need for space for the cradles by containing the entire system at the very highest point in the building, opening up the possibility of side stages on either side.

It is important to locate flyfloors either side of the flytower to provide horizontal access above the nominal height of the scenery.

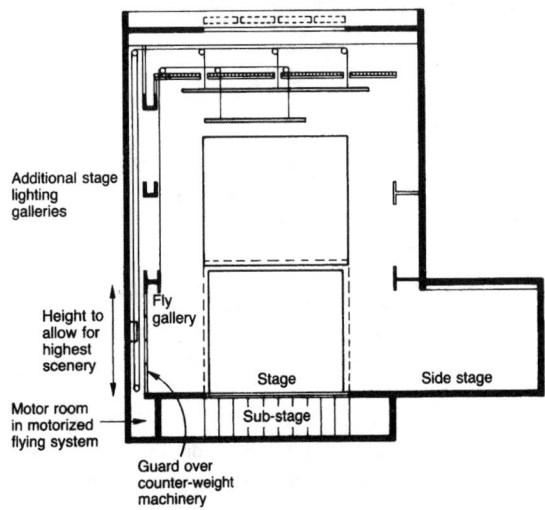

20.49 *Section through flytower showing single-purchase flying system permitting only one side stage*

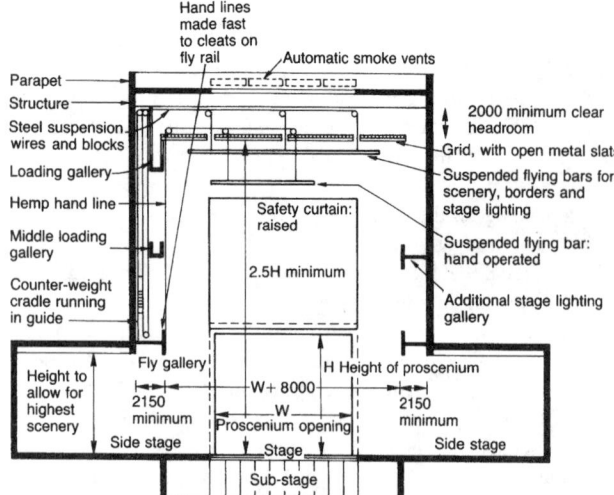

20.50 *Section showing double-purchase flying system and side stages*

This is used by technicians to locate and control horizontal movement of vertically suspended components. If the building is likely to have dedicated usage by a single-occupancy user, then certain suspension positions may be dedicated for lighting systems, in which case a special provision may be made for horizontal access by personnel to reach these positions as well as their raise and lower facility. It will also be possible to feed the necessary electrical supply from directly above the position in a self-monitoring system which caters for the vertical movement. **20.51** shows a flytower stage with a rear stage.

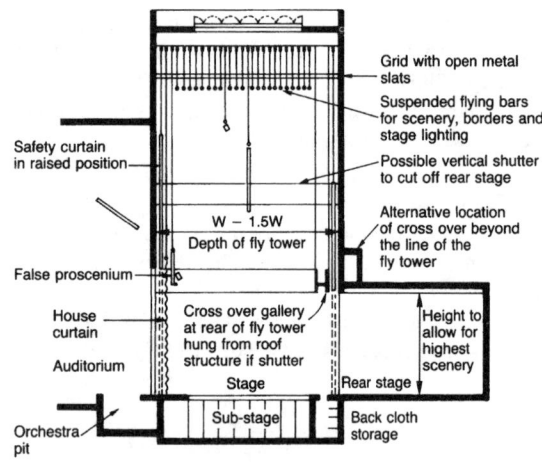

20.51 *Cross-section showing rear stage*

An automatic smoke vent is required at the top of the flytower: regulations require the cross-sectional area of the vent to be a particular proportion of the stage – usually 10%.

4.09 Orchestra pit

A limiting factor is for the conductor to be seen both by the singers and dancers on the stage, and by the musicians in the pit. The audience needs a balance of performance from stage and orchestra.

Allow 3.3 m² average per player, 5 m² for the piano, 10 m² for tympani and percussion, and 4 m² for the conductor. The conductor's eye level must not be lower than stage level when seated on a high stool. To minimise the gulf between stage and audience, the pit can extend under the stage front for a distance no greater than 2 m.

For opera, the pit requires to hold a maximum of 100 musicians, 60 for musicals, 60–90 for dance. The numbers can be less with touring companies. The pit should be horizontally reducible, with the floor level vertically adjustable.

Where there is a multi-use facility orchestra lifts, **20.52**, are common. These can provide:

● A fore stage when elevated
● Two or three extra rows of seating when level with the auditorium floor or
● The orchestra pit when in the down position.

20.52 *Orchestra pit lifts:*

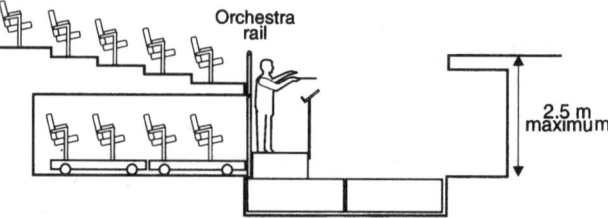

a *Lift in lowest position with seat waggons in store under fixed seating.*

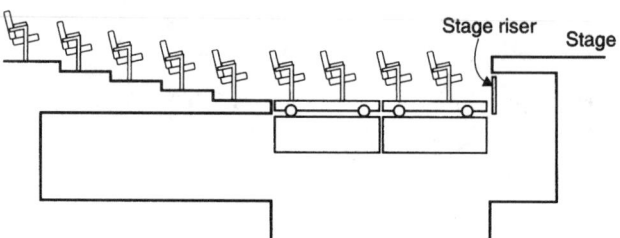

b *Lift partially raised for maximum additional seating.*

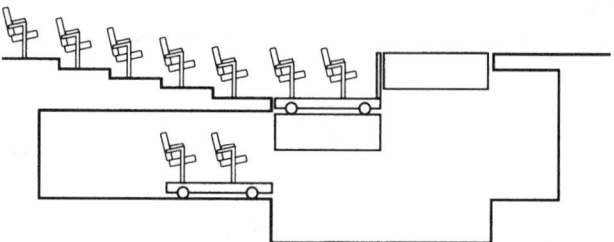

c *Half lift raised for seating and half fully raised for stage extension.*

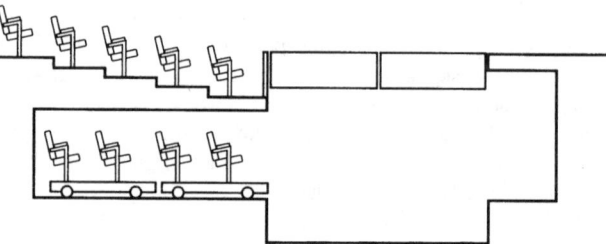

d *Lift fully raised for maximum stage size*

4.10 Open-stage formats

End stage

For dance and opera, the minimum performance area is 10 m × 10 m, for drama 10 m × 8 m. Modest side stages with masking are necessary for the storage of scenery as well as performers' entrances. Orchestra pit can be formed between stage and auditorium.

90° fan

Dimensions vary, based on a circle or faceted circle, with diameters ranging from 8 to 11 m, **20.53**.

Thrust stage

The performance area as a peninsula projecting from rear setting, **20.54**.

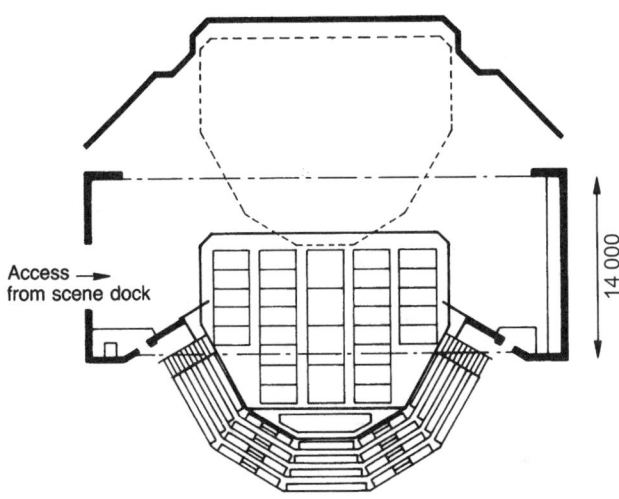

20.53 *West Yorkshire Playhouse, Leeds: plan of a stage where the audience encircles it by 90°. This theatre has a single-purchase flying system and a retractable wagon stage*

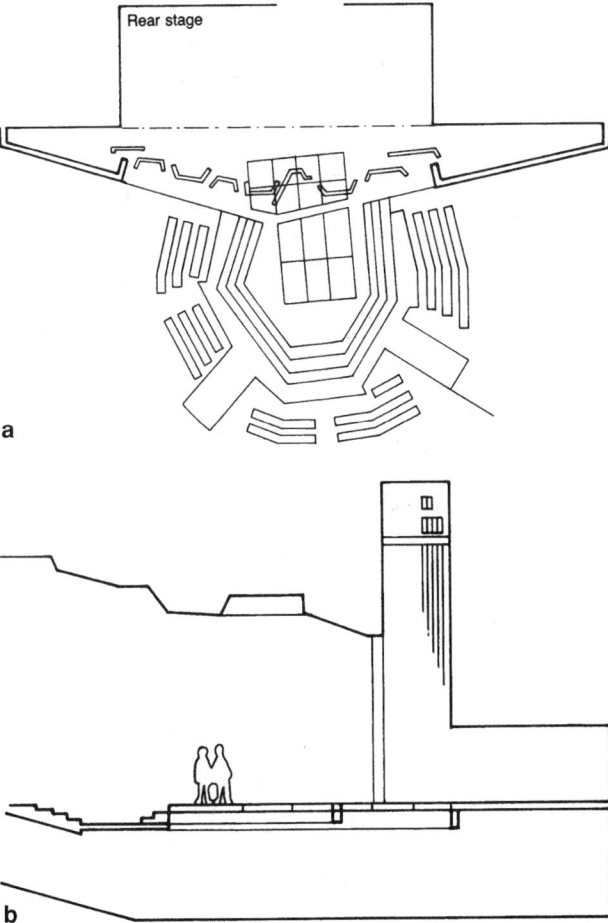

20.54 *Tyrone Guthrie Theatre, Minneapolis: thrust stage with steps at the edge permitting performers to access from various parts of the auditorium. The stage has traps, a rear stage and a backcloth flying system:* **a** *Plan.* **b** *Section*

Theatre-in the-round

The performance area can be circular, square, polygon, rectangular or elliptical, **20.55**. The performers' entry can be combined or separate from the public access.

The stage is usually not raised, but can be 300–750 mm with 600 mm a favourite dimension. The minimum clear height over the stage including scenery suspension grid and stage lighting is 6.5 m. The whole or part of the performance area can receive traps as previously described, with one 'grave' trap 1200 × 2400 mm as a minimum. If there are traps a basement will be needed with access for the performers and minimum ceiling height of 4.4 m.

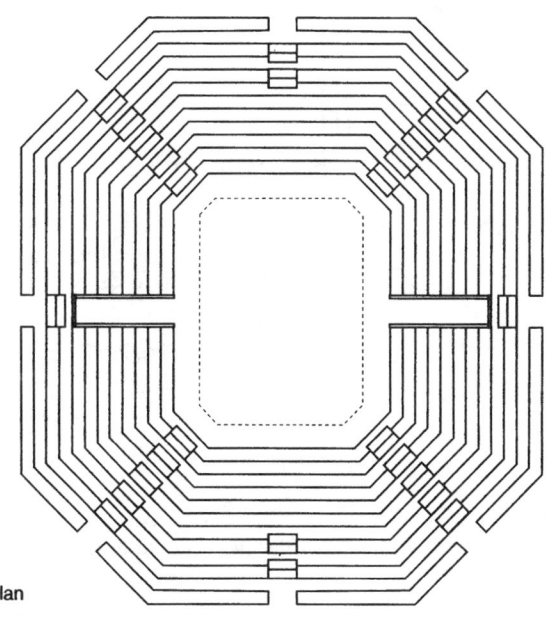

Plan

20.55 *Theatre-in-the-round with a rectangular performance area and performers entering at stage level from vomitories. The audience enters from rear of seating*

4.11 Auditorium lighting positions

There are three main factors governing these positions:

Ease of access is dependent upon the intended use of the auditorium. For intensively used auditoria, staff will require almost daily access to the instruments and this should be provided in such a way that they are not required to use loose ladders in order to carry out their functions. The access needs to be to the rear of the instrument with ample room for the staff to reach around the

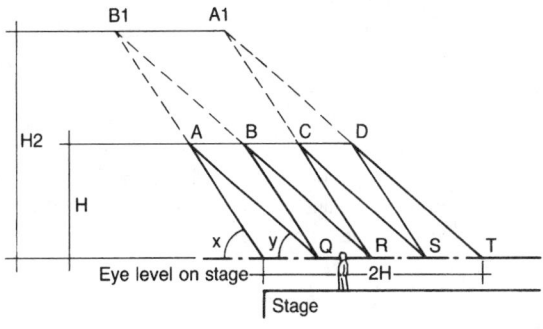

20.56 *Method of locating theoretical positions of spotlights. Spots at A will light a performer at stage edge at 55° in section, about 45° to 50° after crossing, but as the performer moves in from the edge the angle decreases. At Q it is only 40° in section, about 35° after crossing and this is the minimum. Another lighting position B must be provided to cover the area Q to R within the same range of angles, and then C and D to light areas R to S and S to T*

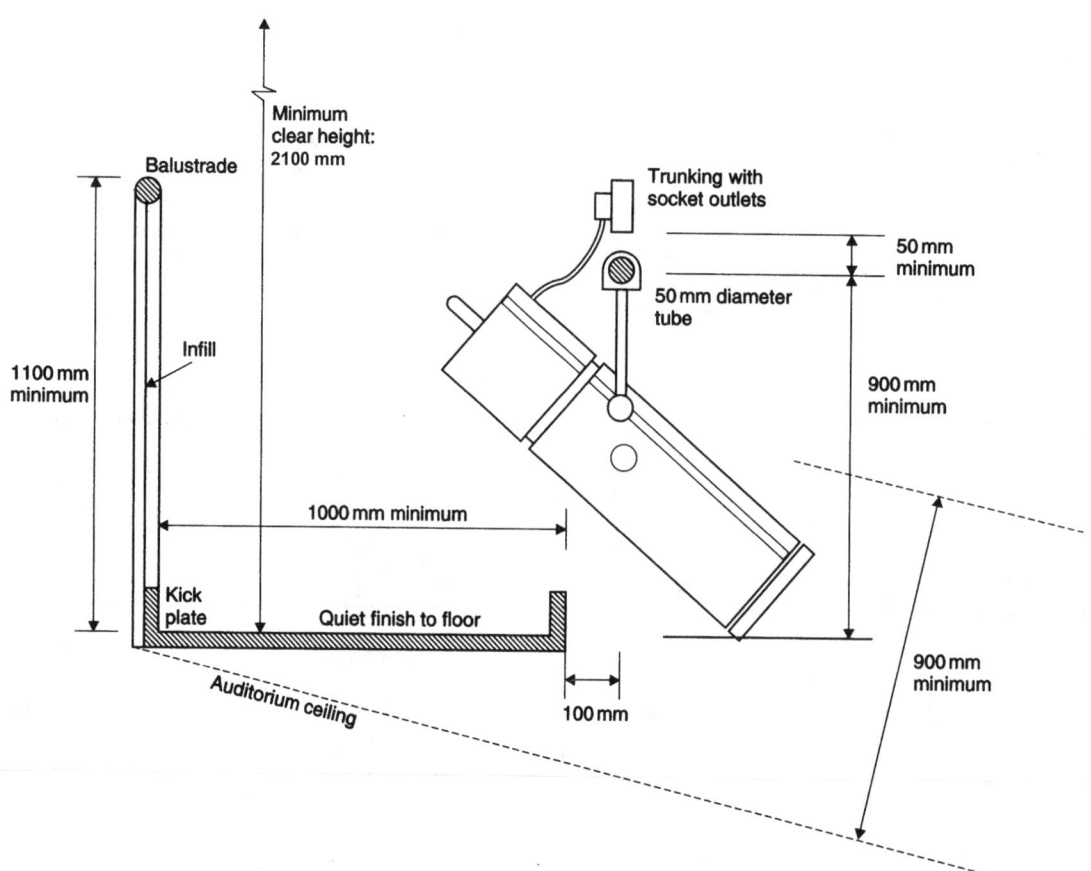

20.57 *Auditorium lighting bridge at ceiling level*

instrument to the front and also sufficient free space for the instrument to be readily demountable should repair be required.

Location. Over a third of the total number of instruments in a modern rig are likely to be located in the auditorium area (front of house), **20.56**. The desired angle is normally between 42° and 44° at an angle to a horizontal plane emanating at the stage front. Lanterns are required at a high angle either side as well as across the main front area of the stage. Depending on auditorium design, lanterns are either housed on bridges which cross the auditorium, **20.57** or are attached to the auditorium structure itself. Provision for instruments on the auditorium side of the proscenium arch in a vertical plane is also recommended. Lighting design for theatre-in-the-round is particularly complex, **20.58**.

Integrity of design. Many people consider lanterns and their relevant bulky cabling and paraphernalia to be unsightly in the context of formal auditorium design and therefore steps need to be taken to provide housings for the instruments such that they are not normally in the view of the majority of the audience. However, auditoria which carry a 'high tech' design ethic will find it just as acceptable to place lanterns in exposed positions, provided they are sympathetically arranged as they then become part of the design integrity. When considering lighting positions, account must be taken of the lanterns themselves intruding into the audience's line of sight, as well as providing a safe means of suspension.

Follow spots

These are an integral part of much musical, ballet and operatic work. An operator directs a movable beam of light onto one or more performers during the course of the performance, **20.59**. Depending on the intended usage of the building, the provision of specific chambers at least 2 m square for this work should be located behind or over seating. The angle of the position to the stage should be around 45° or more, because the whole point of follow spotting is to isolate what is being lit in this way.

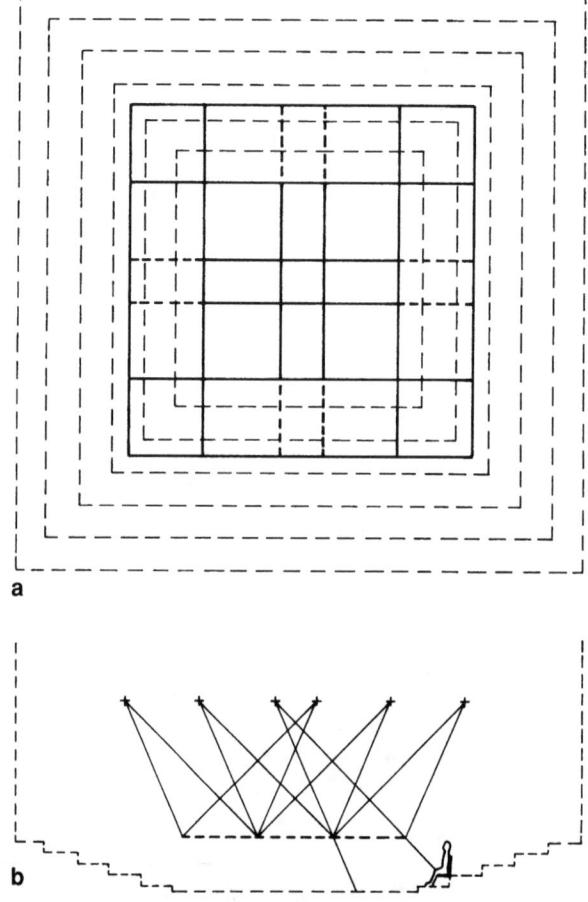

20.58 *On thrust and theatre-in-the-round stages virtually all the lighting comes from overhead to avoid glare in the eyes of the audience:* **a** *Plan.* **b** *Section*

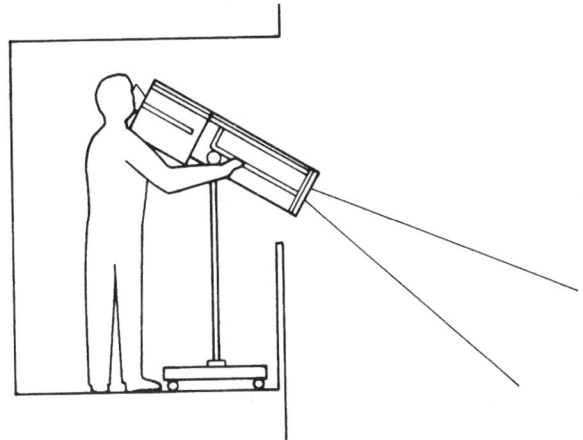

20.59 *Follow spot, minimum size for equipment and operator 1.5 m × 2 m*

A pair of instruments located in a high central position allows the individual operators easy contact, especially if they are separated by glass from the auditorium area. Provision should be considered for two further spotlight positions, either side of the auditorium, at a similarly high angle.

It must be noted that the position should be so that the lantern can reach most of the main acting area of the stage. Sometimes the lanterns are situated within the auditorium on specially constructed platforms at the expense of a number of seats. Provision has to be made for barricading the follow spot position from the audience.

Follow spots as instruments are becoming increasingly powerful and correspondingly larger. Some are more than 2 m in length. Therefore, the overall size of the proposed auditorium will be a factor in determining the size of the follow spot situation. Its position should allow for the instrument, the instrument to swing, and the operator to stand either behind or beside the instrument while this activity is going on. A place for the operator to sit and a local means of isolating the instrument should also be catered for.

4.12 Spaces associated with the audience area

Lighting control room
A room centrally at the rear of the auditorium fully enclosed and sound-proofed with an observation window and space for the lighting control console and for the operator who needs to sit by the console and view the performance through the observation window which has an unrestricted view of the stage, **20.60**. There should also be space for an assistant, a worktop for plans and scripts. A minimum size would be 3 m wide 4.5 m deep and 4.4 m high.

Dimmer rooms
Space is required for the dimmer racks which are the direct means of control for all of the stage lighting instruments. The racks also contain the individual fusing for each stage lighting circuit. Mains cabling runs from the dimmer room to all outlets of the stage lighting installation, and also to the house lights, but the connection between the dimmer racks and the lighting control itself is not a mains voltage line.

The dimmer room should be placed so that quick access may be achieved either from the lighting control position or from the stage

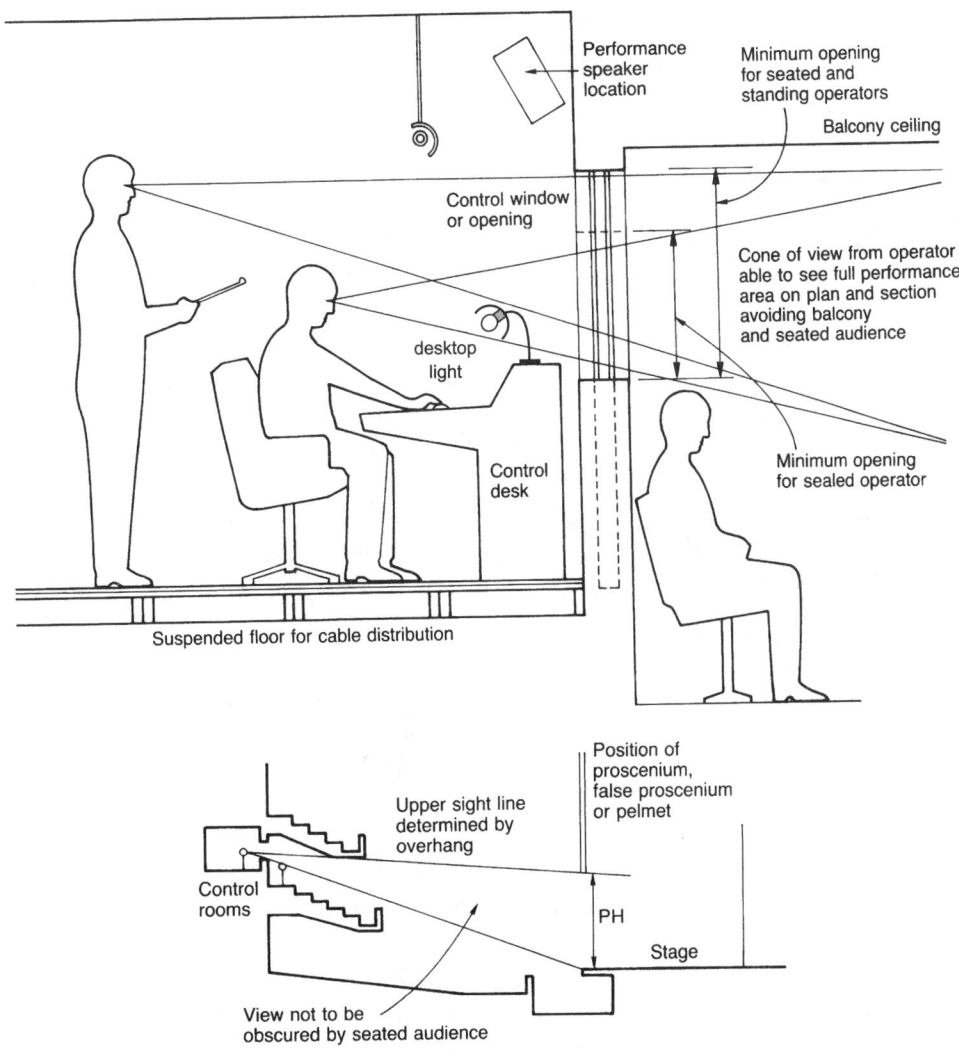

20.60 *Control room with direct view of the stage:* **a** *Section.* **b** *Vertical sightlines*

area. The dimmer room will also normally contain the mains isolation for the stage lighting system. In large installations which have a three-phase supply, each single-phase installation should be physically separated.

Sound control room
An open enclosure in a representative position within the auditorium. The operator requires an interrupted view of the performance area as well as being able to hear the performance. The room contains a control desk, equipment racks, monitor loudspeakers and worktop for scripts. The minimum size is 3 m wide, 4.4 m deep and 4.4 m high.

Auditorium sound-mixing position
For the mixing of amplified sound from the stage by an operator who requires to hear the same sound as the audience. The area requires to be flat, set within the seating area: minimum area of 2 m × 2 m, with mixer pad sound control desk and protective barrier.

TV, radio and recording control room
This is a separate soundproof control room, with observation window and clear view of the stage. It will accommodate announcers, and staff for balancing and directing transmissions and recording. A minimum area of 2 m × 2 m, but should be larger.

Observation room
Those associated with production may need to check activities on the stage from a room at the rear of the auditorium, with a clear view of the stage through an observation window, minimum area, 2 m × 2 m

4.13 Stage-related spaces

Quick change
Separate rooms immediately off the stage, each with two make-up positions and hanging rails.

Properties room
This is a store room, opening directly off a side stage for properties for use during a performance. It requires a sink with hot and cold running water.

Scene dock
At the same level as the stage for storage of scenery.

Loading bay
For the delivery of scenery and properties into the scene dock. Allow for more than one pantechnicon to reverse.

Scenery
A repair and maintenance area at the side of the stage to maintain scenery and properties in use on the stage.

Piano store
For a grand piano when not in use. A separate room kept at a temperature similar to stage conditions; minimum area 4.5 m × 3.5 m.

Lighting equipment
Requires direct access off the side stage for chandeliers, hand properties, etc.

Sound equipment
Storage and maintenance space for such items as microphones, speakers, stands and so on.

Stage manager
Located stage left (facing the audience). Control equipment includes public address, safety curtain and/or drencher release, flytower vent release, and communication with lighting and sound technicians, fly gallery, conductor, etc. as well as cueing performers.

4.14 Spaces for actors, singers and dancers

Dressing rooms
Arrangements are illustrated in **20.61** to **20.69**, covering single shared and communal occupancy rooms.

Green room with kitchen and servery: 3.4 m^2 per occupant.
Laundry for repair and maintenance of costumes, 20 m^2 minimum.
Costume store, including skips and rails
Costume delivery.
Specialist make-up room: 10 m^2 minimum per person.
Pre-performance practice room(s) (singers): 15 m^2 minimum.
Pre-performance dance studio (dancers): 1000 m^2 minimum.
Physiotherapy room (dancers): 15 m^2 minimum.
Wig store and hairdresser's room: 5–10 m^4.
Waiting area for visitors and dressers.
Offices: children's supervisor, company manager, touring manager, etc. 10 m^2 minimum per office.
Toilets.
Performers' assembly areas: at points of entry to stage.

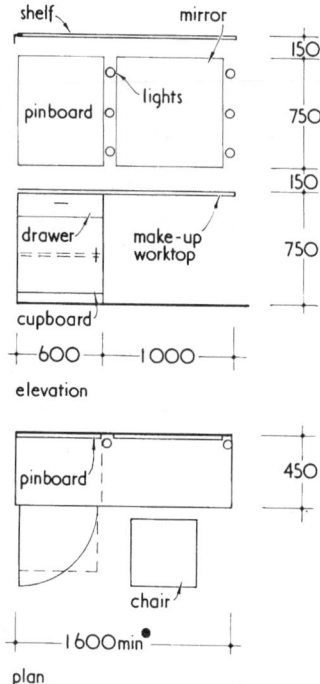

20.61 *Single dressing room:* **a** *Elevation.* **b** *Plan. Dimension marked • is minimum; a greater length is desirable to allow space for flowers, etc*

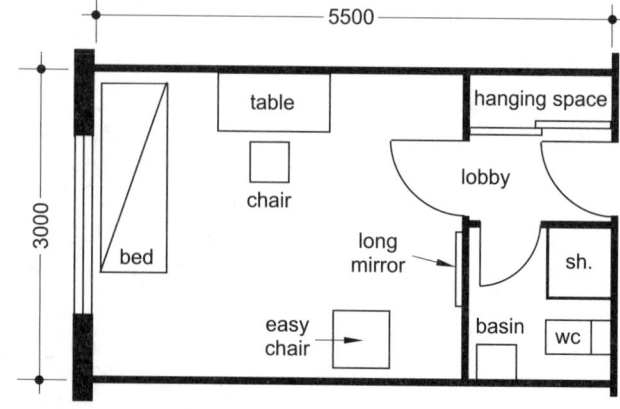

20.62 *Single dressing room with en-suite WC and shower*

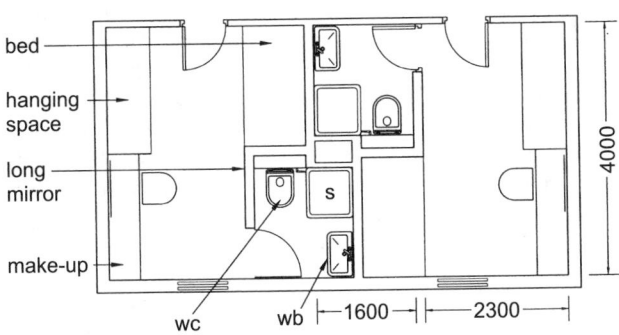

20.63 *A pair of single dressing rooms each 14.4 m²*

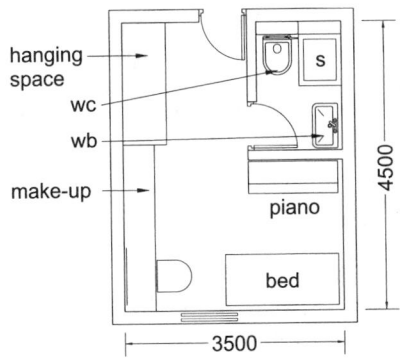

20.64 *Single dressing room with piano, area 15.7 m²*

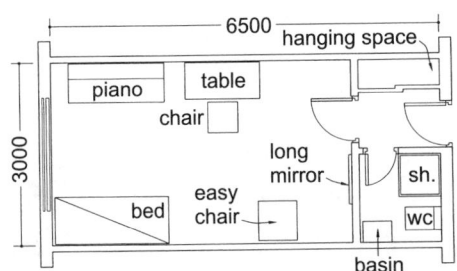

20.65 *Single dressing room with piano and en-suite WC and shower*

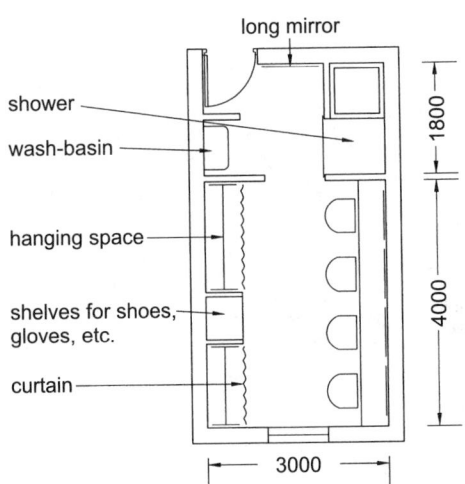

20.66 *Dressing room for four, area 17.4 m²*

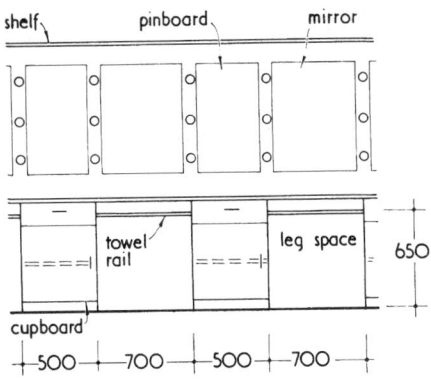

a *Elevation.*

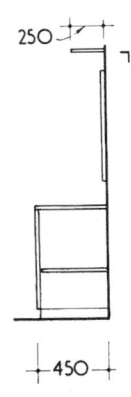

b *Section.*

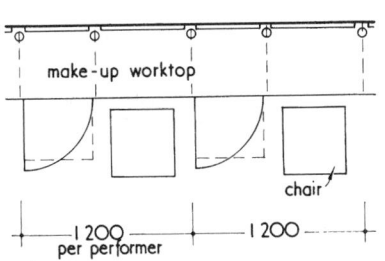

lighting is according to preference or cost; that shown is only a diagrammatic representation

c *Plan*

20.67 a–c *Shared dressing room*

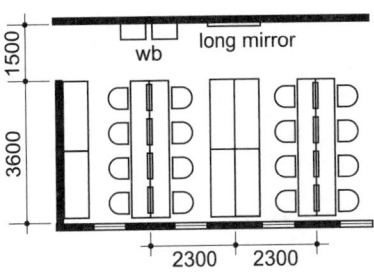

20.68 *Communal dressing room, area of each bay 8.3 m²*

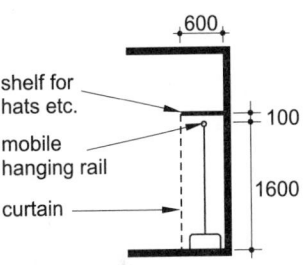

20.69 *Section through hanging space*

4.15 Spaces for musicians

Changing rooms: at least two rooms: area allocated.
Musical instruments store: large instruments and their cases.
Pre-performance practice room(s).
Musicians' common room: 3.4 m² per occupant.
Conductor's room.
Offices: orchestra manager, tour manager, etc.
Musicians' assembly area: at point of entry to orchestra pit.

5 STUDIO THEATRES

5.01 Introduction

Studio theatres, by definition, do not contain moving stage machinery. They usually have some form of mobile or movable seating either to provide for different layouts or to clear the space for other uses at different times.

There are a number of well-developed, flexible seating systems offering great variety and compliance with normal seating regulations, with a foldaway and mobile facility. However, bleacher seating systems demand a dedicated space into which the seating can be concertina-ed when not in use. There is a significant point load factor under the supporting wheels. Bleacher seating arrangements do not offer flexible layout possibilities.

5.02 Access

Studio theatres should have different access points, allowing for seating and performer flexibility. A passage around allows performers to access any entrance. In all cases it is assumed that audience circulation and amenities are located adjacent to designated exits which should have immediate access to further doors on the outer side of the passage leading to the regulatory place of safety. Provision for drapes to be hung and moved around the walls offers the potential for varying the acoustic as well as the colour of the space. Either the walls or the drapes should be black.

Height is a key factor.

5.03 Lighting grid

One of the great selling points for the studio theatre is the speed and ease with which one can move from one production to another. Frequently this is serviced by having a grid made up of 50 mm OD tubing over the whole space from which lighting instruments can be hung in any location. It is doubly advantageous if this can be organised in such a way that there are walk gantries with lighting tubes either side, allowing the personnel to effect all the lighting changes without the use of access equipment and ladders, thereby allowing for completely different functions to be carried out at floor level simultaneously. If the gantry is not possible then it is essential that all of the lighting grid can be accessed from below by a mobile access system. From a desirable lighting point of view, the head of the instrument should not be less than 4 m above the nominal floor level.

6 CONCERT HALL

6.01 Introduction

A relationship diagram for a concert hall is shown in **20.70**. For orchestral and choral classical music in concert hall or recital room there are three broad categories of relationships between audience and platform, **20.71**:

- Audience focused towards the orchestra and choir on the platform, with or without choir stalls, in a single direction, **20.71a**
- Audience on three sides semi-surrounding the platform, **20.71b**, and
- Audience surrounding the platform **20.71c**.

Types of single-direction relationship include the rectangular box as in the diagrams shown, variations on the rectangular box and the fan-shaped auditorium, **20.72**. The rectangular box is a simple well-established form. It allows full cross-reflection of audience, is central to the platform and receives a good sound balance. The fan-shaped auditorium is a particular variation on the rectangular box but suffers from the lack of side- and cross-reflection. Other shapes, **20.73**, include the coffin and elliptical.

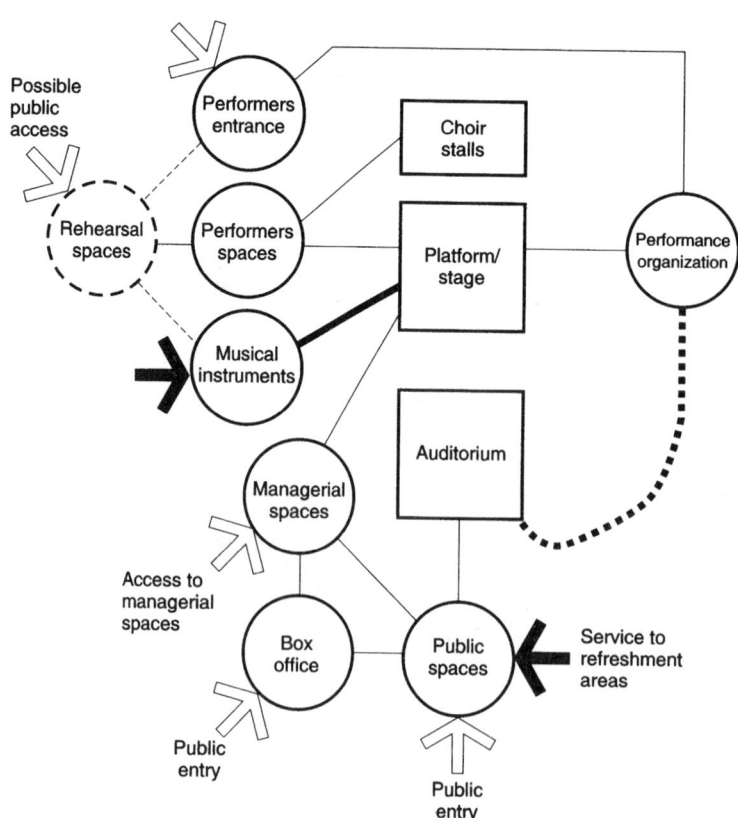

20.70 *Relationship diagram for buildings for orchestral and choral classical music with choir stalls, and for jazz and pop/rock music without choir stalls*

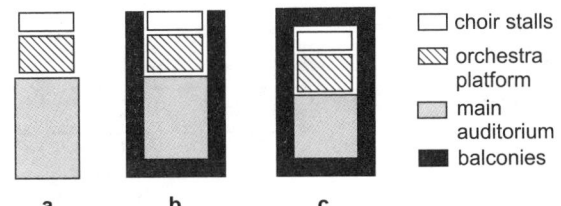

20.71 *Relationships between audience and platform in various rectangular formats:* **a** *Single direction.* **b** *Audience partially surrounding the platform.* **c** *Audience surrounding the platform. With or without rear and side balconies*

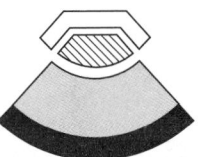

20.72 *90° fan shape, with or without rear and side balconies, in single direction relationship*

20.73 *Orchestral and choral music formats for audience surrounding the platform. With or without rear and side balconies:* **a** *Coffin.* **b** *Elliptical*

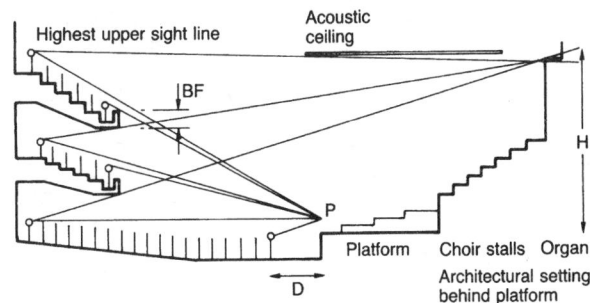

20.74 *Vertical sightlines through auditorium with concert platform. These need to include choir stalls, architectural setting behind the platform as well as the conductor, soloists and orchestra. However, acoustic requirements of direct and reflected sound may override sightline parameters*

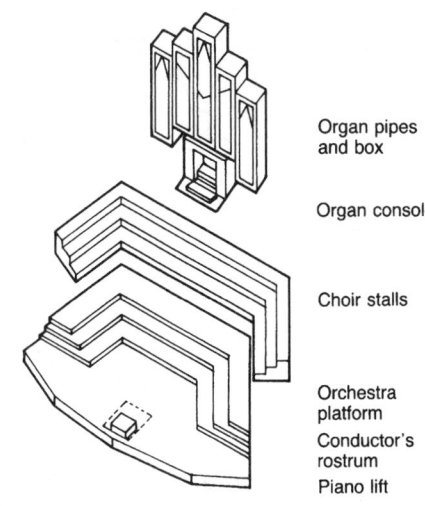

20.75 *Components of the platform for classical music*

6.02 Viewing conditions
For vertical sightlines see **20.74**.

6.03 Platform design
The music components include orchestra platform, choir stalls and organ, **20.75**.

Platform design relates to orchestra size:

- Symphony orchestra and choir
- Symphony orchestra, 80–120 musicians
- Chamber orchestra, 40–50 musicians
- Small ensemble

For a chamber orchestra, the platform can be 6 m deep, 9 m wide and 900 mm high, for a full orchestra an area of 12 m × 12 m, with a platform height of 1000 mm. Various configurations are shown in **20.76** and a section in **20.77**.

6.04 Areas for individual musicians
- Violin players and small wind instruments 1000 × 600 mm; the horns and bassoons, 1000 × 800 mm
- 1200 mm tiers for string and wind players, including cellos and double base
- Tiers up to 2 m for percussion or concert grand piano: 2.75 m × 1.6 m
- Choir: 0.38 m² minimum per singer in choir stalls with seats. The longitudinal section can be flat and stepped transversely, rising from the conductor's rostrum.

6.05 Associated spaces
- Lighting and control room
- Dimmers
- Television and radio transmission and recording control room
- Follow spot
- Observation room

See also para **6.08** below.

6.06 Platform-related spaces
- Piano store
- Storage of musical instruments
- Delivery of musical instruments
- Access for deliveries
- Parking provision for touring vans
- Offices
- Technicians changing
- Electrical workshop
- Electrical store

6.07 Performers' spaces
- Changing rooms: not more than 20 people per room, 3.5 m² each
- Single rooms, **20.62**, 19 m²
- Single room with piano, **20.65**, 23.5 m²
- Single room with space for auditions 40 m²
- Shared rooms 2 m² per occupant.

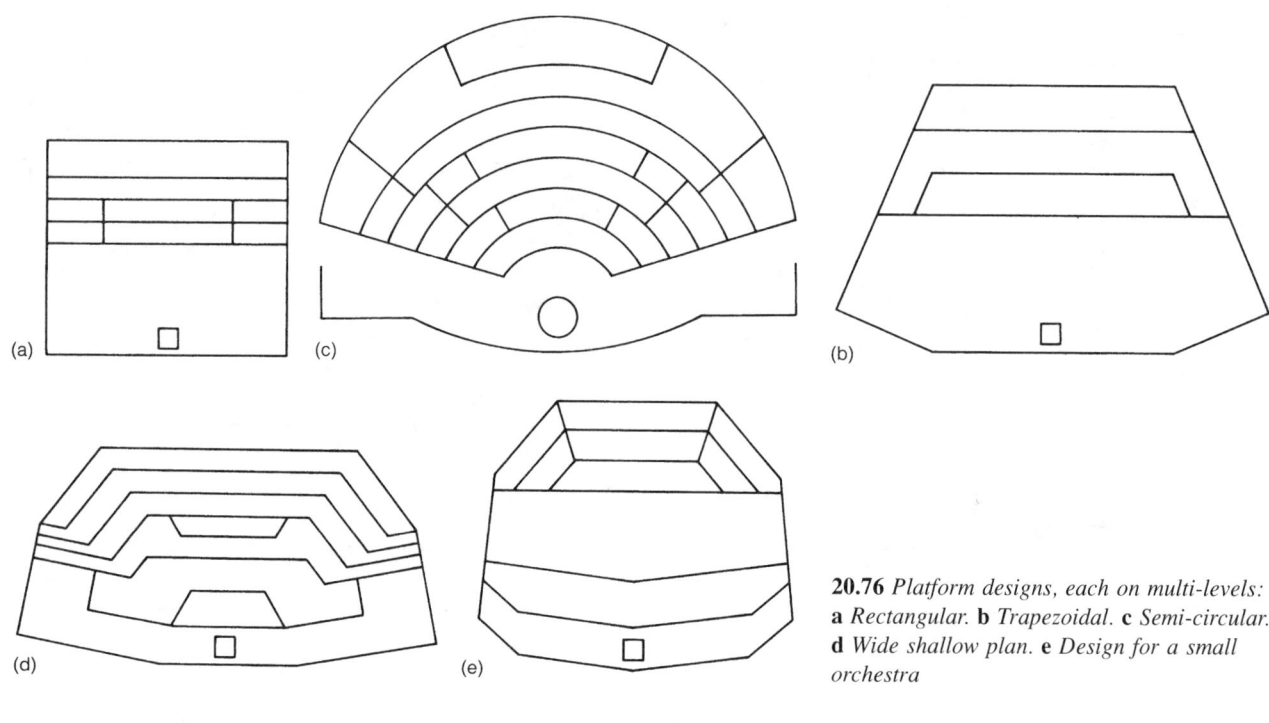

(a)

(c)

(b)

(d)

(e)

20.76 *Platform designs, each on multi-levels:*
a *Rectangular.* **b** *Trapezoidal.* **c** *Semi-circular.*
d *Wide shallow plan.* **e** *Design for a small*
orchestra

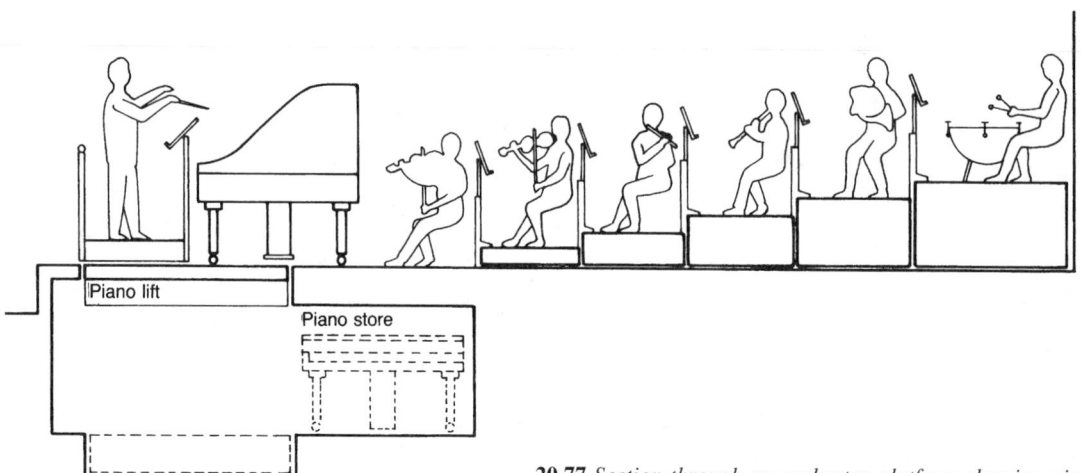

Piano lift

Piano store

20.77 *Section through an orchestra platform showing piano store and lift*

6.08 Associated spaces

- Conductor's green room
- Pre-performance practice room(s)
- Orchestra assembly area
- Choir assembly area
- Musicians' common room
- Orchestra manager's office
- Other offices (e.g. tour manager)
- Toilets

7 CONFERENCE HALLS

7.01 Relationships

20.78 shows the relationships between the parts of a conference suite.

7.02 Formats

Formats depend on use:

- Traditional lecture theatre formats with the audience focused towards a platform on which is provision for a speaker or speakers, possibly served by a range of audio-visual aids, **20.79**. The speaker is the controlling point with audience in a receptive role. Slide, film and video projection limit the extent of encirclement of the platform;

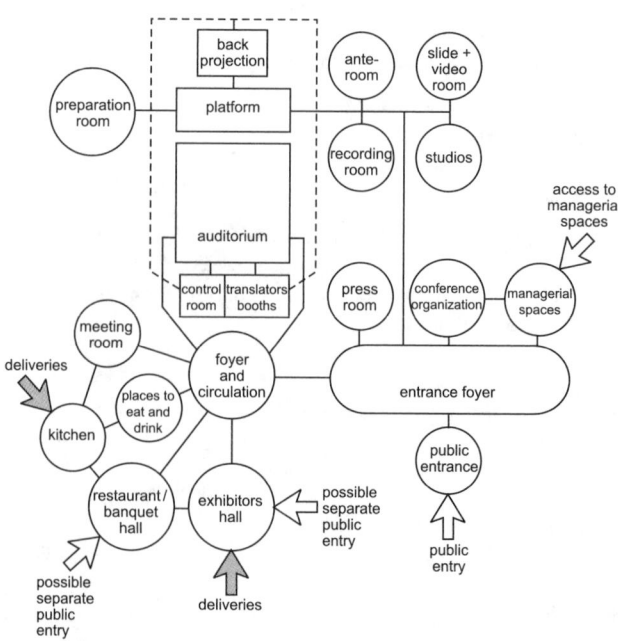

20.78 *Relationship diagram for conference hall*

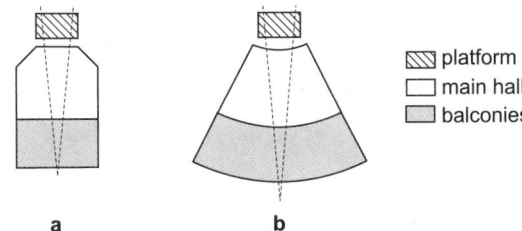
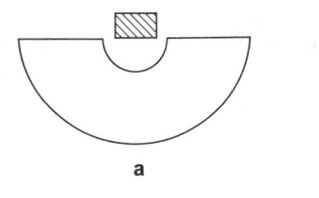
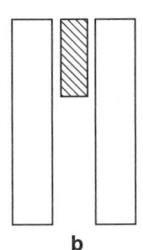

20.79 *Conference hall formats for lectures requiring projection facilities:* **a** *Rectangular with or without rear balcony.* **b** *60° fan with or without rear balcony*

20.80 *Conference hall formats for debating:* **a** *Fan with 180° arc (US Senate).* **b** *Audience in two facing banks (House of Commons)*

- Participation by each member of the audience which suggest the debating formats of semi-circle, U-shape and circle, controlled by a chairman, with little or no audio-visual aids, **20.80**. The need for equal distribution and viewing of all delegates' facial expressions implies a single row only. However, it is possible to have up to six rows where delegates can still be aware of the spoken contribution of each.

The plan shape of the conference hall can be:

- Rectangular
- Fan-shapde, with angles of 135°, 90° or 60°. The last is best for screening
- Hexagonal
- Circular
- Oval, or
- Coffin.

7.03 Functional requirements

With the lecture format the functional requirements include:

- The audience needs to see and hear the speaker, chairman and panel of speakers in the various positions on the platform
- They need a clear view of screens, chalkboard and other visual displays: each has its own physical requirement
- Acoustic clarity of sound listening to speaker and to reproduced sound, and
- Adequate presentation and viewing of any demonstrations.

With the debating format:

- Awareness of the whole audience by every member
- The audience able to hear all speakers and chairman, and
- A clear view of the chairman.

An example of a facility used only for lecturing is shown in **20.81**.

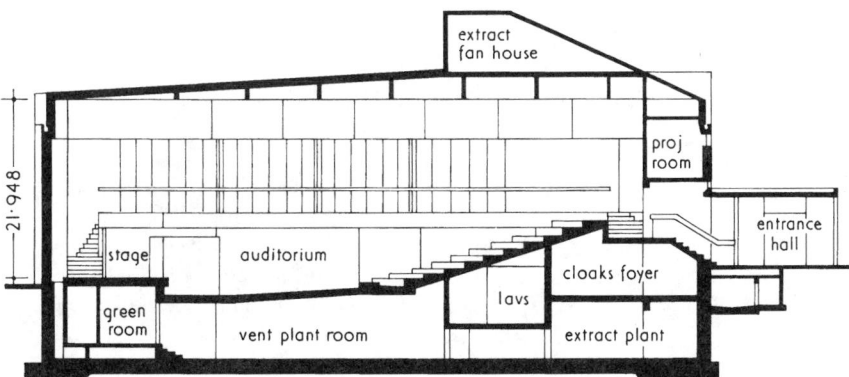

longitudinal section

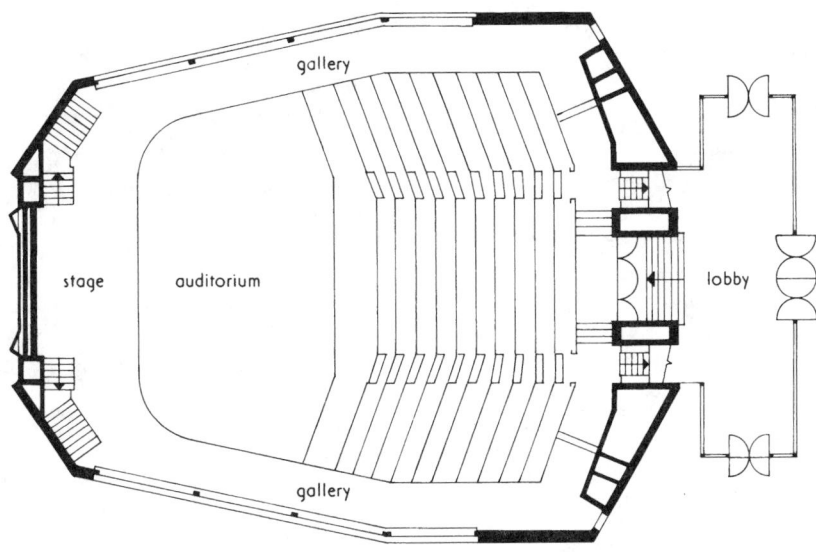

plan

20.81 *Lady Mitchell Hall, Cambridge. A large lecture theatre for 450 students. Architects: Casson, Conder and Partners:* **a** *Longitudinal section.* **b** *Plan of auditorium*

7.04 Audience facilities

Seating design for conference use is covered earlier in this chapter in para **2.05**. In fully equipped conference halls each person in the audience may be provided with:

● Voting buttons: yes, no and abstain
● Simultaneous translation headphones
● Headphones for the hard of hearing, and
● Small individual light.

The following is normally provided to be shared by two adjacent participants:

● Microphone controlled by the chairman from the platform, and
● Button for 'request-to-speak'.

7.05 Platform

Height depends on hall capacity and sightlines:

● 300 mm up to 150 seating capacity
● 600 mm 150–300
● 750 mm over 300.

Steps are required from the auditorium to provide ease of access for speakers onto the platform at ends of gangways and front rows. Ramps may also be needed for wheelchair users.

Size and shape depends on extent of audio-visual aids, lectern, demonstration table, panel table and other equipment as well as sightlines and size and shape of auditorium.

The platform may need to accommodate only a single speaker at one time, with no (or limited) audio-visual aids as the least provision, **20.82**. In other cases it will require to allow for scientific demonstrations, a panel of speakers with or without a lectern, or major presentations as with commercial, political and institutional organisations. For major political conferences there can be as many as fifty people to accommodate on the platform.

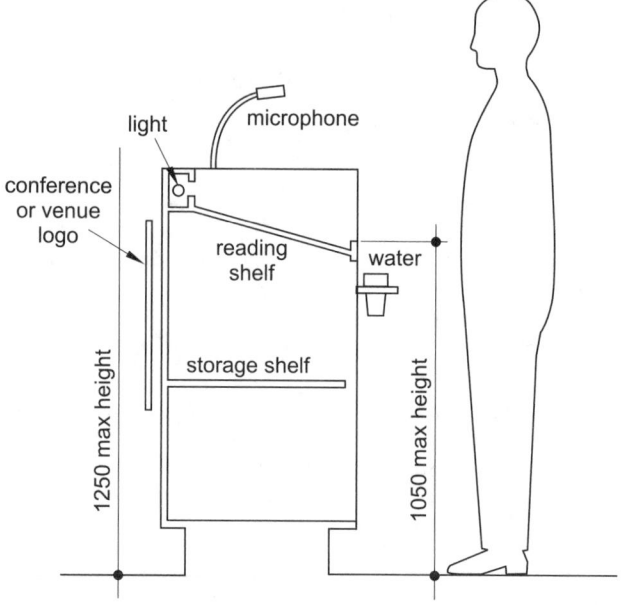

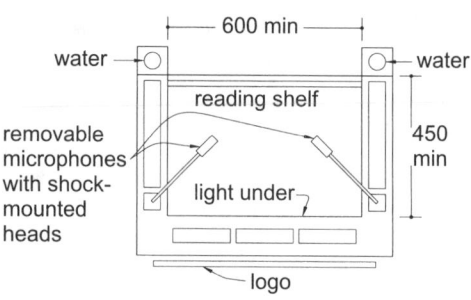

20.83 *Lectern:* **a** *Section.* **b** *Plan*

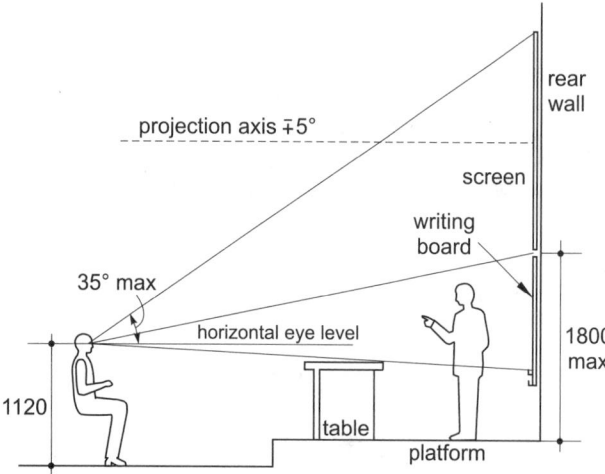

20.82 *Section through lecture theatre showing platform and front wall arrangements*

The setting about the platform can be an architectural setting common to all types of presentations or a shell in which complete new settings can be constructed for each conference.

7.06 Lectern

This is the normal position for the speaker. The lectern, **20.83**, should have:

● A top sloping at 15° large enough for two A4 sheets
● An adjustable screened light to illuminate script
● A mounted microphone with switch
● A jack point for lapel microphone

● A microphone connection to simultaneous interpretation and/or recording systems
● A level surface for pencils and glass of water and jug
● Controls for dimming house lights
● Controls for remote operation of slide and video projectors and screens
● A manual or motorised raise and lower device for lectern stand
● A hand-operated light pointer
● A teleprompter screen (autocue)
● A clock
● Remote cueing
● Possibly red, yellow and green lights visible to both speaker and audience to indicate time available to speaker
● A shelf below the top for brief-case, demonstration items, etc.

7.07 Other platform facilities

The chairman may introduce speakers from the lectern or a separate position elsewhere on the platform, with or without a lectern. It is usual for the chairman to remain in a prominent position on the platform during speaking, questions and discussion, unless slides or films are shown on a screen behind his seat. Anyone on the platform in that case will move to a reserve seat in the body of the hall.

Control panel

It is common to have a separate panel operable by the chairman. Alternatively, it could be duplicated at the lectern. This panel might incorporate:

● A buzzer to the projection room
● A telephone link to the projection room
● Remote operation to black out windows (if any)

- House lights dimmer
- Separate lighting over platform, and
- A teaching board light,

For the chairman only:

- Control for red, yellow and green lights on lectern
- Clock and/or timer
- Panel showing 'request-to-speak' indicators
- On/off control for individual audience microphones
- Voting numbers display (see para **704**), and
- Control of large audience voting number panel.

Demonstration bench
A 'laboratory' fully serviced bench on the platform for the scientific demonstrations, with the supply of electricity, gas, water and drainage. The bench should be able to be wheeled off the platform if to be used for non-demonstration presentations, with plug-in services: the bench can be stored in the adjacent side preparation room.

Panel table
For discussion and presentations by a panel of speakers and a chairman, a long table, parallel to the front edge of the platform, is a recognised format, with a chair and microphone for each panellist, and possibly simultaneous translation earphones. The table should be at least 750 mm deep, allowing 1 m length for each person. The name and details of each panellist may be mounted on the front edge of the table or on a stand in front of each. The lectern may or may not be used.

Rear and side walls of platform
Either a permanent enclosure with all or some of the following (see further details see below, para **7.09**ff):

- Chalkboards
- Projection screens
- Space for conference name, logo and setting
- Clock

- Fixed lectern, overhead projector, table
- Fixed or mobile demonstration table

Curtains, masking, sliding panels may be incorporated to cut off sections of side and rear walls when not in use. Alternatively, there may be a shell with rear and side walls and equipment constructed for a particular conference: similar to theatre open stage with suspension over platform for setting and lighting and lighting.

An easily visible place is needed for a person to stand to translate the speaker's words into sign language.

7.08 Translators' booths

Conferences with international audiences will probably require simultaneous interpretation by translators in booths of those speaking in various languages.

Booths need to be located at the rear or perhaps the side of the auditorium with an unobstructed view by the translator of the speaker, chairman, projection screens and chalkboards as well as any visual display, **20.84**. The booths are soundproofed, with the translator listening to the speech on headphones.

Booths should be located side by side with acoustic isolation and small connecting windows. They should open off a corridor giving discreet but secure access from the public areas. Booth interior should have absorbent material to walls, floor and ceiling, in dark matt colours.

Each booth needs to be able to accommodate two or three seated persons, minimum size 6.5 m wide and 6.4 m deep. The sound-proof observation window can be full width of the booth, 800 mm high, and may be inclined to avoid acoustic reflections on either side. The translators need a clear working surface 500 mm wide in front of the window for scripts, notes, microphone, channel-selection buttons, indicator lights, etc.

Translators' ancillary rooms
A common room for translators should be located near the booths. This should have easy chairs, tables, telephones, cloakroom and toilets.

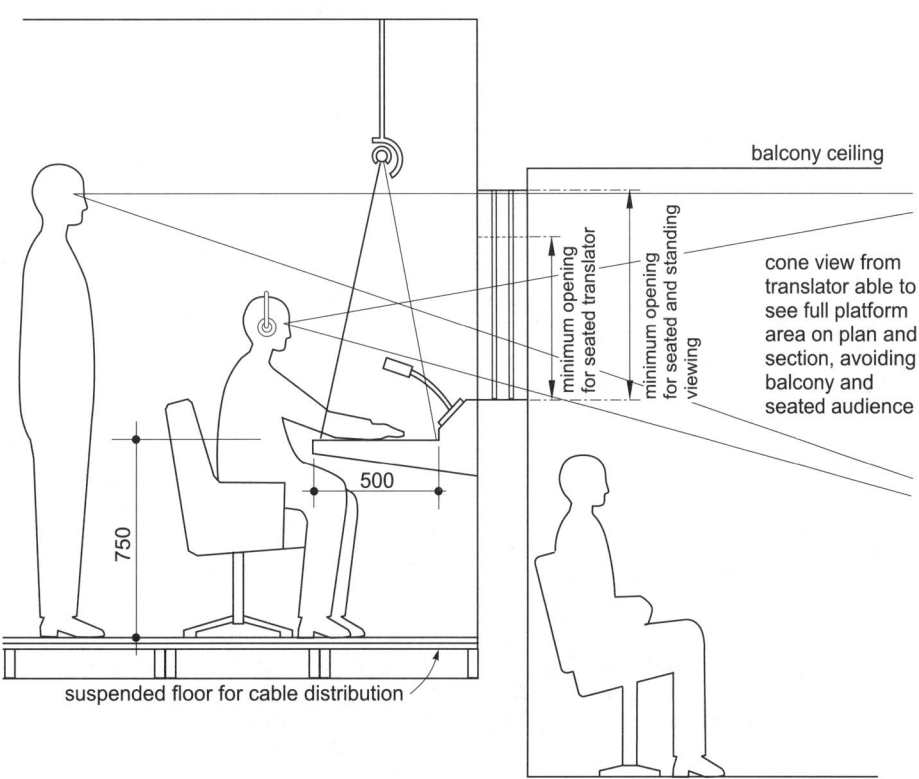

20.84 *Section through translators' booth at rear of auditorium*

Simultaneous translation systems in the auditorium
Available methods are:

● Induction loop: magnetic field transmission generated by a conductor looped around auditorium. Conference delegates have portable receivers.
● Infra-red: modulated light signals radiated from a number of sources. Delegates have portable receivers.
● Hard-wired: cable within underfloor trunking connected to panels in arm rest or back of each seat for heavily used conference facilities.

7.09 Audiovisual facilities

Writing boards

Conventional chalkboards are now uncommon as they have now been superseded by overhead projectors for which material can be pre-prepared. Where they are used they would be a black or white chalkboard, fixed to a rear wall or moveable. The audience viewing angle is critical to avoid glare and reflections. The visibility tends to be restricted to twelve rows. Chalk and pen channel to be incorporated, with a ledge for an eraser.

Boards can slide vertically or horizontally to increase writing surface within a restricted space, **20.85**, or they can revolve vertically or horizontally, if made of a rubber or plastic material.

The extent of chalkboard may be nominal, 1 m × 3.5 m for limited use by a speaker, or, in the case of the presentation of complex and mathematical formulae, a board extending the full width of the platform.

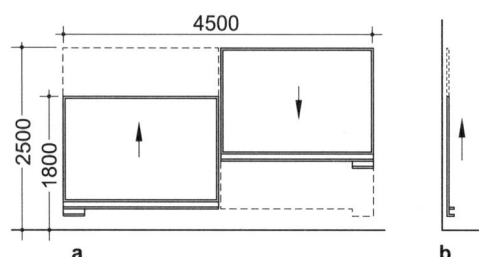

20.85 *Writing boards: vertically sliding:* **a** *Elevation.* **b** *Section*

Small conference rooms are often equipped with whiteboards which are written or drawn on using special felt-tipped pens. These are permanently mounted on a wall, and have a ledge beneath for the pens and the eraser.

Flipcharts

Commonly used in small conferences and seminars, particularly in debating format. A1 size portrait orientation on a board 750 × 900 mm on a loose easel with ledge at 900 mm above platform. A storage space for this and for the pens etc. is useful. Sometimes they are fixed to a rear wall; good visibility is restricted to twelve rows.

Overhead projector

This is now the most useful device used by speakers to illustrate their lectures. **20.86** shows a projector on a stand. The image surface is 250 × 250 mm for writing on or for prepared images. A surface beside the projector is needed for the prepared acetate sheets and pens. The lecturer can be standing or seated. The projector may be located at a lower level in front of the platform to assist sightlines from the front auditorium rows to see the screen over the projector and speaker.

The screen needed to receive the image should be tipped forward to an angle of 20–25° to the vertical to avoid 'keystone'

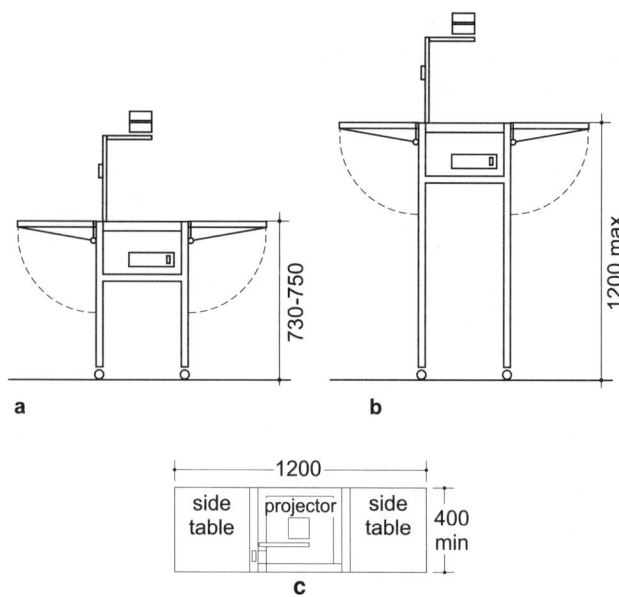

20.86 *Overhead projector:* **a** *Elevation of a projector on a table for a seated speaker.* **b** *Elevation of a projector on a table for a standing speaker.* **c** *Plan of either*

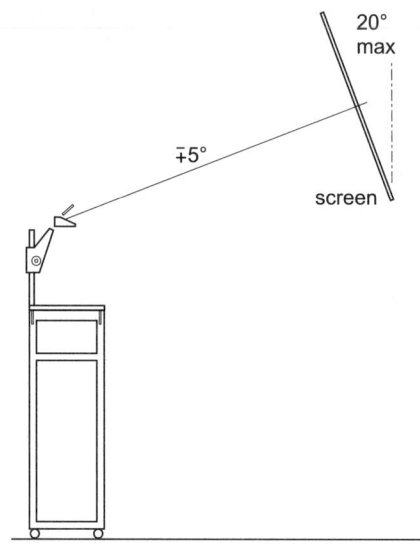

20.87 *Overhead projector screen: tilting helps to avoid the keystone effect*

distortion, **20.87**; the distance from the projector to the screen equals the screen width. Such screens are available that can be swung or rolled away when the main projection screen is used.

Projection room

A projection room, **20.88**, may or may not be needed. Its advantages are that:

● The operator and operations will not disturb the audience
● Noise is reduced or eliminated
● The equipment and the media are more secure from interference and theft
● It is easier to lift the projection beam over the heads of the audience.

The equipment needs to be grouped near the axis of the screen(s). It is more convenient for it to be on loose mobile stands, and the beam should be above the heads of a standing audience. Each port should be provided with a separate black-out shutter. The room should have separate extract ventilation and should open off a ventilated lobby.

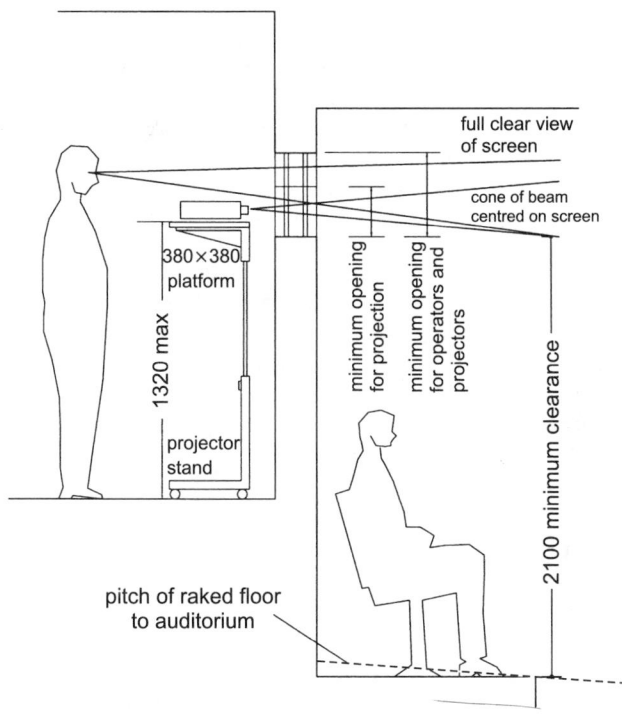

20.88 *Section through projection room at rear of auditorium (projecting slides)*

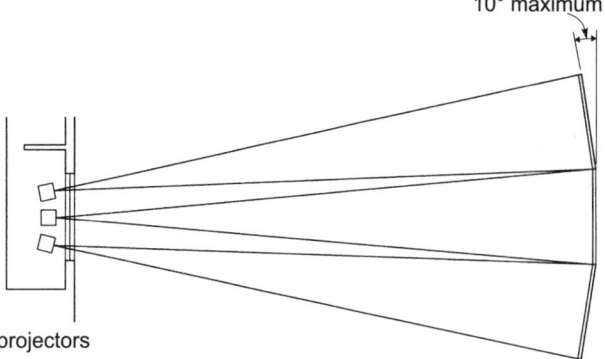

20.89 *Slide projection: multi-screen presentation*

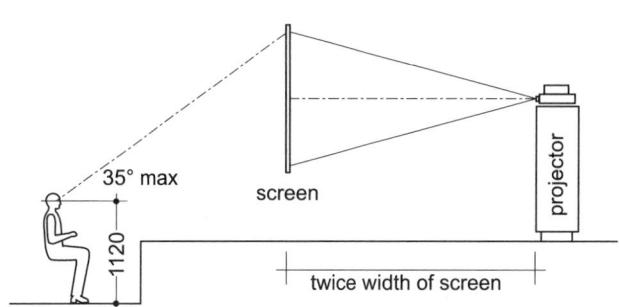

20.90 *Back projection for slides and 16 mm film*

Lighting control room
This is a limited requirement for conferences, but lighting control could be incorporated into a projection room at the rear of the auditorium, minimum size 2 m × 3.5 m. In some cases a dimmer room may be needed (see para **4.10**).

Sound control room
In this case an open room preferably at rear of the auditorium adjacent to the lighting control room, minimum size 2 m × 3.5 m. Here the amplified sound from one or more speakers can be mixed and balanced. The sound control desk may alternatively be situated within the auditorium.

Screens
Increasingly, back-projection screens are being used. In this case the projection room will be behind the platform rather than behind the audience. Back projection for video, film and slide requires wide-angle lenses but allows more freedom for speaker. Where conventional screens are used, they will be mounted above the heads of seated people on the platform. If multiple slide projection is to be used, a wide-screen format is necessary. Sometimes the side screens are angled up to 60°; this tends to limit seating positions with good visibility. Where wide flat screens are used curtains should be provided to reduce the width of these for film and video projection.

Slide projection
One, two and maybe more projected images from 35 mm slides, **20.89–20.91**, able to be used individually or simultaneously; the usual type of projector is the carousel. High-intensity projectors allow some light in auditorium for note taking. Screen areas for projecting slides should be square, as slides may be in portrait or landscape format. For three-screen projection the side screens are sometimes angled as much as 30° from the centre screen.

Video projection
Video projectors are now usually mounted at high level in the auditorium, **20.92**, on stands or behind the screen. Close-range projectors can produce pictures up to 3 m high; they should be 3.5

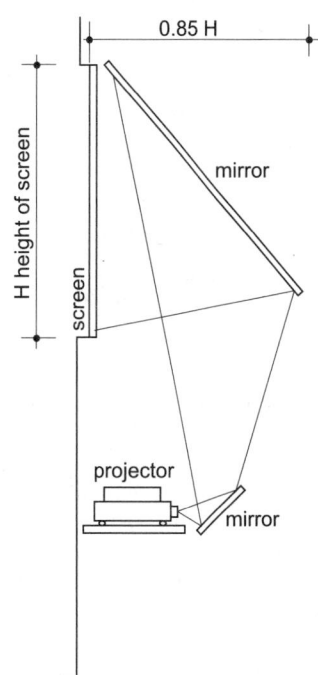

20.91 *Back projection of slides using mirrors*

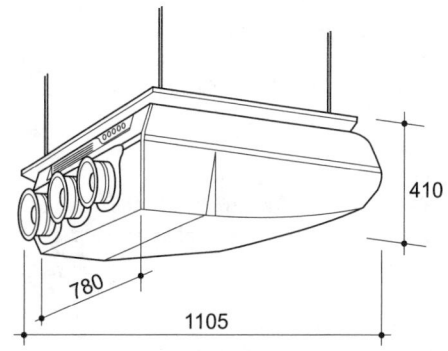

20.92 *Video projector mounted at high level in auditorium*

to 3.6 times the picture width from the screen. Video cassettes may be loaded in a projection room, or from some position on the platform.

For a large screen a long-range projector is used producing a picture up to 7.5 m high. It should be housed in a projection room, with room for control and back-up equipment consisting of racks for VCR equipment, monitor screens, off-air times and ancillary control unit.

For small conference and seminar rooms, conventional TV sets can be used, **20.93**. Sometimes a number of these each serving a section of the audience are suspended at high level in a larger conference facility, but this is a somewhat primitive arrangement.

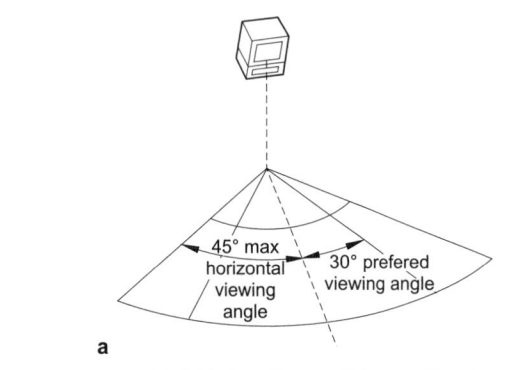

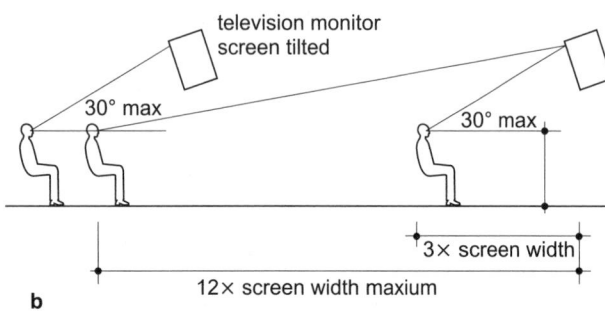

20.93 *Television viewing:* **a** *Horizontal angles.* **b** *Vertical angles*

Film projection

Where films are used they are rarely greater than 35 mm and are usually 16 mm: 8 mm is now uncommon as video has taken its place. Films can be projected from a position within the seating area, but care must be taken that the beam is not interrupted by standing or sitting members of the audience. It is preferable to use a projection room where the beam can be at a higher level, although here the video projector must be avoided. More details in para **8.02** of this chapter.

Television and film cameras

Conferences are frequently televised and recorded. Speakers and demonstrations are often projected oversize on screens both within the main conference hall and in overflow venues. Cameras are usually mobile, but require suitable floor surfaces.

A room may be required for recording and editing purposes, but this may not need direct vision of the conference, and could in fact be a remote studio.

Voting panel

This is a panel indicating electronically the numbers voting by pressing buttons at each seat, mounted above the platform and controlled by the chairman.

7.10 Platform: associated spaces

- Ante-room: reception and waiting areas for conference chairman and speakers, with lounge, changing facilities and toilets;

sound and light lobby onto platform; access for guests from public areas
- Preparation room: preparation of scientific and other demonstrations in room immediately off the platform
- Slide and video room: viewing room for speakers, to sort and check slides, inspect videos and films, check overhead projector material
- Studios: television, film and still photography preparation
- Recording room: separate facility with tape-recording equipment linked to the auditorium and platform amplification system for the recording of the conference proceedings.

7.11 Conference organisation offices

- Offices with desks and chairs
- General office, with desks and chairs, fax machines, telephones, telex, photocopier, computers, typewriters, intercom, translations, secretarial work.

7.12 Press room

- General room: desks and chairs, telephones, fax machines, telex, computers
- Television and radio interview rooms

8 CINEMAS

8.01 Types of film and method of projection

Four standard types of film are described by their width: 8 mm, 16 mm, 35 mm and 70 mm. Each has its appropriate type of employment, screen size and auditorium conditions. These types of film are described in Table IV.

8.02 Methods of projection

There are three methods of film projection:

- Direct projection from the rear of the auditorium onto the screen. The most common method by far
- Indirect projection, where the film projection requires one or more mirrors. This method is used where lack of space or structural difficulties make direct projection difficult to achieve. Mirror projection requires a powerful light source and the screen cannot be wider than 9 m
- Rear projection. Not possible with curved screen, but may be applicable for the smaller auditorium. For this method the picture needs to be reversed, for which mirrors are an economic solution.

8.03 Auditorium design

Functional requirements include

- Every member of the audience requires an unobstructed view of the whole picture area on the screen, without visual and physical discomfort and picture distortion
- Picture sharpness and luminance need to be uniform and satisfactory, and
- An auditorium giving distortion-free sound reproduction.

8.04 Viewing conditions

Viewing criteria are shown in plan, **20.94**, and section, **20.95**. The size and shape of the screen must be related to the shape and rake of the auditorium floor.

Seating rake is less critical than for concert halls and theatres as the screen can be elevated and sound comes from overhead speakers. Nevertheless, a rake of 5° (or less) is recommended. Seating can be well upholstered with a tradition in new commercial cinemas towards comfort, including pullman seats. Short row lengths tend to encourage auditorium roving sales of popcorn, ice-cream and confectionery.

Table IV Film type and application

Film type	Projection	Applications	Print quality	Light source/screen size
8 mm Type 8R – a 'silent' film. There have been several attempts to add sound. Type 8S – more recent. Smaller perforations allow a larger picture area and sound track, magnetically or photographically recorded	Small, portable and (particularly when the film is contained within a cassette or cartridge) very simple to operate	In schools, in aircraft for entertainment and in small auditoria for instruction, demonstration and advertising	Satisfactory where prints made from the original negatives and sound recordings	Low-powered incandescent source satisfactory for screens up to 900 × 655 mm. Tungsten-halogen lamp allows screens up to 1350 × 982 mm (35/40-person audience)
16 mm Silent type – perforations along both edges. Type with sound – perforations along one edge only leave room for either photographic or magnetic sound record	Either relatively light and readily portable, or heavy-duty for permanent installations	For educational, scientific, advertising, entertainment and TV purposes	Many prints made from inferior internegs, so resultant poor quality stopped shows of this gauge	Incandescent source permits screens up to 3 m × 2.2 m. Xenon or carbon arc* screens up to 6 m × 2.4 m. Power of source limited by amount of heat dissipated
35 mm	Portable with incandescent light source, or heavy duty for permanent installations	'Standard' type for commercial cinemas; also for high-quality lecture halls and TV	Good	Incandescent – 7 m × 5 m screen. Xenon or carbon arc* screen size proportional to power of light source; if very high, water-cooled film gates provided
70 mm Space for six magnetic sound tracks	Specially designed, invariably will also accommodate 35 mm	Production costs very high – no films made in 70 mm recently	High-quality photography and sound	

*In licensed premises, xenon and carbon arc projectors must be housed in separate projection rooms

8.05 Acoustics for films

The sound track is an integral part of the audience experience and the quality of sound reproduction has vastly improved. Cinemas are now equipped with stereophonic sound systems which require acoustically dead auditoria; the ideal is a zero reverberation time. Hence all finishes – floor, walls, ceiling and seats – need to be sound absorbent. Side walls should not be parallel, and a fan shape is preferred. The auditorium should be structurally and enclosure-wise insulated from external noise. A suitable ambient noise standard for cinemas is NR30 to NR35. The volume per occupant should be at least 1.25 m³ for large cinemas and 5 m³ per person for small auditoria.

8.06 Screens

Shape

8 mm and 16 mm film is projected with a screen ratio of 1:1.375 and 1:3.135 respectively. With 35 mm the screen ratio is also 1:3.375 but may vary between 1:1.65 and 1:1.85: the international standard is 1:1.75. The ratio of 70 mm film is 1:2.2. Foreign-language films call for 1:1.65 to allow for sub-titles.

Size

Screen size is dependent on light source, screen luminance picture quality, method of projection, viewing conditions and seating capacity. The maximum widths of 0.9 m for 8 mm film, 4 m for 16 mm and 6 m for 35 mm are accepted.

Curvature

For uniform focus a large screen should be curved to keep its surface equidistant from the centre of the lens.

Luminance

As a matt-white surface of A large screen cannot achieve an adequate picture luminance, screen surfaces have been developed with a partial specular reflection to increase luminance.

Position

The centre of the screen should be on the central axis of the auditorium seating, but it may be tilted from the vertical plane and set forward from the structural wall to provide a clear space of at least 3.4 m the loudspeakers.

Masking

Mechanically adjustable black masking to the sides and top of the screen is normally provided to contain the picture surface and obtain maximum apparent brightness. The masking is usually wool serge on metal rails, and the gear should be fixed at floor level for ease of maintenance. Movement is remotely controlled from the projection room.

Construction

Screen material is either PVC or metallised fabric, held by cord lacing to hooks on a metal lattice frame 460 to 920 mm larger than the maximum picture surface. The material needs to be flame-resistant and is replaced at intervals. Sufficient space for manoeuvring a rolled replacement which could be 1 m in diameter will be necessary.

Temporary screens

In some multi-use auditoria screens may require to be easily and conveniently removed. A flat screen up to 6 m wide can be incorporated into a proscenium stage of a theatre form either housed, when rolled, in the stage or flown in the flytower. Curved screens could be flown, but take up much valuable space in the flytower; or they could be stored at the rear of the stage if fitted with rollers or castors for ease of movement.

Speaker installation

The speakers need to be located behind the screen, firmly fixed to the platform or screen frame. One speaker is needed for monophonic sound; for multi-channel and stereophonic sound from 35 mm film, three speaker units are necessary: one centrally placed and the others equidistant from it. 70 mm sound production requires five symmetrically placed about the central speaker.

Platform

The back of the screen frame, including the speaker, needs to be covered with heavy felt to absorb sound. The screen is set over a platform with a forestage, carpeted with black carpet to prevent reflection of sound and light. The forestage edge can be vertical, splayed or stepped.

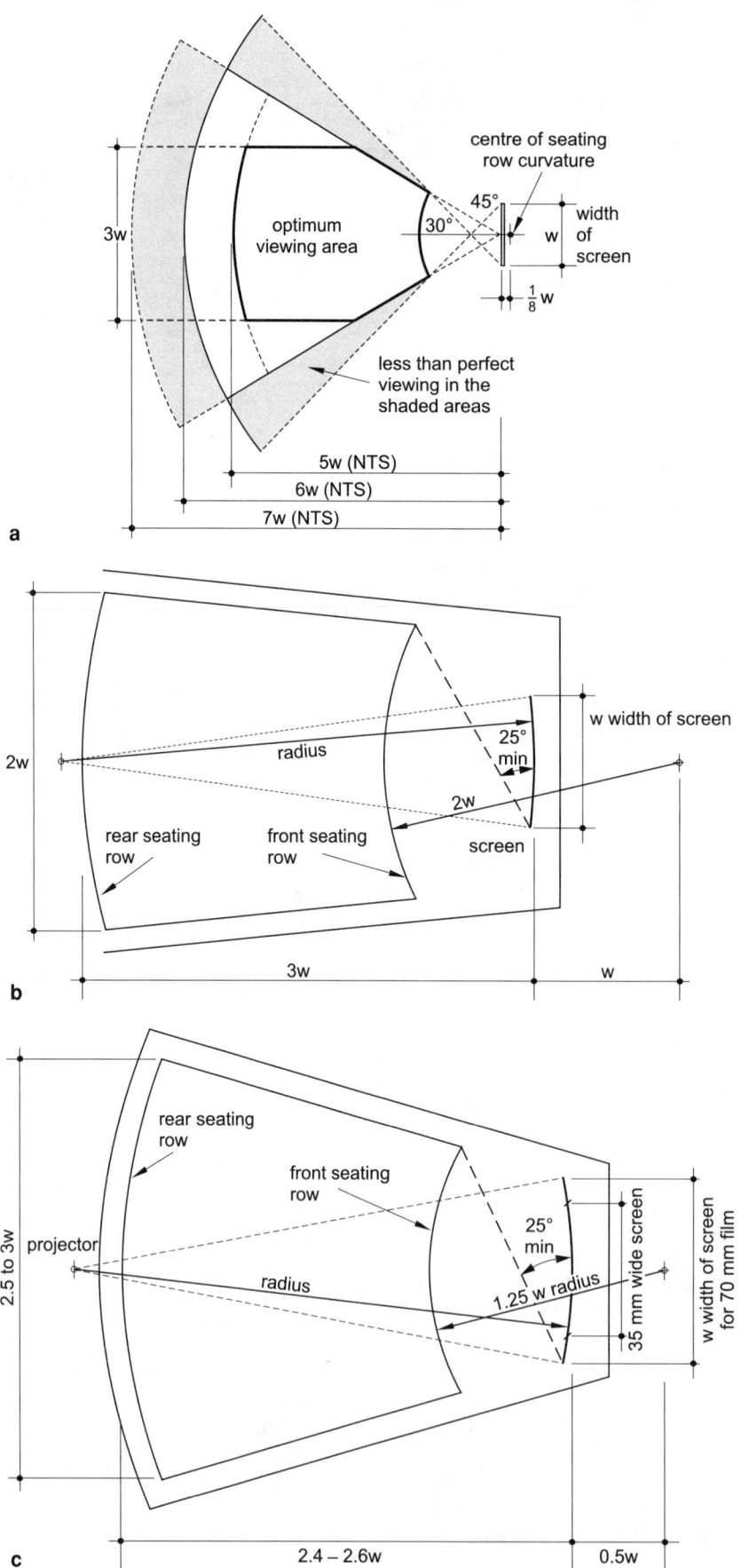

20.94 *Projection criteria for various formats:* **a** *16 mm film.* **b** *35 mm film.* **c** *70 mm film*

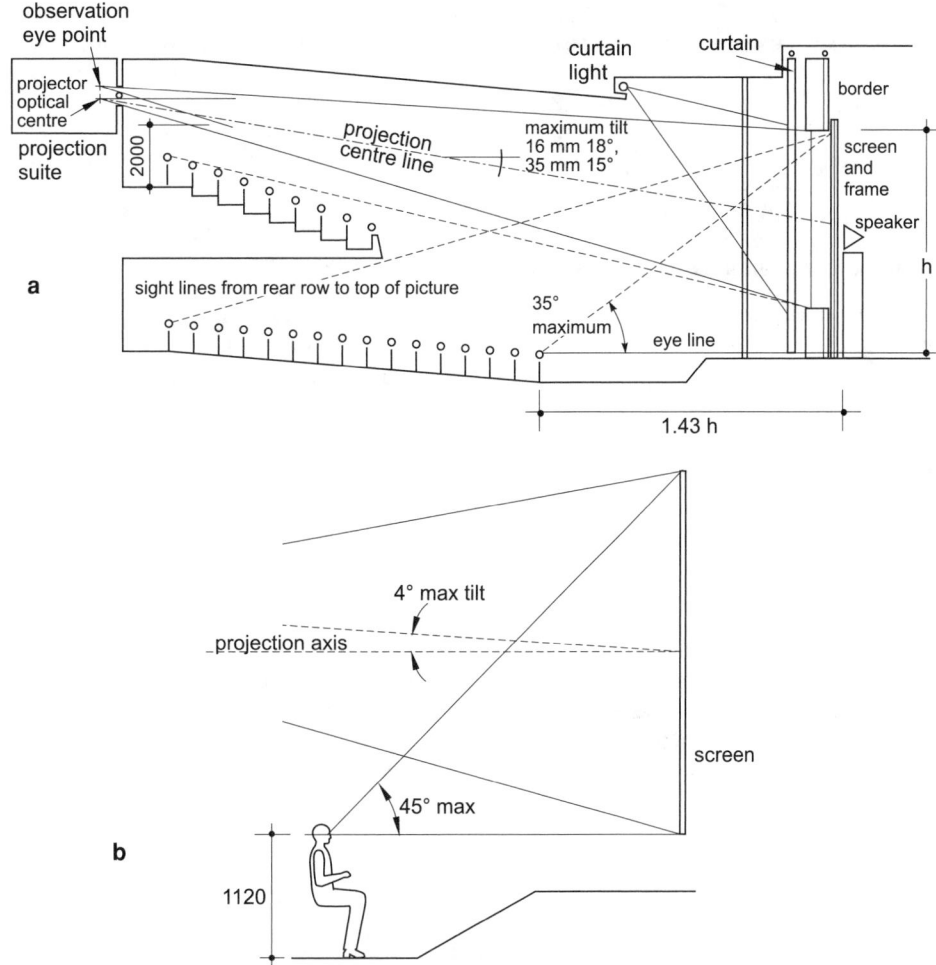

20.95 *Vertical sightlines:* **a** *16 mm and 35 mm film.* **b** *70 mm film*

Curtains

Screen curtains usually move horizontally on rails supported by steel tubes. Curtains overlap at centre when closed, and space is required either side of the screen when open. Alternatively they can be vertical festoon curtains.

8.07 Projection suite

A suite may include the following spaces. Manual operation has been mainly replaced by automatic or remote control in commercial cinemas. New developments will require changes in the layout of equipment and this needs to be considered in the design.

Projection room

A projection room is not required for 8 mm film but is a statutory requirement for 16 mm, 35 mm and 70 mm film. The projectionist:

● Controls the film timing, focusing and direction
● Regulates the volume and tone of sound reproduction
● Adjusts the masking
● Plays music from records or tapes during intervals
● Controls house lights and screen curtains
● Repairs, replaces and rewinds film, and
● Takes charge of all technical equipment.

The minimum sizes of projection rooms are:

● Minimum equipment: 3.9 × 4 m,
● With effects lantern and spotlight: 3.9 × 7.5 m,
● Typical commercial cinema: 6.6 × 7.3 m.

Floor-to-ceiling height should be not less than 6.4 m.

Equipment for commercial cinemas includes:

● Either two projectors or one projector with long-running equipment. Long-running projectors are common in multi-auditorium complexes, with projecting covered by one projectionist moving from one cinema to another
● Effects lantern which may double as a spotlight
● Spotlights
● Music table: non-synchronous music desk with tape-deck, storage and possible record player
● Rewind bench for the rewinding and storage of film having been shown: 600 × 1200 mm minimum and 914 mm high. If inflammable film, then a separate room for re-winding and storing films is necessary
● Switchboard
● Amplifier. Unless there is a remote control system, controls and change-over switches are fitted between projection ports. Racks may be located against side or rear walls with rear access requiring a 500 mm space for maintenance. Three amplifiers may be necessary for stereophonic sound reproduction, with mono-phonic sound only requiring one amplifier and a power pack
● Spares cabinet; and
● Fire extinguishers.

Ports

Each projector, effects lantern and follow spot, needs a separate port with optical quality glass through the wall between projection room and auditorium, **20.96**. Each projectionist also requires an observation port with plate glass. In cinemas with flammable films all ports require fire shutters releasable from either the projection room or the auditorium.

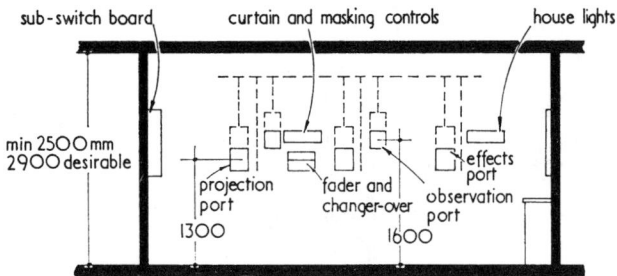

20.96 *Ports in projection room wall. Broken lines show fire shutters, suspension and release bars required when flammable films are shown*

Layout of equipment
A layout is shown in **20.97**. Twin projectors are usually at 1.5 m centres with a 1 m workspace between. Other pieces of equipment are shown in **20.98**.

Services
● Power supplies for projectors. 8 mm and 16 mm portable equipment require a domestic 13 A power socket outlet. For 35 mm equipment with arcs up to 45 A, a single-phase supply is required. Above this, a three-phase supply is necessary.

● Lighting: no light should be directed towards the screen through ports. Task lighting at equipment during performances, general lighting for cleaning and maintenance.
● Ventilation: the projection room, rewinding room and associated lobbies need ventilation systems separate from the auditorium, with steady volumes of air at low velocity.

Associated accommodation
● Staff room: a separate room for projectionist adjacent to projection room, with sink and tea- and coffee-making provision
● Toilet with convenient access for projectionist
● Workroom and store: a separate room for repair and maintenance of films and equipment adjacent to projection room
● Lobby: sound and light lock between projection suite and access corridor

Dimmer and switchroom
If the dissipated power from dimming lights does not exceed 5 kW the dimmers may be in the projection room. If greater, then a separate room will be necessary for the dimmers associated with the switchroom.

Automatic control allows controls to be remote from the projection room, with a separate room located in the auditorium such that the operator has a clear view of the screen: 2 × 2 m minimum size.

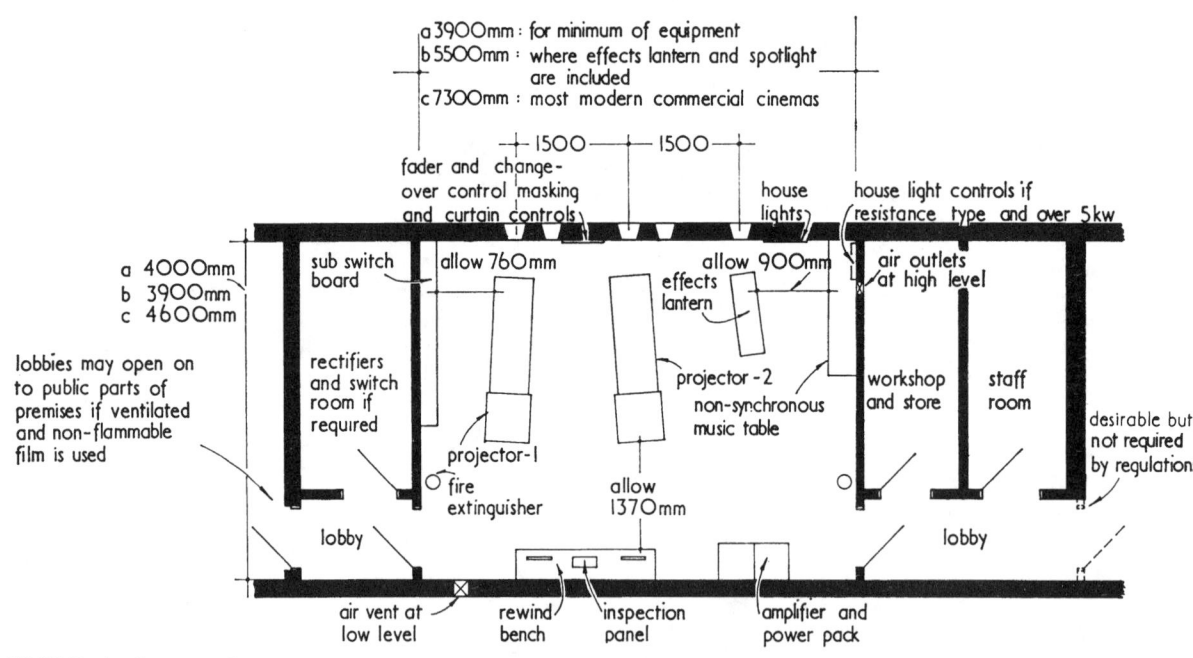

20.97 *Projection room layout*

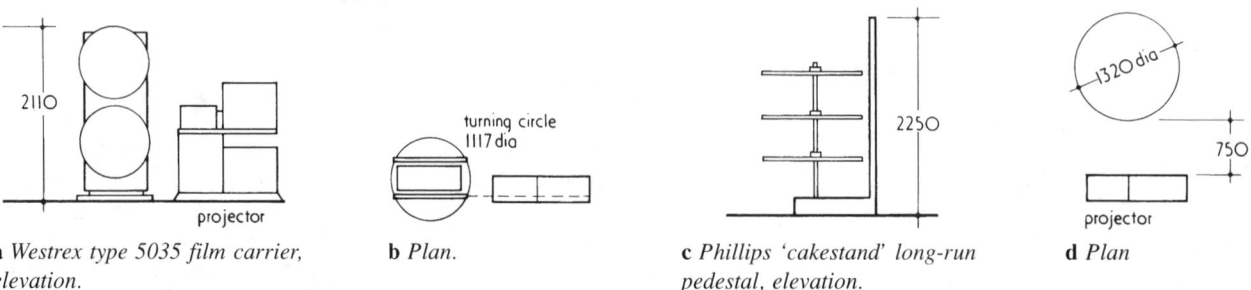

a *Westrex type 5035 film carrier, elevation.* **b** *Plan.* **c** *Phillips 'cakestand' long-run pedestal, elevation.* **d** *Plan*

20.98 a–c *Long-running film projection equipment*

9 MULTI-PURPOSE AUDITORIA

9.01 Requirements

Multi-purpose auditoria refer to an approach where compatible activities are combined within one volume. An example, **20.99**, covers a single form with a modest level of flexibility while combining opera, dance, musicals and drama; as well as concerts, conference and film shows. This is a multi-purpose proscenium stage with flytower and a flexible proscenium zone; the seating in the auditorium can remain constant.

9.02 Physical restraints

Problems can arise in combining different types of production in a single auditorium. Required volumes and reverberation times differ for speech and for music. To adjust the volume, arrangements to lower the auditorium ceiling can be incorporated into the design. Temporary alterations to the surface treatment of walls and ceilings can alter reverberation times, as can electronic 'assisted resonance'.

20.99 *Multi-use stage with flytower and flexible proscenium usable in the following ways:*

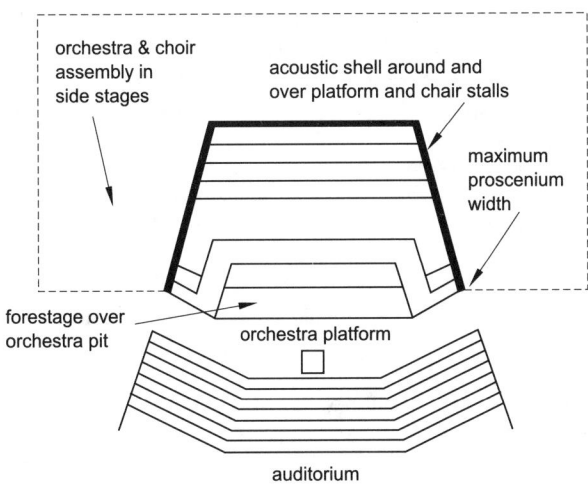

a *For orchestral and choral music.*

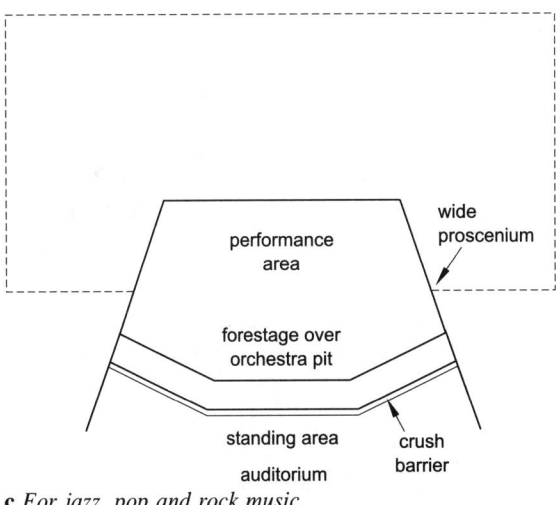

c *For jazz, pop and rock music.*

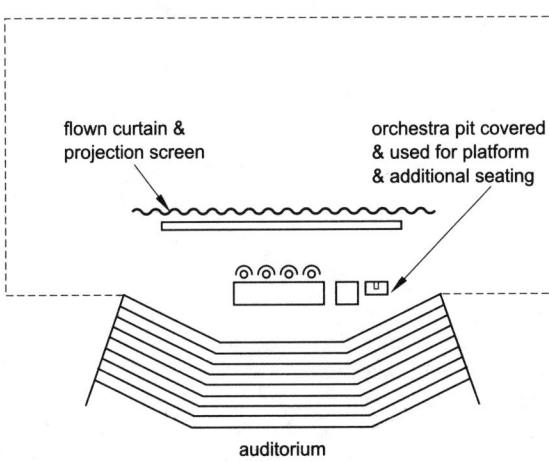

e *For conferences.*

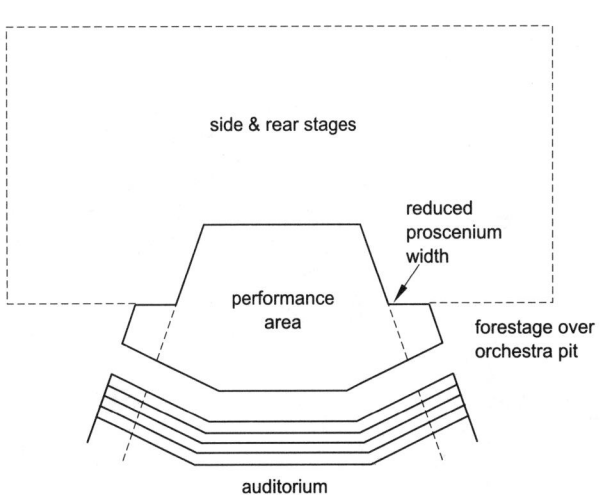

b *For opera, dance and musicals.*

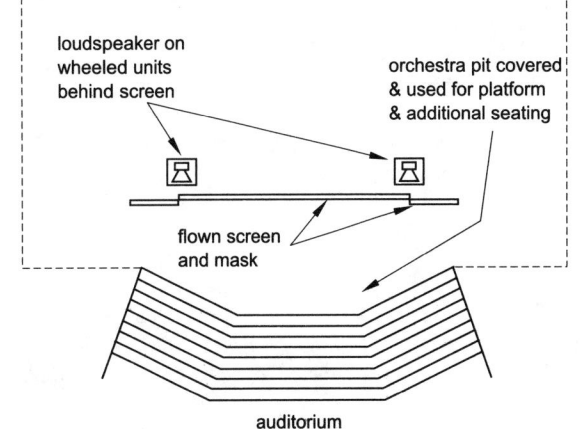

d *For drama.*

f *For cinema*

10 SUPPORT FACILITIES

10.01 Entrance doors and lobbies

These require:

- Ease of access from car parking and public transport
- Canopy: to provide shelter at entrance
- Provision for posters and other information
- Draught lobby
- Automatic sliding doors

10.02 Entrance foyer

Box office, **20.100** (in theatre, concert hall, cinema): counter for the sale of tickets; computer ticket dispenser

Registration (conference hall): counter or table

Reception and information: counter

Cloakroom (not usual in cinema): attended or unattended, see Chapter 3

Creche: at least 6.5 m² per child

First-aid room: bed, washhand basin

Toilets: see Chapter 3

Foyer and circulation: table, chairs, display stands

Performance area: within foyer or separate area

Space and display for exhibitions: see Chapter 31

Auditorium lobbies: barriers to sound and light at entry points into the auditorium; the level of lighting should assist adaptation to and from dark auditorium and the brighter foyer lighting, as with a cinema.

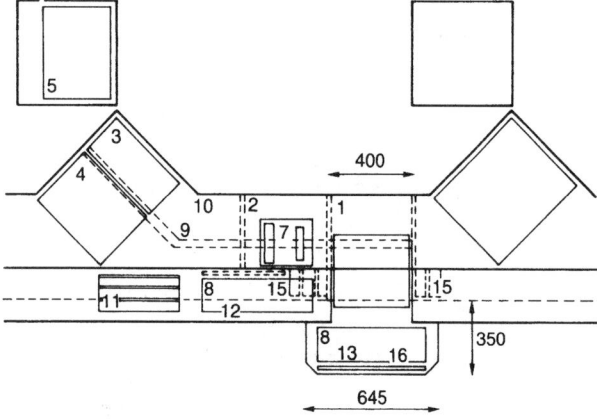

a *Plan.*

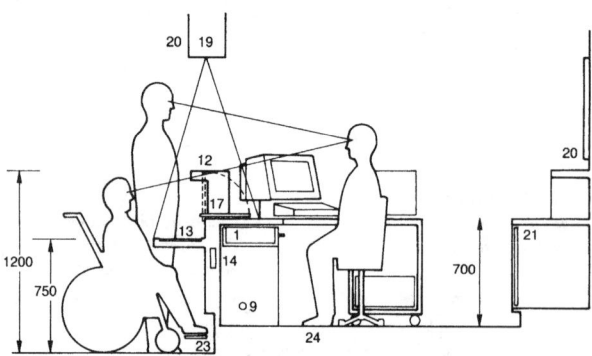

b *Section*

20.100 *Box office. KEY: 1 stationery drawer, 2 till drawer, 3 keyboard, 4 VDU, 5 mobile ticket printer, 7 telephone, 8 seating layout plans, 9 footrest, 10 writing space, 11 leaflets, 12 upper customer counter, 13 lower customer counter, 14 cable trunking, 15 pigeon holes for tickets and messages to be collected, 16 cheque writing upstand, 17 counter flap, 19 counter lighting, 20 display, 21 storage, 24 raised floor*

10.03 Places to eat and drink

- Coffee bar
- Licensed bar
- Cafeteria
- Restaurant
- Banquet room
- Private room
- Associated spaces: bar store, cellar, kitchen, storage, staff rooms, managers offices, delivery, refuse.

See Chapter 18.

10.04 Sales

- Shops and merchandise outlets: display cases, shelving; office, storage, security; see Chapter 13
- Kiosk and other food outlets: display cases, shelving, microwave oven, stockroom (confectionery, drinks, etc.) with possible refrigerator; security.

10.05 Meeting rooms

Break-out rooms, sponsors' rooms; equipped for receptions, and small group lectures, discussions and workshops.

10.06 VIP rooms

Reception rooms for distinguished visitors; lounge and toilets.

10.07 Exhibition hall

Displays including trade exhibitions; storage, deliveries, possible separate public entrance, see Chapter 31.

10.08 Art gallery

Permanent and/or temporary exhibitions, see Chapter 31.

10.09 Office services

Conference halls: access by delegates to fax machines, telephones, photocopiers, translators, secretarial work, see Chapter 11.

10.10 Outdoor areas

Gathering area at front doors; associated with foyer and places to eat and drink as external terraces; store for outdoor furniture; landscaping, see Chapter 6.

10.11 Signage

- External: name of venue, current and future events
- Internal: direction signs to the various public attractions.

10.12 Managerial spaces

Administrative offices

- Offices: functions may include policy, house management, accounts. personnel, marketing, press and publicity, development and community programmes, clerical work; see Chapter 11.
- Associated spaces may include boardroom, storage, strong room, office services and equipment, entrance and reception, toilets.

Box office: room for postal and telephone bookings, storage of sales records and accounts; access to changing, relaxation and toilet facilities.

Men's and women's staff rest rooms: lockers, lounge chairs, refreshments and toilets.

Sales and trays store: refrigerator for ice cream, shelves for confectionery, programmes, documents and other items for sale or distribution; storage of sales trays; table; washhand basin; located directly off the public areas.

Maintenance workshop, office and store: for the maintenance of the building fabric, equipment, emergency services, external works.

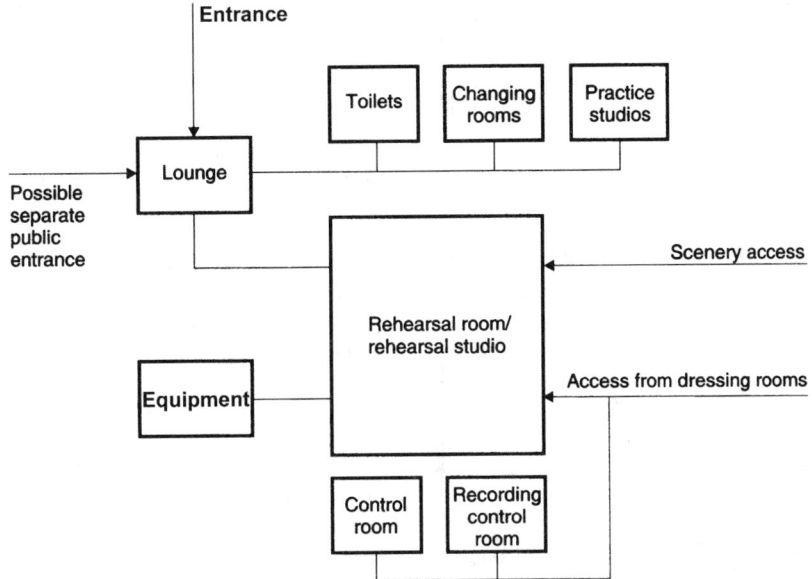

20.101 *Relationship diagram for a rehearsal room or studio*

Cleaners' stores: central storage of materials and equipment; cupboards with sink, cleaning materials and equipment throughout building.

Security control room: surveillance monitors, fire-detection systems, alarms, service monitors, paging systems, locking devices.

Refuse: external provision for dust-bins, well ventilated and easily cleaned.

Catering facilities: the scale of the operation may justify the inclusion of catering facilities for all staff.

10.13 Production spaces

For those opera, dance, musical and drama companies which initiate their own productions, the following spaces are required:

● Offices for the functions of artistic policy, direction, production development, instruction, design, production organisation, business management, development programmes and clerical work

● Associated spaces may include boardroom, library, music room, audition room, working conference room, model-making facilities, dark room, general storage, office services, refreshment areas, toilets, entrance and reception.

10.14 Rehearsal spaces

A relationship diagram for a rehearsal suite is shown in **20.101**.

● Rehearsal room or rehearsal studio able to accommodate largest performing area on the stage plus 2 m on three sides and 3 m on one long side as a minimum

● Practice studios for individual or small group practice, for example for dancers, **20.102**

● Associated spaces may include lounge, changing rooms, toilets, storage of equipment.

10.15 Scenery workshops

The substantial facilities required where the manufacture and maintenance of scenery is involved is well illustrated in **20.103**.

Offices: for head of carpentry workshop, head of paint shop, and head of property department.

Carpentry workshop: for the construction of scenery; power-operated tools (such as woodworking machine, mortise, circular and bandsaws and lathes); benches for carpentry, assembly and canvassing; storage of raw materials such as timber, sheet materials, rolls of materials, nails and screws and so on, including polystyrene sheets which may require a separate fire-resistant enclosure

Paint shop: for the painting of scenery, the method of painting backcloths and flats (flat on the floor, on mobile frame or fixed frame and gantry, and three-dimensional pieces: the extent of benches for mixing paints and other preparation and cleaning brushes; storage requirements for raw materials such as paints and fire-proofing, and equipment such as brushes and spray equipment. Paints may require to be stored in a fire-proof enclosure.

Metalwork shop: the use of metal in the preparation of scenery; provision for welding, cutting and fabricating metalwork items;

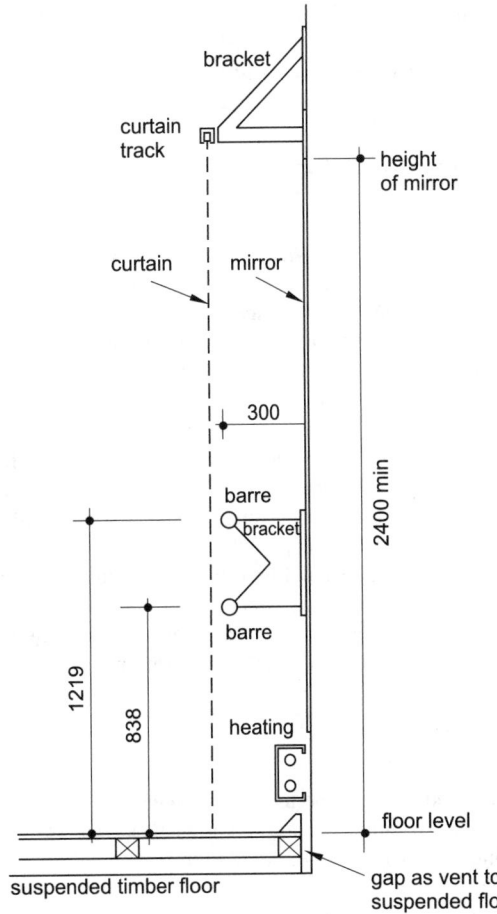

20.102 *Section through wall barres in rehearsal studio for dance practice*

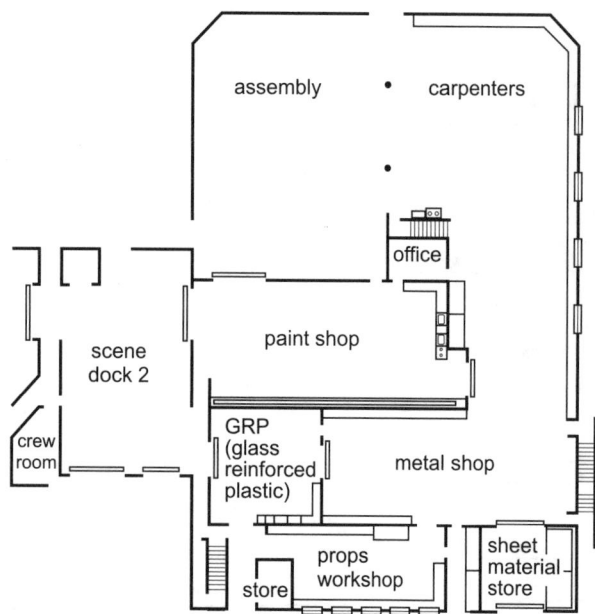

20.103 *Plan of workshops in the West Yorkshire Playhouse, Leeds*

benches, welding screens and bending machinery; storage of raw materials such as sheets, tubes and bars, bolts, nuts and screws.
Trial assembly area: area for the erection of a trial assembly of the set under construction, the size of the performing area of the stage.
Property department: worktops and storage of raw materials. Two separate workshops may be required: one for polystyrene and fibreglass work with associated fire-resistant requirements and extraction of toxic gases, the other for work with other materials.
Delivery and storage of raw materials to the carpentry workshop, paint shop, metalwork shop and property department, including unloading bay and parking of delivery vans and lorries.
Storage of scenery and properties for re-use.

10.16 Layout of workshops
A level floor is required through unloading bays, workshops, scenery store and stage; giving a clear, broad passage of movement of scenery onto the stage. Where a change of level is unavoidable a lift will be inevitable but is not recommended. If touring companies are anticipated, passage from the unloading bay to the stage should be direct without interfering with the workshops.

The paint frame and backcloth storage should be placed so that the rolled backcloths can be moved horizontally into position under the flytower or grid with the painted surface facing the audience. The large doors or roller shutters required for the movement of scenery should not also be used for people. The minimum dimensions of the openings should be determined by the maximum size of scenery expected.

The carpentry shop should be isolated from the paint shop to avoid noise and sawdust penetration, and both areas should be acoustically insulated from the stage. Scenery storage located between workshops and stage acts as a sound barrier.

10.17 Wardrobe
Space is required for:

- Making and fitting of performers' costumes
- Making and fitting associated items such as wigs
- Storing, repairing and cleaning costumes
- Making millinery and accessories
- Dyeing cloth and spraying materials
- Storing rolls of cloth and pattern paper
- Storing small items such as sewing materials, dyestuffs

- Delivery of raw materials including unloading bay and parking of delivery vans
- Office for costume supervisor.

Performers require easy access to the wardrobe for fitting costumes, while the distribution of finished costumes for, and their cleaning during, a production suggests a location close to the dressing rooms.

10.18 Recording studio
For sound effects and music. An isolated space, with control room. Associated areas may include a library of tapes and discs, entry lounge and lobby. Further details may be found in Chapter 19.

10.19 Common facilities
Provision for resting, changing, refreshment, toilets and showers.

10.20 Transport
Van or vans for the collections and delivery of goods, with parking spaces within the curtilage of the site.

10.21 Facilities for people with a disability

Access
- Dedicated car parking spaces at public and staff entrances
- Drop-off points at entrances
- Wheelchair users use main entrance
- External and internal ramped access, handrails and lifts comply with Building Regulations
- Unrestricted access to all levels and non-public areas*
- Dedicated wheelchair spaces in auditorium seating areas
- Accessible toilets complying with Building Regulations
- Box office reception desk and information counter with accessible height and width.

Facilities for people with sensory impairment
- Induction loop system or infra-red hearing provision in auditorium
- Induction loop system in box office, reception desk and information counter
- Visual fire alarm system
- Braille/large print/tactile signs
- Audio description provision
- Facilities for guide dogs.

11 LEGISLATION
The 1968 Theatres Act gives local authorities responsibility for licensing places of public entertainment. There is no national guideline or standard by which they work, and it is essential that contact be made with the appropriate local authority before plans are too far advanced. Before taking any decision they would normally consult the fire authority and the Health and Safety Executive as well as their own safety officer. There is a Home Office Guideline on Safety in Places of Public Entertainment, but it is only a Guideline.

The areas of particular concern will be inflammability of materials, seating layout, emergency lighting levels, escape routes, signage and building services.

12 BIBLIOGRAPHY
Ian Appleton, *Buildings for the performing arts*, Butterworth Architecture, 1996
Roderick Ham (ed.), *Theatre planning*, Architectural Press, 1972

* *Note*: it would not normally be feasible or necessary to provide access for people in wheelchairs to service spaces such as the grid over a stage, or lighting walkways over an auditorium.

21 Community centres

Jim Tanner

Jim Tanner is a partner of Tanner and Partners

CI/SfB 532
Uniclass F532
UDC 725.835

KEY POINTS:
- *There is a need for a community facility in most areas*
- *Existing centres are often inadequate*

Contents

1 INTRODUCTION

1.01 Briefing
By their nature community buildings must serve a variety of functions among which are:

- Meetings
- Child care (creche, day nursery, pre-school playgroup)
- Childrens' activities (scouts, guides)
- Concerts and plays
- Dances
- Parties and receptions
- Exhibitions
- Sporting and leisure activities, and
- Adult education.

The client, such as a church or a local authority, may have its own specific requirements; but the financial viability of community facilities usually depends on letting them out to other organisations. At the briefing and planning stage it is wise to consider activities which could or should be accommodated.

1.02 Space requirement and arrangement
The following points should be borne in mind:

- Meetings can range from committee meetings of half a dozen people to public meetings with an audience of a couple of hundred. If this range is anticipated then accommodation should include one or two smaller meeting rooms as well as the main hall.
- Child care and childrens' activities invariably require storage for furniture and equipment. If scouts use the facilities on a regular basis, for example, they are likely to need permanent storage for camping equipment, such as tents and poles, and cooking as well as games equipment.
- Some indoor sporting activities such as badminton, require generous space provision. See Chapter 25. These are likely to dictate the dimensions of the hall.

2 PLANNING AND DESIGN

2.01 Relationships
The principal plan elements and their relationship to each other are illustrated in **21.1**. **21.2** and **21.3** are typical examples of the type.

2.02 Space requirements
Table I gives recommended floor areas for various functions and activities.

2.03 Design
Community centres are multi-purpose buildings. Needs and priorities will often conflict; the skill of the designer in consultation with the client, statutory authorities and specialists must be exercised so that a balance is struck. All the following factors should be considered.

2.04 Structure and construction
Most new-build self-contained community centres are domestic in scale. The most economic forms of construction are those used in domestic building: solid ground floors, masonry load-bearing walls and lightweight flat roofs or framed pitched roofs. Alternative forms of construction are only occasionally justified: for a difficult site or when only a short-life building is required. In the latter case, it is worth considering proprietary off-the-peg buildings. The appearance of such a building is not always aesthetically pleasing, but there are exceptions. Where the community facilities are to be accommodated in a larger building also used for other purposes, structure and construction will be determined by the wider considerations.

2.05 Materials and finishes
For self-contained community centres it is worth while designing for minimum maintenance, as upkeep funds are always limited. Choice of finishes should be influenced by the following considerations:

Nature of use may dictate forms of construction and finish which are non-standard. For example, when regular provision for dancing (particularly classical ballet) or indoor sport such as badminton or gymnastics is required, the floor should provide some resilience and specialist advice should be sought.

Durability: Some uses, particularly sporting activities, can be exceptionally hard on surface finishes. The main hall may need to be equipped with retractable bleacher seating as used in sports

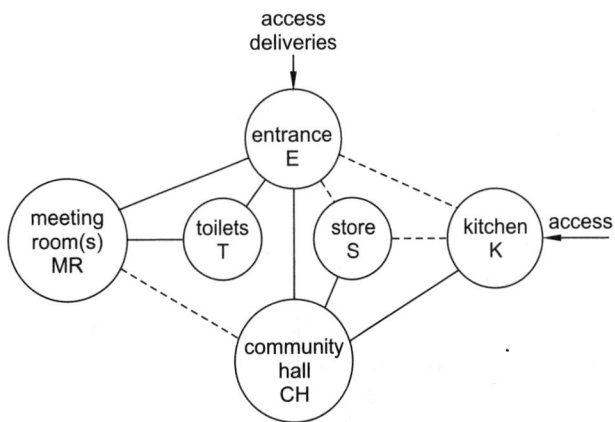

21.1 *Elements of the plan of a community centre*

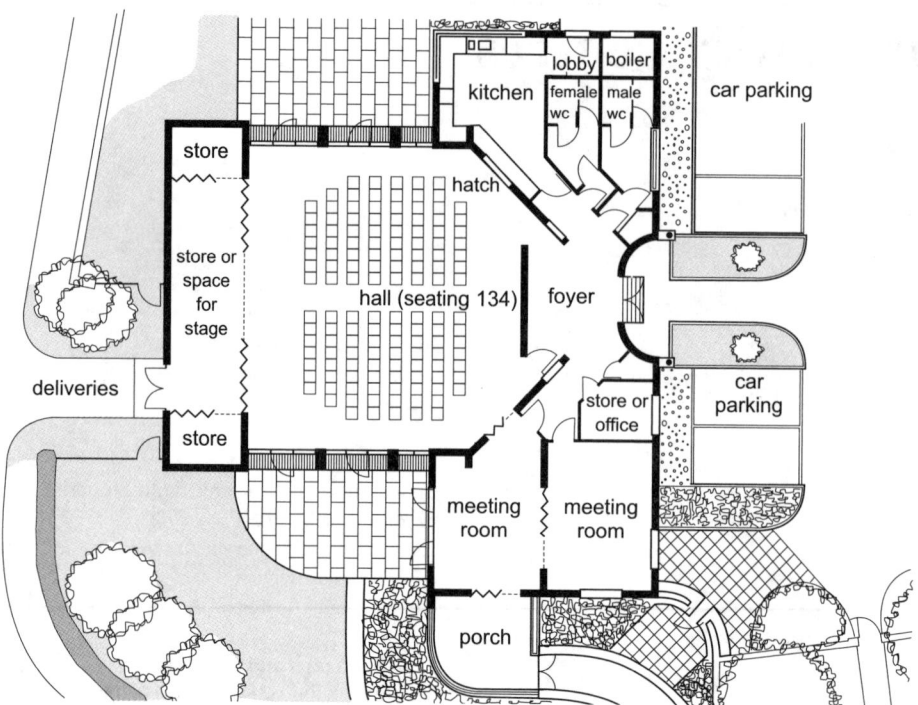

21.2 *Church centre for St James's Church, Finchampstead. Architects: Nye, Saunders & Partners*

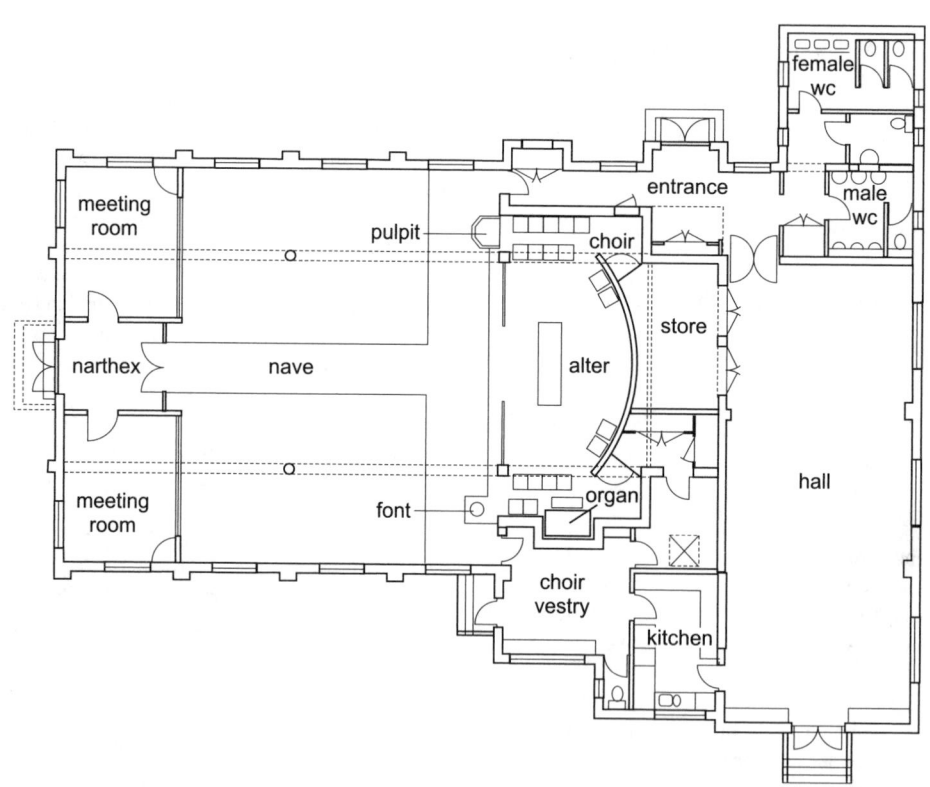

21.3 *Community centre for St Francis Church, Westborough: an example of an addition to an existing building. Architects: Nye, Saunders & Partners*

centres and educational buildings. Pulling out and stacking back such seating creates localised loading and wear. Resilient floors are particularly vulnerable. The manufacturers of the seating and of the floor finishes should be consulted at an early stage.

Safety: Users of a community centre range from small children to elderly and disabled people. Finishes should be chosen with a view to safety, all floors, ramps and steps should be non-slip. Projections, sharp corners and angles should be avoided.

Cleaning: Community facilities get heavy use and limited operating budgets. The building should be easy to clean.

2.06 Means of escape

Care in planning and signposting the means of escape in case of fire is especially important because:

● The users, such as audiences at occasional concerts and meetings. will not be familiar with the building layout.

Table I Minimum floor areas for various activities

Function	Area per person (m²)
Main hall: Closely seated audience	0.46 (based on movable seats, usually armless, 450 mm centre to centre; with fixed seating 500 mm centre to centre will increase to 0.6 m²)
Dances	0.55 to 0.9
Dining	0.9 to 1.1
Creche, day nursery or pre-school playgroup	0–2 years 3.75 2–3 3 3–5 2.5
Children 5–8 years (out of school and holiday schemes, open access projects)	2.5
Meeting rooms	2.25 up to 4 people 2 6 people 1.55 8–12 people 1.25 20 people

Table II Requirements for child care

Item	Comment
Child care: (creche, day nursery, playgroup) Regulation	Child care for children in their early years (generally defined as under-8) usually comes within the Children Act 1989 (see Section 3) and local authorities are responsible for approving and registering facilities. Many of these authorities provide published requirements and guidance on standards.
Staffing ratios	0–2 year olds 1:3 2–3 year olds 1:4 3–5 year olds 1:8 (minimum staff 2)
Outdoor play	A safe area with easy access from the building is a usual requirement
Catering	The Pre-school Playgroups Association recommends that children and adults should sit together during meals and consequently separate dining accommodation for staff is not required

- Small children are likely to be present in a creche or day care centre.
- Elderly and disabled people may use the centre.
- Facilities for leisure or educational purposes may be used by people with learning difficulties.

Early consultation with the local fire authority is essential.

2.07 Licensing
A licence will be required for certain uses and these invariably have conditions attached. See Section 3.

2.08 Noise
A community centre is more likely to generate than to suffer from high noise levels. They are commonly used at night and at the weekend, and are often situated within residential communities. They must therefore be designed to avoid nuisance. Where uses take place simultaneously, sound separation will be necessary between a noisy activity such as a dance and one requiring relative quiet such as a lecture.

The basic principles of acoustic design should be applied:

- Orientation, e.g. location of entrances, exits and windows relative to adjoining buildings
- Layout
- Shape of rooms
- Double glazing, only viable in association with mechanical ventilation
- Sound-absorbent finishes, balanced with requirements of durability and cleanability, and
- Landscaping, including trees, to contain external noise.

Unless unavoidable, noise-producing spaces should not be located alongside quiet spaces. Absorbent surfaces may have to be concentrated at ceiling level or provided by means of drapes and wall hangings. Management can also play a significant part in controlling noise and this should be discussed with the client at an early stage.

2.9 Security
Community centres are more than usually vulnerable to break-ins and vandalism as they do not have resident caretakers or 24-hour surveillance, are not continuously occupied, are visited by a large number of people, contain expensive equipment and are isolated from other buildings. Requirements for security can conflict with those of means of escape, so it is important to consult with experts and local authorities.

2.10 Child care
Table II is a checklist of design considerations where creches, day nurseries or playgroups use the facility.

2.11 Disabled people
There are statutory regulations relating to access for disabled people. These apply not only those using wheelchairs but also include people with visual and auditory impairments and those using other types of walking aids. All these have difficulties with steps and changes of direction, and the design of entrances, circulation spaces and toilets should take this into account.

2.12 Legislation
This is constantly changing. Table III gives some current examples but is not exhaustive. The local authority will advise on the latest requirements. It is particularly important to ensure full conformity if the public are going to be charged for admission.

3 ELEMENTS OF THE PLAN

3.01 Entrance
This should be large enough to accommodate an influx of people, such as prior to a meeting or concert. Signposting should be clear as many will be unfamiliar with the building. Unless there is a separate goods entrance, it should allow for for bulk delivery of food and drink, display material and equipment. Consider the

Table III Legislation

Legislation	Comment
Places of Public Entertainment	Legislation requires that a licence is obtained for premises which are to be used, regularly or occasionally for the following purposes: - Public music or public music and dancing - Public performance of plays - Cinematograph exhibitions to which the public are admitted on payment - Cinematograph exhibitions for children who are members of a cinema club - Indoor sports entertainment Statutory requirements must be satisfied in terms of means of escape in case of fire and other safety considerations. Administered by the local authority
The Children Act 1989	Covers requirements for premises used by children in, for instance, day nurseries, playgroups, creches, out-of-school clubs, holiday play schemes, adventure playgrounds and open-access projects. Administered by the local authority

arrangement of the doors, the durability of surfaces and easy accesses to both the kitchen and the hall.

3.02 Hall

For sports purposes refer to Chapter 25, and for other uses Chapter 20. A rectangular shape is likely to be suitable for a wider range of uses than a square or any other shape. If black-out is required, pay special attention to size and location of windows; mechanical ventilation may be needed.

3.03 Meeting rooms

If more than one, make them different sizes. Aternatively, have one space that can be divided using sliding folding doors; although some of these do not provide adequate sound insulation. At least one meeting room should have direct access to the hall.

3.04 Toilets

Separate toilets will be needed for men, women and disabled people. There may also be a need for smaller toilets for little children. Unisex baby-changing facilities should be provided. If considerable sports usage is expected, showers will be necessary for each sex. See Chapter 3.

3.05 Kitchen

There should be little need for more than a domestic kitchen. If catered functions are expected, provide space for setting out and final preparations. See Chapter 18.

3.06 Storage

A separate store should be provided for each main use:

- Kitchen
- Sports
- Seating and other furniture
- Creche/kindergarden
- Scouts.

The kitchen store should be directly accessible from the kitchen, the others from the hall. Storage space should be as generous as space and budget will allow.

3.07 Furniture

Refer to trade catalogues, and seek specialist advice.

4 BIBLIOGRAPHY

PPA Guidelines, published by the Pre-School Playgroups Association

22 Swimming

Gerald Perrin

Gerald Perrin is senior partner of Perrin Consult, specialist architect in sport and leisure since 1961

CI/SfB 541
Uniclass F541
UDC 725.74

KEY POINTS:
- *Encouraging everyone to learn and enjoy swimming is a priority*
- *Provision divides into leisure and competitive facilities*

Contents

1 INTRODUCTION

There has been a general trend away from pools designed specifically for competition and diving towards shallow water, free-form 'fun' pools with many features including water rides. The introduction of compulsory competitive tendering (CCT) has further increased the emphasis on income-producing dryside provision, in the form of fitness rooms, health and beauty suites, sunbeds, saunas and steam rooms. This dryside space around the fun pool is often themed to represent 'tropical paradises' where dense planting provides the backcloth for steel bands, travel agencies, and poolside refreshments. Indoor/outdoor pools – often seen in European countries – are becoming popular.

Demand for serious swimming facilities in the meantime has reappeared in the form of 25 m pools with six or eight lanes, **22.1**. Many older 33.33 m pools have been converted into combined competition and learner pools by means of causeways at the 25 m

22.1 *25 metre pool complex*

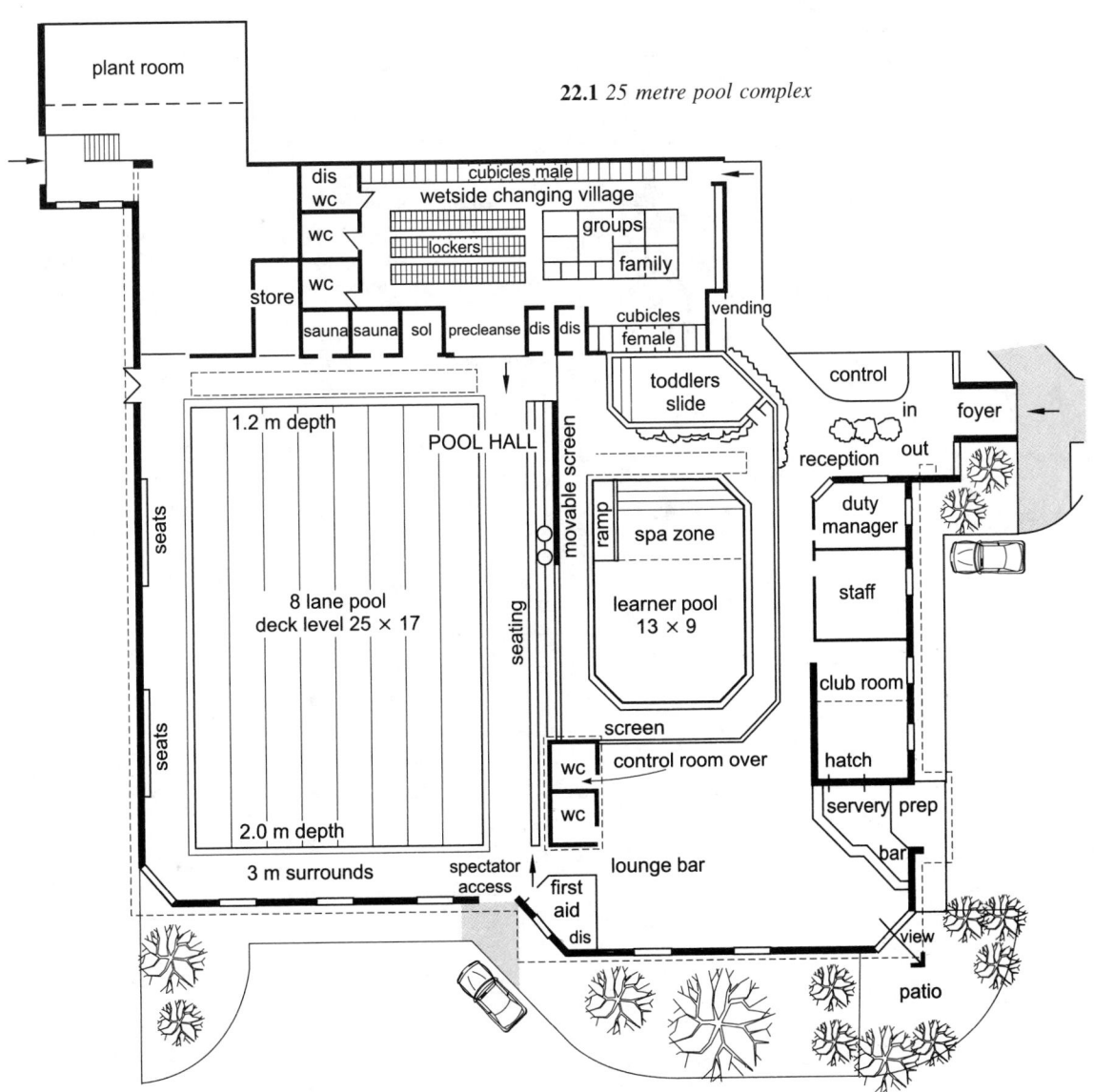

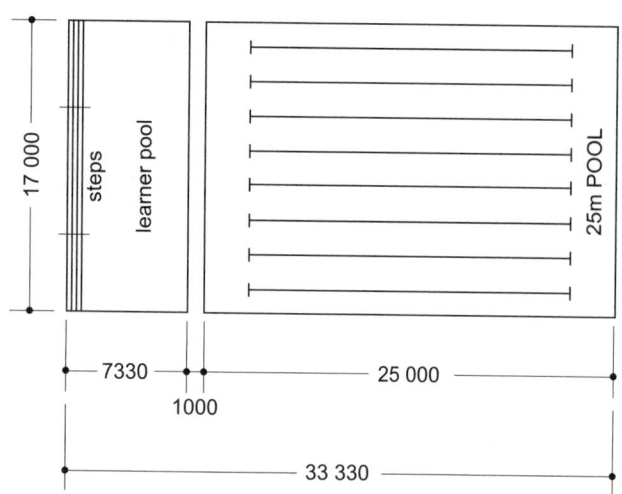

22.2 *Plan of 33⅓₊ metre pool, showing use as 25 metre pool plus learner pool*

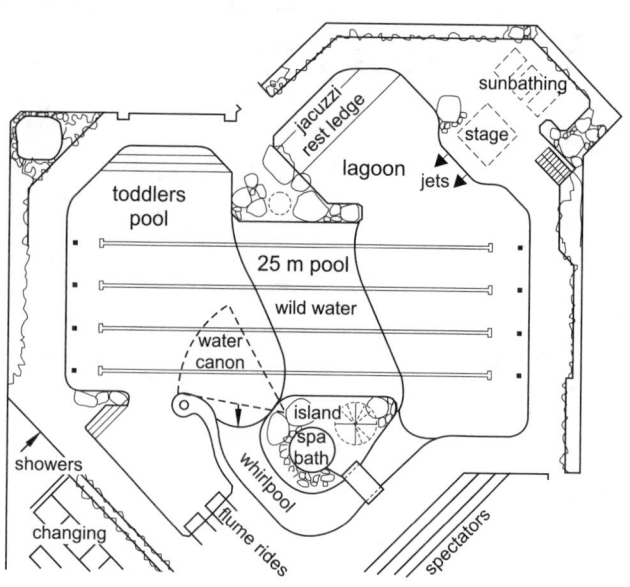

22.3 *Hybrid pool*

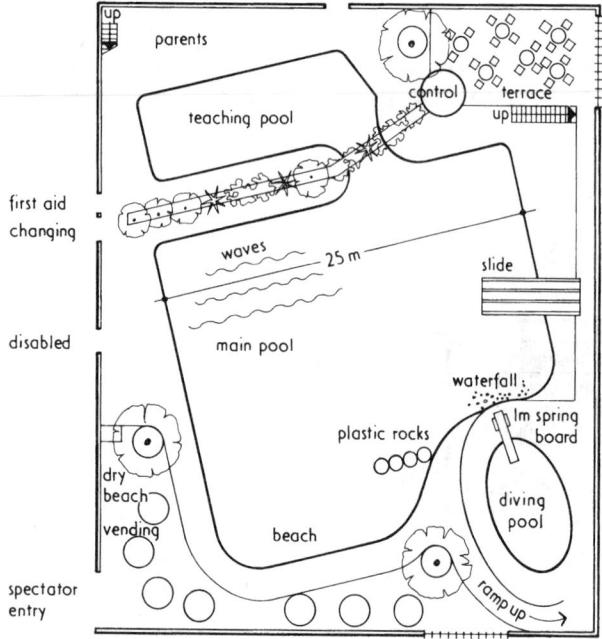

22.4 *Plan of a leisure pool*

mark, **22.2**. Hybrid pools with 25 m training lanes down the centre and free-form sides are becoming increasingly common, **22.3**. Another leisure pool is shown in **22.4**.

The refurbishment of old Edwardian pools and buildings of similar vintage (corn exchanges, sawmills, etc.) has increased the present stock of good pools considerably, especially in the UK and Holland.

2 COMPETITION, LEARNER, TRAINING AND DIVING POOLS

2.01 Dimensions

Dimensions of these pools, are strictly laid down by major governing bodies for swimming (FINA – international: ASA for UK). Changes are made from time to time and it is advisable to seek up-to-date information from the relevant authorities.

2.02 Competition pools

Competition pools are based upon long-course 50 m, **22.5**, or short-course 25 m, **22.6** requirements. Long-course pools have a minimum width of 21 m or 25 m for Olympic competition. The minimum depth of water may be 1 m, although 1.2 m is preferred in 21 m wide pools. Olympic standard pools require a minimum depth of 1.8 m.

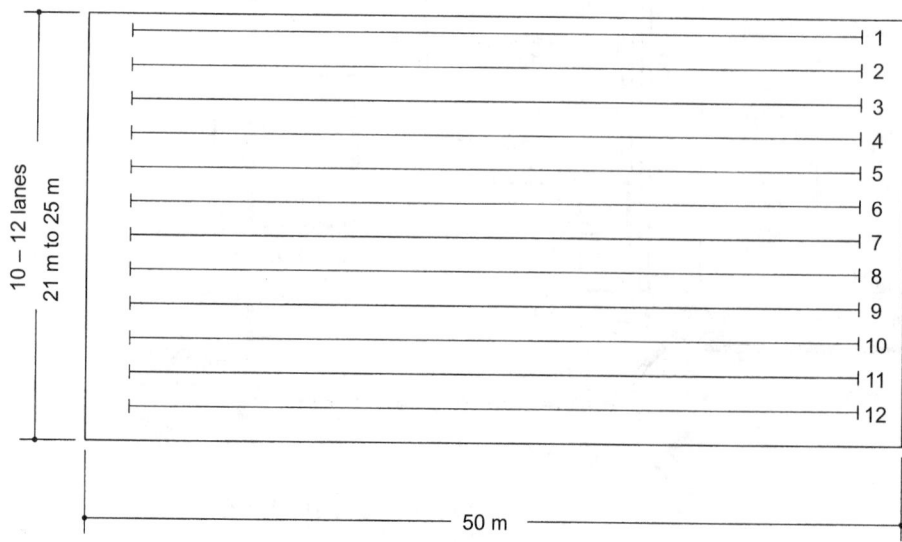

22.5 *Plan of 50 metre pool*

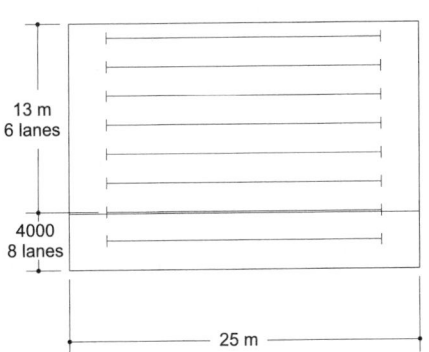

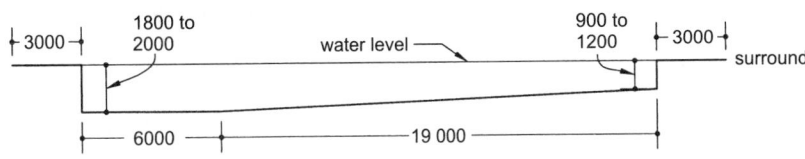

22.6 *25 m pool:*

a *Plan.*

b *Longitudinal section*

2.03 Short-course pools

Short-course, 25 m, pools should have a width of 13 m for six-lane competition, or 17 m for eight-lane. Minimum water depth should be 0.9–1 m (preferably 1.2 m following recent court findings relating to accidents in shallow water pools). Maximum depth may be 1.8–2 m. These pools are suitable for ASA National, District and County standard competitions.

2.04 Training pools

Training pools of 25 m length may have four or five lanes (9 m and 11 m wide). Depths should be as for short-course pools. In both cases the last 6 m of the deep end should be level.

2.05 Learner pools

Learner pools for beginners and non-swimmers, **22.7**, should preferably be separated from the main pool far safety reasons and in order to maintain higher air and water temperatures. Steps along one side form part of the water-acclimatisation process especially for the young. Ramps are sometimes included for disabled non-ambulant users, although with level deck pools these have become largely unnecessary. Handrails should be provided where steps lead down into the water.

Dimensions are based upon class size down one long side (classes are of 30–35 pupils on average), with the width allowing beginners to take at least three or four strokes before reaching the side. Common dimensions are length 12–13 m, width 7–10 m and depth 0.7 m at the foot of steps to 0.9–1.2 m at the deep end.

2.07 Pools for the very young (two months old)

These are frequently provided separately, **22.8**, to acclimatise children to water accompanied by parents. Shallow water, seat/

steps, and water features such as slides and play furniture make up the main characteristics of these pools. There are no fixed dimensions or shapes.

2.08 Hydrotherapy pools

These are commonly seen throughout Europe, particularly in Germany and Austria, for the elderly or infirm, **22.9**. The water is heavily salinated to assist swimming and healing. The increasing number of sports injuries clinics now appearing in the UK suggests a wider role for this type of pool.

2.09 Diving pools

Diving pools attached to main competition pools have been superseded by specialist diving facilities in separate self-contained

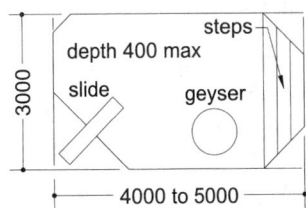

22.8 *Plan of toddlers' pool*

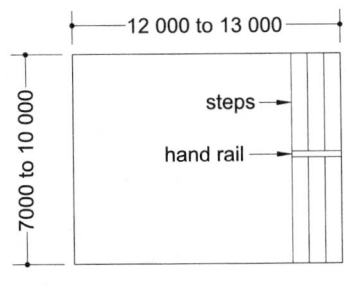

a *Plan.*

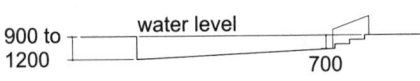

b *Section*

22.7 *Learner pool:*

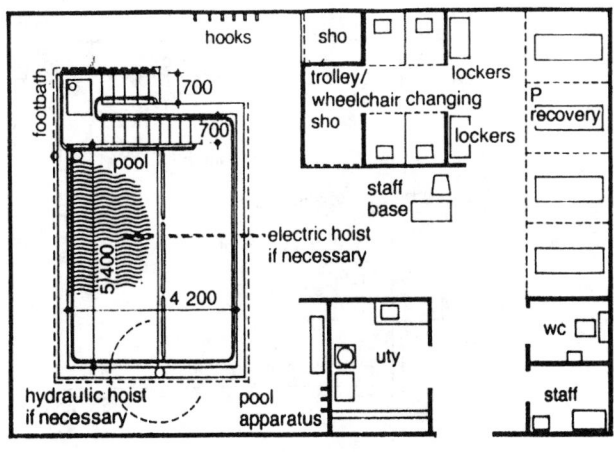

a *Plan.*

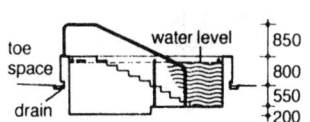

b *Section through pool*

22.9 *Hydrotherapy pool complex:*

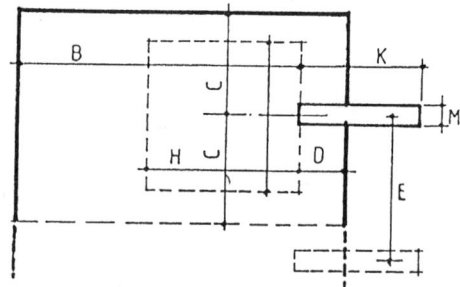

a *Plan.*

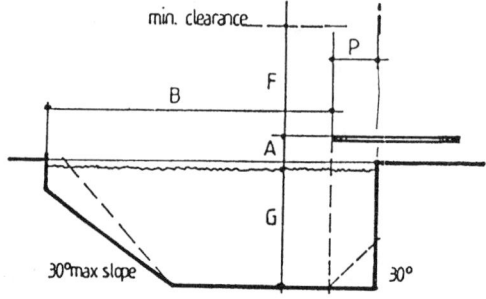

b *Section*

22.10 *Diving pool (see Table I for dimensions):*

spaces where diving can be carried on without interruption. The minimum distance to other pools should be 5 m. The minimum requirements for a diving pool are given in **22.10** and Table I.

Olympic or international standard competition diving requires more rigorous standards, **22.11**, and associated specialist facilities such as sprays to ripple the water surface and lifts to the higher diving boards. The FINA/ASA standards for these are shown in **22.12** and Table II. An example of this type is shown in **22.13**. National training status requires length 30 m, width 25 m and depths as Table I.

All dimensions should be checked with the relevant authorities as they may be amended from time to time.

Table I Minimum dimensions in metres for diving boards

Type of board	Spring	Spring	Fixed	Fixed*	Fixed
A Board height*	1.0	3.0	5.0	7.5	10.0
B Clearance forward	7.5	9.0	10.25	11.0	13.5
C Clearance to sides	2.5	3.5	3.8	4.5	4.5
D Clearance behind	1.5	1.5	1.25	1.5	1.5
E Centre of adjoining board	2.5	2.5	2.5	2.5	2.5
F Clearance overhead	4.6	4.6	3.0	3.2	3.4
G Depth of water	3.0	3.5	3.8	4.1	4.5
H Depth maintained forward	5.3	6.0	6.0	8.0	10.5
J Depth maintained to sides	2.2	2.7	3.0	3.0	3.0
K Board length	4.8	4.8	5.0	6.0	6.0
M Board width	0.5	0.5	2.0	2.0	2.0
N Clearance forwards overhead	5.0	5.0	5.0	5.0	6.0
P Clearance sides and behind overhead	2.75	2.75	2.75	2.75	2.75

*The 7.5 m board is mainly used for training.
A tolerance of ±0.1 is permissible on board height. relate all dimensions to front edge centre of each board.

3 WATER ACTIVITIES

A number of activities are currently associated with deep water in hybrid or competition pools.

3.01 Water polo

Water depth at Olympic standard should be not less than 1.8 m, and for lesser play, 1.2 m. The fields of play are:

- Olympic standard 30 × 20 m
- Club standard 25 × 10 m

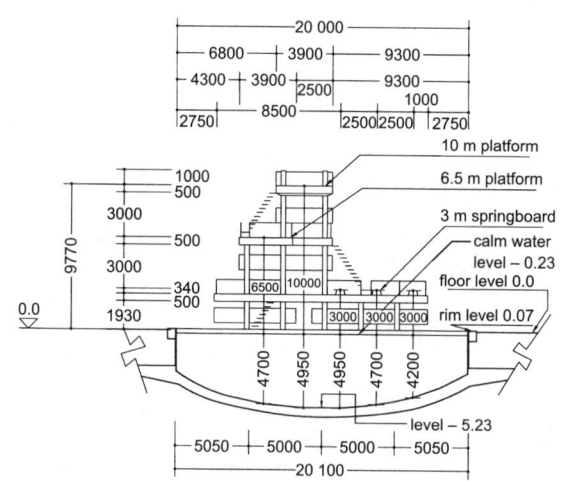

b *Elevation from pool.*

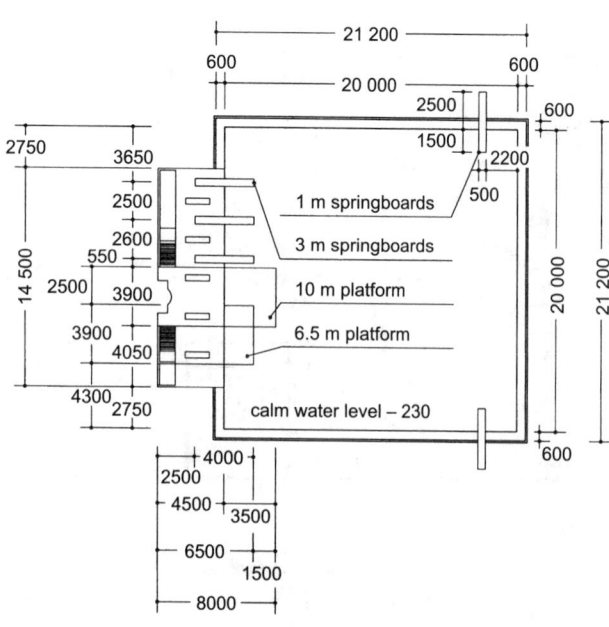

a *Plan.*

22.11 *Olympic regulations diving platform assembly and pool:*

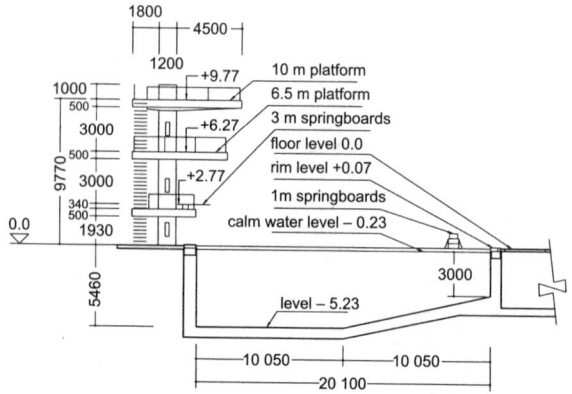

c *Side elevation and pool cross-section*

Table II FINA/ASA dimensions for diving facilities (see 22.12)

			Springboard				Platform									
			1 metre Length 4.80 Width 0.50 Height 1.00		**3 metre** 4.80 0.50 3.00		**1 metre** 5.00 0.60 0.60–1.00		**3 metre** 5.00 0.60 min 1.50 pref. 2.60–3.00		**5 metre** 6.00 1.50 5.00		**7.5 metre** 6.00 1.50 7.50		**10 metre** 6.00 2.00 10.00	
			Horiz.	Vert.	Horiz.	Vert.	Horiz.	Vert.	Horiz.	Vert.	Horiz.	Vert.	Horiz.	Vert.	Horiz.	Vert.
A	From plummet back to pool wall	Designation minimum preferred	A–1 1.50 1.80		A–3 1.50 1.80		A–1 pl 0.75 0.75		A–3 pl 1.25 1.25		A–5 1.25 1.25		A–7.5 1.50 1.50		A–10 1.50 1.50	
A/A	From plummet back to platform plummet directly below	Designation minimum preferred									A/A5/1 0.75 1.25		A/A./5/3,1 0.75 1.25		a/A10/5,3,1/ 0.75 1.25	
B	From plummet to pool wall at side	Designation minimum preferred	B–1 2.50 2.50		B–3 3.50 3.50		B–1 pl 2.30 2.30		B–3 pl 2.80 2.90		B–5 3.25 3.75		B–7.5 4.25 4.50		B–10 5.25 5.25	
C	From plummet to adjacent plummet	Designation minimum preferred	C1–1 2.00 2.40		C3–3, 3–1 2.20 2.60		C 1–1 pl 1.65 1.95		C 3–3 pl, 1 pl 2.00 2.10		C 5–3, 5–1 2.25 2.50		C 7.5–5,3,1 2.50 2.50		C 10–7.5,5,3,1 2.75 2.75	
D	From plummet to pool wall ahead	Designation minimum preferred	D–1 9.00 9.00		D–3 10.25 10.25		D–1 pl 8.00 8.00		D–3 pl 9.50 9.50		D–5 10.25 10.25		D–7.5 11.00 11.00		D–10 13.50 12.50	
E	From plummet to board to ceiling	Designation minimum preferred		E–1 5.00 5.00		E–3 5.00 5.00		E–1 pl 3.25 3.50		E–3 pl 3.25 3.50		E–5 3.25 3.50		E–7.5 3.25 3.50		E–10 4.00 5.00
F	Clear overhead behind and each side of plummet	Designation minimum preferred	F–1 2.50 2.50	E–1 5.00 5.00	F–3 2.50 2.50	E–3 5.00 5.00	F–1 pl 2.75 2.75	E–1 pl 3.25 3.50	F–3 pl 2.75 2.75	E–3 pl 3.25 3.50	F–5 2.75 2.75	E–5 3.25 3.50	F–7.5 2.75 2.75	E–7.5 3.25 3.50	F–10 2.75 2.75	E–10 4.00 5.00
G	Clear overhead ahead of plummet	Designation minimum preferred	G–1 5.00 5.00	E–1 5.00 5.00	G–3 5.00 5.00	E–3 5.00 5.00	G–1 pl 5.00 5.00	E–1 pl 3.25 3.50	G–3 pl 5.00 5.00	E–3 pl 3.25 3.50	G–5 5.00 5.00	E–5 3.25 3.50	G–7.5 5.00 5.00	E–7.5 3.25 3.50	G–10 6.00 6.00	E–10 4.00 5.00
H	Depth of water at plummet	Designation minimum preferred		H–1 3.40 3.50		H–3 3.70 3.50		H–1 pl 3.20 3.30		H–3 pl 3.50 3.60		H–5 3.70 3.80		H–7.5 4.10 4.50		H–10 4.50 5.00
J K	Distance and depth ahead of plummet	Designation minimum preferred	J–1 5.00 5.00	K–1 3.30 3.40	J–3 6.00 6.00	K–3 3.60 3.70	J–1 pl 4.50 4.50	K–1 pl 3.10 3.20	J–3 pl 5.50 5.50	K–3 pl 3.40 3.50	J–5 6.00 6.00	K–5 3.60 3.70	J–7.5 8.00 8.00	K–7.5 4.00 4.40	J–10 11.00 11.00	K–10 4.25 4.75
L M	Distance and depth each side of plummet	Designation minimum preferred	L–1 1.50 2.00	M–1 3.30 3.40	L–3 2.00 2.50	M–3 3.60 3.70	L–1 pl 1.40 1.90	M–1 pl 3.10 3.20	L–3 pl 1.80 2.30	M–3 pl 3.40 3.50	L–5 3.00 3.50	M–5 3.60 3.70	L–7.5 3.75 4.50	M–7.5 4.00 4.40	L–10 4.50 5.25	M–10 4.25 4.75
N	Maximum slope to reduce dimensions beyond full requirements	Pool depth Ceiling ht	30 degrees 30 degrees													

Note: Dimensions C (plummet to adjacent plummet) apply to platforms with widths as detailed. If platform widths are increased then C is to be increased by half the additional width(s).

The standards are shown in **22.14**. However, the game can be played as a recreation in a standard pool, **22.15**. The field is marked above water level at the pool sides. Space should be accessible for the free movement of the referee and goal judges at goal lines.

3.02 Synchronised swimming

This has become progressively popular over recent years and is now performed up to Olympic standard. Water should be not less than 1.8–2 m. Provision should be made for underwater windows, lighting and sound for coaching purposes.

3.03 Sub-aqua diving

Water should be not less than 1.5–2 m in depth with a high degree of clarity. Other requirements are:

- Water depths up to 5.5 m for pressure valuation experience
- Compressor room of approximately 15 m²
- Club room, **22.16**, for approximately 50 people
- Storage space for equipment of approximately 15 m, well drained
- Specialist rooms for advanced training including seminar rooms, club room, compressor store, equipment shop, separate changing rooms and an office

- Snorkelling pool ranging in depth from 1.5 to 5 m, with a diving pit 7 m deep, and
- Access to the pool using suitable ladders, **22.17**.

Details from the British Sub-Aqua Club.

4 LEISURE POOLS AND WATER FEATURES

4.01 Fun pools

Fun pools, **22.18**, with irregularly shaped sides and a considerable amount of shallow water space approximately 350–400 m² in area, may have combinations of the following features:

- Wave-making machinery, **22.19**
- Water cannons
- Underwater massage jets
- Waterfall
- Rapids/wild water, jungle river, lazy river/indoor-outdoor rides
- Whirlpool
- Jacuzzi spa bath
- Plume/water rides
- Slides
- Lagoons with jacuzzi rest ledges
- Underwater lighting and sound.

22.12 *FINA/ASA dimensions for diving facilities (see Table II):*

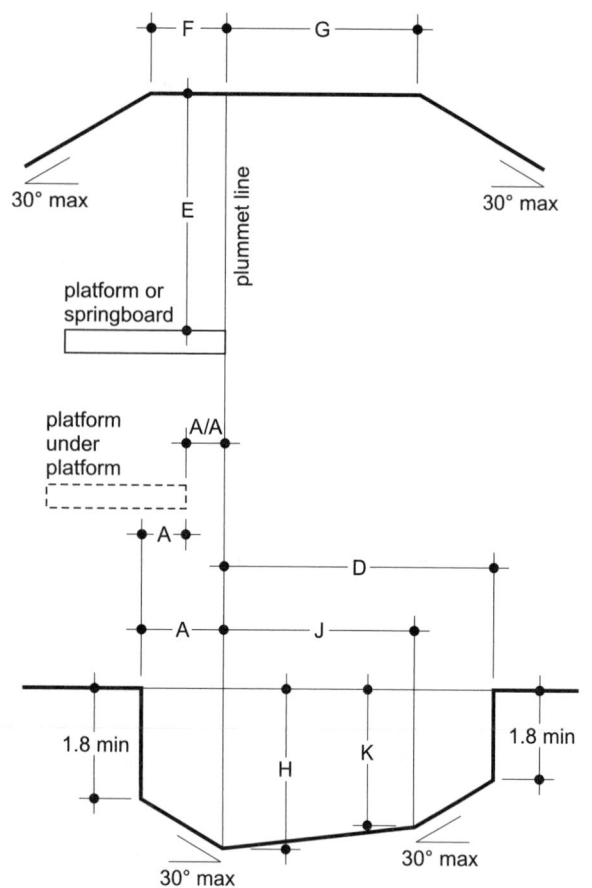

a *Side view.*

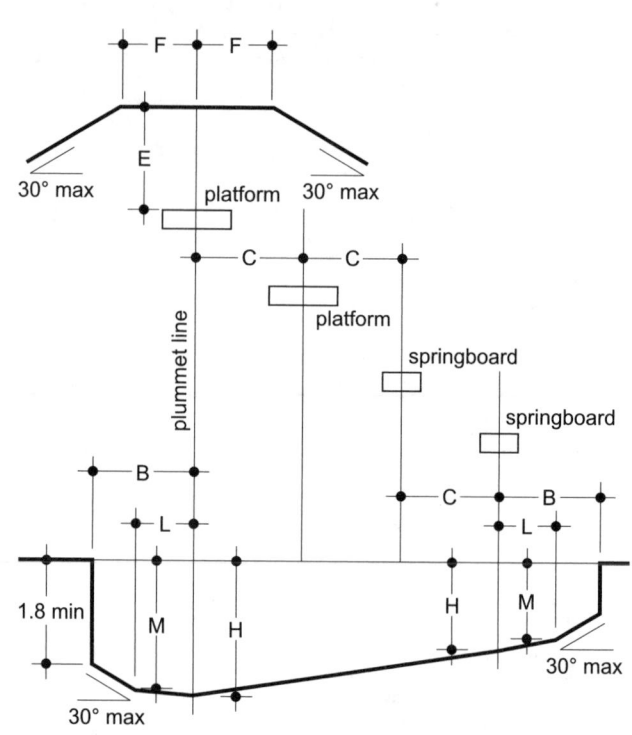

b *Frontal view*

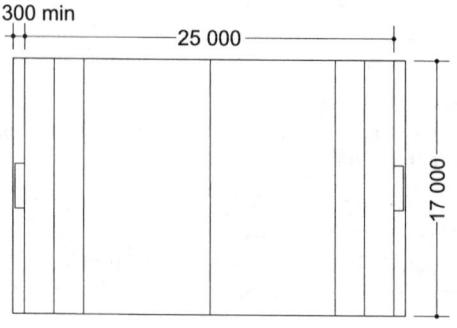

300 min

30 000

mm depth
1.8 m
(2 m pref)

3000

20 000

2 m   4 m   half distance line   4 m   8 m
line   line   line   line

a *For men.*

300 min

25 000

17 000

b *For women*

22.14 *Water polo layouts:*

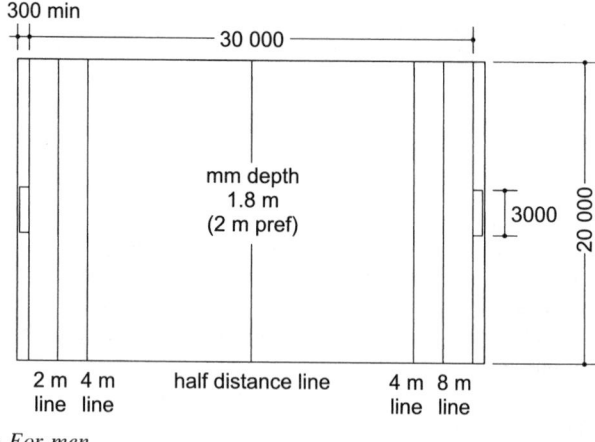

access
ladder to
walway
in roof

10m

7.5m

5m

3m

1m

water level

10m

7.5m

5m

3m

1m

a *Side view.*   **b** *Frontal view*

22.13 *Ponds Forge, Sheffield: diving stages:*

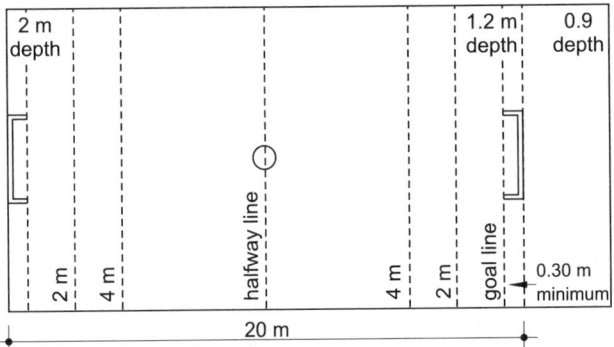

22.15 *Water polo layout for a 25 m × 12.5 m pool*

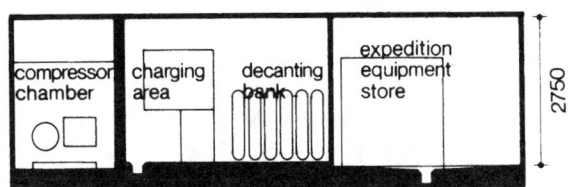

a *Section.*

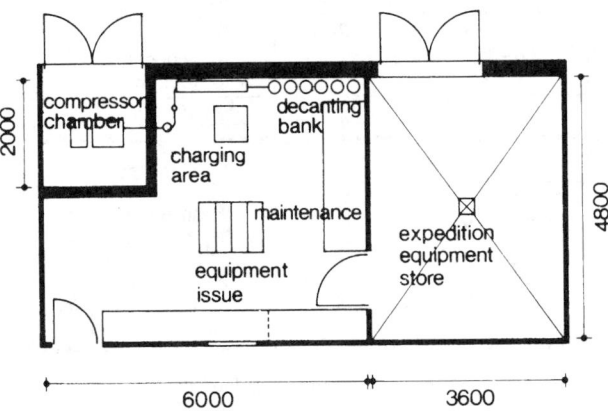

b *Plan*

22.16 *Sub-aqua equipment store and compressor room:*

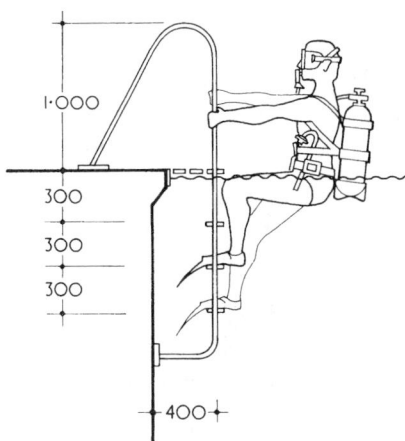

a *Elevation.*

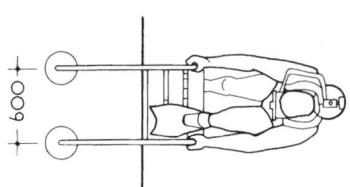

b *Plan*

22.17 *Access to the pool for sub-aqua diving. Specially designed removable steps assist a heavily laden diver:*

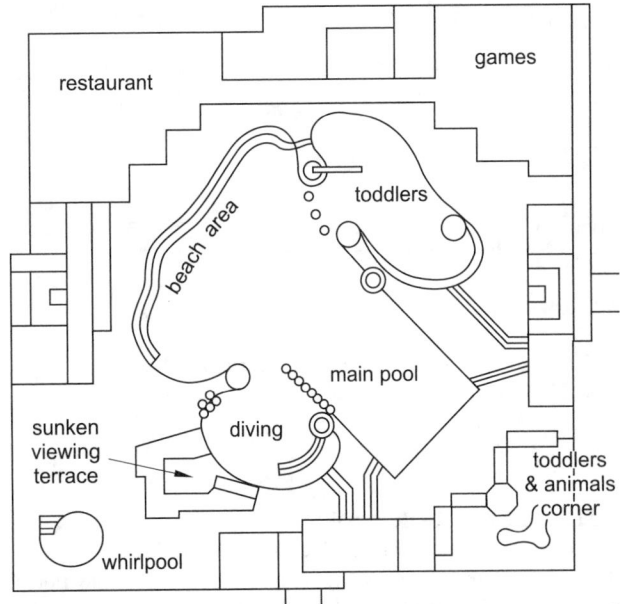

22.18 *Layout of leisure pool De Mirandabad, Amsterdam. Architects: Architektenburo Baanders, Frenken*

4.02 Dryside facilities

Dryside facilities usually associated with the above may include:

- Health and fitness suites plus separate changing, toilets and showers
- Beauty salon – massage, aromatherapy, manicure, hair treatment
- Rapid-tan sunbeds
- Sauna, steam cabins
- Platform for concerts, receptions, fashion shows, steel bands
- Lighting to match
- Themed baths (Turkish, Roman, Japanese, Scandinavian)
- Creche, meetings room
- First aid room
- Equipment store
- Landscape features normally themed to represent a tropical setting
- Food and drinks points
- Administration/supervision/control points
- Travel agency/displays.

4.03 Hybrid pools

These, **22.3**, are similar to leisure pools, but have a central area 25 m in length marked out with four or six training lanes for serious swimming. Depths at either end of this area must be the same as for normal 25 m competition pools. Because the sides may be free-form in shape and other features intrude (e.g. whirlpool, flume rides), competitions cannot be judged properly.

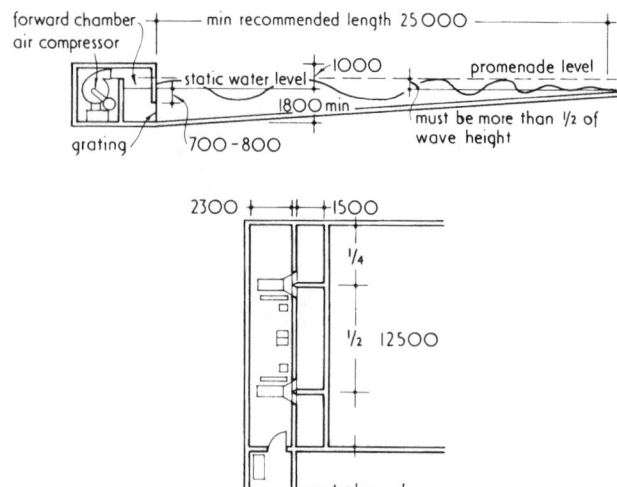

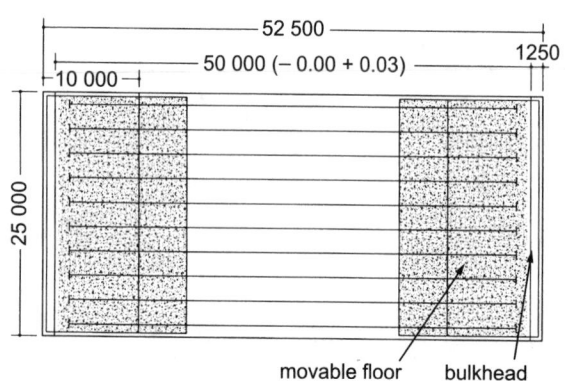

a Plan.

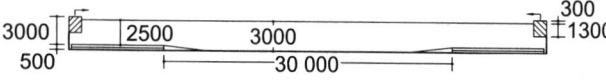

b Cross-section

22.20 A 50 metre pool with ultimate flexibility. This has two movable floors and two laterally moving bulkheads:

5 MOVABLE FLOOR POOLS

22.20 shows a pool with movable floors; while **22.21** shows the flexibility offered to 50 m and 25 m pools by movable floors. Flexibility is further increased by the inclusion of two movable floors and two laterally moving bulkheads.

6 POOL DETAILS AND LANE MARKINGS

6.01 Rest ledges
These are required around pool sides where the water depth exceeds 1.2 m, **22.22**.

6.02 Raised ends and touch pads
Where pools are to be predominantly used for competitions and serious training, raised ends should be provided, **22.23**, equipped with touchpads, **22.24**.

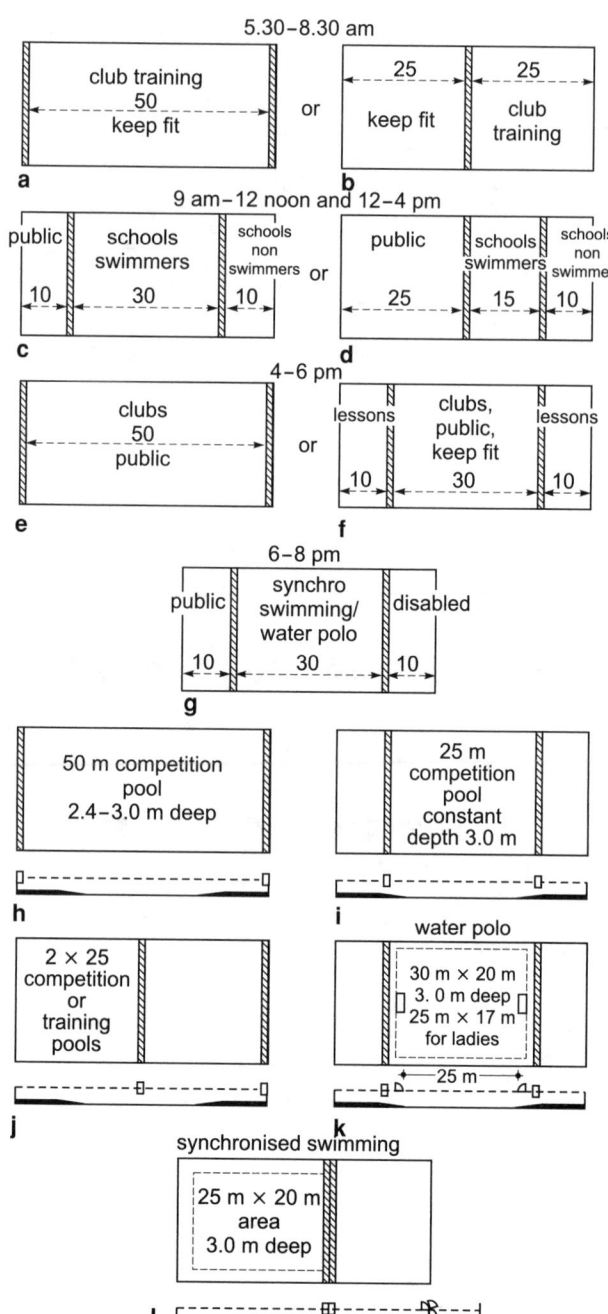

22.19 a Section through a leisure pool showing wave making machine room and 'beaching' of pool **b** Sectional plan of wave-making machine room

22.21 Various arrangements of the pool above: **a** 5:30 to 8:30 am, club training and keep fit. **b** 5:30 to 8:30 am, alternative for club training and keep fit. **c** 9 am to noon, public, school swimmers and school non-swimmers. **d** 9 am to noon, alternative for public, school swimmers and school non-swimmers. **e** 4 to 6 pm, clubs and public. **f** 4 to 6 pm, alternative for clubs, public, keep fit and lessons. **g** 6 to 8 pm, synchro swimming or water polo, public and disabled people. **h** 50 m competition pool 2.4 to 3 m deep. **i** 25 m competition pool constant 3 m depth. **j** Twin 25 m competition or training pools. **k** Water polo: 30 m × 20 m, or 25 m × 17 m for women, 3 m deep. **l** Synchronised swimming: 25 m × 20 m by 3 m deep

6.03 Edge channels
The present preference for deck level pools requires edge channels designed for overflow purposes, finger grip and demarcation between water edge and pool surround, **22.25**.

6.04 Lane rope anchorage
This is for fixing lane booms on level deck pools and is usually behind edge channels on pool surrounds.

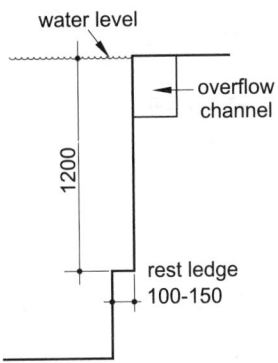

22.22 *Rest ledge*

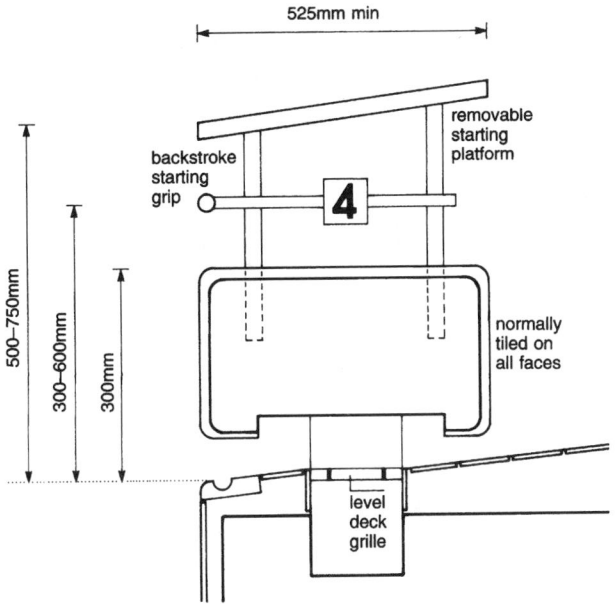

22.23 *Removable starting platform*

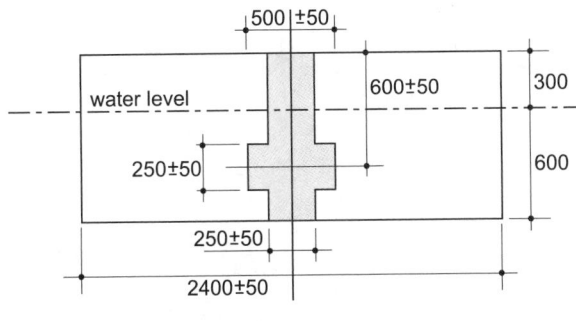

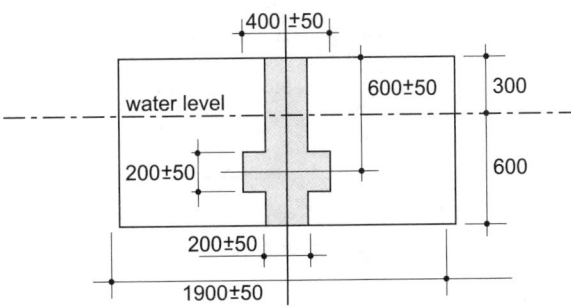

22.24 a *Touch pad to conform to FINA regulations.* **b** *Touch pad for ASA Championship requirements in 25 m pools*

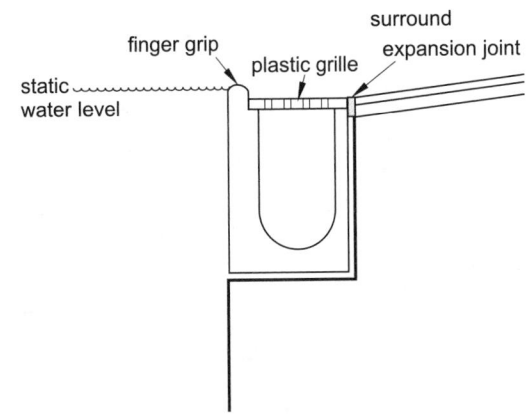

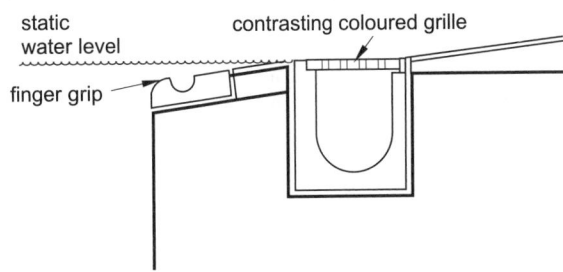

22.25 *Edge details for deck level pools*

6.05 Start–recall
A recall rope and flags are required 15 m in front of the start for competition use.

6.06 Lane markings in competition pools
These should be laid in accordance with FINA/ASA recommendations, **22.26** and Table III.

6.07 Backstroke turn indicators
These are required 5 m from end walls, **22.26**.

6.08 Underwater windows
These may be considered for coaching and video. Underwater lights may be required for environmental purposes.

7 CHANGING PROVISION

7.01 Facilities
Segregated changing facilities, **22.27** have been largely replaced by the changing 'village' arrangement, **22.28**, which is based upon separation of dry and wet footpaths to and from changing cubicles. Minimum cubicles are shown in **22.29**, but it is important to provide a proportion of larger cubicles for the use of families and disabled people.

Table III Dimensions of lane markings in metres

		FINA/ASA 50 m pools	ASA 25 m pools
A	Width of lane markings, end lines, targets	0.25 ± 0.05	0.2 ± 0.05
B	Length of end wall targets	0.5 ± 0.05	0.5 ± 0.05
C	Depth to centre of end wall targets	0.3 ± 0.05	0.3 ± 0.05
D	Length of lane marker cross line	1.0 ± 0.05	0.8 ± 0.05
E	Width of racing lanes	2.5	2.0
F	Distance from cross line to end wall	2.0 ± 0.05	2.0 ± 0.05
G	Touch pad	2.4 ± 0.05	1.9 ± 0.05

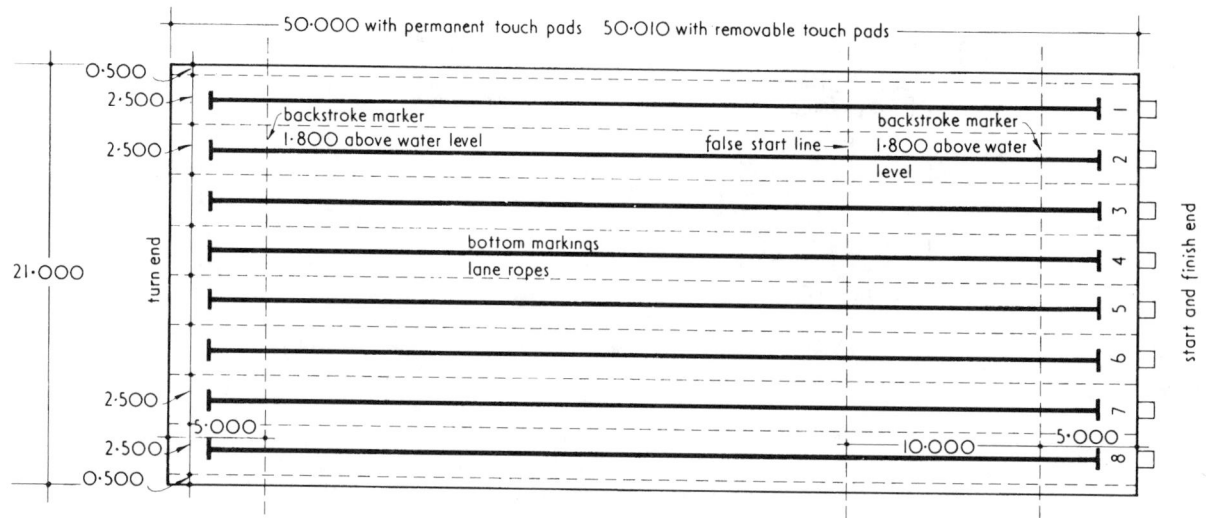

Against the nominal length of 50·000 a tolerance of plus 30mm is allowed 300mm above and 800mm below the surface of the water

a *50 metre pool to Olympic standard;*

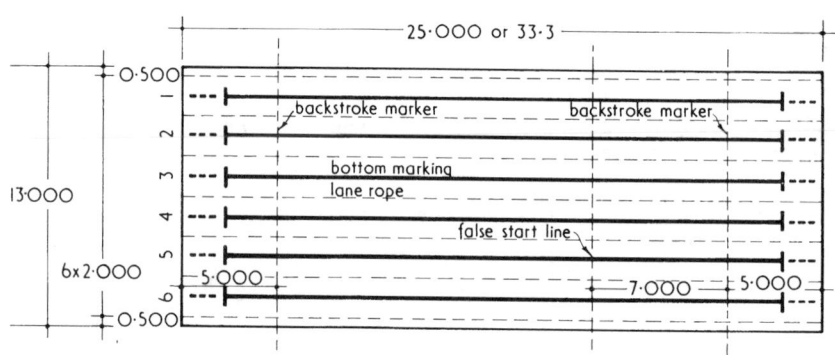

b *25 metre and 33⅓ metre pools*

22.26 *Lane and other marking required for competitive swimming*

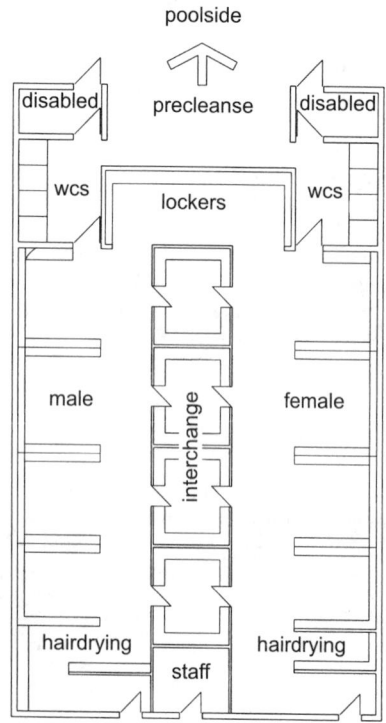

22.27 *Traditional layout of changing rooms*

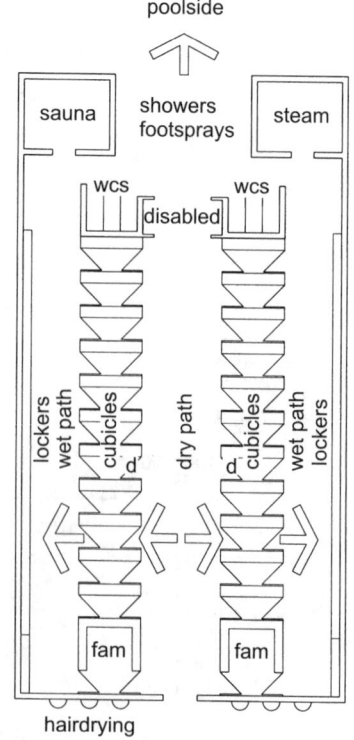

22.28 *Changing village. No segregation. Average cubicle occupancy 4 minutes*

7.02 Other arrangements

Toilets should be positioned between lockers and poolside. Pre-cleanse footbaths are no longer mandatory although foot sprays are still desirable. Showers are largely for after-swim shampooing. Hairdrying facilities are desirable close to changing-room exits.

7.03 Sauna and steam rooms

These may also form part of the 'village', **22.28**.

8 PROVISION FOR DISABLED PEOPLE

8.01 Disabled people

Consideration for disabled people is mandatory. As well as wheelchair users this includes people with impaired vision and those with learning difficulties. Wheelchair users may be provided for either in the changing village or alternatively in rooms around the pool, **22.30** and **22.31**. The disappearance of the footbath has eased wheelchair access to the poolside.

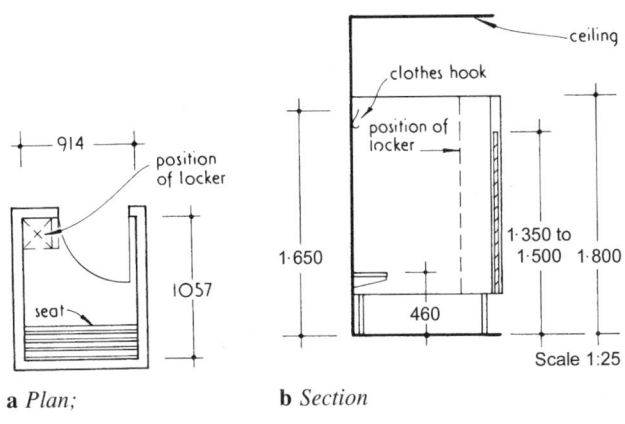

a *Plan;*   **b** *Section*

22.29 *Changing cubicle:*

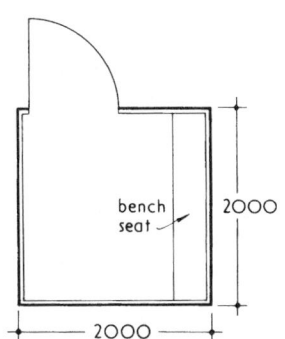

22.30 *Minimum changing provision for disabled people*

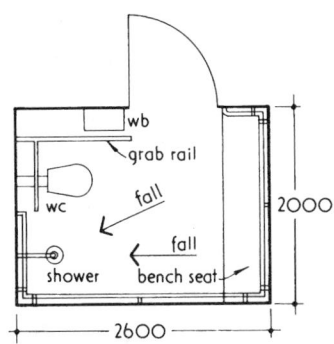

22.31 *Better provision for disabled people*

8.02 Deck level pools

These also improve access into and out of the water for disabled people. Chair hoists are still sometimes provided for this purpose although they are often disliked by users for the attention they cause.

8.03 Other arrangements

Shallow water spa (bubble) areas are much liked by those with learning difficulties.

Large, clearly marked signs, colour-coded footpaths and rails are required for visually impaired people.

9 POOL CAPACITY ANALYSIS

As a rule of thumb, pool capacities may be determined by dividing the water surface area by 2. Thus a $25 \times 13\,m$ pool can accommodate to reasonable comfort standards $325 \div 2 = 162$ bathers.

Changing cubicles, lockers and car parking provision can be based upon the same analysis plus the following allowances:

- Locker allowance based upon pool capacity, with a further 162 changing = 324 lockers, usually in two- to three-tier compartments
- Changing cubicle provision may be based upon a time factor of 5–10-minute occupation per bather. Thus in any one hour 162 bathers in the pool plus a further 162 changing ready to enter the pool = 324 bathers ÷ 10 minutes = 32 cubicles
- Car parking provision may be calculated thus: 324 bathers, 3 persons per car average = 101 spaces + a further allowance for staff, disabled, etc., say 125–150 spaces.

10 BIBLIOGRAPHY

Geraint John and Kit Campbell, *Ice rinks and swimming pools, handbook of sports and recreational building design*, volume 3, 2nd edn, Butterworth Architecture and the Sports Council, Oxford, 1996

23 Boating

John Rawson

John Rawson is an architect

CI/SfB 546
Uniclass F5678
UDC 725.87

KEY POINTS:
- *Boating in all its forms is an increasingly popular pastime*
- *A chronic shortage of facilities tends to make them expensive*

Contents
1 Introduction
2 Water resources
3 Access and transport to the water
4 Boats and waterbody needs
5 On-shore facilities
6 Boat storage
7 Bibliography

1 INTRODUCTION
There is great pressure on the available areas of enclosed and semi-enclosed water. The various uses, which continually increase, are not all compatible (see Table I).

There may be conflict between the wintering needs of wildfowl and all forms of boating, and between the use of powered and unpowered boats. It is possible to resolve this by closed seasons, zoning, or timetabling.

A very large number of people own boats, but usage is variable. Many people trail their boats to races or holiday areas. Weather, tides and currents govern their movements. Facilities that boat owners value are sheltered slipways with easy road access, and with no wash from passing ships.

Boating can be expensive; it is a leisure activity and so can easily be discontinued. Small increases in charges can result in a significant loss of boat owners.

2 WATER RESOURCES
There are a number of types of waterbodies the suitabilities of which are given in Table II.

2.01 Natural lakes
Some areas are seriously overcrowded in the holiday season. It is not easy to acquire waterside land for new facilities.

2.02 Artificial lakes
It is rare to make new lakes specifically for boating due to the amount of earth moving required, but existing areas such as gravel pits can be reshaped, as at the National Water Sports Centre, Holme Pierrepoint, Nottingham. There is a small but steady increase in lakes of this type, such as the recent adoption of a balancing lake at Peterborough for rowing.

Table I Compatibility of watersports

	Fishing	Swimming	Sub-aqua	Wildfowl	Canoeing	Rowing	Sailing	Water ski-ing	Hydroplaning	Power boats	Cruising
Fishing		X	X		PZ	PZ	PZ	X	X	X	PZ
Swimming	X		Z			Z	Z	Z	Z		Z
Sub-aqua	X					PZ	PZ	PZ	PZ	PZ	Z
Wildfowl		Z						X	X	X	
Canoeing	PZ					PZ	PZ	PZ	PZ	PZ	
Rowing	PZ	Z	PZ		PZ		PZ	P	P	P	PZ
Sailing	PZ	Z	PZ		PZ	PZ		PZ	PZ	PZ	Z
Water ski-ing	X	Z	PZ	X	PZ	P	PZ		PZ	PZ	N/A
Hydroplaning	X	Z	PZ	X	PZ	P	PZ	PZ		PZ	N/A
Power boats	X		PZ	X	PZ	P	PZ	PZ	PZ		N/A
Cruising	PZ	Z	Z			PZ	Z	N/A	N/A	N/A	

X incompatible; P programming; Z zoning; N/A not applicable

Table II Areas suitable for watersports

	Lakes	Canal feeders and compensation reservoirs	Water supply reservoirs	Rivers	Canals	Sea
Fishing	X	X	X	X	X	X
Swimming	X			X		X
Surfing	X					X
Sub-aqua	X			X		X
Diving	X	X	X	X	X	
Wildfowl	X	X	X	X		X
Canoeing	X	X	X	X	X	X
Sailing	X	X	X	X		X
Water ski-ing	X	X				X
Hydroplaning	X	X				
Power boats	X	X				X
Cruising	X	X		X	X	X

X incompatible; P programming; Z zoning; N/A not applicable

2.03 Rivers

These are used intensively for purposes from wild-water canoeing to rowing, depending on their characteristics. Few rivers in Britain are wide enough for sailing, except where they become estuaries.

2.04 Reservoirs

Not all reservoirs are yet used for recreation. There is sailing on many; motor boating on fewer. It depends on what the water is used for and the water treatment in use. The water companies have to balance the revenue they might obtain from boating against the cost of water treatment.

2.05 The sea

There is inadequate access. Port and marina facilities are limited, and there are not enough slipways. Wind, currents and the tide all cause difficulties. Areas where there is public access to shorelines will require regular maintenance.

3 ACCESS AND TRANSPORT TO THE WATER

3.01 Facilities

Most foreshore is private and some lakes are private. For light recreational use virtually no built facilities are necessary. The smallest boats, canoes and sailboards, which can be carried, can be launched from any bank or beach. Larger boats need facilities.

3.02 Launching places

These need to have good road access for vehicles towing trailers, with adequate parking nearby. Backing cars with trailers attached needs space and experience. Charging for parking greatly decreases use.

At the seaside, beaches and slipways may not be usable at all states of the tide. The speed of tidal currents may be faster than the top speed of small boats. Craft which do not sail well upwind can be swept out to sea in off-shore winds, unless they carry auxiliary motors.

3.03 Transport on land

For movement on land, weight is more critical than length. The smallest boats, punts, canoes, sailing dinghys, can be man-handled, usually on trailers or trolleys. The next group, both sail and power, up to about 20 ft long, can be moved by a car and trailer. The larger boats need cranes, tractors, winches and low-loaders.

Trailers come in a great range of sizes and designs, to fit all sizes and shapes of boat. Regulations governing their design and dimensions are complex. All new trailers must have automatic brakes, which should not be immersed in water.

3.04 Slipways

There is a severe shortage of direct access from roads to water. Launching, and particularly recovery, takes time and many people may wish to do it at once. For this reason very wide slipways are required. Also, they need parking areas adjacent where cars with trailers attached can be left when boats are launched. There should be space for cars towing trailers to turn in circles where possible, as it is much quicker than backing with them. However large slipways are, speed of throughput is important in busy periods.

Slipway gradients are critical, and about 1:8 is good. Too steep, and vehicles may fail to tow laden trailers up the slope. Too shallow, and it may not be possible to immerse a trailer deep enough to float a boat off it, while it is still attached to a vehicle.

Slipways need to be long, if there is a tide. They need to provide a hard surface to at least 2 m below low water level, or below the lowest draw-down level of a reservoir, as some boats have a quite deep draught. Marine growths at the bottom of a slipway can make launching difficult, or impossible, at low tide.

4 BOATS AND WATERBODY NEEDS

4.01 Types of boat

Boats are found in great variety, but there are two broad types: powered and unpowered. These have different needs.

4.02 Unpowered

This covers rowing boats, punts, canoes, sailing dinghies and sailing cruisers. The first three are human-powered, the others wind-driven.

4.03 Rowing

There are various types of rowing boats, **22.1**. Regulations laid down by FISA (the International Rowing Federation) for international standard events require six rowing lanes for racing, at 13.5 m in width with circulation outside the lanes on each side of the course. The optimum depth to reduce bias in certain lanes should be in excess of 3.8 m, but for economic reasons 3.5 m is considered acceptable to all classes. For domestic events 1000 m at three lanes wide is a basic minimum. **23.2** shows a typical layout.

Coaching can be done in an indoor tank facility, **23.3** or in pair-oared skiffs with the coach as passenger; handling facilities for the skiff may be needed. The modern trend is to start beginners in

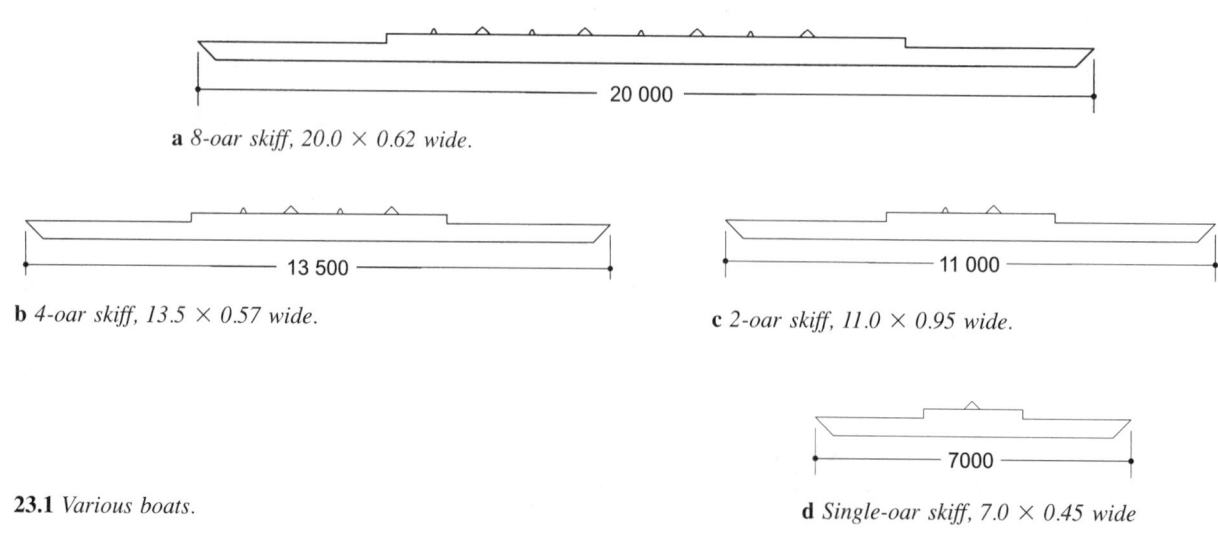

a *8-oar skiff, 20.0 × 0.62 wide.*

b *4-oar skiff, 13.5 × 0.57 wide.*

c *2-oar skiff, 11.0 × 0.95 wide.*

d *Single-oar skiff, 7.0 × 0.45 wide*

23.1 *Various boats.*

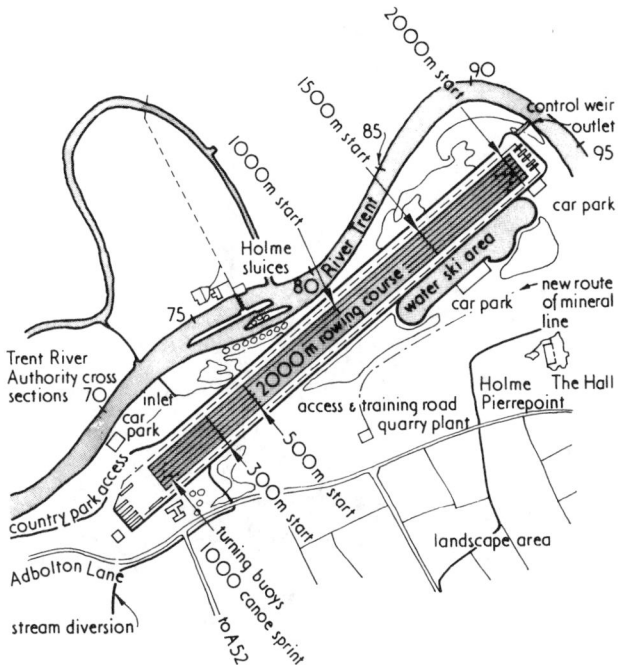

a *Plan.*

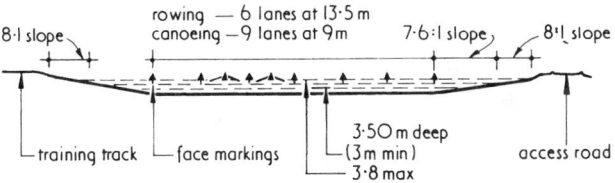

b *Section through the 2000 m rowing course*

23.2 *The National Water Sports Centre at Holmes Pierrepoint:*

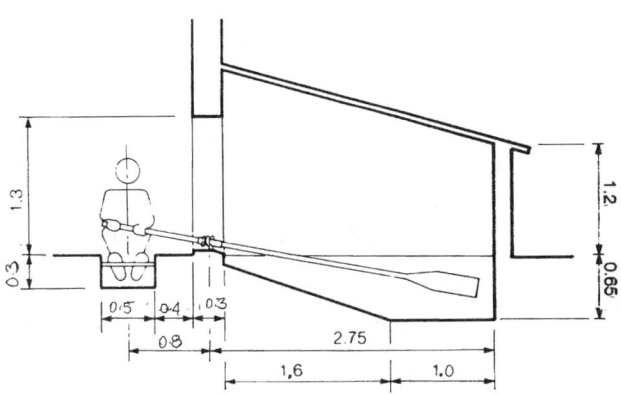

23.3 *Rowing tank*

stable sculling boats and to use indoor rowing machines for basic body movement coaching and fitness. In the past, the coach of an eight used to cycle along the bank adjacent to the boat. However, it is now also possible to use a fast motor boat. Facilities are required for mooring and storing it.

Boats often have to be transported to races in other locations. Many eights are now built with a joint in the middle to reduce the length for transport. Access is required for trucks and/or trailers for boats.

4.04 Canoeing

Kayaks, **23.4**, are the usual form of canoe used. Users are recommended to travel in groups of a minimum of three for safety

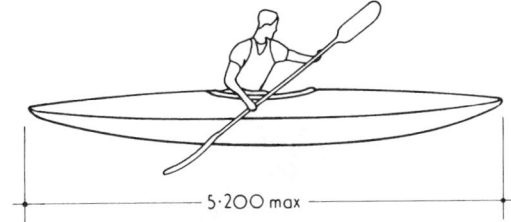

23.4 *Canoe size*

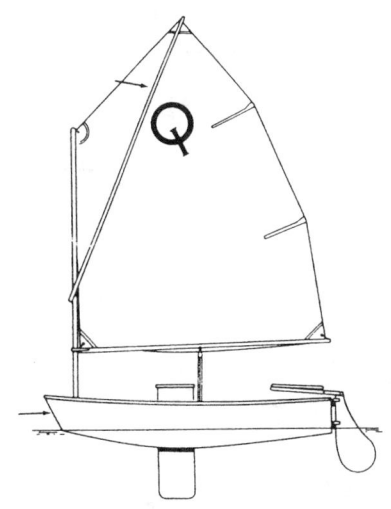

23.5 *Optimist: together with the Mirror dinghy, the most widely used boat for junior training. Length 2.36 m, beam 1.12 m, draught 0.84 m, mass or displacement 35 kg, sail area 3.25 m². For other boats below L/b/d/m/s = 2.36/1.12/0.84/35/3.25*

reasons. Wild-water slalom is a popular form of racing. Kayaks can be transported on car tops or on special trailers that carry up to eight boats. Storage may be required for kayaks on cantilever shelves, and for the special trailers.

4.05 Sailing

Sailing boats vary greatly in size from small dinghies, **23.5** and **23.6**, catamarans, **23.7**, to twin-masted schooners, **23.8**. The larger boats nowadays all include some form of auxiliary power, and have requirements much as power boats.

Dinghy sailing is very popular as it is suitable for all ages, and degrees of athleticism, can be recreational or racing, suitable for large or small lakes, or even the sea, and the boats can always be trailed behind a car.

A large open uninterrupted waterbody is required, well related to the prevailing wind, with as few indentations as possible. Ideally it should be of a shape to allow for a triangular racing course, with one side of the triangle parallel to the prevailing wind. The surrounding landform and buildings should not cause windshadows.

The depth of the water should not be less than 1.5 m, though 1.0 m is acceptable for sailboards. Shallow water can encourage reed growth.

The area of water required is:

- Small boats and training: 1.5 ha
- Club sailing: 6 ha+
- Open competition: 20 ha+

or alternatively

- Dinghies: 0.8 ha per boat
- Small boats such as Optimists: 0.2 ha per boat.

23.6 *470: an Olympic boat. L/b/d/m/s = 4.7/1.68/0.97/120 min/9 main, 3.7 jib, 13 spinnaker*

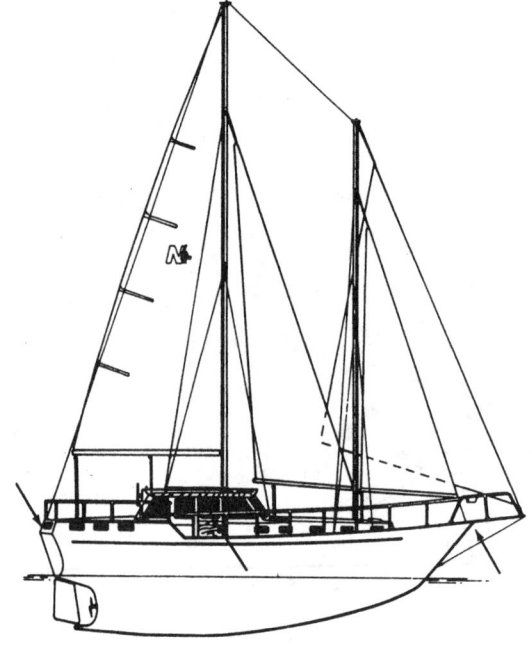

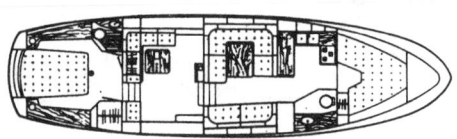

23.8 *Nauticat 44: a big motor sailer with a schooner rig. L/b/d/m/s = 13.28 o/a 11.79 w/1/3.68/1.83/18,000/28.4 main, 11 staysail, 27.5 jib, 8.9 forestaysail*

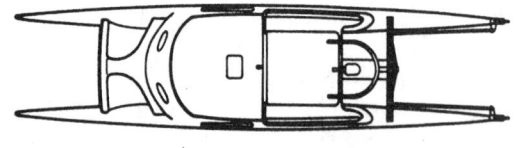

23.7 *Gougeon 32: a big, fast and stable catamaran; sailable single-handed or with two; sleeps two adults and two adults and two children. L/b/d/m/s = 9.75/2.54/1.3 (boards down)/500/17.4 main, 10.1 jib*

An open beach, ideally on a lee shore, is required for instruction and for the launching of sailing boats. Most minerals that are quarried such as sand, gravel and clay make a suitable lake bottom. Excessively alkaline water will cause corrosion of alloy equipment. Algae can be a disadvantage.

One problem can be the occurrence of Weil's disease, associated with rats, that can cause serious illness through the infection of cuts by contaminated water, but it is quite rare.

4.06 Power boats

This covers small motor boats, fast ski boats, jet-skis, inflatables, speedboats, and motor cruisers. They require access to fuel supplies.

Power boats produce noise and wash. This may cause legal or planning restrictions on their use, or prevent the use of lakes nearer than 500 m from noise-sensitive areas for power boating. The wash can damage banks, which should not be vertical; sloping shingle beaches are preferable to prevent backwash. Marginal reedbeds can also absorb backwash.

The area required should be enough to lay out a triangular racing course with 400 m legs, or an oblong space of 800 m × 400 m. A minimum depth of 2.0 m is required.

New EC regulations for pollution and emission control are coming. Boats have already begun to change from petrol to calor gas fuel.

5 ON-SHORE FACILITIES

5.01 Recreational rowing

Commercial boat hire
A stretch of beach or a floating pontoon is all that is needed, but a yard or shed adjacent is required, for gear storage, and an office. Changing facilities may also be appropriate.

Private
Private wet boathouses are sized to accommodate the boats required. Space around moored boats in boathouses has to be generous as they can move in bad weather.

23.9 *Boathouse for a racing club:*

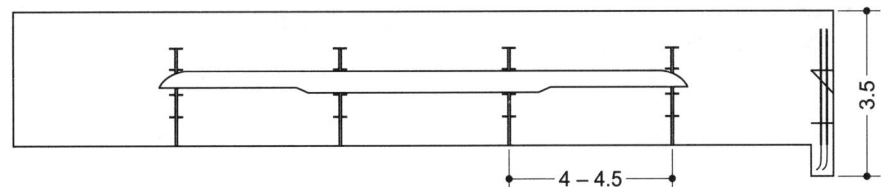

a *Longitudinal section.*

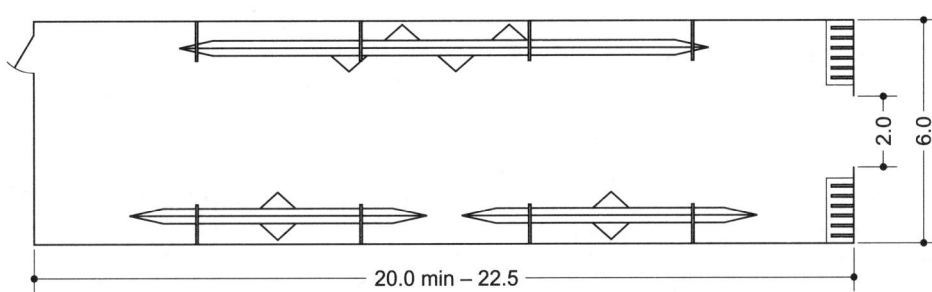

b *Plan.*

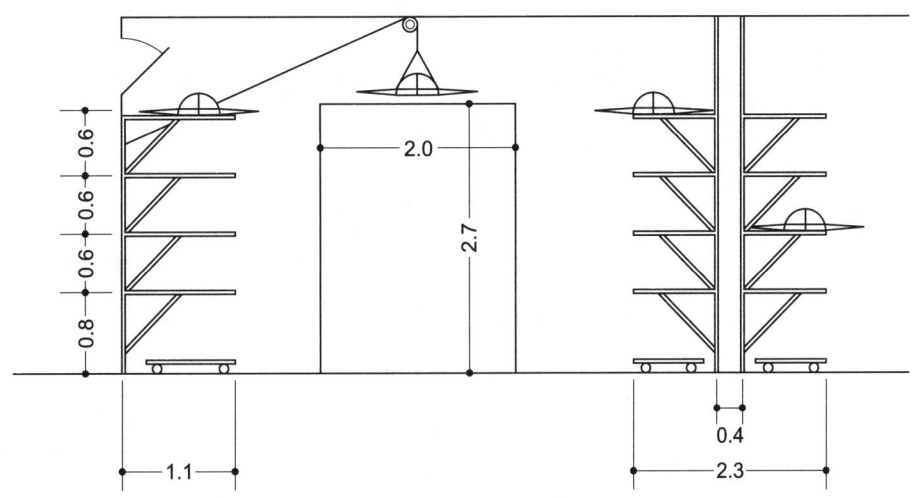

c *Cross-section*

All boats need to be taken out of the water in the winter (even GRP absorbs water). Winter boat storage should be under cover is possible, but good tarpaulins may be enough. Sheds may be required adjacent to the shore for the storage of lifejackets, oars, canoes and sailboards.

5.02 Racing (rowing)

The boathouse

The racing eight, 20 m long, determines the layout of boathouses, **23.9**. The standard storage bay accommodates eight boats on special sliding racks. Several of these bays are usually placed side by side in a suitable building. This needs to be over 20 m from the water so that boats can be turned round. Boats can be launched from a pontoon parallel to the shore by the whole crew moving to one side of the boat. The height of the edge of the pontoon above the water is critical as the riggers and oars of the boat project over it. About 150 mm is acceptable.

Smaller boats – fours, pairs, sculls – can be accommodated on special shelves within a building that is suitable for eights, provided the shelves are spaced correctly. Changing facilities and parking should be adjacent.

Oars can be stored in special racks with the oar handles in a small pit, **23.10**. This saves space and encourages crews to carry oars vertically which is safer than horizontally.

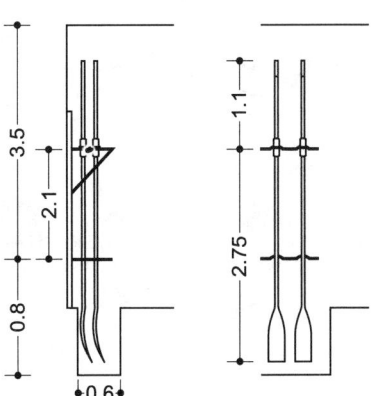

23.10 *Storage of oars*

5.03 Sailing dinghies

Dinghies are too heavy to carry, but on a trailer the smallest can be launched by one or two people. They are normally kept on a simple launching trailer that can be pushed into the water by hand. These trailers cannot be towed.

Road-legal trailers cannot be immersed, hence the double piggyback trailer for boats that have to be driven to a launch site.

Clubhouses and dinghy parks adjacent to launching sites are popular, as towing is obviated, masts can be left erect, and changing facilities are available. Dinghy-sailing, particularly racing, is a wet activity. Only the largest dinghies will lie safely at moorings.

A number of sailing clubs are now buying special trimarans for the use of people with spinal injuries. These require parking adjacent to the boat-launching site, and a hard surface such as concrete (not gravel) right into the water, for wheelchairs.

5.04 Yachts and powerboats

This covers all sail and power boats over about 18 ft long, i.e. larger than dinghies. The smaller ones can be trailed. Larger ones generally move under their own power, racing or cruising from a fixed base.

Sailing cruisers are designed for various degrees of seaworthiness, from inland-only to ocean-going. They have high masts, which conflict with bridges when afloat, and which have to be removed for trailing on land. Many have auxiliary power for use in emergency or in constricted spaces.

5.05 Yacht club buildings

The design of yacht club buildings is not covered here. They have not emerged as a distinctive building type. The facilities required vary considerably in both quantity and quality. Few new ones have been built and most use converted facilities (one uses an old ship). Most need social facilities of some kind, often with a bar. Clubhouses for dinghy sailors need extensive changing facilities, where many crews can change for races. If the location is suitable accommodation for a race officer can be useful.

6 BOAT STORAGE

It is important to note that boats are used for only a very small percentage of their lives. So storage and access to water is the limiting factor in most places. They can be stored wet at:

● Swinging moorings
● Marina berths

or they can be stored dry in:

● Boat parks
● Dry-berthing systems.

6.01 Moorings

The term 'mooring' generally means tying a boat to a fixed point, such a buoy or post, which has no land access, **23.11** (also see Table III).

Traditionally most yachts have been kept at swinging moorings, which consist of single buoys fixed to ground tackle, in natural harbours, lakes and rivers. These are scarce, relatively cheap, space consuming, and not very convenient. Owners will need to row out to the mooring in a dinghy, which they will want to keep nearby.

Boats can be moored bow and stern, between pairs of buoys, for closer packing. Adding further boats alongside the moored one ('rafting-up') can be done only temporarily, and is unpopular with owners.

6.02 Marinas

Marinas have been built in suitable seaside cruising locations. To be successful they must have convenient access from both land and water.

Table III Moorings

References (Figure 23.11)	Type of mooring	Examples	Advantages	Disadvantages	Remarks
A	Stern to quay, jetty or pontoon, bows to piles	Chichester La Grande Motte Rotterdam Kristiansund	Jetty economy	Not as convenient for embarking as alongside jetties or pontoons	
B	Ditto but bows moored to anchors or buoys	Deauville and the majority of Mediterranean marinas	Jetty economy	Not suitable with large tide range as excessive space required for head warps; danger of propellers being entangled in head warps	Particularly suitable for large yachts in basins with little tide range where gangways can be attached to sterns
C	Alongside finger piers or catwalks one yacht on each side of each finger	Cherbourg, Larnaca (Cyprus) and many American marinas	Convenient for embarking and disembarking		
D	Ditto but more than one yacht on each side of each finger	Port Hamble Swanwick Lymington	Ditto, also allows flexibility in accommodating yachts of different lengths	Finger piers must be spaced wider apart than in C though this may be compensated for by the larger number of craft between jetties	Fingers may be long enough for two or three vessels, if more than three then provision should be made for turning at the foot of the berths
E	Alongside quays, jetties or pontoons single banked	Granville	Ditto		
F	Alongside quays jetties or pontoons up to 3 or 4 abreast	St Malo Ouistreham St Rochelle	Economical in space and pontoons	Crew from outer yachts have to climb over inner berthed yachts	This is one of the most economical and therefore most frequently adopted types
G	Between piles	Yarmouth Hamble River Cowes	Cheapest system as no walkways, also high density	No dry access to land; difficulty in leaving mooring if outer yachts are not manned	Not recommended except for special situations such as exist in the examples quoted
H	Star finger berths	San Francisco			

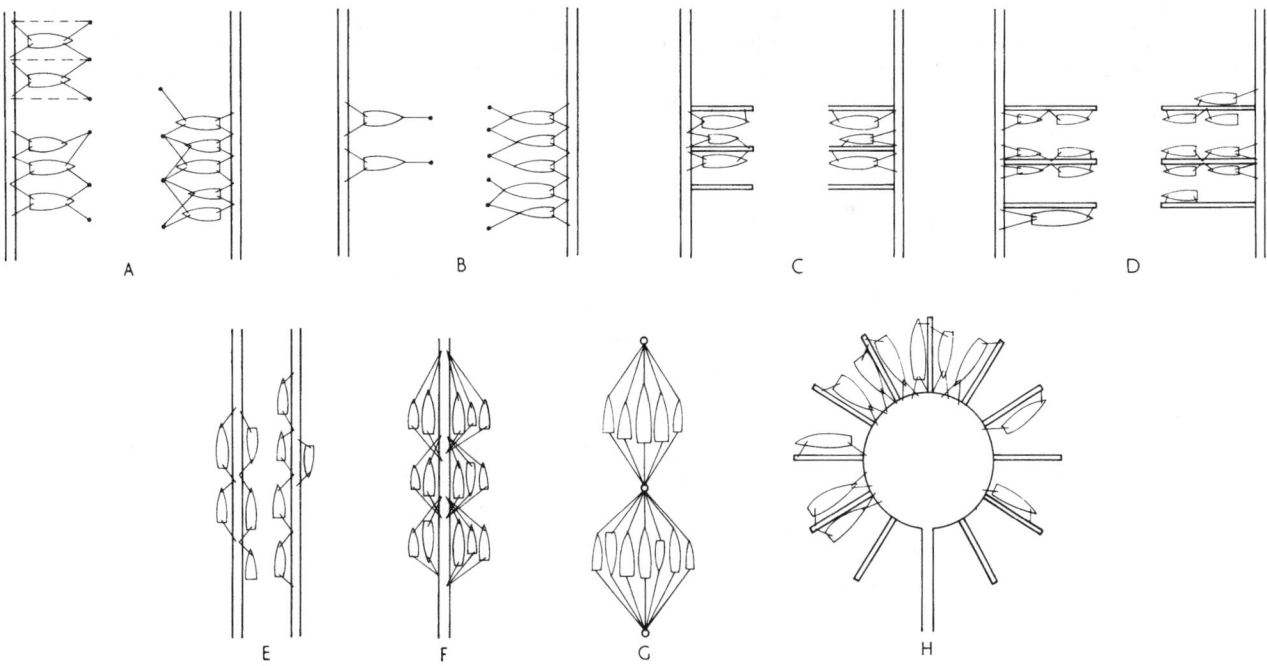

23.11 *Types of mooring (see Table III)*

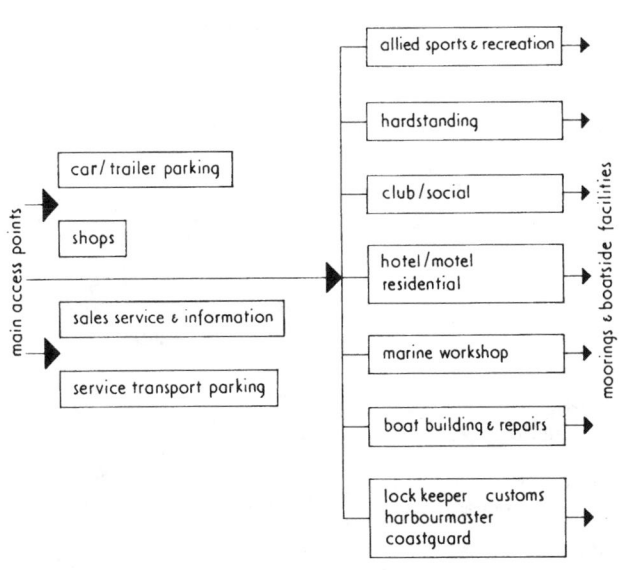

23.12 *Relationship diagram for a marina for development into a basin layout*

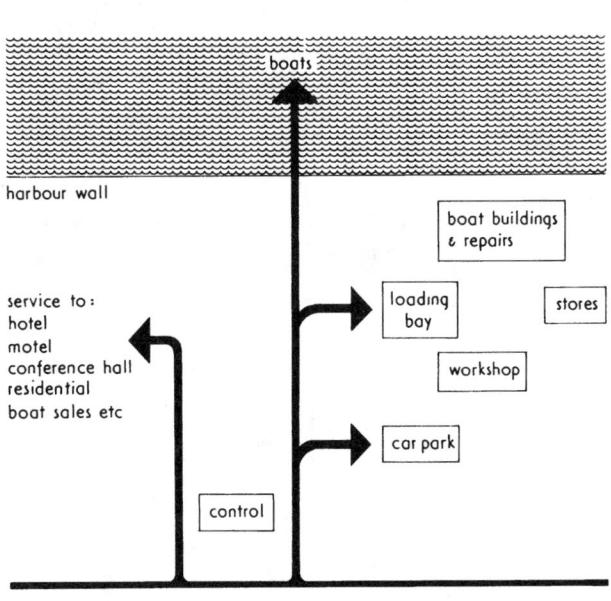

23.13 *Activities in a marina*

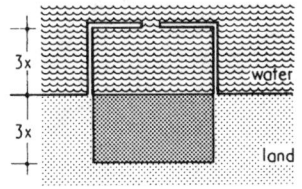

a OFFSHORE
Advantages
minimum quay wall, minimum land take, minimum dredging
Disadvantages
expensive in deep water, vulnerable to weather and currents, navigation hazards, minimum enclosure, silting by litoral drift

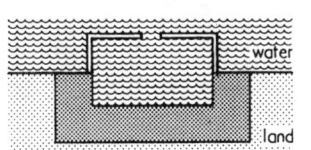

b SEMI-RECESSED
Advantage
good for cut and fill economics
Disadvantage
navigation hazard

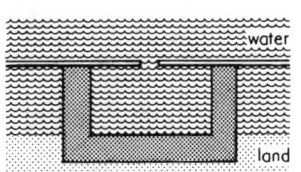

c BUILT-IN
Advantages
uninterrupted shoreline, large land/water interface, considerable enclosure
Disadvantages
large land take, length of quay wall, amount of dredging

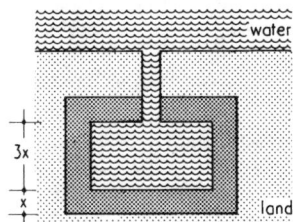

d LAND-LOCKED
Advantages
maximum enclosure, minimum interruption of shoreline
Disadvantages
maximum quay wall, distance from open water

23.14 *Types of land-to-water relationships, all with equal areas of land and water:*

The interrelation between the amenities provided, **23.12**, and the main activities, **23.13**, will control the basic layout. A marina may be off-shore, landlocked or anything in between, **23.14**

There are many possible layouts, but generally, equal amounts of space are allocated to land and water, **23.15** and **23.16**. A detailed breakdown of spaces and ratios is given in Table IV, and a checklist of accommodation and services in Table V.

Marina pontoons are now standard items, **23.17**. They are arranged to rise and fall with changes in water level. Boats are usually moored stern to the pontoon, which often has access

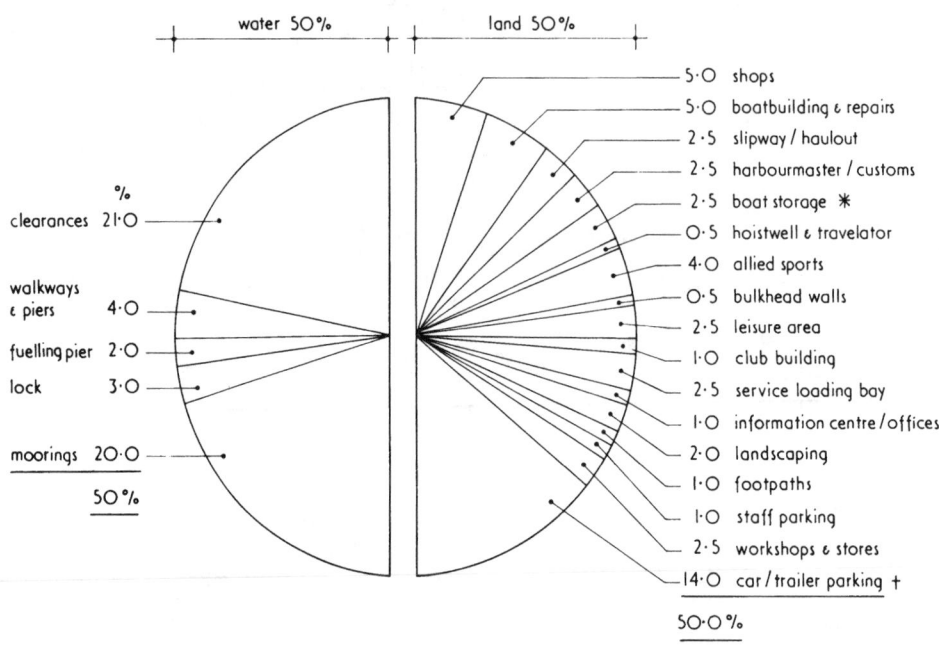

* not including dual use of car parking area
† assumes 4·87 m x 2·43 m (16'x 18') bays

23.15 *One allocation of on- and off-shore space assuming a 50:50 land/water split. This is appropriate to European standards*

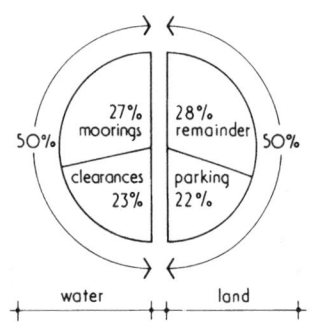

23.16 *Principal space allocations based on the average of ten American marinas. The difference between these figures and those in [23.15] are mainly due to the use of a 2.7 × 5.8 m parking bay*

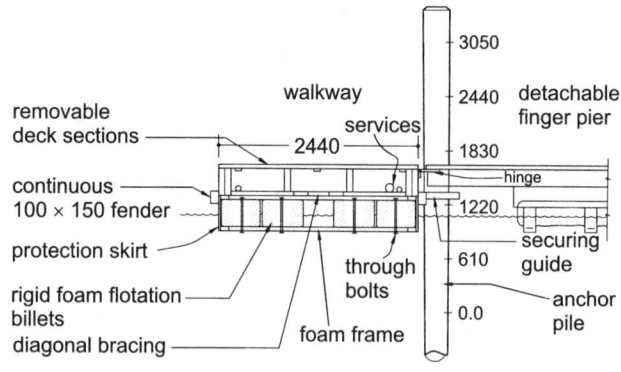

23.17a *Construction detail of floating pier, section A–A*

Table IV Spatial requirements and likely size ranges

	Min.	Max.
Land-to-water ratio	1:1	2:1
Density of boats/hectare (wet moorings)	62	162
Density of boats/hectare on hardstanding	25	75
Car-to-boat ratio	1:1	1:5:1
Density of cars/hectare (2.4 × 5.0 bays)	350	520
Ranges of boat length	4.8–13.7 m	4.3–21.3 m
Ranges of boat beam	1.8–4.3 m	1.5–6.0 m
Ranges of boat draught: inboard	0.64–1.27 m	0.48–1.65 m
outboard	0.30–0.56 m	0.20–0.64 m
sailing boats	1.14–1.77 m	1.00–2.16 m
Average boat length	5.5 m	9 m
Percentage total parking area to total water area	20%	50%
People-to-boats ratio	1.5:1	3:1
People-to-cars ratio	1:1	4.5:1
Cars-to-boats ratio	1:2	2:1

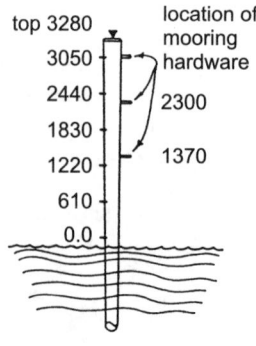

23.17b *Detail of anchor pile*

Table V Checklist of marina accommodation and services

Social activities
Clubhouse, boat-owners' lounge, public house, bar, snack bar, restaurant, offices, committee rooms, starters' post, lookout, viewing terraces, sunbathing, reading room, navigational library, weather forecast board, chart room, television, children's play space, crèche, paddling pool

Shops
Food and general stores, tobacco, stationery, etc.
Bookshop
Chandlery, clothes
Hairdresser, beauty salon
Barber's shop
Sauna
Masseur
Chemist
Laundry, launderette

Services and information
Marina office, information centre, caretaker's maintenance workshop, storage and staffroom
Banking
Post office, Giro
Visitors' information service (e.g. doctors, restaurants, entertainment)
Flagpole, windsock
Weather and tides information
Kennels

Allied activities
Customs house
Harbourmaster's office
Coastguard, weather station and information
Radar, communications mast
Sea Scouts
Lock-keeper's accommodation
Police, security station

Boatside facilities
Storage lockers
Lavatories (public and private)
Showers, baths
Drying rooms, cabinets
Bottled gas service
Electricity, lighting and power
Plug-in telephone service
Dockside laundry service
Tannoy system
Litter bins
Mail service

General services
Gas, main, bottled or in bulk storage
Electricity, lighting and power to piers and grounds (see Safety equipment)
Sewage and refuse disposal
Water supply
Telephones
Centrally controlled security system

Boat services
Boat building, repair, maintenance yard, material store
New and second-hand boat and engine sales and hire
Launching and hauling equipment (fixed and mobile)
Hardstanding
Launching ramps and slips
Dry storage of boats
Covered moorings (wet and dry)
Information board of local services
Brokerage, insurance, marine surveyors
Divers' service
Fuelling station or tender

Allied sporting activities: provision and instruction
Rowing
Scuba, skin-diving equipment and instruction
Water ski-ing, ski-kiting
Swimming
Fishing tackle (hire and sale of bait)
Sail training
Tennis, badminton and squash courts

Allied accommodation
Hotel, motel, holiday flats, public house, holiday inn

Transportation areas and services
Car parking and service (fuel, repairs and hire)
Trailer bays and hire
Bus bay
Transport to and from local centres
Carts for stores and baggage
Motor cycle/bicycle sheds (open and covered)
Boat trips and coach tours
Marina staff electric runabout
Marina workshops and transport areas

Safety equipment
First-aid post and observation platform
Fire-fighting equipment, fireboat
Life-saving equipment and instruction
Warning or flood lights to breakwaters, lock and harbour entrance
General security system, fences and lighting
De-icing or aeration equipment
Weather and tides information

Miscellaneous
Casual recreation area (e.g. picnic and kick-about areas)
Swimming pool
Vending machines, ice dispenser
Paved and grassed areas
Landscaping
Gardeners' stores and sheds etc.

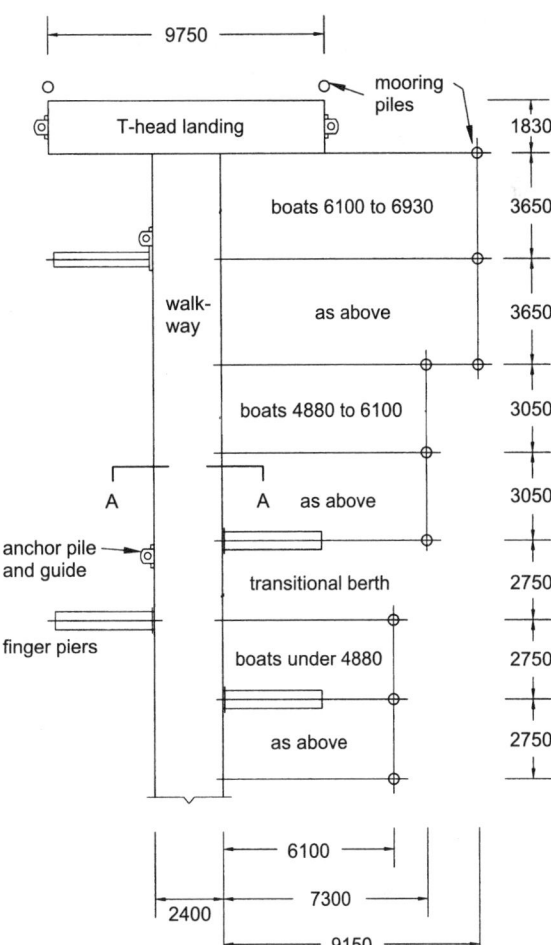

23.18 *Layout of floating pier*

fingers between alternate boats, **23.18**. Services such as electricity and water are supplied to each berth. Boats vary in size and layouts have to accommodate this. Because of the necessity for locks to connect a non-tidal marina to the tidal sea, access may be slow. See the checklist of requirements in Table V. Marinas in non-tidal situations, such as on canals, have fixed piers, **22.19**.

British marinas are expensive; several thousand pounds a year for storage only. Owners are beginning to resist the charges by organising into berth-holder groups, or by berthing abroad. **22.20** shows a large facility.

A development of the marina is the marina village. Essentially this is a housing estate with water frontage to every property. Each boat is moored stern-to in front of a house with the bow tied to a buoy. Houses are often in terraces, with varied shapes and sizes. Car parking is adjacent to the house on the land side. Each house includes a gear store for boat equipment. In spite of the expense of this type of development because of civil engineering costs, these places are even becoming popular with non-sailors who like the marine environment. Adding housing to a marina can have a considerable effect on its financial viability, but brings with it environmental and pollution problems.

New anti-pollution legislation may soon be introduced to force cruising boats to have sewage holding tanks. Marinas will need to provide pumping-out facilities.

6.03 Boat parks

Many yacht clubs and boat builders run some sort of boat park. This consists of an enclosed area of hard-standing adjacent to the water. Dinghies are parked on their launching trailers with erect masts.

Cruisers, both sail and power, are stored on cradles; or are shored up depending on what handling facilities are available. A modern straddle-carrier can carry a boat to a fixed cradle. A tractor can tow a boat on a mobile cradle onto a slipway at low tide ready for it to float off as the tide rises. Cruisers stored in this way are launched in the spring, moored during the season, and recovered in the autumn.

DIY maintenance is commonly done in boat parks. Electricity for power tools, and water supplies are required. A mast crane may be needed. Some sort of catering facility nearby is very popular.

6.04 Dry-berthing

Keeping a boat in the water is not desirable, but it is able to afford instant availability. Storage on land is cheaper and is a sensible

23.19 *Fixed finger pier:*

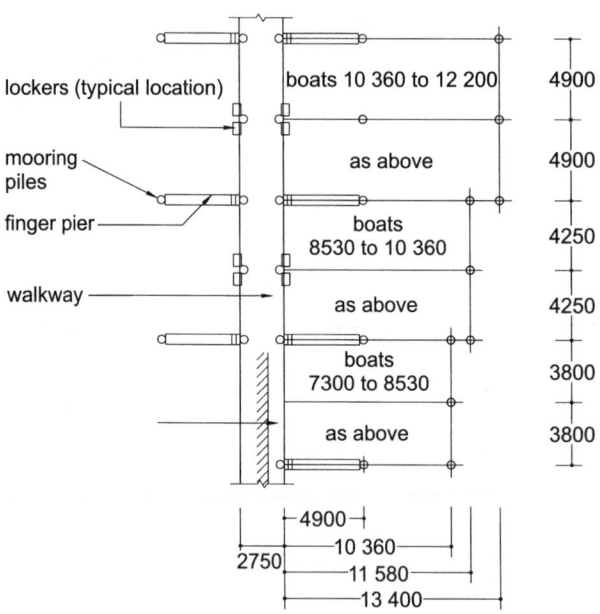

a *Layout*

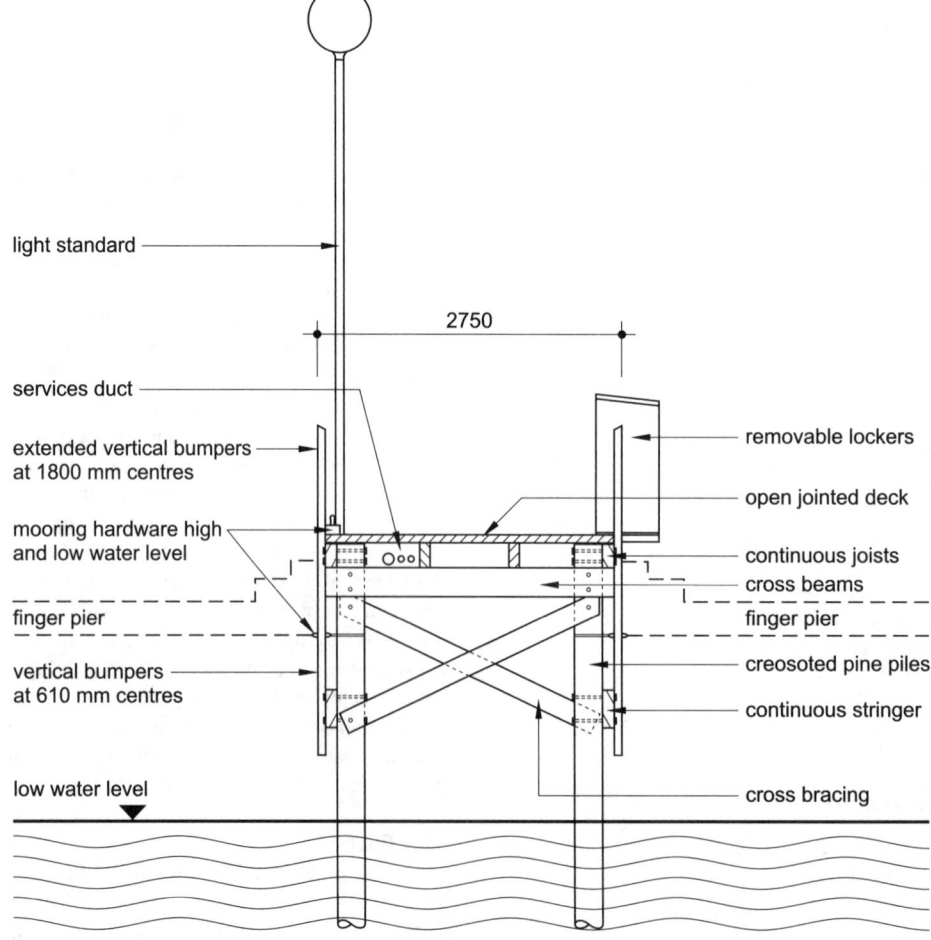

b *Construction detail*

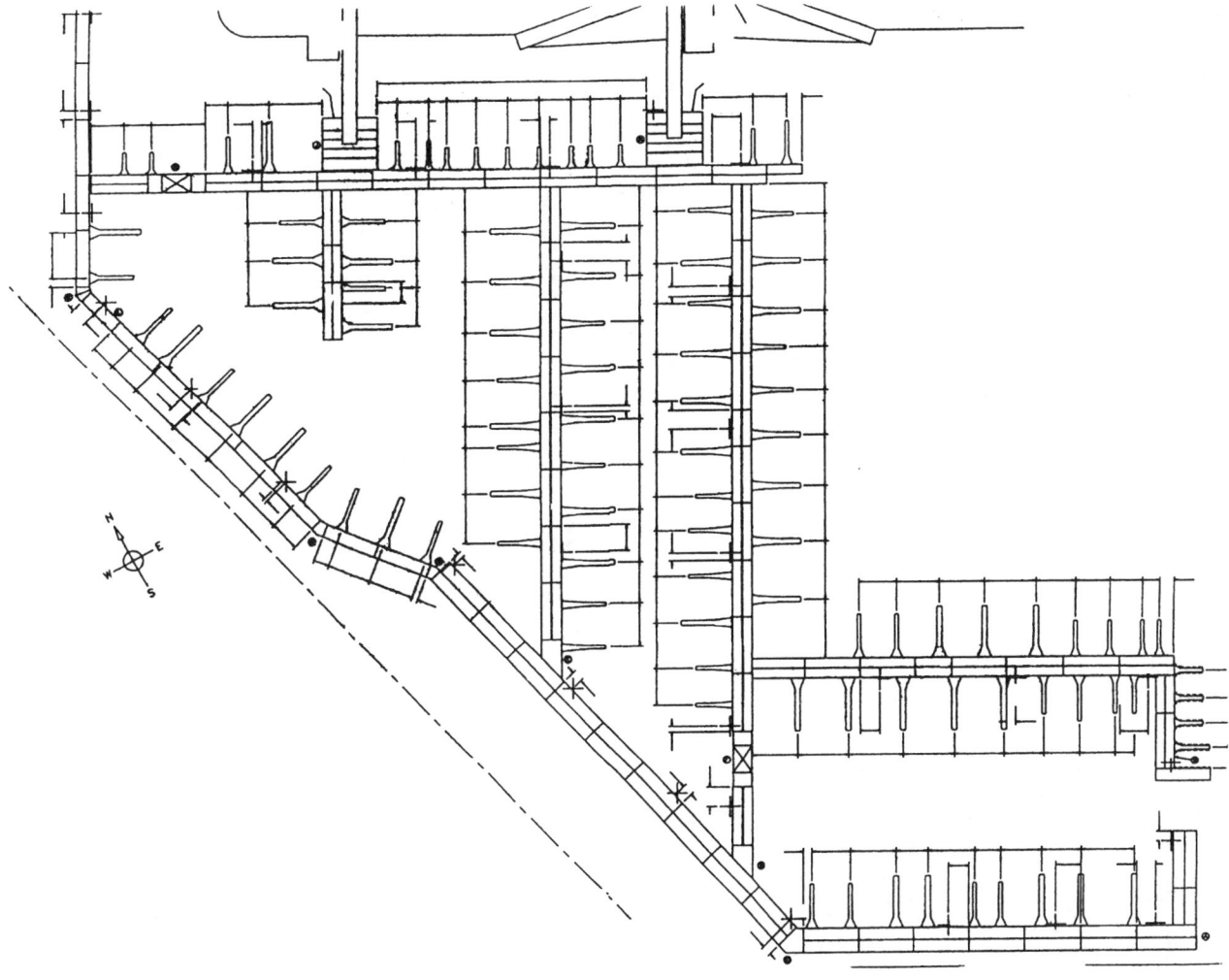

23.20 *Southampton International Boat Show 1992*

alternative provided convenient fast launching facilities can be provided.

Dry-berthing for power boats launching is carried out by a forklift which stacks boats on multi-level racks, rather like a pigeon-hole car park. The operator launches the boats when owners arrive to use them. The current maximum size of boat stored this way in England is 33 ft long/4 tons weight.

Dry-sailing is becoming popular with the owners of racing keelboats up to 30 ft long. The yard owner has launching equipment and puts all the boats in the water every weekend, taking them out during the week.

7 BIBLIOGRAPHY

Donald W Adie, *Marinas, a working guide to their development and design*, Architectural Press, 1975

Geraint John and Kit Campbell, *Outdoor sports, handbook of sports and recreational building design*, vol 1, 2nd edn, Butterworth Architecture and Sports Council, 1993

24 Outdoor sports and stadia

Peter Ackroyd and Geraint John

Peter Ackroyd was until his retirement an architect in the Sports Council Technical Unit, where Geraint John was Chief Architect

CI/SfB: 564
UDC: 796, 725.82
Uniclass: F561

KEY POINT:
● *Standards are constantly changing, so check with sports' governing bodies*

Contents
1 Introduction
2 Sports grounds
3 Athletics
4 Playing field sports
5 Sports requiring special conditions or construction

1 INTRODUCTION

A few sports (mainly those based in the USA) still quote critical dimensions in imperial units. These dimensions are shown here in metric equivalents to the second or third decimal point, which should not be rounded off.

Sports are in alphabetical order under the appropriate classification. Boundary lines are shown by a solid line, safety and other marginal areas by tone, bounded by a broken line, the dimensions of which can vary and should be checked with governing bodies of sport. Court markings are usually indicated by fine lines. For water sports such as rowing and canoeing see Chapter 23, Boating; for water polo see Chapter 22, Swimming. For other information such as detail dimensions, other activities etc. see *Handbook of sport and recreational building design*. A bibliography will be found at the end of Chapter 25.

2 SPORTS GROUNDS AND STADIA

2.01 Facilities

For higher levels of competition in most sports, purpose-built facilities are usually provided. These incorporate special qualities of turf and its sub-grade, together with appropriate facilities for the players and for spectators.

While many sports events can be enjoyed by spectators situated on the sidelines or the boundary of the playing or competing area, there are a number of progressively more elaborate forms:

● Viewing slopes
● Open terraces
● Viewing stands (which despite their name incorporate seating) overlooking part of a playing area and
● Stadia which are generally playing and competing areas completely or substantially surrounded by seating, some even provided with permanent or removable roofing.

2.02 Viewing slopes

These are not suitable for large numbers, and should not be steeper than 17 per cent or 1:6.

2.03 Terraces

Details of a terrace are shown in **24.1**. Barriers are provided at intervals as a protection against crowd surge; the spacings are given in Table I. Gaps are provided in the barriers, but these should

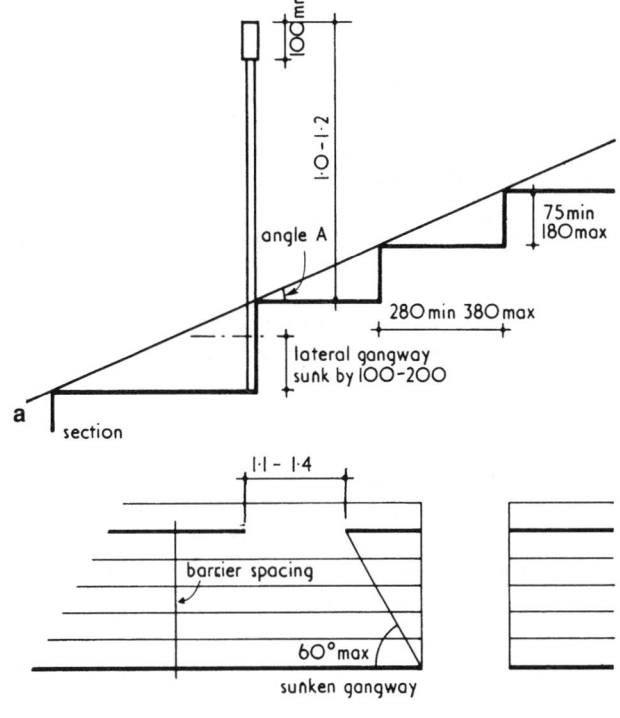

24.1 *Details of terraces for standing spectators.* **a** *Section.* **b** *Plan*

Table I Spacing of barriers on sports grounds (from *Guide to Safety at Sports Grounds*, Home Office, 1973)

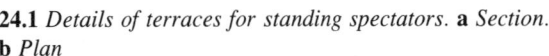

Angle of terrace			Peak areas of ground*		Other areas of ground	
			A	B	A	B
5°	8.8%	1:11.4	5.0	3.3	8.4	5.6
10°	17.5%	1:5.7	4.3	2.9	6.7	4.5
15°	27%	1:3.7	3.8	2.6	5.6	3.7
20°	37%	1:2.7	3.4	2.3	4.8	3.2
25°	47.6%	1:2.1	3.1	2.1	4.2	2.8
30°	58.8%	1:1.7	2.9	1.9	3.8	2.5

*Peak areas of ground are those where the crowd collects thickest, such as behind the goals in association football.
Type A barriers are tested for 6 kN/m loading, or designed for 5 kN/m.
Type B barriers are tested for 4.3 kN/m, or designed for 3.4 kN/m.
Barrier foundations are designed for a factor of safety against overturning of 2.

be staggered as shown on the plan. Gangways should be sunk 100–200 mm below the adjacent terrace to discourage standing in them, and radial gangways should be 'dog-legged' for the same reason. No point on a terrace should be more than 6 m from a gangway; the normal capacity is between 27 and 54 persons per 10 m². The front of the terrace should be no nearer the touchline than:

$(1.75 \pm H)$ cot A or 3 m, whichever is the greater

where 1.75 m is the height of an average male person

H m is the difference in level between the pitch and the bottom of the terrace, and

A is the angle the terrace makes to the horizontal.

2.04 Stands

The design of seating in stands and stadia is similar to that in auditoria (see Chapter 20). The minimum area occupied by a seat is 460 mm wide × 610 mm deep, the preferred 550 × 760. There should be a minimum clearance of 305 mm between front and back of empty seats, although this is included in the above areas. The maximum run of seats with a gangway at each end is 28, half that if only at one end. No seat in a stand should be further than 30 m from an exit.

2.05 Sight-lines and rake of spectator tiers

The rake of spectator tiers is determined either mathematically or graphically in section, where the principal factors are:

● The assumed constant of 'the crown', i.e. the distance from the eye to the top of the head which is known as the C value
● The tread depth or seating row depth
● The point of focus (the middle of the innermost athletics track or the near touchline in football or rugby)
● The height of the spectator's eye in the first row, **24.2**.

In determining the rake, the lines of sight from the eyes of spectators in each row to the focus should be clear of, or at worst tangential to, the top of the head of the spectators in the row in front. This will give a profile which is parabolic, with the rake increasing with the viewing distance. In some countries, this is considered to be uneconomic to construct and unsafe for crowd movement – the stairs in gangways become unequal and therefore unacceptable. Nevertheless, the parabolic approach is acceptable in some countries and was used at the Munich Olympic Stadium.

A straight rake with the necessary elevation between steps will be satisfactory. However, a series of straight rakes tangential to the theoretical parabolic curve is practical and widely used, **24.3**. The effect of lowering the eye level of the front spectator is quite significant.

The following guidelines are suggested for C values:

● 150 mm is an ideal standard capable of giving excellent viewing conditions
● 120 mm is the optimum standard for most spectators, giving very good viewing
● 90 mm should be regarded as the minimum viewing standard
● 60 mm is a figure which means that good viewing can only be achieved between the heads of spectators in the row in front. In very large stadia, there may be some positions where this is the best standard which can be achieved from some seats, but these should be kept to a minimum.

Riser heights

Viewing standards will be affected by the riser height of each seating row. The following calculation is used to determine the riser height:

$$N = \frac{(R + C) \times (D + T)}{D} - R$$

where N = riser height

R = height between eye and point of focus

C = viewing standard (C value)

D = distance from eye to point of focus (typically the near touchline)

T = tread depth, ie depth of seating row.

2.06 Seating

In the move towards all-seated major stadia, it is important to give some consideration to the seat where spectators will spend some time. The time for sitting in the seat will vary with the stadium type. The following are some examples:

Cricket	all day, perhaps even more than one day
Football	1.5–2 hours
Rugby	1.5–2 hours; for seven-a-side tournaments perhaps all day
Pop concerts	3 hours or more
Athletics	sometimes all day, e.g. Olympics
American football	3–4 hours

The need for comfort will vary and multi-purpose stadia should be flexible.

Outdoor stadia seats should be weather-resistant and robust as well as comfortable. Suitable materials include aluminium, some timbers and the most common material for modern stadia, some form of plastic. This has the greatest potential for moulding and shaping for comfort.

Fire retardance also needs to be taken into account. With plastic, additives can be introduced but they often limit colour choice and sometimes will add only delay to fire resistance. The design of the seat is as critical as the material itself in regard to fire resistance. Double-skin forms avoiding edge details which can ignite easily are best.

Colour is important. Some stadias use colour blocks to aid management, but most now use patterns incorporating club insignia which are can be seen when the stadium is not full. Some

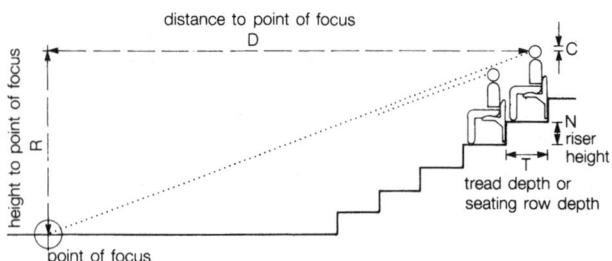

24.2 *Terms for calculating the suitable rake*

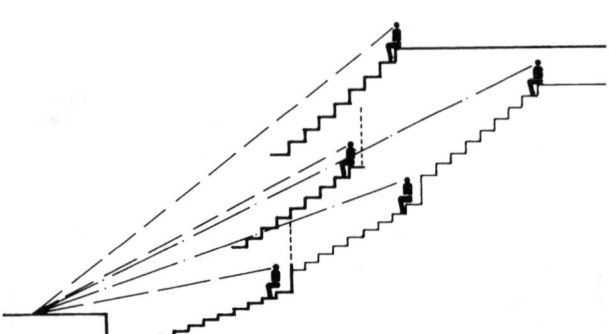

24.3 *Three straight tiers approximately tangential to the theoretical curve in a single tier is economical in cost but not in space. Separating and overlapping the tiers reduces the plan area. The rake angle must not exceed 35° to the horizontal*

colours are better at resisting fading under ultraviolet rays than others.

The seat must be designed to drain and not hold water, and be easy to clean itself, around and underneath. This is important to avoid damage, as dirty seats encourage vandalism.

The fixings must be as few as consistent with strength (to assist cleaning), corrosion resistant and robust. Spectators will occasionally stand on seats, or rest their feet on them from behind, exerting considerable force.

In existing stadia, particularly the older ones, the floor construction will limit the fixing choices available. This can be an important factor in re-equipping an existing stadium with seats, because of the large number of fixing points required.

The life of a seat used to be considered as about twenty years, but it is doubtful whether current models will need to be as long-lasting.

Forms of seating

The quality of the seating will vary depending on the use, but also to produce a range of seats available in the stadium. Standards of comfort demanded by users tend to be rising.

The better quality will be on an individual seat basis with a back, **24.4**. The seat may fold back when not in use. This increases the seat gangway, providing greater convenience and safety. VIP seating in selected areas will require even higher standards. Cheaper seating can be provided by the use of benches or seats with no backs **24.5**. This produces a more economical spacing of rows.

Comfort and event usage

Upholstered versions of standard seats are widely available, while some clubs may wish to upgrade their existing standard seating with the addition of back pads and cushions or full covers. Armrests cannot usually be added to existing standard seats.

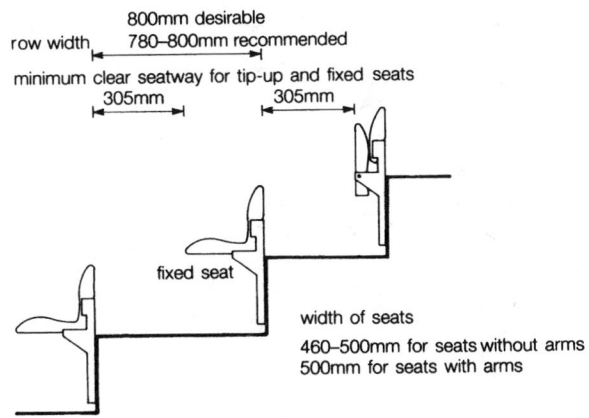

24.4 *Spacing between seating with backs, fixed and fold-up*

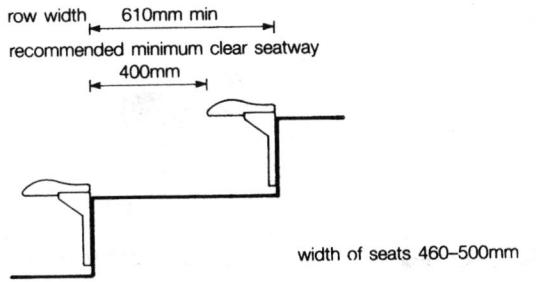

24.5 *Spacing between benches without backs. These allow closer spacing but are less comfortable and are increasingly unacceptable*

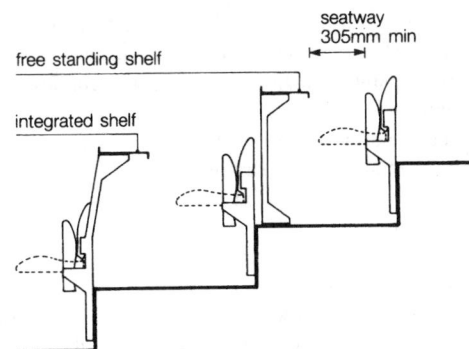

24.6 *Two options for press box seating: integrated or free-standing writing shelf*

If the stadium is to be used for events other than football – for example, pop concerts, American football, public gatherings – it may be worth considering higher-grade seats in sections where customers will sit for a longer period than 90 minutes, perhaps at higher admission prices.

Press box seating

Seats in the press box should be provided with integrated writing shelves or tablets, **24.6**. However, consult with regular press box users to determine how much space they need for computers, monitors, telephones, fax machines or other equipment.

Note that the requirement for a minimum seatway of 305 mm applies in this case to the distance between the rearmost projection on the shelf and the front of the seat.

2.06 Exits from sports grounds

Large numbers of spectators in sports grounds are a source of danger to themselves, particularly from:

● Tripping, slipping and falling
● Crowd pressure on terraces and exits and
● Fire and hooliganism.

All spectators should be able to leave a sports ground within 8 minutes. If there are combustible stands (such as constructed of timber) spectators must be able to be cleared from them within 2½ minutes.

The flow through an exit is about 40 persons per minute per unit of width of 550 mm. Where there are narrowings in the exit route there should be 'reservoir' areas to accommodate those that are waiting to pass. These should not be less than 15 m from an incombustible building, nor 45 m from one that is combustible, and should be designed to hold 54 persons per 10 m². Nowhere should an exit or escape route be less than 1.1 m wide, minimum headroom 2.4 m. Steps should be a minimum of 280 mm going (305 mm preferred). No flight should have less than three or more than 16 risers and two flights with more than 12 risers should have a turn between. Ramps should not be be steeper than 10 per cent (1:10).

3 ATHLETICS

3.01 Athletics stadia

Facilities at a stadium capable of staging national and international meetings should include:

● A 400 m, eight-lane floodlit track with one ten-lane straight of sufficient length to permit a 110 m hurdles to be run with space for the athletes to pull up after passing the tape
● A steeplechase water jump
● Full provision for all field events
● A separate warming-up area (desirable)

- Changing and washing facilities for 200 athletes in the proportion two-thirds male to one-third female
- Additional separate changing accommodation for boys and girls is desirable
- A covered stand to seat least 2000 spectators
- Appropriate toilet and car parking facilities
- An announcer's box and provision for the press, broadcasting and television
- Officials' room
- Equipment rooms and store
- The perimeter of the track not covered by the stand should, if possible, be terraced to provide further spectator accommodation.

Wherever possible, regional athletic stadia should be associated with other sports provision. An indoor sports centre or sports hall alongside the stadium is a distinct advantage. Consult the AAA and NPFA regarding regional and local track gradings with specifications for minimum facilities.

A typical district athletics centre is shown in **24.7**. Athletics centres for national and international level competitions vary with the money available – Olympic facilities now require Croesus's purse! Famous examples of less affluent centres are shown in the *Handbook of sport and recreational building design*.

3.02 All-weather surfacing
- Where surface is all-weather, six lanes are acceptable on circuit.
- Runways for long and triple jumps and pole vault should be all-weather, and a the width may be reduced to 0.9 m. For the high jump an all-weather take-off strip 5 m wide is acceptable.

3.03 Layout
- The layout for the field events may be varied to suit local requirements.
- Where space allows, additional throwing facilities may be sited outside the track, provided there is proper control and safety.

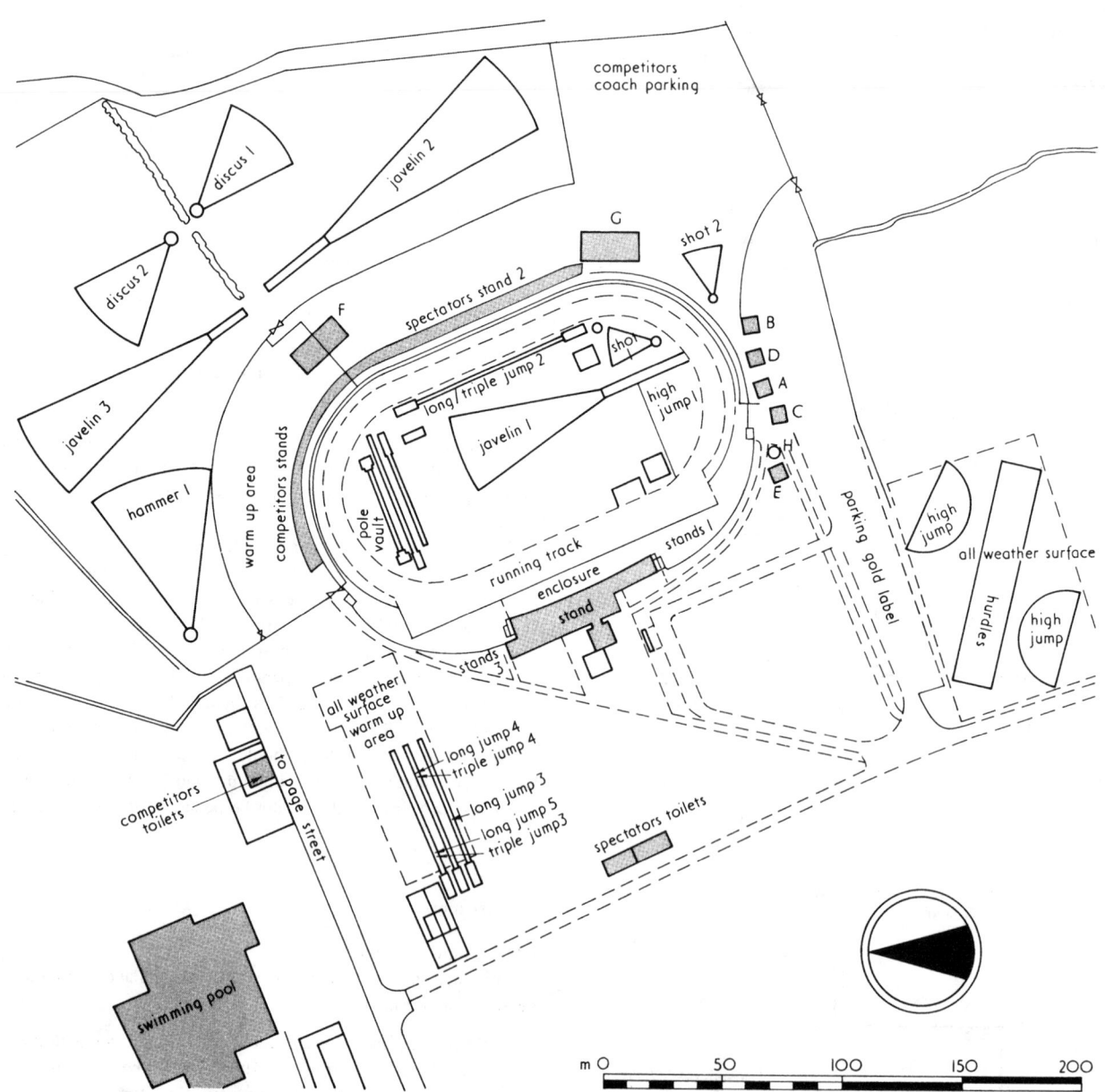

24.7 *Plan of Copthall Sports Centre, courtesy of the London Borough of Barnet. This is an example of a good district athletics centre. KEY: A Transport office, B Public telephones, C Police kiosk, D Billeting enquiries and lost property, E box office, F Souvenir sales, G Refreshments, H First aid*

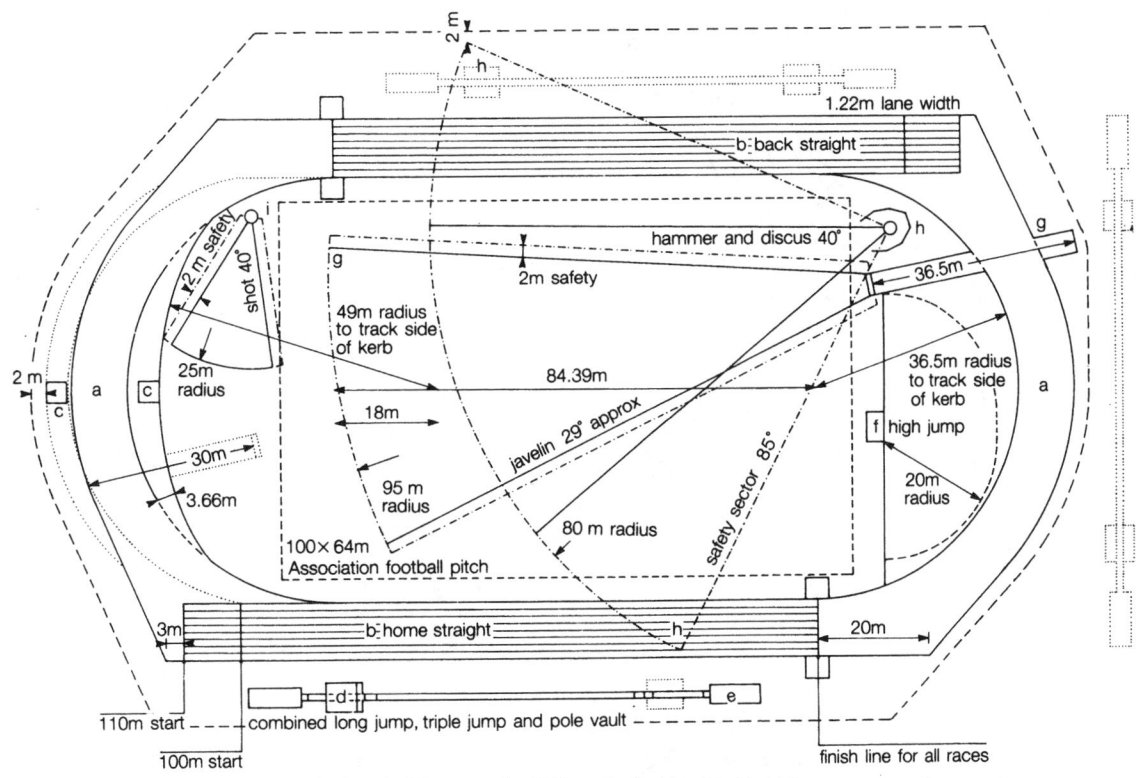

24.8 *Layout guide for 400-metre running tracks and field events. This layout with alternative sitings for field events, is based on NPFA diagram 13b. Different arrangements are possible to suit particular circumstances. For high-level competition, however, alternatives for the throwing circles are limited if maximum distances are to be thrown safely*

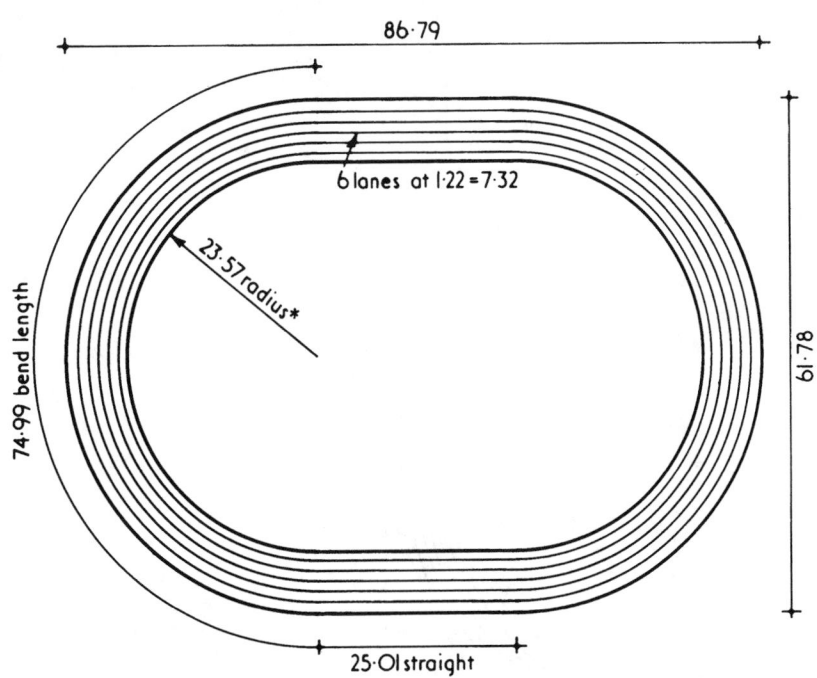

24.9 *200 metre running track. *Radius is measured to the track side of raised or flagged edge. If only a chalk line the radius is 23.67 m*

24.10 *300 metre running track.*
*Radius is measured to the track
side of raised or flagged edge. If
only a chalk line the radius is
34.8 m

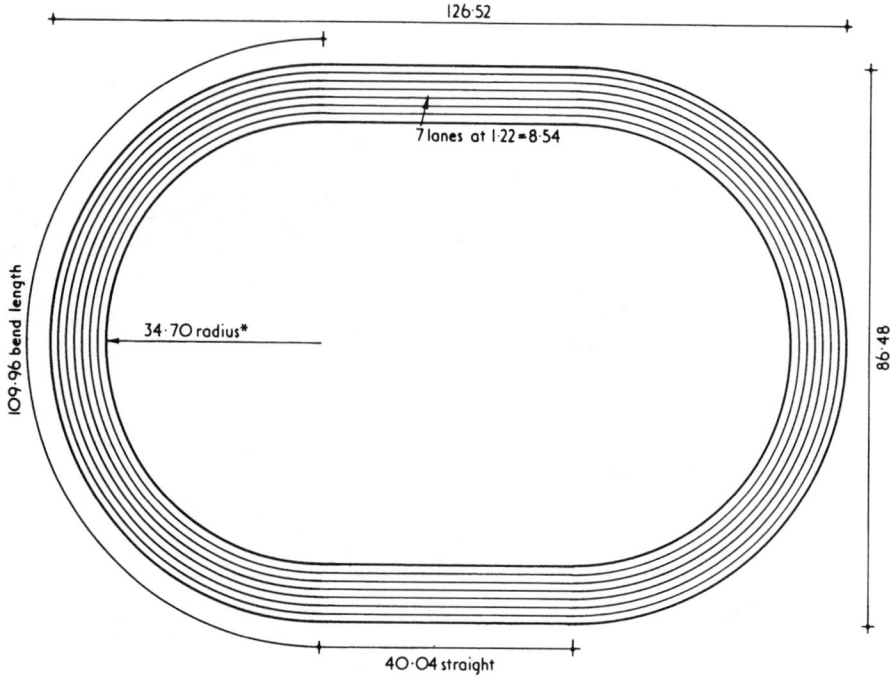

126·52

7 lanes at 1·22 = 8·54

109·96 bend length

34·70 radius*

86·48

40·04 straight

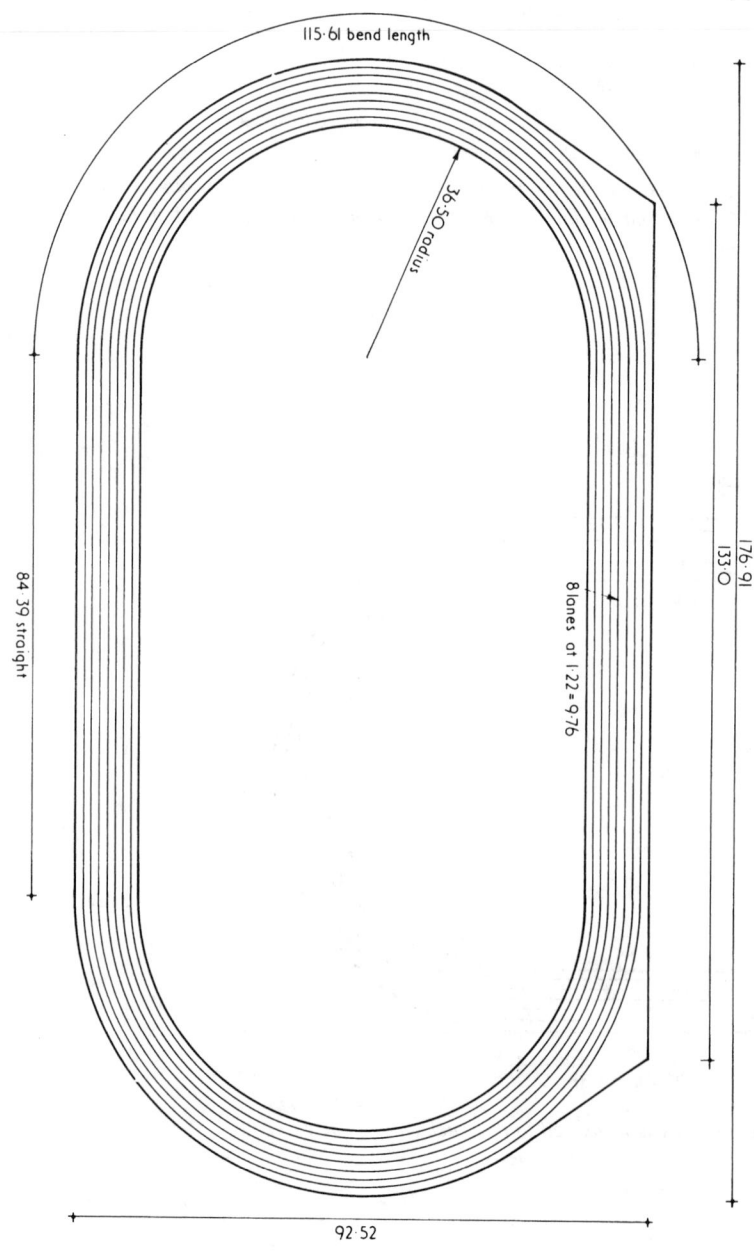

115·61 bend length

36·50 radius

84·39 straight

8 lanes at 1·22 = 9·76

176·91

133·0

92·52

24.11 *400-metre running track: the standard*
7-lane club track. For 6-lane all-weather
surfaces, reduce overall dimensions by 2.44 m.
For major competiton tracks and regional
facilities, 8 all-weather lanes with a 10-lane
sprint straight is required: increase overall
dimensions by 2.44 m, and sprint straight as
shown

- On cinder tracks the straight sprint and hurdle are run on the six outer lanes, thus avoiding the inner lane which is subject to heavy use during long-distance events.
- If the central area is not required for winter games the distances from the shot circle to the inner edge of the track and the javelin runway should be increased to 10 m.
- The safety radius for the throws should be adjusted according to the standards expected to be attained by the competitors.
- The triple jump landing area should be increased to 3.35 m where space and funds permit.

A recommended layout guide is shown in **24.8**.

3.04 Orientation
Siting for pole vault and all jump approaches should be such that the jumpers do not run towards the sun. The arc to be avoided for these events is approximately south-west to north-west (225° to 315°) in the UK. This also applies to grandstand siting.

3.05 Safety precautions
Detailed specifications and safety for field events are set out in the National Handbook. Extension wings should be provided to the safety throwing cage for the protection of the jumps and inner running lanes.

3.06 Discus and hammer circles
Hammer throwers prefer a smoother finish to the concrete than discus throwers. For this reason, also to allow simultaneous training in each event, separate cage-protected circles are often provided.

3.07 Javelin runway
In order not to restrict the use of the running track, the runway should wherever possible be laid down clear of the track by extending it further into the arena. This necessitates the reinstatement of the winter games pitch.

3.08 Tracks without a raised border
Where a track is marked out on grass or on a hard porous area without a raised or flagged border, the track length must be measured along a line 20 cm instead of 30 cm from the track side of the inner edge. This has the effect in the example shown of increasing the radius to the inner edge from 36.50 m to 36.60 m and of reducing the width of the first lane to 1.12 m.

3.09 Formula for other track proportions
Where a track of wider or narrower proportions or of different length is required, the appropriate dimension can be calculated from the following formula:

$$L = 2P + 2(\pi R + 300 \text{ mm})$$

where L = length of track in metres
P = length of parallels or distances apart of centres of curves in metres
R = radius to track side of inner kerb in metres
π = 3.1416 (not 22/7)

The radius of the semicircles should not normally be less than 32 m or more than 42 m for a 400-metre circuit.

3.10 Alternative surfacing for areas
If preferred the spaces at each end of the winter games pitch can be hard surfaced to the same specification as the track with the following advantages:

- Maintenance is simplified
- Runways do not have to be separately constructed and edged and their position can be varied as required

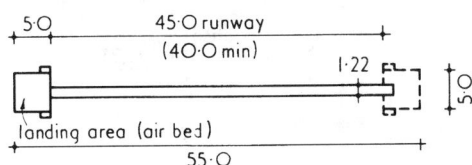

24.12 *High jump*

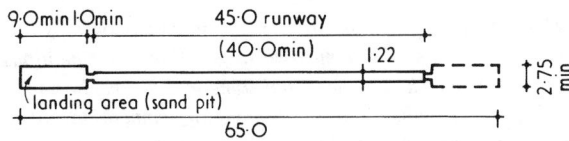

24.13 *Pole vault*

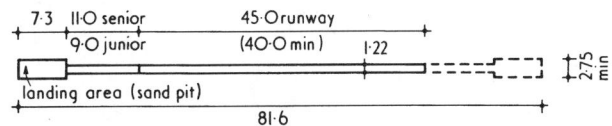

24.14 *Long jump: to avoid adverse wind conditions, landing areas are at both ends*

24.15 *Triple jump*

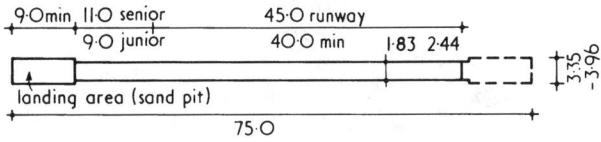

24.16 *Combined triple and long jump*

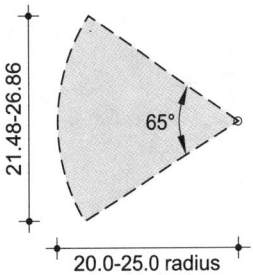

24.17 *Shot*

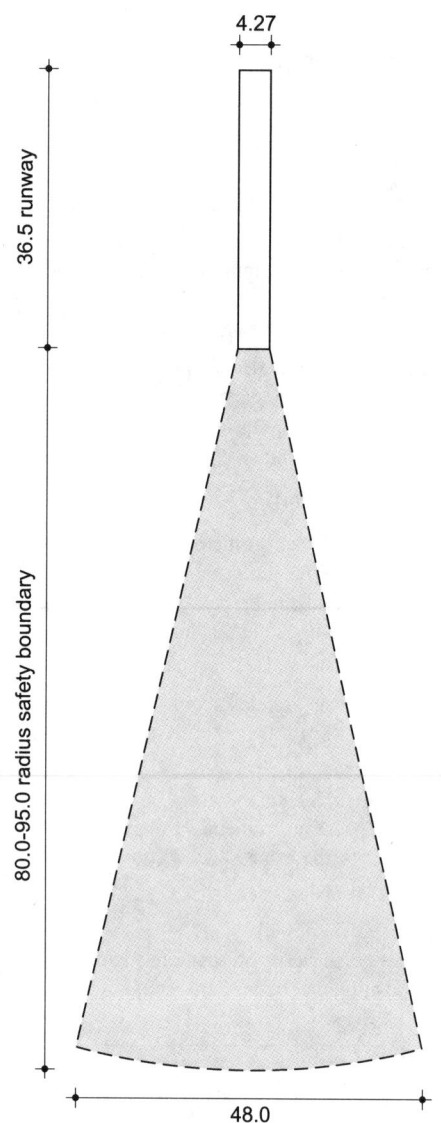

24.18 *Javelin*

24.20 *Archery, clout. The arrows ae shot high into the air to fall into circles marked on the ground, or a circular cloth pegged down, the centre of each being marked by a flag. The various shooting distances are clearly defined on the grass by white lines, tapes or spots and are always measured in yards. Archers move up and back to the distance position, and the waiting line moves accordingly. The overall distance for clout archery is about 230 m*

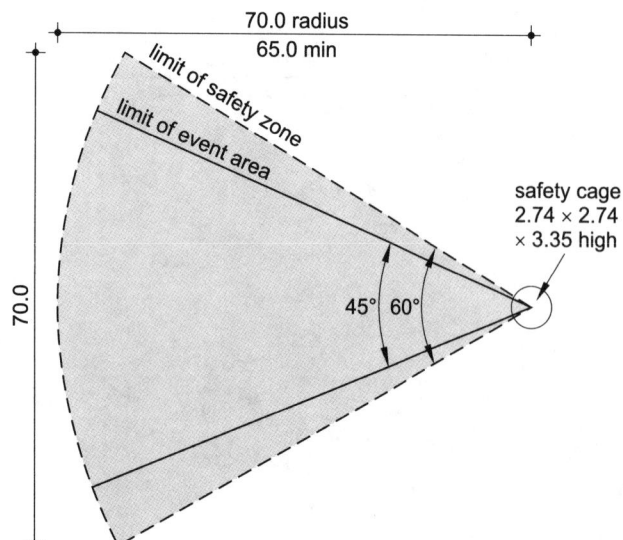

24.19 *Discus and hammer: discus base is 2.5 m dia., hammer base 2.135 m dia.*

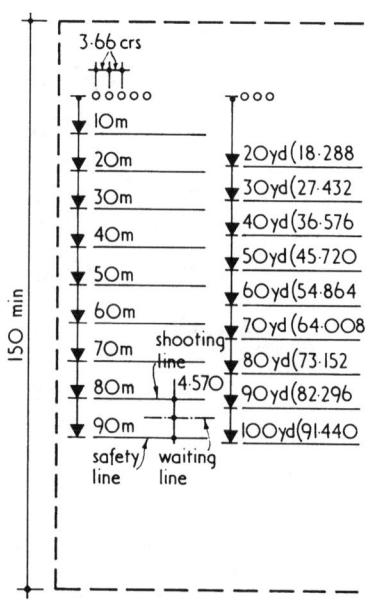

24.21 *Archery, target: club archery 100 m, championships over 150 m depending on the number of targets. Some competitions are shot over metric distances and some will always be shot over imperial lengths. Metric and imperial competitions take place during the same meeting. The waiting and safety lines are moved to positions behind the correct shooting line for each competition. In this example, shooting is over a distance of 50 m*

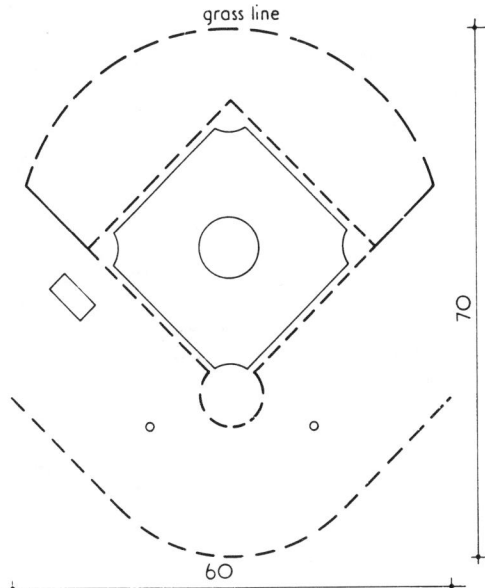

24.22 *Baseball: full-size diamond. Little league, for young players, is two thirds the size*

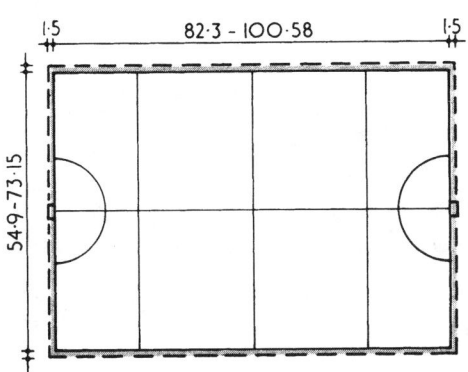

24.23 *Bicycle polo*

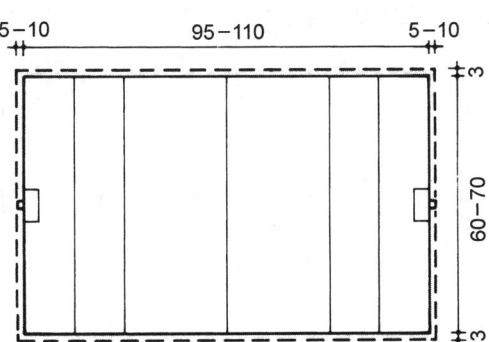

24.24 *Camogie*

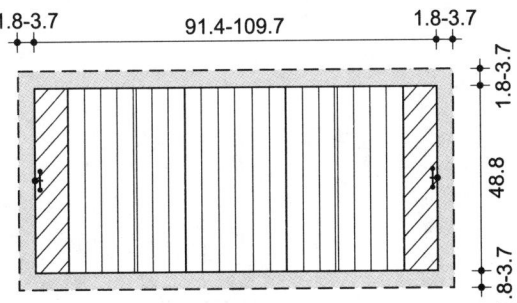

24.25 *Football, American*

● Portable landing areas for high jump practice and coaching can be placed where most convenient.

3.11 Running tracks
Layouts for running tracks scale 1:1000 are given in **24.9** to **24.11**.

3.12 Field events
The important dimensions for the main field events are shown in **24.12** to **24.19** (scale 1:1000).

4 PLAYING FIELD SPORTS

4.01 Playing fields
Games and recreations that take place on ordinary playing fields are shown in alphabetical order in **24.20** to **24.42** (scale 1:2000 except where shown otherwise).

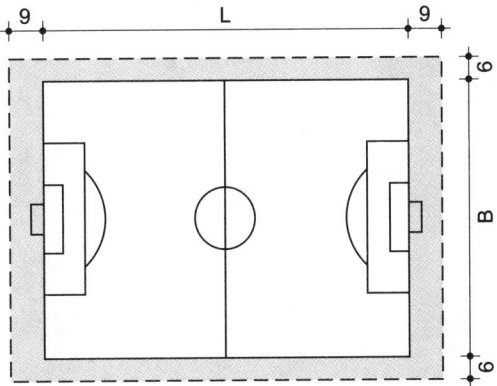

24.26 *Football, Association (Soccer). The NPFA gives the following recommended sizes:*

	L	*B*
International:	*100–110 m*	*64–75 m*
Senior:	*96–100 m*	*60–64 m*
Junior:	*90 m*	*45–55 m*

For five-a-side Association Football see Chapter 25

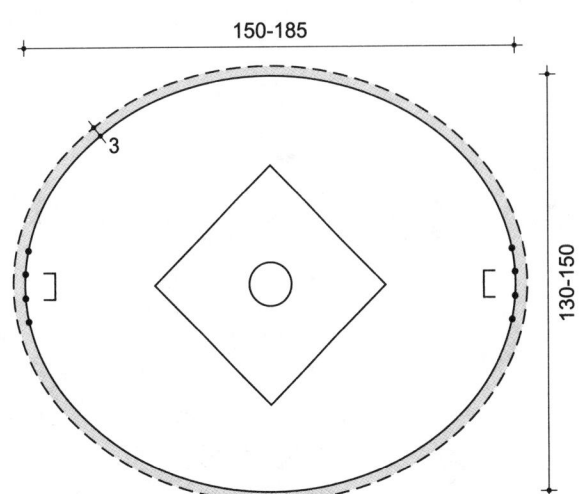

24.27 *Football, Australian*

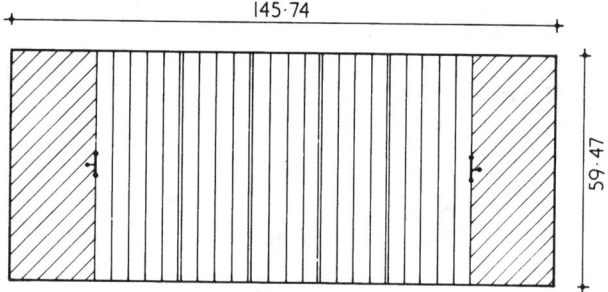

24.28 *Football, Canadian*

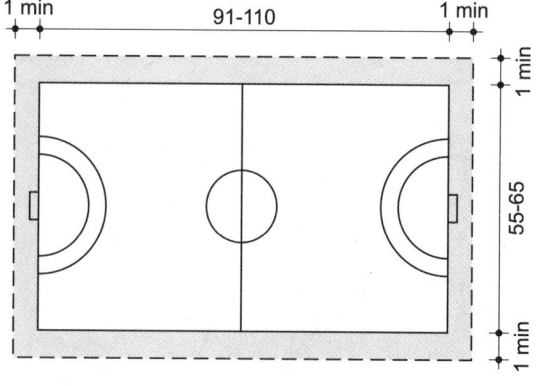

24.32 *Handball*

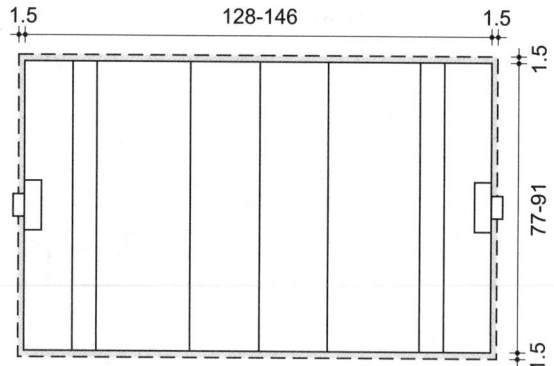

24.29 *Football, Gaelic*

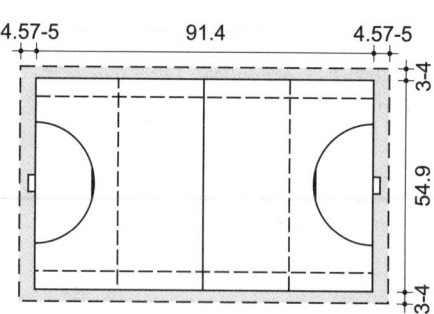

24.33 *Hockey. For county and club matches the NPFA gives a pitch size of 90 × 55 m in an overall space of 95 × 60.4 m, allowing for circulation about the pitch*

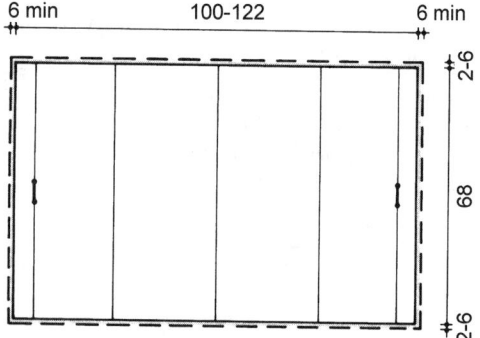

24.30 *Football, Rugby League*

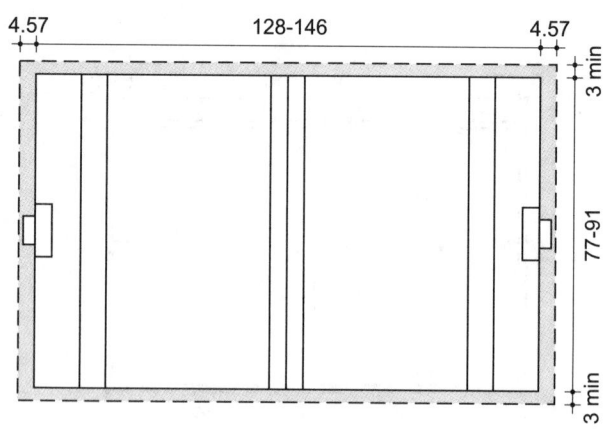

24.34 *Hurling (a similar pitch to that of Gaelic Fotball)*

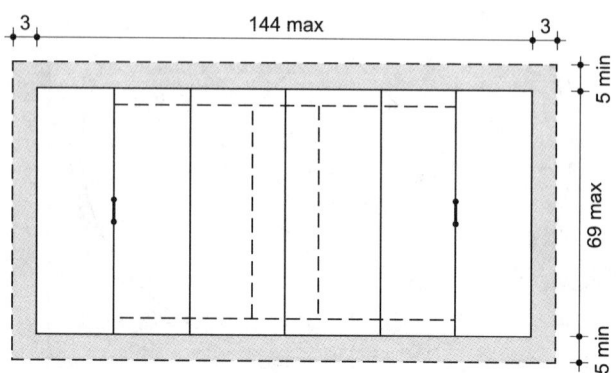

24.31 *Football, Rugby Union*

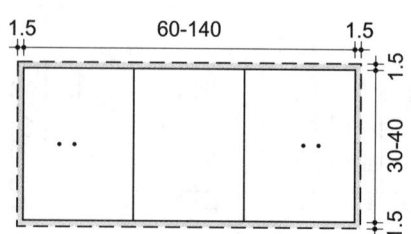

24.35 *Korfball*

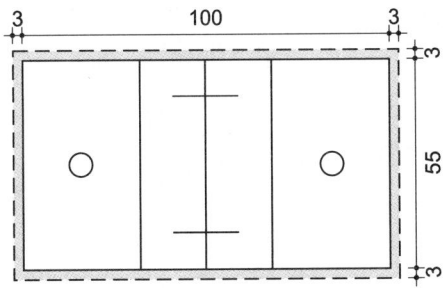

24.36 Lacrosse, men's

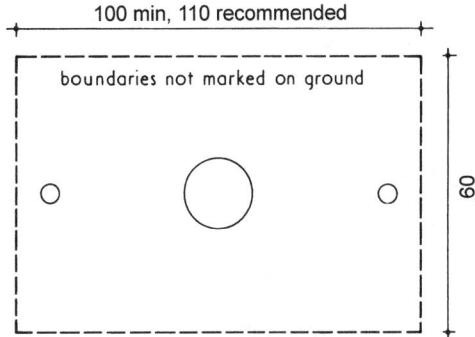

24.37 Lacrosse, women's. The ground has no measured or marked-out boundaries. The women's indoor seven-a-side game has been superseded by Pop-Lacrosse

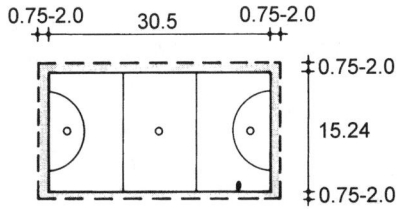

24.38 Netball

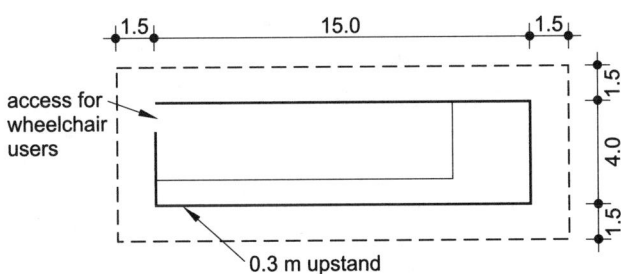

24.39 Petanque. Additional space is needed for competition officials and players' sitting out

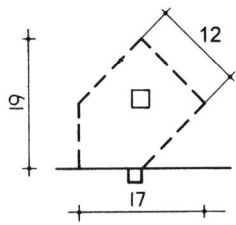

24.40 Rounders. An outfield boundary consisting of a circle about 50 m diameter is used.

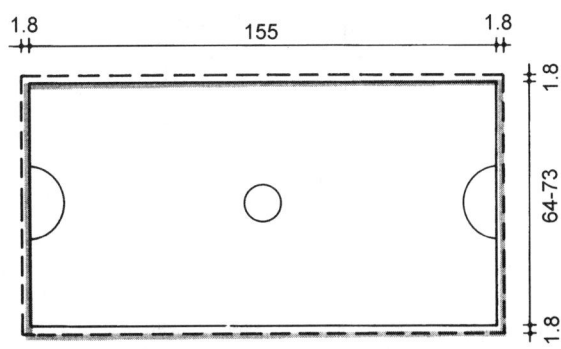

24.41 Shinty

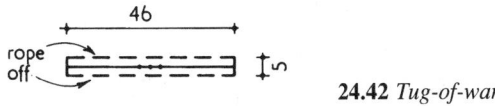

24.42 Tug-of-war

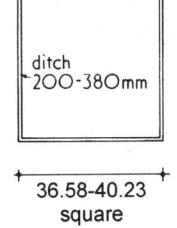

24.43 Bowls. Greens should not be shorter than 30.2 m in the play direction. For domestic play the rink should be a minimum of 4.3 m wide. The square above is suitable for six rinks

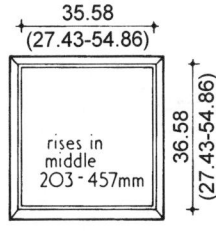

24.44 Crown bowls: played mainly in northern England and Wales and in the Isle of Man. The 'crown', which need not be central, is between 0.25 and 0.46 higher than the edges

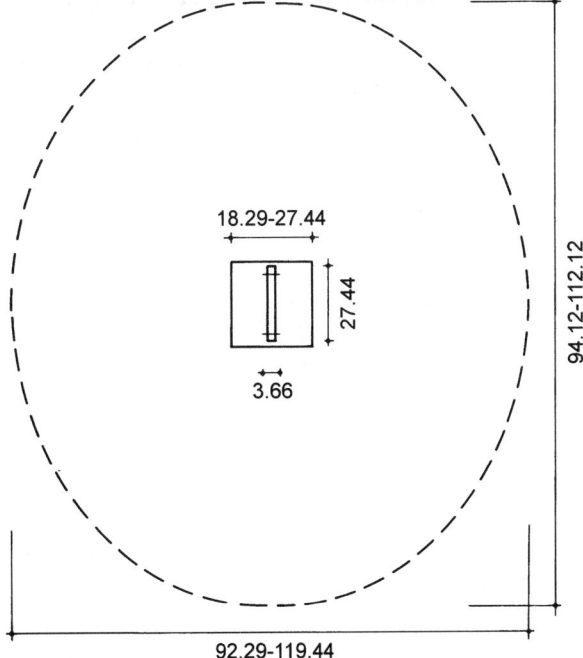

24.45 Cricket. The central square of about 22 m side is able to take the wickets in either direction. This would be special turf and grass species, and is kept roped off when not in use. The outfield, however, can be used for other games when not required for cricket

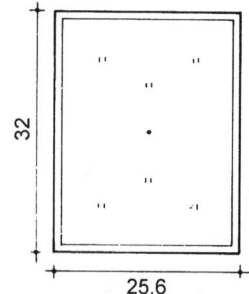

24.46 *Croquet. This can be played on an ordinary field, but the good game demands turf similar to a bowls green*

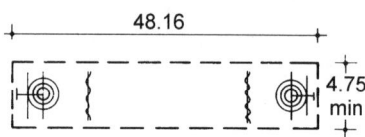

24.47 *Curling. This Scottish game is played on ice*

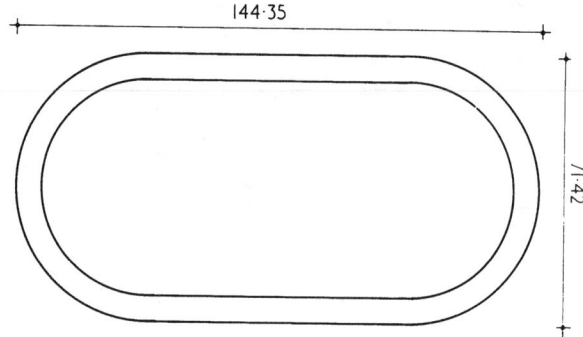

24.48 *Cycle racing 333⅓ metre track*

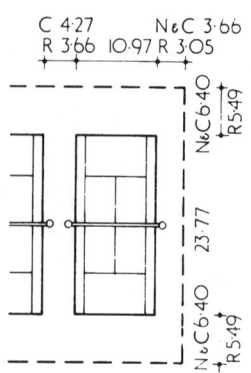

24.49 *Lawn tennis. The surface may be grass, suitable asphalt or a modern composition. The surrounds are of wire netting 3 to 4 m high*

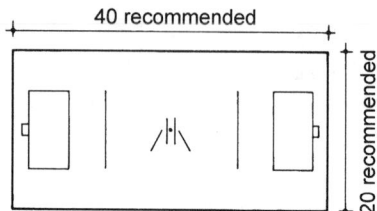

24.50 *Roller hockey. This demands a surface suitable for roller skating: strip wood, terrazzo, smooth concrete or a suitable asphalt*

5 SPORTS REQUIRING SPECIAL CONDITIONS OR CONSTRUCTION

A selection of special constructions are given in **24.43** to **24.50** (scale 1:2000 except where shown otherwise).

BIBLIOGRAPHICAL NOTE

Forthcoming revised edition of AAA/NPFA Facilities for Athletics containing technical requirements and specifications for all grades of outdoor athletics.

25 Indoor sports

Peter Ackroyd

CI/SfB: 562
UDC: 725.85
Uniclass: F562

KEY POINT:

● *Because of the British climate, more and more indoor facilities for sport are needed*

Contents

1 INTRODUCTION

Indoor sporting activity can be competitive, recreational or for training purposes. Most facilities are designed to cater for all three, and are either general-purpose spaces such as sports halls or special to one activity or range of activities, such as a squash court or ice rink. The different sports and activities will be found in alphabetical order in paragraphs **3, 4, 5** and **6**: whichever is appropriate. However, swimming is covered in Chapter 22 and equestrian sports in Chapter 26.

In this chapter the information given about each activity will generally be confined to the required overall sizes at the various recognised levels:

N – international and national competition
C – county and club competition and
R – recreational.

For further information such as detailed dimensions, equipment, environmental installations, etc. refer to the *Handbook of sports and recreational building design.*

2 SPORTS CENTRES

Some sports centres are large complexes encompassing wet and dry sports. **25.1** shows the possible elements of such a complex, some of which are omitted in smaller centres. **25.2** is a plan of a large centre. The essential elements of a small dry sports centre are shown in **25.3**, and a plan of a centre in **25.4**.

3 SPORTS HALLS

3.01 Use of facilities

Sports halls are general-purpose spaces intended to cater for a great variety of activities. Some of these can take place simultaneously, but others need exclusive use for a time. In general, all the activities in paragraphs **3, 4** and **5** and even some of those in paragraph **6** can take place in a suitable sports hall. However, the demand for time in sports halls is so great that those activities that can be carried on in less expensive accommodation tend to be confined to projectile halls and ancillary halls. In this section information about the activities will be found under the most appropriate space.

3.02 Sizes

Only the largest of halls will satisfy all required standards of play for all indoor sports, and therefore it will be necessary to decide on upon the range of sports and levels before determining the floor area. Table I shows what can be accommodated in the various standard sizes of hall.

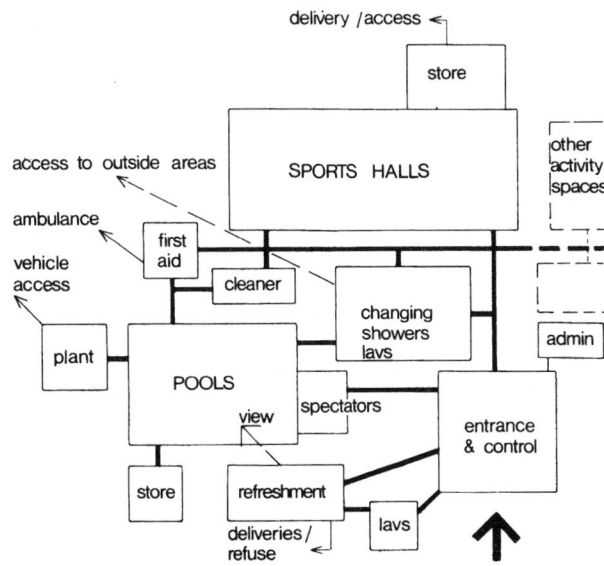

25.1 *Space and circulation diagram of a large wet and dry sports centre*

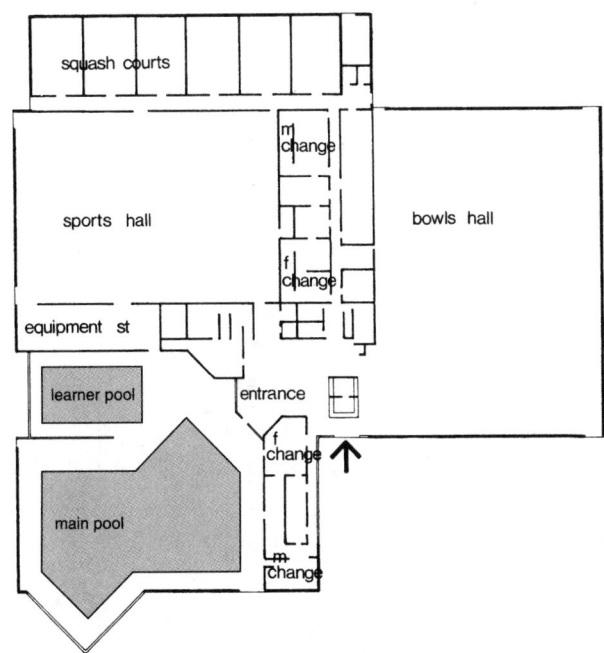

25.2 *Dunstable leisure centre: a leisure pool and dry facilities on a school site*

Table I Definition of sizes: maximum number of courts related to standards of play

	Large hall[fr] 36.5 × 32 × 9.1 m, 1168 m²		Medium halls[fr] 32 × 26 × 7.6–9.1 m, 832 m²		29 × 26 × 7.6–9.1 m, 754 m²		32 × 23 × 7.6–9.1 m, 736 m²		Small halls 32 × 17 × 6.7–7.6 m, 544 m²		29.5 × 16.5 × 6.7–7.6 m, 486.75 m²		26 × 16.5 × 6.7–7.6 m, 429 m²		22.5 × 16.5 × 6.7–7.6 m, 371.25 m²		Community halls 17.0–20.0 × 15.6 × 6.7 m, 265.2–321 m²		17.0–8.5 × 6.7 m, 144.5 m²	
	No.	Standard	No.	Standard	No.	Standard	No.	Standard	No.	Standard	No.	Standard	No.	Standard	No.	Standard	No.	Standard	No.	Standard
Aikido	4 / 6	N / C	4	N	4	N	2 / +3(*)	C / R	2 / 3(1*)	N / R	2	N	2	N	1 / 2	N / R	1	N	–	–
Archery (length of shoot)		≤30 m / 25 m / 18 m / 20 yd		≤25 m / 18 m / 20 yd		18 m / 20 yd		≤25 m		≤25 m / 18 m / 20 yd		18 m / 20 yd		18 m / 15 yd		18 m / 15 yd		–		–
Badminton¹	5 / 6(2*)	N† / R	3/4 / 4	N† / R	3/4 / 4	NC / R*	4 / 6	N¹ / R	4	C**	3 / 4	C** / R*	3	C**	3	R	2	R¹	1	R¹
Basketball	1 / 2	N / C*/R	1 / 2	N / C*/R	1 / 2	N / R*	1	C**	1	C**	1	C**	1	C**	1 / 1	R* / Mini BB	1	Mini BB	–	–
Bowls (portable non-competitive rinks)	7	R	5	R	5	R*	4	R	3	R	3	R*	–	–	–	–	–	–	–	–
Boxing (training rings)	9 / 12	N / R	6 / 12	N / R	4 / 9	N / R	3 / 6	C / R	3 / 6	C / R	3 / 5	C / R	2 / 5	C / R	2 / 4	C / R	2 / 4	C / R	2	R
Cricket six-a-side pitches ns	1 / 2	C / C	1	C	–	–	1	R	1	R	–	–	–	–	–	–	–	–	–	–
Cricket nets	8	N	6	N	6	C	5	N	4	C	4	C	4	R	–	–	–	–	–	–
Fencing (pistes)	12 / 14	N / C	8(3*) / 9	N / C	7 / 8	N / C	6 / 8	N / C	3/4 / 2/3	N/C / R*	3/4 +2	N/C / R*	3/4* +1	N/C / R	3 / 4	N / C*	3	C	2	R
Five-a-side football	1 / 2	N / R*	1	R*	1	R*	1	R*	1	R*	1	R*	1	R*	1	R*	1	R*	–	–
Gymnastics (Olympic)	–	N	–	C	–	P	–	C	–	P	–	P	–	P	–	P	–	P	–	–
Handball	1	N*	1	C	1	N / R*	1	N / R	1	N / R*	1	R* / C	1	C	1	C	1	R*	1	R*
Mini handball	1	C*	1	C	–	–	1	C	1	C	1	C	1	C	1	C	–	–	–	–
Hockey	1	C*	1	C	1	R	1	R	1	R	1	R	1	R	1	R	–	–	–	–
Judo	4 / 6	N / R	2 / 4	N / C	1 / 4	N / C	2 / 3	N / R	2 / 3	N / R	1 / 2	N / C	1 / 2	N / R	1 / 2	N / R	1/2	R	–	–

Activity													
Karate	4 / 12 N R	2/4 / 6 N/C R	2 / 4/6 N* C/R	2 / 6 N R	2 / 6 N R*	2 / 3 N*/C R	1/2 / 3 N/C R	1 / 2 N R	2 R*				
Keep fit; Movement and dance; Yoga. ns	✓	✓	✓	✓	✓	✓	✓	✓	✓				
Kendo	4 / 6 N R*	2 / 4 N C	2 / 4 N C	2 / 4 N R	2 N	2 / 2 N C	2 N* C	1 / 2 N C	1 / 2 N R*	1 P	1 P	–	–
Lacrosse F	1 N	1 C*	1 R	1 C*	1 C*	1 R	–	–	–	–	–	–	–
Lawn tennis	1 / 2 N* R	1 R*	1 R*	1 R*	1 R*	1 R*	–	–	–	–	–	–	–
Micro korfball	1 C	1 C	1 C	1 C	1 R*	1 C	–	–	–	–	–	–	–
Netball	1 / 2 N C*/R	1 R	1 R	1 R	1 R	1 R	–	–	–	–	–	–	–
Table tennis c/c	10 / 15/21 N C/C	6 / 10/15 N C/C	6 / 10/12 N C/C	6 / 10/12 C/C R	7/9 / 14 C/C R	7 / 12 C/C R	6/7 / 10 C/C R	4 / 8 C/C R	3–6 / 6–8 C/C R	4 R	1 R		R*
Trampolining	12 N	8 / 12 N† R	8 N†	4 / 8 N† C*/R	4 / 6 C** R	4 C**	4 C**	4 R	2 R	1 R			
Tug of war	–	–	–	–	–	C	C	–	–	–	–		
Volleyball	2 N	1 N† C	1 N†	1 2* N†/C	1 C**	1 C**	1 C**	1 C**	1 R*			R*	–
Weight lifting contests	–	N	N	N	N	C	C	C	–	–	–	–	–
Wrestling	4 / 12 N C	2 / 6 N C	6 N C	2 / 6 N C	2 / 3 N* C	3 / 8 C R	2 / 6 C R	2 / 4 C R	2 R			2 R	–

Key

N National/international standard
C County/club standard
R Recreational standard
P Practice area only
c/c For table tennis there are two grades of minimum space allowances for inter-county/inter-club standards of play
fr Fire regulations and maximum compartment volumes should be checked. Halls of 7000 m³ or over need a DOE waiver. 'Volume' can include an unenclosed structural roof spaces ns No standards have yet been laid down
S Area behind shooting line is below safety standard recommended. Acceptable space can be provided with a slight lengthening of the hall; or existing spaces may be used for practice purposes
*Below minimum space standard recommended by the governing body concerned, but capable of providing purposeful and enjoyable activity.
**Recreational standard where the hall is less than 7.6 m clear height for badminton and trampolining, or less than 7.0 m for basketball and volleyball 6.7 m height is suitable for mini basketball and mini volleyball
†County/club standard where the hall is less than 9.0 m clear height

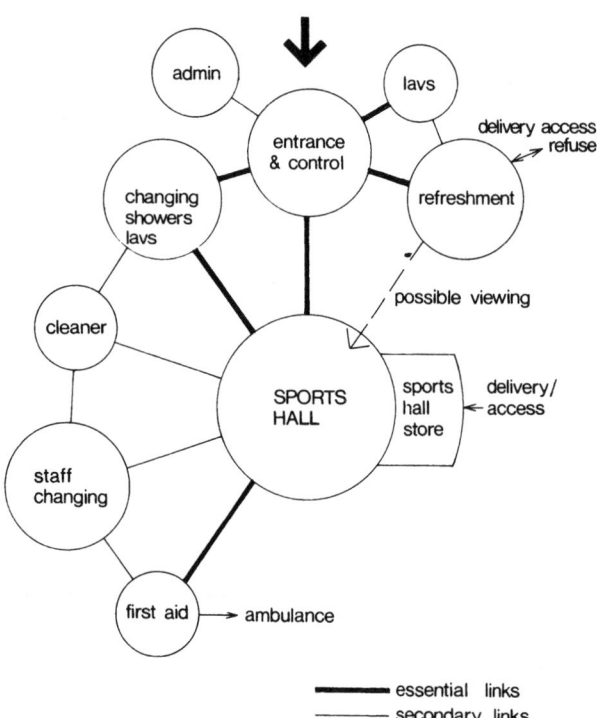

25.3 *Main elements of a dry sports centre*

essential links
secondary links

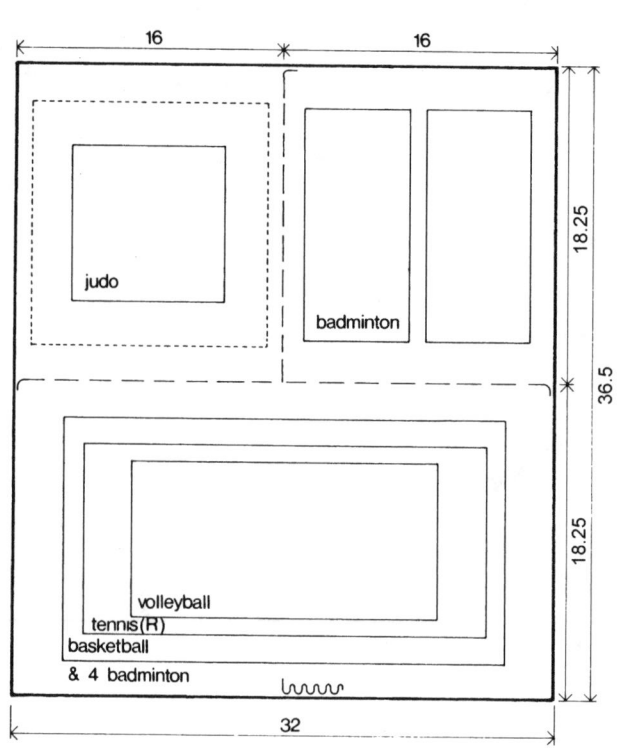

25.5 *Alternative arrangements for large sports halls*

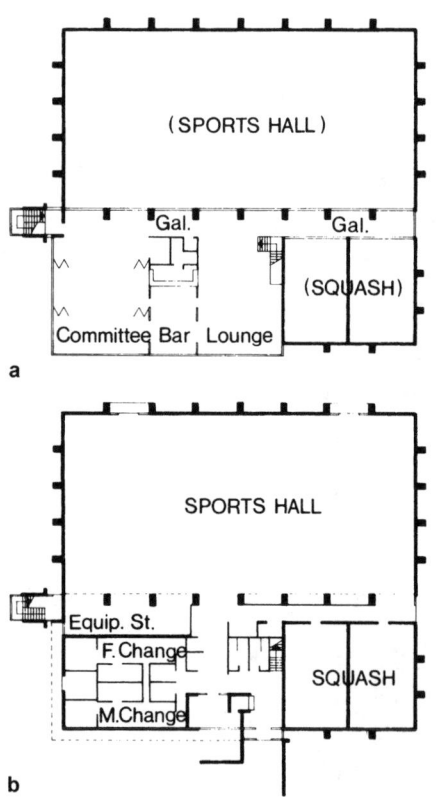

25.4 *Harpenden, a small compactly designed centre. The social areas have been positioned to take advantage of the parkland site.* **a** *First floor.* **b** *Ground floor*

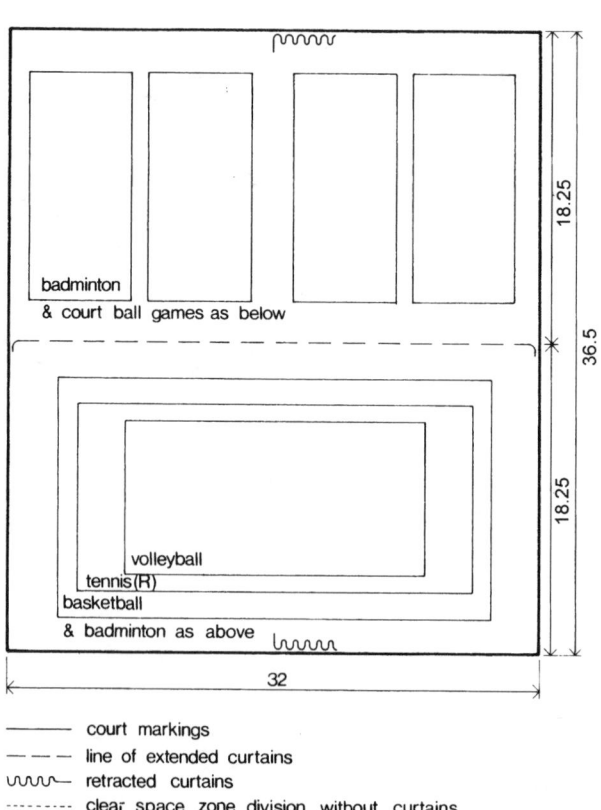

court markings
line of extended curtains
retracted curtains
clear space zone division without curtains

25.6 *Alternative arrangements for large sports halls*

The same floor area may provide for international standard in one or two sports and at the same time offer a wide variety of other activities at a lower standard. Typical arrangements are shown in **25.5** to **25.18**.

3.03 Height

The height of the underside of the roof structure, or the ceiling if there is one, above the floor is specified by each sport's governing body, and this is a critical design factor. Badminton, tennis and

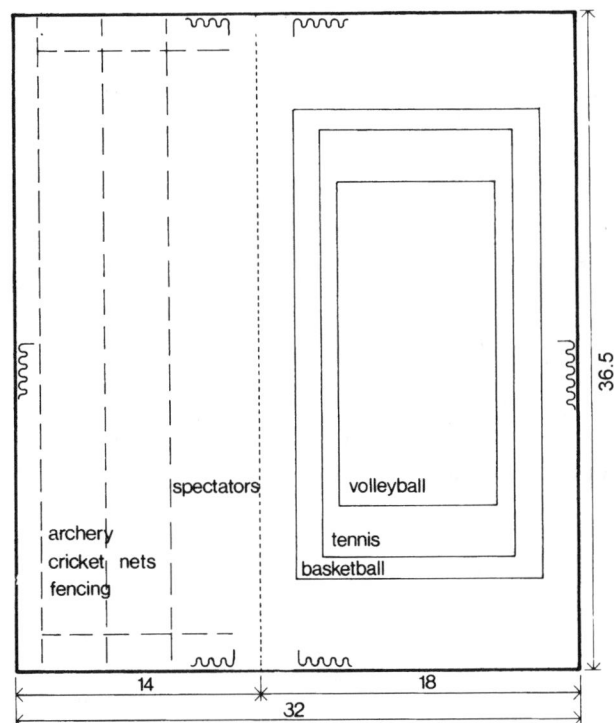

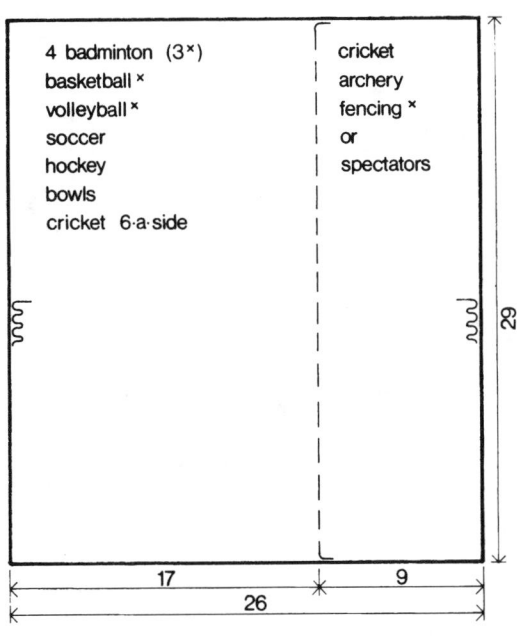

25.7 *Alternative arrangements for large sports halls*

×to N & C standard in given location

25.9 *Alternative arrangements for medium-size halls*

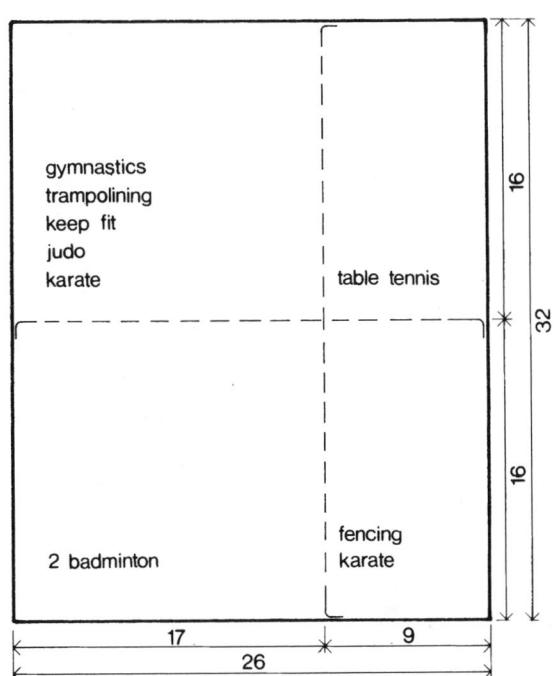

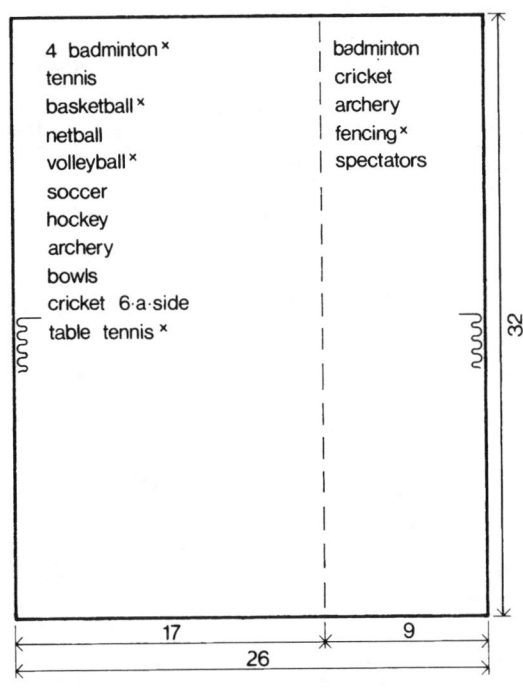

25.8 *Alternative arrangements for medium-size halls*

× to N & C standard in given location

25.10 *Alternative arrangements for medium-size halls*

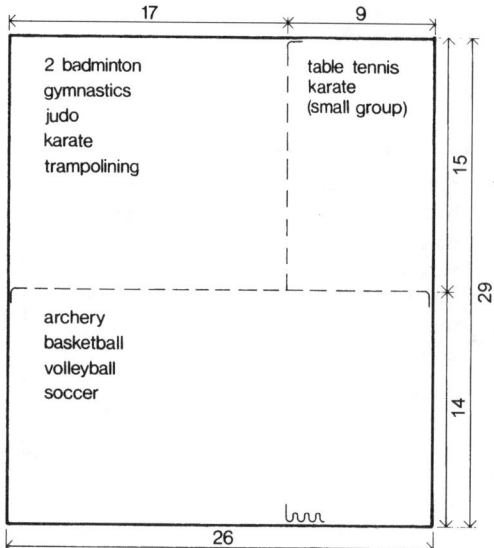

25.11 *Alternative arrangements for medium-size halls*

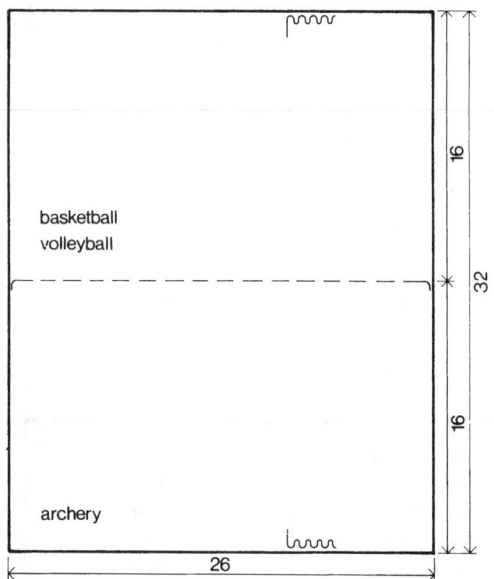

25.12 *Alternative arrangements for medium-size halls*

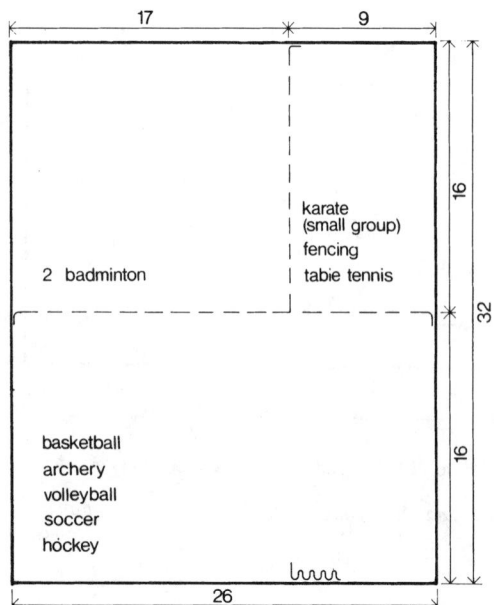

25.13 *Alternative arrangements for medium-size halls*

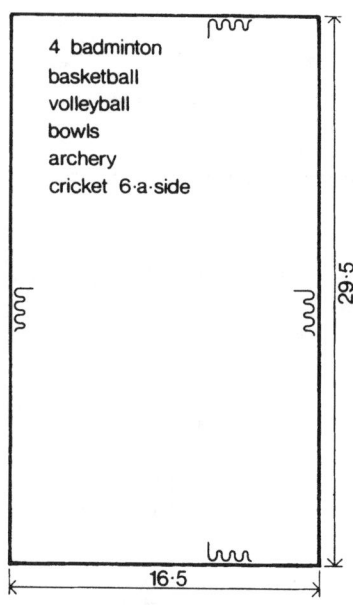

25.14 *For small halls*

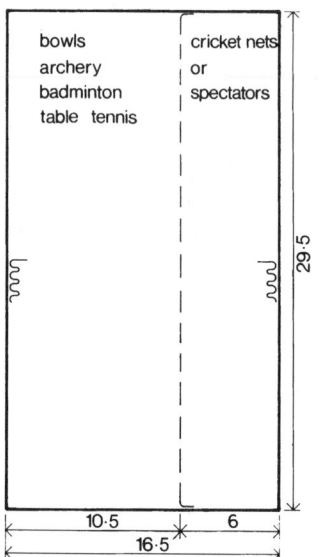

25.15 *For small halls*

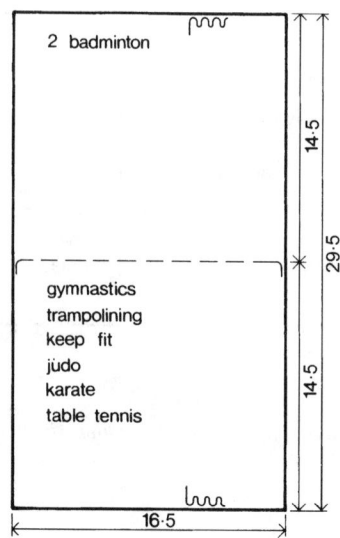

25.16 *For small halls*

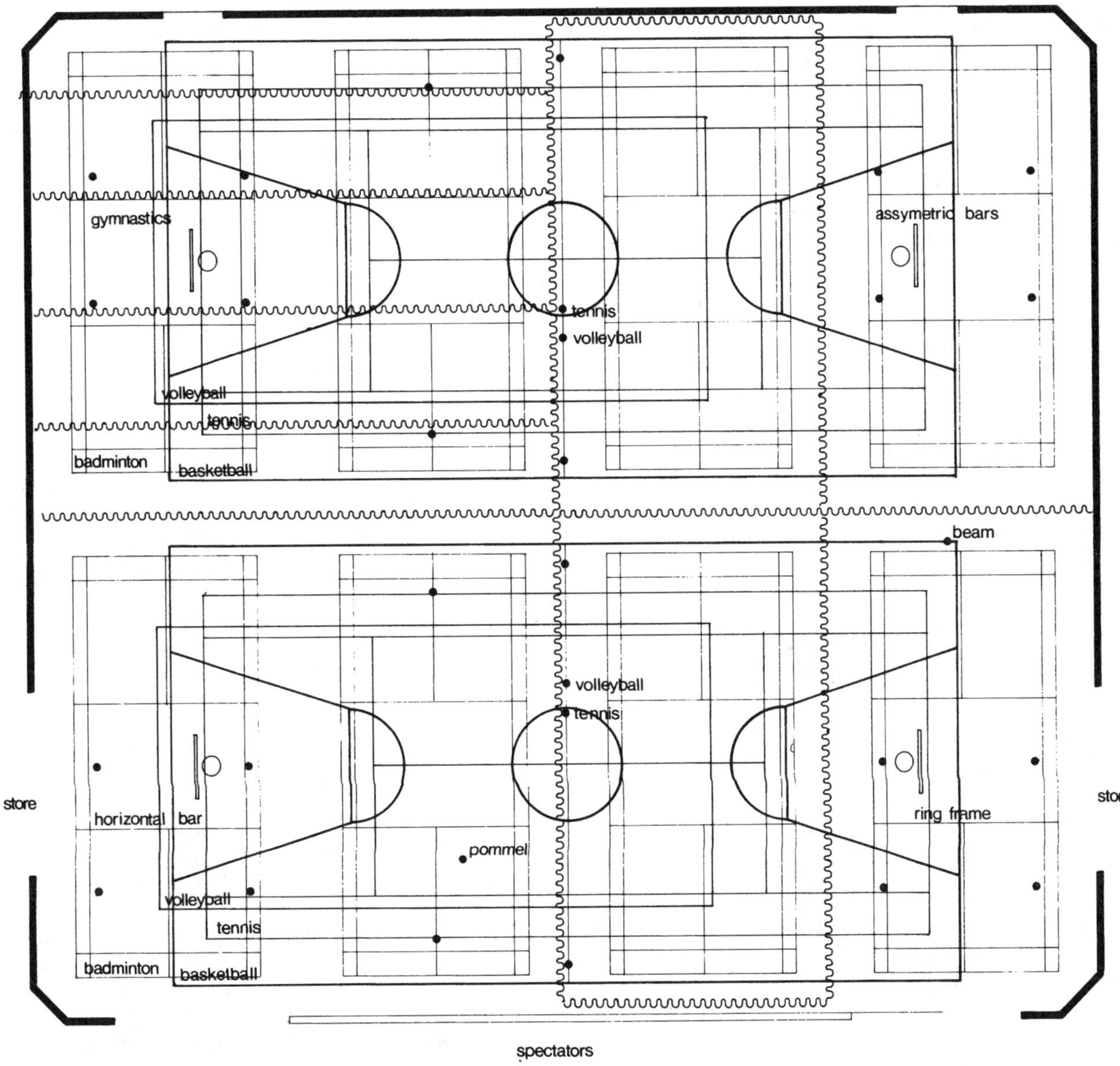

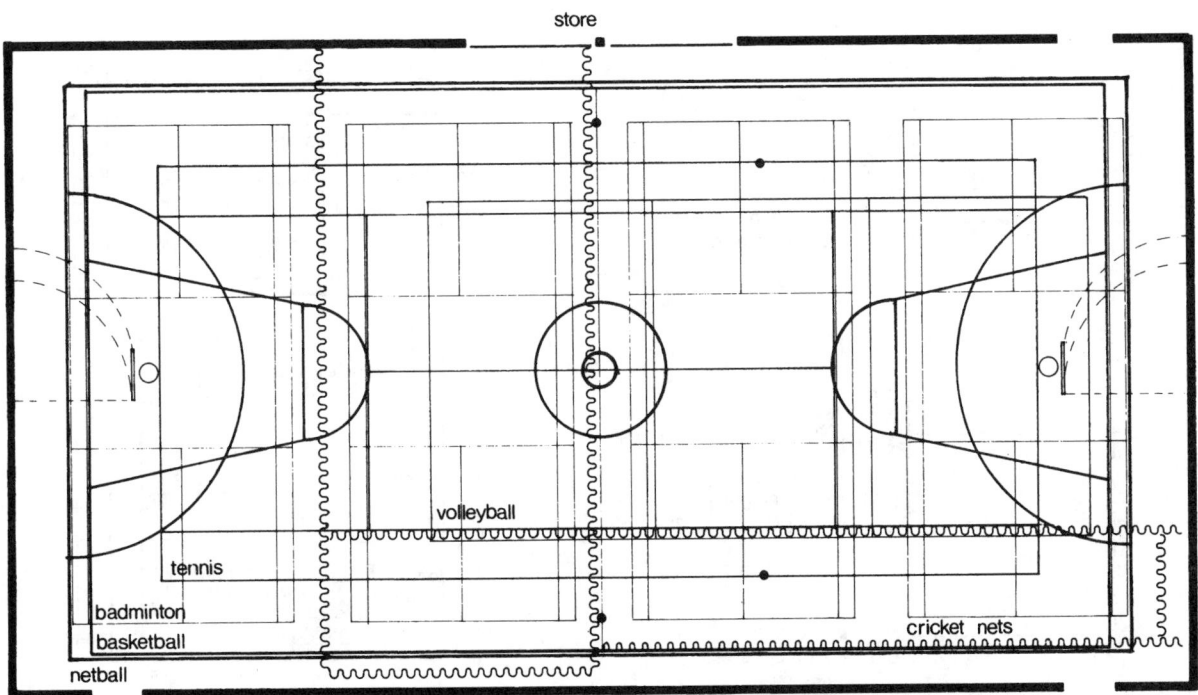

25.17 *Wycombe sports centre: plan of court markings and equipment fixings in sports hall*

25.18 *Tamworth sports centre: plan of court markings and equipment fixings*

trampolining require an unrestricted height of 9.1 m for international competition, while 7.6 is necessary at C level in all sports except those for which height is not critical. However, a height greater than justified by the intended use will increase running costs in heating, lighting and maintenance.

3.04 Construction

The construction and fabric of the hall should be such as to minimise damage, both accidental and from vandalism. Sports halls should only be naturally lit from above; any form of vertical glazing will produce some glare.

3.05 Activities

The sizes required for various activities in the sports hall are shown in **25.19** to **25.32**, (scale 1:500).

4 ANCILLARY HALLS

To economise in the use of the large sports halls, larger centres have practice halls suitable for some smaller-scale activities. The two suggested sizes are:

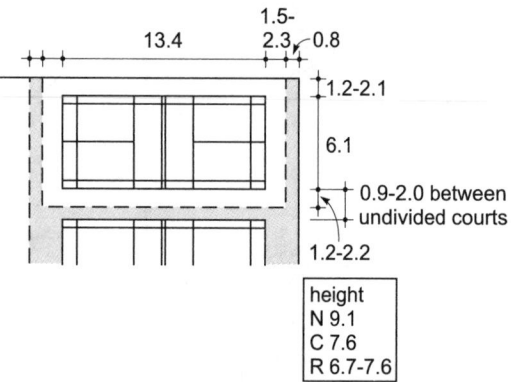

25.19 *Badminton, a doubles court for all standards of play. Where courts are placed side by side, tournaments are held with seating and play on alternate courts. Heights lower than 7.6 m are discouraged by the Badminton Association of England*

- 15 × 12 × 3.5 to 4.5 m
- 21–24 × 12 × 4.5 m with a divider.

Sizes for various activities in this type of hall are given in **25.33** to **25.40** (scale 1:500). For yoga, each person will lie on the floor on a mat or blanket and will ideally need a clear area of 2.5 m diameter.

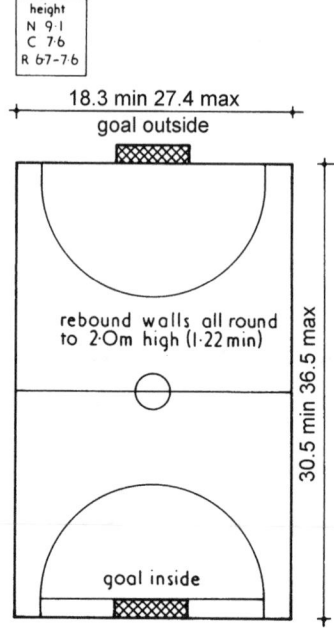

25.21 *Five-a-side football. This needs rebound walls all round to about a height of 2 m, but can be adapted to the available space. In a medium-size sports hall **25.10**, the playing area is the size of the hall. At a recreational level the game may be played in a small size hall, about 30 × 15 m being regarded as a reasonable minimum. Depending on age and sizes of players, their numbers on the pitch could be reduced as necessary for satisfaction. This game can also be played out of doors, but difficulties may be experienced in installing suitably robust rebound walls*

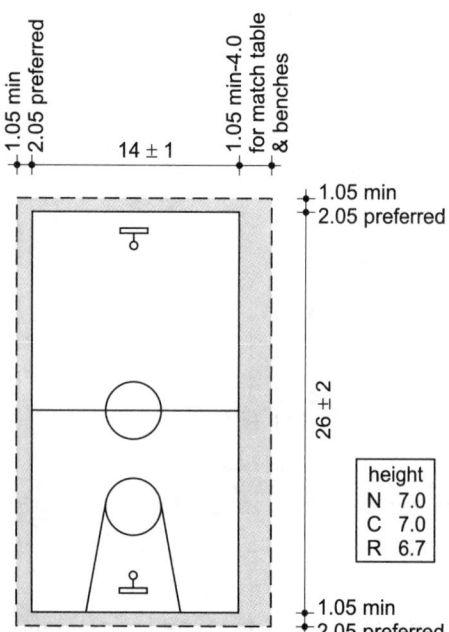

25.20 *Basketball. At a recreational level this game can be played in a school gymnasium 21.3 × 12.2 m*

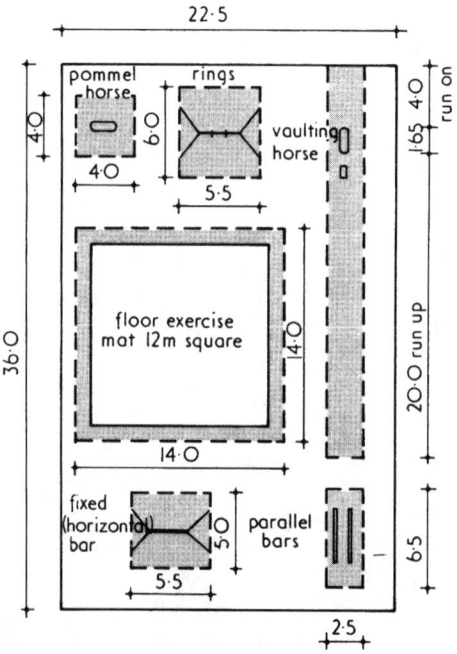

25.22 *Men's gymnastics. See **25.54** for special practice spaces*

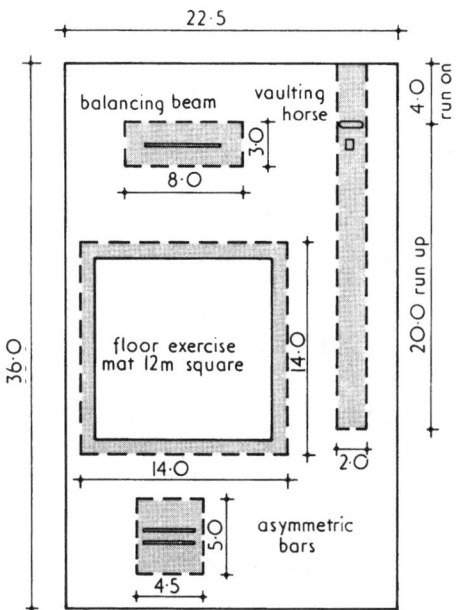

25.23 *Women's gymnastics. See* **25.54**

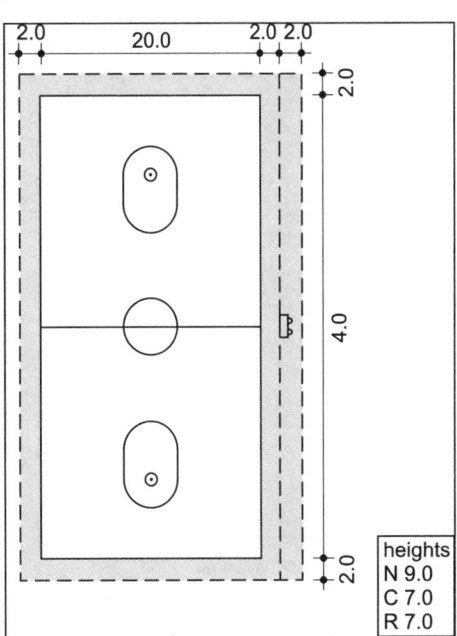

25.26 *Korfball. In halls of smaller dimensions, allow for full safety margins, keep pitch width about 18–20 m, and maximum possible length up to 40 m*

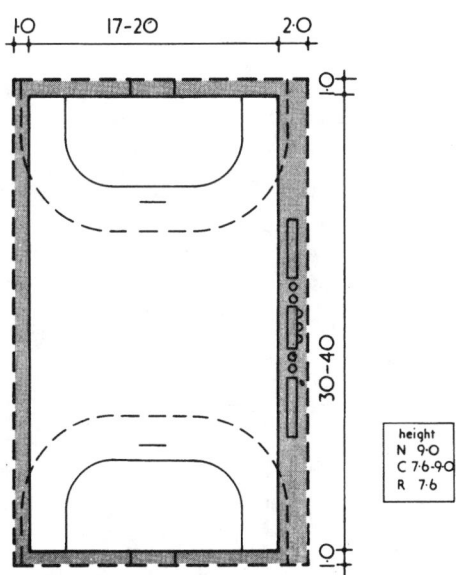

25.24 *Handball, seven-a-side*

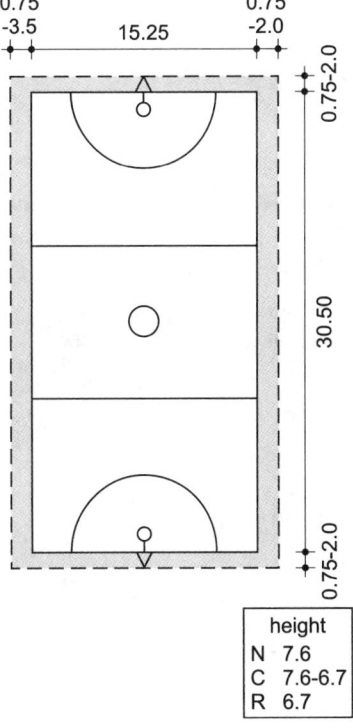

25.27 *Netball*

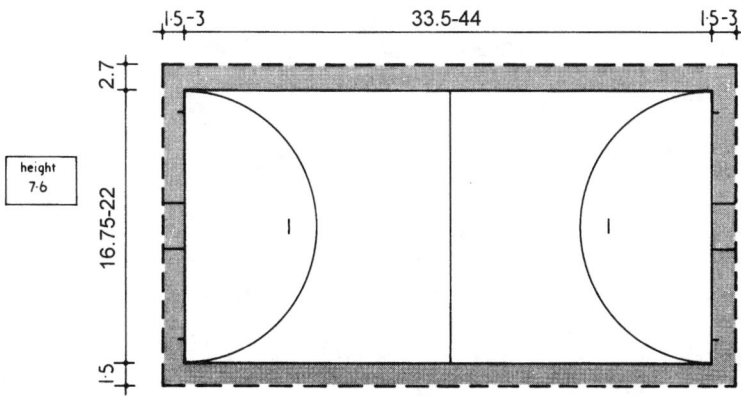

25.25 *Hockey. Team sizes are adjusted according to the size of the available pitch. Side boards should be provided 100 × 100 mm with a 20 mm inward tilt*

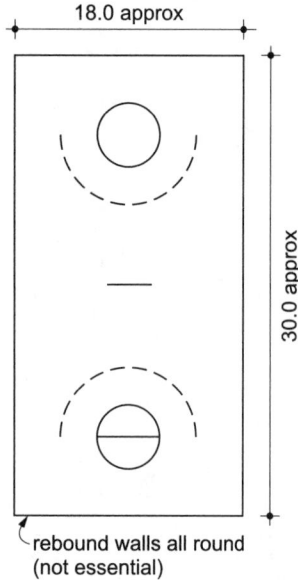

25.28 *Pop Lacrosse. This has superseded indoor women's lacrosse. It can also be played out of doors, when there is no boundary. The size approximates to four badminton courts, and could be played on a five-a-side football pitch. For further details, refer to the English Lacrosse Union, Ashton-under-Lyne, Lancs, or the All England Women's Lacrosse Association, Birmingham*

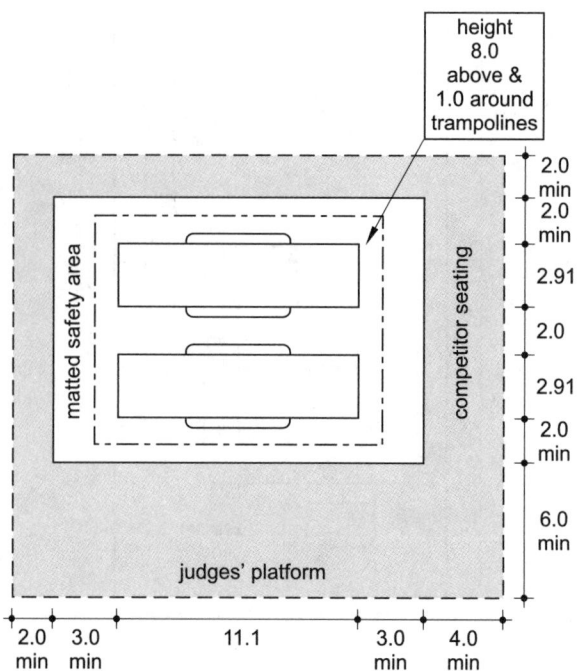

25.30 *Trampoline. The 'bed' is 0.95 to 1.05 m above the ground. Synchronised competitions must be parallel to each other and 2 m apart. Note extended length of end frame units from that previously published*

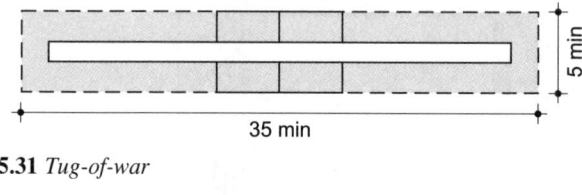

25.31 *Tug-of-war*

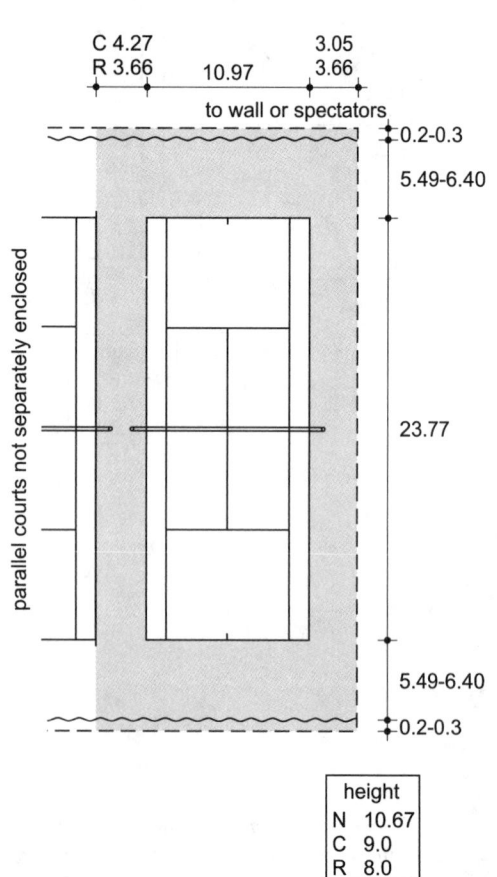

25.29 *Tennis*

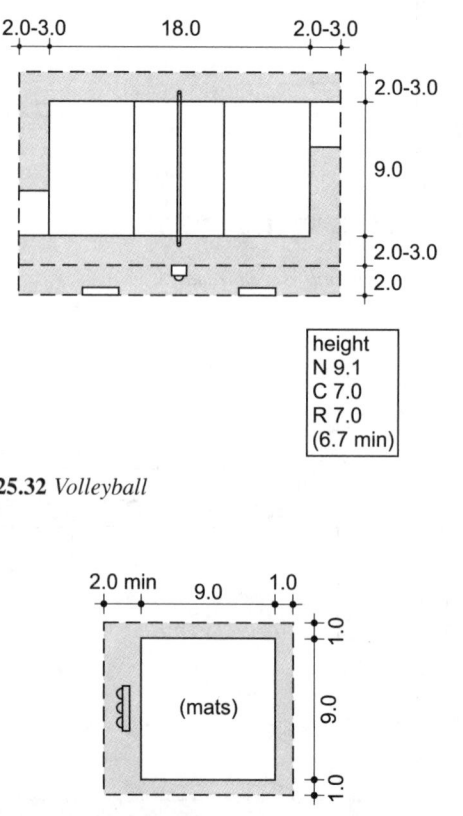

25.32 *Volleyball*

25.33 *Aikido*

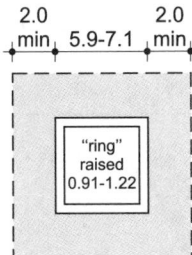

25.34 *Boxing. A ring for recreational purposes may be only 3.6 m square. For competitions, in addition to the ring and spectator accommodation the following are needed:*

● *Medical examination room*
● *Weighing room*
● *Gloving-up room*
● *Administrative facilities*
● *Lighting above the ring*
● *Water supply to each 'corner'*

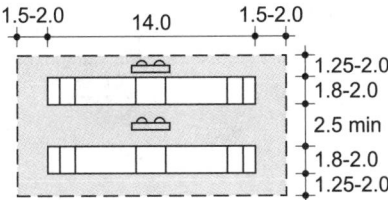

25.35 *Fencing pistes*

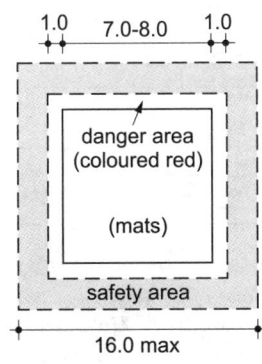

25.36 *Judo*

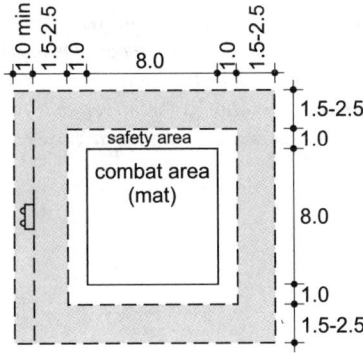

25.37 *Karate. Regional competitions require three international size combat areas*

25.38 *Kendo*

25.39 *Table tennis. See Table III for overall dimensions. The table is 0.76 m high, and normally requires a space 1.4 × 1.6 × 0.5 m for storage. When in use, each table requires individual lighting*

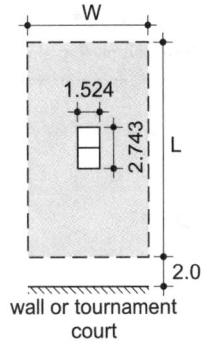

height	
N	7.6
C	4.5
R	3.5

25.40 *Wrestling*

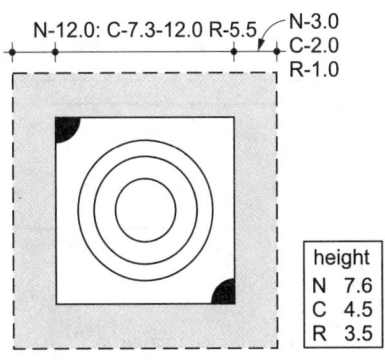

25.41 *Small projectile hall:* **a** *Section.* **b** *Plan*

5 PROJECTILE HALLS

25.41 to **25.43** show plans and sections of a range of projectile rooms, and Table II shows which sports can be covered by them. The spaces required are given in **25.44** to **25.48** (scale 1:500).

Where the projectile room is to be used for firearms shooting, the construction must be to safety standards and robust enough to withstand the use. It may be found that this use will severely restrict the projectile hall's use for other activities.

Table II Projectile halls

	Large 30.3 × 12.8 × 4.6	Medium 30.3 × 9.75 × 3.6–4.6	Small 30.3 × 5.3 × 3.6
Air rifle	12 firing points	8 firing points	4 firing points
Archery	3 details × 6 archers 3 targets	3 details of 4 archers range 18 m	2 details of 4 archers
Bowls	2/4.5 × 27 m roll-up rinks (if no shooting)	1 roll-up rink (if no shooting)	1 rink
Cricket	3 nets 6-a-side cricket	2 nets	1 net
Fencing	1 piste 4 practice pistes	1 piste	1 piste
Golf practice	4 ranges	3 ranges	1 range
Pistol shooting	7 firing points 10 with side screens	5 firing points	3 firing points
Rifle shooting	12 firing points ranges 25 m, 25 yd, 15 yd	9 firing points	4 firing points
Table squash	15 tables	8 tables	4 tables
Table tennis	15 tables	8 tables	4 tables

Table III Dimensions for table tennis playing space (m)

Standard of play	L	W	Ceiling height	Clear height below lights
International matches	14.0	7.0	4.20	4.05
Inter-league and inter-county matches	11.0–14.0 min	5.50–7.0 min	4.20	4.05
Practice and inter-club matches	10.0	5.0	4.20	4.05
Tournaments (more than one table)	8.0	5.0	4.20	4.05
Recreational play	7.6	4.6	–	2.7

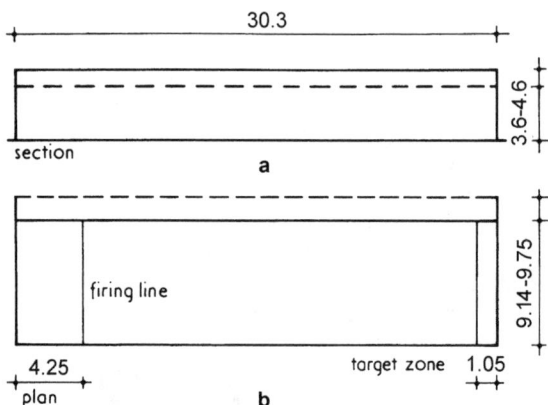

25.42 *Medium-Projectile hall:* **a** *Section.* **b** *Plan*

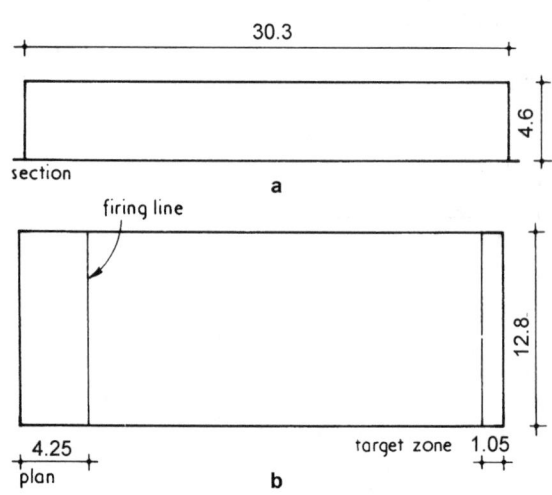

25.43 *Large projectile hall:* **a** *Section.* **b** *Plan*

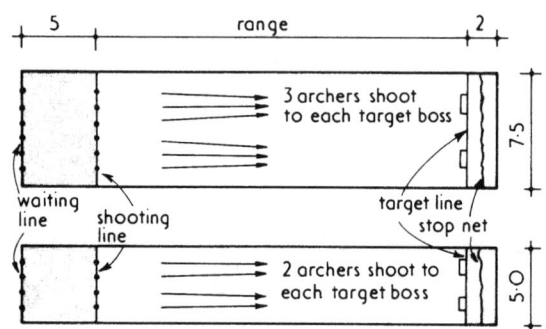

25.44 *Archery. International and national shoots require ranges of 30, 25 and 18 m, and of 20 yards (18.288 m). For club and recreational shoots 15 yards (13.716 m) will do, but 30 m is preferred for competition practice. Archers stand no closer together than 1.25 m when on the shooting line, with two or three to each target. The minimum ceiling height is 3 m. Where there is no public access the distance between the side wall and the first target should be at least 1.2 m. Where spectator accommodation is required, advice should be sought from the Grand National Archery Society. Storage is required for straw bosses and stands, preferably at the target end; and lockable storage for portable bow racks and tackle boxes*

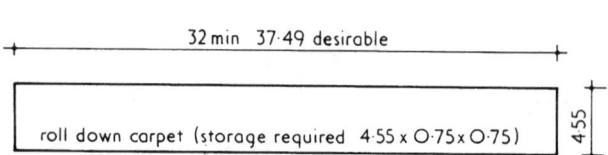

25.45 *Bowling. A single rink in a projectile hall. See also* **25.52**

Table IV Dimensions for indoor athletics tracks (m)

Lap length	Length of straight (s)	Length of bend (B)*	Radius of bend (R)†	Overall length (L₁)		Overall width (W)		Space for sprint straight (L₂)
				6-track	4-track	6-track	4-track	
200	35‡	65	20.49	88	84	53	49	75.98
	50	50	15.716	93.44	89.44	43.44	39.44	81.44
	52.25	47.75	15.0	94.25	90.25	42	38	82.25
	65	35‡	10.94	98.88	94.88	33.88	29.88	86.88
160	35‡	45	14.124	75.25	71.25	40.25	36.25	63.25
	40	40	12.532	77.06	73.06	37.06	33.06	65.06
	45	35‡	10.941	78.88	74.88	33.88	29.88	66.88

*Measured 200 mm from inside of outer white line around flat-edged track, or 300 mm inside a raised border or edge framework.
†Nett radius allowing for 200 mm deduction. The smaller the radius, the greater the inclination of the banking, 10°—18° max.
‡A European Athletic Association regulation minimum dimension.

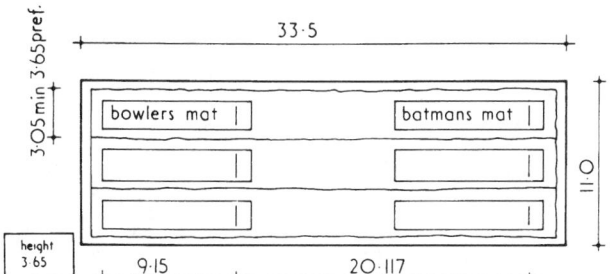

25.46 *Cricket practice nets. For the six-a-side game (not illustrated) the playing area is 30.4–36.5 × 18.9–30.4 × 6.1–7.6 m high*

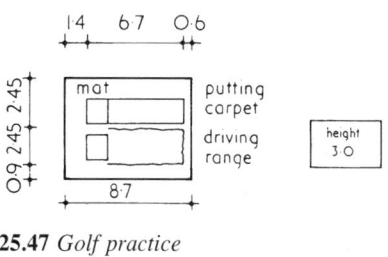

25.47 *Golf practice*

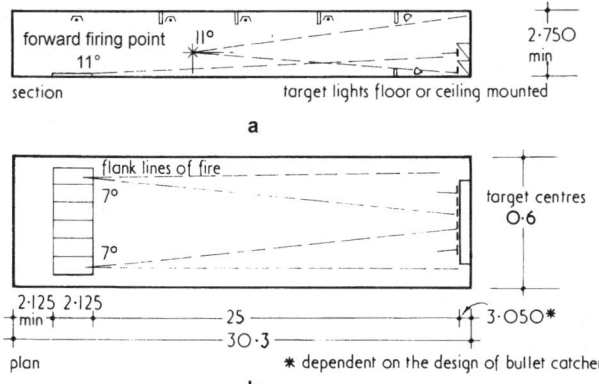

25.48 *Shooting range, small-bore target. For rifle shooting, ranges at 25 m, 25 yd and 15 yd are required at minimum 1.05 m centres. Pistols (where permitted) use 25 m and 25 yd at 1.8 m centres, or 1.15 m with side screens: **a** Section. **b** Plan*

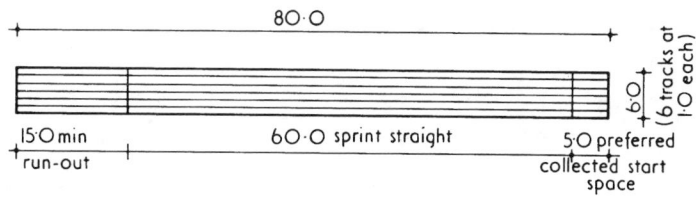

25.49 *Athletics: requirements for straight sprint*

6 SPECIAL SPACES

There are a number of activities that need spaces permanently and exclusively reserved for them. This may be due to the weight or size of the equipment, such as billiards/snooker, or because the playing area is closely defined, such as squash or real tennis. For some of these, semi-portable equipment is now being produced, but these are generally designed for special occasions such as national championships. The critical sizes for these special spaces are given in **25.49** to **25.59** (scale 1:500 except where shown otherwise).

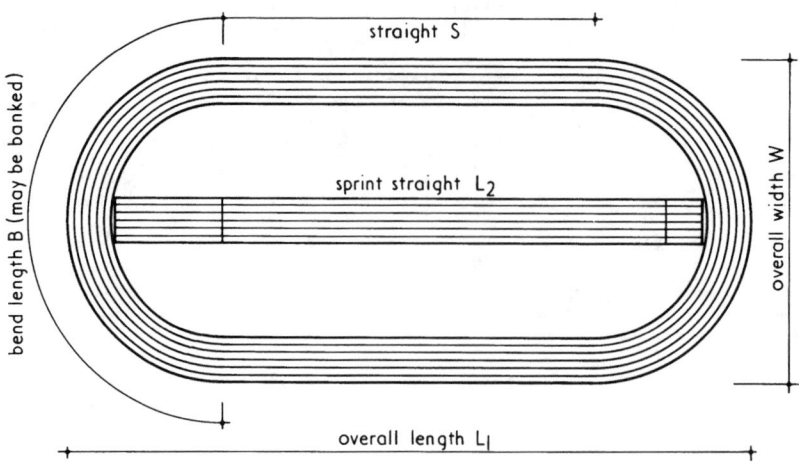

25.50 *Athletics: indoor tracks 200 and 160 metre laps, with straight sprint in centre. See Table IV for dimensions. It is no longer considered satisfactory to fit a running track inside the cycle track in* **25.53**. *If spectator accommodation is needed around the track, a building of considerable clear span is necessary as supports in the central area are not acceptable*

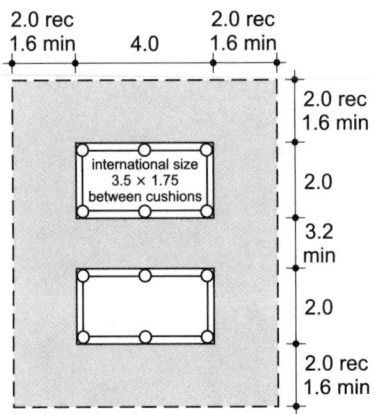

25.51 *Billiards and snooker. The agreed international size, due to become mandatory in 2025, of 3.5 × 1.75 m measured inside the cushions, has had little acceptance, even in major competitions*

25.52 *Bowling. Four rinks are the minimum for recreation, six are required for tournaments*

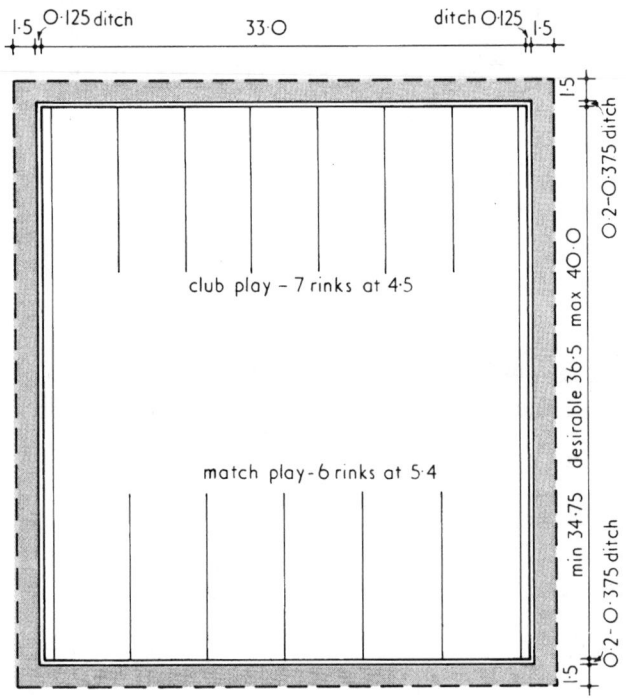

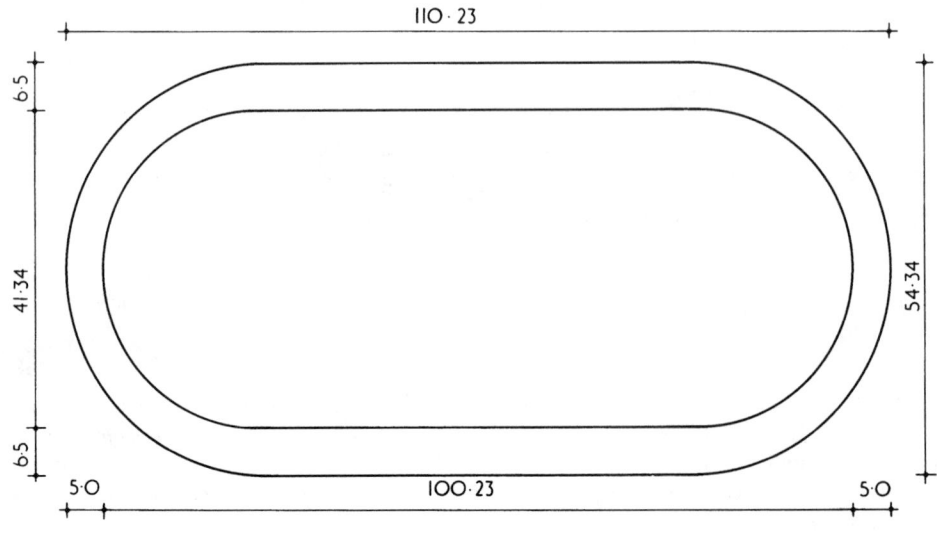

25.53 *Cycling, 250 metre track. This is relatively steeply banked. The 333⅓ m track [24.48] can be used internally*

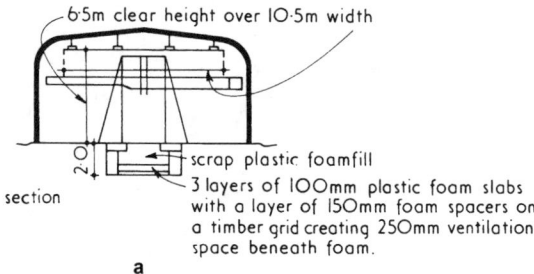

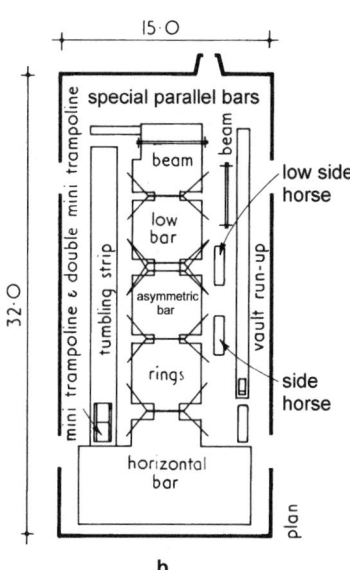

25.54 *Gymnastics practice: training hall at Lilleshall Hall NSC:* **a** *Cross-section.* **b** *Plan*

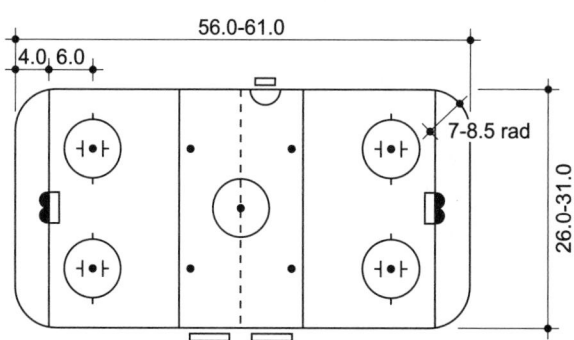

25.55 *Ice hockey. Rinks are usually sized to accommodate the 'pad'; this should be surrounded by a 1.2 m high barrier*

7 BIBLIOGRAPHY

Geraint John and Helen Heard (eds) *Handbook of sports and recreational building design*, Vol. 2, *Indoor Sports*, 2nd edn, Architectural Press 1995

The Oxford Companion to Sports and Games, Oxford University Press, 1976, also as a Paladin paperback

Rules of the Game, Paddington Press, 1974, also as republished by Literary Guild and Bantam Books

Information published by the ruling bodies for each particular sport.

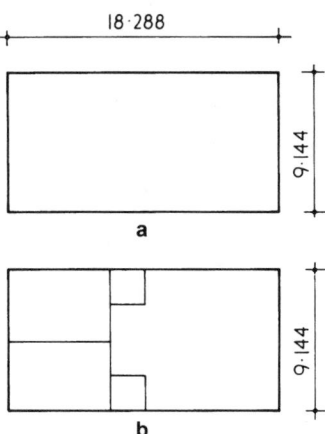

25.56 *Rackets, or racquets:* **a** *Section.* **b** *Plan*

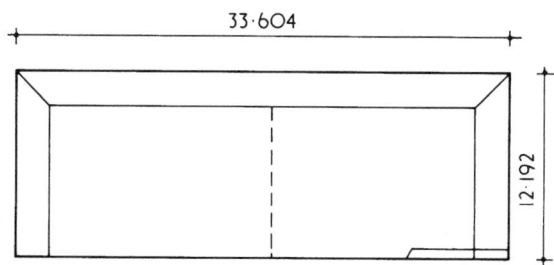

25.57 *Real (or royal) tennis. The dimensions are those at Hampton Court which is reputed to be the widest and among the longest*

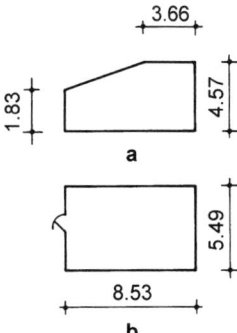

25.58 *Rugby fives:* **a** *Section.* **b** *Plan*

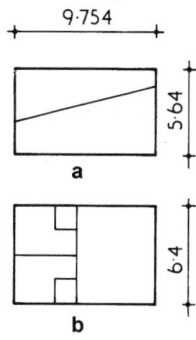

25.59 *Squash. All dimensions are highly critical and are to internal finished surfaces, which are plastered to a special specification:* **a** *Section.* **b** *Plan*

26 Equestrian design

Rod Sheard and Frank Bradbeer

Rod Sheard is Senior Vice President in Hok & Lobb, a practice specialising in leisure facilities. Frank Bradbeer is an architect whose passions include good architecture of all periods, organs and horses

CI/SfB: 565
UDC: 725.88
Uniclass: F5676

Contents

1 GENERAL CONSIDERATIONS

1.01 Horse riding today
Facilities for keeping horses are mainly constructed for recreational riding, equestrian sport and breeding purposes. The use of horses for commercial haulage is unusual nowadays, and together with police or military facilities there is likely to be a specific brief.

1.02 Planning elements in private stables
Private stables range from a stable for one horse to large complexes to accommodate a thousand horses or more, complete with full health and training facilities. The principal elements remain the same, **26.1**, and are based on the physical and psychological requirements of the horses.

1 Boxes
- Loose boxes
- *Sick box/boxes (50 per cent larger)
- *Utility box/boxes

2 Stores
- Feed
- Hay
- Bedding
- Equipment (wheelbarrows, mowers, etc)

3 Housekeeping
- Tack room
- *Cleaning room
- *Drying room
- Staff lavatories/showers
- *Staff rest room
- *Office
- *Vet room

4 External facilities
- Midden
- *Washdown area
- Trailer parking
- Staff parking
- *Carriage store

5 Health/exercise
- Sand roll
- Lungeing yard
- Treadmill
- Weighing machine/weigh bridge
- Equine pool

*In many cases the accommodation will not require these items because of their small-scale activities.

A typical plan is shown in **26.2**.

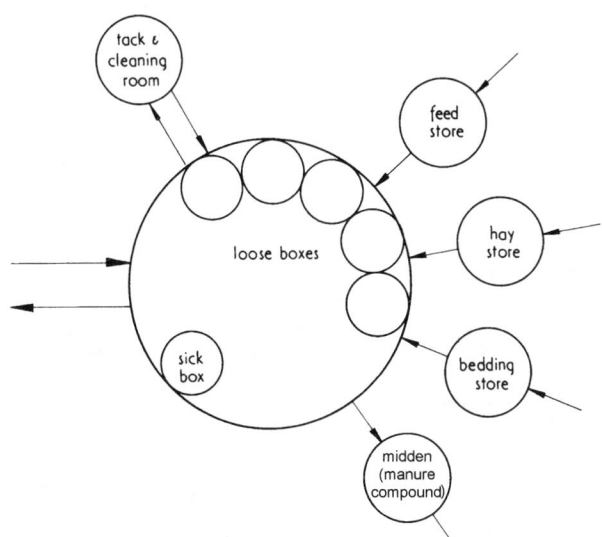

26.1 *Relationships between elements of the plan*

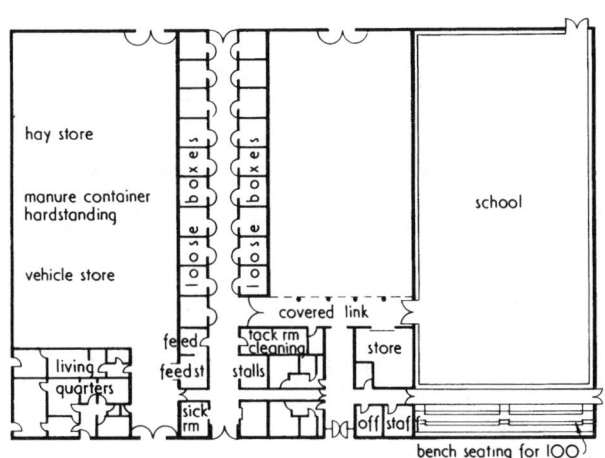

26.2 *Plan of Porter's Field Riding School, Leyton*

1.03 Dimensional criteria

Dimensionally standardised criteria may be applied:

- The size of the horse, with and without rider, **26.3** to **26.5**, Tables I and II
- Stabling and care of the horse, **26.6** to **26.9**
- Tack rooms, **26.10**

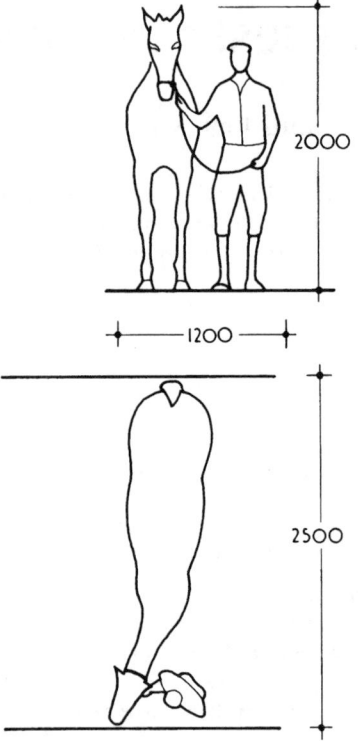

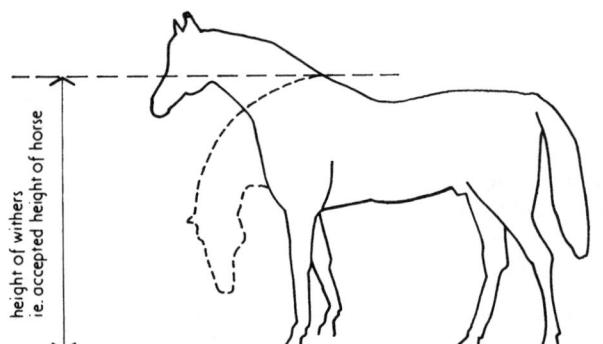

26.3 *Measurement of the height of a horse at the withers. Traditionally the height was measured in hands (4 inches), but a hand is equivalent to a decimeter (100 mm) within the limits of accuracy attainable. Table I gives the heights of a number of breeds of horses and ponies*

26.4 *The led horse.* **a** *Front view.* **b** *Plan*

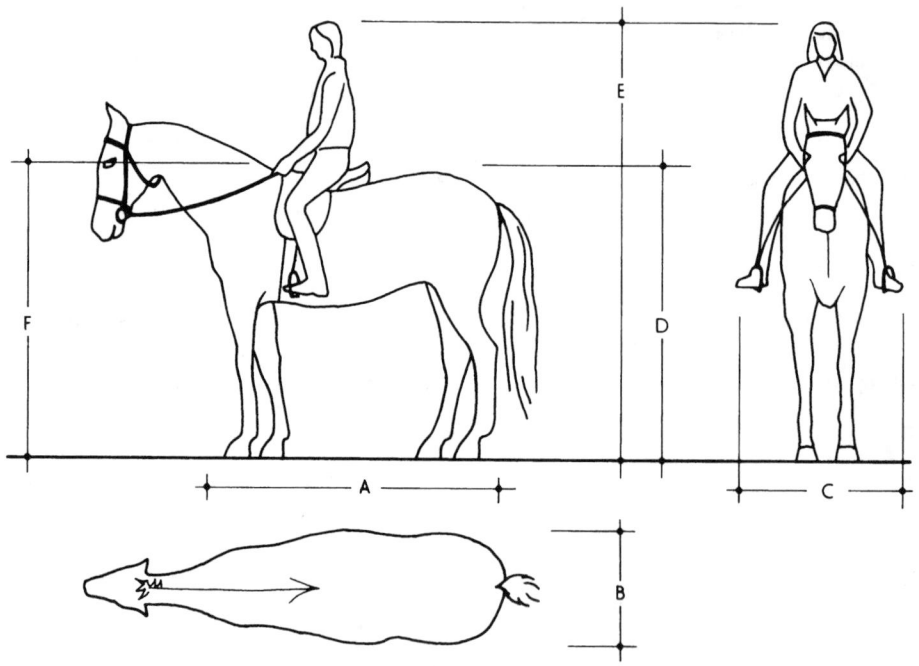

26.5 *Dimensions of the horse and rider, see Table II*

Table I Common breeds of horses and ponies, with heights in hands and equivalent metric measure, 26.3 (*1 hand = 4 inches, 12.2 hands = 12 hands + 2 inches*)

Breed	Height in hands	Height in mm	Breed	Height in hands	Height in mm
Horses			**Ponies**		
Cleveland bay	16	1625	Connemara	14.2	1475
Clydesdale	16	1625	Dartmoor	12	1220
Morgan	14–15	1420–1525	Exmoor	12.2	1270
Percheron	16–16.3	1625–1700	Fell	13.1	1345
Shire	17	1725	Highland	12.2–14.2	1270–1475
Suffolk	16	1625	New Forest	14.2	1475
Tennessee Walker	15.2	1575	Shetland	39 to 42 inches*	990–1065
Thoroughbred	16	1625	Welsh	12	1220

*Shetland ponies are always described in inches.

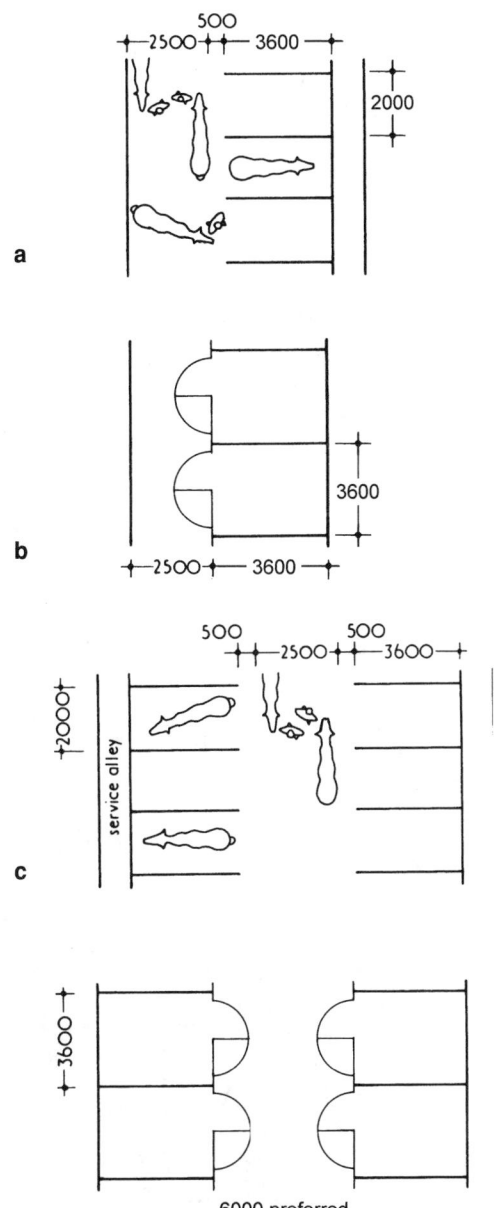

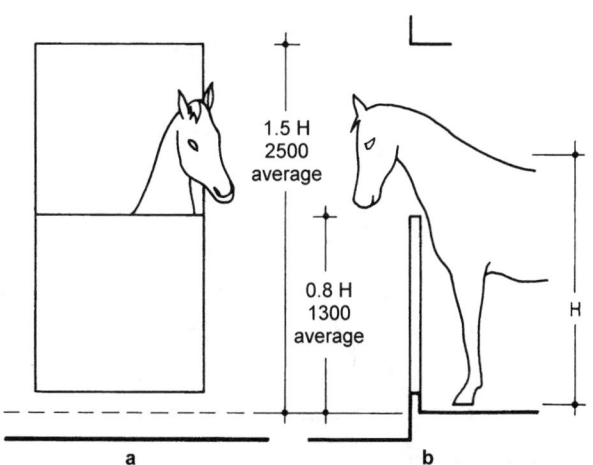

26.6 *Arrangements of stables. **a** Stalls on one side. **b** Loose boxes on one side. **c** Stalls on both sides. **d** Loose boxes on both sides: doors should not be directly opposite one another*

26.7 *The stable door. It is essential for the horse's mental well-being for it to see out – horses are inclined to be very inquisitive! H is the height at the withers (see **26.3**). **a** Front view. **b** Section*

Table II Typical dimensions of horse or pony and rider, 26.5

Dimension	Thoroughbred	New Forest pony	Welsh pony
A	1600	1450	1200
B	550	500	415
C	900	815	675
D	1620	1470	1215
E*	2450	2225	1840
F	1625	1475	1220

* Assuming that the rider is in proportion to the horse or pony

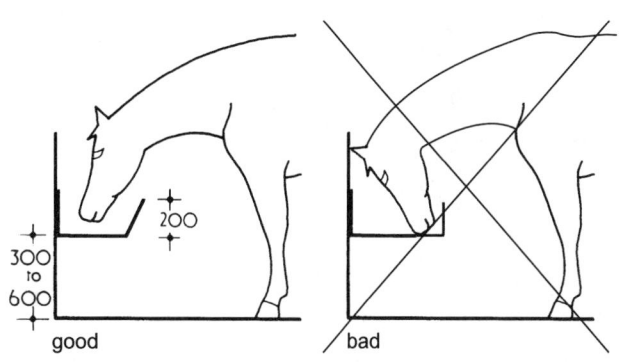

26.8 *Height of the manger*

26.9 *Veterinary box 'Stallapotheke'.*

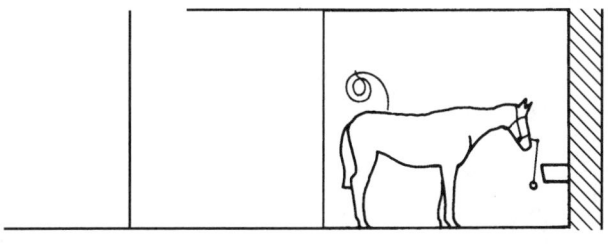

a *section.*

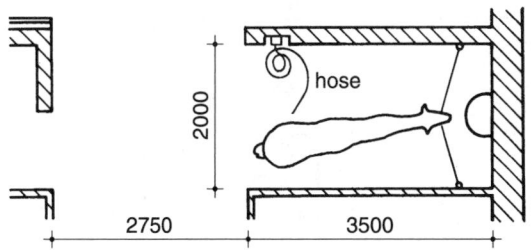

b *Plan*

- Schooling, **26.11** and **26.12**
- The dressage arena, **26.13**
- Polo, **26.14**
- Transportation, **26.15** to **26.17**

2 STABLING AND THE CARE OF THE HORSE

2.01 Environmental conditions

The principal requirements can be identified as follows:

1 Dryness and warmth.
2 Adequate ventilation without draughts
3 Adequate supply of water and good drainage
4 Good daylight and good artificial light

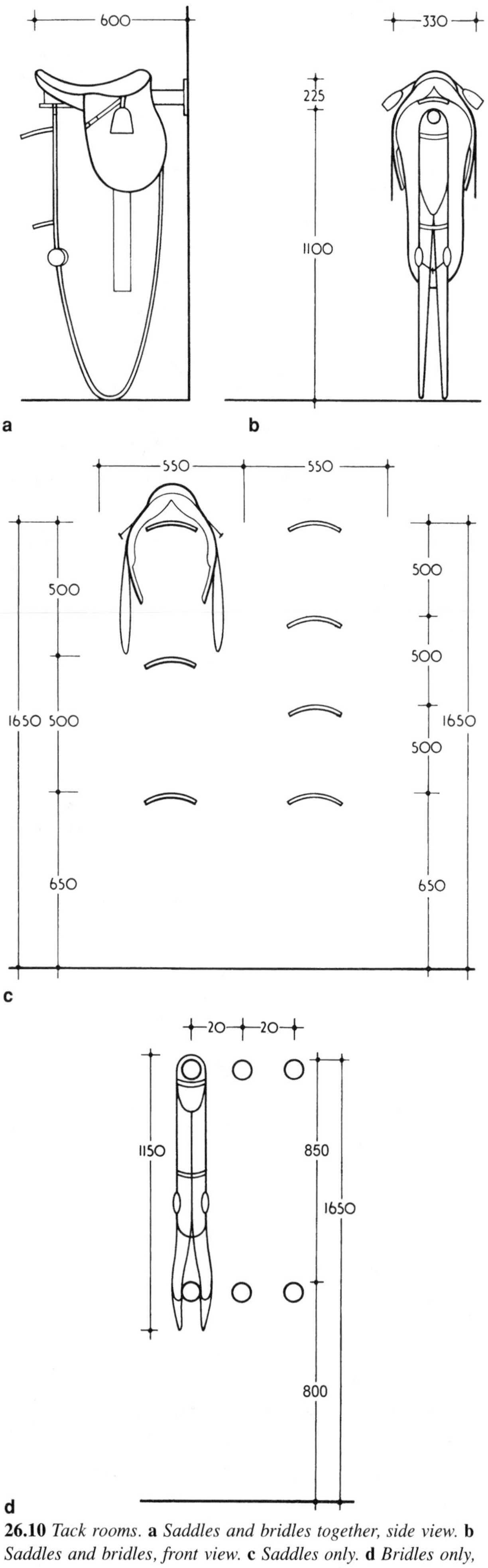

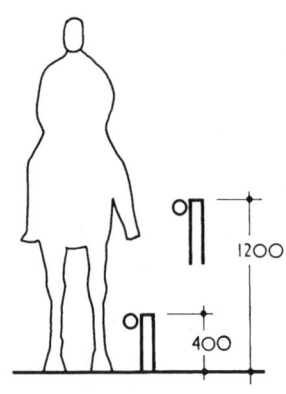

26.11 *Rails for the outside school*

26.10 *Tack rooms.* **a** *Saddles and bridles together, side view.* **b** *Saddles and bridles, front view.* **c** *Saddles only.* **d** *Bridles only, when kept separate*

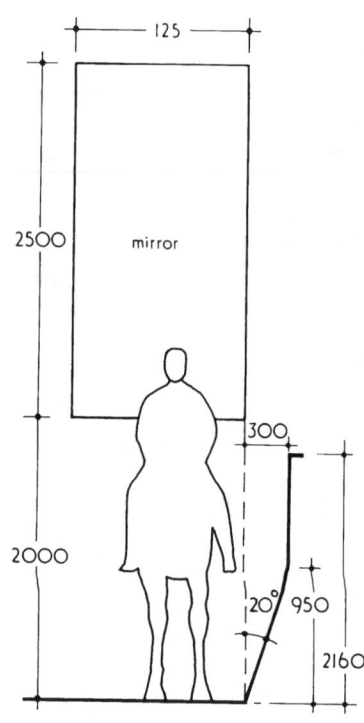

26.12 *Indoor school: batter to walls and arrangement of mirror tilted to give self-vision*

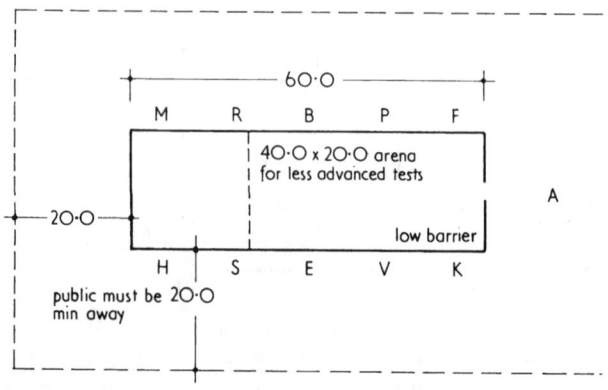

26.13 *Dressage arena*

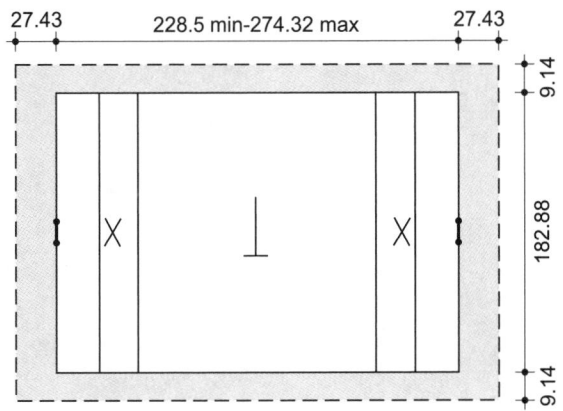

26.14 *Polo*

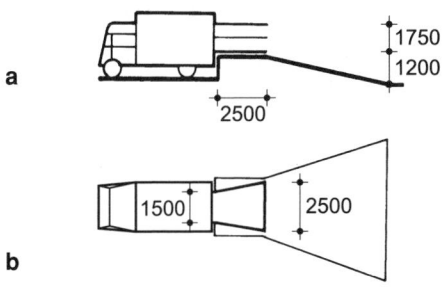

26.15 *Ramp for loading horses into horse-boxes or trailers.* **a** Section. **b** Plan

26.16 *Large trailer*

26.17 *Small trailer*

Siting

- On well-drained ground
- Avoid the tops of hills and hollows
- Protected from severe prevailing winds
- Avoid sites hemmed in without free circulation of air

Temperature

The stable should moderate extremes of exterior conditions. Therefore a degree of air circulation is helpful and adequate ventilation essential. However, care should be taken to avoid draughts.

Size

Unless a particularly small breed is kept the standard dimensions should be adhered to.

Noise

Sudden noise may startle horses and disrupt sleep during the night, therefore relationship to public roads or urban developments requires careful consideration.

2.02 Detail design

Floor

The floor should be impervious to moisture, hard wearing, non-slip, easily cleaned and protect the horse from any ground moisture. Selection of floor finish can vary from dense concrete, granolithic concrete or engineering brick-laid herringbone pattern to proprietary rubber mats and seamless rubber flooring.

Walls

The walls should be smooth for cleanliness and, wherever possible, free from projections. It is preferable that masonry walls are protected up to at least 120 mm by stout timber or plywood panelling on battens. Masonry should be painted white or a light shade to encourage cleanliness. Horses are gregarious animals and therefore it is normal for the partitions to be solid up to 1200–1500 mm and have a metal grille up to 2100 mm above floor level.

Ceilings

The ceiling should not be less than 3050 mm high and care should be exercised in the choice of materials to avoid the build-up of condensation.

Fire resistance

In large installations the fire resistance of the structure and the location of fire separation barriers should be carefully considered bearing in mind the difficulty of evacuating frightened horses and the often rural location.

Doors and windows

Doors to loose boxes should be positioned to one side of the box to allow the horse to keep clear of the draught when the upper half is left open. Doors to two adjoining boxes should not be placed next to each other. The door should open back to 180 degrees and any exposed edges be protected with a galvanised steel capping to avoid 'crib biting'. There should be no sharp arrises and a minimum clear width of 1200 mm. Windows should, where possible, be fitted at high level. Any low-level windows should have Georgian wired glass and a steel protective grille.

Fittings

Usually these will consist of a manger, drinking water receptacle and two tie rings. The exact position of these items will depend to some extent on the management of the stables, and to whether automatic replenishment is incorporated. Tie rings are generally fixed between 1525 and 1800 mm in order to avoid a horse dropping a leg over the tie.

Services

An exterior quality plug socket will be required (one per six stalls maximum) for portable equipment. This should be sited outside the stall. Artificial lighting should provide illumination to both sides of the horse switched from outside the stalls.

Drainage

The floor should be laid to a fall of between 1:80 and 1:60 to a gulley outside the stall or loose box. Channels may be formed to enhance drainage. Good housekeeping is the key to drainage and all gullies should be equipped with a removable perforated bucket to collect bedding and feed that may wash down the gulley.

Midden

The midden must be arranged so that effluent does not run away into groundwater. There should be a gulley and an adjacent water supply to enable regular periodic cleaning. For hygiene reasons it should be sited away from the stables.

27 Places of worship

Leslie Fairweather, Atba Al-Samarraie and David Adler

Leslie Fairweather was editor of The Architects' Journal
Atba Al-Samarraie is Principal Structural Engineer and Consultant in Practice at
Bullen Consultant's Bradford office. His passion is beautiful buildings, architecture
in general and Islamic architecture in particular. He has designed a number of
mosques

CI/Sfb: 6
UDC: 726
Uniclass: F6

Contents

Part A Guide to denominations

1 INTRODUCTION

1.01 Scope
This chapter will cover churches and places of worship for various Christian denominations, synagogues, mosques and Hindu temples. Places of local worship only are dealt with, not larger buildings like cathedrals or those with social spaces, which are not significantly different from social spaces in secular buildings, and for which Chapter 21 (Community Centres) provides further advice.

1.02 History and tradition
In the architecture of places of worship the architect is bound to be more concerned with tradition than in other fields. Users are more conscious of history (and more sensitive about it) than most other clients: they will not allow an architect to ignore established precedents and will expect a full understanding of them.

In recent years, changes in Christian worship have taken place. These are largely connected with the changes in the understanding of ecclesiastical history brought about by the liturgical movement.

Exact details of the forms of worship and building procedures should be discussed with the local religious community, and the architectural implications thoroughly understood. A fairly detailed general guide to the history, procedures and forms of worship (with architectural implications) of the Church of England, the Roman Catholic Church, the Presbyterian Church, the Salvation Army, the Methodist Church and the Society of Friends, is given in *Church buildings*, originally published as a series in *The Architects' Journal* and later in book form (now out of print).

2 CHURCH OF ENGLAND

2.01 The buildings, and how they are used for worship
After the Reformation the Church of England inherited many medieval, mostly Gothic, buildings, strongly directional in their east–west orientation and with the main action remote from the congregation. The people therefore had lost the sense that they were engaged with the clergy in a common action and tended to become spectators with an individualistic rather than a corporate response to the liturgy. The church has now moved into a period of experiment in which it greater fuller expression of the corporate nature of worship and the equal importance of the Word (which must be heard) and of Sacrament within a building which remains true to the Anglican sense of proportion.

2.02 Altar, priest and people
During the period of the Oxford Movement's influence the 'north end position', **27.1**, was largely superseded by the 'eastward position' in which the priest would face the altar with his back to the people, **27.2**. This way of celebrating the Eucharist is contrary to the spirit of the Anglican liturgy. The eastward position has largely been replaced by the one in which the priest faces the people across the altar, **27.3**.

2.03 The main services
The six main services of the Church of England are:

- The Eucharist
- The offices of matins and evensong
- Baptism
- Confirmation
- The solemnisation of matrimony and
- Burial of the dead.

If the architectural requirements of these are catered for, so will those for almost any other service likely to take place in the church.

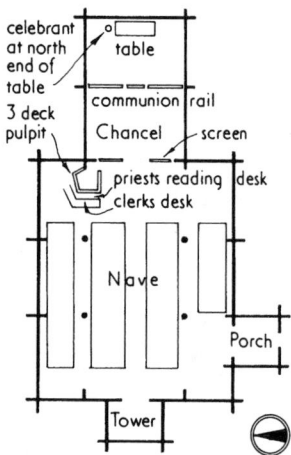

27.1 *Communion table is placed against east wall, priest stands at north end*

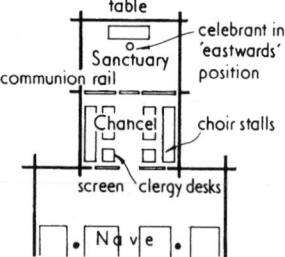

27.2 *Eastward position: priest faces altar with his back to the congregation*

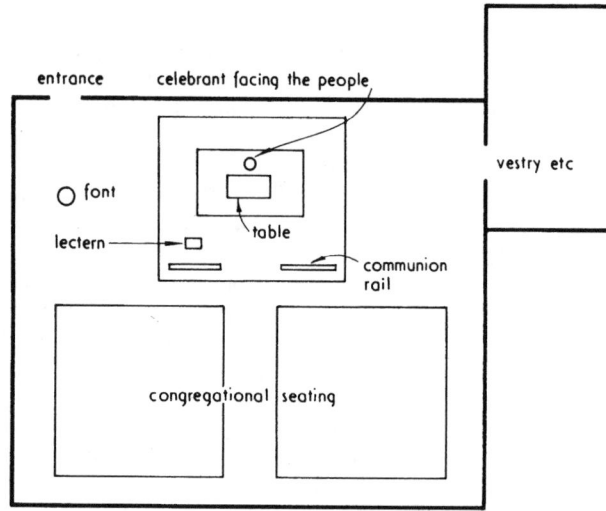

27.3 *One of the many variations of plan where the priest faces the congregation across the altar. The seating may extend around three sides of the altar*

2.04 Church design

Apart from the altar, the general principles of layout and design are the same as for the Roman Catholic Church and the Methodist church. These are shown, with separate altar details, in para **9**.

3 ROMAN CATHOLIC CHURCH

3.01 Worship as a corporate act

The term 'Roman Catholic' (or to members simply 'Catholic') denotes the Christian community which has continuously accepted the authority of the Pope. The chief problem of a community which is building a Catholic church is that, though its building must suit the liturgy as it now is, community and architect must also make some estimate of what the total ultimate change in form of services is likely to be.

The corporate nature of Catholic worship is again now being stressed. Catholic churchgoing has for centuries been highly individualistic. The congregation should participate in the liturgical action and not merely watch it. Baptism is being restored as the corporate act of the local assembly: but it is still conducted as a private ceremony held at a time to suit the parents and which only they and their friends attend. The architect must make corporate baptism possible in a church, even though it may not be practised for some time.

The existence of societies within the parish is always important in its social life and the architect should find out which they are, what they do, and whether they are to be accommodated in any way.

3.02 The main services

The six main services of the Catholic church are:

- Mass
- The Easter liturgy (Holy Week ceremonies)
- Baptism
- Marriage
- Burial of the dead and
- Devotions.

Other liturgical activities include: blessing, dedication, consecration, confirmation, ordination.

3.03 Church design

Apart from the altar, the general principles of layout and design are the same as for the Church of England. These are shown, with separate altar details, in paragraph **9**.

4 UNITED REFORM CHURCH

4.01 Origins and buildings

This is an amalgamation of the Presbyterian Church and the Congregationalists. The Presbyterian Church of Scotland claims to be a continuation of the Celtic church.

During the reformation one of the leaders, John Knox, became greatly influenced by the Swiss, John Calvin, and it was basically his system of church government and structure, as well as much of his theology, which he brought into the church. This system of church government by courts, basically goverment by the members of the church congregation, is known as 'presbyterian'; as opposed to 'episcopalian' which is government by an appointed hierarchy.

The Reformation established the doctrine of 'the priesthood of all believers': it was not necessary for any human being to come between God and a worshipper, and the only mediator accepted was Jesus Christ. There is therefore no good theological reason for a chancel in its literal sense of a 'railed-off area' in a Presbyterian church.

All take part in the full worship and sacramental act. The sanctuary or chancel area is therefore now simply where the central act takes place, but the congregation are essentially participants in that act and the nearer they are to it, the better. There is now a fairly general departure from the earlier rectangular form of church in favour of a more open form where the sense of gathering the people round the Word and sacrament, as represented by the pulpit and communion table, can be expressed.

Present thinking seeks to emphasise the close links between the worship room and the rooms for secular purposes, so that there may not be a complete divorce between the weekday and Sunday activities of the congregation. The economic situation may well lead to multi-purpose buildings where only a portion is kept entirely for worship, while the rest is used for other purposes, with the use of partitions and screens.

4.02 The main services

The types of services normally held are:

- Normal morning public worship
- Evening worship which increasingly is taking a variety of forms, or may be largely a repetition of the morning service
- As above with the addition of one or other of the sacraments, Holy Communion or baptism
- As above, with ordination of elders or admission of new communicants
- Marriages.

Funeral services are very infrequent.

The ordinary conduct of worship is left almost entirely to the minister who may choose to remain in the pulpit for the whole service or may take part of the service from a prayer desk or a lectern, or from behind the table, using the pulpit only for preaching. The minister may move from the pulpit to the communion table to receive the offering, and will certainly do so to administer the sacrament. The font will, of course, be used for administering baptism, and the front of the sanctuary steps for admission of new communicants or for ordination of elders.

4.03 Church design

The Kirk session normally sit among the congregation. While there is great variety in the way services are conducted, most of the speaking is normally done by the minister. The congregation sit for prayers and do not kneel in the pews. The pews are seen as an extension of the communion table, so the congregation is, in effect, sitting around the table. Worshippers remain in their seats throughout the services, the elements of communion being passed around by the elders.

Baptism must take place in the face of the congregation and the font should therefore be visible to all. It should be in advance of, and probably to one side of, the altar and at a slightly lower level. The font can be movable but it should have a permanent site in the sanctuary. It need *not* be at the entrance to the church. There are no special design requirements for Christmas or Easter services.

A central aisle is desirable for marriage ceremonies. The choir should be visible to the congregation but should not be in the sanctuary. There is little social activity connected with worship but ancillary accommodation for social and educational purposes may be needed outside the hours of service.

Many aspects of design are similar to those for the Church of England. The main differences are listed below:

- The communion table is a table and not an altar. It is usually rectangular but other shapes are not precluded. Basic sizes are given in paragraph **9**.
- A large lectern is not essential but where provided should be to the sizes shown in paragraph **10**. Sometimes pulpit and lectern are designed in one piece with upper and lower levels.
- The pulpit may be centrally in front or to one side of the table or, more rarely, behind the table. It should not be more elevated than is required for the congregation to see the preacher. General design is as shown in paragraph **10**.
- A chair for the minister is provided centrally behind the altar with often at least one additional chair on each side for elders. Alternatively, seats for elders may be provided against the back wall of the sanctuary.
- A session room should be provided in addition to a vestry. This is where the elders meet before services and where communion is prepared.

5 THE SALVATION ARMY

5.01 Origins

The Salvation Army arose from evangelical meetings conducted in east London during 1865 by the Reverend William Booth, a minister of the Methodist New Connection. Booth decided to take the church to the people. His services were held in the open air, in tents and in theatres: later he built barracks and citadels in which his converts could hold their meetings. His services were sensational: he used brass bands playing secular tunes to accompany hymns; converts (soldiers) wore uniform. He became a 'general' and directed the organisation in quasi-military style. Men and women had equal rights in office. Booth regarded social work, care of the poor and rehabilitation of the outcast as an essential part of his Christian mission.

The Christian mission, as it was first called, grew beyond all expectations and in 1878 became known as the Salvation Army. In its belief, it is orthodox, evangelical and prophetic. The corps assembles for worship in a hall – a multi-purpose building sometimes called a citadel, temple or barracks. Sometimes within the complex there are two halls, for senior and junior soldiers respectively. Religious services and social activities may be conducted in either or both halls.

5.02 Ceremonies

Ceremonies may be divided into two types:

- Ordinary services held on Sunday – morning, afternoon, and evening
- Ceremonies applicable to marriages, funerals, memorial services, covenants, swearing-in of soldiers and presentation of colours (these may be embodied within one of the ordinary meetings).

The architectural implications are shown in the series of diagrams **27.4** to **27.9**.

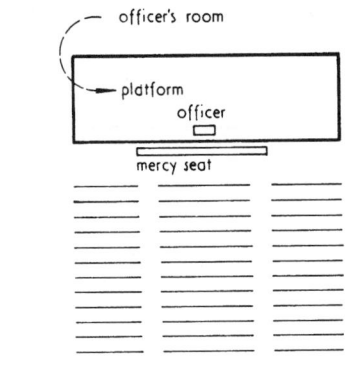

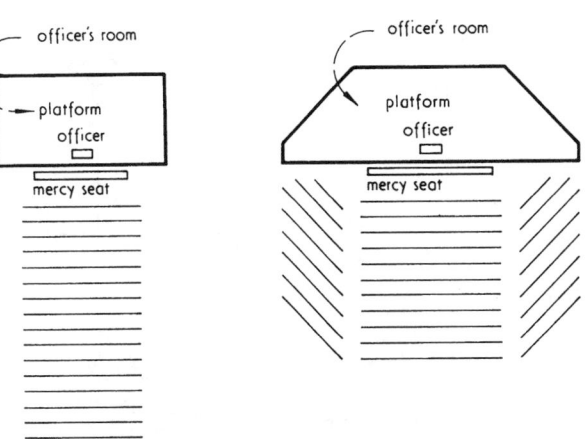

27.4 *Salvation Army: possible basic arrangements. Note that access from officers' room to platform may be on either a side or rear wall*

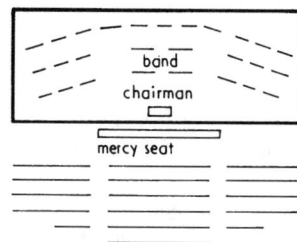

27.5 *Praise meeting or festival*

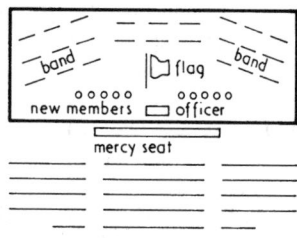

27.6 *Swearing-in ceremony*

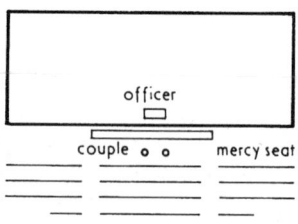

27.7 *Wedding*

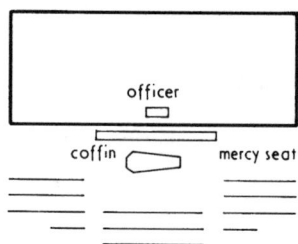

27.8 *Funeral*

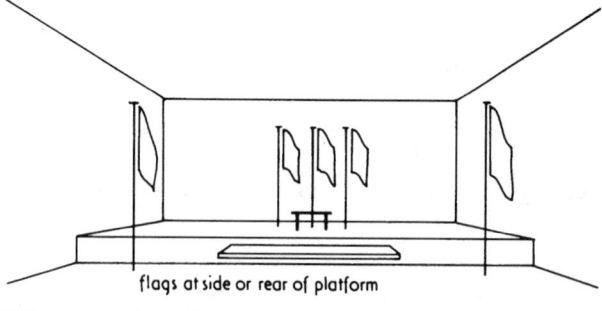

27.9 *Presentation of colurs*

5.03 Design of the assembly hall

There will be no communion service and visually there will be no elevation or placing of the sacred elements in a part of the building. The font, lectern, pulpit, communion table and altar are not essential to the Salvation Army form of worship. In every

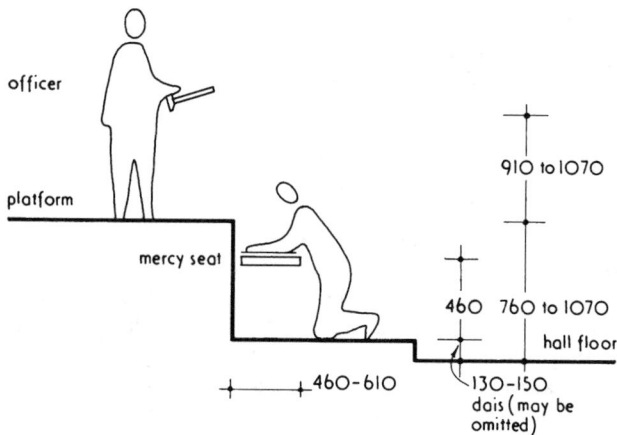

27.10 *Mercy seat*

Salvation Army hall there is a place for the mercy seat, **27.10**. This is a simple wooden form, usually placed at the front of the platform in front of the congregation, and is a place where Christian and non-Christian penitents may kneel at any time.

Platform

The platform will be required to accommodate, at various times, officers taking a leading part in the services; the band (possibly a visiting one which may be larger than that designed for); the songster brigade or a visiting choir.

The size of the platform will depend on local conditions and requirements but approximately 0.5 to 0.6 m² per person (seated in rows) should be allowed. The platform should not be less than about 4–5 m depth, but will normally be more. Its height above the hall floor should not normally be less than 760 mm or more than 1100 mm but sight-lines must be considered in relation to a level floor both on the platform and in the hall.

If there is a gallery there must be a view of the mercy seat from every seat. Movable seats, not fixed pews, are always used both on the platform and in the hall: flexibility is important.

Hall

As a first estimate for the overall area of the hall, allow 0.56 m² for each person to be accommodated. Aisles should not be less than 1.35 m wide. The space between the front edge of the mercy seat and the front face of the congregational seating should not be less than 1.5 m. A wide rectangle, polygon, or square will be a more satisfactory shape than a long narrow rectangle.

The requirements will be for a reasonable standard of acoustics for speech, choral singing and brass band playing. There should be a reasonable level of natural lighting and a reasonable standard of artificial illumination, both on the platform and in the body of the hall. The ventilation in most cases should be natural.

Officers' room

The officers' room (vestry) is used as a meeting-place by leaders or chairmen of meetings and officers of the Census Board who will assemble in the room before taking their place on the platform. The room should accommodate between two and ten persons. Corps records will be kept in this room. Lavatory accommodation will be required, normally one unit for each sex.

Cloakrooms

Lavatory accommodation should be provided for both sexes near or adjacent to the entrance vestibules of the senior or junior halls. This will be required for women in the songster room and for men in the band room.

Storage

Storage will be required in a band room for brass band instruments, music stands and music. The room will also be used for assembly, briefing and cloakroom. Minimum area shown usually be 23–28 m². Instruments are stored in individual lockers to suit sizes of instruments with a small store for reserve instruments and cupboard with shelves for music.

Storage will be required in a songster room for a wind-type portable organ or electric portable organ with amplifier, and music. The room will also be used for assembly, briefing and cloakroom for the women members who would number about 20 to 30 in an average-sized brigade: 18.5 m² would be a minimum area.

Where there are junior and senior corps activities, there may be a junior band and singing company (junior choir). Storage will be required for brass band instruments for this junior band and for music for the singing company.

Where there is a separate junior hall, storage compartments will be contained in that hall. Other social and club activities may also require storage.

6 METHODIST CHURCH

6.01 Origins
The Methodist Church grew out of the Church of England during the eighteenth century and was founded by John and Charles Wesley. A distinct feature of the new movement was the introduction of lay preachers or, as they came to be known, local preachers. The strong emphasis on evangelical preaching is rooted in the Methodist tradition. 'Methodism is nothing if it is not evangelical.'

The church or chapel is normally reserved for worship alone, although meetings, lectures and musical recitals of a specifically religious character may also take place there. A multi-purpose hall, with a sanctuary that can be screened or curtained off, may also be used for public worship during the early stages of the development of a local congregation. There may be other units within the complex such as classrooms, club rooms and assembly halls, both for religious and secular purposes.

6.02 Ceremonies and buildings
The kind of church required today will seat between 100 and 300 people. The influence of the liturgical movement is shown in certain specific ways, and particularly in a new emphasis on the place of the sacraments in the life of the church, and in the increasing use of set prayers and liturgical forms of service. The altar, therefore, is seen again as the Lord's table, used for the family. The font is no longer viewed as making possible a semi-magical act. It is the place at which and the means by which the person baptised, whether child or adult, is sacramentally incorporated into the body of Christ. This rediscovery of the laity, the Lord's table and the font has to be considered in designing a church, for in the end it is the function of the church which is of supreme importance.

These theological rediscoveries will affect the building of a Methodist church:

● In relation to the shape of the church
● In the arrangement of the sanctuary
● In the siting of the choir.

There are normally two services on Sunday, one in the morning and one in the evening. These are conducted by a minister or local preacher from the pulpit, though the earlier part of the service may be conducted from a lectern, the pulpit being used only for the sermon.

Holy Communion is normally celebrated once a month. In order to emphasise the theological statement that the ministry of the Word is of equal importance to the ministry of the Sacrament, pulpit and communion table may be placed close to each other. The minister dispenses the bread and the wine (the latter in small individual glasses) to each of those who have come forward from the congregation to kneel at the communion rail. A small trough or perforated shelf should be fitted to the inside of the communion rail, about 50 mm or 65 mm deep and slightly lower than the top of the rail, where communicants may place the empty wine glasses. See also paragraph **9**, for dimensions of communion rails.

All other main services are similar to Church of England practice and the architectural requirements are the same, although a credence table is not required near the communion table. Specific guidance is contained in *The Methodist Church builders' decalogue* (from the Methodist Property Division, Central Buildings, Oldham Street, Manchester M1 1JQ).

7 SOCIETY OF FRIENDS

7.01 Origins
The Society of Friends (Quakers) originated through the experiences and preaching of George Fox (1624–91). Early Quakers reacted strongly against the current religious practices and liturgy of the established church. All through their history, Quakers have been concerned with a sense of duty to the community.

Because Friends believe that God can communicate with man direct, they do not partake of the outward sacraments. They have no separated priesthood, they do not require their members to subscribe to a creed, and their worship does not make use of a liturgy. They are, however, in broad agreement with the main emphases of Christian belief, and would claim to be both orthodox and evangelical.

7.02 Ceremonies and buildings
In a meeting for worship, Friends gather in silence as a congregation of seeking souls, and 'wait upon the Spirit'. No one directs the worship. Out of the 'gathered' silence of united worship, one or another may be led to engage in vocal ministry or in prayer or to read from the scriptures. There is no music or hymn singing.

The building must be designed to help the quiet worship and the vocal ministry of the participants. There is no observance of the Lord's supper or orthodox communion service; no baptism or initiation ceremonies involving ritual. There will therefore be no need for font, lectern, pulpit or altar.

Sizes of meeting halls vary, but they will mostly be designed to accommodate fifty Friends or less. A square, rectangular or polygonal room may meet the requirements. It is likely that seating will be required in a square or a circle. Meetings may prefer fixed or movable, tiered or level seating.

There is no need for a table in the meeting room, though there normally is one to act as a focal point. The position is not usually literally at the centre of the room; the seating will be arranged in the way felt by the group concerned to be most conducive to a good meeting for worship, and the table, if placed anywhere, will be fitted in with the general arrangement of the room. Its main use is for business meetings.

Society of Friends meeting halls when not required for worship are often used by other denominations, or for secular purposes of an appropriate nature. Other accommodation might include a multi-purpose hall, library, small kitchen foyer and cloakrooms and a caretaker's flat.

8 PASTORAL CENTRES

8.01 Form and function
Pastoral centres are alternatives to conventional church buildings and are increasingly being considered where there is to be a large

new population with non-existent or inadequate ministry and buildings.

A pastoral centre could take many forms – basically it would be a small building or suite of rooms with facilities for consultation, meetings, refreshments and occasional worship. It could be a modified house, a transportable structure or a specifically designed community building: it could even be a converted shop or a caravan. Its purposes would be to shelter a Christian 'presence', comparable to a doctor's surgery or a citizen's advice bureau: ministers would be present for counselling and office work at advertised hours. Small meetings could be held and modest hospitality offered. It could be used for acts of worship though it would be linked to a major worship centre elsewhere. It should be sited in the local centre and could be integrated into a complex of amenity buildings or a shopping centre. If resources were available, and if the population distribution were suitable, two pastoral centres might be provided in a neighbourhood of 6000 to 10 000 people.

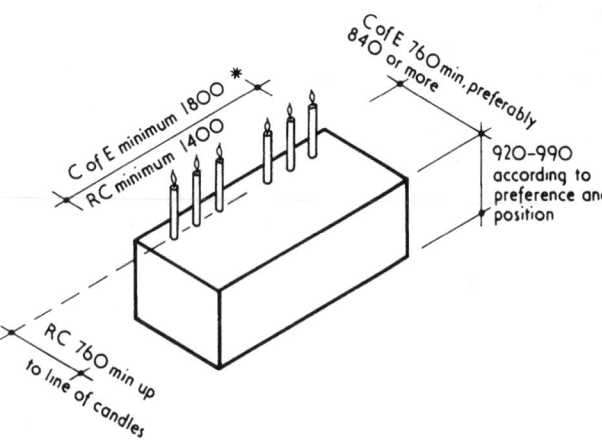

27.11 *Average size of altars. The exact proportions will depend on its position, and whether the priest is facing the congregation or has his back to them. Note that the tabernacle containing the reserved sacrament is not now normally placed on the altar (see section 12)*

Part B Design data

9 ALTAR OR COMMUNION TABLE

9.01 Symbolism
The altar symbolises three things:

- The body of Christ
- The altar of sacrifice
- The table of the last supper.

9.02 Canon law
A Church of England altar may be of wood, stone or other suitable material and may be movable. It should be covered with silk or other 'decent stuff' during divine services and with a fair white linen cloth at holy communion. A Roman Catholic altar must be of natural (not reconstructed) stone with the top member (the mensa) in one piece and containing the relics of two canonised martyrs or saints. However, this requirement may be fulfilled by a small portable altar which is in effect an altar stone often about 300 mm square (or less) and 50 mm deep containing a sealed cavity (the sepulchre) for the relics. The altar may be fixed (stone cemented to the structure) or unfixed (timber with inset portable stone altar as described above). Only a fixed altar may be consecrated. Alternatively, relics may be sunk into floor below altar.

9.03 Position
The altar must be related to congregational seating in such a way that what is done at it is, and is seen to be, a corporate action of the whole assembly. Altars are being brought further forward in the sanctuary and with congregations grouped around, there is less need for the altar to stand so high as in the past, especially when the priest faces the congregation across the altar.

9.04 Size
For liturgical reasons, altars can be less long but possibly slightly deeper than in the past. Average sizes are shown in **27.11** and anthropometric data in **27.12**.

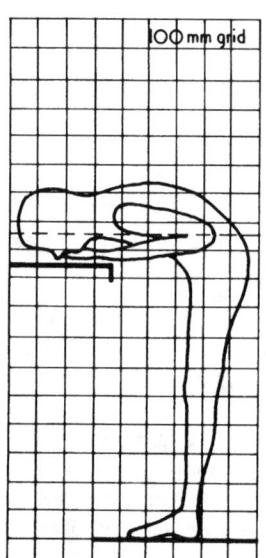 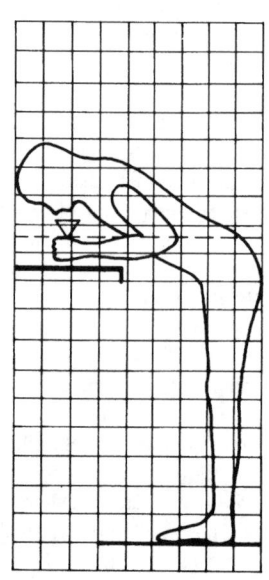 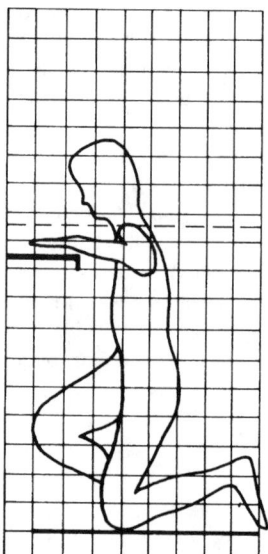 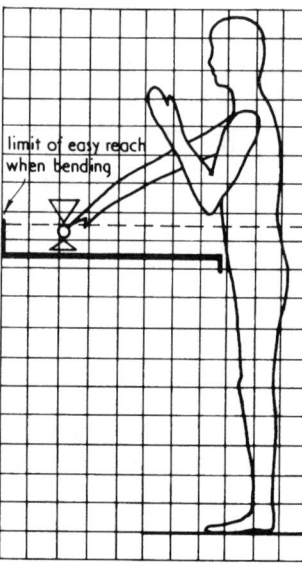

27.12 *Critical actions of priest when standing at the altar. The horizontal dotted lines represents the eye level of the average adult member of the congregation when kneeling. This should preferably not be less than 75 mm above the top of the altar, emphasising the importance of keeping that low. This represents some sacrifice to the priest, since actions a and b are easier if the top is at the traditional height of just over 1 m. a Kissing the surface of the altar. b Saying the words of consecration. c Genuflecting. This position emphasises the value of recessing the altar supports at least on the priest's side, to prevent him bumping his knee. d Reaching forward when standing upright, illustrating the extent of reach*

27.13 Supporting the mensa (altar top). Note that RC altars should not oversail their supports by more than 150 mm, so that the bishop can pass his thumb over the joints at the Consecration.

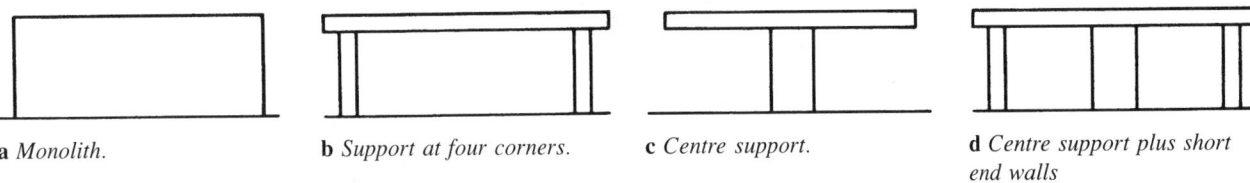

a *Monolith.*   **b** *Support at four corners.*   **c** *Centre support.*   **d** *Centre support plus short end walls*

27.14 Clothing the altar.

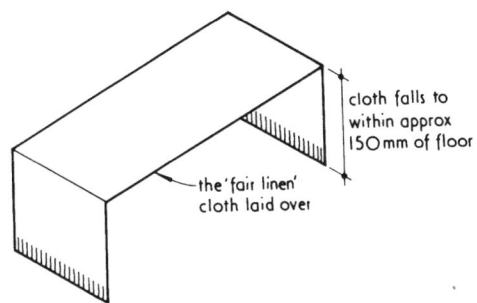

cloth falls to within approx 150 mm of floor

the 'fair linen' cloth laid over

a *Second cloth.*

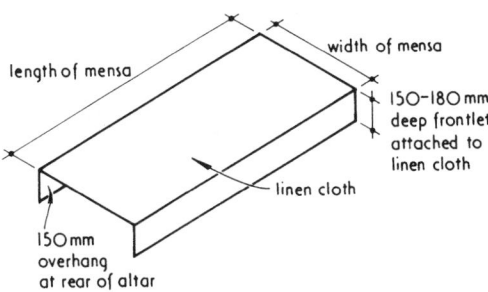

length of mensa

width of mensa

150–180 mm deep frontlet attached to linen cloth

linen cloth

150 mm overhang at rear of altar

b *First cloth.*

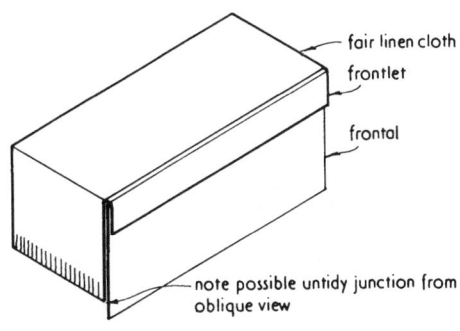

fair linen cloth

frontlet

frontal

note possible untidy junction from oblique view

c Final appearance

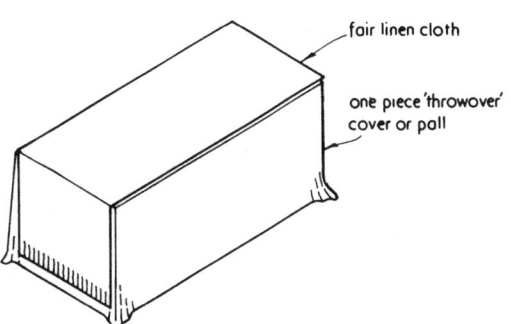

fair linen cloth

one piece 'throwover' cover or pall

27.15 One-piece throwover altar cover. This may have loose draped corners as shown, or tight-fitted corners

9.05 Supports and coverings

Methods of supporting the mensa are shown in **27.13**. With the altar now normally nearer the congregation, the question of clothing the altar may need to be rethought. A traditional Church of England altar covering is shown in **27.14** and **27.15**.

9.06 Footspace

The platform or base on which the altar rests must be large enough for the number of priests expected to stand around while celebrating the Eucharist. It may be raised one or two steps above the level of the congregation, but in general the altar should be kept as low as possible to avoid any sense of separation between it and the people. Possible dimensions are shown in **27.16**.

9.07 Cross and candles

The exact requirements must be discussed with the priest. Candles and cross should not form a barrier between priest and people. Some possibilities for the cross are shown in **27.17** and **27.18**; and for the candles in **27.19**.

9.08 Communion table

A communion table with table lectern as used in Presbyterian churches is shown in **27.20**.

10 SANCTUARY FURNITURE AND PULPIT

10.01 Lectern

This should be in or near the sanctuary but sufficiently apart from the altar to constitute a separate focus, and conveniently sited to be accessible to the congregation to read from, **27.21**. Occasionally two lecterns may be asked for, one each side. The lectern must be in a position where everybody can see the reader's face including those within the sanctuary. It may be fixed or movable, and it may also serve as a pulpit. Dimensions are shown in **27.22**.

10.02 Altar rail

A rail may be dispensed with in some churches, but most will still provide lengths of rail for kneeling to receive communion. It need not be continuous, but must be rigid and firm. Minimum dimensions are given in **27.23** and **27.24**.

10.03 Credence table

This serves as a sort of sideboard for water and wine, but check if anything else is to be placed on it (e.g. offertory money, service books, etc.) in which case a shelf below the table may be needed. It should be to the right of the celebrant within the sanctuary but not where it might cause a visual obstruction. It could be a shelf instead of a freestanding table. Dimensions will vary from about 610 × 760 mm to 1200 × 460 mm, with a minimum height of 820 mm.

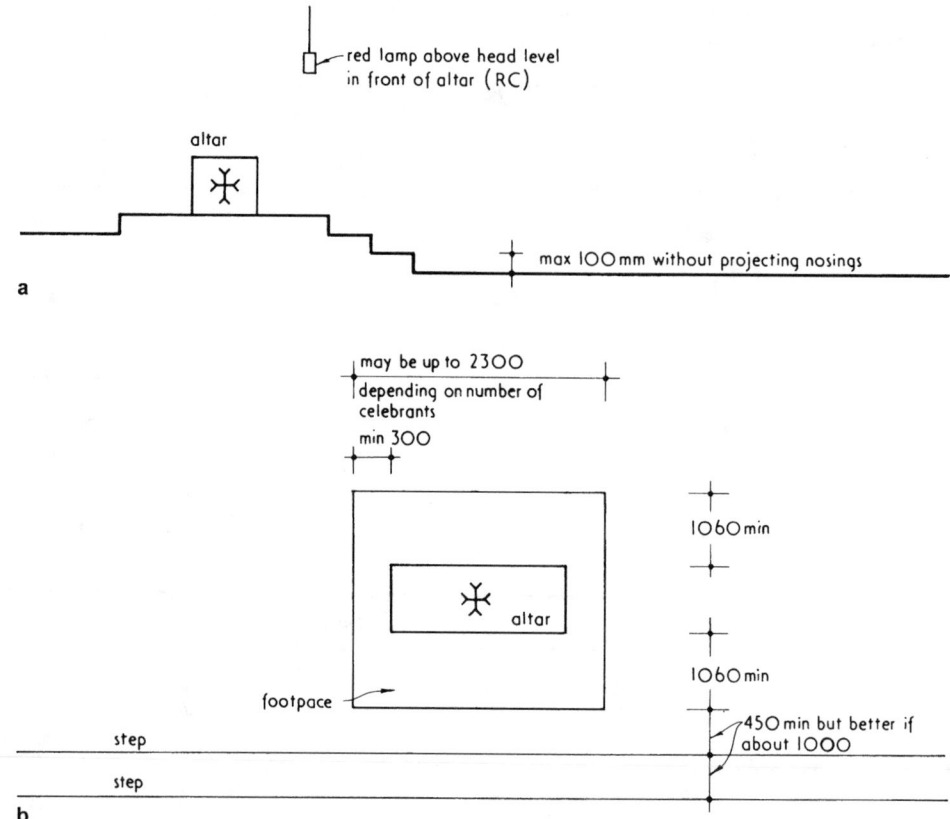

red lamp above head level
in front of altar (RC)

altar

max 100 mm without projecting nosings

a

may be up to 2300
depending on number of
celebrants

min 300

1060 min

altar

1060 min

footpace

step

450 min but better if
about 1000

step

b

27.16 *Space around the altar. Keep altar as low as possible, usual maximum three steps. Position of the altar can also be defined by use of a canopy, structure, lighting, floor pattterns, etc.* **a** *Section.* **b** *Plan*

27.17 *The cross behind the altar at a height where it will not be obscured by the priest. Crosses are not usually placed on the altar in 'facing the people' churches*

27.18 *The cross forward of the altar to one side or suspended above*

max 1700

a　　　　　**b**　　　　　**c**

27.19 *Arrangement of candles.* **a,b** *Six candles.* **c** *Two candles only. Candles may also be placed on a step lower than the altar to reduce height and obstruction to view*

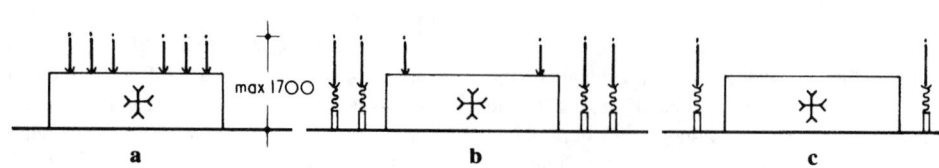

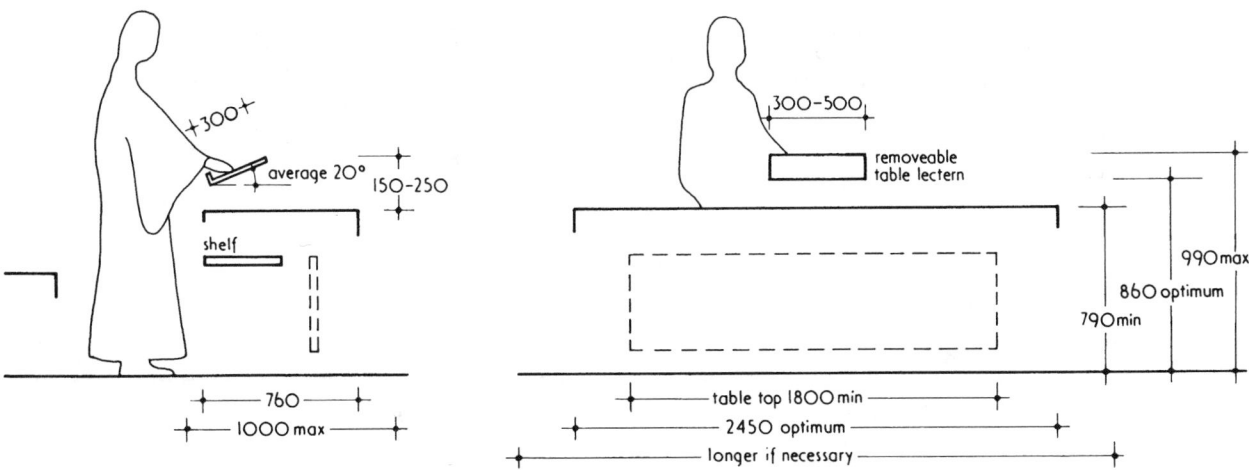

27.20 *Communion table with table lectern for use in Presbyterian churches instead of the altars described above*

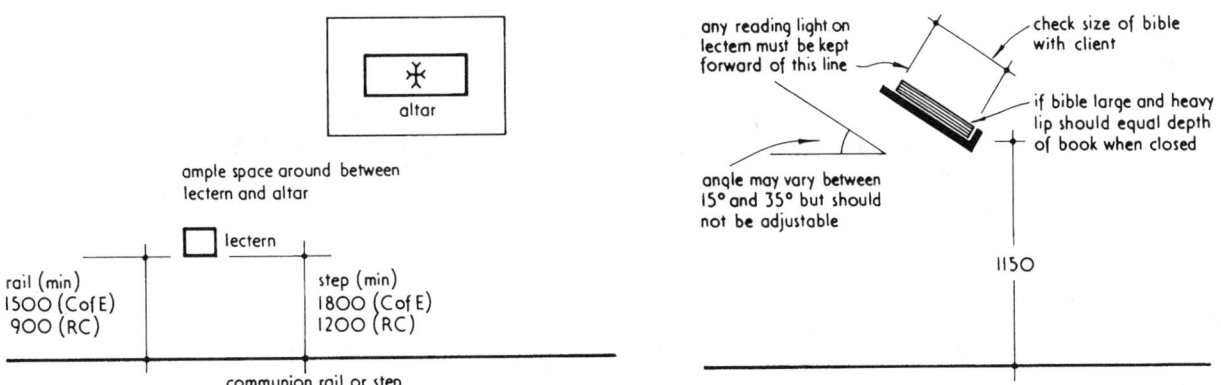

27.21 *Minimum dimensions around lectern depending on whether communion rail or only a communion step is provided*

27.22 *Minimum requirements for lectern*

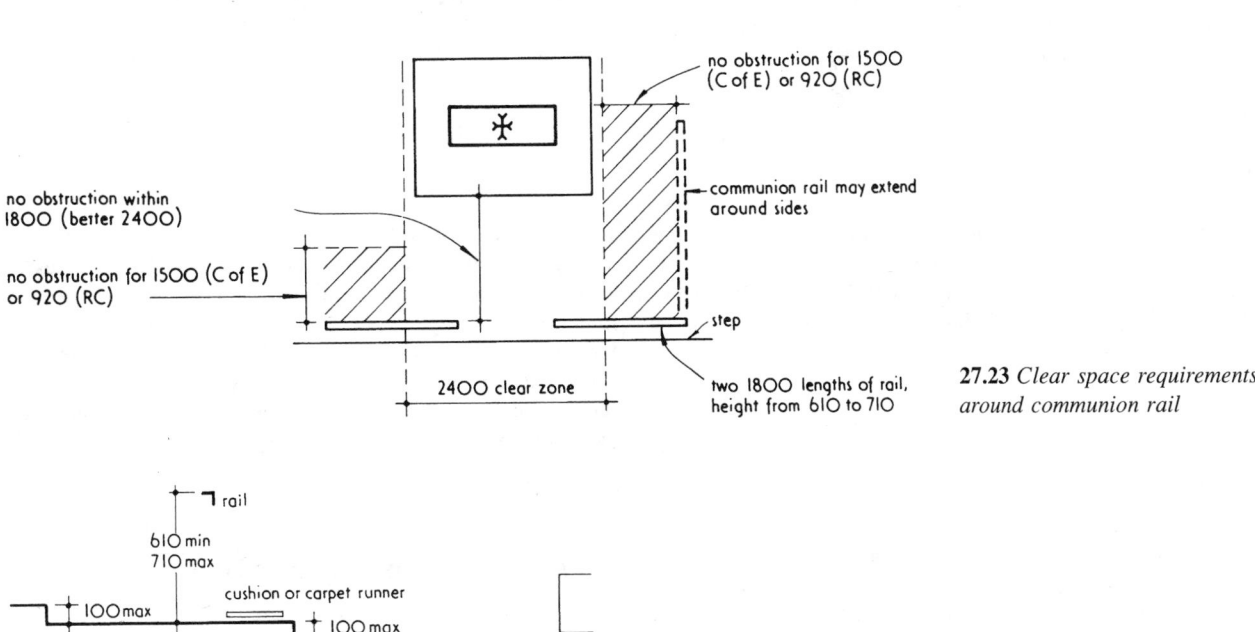

27.23 *Clear space requirements around communion rail*

27.24 *Dimensions for altar rail (i.e. outside central zone of sanctuary). In a new Roman Catholic church there is unlikely to be a second step in the sanctuary, and the minimum unobstructed distance on the sanctuary side of the rail is 920 mm. It is also normal for the whole of the sanctuary to be one step above the nave, but too many steps should be avoided.* **a** *With stepped floor.* **b** *With flat floor*

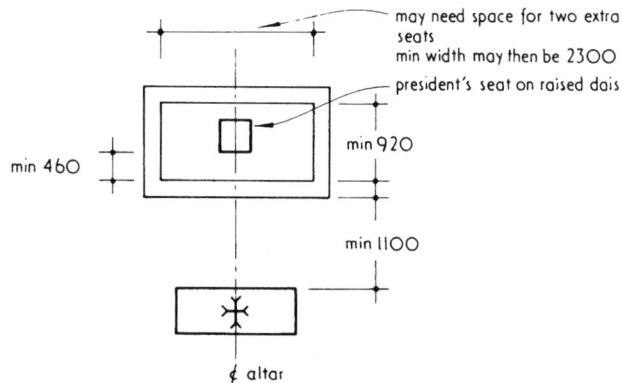

27.25 *Dimensions around the President's seat*

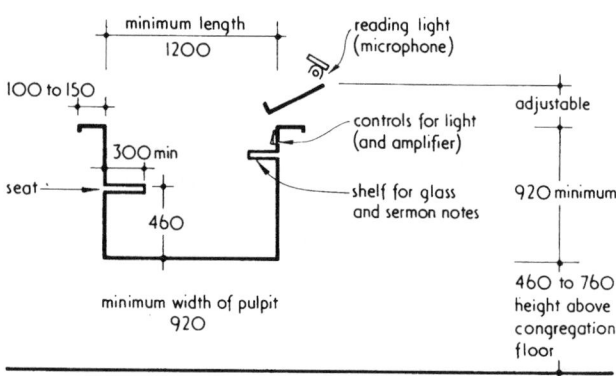

27.26 *Pulpit dimensions*

10.04 Seating for officiants

These will vary considerably and requirements must be established with the local community. Ceremonial seats for priests. In Roman Catholic churches the 'president's seat' will be on the centre line behind the altar, raised up on one or two steps, **27.25**. The seat, which is used by the priest, must not look like a bishop's throne and will usually not have a back to it. The bishop's throne is portable, and placed in front of the altar whenever he visits the church. In Church of England churches it is often better to have the ceremonial seat (which is used by the bishop) at the side of the sanctuary facing the altar.

Incidental seating should be kept to a minimum. It will be needed for additional priests, servers, and lay people on special occasions. It will usually be in the form of benches at the side of the sanctuary.

Stalls will be needed (especially in Church of England churches) for priests at matins and evensong at the side of the sanctuary. Dimensions are similar to those for congregational seating (see paragraph **14**) except that as priests are vested they will need more room to move in and out. Surface for resting a book should be deeper (say, 300 mm) and almost horizontal – not sloping – with a shelf below.

10.05 Pulpit

This should be sited outside but close to the sanctuary. No particular location is now insisted on apart from functional reasons of good sight and sound. Minimum internal area is about 1–2 m². Access should desirably be from the side (if from back, fit a door). Other details are shown in **27.26**. A Presbyterian pulpit may be behind the altar or at either side.

11 FONT

11.01 Description

In Roman Catholic churches movable fonts are not permitted and they are not generally approved of in the Anglican communion. They can be used in Presbyterian and Methodist churches. In Church of England churches fresh water is used for each baptism drained to a separate soakaway. In Roman Catholic churches water is blessed once a year and the baptismal water is stored in the font which has two compartments.

11.02 Dimensions and shape

Anthropometric requirements are shown in **27.27**. Shape is governed by the needs of the priest (space for service book and other small objects); the comfort of the priest in holding the baby; and the safety of the baby (the priest should not have to lean too far over).

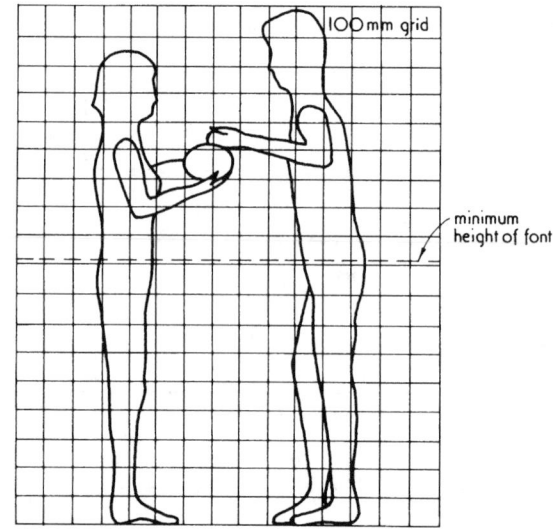

27.27 *Anthropometric diagram showing the critical action at the font*

11.03 Position of font

Various alternative positions are shown in **27.28**. The font must be approached from the church (congregation) side but be divided from it in some way (e.g. by difference in floor or ceiling levels). It must be in a prominent position and be seen by the congregation when seated, or space provided for most of the congregation to stand around. It should be a separate focus from the altar and therefore possibly not in the sanctuary.

12 RESERVATION OF THE SACRAMENT

12.01 Siting

The reserved sacrament in Roman Catholic churches (the consecrated bread of the Eucharist) is not now normally kept in a tabernacle on the altar. It is normally kept:

● In a separate chapel outside the sanctuary
● In a position which is architecturally important
● Where its location will be easily recognised by the congregation.

The requirements are complex and the practice of the local church community must be established and agreed with the Diocesan Advisory Committee. **27.29** and **27.30** show height limitations.

27.28 *Variations on font positioning.*

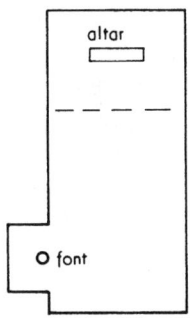

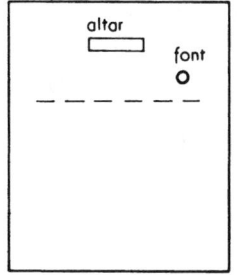

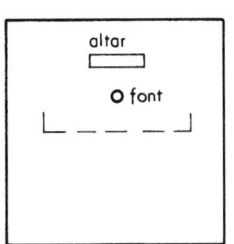

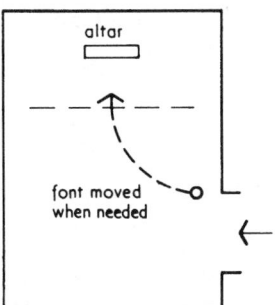

a *In separate baptistery. Acceptable if only baptism proper is performed here with the rest of the service is in the main body of the church.*

b *Font in sanctuary. It may compete with altar, or be made insignificant by it. But in a Prebyterian church, the font is often in this position although lower than the table and possibly on a side extension of the lowest sanctuary step.*

c *As for **b**, but the font is also an obstruction to sight.*

d *Care is needed with a moveable font to retain the dignity of of one of the church's great sacraments.*

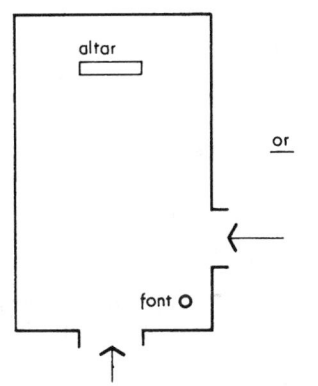

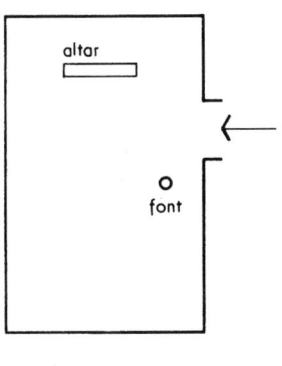

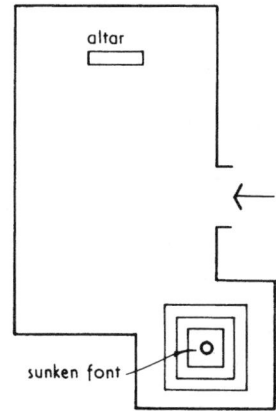

e *and* **f** *When font is placed near the entrance it is important to have the entrance near the font and not the font near the entrance! This may mean that the main entrance is in front of the people's seats and not behind.*

g *The font is sunk into a 'dry pool' with a 'drowning' symbolism*

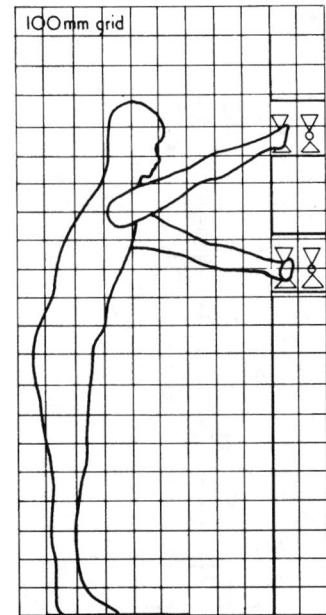

27.29 *Removing ciborium from tabernacle and putting on lower shelf*

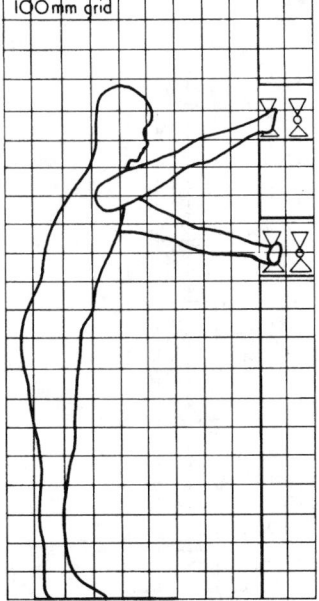

27.30 *Maximum height to give view of back of tabernacle*

The reserved sacrament is occasionally found also in the Church of England, but is more rare and many methods of reservation are practised. For more explanation see the AJ information sheet 1529 contained in *Church buildings*.

13 ENTRANCE AREAS

13.01 Design requirements
- Provide wind lobbies outside entrance doors
- Minimum clear door width (for processions and funerals) should be 1.7 m (1.1 m in a small church); minimum clear height (for processional cross) 2.3 m, otherwise 2.05 m is sufficient
- Provide proper access for disabled people (see Designing for the disabled)
- Provide secondary exit door, especially for weddings
- Provide gathering spaces inside and outside the church as part of the normal exit route where people can naturally gather to talk
- Where needed (especially in Roman Catholic churches) place a holy water stoup on the entrance side of each doorway leading into the church. Rims should be 710 to 760 mm above the floor
- Provide considerable space for notices of all types in a conspicuous position
- Allow space, where required, for one or two small credence tables just inside the entrance
- provide facilities for selling of publications, etc.
- Where possible, provide access from the entrance area to the WC and to the sacristy or vestry
- As a general rule try to keep the purely *secular* activities more in view when the congregation is *leaving* than when entering for a service.

14 CONGREGATIONAL AND CHOIR SEATING

14.01 Arrangement of seating
The congregation should be continuous with the minister with no strong dividing line between them. Equally, the congregation must be united with one another and all must have good access to circulation and to the sanctuary. Seats facing each other around an altar should not be closer than about 6 m, and nobody should look sideways on to anybody else closer than 1.5 to 3.0 m.

14.02 Spacing and dimensioning of seats
Anthropometric details are given in **27.31**. Note also:

- Minimum dimension of seat plus kneeling space front and back is 920 mm. Where congregations do not kneel (e.g. Methodists, Presbyterians), the dimension can be reduced to 760 mm
- Leave a space of about 280 mm between front edge of seat and back edge of kneeler
- Allow minimum width of 510 mm per person
- Maximum length of row is ten persons (5.1 m) with access from both ends, or six persons (3.06 m) with access from one end
- The ledge for hymn books should be about 150 mm wide; (300 mm for the choir).

14.03 Circulation
Basic dimensions are shown in **27.32**. Space must be allowed for invalid chairs during the service where the occupant can participate but not block circulation.

15 VESTRIES AND SACRISTIES

15.1 Accommodation
Accommodation requirements will vary considerably. The most lavish could include:

- Priest's sacristy (sometimes called priest's vestry)
- Server's vestry
- Choir vestry and practice/committee room
- Women's choir vestry
- Churchwardens'/interview room
- Cleaners' room ⎤ sometimes placed together
- Flower arrangers' room ⎦ and called working sacristy
- Priest's WC
- Men's and women's WCs
- General storage
- Small kitchen.

15.02 Planning relationships
The tradition of the vestry/sacristy complex opening directly onto the sanctuary has disadvantages: it emphasises the separation of

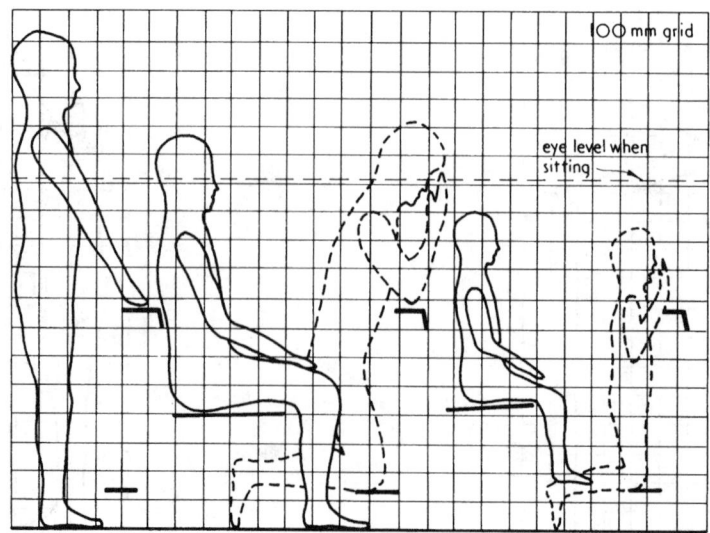

27.31 *Critical dimensions for seating. Black lines indicate one particular solution found very satisfactory in practice. The dotted line indicates 'eye' level when sitting, and concerns the relationship with the altar top*

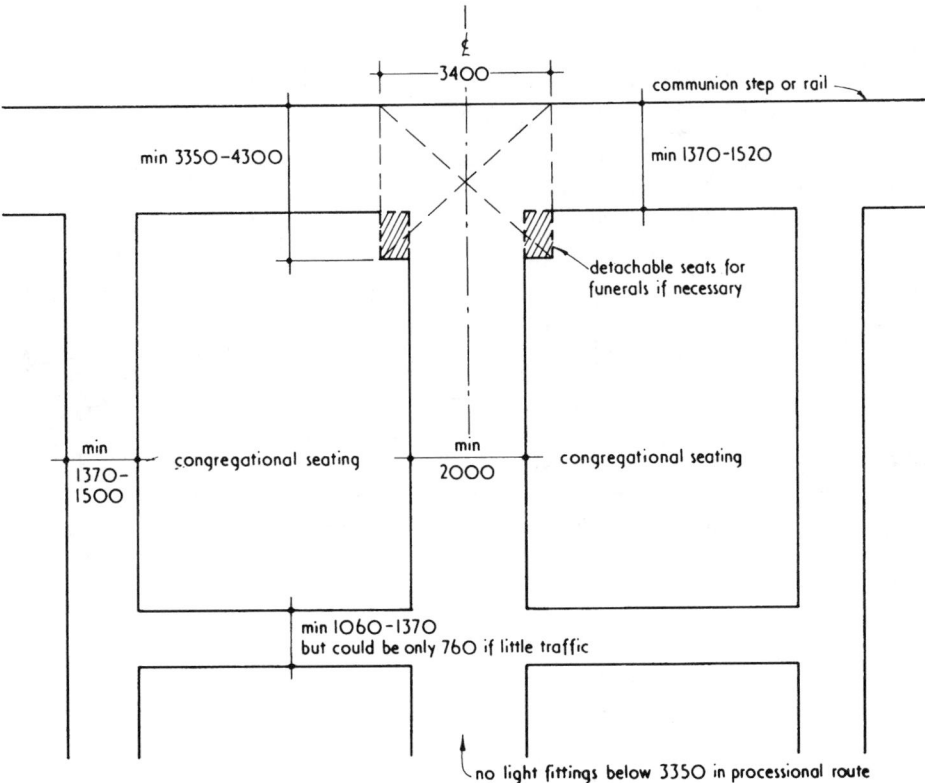

27.32 *Aisle widths. Size and pattern will depend on overall plan and liturgical considerations. Seating may be fan shaped or in blocks around the sanctuary*

priest from the congregation and makes sharing of toilet facilities difficult. The vestry could be near the entrance (but ensure security) so that priest and procession go through the congregation to their place in the sanctuary. Since children often participate in adult worship for only part of its duration, movement between the main worship space and ancillary rooms should be considered.

There should be a lobby with double doors between the choir vestry and the worship room, and a space out of sight of the congregation for processions to form up. A door direct to the outside is essential as priests and choir should not have to go through the worship room to reach their vestries.

15.03 Detailed design
There is a very wide range of objects and vestments to be stored and the precise requirements must be ascertained. A vestment storage cupboard is shown in **27.33**. Doorways should be 1700 mm wide × 2300 mm high. More detailed lists are given in the chapter on Church buildings.

16 CONFESSIONAL

16.01 Design requirements
Priest and penitent must be able to hear what each other has to say without being overheard by others. The bishop's requirements must be established, and the psychological expectations of the parish.

Either priest and penitent may be enclosed in an acoustically isolated box or, more desirably, they may be visible but placed far enough away from other people to make a physical acoustic barrier unnecessary. Basic dimensions are shown in **27.34**.

17 ORGAN AND CHOIR

17.01 Music in church
Use of music in worship can be a highly emotive subject with the type of organ and the placing of the choir two of the most difficult problems. For new churches organs based on the 'werk prinzip' (sometimes called 'neo-classic') should be considered rather than the more traditional Victorian organs with high wind pressures and powerful but muffled tone. The organ builder should be brought in at an early stage of the discussions.

27.33 *Section through vestment cupboard*
Notes:
* These to be fitted with 'trouser bar' under to take stole and maniple of each set of vestments
† Choir vestry: part of bar at 1320 if there are children in the choir

27.34 *Anthropometric study of confessional.*

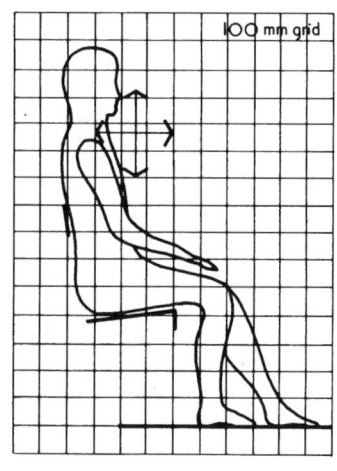

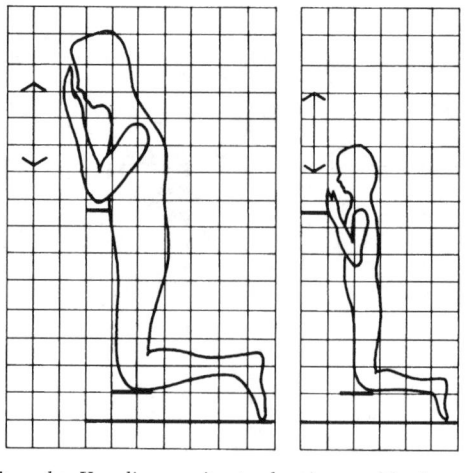

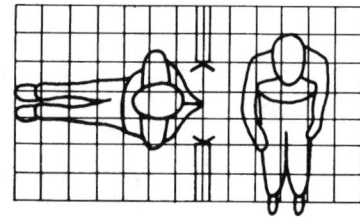

a *Relationship of grille to seated priest.*

b *and* **c** *Kneeling penitents showing positioning of grille where it will serve both adult and child.*

d *Plan view of priest and penitent*

27.35 *Bad organ arrangement. Key: o organ, c organ console, p people, ch choir, m, minister, a altar*

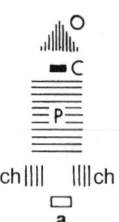

27.36 *Bad position of choir and people, key as for* **27.35**

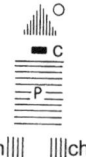

27.37 *Bad position of choir, minister and people, key as for* **27.35**

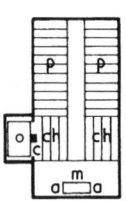
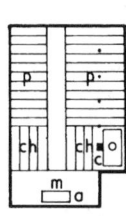
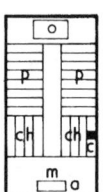
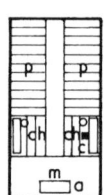
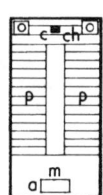
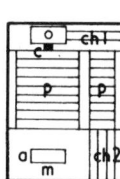
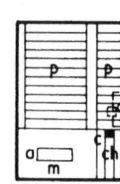

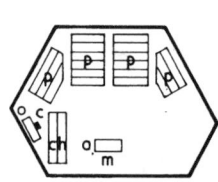
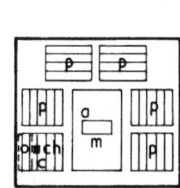
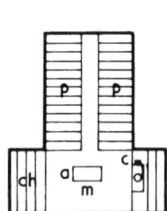
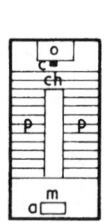
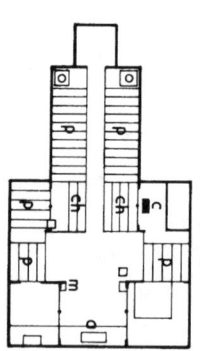

27.38 *Good relationships of organ, choir, congregation and minister/priest. Key as for* **27.35**

17.02 Relationship of musical elements

A few basic principles must be observed:

- The player must be with his or her instrument (i.e. the organ console must be near the pipes), **27.35**
- The choir should be as near as possible to the organ, **27.36**
- Ministers should not be separated from either people or organ, **27.37**
- People should not be placed between the choir and ranks of pipes, **27.36** and **27.37**
- The organ must be in the main volume of the building and raised above the floor so that the pipes are above the heads of the listeners.

Different possible locations of choir, organ and congregation are shown in **27.38**.

C Non-Christian places of worship

18 SYNAGOGUES

18.01 History

The original churches evolved from the synagogues set up to supplement and eventually to supplant the Holy Temple in Jerusalem. It is therefore not surprising that they have many elements in common.

There are two main strands of Judaism: orthodox and progressive. As far as the design of the synagogue is concerned the only difference between them is that in the orthodox tradition men and women are rigidly segregated, and women take no direct part in the service.

18.02 The sanctuary

Holy Ark

The principal architectural feature of the synagogue is the *Aron Kodesh* or Holy Ark, **27.39** which contains the Scrolls of the Law. These scrolls, **27.40**, are hand written on a very long strip of parchment, and are the first five books of the Old Testament, called the *Torah*. Each end of the parchment is fixed to a stave, and the parchment is rolled around the staves. Because the portion to be read is not immediately accessible, as in a conventional book, it is usual to have several scrolls in the Ark, so that the correct place is not having to be found during the service.

Scrolls, when not being read from, are bound, covered with a mantle, and usually adorned with a silver shield, a pointer and *rimonim*. The latter are detachable silver finials, often decorated with small bells, for the top ends of the staves on which the parchment is rolled. The Ark itself is raised and approached up steps from the floor of the synagogue. It should preferably, but not necessarily, be on the eastern wall of the synagogue. It has both

doors and a curtain. It should be able to accommodate at least four scrolls, and may well be large enough for many more. It needs internal lighting, *not* operated by a door switch.

Traditionally the Ark is decorated with particular Hebrew texts, by representations of the Tablets of the Ten Commandments, and often by heraldic beasts.

Bima

The service is conducted from a reading desk raised above the floor of the synagogue. Traditionally this should be in the centre of the space, as in the plan of a synagogue in **27.41**; but some synagogues have been designed with the Bima integrated with the Holy Ark, **27.42**. There is a custom that the Bima should be three steps above the floor.

The Bima contains a reading desk large enough to hold an open Scroll, with at least five people around three sides of it. The Bima should also be able to accommodate two people holding unused scrolls, with sufficient space for dressing them (separately). Facilities are provided for scroll vestments to be kept while that scroll is being read, including pairs of 'spikes' for the rimonim.

Pulpit

A pulpit is provided for the minister or rabbi from which to deliver a sermon. It is usually placed on the longitudinal axis of the synagogue immediately in front of the Holy Ark, and is not raised above the Ark's level. It does not have a door.

Congregational seating

The congregational seating surrounds the Bima. Since services can be very long (on *Yom Kippur* they take the whole day), the seats have to be comfortable. It is common for them to have lockable boxes beneath, as on the Sabbath orthodox people do not carry their prayer books, prayer shawls, etc. In larger synagogues the seating is banked to enable a good view for all.

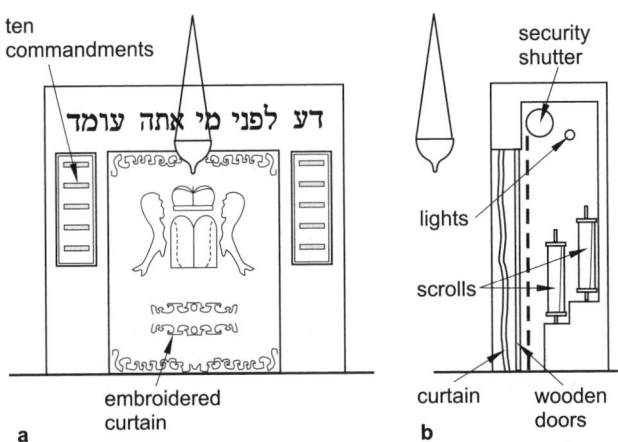

27.39 *Holy Ark.* **a** *Elevation, inscription means 'Know before whom you stand'.* **b** *Section*

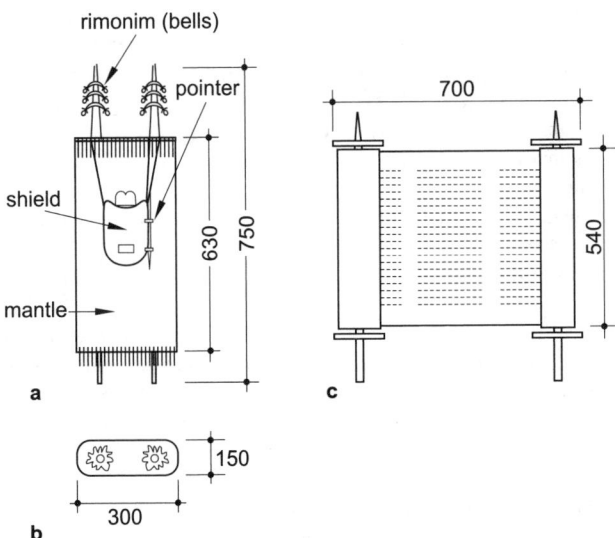

27.40 *Torah scroll.* **a** *Elevation.* **b** *Plan.* **c** *Scroll when open, on reading desk or when elevated*

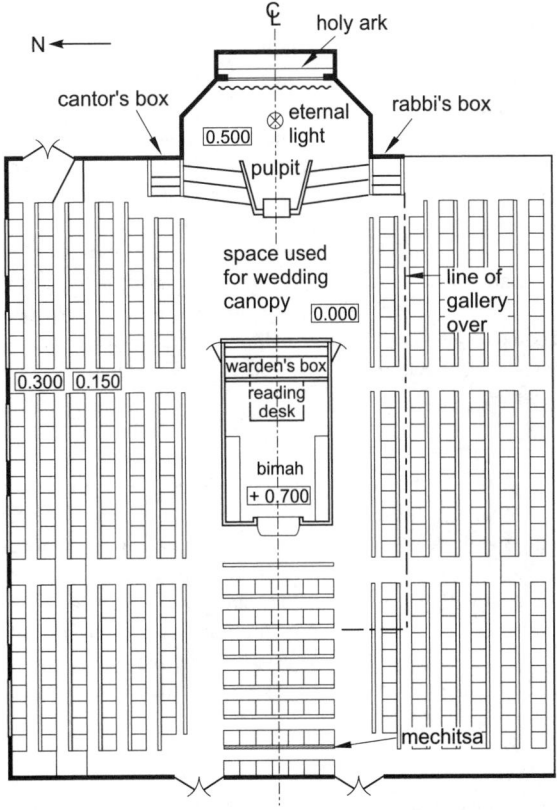

27.41 *Plan of synagogue with central Bima. This would seat 396 men downstairs, 7 women downstairs and 275 women in the gallery*

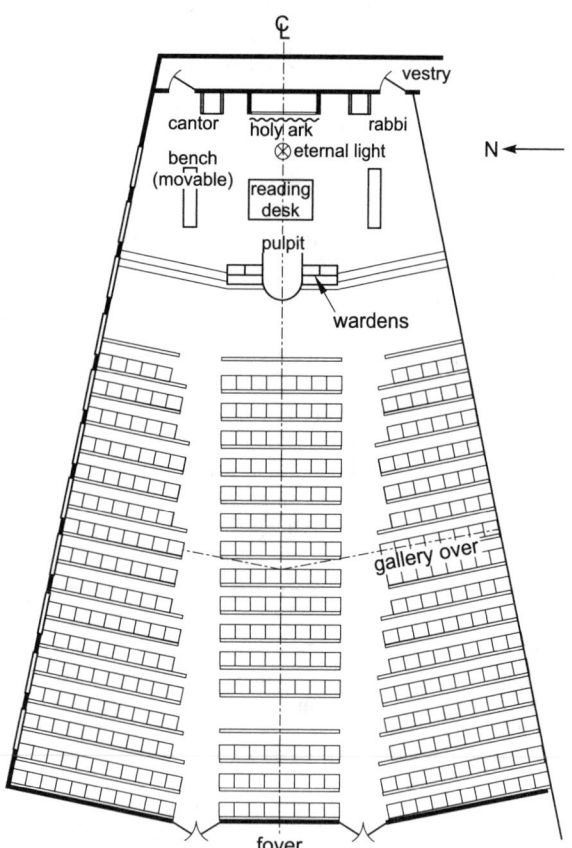

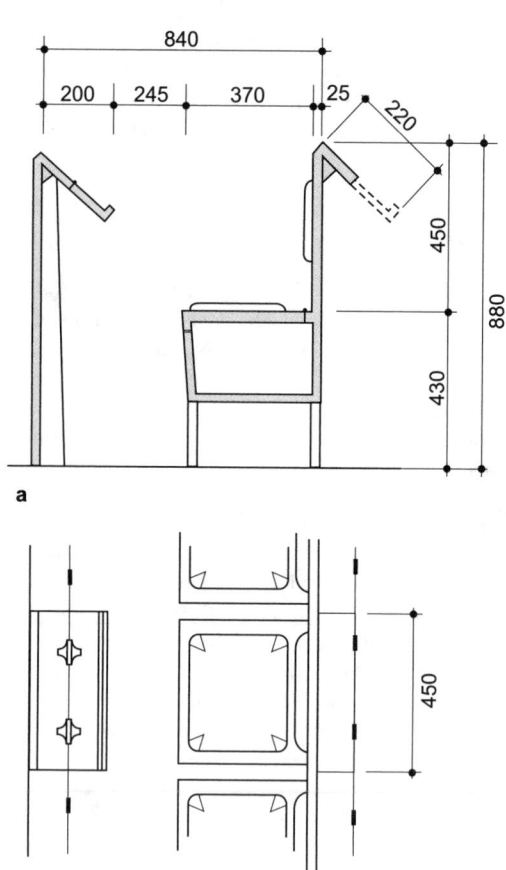

27.42 *Plan of synagogue with Bima before the Holy Ark, seating 376 downstairs and 234 upstairs. For weddings the reading desk and benches are moved aside to accommodate the canopy on the Bima*

27.43 *Seat and bookrest.* **a** *Section. The bookrest folds up to make more clearance. The seat lifts to reveal a locker for prayer book, bible and prayer shawl.* **b** *Plan*

The reading of the scroll is followed by the congregation from Hebrew bibles which are quite large. Each seat, therefore, needs a bookrest, **27.43**. However, some prayers have to be said facing the Holy Ark; this means turning sideways in many seats. It is normal for the bookrests to be hinged to increase the clearance. Prayers are said either standing or sitting. Congregants *never* kneel in a synagogue.

Most larger synagogues have galleries and in orthodox synagogues the women sit here. Since the use of a lift is forbidden on the Sabbath and Holydays, they are not usually provided in orthodox synagogues. Women unable to climb stairs are accommodated in a section of the downstairs behind a curtain (*mechitsah*).

Processions
These are a feature of synagogue servces. At services where readings are given from the Torah, the scroll or scrolls are taken from the Holy Ark and processed to the Bima before the reading, and processed back afterwards. On the Feast of Tabernacles most of the men will process behind the scrolls carrying palm branches and citrons. On the Rejoicing of the Law, all the scrolls that the congregation owns will be processed around the synagogue many times. The aisles must be wide enough for these processions.

Other features
● A *Ner Tamid*, eternal light, hangs before the Holy Ark
● The rabbi or minister has a 'box' normally placed to one side of the Ark, with a seat facing the congregation.
● The *chazan*, or cantor, has a matching box on the other side of the Ark.

● The wardens have a box usually placed just forward of the Bima facing he Ark. It should have room for four wardens.
● Where there is a choir it may be accommodated in a normal seating area, or in a special place such as above the Holy Ark.
● Storage near the entrance should be provided for prayer books, bibles and prayer shawls.
● A display board similar to a hymn board is provided for service details.
● Progressive congregations need an organ. Some orthodox synagogues have a limited musical facility for weddings.
● For weddings, a *chupah* (canopy) is erected on the Bima if there is room, or forward of it on the floor of the synagogue. The couple and the rabbi are accommodated under the chupah, with as many others of the family and witnesses as there are room for.
● Funerals *never* take place in synagogues (it is forbidden for a dead body to remain inside). A special prayer hall, **27.44** is provided at Jewish cemeteries. This is a covered open space with a few benches around the walls for infirm people. The floor is at ground level: the coffin is not carried by bearers but pushed on a wheeled cart. There are doors at both ends to signify the progress of man from birth to death. A small detached building on one side with open windows is provided for *cohanim* who are not permitted to enter any building containing a corpse.
● Purification using water, analagous to Christian baptism, takes place by total immersion not in a synagogue but in a separate facility called a *mikvah*. The design of this can be similar to a hydrotherapy pool. Such purification is not for infants, but is

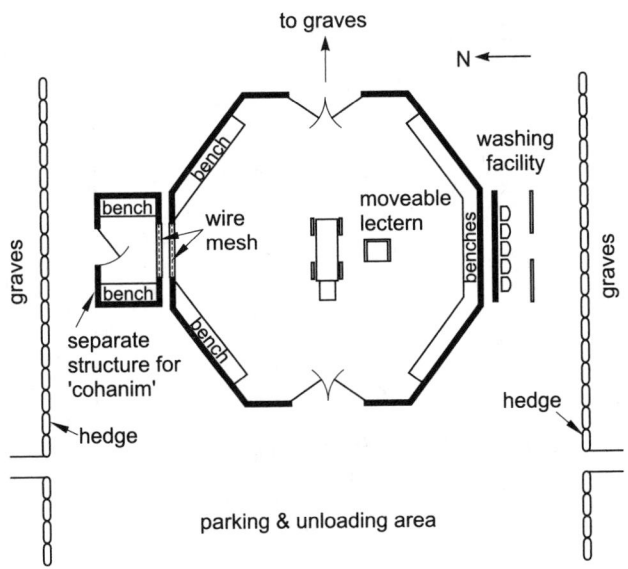

27.44 *Plan of cemetery prayer hall*

used by the orthodox at adult conversions, on certain occasions by women and by some men on a weekly basis.

18.03 Building services

Lighting
Lighting levels should be high as many services take place after dark. It is traditional for all available sources to be used even in daylight. Some may be symbolic, such as a *menorah* near the Holy Ark.

Heating
As services can be long, an efficient heating system is essential. Commonly this comprises hot water radiators; radiant sources such as used in churches are not popular.

Ventilation
This must be efficient as on occasion the synagogue will be packed. Control should preferably be automatic. It should not produce draughts or noise.

Speech reinforcement
This may be required in progressive synagogues, but is not permitted by the orthodox on Sabbaths and Holydays. However, nearly all synagogues are now allowed to use 'loop' systems for deaf people, and this will require microphones to be placed very discreetly on the Bima, pulpit and the Holy Ark controlled automatically.

Large Orthodox synagogues need to be carefully designed for excellent acoustics in view of the lack of any reinforcement system. Even so, this implies a maximum capacity of about 1500.

18.04 Outside the sanctuary

Since services are long, synagogues need adequate cloakroom and lavatory accommodation. A vestry for the rabbi and chazan is often provided at the Ark end of the building with a direct entrance into the sanctuary close to the rabbi's box.

There is a foyer between the street entrance and the sanctuary and there are stairs from this to the ladies' gallery. The foyer should have notice boards to publicise the many activities in conjunction with the congregation. There may also be one or more built-in charity boxes (used only on weekdays). Immediately outside there will be a board giving the times of services, etc.

Most synagogues have additional halls, classrooms for religion school, kitchens, etc. Orthodox synagogues provide no car

parking, as driving on the Sabbath and Holydays is forbidden. However, a very few parking spaces may be provided where land is available for the minister and for weekday use.

18.04 Holydays

The High Holydays occur around September and congregations are much larger than on a normal Sabbath. Some buildings are designed to open up hall and classroom areas to the main sanctuary at this time; alternatively, one or more additional services are provided in detached halls. As Orthodox synagogues use no electrical speech reinforcement, additional services are separately conducted. This usually involves using a mobile Holy Ark with the reading desk on the floors of the hall used; thus special provision in the building design for these occasions need not be made.

19 MOSQUES

19.01 Elements

Muslims actually need no special place to pray – praying can and does take place in the street! Where a purpose-built mosque is provided, it should comprise and conform to particular rules.

Every mosque has four basic elements, **27.45**. These are the *Mihrab*, *Bab Al-Sadir*, dome and minaret. Both the dome and minaret have a symbolic rather than a utilitarian function in contemporary mosque design. (Terms in *italics* are listed in the Glossary section **19.10**).

19.02 The Mihrab

The Mihrab, **27.46**, is indispensable, as it indicates the direction to the *Kaaba* in Mecca, Saudi Arabia. The direction to Kaaba is also

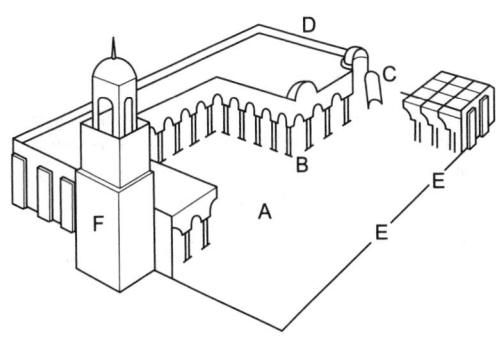

27.45 *Main features of a mosque. Key: A Fountain, B Worship hall, C Mihrab, D Qibla wall, E Entrances, F Minaret*

27.46 *Mihrab*

27.47 *Minbar*

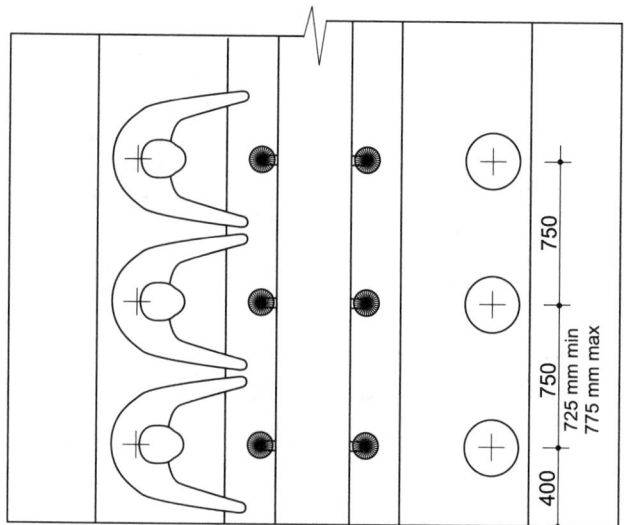

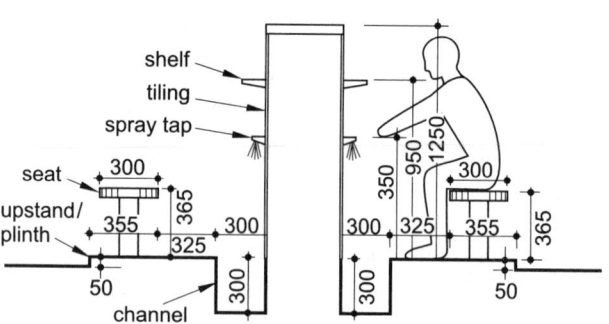

27.48 *Plan and section of ablution*

known as *Qibla*. In symbolic terms, it is the most important element of the modern mosque.

It is essential that this direction is accurately established. The Ordnance Survey office on application can give the precise bearing and distance to Mecca, Saudi Arabia from anywhere in the UK. Generally it is in a south-easterly direction with a bearing of approximately 118° from the north.

The Mihrab is where the Imam leads the congregation for prayer and also houses the *Minbar*, 27.47, a pulpit from which the *Imam* will address the congregation, particularly on Friday. The Minbar might be a low platform, or be at the head of a flight of stairs.

19.03 Bab Al-Sadir

Bab Al-Sadir is the grand entrance. In Arabic, 'Bab' means a gate or door and Al-Sadir meaning the frontal. Traditionally it symbolises the importance of the mosque in the life of the city.

19.04 The dome

The dome is generally centrally located over the main prayer hall and there may be more than one dome to a mosque. It is first and foremost a landmark, indicating the importance of the mosque to the life of the community. In addition, it has two practical functions; one is to echo the words of the Imam inside the mosque and the other is to cool the hot air when it rises upwards and draws in cooler air from outside. Modern technology compensates for the two functions above.

19.05 The minaret

The minaret is used to call the faithful to prayer. It is usually in the form of a circular, octagonal or square tower which projects above the mosque with at least one balcony along its length. It is possible to provide more than one minaret in a mosque and more than one balcony for each minaret.

Traditionally the minaret has an internal staircase leading up to the uppermost balcony, but these days it usually only carries a speaker system so that the Muezzin stays at ground level (sometimes a recording is used).

19.06 Prayers

Prayers are said standing, kneeling and prostrate. There are therefore no seats, but the prayer hall is carpeted and the carpet is marked with imprinted prayer mats pointing to Qibla. Allow at least 0.75 m² per person for praying.

No shoes are allowed past the main entrance, and there are places to leave them, usually in racks, to one or both sides of the entrance.

19.07 Other essentials

Other essentials to be provided are the *Wuzu*, *Wudu* or ablution area, the *Janaza* or morgue, and *Kutub Khana* or library.

19.08 Ablution area

The ablution, 27.48, is where the faithful wash their hands, elbows, faces, behind the ears and their feet in preparation for praying. This is performed under running water. The ablution area also houses the toilets and showers. The number of ablution seats, toilets and showers is governed by the size of the prayer hall.

19.09 Design

Mosque design must conform to particular detail rules, some of which are:

- Male and female entrance/exit, prayer hall and ablution must be separate
- Toilets should be in compartments not cubicles: i.e. must be of solid wall construction not thin partitions or gaps at floor level
- Their orientation is of paramount importance. Compartments must not face or back in the direction of Mecca
- Toilets to be of squatting type (see chapter 3) and have a water tap
- No other habitable enclosure or space should be behind the Mihrab within the confines of the site
- Toilets may not be situated under or over the prayer hall, and no drainage pipes whatsoever should pass under or over it.

It is important for the fulfilling of the client brief that the designer combine the four elements in proportion to each other. 27.49 shows plans of the two levels of a typical mosque.

19.10 Glossary

Bab Al-Sadir	main or grand entrance/gate
Imam	the holy man/preacher/leader of the prayer
Jami or *Jame*	Friday or congregational mosque

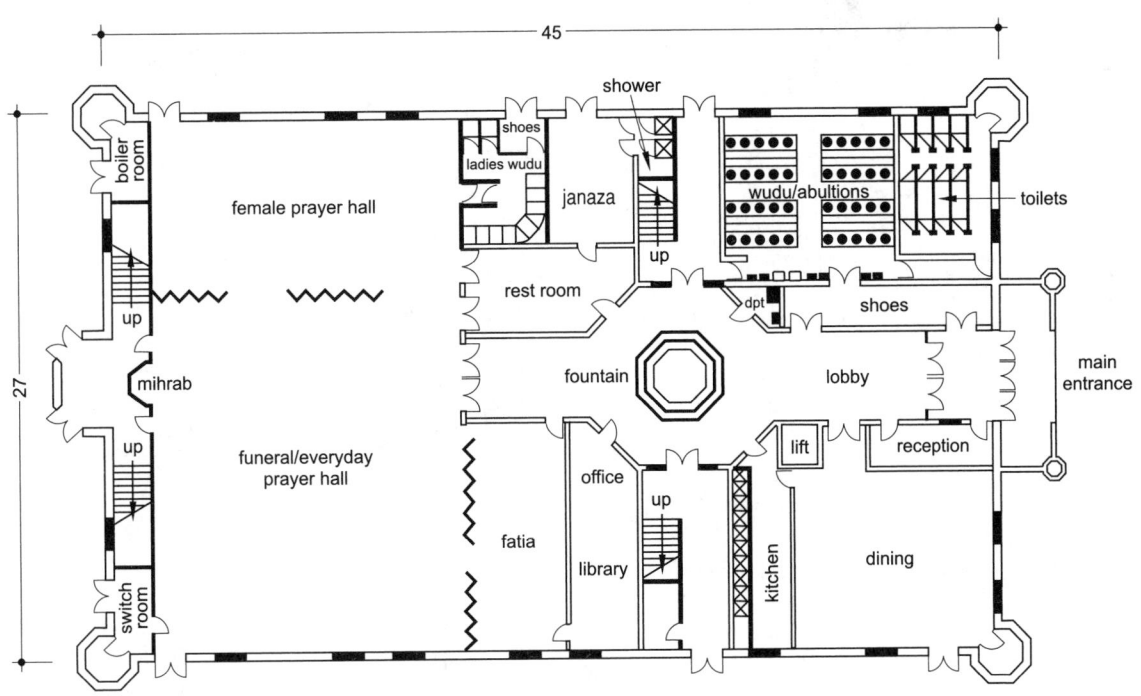

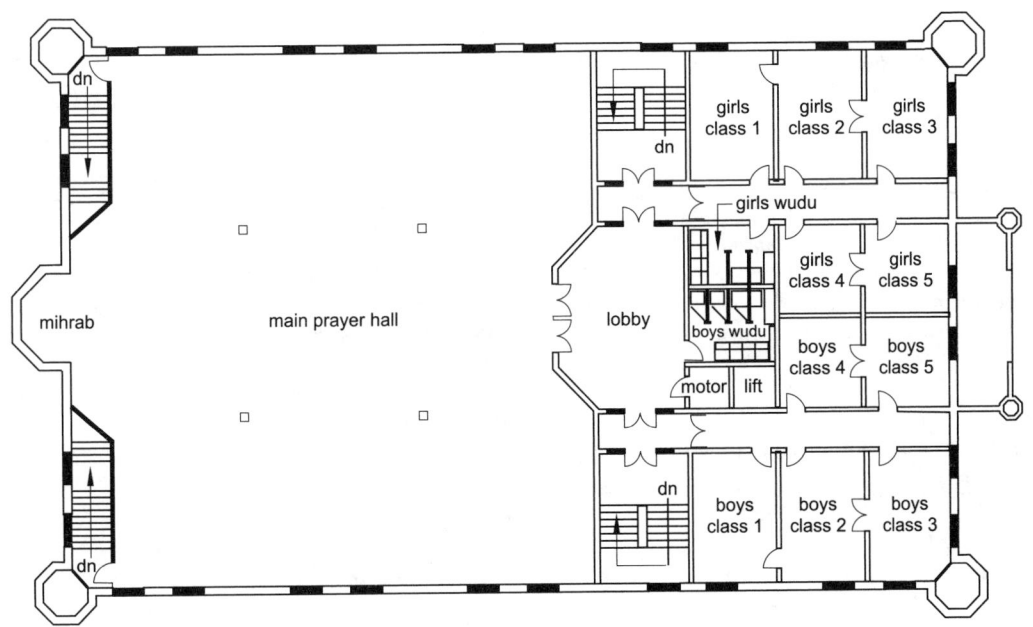

27.49 *Plan of a mosque, ground and first floor*

Janaza	morgue
Kaaba	the holy shrine in Mecca
Kutub Khana	library
Madrasa	school
Masjid	mosque
Mihrab	a niche in the Qibla wall indicating the direction to Kaaba
Minar or *Minara*	minaret
Minbar	pulpit or seat used by the Imam for Friday speech
Muezzin	person calling faithful for prayer
Qibla or *Kibla*	the direction of prayer oriented towards Kaaba in Mecca
Wuzu or *Wudu*	ablution

20 HINDU TEMPLE

20.01 Design

There are three main sections to a Hindu temple, **27.50**:

● The *garbagriha* or shrine room
● The *mandapa* or pillared hall and
● The *ardhamandapa* or porch.

20.02 The garbagriha

This contains the object representing the deity, usually a statue. It may be covered by a canopy, or the roof of the garbagriha itself may be in the form of a pyramid. There should be an ambulatory called the *pradakshina* between the statue and the outer wall.

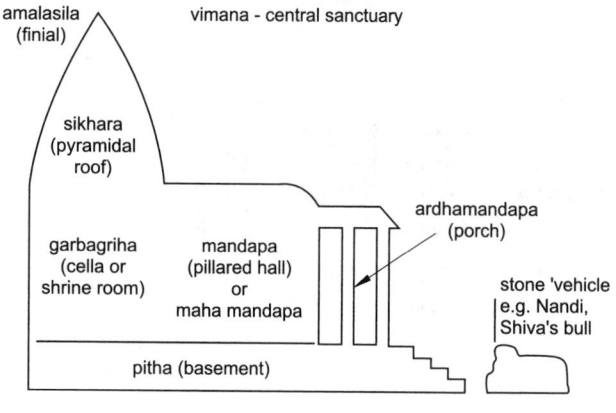

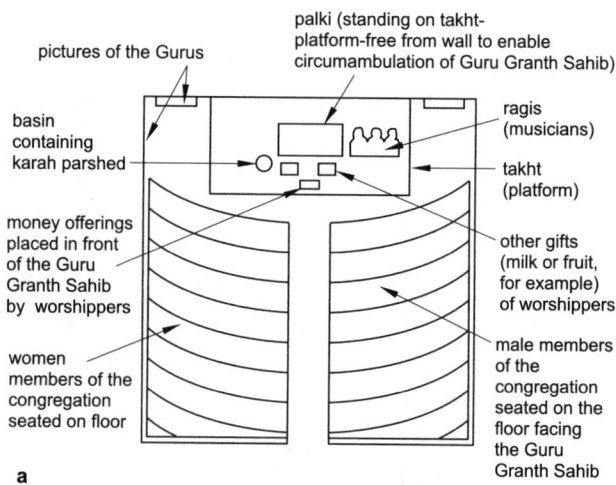

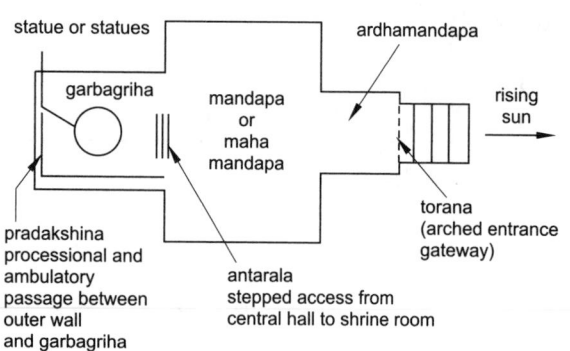

27.50 *Hindu temple, longitudinal section and plan*

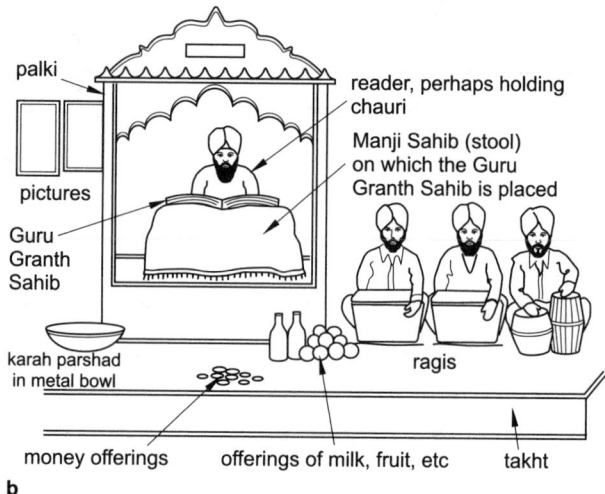

27.51 *Sikh Gurdwara.* **a** *Plan. There is no standard shape but the Guru Granth Sahib must be the focus of attention always visible from all points of the room. The aisle is left free for worshippers to pay their respects to the Guru Granth Sahib before sitting in the congregation. Sometimes separate entrances are required for men and women.* **b** *Elevation of the Takh*

20.03 The mandapa

This is the central hall where the worshippers assemble. They approach the garbagriha through the *antarala* which steps up. Prayers are said here, seated upon the floor. A portable fire altar is brought into the room at the time of worship. Some of the worshippers play musical instruments, others assist the priest.

20.04 The ardhamandapa

This is traditionally orientated towards the rising sun, and also is raised above the ground by steps.

21 SIKH GURDWARA

21.01 Design

The gurdwara, **27.51**, consists of a single large room with the *takh* platform at the end furthest from the entrance. There are no special requirements for orientation. On the takh stands the *palki*, a canopy over the *Guru Granth Sahib* which is the focal point of the gurdwara. The Guru Granth Sahib is the Sikh scripture, and is kept on the *Manji Sahib*, a low reading desk. The palki is free of the wall behind to permit circumambulation.

21.02 Services

Worshippers enter the gurdwara at random times, go directly to the takh and prostrate themselves before the Guru Granth Sahib. They leave offerings of money or of kind on the takh in front of it. They then sit on the floor, men on one side and women on the other, leaving the central aisle for later comers. During the service, verses are read from the Guru Granth Sahib; hymns are sung, music is played by the *ragis*, musicians seated on the takh. The distinguishing feature of a gurdwara externally is the Sikh flag. A tall flagpole is therefore necessary.

Part D

22 CREMATORIA

22.01 Introduction

More people are cremated than buried now due mainly to the scarcity of land for cemeteries and the consequent high cost of grave space. However, some religions such as strict Catholicism and orthodox Judaism do not permit cremation.

In most cases of cremation a ceremony precedes the disposal. This may be religious or it may be a purely secular occasion. After the body has been cremated (which may not be immediately after the ceremony) the ashes may be:

● Deposited in a columbarium associated with the crematorium
● Scattered in a Garden of Remembrance also at the crematorium
or
● Taken away for deposition or disposal elsewhere.

Crematoria may be municipal or commercial. In the former case they are usually situated in or next to a municipal cemetery. Columbaria and Gardens of Remembrance can be provided on the cemetery land. Private crematoria will also provide these facilities, as they can be financially rewarding. The designer must establish a clear brief from a client in these respects.

22.02 Siting

The crematory (i.e. where the furnaces are housed) should not be sited near existing buildings because the effluent from the flue can be unpleasant under certain climatic conditions. The statutory situation requires that crematoria may not be sited closer than 183 m (92 m in inner London) to domestic property. Ideally, crematoria should be located in quiet surroundings, with as much natural landscape as possible.

A minimum site of 1 hectare is required for the crematorium buildings themselves. Further space requirements will depend on whether a Garden of Remembrance is required, when a further hectare at least will be necessary, and more if commercial aspects are to be developed to the full. These areas include the space needed for traffic circulation, parking, a modest amount of room around the building, and the crematorium itself.

Vehicular access to the site should be simple and dignified and free from traffic hazards. The entrance should preferably not be immediately off a principal traffic route. If this is unavoidable, then it should be off a roundabout or where there is space in the central reservation of a dual carriageway for the hearse and mourners' cars to wait in a dignified manner.

22.03 On-site circulation

Clear routes should be provided within the site for vehicular and pedestrian traffic, **27.52**. Only the hearse, principal mourners' and disabled people's vehicles should be allowed beyond the car parking area. These vehicles should arrive at the building under a porte-cochère. The coffin will be transferred to the chapel and then the hearse and other vehicles routed to a waiting area, ready to pick up the principal mourners after the service. One or two parking bays should be provided close to the chapel for disabled people. All other mourners should park their cars in a car park away from the main building.

The entrances to and exits from the building should be located as far as possible from the furnace room so that mourners are not aware of the mechanics of disposal. The pedestrian traffic flow should follow that of the coffin into the chapel. Mourners arriving at the chapel should not meet mourners leaving the previous service. After the service, the people walk from the chapel to a covered way, where floral tributes are displayed, through to the chapel of remembrance (if provided) and then back to the car park via the garden.

22.04 Chapels

Chapels should take into account Christian, non-Christian and secular usage – perhaps separate chapels for Christian and other users; or if the same space is used for all, a system of easily changed symbols installed. Where more than one chapel is provided, one may be small (20 seats) and the other larger (110 seats). Seating should be as described earlier in the chapter for churches. Organs are rarely used, but good facilities for playing recorded music are essential.

The chapel should be designed to reduce emotional disturbance caused by the proceedings, **27.53**. The event can be 'softened' in a number of ways. For example, windows can be provided at a number of levels to enable the mourners to look through the chapel into a restful and attractive external landscape; the designer should avoid a totally introspective environment. Again, the catafalque can be offset from a central position so that the mourners tend to concentrate on the minister conducting the service and not solely on the presence of the coffin.

22.05 Toilets

Many people become emotionally disturbed either before or during the service. The toilets should be easily accessible before the service, immediately after the service and at the point where relatives disperse after the ceremony. At least three groups of toilet facilities are required.

22.06 Coffin circulation

A diagram of the coffin circulation is given in **27.54**.

27.07 The furnace room

The finishes in the furnace room should be impervious and easily maintained. Blow-back on ignition may occur occasionally, and soot deposits can accumulate on walls and ceiling.

22.08 Ancillary accommodation

All or some of the following will be required depending on circumstances:

- Administrative suite
- Manager's office
- Waiting rooms
- Resting place with catafalque
- Vestry for clergy
- Flower room
- Transfer chamber and coffin storage

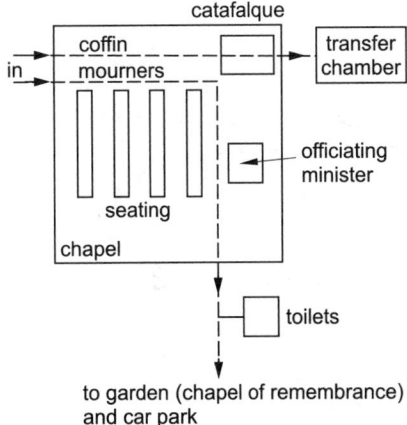

27.53 *Chapel arrangement*

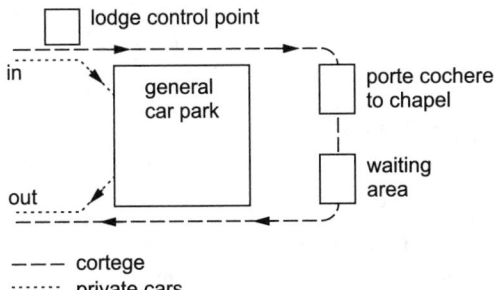

27.52 *Crematorium vehicular flow diagram*

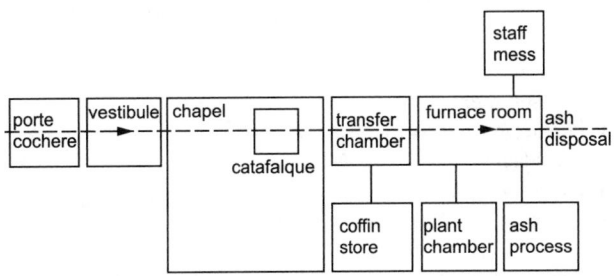

27.54 *Coffin circulation pattern*

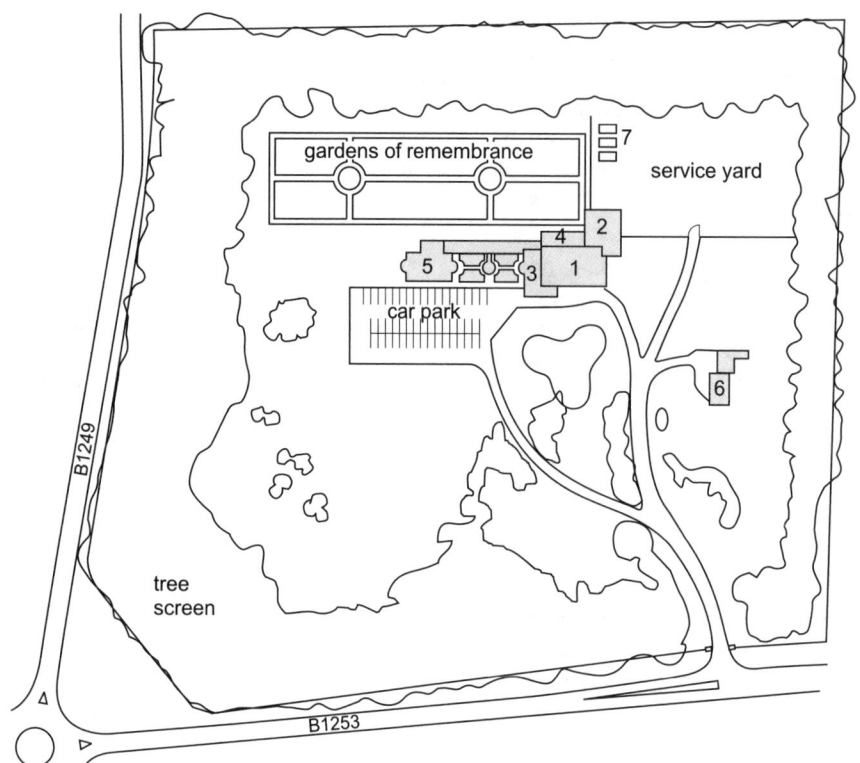

27.55 *Site plan of East Riding Crematorium Architect: R Peter Belt DiplArch RIBA. Key: 1 chapel, 2 cremators, 3 porte-cochère, 4 floral gallery, 5 hospitality suite, 6 superintendant's house, 7 gas tanks*

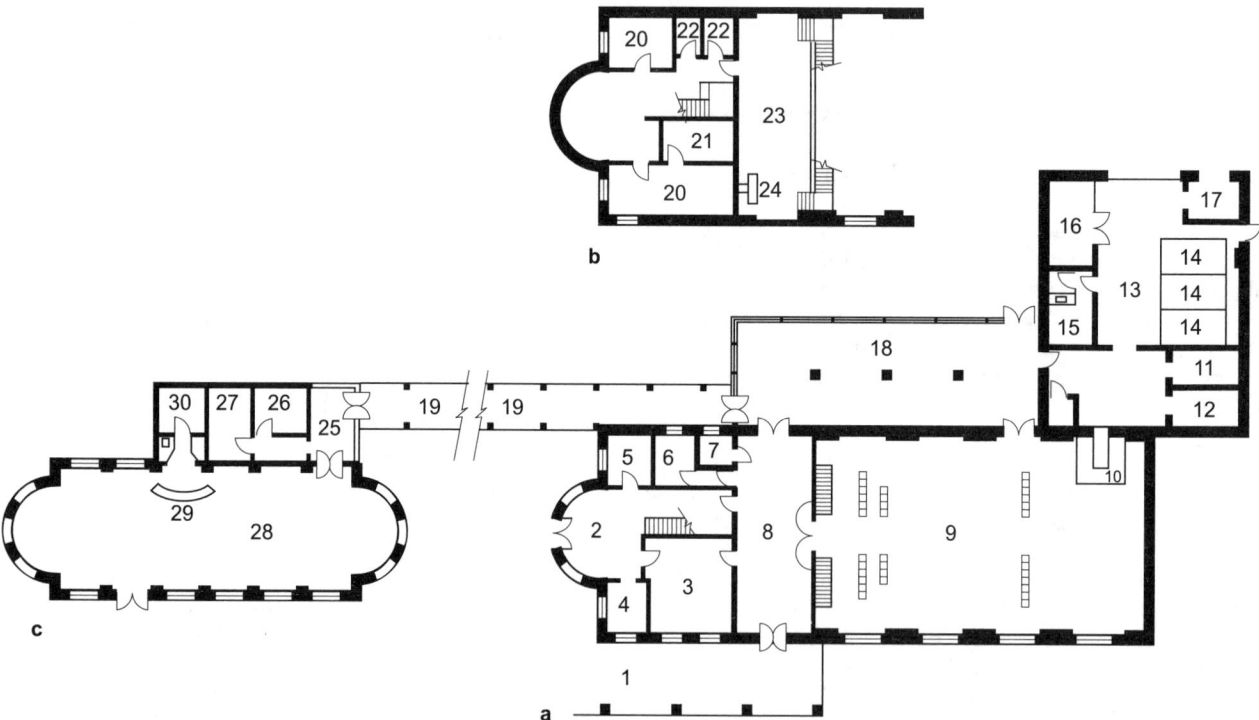

27.56 *East Riding Crematorium: plans of main building complex Architect: R Peter Belt DiplArch RIBA. Key: 1 porte-cochère, 2 entrance hall, 3 waiting room, 4 vestry, 5 enquiries, 6 men's toilets, 7 ladies and disabled people's toilet, 8 foyer, 9 chapel, 10 canopy over catafalque, 11 flower store, 12 cold store, 13 cremation room, 14 creators, 15 staff, 16 workshop, 17 fan room, 18 floral gallery, 19 covered walkway, 20 office, 21 records, 22 toilets, 23 gallery, 24 organ, 25 hospitality porch, 26 men's toilet, 27 women's toilet, 28 reception room, 29 servery, 30 store. **a** Ground floor of main area. **b** First floor. **c** Hospitality suite*

- Viewing room
- Furnace operator's room and storage
- Attendant's room
- Public toilets
- Gardener's store and porter's lodge.

The site plan of a recently constructed crematorium complex is shown in **27.55**. Plans of the main building are given in **27.56**.

23 BIBLIOGRAPHY

Architects' Journal, Church buildings, London, Architectural Press, 1967

Directory of Crematoria, The Cremation Society, Woodcut House, Ashford Road, Hollingbourne, Maidstone, Kent.

The Law of Burial, Cremation and Exhumation, M. R. Davies, Shaw and Sons, London.

Dying, Death and Disposal, Gilbert Cope (ed.), SPCK, London

28 Schools

Guy Hawkins

Guy Hawkins is is an architect and school building consultant. He previously worked in the Architects and Building Branch of the DES, and the Property Services Department of Essex County Council

CI/SfB 71
Uniclass F71
UDC 727.1

KEY POINTS:
- *School building went through a period reflecting advanced theories of education*
- *This period is now ending and schools are reverting to more conventional forms*
- *Security has become an important aspect of school design*

Contents
1 Introduction
2 The builing of schools
3 Detail design considerations
4 Nursery schools and classes
5 Primary schools
6 Middle schools
7 Secondary schools
8 Provision for special needs in education
9 References

1 INTRODUCTION

1.01 This chapter relates specifically to the education system in England and Wales at the time of writing. In other parts of the United Kingdom and elsewhere it varies. Also, education is in a constant state of change, so that what is said will need continual updating. However, at all times and places, the general principles remain.

1.02 Types of school

Full time education is compulsory between the ages of 5 and 16 years. Schools are either independent ('private' and 'public'), run by their owners or by charitable foundations, or maintained ('state' schools). Maintained schools are funded at public expense via the Department for Education and Employment (DfEE), Local Education Authorities (LEAs), Diocesan Boards of Education or special Foundations. Schools are largely defined by their form of government and the ages and sex of the pupils they admit. Most maintained schools are comprehensive – open to all and providing courses for all abilities, but some secondary schools select all or a proportion of their pupils by general or specific ability or interest. Special schools cater for pupils with special needs in education which cannot be met in ordinary schools. Types of school are summarised according to their age range in **28.1**. Within a geographical area there is a common age of transfer from one type of school to another.

1.03 The national curriculum

Maintained schools must teach, as a minimum, the National Curriculum, which specifies ten 'Foundation' subjects plus religious education, organised in four 'Key Stages' up to the age of 16. The curriculum for those over 16 is made up from a range of optional courses leading to specific academic or vocational qualifications.

1.04 The school as a community

Schools have a duty to look after their pupils' welfare (referred to as 'pastoral care'). This is done by formal and informal counselling, and also by the fostering of a school community through assemblies, sport, charitable projects, expeditions, and other shared activities. Each pupil belongs to a basic class or group, and may be part of a larger 'house' or year group. The extent to which this has a direct effect on the provision of space varies, but schools should be designed for a community with a wide range of social needs, activities, and groupings.

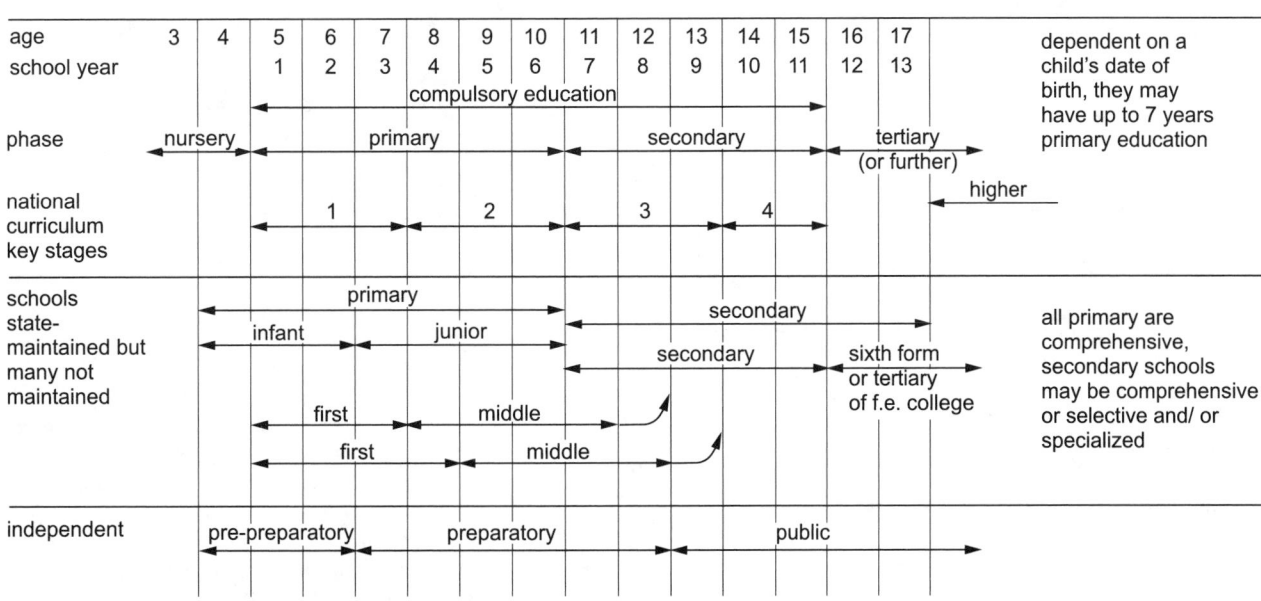

28.1 *Types of school, age range and national Curriculum stages*

2 THE BUILDING OF SCHOOLS

2.01 Funding and promotion of building projects

Most funding for the building, extension, improvement and repair of maintained schools comes from local taxation, controlled according to sector. LEAs, Diocesan Boards, or individual Foundations for CTCs (City Technology Colleges) promote new schools via annual capital programmes, and set design briefs with the aid of specialist advisers. In the case of extensions or improvements at existing schools, the head teacher and governors have an important role, both as users and as carrying financial responsibility for running cost and maintenance under Local Management of Schools (LMS). They may also promote their own locally funded projects. Grant Maintained (GM) schools are fully responsible and independent, receiving grants direct from the Funding Agency for Schools (FAS), for which they must bid, and for which locally generated partnership funding may be required.

2.02 Statutory control, design guidance, and briefing

All new and remodelled buildings must comply with the Education (School Premises) Regulations 1996, and related DfEE standards and procedures conveyed through Circulars and Administrative Memoranda (see references 1 to 5). School building projects must comply with Building Regulations, but are exempt from the usual procedures for obtaining approval. Currently, all projects at GM schools must obtain project approval directly from the DfEE, while the majority of LEA schemes can be self-certified for compliance locally. Procedures change, and advice should be sought from the DfEE.

2.03 Constents

Local Authorities which are both LEAs and Planning Authorities may grant themselves planning consent for educational developments. Independent and GM schools must obtain Planning Consent through normal procedures.

2.04 Regulations

Most general regulations apply to schools – Health and Safety at Work, Food Hygiene, Electricity, Water, Gas, Public Entertainment Licensing.

2.05 The DfEE publishes a series of Building Bulletins on aspects of school design. As the 1996 Regulations are less prescriptive than previous versions, and schools enjoy more autonomy and self-government, the role of non-statutory advice from the DfEE has increased. Most important are the area standards contained in Building Bulletins 82 and 77 which replace the former statutory minimum teaching areas (see references 6 and 28).

2.06 LEAs have standard procedures for commissioning and managing building projects, and many have standard briefs and design guidance for the most common types of school or specialised facility. Advice for GM schools is available from the Grant Maintained Schools Centre (see references 7 and 20).

2.07 Sites for new schools

Completely new schools are only likely to be required in association with large housing developments, for which a full Planning and Highways framework will have been established. This may include provision of sites for schools at no cost, via Section 106 of the Town and Country Planning Act 1990. **28.2** and **28.3** set out a range of

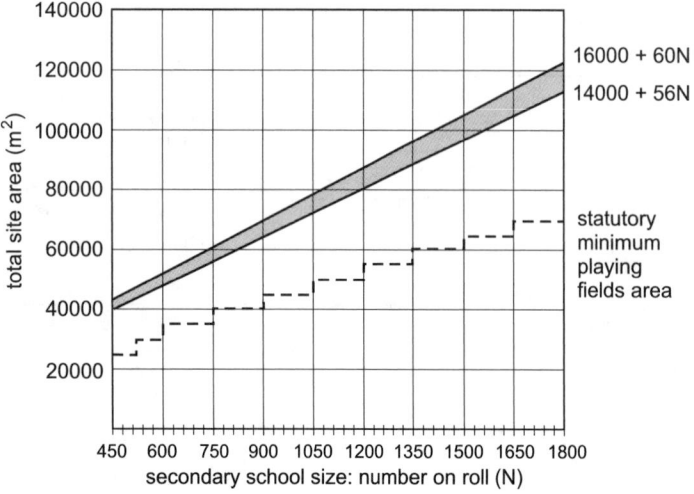

28.2 *Land and playing fields for primary schools. The broken line indicates the statuary requirement for playing fields. The range of total site areas allows for some variety of shape contour, and access arrangements, but more area may be required just above each 'step' in the playing field area*

28.3 *Land and playing fields for secondary schools. The broken line indicates the statutory requirement for playing fields. The range of total side areas allows for some variety of shape, contour, and access arrangements. Schools with wide catchment area and the consequent need to park and turn a number of buses, or schools with significant community use, may require more land, but this may be offset by the use of high-quality all weather games surface*

overall land requirements for schools, but each case requires a full site feasibility study.

Schools may require additional space for parking and turning of buses, for parents' cars, or for community use. Local Planning Authorities will set or agree standards in their area. Space should also be allowed for the retention and enhancement of existing landscape features. (See references 6 and 8.)

2.08 Community use

Most schools are used outside school hours, and many are specifically planned and funded as community schools or joint-use centres incorporating educational, sports, and leisure facilities; possibly with day as well as evening use. Alternatively, falling school rolls may release space to be let out for such purposes. The National Lottery Sports and Arts Funds have had a major impact in this area, and many school and community projects are being developed with their aid. Lottery grants are dependent on a proportion of the cost being raised locally.

All such joint use schemes require careful design for premises management – heating and lighting must be zoned, and possibly separately metered, and the conflicting demands of security and fire escape resolved. Halls need to be licensed for public entertainment. Outdoor areas must be secure and well lit, parking adequate and easy to control, and signposting and routes clear. Large joint-funded schemes require good financial and management planning to be successful. Where there is no outside source of finance, all income from lettings of premises goes to the school governors, who must be able to cover their costs. (See references 9 and 10.)

2.09 Growth and change, flexibility and adaptability

Schools are vulnerable to changes in population and popularity, curriculum and teaching methods. The potential for growth, change, and possible contraction and change of use must be considered seriously at all stages and levels of design. Short-term flexibility of use can be maximised by good standards of space and services provision, and appropriate furniture. Adaptability in the medium term is assisted by good site development strategy, buildings with regular planning grids and simple shapes, and the positioning of fixed elements such as staircases and lavatory blocks to give maximum freedom in relocating partitions. In the longer term, change of use of part or all of the buildings for non-education purposes requires fresh planning consent and may have major implications for road access and on-site parking provision.

3 DETAIL DESIGN CONSIDERATIONS

3.01 Anthropometrics

School buildings and furniture need to be designed with regard to the childrens' body dimensions. The chart **28.4** shows the ranges to be found for four basic dimensions at ages from 2 to 18. This should assist the architect in regard to such items as bench seating and stand-up worktops. Vertical grip reach controls the shelving for children to be able to reach, and also for the height to put shelves which need to be out of their reach.

3.02 Furniture

Ranges of undersize furniture have long been produced for use in schools. There are at present three standard ranges which may be encountered:

- Commercial, Table I
- British Standard 5873: Part 1: 1980, Table II and
- BS EN 1729 (Draft), Table III.

The relevant dimensions are shown in **28.5**.

Since school budgets are limited, furniture tends to be retained until it becomes unusable, so it is likely that for some time ahead

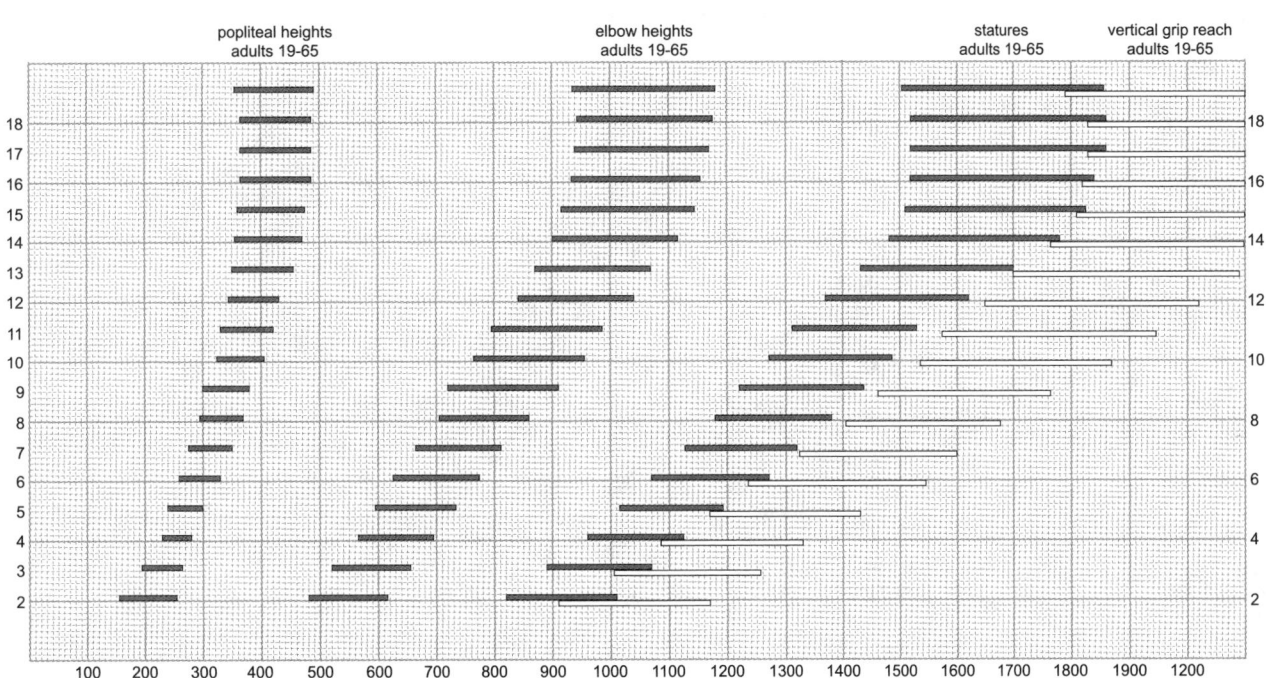

28.4 *Diagram of four main dimensions for children from two to eighteen, from left to right:*

- *popliteal high for seating*
- *elbow height, standing worktop 75 mm below elbow*
- *stature*
- *vertical grip reach, for shelving.*

This diagram covers children of both sexes between the 5th and 95th percentiles. Allow for increase due to footware of 20 mm for young children, 25 mm for older children and 45 mm for older girls.

As an example, 5 year-old child can sit comfortably on a seat less than 260 mm high. It can reach an item on a shelf less than 615 mm high, and a shelf over 755 mm is likely to be out of reach

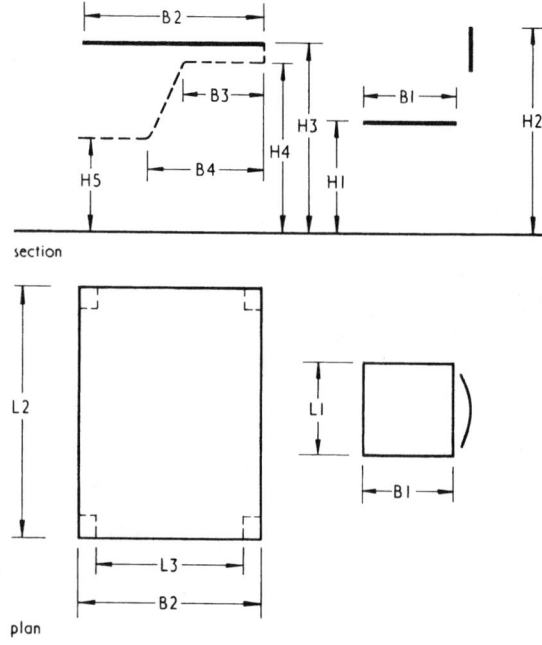

section

plan

28.5 *Critical dimensions for school furniture, see Table II*

Table I Furniture size available through a commerical supplier (see 28.5)

	A	B	C	D	E
Colur code	White	Yellow	Red	Blue	Green
Stature range					
Approx. ages	3–5	5–8	7–11	10–14	11+
Chair seat height H1	280	320	355	390	430
Table top height H3	500	550	600	650	700

any of the standard ranges could be found in a school. The fact that two ranges have similar sizemarks and all have similar colour codes although each applies to a different actual size is likely to cause endless confusion.

The commercial ranges with sizemarks A to E is currently the commonest. The EN BS range, being a product of CEN, will take its place; as by the Construction Products Directive the furniture produced under it will almost certainly become mandatory for all maintained schools. This range is similar to the superseded BS 5873 range, but has an additional small size to satisfy continental Europe's demand for furniture for the very young.

3.03 Furniture of various types are shown in **28.6** to **28.20**. **28.21** shows a free standing study carrel, **28.22** a study bay for senior

Table II Furniture sizes to BS 5873-Part 1:1980 (see 28.5)

		1	2	2.5	3	4	5
Colour code		Orange	Violet	Black	Yellow	Red	Green
Stature range		1000–1120	1120–1300	1880–1360	1300–1480	1480–1620	1620+
Approx age		3–5	5–11	5–12	5–13	8–18	11+
Chair seat height	H1	260	300	302	340	380	420
Chair seat depth	B1	250	280	280	320	350	370
Chair min width	L1	250	270		290	320	340
Chair max width	L1	380	380	380	380	430	430
Backrest height	H2	448–513	526–583	546–603	592–653	661–713	720
Table top height	H3	460	520	540	580	640	700
Table min depth	B2	550	550	550	550	550	550
Table min length for one person	L2	550	550	550	550	550	550
Table min length for two people	L2	1100	1100	1100	1100	1100	1100
Min thigh height	H4	400	460	460	520	580	640
Min tibia height	H5	250	250	250	300	300	350
Min knee depth	B3	300	300	300	300	350	400
Min Tibia depth	B4	400	400	400	400	450	500
Min width for one person	L3	470	470	470	470	470	470

Table III Furniture sizes to BS EN 1729 (draft)—simplified (see 28.5)

		1	2	3	4	5	6	7
Colour code		Orange	Violet	Black	Yellow	Red	Green	White
Sature range		800–100	950–1150	1100–1350	1250–1550	1400–1700	1600–1900	1850+
Popliteal range		210–260	260–320	310–380	260–440	410–500	450–550	500+
Approx ages								
Chair seat height	H1	210	260	310	360	410	450	500
Chair seat depth	B1		240	380	330	380	420	450
Chair min width	L1		240	300	340	380	400	420
Backrest height	H2		510	590	670	740	810	900
Table top height	H3	400	470	540	610	680	750	830
Table min depth	B2		500	500	500	500	500	500
Table min length for one person	L2		600	600	600	600	600	600
Table min length for two people	L2		1200	1200	1200	1300	1300	1300
Min thigh height	H4	150	200	250	300	350	390	440
Min tibia height	H5		400	480	550	620	670	720
Min knee depth	B3		300	300	350	400	450	450
Min tibia depth	B4		400	400	450	500	550	550

28.6 *Square table for primary schools (and alternative seating arrangements):*

A 900 × 900 × 455
B 1200 × 1200 × 455
C 1200 × 1200× 510

28.7 *Oblong table for primary schools:*

A 900 × 450 ×455
A 1200 × 600 × 455
B 1200 × 600 × 510
C 1350 × 700 × 565

28.8 *Round table for primary schools:*

A 850 dia × 455
B 850 dia × 510
C 1270 dia × 565

28.9 *Square pedestal table:*

B 1200 × 1200 × 510
C 1350 × 1350 × 565

28.10 *Teacher's table:*

1200 × 750 × 700

28.11 *Workbench:*

1200 × 600 × 550, 600, 650 or 700

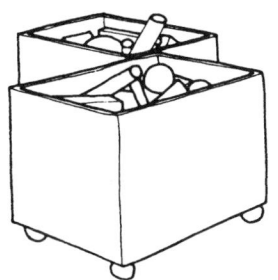

28.12 *Mobile storage bins:*

600 × 450 × 500

28.13 *Trolley locker:*

900 × 450 × 600, 650 or 700

28.14 *Book storage and display trolleys:*

900 × 450 × 900

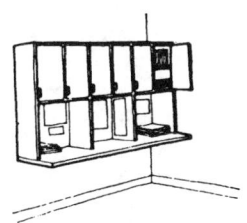

28.15 *Staff locker and writing unit: 2400 × 350, writing flap overall width 500 mm, height 1200 mm*

28.16 *Coat trolley:*

1400 × 1000 × 650

28.17 *Easel:*

800 × 1200 high

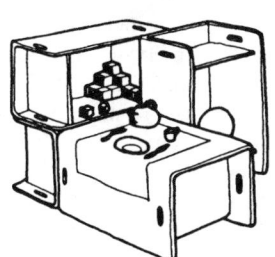

28.18 *Flexible combination units for primary schools:*

900 × 450 × 225

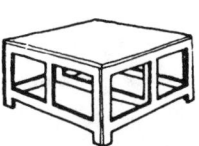

28.19 *Folding rostrum unit:*

900 × 900 × 450

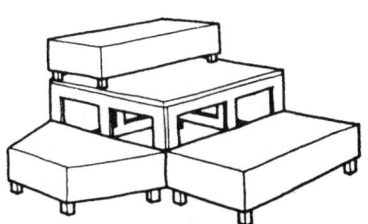

28.20 *Oblong and trapezoidal rostrum units in combination with the previous unit*

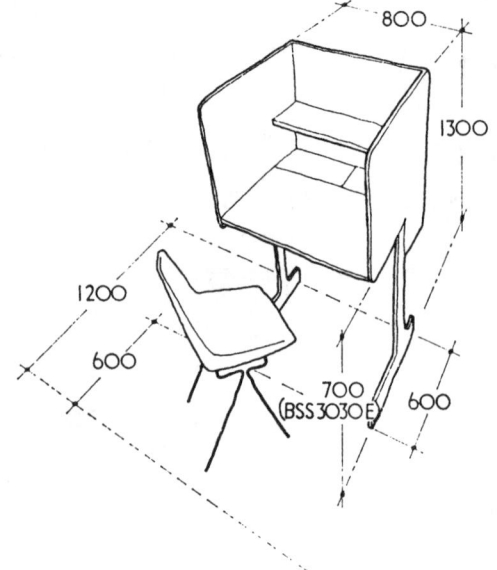

28.21 *Study carrel*

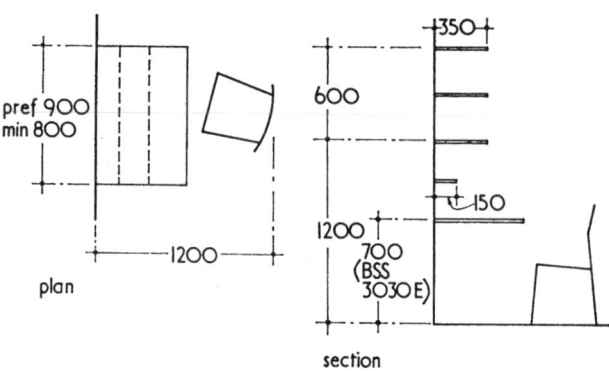

28.22 *A study bay: dimensions for individual work spaces for senior pupils*

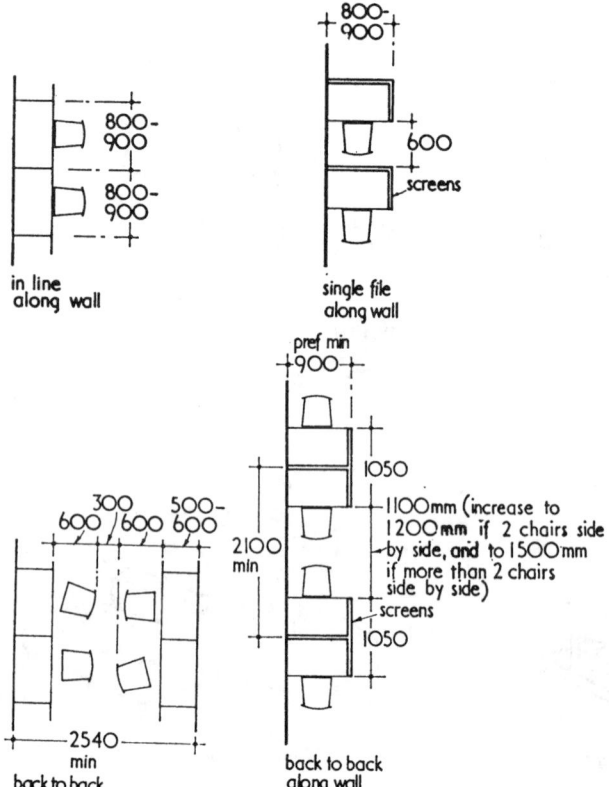

28.23 *Various arrangements of study bays*

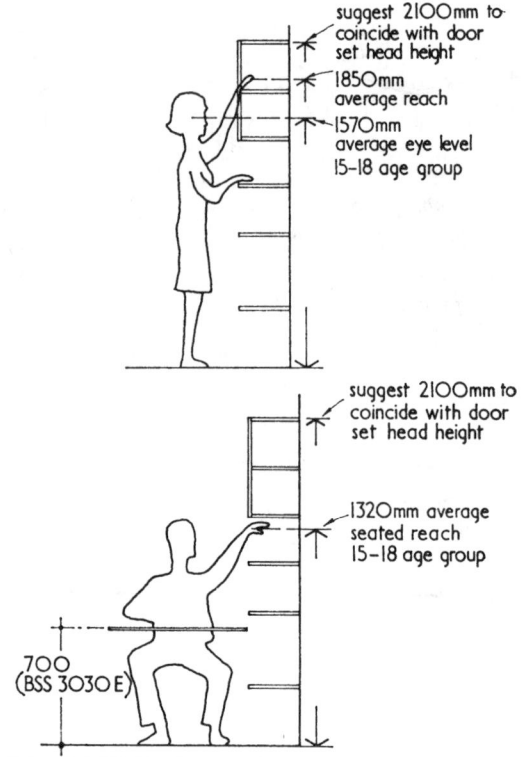

28.24 *Average height and reach of a pupil in year 12 and upwards (sixth-formers)*

pupils and **28.23** various arrangements for private study. **28.24** indicates height and reach for secondary school pupils.

3.04 Provision for disabled people

New schools must be designed for use throughout by disabled pupils, staff and visitors. Design parameters for this will be found in Chapters 2, 3 and 4.

Arrangements for safe escape in case of fire are the most difficult part of the exercise. These require combinations of design provision together with management procedures involving assistance by able bodied persons. The means of escape for disabled people in some existing buildings may be extremely difficult and expensive to organise. Current thinking is that a small risk is acceptable when otherwise a disabled person would be totally denied access. (See references 5 and 11.)

When referring to the needs of disabled people the tendency is to concentrate on requirements for wheelchair users. The needs of people on crutches, with visual or aural impairments or with other disabilities should not be ignored. In particular, adequate guidance for blind pupils, staff and visitors should be provided. Blind people may also have assistance from guide dogs.

3.05 Construction and environment

School building has pioneered much technical innovation, originally in the interest of low capital cost and rapid production, more recently in the quest for energy conservation; some design solutions have resulted in problems of maintenance, and environmental discomfort. The 'deep plan' remains an important means of creating appropriate planning relationships, and attention is currently focused on use of appropriate sections, control of ventilation, and use of passive solar energy. Room acoustics remain a crucial element in the success of any school building. (See references 4, 12 and 13)

Compliance with COSHH regulations may require upgrading of those areas where fumes and dust are created, including replacement of convectors by radiators, and the provision of fume and dust extraction to individual appliances. (See reference 14.)

3.06 Services

In the provision of services, the widespread use of computers gives rise to the need for glare-free lighting as well as increased power outlet and network cabling provision.

3.07 Security

Security is a major recent issue in schools, and many have installed sophisticated external lighting, intruder alarm and TV surveillance systems. However, the most elaborate technological systems are of no value if not backed up by appropriate management procedures.

The hazards emanate from several directions:

● Externally from burglary, particularly of computer equipment
● Also externally, attacks on staff and pupils
● Internally from vandalism and pilfering.

The design of the school can make a substantial contribution in all these areas. If possible, multi-computer installations should be located on upper floors, from which it would be more difficult to remove items. Doors and windows must be sufficiently secure. Flat roofs making external access to upper floors easier should be avoided. Despite some design trends which deprecate them, straight corridors without local widening are easier to keep under observation, and prevent places where people can lurk unseen.

There should be a minimum of entrances to the school, and all should be able to kept under observation at all times. In any case, only one entrance should be usable by the general public, parents, etc. and this should lead directly to a reception area covered by the school office. It should not be possible to penetrate from here into the main school without permission. Any service entrance for kitchen supplies, etc. should be similarly organised so that the main school is not easily accessible from here.

3.08 Fire

In some schools, particularly secondary, problems are caused by letting off fire alarms, and interference with fire point installations. As a result, these are no longer situated in corridors. They are placed within classrooms and offices so that they can be kept under observation.

4 NURSERY SCHOOLS AND CLASSES

4.01 Age range and typical sizes

Nursery classes provide education for those below the compulsory school age of 5 years, who usually attend part-time. They should not be confused with play groups or day nurseries, both of which operate under Social Services regulations, even if using school buildings. Provision is not statutory, and varies widely between areas. There are relatively few self-contained nursery schools, more often one or two classes of around 26 children are attached to infants or primary schools, making some use of their common facilities. **28.25** illustrates a two-class nursery unit designed as a free-standing building but which would probably be attached to a primary school. (See references 19 and 27.)

4.02 Accommodation

Playroom
Around 2.3 m² per place. About two thirds of the floor area should be suitable for practical and messy activities, the remainder carpeted for listening to stories or playing on the floor. Adjacent store of 6–8 m² for large play equipment and wheeled toys, accessible from inside or outside play areas.

Outdoor play area
Around 9 m² per place, of which at least two thirds to be paved. The area should be fully enclosed by a fence with a child-proof latch, and open to the sun, but sheltered from wind, with some fixed seating perhaps on a low wall. A variety of fixed play equipment can be provided, with a safety surface below. Sand pits should be fitted with a removable cover.

Lavatories and coat hanging
One WC and washbasin per 10 children, usually unisex. One cubicle should be fitted with a shower tray and be large enough to admit an adult to help after 'accidents', and to clean and change the patient in privacy. Coat area, with rack for wellingtons in a draught lobby to outside area.

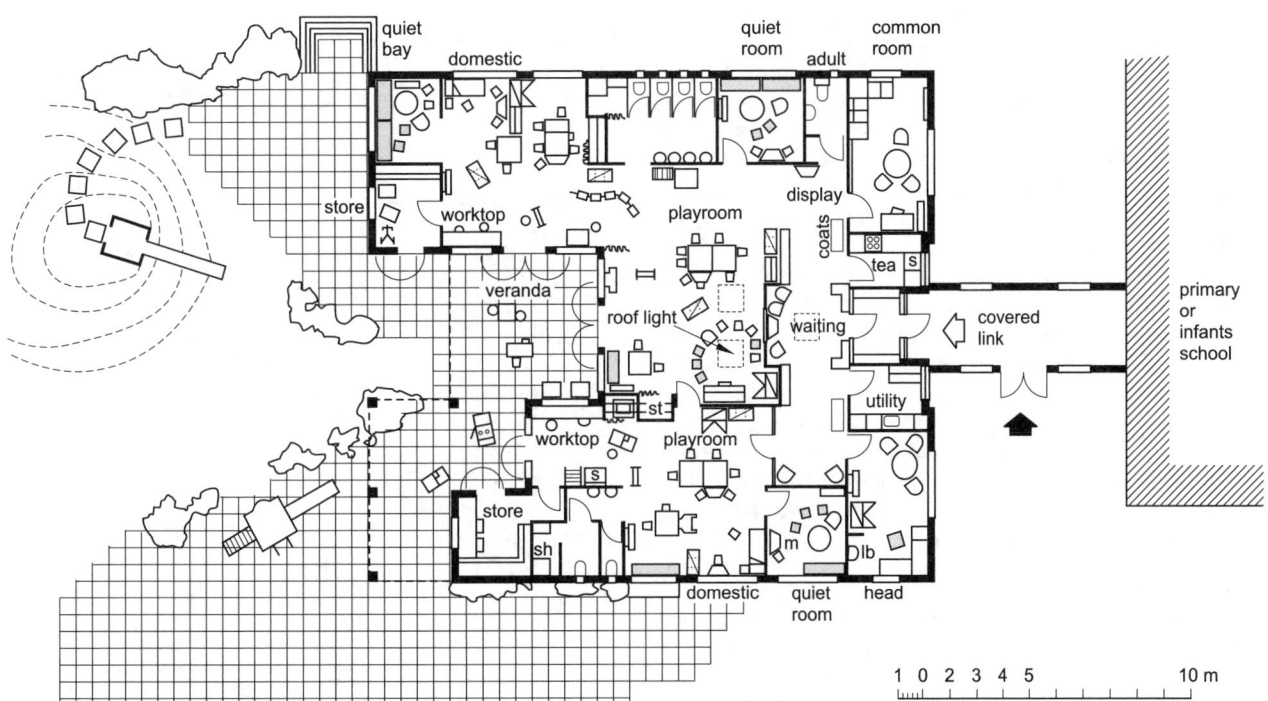

28.25 *A two-class nursery unit. This unit, for up to 60 children, would probably be attached to a large primary school or infants school. It has a full range of teaching and support facilities which would make it particularly suitable for integrating a small number of children with special needs*

Staffroom/quiet room/parents room
This should be 9–10 m² for a nursery class attached to a primary school. A nursery school or unit of two or three classes will also need an office, head teacher's room, staff room, adult lavatories, and a kitchenette for preparing drinks and mid-session snacks for children.

4.03 Security
Recent events have focused attention on the need to ensure both that children cannot wander out of the school enclosure and that they are protected inside the enclosure from those that might wish to harm them.

5 PRIMARY SCHOOLS
This term includes Infant, Junior, and First schools.

5.01 Age range and typical sizes
Pupils aged from 5 to 11 (Years 1–6). Children just under 5 ('Rising Fives') are usually admitted, so that the full primary school age range is actually 7 years, the first year being called 'reception'. Primary schools typically range from 90 to 420 pupils. In densely populated areas, separate infants' (Years 1–2), and Junior schools (Years 3–6) are often provided to avoid having schools which are too large. Infants schools range from 120 to 240 pupils, Juniors from 180 to 360. First schools, age range 5–8 or 5–9, are provided in areas which have Middle schools.

5.02 Curriculum and organisation
The National Curriculum at Key Stages 1 and 2 forms the basis of primary school work. Pupils spend most of their time in a group of around 30, with one class teacher; but pairs or groups of class spaces are often clustered together to allow sharing of specialist teacher skills or resources, and variation of group sizes for different activities.

Once or twice a day each group will go the the hall, or a group room for assembly, physical education, music, or drama. At any time small groups could be working in a library or resource area accessible to the whole school. More than half the children will probably stay to lunch, either bringing sandwiches or having a hot school meal.

5.03 Site planning – access and road safety
Most children arrive on foot accompanied by parents. In the past, several pedestrian entrances were often provided, and these were kept well away from the vehicular access and led straight onto the playgrounds from which the children could go into their class bases via coat and lavatory areas. However, security considerations now tend to restrict the number of entrances so that they can be closely monitored.

In some areas many children are brought to school by car; setting down and picking up can cause congestion and contribute to road safety problems. It may be necessary to provide turning and waiting areas in order to obtain planning consent for a new or enlarged school.

In many cases children are brought from outlying districts by school bus. It is not altogether desirable for these to set down or pick up on the road outside the school, and space within the school grounds may have to be provided. Space may also have to be provided for the parking of staff cars.

5.04 Community use
Joint use of primary schools is generally confined to the hall, any large room not used as a class base, and possibly the outdoor play areas and changing rooms. The design needs to ensure that these can be used as self-contained areas without risking disturbance to materials and displays left out in class bases, and can be heated and serviced in such a way that the running cost can be controlled and correctly apportioned. (See references 10 and 22.)

If meetings of adults are to take place frequently in these spaces, normal size chairs will have to be available. Storage for these will be necessary.

5.05 Recreation areas, playing fields, and landscape
Both paved and grass recreation areas are needed. For infant schools the paved area need not be laid out for formal games. **28.26** shows the range of paved area which should be marked out for games, and **28.27** shows the additional informal recreation area needed, of which half should be paved. The remainder is usually grass and can be developed to provide a variety of work and play facilities, including wild area, pond or animal enclosures.

Playing fields are required at schools having pupils over 8 years of age. **28.2** shows the regulation areas. A junior football pitch size is around 75 m × 45 m, but training grids and running tracks are probably more useful than a second pitch at the larger junior schools. The fullest use of outdoor areas depends on comfort and protection from wind, and the role of landscaping in providing this is as important as its visual or educational function. (See references 6 and 8.)

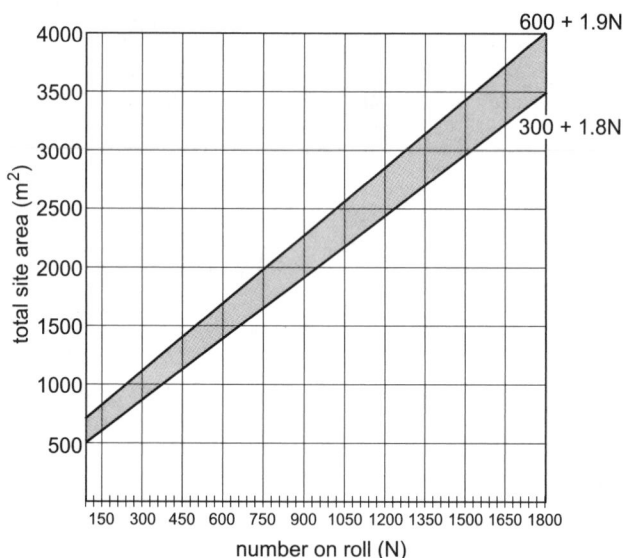

28.26 *Hard paved areas for games. The areas shown indicate the area to be laid out and marked for formal games in schools for all age ranges, except in infants schools, where no formal arrangement is needed*

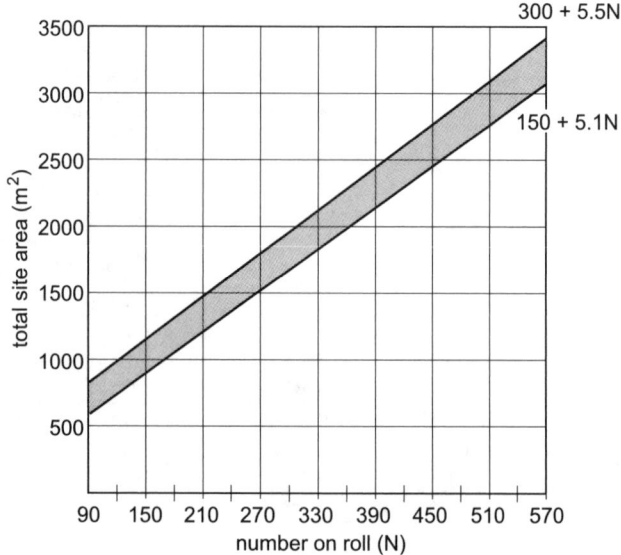

28.27 *Informal recreation areas for primary schools. About half the area should be paved, the remainder can be grass*

5.06 Design strategy for new schools

Primary school buildings are usually single storey, to allow flexibility in organisation, easy access to common resources and outdoor areas, and easy movement of disabled people and trolleys carrying teaching equipment. Changes of floor level appropriate to steep sites require ramps to provide for these. The main elements, the class bases, are grouped to allow the sharing of resources, quiet rooms and practical areas; with easy access to the library and other common areas such as the hall. The visitors' entrance, the staff areas and the the kitchen should be closely associated with the hall.

28.28 and **28.29** show two appropriate designs. Similar organisational structures underlie many other schemes, including those in non-rectilinear form. (See references 20, 21 and 23.)

5.07 Extending and remodelling existing schools

Primary schools tend to have strong design characteristics according to their date of construction, and the adaptability of their form varies widely. In consequence, many extension projects include an element of remodelling, to remedy the revealed problems of the original plan, and to ensure the coherence of the overall scheme.

5.08 Schedules of accommodation

Building Bulletin 82 sets standards for teaching and total floor areas for all types of primary schools. **28.30** shows the possible range of these areas according to the number of pupils on roll, and individual promoters have to decide an appropriate balance between space and cost. (See references 6, 20 and 21.)

5.09 Design requirements

Class bases

Each class will require a definable 'home base', but this can be achieved with a variety of forms from fully open plan to enclosed rooms, and all variations continue to be built. Commonly two or more class areas are closely associated, with some sharing or intercommunication. **28.28** and **28.29** show a range of design approaches.

About two thirds of the floor area should be carpeted for work sitting at tables, the remainder being suitable for practical activities including science and technology, with a sink with hot and cold water, standing-height worktop, and direct access to an outside paved area for summer use. However, to use such a door for general access all year round, though tempting, can easily negate all other energy-saving strategies, to say nothing of possible security problems.

Children generally keep their books, pencils, etc. in mobile plastic tray units within the class base. A teaching materials' store is needed for each class base, either 'walk-in' with a door or open shelving. Two classes might share a double size store.

Hall

Used for assembly, physical education, music, drama, and for parents' meetings and social events. It may also be used for dining. It should be easily accessible from the visitors' entrance. The hall should not used for general circulation and should be acoustically isolated from teaching areas. Height 4.8 m over most of the area to permit climbing frames pivoted to one wall. A sprung floor is desirable, if seldom affordable. It may be licensed for public entertainment. Stores for PE equipment and dining furniture

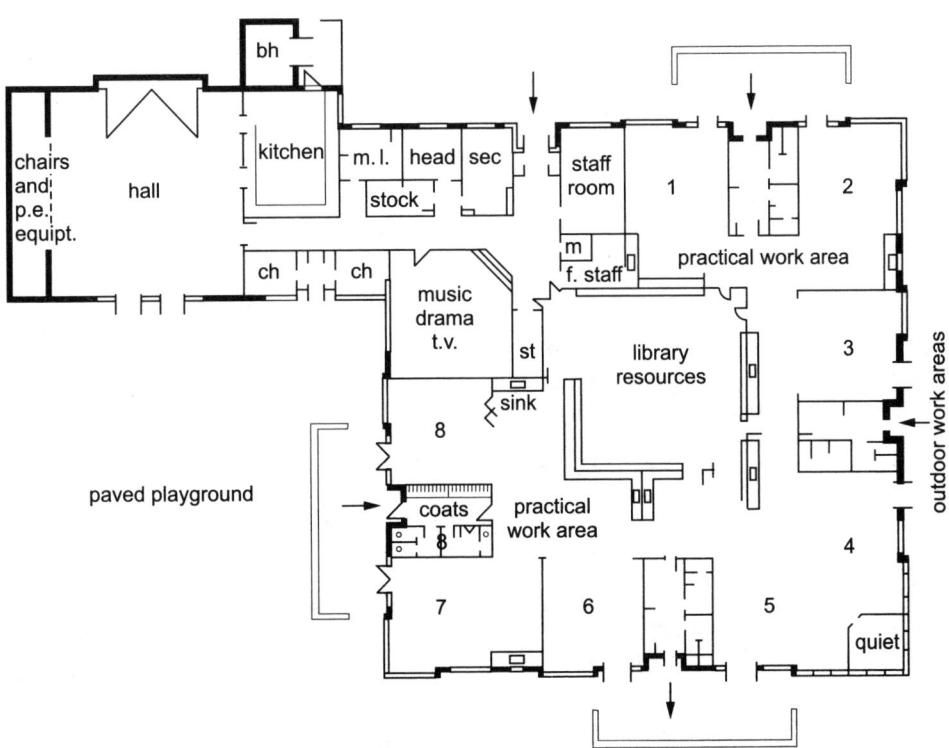

28.28 *Primary school development plan strategy 1: a typical 'doughnut' form with a central atrium, and teaching areas facing in all directions. The hall is removed from the main teaching areas for acoustic privacy, and for evening use the doors to the library/resource area can be locked, leaving a self-contained unit with entrance, adult lavatories, hall, music room, and changing rooms. The plan has practical areas towards the core, and quieter carpeted areas around the perimeter. Each pair of bases shares an entrance direct from the outdoor play area, with lavatories and coat hanging in a large draught lobby. One side of the plan (Bases 1–4) shows a large central library/resource area, with through circulation; the other side (Bases 5–8) has circulation through the practical areas, with an enclosed library/resource area*

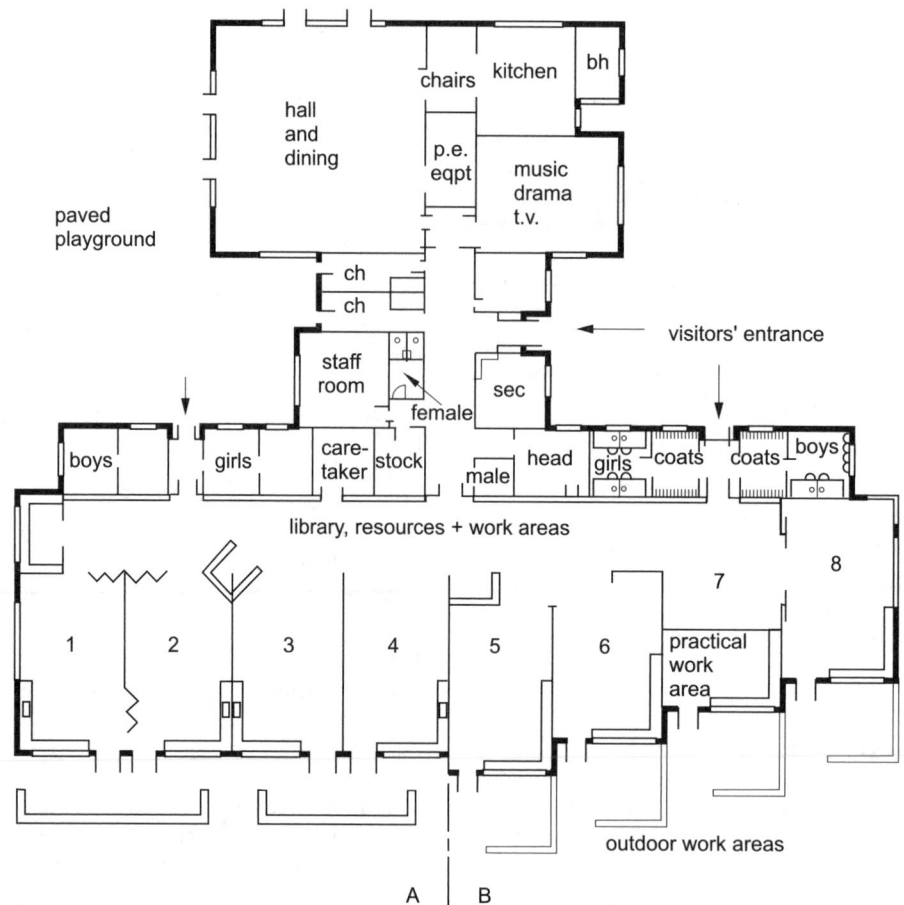

28.29 *Primary school development plan strategy 2: a typical linear plan, with the teaching areas facing predominantly in one direction, usually south, or towards the main view and outdoor play areas. As in **28.28** the hall and related areas can be closed off for evening use, with services zoned to suit. In this case the plan is 'soft centred', with shared areas being predominantly quiet, and practical areas related to outdoor work areas on the perimeter. Pupils' entrances, coat lobbies and lavatories are concentrated at two points, which may be more congested than the arrangement shown in **28.28**, but leaves the main run of teaching space free of large fixed elements. The two sides of the plan, A and B, show a variety of detailed design, and more variations from fully open to fully enclosed bases are obviously possible within the main format, or by alteration over time*

should have full width access directly from the hall, and preferably full-size chairs.

Other teaching areas
- A group room may be provided in larger schools. This is an enclosed, acoustically isolated area, used for drama, music, or TV. It will have a carpeted floor and dimmable lighting.
- One or two small enclosed quiet rooms may also be provided.
- The library may be planned as as a central area, or as part of a widened corridor, accessible to the whole school.
- Resource areas for science, technology, cooking, or clay work in larger schools, possibly in the form of bays of around 8 m² accessible to the whole school.

However, it may be necessary to be able to close off library and resource areas if pilfering from them is likely to be a problem.

Lavatories, changing rooms, coat storage
A minimum of 1 WC and washbasin per 20 pupils, but often two per class are provided. Easily supervisable from the class bases and accessible from out of doors via a draught lobby without entering the class areas. Separate lavatories for each sex are required where children are over 8 years old. Coat areas may be conveniently combined with an entrance lobby shared by a pair of bases, possibly incorporating the lavatories. Shelves or racks should be provided for lunch boxes, and sports bags. Changing

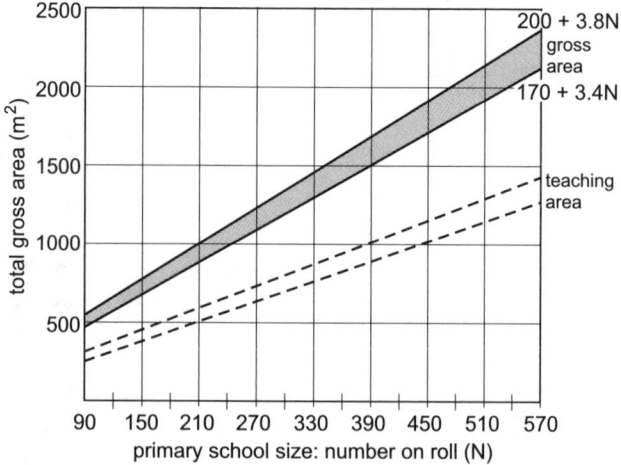

28.30 *Floor areas for primary schools. The main graph shows the range of gross floor areas, with broken lines showing teaching area at 60% of gross. Smaller schools may not achieve this, larger ones may do better. Areas required by infants and juniors are not very different – the infants are smaller, but use larger equipment and more space than juniors. Factors such as whether a full school meals kitchen or only a servery is provided have considerable influence on final areas and proportions*

rooms are no longer a statutory requirement for those aged under 11, but may be considered appropriate, and may be combined with one set of lavatories.

Non-teaching areas

- Visitors' entrance and waiting area with space for displays of school work
- School office, including a reception counter overlooking the entrance. The management information computer will be housed here, and some privacy is necessary for this. A curtained corner with a chair or bed for sick children to rest under supervision is often thought more convenient than using the medical room for this purpose
- Stock room
- Head teacher's room, near school office, but not too isolated from teaching areas. In small schools this room may also have to serve for medical inspection, and should be fitted with a washbasin
- A deputy head's room may be required in larger schools, and this usually serves for medical inspection
- Staff room for relaxing and some preparation of teaching material
- Staff lavatories are more flexible if unisex, each with a washbasin
- A lavatory for disabled use can be provided for use by children and adults in a small school; in a larger school two may be justified
- Caretaker's store and separate office.

6 MIDDLE SCHOOLS

6.01 Age range and typical sizes
May take pupils aged 8–12, whereupon treated as a primary school by the DfEE. Sizes range from 240 to 360 pupils. Alternatively, takes pupils aged 9–13, and is treated as a secondary school by the DfEE. Their sizes range from 360 to 600 pupils.

6.02 Curriculum, organisation, and accommodation
Years 8–12 middle schools are generally similar to primary schools, but are now faced with the challenge of covering the start of Key Stage 3 of the national curriculum; 9–13 schools have in any case included more specialised spaces, but are faced with the same problem. The range of teaching and total floor areas and the schedule of individual areas for middle schools can be calculated by the methods given in Building Bulletin 82, and the design features determined from an appropriate combination of elements of primary and secondary practice.

7 SECONDARY SCHOOLS

7.01 Age range and typical sizes
Contains pupils 11 years of age and over. Sizes range from 450 to 1200 pupils in years 7–11. Secondary schools are usually described as having so many 'forms of entry' (fe). For example a four fe school has four forms of thirty pupils in each of its five year groups = 600 pupils under 16 years.

Those who wish to continue full-time education beyond the age of 16 can do so at the same school, or at a tertiary college, sixth form college, or college of further education. It is difficult in a school sixth form of under 100 students to ensure variety of choice and viable teaching group sizes, so schools of less than four fe are often 11–16 only.

7.02 Curriculum and organisation
Secondary schools must cover the national curriculum at Key Stages 3 and 4. The curriculum for those over 16 years old is largely determined by national examination requirements: 'A' levels and vocational qualifications, plus general studies.

Pupils are based in a form or tutor group for pastoral care purposes, but move to specialist rooms and teachers for most subjects. The sixth form may have their own social base with a common room.

Schools are generally organised in subject departments or faculties of related subjects, and this is reflected in the layout of the buildings. Larger schools may also be divided into lower and upper schools, usually after year 9, and commonly where the school has been formed by reorganisation from several sets of buildings.

7.03 Site planning – access, roads, and parking
Secondary schools are substantial land users and traffic generators. A new school may require extensive off-site road works, on-site turning facilities for buses, and large car parks; particularly if community use during the day is involved. Vehicular access will be required to the rear of the buildings for service deliveries, playing field maintenance, and fire-fighting.

7.04 Recreation areas, playing fields, and landscape
The possible range of area of hard surfaced games courts required is shown in **28.26**. This should be appropriately shaped, marked and possibly fenced for a variety of games. It may be a joint use area with floodlighting for evening use. Additional informal areas required are shown in **28.31**. About half of this should be paved, and can include smaller social areas or courtyards. The remainder can be grass, possibly including environmental study areas.

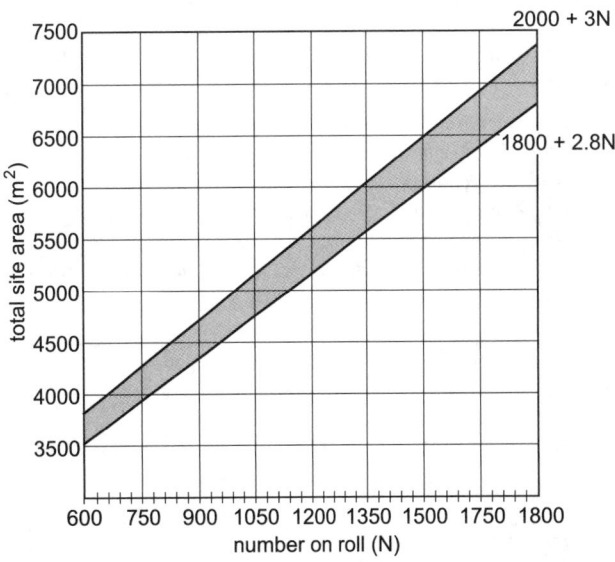

28.31 *Informal recreation areas for secondary schools. About half the area should be paved, the remainder can be grass*

The regulations specify minimum areas of playing fields to be provided, **28.3**, not necessarily on the main school site when that is in a built-up area. They must be capable of sustaining seven hours play per week in term time without detriment. Modern methods of construction, using a partial sand bed, are capable of sustaining considerably more use than this, and are thus eminently suitable for joint use. The porous 'redgra' type pitches have been largely superseded by sand-filled plastic mat surfaces which are expensive but often jointly financed for additional community use. Both types of surface count as twice their actual area in terms of playing field regulations. The floodlighting which is an essential element to maximise use of such facilities can be a problem in residential areas. (See references 6, 8 and 10.)

7.05 Design and development strategy for new schools

The major components of a secondary school plan are the subject departments with different needs in regards to size, shape, location and environment. Frequently where there is new housing development, there is a requirement to develop in phases. As each successive phase of new building is added, some remodelling of existing areas is needed to preserve departmental suitabilities.

The result of addressing these factors may be a campus of linked buildings, often incorporating a central mall or pedestrian street. This allows new buildings to be attached to an extendible circulation core. The basic planning unit may consist of several departments, each with a cluster of specialised and general teaching spaces around a common resource centre, as shown in more detail in **28.32** to **28.34** (See references 24 and 25.)

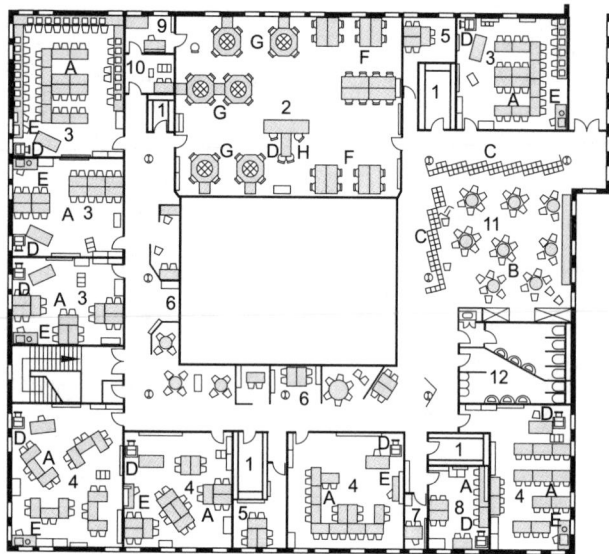

28.32 Secondary school design 1: humanities and languages. A two-storey block with a central well houses a large faculty including the departments of English, modern languages, history, geography, and religious studies. The first floor shown includes a large 'open-learning' language centre, teaching rooms of various sizes, staff offices, storage, and shared study or social areas surrounding the central glazed well

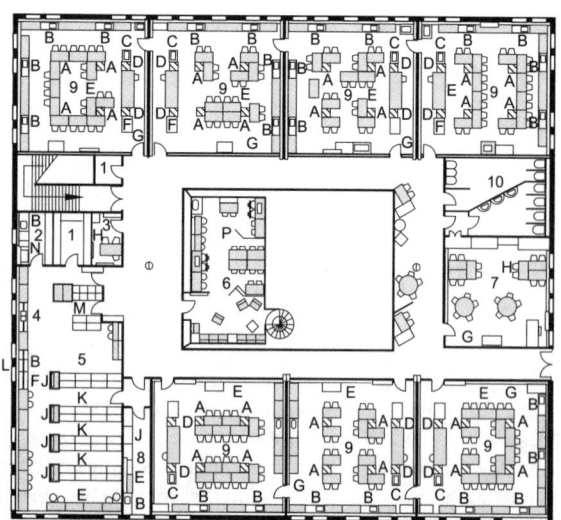

28.33 Secondary school design 2: science. The first floor of a two-storey block houses the science department. A single large prep room and store serves all laboratories, which are equipped with service bollards and loose worktables to allow a variety of arrangements. The central mezzanine study and work area is accessible from a similar central area on the floor below, which houses technology, **28.34**

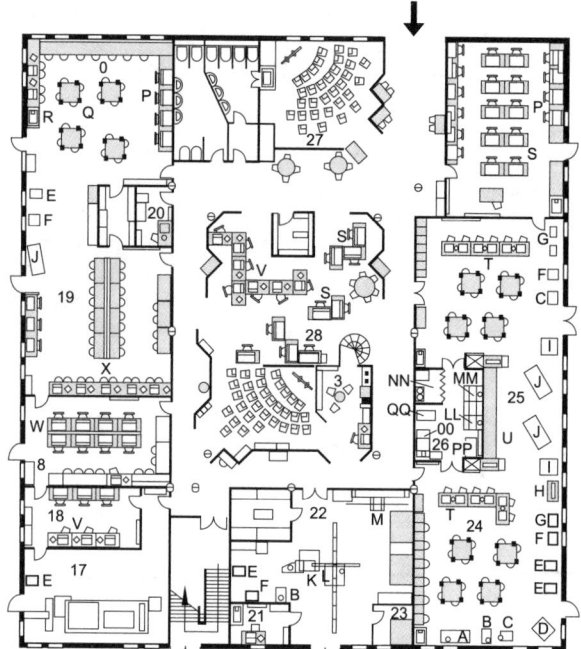

28.34 Secondary school design 3: design and technology. The ground floor of a two-storey block, with central resource/work/display area, large materials prep room and store, and paired technology areas for work with a range of materials and components

7.06 Community use

Many secondary school facilities are suitable for joint use, particularly those for sport and the performing arts. Other areas are suitable for evening classes and for youth and community organisation lettings.

Any large joint-use scheme will be jointly funded, possibly by the National Lottery, and promoters will expect to see these areas prominent on the most visible part of the site, designed to attract the general public. Large-scale adult use implies large areas for parking.

Security is an important issue, to prevent crime against persons and property, and to ensure that the users feel safe, especially at night. This is a matter of basic design as much as sophisticated electronic systems or hostile-looking railings. **28.35** shows the site plan of a large secondary school with extensive indoor and outdoor community use. (See reference 10.)

7.07 Extending and remodelling existing schools

Most existing secondary schools have reached their present form over many years, via reorganisation and multi-phased extension. Pressures of cost and time favoured the addition of detached 'blocks', usually resulting in departments being split between several buildings, a good deal of external circulation, and generally haphazard organisation and appearance.

Projects for rationalising existing buildings to improve departmental suitability and to upgrade individual facilities involve a complex mix of remodelling, linking and small-scale extension. The design process involves extensive consultation with the users and managers, who will have strong views on historic features which do not work, and may be prepared to cooperate in facilitating complex on-site working arrangements in order to get the right end result. The age of the buildings may mean that substantial maintenance and energy conservation work, including rezoning of heating systems may also be required, involving synchronisation of capital and revenue budgets. **28.36** shows such a project.

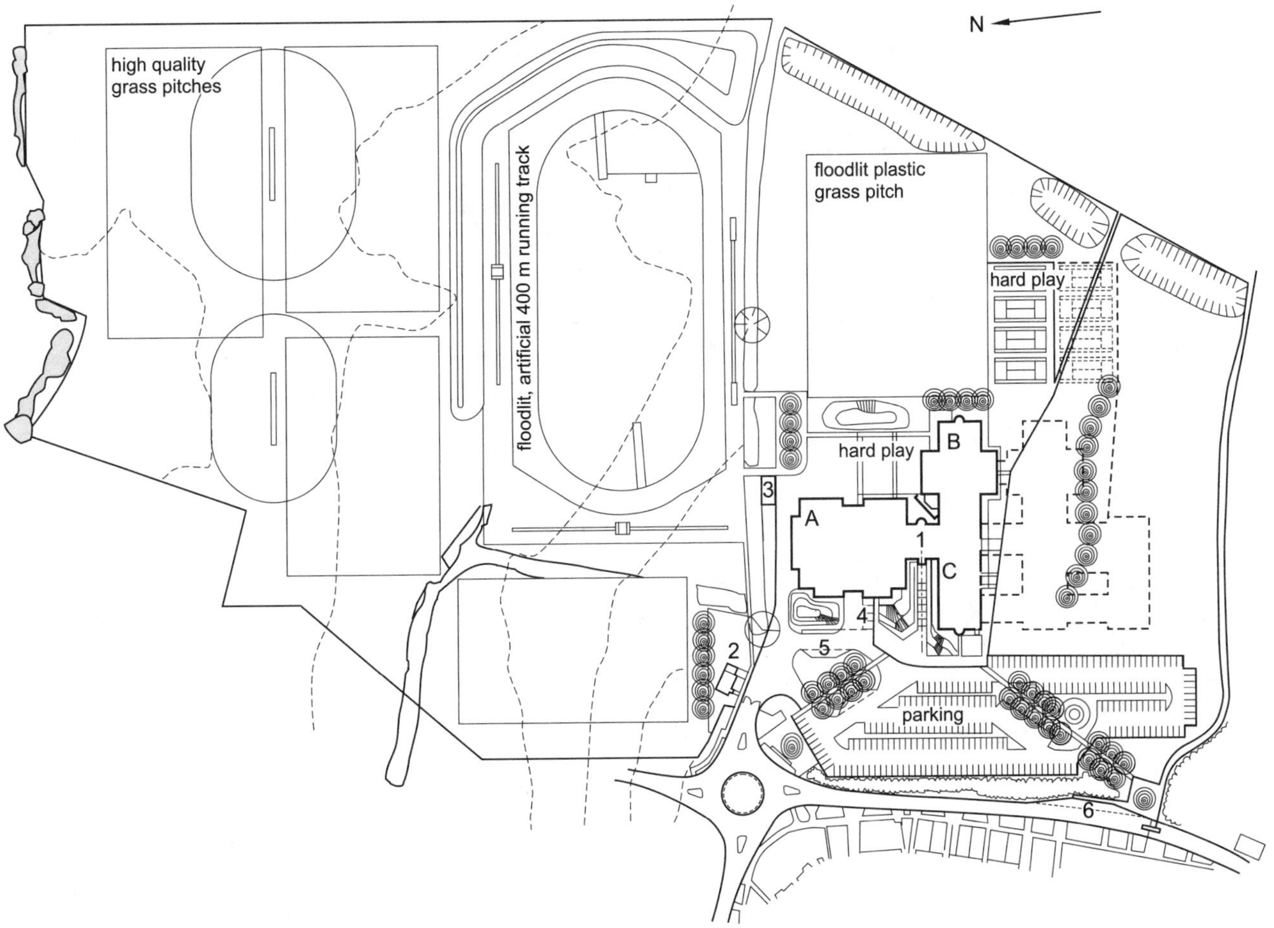

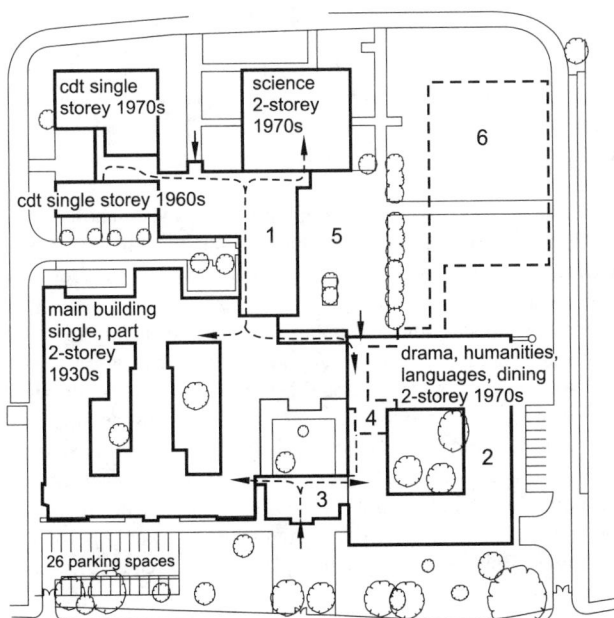

N ←

high quality grass pitches

floodlit, artificial 400 m running track

floodlit plastic grass pitch

hard play

hard play

A   B

3

1   C

4

5   2

parking

6

28.35 *Tabor High School, Essex, a secondary school site layout. A school with a large amount of community use, including daytime use. The joint-use sports centre, run by the District Council recreation department, is to the left of the entrance hall, other school areas to the right, with potential for expansion*

cdt single storey 1970s

science 2-storey 1970s

6

cdt single storey 1960s

1   5

main building single, part 2-storey 1930s

drama, humanities, languages, dining 2-storey 1970s

4

3   2

26 parking spaces

28.36 *Shoeburyness High School, rationalisation plan*

1 *New art/link block unites departments and reduces energy losses*
2 *Former art rooms converted to general teaching space*
3 *New link classrooms and pupils' entrance*
4 *Open area at ground level filled in to form link and extra classroom*
5 *Landscaped courtyard*
6 *Site for future expansion*

This school consisted of separate single-and two-storey blocks built between the 1920s and the 1970s. The most recent phase, to replace a number of demountable classrooms, knits the disparate parts together by means of a new art block and a further iinking classroom block, together with some infilling of open areas at ground floor level, and internal remodelling. Besides relating departments more closely and providing fully internal circulation, energy use and security are improved, and more attractive outdoor areas created. The joint-use sports centre is separate from the main buildings

7.08   Schedules of accommodation

The schedule of individual teaching spaces is derived from the analysis of proposed curriculum and pupil numbers, plus communal or untimetabled areas such as the library, study areas, and halls. DfEE Building Bulletin 82 explains the calculation process fully. **28.37** shows the possible range of gross floor and teaching areas. (See reference 6.)

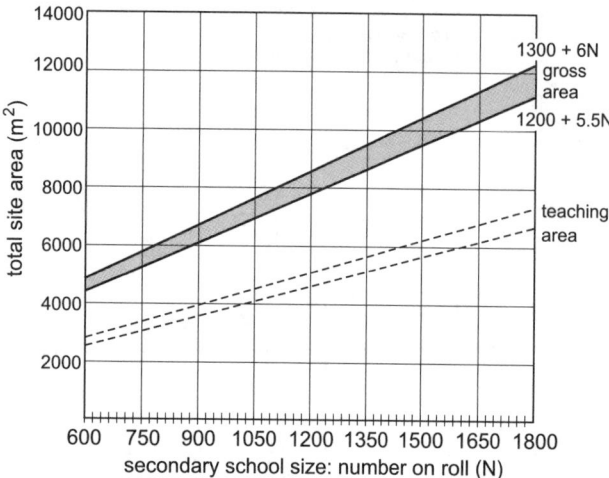

28.37 *Floor areas for secondary schools. The main graph shows the range of gross floor areas, with broken lines showing teaching area at 60% of gross, for 11–16 schools of more than 600 pupils. For schools with a sixth form the range of total area can be determined by the formula 1300 + 6N 3n (upper limit) or 1200 + 5.5N + 2.5n (lower limit) where N is the total number of pupils of all ages, and n is the number aged over 16*

7.09   Design requirements

English, maths, humanities, languages

All require a mix of general classrooms, seminar and tutorial rooms, for groups of 15–30 pupils, sitting formally at tables, for 'chalk and talk' or less formally around grouped tables for discussion. Some larger rooms will also be required for teaching which includes practical work in a classroom context, with larger tables and extra work surfaces, for example using large maps, recording equipment, or a small number of computers. Rooms for teaching can be grouped round a common resource and study area, as in **28.32**.

Information technology and business studies

Use of information technology (IT) will be possible throughout the school, but teaching of basic techniques will require one or two dedicated rooms possibly associated with business studies. These range from word processing to management and 'mini enterprise' activity, and require seminar and group work space with furniture and IT facilities which can be easily rearranged, as in real business and industrial environments. A business studies suite may have extended functions: careers advice, industry liaison or a conference centre, perhaps jointly financed and used by local enterprises. This could comprise a display area, library and reference area, and one or two small interview rooms.

Science

Laboratories are seldom devoted to one science, and need to be internally flexible (see Chapter 30). Service bollard systems and overhead boom systems with movable standing-height tables provide for this need. A single central preparation and storage area is more practical, and economical in use of support staff than the traditional small prep rooms shared by two labs, and is

conveniently associated with the faculty staff room. A separate external store is needed for flammable materials in bulk. The provision of outdoor areas – ponds, greenhouses, growing plots, or animal farms – is a matter of local tradition rather than curriculum requirement, but is very strong in some areas not all of which are rural. **28.33** shows a typical new science department with single preparation and storage area, central pupils' reference and computing area, and laboratories with service bollards and movable workbenches. (See reference 25.)

Design and technology

Pupils will be involved in design and construction in metals, wood, plastics, and fabrics. Design takes place in close proximity to making and testing. Washbasins and warm-air hand driers are essential whether designing on paper or with computer-aided design (CAD) systems. Heat treatment and other processes produce fumes and dust, which must be extracted at the point of origin.

A central resource area is needed for display and reference, supervisable from the work areas, as shown in **28.34**. In remodelling of existing premises, the existing 'industrial workshop' image may be a problem. The creation of such a central area, perhaps by infilling between blocks, can be the key to the visual transformation of the suite, as well as providing an extra facility.

Secure storage is required for pupils' work in progress, and this might be associated with the faculty room used by teaching staff and technicians. A central storage and preparation area for bulk materials is required, but small electronic components and the like are best kept in a separate clean store. (See reference 26.)

Food technology may be part of general technology, and this will include experimental work and testing as well as cookery.

Art and design

Planning can be similar to that for technology suites, possibly with more flexible open plans, and with similar careful separation of more messy activities – sculpture and ceramics – from cleaner areas. Work with fabrics will take place here as well as in technology. Daylight remains a valued commodity in these areas.

Physical education

Most schools will require two spaces. These have traditionally been a sports hall and a gymnasium, but rising standards in sports halls – sprung floors, heating and lighting as found in public and joint-use sports centres – make it possible to perform most activities in the same space, (see Chapter 25). Separate dance studios and multi-gyms are then often provided instead of a gym.

Community use is an essential element of most school sports and PE provision, and may have a radical influence on the amount and type of space and facilities provided. Typically, additional joint funding would allow a larger sports hall, a multi-gym, separate exercise studio and improved quality changing rooms to conform to adult expectations and to withstand constant use.

Swimming pools (see Chapter 22) are unlikely to be provided except by joint funding for community use. The most common and workable scenario is for the school to provide the site in exchange for agreed hours of use. The major financing and management will lie with the local authority recreation department, or with a commercial enterprise. Where a swimming pool is readily available to pupils, the regulation playing field requirement may be abated.

Music and drama

These subjects may well share a suite. Dance activity also overlaps with physical education. In music, a good deal of emphasis is placed on individual and small-group work, often involving advanced electronic instruments. Consequently, security and extensive provision of electrical power is important, as well as acoustic isolation from the remainder of the school. Drama studios need not be elaborate, and may take the form of a large classroom, or a multipurpose hall, with blackout and simple lighting system (see Chapter 20). Secure storage is necessary for all areas.

Library, resource, and study areas
Developments in information technology reinforce the library's importance as information centre rather than rendering it unnecessary; books and printed material remain important alongside CD-ROM and programs networked from central file servers. However, both resources and study areas may also be dispersed around the school in faculty centres. If the school is appropriately located and planned, the school's library may be combined with a public library jointly financed (see Chapter 32).

Halls
Full assemblies of large schools are seldom practicable, and all main large spaces will be used for assemblies of year or house groups, and for other functions – dining, drama, music, parents' meetings. This gives rise to the usual design problems of multi-purpose halls – floors, seating, stages, acoustics (see Chapters 20 and 21).

Common rooms and social areas
Common rooms are usually provided for sixth forms, and sometimes for other groups. Casual social areas may be situated about the school by widening corridors, providing seating and a drinks vending machine.

7.10 Non-teaching areas

Lavatories and changing rooms
These follow normal adult practice (see Chapter 3). Changing rooms should be designed to reflect the different demands of indoor and outdoor activities. If possible, provide access from outside via a boot-cleaning area to a single set of changing rooms which is also directly accessible from inside should be provided.

Coat hanging and lockers
The recent tradition is for coats and school bags to be carried around all day, allowing the former cloakrooms to be converted to teaching accommodation. There is some sign of a reverse in this trend, owing to concern about the physical effects on children carrying heavy loads around. Only a high-quality industrial locker system will withstand the likely vandalism and criminality. Lockers should be fully visible in corridors, not in separate areas. Even in corridors, lockers are not perceived to be totally secure, and they may need to be in the class bases. There is a disadvantage to this where such bases are used by other classes during the day, with locker users wanting access.

Dining rooms and kitchens
Dining rooms may be dedicated or dual purpose (see Chapter 18). The proportion of pupils who take a cooked meal varies very widely, but staggered lunches with up to four starting times are universal. Pupils who bring sandwiches are often accommodated away from the dining room in halls, or even in classrooms. The latter should not be encouraged owing to the the likelihood of rodent infestation as a result.

Dual-purpose rooms require adjacent storage for the dining tables and chairs, and they cannot be fully timetabled because of the time required to set out and clear away furniture. School catering arrangements are undergoing radical change, with a

variety of outside contractors being employed. 'Fast food' is universal and many large old kitchens are being reduced in size, with the surplus space being adapted for other purposes.

Staff rooms
Where staff preparation and resource facilities are provided in faculty areas, the central staff room is largely social in character. It should be adaptable for meetings, staff conferences, and in-service training events. A separate room for smokers may be requested.

Staff offices
Individual rooms will be required for the head teacher, possibly a bursar, and for deputy heads, year heads and any staff who need to interview pupils, staff, and parents, and to keep confidential records. Heads of faculty or department may have their own rooms or may use the faculty staff room.

Administrative and service staff offices
A reception and waiting area with display facilities is required for visitors adjoining the main office. The computers for the management information system should be in a separate room, as confidential information is often on-screen. The office for the caretaker, school keeper or site manager (whatever his or her title), should also be in this area and not adjoining the boiler house.

8 PROVISION FOR SPECIAL NEEDS IN EDUCATION
8.01 Some children have special needs in education: physical or mental difficulties which mean they cannot cope with the normal curriculum or school activities. Wherever possible these pupils are provided with extra assistance or facilities within ordinary schools, or in support units attached to them.

There remains a requirement for special schools for some pupils, with a very high level of specialist teaching and care staff, curricula geared to their individual needs, and purpose-built space and facilities. In addition to the education authority, the local health authority provides some services including speech and physiotherapy, and may contribute capital for hydrotherapy pools or other facilities. Social services departments also have an overall duty towards children with disabilities, and may be involved in briefing and provision of capital.

8.02 Provision in mainstream schools
Some children, mostly those with moderate learning difficulties, mobility problems, vision or hearing impairment, or speech and language disorders, can attend normal schools given staff support, some minor building adaptations, and the use of special facilities for part of the time. Building Bulletin 61 gives very full design guidance.

In the case of wheelchair users, it is often difficult to make entire secondary schools accessible and with adequate means of escape. It has been the practice to designate one school in an area and concentrate provision there. This policy has come in for a lot of criticism as it limits the choice for pupils who may have to use wheelchairs but are otherwise fully capable of taking advantage of facilities which may not be available in such a designated school. There are very few buildings that cannot, in fact, be made accessible to such people, given the will to do so, with a combination of physical adaptations and management organisation. (See references 3, 5, 7 and 27.)

8.03 Special schools in general
The types of special school which are widely found are detailed below. Although described as having a specific role, each

special school is different and tends to follow the needs which emerge in a particular locality. Building Bulletin 77 gives full design guidance. Very specialised schools for the visually and aurally impaired, or for accident victims are very small in number and generally run by charitable foundations. (See reference 28.)

8.04 Schools for pupils with moderate learning difficulties

Typically these are for the secondary age range for those who cannot keep up in normal school work. School size is from 60 to 120 pupils, using a modified mainstream curriculum with class sizes of around 12 pupils. To provide adequate specialised facilities in a school of this size is difficult and these schools benefit from being near mainstream schools for mutual support, exchange of expertise, and a variety of schemes for part-time integration.

Some children have multiple disabilities and may have mobility problems in addition to mental or behavioural difficulties. **28.38** shows a school for pupils with physical disabilities and/or moderate learning difficulties adapted from a redundant primary school. Where no such need exists, detailed design requirements are similar to those for mainstream schools.

The fact that a school for pupils with moderate learning or behavioural difficulties has provision for wheelchair users should not be a reason for sending pupils there who have only physical disabilities.

8.05 Schools for pupils with severe learning difficulties (SLD)

These are all-age schools for children with permanent severe brain damage which affects physical functions as well as learning. The range of ability is wide, the curriculum is developmental. It focuses on independence, self-care, and social living together with National Curriculum work at a level appropriate to the pupils' abilities. Schools are typically of 50–80 pupils divided into primary and secondary sections, and probably with a separate unit for 16–19-year-olds.

Class sizes are around 8 pupils. Detailed design requirements can be very specific: non-teaching areas are extensive, requiring special lavatory and hygiene facilities, storage for special supports and equipment, therapy and treatment rooms, and facilities for a large number of teaching and ancillary staff. Many pupils come in taxis or special buses, and there may be a need for on-site turning and unloading with a canopy for wet weather. Outdoor areas for

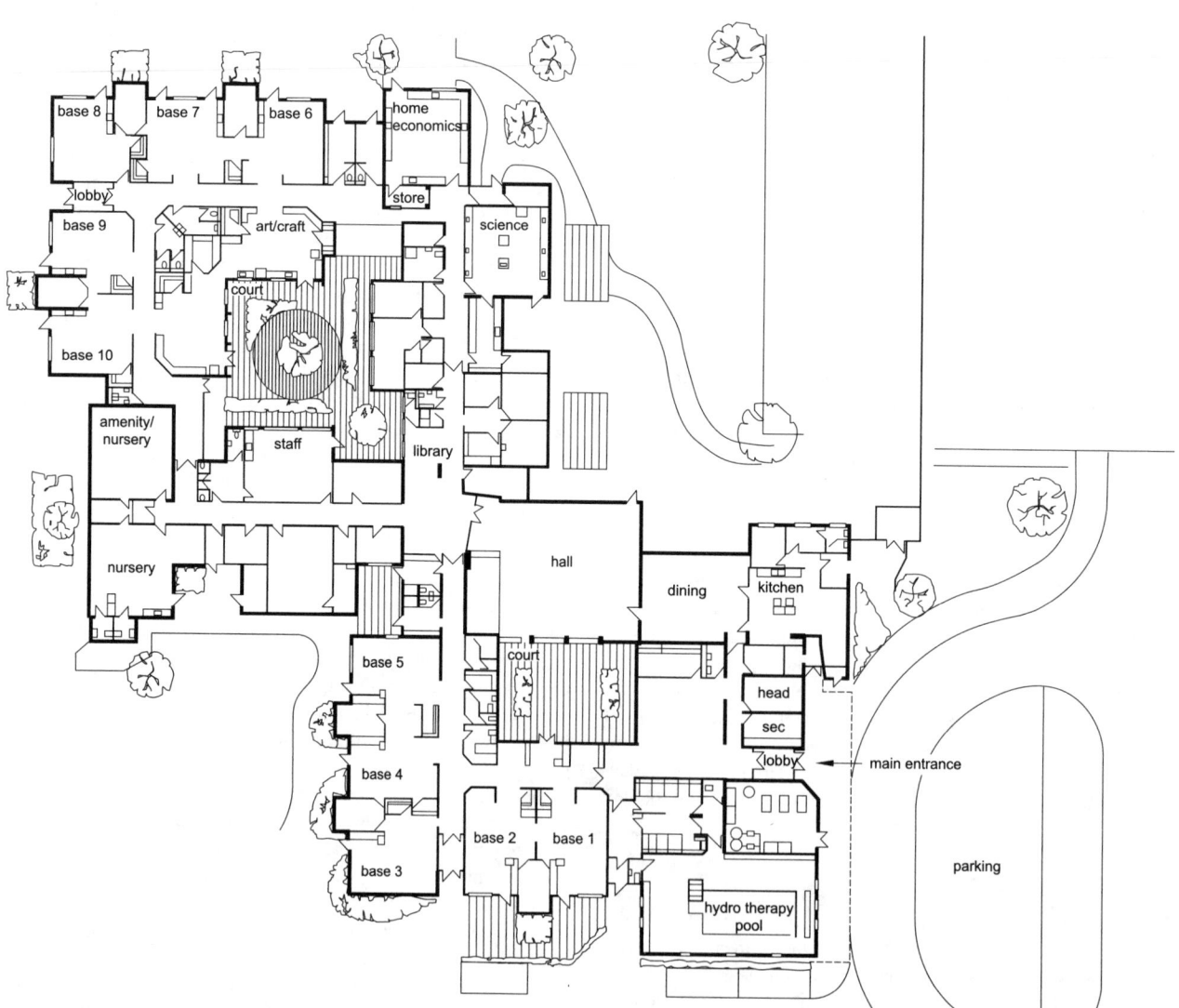

28.38 *Woodacre School (MLD and PH), Essex. A special school in a former junior school built in the 1950s (the central X of the plan) extended on two sides to create a school for pupils with moderate learning difficulties or physical handicaps aged from 3 to 16. The school is broadly divided into primary and secondary sections and shows characteristics common to most types of special school – class bases for small groups, quiet rooms for one-to-one help, spacious circulation, specialist therapy facilities, sheltered courtyards, and canopied entrance for setting down from cars, or minibuses. The school adjoins a mainstream secondary school which is adapted for physically handicapped pupils*

some relatively inactive children need to be very sheltered, and large internal courtyards have many advantages.

8.06 Schools for pupils with physical and neural impairment

These are all-age schools, for those who cannot cope physically with a normal school environment: some of those in wheelchairs, some with brittle bones or weak hearts, or who cannot perform basic physical tasks such as writing. The range of ability can be very wide up to mainstream curriculum standards; but requiring extra support or equipment such as personal computer interface devices. Typically all-age schools are of 50–80 pupils, with class groups of around 8. Extensive non-teaching areas are required similar to SLD schools.

8.07 Schools for pupils with emotional and behavioural difficulties

Separate primary and secondary schools for children who are aggressive, withdrawn, or insecure. A mainstream curriculum may be followed, but the main function of the school is to modify behaviour by social means as much outside the classroom as within it. Class groups are of around eight pupils. These schools are often weekly boarding schools. (See reference 29.)

9 REFERENCES

General

1. *The Education School Premises Regulations 1996*, The Stationery Office
2. *Circular 10/96 – The School Premises Regulations*, DfEE
3. *Fire and the design of educational buildings* (6th edn), Building Bulletin 7; The Stationery Office
4. *Guidelines for environmental design and fuel conservation in education buildings*, Design Note 17, DfEE (to be superseded during 1997)
5. *Access for disabled people to educational buildings*, Design Note 18 (2nd edn), DfEE
6. *Area guidelines for schools*, Building Bulletin 82, The Stationery Office, 1996
7. *Capital building bids – procurement and commissioning*, The Grant Maintained Schools Centre, revised edition 1996
8. *The outdoor classroom*, Building Bulletin 71, The Stationery Office, 1990
9. *Our school your school*, DfEE
10. *Educational facilities – design for community use*, The Sports Council, 1994
11. *Fire precautions in the design and construction of buildings, Code of practice for means of escape for disabled people*, BS 5588: Part 8: 1988
12. *Schools' environmental assessment method (SEAM)*, Building Bulletin 83, The Stationery Office, 1996
13. *Passive solar schools: a design guide*, Building Bulletin 79, The Stationery Office, 1995
14. *Fume cupboards in schools*, Design Note 29, DfEE (to be superseded during 1997)
15. *Security lighting*, Building Bulletin 78, The Stationery Office, 1993
16. *Closed circuit TV surveillance systems in educational buildings*, Building Bulletin 75, The Stationery Office, 1991

17. *Crime prevention in schools: specification, installation and maintenance of intruder alarm systems*, Building Bulletin 69, The Stationery Office, 1989
18. *Crime prevention in schools: practical guidance*, Building Bulletin 67, The Stationery Office, 1987

Nursery schools

19. *Building for nursery education*, Design Note 1, DfEE

Primary schools

20. *Design for learning: designing an infant, junior, or primary School*, Hampshire County Council Education Department, 1996
21. *St Johns School, Sefton: the design of a new primary school*, Design Note 47, DfEE
22. *Community use of primary schools*, Datasheet 62, The Sports Council, 1992
23. Richard Weston, *Schools of thought*, Hampshire County Council, 1991

Secondary schools

24. *New initiatives in City Technology Colleges*, Building Bulletin 72, The Stationery Office, 1991
25. *Science accommodation in secondary schools, a design guide*, Building Bulletin 80, The Stationery Office, 1995
26. *Design and technology accommodation in secondary schools: a design guide*, Building Bulletin 81, The Stationery Office, 1996

Special needs in education

27. *Designing for pupils with special educational needs: ordinary schools*, Building Bulletin 61, The Stationery Office, 1992
28. *Designing for pupils with special educational needs: special schools*, Building Buletin 77, The Stationery Office, 1992

Boarding schools

29. *School boarding accommodation: a design guide*, Building Bulletin 84, The Stationery Office, 1997

General notes

The Architects and Building Branch of the Department for Education and Employment is the main source of design information in this area. Its list of publications is obtainable free from DfEE. Further Building Bulletins are in preparation, and those on the following subjects are expected to be published during 1997:

School grounds
Art accommodation in secondary schools
Music accommodation in secondary schools
Guidelines for environmental design in schools (to replace Design Note 17) Fume cupboards in Schools (to replace Design Note 29)
Guidance for Governors on initiating capital projects

The Sports Council and the Arts Council publish a range of guidance notes for their areas of interest which are relevant to joint school and community projects, in particular where Lottery funding is imvolved.

29 Higher education

CI/SfB: 72
UDC: 727.3
Uniclass: F72

KEY POINTS:
- *Ex-polytechnics are being upgraded to reflect their current university status*
- *Training facilities for in-service education are increasingly demanded*

Contents

1 INTRODUCTION

Higher education is taken to mean all post-secondary education. Table I gives the main types of institution covered in this section, although the Open University will not be specifically detailed. No particular institution is without its peculiarities of one sort or another: siting, constituents or functions. What follows, therefore, is a series of generalisations which may or may not apply in another time or place.

Many of the building types found in higher education have their counterparts elsewhere. Factors controlling their design will therefore be found in other sections of this Handbook, and will not be repeated here.

2 UNIVERSITIES

2.01 Since 1993 all the former polytechnics in the UK have become universities. It is to hoped that in years to come they will be able to upgrade their buildings: originally they were subject to lower standards than university buildings.

Table I Categories of higher educational institutions

UK designation	Features	Designations elsewhere for institutions with similar features
University	Full-time courses to first and succeeding degrees Research	University University College Polytechnic Technical University Specialist academy
College of further education	Full- and part-time courses to diploma level for vocational and recreational subjects	Technical college Technical high school Sixth form college Vocational training college Non-advanced further education centre Adult education centre
College of Education	Full-time course for non-graduates for Bachelor of Education or equivalent Full-time course for graduates for Certificate of Education	Teacher training college
Open University	Courses by correspondence, also using radio and television Summer schools and evening tutorials at other educational establishments borrowed for the purpose Staff accommodation as for universities No student accommodation	Correspondence colleges

2.02 All over the world new universities are being established, and existing ones enlarged. The criteria developed and published by the UK, USA and other Western government agencies for the design and management of their institutions of higher education can be used as a basis for other parts of the world. However, local considerations may necessitate modifications:

- Climatic
- Socio-religious, e.g. segregation of the sexes in Moslem countries
- Standard of living.

Caution is therefore needed in transposing Western source data to projects elsewhere. It is recommended that where doubt exists to re-synthesise space planning data from detailed net workstation areas, in consultation with the future users or other experienced local equivalents.

2.03 Types of university

There are three basic types of university, illustrated in UK practice as:

- *Oxbridge*, consisting of a number of semi-autonomous colleges providing residential and catering facilities for students and staff together with some small-scale teaching space; with an amount of central shared facilities jointly administered. This type is unique to Oxford and Cambridge.
- *London*, consisting of a number of almost independent colleges, many of a specialist nature, each virtually self-contained universities. There are some central services, nearly all duplicating college facilities. This type is unique to London.
- *Provincial*, consisting of a number of subject departments or faculties, and various central facilities including usually an element of residential accommodation. This is the archetype, and most of what follows applies to this type of university.

2.04 A provincial type of university can be built in one of two ways, or a combination of them:

- Integrated and dispersed, where separate buildings and facilities are found among the local community, as and where sites become available. Often facilities are fitted into converted existing buildings, when space standards as described later may have to be modified. Otherwise, the design principles are not different from:
- Campus, where the buildings, or most of them, are arranged on one large site.

2.05 Types of campus

When a new university or polytechnic is to be built, a development (or master) plan is drawn up, showing how it is intended for the institution to cope with the expected expansion over the years to come. Expansion usually occurs by increasing the sizes of existing departments, rather than by the establishment of many new ones (although some new departments may be set up). There are three ways in which a department can expand:

- Extension to its existing buildings externally, for which space must be available

- Displacement of adjoining departments, for which the buildings must have been designed with flexibility in mind and
- Fragmentation over a series of separated buildings, which is normally deplored.

2.07 Forms of development
The form of the initial development of the campus will reflect the decision on methods of expansion. The common forms are:

- Molecular, as at York, **29.1**, where departments and facilities are in widely separated buildings, leaving ample space for expan-

sion. The disadvantage of this scheme is that there are long distances to be covered between facilities, and some minor functions such as parking, lavatories and refreshments have to be repeated at each 'nucleus',

- Linear, as at Surrey, **29.2**, which is designed with three strips containing residential, general and academic accommodation respectively. These strips can be extended at either end, and the academic accommodation is designed for easy conversion, enabling displacement to be facilitated
- Radial, such as Essex, **29.3**, where expansion takes place all round.

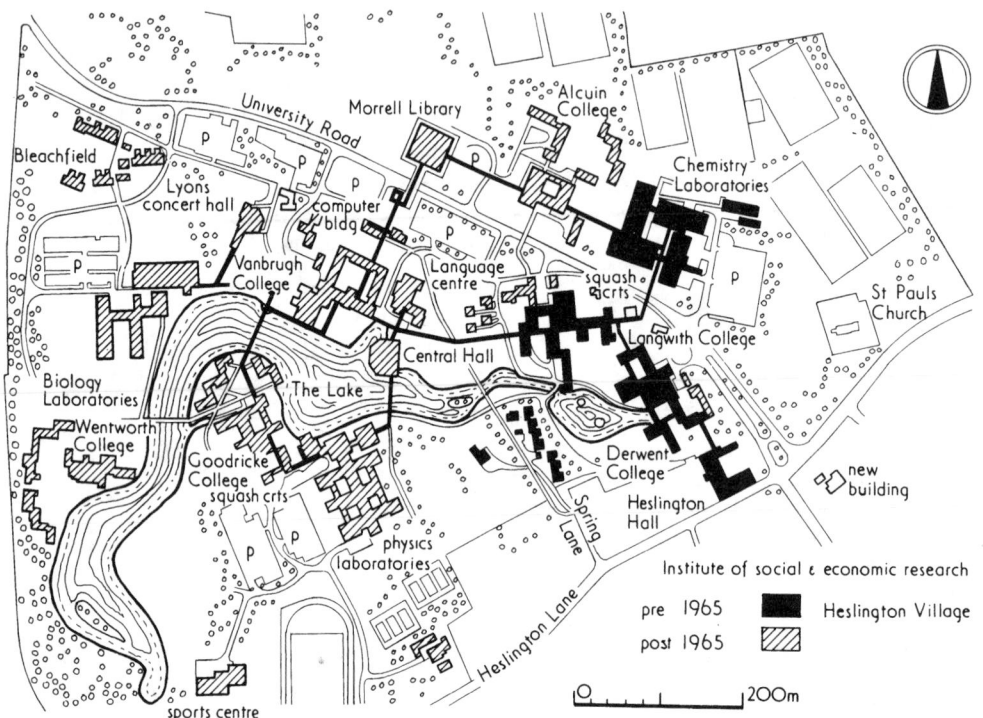

29.1 *York University, a molecular type of development plan.* Architects: Robert Matthew, Johnson-Marshall and Partners

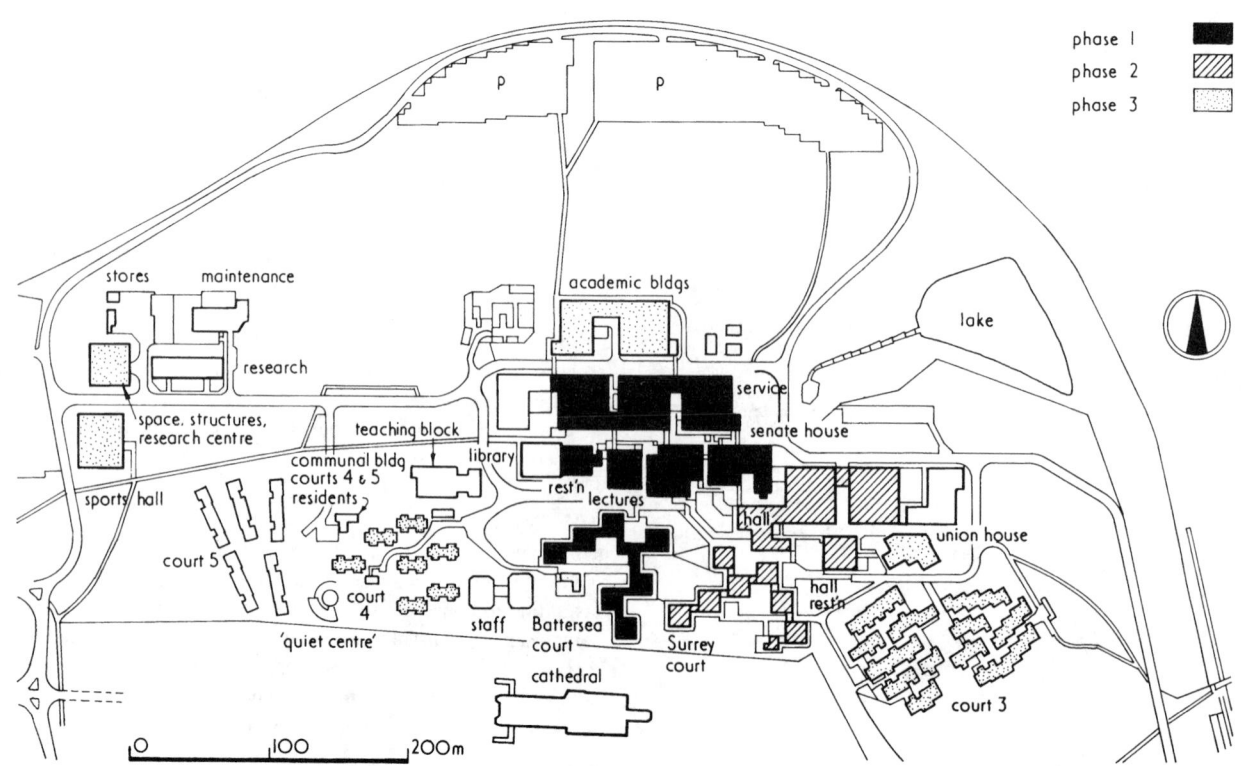

29.2 *Surrey University at Guildford, a linear development.* Architects: Building Design Partnership

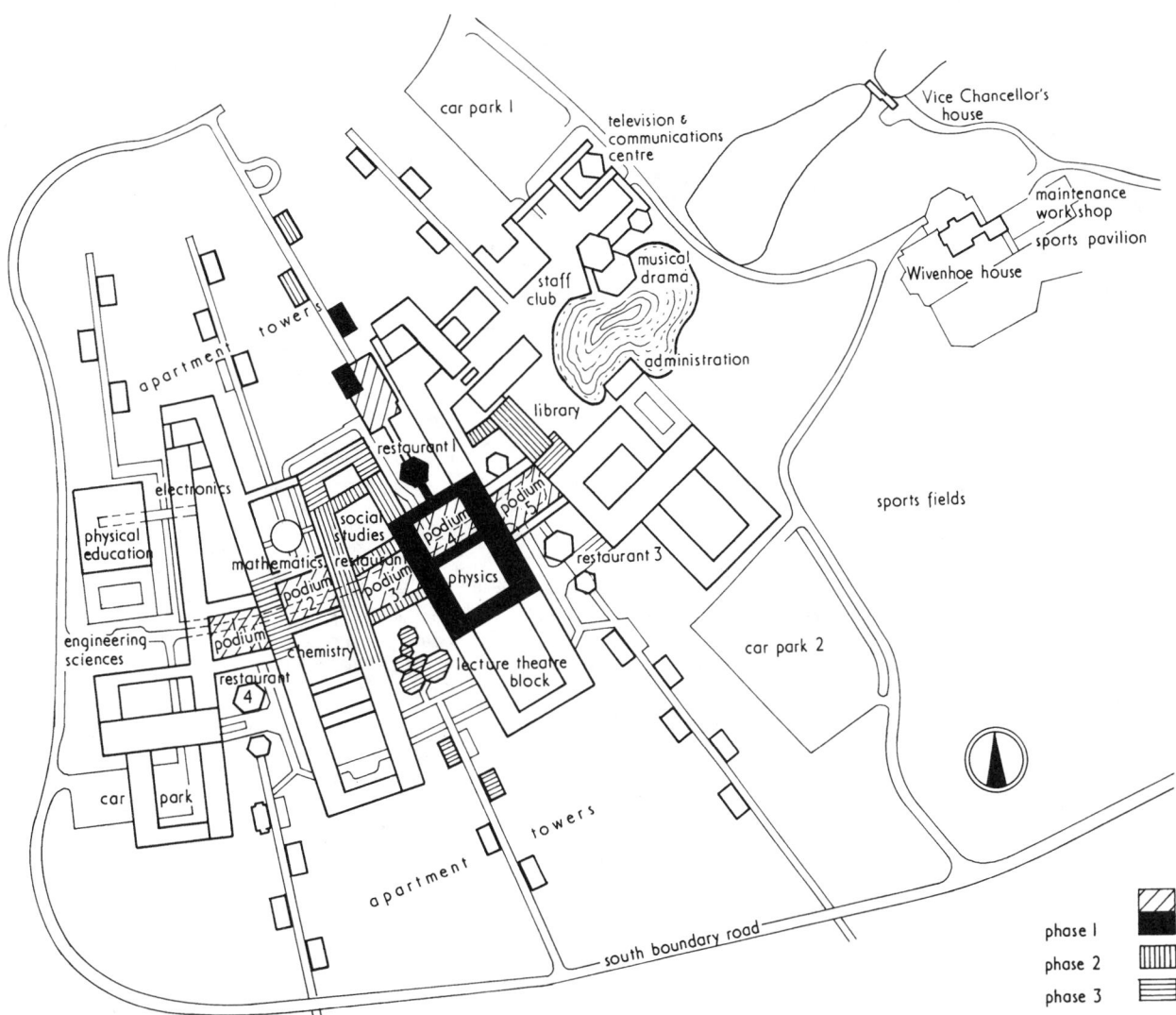

29.3 *Essex University at Colchester, radial development.* Architects: Architects' Co-Partnership

2.08 Building types
The main types of buildings are shown in **29.4**, which also indicates where information can be found elsewhere in the Handbook. The form of the campus will also be determined by a number of important policy decisions regarding these buildings.

2.09 Non-specialist teaching building policy
Most departments will have their own seminar and tutorial rooms, and may even use academic staff offices for such functions. A policy on whether departments should have their own lecture theatres, classrooms or even libraries must be established. In most new universities such facilities are usually shared between some or all departments for more economy of usage.

2.10 Residential accommodation policy
Students may live:

- In accommodation provided by the university on-campus
- In accommodation provided by the university off-campus
- In lodgings, with or without meals
- In privately rented accommodation, usually shared between a number
- At home (in their parents' house).

Before constructing students' accommodation it is usual to conduct a survey of lodgings and rentable accommodation in the locality. When doing this it is important to estimate other demands on such resources: other higher educational establishments, specialist industrial enterprises, etc. From such surveys, it can be

determined what number of students will need to have accommodation provided directly or indirectly by the university. Of this number, some may be situated on-campus, although there are arguments for and against such accommodation:

Advantages
- Savings of time and money in travel
- Ability to prepare all meals oneself
- Reduction in private study facilities in other university buildings
- Propinquity to library, etc. over weekends.

Disadvantages
- Mutual disturbance by noise, etc.
- Lack of contact with locality
- Need for parking facilities for students' vehicles on campus.

The types of accommodation that might be provided are given in **29.4**. Further information on this can be found in Chapter 34.

2.12 Catering policy
The third policy decision affecting campus shape is concerned with the communal catering service. This can be:

- Completely centralised preparation and consumption (one large kitchen and dining room)
- Centralised preparation, dispersed consumption (one large kitchen, separated dining accommodation)
- Dispersed preparation and consumption (separate dining rooms, often specialising in different kinds of food and catering, each with its own kitchen).

```
┌─────────────────────────────────────────────────────────────────────────────────┐
│ Campus                                                                            │
│ ┌───────────────────────────────────────────────────────────────────────────┐   │
│ │ Academic Buildings                                                        │   │
│ │ ┌─────────────────────────────────────────────────────┐ ┌──────────┐ ┌──────────┐ │
│ │ │ Teaching Spaces                                     │ │ Library  │ │Staff offices &│
│ │ │ ┌─────────────────────────┐ ┌────────────────────┐ │ │(see Chapter│ │research spaces│
│ │ │ │Specialised accommodation│ │Non-specialised     │ │ │32-Libraries)│ │(see Chapter 11-│
│ │ │ │                         │ │accommodation       │ │ │          │ │Offices)  │
│ │ │ │laboratories for science,│ │tutorial rooms      │ │ │          │ │          │
│ │ │ │technology & engineering │ │seminar rooms } (see│ │ │          │ │          │
│ │ │ │(see Chapter 30-Labora-  │ │classrooms    3.04) │ │ │          │ │          │
│ │ │ │tories) workshops for    │ │lecture theatres    │ │ │          │ │          │
│ │ │ │crafts & engineering     │ │(see 3.05 and       │ │ │          │ │          │
│ │ │ │art studios drawing      │ │Chapter 20-Auditoria│ │ └──────────┘ └──────────┘
│ │ │ │offices (see Chapter 11- │ │)                   │ │ ┌──────────┐            │
│ │ │ │Offices) language        │ │                    │ │ │Computer  │            │
│ │ │ │laboratories             │ │                    │ │ │centre    │            │
│ │ │ └─────────────────────────┘ └────────────────────┘ │ └──────────┘            │
│ │ └─────────────────────────────────────────────────────┘                        │
│ │                                                                                 │
```

Campus

Academic Buildings

Teaching Spaces

Specialised accommodation

laboratories for science, technology & engineering (see Chapter 30–Laboratories) workshops for crafts & engineering art studios drawing offices (see Chapter 11–Offices) language laboratories

Non-specialised accommodation

tutorial rooms
seminar rooms } (see 3.04)
classrooms
lecture theatres (see 3.05 and Chapter 20–Auditoria)

Library

(see Chapter 32–Libraries)

Computer centre

Staff offices & research spaces

(see Chapter 11-Offices)

Administrative buildings

'Senate House'
(see Chapter 11–Offices)

Residential buildings

(may be wholly or off-campus)

study bedrooms + shared sanitary & kitchen/utility accommodation
(see Chapter 34 Student housing)
2 person flats for married students

2 & 4 person flats for sharing

family dwellings for students & /or staff with children (preferably off-campus)
(see Chapter 33–Houses and flats)

Amenity buildings & spaces

(some may be off-campus)

cafeterias & restaurants } (see Chapter 18–
student union & bars } Eating & drinking)
sports centres (see Chapter 25–Indoor sports)
sports fields (see Chapter 24–Outdoor sports)
swimming pool (see Chapter 22–Swimming)
boathouse (see Chapter 23–Boating)
cultural centre for music/drama (see Chapter 20–Auditoria/theatres)

chapel & chaplaincy centre (see Chapter 27–Places of worship)
shops (see Chapter 13–Retail trading)
health centre (see Chapter 16 –Primary health care)
bank (see Chapter 14–Payment offices)

29.4 *Schematic diagram of a university campus*

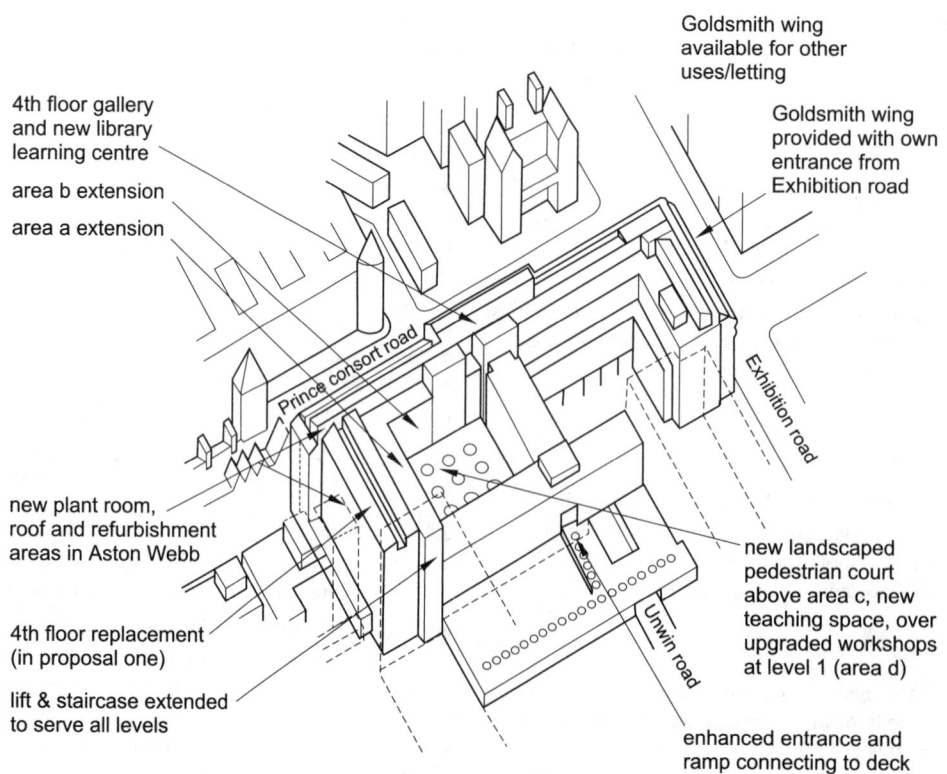

Goldsmith wing available for other uses/letting

Goldsmith wing provided with own entrance from Exhibition road

4th floor gallery and new library learning centre

area b extension

area a extension

new plant room, roof and refurbishment areas in Aston Webb

4th floor replacement (in proposal one)

lift & staircase extended to serve all levels

new landscaped pedestrian court above area c, new teaching space, over upgraded workshops at level 1 (area d)

enhanced entrance and ramp connecting to deck

Prince consort road

Exhibition road

Unwin road

29.5 *Royal School of Mines, Imperial College, London. A feasibility study.* Architects: RMJM

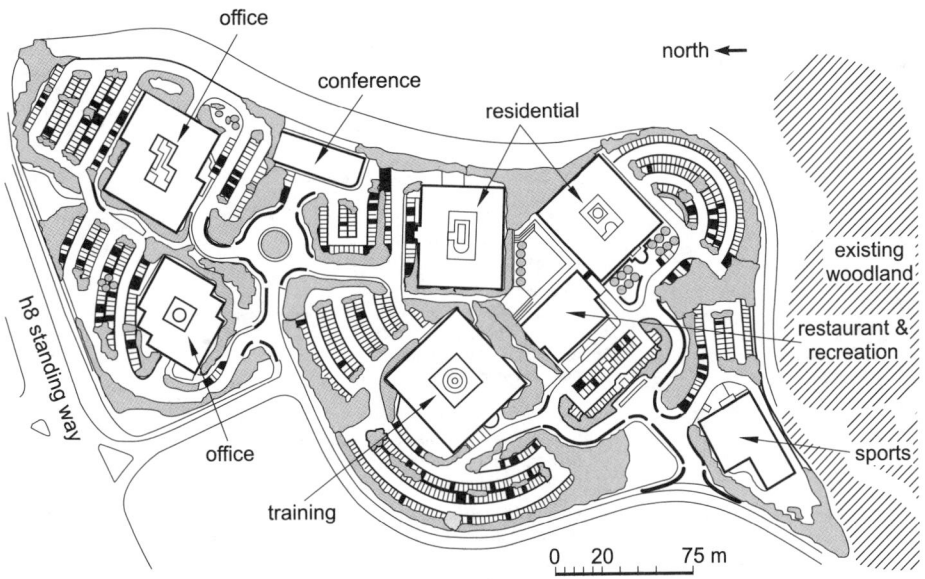

29.6 *British Telecom Training Centre, Milton Keynes.* Architects: RMJM

Table II Space standards for universities

	Staff offices and research spaces	Administrative, technical and secretaries	Classrooms, seminar rooms, etc.
TEACHING AREAS			
1 Arts, social sciences, mathematics, architecture	1.55 m^2/student	0.5 m^2/student	0.65 m^2/course student
2 Science, engineering science, electronics	4.35	0.45	0.35
3 Engineering	4.50	0.45	2.4
4 Preclinical medicine	3.80	0.45	0.35
5 Clinical medicine	6.15	1.0	0.35
6 Clinical dentistry	5.05	1.0	0.35
Additional areas for specialised accommodation:			
1 Languages and social psychology		0.8 m^2/course student	0.8 m^2/research student
Mathematics		1.1	1.1
Education, traditional geography, archaeology		2.7	2.7
Scientific geography		5.5	5.5
Experimental psychology		6.9	6.9
Architecture		6.55	6.55
Music (departments of 50 students only)		7.5	7.5
2 Laboratories and ancillary accommodation for:			
Biology		5.0 m^2/course student	15.2 m^2/research student
Physics, engineering science, electronics		4.9	13.8
Chemistry		5.0	14.25
3 Engineering laboratories, workshops, preparation, storage		3.95 m^2/course student	14.3 m^2/research student
4 Preclinical medicine teaching laboratories: multi-disciplinary		7.50 m^2/course student	
anatomy		1.88 m^2/course student	
5 Clinical medicine reasearch space including ancillaries			16.0 m^2/research student
6 Clinical dentistry: teaching laboratories including ancillaries		5.0 m^2/course student	
research and writing-up space including ancillaries			11.0 m^2/research student
Additional space in association with lecture theatres for audio-visual facilities: allow for TV studio accommodation and ancillaries (see Chapter 19)	for between 3000 and 6000 students		450 m^2
	over 6000 students (provides second studio)		40 m^2
Balance areas	for general teaching areas excluding workshops		40%
	for workshops		25%
	for academic staff workrooms		50%
	for non-academic staff workrooms		40%
LIBRARIES			
Basic provision:	1 reader space for 6 students		0.40 m^2/student
	books: 3.8 m run of shelving/student		0.62 m^2/student
	administrative and support facilities		0.2 m^2/student
		Total (say)	1.25 m^2/student
Additional area in law schools to provide	1 reader space for 2 students		0.80 m^2/student
	Additional area for book stacks to accommodate excess of accessions over withdrawals for ten years		0.20 m^2/student
	Additional area for special collections of books, manuscripts or pamphlets		as required
	Addition for reserve store, separate from main library		50 m^2 plus 3.5 m^2/1000 volumes
	Balance area		25%
ADMINISTRATION			
For central administration, including Senate House, conference room, committee rooms	up to 3000 students		450 m^2
	additional students		0.35 m^2/student
For maintenance depot, including central stores and workshops, but excluding furniture stores	up to 3000 students		0.25 m^2/student
	additional students		0.15″
	Balance area		50%

Table II (*Continued*)

AMENITY BUILDINGS		
Restaurants and cafeterias	Dining areas (based on 60% usage)	0.2 m²/student
	Kitchens, etc	0.17 m²/student
	or can be calculated:	
	Kitchen area:	
	for 3 main meals including breakfast	0.45 m²/meal/sitting
	1 meal per day	0.4 m²/meal
	cooked snacks	0.3 m²/snack
	coffee and sandwiches	0.1 m²/snack
	balance area for catering spaces	25%
Communal and social areas	students	0.7 m²/student
	academic, senior administrative and research staff (excluding medical schools)	0.19 m²/student
	ditto in medical schools	(0.30)
	non-academic staff	0.16
	Total	1.05 m²/student
	Total in medical schools	1.16 m²/student
	large hall or space for use in conjunction with social space between 3000 and 6000 students	450 m²
	balance area for communal spaces	30%
Students' Union offices and administration	up to 3000 students	0.15 m²/student
	additional students	0.02 m²/student
Sports facilities		
Indoor sports (see section 27)	up to 3000 students	0.47 m²/student
	additional students up to 6000	0.13 m²/student
	additional students	0.02 m²/student
Outdoor sports (see section 28)		
Grass pitches, playing fields	up to 3000 students	28 m²/student
	additional students	14.5 m²/student
Pavilion and groundsman's store	up to 3000 students	0.18 m²/student
	additional students	0.10 m²/student
Health services (see Chapter 16)		
Simple consultancy suite for doctor and nurse treatment based on NHS provision for a group practice to service an equivalent number of patients	up to 3000 students	0.03 m²/student
	additional students	0.015 m²/student
Dental services are only provided if unavailable locally		
A central sickbay may be provided unless located within residential accommodation		2 beds/1000 students
Complete health service, including dentistry	up to 3000 students	0.10 m²/student
	additional students	0.03 m²/student
RESIDENTIAL ACCOMMODATION where provided (for students)		
Medium-rise buildings with no lifts		420 students/hectare
High-rise buildings		600 students/hectare
Allocations of space	study bedrooms	8.4–13 m²/place
	ablutions	1.21 m²/place
	storage	0.54 m²/place
	amenities	1.0 m²/place
	utilities	0.5 m²/place
	communal space	0.65 m²/place
	balance area for circulation	25%
	additional area for self-catering dining and kitchens	1.2–1.7 m²/place
Where a warden is in residence, allow for warden's residence offices for		107–120 m²/place
	warden	9.3 m²
	domestic bursar	9.3 m²
	secretary	7.0 m²
	porter	6.5 m²
	records	5.6 m²
In independent housing with self-catering	study bedroom	9.3 m²
	ancillary	1.5 m²
	amenity	2.2 m²
	balance	3.0 m²
	Total	16.0 m²

Dispersed facilities can be centred on residential buildings to resemble Oxbridge colleges, as at York; or can be distributed at random as at Surrey. Design details for catering can be found in Chapter 18.

2.13 Existing buildings
Much work needs to be done on refurbishing, converting and extending existing buildings for university and other educational use. **29.5** shows one such scheme.

2.14 Training centres
There is an increasing requirement for facilities for in-service training of staff in industrial, commercial and governmental organisations. The buildings for the BT Training Centre are shown in **29.6**.

2.13 Space standards
Allocations of space for different functions cannot be made to rigid rules, as each circumstance will be specific. However, the figures in Table II can be used as an initial design guide.

2.14 Part-time students
Not all students, even in universities, will be full time. Various forms of higher education are intended to keep the student from becoming completely divorced from the real world of industry and commerce to which he or she will return at the end of his course. Table III gives the forms of part-time involvement common in the UK, and the equivalent full-time student (FTE) factor to be taken in connection with the space standards in Tables II, VI and VII.

Table III Part-time students

Type of student/description	Full-time equivalent (FTE) for planning purposes
Full-time student Has no other occupation. Probably attends minimum 20 hours a week. May live in	1
Thick sandwich student Attends full-time for three academic years in rota but works in industry for at least a year during the period	1
Thin sandwich student Attends full-time for six months, works in industry the other six months including the long vacation. Repeats as long as necessary	1
Block release student While being trained in industry (eg an apprentice) attends full-time for a block of three or four months	1/3
Part-time day student Attends one day a week plus two or more evenings	2/9
Evening student Only attends in evening	No allowance

2.11 Balance area

The areas given in Table II are mainly net usable areas. To these have to be added balance areas, given as a percentage of the net usable area:

Net usable area + balance area = gross area

Balance area includes allowance for corridors and stairs, entrance foyer, enquiry counter, cloakrooms, locker spaces, lavatories, cleaners' stores, maintenance workshops, gardeners' stores, boiler rooms, electricity sub-stations and meter rooms, delivery bays, porters' rooms, plant rooms, service ducts. The percentage allowances for balance area are given in the appropriate places in Table II.

3 TEACHING SPACES

3.01 Density of academic development

The numbers of students that can be accommodated on a campus are given in Table IV.

Table IV Density of facilities for academic areas

Plot ratio	Number of students per hectare	
	Art based	Science and technology
0.5:1.0	395	200
1.0:1.0	790	400
1.5:1.0	1185	600
2.0:1.0	1580	800
2.5:1.0	1975	1000

3.02 Teaching places

The numbers of teaching places that will be required for any type of institution can be calculated from the following formula:

$$N_t = N_s \times H_s/H_w \times 100/F$$

where N_t = number of teaching places required
  N_s = number of students
  H_s = hours per week per student in the accommodation
  H_w = total number of available hours a week for the accommodation
  F = net utilisation factor

Example:

200 students require an average of 10 hours a week of lectures in a working week of 40 hours and assuming a net utilisation factor of 80 per cent. What number of teaching spaces should be provided?

$N_s = 200$, $H_s = 10$, $H_w = 40$ and $F = 80$

hence $N_t = 200 \times 10/40 \times 100/80 = 63$ spaces.

3.03 Areas of teaching spaces

The areas required for various forms of teaching accommodation, related to teaching spaces rather than to total student population, are given in Table V.

3.04 Tutorial and seminar rooms

Tutorials often take place in academic staff offices. Some prefer special rooms for the purpose, **29.7**. Seminar rooms are shown in **29.8**.

Table V Usable area per working space for teaching accommodation (for balance areas see Table VII under 'Teaching Space')

Non-specialised	
Tutorial rooms	
Rooms with informal seating	1.85 m²/space
Rooms with tables or desks	2.30 m²/space
Rooms with demonstration area	2.50 m²/space
Lecture theatres	
Rooms with close seating	1.00 m²/space
Drawing offices: A1 and smaller	3.70 m²/space
A0 and bigger	4.60 m²/space
Laboratories	
Advanced science and engineering	5.60 m²/space
Non-advanced science and engineering	4.60 m²/space
Management and Business Studies	
Work study	4.60 m²/space
Typewriting	3.20 m²/space
Accounting	2.80 m²/space
Workshops	
Crafts involving large-scale machines and equipment, eg welding, motor vehicles, machine tools	8.40 m²/space
Crafts requiring workbenches and smaller scale machines and equipment, e.g. carpentry, plumbing, electrical	5.60 m²/space
Craft rooms, e.g. dressmaking, cookery	5.60 m²/space

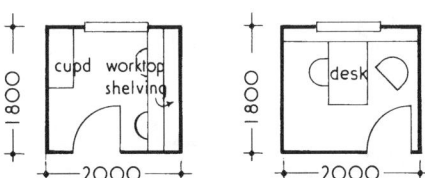

29.7 *Two types of tutorial rooms*

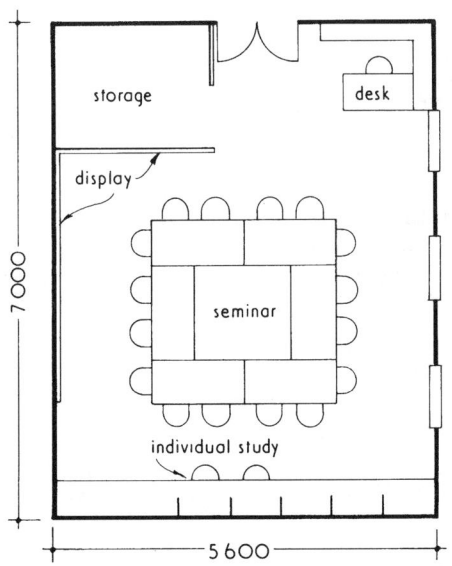

29.8 *A seminar room*

Table VI Space standards for colleges of further education

Teaching spaces
see para **3**

Libraries

	colleges with 30% advanced work	colleges with less than 30% advanced work
first 500 FTE students	390 m²	300 m²
additional FTE students	0.44 m²/student	0.38 m²/student
balance area	25%	

Non-teaching areas for the following:
principal's and vice-principal's rooms
registrar's and departmental heads' rooms
main offices
rooms for principal's and departmental heads' secretaries
offices for welfare and advisory services
building maintenance officer's room
interview room
enquiry kiosk
porter's room
bookshop
medical room
storage for the above at 15%

*up to 500 FTE students	255 m²
500 to 2500 FTE students	0.128 m²/student
additional students	0.05 m²/student
academic staff rooms (other than departmental heads)	0.36 m²/student
non-academic staff allocated to departments	0.20 m²/student
Balance areas: administrative	50%
academic staff workroom	50%
non-academic staff workroom	40%
communal	30%

Communal accommodation
for the following:
physical recreation including changing rooms
student and staff common rooms
students' union/staff association
music/indoor sports
storage for the above

*up to 500 FTE students	590 m²
500 to 2000 FTE students	0.42 m²/student
additional FTE students	0.14 m²/student
additional area for full-time and sandwich course students who make fuller use of the facilities	0.5 m²/full-time/ sandwich student
dining rooms, allow for quarter to half of student body	1.12 m²/space
cooking and service areas, see universities	
Student common rooms	0.75 m²/student
Staff common rooms	1.85 m²/member
Lockers, baths, showers, laundry/drying space for day/lodging students	0.9 m²/student
(A single-sex changing room is about 74 m²)	
Balance areas: communal	30%
catering	25%

Residential accommodation
see universities and polytechnics

*approximation to complex formula

Table VII Space standards for colleges of education

Teaching space

Total space provided	4.65 m²/student
tutorial/seminar rooms	13.5 m²/staff member excluding principal and vice-principal
lecture rooms: first 100 places	1.1 m²/student
additional spaces	0.9 m²/student
general teaching rooms	1.85 m²/student
additional area for storage	10%
balance areas: general teaching spaces	40%
academic staff workrooms	50%
non-academic staff workrooms	40%

Libraries
including private study areas

*first 200 students	1.1 m²/student
additional students	0.95 m²/student
balance area	25%

Non-teaching areas see colleges of further education

Communal areas
students' residences } see universities and polytechnics

*approximation to complex formula

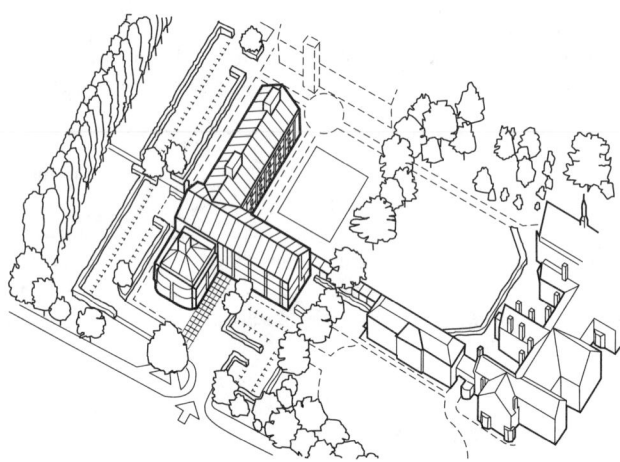

29.9 *Homerton College, Cambridge, Teacher Training Facility.*
Architects: RMJM

3.05 Lecture theatres

These are expensive facilities which are often under-used. They range in size from large classrooms accommodating 50 students to large theatres for 500. However, investigation has shown that the common lecture group is between 30 and 60, so the larger sizes are appropriate only when conference facilities are needed, or where use as an assembly hall or cinema is also envisaged. Further details of lecture facilities will be found in Chapter 20.

4 COLLEGES OF FURTHER EDUCATION

These have a higher proportion of part-time and evening students. Areas for teaching spaces must therefore be calculated by the method in para **3.02**. Areas for other facilities will be found in Table VI.

5 COLLEGES OF EDUCATION

Space standards for institutions training teachers are given in Table VII. One such is shown in **29.9**.

30 Laboratories

Tony Branton with Chris Bissell

Tony Branton is co-director of the Laboratories Investigation Unit. Chris Bissell is an architect formerly with the DES

CI/SfB 732
UDC 727.3
Unicode F739

KEY POINT:

● *The principal concern in the design of a laboratory relates to the building services needed*

Contents

1 INTRODUCTION

1.01 Type of laboratory – changing requirements

All laboratories must be designed to cope with growth and change irrespective of the scale of the work, or the scientific discipline involved. The three major types of laboratory are:

● Research
● Teaching
● Analytical

Of these, the need to cater for rapidly changing requirements is most evident in research work.

With teaching, an increasing diversity of educational methods coupled with multi-disciplinary use of laboratory space has produced similar needs for adaptable layouts. Analytical work is changed by developments ln analytical equipment and procedures associated with it. Requirements in all laboratories will change during the life of the building and this must be anticipated in the initial design. The designer must encourage users to think beyond immediate needs when the brief is being prepared.

1.02 Scope

The information contained in this chapter is related primarily to bench-scale laboratories. Standards common to all scientific disciplines are stressed to highlight areas where interchange of use is viable. While special requirements must be met, they should, wherever possible, be catered for within an adaptable building framework based on common requirements. The designer must develop a basic structure and service distribution system within which a variety of alternative layouts is possible. In the case of a laboratory building, the dimensional requirements of laboratory spaces and their associated services should primarily determine this system, other spaces, such as lecture rooms, offices and stores, being co-ordinated into the system as necessary. Where the laboratory is only a small part of a larger scheme, as in a hospital or school, other constraints will predominate. Whatever the context, design decisions on the size of laboratory spaces, frequency of services, etc. must be based on a general analysis of detailed requirements for all present and future likely activities in the laboratory.

2 AREAS

2.01 Areas per workplace

The figures given in Tables I to IV are expressed as areas per workplace. In most cases this includes an allowance for shared facilities within the laboratory, e.g. instrumentation, wash-up sinks, fume cupboards, which are additional to the basic area required for the student or scientist's workstation. If some of these facilities are centralised in order to allow multidiscipline or multipurpose use of basic laboratory space, an appropriate portion of calculated area must be transferred to the centralised space and the laboratory area reduced accordingly. Areas per workplace are given as 'usable areas', i.e. the area needed exclusively for research, teaching or routine laboratory purposes. The percentage addition for 'balance areas' is accounted for by ducts, lavatories, cloakrooms, boiler houses, plant rooms, lifts and general circulation space.

Tables I to IV give area guidelines for schools, colleges, universities and research. In addition, there are:

● Analytical (industrial or hospital) laboratories. Private industrial firms may have their own standards. Simple analytical work can have requirements similar to teaching, e.g. $5.6\,m^2$ per workplace. More complex routines may be better related to the research standards given in table IV.
● Machine- or equipment-orientated laboratories. In this type of laboratory (or workshop), whether teaching, research or routine, the sizes of spaces will be determined by the shape, size and number of machines, rigs or pieces of equipment rather than by the number of workplaces. In general these areas must be assessed on an *ad hoc* basis. The following standards are given for further education colleges: workshops, machine laboratories – 7.5 to $8.4\,m^2$ per workplace plus 25 per cent addition for storage plus 25 per cent addition for balance area.

Table I Schools
These areas, derived from DES bulletins, distinguish levels and scale of work, but not subjects

Level of work		Scale of work*	
General science	$2.8\,m^2$	Benchscale work	$3.2\,m^2$
Individual projects	$3.6\,m^2$	Workshop scale	$4.6\,m^2$

*For calculating overall laboratory areas, including storage and preparation

Table II Colleges of further education *Individual subjects are not distinguished*

Level of work	Area per workplace	% addition for service rooms	Balance area addition*
Advanced science and engineering	$5.6\,m^2$	25	40%
Non advanced science	$4.6\,m^2$	15	40%

*The balance area is a percentage addition to the area per workplace and the percentage addition for service rooms

Table III Universities

	Area per workplace	Addition for storage and preparation	Addition for other teaching and research ancillaries	Balance area addition†	
	m²	%	%	%	
Pure sciences*					
Teaching laboratories					
Biological sciences (general purpose labs)	4.0	15	*Ad hoc* in accordance with needs (say, 15%)	30*	
Biological sciences (other than gen purpose)	5.0	15	,,	30*	
Physics	5.0	15	,,	30*	
Chemistry	5.0	15	,,	30*	
Research laboratories					
Individual or advanced research	11.0	15	,,	30*	
MSC courses	7.5	15	,,	30*	
Other technological and scientific subjects					
Teaching laboratories					
Elementary or intermediate	3.7	15	15	45	⎫
First and second year honours and general	4.2–4.6	15	15	45	⎪
Final year honours	5.6–6.5	15	15	45	⎪ balance area % includes allowance for plant rooms, etc
Research laboratories					⎬
Research students in groups of 4 or more	7.4	15	15	45	⎪
Individual or advanced research	11.0	15	15	45	⎭

*Additional balance area allowances will be needed for plant rooms, ducts, boiler houses and entrance halls: physics – up to 12½ % of workplace, storage/prep and ancillary areas; chemistry and biological sciences – up to 20% of workplace, storage/prep and ancillary areas
†The balance area is a % addition to the workplace, storage/prep and ancillary/areas

3 FURNITURE AND EQUIPMENT DIMENSIONS

3.01 Worktop height

Most laboratory work takes place in a vertical zone above the worktop. The lowest convenient worktop height should be specified as this increases the volume with easy reach, **30.1a**. In addition to catering for prolonged periods of written work in the laboratory, a seated worktop height, **30.1b**, can also be specified for small-scale work involving fine manipulations, e.g. fine electronics assembly or work at the microscope. In some cases a further lowering of the supporting surface can usefully increase the vertical zone within easy reach. An extreme example of this is the low chemistry bench for tall glassware rigs, **30.1c**.

Worktop heights for school science must be considered in relation to other non-science subjects. The heights given in **30.2** are for general use and thus allow for an interchange of use in practical work areas. The relationship of seat height to worktop height is critical and these should be related as shown in **30.2**.

3.02 Worktop depth

If the worktop is too deep the back of it will be used for dead storage, making access to services controls difficult. The depth should be based on maximum convenient reach. A 600 mm depth will meet most requirements but there may be cases where 700 or 750 mm will be needed for large bench-mounted instruments.

3.03 Height of services controls

Services controls should be as near to shoulder height as is possible. This is the shortest distance in terms of reach and controls are less likely to be concealed by apparatus.

3.04 Sinks

For comfortable working the rim of wash-up sinks should be slightly higher than the general worktop, **30.3a**. The same applies to any associated draining top. As an alternative, a shallow tray with rim at worktop height can be specified and a deep bowl used with it when a greater depth of water is required for soaking, washing or cooling larger apparatus, **30.3b**. Smaller sinks, drip cups or continuous troughs used for the disposal of liquids are not critical and can be set at worktop height. As an alternative to the small sink a shallow tray can be placed on the worktop to drain

Table IV Research (government and industrial) An individual scientist's or research assistant's area requirements can vary considerably depending on the sizes and amounts of equipment used for experiments. The figures give a likely range*

Chemistry	8–12 m²
Physics	6–8 m²
Biology	6–8 m²

*University figures for storage and preparation, and ancillary laboratory areas may be used as guidelines for research accommodation but *ad hoc* requirements are more likely to occur in ancillary laboratory areas and must be allowed for on an individual job basis

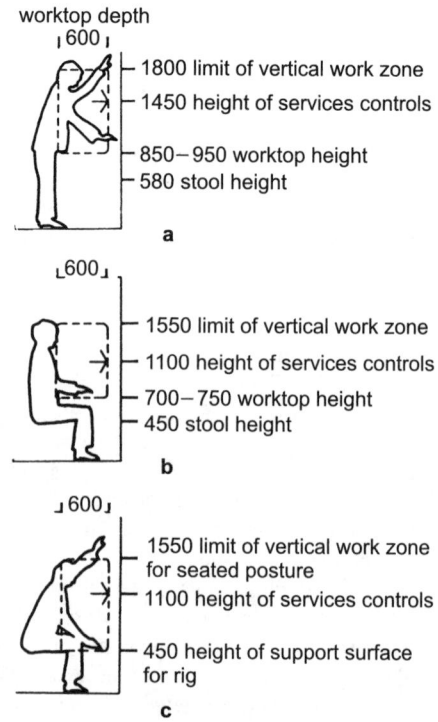

30.1 *Limits of reach in various situations. The heights of service controls specified may have to be reduced in practice, but the reduction should be minimised.* **a** *Standing or sitting on a high stool.* **b** *Seated on a chair.* **c** *Seated and working on a high rig*

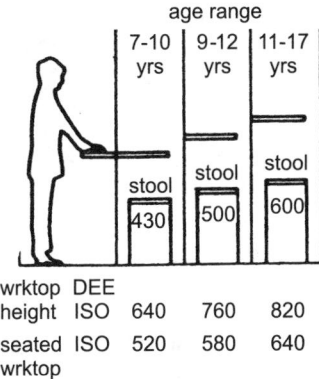

30.2 *Standing and sitting heights for schools*

	age range		
	7-10 yrs	9-12 yrs	11-17 yrs
	stool 430	stool 500	stool 600
wrktop height	DEE ISO 640	760	820
seated wrktop	ISO 520	580	640

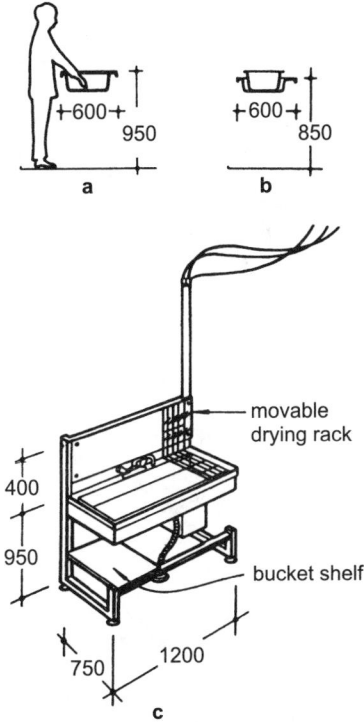

30.3 *Wash-up sink heights for adults (over 18 years of age).* **a** *Sink at 950 worktop height for comfortable working.* **b** *Shallow tray at lower worktop height with a loose, taller washing-up bowl.* **c** *General-purpose moveable wash-up sink with heater*

into a drip cup or trough. The tray can be stored when not in use. For use with large free-standing rigs, or for demonstration purposes, a movable sink **30.3c**, can be employed.

3.05 Storage

The maximum height and lowest level of storage which is frequently used should be based on convenient reach. Extreme high and low zones tend to be used for dead storage, **30.4**.

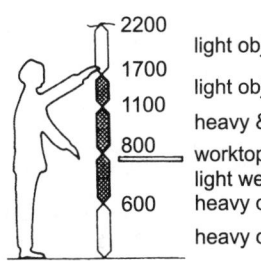

30.4 *Vertical storage zones based on common patterns of use*

Underbench storage should not exceed 50 per cent of the underbench space and must be movable. At least 600 mm width of knee-hole space must be provided under the bench at each workstation. In schools with a small bench length requirement, virtually all underbench space will be required for knee-hole space.

The depth of storage cupboards should not normally exceed 500 mm. Access to the back of shelves deeper than 500 mm is difficult particularly in the case of underbench units. The 500 mm depth will fit neatly under a 600 mm deep worktop (allowing for a back rail to the table).

Shelves and trays within storage units should be adjustable in height. Drawers are not recommended as they cannot be adjusted. Comfortable reach into a 300 mm deep cupboard above floor level is as follows:

```
 7 years – 1100 mm
 9 years – 1170 mm
10 years – 1260 mm
11 years – 1300 mm
12 years – 1375 mm
17 years – 1640 mm
18 years – 1675 mm
```

3.06 Storage units

A number of science storage systems now available, based on a standard tray size, **30.5**, are intended for the storage of small equipment and experimental kits. Tall cupboard units, **30.6**, should be used in preference to underbench storage as these give the range of choice as to storage level referred to in **30.4**. If underbench units are required they must be related to bench unit sizes. The unit shown in **30.7** is dimensioned to suit a 600 × 1200 bench unit. Trolleys are available for serving laboratories from storage and preparation areas, **30.8**. All units should be based on standard tray and shelf sizes and the interior of units should be capable of taking any combination required with full vertical adjustment.

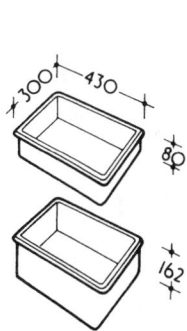

30.5 *Standard storage tray sizes*

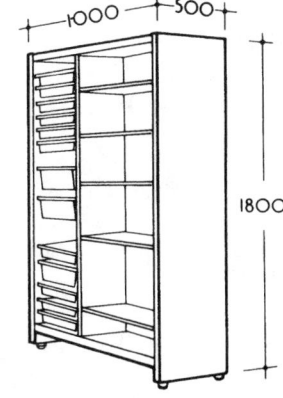

30.6 *Tall storage cupboards, preferred to underbench storage*

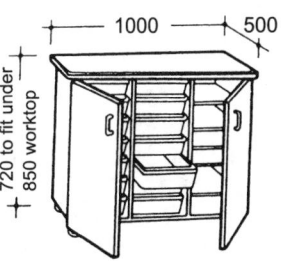

30.7 *Mobile underbench unit*

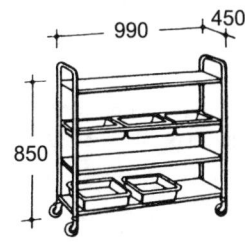

30.8 *Service trolley*

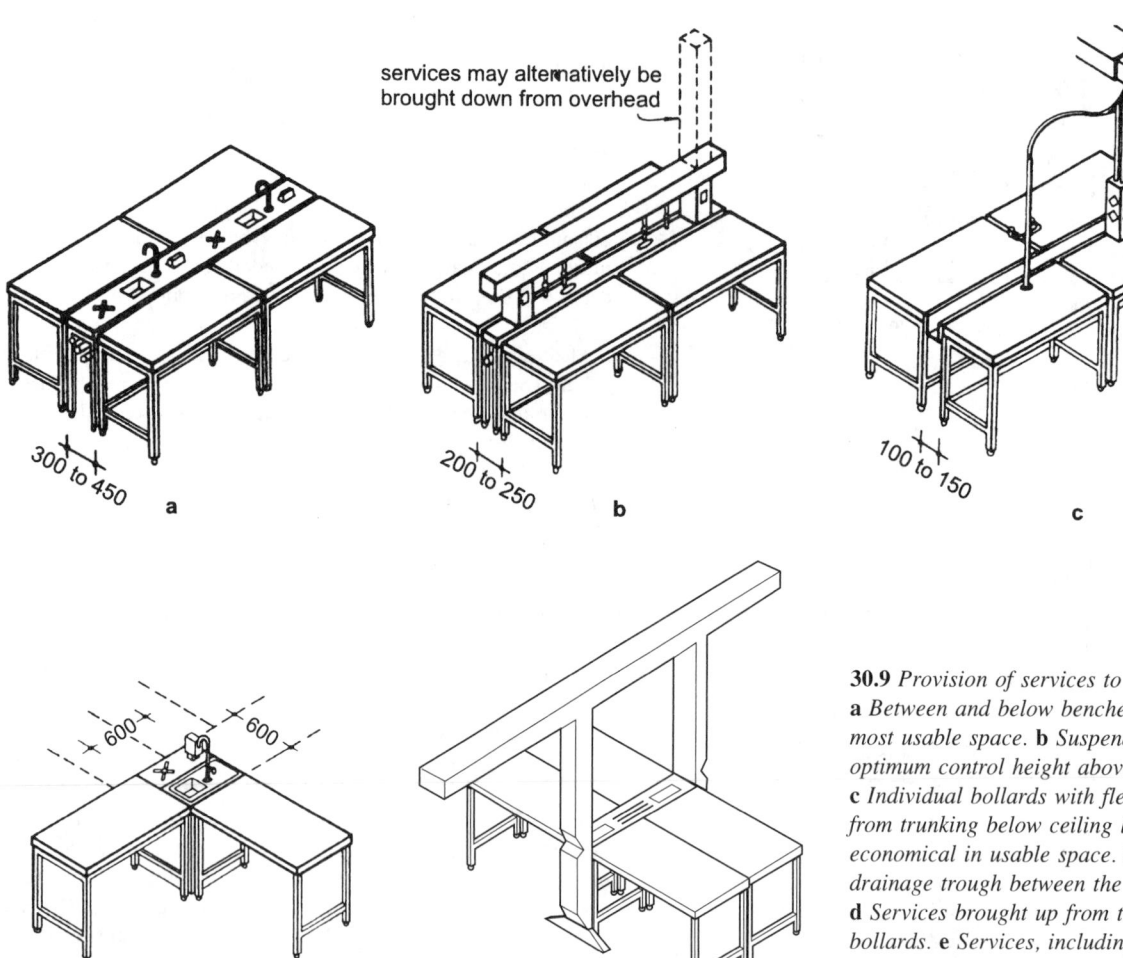

services may alternatively be brought down from overhead

300 to 450 **a**

200 to 250 **b**

100 to 150 **c**

600   600

d

e

30.9 *Provision of services to worktops.* **a** *Between and below benches: taking most usable space.* **b** *Suspended at optimum control height above the worktop.* **c** *Individual bollards with flexible links from trunking below ceiling level: most economical in usable space. Note the drainage trough between the worktops.* **d** *Services brought up from the floor in bollards.* **e** *Services, including vacuum drainage, provided through linked workstation frames*

3.07 Services space related to worktop

When assessing floor area for worktop and equipment, the area taken up by associated services must be included. This area should be kept to a minimum in order to give as much floor space as possible for laboratory work. The arrangement shown in **30.9a** is most wasteful of space. By raising the service runs apart from drainage above the worktop (see recommendations for the height of controls), as shown in **30.9b**, the width of services spine can be usefully reduced. Further savings can be made by raising the local service runs into a boom below the ceiling with flexible connections to bollards on the worktop; the space between the worktops having to accommodate a drainage trough only, **30.9c**. The dimensions of floor-mounted service bollards, **30.9d**, are commonly related to the width of benching, allowing worktop to abut any side as requirements dictate.

3.08 Mobile services units

Where the requirement for laboratory services is infrequent or where centralised piped services are unable to supply the quality of service required, localised mobile sources provide a highly adaptable solution to the problem, **30.10** and **30.11**. If they are used floor space must be allocated.

3.09 Fume cupboards

Fume cupboards, **30.12** to **30.14**, are costly items and demands for them vary between scientific disciplines (Table V). The facility to reposition them and build up concentrations in different parts of a building will help to ensure their full use when changes in the use of laboratory space occur. Critical dimensions are given in Table VI; linear air velocities in Table VII.

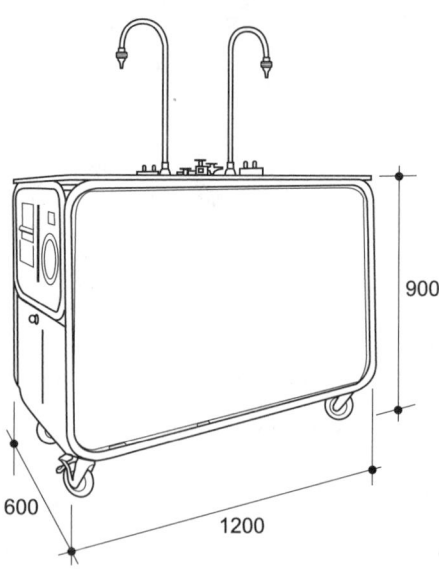

900

600

1200

30.10 *Mobile trolleys, developed for use in schools. These contain their own water supplies and drainage in tanks under the sink. The unit is plugged into a 13 amp socket outlet to enable demonstrations and simple tests to be carried out in otherwise unserviced areas*

3.10 Floor mounted equipment

In many cases space must be allocated for floor-mounted equipment. Typical examples are shown in **30.15** to **30.18**, but sizes will vary with different performance requirements and manufacturers' models. Space allocated on plans should never be

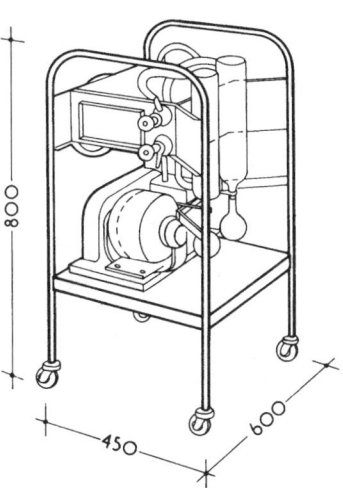

30.11 *Mobile vacuum pump, operable on a 13 amp supply and adjustable to individual requirements*

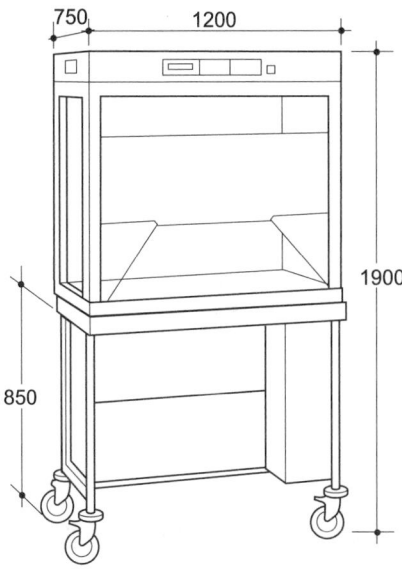

30.14 *Mobile recirculation fume cupboard incorporating filters*

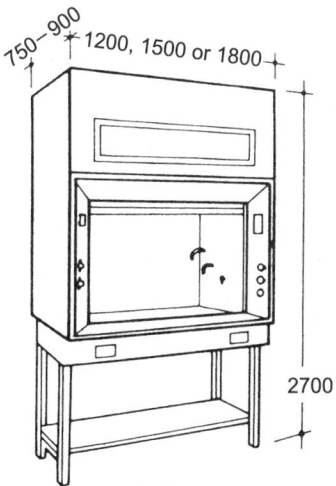

30.12 *Relocatable fume cupboard with aerofoil front and bypass air grille over sash*

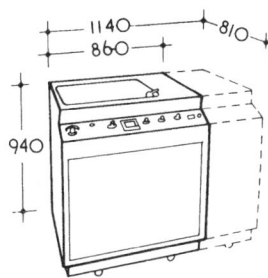

30.15 *Floor-mounted centrifuge*

Table V Numbers of cupboards required (rough guide)

FE, university teaching	
Physics	1 to 30 students
Organic chemistry	1 to 2 students
Inorganic chemistry	1 to 2 students
Physical chemistry	1 to 10 students
Biology	1 to 10 students
Biochemistry	1 to 10 students
Research work	
Chemistry	1 to 1 or 2 workers
Biochemistry	1 ro 2 or 4 workers
Biology	small demand ad hoc to individual needs
Physics	small demand ad hoc to individual needs

Table VI Critical dimensions of fume cupboards

	Schools	FE, university, industrial
Worktop height	as 30.4	as 30.1
Clear width of front opening	750–1200	900+
Height of front opening	750	840–900
Worktop to top of cupboard	1050+	1050–1800
Depth of clear working space	600–750	600–900

Table VII Linear air velocities required through open fronts

Schools	0.3 m/s
FE, university, industrial including special toxic hazards	velocity required dependent on risk assessment (see BS7258: part 3: 1990)

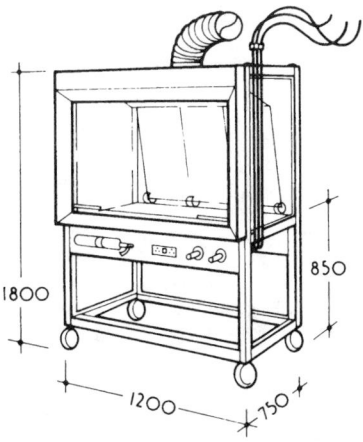

30.13 *Mobile fume cupboard which has glazed baffle, back and sides for demonstration purposes*

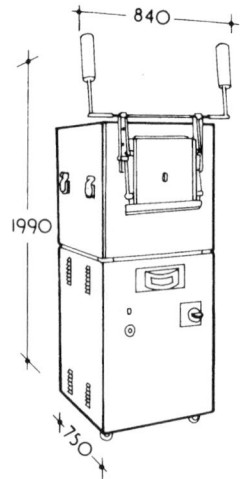

30.16 *Box furnace*

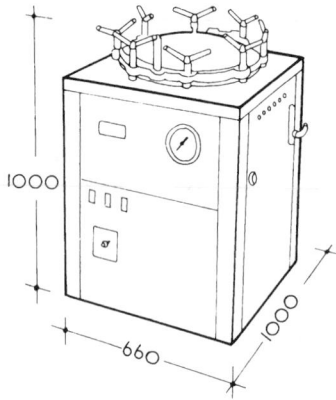

30.17 *Autoclave*

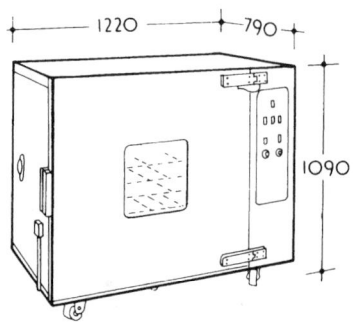

30.18 *Humidity oven*

precise and laboratory furniture should be movable to accommodate changes in the quantity and sizes of such equipment during the life of the laboratory.

3.11 Layout at the workstation

Where more than one worktop unit is required, the opportunity to create workbays should be allowed for. This more readily defines an individual's territory and puts a greater area of worktop or equipment space within convenient reach from a single position, **30.19**. Worktop lengths are given in Table VIII.

3.12 Space requirements for personnel

The application of the dimensions given in **30.20** will depend on the form of layout adopted in a given situation. The lower figures are suitable for short peninsula or island layouts (up to 2400 mm in length). Longer runs of worktop will require the maximum shown (4800+lengths). These situations shown in **30.20** are related primarily to linear worktop layouts and necessarily indicate (as in 30.20b and 30.20e) workspace and circulation intermixed. Where possible this should be avoided. This can be done if short peninsula or island layouts, or workbays, **30.19**, are used. Separation of workspace and circulation will reduce the likelihood of accidents and ease the problem of escape from hazards (see para **4**).

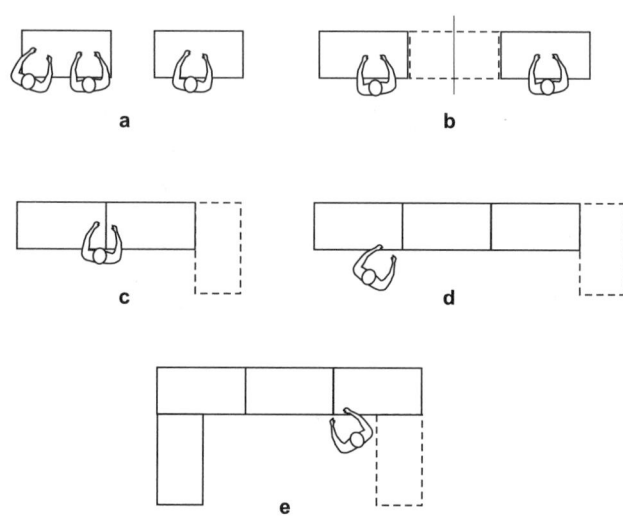

30.19 *Worktop/equipment areas based on 1200 × 600 mm units.*
a *School teaching.* **b** *University teaching.* **c** *Research with low space requirement.* **d** *Research with medium space requirement.*
e *Research with high space requirement*

Table VIII Space requirements at the workstation for worktop/equipment*

Level of work	Worktop length per person	Activity
Teaching (school) all subjects	600	Working in pairs
	900	Individual working
	1200	Advanced work
Teaching (college, university)		
Physics	900–1800	Elementary to advanced
Chemistry	1200–1800	1800 includes a 50% contribution of space for a small
Biochemistry	1200–1800	sink between 2 persons
Biology	1200	
Research (low requirement)	2400–3600	
Research (medium requirement)	3600–4800	For overall calculation a mean length should be taken
Research (high requirement)	4800–6000	

*The requirements above do not include space for shared equipment, fume cupboards, wash-up sinks, etc.

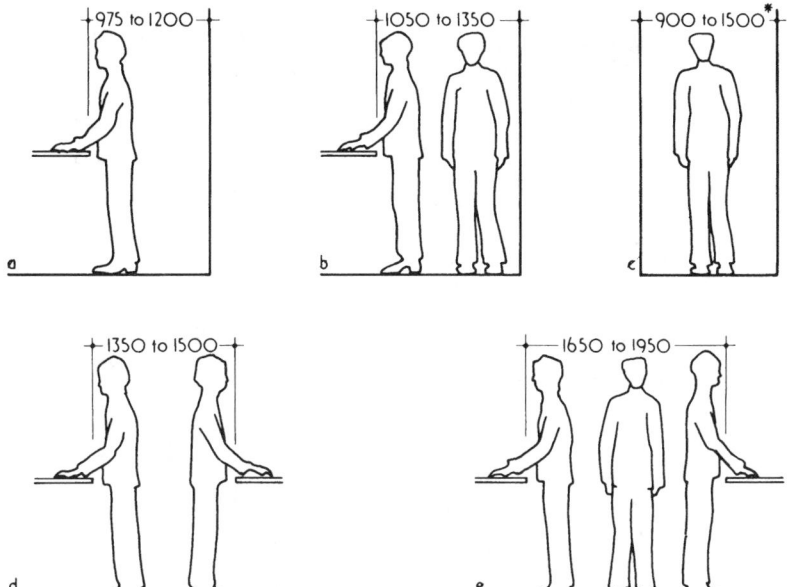

30.20 *Space required between worktops or equipment.* **a** *One worker, no through traffic.* **b** *One worker plus passageway.* **c** *Passageway only.* 1500 mm allows two to pass each other.* **d** *Two workers back to back, no through traffic.* **e** *Two workers back to back plus passageway*

4 LABORATORY LAYOUTS

4.01 Planning for variety
Furniture will normally have a minimum useful life of 15 years and over such a period changes in requirements will demand adjustments or even total rearrangements. All laboratory furniture should be movable.

There are no ideal layouts which suit a wide range of needs. Requirements will vary according to the educational research or routine needs of the moment. The shape of the laboratory should not therefore be based on a single layout of furniture and equipment but should rather be assessed on its ability to accommodate a variety of layouts. Long and narrow, or irregular shapes are less satisfactory than the squarer shapes in **30.21**.

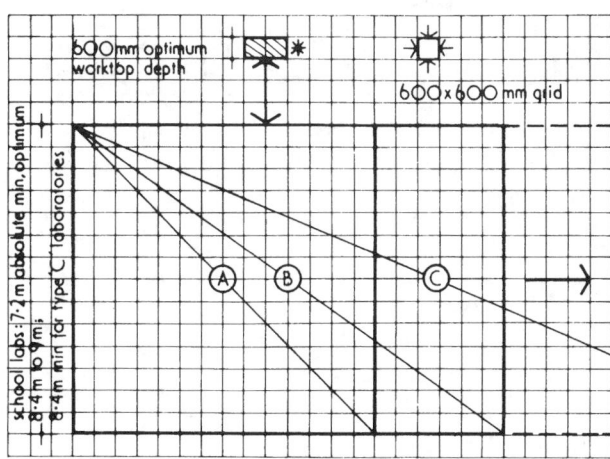

30.21 *Laboratory space for teaching. Where constant voice and visual contact between teacher and all students is important, the laboratory space should be designed within a plan proportion of 1 × 1 to 1 × 1½, ie between A and B. In universities and further education, classes as large as 100 students with intermittent contact with the lecturer may have extended proportions (C). Furniture units * should be sized to fit the available area. Larger furniture means less circulation space with consequent lower safety standard*

4.02 Effective space and access
In addition to providing a suitable shape of space, it is vital that full use is made of the floor area for laboratory purposes. Irregularities on the perimeter of a space will reduce the effective area, and environmental as well as laboratory services elements require careful co-ordination with the building structure, **30.22**. If such irregularities are unavoidable, as is often the case when converting existing buildings, the perimeter can be smoothed out with a continuous rail at benchtop height. This then provides a straight abutment for benching and defines the effective area.

An alternative way out of the laboratory should be provided for escape purposes. Doors to laboratories should be 1½-leaf minimum to cater for the periodic movement of items of equipment which are wider than the normal single-leaf door opening.

4.03 The location of storage
The efficient storage and distribution of apparatus and equipment is critical to the effective use of teaching laboratories. The traditional practice of distributing storage round the laboratory in underbench units, **30.23a**, is no longer appropriate in school laboratories. The wide range of experimental work undertaken by different classes in the same laboratory necessitates centralising

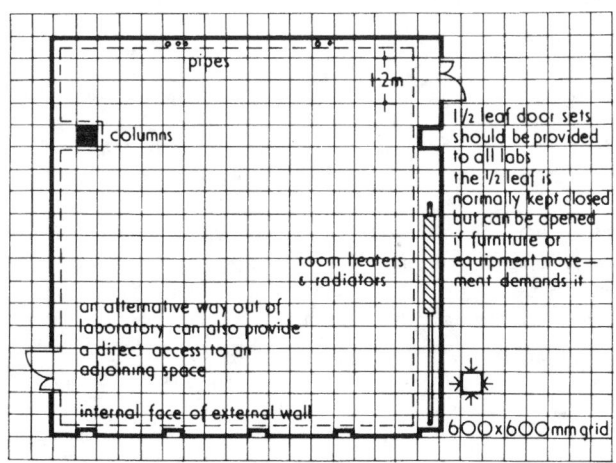

30.22 *Effective space and access*

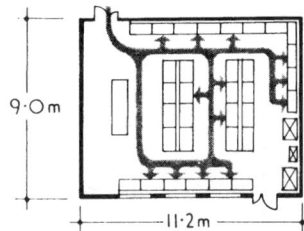 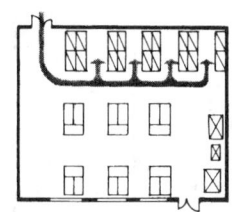

30.23 *Distribution of storage within a teaching laboratory.*
a *Traditionally dispersed.* **b** *Centralised for more efficient management and access*

storage within the laboratory, **30.23b**. This approach enables apparatus and experimental kits to be checked by the teacher or technician without interfering with the class. Also the class can visit the storage in a controlled manner. Organising storage within the laboratory in this way is also appropriate in higher and further education where the multidisciplinary use of laboratories by various groups of students is proposed. Centralised storage/ preparation is possible for groups of laboratories if there is adequate technical/management assistance available, **30.24**. Experimental kits can be trollied from the central area to any teaching laboratory to meet individual class needs. This leads to more intense use of equipment, reduces the need for duplication and allows teachers and lecturers to devote more time to personal contact with the students.

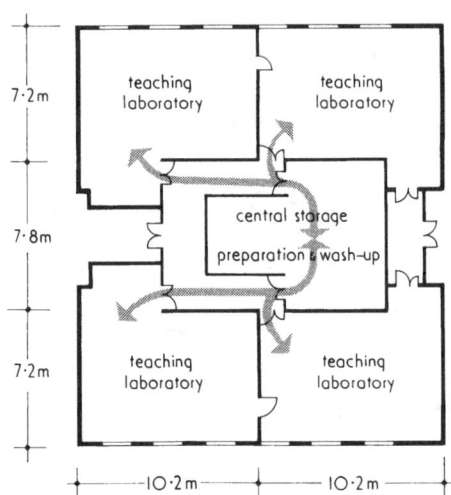

30.24 *Centralised storage for a group of laboratories*

4.04 School laboratories

The layout of the laboratory should provide:

- Good pupil/teacher contact
- Safe movement
- Convenient access to equipment and materials.

30.25 and **30.26** show alternative layouts for general science work using the same furniture units. Both layouts will accommodate up to 36 pupils for general work (or 22 for advanced studies). In both cases storage is organised as shown in **30.23b**. The long linear arrangement of benching requires wide gangways to ensure safe back-to-back working and allow the teacher to circulate safely while work is in progress. The short peninsula and island benching, **30.26**, provides a clearer separation between individual workspace and general circulation. Gangways between benching can be reduced and space for a central group area gained. Both **30.25** and **30.26** are serviced from overhead supplies as shown in **30.9c** (refer to later notes on services distribution for further information **30.38**.

4.05 An alternative method of servicing from under the floor using free-standing bollards (see **30.9d** with wall-mounted spines is shown in **30.27**. Although this layout meets the requirement of separating workspace and general circulation, it is less adaptable than overhead booms due to the fixed nature of the bollard, which while allowing alternative arrangements of benching nevertheless predetermines their basic spacing.

No fixed position for demonstration is indicated on any of the layouts. To fix the use of floor area with demonstration facilities which will have only intermittent use is wasteful. It is more efficient to use any suitably located bench or a trolley (see **30.10**) of a height to suit the age range using the laboratory, ie normal worktop height as specified for general laboratory work.

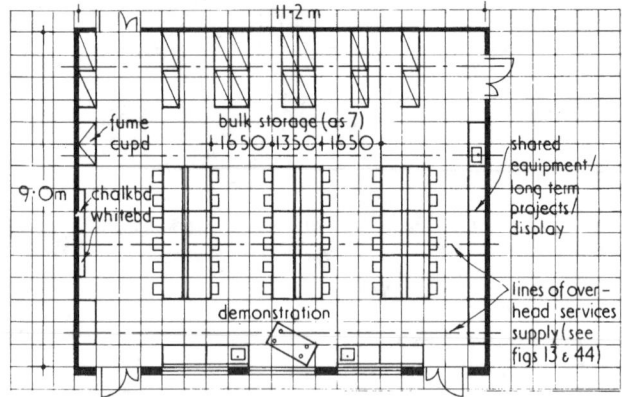

30.25 *School laboratory layout with linear bench arrangement accommodating 36 pupils at 2.8 m² each, or 28 pupils at 3.6 m² each*

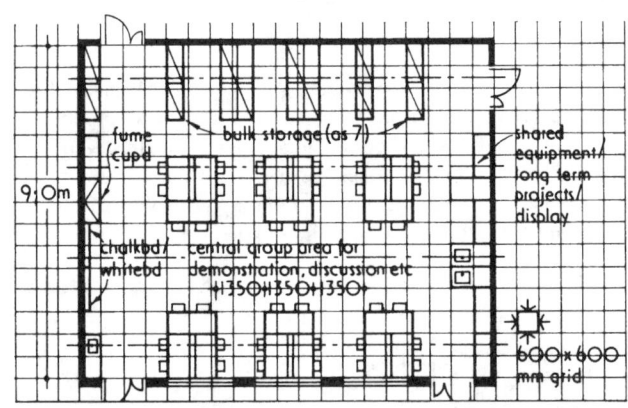

30.26 *The same numbers as* **30.25** *are accommodated at short peninsular and island benching. Both schemes have overhead servicing*

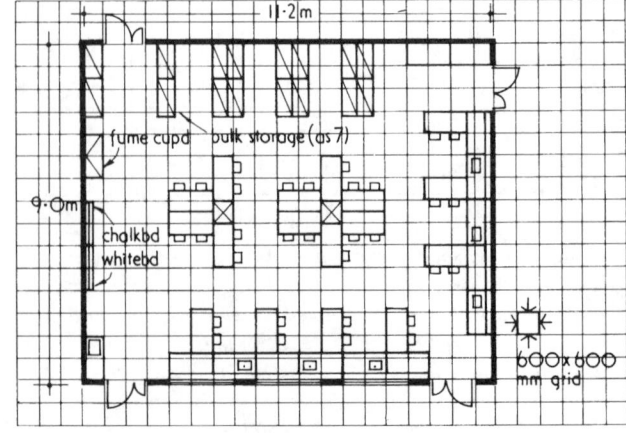

30.27 *The same capacity with perimeter servicing and underfloor servicing to free-standing bollard (see* **30.9d***)*

4.06 University and college teaching laboratories

Planning for safe movement and convenient access to shared equipment is vital (as for school laboratories). The need to plan for direct contact with the lecturer will vary depending on the level of work undertaken. Large laboratories make constant direct contact impossible but this is educationally acceptable with the use of project-orientated teaching methods. **30.33** and **30.34** show typical layouts suitable for a wide range of subjects with some variations, e.g. fume cupboard provision would increase for some chemistry subjects (see para **3.09**). The extended linear layout of **30.28** and the short peninsula and island arrangements of **30.29** are generically related to **30.25** and **30.26** respectively and the same observations apply. Discussion and demonstration should be catered for, but continuous lecturing should be provided for in an appropriate space. If storage and shared equipment are centrally located (as in **30.24**) multipurpose use of the laboratories shown is feasible, leading to a possible higher utilisation of their high cost facilities. For larger groups the layouts illustrated can be repetitively extended based on the areas per student given.

Multipurpose use of teaching laboratories requires convenient access to and rapid changes of special equipment and apparatus. **30.30** shows a reversal of the traditional layout, i.e. space for special apparatus which is to be shared is concentrated in a central area as opposed to being distributed around the perimeter. If mounted on trollies, apparatus and experimental kits for a whole variety of subjects can be conveniently brought into the laboratory from an adjoining preparation/storage area.

4.07 Research laboratories

Research is commonly carried out by small teams of workers and lends itself to accommodation within repetitive units of space. The range of area requirements (para **2.01**) indicates a useful unit size of 24 m². This will accommodate four workers at 6 m² each, three at 8 m² and two at 12 m², in the science disciplines listed.

The degree of adaptability within the unit is dependent on the shape adopted. The rectangular unit, **30.31**, provides for straight runs of worktop and equipment. The square unit, **30.32**, provides for straight runs of worktop and equipment layout including the creation of individual workbays as previously recommended (para **3.11**).

The rectangular unit provides the most economical plan form if a central corridor only is used, **30.33a**. Growth in the use of shared equipment has led to the planning of central areas for accommodating such items which, when combined with the square unit, provide highly adaptable laboratory buildings, **30.33b** and **30.33c**. Both laboratory units illustrated can be sub-divided to provide offices, darkrooms, coldrooms, etc. The alternative layouts shown in **30.34** are not exhaustive but indicate the ability of the square

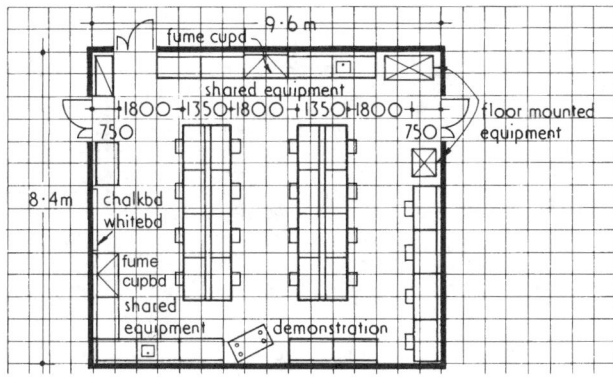

30.28 *University laboratory layout accommodating 20 students at 4.0 m² each, or 16 students at 5.0 m² each*

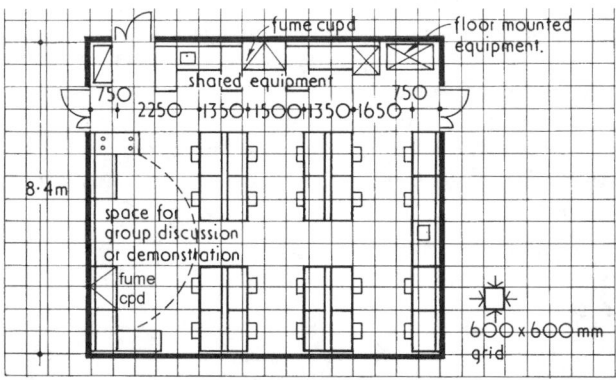

30.29 *The same capacity as* **30.28** *with shorter bench arrangements and a discussion/demonstration area*

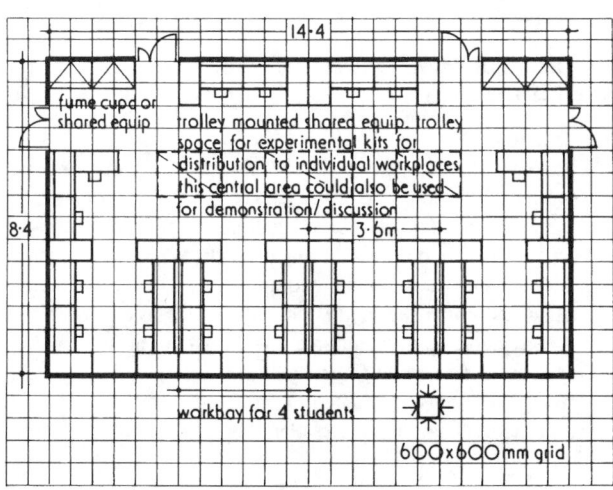

30.30 *University layout for 24 students at 5.0 m² each with shared equipment centrally located*

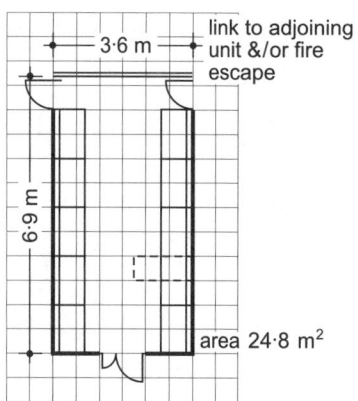

30.31 *Research laboratory based on a rectangular unit of space*

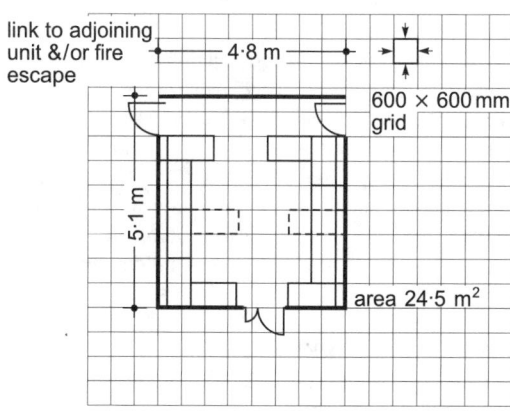

30.32 *Research laboratory based on a square unit of space*

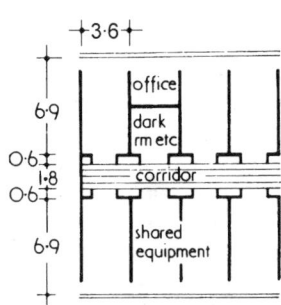 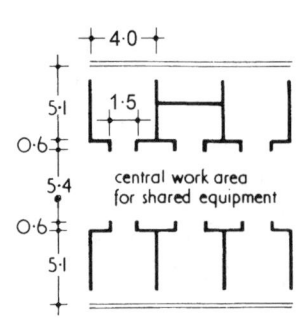 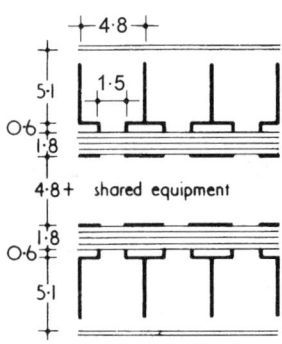

30.33 *Plans incorporating both laboratory types.* **a** *Rectangular units with central corridor on a 3.6 m module.* **b** *Square units with a shared central work area on a 4.8 m module.* **c** *Square units with a double corridor, the core holding shared equipment, also on a 4.8 m module*

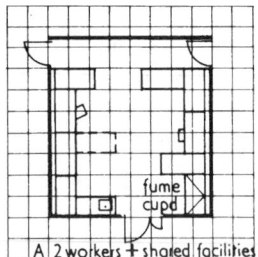 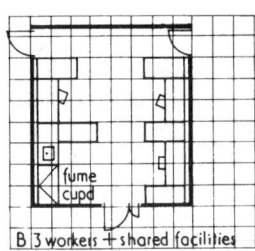 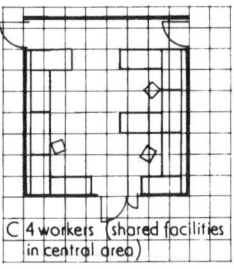 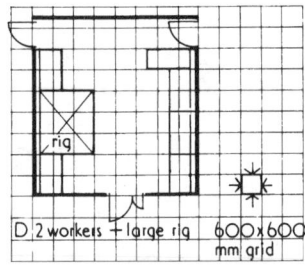

30.34 *Alternative layouts within the square laboratory unit shown in* **30.32.** **a** *Two workers + shared facilities.* **b** *Three workers + shared facilities.* **c** *Three workers, shared facilities in central area.* **d** *One worker + large rig*

unit to accommodate large experimental rigs and more importantly to allow definition of individual workers' territories at different densities of occupation. The opportunity to provide a clearer separation between personal circulation through the laboratory should be noted (cf. recommendations in para **3.12**).

4.08 Analytical laboratories
The layout of laboratories for analytical work may follow recommendations for research if closely related to it, thereby permitting change of use. Large laboratories with a high density of occupation are closer to those found in high-density teaching, **30.28**, **30.29**, and **30.30**, and similar layouts can be applied. Growth in the use of large-scale electro-analytical equipment (as in hospital pathology laboratories) has made the ability to exchange the use of floor space between furniture and floor-mounted equipment of greater importance.

4.09 The layout of ancillary laboratory spaces
Spaces containing special equipment and/or routine processes necessary to support general laboratory activities are too numerous in type to be dealt with here. The references in section 10 provide detailed information.

Note that many of the design solutions for fitting out spaces illustrated in the information listed above are of the 'built-in' type. 'Building-in' should be avoided wherever possible and preference given to an adaptable design approach, e.g. relocatable laboratory furniture and services fittings are more readily adjustable by users when new equipment has to be accommodated; coldrooms and temperature controlled rooms can be purchased as prefabricated movable enclosures as an alternative to building them in.

5 SERVICES REQUIREMENTS
The demand for services outlets depends on the nature and level of work. Table IX gives only general assessments of need; requirements in individual situations should be checked. If the number

provided is fixed, a large number will have to be installed to meet maximum demand, but if outlets can be added or subtracted easily at any time, a smaller initial provision may be made. It is more important to ensure that the services distribution system has the capacity to meet maximum demands. Accepted diversity factors are 20 per cent for electrical outlets and 40 per cent for all other outlets. Earlier studies of laboratory electrical demands give the following:

- Physical work – up to 20 watts/m^2
- Biological work – up to 30 watts/m^2
- Chemical work – up to 50 watts/m^2.

Requirements for other services – steam, vacuum, compressed air, special gases and special electric supplies – should be assessed for frequency and quality needed. Where the demand is intermittent or a particular quality is required, localised sources may provide the best answer, **30.11**

6 STRUCTURAL AND ENVIRONMENTAL REQUIREMENTS

6.01 Structure
- *Loadings (superimposed)*: For bench-scale laboratories design for 5.0 kN/m^2 + point loads of 3.6 kN to 5.0 kN. Average loads from suspended services (including ventilation ductwork) 0.25 kN/m^2. The point load capacity will deal with most bench-scale items of floor-mounted equipment (up to, say, 1 tonne in weight, assuming the load is spread). Loads in excess of this, i.e. heavy engineering equipment and rigs, are most economically located on ground floors.
- *Spans*: These must be related to preferred laboratory sizes, see **30.21** and **30.34**, the basic planning grid adopted (600 mm preferred) and the spacing of services distribution. Rectangular column grids may be utilised for linear building development but square grids are preferred if two-way development is envisaged, i.e. if the building form turns through 90°.

Table IX Average numbers of outlets per person

Laboratory	Electric* (13 amp double socket outlet)	Cold water	Natural or town gas (double gas tap)	Additional notes
Teaching				
School				
Elementary level	1†	1	1	If a laboratory is set aside for physics use only, cold water and gas outlets should be reduced in number
University/college				
Physics	2	1 per 4 people	1 per 4 people	Gas requirement minimal, bottled gas may be used as an alternative
Chemistry	2	1–2	2	
Biology	2	1–2	1	
Research				
University/College	2–6	1–3	Up to 4	Chemistry subjects have a high requirement for water and gas (if used as a heating medium). Physics subjects have a high requirement for electrics

* Socket outlets – all scientific work is using increasing numbers of electrical instruments. This results in high demands for socket outlets. In most cases the loads involved are small and these demands can be met by using plug-in splitter boards used at 13-amps.

† For schools the use of low voltage (110 V AC) is recommended by some authorities for safety reasons. However, not all electrical instrumentation is readily available in low voltage ratings. An alternative is a 240 V supply with earth leakage protection rated at 10 milliamps.

6.02 Environment

● *Heat*: 18°C required for comfort conditions. Special requirements for experimental work, e.g. coldrooms, temperature-controlled rooms should be dealt with on a local basis (complete package rooms are available).

● *Ventilation*: Rate of air change: at least 30 m³ of fresh air per person per hour for general work. Rates above two air changes per hour will require mechanical ventilation or full air conditioning. Extract must be balanced if fume cupboards are provided in laboratories. Certain activities may require higher air-change rates and/or special filtration.

● *Lighting*: General laboratories 350 lux on the working plane; glare index 19. In analytical laboratories constant reading of instruments may demand 600 lux; glare index 19. Where such activity is intermittent local additional lighting provides a more economical solution.

● *Sound*: Background noise levels in individual spaces, e.g. office, research laboratory or teaching laboratory (up to 36 places) NC 35. For larger multipurpose laboratories (teaching, research or routine) NC 45.

7 LABORATORY SERVICES DISTRIBUTION RELATED TO THE BUILDING SHELL

Routes for the distribution of services must be co-ordinated with the structural design of the laboratory building shell. Sub-main distribution is commonly based on one of two variants, vertical sub-mains, **30.35**, or horizontal sub-mains, **30.36**. Vertical sub-mains incorporated into a regular provision of builders' work ducts tend to be used in conjunction with repetitive laboratory units as shown in **30.31** and **30.32** or where standardisation of bench spacing is imposed throughout the building. While readily accommodating fume extract ductwork, the floor area taken up by the vertical ducts (around 4 per cent of the gross area) is higher than for the horizontal method (between 1 and 2 per cent

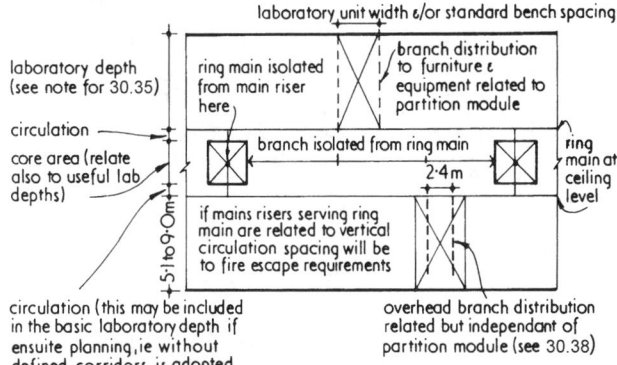

30.36 *Horizontal sub-main distribution incorporating the ring-main principle*

depending on fume extract requirements). The horizontal method with its limited number of vertical mains risers allows a high degree of planning flexibility. Horizontal sub-mains can be designed on the ring main principle which is better able to deal with high demands for piped supplies in any part of the building. Both methods of distribution enable branches to be isolated on the floor that is being served (i.e. without interference to floors above and below), but the horizontal method allows the isolation of large areas on one floor by isolating the sub-mains from the mains riser at the same floor.

8 SERVICES DISTRIBUTION IN THE LABORATORY

The method of distributing services from the sub-mains to furniture and equipment has a major influence on the flexibility of layout possible during the laboratory's total life. Where fixed service runs are integrated into the furniture, **30.37**, the spacing and configuration of furniture must necessarily be standardised if the initial economic advantages of repetitive service runs are to be gained. **30.37** shows a selection of typical configurations, each of which requires some variation in the routing of services to and from them. Where layouts abut vertical ducting as in A, the route is simple and direct. Island layouts as in B involve more indirect routes, the introduction of doors as in D adding similar complications. Peninsular layouts from the external wall as in C require distribution along the external wall. If this is extended along the whole building it becomes a horizontal sub-main (a variation on **30.36**). This sub-main location takes up space below windows and for ease of maintenance and adaptation, perimeter heating must be independently located at ceiling level. Service runs in furniture may be based on **30.9a**, **30.9b** or **30.9c**.

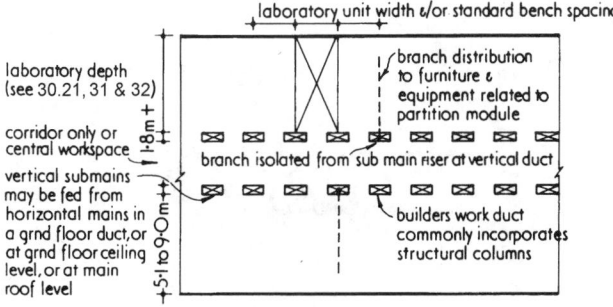

30.35 *Vertical sub-main distribution (relate to* **30.33***)*

Although loose worktop and storage units (or equipment) can be associated with rigid service runs, **30.37**, any major change in layout will involve adaptation or extension of the service runs. If, however, the distribution of rigid service runs within the laboratory can be separated from furniture, equipment and partitions, and flexible connections made to loose services units, **30.38**, layouts can be adjusted directly by users to meet new requirements. Standardisation of furniture layouts is no longer critical.

Island, perimeter and peninsular arrangements can be accommodated and gangways adjusted to meet safe requirements for individual situations (see **30.25**). While a wide variety of layouts

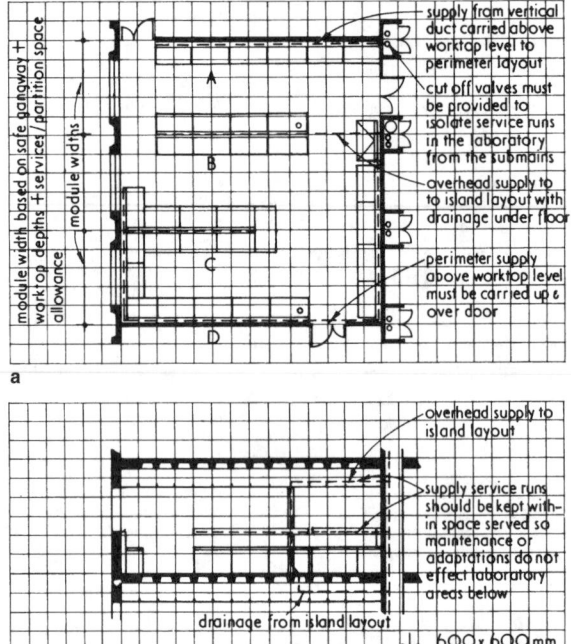

30.37 *Rigid services distribution integrated with furniture layout.* **a** *Plan. Although vertical sub-mains are shown, service runs could alternatively be supplied from horizontal sub-mains as in* **30.38**. **b** *Section*

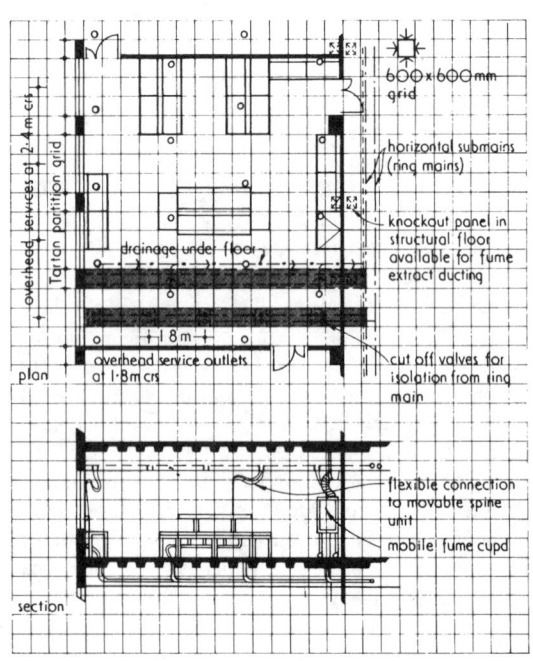

30.38 *Rigid overhead services distribution linked via flexible connections to loose furniture equipment*

can be provided, the rigid services distribution in the laboratory is completely standardised, i.e. both supply services and drainage are provided on a regular grid. Loose services units associated with furniture can be based on **30.9b** or **30.9c**.

9 VERTICAL DIMENSIONS AND SPACE FOR SERVICES

9.01 Vertical dimensions
The clear height in bench-scale laboratories should not be less than 2.7 m. If a height approaching 4.8 m is required for tall equipment or rigs, this may be increased as indicated in **30.39** to allow the possibility of introducing a mezzanine floor for work which does not require the double height, thereby achieving a more effective use of volume.

9.02 Horizontal space for services
Variations are shown in **30.40**, **30.41** and **30.42**. The space shown in **30.42** is expensive to provide and can be justified only if intensive use of the laboratory is predicted 24 hours a day, every day and services require constant adaptation and maintenance. Suspended ceilings are not always essential but may be necessary for cleanliness, acoustic or aesthetic reasons (or to support services); 50 to 75 mm should be allowed for their construction.

Suspended ceilings which allow direct access to services above should not form the fire protection for the structural floor above – the access requirement will compromise the fire resistance function.

9.03 Vertical space for services
If vertical sub-main ducting is used, horizontal space requirements will be minimal. Minimum size to accommodate fume ducting plus pipework would be 600 × 1200 mm.

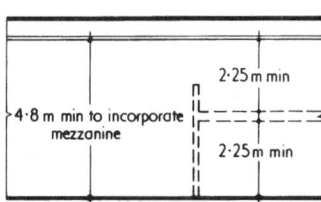

30.39 *Double height laboratory incorporating a temporary mezzanine floor*

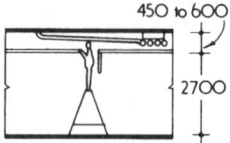

30.40 *Space for pipework, electrics and drainage*

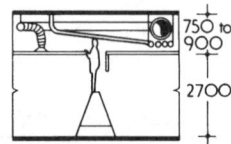

30.41 *Space for pipework, electrics, drainage and ventilation ductwork*

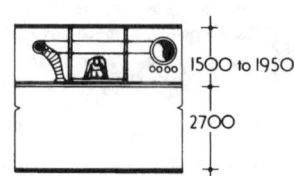

30.42 *All services, plus space for a crawl- or walkway*

10 BIBLIOGRAPHY

10.01 Legislation and Standards

Author, title, publisher	Brief summary	Author, title, publisher	Brief summary
BENCH AND EQUIPMENT SPACE BS 3202: Parts 1–4: 1991 Laboratory furniture, British Standards Institution, London	Part 1 defines the scope and relevant statutes Part 2 defines strength, specification and performance requirements for samples Part 3 contains recommendation for design, storage services Part 4 covers the installation of laboratory furniture	Offices, Shops & Railway Premises Act 1965, HMSO, London	This will apply for office staff employed more than 21 hours/week
		The Factories Act 1961, HMSO, London	May affect laboratory building. Relevance should be checked when workshops for repair are provided
BS 7258: Parts 1 & 2: 1990 Laboratory fume cupboards British Standards Institution, London	Part 1 specification for the minimum safety requirements and test method (does not cover special applications) Part 2 minimum information to be exchanged between parties to supply contracts, and recommendation for siting/ventilation	Petroleum (Consolidation) Act 1928, HMSO, London	May apply when spirit in excess of 3 gallons are stored or compressed gases, calcium carbide or calcium disulphide.
		Radioactive Substances Act 1960, HMSO, London	Explanatory memorandum to explain control on the use and disposal of radioactive material
SERVICES: ELECTRICAL BS 5501: 1977, Electrical apparatus for potentially explosive atmosphere, British Standards Institution, London	Incorporates both BS 229 and 1259; generally covering circuits of equipment which do not create sparks etc.	Public Health Act 1961, HMSO, London	
		Dangerous Drugs Acts 1965, 1967 Pharmacy & Poisons Act 1933 Therapeutic substances Act 1956 All from HMSO, London	All of these Acts make provisions to ensure security in the storage of drugs
BS 5345: 1990, Selection of installation of electrical equipment for use in potentially explosive situations, British Standards Institution, London	Now incorporates CP 1003	Control of Pollution Act 1974, HMSO, London	
		Clean Air Act 1956	
BS 7671: 1992, Regulation for Electrical Installations British Standards Institution, London	Exact copy of IEE, 16th Edition, Wiring Regulations	Public Health Acts 1925, 1936, 1937 Public Health (London) Act 1936 All from HMSO, London	These Acts may affect disposal of laboratory waste products either by incineration or as effluents
ENVIRONMENT: VENTILATION CP 352:1958, Code of Practice for mechanical ventilation and air conditioning in buildings, British Standards Institution, London		Health & Safety (Dangerous Pathogens) Regulations 1981, No. 1011, 1981, HMSO, London	Covers the keeping and storage of listed pathogens including notification periods for keeping and transportation
BS 4194: 1984, Specification for design requirements of testing of controlled atmosphere laboratories.	Applies to laboratories having controlled temperature and humidity	Control of Substances Hazardous to Health Regulations 1988, No. 1657, 1988 HMSO, London	Covers the duty to protect those working in premises where health risks may arise from work involving hazardous substances
BS 5295: parts 0–4: 1989, Environmental cleanliness in enclosed spaces, British Standards Institution, London	Covers clean room specification, and the design, construction, operation and monitoring of clean rooms.	Supplemented by 1990, No. 2026, also HMSO, London	Includes risk assessment test and examination of control measures, exposure monitoring health surveillance
		The Electricity at Work Regulations, 1989, No. 635, HMSO, London	Covers the general requirements for safety of equipment, including in hazardous environments and work on equipment.
HEALTH AND SAFETY Health and Safety at Work Act 1974, Chapter 37, HMSO, London (1975 reprint)	Brings together most relevant legislation under one Act and establishes Health and Safety Commission and Executive	Health & Safety Executive, Health & Safety in Departments of Electrical Engineering, H&SE Guidance Note, GS34, January 1986	

Author, title, publisher	Brief summary	Author, title, publisher	Brief summary
MICROBIOLOGICAL PROTECTION		*FIRE PROTECTION*	
BS 5726: 1992, Microbiological safety cabinets, British Standards Institution, London	Adjusts 1979 BS, Lifts, dimensional restraints and air exhausting. Tightens regulations on chemical filtration resistance, vibration, protection	BS 5588, Fire Precautions in Design and construction of buildings, British Standards Institution, London, 1990	Part 3 deals with offices, Part 4 with smoke control in escape routes, Part 5, fire-fighting, lifts and stairs, Part 6, places of assembly, Part 8, disabled escape, Parts 1 and 9 deal with ventilation and air conditioning
Advisory Committee on Dangerous Pathogens: Categorisation of Pathogens according to hazard and categories of containment (second edition 1990), HMSO, London	Under Health & Safety at Work Act, general duty applies where there is exposure to pathogens. New regulation and guidance under COSHH have come into force. These regulations require a need to assess risks and to implement and maintain appropriate control measures, publication lists, micro organisers and recommendations for containment	BS 5908: 1990, Fire precautions in the chemical and allied industries, British Standards Institution, (London)	Guidance on the nature of fire hazards
		BS 5306, Fire extinguishing installations, British Standards Institution, London	Cover selection of systems, hydrants, sprinklers, fire extinguishers, carbon dioxide and halon systems, foam, and powder systems
Health & Safety Executive, Proposed control of substances hazardous to health	Draft, covering duties, prohibitions, health risks, control measures, monitoring	BS 5266: 1988, Emergency lighting, British Standards Institution, London	Specification for small power relays (electromagnetic) for emergency lighting application
RADIOLOGICAL PROTECTION		CP 402: Fire Fighting installations, British Standards Institution, London	
BS 4094 Part 1 (1966): 1988, Data on shielding from ionising radiation, British Standards Institution London	Part 1 deals with shielding of gamma radiation including data for calculation. Part 2 deals with X-ray shielding	CP 153: Part 4, Fire hazards Associated with glazing in buildings, British Standards Institution, London	
Radio-active substances Act, HMSO, London 1960 (See also above)		CP 3: Precautions against fire, British Standards Institution, London	
Ionising Radiation (sealed sourced) Regulations 1969, SI No. 808, HMSO, London		CP 95: 1970, Fire protection for electronic data processing, British Standards Institution, London	
Code of Practice for protection of persons against ionising radiations arising from medical and dental use, DHSS, 1972		CP 1019: 1972, Installation and servicing for electrical fire alarm systems, British Standards Institution, London	
Radiochemical Centre Manual, The Radiochemical Centre, Amersham, Bucks, HMSO, London (1966)		DES Building Bulletin No. 7, Fire and the Design of Schools	Useful information related to statutory requirements. Although this deals with school requirements, the general principles have wider application
Safe Handling of Radioisotopes, Safety Series No. 1, International Atomic Energy Agency, Vienna, HMSO (1962)			
World Health Organisation, Protection against Ionising Radiation, A Survey of current world legislation, Geneva (1972)		DES Safety Series No 2, Safety in Science Laboratories, London, HMSO.	

10.02 Other references
W. Schramm, *Chemistry and Biology Laboratories: design, construction, equipment,* Pergamon Press, Oxford 1965. (Gives layout information on a wide range of special laboratory equipment.)

AJ Information Sheets:
1312 No. 2 (3, February 1965)
1547 (13, December 1967) Chromatography rooms
1548 (13, December 1967) Controlled temperature rooms
1549 (13, December 1967) Electron microscope rooms
1550 (29, November 1967) Glass washing facilities
1551 (29, November 1967) Solvent stores
1552 (29, November 1967) Balance rooms
1597 (29, May 1968) Animal house space – general design
1598 (29, May 1968) Animal house space – rabbits and small rodents
1599 (29, May 1968) Animal house space – dogs
1600 (12, June 1968) Animal house space – cats and primates
1601 (12, June 1968) Animal house space – specific pathogen free and gnotobiotic units.

K. Everett and D. A. Hughes, *Guide to Laboratory Design,* Butterworths, London 1975. (Contains recommendations on the layout and specification of laboratories for radioactive and biohazard work.)
ABS Information manual, Universities of Indiana and California, EFL and US Department of Health, Education and Welfare, 1971

Architecture Research Unit, *An extension of the Department of Zoology laboratories,* University of Edinburgh, 1968
BS 3202, Laboratory furniture and fittings, London, British Standards Institution, 1959
DES Building Bulletin No. 45 JDPCLASP System building for higher education, HMSO, London, 1970
DES, Guidelines on environmental design in educational buildings, DES, 1974
Electrics 72/73, Educational and scientific laboratories, Electricity Council, 1973
Laboratories Investigation Unit paper No. 3, Growth and change in laboratory activity, LIU, 1971
Laboratories Investigation Unit paper No. 6, Adaptable furniture and services for education and science, LIU, 1972
Laboratories Investigation Unit paper No. 9, The Charles Darwin Building, Bristol Polytechnic, HMSO, London, 1977
Nuffield Foundation, *The design of research laboratories,* Oxford University Press, London, 1961
University Grants Committee, *Notes on procedure,* HMSO, London, 1971
Strategic Estate Management, HEFCE, 1992
Laboratories Investigation Unit, *Design guidance for research laboratories,* forthcoming publication, HMSO

Acknowledgements
Particular thanks are due to Frank Drake for contributions to the section on school laboratory layouts, and other helpful comments.

31 Museums, art galleries and temporary exhibition spaces

Geoffrey Matthews

Geoffrey Matthews is a museum consultant

CI/Sfb:75
UDC: 727.7
Uniclass: F754 & F755

KEY POINTS:
- *The expansion policy*
- *The circulation system*
- *The storage system*
- *Environmental control*

Contents

1 INTRODUCTION

1.01 'A museum is an institution which collects, documents, preserves, exhibits and interprets material evidence and associated information for the public benefit' (Museums Association (UK), 1984).

1.02 The design of museums, art galleries and the temporary exhibition spaces associated with similar organizations involves the housing of a wide range of functions broadly indicated in the common definitions of a museum. Museums, however, vary considerably in size, organization and purpose. It is important therefore to consider the particular context and features that characterize a museum in the process of developing concepts.

1.03 Collections in national museums are very large and varied in material and generally of international importance. The National Maritime Museum in Greenwich, for example, houses collections of machinery, boats, costumes, medals, ship models, paintings, silver, weapons, and scientific instruments, among many other types of material. Such museums are staffed by a wide range of highly qualified experts in collection management, research, conservation, public relations and marketing.

In some local and private museums collections are small, specific in material content and of specialist or local interest. Many such museums have only one qualified curator to oversee management of the collections and public services, and many of the specialist functions may be provided by outside bodies such as the Area Museum Councils. **31.1** shows a typology of museums based on subject/museological approach, collection characterization, and type of institution.

2 AREA DATA

2.01 There is no convenient formula for determining the areas to be devoted to the different functions. The client's intentions in respect of public access to collections, information and staff, and

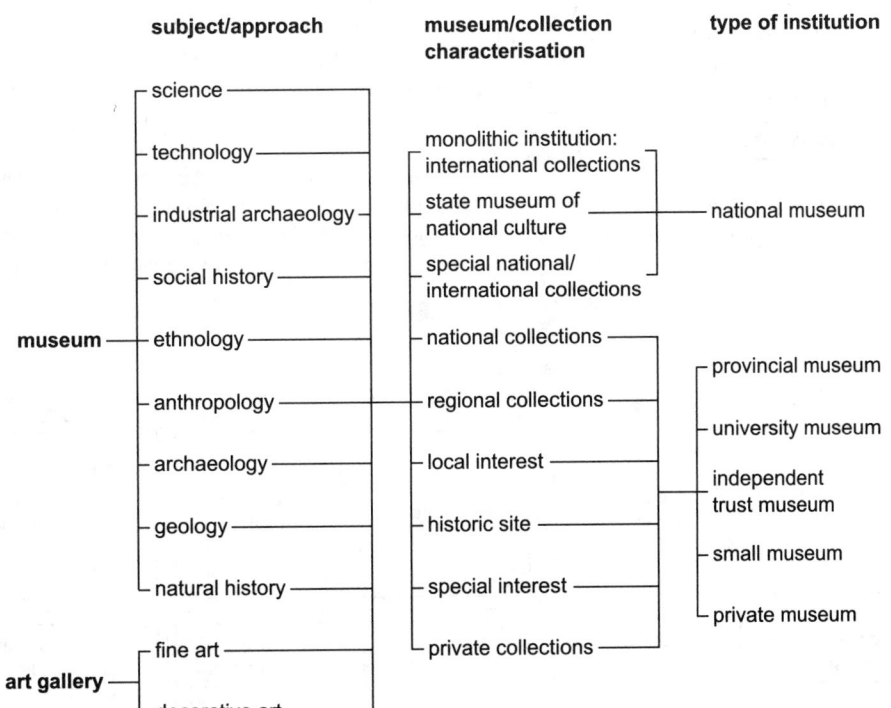

31.1 *A museum typology based on: museological approach/interpretive discipline; collection characterization; and institution characterization*

of commitment to research and conservation will provide an initial guide.

2.02 Some museums may have only a small proportion of the permanent collections on public exhibition at any one time, the bulk remaining in storage and accessible for research and conservation purposes only. Well-serviced temporary exhibition space may be a priority in such cases. Other museums may have smaller collections attractive enough to the visiting public to warrant the development of sophisticated exhibitions with a designed life of several years. In such cases storage space may be needed primarily for the expansion of the collections, and considerable effort may be made to develop educational programmes.

3 GENERAL PLANNING

3.01 The relationships between functions are common to all museums and art galleries. The flow diagram **31.2** shows collection item movements in the operation of collection services, but note that not every operation necessarily requires a separate space, and some services may be provided by outside agencies. As far as possible, collection movement and public circulation should be kept separate. **31.3** shows one approach to zoning and expansion based on this principle. **31.4** shows a possible layout for a small museum in which interpretive exhibitions and educational

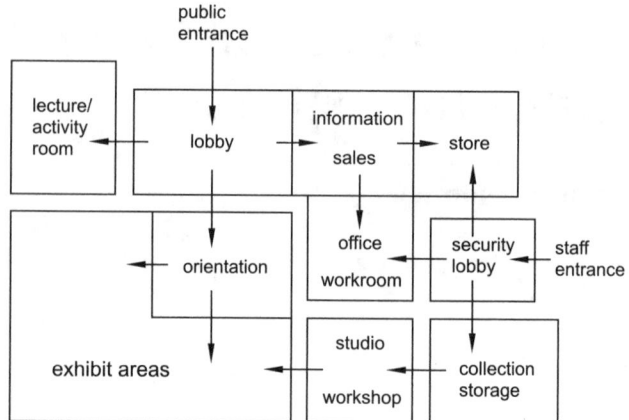

31.4 A possible layout diagram for a small museum

programmes are central to its operation. Where a museum is to be developed around a large-scale permanent installation this should be integrated into the interpretive scheme at an early stage. Examples are Jorvik Viking Centre's archaeological site and the National Railway Museum's turntables.

3.02 Museums are long-term developments: concepts for layout and massing should therefore be capable of expansion in all areas and a degree of internal rearrangement, particularly in work and ancillary areas. **31.5** shows possible massing concepts, and **31.6** illustrates the three methods of expansion.

4 EXHIBITION AND COLLECTION STORAGE SPACES

4.01 The layout of public areas in a museum, **31.7**, may be based on a simple concept of free circulation around a single open-plan exhibition space, **31.7a**, or on more complex concepts related to generic interpretive structures. It is important to consider the nature of the narratives appropriate to the museum's objects of interest. The storyline of an exhibition may be translated into:

- A *linear* arrangement of spaces with beginning, middle and end, **31.7b**
- A *loop* where the essentially linear storyline leads naturally back to the beginning, **31.7c**
- An arrangement of *core and satellites* where each theme or detailed treatment of a subject leads back to a central introductory or orientational area, **31.7a**
- A more *complex* scheme combining linear, loop and core–satellite arrangement of spaces which is specifically structured to account for more or less stable relationships between collections and interpretive themes, **31.7d** or

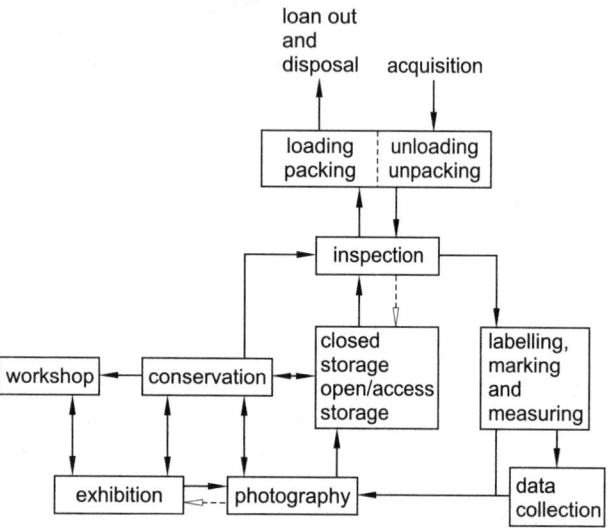

31.2 Flow diagram of collection item movements in the operation of collection services: exhibitions, conservation and collections management

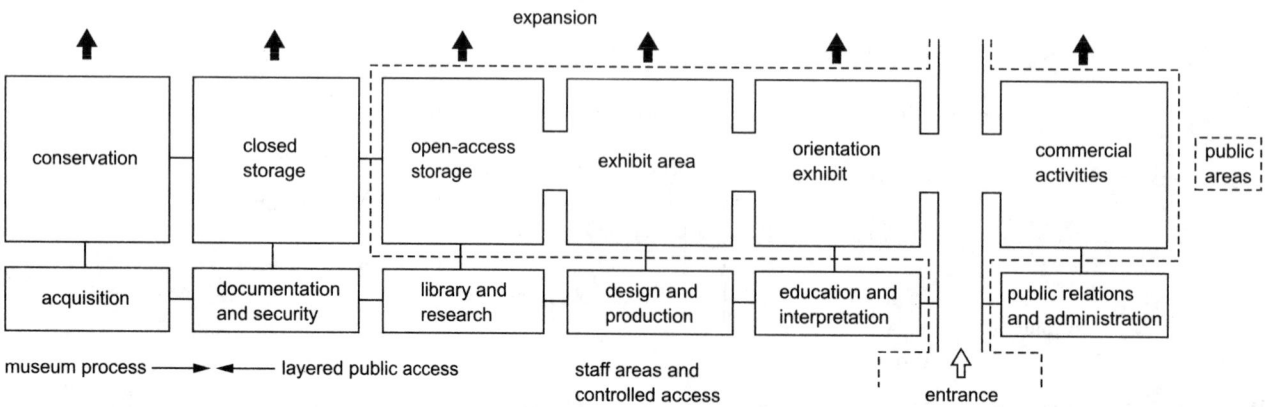

31.3 A layout concept showing a clear relationship between museum functions and an approach to zoning and expansion

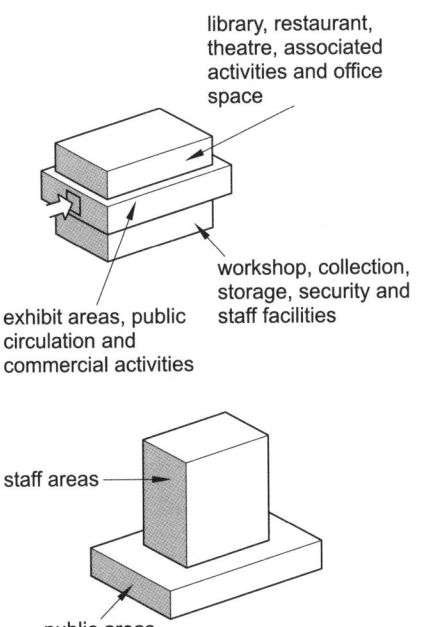

library, restaurant, theatre, associated activities and office space

exhibit areas, public circulation and commercial activities

workshop, collection, storage, security and staff facilities

staff areas

public areas

31.5 *Two basic massing concepts that allow public areas to be organised on one level*

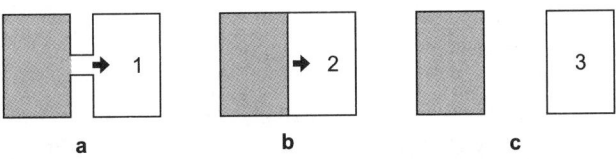

a

b

c

31.6 *Three modes of expansion:* **a** *Block addition;* **b** *Extension;* **c** *New building*

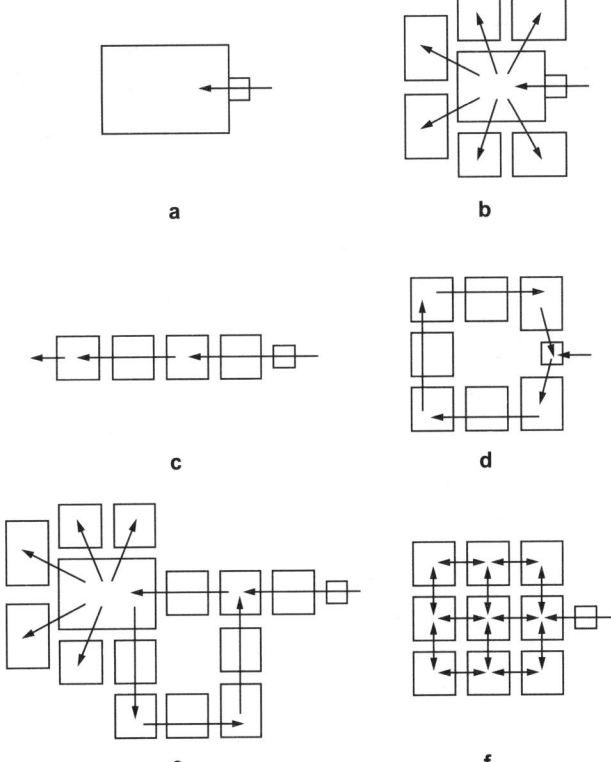

31.7 *Genetic plans for exhibit and open-access storage areas:* **a** *Open plan;* **b** *Core + satellites;* **c** *Linear procession;* **d** *Loop;* **e** *Complex;* **f** *Labyrinth*

- A *labyrinthine* arrangement where the relationships between areas can be varied from exhibition to exhibition by managing the public circulation, **31.7e**.

4.02 In any arrangement of exhibition spaces consider the problem of orientation, at the entrance to the museum and at key decision points in the museum information and visible clues should be provided to enable the visitor to grasp the organization of the collections, the interpretive scheme, and the public services offered by the museum. The aim of orientation is not only easy understanding of the building layout but more crucially to facilitate access to collections, information and museum services.

Many museums carefully control access to all collection storage spaces. However, it is increasingly worth considering the provision of open-access storage areas particularly for collection study. The former requires that storage areas are made secure and that visitors are closely supervised. Open access, on the other hand, requires that secure forms of storage equipment and furniture are arranged in very compact layouts. **31.8** shows a typical layout for a storage area fitted out with ranks of secure display cases. **31.9** shows a secure storage area with open-floor storage for larger collection items.

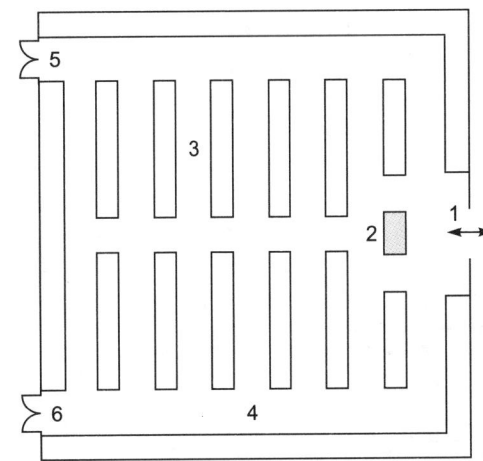

31.8 *Method of layout in open-access storage areas*

1 *Entrance from main exhibit areas*
2 *Orientation point*
3 *Ranks of cases glazed on all sides*
4 *Full-height wall cases*
5 *Fire exit*
6 *Controlled access to staff areas and secure storage*

5.0 INTERPRETATION, COMMUNICATION AND DISPLAY

5.01 At an early stage the communications strategy of the museum should be determined. The relative importance and coordination of exhibition, education, publication, live interpretation and other forms of direct communication with the public are the essential factors that will determine the interface between staff and public. It is not sufficient to consider only the relationship between visitor and displayed collections, a wide variety of media are now used in museum exhibitions to facilitate communication with the visiting public – graphic display, audio-visual, theatre, video, computer graphics, animatronics, tableau and reconstruction, and working environments. Once beyond the stage of producing a general scheme it is important to consult an exhibition designer and a museum consultant to explore the matrix of interactions between people, information and collections that must be accommodated.

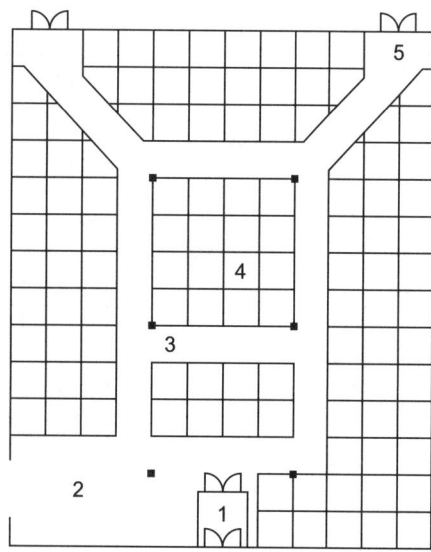

31.9 *Grid system for open-floor secure storage area*

1 *Controlled entrance lobby*
2 *Inspection area*
3 *Clear aisles*
4 *Grid marked on floor, eg 1.5 m squares lettered in one direction, numbered in the other*
5 *Fire exit*

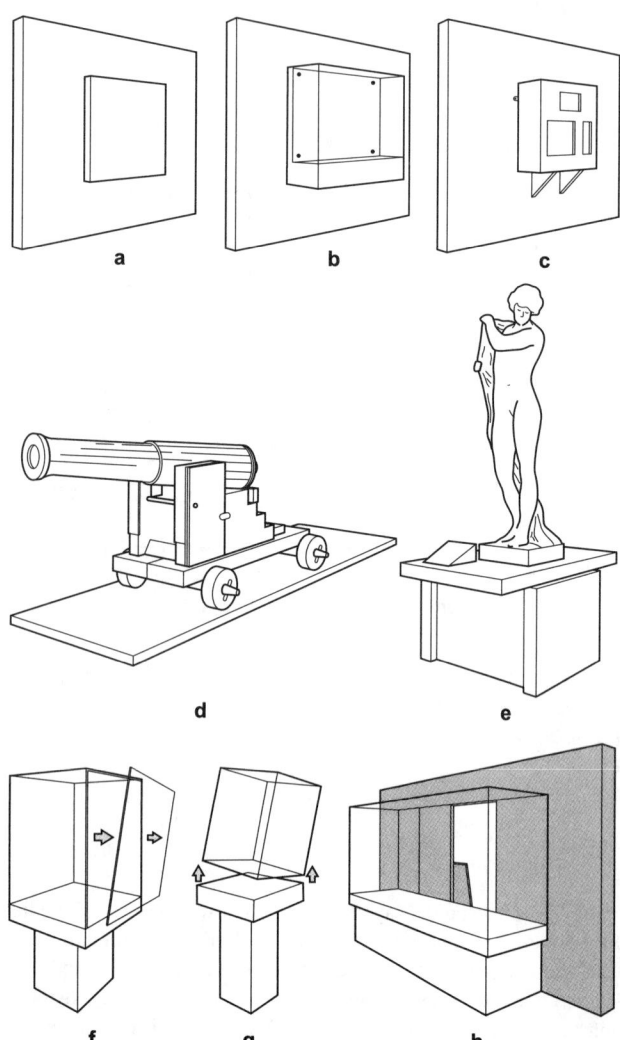

31.10 *Exhibits may be of four basic types:* **a,b,c** *Hanging or wall mounted;* **d,e** *Free-standing and open exhibits;* **f,g,h** *Contained exhibits and display cases*

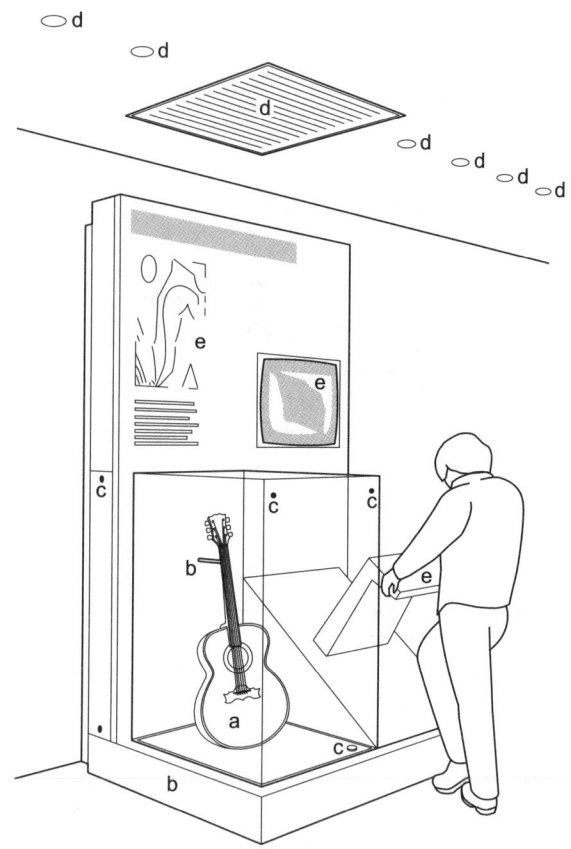

31.11 *Each of exhibit types in* **31.10** *may have any combination of the following elements:* **a** *Item or items from the collection;* **b** *Fixing mount, support or plinth;* **c** *Preservation: protection of vulnerable or removeable parts, lock, alarm, barrier, glazing, thermo-hydrometer (contained exhibits may have buffering material against changes in relative humidity);* **d** *Lighting;* **e** *Interpretive material: label, graphic information, sound, audio-visual, kinetic device, interactive device*

A wide range of academic expertise may be brought to bear in the interpretation of collections for exhibition purposes. Within the framework that the initial consultations provide, informed decisions may be made regarding the interpretive process and techniques, and the choice of media and types of exhibit to be employed. **31.10** shows a broad typology of exhibit and media installations, and **31.11** indicates the physical elements associated with exhibits. Reference should be made to the anthropometric data in Chapter 2 in determining coordinating dimensions; for example, the range of eye levels represented in the visiting population.

6 ANCILLARY ACCOMMODATION

6.01 For guidance on space requirements and design criteria for offices, catering facilities, sanitary installations and cloakrooms, circulation spaces, loading bays, retail areas, auditoria, educational facilities, laboratories, and libraries reference should be made to other chapters in this book.

7 ENVIRONMENT AND CONSERVATION

7.01 Relative humidity and temperature

Special consideration must be given to proper control of relative humidity, temperature and air pollution in all collection areas of a museum or art gallery. This includes: exhibition areas; collection storage; and conservation, display and photographic work areas.

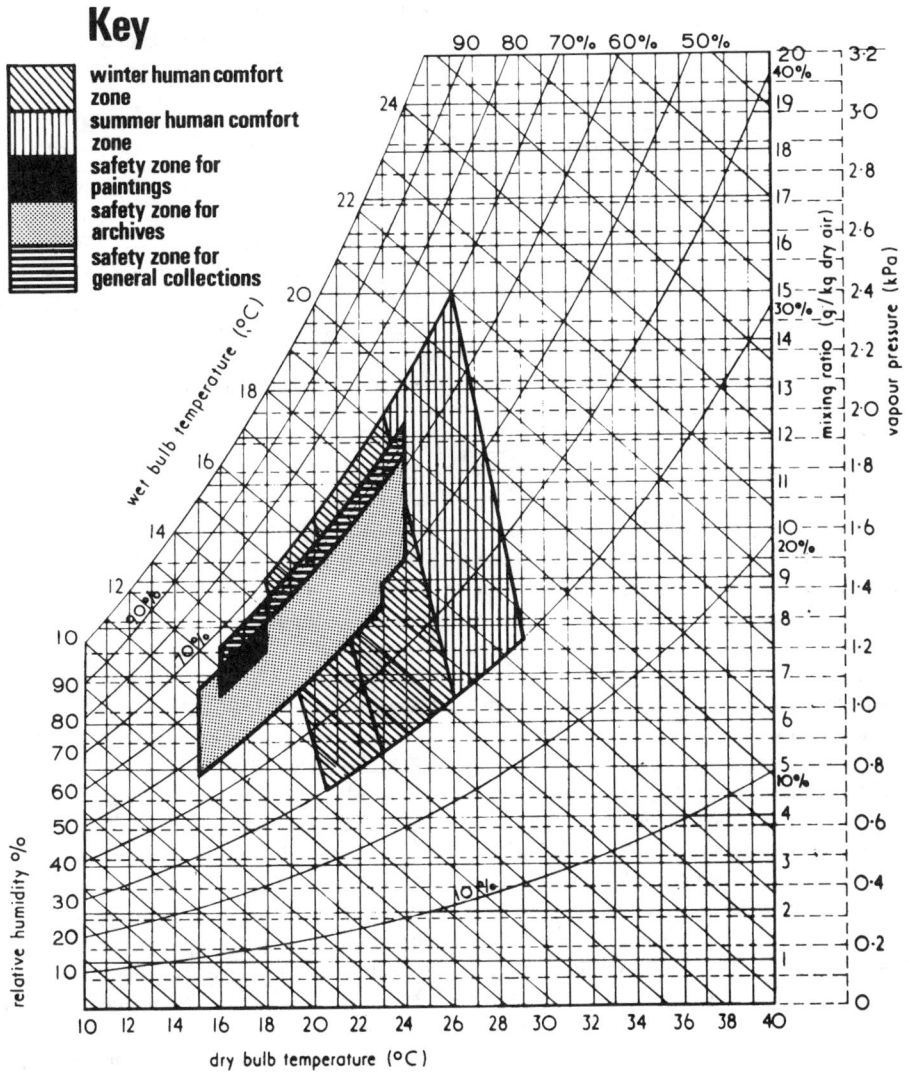

31.12 *Psychrometric chart (see Chapter 38) showing safety and comfort zones for museums, art galleries and archives*

Passive, low-tech approaches may be considered where climate and the inertia of the building allow. Full air conditioning may be required to cope with climatic extremes, even in this case the building envelope should provide a sufficient buffering effect to prevent sudden changes in relative humidity during periods of repair or maintenance. **31.12** shows suitable conditions in museums, while Table I gives the ranges of museum interior temperature and relative humidity recommended in various climatic zones.

7.02 Air pollution
Information about local air quality should be sought and used to decide on the appropriate approach to control. If air filtration is necessary it should not be of the electrostatic type, as malfunction can result in the generation of highly damaging ozone levels.

7.03 Light and lighting
Museum lighting is a complex subject. It is important, particularly in art museums, to determine a clear policy on the approach to natural and artificial lighting. Direct sunlight should not fall on any collection item and UV radiation must be effectively eliminated from all light reaching a collection item: at the higher energy end of the spectrum light is very effective in initiating chemical change in vulnerable materials. The maximum light dosage recommended for different categories of collection item is summarised in Table II. These dosages are normally achieved by limiting the level of illumination on collection items during visiting hours to 50 lux per annum on the most sensitive material such as paper, textile, watercolour and 200 lux on other sensitive materials such as wood, leather, oil paint.

The eye has a limited ability to adapt to changes in brightness, and as the visitor moves through the museum sudden changes in lighting levels and extreme contrasts of brightness in the field of

Table I Recommended temparatures and relative humidities in various climatic zones

Climate	Temp (°C)	RH (%)	Notes
Humid tropics	20–22	65	Acceptable for mixed collections. However, RH too high for iron and chloride-containing bronzes. Air circulation very important
Temperate coastal and other non-arid regions	20–22	55	Widely recommended for paintings, furniture, wooden sculpture in Europe, satisfactory for mixed collections. May cause condensation and frosting difficulties in old buildings, especially inland Europe and northern North America
Temperate inland regions	20–22	45–50	A compromise for mixed collections and where condensation may be a problem. May be best level for textiles and paper exposed to light
Arid regions	20–22	40–45	Acceptable for display of local material. Ideal for metal-only collections

Table II Recommended maximum light dosages

Type of collection	Dosage (kilolux-h)	Notes
Objects specially sensitive to light, e.g. textiles, costumes, watercolours, tapestries, prints and drawings, manuscripts, miniatures, paintings in distemper media, wallpapers, gouache, dyed leather. Most natural history items, including botanical specimens, fur and feathers	200	Usually only possible to achieve with artificial lighting
Oil and tempera paintings, undyed leather, horn, bone and ivory, oriental lacquer	650	If a daylight component is used great reduction of UV is necessary
Objects insensitive to light, e.g. metal, stone, glass, ceramics, jewellery, enamel, and objects in which colour change is not of high importance	950	Higher dosage is possible but usually unnecessary

view should be avoided. However, a reasonable range of contrast should be maintained in conditions of low illumination to prevent a dull effect and possible problems of visual accommodation.

7.04 Acoustics and zoning

The transport of sound through structure should be controlled. Functional zones should be provided with surface or sub-surface materials that dampen impact sounds and isolating cavities to interrupt the structural transmission of sound. Noise levels should be controlled within zones by appropriate choices of material finishes on floors, walls and ceilings, and the shaping of interior spaces to prevent flutter and unwanted amplifying effects. To generalise and simplify, the penetration of low-frequency sound is lessened by structural mass, of middle frequencies by diffusing and absorbing surfaces, and of high-frequency sound by the elimination of small-scale air gaps in doors, windows and partition walls.

8 SECURITY AND SERVICES

8.01 Security

Many security problems can be avoided by keeping the number of access points to the site and to the building to a minimum. The ideal is one public entrance monitored by information staff and/or attendants, and one staff entrance controlled by the security staff responsible for key control and the checking of deliveries and outside contractors.

8.02 Secure areas

The health and safety of the public and the staff and collection security are the prime considerations in determining the zoning of the museum into secure areas. During open hours it may be sufficient to separate public and staff areas. When the museum is closed to the public it is normal to secure more specific zones, for example:

1 Entrance, orientation/information, shop, café and toilets/cloakrooms
2 Temporary and permanent exhibitions – in larger museums sub-divided into several secure exhibit areas
3 Educational facilities, lecture theatre, study collections
4 Offices: administration, curatorial, conservation, design, etc.
5 Conservation workshops, laboratories, photographic facilities
6 Collection storage, security staff areas, collection packing and inspection areas
7 Exhibition and maintenance workshops.

8.03 Security staffing is also considerably more effective and economic if all exhibition and open storage areas are on one level.

8.04 Services

For general guidance see appropriate chapters in this book. In addition, special consideration should be given to minimising the risk to the collections when locating service installations and routing service ducts. For example, water and waste pipes should not be routed near collection storage and exhibition areas.

8.05 Risk management is also greatly enhanced if a separate heating/air conditioning system or independent control system is provided in collection areas.

9 BIBLIOGRAPHY

Edward P. Alexander, *Museums in Motion*, American Association for State and Local History, Nashville, 1979

Timothy Ambrose, *New Museums: A Start-up Guide*, HMSO, London, 1987

Timothy Ambrose, and Sue Runyard (eds), *Forward Planning: a handbook of business, corporate and development planning for museums and galleries*, Routledge, London, 1991

Michael Belcher, *Exhibitions in Museums*, Leicester University Press, 1991

Patrick Boylan, (ed.), *Museums 2000: Politics, People, Professionals and Profit*, Museums Association/Routledge, London, 1992

Douglas Davis, *The Museum Transformed*, Abbeville Press, New York 1990

Margaret Hall, *On Display*, Lund Humphries, London, 1987

Kenneth Hudson, *Museums of Influence*, Cambridge University Press, Cambridge, 1987

Lighting, A Conference on lighting in Museums, Galleries and Historic Houses (Bristol University, 9–10 April 1987) Museums Association/United Kingdon Institute for Conservation/Group of Designers and Interpreters in Museums, 1987

Gail Dexter Lord, and Barry Lord (eds), *The Manual of Museum Planning*, HMSO, London, 1991

Robert Lumley, (ed.), *The Museum Time-Machine*, Routledge, London, 1988

Geoff Matthews, *Museums and Art Galleries: A Design and Development Guide*, Butterworth Architecture, Oxford, 1991

R. S. Miles, *et al.*, *The Design of Educational Exhibits*, Unwin Hyman, London, 1982

Susan M. Pearce, *Museums, Objects and Collections: A Cultural Study*, Leicester University Press, 1992

David R. Prince, and Bernadette Higgins-Mcloughlin, *Museums UK: The Findings of the Museums Data-Base Project*, Museums Association, 1987

Royal Ontario Museum, *Communicating with the Museum Visitor: Guidelines for Planning*, ROM, 1976

Nathan Stolow, *Conservation and Exhibitions*, Butterworth, London, 1987

John. M. A. Thompson, (ed.), *Manual of Curatorship*, 2nd edn, Butterworth/Museums Association, London, 1992

Gary Thomson, *The Museum Environment*, 2nd end, Butterworth, London, 1986

David Uzzell, (ed.), *Heritage Interpretation (Vol. 2.): The Visitor Experience*, Belhaven Press, London, 1989

Giles Velarde, *Designing Exhibitions*, Design Council, London, 1988

32 Libraries and information centres

CI/SfB(1976): 76
UDC: 727.8
Uniclass: F76

This chapter is an updated version of that in the previous edition which was written by Godfrey Thompson. He was until his retirement Guildhall Librarian and Director of Art Gallery, City of London

KEY POINTS:
- *Libraries are increasingly becoming places from which to obtain information rather than only books.*
- *Information accessible in future libraries will be less from conventional books are more from other forms of media.*
- *Libraries in future may not be visited in person, but accessed remotely.*

Contents
1 Introduction
2 Design checklist
3 Design criteria
4 Area allowances
5 Book storage capacity
6 Readers' facilities
7 Storage for other media
8 Control counters
9 Bibliography

1 INTRODUCTION

About 50 000 new books are now published in the UK each year, and libraries are expected to try to absorb this growth. Academic and research libraries tend to grow by about 5 per cent per year. Public libraries, because they weed out as well as replenish and extend stocks, do not grow so quickly, if at all. Much depends on the size and style of readership in the catchment area. Libraries deal with films, sound recordings, CD-ROMS, microforms of information as well as books. However, books are likely to form the bulk of library stock for some time to come.

2 DESIGN CHECKLIST

The following checklist covers the kinds of information that may be needed to draw up a design brief. It is relevant mainly (but not only) to public libraries.

User services
Opening hours
Peak-use times
Hours
Days of the week
Times of the year (particularly for educational libraries)

Numbers of readers (preferably separate figures for each part of the library)
Bibliographical
General reference
Adult lending
Children's lending
Periodicals, newspapers
Music
Special reference (e.g. commercial, technical)
Local history
Arts
Other departments

Associated activities
Meeting rooms
Lecture rooms
Typing room
Exhibition area

Reader facilities
Catalogue reference
Document copying
CD-ROM viewing/listening
Accessing remote databases
Microform viewing
Video cassette viewing/listening
Audio reproduction
Poster display

Refreshments
Storage of readers' belongings
Coats
Bags
Umbrellas

Lavatories
Telephones
Bookshop
Vending machines

Staff services to user
Number of staff on duty at the following points
Security points
Book issue and return
Reader enquiries

External activity for which the library is the headquarters
Branch library supply and services
School library supply and services
Welfare libraries (handicapped readers, prisons, etc.)
Privileged readers (school teachers to select books from a display range)
Mobile libraries (garaging, servicing)

Technical services
Number and types of staff
Offices
Administrative
Executive
Network manager

Areas for
Accessioning
Cataloguing
Processing
Receipt and despatch
Post and packing
Printing
Photography

CD-ROM making
Binding
Poster drawing

Staff rooms
Lounge
Tea room and kitchen
Lavatories

Storage
Strong room
Stationery
Furniture
Cleaning materials

Car parking

3 DESIGN CRITERIA

3.01 Types of library
Libraries are of three basic types:

● Lending libraries with minimal or no reader areas
● Reference libraries with large reader areas and few or no lending facilities
● Libraries with reference/study areas plus lending facilities.

Most public libraries have separate sections of both main types. The British Library is purely for reference – its lending facilities are elsewhere. University libraries usually combine the types, but may lend for periods of only a few hours.

3.02 Book storage
There are two forms of library in relation to book and other material storage:

● Closed access, where the general users have to ask for the material they need and
● Open access, where some or most of the material is on open shelves on which the users may browse. Even in this type of library, however, some closed storage will be required for valuable stock and for obsolescent material.

3.03 Catalogue
An essential part of any library is the catalogue. In the past this was kept almost invariably in the form of index cards, usually 6 in × 4 in, kept captive in drawers in cabinets. Some libraries used paper slips in binders as an alternative method. The design criteria for such facilities shown in previous editions have been omitted as they are now completely obsolete.

Nowadays, catalogues are kept on computer and this can be combined with monitoring the lending and acquisition functions. Monitors and keyboards will be required for all staff positions, and additional ones for the use of the public. These can be dumb terminals for a central computer, or more commonly standard workstations on a network. Such a network will require a network manager and storage for back-up material which may be tapes or CD-ROMS.

A computer workstation is shown in **32.1**. This would be suitable for both staff and for the public to use. However, technology is progressing all the time, and new facilities are using flat liquid crystal screens, obviating the need for bulky cathode-ray tube monitors.

3.04 Viewing facilities
Although the technology moves on all the time, it leaves its detritus in its wake. As many libraries are archive depositories, they will need to be able to access many obsolete forms of record. In particular, microform readers and printers of different types will

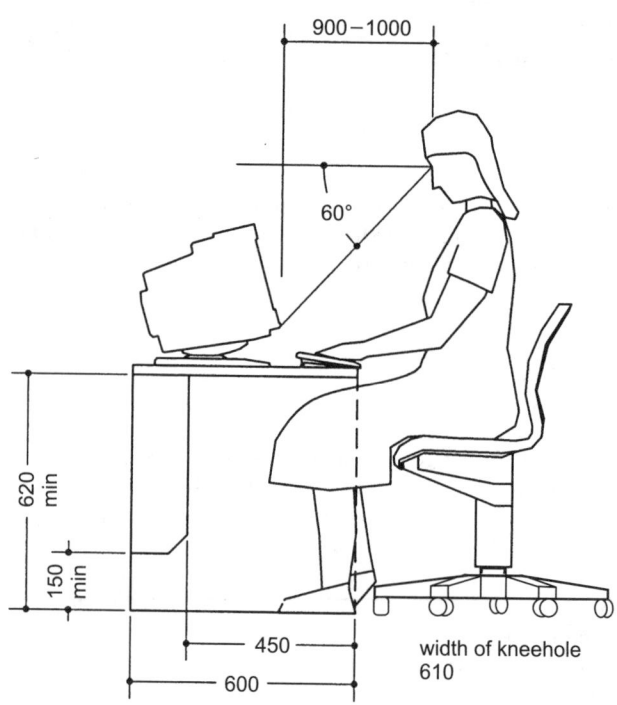

32.1 *A workstation with keyboard and standard monitor suitable for a library*

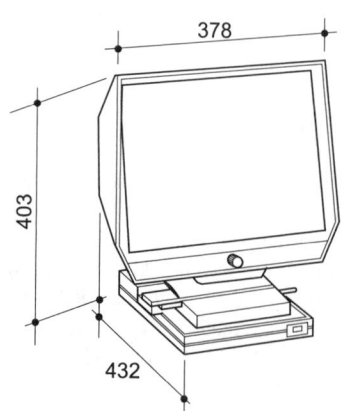

32.2 *A simple microfiche reader*

be needed. **32.2** shows a simple microfiche viewer and **32.3** a type of printer/reader suitable for both microfiche and microfilm.

3.05 CD-ROM
The current preferred media for storage is the CD-ROM, which consists of a thin disk 120 mm in diameter. This can store up to 650 megabytes of information, which can be text, pictures, sound, or a mixture of all three. To understand this, consider that a page of this book of pure text would need about 7 kilobytes to store. One CD-ROM is therefore able to store about 100 000 such pages – something like three *Encyclopedia Britannicas*! However, graphics and sound are much less economical in space.

To view the contents of a CD-ROM, the same public workstation as for viewing the catalogue may be used, provided it has a CD-ROM drive incorporated, or if the CD-ROM is loaded by staff somewhere else on the network. Unless it is situated in a closed carrel, it should be provided with earphones so that the sound the CD-ROM may include does not disturb others.

3.06 Networking facilities
Much information is readily and often cheaply available through the Internet and other network facilities. Again, the same

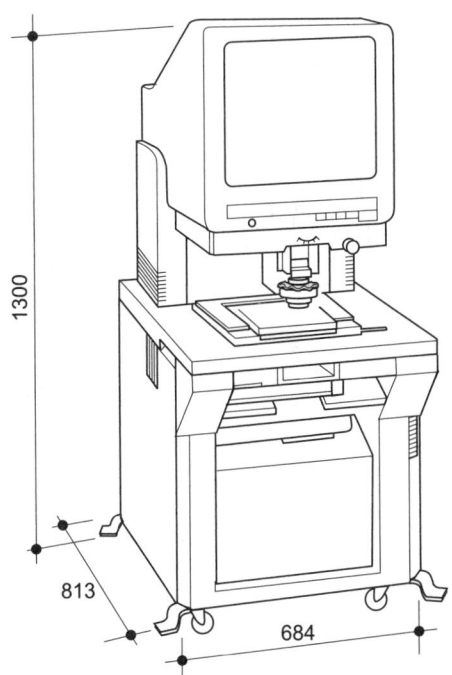

32.3 *A reader/printer for microfiche and microfilm*

workstations may be used for this purpose, although they will need to be fitted with an appropriate monitoring and metering device to ensure that any fees incurred can be correctly attributed.

3.07 Note-taking
Information derived from CD-ROM, or network databases, may need to be recorded by the user for later consultation. This could be by hand in a notebook. Alternatively, it can be transferred to removable electronic media such as a $3\frac{1}{2}$-in floppy disk. It would not be appropriate to fit a floppy drive to a publicly accessed workstation, as this would permit a computer virus to be introduced into the network with potentially disastrous results. The staff therefore need a facility to provide this service for the user. Incidentally, a CD-ROM brought in from outside could also be used for nefarious purposes, so some form of control to prevent this is also necessary.

3.07 Numbers of computer workstations
It will not be possible during the design period to predict how many of these will be needed, either now or in the future. Therefore provision should be made in accommodation and cabling to allow for expansion of these at the expence of conventional reading spaces which will be less required.

4 AREA ALLOWANCES

4.01 Public libraries
Space requirements vary considerably, but the International Federation of Library Associations has worked out averages based on actual libraries. These are given in Table I.

4.02 University and college libraries
Published space recommendations also vary but an approximate guide would be:

- One seat for each of 30 per cent of students
- 2.3 to 3.5 m^2 floor area per seat – overall area
- 50 to 65 volumes per m^2 of overall floor area.

For libraries in educational establishments under the control of the Department of Education and Employment allowances in the past have been:

Table I Public library serving population of 100 000

Function*	Floor area m^2	Comment
Adult lending	750	Plus 10% if exhibition area needed
Adult reference		
Book stock	200 ⎫	Plus 20% overall for
Seating	375 ⎬	staff workrooms and
Periodicals	100 ⎭	offices
Children's library	350 ⎫	Plus 20%
Stack	100 ⎬	overall for
Staff rooms	180 ⎭	circulation area
Total	2945	

*These areas exclude music library, audio-visual material and administrative offices if the library is headquarters for branches of mobile libraries, etc.

Colleges with at least 30 per cent of advanced work
390 m^2 for the first 500 full-time students and then 0.44 m^2 for each additional student

colleges with less than 30 per cent advanced work
300 m^2 for the first 500 students and then 0.38 m^2 for each additional student.

Spaces taken by library readers are given in Table II.

5 BOOK STORAGE CAPACITY
5.01 There is no doubt that in most libraries there will be a continuing need for accommodation of conventional books for some time to come.

5.02 Structural grid
Book stacks and shelving systems are rigidly standardised on a length of 900 mm. Spacing of book stacks, and therefore the capacity of the library, will be radically affected by the chosen structural grid, and also by the dimensions of the vertical structural elements and other facilities such as service ducts. In this building type, if in no other, careful integration of all structural and service items is essential.

5.03 Layout
A layout for stacks within a 6900 mm structural grid is given in **32.4** and Table III lists the book capacity of structural grids ranging from 5.6 to 8.4 m.

Table II Reader space requirements

User	Floor area m^2
Student or general reader	2.3
Research worker	3.25
Carrel user	3.70
Actual floor area occupied by reader at table	0.93 to 1.20

Table III Books per 300 mm run of shelf

Type	Number	Recommended shelf depth
Children's books	10–12	200–300
Loan and fiction stocks in public libraries	8	200
Literature and history, politics and economics	7	200
Scientific and technical	6	250
Medical	5	250
Law	4	200

NB: Various space-saving devices, most of them proprietary, are available, eg hinged shelf, sliding drawer, parallel rolling and right-angled rolling stacks.

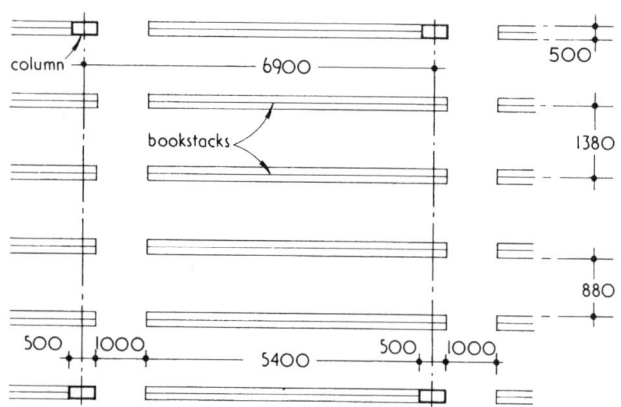

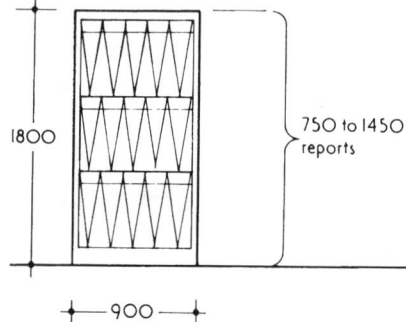

32.7 Capacity of lateral filing cabinets to hold reports

32.4 *Capacity of bookstacks within a 6900 mm structural grid:*

2 stacks on grid line = 10 800
8 stacks in bay = 47 200
= 58 m run of shelves
58 m of shelves 7 high = 406 m run of books
406 m at 20 books/m = 8120 books per bay
or 169 books/m² floor area

Table IV Book capacity at various sizes of structural grid

Grid size m	Spacing of stacks	No. of double-sided stacks	Books per structural bay
5.6	1.4	3	5012
6.0	1.5	3	5460
6.0	1.2	4	6860
6.5	1.1	4	6160
7.0	1.55	4	8310
7.25	1.45	4	8610
7.2	1.2	5	10276
7.5	1.25	5	10780
7.7	1.1	6	12992
7.8	1.56	4	9380
7.8	1.30	5	11290
8.4	1.68	4	10220
8.4	1.2	6	14364
8.4	1.4	5	12292

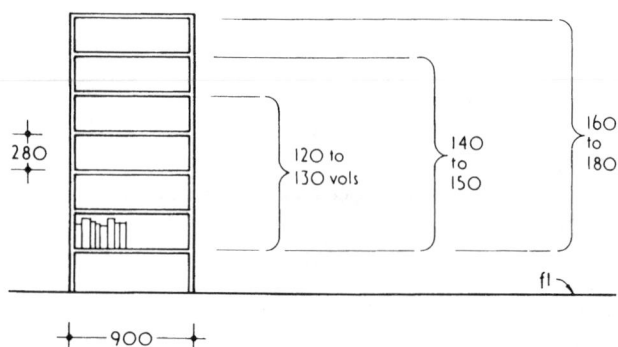

32.5 Capacity of shelves to hold books, three quarters full to allow for expansion and movement

Table V Shelf depth and spacing

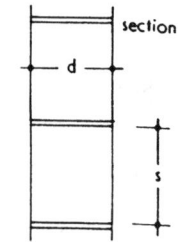

Type of book	% of total	Spacing mm	Depth mm
Popular (light novels)	50	225	230
General	97	280	230
Bound periodicals	—	300	230
Oversize books	3	500	300–400

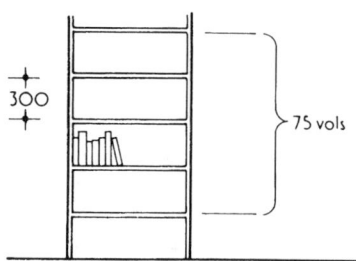

32.6 Capacity of shelves to hold periodicals in bound volumes

5.04 Bookshelf capacity

The capacity of standard 900 mm bookshelves to hold books periodicals and reports is indicated in **32.5** to **32.7**. These shelves are assumed to be only three-quarters full to allow for expansion and book movement. The average space requirements of each type of book are given in Table IV.

5.05 Shelf depth and spacing

Table V gives the recommended shelf depth and the average spacing along the shelf for the main types of book.

5.06 Closed access systems

32.8 shows the limitations of various narrow aisle widths. Anything less than 610 mm makes it difficult to bend to reach the lower shelves. 810 mm is the minimum if a trolley is to be used.

As space is often at a premium, sliding stacks may be used. These provide for only one such 900 mm aisle for, say, ten stacks, depending on the frequency of use and the numbers of staff. Sliding stacks are generally confined to the lowest level of the building due to the heavy structural load involved. If used on suspended floors there are also onerous limitations of deflection which could cause jamming.

5.07 Open-access systems

Where the public are given access to the shelves the dimensions must take account of the length of stack. If long, two people must be able to pass in comfort, **32.9**. Someone in a wheelchair must also be able to pass a standing person. However, if the distance between cross-aisles is no more than about 8 m it may be acceptable to make the aisle width no more than will comfortably pass a wheelchair, say 900 mm. Recommended minimum dimensions are given in **32.10**.

Libraries often have their shelves arranged to form alcoves with books shelved on three sides. **32.11** shows dimensions for these. **32.12** is for use where the alcoves also accommodate reading tables.

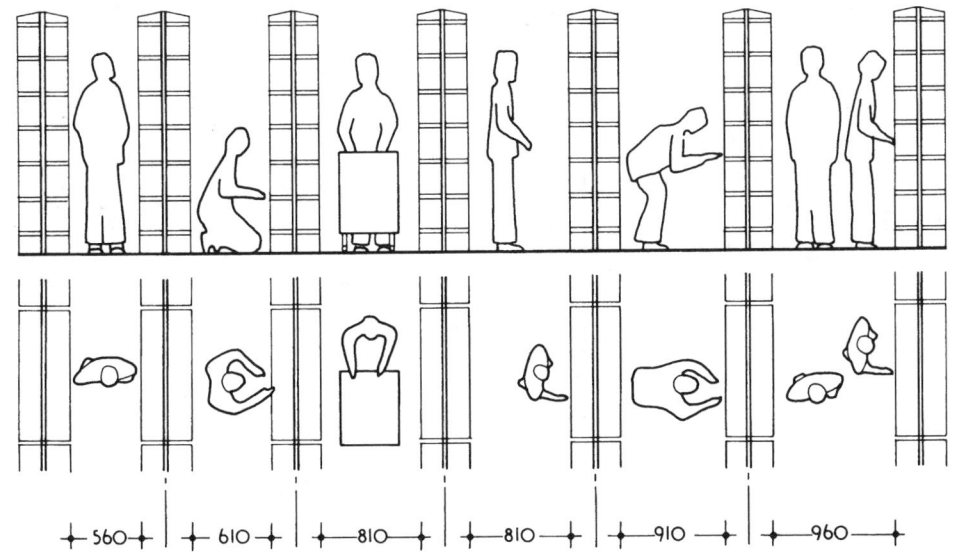

32.8 *Minimum clearances in shelving areas for various attitudes: narrow aisles*

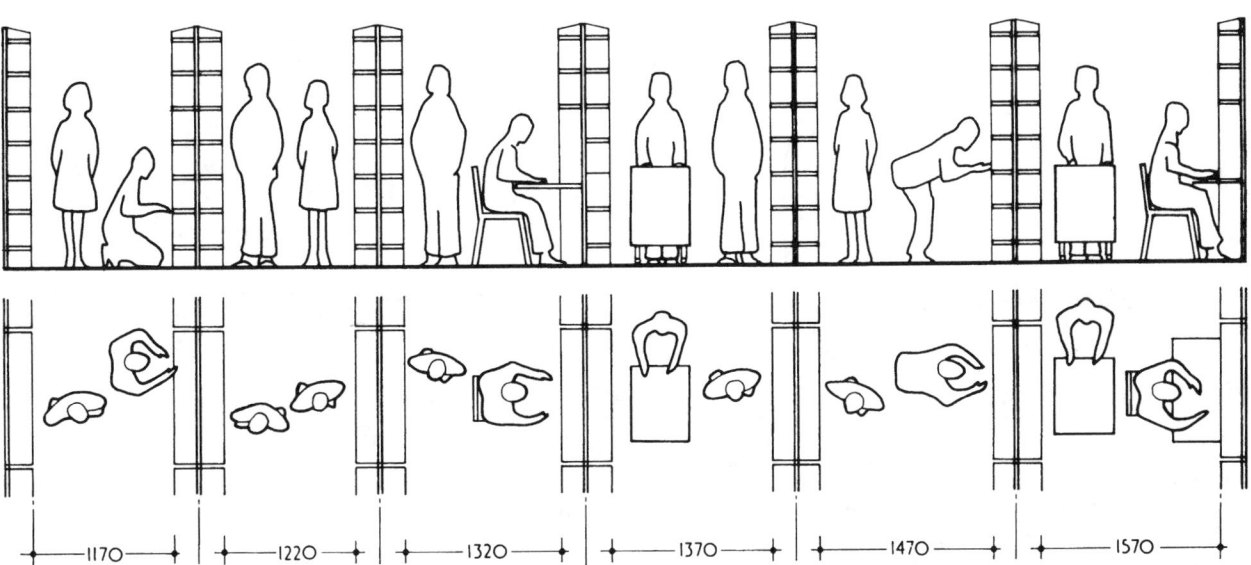

32.9 *Minimum clearances in shelving areas for various attitudes: wide aisles*

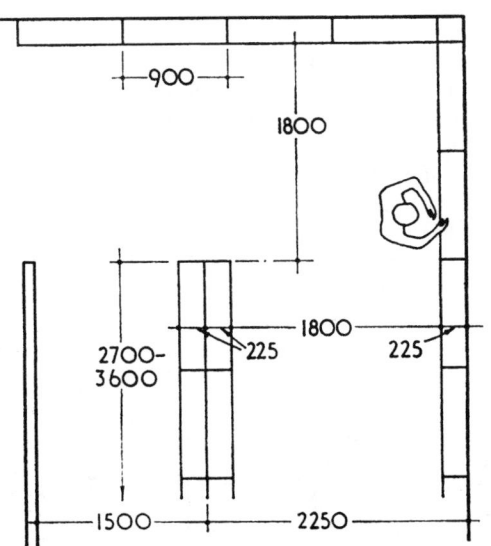

32.10 *Recommended minima in open-access bookshelf areas*

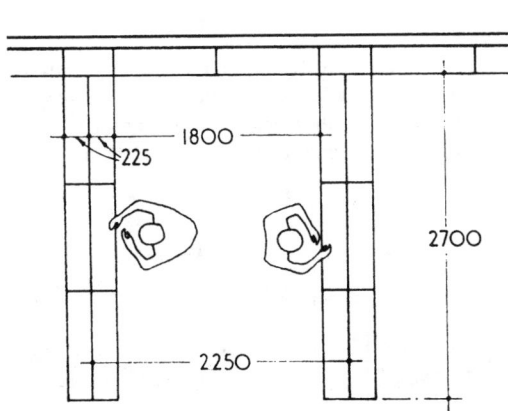

32.11 *Recommended minima for open-access bookshelf areas arranged as alcoves*

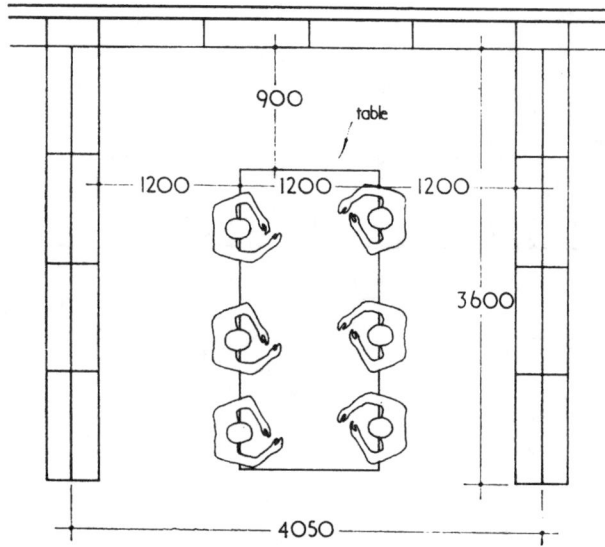

32.12 *Recommended minima for open-access bookshelf areas arranged as alcoves containing reading tables*

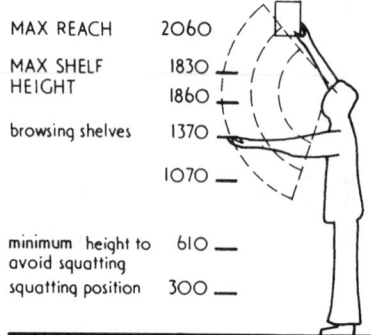

32.13 *Optimum shelf heights for adults*

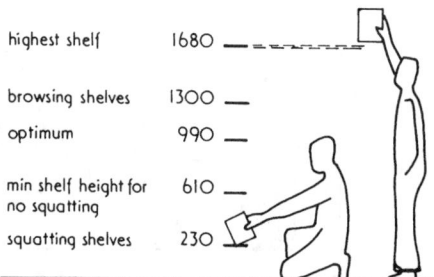

32.14 *Optimum shelf heights for teenagers*

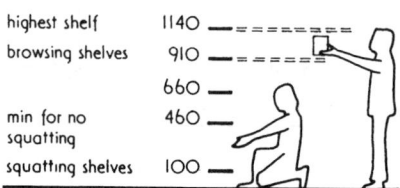

32.15 *Optimum shelf heights for children*

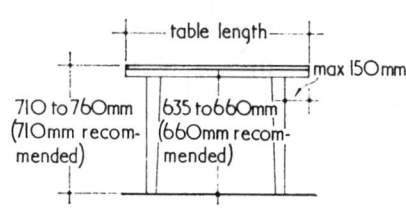

32.16 *Reading table height for adults*

5.08 Shelf heights

The easiest shelves to access are those at the user's eye height. **32.13** gives height criteria for adults. For libraries, such as in schools, used mainly by teenagers **32.14** should be followed, and **32.15** for small children. People in wheelchairs will need assistance from staff in normal libraries to reach the higher and possibly the lower shelves. In libraries designed to cater particularly for wheelchair users, only shelves between 400 and 1200 mm above the floor should be used.

6 READERS' FACILITIES

6.01 Tables

Most readers are expected to use communal tables, **32.16**. The design parameters for these are given in **32.17**.

In reference libraries tables are commonly arranged in rows in areas separate from the bulk of the books. **32.18** to **32.20** show reading tables for up to eight people at a table. Double-sided tables are not popular unless there is a low screen down the middle to ensure a measure of privacy. The size of table must reflect the material likely to be consulted – obviously maps and newspapers require more space.

6.02 Carrels

Where users will require more privacy they can be accommodated in:

- Individual tables, **32.21**
- Dual reading tables with screens, **32.22**
- Open carrels, **32.23**; these can be placed within bookstack areas, **32.24**, or
- Closed carrels, **32.25**.

6.03 Children

For children's use lower tables are used, **32.26**. Round tables, **32.27** are commonly used.

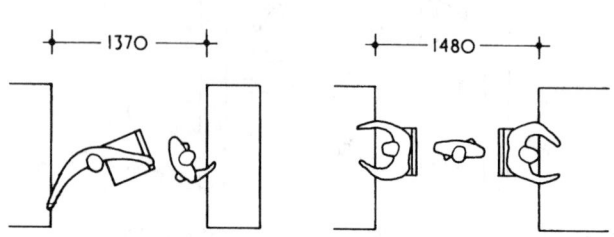
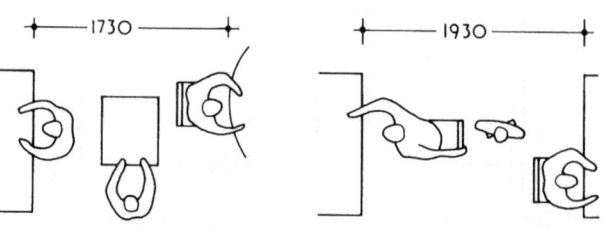

32.17 *Minimum clearances in reading areas*

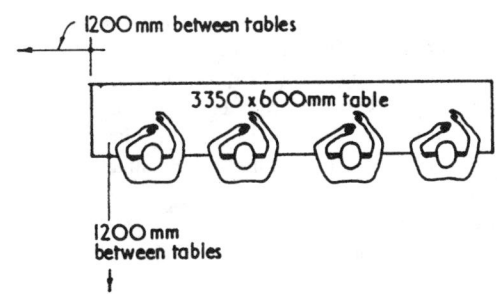

32.18 *Minima for single-sided tables for four people*

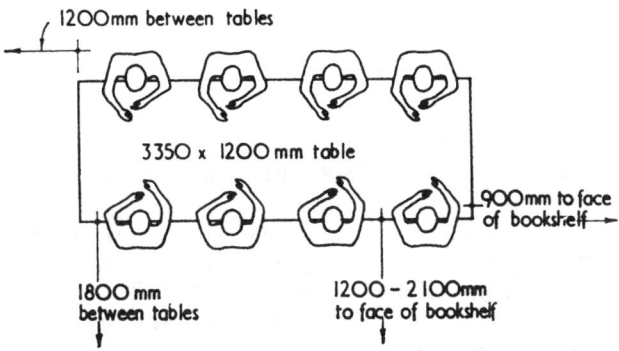

32.19 *Minima for eight-person reading tables*

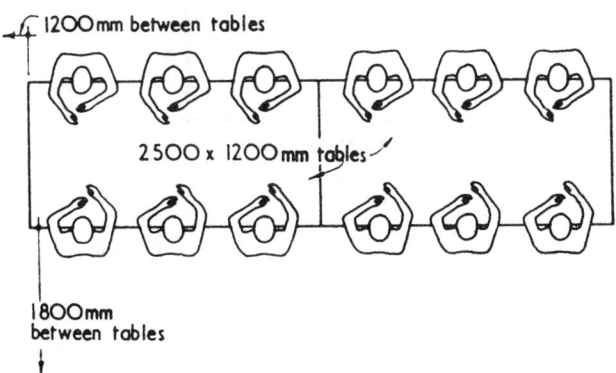

32.20 *Minima for six-person reading tables*

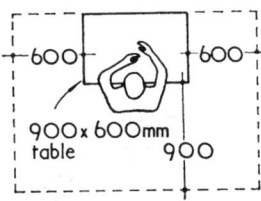

32.21 *Recommended minima for one-person reading tables*

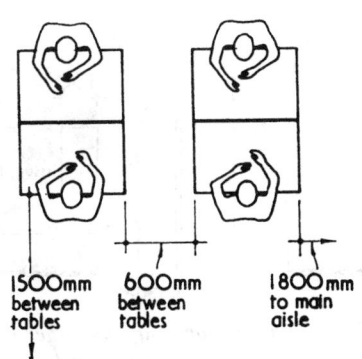

32.22 *Minima for dual-reading tables*

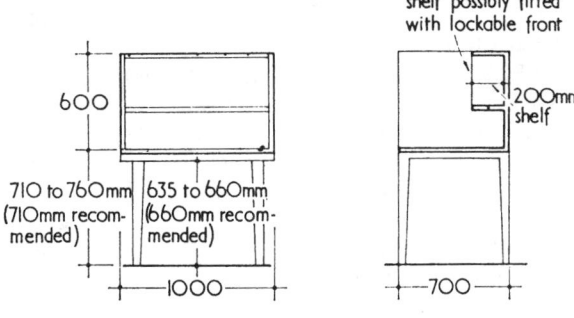

32.23 *Open carrel*

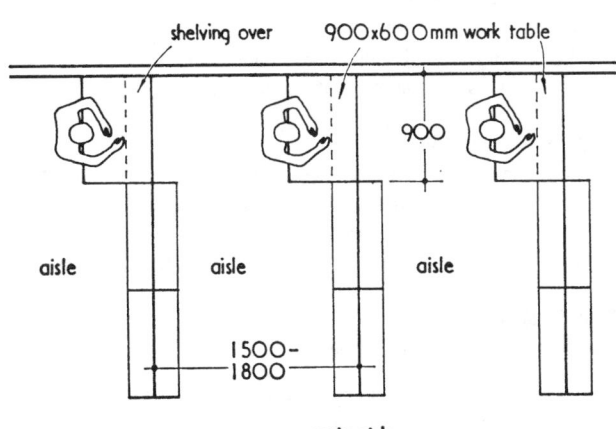

32.24 *Arrangement for open carrels in bookshelf areas*

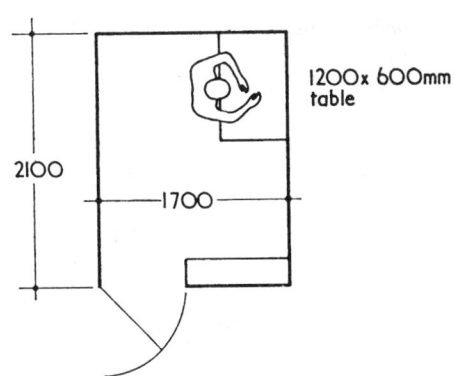

32.25 *Recommended single-person enclosed carrel*

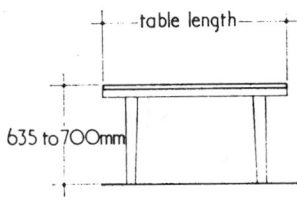

32.26 *Reading table height for children*

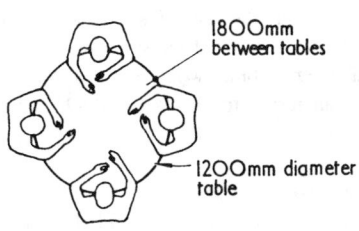

32.27 *Round reading tables*

7 STORAGE FOR OTHER MEDIA

7.01 CD-ROM storage
A CD-ROM disk is often supplied in a 'jewel case'. This is a transparent plastic box 140 × 125 × 10 mm. When stored in these, the disks take up substantial additional space. They may be more economically kept in paper or plastic envelopes, and these can be stored in drawers in cabinets. Those originally intended for the now obsolete 5¼-in floppy computer disk could be used for this purpose! An alternative form of storage is in pocketed albums holding up to 48 disks in a space 320 × 160 × 45 mm. Such albums may be easily accommodated on standard bookshelves of suitable depth and spacing.

7.02 Video cassette storage
Concerns have been expressed over the bulk storage of video cassettes with a risk of spontaneous combustion. They are usually kept in cabinets with shelves of shallow depth.

7.03 Other electronic media
A limited number of 3½-in floppy disks may need to be kept, together with backup tapes of various types and sizes. None of this material is likely to be required by library users, so its storage may conveniently be in or close to the network manager's office.

7.04 Microforms
Microforms are:

- *Microfilm* stored in cabinets, **32.28**. These cabinets will hold 675 reels of 35 mm film, or 125 reels of 16 mm film.
- *Microfiche*, previously in a number of sizes varying from 75 × 125 to 100 × 150 mm but the current ISO Standard specifies only 105 × 148 mm. However, storage for older sizes may also be necessary.
- *Micro-opaques*, the usual sizes of which are 125 × 75, 225 × 150 and 215 × 165 mm.

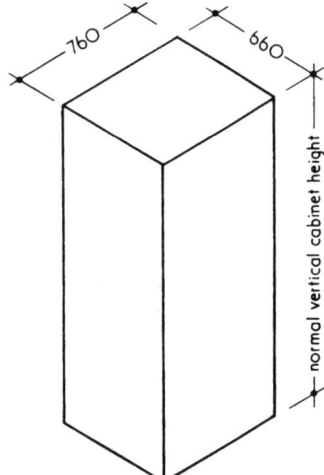

32.28 *Storage cabinet for microfilms*

7.05 Films
Cinema film tends to deteriorate unless kept in a controlled environment, although the risk of spontaneous combustion that was associated with original film stock no longer applies. It is unlikely that a general library would wish to store cinema film – it is now easily transferred to videotape which make its use much simpler.

7.06 Audio cassettes
The predominant cassette format is still the 'compact cassette' enclosed in a box that is 109 × 70 × 17 mm. Boxes containing twin cassettes are 109 × 70 × 34 mm. Both these formats are used principally for music. 'Talking books' are available in many public libraries for people with impaired vision among others. These, even when a single cassette, are often in double boxes 139 × 107 × 17 mm. All formats have their titles on 'spines' designed to be visible when on the shelf with the longest dimension vertical.

7.07 Sheet music
Sheet music can be bound into books placed on normal shelving. The standard size is A4, but older music is often found in a slightly larger format of 311 × 242 mm. The traditional method of storge of single sheets and thin items is in shallow drawers with drop-down fronts, internal dimensions 393 × 300 × 73 mm.

8 CONTROL COUNTERS

8.01 Shape
- In the smallest library a single control, **32.29**, covers both issue and return. A desk may be used, but a counter has the advantage that it is at standing height and can have cupboards fitted. This layout has the disadvantage that the inevitable crossing of traffic routes can be troublesome at peak times.
- The layout in **32.30** offers more security control and fewer traffic problems, but two members of staff are necessary at all times to operate it.

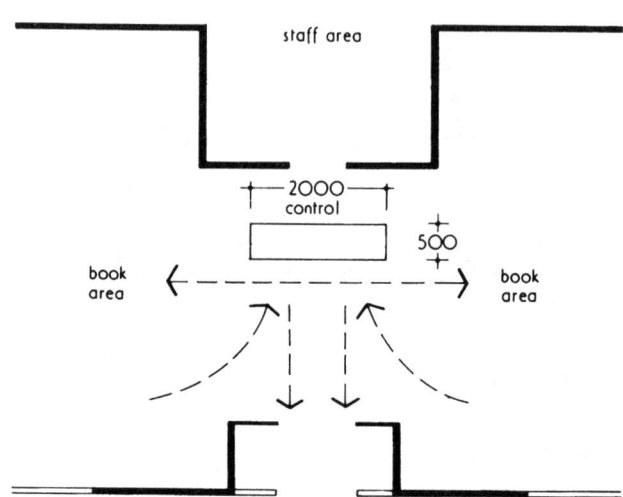

32.29 *Control counter for a small library, suffers from congestion at busy times*

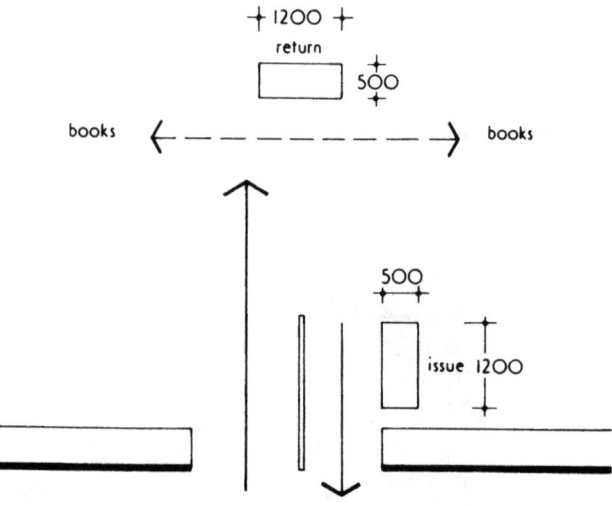

32.30 *Control arrangements for a slightly larger library: more security and less congestion, but requires at least two staff at all times*

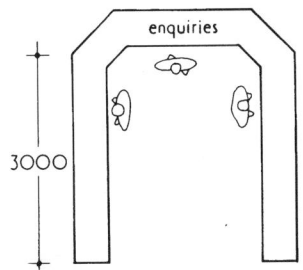

32.31 *Most common type of control counter: can be operated by one person during quiet periods*

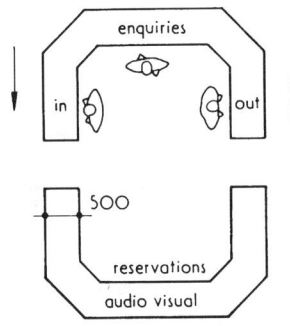

32.32 *Variation of* **32.31** *for larger libraries – can still be operated by one person*

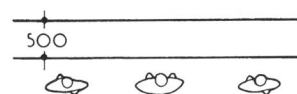

32.33 *Type of control counter preferred in very large libraries, universities, etc.*

- This shape, **32.31**, with slight variation, is the commonest of all. It shields the staff and allows one person to serve at quiet periods. In larger libraries, a variation can be this shape doubled so that a reserved book and enquiry area can be manned at quiet times with minimal staffing, **32.32**.
- In the largest libraries, particularly in universities, the counter acts as a barrier between readers and staff working areas. Here the shape can fit in with that of the building, but it is usually straight, **32.33**. In some university libraries such a counter can be more than 20 m long.

8.02 Width

Counters are usually 500 mm wide and sometimes also have a 150 mm bag rail on the outside of the in-counter.

8.03 Height

Both readers and staff will stand, so height should be 1.20 m. A popular variation has a slope on the in-counter where books can be placed while being checked in, **32.34**. Alternatively, the same design can be used, but with a counter 750 mm high, with an

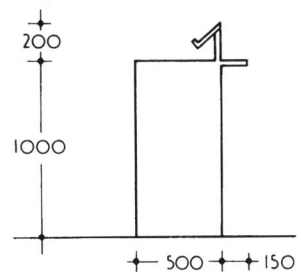

32.34 *Section through a control counter*

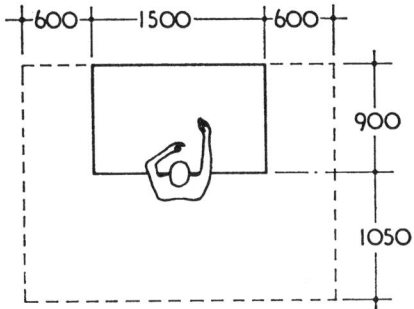

32.35 *Recommended minima for library staff*

overall height of 950 mm. Staff can then sit to receive books. Where staff need working space away from the control counter **32.35** gives recommendations.

8.05 Security

Unfortunately all libraries need to take precautions against theft. Exits incorporate the kind of electronic monitoring used in shops to detect books and other items not checked out at the counter. The devices inside the books can be neutralised at the counter, or can be passed back to borrowers once they have passed the barrier.

Libraries need special control arrangements in case of fire, otherwise the exit controls could be by-passed by simply setting off a fire alarm!

One problem that has yet to be solved is dealing with the person that tears out pages from a book. Copying machines at reasonable prices and change readily available can help to reduce this. Video surveillance will be necessary where there is valuable material.

9 BIBLIOGRAPHY

AJ Information sheet 1318, Library planning 2: Space standards, *The Architects' Journal*, 24.2.65
AJ Information sheets 1319 and 1320, Library furniture and equipment 1: Book storage, 2: General, *The Architects' Journal*, 3.3.65
AJ Information sheet 1593, Library planning: structural modules, *The Architects' Journal*, 28.2.68
Godfrey Thompson, *Planning and Design of Library Buildings*, Architectural Press, London, 1973; 2nd edn 1977

33 Houses and flats

Ian Chown

Ian Chown is an associate at PRP Architects, a practice specialising in socially conscious housing

CI/SfB: 81
UDC: 728
Uniclass:F81

KEY POINTS:
- *There are less statutory controls than in the past, but*
- *Low space standards lead to dissatisfaction, and*
- *Accommodation has to be tailored to numbers and characteristics of expected residents.*

Contents

1 INTRODUCTION

1.01 Housing standards

Governments have made a number of attempts during this century to influence or impose standards in housing. The Tudor Walters Report of 1918 and the Dudley Report in 1944 reflected the 'homes fit for heroes' feeling of social optimism following each world war.

In 1961 the report 'Homes for Today and Tomorrow' was published by the Parker Morris Committee, appointed as a subcommittee of the Central Housing Advisory Committee of the Ministry of Housing and Local Government (MHLG). The standards in this report, which have subsequently become universally known as Parker Morris Standards, were imposed as mandatory on local authority housing in 1967 by MHLG Circular 36/67, and were converted to metric in circular 1/68. They ceased to be mandatory in 1981.

It was the hope of the Parker Morris (PM) Committee that their standards would apply to all housing, whether publicly or privately funded. However, although the standards become the minimum for, initially, all local authority and, later, all housing association new-build schemes, the private sector remained aloof.

1.02 Public and private sector housing

In Britain, as in many other countries, housing is divided into privately and publicly funded sectors. In the early years of the century, the new local authorities increasingly took over from charitable foundations (such as the Peabody and Guinness Trusts) the provision of *social housing*. Such housing was promoted to keep the poor out of insanitary slums or even off the streets. It also had a side-benefit for the wealthy by helping to provide a nearby pool of labour.

The growth of municipal housing became such that in some urban boroughs most of the housing was in their ownership. This has been reversed in the last twenty years by a number of government measures: *right-to-buy*, restriction of LA expenditure, and by the growth (or regrowth) of charitable Housing Associations (HAs), funded and subsidised through the Housing Corporation (HC).

While the privately funded sector used to be geared to the provision of housing for rent, it now almost exclusively provides for purchase through mortages, mainly from the banks and building societies. With the volatility of interest rates, the level of affordable payments is crucial for most of its customers; there is a therefore a tendency for standards in the 'spec housing' market to be cut to the bone.

There has until recently been a constant demand for small 'starter homes' – both flats and houses – at affordable prices. This reflects the demographic changes this century: household sizes have fallen dramatically, but the numbers of independent households have exploded; partly due to the steady growth of failed marriages and partnerships. Later, some of these initially small households, when they have more money, and perhaps a family, are able to sell and buy somewhere bigger. This may be a large, older house; or it may be one of the superior quality speculative houses that some developers are building at or even above PM standards. It is uncertain whether the demand for starter homes will continue. In some cases they have been found difficult to sell when the original owners have required more space. Even people living on their own are beginning to demand more generous accommodation.

The public sector is very different. It is a baleful symptom of the two very distinct systems of providing housing in the UK that tenants of social housing have less choice in their dwellings. Also, once the household is accommodated, their ability to move home is limited. Often the only opportunity is likely to be a mutual swap with another household. Clearly this does not happen very often, so the tenant is likely to be in his or her flat or house for a long time. Babies may be born, children may grow up, grannies may die, but the harassed LA Housing Department or small Housing Association Management Team is unlikely to have a larger (or smaller), dwelling coming available for a requested transfer. This is the argument for ensuring especially in the publicly funded sector that reasonable standards are maintained.

People must have the room to settle satisfactorily into what is likely to be their long-term home. Since 1981 the Parker Morris standards are no longer mandatory for new-build schemes. The Housing Corporation does not lay down space standards, preferring to leave these to the experience and judgement of the housing associations, and to their architects.

Instead, the HC funds HA schemes according to its Total Cost Indicators (TCI), which lays down cost allowances based upon $5\,m^2$ increment bands. These bands (see Table I) are related to probable occupancies, but these are also very broad and approximate, so that the bands vary from well below to well above PM dwelling sizes. The use of HC *TCI space standards* does not therefore mean that housing associations can no longer build to PM standards, as is sometimes suggested. Larger dwelling plans tend to attract greater cost allowances (but higher rents can then follow).

1.03 Housing for different users

A significant proportion of the population is disabled in some way. While many of these people are able to cope in normal dwellings, other people such as those in wheelchairs require substantial modifications to enable them to live satisfactorily. It is unlikely that all new housing will ever have to be totally accessible to

Table I Housing Corporation floor area bands, for use with Total Cost Indicators (1998)

NB: Probable occupancies in persons are noted, but this table is *not* intended to be used as a guide to appropriate floor areas for households of given numbers. It includes accommodation for frail and elderly.

Dwelling floor area	Probable occupancy
Up to 25 m²	1 person
Exceeding 25 m² and not exceeding 30 m²	1 person
Exceeding 30 m² and not exceeding 35 m²	1 and 2 persons
Exceeding 35 m² and not exceeding 40 m²	1 and 2 persons
Exceeding 40 m² and not exceeding 45 m²	2 persons
Exceeding 45 m² and not exceeding 50 m²	2 persons
Exceeding 50 m² and not exceeding 55 m²	2 and 3 persons
Exceeding 55 m² and not exceeding 60 m²	2 and 3 persons
Exceeding 60 m² and not exceeding 65 m²	3 and 4 persons
Exceeding 65 m² and not exceeding 70 m²	3 and 4 persons
Exceeding 70 m² and not exceeding 75 m²	3, 4 and 5 persons
Exceeding 75 m² and not exceeding 80 m²	3, 4 and 5 persons
Exceeding 80 m² and not exceeding 85 m²	4, 5 and 6 persons
Exceeding 85 m² and not exceeding 90 m²	4, 5 and 6 persons
Exceeding 90 m² and not exceeding 95 m²	5 and 6 persons
Exceeding 95 m² and not exceeding 100 m²	5 and 6 persons
Exceeding 100 m² and not exceeding 105 m²	6 and 7 persons
Exceeding 105 m² and not exceeding 110 m²	6 and 7 persons
Exceeding 110 m² and not exceeding 115 m²	6, 7 and 8 persons
Exceeding 115 m² and not exceeding 120 m²	6, 7 and 8 persons

Table II Parker Morris minimum floor areas (square metres) (mandatory for publicly funded housing from 1967 to 1981)

		Number of persons (i.e. bedspaces)						
		1	2	3	4	5	6	7
HOUSES								
1 storey	N	30	44.5	57	67	75.5	84	–
	S	3	4.0	4	4.5	4.5	4.5	–
	Total	33	48.5	61	71.5	80	88.5	–
2 storey	N	–	–	–	72	82	92.5	108
(semi or end	S	–	–	–	4.5	4.5	4.5	6.5
terrace)	Total	–	–	–	76.5	86.5	97	114.5
2 storey	N	–	–	–	74.5	85	92.5	108
(intermediate	S	–	–	–	4.5	4.5	4.5	6.5
terrace)	Total	–	–	–	79	89.5	97	114.5
3 storey	N	–	–	–	–	94	98	112
(excluding garage	S	–	–	–	–	4.5	4.56	6.5
if built-in)	Total	–	–	–	–	98.5	102.5	118.5
FLATS	N	30	44.5	57	70	79	86.5	–
	S	2.5	3.0	3	3.5	3.5	3.5	–
	Total	32.5	47.5	60	73.5	82.5	90	–
MAISONETTES	N	–	–	–	72	82	92.5	108
	S	–	–	–	3.5	3.5	3.5	3.5
	Total	–	–	–	75.5	85.5	96	111.5

Net space is the area enclosed by the walls of the dwelling, measured to unfinished faces, including the area occupied in every floor by staircases, partitions, chimney breasts, flues and heating appliances. It excludes the area of general storage space, dustbin stores, fuel stores, garages, balconies, areas with sloping ceilings below 1.5 m height, and porches or lobbies open to the air.

General storage space should be provided in addition to the net space. It excludes the areas of dustbin stores, fuel stores, pram space, and, in a single-access house, any space within a store required as access from one side of the house to the other (taken as 700 mm wide).

In houses, at least 2.5 m² should be at ground level, and on upper floors it should be separated from linen or bedroom cupboards or wardrobes. If there is an integral or adjoining garage, any area over 12.0 m² can count as general storage space.

In flats and maisonettes no more than 1.5 m² may be outside the dwelling (e.g. in a lockable store off a common area) and, if there is an integral or adjoining garage, any area over 12.0 m² can count towards the 1.5 m².

Fuel storage is excluded from the table. If it is needed, then the following areas should be provided in addition to Net space and General storage space:

For houses	1.5 m² if there is only one appliance
	2.0 m² if there are two appliances or in rural areas
For flats and maisonettes	1.0 m² if there is no auxiliary storage

N = Net space
S = General storage space

people in wheelchairs, but housing to *special needs* standards is now being built, both for *mobility* and more onerous *wheelchair* use. Housing not specifically designed for people with disabilities is known as *general needs* housing. A new Part M of the Building Regulations is likely to extend the requirements for wheelchair access to a substantial proportion of new dwellings, although it is understood that some will still be exempt.

1.04 Parker Morris standards
For the reasons given above, it is important that public sector housing, at least, is not allowed to slip below the standards that came to be accepted as reasonable during the period when Parker Morris ruled by statute. Research into housing built to PM standards has shown that, while there may be much wrong with other aspects of estate design, such as the confused and insecure arrangement of external spaces, there is usually a good level of satisfaction with the internal layout and space standards. And, conversely, where public sector housing has been designed to lower than PM standards, or where PM housing has been over-occupied, the tenants have responded by consistently expressing dissatisfaction.

This edition of the *Metric Handbook* therefore continues to include the essential parts of the Parker Morris standards as its basic minimum recommendations. These recommendations start with the areas of net floor space and general storage space, given in Table II. Other important recommendations included by Parker Morris are integrated into the following subsections of this chapter.

It should be stressed that Parker Morris did *not* lay down minimum areas for *rooms*. The report simply stated that the dwelling had to be furnishable with a specified amount of furniture (Table III) which had to be shown on the plans. It also required reasonable storage space, and this has proved to be a popular and successful feature of Parker Morris housing.

1.05 Room area standards
In the housing association sector an additional set of space standards has come to be widely accepted for the minimum sizes of individual rooms. These are quite commonly but erroneously referred to as 'Parker Morris'. As stated above, the PM committee went out of their way to avoid being prescriptive about individual rooms. The origin of these figures given in the table of room areas (Table IV) is understood to have been the Greater London Council,

which funded many housing association projects in the capital in the 1970s and early 1980s. They were particularly applied to refurbishment or rehabilitation projects, to which Parker Morris standards were never mandatorily applied.

Since the demise of Parker Morris as statutory minima, these room sizes have been increasingly seen as reasonable minimum design standards for social housing; many housing associations now include them in their briefing documents to architects. It is our opinion that these should be taken as *absolute minima* for public sector houses and flats. In addition, if total dwelling areas are based on PM standards, these room sizes can be exceeded. Some London boroughs have included these room areas in the standards sections of their Unitary Development Plans, published in the early 1990s, as minima which must be achieved in any housing schemes, public or private, for which planning approval is being sought. This is potentially controversial, as it is debatable whether planning authorities have the power under Town and Country Planning Acts to lay down minimum space standards. Private developers have a long tradition of resisting space standards imposed other than by the market.

1.06 Room-by-room commentary on room area standards
Table IV, in addition to these minimum standards, gives recommended areas based on experience, the Housing Commission's lists of required furniture and also the NHBC minimum requirements.

Table III Parker Morris standards for fittings and space for furniture
(Mandatory for publicly funded housing from 1967 to 1981)

1   WCs and washbasins
(a) 1–2-and 3-person dwellings: 1 WC (may be in bathroom)
(b) 4-person houses and maisonettes, and 5-person flats and single-storey houses:
    1 WC in a separate compartment
(c) 5-or more person houses and maisonettes, and 6-or more person flats and
    single-storey houses: 2 WCs (1 may be in bathroom)

(PM also required a separate WC to have a washbasin; this is now required under
Building Regulations)

2   Linen storage (not counting as general storage space)
(a) 1–2-or 3-person dwelling: $0.4 \, m^3$
(b) 4-or more person dwelling: $0.6 \, m^3$

3   Kitchen fitments
(a) 1-or 2-person dwellings: $1.7 \, m^3$
(b) 3-or more person dwelling: $2.3 \, m^3$

including ventilated 'cool' cupboard (now less relevant) and broom cupboard (need
not be in kitchen). Standard fittings measured overall for depth and width, and
from underside worktop to top of plinth for height.

Kitchens should provide an unbroken sequence: worktop/cooker
position/worktop/sink/worktop

4   Electric socket outlets
(a) Working area of kitchen	4
(b) Dining area	1
(c) Living area	3
(d) Bedroom	2
(e) Hall or landing	1
(f) Bedsitting room in family dwelling	3
(g) Bedsitting room in 1 person dwelling	5
(h) Integral or attached garage	1
(i) Walk-in general store (in house only)	1

(These standards would now be considered low, but would be roughly appropriate
if each number represented a double socket)

5   Space heating
Minimum installation should be able to maintain kitchen and circulation spaces at
13°C, and living and dining areas at 18°C, when outside temperature is –1°C.

(This standard would now be considered far too low, and all new and refurbished
general needs housing should be able to be maintained at 18°C, with 21°C for day
rooms, when outside temperature is –1°C.)

6   Furniture
All plans should be able to show the following furniture satisfactorily
accommodated:

(a) *Kitchen:*   a small table, unless one is built in

(b) *Dining area:*   dining table and chairs

(c) *Living area:*   2 or 3 easy chairs
                     a settee
                     a TV set
                     small tables
                     reasonable quantity of other possessions such as radiogram
                     (sic) and bookcase

(d) *Single bedroom:* bed or divan 2000 × 900 mm
                     bedside table
                     chest of drawers
                     wardrobe, or space for cupboard to be built in

(e) *Main bedroom:* double bed 2000 × 1500 mm or, where possible:
                     2 single beds* 2000 × 900 mm as alternative
                     bedside tables
                     chest of drawers
                     double wardrobe or space for cupboard
                     to be built in
                     dressing table

(f) *Other double   2 single beds 2000 × 900 mm each
    bedrooms:*   bedside tables
                     chest of drawers
                     double wardrobe or space for cupboard to be built in**
                     small dressing table

*Where single beds are shown, they may abut, or where alongside walls should
have 750 mm between them.
**May be outside the room if easily accessible.

Table IV Room sizes, minimum and recommended (see text, areas in m^2)

Number of residents	1	2	3	4	5	6	7
Living room in a dwelling with a dining kitchen							
recommended	11	12	13	14	15	16	17
minimum	11	12	13	14	15	16	17
Living room in a dwelling with a galley kitchen:							
recommended	13	14	16	17	19	20	21
minimum	13	14	15	16	17.5	18.5	19.5
Dining kitchen							
recommended	8	9	10	11	12	13	14
minimum	8	9	10	11	12	13	14
Galley kitchen							
recommended	5.5	6.5	6.5	7	8	8	9
minimum	5.5	5.5	5.5	7	7	7	9
Main bedroom (double)							
recommended	9	12	12	12	12	12	12
minimum	8	11	11	11	11	11	11
Other double bedrooms							
recommended	–	–	–	12	12	12	12
minimum	–	–	–	10	10	10	10
Single bedrooms							
recommended	–	*9	8	8	8	8	8
minimum	–	*8	6.5	6.5	6.5	6.5	6.5

*A flat for two single people should have two single bedrooms of recommended
$9 \, m^2$, minimum $8 \, m^2$ each.
Notes: 'Minimum' room areas shown are those commonly required in social
housing. They are sometimes but erroneously referred to as 'Parker Morris' room
areas. PM in fact made a point of *not* laying down requirements for room areas.
'Recommended' room areas are shown as guidance for better provision, especially
in social housing.

- *Living rooms:* Provided a proper dining kitchen is included,
  the sizes given in the 'absolute minimum' table can be
  acceptable.
- *Kitchens:* These are no longer places solely for the preparation
  of food and washing up. Most households now spend a
  considerable time in their kitchens, and they tend increasingly
  to be treated as living rooms. Just watch one episode of a TV
  soap opera! We do not therefore recommend galley kitchens
  except for single-bedroom dwellings. The minimum sizes
  recommended for dining kitchens are reasonable, however.
- *Main bedroom:* Master bedrooms of less than $12 \, m^2$ should be
  considered tight, for double bed and large wardrobe, etc. Great
  care needs to be taken over single-person flats, especially for
  elderly people; a widow may well not want to dispose of her
  double bed and other familiar furniture.
- *Other double bedrooms:* The minimum of $10 \, m^2$ can be
  acceptable in some circumstances, as this size of room can be
  used flexibly by a single person, by children in bunks or by two
  single beds set against walls. However, the furniture list now
  published by the HC for social housing makes $11 \, m^2$ or $12 \, m^2$
  necessary, depending on shape.
- *Single bedroom:* There is evidence that $6.5 \, m^2$ is too small for
  most single bedrooms. $8 \, m^2$ is a more reasonable standard, and
  $6.5 \, m^2$ should be regarded as the absolute minimum. The NHBC
  area would barely accommodate a bed, a wardrobe and a chair.

2 OTHER PUBLISHED SPACE STANDARDS
2.01 The MHLG, followed by the DOE published a number of
Design Bulletins in the 1970s, a number of which refer specifically
to housing. Additionally, the Housing Development Directorate of
the DoE produced a number of Occasional Papers. All the useful
publications are listed in the Bibliography at the end of this
chapter, although you may have difficulty tracking down copies of
some of them.

2.02 The Housing Corporation used to control development
by housing associations through its published 'Design and

Table V Housing Corporation standards, for housing association dwellings (from HC Scheme Development Standards, August 1995)

1 EXTERNAL ENVIRONMENT

1.1 Location, site layout and orientation

Essential:

(a) location convenient for public transport, services and other general and social facilities, and
(b) location readily accessible, when wheelchair user housing is provided.

Recommended:

(c) orientations to give privacy and freedom from noise
(d) main pathways convenient and well lit
(e) drying facilities
(f) canopy or porch
(g) directional signs and numbering
(h) convenient, accessible and inconspicuous refuse areas and
(i) lockable external storage

1.2 Vehicular access and parking

Essential:

(a) convenient access for deliveries and public services
(b) shared surface cul-de-sacs should serve no more than 25 dwellings, and
(c) shared driveways should serve no more than 5 dwellings.

Recommended:

(d) convenient off-road hardstanding, and
(e) car parking located to enable natural surveillance.

2 INTERNAL ENVIRONMENT

2.1 General convenience, and accommodation of specified furniture etc. (The Corporation also refers to Sections 15 to 18 of BRE's Housing Design Handbook).

2.1.1 General within dwellings

Essential:

(a) layout to minimise noise transmissions
(b) convenient relationships between rooms
(c) sensible circulation space for room activities
(d) adequate space for sensible furniture arrangement (see Table VI for Housing Corporation's required list of furniture)
(e) space to move larger items of furniture
(f) space for whole family and occasional visitors to gather
(g) space for a small worktop or similar in single bedrooms
(h) space for an occasional cot in main bedroom (family units)
(i) space for a pram or pushchair (family units)
(j) adequate and sensibly placed electrical outlets
(k) aerial point with appropriate coaxial cable links
(l) enclosed storage space for food, utensils, washing and cleaning items
(m) enclosed storage for brooms and tall equipment
(n) hanging space for outdoor clothes
(o) enclosed storage for airing clothes and linen
(p) a bath, WC and basin
(q) additional separate WC and basin in units for 5 p and over
(r) space and connections for cooker, fridge/freezer and washer
(s) whole dwelling heating
(t) heating to provide suitable temperatures for room use
(u) individual tenant control of heating output, and
(v) additional sanitary and kitchen provisions in extended family accommodation, where appropriate.

Recommended:

(w) space for two people to have casual meals in kitchen
(x) space for extra kitchen equipment such as microwave, dishwasher, etc.
(y) principles of 'Accommodating Diversity' to be incorporated, and
(z) shower.

2.1.2 Communal areas and landings

Essential:

(a) passenger lift(s) if required for user group
(b) passenger lift(s) should be able to take wheelchair, and
(c) lift controls should be operable from a wheelchair.

2.1.3 Housing for the elderly

Essential:

(a) bathroom/WC doors to open out, where internal space is limited
(b) bathrooms to have external override door locks and handholds
(c) as an alternative to a bath, a shower with non-slip surface and side seat
(d) thermostatic mixing valves in Category 2 housing
(e) easy-rise staircase with handrails to both sides in Category 2 housing
(f) electrical outlets and switches positioned for convenient use by the elderly, and
(g) 24-hour alarm facilities.

Table V (*Continued*)

2 INTERNAL ENVIRONMENT (*Continued*)

2.1.4 Communal facilities in housing for the elderly and special needs

Essential in Sheltered Category 2 and Frail elderly schemes, but Optional in Sheltered Category 1 and Special needs schemes:

(a) accommodation for a resident warden
(b) common room, with space for sensible furniture for residents and visitors
(c) common room to be heated, comfortable and appropriately furnished
(d) common room to be wheelchair accessible
(e) WC and basin near to common room
(f) chair store for common room
(g) tea kitchen for common room
(h) laundry room, with automatic washing machine, tumble-dryer, sink, bench and extract ventilation
(i) twin bed guest room with basin, heated and comfortably furnished, and near to a WC,
(j) circulation areas to be heated and appropriately furnished, and
(k) office, close to main entrance.

2.1.5 Frail elderly schemes

Essential:

(a) individual parts or dwellings should meet sheltered Category 2 standards
(b) all parts should be wheelchair user accessible (see section 3.2)
(c) communal facilities to include all those in list above (section 2.1.4)
(d) a communal side-entry bath or similar
(e) a communal wheelchair-entry shower
(f) communal toilets near the common room and dining room
(g) communal laundry
(h) central linen store
(i) sluice room
(j) catering facilities, central and/or dispersed
(k) catering facilities to be wheelchair usable if dispersed, and
(l) furniture, fittings, fixtures and floor coverings.

2.1.6 Shared housing, and special needs housing

Essential:

(a) individual bedrooms
(b) 1 bath, 1 WC and 1 basin per 5 persons maximum
(c) separate WC, if bathroom shared by more than 2 people
(d) bathrooms and WCs must be conveniently located
(e) cooker, fridge/freezer and washer
(f) appropriate balance of private and shared spaces
(g) catering facilities, central and/or dispersed
(h) furniture, fittings, fixtures and floor coverings
(i) in large shared schemes, located near main communal area: central laundry with coin-operated machine, small interview/reception room, pay phone and cloakroom, and WC with basin.

3 ACCESSIBILITY

3.1 General access, allowing for people with limited mobility

The Housing Corporation requires compliance with the Essential Criteria from 'Building Homes for successive generations', by the Access Committee for England (ACE) in general needs housing (see Table XI) although with relaxations:

1 front entrance doors minimum clear opening width of 775 mm, and
2 entrance-level WC not essential in dwellings for less than 5 persons.

Essential:

(a) entrance path gateways minimum 850 mm clear width
(b) dropped kerbs where main paths meet roads and drives
(c) dwelling approaches level or gently sloping
(d) lifts, where provided, to be sized for wheelchair access
(e) main paths minimum 900 mm wide, with firm, even surface
(f) level area outside front door, at threshold level
(g) entrance door flush threshold (i.e. max. 15 mm upstand)
(h) entrance door minimum clear opening width 775 mm
(i) internal doors minimum clear opening width 750 mm
(j) corridors at entrance level wide enough for wheelchair access
(k) staircase suitable for future stair-lift, and
(l) entrance-level WC and basin, in 5 person units and larger

Recommended:

(m) entrance door minimum clear opening width 800 mm
(n) entrance-level WC and basins in units smaller than 5 persons, and
(o) other 'desirable' or 'optional' features from ACE guide.

NB: *Description of clear door opening width: a clear opening for accessibility purposes is measured between the inside face of the door stop and the inside of the door, when opened at 90 degrees.*

Table V (*Continued*)

2 ACCESSIBILITY (*Continued*)

3.2 Dwellings designed for wheelchair users

Essential:
(a) essential items a-d from section 3.1 above
(b) additional external features:
   level paved areas outside all external doors
   main paths minimum 1 200 mm wide, with firm even surface,
   ramps to have handrails and safety edges to both sides,
   linked car port for individual self-contained units, and
   car parking spaces no further away than 30 m for shared units;
(c) additional internal features:
   entrance door minimum clear opening width 800 mm
   wheelchair circulation space between furniture in all rooms
   wheelchair manoeuvring space in all rooms (1500 mm clear diameter circle)
   all rooms to be on one level or accessible by wheelchair vertical lift
   heating to be able to maintain all habitable rooms at 22°C
   space for wheelchair storage and charging, and
   wheelchair charging area to be ventilated either naturally at high level or mechanical extract;
(d) wheelchair user kitchen, including:
   full range of units and worktop
   accessible storage
   waist-level oven
   built-in hob
   fridge/freezer
   fittings accessible from wheelchair
   knee space for safe wheelchair manoeuvre, and
   slip-resistant floor finish;
(e) bathrooms/WCs:
   WC and basin at entrance level
   second separate WC in dwellings for 4 or more persons
   walls robust enough to take support rails
   ceilings robust enough to take track and hoist
   slip-resistant floor finish
   WCs to allow front, diagonal and side transfer
   space for safe wheelchair manoeuvre
   400 mm wide transfer platform at head of bath, and
   floor gully in bathroom, or WC where separate;
(f) living rooms, dining rooms, bedrooms:
   windows to maximise views out while seated,
   bedroom ceiling robust enough to take track and hoist,

The Scheme Development Standards include an appendix giving further requirements for accommodation for wheelchair users, see Table X.

4 SAFETY AND SECURITY

4.1 Safety, internally and externally

(The Corporation also refers to the relevant sections of the BRE's Housing Design Handbook.)

Essential:
(a) windows to be safely openable and cleanable
(b) stairs and steps to be safely negotiable
(c) lighting to be adequate for safety
(d) opened doors and windows not to be obstructive or hazardous
(e) kitchen and bathroom to be safely laid out
(f) min. 1000 mm clear in front of all kitchen equipment, and
(g) min. 1200 mm clear in front of kitchen equipment in shared housing.

4.2 Security, internally and externally

(The Corporation requires advice to be sought from the Local Police Architectural Liasion officers or Design Advisers, and from the Police 'Secured by Design' initiative.)

Essential:
(a) side or rear gates to be lockable
(b) rear fencing to deter climbing
(c) layout to avoid through-routes and minimise hiding places
(d) layout to maximise natural surveillance
(e) opening window lights to be secure, and
(f) external doors to be sturdy and have mortice deadlocks.

5 ENERGY EFFICIENCY

The Corporation refers to the Energy Efficiency Office's Good Practice Guides: 79 Low energy design for housing associations (for new-build), and 155 Energy efficient refurbishment of existing housing (for refurbishment).

Essential:
(a) SAP rating to meet minimum standards (see Table VI), or in buildings which cannot be SAP assessed (certain types of multi-residential buildings) evidence that energy-efficient measures have been incorporated, and
(b) housing for vulnerable users to allow for higher temperatures and extended heating periods as appropriate.

Recommended:
(c) SAP rating to exceed minimum standards by at least 6 (see Table VI), and
(d) BRE Environmental Standard Award.

Table V (*Continued*)

6 BUILDING PRACTICE AND MAINTENANCE

6.1 Service installations

Essential:
(a) service installations to be readily accessible for inspection, and
(b) service installations to be accessible for routine maintenance and repair.

Recommended:
(c) pipework and ductwork to be unobtrusive, and
(d) pipework and ductwork to be economical in layout.

6.2 Suitability and durability of components and materials

Essential:
(a) durability and suitability to be appropriate for position of use.

Recommended:
(b) finishings, fittings and equipment to be good quality
(c) new fittings and equipment to be compatible with any existing
(d) housing management and maintenance departments to be consulted, and
(e) availability of replacement parts and components to be taken into account.

Contract Criteria'. These were replaced by less prescriptive documents: the HC Procedure Guide (with mandatory requirements) and HC Good Practice Guide (advisory). In 1993 the Housing Corporation published new Scheme Development Standards. They were revised in 1995. These replaced the previous standards as mandatory requirements for housing association developments.

Although the SDSs do not lay down space standards, either for overall dwellings or for individual rooms, they do include a schedule of furniture requirements which impinges on room sizes. They also refer to the recommendations in the BRE's Housing Design Handbook, for furniture and activity spaces, as well as to the Access Committee for England's recommendations for accessibility (see para **3.04** below). They also cover issues such as general accessibility and mobility standards (requiring level thresholds and front doors giving minimum 775 mm clear openings) as well as standards for insulation that may exceed those in the Building Regulations. See Tables V, VI and VII for extracts from the HC Scheme Development Standards.

2.03 The National House Building Council publishes a comprehensive set of standards for private house builders. Most of these concern standards for construction, but they also include a limited number of specific space standards. Ones to watch out for are minimum kitchen dimensions and minimum loft hatch dimensions. The NHBC minimum standards for bedrooms are very small indeed, and generally unsuitable for the public sector. Some of the NHBC space and dimensional standards are given in Table VIII.

Table VI SAP ratings referred to in Table V, section 5

Floor area (m²)	New-build SAP		Rehabilitation SAP	
	minimum	recommended	minimum	recommended
≤35	71	77	56	62
>35/≤40	72	78	57	63
>40/≤45	73	79	58	64
>45/≤50	74	80	59	65
>50/≤55	75	81	60	66
>55/≤60	76	82	61	67
>60/≤65	77	83	62	68
>65/≤70	78	84	63	69
>70/≤75	79	85	64	70
>75/≤80	80	86	65	71
>80/≤90	81	87	66	72
>90/≤100	82	88	67	73
>100/≤110	83	89	68	74
>110/≤120	84	90	69	75
>120	85	91	70	76

Table VII Housing Corporation requirements: furniture list from Appendix 1 to Scheme Development Standards, August 1995 (see Table V, section 2.1.1)

Living room:
- armchair/settee for occupiers plus seating for two visitors
- television
- coffee table, and
- storage units.

Dining area:
- dining table and chairs for occupiers, and
- storage unit (unless dining area within kitchen).

Double bedroom:
- double bed or two single beds
- two bedside tables
- chest of drawers
- dressing table with stool
- double or two single wardrobes, and
- cot space – occasional (main bedroom of family units).

Single bedroom:
- single bed
- bedside table
- chest of drawers
- single wardrobe, and
- desk with stool.

Bathroom:
- wc and cistern,
- bath, and
- washhand basin.

Internal and external storage (see kitchen also):
- hanging space for outside clothes
- space for pram/pushchair/buggy (family units only)
- enclosed storage: airing and linen
- secure storage: medicines and hazardous substances
- space for bulk-buy food, household steps, suitcases, ironing board, sewing machine, broom, etc. and
- bicycles, tools and gardening equipment (as appropriate to user group and dwelling type).

Kitchen:
- a range of built-in kitchen fitments incorporating cupboards for pans, crockery, etc. (should reflect number of persons in household)
- cupboards for cleaning materials
- broom cupboard
- larder unit (may be within additional cupboards and/or wall units)
- drawers for cutlery, utensils, towels, etc,
- tray space
- wall units (should reflect number of persons in household)
- worktops, and
- sink top and drainer/s;

Serviced spaces (to include all electrical and plumbing connections) for:
- cooker
- refrigerator (space with removable worktop over and co-ordinated with wall units to allow option of fridge–freezer),
- washer–drier (unless provided for in laundry/utility room), and
- additional electrical socket outlets for at least six worktop appliances (toaster, kettle, etc.) (should be positioned to reflect relevant zones of activity).

Table VIII National House Building Council requirements for private sector dwellings
(normally those for which a mortgage is needed) summarised from NHBC Standards, chapter 12, operative 1995.

The NHBC does not set space standards, but requires that purchasers are provided with floor plans showing that bedrooms can accommodate bed or beds without obstructing the door swing. Other free-standing furniture such as wardrobes, chests of drawers etc. may be shown at the builder's discretion.

Furniture and activity spaces (mm)

Furniture	Furniture size	Activity space
Double bed	2000 × 1350	400 to sides, 450 at foot
Single bed	2000 × 900	400 to side, 250 at foot
Large chest of drawers	950 × 600	1000 deep (700 if space bounded by low furniture such as a bed)
Small chest of drawers	750 × 450	
Dressing table	1100 × 400	600 deep
Large wardrobe	950 × 600	1000 deep (700 if space bounded by low furniture such as a bed, or if wardrobe has sliding doors)
Small wardrobe	600 × 600	
Bedside table	400 × 400	None

Table IX Building Regulations (England and Wales) applying to dwellings

Approved Document		Last revision	Applies to housing	Relevant to planning of housing
A	Structure	1992	*	
B	Fire Safety (Means of Escape, etc.)	1992	*	*
C	Site preparation (resistance to moisture)	1992	*	
D	Toxic substances (cavity insulation)	1985	*	
E	Resistance to passage of sound	1992	*	*
F	Ventilation	1995	*	*
G	Hygiene (bathrooms, etc)	1992	*	*
H	Drainage and waste disposal	1990	*	*
J	Heat producing appliances	1990	*	*
K	Stairs, ramps and guarding	1998	*	*
L	Conservation of fuel and power	1995	*	*
M*	Access and facilities for disabled people	1992		
N	Glazing materials and protection	1998	*	

*The government is currently (1998) considering extending Part M to cover all or some dwellings. This will have important effects on the planning and construction of housing.

2.04 Building Regulations

Now that the Regulations are published in 'Approved Document' format, they are clear and easy to understand. No general guide is included here. However, we draw attention to the main parts affecting the planning of housing (see Table IX). All the parts except M (Access and Facilities for the Disabled) apply to housing, and it is likely that this part will be extended to apply to some housing quite soon. It is therefore prudent to aim to satisfy its requirements where possible.

2.05 Other statutory controls

The *Underground Rooms Regulations*, published by some local authorities under the Housing Acts, cover lighting and ventilation of basement habitable rooms.

Planning Authorities are now publishing Unitary Development Plans, including standards for housing which are imposed through development control. These cover such areas as housing density, external design, car parking, and, in some cases, minimum room sizes.

Planning densities are normally expressed in *habitable rooms per hectare* (or acre). The definition of habitable rooms is normally taken to be all living rooms, bedrooms and dining kitchens (the latter commonly only if more than 13 m²). Densities for new housing commonly vary from around 150 habitable rooms per hectare (60 habitable rooms per acre) to 250 habitable rooms per hectare (100 habitable rooms per acre), **33.1**, **33.2** and **33.3**. Some authorities allow higher densities for non-family housing, or for areas close to urban centres or good transport links. External design generally covers minimum dimensions between habitable rooms facing each other directly or obliquely, and sizes of gardens and other external spaces, **33.4**.

Car-parking requirements vary considerably between planning authorities. Inner-city planners may require only one space per house and less for a flat, but suburban areas may demand two or more spaces per house. Visitors' spaces need to be added at 10 to 20 per cent. Some authorities at present allow considerable relaxation of their requirements for social housing, on the basis of lower than average recorded car ownership, but this may change.

3 OTHER DESIGN DATA

Several important dimensions and spatial requirements are not covered by statutory control.

3.01 Ceiling heights

These have not been covered by the Building Regulations since 1985, as the DoE has decided that they do not significantly affect health and safety. Despite this, the old standard of 2.3 m should

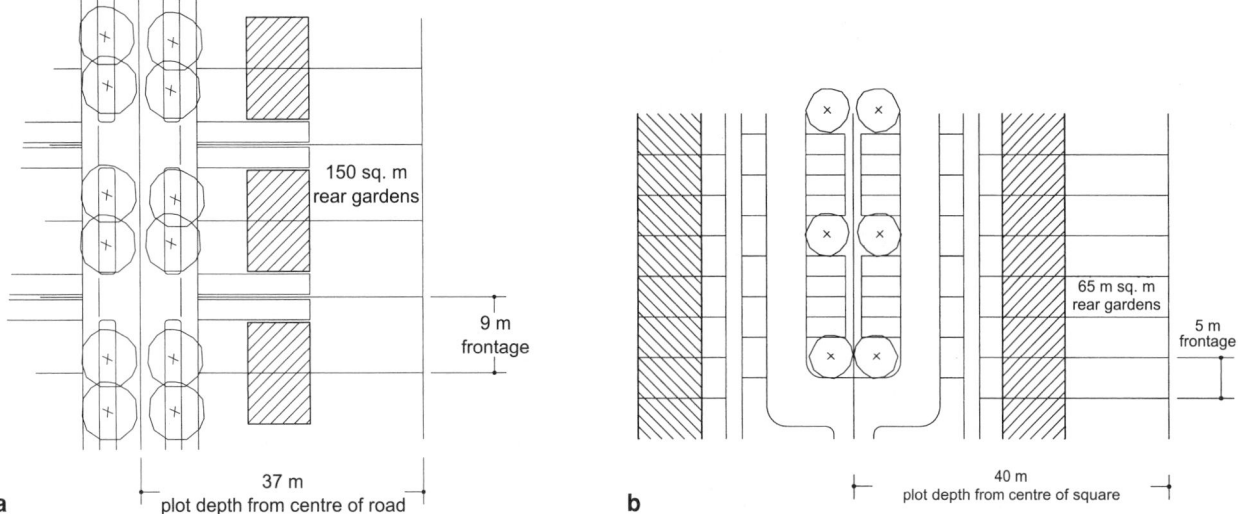

33.1 *National housing layouts at 150 and 250 hr/ha based upon typical houses of five habitable rooms.* **a** *Semi-detached houses with in-curtilage car parking: 30 dwellings per hectare (12 per acre); 150 habitable rooms per hectare (60 per acre).* **b** *Terraced houses around an urban square: 50 dwellings per hectare (20 per acre); 250 habitable rooms per hectare (100 per acre)*

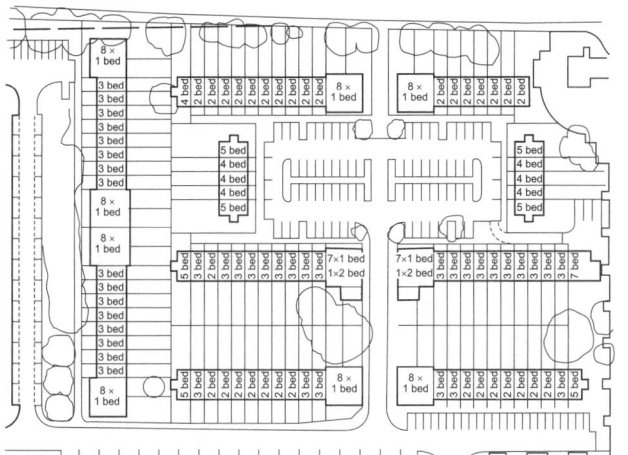

33.2 *Housing layout at 250 hr/ha (100 hr/acre) in a typical urban location with open car-parking area*

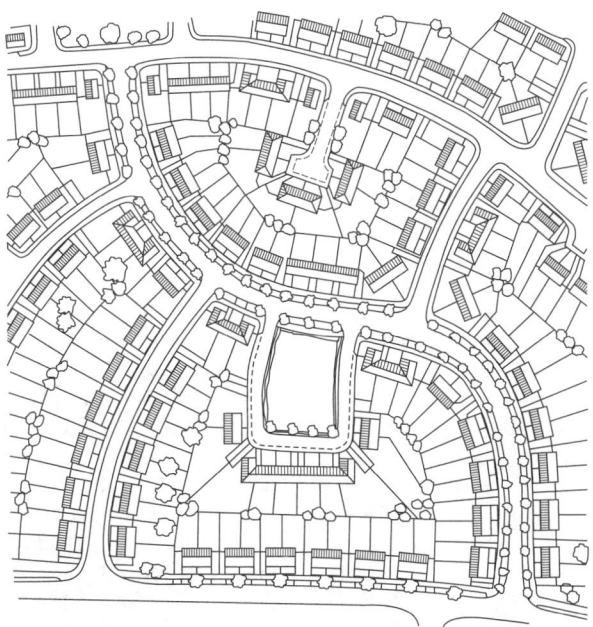

33.3 *Housing layout at 150 hr/ha (60 hr/acre) in a suburban location*

still be considered the minimum reasonable ceiling height for domestic buildings. 2.4 m is preferable, **33.5**. For rooms in the roof, floor areas are calculated to include only those parts where the ceiling height exceeds 1.5 m.

3.02 Staircase widths

These have not been included in part K of the Building Regulations since 1992. For means of escape purposes, widths of staircases to blocks of flats are covered in part B; but this does not cover the majority of single family-houses. The movement of furniture should be considered, and 800 mm should be the minimum reasonable clear stair width in domestic building.

3.04 Kitchen units

The previous edition of this Handbook included detailed graphs on comfortable heights for kitchen worktops, demonstrating that the common standard height of 900 to 914 mm is too low for the majority of both men and women. This height generally suits only women over 60. For the majority of women, worktops at 950 mm and sinktops at 975 mm are the most comfortable. For men, these heights can be increased further. So for fixed kitchens used by both sexes of able-bodied people, 950 to 975 mm is recommended. The use of lower worktops, at 850 mm, for housing for the elderly is not recommended, especially as 'white goods' will rarely fit underneath this height. For further information see Chapter 2, section 3.

3.04 Space standards for housing in relation to people with disabilities

When planning dwellings for regular occupation by users of wheelchairs or walking frames, it might be supposed that recommended room areas would need to be augmented. This is not necessarily always the case. Much more important are linear dimensions across circulation areas and between fixed appliances or obstructions. For this reason the planning of kitchens and bathrooms is especially important. Ample guidance is given in Selwyn Goldsmith's *Designing for the Disabled*. A much-distilled summary of some of the main requirements is given in Table X. These recommendations will tend to lead to increases in the floor areas of kitchens and bathrooms, and widths of circulation spaces, which may in turn cause the overall dwelling area to exceed Parker Morris standards. PM standards should therefore be considered the absolute minimum. (See also Chapter 2 for wheelchair data, and Chapter 3 for sanitary installations for disabled people.)

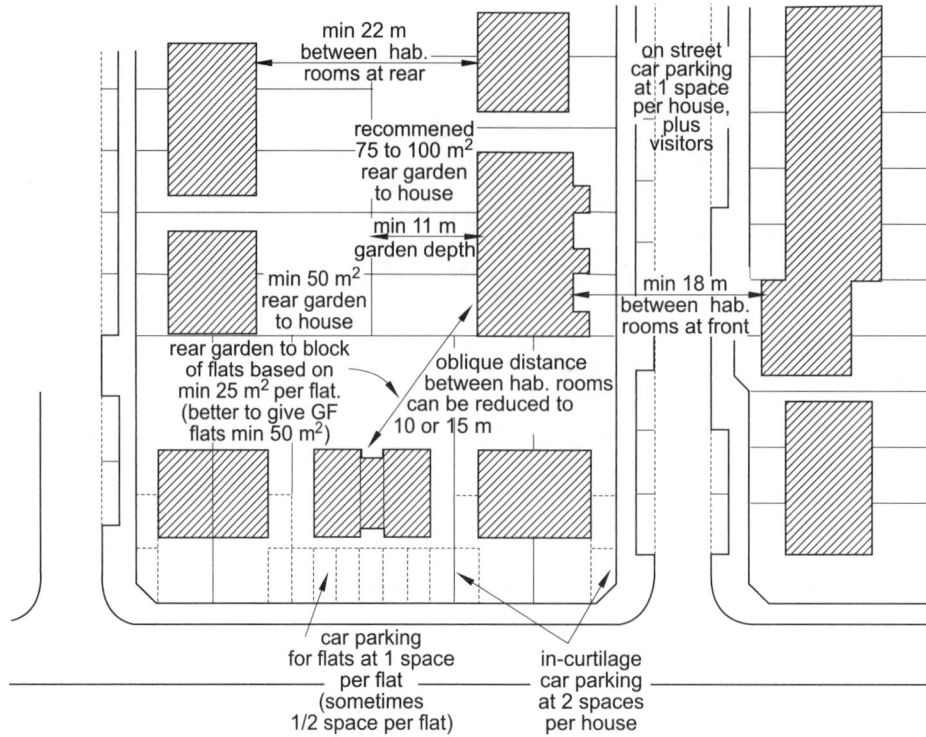

33.4 *Typical planning standards. NB: Different planning authorities have widely differing minimum dimension requirements*

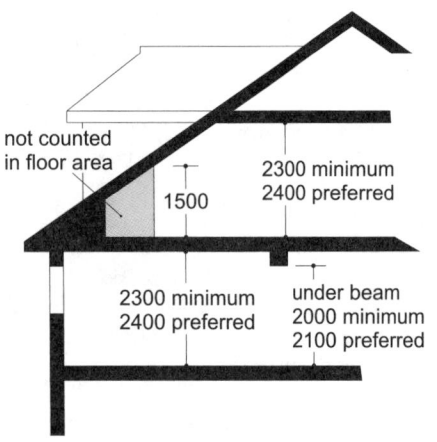

33.5 *Ceiling heights and rooms in the roof, no longer covered by Building Regulations*

Table X Key dimensional requirements for wheelchair and mobility housing: recommended minima in millimetres

	Wheelchair housing	Mobility housing
Entrance doorway clear width	800	775
Level threshold maximum upstand	15	15
Internal doorway clear width	750	750
Space to side of door (on lock/latch side)	300	300 recommended 100 minimum
Corridor width	1200	1050 recommended 900 minimum
Turning-circle diameter	1500	–
Space between bathroom and kitchen fittings	1500 recommended 1200 minimum	1200 recommended 1000 minimum
Bedroom width	3000	2800
Wheelchair storage (may overlap hall space)	1200 × 700	–
Transfer space for WC: front diagonal side	1200 750 750	– – –
WC pan centre to adjacent wall	400	400

There has been a radical change in thinking in the last few years. There is now an increasing view that *all* housing should be accessible to people in wheelchairs, not least to permit them to visit friends and relations. This will also permit people to remain in their dwellings well into old age or infirmity, instead of having to move to more accessible accommodation. The Access Committee for England (a semi-govermental body) has published *Building homes for successive generations* giving data for this, and there is good reason for believing that the Building Regulations on accessiblity will soon be extended to general needs housing on similar lines. Table XI gives these criteria.

3.05 Lifetime Homes

A further recent initiative has been published and promoted by the Joseph Rowntree Foundation, in their concept of 'Lifetime Homes'. As in the ACE recommendations, the idea is to construct dwellings that can be more easily adapted to cope with residents' future disabilities, should these arise. Such disabilities

could be either temporary, such as resulting from an accidental injury, or permanent, from accident or illness. JRF's recommendations take the form of 16 points covering the planning and construction of new dwellings. These 16 points are listed in Table XII. The standards for Lifetime Homes are not mandatory, but it is possible that some of the recommendations for accessibility may be reflected in the forthcoming revised Part M of the Building Regulations, which is expected to cover dwellings for the first time. The information currently available suggests that there will be exceptions: for example, blocks of flats under five storeys without lifts are still likely to be permitted; and there will probably be special consideration for houses in very hilly areas.

Table XI Recommendations for accessible general needs housing from *Building homes for successive generations*

PRINCIPLES:	ESSENTIAL CRITERIA:
1 The approaches and entrances to dwellings should be accessible to disabled people, including wheelchair users.	1 Entrances to dwellings should, wherever possible, have a level or gently sloped approach.
	2 Where dwellings (usually flats) are accessed by lifts, the lifts should be accessible to wheelchair users.
	3 Entrances to dwellings should have flush thresholds, and a minimum clear opening door width of 800 mm.
2 Areas normally used by visitors, e.g. hall, WC and living room, should be accessible to disabled people, including many wheelchair users.	4 Internal doorsets should have a minimum clear opening width of 750 mm.
	5 Circulation spaces at entrance level, (e.g. halls and corridors) should have a minimum width of 900 mm, and allowances should be made so that wheelchair users can turn into rooms and corridors.
	6 There should be a WC and a living room at entrance level
	7 The entrance-level WC should allow for access by a wheelchair user who has sufficient mobility to make either a front, diagonal or lateral transfer to the WC unaided.
3 Dwellings on more than one storey or level should be designed internally for easy movement and be amenable to modification, if necessary, for persons of limited mobility.	8 For dwellings on more than one storey or level, a staircase should be designed to allow for possible future installation of a stairlift.

See Table V, section 3, for Housing Corporation's requirements relating to the above. Also refer to the Access Committee for England's guide for other details.

Table XII Lifetime Home standards, published by Joseph Rowntree Foundation

Access
1 Where car-parking is adjacent to the home, it should be capable of enlargement to attain 3.3 m width.*
2 The distance from the car-parking space to the home should be kept to a minimum and should be level or gently sloping.*
3 The approach to all entrances should be level or gently sloping.* (Gradients for paths should be the same as for public buildings in the Building Regulations.)
4 All entrances should be illuminated*** and have level access over the threshold,* and the main entrance should be covered.
5 Where homes are reached by a lift, it should be wheelchair accessible.*

Inside the home
6 The width of the doorways and hallways should accord with the Access Committee for England's standards.* (See Table XI)
7 There should be space for the turning of wheelchairs in kitchens, dining areas and sitting rooms and adequate circulation space for wheelchair users elsewhere.***
8 The sitting room (or family room) should be at entrance level.*
9 In houses of two or more storeys, there should be space on the ground floor that could be used as a convenient bed space.
10 There should be a downstairs toilet** which should be wheelchair accessible, with drainage and service provision enabling a shower to be fitted at any time.
11 Walls in bathrooms and toilets should be capable of taking adaptations such as handrails.
12 The design should incorporate provision for a future stairlift* and a suitably identified space for potential installation of a house lift (through-the-floor lift) from the ground to the first floor, for example to a bedroom next to the bathroom.***
13 The bath/bedroom ceiling should be strong enough, or capable of being made strong enough, to support a hoist at a later date.*** Within the bath/bedroom wall provision should be made for a future floor to ceiling door, to connect the two rooms by a hoist.
14 The bathroom layout should be designed to incorporate ease of access, probably from a side approach, to the bath and WC. The wash basins should also be accessible.***

Fixtures and fittings
15 Living room window glazing should begin at 800 mm or lower, and windows should be easy to open/operate.***
16 Switches, sockets and service controls should be at a height usable by all (i.e. between 600 mm and 1200 mm from the floor).***

Notes: See Table V for Housing Corporation SDS requirements:
*essential
**essential for 5-person dwellings and above, recommended for others
***recommended

4 SINGLE FAMILY HOUSES

4.01 There is now a large consensus that families with children should be housed at ground level in single-family houses, or in ground-floor flats or ground- and first-floor maisonettes with direct entrances. It is not just that children need private gardens. Equally, if not more importantly, the shared entrances, staircases and corridors in blocks of flats, and the external spaces around them, have proved to be largely incompatible with family life. This is especially true in the public sector, where the resources to overcome the management and maintenance problems of communal areas are very limited.

4.02 Orientation and gardens

The relationship between the single-family dwelling and the adjacent public domain (i.e. the highway, the street, court, or – much less satisfactorily – the footpath) should be as clear and simple as possible. A private front garden, with front gate and front path leading to the front door, and with minimum depth of 2 to 3 m has proven benefits as *defensible space*, as promulgated by Oscar Newman and Alice Coleman. This is not to say that successful houses have not been built with no front garden, and the front door opening directly, or via an inset porch, from the public pavement. There are many thousands of quite satisfactory houses planned like this in the Victorian inner cities; but in these cases the pavement is clearly part of the publicly maintained highway. When there is an intervening 'confused' space that is neither public nor private but needs to be communally managed, this is rarely satisfactory, and often leads to tangible neglect. Similarly, rear gardens benefit from simplicity and clarity of relationship to the house and of enclosure. Communal space is best kept to a minimum or omitted altogether. Such is the concern about security these days that opinion is generally against any provision of rear access, especially from unsupervised rear pathways, even when these are of practical convenience, such as in uninterrupted terraces.

Orientation of the dwelling for best sunlight is probably taken less seriously now than twenty years ago, and should not normally take precedence over achieving simple clear relationships of private and public domains. However, within the dwelling it should normally be possible to arrange for one of the two day rooms (living room or dining kitchen) to get direct sunlight for a large part of the day. It is preferable for one day room to face the front permitting supervision of the street; and for the other to face the rear giving direct garden access. Another factor is the potential for passive solar gain in the winter through the simple expedient of larger double-glazed windows on the southern elevation.

4.03 Height

Although the majority of family houses are of two storeys, three storeys can be appropriate in urban areas. The expense of building taller is usually more than compensated for by savings in foundations and roofs, making this an economical type. Four-storey houses, however, are difficult to plan, because of the need for an alternative escape route from the upper floors (Building Regulations Part B1). Mutual escape is normally provided between adjacent houses via adjoining rooms or balconies; but this leads to potential security risks.

4.04 Frontage widths

Because of the costs of providing roads and services infrastructure, there is often pressure to build narrow-frontage houses – especially in urban areas. Anything less than 5.0 m width can be considered narrow frontage, **33.6**. This scheme, dating from the late 1980s, would not be built now as there is no entrance-level WC. Although reasonably satisfactory houses have been built with frontages of

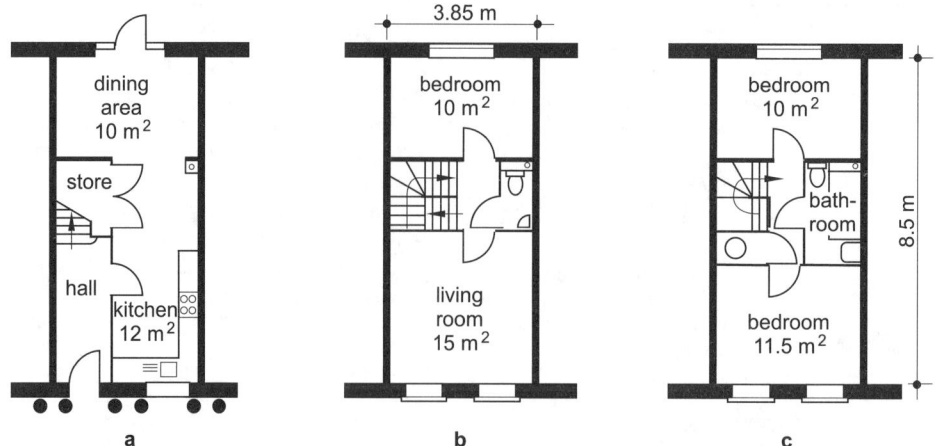

33.6 *Example of narrow-frontage terraced house for an inner-city site, 98 m², equivalent to a Parker Morris five-person house. The centre-to-centre frontage width of 4.05 m is very narrow and close to the minimum possible. The staircase is very tight and only feasible with winders.* Architects: Hunt Thompson Associates. **a** *Ground floor;* **b** *First floor;* **c** *Second floor*

4.0 m or even 3.5 m, the stresses on internal planning start to build up below approximately 4.5 m. A reasonable minimum could be taken to be 4.25 m frontage. Below this width, rear gardens also become apologetic. **33.7** shows a five-person, three bedroom, three-storey terrace house with a 4.5 m frontage.

It is not generally realised that high ceiling heights in some larger Victorian houses result from a combination of narrow frontage and substantial plan depth. The need for adequate daylighting means that frontage, depth and ceiling height are interdependent.

Taking 5.0 m as the normal terrace house frontage, **33.8** shows a two-bedroom, four-person, two-storey house; **33.9** a three-bedroom, five-person, two-storey house; **33.10** a three-bedroom, six-person, two-and-a-half-storey house.

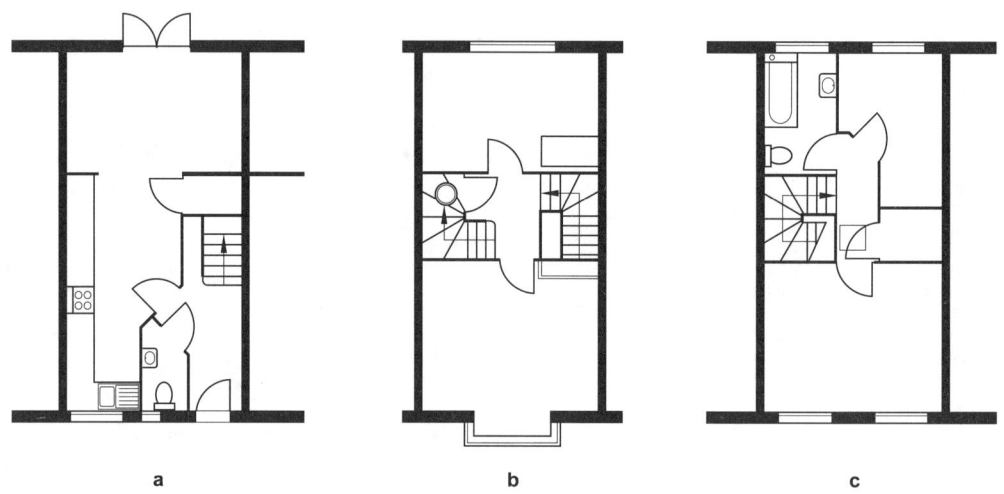

33.7 *A five-person, three-bedroom, three-storey terrace house with a 4.5 m frontage of 17 m².* **a** *Ground floor;* **b** *First floor;* **c** *Second floor*

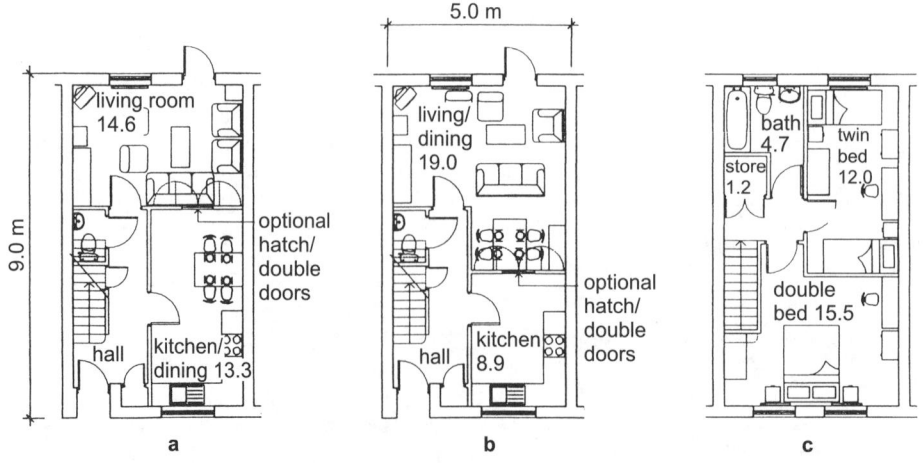

33.8 *A two-bedroom, four-person, two-storey terrace house of 79 m².* Architects: PRP Architects. **a** *Ground-floor plan with kitchen/diner;* **b** *Alternative ground floor with living/dining room;* **c** *First-floor plan*

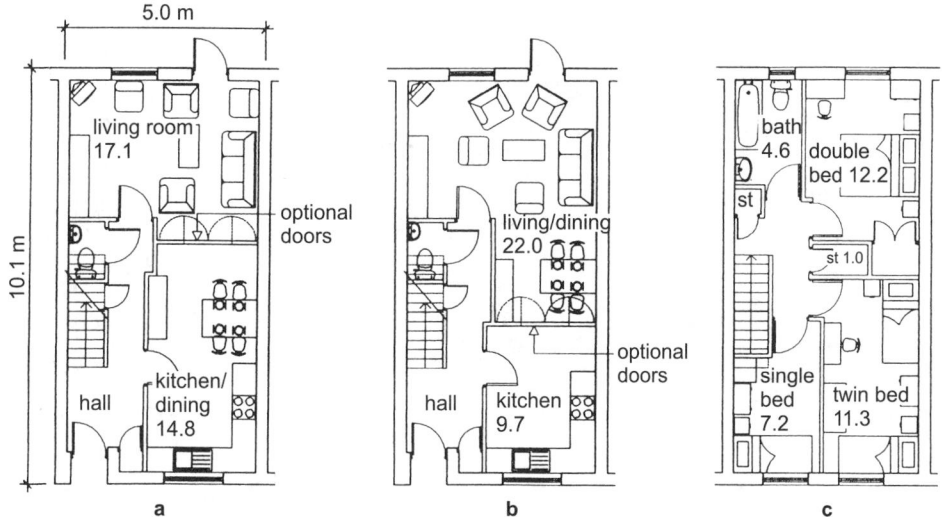

33.9 *A three-bedroom, five-person, two-storey terrace house of 85.9 m². Architects: PRP Architects.* **a** *Ground-floor plan with kitchen/diner;* **b** *Ground-floor plan with living/dining room;* **c** *First-floor plan*

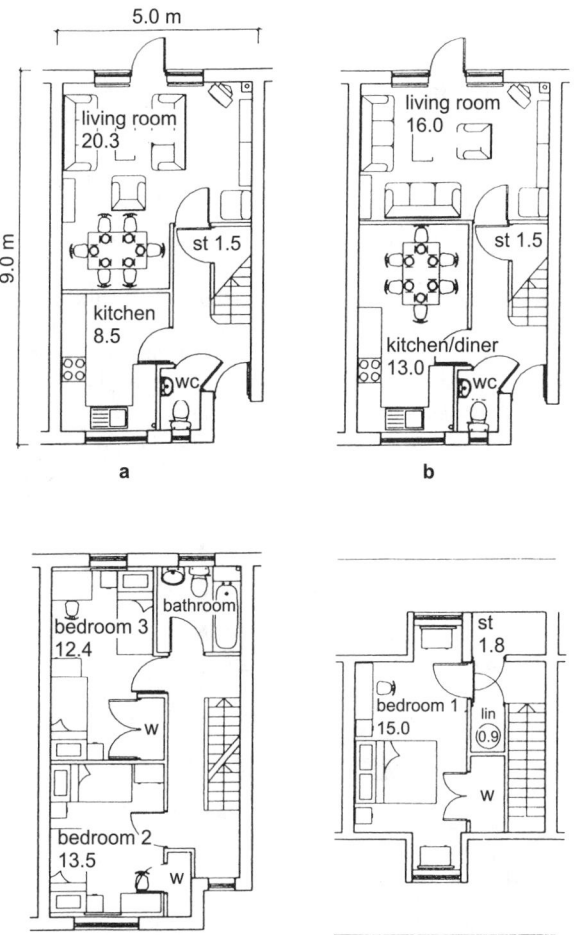

33.10 *A three-bedroom, six-person, two-and-a-half-storey terrace house of 99 m².* **a** *Ground-floor plan with living/dining room;* **b** *Ground floor with kitchen/diner;* **c** *First-floor plan;* **d** *Second-floor plan*

4.05 Internal planning

Opinions continue to differ over the relative positions of living room and kitchen, and therefore no recommendation is given here as to whether the kitchen is best at the front or the back. It is, however, rarely satisfactory for the only access to the rear garden to be via the living room: in fact Parker Morris ruled this out. In narrow-frontage houses where the living room needs to occupy most of the full width of the front of the house, the dining kitchen will almost certainly be at the rear. In three-storey houses this sometimes works well in combination with a front living room at first-floor level as in **33.7**. Rooms can then be full width, and offer good outlook and supervision to both front and rear, as well as benefiting from sunlight with almost any orientation. **33.11** shows a seven-person semi-detached or end-of-terrace house; this achieves a full-width ground-floor front room by placing the entrance in the side wall.

4.06 Living/dining versus kitchen/diner

Several of the examples shown in this chapter give alternative ground-floor plans with the dining space in either the living room or the kitchen; also the possibility of opening the two spaces into one.

4.07 The main bathroom

This should preferably be located on the floor with the most bedrooms. In three-storey houses this might be the first or the second floor. A ground-floor WC is very desirable in all family houses, however small. Although there is no longer a legal prohibition of WCs opening directly from kitchens, this arrangement is not normally either popular or advised. An exception might sometimes be a utility room containing a WC and forming the route to the garden. WC compartments should have a handbasin, although where it is adjacent to a bathroom or a utility room this is often omitted.

In larger family houses with four or more bedrooms, a second bathroom, or shower room, is recommended. This can be useful in three-storey houses, as it can mean having a WC on each floor. One bathroom or shower room can be en-suite with the main bedroom; however, this has not normally been considered to be appropriate in social housing. The Parker Morris standards for WCs were not especially generous: one WC in the bathroom for up to three-person dwellings; one separate WC for four-person houses; and two WCs; one of them in the bathroom, when the floor area of the house exceeded the minimum for five persons. These should be considered the *absolute* minima.

4.08 Storage

Where Parker Morris scored highly was in specifying good standards for storage. This has proved popular, and with people becoming more acquisitive all the time, real needs for storage space are increasing. General storage space is laid down in PM standards, over and above net floor space (see Table II). PM was

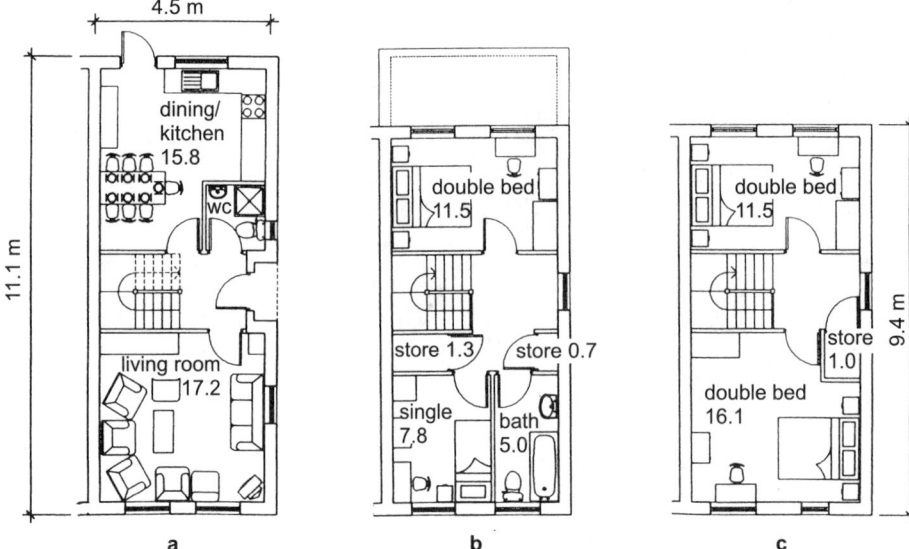

33.11 *Seven-person four-bedroom house of 118.5 m². Architects: PRP Architects.* **a** *Ground floor;* **b** *First floor;* **c** *Second floor*

specific that a large part (minimum 2.5 m²) of the general storage space should be at ground level. All of it should normally be accessible from circulation areas rather than from rooms. It was not intended that the loft space should count, as this is not normally conveniently accessible (though a good-quality loft ladder will make it more so) and trussed rafter construction makes the space much less usable. Having said this, boarding to at least part of the loft will create valuable extra storage space for light objects such as empty packing cases, etc.

In addition to general storage space, Parker Morris stipulated the following storage spaces, *included* in the net floor area of the dwelling:

1 Space for hanging outdoor clothes in the entrance hall
2 Space for a pram (1400 × 700) in houses for three persons or more
3 Linen cupboard: 0.6 m²
4 Kitchen storage: 2.3 m² (Parker Morris stipulated that part of this should be in a ventilated 'cool' cupboard, but this is less necessary now that virtually all households possess a refrigerator).

Bedroom cupboards such as built-in wardrobes were not stipulated. These can be valuable especially for low-income families; however, they need to be carefully planned in order to prevent them making the bedrooms less furnishable. If provided, built-in wardrobes also come out of the net floor space, and do not count towards general storage space. The figures in Table II should not include dustbin stores or spaces (which should be at the front of single-family houses), fuel stores if these are required, nor any space within a store which is needed for through access, such as to get to the rear of a single-access house. For this purpose Parker Morris stipulated a 700 mm width. Space in an integral or adjoining garage over and above 12.0 m² can count towards general storage space.

4.09 Stair configuration

Although the Building Regulations do not rule out winders provided certain minimum dimensions are met, winders are intrinsically less easily negotiated and more hazardous, especially for young children and older people. It is important that large wardrobes and other furniture can be taken up and down the stairs. This needs to be carefully planned for, especially in three-storey houses, where the soffit of the upper flight can restrict the head height over the lower flight, and winders make the problems worse.

4.10 External design

Refuse storage space is almost always needed at the front of the house, **33.12**. This can be over-designed, and there are many examples of ugly dustbins concealed inside even more ugly bin enclosures – sometimes little temples which make an inappropriate celebration out of storing refuse, with intricate and flimsy doors, hinges and catches that hardly survive the first visit by the dustman. The location for the dustbins or *wheelybin* needs to be clearly identified, for example by partial enclosure or change of paving surface. It needs to be close to the highway, the front gate and path, and not too far from the front or kitchen door. It should not be where smells would cause a problem, such as immediately under the window of a habitable room. It should always be copiously ventilated, and from this point of view the best form of enclosure is none at all.

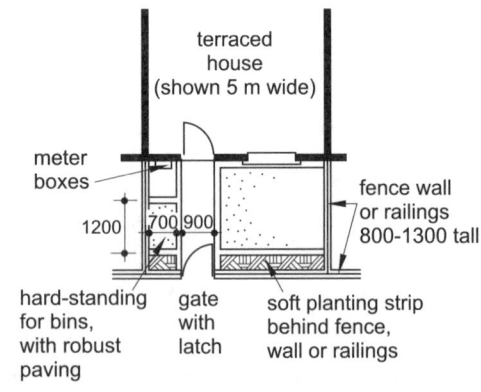

33.12 *Front garden of a terraced house showing refuse storage*

Meter positions can sometimes be integrated with that of dustbins, so that one can partially mask the other. This is more the case now that the service companies increasingly ask for external or externally readable meters.

External enclosure by fences, walls or railings can dramatically influence the look of a housing development. The function of a front garden enclosure is different from that of the rear garden, and this should be reflected in the design, **33.12**. Front fences, railings or walls should allow easy visual surveillance, both ways. A height of between 800 mm and 1300 mm is usually appropriate, and it is useful if the enclosure can be seen through below this level, but does not let dogs through. Thus railings and paling fences score over walls. Front gates should be of roughly the same height. A closed gate effectively excludes dogs and makes a *defensible* space feel rather more so; but gates, gate posts and catches need to be sturdy and carefully designed. Probably a majority of existing front gates do not shut properly, because of historical movement of the posts.

Enclosure of rear gardens is simpler. An impermeable wall or fence of approximatley 1.8 m height is normally recommended at the far end. The side (party fence) enclosures can be reduced to approximately 1.2 m. Most people seem to welcome some garden-to-garden contact with their neighbours, though not immediately next to the house, where a greater height is preferred. If gates *are* provided in rear garden walls or fences, these should be full height (at least 1.8 m) and lockable with security grade dead locks.

5 PURPOSE-BUILT FLATS

5.01 A block of flats nearly always involves shared entrances, stairs, landings, balconies or lobbies, and often one or more lifts. It is these that make flats more difficult to manage, because someone has to clean and look after these common spaces. These features tend to make flats unsuitable for families with children, as already said above. Flats should therefore normally be considered only for single people and childless couples, In many developments, one would expect most flats to be single-bedroom, with a lesser number of double-bedroom. The latter can be popular with couples whose children have grown up, or are just being born; and with other smaller households.

The common areas and facilities become exponentially more difficult to manage with increasing numbers of flats in the block. Small blocks of four or six flats are easier to manage than those where the numbers get into double figures. Shared systems such as entryphones rely upon responsible behaviour; this is more achievable with a small number of households who know each other.

5.02 Height of blocks

Parker Morris stipulated the maximum walk-up to a flat front door to be two storeys. Although the Housing Corporation no longer rules out four-storey blocks without lifts, these are on the limit of acceptability. For five storeys and above, a lift is essential. The whole question of lifts awaits a decision by the DoE on the extension of access requirements for disabled people to all new residential property.

5.03 Common stairs, corridors and balconies

Essential criteria for common parts of blocks of flats are laid down clearly in the Building Regulations Part B1 and in BS 5588 Part 1. Direct entry to flats is permitted without intervening lobbies in low blocks (up to four storeys) with no more than two flats per floor if the entrance halls within the flat are fire-protected routes with fire doors and door closers. If lobbies are provided, then within small flats (less than 9 m maximum travel distance from the furthest point in the flat to the front door) a protected route is not stipulated.

Common, or semi-public, staircases are usually best located at the front of the block, where the stair windows can look over the highway or public domain, rather than over private gardens provided for the ground-floor flats.

5.04 Stacking of similar rooms

All party floors have to provide sound insulation; but the levels of insulation that are mandatory cannot prevent all noise nuisance, and it is best if similar rooms are stacked one above the other. The worst combination is one flat's living room directly above another flat's bedroom.

5.05 Configuration of rooms around the common stairs

The minimum levels of sound insulation specified in the Building Regulations between all habitable rooms in flats and the common

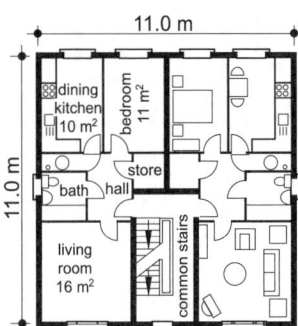

33.13 *Small block of one-bedroom, two-person flats, bedrooms located away from stairs. Each flat 52 m². Lobbies between stairs and flats are required in larger blocks*

parts of the block are less than fully satisfactory. It is preferable therefore to situate bedrooms away from the common stairs **33.13**; and particularly, well away from any liftshaft.

Day rooms are best at the front and bedrooms at the quieter rear, perhaps alongside the kitchen. There are however, many examples of small blocks of flats with bedrooms at the front alongside the stairs, and living rooms at the rear. The banal reason for this is that the bedrooms are narrower than the living rooms which make use of the extra width behind the stairs. This plan form combines the worst exposure of the bedrooms to noise nuisance from the common stairs with the least satisfactory orientation of day and night rooms.

5.06 Balcony access

This is no longer common, having been discredited by the social failures of much of the deck-access medium-rise local authority housing built in the 1960s and 1970s. However, some of the smaller self-contained balcony access flat blocks built between the wars have proved quite satisfactory in long-term use. Open-air balconies can sometimes avoid the squalor associated with wholly internal common circulation areas, but open balconies enable the planning of large extended blocks, with too many flats using a single entrance and stair. This should be resisted.

A problem with balcony access flats is the dual aspect; some windows are directly onto the balcony. These are not popular, owing to lack of privacy and the security risks. Kitchens and bathrooms tend to be placed on the balcony side, but residents dislike strangers passing the kitchen sinks.

5.07 Lifts

In blocks of flats these should always be capable of taking a wheelchair; and this means at least an eight-person lift as defined by BS 5655 (see Chapter 5). A thirteen-person lift should also be capable of taking a horizontal stretcher. Lifts in medium-rise flat blocks have become rather easier to plan, using hydraulic lifts with pump rooms at or near the base, as opposed to electric lifts with motor rooms at the top. Hydraulic pump rooms can be very compact and flexibly positioned, as shown in **5.3**. Also refer to **5.6** for dimensions for an electric traction lift.

5.08 Refuse

This is always a problem with flats. Traditionally, public sector housing has used chutes. These cause a noise nuisance, tend to get blocked, and the inlet points can become particularly unsavoury. Additionally, the chambers at the base of the chutes, with paladins or skips, collect overflowing rubbish, vermin, and general mess and squalor. lf blocks of flats can be kept small (up to six or eight flats) then it is quite possible to provide a discreet but easily accessible area containing a separate rubbish bin for each flat, clearly and individually marked, **33.14**.

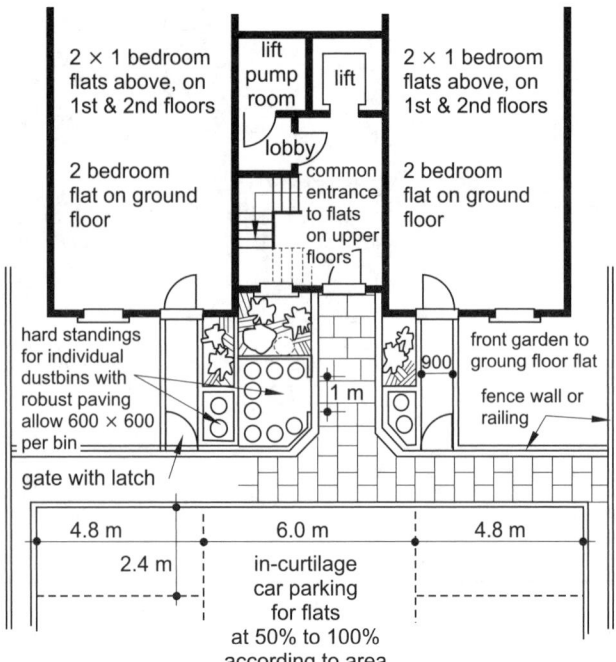

33.14 *External planning for typical three-storey block of ten flats showing refuse storage*

For large or tall blocks, there is little alternative to refuse chutes – in fact, they are required under the Building Regulations for blocks of more than five storeys. The base area needs to be carefully designed, with robust and easily cleaned surfaces, good access for cleaning and copious ventilation.

5.09 External areas
Unless there is a very competent management regime, shared external areas should be minimised or abolished. Clearly the latter is not entirely possible, as access is needed to the common front door. The route to this entrance should be as simple as possible: broad and short. Areas to the sides of this access can be given to the ground-floor flats as front gardens; and these will be much more successful if these flats have separate front doors independent of the common entrance. Similarly, the best use for the ground behind the block is normally as rear gardens for the ground-floor flats. Communal gardens sound good but rarely work, unless there is an exemplary system of management by residents' association or landlord. (As residents of Georgian squares know, this does not come cheap!) External space for upper-floor flats is often provided by private balconies, although these are not without their own problems. The enclosure of front and rear gardens to ground-floor flats should be similar to that for single-family houses (see para **4.09**). The shared approach to the main entrance door should be treated rather differently. In larger blocks, many people would not bother to shut a gate, so it may be omitted. If there is no unallocated garden space there will, naturally, be no fencing except on either side of this approach.

If there is any soft landscaping along the shared approach route, it needs to be carefully planned to withstand rather less tender loving care than in private gardens. If flanked by well cared-for private gardens, then the common approach path is best left as good quality hard landscaping and paving.

6 HOUSE CONVERSIONS
6.01 The conversion of large houses into self-contained flats in the 1970s and 1980s used to be the stock-in-trade of inner city housing associations, as well as private developers. There is evidence of a falling off of this type of rehabilitation project, partly because of a gradual shift in demand, but also because housing associations have been turning more towards new-build schemes since the Housing Act 1988.

6.02 Planning
Splitting up a single-family house involves creating at least one new dwelling, and thereby constitutes 'Development' under the Planning Acts. Unlike extending a single-family house by an allowed percentage of its volume, this is not 'Permitted Development', as defined by the General Development Order and its various amendments. Therefore house conversions require planning permission, and this allows planning authorities to control this type of development if they feel that it is eroding the balance of single-family houses in the district.

Houses that are statutorily listed have more onerous constraints; for example, requiring Listed Building Consents for any demolition (however small). Certain restraints also apply to all properties within Conservation Areas, possibly depending on what Article 4 directions have been approved. Conservation Area Approval is no longer required for a small amount of demolition, such as of an outhouse; but a proposal of this nature might well lead to a spot-listing, when a Listed Building Consent would then be required. In many of these cases the planning authority and/or English Heritage may then get very involved in detailed design and aesthetics.

This introduces the first discipline when dealing with an existing house, which is to respect its existing qualities and character. A natural conversion should aim to keep well-proportioned rooms intact wherever possible. This commonly means at least the main front rooms at ground- and first-floor levels. Avoid boxed-in lobbies in the corners of previously good rooms: they can make nonsense of original decorative elements such as cornices and picture rails, and also make the rooms more difficult to furnish. Another implicit aspect of natural conversions is the aim to keep similar rooms stacked over each other. Day rooms of one flat should not be planned over bedrooms of another flat; and bathrooms and kitchens are best stacked, thereby simplifying drainage and plumbing.

The same considerations about accommodation for families with children apply as for new-build. Family dwellings should be at ground and/or basement level, or at least have direct street entry and garden access. This will usually mean only one large unit in the conversion of a house, with one or more smaller units (preferably one-bedroom) over it. In an understandable wish to reduce the common areas, many conversions have been built the 'wrong way up' with a large unit over a one-bedroom flat at ground-floor level. This is unsatisfactory, especially in social housing. Family life is noisy, and does not fit well over single people or couples.

Having said this, common areas and stairs should be minimised or abolished if at all possible, as these cause continuing management problems. New external stairs may be added in some cases to achieve the objective of a separate direct entrance for each dwelling.

6.03 Building Regulations
Creating new dwellings constitutes building work and is controlled by the Building Regulations. Most of the same parts (see Table IX) apply to conversions as to new-build. The main exception is Part L, in recognition of the fact that it may not be reasonably possible to add thermal insulation to all elements of the existing fabric to the standards required for new buildings.

Some elements such as top-floor ceilings, though, are quite simple to insulate, and could be upgraded to a higher level than required for new-build to compensate for not insulating the walls. Thermal insulation can also often be added to the walls of rear extensions, where there is a greater proportion of exposed wall surface to floor area, and decorative features, which would be lost, are absent. The replanning of rear parts of the house to provide new service rooms may also give opportunities to add insulating linings. Also worth considering (subject to planning restrictions) is external insulation, as this gives a better thermal performance and reduces cold bridging. Parts B1 (Means of Escape) and E (Resistance to the Passage of Sound) apply to conversions as for new-build, and are most likely to affect the final design.

6.04 Loft conversions

If habitable rooms are converted out of loft space, the resulting floor area is measured over those parts that are more than 1.5 m high. A two-storey house is covered by Part B1 of the Building Regulations only as far as controlling *inner rooms*. However, when its loft is converted, extra requirements of Part B1 come into force.

Under Part K, alternating-tread stairs are specifically allowed up to single rooms and bathrooms in a loft. Despite this, there are considerable reservations about the safety of alternating-tread stairs, and they are not recommended, especially in social housing. A reasonable width for a staircase leading to a single habitable room in a loft is 800 mm, with a minimum of 700 mm.

6.05 External areas

Similar considerations apply as to purpose-built flats. The best answer is often the simplest: to give both front and rear gardens to the lowest dwelling, which is likely to be the largest. Balconies to upper-floor units are less likely to be feasible than with new-build, unless a low rear extension provides an opportunity for a roof terrace. Some planning authorities deprecate these as prejudicing the privacy of neighbouring gardens. In cases of detached, semi-detached and end-of-terrace properties with easy access to the rear, plots for the upper flats can be provided by dividing the rear garden. There are also examples where a first-floor flat has been given access by means of an external stair.

7 ACCOMMODATION FOR SINGLE PEOPLE

7.01 In DoE Design Bulletin DB29 *Housing single people*, published in 1975, a distinction was drawn between the space requirement for *middle-aged permanent* residents and for *young mobile workers*. This led to a recommendation for small (25 m²) bedsitting room flats for the latter category. The trouble is young mobile tenants turn into middle-aged permanent ones quicker than housing managers can respond. This has resulted in a great degree of dissatisfaction with bed-sit flats for single people.

The four principal types of accommodation provided for single people are:

- Self-contained one-bedroom flats, for which Parker Morris standards are recommended without change
- *Cluster flats* providing a number of bedsitting rooms for individuals, with shared dining kitchens, living rooms and sanitary facilities, **33.15**, and
- Sheltered housing for elderly single people (see para **8** below)
- That which is suitable for students, nurses, etc. This is fully covered in Chapter 34.

7.02 Cluster flats

Because of the space needed for the individual bedsitting rooms, the floor areas for cluster flats should be rather greater than for the equivalent size of a general needs household, for three-person units and larger (see Table XIII).

Even more than with Parker Morris general needs housing, storage space is important for single persons sharing a dwelling. DB29 therefore laid down minimum storage spaces, distinguishing between that for individuals and that for the dwelling as a whole (see Table XIII). The minimum area for the individual bedsitting rooms within a cluster flat was not laid down in DB29, and does not equate directly with any classification in Table IV. A minimum bedsitting room is 12 m², the recommended size for a medium to long-stay resident is 15 m², and a washbasin should be provided in each.

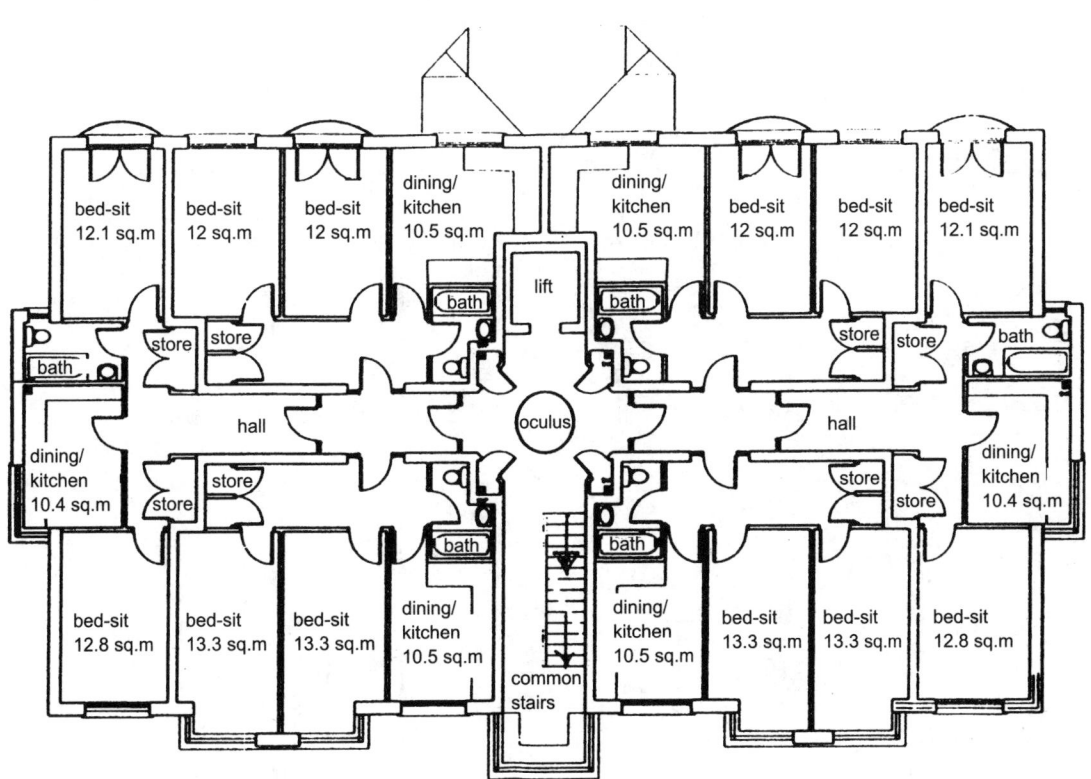

33.15 *First floor of a block containing six flats of 51 m², each with two bed-sitting rooms for single people sharing (see **33.16** and **33.18** for other floors of this block)*

Table XIII Housing for single people from DB29

Numbers of single people sharing	1	2	3	4	Each additional person
Minimum areas (including storage) in:					
single-storey houses	33 m²	48.5 m²	65 m²	85 m²	20 m²
houses more than 1 storey				90 m²	
flats	32.5 m²	47.5 m²	65 m²	85 m²	20 m²
maisonettes				90 m²	
Personal storage	3 m³	6 m³	9 m³	12 m³	3 m³
including shelves or drawers with area not less than:	2 m²	4 m²	6 m²	8 m²	2 m²
Dwelling storage	0.5 m³	0.5 m³	0.5 m³	0.5 m³	
including shelves or drawers with area not less than:	0.8 m²	0.8 m²	0.8 m²	0.8 m²	
Kitchen storage	1.4 m³	2.1 m³	2.8 m³	3.5 m³	0.7 m³
including shelves or drawers with area not less than:	5 m²	7 m²	9 m²	11 m²	2 m²
Electric socket outlets	9	12	15	18	3
Bath or shower	1	1	1	1	
Washbasin	1	1	1	2	
WC separate	1*	1*	1	2*	

*one may be in the bathroom

7.03 Common rooms

Where these are provided, the areas should be at least 20 m² for the first 25 persons (*young mobile*) plus 0.4 m² for each additional person. However, it is now less common to provide common rooms, as schemes tend to consist of self-contained flats, either for one-person households, or of clusters, who share integral day rooms. There is one exception that should be noted.

7.04 Foyers

A concept introduced from France in the early 1990s is the *foyer*, consisting of a complex containing accommodation for young single people either in one-person flats or more usually a number of cluster flats, or a mixture of the two types. It also includes substantial training and other facilities such as cafeterias, laundries and common rooms. To make it economically feasible, a foyer may need to house about 100 young people. Although successful in France, it is still too early to assess how well foyers work in the UK.

8 SHELTERED HOUSING

8.01 The design standards for accommodation specially designed for elderly people were first set down in the forms of *Category 1* and *Category 2* in MLHG Circular 82/69. This did not refer to *sheltered housing*, which is the name now generally employed for separate flats or bungalows for the elderly within a scheme that also has shared facilities such as common rooms and a warden.

8.02 The standards in Circular 82/69 were mandatory for publicly funded sheltered housing schemes from 1969 until the parallel demise of Parker Morris in the early 1980s. The circular has now been withdrawn, but the standards in its Appendix 1 remain a reasonable guide to what should normally be included in a sheltered scheme. The one exception is the small one-person *grouped flatlets*, which have proved neither popular nor suitable for elderly people.

8.03 The Housing Corporation, in its Scheme Development Standards for Housing Associations, continues to define sheltered housing as *Category 1* and *Category 2*, with an intermediate *Category 1 plus* which would incorporate some but not all of the facilities needed for a full Category 2 scheme. These Standards require most of the facilities listed in Circular 82/69, but give no space standards. The following guidance is taken from Circular 82/69 (Tables XIV and XV) and from the Housing Corporation current Standards (Table V).

8.04 Category 1

It will be seen from Tables XIV and XV that Category 1 dwellings need not be radically different from general needs one- and two-person units, **33.16**. The minimum recommended floor areas (Table XIV) are identical to Parker Morris equivalents (Table II). The main additional requirements concern access (maximum of one storey up enclosed stairs with a gentle pitch unless a lift is provided), full central heating (which should be universal in any case), and baths suitable for the potentially infirm.

It should be said that the stipulation of short (1550 mm long) baths, previously made by the Housing Corporation, is questioned by some physiotherapists. Nowadays many types of special baths are available, some with mechanically assisted immersion. Some of these are based on normal domestic sizes, of approximately 1700 × 700 mm, and are designed to replace ordinary baths without much difficulty.

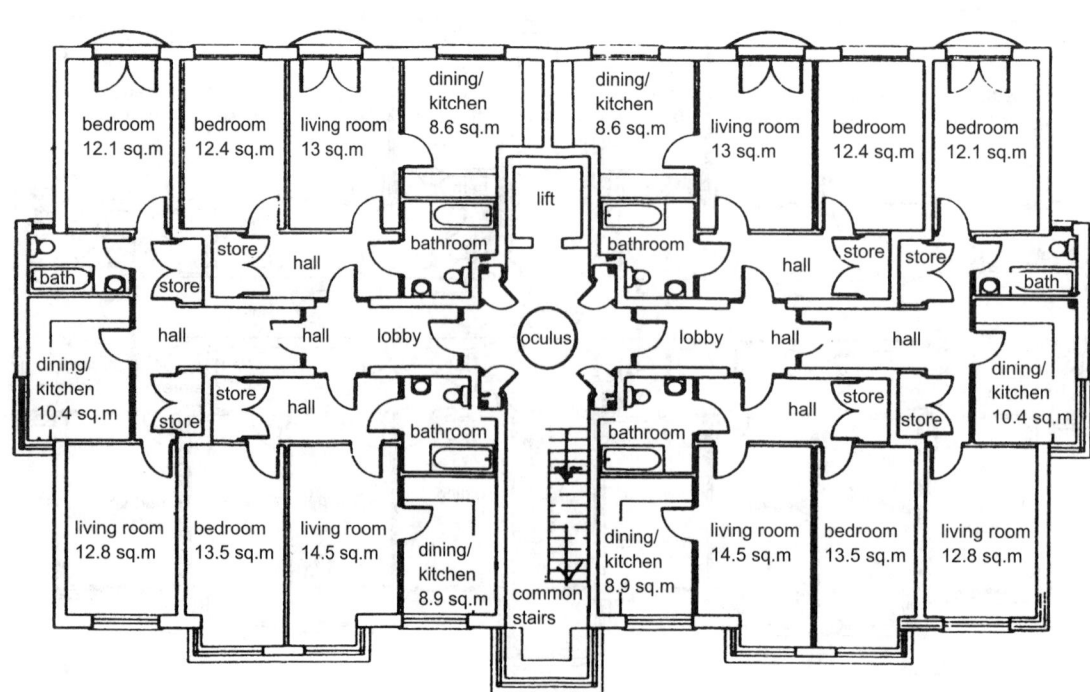

33.16 *Second floor of same block as* **33.15** *with six one-bedroom Category 1 sheltered flats of 51 m². The third floor is similar*

Table XIV Sheltered housing for the elderly Minimum floor areas in m² from Circular 82/69. Mandatory for publicly funded schemes from 1969 until 1981.

	No. of persons (bedspaces)	Net area	General storage area	Total
Category 1 bungalows	1	30.0	3.0	33.0
	2	44.5	4.0	48.5
Category 1 flats	1	30.0	2.6	32.6
	2	44.5	3.0	47.5
Category 2 'flatlets'	1	28.1	1.9	30.0
	2	39.0	2.5	41.5

Notes:

1 Category 1 standards were the same as in Parker Morris, Table II.

2 In Category 1 bungalows no more than 1.5 m² of general storage space should be outside the dwelling. In Category 1 flats, all should be inside.

3 In Category 2 flatlets for one person, up to 0.8 m² of the general storage space may be outside the flatlet in internal communal storage; in two person flats, up to 1.2 m².

4 The Circular recommended caution in providing a bath in a one-person flatlet. It suggested a very short 1350 mm bath. This excessive caution was probably misplaced.

5 The Circular also recommended smaller 'grouped flatlets' for single persons with bedsitting rooms and small kitchens sharing a bathroom. These proved neither popular nor suitable and the Housing Corporation now requires every flat to be self-contained with its own bath or shower.

Table XV Sheltered housing for the elderly Minimum standards from Circular 82/69 for plans, fittings and facilities. Mandatory for publicly funded schemes from 1969 until 1981.

1 Plan arrangements
(a) enclosed staircases
(b) maximum climb of 1 storey, without a lift
(c) 2 lifts, and all access enclosed, if more than 4 storeys high
(d) convenient, covered and lit access to refuse storage
(e) entrance lobbies or halls with clothes hanging space
(f) kitchens should provide unbroken sequence: worktop/cooker/worktop/sink/draining board
(g) in 2- and 3-person dwelling; space in kitchen for 2 persons to eat

2 Furniture
Plans should be able satisfactorily to accommodate the following:

(a)	Kitchen	in Category 1, a small table
(b)	Living room	small dining table and chairs
		2 easy chairs, or 1 settee and 1 chair
		TV set
		small table
		reasonable quantity of other possessions, e.g. bookcase
(c)	Bedroom (single)	single bed
		bedside table
		small dressing table and chair
		built-in cupboard 600 mm wide, or space for single wardrobe
(d)	Bedroom (double)	2 single beds (or double bed alternative)
		2 bedside tables
		small chest of drawers
		small dressing table and chair
		built-in cupboard 1200 mm wide, or space for a double wardrobe
(e)	Bed recess	same as single bedroom

3 Kitchen fitments
(a) Storage capacity minimum 1.7 m³ including refrigerator minimum capacity 0.07 m³ or space for a refrigerator, and a broom cupboard.
Fittings measured overall for depth and width, and from underside of worktop to top of plinth for height. Maximum height of worktops 850 mm (Note: this is no longer recommended, see sections above)
(b) In Category 2 flatlets; a gas or electric cooker, adapted for safe use by elderly people.

4 Linen cupboard
(a) storage capacity 0.4 m³
(b) at least 2 shelves, at minimum height 300 mm, and maximum height 1520 mm.

5 Electric socket outlets
4 (a) Kitchen
(b) Living room 3
(c) Bedroom 2
(d) Hall or lobby 1
(e) Bedsitting room 5

(These standards would now be considered low, but would be roughly appropriate if each number represented a double socket.)

6 Space heating
(a) The installation should be able to maintain:
flats and communal rooms (if provided) at 21°C
circulation areas in Category 2 schemes at 15.6°C
when outside temperature is −1°C
(b) The temperature should be controllable by the resident.

7 Bathrooms
(a) Baths should be flat bottomed and short (1550 mm) to prevent an elderly person becoming competely immersed. (*Note: this guidance on short baths is not agreed with by all occupational therapists.*)
(b) All baths and Wcs should have at least one hand-hold in a convenient position.
(c) Doors to bathrooms should open outwards and have locks openable from outside in an emergency.
(d) One in four bathrooms may be replaced by a shower room. The shower compartment floor should be non-slip and free of hazards, with a secure hand-hold and wall-mounted seat. The hot water should be thermostatically controllable to a maximum 49°C, with a height adjustable outlet.

(Note: All Category 1 and 2 flats should now be provided with a full bathroom, with WC, washbasin and bath or shower.)

8 Communal facilities for Category 1 schemes
Common rooms (e.g. lounge, TV room, workshop or hobbies room) are optional in Category 1 schemes. If they are included, then the following should be provided:

(a) floor area 0.95 m² per resident
(b) short route from the dwellings (not necessarily covered)
(c) one WC and handbasin, near the common room
(d) small tea kitchen, next to the common room
(e) space for hats and coats
(f) small cupboard for cleaning materials
(g) store next to the common room, at least 2 m².

A Category 1 scheme may have an emergency call system, which should be linked to a reception point. (It is general to include this in current schemes.)
A Category 1 scheme may also include a guest bedroom. This should be near a communal toilet. (An en-suite bathroom is preferable.)

9 Communal facilities of Category 2 schemes
The following should be provided:

(a) a common room or rooms, floor area 1.9 m² per resident
(b) a WC and handbasin, near each common room
(c) a small tea kitchen, next to the common room
(d) space for hats and coats
(e) a store next to common room, at least 2 m²
(f) a warden's self-contained dwelling, designed to general needs standards (see Tables II to V) (or, for schemes of less than 15 flats, adjoining a residential home, a warden service provided from the home)
(g) an emergency call system linked to the warden,
(h) a laundry room, with minimum of:
1 automatic washing machine
1 tumble-drier
1 sink
1 table or bench for folding clothes
(j) a cleaner's cupboard, minimum 1 m³
(k) a telephone and seat
(l) enclosed and heated circulation areas
(m) the possibility of door-to-door goods delivery
(n) a warden's office near the main entrance
(p) a Category 2 scheme may also include a guest bedroom, which should be near a communal toilet. (An en-suite bathroom is preferable.)

It would be normal for a larger Category 1 scheme to include a number of two-bedroom units, which should be to Parker Morris three- or four-person size. Category 1 dwellings tend to follow certain recognised patterns:

1 Small two-storey blocks of flats, containing, for example, from four to eight dwellings

2 The lower two storeys of a general needs block of flats, up to four storeys tall, without lifts. (This can conflict with the policy of putting family housing at ground-floor level)

3 A group of bungalows, perhaps forming part of a larger sheltered scheme.

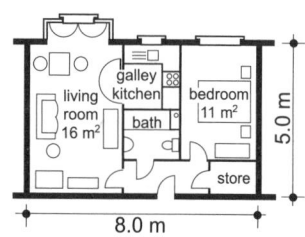

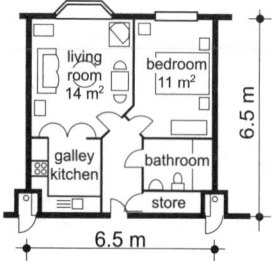

33.17 *Category 2 sheltered flats, two-person one-bedroom flats at 41.5 m² each*

8.05 Category 2

These dwellings are more clearly distinguished from general needs housing by their need to be grouped in a single scheme or block. The size of the scheme will be constrained by the the requirement for a resident warden in his or her own dwelling on the site. It will need to have enough flats to contribute to the salary and costs of the warden; this means a minimum of about 20 flats. But the scheme should not be so large that the warden's time and care are too stretched to cope; and this imposes a maximum size of 40 flats. Category 2 schemes therefore tend to contain about 30 flats, **33.17**.

A number of the ground-floor flats (between two and six of them) are normally designed for residents in wheelchairs, **33.18**. Also, although most Category 2 flats have one bedroom, a small number of two-bedroom flats can be included. These are valuable for elderly siblings, for example. Such flats should be approximately 10 m² larger than the standard one-bedroom two-person flatlets in Table IV, i.e. 50 to 55 m².

Of one-bedroom flats, it has been found that the greatest demand is for nominal two-person units. Many single elderly people are fairly recently widowed, and still have furniture, e.g. double beds, from their marriages. For these, a double bedroom is very desirable (see Table IV).

Sheltered flats' bathrooms should be better equipped and rather larger than for general needs, to allow space for assistance with bathing or showering, when necessary.

Category 2 schemes should include the communal facilities listed in Tables V and XV, all accessible indoors, via heated common circulation areas. The planning of the communal facilities will vary greatly from scheme to scheme, but some general principles apply. If more than one common room is provided, one should preferably be at the front of the building to face the street and approaching visitors; and another can usefully overlook the rear garden. One might be planned as an evening room; and the other to suit more daytime activities, with perhaps a conservatory linking it to the garden. Every common room should have a WC to mobility or wheelchair standard (see Chapter 3) as close as

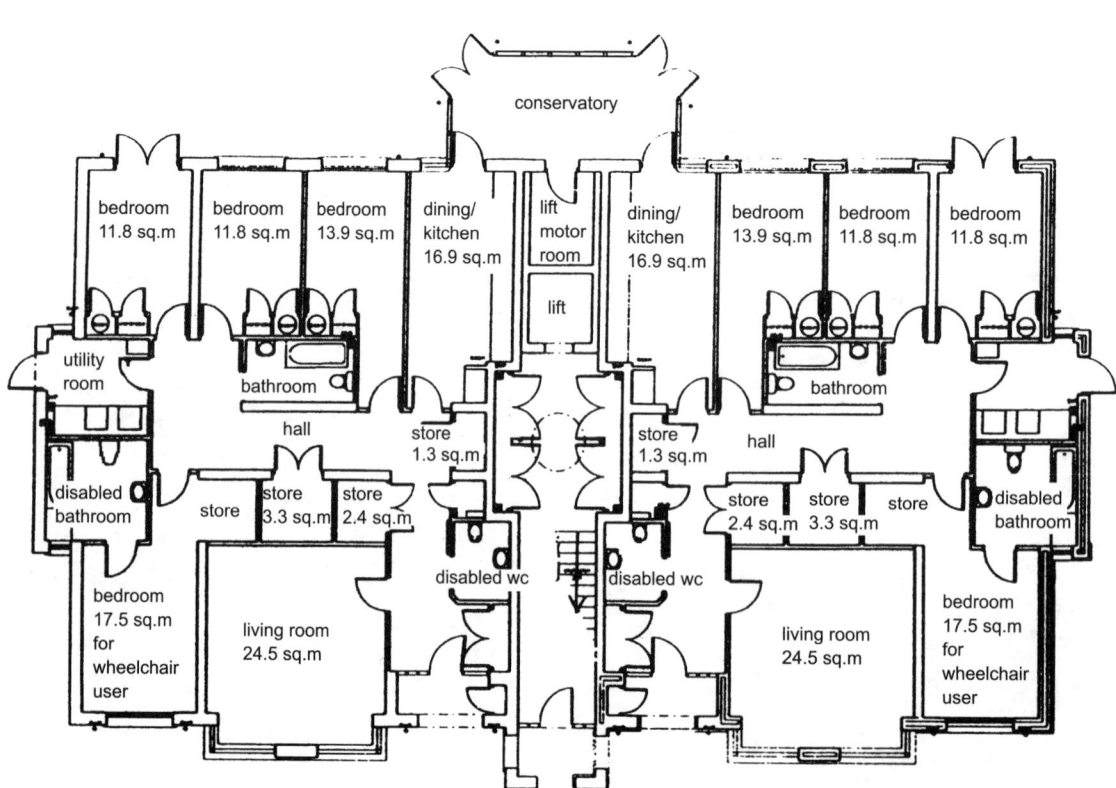

33.18 *Ground floor of same block as* **33.15** *and* **33.16** *containing two flats each of 165 m² with four bedrooms, one of which is for a wheelchair user*

possible, and a furniture store. One of the common rooms should have a kitchen. The laundry is best sited at ground-floor level, with direct access to a drying area in the garden, even if it is equipped with tumbler-driers.

Most Category 2 sheltered schemes have a bathroom suitable for assisted use, as some residents will be or become too frail to bathe themselves. This is not necessary where the sheltered scheme is linked to a adjacent residential home whose facilities can be used.

The warden's dwelling may be a flat, a house or a maisonette, and should be to general needs standards (see Tables II–VIII). Since the warden may well have a family, it should preferably be a three-bedroom family unit meeting all the normal criteria for family dwellings (see above), i.e. be at ground level, with its own independent front and rear gardens and separate front door. Additionally, there should be a discreet direct link to the common circulation area of the flats. The warden's dwelling need not be near the warden's office, which should be close to the main entrance of the scheme. Indeed, it is preferable if the dwelling is in a more private location.

Some residents of sheltered housing will be or become frail, while others will retain their full fitness for many years. To cater flexibly with a varied population of elderly people, a larger development could contain a mixture of Category 1 dwellings (perhaps free-standing bungalows), a Category 2 scheme of around thirty flats, and a Frail and Elderly Home (see Chapter 35).

Against this, geriatric ghettos should be avoided. A comprehensive housing development should aim sensitively to integrate housing for older citizens together with general needs family houses and flats. While some elderly people enjoy the noise and activities of children, others are irritated by them. A proportion of units for elederly people should be located at a distance from general needs housing. When shops and other facilities are included or nearby, the sheltered housing should be sited close to them.

8.06 Private sector
Housing for elderly couples and singles provided by the private sector are referred to as *retirement homes*. The facilities are similar to Category 1. Usually, there is no resident warden although there

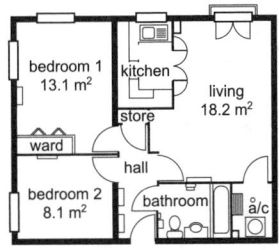

33.19 *Private sector retirement home with two bedrooms, Note the tiny kitchen and the lack of adequate storage space*

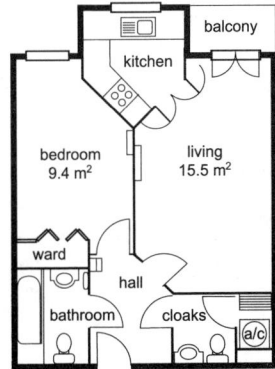

33.20 *Single-bedroom retirement home. For one bedroom, this has very generous sanitary arrangements, but again a singular lack of space to store a lifetime's possessions*

may be a manager on-site during office hours, and a system of calling a private emergency service when he or she is not there. Typical examples are shown in **33.19** and **33.20**.

9 ESTATE MODERNISATION
9.01 Local authorities have recently been building little new housing, but they still own an enormous stock of existing estates built over the last hundred years. Many of these are now decrepit and out of date. Significant funds and initiatives are therefore being directed towards the special problems of these estates. These initiatives include government-financed Estate Action Programmes, City Challenge projects, and Housing Action Trusts; as well as funding via the Housing Corporation for stock transfers to housing associations.

9.02 Many flat blocks built before the First World War, often by philanthropic organisations or Model Dwelling Companies, are characterised by too small floor areas, outdated internal planning with inadequate kitchens and bathrooms, and unsatisfactory means of escape. The building services are probaby obsolete, and central heating and thermal insulation absent. Some of these blocks, however, possess considerable architectural character, and have stable and supportive communities of residents.

9.03 Blocks built between the wars may also be lacking in modern services, heating, and insulation; but can be better planned internally and well-built structurally. Floor areas improved between the wars, but kitchens were usually still too small for modern requirements. External planning was simple, but with more communal space than is now desirable. Blocks from this period represent a vast investment in housing stock, with enormous potential for improvement into good-quality modern housing.

9.04 Since the Second World War, social housing has suffered from too many well-intentioned attempts to rethink design and planning from scratch. Consequently the last fifty years have seen widely differing forms of housing, many of which have proved dramatically unsuccessful. High-rise blocks of flats are only the most prominent and publicised of mistakes. Some of the medium-rise (five or six storey) deck access estates have proved even less satisfactory.

It is ironic that the dwellings in these large inner-city estates were built to comply with the good internal standards of Parker Morris. It is the external estate design that is hated and feared by the residents. Over-imaginative networks of decks, footpaths and confused and potentially dangerous open spaces present intractable problems of estate management, and fail to provide private and public open spaces appropriate for families with children.

9.05 Estate modernisation presents many varied, peculiar and acute problems. First, an investigation to establish what the problems really are has to be carried out. These are rarely simple, and vary widely from estate to estate. The people who understand the problems best are the residents, but they may need help to articulate them. Careful approaches and techniques under the general description of *community architecture* should be adopted to identify and address the tenants' concerns.

Architectural teams usually move onto the estate to conduct surveys, set up design surgeries, hold open meetings and distribute newsletters to reach their social clients.

9.06 After this consultation, designs and proposals can be worked up in close collaboration with the residents. The works needed to improve estates will be different in each case; but may include some or all of the following:

- Moving family units down to ground level, perhaps by combining flats on ground and/or first floors into larger flats or maisonettes, and subdividing large flats on upper floors into small ones
- Using unwanted external space to provide private gardens for the ground-floor units, with separate direct access from the public highway or estate road
- Remodelling the flat interiors, giving larger dining/kitchens and better bathrooms
- High-rise blocks that cannot be split up or effectively use entryphones can be provided with *concierge* systems; using a combination of electronic and human portering to provide 24-hour security
- Improving refuse arrangements, aiming to disperse rather than concentrate collection points
- Improving the fabric; adding thermal and sound insulation; adding pitched roofs on top of flat roofs; replacing windows with double glazing and controllable trickle ventilation
- Renewing the mechanical and electrical services; adding central heating; improving ventilation by putting extract fans into kitchens and bathrooms. Where there is district heating with a central boiler house and a history of problems, replacing with unit systems in each dwelling. Consider heat-retrieval systems
- Consider converting some blocks to integrated sheltered housing. In these cases, entrances and gardens must be clearly distinguished and separated
- Communal external spaces to be reduced to a minimum or abolished
- If all family flats and maisonettes have their own private gardens, communal children's play space is unnecessary. If not, it must be carefully sited as it may cause nuisance to neighbouring dwellings. Playspace in local parks is preferable if they are nearby; or situated in clearly public spaces such as the squares in some large estates. However, in all these cases a lack of security is often perceived; ideally, family accommodation without sufficient private open space should be avoided
- Estate roads, car parking and emergency vehicle access need to be replanned. Parking within the curtilage may be possible if the front gardens are deep enough; otherwise provide small parking bays in clear view of the dwellings they serve. Basement parking and car courts at the rear of blocks are to be avoided on grounds of inadequate security
- Replan pedestrian routes in order to eliminate unnecessary footpaths and to maximise natural supervision from the dwellings of all routes
- Adding lifts if over three storeys high
- Perhaps enclosing open balconies and staircases, and splitting up long balcony access buildings into smaller blocks, preferably with no more than 10 or 12 flats in each. This will make them more secure and manageable
- Adding entryphones to privatise staircases

10 BIBLIOGRAPHY

Homes for today and tomorrow ('The Parker Morris Report') HMSO 1961

MHLG/DoE Circulars
36/67 Housing Standards
1/68 Metrication of Housebuilding
82/69 Housing Standards for Old People

DoE Bulletins and Papers

Design Bulletins
DB1   Some aspects of designing for old people (1968)
DB36   Space in the home (1968)
DB12   Cars in housing (1971)
DB13   Safety in the home (1976)
DB14   House planning; a guide to user needs (1968)
DB23   Housing for single people 1 (1971)
DB24   Pts 1 & 2 spaces in the home, bathrooms, WCs and kitchens (1972)
DB25   The estate outside the dwelling (1972)
DB26   New housing and road traffic noise (1972)
DB27   Children at play (1973)
DB29   Housing for single people 2 (1974)
DB30   Services for housing; sanitary plumbing & drainage (1974)
DB31   Housing for the elderly; the size of grouped schemes (1975)
DB32   Residential roads and footpaths. Second edition (1992)
DB33   Housing single people (1978)

HDD Occasional papers
2/74   Mobility housing
2/75   Wheelchair housing

Housing Corporation
Scheme Development Standards (1995)
Good practice guide, incorporating design & contracting Guidance (1990)

National House Building Council
Standards, vol 1, chapter 1.2
The home – its accommodation and services (1991)

The Building Regulations 1991
See Table IX for a list of Approved Documents and their relevance to housing.

British Standards
Many British Standards are cited in the Approved Documents to the Building Regulations. Many more BSs that are not statutorily cited apply to housing. These cannot all be listed here, but especially important (and cited in Approved Document B) is:

BS 5588 Part 1 1991: Means of escape in case of fire for houses and flats.

Local Authorities
Each planning authority is obliged to publish a Unitary Development Plan. The first of these have been published and many others are in Draft consultative form. UDPs incorporate planning standards for housing density and other matters.

Selwyn Goldsmith, *Designing for the disabled*, third edition, RIBA, 1984
Alice Coleman, *Utopia on trial*, Hilary Shipman Ltd, 1985
Oscar Newman, *Defensible space*, The Architectural Press Ltd, 1973
Building Research Establishment, *Housing design handbook*, 1993
Access Committee for England, *Building homes for successive generations: criteria for accessible general housing*, 1992
Joseph Rowntree Foundation, *Designing lifetime homes*, 1997

34 Student housing and housing for young people

Liz Pride

CI/SfB: 856
UDC: 728.4
Uniclass: F856

Liz Pride is an architect, and an associate of MacCormac, Jamieson, Pritchard

KEY POINTS:
- *Student housing is often designed down to a price.*
- *Sometimes it is needed for conference accommodation, so has to be more luxurious.*
- *There is a growing demand for single-person housing.*

Contents

1 INTRODUCTION

1.01 This chapter deals with the design of accommodation for students, but is also relevant for other groups who are typically mobile (in respect of the length of time they stay in accommodation) and are young. The term 'college' is used to include universities and colleges of higher education.

1.02 Recent government legislation has resulted in considerable expansion in the provision of student housing, and a reassessment of the traditional design forms of accommodation. The trend is towards creating a varied accommodation portfolio which offers students choice in the type, standard and cost of housing. It also allows the college flexibility in the event of changes in course structure, the form of the academic year and, ultimately, the need to sell or lease out housing which becomes surplus to requirements.

1.03 The government no longer provides money for student accommodation; colleges generally require schemes to be self-funding through rents, and to act as collateral to raise development funds for future projects. The emphasis is consequently on reducing financial risk to the college, often reinforced by the need to complete construction in time for a new academic year.

1.04 The government offers no advice on the design of student accommodation, on the basis that colleges are so varied in character that any guidance would be too inflexible, and that policy should be developed at a local level.

2 STUDENTS

2.01 Conventionally, students are perceived as young, single, mobile, adaptable and have low incomes. Increasingly there is a need to cater for a broader range of people – for students with disabilities, for mature and married students and those with families, including single-parent families.

2.02 The characteristics which differentiate student accommodation from other housing are:

- Providing an appropriate environment in which to study as well as to live
- Providing opportunities for informal academic and social interchange
- Providing privacy and quiet where people are living in close proximity and are sharing facilities – most students will not have the opportunity to choose their neighbours
- There will be a proportion of foreign students and those attending short courses, who need to be helped to settle in quickly
- For many students it will be their first experience of living away from home and managing for themselves
- Most students dislike the sense of living in institutional surroundings, but many value the sense that they are a part of the college with a shared purpose and interests, and
- Lastly, the design of student accommodation offers the opportunity to give young people an experience of good-quality architecture which may create an awareness for the rest of their lives.

2.03 In the past much accommodation has been built with little reference to the views of the students themselves. Recent research reveals the following unsurprising preferences and concerns:

- Rent levels and value for money
- Safety and security
- Location in relation to other parts of the college, the town and to friends
- Comfort on a basic level – heat, light, hot water, clean communal facilities
- Reasonable room size
- Facilities for self-catering
- Private bathrooms, and
- Low noise levels.

3 TYPES OF ACCOMMODATION
Two issues define the character of the accommodation.

3.01 The number of students in each unit
In traditional 'halls of residence' or hostels, several hundred students might be accommodated in one building, usually in rooms off a common corridor. In the 'Oxbridge' model, buildings are divided into staircases each accommodating some four to ten students.

It is generally agreed that groups of five or six students function best socially, and so reduce potential management problems. Smaller groups may not get on where they have not chosen to live together; larger numbers are unlikely to form a cohesive social group.

3.02 The facilities provided in each unit
This relates particularly to catering facilities. In halls of residence central catering is provided elsewhere in the college. However,

many students prefer not to use such facilities all or some of the time; either because they dislike the fare provided or for reasons of economy. In hostels, flats and houses kitchens are provided for self-catering. Bathroom arrangements in student accommodation depend on whether the rooms are also intended for conference use; for this en-suite bathrooms are virtually obligatory.

Other facilities – laundries, bars, leisure facilities, etc. – will be provided where the student numbers are large enough to support them; or may reflect whether the rooms are let just for the academic terms or for the whole year. In halls and hostels there may be aspects of pastoral care by a warden, or of provision of services such as cleaning or bed linen.

3.03 Taken together, these two factors largely determine the degree to which the accommodation feels institutionalised or independent, **34.1**.

Note: A hostel is defined in the Housing Act of 1985 as:

'(a) residential accommodation otherwise than in separate and self-contained sets of premises, and
(b) either board or facilities for the preparation of food ... or both.'

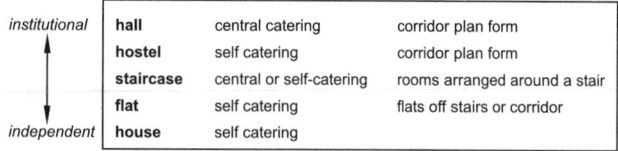

institutional	**hall**	central catering	corridor plan form
	hostel	self catering	corridor plan form
	staircase	central or self-catering	rooms arranged around a stair
	flat	self catering	flats off stairs or corridor
independent	**house**	self catering	

34.1 *Types of accommodation*

4 BUILDING FORM

4.01 Principal types
As stated above there are three basic forms of student residences, two of which can be further subdivided:

- Staircase, where a limited number of units at each level are served by a single staircase, **34.2**
- Linear corridor, where the number of study bedrooms served depend only on fire escape arrangements, **34.3**
- Corridor wrapped around a service core, **34.4**
- Flat or maisonette, **34.5** and
- House, **34.6**.

4.01 Circulation area
Corridor access schemes tend to have a higher proportion of circulation area than staircase schemes. In addition, it is difficult to bring natural light and ventilation into the corridors, and their design requires careful handling to avoid monotony.

4.02 Depth of plan
Deeper plans are more economical and are achieved by increasing the depth of the student room, or by providing internal bathrooms in the centre of the plan. Depending on the overall area, the use of the study bedroom may be restricted if it becomes too narrow – 2.4 m is a practical minimum.

5 STANDARDS AND REGULATIONS

5.01 The way in which standards are interpreted and applied to student accommodation varies in different parts of the country. There is also some duplication in legislation and confusion about the categories which apply to different types of accommodation.

5.02 Clarify the local authority's exact requirements at an early stage in the project. Standards have been rising over the years and colleges are beginning to look towards the future. Points to note are as follows.

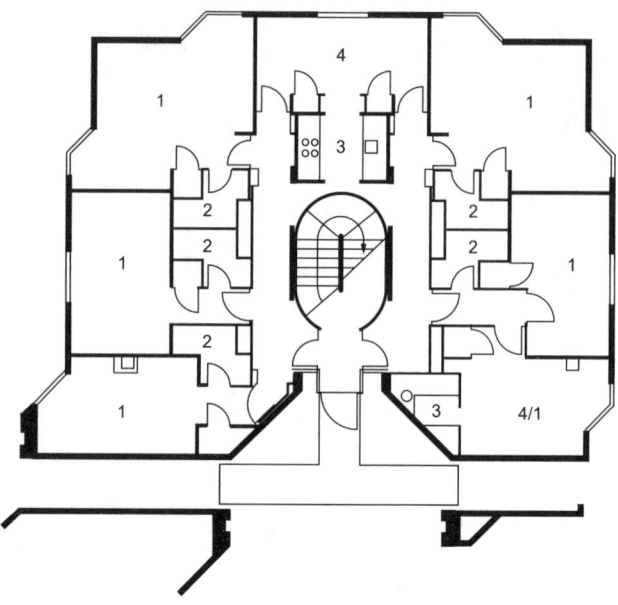

a *Ground-floor plan.*

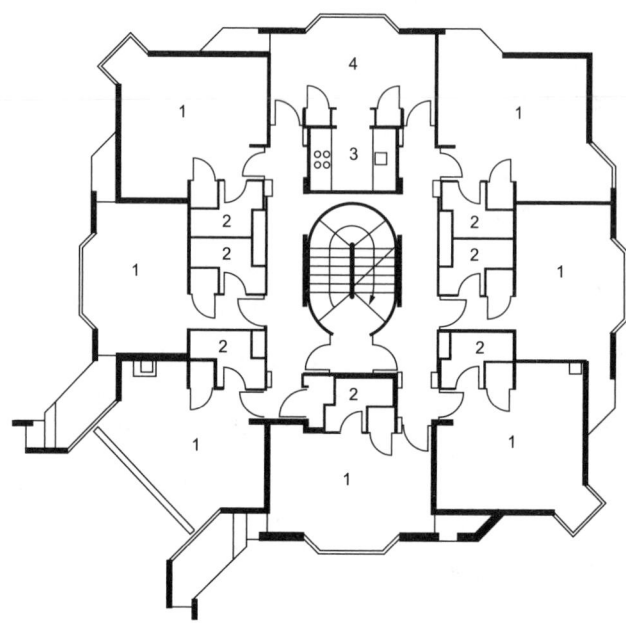

b *Plan of first floor, upper floors similar*

34.2 *Generic type: Hall with staircase arrangement. Jowett Building, Balliol College, Oxford. Architects: MacCormac Jamieson Prichard.*

Key: 1 study bedroom, 2 bathroom with shower (prefabricated unit), 3 kitchen, 4 dining room.

5.03 The Building Regulations: Part B: Fire Safety
Most schemes will be classed as 'other residential'. A typical project of three storeys requires stairs to be protected and lobbied from the bedsitting rooms, and to be ventilated. There will be a fire-detection system with smoke detectors in student rooms and heat detectors in kitchens; provision of extinguishers and fire blankets. If there is wheelchair access to upper floors, refuge lobbies are required adjacent to stairs to allow wheelchair users to wait for rescue in relative safety.

5.04 Consider at an early stage the design of fire doors and fire glazing, positions for extinguishers, detectors, call points, etc. to avoid an institutional feel and to reduce potential vandalism (extinguishers being let off, fire doors wedged open, etc.). The

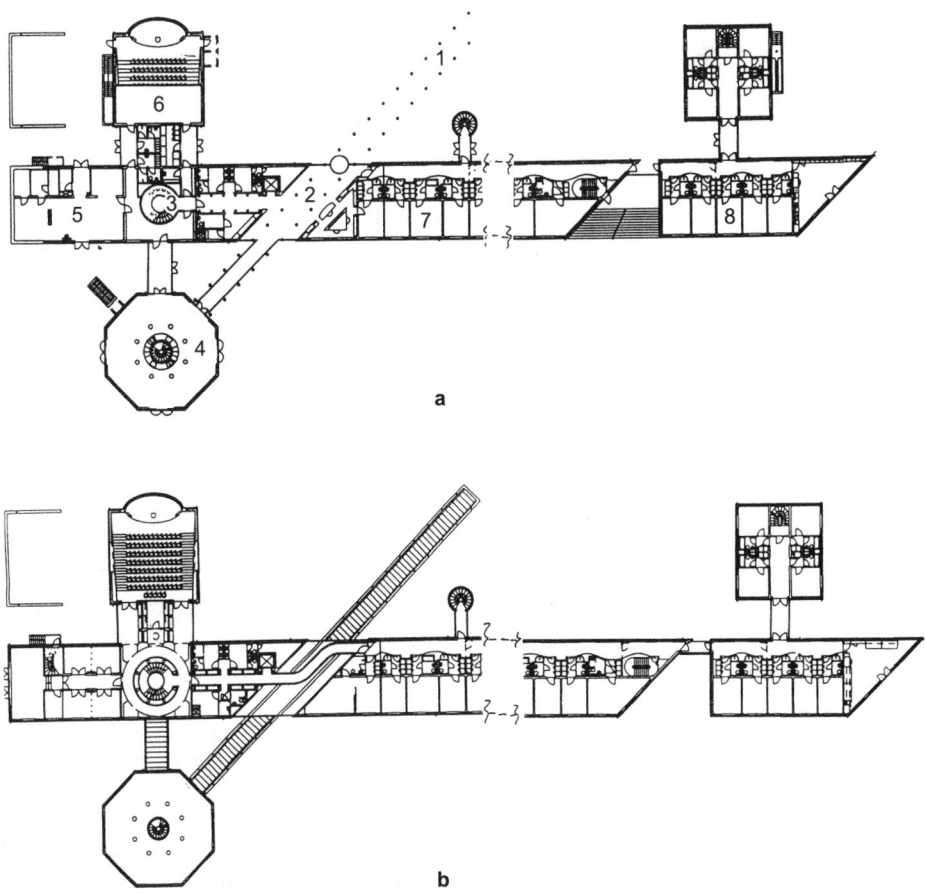

34.3 *Generic type: Hall of residence with a corridor arrangement. The Maersk McKinney Møller Centre, Churchill College, Cambridge. Architects: Henning Larsens Tegnestue Key: 1 entrance colonnade, 2 double-height entrance lobby, 3 stairs, 4 dining room, 5 kitchen, 6 lecture theatre, 7 student rooms for Møller Centre, 8 student rooms for Churchill College.* **a** *Ground-floor plan.* **b** *First-floor plan*

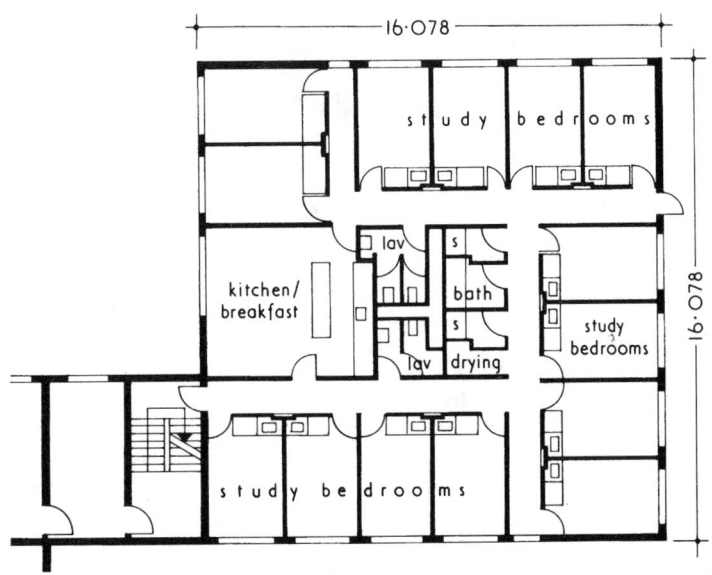

34.4 *Generic type, hall with corridor around a central sanitary core. Plan is repeated on four levels and in a number of blocks. Staircases are shared between each pair. This shows 14 study bedrooms with associated kitchen/breakfast and sanitary accommodation. Battersea Court, University of Surrey, Guildford. Architects: Building Design Partnership*

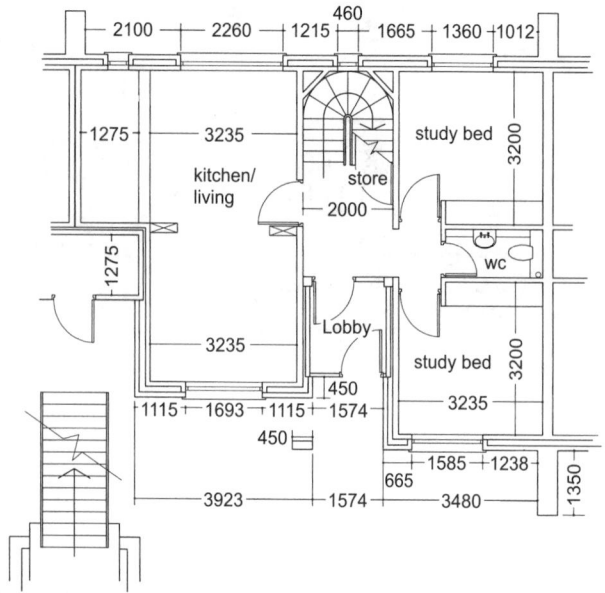

a *Ground-floor plan.*

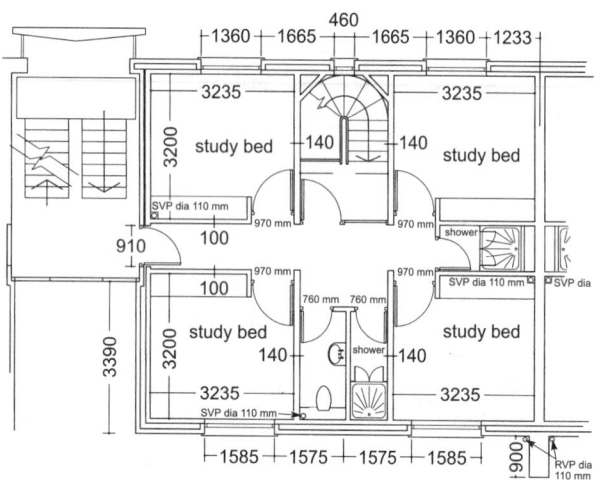

b *First-floor plan*

34.5 *Generic type: student flats/maisonettes. Six study bedrooms on two floors sharing kitchen/living rooms. Each maisonette has its own front door. Panns Bank, Sunderland University. Architects: Feilden Clegg Design.*

college should also consider its management arrangements in regard to fire safety in relation to the design proposals.

5.05 If it is planned to use accommodation for conferences, a Fire Certificate will be required and more onerous standards will apply. This is because the conference attendees, unlike the students, will not be familiar with the layout of the building. It is arguable that the Fire Certificate Standards provide for an appropriate safety level and should be met in any case.

Means of escape in case of fire is also covered by legislation for Houses in Multiple Occupation (see below). However, Department of Environment Circular 12/92 states that compliance with Building Regulations will ensure adequate provision for Means of Escape for normal use.

5.06 Part E: Resistance to the passage of sound

Part E applies only to 'dwellings', which include self-contained houses or flats designed for student use, but does not apply to more institutional forms of student residences such as halls or hostels. Noise is a major source of annoyance in student residences, because the use of bedsitting rooms for leisure, study and sleep contains inherent conflict. In nurses' accommodation shift working exacerbates the problem. There may be noise from other students, both inside and outside the building, from service ducts, lifts, badly adjusted door closers, common areas, telephones, etc. It is important to insulate each room to a high standard – 40 dB is appropriate.

5.07 Part F: Ventilation

The regulations apply to student accommodation. Shared bathrooms and kitchens are used intensively. In student accommodation bathrooms are often internal, so problems of condensation are common. Student bedrooms may be left unoccupied for long periods during the holidays, and adequate background ventilation is important.

Part M: Access and Facilities for Disabled People

Part M covers access and use of a building by disabled people and provision of sanitary conveniences. This includes people with mobility, auditory or visual disabilities. The 1999 amendment of Part M includes requirements for student accommodation in the form of 'traditional halls of residence' and in the form of 'dwellings' (e.g. houses and flats). Reference is also made to use of accommodation for conferences.

The Disabilities Discrimination Act 1995 and the Disability Discrimination (Employment) Regulations 1996 also impose obligations on Colleges which must be addressed.

Disabled people may be discouraged from attending college at all if there is insufficient provision for them. Ideally, their accommodation should be integrated with other students, and the need to visit friends should also be considered. This can be achieved, at least in part, if all ground-floor areas are made accessible to wheelchair users. Wheelchair lifts are only required to floors above a certain area, so they are often not required in 'flat' or 'staircase' forms of accommodation. Provision for ambulant disabled people will increase the area required for stairs and corridors. The local authority may require provision for disabled people under the Chronically Sick and Disabled Persons Act, which can be enforced through the statutory planning process. Early consultation regarding their requirements is essential.

5.08 Houses in Multiple Occupation (HMOs)

An HMO is defined by the Housing Act 1985 as 'a house which is occupied by persons who do not form a single household'. It is normally assumed that a single household is one whose members eat together; although if they are not related to each other this might not be accepted.

Department of Environment Circular 12/86 gives further advice on the definition and confirms that hostels are HMOs. Other types of student accommodation may not be, but this can only finally be determined with reference to case law. The local authority's Environmental Health Officer (who would be responsible for this area of legislation) should be consulted at an early stage. DoE Circular 12/92 gives guidance on standards which would meet requirements for HMOs under the Housing Act 1985. The guidance is 'advisory' only to allow local authorities to develop their own codes of practice. Even where student accommodation is not an HMO, the standards generally provide a good yardstick. One aspect of the requirements is that they increase where there are more than five students, and this may influence the size of units which the college chooses to provide.

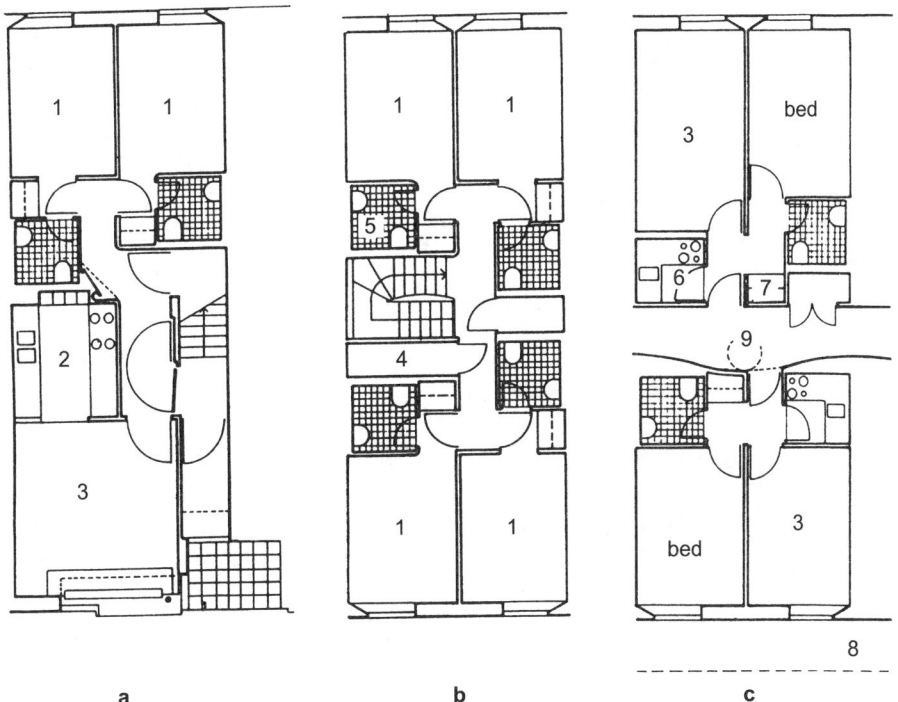

a   b   c

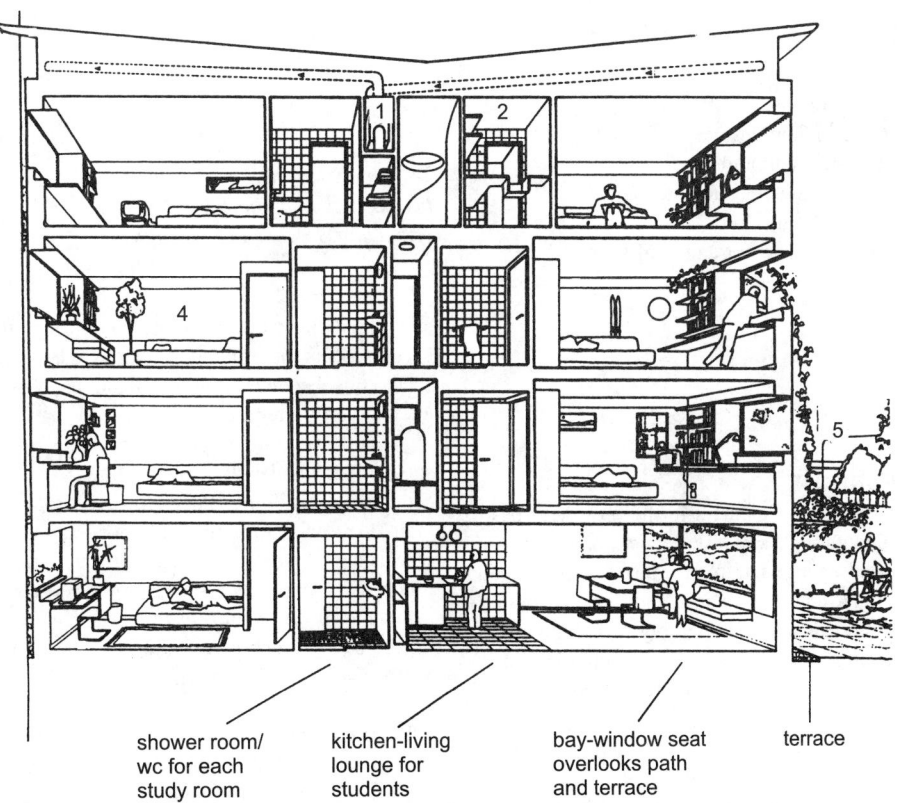

shower room/   kitchen-living   bay-window seat   terrace
wc for each   lounge for   overlooks path
study room   students   and terrace

d

34.6 *Generic type: terrace house plus self-contained flats Constable Terrace, University of East Anglia. Architects: Rick Mather Architects. Key:* **1** *study bedroom,* **2** *kitchen,* **3** *living/dining room,* **4** *services/storage/cleaners,* **5** *shower/WC,* **6** *kitchenette,* **7** *ventilated cupboard,* **8** *line of roof overhang,* **9** *rooflight to continuous corridor.* **a** *Ground-floor plan.* **b** *Plan of first and second floors.* **c** *Plan of third floor containing corridor accessed self-contained flats for two persons.* **d** *Isometric sectional view*

5.09 Local Authority requirements in relation to HMOs

These are likely to cover:

Storage and preparation of food – safety, convenience and hygiene:

- One sink and one full-size cooker are required for up to five students. The sink should have a bowl and drainer, or two bowls. The cooker should have an oven, grill and four rings. Smaller cookers can be provided if they are used by only one person
- Number of sockets
- Storage: $0.13\,m^3$ of refrigerator space per person
  $0.30\,m^3$ of storage for dry goods per person
- Provision and arrangement of worktops.

Small kitchens may be needed even if there is a central catering facility.

WCs, baths and showers – proximity to rooms, privacy and hygiene:

- Provide one WC, one washbasin and one bath or shower for each unit (i.e. each flat) or for up to five individuals. If five people share a WC it should be separate from the bathroom unless the HMO is small and the occupants tend to live as a single household.
- If there are washbasins in the rooms, the other amenities should not be more than one floor away.
- A WC and washbasin should not be further away than one floor or 30 m horizontally.

Means of escape and fire precautions
See above.

Space standards – fitness for human habitation, over-crowding:

- Room areas:
  Bedrooms/bedsitting rooms:
    one person: $6.5\,m^2$ minimum
    two people: $10.2\,m^2$ minimum
  Bedsitting rooms with cooking facilities: add $3.7\,m^2$
  Kitchen/dining room: $6.5\,m^2$
- Appropriate supplies of mains, hot and cold water
- Drainage
- Space heating
- Natural lighting
- Artificial lighting
- Refuse

6 THE STUDY BEDROOM

6.01 This is the most important element in the project; it has to facilitate a range of functions in a small space – sleeping, studying, relaxing, socialising and eating. The room must feel private and secure, with good light and ventilation and, ideally, with a reasonable view. The student should preferably be able to control the environment – heating, lighting, etc. – and should be able to impose her or his own personality on the room without damaging it.

Virtually all colleges now admit students of both sexes. While residential accommodation may be segregated, all should be suitable for either sex to allow for changes during the life of the building. Particular differences relating to this aspect include size and position of mirrors and provision of shaver points.

6.02 Room size and shape

The minimum practical area for one person, excluding any unusable circulation area by the door, is $10\,m^2$, **34.7**. Carefully consider the proportions of the room, alternative furniture layouts, positions of door, window, washbasin, built-in cupboard, sockets

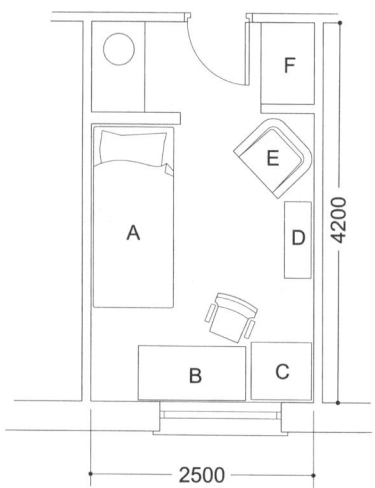

a *Without bathroom (area 10.5 m²).*

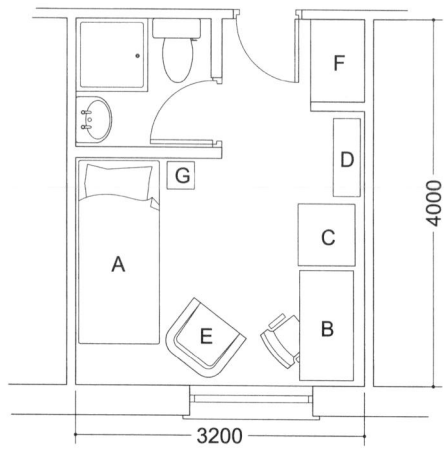

b *With en-suite shower/WC/basin (12.8 m²)*

34.7 *Study bedrooms: minimum planning dimensions. Key: A bed, B desk and chair, C chest of drawers, D bookshelves, E easy chair, F wardrobe, G table.*

and fixed lighting positions to ensure that the room will accommodate the different functions. The larger the floor area, the easier this becomes, but it should be possible to provide two alternative furniture layouts even with a room of minimum area. A rectangular proportion provides a better furniture layout than a square room and will tend to allow for a deeper (and so more economical) building plan. However, rooms should not be less than 2.4 m wide and preferably not less than 2.5 m to allow for a wheelchair's turning circle. Provide variety by changing the proportions, orientation or window positions in the rooms, and so avoid the institutional feel that identical small rooms inevitably have. Features such as window seats, balconies, alcoves, etc. add to the character of the room.

6.03 Furniture

Choose the furniture to allow units to work together – for example, a chest of drawers the same height and depth as the desk can be used as an extension to it.

Typical provision:

Bed: 900 mm × 2000 mm
May have storage drawer under. It usually doubles as a sofa. In some projects, a padded wall unit acts as a back rest, but this restricts changing the bed position.

Desk:	700 mm × 1200 mm minimum, 1800 mm length preferred. With drawers to one side, at least one large enough for A4 files. If the window cill is at, or slightly above, desk height it can be used as an extra shelf.
	If the student is using a laptop computer a standard desk should be adequate. However, a desktop computer needs a desk of 800 mm minimum depth.
Chest of drawers:	Height and depth as desk – 800 mm wide with three full depth drawers.
Wardrobe:	Often built-in and combined with a unit containing a washbasin. Full-height hanging space 600 mm × 900 mm minimum, with storage above. Lockable storage space at high level for belongings during holidays when rooms let out for conference use. A separate central trunk room should be provided for suitcases unless the wardrobe can accommodate these.
Shelving:	For books and possessions: 300 mm × 3600 mm total run – can be dimensioned to stack on top of the chest of drawers.
Bedside table:	May not be needed if shelves can serve the purpose.
Easy chair:	For reading.
Desk chair:	A comfortable chair, without arms.
Pinboard:	Generous provision to discourage use of walls.
Washbasin:	Separate the basin from the main area of the room, e.g. place it in a cupboard or a room divider. Provide sufficient storage for washing kit, make-up, a mirror, a light and shaver socket.

6.04 En-suite bathrooms

Colleges who are able to attract conference trade generally provide en-suite shower/WC/washbasin for the student rooms used for this. Students like these facilities but are often unable to afford the extra rent that they require. They add as much as 2.5 m² to the room area. **34.8** shows a particularly generous scheme of the staircase

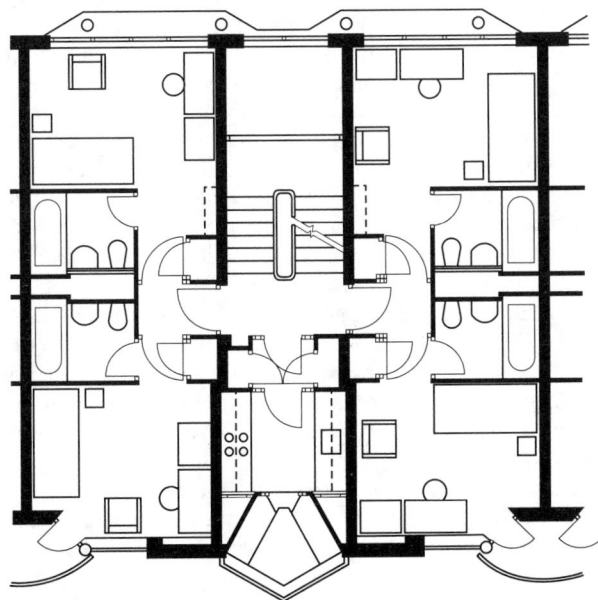

34.8 *Rooms designed to allow for alternative furniture arrangements, average size 11.5 m² excluding bathroom. Queen Mary and Westfield College, University of London. Architects: MacCormac Jamieson Prichard*

type. The cost of full bathrooms for each room is partly offset by providing a very minimum kitchen. Bathrooms can be supplied as finished 'pods', to be slotted into the bedsitting rooms. This allows the intricate work involved in the finishes and in waterproofing showers and floors to be carried out under factory conditions, and avoids delays to other trades on-site.

6.05 En-suite kitchen facilities

These are rarely provided. They would add approximately 3.3 m² to the room area.

6.06 Services

- *Lighting* General lighting should be supplemented by task lighting to serve desk, easy chair and bed positions.
- *Electric power* A minimum of three double sockets will be required for equipment, which may include television, kettle, computer, stereo, hair drier, light fittings, radio, clock, etc. Sometimes there is a limitation on the maximum allowable current to prevent electric fires being used. Alternatively, the supply may be via a prepayment meter. In any case, the supply to the building should be adequate for any foreseeable load.
- *Heating* The provision and control of heating will depend on the college's strategy for energy conservation and for charging. Background heating may be provided within the rent, with the facility to boost heat within each room for an extra charge.
- *Communications* Provision of television aerial sockets, data sockets, cable trunking and telephone sockets are increasingly common.

With all services, access for maintenance and meter reading should be arranged, where possible, without the need for access to the student rooms.

6.07 Students with special needs

There are two aspects to be considered:

- Accommodation for disabled students, preferably integrated with other students
- Access for disabled students to other areas, to allow them to visit friends etc. Current legislation is discussed above.

Some rooms will be more appropriate for accommodation by disabled students than others, e.g. those close to teaching and other central facilities and rooms on the ground floor. Most projects will not include lifts for wheelchair access, but can still be designed to give wheelchair access to the ground floor.

A room designed specifically for wheelchair users should allow a free turning circle of 1500 mm. Such rooms should be designed with space to store the unused wheelchair without obstruction.

Other variations to standard rooms include:

- Desk height to clear wheelchair, i.e. minimum 760 mm clearance to underside
- Shelving between 700 mm and 1300 mm above floor level
- Sockets, switches and ironmongery at 1000 mm above floor level
- Sinks to clear wheelchairs at 760 mm above floor level, or adjustable
- Window-opening gear
- Good lighting and bold colours for the partially sighted
- Minimum clear door openings 900 mm, and
- Telephone socket.

6.08 Larger study bedrooms

Where cost is not so much a consideration, a larger study bedroom has the advantage of greater adaptability and zoning, **34.9**.

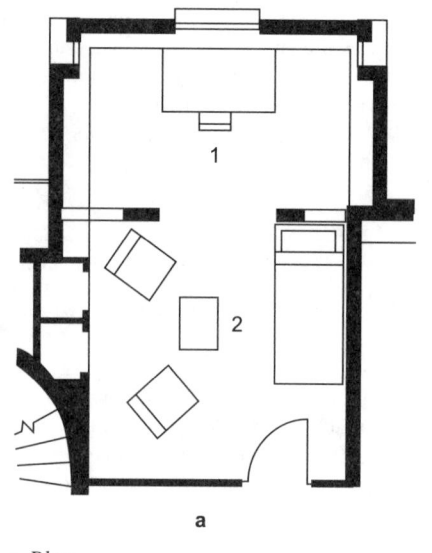

a *Plan.*

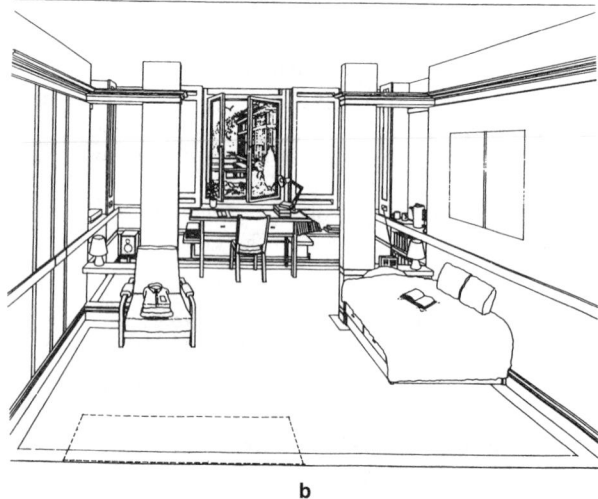

b *Perspective*

34.9 *The larger study bedroom can be zoned: 1 study area, 2 sleep and relaxation. The Garden Quadrangle. St John's College, Oxford. Architects: MacCormac Jamieson Pritchard.*

7 KITCHEN/DINING ROOMS

7.01 Kitchens provide opportunities for casual encounters, conversation and friendship; they play a crucial part in helping social groups to form. This in turn leads to a sense of ownership of the accommodation, so that greater care is taken of it. In staircase schemes, kitchens can be arranged to overlook stairs and halls, providing further opportunities for interaction and a degree of security/informal policing. Kitchens are more likely to be used for socialising than common rooms; the dining areas should be designed to allow all the students in the unit to eat at the same time, preferably with some room for guests.

7.02 The area needs to be functional, easy to clean and to permit several people to prepare food simultaneously. The size provision of kitchen units will depend on the number of students and the intensity of use – students resident throughout the year or those in accommodation far from central facilities will use kitchens more intensively. The trend is towards self-catering. As a guide, a minimum length of work surface of 3600 mm, including cooker and sink, will be sufficient for six people. Circulation space between units should be 1200 mm minimum. Provide cookers and sinks in line with HMO guidance (see above). A microwave oven

should be provided as well as a conventional cooker, and a freezer in addition to a refrigerator. Each person will need one shelf. Lockable cupboards should be provided for each student for storage of tins, dry goods, etc.

7.03 Services
● *Electric power* Provide sockets at worktop and at low level. Some colleges meter and charge for cookers separately from rents to discourage wasteful use of energy (a lone potato baking in the oven for an hour). Incorporate a time switch with cookers and hobs in case they are left on by mistake.
● *Lighting and mechanical extract* These should be good. Also provide generous opening windows positioned to avoid noise and smell annoyance to neighbouring study bedrooms.
● *Fire* Use heat detectors not smoke detectors (which would go off as soon as cooking starts!), and provide a fire blanket and extinguisher.
● *Refuse* Place bins for easy cleaning and emptying.

7.04 Kitchen/dining rooms may be extended to incorporate a living area. This should be large enough to allow each of the residents an easy chair, and to provide coffee table(s) and a television.

7.05 Special needs
Where the kitchen serves disabled/wheelchair accommodation, it should be designed accordingly, with appropriate types of sink, worktop, cooker, taps, handles and storage etc. Provide sufficient area for the wheelchair's turning circle of 1500 mm and at the dining table. If this kitchen is also used by students without special needs, some duplication may be necessary.

7.06 Sanitary accommodation
Bathrooms, showers and WCs are usually designed to the minimum practical area. Simpler arrangements will be easier to construct to a good standard and are less likely to cause problems in cleaning and maintenance. Students are not always careful in the way they use the facilities; overflowing and leaking showers are a common problem. Service ducts should be carefully located and detailed, with access from corridors. Factory-assembled bathroom 'pods' have been used successfully (see above).

Consider proximity to study bedrooms and acoustic and visual privacy. Provide good mechanical ventilation, especially in showers, and moisture-resistant light fittings (avoid glass). Include a shelf, towel rail and hooks for clothes and wash kit in the shower area but out of the way of the shower itself. A mirror, with a light/shaver socket over may also be required. The layout of WCs should take account of the type of toilet rolls and holders and sanitary towel disposal units used by the college, all of which can be bulky (see Chapter 3). Even where a shower tray is used, the floor in any shower room should drain to a floor gully. Thermostatic balanced pressure mixers should be provided to showers, to avoid risk of scalding.

Numbers of facilities should generally be at least in accordance with HMO guidance: one WC, washbasin and bath or shower for every five students. A provision of one to every three students would be better. Some people prefer baths to showers: provide a mixture to allow choice. WCs should be separate from bathrooms unless serving very few people. These facilities are in addition to washbasins in student rooms. Any facilities to be used by people in wheelchairs should have WCs to BS 5810 and showers either without trays or with sunken trays fitted with duckboards.

8 OTHER FACILITIES
Provision will depend on the number of students living in the accommodation and on the availability of facilities elsewhere. They may include the following.

8.01 Laundry

Where accommodation is in 'houses', provide a washing machine in the kitchen. Elsewhere, include a laundry with washing and drying machines of a robust commercial type, coin operated with emergency cut-off switch, plus a sink for hand-washing clothes, facilities for ironing and folding clothes and seats for waiting.

Laundries can be noisy, smelly and humid and are liable to flooding. There is also a risk of theft where clothes are left unattended. Choose the location carefully and provide good lighting, ventilation and a floor gully. Fittings and equipment should allow easy maintenance. Services such as electricity supply, hot water, etc. must be adequate for the level of use.

8.02 Cleaners' storage

In 'flat' or in 'house' type accommodation, where cleaning is the students' responsibility, a tall cupboard will be sufficient. Where the college arranges cleaning provide central stores for the cleaners within a reasonable distance from all the accommodation. In larger schemes there should be a store on each floor. Stores contain a sink and slop hopper, shelves for storage, space for cleaning equipment and materials, a refuse bin and a place for the cleaners' coats and belongings.

8.03 Telephones

An adequate number should be provided on both external and internal networks. Locate them so that they do not cause annoyance to the occupants of neighbouring rooms. Provide space for a small seat/shelf.

8.04 Other possible facilities

- Central common room/television room/party room (these tend to be little used)
- Central computer room (less likely now that more students have direct network access)
- Music practice room
- Games room
- Trunk store
- Porters' lodge, and
- Guest bedrooms.

8.05 Refuse collection

Consult the refuse collectors at the preliminary design stage; and include their separation requirements for recycling. The size of any bin store will depend on the number of students and the frequency of collection. Bins filled by staff may be cleaner and tidier than those used by students, but all are potentially untidy, smelly and attract vermin. Stores should be easy to access, especially by refuse collectors, and to clean and maintain. Locate to reduce nuisance to residents, and provide good ventilation. Provide the equivalent of a domestic bin for each three students.

8.06 Parking, loading and unloading

Both the local planning authority and the college are likely to have parking policies. Each situation has its appropriate provision. Students attending an out-of-town campus are more likely to have cars. Security is important: both for guarding against theft and for personal safety. Parking areas should be overlooked and relatively close to entrances. Inconvenient locations lead to management problems with students and staff. Soft and hard landscaping should be used to improve the appearance of parking.

Each student arrives at the start of the academic year with large quantities of luggage. They nearly all arrive on the same day; provide sufficient space near to the building entrance for unloading several vehicles simultaneously.

8.07 Security

This is a major issue in student housing, especially in women's hostels, nurses' accommodation and in higher education colleges. Design to address issues of personal attack, vandalism and theft. Provide overlooking of parking areas, paths and entrances, and of common areas within the building (for example, from kitchens) giving informal checks on intruders. Nurses are particularly vulnerable because they work shifts and may return home late at night. Good external lighting is essential.

Provide both the entrance doors to blocks and the doors to study bedrooms with security locks. Swipecard systems are used instead of keys, although they are more expensive. Each student has a card programmed to pass the appropriate doors which expires at the end of their stay. There are always problems with lost keys; choose a system where replacements are readily available and where stolen keys can be rendered unusable.

Entryphones are increasingly common, with handsets in each room. Provide spy holes in study bedroom doors.

9 CONFERENCE USE

9.01 Some colleges attract conference trade during the vacations and this affects the design of accommodation, especially that located near other college facilities – central dining, lecture halls, etc.

- En-suite bathrooms will be preferred
- A Fire Certificate will be required and higher fire standards will apply
- A higher standard of fittings and finishes may be required, including provisions for telephone and connection to data networks
- Lockable storage provided for students' possessions, and
- Central linen stores.

35 Homes for old people

Ian Smith

Before his retirement Ian Smith was a partner in Hubbard Ford and Partners

CI/SfB 44
Uniclass: F442
UDC: 725.513

KEY POINTS:
- *Because of other available accommodation, the people needing care are increasingly infirm*
- *There is a need for activities for residents other than watching TV*

Contents
1 Main elements of the plan
2 Relationship between elements of the plan
3 Planning allowances
4 Planning examples
5 Room data and space requirements
6 Building equipment and fittings
7 Furniture
8 Bibliography

1 MAIN ELEMENTS OF THE PLAN

The design of homes for old people should create a homely, comfortable and friendly atmosphere. The importance of avoiding an institutional character is stressed in most design guides and instructions to architects.

This chapter deals with the design of homes in which the residents are in need of special care and attention. Sheltered housing and grouped flatlets for old people are described in Chapter 33 on general housing. The special facilities provided may vary, depending on the degree of infirmity and mobility of the residents, but the basic relationship between the main elements of the plan are common to all homes for old people.

The main areas of the home are:

- The residents' rooms and closely linked bathrooms and lavatories
- Dining room, lounges and rooms for other communal activities
- Kitchen, storage, washing up and service areas
- The administrative rooms, matron's office and medical room, and
- Staff accommodation for both resident and day staff.

2 RELATIONSHIP BETWEEN ELEMENTS OF THE PLAN

35.1 shows how the main areas of the building are interrelated. The aim should be to encourage social contact, but at the same time to preserve individual privacy. The residents' rooms are often grouped round a small sitting room and services area containing a bathroom and lavatories. Circulation routes to the communal lounges and dining room should be as short as possible, although routes through the residents' groups should be avoided. Communal areas may either be centralised or divided between the residential groups, but most homes have a main dining room, which should be close to a sitting area. The administrative offices should be close to the entrance hall, and, if possible, within easy reach of the kitchen. Staff accommodation should be provided in self-contained flats with separate outside entrances.

3 PLANNING ALLOWANCES

Typical accommodation allowances are given in Table I.

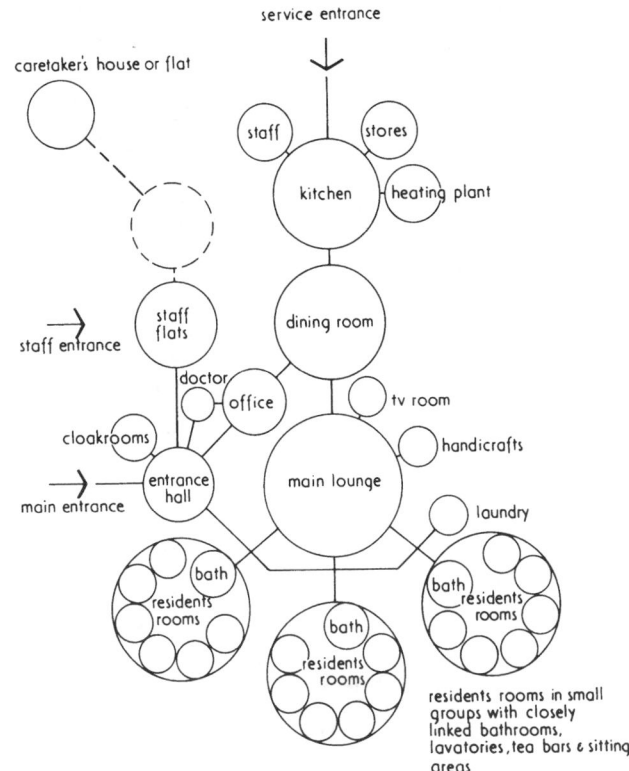

35.1 *Relationships between elements of the plan*

Table I Planning allowances

Accommodation and facilities		
Residents	Single bedsitting rooms	9.6 m² — 12 m²
	including private WC	15.3 m²
	Double bedsitting rooms	14.8 m² — 16 m²
	Bathrooms and lavatories	
	Sitting areas and tea bars	8.8 m²
	Stores	
Communal rooms	Entrance hall and visitors' cloakroom	
	Lounges	2.3 m² per person
	Dining room	1.5 m² per person
	Handicrafts or sewing room	15 m²
Kitchen	Larder and dry store	12.15 m²
	Food preparation and cooking	42.50 m²
	Washing up	15 m²
	Cloakroom and non-resident staff room	12 m²
Administration	Matron's office	11 m²
	Doctor's room	10 m²
	Visitors' room	10 m²
Ancillary rooms	Sluice rooms	6 m²
	Laundries	20 m²
	Linen storage	8 m²
	Cleaners' stores	4 m²
	Box rooms	8 m²
	Boiler and plant room	25.30 m²
	Garden store and WC	10 m²
Staff accommodation		
Self-contained flat for matron		70 m²
Self-contained flat for assistant matron		60 m²
2 staff bedsitting rooms		12 m²
Staff bathroom		
Staff kitchen		6 m²
2 staff garages		
Staff lounge		12 m²

NB: Room areas based on typical 40-person home

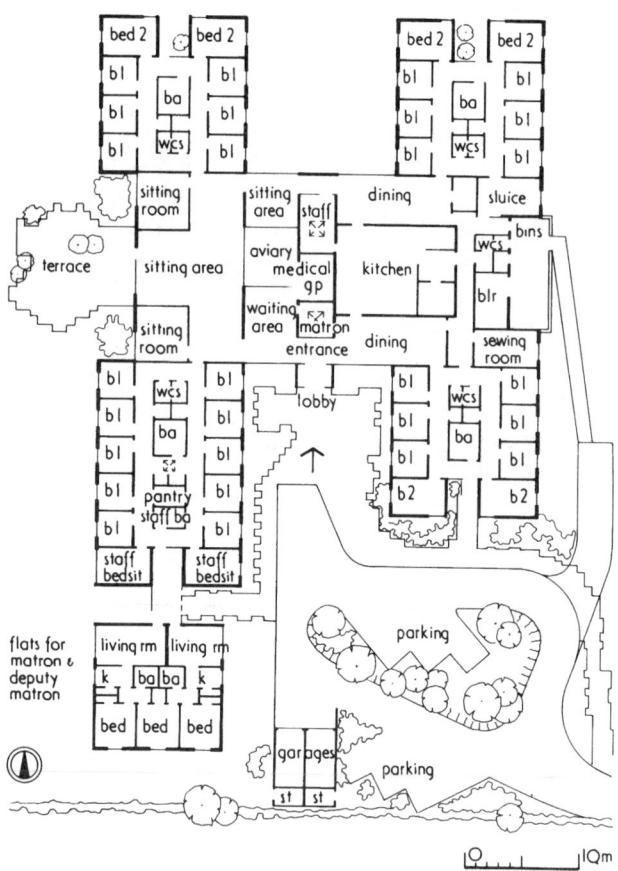

35.2 *Plan of Glebe House, Southbourne*

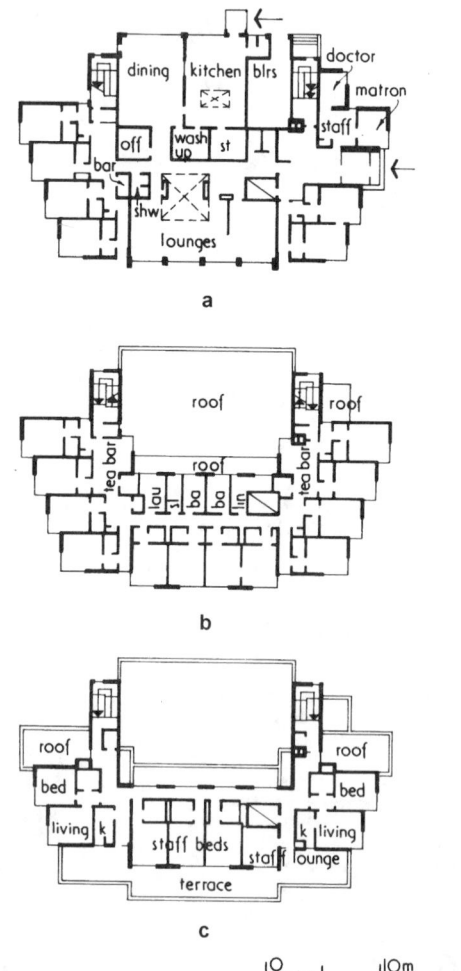

35.3 *Maidment Court, Dorset.* **a** Ground-floor plan. **b** Plan of first and second floors. **c** Third-floor plan

4 PLANNING EXAMPLES

The plans of two typical homes are shown in **35.2** and **35.3**.

5 ROOM DATA AND SPACE REQUIREMENTS

Typical layouts are given for single rooms, **35.4**, and double rooms, **35.5**. These layouts, from DHSS Building Note 2, with rooms of varying proportion, show ways of providing a flexible arrangement within clearly defined sleeping/sitting areas. With narrow rooms, corridor circulation is reduced to a minimum, but other types may well be suitable where a different overall plan-form is chosen.

6 BUILDING EQUIPMENT AND FITTINGS

6.01 Some of the information below repeats material in previous chapters. It is also included here because of its importance for this building type.

6.02 Elderly people should be encouraged to do as much as possible for themselves. To facilitate this, the design of the accommodation and appliances should take into account the limitations imposed by age.

6.03 Taps

Choose taps that can be manipulated by arthritic fingers. Surgeon's taps are not recommended, however, as in extreme cases ordinary taps can be modified to provide a similar facility. Within one building, it is sensible to maintain consistency as to the location of

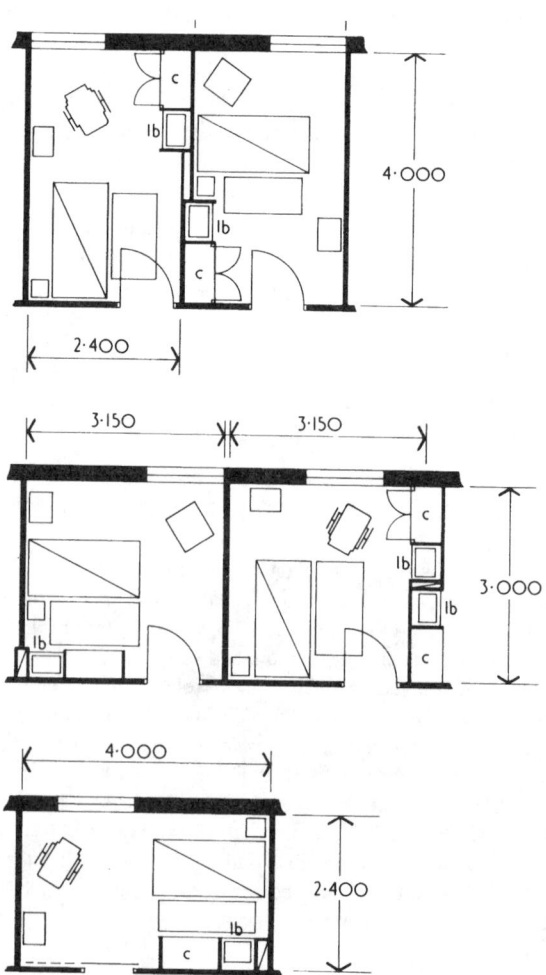

35.4 *Room data and space requirements for single rooms*

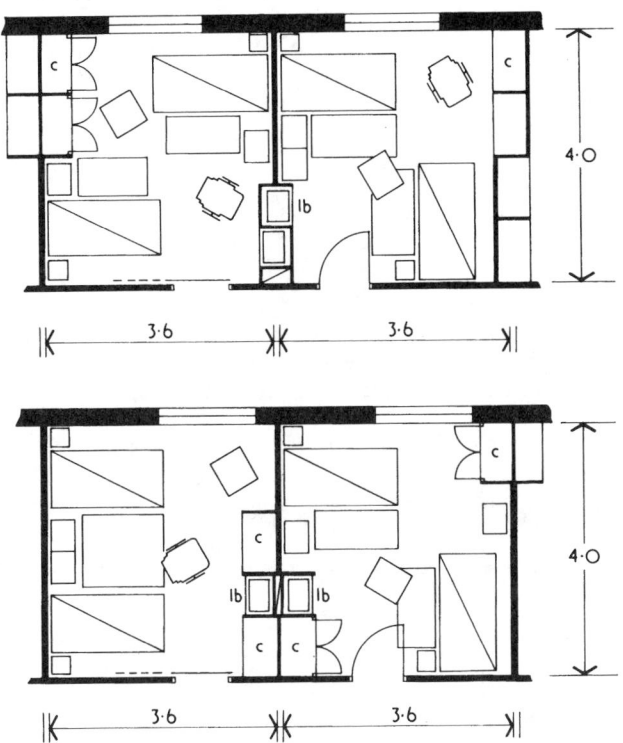

35.5 *Double room requirements*

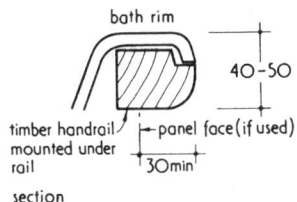

35.6 *Bath rim adapted for easy gripping*

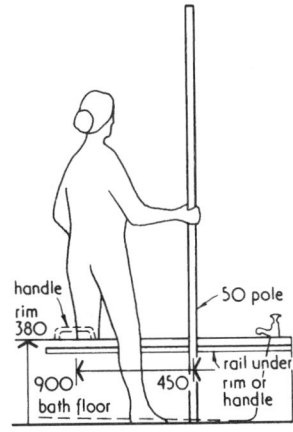

35.7 *Aids for getting in and out of the bath: pole, handle and rim. Maximum height of rim from floor 380 mm*

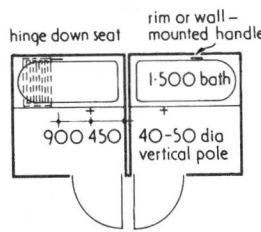

35.8 *Plan of bathrooms showing handing to suit people with disability of either right or left leg, and position of pole aid*

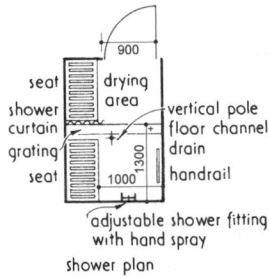

35.9 *Plan of shower room showing seats and aids*

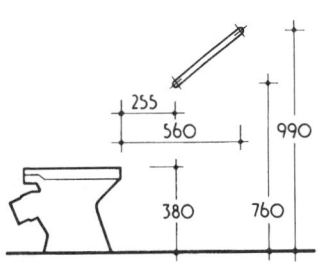

35.10 *Inclined rails mounted on walls of WC*

hot and cold, e.g. hot always on the right as is now provided in current standards. In addition, the tops should always be boldly colour-coded. It is hoped that in the near future a standard for additional tactile identification will be introduced.

6.04 Washhand basins and baths

Washhand basins should be fitted with their rims between 800 and 850 mm high. Bathrooms should be large enough for undressing and dressing, and for someone else to lend a hand. Low-sided baths are available, as the rim, which should be easy to grip, **35.6**, should not be higher than 380 mm from the floor. Alternatively, the bath may be set with the trap below floor level. It should have as flat a bottom as possible and should not be longer than 1.5 m; lying down is not encouraged. Grab handles and poles should be provided as in **35.7** to help getting in and out. A seat at rim height is useful for sitting on to wash legs and feet. Bathroom and lavatory doors should open out, with locks operable from the outside in emergencies, **35.8**.

6.05 Showers

Some old people find showers more convenient to use than baths, **35.9**. If the floor of the compartment is of smooth non-slip material with a fall to a drain of 1:40, there is no need for a tray with an upstand to be stepped over. The compartment should be well heated, with pegs for clothes on the dry side, divided from the wet with a shower curtain. The water supply should be automatically controlled to supply only between 35°C and 49°C. The shower head should be on the end of a flexible hose, with a variety of positions available for clipping it on. WCs should have a seat height of 380 mm, and handles provided as in **35.10**.

6.06 Cupboards

Shelves and cupboards should acknowledge the limitations of elderly people. The clothes cupboard rail should be mounted 1.5 m from the floor, and the cupboards should be at least 550 mm deep, **35.11**, **35.12**.

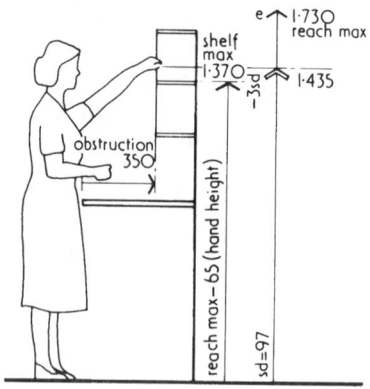

35.11 Maximum reach over worktop

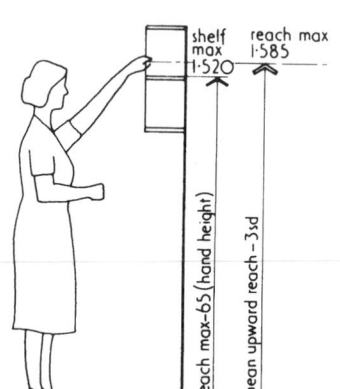

35.12 Maximum reach to unobstructed wall-mounted cupboard

35.13 Table and sitting worktop design, giving height and thigh clearance

35.14 Standing worktop design, giving height of working surface and reach forward to fittings [scale consistent with 3613]

7 FURNITURE

7.01 Easy chairs

A variety of chair types should be provided in sitting and common rooms, to ensure maximum comfort for all the old people. Seats should not be too low, as this makes the chair difficult to get out of; but if too high, the feet may end up off the floor. A height between 400 mm and 430 mm is about right, with footstools available for those with extra-short legs. A seat depth between 410 mm and 470 mm is ideal: any more and cushions become necessary. The back should be angled at 28° to the vertical, and high enough to support the head, for which an adjustable pad is useful. Armrests 230 mm above the seat at the front facilitate getting up, but if lower at the back, make sewing and knitting easier. There should be a gap under the seat to allow the heels to be drawn right back when rising. Generally, the padding should not be too soft and generous, as this can put strain on the tissues rather than allowing the bone structure to support the body.

7.02 Tables and dining chairs

Occasional tables in common rooms should not be lower than chair seat height. Dining tables should be 700 mm high, and used with chairs having a seat height of 430 mm and a depth of 380 mm. There should be a gap for the thigh between the chair seat and the underside of the table top of at least 190 mm, **35.13**.

7.03 Worktops

Comfortable reach to worktops are shown in **35.14**.

8 BIBLIOGRAPHY

David M. Boswell and Janet M. Wingrove, *The handicapped person in the community*, Tavistock Publications and Open University Press, London, 1974

BS CP 96 *Access for the disabled to buildings, Part 1 General recommendations*, BSI, London, 1967

Cheshire County Council, Department of Architecture, *Made to measure: domestic extensions and adaptation for handicapped persons*, Chester 1974

Chronically Sick and Disabled Persons Act 1970

DHSS Joint Circular 12/70

Chronically Sick and Disabled Persons Act 1970, HMSO, London, 1970 (explanatory circular)

DOE Joint Circular 92/75, *Wheelchair and mobility housing, standards and cost*, HMSO, London, 1975

Julia Farrant and Alice Subiotto, *Planning for disabled people in the urban environment (research study by the Planning Research Unit, Department of Urban Design and Regional Planning, University of Edinburgh)*, Central Council for the Disabled, London, 1969

Selwyn Goldsmith, *Designing for the disabled*, 3rd edn, RIBA Publications, London, 1976

Selwyn Goldsmith, DOE, HDD Occasional Papers 2/74 and 2/75

Mobility housing and wheelchair housing (*The Architects' Journal* 3.7.74 and 25.6.75)

36 Hotels

Fred Lawson and John Rawson

CI/SfB: 85
UDC: 728.51
Uniclass: F852

KEY POINTS:
- *Standards are tending to rise all the time*
- *Value for money is a prime concern*
- *Ancillary facilities are a major generator of business*

Contents

1 INTRODUCTION

1.01
Hotels provide a service to their customers whose requirements are:

- Clean, quiet and comfortable rooms
- Good food
- Good service, and
- Value for money.

The financial viability of the project depends on keeping capital requirements and operating costs to a minimum. This depends largely on the standards of planning, construction and equipment of the building. For the architect the two most important technical decisions are:

- Location of the main kitchen, and
- Provision of an efficient duct system.

Hotel staff requirements are substantial and the payroll absorbs about one third of the turnover. The designer must ensure maximum working efficiency in order to minimise their number. The ratio of staff to guests varies from 1:10 in a budget hotel to 1:2 or more in a luxury hotel. Facilities are required for staff changing, toilets, canteen, security and personnel offices; in some cases even some living accommodation may be required. Designing the hotel needs to be done in the closest consultation with those who will run it, in order to maximise their efficiency.

1.02 Hotel classification
Virtually all countries classify hotels but in different ways: most have some sort of symbol or 'star' system, as proposed by the World Tourism Organisation. The grading defines the space and facilities available. There are several broad categories:

- Hotel: including city, resort and sport hotels, defined by star category
- Motel: originally simple low-rise developments suitable for the motorist
- Inn, auberge, gasthof: originally a bar with some rooms attached
- Boarding house: with simple rooms generally let for a week or more

- Bed and breakfast establishment: accommodation with no restaurant and
- Holiday villages: often with self-catering accommodation.

2 GENERAL CONSIDERATIONS

2.01 Orientation
During the preliminary design stage consider the relationships of different parts of the hotel and the effects of noise and pollution. However, restrictions imposed by the site, particularly in a town, may determine the building's orientation regardless of other considerations. See para **3.04** for orientation of bedrooms.

2.02 General arrangement
Determine and agree pedestrian and vehicular access at an early stage. The main hotel entrance is a critical commercial feature determining the location of the main frontage.

Site value usually determines the height of the development. In a cheap rural setting, costs favour a low building. There are savings in foundation and structural work, lifts are not currently obligatory up to three storeys (although this may change with disabled access regulations, and could incur considerable later costs). There may be also be savings in maintenance costs. On the other hand, long corridors with more staircases are needed, and engineering services may be more expensive. On a town site, cost may dictate a high building. A compromise has to be arrived at, taking into account planning restrictions, rights of light and any legal restrictions caused by adjacent properties. The most common arrangement is a tall bedroom block over a larger area of low public rooms. High site costs may lead to the high-value frontage being let as commercial space such as shops. Bedrooms can be located above another such as offices or flats. Various relationships between the two sorts of accommodation – bedrooms and public areas – are shown diagrammatically in **36.1** to **36.4**.

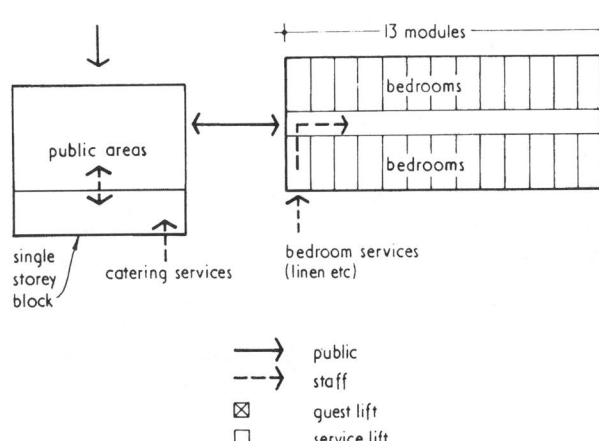

36.1 *Simple bedroom block with detached single-storey catering building as in primitive motels. No cohesion or rationalisation of circulation*

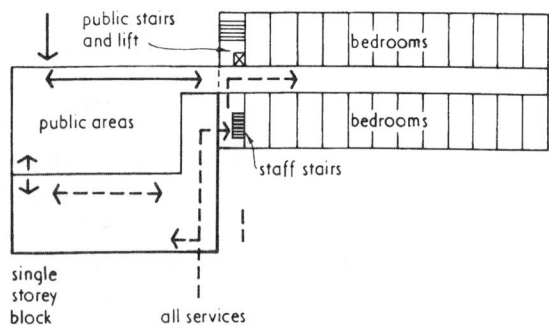

36.2 *Simple rationalisation of circulation. All bedroom and catering services collected in controllable zones and routes. Public areas are single storey*

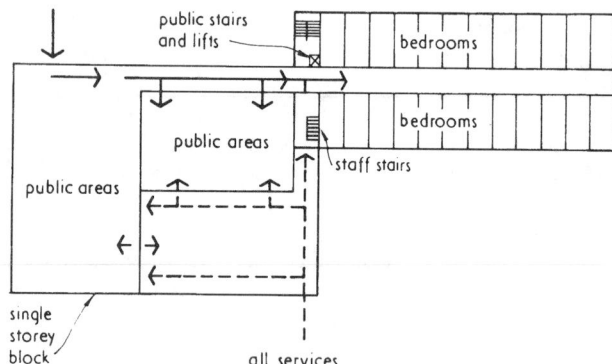

36.3 **36.2** *after extension. More public and function rooms added, still single-storey. These may be appropriately subdivided. Guest and staff circulations should not mix*

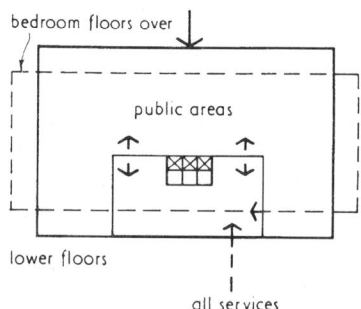

36.4 *The same circulation principles apply where bedrooms are built over public areas. It is simpler to plan with vertical rather than horizontal circulation. Note grouping of lifts to serve guests on one side and staff on the other*

2.03 Circulation

The general circulation layout should facilitate movement and, as far as possible, provide for the separation of guests, staff and maintenance personnel. This is not just to avoid disturbing the guests, but also to enable efficient servicing. Separate the circulation of resident and non-resident guests; for instance, by providing direct access to restaurants and banqueting halls. This avoids congestion in the main reception area and gives better control and supervision. A diagram of main circulations is given in **36.5**, although this is not to be taken as a layout in itself. General relationships covering the whole hotel are shown in **36.6**.

Corridors are wasted space. Circulation in public spaces should wherever possible be through areas of other use such as lounges or shopping precincts, or have a special use, such as lobbies.

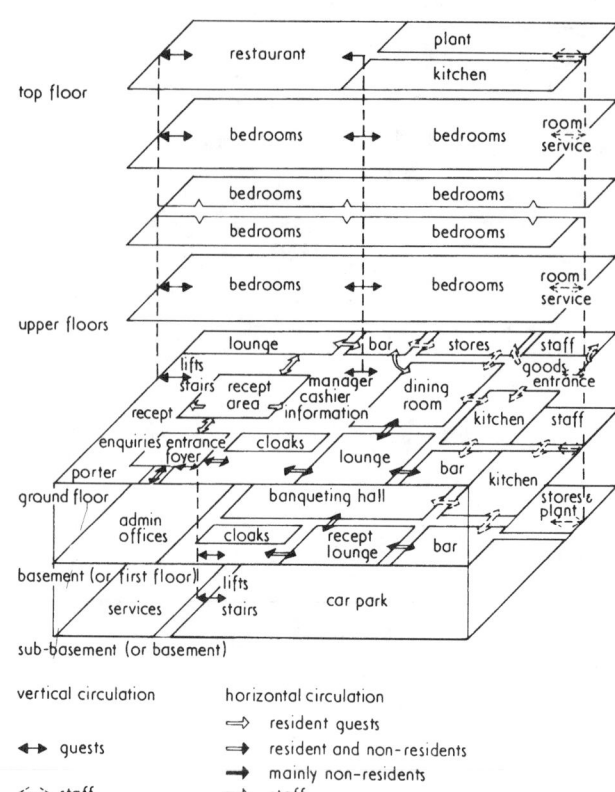

36.5 *Circulation diagram showing desirable relationships, not intending to imply any particular layout*

2.04 Staircases

Staircase design is dictated by fire escape requirements. The main stairs should be beside the lift bank to enable guests to find them easily, with secondary stairs at the end of each corridor. Some ramps may be required for guests using wheelchairs.

2.05 Lifts

Lifts are expensive. They should be wider than they are deep to facilitate entry. Tough surfaces are required to resist damage by baggage. The main lift bank must be visible on entering the reception area. Specialist design of the lift system may be necessary. Additional service lifts may also be required for housekeeping and room service. There are often one or two service lifts to every three guests' lifts, and these open onto service lobbies on each floor. At least one lift should be large enough to take furniture such as a bed or bath, or a stretcher case as accidents and illness occur in hotels, and it may be preferable not to use the public areas in such event.

2.06 Environment

The internal environment must be attractive, engender confidence in the operation and leave a memorable impression. It must be safe, resist damage and be easy to clean and repair. It must provide maximum space and facilities at minimum cost.

2.07 Lighting

Lighting should assist in providing the appropriate environment, differentiate spaces, and illuminate signs and hazards, etc. as appropriate. It may change with time of day. Light sources are likely to be incandescent in areas used by guests. Spotlights and coloured sources may be used. Fluorescent tubes will be used in work areas for economy.

2.08 Noise

Noise will be generated both outside and inside a hotel, and the rooms within will need to be protected from it. External noise

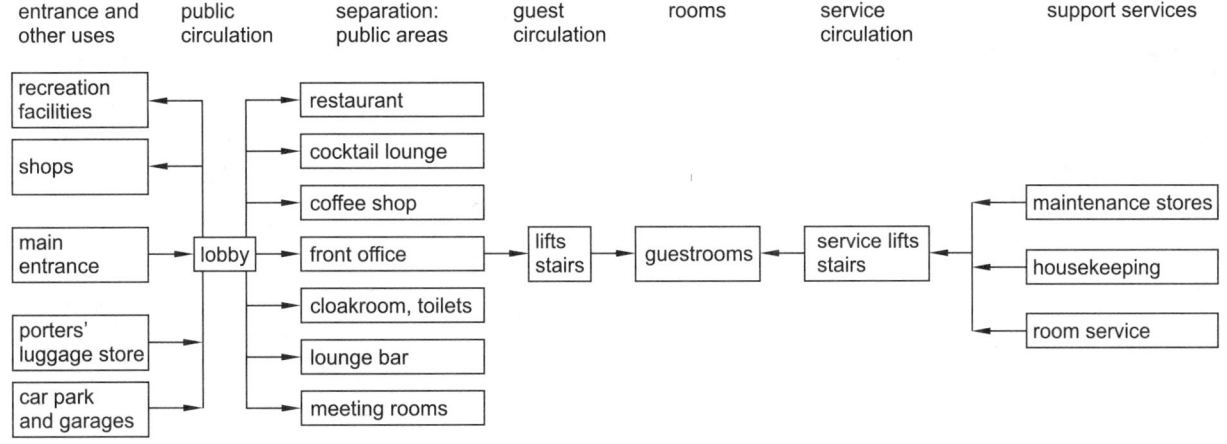

36.6 *Circulation and relationship diagram*

comes from highways, low-flying aircraft (near airports), building sites, car parks, swimming pools and play areas, and hotel servicing such as refuse collection and even guests arriving to stay or to attend conferences, etc. Internal noise comes from public rooms such as discos, service areas such as kitchens, televisions and telephones in bedrooms, and from mechanical services. Doors can bang and keys are rattled in locks. All piped services are liable to create or transmit noise, ventilation ducting such as bathroom ventilation can reduce sound insulation, and lifts should not be next to bedrooms.

The first line of defence against noise is careful planning: placing noisy areas away from quiet ones. The second, insulation, generally depends on heavy construction of walls and double windows. The third is the reduction of reverberation to lower sound levels, the absorption of impact noise with soft finishes, and the prevention of door slamming. Machinery should be on resilient mountings.

2.09 Safety
Safety covers not only design but also how buildings are maintained and used. Accidents are likely to occur when these are poor. As hotels are used by the young, old and infirm, designers must be specially careful in detailing and in choice of materials. Some points to check are:

● Planning: safe positioning of equipment, with adequate working space
● Floors: non-slip, easily cleanable, effective marking of steps and edges
● Doors: check door swings for clearance and visibility
● Windows: must be safe to clean, and not open accidentally
● Lifts: level properly, landings adequate
● Bathrooms: correct positions of fixings, non-slip floors, electrical safety
● Kitchens: ditto, work areas to be well lit, and
● Machinery: properly guarded, and maintained.

2.10 Fire precautions
There have been many tragic accidents in hotels in recent years. Take fire precautions very seriously for the following reasons:

● The occupants will be transient, and unfamiliar with the building
● Many guests will be elderly, very young, disabled, tired or inebriated
● Large numbers of people will be asleep in separate bedrooms, each needing to be warned and evacuated separately
● There may be large numbers of people in the public rooms, creating crowd-control problems

● Fire loading may be high, due to the furnishings present, and kitchens, garages, boiler houses, etc. are high risks, and
● Staff are on duty intermittently, and few may be there at night.

The common causes of hotel fires are kitchens, smoking, and electrical. The three principal precautions are as follows.

Structural protection
This is to ensure that the building does not collapse before people can escape from it; also that escape routes are protected from fires in adjacent rooms. Combustible materials may be prohibited in escape routes.

Active protection
This covers the installation of fixed equipment to detect fires, raise the alarm, and put them out. There must be access for fire brigade vehicles and appliances, and provision of firemen's lifts. Special water storage tanks and fixed fire mains and hydrants may be required. Automatic sprinklers, electromagnetic door releases, dampers in ventilation ducts and portable fire extinguishers may all be required.

Means of escape
Current building regulations require:

● Maximum travel distances from bedrooms or points in public rooms to a protected escape route
● Alternative directions of escape, normally at least two from any point
● Protected escape routes to be of adequate width and unobstructed
● Final escape must be free; not into a closed courtyard, and
● Maximum times are laid down for the complete evacuation of the building.

36.7 illustrates the main requirements of the regulations.

2.11 Security
Security involves the protection and control of property, and the safety and supervision of all persons occupying, entering or leaving. In planning, consider the following:

● Control of property, i.e. prevention of theft. This covers strength of construction of doors and walls, burglar alarms, CCTV, and controlling unauthorised exit through fire escapes
● Control of entry to bedrooms. This covers access to windows and balconies, and the lock mastering system. Access of guests, cleaners, manager and security personnel have to be controlled, and locks have to be changed regularly to prevent later access

36.7 *Requirements for means of escape (see also Chapter 42).*

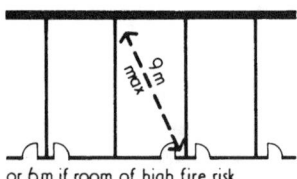

a *Maximum allowable travel distance to the doorway from the most remote corner of the room.*

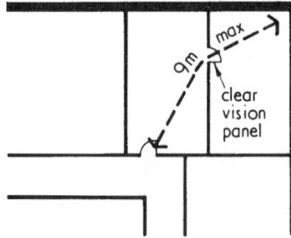

b *In multi-room suites no single cross-room dimension should exceed 9 m.*

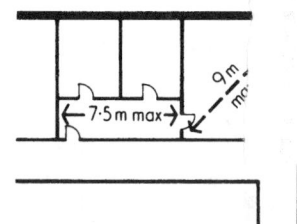

c *In multi-room suites any associated private corridor limited to 7.5 m long.*

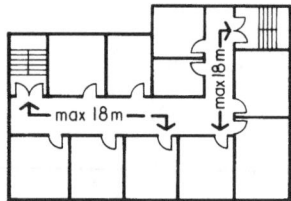

d *Stage 2 escape; no room exit further than 18 m from entrance to protected escape route.*

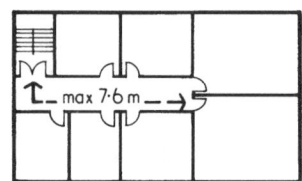

e *Dead-end corridors limited to 7.6 m long*

using old keys. Electronic card key systems facilitate frequent code changes

- Provision of safes and strongrooms for valuable items, both in bedrooms and centrally
- Surveillance of everyone entering or leaving. Entrances must be planned so that they are always watched. Side or garage entrance routes must not by-pass reception desks. Goods entrances should have roll-down shutters
- Baggage handling and checking. Baggage rooms should be isolated and have explosion relief
- Security of hotel grounds. Motels, holiday village or condominium developments may have substantial grounds. Unclimbable perimeter fences and floodlighting are common. Intruder detection appliances may be used
- Ensure that criminals cannot escape by setting off fire alarms and using unsupervised fire exits.

2.12 Hygiene

Failure to maintain a proper standard of hygiene can lead to a hotel being closed down. The designer should specify:

- Impervious easily cleaned surfaces
- Facilities to prevent cross-contamination of food
- Control of ventilation and temperature
- Protection against flies, rodents or smells
- Means of washing food, utensils, and surroundings
- Sanitary, washing and changing facilities for staff, and
- Proper refuse storage and disposal.

2.13 Piped services

A hotel depends on having an economical ducting system. It must be of generous size, as short as possible, and with easy access to every part without going into bedrooms.

Large quantities of water are used for catering, boilers, swimming pools, cleaning, fire fighting and irrigation of grounds. Storage equal to 100 per cent of daily use is recommended. Drainage must be provided to carry all this away. The repetition of bathrooms lends itself to prefabrication of pipework. Heating systems for bedrooms must have local control. Refer to Chapter 44.

2.14 Communications

Space requirements for communications equipment are constantly changing. Equipment tends to get smaller, but services provided increase in number.

Telephones

A hotel will have separate groups of lines for guests and administration. They will normally go to a private automatic branch exchange (PABX). All bedrooms usually have a telephone; incoming calls via the operator, outgoing calls direct dialled, but metered and charged for by the hotel. There will be payphones in public areas and staff rest rooms. Internal extensions will be located in plant rooms, kitchens, serveries and bars, etc. and in escape routes. A direct line will be required for a fax machine. Phone systems will provide automatic morning alarm calls.

Public address

Public areas are often covered by a public address system for paging guests. Individual public rooms, such as discos or conference spaces need their own equipment. These can be used for background music.

Radio and TV

Normally by a central aerial system and coaxial cables to all rooms.

Computer systems

These are constantly changing, but many hotels have terminals in restaurants, room service areas, etc. so that the guest's bill is constantly updated and immediately available. Quick settlement of guests' bills is very important in business executives' hotels, where most of the guests check out at the same time in the morning.

Staff paging

There is usually some radio-based method of locating and contacting staff.

3 BEDROOMS

3.01 Bedrooms are the core of the hotel industry. For flexibility most rooms have a double bed or twin beds. Bedrooms normally have en-suite bathrooms. It may be assumed in preliminary calculations that the capital cost of a room will approximate to 1000 times its nightly rate.

3.02 Areas

Corridor widths and bedroom sizes are greater in more expensive hotels. In the preliminary design stage allow the following overall bedroom areas:

2-star: 20–22 m²
3-star: 25–27 m²
4-star: 30–34 m²
5-star/exclusive 36 m² min.

The ancillary areas that will be required to service these rooms are shown in Table I.

3.03 Bedroom corridors

Corridors in bedroom areas should be minimised. Widths vary from 1.3 m wide for 2-star to 1.8 to 2.0 m wide for 5-star. Costs usually dictate bedrooms both sides of corridors. Though a number of city hotels have been built high with central service cores surrounded by bedrooms, this is not economical owing to the quantity of circulation space.

To avoid an institutional appearance corridors should not appear too long. Fire regulations determine the positioning of escape stairs.

Access to all guests' bedrooms should be free of steps. At least 50 per cent should be accessible to disabled people.

3.04 Orientation

Take account of sunlight. Bedroom blocks with the long axis nearer north–south than east–west are preferable. Position bed-

Table I Service areas in m² according to number of guest rooms

	100 rooms	250 rooms	500 rooms	1000 rooms	Notes
Housekeeping and general storage	1.40	1.11	0.93	0.74	Hotel laundry requires a similar area. Most hotels use off-site laundry services
Administration department	0.46	0.46	0.37	0.28	

36.8 *Generic block plan forms:*

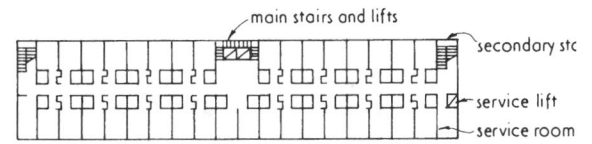

a *Linear room arrangement;*

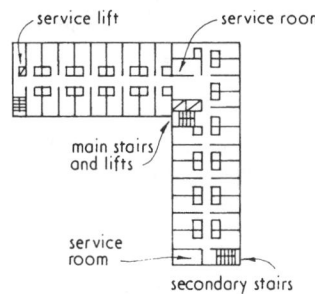

b *L-shaped room arrangement;*

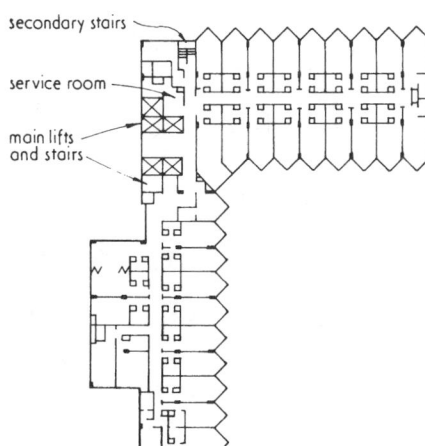

c *A US example of L-shape at Chicopee Motor Inn;*

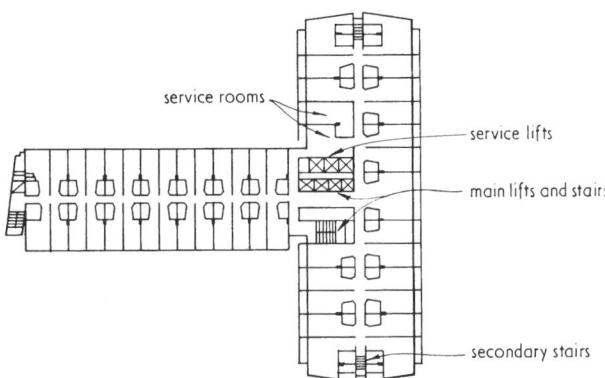

d *T-shaped arrangement at Royal Garden Hotel, London;*

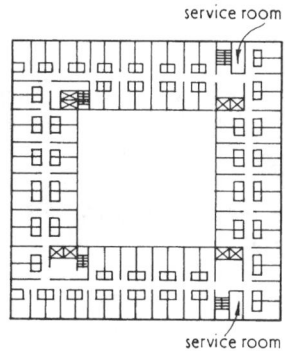

e *Rooms around a square court;*

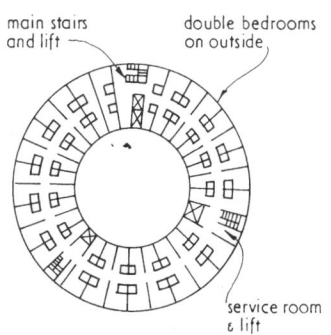

f *Rooms around a circular court at Ariel Hotel, Heathrow*

rooms to minimise noise from traffic, machinery, kitchens, and the hotel's public rooms.

3.05 Form

The bedroom areas are formed from relatively small units divided by separating walls, with many service ducts. On plan the block often forms an elongated rectangle, which can be straight or curved, or bent around a corner, or surrounding a rectangular or round courtyard. Various forms of bedroom blocks are shown in **36.8**.

3.06 Structural grid

Apart from site constraints, the structural framework and vertical services (including lifts) have to be related to the public rooms below, which will have a quite different structural grid. The structural module for the bedroom block will depend on the bedroom sizes required.

Bedroom layout should be related to staff capacities. One chambermaid can cope with about six bedrooms in luxury hotels and up to twenty or even more in lower-grade premises. Designing in multiples of her capacity per floor will minimise staff costs.

The length of each wing will be determined by the maximum escape distance in case of fire to a protected stair. Lifts and stairs are usually placed together as structural cores. Do not have lifts against bedroom walls because of noise transmission.

Bedroom sizes must be correct as they cannot be altered after construction. The structural design of high blocks is usually post and beam, while low blocks are usually cross-wall. Cross-walls have good inherent sound insulation, while post and beam save weight and therefore foundation costs.

3.07 Services

As standards are constantly rising, provide easily renewable fixed services in generously sized ducts. Preferably design bedrooms in handed pairs, so that the bathrooms are adjacent. This saves on duct space and reduces noise transmission, but take care to avoid noise through adjacent bathroom vent extracts or details such as recessed soap dishes.

3.08 Types of room

The ratio of singles to doubles will be decided by the client depending on expected use. Most hotels have 100 per cent doubles, but some hotels for business executives require many singles. Communicating doors between rooms maximise flexibility as suites can be formed; but fit two lockable doors in each wall for sound insulation. Ease planning problems at corners of blocks by having suites with a common lobby for two or more rooms.

Five per cent of rooms must be suitable for wheelchair users. This includes providing a much larger bathroom so that there is room to turn inside it in a wheelchair and transfer to the WC.

Be aware of the terminology used:

- Module: a single space, based on the structural grid, which can be used for any purpose including business. Used for financial feasibility calculations
- Bedroom: a single module containing a bedroom with its own bathroom
- Suite: two or more modules incorporating bedrooms, bathrooms and a separate sitting room
- Keys: total number of bedrooms and suites.

3.09 Bedroom planning

Rooms must be designed and furnished to facilitate access, cleaning, making up and servicing. The shape and to some extent the size will be governed by the placing of the bathroom. Most new hotels have individual bathrooms for each bedroom. There are three common arrangements:

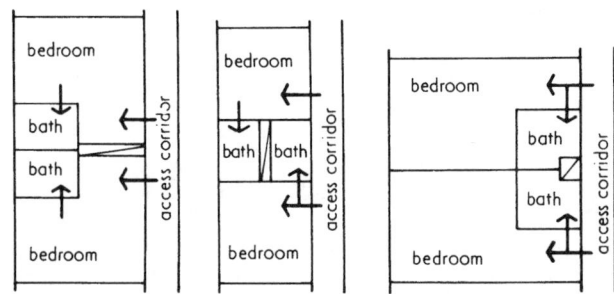

36.9 *Generic plan arrangements:* **a** *Bathrooms on external walls;* **b** *Bathrooms between bedrooms;* **c** *Internal bathrooms*

- *Bathroom on external wall* This gives natural ventilation to the bathroom, **36.9a**. The greatest disadvantage is that the service duct can only be inspected by passing through the bedroom. Also with bedrooms on both sides of the corridor two separate drainage systems are necessary. The amount of external walling is increased, the bedroom window is often recessed and light to the bedroom may be lost.
- *Bathrooms between bedrooms* The main disadvantage is the elongation of the corridor and the increased external wall, **36.9b**. If the bathrooms are adjacent one of them is internal, so the ventilation problem is only half solved, and access to the service duct is still through a bedroom. Few arguments commend this arrangement, but it may be unavoidable in conversions.
- *Internal bathrooms* These necessitate a lobby, **36.9c**, but it is generally used for the furnishings and so can be subtracted from the bedroom area. It can help with sound insulation from corridor noise. The bathrooms will require artificial lighting and ventilation. But the external walling and the corridors are minimised. This is the most common layout.

36.10 and **36.11** show typical double and single rooms in more detail, while **36.12** shows a twin-bedded room of non-conventional shape.

3.10 Terraces and balconies

These are pleasant but costly. They lead to an increase in the volume of the building, and to problems of security, wind and waterproofing. A raised threshold is always needed, and guests

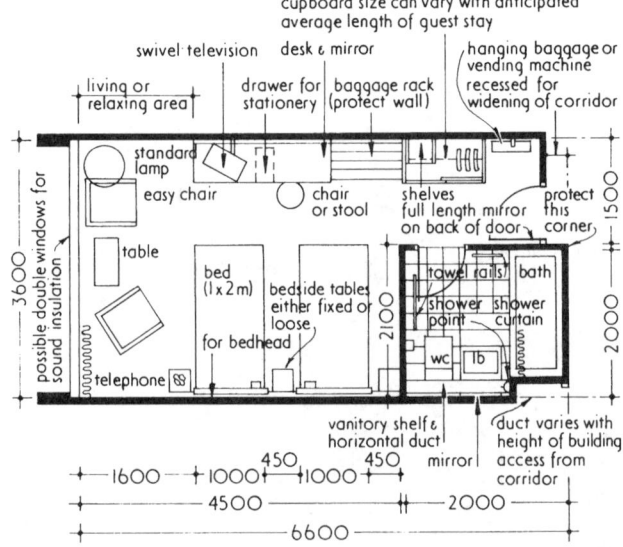

36.10 *Twin-bedded room with with clothes storage and dressing table along party wall. Size varies according to site constraints and standard of accommodation*

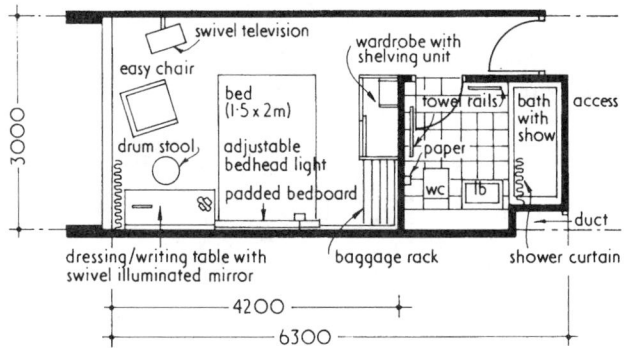

36.11 *Layout for single bedroom. Note double bed for use as double room if required*

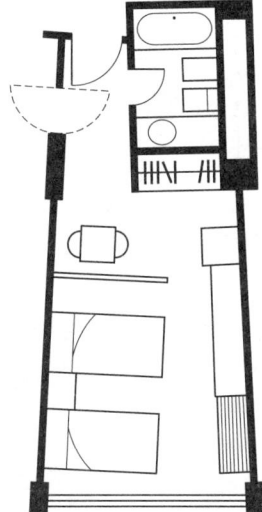

36.12 *Twin-bedded room*

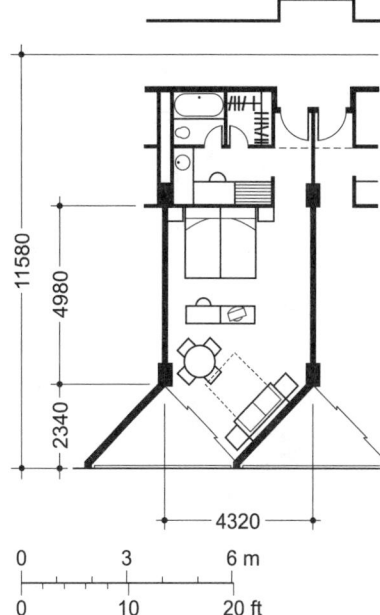

36.13 *Bedroom in a saw-tooth facade hotel*

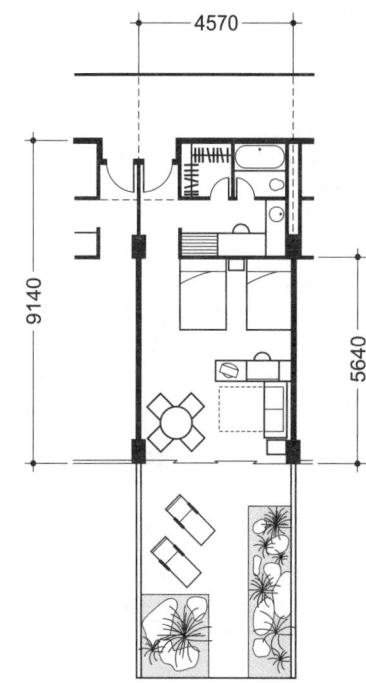

36.14 *Bedroom with large terrace*

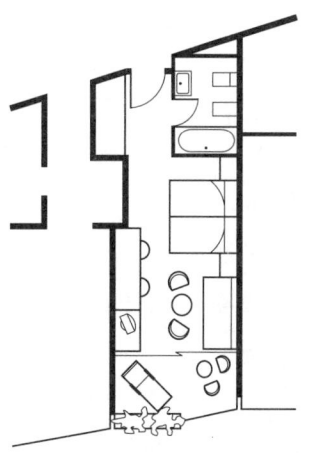

36.15 *Bedroom with small terrace*

may slip or trip, causing claims for damages. It is wise to restrict them to rooms with outstanding views, and to those in higher price ranges only. **36.13** to **36.15** shows examples of hotel rooms with such features.

3.11 Furniture and fittings

General

Furniture can be free-standing or built-in, and it can be bought from the domestic market or specially commissioned. Requirements will vary depending on the length of stay of the guests, and on the prices to be charged.

Free-standing furniture, particularly if of standard design, is cheap, flexible, easy to maintain and available in many varieties. Fixed furniture saves space and can facilitate cleaning by being fixed clear of the floor. It can help with sound insulation between rooms, but, on the other hand, it may transmit noise from doors, drawers and hangers being moved. It is regarded as a fixture and hence as a capital investment.

Hotel furniture must be robust, and if fixed, firm. Moveable fitments should be few, particularly in motels where control is more difficult than in conventional hotels with one entrance. It has been known for everything to be stripped from a room including the television set and beds. In any case electrical equipment, such as hair-driers, are usually permanently wired-in, and television sets can have all their controls in bedside fitments. **36.16** shows the space requirements of all the common items of furniture.

When a room needs to be redecorated it will be out of commission. Walls and ceilings should be of materials that can be

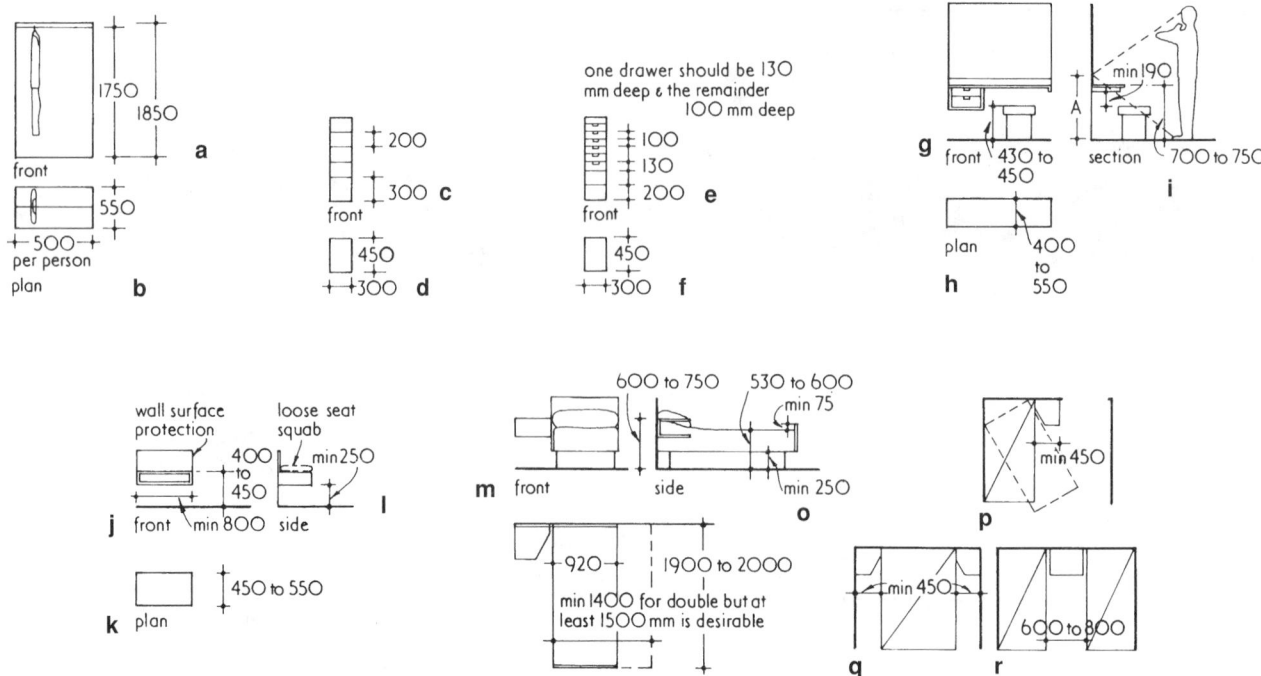

36.16 *Space requirements for hotel bedroom furniture. Note: the dimensions for wardrobe, shelf and drawer units are minimum clear internal dimensions. **a** Wardrobe front – per person; **b** Wardrobe plan; **c** Shelf unit front; **d** Shelf unit plan; **e** Drawer unit front; **f** Drawer unit plan; **g** Dressing/writing table front; **h** Dressing/writing table plan; **i** Dressing/writing table section. Dimension A must not exceed half eye height to achieve full-length view. For combined dressing and writing use the minimum table top area is 0.6 m²; **j** Luggage rack front; **k** Luggage rack plan; **l** Luggage rack side; **m** Bedside table and single bed front; **n** Bedside table and single bed plan; **o** Bedside table and single bed side; **p** Bedside table for single bed; **q** Bedside tables for a double bed; **r** Bedside table for twin beds*

easily cleaned. Carpets can be of modular squares so that worn areas can be replaced. A small increase in the cost of furnishings can be a good investment. The main types of accidental damage are cigarette burns and people sitting on wall-hung fixtures. Horizontal surfaces should be as heat-resisting as possible, and fixtures should be very firmly fixed, or provided with legs. Catches should be strong and simple, and doors may have to be prevented from opening too far. A large proportion of a hotel's income is spent on staff and maintenance. The designer should seek to reduce these.

One of the chief reasons for needing cleaning and eventual redecoration is smoking by the guests. Modern practice is to maintain some rooms solely for smokers, to minimise the problem for the other rooms.

Beds
These must satisfy a number of requirements:

● Comfort
● Adequate dimensions
● Durability
● Ease of movement for making up
● Ease of dismantling for storage
● Absence of creaking, and
● Good appearance, including bedhead which may be a fixture.

Positioning is important: generally singles are located parallel to a wall and doubles have the bedheads against one of the party walls. The opposite, singles with the head to the party wall, or doubles with the beds parallel to walls, the so-called studio room layout, use more space.

Beds are now 1 m wide for a single and 2 m × 1.5 m for a double, but the size varies with the degree of luxury. For appearance, a height of 300 to 400 mm, including mattress, is best. For ease of making, however, as low beds cause fatigue and

backache, a height of 530 to 600 mm or even 700 mm is better. Including the bedhead the bed is therefore 2.10 m long. A minimum of 0.8 m is needed as passageway at the foot of the bed, so the minimum width of a double bedroom is 2.9 m.

If the associated bathroom has a full-length bath, basin and a WC it also needs to be 2.1 m overall. There is consequently no space in the entrance lobby for furnishings, so wasting this space completely. If a further 0.6 m is allowed in the lobby for furnishing, the room width becomes 3.5 m. This is a fairly common module in modern medium-priced bedroom wings. It balances the need for shortening corridors with the provision of reasonable space in individual rooms.

Fittings
A long hanging wardrobe space with between 300 mm and 500 mm width is required for the first person, plus 300 mm more for each extra person, with preferably a short hanging space somewhat smaller. Provide at least two shelves or drawers for the first, and one more for each extra person, with a width of 300 mm and a depth of 450 mm.

A luggage rack, which could have a space for a trolley underneath, 800 to 900 mm long, is needed. There must be guards against abrasion by metallic objects such as studs on suitcases, and it should be high enough to avoid fatigue for those packing.

Provide a dressing table at least 900 mm long, doubling as a writing table, and with at least one drawer. Fix a mirror above it, ideally with two side mirrors. It must have a good light, with separate switches. There should also be a full-length mirror with suitable lights.

There should be separate reading lights over the bed or beds, a general light and a light in the entrance lobby as well as those in the bathroom.

The bedhead is normally built in, but may need to be moveable to allow change of bed position. It holds bedside tables large enough for books, spectacles, water and a telephone. All lights, radio and television should be controlled from the bedhead, also any mechanical equipment such as curtain controls, heating and ventilation or tea maker. In the best hotels there will be a drink dispenser, a refrigerator, and sometimes a safe.

Loose furniture

Each bedroom should have one or two occasional chairs, at least one easy chair per person, a swivel dressing table chair, an occasional table, standard or table lamps, ashtrays, maybe a trouser press, and usually a television set.

4 PUBLIC AREAS

4.01

These areas usually need long-span construction and vary greatly from one hotel to another. They are usually located at ground level for convenience. Roof-top restaurants are only built to take advantage of quite exceptional views – the costs of servicing them can be substantial.

4.02 Entrance

The impression created by the main entrance is important and defines the type of hotel. It must always be obvious and lead directly to reception. Something more than a canopy is desirable to provide protection from wind and rain. A porte-cochère should be wide enough to allow two cars to pass and possibly high enough for coaches. Special lighting may be needed to accentuate the entrance.

Provide doors wide enough for a porter with bags, 900 mm clear. With revolving doors, side-hung escape doors will also be required. A draught lobby should normally be provided. Consider automatic doors.

All public entrances must be accessible to ambulant disabled people, and at least one to those in wheelchairs. At least one entrance from the hotel garage must be accessible to wheelchair users.

A transition area of flooring is required at the entrance before fine floor finishes are approached. There will be dirt and wear from foot traffic.

4.03 Reception

The reception desk should be visible to the guest immediately on entry, and it should be on the route to the lifts and stairs. Sometimes clients will require it to be visible from the street, alternatively they may decide that privacy for guests may be more important. This will influence the type of glazing and curtains. Occasionally a hotel is located above another street-level use. If the reception itself is on an upper floor, the stairs and lifts must be exclusive to the hotel.

In any reception, the following facilities are required:

- Counter, suitable for writing, with a 'bag shelf'
- Space for receptionist
- Key racks, often associated with letter racks behind counter
- Cashier and accounting equipment, computer, etc. Foreign currency service may affect storage requirements
- House telephone, for visitors to speak to guests in their rooms
- Call boxes: if there are phones in rooms only a few will be needed. They must be visible to reception staff but have some privacy
- Space for timetables, tourist leaflets, brochures, etc.
- Postbox, stamp machines, etc.
- Telephone meters for recording the cost of calls from guests' rooms
- Clocks and calendars visible to staff and guests
- Stationery and records store
- Strongroom or safe
- Parcel or baggage storage
- Room call system, and
- CCTV monitors, etc.

The relationships between the reception desk and other facilities are shown diagrammatically in **36.17**.

There is often a separate head porter's station, which may include an enquiry counter. It should be in a strategic position to control the entrance, the coming and going of guests, call boxes, and any external taxi rank or valet parking system. The head porter will control porters and messengers, and will look after baggage. He or she will be able to communicate with the garage, luggage room, reception, and cashier and will monitor fire alarms and service bells.

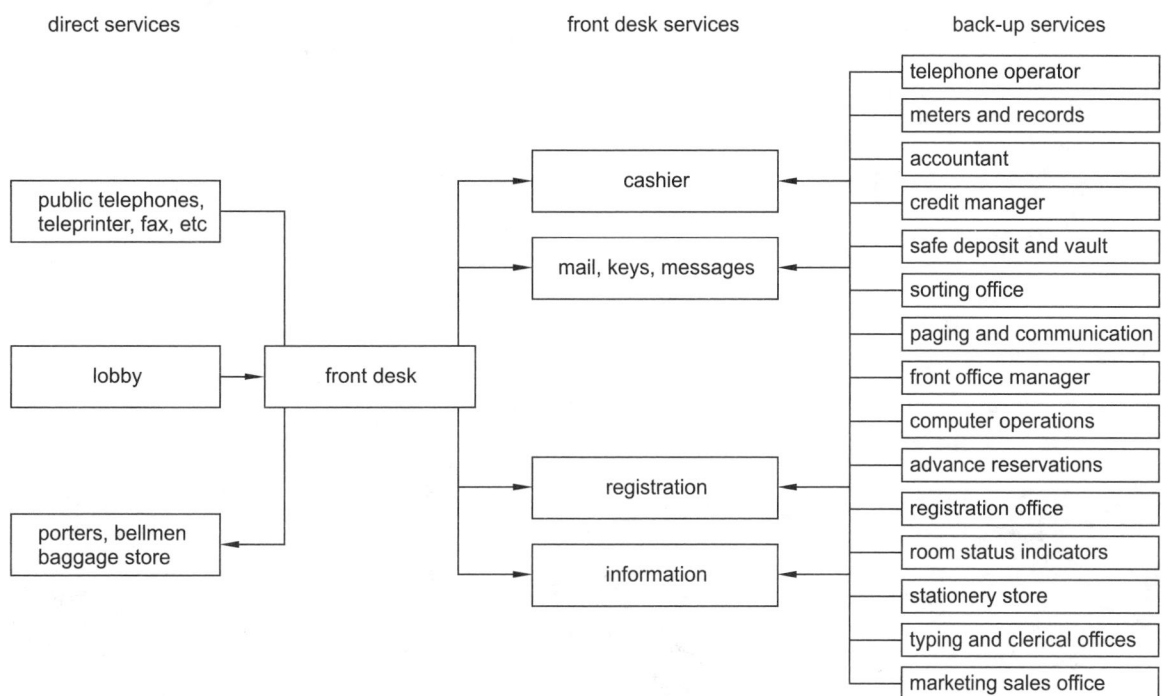

36.17 *Relationship diagram for administration services*

The client must decide on baggage handling. If not carried by the guest, there may be a separate baggage entrance, especially if tour buses bring mass deliveries of luggage. A lift, baggage room and a foolproof method of identifying luggage may be necessary; guests are nervous if they are separated from it. Provide some space for trolleys. Access to those public rooms mainly for non-residents (including conference, banqueting suites, etc.) is often separate from the main reception. Another entrance foyer will be needed, plus cloakrooms.

4.04 Lounges

The traditional image of a lounge as a separate room is changing. Isolated lounges earn no revenue. They are more likely to be part of an irregular area joining public rooms to the entrance area, or part of a bar. If there is a bar the room should not look dead when the bar is closed. Resort hotels may have a lounge for entertaining guests' friends. A rough planning figure is 1.1 to 1.4 m^2 per seat. Furniture is normally easy chairs and low coffee tables, and the atmosphere should be informal and relaxing.

The design of bars is influenced by the areas that they serve: lounge, restaurant, coffee shop, banqueting rooms, room service, etc. and the degree to which waiter service is employed. Bar design is dealt with in detail in Chapter 18.

4.05 Dining rooms

The dining room is usually open to non-residents, so there should be convenient access from outside the hotel in addition to access for resident guests. Most larger hotels will have dining rooms on several levels, such as a breakfast room on the first floor. The main dining room must be directly adjacent to the main kitchen. Details are in Chapter 18. Table II gives areas required according to the number of seats, and includes the areas that are more fully covered in section 5 below.

4.06 Function rooms

Function rooms tend to be linked to the business facilities as they are also used for conferences, etc. But these large rooms have to be designed to be multi-functional as the cost of providing them is high and so they have to be in frequent use.

They may need to be adaptable for banqueting, dancing, conferences or exhibitions. Floors may have to be changed, e.g. by changing the covering. Considerable space adjacent will be needed for furniture storage. It may be necessary to be able to divide the room with sliding screens, but ineffective soundproofing may not allow use of both parts at the same time. A separate entrance from outside is usually needed. There must be at least two emergency exits. Very good sound insulation is vital both to prevent sound

Table II Food service areas in m^2 according to numbers of seats

	Area per seat (m^2)	Notes
a Food services		
A-la-carte restaurant	1.8 to 2.0	Seating area in restaurant
Brasserie Coffee shop	1.7 to 1.8	Gross factor, allowing for circulation
Lounge and bar	1.8 to 2.0	Cloakrooms, etc. typically add 20%
Functions, banquet style	1.2	
Functions, conference style	1.6	
Foyer to banquet hall	0.3	
Staff canteens	0.7 to 0.9	
b Service facilities		
Main kitchen	0.9 to 1.0	or 60% of dining room
Coffee shop kitchen	0.6	or 45% of coffee shop
Food, liquor and china storage	0.5 for diners 0.3 for coffee shop	or 50% of kitchen
Banquet kitchen	0.24	or 20% of banquet room
Banquet storage	0.05	or 8% of banquet room

entering and escaping to bedrooms, etc. Excellent environmental services are necessary.

4.07 Checklist of requirements

- Ante-rooms
- Food and liquor service
- Method of dividing room
- Soundproofing and acoustic treatment
- Storage of moveable walls
- Furniture storage
- Crockery and equipment storage
- Dance floor, with removable carpet
- Protection of walls against chair damage
- Air-conditioning
- Toilet and cloakroom facilities
- Cine projection
- External access for heavy equipment for exhibitions
- Exhibition services, e.g. gas, water, drainage, phones
- Dimmable lights
- Electronic equipment: TV, audio
- Changing rooms for temporary staff or performers
- Bandstand or dais, temporary or permanent
- Theme motif or name
- Press box
- Fire exits, lighting, etc.

A diagrammatic representation of these relationships is shown in **36.18**.

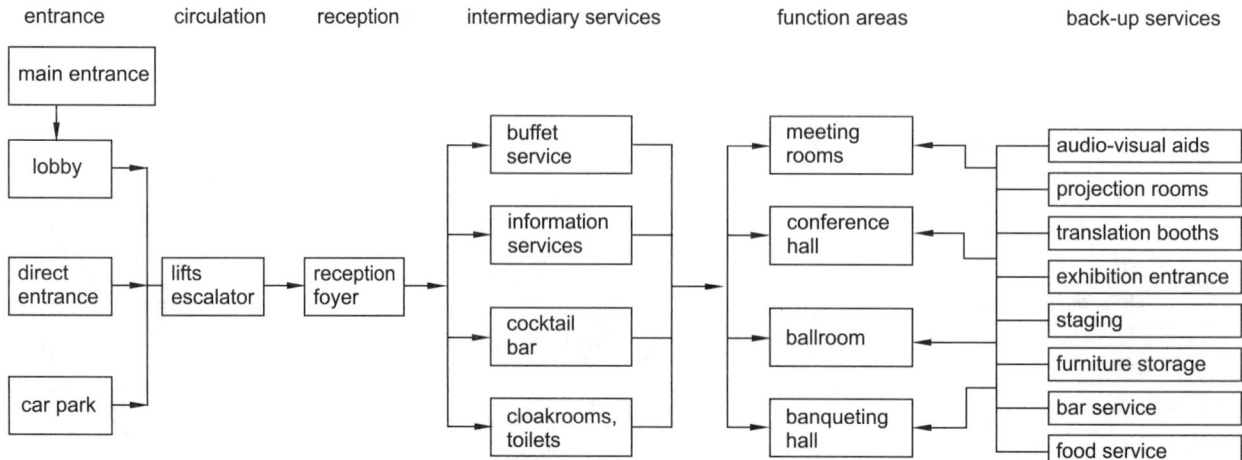

36.18 *Relationship diagram for non-residential functions*

5 SERVICE AREAS

36.19 is a relationship diagram for the service functions.

5.01 Bedroom servicing

Table I gives service areas required according to number of guest rooms. Take particular care where room service areas are concerned, as much work is done while guests are still asleep.

5.02 Catering servicing

The most important element to get right is the location of the main kitchen. This has to serve the main restaurant three times a day, 365 days a year, and needs to be immediately adjacent. It also serves, directly or by satellite kitchens, other catering outlets, functions, banquets, bar food, room service, staff restaurant, etc. Its location is critical for back-of-house circulation. Site kitchens and rooms used for food and wine storage on the north or northeast side if possible, to facilitate temperature control. Areas required are given in Table II.

5.03 Offices

The manager's office is usually adjacent to reception for reasons of control. Other offices, accounting, records, etc. can be elsewhere as long as communication to reception is good. In a large hotel accounting is computerised for speed and staff economy. While office sizes vary greatly, a rough indication is 7.5 to $20\,m^2$, and Table III gives some further details.

6 OTHER SPACES

Table IV covers area requirements for various other spaces.

6.01 Special accommodation

The other facilities that may be required are:

- Staffroom for guests' chauffeurs or other staff
- Day nurseries (especially in resort hotels)
- House doctor or nurse, and sick bay (see Chapter 16)

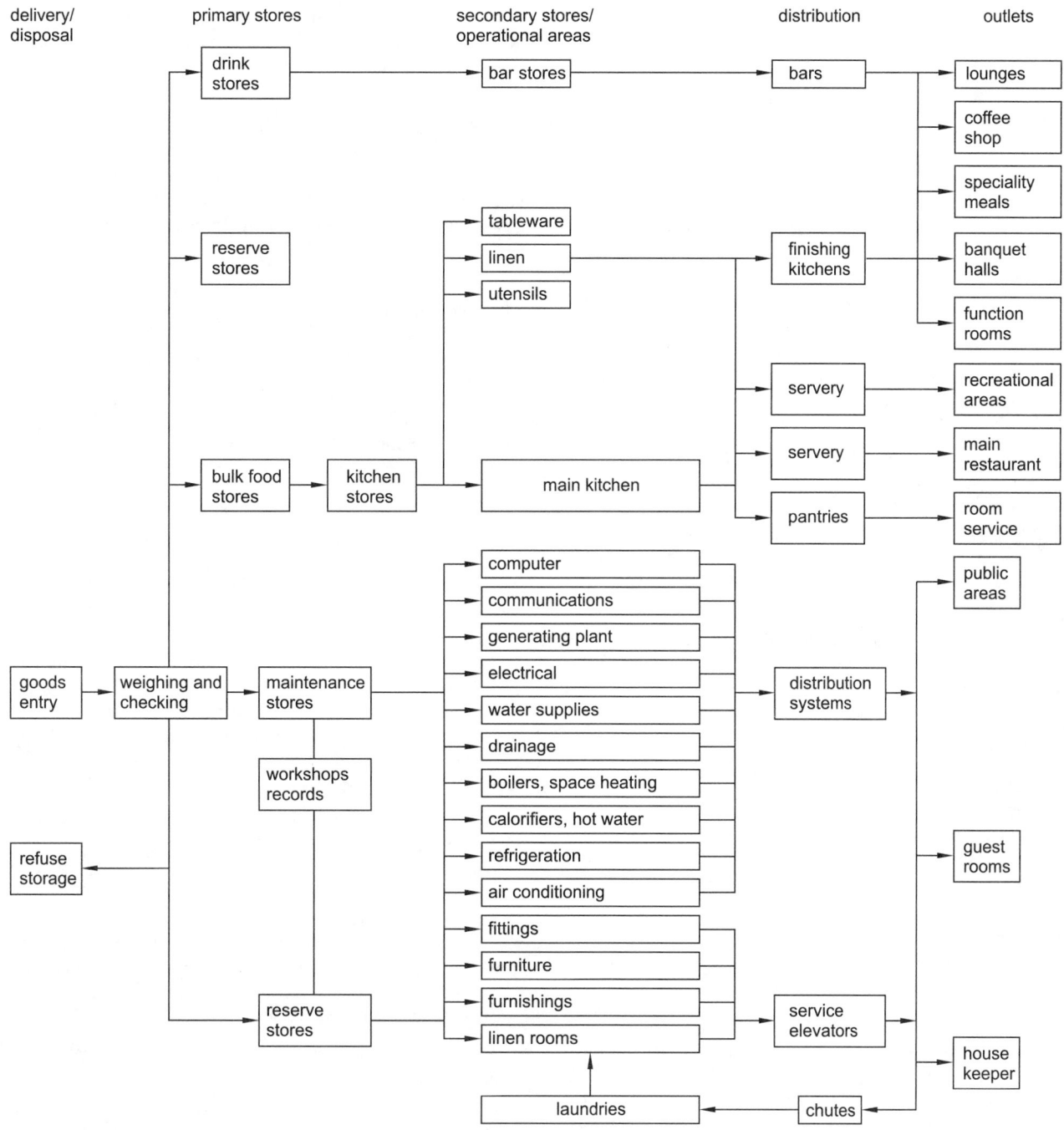

36.19 *Relationship diagram for technical and catering services*

Table III Office areas required in m²

	100 guest rooms	200 guest rooms
a Administrative		
Manager	9.5 to 11.5	11.5 to 14.0
Assistant manager	7.5 to 9.5	9.5 to 11.5
Financial	not required	7.5 to 9.5
Secretaries (area for each, two required)	7.5 to 9.5	11.5 to 14.0
Sales and catering	not required	11.5 to 14.0
Purchasing	not required	11.5 to 14.0
Personnel and auditing	not required	7.5 to 9.5
General office	14.0 to 18.5	18.5 to 23.0
b Food and beverage department		
Catering manager	7.5 to 9.5	9.5 to 11.5
Chef	not required	9.5 to 11.5
Banquet manager and waiter	not required	7.5 to 9.5
Room service	not required	7.5 to 9.5
c Housekeeping		
Housekeeper	7.5 to 9.5	7.5 to 9.5
Receiving clerk and timekeeper	7.5 to 9.5	7.5 to 9.5
Engineer	7.5 to 9.5	7.5 to 9.5

Table IV Areas for various spaces

Function	Area
a Circulation and reception	
General allowance	Gross factors: 25–35% added to room areas
Lobby areas	2-star 0.6 m² per room to 5-star 1.2 m² per room
b Cloakrooms	
Fixed rows of hooks	0.1 m² per user including staff circulation and and space around counter
Hooks plus seats or lockers	0.2 to 0.3 m² per user
c Health and fitness clubs	
Swimming pool	15.0 × 7.0 × 1.4 m plus 2 m surround plus changing rooms
Gymnasium	15 m² for a small fitness room to 65 m² for a large complex
d Public assemblies	
Conferences (theatre style)	0.6 to 1.0 m² per person plus stage, plus translation booth or 1.0 to 1.2 m² overall (see Chapter 20)
Dances	0.6 to 0.9 m² per person plus band space up to 12 m² for a 6-piece band
Recreations	See Chapter 25

- Business executives secretarial facilities or offices (see Chapter 11)
- Gymnasium or fitness centre (see Chapter 25)
- Sauna or Turkish baths (see Chapter 3)
- Cinema (see Chapter 20)
- Meeting rooms (see Chapter 11)
- Press, interview or lecture rooms
- Casino or card rooms
- Changing rooms for swimming pools
- Night clubs
- Kosher kitchens
- Manager's flat
- Service flats or suites
- VIP rooms, and
- Chapels (see Chapter 27).

6.02 Cloakrooms and lavatories

These should be on main circulation rooms near public rooms. They must be discreetly conspicuous, and male and female must be separate. It must not be possible to see in even when all the doors are open, nor must they communicate directly with rooms used for food.

Women's lavatories should include a powder room of appropriate size. Women prefer the cloakroom to be within the lavatory area, but men prefer it to be outside. The number of fitments depends on the maximum number of people to be served. For details see Chapter 3.

7 ACCESS AND CAR PARKING

7.01 Access

Pedestrian and vehicular access to the hotel needs to be determined and agreed at an early stage. Access for guests and hotel servicing must be clearly separate. Provision must be made for:

- Guests: arriving by private car, taxi, public buses, coaches or on foot
- Staff: arriving by car or public transport
- Goods deliveries: food, laundry, furniture may need to be separate.
- Refuse: separate from food supplies

Roads must have curvatures related to the size of vehicle, space must be available for waiting, and approaches should be visible from inside the building.

7.02 Signage

External signage is always required. Consider the proper integration of illuminated signs on the building at the design stage, not as an afterthought. Flagpoles, floodlighting and other feature entrance signage may be required, as well as remote off-site direction signs.

7.03 Lighting

External lighting needs to draw attention to the hotel and highlight an inviting entrance. It should banish dark corners and enhance security.

7.04 Car parking

Planning requirements vary according to the type and size of hotel and its location. The planning authority will advise. Refer to Chapter 4.

A common operational requirement is 1.2 to 1.3 spaces per room. Inside London it may be less, but space for conference parking may be greater. The biggest problem is usually fly-parking by outsiders where the site is desirable.

Provision must be made for cars to drop off passengers easily at the main entrance, and then go to the car park; the driver must then be able to return easily on foot to the entrance to rejoin guests. Afterwards, it must be equally easy for the car to return to pick up at the entrance. In a town the parking may have to be in the basement, and mechanical plant may be displaced to a sub-basement or upper floor.

7.05 Servicing

Secondary access is required for goods and service vehicles with adequate provision for turning, loading and unloading. It is normally from a road different from the main entrance. Staff access is usually through the service entrance to simplify control. It is necessary to make separate provision for receiving and handling different types of goods, taking into account their nature and storage requirements. The main divisions are:

- Beers, wines, spirits: needing beer and wine cellars, spirit stores and crate storage
- Food: needing cold stores, vegetable stores and dry goods stores
- Laundry and soft furnishings: linen stores

- General: crockery and cutlery stores, cleaning equipment stores, storage for maintenance plant, furniture and general goods and
- Fuel: oil storage tanks and solid fuel enclosures.

7.06 Refuse
Refuse collection vehicles will normally use the service entry. There must be space for:

- A compactor, about the size of one car-parking bay
- Crushing machines and containers for glass bottles
- Containers or skips for large dry items
- Bins for food waste intended for animals
- Space for returnable containers
- Material intended for incineration

Rubbish is a potential source of nuisance as decaying residues of food attract rats and flies, and rubbish clearance operations can be noisy. Bins and containers should be situated in an impervious enclosure equipped with means of hosing down and drainage.

37 Tropical design

Martin Evans

Martin Evans is an architect and an author of a number of books

CI/SfB: (H11)
UDC: (213)
Unicode: U214

KEY POINT:
- *check all local conditions and methods*

Contents

1 INTRODUCTION

The purpose of this chapter is to collect data and assemble checklists to assist readers designing for tropical conditions. There is a shortage of textbooks on tropical design both for designers trained and living in temperate climates and for nationals of tropical climates who find they are aware of the problems but do not have any realistic data. This chapter concentrates on environmental comfort, giving general parameters, but these must be supplemented by local knowledge or research – the designers must ensure that they comply with local requirements, legislation and building controls, and consider the merits of traditional local solutions before adopting any of the recommendations made here.

2 CLIMATIC ZONES

2.01 Critical data

The main climatic zones of the tropics are shown in Table I, together with the latitudes in which they are found, typical

Table I Occurrence and characteristics of main climatic zones

Zone	Approximate latitude range	Natural vegetation	Typical cultivation	Climate	Problems	Requirements
Warm humid equatorial	7½N—7½S	Tropical rain forest	Banana, palm oil	Warm with high humidity and rainfall	Humidity prevents sweat evaporation; hot nights make sleep difficult; high rainfall and glare from overcast sky, sun on east and west facades	Air movement from fans or cross ventilation, low thermal capacity construction, sloping roofs and large overhangs, windows facing north and south
Tropical island	5–30°N 5–30°S	Rain forest	Sugar cane	Warm, humid but less cloud than warm humid zone	Similar to warm humid equatorial, but clear skies and bright sun more frequent	Similar to warm humid but with additional care in the design of shading the south facing windows in the northern hemisphere (vice versa in the southern)
Hot dry tropical	15–32°N 15–32°S	Desert, steppe	Palms, grazing (nomadic)	Hot and dry with high annual and daily variation of temperature	High diurnal range, very hot days in summer, cool winter days, low rainfall, very strong solar radiation and ground glare, sandy and dusty environment	High heat capacity construction, shading devices which allow solar heating in winter, small windows, flat roofs (often used for sleeping), small courtyards to give shade and protection
Maritime desert	15–30°N 15–30°S	Desert	Palms, grazing	Hot, humid with low rainfall	Similar to hot dry climates but with higher humidity causing discomfort by preventing sweat evaporation	Similar to hot dry but air movement is desirable at times
Intermediate composite or monsoon	5–20°N 5–20°S	Monsoon forest, dry tropical forest or scrub, savannah	Paddy rice, sugar cane, millet	Warm humid and hot dry seasons often with cool season	Combines the problems of warm humid and hot dry climate	Compromise between the requirements of warm humid and hot dry climate or ideally (but more expensively) two buildings or parts of buildings for use at different times of the year
Equatorial upland	10°N—10°S	Broadleaf forest, mountain vegetation	Millet	Temperate to cool depending on altitude	Combine the problems of warm humid and hot dry climates with those of a temperate or cold climate for all or part of the year	Design to take advantage of solar radiation when cool or cold. Heating and additional insulation may be required
Tropical upland	10–30°N 10–30°S	Steppe, cedars	Wheat	Hot summers, cold winters	Do	Do
Mediterranean	32–45°N 32–45°S	Mediterranean scrub	Vines, olives, citrus fruits	Hot dry summers, cool wet winters	Summers have some of the problems of a hot dry climate while winters are cold and humid with moderate rainfall	Design with high thermal capacity, medium to small openings, and courtyards to give shade and protection

Table II Climatic data

Data required	Units	Relevance
Monthly mean max temperature	°C	thermal comfort analysis
Monthly mean min temperature	°C	
Monthly mean max humidity	%	
Monthly mean min humidity	%	
Monthly mean rainfall	mm	vegetation
Peak rainfall intensity and duration	mm/unit of time	storm damage
(Daily or hourly rainfall may be the only data available)	mm	rainwater drainage
Sunlight	hours	natural lighting
Cloud cover	oktas* or %	
Absolute max temperature	°C	thermal expansion
Absolute min temperature	°C	and effect on building materials
Frequency distribution of wind for different speeds and directions	% m/s	siting and orientation
Frequency of special phenomena, ie sandstorms, fog, hail, thunder	days per year	provision of special precautions

*1 okta = 1 eighth of the sky

Table IV Indicators of requirements for comfort for each month

Humid indicators

H1	Air movement essential	mean monthly maximum temperature above the day comfort limits combined with humidity over 70% or humidity between 30–70% and a diurnal range of less than 10°C
H2	Air movement desirable	mean monthly maximum temperatures within the comfort limits combined with humidities over 70%

Arid indicators

A1	Thermal storage required	diurnal range of temperatures over 10°C and humidity less than 70%
A2	Space required for outdoor sleeping	mean monthly minimum temperatures above the night comfort limits and humidity below 50%. Outdoor sleeping may also be indicated where maximum temperatures are above the day comfort limits and diurnal range is above 10°C with humidities less than 50%.

Cold indicators

C1	Solar radiation desirable	mean monthly maximum temperatures below day comfort limits
C2	Additional heating required	mean monthly maximum temperature below 15°C

vegetation and climatic characteristics and the problems requiring special design solutions to ensure comfort. The main climatic data required for tropical design will include the criteria listed in Table II. Mean figures may be calculated over short periods (five years or more), but it can be dangerous to assume peaks from records of such a short period.

indicators are shown in Table IV. The total number of indicators for each month for the whole year can be used in Table V to find the requirements for plan form and building elements. This method takes into account the possibility of conflicting requirements over the year and the requirements shown in Table V are optimised over the whole year. Some flexibility in interpretation may be required in borderline cases.

3 COMFORT AND REQUIREMENTS FOR COMFORT

3.01 Thermal comfort

Thermal comfort is dependent on temperature, humidity, radiation and air movement as well as type of activity, clothing and degree of acclimatisation. A guide to the range of bulb temperatures which are likely to be perceived as comfortable is given in Table III. These thermal comfort limits apply when there is no loss or gain of heat by radiation or air movement. The first step in the climatic design process is to compare the comfort limits with the meteorological data.

3.02 Meteorological data

Annual average temperature is the average of the mean monthly maximum and minimum temperatures. The average of the highest mean monthly maximum and lowest mean monthly minimum gives a close approximation.

A comparison of the monthly mean maximum temperature with the appropriate day comfort limit indicates whether days are hot, comfortable or cold. Similarly, a comparison of the mean monthly minimum temperature with the appropriate high comfort limits indicates whether nights are hot, comfortable or cold. The degree of thermal stress can be used to indicate the design features required to achieve comfort during a particular month. These

4 THERMAL PERFORMANCE REQUIREMENTS

4.01 Parameters

The thermal characteristics for walls and roofs in tropical climates should be defined not only by the insulation they provide (i.e. U-value or air-to-air transmittance) but also by their ability to reflect solar radiation and to delay the flow of heat through the construction. In addition to the U-value, two other useful parameters of thermal performance are:

● Solar heat factor: the proportion of incident solar radiation transmitted through a construction
● Time lag: the response of a construction to temperature change.

The requirements for U-value, solar heat factor and time lag are given in Table VI which uses the indicators from Table IV. The following paragraphs explain the solar heat factor and time lag in greater detail.

4.02 Sol air temperature

Sol air temperature is defined as the temperature of the outside air which would give the same rate of heat transfer and the same distribution of temperature through a construction as the combined

Table III Thermal comfort limits (°C)

Monthly average relative humidity	Annual average temperature					
	over 20°C		15–20°C		under 15°C	
	Day	Night	Day	Night	Day	Night
0–30%	26–34	17–25	23–32	15–23	21–30	14–21
30–50%	25–31	17–24	22–30	15–22	21–27	14–20
50–70%	23–29	17–23	21–28	15–21	19–26	14–19
70–100%	22–27	17–21	20–25	15–20	18–24	14–18

Table V Building and planning requirements*

Requirements	Indicators (From Table IV)
Layout alternatives	
1 Buildings orientated on E–W axis	A1 for up to 10 months and C1 for up to 2 months and/or H1 for over 6 months
2 Compact courtyard planning	A1 for 11 or 12 months and C1 for up to 4 months
3 Compact forms	All other cases
Spacing for breeze	
1 Open spacing of 5 times building height for breeze penetration (see 9)	H1 for 11 or 12 months
2 Open spacing with some precautions against cold or hot dry winds	H1 for between 2–10 months
3 Compact planning	H1 for one month or less
Spacing for solar radiation	
1 Spacing not dependent on solar radiation	C1 for up to 3 months
2 Spacing to allow solar radiation (but high sun angles may still allow close spacing)	C1 for 4 months or more
Building form for air movement	
1 Rooms single banked with permanent provision for cross-ventilation	H1 for over 3 months; or H1 for one or two months and A1 for 5 months or less
2 Cross-ventilation not essential	Never H1 and H2 for one month or less
3 Double-banked rooms with temporary provision for cross-ventilation	All other cases
Outdoor sleeping	
Space required for outdoor sleeping	A2 for two months or more
Openings	
1 Large openings 40–80% of north and south walls	A1 one month or less and C1 never
2 Medium sized openings 20–40% of area of external walls	A1 one month or less and C1 one month or more or A1 for 2–5 months
3 Composite 15–30% of area of external walls	A1 for between 6 and 10 months
4 Small 10–20% of external wall area	A1 for 11 or 12 months C1 for up to 3 months
5 Medium 15–25% of external wall area	A1 for 11 or 12 months C1 for 4 months or over A1 for 11 or 12 months

*This table is intended for housing or similar buildings

Table VI Thermal performance recommendations

Structure	Performance	Indicator (Table IV)
External walls		
1 Light walls	U value: 2.8 W/(m²K) max Solar heat factor: 4% max Time lag: 3 hours max	A1 for up to 2 months
2 Heavy walls	U value: 2.0 W/(m²K) max Solar heat factor: 4% max Time lag: 8 hours minimum	A1 for 3 months or more
Roofs		
1 Light roof	U value: 1.1 W/(m²K) max Solar heat factor: 4% max Time lag: 3 hours max	H1 for 10 months or over and A1 for up to 2 months
2 Heavy roofs	U value: 0.85 W/(m²K) max Solar heat factor: 3% max Time lag: 8 hours minimum	H1 for 9 months or less and A1 for 6 months and more
3 Well insulated roofs	U value: 0.85 W/(m²K) max Solar heat factor: 3% max Time lag: 3 hours max	All other cases

effects of solar radiation and air temperature. The sol air temperature will be higher than the air temperature when a surface is subject to solar radiation:

$$\theta_{sa} = \frac{\alpha I}{f_o} + \theta_o$$

where θ_{sa} = sol air temperature (°C)
  α = absorptivity of surface to solar radiation
  f_o = outside surface conductance (W/m²K)
  I = intensity of solar radiation (W/m²)
  θ_o = outside air temperature (°C).

4.03 Solar heat factor
The solar heat factor is defined as the heat flow through the construction due to solar radiation, expressed as a proportion of the total solar radiation incident on the surface of the construction. When a building has large openings and is well ventilated to the exterior (as is often the case in the tropics), the solar heat factor is dependent on the U-value and absorptivity the external surface conductance (f_o can be taken as a constant):

$$\frac{q}{I} = \frac{U\alpha}{f_o}$$

Surfaces heated by solar radiation will get hottest when wind velocities are low. Therefore external surface resistances for cold conditions should not be used. In hot conditions with low wind speeds a recommended value for f_o is 20 W/(m²K). If the solar heat factor is expressed as a percentage then:

$$\frac{q}{I} = \frac{U\alpha}{20} \times 100 = 5\,U\alpha$$

U-values may be increased if absorptivities are proportionately reduced, while still maintaining a constant solar heat factor. Most reflective surfaces require good maintenance if they are to remain effective. In many situations it is not prudent to rely on maintenance or repainting of surfaces, and therefore U-values should be decreased to obtain the required thermal performance standard. A solar heat factor of less than 4 per cent will ensure that ceiling temperatures will not be more than 5°C above air temperatures and will not add to discomfort.

4.04 Solar radiation
Wide variations may occur according to the colour and weathering of the surface. Surfaces exposed to solar radiation should have low absorptivities and high emissivities to reflect solar radiation and to reradiate absorbed solar radiation. Surfaces facing cavities, however, will transmit less heat by radiation across the cavity if the 'low-temperature' emissivity is low. Table VII gives the percentage absorptivity and emissivity of surfaces.

Table VII Percentage absorptivity and emissivity of surfaces

Material of surface	Absorptivity of solar radiation (short wave 0.3–2.5 microns)	Emissivity of low temperature radiation (long wave 5–20 microns)
Aluminium polished	5–15	5–10
Aluminium weathered	15–40	10–15
Whitewash new	10–15	80–90
Whitewash weathered	20–30	80–90
White paint	25–30	80–90
Aluminium paint	55	55
Pinewood	40	95
Asbestos cement weathered	70	95
Galvanised iron: new	25	25
Galvanised iron: rusty	90	28
White marble	50–60	95
Red brick	75–85	65–80
Black non-metalic surface ie bitumen	85–90	65–80

For all materials:

Reflectivity = 1 – absorptivity (for radiation of a given wavelength)

Absorptivity = emissivity (for radiation of a given wavelength).

The approximate absorptivity of solar radiation of paints can be calculated if the Munsell value is known (as it is for colours in the BS range of paints for building purposes). The 'value' of the colour is given by the number which appears after the 'hue' letter in the Munsell number. This should be substituted for V in the formula:

Absorptivity = $100 - [V (V - 1)]$ (for solar radiation)

Example: Munsell number 6.25Y8.5/13 (Yellow)

$V = 8.5$ Absorptivity = 36 per cent

At low temperatures most paints have an emissivity of 80–90 per cent.

4.05 Time lag
Time lag is defined as the phase difference (delay) between external periodic variations in temperatures and the resulting internal temperature variations. The period of variations is 24 hours and the lag is measured in hours. Table VIII gives time lag for homogeneous materials.

Table VIII Time lag for homogeneous materials (in hours)

Materials		Thickness of material (mm)					
		25	50	100	150	200	300
Dense concrete	min	–	1.5	3.0	4.4	6.1	9.2
	max	–	1.1	2.5	3.8	4.9	7.6
Brick	min	–	–	2.3	–	5.5	8.5
	max	–	–	3.2	–	6.6	10
Wood	min	0.4	1.3	3.0	–	–	–
	max	0.5	1.7	3.5	–	–	–
Fibre insulating board	ave	0.27	0.77	2.7	5.0	–	–
Concrete with foamed slag aggregate	ave	–	–	3.25	–	8	–
Stone	ave	–	–	–	–	5.5	8.0
Stabilised soil	ave	–	–	2.4	4.0	5.2	8.1

Table IX Time lag for composite roof constructions

Construction (described from the external surface inwards)		Time lag (hours)
40 mm 100 mm	Mineral wool Concrete	11.8
100 mm 40 mm	Concrete Mineral wool	3 (same as concrete alone)
14 mm 165 mm 14 mm	Cement plaster Concrete Cement plaster	3.8
14 mm 50 mm 115 mm 14 mm	Cement plaster Vermiculite concrete Concrete Cement plaster	13
Any finish 25 mm	Expanded polystyrene any structural concrete slab	over 8
Any finish 75 mm 100 mm	Lightweight concrete screed Concrete slab	over 8
30 mm 20 mm 60 mm 240 mm 14 mm	Concrete tiles Mortar bed waterproof membrane Screed Hollow pot slab Render	12

For non-homogeneous construction, the order in which different layers are placed can change the time lag considerably. If insulation is placed on the external surface of a dense material, the time lag is considerably increased. Table IX gives the time lag of constructions.

Although the time lag indicates when the thermal impact of outside temperature swings will affect the interior, the actual internal conditions can only be calculated when the heat flow into and through all room surfaces is considered.

5 SOLAR RADIATION

5.01 Criteria
The intensity of solar radiation on a surface depends on the altitude of the sun, the orientation of the surface in relation to the sun and the absorption of solar radiation by the atmosphere, pollution, cloud, etc, **37.1**.

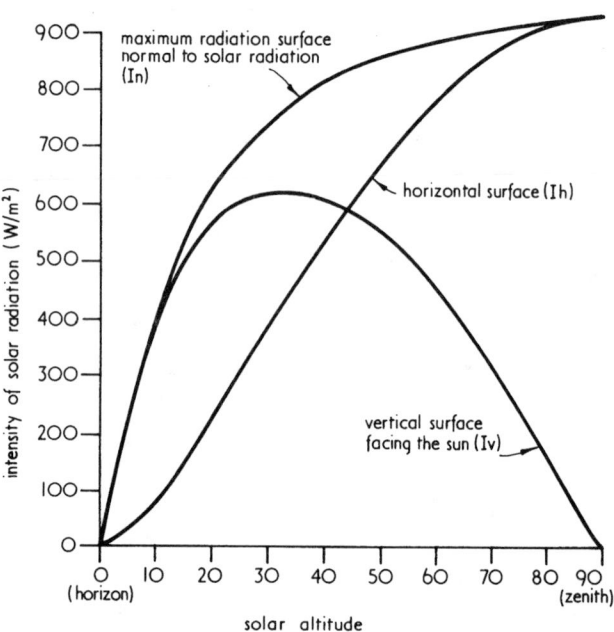

37.1 *Intensity of solar radiation*

5.02 Calculation
For vertical surfaces inclined at an angle θ to the azimuth (horizontal angle of sun on plan), the intensity of radiation on surface I will be:

$$I_{v\theta} = I_v \times \cos \theta$$

where I_v is taken from **37.1**. The altitude and azimuth of the sun can be found from sunpath diagrams. A list of sources of these appears below. The radiation from **37.1** should be multiplied by the values from Tables X and XI to give total radiation at the appropriate altitude and/or for appropriate atmospheric conditions.

Table X Increase in solar radiation with altitude

Height above sea level	Altitude of sun in degrees				
	20°	30°	40°	60°	80°
900	1.14	1.12	1.10	1.08	1.08
1500	1.26	1.20	1.17	1.15	1.15
3000	1.30	1.31	1.28	1.25	1.23

Table XI Effect of cloud and atmospheric pollution on radiation*

Very low humidities and clear skies	1.1 (increase)
High humidities and pollution 'clear sky'	0.9 (decrease)
Overcast sky	0.1–0.3 (decrease)

*Varies greatly with cloud and solar altitude

6 SHADING AND GLAZING

6.01 Solar control glass

Special glasses for solar control absorb a considerable proportion of solar radiation. This heats the glass and special precautions must be taken to avoid problems resulting from thermal movement. About a third of the absorbed heat is transmitted indirectly to the interior and two-thirds to the exterior, so the total proportion of transmitted solar radiation may be considerably greater than the directly transmitted solar radiation. The high temperature of the glass may also cause discomfort. For comparison, a sheet of aluminium or an uninsulated concrete slab has been shown in Table XII. Almost all special glasses will get as hot as these materials.

6.02 Reducing solar gain

The best way to reduce solar radiation heat gain is to reduce window size (or provide external shading) for windows receiving direct solar radiation, though precautions may be required against glare from bright cloudy sky or the ground.

6.03 External shading

If a view is not required, a coat of white paint on glass will give reduced light and solar radiation transmission at considerably less cost than special glasses. The best way to control solar radiation, however, is to use external shading design with the aid of a sunpath diagram. When the sunpath diagrams for the northern hemisphere are used for the southern hemisphere, changes should be made to the time, month, azimuth, direction as shown in Table XIV. Shading coefficients are given in Table XIII.

Internal shades are comparable with special glasses. Most forms of external shading are better than special glasses or internal shades.

Sources for sunpath diagrams
1. *Manual of tropical housing and building* Part 1. Climate design, Koenigsberger, Ingersol, Mayhew, Szokolay. Longmans, 1974.

2 Sharma, M. R. and Rao, K. R. *Solar radiation protractors*, Central Building Research Institute. Rorkee, India. Equidistant projection 15°N–15°S; 15°N–35°N at 5-degree intervals (reproduced in Givoni, *Man, climate and architecture*, Elsevier, 1969).

3 *Solar charts and shadow angle protractor for daylight planning*, Catalogue no. 374, Henry Hope & Sons, London, 1969. Stereographic projection 32°N–28°S at 4-degree intervals.

4 Richards, S. J. *South African architectural record*, Vol. 36, No 11. Stereographic projection 20°S–34°S at 2-degree intervals (reprinted by South African Council for Scientific and Industrial Research, Pretoria 1952).

Table XIII Shading coefficients: the quantity of solar radiation transmitted as a proportion of that transmitted through clear glass

Fenestration	Shading coefficient
Clear 6 mm glass	1.00
Glass with internal dark roller blind	0.70–0.80
Glass with internal dark venetian blind	0.75
Glass with internal medium venetian blind	0.55–0.65
Glass with internal white venetian blind	0.45–0.55
Glass with external miniature louvres	0.50–0.10 (depends on angle of incidence)
Glass with dark canvas external awning	0.20–0.28
Glass with dense trees providing shade	0.20–0.30
Glass with movable louvres	0.10–0.20
Heat absorbing glasses	0.45–0.80

Table XIV Changes for sunpath diagrams in southern latitudes

Time (solar time)		Date		Azimuth degrees clockwise		Direction
North→South		North→South		North→South		North→South
4	20	28 Jan	30 July	0	180	
5	19	28 Feb	30 Aug	30	210	
6	18	21 Mar	23 Sept	60	240	North—South
7	17	15 April	15 Oct	90	270	
7	17	15 May	15 Nov	120	300	
11	13	22 June	22 Dec	150	330	East—West
12	12	30 July	28 Jan	180	360	
13	11	30 Aug	28 Feb	210	30	
13	11	23 Sept	21 Mar	240	60	South—North
17	7	15 Oct	15 April	270	90	
18	6	15 Nov	15 May	300	120	
19	5	22 Dec	22 June	330	150	West—East
20	4			360	180	

Table XII Solar heat gains through glass*

Fenestration	Visible radiation transmitted %	Direct solar radiation transmitted %	Total solar radiation transmitted %	Index of increase of surface temp. above air temp (clear glass = 1)
Clear float glass	85	80	84	1
Glass with reflective polyester film	18	17	25	2
	33	31	39	2
Solar energy reflecting glass	42	47	52	2.5
	58	59	62	4
Surface modified heat absorbing glass	50	56	67	3
	50	48	62	4
Tinted solar control glass grey	42	45	62	4
	42	40	58	4
	24	22	47	4
	19	16	43	4.5
green	76	52	66	4
	74	45	61	4
	62	30	51	4
Clear glass with open weave curtain internally	40	70	82	1
Corrugated aluminium (new)	0	0	9	2
100 mm concrete	0	0	15	4

Sources: Manufacturers' data; heat gains through fenestration F.J. Lotz and J.F. van Straaten, CSIR: R/Bov 223.
*Ranges of products are given. Consult manufacturers for specific data.

5 *AJ Handbook of Building Environment.* Information Sheet – Sunlight 5, 30.10.68 pp 1024–1035. Gnomic projection 040° (N or S) at 2-degree intervals.

All sunpath diagrams for the northern hemisphere can be used for the southern hemisphere by reversing the hours and months and rotating the azimuth scale by 180°.

7 AIR MOVEMENT AND VENTILATION

7.01 Wind velocities
The conversion of wind velocities from imperial to metric with the Beaufort scale and the corresponding wind pressures on a flat plate normal to the wind are given in **37.2**.

7.02 Urban areas
Wind velocities in urban or suburban areas may be estimated in relation to wind velocities in open country, **37.3**.

7.03 Effect of wind speed
Table XV shows the effect of different wind speeds in warm humid climates.

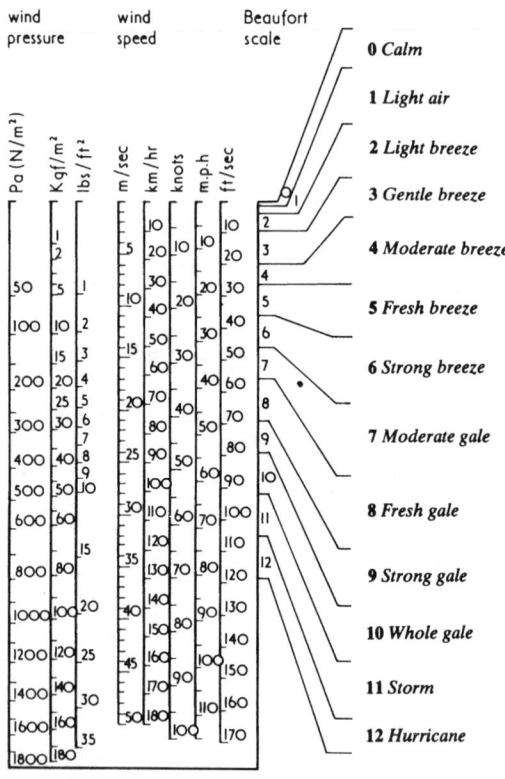

37.2 *Conversion chart for wind velocities and the corresponding wind pressures. Reference: BRS Digest No 101, Jan 1969, fig 13; HMSO.* **Key** *0 Calm: smoke rises vertically; 1 Light air: direction shown by smoke but not wind vanes; 2 Light breeze: wind felt on face, leaves rustle; 3 Gentle breeze: wind extends light flags, leaves in constant motion; 4 Moderate breeze: raises dust and loose paper, small brances are moved, onset of mechanical discomfort; 5 Fresh breeze: small trees in leaf begin to sway, uncomfortable in urban areas; 6 Strong breeze: large branches in motion, telegraph wires whistle, umbrellas difficult to use; 7 Moderate gale: whole trees in motion, difficult to walk against wind; 8 Fresh gale: breaks twigs off trees, generally slows down walking; 9 Strong gale: slight structural damage occurs, tiles and slates dislodged; 10 Whole gale seldom experienced inland; 11 Storm: trees uprooted; 12 Hurricane: rarely experienced, accompanied by widespread damage.*

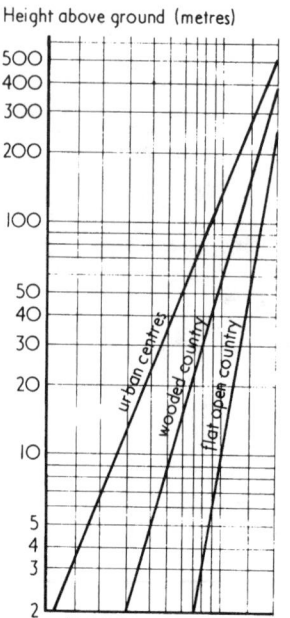

37.3 *Wind speed at different elevations and environments expressed as percentages of the wind speed at 10 m in flat open country, i.e. at an airport wind recording tower. For example, if the wind speed at the airport is 3 m/s, at the top of a building 35 m high in an urban centre the wind speed will be 50% of this: 1.5 m/s. Reference: Paper 2 'Wind effects on building and structure', HMSO 1965, fig 5*

Table XV Effect of internal wind speeds in warm humid climates

Range of speeds m/min	Effect
0–15	Not noticeable, less than 1°C of apparent cooling as air passes over skin
15–30	Just noticeable cooling effect equivalent to 1–2°C
30–60	Effective and pleasant cooling effect
60–100	Maximum windspeed for cooling without undesirable side effects
100–200	Too fast for desk work; papers start to blow around
over 200	Too fast and uncomfortable for internal conditions.

7.04 Wind shadow
The length of the wind shadow for various shapes of building is given in **37.4**. Example: a two-storey building 6 m high, 3 m wide and 24 m long ($A = 3$ m). The wind shadow will be $11\frac{3}{4} \times A$, that is, 35 m long.

The variations in wind direction will alter the direction of the wind shadow, and allowance must be made for these variations. As a rough guide the wind shadow will be $5 \times$ height of building (including the pitched roof).

8 MECHANICAL AIDS TO COMFORT

8.01 Ceiling fans
Ceiling fans give a wide distribution of blown air, **37.5**. Since the diameter of the fan is large, the fan can have a relatively low speed, reducing noise. Typical installation:

Ceiling height   3.0 m min
Blade height   2.5 m
Fan diameter   1.0 m

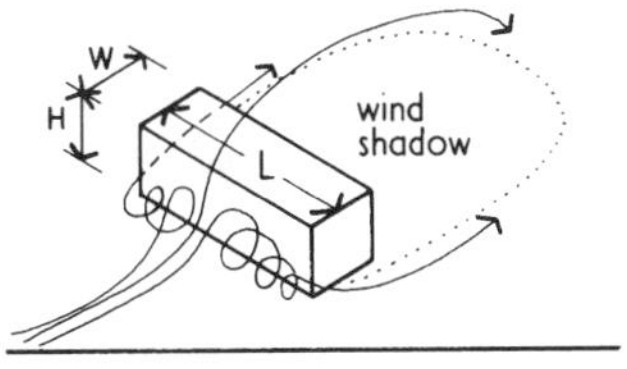
W
H
L
wind
shadow

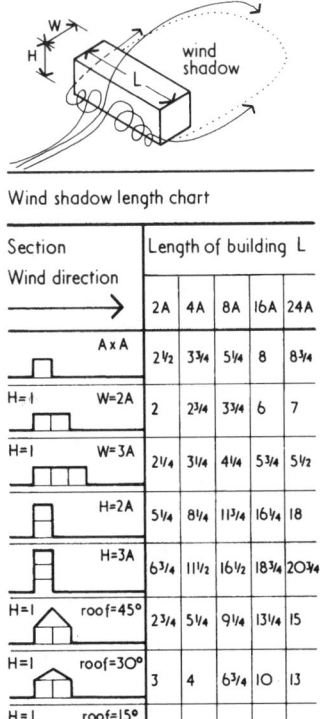

Wind shadow length chart

Section / Wind direction →	Length of building L 2A	4A	8A	16A	24A
A x A	2½	3¾	5¼	8	8¾
H=1 W=2A	2	2¾	3¾	6	7
H=1 W=3A	2¼	3¼	4¼	5¾	5½
H=2A	5¼	8¼	11¾	16¼	18
H=3A	6¾	11½	16½	18¾	20¾
H=1 roof=45°	2¾	5¼	9¼	13¼	15
H=1 roof=30°	3	4	6¾	10	13
H=1 roof=15°	3	5¼	8¼	11½	14½
H=1 roof=15°	2½	4¼	6½	11	13¾

37.4 *Wind shadow length chart. Reference: B. H. Evans, Research Report 59, Texas Engineering Station 1957. See also overseas Building Note 112*

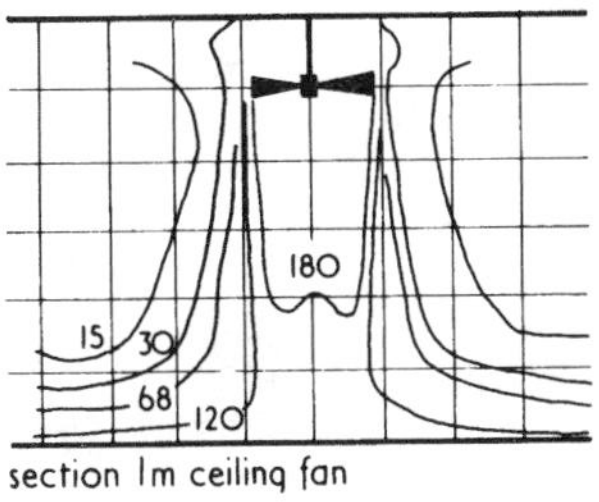
180
15
30
68
120
section 1m ceiling fan

37.5 *Ceiling fans are fairly slow moving and quiet. Blades must be higher than an outstretched arm (2.4 m)*

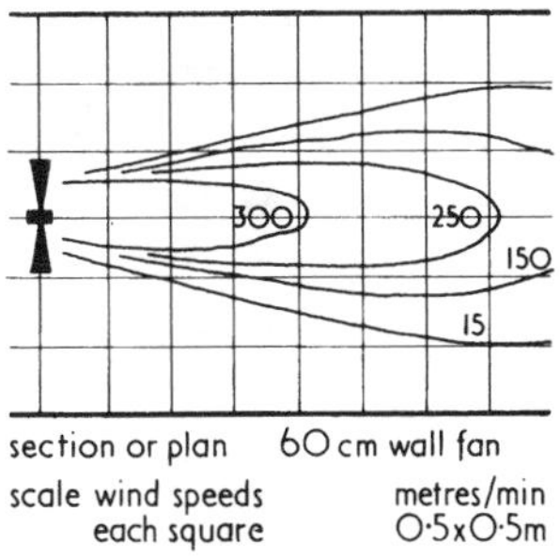
300
250
150
15
section or plan
60 cm wall fan
scale wind speeds
each square
metres/min
0·5x0·5m

37.6 *Wall fans rotate at speed and may be noisy. Those swinging from side to side cover a larger area with less regular air movement. Reference: L.G. Wood 'Performance of ceiling and desk fans', Electrical Energy, March 1957*

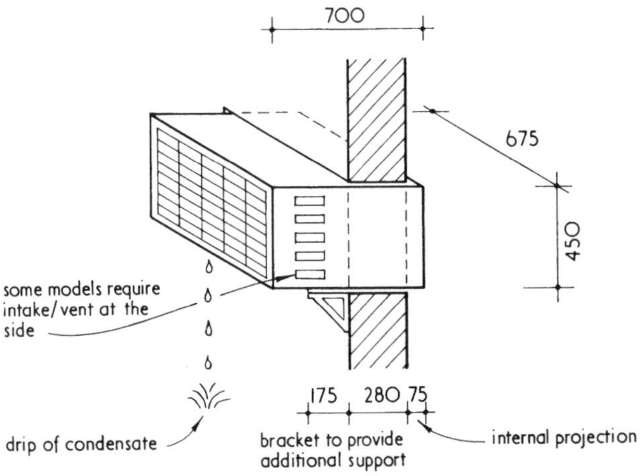
700
675
450
some models require
intake/vent at the
side
drip of condensate
175
280
75
bracket to provide
additional support
internal projection

37.7 *Unit air conditioner mounted in external wall*

8.02 Wall-mounted fans

These give higher air speeds and a more concentrated air stream, **37.6**. They are often arranged to swing from side to side. Typical data:

Mounting height	1.5–2.0 m
Angle of swing	up to 60°
'Reach' of blown air	3–4 m

8.03 Roof extract fans

With light roof constructions, extract fans are used to remove hot air from the ceiling void. Internal air temperatures may be reduced by 3–5°C in climates where high solar radiation is combined with moderate air temperatures. The extract fan does not give perceptible air movement within the building.

8.04 Unit air conditioners

Room air conditioners are available with a cooling capacity of from about 1.5 to 7 kW (Btus/h are commonly used to measure capacity as many manufacturers and designs originate in the USA). Specifications vary considerably and may include additional features such as heaters. They are usually accommodated in walls or under windows (often as afterthoughts). Table XVI shows typical dimensions for a range of cooling capacities based on six widely available makes. Unit air conditioners require external air for removing excess heat, fresh air inlet and drainage for water removed from the air during cooling, **37.7**.

8.05 Split air conditioning units

Split air conditioning units have the following advantages over unit (or 'room') air conditioners:

- Minimal structural alterations if installed in an existing building or minimal requirements for new buildings: the two pipes connecting the condenser to the air handler will fit through a 100 mm hole
- Greater security; important for banks, shops, etc.
- Reduced noise due to external position of condenser
- Greater flexibility internally as air handler may be placed on internal wall or even ceiling
- Improved external appearance as condenser may be placed on the roof, reducing problems of dripping condensate.

The air cooler and fan are not usually designed to provide ventilation by the exchange of internal air for external air.

8.06 Traditional aids to comfort

There are many traditional aids to comfort which may still be cheaper and as effective as mechanical aids. These include:

Cooling towers which catch the breeze and bring it down a vertical shaft into the interior of the building, often passing an earthenware water jar which cools and humidifies the air. They are used in desert and maritime desert climates.

Table XVI Unit air conditioners: typical data

Capacity BTUs per hour (or kilojoules/hour)	Capacity kW	Height mm	Width mm	Depth mm	Weight kg	Air handled m³/min	Moisture removed litres/hour
Domestic and small rooms							
5 000	1.47	320	485	490	24	4.6	0.6
6 500	1.90	360	500	360–500	42–47	5.4	0.7
7 200	2.11	360	500	360–500	42–47	5.4	0.8
7 600	2.23	379	618	587	57	8.3	0.9
Small shops, small to medium offices, small apartments							
9 000	2.64	367–380	618	570	53	8.3	1.1
9 300	2.73	367–380	560–620	517–586	47–60	8.0–8.3	0.9–1.2
10 500	3.08	367–380	615	570	55	9.0–10.5	1.5
12 000	3.52	380–460	650–677	609–700	65–78	9.5–10.5	1.3–1.5
13 600	4.00	380–460	615	570	54–58	10.5	1.9
15 000	4.40	380–470	650–677	630–750	73–80	11.7	1.9
16 000	4.67	380–470	615	570–700	55–59	11.7	2.4
16 500		400–470	660	700	90–92	11.4–11.8	1.6–1.8
Larger offices, large apartments							
17 000	5.00	450	600	700–792	90–92	8.7–12.8	1.9–2.3
18 000	5.28	380	615	570	69	11	2.7
20 000	5.86	535	693	783	108	18.5	2.8
23 500	6.89	452	660	792	107	20.0	3.0

Sources: manufacturers' data *1 BTU = 1.055 kJ

Air coolers Water is thrown at or dripped onto brushwood branches hung over a window to cool the air and filter out the dust. A modern version is the desert cooler – an electric fan which blows air over a damp fabric cooling and humidifying as it passes.

Planting Many plants, climbers and trees provide shade during hot summer months and drop their leaves during the cool winter allowing the sun to provide welcome heating; an automatic adjustable shading device used in composite, desert, Mediterranean and even temperate climates.

It should be realised, however, that some traditional aids have undesirable side effects (such as attracting or harbouring insects), high capital cost, as well as being regarded as symbols of the past (like thatched roofs in Northern Europe).

9 ILLUMINATION FROM SUN AND SKY IN THE TROPICS

9.01 Illumination at work surfaces
The illumination required at the work surface for a given task is the same regardless of latitude. However, since light is associated with heat (both physically and psychologically), there is a case for adopting slightly lower lighting standards to achieve higher levels of thermal comfort. In some countries, the cost of achieving high lighting standards may also be a factor.

The illumination from the sky is greater in tropical and sub-tropical regions so that a lower daylight factor can be used to achieve the same illumination at the work surface. The illumination from an overcast sky varies with latitude, altitude, degree of cloudiness and pollution. A guide is given in Table XVII.

9.02 Position of windows
With an overcast sky, the sky below 35° has below-average brightness and windows which allow a view of this part of the sky

Table XVII Illumination from a design sky

Latitude (N or S)	Design sky illumination
0°	17 000 lux
10°	15 000 lux
20°	13 000 lux
30°	9 000 lux
40°	6 000 lux
50°	5 000 lux

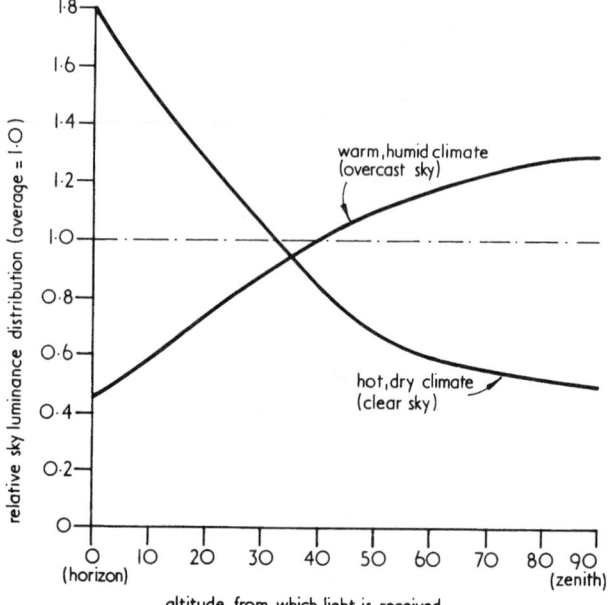

37.8 *Sky luminance distribution*

will avoid glare from the brighter overcast sky at higher angular altitudes, **37.8**. Conversely, in hot dry conditions windows should allow a view of the deep blue sky at high altitudes rather than the horizon, as this may be a source of glare from haze on the horizon (and glare from the sunlit ground). In this case, the window must be protected from direct solar radiation.

In the equatorial regions, however, the warm humid climate is often associated with a bright but constant overcast sky with a luminance which may drop to 10 000 lux or below. The hot dry desert regions receive light mainly from direct sunlight and considerably less from the (usually) deep blue sky.

9.03 Incidence of light
Table XVIII gives a very rough comparison of the relative amount of light from different sources. **37.8** shows the relative sky luminance distribution in hot dry desert climates with a clear sky, and for warm humid climates with an overcast sky. (It is assumed that the warm, humid climate has a similar distribution to the CIE standard overcast sky.)

Table XVIII Sun, sky and ground brightness

Hot dry desert conditions	Sky (away from sun)	3 000 lux
	Sun	50 000 lux
	Ground (20% reflectivity)	11 000 lux
Warm humid equatorial conditions	Sky (overcast)	10 000 lux
	Ground (20% reflectivity)	2 000 lux

10 PUBLIC UTILITIES IN THE TROPICS

Principles of design of public utilities are similar to those used in temperate regions but there are a number of differences due to climate, economic conditions and social factors, some of which are mentioned below.

10.01 Water supply

Table XIX gives standards which have been recommended by international organisations. However, the standards actually adopted must be related to local resources and conditions. In some countries, brackish water for irrigation is supplied by an independent system to conserve drinking water. Table XX shows the large amounts of water required to maintain lawns and Western-style gardens.

10.02 Foul sewerage

The capacity of piped systems will be related to the water supply standard. Where sewers are laid with low falls and where high soil temperatures exist, sewage may become septic and attack asbestos cement and cement pipes. Sewage disposal may be by pit latrine, aqua privy or septic tank in low-density development. Pit latrines require adequate space for replacements after the average life of five years, although this depends on soil conditions etc. They should be at least 7 m away from any building.

10.03 Surface water drainage

In many parts of the world design rainfall intensities are unestablished. Frequently, very heavy rain follows a long dry period during which drainage channels become blocked with sand and soil. In these zones, open or openable monsoon drains are used to provide adequate capacity and ease of cleansing. Where piped systems are employed large sand traps are needed at each gulley, and a minimum pipe size of 150 mm (sometines 200 mm pipes are mandatory). Gradients should give a minimum self-cleansing velocity of 1 m/s. Roof gutters are rarely provided at the eaves where torrential rains are experienced, as they cannot cope with

Table XIX Daily domestic water supply standards (litres per capita)*

Distribution	Minimum or temporary	Normal	With wastage allowance
Standpipe for up to 100 persons	20	40	60
Single tap connection	120	160	180
Multiple tap connection	160	200	240
Multiple tap connection in areas of water shortage	100	150	–

Sources: WHO, World Bank

Table XX Water supply for irrigation in hot dry climates

Type of vegetation		Water supply requirement
Private gardens	maximum	350 000 litres/hectare/day
	average	225 000 do
		170 000 do
Private gardens without grass	average	80 000 do
Irrigated vegetables		
Public parks		60–140 000 do
Tree plantations		2–7 000 do

the flows and water lying in them encourages mosquitoes. Water discharges straight off the roof into open dish drains, or onto a wide concrete apron with a fall away from the house to avoid soaking the walls from the rebound. Porches are needed to protect people using the entrance.

10.04 Electricity

Standards for voltage, demand, etc. vary widely. The design of the distribution system is as for temperate climates except that high soil temperatures may lead to a requirement for cable sizes to be larger to avoid over-heating.

11 HOUSING STANDARDS

Housing standards vary widely. Some may be unrealistically high in relation to national or family income. Others may be considered too low in relation to basic needs. Tables XXI and XXII give some guide to the range of plot and dwelling size. Table XXIII gives requirements affecting ceiling height.

Table XXI Plot sizes and densities

Type of plot	Minimum frontage: m	Size: m²	Minimum net density: plots/ha
Site and service projects:			
minimum	5	60	100
recommended minimum	7.5	100	66
(USAID and UNRWA):			
low density	–	200	33
very low density	–	400	18
OPEC country standard:			
minimum	9	200	25
normal minimum	12	300	17
medium density	–	400	14
low density	–	1000	7

Table XXII Dwelling size

Type of dwelling	Area m²		
	low	medium	high*
Core house (for self-build expansion)	8	18	–
Core house with one room	20	30	–
Bachelor units	22	–	–
Family dwellings:			
2 room units	36	50	–
3 room units	52	65	82
4 room units	65	85	100
5 room units	78	100	120
6 room units	–	–	140

*High, medium and low refers to the GNP of the countries selected

Table XXIII Floor to ceiling height*

To allow for ceiling beyond reach (in some regions 95 percentile reach is less than 2.264 found in Britain)	2.300 (ISO recommendation)
To allow for floor to ceiling as multiple of 200 (concrete block) or 300 (less usual vertical module)	2.400 (ISO recommendation)
To allow for ceiling mounted fan (2.400 + fan) (avoid mounting below light to avoid flicker)	3.000
Common requirement in tropical regions	3.000

*High ceiling heights have little effect on thermal comfort. See Givoni, *Man, climate and architecture*, Elsevier, 1969; United Nations, *Modular co-ordination of low cost housing*, New York, 1970; and BRE Overseas Building note 155

12 HAZARDS

12.01 Earthquakes

Data on the location and severity of significant earthquakes between 1900 and the present day for all tropical regions can be obtained from the Institute of Geological Sciences, Edinburgh and other centres. The maps give data on date, magnitude (on the Richter scale) and depth of epicentre.

Structures must be designed to resist seismic forces. The severity of these forces will depend on the type of structure, the dead and live load, the location (seismic zone) and soil conditions. In general, building plans and massing should be simple, avoiding T, X, or similar forms. Expansion joints and adjoining structures should be avoided as buildings may knock one another during minor tremors. For all but the simplest structures in minor seismic areas, a structural engineer's advice should be sought.

12.02 Hurricanes

In addition to the abnormally high wind loads, precautions are required to resist or reduce loads resulting from differences between internal and external pressures. Countries experiencing hurricanes and typhoons have appropriate building regulations concerning fixing for roofs, windows and structural design loadings.

12.03 Sandstorms

Table XXIV shows the effect of wind on sand movements. Tight closing of all openings is required to reduce nuisance from blown sand. Complete protection is not usually practical.

12.04 Termites

There are two main types of termites:

- *Drywood termites* are similar to wood-boring beetles found in temperate climates. They can fly into buildings or be introduced in previously infested timber. Prevention by use of (expensive) naturally resistant timbers or by pre-treatment of timber with a wood preservative and by screening of openings and roof cavities.

- *Subterranean termites* need to maintain contact with the ground and can survive in drier conditions than the drywood termites.

Table XXIV Effect of wind on sand

Windspeed m/min	Effect*
200	Sweeping sand. Visibility not impaired. Sand blown along the surface or up to 1 m from the ground
300	Driving sand. Visibility impaired. Sand rises up to 2 m high
600	Sandstorm. Particles of sand remain suspended in the air

*Depends on size of sand grains, humidity of ground, etc.

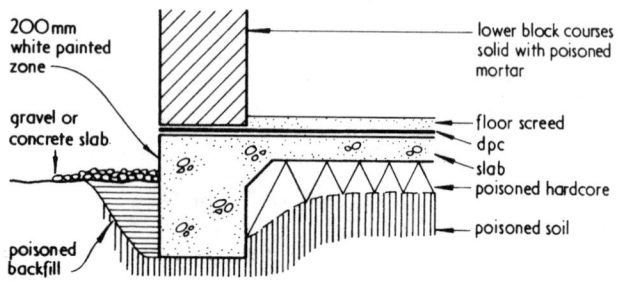

37.9 *Protection against termites when using a concrete slab floor*

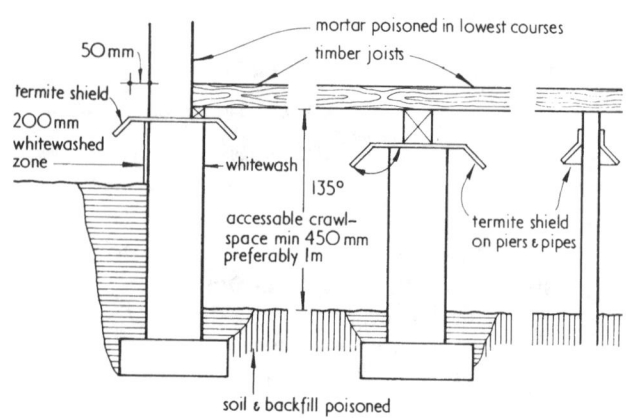

37.10 *Metal termite shields protecting a suspended timber floor over a crawl space*

Prevention by a general soil poison over the entire ground slab combined with poisoning of soil around the building perimeter and the poisoning of materials used in ground-floor slab and lower courses of walls, including hardcore, building sand, mortar and render and effective sealing of cracks, joints and holes with pitch-based sealing compound, or the use of termite shields where suspended timber floors are used. In addition, regular inspection is required, **37.9** and **37.10**.

12.05 Mosquitoes

Nuisance can be reduced by:

1 Cutting back undergrowth near buildings
2 Avoiding standing water on or near buildings, i.e. gutters
3 Screening of all openings with 16 mesh, 30 gauge wire screen or plastics mesh where windows open. Screening of bedrooms should have priority.
4 Avoid lighting which attracts mosquitoes (and other flying insects indoors, especially over dining tables, beds, etc.
5 Use external lighting to divert mosquitoes and other insects way from openings.

12.06 Diseases

Bad housing conditions contribute to many diseases common in the tropics. The main factors required to avoid conditions which encourage the spread of disease are:

- Safe water supply
- Safe sewage treatment and disposal
- Easily cleaned WC and bathroom, **37.11**
- Sound construction without cracks or crevices

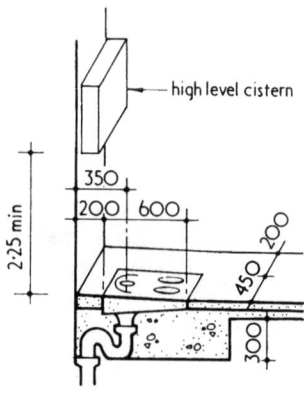

37.11 *Easily cleaned squatting WC, preferable in hot climates*

- Fly screening of kitchen and food storage areas
- Adequate natural light
- Adequate space standards
- Clearing of vegetation around the dwelling and
- Avoiding standing water on badly drained surfaces, gutters and vegetation.

13 BIBLIOGRAPHY

13.01 Comfort and requirements for comfort
Design of low cost housing and community facilities, vol 1, *Climate and house design*, New York, United Nations, 1971

13.02 Thermal performance requirements
Givoni, (ed.,) *Man, climate and architecture*, Elsevier, 1969
Institute of Heating and Ventilating Engineers, *Guide 1970*, Book A, London, 1970
H. Koenigsberger, T. G. Ingersol, A. Mayhew and S. V. Szokolay, *Manual of tropical housing and design, Part 1 Climate design*, Longmans, Harlow, Essex, 1973
A. G. Loudon, *Summertime temperatures in buildings without air-conditioning*, BRS CP 47/68

13.03 Solar radiation
P. Petherbridge, *Sunpath diagrams and overlays*, HMSO, London, 1969
H. Ransom, Tropical Building Studies 3, *Solar radiation thermal effects on building materials*, HMSO, London, 1962

13.04 Illumination from sun and sky
C. G. H. Plant, *Windows: design and function under tropical conditions*, Overseas Building Note 142, BRE, 1972
C. G. H. Plant, J. Longmore and R. G. Hopkinson, A study of interior illumination due to skylight and reflected sunlight under tropical condition, Proceedings of the CIE conference *Sunlight in buildings* (1965), Bouwcentrum, Rotterdam, 1967

13.05 Public utilities
B. H. Dietrich and J. M. Henderson, *Urban water supply conditions in 75 developing countries*, WHO, 1963
E. G. Wagner and J. Lanoix, *Water supply for rural areas and small communities*, WHO
E. G. Wagner and F. Lanoix, *Excreta disposal for rural areas and small communities*, WHO, 1958

13.06 Hazards
Building Research Station, *Tropical building legislation: model building regulations for small buildings in earthquake and hurricane areas*, 1966
W. Victor Harris, *Termites: their recognition and control*, Longmans, Harlow, 1971
Preservation of personal health in warm climates, Ross Institute of Tropical Hygiene, London, 1970
Termites and tropical building, Overseas Building Note 170, BRE, 1976

38 Thermal environment

Phil Jones

Professor Phil Jones occupies the chair in Architectural Science at the University of Wales, Cardiff

CI/SfB: (M)
UDC: 644.1, 644.5
Uniclass: U35

KEY POINTS:

● *Safety and comfort for the inhabitants are the main considerations for an internal environment*
● *Conservation of energy and reduction of emissions come a close second*

Contents

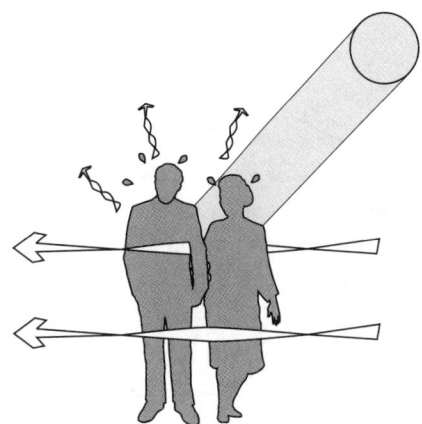

38.1 *Thermal design to achieve comfort for a given climatic condition. Passive design is related to building form and fabric. Active design is related to mechanical services, energy use and environmental impact*

1 INTRODUCTION

1.01

Thermal design is concerned with the heat transfer processes that take place within a building, and between the building and its surroundings and the external climate, **38.1**. It is primarily concerned with providing comfort and shelter for the building's occupants and contents. Thermal design therefore includes consideration of the

● Climate
● Building form and fabric
● Building environmental services, and
● Occupants and processes contained within the building.

It is also concerned with the energy used to provide heating, cooling and ventilation of buildings, and the local and global impact of energy use. The thermal design should be integrated with the visual and acoustic aspects of the design in order to achieve an overall satisfactory environmental solution.

1.02 Three stages to thermal design

Stage 1: Internal conditions for occupants or processes
The prime aim is to create spaces that are comfortable and healthy for their occupants, **38.2** People will typically spend 90% or more of their time in buildings. The environments people live and work in must promote a good quality of life. Thermal conditions should be within acceptable comfort limits and the indoor air quality should be free from any harmful pollutants. Buildings must also provide appropriate thermal conditions for their contents, processes and for maintaining the building fabric itself. The required environmental conditions of all spaces should be clearly defined at the initial design stage in relation to the activities and contents of the space.

Stage 2: Climate modification through the building envelope
Buildings can be designed to interact with the external environment in order to benefit from the natural energy of the sun and wind, **38.3**. The envelope of the building can be used to 'filter'

38.2 *Thermal comfort is influenced by air temperature, air movement, relative humidity and the surrounding radiant environment*

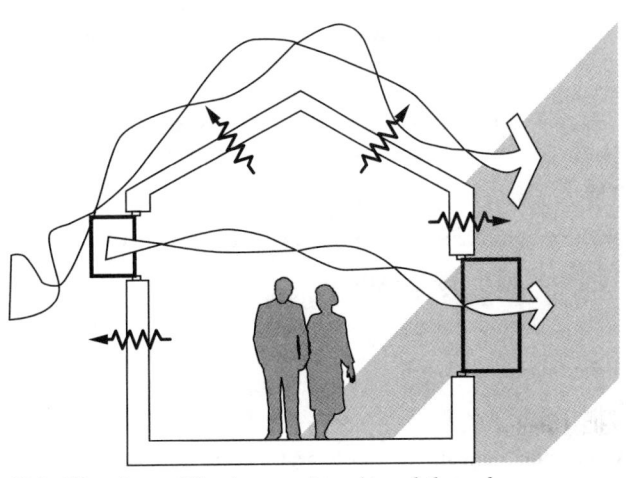

38.3 *Climatic modification can be achieved through manipulation of a building's form and construction*

or 'modify' the external climate to provide internal comfort conditions for much of the year without the use of fuel. The heat from the sun can be used to heat spaces in winter or to drive air movement for ventilation and cooling through buoyancy forces. The wind can also be used to provide ventilation and cooling. The fabric of the building can be used to insulate against heat loss or gain, and to stabilise the internal environment against extremes of external temperatures (hot or cold). The form, mass, orientation and construction of the building need to be designed in response to the climate and specific location.

Stage 3: Mechanical services

If a building is designed to respond positively to the climate then its dependence on mechanical services to heat, cool and ventilate spaces will be minimised, **38.4**. However, there are few climates in the world where mechanical systems can be eliminated altogether. In temperate climates such as the UK a heating system will still generally be required during the winter period. In hot climates, mechanical cooling is often needed, sometimes the whole year round, for commercial buildings. These services should be provided in an energy-efficient way in order to minimise energy use from fossil fuels, and to reduce the impact that buildings have on polluting the environment. Wherever possible, renewable energy sources, such as wind power, photovoltaics and solar heating, should be considered. The mechanical systems and their controls should be designed to be able to respond to the specific needs of the occupants.

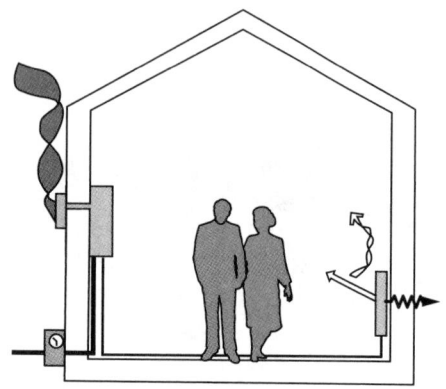

38.4 *Mechanical services should be designed to minimise energy use and environmental impact*

2 HEAT TRANSFER MECHANISMS

2.01 There are four types of heat transfer that relate to thermal environmental design, **38.5**. These are conduction, convection, radiation and evaporation. They are described below with examples of how they relate to building thermodynamics.

Heat is a form of energy, measured in joules (J). The rate of energy use per second (s) is measured in watts (W), where;

$$1\,W = 1\,J/s\ (1\,kW = 1000\,J/s)$$

Another unit of energy is the kilowatt-hour (kWh), where:

$$1\,kWh = 3600\,J\ (or\ 3.6\,MJ)$$

and the therm, where:

$$1\ therm = 29.3\,kWh$$

2.02 Conduction

Conduction normally applies to heat transfer through solids. It is the transfer of heat from molecule to molecule form relatively warm to cool regions. The rate of heat transfer through a solid is

dependent on its thermal conductivity, or *k*-value. The *k*-value is loosely related to the density of the material, **38.6** (See Table I). High-density materials generally have high *k*-values – they are termed 'good conductors' of heat (eg high-density concrete, metals). Low-density materials have low *k*-values – they are termed 'good thermal insulators' (eg mineral fibre batts, low-density concrete blocks). The thermal resistance of a given thickness of material in a construction is calculated by dividing its thickness by its *k*-value. The higher the resistance the better its insulation.

$$R = x/k \tag{1}$$

where R = thermal resistance (m^2.K/W)
 x = thickness (m)
 k = thermal conductivity (W/m.K)

The conductivity k of a material is the inverse of its resistivity r, that is,

$$k = 1/r$$

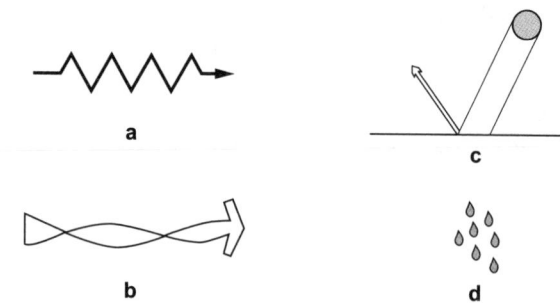

38.5 *Heat is transferred by:* **a** *Conduction;* **b** *Convection;* **c** *Radiation;* **d** *Evaporation*

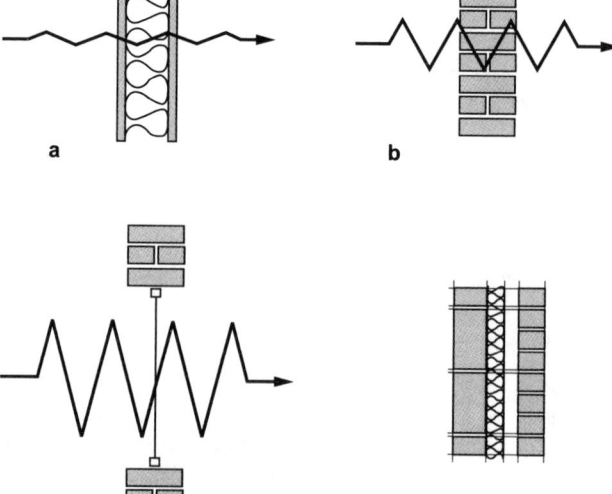

38.6 *Comparison of thermal conduction properties of different constructions.* **A** *Mineral wool has a low density (25 kg/m^3) and is a good thermal insulator (k = 0.035 W/mK).* **b** *Bricks have a relatively high density (1700 kg/m^3) and a low thermal resistance (k = 0.84 W/mK).* **c** *Glazing has a relatively high density (1700 kg/m^3) and a low thermal resistance (k = 1.05 W/mK).* **d** *Walls need to have structural and weatherproofing properties as well as thermal insulation properties. Most wall constructions are therefore composed of a number of layers, the resistances of which can be added to give an overall wall thermal resistance*

Table I Thermal conductivity and density of common building materials

Material	Density (kg/m³)	Thermal conductivity (W/m.K)
Walls		
Brickwork (outer leaf)	1700	0.84
Brickwork (inner leaf)	1700	0.62
Cast concrete (dense)	2100	1.40
Cast concrete (lightweight)	1200	0.38
Concrete block (heavyweight)	2300	1.63
Concrete block (medium weight)	1400	0.51
Concrete block (lightweight)	600	0.19
Normal mortar	1750	0.80
Fibreboard	300	0.06
Plasterboard	950	0.16
Tile hanging	1900	0.84
Timber	650	0.14
Glass	1700	1.05
Surface finishes		
External rendering	1300	0.50
Plaster (dense)	1300	0.50
Plaster (lightweight)	600	0.16
Calcium silicate board	875	0.17
Roofs		
Aerated concrete slab	500	0.16
Asphalt	1700	0.50
Felt/bitumen layers	1700	0.50
Screed	1200	0.41
Stone chippings	1800	0.96
Tile	1900	0.84
Wood wool slab	500	0.10
Floors		
Cast concrete	2000	1.13
Metal tray	7800	50.0
Screed	1200	0.41
Timber flooring	650	0.14
Wood blocks	650	0.14
Insulation		
Expanded polystyrene (EPS) slab	25	0.035
Mineral wool quilt	12	0.040
Mineral wool slab	25	0.035
Phenolic foam board	30	0.020
Polyurethane board	30	0.025

Example 1

What is the thermal resistance of a wall comprising 100 mm brick, 50 mm mineral wool slab insulation, 100 mm medium-density concrete block?

Material	Thickness (m)	k-value (W/mK)	Resistance (m²K/W)
Brick	0.1	0.84	0.12
Insulation	0.05	0.055	1.43
Block	0.1	0.51	0.02
Total thermal resistance			1.73

Notes:

(1) Values for conductivity are from Table 1.
(2) The thermal resistance of each layer is calculated according to formula 1:
   $R = x/k$.
(3) The main contribution to the total thermal resistance is from the mineral wool slab insulation.
(4) Thermal resistance will be used later in the calculation of U-values (in Section 5).

2.03 Convection

Convection takes place in a fluid such as air or water. Once heated it becomes less dense and more buoyant. Fluids are normally heated by conduction from a warm surface such as the electric element in a hot water cylinder, or the hot surface of a panel heater. A cold surface will conduct heat from the adjacent fluid, thereby cooling the fluid. This will make it more dense and cause the fluid to become less buoyant, for example causing a downdraught under a cold window. For a typical room, the relatively warm and cool surfaces set up a series of interacting convective flow patterns. The convection of air in a room is an integral part of most heating systems.

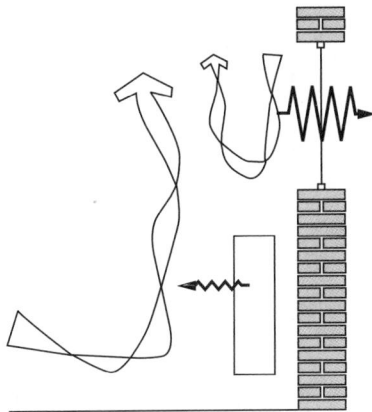

38.7 *Typical convection patterns generated by relatively warm (panel heater) and cool (glazing)*

In the example, **38.7**, heat is conducted from the air to the cooler surface of the glazing, causing a downdraught. Heat is conducted to the air from the warmer surface of the panel heater, causing an updraught. Although panel heaters are usually called radiators they mainly provide heat (typically 60–70%) through convection. The formula for convective heat transfer from a surface to air is:

$$Q_c = h_c \times (t_a - t_s) \tag{2}$$

where Q_c = convective heat transfer (W)
h_c = convective heat transfer coefficient ($\text{Wm}^{-2}\text{K}^{-1}$)
t_a = air temperature (°C)
t_s = surface temperature (°C)

Heat flow upwards: $h_c = 4.3\,\text{Wm}^{-2}\text{K}^{-1}$
Heat flow downwards: $h_c = 1.5\,\text{Wm}^{-2}\text{K}^{-1}$
Heat flow horizontally: $h_c = 3.0\,\text{Wm}^{-2}\text{K}^{-1}$

Note: Values of h_c are at room temperature (21°C). They will increase with higher surface temperatures.

2.04 Radiation

Radiation is the transfer of heat between two surfaces. It is independent of the air between them. For example, heat travels by radiation from the sun to the earth through the vacuum of space. Radiant heat is in the infrared part of the electromagnetic spectrum (which includes X-rays, ultraviolet, visible light, infrared, microwaves and radio, waves – which differ from each other by their wavelength and frequency). The sun emits radiation with wavelengths between 0.29 and 3.0 μm, which includes the visible spectrum (0.38 and 0.78 μm), **38.8**. The hotter the emitting body, the shorter the wavelength. Infrared radiation below a wavelength of 3.0 μm is termed short-wave; above this it is termed long-wave. The sun emits most of its heat energy as short-wave radiation, while lower-temperature surfaces, such as buildings, tend to emit only long-wave radiation.

Glass is relatively transparent to short-wave radiation while opaque to long-wave radiation. This is the principle of the 'greenhouse effect', **38.9**, which is important in 'passive solar design'. The short-wave radiation from the sun passes through glass and warms up the internal surfaces, which in turn emit long-wave radiation which is 'trapped' within the space. The only heat loss therefore takes place through conduction.

Solar radiation incident on solid walls will heat up the external wall surface, **38.10**. This heat is conducted through the wall where it will result in a rise in the internal surface temperature. The internal surface will then radiate long-wave radiation in proportion to its surface temperature and emissivity (see below). Glazing, however, is transparent to 'short-wave' solar radiation and radiative heat is transmitted directly through the glass, **38.11**.

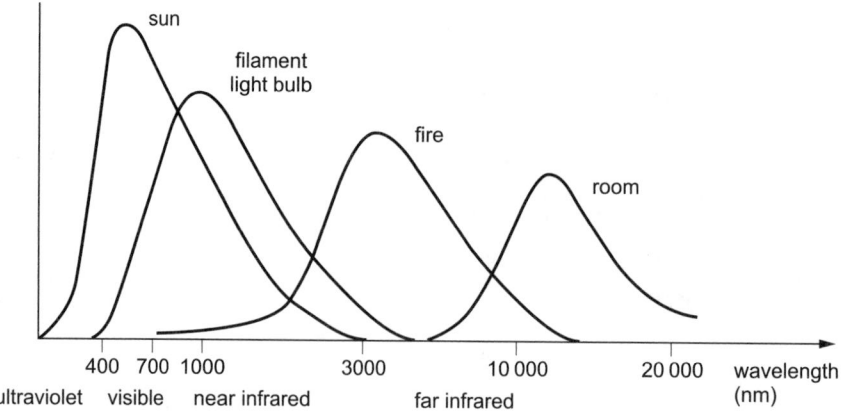

38.8 *Spectrum of long-wave (low-temperature) and short-wave (solar) radiation; Vertical axis is not to scale*

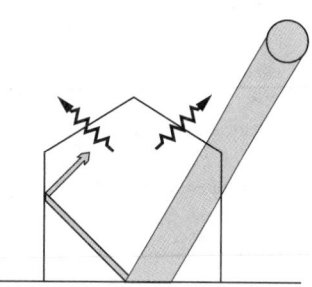

38.9 *Heat transfer process in a greenhouse, which forms the basis of passive solar design*

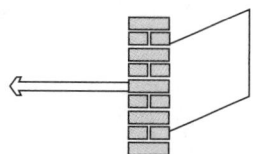

38.10 *Radiation absorption and emission at surfaces*

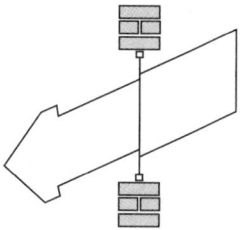

38.11 *Radiation transmission through glass*

Table II Surface emissivities/absorptivities

Finish	Thermal absorptance and emittance
Aluminium paint	0.55
Aluminium, polished	0.08
Asbestos cement, aged	0.95
Black matt	0.95
Chromium plate	0.20
Galvanised iron, aged	0.28
Grey paint	0.95
Light green paint	0.95
Limestone	0.95
Red clay brick	0.94
White marble	0.95
White paint	0.89
Wood, pine	0.95

Source: Coblenz, Cammerer and Drysdale, *Handbook of Chemistry and Physics*

2.05 The Stefan–Boltzmann law

The amount of radiation emitted by a surface is related to its temperature and emissivity according to the Stefan–Boltzmann law:

$$Q_r = (5.673 \times 10^8) \times S \times T^4 \tag{3}$$

where Q_r = radiation emitted by the surface
  E = surface emissivity
  T = surface temperature (°C)
  5.673×10^{-8} = Stefan–Boltzmann constant (W/m² K⁴)

2.06 Emissivity and absorptance

The emissivity of a surface is the amount of radiation emitted by the surface compared to that radiated by a matt black surface (a 'black body') at the same temperature. The best emitters are matt dark surfaces and the worst are silvered surfaces (although they are good reflectors of radiation). The emissivity of a surface varies between 0 and 1, with most common building materials, such as bricks and plaster, having an emissivity of about 0.95. The absorptance is the amount of radiation absorbed by a surface compared to that absorbed by a black body. For low-temperature surfaces the absorptance and emittance are the same (Table II).

2.07 Evaporation

Evaporation takes place when a liquid such as water changes state to a vapour. A vapour is a mixture of gases which exerts a vapour pressure. The water molecules that escape from the liquid tend to have a higher energy content than those left behind and so the average energy content of the liquid is reduced, and therefore its temperature is also reduced. In order for evaporation to take place, the vapour pressure of water (in the form of droplets or a wetted surface) must be greater than the partial pressure of the water vapour in the surrounding atmosphere. The lower the relative humidity of the air, the greater the evaporation that will take place. The evaporation rate can be calculated as follows:

$$W = \frac{(8.3 \times 10^{-4})}{135} h_c \times (p_{va} - p_s) \tag{4}$$

where W = rate of evaporation from the surface
  h_c = convective heat transfer coefficient
  p_{va} = vapour pressure in air
  p_s = saturation vapour pressure at surface temperature.

Evaporation produces local cooling on wetted surfaces. This can be used to advantage in hot countries where roof ponds, cooled by evaporation, can be used to cool the roof construction. The tradition in some hot dry countries is to simply spray the floors of courtyards with water to cool the floor surface. Air passed over wetted surfaces is cooled and its moisture content raised. The rate of evaporation increases with increased liquid temperature, reduced vapour pressure of the surrounding atmosphere, or increased air movement across the wetted surface.

Condensation is the reverse of evaporation and takes place when air comes into contact with a relatively cold surface. The air adjacent to the cold surface is cooled and becomes saturated and the vapour condenses into a liquid forming droplets on the surface (condensation is dealt with in detail in Section 5).

2.08 Thermal capacity

The thermal capacity of a material is a measure of its ability to store heat from the surrounding air and surfaces. Generally, the more dense a material, the greater its capacity to store heat (Table III). Therefore, high-density materials, such as concrete, will store more heat than low-density materials, such as mineral wool. The thermal capacity of a material can be calculated from the formula:

$$\text{Thermal capacity} = \text{volume (m}^3) \times \text{density (kg/m}^3)$$
$$\text{(J/K.m}^3) \qquad\qquad \times \text{specific heat (J/kg.K)} \qquad (5)$$

Dense masonry materials have 100 times the thermal capacity of lightweight insulating materials (Table III).

2.09 Thermal capacity and response

Lightweight buildings will respond quickly to heat gains, **38.12**, from either internal sources (people, lights, machines) or external sources (solar radiation, high external air temperatures). They have a relatively low thermal capacity. The internal air will therefore warm up quickly as the mass of the building will have a relatively low capacity to absorb internal heat. They will also cool down quickly when the heat source is turned off, as there is little residual heat in the construction to retain air temperatures. They are more likely to overheat during warm weather and be cool during colder weather. They therefore require a more responsive heating/cooling system, and are more suited to intermittent occupancy.

Heavyweight buildings are slower to respond to extremes of temperature, **38.12**, and therefore have the potential to maintain a more stable internal environment. Buildings constructed of heavyweight materials will have a high thermal capacity. They will be slow to heat up as the mass of the building will absorb heat from the space. However, they will also be slow to cool down and are able to retain relatively high internal air temperatures between heating periods. Heavyweight buildings can maintain relatively cooler internal environments in warmer weather by absorbing peaks in heat gains. Typical cooling effects may be up to 3°C reduction in internal air temperature peaks due to thermal mass effects. In addition, the mean radiant temperature will be lower due to the lower surface temperatures.

The thermal mass effect is related to the exposed surface area of material and its thickness and heat capacity. Surface area is relatively more important that thickness of material. For example, for absorbing short-term (diurnal) peaks in heat gain the thermal mass thickness need only be about 40 mm.

3 THERMAL COMFORT

3.01 The body produces heat through metabolic activities and exchanges heat with its surroundings by conduction, convection and radiation (typically 75%), and evaporation (typically 25%). Thermal comfort is achieved when there is a balance between metabolic heat production and heat loss. It is mainly dependent on the thermal environmental conditions and the activity and clothing of the person in that environment.

3.02 Metabolic activity

The human body produces metabolic heat as a result of its muscular and digestive processes. It has to maintain a constant core temperature of 37°C. If the core body temperature is reduced by more than about 1°C hypothermia sets in; if it increases by

Table III Density, specific heat and thermal capacity of common materials

Material	Density (kg/m³)	Specific heat (J/kg.K)	Thermal capacity (J/K.m³)
Granite	2600	900	2340 × 10³
Brick	1700	790	1343 × 10³
Concrete (dense)	2100	820	1722 × 10³
Concrete (light)	500	1000	500 × 10³
Mineral fibre	25	960	24 × 10³
Polystyrene board	15	1400	21 × 10³

Table IV Metabolic heat generation for different activities at 20°C in MET and in watts (W) for sensible (S) and latent (L) heat loss

Activity	MET	S(W)	L(W)
Seated at rest (theatre, hotel, lounge)	1.1	90	25
Light work (office, dwelling, school)	1.3	100	40
Standing activity (shopping, laboratory)	1.5	110	50
Standing activity (shop assistant, domestic)	2.2	130	105
Medium activity (factory, garage work)	2.5	140	125
Heavy work (factory)	4.2	190	250

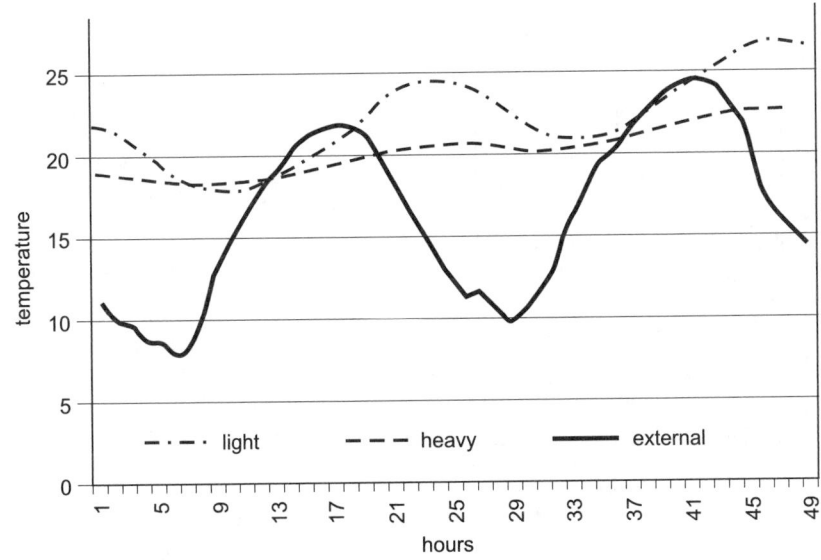

38.12 *Thermal responses of lightweight and heavyweight buildings against external temperature over a two-day period*

more than about 1°C the person may suffer a heat stroke. The body must therefore lose the metabolic heat it generates in a controlled way. Clothing is one way of controlling heat loss. There are also physiological control mechanisms: for example, shivering when cold increases metabolic activity; the formation of 'goose-pimples' increases the body's surface resistance to heat loss; sweating when warm increases heat loss by evaporation. The heat generated by metabolic activity is measured in units of MET (1 MET = 58.2 W/m² of body surface area; the average surface area of an adult is 1.8 m²). Typical values of MET for different activities are given in Table IV.

3.03 Clothing provides insulation against body heat loss. The insulation of clothing is measured in units of CLO (1 CLO = 0.155 m²K/W; the units are those of internal resistance). Values of CLO for typical clothing ensembles are given in Table V.

3.04 Air temperature is often taken as the main design parameter for thermal comfort. The CIBSE recommended range for internal air temperature is between 19°C and 23°C in winter and less than 27°C in summer. The air temperature gradient between head and feet is also important for comfort; the temperature at feet should generally not be less than 4°C below that at head.

38.13 *Psychrometric chart (from figures in CIBSE Guide). This relates dry bulb temperature, wet bulb temperature and moisture content to relative humidity (RH)*

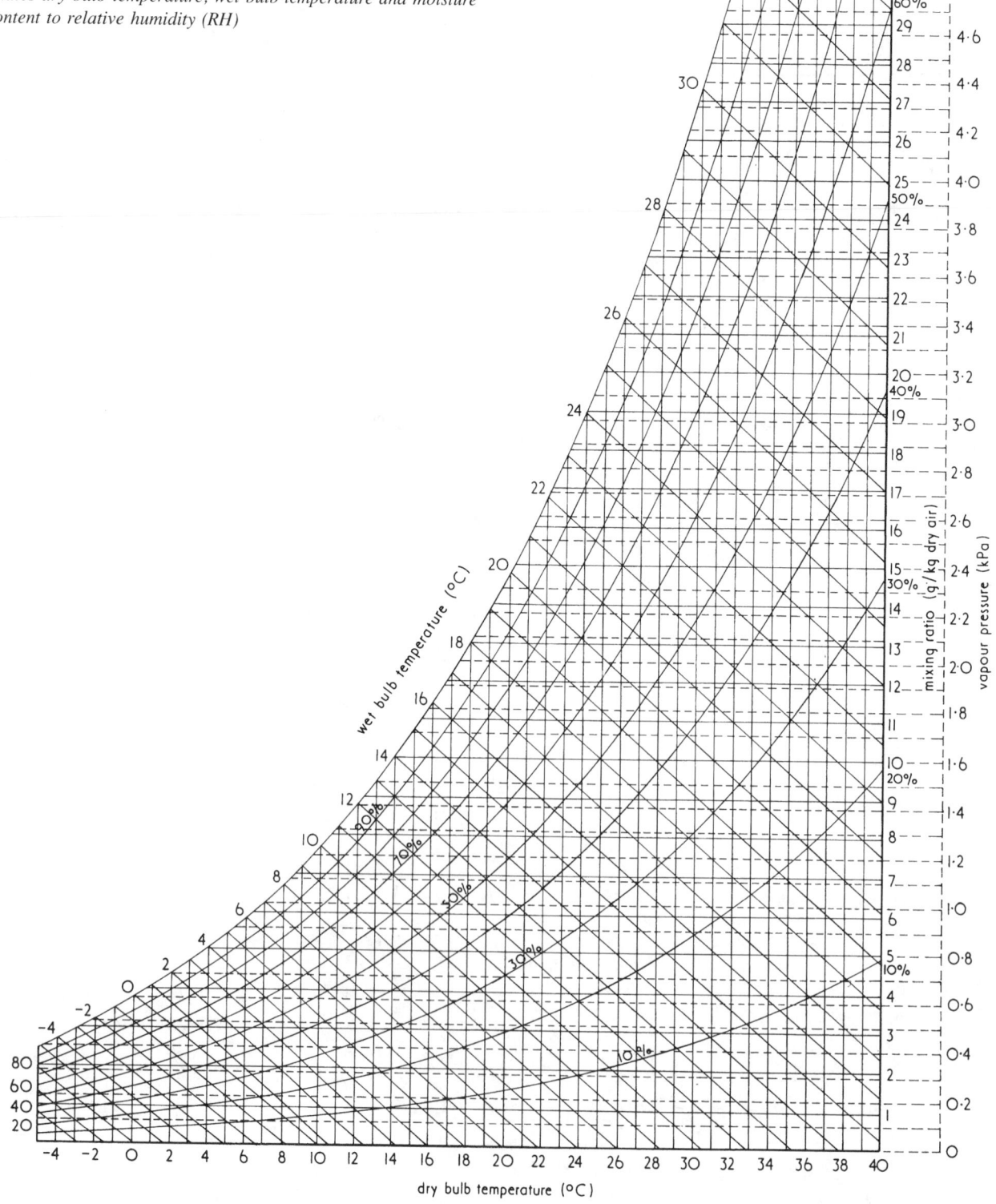

Table V Clothing resistance in CLO and
thermal resistance

	CLO	(m²K/W)
Nude	0	0
Light summer clothes	0.5	0.08
Light working ensemble	0.7	0.11
Winter indoor	1.0	0.16
Heavy business suit	1.5	0.23

3.05 Radiant temperature is a measure of the temperature of the surrounding surfaces, together with any direct radiant gains from high temperature sources (such as the sun). The *mean radiant temperature* is the area-weighted average of all the surface temperatures in a room. If the surfaces in a space are at different temperatures then the perceived radiant temperature in a space will be affected by the position of the person in relation to the various surfaces, with the closer or larger surface areas contributing more to the overall radiant temperature. Comfort can be affected by radiant asymmetry, and people are especially sensitive to warm ceilings (a 10°C radiant asymmetry from a warm ceiling can give rise to 20% comfort dissatisfaction). The *vector radiant temperature* is a measure of the maximum difference in a room between the radiant temperatures from opposite directions.

3.06 Relative humidity (RH) of a space will affect the rate of evaporation from the skin. The RH is a percentage measure of the amount of vapour in the air compared to the total amount of vapour the air can hold at that temperature. When temperatures are within the comfort range (19–23°C) the RH has little effect on comfort as long as it is within the range 40–70%. At high air temperatures (approaching average skin temperature of 34°C) evaporation heat loss is important to maintain comfort. Wet bulb temperature is a measure of the temperature of a space using a wetted thermometer. A 'dry bulb' temperature sensor will exchange heat with the surrounding air by convection. A wet bulb thermometer loses additional heat by evaporation and can be used in combination with a dry bulb, to obtain a measure of RH by referring to the *psychrometric chart*, **38.13**. An example of the use of this is shown in **38.14**, where a dry bulb temperature (dbt) of 19°C and a wet bulb temperature (wbt) of 14°C indicates a relative humidity (RH) of 60%.

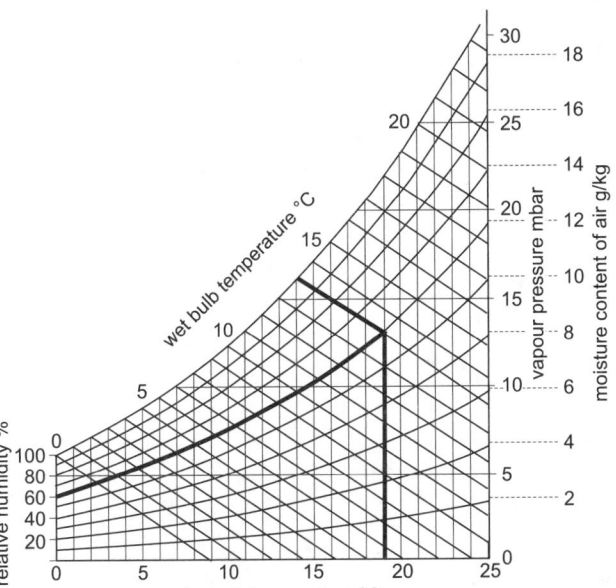

38.14 A psychrometric chart showing that a dry bulb temperature of 19°C and a wet bulb temperature of 14°C relates to an RH of 60%

3.07 Air speed is a measure of the movement of air in a space. People begin to perceive air movement at about 0.2 m/s. Air speeds greater than 0.2 m/s produce a 20% and greater comfort dissatisfaction due to perceived draught. For most naturally ventilated spaces the air speed will be less than 0.1 m/s, away from the influence of open windows. For mechanically ventilated spaces, the air speed is generally greater than 0.1 m/s and could be greater than 0.2 m/s in areas close to air supply devices or where supply air jets are deflected by downstand beams or other geometric features of the space, and such speeds should be avoided. It is possible to counter draught discomfort to a certain extent by increasing air temperatures, as indicated in **38.15**.

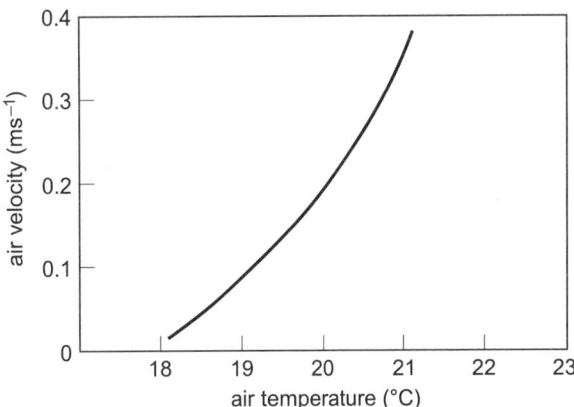

38.15 The interaction of air temperature and air movement on perceived comfort

3.08 Thermal comfort: compensation and adaption
The perception of thermal comfort is a function of the combination of the physical environment (air and radiant temperature, air movement and relative humidity) and the activity and clothing level of the person. To some extent these factors are compensatory. For example, during cool conditions, an increase in air movement can be compensated by an increase in air temperature, while in warm conditions, an increase in relative humidity can be compensated for by an increase in air movement. People can also adapt their clothing levels, activity levels and posture in response to the prevailing thermal conditions. In this way they are varying either their rate of metabolic heat production or their rate of body heat loss. Thermal indices use combinations of the comfort parameters in a compensatory way to provide a single measure of thermal comfort.

The *resultant temperature*, sometimes called *globe temperature*, is a combination of air temperature and mean radiant temperature, in a proportion comparable to that of the body's heat loss. At low air speeds (<0.1 m/s) the following relationship can be applied:

$$t_{res} = 0.5\ t_{mrt} + 0.5\ t_a \tag{6}$$

where t_{res} = resultant temperature (°C)
  t_{mrt} = mean radiant temperature (°C)
  t_a = air temperature (°C)

The resultant temperature can be measured at the centre of a black globe of 100 mm diameter (although globes between 25 mm and 150 mm will give acceptable results).

The *corrected effective temperature (CET)* relates globe temperature, wet bulb temperature and air speed. It is equivalent to the thermal sensation in a standard environment with still, saturated air for the same clothing and activity. CET can be represented in nomogram form as shown in **38.16**.

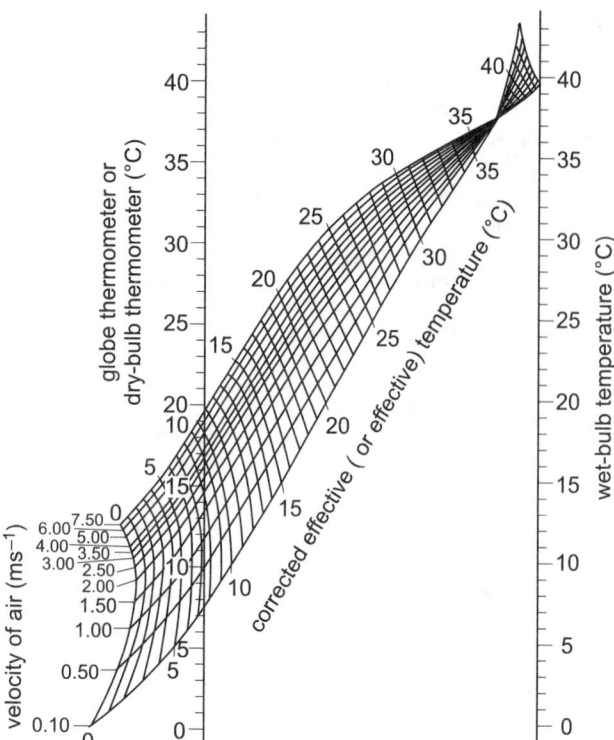

38.16 *Nomogram for estimating corrected effective temperature (CET)*

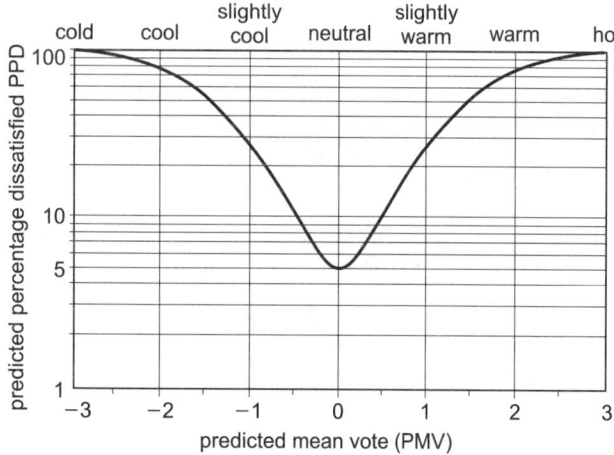

38.17 *PPD as a function of PMV*

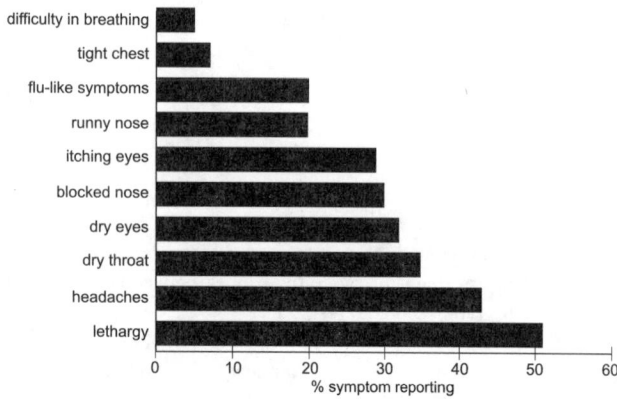

38.18 *Sample percentage symptom reporting for air conditioned offices*

3.09 PMV and PPD

The *predicted mean vote (PMV)* is a measure of the average response from a large group of people voting on the scale below:

hot	+3
warm	+2
slightly warm	+1
neutral	0
slightly cool	−1
cool	−2
cold	−3

The PMV can be calculated from *Fanger's comfort equation* which combines air temperature, mean radiant temperature, RH and air speed together with estimates of activity and clothing levels. The *percentage people dissatisfied (PPD)* provides a measure of the percentage of people who will complain of thermal discomfort in relation to the PMV. This is shown graphically in **38.17** and can be calculated from:

$$PPD = 100 - 95 \exp(10.03353 \, PMV^4 - 0.2179 \, PMV^2) \quad (7)$$

The implication of PPD is that there is no condition where everyone will experience optimum comfort conditions. It predicts that there will always be 5% of people who will report discomfort.

3.10 Sick building syndrome is a term used to describe a set of commonly occurring symptoms that affect people at their place of work, usually in office-type environments, and which disappear soon after they leave work. These symptoms include dry eyes, watery eyes, blocked nose, runny nose, headaches, lethargy, tight chest, and difficulty with breathing, typical percentage symptom reporting for air-conditioned offices is shown in **38.18**. The *personal symptom index (PSI)* is often used as a measure of the average number of symptoms per person for a whole office or zone.

Workers who report high levels of symptoms also often report problems associated with thermal comfort, and in general perceive the air quality as stale, dry and warm. Studies have indicated that air-conditioned buildings appear to have a higher level of complaint than naturally ventilated buildings – possible reasons include cost cuts in their design, difficult to maintain and operate, difficult to keep clean (especially the air-distribution ductwork) and low ventilation effectiveness due to short-circuiting between supply and extract. Workers with a higher risk of symptoms are those in open-plan offices more than those in cellular ones, clerical workers more than managerial, women more than men, those in public sector buildings more than private, those in air-conditioned offices more than naturally ventilated ones, and those buildings where there is poor maintenance and poor operation of controls.

3.11 Ventilation

Ventilation is required to maintain good air quality for health and comfort. Tables VI to VIII give recommended ventilation rates. Ventilation is considered in detail in Section 6.

4 SITE AND CLIMATE

4.01 The site and climatic conditions have a major impact on the thermal design of a building, and should be considered in the early stages of design. Also, the building will modify the existing climate of the site to create a specific microclimate surrounding itself. Climate data is available for many parts of the world, often as hourly values compiled into a standard *Test Reference Year (TRY)* format.

Table VI Recommended design values for internal environmental temperatures and empirical values for air infiltration and ventilation allowance (for normal sites and winter heating)

Type of building	Air t_{ei} (°C)	Ventilation infiltration rate (h^{-1})	Allowance (W/m^2 °C)
Art galleries and museums	20	1	0.33
Assembly halls, lecture halls	18	½	0.17
Banking halls:			
Large (height > 4 m)	20	1	0.33
Small (height < 4 m)	20	1½	0.50
Bars	18	1	0.33
Canteens and dining rooms	20	1	0.33
Churches and chapels:			
Up to 7000 m³	18	½	0.17
> 7000 m³	18	¼	0.08
Vestries	20	1	0.33
Dining and banqueting halls	21	½	0.17
Exhibition halls:			
Large (height > 4 m)	18	¼	0.08
Small (height < 4 m)	18	½	0.17
Factories:			
Sedentary work	19		
Light work	16		
Heavy work	13		
Fire stations, ambulance stations:			
Appliance rooms	15	½	0.17
Watch rooms	20	½	0.17
Recreation rooms	18	1	0.33
Flats, residences and hostels:			
Living rooms	21	1	0.33
Bedrooms	18	½	0.17
Bed-sitting rooms	21	1	0.33
Bathrooms	22	2	0.67
Lavatories and cloakrooms	18	1½	0.50
Service rooms	16	½	0.17
Staircase and corridors	16	1½	0.50
Entrance halls and foyers	16	1½	0.50
Public rooms	21	1	0.33
Gymnasia	16	¾	0.25
Hospitals:			
Corridors	16	1	0.33
Offices	20	1	0.33
Operating theatre suite	18–21	½	0.17
Stores	15	½	0.17
Wards and patient areas	18	2	0.67
Waiting rooms	18	1	0.33
Hotels:			
Bedrooms (standard)	22	1	0.33
Bedrooms (luxury)	24	1	0.33
Public rooms	21	1	0.33
Corridors	18	1½	0.50
Foyers	18	1½	0.50
Laboratories	20	1	0.33
Law courts	20	1	0.33
Libraries:			
Reading rooms			
(height > 4 m)	20	½	0.17
(height < 4 m)	20	¾	0.25
Stack rooms	18	½	0.17
Store rooms	15	¼	0.08
Offices:			
General	20	1	0.33
Private	20	1	0.33
Stores	15	½	0.17
Police stations: Cells	18	5	1.65
Restaurants and tea shops	18	1	0.33
Schools and colleges:			
Classrooms	18	2	0.67
Lecture rooms	18	1	0.33
Studios	18	1	0.33
Shops and showrooms:			
Small	18	1	0.33
Large	18	½	0.17
Department store	18	¼	0.08
Fitting rooms	21	1½	0.50
Store rooms	15	½	0.17
Sports pavilions: Dressing rooms	21	1	0.33
Swimming baths:			
Changing rooms	22	½	0.17
Bath hall	26	½	0.17
Warehouses:			
Working and packing spaces	16	½	0.17
Storage space	13	¼	0.08

The values quoted for rates of air infiltration in this table should not be used for the design of mechanical ventilation, air conditioning or warm air heating systems.

Table VII Mechanical ventilation rates for various types of building

Room or building		Recommended air change rates* (h^{-1})
Boilerhouses and engine rooms		15–30
Banking halls		6
Bathrooms, internal		6†
Battery charging rooms		up to 5†
Canteens		8–12‡
Cinemas		6–10‡
Dance halls		10–12‡
Dining and banqueting halls, restaurants		10–15‡
Drying rooms		up to 5
Garages:	public (parking)	6† minimum
	repair shops	10† minimum
Hospitals:	treatment rooms	6
	operating theatre	15–17
	post-mortem room	5
Kitchens:	hotel and industrial	20–60†
	local authority	up to 10†
Laboratories		4–6
Laundries		10–15
Lavatories and toilets, internal		6–8†
Libraries:	public	3–4‡
	book stacks	1–2
Offices, internal		4–6‡
Sculleries and wash-ups, large-scale		10–15†
Smoking rooms		10–15
Swimming baths:	bath hall	
	changing areas	10
Theatres		6–10‡

*The recommended air change rates do not apply in cases of warm-air heating, when the rate may be dictated by the heat requirements of the building or room.
†Refers to extract ventilation.
‡The supply air at the recommended rate will not necessarily be all outdoor air, the required quantity of outdoor air must be checked against the number of occupants at a desirable rate per person.

Table VIII Recommended outdoor air supply rates for air-conditioned spaces

Type of space	Smoking	Outdoor air supply (litre/s)		
		Recommended	Minimum (take greater of two)	
		Per person	Per person	per m² floor area
Factories*†	None			0.8
Offices (open plan)	Some			1.3
Shops, department stores and supermarkets	Some	8	5	3.0
Theatres*	Some			–
Dance halls*	Some			–
Hotel bedrooms†	Heavy			1.7
Laboratories†	Some	12	8	–
Offices (private)	Heavy			1.3
Residences (average)	Heavy			–
Restaurants (cafeteria)†‡	Some			–
Cocktail bars	Heavy			–
Conference rooms (average)	Some			–
Residences (luxury)	Heavy	18	12	–
Restaurants (dining rooms)†	Heavy			–
Board rooms, executive offices and conference rooms	Very heavy	25	18	6.0
Corridors				1.3
Kitchens (domestic)†	A per capita basis is not			10.0
Kitchens (restaurant)†	appropriate to these			20.0
Toilets*				10.0

*See statutory requirements and local bye-laws.
†Rate of extract may be over-riding factor.
‡Where queuing occurs in the space, the seating capacity may not be the appropriate total occupancy.
For hospital wards, operating theatres, see Department of Health and Social Security Building Notes.

The climate conditions that relate directly to thermal design include:

- Solar radiation, sun path and cloud cover
- Wind speed and direction
- Air temperature
- Relative humidity; and
- Rainfall and driving rain index.

4.02 Solar radiation and sun path

Solar radiation impacts on the building in three forms, **38.19**:

- Direct radiation, from the position of the sun in the sky
- Diffuse radiation, from the whole of the visible sky; and
- Reflected radiation (*albedo*) from adjacent surfaces.

All three components will vary according to time of day, time of year and cloud cover, and how much sky is seen by the building depending on natural and man-made obstructions. The solar path can be determined from the altitude and azimuth angles of the sun as in **38.20**. Typical values of solar radiation are given in Tables IX and X, and the effect of sun angle and overshadowing in **38.21**. The annual variation of possible hours of sunshine for the UK is presented in **38.22**.

The main component is the direct radiation, but the reflected radiation can be significant where there are hard light-coloured reflective surfaces adjacent to the building, either from the built form itself or from existing buildings and landscaping. Table XI contains data on reflected radiation for different angles and surfaces (the solar absorption of a surface is 1 – reflectance).

Cloud cover is measured in octals on a scale of 0 to 8, with 0 being completely cloudless and 8 completely overcast. The diffuse radiation component will be higher for an overcast sky as shown in Table IX. Cloudiness (C) is a measure of the proportion of cloud in the sky. C is zero for a clear sky and 1 for an overcast sky.

Table IX Solar altitude, and direct and diffuse solar radiation (cloudy and clear sky) at mid-day for South-east England

Month	Altitude	Direct Normal (W/m²)	Diffuse (W/m²)	
			Cloudy	Clear
June	64	900	310	100
July/May	60	895	295	100
August/April	52	865	255	95
September/March	40	815	195	85
October/February	29	700	140	75
November/January	20	620	90	60
December	17	560	75	50

Table X Daily mean solar irradiances (W/m²) on vertical and horizontal surface. Diffuse radiation for cloudy/clear sky conditions

	S	SE/SW	E/W	NE/NW	N	H	Diffuse
June	105	135	140	85	35	295	120/50
July/May	115	140	135	75	20	270	110/45
August/April	150	150	115	45	5	215	90/40
September/March	175	145	80	20	0	140	60/30
October/February	165	120	50	5	0	80	35/20
November/January	125	90	25	0	0	35	20/15
December	100	70	20	0	0	25	15/10

Table XI Reflected radiation for different surfaces

Surface	Reflectance
Concrete	0.2–0.45 (weathered to clean)
Polished aluminium	0.7
White paint	0.6–0.75
Aluminium paint	0.45
grass	0.33
Desert ground	0.25
Sand	0.18
Water	0.02–0.35 (for angle of incidence = 0–80°)

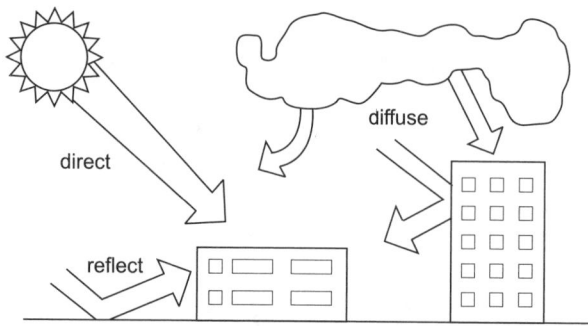

38.19 *Direct, diffuse and reflected solar radiation*

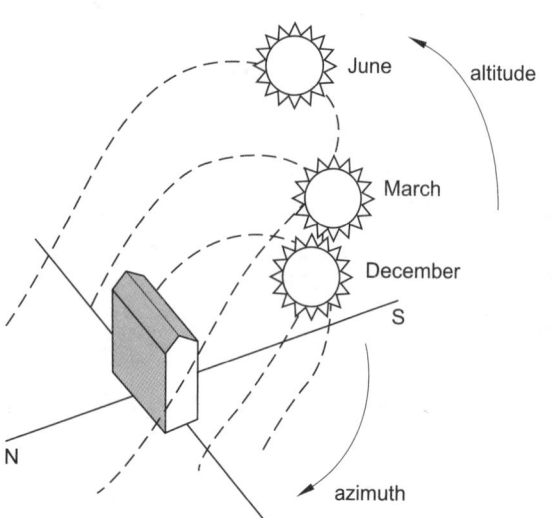

38.20 *Sun angles indicating azimuth and altitude*

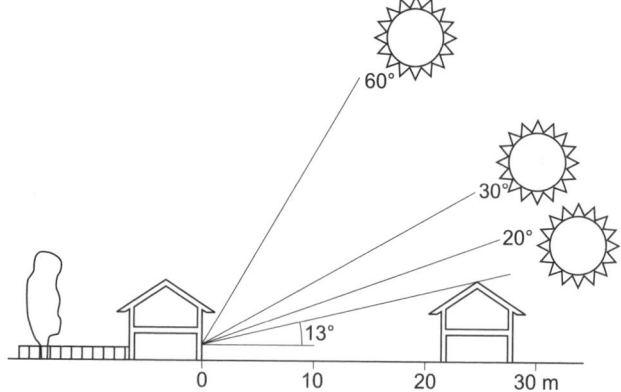

38.21 *Sun angle and overshadowing*

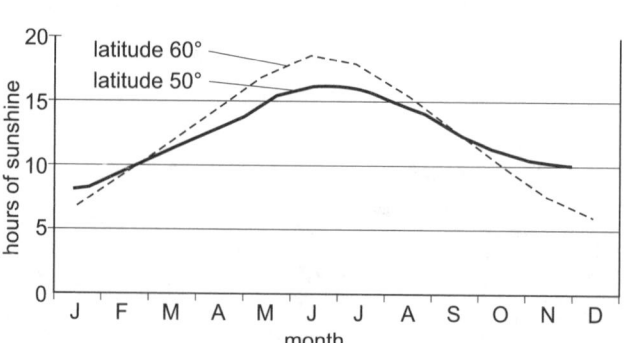

38.22 *The annual variation of possible hours of sunshine for the UK. Northern regions receive more hours in summertime*

4.03 External air temperature

The external air temperature will affect the rate of transmission and convective heat loss from a building. It will typically vary over a 24-hour period (the diurnal variation) and over a year (seasonal variation). It will also vary with location. Table XII presents the average monthly external air temperature for different locations within the UK. **38.23** shows the typical diurnal temperature variations for southern England.

4.04 Sol-air temperature

When solar energy is absorbed by an external wall it has the same effect, in relation to heat loss, as a rise in external air temperature. The sol-air temperature is the external air temperature which in the absence of solar radiation. would give rise to the same heat transfer through the wall as takes place with the actual combination of external temperature and incident solar radiation.

$$t_{sa} = (\alpha I_s + \varepsilon I_1) R_{so} + t_{ao} \qquad (8)$$

where t_{sa} = sol-air temperature
$\quad\quad\ t_{ao}$ = sol-air temperature
$\quad\quad\ \alpha$ = solar absorptance
$\quad\quad\ \varepsilon$ = long-wave emissivity
$\quad\quad\ R_{so}$ = external surface resistance
$\quad\quad\ I_s$ = solar irradiance (W/m^2)
$\quad\quad\ I_1$ = long-wave radiation loss (W/m^2)
$\quad\quad\quad$ = 93–79 C (horizontal surfaces)
$\quad\quad\quad$ = 21–17 C (vertical surfaces)
$\quad\quad\ C$ = cloudiness (see para **4.02**)

4.05 External relative humidity

The external RH will vary with external air temperature and moisture content of the air. During periods of warmer weather, the RH may be relatively low due to the higher external air temperatures, although at night it will rise as the air temperature falls, **38.24**. During cold weather the external RH can rise typically to over 90%. **38.25** presents seasonal average RH values.

4.06 Rainfall and driving rain index

Rainfall can affect thermal performance. If an external surface is wet then it will lose heat by evaporation and this will reduce the external surface temperature, sometimes to below air temperature, increasing heat loss. Wind-driven rain ('driving rain') can penetrate some constructions, causing a reduction in thermal resistance. In areas of high incidence of driving rain, care must be taken to select constructions that provide protection against rain penetration.

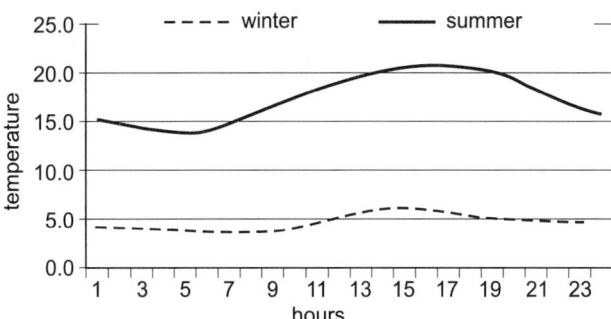

38.23 *Diurnal UK variations for winter (January) and summer (June) for south-east England*

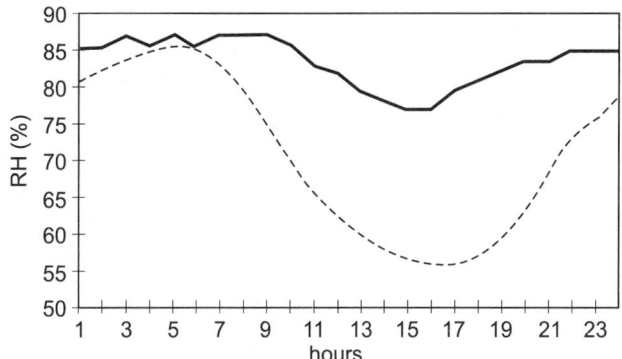

38.24 *Diurnal RH variation for January (solid) and June (dotted)*

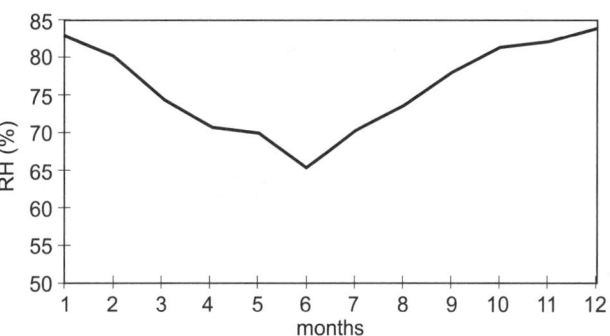

38.25 *Seasonal average daily RH values for the UK*

Table XII UK average daily temperatures (1941–1970)

		J	F	M	A	M	J	J	A	S	O	N	D	Annual
Belfast														
	Max	5.8	6.5	9.0	11.8	14.7	17.4	18.1	18.0	16.0	12.9	8.9	6.7	12.1
	Min	1.3	1.1	2.4	3.9	6.1	9.2	10.7	10.5	9.3	7.2	3.9	2.5	5.7
	Mean	3.5	3.8	5.7	7.9	10.4	13.3	14.4	14.3	12.7	10.1	6.4	4.6	8.9
Glasgow														
	Max	5.5	6.3	8.8	11.9	15.1	17.9	18.6	18.5	16.3	13.0	8.7	6.5	12.3
	Min	0.8	0.8	2.2	3.9	6.2	9.3	10.8	10.6	9.1	6.8	3.3	1.9	5.5
	Mean	3.1	3.5	5.5	7.9	10.7	13.6	14.7	14.5	12.7	9.9	6.0	4.2	8.9
London														
	Max	6.1	6.8	9.8	13.3	16.8	20.2	21.6	21.0	18.5	14.7	9.8	7.2	13.0
	Min	2.3	2.3	3.4	5.7	8.4	11.5	13.4	13.1	11.4	8.5	5.3	3.4	7.0
	Mean	4.2	4.5	6.6	9.5	12.6	15.9	17.5	17.1	14.9	11.6	7.5	5.3	10.0
Cardiff														
	Max	6.8	6.9	10.0	13.2	16.2	19.2	20.4	20.1	18.0	14.5	10.2	8.0	13.0
	Min	1.5	1.5	2.8	5.0	7.7	10.7	12.3	12.3	10.7	8.0	4.7	2.7	6.0
	Mean	4.1	4.2	6.4	9.1	11.9	14.9	16.3	16.2	14.3	11.3	7.5	5.3	10.0

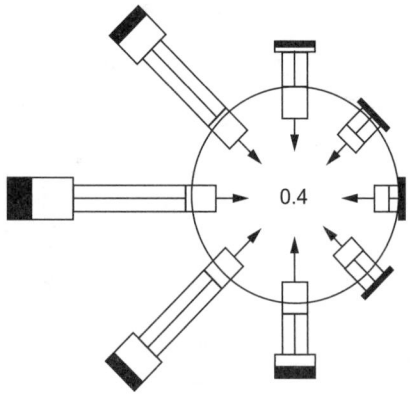

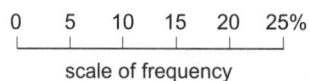

scale of frequency

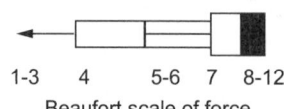

Beaufort scale of force

38.26 *Standard wind rose*

4.07 Wind

The impact of wind on a building has two main consequences for thermal design. It affects the connective heat loss at the external surfaces, as well as the ventilation and infiltration rate and the associated heat loss.

4.08 Wind speed and direction

Wind speed is measured in m/s or sometimes in knots where 1 knot equals 0.4 m/s. Wind direction is usually measured at eight points of the compass or, when required in more detail, in degrees clockwise from south. The wind speed and direction can be represented by a *wind rose*, **38.26**, which indicates the relative frequency and speed of wind from different directions.

Wind speed increases with height due to the frictional drag of the ground. The profile of variation with height is called the *boundary layer*, and it will vary from town to open country locations, as shown in **38.27**, and according to the relationship:

$$v/v_r = k\,H^a \qquad (9)$$

where v = mean wind speed (m/s) at height H (m)
v_r = mean wind speed (m/s) at height 10 m
values of k and a from Table XIII

Table XIII Values of coefficients for formula (9)

Terrain	k	a
Open country	0.68	0.17
Urban	0.35	0.25
City	0.21	0.33

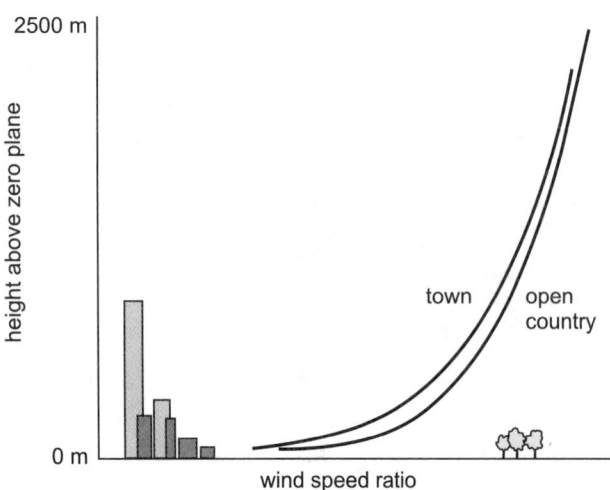

38.27 *Boundary layer wind profile*

4.09 Dynamic and static wind pressures

The static pressure (P_s) of the air is the pressure in the free-flowing air stream (as shown on the isobars of a weather map). Differences in static pressure arise from global thermal effects and cause wind-flow. The dynamic pressure (P_d) is the pressure exerted when the wind comes into contact with an object such as a building, **38.28**. The total or stagnation pressure (P_t) is the sum of the static and dynamic pressures. In most cases P_s can be ignored in thermal design as it is usual to deal with pressure differences across a building, ie the difference in P_d. The dynamic wind pressure is related to the air density (r) and the square of the wind speed (v).

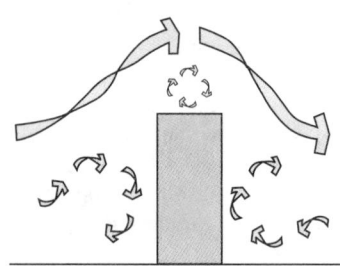

38.28 *Typical wind flow pattern around a high-rise building*

4.10 Pressure coefficients

The impact of wind on the building form generally creates areas of positive pressure on the windward side of a building and negative pressure on the leeward and sides of the building. The pressure coefficient is the relative pressure at a specific location on the building and it can be used to calculate the actual dynamic pressure for a given wind speed.

$$P_d = C_p \times 0.5\,\rho v^2 \text{ (Pa)} \qquad (10)$$

where ρ = density of the air (kg/m^3)
v = wind speed (m/s) at a reference height, h (m)
C_p = pressure coefficient measured with reference to the wind speed at the height h.

The pressure coefficients are dependent on general building form, as shown in the example in **38.29**. A scale model of the building can be placed in a wind tunnel to predict C_{ps}. Building form is the main determinant of pressure distribution for a given wind direction. Openings should then be located to produce the required 'cross-ventilation' from pattern, **38.30**.

4.11 External sheltered areas

There are 'rules of thumb' which can be applied to estimate the impact of wind on buildings, in relation to creating external sheltered areas (for example, courtyards). These are shown in **38.31**. The figures show that distances between buildings should

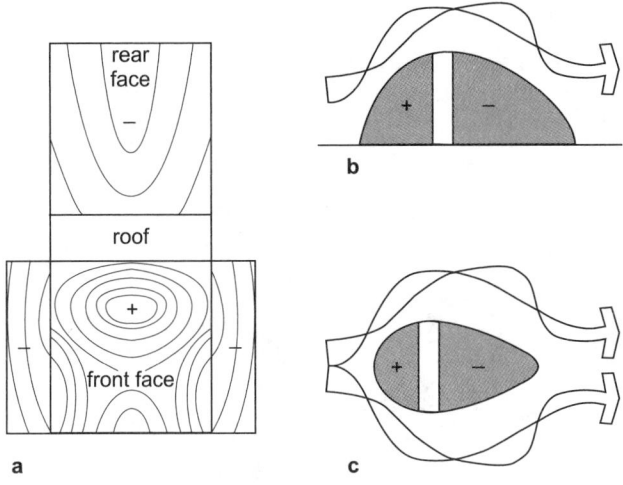

38.29 *Wind pressure over a building envelope:* **a** *Pressure distribution;* **b** *Section;* **c** *Plan*

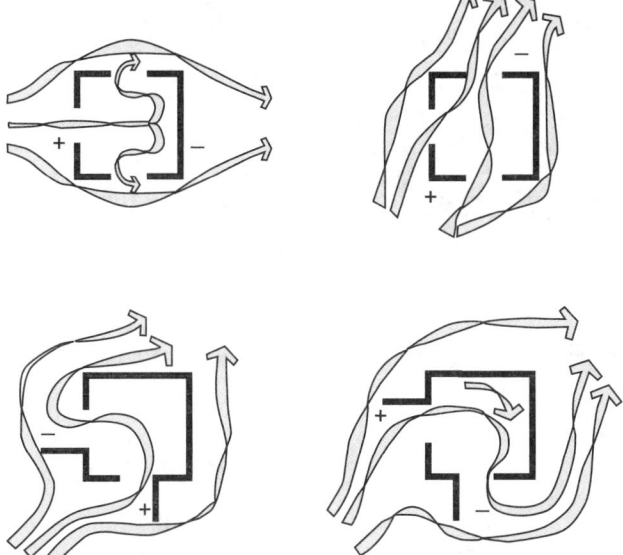

38.30 *Pressure coefficients can be manipulated by the form of the building*

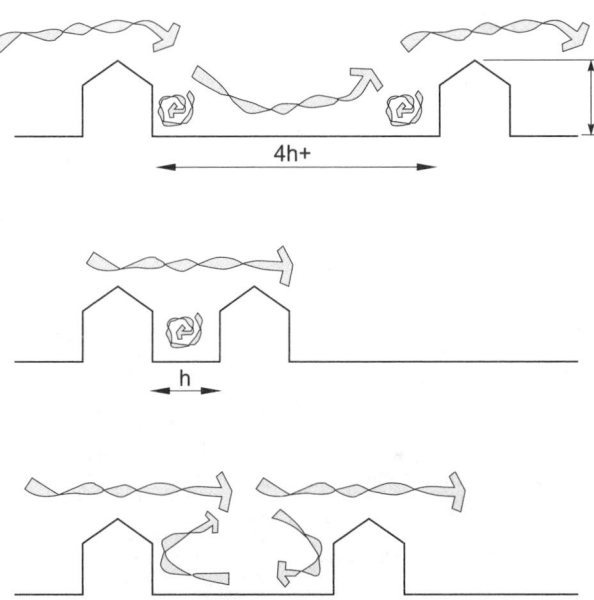

38.31 *Building spacing and provision of sheltered external spaces*

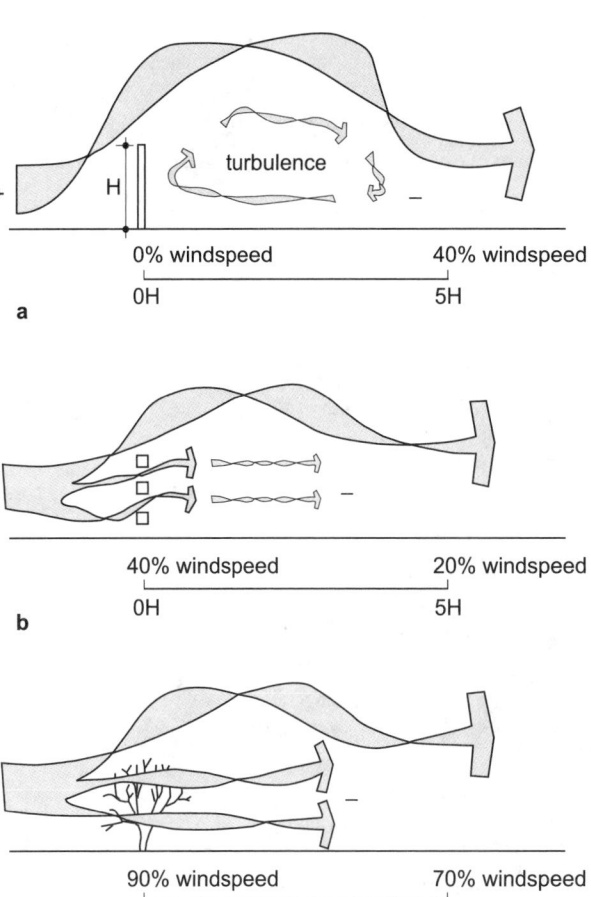

38.32 *Barriers and their effect on wind flow:* **a** *Dense barrier;* **b** *Medium barrier;* **c** *Loose barrier*

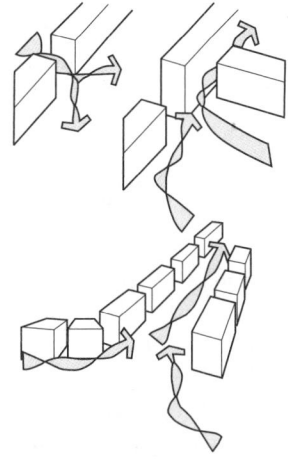

38.33 *Localised high wind speeds can be caused by 'canyon' effects and acceleration around corners*

be less than about 3.5 times the building height, in order to create shelter from the prevailing wind.

Barriers can be used to reduce wind speed and create external sheltered areas. Porous barriers are often more suitable than 'hard' barriers as they reduce wind speed and do not induce counter wind flow areas as shown in **38.32**. High wind conditions can be created by downdraughts from tall buildings (as in **38.28**), wind 'canyons' or acceleration around corners **38.33**.

4.12 Site analysis

An overall site analysis should identify the prevailing wind, the seasonal sun paths, and existing shelter and obstructions, well as other aspects, such as noise sources and views, as in **38.34**.

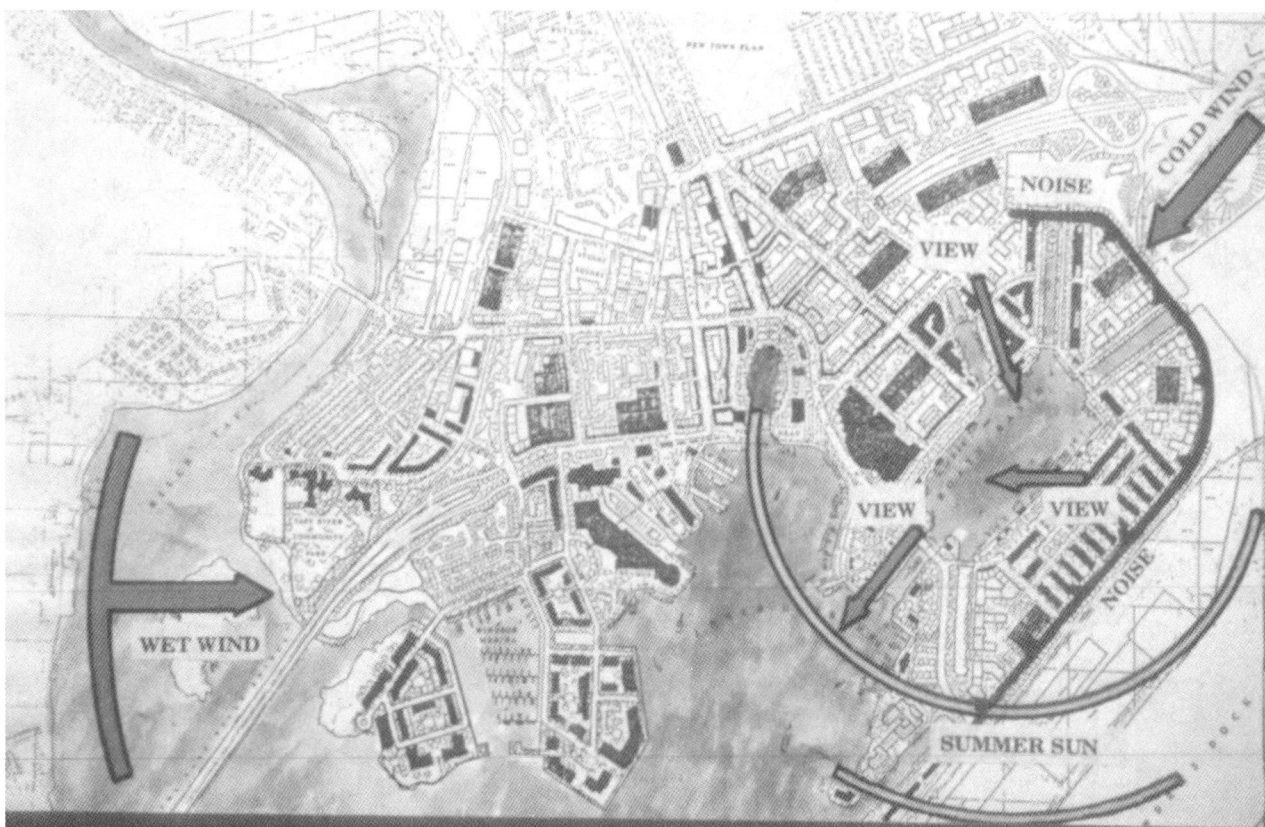

38.34 *Example of environmental site analysis*

5 BUILDING FABRIC

5.01 *U*-values

The *U*-value of the wall, roof or floor element of a building can be used to provide an estimate of its heat loss. The *U*-values of typical construction types are given in Table XIV. The *U*-value of a wall construction can be calculated using the following procedure:

1 Calculate the resistance of the individual layers of the construction (see Section 2 and refer to *k*-values in Table I).

$$R_{1,2,3...} = x/k \qquad (11)$$

where $R_{1,2,3...}$ = thermal resistance of element 1,2,3 . . . $(\text{m}^2.\text{K}.\text{W}^{-1})$
x = thickness (m)
k = thermal conductivity $(\text{W}.\text{m}^{-1}.\text{K}^{-1})$

2 Select the appropriate values for the internal and external surface resistances (R_{si} and R_{se}) by referring to standard tables (Tables XV and XVI).

3 Select the appropriate resistance of any air cavities (R_{cav}) by referring to the standard Table XVII.

4 Calculate the total thermal resistance (R_{total}) of the wall using the following formula:

$$R_{total} = R_1 + R_{su} + R_3 + \ldots + R_{si} + R_{se} + R_{cav} \qquad (12)$$

5 Calculate the *U*-value, that is, the conductance, of the wall using the following formula:

$$U\text{-value} = 1/R_{total} \qquad (13)$$

The heat loss (Q_f) associated with an element of the construction of area (A) and with a temperature difference (D_T) across it can be estimated as follows:

$$Q_f = U \times \text{area} \times \text{temperature difference} \qquad (14)$$

Example 2

U-value calculation

Calculate the *U*-value of the insulated cavity wall construction shown in **38.35** for an exposed site. Estimate the rate of heat loss through $10\,\text{m}^2$ of the fabric for a 20°C temperature difference across the wall.

The calculation is carried out in Table XVIII; giving a total resistance of $2.96\,\text{m}^2\text{K/W}$.

Hence *U*-value = $1/2.96$ = $0.34\,\text{W/m}^2\text{K}$

and heat loss Q_f = $0.34 \times 10 \times 20$ = $68\,\text{W}$

5.02 Thermal insulation

A high standard of thermal insulation in buildings in a temperate climate such as in the UK has the following benefits:

● It reduces the rate of heat loss, and therefore buildings use less energy to maintain comfortable internal thermal conditions. This also means that people are more able to afford to heat their buildings to comfortable conditions, and

● It raises internal surface temperatures and therefore reduces the risk of surface condensation.

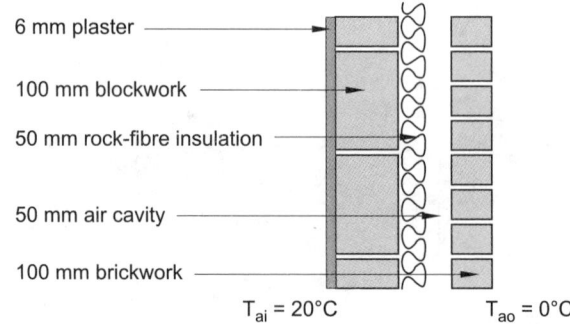

6 mm plaster
100 mm blockwork
50 mm rock-fibre insulation
50 mm air cavity
100 mm brickwork

$T_{ai} = 20°C$ $T_{ao} = 0°C$

38.35 *Construction of wall in Example 2*

Table XIV Typical constructions and their *U*-values

Construction type	Element	x	k	R	Drawing
Cavity wall construction with lightweight block	Ri	–	–	0.123	
	Plaster	0.06	0.16	0.38	
	Blockwork	0.1	0.15	0.67	
	Cavity	0.05		0.18	
	Brickwork	0.01	0.84	0.12	
	Ro	–	–	0.055	
	TOTAL			1.53	
					U-value = 0.65 W/m²K
Cavity wall with 50 mm cavity filled with insulation	Ri	–	–	0.123	
	Plaster	0.06	0.16	0.38	
	Blockwork	0.1	0.15	0.67	
	Insulation	0.05	0.035	1.43	
	Brickwork	0.1	0.84	0.12	
	Ro	–	–	0.055	
	TOTAL			2.78	
					U-value = 0.36 W/m²K
Cavity wall construction with 220 mm insulating block	Ri	–	–	0.123	
	Plaster	0.06	0.16	0.38	
	Blockwork	0.22	0.15	1.37	
	Cavity	0.05		0.18	
	Brickwork	0.1	0.84	0.12	
	Ro	–	–	0.055	
	TOTAL			2.23	
					U-value = 0.45 W/m²K
Timber frame construction with 100 mm insulation	Ri	–	–	0.123	
	Plasterboard	0.06	0.16	0.38	
	Insulation	0.10	0.035	2.86	
	Cavity	0.05		0.18	
	Brickwork	0.1	0.84	0.12	
	Ro	–	–	0.055	
	TOTAL			3.7	
					U-value = 0.27 W/m²K
Roof construction with 100 mm insulation	Ri	–	–	0.104	
	Plasterboard	0.06	0.16	0.38	
	Insulation	0.10	0.035	2.86	
	Cavity	0.05		0.18	
	Ro	–	–	0.055	
	TOTAL			3.52	
					U-value = 0.28 W/m²K

Table XV Internal surface resistance (m²K·W⁻¹)

Walls	0.123
Floors or ceilings	
upward heat flow	0.104
downward heat flow	0.148
Roofs	0.104

Table XVI External surface resistance (m²K.W⁻¹)

	Sheltered	Normal	Exposed
Walls	0.08	0.055	0.03
Roofs	0.07	0.045	0.02

Table XVII Wall cavity resistance

	Width (mm)	Resistance (m²K.W⁻¹)
Sealed	6	0.11
Reflective surface	6	0.18
	>19	0.18
Reflective surface	>19	0.35

Table XVIII Calculation for Example 2

Element	Thickness (m)	k-value (W/mK)	Resistance (m²K/W)
Ri	–	–	0.123
Plaster	0.06	0.16	0.38
Blockwork	0.1	0.15	0.67
Insulation	0.05	0.035	1.43
Cavity	0.05		0.18
Brickwork	0.1	0.84	0.12
Ro	–	–	0.055
Total			2.96

5.03 Types of insulation

Most thermal insulating materials have k-values of 0.3–0.4 W/m.K. The most common types are:

- Mineral fibre – this can be glass fibre or rock fibre and is available in lower-density roll form or higher-density batt form. The roll form is usually used to insulate roofs, while the batt form is often used in walls where, because of its greater rigidity, it is more appropriate to vertical fixing. Mineral fibre insulation forms a good attachment to the inner skin of the construction, leaving no air gap. It is often used in wall and roof industrial cladding type constructions. Mineral fibre may also be in a loose form that can be 'blown' into a cavity, to 'cavity fill' an existing or new construction (see below).
- Rigid board – this is usually made from foamed plastic or foamed glass. k-values are typically 0.037 W/m.K. It can be gas filled to give lower k-values, although boards which use ozone-depleting gases should be avoided. If rigid board insulation is used, it is essential to achieve a good attachment to the inner skin of the construction in order to avoid airflow between the inner skin and the insulation layer, which will detract from its U-value performance. The cavity should be kept clean and mortar 'snobs' and other sources of blockage on the inner skin should be eliminated before the insulation is fixed. Rigid board insulation is often used in composite 'factory made' cladding system constructions, where it is installed between two layers of metal sheeting.
- Blown insulation cavity fill, including mineral or cellulose fibres or plastic granules. Insulation is blown into the cavity after completion of construction. Care is needed in installing blown insulation in order to avoid any voids in the insulation in areas where the insulation has difficulty in penetrating, for example, blocked areas of the cavity. This method of cavity insulation has the advantage that it can be applied to existing constructions.
- Recycled paper insulation, such as 'Warmcel'. This is produced from 100% recycled newspaper, and has very low embodied energy compared to most other insulation materials. It has a k-value of 0.035 W/m.K. It can be applied in a 'breathing wall' construction, where sufficient vapour resistance is provided by the materials on the inside of the construction to prevent the risk of interstitial condensation. Materials in the middle and outside have low vapour resistance to allow moisture to freely transfer to the outside, or
- Low-density concrete blocks. Blocks with densities down to 480 kg/m³ give thermal insulation with k-values of 0.11 W/m.K. Such blocks are normally 210 mm in thickness and are used for the inner skin of a construction; this may be an infill panel or a loadbearing wall. They contribute to the thermal insulation of cavity construction, especially when the cavity needs to be left empty for weather resistance in exposed locations. Lightweight blockwork requires sufficient expansion joints to avoid cracking.

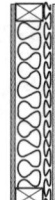

38.36 A combination of low-density insulation in a timber frame construction with a higher density insulation applied outside with an external render

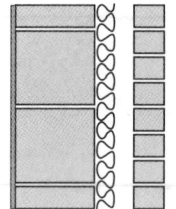

38.37 A combination of insulating block inner skin with part-filled cavity insulation

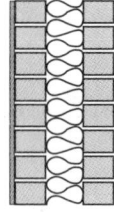

38.38 A construction with a heavyweight inner skin to provide thermal stability

Some constructions might use a combination of insulating materials to achieve its required U-value, **38.36** and **38.37**. In addition, thermal insulation may need to be integrated with a thermal mass layer to provide the required thermal performance, **38.38**.

5.04 Thermal bridging

Thermal bridging takes place through details of construction that have a relatively low thermal resistance to heat flow; they have a high U-value in comparison with the rest of the construction. Common areas of thermal bridging are around windows, doors and structural elements. Heat will flow from high to low temperatures by conduction along the path of 'least thermal resistance'. In the case of jambs, sills, lintels and floor edges, the least resistance path will generally be along the highly conductive materials such as metal and dense concrete. Heat loss at thermal bridges can be reduced by adding insulation and thermal breaks, and ensuring that the insulation is continuous over the building envelope. If thermal bridging occurs it will result in increased heat loss and increased risk of condensation. The heat loss through floors is a specific case where heat will follow the three-dimensional line of least thermal resistance as shown in **38.39**. The U-value of floors is therefore taken as an average value accounting for the high 'edge losses' and slab dimensions.

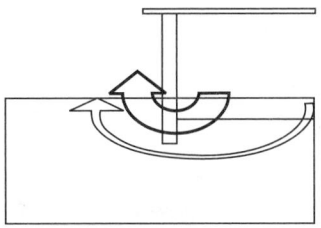

38.39 The edge losses are dominant in floor heat loss

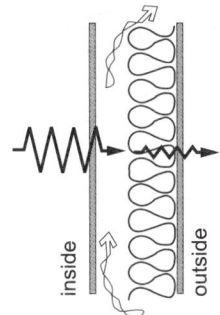

38.40 Insulation on the cold side of a ventilated cavity has a considerably reduced effect due to the cavity's convective heat loss

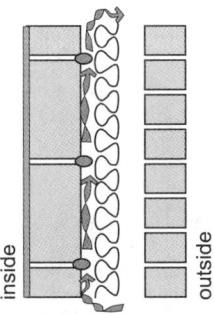

38.41 Mortar snobs may distance the insulation from the inner skin introducing airflow on the warm side of the insulation and shortcircuiting the heat flow through convective losses

5.05 Installation of insulation

The following guidelines should be followed when designing an insulated construction:

- Insulation should always be located on the 'warm and dry side' of a ventilated cavity (unless informed otherwise, it is usual to assume that all cavities are ventilated). If a cavity or air gap is ventilated on the warm side of the insulation this could provide a 'short circuit' for heat loss as indicated in **38.40**.

- Avoid air infiltration through or around the insulation material as indicated in **38.41**. Ensure continuity of insulation at design details, eg eaves and floor junctions.
- Ensure that there is a vapour barrier on the warm side of the insulation to guard against negation of its insulation property by moisture penetration from condensation,
- Avoid compression of low-density insulation.

5.06 Glazing

Glass is the main material used for glazing. It is available in a wide range of configurations with different thermal properties.

5.07 Thermal performance of glass

Glass is transparent to short-wave infrared radiation and opaque to long-wave radiation (see para **2.04**). It is also a good conductor of heat. Although glass transmits the short-wave infrared part of the solar radiation spectrum, it will also reflect and absorb a proportion of the radiation as shown in **38.42**.

5.08 *U*-Value of glass

The main thermal resistance in glass results from the surface resistances. The glass material itself has practically no thermal resistance.

Example 3
Calculate the U-value of a single layer of glass

Total resistance (R) = 0.118 m^{2}K/W
Internal surface resistance is 0.123
External surface resistance is 0.055
k-value of glass is 1.05 thickness 6 mm
$R = 0.123 + 0.006/1.05 + 0.055$
Total resistance $(R) = 0.1837$ m^{2}K/W
U-value is $1/R = 5.4$ W/m^{2}K

Adding layers of glass will improve the insulating properties of glazing due to the resistance of the trapped layer of air (or another gas). The thermal resistance of an air- or gas-filled cavity increases in proportion to its width up to about 20 mm and remains constant up to 60 mm, after which it decreases slightly. Increasing the layers of glass will reduce the solar transmittance by about 80% per layer (see Table XIX).

The glazing frame can provide a thermal bridge, which will increase the overall *U*-value of the glazing system. Other properties of glazing systems are given in Table XX.

5.09 Glazing treatment

The transmission of solar radiation can be reduced by different glazing treatment or the use of blinds or solar shading. Internal blinds convert short-wave radiant heat gains to convective and

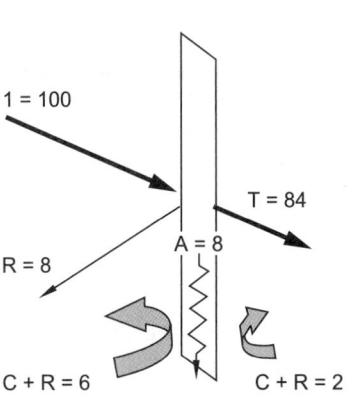

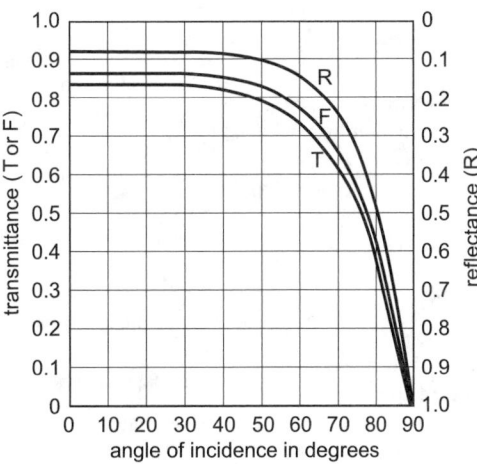

38.42 Transmitted, reflected, absorbed and re-emitted solar radiation as a percentage of incident value for 4 mm single glazing, and graph indicating variation of solar transmittance with angle of incidence:

Incident (I)   = *100%*
Reflected (R) = *8%*
Transmitted (T) = *84%*
Absorbed (A) = *8%*

Convected and radiated inside (C+R) = 2%
Convected and radiated outside (C+R) = 6%

Table XIX Solar transmission, total heat gains and light transmission for different glazing systems

	Transmission	Total heat gain	Light
6 mm clear glass (×1)	84	86	87
6 mm clear glass (×2)	64	73	76
6 mm Spectrafloat (×1)	56	66	49
6 mm Antisun (×1)	45	60	75
6 mm Solarshield (×1)	9	22	16
Insulight Gold (×2)	14	22	26
6 mm clear glass+blind (×1)	9	47	–
6 mm clear glass+blind between layers of glass (×2)	8	24	–

Table XX U-values of different glazing systems

	U-value (W/m²K)			
	wood	metal	PVC-U	Thermal break
Single glazing	4.7	5.8	4.7	5.3
Double glazing	3.3	4.2	3.3	3.6
Double glazing, argon fill	3.1	4.0	3.1	3.4
Double glazing, low-E	2.6	3.4	2.6	2.8
Triple glazing	2.6	3.4	2.6	2.9

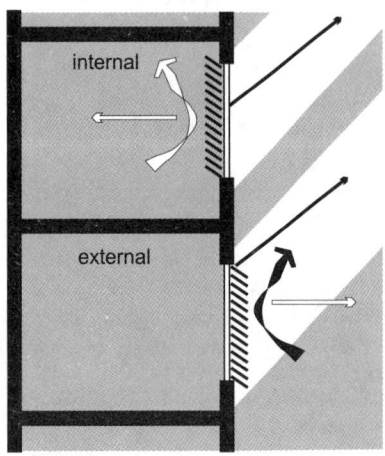

38.43 *Comparison of heat gains through external and internal shading. Solar gain of 12% for external white louvres, and 46% for internal white louvres*

long-wave radiant heat gains. Blinds located externally **38.43** or between layers of glass (provided the cavity is ventilated) are more effective in reducing solar heat gains.

5.10 Low-emissivity glass
A coating of metal oxide can be applied to a glass surface to reduce its emissivity This will reduce its long-wave radiation loss, which will reduce the overall transmission loss by about 30%. The low-emissivity coating is usually applied to the inside surface of the inner pane of a double-glazed unit.

5.11 Matrix glazing systems
Matrix glazing systems are designed to make maximum use of daylight, while at the same time controlling solar heat gain. They usually consist of a reflective matrix located between two layers of glass. The blades of the reflector are angled to respond to the particular orientation of the glass and the requirement accepting or rejecting the solar heat gains, **38.44**.

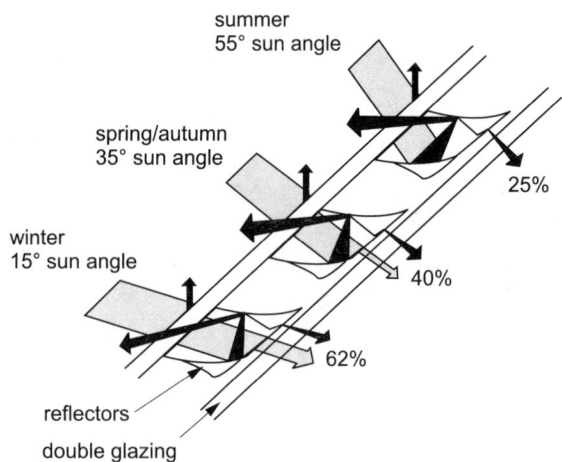

38.44 *Matrix glazing system*

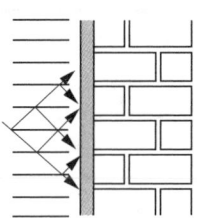

38.45 *Transparent insulation material (TIM)*

5.12 Transparent insulation material (TIM)
This can be applied to the face of an opaque south-facing facade to provide insulation while at the same time allowing the passage of solar gains to the solid wall behind, **38.45**. It can also be installed between two layers of glass where light but not view is required.

6 CONDENSATION

6.01 Condensation occurs when moist air meets a relatively cool surface. Water condenses out of the air and is deposited on the cool surface. It can result in dampness, surface mould growth, and deterioration of the building fabric.

6.02 Terminology
● The amount of water vapour that the air can contain is limited and when this limit is reached the air is said to be *saturated*.
● The saturation point varies with temperature. The higher the air temperature, the greater the amount of water vapour it can contain.
● Water vapour is a gas, and in a mixture of gases such as air, the water vapour contributes to the total vapour pressure exerted by the air.
● The ratio of the vapour pressure in any mixture of water vapour and air to the vapour pressure of saturated air at the same temperature is the *relative humidity* (RH).
● If air is cooled it will eventually reach saturation point, that is, 100% RH, and any further cooling will cause the vapour to condense. The temperature at which condensation occurs is called the *dewpoint* temperature.

6.03 Surface condensation
When air with a relatively high RH comes into contact with a cold surface condensation can take place. The risk of surface condensation depends on:

● Air and surface temperature, and
● Moisture content of the air.

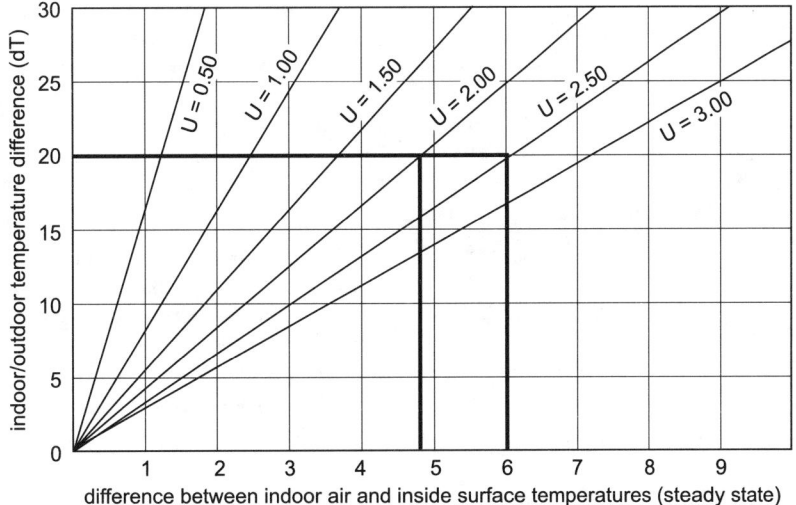

38.46 *Internal air-to-surface temperature versus inside/outside temperature difference for different* U-*values*

6.04 Mould growth
Surface condensation can cause mould growth. Mould spores can germinate at RHs above 80%. If the RH is generally greater than 70% for long periods mould will spread.

6.05 Estimating surface temperature
The following formula can be used to estimate the surface temperature:

$$\text{Temperature drop between the air and the surface} = \Delta T \times U \times R_{si} \quad (15)$$

where ΔT = inside/outside air temperature difference
U = wall U-value
R_{si} = internal surface resistance

Example 4
What is the internal surface temperature of single glazing (U-value – 5.8 W/m²K), if the internal air temperature is 20°C and the external air temperature is 0°C? The internal surface resistance is 0.123 m²K/W.

$D_T = 20$ $U = 5.8$ $R_{si} = 0.123$

Temperature drop (air to wall surface) $= 20 \times 5.8 \times 0.123$
$= 13.9°C$

Therefore the internal surface temperature $= 20 - 13.7 = 6.1°C$

6.06 Surface temperature and U-value
The internal surface temperature is affected by the U-value of the construction element, **38.46**. The higher the U-value, the lower the internal surface temperature for a given heat input to the space. Thermal bridging constitutes a localised increase in U-value which will result in a lower surface temperature. High U-value elements at risk include single glazing and thermal bridging.

6.07 Moisture content of the air
Moisture is contained in the external air and this is added to by various building use activities (Table XXI). The main moisture sources are:

External air: external air enters the building through ventilation. Its RH will depend on its moisture content and temperature. For example, on a typical winter's day external air at 90% RH and 5°C will contain about 5 g/kg (dry air) of water vapour. Saturated air at 0°C will contain 3.8 g/kg. These values can be obtained from the psychrometric chart, **38.13**; see para **3.06**.

Table XXI Moisture addition to internal air

	kg/kg dry air
Dwelling	0.0034
Offices shops, classrooms	0.0017
Catering	0.0068

Table XXII Moisture content of materials

Material	Water content (litres/m²)
105 mm brickwork	33
100 mm blockwork	40
150 mm in-situ concrete	30

Table XXIII Moisture emission rates (four-person house)

Source	Litres per 24-hour period
4 persons asleep (8 hours)	1.0–2.0
2 persons active (16 hours)	1.5–3.0
Cooking	2.0–4.0
Bathing, dishwashing, etc	0.5–1.0
Drying clothes	3.0–7.5
Pariffin heater	1.0–2.0
Daily total	5.0–10.0 (max 10–20)

Drying out: building materials contain moisture (Table XXII). A building could take a year to dry out after construction. A new house might contain 4000 litres of water which will be released during the drying-out period.
Occupants: moisture is produced as a result of occupants' activities (Table XXIII). On average, 3.4 g/kg of moisture is added to the air by internal activities in a house.

6.08 Causes of surface condensation
Minimising the risk of surface condensation requires a balanced approach to heating, ventilation and insulation, together with minimising moisture production:

Heating: inadequate heating can result in low air temperatures and higher levels of RH. It also means colder surface temperatures. Intermittent heating can result in the fabric and surface temperatures significantly cooler than the air temperature (during warm-up). Warm moist air coming into contact with cool surfaces can then result in condensation. Partial heating of a house can result in warm, moist air convecting to cooler rooms with cooler surfaces. Surface areas shielded from heating (eg behind wardrobes) will be more at risk.

Ventilation: low ventilation rates will result in a build-up of moisture in the air causing higher RHs. Too much ventilation could give rise to lower internal air temperatures which will again increase the RH, and also reduce surface temperatures. Ventilation should therefore be balanced as illustrated in **38.47**

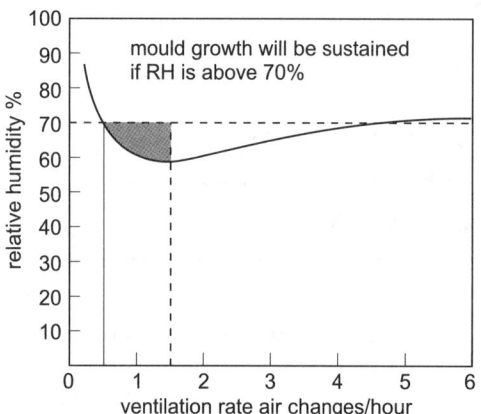

38.47 *Ventilation rate versus RH, indicating that low and high rates can give rise to higher RHs*

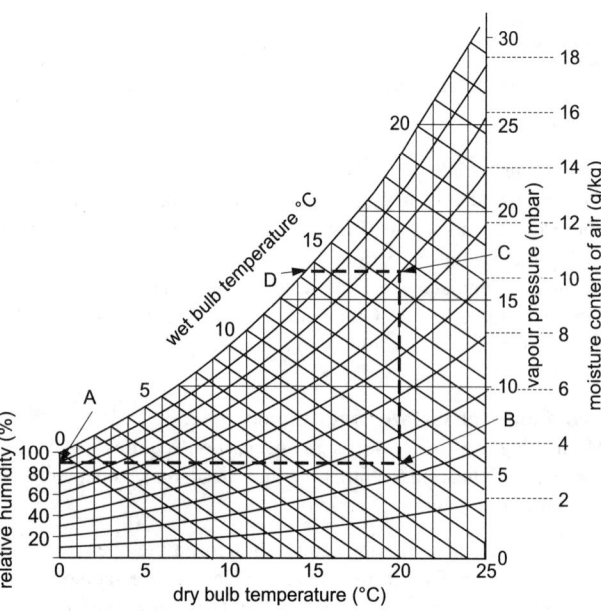

38.48 *Illustration to Example 5: predicting the risk of surface condensation using a psychrometric chart*

6.09 Estimating risk of surface condensation
The risk of surface condensation can be estimated if the RH and air and surface temperatures are known.

Example 5
Predict the risk of surface condensation using the psychrometric chart **38.48**

- The outdoor dry-bulb air temperature is 0°C and contains 3.8 g/kg of moisture, which gives an RH of 100% (point A).
- On entering the building the air warms to 20°C. If its moisture content remains the same, its RH will reduce to 27% (point B).
- Internal activities are assumed to generate additional moisture of 7 g/kg, increasing the RH to 70% (point C).
- The dewpoint temperature for air at 70%RH is 15°C (point D).

This means that condensation will occur if the air comes into contact with a surface at a temperature of 15°C or less.

Referring to the graph in **38.46** for an internal/external air temperature difference of 20°C, surface condensation will occur if the *U*-value is greater than 2 W/m²K, in which case the internal surface temperature will be 15°C, ie 5°C less than the air temperature.

6.10 Interstitial condensation
Condensation can occur within a construction. The dewpoint temperature profile of a wall can be predicted. If the actual temperature at any point within the construction falls below the dewpoint temperature then there is a risk of interstitial condensation taking place, as shown in **38.49**.

6.11 Vapour resistance
A material will resist the passage of vapour depending on its vapour resistivity or vapour resistance (Tables XXIV and XXV) (analogous to thermal resistance). The vapour resistance of a given thickness of material within a construction is:

$$V_r = x \times v_r \tag{16}$$

where v_r = vapour resistivity (Ns/kg.m)
  x = thickness of material (m)
  V_r = vapour resistance (Ns/kg)

6.12 Vapour pressure
The vapour pressure can be estimated from the moisture content using a psychrometric chart. The dewpoint temperature for a given

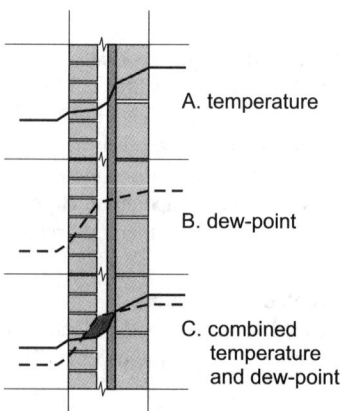

38.49 *Set of three diagrammatic representations of:*

A *Temperature profile through wall,*
B *Dewpoint temperature profile, and*
C *Overlap of these two profiles indicating area of interstitial condensation risk*

Table XXIV K-value and vapour resistivity and resistances

Material	K-value (W/mK)	Vapour resistivity (MNs/gm)
Brickwork	0.84	25–100
Concrete	1.4	30–100
Render	1.3	100
Plaster	0.5	60
Timber	0.14	45–75
Plywood	0.14	1500–6000
Fibreboard	0.07	15–60
Hardboard	0.14	450–750
Plasterboard	0.17	45–60
Compressed strawboard	0.1	45–75
Wood-wool slab	0.11	15–40
Expanded polystyrene	0.04	20–30
Glass wool (open cell)	0.04	15–40
Glass wool (closed cell)	0.02	30–1000
Expanded ebonite	0.03	1000–6000

Table XXV Vapour resistance of membranes

Membranes	Vapour resistance (MNs/g)
Average gloss paint	7.5–40
Polythene sheet	110–120
Aluminium foil	4000

vapour pressure will be the dry bulb temperature at 100% RH. The drop in vapour pressure across a given thickness of material in a construction is:

$$dV_p = (V_r/V_R) \times dV_p \tag{17}$$

where dV_p = drop in vapour pressure across a given thickness of material (kPa)

V_r = vapour resistance of material (Ns/kg)

V_R = vapour resistance of construction (Ns/kg)

dV_p = vapour drop across construction (kPa)

Example 6

Calculate the dewpoint temperature and actual temperature across a construction, **38.50**.

1 Calculate thermal resistance of each layer.
2 Calculate temperature drop across each layer:

$$\Delta t = \Delta T \times U \times R_s \text{ (formula (15))}$$

3 Plot temperature profile.
4 Calculate vapour resistance for each layer from formula (16).
5 Calculate vapour pressure drop across each layer from formula (17).
6 Calculate vapour pressure at the interface of each layer.
7 Look up dewpoint temperature on psychrometric chart, **38.13**
8 Plot dewpoint temperature profile.
9 CHECK CROSSOVER FOR CONDENSATION RISK.

The calculation and results are shown in Table XXVI.

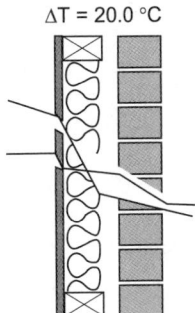

ΔT = 20.0 °C

38.50 *Construction of wall in Example 6*

7 INFILTRATION AND VENTILATION

7.01 Ventilation

Ventilation is the process of supplying and removing air by natural or mechanical means to and from any space. It is a combination of infiltration and purpose ventilation. Purpose ventilation can be either natural (opening windows), or mechanical (turning on a fan), or a combination of each. Ventilation rate is measured in air changes per hour (ac/h), m^3/s or litres per second per person (l/s/p). Typical ventilation rates are given in Table XXVII; a more comprehensive list is given in Tables VI to VIII.

7.02 Air infiltration

Air infiltration is the term used to describe the fortuitous leakage of air through a building due to imperfections in the structure, such as:

● Cracks around doors, windows, infill panels
● Service entries, pipes, ducts, flues, ventilators and
● Through porous constructions, bricks, blocks, mortar joints.

7.03 Natural ventilation

Natural ventilation is the movement of outdoor air into a space through intentionally provided openings, such as windows, doors and non-powered ventilators. This is in addition to the ventilation due to air infiltration. In many cases, for much of the year infiltration alone will provide sufficient outdoor air to ventilate the building. However, it is uncontrollable, and if excessive, it can incur a high-energy penalty and/or make the building difficult to heat (or cool) to comfort levels.

7.04 Mechanical ventilation

Mechanical ventilation is the movement of air by mechanical means to and/or from a space. It can be localised using individual wall or roof fans, or centralised with ducted distribution. It is controllable and can, for example, incorporate a heat-recovery system to extract heat from exhaust air and use it to pre-heat supply air.

7.05 Build tight, ventilate right!

Infiltration is present in both naturally ventilated and mechanically ventilated spaces. It is considered 'best practice' to reduce the

Table XXVI Calculation for Example 6

	Temp.	Inside surface		Plaster-board		Insuta-tion		Cavity		Brick		Outside surface	Temp.
Thickness				0.15		0.05		0.05		0.1			
Thermal resistance		0.12		0.9		2.5		0.18		0.12		0.055	2.1
Temperature drop		0.78		0.59		16.31		1.17		0.78		0.36	
Temperature	20.0		19.2		18.6		2.3		1.2		0.4		**0.0**
Vapour resistance (X × V_r)				7.9		2.8				6.3			
Vapour pressure crop				0.3		0.1				0.25			
Vapour pressure					1.0		0.9		0.9				0.65
Dewpoint temperature	**10.7**				**7.0**		**6.0**		**6.0**				**0.8**

Table XXVII Typical ventilation rates

Building type	l/s/person	ac/h
Domestic:		
Habitable rooms	–	1
Kitchens bathrooms	–	3
Offices	8	1 to 2
Schools	8.3	2 to 5
Bars	15	10 to 15

infiltration as much as possible by sealing measures, and then to depend on controllable natural or mechanical means to provide the main ventilation.

7.06 Ventilation effectiveness and efficiency

The term *ventilation effectiveness* is used to describe the fraction of fresh air delivered to the space that reaches the occupied zone. It should ideally be 100%. However, if air short-circuits between supply and extract points then it could be greatly reduced, often down to as low as 50%, **38.51**.

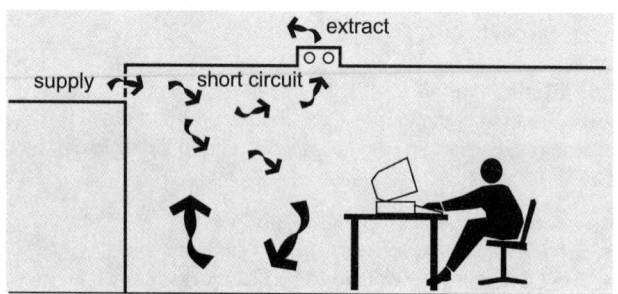

38.51 *Short-circuiting of air between supply and extract reduces ventilation effectiveness and efficiency*

The term *ventilation efficiency* is used to describe the ability of a ventilation system to exhaust the pollutants generated within the space. For a specific pollutant, it is the mean concentration level of the pollutant throughout the space in relation to its concentration at the point of extract. The ventilation efficiency at a single location is the ratio of pollutant concentration at that location in the space to its concentration at the point of extract:

$$\text{Ventilation efficiency } E = (C_e - C_s)/(C_e - C_s) \qquad (18)$$

where E = ventilation efficiency
C_e = concentration of pollutant at exhaust
C_s = concentration of pollutant in supply

If there is a significant level of the pollutant in the supply air then this should be subtracted from the internal and exhaust concentration levels.

7.07 Metabolic carbon dioxide as an indicator of air quality

Metabolic carbon dioxide is often used as an indicator of air quality. For naturally ventilated spaces in winter when windows are closed, the carbon dioxide level may rise to typically 1500 ppm for offices, and 2500 ppm for school classrooms. For mechanically ventilated buildings the carbon dioxide level should not rise above 1000 ppm and will generally be less than 800 ppm. Metabolic carbon dioxide can also be used to estimate ventilation efficiency using formula (18).

7.08 Ventilation heat loss

The air supplied to a space has to be heated in winter and sometimes cooled in summer. In a mechanical ventilation system this is achieved by pre-heating or cooling the air before it is delivered to the space. For natural ventilation it is usually achieved by incoming fresh air mixing with air already in the space and then this mixture is heated by the heating system, for example by contact with 'radiator' surfaces.

The air that is exhausted from the space, through natural or mechanical means, contains heat energy. For a mechanical ventilation system this heat is sometimes recovered through a heat exchanger – otherwise it is wasted. The ventilation component of heat loss can be a significant and sometimes major proportion of the total building heat loss. It can also be very variable, especially in naturally ventilated buildings, as it depends on external wind velocity and air temperature.

The heat lost or gained through ventilation can be estimated from:

$$Q_v = V_a \times \text{volume} \times \Delta T \times \rho C/3600 \qquad (19)$$

or

$$Q_v = V_l \times \text{number of people} \times \Delta T \times \rho C/1000 \qquad (20)$$

where Q_v = heat loss or gain in watts
V_a = ventilation rate in air changes per hour (ac/h)
V_l = ventilation rate in litres per second per person (l/s/p)
ρC = volumetric heat capacity of air = $1200\,\text{Jm}^{-3}\text{K}^{-1}$
ΔT = internal/external air temperature difference (°C).

An increase in internal/external temperature difference causes an increase in ventilation rate and an increase in heat loss or gain.

When designing a heating system the ventilation rate used to calculate the design heat loss should correspond to a design ventilation rate. However, when estimating seasonal energy performance the ventilation rate will be the average ventilation rate over a heating season.

7.09 Natural ventilation design

Natural ventilation through leakage and purpose ventilation is a result of two processes, termed *stack effect* and *wind effect*.

7.10 Stack effect

Stack effect occurs when there is a difference between the inside and outside air temperature. If the inside air temperature is warmer than the outside air it will be less dense and more buoyant. It will rise through the space escaping at high level through cracks and openings. It will be replaced by cooler, denser air drawn into the space at low level. Stack effect increases with increasing inside/outside temperature difference and increasing height between the higher and lower openings. The neutral plane, **38.52**, occurs at the location between the high and low openings at which the internal pressure will be the same as the external pressure (in the absence of wind). Above the neutral plane, the air pressure will be positive relative to the neutral plane and air will exhaust. Below the neutral plane the air pressure will be negative and external air will be drawn into the space.

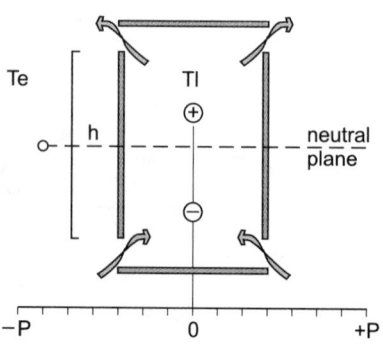

38.52 *Pressure gradient due to stack effect, indicating the location of the neutral plane*

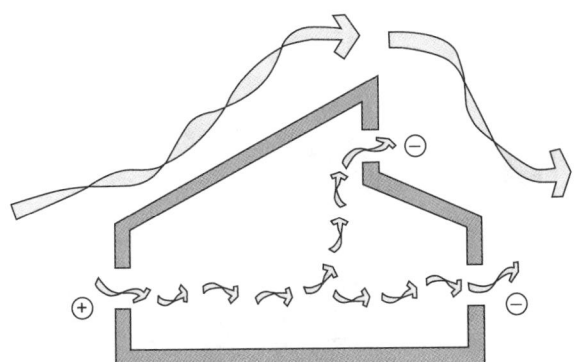

38.53 *Wind driven cross-ventilation*

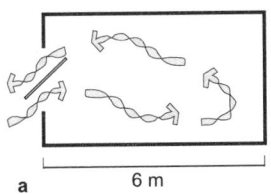

a

6 m

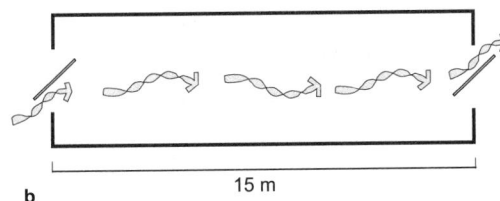

b

15 m

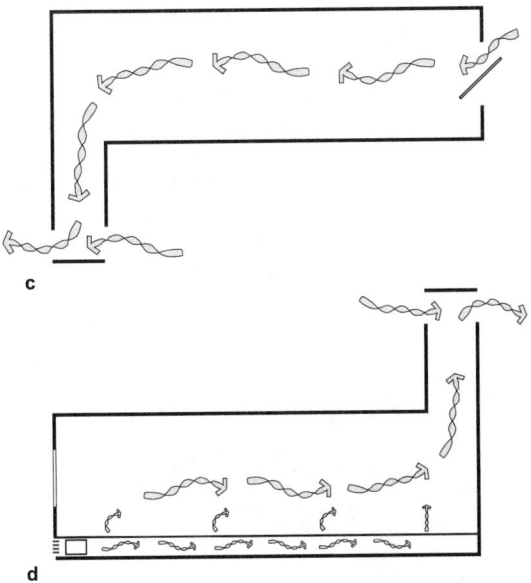

c

d

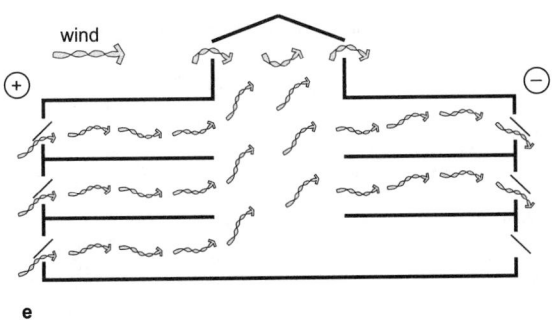

wind

e

38.54 *Natural ventilation strategies:* **a** *Single-sided;*
b *Cross-ventilation;* **c** *Cross-ventilation with chimney;*
d *Cross-ventilation with underfloor supply;* **e** *Atrium: stack and wind effects*

The pressure difference due to stack is estimated from:

$$P_s = -\rho \times T \times g \times h \times (1/T_e - 1/T_i) \qquad (21)$$

where P_s = pressure difference in pascals (Pa)
  ρ = density of air at temperature T
  g = acceleration due to gravity = 9.8 m/s^2
  h = height between openings (m)
  T_i = inside temperature in kelvins, and
  T_e = external temperature in kelvins.

7.11 Wind effect

Wind effect ventilation, sometimes referred to as *cross-ventilation*, is caused by the pressure differences on openings across a space due to the impact of wind on the external building envelope, **38.53** Pressure differences will vary, depending on wind speed and direction and location of the openings in the envelope. The pressure at any point on a building envelope can be calculated for a given wind speed and direction if the pressure coefficient at the point is known (see para. 4.10). Pressure coefficients are usually derived from wind tunnel tests. The pressure difference across a building due to wind can be estimated from:

$$P_w = 1/2\ \rho v^2\ (Cp_1 - Cp_2) \qquad (22)$$

where P_w = pressure difference across the building (Pa)
  Cp_1 and Cp_2 = pressure coefficients across the building in relation to the wind speed (v) and air density (ρ).

7.12 Ventilation strategies

38.54 presents a range of natural ventilation strategies with depths limits for single-sided and cross-ventilated spaces. **38.55** illustrates *passive stack ventilation (PSV)* used in domestic buildings and **38.56** shows on typical domestic mechanical ventilation system.

38.55 *Passive stack ventilation (PSV) can be used instead of mechanical ventilation for local extract, for example in kitchens and bathrooms*

8 HEATING AND COOLING SYSTEMS

8.01 The purpose of heating systems is to maintain internal air and radiant temperatures within the comfort zone. During the 'heating season' a building will lose heat through the fabric and through air infiltration and ventilation. However, a building will also gain heat from internal sources (cooking, electric power and people) and from external solar heat gains. A heating system is required to make up the difference between the heat gains and the heat losses. If a building is well insulated, has a low air infiltration rate and controlled ventilation, then it can be heated mainly from the incidental heat gains. A heating system should be sized and controlled such that it can provide the appropriate amount of heat input in an efficient and effective way.

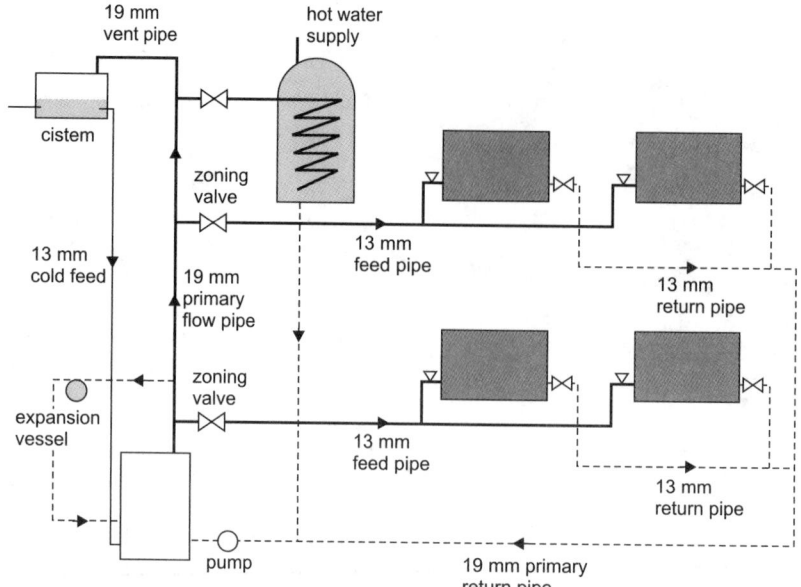

38.56 *Domestic two-pipe wet central heating system with flow and return to each radiator. The system can either be pressurised using an expansion vessel (dotted circuit); or gravity feed, in which case it requires a header tank located above the top radiator*

8.02 Types of heating systems

There are direct and indirect heating systems. Direct systems are located in the space, and include open coal fires, gas fires, electric storage heaters and paraffin heaters. For industrial applications there are high-temperature gas-fired radiant tubes and plaques. The main types of indirect systems are wet central heating systems, **38.56**, and ducted warm air systems, **38.57**. There are also low-temperature 'surface' heating systems such as under-floor heating, and ceiling and wall systems, where heat is input to the building mass.

8.03 Heat distribution

Heat can be distributed in water or in air. As water has a higher specific heat capacity than air, it requires smaller pipes in comparison to air ducts for the same heat transfer (Table XXVIII).

Water distribution can be 'gravity' feed or pressurised. An open system will require a header tank, whereas a pressurised system is sealed and requires a pressurisation unit. Pressurised systems can be used to carry water at temperatures higher than 100°C, and are sometimes used for commercial and industrial systems.

8.04 Heat emitters

Surface panel or tube heater emit heat by a mixture of convection and radiation. The balance changes with surface temperature and finish. For low-temperature emitters the heat output is mainly convection, whereas for high-temperature emitters the radiant component of heat output increases (see Table XXIX). In some cases the convective heat component may not be useful, as in overhead industrial localised heating. Some emitters, for example electric storage heaters, use a combination of heated surface plus forced convection.

8.05 Boilers convert fuel to heat. In doing so they produce products of combustion which must be flued. The boiler efficiency (see Table XXX) is a measure of the conversion of the energy in the fuel (its calorific value) to the useful heat extracted. Condensing boilers are able to recover latent heat from the flue gases. Boiler efficiency is usually reduced at part-load operation. In larger buildings, modular boilers allow maximum efficiency

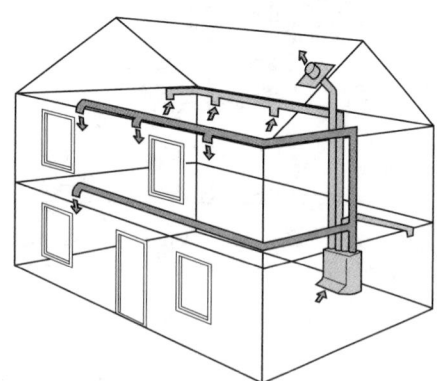

38.57 *Domestic mechanically ventilated heat recovery system with extract in kitchen and bathroom and supply in living spaces, with heat recovery in cooker hood*

Table XXVIII Water is more efficient than air in transferring heat because it has a higher volumetric specific heat capacity (ie energy content per unit volume)

	Specific heat capacity (kJ/kg.K)	Volumetric specific heat capacity (kJ/m³.K)
Water	4.2	415
Air	1.01	1.2

Table XXIX Radiant and convective output from heated surfaces, based on heating surface emissivity of 0.9

Type	Surface temperature (°C)	Direction of heat flow	Heat output (W/m²)	
			Convective	Radiant
Underfloor heating	24	up	18	27
Low temperature radiators	40	vertical	75	114
Domestic radiators	70	vertical	255	330
Medium pressure hot	110	down	178	727
water panels		vertical	558	727
Gas-fired radiant tubes*	150		1709	1 078
	300		4414	4 367
	500		8627	15 184

*Gas radiant tubes are usually mounted at a high level and operate between 150°C and 500°C. The convective component is generally lost to the high level; the radiant component is based on a floor level temperature of 18°C.

Table XXX Boiler efficiencies

Type	Full load	50% load	Seasonal average
Gas conventional	70–75%	65–75%	65%
Gas high efficiency	80–85%	77–82%	78%
Gas condensing	85–95%	85–95%	88%
Oil	65–85%	–	–
Coal	55–65%	–	–

Table XXXI Heat losses from pipes and ducts

Type	Fluid temperature (°C)	Heat loss (W/m)	
		Uninsulated	With 25 mm insulation
15 mm dia pipe	50	32	6
	70	62	11
500 mm dia duct	40	333	47

Table XXXII Seasonal energy design temperatures

Region	Seasonal average temperature T_{sa} (°C)	Annual Degree Days
Thames Valley	7.5	2120
South Eastern	6.7	2427
Southern	7.8	2265
South Western	8.3	1949
Severn Valley	7.2	2211
Midland	6.7	2507
West Pennines	6.7	2362
North Western	6.4	2532
North Eastern	5.9	2510
East Pennines	6.6	2373
East Anglia	6.7	2451
Borders	6.1	2709
West Scotland	5.8	2585
East Scotland	6.0	2719
North-east Scotland	5.5	2886
Wales	7.2	2244
Northern Ireland	6.4	2522

with sequencing a number of smaller boilers instead of a few large ones so that the majority operate at full-load. Combination boilers allow for direct heating of domestic hot water, thus avoiding the need for storage and reducing the standing heat losses.

8.06 Distribution losses

There will be heat loss associated with the distribution system. Pipes and ducts should be well insulated (Table XXXI). There will also be standing 'case' heat losses associated with the boiler, which may be considered useful (although it is uncontrolled) if they contribute to space heating.

8.07 Building 'design heat loss'

Fabric and ventilation heat loss has been explained in Sections 5 and 6. The *design heat loss* of a building is its heating demand for a given external air temperature, which will vary for different parts of the UK. It can be estimated as follows:

Fabric heat loss rate Q_f (W/°C)
Ventilation heat loss rate Q_v (W/°C)
Total heat loss rate $Q = Q_f + Q_v$ (W/°C)
Design internal air temperature T_i (°C)
Design external air temperature T_e (°C)

Design heat loss $= Q \times (T_i - T_e)$ (W)   (23)

8.08 Seasonal energy use

The seasonal energy use can be calculated from the design heat loss, but using some form of seasonal temperature instead of a design temperature. Also, an allowance has to be made for system efficiency and incidental heat gains. The seasonal temperature can be in the form of a heating season average temperature or *degree days* (Table XXXII). If average temperature is used, then some account of seasonal heat gains are required. Degree days already assume some level of useful heat gains in relation to a *base temperature*; which is the temperature below which heating is required. The standard base temperature is 15.5°C, which takes account of typical internal heat gains.

8.09 Heat gains

There will be heat gains from internal activities and solar effects (Table XXXIII). For domestic buildings, the internal gains can be estimated depending whether the household has high, medium or low activities (Table XXXIV). Not all the internal gains will usefully supplement the heating. Some may cause overheating and some may occur where or when they are not required.

Table XXXIII Solar heat gains

	Single glazing			Double glazing		
	S	SE/SW	E/W	S	SE/SW	E/W
J	14	12	6	12	10	5
F	19	16	11	16	13	9
M	35	31	23	30	26	19
A	35	34	30	29	29	26
M	42	44	42	35	37	35
J	41	45	46	35	38	39
J	39	43	42	33	36	35
A	40	41	37	34	34	31
S	39	36	29	33	30	24
O	31	27	18	26	22	15
N	19	16	9	16	13	7
D	14	12	5	12	10	4

Table XXXIV Domestic internal heat gains

Heat source	Total heat gain (kWh/day)	
	low	high
Occupants	4.02	5.46
Lighting	2.17	2.50
Cooker	2.89	4.25
Refrigerator	1.44	1.44
Television	0.45	0.54
Hot water	3.70	4.70
TOTAL	14.67	18.89

8.10 Environmental temperature

It is more accurate in cases where the radiant temperature is significantly different from air temperature to calculate the heat transfer to the internal surface of a wall using the *environmental temperature* which combines air temperature and mean radiant temperature:

$$t_{ei} = 2/3\ t_{mrt} + 1/3\ t_{ai}$$ (24)

where t_{ei} = environment temperature
t_{mrt} = mean radiant temperature, and
t_{ai} = air temperature.

38.58 illustrates the use of resultant temperature (formula (6)), environment temperature (formula (24)) and sol-air temperature (formula (8)).

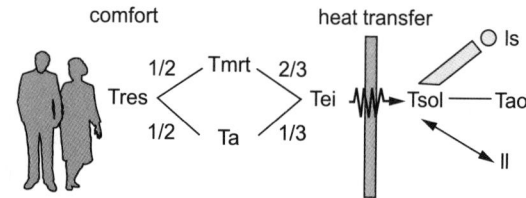

38.58 *Resultant temperature, environmental temperature and sol-air temperature*

8.11 Seasonal energy use (*E*)

To calculate the seasonal energy use for space heating; firstly using average temperature:

$$E = ((Q_f + Q_v) \times (T_i - T_{sa})$$
$$\times \text{ number of hours} - \text{seasonal heat gains}) \times \textit{eff} \quad (25)$$

where E = the seasonal energy use (W)
Q_f = fabric heat loss
Q_v = ventilation heat loss
T_i = average internal temperature
T_{sa} = seasonal average temperature (Table XXXII)
$\textit{eff}$ = efficiency of heating system.

Using degree days:

$$E = (Q_f + Q_v) \times \text{degree-days} \times 24 \times \textit{eff} \quad (26)$$

8.12 Carbon dioxide emissions

Table XXXV gives the carbon dioxide emissions associated with fuel use.

Table XXXV Carbon dioxide emissions associated with fuels

Fuel	Mass of carbon dioxide	
	kg/Gj	kg/kWh
Gas (mains)	52	0.0144
Liquid petroleum gas (LPG)	76	0.0211
Heating oil	75	0.0208
House coal	83	0.0231
Anthracite	90	0.0250
Smokeless solid fuel	116	0.0322
Electricity	188	0.0522

Example 7

Calculation of seasonal heating, fuel use and carbon dioxide emission from a modern detached house located in Cardiff, and heated by a gas condensing boiler.

Fabric heat loss

Element	Area (m²)	U-value (W/m²/°C)	Heat loss (W/°C)	
Walls	115	0.27	31	Table XIV
Roof	35	0.28	10	Table XIV
Floor	35	0.40	14	
Windows	30	2.60	78	Table XX
Total			133	

Ventilation heat loss Formula (19)

Air change rate (/h)	Volume (m³)	Heat loss (W/°C)	
1	210	69	Table XXVII
Total heat loss		202	

Seasonal heat loss (October-May) Formula (25)

Example 7 *continued*

External temperature	7	Table XXXII
Internal temperature	17	
Hours of use	5 760	
Seasonal heat loss (kWh)	11 411	

Heat gains

Windows	Area (m²)	Unit gains (kWh/m²)	Total gains (kWh)	
Solar gains				Table XXXIII
South	10	190	1900	
North	5	0	0	
East	5	110	550	
West	10	110	1100	
Total			3550	
Internal gains				Table XXXIV
People	4	370	1480	
Hot water			450	
Electrical			1100	
Cooking			950	
Total			3980	

Total heat gains (kWh)	7530	
Heating system load (kWh)	3881	Formula (25)
Heating system efficiency (%)	88	Table XXX
Heating system fuel use (kWh)	4410	
Carbon dioxide emission (kg/annum)	838	Table XXXV

8.13 Mechanical ventilation may be required in buildings as an alternative or in addition to natural ventilation. Specific applications include:

- Deep plan spaces which cannot be ventilated from the side by natural means
- Spaces with a high occupancy or high heat gain
- Spaces with high source levels of pollution, including industrial processes and moisture in kitchens and bathrooms
- Where the external air quality may be poor and so the external air needs to be filtered or taken in at high level and
- Where high ventilation rates are required in winter, mechanical ventilation (with pre-heated air) can be used without incurring cold draughts.

8.14 Mechanical extract

Local mechanical extract can be used to exhaust pollutants at source (for example, in kitchens, bathrooms and toilets; and locally for industrial processes such as solder baths and welding booths).

8.15 Mechanical supply systems can be used in situations where a positive flow needs to be established between a space and its surroundings. Examples are:

- In a house or apartment to maintain a minimum ventilation rate and reduce condensation risk
- Mechanical induction systems where high-velocity warm air is supplied to a space, and extract is through natural leakage and
- Mechanical supply to an office and extract naturally, perhaps through an atrium or chimney/tower.

8.16 Balanced supply and exhaust

Mechanical ventilation systems in larger buildings usually have a balanced supply and extract, **38.59**. This allows:

- Control of higher ventilation rates
- Heating and/or cooling of incoming air
- Filtration of incoming air
- Humidity control of air and
- Heat recovery from exhaust to supply air.

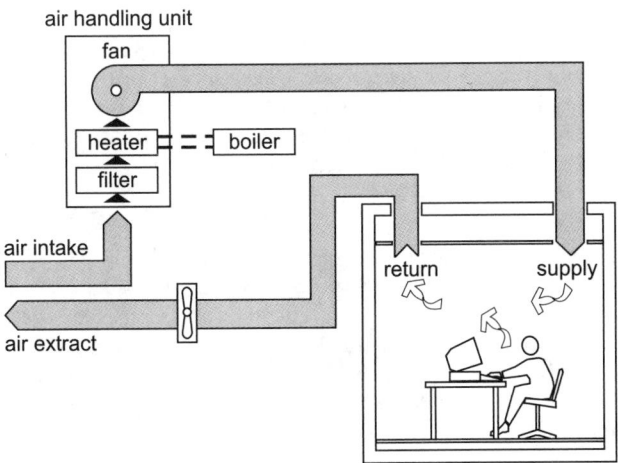

38.59 *Components of one type of balanced supply and extract mechanical ventilation system*

8.17 Air supply rates

If the air supply is for ventilation, then the volume flow rate can be estimated from the number of occupants in the space. This will be typically 8 litres/second person unless there is smoking, in which case it will be 16 or 32 l/s/p for light and heavy smoking respectively. If air is required as the sole source of heating then the volume flow rate can be estimated from the following formulae:

Volume flow rate = design heat loss/$((T_{su} - T_{ex}) \times C_p))$ (27)

where T_{su} = supply air temperature
$\quad\quad T_{ex}$ = extract air temperature, and
$\quad\quad C_p$ = volumetric specific heat of air

Example 8

Calculate the volume flow rate of air to ventilate a 1000 m² office space, height of 2.5 m, occupied by 100 people. If the design heat loss of the space is 15 kW, what is the volume flow rate required to heat the space if the supply air temperature is 30°C and the extract is 23°C?

Ventilation volume flow rate = $(100 \times 8)/1000$
$\quad\quad\quad\quad\quad\quad\quad\quad\quad$ = 0.8 m³/s
$\quad\quad\quad\quad\quad\quad\quad\quad\quad$ = 0.8 × 3600/2500
$\quad\quad\quad\quad\quad\quad\quad\quad\quad$ = 1.12 ac/h

Heating volume flow rate $\quad$ = 15000/((30 − 23) × 1200)
$\quad\quad\quad\quad\quad\quad\quad\quad\quad$ = 1.8 m²/s
$\quad\quad\quad\quad\quad\quad\quad\quad\quad$ = 1.8 × 3600/2500
$\quad\quad\quad\quad\quad\quad\quad\quad\quad$ = 2.6 ac/h

8.18 Air distribution

Air is distributed from the air handling unit (AHU) to the space through a system of ducts, **38.60**. The cross-section area of the AHU and ducts depends on the air speed for a given volume flow rate, and can be calculated from:

csa = volume flow rate/air speed (28)

where *csa* is the cross-sectional area in m₂.

The velocity through the AHV would typically be 2 m/s. The velocity through the main riser ducts will vary from 3 m/s (low velocity) to 7 m/s (medium velocity)

8.19 Fan power

The fan power required to supply the air through the ducted system depends on the volume flow rate and the pressure drop in the system, which are related to the air speed. For an energy-efficient mechanical ventilation system with low duct velocity, the *specific fan power* could be less than 1 kW/m³ of air supply. This compares to about 4 kW/m³ of air supply in standard systems.

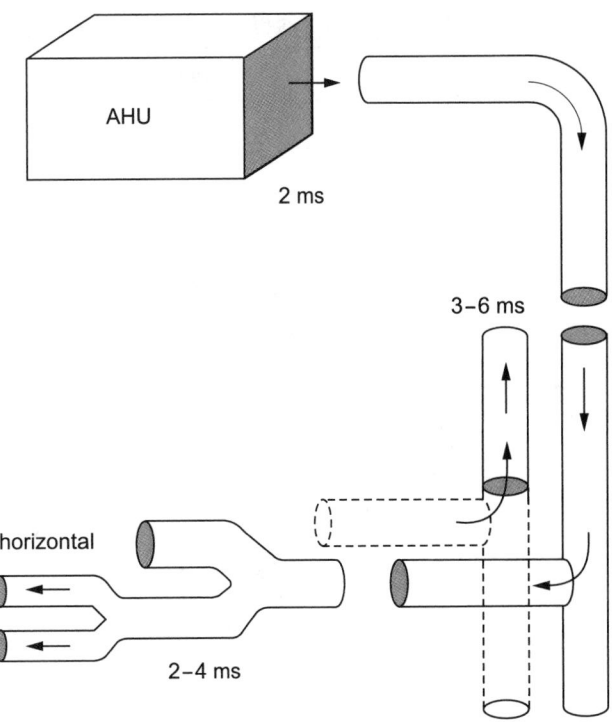

38.60 *Ducted air distribution system indicating velocity ranges*

Table XXXVI Heat recovery systems and typical efficiencies

Heat recovery system	Efficiency
Plate heat exchangers	40% and 60%
Thermal wheels	79–82%
Run-around coils	45% and 60%
Double accumulators	85–95%

8.20 Heat-recovery systems

An advantage of mechanical ventilation is that it can use heat recovery. This can be applied at all scales of building from domestic to large-scale commercial. It is especially appropriate to maintaining energy efficiency in full fresh-air systems. Heat recovery is only worth while if the recovered heat is useful and is greater than the energy used due to the increase in fan power from the increase pressure drop of the heat-recovery equipment. Table XXXVI lists the efficiency ranges of heat-recovery systems.

8.21 Cooling systems

Some buildings require cooling in addition to what can be achieved from ventilation alone. Such buildings may have a high internal heat gain, where mechanical ventilation will not provide sufficient cooling, especially during warm weather. The building itself may be designed for a hot climate, where air-conditioning with cooling and humidity control is necessary. Cooling of air is achieved by passing the air over cooling coils in the AHU.

8.22 Heat gains

The main reason for mechanical cooling is in response to heat gains from people, office machinery, lighting, solar gains and high external air temperatures. Solar gains have been discussed in para **4.02**. Internal gains from lighting and machines can be high (Table XXXVII), but they are often overestimated, which can result in over capacity of the system design.

8.23 Room air delivery

Chilled air can be delivered to the space, either in a mixing mode or a displacement mode.

Table XXXVII Internal heat gains for a typical office

Factor	Heat gain (W/m^2)
People	10
Equipment (computers, copiers, etc)	15–25
Lighting	10–25
TOTAL	35–60

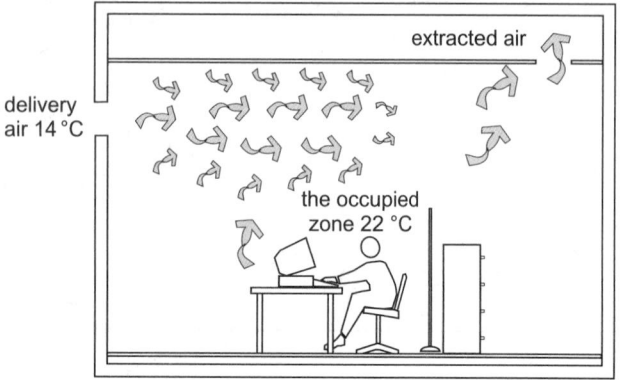

38.61 *Mixing mode of air delivery*

8.24 Mixing mode of air delivery

The air supplied to the space is typically about 13°C at the design cooling load. The air is jetted into the space such that it mixes with air already in the space by entrainment and when the air enters the occupied zone it is at the appropriate temperature, speed and RH for comfort, **38.61**. Air may be supplied from the perimeter, the ceiling or even the floor.

8.25 Coanda effect

Ceiling systems often rely on the *coanda effect*, **38.62a**, to ensure that the cool supply air remains at high level ('sticks' to the ceiling) until it is mixed. The coanda effect does not work at low jet velocities and the jet becomes 'unstuck' and can cause cold air 'dumping', **38.62b**.

8.26 Displacement air delivery

Air is supplied to the space at a low velocity such that it displaces the air already in the space towards the ceiling extract, **38.63**. Air is usually supplied at the floor or through low-level diffusers. However, some floor systems, that use *swirl* diffusers, are assumed to be displacement but are really mixing systems.

8.27 Air supply

The temperature and volume flow rate of the supply air will often determine the type of system used. Displacement systems should have air delivery temperatures greater than 18°C or they are likely to cause cool draughts. So if low-temperature supply is needed for a high heat load, then mixing systems are usually more suitable. **38.64** shows the relationship between air supply temperature, volume flow and internal heat gains.

8.28 Central air-conditioning systems

38.65 illustrates a typical central air-conditioning system layout.

8.29 Variable air volume (VAV)

In this system the volume of air is controlled in response to the cooling load. As the cooling load is reduced the volume of air is also reduced until a minimum air supply is reached, after which the supply air temperature is increased.

8.30 Constant air volume (CAV)

With this the air is supplied at a constant volume and the temperature of the air is varied in response to the space cooling or heating load.

8.31 Localised systems

are usually either fan coil units or heat pump units. They can be located around the perimeter of a space or in the ceiling void, **38.66**. A space may have multiple units, or one unit may supply a single floor. They need access to outside air, which can either be supplied directly to the unit from outside or be ducted separately from a central unit which only supplies ventilation air requirements and not heating and cooling requirements. Fan coil units are served by hot and cold water systems that supply the main heating and cooling load.

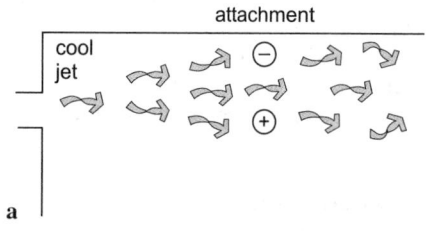

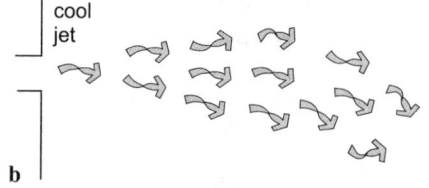

38.62 *Coanda effect*

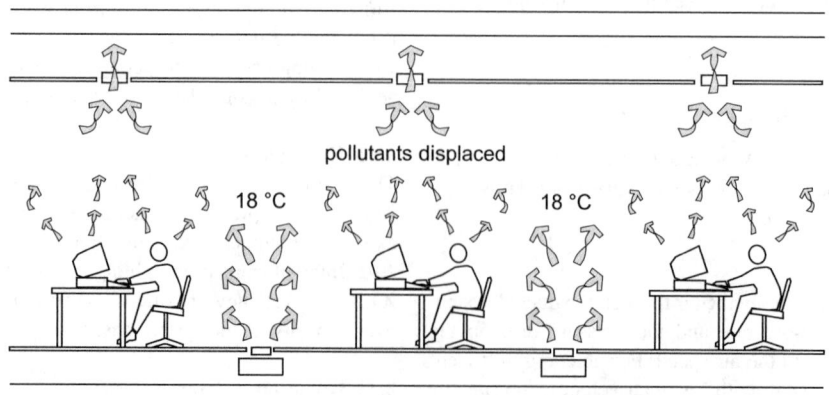

38.63 *Air displacement system*

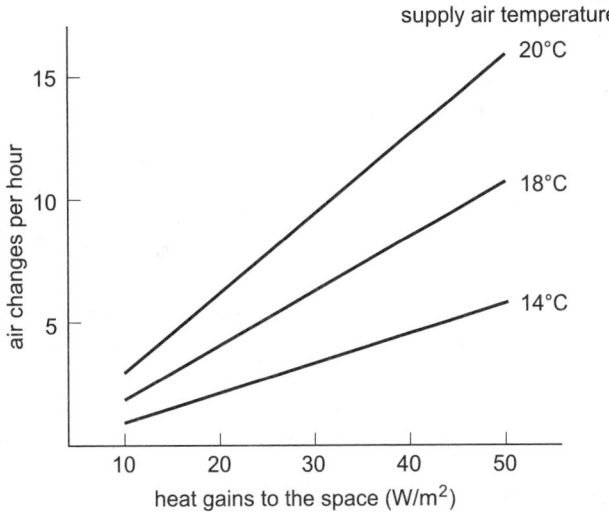

38.64 *Relation between volume flow, supply air temperature and cooling load*

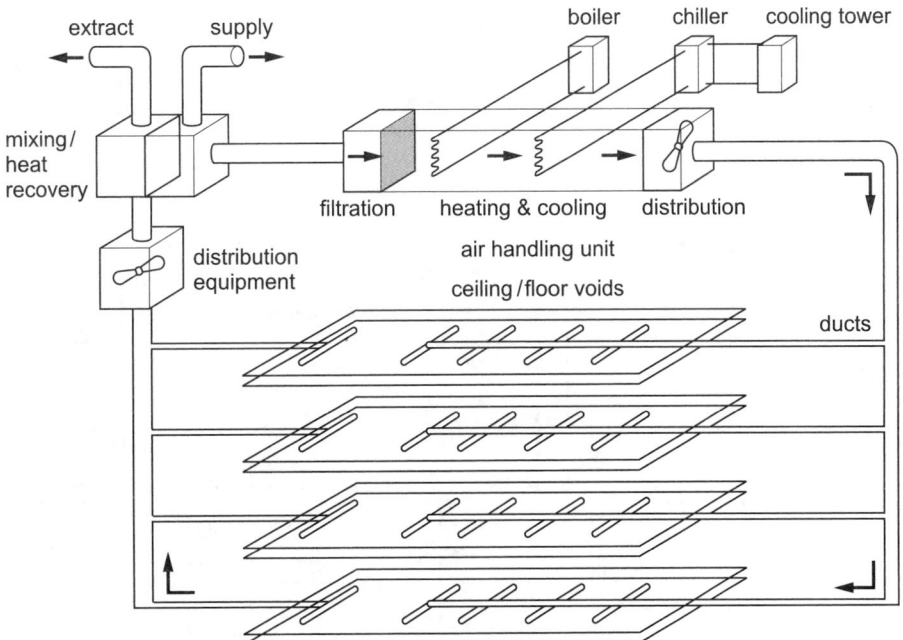

38.65 *Layout of a central air conditioning system*

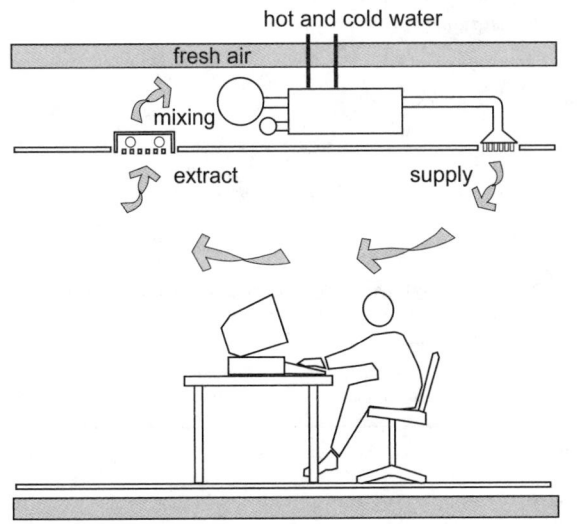

38.66 *Ceiling fan coil system*

8.32 Passive cooling systems

Passive cooling is achieved by means of introducing chilled surfaces in a room, the opposite of radiators for heating, **38.67**. These surfaces absorb heat from the space by convection/conduction and radiative heat exchange. Passive cooling devices can be in the form of fins, panels or beams. Sometimes the whole surface is cooled. Surface temperatures are about 15°C and cooling loads of typically up to 40 W/m² can be achieved. To avoid the risk of condensate forming on the chilled surfaces in situations of high relative humidity, sensors can be incorporated into the design to raise the surface temperatures. Alternatively, if mechanical ventilation is used the ventilation air can be dehumidified at the AHU.

8.33 Refrigeration

Cooling systems require some form of refrigeration equipment in order to extract heat from the cooling fluid that flows in the cooling coils in the air handling unit, or in the passive cooling system. A standard heat pump circuit is shown in **38.68** and an absorption circuit in **38.69**.

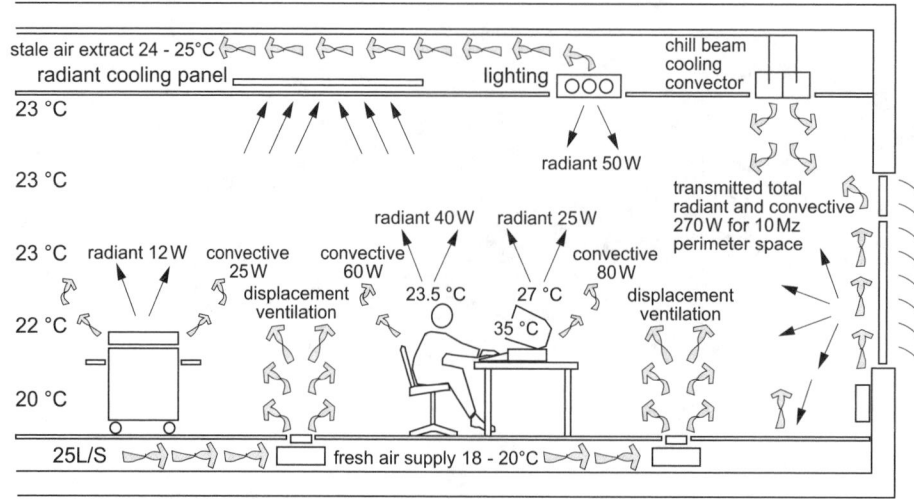

38.67 *Passive cooling systems (chilled beams or panels) can be combined with displacement ventilation*

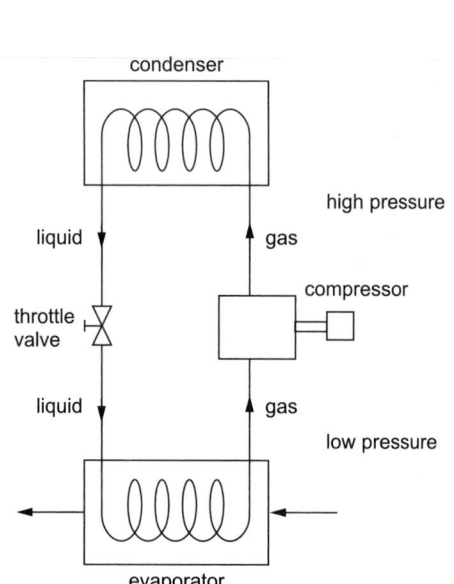

38.68 *Diagrammatic heat pump circuit. The refrigerant is in a liquid state as it enters the evaporator where it absorbs heat and changes state to gas. It is compressed to a hot gas and enters the condenser where it gives out heat and returns to liquid state. In reverse operation it can be used to cool*

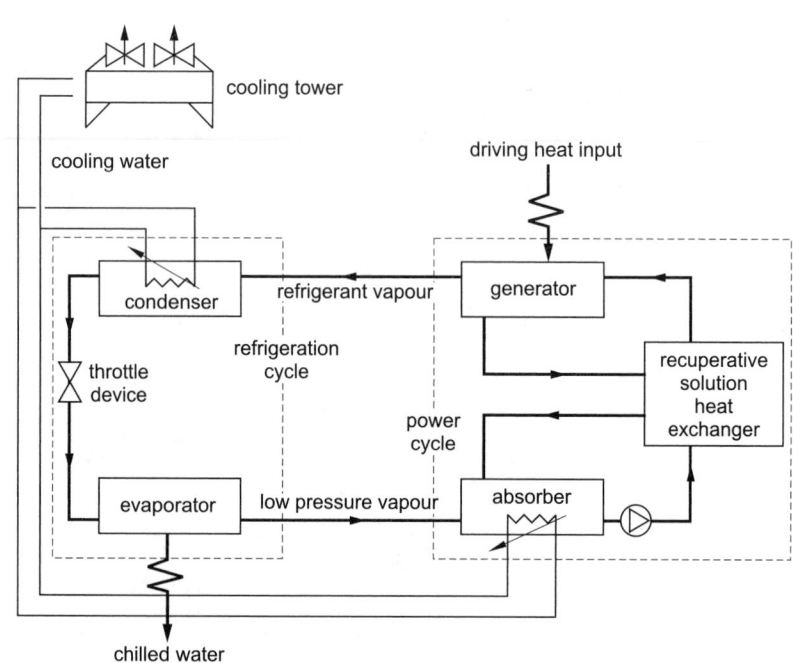

38.69 *Schematic diagram of an absorption cooling system. Refrigerant vaporised in the generator passes to the condenser where it rejects heat and condenses, Its pressure (and temperature) is then reduced by a throttling device before it enters the evaporator, here it absorbs heat from the chilled water circuit and becomes a low-pressure vapour. It then returns to the absorber*

8.34 Hybrid systems

Hybrid, or mixed-mode, systems combine mechanical and natural ventilation in either a spatial or a seasonal mix. Seasonal hybrid buildings may be naturally ventilated in summer and mechanically ventilated in winter. Spatial hybrid buildings may have spaces that are both naturally ventilated (say, at the perimeter) and mechanically ventilated (say, in the depth of space).

8.35 Space for services

The space requirements for the location of mechanical services and their distribution systems can be considerable: typically 2–15% depending on building type, and must be considered early in the design process (Table XXXVIII).

Table XXXVIII Typical space requirements for different systems for an office building as a percentage of total floor space

	Natural ventilation	Mechanical ventilation	Air conditioning
AHUs	–	2	4
Boilers	1.5	1.5	1.5
Chillers	–	–	2
Total	1.5	3.5	7.5

9 PREDICTION AND MEASUREMENT

9.01 There are a number of prediction and measurement techniques now available that the designer can use to help achieve a good thermal design. Prediction techniques can be used during the design to inform the design process. Measurement techniques can be applied after construction, during the 'hand-over' period, in order to check the thermal design performance. Some of the more common techniques are introduced below.

9.02 Building energy models

Computational dynamic building energy models can be used to predict the time-varying thermal performance of a building. They are able to predict the dynamic performance of a building and can account for the thermal capacity of the structure as well as time-varying response to internal heat gains and solar radiation. They will predict on a regular time interval (usually hourly) the following parameters:

- Internal air temperature
- Internal mean radiant temperature
- Internal relative humidity
- Energy used for space heating or cooling and
- Temperature profiles through the construction

These values can be predicted for each space in the building over any time period (eg day, week, year). The models require the following input data:

- Meterological data: temperature, solar, wind. This is available in standard *test reference year (TRY)* format for various sites

- Construction data: *k*-values, density, specific heat capacity, and dimensions for materials used
- Building geometry: areas and locations of walls, floors, etc
- Occupancy patterns: hours of use, energy use, activities and
- Heating, ventilating and cooling operation: times of use, system and control details.

Examples of available building energy models include HTB2, **38.70**, ESP, EASICALC and SERIRES.

9.03 Ventilation and airflow models

Network models

Network or *zonal* models can be used to calculate the flow of air between one or more zones in a building and between the spaces and outside. They are computer based and calculate the flows between pressure nodes both within and outside the building. Their main advantage is that they can be used to calculate inter-zone flows and therefore air change rates, ventilation heat transfer and the transfer of contaminants. They can be used to study new building forms, can handle a wide range of opening and crack types and can predict the interaction of buoyancy and wind-driven effects. Current examples of such models include the BRE model BREEZE and the US model CONTAM93.

Computational fluid dynamics (CFD) models

CFD can be used to predict the internal airflow patterns driven by the combination of the external forces of wind and stack and the internal forces from buoyancy (warm or cold surfaces) and momentum (airjets) sources, **38.71**. It can also be used to predict

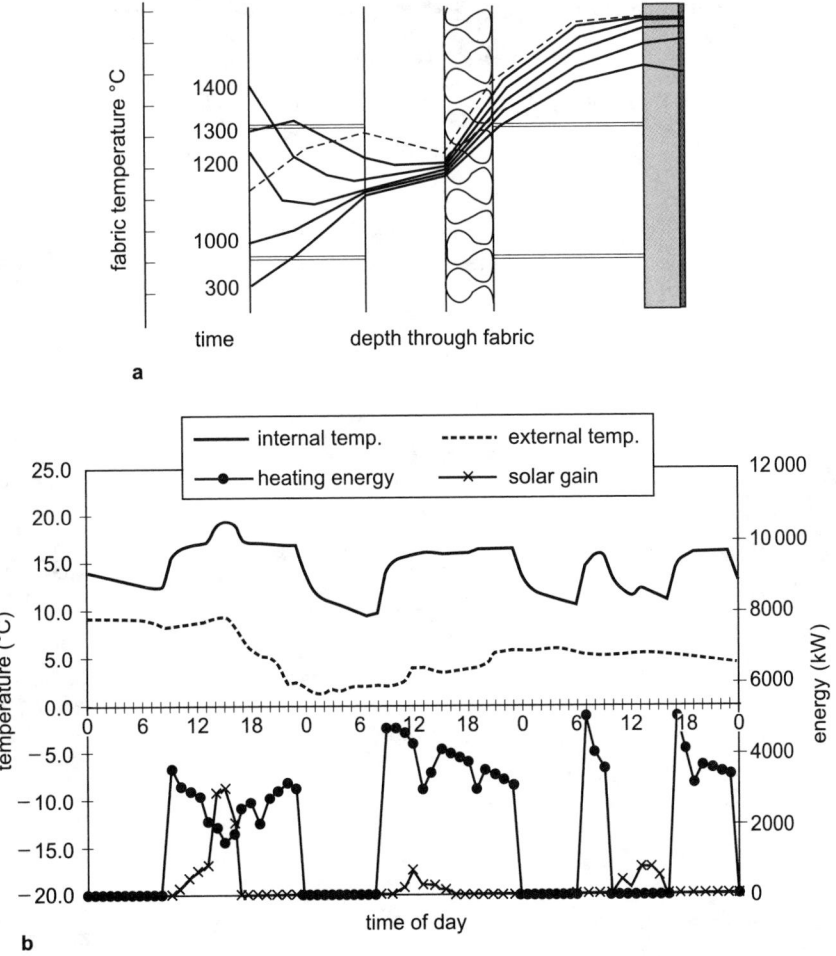

38.70 *Example of the results of the building energy model HTB2:* **a** *Predicting the temperature profile through a wall over time;*
b *Forecasting the internal air temperature and energy use as they vary with external temperature and solar gain over a three-day period*

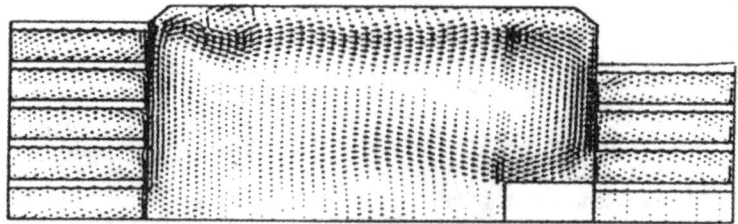

38.71 *Example of the use of computational fluid dynamics (CFD) to predict air movement in an atrium atrium*

38.72 *Boundary layer wind tunnel and model at the Welsh School of Architecture used for measuring* C_{ps}

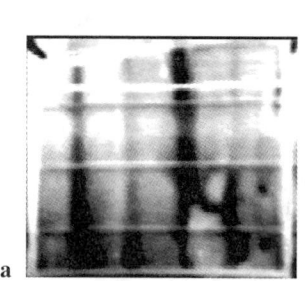

38.73 *Examples of thermographic images:*
a *Finding missing insulation;* **b** *Showing air leakage when viewed from inside;* **c** *Air leakage viewed from outside*

the ventilation rate and the dispersal of a pollutant through the space or smoke movement in the event of a fire. CFD can be used to predict the external wind flow around a building and the resulting pressure field from which the pressure coefficients (C_p) can be calculated. It is therefore an extremely versatile and useful technique in the field of ventilation and air quality prediction. It is, however, highly complex and requires a level of skill and understanding of ventilation design, building physics and computational numerical techniques in order to obtain credible solutions. However, models are becoming easier to use by the non-specialist and the need to use such models in ventilation design will eventually result in their widespread use.

Wind tunnel modelling

A physical model of a building and its surroundings can be constructed and placed in a wind tunnel, **38.72**, where it is subjected to a controlled wind flow. Pressure sensor taps can be installed at various points on the building envelope, corresponding to ventilation openings. The pressure at each opening can be measured. This can then be related to the free wind pressure, at a point of known height above the surface, in order to obtain the C_p value as described in Section 4.

9.04 Thermographic surveys

All objects emit heat energy (ie infrared radiation), the amount being dependent on the surface temperature and its emissivity. *Thermography* is the term used to describe the process of making this heat energy visible and capable of interpretation. An infrared camera can be used to scan the surfaces of a building and produce a 'live' heat energy picture that can be viewed. The picture appears in colour or greyscale. The differences in colour or tones of grey correspond to differences in surface temperature across the surface being viewed. Surface temperature differences of the order of 0.5°C can be identified. Areas of defective or missing insulation can be detected by identifying locally warm (viewed from the outside) or cool (viewed from the inside) surface areas. If there is air leakage into a building it can produce a locally cooled area on the internal surface which can be detected by the camera. If there is air leakage to the outside this can produce a locally heated area. **38.73** presents some examples of thermographic images.

Table XXXIX Air leakage standards, for 50Pa internal/external pressure difference of 50Pa (from BSRIA).

	m³/h/m² @ 50Pa
Domestic	7
Commercial	
Natural ventilation	10
Air conditioning	5
Industrial	15
Stores	5

9.05 *U*-value measurement

The *U*-value of a construction can be estimated from measurements of internal and external surface temperature and heat flux. These measurements need to be carried out over a period of time to minimise the effects of thermal capacity. For lightweight cladding constructions an estimate of the *U*-value can be achieved in about eight hours. In heavyweight masonry construction a period of a week to ten days may be needed. Measurements should be carried out on a north-facing wall or roof to avoid interference from solar gains.

9.06 Air leakage measurements offer a means of assessing the relative airtightness of different buildings by comparison with standard values. The air leakage of a building can be measured by pressurising the building using a fan and measuring the volume flow of air needed to maintain a fixed pressure difference between inside and outside.

Air leakage rate standards are normally specified either for whole buildings (in air changes per hour) or in normalised form relating to envelope area ($m^3 \cdot s^{-1}$ per m^2 of envelope area). Table XXXIX presents typical design air leakage values.

If there is air leakage into a building it can produce a locally cooled area on the internal surface which can be detected by the camera. If there is air leakage to the outside this can produce a locally heated area.

39 Light

Joe Lynes

Joe Lynes is a consultant

CI/SfB: (63)
UDC: 644.3
Uniclass: U631

KEY POINTS:

● *Increased emphasis on energy conservation with sophisticated controls*
● *Good maintenance is essential*

Contents

1 A PASSIVE SOLAR RESOURCE

1.01 Siting and orientation

Thermal applications of solar energy have long been recognised. The potential of sunlight, direct and diffused, in saving electrical energy by reducing the demand for artificial lighting, is less obvious. Here early decisions on siting and orientation may be more effective than later decisions on fenestration. Detailed guidance on the strategy of daylighting is contained in Littlefair (1991).

High-rise buildings should ideally be sited to the north, and low-rise or low-density buildings to the south of a new development, taking care not to overshadow existing buildings. Full advantage should be taken of south-facing slopes. Terraced housing should run east-to-west, so that one wall can face south. Detached or semi-detached dwellings can be on north–south link roads. Courtyards should be open to the southern half of the sky. Garages should face north. The pitch of north-facing roofs should be shallow to minimise overshadowing.

1.02 Site planning criteria

The daylight illumination reaching any point depends largely on how much sky is visible from the point in question. The amount of light striking a window (and hence entering a room) on a densely overcast day is roughly proportional to the angle θ, **39.1**, i.e. to the effective angle in degrees subtended in a vertical plane by the sky visible from the centre of the window.

The BRE Report expresses the daylight reaching a vertical wall or window, on a densely overcast day, in terms of the *vertical sky component* SC_v. This is the direct *illuminance* (lux) on the vertical surface, expressed as a percentage of the simultaneous horizontal illuminance under an unobstructed overcast sky. An unobstructed vertical wall would have a vertical sky component of 39 per cent.

An additional check on the penetration of daylight is provided by the *no-sky line*, **39.2**. This is a 'line' (actually a surface in three-dimensional space) which divides a room into two parts: one part is exposed to a view of the sky, the other part receives no direct daylight at all. The latter zone is disadvantaged with regard to both view and natural lighting.

Incident sunlight is expressed in terms of probable sunlight hours. These are the total number of hours per year when the sun would, under typical cloud conditions, shine directly onto a given point. The recommendations in the BRE Report are summarised below in paras **1.03** to **1.07**.

1.03 New developments – daylight potential

Two alternative checks are recommended to ensure that surrounding obstructions do not unduly detract from the natural lighting in a room. First, from a standard reference height 2 m above ground level, check whether any visible obstruction projects above the 25° horizontal roofline limit, **39.3**. Odd trees may be ignored. If the

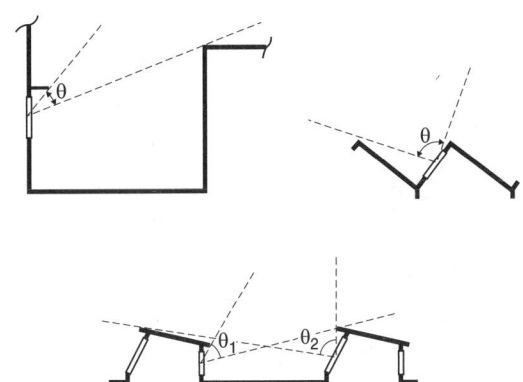

39.1 θ *is the angle subtended at the window by the visible sky*

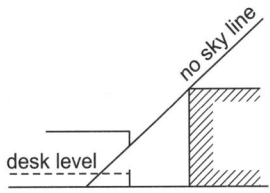

39.2 *No sky is directly visible from indoors to the left of the no-sky line*

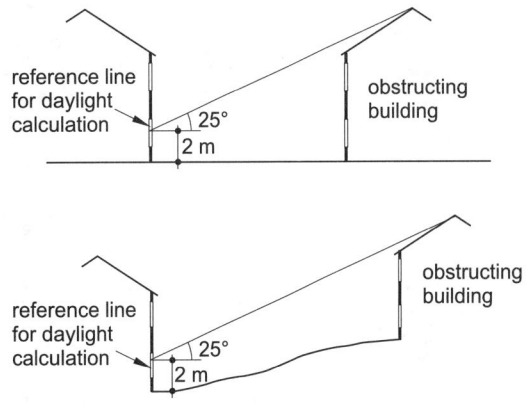

39.3 *The 25° criterion*

25° line is substantially clear of obstruction then a target vertical sky component of at least 27 per cent should be achieved. If this first check fails, the obstruction may still be narrow enough to allow adequate daylight around its sides. To check this, it is necessary to ensure that every point along the standard 2 m reference line is within 4 m (measured sideways) of a point which does have a vertical sky component of 27 per cent or more. The BRE Report contains a *skylight indicator* for estimating vertical sky components on an obstructed site.

1.04 New developments – sunlight potential

In a new dwelling, and in any other new buildings in which sunlight would be desirable, two recommendations for incident sunlight should both be met:

(a) One principal window wall should face within 90° of due south, and
(b) Along this window wall, every point on the standard 2 m reference line should be within 4 m (measured sideways) of a point exposed to at least one quarter of the annual probable hours of sunlight on an open site. These hours of exposure should include at least 5 per cent of probable hours of sunlight in the six winter months between 21 September and 21 March.

The BRE Report contains *sunlight availability indicators* for three latitudes: 51.5°N (London), 53.5°N (Manchester) and 56°N (Glasgow). These can be used for estimating hours of probable sunlight on an obstructed site.

1.05 Existing buildings – daylight protection

If any part of a new building or extension, seen from the lowest window of an existing building, projects above the 25° horizontal reference limit, **39.3**, then two further tests must be applied:

(a) The vertical sky component at the centre of each existing main window must be not less than 27 per cent, and not less than 0.8 times its previous value, and
(b) The area of the *working plane* within the *no-sky line*, **39.2**, must not be less than 0.8 times its previous value.

The BRE *skylight indicator* is designed for checking vertical sky components.

In some cases, legal rights to light may supplement the BRE recommendations. A right to light may be gained either by legal agreement or if a window has received the light without interruption for 20 years or more. Infringement of a right to light is judged by comparing *sky factor* contours indoors before and after the infringement.

1.06 Existing buildings – sunlight protection

If an existing living room has a main window facing within 90° of due south, one of two alternative conditions should be met: either

(a) No part of a new building, seen from the centre of the window and projected onto a vertical plane perpendicular to the window wall, is more than 25° above the horizon, or
(b) The point at the centre of the window, on the indoor plane of the window wall, must be exposed to at least a quarter of annual probable sunlight hours, including at least 5 per cent of annual probable sunlight hours in the six winter months between 21 September and 21 March, and not less than 0.8 times its previous sunlight hours in either period.

1.07 Adjoining development land

For a building to be a 'good neighbour', it should stand well back from the plot boundary to avoid unduly restricting well-daylit development on adjoining properties. A neighbouring site will have acceptable daylight protection if, along each common boundary line, one of the following alternative criteria is met: either

(a) No new building, seen from a point 2 m above ground level and projected onto a vertical plane perpendicular to the boundary, is more than 43° above the horizon, or
(b) Every point 2 m above the boundary line should lie within 4 m (measured along the boundary) of a point which has a vertical sky component (facing the new obstruction) of 17 per cent or more.

Note: There is no protection for sunlight (or view), as distinct from daylight, along boundaries.

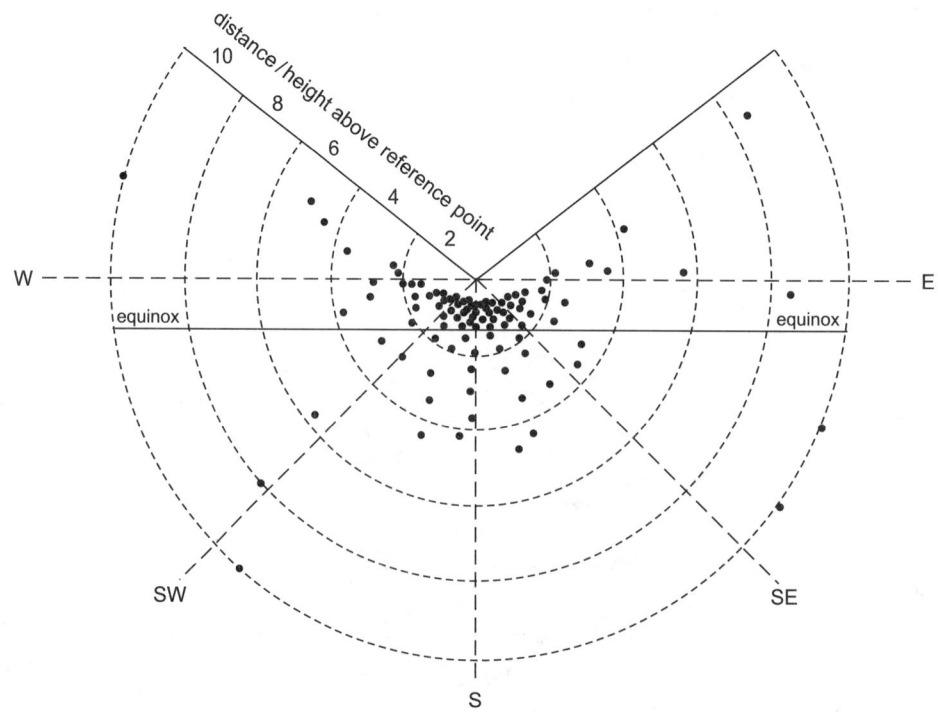

39.4 *Sunlight availability indicator for latitude 53.5°N. The annual total of unobstructed hours of probable sunlight would be 1392 hours*

1.08 BRE site planning aids

The Building Research Establishment has issued a number of indicators to assist designers in meeting their site planning recommendations:

- *Skylight indicator*, **39.3**
- *Sunlight availability indicator*, **39.4**
- *Sun-on-ground indicator*, **39.5**
- *Sunpath indicator*, **39.6**
- *Solar gain indicator*, **39.7**

Table I summarises the BRE criteria, indicating which planning aid is applicable to each criterion.

1.09 Solar geometry

The sun's apparent position in the sky is specified in terms of two angular coordinates:

- The *altitude* γ in degrees above the horizon
- The *azimuth* α in degrees clockwise in plan, measured from due north

These coordinates are given by the equations:

$$\gamma = \arcsin\,(\sin\phi\,\sin\delta - \cos\phi\,\cos\delta\,\cos 15t) \qquad \text{equation (1)}$$

$$\alpha = \arccos\,[(\sin\delta - \sin\phi\,\sin\gamma)/(\cos\phi\,\cos\gamma) \qquad \text{equation (2)}$$

where

ϕ = geographical latitude of site (positive in the northern hemisphere)

δ = *solar declination* (north is positive, south negative)

t = hours since midnight (note that the term $15t$ is in degrees)

The *altitude* of the sun at noon is $(90° - \phi - \delta)$.

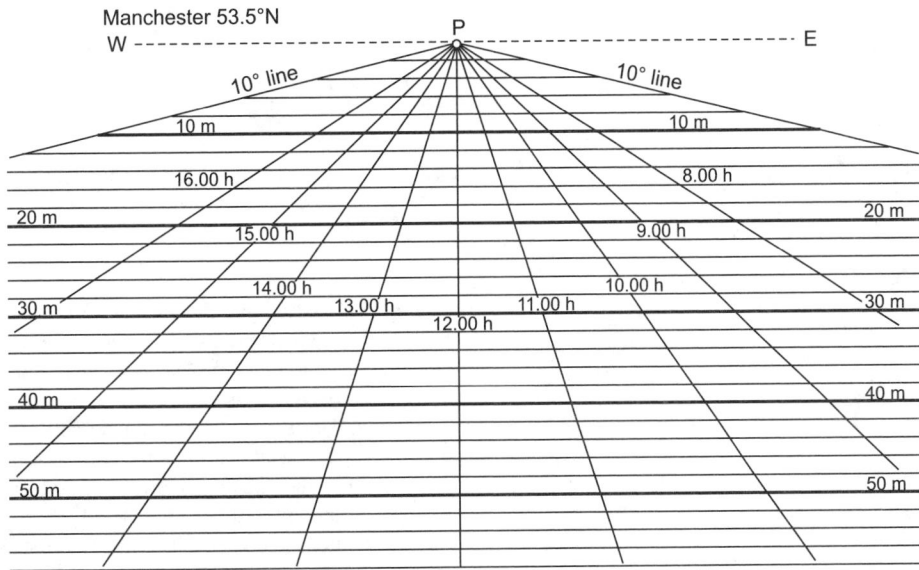

39.5 *Sun on ground indicator for 21 March, latitude 53.5°N*

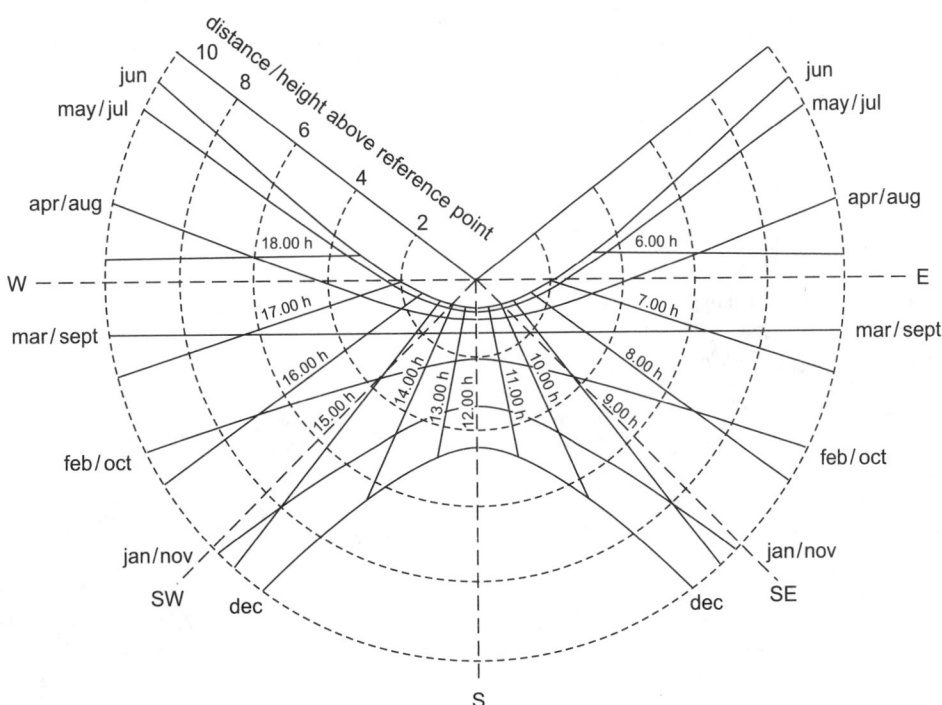

39.6 *Sunpath indicator for latitude 53.5°N*

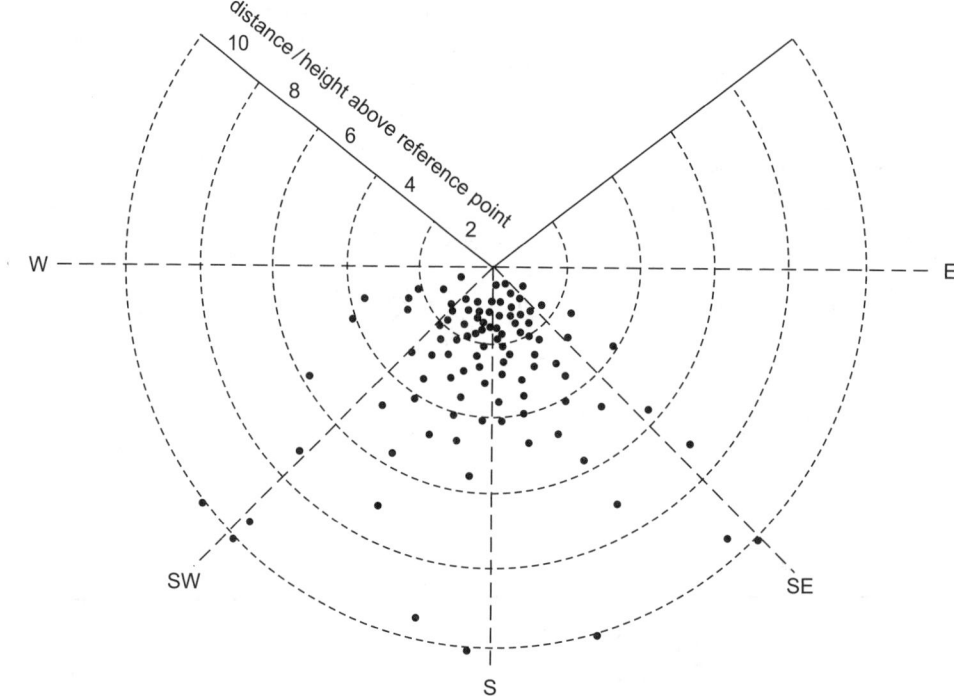

39.7 *Solar gain indicator for latitude 53.5°N. Solar radiation on unobstructed south-facing window = 322 kWh/m² during the heating season*

Table I Solar declination

Date	Solar declination
22 June	23.4°N (Summer solstice)
21 May/24 July	20°N
26 April/28 Aug.	10°N
21 March/23 Sept.	0° (Equinox)
23 Feb./20 Oct.	10°S
21 Jan./22 Nov.	20°S
22 Dec.	23.4°S (Winter solstice)

1.10 Sunlight – the use of models

A simple block model is adequate for most studies of solar penetration. It can be illuminated by a pearl household lamp located as far from the model as possible to ensure near-parallel 'sunlight'. Better still, in conjunction with the matchbox sundial, one can use the real sun outdoors as a light source. The relative positions of source and model are so arranged that the direction of the incident light will replicate the direction of the sun's rays at the time and season under investigation.

One way of bringing the correct angles of sunlight to bear on the model is to mount it on a *heliodon*, **39.8**. A simple turntable carries a platform which is tilted so as to be parallel to the earth's surface at the relevant latitude, ground at the north pole usually being taken as horizontal. The artificial sun is moved above or below this horizontal datum plane, depending on the season; it may slide up and down a vertical scale, **39.9**, whose solstice-to-solstice height subtends 23.4° at the centre of the tilted heliodon platform. The centre of the vertical scale should be level with the platform. The earth's daily rotation is simulated by spinning the tilted platform so that the movement of shadows throughout a chosen day can be observed.

The matchbox sundial, **39.10**, has been described as the beggar's heliodon. It comprises a stick (the 'gnomon') standing in a folded tray which fits inside a matchbox. A grid of lines on the tray traces the the position of the shadow of the tip of the gnomon at different hours and seasons. The seven monthly shadow orbits correspond to the dates and *solar declinations* shown in Table I.

The matchbox sundial illustrated is suitable only for latitude 53.5°N. To use it elsewhere, tilt it about an east–west axis through an angle equal to the difference in latitude, shadows being shorter as you approach the equator.

Align the north point on the sundial with the north point of the model. Shine a distant lamp on the sundial, casting the shadow of the gnomon at the month and time of day under consideration. The pattern of sunlight and shadow should be correct on the model. Ideally this is a three-person activity. The first person – the tallest! – holds the lamp as far from the model as possible. The second watches the sundial and directs the first accordingly. The third

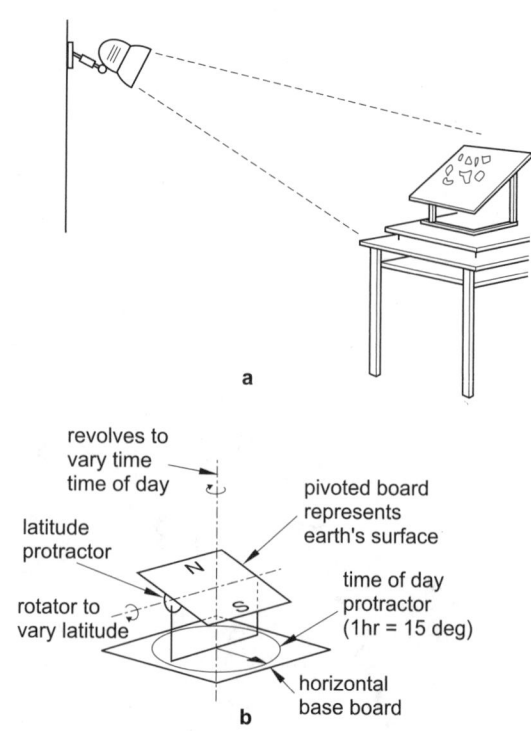

39.8 *The heliodon:* **a** *In use;* **b** *Explanatory diagram*

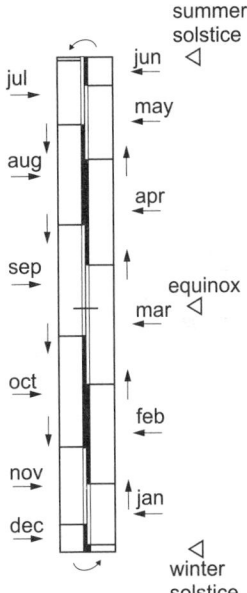

39.9 *Graduated season scale for heliodon. A lamp slides up and down this scale to simulate the sun's position month by month*

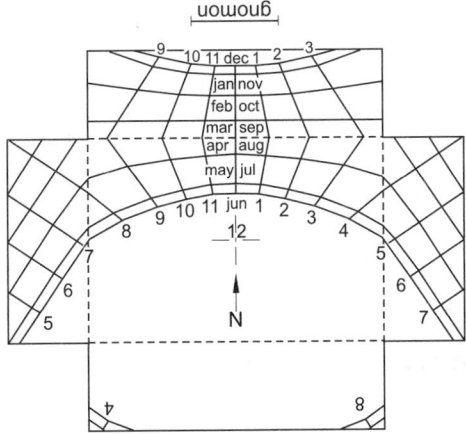

39.10 *'Matchbox' sundial for latitude 53.5°N*

takes photographs – always from due north in the northern hemisphere, otherwise the shadow of the photographer, camera and tripod will appear in the photograph. Remember to include in each photograph a card to show the time and date under investigation. Otherwise you may not be sure afterwards which photograph is which!

The alternative 'aviator method' avoids the need for colleagues, and for plunging your environment into darkness, but there are no photographs to show for it. This approach depends on the fact that the sun never 'sees' a shadow. Solar shadows are cast only on surfaces hidden from direct sunlight. Place a matchbox sundial, correctly orientated, beside a model. Align your eye with the tip of the gnomon, and with the chosen time and date marks. Those parts of the model which you can see from that position will be sunlit at the chosen time. Those parts which are concealed will be in shadow. The aviator method also works with a heliodon if you place your eye in the position of the 'sun'.

Model studies are useful for three types of sunlight investigation:

1 Seeing how far direct sunlight can penetrate inside a modelled room, and how effectively it is controlled by sunbreaks.
2 Seeing how adjacent buildings intercept each others' sunlight.

3 Measuring the sunlight illumination received indoors after reflection from the ground and from nearby sunlit buildings; this is applicable to dry tropical areas, not to the UK.

2 DAYLIGHT INDOORS

2.01 Daylight factors
Daylight design in the UK has traditionally been based on the convention of a Standard Overcast Sky for three reasons:

(a) Prudence: if the natural lighting is sufficient on an overcast day it is likely to be more than adequate when the sun shines.
(b) Convenience: a densely overcast sky looks the same whichever direction (in plan) one faces – north, south, east or west. The effect of orientation vanishes from the calculation but not, one hopes, from the designer's awareness!
(c) Given the overall brightness profile of a Standard Overcast Sky, the *illuminance* at any given point indoors must be directly proportional to the simultaneous outdoor illuminance under the unobstructed overcast sky vault, whether the sky itself is bright or dull.

The constant ratio of indoor to unobstructed outdoor illuminance is usually expressed as a percentage, and is referred to as the *daylight factor*. Thus the daylight factor at a given point may be defined as the *illuminance* (lux) at that point, expressed as a percentage of the simultaneous horizontal illuminance under an unobstructed overcast sky.

Until recently it was customary to specify natural lighting levels in terms of the minimum daylight factor in a given interior. This involved a painstaking calculation at the end of which there was little assurance that people's impression of daylit spaces would actually correlate with the minimum daylight factors. The current trend is to express the natural lighting of a room in terms of the average (as distinct from the minimum) daylight factor. This requires only a back-of-the-envelope calculation (see para **2.03** below), and yields, for each room, a single figure which characterises the daylight level.

Limitations of the average daylight factor must not be overlooked. In a medium-sized room we can usually form a unitary impression of the daylighting: we sum it up as 'bright', 'adequate', 'dim', etc. as the case may be. But in a deeper side-lit space our impression is more complex; one side of a room may look bright, the other side dim by comparison. To interpret an average daylight factor with discernment we need to know at what point the concept will break down.

Broadly speaking, a side-lit room is too deep – or the daylighting unbalanced – when either the *no-sky line*, **39.2**, cuts off a substantial area of the working plane, and/or

when $l/w + l/h > 2/(1 - R_b)$ equation (3)

where l = depth of room from window to back wall
w = width of room measured across the window wall
h = height of window head above floor
R_b = area-weighted average *reflectance* in back half of room

Unless the average daylight factor has been ruled out by one of the above considerations, it may be quoted with confidence to characterise the daylit appearance of a room. Thus an average daylight factor greater than 5 per cent will generally give the impression of generous daylighting (except, of course, on a dull day or in the evening), while an average below 2 per cent would be judged gloomy; electric lighting would be switched on as soon as an occupant entered.

2.02 The use of models
Scale model rooms have often been used for the prediction of daylight factors. The basic laws of illumination (the additivity,

inverse square and cosine laws) dictate that daylight factors in a perfectly scaled model must agree with those in the full-scale building. Unfortunately immediate application of this principle is fraught with pitfalls for the unwary.

Architectural models commissioned for other purposes are unlikely to be suitable. Joints and corners must be perfectly light-tight. Walls must be opaque: balsa and white card are out. Surface colours, and especially *reflectances*, must be correctly simulated. Glass *transmittance* must also be correct or, failing that, must be offset by applying a correction factor to the end result. Outdoor obstructions must be properly scaled, at least with regard to angular subtense, and also finished appropriately. Finally the measured daylight factor must be adjusted to take account of dirt on the glass and on room surfaces, and to allow for any curtains or glazing bars, and for absorption of light by furniture and other impediments.

In principle the daylight factor inside a model can be obtained by measuring the indoor illuminance at some chosen position with a lightmeter, and expressing it as a percentage of the illuminance on the roof of the model. This assumes that the roof is exposed to the whole sky vault; otherwise it will be necessary to take directional readings of sky brightness. It assumes too that the sky is densely overcast; this requirement follows from the definition of a *daylight factor*.

The necessity of waiting for overcast conditions to occur unaccompanied by rain, snow or gusty winds has led, logically enough, to the development of artificial skies, providing a Standard Overcast brightness profile at the flick of a switch. These too have their pitfalls. Mirror-box skies produce multiple reflections of the model at horizon level. Those too small to accommodate a model inside will be unsuitable for testing rooflights. Sky domes suffer from parallax and horizon errors unless they are very large compared with the model under test.

Since most of the potential errors would cause daylight measurements in models to be overestimated, one can anticipate that, unless exceptional precautions are taken, the measured daylight factors will considerably exceed those in the real building. This need not discourage the use of models. Indeed one may wonder why a designer should bother with daylight factors when he or she can judge and fine-tune the daylit appearance of his or her model by eye. The best advice must be to formulate in advance the questions – they may be qualitative rather than numerical – which the model study is designed to answer. Analysis of these key questions may well reveal that specific daylight factors are unimportant, and that more may be learned by studying a model under real sky conditions, facing alternately towards and away from the sun, than by leaving the overcast sky convention to dictate a programme of expensive measurements which may turn out to be irrelevant.

2.03 Calculating the average daylight factor
The average daylight factor df is given by the following equation:

$$df = (T \times W \times q \times M)/[A(1 - R2)] \text{ per cent} \quad \text{equation (4)}$$

where T = transmittance of glazing material (clear single glazing = 0.85; clear double glazing = 0.75)

W = net area of glazing material

θ = vertical angle of sky seen from centre of window, **39.1**

M = maintenance factor, Table II

A = total area of interior surfaces: floor + ceiling + walls, including windows

R = area-weighted average reflectance of interior surfaces

2.04 Shaping a window
Increasingly the prime function of a window is as much to provide a view as to illuminate the interior. In principle the analysis of

Table II Maintenance factors for natural lighting (from BS 8206 Part 2 and the CIBSE Window Design Guide)

Location of building	Inclination of glazing	Non-industrial or clean industrial work	Dirty industrial work
Non-industrial or clean industrial area	Vertical	0.9	0.8
	Sloping	0.8	0.7
	Horizontal	0.7	0.6
Dirty industrial area	Vertical	0.8	0.7
	Sloping	0.7	0.6
	Horizontal	0.6	0.5

view presents no great problem. A straight line can be drawn from the eye of an occupant to an object of regard outside the building. If the straight line passes through a window opening, in both plan and section, then the object will be visible; if not it may be necessary to alter the shape or position of the window.

In practice, occupants move around, and the indoor end of the straight line moves with them; usually a good view from the back of a room is harder to accommodate than a view from just inside a window. The choice of desirable objects of regard is usually easier in reality than in theory; but it is a choice that needs to be made consciously and deliberately if the window is to be optimised.

The skyline plays a key role. Ideally the view of the skyline should not be interrupted by the window head. Should this be impracticable, some direct view of the sky remains desirable, if only to reveal the clarity or cloudiness of the sky.

But the need for a view interacts with other aspects of the environment. A direct view of the sky can be a source of discomfort ('glare'), especially if the patch of sky is close to the direction of the sun. On the other hand, the daylight factor at the back of a room depends largely on the amount of sky directly visible, see para **1.02**. Thus there is a potential conflict between the imperatives of view, comfort and uniform daylighting. This conflict can be resolved only by prioritising. The relative importance of the three factors will largely determine the right shape and position for each window.

3 WINDOW DESIGN

3.01 A sequence for window design
We return to equation (4) for the average daylight factor in para **2.03**. Inspection of the expression suggests a natural sequence for window design decisions.

Stage 1
The first item to be fixed in the equation is the angle θ defining the position of exterior obstructions. This depends mainly on the spacing and massing of surrounding buildings. The block layout is effectively fixed quite early in the design process, well before fenestration has been thought about. Access, prospect, privacy, site utilisation and microclimate are some of the formative factors at this stage. Because these will act as constraints on the daylight factor, the determination of the angle θ is identified as the first stage in window design. Some relevant criteria and design aids are listed in Table III.

Stage 2
A side-lit room may be too deep to be satisfactorily daylit. This outcome was discussed in para **2.01** above. It occurs when the no-sky line seriously encroaches on the working plane, or when equation (3) in para **2.03** is true.

If the room is indeed too deep for stand-alone natural lighting, the average daylight factor cannot be a valid design criterion. Instead the windows should be optimised mainly for view and for

Table III BRE criteria and planning aids

Criterion	Where	Standard	Indicator	Short cut	Count
Daylight potential	New-build	Within 4 m of SC_v 27%	Skylight indicator	Clear above 25°	54 crosses
Daylight protection	Existing window	SC_v at window at least 27%	Skylight indicator	Clear above 25°	54 crosses
Daylight protection	Boundary	Within 4 m of SC_v 17%	Skylight indicator	Clear above 43°	34 crosses
Sunlight potential	New-build	1 principal wall within 90° of due south. Within 4 m of exposure to 25% of probable sunlight hours, including at least 5% in winter 6 months.	Sunlight availability indicator		25 and 5 dots
Sunlight protection	Existing window	25% of probable sunlight hours, including at least 5% in winter 6 months.	Sunlight availability indicator	Clear above 25°	25 and 5 dots
Sunlight protection	Open space	Not more than 2 fifths totally shaded at equinoxes.	Sun-on-ground indicator		Area shaded
Planning for sunlight			Sunpath indicator		
Passive solar gains	Passive solar buildings	Optimise, and watch summer overheating	Solar gain indicator		Each dot is 1% of available kWh

thermal factors and, if daylight linked controls, as in section **9**, are contemplated, for the dimming and extinction of the row of luminaires closest to the window wall. Unless the room survives the two tests in Stage 2 the designer should proceed straight to Stage 4, omitting Stage 3 of the window design sequence.

Stage 3
The window area W is estimated by inverting equation (4):

$$W = df \times A (1 - R^2)/(T \times \theta \times M)$$

At this point there is the usual conflict between visual and thermal considerations. The average daylight factor *df* is proportional to the window area *W*, but so is the winter heat loss through the windows, and so (other things being equal) is the daily mean solar cooling load. Passive solar design, harnessing both daylight and solar gain, will optimise by reducing heat loss through the glazing. Other approaches to design must face and resolve a three-way conflict. It is important to reconcile these pressures on the window area at this stage, before proceeding to Stage 4 which is concerned with optimising window shape and position for a given window area.

Stage 4
By this stage either the window area is established and the average daylight factor settled in Stage 3 or the room has been identified in Stage 2 as too deep for stand-alone natural lighting. In either case the shape and position of the windows have yet to be finalised, but the completion of the design is obviously simplified by the prior decisions in Stages 2 and 3.

The competing claims of view, visual comfort and daylight uniformity were reviewed in para **2.04** above. They centred on the visibility of the skyline. The avoidance of glare required as little visible sky as possible. A good view implied a good sight of the skyline itself but no additional access to the sky. Uniform daylighting mandated as much sky as possible visible from the depths of the room. The conflict must be resolved, in Stage 4 as in Stage 3, by identifying and balancing the relevant priorities.

Also in Stage 4 the possible advantages of multilateral fenestration may merit review. Windows in more than one wall may improve the natural lighting in two respects: by increasing the area of sky seen from the worst-lit parts of the room, and by reducing the brightness contrast between the sky and the window walls. In a naturally ventilated building they will also promote cross-ventilation, mitigating summertime overheating.

Applicability
Obviously the above idealised sequence is remote from the reality of window design. The results of applying it slavishly window-by-window would be a chaotic elevation, maybe unbuildable. A design sequence should provide a safety-net for an architect in

trouble. He or she can retrace his or her steps and recognise false turns if need be. The key to good daylighting design is to identify significant crunch points: What is the most important or the most demanding room on a given facade? Design its windows properly. Propagate variants of the solution up and down the elevation. Then the windows will do their job, both as external visual elements and as components of the interior environment.

4 ELECTRIC LAMPS

4.01 The 1995 Building Regulations
Part L of the 1995 Building Regulations for England and Wales lays down limits on the fuel consumed for electric lighting in non-domestic buildings. It offers two alternative methods of compliance:

● A shortlist of acceptable lamps in (Table IV)
● A limit on lamp efficacy (para **4.02** below).

Table IV Building Regulations requirements Satisfied if at least 95 per cent of the installed lighting circuit wattage is for lamps in this table

Lamps	Types permitted
High-pressure sodium Metal halide Induction lamps	All types and sizes
Fluorescent tubes	All 25 mm diameter (T8) lamps with low-loss or high-frequency control gear
Compact fluorescent	All sizes above 11 W

4.02 Lamp efficacy
The efficacy of an electric lamp is defined as its *luminous* flux output (lumens) divided by the electrical power consumed (watts). Efficacy is expressed in lumens per watt (lm/W). Lamp manufacturers use a number of different conventions in declaring lamp efficacies. The lumens may be '*initial lumens*' or '*average-through-life*'. The wattage may be '*lamp watts*' – those consumed by the lamp itself – or '*circuit watts*' which include losses in control gear, ballasts, etc.

Part L of the Building Regulations specifies efficacy in terms of **initial** lumens per **circuit** watt. The initial lumen output of an electric lamp is the output of a clean lamp once its output is reasonably stable. For fluorescent and other discharge lamps this condition is said to be reached after 100 hours of normal operation.

Circuit efficacies for various lamps are listed in Tables V to X. As yet, agreed values of lamp lumens per circuit watt have not

Table V Circuit efficacy of mains voltage filament lamps

Lamp type	Rating (W)	Efficacy (lm/W)
General lighting service (GLS)	60	12
	100	14
	150	15
	200	15
	300	16
	500	17
	1000	18
Double-ended linear halogen lamps	100	14
	150	15
	200	16
	250	18
	300	16
	500	20
	750	20
	1000	22
	1500	22
	2000	22

Table VI Circuit efficacy of krypton-filled (T8) fluorescent tubes

Lamp type	Rating (W)	Circuit wattage Conventional ballast (W)	Circuit wattage High frequency (W)	Circuit efficacy Conventional ballast (lm/W)	Circuit efficacy High frequency (lm/W)
Triphosphor	70	82	66	80	99
	58	70	55	77	98
	36	46	36	75	96
	18	29	19	50	76
Multiphosphor	58	70	55	54	68
	36	46	36	51	65
	18	29	19	34	53

Table VII Circuit efficacy of compact fluorescent lamps

Lamp type	Rating (W)	Circuit wattage Conventional ballast (W)	Circuit wattage High frequency (W)	Circuit efficacy Conventional ballast (lm/W)	Circuit efficacy High frequency (lm/W)
Two-limb lamps (2L)	7	12	–	33	–
	9	13	12	46	50
	11	15	14	60	64
	18	23	19	54	66
	24	35	27	51	67
	36	48	37	60	78
	40	46	44	76	80
	55	–	63	–	76
Four-limb lamps (4L)	10	16	–	38	–
	13	18	14	50	64
	18	23	20	52	60
	26	34	29	53	62
Flat 4-limb	36	–	39	–	72
Square lamps (2D)	16	21	–	50	–
	28	36	–	57	–
	38	48	–	59	–

Table VIII Circuit efficacy of metal halide lamps (MBI)

Lamp type	Rating (W)	Circuit wattage (W)	Circuit efficacy (lm/W)
Fluorescent coating (MBIF)	250	288	68
	400	410	83
Tubular (MBI-T)	250	288	71
	400	410	85

Table IX Circuit efficacy of high-pressure mercury lamps with phosphor coating (MBF)

Lamp rating (W)	Circuit wattage (W)	Circuit efficacy (lm/W)
50	62	29
80	94	43
125	142	46
250	275	47
400	430	51

Table X Circuit efficacy of high-pressure sodium lamps

Lamp type	Rating (W)	Circuit wattage (W)	Circuit efficacy (lm/W)
Elliptical bulb (SON-E)	50	62	56
	70	86	67
	100	114	81
	150	172	90
	250	280	95
	400	432	106
Tubular (SON-T)	70	86	70
	100	114	84
	150	172	93
	250	280	102
	400	432	111
Increased output (SON-XL)	50	62	65
	70	86	76
	100	114	88
	150	172	102
	250	280	118
	400	432	131
Improved colour, elliptical bulb (SONDL-E)	150	172	67
	250	280	79
	400	432	83
Improved colour, tubular (SONDL-T)	150	172	70
	250	280	82
	400	432	86
'White' SON (SDW-T)	50	62	37
	100	113	42

been published by the Lighting Industries Federation, the Electricity Association or the Chartered Institution of Building Services Engineers. In borderline cases users would be well advised to confirm values from these tables with their suppliers.

The 1995 Building Regulations will be satisfied if the overall efficacy of the lighting installation is not less than 50 lumens per watt. Note that the overall efficacy is the total lamp lumens divided by the total circuit watts. The overall efficacy is not weighted with respect to the number of lamps, but to their contributions to the overall wattage.

4.03 Lamp colour

Two aspects of lamp colour may be distinguished:

- The appearance of the source itself: warm, intermediate or cool
- Its effect on critical objects such as food or the human complexion: 'colour rendering'.

Colour characteristics of some lamp families are summarised in Tables XI and XII.

5 LUMINAIRES

5.01 Specification

The term 'luminaire' describes a complete lighting unit including lamp(s), optical components and control gear. It largely replaces the older term 'lighting fitting', which sometimes failed to

Table XI Colour properties of tubular fluorescent lamps

Appearance of lamps	Colour inspection	Colour rendering suitable for		Factories
		Shops & offices	Offices	
Warm	Colour 93 Lumilux de Luxe 32 Polylux Deluxe 930	Colour 82 and 83 Energy Saver 183 Lumilux 31 and 41 Polylux 827 and 830	Deluxe Warm White	Colour 29 Warm White 29 Warm White 30
Intermediate	Chroma 50 Colour 94 Deluxe Natural 36 Lumilux de Luxe 22 Polylux Deluxe 940 Polylux Deluxe 950	Colour 84 Energy Saver 84 Lumilux 21 and 26 Kolor-Rite 38 Polylux 835 and 840	Colour 33 Cool White 20 and 33 Natural 25 Universal White 25	Colour 35 White 23 White 35
Cool	Artificial Daylight Biolux Colour 95 and 96 Colour Matching Lumilux de Luxe 12 Northlight 55	Colour 85 and 86 Lumilux 11 Polylux 860	Daylight 54	

Table XII Colour properties of other lamps

Lamp family	Appearance of lamp	Colour rendering
Filament	Warm	Excellent

High-pressure sodium
    Standard
    Improved colour
	
	Warm
	Warm
		
		Suitable for factories
		Suitable for offices

Metal halide	Cool	Suitable for offices

Table XIII Ingress protection system (IP)

First numeral	Protection	Solid objects excluded
0	Unprotected	No special protection
1	Protected against solid objects exceeding 50 mm in diameter	Human hands (but no protection against tampering)
2	Protected against solid objects exceeding 12 mm in diameter	Human fingers
3	Protected against solid objects exceeding 2.5 mm in diameter	Large tools
4	Protected against solid objects exceeding 1 mm in diameter	Small tools
5	Dust-protected	Dust penetration does not stop the equipment from working properly
6	Dust-tight	No dust can penetrate

Second numeral	Protection	Liquids excluded
0	Unprotected	No special protection
1	Protected against dripping water	Vertically falling drips have no effect
2	Protected against dripping water when tilted up to 15°	Vertically falling drips have no effect when luminaire is tilted up to 15° from its normal position
3	Protected against spraying water	No harm from water falling as spray at angles up to 60° from the vertical
4	Protected against splashing water	No harm from water splashed from any direction
5	Protected against water jets	No harm from water jets from any direction
6	Protected against heavy seas	Water from heavy seas or powerful jets shall not enter in harmful quantities
7	Protected against immersion	No harmful entry of water under defined conditions of pressure and time
8	Protected against submersion	Suitable for continuous submersion in water, under conditions to be specified by manufacturer

embrace the necessary lamp. Manufacturers may include the following items in a luminaire specification:

- IP classification
- Light output ratio
- Flux fraction ratio
- Polar curve and/or intensity distribution data
- Spacing-to-height ratio
- Utilization factors
- Glare index table

5.02 IP Classification

The Ingress Protection (IP) system classifies the protection of luminaires against solids and moisture in terms of a two-digit number, e.g. IP54. The first digit covers the entry of solid objects, the second covers moisture penetration (see Table XIII).

5.03 Light output ratio

The *light output ratio* (LOR) of a luminaire is the proportion of luminous flux (lumens) from the lamp(s) which emerges from the luminaire. The LOR for a bare lamp would be 1.00. The light output ratio for a fluorescent luminaire depends on the ambient temperature, so values are standardised at 25°C.

The light output ratio is sometimes split into two components. The downward light output ratio (DLOR) is the proportion of lamp flux which emerges from the luminaire in directions below the level of the luminaire. The upward light output ratio (ULOR) is the proportion of lamp flux which emerges from the luminaire in directions above the level of the luminaire.

Other things being equal, a luminaire having a high light output ratio is more efficient than one with a lower LOR.

Typical values:	Open reflector	0.7 to 0.8
	Enclosed diffuser, suspended or	
	surface-mounted	0.6 to 0.7
	Recessed diffuser	0.5 to 0.6

5.04 Flux fraction ratio

The *flux fraction ratio* (FFR) of a luminaire is the ratio of the flux (lumens) emerging in directions above the level of the luminaire to the flux directed below the level of the luminaire. For a downlight, the flux fraction ratio is zero; for an uplighter, infinity.

With a high FFR the ceiling may be more brightly lit than the working plane. With a low FFR the ceiling may look dark; so low-

FFR luminaires work best when the ceiling and the floor both have a reasonably high reflectance. See also Table XVI below.

5.05 Intensity distribution

The luminous intensity of a given luminaire depends on the direction from which it is viewed. An uplighter has zero intensity except when seen from above. A downlight has zero intensity except from below. The distribution of intensity is usually plotted in polar co-ordinates, in the form of a polar curve or an iso-candela diagram. In a polar curve the radial distance in each direction is proportional to the corresponding intensity. In an iso-candela diagram loci of constant intensity are plotted on a spherical web analogous to the lines of latitude and longitude on a map of the world.

Polar curves are tricky to interpret. The flux in different angular zones is not proportional to the areas swept out on the intensity distribution. Study a globe: the area within the Arctic and Antarctic circles is far less than the area within the tropics, though the respective angular limits are the same size. So a given intensity near the vertical axis of a polar curve would contain less flux than the same intensity directed sideways.

Where polar curves and iso-candela diagrams come into their own is in predicting the direct horizontal *illuminance E* (lux) at different positions on a working plane. This is given by the 'cosine cubed' law:

$$E = (I \times \cos^3\theta)/h^2 \qquad \text{equation (5)}$$

where I is the intensity (candelas) in the direction of the chosen reference point

θ is the angle of incidence of light from a luminaire

h is the height (metres) of the luminaire above the working plane.

The cosine-cubed law is directly applicable only to a luminaire whose maximum dimension is less than one fifth of its distance from the reference point. If the luminaire is closer than this, divide it (conceptually) into n equal elements each sufficiently small to satisfy the cosine cubed law. The intensity of each element should be taken as one nth of the intensity from the whole luminaire, and each will have a different angle of incidence θ. The total direct illuminance is obtained by summing the contributions from the separate elements. Clearly this exercise is best left to the computer.

5.06 Spacing-to-height ratio

The spacing-to-height ratio (SHR) of a lighting installation is the ratio of the centre-to-centre distance between adjacent luminaires to their height above the *working plane*, **39.11**. The evenness of electric lighting depends on the spacing-to-height ratio: in general – there are exceptions – the closer the spacing, the more uniform the illumination.

Maximum SHRs should be found in luminaire catalogues. For axially symmetric luminaires a single value – SHR_{max} – is usually

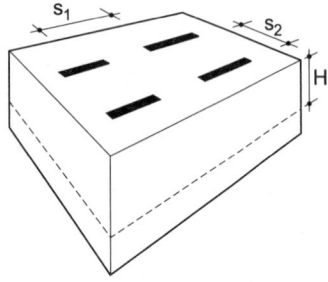

39.11 *Diagrammatic arrangement of a lighting installation.*
Key: S_1 = *axial spacing*, S_2 = *transverse spacing*, *S/H = the spacing-to-height ratio (SHR)*

quoted. For disymmetrical luminaires (i.e. symmetrical about two vertical planes) two values, axial (SHR_{max}) and transverse ($\text{SHR}_{max\,tr}$), are often given. In this case the spacing is subject to three constraints:

(a) Axial spacing must not exceed SHR_{max}
(b) Transverse spacing must not exceed $\text{SHR}_{max\,tr}$
(c) (Axial SHR × transverse SHR) must not exceed $(\text{SHR}_{max})^2$.

Luminaires with very sharp gradients in their polar curves of transverse intensity may have additional spacing constraints. These are usually presented in a spacing chart showing acceptable combinations of transverse and axial spacing-to-height ratio.

Typical SHR_{max}:   Trough reflectors   1.5 to 1.8
                Enclosed diffusers   1.3 to 1.5
                Louvrered fittings   1.0 to 1.3

5.07 Utilization factors

The average *illuminance E* (lux) on the *working plane* is given by the expression:

$$E = (N \times n \times F \times UF \times MF)/A \text{ lux} \qquad \text{equation (6)}$$

where N = number of luminaires
n = number of lamps per luminaire
F = initial flux (lumens) from one lamp
UF = *utilization factor*
MF = *maintenance factor*
A = is the area of the working plane in m^2

Alternatively the lamp flux ($N \times n \times F$) required to supply a given illuminance E is given by the expression:

$$N \times n \times F = (E \times A)/(UF \times MF) \text{ lumens} \qquad \text{equation (7)}$$

Utilization factors are tabulated by luminaire manufacturers. They depend mainly on the choice of luminaire, on the shape and size of the interior, and on the reflectances of the bounding surfaces of the interior. The shape of the interior is embodied in the *room index*, K, so this is one of the parameters in every utilization factor table.

5.08 Maintenance category

The maintenance category of a luminaire is an alphabetical classification which indicates how rapidly the *luminaire maintenance factor* will decrease in a given environment. Examples from each category are listed in Table XIV.

The concept of *luminaire maintenance factor* is still in its infancy. It is envisaged that in due course manufacturers will be in a position to quote LMF profiles for their products. The maintenance category should therefore be regarded as a stop-gap grading system.

5.09 Glare index

The glare index of a lighting installation predicts the incidence of discomfort or distraction by bright luminaires. Maximum limits recommended in the CIBSE Code for Interior Lighting range from 16 for a drawing office to 28 for heavy industry (see Bibliography and References).

Table XIV Luminaire maintenance categories

Maintenance category	Typical luminaire
A	Bare lamp batten
B	Open top reflector (ventilated self-cleaning)
C	Closed top reflector (unventilated)
D	Enclosed (IP2X)
E	Dustproof (IP5X)
F	Uplighter

Manufacturers have been encouraged to publish tables of 'uncorrected' glare index for each of their luminaires. These are given as a function of the direction of view (endwise or crosswise in relation to a linear luminaire), the surface reflectances and the room dimensions (length and width expressed as multiples of the height of the luminaires above eye level). Uncorrected glare indices relate to luminaires, 2 m above eye level, powered by lamps emitting 1000 lumens per luminaire. The correction to be added for other mounting heights and lamp outputs is:

$$4 \times \log_{10}H + 6 \times \log_{10}(n \times F) - 19.2 \qquad \text{equation (8)}$$

where H = height of luminaires above eye level (metres)

n = number of lamps in each luminaire

F = luminous flux from each bare lamp (lumens)

The current glare index system will shortly be replaced by an internationally accepted unified glare rating (UGR) system. The form in which luminaire data is to be presented is still under discussion, but present-day limiting glare indices are unlikely to change.

6 PLANNING AN OVERALL LIGHTING SYSTEM

6.01 The lumen method

The vast majority of lighting systems are planned by the lumen method, using equations (6) and (7) from para **5.07** above. These equations suggest a natural sequence for electric lighting design decisions:

Stage 1

The first decision is the choice of target illuminance *E*. The CIBSE code (1994) recommends values of *standard maintained illuminance* for over 700 different locations or activities. A few examples are given in Table XV.

The flow chart, **39.12**, is used when the circumstances or demands of the task in hand are more relaxed or more severe than usual. The dashed lines in the figure offer a compromise expedient when this is appropriate. The target illuminance thus obtained is known as the *design maintained illuminance*.

Table XV Standard maintained illuminance (from CIBSE Code for Interior Lighting)

Walkways	50 lux
Corridors	100
Loading bays	150
Turbine halls	200
Classrooms	300
General offices	500
Drawing offices	750
General inspection	1000
Precision assembly	1500
Minute assembly	2000

In many cases, especially in dwellings or in public areas, the visual task is hard to identify, and the illuminance is calculated to provide the right atmosphere for getting together or for relaxing. Especially where this is the case, listed values of standard maintained illuminance should be treated as a point of departure, not as a target. If a designer seeks a subdued atmosphere a lower value would be right; if a brighter ambience is envisaged, a higher illuminance would be justified.

Stage 2

The second decision is the broad choice of lamp type. Apart from cost, three factors dominate this choice:

(a) Efficacy (lumens per watt). Efficacy values are shown in Tables V to X.

(b) Lamp colour balance: warm, intermediate or cool. See Tables XI and XII.

(c) Colour rendering: see columns in Tables XI and XII.

A high efficacy will reduce energy consumption and hence running costs, air pollution and greenhouse gas emissions. The 1995 Building Regulations prescribe an upper limit on lighting circuit efficacies for non-domestic buildings; see para **4.01** above.

Stage 3

The third decision is the broad choice of luminaire family. To a large extent the character of the space will dictate the character of

39.12 *Design maintained illuminance flow chart*

Table XVI The effect of luminaire intensity distribution on the atmosphere in a room

Flux fraction ratio	Spread of downward light		
	Tight	Medium	Widespread
0 to 0.1	Concentration on task in hand	Dark ceiling may look oppressive	Danger of glare?
0.1 to 0.8	Well-mannered, formal	Safe, characterless?	Welcoming, expansive
over 0.8	Dignified	Safe, relaxing	Relaxing

the luminaire. A utilitarian space demands a utilitarian luminaire while a reassuring space calls for a domestic style of luminaire. The principal photometric quantities governing the choice of luminaire are

(a) The intensity distribution (polar curve); see para **5.05** above. The general effect of alternative distributions is listed in Table XVI. Do not read too much into this table. Lighting alone has only a modest effect on the environment; it is psychologically powerful only as a reinforcement to the other resources of interior design. Colour, texture, furnishings and lighting should be designed hand in hand for the best effect.

(b) The light output ratio; see para **5.03** above. A high light output ratio will reduce energy consumption, but it generally has much less effect on energy costs than the choice of illuminance in Stage 1 or the choice of lamp efficacy in Stage 2.

If a wise choice is made at this Stage there should be little problem in satisfying the glare check in Stage 7.

Stage 4
The fourth decision relates to cleaning and maintenance. The various components of the *maintenance factor* – the *lamp lumen maintenance factor*, the *lamp survival factor*, the *luminaire maintenance factor* and the *room surface maintenance factor* – must be separately evaluated and subsequently combined. This is no mere mechanical chore. It involves the consideration of alternative maintenance regimes and cleaning schedules, and may well call for retrospective changes in Stages 2 and 3.

Stage 5
The fifth decision involves sizing the lighting installation. The principal terms in the equation for the lumen method have been settled in Stages 1 to 4. The total required lamp flux ($n \times N \times F$) is now calculated using equation (7).

Stage 6
The sixth decision decomposes the lamp flux $n \times N \times F$ into its three components:

n: In most non-fluorescent luminaires, n (the number of lamps per luminaire) = 1. In the case of fluorescent luminaires it is wise to standardise on a single size and colour of lamp throughout a given project. This simplifies lamp replacement, minimises storage difficulties and helps to obviate the 'strawberry and vanilla' effect of different tube colours side by side in the same room or even the same luminaire. Different lighting levels in different rooms are then achieved by using different numbers of tubes in each luminaire.

N: *Where an even overall spread of light is wanted, the spacing-to-height ratio* imposes a lower limit on N (the number of luminaires); see para **5.06** above. In practice the spacing-to-height ratio should play only a minor part in determining N. Where the layout of workstations is known it should logically dictate the luminaire layout. Where the activity involves some focus of emphasis, that focus should be selectively illuminated,

and the geometry of the lighting layout might revolve about the focus. In any case the layout should respect the structural grid.

A lighting calculation is sometimes held to justify an excessive number or an aggressive layout of luminaires. This is nonsense: no lighting calculation should ever be permitted to dictate design priorities, and no designer should ever offer such an excuse for abdication.

F: Once n and N are fixed, the lamp flux F will determine the wattage of each lamp. Available lamps will never provide the precise lamp flux mandated by a lumen calculation. A neighbouring value should be selected and, if the lighting level has been wrongheadedly specified too tightly, it may be necessary to rerun the lumen method equation and check the illuminance.

Stage 7
The final stage comprises a check on the glare index of the installation; see para **5.09** above. In the case of linear luminaires, this stage provides an opportunity to optimise their orientation. Glare is not the only factor which should govern the way they are aligned. The orientation may also be chosen to minimise the shadow cast by the body onto the desk or table, to reduce shiny reflections in the task, to emphasise one or other dimension of a room, to guide visitors along a preferred route and/or to signal their arrival by a change of layout, illuminance, mounting height, etc.

Applicability
This idealised sequence, like its counterpart for window design, para **3.01**, bears little resemblance to the everyday practice of lighting design, where many decisions are justifiably based on precedent, experience or habit. The advantage of a step-by-step procedure appears when a designer is stuck. He or she can then reassess earlier decisions in their logical sequence, identifying and correcting the blockage.

7 DISPLAY LIGHTING

7.01 Luminaires for display lighting
The effectiveness of display lighting depends as much on the skill of the person responsible for aiming it as on the accuracy of the specifier. The latter would be well advised to consider who is likely to take charge of it once his or her back is turned. It may well be a caretaker, a shop assistant or a clerk of works, with no training in display lighting techniques. If so, any track lighting is likely to become poorly positioned and wrongly aimed. Fixed lighting, perhaps above egg-crate louvres, may well be preferable. The following notes relate mainly to track lighting, but the same principles apply to fixed lighting.

In a space where visitors are free to move around it is virtually impossible to light vertical surfaces without shining light straight into somebody's eyes. To avoid this, start from the principal entrance and plan a route through the exhibits. Run lighting track across, not along, this route. Arrange spotlights to shine over the shoulders of visitors following the preferred route. At each point along the route, make sure that the next stopping point is attractively lit, to encourage circulation in the right direction. Visitors moving the opposite way will face darker surfaces and will have to brave the dazzle of spotlights planned for their more accommodating brethren. They may take the hint.

Track lighting should preferably be 2.5 to 3 m high. Lower mounting would invite glare, tampering, and discomfort from heat radiated from the lamps. Higher mounting would make aiming more difficult, and spotlights might remain unadjusted month after month.

Spotlights are available with widely varying degrees of 'punch'. Some are tightly concentrated; others diffuse their output more widely. Published *performance cones* give a graphic indication of the angles at which the beam intensity from a spotlight is at 50 per cent of its peak value. Beam diameters and maximum illuminances are often shown for surfaces facing the spotlight at various distances. Illuminances at other distances and inclinations may be estimated fom the cosine cubed law, para **5.05** equation (5) above.

Do not confuse the performance cone with the *cutoff line*. The latter may also be a cone, and can register as a conic section, usually a hyperbola, dividing directly lit from unlit areas of a wall. It is wise to anticipate the nature and position of cutoff lines. They can show up as scallops disconcertingly unrelated to the illuminated target.

7.02 Planning display lighting

Effective display lighting depends as much on darkness as on illumination. Objects will stand out only if they look significantly brighter than their surroundings. Brightness has two aspects:

(a) *Illuminance*: to appear noticeably brighter the illuminance on a surface should be at least three times the background illuminance; to stand out strongly would require a ratio of 10:1 or more.
(b) *Reflectance*: if an object has a lower reflectance than its background it will respond much less to an increase in illuminance; spotlighting may well be inappropriate, and the profile of the beam may need careful trimming to the profile of the target.

The overall pattern of light and shade deserves careful consideration. To pick out a single focus of attention is simple and always effective. To highlight two objects risks an impression of disunity. To spotlight more than three requires some skill, and invites confusion.

The predominant direction of the lighting is also important. Illumination has vectorial properties. Ignoring interreflected light, the *illumination vector* due to each spotlight is equal to the illuminance on a surface facing the source. However, the illumination vector must not be confused with the illuminance. Illuminances from different sources are added together by simple arithmetic, but illumination vectors obey the parallelogram law for vectorial addition, **39.13**. The vector resultant of two sources is represented in magnitude and direction, by the diagonal of a parallogram of illumination vectors. Spotlights shining from opposite directions may produce a zero resultant: the lighting would have no clear direction. Most objects look more attractive under a sideways vector than under a vector from straight overhead or from below; compare a side-lit room with a room lit by an overhead array of luminaires. However, a vector shining along the

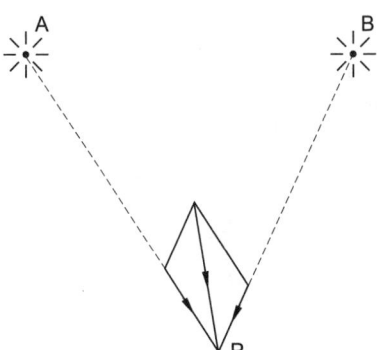

39.13 *The illuminance vector at P due to sources A and B is the diagonal of the parallelogram whose sides are the vectors due to A and B*

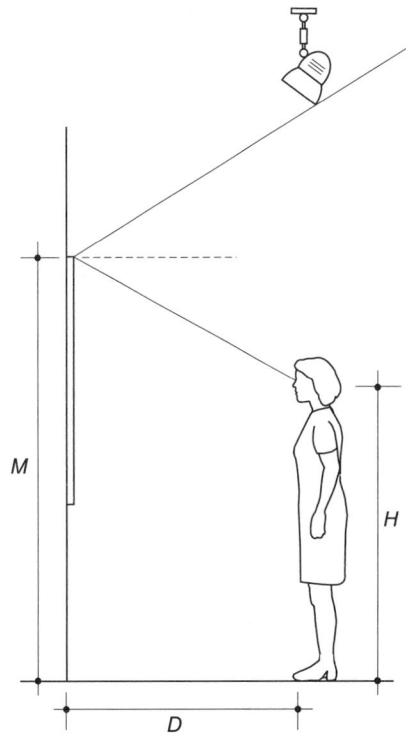

39.14 *For picture lighting assume* D = *length of picture diagonal,* M *height of top of tallest picture frame,* H = *eye level of short adult, say 1.5 m*

direction of view tends to flatten the object, and a vector in the opposite direction tends to show the object in silhouette. The direction of the illumination vector, and the strength of the directional flow of light, are under the designer's control, and should be part of his or her vocabulary.

The lighting of paintings, notice-boards, chalk-boards, etc. must meet two constraints:

(a) It must not produce shiny reflections, which reduce legibility, and
(b) It must provide reasonably even illumination over the target surface.

The best position for the luminaire is shown in **39.14**. If it were mounted closer to the target surface, the foot of the target would look dimly lit compared with the top. If it were further back, a visitor would see shiny reflections.

In conclusion, the Golden Rule for successful spotlighting is 'Light objects, not people'. The positioning of luminaires should be constrained as much by the need to avoid glare and distraction as by the need to reveal an illuminated object.

8 VISUAL DISPLAY TERMINALS

The front surface of a visual display terminal (VDT) acts as a partial mirror. Screen visibility is impaired when specular reflections approach or exceed the brightness of the luminous pixels.

Side windows present a double problem. If operators face a window they suffer because it is much brighter than the VDT. If their backs are to the window they will pick up its reflection in the VDT screen. The face of the VDT should ideally be at right angles to the face of the window. If there are windows on two adjacent walls this remedy may fail, and solid screens might be considered.

In a private office the choice of luminaire is seldom critical; a ceiling-mounted fitting would not normally be reflected in the display screen. In an open-plan office the choice is more restricted.

Table XVII VDT luminaire categories from CIBSE Lighting Guide 3

Category	VDT use	Brightness limitation angle
1	Intense	55°
2	General	65°
3	Minimal	75°

If the height of the ceiling is greater than 2.5 m uplighters containing metal halide or high-pressure sodium lamps, possibly integrated into the office furniture, should be suitable. If the ceiling height exceeds 3.5 m, one might consider direct-indirect lighting, suspended uplighters or column-mounted uplighters. For ceiling heights below 2.5 m the best solution is a modular VDT luminaire providing a suitable illuminance (perhaps 300 lux) on the desk, with restricted light sideways to reflect in the screen.

CIBSE LG3 (1993) defines three categories of VDT luminaire, whose photometric performance is characterised by the angle, from the downward vertical, above which a brightness limit (200 candelas per square metre of projected area) is not exceeded. Category 1 provides the tightest control: see Table XVII.

9 LIGHTING CONTROLS

Five families of electric lighting controls may be distinguished as follows.

9.01 Constant illuminance control

Dimmable high-frequency fluorescent luminaires can be linked to indoor photocells set to sustain the *design maintained illuminance*. Otherwise a clean installation of new lamps would provide a substantially higher illuminance, with a correspondingly high energy consumption. As time passes the controls will gradually pass additional power to the lamps, to compensate for the effects of dirt and deterioration. When the lamps are fully loaded the time is overdue to alert the maintenance staff to clean the luminaires. This system has an additional advantage when the room changes from one use to another which permits a lower task illuminance: the setting can be adjusted to maintain the reduced lighting level.

9.02 Daylight linking

One or more rows of luminaires along a window wall may be linked to either interior or exterior photocells which monitor daylight levels and adjust the electric lighting accordingly, either by top-up (dimming) or by simple on/off switching. Note that high-intensity discharge lamps are unsuitable for dimming. Control zones should be parallel to the windows. Daylight linking can be combined with the occupancy detection system below.

9.03 Manual switching

Manual switching is particularly suitable for intermittently occupied spaces. Switches should be close to the luminaires they control. As a rule of thumb, the number of switches in a space should be not less than the square root of the number of luminaires. Thus twelve luminaires would require at least four switches. Options include low-voltage switching, pull-cords and remote 'wireless' switches such as ultrasonic or infrared; or a telephone signal to an energy-management system.

9.04 Time switching

Electric lighting is switched off automatically at a control panel at the same time each day, to coincide with work breaks, e.g. at mid-day. It is better to switch half the lights at first, the rest 10 minutes later. Users are then free to relight the lamps they still need. This system shares the responsibility for energy saving with the occupants, whose understanding and co-operation should be assured in advance.

There are several alternative methods for implementing a synchronised or staggered switch-off:

- Low-voltage wiring to a relay in each lighting circuit
- A mains-borne signalling system
- A one-second interruption of the mains supply to each luminaire, causing latching relays to switch off.

In each case pull-switch or other manual overrides should be provided, for occupants to switch lamps straight back on if needed.

9.05 Occupancy-linked switching

The aim of occupancy-linked lighting controls (presence detectors) is to operate the lighting when, but only when, somebody is there to make use of it. The best application is where occupancy is infrequent or unpredictable, e.g. private offices, conference rooms, toilets, warehouse storage aisles, photocopy rooms, and bookcase lighting in libraries.

Some units beep or flash a warning signal just before lights are turned off, so that an undetected occupant can wave an arm and avoid being left in the dark. Fluorescent lamps require a time delay before switching off, as repeated switching shortens lamp life. Occupancy-linked discharge lamps with long restrike times should be supplemented by separate background lighting.

Occupancy detectors are particularly suited to daylit spaces, and may be combined with daylight sensors. Presence detectors can double as part of a security system. At night or at weekends they can activate an alarm instead of working the lights. They can also assist security patrols at night. However, since they react to movement a motionless occupant may escape detection.

Occupancy detectors may be triggered by air movement, by a flapping curtain, or by events in a corridor outside the monitored space. Ultrasonic detectors seem more prone than passive infrared detectors to these extraneous stimuli. The sensitivity of some units can be adjusted to minimise these failings, at the price of their effective surveillance area. But the best arrangement is always to insist on manual-on/automatic-off occupancy controls with a manual override.

10 GLOSSARY

Altitude
The angle in degrees, subtended at a viewpoint, between a chosen point and the horizon. The solar altitude is the altitude of the sun above the horizon.

Azimuth
An angle in plan, also called *bearing*. The solar azimuth is usually measured from due north.

Candela see *luminous intensity*.

Circuit wattage
The power consumed by the lamps in an electric lighting system, by their control gear, and by associated equipment for power factor correction.

Cutoff line
The line above (or in the case of an uplighter, below) which a lamp is not visible. Strictly speaking, the cutoff line is a surface in three dimensions. The cutoff line for a window is the *no-sky line*, see para **7.01**.

Daylight factor
Equal to the illuminance (lux) at an indoor point, expressed as a percentage of the simultaneous horizontal illuminance under an unobstructed overcast sky outside, see para **2.01**.

Design maintained illuminance
The target value for lighting design. It is derived from the *standard maintained illuminance* by following the flow chart **39.12**, see para **6.01**.

Direct-indirect lighting
Provided by a luminaire designed to combine the photometric characterictics of an uplighter and a downlight. It provides upward and downward illumination, sometimes in variable proportions, but little or no light sideways. Direct–indirect lighting has recently undergone a revival for VDT lighting, see Section **8**.

Efficacy (h)
For an electric lamp, equal to its luminous flux output (lumens), divided by the electric power consumed (watts). The 1995 Building Regulations specify lamp efficacy in terms of initial lumens per circuit watt. See para **4.02**.

Flux, see *luminous flux*.

Glare index
Predicts the incidence of discomfort or distraction by bright luminaires, see para **5.09**.

Illuminance (E)
The degree of concentration of light in lux striking a surface. Illuminance is measured by a special lightmeter – an illumination photometer; photographic lightmeters are unsuitable.

Illumination vector
The difference in *illuminance* at a point between opposite sides of a small flat surface so orientated that this difference is a maximum. The direction of the vector is then normal to the surface; the positive direction is from higher to lower illuminance. Illumination vectors obey the parallelogram law for vector addition. See para **7.02**.

Initial lumens
The flux from a clean lamp once its output is reasonably steady; for fluorescent and other discharge lamps this condition is said to be reached after 100 hours of normal operation.

Intensity see *luminous intensity*.

IP (Ingress Protection) classification
Provides a two-digit classification of the protection of luminaires against solid objects and moisture, e.g. IP54. The first digit refers to solids, the second to moisture. See Table XIII.

Lamp life survival factor (LSF)
The proportion of lamps in an installation still operating after a given interval. In calculating the *maintenance factor*, assume LSF = 1.0 unless bulk relamping is to be carried out without previous spot replacement of failed lamps.

Lamp luminous flux maintenance factor (LLMF)
The output (in lumens) of the lamps in an installation after a given interval, expressed as a fraction of their initial output. Curves of LLMF for different lamp types are available from manufacturers.

Lumen see *luminous flux*

Luminaire maintenance category
An alphabetical classification indicating the speed at which the luminaire maintenance factor will depreciate in a given environment. See Table XIV.

Luminaire maintenance factor (LMF)
The light output ratio of a luminaire after a given interval, expressed as a fraction of its light output ratio when clean. The LMF includes the effect of dirt deposited on or inside the luminaire, but not the regular lamp lumen depreciation which is monitored separately by the lamp luminous flux (lumen) maintenance factor. Luminaire manufacturers should be approached for this information. If it is not available, one can refer to standard values for different luminaire maintenance categories.

Luminous flux (ϕ)
The rate in lumens at which light energy is emitted from a source or received by a surface. For a given illuminance E lux, the flux striking a surface will be proportional to the area A (m^2):

$$\phi = E \times A \text{ lumens} \qquad\qquad \text{equation (9)}$$

Hence 1 lux = 1 lumen per square metre.

Luminous intensity
Light from a point source obeys the inverse square law: the illuminance E lux on an element facing the source is inversely proportional to the square of the distance d metres between the source and the element. In other words, the product $E \times d^2$ is constant. The constant $E \times d^2$ is known as the luminous intensity, or simply the intensity, of the source. It is expressed in candelas (formerly candle-power). The product $E \times d^2$ will not be constant unless the distance d is quite large compared to the maximum dimension of the luminaire in question. In practice the distance should be at least five times the longest dimension of the luminaire. See also para **5.05**.

Lux see *illuminance*.

Maintenance factor (MF)
The ratio of the illuminance (lux) of a lighting system, or, in the case of natural lighting, the daylight factor, after a given interval, expressed as a fraction of the illuminance or daylight factor when the same installation was clean and newly commissioned. The maintenance factor for electric lighting may be decomposed into four components:

$$\text{MF} = \text{LLMF} \times \text{LSF} \times \text{LMF} \times \text{RSMF}$$

where LLMF = *lamp luminous flux (lumen) maintenance factor*
  LSF = *lamp survival factor*
  LMF = *luminaire maintenance factor*
  RSMF = *room surface maintenance factor*

See Table II for maintenance factors for natural lighting.

No-sky line
The dividing line, **39.2**, in a room between the area which is exposed to a direct view of the sky, and the area which receives no direct daylight at all.

Performance cone
Gives a graphical indication of the angles at which the beam luminous intensity from a reflector lamp or a downlighter falls to 50 per cent of its peak value. Performance cones often include values of beam diameter and maximum illuminance at various distances from the luminaire. They are a convenient way to compare different forms of spotlight. See para **7.01**.

Probable sunlight hours
The long-term average number of hours per year when direct sunlight is visible from a given point. Typical cloud conditions are taken into account.

Table XVIII Approximate reflectances of typical building finishes from CIBSE Code for interior lighting interior lighting

Building surface	Material or finish	Reflectance
Ceilings	White emulsion paint on plain plaster surface	0.8
	White emulsion paint on acoustic tile	0.7
	White emulsion paint on no-fines concrete	0.6
	White emulsion paint on wood-wool slab	0.5
Walls	White emulsion paint on plain plaster surface tiles, white glazed	0.8
	Brick, white gault	0.7
	Plaster, pink	0.65
	White asbestos cement Brick, concrete, light grey Portland cement, smooth	0.4
	Stainless steel	0.35
	Brick, fletton	0.3
	Concrete, light grey Portland cement, rough (as board marked) Brick, London stock Timber panelling: light oak, mahogany, gaboon	0.25
	Timber panelling: teak, afromosia, medium oak brick, concrete, dark grey	0.2
	Brick, blue engineering	0.15
	Chalkboard, painted black	0.05
Floors and furniture	Paper, white	0.8
	Cement screed PVC tiles, cream Carpet: light grey, middle buff	0.45
	Timber: birch, beech, maple	0.35
	Timber: oak PVC tiles, brown and cream marbled Carpet: turquois, sage green	0.25
	Timber: iroko, keming, medium oak Tiles, cork, polished	0.2
	Quarry tiles: red, heather brown Carpet, dark, 'low maintenance' PVC tiles, dark brown Timber, dark oak	0.1

Reference plane see *working plane.*

Reflectance (R)

The proportion of incident light which a surface reflects. A perfectly white surface would have a reflectance of 1.00, a perfectly black surface would have zero. Table XVIII gives some values for typical surfaces.

Room Index (K)

Specifies the proportions of a room, insofar as they affect the utilisation factor. Other things being equal, two interiors having the same room index will have the same utilisation factor for a given luminaire, whatever their geometrical differences.

For a square room *l* metres square $K = l/2h$

For a rectangular room *l* metres long and *w* metres wide $K = (l \times w)/[(l + w)h]$ where h = height (m) of centroid of luminaires above the working plane. For a non-rectangular interior K = (floor area + ceiling area) / (wall area between the working plane and the plane of the luminaires).

Room surface maintenance factor (RSMF)

The illuminance after a set time expressed as a fraction of the illuminance when the room was newly decorated. Depreciation of lamp and luminaire outputs are not included in the RSMF; they are monitored separately by the lamp luminous flux maintenance factor and the luminaire maintenance factor respectively.

Sky factor

The horizontal illuminance (lux) at a given point due to light received directly through an unglazed window opening from a sky of uniform brightness, expressed as a percentage of the horizontal illuminance under an unobstructed vault of the same sky. See para **1.05**.

Skylight indicator

39.15, for checking the daylight potential of new buildings and daylight protection for existing buildings. It provides an estimate of the vertical sky component on a built-up site. The centre of the semi-circular indicator corresponds to the position in plan of the reference point. Its base should run along the plane of the window wall. Radial distances correspond to the ratio (distance of obstruction on plan) / (height of obstruction above reference point). Each little cross stands for a vertical sky component of 0.5 per cent. Count how many crosses fall within the outline of the sky. Divide by 2. The answer equals the vertical sky component, expressed as a percentage.

Solar declination

At any moment the sun is precisely overhead at some point on the earth's surface. The latitude of this point depends on the season, and is known as the solar declination. Some values of solar declination are shown in Table I.

Solar gain indicator

39.7, checks solar radiation (direct and diffuse, but not reflected), striking a vertical south-facing wall or window. Values are summed over the heating season (1 October to 30 April). They do not cover the summer months, so provide no check on summertime overheating. With this limitation in mind, they provide valuable

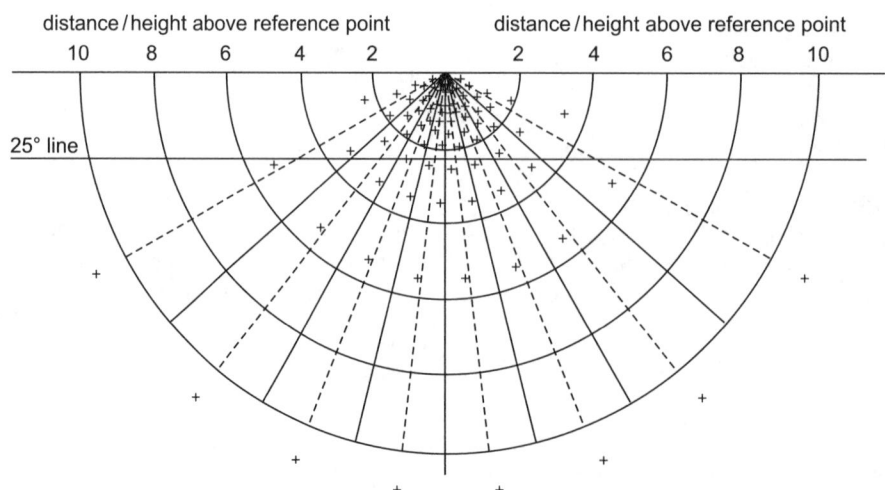

39.15 *Skylight indicator*

data for passive solar design, indicating the potential contribution of solar radiation to space heating. The indicator is strictly applicable only to a south-facing vertical wall. Do not use it for sloping windows, or for vertical planes facing more than 30° away from due south. The indicator, for the appropriate latitude, is aligned in the same way as the *sunlight availability indicator*. Each of the 100 dots stands for 1 per cent of incident solar radiation during the heating season. The total incident radiation is one hundredth of the exposed dots, multiplied by the maximum value, in kWh/m², which is marked on the caption of each indicator.

Spacing-to-height ratio (SHR)
The ratio of the centre-to-centre distance between adjacent luminaires to their height above the working plane, **39.11**. See para **5.06**.

Standard maintained illuminance
The illuminance in lux recommended for a given task under standardised conditions. Values of standard maintained illuminance are published in the CIBSE Code. They should be translated into design maintained illuminance values when a new lighting system is envisaged. See para **6.01**.

Sunlight availability indicator
39.4 for checking sunlight protection for existing buildings and sunlight potential for new buildings. It provides a measure of the *probable sunlight hours* on a built-up site. The centre of the indicator corresponds to the position in plan of the reference point. Radial distances correspond to the ratio (distance of obstruction on plan)/(height of obstruction above reference point). Align the south-point of the indicator with the south-point of the site plan. Each of the 100 dots on the indicator stands for 1 per cent of the annual probable hours of sunlight. Choose the indicator whose stated latitude (51.5°, 53.5° or 56°) is closest to the geographical latitude of the site. If a dot is closer to the centre than any obstruction in that direction, then sunlight from that dot is unobstructed (unless, of course, it comes from behind the facade). Count the unobstructed dots. The total is the percentage of probable sunlight hours. Littlefair (1991) recommends an annual exposure to at least 25 unobstructed dots, including at least five from beyond the equinox line.

Sun on ground indicator
39.5, designed for site planning, and shows the length and direction of shadows at the equinox. The Building Research Establishment has issued indicators for the following latitudes – 51.5°, 53.5° and 56° – each at scales of 1:100, 1:200, 1:500 and 1:1250. Place the point P of the indicator over a reference point at ground level on plan. Line the south point of the indicator with the south point on the plan. Parallel east–west lines on the indicator show the heights of obstructions which would just intercept direct sunlight at the time indicated. Hence one can estimate the hours of potential sunlight reaching any point on the ground at the equinox. Sunlight less than 10° above the horizon is ignored.

Sunpath indicator
39.6, for checking times and seasons when direct sunlight strikes a given reference point on a built-up site. It is aligned and scaled in the same way as the *sunlight availability indicator*. Choose the indicator whose stated latitude (51.5°, 53.5° or 56°) is closest to the geographical latitude of the site. If a point on one of the

sunpath lines is closer to the centre than any obstruction in that direction, then the sunlight at that moment is unobstructed (unless, of course, it comes from behind the facade).

Transmittance (T)
The proportion of luminous flux in lumens striking the upper surface of a transparent or translucent sheet which emerges from the lower surface. The transmittance of clear window glass is taken as 0.85; double glazing 0.75.

Utilisation factor (UF)
The fraction of luminous flux in lumens generated by the lamps in an installation which eventually, after multiple reflection by surrounding surfaces, strikes the working plane. It does not include any allowance for the effect of dirt; this is embodied in the maintenance factor. See para **5.07**.

Vertical sky component (SC_v)
The illuminance in lux on a vertical element at a point due to direct light from the overcast sky vault, expressed as a percentage of the simultaneous horizontal illuminance under the whole unobstructed sky vault.

Working plane, or reference plane
The flat plane on which the visual task is located. In a corridor this would be at floor level. In a shop, at counter height. In an office 0.7 m, a factory or kitchen 0.85 m above floor level. Unless otherwise stated the working plane is assumed to be horizontal.

11 BIBLIOGRAPHY AND REFERENCES

British Standards Institution (BSI)
BS 8206: Part 1:1985 *Code of practice for artificial lighting*
BS 8206: Part 2:1992 *Code of practice for daylighting*

Building Research Establishment (BRE)
Digest 309: *Estimating daylight in buildings – 1*, Garston, 1986
Digest 310: *Estimating daylight in buildings – 2*, Garston, 1986
P. J. Littlefair, Information Paper IP 15/88: *Average daylight factor: a simple basis for daylight design*, Garston, 1988
P. J. Littlefair, Report BR209: *Site layout planning for daylight and sunlight: a guide to good practice*, Garston, 1991

Chartered Institution of Building Services Engineers (CIBSE)
Applications manual: window design, London, 1987
Code for interior lighting, London, 1994
Lighting Guide No. 1: The industrial environment, London, 1989
Lighting Guide No. 2: Hospitals and health care buildings, London, 1989
Lighting Guide No. 3: Areas for visual display units, London, 1993
Lighting Guide No. 4: Sports, London, 1990
Lighting Guide No. 5: The visual environment in lecture, teaching and conference rooms, London, 1991
Lighting Guide No. 6: The outdoor environment, London, 1992
Lighting Guide No. 7: Lighting for offices, London, 1993
Lighting Guide No. 14: Museums and art galleries, London, 1994

40 Sound

Neil Spring

Sandy Brown Associates

Neil Spring is an acoustic consultant

CI/SfB: (P)
UDC: 534.84
Uniclass:U37

KEY POINTS:

● *Current Building Regulations are less legalistic than before*
● *Insulation requirements now extend to conversions*

Contents

1 INTRODUCTION

Sound affects the occupants of a building in two distinct ways:

● The quality of sounds generated within, e.g. a concert hall
● Annoyance with loud noise. (*Noise* is a term used to describe unwanted sound.)

The factors that determine sound quality are still imperfectly understood, despite much recent research and experience. The same is true to a lesser extent of the factors affecting noise. Part of the difficulty is that asking someone how he feels about his environment may itself modify his reactions. Very loud prolonged sounds, such as occur in some industries, can result in permanent damage to the ear. The fear that they can damage buildings has been exaggerated, and need not normally be considered by the architect. Many acoustical problems in buildings can be avoided by considering the broad requirements early in the design process. Later on, rectification is rarely satisfactory or economical.

2 FUNDAMENTAL ACOUSTICS

Sound is perceived when the ear-drum is set vibrating by variations in the air pressure just outside the ear. These pressure variations will have been caused by some vibrating object, said to radiate sound. The simplest kind of sound is a single pure tone, for which the graph of air pressure plotted against time produces a sine wave, **40.1**. The greater the *amplitude A* of the pressure variation, the louder the tone. The more rapid the variation (i.e. the higher the *frequency*), the higher the pitch of the tone.

2.01 Sound pressure level

The *sound pressure* of a pure tone generally means the root mean square value of the variation in pressure of the air due to the sound, not the amplitude or peak value A. This is because the rms value is the best measure of energy whether the sound is a pure tone or not. For a sine wave, the rms value is the amplitude divided by $\sqrt{2}$.

Audible sound pressures extend approximately from 2×10^{-5} Pa (the quietest sound that most people can hear – the *threshold of hearing*) to 100 Pa (sound so loud that it starts to be actually painful). This enormous range is telescoped by using a logarithmic notation employing the *decibel*.

The *sound power* of a pure tone is proportional to the square of the pressure. The ratio of the powers of two sounds is therefore the square of the ratios of the pressures. The *sound pressure level*, L_p of a given sound expressed in decibels is ten times the common logarithm of the ratio of its power and that of the internationally recognised threshold of hearing: i.e.

$$L_p = 10 \log_{10}\left(\frac{p_1^2}{p_0^2}\right) = 20 \log_{10}\left(\frac{p_1^2}{2 \times 10^{-5}}\right) \text{ decibals (dB)}$$

Expressed in this way, the audible range extends roughly from 0 dB SPL to 134 dB SPL. A sound usually seems twice as loud when its pressure has trebled, i.e. it has increased by 10 dB.

2.02 Sound power level

The sound power of a source, measured in watts, is deduced from measurements of sound pressure in a well-defined acoustical environment, such as an *anechoic chamber* or a *reverberation room*. The range of powers being even greater than that of pressure levels, decibel notation is again used. The international reference level for sound power is 1 picowatt, so the sound power level L_W is given by:

$$L_W = 10\log_{10}\left(\frac{W_1}{10^{-12}}\right) \text{dB}$$

where W_1 is the sound power in watts.

The SPL produced at a particular place will depend on the distance, orientation and sound power level of the source; and also on the amount of acoustical absorption present. It is important in any application to distinguish between sound pressure level and sound power level as they are usually numerically quite different.

2.03 Frequency

The frequency of a pure tone is measured in hertz (Hz), equal to and formerly called cycles per second, **40.1**. The human range of audible frequencies varies, but is roughly from 20 to 20 000 Hz. The ability to hear higher-frequency sounds progressively deteriorates with age.

Any steady sound, however complex, can be reproduced by combining enough pure tones of the right amplitudes and

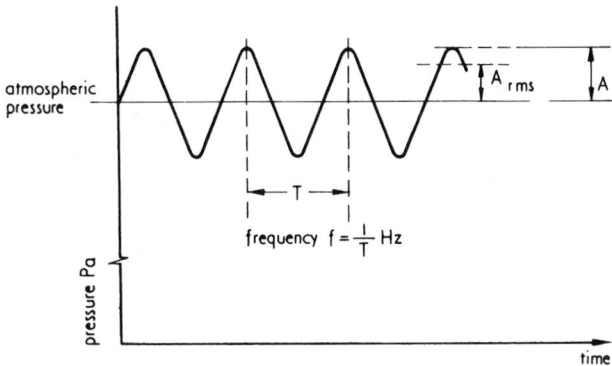

40.1 *Sinusoidal variation of air pressure at a point, due to a pure tone*

frequencies. Thus, if we know the behaviour of a material, wall or room, etc. with regard to the audible spectrum of pure tones, we can predict the behaviour with any steady sound.

The acoustical properties of materials or rooms are described in relation to contiguous frequency bands. Octave-band measurements are carried out where economy is needed. One-third octave bands are used when greater accuracy is required.

Octave-band centre frequencies: 63, 125, 250, 500, 1000, 2000, 4000 Hz

One-third-octave band centre frequencies: 50, 63,80,100,125, 160, 200, 250, 315, 400, 500, 630, 800, 1000, 1250, 1600, 2000, 2500, 3150, 4000, 5000, 6300, 8000 Hz

2.04 Reverberation time

The reverberation time is defined as the time taken for an interrupted sound to fall in level by 60 dB. The reverberation time and its variation with frequency is probably the most significant measurable factor determining the acoustical character of a room, and it can be calculated from Sabine's formula:

$$T = \frac{0.16}{S_\alpha + xV}$$

where V = room volume in m^3
S_α = total surface absorption in m^2
x is a coefficient related to the sound attenuation of air.

The total surface absorption is obtained by adding together the separate areas of absorbent:

$$S_\alpha = S_1\alpha_1 + S_2\alpha_2 + S_3\alpha_3 + \ldots\ldots + S_n\alpha_n$$

where S_1 is the area in m^2 with absorption coefficient α_1, etc. Table I gives examples of typical absorption coefficients.

The Norris–Eyring formula is accepted as more accurate for rooms with a high average absorption coefficient:

$$T = \frac{0.16\ V}{S[-2.30\ \log(1 - \alpha)] + xV}$$

The range of T varies from 0.25 seconds (s) for a small pop recording studio, to over 10 s for a large cathedral. For clear speech in a lecture hall or theatre, T should be between 0.7 and 1.0 s. Outside these limits, a specially designed speech reinforcement system will be required.

For most uses the reverberation time should be the same for low, middle and high frequencies. A moderate rise in the bass reverberation time is acceptable for speech, and is often considered preferable for music. In large auditoria the high-frequency reverberation time inevitably falls because the enclosed air has a high absorption value. In any case allowance must be made for the absorption of the audience, usually the greatest single component.

The acoustical shortcomings inevitable in multi-purpose auditoria can be alleviated by installing an electroacoustic enhancement system such as the assisted resonance system at the Royal Festival Hall in London. A variety of competing systems are now available.

Table I Absorption coefficients

	Frequency Hz						
	63	125	250	500	1000	2000	4000
Air, x (per m^3)	0	0	0	0	0.003	0.007	0.023
Audience seated in fully upholstered seats (per person) m^2	0.15	0.18	0.40	0.46	0.46	0.51	0.46
Orchestral player with instrument (average), m^2	0.18	0.37	0.8	1.1	1.3	1.2	1.1
Carpet, pile over thick felt on concrete floor	0.05	0.07	0.25	0.5	0.5	0.6	0.65
Plaster, on solid backing	0.05	0.03	0.03	0.02	0.03	0.04	0.05

3 ROOM SHAPE AND QUALITY

3.01 Preferred dimensions – large auditoria

The size of a room is usually determined by factors other than the acoustics. Very large auditoria are difficult to fill with sound. Most of the direct sound will never reach the remoter parts, and the large surface area produces a corresponding absorption resulting in a weak level of reverberant sound. Little evidence for an ideal set of proportions exists for auditoria of conventional shape. Unconventional shapes introduce the risk of incorporating intolerable defects which prove impracticable to correct.

Successful traditional concert halls are usually rectangular both in plan and section, e.g. Symphony Hall, Boston. This shape is convenient, and produces the reverberation time of up to two seconds preferred for symphonic music. With careful design, modern halls of non-rectangular shape can be extremely successful, a particular example being St David's Hall, Cardiff. Where a shorter reverberation time is desired, other shapes are satisfactory, such as the horseshoe of the traditional opera house, and the fan for a theatre. The likelihood of audible echoes in large auditoria can usually be predicted, but conditions producing them are too various to summarise. Elimination of echoes is often expensive rather than technically difficult, an elegant example being the 'flying saucers' in the Royal Albert Hall, London.

Auditoria for speech and drama have clarity as a prime requirement. The shape should ensure that the audience receives strong sound reflections immediately after the direct sound. For musical performances many prefer early sound reflections arriving at the listener from a lateral direction.

3.02 Preferred dimensions – small rooms

Small rooms can present serious acoustical problems, being often bedevilled with colouration, that is, the excessive accentuation of one or more notes of particular pitches. We particularly notice this phenomenon in bathrooms and telephone boxes, and it comes from the fact that the dimensions of these small rooms are comparable with the wavelengths* of speech. Colourations are particularly evident in rectangular rooms where the length, breadth and height bear a simple numerical ratio to each other; the theory for this is well understood. However, the ideal proportions have still to be discovered.

3.03 Acoustical models

It has become quite usual to build a scale model of a proposed auditorium for acoustical testing. Any defects revealed by the tests can be dealt with before the full-scale auditorium is built. Models are particularly useful where an auditorium of novel shape is being considered.

The scale factors range from 1:50 to 1:8. The 1:50 model gives less accurate results than models of larger scale, but this disadvantage is generally outweighed by the lower costs of building, testing and modifying the smaller model.

An alternative is to build a digital computer model of the proposed auditorium. A number of programs are available which claim adequately to simulate the behaviour of sound in a mathematical model of the room. More recent digital simulation programs claim to enable the designer to listen to sounds processed by the computer as though the listener were present in the completed hall.

4 NOISE

4.01 Noise criteria

As the human ear is most sensitive to frequencies between 1 and 3 kHz, a 1 kHz tone will sound much louder than a 100 Hz

---

*The wavelength λ in metres of a tone of frequency f in hertz is given by $\lambda = c/f$ where c is the velocity of sound (approximately 340 m/s in air).

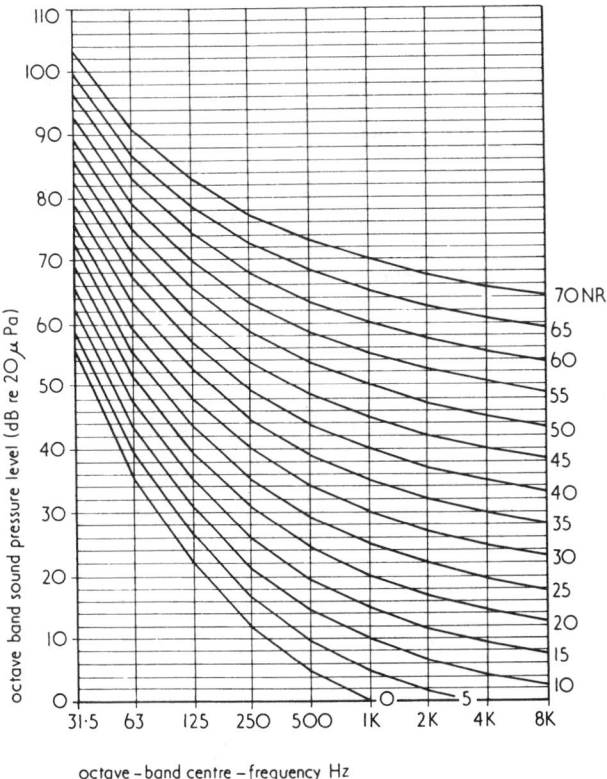

40.2 *Noise rating curves*

tone of the same sound pressure level. Any measuring of loudness must take this frequency sensitivity into account, and the simplest of sound-level meters has a device which roughly compensates for it called the A-weighting network. Readings from such a meter are designated A-weighted sound pressure levels (symbol L_{pA}) to distinguish them from plain unweighted dB SPL (symbol L_p). Although the loudness and annoyance of a sound can depend on other factors than the A-weighted sound pressure level, it is a useful measure for many of the sounds encountered in and around buildings.

A building performance specification may contain criteria expressed in A-weighted sound pressure levels for various areas, but where ventilation noise is likely to be significant, it is more usual for them to be given in Noise Criteria (NC) curves, or the similar Noise Rating (NR) curves, **40.2**. These plot octave-band SPL against frequency. If NR-35 is specified, for example for a private office, then the noise level in any octave band should not exceed that indicated for the NR-35 line on the graph. The preference for the NC and NR criteria rather than the A-weighted SPL criterion arises from the octave-band data used in the design of mechanical services systems.

Noise criteria are commonly specified as maxima rather than optimal levels, and this is a reflection of frequent failures to meet the criteria many years ago. Unexpectedly noisy systems are now much less likely and the consequences of systems which are too quiet are now often a matter of some concern. An office may be so quiet that private conversation can easily be overheard and occasional outside noises may be particularly distracting. In such a circumstance, a continuous masking (sometimes called *white*) noise may be deliberately introduced to help to drown other sounds, using loudspeakers or by increasing the ventilation system noise.

Apart from A-weighted SPL, NC and NR ratings for noise, there are others the architect may encounter. Each has its merits, but most require rather more than a simple sound level meter for measurement. Some of these are:

$L_{A10,T}$ The A-weighted sound pressure level of a noise exceeded for 10 per cent of a given time interval T

$L_{A10,(18 hour)}$ The average of the values of L10 measured hourly between 06.00 and 24.00 hours on a normal working day. Used for planning and design as an index of road traffic noise.

$L_{Aeq,T}$ The equivalent continuous A-weighted sound pressure level. This is the notional constant sound level which would give the same A-weighted sound energy as that of the actual varying sound over a specified period of time, T. This has become the preferred index for characterising a wide range of different kinds of sounds which are not steady. $L_{Aeq,T}$ is used in a number of countries for rating industrial and transport noise.

$L_{Ar,T}$ *rating level*   The measured equivalent continuous A-weighted sound pressure level plus any adjustment for the character of the noise. An adjustment would commonly be made for whines, hisses, screeches, hums, bangs, clicks, clatters or thumps.

All the above are measured in decibels. Considerable confusion may arise if the particular index is not identified in each case.

4.02 Internal noise sources

Because effective noise insulation is often impractical and usually costly, noise-producing areas should be sited away from noise-sensitive areas. In modern non-industrial buildings, the mechanical plant room is likely to be the noisiest area, especially if it contains heavy and inherently unbalanced plant. Chillers and large boilers can present severe noise problems particularly at low frequencies where curative measures are difficult. A buffer zone formed by a corridor or storage area around the plant room is a useful noise control measure.

The airborne noise radiated by industrial machinery can usually be calculated sufficiently accurately using the manufacturer's sound power level data. If the calculated noise level is too high, the reverberant noise level can be reduced by lining part of the plant room surfaces with an efficient acoustical absorbent; otherwise more costly measures may be necessary. The noise transmitted into the structure of the building via the machinery mounts, etc. is much more difficult to estimate. This is because the basic mechanical noise-generating characteristics of the machine are generally not known, and also because the ways in which sound propagates through building structures are imperfectly understood. In designing noise-isolation measures, rule-of-thumb methods are frequently used. They do not always work, and a long and expensive investigation is then needed to discover why; sound may easily propagate through structures with relatively little attenuation.

Many structure-borne noise problems are avoided by siting the plant room in a basement. When specifying ventilation noise levels, etc., the designer should take into account the noise arising from activities within the areas served, so that the criteria are compatible. In some circumstances, impact noise from footsteps can be a problem.

As well as the effects on people within the building, due consideration must be given to the effects on the neighbourhood. Roof-mounted cooling towers may produce a noise problem in residential areas. Discotheques, night clubs and other performance venues employing high-powered amplification systems are a potential noise nuisance. Planning conditions are often imposed on such developments and the planning authority may need convincing that adequate sound-insulation measures will be incorporated.

4.03 External noise sources

The most important kind of external noise affecting buildings is transport noise from road traffic, aircraft and railways. An essential characteristic of such sources is that they are not generally under the control of those affected by their noise. It is therefore essential to assess the likely level of external noise to which a proposed building is to be subjected. If this is done early enough in the design process, the scheme can be economically produced to alleviate the effects of the noise.

An example of planning against noise profoundly influencing the design is the five- to eight-storey Byker Wall in Newcastle-upon-Tyne. Here, a barrier against the noise from an adjacent motorway is formed by a long block of flats. The flats all have small windows facing the motorway and the noise-sensitive rooms are on the quiet side of the barrier. The whole structure protects more conventional dwellings on the side remote from the traffic.

Where the source of noise is known it is often possible to calculate the likely noise level from its characteristics and the geometry of the site. In the UK there is now an official procedure for calculating the noise from motor vehicles, and this is recommended as preferable to measurement. At first sight this seems strange, but in practice it can be difficult to achieve a valid measurement. Some cynics have suggested that in the British Isles the prevailing wind direction and speed and the rainfall are such that valid 18-hour traffic noise measurements are impossible except on a few days in the year!

Other sources of transport noise, such as railways, are not so well documented; direct site measurements may be the only course to take. In the case of the International Conference Centre in Birmingham with its concert hall and a railway line underneath, the main problem was structure-borne sound. A major part of the building was constructed on foundations incorporating vibration-isolating elements.

Aircraft are a well-publicised source of serious noise, and there are usually severe planning restrictions on dwellings close to airports. However, hotels are often built here, and with care in siting and design the noise problems can be successfully overcome. Public concern about jet engine noise has led to the development of quieter engines, and we can look forward to a diminution of the problem as the older aircraft are replaced. Other sources of noise that may have to be considered in particular situations include helicopters, hovercraft and industrial plant.

5 SOUND INSULATION

When a sound wave strikes a wall only a fraction of the incident sound energy is transmitted through the wall. The ratio of the incident to the transmitted sound energy, expressed in decibels, is called the sound reduction index. It can be properly measured only in a laboratory. The reduction in sound pressure level between adjacent rooms in an actual building depends not only on the sound reduction index of the separating wall, but also upon its area, the acoustic absorption present in the receiving room and the amount of transmission by *flanking paths* (see para 5.04). Neglecting flanking transmission, the relation between the average sound level difference between two rooms and the sound reduction index of the separating wall is:

$$L_{p1} - L_{p2} = R + 10\log(A/S)$$

where L_{p1} = sound pressure level averaged over the room containing the source

L_{p2} = sound pressure level averaged over the receiving room

R = sound reduction index of the separating wall

S = area of separating wall in m^2

A = acoustic absorption of receiving room in m^2 units.

Often A is comparable in size to S, making the level difference $L_{p1} - L_{p2}$ vary little from the sound reduction index R so that it is commonly referred to simply as the 'sound insulation'.

5.01 Composite insulation

40.3 is an aid for calculating the sound insulation of a partition composed of two different materials. Consider a wall consisting of brickwork with insulation 45 dB and a glazed area amounting to one-fifth the total wall area of insulation 25 dB. On the vertical axis of **40.3** the area ratio 1:4 meets the 20 dB difference curve at 13 dB on the horizontal axis. The composite insulation is therefore $45 - 13 = 32$ dB.

5.02 Mass law

To a first approximation the insulation of a single leaf wall or floor depends on its mass per unit area. From **40.4** the insulation averaged over the frequency range 100 to 3150 Hz increases by about 5 dB for each doubling of mass (the *mass law*).

5.03 Coincidence effect

The sound insulation also increases by 5 to 6 dB for each doubling of frequency provided the partition is very limp, for example a lead sheet. However, most partitions are fairly stiff. With some materials the stiffness combines with the mass in such a way as to produce a resonance effect, seriously reducing the insulation below the mass-law value. This resonance, called the coincidence effect, is caused by flexural waves in the partition, and its significance depends on its nature and thickness. For a 215 mm brick wall the effect occurs at about 100 Hz, which is generally too low to matter. Window glass has coincidence frequencies in the upper audible range.

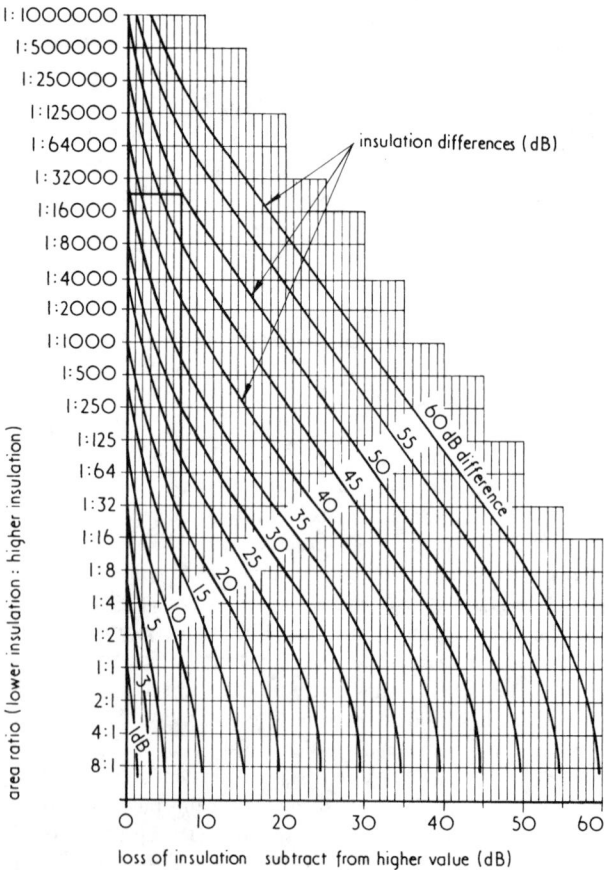

40.3 *Variation in construction. An extreme example: a storey-height crack 0.2 mm wide in a wall of 10 m^2 could result in an insulation loss of 7 dB (From Guidance Note: Sound Insulation, HMSO, 1975)*

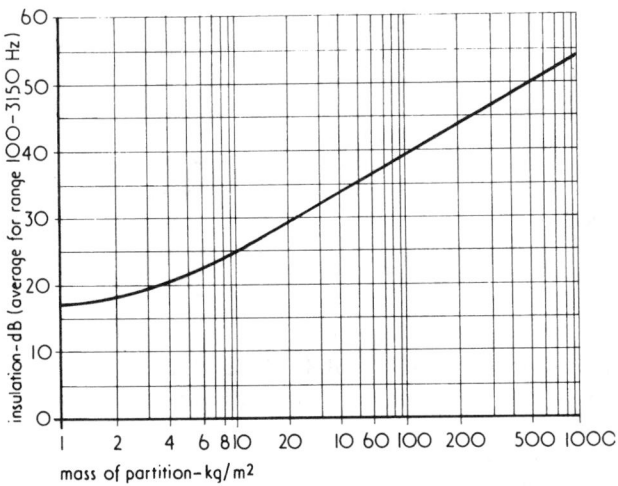

40.4 *Relationship of sound insulation to mass per unit area (from same as*

5.04 Flanking transmission

In real buildings, sound is transmitted from one room to an adjacent room via many paths, **40.5**. Where the separating wall has a sound reduction index of 35 dB or less, most of the sound is transmitted through the wall. If, however, we try to improve the insulation by using a heavier wall, the *flanking paths*, or indirect transmission routes, become more important. In fact, it is difficult to achieve better than 60 dB sound level difference without special measures, such as carefully designed structural discontinuities, to reduce the flanking transmission.

5.05 Openings

Any kind of opening in a partition will seriously impair the sound insulation. The effect can be assessed by using **40.3**, and assigning a value of 0 dB for the insulation of the opening.

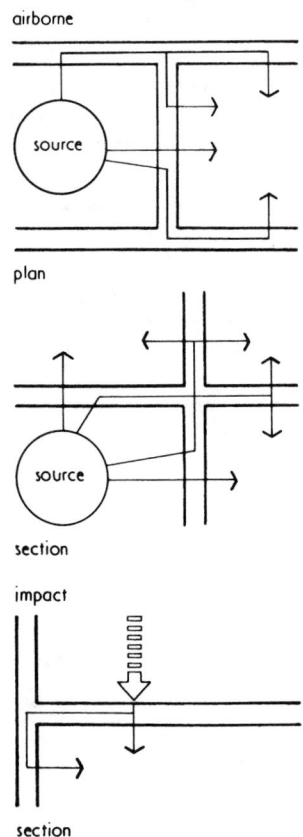

40.5 *Sound transmission paths (from same as* **40.3***)*

5.06 Double walls

Two single walls, each of 30 dB sound insulation, when combined would not produce 60 dB but only about 35 dB; the doubling of the mass per unit area adding 5 dB by the mass law. However, separating the two walls several metres apart would, if there were no flanking transmission, approach 60 dB. Practical double walls lie between these extremes, but it is difficult to theorise how a particular combination will actually behave.

Double walls and multi-leaf partitions are used where the required mass of a single leaf would be excessive. They improve dramatically on the mass law at middle and high frequencies, but at low frequencies the insulation is usually little better, and sometimes worse than a single leaf of the same mass per unit area.

5.07 Floors

The insulation of floors against airborne sound follows the same laws as for walls. An additional problem is the direct structural excitation of a hard-surfaced floor by footsteps, **40.5c**. If a carpet is unacceptable, a floating floor must be used if footstep noise is to be reduced in the room underneath. The resilient element for such a floor may be of mineral wool, slab or blankets, rubber, expanded polystyrene or springs, but it is essential that the particular material that is chosen is known to be effective and durable. Care must be taken not to bridge this resilient element with any rigid connection to the base floor.

The airborne sound insulation of a floor can be improved by suspending an impermeable ceiling below it, but the improvement is often limited by structural limitations on its weight and by height considerations.

5.08 Windows

The windows are usually the weakest part of the envelope where sound insulation is concerned. The mass per unit area of the glazing is generally small compared with the rest of the envelope. Table II is a guide to the sound insulation of different windows. In order to obtain the highest insulation double glazing will be required, at least one pane of which is sealed. Specially designed sound-attenuated ventilation will then be required.

Table II Sound insulation of windows (from BRE Digest 140)

Description	Sound reduction (av. 100–3150 Hz)
Any type of window when open	about 10 dB
Ordinary single openable window closed but not weather-stripped, any glass	up to 20 dB
Single fixed or openable weather-stripped window, with 6 mm glass	up to 25 dB
Fixed single window with 12 mm glass	up to 30 dB
Fixed single window with 24 mm glass	up to 35 dB
Double window, openable but weather-stripped, 150–200 mm air space, any glass	up to 40 dB
Double window in separate frames, one fixed, 300–400 mm air space, 6–10 mm glass, sound-absorbent reveals	up to 45 dB

5.09 Doors

Single doors having a sound insulation greater than 35 dB are expensive and difficult to install. Seals are required around the edge to prevent leakages, and where these are effective they make the door hard to open and close. Magnetic door seals similar to those on refrigerators are a small improvement. The most effective solution where the space is available is the use of two moderately insulating doors separated by an absorbent-lined 'sound lock'.

5.10 Barriers

Barriers that intercept the line-of-sight between a sound source and the receiver are a common method of reducing a noise level. Outdoors they are used as a shield against traffic and aircraft noise, and some types of machinery. Indoors, they are used in open-plan offices and schools, and for altering the acoustics of broadcasting and recording studios.

The psychological effect of a visually opaque barrier can be very strong, giving a misleading impression of its acoustical effectiveness. For example, a line of trees is often proposed as a sound barrier although the measured acoustical effect is small. A bank of trees about 9 m in depth would be needed to provide an adequate acoustic screen for a motorway, for example.

There have been extensive theoretical studies on the effectiveness of barriers in idealised situations, but not much has resulted which can be applied in practice. Quite apart from the nature and geometry of the barrier itself, its performance can depend appreciably on the frequency of the sound, the weather and the nature of the ground between source and receiver. As a rough guide, screen-type barriers 1 to 4 m high and mass about 10 kg/m^2 can give transmission losses of 5 to 20 dB.

5.11 Enclosures

Enclosures are used to suppress the noise from a stationary machine or item of plant such as a diesel generator. For them to be effective, they should have few or no openings. Where this is not possible because of the need to ventilate, properly designed attenuated air routes are required. The effectiveness of the enclosure is enhanced by lining internally with an acoustical absorbent. Telephone hoods are an example of a partial enclosure, the effectiveness of which depends on how well the user obstructs the opening.

5.12 Cost and the designer

Structures designed to give a higher-than-average degree of sound insulation, such as broadcasting studios, are usually costly. The mass law, providing only a 5 dB increase for doubling the material used, illustrates how quickly the law of diminishing returns sets in. Attempts to beat the mass law by installing double or multi-leaf partitions incur the penalty of loss of usable space.

It is usually difficult to increase the sound insulation of an existing modern building. Older buildings of heavy construction have been successfully converted into broadcasting and recording studios. Several local radio stations in the UK can bear witness to this.

Because it is generally costly to increase sound insulation, the acoustical designer is rarely allowed the luxury of a safety margin. Unfortunately, the design of sound-insulating structures is still an imprecise science, and an economically designed building can fail to meet the expected performance. No reputable and knowledgeable acoustical consultant will guarantee the success of his or her design, any more than a doctor would guarantee to cure a patient. The acoustical consultant's task is to achieve the right balance between a design that is too costly initially and one for which failure would be disastrous.

6 ACOUSTICAL TEST DATA

One of the problems often facing the designer is the lack of reliable acoustical data on materials and products. Some well-established manufacturers still supply information that is quite meaningless, although appearing authentic to the uninitiated. The situation has improved appreciably in recent years with the NAMAS accreditation of test laboratories and the expansion and refinement of standards for measuring the acoustical properties of building elements and materials.

7 STANDARDS AND CODES OF PRACTICE

There are a growing number of national, European and international standards and codes of practice, some of which are listed in the Bibliography at the end of this chapter. These are invaluable in defining the methods used in testing acoustical materials, measuring environmental noise, traffic noise, etc. These advances enable a more objective assessment to be made of an acoustical material, device or situation and coloured less by an over-enthusiastic sales department.

8 LEGISLATION

The architect has now to take into account a growing body of legislation concerned with reducing the objectionable effects of noise generated within his or her building, and the effects of external noise sources on the occupants. The Building Regulations lay down the requirements for sound transmission of walls, floors and stairs in dwellings. The general requirement is that the relevant element shall resist the transmission of airborne/impact sound. Useful guidance on methods to achieve the requirements is given in Approved Document E.

Compliance may be demonstrated by adopting the widely used forms of construction described in the Approved Document and summarised in Tables III and IV. Refer to the AD for fuller details, particularly essential for the junctions which, if not properly constructed, can negate the whole purpose of the exercise.

Alternatively, one may adopt a form of construction that is similar to one that has been shown by field tests to comply with the requirements. Failing these two methods of demonstrating compliance, one may test the construction in a specified type of acoustic chamber to the standards shown in Table V. Unlike earlier regulations, the current regulations apply to conversions as well as to new constructions.

In other countries other forms of legislative control apply. In the USA, the Environmental Protection Agency demands that a proposed development is preceded by an Environmental Impact Statement to show that no noise nuisance will result from it. European countries have specific noise limits for sanitary facilities such as WCs. Many countries have strict planning controls near known noise sources such as airports, and some provide financial assistance to insulate against sound in the proximity of motorways, etc.

Table III Construction of separating walls in new buildings, based on Approved Document E 1992 to the Building Regulations 1991

Type	Specification	Example	Drawing
1 Solid masonry			masonry
A	Brick plastered on both room faces. Mass including plaster 375 kg/m², 13 mm plaster. Lay bricks in bond including headers.	215 mm brick, lightweight plaster, 75 mm coursing; brick density of 1610 kg/m³	
B	Concrete block, plastered on both room faces. Mass including plaster 415 kg/m², 13 mm plaster. Use blocks which extend to the full thickness of the wall.	215 mm block, lightweight plaster, 110 mm coursing; block density of 1840 kg/m³	
C	Brick, plasterboard on both room faces. Mass including plasterboard 375 kg/m². 12.5 mm plasterboard, any normal fixing method. Lay bricks in bond including headers.	215 mm brick, 75 mm coursing; brick density of 1610 kg/m³	
D	Concrete block, plasterboard on both room faces. Mass including plasterboard 415 kg/m². 12.5 mm plasterboard, any normal fixing method. Use blocks which extend to the full thickness of the wall.	215 mm block, 150 mm coursing, block density of 1840 kg/m³	
E	Concrete *in-situ* or large panel, minimum density 1500 kg/m³, plaster optional. Mass including plaster if used, 415 kg/n². Fill joints between panels with mortar.	An unplastered wall of density 2200 kg/m³; 190 mm thickness.	
2 Cavity masonry			masonry cavity masonry
A	Two leaves of brick with 50 mm cavity, plastered on both room faces. Mass including plaster 415 kg/m². 13 mm plaster.	102 mm leaves, lightweight plaster, 75 mm coursing; brick density of 1970 kg/m³	50mm
B	Two leaves of concrete block with 50 mm cavity, plastered on both room faces. Mass including plaster 415 kg/m². 13 mm plaster.	100 mm leaves, lightweight plaster, 225 mm block coursing; block density 1990 kg/m³	50mm

Table III (*Continued*)

Type	Specification	Example	Drawing
C	Two leaves of lightweight aggregate block, maximum density 1600 kg/m³, with 75 mm cavity, plastered or dry lines on both room faces. Mass including finish 300 kg/m². 13 mm plaster or 12.5 mm plasterboard. (Depends on composition of aggregate, may not give reasonable insulation if a *denser* block is used.)	100 mm leaves with lightweight plaster, 225 mm coursing; block density of 1371 kg/m³.	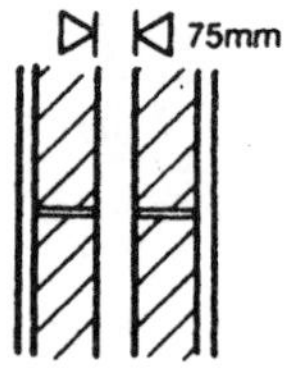 75mm

Constructions where a step and/or stagger of at least 300 mm is used

Type	Specification	Example	Drawing
D	Two leaves of concrete block with 50 mm cavity, plasterboard on both room faces. Mass of masonry alone 415 kg/m². 12.5 mm plasterboard, use any normal fixing method.	100 mm leaves, 225 mm coursing; block density 1990 kg/m³	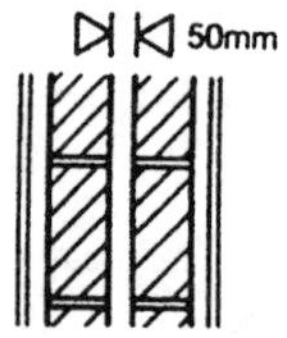 50mm
E	Two leaves of lightweight aggregate concrete block, maximum density 1600 kg/m³, 75 mm cavity, plastered or drylines on both room faces. Mass including finish 250 kg/m². 13 mm plaster or 12.5 mm plasterboard.	100 mm leaves, lightweight plaster, 225 mm coursing; block density 1105 kg/m³.	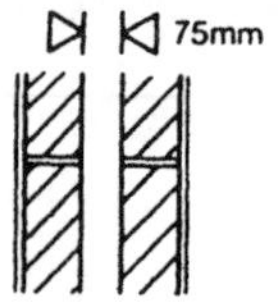 75mm

3 Masonry between isolated panels

Four types of masonry cores (A to D), and two panels (E and F) which in any combination of core plus panels will give reasonable resistance to direct transmission

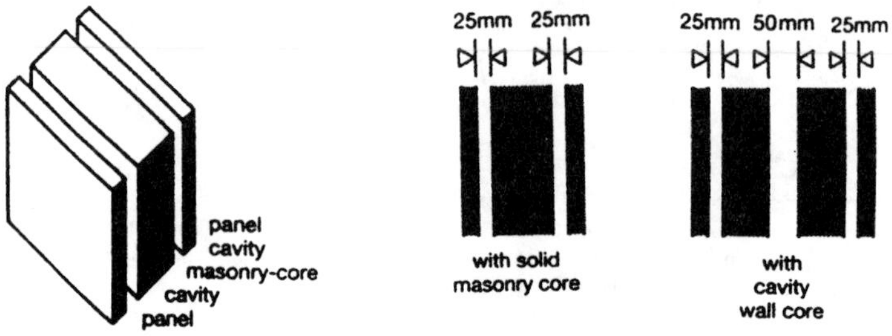

panel
cavity
masonry-core
cavity
panel

25mm 25mm
with solid masonry core

25mm 50mm 25mm
with cavity wall core

Masonry cores:

Type	Specification	Example	Drawing
A	Brick mass 300 kg/²	215 mm core, 75 mm coursing, brick density of 1290 kg/m³	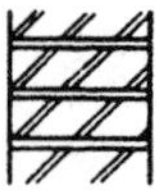
B	Concrete block mass 300 kg/m²	140 mm core, 110 mm coursing, block density 2200 kg/m³	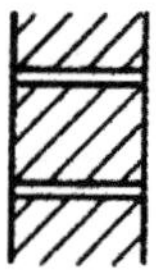
C	Lightweight concrete block mass 160 kg/m²	200 mm core, 225 mm coursing, block density 730 kg/m³.	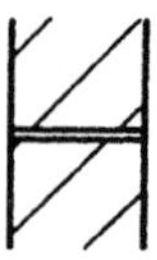
D	Cavity brickwork or blockwork of any mass	Two leaves of brickwork or blockwork, each leaf at least 100 mm thick with a cavity at least 50 mm wide and only butterfly type ties to connect the leaves.	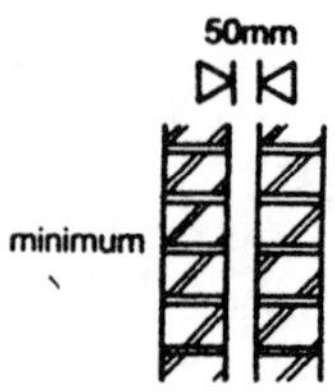 50mm minimum

Panels:

E	Two sheets of plasterboard joined by a cellular core, mass including plaster finish if used 18 kg/m²; fix to ceiling and floor only, tape joints between panels
F	Two sheets of plasterboard with joints staggered, thickness of each sheet 12.5 mm if a supporting framework is used, or total thickness of 30 mm if none.

Table III (*Continued*)

Type	Specification	Example	Drawing
			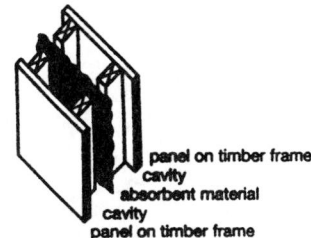 panel on timber frame / cavity / absorbent material / cavity / panel on timber frame

4 Timber frames with absorbent material

Two constructions (A and B), lining (C) and absorbent material (D)

Type	Specification	Drawing
A	Timber frames, 200 mm between linings, plus absorbent material in cavity. Plywood sheathing may be used in the cavity for structural purposes	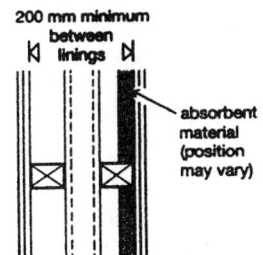 200 mm minimum between linings — absorbent material (position may vary)
B	Timber frames, masonry core, aborbent material in cavity, claddings 200 mm apart, framing clear of core	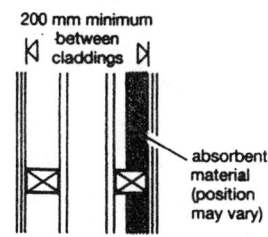 200 mm minimum between claddings — absorbent material (position may vary)
C	Lining on each side: two or more layers of plasterboard combined thickness 30 mm, joints staggered	
D	Absorbent material:unfaced mineral fibre batts or quilt (may be wire reinforced), density at least 10 kg/m³ thickness 25 mm if suspended in the cavity between frames, 50 mm if fixed to one frame or 25 mm per quilt if one fixed to each frame.	

Table IV Construction of separating floors in new buildings, based on Approved Document E 1992 to the Building Regulations 1991

Type	Limitations	Points to watch	Constructions	Figure

Floor type 1: Concrete base with soft covering
The resistance to airborne sound depends on the mass of the concrete base and on eliminating air paths. The soft covering reduces impact sound at source.

Type	Limitations	Points to watch	Constructions	Figure
General	Where resistance to airborne sound only is required the soft covering may be omitted. No other part of the construction may be omitted as this would reduce airborne sound resistance.	Fill all joints between parts of the floor to avoid air paths. Control sound paths around the floor to reduce flanking transmission. Workmanship and detailing must be given special attention at the perimeter and wherever the floor is penetrated by a pipe or duct (to reduce flanking transmission and to avoid air paths).	Four examples of floor bases (A, B, C & D) which give suitable resistance to direct transmission of airborne sound are shown, followed by examples of soft covering (E) which should be added to give suitable resistance to impact sound transmission. Details of how junctions should be made to limit flanking transmission follow.	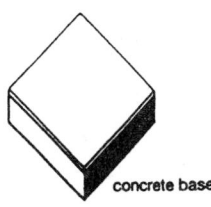 concrete base

Floor bases

Type	Constructions	Figure
A	Solid concrete slab (*in-situ*) Floor screed and/or ceiling finish optional. Mass (including any screed and/or ceiling finish) 365 kg/m².	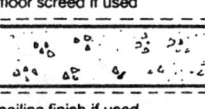 floor screed if used / ceiling finish if used
B	Solid concrete slab with permanent shuttering Floor screed and/or ceiling finish optional. Mass (including shuttering only if it is solid concrete or metal and including any screed and/or ceiling finish) 365 kg/m².	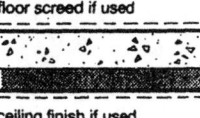 floor screed if used / ceiling finish if used

Table IV (*Continued*)

Type	Limitations	Points to watch	Constructions	Figure
C			Concrete beams with infilling blocks Floor surface should be level and a levelling screed may be necessary. Ceiling finish optional. Mass of beams, blocks, screed and ceiling finish 365 kg/m².	floor screed if used ceiling finish if used
D			Concrete planks (solid or hollow) Floor surface should be level and a levelling screed may be necessary. Ceiling finish optional. Mass of planks screed and ceiling finish 365 kg/m².	floor screed if used ceiling finish if used

Soft covering

Type	Limitations	Points to watch	Constructions	Figure
E			Any resilient material, or material with E a resilient base, with an overall uncompressed thickness of at least 4.5 mm Suitable resilience will also be provided by a floor covering with a weighted impact sound improvement (ALw) of not less than 1 7dB as calculated in Annex A to BS 5821: Method for rating the sound insulation in buildings and building elements Part 2:1984. Method for rating the impact sound insulation.	

Floor type 2: Concrete base with floating layer

The resistance to airborne sound depends partly on the mass of the concrete base and partly on the mass of the floating layer. Resistance to impact sound depends mainly on a resilient layer isolating the floating layer from the base and from the surrounding construction.

Type	Limitations	Points to watch	Constructions	Figure
General	Where resistance to airborne sound only is required the full construction should still be used.	Fill all joints between parts of the floor base to avoid air paths. Control sound paths round the floor to reduce flanking transmission. Workmanship and detailing should be given special attention at the perimeter and wherever the floor is penetrated (to reduce flankin transmission and to avoid air paths). Take care not to create a bridge between the floating layer and the base, surrounding walls, adjacent screed. With bases C and D a screed may be required to seal the floor and to accommodate surface irregularities.	Four floor bases (A,B,C & D) two floating layers (E & F) and one resilient layer (G) are shown. Any combination of base, resilient layer and floating layer will give suitable resistance to direct transmission. Two additional resilient layers which may be used under screeds only are also specified (H and 1). Details of how junctions should be made to limit flanking transmission follow.	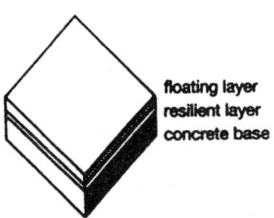 floating layer resilient layer concrete base

Floor bases

Type	Limitations	Points to watch	Constructions	Figure
A			Solid concrete slab (*in-situ*) Floor screed and/or ceiling finish optional. Mass (including any bonded screed and/or ceiling finish) 365 kg/m².	floor screed if used ceiling finish if used
B			Solid concrete slab with permanent shuttering. Floor screed and/or ceiling finish optional. Mass (including shuttering only if it is solid concrete or metal, and including any bonded screed and/or ceiling finish) 300 kg/m².	floor screed if used ceiling finish if used
C			Concrete beams with infilling blocks The floor base should be reasonably level (maximum 5 mm step between units). A levelling screed may be required. Ceiling finish is optional. Mass of beams, blocks and any bonded screed or ceiling finish 300 kg/m².	floor screed if used ceiling finish if used

Table IV (*Continued*)

Type	Limitations	Points to watch	Constructions	Figure
D			Concrete planks (solid or hollow) The floor base should be reasonably level (maximum 5 mm step between units). A levelling screed may be required. Ceiling finish is optional. Mass of planks and any bonded screed or ceiling finish 300 kg/m².	floor screed if used ceiling finish if used

Floating layers

Type	Limitations	Points to watch	Constructions	Figure
E			Timber raft. Timber boarding or wood based board. 18 mm thick with tongued and grooved edges, fixed to 45 × 45 mm battens. The raft should be laid loose on the resilient layer.	timber raft timber batten
F			Screed 65 mm cement sand screed, with 20–50 mm wire mesh to protect the resilient layer while the screed is being laid.	screed wire mesh

Resilient layers

Type	Limitations	Points to watch	Constructions	Figure
G			25 mm mineral fibre density 36 kg/m³. A 13 mm thickness may be used under a timber raft if the battens used have an integral closed cell resilient foam strip. Lay the fibre tightly butted and turned up at the edges of the floating layer. Under a timber raft, the fibre may be paper faced on the underside. Under a screed, fibre should be paper faced on the upper side to prevent screed entering the layer.	

Additional resilient layers for use under screeds only.

Type	Limitations	Points to watch	Constructions	Figure
H			13 mm pre-compressed expanded polystyrene board (impact sound duty grade). Lay boards tightly butted. Use board on edge as a resilient strip at edges of floating screed.	
I			5 mm extruded (closed cell) polyethylene foam, density 30–45 kg/m³. To protect the material from puncture it should be laid over a levelling screed. Lay with joints lapped and turn up at edges of the floating screed.	

Floor type 3: Timber base with floating layer

The resistance to airborne sound depends partly on the structural floor plus absorbent material or pugging, and partly on the floating layer. Resistance to impact sound depends mainly on a resilient layer isolating the floating layer from the base and the surrounding construction.

Type	Limitations	Points to watch	Constructions	Figure
General	Where resistance to airborne sound only is required the full construction should still be used.	Control sound paths around the floor to reduce flanking transmission. Workmanship and detailing should be given special attention at the perimeter and wherever the floor is penetrated (to reduce flanking transmission and to avoid air paths). Use the correct density of resilient layer and ensure it can carry the anticipated load. Take care not to bridge between the floating layer and the base or surrounding walls (e.g. with services or fixings which penetrate the resilient layer). Allow for movement of materials, e.g. expansion of chipboard after laying (to maintain isolation).	Three complete constructions (A, B & C) which give suitable resistance to direct sound transmission are shown. Note that there are some options within each of these constructions. Types of pugging are described (D). Details of how junctions should be made to limit flanking transmission follow.	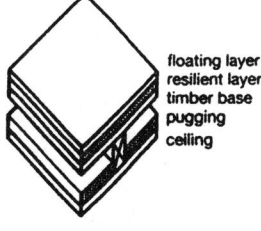 floating layer resilient layer timber base pugging ceiling

Table IV (*Continued*)

Type	Limitations	Points to watch	Constructions	Figure

Floors

Type	Constructions	Figure
A	Platform floor with absorbent material. Either a floating layer of timber or wood-based board 18 mm thick with tongued and grooved edges, all joints glued, spot bonded to substrate of 19 mm plasterboard; or a floating layer of two thicknesses of cement bonded particle board with joints staggered, glued and screwed together, total thickness 24 mm. Resilient layer of 25 mm mineral fibre, density 60–100 kg/m³ (Note that the low figure gives the best insulation but a 'softer' floor, in such cases additional support can be provided around the perimeter of the floor by a timber batten with a foam strip along the top attached to the wall.) Floor base of 12 mm timber boarding or wood-based board nailed to timber joists (size to suit structure). Ceiling of two layers of plasterboard with joints staggered, total thickness 30 mm with an absorbent material, 100 mm unfaced mineral wool, density at least 10 kg/m³ laid on the ceiling.	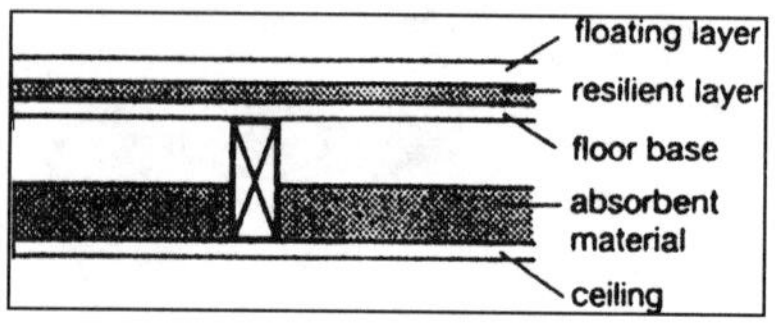
B	Ribbed floor with absorbent material Floating layer of timber or wood-based board 18 mm thick with tongued and grooved edges and all joints glued, spot bonded to substrate of 19 mm plasterboard, nailed to 45 mm × 45 mm timber battens placed over the joists. Resilient strips of 25 mm mineral fibre, density 80–140 kg/m³ laid on joists. Floor base of 45 mm wide timber joists. Ceiling of two layers of plasterboard with joints staggered, total thickness 30 mm, with an absorbent blanket of 100 mm unfaced rock fibre, density at least 10 kg/m³ laid on the ceiling.	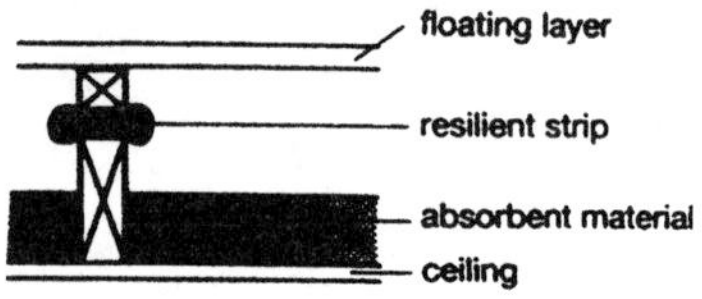
C	Ribbed floor with heavy pugging Floating layer of timber or wood-based board 18 mm thick with tongued and grooved edges and all joints glued, nailed or screwed to 45 mm × 45 mm timber battens placed either on or between joists (for sheet materials, placing on joists is recommended). Resilient strips of 25 mm mineral fibre density 80–140 kg/m³ laid on joists. Floor base of 45 mm wide timber joists. Ceiling of either 19 mm dense plaster on expanded metal lath or 6 mm plywood fixed under the joists plus two layers of plasterboard with joints staggered, total thickness 25 mm. Both types of ceiling to have pugging of mass 80 kg/m² laid on a polyethylene liner.	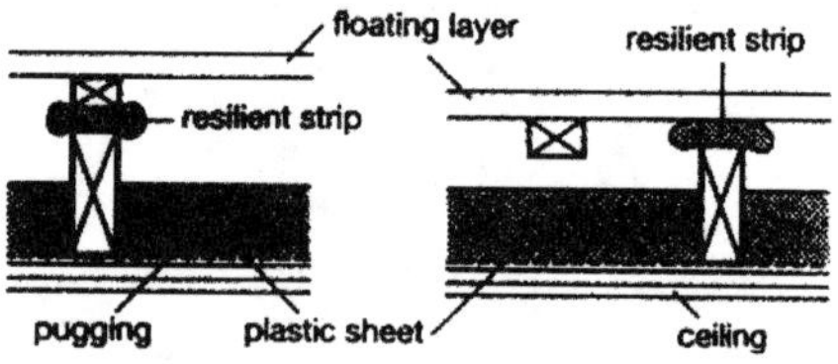
D	The pugging between joists may be of the following types: Traditional ash (75 mm), or 2 mm–10 mm, limestone chips (60 mm), or 2 mm–10 mm whin aggregate (60 mm), or dry sand (50 mm). Figures in brackets show approximate thickness required to achieve 80 kg/m² (other figures denote sieve size). Do not use sand in kitchens, bathrooms, shower rooms or watercloset compartments where it may become wet and overload the ceiling.	

Table V Sound insulation values for testing, based on Approved Document E 1992 to the Building Regulations 1991

	Walls		Floors	
	Mean value	Individual value	Mean value	Individual value
a1 Airborne sound tests in up to four pairs of rooms, minimum values of weighted standardised level difference ($D_{nT,w}$) as defined in BS 5821: Part 1: 1984	53	49	52	48
a2 Impact sound tests in up to four pairs of rooms, maximum value of weighted standardised level difference ($L'_{n,w}$) as defined in BS 5821: Part 2: 1984			61	65
b1 Airborne sound tests in at least eight pairs of rooms, minimum values of weighted standardised level difference ($D_{n,w}$) as defined in BS 5821: Part 1: 1984	52	49	51	48
b2 Impact sound tests in at least eight pairs of rooms, maximum value of weighted standardised level difference ($L'_{n,w}$) as defined in BS 5821: Part 2: 1984			62	65

9 BIBLIOGRAPHY

BS 5228 *Code of Practice for noise control on construction and open sites*

BS 8233 *Code of Practice for sound insulation and noise reduction for buildings*

BS 2750 *Acoustics – Measurement of sound insulation in buildings and of building elements*

BS 5821 *Methods for rating the sound insulation in buildings and of building elements*

BS 3638 *Method for measurement of sound absorption in a reverberation room*

BS 6864 *Laboratory tests on noise emission from appliances and equipment intended for use in water supply installations*

BS 4142 *Method for rating industrial noise affecting mixed residential and industrial areas*

ISO 6242–3 *Building construction – Expression of user's requirements – Part 3: Acoustical requirements*

ISO 1996 *Acoustics – Description and measurement of environmental noise*

   Part 1 Basic quantities and procedures

   Part 2 Acquisition of data pertinent to land use

   Part 3 Application to noise limits

Department of the Environment and the Welsh Office, *The Building Regulations 1991 – Approved Document E Resistance to the passage of sound*, HMSO, London

Building Standards (Scotland) Regulations

Department of the Environment, *Calculation of road traffic noise*, London, 1988

Noise Insulation Regulations 1975, HMSO, London

Department of Transport, *Railway noise and the insulation of dwellings*, HMSO, London, 1991

Department of the Environment, *Planning Policy Guidance – PPG24*, HMSO, London, 1994

Department of the Environment, *Digests, Information Papers*, Building Research Establishment, Garston, Watford, WD2 7JR.

41 Structure

David Adler

CI/SfB (J)
Uniclass: U31
UDC: 624

KEY POINTS:
- *Current codes of practice require experts in design of the specific type of structure and material*
- *Simplified design methods do exist, but only for very basic structures*

Contents

1 INTRODUCTION

1.01 Structural engineering ensures that the loads of the building and its contents are transmitted safely and economically to the ground, allowing for considerations of function, aesthetics, internal and external environment, and restraints imposed by other members of the building team, legislation, etc.

The subject is compounded of roughly equal amounts of experience and investigation. Most of the latter involves the use of mathematics, although model testing is occasionally employed.

1.02 In recent years mathematical methods prescribed in new Codes of Practice, particularly the Eurocodes, have become more complex. These make the use of computer programs essential, although whether the methods produce more economical and safer structures is a matter of some controversy.

In fact, some engineers still prefer to use the simpler methods that were common in the past. These are quite satisfactory in many cases such as traditional-type housing and smaller structures. In order to facilitate this, and in particular to avoid errors that did exist in the past, there are unofficial codes published under the auspices of one or more of the engineering institutions, and which are listed in the Bibliography. The methods in these documents are often acceptable to building inspectors to show conformity with the Building Regulations.

1.03 The treatment of the subject in this chapter is necessarily brief. It will be even less comprehensive than in previous editions, but will still try to give the architect something of a feel for structure, and help him or her in discussions with a structural engineer. Because of the complexity of the methods now used, building inspectors are increasingly insisting on calculations by chartered engineers.

1.04 There are three important factors in structural design:

- Accurate assessment of the behaviour of the structural form
- Accurate identification and calculation of all the forces acting
- Full knowledge of the properties of the structural materials.

An outline of the methods used is given below.

2 BASIC STRUCTURAL THEORY

2.01 This section will summarise basic structural concepts and the terms that might be met in dealing with structural matters. Examination in greater depth may be found in the *Handbook of building structure* and in the other references at the end of the chapter.

2.02 Limit state

Current techniques in structural engineering and their Codes of Practice are based on the concept of the limit state. Traditionally, design involved calculating the maximum stress and deflection in a member under working load. That stress was compared with the stress in that material known, through experiment, to lead to failure. Safe design included a margin, called the *factor of safety*, between the working and failure stress values. This traditional method is generally referred to as *permissible stress* design.

As already mentioned, it is important to anticipate how the form of the structure will behave under increasing load. Other factors than excessive stress can cause building failure: *instability* in particular. A child building a tower of wooden blocks soon learns that beyond a certain height it will collapse, even though none of the blocks is crushed. This is one reason for the change to limit state design.

A structure may become unserviceable or unsatisfactory in very many ways. Apart from collapsing completely, it may crack locally so badly as to let in the weather, it may deflect until the users feel unsafe. These are all limit states. The task of the structural designer is to ensure that none of the possible limit states is ever reached. This is done by calculating, for example, the load at which the collapse limit state is reached; a *load factor* is then applied to determine the safe working load: usually about half the collapse load. A similar procedure is adopted for the other limit states. The method is not fundamentally different from the traditional way, it is simply more organised.

2.03 Loads

In para **2.02** above, reference was made to loads. A load is an example of a force, and the term is usually used to describe those outside forces that act on a building structure. In Eurocodes all loads and factors producing stress or deflection are called *actions*, and this term is becoming more common. Actions are of four types:

- Dead loads: from the weight of the structure itself and that of other fixed parts of the building such as cladding, finishes, partitions etc.
- Imposed loads: of people, furniture and of materials stored in the building
- Dynamic loads: these are of many origins. The commonest dynamic load on a building is that caused by wind, which can produce horizontal and vertical pressures, and also suctions. Other horizontal dynamic loads are produced by earthquakes, and by moving machinery such as overhead cranes in large workshops. For the purposes of design, dynamic loads are often transformed into equivalent static loadings
- The fourth type of action is one that is not produced by an outside force, but by internal factors such as thermal expansion.

2.04 Force units

Forces, including loads, are measured in newtons (N). 1 N is the force required to give a mass of 1 kg an acceleration of 1 m/s^2. A tip to remember is that a newton is about the weight of an apple. Most forces in structural engineering are expressed in KN (kilonewtons). Table I gives conversions from and to SI, MT and FPS units for loadings of all types.

2.05 Mass and weight

Confusion often arises between the terms *mass* and *weight*. Outside nuclear physics, the *mass* of an object is a fixed quantity which is a basic property of that object. Its *weight* will depend on the mass, but also on the value of the gravitational effect on the object. This is not a constant, but can vary, not only in extra-terrestrial conditions but even very slightly on different places on earth. However, for all practical purposes the acceleration of gravity is taken as 9.80665 m/s^2, so that the weight of a kilogram mass is 9.80665 N.

2.06 Loads

Perhaps the most important calculations the engineer does relates to the accurate assessment of loading. In Table II you will find the loads of various materials which may comprise the fabric of a building and be included in the dead load as described above. It also gives the densities of materials that may be stored within it: part of the imposed loads. The figures are given both in the usual mass density form: kg/m^3, and also in the more convenient weight density Kn/m^3. Some loadings are more conveniently calculated from superficial or linear unit weights, and a few are given in Tables III and IV.

Table V indicates minimum imposed loads that should be allowed for in designing buildings for various purposes. These figures are intended to cover for the people in the building, and the kind of material normally stored. However, these loads sometimes

Table I Various conversions for loadings

Point loads
1 N = 0.102 kgf = 0.225 lbf
1 kN = 101.972 kgf = 224.81 lbf = 0.1004 tonf
1 MN = 101.972 tf = 224.81 kipf = 100.36 tonf
1 kgf = 9.807 N = 2.205 lbf
1 tf = 9.807 kN = 2.205 kipf = 0.9842 tonf
1 lbf = 4.448 N = 0.4536 kgf
1 kipf = 4.448 kN = 453.59 kgf = 0.4536 tf
1 tonf = 9.964 kN = 1.016 tf

Linearly distributed
1 N/m = 0.0685 lbf/ft = 0.206 lbf/yd
1 kN/m = 68.5 lbf/ft = 0.0306 tonf/ft
1 kgf/m = 9.807 N/m = 0.672 lbf/ft = 2.016 lbf/yd
1 tf/m = 9.807 kN/m = 0.672 kipf/ft = 2.016 kipf/yd = 0.3 tonf/ft = 0.9 tonf/yd
1 lbf/ft = 14.59 N/m = 1.488 kgf/m
1 kipf/ft = 14.58 kN/m = 1.488 tf/m
1 tonf/ft = 32.69 kN/m = 3.33 tf/m
1 tonf/yd = 10.90 kN/m = 1.11 tf/m

Superficially distributed
1 N/m^2 = 0.0209 lb/ft^2
1 kN/m^2 = 20.89 lb/ft^2
1 MN/m^2 = 9.324 tonf/ft^2
1 kgf/m^2 = 9.80665 N/m^2 = 0.2048 lbf/ft^2 = 1.843 lbf/yd^2
1 tf/m^2 = 9.80665 kN/m^2 = 0.2048 kipf/ft^2 = 0.0914 tonf/ft^2 = 0.823 tonf/yd^2
1 lb/ft^2 = 47.88 N/m^2 = 4.88 kgf/m^2
1 kipf/ft^2 = 47.88 kN/m^2 = 4.88 tf/m^2
1 tonf/ft^2 = 107.25 kN/m^2 = 10.93 tf/m^2
1 tonf/yd^2 = 11.92 kN/m^2 = 1.215 tf/m^2

Densities
1 N/m^3 = 0.00637 lbf/ft^3
1 kN/m^3 = 6.37 lbf/ft^3
1 MN/m^3 = 2.844 tonf/ft^3
1 kg/m^3 = 0.0624 lb/ft^3 (mass density)
1 t/m^3 = 62.4 lb/ft^3
1 lb/ft^3 = 16.02 kg/m^3 1 lbf/ft^3 = 157 N/m^3
1 ton/ft^3 = 35.88 t/m^3 1 tonf/ft^3 = 351.9 kN/m^3
1 ton/yd^3 = 1.33 t/m^3

Table II Densities of bulk materials

	kg/m^3	kN/m^3
Adamantine clinkers, stacked	208	220.4
Aggregates		
Coarse		
Normal weight, eg natural aggregates	1600	15.7
Lightweight, eg clinker, foamed slag, expanded clay and sintered pulverised-fuel ash	320.4–800.9	3.14–7.85
Heavyweight, eg barytes, magnetite and ilmenite	2400	23.5
Steel shot	4325	42.4
Fine		
Normal weight, eg sand	1760	17.3
Lightweight, eg clinker, foamed slag expanded clay and sintered pulverised-fuel ash	560.6–1041	5.5–10.2
Heavyweight, eg barytes, magnetite and ilmenite	2565	25.2
Steel shot	4325	42.4
Combined ('all-in' ballast)	2080	20.4
Alcohol	785	7.7
commercial proof spirit	913	9.0
wood-barrels	449	4.4
Alluvium, undisturbed	1602	15.7
Animal food, cases	400	3.9
Anthracite, broken	805	7.9
Apples, barrels	400	3.9
Argentine	7208	70.7
Asbestos		
crude	897	8.8
fibre, cases	673	6.6
fibres, sprayed (including binder)	80–240	
natural	3044	29.8
pressed	961	9.4
cement	1922–2082	18.8
sand	961	9.4
felt	150	1.5
Ashes, dry	641	6.3
Asphalt:		
natural	1009	9.9
paving	2082	20.4
Automatic machines, cases	160	1.6
Automobiles, cases	128	1.2
Aviation spirit	753	7.4
Axles and wheels	513	5.0
Baggage	128	1.2
Barium oxide, solid	4645–5446	45.5–53.4
Barley		
grain	705	6.9
bags	593	5.8
ground	529	5.2
Barrels, empty	128	1.2
Basic slag, crushed	1794	17.6
Baths, iron, cases	208	2.0
Beer	1025	10.0
bottled, cases	449	4.4
barrels	529	5.2
Beeswax	961	9.4
Benzene	881	8.6
Benzol	881	8.6
Bicycles, crates	128	1.2
Bitumen		
natural	1089	10.7
prepared	1362	13.4
emulsion	1121	11.0
Blood	1057	10.4
dried, casks	561	5.5
Bone	1762–2002	17.3–19.6
manure, bags	513	5.0
meal, bags	801	7.8
Books:		
on shelves	641	6.3
bulk	961	9.4
Boots and shoes, cases	384	3.8
Bottled goods, cases	897	8.8
Bottles, empty crates	416	4.1
Brewer s grains		
wet	497	4.9
desiccated	256	2.5
Bricks (common burnt clay)		
stacked	1602–1920	15.7–18.8
sand cement	1840	18.0
sand lime	2080	20.4
ballast	1200	11.8
brickwork	1920	18.8
Calcium carbide, solid	2211	21.7
Canvas, bales	769	7.5
Carpets, rolls	256	2.5
Casein	1346	13.2
Casks, empty	128	1.2
Cast stone	2243	

Table II *Continued*

	kg/m³	kN/m³
Celluloid	1346–1602	13.2–15.7
goods, cases	160	1 f
Cement		
bags	1281	12.6
bulk	1281–1442	12.6–14.2
casks	961	9.4
slurry	1442	14.7
Cheese, cases	513	5.0
Cigarettes, cases	240	2.4
Cinders	641	6.3
Clay		
dry, lumps	1041	10.2
dry, compact	1442	14.1
damp, compact	1762	17.3
wet, compact	2082	20.4
undisturbed	1922	18.8
undisturbed, gravelly	2082	20.4
china, compact	2243	22.0
Clinker, furnace	1025	10.0
Concrete cement, plain		
aerated	480–1600	
brick aggregate	1840–2160	
clinker	1440	14.1
stone ballast	2240	22.0
natural aggregates	2307	
lightweight aggregates		
normal	640–1600	
structural	1600–2000	
Heavy weight aggregates		
eg barates, ilmenite, magnetite, etc	3045–3365	
Steel shot	5045–5525	
No-fines	1840	
Organic aggregate	720–1840	
Diatomaceous earth	1220–1400	
Concrete cement, reinforced		
1 per cent steel	2370	23.2
2 per cent steel	2420	23.7
5 per cent steel	2580	25.3
Cork, granular, 4.8 mm size, loosely packed	120	
Corn, bulk	721	7.1
Cotton		
raw, compressed	400–577	3.9–5.7
bales, American	272	2.7
pressed bales, Egyptian	529	5.2
Diatomaceous brick	481	4.7
Diesel oil	881	8.6
Doors, crates	320	3.1
Dry goods, average	481	4.7
Dutch clinkers, stacked	1602	15.7
Dynamite	1233	12.1
Earth		
dry, loose	1280	12.6
dry, compact	1550	15.2
moist, loose	1440–1600	14.1–15.7
moist, compact	1760–1840	17.2–18.1
Earthenware, packed	320	3.1
Ebonite	1201–1281	11.8–12.6
Felt		
hair	272	2.7
roofing, rolls	593	5.8
Fibreboard	160–400	1.5–4.0
Files, etc, cases	897	8.8
Firebrick, Stourbridge	2002	19.6
Fish, boxes	721	7.1
Flour	705	6.9
sacks	641	6.3
barrels	545	5.3
Foam slag	700	6.9
Fuller's earth, natural	1762–2403	17.3–23.6
Glass		
bottle	2723	26.7
common green	2515	24.7
crown, extra white	2451	24.0
silicate	2195	21.5
flint, best	3076	30.2
heavy	4966–5927	48.7–58.1
optical	3524	34.6
plate	2787	27.3
crates	801	7.8
Pyrex	2243	22.0
bottles, crates	416	4.1
refuse (broken)	1522	14.9
silk	160–208	1.6–2.0
Grain		
barley	625	6.1
oats	416	4.1
rye	721	7.1

Table II *Continued*

	kg/m³	kN/m³
Granolithic	2243	22.0
Gravel		
loose	1602	15.7
undisturbed	1922–2162	18.8–21.2
Gunpowder	897	8.8
Gypklith	449	4.4
Gypsum		
crushed	1041–1602	10.2–45.7
bags	833	8.2
solid	2563	25.1
plaster	737	7.2
Hardcore	1922	18.8
Hoggin	1762	17.3
Hosiery, cased	224	2.2
Ice	913	9.0
Implements, agricultural, bundles	256	2.5
Indiarubber	1121	11.0
Ironmongery, packages	897	8.8
Ivory	1842	18.1
Jointing compound for tanks	801	7.8
Jute		
bales	481	4.7
bales, compressed	641	6.3
Leather	961	9.4
hides, compressed	368	3.6
rolls	160	1.6
Lime:		
acetate of, bags	1281	12.6
Blue Lias,		
ground	849	8.3
lump		
carbonate of, barrels	1281	12.6
chloride of, lead-lined cases	449	4.4
grey chalk, lump	705	6.9
grey stone, lump	881	8.6
hydrate, bags	513	5.0
hydraulic	721	7.1
quick, ground	1025	10.0
slaked,		
ground, dry	561	5.5
ground, wet	1522	14.9
Lime mortar		
dry	1650	16.2
wet	1746	17.1
Linoleum, rolls	481	4.7
Loam (sandy clay):		
dry, loose	1201	11.8
dry, compact	1602	15.7
wet, compact	1922	18.8
Macadam	2082	20.4
Magnesia, solid	2403	23.6
Mastic	1121	11.0
Metals:		
Aluminium		
cast	2771	27.2
rolled	2675	26.2
bronze	7545	74.0
DTD alloys	2675–2787	26.2–27.3
paint	1201	11.8
paste	1474	14.4
powder	721–801	7.0–7.9
sulphate, bags	721	7.1
wrought	2771	27.2
Antimony		
pure	6680	65.5
ore, bags	1442	14.1
Barbed wire	384	3.7
Bars, steel, bundles	2723	26.7
Bell metal	8490	83.2
Bolts and nuts, bags	1201	11.8
Brass		
copper 60 per cent, zinc 40 per cent (CZ 123 of BS 2870)	8426	
copper 70 per cent, zinc 30 per cent (CZ 106 of BS 2870)	8522	
cast	8330	81.7
rolled	8570	84.0
casks	721	7.1
tubes, bundles	897	8.8
Bronze		
phosphor, wrought (BS 369 and 407)	8938	
cast	8330	81.7
drawn, sheet	8794	86.2

Table II *Continued*

	kg/m³	kN/m³
Metals, *continued*		
Cadmium	8618	84.5
Chromium	7096	69.6
Cobalt	8586	84.2
Copper		
cast	8762	85.9
drawn or sheet	8938	87.6
ingots	3588	35.2
Cupro-nickel (60 per cent to 80 per cent Cu)	8938	87.6
Delta metal	8602	84.4
Duralumin	2787	27.3
Galvanised sheets, bundles	897	8.8
Gold	19318	189.4
Gunmetal		
cast	8458	82.9
rolled	8794	86.2
Hiduminium	2803	27.5
Iron		
cast	7208	70.7
malleable cast	7368–7497	72.2–73.5
wrought	7689	75.4
corrugated, bundles	897	8.8
pig		
random	2723	26.7
stacked	4485	44.0
pyrites, ground	2883	28.3
solid (60 per cent Fe)	4806–5128	47.1–50.3
sulphate, powdered	1121	11.0
wire, coils	897	8.8
Kupfernickel	7208–7609	70.6–74.6
Lead:		
cast or rolled	11325	111.1
pigs	3588	35.2
bronze (Cu 70 Pb 30)	9771	95.8
red, powder	2082	20.4
white, powder	1378	13.5
paste in drums	2787	27.3
Magnesium	1730	17.0
alloys, about	1842	18.1
Manganese	7368	72.2
bronze	8602	84.4
Mercury	13536	132.7
Molybdenum	9980	97.9
Muntz metal:		
cast	8394	82.3
sheet	8922	87.5
Nails, wire, bags	1201	11.8
Nickel	8810	86.4
silver	8730	85.6
Phosphor-bronze:		
cast	8650	84.8
drawn	8810	86.4
Platinum	21465	210.5
Rails, railway	2403	23.6
Screws, iron, packages	1602	15.7
Silver		
cast	10444	102.4
pure	10492	102.9
glance	7208	70.7
Solder, pigs	2723	26.7
Steel	7833	76.8
balls, barrels	1201	11.8
punchings	4806	47.1
mild, solid or cast	7849	
Titanium	4485	44.0
oxide, solid	3684	36.1
Tungsten	19222	188.5
Vanadium	5991	58.8
White lead		
powder	1378	13.5
paste in drums	2787	27.3
paint	2803	27.5
White metal	7368	72.2
Wire		
iron,coils	1185	11.6
nails, bags	1201	11.8
rod, coils	801	7.8
rope, coils	1442	14.1
Zinc		
cast	6804	66.7
rolled	7192	70.5
sheets packed	897	8.8
solid	7144	
Mortar		
cement, set	1922–2082	18.8–20.4
lime, set	1602–1762	15.7–17.3
Mud	1762–1922	17.3–18.8
Neoprene	1201	11.8

Table II *Continued*

	kg/m³	kN/m³
Ores:		
Bauxite	2563	25.1
crushed	1281	12.6
ore, bags	1201	11.8
Coal		
loose lumps	897	8.8
slurry	993	9.7
Coke	481–561	4.7–5.5
Magnesite	3044	29.8
Magnetic oxide of iron	4966	48.7
Magnetite	4966	48.7
Manganite	4325	42.4
Mica	2723–3044	26.7–29.8
Porphyry	2803	27.5
Pyrites:		
Iron		
ground	2883	28.3
solid (60 per cent Fe)	4806–5126	47.1–50.3
copper, solid	4085–4325	40.0–42.4
Quartz	2643	25.9
loose	1442–1682	14.1–16.5
Quartzite	2723	26.7
Shale	2563	25.1
granulated	1121	11.0
oil, Scottish	945	9.3
Silica, fused transparent	2211	21.7
translucent	2050	20.1
Silicon, pure	291	2.8
Spar		
calcareous	2723	26.7
feld	2691	26.4
fluor	3204	31.4
Wolfram (Wolframite)	7368	72.2
Zincblende	4085	40.1
Paint:		
aluminium	1201	11.8
bituminous emulsion	1121	11.0
red lead	3123	30.6
red lead dispersed	1522	14.9
white lead	2803	27.5
zinc	2403	23.6
Paper:		
blotting, bales	400	3.9
printing, reels	897	8.8
wall, rolls	384	3.8
writing	961	9.4
Paraffin:		
oil	801	7.8
wax	897	8.8
Peat:		
dry, stacked	561	5.5
sandy, compact	801	7.8
wet, compact	1362	13.4
Perspex	1346	13.2
Petrol	689–769	6.7–7.5
cans or drums	721–801	7.0–7.8
Phosphates:		
ground	1201	11.8
bags	849	8.3
Pipes:		
brass, bundles	897	8.8
cast iron, stacked	961–1281	9.4–12.6
earthenware, loose	320	3.1
salt-glazed, stacked	400	3.9
wrought iron,		
stacked 3/8 in (9.5 mm)	3204	31.4
3 m (76.2 mm)	1442	14.1
6 m (152.4 mm)	801	7.8
Pitch	1089	10.7
Plaster of Paris:		
loose	929	9.1
set	1281	12.6
Polystyrene	1057	10.4
Polvinyl chlor. acetate	1201–1346	11.8–13.2
Porcelain	2323	22.8
Portland cement:		
loose	1201–1362	11.8–13.4
bags	1121–1281	11.0–12.6
drums	1201	11.8
Potatoes	641	6.3
Quicklime, ground, dry	1025	10.0
Quilt, eel grass	176	1.72
Resin		
lumps	1073	9.0
barrels	769	7.5
Resinoil	993	9.7

Table III Continued

	kg/m²	N/m²
Lead sheet (BS 1178)		
0.067 in (1.7 mm)	19.5	191
0.084 in (2.1 mm)	24.4	239
0.101 in (2.6 mm)	29.3	287
0.118 in (3.0 mm)	34.2	335
Linoleum		
3.2 mm	4.4	43
4.5 mm	5.9	58
6.7 mm	9.8	96
Metal-faced plywood		
Aluminium		
4.8 mm thick		
Faced 1 side	3.9	38
Faced 2 sides	5.4	53
6.4 mm thick		
Faced 1 side	4.9	48
Faced 2 sides	6.3	62
9.5 mm thick		
Faced 1 side	6.3	62
Faced 2 sides	7.3	72
12.7 mm thick		
Faced 1 side	8.3	81
Faced 2 sides	9.8	96
19.1 mm thick		
Faced 1 side	12.2	120
Faced 2 sides	13.7	134
Galvanized steel		
4.8 mm thick		
Faced 1 side	4.9	48
Faced 2 sides	7.8	76
6.4 mm thick		
Faced 1 side	6.3	62
Faced 2 sides	8.8	86
9.5 mm thick		
Faced 1 side	7.3	72
Faced 2 sides	9.8	96
12.7 mm thick		
Faced 1 side	9.3	91
Faced 2 sides	12.2	120
19.1 mm thick		
Faced 1 side	13.7	134
Faced 2 sides	16.1	158
Pavement lights, glazed		
Cast iron or reinforced concrete	122.1 ± 24.4	1200 ± 240
Pitchmastic flooring		
25 mm thick	16.2 ± 1.6	159 ± 16
Plaster		
Gypsum		
Two coat, 12 mm thick		
Normal sanded undercoat and neat finishing	20.8	204
One coat, 5 mm thick, neat gypsum	6.7	66
Lime (non-hydraulic and hydraulic) 12 mm thick	23.1	227
Barium sulphate 12 mm thick	36.9	362
Lightweight		
Perlite aggregate, 2 coat, 12 mm thick	9.6	94
Vermiculite aggregate, 2 coat, ditto	10.5	103
Plasterboard, gypsum		
Solid core		
9.5 mm	8.3	81
12 mm	10.6	104
18 mm	16.1	158
Perforated lath		
9.5 mm	7.8	76
12 mm	10.1	99
Plastics		
Flooring		
Flexible PVC		
1.6 mm	2.4	24
2.0 mm	3.4	33
2.5 mm	3.9	38
3.2 mm	4.9	48
PVC vinyl tiles		
1.6 mm	3.4	33
2.0 mm	4.4	43
2.5 mm	5.9	58
3.2 mm	6.8	67
4.8 mm	10.3	101

Table III Continued

	kg/m²	N/m²
Plastics, continued		
Flat sheet		
Acrylic		
3.2 mm	3.9	38
6.4 mm	7.3	72
Cellulose acetate		
1.6 mm	2.0	20
3.2 mm	4.4	43
Synthetic resin bonded paper		
Melamine faced 1.6 mm thick	2.0–2.4	20–24
Corrugated (including allowance for laps)		
Acrylic	4.4	43
Glass-fibre reinforced polyester	3.9	38
PVC	3.9	38
Expanded and foamed (each per 25 mm thick)		
Expanded PVC	1.5 ± 1.0	15 ± 10
Expanded polystyrene	0.5	5
Foamed polystyrene	0.5 ± 0.1	5 ± 1
Foamed polyurethane	2.4 ± 1.5	24 ± 15
Foamed phenolic resin	1.5 ± 0.5	15 ± 5
Domelights		
Acrylic		
4.8 mm	5.4	53
6.4 mm	7.3	72
Damp-proof course		
Polythene 0.5 mm nom thickness	0.5	5
Plywood		
Per mm thick	0.6 ± 0.1	6 ± 1
Quilt each per 25 mm thick		
Eelgrass	1.5–2.0	15–20
Glass fibre	1.0	10
Hair	4.9 ± 0.5	48 ± 5
Kapok	0.5	5
Mineral wool	3.4 ± 1.5	33 ± 15
Rendering		
Portland cement:sand (1:3) 12 mm thick	27.7	272
Rubber		
Flooring		
Sheet or tiles		
3 mm	5.1	50
5 mm	8.6	84
6.5 mm	10.9	107
10 mm	16.9	166
Latex-hydraulic cement 6.5 mm thick	12.9 ± 1.5	127 ± 15
Cellular, each per 25 mm thick		
Expanded		
Light density (max static load 10 kN/m²)	5.3	52
Standard density (max static load 15 kN/m²)	7.7	76
Heavy density (max static load 50 kN/m²)	12.0	118
Expanded ebonite	2.0	20
Screeding		
Portland cement:sand (1:3) 12 mm thick	27.7	272
Shingles		
Cedar wood	7.3	72
Slate		
Slab (Westmorland etc) 25 mm thick	72.0	706
Slating (including 75 mm laps and nails)		
Welsh		
Thin	24.4	239
Thick	48.8	479
Westmorland		
Thin	48.8	479
Thick	78.1	766
Cornish		
Thin	29.3	287
Thick	48.8	479
Steel		
Mild, sheet		
Corrugated (including 20 per cent for laps 'as laid') 1.25 mm	13.7	134
Flat 1.25 mm	9.8	96
Protected		
Corrugated (including 20 per cent for laps 'as laid') 1 mm	15.6	153
Flat 1 mm	10.7	105

Table II Continued

	kg/m³	kN/m³
Rubber		
crepe, cases	400	3.9
processed sheet	1121	11.0
raw	929	9.1
sponge	48–1600	4.7–15.7
vulcanised	1201	11.8
Salt, bulk	961	9.4
Salt-glazed ware	2243	22.0
Sand		
saturated	1922	18.8
undisturbed dry	1682	16.5
saturated	2002	19.6
Sea water	1009–1041	9.9–10.2
Silk, bales	352	3.4
Sirapite, powder	1025	10.0
Slag		
coarse	1442	14.1
granulated	961	9.4
Slag wool	224–288	2.2–2.8
Sludge cake, pressed, 50 per cent water	929	9.1
Snow		
fresh	96	0.94
wet compact	320	3.1
Soap, boxed	913	9.0
Soda, bags	657	6.4
Soils		
non-cohesive (or granular), ie sands and gravels		
loose	1840 ± 160	
dense	2080 ± 160	
cohesive, ie silts and clays		
soft	1600 ± 240	
firm	1760 ± 160	
stiff	2000 ± 160	
Soot	352	3.4
Spirits of wine	785	7.7
Sponge rubber	48–1600	0.47–15.7
Stationery cases	513	5.0
Stone (for cramps in stonework add 80 kg/m³)		
Aggregates:		
coarse	152	14.9
fine	50	8.3
Alabaster	2691	26.4
Ancaster	2499	24.5
Ballast		
loose, graded	1602	15.7
undisturbed	1922	18.8
Bath	2082	20.4
Caen	2002	19.6
Chalk	1602–2723	15.7–26.7
broken, barrels	9261	9.4
Darley Dale	2371	23.2
Flint	2563	25.1
Forest of Dean	2435	23.9
freestone	2243–2483	22.0–24.3
masonry, dressed	2403	23.6
rubble	2243	22.0
granite	2643	25.9
chippings	1442	14.1
dressed, cases	2243	22.0
Peterhead	2595	
Cornish	2643	
Guernsey	2931	
Ham Hill	2162	21.2
Hopton Wood	2531	24.8
Ironstone:		
Cleveland, lumps	2162	21.2
Spanish, lumps	2403	23.6
Swedish, lumps	3684	36.1
Kentish rag	2675	26.2
crushed	1602	15.7
Mansfield	2259	22.2
Mansfield red	2403	
marble	2595–2835	25.4–27.8
millstone grit	2323	22.8
Portland	2243	22.0
Pumice stone	481–913	4.7–9.0
Purbeck	2707	26.5
ragstone	2403	23.6
slate:		
Welsh	2803	27.5
Westmorland	2995	29.4
Soapstone	2723	26.7
Terracotta	1794–2114	17.6
Tinstone	6407–7048	62.8–69.1
Woolton	2195	
York	2243	22.0
Stoneware	2243	22.0

Table II Continued

	kg/m³	kN/m³
Straw		
pressed	96	0.94
compressed bales	304	3.0
Strawboards, bundles	593	5.8
Strontium white		
solid	3844	37.7
ground	1762	17.3
Sulphate of		
aluminium, bags	721	7.1
ammonia, bags	641	6.3
copper, cast	1346	13.2
iron, powder	1121	11.0
Sulphur, pure solid	1922–2082	18.8–20.4
Sulphuric acid, 100 percent	1970	193
commercial	1682–1794	16.5–17.6
Tar	1137–1233	11.2–12.1
barrels	801	7.8
Tarmacadam	2082	20.4
Tarpaulins, bundles	721	7.1
Tetraethyl lead	1602	15.7
Timbers:		
Ash		
English	689	6.8
Canadian	737	7.2
Balsawood	112	1.1
Bamboo	352	3.4
Beech	769	7.5
Birch		
American	641	6.3
logs	449	4.4
squares	625	6.1
yellow	705	6.9
Boxwood	929	9.1
Cedar, western red	384	3.8
Cherry wood	721	7.1
Chestnut		
horse	513	5.0
sweet	561	5.5
Cork	128–240	1.2–2.4
bales	80	0.78
Cypress wood	593	5.8
Deal, yellow	432	4.2
Ebony	1185–1330	11.6–13.1
Elm		
American	673	6.6
Canadian	673	6.6
Dutch	577	5.6
English	577	5.6
wych	689	6.8
Fir:		
Douglas	529	5.2
silver	481	4.7
Hemlock, western	497	4.9
Iroko	657	6.4
Ironwood	1137	11.2
Larch	593	5.8
Lime	561	5.5
American	416	4.1
Logwood	913	9.0
Mahogany:		
African	561	5.5
Honduras	545	5.3
Spanish	689	6.8
Maple:		
Canadian	737	7.2
English	689	6.8
Oak:		
African	961	9.4
American red	721	7.1
white	769	7.5
Austrian	721	7.1
English	801–881	7.8–8.6
Padauk	785	7.7
Peruvian bark, bales	240	2.4
Pine:		
American red	529	5.2
British Columbian	529	5.2
Christiania	689	6.8
Columbian	529	5.2
Dantzig	577	5.6
Memel	545	5.3
Kauri, Queensland	481	4.7
New Zealand	609	6.0
Oregon	529	5.2
pitch	657	6.4
Riga	545–753	5.3–7.4

Table II Continued

	kg/m³	kN/m³
Timbers, *continued*		
Plywood	481–641	4.7–6.3
plastic bonded	721–1442	7.0–14.2
resin bonded	721–1362	7.0–13.4
Poplar	449	4.4
Pulp, wood:		
dry	561	5.5
wet	721	7.1
Redwood:		
American	529	5.2
Baltic	497	4.9
non-graded	432	4.2
Zimbabwian	913	
Satinwood	961	9.4
Sawdust	208	2.0
Spruce		
Canadian	465	4.6
Norway	465	4.6
Sitka	449	4.4
Sycamore	609	6.0
Teak, Burma or African	657	6.4
Walnut	657	6.4
Whitewood	465	4.6
Willow		
American	577	5.6
English	449	4.4
Wood block paving	897	8.8
Yew	673–801	6.6–7.8
Tinned goods, cases	481–641	4.7–6.3
Tinplate, boxes	3204–4485	31.4–44.0
Tinware, cases	192	1.88
Tools, hand, cases	897	8.8
Treetex	208	2.0
Tubes, see 'Pipes'		
Tyres, rubber	176–268	1.7–2.5
Varnish		
barrels	593	5.8
tins in cases	721	7.1
Vermiculite		
Exfoliated		
Fine aggregate for plaster	128–160	
Coarse aggregate for plaster	88–112	
Fine aggregate for concrete	72–88	
Coarse aggregate for concrete and loose fill	64–80	
Crude	576–881	
Waste paper	352	3.4
pressed packed	449–513	4.4–5.0
Water		
fresh	1001	9.8
salt	1009–1201	9.9–11.8
Wax		
bees'	961	9.4
Brazil	993	
cases or barrels	593	5.8
paraffin	897	8.8
Wine		
bulk	977	9.6
bottles in cases	593	5.8
Wool		
compressed bales	769	7.5
uncompressed	208	2.0

need to be checked against the figures in Tables II, III and IV for more unusual circumstances.

2.07 Structural elements

For convenience of design, large structures are broken up into elements. These are of different types according to the function they perform in the building. Before describing each type, it will be necessary to go deeper into the forces that are found internally in the materials of the structure.

2.08 Stress and strain

If a bar of uniform cross-section has a force applied at each end, **41.1**, it will stretch slightly. This stretch is called the *strain* in the bar, and is defined as the extension divided by the original length.

Table III Superficial masses of materials in kg/m² and weights in N/m² This is based on figures in BS 648:1964, and should be taken as approximate.

	kg/m²	N/m²
Aluminium sheet		
Flat		
1.22 mm	3.4	33
0.91 mm	2.4	24
0.71 mm	2.0	20
0.56 mm	1.5	15
Corrugated (BS 2855) (including 20 per cent added weight for laps 'as laid')		
1.22 mm	4.4	43
0.71 mm	2.9	28
0.56 mm	2.0	20
Asphalt		
Roofing 2 layers, 20 mm	43.9	431
Damp-proofing		
20 mm	42.4	416
25 mm	52.9	519
30 mm	63.5	623
Flooring 25 mm thick	52.9 ± 4.9	519 ± 48
Road and footpaths		
12 mm	27.7	272
20 mm	46.0	451
Battens		
Slating and tiling, 40 × 20 mm softwood		
100 mm gauge	3.4	33
Bitumen damp-proof courses		
Hessian base	3.9	38
Fibre felt	3.4	33
Hessian base and lead	4.4	43
Fibre felt and lead	4.4	43
Bitumen roofing felts		
Bitumen felts (fibre base)		
Saturated bitumen	0.5	5
	1.0	10
Sanded bitumen	2.0	20
	2.4	24
	2.9	28
Self-finished bitumen*	1.0	10
	1.5	15
	2.0	20
	2.4	24
	2.9	28
Coated and sanded bitumen felt	2.0	20
	2.4	24
	2.9	28
Mineral surfaced bitumen	3.4	33
Reinforced bitumen felt	1.0	10
Fluxed pitch felts (fibre base)		
Saturated fluxed pitch	0.5	5
	1.0	10
Sanded fluxed pitch	2.0	20
	2.9	28
Impregnated flax felts and hair felts		
Impregnated flax		
Black		
Roofing	2.0	20
Sarking	1.5	15
Black sheathing	1.0	10
Brown		
No 1 Inodorous	1.5	15
No 2 Inodorous	1.0	10
Brown sheathing	1.0	10
Impregnated hair		
Black		
Black hair sheathing	2.0	20
Brown		
Brown bituminous hair	2.0	20
Bitumen felts (glass fibre base)		
Bitumen glass fibre	1.5	15
	2.0	20
Mineral surfaced bitumen glass fibre	2.9	28

*When fine sand is used in lieu of talc this weight is increased by approximately 0.5 kg/m², 5 N/m².

	kg/m²	N/m²
Blockwork, walling (all except diatomenous earth per 25 mm thickness)		
Clay		
Hollow	25.5	250
Perforated (approximately 50 per cent perforated)		
Medium density	27.9	274
High density	32.2	316

Table III Continued

	kg/m²	N/m²
Blockwork, walling, *continued*		
Concrete		
Ballast and stone aggregate		
Cellular	40.0	392
Hollow	34.2	335
Solid		
Stone aggregate	53.8	528
Slate aggregate	48.0	471
Lightweight aggregate		
Cellular	28.3	278
Hollow	25.5	250
Solid	31.7	311
Aerated		
Based on 560 kg/m³	14.4	141
Based on 800 kg/m³	19.2	188
Organic aggregates eg sawdust, peat etc		
Based on 1280 kg/m³	33.7	330
Diatomaceous earth		
50 mm thick	32.7	321
65 mm thick	39.5	387
75 mm thick	43.2	424
100 mm thick	52.4	514
115 mm thick	56.9	558
Board, laminated (ie battenboard, blockboard and laminboard)		
Per 25 mm thick	11.0 ± 1.0	108 ± 10
Brickwork (all per 25 mm thick)		
Clay		
Solid,		
Low density	50.0	490
Medium density	53.8	528
High density	58.2	571
Perforated		
Low density, 25 per cent voids	38.0	373
Low density, 15 per cent voids	42.3	415
Medium density, 25 per cent voids	39.9	391
Medium density, 15 per cent voids	46.2	453
High density, 25 per cent voids	44.2	433
High density, 15 per cent voids	48.0	471
Concrete	57.7	566
Lightweight/Flue		
Diatomaceous earth	16.3	160
Calcium silicate (sand lime and flint lime)	50.0	490
Carpet	2.9 + 0.5/–1.0	28 + 5/–10
Copper sheet and strip		
1.2 mm	10.8	106
0.9 mm	8.1	79
0.7 mm	6.3	62
0.6 mm	5.4	53
0.45 mm	4.0	39
Cork board per 25 mm thickness		
Normal	4.3	42
Semi-compressed	4.8	47
Compressed	7.2	71
Flooring	9.6	94
Felt		
Insulating per 25 mm thick	4.8	47
Fibre building board		
Insulating boards 12 mm	3.4	33
Hardboard 3 mm	3.4	33
Laminated 5 mm	3.4	33
Acoustic (unfaced)		
12 mm	3.4–4.9	33–48
20 mm	4.4–6.8	43–67
Flagstones		
Concrete		
50 mm thick	115	1130
60 mm	138	1350
63 mm	145	1420
65 mm	150	1470
70 mm	161	1570
Natural stone		
50 mm thick	56	549
65 mm	73	716

Table III Continued

	kg/m²	N/m²
Floors		
Hollow clay blocks		
Without ribs (including reinforcement and mortar jointing between blocks but excluding any concrete topping)		
100 mm	144	1410
125 mm	168	1650
150 mm	187	1830
175 mm	225	2210
200 mm	255	2500

Note: These weights are based on the use of hollow blocks of varying size and depth. For each 25 mm of thickness of concrete topping add 60 kg/m², 590 N/m².

	kg/m²	N/m²
With concrete ribs between blocks (including reinforcement but excluding any concrete topping)		
75 mm	91	890
90 mm	108	1060
100 mm	120	1180
115 mm	133	1300
125 mm	140	1370
140 mm	151	1480
150 mm	168	1550
175 mm	178	1750
200 mm	197	1930

Note: These weights are based on the use of blocks of varying size and depth and of lesser density than those used without concrete ribs between the blocks. For each 25 mm thickness of concrete topping add 60 kg/m², 590 N/m².

	kg/m²	N/m²
Hollow concrete units (including any concrete topping necessary for constructional purposes)		
100 mm	168	1650
125 mm	192	1880
150 mm	217	2130
175 mm	240	2350
200 mm	285	2800
225 mm	312	3060
Glass		
Float		
4 mm	11.1	109
5 mm	13.9	136
6 mm	16.7	164
8 mm	22.3	219
10 mm	27.9	274
12 mm	33.4	328
15 mm	41.8	41(
19 mm	53.0	52
Wired cast		
6 mm thick	16.0	
Glass blocks		
Hollow 100 mm thick		
200 mm (25 blocks per m²)	84.3	
150 mm (44.44 blocks per m²)	99.2	
Glass fibre all per 25 mm thick		
Thermal insulation of roofs and walls	0.5	
Acoustic insulation of floating floors	1.0	
Slab	2.0–4.9	
Formboard	5.4	
Roof board	6.3	
Glazing, patent		
(Bars at 0.6 m centres and wired cast glass 6 mm thick)		
Lead-covered steel bars		
Spans up to 1.8 m	25.9	
Spans 1.8–3.4 m	29.3	
Aluminium bars		
Spans up to 3.4 m	19.	
Gypsum panels and partitions		
Building panels		
75 mm thick		
100 mm thick		
125 mm thick		
150 mm thick		
Dry partition		
55 mm thick		
65 mm thick		
Lathing		
Wood		
Clay		

Table III *Continued*

	kg/m²	N/m²
Stonework, natural		
Note: For cramps add 5 lb/ft³ (80.1 kg/m³)		
Limestone		
Light, eg Bathstone		
100 mm thick	206.6	2026
150 mm thick	312.4	3064
Medium, eg Portland stone		
75 mm thick	168.2	1650
100 mm thick	225.9	2215
Heavy, eg marble		
20 mm thick	53.7	527
40 mm thick	107.6	1055
Sandstone		
Light, eg Woolton		
100 mm thick	221.1	2168
150 mm thick	331.6	3252
Medium, eg Darley Dale		
100 mm thick	230.7	2262
150 mm thick	350.8	3440
Heavy, eg Mansfield Red		
100 mm thick	240.3	2357
150 mm thick	360.4	3534
Granite		
Light, eg Peterhead		
50 mm thick	129.7	1272
75 mm thick	192.2	1885
Medium, eg Cornish		
50 mm thick	134.5	1319
75 mm thick	197.0	1932
Heavy, eg. Guernsey		
50 mm thick	144.2	1414
75 mm thick	221.1	2168
Tarmacadam		
Roads and footpaths 25 mm thick	57.7	566
Terrazo		
Paving 16 mm	32.9 ± 3.4	323 ± 33
Tiles 25 mm	48.0 ± 4.9	471 ± 48
Partitions 40 mm	85.8 ± 8.3	841 ± 81
Thatching		
Reed (including battens) 300 mm thick	41.5	407
Thermal capacity roof coverings		
Shingle and felspar per 25 mm thick	36.0	353
Tiling, floor		
Asphalt 3 mm thick	5.9	58
Clay		
12 mm thick	25.8	253
20 mm thick	40.4	396
Cork compressed		
6 mm thick	2.3	23
Hardboard faced, bitumen based		
3 mm thick	3.7	36
PVC flexible		
1.6 mm thick	2.4	24
2.0 mm thick	3.4	33
2.5 mm thick	3.9	38
3.2 mm thick	4.9	48
PVC vinyl		
1.6 mm thick	3.4	33
2.0 mm thick	4.4	43
2.5 mm thick	5.9	58
3.2 mm thick	6.8	67
4.8 mm thick	10.3	101
Concrete 16 mm thick	38.1	374
Tiling, roof		
Clay		
Plain		
Machine made, 100 mm gauge	63.5	623
Hand made, 100 mm gauge	70.8	694
Single lap (interlocking)	39.1 ± 4.9	383 ± 48
Concrete		
Slate aggregate 300 mm gauge	43.9	431
Stone aggregate		
Plain		
75 mm gauge	92.8	910
100 mm gauge	68.4	671
115 mm gauge	61.0	598
Interlocking (single lap)	48.8 ± 7.3	479 ± 72

Table III *Continued*

	kg/m²	N/m²
Tiling, wall		
Clay 10 mm thick	20.5	201
Fibre acoustic 20 mm thick	5.7	56
Plastics		
Polystyrene		
Dense 1.8 mm	2.0	20
Expanded 4.8 mm	2.0	20
PVC 1.5 mm	3.4	33
Weather boarding		
0.75 in (19.1 mm)	7.3	72
1 in (25.4 mm)	8.8	86
Wood floors, strip		
Note: All thicknesses are 'finished thicknesses'.		
Softwood		
22 mm	11.2	110
28 mm	13.7	134
Pitchpine		
22 mm	15.1	148
28 mm	19.0	186
Hardwood		
22 mm	16.1	158
28 mm	21.0	206
Wood floors, block (including mastic)		
Softwood		
22 mm	12.7	125
28 mm	15.1	148
Pitchpine		
22 mm	16.6	163
28 mm	20.5	201
Hardwood		
22 mm	17.6	173
28 mm	22.5	221
Wood chipboard		
Uniform		
12 mm	9.3	91
20 mm	15.3	150
Three-layer boards		
Light		
12 mm	6.9	68
20 mm	10.3	101
Heavy		
12 mm	9.3	91
20 mm	15.3	150
Zinc sheet		
0.6 mm	4.2	41
0.65 mm	4.5	44
0.7 mm	5.2	51
0.8 mm	6.0	59
1.0 mm	7.5	74

The *stress* on this bar is the force on the cross-section divided by its area. The relationship between the strain and the stress is a crucial factor in structural engineering. **41.2** shows a graph of this relationship for steel. The length OA is a straight line and is called the *elastic* zone. In the elastic zone the stress/strain is a constant called *Young's Modulus*. At A there is a sudden change called the *yield point*. Beyond this point along the curve AB there is no constant relationship between the stress and the strain. In fact, even if there is no increase in stress, the strain can increase over time until the bar breaks at B. This length of curve is known as the *plastic zone*. While *Hooke's Law*, which says that stress and strain are proportionate, only applies in the elastic zone, the more general law states that there can be no stress without some strain, and no strain without stress.

In **41.3** OAB shows the actual stress/strain relationship for a typical concrete. This, for many practical purposes can be substituted by OCD. OC is the elastic and CD the plastic zones.

2.09 Units of stress

The basic SI unit of stress is the N/m² (which is also called the pascal, Pa), but this is too small a unit for practical purposes. The correct form for the normal unit is MPa or MN/m² but this is often

Table IV Linear masses of materials in kg/m and weights in N/m This is based on figures in BS 648:1964, and should be taken as approximate.

	kg/m	N/m
Gutters		
Cast iron		
Half-round		
76 mm	2.7	26
102 mm	3.1	30
127 mm	4.0	39
152 mm	4.8	47
Ogee		
114 mm	4.2	41
127 mm	4.6	45
PVC		
100 mm	0.6	5.9
Aluminium		
Half-round, 1.8 m lengths		
108 mm		
Cast	1.2	12
Wrought 2 mm	0.9	9
115 mm		
Cast	1.3	13
Wrought 2 mm	1.0	10
125 mm		
Cast	1.5	15
Wrought 2 mm	1.2	12
150		
Cast	1.6	16
Wrought 2 mm	1.3	13
Ogee, 1.8 m length,		
100 mm		
Cast	1.3	13
Wrought 2 mm	1.2	12
115 mm		
Cast	1.6	16
125 mm		
Cast	1.9	19
Wrought 2 mm	1.3	13
Rectangular, 1.8 m lengths		
100 × 50 mm		
Wrought	1.2	12
100 × 75 mm		
Cast	2.2	22
125 mm × 65 mm		
Wrought	1.5	15
125 × 100 mm		
Cast	3.0	29
150 × 75 mm		
Wrought	1.8	18
Precast concrete		
560 mm on bed and 175 mm high	92 ± 3	900 ± 30
Pipes		
Cast iron		
Rainwater		
65 mm nominal size	4.9	48
75 mm nominal size	6.0	59
100 mm nominal size	7.7	76
Flue or smoke		
100 mm nominal size	8.9	87
115 mm nominal size	10.0	98
125 mm nominal size	12.4	122
150 mm nominal size	16.8	165
175 mm nominal size	22.6	222
200 mm nominal size	29.3	287
225 mm nominal size	37.7	370
250 mm nominal size	46.6	457
300 mm nominal size	63.5	623
Soil, waste and ventilating		
Medium		
75 mm nominal size	9.2	90
100 mm nominal size	11.9	117
150 mm nominal size	18.2	178
Heavy		
75 mm nominal size	10.1	99
100 mm nominal size	13.4	131
Extra heavy		
100 mm nominal size	15.9	156
150 mm nominal size	23.5	230
Drainage		
100 mm nominal size	26.0	255
150 mm nominal size	37.2	365
Copper		
Water supply average weights of tube, fittings and clips		
12 mm nominal size	0.4	4
18 mm nominal size	0.7	7

Table IV *Continued*

	kg/m	N/m
Pipes, *continued*		
Copper, *continued*		
Rainwater, soil, waste and ventilating		
75 mm nominal size	3.1	30
100 mm nominal size	4.9	48
150 mm nominal size	8.0	78
Half-hard tube EN1057-R25		
6 mm dia 0.6 mm thick	0.10	1.0
6 mm dia 0.8 mm thick	0.13	1.3
8 mm dia 0.6 mm thick	0.13	1.3
8 mm dia 0.8 mm thick	0.18	1.8
10 mm dia 0.7 mm thick	0.20	1.9
10 mm dia 0.8 mm thick	0.22	2.2
12 mm dia 0.6 mm thick	0.20	2.0
12 mm dia 0.8 mm thick	0.27	2.6
15 mm dia 0.7 mm thick	0.29	2.9
15 mm dia 1.0 mm thick	0.42	4.1
22 mm dia 0.9 mm thick	0.56	5.4
22 mm dia 1.2 mm thick	0.74	7.2
28 mm dia 0.9 mm thick	0.71	6.9
28 mm dia 1.2 mm thick	0.94	9.2
35 mm dia 1.2 mm thick	1.17	11.5
35 mm dia 1.5 mm thick	1.47	14.4
42 mm dia 1.2 mm thick	1.41	13.8
42 mm dia 1.5 mm thick	1.76	17.3
54 mm dia 1.2 mm thick	1.8	18
54 mm dia 2.0 mm thick	3.0	30
66.7 mm dia 1.2 mm thick	2.2	22
66.7 mm dia 2.0 mm thick	3.7	37
76.1 mm dia 1.5 mm thick	3.2	31
76.1 mm dia 2.0 mm thick	4.3	42
108 mm dia 1.5 mm thick	4.5	44
108 mm dia 2.5 mm thick	7.5	74
133 mm dia 1.5 mm thick	5.6	55
159 mm dia 2.0 mm thick	8.9	87
Steel, add 5 per cent extra if galvanized		
Screwed and socketed		
Light		
32 mm nominal bore	2.7	26
38 mm nominal bore	3.3	32
50 mm nominal bore	4.2	41
75 mm nominal bore	7.0	69
100 mm nominal bore	10.1	99
Medium		
32 mm nominal bore	3.1	30
38 mm nominal bore	3.7	36
50 mm nominal bore	5.2	51
75 mm nominal bore	8.6	84
100 mm nominal bore	12.4	122
150 mm nominal bore	19.8	194
Heavy		
32 mm nominal bore	3.9	38
38 mm nominal bore	4.5	44
50 mm nominal bore	6.3	62
75 mm nominal bore	10.3	101
100 mm nominal bore	14.7	144
150 mm nominal bore	21.9	215
Soil, waste and ventilating		
75 mm nominal	3.0	29
100 mm nominal	3.7	36
Plastics		
Polythene		
General purposes		
Light		
12 mm nominal	0.06	0.6
25 mm nominal	0.3	3
50 mm nominal	0.6	6
Medium		
10 mm nominal	0.09	0.9
20 mm nominal	0.4	4
60 mm nominal	1.0	10
Heavy		
12 mm nominal	0.1	1
25 mm nominal	0.6	6
50 mm nominal	1.3	13
High density		
Class B		
12 mm nominal	0.09	0.9
25 mm nominal	0.1	1
50 mm nominal	0.6	6
Class C		
12 mm nominal	0.1	1
25 mm nominal	0.3	3
50 mm nominal	0.9	9
Class D		
12 mm nominal	0.1	1
25 mm nominal	0.3	3
50 mm nominal	0.6	6

Table IV *Continued*

	kg/m	N/m
Pipes, *continued*		
Plastics, *continued*		
Polythene, *continued*		
Cold water		
Normal		
12 mm nominal bore	0.1	1
25 mm nominal bore	0.3	3
50 mm nominal bore	0.7	7
Heavy		
12 mm nominal bore	0.1	1
25 mm nominal bore	0.4	4
Rainwater		
65 mm nominal size	0.6	6
Soil		
100 mm nominal size	3.0	29
PVC		
Cold water supply		
Class AA		
150 mm nominal size	3.1	30
Class B		
50 mm nominal size	0.6	6
75 mm nominal size	1.2	12
100 mm nominal size	1.8	18
150 mm nominal size	3.9	38
Class C		
25 mm nominal size	0.3	3
50 mm nominal size	0.7	7
75 mm nominal size	1.5	15
100 mm nominal size	2.5	25
150 mm nominal size	5.5	54
Class D		
12 mm nominal size	0.1	1
25 mm nominal size	0.3	3
50 mm nominal size	0.9	9
75 mm nominal size	1.9	19
100 mm nominal size	3.3	32
150 mm nominal size	7.1	70
Clay salt-glazed		
75 mm	11.9	117
100 mm	16.4	161
150 mm	25.3	248
225 mm	40.2	394
300 mm	68.5	672

Concrete, unreinforced or reinforced, spigot and
socket

Note: For pipes with ogee joints, i.e. without a collar, deduct 10 per cent from the weights below.

100 mm nominal	31.3–32.7	307–321
150 mm nominal	41.7–47.6	409–467
225 mm nominal	67.0–74.4	657–730
300 mm nominal	104.2–116.1	1022–1139
380 mm nominal	141.4–151.8	1385–1489
450 mm nominal	186.0–197.9	1824–1941
600 mm nominal	300.6–312.5	2948–3065
750 mm nominal	418.2–468.8	4101–4598
900 mm nominal	550.6–583.4	5400–5721
1200 mm nominal	937.5–958.4	9194–9399
1400 mm nominal	1168–1347	11450–13210
1500 mm nominal	1377–1451	13500–14230
1800 mm nominal	1929	18920

Aluminium		
Rainwater, with ears		
50 mm nominal		
Cast	1.2	12
Wrought		
Heavy, 1.2 mm thick	0.7	7
Light, 0.7 mm thick	0.4	4
65 mm nominal		
Cast	1.5	15
Wrought		
Heavy, 1.2 mm thick	0.9	9
Light, 0.7 mm thick	0.6	6
75 mm nominal		
Cast	2.4	24
Wrought		
Heavy, 1.2 mm thick	1.0	10
Light, 0.7 mm thick	0.7	7
100 mm nominal		
Cast	2.5	25
Wrought		
Heavy, 1.2 mm thick	1.5	15

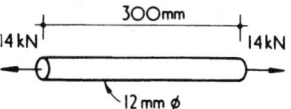

41.1 *A bar of uniform cross-section under a tensile force*

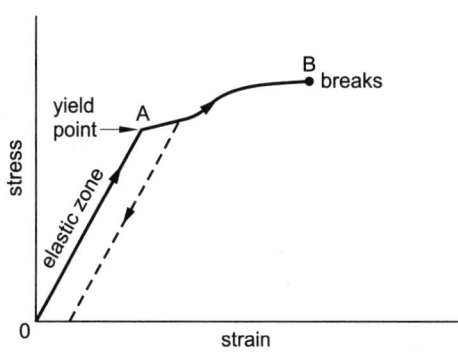

41.2 *Stress–strain diagram for steel showing the yield point where Hooke's Law (stress is proportional to strain) no longer operates. Dotted line shows deformation caused when stress is reduced after the yield point, material does not return to its original form*

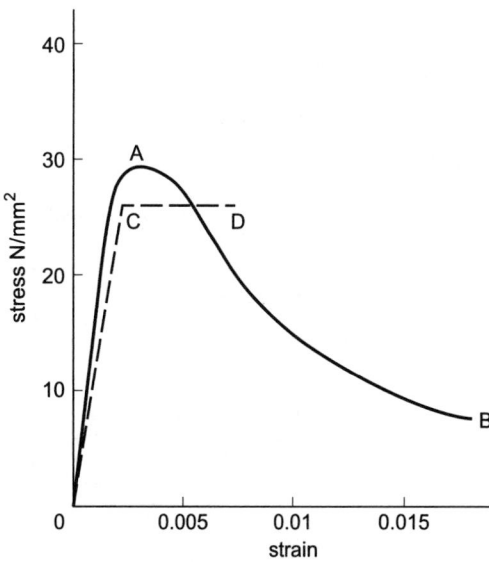

41.3 *Stress–strain diagram for a typical concrete*

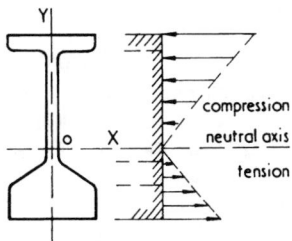

41.4 *Structural member under pure bending*

Table V Design imposed loads from BS 6399-Part 1:1996

Type of activity or occupancy for part of the building or structure	Examples of specific use		Uniformly distributed load (kN/m²)	Concentrated load (kN)
A Domestic and residential activities (also see category C)	All usages within self-contained dwelling units. Communal areas (including kitchens) in blocks of flats with limited use (see note 1) (for communal areas in other blocks of flats see C3 and below)		1.5	1.4
	Bedrooms and dormitories exeept those in hotels and motels		1.5	1.8
	Bedrooms in hotels and motels Hospital wards Toilet areas		2.0	1.8
	Billiard rooms		2.0	2.7
	Communal kitchens except in flats covered by note 1		3.0	4.5
	Balconies	Single-dwelling units and communal areas in blocks of flats with limited use (see note 1)	1.5	1.4
		Guest houses, residential clubs and communal areas in blocks of flats except as covered by note 1	Same as rooms to which they give access but with a minimum of 3.0	1.5/m run concentrated at the outer edge
		Hotels and motels	Same as rooms to which they give access but with a minimum of 4.0	1.5/m run concentrated at the outer edge
B Offices and work areas not covered elsewhere	Operating theatres, X-ray rooms, utility rooms		2.0	4.5
	Work rooms (light industrial) without storage		2.5	1.8
	Offices for general use		2.5	2.7
	Banking halls		3.0	2.7
	Kitchens, laundries, laboratories		3.0	4.5
	Rooms with mainframe computers or similar equipment		3.5	4.5
	Machinery halls, circulation spaces therein		4.0	4.5
	Projection rooms		5.0	To be determined for specific use
	Factories, workshops and similar buildings (general industrial)		5.0	4.5
	Foundries		20.0	To be determined for specific use
	Catwalks		–	1.0 at 1 m centres
	Balconies		Same as rooms to which they give access but with a minimum of 4.0	1.5/m run concentrated at the outer edge
	Fly galleries		4.5 kN/m run distributed uniformly over width	–
	Ladders		–	1.5 rung load
C Areas where people may congregate	Public, institutional and communal dining rooms and lounges, cafes and restaurants (see note 2)		2.0	2.7
C1 Areas with tables	Reading rooms with no book storage		2.5	4.5
	Classrooms		3.0	2.7
C2 Areas with fixed seats	Assembly areas with fixed seating (see note 3)		4.0	3.6
	Places of worship		3.0	2.7
C3 Areas without obstacles for moving people	Corridors, hallways, aisles, stairs, landings etc in institutional type buildings (not subject to crowds or wheeled vehicles), hostels, guest houses, residential clubs, and communal areas in blocks of flats not covered by note 1. (For communal areas in blocks of flats covered by note 1, see A)	Corridors, hallways, aisles etc (foot traffic only)	3.0	4.5
		Stairs and landings (foot traffic only)	3.0	4.0
	Corridors, hallways, aisles, stairs, landings, etc in all other buildings including hotels and motels and institutional buildings	Corridors, hallways, aisles, etc (foot traffic only)	4.0	4.5
		Corridors, hallways, aisles, etc, subject to wheeled vehicles, trolleys etc	5.0	4.5
		Stairs and landings (foot traffic only)	4.0	4.0
	Industrial walkways (light duty)		3.0	4.5
	Industrial walkways (general duty)		5.0	4.5
	Industrial walkways (heavy duty)		7.5	4.5
	Museum floors and art galleries for exhibition purposes		4.0	4.5
	Balconies (except as specified in A)		Same as rooms to which they give access but with a minimum of 4.0	1.5/m run concentrated at the outer edge
	Fly galleries		4.5 kN/m run distributed uniformly over width	–

Table V *Continued*

Type of activity or occupancy for part of the building or structure	Examples of specific use	Uniformly distributed load (kN/m²)	Concentrated load (kN)
C4 Areas with possible physical activities (see clause 9)	Dance halls and studios, gymnasia, stages	5.0	3.6
	Drill halls and drill rooms	5.0	9.0
C5 Areas susceptible to overcrowding (see clause 9)	Assembly areas without fixed seating, concert halls, bars, places of worship and grandstands	5.0	3.6
	Stages in public assembly areas	7.5	4.5
D Shopping areas	Shop floors for the sale and display of merchandise	4.0	3.6
E Warehousing and storage areas. Areas subject to accumulation of goods. Areas for equipment and plant	General areas for static equipment not specified elsewhere (institutional and public buildings)	2.0	1.8
	Reading rooms with book storage, eg libraries	4.0	4.5
	General storage other than those specified	2.4 for each metre of storage height	7.0
	File rooms, filing and storage space (offices)	5.0	4.5
	Stack rooms (books)	2.4 for each metre in storage height but with a minimum of 6.5	7.0
	Paper storage for printing plants and stationery stores	4.0 for each metre of storage height	9.0
	Dense mobile stacking (books) on mobile trolleys, in public and institutional buildings	4.8 for each metre of storage height but with a minimum of 9.6	7.0
	Dense mobile stacking (books) on mobile trucks, in warehouses	4.8 for each metre of storage height but with a minimum of 15.0	7.0
	Cold storage	5.0 for each metre of storage height but with a minimum of 15.0	9.0
	Plant rooms, boiler rooms, fan rooms, etc, including weight of machinery	7.5	4.5
	Ladders	–	1.5 rung load
F	Parking for cars, light vans, etc. not exceeding 2500 kg gross mass, including garages, driveways and ramps	2.5	9.0
G	Vehicles exceeding 2500 kg. Driveways, ramps, repair workshops, footpaths with vehicle access, and car parking	To be determined for specific use	

Note 1. Communal areas in blocks of flats with limited use refers to blocks of flats not more than three storeys in height and with not more than four self-contained dwelling units per floor accessible from one staircase.

Note 2. Where these same areas may be subjected to loads due to physical activities or overcrowding, e.g. a hotel dining room used as a dance floor, imposed loads should be based on occupancy C4 or C5 as appropriate. Reference should also be made to clause 9.

Note 3. Fixed seating is seating where its removal and the use of the space for other purposes is improbable.

expressed as N/mm², and this form is allowable and the most commonly used.

2.10 Tension members

If the stress in the member tends to lengthen it, it is said to be in *tension*. Elements in tension are called *ties*. In many ways, this is the simplest kind of stress. Some materials are ideal for resisting it: steel in particular. Cables, wires and chains can be used to carry tension, but no other kind of force. Other materials have little or no resistance to tension: stone, cast iron and unreinforced concrete fall into this category.

2.11 Compression members

If the stress in the member tends to shorten it, it is in *compression*. Elements in compression are called *struts* if they are small; or sometimes *columns*, *piers* or *stanchions*. The term used depends on the position and the material of which they are composed.

Most materials other than cables, wires and chains can be used to carry compression. However, there is an instability phenomenon that occurs with compression called *buckling*. For some members, particularly those that are slender in comparison with their length, increase of compressive load will cause it to bend until failure occurs in tension on one side. It is this buckling effect that causes the collapse of towers and high walls of masonry construction.

2.12 Pin-jointed frames

Some structures are designed and constructed completely of members that are either in pure tension or compression. The familiar roof truss is of this type; the general term for which is *pin-jointed frame*. Methods for finding the magnitude of the forces in each member can be found in the standard textbooks. In practice, very few such structures are actually physically pin-jointed (although some have been built), but the use of conventional jointing has not been found significantly to affect the performance calculated from the theoretical assumptions.

2.13 Bending

Struts and ties transmit forces along their length without changing the magnitude or direction of those forces. However, the purpose of most structures is to make some change in the disposition of the forces carrying their loads: as for example, to provide a large open space beneath it. This change could be accomplished by using pin-jointed frames, but most commonly bending members, or *beams*, are used.

Bending is the phenomenon by which a single member has both compression and tension within it. For the normal case of a beam supported at each end with a load in the centre of the span, there will be compression in the top layers of the beam, and tension in the bottom layers. Somewhere in the middle of the beam will be layer with no stress at all. This layer is known as the *neutral axis*, **41.4**.

A cross-section of a beam will have imposed on it a combination of forces known as a *bending moment*. A bending moment is to a beam what a load is to a column.

2.14 Materials in bending

Since bending includes both compression and tension, only materials that are strong in both are generally suitable for beams. Steel and timber are good examples of such materials. Stone, being weak in tension, makes poor bending members. This is the reason why the ancient Greeks had to build their columns so close together. Only when the arch had been invented could the spans be increased, because the arch is wholly in compression. Cast iron is another material weak in tension, although not as weak as stone. Beams of this material have lower flanges larger than the upper to allow for this. Concrete is also poor under tensile force, so steel is used to reinforce the bottom of concrete beams.

2.15 Beams

Beams are of a number of different types:

● *Simply supported*, **41.5**. Each end is assumed to be completely free to move rotationally and one end is also free to move in the direction of the beam length. The bending moments will then be zero at the ends, and if the loading is uniformly distributed along the length of the beam it will be a maximum at mid-span.

● *Cantilever*, **41.6**. This type is supported only at one end where it is fixed in both position and rotationally. The bending moment will be zero at the free end and a maximum at the support.

● *Encastré* or built-in at both ends, **41.7**. This type of beam is called *statically indeterminate* as the values of the bending moments are not calculable by normal statical methods. These values actually depend on a number of imponderables, such as how much fixity there is. However, engineers by-pass these problems by making assumptions. Since the basic principle of structural engineering borne out by experience is that a structure will only fail when all possible modes of support have been exhausted, any reasonable assumption followed through would be sufficient to carry the loading. Maximum moments will occur in encastré beams either at midspan or at one, other or both ends.

● *Continuous*, **41.8**. A beam on several supports can be seen as a number of contiguous encastré beams – in fact one method of calculation for these starts with this assumption. Generally the maximum moments occur over the supports.

● *Lintols*, **41.9**. Beams that are supported on brickwork, such as lintols over doorways and windows, are not considered structurally encastré, and are normally designed as simply supported.

2.16 Bending moments

In order to design a beam an engineer first calculates the bending moments at critical sections, and from these derives the maximum stresses at those sections. This can be a time-consuming and complicated matter. For a large number of the simpler cases the midspan of an assumed simply supported beam will suffice to give

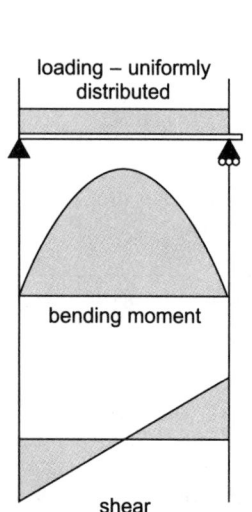

41.5 *Simply supported beam under uniform loading*

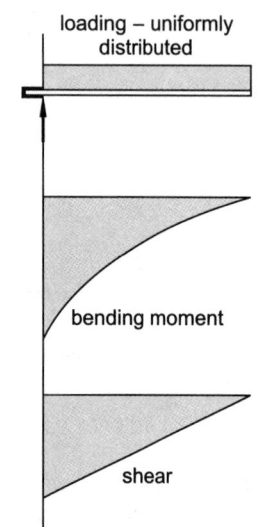

41.6 *Cantilever beam*

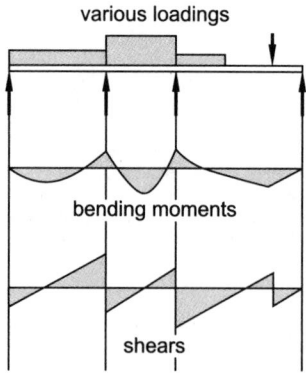

41.8 *Continuous beams*

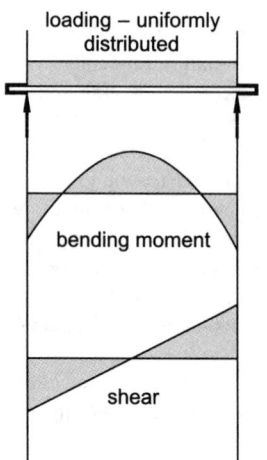

41.7 *Encastré beam*

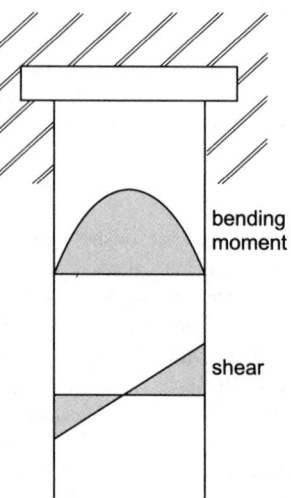

41.9 *Lintol*

Table VI Standard beam conditions

1 Cantllevers

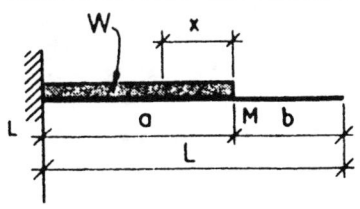

$$M_x = \frac{Wx^2}{2a} \quad M_{max} = \frac{Wa}{2}$$

$$S_{max} = R_L = W$$

$$\delta_M = \frac{Wa^3}{8EI}$$

$$\delta_{max} = \delta_R = \frac{Wa^3}{8EI} \times \left(1 + \frac{4b}{3a}\right)$$

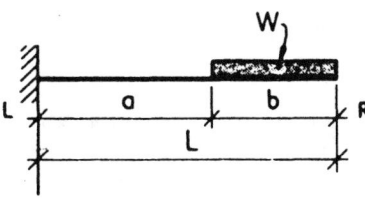

$$M_{max} = W\left(a + \frac{b}{2}\right)$$

$$S_{max} = R_L = W$$

$$\delta_{max} = \delta_R$$

$$= \frac{W}{24EI}(8a^3 + 18a^2b + 12ab^2 + 3b^3)$$

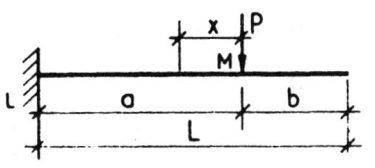

$$M_x = P_x \quad M_{max} = Pa$$

$$S_{max} = R_L = P$$

$$\delta_M = \frac{Pa^3}{3EI}$$

$$\delta_{max} = \delta_R = \frac{Pa^3}{3EI} \times \left(1 + \frac{3b}{2a}\right)$$

2 Free support beams

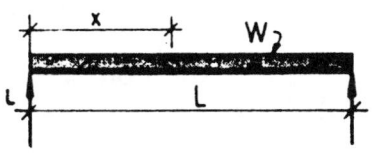

$$M_x = \frac{Wx}{2}\left(1 - \frac{x}{L}\right)$$

$$M_{max} = \frac{WL}{8}$$

$$R_L = R_R = \frac{W}{2}$$

$$\delta_{max} \text{ at centre} = \frac{5}{384} \times \frac{WL^3}{EI}$$

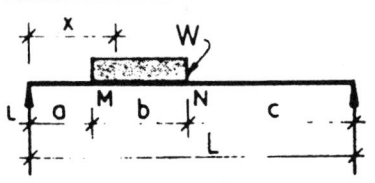

$$M_{max} = \frac{W}{b}\left(\frac{x^2 - a^2}{2}\right)$$

when

$$x = a + R_L \times \frac{b}{W}$$

$$R_L = \frac{W}{L}\left(\frac{b}{2} + c\right)$$

$$R_R = \frac{W}{L}\left(\frac{b}{2} + a\right)$$

if $a = c$

$$M = \frac{W}{8}(L + 2a)$$

$$\delta_{max} = \frac{W}{384EI} \times (8L^3 - 4Lb^2 + b^3)$$

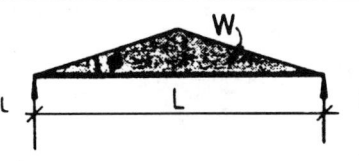

$$M_x = W_x\left(\frac{1}{2} - \frac{2X^2}{3L^2}\right)$$

$$M_{max} = \frac{WL}{6}$$

$$R_L = R_R = \frac{W}{2}$$

$$\delta_{max} = \frac{WL^3}{60EI}$$

If $\phi = 60° \quad M = 0.0725 \, wL^3$

$$R = 0.217 \, wL^2$$

Table VI *Continued*

2 Free support beams, *continued*

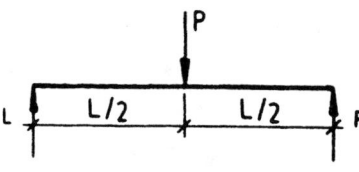

$$M_{max} = \frac{PL}{4}$$

$$R_L = R_R = \frac{P}{2}$$

$$\delta_{max} = \frac{PL^3}{48EI}$$

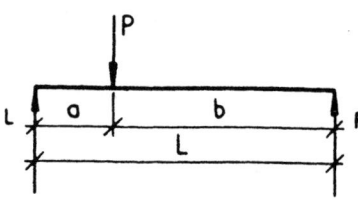

$$M_{max} = P\frac{ab}{L} = M_p$$

$$R_L = \frac{Pb}{L} \quad R_R = \frac{Pa}{L}$$

δ_{max} always occurs within 0.0774L of the centre of the beam.
When b > a

$$\delta_{centre} = \frac{PL^3}{48EI} \times \left[3\frac{a}{L} - 4\left(\frac{a}{L}\right)^3\right]$$

This value is always within 2.5 per cent of the maximum value.

$$\delta_p = \frac{PL^3}{3EI}\left(\frac{a}{L}\right)^2\left(1 - \frac{a^2}{L}\right)^2$$

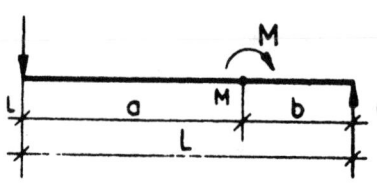

$$M_{ML} = M\frac{a}{L} \quad M_{MR} = M\frac{b}{L}$$

$$R_A = R_B = \frac{M}{L}$$

when a > b

$$\delta_M = -\frac{Mab}{3EI}\left(\frac{a}{L} - \frac{b}{L}\right)$$

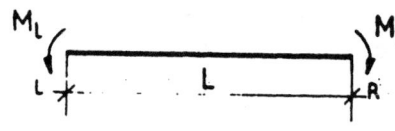

$$R_L = -R_R = \frac{M_L - M_R}{L}$$

when $M_L = M_R$,

$$\delta_{max} = -\frac{ML^2}{8EI}$$

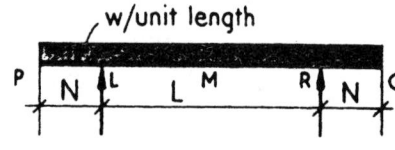

$$M_L = M_R = -\frac{wN^2}{2}$$

$$M_{max} = \frac{WL^2}{8} + M_L$$

$$R_L = R_R = w\left(N + \frac{L}{2}\right)$$

$$\delta_p = \delta_q = \frac{wL^3N}{24EI} \times (1 - 6n^2 - 3n^3)$$

$$\delta_{max} = \frac{wL^4}{384EI}(5 - 24n^2)$$

$$n = \frac{N}{L}$$

3 Fixed-end beams

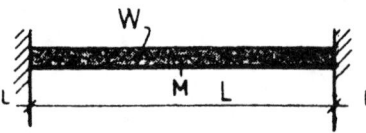

$$M_L = M_R = -\frac{WL}{12}$$

$$M_M = \frac{WL}{24}$$

$$R_L = R_R = \frac{W}{2}$$

points of contraflexure 0.21L from each end

$$\delta_{max} = \frac{WL^3}{384EI}$$

Table VI *Continued*

3 Fixed-end beams, *continued*

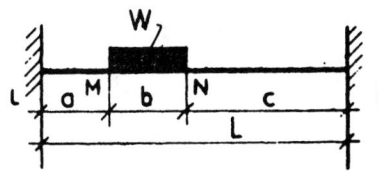

$$M_L = -\frac{W}{12L^2b}$$

$$[c^3(4L - 3c) - c^3(4L - 3c)]$$

$$M_R = -\frac{W}{12L^2b}$$

$$[d^3(4L - 3d) - a^3(4L - 3a)]$$

$$a + b = d$$

$$b + c = e$$

when r = reaction if the beam were simply supported.

$$R_L = r_L + \frac{M_L - M_R}{L}$$

$$R_R = r_R + \frac{M_R - M_L}{L}$$

when a = c,

$$\delta_{max} = \frac{W}{384EI} \times (L^3 + 2L^2a + 4La^2 - 8a^3)$$

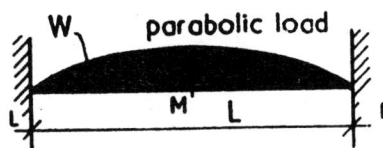

$$M_L = M_R = -\frac{WL}{10}$$

$$M_M = \frac{5WL}{32} - \frac{WL}{10} = \frac{9WL}{160}$$

$$R_L = R_B = \frac{W}{2}$$

$$\delta_{max} = \frac{1.3WL^3}{384EI}$$

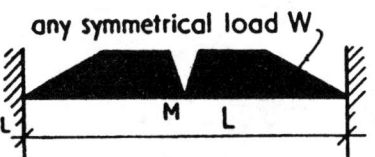

$$M_L = M_R = -\frac{A_s}{L}$$

where A_S is the area of the free bending moment diagram

$$R_L = R_R = \frac{W}{2}$$

$$\delta_{max} = \frac{A_Sx - A_1x_1}{2EI}$$

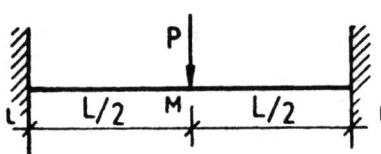

$$M_L = M_R = -\frac{PL}{8}$$

$$M_M = \frac{PL}{8}$$

$$R_L = R_R = \frac{P}{2}$$

$$\delta_{max} = \frac{PL^3}{192EI}$$

Table VI *Continued*

3 Fixed-end beams, *continued*

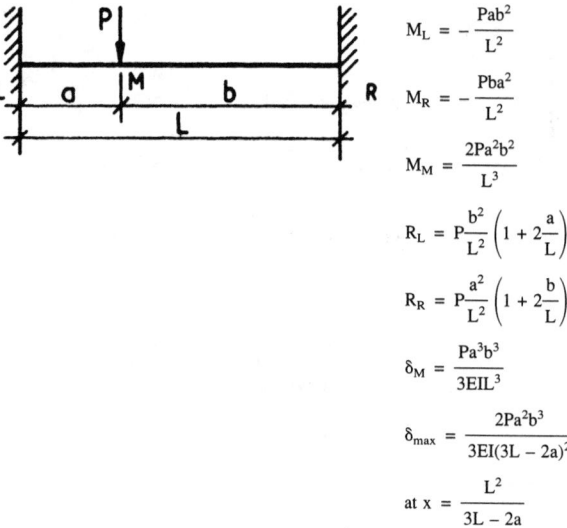

$$M_L = -\frac{Pab^2}{L^2}$$

$$M_R = -\frac{Pba^2}{L^2}$$

$$M_M = \frac{2Pa^2b^2}{L^3}$$

$$R_L = P\frac{b^2}{L^2}\left(1 + 2\frac{a}{L}\right)$$

$$R_R = P\frac{a^2}{L^2}\left(1 + 2\frac{b}{L}\right)$$

$$\delta_M = \frac{Pa^3b^3}{3EIL^3}$$

$$\delta_{max} = \frac{2Pa^2b^3}{3EI(3L - 2a)^2}$$

$$\text{at } x = \frac{L^2}{3L - 2a}$$

4 Propped cantilevers

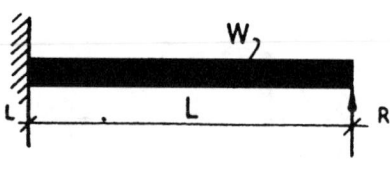

$$M_L = -\frac{WL}{8}$$

$$M_{max} = \frac{9WL}{128} \text{ at } x' = \tfrac{5}{8}$$

$$M = 0 \text{ at } x' = \tfrac{1}{4}$$

$$R_L = \tfrac{5}{8}W$$

$$R_R = \tfrac{3}{8}W$$

$$\text{if } m = 1 - X'$$

$$\delta = \frac{WL^3}{48EI} \times (m - 3m^3 + 2m^4)$$

$$\delta_{max} = \frac{WL^3}{185EI}$$

$$\text{at } X' = 0.5785$$

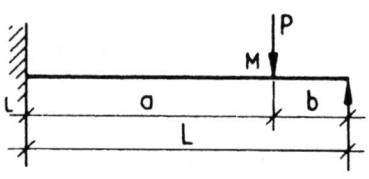

$$M_L = -\frac{Pb}{2}(1 - b^{12})$$

(maximum 0.193PL if b′ = 0.577)

$$M_M = \frac{Pb}{2}(2 - 3b' + b^{13})$$

(maximum 0.174PL if b′ = 0.366)

$$R_R = \tfrac{1}{2}Pa^{12}(b' + 2)$$

$$\delta_m = \frac{Pa^3b^2}{12EIL^3} - (4L - a)$$

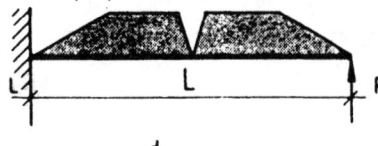

any symmetrical load W

centre of gravity of s

If A_s = area of free bending moment diagram

$$M_L = \frac{3A_s}{2L}$$

$$R_L = \frac{W}{2} + \frac{M_L}{L}$$

$$R_R = \frac{W}{2} - \frac{M_L}{L}$$

δ_{max} at X where area Q = area R

$$\delta_{max} = \frac{\text{area } S \times X \times d}{EI}$$

Table VII Properties of sections

Section shape	Area of section A	Distance (y_1) of extremity of section from neutral axis	Moment of inertia about neutral axis $X \times (I_x)$	Modulus $Z_x = \left(\dfrac{I_x}{Y_1}\right)$	Radius of gyration $k = \sqrt{\dfrac{I_x}{A}}$
	a^2	$\dfrac{a}{2}$	$\dfrac{a^4}{12}$	$\dfrac{a^3}{6}$	$\dfrac{a}{\sqrt{12}} = 0.289a$
	bd	$\dfrac{d}{2}$	$\dfrac{1}{12}bd^3$	$\dfrac{1}{6}bd^2$	$\dfrac{d}{\sqrt{12}} = 0.289d$
	a^2	$\dfrac{a}{\sqrt{2}} = 0.707a$	$\dfrac{a^4}{12}$	$\dfrac{\sqrt{2}}{12}a^3 = 0.118a^3$	$\dfrac{a}{\sqrt{12}} = 0.289a$
	$\dfrac{bd}{2}$	$\dfrac{d}{3}$	$\dfrac{bd^3}{36}$	$\dfrac{bd^2}{24}$	$\dfrac{d}{\sqrt{18}} = 0.236d$
	$\dfrac{a+b}{2}d$	$\dfrac{a+2b}{a+b}\dfrac{d}{3}$	$\dfrac{a^2+4ab+b^2}{36(a+b)}d^3$	$\dfrac{a^2+4ab+b^2}{12(a+2b)}d^2$	$d\sqrt{\dfrac{a^2+4ab+b^2}{18(a+b)^2}}$
	$\dfrac{\pi d^2}{4} = 0.7854d^2$	$\dfrac{d}{2}$	$\dfrac{\pi d^4}{64} = 0.0491d^4$	$\dfrac{\pi d^3}{32} = 0.0982d^3$	$\dfrac{d}{4}$
	$\dfrac{\pi}{4}(d^2 - d_1^2)$	$\dfrac{d}{2}$	$\dfrac{\pi}{64}(d^4 - d_1^4)$	$\dfrac{\pi}{32}\dfrac{d^4 - d_1^4}{d}$	$\dfrac{\sqrt{d^2 + d_1^2}}{4}$
	$\dfrac{\pi d^2}{8} = 0.3927d^2$	$\dfrac{2d}{3\pi} = 0.212d$	$\dfrac{9\pi^2 - 64}{1152\pi}d^4 = 0.007d^4$	$\dfrac{(9\pi^2 - 64)d^3}{192(3\pi - 4)} = 0.024d^3$	$\dfrac{\sqrt{9\pi^2 - 64}d}{12\pi} = 0.132d$
	$\dfrac{\pi bd}{4} = 0.7854bd$	$\dfrac{d}{2}$	$\dfrac{\pi bd^3}{64} = 0.0491bd^3$	$\dfrac{\pi bd^2}{32} = 0.0982bd^2$	$\dfrac{d}{4}$
	$\dfrac{\pi}{4}(bd - b_1 d_1)$	$\dfrac{d}{2}$	$\dfrac{\pi}{64}(bd^3 - b_1 d_1^3)$	$\dfrac{\pi}{32}\dfrac{bd^3 - b_1 d_1^3}{d}$	$\tfrac{1}{4}\sqrt{\dfrac{bd^3 - b_1 d_1^3}{bd - b_1 d_1}}$
	$(bd - b_1 d_1)$	$\dfrac{d}{2}$	$\dfrac{1}{12}(bd^3 - b_1 d_1^3)$	$\dfrac{bd^3 - b_1 d_1^3}{6d}$	$\sqrt{\dfrac{bd^3 - b_1 d_1^3}{12(bd - b_1 d_1)}}$
	$(bd - b_1 d_1)$	$\dfrac{d}{2}$	$\dfrac{1}{12}(bd^3 - b_1 d_1^3)$	$\dfrac{bd^3 - b_1 d_1^3}{6d}$	$\sqrt{\dfrac{bd^3 - b_1 d_1^3}{12(bd - b_1 d_1)}}$
	$(bd - b_1 d_1)$	$\dfrac{d}{2}$	$\dfrac{1}{12}(bd^3 - b_1 d_1^3)$	$\dfrac{bd^3 - b_1 d_1^3}{6d}$	$\sqrt{\dfrac{bd^3 - b_1 d_1^3}{12(bd - b_1 d_1)}}$

Table VII *Continued*

Section shape	Area of section A	Distance (y_1) of extremity of section from neutral axis	Moment of inertia about neutral axis $X \times (I_x)$	Modulus $Z_x = \left(\dfrac{I_x}{Y_1}\right)$	Radius of gyration $k = \sqrt{\dfrac{I_x}{A}}$
	$(bd - b_1 d_1)$	$\dfrac{bd^2 - 2b_1 d_1 d + b_1 d_1{}^2}{2(bd - b_1 d_1)}$	$\dfrac{(bd^2 - b_1 d_1{}^2)^2 - 4bdb_1 d_1(d - d_1)^2}{12(bd - b_1 d_1)}$	$\dfrac{(bd^2 - b_1 d_1{}^2)^2 - 4bdb_1 d_1(d - d_1)^2}{6(bd^2 - 2bdd_1 + b_1 d_1{}^2)}$	—
	$(bd - b_1 d_1)$	$\dfrac{bd^2 - 2b_1 d_1 d + b_1 d_1{}^2}{2(bd - b_1 d_1)}$	$\dfrac{(bd^2 - b_1 d_1{}^2)^2 - 4bdb_1 d_1(d - d_1)^2}{12(bd - b_1 d_1)}$	$\dfrac{(bd^2 - b_1 d_1{}^2)^2) - 4bdb_1 d_1(d - d_1)^2}{6(bd^2 - 2bdb_1 + b_1 d_1{}^2)}$	—
	$(bd - b_1 d_1)$	$\dfrac{bd^2 - 2b_1 d_1 d + b_1 d_1{}^2}{2(bd - b_1 d_1)}$	$\dfrac{(bd^2 - b_1 d_1{}^2)^2 - 4bdb_1 d_1(d - d_1)^2}{12(bd - b_1 d_1)}$	$\dfrac{(bd^2 - b_1 d_1{}^2)^2) - 4bdb_1 d_1(d - d_1)^2}{6(bd^2 - 2bdb_1 + b_1 d_1{}^2)}$	—
	$(bd_1 + b_1 d)$	$\dfrac{d}{2}$	$\dfrac{1}{12}(bd_1{}^3 + b_1 d^3)$	$\dfrac{b_1 d^3 + bd_1{}^3}{6d}$	$\sqrt{\dfrac{bd_1{}^3 + b_1 d^3}{12(bd_1 + b_1 d)}}$
	$(bd_1 + b_1 d)$	$\dfrac{d}{2}$	$\dfrac{1}{12}(bd_1{}^3 + b_1 d^3)$	$\dfrac{b_1 d^3 + bd_1{}^3}{6d}$	$\sqrt{\dfrac{bd_1{}^3 + b_1 d^3}{12(bd_1 - b_1 d)}}$
	$(bd_1 + b_1 d)$	$\dfrac{d}{2}$	$\dfrac{1}{12}(bd_1{}^3 + b_1 d^3)$	$\dfrac{b_1 d^3 + bd_1{}^3}{6d}$	$\sqrt{\dfrac{bd_1{}^3 + bd_1 d^3}{12(bd_1 + b_1 d)}}$

a safe answer, if not perhaps the most economical. Table VI gives maximum bending moments for the common cases likely to be met.

2.17 Bending stresses

Once the bending moment M is known, the stress f at any layer distance y from the neutral axis can be found from:

$$\frac{M}{y} = \frac{f}{I}$$

It is seen that the stress in the extreme fibre of a beam depends on the *second moment of area (I)* of the cross-section. While a full exposition of this parameter is beyond the scope of this chapter, values for a number of common cross-sectional shapes can be found in Table VII. Suffice it to say that the larger the second moment of area is, the smaller will the maximum stress be. It is therefore beneficial to choose cross-section shapes that have large *I*-values for the given area of material. The most common shape of cross-section for a steel beam is an *I* for this reason. The further away from the neutral axis that the flanges can be, the less they need be in area to give a required second moment of area.

There is a limit to this, however. Since the top flange is in compression, if it becomes too small in itself, and too divorced from the rest of the beam, it can buckle. This is particularly significant in the design of steelwork, and is the reason that bending stresses in the extreme fibres of steel beams are reduced well below the ultimate strength of the material.

2.18 Shear

A section of a beam is not only acted on by a bending moment. Most cross-sections will also have to carry a force in the plane of the section, called a *shear force*. Generally, the shear will be greatest at the supports of a beam, and least at midspan.

In the case of an I-section, the shear force acts mainly within the web connecting together the two flanges that are in compression

Table VIII Maximum span/depth ratios (rule-of thumb)

Concrete beams	20
Concrete slabs	30
Steel beams (I-section)	25
Timber joists	20

and tension. If the web becomes too slender it can buckle under the influence of the shear force.

2.19 Deflection

In para **2.06** it was said that there could be no stress without strain. Since the top of the beam is in compression, it must reduce in length; the bottom, in tension, must stretch. This will lead to the beam taking up a curved form: in the case of a simply supported beam with vertical loading, it will sag. Excessive sagging is not only unsightly, it may cause damage to finishes such as plaster ceilings, or cause load to be transferred onto partitions that are not designed to carry such load. Formulæ are published giving the deflections of various kinds of beams under different loadings (some included in Table VI).

As a guide to probable deflection characteristics, rule-of-thumb span-to-depth ratios are often used. Provided the use in confined to preliminary investigation, and the actual deflections are later checked, the ratios in Table VIII will be found of value.

3 STRUCTURAL MATERIALS

3.01 The third major factor in structural design is a knowledge of the behaviour of the materials used. These have remained almost unchanged over the years. The basic palette consists of masonry (stone, brick and block), timber, steel and reinforced concrete. New materials such as plastics are unlikely to have more than a marginal effect in the immediate future. Table IX compares some properties of structural interest of these materials.

Table IX Comparison of material properties

Property	Masonry (clay brickwork)	Reinforced concrete (with 4% reinforcement)	Steel (mild steel)	Wood (whitewood)	Glass reinforced plastic (polyester)	Glass (annealed soda glass)	Fabric (polyester yarn with pvc coating)
Type of material	Ceramic	Ceramic with metal	Metal	Natural Composite	Synthetic Composite	Glass	Polymer
Specific gravity (w)	2.2	2.4	8.0	0.46	1.8	2.4	1.4
Weight (p) kN/m³	22	24	78	4.5	18	24	14
Tensile strength (σ_{TS}) N/mm²	1	18	400	75	250	50 (1500 for unflawed glass)	1000
Compressive strength (σ_c) N/mm²	15	45	400	25	150	200	none
Flexural strength – modulus of rupture (σ_b) N/mm²	1.5	18	400	50	300	55	none
Elastic modulus (E) kN/mm²	20	35	210	10	15	74	14
Fracture toughness (K_c) MN/m$^{3/2}$	0.9	(0.6 for unreinforced concrete)	140 (low-carbon steel) 50 (medium-carbon steel)	12	20	0.7	Tear strength can be high
Toughness (G_c) kJ/m²	0.02	(0.03 for unreinforced concrete)	100 (low-carbon steel) 12 (medium-carbon steel)	10	10	0.01	…
Impact strength	negligible	tolerable if reinforced	good	moderately good	moderately good	negligible	good
Elongation % ductility	none	5 (but cracks develop)	22	…	…	none	14
Creep factor – final creep strain to elastic strain at working stresses	2	2	negligible at normal temperatures	1	1–10 (high at high temperatures)	negligible at normal temperatures	significant at high stresses
Fatigue ratio in reversed bending – working stress as a proportion of flexural strength below which fatigue does not affect life of material (10⁷ cs)	…	…	0.42	0.30	0.20	…	…
Damping – damping ratio	…	high	negligible	moderate	high	negligible	…
Reversible moisture movement	+0.05	0.02	none	1.50	small	none	small
Movement % initial expansion (+) or shrinkage (–) %	0.02	–0.02	none	…	small	none	…
Coefficient of thermal expansion (α) × 10⁻⁶/°C	6	12	12	4	14	8	…
Thermal conductivity at 5% moisture content (λ) W/m°C	0.70	2.00	45.00	0.13	0.20	1.00	…
Temperature held 1 hour at which material begins to soften or has lost half its strength °C	…	300–800	480	180	150	500	70 (failure at joints)
Energy required to make material GJ/m³ (1 tonne of oil is energy equivalent of 40 GJ)	9	5	260 (320 aluminium)	0.3	100	50	…
Strength to weight ratio (σ_{TS}/w or σ_b/w) N/mm²	0.5	8	60	150	145	22	780
Elastic modulus to weight ratio (E/w) kN/mm²	9	15	27	22	8	30	10
Efficiency of material for making light column elements of solid section ($E^{1/2}/w$) kN$^{1/2}$/mm	2	2.5	1.8	7	2.5	…	…
Efficiency of material for making light wall panels of solid section ($E^{1/3}/w$) kN$^{1/3}$/mm$^{5/3}$	1.2	1.4	0.8	4.8	1.5	1.8	…
Bulk cost	low	low	high	very low	very high	high	very high
Tensile strength to bulk cost	very low	low	high	high	low	very low	high
Compressive strength to bulk cost	high	high	high	moderate	very low	low	…
Elastic modulus to bulk cost	high	high	high	moderate	very low	low	very low
Fire resistance of individual elements	very high	high	very low	high	very low	very low	…
Combustibility of untreated material	non-combustible	non-combustible	non-combustible	combustible	combustible	non-combustible	combustible
Flame spread of untreated material	none	none	none	flame spread	flame spread	none	flame spread
Smoke generation	none	none	none	toxic fumes	toxic fumes	none	toxic fumes
Durability of treated material in temperate climate	indefinite	indefinite	>50 years	variable	<50 years	indefinite	15 years

4 MASONRY

4.01 Masonry is the general term used for loadbearing construction in brick, block and stone; these are materials of interest to architects. Since they and the mortar that is used to fill the gaps between their elements are all weak in tension, such construction is normally used to carry only simple compressive forces in vertical elements such as walls and piers, sometimes in arches. Nevertheless, tensile stresses up to 0.1 N/mm^2 may be acceptable in certain circumstances.

4.02 Design

The *Manual for the design of plain masonry in building structures* (the Red Book) should be useful to non-experts using simple structural masonry (see Bibliography).

4.03 Table X gives properties of common masonry materials.

4.04 Vertical loadbearing elements

A *wall* is a vertical load-carrying element whose length in plan is at least four times its width, otherwise it is a *column*. A *pier* is a column integral with a wall. References to walls apply also to columns and piers unless stated otherwise.

The load-carrying capacity of a wall depends on:

- The crushing strength of the brick, block or stone
- The composition of the mortar
- The size and shape of the brick, block or stone
- The height of the wall relative to its width – its slenderness ratio
- The eccentricity of the loading

Details of design methods will be found in the publications listed in the Bibliography.

Tables XI to XV give information on typical masonry designs. Although popular in the past, masonry is rarely used for floors nowadays. However, vaults and domed roofs continue to be built in traditional types of buildings such as churches.

5 TIMBER

5.01 Structure of timber

Timber is probably the oldest building material used by humans. Wood is composed of hollow tubular fibres of cellulose impregnated with the resin lignin, packed closely together not unlike a bundle of drinking straws. The result is that the material is strong

Table X Properties of masonry as built

Property	Clay brickwork	Calcium silicate brickwork	Dense concrete blockwork	Aerated concrete blockwork	Natural limestone
Specific gravity	2.2	2.0	2.1	0.9	2.2
Weight kN/m³	22	20	21	9	22
Compressive strength N/mm²	3–24	3–8	3–24	6	10
Flexural strength N/mm² – parallel to bed joints – perpendicular to bed joints	2.0 0.8	1.2 0.4	1.0 0.4	0.5 0.3	...
Elastic modulus kN/mm²	5–25	14–18	5–25	2–8	15
Creep factor – final creep strain to elastic strain at working stresses	1.2–4.0	...	2.0–7.0	2.0	
Reversible moisture Movement %	0.02	0.01–0.05	0.02–0.04	0.02–0.03	0.01
Initial moisture expansion (+) or Drying Shrinkage (–) %	+0.02–+0.08	–0.01––0.05	–0.02––0.06	–0.05––0.09	+0.01
Coefficient of thermal expansion × 10⁻⁶/°C	5–8	8–14	6–12	8	4
Thermal Conductivity at 5% moisture content W/m°C	1.3	1.2	1.2	0.3	1.3

Table XI Masonry – vertical support elements

Element	Horizontal and vertical section	Typical heights (h) (m)	h/d between lateral supports	Critical factors for sizing	Remarks
Masonry column		1–4	15–20	Buckling and crushing (h/d>6) Crushing (h/d<6) Bending	h is vertical distance between lateral supports and d is thickness of column
Masonry wall		1–5	18–22	Buckling and crushing (h/d>6) Crushing (h/d<6) Bending	h is vertical distance between horizontal lateral supports; wall may also have vertical lateral supports
Reinforced and prestressed masonry columns and walls		2–7	20–35	Bending	h is vertical distance between horizontal lateral supports; wall may also have vertical lateral supports

Table XII Masonry – floors

Element	Section and plan	Typical depths (d) (mm)	Typical spans (L) (m)	Typical L/d	Critical factors for sizing/remarks
Masonry arch and fill		50–225	2–5	20–30	Bending or cracking from loads at quarter points Fill above arch crown helps to prestress arch L/h ratio about 10–20
Reinforced brick beam		300–600	4–12	10–16	Deflection and splitting at brick joints. Bending

Table XIII Masonry – roofs

Element	Section and plan	Typical depths (d) (mm)	Typical spans (L) (m)	Typical L/d	Critical factors for sizing/remarks
Masonry shells		75–125	6–15	80–120	Bending at edge of shell Shell has funicular shape for major load so as to reduce tension and shear stresses Reinforcement may be necessary for larger spans
Masonry arch		70–600	8–50	30–60	Bending or cracking Arch requires funicular shape for load due to self-weight Flat arches cause high sidethrust L/h ratio about 5
Vaults and domes		50–150	5–40	30–80	Domes have been built spanning up to 40 m and stone vaults up to 20 m Vaults built at high level require buttresses

in the longitudinal direction – in tension and compression – but weak in the interface between the fibres.

5.02 Advantages of timber
Consequently, timber has the supreme virtue of 'toughness'. It usually gives a forewarning of imminent failure, as the weakness between the fibres inhibits the progress of transverse cracks. Even when failure has occurred, there is often enough residual strength to carry a substantial load. Its principal drawbacks are susceptibility to insect and fungal attack and vulnerability to fire. Biological resistance can be fortified by treatment, and fire-resistance, particularly in the larger section sizes, is greater than generally realised.

Timber is one of that minority of materials that is almost equally strong in tension and compression. This strength is such that buckling of the compression flange of bending members is rarely a problem. Rectangular sections are easily formed and used for this purpose. Timber is easily worked by hand and machine tools, and it is simple to connect with other members, both other timber members and those of steel, masonry and concrete.

5.03 Timber sources and grades
Timber can be home-produced or imported from many places. There is a degree of standardisation, but the designer can encounter a wide variation in qualities. The structural properties of some common types are given in Table XVI.

Table XIV Masonry – wall/roof systems

Element	Section and plan	Typical heights (H) (storeys)	Typical H/W	Remarks
Multistorey loadbearing walls with concrete slabs		5–25 storeys	1.5–3.5	Most economic for buildings with small room areas Lateral forces resisted by walls in plane of forces
Masonry towers		5–25 storeys	3–6	Sections may require stiffening with rings or horizontal slabs at intervals Lower heights permit higher values of L/d Wind forces are lower on towers of circular section

Table XV Masonry – elements carrying gravity loads

Element	Section	Typical heights (H) (m)	Typical H/d	Remarks
Reinforced masonry retaining wall		1–6	10–15	Wall made of reinforced hollow blocks or units with reinforced concrete pockets w about $H/2$–$2H/3$
Masonry rubble in baskets		1–3	1–2	Rubble masonry block walls usually more economic than thick mass concrete retaining wall

Plan/on element	Vertical section	Sizing formulae	Remarks
Single wall		$\dfrac{h}{t} < 20$	Formula valid when lateral movement is prevented at top and bottom of wall, at right angles to wall; such restraint usually provided by floor and roof construction Wall has greater bending strength in the horizontal direction so that vertical supports would be preferred to horizontal supports Walls fail by crushing if $h/t < 10$ or by buckling and crushing if $h/t > 10$
Column $t < w < 4t$		$\dfrac{h}{t}$ and $\dfrac{2h}{w} < 20$ $P < \dfrac{t.w.u.}{5}$ where u is ultimate compressive strength of small masonry sample	Column illustrated given lateral restraint at top in one direction only and effective height of column in that direction taken as actual height; effective height in direction at right angles taken as twice actual height Columns fail by crushing if slenderness ratio, $h_{cf}/t < 10$ where h_{cf} is effective height and t is thickness of column P is working value of load applied near centre of column t_1 and t_2 are thicknesses of leaves of cavity wall which are tied together Wall illustrated has vertical load from floor taken by inner leaf only
Cavity wall		$\dfrac{h}{t_{cf}} < 20$ where t_{cf} is greater of t_1, t_2 or $2/3(t_1 + t_2)$	
Single wall with piers or intersecting walls	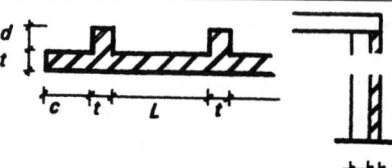	$\dfrac{L}{t} < 20$ $\dfrac{2.5c}{t} < 20$	Vertical piers or intersecting walls used to restrain walls as alternative to horizontal supports at top and bottom of wall Dimension c is distance of outhang from last vertical support d is depth of pier of intersecting wall which should be greater than 500 mm

Table XVI Properties of wood

Property at 12% moisture content	Hem-fir softwood	Kapur hardwood	Hem-fir glulam timber	Douglas fir plywood	Wood chipboard
Specific gravity	0.40	0.73	0.41	0.56	0.71
Weight kN/m³	3.9	7.2	4.0	5.5	7.0
Mean 7-day tensile strength of good quality working size sample N/mm²					
– along grain	60	115	75	40	15
– across grain	2	4	2		
Mean 7-day compressive strength of good quality working size sample N/mm²					
– along grain	24	45	30	25	
– across grain	3	6	3	3	
Mean 7-day flexural strength of good quality working size sample – modulus of rupture N/mm²	42	85	50	60 (face parallel to grain)	15
Elastic modulus in bending kn/mm²	9–10	12–20	10	10–12	2–3
Creep factor – final creep strain to elastic strain at working stresses	0.5–1.5	0.5–1.5	0.5–1.5	0.5–1.5	
Reversible movement for 30% change in relative humidity %					
– along grain	0.05	0.05	0.05	0.25 (in plane)	0.25 (in plane)
– across grain	1.0–2.5	1.0–4.0	1.0–2.5	2.00 (across plane)	4.50 (across plane)
Coefficient of thermal expansion × 10⁻⁶/°C					
– along grain	3.5	4	3.5		
– across grain	34	40	34		
Thermal conductivity across grain W/m °C	0.14	0.21	0.14	0.16	0.14
Variation in strength with temperature – % strength compared to 20°C (68°F) strength					
–50°C (–58°F)	150	150	150	150	
20°C (68°F)	100	100	100	100	
50°C (122°F)	75	75	75	75	

5.04 Large timber sections

Because of the shape and composition of the tree trunks from which timber comes, it is difficult to produce directly the larger size sections often required for modern contruction, particularly for beams. For such larger sections smaller timbers are glued together to form *laminated beams*, **41.10**. These are extremely useful for many purposes, and their manufacturers produce handbooks giving comprehensive data for their use.

5.05 Design methods

The advanced technology of timber started in the railway era when it was used for elaborate viaducts and bridges. These were generally constructed by trial and error, calculation methods being developed later. In recent years these methods of calculation have been taken to the point where it has become an extremely specialised field. The use of the current Codes of Practice by non-specialists (even if they are engineers) is not recommended, and there is yet no simpler manual published by the Institution of Structural Engineer. In complicated timber structures, the sizes of the members tend to depend more on the design of the connections than on the internal stresses.

5.06 Timber frame

Over 80% of the world's housing is composed of timber frame. It is uncommon in the UK, but Tables XVII to XXII give information relating to vertical support in timber and on frame and wall systems.

5.07 Roof trusses

The average UK architect meets timber in two common places: roof trusses and floor joists. Nowadays, most trusses are of the gang-nail type supplied to order for the required conditions. The manufacturer will supply calculations based on the Code of Practice for submission to the local building inspector. For preliminary design purposes, the data in Tables XXIII-XXV will be found of value for trusses of the shapes in **41.11** and **41.12**.

5.08 Floor joists

For the design of floor joists the information in Approved Document A should be sufficient for most purposes. Table XXVI (from this source) gives maximum spans of joists for timber of the most common type.

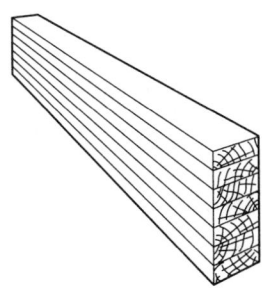

41.10 *A laminated timber beam*

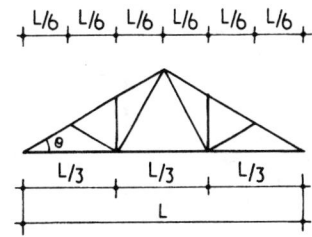

41.11 *Diagram of a fan trussed rafter*

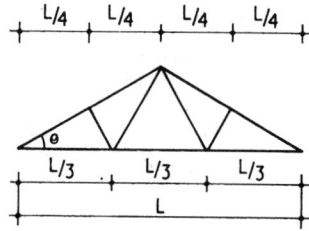

41.12 *Diagram of a fink or 'W' trussed rafter*

6 REINFORCED CONCRETE

6.01 Composition
Reinforced concrete is probably the most prolific and versatile structural material. It is composed of two distinct materials: concrete and reinforcement, each of which can be varied in quality, disposition and quantity to fulfil almost any requirement.

The concrete component is itself an amalgam of at least three constituents: aggregate, cement and water. These are mixed together into a homogeneous mass, and are then put in place and left for the chemical and physical changes to occur that result in a hard and durable material. The strength and durability will depend on the quality and quantity of each of the constituents; and whether any other material, such as an additive, has been added to the wet mix. Since the mixing of concrete has now in the majority of cases been taken off the building site and is done by the ready-mix companies, control over this aspect, as far as the architect is concerned, has become less direct. The strength of the hardened material as demonstrated by the ubiquitous cube crushing test will not necessarily indicate that sufficient cement has been included to fulfil the requirement for long-term durability. Sometimes additives are included in the mix to promote workability and early strength. Deterioration in the material due to these may not become evident for some years, but may then be disastrous. The properties of various types of concrete are summarized in Table XXVII.

Table XVII Wood – vertical support elements

Element	Horizontal and vertical section	Typical heights (h) (m)	h/d between lateral supports	Critical factors for sizing	Remarks
Glued laminated timber column		2–4	15–30	Splitting and crushing (h/d<15) Crushing and buckling (h/d>15)	Ratio $w/d \approx$ 2–3 Multistorey columns may require lower h/d ratios than those given.
Stud frame wall panel		2–4	20–35	Crushing and buckling Thickness of insulation required	Studs usually at about 400 mm centres with plywood or other sheeting nailed to it.
Solid timber column		2–4	15–30	Warping or distortion of timber	Multistorey columns may require lower h/d ratios than those given

Table XVIII Wood – floors

Element	Section and plan	Typical depths (d) (mm)	Typical spans (L) (m)	Typical L/d	Critical factors for sizing/remarks
Particle boards		12–30	0.3–0.6	24	Strength Creep deflection
Plywood floor decking		12–30	0.3–0.9	30–40	Deflection Point loads Strength
Softwood floor boards		16–25	0.6–0.8	25–35	Deflection Strength
Joists with floor board – softwood – hardwood		200–300 100–250	2–6 2–7	12–20 22–28	Deflection Spacing of joists is about 450–600 mm
Glued laminated timber beam		180–1400	5–12	14–18	Deflection Ratio d/b about 3–5 to prevent instability of unrestrained section.
Open web joist with wood flanges and steel tube diagonals		500–2000	5–18	8–10	Deflection Vibration

6.02 Specification

Provided a clear specification is laid down and checked by site staff, the concrete should fulfil its function indefinitely. This specification should now be in accordance with BS 5328: Part 2, Methods for specifying concrete, which includes not only for strength but also for minimum cement content, aggregate size, cement type and other relevant aspects. A number of standard mixes are specified in BS 5328, and these are detailed in Table XXVIII.

A slightly different approach is taken in the Orange Book. This refers to the traditional nominal mixes as detailed in **Table XXIX**. This source also gives recommendations for working permissible stresses for various concrete grades: these are shown in Table XXX.

Table XIX Wood – roofs, beam and deck

Element	Section and elevation	Typical depths (d) (mm)	Typical spans (L) (m)	Typical L/d	Critical factors for sizing/remarks
Roof planks		25–75	2–6	45–60	Deflection Planks assumed to be simply supported
Plywood roof decking		10–20	0.3–1.2	50–70	Deflection Decking assumed to be continuous
Stressed skin plywood roof panels		100–450	3–7	30–35	Deflection Panel assumed to be simply supported Dimension a is about 300–500 mm
Trough decking with plywebs		225–400	5–12	25–30	Decking assumed to be simply supported
Joists with roof deck – softwood – hardwood		100–225 100–250	2–6 3–8	20–25 30–35	Deflection Joists assumed to be simply supported and spaced at 600 mm
Roof purlins – softwood – hardwood		150–300 200–400	2–5 3–8	10–14 15–20	Available length and depth of wood Bending strength Purlin assumed to be simply supported and carrying about 2 m width of roof
Glued laminated timber beam with roof deck		180–1400	4–30	15–20	Deflection Beams assumed to be simply supported with spacing $L/3$–$L/5$ Ratio d/b about 5–8
Glued plywood box beam		200–2000	6–20	10–15	Deflection Bending strength Longitudinal shear Web buckling Beams assumed to be simply supported
Open web joist with wood flanges and steel tube diagonals		500–2000	9–30	10–15	Webs bolted to flanges
Trussed rafter without purlins		1200–2000	6–10	4–6	Strength of joints Bending in rafter Assumed spacing 600 mm
Sloping trusses with purlins		1000–3000	6–20	5–7	Strength of joints Assumed spacing is 2–5 m
Flat top timber girders		1500–3000	12–25	8–10	Strength of joints Assumed spacing is 4–6 m

Table XX Wood – roofs, beam and surface

Element	Section and plan	Typical spans (L) (m)	Typical L/d	Remarks
Stressed skin panel folded plate roof		9–20	8–15	Panel has 2 skins with w/d ratio of 20–30 and thickness of about 75–200 mm
Three-layer stressed skin ply hyperbolic paraboloid		12–30	2–8	Shell has edge beams with L/d ratio of about 60–80
Three-layer stressed skin ply barrel vault		9–30	4–8	Shell has edge beams. Ratio w/h about 2–4
Pyramid roof		12–35	2–6	Simple to construct. Often used with steel tension members at base
Glued laminated timber dome		12–100	5–7	Typically, dome members have three-way grid, radial lines or lamellar curve patterns when projected on plan. Connections semi-rigid or pinned
Lamellar arch roof		15–25	5–7	Typically, members on two intersecting parallel lamellar lines making diamond shapes when projected on plan
Warped rectangular grid (hyperbolic paraboloid)		12–80	5–10	Grid covered with ply panels. Ratio L/d about 60–80
Domed grid shell		12–30	5–7	Grid members flexible to allow shaping to curve. Shape reasonably close to funicular shape for dead load

6.03 Design

As mentioned above, there are two main methods of design. The Eurocode is not recommended to non-experts. A method based on BS 8100 is given in the *Manual for the design of reinforced concrete building structures* (the Green Book). An even simpler method is given in the *Recommendations for the permissible stress design of reinforced concrete building structures* (the Orange Book), and this should be understandable by and useful to many architects (see Bibliography).

6.04 Reinforcement

Reinforcement is rarely other than steel, although other materials such as glass fibre have been tried (mainly in cladding units). The steel may be smooth round steel, in which case the bars are referred to as R25, etc, the numbers indicating the diameter in millimetres. Only those sizes in Table XXXI are available.

The other type of bar reinforcement is a high-yield deformed bar referred to as Y25 etc. In this case the numbers refer to the plain bar diameter of equivalent cross-sectional area. The actual bar size will be about 10% greater than this due to the deformation. The two kinds of high-yield bar used are hot-rolled and cold-worked, but for practical purposes the difference is rarely significant.

6.05 Mesh reinforcement

For many positions, such as in slabs and walls, it is convenient to use reinforcement in the shape of a sheet or mesh composed of bars in both directions. Table XXXII gives the standard sizes of available meshes.

6.06 Reinforcement position

Concrete is strong in compression, but weak in tension. The reinforcement is used to compensate for this weakness. There must be some reinforcement wherever any tension is likely to occur, and sufficient at places of maximum tension. Simply spanning beams are reinforced near the bottom, with most reinforcement at midspan. Shear forces also produce tensile stresses – links or stirrups are used to reinforce the concrete against the effects of these stresses. Sometimes the compressive strength of the concrete is insufficient for the loading, and in this case reinforcing bars can be used to help take the compression as well. Such use for reinforcement is expensive, and is only used when increasing the size of the beam is not possible.

In cantilever beams the tension occurs near the top. These beams have their heaviest reinforcement at the top, with most near the root.

Table XXI Wood – frame and wall systems

Element	Section and plan	Typical spans (L) (m)	Typical L/d	Remarks
Rigid glued laminated timber frame		12–35	30–50	Spacing of frames about 4–6 m Laminated frame may be curved and of varying depth but more expensive than uniform straight members Ratio L/h about 5–7
Glued laminated beam and post		4–30	18–22	Frame not rigid in its own plane so vertical bracing necessary, eg with rigid gables connected to roof plane
Plywood box portal frames		9–45	20–40	Box beams made of solid section timber flanges, glued and nailed to plywood side pieces, acting as webs Spacing of frames about 4–6 m
Glued laminated arch		15–100	30–50	Maximum convenient transportable lengths 15–25 m Arch shape is nearly funicular for important load case Arches may have rectangular or circular plan Ratio L/h about 5–7
Plywood floor and wall panels		Height, H 2 – 4 storeys		Enclosures usually built in platform construction in which vertical framing members are not continuous
Braced frame		2 – 4 storeys		Frame may be braced with diagnol steel rods or plywood panels acting as diaphragms

6.07 Effective depth

The effective depth of the beam is the distance from its top (or compression flange) to the centroid of area of the tensile steel reinforcement. It is indicated by the symbol d.

6.08 Minimum reinforcement

Stresses arise in concrete not only from the applied loads but also from a variety of other causes. For example, when concrete dries and sets it tends to shrink slightly. If it cannot move it will tend to crack. Similar cracking will occur if movement induced by thermal expansion and contraction is inhibited. Consequently, to reduce the tendency to form large cracks, a modicum of reinforcement is used throughout: this causes the formation of a multitude of fine cracks instead.

6.09 Deflection

In addition to limiting the working stresses below the permissible values, reinforced concrete must possess sufficient stiffness to prevent deflection or deformation which might impair the strength or efficiency of the structure, or produce cracks in finishes or partitions. For all normal cases it may be assumed that the stiffness will be satisfactory if the ratio of span to overall depth does not exceed the appropriate value from Table XXXIII.

6.10 Concrete cover to reinforcement

In all cases there must be sufficient concrete cover to reinforcement. This is:

● To preserve it from corrosion
● To ensure an adequate bond with the concrete and
● To ensure sufficient protection in case of fire.

The Orange Book gives tables of minimum cover depending on the type of concrete, the exposure conditions and the degree of fire protection required. In no case should the cover be less than the nominal maximum aggregate size, or, for the main reinforcement, the bar size.

6.11 Details of various kinds of concrete structure are given in Tables XXXIV to XXXIX.

7 STRUCTURAL STEELWORK AND OTHER METALS

7.01 Metals

Steel is by far the majority metal used structurally, but other materials are used in ancillary elements. Table XL gives properties of various steels and aluminium alloy.

Table XXII Softwood timber – elements carrying gravity load

Element and horizontal section	Elevation and section on element	Sizing formulae	Remarks
Solid timber tie		$\dfrac{P}{0.84A} < p_t$ where P is working value of tie force A is gross area of tie p_t is allowable working stress of timber softwood in tension = 3.5 N/mm² $\dfrac{L}{t} < 70$ where t is least dimension of tie cross-section L is length of tie between supports	Area of tie at connection assumed to be 80% of gross area Given span to width ratio assumes tie may take small amount of compression Actual area of tie usually decided by type of connection detail; because of difficulty of tension connections steel rods often used in place of timber ties Given allowable stress is for long-term (2 month) load on construction grade softwood
Solid timber column		$\dfrac{P}{A} < p_c$ where P is working value of compression in column P_c is allowable working stress of timber in compression which depends on slenderness ratio h_{cf}/t see below, where h_{cf} is effective height of column; slenderness ratio should not normally exceed 50 $\dfrac{h_{cf}}{t} = \quad p_c =$ 10 9.0 N/mm² 20 6.0 N/mm² 30 2.8 N/mm² 40 1.5 N/mm² 50 1.0 N/mm²	For buildings which are laterally braced for example by cross-bracing, effective height of columns h_{cf} is not greater than actual height h between floors Given formula valid for columns carrying axial load Given allowable stress is for long-term (2 month) load on construction grade softwood
Simply supported solid timber beam		$\dfrac{M}{Z} < p_{bc}$ where M is working value of bending moment on beam Z is the section modulus of the beam p_{bc} is allowable working stress of softwood in bending = 7 N/mm² $\Delta = \dfrac{5W.L^3}{384E.I} = \dfrac{5f_{bc}.L^2}{24E.d}$ where W is total u.d. load on beam L is span and d is depth of beam Δ is midspan deflection I is moment of inertia of beam E is elastic modulus of timber including effects of creep which depends on duration of load f_{bc} is actual bending stress in beam at midspan To prevent ponding on flat roofs $E.I > c.\rho_w.L^4/50$ where I is moment of inertia of roof beams at spacing c E is short-term elastic modulus of softwood = 11 kN/mm² ρ_w is density of water = 10 kN/m³ L is span of roof beams given camber > $2.5\Delta_d$ where Δ_d is dead load deflection of beams at midspan	Formulae assume top of beam is laterally restrained or has ends held in position; in general $d/b < 7$ and if $d/b > 6$ beam requires bridging as well as lateral restraint where b is width of beam Given allowable stress is for long-term (2 month) load on construction grade softwood Typical spacing of beams in floors, c, is 450–600 mm If total deflection limited to $L/330$ then $E.I > 4.34\,W.L^2$
Simply supported glued-laminated timber beam 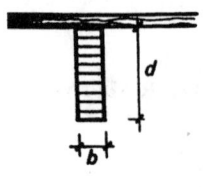	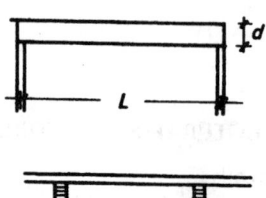	$\dfrac{M}{Z} < p_{bc}$ where p_{bc} is allowable – working stress in bending = 12.5 N/mm² To prevent ponding on flat roofs $E.I > c.\rho_w.L^4/50$ where E is short-term elastic modulus of laminated softwood = 12 kN/mm²	Notes and formula for deflection as for solid timber beams

Table XXIII Maximum permissible spens for rafters for fan trussed rafters

Basic size mm	Actual size mm	Pitch (degrees)								
		15 m	17½ m	20 m	22½ m	25 m	27½ m	30 m	32½ m	35 m
38 × 75	35 × 72	8.03	8.38	8.64	8.87	9.08	9.27	9.46	9.65	9.85
38 × 100	35 × 97	9.89	10.37	10.67	10.96	11.00	11.00	11.00	11.00	11.00
38 × 125	35 × 120	11.00	11.00	11.00	11.00	–	–	–	–	–
44 × 75	41 × 72	8.65	9.00	9.25	9.48	9.73	9.89	10.08	10.30	10.48
44 × 100	41 × 97	10.71	11.00	11.00	11.00	11.00	11.00	11.00	11.00	11.00
44 × 125	41 × 120	11.00	–	–	–	–	–	–	–	–
50 × 75	47 × 72	9.26	9.62	9.86	10.10	10.36	10.53	10.70	10.93	11.00
50 × 100	47 × 97	11.00	11.00	11.00	11.00	11.00	11.00	11.00	11.00	–

Table XXIV Maximum permissible spans for rafters for fink trussed rafters

Basic size mm	Actual size mm	Pitch (degrees)								
		15 m	17½ m	20 m	22½ m	25 m	27½ m	30 m	32½ m	35 m
38 × 75	35 × 72	6.03	6.16	6.29	6.41	6.51	6.60	6.70	6.80	6.90
38 × 100	35 × 97	7.48	7.67	7.83	7.97	8.10	8.22	8.34	8.47	8.61
38 × 125	35 × 120	8.80	9.00	9.20	9.37	9.54	9.68	9.82	9.98	10.16
44 × 75	41 × 72	6.45	6.59	6.71	6.83	6.93	7.03	7.14	7.24	7.35
44 × 100	41 × 97	8.05	8.23	8.40	8.55	8.68	8.81	8.93	9.09	9.22
44 × 125	41 × 120	9.38	9.60	9.81	9.99	10.15	10.31	10.45	10.64	10.81
50 × 75	47 × 72	6.87	7.01	7.13	7.25	7.35	7.45	7.53	7.67	7.78
50 × 100	47 × 97	8.62	8.80	8.97	9.12	9.25	9.38	9.50	9.66	9.80
50 × 125	47 × 120	10.01	10.24	10.44	10.62	10.77	10.94	11.00	11.00	11.00

Table XXV Maximum permissible spans for celling ties for fink and fan trussed rafters

Basic size mm	Actual size mm	Pitch (degrees)								
		15 m	17½ m	20 m	22½ m	25 m	27½ m	30 m	32½ m	35 m
38 × 75	35 × 72	5.07	5.31	5.53	5.74	5.94	6.12	6.31	6.50	6.67
38 × 100	35 × 97	7.03	7.36	7.68	7.99	8.27	8.54	8.81	9.06	9.33
38 × 125	35 × 120	8.66	9.10	9.49	9.88	10.24	10.59	10.93	11.00	11.00
38 × 150	35 × 145	10.17	10.71	11.00	11.00	11.00	11.00	11.00	–	–
44 × 75	41 × 72	5.53	5.78	6.03	6.26	6.48	6.69	6.89	7.08	7.28
44 × 100	41 × 97	7.53	7.90	8.25	8.59	8.90	9.19	9.48	9.75	10.04
44 × 125	41 × 120	9.13	9.60	10.04	10.46	10.86	11.00	11.00	11.00	11.00
44 × 150	41 × 145	10.52	11.00	11.00	11.00	11.00	–	–	–	–
50 × 75	47 × 72	5.92	6.20	6.46	6.72	6.94	7.17	7.39	7.60	7.81
50 × 100	47 × 97	7.93	8.33	8.71	9.06	9.38	9.70	10.02	10.32	10.62
50 × 125	47 × 120	9.42	9.94	10.40	10.86	11.00	11.00	11.00	11.00	11.00
50 × 150	47 × 145	10.59	11.00	11.00	11.00	–	–	–	–	–

Table XXVI Maximum clear span of floor joists (m)

| Size of joist (mm × mm) | Dead load kN/m² excluding the self-weight of the joist | | | | | | | | |
| | Not more than 0.25 Spacing of joist (mm) | | | More than 0.25 but not more than 0.50 Spacing of joist (mm) | | | More than 0.50 but not more than 1.25 Spacing of joist (mm) | | |
	400	450	600	400	450	600	400	450	600
38 × 97	1.83	1.69	1.30	1.72	1.56	1.21	1.42	1.30	1.04
38 × 122	2.48	2.39	1.93	2.37	2.22	1.76	1.95	1.79	1.45
38 × 147	2.98	2.87	2.51	2.85	2.71	2.33	2.45	2.29	1.87
38 × 170	3.44	3.31	2.87	3.28	3.10	2.69	2.81	2.65	2.27
38 × 195	3.94	3.75	3.26	3.72	3.52	3.06	3.19	3.01	2.61
38 × 220	4.43	4.19	3.65	4.16	3.93	3.42	3.57	3.37	2.92
47 × 97	2.02	1.91	1.58	1.92	1.82	1.46	1.67	1.53	1.23
47 × 122	2.66	2.56	2.30	2.55	2.45	2.09	2.26	2.08	1.70
47 × 147	3.20	3.08	2.79	3.06	2.95	2.61	2.72	2.57	2.17
47 × 170	3.69	3.55	3.19	3.53	3.40	2.99	3.12	2.94	2.55
47 × 195	4.22	4.06	3.62	4.04	3.89	3.39	3.54	3.34	2.90
47 × 220	4.72	4.57	4.04	4.55	4.35	3.79	3.95	3.74	3.24
50 × 97	2.08	1.97	1.67	1.98	1.87	1.54	1.74	1.60	1.29
50 × 122	2.72	2.62	2.37	2.60	2.50	2.19	2.33	2.17	1.77
50 × 147	3.27	3.14	2.86	3.13	3.01	2.69	2.81	2.65	2.27
50 × 170	3.77	3.62	3.29	3.61	3.47	3.08	3.21	3.03	2.63
50 × 195	4.31	4.15	3.73	4.13	3.97	3.50	3.65	3.44	2.99
50 × 220	4.79	4.66	4.17	4.64	4.47	3.91	4.07	3.85	3.35
63 × 97	2.32	2.20	1.92	2.19	2.08	1.82	1.93	1.84	1.53
63 × 122	2.93	2.82	2.57	2.81	2.70	2.45	2.53	2.43	2.09
63 × 147	3.52	3.39	3.08	3.37	3.24	2.95	3.04	2.92	2.58
63 × 170	4.06	3.91	3.56	3.89	3.74	3.40	3.50	3.37	2.95
63 × 195	4.63	4.47	4.07	4.44	4.28	3.90	4.01	3.85	3.35
63 × 220	5.06	4.92	4.58	4.91	4.77	4.37	4.51	4.30	3.75
75 × 122	3.10	2.99	2.72	2.97	2.86	2.60	2.68	2.58	2.33
75 × 147	3.72	3.58	3.27	3.56	3.43	3.13	3.22	3.09	2.81
75 × 170	4.28	4.13	3.77	4.11	3.96	3.61	3.71	3.57	3.21
75 × 195	4.83	4.70	4.31	4.68	4.52	4.13	4.24	4.08	3.65
75 × 220	5.27	5.13	4.79	5.11	4.97	4.64	4.74	4.60	4.07
38 × 140	2.84	2.73	2.40	2.72	2.59	2.17	2.33	2.15	1.75
38 × 184	3.72	3.56	3.09	3.53	3.33	2.90	3.02	2.85	2.47
38 × 235	4.71	4.46	3.89	4.43	4.18	3.64	3.80	3.59	3.11

Note 1. Softwood tongued and grooved floorboards if supported at a joist spacing of up to 500 mm should be at least 16 mm finished thickness; and if supported at wider spacings up to 600 mm should be 19 mm finished thickness.

Note 2. The sizes, spacings and spans given will support the dead loads stated in the tables, and an imposed load not exceeding 1.5 kN/m². (These tables can be used when a bath is to be installed provided joists supporting the bath are duplicated.)

Table XXVII Properties of concrete

Property	Structural concrete	Lightweight concrete	No-fines concrete	Autoclaved aerated concrete	Polymer concrete (Polyester mortar)	Glass-fibre reinforced cement (5% fibre)	Sprayed concrete without fibre reinforcement
Specific gravity	2–4	0.4–2.0	1.5–1.9	0.6–0.9	2.4	2.5	2.3
Weight kN/m³	24	4–20	15–19	6–9	24	25	23
Long-term compressive strength N/mm²	20–100	5–60	4–9	3–6	50–100	30–100	30–60
Long-term flexural strength-modulus of rupture N/mm²	3	3	1	1	10–40	15–20 (10 years)	3
Elastic modulus in compression kN/mm²	15–40	5–25	15	1.5–9	3–15	20–30 (10 years)	20–30
Impact strength	very low	low	very low	very low	high	high but decreases	low
Tensile strain capacity % – elongation before cracking	0.004–0.012	–	–	–	1–5	0.05	–
Creep factor – final creep strain to elastic creep strain at working stresses at 20°C (68°F)	1–3	2–4	2–4	1–3	4–7	2–5	2–5
Reversible moisture movement %	0.02–0.10	0.03–0.20	–	0.02–0.03	–	0.15–0.30	0.15–0.30
Initial drying shrinkage %	0.02–0.08	0.03–0.04	0.01–0.03	0.02–0.09	1.00	0.15–0.30	0.15–0.30
Coefficient of thermal expansion × 10^{-6}/°C	7–14	6–12	4–8	8–10	20–40	7–11	7–14
Thermal conductivity at 5% moisture content W/m °C	1.6–2.2	0.2–0.9	0.8 (dense aggregate)	0.3	–	0.5–1.2	1.6–2.2

Table XXVIII Standard mixes to BS 5328: 1990

Standard mix (1)			ST1	ST2	ST3	ST4	ST5
Cement (kg) (2)	Nominal aggregate 40 mm	Slump 75 mm	180	210	240	280	320
		Slump 125 mm	200	230	260	300	340
	Nominal aggregate 20 mm	Slump 75 mm	210	240	270	300	340
		Slump 125 mm	230	260	300	330	370
Total aggregate	Nominal aggregate 40 mm	Slump 75 mm	2010	1980	1950	1920	1820
		Slump 125 mm	1950	1920	1900	1860	1860
	Nominal aggregate 20 mm	Slump 75 mm	1940	1920	1890	1860	1830
		Slump 125 mm	1880	1860	1820	1800	1770
Percentage of total aggregate for fine aggregate (3)	Nominal aggregate 40 mm		30–45	30–45	30–45		
	Nominal aggregate 20 mm		35–50	35–50	35–50		
	Nominal aggregate 40 mm	Grading limits C				30–40	30–40
		Grading limits M				25–35	25–35
		Grading limits F				25–30	25–30
	Nominal aggregate 20 mm	Grading limits C				35–45	35–45
		Grading limits M				30–40	30–40
		Grading limits F				25–35	25–35
Characteristic strengths to be assumed for design (N/mm²)			7.5	10.0	15.0	20.0	25.0

Notes:
(1) When a mix is required with a very low slump the proportions shall be taken from the 75 mm line.
(2) These proportions should produce approximately 1 m³ of wet concrete.
(3) Aggregate quantities may need adjustment depending on particular characteristics. For ST1, ST2 and ST3 they may be volume batched.

Table XXIX Proportions and strength requirements for nominal concrete mixes with Portland cement or Portland-blastfurnace cement and with aggregates complying with BS 882

(1) Mix proportions	(2) Cubic metres aggregate per 50 kg of cement		(3) Cube strength within 28 days after mixing N/mm²		(4) Alternative cube strength within 7 days after mixing N/mm²	
	Fine	Coarse	Preliminary test	Works test	Preliminary test	Works test
1:1:2	0.035	0.07	40	30	26.7	20
1:1½:3	0.05	0.10	34	25.5	22.7	17
1:2:4	0.07	0.14	28	21	18.7	14

Table XXX Basic permissible concrete stresses and moduli of elasticity

Grade of concrete f_{cu}(1)	Nominal mix	Standard mix	Basic permissible concrete stress, N/mm²		Mean *E*-values (short term) (5) kN/mm²
			Compression P_{cc}	Average bond (4)* P_b	
15 (2)	–	ST3	4.1	1.3	23
20	1:2:4	ST4	5.5	1.5	24
25	1:1½:3	ST5	6.9	1.7	25
30	1:1:2	–	8.2	1.8	26
35			9.6	2.0	27
40			11.0	2.1	28
45 (3)			12.4	2.2	29
50			13.7	2.4	30
55			15.1	2.5	31
60			16.5	2.6	32

Notes
*The basic stresses for bond relate to type 2 deformed bars in tension.
(1) F_{cu} is the characteristic strength of the concrete: ie that value below which 5% of the population of all possible strength measurements are expected to fall.
Alternatively, this may be assumed to be the 28-day works cube strength.
(2) Grade 15 may be used only for lightweight aggregate concrete.
(3) For normal building structures grades 45 and above are rarely used.
(4) For type 1 deformed bars the values are 80% of those quoted.
For plain bars they are 55% of those quoted. In a beam where nominal links have not been provided, the bond stress should be taken as that for plain bars, irrespective of the type of bar used.
For fabric to BS 4483 the permissible bond stress is 1.3× the value of average bond stress provided that:
   (*a*) the fabric is welded in a shear resistant manner complying with BS 4483, and
   (*b*) the number of welded intersections within the anchorage length is at least equal to a value of 4 × area of steel required/area of steel provided.
When condition (*b*) is not satisfied, the anchorage bond should be taken as that appropriate to the individual wires or bars in the sheet.
(5) The quoted short-term elastic moduli are average values. For long-term loads, creep effects will produce higher deformations, so that the total can be 2 to 4 times the short-term value. Where this is critical, specialist literature on the subject should be consulted.

Table XXXI Areas of round bar reinforcement (mm²)

Diam (mm)	Weight (kg/m)	Areas in mm² for numbers of bars											
		1	2	3	4	5	6	7	8	9	10	11	12
6	0.222	28	57	85	113	142	170	198	226	255	283	311	340
8	0.395	50	101	151	201	252	302	352	402	453	502	552	604
10	0.617	79	157	236	314	393	471	550	628	707	785	864	942
12	0.888	113	226	339	452	565	678	791	904	1 017	1 130	1 243	1 356
16	1.58	201	402	603	804	1 005	1 206	1 407	1 608	1 809	2 010	2 211	2 412
20	2.47	314	628	942	1 256	1 570	1 884	2 198	2 512	2 826	3 140	3 454	3 768
25	3.86	491	983	1 474	1 966	2 457	2 948	3 439	3 932	4 423	4 915	5 406	5 896
32	6.31	804	1 608	2 412	3 216	4 020	4 824	5 628	6 432	7 236	8 040	8 844	9 648
40	9.87	1 260	2 520	3 780	5 040	6 300	7 560	8 820	10 080	11 340	12 600	13 860	15 120

Diam (mm)	Areas in mm²/m for spacings in mm								
	50	75	100	125	150	175	200	250	300
6	566	376	283	226	188	162	141	113	94
8	1 006	670	503	402	335	287	251	201	168
10	1 570	1 048	785	628	524	449	393	314	262
12	2 262	1 508	1 131	904	754	646	565	452	377
16	4 020	2 680	2 010	1 608	1 340	1 149	1 005	804	670
20	6 284	4 190	3 142	2 514	2 095	1 795	1 571	1 257	1 047
25	9 830	6 552	4 915	3 932	3 276	2 809	2 457	1 966	1 638
32		10 720	8 040	6 432	5 360	4 594	4 020	3 216	2 680
40			12 600	10 080	8 400	7 200	6 300	5 040	4 200

Table XXXII Sizes of reinforcing meshes

BS reference	Mesh sizes Nominal pitch of wires (mm)		Size of wires (mm)		Cross-sectional area (mm²) per metre width		Nominal mass kg per m²
	Main	Cross	Main	Cross	Main	Cross	
Square mesh fabric							
A 393	200	200	10	10	393	393	6.16
A 252	200	200	8	8	252	252	3.95
A 193	200	200	7	7	193	193	3.02
A 142	200	200	6	6	142	142	2.22
A 98	200	200	5	5	98	98	1.54
Structural fabric							
B 1131	100	200	12	8	1131	252	10.90
B 785	100	200	10	8	785	252	8.14
B 503	100	200	8	8	503	252	5.93
B 385	100	200	7	7	385	193	4.53
B 283	100	200	6	7	283	193	3.73
B 196	100	200	5	7	196	193	3.05
Long mesh fabric*							
C 785	100	400	10	6	785	70.8	6.72
C 636	80–130	400	8–10	6	636	70.8	5.55
C 503	100	400	8	5	503	49.0	4.34
C 385	100	400	7	5	385	49.0	3.41
C 283	100	400	6	5	283	49.0	2.61
Wrapping fabric							
D 49	100	100	2.5	2.5	49.0	49.0	0.760

*Cross wires for all types of long mesh may be of plain hard drawn steel wire.

Table XXXIII Spans to depth ratios

	A	B	C
Beams			
Simply supported beams	20	18	17
Continuous beams	25	23	21
Cantilever beams	10	9	8
Slabs			
Slabs spanning in one direction, simply supported	30	27	25
Slabs spanning in one direction, continuous	35	31	30
Slabs spanning in two directions, simply supported	35	31	30
Slabs spanning in two directions, continuous	40	36	34
Cantilever slabs	12	11	10

Notes:

Column A Members with steel stresses not more than 140 N/mm² and concrete stresses not more than 10.0 N/mm²

Column B Members with either steel stresses greater than in column A or concrete stresses greater, but not both

Column C Members with both steel and concrete stresses greater than in column A

7.02 Grades of steel

Steel for structural purposes is available in the United Kingdom in three grades increasing in strength: grade 43, which corresponds to the previous description of 'mild steel', grade 50 and grade 55.

7.03 Handbooks

Books of design tables are issued by the Steel Construction Institute. However, non-experts would find these very much more difficult to understand than the old handbooks that were issued by the steel companies. The tables in the old edition relating to ordinary mild steel are therefore reproduced in this edition as far as the sections in them are still available. These are Tables XLI to XLIV, and they may be used for rough sizing purposes, but building inspectors may require more rigorous calculations for final design. They may accept designs to the *Manual for the design of steelwork building structures* (the Grey Book) instead of the more complex Eurocode.

Table XXXIV Concrete – vertical support elements

Element	Horizontal and vertical section	Typical heights (h) (m)	h/d between lateral supports	Critical factors for sizing	Remarks
Cast-in-place column – single storey – multistorey		2–8 2–4	12–18 6–15	Buckling and crushing ($h/d>10$) Crushing ($h/d<10$) Bending	Columns rigidly connected to beams form frames which act as a vertical bracing system
Cast-in-place wall		2–4	18–25	Buckling Construction method	
Cast-in-place no-fines wall		2–3	10–15	Crushing	Often used for housing Dimension $d>200\,mm$
Precast column – single storey – multistorey		2–8 2–4	15–30 6–20	Buckling and crushing ($h/d>10$) Crushing ($h/d<10$) Bending Connections	Variety of high-quality finishes available with precast products
Precast loadbearing panel		2–3	20–25	Buckling Connections Handling stresses	
Precast tilt-up panel		4–8	15–25	Handling stresses	
Prestressed concrete columns – single storey – multistorey		4–8 2–4	15–25 10–20	Buckling	Prestressing helps to eliminate tensile stresses due to bending
Prestressed concrete hangers		1–40	1–150	Variation in load	Stiffer and more resistant to corrosion than the steel tie

7.04 Details of various kinds of steel structure are given in Tables XLV to LI.

8 OTHER MATERIALS

8.01 Plastics
Properties of some plastics materials are shown in Table LII. The use of these in roofs is given in Table LIII.

8.02 Fabric
Plastics are used in the manufacture of many structural fabrics which are finding increasing uses. Table LIV gives properties of some of these, and Table LV covers their use in roofs.

9 FOUNDATIONS

9.01 Nature
The purpose of a foundation is to transmit the loads of and contained by a building structure to the ground. The nature of the foundation will depend on:

- The characteristics of the soil
- The magnitude of the loads of the structure
- The nature of the loads of the structure.

In the majority of buildings, the loads transmitted to the ground will arrive either as point loads down columns or line loads down walls. For the type of building with which these notes deal, the magnitudes of these loads will not be so great as to significantly affect the choice of foundation system.

9.02 Soil
This will basically depend on the strength of the soil to carry the load. The term 'soil' in this context means not vegetable material suitable for growing crops, but the material forming the surface of the earth to a depth of about 100 m, which is not so hard in nature as to be classified as a 'rock'.

The technology of the physical properties of soil is called soil mechanics. It is not appropriate to deal in depth with this subject, but some simple principles are necessary to understand the design of foundations.

Table XXXV Concrete – floors

Element	Section and plan	Typical depths (d) (mm)	Typical spans (L) (m)	Typical L/d	Critical factors for sizing/remarks
One-way solid slab – reinforced – prestressed		100–250 125–200	2–7 5–9	22–32 38–45	Deflection Bending Simply supported slabs have the lower values of L/d in given range.
Reinforced two-way slab		100–250	6–11	28–35	Deflection Bending Suitable for heavy loading and concentrated loads $L < L_1 < 1.4L$
One-way ribbed slab (pan joist) – reinforced – prestressed		225–600 300–450	4–12 10–18	18–26 30–38	Deflection Bending Shear Most suitable for long spans with light loads Dimensions a, b and c as below
Two-way waffle slab – reinforced – prestressed		350–650 450–650	9–15 10–22	18–24 25–32	Deflection Bending Form moulds of standard size available More costly to form than ribbed slab Dimensions for a are 100–200 mm, b are 900–1800 mm, c are 60–100 mm approximately
Reinforced one-way joists with hollow blocks (filler blocks)		150–300	3–7	20–25	Bending Shear Small holes in the floor easily made for services
Partially prestressed ribbed floor		300–500	10–15	35–40	Live load Deflection Bending Less creep and upward deflection than fully prestressed floor
Block and joist floor (joists prestressed)		150–200	3–7	30–35	Bending Deflection Block and joist are precast but have cast-in-place topping 50–75 mm thick
Precast prestressed planks		100–200	6–9	35–45	Live load deflection Bending Slabs more than 175 mm deep often built with voids Topping depth, a, is 50–75 mm thick
Prestressed hollow core slab		100–350	6–10	35–40	Bending Joists are precast but have cast-in-place topping of depth, a, 35–50 mm thick
Widespan slab – reinforced – prestressed		100–300 100–225	3–7 4–9	26–32 35–45	Bending Deflection Slabs are precast with cast-in-place topping Slab often propped during construction.
Precast prestressed double-T beams		350–800	9–18	20–30	Live load Bending Shear Handling stresses Beams have cast-in-place topping 50–75 mm thick

Table XXXV *Continued*

Element	Section and plan	Typical depths (d) (mm)	Typical spans (L) (m)	Typical L/d	Critical factors for sizing/remarks
Flat slab without drop panels (flat plates) – reinforced – prestressed		125–200 200–225	4–8 9–10	28–36 40–48	Shear round columns Deflection Bending Compared to beam and slab, flat slabs save depth and formwork costs but have lower resistance to lateral forces
Flat slab with drop panels – reinforced – prestressed		125–300 200–225	5–10 12–14	28–36 40–48	Shear at drops Deflection Bending Dimension d_d is about $1.25d$–$1.45d$; b is about $L/3$
T or L Beam – reinforced – prestressed		400–700 300–850	5–15 9–24	14–20 20–30	Beams usually spaced at about 3–7 m giving slab depth between 100–175 mm Simply supported beams have the lower values of L/d in the given range
Wide beam – reinforced – prestressed		350–650 300–500	6–12 9–15	16–22 22–32	Deflection Bending Used where height is limited Simply supported beams have the lower values of L/d in the given range Dimension a is about 600–1200 mm

Table XXXVI Concrete – roofs

Element	Section and plan	Typical depths (d) (mm)	Typical spans (L) (m)	Typical L/d	Critical factors for sizing/remarks
Reinforced one-way solid slab		125–500	3–6	20–30	Deflection Bending
Reinforced one-way ribbed slab (pan joist)		500–1200	6–14	25–30	Deflection Shear Bending Dimensions for a are 100–150 mm; c are 50–100 mm.
Reinforced two-way waffle slab		625–1500	9–16	20–25	Deflection Bending Dimensions as above
Reinforced flat slab without drop panels		400–900	4–8	32	Shear round columns Deflection Bending

Table XXXVI *Continued*

Element	Section and plan	Typical depths (d) (mm)	Typical spans (L) (m)	Typical L/d	Critical factors for sizing/remarks
Prestressed hollow core slabs		100–200	6–10	40–50	Compressive strength of unit Live load variation Slabs are precast but have 50–75 mm cast-in-place topping
Prestressed double-T beam		350–800	12–25	30–35	Bending Shear Handling stresses
Prestressed single-T beam		750–2500	15–25	30–35	Bending and shear Handling stresses Beams are precast but have 50–75 mm cast-in-place topping
Reinforced aerated concrete slabs		100–200	2–5	20–25	Bending Slabs connected by strip of cast-in-place concrete
Reinforced inverted hyperbolic paraboloids (umbrellas)		75–100	9–15	120–200	Cover to bars Tension reinforcement required at top of umbrella Umbrellas are independent and may be at different heights L/h ratio about 6–12.
Reinforced hyperbolic paraboloid shell		75–100	15–55	200–450	Deflection at tips Cover to bars Edge beams may be prestressed to overcome tensile stresses L/h ratio about 4–7
Domes		75–300	15–120	300–450	Shell buckling Cover to bars Minimum thickness, d, about 60 mm Tension ring at base often prestressed
Reinforced concrete folded plates		75–125	9–36	40–50(w/d)	Bending in slab Tie force in valley Minimum thickness about 60 mm L/h ratio about 8–15
Reinforced long barrel shell		75–100	25–40	50–65(w/d)	Cover to bars Minimum thickness about 60 mm Shell often prestressed to overcome tensile stresses L/h ratio about 10–15.
Reinforced skew grid		300–700	10–20	25–35	Deflection Bending Corners stiffer with skew grid than with grid parallel to sides thus allowing larger spans

Table XXXVII Concrete – wall and frame systems

Element	Section and plan	Typical spans (L) (m)	Typical L/d	Remarks
Single storey precast frames		12–24	22–30	Joints in horizontal member usually at corner or about L/4 from corner if frame is large

Table XXXVII *Continued*

Element	Section and plan	Typical spans (L) (m)	Typical L/d	Remarks
Arches		15–60	28–40	Arches usually continuous and fully rigid between springing points L/h ratio about 4–12
Precast exterior frames with interiors cast-in-place		6–12	22–30	Connections between precast components done with cast-in-place concrete Interior frame may also use precast elements or be cast against precast permanent formwork System used for buildings up to about 20 storeys high Spans given indicative only
Cast-in-place floor and wall panel systems		6–12	25–30	This system usually uses a standard rapid formwork system System is inherently rigid and used for buildings up to about 20 storeys high
Precast floor and wall panel systems		6–12	22–25	Usually no rigid joint between floor and wall panels; hence system similar in many respects to load bearing masonry with floor slab System economic up to about 15 storeys
Precast beams and columns with precast floor units		6–12	14–16	With rigid connections, system can only go up to about two storeys without extra vertical bracing
Multistorey cast-in-place frames		5–15 storeys	1–5	Cast-in-place frames without extra vertical bracing are economic up to about 15 storeys L/d ratio about 20–40
Shear walls or cores with rigid frame		10–55 storeys	4–5	Shear wall or core interacts with rigid frame to provide a vertical bracing system which is stiff over height of building Given values of height ratio (H/W) larger for buildings less than about 20 storeys high
Framed tubes and core		40–65 storeys	6–7	Also known as tube in tube system Framed tube interacts with core
Core structures with suspended floors or semi-rigid frame		10–30 storeys	8–12	Core provides all lateral stability Only limited plan areas with suspended floors

Table XXXVIII Concrete – below grand

Element	Section	Typical heights (H) (m)	Typical L/d	Remarks
Retaining wall		2–6	10–12	Dimension B is about H/2–2H/3 Toe helps to prevent sliding
Shell and box enclosures		1–4	25–30	Used for subways, culverts etc Loading depends on soil type and depth

Table XXXIX Concrete – elements carrying gravity load

Horizontal section on element	Elevation on element	Sizing formulae	Remarks
Prestressed tie 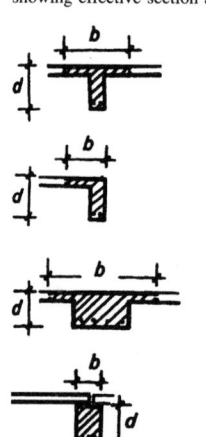		$P < \dfrac{A.u}{3}$ where A is area of tie P is working value of tie force u is ultimate compressive strength of concrete by standard cylinder test ($= 0.8 \times$ ultimate strength by standard cube test)	Minimum working force in prestressing cables is at least equal to P
Reinforced column		$P < \dfrac{A.u}{3}(1 + 0.14n)$ where A is area of column P is working value of axial load n is percentage of mild steel longitudinal reinforcement $\dfrac{h}{t} < 15$ where t is least width of column and h is height between lateral supports	Concrete columns in buildings are usually 'short' ie $h_{cf}/t < 15$; formulae given for 'short' columns, axially loaded with longitudinal reinforcement and link bars With more reinforcement reduction in area possible eg with 4% reinforcement there is a possible 20% reduction in area compared to 2% reinforcement; typical percentages vary from 2% to 6% For building laterally braced, for example by stair or elevator shafts, the effective height of columns h_{cf}, is not greater than the actual height; for slender columns, those with h_{cf}/t >15, there is a decrease in load compared to that for 'short' columns eg for column with $h_{cf}/t = 30$ area required is double that for same load on 'short' column To take account of bending, if present, as well as the compression in columns, multiply vertical load on column by $\dfrac{s + x}{s + 1}$ and treat factored amount as axial vertical load where s is the number of storeys above the column considered and $x = 1.25$ for interior columns, $x = 2.00$ for corner columns and $x = 1.50$ for all other exterior columns For 1 h fire rating, minimum length of side of column = 200 mm and for 2 h rating length = 300 mm
Simply supported reinforced beam showing effective section at midspan	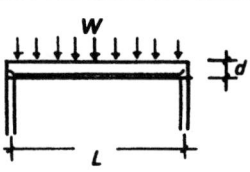	$\dfrac{L}{d} = 18$ (rectangular beams) or $\dfrac{L}{d} = 15$ (T and L beams) giving $\Delta \approx L/240$ where d is overall depth of beam and L is span Economic value of d given when $\dfrac{M}{u.b.d^2} = 0.03$ to 0.05 with maximum value ≈ 0.09 where M is working value of bending moment b is width of top of beam $\dfrac{V}{u.b_1.d} < 0.06$ with maximum value ≈ 0.15 where V is working value of shear force at supports b_1 is width of web of beam	Span to depth ratios given for beams with about 1% tension reinforcement at a stress of 240 N/mm²; higher values of L/d up to about 1.5 those given are possible for wide beams or those with heavier reinforcement; for long spans L/d should be reduced Span to depth ratios given are for rectangular and T and L beams having similar flange widths; T and L beams give considerable savings in concrete section and weight, compared to rectangular beams designed for same task, and can be assumed to have same L/d ratio as a narrow rectangular beam For T beams at midspan $b = L/5$ and for L beams $b = L/10$ Typical total percentages of reinforcement in beam are between 2.5% and 4.5% More efficient use of material is had with high values of L/d; however, to prevent lateral instability restraints required, usually by floor or roof construction, eg for a beam with $d/b = 4$ maximum span between lateral restraints = $60\,b$ Bending moment in middle of beam, $M = W.L/8$ where W is total u.d. load on beam and shear at supports = $W/2$ Required area of steel in tension $= \dfrac{M}{p \times 0.8\,d_1}$ where p is allowable working stress in steel d_1 is the effective depth of the beam equal to the distance from the centre of the reinforcement to the top of the beam For 1 h fire rating minimum width of beam = 120 mm and for 2 h fire rating width = 200 mm

Table XXXIX *Continued*

Horizontal section on element	Elevation on element	Sizing formulae	Remarks
Continuous reinforced beam showing effective section at midspan, left, and at support, right 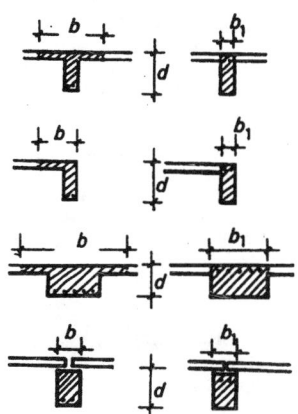	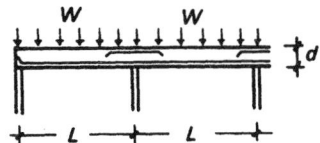	$\dfrac{L}{d} = 22$ (rectangular beams) or $\dfrac{L}{d} = 18$ (T and L beams) giving $\Delta \approx L/240$ where d is overall depth of beam and L is span Economic value of d given when $\dfrac{M}{u.b.d^2}$ or $\dfrac{M}{u.b_1.d^2} = 0.03$ to 0.05 with maximum value ≈ 0.09 where M is working value of bending moment b is width of top of beam at midspan and b_1 is width of beam web at support u is ultimate strength of concrete by standard cylinder test $(= 0.8 \times$ ultimate strength by standard cube test) $\dfrac{V}{u.b_1.d} < 0.06$ with maximum value $= 0.15$ where V is working value of shear force at supports	At support points T and L beams have an effective section which is rectangular For T-beam at midspan $b = L/7$ and for L-beams $b = L/14$ Bending moment at middle of end span $= W.L/11$ and at first interior support $= W.L/9$ where W is total working u.d. load on span, all spans are equal and dead load is greater than live load Shear at supports $= 0.6\,W$ Required area of steel in tension $= \dfrac{M}{p \times 0.8d_1}$ where p is allowable working stress in steel and d_1 is the effective depth of the beam Notes on span to depth ratios as for simply supported beams For 1 h fire rating minimum width of beam $= 120$ mm and for 2 h fire rating width $= 150$ mm
Cantilevered reinforced beam showing effective section at support 	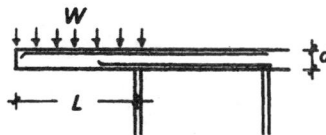	$\dfrac{L}{d} = 8$ where d is overall depth of cantilever L is length of cantilever Economic value of d given when $\dfrac{M}{u.b_1.d^2} = 0.03$ to 0.05 with maximum value ≈ 0.09 where M is working value of bending moment b_1 is width of web of beam $\dfrac{V}{u.b_1.d} < 0.06$ with maximum value $= 0.15$ where V is working value of shear force at supports	For cantilever beam with $d/b = 4$, maximum distance between end and last lateral restraint $= 25\,b$ Bending moment at support $= W.L/2$ where W is total u.d. load on cantilever and shear is W Notes on fire resistance and on span to depth ratio as for simply supported beams
Simply supported prestressed beam 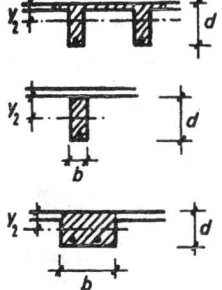	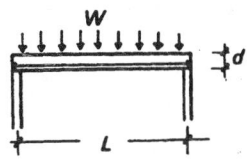	$\dfrac{L}{d} = 34$ (rectangular beams) or $\dfrac{L}{d} = 28$ (T and L beams) $Z = \dfrac{l}{y_2} = \dfrac{1.40M}{u}$ (rectangular section) or $Z_2 = \dfrac{l}{y_2} = \dfrac{1.45M}{u}$ (double T-section)	y_2 is the distance from the centroid to the top of the concrete section l is the moment of inertia of the section about the centroid Z is the section modulus, which, for rectangular sections, is equal to $b.d^2/6$ M is the working value of the banding moment Depth of prestressed beams are about 65% of those required in reinforced concrete Minimum working values of the prestressing force in cables are $M/0.5d$ for rectangular sections or $M/0.6d$ for double T sections, where M, as above, is the maximum working value of the bending moment in the beam

Table XXXIX *Continued*

Plan on element	Vertical section	Sizing formulae	Remarks
Simply supported one-way solid slab 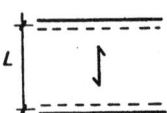	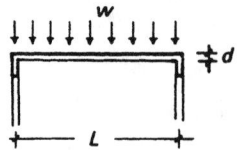	$\dfrac{L}{d} = 20$ giving $\Delta \approx L/240$ where d is overall depth of slab and L is span	Span to depth ratio given for slabs with about 0.5% tension steel reinforcement working at a stress of 240 N/mm². With effective depth of slab = 0.85d; higher values of L/d up to about 30 possible with more reinforcement. Typical percentages of reinforcement in one-way slabs ≈ 1% Bending moment at middle of slab = $w.L^2/8$ per unit width where W is load per unit area For cantilever slabs span to depth ratio $L/d = 9$ with bending moment = $w.L/2$ Required area of steel in tension $$= \frac{M}{p \times 0.8 d_1}$$ where M is working value of bending moment, p is allowable working stress in steel, d_1 is the effective depth of the slab For 1 h fire rating minimum, depth of slab $d = 95$ mm and for 2 h fire rating $d = 125$ mm
Continuous one-way solid slab 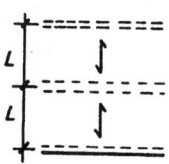	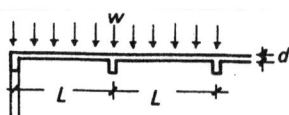	$\dfrac{L}{d} = 25$ giving $\Delta \approx L/240$	Span to depth ratio given for slabs with about 0.5% tension steel reinforcement working at a stress of 240 N/mm². With effective depth of slab = 0.85d; higher values of L/d up to about 35 possible with more reinforcement For 1 h fire rating minimum depth of slab $d = 95$ mm and for 2 h rating $d = 125$ mm Bending moment in middle of slab = $w.L^2/12$ per unit width and bending moment at interior supports = $w.L^2/9$ where w is total load per unit area and dead load is greater than live load
Continuous two-way solid slab 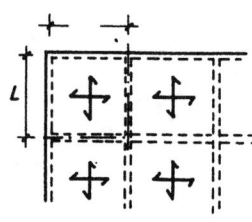	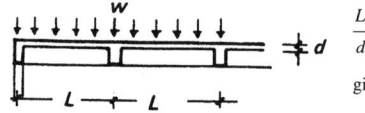	$\dfrac{L}{d} = 32$ giving $\Delta \approx L/240$	Span to depth ratio given for square slabs supported along the edges with 0.25% tension steel reinforcement, in two directions, working at stress of 240 N/mm². With effective depth of slab = 0.8d; higher values of L/d up to about 40 possible with more reinforcement Typical percentages of reinforcement in two-way slabs ≈ 0.8% Bending moment at middle of slab = $w.L^2/24$ per unit width and bending moment at interior supports = $w.L^2/18$ where w is total load per unit area and dead load is greater than live load Notes on fire resistance as for one-way slabs
Continuous one-way ribbed slab	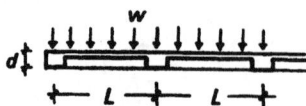	$\dfrac{L}{d} = 16$ giving $\Delta \approx L/240$ where d is overall depth of slab and L is span $\dfrac{V}{u.b_1.d} < 0.014$ where V is working value of shear force on each rib, b_2 is width of rib and d is overall depth of slab	Span to depth ratio given for slab with about 0.5% tension reinforcement, based on gross cross-sectional area including voids, working at a stress of 240 N/mm². With effective depth of slab = 0.85d; higher values of L/d up to about 30 possible with more reinforcement. Bending moment on each rib at centre of slab = $c.w.L^2/12$ and bending moment on each rib at support = $c.w.L^2/30$ with wide support beam or = $c.w.L^2/9$ with narrow support beam where c is spacing of ribs and w is load per unit area For 1 h fire rating minimum width of ribs and depth of slab between ribs = 90 mm and for 2 h rating these dimensions = 115 mn

Table XXXIX *Continued*

Plan on element	Vertical section	Sizing formulae	Remarks
Continuous two-way waffle slab	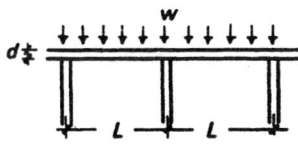	$\dfrac{L}{d} = 26$ giving $\Delta \approx L/240$ $\dfrac{V}{u.b_1.d} < 0.014$ where V is working value of shear force on each rib of waffle slab	Span to depth ratio given for slab with 0.25% tension reinforcement in two directions, based on gross cross-sectional area including voids, working at a stress of 240N/mm². With effective depth of slab = 0.80d; higher values of L/d up to about 35 possible with more reinforcement Bending moment on beams with the same depth as the slab are as for T-beams in two-way beam and slab systems M at midspan $= \dfrac{2w.L^2}{3} \cdot \dfrac{L}{12}$ and at support $= \dfrac{2w.L^2}{3} \cdot \dfrac{L}{9}$ where w is total load per unit area with dead load greater than live load Bending moment on each rib at centre of slab $= c.w.L^2/24$ and at support $= c.w.L^2/18$ where c is spacing of ribs of waffle slab
Flat slabs without drop panels		$\dfrac{L}{d} = 29$ $\dfrac{w.L^2}{u.d(4t + 12d)} < 0.014$ where t *is* diameter of round column or length of side of square column	Span to depth ratio given for square panels having three equal bays in each direction with 0.25% tension reinforcement in two directions working at stress of 240 N/mm² Higher values of L/d up to 32 possible with more reinforcement Bending moments on column strip at midspan $= w.L^2/8$ per unit width and over columns, without redistribution, $= w.L^2/6$ per unit width where w is full load per unit area and dead load is greater than live load; bending moments on middle strip as for two-way solid slabs
Flat slab with drop panels		$\dfrac{L}{d} = 32$ $\dfrac{w.L^2}{u.d_d(4t + 12d_d)} < 0.014$ where d_4 is depth of slab plus depth of drop panel	Span to depth ratio given for square panels having three equal bays in each direction with 0.25% reinforcement in two directions working at stress of 240 N/mm² Higher values of L/d up to 36 possible with more reinforcement Bending moments as for flat slabs without drop panels Typical value of length of side of drop panel, m, is between 0.3L and 0.5L

Table XL Properties of steel and aluminium.

Property	Prestressing strand	High strength low-alloy steel	Structural carbon steel	Coldformed steel	Casting steel	Wrought iron	Grey cast iron	Wrought aluminium Alloy
Carbon content %	0.60–0.90	0.10–0.28	0.10–0.25	0.20–0.25	0.15–0.50	0.05	2.50–4.50	..
Specific gravity	7.8	7.8	7.8	7.8	7.8	7.6	7.2	2.8
Weight kN/m³	77	77	77	77	77	75	71	27
Tensile strength N/mm²	1200–1800	400–700	400–560	280–600	400–600	300–350 (in r. line)	150–350	200–550
Yield stress or 0.2% proof stress N/mm² – stress at or near which permanent deformation starts	1100–1700	340–480	240–300	200–500	200–400	180–200 (in line of rolling)	..	120–500
Elastic modulus kN/mm²	165	210	210	210	210	190	210	70
Fracture toughness at 20° C MN/m^½ – resistance to brittle failure	10–150	10–150	50–400	20–400	20–200	100–300	5–20	25–50
Temperature at which alloys have Charpy V-notch value >27J °C	..	−15	−50	−15	−30	..	+20	−50
Elongation % – ductility	4	15	15–25	12–25	15–20	8–25	2	8–20
Fatigue ratio in reversed tension – working stress as a proportion of tensile strength below which fatigue does not affect life of part (10^7 cycles)	0.3	0.5	0.4	0.4	0.3	0.2–0.5	0.4	0.3
Weldability	not suitable for welding	good with right alloys	good if low-carbon steel	generally good	moderate	generally poor	poor	good if right alloys
Coefficient of thermal expansion × 10^{-6}/°C	12	12	12	12	12	12	12	24
Thermal conductivity W/m °C	45	45	45	45	45	45	45	205
Temperature at which metal has 50% of room temperature strength °C	350–500	500	500	500	500	500	can crack at high temperatures	190
Corrosion resistance of untreated metal	poor	moderate to good	poor	poor to moderate	moderate	good	good	very good

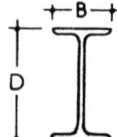
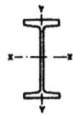

Table XLI Universal beams

1 Dimensions and properties

Serial size mm	Mass per metre kg	Depth of section D mm	Width of section B mm	Area of section cm²	Moment of inertia			Radius of gyration		Elastic modulus		Ratio $\dfrac{D}{T}$
					Axis x–x		Axis y–y cm⁴	Axis x–x cm	Axis y–y cm	Axis x–x cm³	Axis y–y cm³	
					Gross cm⁴	Net cm⁴						
305 × 165	54	310.9	166.8	68.4	11 710	10 134	1 061	13.09	3.94	753.3	127.3	22.7
	46	307.1	165.7	58.9	9 948	8 609	897	13.00	3.90	647.9	108.3	26.0
	40	303.8	165.1	51.5	8 523	7 384	763	12.86	3.85	561.2	92.4	29.9
305 × 127	48	310.4	125.2	60.8	9 504	8 643	460	12.50	2.75	612.4	73.5	22.2
	42	306.6	124.3	53.2	8 143	7 409	388	12.37	2.70	531.2	62.5	25.4
	37	303.8	123.5	47.5	7 162	6 519	337	12.28	2.67	471.5	54.6	28.4
305 × 102	33	312.7	102.4	40.8	6 487	5 800	193	12.46	2.15	415.0	37.8	29.0
	28	308.9	101.9	36.3	5 421	4 862	157	12.22	2.08	351.0	30.8	34.8
	25	304.8	101.6	31.4	4 387	3 962	120	11.82	1.96	287.9	23.6	44.6
254 × 146	43	259.6	147.3	55.1	6 558	5 706	677	10.91	3.51	505.3	92.0	20.4
	37	256.0	146.4	47.5	5 556	4 834	571	10.82	3.47	434.0	78.1	23.4
	31	251.5	146.1	40.0	4 439	3 879	449	10.53	3.35	353.1	61.5	29.1
254 × 102	28	260.4	102.1	36.2	4 008	3 569	178	10.52	2.22	307.9	34.9	26.0
	25	257.0	101.9	32.2	3 408	3 046	148	10.29	2.14	265.2	29.0	30.8
	22	254.0	101.6	28.4	2 867	2 575	120	10.04	2.05	225.7	23.6	37.2
203 × 133	30	206.8	133.8	38.0	2 887	2 476	384	8.72	3.18	279.3	57.4	21.5
	25	203.2	133.4	32.3	2 356	2 027	310	8.54	3.10	231.9	46.4	26.0

2 Safe loads for grade 43 steel (ordinary mild steel)

Serial size	Mass per metre	Safe distributed loads in kilonewtons for spans in metres and deflection coefficients													Critical span L_c
		2.00	2.50	3.00	3.50	4.00	4.50	5.00	5.50	6.00	7.00	8.00	9.00	10.00	
mm	kg	112.0	71.68	49.78	36.57	28.00	22.12	17.92	14.81	12.44	9.143	7.000	5.531	4.480	m
305 × 165	54	479*	398	331	284	249	221	199	181	166	142	124	110	99	3.69
	46	412*	342	285	244	214	190	171	155	143	122	107	95	86	3.53
	40	370	296	247	212	185	165	148	135	123	106	93	82	74	3.38
305 × 127	48	404	323	269	231	202	180	162	147	135	115	101	90	81	2.59
	42	351	280	234	200	175	156	140	127	117	100	88	78	70	2.45
	37	311	249	207	178	156	138	124	113	104	89	78	69	62	2.37
305 × 102	33	274	219	183	158	137	122	110	100	91	78	68	61	55	1.90
	28	232	185	154	132	116	103	93	84	77	66	58	51	46	1.79
	25	190	152	127	109	95	84	76	69	63	54	47*	42	38	1.64
254 × 146	43	333	267	222	191	167	148	133	121	111	95	83			3.41
	37	286	229	191	164	143	127	115	104	95	82	72			3.22
	31	233	186	155	133	117	104	93	85	78	67	58			2.96
254 × 102	28	203	163	135	116	102	90	81	74	68	58	51			2.01
	25	175	140	117	100	88	78	70	64	58	50	37			1.87
	22	149	119	99	85	74	66	60	54	50	43	37			1.75
203 × 133	30	184	147	123	105	92	82	74	67	61	53				3.03
	25	153	122	102	87	77	68	61	56	51					2.80

Notes: In calculating the net amount of inertia, each flange is reduced by one hole. other sizes are available
Loads printed in *italic* type do not cause overloading of the unstiffened web, and do not cause deflection exceeding span/360.
Loads printed in ordinary type should be checked for deflection.
*Load is based on allowable shear of web and is less than allowable load in bending.

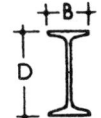

Table XLII Joists

1 Dimensions and properties

Nominal size mm	Mass per metre kg	Depth of section D mm	Width of section B mm	Area of section cm²	Moment of inertia Axis x–x Gross cm⁴	Moment of inertia Axis x–x Net cm⁴	Axis y–y cm⁴	Radius of gyration Axis x–x cm	Radius of gyration Axis y–y cm	Elastic modulus Axis x–x cm³	Elastic modulus Axis y–y cm³	Ratio $\dfrac{D}{T}$
254 × 203	81.85	254.0	203.2	104.4	12 016	10 527	2 278	10.7	4.67	946.2	224.3	12.8
254 × 114	37.20	254.0	114.3	47.4	5 092	4 243	270.1	10.4	2.39	401.0	47.19	19.8
203 × 152	52.09	203.2	152.4	66.4	4 789	4 177	813.3	8.48	3.51	471.3	106.7	12.3
152 × 127	37.20	152.4	127.0	47.5	1 818	1 627	378.8	6.20	2.82	238.6	59.65	11.5
127 × 114	29.76	127.0	114.3	37.3	979.0	866.9	241.9	5.12	2.55	154.2	42.32	11.0
127 × 114	26.79	127.0	114.3	34.1	944.8	834.6	235.4	5.26	2.63	148.8	41.19	11.1
127 × 76	16.37	127.0	76.2	21.0	569.4	476.1	60.35	5.21	1.70	89.64	15.90	13.2
114 × 114	26.79	114.3	114.3	34.4	735.4	651.2	223.1	4.62	2.54	128.6	39.00	10.7
102 × 102	23.07	101.6	101.6	29.4	486.1	425.1	154.4	4.06	2.29	95.70	30.32	9.9
102 × 44	7.44	101.6	44.4	9.5	152.3	126.9	7.91	4.01	0.91	29.99	3.44	16.7
89 × 89	19.35	88.9	88.9	24.9	306.7	263.7	101.1	3.51	2.01	68.99	22.78	9.0
76 × 76	14.67	76.2	80.0	19.1	171.9	144.1	60.77	3.00	1.78	45.06	15.24	9.1
76 × 76	12.65	76.2	76.2	16.3	158.6	130.7	52.03	3.12	1.78	41.62	13.60	9.1

2 Safe loads for grade 43 steel (ordinary mild steel)

Nominal size mm	Mass per metre kg	Safe distributed loads in kilonewtons for spans in metres and deflection coefficients 1.00 448	1.25 287	1.50 199	1.75 146	2.00 112	2.25 88.5	2.50 71.7	2.75 59.2	3.00 49.8	3.25 42.4	3.50 36.6	4.00 28.0	4.25 24.8	Critical span L_c m
254 × 203	81.85						518*	500	454	416	304	357	312	294	5.80
254 × 114	37.20		386*	353	302	265	235	212	192	176	163	151	132	125	2.35
203 × 152	52.09			362*	356	311	277	249	226	207	191	178	156	146	4.47
152 × 127	37.20	315	252	210	180	158	140	126	115	105	97	90	79	74	3.79
127 × 114	29.76	204	163	136	116	102	90	81	74	68	63	58	51	48	3.55
127 × 114	26.79	188*	157	131	112	98	87	79	71	65	60	56	49	46	3.61
127 × 76	16.37	118	95	79	68	59	53	47	43	39	36	34	30	28	2.06
114 × 114	26.79	170	136	113	97	85	75	68	62	57	52	49	42	40	3.63
102 × 102	23.07	126	101	84	72	63	56	51	46	42	39	36	32	30	3.48
102 × 44	7.44	40	32	26	23	20	18	16	14	13	12	11	10	9	0.95
89 × 89	19.35	91	73	61	52	46	41	36	33	30	28	26	23	21	3.33
76 × 76	14.67	60	48	40	34	30	26	24	22	20	18	17	15	14	2.91
76 × 76	12.65	55	44	37	31	27	24	22	20	18	17	16	14	13	2.95

Notes: In calculating the net moment of inertia, one hole is deducted from each flange.

Sections with mass shown in italics, although frequently rolled were not in BS.4. Availability should be checked with BSC Sections Product Unit. Flanges of BS4 joists have a 5° taper; all others taper at 8°.

The loads listed are based on bending stresses of 165N/mm² in section 2 and 230N/mm² in section 3 and assume adequate lateral support. Without such support the span must not exceed L_c unless the compressive stress is reduced in accordance with clause 19a of BS 449.

Loads printed in **bold** type may cause overloading of the unstiffened web, the capacity of which should be checked.

Loads printed in *italic* type do not cause overloading of the unstiffened web, and do not cause deflection exceeding span/360.

Loads printed in ordinary type should be checked for deflection.

*Load is based on allowable shear of web and is less than allowable load in bending.

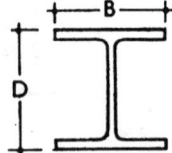

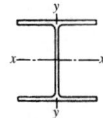

Table XLIII Universal columns used as beams

1 Dimensions and properties

Serial size mm	Mass per metre kg	Depth of section D mm	Width of section B mm	Area of section cm²	Moment of inertia			Radius of gyration		Elastic modulus		Ratio D/T
					Axis x–x		Axis y–y cm⁴	Axis x–x cm	Axis y–y cm	Axis x–x cm³	Axis y–y cm³	
					Gross cm⁴	Net cm⁴						
254 × 254	167	289.1	264.5	212.4	29 914	27 171	9 796	11.9	6.79	2070	740.6	9.1
	132	276.4	261.0	167.7	22 416	20 350	7 444	11.6	6.66	1622	570.4	11.0
	107	266.7	258.3	136.6	17 510	15 889	5 901	11.3	6.57	1313	456.9	13.0
	89	260.4	255.9	114.0	14 307	12 973	4 849	11.2	6.52	1099	378.9	15.0
	73	254.0	254.0	92.9	11 360	10 299	3 873	11.1	6.46	894.5	305.0	17.9
203 × 203	86	222.3	208.8	110.1	9 462	8 373	3 119	9.27	5.32	851.5	298.7	10.8
	71	215.9	206.2	91.1	7 647	6 756	2 536	9.16	5.28	708.4	246.0	12.4
	60	209.6	205.2	75.8	6 088	5 383	2 041	8.96	5.19	581.1	199.0	14.8
	52	206.2	203.9	66.4	5 263	4 651	1 770	8.90	5.16	510.4	173.6	16.5
	46	203.2	203.2	58.8	4 564	4 035	1 539	8.81	5.11	449.2	151.5	18.5
152 × 152	37	161.8	154.4	47.4	2 218	1 931	709	6.84	3.87	274.2	91.78	14.0
	30	157.5	152.9	38.2	1 742	1 516	558	6.75	3.82	221.2	73.06	16.8
	23	152.4	152.4	29.8	1 263	1 104	403	6.51	3.68	165.7	52.95	22.3

2 Safe loads for grade 43 steel (ordinary mild steel)

Serial size	Mass per metre	Safe distributed loads in kilonewtons for spans in metres and deflection coefficients														Critical span L_c
		1.5	2.0	2.5	3.0	3.5	4.0	4.5	5.0	5.5	6.0	6.5	7.0	7.5	8.0	
m	kg	199.1	112.0	71.68	49.78	36.57	28.00	22.12	17.92	14.81	12.44	10.60	9.143	7.964	7.000	m
254 × 254	167		1110*	1093	911	781	683	607	546	497	455	420	390	364	342	11.094
	132		862*	856	714	612	535	476	428	389	357	329	306	285	268	9.265
	107		694*	693	578	495	433	385	347	315	289	267	248	231	217	8.068
	89			546*	484	414	363	322	290	264	242	223	207	193	181	7.280
	73			436*	394	337	295	262	236	215	197	182	169	157	148	6.611
203 × 203	86	578*	562	450	375	321	281	250	225	204	187	173	161	150	140	7.511
	71		444*	374	312	267	234	208	187	170	156	144	134	125	117	6.665
	60	390*	384	307	256	219	192	170	153	139	126	118	110	102	96	5.864
	52		330*	269	225	192	168	150	135	122	112	104	96	90	84	5.491
	46	297*	296	237	197	169	148	132	119	108	99	91	85	79	74	5.154
152 × 152	37	241	181	145	121	103	90	80	72	66	60	56	52	48	45	4.504
	30	195	146	117	97	83	73	65	58	53	49	45	42	39	36	4.028
	23	146	109	87	73	62	55	49	44	40	36	34	31	29	27	3.462

Notes: In calculating the moment of inertia, each flange is reduced by one hole.
The loads listed are based on bending stresses of 165N/mm² in section 2 and 230N/mm² in section 3 and assume adequate lateral support. Without such support the span must not exceed L unless the compressive stress is reduced in accordance with clause 19a of BS 449.
Loads printed in **bold** type may cause overloading of the unstiffened web, the capacity of which should be checked.
Loads printed in *italic* type do not cause overloading of the unstiffened web, and do not cause deflection exceeding span/360.
Loads printed in ordinary type should be checked for deflection.
*Load is based on allowable shear of web and is less than allowable load in bending.

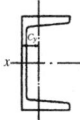

Table XLIV Channels

1 Dimensions and properties

Nominal size mm	Mass per metre kg	Depth of section D mm	Width of section B mm	Area of section cm²	Dimension Cy cm	Moment of inertia			Radius of gyration		Elastic modulus		Ratio $\dfrac{D}{T}$
						Axis x–x		Axis y–y cm⁴	Axis x–x cm	Axis y–y cm	Axis x–x cm³	Axis y–y cm³	
						Gross cm⁴	Net cm⁴						
305 × 102	46.18	304.8	101.6	58.83	2.66	8214	6583	499.5	11.8	2.91	539.0	66.59	20.5
305 × 89	41.69	304.8	88.9	53.11	2.18	7061	5826	325.4	11.5	2.48	463.3	48.49	22.3
254 × 89	35.74	254.0	88.9	45.52	2.42	4448	3612	302.4	9.88	2.58	350.2	46.70	18.7
254 × 76	28.29	254.0	76.2	36.03	1.86	3367	2669	162.6	9.67	2.12	265.1	28.21	23.2
229 × 89	32.76	228.6	88.9	41.73	2.53	3387	2732	285.0	9.01	2.61	296.4	44.82	17.2
229 × 76	26.06	228.6	76.2	33.20	2.00	2610	2041	158.7	8.87	2.19	228.3	28.22	20.5
203 × 89	29.78	203.2	88.9	37.94	2.65	2491	1996	164.4	8.10	2.64	245.2	42.34	15.8
203 × 76	23.82	203.2	76.2	30.34	2.13	1950	1508	151.3	8.02	2.23	192.0	27.59	18.2
178 × 89	26.81	177.8	88.9	34.15	2.76	1753	1397	241.0	7.16	2.66	197.2	39.29	14.5
178 × 76	20.84	177.8	76.2	26.54	2.20	1337	1028	134.0	7.10	2.25	150.4	24.72	17.3
152 × 89	23.84	152.4	88.9	30.36	2.86	1166	924.1	215.1	6.20	2.66	153.0	35.70	13.2
152 × 76	17.88	152.4	76.2	22.77	2.21	851.5	653.6	113.8	6.12	2.24	111.8	21.05	16.9
127 × 64	14.90	127.0	63.5	18.98	1.94	482.5	367.1	67.23	5.04	1.88	75.99	15.25	13.8
102 × 51	10.42	101.6	50.8	13.28	1.51	207.7	167.8	29.10	3.95	1.48	40.89	8.16	13.3
76 × 38	6.70	76.2	38.1	8.53	1.19	74.14	54.48	10.66	2.95	1.12	19.46	4.07	11.2

2 Safe loads for grade 43 steel (ordinary mild steel)

Nominal size mm	Mass per metre kg	Safe distributed loads in kilonewtons for spans in metres and deflection coefficients													Critical span L_c m
		1.50 199.1	2.00 112.0	2.50 71.68	3.00 49.78	3.50 36.57	4.00 28.00	4.50 22.12	5.00 17.92	5.50 14.81	6.00 12.44	7.00 9.143	8.00 7.000	9.00 5.531	
305 × 102	46.18	*474*	*356*	*285*	*237*	*203*	*178*	*158*	142	129	119	102	89	79	3.077
304 × 89	41.69	*408*	*306*	*245*	*204*	*175*	*153*	*136*	122	111	102	87	76	68	2.537
254 × 89	35.74	*308*	*231*	*185*	*154*	*132*	*116*	103	92	84	77	66	58		2.842
254 × 76	28.29	*233*	*175*	*140*	*117*	*100*	87	78	70	64	58	50	44		2.142
229 × 89	32.76	*261*	*196*	*156*	*130*	*112*	98	87	78	71	65	56			3.005
229 × 76	26.06	*201*	*151*	*121*	*100*	86	75	67	60	55	50	43			2.317
203 × 89	29.78	*216*	*162*	*129*	*108*	92	81	72	65	59	54				3.190
203 × 76	23.82	*169*	*127*	*101*	*84*	72	63	56	51	46	42				2.497
178 × 89	26.81	*174*	*130*	*104*	*87*	74	65	58	52	47	43				3.388
178 × 76	20.84	*132*	*99*	*79*	*66*	57	50	44	40	36	33				2.577
152 × 89	23.84	*135*	*101*	*81*	67	58	50	45	40						3.629
152 × 76	17.88	*98*	*74*	*59*	49	42	37	33	30						2.591
127 × 64	14.90	*67*	*50*	40	33	29	25								2.477
102 × 51	10.42	*36*	*27*	22	18										1.993
76 × 38	6.70	*17*	13	10											1.724

Notes: In calculating the moment of inertia, each flange is reduced by one hole.
The loads listed are based on bending stresses of 165N/mm² in section 2 and 230N/mm² in section 3 and assume adequate lateral support. Without such support the span must not exceed L_c unless the compressive stress is reduced in accordance with clause 19a (ii) of BS 449.
Loads printed in *italic* type do not cause overloading of the unstiffened web, and do not cause deflection exceeding span/360.
Loads printed in ordinary type should be checked for deflection.

Table XLV Steel – vertical support elements

Element	Horizontal and vertical section	Typical heights (h) (m)	h/d between lateral supports	Critical factors for sizing	Remarks
Rolled steel of open section – single storey – multistorey		2–8 2–4	20–25 7–18	Buckling ($h/d > 14$) Buckling and compression ($h/d < 14$)	Standard rolled sections usual but special shapes may be made by welding Connections easier with open rather than closed sections
Rolled steel of hollow section – single storey – multistorey		2–8 2–4	20–35 7–28	Buckling ($h/d < 20$) Buckling and compression ($h/d > 20$)	Closed sections have smaller exposed surface and greater torsional stiffness than open sections of same weight.
Lattice column		4–10	20–25	Buckling	Lattice may be used if large column required
Steel and concrete composite column		2–4	6–15	Buckling and crushing ($h/d > 10$)	Concrete increases stiffness and fire resistance
Cold-formed steel studs with steel panels		2–8	15–50	Buckling	Steel studs can also be stiffeners for gypsum, GRC or plywood panels
High strength steel hangers		1–40	–	Axial stiffness	Hangers usually solid rods, strand or rope cables. Rods have less tensile strength but axially stiffer than cable

Table XLVI Steel – floors

Element	Section and elevation	Typical depths (d) (mm)	Typical spans (L) (m)	Typical L/d	Critical factors for sizing/remarks
Steel decking		50–75	2–3	35–40	Deflection
Cold-formed steel deck with composite concrete topping		100–150	2–4	25–30	Deflection of deck when used as formwork Thickness of concrete for fire protection Dimension $a \approx 40$–80 mm
Wide flange rolled steel section		100–500	4–12	18–28	Deflection
Deep rolled steel section		200–500	6–30	15–20	Deflection Bending strength
Rolled steel truss		1000–4000	12–45	8–15	Axial compression of members Joints Deflection
Vierendeel girder		1000–3000	6–18	4–12	Bending strength of members near supports Deflection
Composite concrete steel girder		300–1000	7–15	20–25	Often used with secondary steel joists between girders Saving of about 25% in steel compared to non-composite section

Table XLVII Steel – roofs, beam and deck

Element	Section and elevation	Typical depths (*d*) (mm)	Typical spans (*L*) (m)	Typical *L/d*	Critical factors for sizing/remarks
Cold-formed steel deck		25–120	2–6	40–70	Deflection
Steel sandwich panel		75	2–3	25–30	Sheet has injected plastic foam insulation Good bond of insulation to steel sheet is important.
Channel reinforced woodwool deck		50–150	2–4	20–25	Deflection Strength
Cold-formed steel sections		120–300	3–12	25–35	Deflection Often very flexible about minor axis
Cold-formed open web steel joist		300–1000	5–20	15–25	Deflection Buckling
Wide flange rolled steel section		100–500	6–14	20–30	Deflection
Deep rolled steel section		200–1000	6–60	18–26	Deflection Bending strength Buckling of top flange

9.03 Bearing pressure

The bearing pressure that can be carried by the soil is the *additional* load that can be carried on a unit area. A soil stratum at a depth of, say, 3 m is already carrying the weight of that 3 m of soil, **41.13**. In fact, the bearing capacity of many soils increases substantially with depth. This is because a common mode of failure under excessive load is sideways spillage of the soil, often accompanied by upward heave of the material around the area of application, **41.14**. Obviously this is much less likely where the load is carried at some depth, **41.15**.

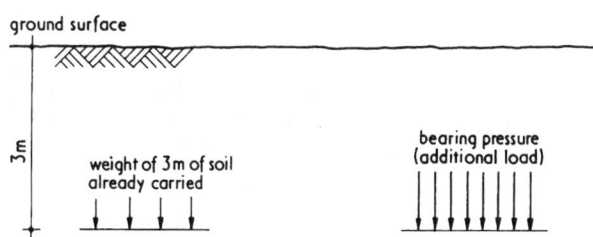

41.13 *Bearing pressure on formation level of soil*

Since the bearing capacity represents the additional load the soil can carry, the greater the depth, the smaller proportion of the total (or gross) pressure this will form. In fact, it is even possible to produce zero or negative net pressure by removing the overburden, and replacing it with something weighing much less, for example a hollow box. This is the principle by which loads can be carried on soft marshy soil; the extreme case is a boat! In many cases, the architect will be told what the bearing capacity of the soil is at normal foundation depth – about 1 m. Table LVI gives figures for common soils but should be used with caution.

9.04 Pad and strip foundations

These are the types of foundation most commonly met by architects, and their design should only require the use of an engineer if there are complications. Simple pad and strip foundation calculation is best shown from an example.

Example 1

A brick wall forming the outside of a house carries a load of 85 kN/m. What width of foundation will be required at a depth of 1.5 m, given a bearing capacity of the soil at that depth of 60 kN/m²? Ignore the weight of the foundation itself:

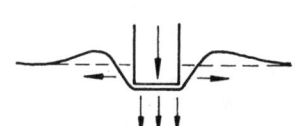

41.14 *Shallow foundation carrying excessive load can cause heave*

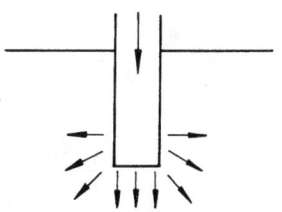

41.15 *A deeper foundation is restrained*

Table XLVIII Steel – roofs, beam and surface

Element	Section and elevation or plan	Typical spans (L) (m)	Typical L/d or L/b	Remarks
Rolled steel castellated beam		6–18	10–18	Web buckling Shear
Flat rolled steel truss		12–75	10–18	Bending strength Deflection Typical spacings of trusses 6–12 m Truss cambered for spans >25 m
Sloping rolled steel truss		8–20	5–10	Truss often bolted up from steel angle sections
Two-layer space frame		30–150	15–30	Space frame has pinned or semi-rigid joints and works as three-dimensional reticulated structure Plan geometry based on rectangular, triangular or hexagonal grids Size of grid, d, about 1.4 h and about 5–12% of span, L, $L < L_1 < 1.4L$
Braced barrel vault		20–100	55–60	Vaults may have single or double layer of steelwork L/h ratio about 5–6
Corrugated arch		30–45	4–5	Made with two layers of cold-formed corrugated sheet bolted together with insulation between
Cable-stayed roof beams		60–150	5–10	Cables serve to support horizontal beams and increase the span
Hanging cable roof		50–180	8–15	Roofs have single curvature (gutter) shape or synclastic double curvature (saucer) shape
Net roof with rigid covering		30–180	6–12	Roofs have anticlastic double curvature (saddle) shape
Single-layer domed grid		15–100	5–7	Double-layer domes also constructed spanning up to 200 m
Double-layer stressed skin folded plate		9–30	10–20	Single-layer skin construction possible spanning up to about 25 m Failure usually caused by connections or buckling
Double-layer stressed skin hyperbolic paraboloid shell		9–30	6–12	Steel sheets are laid along the straight line generators on the hp surface and slightly twisted across their width
Air supported stainless steel membrane		80–300	25–30	Low L/H ratio gives roof wind uplift and requires only small change in shape from flat plan shape

Table XLIX Steel – frame systems

Element	Section and plan	Typical spans (L) (m)	Typical L/d	Remarks
Single-storey rigid frame		9–60	35–40	Frame is rigid in its own plane Typical spacing of frames L/4–L/6
Arch		60–150	40–50	Buckling often critical Arch usually has pinned connections at base and sometimes at apex too Typical L/h ratio about 5–15
Single-storey beam and post		6–40	12–20	Frame not rigid in its own plane so vertical bracing necessary, eg with rigid gables connected to roof plane
Multistorey rigid frame		6–20	20–35	Sidesway at top and between storeys often critical Rigid joints between beams and columns obtained by welding or welding and bolting System economic up to about 25 storeys With moment joints between beams and columns, obtained by bolting, building may go up to about 15 storeys without the use of extra vertical bracing
Shear truss and simple frame		typical height, H 5–20 storeys	H/W 6–8	Frame is not rigidly connected to shear truss Shear truss more efficient as vertical bracing than rigid frame

Element	Section and plan	Typical heights (H) (storeys)	Typical H/W	Remarks
Shear truss and rigid frame		10–40 storeys	3–4	Frame is rigidly connected and interacts with shear truss Frame provides ductile strength in earthquake areas
Shear truss and rigid frame with belt trusses		40–60 storeys	5–7	Horizontal belt trusses reduce sidesway
Framed tube		30–80 storeys	5–7	Deep column and beam sections stiffen frame so that it can behave like a perforated tube
Diagonal truss tube		60–110 storeys	5–7	Diagonals take horizontal and vertical loads and stiffen frame

Table L Steel—below ground

Element	Section	Typical spans (L) (m)	Typical L/d	Remarks
Steel corrugated shells		2–8	30–80	Pipe arches usually made from galvanised cold-formed steel sheets with corrugations about 50–100 mm deep and bolted together with high-strength bolts Compression in sheet depends on soil and depth of cover

Table LI Steel – elements carrying gravity load

Element	Section and elevation on element or plan	Sizing formulae	Remarks
	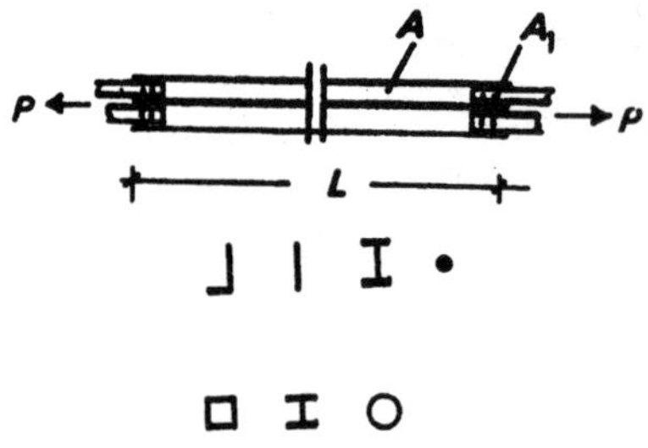	$\frac{P}{A_1} < p_1$ where P is working value of tie force A_1 is net area of tie p_1 is allowable working stress of steel in tension = 110 N/mm^2 $\frac{L}{r_{min}} < 240$ where r_{min} is minimum radius of gyration of tie section L is length of tie between supports Extension $e = \frac{P.L}{A.E}$ should be checked where A is gross area of tie E is elastic modulus of steel = 2.1×10^5 N/mm^2	At bolted connections, area of tie is reduced by holes and this is the net area, A_1 Area of tie usually decided by connection detail and need to limit extension If connection points markedly eccentric to centroid of tie, area of tie may need to be increased Increasing the width of the joint, whether bolted or welded, increases strength more than increasing overlap of joint Joints subject to alternating tension and compression need special consideration to prevent fatigue
Column r_y/b = r_x/d = 0.22 0.38 0.25 0.42 0.38 0.38 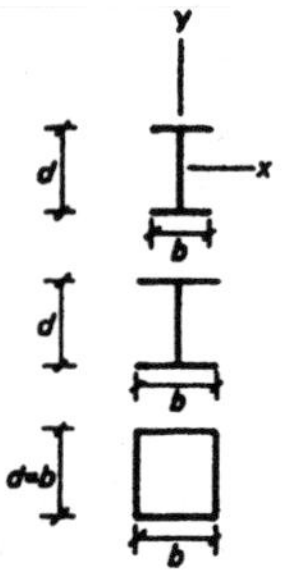	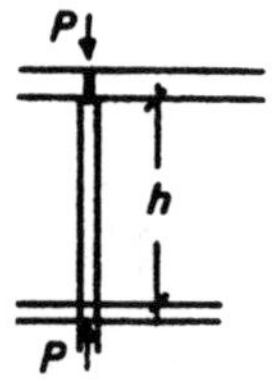 r_y/b = r_x/d = 0.41 0.35 0.35 0.35 0.60 0.35 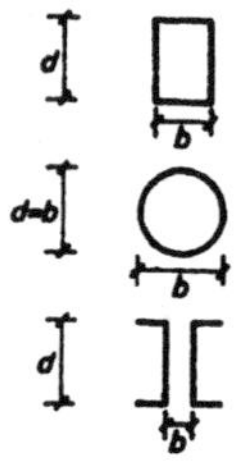	$\frac{P}{A} < p_c$ where P is axial load in column A is area of column p_c is allowable working stress of steel in compression which depends on slenderness ratio h_{ef}/r_{min} see below, where h_{ef} is effective height of column; slenderness ratio must not exceed 200 and should normally be less than 180 $\frac{h_{ef}}{r_{min}}$ = p_c = 10 150 N/mm^2 50 120 N/mm^2 80 100 N/mm^2 150 40 N/mm^2 200 20 N/mm	Dimension b is width of column along x axis, d is depth of column along y axis and c is width of column at right angles to v axis (axis of minimum moment of inertia and radius of gyration) For buildings which are laterally braced for example by cross-bracing or cores, effective height of columns, h_{ef} is not greater than actual height between floors h. Given formula valid for columns carrying axial load; for columns carrying bending moment as well as axial load Steel columns are usually slender and more efficient use of column material is had by collecting loads into one rather than several columns; an efficient section shape for each individual column is one with a low value of A/r_{min}^2 e.g. A/r_{min}^2 for square or circular sections varies from 0.8 to 2.5 and for 1-sections varies from 2 to 7
Simply supported rolled steel beam	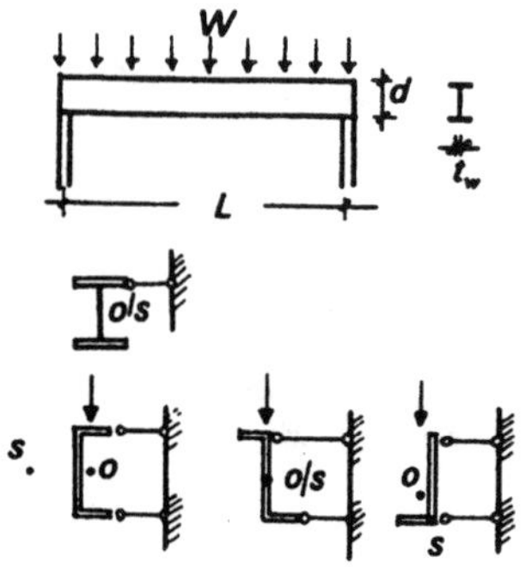	$\frac{M}{Z} = f_{bc} < p_{bc}$ where M is working value of bending moment on beam Z is the section modulus of the beam p_{bc} is allowable working stress of steel in bending = 165 N/mm^2 $\Delta = \frac{5W.L^3}{384E.I} = \frac{5f_{bc}.L^2}{24E.d}$ where W is u.d. load on beam L is span Δ is midspan deflection I is moment of inertia of beam E is elastic modulus of steel = 2.1×10^5 N/mm^2 f_{bc} is actual bending stress in beam at midspan Typical maximum span to depth ratios, L/d, are 28 for roof purlins 25 for roof beams in flat roofs 22 for floor beams giving total dead and live load deflections $\Delta = L/220$, $L/250$ and $L/280$ respectively if beam fully stressed, from above formule If live load deflection limited to $L/360$ then $E.I > 3.98 W_l.L^2$ where W_L is u.d. live load on beam $\frac{V}{d.t_w} < p_v$ where V is working value of shear force on beam t_w is the thickness of web of beam P_v is allowable working stress of steel in shear = 105 N/mm^2	Given allowable stress in bending p_{bc} assumes top flange restrained against buckling, and horizontal forces if any, with maximum distance between lateral restraints = $85r_{min}$; if distance between restraints = $150r_{min}$ then p_{bc} = 100 N/mm^2, where r_{min} is minimum radius of gyration of top flange spanning between any lateral restraints Steel sections symmetrical about the y axis have shear centre (O) in vertical line with centroid of section (S) for sections not symmetrical about y axis, loading along vertical line through centroid requires lateral restraint to prevent twist and/or lateral deflection of the section eg channel sections twist, Z-sections deflect laterally and angle sections twist and deflect laterally without such restraints; normally restraints provided by floor or roof construction Bending moment in middle of beam, M, = $W.L/8$ and shear force at supports = $W/2$

Table LI *Continued*

Element	Section and elevation on element or plan	Sizing formulae	Remarks
Continuous rolled steel beam	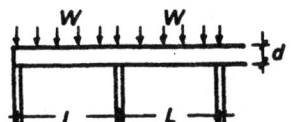	$\dfrac{M}{Z} = f_{bc} < p_{bc}$ where M is working value of bending moment on beam Z is the section modulus of the beam pbc is allowable working stress of steel in bending = 165 N/mm² $\Delta = \dfrac{5f_{bc}.L^2}{24E.d}$ or less where L is span of beam Δ is midspan deflection E is elastic modulus of steel = 2.1×10^5 N/mm² f_{bc} is actual bending stress in beam at midspan $\approx \dfrac{1}{Z}\left(M_s - \dfrac{M_A + M_B}{2}\right)$ where M_s is W.L/8, M_A and M_B are moments at supports, all at working values, W is u.d. load on beam, Z is section modulus of beam $\dfrac{V}{d.t_w} < P_V$ where V is working value of shear force on beam t_w is the thickness of web of beam p_v is the allowable working stress of steel in shear = 105 N/mm²	Assuming W is total u.d. load on each span, all spans are equal and dead load is greater than live load, bending moment in span of beam, M_t, = W.L/12 and bending moment at interior supports = W.L/9 except first interior support for which bending moment = $W.L/8$ Shear at supports $V = 0.6\,W$ Notes on allowable stress and unsymmetrical sections as for simply supported beams
Simply supported composite steel and concrete beam	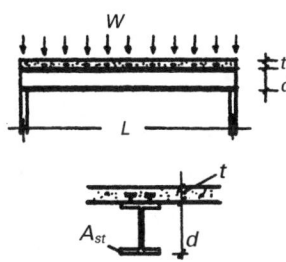	$\dfrac{M}{A_{st}\,(0.5\,d + 0.8\,t)} < p_t$ and $\dfrac{M_d}{Z_{st}} < p_{bc}$ where M is working value of total bending moment on beam $\dfrac{M}{Z_{comp}} < P_{bc}$ where $\dfrac{Z_{comp}}{Z_{st}} < 1.35 + 0.35M_t/M_d$ and M_t is working value of bending moment due to live load $\Delta_d = \dfrac{5W_d.L^3}{384E.l_{st}}$ and $\Delta_t \approx \dfrac{5r.W_t.L^3}{384E.l_{st}}$ where r has a value between 0.3 and 0.5	Typical values of $\dfrac{L}{t + d}$ are 24 or 20 for those with vibration Given formulae assume that steel beam is not propped during construction and carries dead load alone but the live load is carried by composite action M_d is working value of bending moment due to dead load A_{st}, Z_{st} and d are area, section modulus and depth of steel beam and t is depth of concrete slab P_t and P_{bc} are allowable working stresses for steel in tension = 125 N/mm² and for steel in bending = 165 N/mm² Z_{comp} is section modulus of composite section Δ_d and Δ_t are deflections due to dead and live loads W_d and W_t are working values of dead and live u.d. load on span l_{st} is the moment of inertia of the steel section
Simply supported truss	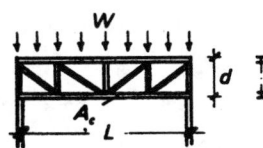	$\dfrac{M}{d.A_v} < p_c$ where M is working value of bending moment on truss at midspan A_v is area of top or bottom chord of truss at midspan d is depth of truss between chord centre lines p_c is allowable working stress of steel in compression $\approx$ 150 N/mm² $\Delta \approx \dfrac{10W.L^3}{384E.l}$ where l is moment of inertia of top and bottom chords about centreline of truss = $A_c.d^2/2$ If live load deflection limited to $L/360$ then $E.l > 7.96\,W_t.L^2$ Economic value of L/d = 10 to 14	Given formulae apply to trusses with top chord restrained against buckling Forces in truss members largely axial and are checked under tension or compression Deflection in truss is greater than that of beam with same moment of inertia because of shear deflection in truss due to change in length of diagonal and vertical members

Table LI *Continued*

Element	Section and elevation on element or plan	Sizing formulae	Remarks
Simply supported vierendeel girder	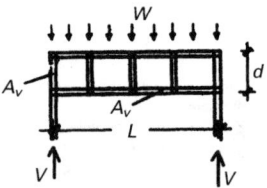	$\dfrac{M}{d.A_v} < p_c$ where M is working value of bending moment on girder at midspan A_v is area of top or bottom chord of girder at midspan d is height of girder between chord centre lines equal to horizontal panel dimension $\dfrac{V}{2A_v} + \dfrac{M}{Z} < P_c$ where A is area of vertical member above support and of adjacent top and bottom chord members M_v is working value of bending moment on end chords and verticals $= V.d/4$ where V is equal to vertical reaction at each support Economic value of $L/d = 6$ to 10	Given formulae apply to girder with top chord restrained against buckling Members in vierendeel girder subject to shear forces, axial forces and bending moments; although vierendeel girder inefficient form becomes relatively more efficient with increase in size Estimate of deflection of truss established by frame analysis of girder taking account of flexibility of members in bending and shear
Double layer space frame	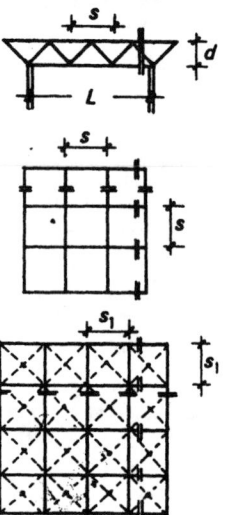	Economic value of $\dfrac{L}{d} < 15$ for space frame supported at corners or $\dfrac{L}{d} < 20$ for space frame supported around perimeter where L is span and d is depth of frame $s \approx \sqrt{2}d$ to $2d$ and $s \approx L/10$ for L up to $50\,\text{m}$ or $s \approx L/10$ to $L/15$ for L above $5\,\text{m}$ where s is module size of bottom layer of frame $s_1 \approx s$ to $\dfrac{s}{\sqrt{2}}$ where s_1 is module size of top layer of frame	Wide variations in span to depth ratios from those given are possible The number of joints and members in a space frame is proportional to the inverse of the square of the module size; therefore economy of space frame increased by larger number of supports, moderate span to depth ratio as well as by larger module size

If B = the width of the foundation in metres, the pressure transmitted to the soil will be

$$\frac{85}{B}\ \text{kN/m}^2$$

Put this equal to the capacity to obtain the minimum allowable value of B:

$85/B = 60$,   hence $B = 1.417\,\text{m}$

The practical width of foundation is therefore 1.5 m, **41.16**.

Example 2

A column carries a load from a warehouse building of 1000 kN. The soil is poor in quality down to a depth of 2.5 m, where a gravel seam is capable of carrying 185 kN/m². A square concrete pier is to be constructed from the bearing layer up to ground level. What should the size of the pier be? **41.17**.

    The gravel will have to carry the weight of the concrete pier as well as the column load. The load imposed by any material will be

Density × height

The density of concrete is assumed to be 24 kN/m³ (Table II). The pressure at the gravel due to this concrete will therefore be

$24 \times 2.5 = 60\,\text{kN/m}^2$

However, the same depth of soil will have been removed to construct the pier. The pressure this exerted on the gravel layer was $2.5 \times 16\,\text{kN/m}^2$ (generally assumed density of soil)

$= 40\,\text{kN/m}^2$

Consequently the pressure capacity available to carry the load of the column will be:

Bearing capacity + soil pressure − pier weight

     1.85   +   40   −   60 $= 165\,\text{kN/m}^2$

The required pier area is hence

$$\frac{1000}{165} = 6.06\,\text{m}^2$$

The side of the pier will be $\sqrt{6.06} = 2.46\,\text{m}$, say 2.5 m

9.05 Other foundation types

It is frequently found that the loads of the building are so large, or the bearing capacity of the soil is so poor, that suitable pad or strip foundations will be either very deep, or required to be so large that

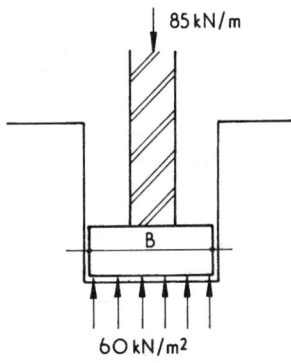

41.16 *Width of a strip foundation, section (Example 1)*

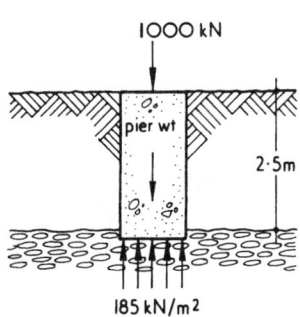

41.17 *Concrete pier of gravel layer (Example 2)*

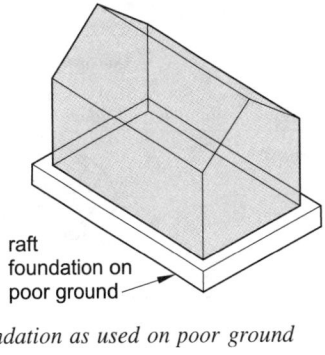

41.18 *Raft foundation as used on poor ground*

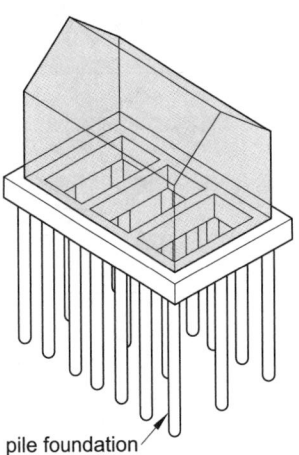

41.19 *Alternative pile foundation*

Table LII Properties of structural plastic

Property	Polyester resin (thermosett.)	Polyester with chopped strand glass mat	Polyester with woven glass rovings	Polyester with glass unidirectional reinforced glass rovings epoxy		Polycarbonate (Thermopl.)	Acrylic (thermopl.)
Glass content by weight %	nil	25–50	50	60	60		
Specific gravity	1.1–1.5	1.4–1.6	1.7–1.8	1.8–1.9	2.1	1.2	1.2
Weight kN/m^3	12	15	18	19	21	12	12
Short-term tensile strength at 20°C N/mm^2	40–80	80–175	210–250	660	350–550	60	50–70
Short-term flexural strength at 20°C modulus of rupture (N/mm^2)	50–90	125–210	220–300	700	500–825	80	90–100
Short-term elastic modulus in bending in direction of fibres at 20°C(68°F)	2–5	6–10	15	30	35	2.6	3.2
Fracture toughness at 20°C MN/m$^{3/2}$	0.5	10–20	10–30	10–40	40–50	1–2	1–1.5
Long-term tensile strength (10 years) at 20°C put as proportion of short-term strength		0.5	0.5	0.5	0.5–0.65	0.20	0.25
Creep factor – final tensile creep strain (10 yr) to short-term elastic strain at 20°C at stress of 33% of short-term tensile strength	–	1	1	1	1	1.5–2	1.5–2
Shrinkage %	0.004–0.080						
Water adsorption over 24 hours %	0.15–0.60			0.20	0.15	0.30–0.40	
Coefficient of thermal expansion × 10^{-6}/°C	100–180	20–30	10–15	10–15	10–15	70	60–70
Thermal conductivity W/m °C	0.2	0.2	0.2	0.2	0.25	0.2	0.2
Softening temperature or maximum operating temperature °C	70	70	70	70	110	120	75
Visible effect of weathering	yellows	yellows	yellows	yellows	no effect	yellows and becomes brittle	no effect

Table LIII Plastics – roofs, surface

Element	Axonometric	Typical spans (L) (m)	Critical factors for sizing	Remarks
Domes using shaped panels		5–20	Thickness affected by size and shape of panel	Domes may have rectangular or circular base. Made by bolting together shaped panels. Plastic panels typically 2–6 mm thick but thicker than this at edges
Folded plate structures using shaped panels		5–20	Thickness affected by size and shape of panel	Made by bolting together two or three different types of shaped panel. Panels may be double skin with insulation between
Shaped roof panels		1–5	Deflection	Panels must be shaped or have stiffeners to overcome flexibility
Laminated panel		4–6	Deflection	Made from good quality grp with 40–60 mm insulation between skins. Used for roofs but also as load-bearing panels and for floors in two or three storey buildings of small plan area

Table LIV Properties of fabric

Property	PVC-coated polyester fabric	PTFE-coated glass fabric	Silicone-coated glass fabric	Neoprene-coated nylon fabric
Specific gravity of fabric yarn	1.38	2.55	2.55	1.14
Weight of fabric yarn kN/m^3	13.5	25.0	25.0	11.2
Short term tensile strength of fabric yarn N/mm^2	1100	1500–2400	1500–2400	500–960
Tenacity N/tex short-term strength to linear density in tex of fabric yarn	0.90	1.10	1.10	0.95
Elastic modulus of fabric yarn kN/mm^2	14	65	65	6
Elastic modulus to linear density of fabric N/tex (a tex is the mass in gm of 1 km of yarn)	12	30	30	5
Weight of a typical fabric N/m^2	8 (0.7 mm thick)	15 (1 mm thick)	11 (0.9 mm thick)	7 (0.8 mm thick)
Short-term tensile strength of fabric N/50 mm width – warp direction – weft (fill) direction	1800 (0.7 mm thick) 1700	6500 (1 mm thick) 5500	6500 (0.9 mm thick) 6000	2000 (0.8 mm thick) 1600
Long-term tensile strength of Coated Fabric (2 years) under continuous load as proportion of short-term strength	0.5	0.6	0.6	–
Tear strength of fabric N – warp direction – weft (fill) direction	300 (0.7 mm thick) 350	270 (1 mm thick) 350	400 (0.9 mm thick) 450	500 (0.8 mm thick) 700
Elongation of fabric % – warp direction – weft (fill) direction	14 20	6 7	5 5	25 30
Shear strength of fabric N/degree	small	450 (1 mm)	–	small
Combustibility of untreated fabric	flammable	hardly flammable	hardly flammable	flammable
Durability years	10–15	25	25	8–12

Table LV Fabric – roofs

Element	Axonometric	Typical spans (L) (m)	Typical curvatures (m)	Critical factors for sizing	Remarks
Fabric tent		9–18	25–35	Radius of curvature Tear strength Wind or snow loads	Surface of tent has anticlastic (saddle) shape at each point and is prestressed Typical prestress in fabric 5–10 kN/m Prestress determined by loads and curvature.
Cable reinforced fabric tent		18–60	80–100	Tear strength of fabric, spacing of cables, radius of curvature and wind and snow loads	Surface of tent has anticlastic shape and is prestressed by pulling on cables Prestress in fabric and cables determined by loads and curvature.
Prestressed steel net with fabric covering		25–100	–	Radius of curvature Wind or snow load	Size of cable mesh about 500 × 500 mm Surface of net has anticlastic shape Typical average stress in net 40–60 kN/m High strength of net allows large radius of curvature
Air-supported membrane		15–45	–	Radius of curvature Tear strength Wind or snow loads	Inflation pressure low Surface of membrane has synclastic (dome shape at each point and is prestressed.
Cable stayed air supported membrane		90–180	80–100	Tear strength of fabric, spans, spacing of cables and snow loads	Cables anchored to ring beam that has funicular shape Low rise of roof gives wind uplift on it
Pneumatic frame (prestressed tube)		6–45	–	Tear strength Shape and diameter of tube Wind or snow loads	Tubes require large diameters and high pressures to achieved sufficient stiffness

Table LVI Safe bearing capacities of soils

Group	Class	Types of rocks and soils	Presumed bearing value kN/m²	Remarks
I Rocks	1	Hard igneous and gneissic rocks in sound condition	10 000	These values are based on the assumption that the foundations are carried down to unweathered rock
	2	Hard limestones and hard sandstones	4000	
	3	Schists and slates	3000	
	4	Hard shales, hard mudstones and soft sandstones	2000	
	5	Soft shales and soft mudstones	600 to 1000	
	6	Hard sound chalk, soft limestone	600	
	7	Thinly bedded limestones, sandstones, shales	To be assessed after inspection	
	8	Heavily shattered rocks		
II Non-cohesive soils	9	Compact gravel, or compact sand and gravel	>600	Width of foundation (B) not less than 1 m Ground-water level assumed to be a depth not less than B below the base of the foundation
	10	Medium dense gravel, or medium dense sand and gravel	200 to 600	
	11	Loose gravel, or loose sand and gravel	<200	
	12	Compact sand	>300	
	13	Medium dense sand	100 to 300	
	14	Loose sand	<100	
III Cohesive soils	15	Very stiff boulder clays and hard clays	300 to 600	Group III is susceptible to long-term consolidation settlement
	16	Stiff clays	150 to 300	
	17	Firm clays	75 to 150	
	18	Soft clays and silts	<75	
	19	Very soft clays and silts	Not applicable	
IV	20	Peat and organic soils	Refer to engineer	
V	21	Made ground or fill	Refer to engineer	

adjoining bases impinge on one another. The two common solutions to this problem are:

- Raft foundations, **41.18**, where the bases are combined together to form one large base. This has to be so reinforced as to allow for the stresses induced by inequalities of loading and bearing capacity,
- Piles, **41.19**, which are devices for carrying loads down to deeper levels than would otherwise be practical.

Raft foundations are beyond the scope of this section, but some knowledge of piles will be useful.

9.06 End-bearing piles

Piles can be divided into those that carry their loads into the soil mainly by the pressure of their lower ends, **41.20** and those that act by virtue of the friction between the soil and their shaft lengths, **41.21**. End-bearing piles normally sit on rock or gravel strata with high bearing capacities. They may consist of a precast concrete shaft, driven into place with a large mechanical hammer. Alternatively a hollow shell is driven and afterwards filled with wet concrete to form the pile. In either of these cases, the amount of penetration achieved at each hammer blow is an indication of the carrying capacity of the pile. A design method for simple end-bearing piles in the shape of the short-bored variety sometimes used in housing is illustrated in the following example.

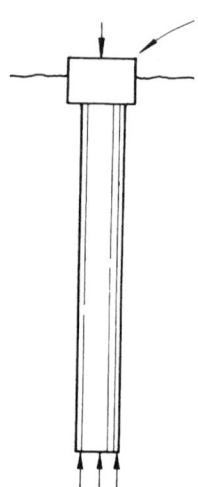

41.20 *End-bearing pile*

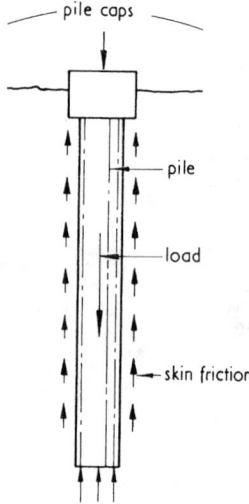

41.21 *Friction pile*

Example 3

The brick wall in Example 1 above is to be carried on short-bored piles taken down to a gravel seam 4 m deep. The gravel has a capacity of 400 kN/m², and the piles are 650 mm diameter. What is the required spacing of the piles? **41.22**

The area of the pile base is

$$\pi \times (\tfrac{1}{2} \times 0.65)\, m^2 \; = \; 0.332\, m^2$$

The load that can be carried by each is therefore

$$400 \times 0.332 \; = \; 133\, kN$$

The length of wall loaded at 85 kN/m carried on one pile is hence

$$\frac{133}{85} \; = \; 1.56\, m$$

Therefore, piles should be at, say, 1.5 m centres.

The minimum permissible spacing is 3 × diameter or 1.35 m in this case.

9.07 Skin-friction piles

Skin-friction piles, mostly appropriate for cohesive soils such as clays, are usually bored. In this method a hole is constructed in the ground by augering or other methods. If necessary, the sides of the hole are temporarily sleeved. When the necessary depth has been reached, reinforcement is lowered into the hole and concrete is poured in. Some method of compacting the concrete is employed, so that all cavities in the ground are properly filled. The sleeve is withdrawn as the concrete goes in, to ensure intimate contact between pile and soil, **41.21**.

The capacity of this type of pile is not self-evident as in the case of driven piles. Calculation is used to determine the length of pile required, based on the shear strength of the clay at various depths below the ground. This information is gained by carrying out a site investigation prior to the design.

While the calculations themselves are not particularly difficult, the subject is one where engineering judgment is required in their interpretation. It is recommended that this type of pile should be installed either under the supervision of a consulting engineer, or to a design guaranteed by the piling firm.

9.08 Pile testing

In both driven and bored piles it is usual to carry out one or more tests on the actual piles on each contract. On very large contracts additional piles are tested to failure, but normally one of the working piles is simply loaded to 1½ times the working load to prove the efficacy of the design.

9.09 Under-reamed piles

There is a third type of pile which is a bored end-bearing pile. The shaft is augered in the usual way, but when the required depth has

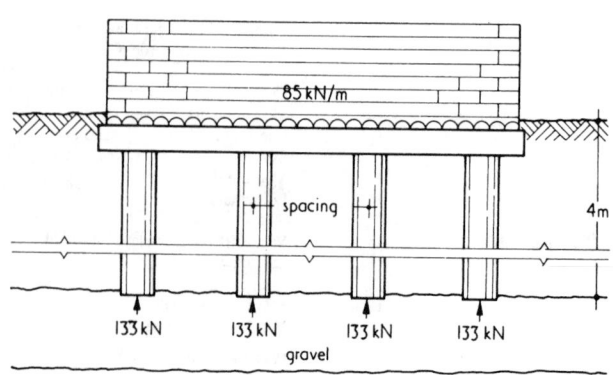

41.22 *Short-bored piles (Example 3)*

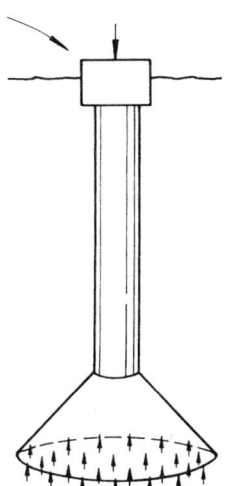

41.23 *Under-reamed pile*

been reached a special tool is used to enlarge the base to a bell-shape, **41.23**. These piles are substantial in size, and men are lowered to clean out the base prior to concreting, and also to inspect and approve the soil on which the load will rest. It is not often possible to test this type of pile in view of the magnitude of the loads carried.

10 BIBLIOGRAPHY

10.01 General
Allan Hodgkinson (ed.) *AJ Handbook of Building Structure*, Architectural Press, London, 1974
Andrew Orton, *The Way We Build Now*, E & F N Spon, London, 1988
Bryan J B Gauld, *Structures for Architects*, Longman Scientific & Technical, 1995
Building Regulations, 1991, *Approved Document A, Structure*
Institution of Structural Engineers, *Aims of structural design*, 1987
Institution of Structural Engineers, *Stability of buildings*, 1989
Institution of Structural Engineers, *The achievement of structural adequacy in buildings*, 1989

10.02 Loading
BS 648: 1964, *Schedule of weights of building materials*
BS 6399: Part 1: 1984, *Code of practice for dead and imposed loads*
BS 6399: Part 2: 1995, *Code of practice for wind loads*
BS 6399: Part 3: 1988, *Code of practice for imposed roof loads*

10.03 Masonry
BS 5628: Part 1: 1992, *Structural use of unreinforced masonry*
BS 5628: Part 3: 1985, *Masonry, materials and components, design and workmanship*
Institution of Structural Engineers, *Manual for the design of plain masonry in building structures* (Red Book), 1997

10.04 Timber
BS 5268: Part 2: 1991, *Code of practice for permissible stress design (of timber structures)*
BS 5268: Part 3: 1985, *Code of practice for trussed rafter roofs*
Ozelton and Baird, *Timber designers' manual*, CLS, 1976

10.05 Concrete
BS 5328: Part 1: 1991, *Guide to specifying concrete*
BS 5328: Part 2: 1991, *Methods for specifying concrete mixes*
BS 8110: Part 1: 1985, *Code of practice for design and construction (the structural use of concrete)*
The Institutions of Civil and of Structural Engineers, *Manual for the design of reinforced building structures* (Green Book), 1985
The Institution of Structural Engineers, *Recommendations for the permissible stress design of reinforced concrete building structures* (Orange Book), 1991
Reynolds and Steedman, *Reinforced concrete designer's handbook*, 1988

10.06 Steel
BS 5950: Part 1: 1990, *Code of practice for design in simple and continuous construction: hot rolled sections (structural use of steelwork in building)*
The Institutions of Civil and of Structural Engineers, *Manual for the design of steelwork building structures* (Grey Book), 1989
Steel Construction Institute, *Steel designers' manual*, 1992

10.07 Foundations
BS 8004: 1986, *Code of practice for foundations*
Institutions of Civil and of Structural Engineers, *Soil–structure interaction*, 1989

42 Fire

Beryl Menzies

Beryl Menzies is a consultant in fire safety

CI/Sfb (K)
UDC: 614.84
Uniclass: U32

KEY POINTS:
● *Consider from first principles how a fire can start*
● *Then how can it grow?*
● *Will it threaten life, property or both?*
● *How can it be fought?*
● *How will people escape?*
● *Only after considering all these points, refer to regulations.*

Contents

1 INTRODUCTION

When designing a building with fire safety in mind, particularly ease of escape, it is important not to forget the needs also for usability and security. If the fire measures are seen to be too onerous (for example, a multiplicity of fire doors) they will be circumvented (propped open) and their purpose will be frustrated. Fire escape doors are often weak points when it comes to unauthorised ingress, particularly in places of public assembly.

2 COMPONENTS OF FIRE

2.01 Fire is combustion producing heat and light. Combustion will occur and continue if three factors are present: oxygen, heat and fuel. These are generally referred to as the combustion triangle, **42.1**.

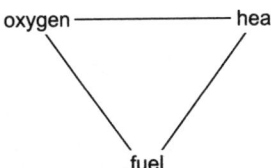

42.1 *Triangle of fire*

2.02 Fire can be extinguished by removing one side of the combustion triangle:

● Starve or limit the fuel by removing it
● Smother by limiting or stopping the further supply of oxygen, or
● Cool by dissipating the heat faster than it is generated.

2.03 A source of heat comes into contact with a combustible material (the fuel) which ignites and supports combustion while oxygen is present. The heat sources within a building are many –

cooking, smoking, heating equipment, overheating/faulty equipment (particularly electrical).

2.04 Three kinds of fuel have been identified:

● Tinder, material ignitable by a match which will continue to burn after its removal
● Kindling, material which will ignite and burn if associated with sufficient tinder, but in which a match will not produce a continuing fire, and
● Bulk fuel, which needs kindling to cause to burn.

2.05 The fuel may be present in the building structure, fittings and/or contents and can be in the form of solids, liquids or gases. Most organic materials will burn. Certain materials spontaneously combust and care is required in their storage, eg linseed oil, certain chemicals, grains. Certain industrial processes involving high levels of dust, eg printing, flour mills, can result in flash fires. Specialist advice should be sought in respect of these matters.

2.06 The initial source of heat cannot ignite most bulk fuels unless the fire is able to follow the tinder-kindling chain. Of course, this does not apply when the bulk fuel is itself highly combustible; but it does apply to elements of building construction and to many stored materials.

This leads to the point that fire risks in most buildings can be greatly reduced if measures are taken to avoid build-ups of tinder. Dust, waste paper, sawdust, rags, etc are materials which will act as tinder; so will a number of man-made organic materials which are now coming under stricter control.

2.07 Smoke

This is formed when organic materials decompose by heat giving off tarry and sooty decomposed materials. It is likely that most smoke will be generated by the building contents.

2.08 Heat

This can be transmitted in three forms:

● Conduction – heat energy is passed from one molecule to the next. The conductivity of a material (which varies with the material) may affect the fire resistance of a component or structure. A steel member in contact with combustible materials may transfer the heat generating a fire or damage away from the original source.
● Radiation – heat is transmitted in straight lines without any contact between the radiating material and the target which may absorb or reflect the heat. The intensity reduces inversely as the square of the distance from the source of radiation. Combustible materials placed in close proximity to a radiant fire will ignite.
● Convection – only occurs in liquids and gases. The heated combustion gases become buoyant and rise through voids and shafts with the potential of causing ignition in other areas of a building.

3 PRINCIPLES OF FIRE PROTECTION

Note: specific recommendations relating to periods of fire resistance for specific uses, structural elements etc are given in various codes only some of which are referred to here.

3.01 Potential problems

- Unrestricted growth and spread of a fire within a building that will cause extensive damage and may result in its collapse,
- Rapid spread of fire across surfaces within the building, ignition of adjacent fuels, means of escape prejudiced,
- Spread of fire, smoke and hot gases in a building through ducts, voids and shafts affecting the means of escape, access for firefighters and causing extensive damage to decorations and property,
- Spread of fire to adjacent buildings affecting life safety and property,
- Loss of contents, disruption of work, loss of trade/production.

3.02 The aim of fire precautions within a building is to inhibit the growth and to restrict the spread of any fire. The influencing factors are:

- The size of building – area, height, volume
- The layout and configuration within the building
- The uses accommodated, and the requirements of the occupants
- The construction materials, linings and claddings
- The type of construction
- The services installed
- The furniture.

3.03 the precautions are:

- Protection of loadbearing structure to prevent untimely collapse, limitation of combustibility of key structural elements
- Adequate and appropriate provisions for means of escape
- Access for fire-fighters up to and through the building to reach the seat of the fire and promptly extinguish it
- Compartmentation and separation to restrict spread of fire, maintenance of these by protection of openings, fire stopping and cavity barriers within concealed spaces
- Safe installation and maintenance of services, heat-producing equipment and user equipment
- Separation of different uses to protect, for example, a risk to sleepers from commercial uses
- Enclosure of high risks with fire-resisting construction to protect adjacent areas
- Active fire-extinguishing installations to detect and/or contain fire in its early stages and restrict its spread and growth
- Limitation of flame spread by selective use of materials
- Fire-resisting external walls and/or space separation to prevent spread of fire to adjacent properties, protection of openings in external walls, limited flame spread across external walls and roofs, use of insulation with limited combustibility to restrict ignition and spread
- The provision of natural or mechanical ventilation, smoke extraction and/or smoke control measures to facilitate means of escape and firefighting
- Management training and procedures for evacuation, maintenance of fire precautions, risk analysis, management policy.

3.04 Growth and spread

An analysis of the growth and spread of fire is explained in detail and substantiated by Malhotra in BRE publication BR 96 *Fire Safety in Buildings*.

3.05 Fire load and ignitability

The majority of a fire load within a building will be its contents, over which a designer may have no influence. Some types of occupancies have controls relating to the ignitability of furniture (domestic and assembly buildings under licensing legislation,

Table I Classification of purpose groups (from Approved Document B, Table D1)

Title	Group	Purpose for which the building or compartment of a building is intended to be used
Residential* (dwellings)	1(a)	Flat or maisonette.
	1(b)	Dwellinghouse which contains a habitable storey with a floor level which is more than 4.5 m above ground level.
	1(c)	Dwellinghouse which does not contain a habitable storey with a floor level which is more than 4.5 m above ground level
Residential (Institutional)	2(a)	Hospital, nursing home, home for old people or for children, school or other similar establishment used as living accommodation or for the treatment, care or maintenance of people suffering from illness or mental or physical disability or handicap, place of detention, where such people sleep on the premises.
(Other)	2(b)	Hotel, boarding house, residential college, hall of residence, hostel, and any other residential purpose not described above.
Office	3	Offices or premises used for the purpose of administration, clerical work (including writing, book keeping, sorting papers, filing, typing, duplicating, machine calculating, drawing and the editorial preparation of matter for publication, police and fire service work), handling money (including banking and building society work), and communications (including postal, telegraph and radio communications) or radio, television, film, audio or video recording, or performance [not open to the public] and their control.
Shop and Commercial	4	Shops or premises used for a retail trade or business (including the sale to members of the public of food or drink for immediate consumption and retail by auction, self-selection and over-the-counter wholesale trading, the business of lending books or periodicals for gain and the business of a barber or hairdresser) and premises to which the public is invited to deliver or collect goods in connection with their hire repair or other treatment, or (except in the case of repair of motor vehicles) where they themselves may carry out such repairs or other treatments.
Assembly and Recreation	5	Place of assembly, entertainment or recreation; including bingo halls, broadcasting, recording and film studios open to the public, casinos, dance halls; entertainment-conference, exhibition and leisure centres; funfairs and amusement arcades; museums and art galleries; non-residential clubs, theatres, cinemas and concert halls; educational establishments, dancing schools, gymnasia, swimming pool buildings, riding schools, skating rinks, sports pavilions, sports stadia; law courts; churches and other buildings of worship, crematoria; libraries open to the public, non-residential day centres, clinics, health centres and surgeries; passenger stations and termini for air, rail, road or sea travel; public toilets; zoos and menageries.
Industrial	6	Factories and other premises used for manufacturing, altering, repairing, cleaning, washing, breaking-up, adapting or processing any article; generating power or slaughtering livestock
Storage and other non-residential†	7(a)	Place for the storage or deposit of goods or materials [other than described under 7(b)] and any building not within any of the purpose groups 1 to 6.
	7(b)	Car parks designed to admit and accommodate only cars, motorcycles and passenger or light goods vehicles weighing no more than 2500 kg gross.

* Includes any surgeries, consulting rooms, offices or other accommodation, not exceeding 50 m² in total, forming part of a dwelling and used by an occupant of the dwelling in a professional or business capacity.

† A detached garage not more than 40 m² in area is included in purpose group 1(c); as is a detached open carport of not more than 40 m², or a detached building which consists of a garage and open carport where neither the garage nor open carport exceeds 40 m² in area.

hospitals and prisons under government directives), Table I. Electricity, often cited as the cause of fires, while not it itself a risk presents a potential hazard when brought into contact with combustible material; all new electrical installations should be installed in accordance with the current edition of the regulations of the Institution of Electrical Engineers and existing installations periodically examined and tested for potential risks.

3.06 Smoke
The limitation of smoke spread is considered mainly as an aspect of safe means of escape. Specific limitations of smoke production are not, to date, generally specified. There is no generally accepted test related to smoke emission. The production of toxic gases which accompanies all fires would be very difficult to specify.

3.07 Combustibility
While it would be possible to construct a totally non-combustible building, it is not practical and not required by legislation; although some codes do relate means of escape to a classification based on the 'combustibility' of a building. Non-combustible materials should be used where hazardous conditions are anticipated or there is a need to maintain the integrity of a structure for the maximum time, eg a compartment wall or floor, or an escape stair in a high building.

3.08 Fire resistance
The need for and degree of fire resistance within a structure may be dictated by Building Regulations, insurance or damage-limitation requirements. The prevention of untimely collapse allows evacuation, containment of a fire and therefore protection of adjacent areas, and access for firefighters. This is essential in high-rise buildings. Factors relating to the need for fire resistance are building height and size, occupancy and anticipated fire severity; although it should be noted that the current recommendations under the Building Regulations do not consider capacity, ie volume, relevant, Table II. While a specific period of fire resistance may be specified and an element constructed accordingly, it should not be assumed that the period will be attained; it may be longer or shorter due to, among other factors, interaction with other elements or non-maintenance, or more severe fire conditions than those anticipated in the test.

3.09 Fire compartments
These are formed around areas of different uses or hazards, or to divide an area into a size in which it is considered a fire could be contained and dealt with by firefighters, and thereby protecting adjacent areas. The addition of automatic active measures such as sprinklers to contain and control the growth of a fire allows larger compartments or, in some cases, their omission. If the only consideration is life safety, it can be argued that if all persons can safely escape there is no need for compartmentation, and the potential exists for reduced fire resistance. This principle is often adopted in low-rise or single-storey buildings. However, in the case of high-rise or buildings with phased or staged evacuation, compartmentation is an essential part of the safety package. Flats and maisonettes are constructed such that every unit is a compartment; in the event of a fire it is only necessary initially to evacuate the unit on fire.

Table II Minimum periods of fire resistance (from Approved Document B, Table A2)

Purpose group of building	Minimum periods (minutes) for elements of structure in a:					
	Basement storey[1] including floor over		Ground or upper storey			
	Depth (m) of a lowest basement		Height (m) of top floor above ground, in building or separating part of building			
	more than 10	not more than 10	not more than 5	not more than 20	not more than 30	more than 30
1 Residential (domestic):						
(a) flats and maisonettes	90	60	30[2]	60[3,7]	90[3]	120[3]
(b) and (c) dwellinghouses	not relevant	30[2]	30[2]	60	not relevant	not relevant
2 Residential:						
(a) Institutional[4]	90	60	30[2]	60	90	120[5]
(b) other residential	90	60	30[2]	60	90	120[5]
3 Office:						
– not sprinklered	90	60	30[2]	60	90	not permitted
– sprinklered	60	60	30[2]	30[2]	60	120[5]
4 Shop and commercial:						
– not sprinklered	90	60	60	60	90	not permitted
– sprinklered	60	60	30[2]	60	60	120[5]
5 Assembly and recreation:						
– not sprinklered	90	60	60	60	90	not permitted
– sprinklered	60	60	30[2]	60	60	120[5]
6 Industrial:						
– not sprinklered	120	90	60	90	120	not permitted
– sprinklered	90	60	30[2]	60	90	120[5]
7 Storage & other non-residential:						
(a) any building or part not described elsewhere:						
– not sprinklered	120	90	60	90	120	not permitted
– sprinklered	90	60	30[2]	60	90	120[5]
(b) car park for light vehicles:						
(i) open sided park	not applicable	not applicable	15[2,6]	15[2,6]	15[2,6]	60
(ii) any other park	90	60	30[2]	60	90	120[5]

[1] The floor over a basement (or if there is more than 1 basement, the floor over the topmost basement) should meet the provisions for the ground and upper storeys if that period is higher.
[2] Increased to a minimum of 60 minutes for compartment walls separating buildings
[3] Reduced to 30 minutes for any floor within a maisonette, but not if the floor contributes to the support of the building
[4] Multi-storey hospitals designed in accordance with the NHS Firecode documents should have a minimum 60 minutes standard
[5] Reduced to 90 minutes for elements not forming part of the structural frame
[6] Increased to 30 minutes for elements protecting the means of escape
[7] Refer to Approved Document B regarding the acceptability of 30 minutes in flat conversions

Table III Maximum dimensions of multi-storey non-residential buildings and compartments (from Approved Document B, Table 12)

Purpose group of building (or part)	Height of floor of top storey above ground level (m)	Floor area of any one storey in the building or compartment (m²)
Office	no limit	no limit
Assembly & Recreation Shop & Commercial:		
not sprinklered	no limit	2 000
sprinklered[1]	no limit	4 000
Industrial:[3]		
not sprinklered	not more than 20	7 000
	more than 20	2 000[2]
sprinklered[1]	not more than 20	14 000
	more than 20	4 000[2]

	Height of floor of top storey above ground level (m)	Maximum compartment volume (m³)
Storage[3] & Other non-residential:		
(a) car park for light vehicles	no limit	no limit
(b) any other building or part:		
– not sprinklered	not more than 20	20 000
	more than 20	4 000[2]
– sprinklered[1]	not more than 20	40 000
	more than 20	8 000[2]

[1] 'Sprinklered' means that the building is fitted throughout with an automatic sprinkler system meeting the relevant recommendations of BS-5306 Part 2, ie the relevant occupancy rating together with the additional requirements for life safety.
[2] This reduced area limit applies only to storeys that are more than 20 m above ground level.
[3] There may be additional limitations on floor area and/or sprinkler provisions in certain industrial and storage uses under other legislation, for example in respect of storage of LPG and certain chemicals.

Effective compartmentation requires attention to detail. Openings, including those for ventilation and services, must be protected; where shafts perforate compartment floors 'protected shafts' should be detailed, Table III.

3.10 Compartments within residential, institutional and health buildings require careful consideration as they form an essential part of the scheme for means of escape. All floors should be compartment floors. It is recommended that compartments do not exceed 2000 m² in multi-storey hospitals and 3000 m² in single-storey hospitals. In non-residential buildings floors over and generally within basements and any floor at a height of 30 m above ground level should be constructed as compartment floors.

3.11 Growth

To limit the growth of fire within the main structural elements is generally relatively easy provided that they do not contain large voids. The addition of linings and claddings can facilitate the rapid spread of fire beyond its area of origin. Flame can spread quickly in all directions and fixings are important. It has been found by experiment that the better the material is as an insulator, the greater the likelihood that flame spread will be more rapid and further.

3.12 Surface spread of flame

This is generally tested in accordance with BS 476 Part 7 1971, the results being classified 1 to 4 (Class 1 being very good, Class 4 very poor) on the basis of flame spread from the point of ignition. Class 0 is a classification defined for the purposes of recommendations under the building Regulations (not a British Standard). Current codes vary in their recommendations but generally all escape routes and circulation spaces should have Class 0, all other areas other than small rooms Class 1.

3.13 Ventilation to release heat and control and/or dispel smoke from a fire will allow easier and rapid access by fire fighters to extinguish a fire. Its relationship to means of escape is outlined elsewhere.

Ventilation can be natural or mechanical. The latter is preferable as it is controllable, can be activated automatically and, when designed correctly, not influenced by wind, internal layout and configurations, outside temperature or stack effect. It does, however, add considerable cost, as it is necessary to safeguard its operation by using fans tolerant of high temperatures, protected wiring, fire and smoke dampers, automatic detection, secondary power supplies and monitoring. It may require sophisticated computerised controls.

3.14 Opinions vary on the design of mechanical smoke extract systems, and the need or otherwise to incorporate fail-safe measures. It is necessary to determine if the system is for smoke extraction or smoke control. There is no generally accepted comprehensive code for mechanical smoke control systems; specialist advice should be sought.

3.15 Natural ventilation by the provision of open, openable or breakable vents, is usually intended for operation by the firefighters who will take into consideration aspects of wind etc. Openings should aggregate not less than 5% of a total floor area within basements and areas of high or special risk, and 2.5% above ground. If vents are not accessible, they should be permanent, open automatically or open by remote control.

3.16 The use of natural ventilation in large open areas such as single-storey factories, auditoria, exhibition halls and the like will necessitate the formation of smoke reservoirs to restrict the spread of smoke. See BRE publications Digest 260, *Smoke control in buildings: design principles* and BR 186 *Design principles for smoke ventilation in enclosed shopping centres.*

3.17 Specific access for firefighters will allow their prompt action. Access is required up to, into, and through a building. Various dimensional information is given below but it should be remembered that fire equipment is not standardised; it is also constantly changing, giving many variations in sizes and weights.

If a building is provided with a fire main, access is required to within 18 m of the inlet to a dry riser or the access to a firefighting shaft containing a wet riser. The setdown point should be within sight of the dry riser inlet or shaft access.

Table IV Fire service vehicle access to buildings not fitted with fire mains (from Approved Document B, Table 19)

Total floor[1] area of building (m²)	Height of floor of top storey above ground[2]	Provide vehicle access to:	Type of appliance
up to 2 000	up to 9	see paragraph 16.2	pump
	over 9	15% of perimeter[3]	high reach
2 000–8 000	up to 9	15% of perimeter	pump
	over 9	50% of perimeter[3]	high reach
8 000–16 000	up to 9	50% of perimeter[3]	pump
	over 9	50% of perimeter[3]	high reach
16 000–24 000	up to 9	75% of perimeter[3]	pump
	over 9	75% of perimeter[3]	high reach
over 24 000	up to 9	100% of perimeter[3]	pump
	over 9	100% of perimeter[3]	high reach

Notes:
Provisions about the design of vehicle access routes are given in paragraphs 16.8 to 16.10 and Diagram 44 of Approved Document B.
[1] The total floor area is the aggregate of all the floors in the building.
[2] In the case of purpose group 7(a) (storage) buildings, height should be measured to mean roof level, see methods of measurement in Appendix C of Approved Document B
[3] Perimeter is described in Diagram 43 of Approved Document B.

Table V Typical vehicle access route specification (from Approved Document B, Table 20)

Appliance Type	Minimum width of road between kerbs (m)	Minimum width of gateways (m)	Minimum turning circle between kerbs (m)	Minimum turning circle between walls (m)	Minimum clearance height (m)	Minimum carrying capacity (tonnes)
Pump	3.7	3.1	16.8	19.2	3.7	12.5
High Reach	3.7	3.1	29.0	29.0	4.0	17.0

Notes:
(1) Fire appliances are not standardised. Some fire services have appliances of greater weight or different size. In consultation with the Fire Authority, Building Control Authorities and Approved Inspectors may adopt other dimensions in such circumstances.
(2) Because the weight of high-reach appliances is distributed over a number of axies, it is considered that their infrequent use of a carriageway or route designed to 12.5 tonnes should not cause damage. It would therefore be reasonable to design the roadbase to 12.5 tonnes, although structures such as bridges should have the full 17 tonnes capacity.

Table VI Dimensions required for fire appliances (see 42.3)

Dimension	Description	Type of appliance	
		Turntable ladder	Hydraulic platform
A	Maximum distance of near edge of hardstanding from building	4.9 m	2.0 m
B	Minimum width of hardstanding	5.0 m	5.5 m
C	Minimum distance of further edge of hardstanding from building	10.0 m	7.5 m
D	Minimum width of unobstructed space for swing of appliance platform	NA	2.2 m

No appliances should have to reverse more than 20 m. Dead-end roads should be provided with hammerhead turning spaces if longer than this, Tables IV, V and VI, **42.2** to **42.5**

3.18 Firefighting shafts

Access into the building should be provided via a firefighting shaft. In the cases of tall buildings and those with deep basements this should incorporate a firefighting lift to transport equipment and personnel at speed. In all cases it should include a staircase 1.1 m in width between walls or balustrades, ventilated or pressurised, entered from the floor areas via a lobby, both of which are separated from the remainder of the building by 2-hour fire-resisting construction. BS 5588 Part 5 details the technical and dimensional specification for a firefighting shaft. The criteria for the provision and number of shafts in any particular building is set out in that Part of the BS 5888 series relating to the specific use or within Building Regulations. A firefighting lift can be one normally used for passengers; it should not be one used as a goods lift, **42.6**, **42.7**.

3.19 The spread of fire to adjacent buildings can be prevented by:

● Clear space
● Fire-resisting walls,
● External walls of limited combustibility and limited surface spread of flame, and/or
● Roof coverings resistant to penetration of fire.

If precautions are taken within a building to limit a fire's growth and spread, it can be assumed that its effects on an adjacent building are reduced. Openings in an external wall or walls having no fire resistance present weaknesses to an adjoining building by radiation and convection. If property protection in addition to life safety is a consideration, then all buildings should be considered as being of equal risk.

If life safety is the only factor, then residential, assembly and recreational uses are at greater risk from external fire sources, and warrant additional safeguards. It is generally assumed that only one compartment is involved in a fire and as such the risk emanates only from its external enclosures.

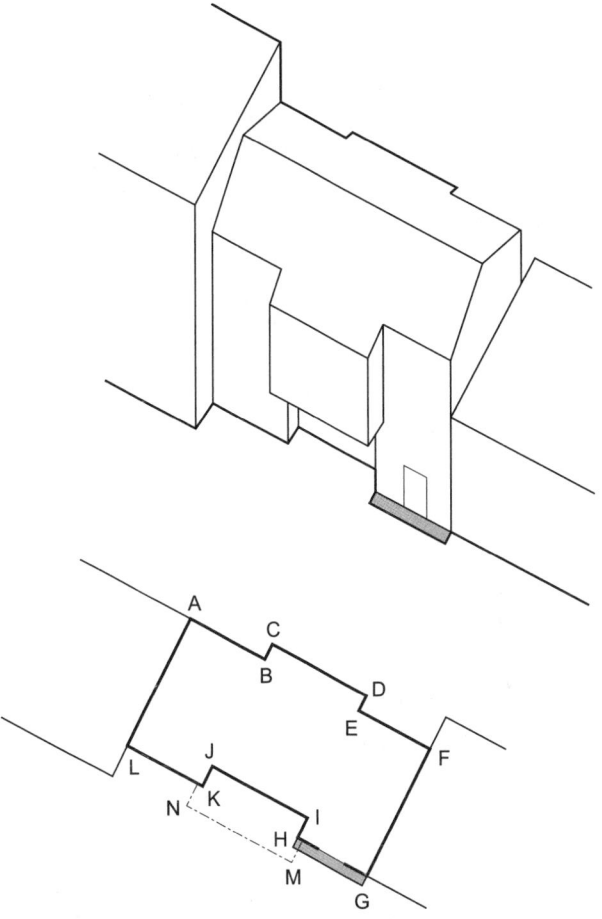

42.2 *Example of building footprint and perimeter. The building is AFGL where walls AL and FG are shared with other buildings. The footprint is the maximum aggregate plan perimeter found by the vertical projection of any overhanging storey onto a ground storey: ie ABCDEFGHMNKL. The perimeter for the purposes of the table is the sum of the lengths of the two external walls taking account of the footprint, ie (A to B to C to D to E to F) + (G to H to M to N to K to L). If the dimensions of the building require vehicular access by the table, the shaded area illustrates a possible example of 15% of the perimeter. Note the there should be a door into the building in this length. If the building has no walls common with other buildings, the lengths AL and FG would be included in the perimeter*

3.20 Methods generally used for determining the necessary degrees of protection are based on acceptable percentages of 'unprotected areas' (openings, non-fire-resisting walls, combustible claddings and insulation) having regard to heat radiation exposure from a known use. The basis of the necessary calculations are set out in BRE document BRE 187 *External fire spread: building separation and boundary distances*; Approved

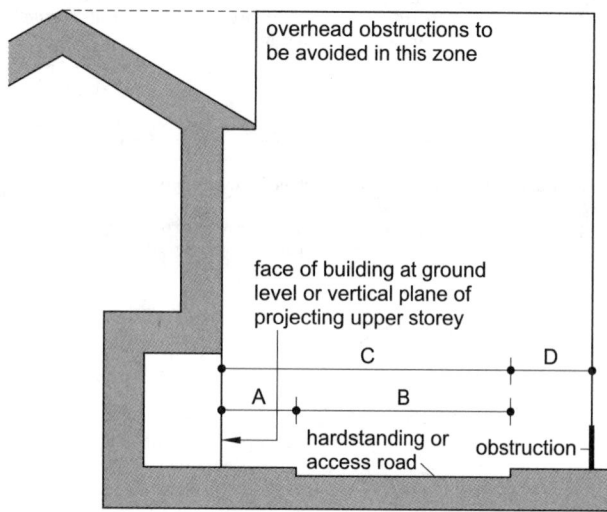

42.3 *Relationship between building and hardstanding or access roads for high-reach fire appliances. For key, see Table VI*

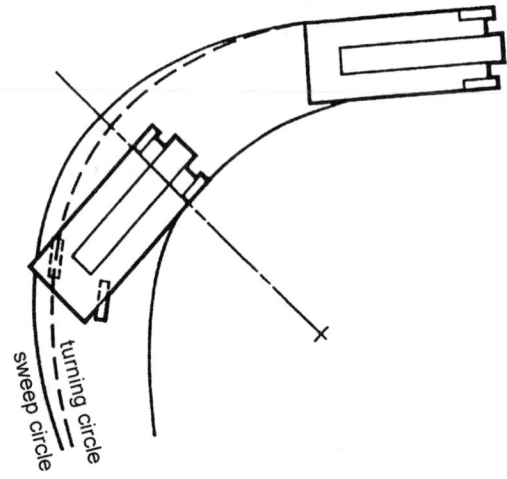

42.4 *A pumping appliance (drawing not to scale)*
Max length 8.5 m, max height 3.3 m, max width 2.3 m, max weight 13.21 ts, on front axle 5.5 ts, on rear axle 6.1 ts, max wheelbase 3.81 m, rear wheel track 2 m, ground clearance 229 mm, roadway width required 3.66 m, turning circle 16.75 m, sweep circle 18.3 m

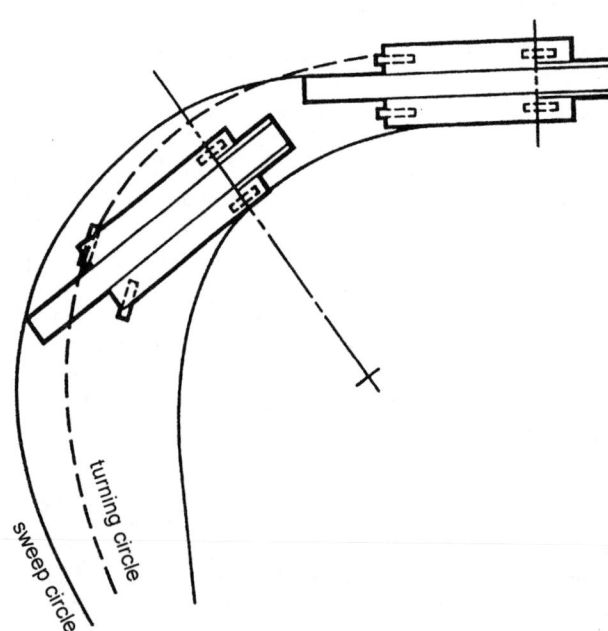

42.5 *A hydraulic platform and turntable ladders (drawing not to scale)*
Max length 10 m, max height 3.5 m, max width 2.5 m, max width with jacks out 4.4 m, laden weight 16.25 t, av. weight front axle 6 t, av. weight rear axle 10 t, max wheelbase 5.33 m, rear wheel track 2 m, min ground clearance 229 mm, road width required 6 m, turning circle 21.5 m, sweep circle 24.5 m. The overhang of the booms on the headrest do not exceed 1.83 m from foremost part of the vehicle. Turntable ladders and hydraulic platforms ('cherry-pickers') are fitted with four ground jacks as stabilisers, for which the working load is normally less than 7.5 t.

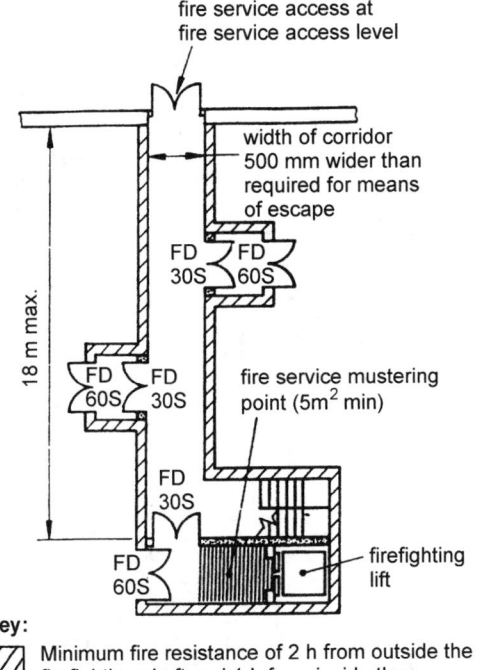

fire service access at
fire service access level

width of corridor
500 mm wider than
required for means
of escape

FD 30S   FD 60S

FD 60S   FD 30S

fire service mustering
point (5m² min)

FD 30S

FD 60S

firefighting
lift

18 m max.

Key:

▨ Minimum fire resistance of 2 h from outside the
firefighting shaft and 1 h from inside the
firefighting shaft

▦ Minimum fire resistance of 1 h from both sides

42.6 *Typical firefighting shaft layout at fire service access level,
access via a corridor*

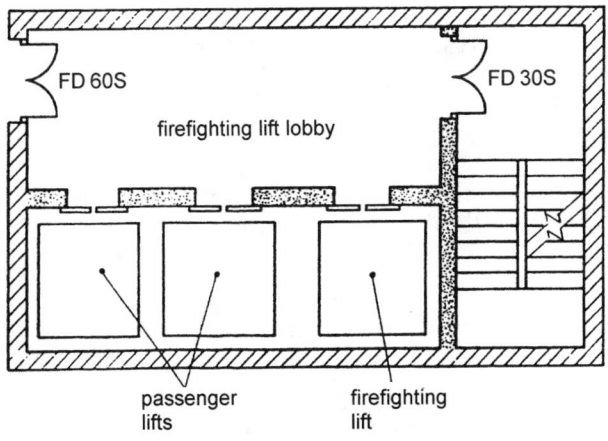

FD 60S

firefighting lift lobby

FD 30S

passenger
lifts

firefighting
lift

42.7 *Passenger lifts within the firefighting shaft. Firefighting
lobbies should have a clear floor area of not less than 5 m². The
clear floor area should not exceed 20 m² for lobbies serving up
to four lifts, or 5 m² per lift for lobbies serving more. All
principal dimensions should be not less than 1.5 m and should
not exceed 8 m in lobbies serving up to four lifts, or 2 m per lift
in lobbies serving more*

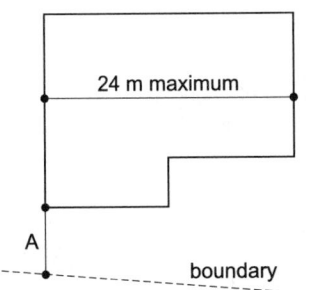

24 m maximum

A

boundary

42.8 *Permitted unprotected areas in small residential buildings*

Table VII Unprotected areas for small residential buildings. See **42.8** (from
Approved Document B, Diagram 41)

Minimum distance (A) between side of building and relevant boundary (m)	Maximum total area of unprotected areas (m²)
1	5.6
2	12
3	18
4	24
5	30
6	no limit

Table VIII Permitted unprotected areas in small buildings or compartments
(from Approved Document B, Table 16)

Minimum distance between side of building and relevant boundary (m)		Maximum total percentage of unprotected area (%)
Purpose groups Residential, Office, Assembly and Recreation (1)	Shop & Commercial Industrial, storage & other Non-residential (2)	(3)
n.a.	1	4
1	2	8
2.5	5	20
5	10	40
7.5	15	60
10	20	80
12.5	25	100

Notes:

n.a. = not applicable

(1) intermediate values may be obtained by interpolation.

(2) For buildings which are fitted throughout with an automatic sprinkler system,
meeting the relevant recommendations of BS-5306 Part 2, the values in
columns (1) & (2) may be halved, subject to a minimum distance of 1 m being
maintained.

(3) In the case of open-aided car parks in purpose group 7(b) the distances set out
in column (1) may be used instead of those in column (2).

Document B makes recommendations in relation to small
buildings or compartments, both residential in Table VII and **42.8**
and non-residential in Table VIII.

3.21 Combustible claddings and insulation present a risk, especially in tall buildings. While claddings and their supports are not
always required to be fire-resisting, insulation at a height
exceeding 15 m is recommended to be of limited combustibility,
42.9

3.21 Roof coverings (not structures) in close proximity to
boundaries should have limited flame spread and penetration to
fire. The performance of coverings is designated by reference to
BS 476 Part 3 which classifies the results on the flame spread and
time taken to penetrate; AA being the best (specimen not
penetrated within one hour, no spread of flame), DD the worst
(penetrated in preliminary flame test, extensive and continuing
spread of flame). The addition of a suffix 'x' denotes one or more
of dripping from the underside, mechanical failure, development
of holes. Approved Document B sets out specific classification
recommendations relating to distances from the boundary, Table
IX together with recommendation for plastic rooflights, **42.10** and
Table X.

4 MEANS OF ESCAPE

4.01 There are numerous codes and guides relating to means of
escape from various uses, some of which, as they have evolved,
have overlapped and derived different recommendations for the

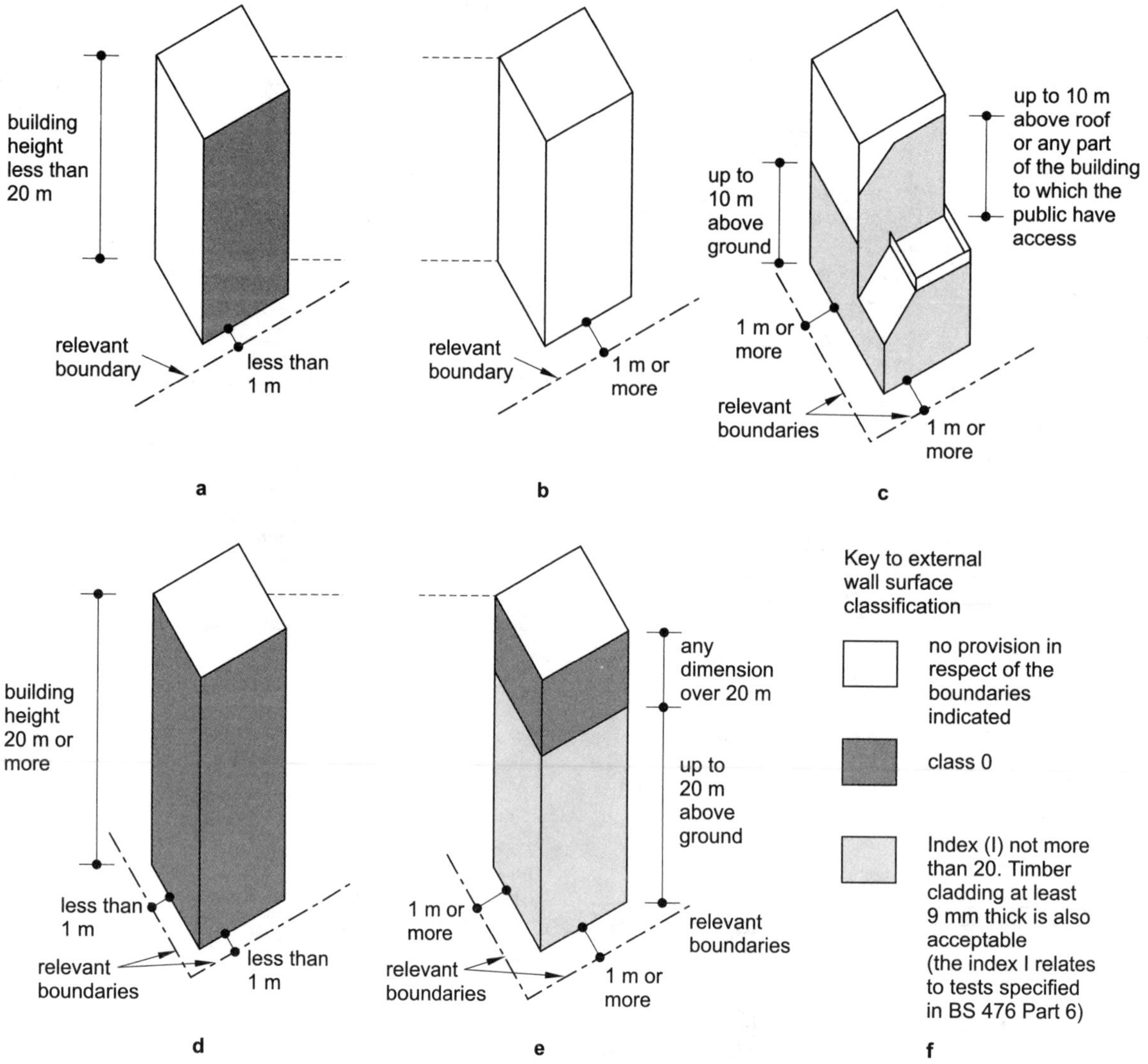

building height less than 20 m

relevant boundary → less than 1 m

a

relevant boundary → 1 m or more

b

up to 10 m above ground

up to 10 m above roof or any part of the building to which the public have access

1 m or more

relevant boundaries → 1 m or more

c

building height 20 m or more

less than 1 m

relevant boundaries → less than 1 m

d

any dimension over 20 m

up to 20 m above ground

1 m or more

relevant boundaries → 1 m or more

relevant boundaries

e

Key to external wall surface classification

□ no provision in respect of the boundaries indicated

■ class 0

▨ Index (I) not more than 20. Timber cladding at least 9 mm thick is also acceptable (the index I relates to tests specified in BS 476 Part 6)

f

42.9 *Provisions for external surfaces of walls.* **a** *Any building.* **b** *Any building other than as shown in* **c**. **c** *Assembly or recreational building of more than one storey.* **d** *Any building.* **e** *Any building.* **f** *Key to external wall surface classification*

Table IX Limitations on roof coverings (from Approved Document B, Table 17)

Designation of covering of roof or part of roof	Minimum distance from any point on relevant boundary			
	Less than 6 m	At least 6 m	At least 12 m	At least 20 m
AA, AB, or AC	–	–	–	–
BA, BB, or BC	×	–	–	–
CA, CB, or CC	×	(1)	(2)	–
AD, BD, or CD	×	(1)	(2)	(2)
DA, DB, DC, or DD	×	×	×	(1)
Thatch or wood shingles, if performance under BS 476, Part 3: 1958 cannot be established	×	(1)	(2)	(2)

Notes:
Unwired glass in, rooflights at least 4 mm thick can be regarded as AA. See Table IX for limitations on plastic rooflights
– Acceptable
× Not acceptable
(1) Not acceptable on any of the following buildings:
   (a) Houses in terraces of three or more houses,
   (b) Industrial, Storage or Other non-residential purpose group buildings of any size,
   (c) Any other buildings with a cubic capacity of more than 1500 m³
   And only acceptable on other buildings if the part of the roof is no more than 3 m² in area and is at least 1.5 m from any similar part, with the roof between the parts covered with a material of limited combustibility.
(2) Not acceptable on any of the buildings listed under (a), (b) or (c) above.
Separation distance considerations do not apply to roofs of a pair of semi-detached houses.

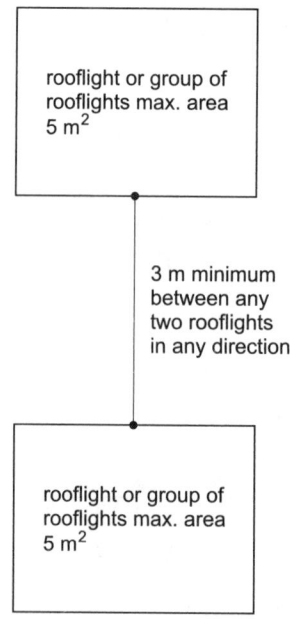

rooflight or group of rooflights max. area 5 m²

3 m minimum between any two rooflights in any direction

rooflight or group of rooflights max. area 5 m²

42.10 *Limitations on spacing and size of plastic rooflights having a Class 3 or TP(b) lower surface: see Table IX.* Note: *the surrounding roof covering should be of limited combustibility for at least 3 m*

Table X Plastics rooflights: limitations on use and boundary distance (from Approved Document B, Table 18)

Minimum classification on lower surface[1]	Space which rooflight can serve	Minimum distance from any point on relevant boundary to rooflight with an external surface classification[2] of:		
		TP(a)	AD BD CA CB CC CD OR TP(b)	DA DB DC DD
1 TP(a) rigid	any space except a protected stairway	6 m[3]	n.a.	n.a.
2 Class 3 or TP(b)	(a) balcony, verandah, carport, covered way or loading bay, which has at least one longer side wholly or permanently open (b) detached swimming pool (c) conservatory, garage or outbuilding, with a maximum floor area of 40 m²	n.a.	6 m	20 m
	(d) circulation space[4] (except a protected stairway) (e) room[4]	n.a.	6 m[5]	20 m[5]

Notes:

n.a. Not applicable

[1] See also the guidance to Table VIII.

[2] The classification of external roof surfaces is explained in Appendix A of Approved Document B.

[3] No limit in the case of any space described in 2(a) (b) and (c).

[4] Single-skin rooflight only, in the case of non-thermoplastic material.

[5] The rooflight should also meet the provisions of Polycarbonate and PVC rooflights which achieve a Class 1 rating by test, may be regarded as having an AA designation.

None of the above designations are suitable for protected stairways.

same matters. Occasionally, they include matters outside those of life safety. Generally, means of escape is the provision of safe routes for persons to travel from any point in a building to a place of safety.

4.02 At the time of writing, various aspects of fire safety, particularly the basis on which adopted standards and practices are founded, are under review. However, there is nothing to stop an alternative, innovative or unorthodox approach to means of escape being adopted. Fire-engineering solutions may be used where the established practices are unsuitable; here methods such as smoke control and automatic detection and suppression are used to evolve a package of safety measures for a specific user and building design requirements. It should be noted that a change in specific user may require a reassessment of the fire safety provisions.

4.03 Whatever method is adopted, the means of escape must be tailored to the individual occupancy and building. Where a project is speculative a judgement must be made as to the necessary provisions for means of escape: to assume the worst case may not be feasible, although it will result in a level of provision acceptable for the majority of occupancies. In the case of designs such as atria, persons should be at no greater risk than those in a non-atrium building.

4.04 The aim is to make provision such that escape can take place unaided. The occupants of some buildings, however, will not be able to achieve this. There are certain basic principles and provisions accepted as necessary for the provision of minimum means of escape. These are:

- Exits and escape routes of adequate number and width within a reasonable distance of all points in the building
- An alternative means of escape (in the majority of cases)
- Protected escape routes where necessary
- Lighting and directional signage
- Readily openable exit doors
- Smoke control to safeguard escape routes
- Separation of high or special risks
- Access for fire brigade to attack the seat of a fire swiftly for protection of life
- Audible/visual warning of fire and active measures
- First aid fire appliances, and
- Instruction of action to be taken in the event of a fire and evacuation procedure.

4.05 The last three items are additional to structural provision for means of escape. However, some procedures for evacuation and the life safety systems associated with certain designs of building, eg atria and shopping malls, and certain uses, eg hospitals, necessitate the utilisation of active measures to provide effective means of escape–pressurisation/depressurisation of escape routes to control smoke, automatic detection by heat and smoke detectors, etc.

4.05 The concept for escape from flats and maisonettes differs from that of other uses. This is based on the high standard of compartmentation and separation recommended in Approved Documents Part B, in particular B3 Internal Fire Spread (structure). Major factors are difficulties in alerting the population of the block to a fire (fire alarms in this situation being a potential source of acute nuisance), and also in ensuring that everyone in fact is evacuated.

4.06 Each residential unit is a separate fire compartment, and it is considered only necessary initially to evacuate the unit on fire. Consequently the necessary width of escape exits and routes may be minimalised. The spread of fire and smoke is controlled under the principles of smoke containment. As it has been shown that most fires are containable within the room of origin, the current edition of BS 5588 Part 1 (Code of practice for residential buildings) and Approved Document B have reduced the recommendations relating to fire separation within the unit from those previously given. The travel distance, any alternative means of escape, and the layout dictate the level of internal protection necessary, which influences the common area protection, **42.11** to **42.35**.

4.07 Parts 2 and 3 of BS 5588 (fire precautions in the design, construction and use of buildings) deals with offices and shops respectively. Part 11 of the 5588 series is currently being drafted; this will relate to shops, offices, factories, warehouses and similar workplaces. The recommendations within Part 11 will reflect modern practices and research, and will replace many of the recommendations currently within Parts 2 and 3 which are some 11 years old. They will accord more closely with Approved Document B issued with the Building Regulations. Data currently within Parts 2 and 3 has not generally been reproduced within this chapter.

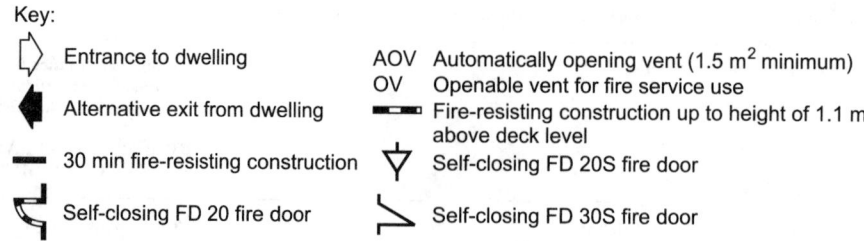

Key:

⬪ Entrance to dwelling

◀ Alternative exit from dwelling

— 30 min fire-resisting construction

Self-closing FD 20 fire door

AOV   Automatically opening vent (1.5 m² minimum)
OV   Openable vent for fire service use

▬ Fire-resisting construction up to height of 1.1 m above deck level

Self-closing FD 20S fire door

Self-closing FD 30S fire door

42.11 *Key to following drawings* **42.12 to 42.35**
The entrance and alternative exit doors may need to be fire doors, and compartment walls need to be fire-resisting

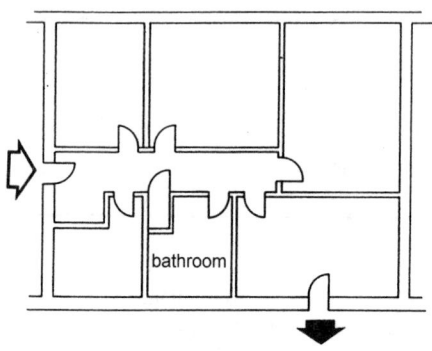

42.12 *Flat with alternative exit and where all habitable rooms have direct access to an entrance hall*

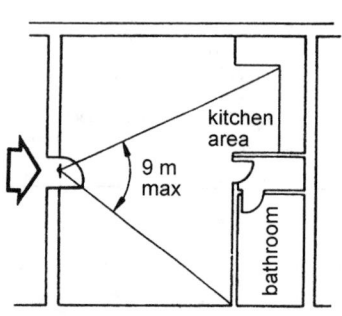

42.15 *Open-plan flat (bed-sitter) with restricted travel distance*

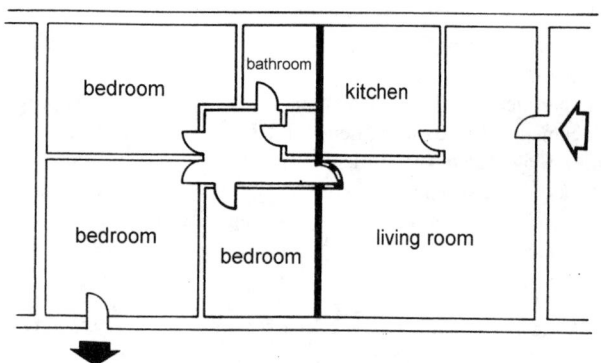

42.13 *Flat with alternative exit and where all habitable rooms do not have direct access to an entrance hall. The fire-resisting partition separates living and sleeping accommodation*

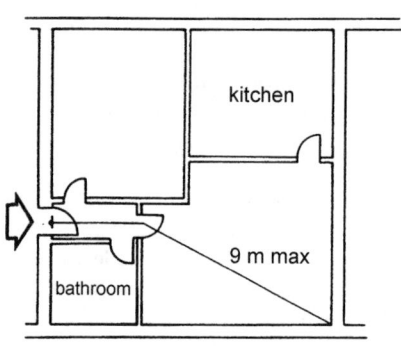

42.16 *Flat with separate habitable rooms and restricted travel distance*

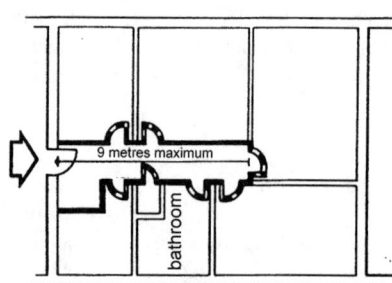

42.14 *Flat with a protected entrance hall and restricted travel distance. If the partitions between bathroom and adjacent rooms have 30 minutes fire resistance, then the partition between it and the entrance hall need not be fire-resisting and its door need not be a fire door. The cupboard door need not be self-closing*

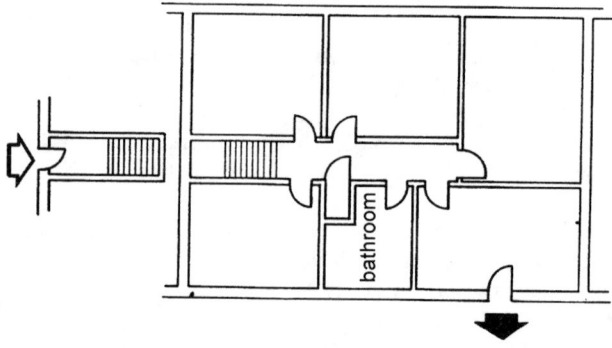

42.17 *Flat entered from above or below with an alternative exit and where all habitable rooms have direct access to an entrance hall*

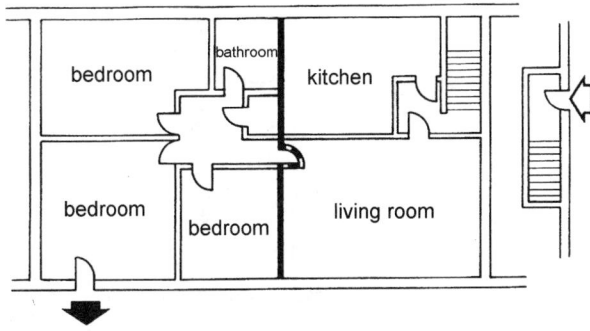

42.18 *Flat entered from above or below with an alternative exit and where all habitable rooms do not have direct access to an entrance hall. The fire-resisting partition separates living and sleeping accommodation*

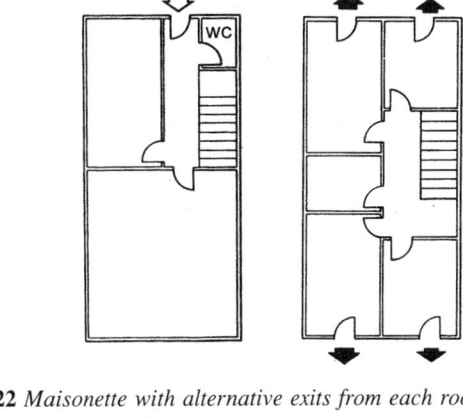

42.22 *Maisonette with alternative exits from each room not on the entrance floor level*

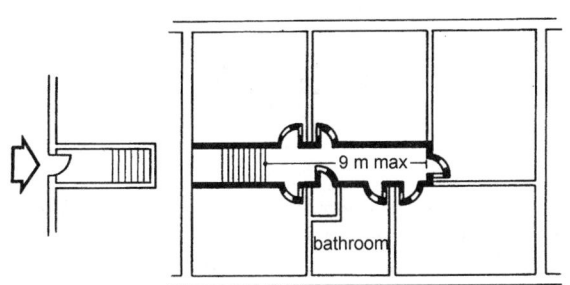

42.19 *Flat entered from below with a protected entrance and restricted travel distance. If the partitions between bathroom and adjacent rooms have 30 minutes fire resistance, then the partition between it and the entrance hall need not be fire-resisting and its door need not be a fire door. The cupboard door need not be self-closing*

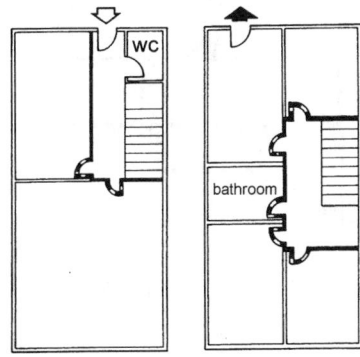

42.23 *Maisonette with protected entrance floor and landing. If the partitions between bathroom and adjacent rooms have 30 minutes fire resistance, then the partition between it and the entrance hall need not be fire-resisting and its door need not be a fire door.*

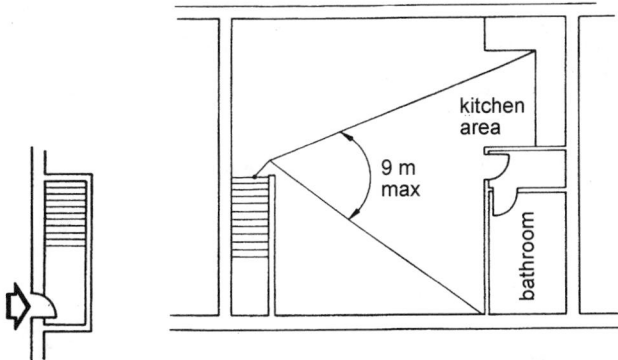

42.20 *Open-plan flat (bed-sitter) entered from below with a restricted travel distance*

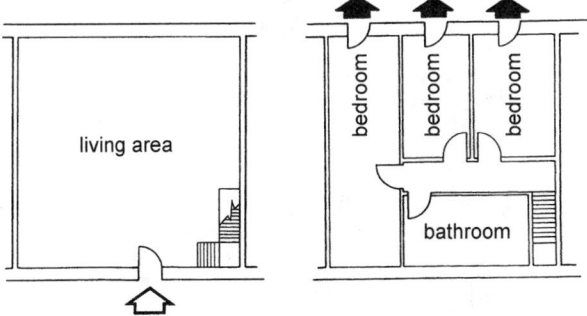

42.24 *Open-plan maisonette*

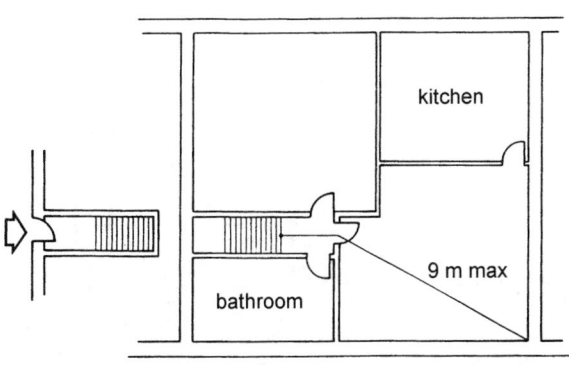

42.21 *Flat with separate habitable rooms entered from below with a restricted travel distance*

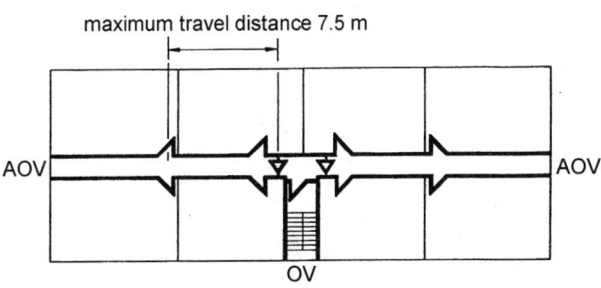

42.25 *Common escape routes in single stair buildings more than 11 m high with corridor access dwellings. Where all dwellings on a storey have independent alternative means of escape, the maximum travel distance may be increased to 30 m. Where a firefighting lift is required, it should be sited not more than 7.5 m from the door to the stair. The openable vents (OVs) to the stairway may be replaced by an openable vent over the stair*

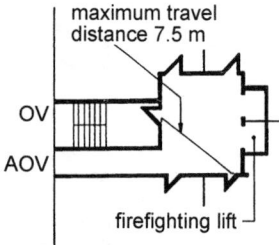

42.26 *Common escape routes in single stair tower blocks more than 11 m high, with the stair adjacent to an external wall. See riders to* **42.25**

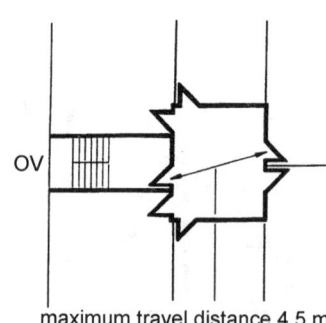

42.31 *Common escape routes in small single-stair buildings*

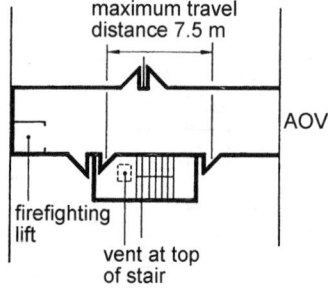

42.27 *Common escape routes in single stair tower blocks more than 11 m high with internal stair. See riders to* **42.25**

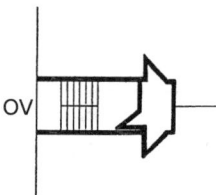

42.32 *Common escape routes in small single-stair buildings with not more than two dwellings per storey. The door between the stair and lobby should be free from security fastenings. Where the dwellings have protected entrance halls, the separation between the stair and the dwelling entrance doorts is not necessary*

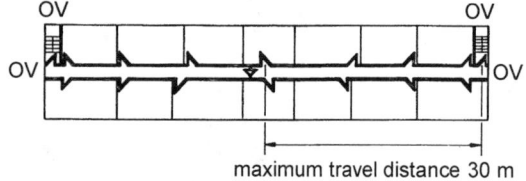

42.28 *Common escape routes in multi-stair buildings with corridor access dwellings and no dead-ends*

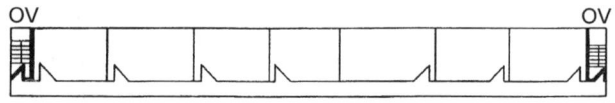

42.33 *Common escape routes in balcony/deck approach multi-stair buildings*

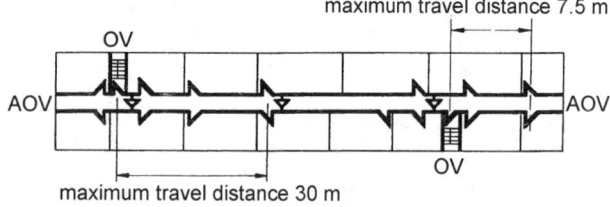

42.29 *Common escape routes in multi-stair buildings with corridor access dwellings and with dead-ends. The central fire door may be omitted where the maximum travel distance does not exceed 15 m*

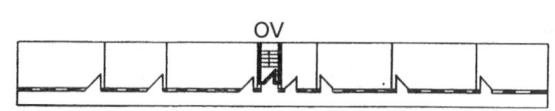

42.34 *Common escape routes in balcony/deck approach single-stair buildings*

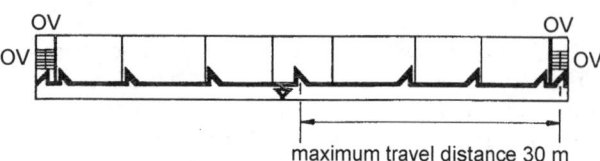

42.30 *Common escape routes in multi-stair buildings with corridor access dwellings on one side only*

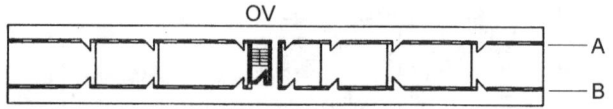

42.35 *Common escape routes in balcony/deck approach single-stair buildings with an alternative exit from each dwelling. One of the external enclosures A or B must be fire resisting*

4.08 Number of exits and escape routes

In order to determine the number of exits from a room or storey, their occupancy must be established. This may be known, or it can be assessed by the use of recognised space factors for specific uses. These are only indicators and can be varied. These numbers will also affect the width of escape routes. In existing buildings the width of doors, stairways, passages etc, if not to be altered, will dictate the numbers of people that can be accommodated, Tables XI, XII and XIII:

$$\text{Occupancy} = \frac{\text{Area of room or storey (m}^2)}{\text{Floor space per person (m}^2)}$$

4.09 Once the occupancy factor for an area is known the number of exits must equate to the necessary total width of escape required, although a minimum number of exits is specified within Approved Document B and Part 6 of BS 5588 (assembly buildings). Not less than two exits should be provided, except in the case of an occupancy of less than 50, or a small storey with a limited travel distance ('dead end').

4.10 The capacities of exits are given in various tables. Most recommendations equate to approximately 40 persons passing through a unit width of 500 mm in $2\frac{1}{2}$ minutes. While not all exits need be of equal width, they should be evenly distributed to provide alternatives. Where there are two or more exits, it is

assumed that fire may affect one of them, therefore the largest exit should be discounted. Hence the total number of exits = calculated number + 1, Table XIV

4.11 Alternatively, the number of exits may be determined by recommended travel distances, ie the actual distance to be travelled to the nearest exit, having regard to obstructions such as partitions. The distances currently recommended are historical,

Table XII Floor space factors for assembly buildings (from BS 5588: Part 6, Table 3)

Description of floor space	Floor space per person (m^2)
1 Individual seating	0.4 to 0.5
2 Bench seating	0.3[1]
3 Dance area	0.5
4 Ice rinks	1.2
5 Restaurants and similar table and chair arrangements around a dance area	1.1 to 1.5
6 Bars without seating and similar refreshment areas	0.3
7 Standing spectator areas	0.3
8 Exhibition	1.5[2]
9 Bowling alley billiard or snooker hall	9.5
10 Museum/art gallery	5.0
11 Studio (radio, television, film, recording)	1.4

[1] If the number and length of benches is known, a factor of 450 mm per person should be used.
[2] Alternatively, a factor of 0.4 m^2 may be used over the gross area of gangways and other clear circulation space between stalls and stands.
Note. These floor space factors are for guidance only and should not be taken as the only acceptable densities. Where the number of seats is known this should be used in preference to the floor space factors.

Table XI Floor space factors (from Approved Document B, Table 1)

Type of accommodation[1,6]	Floor space factor m^2/person
1 Standing spectator areas	0.3
2 Amusement arcade, Assembly hall (including a general-purpose place of assembly) Bar (including a lounge bar), Bingo hall, Dance floor or hall, Club, Crush hall, Venue for pop concert and similar events, Queuing area	0.5
3 Concourse or shopping mall[2]	0.75
4 Committee room, Common room, Conference room, Dining room, Licensed betting office (public area), Lounge (other than a lounge bar), Meeting room, Reading room, Restaurant, Staff room, Waiting room[3]	1.0
5 Exhibition hall	1.5
6 Shop sales area[4] Skating rink	2.0
7 Art gallery, Dormitory, Factory production area, Office (open-plan exceeding 60 m^2) Workshop	5.0
8 Kitchen, Library, Office (other than in 7 above), Shop sales area[5]	7.0
9 Bedroom or Study-bedroom	8.0
10 Bed-sitting room, Billiards room	10.0
11 Storage and warehousing	30.0
12 Car park	two persons per parking space

Notes:
[1] Where accommodation is not directly covered by the descriptions given, a reasonable value based on a similar use may be selected.
[2] Refer to section 4 of BS 5588: Part 10 for detailed guidance on the calculation of occupancy in common public areas in shopping complexes.
[3] Alternatively the occupant capacity may be taken as the number of fixed seats provided, if the occupants will normally be seated.
[4] Shops excluding those under item 8, but including – supermarkets and department stores (all sales areas), shops for personal services such as hairdressing and shops for the delivery or collection of goods for cleaning, repair or other treatment or for members of the public themselves carrying out such cleaning, repair or other treatment.
[5] Shops (excluding those in covered shopping complexes, and excluding department stores) trading predominantly in furniture, floor coverings, cycles prams, large domestic appliances or other bulky goods, or trading on a wholesale self-selection basis (cash and carry).
[6] If there is to be mixed use, the most onerous factor(s) should be applied.

Table XIII Capacities of exits in shopping complexes other than from mally (from BS 5588 Part 10, Table 3)

Maximum number of persons	Width (mm)
50	800
110	900
220	1100
240	1200
260	1300
280	1400
300	1500
320	1600
340	1700
360	1800

Note 1. Other values of width for a maximum number of persons greater than 220 may be obtained by linear interpolation or extrapolation.
Note 2. For the purposes of this table, the width of a doorway is that of the leaf or leaves, and the width of a passage is between the sides at shoulder level (that is about 1.5 m above finished floor level).

Table XIV Widths of escape routes and exists (from Approved Document B, Table 5)

Maximum number of persons	Minimum width mm[1]
50	800[2]
110	900
220	1100
more than 220	5 per person

Notes:
[1] Refer to the guidance in the Approved Document to part M on minimum widths for areas accessible to disabled people.
[2] May be reduced to 530 mm for gangways between fixed storage racking, other than in public areas of Purpose Group 4 (shop and commercial).

based on experience and accepted practice. They are not sacrosanct, but should be shorter rather than longer. Extension of travel distances may be justified where compensatory factors such as smoke control systems or early warning of fire is provided. Only one exit need be within the travel distance, alternatives may be at any distance, Tables XV to XVIII.

4.12 Alternative means of escape

A person should be able in most circumstances to turn their back on a fire and walk to an alternative exit. If escape is in one direction only, an exit or alternative escape route should be near enough for people to reach it before being affected by heat and smoke. The Scottish Building Regulations and the Home Office Guide for premises requiring a fire certificate recommend that the angle of divergence should be not less than 45° plus 2½° for every metre travelled in one direction, **42.36**, **42.37** and **42.38**.

4.13 Width of escape routes and exits

An escape route should be as wide or wider than an exit leading to it, and should be of uniform width. The width of a final exit should equate to the route or routes it serves. This may comprise the total number of persons descending a stair plus a ground-storey population plus those ascending from a basement.

4.14 Unfortunately to date there is no agreed method of measuring width. In addition to means of escape, access for the disabled may be a consideration with specific details for projection of handrails. The variations should be accommodated by measuring an absolute clear width with no allowances for the projection of handrails, door thickness, etc, except door furniture with a maximum intrusion of 100 mm. The safe and rapid use of a stair is dependent on all persons being within reach of a handrail, therefore no staircase should exceed 1.4 m in width unless additional central handrails are provided.

4.15 The capacity and therefore the width of the a stair differ from that of a horizontal escape route being influenced by the rate of decent and the standing position on the stairs. The width necessary is also influenced by the type of evacuation – total or phased – the stair having to accommodate only the population of a phase in the latter instance:

Total evacuation: on the raising of the alarm the total population moves to evacuate the whole of the building in a single phase.
Phased evacuation: on the discovery of a fire the alarm is given in the following manner. The fire floor and the floor above are given the signal to evacuate immediately, all other floors are given the alert signal to stand by to evacuate. If the fire is extinguished no further evacuation is necessary; if not, the next two floors immediately above the initial phase are evacuated; and so progressively in separate phases of two floors up the building to the top. Evacuation then proceeds down the building, starting with the floors nearest the fire, until it is complete or the fire extinguished. As the population of only two floors are evacuated at a time, the stair width dimensions can be decreased.

4.16 As people remain in the building during the fire-phased evacuation, it can take place only if additional protective measures are incorporated:

● All compartment floors with openings through them protected to maintain compartmentation
● All stairs protected by lobbies or corridors of fire-resisting construction
● A fire alarm system incorporating a personal address system operated from a central control point from where occupants can be instructed and orderly evacuation directed
● An automatic sprinkler installation (although this may not be necessary in a low-rise building with, say, three phases of evacuation which would be complete within 30 minutes).

Table XV Limitations on travel distance (from Approved Document B, Table 3)

Purpose Group	Use of the premises or part of the premises	Maximum travel distance[1] where travel is possible in:	
		one direction only (m)	more than one direction (m)
2(a)	Institutional[2]	9	18
2(b)	Other residential:		
	(a) in bedrooms[3]	9	18
	(b) in bedroom corridors	9	35
	(c) elsewhere	18	35
3	Office	18	45
4	Shop and Commercial[4]	18	45
5	Assembly and Recreation:		
	(a) buildings primarily for the handicapped except schools	9	18
	(b) elsewhere	15	32
6	Industrial (5)	25	45
7	Storage and other non-residential[5]	18	45
2–7	Place of special fire risk[6]	9(3)	18(3)
2–7	Plant room or rooftop plant:		
	(a) distance within the room	9	35
	(b) escape route not in open air (overall travel distance)	18	45
	(c) escape route in open air (overall travel distance)	60	100

Notes:
[1] The dimensions in the table are travel distances. If the internal layout of partitions, fittings, etc is not known when plans are deposited, direct distances may be used for assessment. The direct distance is taken as 2/3rds of the travel distance.
[2] If provision for means of escape is being made in a hospital or other health care building by following the detailed guidance in the relevant part of the Department of Health 'Firecode', the recommendations about travel distances in the appropriate 'Firecode' document should be followed.
[3] Maximum part of travel distance within the room.
[4] Maximum travel distances within shopping malls are given in BS 5588: Part 10: 1991. Guidance on associated smoke control measures is given in a BRE report *Design principles for smoke ventilation in enclosed shopping centres*, BR 186.
[5] In industrial buildings the appropriate travel distance depends on the level of fire risk associated with the processes and materials being used. Control over the use of industrial buildings is exercised through the Fire Precautions Act. Attention is drawn to the guidance issued by the Home Office *Guide to fire precautions in existing places of work that require a fire certificate, Factories Offices Shops and Railway Premises*. The dimensions given above assume that the premises will be of 'normal' fire risk, as described in the Home Office guidance. If the building is high risk, as assessed against the criteria in the Home Office guidance, then lesser distances of 12 m in one direction and 25 m in more than one direction, would apply.
[6] Places of special fire risk are listed in the definitions in Appendix E, of Approved Document B.

Table XVI Maximum travel distances in assembly buildings (from BS 5588: Part 6, Table 2)

Available direction of escape	Areas with seating in rows (m)	Open floor areas (m)
(a) In one direction only	15	18
(b) In more than one direction	32[1]	45[2]

[1] This may include up to 15 m in one direction only.
[2] This may include up to 18 m in one direction only.

Table XVII Maximum travel distances in stopping malls (from BS 5588: Part 10, Table 1)

Available direction of escape	Uncovered malls (m)	Covered malls (m)
(a) In one direction		
(1) malls at ground level	25	9
(2) malls not at ground level	9	9
(b) In more than direction		
(1) malls at ground level	not limited	45
(2) malls not at ground level	45	45

Table XVIII Maximum travel distances in shopping complexes other than in malls (from BS 5588: Part 10, Table 2)

Accommodation	Maximum part of travel distance within room or area		Maximum travel distance to nearest storey exit	
	Escape in one direction only (m)	Escape in more than one direction (m)	Escape in one direction only (m)	Escape in more than one direction (m)
Accommodation other than the following list	18	45[1]	18	45[1]
Engineering services installation rooms Boiler rooms Fuel storage spaces Transformer, battery and switchgear rooms Rooms housing a fixed internal combustion engine	9	18	18	45[1]

[1] This may include up to 18 m with escape in one direction only.

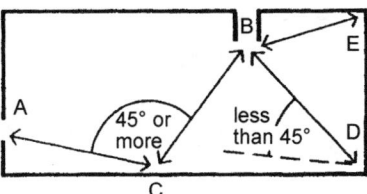

42.36 Alternative escape routes are available from C because angle ACB is at least 45°, so that either CA or CB should be less than the maximum travel distance given in Table XV. Alternative routes are not available from D because angle ADB is less than 45°, so that DB should not exceed the distance for travel in one direction. There is also no alternative route from E

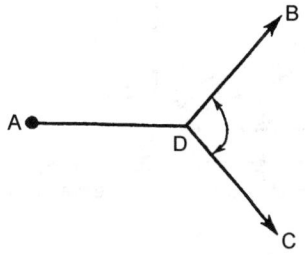

42.37 Alternative escape routes in principle, A being the point of origin and D the point of divergence of alternative routes. Angle BDC = 45° + 2½° for each metre travelled from A to D

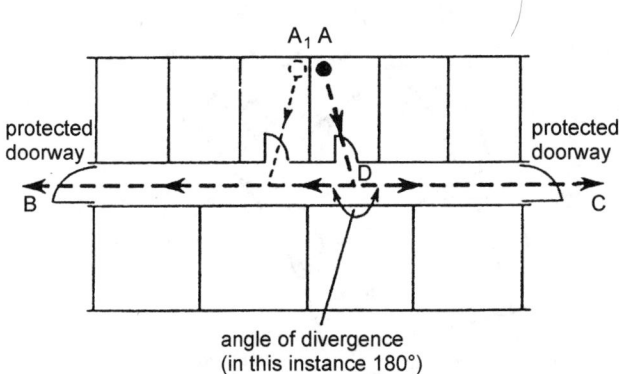

angle of divergence
(in this instance 180°)

42.38 Alternative escape routes in practice

4.17 Phased evacuation is not generally accepted for any basements, assembly, hotel, recreational and similar buildings, and, to date, the majority of shops. However, in the case of mixed user and large complexes total evacuation may not be necessary or prudent and enforcing authorities should be consulted at an early stage.

Table XIX Minimum width of escape stairs (from Approved Document B, Table 6)

Situation of stair	Max number of people served[1]	Minimum stair width (mm)
1 In an institutional building (unless the stair will only be used by staff)	150	1000
2 In an assembly building and serving an area used for assembly purposes (unless the area is less than 100 m²)	220	1100
3 In any other building and serving an area with an occupancy of more than 50	over 220	note[2]
4 Any stair not described above	50	800

[1] Assessed as likely to use the stair in a fire emergency.
[2] See Table 7 for sizing stairs for total evacuation, and Table 8 for phased evacuation.

4.18 Where two or more stairs are provided, it is reasonable to assume that one will not be available for use due to fire or smoke unless a sufficiently high degree of protection is afforded. If a stair is approached through a lobby, or protected by a pressure-differential smoke control system, it can be assumed that it will be available. Where such protection is not provided, a stair should be discounted (number of stairs required = calculated number plus 1). Each stair should be discounted in turn, to ensure that the capacity of the remaining stairs in total is adequate, Tables XIX and XX.

4.19 Stair design should accord with Approved Document K or BS 5395, Stairs, ladders and walkways, **42.39, 42.40** and **42.41,** and Table XXI.

For buildings over 10 storeys Approved Document B recommends the use of the following formula to assess the capacity of stairs:

$$P = 200w + 50(w-0.3)(n-1)$$

where P is the number of people that can be accommodated
w is the width of the stair in metres
n is the number of storeys in the building

Where phased evacuation is envisaged, the minimum widths in Table XXII may be adopted.

Small buildings occupied by a limited number of persons and satisfying the criteria for travel distance and a single exit can have a single stairway, Tables XXIII and XXIV.

4.20 The recommended widths assume a uniform distribution of population. If any floor within a building has a higher population, eg a conference room or restaurant, extra or wider stairs necessary to accommodate the increased population should extend down to the final exit.

4.21 Separate stairs should be provided for use by residential or assembly occupancies independent of any other use. Where a

Table XX Capacity of a stair for basements and for total evacuation of the building (from: Approved Document B, Table 7; also BS 5588: Part 6, Table 5)

No. of floors served	Maximum number of persons served by a stair of width:								
	1000 mm	1100 mm	1200 mm	1300 mm	1400 mm	1500 mm	1600 mm	1700 mm	1800 mm
1	150	220	240	260	280	300	320	340	360
2	190	260	285	310	335	360	385	410	435
3	230	300	330	360	390	420	450	480	510
4	270	340	375	410	445	480	515	550	585
5	310	380	420	460	500	540	580	620	660
6	350	420	465	510	555	600	645	690	735
7	390	460	510	560	610	660	710	760	810
8	430	500	555	610	665	720	775	830	885
9	470	540	600	660	720	780	840	900	960
10	510	580	645	710	775	840	905	970	1035

Notes:
The capacity of stairs serving more than 10 storeys may be obtained by using the formula in para **419**.
This table can also apply to part of a building.

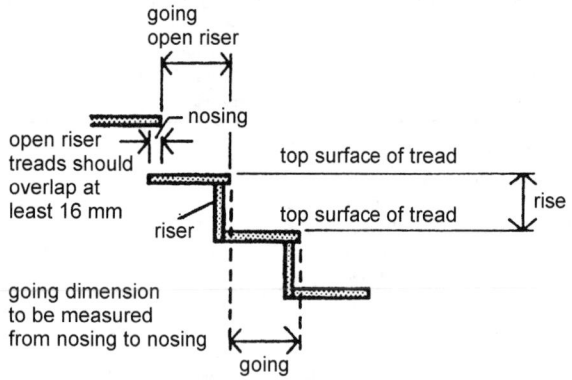

42.39 *Measuring rise and going on staircases*

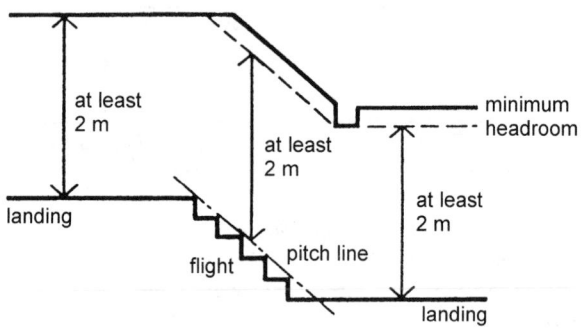

42.40 *Measuring headroom on staircases*

Table XXI Rise and going (from Approved Document K, Table 1)

	Maximum rise (mm)	Minimum going (mm)
1 Private stair	220†	220*
2 Institutional and assembly stair	180‡	280†
3 Other stair	190‡	250

* The maximum pitch for a private stair is 42°.
† If the area of a floor of the building is less than 100 m², the going may be reduced to 250 mm.
‡ For maximum rise for stairs providing the means of access for disabled people reference should be made to Approved Document M: Access and facilities for disabled people.

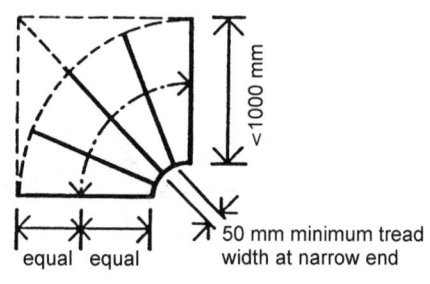

Table XXII Minimum aggregate width of stairs designed for phased evacuation (from Approved Document B, Table 38)

Maximum number of people in any storey	Stair width¹ (mm)
100	1000
120	1100
130	1200
140	1300
150	1400
160	1500
170	1600
180	1700
190	1800

¹ Stairs with a rise of more than 30 m should not be wider than 1400 mm unless provided with a central handrail (see para **4.6**)
As an alternative to using this table, provided that the minimum width of a stair is at least 1000 mm, the width may be calculated from: [(P × 10) – 100 mm where P = the number of people on the most heavily occupied storey.

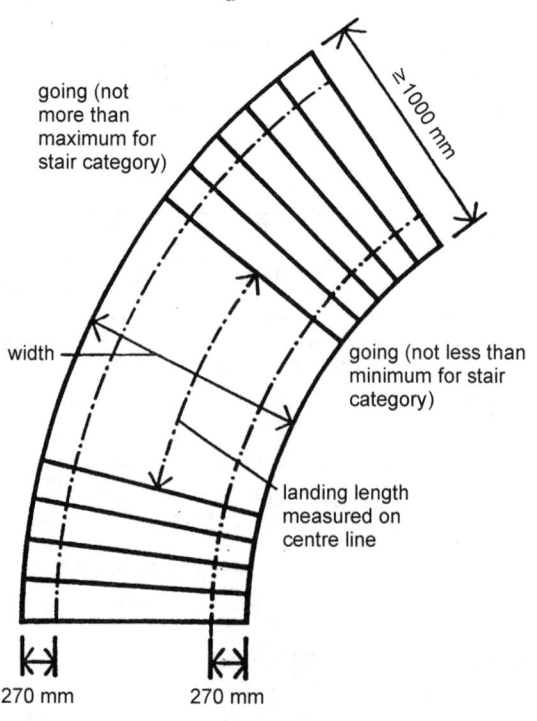

42.41 *Measuring tapered treads.* **a** *Stair width less than 1 m.*
b *Stair width equal to or greater than 1 m*

Table XXIII Maximum permitted distances of travel* in small shops (from BS 5588: Part 2, Table 6)

	Maximum travel distance (m)	Maximum direct distance (m)
Ground storey with a single exit	27	18
Basement or first storey with a single stairway	18	12
Storey with more than one exit/stairway	45	30

* See footnote to **9.2.3** in BS 5588.

Table XXIV Capacity of a stairway for an office building permitted to be served by a single stairway (from BS 5588: Part 3, Table 6)

Maximum number of persons per storey	Width of stairway (mm)
50	900
more than 50	1100

totally independent escape can be provided from these higher risk uses, eg using an access deck or walkway, it is reasonable that some stairs may be shared.

4.22 The use of external stairs should be avoided if possible, due to the psychological effect of using unfamiliar external stairs at high levels and the effects of bad weather. The width and design of external stairs is the same as for internal ones. External stairs are not considered suitable for use by the general public, nor for nor hospital or similar uses. They should only be used as an alternative escape unless they are the only stair, **42.42**.

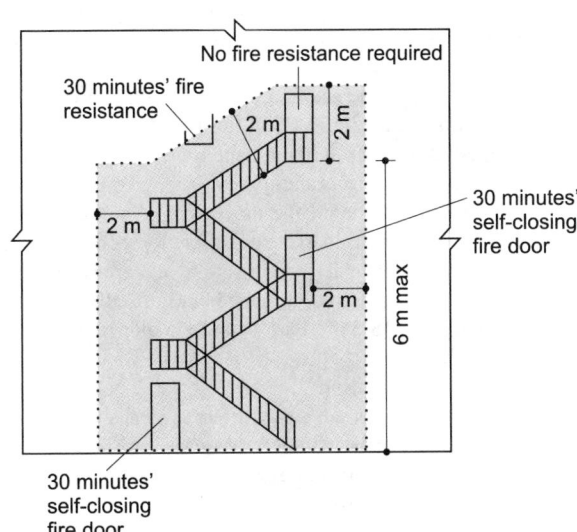

42.42 *Enclosure of escape stairs and ramps, not drawn to scale. The shaded area should have not less than 30 minutes fire resistance*

An external escape route should be protected against the accumulation of ice and snow. This may be in the form of an enclosure, partial shielding or trace heating.

4.23 Escape routes
Recommendations related to means of escape are generally based on a 30-minute period of fire resistance. Higher periods may result by reason of the need to maintain compartmentation or provide firefighting shafts.

Escape stairs, other than external, should be enclosed by fire-resisting construction to protect against the effects of smoke, heat and fire, and to retard the progress of fire and smoke affecting escape routes. Escape routes should lead to final exits.

4.24 Additionally, lobbies or corridors of fire-resisting construction should be provided to give additional protection to stairs in the following positions:

● Between a floor area and stair in all buildings over 20 m in height at all levels
● Between a stair and a basement storey as the stair is at greater risk from heat and smoke
● Between a stair and an enclosed car park
● Between a stair and a higher risk area, eg a boiler room
● Between a stair and a floor area in a single-storey building other than a small shop (see BS 5588 Part 2) to protect the stair from smoke
● In assembly buildings to protect the public and performers – where an opening occurs in a proscenium wall, and between stage and dressing-room corridors
● Where phased evacuation is used, and
● Where a stair is not discounted.

4.25 Escape routes do not necessarily have to be enclosed; in some situations this would create great problems – open-plan offices, exhibition halls, warehouses, factories.

4.26 Where a corridor dead-end situation exists, the escape route must be protected against fire, heat and smoke by fire-resisting construction, as it may be necessary to pass the room on fire to reach the exit, **42.43**.

4.27 Where a corridor connects escape routes, it should be protected against the ingress of smoke. To be effective, the construction should be from structural floor to structural floor or imperforate suspended ceiling. The corridors should also be subdivided by cross-corridor doors to inhibit the progress of smoke. These doors do not necessarily require fire resistance. Their purpose is to make it possible to take an alternative means of escape, not to subdivide the corridor at given intervals. Corridors exceeding 12 m should be subdivided (not subdivided at 12 m intervals), **42.44**.

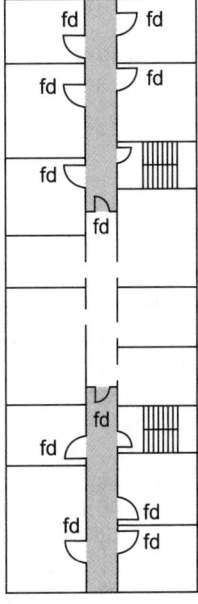

42.43 *Dead-end corridors continued past stairway*

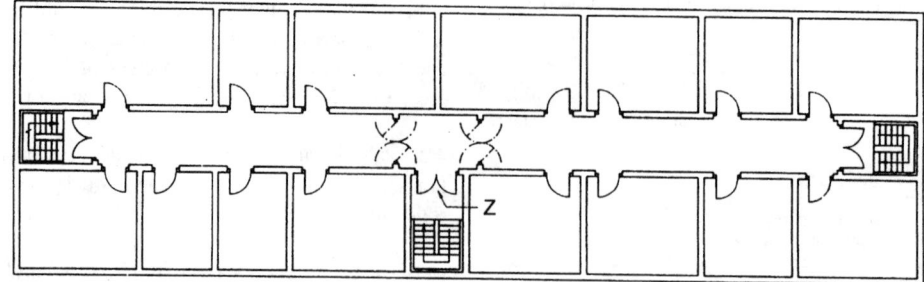

42.44 *Corridors connecting alternative exits. Doors to central stairway should be at position Z, doors may also be required across the corridors*

4.28 Lighting and directional signage
General artificial lighting should be provided for persons to move about a building effectively and safely.

4.29 Emergency lighting
This should be provided in the those areas necessary for escape purposes in case the artificial lighting fails. It may be a maintained system (continuously illuminated in conjunction with the general lighting) or be non-maintained; only coming into operation on the failure of the general lighting. Maintained systems are usually provided in areas with large numbers of the public unfamiliar with their surroundings, and where darkened situations may be common.

Escape lighting should be provided in:

● Areas occupied or used by the public
● Windowless accommodation
● Escape routes, including internal corridors without borrowed light
● Basements
● Areas used outside normal daylight hours, and
● Rooms containing essential equipment.

4.30 Signs
These are required to indicate the way to exits, and the exits themselves. Preferred colours, sizes, typeface and graphics are set out in BS 5499. The criterion is that signs should be distinguishable against their background and surroundings and be of a size that can be read at the required distance. If the use of the building warrants, the signs may have to be in more than one language. Signs should also be provided to indicate fire doors, and those that should be kept locked shut. In public assembly areas, signs are usually internally illuminated; elsewhere it is normally sufficient for escape lights to be positioned so as to illuminate a sign.

4.31 Fastenings
Fastenings on exit doors should allow exit without the use of a key or other device. Unless careful consideration is given to fastenings security may be undermined. The degree of security required will depend on the use of the building and user requirements. Access *into* a building is not required for escape purposes: re-entry into a floor area is neither necessary nor desirable. Fastenings that prevent a person entering a floor area from a staircase are acceptable. This is often a necessity to prevent theft in offices, factories and hotels and the like. The use of electronic fastenings and the use of card systems or similar to gain entry are acceptable provided that on the raising of the fire alarm or failure of the electrical system all locks 'fail-safe' in the unlocked position. However, consideration should also be given to the possibility of criminals setting off a false fire alarm in order to circumvent security arrangements.

4.31 Panic bolts and latches are most suitable where there are large numbers of persons. Turnbuckle locks with lever handles are commonly used where no public is involved. These may not be suitable in some institutional buildings, or places used predominantly by the elderly or disabled who may find a small turnbuckle difficult to operate; appropriate door ironmongery should be fitted in these circumstances.

4.32 Smoke control
If a smoke control system is for life safety purposes, it is essential that its initiation is automatic on the detection of smoke; and if mechanical, that it remains operational at all times by the use of duplicate equipment and secondary power supplies etc. Specialist advice should be sought regarding the type, design and installation of a life safety system.

4.32 The measures required to protect a means of escape from the effects of smoke will depend on the escape scheme adopted. Where escape is over a reasonable travel distance, the enclosure of the routes by partitions constructed to resist smoke, ie to maintain their integrity, should be adequate. Some smoke will enter escape routes, but should not reach a level to make their use untenable in the time it takes to reach an exit.

As described earlier, the addition of lobbies will retard the entry of smoke. Ventilating the lobbies will further dilute the smoke and hopefully direct it away from the escape route. It is also possible to protect escape routes from the ingress of smoke by the use of pressure differentials to retard the movement of smoke whereby fans, ducts and vents are used to create different pressures between the fire and protected area (pressurisation or depressurisation). Any such system should be designed and installed with the recommendations of BS 5588 Part 4 (under major revision).

4.33 Mechanical ventilation
These systems should not adversely affect a means of escape by perforation of enclosures without adequate protection, or by directing smoke into escape routes. Systems should have regard to BS 5720 and BS 5588 Part 9.

4.34 Ancillary accommodation
Service areas such as boiler and switch rooms should include provision in accordance with Tables XXV and XXVI.

4.35 Escape for people with disabilities
Escape for disabled people should be provided from all buildings to which they have access. BS 5588 Part 8 gives guidance on means of escape for them. Buildings designed particularly for use by persons with disabilities will require specific additional facilities and protection to escape routes depending on the disability. In any case, controlled escape by effective management is vital and assistance should be available.

The Building Regulations require access for disabled persons to the majority of buildings; therefore a number of factors to facilitate

Table XXV Maximum permitted part of travel distance in certain areas of ancillary accommodstion (from BS 5588: Part 3, Table 8)

Areas of ancillary accommodation	Cross-reference	Maximum part of travel distance within the room (m)	
		For escape in one direction only, or in directions less than 45° apart that are not separated by fire-resisting construction	For escape in more than one direction in directions 45° or more apart, or in directions less than 45° apart but separated by fire-resisting construction
1 Higher fire risk areas other than items 2, 3, 4 and 5	11.6		
2 Transformer and switchgear rooms	12.2		
3 Boiler rooms	14.6.2	6	12
4 Some fuel storage spaces	14.7		
5 Room housing a fixed internal combustion engine	14.8		

See 1

Table XXVI Structural fire protection of areas of ancillary accommodation (from BS 5588: Part 3, Table 9)

Area of ancillary accommodation	Cross-reference	Structural fire protection: the area of ancillary accommodation should be separated from other parts of the building by:
1 Storage area not greater than 450 m² (see notes 1 and 2)	18	Robust construction having a minimum standard of fire resistance of 30 min (see note 3)
2 Repair and maintenance workshops and reprographic rooms (see note 1)	20	
3 Kitchens (separately or in conjunction with an associated restaurant/canteen)	21	
4 Transformer, switchgear and battery rooms, for low voltage or extra low voltage equipment	12.2	
5 Loading bays	18	Robust construction having a minimum standard of fire resistance of 60 min (see note 3)
6 Storage areas greater than 450 m² (see notes 1 and 2)	18	
7 Service installation rooms other than those covered by items 4 and 10 to 14 inclusive		
8 Car parks within or adjoining an office building and not greater than 450 m² in area	19	
9 Car parks within or adjoining an office building and greater than 450 m² in area	19	Robust construction having a minimum standard of fire resistance equivalent to that required of the elements of construction of the building and in no case less than 60 min (see note 3)
10 Boiler rooms (see note 4)	14.6	
11 Fuel storage spaces (see notes 4 and 5)	14.7	
12 Transformer and switchgear rooms for equipment above low voltage	12.2	
13 Rooms housing fixed internal combustion engines	14.8	
14 Any higher fire risk area other than items 10 to 13	11.6	

Notes:
(1) Not higher fire risk areas.
(2) Other than refuse storage...
(3) Any openings in the required construction should be protected by doors having a similar standard of fire resistance.
(4) Other than oil fired boiler installations and oil storage.
(5) Other than liquefied petroleum gas storage.

their escape will exist – additional width escape routes to accommodate wheelchairs, position and height of guarding on stairs and ramps. Also, in some cases lifts, if adequately protected, may be used by them in the event of fire. It may be necessary to construct protected refuges adjacent to lifts and stairs for those in wheelchairs and with limited mobility to await the use of a lift or assistance to evacuate the building.

When assessing escape arrangements for disabled people it is important not to consider only those that are in wheelchairs. Among others, blind people need help to find the exits, and deaf people require audible warnings to be duplicated by visual ones.

4.36 Fire safety management

This is the prevention and control of a fire, and the maintenance of the fire safety facilities. The understanding and maintenance of these is essential, particularly in a large or complex building; therefore the occupier/management should have comprehension of the safety measures incorporated into the design of the building. This means that the designer must supply all relevant information in a fire safety manual. Details should include:

- The basis on which the means of escape was planned
- The type of management structure and staff responsibilities envisaged
- Operational details of mechanical and electrical systems, and
- Record drawings of active and passive protection measures.

5 MATERIALS

5.01 The materials forming a building should be chosen having regard to the safety of the structure and occupants. The adequacy of their resistance or their ability to sustain load for any particular period may necessitate their protection to prevent the premature failure of the structure by collapse or failure of loadbearing capacity. Additional resistance may be achieved by protective coverings, casings or membranes.

5.02 Fire resistance relates to the form of construction, not the material, and is stated in terms of performance in relation to British Standards methods of test:

- Loadbearing capacity (resistance to collapse)
- Integrity (resistance to fire penetration), and
- Insulation (resistance to transfer of excessive heat).

5.03 The criterion *loadbearing capacity* has replaced stability. In line with international practice, under BS 476 Part 22, non-loadbearing elements are assessed only for integrity and insulation. Loadbearing elements are tested in accordance with Part 21. BS 476 Part 8 is still often referred to, although superseded in 1987 by Parts 20, 21, 22 and 23. When tested specifications are used, the construction must replicate that tested in total. Consideration of products or systems having an Agrément Certificate issued by the British Board of Agrément or a product complying with a European Technical Approval (refer to the EEC Construction Products Directive) may be of use.

5.04 Regard should be given to the ease of acquiring the required fire protection, ease of construction, and durability. Although the last is not required under the Building Regulations, a material should be 'fit for the purpose'. There are several terms used in Approved Document B issued in support of the Building regulations specifically relevant to materials and their choice.

5.05 Restriction of the spread of flame across the surface of a material is an important factor of fire safety, as it affects fire growth and spread, and means of escape. The surface spread is referred to in terms of class classification in accordance with BS 476 Part 7 1971 and reference to Class 0. Flame spread can be reduced by the application of chemicals in the form of a surface application or pressure impregnation. In the latter case mechanical damage to the surface exposing a substratum will not be detrimental to the material. Materials chosen for low spread of flame properties may later be compromised by inappropriate painting.

5.06 Steel

Exposed steel can lose strength very quickly when exposed to fire; buckling and collapsing in as little as 10 to 15 minutes. The actual temperature at which it starts to lose strength depends on the type of steel, whether it is in tension or compression, and its restraint if any. Encasing the steel insulates it against temperature rise. Protection can be in the form of concrete, fire-retardant boards, fibrous sprayed or intumescent coatings; or suspended ceilings. Water cooling has been used to protect columns.

5.07 Aluminium

Some forms fail structurally at quite low temperatures but it has good properties for flame spread.

5.08 Concrete

This loses its crushing strength in fire, Table XXVII. The heat of the fire also affects the strength of steel reinforcement. Adequate concrete cover is essential, and may require the addition of mesh reinforcement to restrict spalling; this is caused by the reinforcement expanding with heating.

5.09 Clay masonry, brickwork

As a form of ceramic clay performs well at high temperatures albeit some expansion may take place. Any steel in clay can expand causing failure and should be protected.

5.10 Timber

This performs better than steel in a fire. It is a low conductor of heat; it progressively chars, protecting itself with a charcoal layer. The charring rate can be assessed, and the ability of the residual timber to sustain the required loads calculated – see BS 5268 Part 4 Section 4.1 Method of calculating fire resistance of timber members. Timber studwork with plasterboard can easily achieve 30 minutes' fire resistance, one hour with additional protection. Existing timber floors can be upgraded to improve their fire resistance by the addition of soffit protection and insulation – see BRE Digest 208, *Increasing the fire resistance of existing timber floors*.

5.11 Asbestos

This is no longer used in its basic form for health reasons.

5.12 Protective board, eg plasterboard, mineral fibre boards.

This is used to protect structural members, and form fire-resisting enclosures on suitable frames. Some forms of construction and systems can achieve in excess of 2 hours, fire resistance when constructed correctly. Care is necessary when cutting for services, etc to maintain the fire resistance. There are many proprietary systems utilising protective boards on timber and metal frames.

5.13 Glass

Plain glass (also depending on whether it is toughened or laminated) offers negligible fire resistance. Wired glass can

Table XXVII Behaviour of concrete in fire

Temperature (°C)	Permanent loss of compressive strength as demonstrated by crushing test
250	5%
600	64%
1200 and above	collapse

Table XXVIII Provisions for fire doors (from Approved Document B, Table B1)

Position of door	Minimum fire resistance of door in terms of integrity (minutes)[1]
1 In a compartment wall separating buildings	As for the wall in which door is fitted, but a minimum of 60
2 In a compartment wall: (a) if it separates a flat or maisonette from a space in common use,	FD 30S
(b) enclosing a protected shaft forming a stairway situated wholly or partly above the adjoining ground in a building used for Flats, Other Residential, Assembly & Recreation, or Office purposes,	FD 30S
(c) enclosing a protected shaft forming a stairway not described in (b) above.	Half the period of fire resistance of the wall in which it is fitted but 30 minimum and with suffix S
(d) not described in (a), (b) or (c) above.	As for the wall it is fitted in, but add S if the door is used for progressive horizontal evacuation under guidance to B1
3 In a compartment floor	As for the floor in which it is fitted
4 Forming part of the enclosures of: (a) a protected stairway (except where described in item 9),	FD 30S
(b) lift shaft, or	FD 30
(c) service shaft, which does not form a protected shaft in 2(c) above	FD 30
5 Forming part of the enclosures of: (a) a protected lobby approach (or protected corridor) to a stairway	FD 30S
(b) any other protected corridor	FD 20S
6 Affording access to an external escape route	FD 30
7 Sub-dividing: (a) corridors connecting alternative exits,	FD 20S
(b) dead-end portions of corridors from the remainder of the corridor	FD20S
8 Any door: (a) within a cavity barrier,	FD 30
(b) between a dwellinghouse and a garage,	FD 30
(c) forming part of the enclosure to a communal area in sheltered housing.	FD 30S
9 Any door: (a) forming part of the enclosures to a protected stairway in a single family dwellinghouse,	FD 20
(b) forming part of the enclosure to a protected entrance hall or protected landing in a flat or maisonette,	FD 20
(c) within any other fire resisting construction in a dwelling not described elsewhere in this table.	FD 20

Notes
[1] To BS 476: Part 22 (or BS 476: Part 8 subject to paragraph A5).
S Unless pressurisation techniques complying with BS 5588: Part 4 are used, these doors should also have a leakage rate not exceeding 3 m³/m/hour (head and jambs only) when tested at 25 Pa under BS 476: Section 31.1.

achieve a 1 hour standard of fire resistance in terms of integrity but with little insulation. Recent developments have resulted in plain glass giving 15 minutes, insulation. Insulating fire-resisting glazing can achieve in excess of 2 hours; the size of glazing panels may be restricted.

5.14 Plastics

Thermosetting (harden when heated) and thermoplastic (soften on heating). Plastics often fall from their supports, making an assessment of their action in fire difficult under test conditions. The material may not burn, but can drip flaming droplets and spread fire. See Approved Document B regarding the acceptable use of thermoplastic materials for ceilings, rooflights and lighting diffusers.

5.15 Doors and shutters: wooden, glass, metal or composite,

Table XXVIII. Some can achieve a fire resistance in excess of 4 hours. They are tested with regard to their integrity and insulation; most do not require insulation. Shutters are generally held open and close on the actuation of a fusible link, or automatically following detection of heat or smoke. Doors are designated according to their performance in minutes in terms of their integrity. Doors forming part of a protected enclosure (stair, lobby or corridor) for means of escape should have not less than a 30-minute standard of fire resistance. Additionally these doors should be able to resist the passage of smoke at ambient temperatures; these are generally denoted by the suffix 'S', ie FD30S.

Most door sets require the addition of an intumescent strip to attain a 30-minute standard of fire resistance. The seal intumesces at high temperature swelling to seal any imperfections of fit or gaps and thereby protecting the edges of the door to maintain its integrity. The ambient temperature seal, which may be in the form of a brush, retards the passage of smoke around the door when the fire is at a lower temperature but possibly producing large quantities of smoke. Various codes require 'S' doors in different situations.   To be effective for means of escape doors must be self-closing. Where a door is in constant use it may be acceptable to use a hold-open device (usually electromagnetic) to avoid it being edged open or damaged.

5.16 Materials for fire stopping and cavity barriers

These must effectively close a concealed cavity, and stop spread of fire and smoke around a service or element, by sealing an imperfection of fit. The material must be capable of sustaining movement, including expansion, be adequately fixed, and, in the case of barriers, have fire resistance. Materials include intumescent mastics, fire-protective boards, cement mortar, gypsum plaster and glass fibre; there are numerous proprietary systems.

5.17 Intumescent coatings

These are formed of differing materials with varying characteristics and foam on exposure to heat to form a protective coating. They can be used to improve fire resistance and reduce surface spread of flame. If adopted the following points should be considered:

- The intumescent system must be compatible with the material to be protected.
- The system must suit site conditions by virtue of the necessary mode of application, and in accordance with that tested and achieving the required standard. This includes atmospheric conditions,
- Not all are suitable in areas of high humidity
- Protection against mechanical damage may be necessary
- The possible damage of the protection by secondary fixings, follow-on trades or water damage.

6 FIRE PROTECTION APPLIANCES AND INSTALLATIONS

6.01 Fire protection appliances and installations are increasingly forming a part of an overall fire protection system. Active extinguishing systems are often installed to compensate for inadequate structural protection, or to facilitate an innovative concept or design which would be hampered by protective construction or division by fire walls.

6.02 The following brief descriptions give an indication of some of the appliances and systems available, and their application. The adoption of any particular system requires careful consideration – the nature of the risk, effectiveness of protection, reliability, ease of maintenance. Specialist advice should be sought. Reference should be made to the relevant British Standards – see Section 9. Although the use of a foreign system or component is not prohibited, the prior agreement and approval of any enforcing authority, insurer or water undertaker should be obtained.

6.03 Hand fire appliances: extinguishers, fire buckets, fire blankets. First aid appliance for use by general public. The extinguishing medium of hand-held extinguishers varies to suit the risk; they are colour coded for quick reference.

6.04 Hose reels

First aid appliance for use by occupants and firefighters; connected to a pressurised water supply.

6.05 Automatic sprinklers provide an automatically released water spray above a fire to contain its growth and inhibit its spread. There are various types and systems for specific areas, applications and risk categories. It should be noted that some systems are meant for property protection only, and that special provisions relate to life safety. Certain situations are not considered suitable for protection by sprinklers because of the potential water damage (art galleries, museums, historical libraries), the risk of accidental discharge or the unsuitability of water as the extinguishing medium for certain processes and materials. There may also be a need to provide large volumes for on-site water storage.

6.06 Water drenchers: a curtain of water, usually to protect the outside of a building or the safety curtain of a theatre.

6.07 Water spray projector systems: for fires involving oils or similar flammable liquids.

6.08 Hydrant systems (sometimes known as mains). A rising main to deliver water for firefighting onto the floor of a building via landing valves. A wet rising main is a pipe permanently charged with water and is generally installed in buildings above 60 m in height; beyond the pumping capabilities of a fire service pumping appliance; it requires water storage. A dry riser is a pipe charged by a fire service pump at ground/access level; it can be at any height but is generally provided in a building over 18 m. Any horizontal section should not exceed 12 m in length unless the delivery of the required rate of water at each outlet can be proven hydraulically. Falling or dropping mains deliver water to low levels. Private hydrants are provided within the curtilage of a site where statutory hydrants are too distant or where the risk is such as to require large volumes of water immediately.

6.09 Foam installations

Of limited application; generally for the extinction of flammable liquid fires. May require space for on-site foam-making equipment. There are various forms; specialist advice will be needed. A foam inlet is a fixed pipe through which foam can be pumped to protect rooms containing oil fuel, oil fired boilers etc.

6.10 Gaseous and vaporising liquid installations

These can be:

Carbon dioxide to protect an enclosed area acting in the main by dilution of the atmosphere. Not suitable for all fires. Satisfactory for electrical, computer and telephone equipment, flammable liquids, some chemicals, libraries, archives, art stores, diesel engines and textiles.

Vaporising liquids (halogenated hydrocarbons). Because of the stated detrimental effects of halon on the atmosphere alternatives are being developed; the Building Research Establishment should be consulted for information on acceptable alternatives.

Dry powder installations are suitable for use on flammable liquid and metal fires. Clearance after use is a problem.

6.11 Automatic detectors (note that their effectiveness is dependent upon the correct selection and siting – see the various Building Research Establishment reports):

Smoke detectors detect the presence of smoke by optical (obscuration) or ionisation methods and raise an alarm. Ionisation detectors are sensitive in the early stages of a fire when smoke particles are small; most suitable in a controlled environment such as a computer suite. Optical detectors react to the visible products of combustion and are the most effective.

Heat detectors detect heat at a pre-selected temperature or on a rapid rise in temperature. Use where smoke may be present as part of process or function but regard should be had to normal temperature of area where sited.

Radiation and ultraviolet detectors respond to distinctive flame flicker. Suitable for large open areas and can detect certain chemical fires.

Laser beam detectors: rising hot air affects laser beam being projected onto receiver by obscuration or movement. Suitable for covering large open areas but note that the receiver may be subject to building movement; beware of false alarms from falling objects or birds.

6.12 Fire alarms manual and automatic (as defined in BS 5839 Part 1). The system must be carefully chosen to meet specific needs – property or life safety; special needs of those with impaired hearing or sight; public entertainment application (possibly muted alarms) or a specific evacuation procedure (two stage/phase evacuation).

6.13 A manual system (gongs, handbells, etc) is only to be used in exceptional cases for very small buildings or specific areas. An automatic system in which an alarm of fire can be initiated automatically by the breaking of a call point or by a detector is the more common form. The complexity of the evacuation may require a message relayed via a public address system, initial alarms and alert signals, or the provision of fire telephones. Modern systems can be highly technical, incorporating computers and other data-processing equipment; specialist advice should be obtained at an early stage in any design.

7 STATUTORY REQUIREMENTS

7.01 The statutory requirements to provide fire precautions almost without exception relate to life safety and the dimmution of fire, although in consequence a degree of property protection is achieved. Some counties and most major conurbations have local Acts or bylaws in relation to access for firefighting. Many large towns and cities have provisions relating to 'large' buildings. At the time of writing the legislation relating to fire is under major review, with a view to rationalisation and streamlining aimed at deregulation. This will involve the repeal of many Acts and Regulations where the Building Regulations have a similar requirement, and extension of existing fire safety legislation to encompass uses such as public entertainment currently dealt with under numerous statutes. A list of national legislation relating to fire is contained in Section 8.

7.02 The Building Regulation (England and Wales) are substantive; the Scottish Building Regulations are currently prescriptive (but are under review); the Building Regulations (Northern Ireland) are currently prescriptive.

7.03 The fire safety aspect of the Regulations in England and Wales (Part B) applies to all buildings other than certain prisons. While there is an Approved Document of technical standards to Part B there is no obligation to adopt its recommendations. Provided that the substantive requirement is fulfilled any solution acceptable to the enforcing authority (or Approved Inspector) may be used. If a recognised code is used it is only necessary for the purposes of fulfilling the statutory requirement to adopt the recommendations pertaining to the requirement. However, care should be exercised, as any one recommendation may be reliant on the adoption of another. Section 9 details current codes and guides.

7.04 The requirements for fire safety under the building Regulations of England and Wales are:

BI: Means of escape. The building shall be designed and constructed so that there are means of escape in case of fire from the building to a place of safety outside the building capable of being safely and effectively used at all material times.

B2: Internal fire spread (linings)

(1) To inhibit the spread of fire within the building the internal linings shall
    (a) resist the spread of flame over their surfaces; and
    (b) have, if ignited, a rate of heat release which is reasonable in the circumstances
(2) In this paragraph 'internal linings' means the materials lining any partition, wall, ceiling or other internal structure.

B3: Internal fire spread (structure)

(1) The building shall be designed and constructed so that, in the event of fire, its stability will be maintained for a reasonable period.
(2) A wall common to two or more buildings shall be designed and constructed so that it resists the spread of fire between those buildings. For the purposes of this subparagraph a house in a terrace and a semi-detached house are each to be treated as a separate building.
(3) To inhibit the spread of fire within the building, it shall be subdivided with fire-resisting construction to an extent appropriate to the size and intended use of the building.
(4) The building shall be designed and constructed so that the unseen spread of fire and smoke within concealed spaces in its structure and fabric is inhibited.

B4: External fire spread

(1) The external walls of the building shall resist the spread of fire over the walls and from one building to another, having regard to the height, use and position of the building.
(2) The roof of the building shall resist the spread of fire over the roof and from one building to another, having regard to the use and position of the building.

B5: Access and facilities for the fire service

(1) The building shall be designed and constructed so as to provide facilities to assist firefighter in the protection of life.
(2) Provision shall be made within the site of the building to enable fire appliances to gain access to the building.

7.05 B2, B3(1),(2) and (4), B4 and B5 apply to all buildings; certain prisons are exempt from the other requirements.

7.06 The Building Regulations relate to a building under construction, certain changes of use, and certain extensions and alterations. Once occupied the Fire Precautions Act may be applicable. To avoid any potential conflict, the Department of the Environment and the Home Office have issued an advice document to enforcing authorities on how the required consultation process should take place. The document, *Building Regulation and Fire Safety Procedural Guidance*, also provides a guide for an applicant through the approval procedure outlining the aims and varying responsibilities of the authorities concerned.

7.07 Section 13 of the Fire Precautions Act 1971 imposes a 'statutory bar' on a Fire Authority preventing them making the issue of a fire certificate conditional on works to the means of escape approved under the Building Regulations, provided that such matters were shown on deposited plans, and circumstances have not changed. If such matters did not have to be shown the statutory bar does not apply.

8 LEGISLATION

Building Act 1984
Building Regulations 1991 (England and Wales)
The Building Standards (Scotland) Regulations 1990
The Health and Safety at Work etc Act 1974
The Building (Inner London) Regulations 1985 and 1987
The Construction Products Regulations 1991
The Fire Precautions Act 1971
The Fire Precautions (Hotels and Boarding Houses Order 1972
The Fire Precautions (Factories, Offices, Shops and Railway Premises) Order 1989
Fire Safety and Safety of Places of Sport Act 1987
   (Commencement No. 1) Order 1987
   (Commencement No. 5) Order 1989
   (Commencement No. 7) Order 1993
Local Government and Housing Act 1989 Section 352
Education Act 1944 (as amended)
Licensing Act 1964
The Cinemas Act 1985
The Theatres Act 1968
The Sunday Theatres Act 1972
The Local Government Act 1985
Private Places of Entertainment (Licensing) Act 1967
The London Government Act 1963
The Greater London (General Powers) Act 1966 and 1978]
Petroleum (Consolidation) Act 1928

9 BIBLIOGRAPHY

9.01 Building Regulations
The Building Regulations 1991 Approved Document B – Fire Safety (with 1992 amendments).
Building Regulations and Fire Safety. Procedural Guidance 1992.

9.02 Fire precautions: guides and codes
Fire Precautions Act 1971, Guide to fire precautions in premises used as hotels and boarding houses which require a fire certificate (Home Office/Scottish Office, 1991, ISBN 0 11 341005 0)
Fire Precautions Act 1971, Fire Safety Management in Hotels and Boarding Houses (Home Office/Scottish Office/Fire Protection Association, 1991, ISBN 0 11 340980 X)
Houses in multiple occupation. Guidance to local authorities on standards of fitness under Section 352 of the Housing Act 1985

Department of the Environment Circular 12/92 1992 ISBN 0 11 752640 1
Guide to means of escape and related fire safety measures in certain existing houses in multiple occupation (Home Office/Department of the Environment/Welsh Office, ISBN 0 862526369 9)
Guide to fire precautions in existing places of entertainment and like premises (Home Office/Scottish Office and Health Department, 1990, ISBN 0 11 340907 9)
Model rules of management for places of public entertainment
Model technical regulations for places of public entertainment
Rules of management for occasional licences (London District Surveyors Association in conjunction with Association of London Chief Environmental Health Officers, 1989)
From the London District Surveyors Association:
   Fire Safety Guide No. 1, Fire Safety in Section 20 Buildings
   Fire Safety Guide No. 2, Fire Safety in Atrium Buildings
   Fire Safety Guide No. 3, Phased evacuation from office buildings
Guide to safety at sports grounds (Home Office/Scottish Office, 1990, ISBN 0 11 341001 8)
Code of practice for fire precautions in factories, offices, shops and railway premises not required to have a fire certificate (Home Office/Scottish Home and Health Department, 1989, ISBN 0 11 340904 4)
Fire Precautions Act 1971, Guide to fire precautions in existing places of work that require a fire certificate (Home Office/Scottish Home and Health Department, 1989, ISBN 0 11 340906 0)
Fire and the design of schools: Building Bulletin 7 (Department of Education and Science, 1975)
Draft Guide to fire precautions in existing residential care premises (Home Office/Scottish Home and Health Department, 1983, ISBN 0 86 252084 3)
Draft guide to fire precautions in hospitals (Home Office/Scottish Home and Health Department, 1982)

9.03 British Standards
BS 476 Fire tests on building materials and structures
   Part 3: External fire exposure roof test
   Part 4: Non-combustibility test for materials
   Part 6: Method of test for fire propagation for products
   Part 7: Method for classification of the surface spread of flame of products
   Part 10: Guide to the principles and application of fire testing
   Part 11: Method for assessing the heat emission from building materials
   Part 13: Method of measuring the ignitabilty of products subjected to thermal irradiance
   Part 20: Method for determination of the fire resistance of elements of construction (general principles)
   Part 21: Methods for determination of the fire resistance of loadbearing elements of construction
   Part 22: Methods for determination of the fire resistance of non-loadbearing elements of construction
   Part 24: Methods for determination of the fire resistance of ventilation ducts
   Section 31.1: Methods for measuring smoke penetration through doorset and shutter assemblies. Method of measurement under ambient temperature conditions
BS 1635: Recommendations for graphic symbols and abbreviations for fire protection drawings
BS 2782: Methods for testing plastics, Parts 1 Thermal properties (various methods)
BS 4422: Glossary of terms associated with fire, Parts 1 to 6
BS 5266: Part 1: Emergency lighting Code of practice for the emergency lighting of premises other than cinemas and certain other specified premises used for entertainment.
BS 5268: Structural use of timber, Part 4 Fire resistance of timber structures

BS 5306: Fire extinguishing installations and equipment on premises

Part 0: Guide for the selection of installed systems and other fire equipment

Parts 1 to 7 deal with various installations and systems

BS 5378: Part 1: Safety signs and colours, specification for colour and design

BS 5395: Stairs, ladders and walkways

Part 1: Code of practice for the design of straight stairs

Part 2: Code of practice for the design of helical and spiral stairs

Part 3: Code of practice for the design of industrial type stairs, permanent ladders and walkways

BS 5499: Fire safety signs, notices and graphic symbols

Part 1: Specification for fire safety signs

Part 2: Specification for self-luminous fire safety signs

Part 3: Specification for internally-illuminated fire safety signs

BS 5502: Part 23: Buildings and structures for agriculture. Code of practice for fire precautions

BS 5725: Emergency exit devices

BS 5588: Fire precautions in the design and construction and use of buildings

Part 1: Code of practice for residential buildings

Part 2: Code of practice for shops (being revised and incorporated into Part 11)

Part 3: Code of practice for office buildings (being revised and incorporated into Part 11)

Part 4: Code of practice for smoke control in protected escape routes using pressurization (under revision).

Part 5: Code of practice for firefighting lifts and stairs

Part 7: Code of practice for atrium buildings (in preparation)

Part 8: Code of practice for means of escape for disabled people

Part 9: Code of practice for ventilation and air conditioning ductwork

Part 10: Code of practice for shopping complexes

Part 11: Code of practice for shops, offices, factories, warehouses and similar workplaces (in preparation)

BS 5839: Fire detection and alarm systems for buildings

BS 5852: Fire tests for furniture

BS 8202: Coatings for fire protection of building elements

BS 8313: Code of practice for accommodation of building services in ducts

PD 6512: Use of elements of structural fire protection with particular reference to the recommendations given in BS 5588, Fire precautions in the design and construction and use of buildings

Part 3: Guide to the fire performance of glass

9.04 There are a number of ISO (International Organisation for Standardisation) standards being developed which do not currently agree with British Standards but an increasing number being revised and developed that do and can be found in the same document. ISO documents have wider recognition abroad and use in many EC countries.

9.05 Books

Bird and Docking, *Fire in Buildings*, Adam & Charles Black, 1949 (out of print and rare)

E W Marchant (ed.), *Fire and Buildings*, MTP, 1972

Stollard and Abrahams, *Fire From First Principles*, E & F N Spon, 1991

S Barlay, *Fire, An International Report*, Hamish Hamilton, 1972

43 Security

David Adler

The editor acknowledges assistance from the Metropolitan Police Crime Prevention Design Department in updating this chapter

CI/SfB (68)
UDC: 343.7
Uniclass U547

1.01 Crimes
The main types of crime are:

1 Pilferage by staff or other insiders
2 Pilferage by public (shoplifting)
3 Vandalism without gain to the perpetrator
4 Casual break-ins
5 Planned break-ins
6 Attacks on persons for immediate gain (muggings, etc)
7 Various types of kidnapping, hijacking, etc, mainly for ransom
8 Bomb attacks, etc, for political objectives.
9 Fraud
10 Assaults for other than immediate gain (racism, 'fun', vengeance, etc)
11 Arson
12 Motor vehicle crime
13 Anti-social behaviour

Table I indicates which particular building types are subject to these crimes and suggests suitable precautionary measures. Most combative measures are designed either to slow up criminals until they feel vulnerable to discovery or else makes it difficult for them to remain unobserved.

1.02 Fences
Where commercial or industrial site perimeter protection is indicated a fence is better than a wall as one can see through it. It should be not less than 2.5 m high and topped with two strands of barbed wire. Fences higher than 2 m will require planning approval, and a form of protection such as barbed wire may possibly be the subject of a public liability claim. If a wall has to be used, it should have barred openings in it.

In the domestic situation, openings in walls may be inappropriate. Walls and wooden fences can successfully be protected with trellis topping.

1.03 Windows
Window panes less than $0.05\,m^2$ in area cannot be climbed through. Larger panes should be as large as possible. Laminate glass may be used, particularly near door locks.

For more security windows should be barred or fitted with grilles. Vertical bars are more effective than horizontal. Ideally, the bars should be of square cross-section minimum 20 mm at a maximum spacing of 125 mm and built in 75 mm. Transverse tie-bars should be provided at 600 mm centres.

1.04 Front doors
The 'last door out' (which cannot be barred or bolted from inside) should be as stout as possible, in any case more than 44 mm thick. It should be solid (not of hollow construction) and the hinge should be internal. When opening in, the stop should be formed by rebating the solid and not planted; otherwise the tongue of the lock is readily accessible. The lock should be a mortice lock to BS 3621: 1963 or equivalent, although some

prefer rim locks as mortice locks can weaken a door. If more than one lock is fitted they should be well spaced apart (approximately one third the door height).

Fire regulations require door locks to be openable from inside without a key: this conflicts with security as it facilitates an intruder's escape. In cases when there are more than a few people inside the building, or where the occupiers are unfamiliar with it, the fire escape requirements are paramount. This does not generally apply to most small domestic premises, where it is usually possible to secrete a key in proximity to the door. Locks that are key lockable from outside but have no keyhole inside and are not unlockable in any other way should not be used as legitimate occupiers may be inadvertently locked in.

Security experts also recommend non-key-operated bolts and chains in addition to locks. The disadvantage of these is that a successful intruder will use them to avoid being interrupted. However, such an interruption may lead to violence; the balance of opinion favours their provision and use.

A letter plate in the door should be sized and positioned so that it cannot be used to gain entrance: the minimum distance between it and the lock should be more than 400 mm. There have been disquieting examples of arson using letter boxes. Consideration may be given to to the provision of a letter box separate from the house on the Continental pattern.

Unless there is another method of identifying callers, a lensed spyhole should be provided. Glass in doors or adjacent to them should be laminated.

1.05 Other doors
All external doors should be of similar construction to front doors. Doors that are outward opening should be fitted with hinge-side bolts to prevent ingress by hinge removal. Patio doors are particularly vulnerable, and a supplementary steel roller-shutter may be necessary. Other than this, ensure minimum three-point locking, an anti-lift device and laminated glass in the outside layer of sealed units. French windows may also need supplementary shutters, but espagnolette locking bolts are a minimum requirement, on each leaf if double. Doors from integral garages should be as secure as external doors. Other internal doors are best left unlocked to avoid unnecessary damage.

1.06 Defensible space
The layout of any site, industrial, commercial, residential or otherwise should be considered from a security point of view. If possible, ensure that all normal and possible entry and exit points to buildings are under casual observation from neighbours or passers-by. In flats, restrict access to the rear of the building, and provide all footpaths with good lighting. Additional external lighting incorporating passive infrared detectors can be most useful.

Appropriate planting can reinforce barriers, but make sure that vegetation does not affect visibility, or trees provide easy ways over barriers.

Table I Relationship between crime and building type

Type of building	Principal risks	Vulnerable points	Design solutions
Single person/family dwellings	4, 5, 11	Ground-floor doors and windows	Doors and windows fitted with security locks that cannot be opened by merely breaking the glass
			Overlooking of all doors and windows from neighbouring properties, with adequate lighting from street lights etc
		Upper windows near to low-level roofs, drainpipes, etc	Anti-climb paint or barbed wire on drainpipes
			Locks and visibility as above
Flats	3, 4, 5, 6, 11, 13	Door to flat, particularly where this opens off internal lobby, as no window is allowed by fire regulations. This means that criminals can often proceed without the possibility of being seen from a neighbouring flat	Solid door with bolts at hinge side in addition to security locks, bolts and spyhole
			Good lighting, proof against interference
			Minimum length of corridors, few corners
Multi occupancy dwellings	3, 4, 5, 6, 11, 13	Generally as flats	Generally as flats
Hostels	1, 4, 11	Communal areas	No architectural measures other than ensuring that fire exits cannot be used for unauthorised ingress
		Rooms	
Hotels	1, 4, 5, 13	Kitchens, linen stores, rooms	Ensure that all exits are under constant casual observation at all times. This makes it difficult for staff or intruders to remove their booty
			A substantial safe should be provided near the reception for guests' valuables. Safe less than 600 kg weight must be secured against bodily removal
			Master key system for rooms under good control
Shops	1, 2, 4, 5, 8, 9, 10, 11, 13	Ground-floor doors and windows	Security locks and easy observation
		Back-up stores and rear corridors	Should be designed to be under constant casual observation. If not architecturally possible closed-circuit television can be used, although this may affect trade by alienating customers
		Unfrequented areas of sales floor, fitting rooms in garment shops	
Offices	1, 4, 5, 8	Ground-floor doors and windows, particularly rear fire escapes	Panic-type locks on rear escape doors. All areas under constant casual observation
			Supply all staff with lockable furniture for personal valuables
			Consider a secure store for expensive items
			Computers to be fitted with anti-theft devices
Factories and storage buildings	1, 4, 5, 8, 9, 11, 13	Ground-floor doors and windows, lorry-loading banks	Doors barred with heavy-duty locks-in many cases machinery for cutting through such devices will be to hand
			Constant casual observation, including security patrolling at night
			Good fencing around the site, with permanent lighting of the area between fence and building
Sports buildings	1, 3, 5, 6, 8, 9, 10, 11, 13	Changing rooms, cash desk	Stout lockers, good observation, substantial safe for takings, if must be left on premises
Restaurants	1, 8, 9, 13	Kitchens, stores, cash desk	Constant casual observation
Banks	5, 7, 8, 9	Almost everything	Sophisticated security measures that are not generally known outside the particular organisation
Car parks	1, 2, 3, 4, 6, 8, 9, 10, 12, 13		Observation at all times, including the use of lighting and closed-circuit television. In this case public acceptance is universal

1.07 References

BS 8220: Guide for security of buildings against crime
BS 8220: Part 1: Dwellings
BS 8220: Part 2: Offices and shops
BS 8220: Part 3: Warehouses and distribution units

Oscar Newman, *Defensible space*, Architectural Press, 1972
Secured by design, new homes security scheme (Association of Chief Police Officers Project and Design Group, 1994)
Secured by design, commercial (Association of Chief Police Officers Project and Design Group)

44 Access for maintenance

CI/Sfb: (75)
UDC: 624.059
Uniclass: MX22

KEY POINTS:
- *Health and safety considerations are of the highest priority*
- *Design that does not take maintenance into account is unacceptable*

Contents
1 Method and frequency of cleaning
2 Access
3 Internal access
4 External access
5 Roof suspension systems
6 Bibliography

1 METHOD AND FREQUENCY OF CLEANING

1.01 Method
The methods by which windows and facades are to be regularly cleaned and maintained must be considered at an early stage of design, and the necessary equipment incorporated into the structure. Recent incidents and subsequent legislative measures reinforce this, and failure to ensure proper provision may result in very expensive remedial work.

Regular washing with cold or warm water (sometimes with a mild detergent) is normally adequate, applied either by swab with chamois leather to dry and scrim to polish; or by squeegee, which is much quicker over large areas and when used from cradles. Between $400\,m^2$ and $500\,m^2$ in eight hours is average, using a squeegee in ideal conditions.

1.02 Frequency
Table I shows some recommendations for frequency of washing according to locality, and Table II gives frequency of washing particular building types in non-industrial areas. For industrial areas and cities the interval between cleans should be halved.

2 ACCESS

2.01 Internal or external access?
Type of access is decided by:

- Method and frequency of cleaning
- Capital and running costs
- Whether cleaned by tenants or professional window cleaners
- Safety requirements
- Appearance of equipment when not in use.

Table I Recommended frequency of cleaning per year

Location	Ground floor facing street	Other windows	Rooflights
London postal area and smoky industrial areas of large cities	16	8	2
Semi-industrial towns	12	6	2
Non-industrial towns	8	4	1

Table II Recommendations for frequency of washing of particular building types

Type of building	Side windows	Rooflights
Offices	Every 3 months*	Every 12 months
Public offices, banks, etc	2 weeks	3 months
Shops	Outside every week Inside every 2 weeks	6 months
Shops (in main streets)	Outside daily Inside every week	3 months
Hospitals	3 months	6 months
Schools	3–4 months	12 months
Hotels (first class)	2 weeks	3 months
Factories (precision)	4 weeks	3 months
Factories (heavy work)	2 months	6 months
Domestic (by contract)	4–6 weeks	–

* Ground-floor windows facing streets should be cleaned at twice this frequency

A general guide to selecting external types of access is shown in **44.1**. When selecting internal types of access, take into account possible problems:

- Type of window (especially high-rise housing)
- Method of cleaning adjacent exterior cladding
- Freak draughts and disruption to air-conditioning when opening windows
- Disruption to furniture and activities; possible damage to property
- Relative cost of providing opening windows (for cleaning from inside) against cost of cradle (for cleaning from outside)
- Safety (beware cleaners, especially tenants, having to lean out to clean adjacent fixed lights).

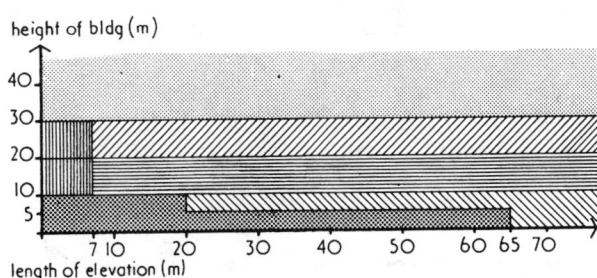

▨	Traditional methods (specialist equipment not usually required)
◩	Travelling ladder or manual cradle systems
▥	Removable runway system
▤	Manual cradle system
▨	Manual cradle system, semi-powered cradle system or powered cradle system
▢	Powered cradle system with cradle restraint

44.1 *Chart for selecting system for external access*

Cleaning the internal glass face is usually no problem unless inaccessible.

Often two separate contractors are given the work of cleaning the inside and outside faces. Cleaning the outside from the outside will usually give better results, and can effect long-term savings over the extra cost of providing opening windows to allow cleaning from inside.

3 INTERNAL ACCESS

3.01 Ergonomics
Human dimensions related to window cleaning are shown in **44.2** to **44.5** and **Table III**.

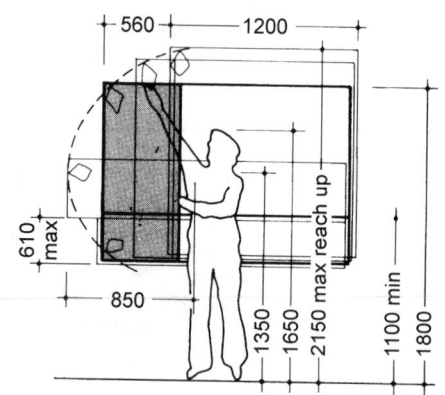

44.2 *Exterior reach to adjacent fixed light through opening light. Shaded area is average acceptable size for ease of cleaning*

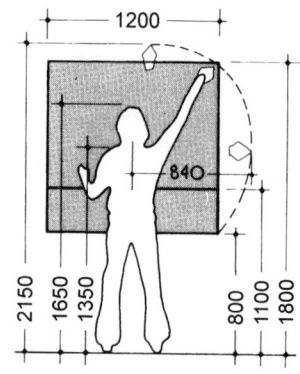

44.3 *Interior reach to fixed, reversible or pivot window*

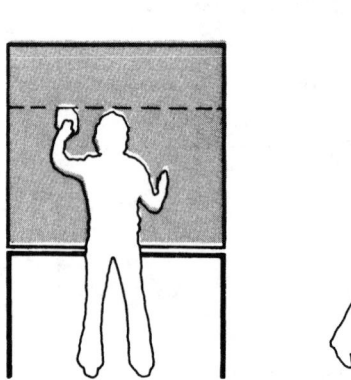 

44.4 *Reach becomes less over bench or worktop*

3.02 Types of window
To avoid accidents with small children, all opening windows, except possibly those less than 1.5 m above the ground outside, should now be fitted with devices to prevent them normally opening to leave a gap more than about 100 mm. This device has to be removeable for cleaning purposes, but the method should obviously be child proof. When any degree of leaning-out to clean windows is involved, a safety harness linked to an internal anchorage must be used. Two such examples are shown in **44.6**.

- Side-hung casements should have offset pivot hinges to give minimum 100 mm gap, set well forward of the frame which should not be fixed more than 100 mm in from the external face. Consider using Continental-type inward-opening casements which solve most window-cleaning problems.
- Double-opening windows have both side hinges and hopper hinges allowing for easy cleaning and safety.
- Hopper windows opening inwards must be low and narrow for easy cleaning. If high and large, they can be dangerous.
- Vertical and horizontal sliding sash windows should not be used for internal cleaning.
- Horizontal and vertical pivot windows are satisfactory for internal cleaning if they can be fully reversed and securely fixed with locking bolts both when reversed for cleaning and open normally for ventilation.

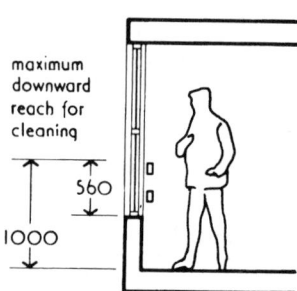

44.5 *Dimensions of fixed light heights and guard rails for domestic buildings*

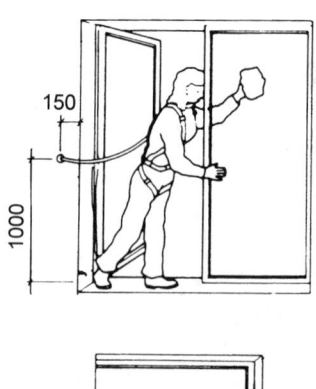

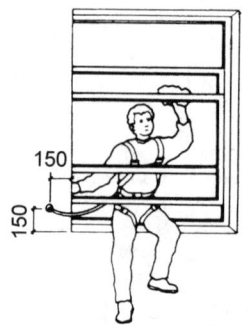

44.6 *Two situations where cleaning access is from the inside, but when a properly anchored safety harness should be used*

Table III Access to external faces from the inside Note: shaded area indicates glass face

Good	Satisfactory	Bad

Casement

(1) Inward opening

(2) Outward opening with extending hinges

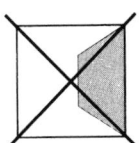

(3) Outward opening

Double opening hopper

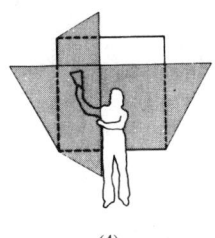

(4)

(5) Inward opening

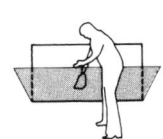

(6)

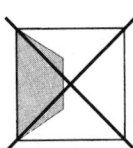

(7) Outward opening

Vertical slide

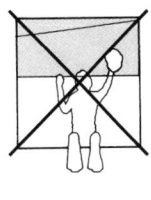

(8)

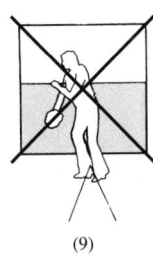

(9)

Horizontal slide

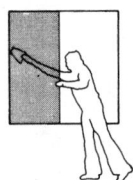

(10) Top corner reach possible (see **44.2**)

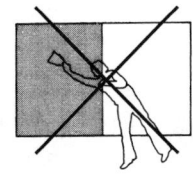

(11) Corner reach not possible

Horizontal pivot

(12) Completely reversible

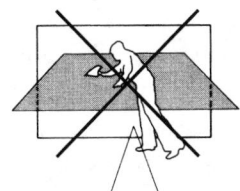

(13) Not completely reversible and too high (see 3)

Vertical pivot

(14) Completely reversible

(15) Not reversible but at correct height (see **44.3**)

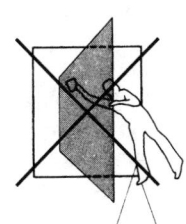

(16) Not reversible and too high (see **44.3**)

Table III Access to external faces from the inside Note: shaded area indicates glass face

Good	Satisfactory	Bad
Top hung		

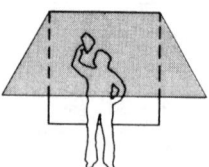

(17) Top-hung opening in

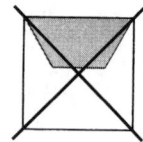

(18) Top-hung opening out is impossible to clean

Fixed adjacent

(19) Corner reach possible

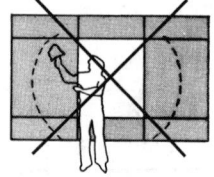

(20) Corner reach impossible

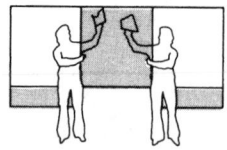

(21) Centre reach possible

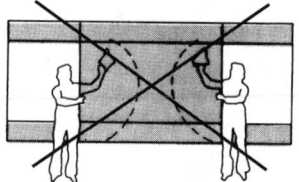

(22) Centre reach impossible

Access to internal faces

Double glazing

 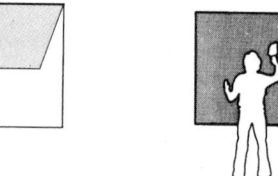

(23) Fully reversible pivot

(24) Inward opening casement

(25) Top-hung opening. Too large and distorts when held by corner

---

- Sliding projecting windows can be dangerous for internal access cleaning unless maximum depth is 750 mm, but even then cleaning can be hazardous.

4 EXTERNAL ACCESS

4.01 Manual cleaning: access from ground

Type of access can be initially assessed from **44.1**. Manual cleaning methods with access from the ground include:

- On foot: maximum window height 1.8 m providing there are no awkward projections.
- Single part ladder: up to 3 m, but awkward with long horizontal windows (use travelling ladders – see para **4.02**. Long-handled squeegee can sometimes be used instead.
- Ladders over 3 m must be secured. Maximum 9 m, safe inclination 83°. Securing can be with mechanical anchorage, as to the ground, **44.7**. The top of the ladder can be restrained using proprietary 'D' wheels, **44.8a**. These rubber wheels with hollows between the rib and the hub are stiff enough to stay round, **44.8b**, when the ladder top to which they are fixed is

moved up or down the wall. When the ladder is in use, the wheel is pressed against the wall and becomes the D-shape that holds it securely, **44.8c**.

- Mechanical ladder on mobile chassis. Can be either free-standing or leant against a wall. More rigid than simple ladders but still only gives access to limited areas.
- Single stepladder in the form of a mobile trestle. Maximum height is 5.4 m.
- Lightweight portable scaffolding. Height is maximum three times least base dimension unless weighted, tied back to building, or outriggers fitted. Special scaffolds can be made to suit building design. Provides safe, rigid platform leaving both hands free.
- Zip-up staging in light, hinged aluminium alloy sections each 2.14 m high × 1.6 m long × 1.35 m wide. Height is maximum four times least base dimension, but outriggers and restraint can increase this ratio. Again, variations are possible to suit building design.
- Mobile folding and telescopic platforms, only for use as secondary access for difficult areas. Generally of fixed height between 12 m and 15 m.

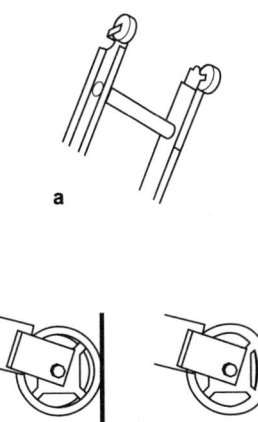

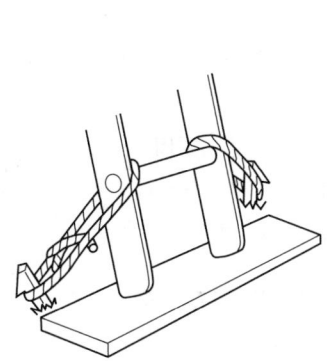

44.7 *Ladder with feet supported and fixed in natural ground*

44.8 *Ladder with top restraint* (Ladderfix Ltd). **a** *'D' wheels fitted to ladder.* **b** *D wheel able to roll.* **c** *D wheel under load*

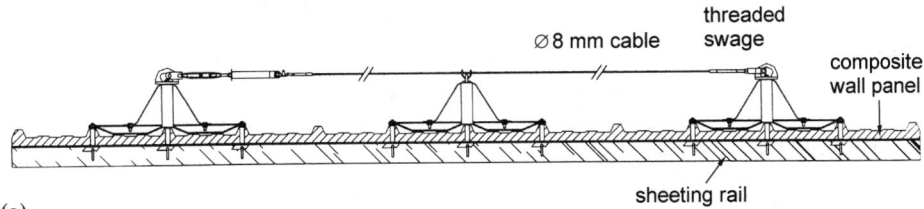

(a)

(b)

44.9 *A continuous wire cable with harness-clip that rides through the anchor fixings* (Latchways plc). **a** *Fixing to a wall.* **b** *In use*

4.02 Manual cleaning using permanent access

There are five main possibilities:

- Balconies: but only if all windows can be reached, otherwise some other forms of access will be needed.
- Sills and ledges: if continuous, more useful to a professional window cleaner than a balcony. Construction Regulations 1966

44.10 *Fixed ladder leading to interior catwalk*

suggest 630 mm as minimum width, but some cleaners will accept 300 to 500 mm width. A ledge from which a fall of 2 m or more is possible must be provided with either a guard rail or a continuous safety harness anchorage, as in **44.9**. Ledges requiring the operative to clip, unclip or reclip his safety harness while on the ledge are not acceptable.

- Catwalks: mainly for lateral movement. Must be level and non-slip. Maximum gradient of 20° with regularly spaced stepping laths for sloping roofs; above 20° needs steps. Internal catwalks need 2 to 2.15 m headroom. Minimum footing width 630 mm (870 mm if materials put on gangway): guard rails between 900 mm and 1150 mm above platform when more than 2 m above ground; toe boards 150 mm deep with maximum distance of 750 mm between the board and lowest guard rail.

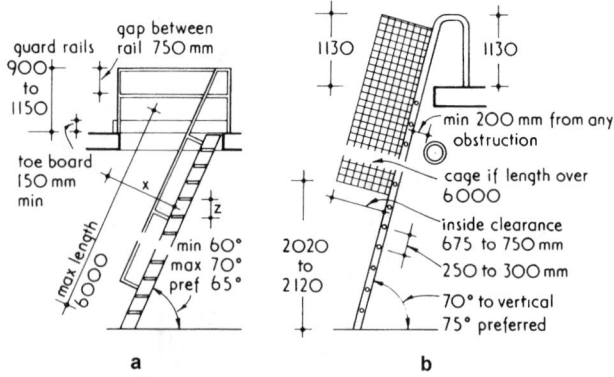

44.11 *Recommended dimensions for fixed ladders and landings, based on Construction Regulations 1966 (with additional information from Industrial Data Sheet 53) (Australian Department of Labour).* **a** *up to 70°*
x = head clearance, min 1050 mm for 60° slope, 950 mm for 70° slope
z = steps, minimum width 100 mm, 200 to 250 mm rise flight width 450 to 750 mm. **b** *over 70° with cage*

- Fixed ladders: use steps up to 70°, rungs over 70° pitch, **44.10** and **44.11**. Vertical ladders not recommended, but where necessarily used must be caged. Use landings every 6 m height positioned to break fall, or use metal mesh safety cage over the ladder.
- Travelling ladders: with top and bottom fixings on continuous rail or channel to allow ladder to slide along and round the facade. Useful for long bands of glazing up to 4.5 m high; can be fixed at almost any angle.

5 ROOF SUSPENSION SYSTEMS

5.01 Temporary systems
These are usually hired and erected and dismantled each time. There are two systems:

- Counterweighted system as shown in **44.12**. Rather unwieldy and limited; roof structure and parapet must be capable of taking load.
- Fixed davits as shown in **44.13**. Same problems as the counterweight system but safer, although horizontal traverse is more difficult.

There are also a few proprietary portable gantry systems.

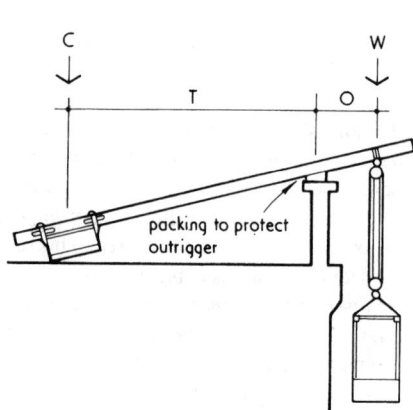

44.12 *Cradle using counterweight system*
To balance $C \times T = W \times O$
for safety $C \times T$ *should not be less than three times* $W \times O$

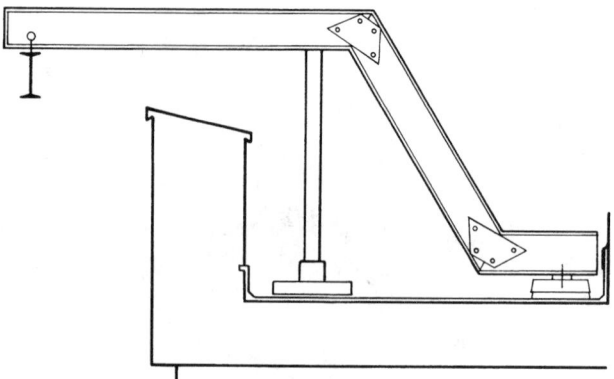

44.13 *Fixed davits on a roof with parapet*

5.02 Permanent systems: trolley units
A permanent system is usually desirable and for frequent cleaning soon covers the extra initial cost; but unless carefully designed and integrated with the structure and facade it can look very unsightly. In all cases roof structure and finishes must be able to carry the imposed loads. There are two elements to consider: the roof trolley system and the suspended chair or cradle (see para **5.03**) There are two trolley systems:

- Manual roof trolley consisting of a continuous rail, often RSJ, positioned about 450 mm in front of the wall face, to which the cradle is attached by ropes and castors. The most common is a pair of continuous rails, fixed to the roof about 750 mm apart, on which runs a cantilevered trolley, **44.14**.
- Powered roof trolley is the most efficient and safest and is essential for heights of over 45 m. It is also the most expensive, but can be relatively cheap for large buildings. It must be considered at the very earliest design stages. The general principle is the same as the manual trolley except that the unit is powered. Power supply needed is 440 V three-phase.

5.03 Suspended units
There are two basic types: chairs and cradles:

- Bosun's chair, **44.15**, extensively used for awkward areas and always used with manual gantries. A modern version is the facing bicycle, with pedals to work the winch.
- Manually operated cradle. A typical standard timber cradle is shown in **44.16**. Not recommended for heights over 30 m.

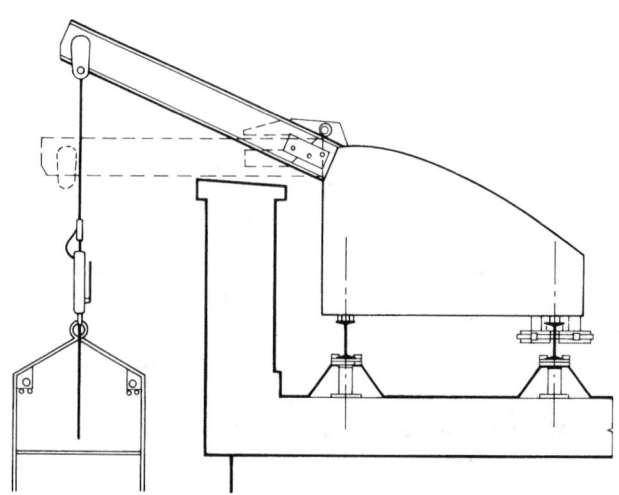

44.14 *Hand-operated roof trolley travelling on twin track. The boom can be lowered to the horizontal to deal with projections on the face of the building*

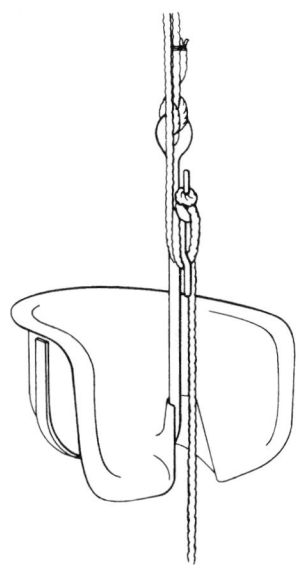

44.15 *Bosun's chair in performed plastic*

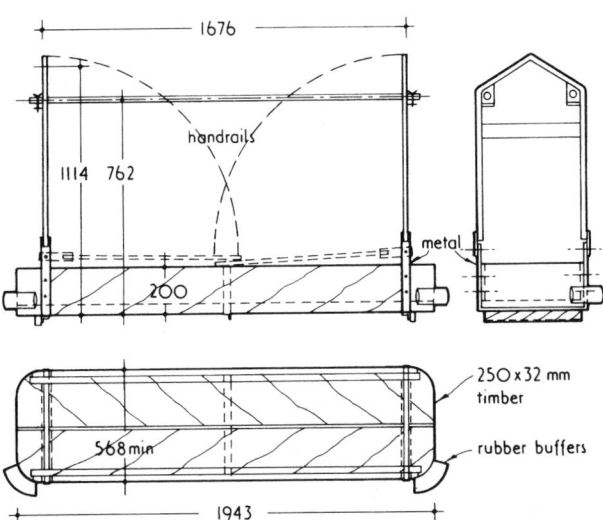

44.16 *Standard timber cradle.* **a** *Side elevation.* **b** *End elevation.* **c** *Plan*

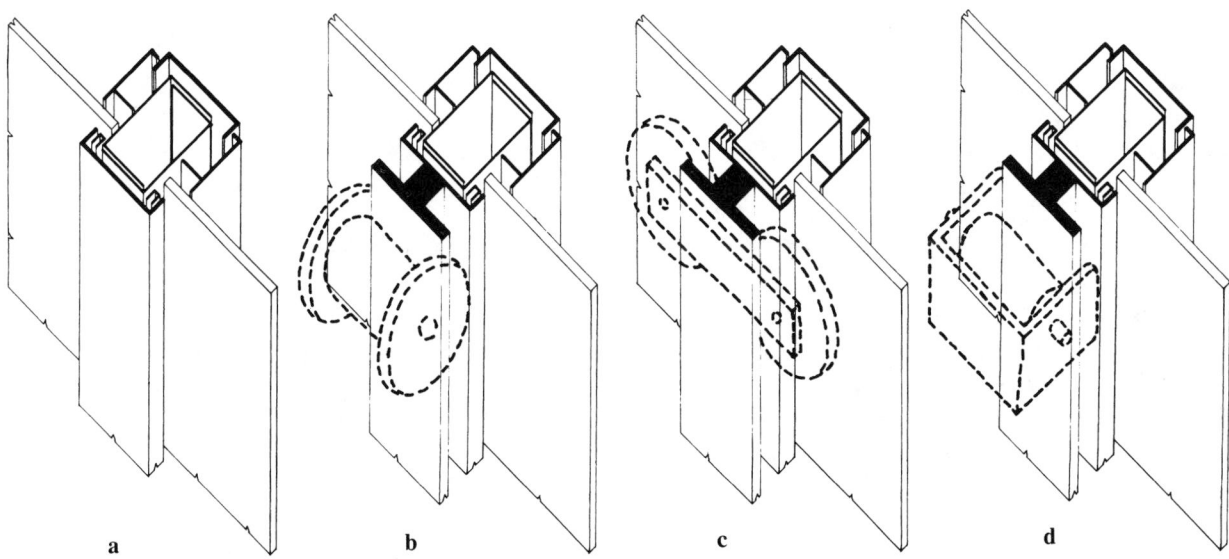

44.17 *Mullion guides.* **a** *Standard mullion.* **b** *Roller on guide to prevent lateral movement.* **c** *Casters on guide to prevent outward movement.* **d** *Standard roller*

● Power-operated cradle. Sizes range from 1.8 to 9 m width; materials can be steel, aluminium or GRP.

In all cases some form of manual or mechanical chair or cradle restraint, and of independent safety harness for the occupants, must be provided. The only method to provide continuous restraint is a mullion guide, **44.17**.

6 BIBLIOGRAPHY

Handbooks

AJ Handbook: Design and cleaning of windows and facades. Published in *The Architects' Journal* from 7 March 1973 to 2 May 1973 (AJ, 7.3.73; 4.4.73; 18.4.73; 2.5.73) (Now somewhat outdated)

General

The Construction (Health, Safety and Welfare) Regulations 1996
BS 5974: 1990, *Code of practice for temporarily installed suspended scaffolds and access equipment*
BS 6037: 1990, *Code of practice for permanently installed suspended access equipment*
BS 8213: Part 1: 1991, *Code of practice for safety in use and during cleaning of windows and doors*

Health and Safety Executive publications

HSG 150 *Health and safety in construction*
GS 42 *Tower scaffolds*
CIS No 5 *Temporarily suspended access cradles and platforms*
GS 31 *Safe use of ladders, step ladders and trestles*

Trade

The Worshipful Company of Environmental Cleaners
HCL Safety Ltd
Ladderfix Ltd
Total Access (UK) Ltd

45 Service distribution

The editor acknowledges help from Don Montague's chapter on Planning and from Ove Arup & Partners

CI/Sfb (28.8)
UDC: 696, 697
Uniclass: L782

KEY POINT:
● *The space required by services is often under-estimated in sketch designs*

Contents

1 INTRODUCTION

It is said that many modern buildings are in effect enclosures for the building services. Even in modest houses the space needed to provide those services now considered essential has become a significant quantity. The methods to be used in distributing services needs to be considered in the early design stage, as this may well control the final concept.

2 SERVICE ENTRIES/EXITS AND DISTRIBUTION

Table I lists the services that are to be provided with entries or exits into different types of buildings. Table II lists those that will be distributed around the building.

3 PLANT ROOMS AND DISTRIBUTION ZONES

3.01 Plant to service the building itself can be a major space-user. Some equipment can be accommodated within general areas; but some, for one reason or another, requires dedicated and segregated

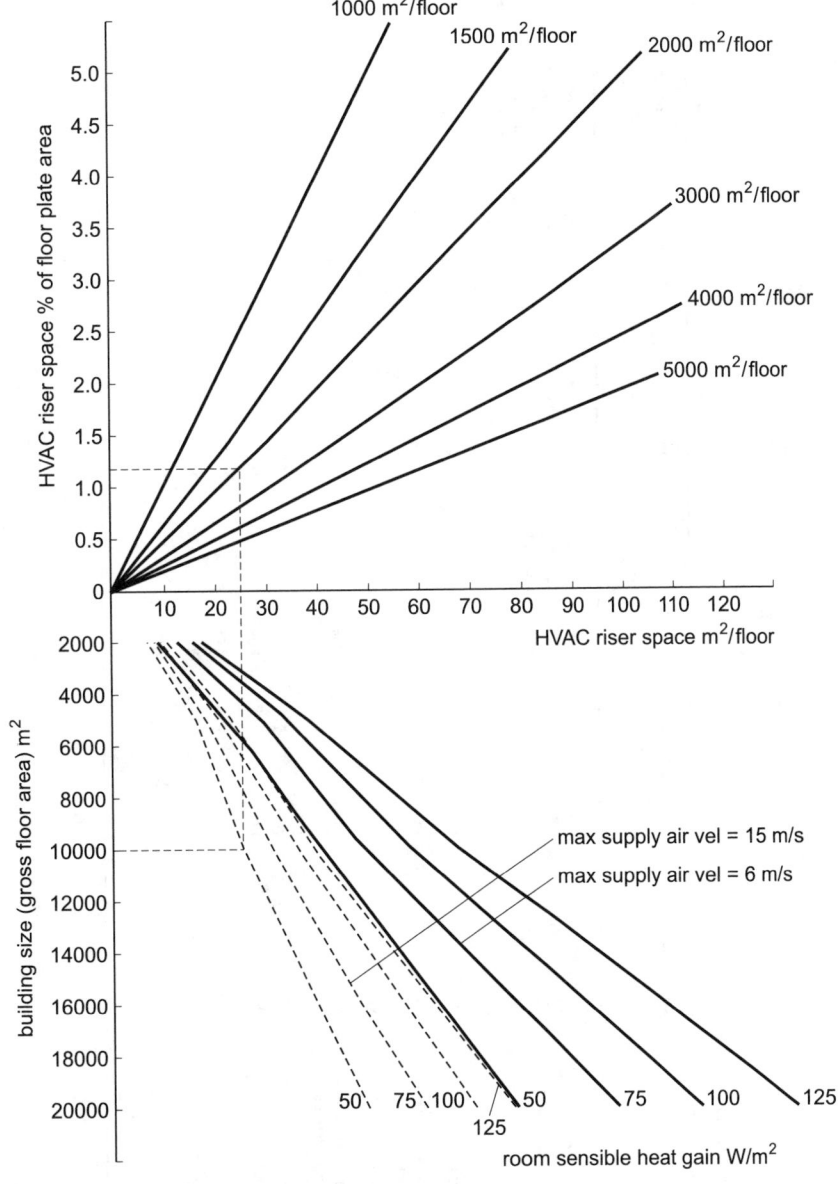

45.1 *HVAC riser space for VAV plus perimeter heating in two-storey buildings*

Table I Service entries and exits

Services	Industrial transport	Offices, shops, administration	Health	Catering	Recreation	Religious	Education, laboratories, art galleries, museums	Houses	Flats	Hostels, hotels
Electricity	High voltage Medium voltage Low voltage three-phase	Low voltage three-phase	Medium voltage Low voltage three-phase	Low voltage three-phase	Low voltage three-phase	Low voltage three-phase	Low voltage three-phase	Low voltage single-phase	Low voltage three-phase for lifts	Low voltage three-phase
Gas	Yes	Yes	Yes	Yes	Yes	Possibly	Yes	Yes	Yes	Yes
Heating oil	Possibly	Possibly	Possibly	Possibly	Possibly	Possibly	Possibly	Possibly	Possibly	Possibly
Hot water or steam for heating		Possibly	Possibly	Possibly					Possibly	Possibly
Fresh water	Yes	Yes	Yes	Yes	Yes	Yes	Yes	Yes	Yes	Yes
High pressure water for sprinklers etc	Yes	Probably	Possibly	Possibly	Possibly	No	Possibly	No	No	Possibly
Sewerage	Yes	Yes	Yes	Yes	Yes	Yes	Yes	Yes	Yes	Yes
Separate rainwater	Possibly	Possibly	Possibly	Possibly	Possibly	Possibly	Possibly	Possibly	Possibly	Possibly
Flue or flues	Yes	Yes	Yes	Yes		Only crematoria	No	Yes	Possibly	Possibly
Telephone	Many lines	Possibly many lines	Yes	Yes	Yes	Yes	Yes	Yes	Yes	Yes
Cable	Possibly	Unlikely	Possibly	Yes	Yes	Yes	Yes	Possibly	Yes	Yes
TV aerial feed									Yes	Yes

Table II Services to be distributed in buildings

Services	Industrial, transport	Offices, shops, administration	Health	Catering	Recreation	Religious	Education, laboratories, art galleries, museums	Houses	Flats	Hostels, hotels
Electricity	Medium voltage Low voltage three-phase Low voltage single-phase for power Low voltage single-phase for lighting	Low voltage three-phase Low voltage single-phase for power Low voltage single-phase for lighting Uninterruptible and protected power supply (UPS)	Low voltage three-phase Low voltage single-phase for power Low voltage single-phase for lighting Possibly UPS	Low voltage three-phase Low voltage single-phase for power Low voltage single-phase for lighting	Low voltage three-phase Low voltage single-phase for power Low voltage single-phase for lighting	Low voltage single-phase for power Low voltage single-phase for lighting	Low voltage three-phase Low voltage single-phase for power Ultra-low voltages (12 V DC, 6 V DC etc) UPS	Low voltage single-phase for power Low voltage single-phase for lighting	Low voltage three-phase Low voltage single-phase for power Low voltage single-phase for lighting	Low voltage three-phase Low voltage single-phase for power Low voltage single-phase for lighting Possibly UPS
Gas (for heating etc)	Yes	Probably	Probably	Yes	Probably	Possibly	Possibly	Yes	Probably (depending on construction)	Probably
Fresh water from mains	Yes	Yes	Yes	Yes	Yes	Yes	Yes	Yes	Yes	Yes
Water from tank	Yes	Yes	Yes	Yes	Possibly	Possibly	Yes	Yes, as long as regulations insist	Yes, as long as regulations insist	Yes
Hot water for washing etc	Yes, or may be locally heated	Yes, or may be locally heated	Yes	Yes, or may be locally heated	Yes, or may be locally heated	Not likely	Yes, or may be locally heated	Yes	Yes	Yes
Dry riser	Possibly	Possibly	Possibly	No	No	No	Possibly	No	Yes	Possibly
Sewerage	Yes	Yes	Yes	Yes	Yes	Yes	Yes	Yes	Yes	Yes
Rainwater drainage	Yes	Yes	Yes	Yes	Yes	Yes	Yes	Yes	Yes	Yes
Special drainage for contaminated water	Probably	No	Possibly	Possibly	No	No	Possibly	No	No	No
Hot water/steam for heating	Possibly	Possibly	Probably	Possibly	Probably	Possibly	Probably	Most probably	Most probably	Most probably
Fresh air/exhaust (ventilation)	Yes	Yes	Yes	Yes	Yes	Yes	Yes	Limited to bathrooms and kitchens	Limited to bathrooms and kitchens	Possibly
Conditioned air	Possibly	Probably	Probably	Probably	Possibly	No	Possibly	Unlikely	Unlikely	Possibly
Compressed air	Possibly	No	Possibly	No	No	No	Possibly	No	No	No
Gases such as oxygen, nitrous oxide etc	Possibly	No	Yes	No	No	No	Possibly	No	No	No
Telephone	Yes	Yes	Yes	Yes	Yes	Yes	Yes	Yes	Yes	Yes
Cable	Possibly	Possibly	Yes	Yes	Yes	Possibly	Yes	Possibly	Yes	Yes
TV aerial	No	No	Yes	Yes	Possibly	Possibly	Yes	Yes	Yes	Yes
Computer network	Yes	Yes	Yes	Possibly	Possibly	No	Yes	No	No	Possibly
Other communications	Public address Fire alarms Intruder alarms	Public address Fire alarms Intruder alarms	Fire alarms Possible intruder alarms	Fire alarms Intruder alarms	Public address Fire alarms Intruder alarms	Fire alarms	Public address Fire alarms Intruder alarms	Intruder alarms	Intruder alarms Entryphone systems	Public address Fire alarms Intruder alarms
Lamson tubes	Possibly	Possibly	Possibly	No	No	No	No	No	No	No

Table III Relationship of plant rooms and risers to building form

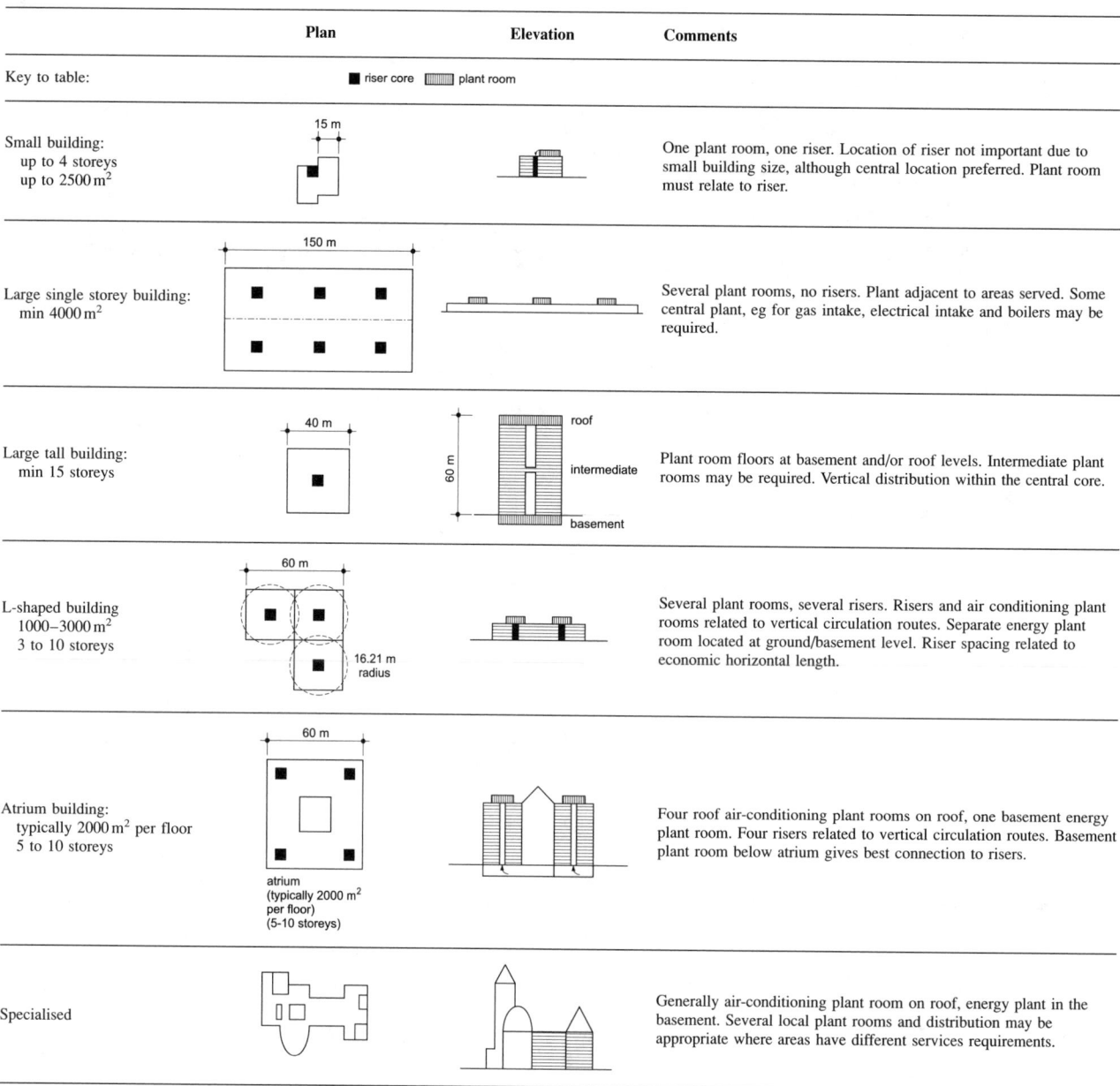

	Plan	Elevation	Comments
Key to table:	■ riser core ▦ plant room		
Small building: up to 4 storeys up to 2500 m²	15 m		One plant room, one riser. Location of riser not important due to small building size, although central location preferred. Plant room must relate to riser.
Large single storey building: min 4000 m²	150 m		Several plant rooms, no risers. Plant adjacent to areas served. Some central plant, eg for gas intake, electrical intake and boilers may be required.
Large tall building: min 15 storeys	40 m	roof intermediate basement 60 m	Plant room floors at basement and/or roof levels. Intermediate plant rooms may be required. Vertical distribution within the central core.
L-shaped building 1000–3000 m² 3 to 10 storeys	60 m / 16.21 m radius		Several plant rooms, several risers. Risers and air conditioning plant rooms related to vertical circulation routes. Separate energy plant room located at ground/basement level. Riser spacing related to economic horizontal length.
Atrium building: typically 2000 m² per floor 5 to 10 storeys	60 m / atrium (typically 2000 m² per floor) (5-10 storeys)		Four roof air-conditioning plant rooms on roof, one basement energy plant room. Four risers related to vertical circulation routes. Basement plant room below atrium gives best connection to risers.
Specialised			Generally air-conditioning plant room on roof, energy plant in the basement. Several local plant rooms and distribution may be appropriate where areas have different services requirements.

space. The main plant areas which may be needed in all kinds of buildings are:

- Intake rooms, for water, gas, electricity, communications
- Transformer chambers and switch rooms
- Tank rooms for water and oil
- Standby generator rooms
- Boiler and calorifier rooms
- Sewage pump rooms
- Lift motor rooms
- Air handling and conditioning plant rooms and
- Building management system control rooms

3.02 The relationships of plant rooms and risers to the forms of particular building types are summarized in Table III.

3.03 Heating, ventilation and air conditioning
Figures for estimating the amount of space to be allocated to HVAC plant are given in Table IV. The graphs in **45.1** to **45.5** indicate the space needed for HVAC risers.

3.04 Air ducts and plenums
Table V summarizes the factors to be taken in account **45.6** to **45.8** illustrate the importance of good early planning.

3.05 Boiler and calorifier plant
45.9 illustrates a boiler room and the dimensions are given in Table VI. **45.10** shows a calorifier installation with dimensions in Tables VII and VIII.

3.06 Air handling and conditioning plant
Table IX summarises the different possible arrangements for air handling units. **45.11** shows an air handling plant room. **45.12** is a full air air-conditioning plant with dimensions in Table X.

3.07 Fan coils
Fan coil units are approximately 250 mm deep. Their lengths depend on their ratings as follows:

1.0–1.2 kW sensible cooling, 820 mm
1.2–2.4 kW, 1135 mm
2.4–3.0 kW, 1335 mm
3.0–4.4 kW, 1925 mm

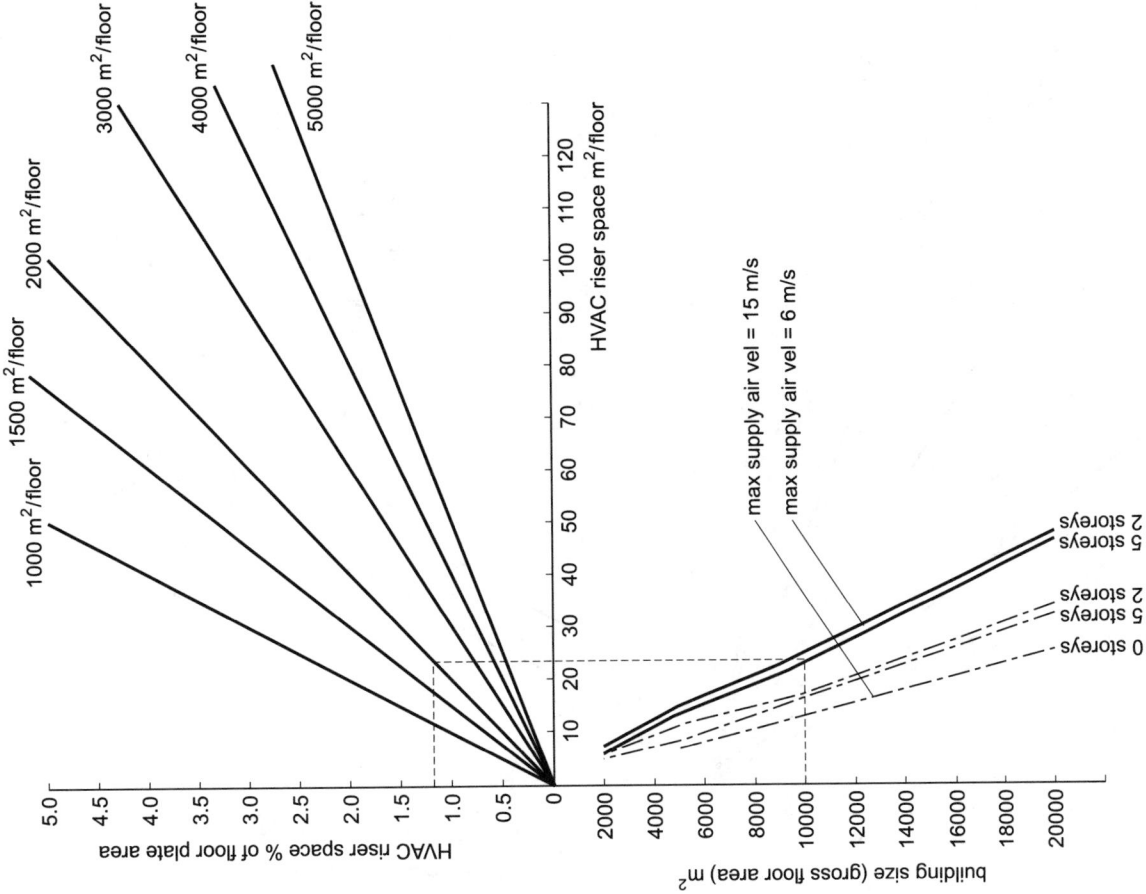

45.3 *HVAC riser space for four-pipe fan coil systems (primary air 3 ac/h)*

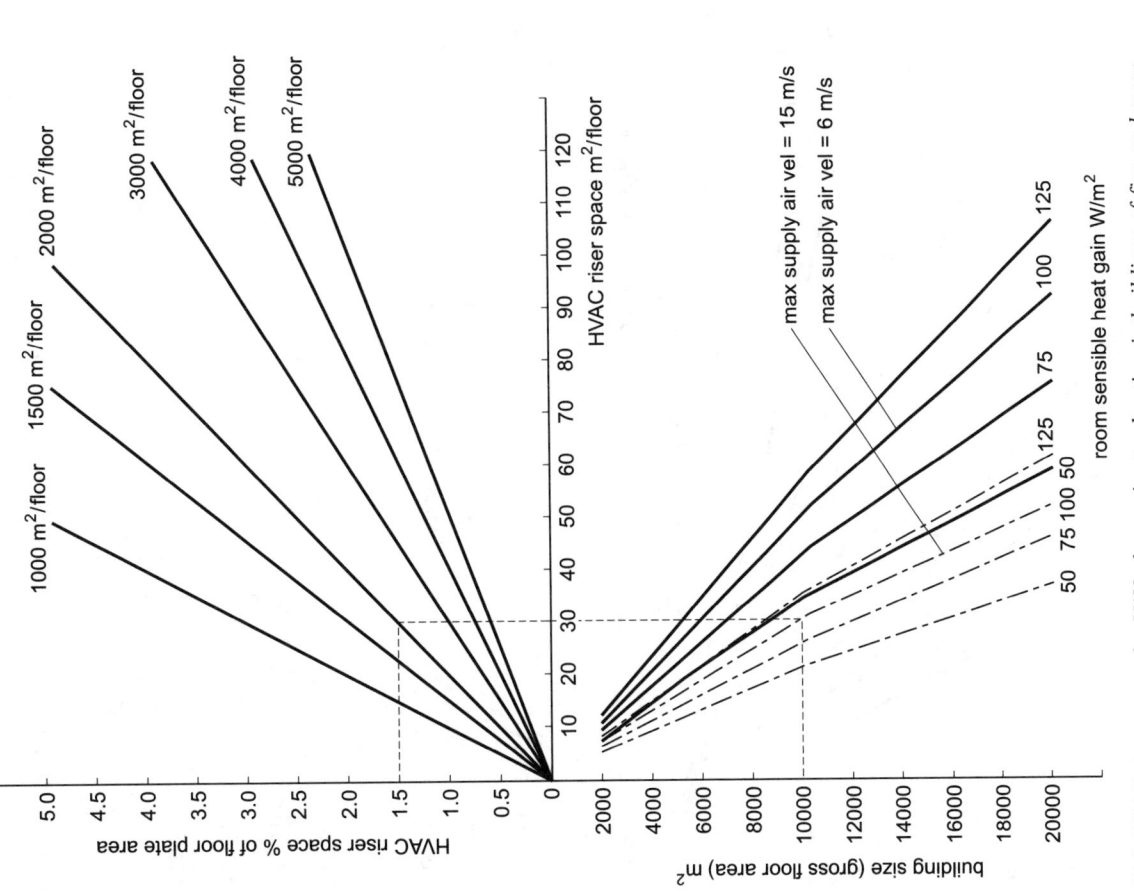

45.2 *HVAC riser space for VAV plus perimeter heating in buildings of five and more storeys*

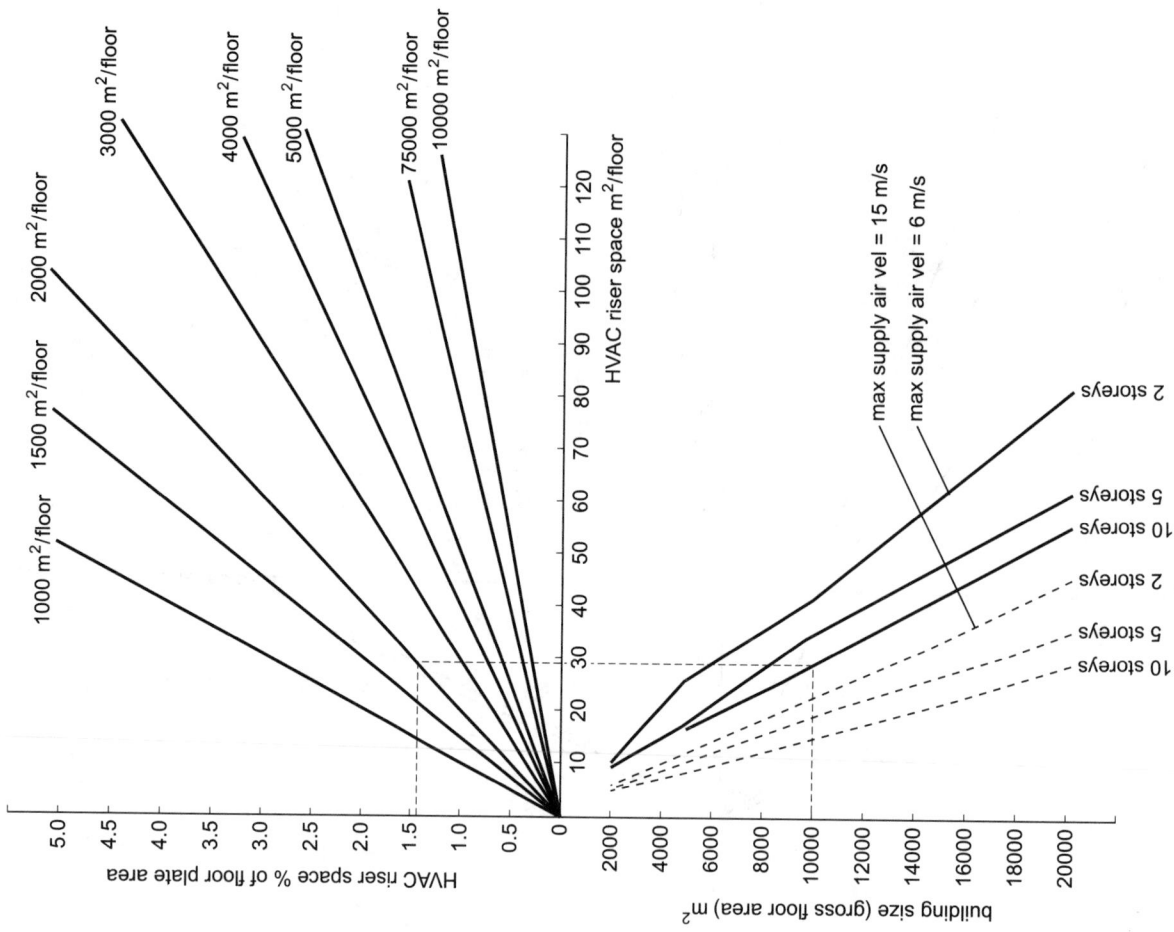

45.5 *HVAC riser space for heating only and 6 ac/h mechanical ventilation*

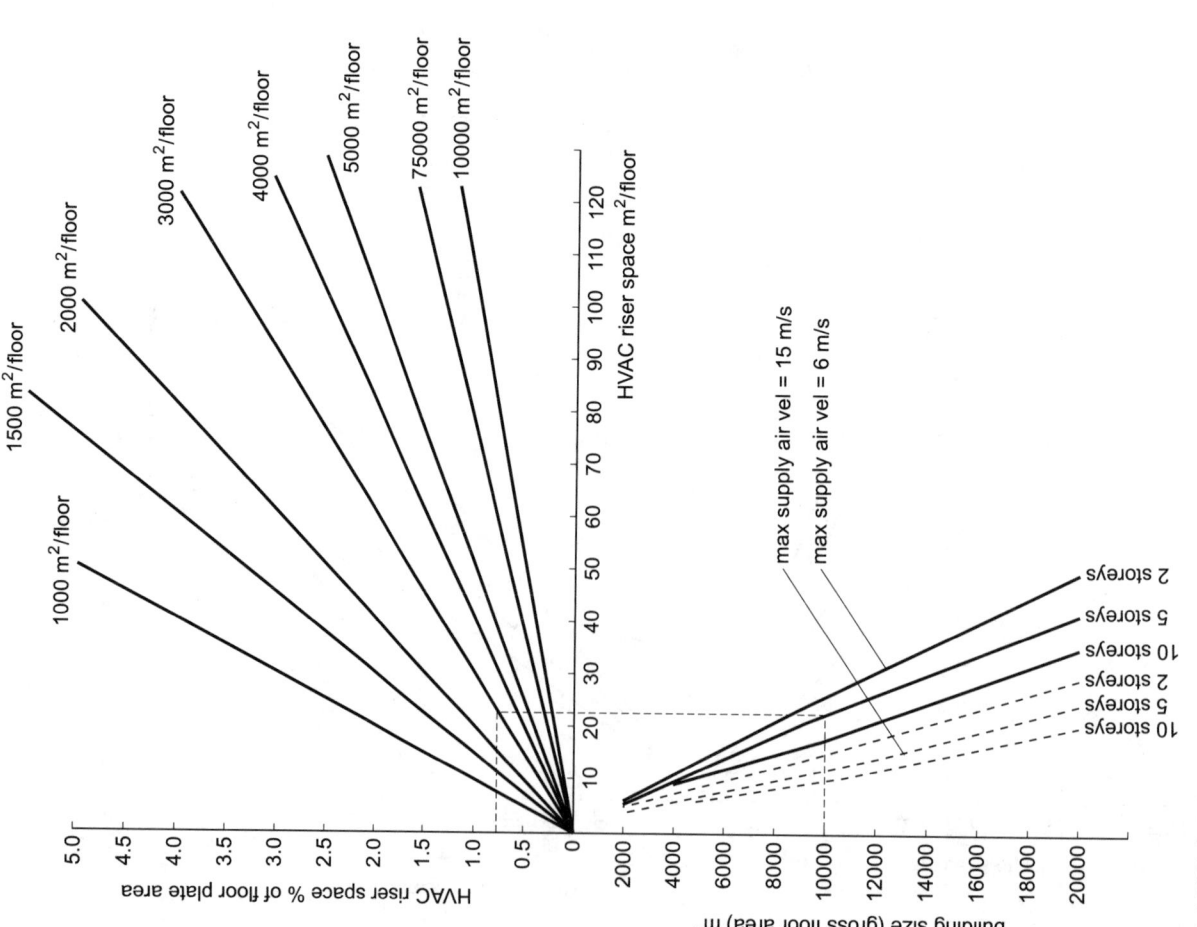

45.4 *HVAC riser space for heating only and 3 ac/h mechanical ventilation*

Table IV Floor area percentages occupied by HVAC plant

System type	Building size (m²)			
	2000	5000	10 000	20 000
OFFICES				
Heating only, natural ventilation:				
Central plant	1.1–1.4	0.7–0.8	–	–
Terminals: radiators	0.6–0.7	0.6–0.7	–	–
Heating only, mechanical ventilation:				
Central plant	1.1–1.4	0.7–0.8	–	–
Air handling plant	4.6–6.4	3.6–5.1	–	–
Terminals: radiators	0.4–0.5	0.4–0.5	–	–
Four-pipe fan coil system (3 ac/h primary air):				
Central plant	3.8–4.2	2.0–2.3	1.1–1.5	0.8–1.2
Air handling plant	4.6	2.7	1.6	1.6
Heat rejection cooling towers	1.2–1.4	0.6–0.8	0.4–0.6	0.3–0.5
Variations:				
Floor by floor AHU 5-storey	–	3.6	2.7	2.6
Floor by floor AHU 10-storey	–	5.4	3.5	2.6
Heat rejection by air-cooled condenser	3.2–4.3	1.8–2.8	1.2–2.4	0.7–2.4
Floor-mounted terminals	1.0	1.0	0.5	0.4
VAV and perimeter heating:				
Central plant	3.8–4.2	2.0–2.3	1.1–1.5	0.8–1.2
Air handling plant	7.5–10.8	6.0–9.0	4.0–8.7	2.3–7.7
Heat rejection cooling towers	1.2–1.4	0.6–0.8	0.4–0.6	0.3–0.5
Terminals: radiators	0.4–0.5	0.4–0.5	0.4–0.5	0.4–0.5
Variations:				
Floor by floor AHU 5-storey	–	6.0–12.0	4.8–10.4	3.7–9.2
Floor by floor AHU 10-storey	–	7.8–15.6	7.8–10.4	3.7–9.0
Heat rejection by air-cooled condensers	3.2–4.3	1.8–2.8	1.2–2.4	0.7–2.4
RETAIL				
Four-pipe fan coil system:				
Central plant	–	2.5–2.8	1.5–2.1	1.0–1.3
Air handling plant	–	3.4–3.5	3.2–3.3	3.1–3.2
Heat rejection cooling towers	–	0.8–1.0	0.5–0.7	0.5–0.7
Variations:				
Floor by floor AHU 2-storey	–	6.0–12.0	3.1	3.0
Floor by floor AHU 5-storey	–	7.8–15.6	3.9	3.0
Heat rejection by air-cooled condenser	3.2–4.3	1.8–2.8	2.0–3.7	1.9–3.3
VAV and terminal reheat:				
Central plant	–	2.5–2.8	1.5–2.1	1.0–1.3
Air handling plant	–	6.7–12.9	6.4–11.1	5.5–9.9
Heat rejection cooling towers	–	0.8–1.0	0.5–0.7	0.5–0.7
Variations:				
Floor by floor AHU 2-storey	–	6.5–12.2	6.1–12.0	5.9–11.8
Floor by floor AHU 5-storey	–	7.8–13.8	7.1–11.8	5.9–11.8
Heat rejection by air-cooled condenser	–	2.5–3.7	2.0–3.7	1.9–3.3
HOTELS				
Heated only, mechanical ventilation:				
Central plant		2.5–3.0	1.6–2.1	1.2–1.3
Air handling plant		5.0	4.8	4.7
Terminals: radiators		0.4	0.4	0.3
Four-pipe fan coil system:				
Central plant	–	2.5–3.0	1.6–2.1	1.2–1.3
Air handling plant	–	2.7	2.7	2.6
Heat rejection cooling towers	–	2.0–2.6	1.5–2.0	1.5–2.0
Variations:				
Floor by floor AHU 2-storey	–	3.3	2.8	2.6
Floor by floor AHU 5-storey	–	3.3	2.6	2.6
Heat rejection by air-cooled condenser	–	1.5–2.0	1.5–2.0	1.5–2.0
VAV and perimeter heating:				
Central plant	–	2.5–3.0	1.6–2.1	1.2–1.3
Air handling plant	–	6.0–7.0	4.4–6.0	4.7–5.9
Heat rejection cooling towers	–	0.6–0.7	0.4–0.5	0.3–0.4
Variations:				
Floor by floor AHU 2-storey	–	4.7–7.5	4.7–7.4	4.7–6.8
Floor by floor AHU 5-storey	–	5.0–8.4	5.0–7.2	4.6–6.5
Heat rejection by air-cooled condensers	–	2.0–2.6	1.5–2.0	1.5–2.0

Table IV *Continued*

System type	Building size (m²)			
	2000	5000	10 000	20 000
HOTELS, *continued*				
Two pipe fan coils to bedrooms, VAV and terminal reheat to public rooms:				
Central plant		2.5–3.0	1.6–2.1	1.2–1.3
Air handling plant		5.8–6.6	3.9–4.5	3.2–4.2
Heat rejection cooling towers		0.6–0.7	0.4–0.5	0.3–0.4
Variations:				
Floor by floor AHU 2-storey		4.7–5.7	4.2–5.2	4.0–4.9
Floor by floor AHU 5-storey		5.7–6.7	4.4–5.4	4.2–5.1
Heat rejection by air-cooled condenser		2.0–2.6	1.5–2.0	1.5–2.0
PLACES OF ASSEMBLY				
VAV and terminal reheat:				
Central plant	5.3–6.1	2.7–3.4	–	–
Air handling plant	7.8–11.4	6.5–3.4	–	–
Heat rejection cooling towers	1.3–1.8	0.8–1.2	–	–
Variation:				
Heat rejection by air-cooled condenser	4.2–5.9	2.7–3.7	–	–

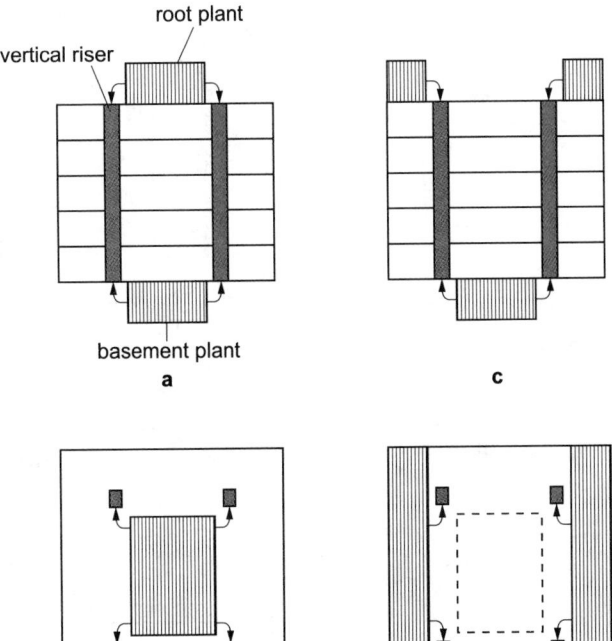

45.6 *Examples of showing good connection of plant areas to vertical risers.* **a** *Section.* **b** *Plan.* **c** *Section.* **d** *Plan*

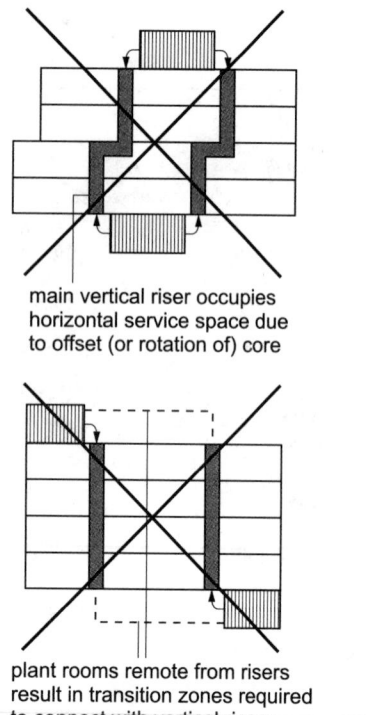

main vertical riser occupies
horizontal service space due
to offset (or rotation of) core

plant rooms remote from risers
result in transition zones required
to connect with vertical risers

45.7 *Examples of poor distribution efficiency: avoid these*

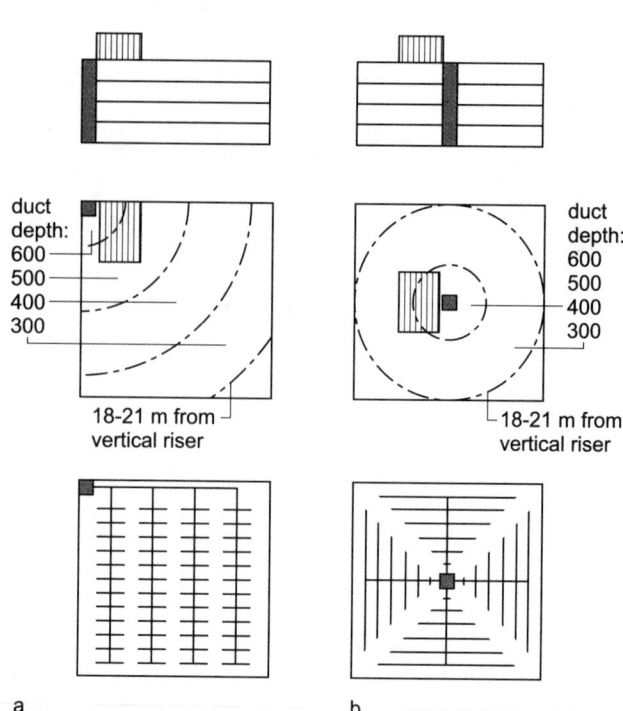

duct
depth:
600
500
400
300

18-21 m from
vertical riser

duct
depth:
600
500
400
300

18-21 m from
vertical riser

a   b

45.8 *Effects of riser location on duct depths.* **a** *A building 40 m square with air duct located at the corner. The longer the duct, the deeper it must be where it joins the riser. This increases the size of the suspended ceiling or raised floor zone.* **b** *With the riser located centrally the duct runs are shorter and their depths are reduced*

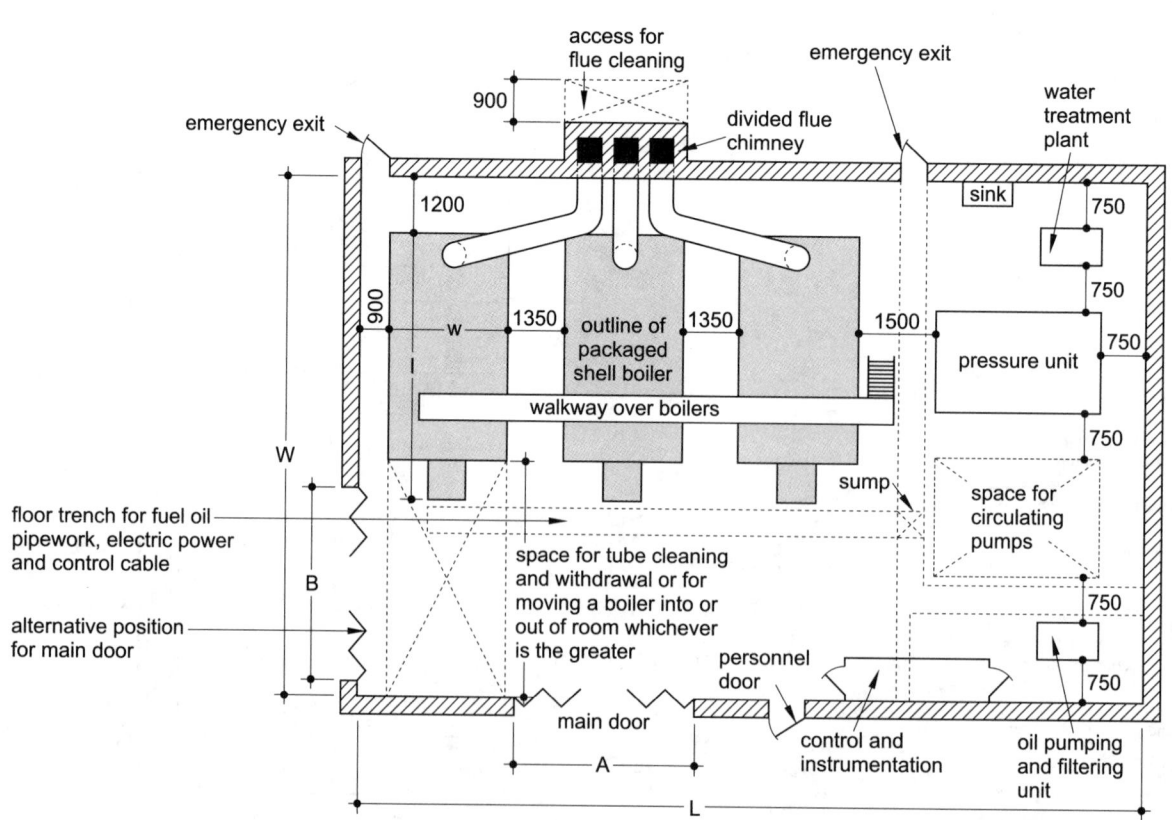

45.9 *Plant room space using oil-fired, three boiler installation*

Table V Builder's work air ducts and plenums

Notes on Use

1 The use of builders' work enclosures as air ducts and plenums should be very carefully evaluated at the early stages of design. In many cases, they do not represent a cheaper solution in terms of overall building costs. Sheet metal and building materials should be compared in terms of costs, performance and construction aspects.

2 The use of builder's work supply ducts should be generally avoided. Filtered and thermally treated air requires careful handling. If such ducts are used, the expected standards of air tightness, insulation and moisture control are difficult and costly to achieve. Standards of workmanship should be very high and require great care to enforce in practice.

Summary of technical considerations

Energy implications	Increased fan power; friction coefficient increases for brick/block/concrete ducts when compared to sheet steel: × 1.4 for fair-faced brickwork × 2.0 for rough-finished brickwork Fan power is directly proportional to friction coefficient.
Thermal losses/gains	Thermal losses increase; greater absorption of heating or cooling energy by thermally heavy containing walls. System time constants increase, can impose control problems. Duct lining to reduce losses, must be considered with care to avoid introducing fine fibres into the air stream. Regular inspection and maintenance is required.
Leakage and filtration	Brick and blockwork is porous; settlement, expansion and contraction will result in significant leakage, particularly through mortar joints; not recommended without a generous allowance for leakage. Brick or blockwork must be rendered or plastered, preferably both sides. Access for personnel is required to allow for resealing of the duct. Adverse effect on the standard of filtration. Full consideration should be given to differential pressures across containing walls; if supply and extract ducts run adjacent, pressure differentials can be appreciable.
Construction constraints	Branches leaving large vertical risers can be problematic: (a) Detail of sheet steel duct connections is crucial. (b) Structurally, passing the branch through a highly stressed element of the building.
Specification	Involvement in the design of builders work ducts maybe outside the scope of the standard HVAC services, eg defined by ACE agreements. It is important to establish early in the design who will take responsibility for design and site supervision.

Table VII Calorifier capacity and dimensions

Capacity litres	Dimensions including insulation, mm		Heater battery withdrawal (max) 8 mm	Dimensions Z mm
	Diameter d	Height h		
500	700	1800	800	750
650	800	1800	1000	750
800	850	1900	1000	750
1000	950	1900	1150	750
1200	1000	2100	1150	750
1500	1150	2100	1300	850
2000	1150	2500	1300	850
2500	1300	2600	1450	950
3000	1350	2700	1500	1050
4000	1450	3100	1600	1050
5000	1600	3100	1750	1150
6500	1700	3400	1850	1300

Dimension Z has been determined on the basis of angled withdrawal of the heater battery.

If battery withdrawal normal to the wall is required, dimension W should be increased by B-Z.

Inspection holes should be easily accessible.

Vertical spindle glandless in-line pumps can be accommodated within the overall space.

When horizontal direct-driven pumps are required, dimension W should be increased by 300 to 600 mm depending on the make of pump. Dimensions are based on conventional storage calorifiers.

Key to symbols used in Figure 45.10

X Space at sides and rear of calorifiers, nominal allowance 750 mm with a minimum of 700 mm.

Y Space between adjacent calorifiers, nominal allowance 600 mm with a minimum of 550 mm.

Z Space for withdrawal of heater battery.

R Minimum space above calorifier, dimensions allowed:
    up to 1000 litres 750 mm
    1200 to 3000 litres 1050 mm
    4000 to 6500 litres 1350 mm

S Space for supporting feet or plinth, 100–300 mm depending on method of support.

Table VI Boiler and boiler room sizes

Total installed Boiler power kW	Clear dimensions of boiler room (mm)			Boiler dimensions (mm)			Boiler masses t	Minimum dimensions of door openings, (mm)		
	Length L	Width W	Height H*	Length l	Width w	Height h		Width A	Width B	Height
9000	19500	12000	5400	6325	3175	3475	22	4200	3900	4200
7500	19200	11100	5100	5850	3125	3175	19	4200	3900	3900
6000	17400	10300	5100	6000	2700	3150	16	3600	3300	3900
4500	16800	10200	5100	5075	2650	3150	14	3600	3300	3900
3600	16200	9300	4500	4475	2450	2475	11	3300	3000	3000
3000	15600	9300	4500	5050	2375	2350	9	3300	3000	3000
2400	15300	9000	4500	4425	2300	2275	8	3300	3000	3000
1950	15000	8400	4200	4000	2275	2150	7	3300	3000	2700
1500	14400	7800	4200	3525	2000	1950	5	3000	2700	2700
1200	14400	7800	4200	3900	1950	2075	5	3000	2700	2700
900	14400	7800	3900	3750	1950	1975	4	3000	2700	2700
750	14100	7200	3900	2825	1800	1750	3	2700	2400	2400
600	14100	7200	3900	3075	1950	1975	3	3000	2700	2700
450	12900	6000	3900	2675	1500	1725	2	2400	2100	2400

* A nominal 2100 mm has been allowed between walkway and ceiling. This dimension may be reduced to 1500 mm locally under beams

Location depends on building design

Some boilers require additional space, eg rear access doors, tube cleaning and withdrawal

Table VIII Spaces for multiple calorifiers

Total storage capacity and dimensions of spaces for two calorifiers				For each additional calorifier *add L* mm	Minimum width of door opening mm
Capacity litres	L mm	W mm	H (min) mm		
1000	3600	2400	3000	1500	800
1300	3600	2400	3000	1500	900
1600	3900	2400	3000	1500	900
2000	3900	2700	3000	1500	1200
2400	4200	2700	3600	1800	1200
3000	4500	2700	3600	1800	1200
4000	4500	2700	3900	1800	1200
5000	4800	3000	3900	2100	1600
6000	4800	3300	4200	2100	1600
8000	5100	3300	4800	2100	1600
10 000	5400	3600	4800	2400	1800
13 000	5700	3900	5100	2400	1800

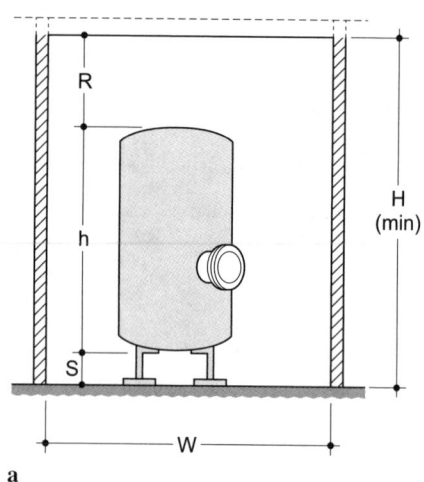

a

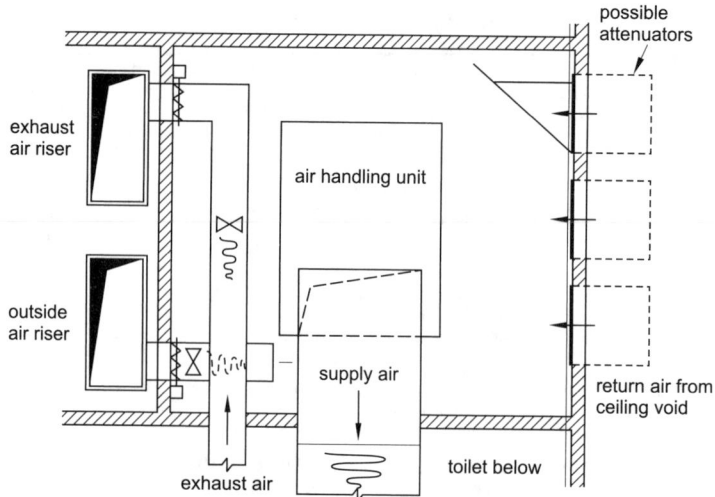

45.11 *Plant room for floor-by-floor VAV AHU*

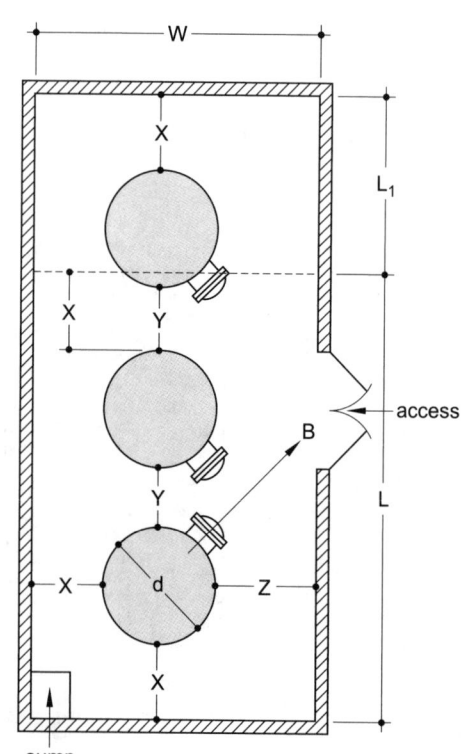

b sump

45.10 *Vertical storage calorifier space requirements.* **a** *Section.* **b** *Plan. See Tables VI and VII and key on p. 45-9*

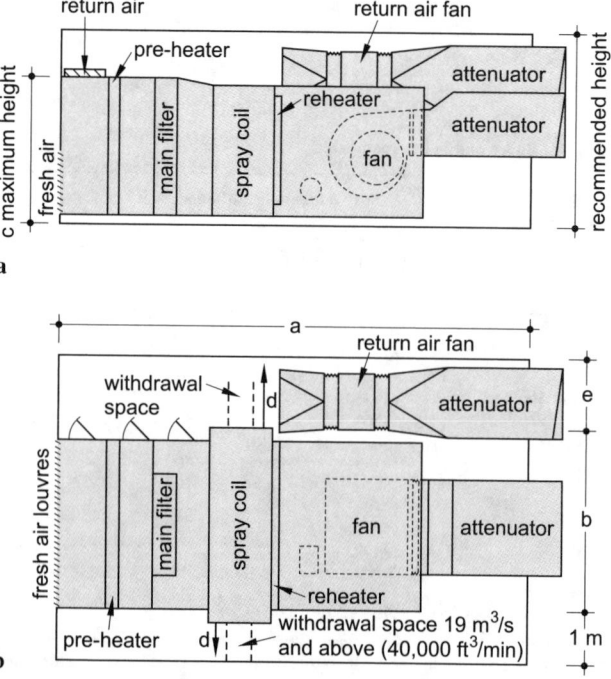

a

b

45.12 *Built-up single duct air-conditioning plant room. Space additional to this will be required for withdrawing the coils, depending on the size and position of the equipment.* **a** *Elevation.* **b** *Plan*

Table IX Floor-by-floor AHU arrangements

Configuration	Comments
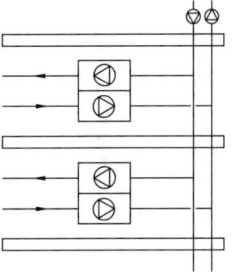	Central fans serving main outdoor air and exhaust air risers. Size of risers can be minimised if only minimum fresh air supplied. Effectiveness of free cooling reduced.
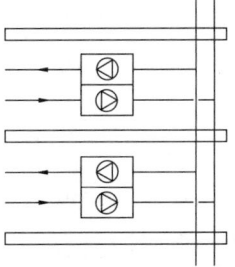	Outdoor air and exhaust air shafts, no rooftop air handling plant.
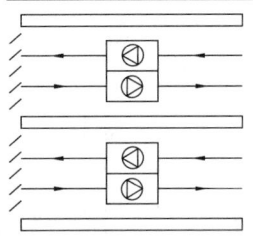	Floor by floor air and exhaust air. No rooftop air handling plant required and avoidance of risers within the building. Improves nett to gross floor area ratio. Problems could be experienced in siting outdoor air and exhaust air louvers on the building elevation.

Table X Air-conditioning plant sizes

Air volume m³/s	Dimension (m)						Plant room			% of Building at OA m³/min per m²
	a	b	c	d	e	h	Area m²	Minimum access m × m	m² per m³/s	
9.438	9.40	3.12	2.55	2.85	1.15	3.50	49.60	2.00 × 2.00	5.25	3.50%
14.157	10.20	4.10	2.55	3.75	1.15	3.80	63.75	2.30 × 2.30	4.50	3.00%
18.875	10.60	4.10	3.20	1.90	1.40	4.20	68.80	2.60 × 2.60	3.65	2.40%
23.595	10.90	5.00	3.20	2.30	1.40	4.60	80.70	2.75 × 2.75	3.32	2.25%
28.314	11.20	5.00	3.80	2.30	1.70	5.10	86.20	3.10 × 3.10	3.05	2.00%

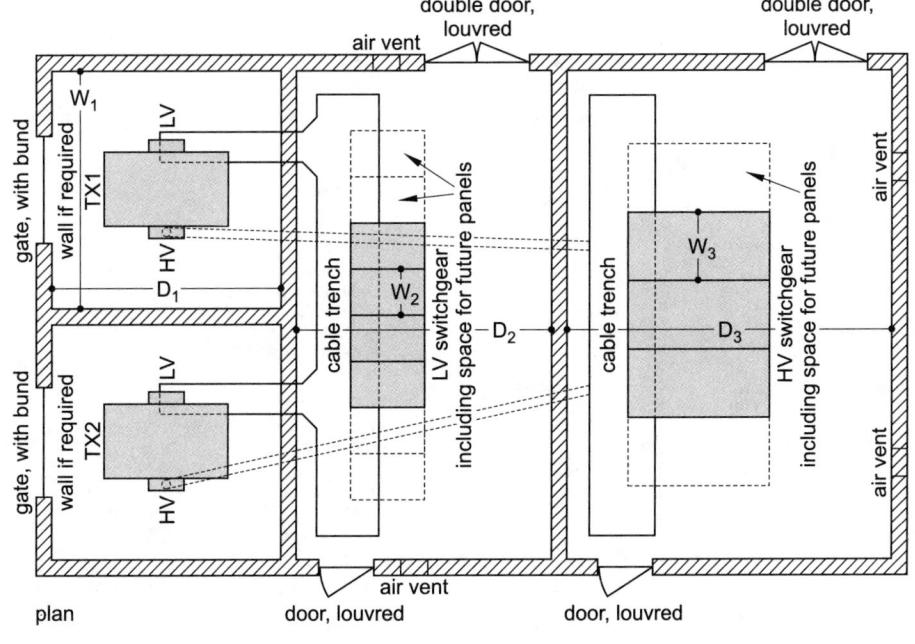

45.13 *Electrical sub-station space requirements*

Table XI Percentage of gross floor area occupied by electrical plant

Installation	Building size (m²)			
	2000	5000	10 000	20 000
GENERAL-PURPOSE OFFICE				
Electrical load (kVA)	40–110	100–280	200–560	400–1100
1 Transformer				
Liquid × 1	–	–	0.25	0.12–0.15
× 2	–	–	–	0.25
Cast resin × 1	–	–	0.22	0.10–0.14
× 2	–	–	–	0.17
2 HV switchroom				
RMU 1	–	–	0.28	0.14
2	–	–	–	0.21
Panels 1	–	–	0.33	0.17
2	–	–	–	0.22
3 LV switchroom				
rear access	1.67	0.67	0.33	0.17–0.18
front access	1.20	0.48	0.24	0.12–0.13
4 Packaged substation (1000 kVA)	–	–	0.69	0.35–0.42
GENERAL-PURPOSE OFFICE WITH AIR CONDITIONING				
Electrical load (kVA)	80–280	200–700	400–1400	830–2800
1 Transformer				
Liquid × 1	–	0.50	0.24–0.33	0.14–0.17
× 2	–	–	0.50	0.22–0.30
Cast resin × 1	–	0.44	0.20–0.27	0.12–0.15
× 2	–	–	0.34	0.14–0.21
2 HV switchroom				
RMU 1	–	0.56	0.28	0.14
2			0.42	0.21
Panels 1	–	0.46	0.33	0.17
2			0.44	0.22
3 LV switchroom				
rear access	1.67	0.67	0.37	0.25
front access	1.20	0.48	0.27	0.19
4 Packaged substation(s) (1000 kVA)	–	1.46	0.6–0.91	0.37–0.82 (2 no)
HIGH-TECH OFFICE				
Electrical load (kVA)	190–460	730–1600	1400–3300	2900–6500
1 Transformer				
Liquid × 1	–	0.55–0.66	0.33	–
× 2	–	1.10	0.55–0.60	0.30
× 3	–	–	1.00	1.00–1.05
Cast resin × 1	–	0.49–0.54	0.27–0.30	–
× 2	–	0.76	0.34–0.41	0.21–0.23
× 3	–	–	0.68	0.34–0.40
2 HV switchroom				
RMU 1	–	0.56	0.28	0.14
2			0.42	0.21
3		0.56	0.28	
Panels 1	–	0.66	0.33	0.17
2			0.44	0.22
3			0.55	0.28
3 LV switchroom				
rear access	1.65	0.74	0.51	0.46
front access	1.20	0.54	0.38	0.32
4 Packaged substation(s) (1000 kVA)	–	1.46–1.61	0.80–1.64 (2 no)	0.82 (2 no)–1.48 (4 no)
RETAIL				
Electrical load (kVA)	400–650	1000–1700	2000–3200	4000–6500
1 Transformer				
Liquid × 1	1.40	0.61–0.66	0.33	–
× 2	–	1.10	0.44–0.60	0.30
× 3	–	–	1.00	0.50–0.52
Cast resin × 1	1.10	0.54–0.60	0.30	–
× 2	–	0.67	0.38–0.41	0.45
× 3	–	–	0.68	0.36–0.41
2 HV switchroom				
RMU 1	1.40	0.56	0.28	–
2		–	0.42	0.21
3			0.56	0.28
Panels 1	1.70	0.66	0.33	–
2		0.88	0.44	0.22
3			0.55	0.28
3 LV switchroom				
rear access	1.65	0.74	0.51	0.46
front access	1.20	0.54	0.38	0.32
4 Packaged substation(s) (1000 kVA)	3.51	1.46–1.61	0.89–1.64 (2 no)	1.08 (4 no)–1.48 (6 no)

Table XI *Continued*

Installation	Building size (m²)			
	2000	**5000**	**10 000**	**20 000**
HOTEL				
Electrical load (kVA)	250	700	1500	3000
1 Transformer				
Liquid × 1	–	0.55	0.33	0.17
× 2	–	–	–	0.30
Cast resin × 1	–	0.49	0.27	0.15
× 2	–	–	–	0.19
2 HV switchroom				
RMU 1	–	0.56	0.28	0.14
2			0.42	0.21
Panels 1	–	0.66	0.33	0.17
2			0.44	0.22
3 LV switchroom				
rear access	1.67	0.73	0.51	0.46
front access	1.20	0.53	0.38	0.32
4 Packaged substation(2) (1000 kVA)	–	1.46	0.91	0.82 (2 no)

Table XII Percentage of gross floor area occupied by standby electrical plant

Electrical load (kVA)	Space required (m²)		
	200	**500**	**1250**
1 Generator single machine, water cooled −15 dBA enclosure	–	33	46
2 UPS: (a) static	17	25	
(b) rotary	56	71	
(c) battery	13	22	

Table XV Switchgear, air circuit breaker, space requirements

Current rating A	Dimensions (m)			Area m²	Weight kg
	D_2	W_2	H_2		
600	3.65	0.65	2.25	2.40	438
800	3.65	0.65	2.25	2.40	438
1200	3.85	0.70	2.30	2.70	535
1600	3.85	0.75	2.30	2.90	463
2400	3.85	0.95	2.30	3.65	590

Table XIII Riser space for power distribution

Building type	Allowance	Comments
Speculative office	0.23–0.29	This includes provision for Landlord riser
High tech, dealing office	0.25–0.29	Applies where local PDUs are in use
	0.50–0.55	Applies where duplicate UPS distribution system is installed alongside a normal power distribution system
Hotels		For prestige high star-rated hotels, it is recommended that each room has its own separate lighting and power circuits. This will influence distribution board sizes and consequently riser space.
		Two cable trays should be installed per riser: one to support sub-mains distribution and the other to carry the numerous telecommunications cable, video, PA and other services found in a modern hotel. The latter tray should be sized at 300 mm per 150 bedrooms

Table XVI HV switchgear, oil circuit breaker, space requirements

Max s/c rating MVA	Current rating A	Dimensions (m)			Area m²	Weight kg
		D_2	W_2	H_2		
250/350	400	4.20	0.65	2.95	2.75	680
	800	4.20	0.60	2.25	2.55	680
	1200	4.20	0.65	2.95	2.75	680
	1600	4.65	0.95	2.30	4.45	1190
	2000	4.65	0.95	2.30	4.45	1220

Transformer height H_1 includes necessary height clearance, H_2 and H_3 exclude clearances

Table XIV 116 V/433 V oil-filled transformer space requirements

Transformer rating kVA	Dimensions (m)			Area m²	Weight kg
	D_1	W_1	H_1		
300	3.35	2.90	3.10	9.75	1439
500	3.50	3.00	3.30	10.50	2245
750	3.55	3.05	3.25	10.85	2910
1000	3.80	3.20	3.45	12.25	3590
1500	4.00	3.50	3.70	14.00	5180

Table XVII Cross-sectional zones

Zone	Letter	Comment
Structural	A	Specified by structural engineer
Services	B	50 mm deflection and tolerance
	C	Approximately 500 mm HVAC duct or terminal device
	D	50 mm support and tolerance
	E	50–150 mm sprinkler sub-zone
	F	150 mm lighting and ceiling sub-zone
Headroom	G	Specified by client and architect
Raised floor	H	Data, communications, small power

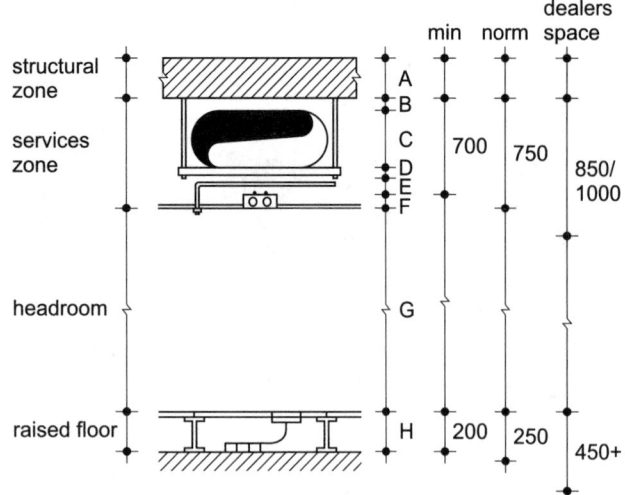

45.14 *Typical cross-section for structure and services*
Key for **45.14** *to* **45.18** *is given in Table VII*

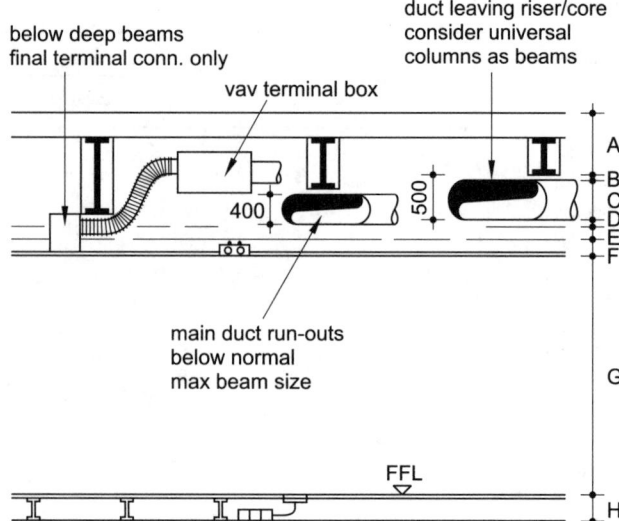

45.15 *Horizontal service distribution with universal steel beams*

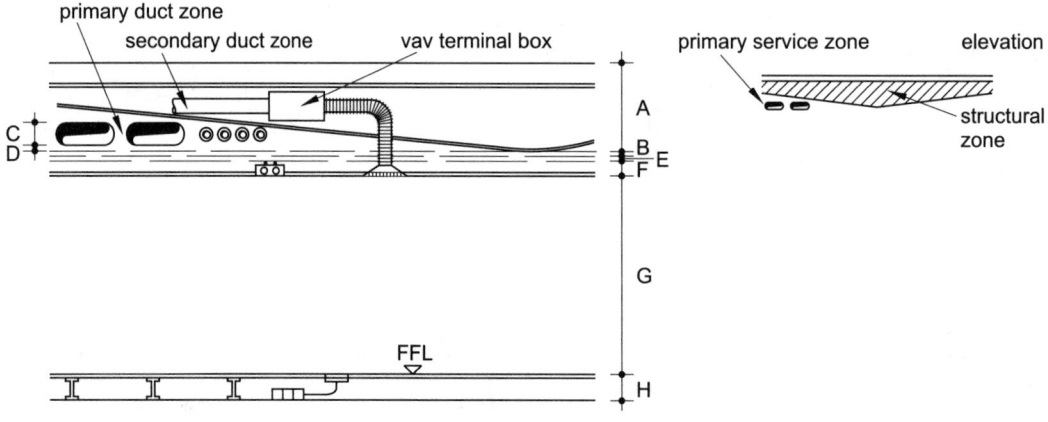

45.16 *Horizontal service distribution with tapered beams*

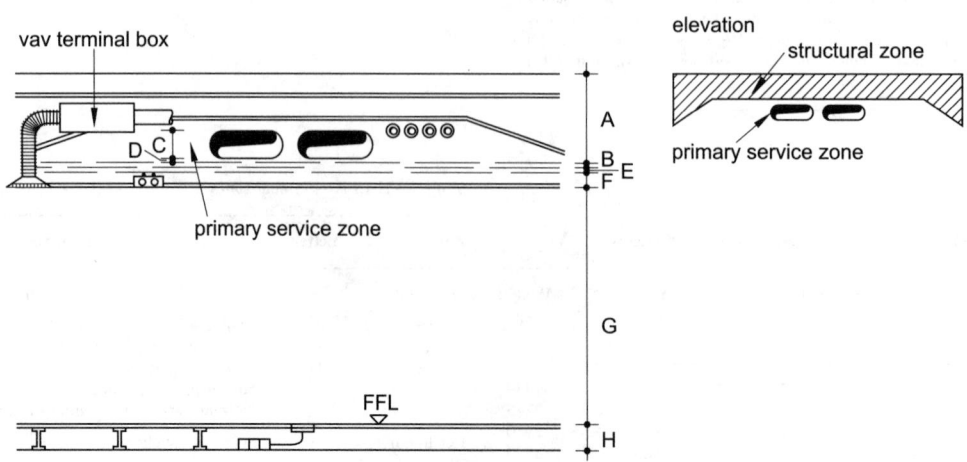

45.17 *Horizontal service distribution with haunched tapered beams*

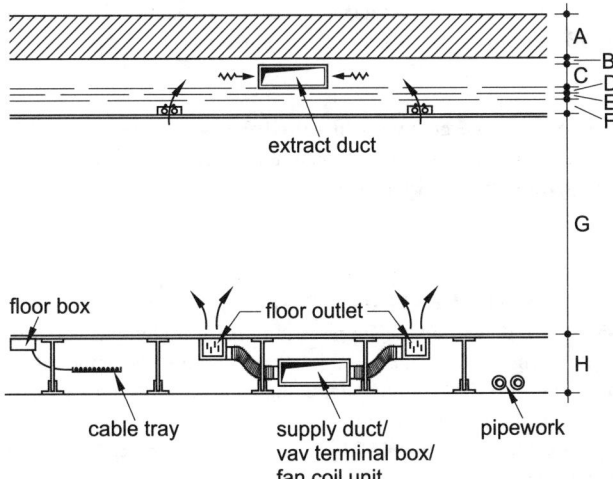

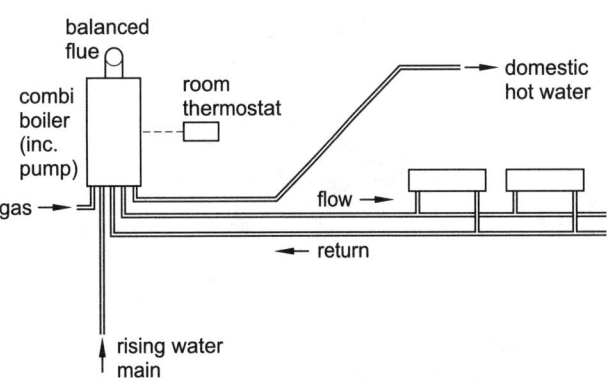

45.21 *Domestic central heating and hot water system using gas-fired combination boiler*

45.18 *Horizontal service distribution with floor supply system*

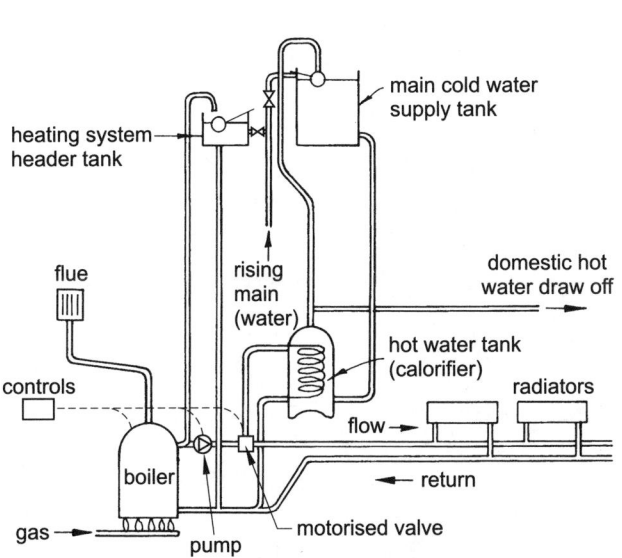

45.19 *Domestic central heating system using conventional gas boiler, small bore pumped supply to radiators on two-pipe system, and gravity circulation to heat domestic hot water*

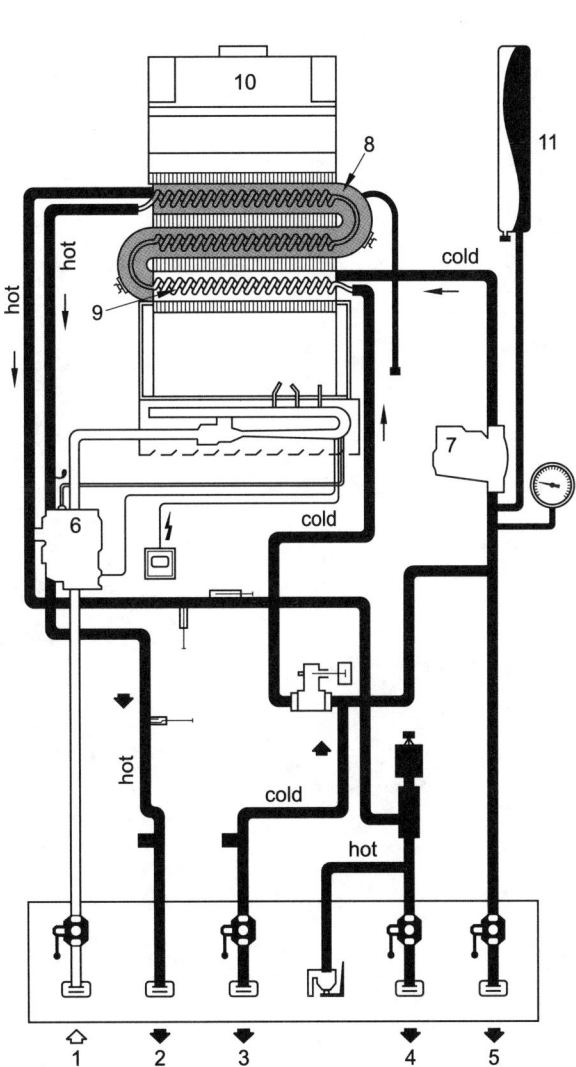

45.22 *Combination boiler*

Key:
1 *Gas inlet*
2 *Domestic hot water supply*
3 *Water inlet*
4 *Heating water flow*
5 *Heating water return*
6 *Combination gas valve*
7 *Heating circulating pump*
8 *Heating element*
9 *Hot water coil*
10 *Balanced flue*
11 *Expansion vessel*

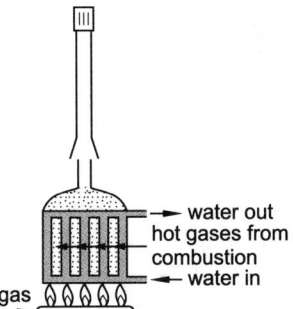

45.20 *Diagrammatic representation of a water boiler, in this case using gas*

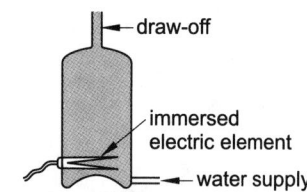

45.23 *Diagram of electric immersion heater in hot water cylinder*

3.08 Electrical equipment
Table XI gives information enabling the allocation of space required for general electrical services, while Table XII covers the provision of stand-by plant that might be required in buildings such as hospitals. The space required for the electrical risers is given in Table XIII.

A transformer and associated switchgear chamber is shown in **45.13**, the dimensions for which are given in Tables XIV, XV and XVI.

3.09 Suspended ceilings and raised floors
45.14 to **45.18** show spaces required for horizontal distribution with explanation in Table XVII.

4 DOMESTIC HEATING AND HOT WATER
45.19 is a diagrammatic representation of a traditional domestic water-borne heating and stored hot water system. A diagram of the workings of this gas-fired boiler is shown in **45.20**. A more modern system using a combination boiler, which generates the hot water on demand, is shown in **45.21**, and the boiler in **45.22**. A domestic electric hot water storage heater is shown in **45.23**.

46 Materials

CI/Sfb: Ya
Uniclass: V

KEY POINTS:
- *Changes are occurring all the time, always refer to manufacturers*
- *Not all materials are, or perhaps ever will be, totally metricated*

Contents

1 INTRODUCTION

In the very first edition of this handbook, this chapter gave information about the metrication of materials which up until then had always been supplied to imperial dimensions, quantities and weights. Now that the metrication process has almost been completed (with exceptions noted below), this chapter is intended to give information about the dimensions of materials which may affect the planning of a building. Of necessity it is neither totally complete, nor can it always be completely up to date.

It has now become evident that some materials, mainly those with a long history behind them and possibly a phasing-out in the future, will not be metricated; although their parameters may be expressed in metric units. Attention may also be drawn to the case of water pipes and fittings mentioned below.

The editor would be particularly grateful for notification of any changes that need to be made in this chapter in subsequent reprintings.

2 STEEL

2.01 General

BS 6722: 1986 lays down the preferred metric dimensions to size all kinds of metal wires, bars and flat products, both ferrous and non-ferrous. These preferred dimensions are as below, with the first preferences in ordinary type and the second in italics.

The preferences (in mm) for bars and the thickness of flat products are:

0.10, *0.11*, 0.12, *0.14*, 0.16, *0.18*, 0.20, *0.22*, 0.25, *0.28*, 0.30, *0.35*, 0.40, *0.45*, 0.50, *0.55*, 0.60, *0.70*, 0.80, *0.90*.

1.0, *1.1*, 1.2, *1.4*, 1.6, *1.8*, 2.0, 2.2, 2.5, *2.8*, 3.0, *3.5*, 4.0, *4.5*, 5.0, *5.5*, 6.0, *7.0*, 8.0, *9.0*.

10.0, *11.0*, 12.0, *14.0*, 16.0, *18.0*, 20.0, *22.0*, 25.0, *28.0*, 30.0, *35.0*, 40.0, *45.0*, 50.0, *55.0*, 60.0, *70.0*, 80.0, *90.0*.

100.0, *110.0*, 120.0, *140.0*, 160.0, *180.0*, 200.0, *220.0*, 250.0, *280.0*, 300.0.

The preferences for the widths and lengths of flat products are:

400, 500, 600, 800, 1000, 1200, 1250, 1500, 2000, 2500, 3000, 4000, 5000, 6000, 8000, 10 000.

2.02 Plate, strip and bars

The tables of commonly available sizes from the previous edition are here reprinted: Table I for steel plates, Table II for hot-rolled flats and Tables III to V for rounds, squares and hexagons.

Table I Mild steel plate sizes

Thickness	2000 × 1000	2500 × 1250	3000 × 1500	4000 × 1500	4000 × 1750	4000 × 2000	4000 × 2500	5000 × 1500	5000 × 2000	5000 × 2500	6000 × 1500	6000 × 2000	6000 × 2500	8000 × 1500	8000 × 2000	8000 × 2500	10 000 × 2000	10 000 × 2500
6		×	×	×	×			×			×			×				
8		×	×	×	×			×			×			×				
10		×	×	×	×		×	×	×	×	×	×	×	×	×	×		
12.5		×	×	×	×	×	×	×	×	×	×	×	×	×	×	×	×	×
15		×	×	×		×	×		×	×	×	×	×	×	×	×	×	×
20		×	×	×		×	×		×	×	×	×	×	×	×	×	×	×
25		×	×	×		×	×		×	×	×	×	×	×	×	×	×	×
30		×	×	×		×	×		×	×	×	×	×	×	×	×	×	×
35		×	×	×		×	×	×	×	×	×	×	×	×	×	×	×	×
40		×	×	×		×	×	×	×	×	×	×	×	×	×	×	×	×
45		×	×	×		×	×	×										
50	×	×	×	×		×	×	×										
60	×	×	×	×		×	×											
65	×	×	×	×		×												
70	×	×	×	×		×												
75	×	×	×	×		×												
80	×	×	×	×		×												
90	×	×	×	×		×												
100	×	×	×	×		×												
110	×	×	×	×		×												
130	×	×	×	×		×												
150	×	×	×	×		×												

Table II Hot rolled flats

Width (mm)	Standard thickness (mm)																	
	3	5	6	8	10	12	15	18	20	25	30	32	35	40	45	50	60	65
25	×	×	×	×	×	×			×									
30	×	×	×	×	×	×	×		×	×								
35	×		×	×	×	×	×		×	×								
40	×	×	×	×	×	×	×		×	×								
45	×		×	×	×	×	×		×	×								
50	×	×	×	×	×	×	×	×	×	×	×		×	×				
55			×	×	×	×			×	×	×							
60	×		×	×	×	×	×		×	×	×		×	×	×	×		
65	×	×	×	×	×	×	×	×	×	×	×		×	×	×	×		
70		×	×	×	×	×	×		×	×	×			×				
75			×	×	×	×	×	×	×	×	×	×	×	×		×		×
80		×	×	×	×	×	×		×	×	×		×	×	×	×		
90			×	×	×	×	×		×	×	×		×	×	×	×	×	×
100		×	×	×	×	×	×		×	×	×		×	×	×	×	×	×
110					×	×	×		×	×	×			×				
120						×	×		×	×				×				
130		×	×	×	×	×	×		×	×	×			×	×	×	×	
140					×	×												
150			×	×	×	×	×		×	×	×		×			×		
160					×	×	×		×	×	×		×	×				
180					×	×	×		×	×	×		×	×				
200						×	×		×	×	×		×	×	×	×	×	
220						×	×		×	×	×		×	×	×	×	×	
250						×	×		×	×	×		×	×	×	×	×	
275						×	×		×	×	×		×	×	×	×	×	
300						×	×		×	×	×		×	×	×	×	×	
325							×		×	×	×		×	×	×	×	×	
350							×		×	×	×		×	×	×	×	×	
375									×	×	×		×	×	×	×	×	
400									×	×	×		×	×	×	×	×	
425									×	×	×		×	×	×	×	×	
450									×	×	×		×	×	×	×	×	
475										×	×		×	×	×	×		
500										×	×		×	×	×	×		
525										×	×		×	×	×	×		
550										×	×		×	×	×	×		
575										×	×		×	×	×	×		
600										×	×		×	×	×	×		

Table III Rounds for all purposes

Diameter Standard mm	Mass/length kg/m	Diameter Standard mm	Mass/length kg/m	Diameter Standard mm	Mass/length kg/m	Diameter Standard mm	Mass/length kg/m
5.5	0.187	20.5	2.59	58.5	21.1	170.0	178
6.0	0.222	21.0	2.72	60.0	22.2	175.0	189
6.5	0.260	21.5	2.85	62.0	23.7	180.0	200
7.0	0.302	22.0	2.98	65.0	26.0	185.0	211
7.5	0.347	23.0	3.26	67.0	27.7	190.0	223
8.0	0.395	23.5	3.40	68.0	28.5	195.0	229
8.5	0.445	24.0	3.55	70.0	30.2	200.0	247
9.0	0.499	25.0	3.85	71.5	31.5	210.0	272
9.5	0.556	25.5	4.01	75.0	34.7	220.0	298
10.0	0.617	26.0	4.17	78.0	37.5	230.0	326
10.5	0.680	26.5	4.33	80.0	39.5	240.0	356
11.0	0.746	27.0	4.49	85.0	44.5	250.0	385
11.5	0.815	28.5	5.01	90.0	49.9	260.0	417
12.0	0.888	32.0	6.31	95.0	55.6	270.0	449
12.5	0.963	35.0	7.55	100.0	61.7	280.0	483
13.0	1.04	38.0	8.90	105.0	68.0	290.0	518
13.5	1.12	40.0	9.86	110.0	74.6	300.0	555
14.0	1.21	42.0	10.9	115.0	81.5	320.0	631
14.5	1.30	43.0	11.4	120.0	88.0	330.0	672
15.0	1.39	45.0	12.5	125.0	96.3		
16.0	1.58	46.0	13.1	130.0	104		
16.5	1.68	50.0	15.4	135.0	112		
17.0	1.78	51.0	16.0	140.0	121		
17.5	1.88	52.0	16.7	145.0	130		
18.0	2.00	52.5	17.0	150.0	139		
18.5	2.11	55.0	18.7	155.0	148		
19.0	2.23	55.5	19.0	160.0	158		
20.0	2.47	57.0	20.0	165.0	168		

Table IV Squares

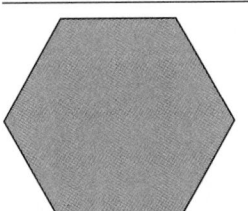

Side Standard mm	Mass/length kg/m
7.0	0.385
8.0	0.502
10.0	0.785
12.0	1.13
13.0	1.33
15.0	1.77
20.0	3.14
25.0	4.91
30.0	7.07
35.0	9.62
40.0	12.6

Table V Hexagons

A/F Standard mm	Mass/length kg/m
9.5	0.61
11.0	0.82
12.5	1.06
14.5	1.43
15.0	1.53
16.	1.85
20.5	2.86

Table VI British Standard structural steel sections to BS4: Part 1: 1993

Nominal size	Available masses per m run

Universal beams

Nominal size	Available masses per m run
914 × 419	388, 343
914 × 305	289, 253, 224, 201
838 × 292	226, 194, 176
762 × 267	197, 173, 147, 134
686 × 254	170, 152, 140, 125
610 × 305	238, 179, 149
610 × 229	140, 125, 113, 101
533 × 210	122, 109, 101, 92, 82
457 × 191	98, 89, 82, 74, 67
457 × 152	82, 74, 67, 60, 52
406 × 178	74, 67, 60, 54
406 × 140	46, 39
356 × 171	67, 57, 51, 45
356 × 127	39, 33
305 × 165	54, 46, 40
305 × 127	48, 42, 37
305 × 102	33, 28, 25
254 × 146	43, 37, 31
254 × 102	28, 25, 22
203 × 133	30, 25
203 × 102	23
178 × 102	19
152 × 89	16
127 × 76	13

Universal columns

Nominal size	Available masses per m run
356 × 406	634, 551, 467, 393, 340, 287, 235
356 × 368	202, 177, 153, 129
305 × 305	283, 240, 198, 158, 137, 118, 97
254 × 254	167, 132, 107, 89
203 × 203	86, 71, 60, 52, 46
152 × 152	37, 30, 23

Joists

Nominal size	Available masses per m run
254 × 203	82
254 × 114	37
203 × 152	52
152 × 127	37
127 × 114	29, 27
127 × 76	16
114 × 114	27
102 × 102	23
102 × 44	7
89 × 89	19
76 × 76	15, 13

Universal bearing piles

Nominal size	Available masses per m run
356 × 368	174, 152, 133, 109
305 × 305	223, 186, 149, 126, 110, 95, 88, 79
254 × 254	85, 71, 63
203 × 203	54, 45

2.03 Structural steel sections

Most steel sections of British origin are still based on the old Imperial sizes although sized in metric dimensions and billed in kilograms or tonnes. Table VI summarises the dimensions available.

However, some are made in metric co-ordinated sizes, and these are also available from the Continent, as they have been ever since steel construction started at the end of the nineteenth century. Some of these are listed in Table VII.

2.04 Steel reinforcement for concrete

For details of sizes of these refer to Chapter 41, Structure.

3 TIMBER

3.01 Timber used in building is either softwood or hardwood, depending on species; each may be supplied sawn or finished. Sizes are usually quoted 'ex', meaning the sawn size, and Table VIII gives the normal reductions to find the finished size.

3.02 Softwood

Standard sizes for sawn softwood have been agreed to cover all European countries, but with provision for some special sizes for each country. These are summarised in Table IX.

To the figures given in the tables a tolerance of ±0.5 mm should be allowed. Joinery standard allows for a high degree of straightness, and both back and front are finished. Trim standard allows for the back to be rough as concealed, and a lower requirement for straightness.

Standard softwood and hardwood profiles are available in a number of varieties, of which tongue-and-groove floorboarding is the commonest. Table X gives the standard dimensions of these.

Wood is normally supplied in lengths varying from 1.8 m in increments of 0.3 m up to a maximum of 6.3 m. The maxima vary for different species and size of section.

3.03 Hardwood

Hardwood is normally supplied in planks of specified thickness but arbitrary width and length, depending on species and thickness. The standard thicknesses are: 19, 25, 32, 36, 38, 44, 50, 63, 75, 100, 150, 200, 250 and 300 mm.

Table VI *Continued*

Nominal size	Available masses per m run

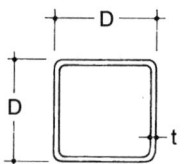

Circular hollow sections

660 dia	752, 612, 496, 392, 216
610	691, 562, 456, 361, 291
559	628, 512, 416, 329, 266
508	565, 462, 376, 298, 241, 194, 153, 123, 99, 78
457	411, 335, 266, 216, 174, 137, 110, 89, 70
406.4	295, 235, 191, 154, 121, 98, 79, 62
355.6	204, 166, 134, 106, 85, 69, 54
323.9	184, 150, 121, 96, 77, 62, 49, 39
273	153, 125, 101, 80, 65, 52, 41, 33
244.5	135, 111, 90, 72, 58, 47, 37, 30
219.1	98, 80, 64, 52, 42, 33, 26, 24
193.7	70, 56, 45, 37, 29, 23
168.3	48, 39, 32, 25, 20
139.7	32, 26, 21, 17
114.3	17, 14, 10
88.9	10, 8, 7
76.1	8.8, 7.1, 5.8
60.3	6.8, 5.6, 4.5
48.3	5.3, 4.4, 3.6
42.4	3.8, 3.1, 2.6
33.7	2.9, 2.4, 2.0
26.9	1.9
21.3	1.4

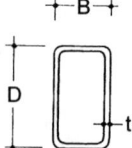

Square hollow sections

600 × 600	671, 611, 550, 487, 439
550 × 550	608, 555, 500, 443, 399, 355, 309, 263
500 × 500	498, 450, 399, 360, 320, 280, 238, 181
450 × 450	399, 355, 321, 286, 250, 213, 162
400 × 400	282, 251, 235, 191, 151, 122, 98
350 × 350	242, 217, 190, 166, 131, 106, 85
300 × 300	141, 112, 90, 73, 58
260 × 260	96, 78, 63, 50
250 × 250	115, 92, 75, 60, 48
200 × 200	90, 72, 59, 48, 38, 30
180 × 180	80, 64, 53, 43, 34, 27
160 × 160	70, 57, 46, 38, 30, 24
150 × 150	65, 53, 43, 35, 28, 23
140 × 140	49, 40, 33, 26, 21
120 × 120	41, 34, 28, 22, 18, 14
100 × 100	27, 23, 18, 15, 12
90 × 90	20, 16, 13, 10
80 × 80	18, 14, 12, 9, 7
70 × 70	15, 12, 10, 7.4, 6.2
60 × 60	12.5, 10.3, 8.4, 6.9, 5.6, 5.3
50 × 50	8.3, 6.9, 5.6, 4.6, 4.4, 3.7
40 × 40	5.3, 4.4, 3.6, 3.4, 2.9

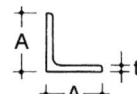

Rectangular hollow sections

500 × 300	235, 191, 151, 122
500 × 200	166, 131, 106, 85
450 × 250	166, 131, 106, 85
400 × 300	166, 131, 106, 85
400 × 200	141, 112, 90, 73, 58

Table VI *Continued*

Nominal size	Available masses per m run

Rectangular hollow sections, *continued*

400 × 150	128, 102, 83, 67, 53
400 × 120	96, 78, 63, 50
350 × 250	141, 112, 90, 73
350 × 150	115, 92, 75, 60, 48
300 × 250	128, 102, 83, 67, 53
300 × 200	115, 92, 75, 60, 48
300 × 100	90, 72, 59, 48, 38
260 × 140	90, 72, 59, 48, 38
250 × 150	90, 72, 59, 48, 38, 30
250 × 100	78, 63, 51, 41, 33
200 × 150	78, 63, 51, 41, 33, 27
200 × 120	70, 57, 46, 38, 30, 24
200 × 100	65, 53, 43, 35, 28, 23
160 × 80	41, 34, 28, 22, 18, 14
150 × 100	43, 35, 29, 23, 19, 15
120 × 80	27, 23, 18, 15
120 × 60	20, 16, 13, 10
100 × 60	18, 14, 12, 8.5, 7.2
100 × 50	16, 13, 11, 8.8, 7.1, 6.7
90 × 50	15, 12, 10, 7.4, 6.2
80 × 40	13, 10, 8.4, 6.9, 5.6, 5.3
60 × 40	8.3, 6.9, 5.6, 4.6, 4.4, 3.7
50 × 30	5.3, 4.4, 3.6, 3.4, 2.9

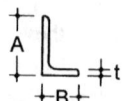

Channels

432 × 102	66
381 × 102	55
305 × 102	46
305 × 89	42
254 × 89	36
254 × 76	28
229 × 89	33
229 × 76	26
203 × 89	30
203 × 76	24
178 × 89	27
178 × 76	21
152 × 89	24
152 × 76	18
127 × 64	15
102 × 51	10.4
76 × 38	6.7

Equal angles

250 × 250	128, 118, 104, 94
200 × 200	71, 60, 54, 49
150 × 150	40, 34, 27, 23
120 × 120	27, 22, 18, 15
100 × 100	22, 18, 15, 12
90 × 90	16, 13, 11, 9.6, 8.3
80 × 80	12, 9.6, 7.3

Unequal angles

200 × 150	47, 40, 32
200 × 100	34, 27, 23
150 × 90	27, 22, 18
150 × 75	25, 20, 17
137 × 102	17, 15, 12
125 × 75	18, 15, 12, 10

Table VI *Continued*

Nominal size	Available masses per m run
Unequal angles, *continued*	
100 × 75	15, 13, 11
100 × 65	12, 10, 8.8
80 × 60	8.3, 7.4, 6.4
75 × 50	7.4, 5.7
65 × 50	6.8, 5.2, 4.4
60 × 30	4.0, 3.4
40 × 25	1.9
Parallel flange channels	
430 × 100	64
380 × 100	54
300 × 100	46
300 × 90	41
260 × 90	35
260 × 75	28
230 × 90	32
230 × 75	26
200 × 90	30
200 × 75	23
180 × 90	26
180 × 75	20
150 × 90	24
150 × 75	18
125 × 65	15
100 × 50	10

4 BRICKS AND BLOCKS

4.01 Bricks

The work size of the standard clay brick is 215 × 102.5 × 65 (co-ordinating size 225 × 112.5 × 75), and this brick is supplied in an enormous variety of face colours and textures, strengths and other properties. Other brick sizes are made, mostly as specials in limited selections. Metric modular sizes have not achieved the popularity envisaged in the previous edition.

Concrete bricks are covered in BS 6073:Part 2: 1981; the following standard work sizes are given:

$(L \times H \times t)$ 290 × 90 × 90,

215 × 65 × 103,

190 × 90 × 90 and

190 × 65 × 90.

4.02 Building blocks

The standard sizes of blocks are laid down in BS 6073 Part 2: 1981 and given in Table XI. However, manufacturers should be contacted to establish whether blocks of the size, quality and price desired can be readily obtained.

5 PRECAST CONCRETE

5.01 Paving flags

These are manufactured to the requirements of BS 7263 Part 1: 1994 in the dimensions given in Table XII. Tactile flags are used in the pedestrian pavement adjacent to pedestrian crossings to indicate their presence to people who are visually impaired and their dimensions are shown in Table XIII. **46.1** shows details of their construction.

5.02 Concrete kerbs and edgings

46.2 shows the now-standard kerbs and channels from BS 7263: Part 1: 1994 which supersede those unmetricated sizes given in the previous edition. **46.3** shows edgings and quadrants from the same standard.

Table VII Metric steel structural sections
Sizes may be slightly larger or smaller than listed, varying for the different masses given. For details see British Steel publication: *Structural sections in accordance with European specifications*

Nominal size	Mass (kg/m run) – approximate
Beams with parallel flanges to Euronorm 19–57	
750 × 265	222, 210, 196, 185, 173, 160, 147, 137
600 × 225	184, 154, 144, 122, 108
550 × 210	159, 134, 123, 106, 92
500 × 200	129, 111, 107, 91, 79
450 × 190	104, 95, 92, 78, 67
400 × 180	84, 82, 76, 66, 57
360 × 170	70, 66, 57, 50
330 × 160	60, 57, 49, 43
300 × 150	52, 49, 42, 37
270 × 135	44, 42, 36, 31
240 × 120	37, 34, 31, 26
220 × 110	32, 29, 26, 22
200 × 100	27, 25, 22, 18
180 × 90	22, 21, 19, 15
160 × 80	18, 16, 13
140 × 75	14, 13, 11
120 × 65	10, 8.7
100 × 55	8.1, 6.9
Parallel wide flange beams to Euronorm 53–62	
1000 × 300	349, 314, 272, 222
900 × 300	333, 291, 252, 198
800 × 300	317, 262, 224, 172
700 × 300	301, 241, 204, 166, 150
650 × 300	293, 225, 190, 138
600 × 300	285, 212, 178, 174, 151, 137, 129
550 × 300	278, 199, 166, 120
500 × 300	270, 187, 155, 107
450 × 300	263, 171, 140, 123, 100
400 × 300	256, 155, 125, 107, 92
360 × 300	250, 142, 112, 84
340 × 300	248, 134, 105, 79
320 × 300	245, 127, 98, 74
300 × 300	238, 177, 117, 88, 70
280 × 280	189, 103, 76, 61
260 × 260	172, 93, 68, 54
240 × 240	157, 83, 60, 47
220 × 220	117, 72, 51, 40
200 × 200	103, 61, 42, 35
180 × 180	89, 51, 36, 29
160 × 160	76, 43, 30, 24
140 × 140	34, 25, 18
120 × 120	27, 20, 15
100 × 100	20, 17, 12
Equal angles to Euronorm 56–77 and DIN 1028	
200 × 200	71, 60, 54, 49
180 × 180	54, 51, 49, 46, 44, 41, 38, 36
160 × 160	45, 43, 41, 38, 36, 34
150 × 150	40, 34, 32, 27
130 × 130	28, 24, 20
120 × 120	27, 22, 20, 18, 15
110 × 110	20, 17, 14
100 × 100	18, 15, 12, 9.3
90 × 90	21, 16, 12, 9.6
Unequal angles to Euronorm 57–78 and DIN 1029	
200 × 100	32, 27, 23
150 × 100	33, 29, 24
150 × 90	27, 22, 18
150 × 75	22, 19, 15
125 × 75	19, 16, 14, 12
120 × 80	18, 15, 12
100 × 75	15, 14, 13, 12, 11, 9.3
100 × 65	13, 12, 11, 10, 8.8

Table VIII Reduction from basic size to finished size of sawn softwoods

Purpose	For sawn sizes of width or thickness (mm)				
	15 to and inc 22	Over 22 to and inc 35	Over 35 to and inc 100	Over 100 to and inc 150	Over 150
Trim	5	5	7	7	9
Joinery and cabinet work	7	7	9	11	13

Table IX Standard sizes of softwood

Thickness	50	60	63	75	80	90	100	115	120	125	138	140	150	160	175	180	200	220	225	240	250	260	275	300
35				e			e	e		e			e		e		e	e					e	
38	h		f	fnu			*	fu		*	u		*		fhinsuw		fhinuw		fhinuw		uw		hu	uw
40		g																						
44				eh			ehsw					ehsw			ehw		ew		e					
47				uw			uw			uw			uw		uw		uw		uw		uw		w	uw
50	h		h	ehuw	a		*	f	a	*		a	*	af	*	a	*	a	*	a	u	a		u
58													i		i		i		i					
60					g		a		ag			ag	*	ag		ag	g			g				
63				efhi		i	*			*			*	fh	*		ehinswu		ehiswu		h		h	
75				fhw		i	efhw			ehiw			*		*		*		*		h	h	ehw	w
80					ag		ag		acg			acg		g		acg	acg			g				
95							h			h			h											
100				a			acfghuw		acg	h		c	huw	ac	fw	ac	*	c	huw	a	huw		u	cuw
115								f																
120									cg							c	cg	c			c			
125										f														
140				a			a					ac				a		c			c	c		
150													fu				u							
160				a			a		a					acg			a				a	cg		
250																					fu			
300																								fu

Key: *Eurostandard preferred sizes
Additional sizes in the following countries:
a Austria, c Switzerland, e Ireland, f France, g Germany, h Netherlands, i Italy, n Norway, s Finland, u United Kingdom, w Sweden.

Table X Floor boards in mm from BS 1297: 1987

	65	90	113	137
16				
19				
21				
28				

Table XI Standard sizes of building blocks from BS 6073: Part 2: 1981

Work thickness →	60	75	90	100	115	125	140	150	175	190	200	215	220	225	250
Face size: L × H															
590 × 215		*	*	*		*	*	*	*		*	*	*	*	*
590 × 190		*	*	*			*	*		*	*	*	*		
590 × 140		*	*	*			*	*		*	*	*	*		
440 × 290	*	*	*	*			*	*		*	*				
440 × 215	*	*	*	*	*	*	*	*	*	*	*	*	*	*	*
440 × 190	*	*	*	*			*	*		*	*		*	*	
440 × 140	*	*	*	*			*	*		*	*			*	
390 × 190	*	*	*	*	*		*	*		*	*				

Table XII Sizes and types of paving flags from BS 7263: Part 1: 1994

Flag type	Nominal (co-ordinating) size	Work size	Thicknesses
A plain	600 × 450	598 × 448	50, 63
B plain	600 × 600	598 × 598	50, 63
C plain	600 × 750	598 × 748	50, 63
D plain	600 × 900	598 × 898	50, 63
E plain / TA/E tactile	450 × 450	448 × 448	50, 70
F / TA/F tactile	400 × 400	398 × 398	50, 65
G / TA/G tactile	300 × 300	298 × 298	50, 60

When ordering use type letter(s) and thickness, eg 'A 50'

Table XIII Tactile slab dimensions for 46.1

Type of tactile crossing flagstone	Dimension (mm) tolerance ±2 mm	
	X	Y
TA/E	64	33
TA/F	66.8	33
TAG	75	37.5

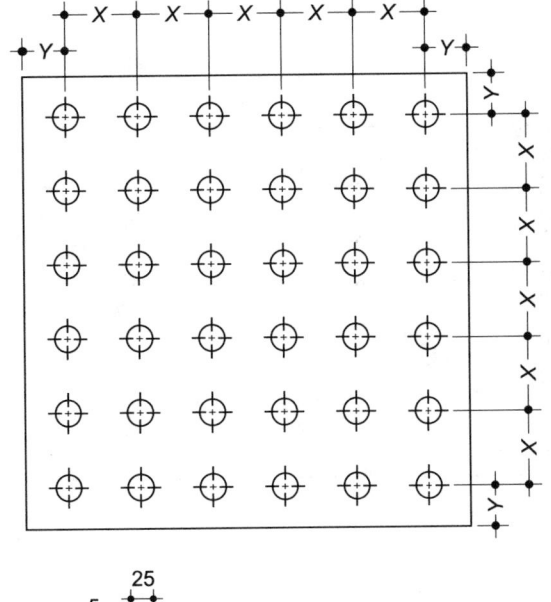

a

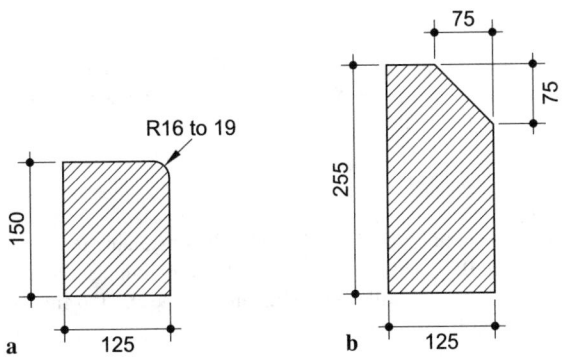

b

46.1 *Construction of tactile paving slabs. For X and Y dimensions see Table XIII*
a *Plan.* **b** *Elevation*

6 ALUMINIUM

6.01 Aluminium bars and flats

Aluminium bars are now made to the requirements of BS 6722: 1986, for details of which see para **2.01** above. Tables XIV to XVI are reprinted from the previous edition to indicate the commonly available sizes.

6.02 Aluminium structural sections

Table XVII based on BS-1161: 1977 gives the sizes of available sections, but does not cover lipped or bulbed sections, for which refer to the BS.

7 ROOFING

7.01 Aluminium sheet for roofing

The standard for aluminium for roofing (CP143 Part 15: 1973) has not changed since the previous edition. Sheeting comes to site in coils 457 mm wide, and are passed through a machine to run up the edges to form seams when applied *in situ*. Because of the supply in coils it is not usually necessary to form joints transverse to the standing seams. The material is available in thicknesses of 0.71 and 0.91 mm, and the seams will be at 365 mm centres.

7.02 Copper

Copper is now covered by BS EN 1172: 1996. Standard thicknesses are 0.5, 0.6, 07, 0.8 and 1.0 mm. Widths less than or equal to 1250 are supplied in lengths of 2 or 3 metres.

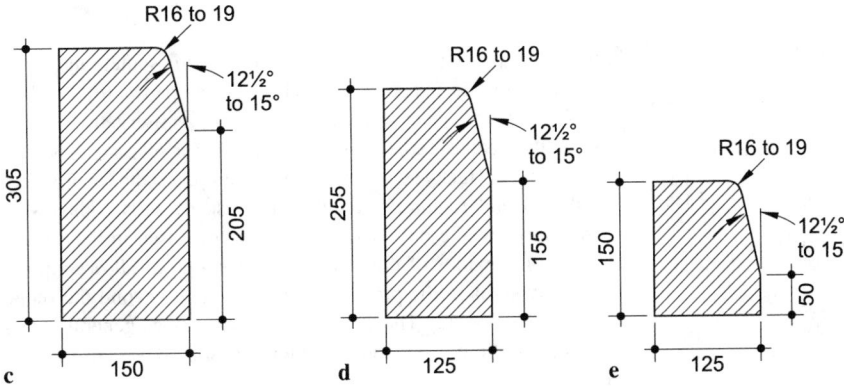

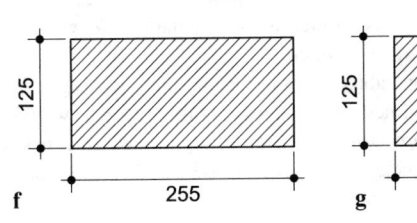

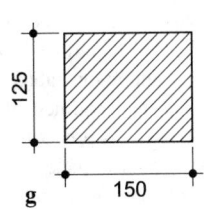

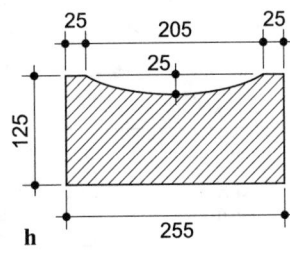

46.2 *Precast concrete kerbs and channels to BS7263 Part 1: 1994*
a *Bullnose kerb type BN.* **b** *45° splayed kerb type SP.* **c** *Half battered kerb type HB1.* **d** *Half battered kerb type HB2.* **e** *Half battered kerb type HB3.* **f** *Channel square type CS1.* **g** *Channel square type CS2.* **h** *Channel dished type CD*

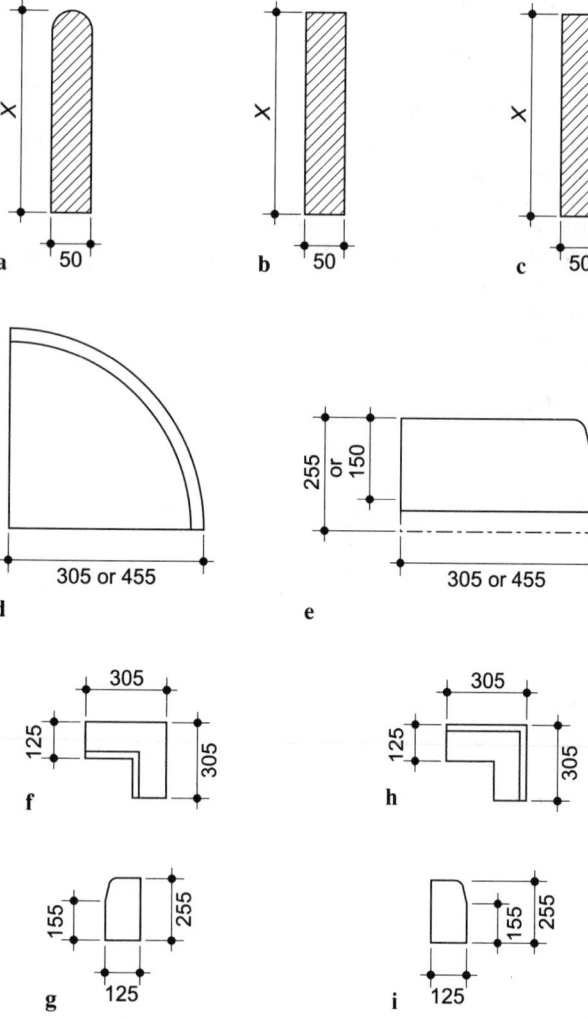

46.3 *Edgings quadrants and angle kerbs to BS 7263: Part 1: 1994.* **a** *Round top edging type ER.* **b** *Flat top edging type EF.* **c** *Bullnose edging type EBN.* **d** *Quadrants may have different profiles to match kerb types: types QBN, QHB or GSP plan.* **e** *Elevation of quadrant.* **f** *Internal angle kerb type IA, plan.* **g** *Internal angle kerb type IA, elevation.* **h** *External angle kerb type XA, plan.* **i** *External angle kerb type XA, elevation*

Table XVI Aluminium flat bars

Width mm	Thickness (mm)								
	1.6	2.5	3	4	6	10	12	16	25
10	–	–	X	–	X	–	–	–	–
12	–	X	X	X	X	X	–	–	–
16	–	X	X	X	X	X	–	–	–
20	–	X	X	X	X	–	–	–	–
25	X	X	X	X	X	X	X	X	–
30	–	X	X	X	X	X	X	–	–
40	–	X	X	X	X	X	X	–	–
50	–	–	X	X	X	X	X	–	X
60	–	–	X	–	X	X	X	–	–
80	–	–	X	–	X	X	X	–	X
100	–	–	X	–	X	X	X	X	X
120	–	–	–	–	X	X	–	X	–
160	–	–	–	–	X	X	–	X	–
200	–	–	–	–	–	X	–	X	–
250	–	–	–	–	–	X	–	X	–

Two methods of copper roofing are available: traditional and long-strip. Fully annealed copper strip conforming to BS 2870: 1980 C101, C102, or preferably C104 or C106 is used in traditional roofing as detailed in Table XVIII. For long-strip roofing the material used is 1/8 to 1/4 hard temper copper strip, also in conformity with the above specification, and as shown in Table XIX.

7.03 Lead
Sizes of milled lead sheet and strip are laid down in BS 1178: 1982, summarised in Table XX. The Code of Practice for roof covering is BS 6915: 1988.

7.04 Zinc
Zinc is now covered by BS EN 988: 1997. It is available in metric thicknesses of 0.6, 0.65, 0.7, 0.8 and 1.0 mm, but as the old traditional gauge may still be encountered Table XXI from the previous edition is reprinted here.

8 GLASS
Since our previous edition there has been something of a revolution in the use of glass. This is due partly to Building Regulations and their influence on energy conservation which makes the use of solar control and similar glasses virtually mandatory in many situations. In addition, health and safety legislation and regulation requires the use of safety glasses in many places where ordinary glazing has been used in the past.

The complexities of this situation means that a full description of each type (as in the previous edition) is now beyond the scope of this handbook. There is really only one general glass manufacturer in Britain, and their literature should be consulted for details.

A summary of the different functions is given in Table XXII, and the different types of glass related to these functions is covered by Table XXIII. Many of the types have proprietary names which will be found in the trade literature, particularly *Glass* from Pilkington United Kingdom Limited.

A general point on this table relates to the maximum sizes given. It should not be assumed that panes of these sizes would necessarily be safe. A procedure for determining the safe thickness of glass for a specific pane size is given in BS 6262: 1982, Code of practice for glazing for buildings.

Table XIV Recommended metric sizes for aluminium and aluminium alloy round bars

Diameter (mm)				
3.0	12.0	30.0	65.0	130.0
4.0	14.0	32.0	70.0	140.0
5.0	16.0	35.0	75.0	160.0
6.0	18.0	40.0	80.0	180.0
7.0	20.0	45.0	90.0	200.0
8.0	22.0	50.0	100.0	
9.0	25.0	55.0	110.0	
10.0	28.0	60.0	120.0	

Table XV Recommended metric sizes for aluminium and aluminium alloy square bars

Side (mm)				
3.0	8.0	20.0	50.0	120.0
4.0	10.0	25.0	60.0	160.0
5.0	12.0	30.0	80.0	200.0
6.0	16.0	40.0	100.0	

Table XVII Aluminium structural sections to BS 1161: 1977

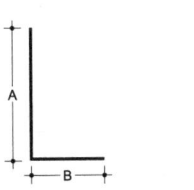

Equal angles

Nominal size	Thickness	Mass (kg/m)
120 × 120	10	6.47
	7	4.68
100 × 100	8	4.31
	6	3.34
80 × 80	6	2.59
	5	2.23
60 × 60	3.5	1.17
50 × 50	5	1.62
	3	0.836
40 × 40	3	0.647
30 × 30	2.5	0.404

Unequal angles

Nominal size	Thickness	Mass (kg/m)
140 × 105	11	7.26
	8.5	5.83
120 × 90	10	5.65
	7	4.11
100 × 75	8	3.77
	6	2.94
80 × 60	6	2.26
	5	1.96
60 × 45	5	1.41
	3.5	1.03
50 × 38	4	0.947
	3	0.738

Table XVII *Continued*

Channels

Nominal size	Thickness		Mass (kg/m)
	Web	Flange	
240 × 100	9	13	12.5
200 × 80	8	12	9.19
180 × 75	8	11	8.06
160 × 70	7	10	6.58
140 × 60	7	10	5.66
120 × 50	6	9	4.19
100 × 40	6	8	3.20
80 × 35	5	7	2.29
60 × 30	5	6	1.69

I-section

Nominal size	Thickness		Mass (kg/m)
	Web	Flange	
160 × 80	7	11	7.64
140 × 70	7	10	6.33
120 × 60	6	9	4.77
100 × 50	6	8	3.72
80 × 40	5	7	2.54
60 × 30	4	6	1.59

Tees

Nominal size	Thickness	Mass (kg/m)
120 × 90	10	5.68
100 × 75	8	3.79
80 × 60	6	2.27
60 × 45	5	1.42
50 × 38	4	0.952

Table XVIII Thicknesses and sizes of copper sheet for traditional roofing

Thickness mm	Bay width Standing seam mm	Roll mm	Standard width of sheet to form bay mm	Length of each sheet m	Mass kg/m²
0.45	525	500	600	1.8	4.0
0.60	525	500	600	1.8	5.4
0.70	675	650	750	1.8	6.3

Table XIX Maximum widths and lengths of copper strip for the long strip system

	Thickness mm	Width of strip mm	Centres of standing seams mm	Length of each panel m
Normal conditions	0.6	600	525	8.5
Exposed conditions	0.6	450	375	8.5

9 WINDOWS AND DOORS

9.01 Windows and door frames are generally available in four materials:

- Wood
- Steel
- Aluminium
- Unplasticised vinyl chloride (UPVC)

As much work of the industry is in the field of replacements for deteriorated existing windows and doors, it has tended to retain imperial rounded dimensions, although they may be expressed in millimetres. Co-ordinated dimensions do exist for new construction, and the drawings in the previous edition are here reproduced as Tables XXIV to XXVI.

9.02 Doors

Although doors of steel and of aluminium construction are manufactured for mainly external use, these are usually classified as windows, and will be found in that section. Doors of basically timber construction are available in old imperial sizes for replacement purposes. Metrically co-ordinated sizes are shown in

Table XX Milled lead sheet and strip sizes to BS 1178: 1982

BS Code no.	Thickness (mm)	Average weight (kg/m²)	Colour marking
3	1.32	14.97	green
4	1.80	20.41	blue
5	2.24	25.40	red
6	2.65	30.06	black
7	3.15	35.72	white
8	3.55	40.26	orange

Table XXI Traditional Zinc gauges

Gauge	Thickness mm	Mass kg/m²
1	0.102	0.73
2	0.152	1.10
3	0.178	1.28
4	0.203	1.16
5	0.254	1.83
6	0.279	2.01
7	0.330	2.38
8	0.381	2.74
9	0.432	3.11
10	0.483	3.48
11	0.559	4.02
12	0.635	4.57
13	0.711	5.12
14*	0.787	5.67
15*	0.914	6.58
16*	1.041	7.50
17	1.168	8.41
18	1.295	9.33
19	1.448	10.43
20	1.600	11.52
21	1.778	12.80

*Normal gauges for external building work nos 14, 15 and 16

Tables XXVII to XXVIII. Standard door leaf thicknesses are 40 or 44 mm, and heights 2040 mm internally, 1994 mm for external situations.

Doors come in a variety of patterns, principally those shown in **46.4** and **46.5**. The different ways that these are used are covered in Tables XXIX and XXX.

9.03 Disabled people

When specifying or designing doors and windows, consideration should be given to the needs of disabled people. For wheelchair

Table XXII Functions of glazing from Pilkington United Kingdom Limited

Orientation of glazing	Principal requirement	Primary function						
		Environmental control			Fire resistance	Safety and security	Privacy and appearance	Structural strength
		Solar control	Thermal insulation	Acoustic insulation				
Factor		A	B	C	D	E	F	G
Vertical	Curtain walling	*	*	*				*
	Window	*	*	*		*	*	
	Door				*	*	*	
	Barrier					*		*
	Partition			*	*	*	*	*
	Vision panel				*	*	*	
Horizontal or sloping	Sloping wall	*	*			*		*
	Roof glazing	*	*			*		*
	Canopy					*	*	*
	Floor				*	*		*

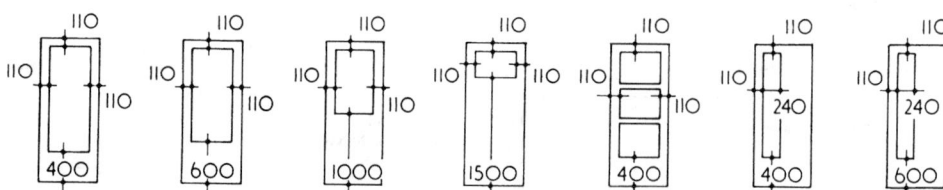

46.4 *Standard glazing in flush doors to BS 4787*

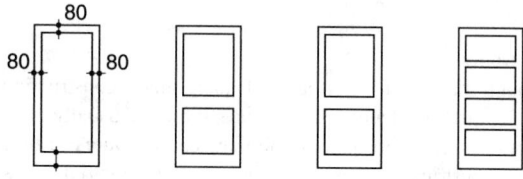

46.5 *Standard glazing in panelled doors to BS 4787*

users clear door openings should never be less than 750 mm, and should preferably be 800 mm or greater, particularly when the wheelchair may need to turn into the opening. It will be seen from Tables XXVII and XXVIII that internal door sets of 900 mm with single leaf, and external door sets of 1000 mm are minimum requirements. Narrower doors should only be used for cupboards or service spaces into which wheelchairs will not ever be required to enter.

Table XXIII Types of glass and glazing from Pilkington United Kingdom Limited

No.	Type	Functions (see Table XXII)	Thicknesses (mm)	Maximum size (mm)	Minimum size when supplied toughened (mm)
1	Clear float glass		4 5, 6, 8, 10, 12 15 19	1500×2200 2000×4200 1700×4200 1500×4200	300×500
2	Insulating units	B C	various	check with manufacturer	
3	Low emissivity (<0.2) glass	B	4 6	1500×2200 2000×4200	300×500
4	Clear float glass with low E coating	B	6, 10	2000×3500	300×750
5	Tinted float glass with very low E coating	A B	6	2000×3500	300×750
6	Tinted float glass with very low external reflection	A	6	1500×2200 2000×3500	300×750
7	High-performance reflective solar control coated float glass	A	6	1500×2200 2000×3500	300×750
8	Medium-performance reflective solar control coated float glass	A	6	2000×4200	300×500
9	Medium-performance silver/bronze reflective solar control coated clear float glass	A	4 5, 6	1500×2200 1800×3300	300×500
10	Low/medium solar control body tinted glass	A	4 (bronze, grey, green) 5, 6, 8, 10, 12 (bronze, grey) 6 (blue) 6, 10 (green)	1500×2200 2000×4200 2000×300 2000×4200	300×500
11	Spandrel panel of toughened glass with coloured ceramic coating	A B	6, 8, 10, 12	1500×3000	300×500
12	Spandrel panel of solar control glass of one of the above types treated with a silicone opacifier	A B	6, 10	1500×2600	300×750
13	Laminated glass with a special acoustic cast-in-place (CIP) resin interlayer	C	7, 9, 11, 13 and 17	2100×3500	300×300
14	Clear glass with a 13 mm square electrically welded, chemically treated steel wire mesh sandwiched in the centre during the continuous rolling manufacturing process	D G	6	1985×3300	
15	As 14 but with a stronger and thicker steel mesh	D E G	6	1985×3300	
16	As 14 but with using a textured glass	D G	7	1985×3500	
17	As 15 using a textured glass	D E G	7	1985×3500	
18	A product with three glass layers, an intumescent interlayer and an ultraviolet interlayer giving Class B impact performance to BS 6206 and 30 min fire integrity	D	10	1400×2000 (as tested)	
19	As 18, but with four glass layers and two intumescent layers giving Class A impact performance and 60 min fire integrity	D	13	1400×2000 (as tested)	
20	A product with four glass layers and three intumescent interlayers for internal use	D	15	1600×2600 (as tested)	
21	As 20 but with five glass layers and four intumescent layers	D	21	1600×2200 (as tested)	
22	Combinations of 20/21 or 21/21 with an 8 mm cavity between	D	44, 50	1400×2000 (as tested)	
23	A range of products as 20 to 22 but with additional glass layers incorporating a UV filter layer. These are for external use where sunlight may degrade the intumescent interlayers	D	18 27 47, 56	1600×2600 (as tested) 1600×2200 (as tested) 1400×2000 (as tested)	
24	Toughened glass: a range of glass products manufactured by subjecting final size edgeworked panes to a heating and cooling treatment	E G	Details in the various types		
25	Laminated glass: a range of products made by combining two or more glass sheets with one or more plastic interlayers, which may be of polyvinalbutyral (PVB) or of resin CIP. See Table XXII	C E F G	6.4	3210×2500	
26	A product specifically for shop doors and windows using laminated anti-bandit glass permanently bonded to steel beading to be internally fixed to conventional openings	E			
27	A series of glasses having specially formulated coatings which resist the transmission of electromagnetic radiation using the Faraday cage principle. These are for use where interference with computer or communication equipment must be avoided	E	various	1300×2400 (laminated) 2000×3500 (insulating)	
28	One-way glass having a partial mirror coating which allows vision only from a dark side to a light one	E	6 mm annealed or 6.4 mm laminated	2100×3210	
29	One-way glass with vertical mirror stripes for where lighting levels are similar on each side	E	4	1220×1840	
30	A frame containing two striped panes and an internal louvred glass allowing adjustment for vision or obscuration.	E		400×400 only size available	
31	Textured glass in a variety of patterns	F	3 (not available toughened) 4 and 6	1200×1200	300×500
32	Acid etched glass	F	4 and 6	1320×1840	
33	Sand blasted glass	F	various		

Table XXIII *Continued*

No.	Type	Functions (see Table XXII)	Thicknesses (mm)	Maximum size (mm)	Minimum size when supplied toughened (mm)
34	Float glass printed with a ceramic ink design and subsequently fired and toughened	F	4–15	1500 × 2700	200 × 350
35	Two sheets of float glass with a CIP resin layer formulated to reduce ultraviolet transmittance (three grades available)	A	8	2100 × 3500	300 × 500
36	An on-line pyrolitically coated float glass with a very high reflectance and a low light transmittance. This, depending on the lighting conditions will act either as a mirror or as a viewing mirror	F	3, 4 and 6	2240 × 3300	
37	Silvered float glass for mirrors	F	various	as for float	
38	As 37 but decorated for advertisement purposes	F	various	as for float	
39	Stained glass	F	bespoke		
40	Glass with self-adhesive coloured film	F	various		
41	Glass with fired-on transfer	F	4–12	1000 × 1500	
42	Leaded glass: small individual pieces joined using lead cames. The glass can be float or more commony textured	F	4 or less	2000 × 3500	
43	Bevelled glass	F	4 or more	1200 × 1800	100 × 100
44	Brilliant cut glass	F	4–12	1400 × 2500	
45	Shaped cut glasses, panes with non-rectangular and curved sides	F			
46	A total system combining superior engineering, fittings and glass.	G	10, 12		
47	Another high performance cladding system with a flush all-glass exterior surface	G			
48	Thick float glass	C G	10–25		

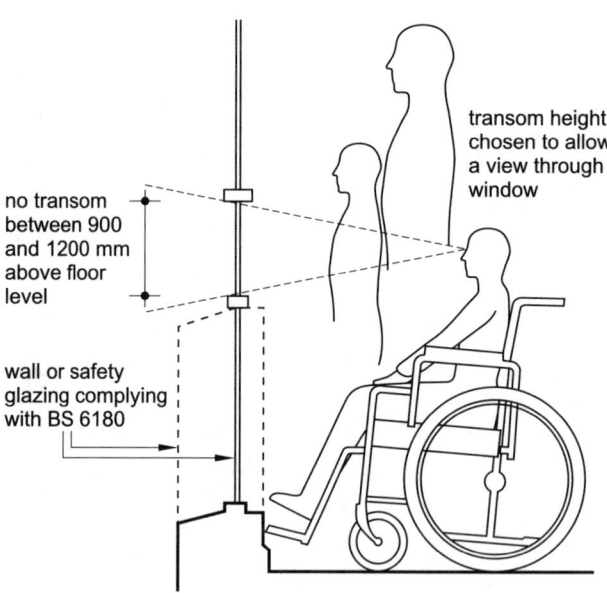

46.6 *Height of window opening to allow a view from a wheelchair or a chair*

Windows also need to be carefully designed so that a transom interrupting vision for a seated person should not be between 900 and 1200 mm from the floor, **46.6** Safety considerations also dictate that no opening in a window (other than a french window) should be less than 800 mm from the floor; also it is desirable that all glazing below this level should be of a safety type. The height for window controls to be used by people in wheelchairs should be between 800 and 1000 mm from the floor, and no window control should be above 1650 mm from the floor.

10 PIPES FOR PLUMBING AND DRAINAGE

10.01 Pipes for the conveyance of liquids and gases vary widely in material, quality, size and jointing methods. Many types are still based on inch measures and Whitworth screw threads, particularly as these were and are widely used not just in the United Kingdom but also in continental Europe. Even where pipe sizes are metricated, they do not always conform to the recommended series of dimensions. This series requires the outside diameter of a pipe

Table XXIV Co-ordinating sizes of timber windows

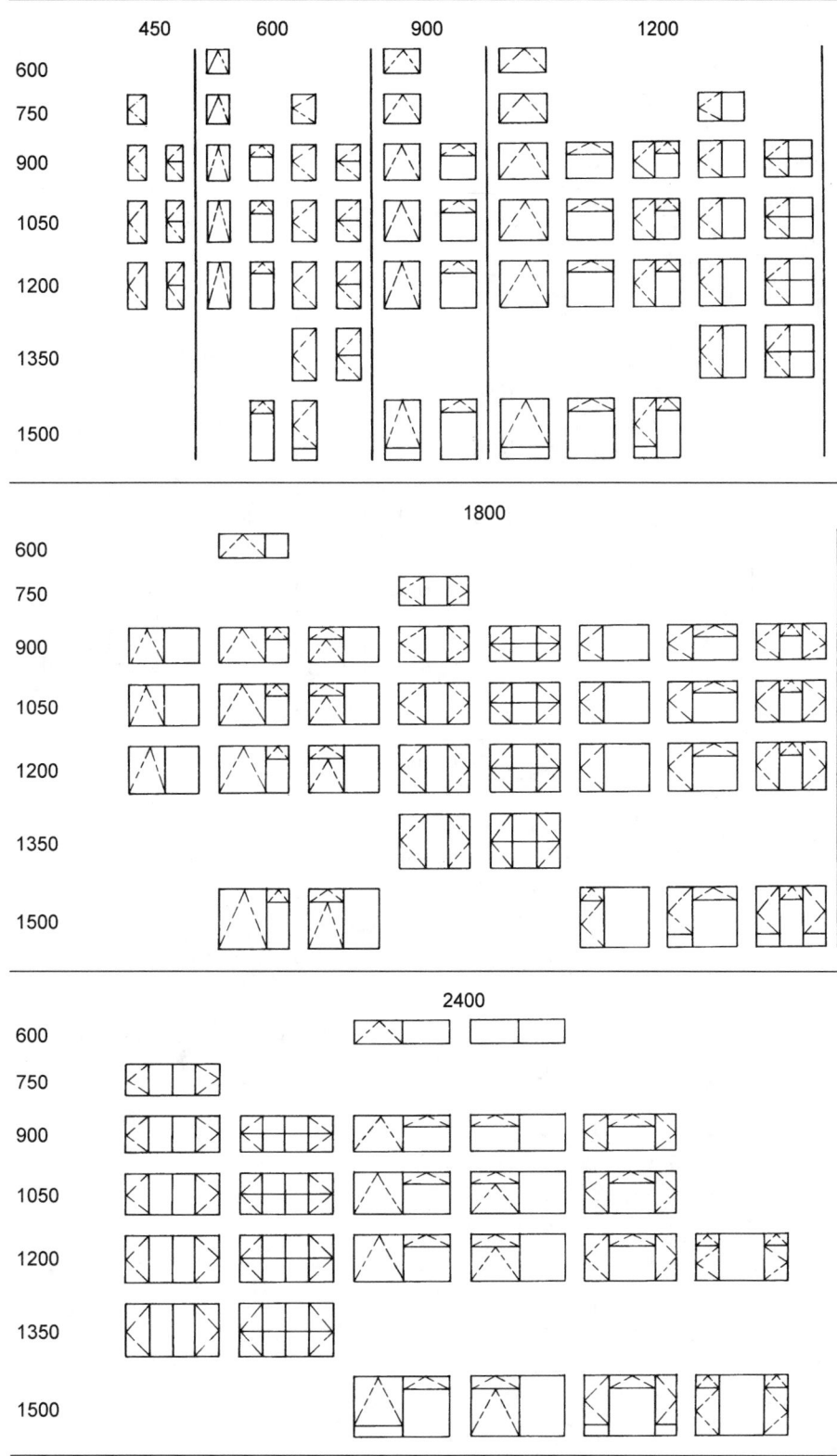

to be one of the following (in mm): 2.5, 3, 4, 5, 6, 8, 10, 12, 16, 20, 25, 32, 40, 50, 63, 75, 90, 110, 125, 140, 160, 180, 200, 225, 250, 280, 315, 355, 400, 450, 500, 560, 630, 710, 800, 900, 1000, 1200, 1400, 1600, 1800 or 2000.

10.02 Pipe materials

Pipes are made of the following materials:

● Steel
● Copper
● Stainless steel
● Cast iron
● Plastics
● Glass (for specialist laboratories, etc)
● Vitrified clay.

Steel and copper are used in thick- and thin-walled versions, depending on the system of connection.

Table XXV Co-ordinating sizes of steel windows

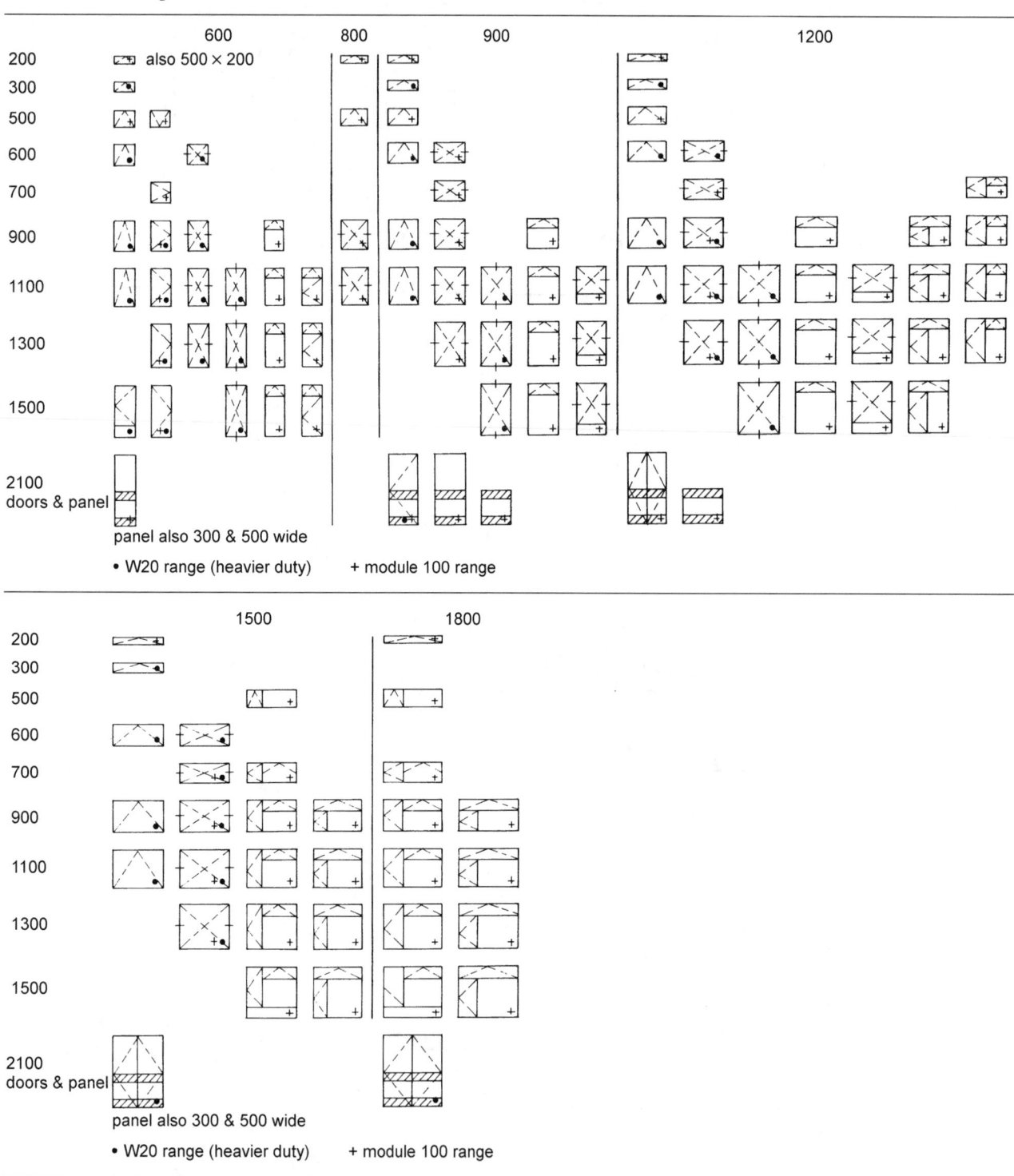

panel also 300 & 500 wide

• W20 range (heavier duty)   + module 100 range

Table XXVI Co-ordinating sizes of aluminium windows

Table XXVII Co-ordinating sizes of internal doorsets

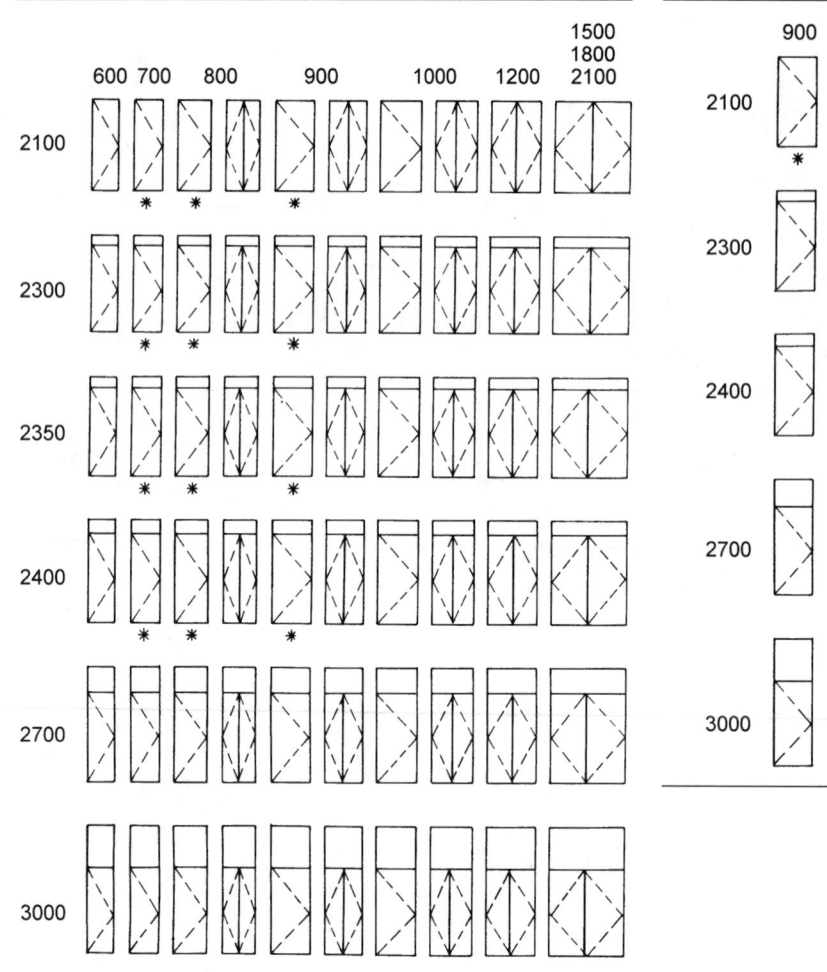

Table XXVIII Co-ordinating sizes of external doorsets

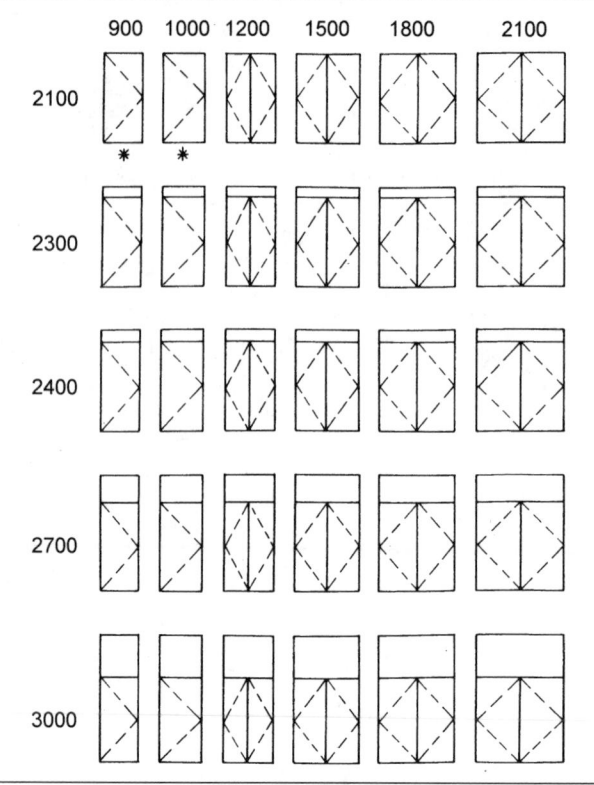

10.03 Pipe joints
The methods in general use are:

- Screwed joints – steel, plastic and copper (rarely nowadays)
- Welding – steel
- Spigot and socket dry (push-fit)
- Spigot and socket with cementitious material – cast iron
- Spigot and socket with solvent cement – plastics
- Compression fittings – copper, stainless steel, light-gauge steel, plastics
- Capillary soldering – copper.

10.04 Insulation
Pipes carrying hot or chilled liquids, or in exposed conditions, will be insulated. The thickness of insulation will be between 25 and 75 mm depending on material used and the size of the pipe. After allowing for any such insulation, the space allowed for any pipe should be between two to three times the actual diameter of the barrel. This will allow for sockets, joints, bends and clearances.

10.05 Steel pipes for screwed joints
These are available in light, medium and heavy qualities. The sizes given in Table XXXI are to international standard ISO/65, and are based on nominal inch sizes.

10.06 Copper
Copper pipes are specified in accordance with EN 1057-R25. Joints in these pipes are made with compression fittings or capillary soldered fittings. There are three quality grades:

EN 1057-R220 soft
EN 1057-R250 half-hard
EN 1057-R290 hard

Sizes and thicknesses are given in Table XXXII.

10.07 Stainless steel
These are used as a lower-cost substitute for copper pipe. They are supplied in the same sizes corresponding to external diameter, as above.

10.08 Cast iron
Cast iron pipes are still made to the following three specifications:

- BS 460: 1964 Light grade rainwater pipes
- BS 416 Part 1: 1990 for soil waste and vent pipes with spigots and sockets above ground
- BS 416 Part 2: 1990 for socketless systems
- BS 437: 1978 for underground pipework, whether buried or in ducts.

They are made in nominal inch sizes, the external diameters of which are given in Table XXXIII.

10.09 Plastics
The types of plastic used for pipes, and the uses of the pipes, are both numerous. Consequently, there are a considerable number of British and European Standards governing this material. BS 3867: 1987 lays down some general information on sizing and pressure

Table XXIX Types of internal doors

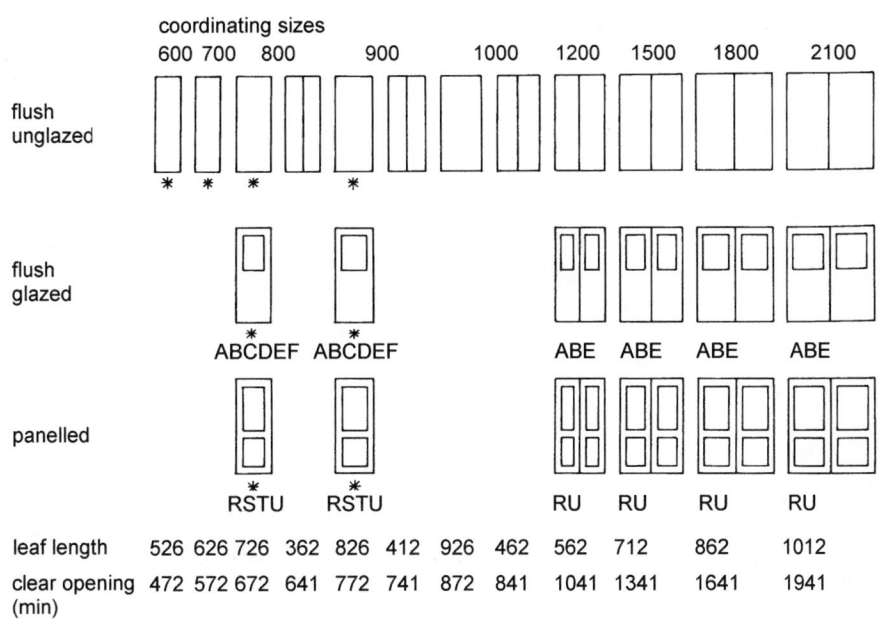

leaf length 526 626 726 362 826 412 926 462 562 712 862 1012

clear opening (min) 472 572 672 641 772 741 872 841 1041 1341 1641 1941

Table XXX Types of external doors

coordinating sizes
900 1000 1200 1500 1800 2100

flush unglazed

flush glazed
BCDG BCDG B B B B

panelled
RSTU RSTU RU RU RU RU

leaf length 807 907 552 702 825 1002

clear opening (min) 751 851 1018 1318 1618 1918

Table XXXII Sizes of copper pipes to BS EN 1057

Size; external diameter	Thicknesses
R220 and R250	
6	0.6, 0.8
8	0.6, 0.8
10	0.7, 0.8
12	0.6, 0.8
15	0.7, 1.0
22	0.9, 1.2
28	0.9, 1.2
35	1.2, 1.5
42	1.2, 1.5
54	1.2, 2.0
66.7	1.2, 2.0
76.1	1.5, 2.0
108	1.5, 2.5
R250	
133	1.5
159	2.0

Table XXXI Mean outside diameters of steel pipes (mm)

Nominal bore in	mm	Light	Medium and heavy
⅓	6	9.9	10.1
¼	8	13.4	13.6
⅜	10	16.9	17.1
½	15	21.2	21.4
¾	20	26.6	26.9
1	25	33.5	33.8
1¼	32	42.2	42.5
1½	40	48.1	48.4
2	50	59.9	60.3
2½	65	75.6	76.0
3	80	88.3	88.8
4	100	113.4	114.1
5	125	–	139.6

Table XXXIII Maximum external diameters of cast iron pipe (mm)

Nominal bore		BS 460 rainwater pipes		BS 416 above ground s, w and v		BS 437 below ground	
in	mm	pipe	socket	pipe	socket	pipe	socket
2	50	54	69	64	89	65	117
2½	65	67	89	76	103	–	–
3	75	79	94	89	116	92	150
3½	90	–	–	102	130	–	–
4	100	105	120	114	143	119	185
5	125	130	146	140	171	–	–
6	150	156	175	165	197	173	239
9	225	–	–	–	–	256	337

Table XXXIV Sizes of plastic pipes to BS 3867: 1987 (More larger sizes are also included in the standard)

Size: nominal inches	Mean external diameter (mm)
⅛	10.2
¼	13.5
⅜	17.2
½	21.3
¾	26.9
1	33.7
1¼	42.4
1½	48.3
2	60.3
2½	75.3
3	88.9
4	114.3
6	168.3

Table XXXV Sizes of polypropylene and thermoplastic waste pipes to BS 5254: 1976 and BS 5255: 1989

Nominal size: in/mm	Outside diameter (mm)
1¼/32	38.25 ± 0.15
1½/40	44.60 ± 0.15
2/50	57.30 ± 0.15

Table XXXVI Dimensions of PVC insulated, PVC sheathed electric cables (mm)

Cross-sectional area of single conductor (mm²)	Approximate normal rating (amps)	Single (dia)	Flat twin	Flat three	Flat twin + earth	Flat three + earth
1.0	6	4.2	6.7 × 4.4	9.0 × 4.4	7.8 × 4.4	10.2 × 4.4
1.5	8	4.4	7.2 × 4.6	9.8 × 4.6	8.3 × 4.6	11.0 × 4.7
2.5	11	5.0	8.6 × 5.4	11.9 × 5.5	9.7 × 5.4	13.0 × 5.5
4.0	15	6.2	10.7 × 6.5	15.0 × 6.7	12.0 × 6.5	
6.0	19	6.8	12.0 × 7.3	16.7 × 7.3	13.8 × 7.3	
10.0	26	8.1	14.9 × 8.8	21.0 × 8.9	17.4 × 8.8	

Table XXXVII Dimensions of flexible electric cords (for connection of mobile appliances to outlets)

Cross-sectional area of single conductor (mm²)	Suspension capacity (kg)	Approximate normal rating (amps)	Tough rubber sheathed			Circular cotton braided		PVC sheathed			
			twin	three-core	four-core	twin	three-core	twin flat	twin round	three-core	four-core
0.5	2	3	6.2	6.6	7.3	5.1	5.5	4.0 × 6.1	6.1	6.5	7.0
0.75	3	6	6.6	7.2	7.8	6.3	6.8	4.2 × 6.5	6.5	6.9	7.5
1.0	5	10	7.2	7.8	8.3	6.7	7.2		6.9	7.3	8.2
1.5	5	15	8.8	9.3	10.3	7.3	7.8		7.5	8.1	9.0
2.5	5	20	10.2	10.9	12.1					9.8	10.8
4.0	5	25	12.1	12.8	14.2					11.6	12.7

gradings for inch-series pipes, as given in Table XXXIV. BS 5254: 1976 covers polypropylene waste pipes and fittings and BS 5255: 1989 those of thermoplastic material. Table XXXV gives the dimensions of these limited ranges.

10.10 Pipes of vitrified clay
These pipes are covered in BS EN 295. The series of sizes is as follows, with the first preference in ordinary type and the second in italics:

75, 100, *125*, 150, *175*, *200*, *225*, *250*, 300, 375, 450, 525, 600, 675, 750, 825, 900 mm

11 MATERIALS FOR ELECTRICITY SUPPLY AND DISTRIBUTION

11.01 Electricity supply and distribution cables are mainly:

● Armoured cable for intake (not covered here, see the technical literature)
● PVC insulated, in conduits of steel or plastic
● PVC insulated, PVC sheathed
● Mineral insulated copper (or aluminium) conductors

● Wiring harnesses (manufactured for specific locations, hence non-standard).

11.02 PVC double-insulated cables
These are normally used in electrical distribution for the smaller building types. Table XXXVI gives the dimensions of these, which are often accommodated in small ducts or voids in the construction. Conductor cross-sectional areas of 1 and 1.5 mm² are used for lighting circuits, while ring mains are composed of cables with conductors of 2.5 mm². Since earth-continuity conductors are now used in all circuits, all cable types have integral earth conductors. Cables with three insulated cores plus earth are used for circuits with two-way switching of lights. Flexible electrical cords for the connection of mobile and portable equipment are detailed in Table XXXVII.

11.03 Mineral insulated cables (MICC or 'pyro')
These are used mainly when space is at a premium, or in external situations. Table XXXVIII gives the dimensions of these.

11.04 Steel conduits
These are covered in BS 4568: Part 1: 1970, and conduits of plastics in BS 4607: Part 1: 1984; summarised in Table XXXIX.

Table XXXVIII Sizes of mineral insulated cables

No of conductors	Cross-sectional area of single conductor (mm²)	Copper sheathed			Aluminium sheathed		
		Approximate normal rating (amps)		Cable diameter over copper sheath (mm)	Approximate normal rating (amps)		Cable diameter over aluminium sheath (mm)
		single-phase	three-phase		single-phase	three-phase	
1	1.0	22	18	3.1			
	1.5	27	23	3.4			
	2.5	36	31	3.8			
	4.0	46	41	4.4			
	6	63	56	6.4			
	10	85	75	7.3			
	16	112	99	8.3	100*	88*	8.6
	25	146	128	9.6	130*	114*	9.9
2	1.0	17		5.1	19		5.4
	1.5	22		5.7	24		5.4
	2.5	29		6.6	33	6.8	
	4.0	38		7.7	44		7.9
	6	53		10.9	55		9.0
	10	71		12.7			
	16	94		14.7	84*		15.0
	25	124		17.1	113*		18.8
3	1.0	14	14	5.8	16	16	6.0
	1.5	18	18	6.4	21	21	6.6
	2.5	26	26	9.3			
	4.0	34	34	10.4			
	6	44	44	11.5			
	10	59	59	13.6			
	16	78	78	15.6	71*	71*	16.0
	25	103	103	18.2	94*	94*	20.0
4	1.0	15	15	6.3	16	16	6.0
	1.5	19	19	7.0	21	21	7.3
	2.5	27	27	10.1			
	4.0	35	35	11.4			

* Aluminium conductors

Table XXXIX Electrical conduits

Nominal size corresponding to maximum external diameter d₁	Minimum internal diameter d_2					Non-circular conduits	
	Steel		Rigid PVC	Pliable plastic self-extinguishing		Maximum outside dims	Minimum inside dims
	Light gauge plain ends	Heavy gauge screwed ends		Plain	Corrugated		
13	–	–	–	–	–	13.0 × 8.1	11.0 × 6.1
16	13.5	12.7	13.0	10.7	11.7	16.3 × 9.9	14.3 × 7.9
20	17.5	16.2	16.9	14.1	15.5	22.6 × 11.4	20.6 × 9.4
25	21.9	21.1	21.4	18.4	19.8	28.7 × 11.4	26.5 × 9.2
32	28.9	28.1	27.8	24.4	26.4	32.5 × 11.4	30.3 × 9.2
40	–	–	–	31.2	34.0	–	–
50	–	–	–	39.7	43.5	–	–
63	–	–	–	49.6	56.0	–	–

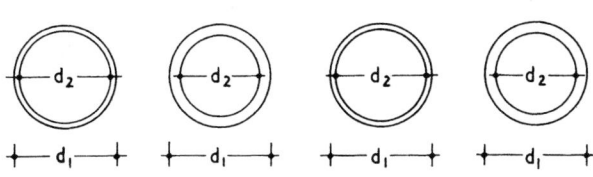
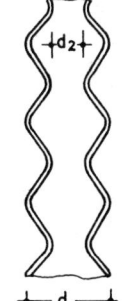
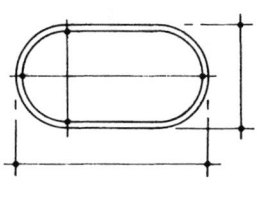

Table XL Circular boxes for electrical conduit systems: minimum outside dimensions (diameter × depth)

Box type	Nominal conduit size	Rigid PVC	Cast iron	Steel
Small circular box	16	64.4 × 28.6	64.3 × 27.0	63.2 × 26.5
	20	64.4 × 28.6	64.3 × 27.0	63.2 × 26.5
	25	64.4 × 31.8	64.3 × 30.0	63.2 × 29.5
Cover thickness		–	2.4	1.15
Circular looping box	16	64.6 × 32 (nom)	67.5 × 34.0	66.4 × 33.5
	20	64.6 × 32 (nom)	67.5 × 34.0	66.4 × 33.5
	25	–	67.5 × 34.0	66.4 × 33.5
Cover thickness		–	2.0	1.47
Large circular box	20		86.6 × 37.8	85.7 × 36.5
	25		86.6 × 37.8	85.7 × 36.5
	32		86.6 × 40.8	85.7 × 39.5
Cover thickness			3.2	1.47
Extension rings	20	nominal depths of 13, 20, 25 and 32 mm	–	–

Table XLI Rectangular boxes for the accommodation of electrical wiring accessories

Box type	Nominal conduit sizes	External face dimensions	Nominal external depth Insulating material	Cast iron	Steel
UA1	16, 20 and 25	75 × 75	17.5	18.0	17.0
			27.0	27.3	26.2
			37.0	37.3	36.2
			43.0	43.3	42.2
			49.0	49.3	48.2
UA2	16, 20 and 25	135 × 75	17.5	18.0	17.0
			27.0	27.3	26.2
			37.0	37.3	36.2
			43.0	43.3	42.2
			49.0	49.3	48.2
UA3	20 and 25	195 × 75	43.0	43.3	42.2
UA4	20 and 25	135 × 135	43.0	43.3	42.2
UA6	20 and 25	195 × 135	43.0	43.3	42.2

These British Standards also give details of the round connection boxes used for junctions, looping and for the attachment of ceiling roses (known colloquially as 'beezer' boxes). Table XL summaries the dimensional information about these in the standards. As far as steel conduits are concerned, it is worth noting that these are obtainable in four classes of protection:

● Class 1: Light protection inside and out (priming paint)
● Class 2: Medium protection inside and out (stove enamel, air-drying paint)
● Class 3: Medium heavy protection, inside as class 2, outside as class 4
● Class 4: Heavy protection inside and out (hot-dip zinc coating, sherardised).

11.05 Rectangular boxes
Boxes of the type used to accommodate wiring accessories such as switches, socket outlets, cooker points etc are covered by BS 4662: 1970. These are summarised in Table XLI.

Appendix A
The SI system

Table I Base units of the SI system

Quantity	Name of unit	Unit symbol
Length	metre	m
Mass	kilogram	kg
Tme	second	s
Electric current	ampere	A
Thermodynamic temperature	kelvin*	K
Amount of substance	mole	mol
Luminous intensity	candela	cd
Supplementary units		
Plane angle	radian	rad
Solid angle	steradian	sr

Table II Derived SI units

Quantity	Name of unit	Symbol	Remarks
Frequency	hertz	Hz	$1\,Hz = s^{-1}$
Force	newton	N	$1\,N = 1\,kg.m/s^2$
Pressure Stress	pascal	Pa	$1\,Pa = 1\,N/m^2$
Energy Work Quantity of heat	joule	J	$1\,J = 1\,N._m$
Power Radiant flux	watt	W	$1\,W = 1\,J/s$
Electric charge Quantity of electricity	coulomb	C	$1\,C = 1\,A._s$
Electric potential Potential difference Tension Electromotive force	volt	V	$1\,V = 1\,W/A$
Capacitance	farad	F	$1\,F = 1\,C/V$
Electrical resistance	ohm	Ω	$1\,\Omega = 1\,V/A$
Electrical conductance	siemens	S	$1\,S = 1\,\Omega^{-1}$
Magnetic flux	weber	Wb	$1\,Wb = 1\,V.s$
Magnetic flux density	tesla	T	$1\,T = 1\,Wb/m^2$
Inductance	henry	H	$1\,H = 1\,Wb/A$
Celsius temperature	degree Celsius	°C	$1\,°C = 1\,K$
Luminous flux	lumen	lm	$1\,lm = 1\,cd_{sr}$
Illuminance	lux	lx	$1\,lx = 1\,lm/m^2$

Table III Multiples and submultiples of SI units

Power of 10	Prefix	Symbol
24	yetta	Y
21	zetta	Z
18	exa	E
15	peta	P
12	tera	T
9	giga	G
6	mega	M
3	kilo	k
2	hecto	h
1	deca	da
−1	deci	d
−2	centi	c
−3	milli	m
−6	micro	μ
−9	nano	n
−12	pico	p
−15	femto	f
−18	atto	a
−21	zepto	z
−24	yocto	y

Table IV Approved SI units, multiples and submultiples together with other units commonly in use. Based on BS 5555:1981 An asterisk indicates a unit outside the SI system currently recognised by the CIPM for a specific use

Item no in ISO 31:1992	Quantity	SI unit	Recommended multiples and sub-multiples	Other units which may be used	Remarks
1 Space and time					
1-1	Plane angle	rad (radian)	mrad µrad	degree (°) = π/180 rad minute (′) = (1/60)° second (″) = (1/60)′ grade (^{G}) = π/200 rad	Radians are principally used in purely mathematical situations. In practice, degrees and its subdivisions are normally used in the UK. The symbols ° ′ and ″ are exceptions in that there is no space between the value and the symbol. Decimal subdivisions of the degree are preferred to minutes and seconds; this facilitates the using of pocket calculators. On continental Europe, the grade (or its alternative name, the gon) is often used, always decimally subdivided.
1-2	Solid angle	sr (steradian)			
1-3	Length	m (metre)	km, cm, mm, µm, nm, pm, fm	*nautical mile 1 n mile = 1852 m exactly	The statute mile is currently intended to stay for the moment on road signs in the UK 1 mile = 1.609 344 km exactly On road signs the mile is confusingly abbreviated m, ml is preferred
1-4	Area	m^2	km^2, dm^2, cm^2, mm^2	*hectare (ha), *are (a) 1 ha = 10^4 m^2 1 a = 10^2 m^2	The square foot is still used by commercial estate agents in the UK 1 sq ft = 0.092 290 304 m^2 exactly The acre is also commonly found in the UK 1 acre = 0.404 685 6422 ha exactly
1-5	Volume	m^3	dm^3, cm^3, mm^3	*litre (l), *hl, *cl, *ml 1 hl = 10^{-1} m^3 1 l = 10^{-3} m^3 = 1 dm^3 1 cl = 10^{-5} m^3 1 ml = 10^{-6} m^3 = 1 cm^3	The abbreviations l and L may each be used for litre; the full name is often used to avoid confusion. The imperial pint (pt) has been approved for continuing use in the UK, but only for draught beer and for milk in bottles (not cartons!). 1 pt = 0.568 245 l
1-6.1	Time	s (second)	ks, ms, µs, ns	minute (min) 1 min = 60 s exactly hour (h) 1 h = 60 min exactly day (d) d = 24 h exactly	Other units such as week, month and year (a) are in common use; definitions of month and year often need to be specified
1-8.1	Angular velocity	rad/s			
1-10.1	m/s	m/h kilometre per hour (km/h) 1 km/h = (1/3.6) m/s			1 *knot = 1.852 km/h exactly (no abbreviation approved) Miles per hour (mph) are continuing on UK road signs 1 mph = 1.609 344 km/h exactly
1-11.1	m/s^2				
2 Periodic and related phenomena					
2-3.1	Frequency	Hz (hertz)	THz, GHz, MHz, kHz		
2-3.2	Rotational frequency	s^{-1}		min^{-1}	revs per min (r/min) and revs per sec (r/s) are also used
2-4	Angular frequency	rad/s			
3 Mechanics					
3-1	Mass	kg (kilogram)	Mg, g, mg, µg	tonne (t) unified atomic mass unit (u)	1 t = 10^3 kg tonne in the UK also called metric ton 1 u approx = 1.660 540 × 10^{-27} kg
3-2	Volumic mass Density Mass density	kg/m^3	Mg/m^3 kg/dm^3, g/cm^3 (all the same)	t/m^3, kg/l (kg/litre), g/ml, g/l	
3-5	Lineic mass Linear density	kg/m	mg/m		1 tex = 10^{-6} kg/m = 1 g/km The tex is used for textile filaments
3-7	Moment of inertia	$kg.m^2$			
3-8	Momentum	kg.m/s			
3-9	Force	N (newton)	MN, kN, mN, µN		
3-11	Moment of momentum Angular momentum	$kg.m^2$			
3-12.1	Moment of force	N.m	MN.m, kN.m, mN.m, µN.m		Moment of force is often called simply moment or bending moment
3-15.1	Pressure	Pa (pascal)	GPa, MPa, kPa, hPa, mPa, µPa	*bar = 100 kPa exactly 1 mbar = 1 hPa bars are used only in fluid pressures	
3-15.2	Normal stress	Pa	GPa, MPa, kPa		1 MPa = 1 N/mm^2

Table IV *Continued*

Item no in ISO 31:1992	Quantity	SI unit	Recommended multiples and sub-multiples	Other units which may be used	Remarks
3 Mechanics, *continued*					
3-23	Dynamic viscosity	Pa.s	mPa.s		poise (P) $1\,cP = 1\,mPa.s$ The poise is only used in conjunction with CGS units
3-24	Kinematic viscosity	m²/s	mm²/s		stokes (St) $1\,cSt = 1\,mm^2/s$ The stokes is used only in conjunction with CGS units
3-25	Surface tension	N/m	mN/m		
3-26.1 3-26.2	Energy Work	J (joule)	EJ, PJ, TJ, MJ, kJ, mJ	electronvolt (eV) $1\,eV = (1.602\,10 \pm 0.000\,07) \times 10^{-19}\,J$ eV, MeV and GeV are used in accelerator technology	kilowatt-hour (kW.h) $1\,kWh = 3.6 \times 10^6\,J = 3.6\,MJ$ W.h, kW.h, MW.h, GW.h and TW.h are used in the electrical power industry
3-27	Power	W (watt)	GW, MW, kW, mW, µW		$1\,W = 1\,J/s$
4 Heat					
4-1	Thermodynamic temperature	K (kelvin)			
4-2	Celsius temperature	°C (no space beween value and sumbol)			$1\,°C = 1\,K$ The temperature in °C is the temperature expressed in kelvins minus exactly 273.15 K
4-3.1	Linear expansion coefficient	K⁻¹			
4-6	Heat, quantity of heat	J	EJ, PJ, TJ, GJ, MJ, kJ, mJ		
4-7	Heat flow rate	W	kW		$1\,W = 1\,J/s$
4-9	Thermal conductivity	W/(m.k)			
4-10.1	Coefficient of heat transfer	W/(m.K)			
4-11	Thermal insulance	m.k/W			
4-15	Heat capacity	J/K	kJ/K		
4-16.1	Massic heat capacity (was specific)	J/(kg.K)	kJ/(kg.K)		
4-18	Entropy	J/K	kJ/K		
4-19	Massic entropy	J/(kg.K)	kJ/(kg.K)		
4-21.2	Massic thermodynamic energy (was specific energy)	J/kg	MJ/kg, kJ/kg		
5 Electricity and magnetism					
5-1	Electric current	A (ampere)	kA, mA, µA, nA, pA		
5-2	Electric charge, quantity of electricity	C (coulomb)	kC, µC, nC, pC		$1\,A.h = 3.6\,kC$
5-3	Volumic charge, charge density	C/m³	C/mm³ or GC/m³, MC/m³ or C/cm³, kC/m³, mC/m³, µC/m³		
5-4	Areic charge, surface density of charge	C/m²	MC/m² or C/mm², C/cm², kC/m², mC/m², µC/m²		
5-5	Electric field strength	V/m	MV/m, kV/m or V/mm, V/cm, mV/m, µV/m		
5-6.1 5-6.2 5-6.3	Electric potential Potential difference tension Electromotive force	V (volt)	MV, kV, mV, .V		
5-7	Electrical flux density	C/m²	C/cm², kC/m², mC/m², µC/m²		
5-9	Capacitance	F (farad)	mF, µF, nF, pF		
5-33	Resistance to direct current	Ω (ohm)	GΩ, MΩ, kΩ, mΩ, µΩ		
5-34	Conductance of direct current	S (siemens)	kS, mS, µS		$1\,S = 1/\Omega$
5-36	Resistivity	Ωm	GΩm, MΩm, kΩm, Ωcm, mΩm, µΩm, nΩm		$\mu\Omega m = 10^{-2}\,\Omega m$ $(\mu\Omega mm^2)/m = 10^{-6}\,\Omega m = \mu\Omega m$ are also used
5-37	Conductivity	S/m	MS/m, kS/M		
5-38	Reluctance	H⁻¹			
5-39	Permeance	H (henry)			
5-49	Active power	W	TW, GW, MW, kW, mW, µW, nW		In electric power technology active power is expressed in watts, apparent power in volt amperes V.A and reactive power in vars (var)
5-52	Active energy	J	TJ, GJ, MJ, KJ		$1\,W.h = 3.6\,kJ$ exactly TW.h, GW.h, MW.h, kW.h

Table IV *Continued*

Item no in ISO 31:1992	Quantity	SI unit	Recommended multiples and sub-multiples	Other units which may be used	Remarks
6 Light					
6-3	Wavelength	m	μm, nm, pm	*ångström (Å)	$1\ \text{Å} = 10^{-10}\,\text{m} = 10^{-4}\,\mu\text{m} = 10^{-1}\,\text{nm}$
6-7	Radiant energy	J			
6-10	Radiant power energy flux	W			
6-13	Radiant intensity	W/sr			
6-15	Radiant exitance	w/m^2			
6-29	Luminous intensity	cd (candela)			
6-30	Luminous flux	lm (lumen)			
6-31	Quantity of light		lm.h	1 lm.h = 3600 lm.s exactly	
6-32	Luminance	cd/m^2			
6-33	Luminous exitance	lx (lux)			
6-35	Light exposure	lx.s			
6-36.1	Luminous efficacy	lm/W			
7 Acoustics					
7-1	Period, periodic time	s	ms, μs		
7-2	Frequency	Hz	MHz, kHz		
7-5	Wavelength	m	mm		
7-8	Volumic mass Mass density Density	kg/m^3			
7-9.1	Static pressure	Pa	nPa, μPa		
7-9.2	(Instantaneous) sound pressure				
7-11	(Instantaneous) sound particle velocity	m/s	mm/s		
7-13	(Instantaneous) volume flow rate	m^3/s			
7-14.1	Velocity of sound	m/s			
7-16	Sound power	W			
7-17	Sound intensity	W/m^2	mW/m^2, μW/m^2, pW/m^2		
7-18	Acoustic impedance	Pa.s/m^3			
7-19	Mechanical impedance	N.s/m			
7-20.1	Surface density of mechanical impedance	Pa.s/m			
7-21	Sound pressure level		bel (B), dB	1 dB = 10^{-1} B	
7-28	Sound reduction index		B, dB		
7-29	Equivalent absorption area of surface or object	m^2			
7-30	Reverberation time	s			

Appendix B
Conversion factors and tables

Table 1 Conversion factors Bold type indicates exact conversions. Otherwise four or five significant figures are given.

Quantity	Conversion factors	
General purposes		
Length	1 mile	= 1.609 km
	1 chain	= **20.1168** m
	1 yard	= **0.9144** m
	1 foot	= **0.3048** m = **304.8** mm
	1 inch	= **25.4** mm = **2.54** cm
Area	1 square mile	= 2.590 km^2 = 259.0 ha
	1 hectare	= **10 000** m^2
	1 acre	= 4 046.9 m^2 = 0.40469 ha
		= **4840** yd^2
	1 square yard	= 0.8361 m^2
	1 square foot	= 0.09290 m^2 = 929.03 cm^2
	1 square inch	= 645.2 mm^2 = 6.452 cm^2
Volume	1 cubic yard	= 0.7646 m^3
	1 litre	= **1** dm^3 = **1000** cm^3
	1 m^3	= **1 000** litres
	1 millilitre	= **1** cm^3 = **1000** mm
	1 cubic foot	= 0.02832 m^3 = 28.32 litre
	1 petrograd standard	= 4.672 m^3
	1 cubic inch	= 16 387 mm^3 = 16.387 cm^3
		= 16.387 ml = 0.016387 litre
Capacity	1 UK gallon	= 4.546 litre
	1 UK quart	= 1.137 litre
	1 UK pint	= 0.5683
	1 UK fluid ounce	= 28.413 cm^3
	1 US barrel (for petroleum)	= 159.0 litre
	1 US gallon	= 3.785 litre
	1 US liquid quart	= 0.9464 litre
	1 US dry quart	= 1.101 litre
	1 US liquid pint	= 0.4732 litre
	1 US dry pint	= 0.5506 litre
	1 US liquid ounce	= 29.574 cm^3
Mass	1 UK ton	= 1.016 tonne = 1016.05 kg
	1 US (or short) ton	= 0.9072 tonne = 907.2 kg
	1 kip (1000 lb)	= 453.59 kg
	1 UK hundredweight	= 50.80 kg
	1 short (US) hundred-weight	= 100 lb = 45.36 kg
	1 pound	= 0.4536 kg
	1 ounce avoirdupois	= 28.35 g
	1 ounce troy	= 31.10 g
Mass per unit length	1 UK ton per mile	= 0.6313 kg/m = 0.6313 t/km
	1 lb per yard	= 0.4961 kg/m
	1 lb per foot	= 1.4882 kg/m
	1 lb per inch	= 17.86 kg/m
	1 oz per inch	= 1.1161 kg/m
Length per unit mass	1 yd per lb	= 2.016 m/kg
Mass per unit area	1 ton per square mile	= 392.3 kg/km^2 = 0.3923 g/m^2
		= 3.923 kg/ha
	1 ton per acre	= 0.2511 kg/m^2
	1 hundred weight per acre	= 0.01255 kg/m^2
	1 lb per square foot	= 4.882 kg/m^2
	1 lb per square inch	= 703.07 kg/m^2
	1 oz per square yard	= 33.91 g/m^2
	1 oz per square foot	= 305.15 g/m^2
	1 kg/cm^2	= 10 t/m^2
Mass density (mass per unit volume)	1 ton per cubic yard	= 1329 kg/m^3 = 1.3289 t/m^3
	1 lb per cubic yard	= 0.5933 kg/m^3
	1 lb per cubic foot	= 16.02 kg/m^3
	1 lb per cubic inch	= 27.68 g/cm^3 = 27.68 t/m^3

Table 1 *Continued*

Quantity	Conversion factors	
Area coverage	x square yards per ton	$= \dfrac{1}{x} \times 1215$ kg/m^2
	x square yards per gallon	$= \dfrac{1}{x} \times 5.437$ litre/m^2
Volume rate of flow	1 cubic feet per minute	= 0.4719 litre/s
		= 471.9 cm^3/s
		= 0.0004719 m^3/s
	1 cusec (cu ft per sec)	= 0.02832 m^3/s ('cumec')
	1 cu ft per thousand acres	= 0.06997 litre/ha
		= 0.006997 m^3/km^2
		= 6997 cm^3/km^2
	1 cubic inch per second	= 16.39 ml/s
	1 gallon per year	= 4546 cm^3/a* = 0.004546 m^3/a
	1 gallon per day	= 4546 cm^3/d
	1 litre/s	= **86.4** m^3/d
	1 million gallons per day	= 0.05262 m^3/s
	1 gallon per person per day	= 4.546 litre/(person day)
	1 gallon per sq yd per day	= 0.005437 m^3/(m^2.d)
		= 0.000062928 mm/s
	1 gallon per cu yd per day	= 0.005946 m^3/(m^3.d)
	1 gallon per hour	= 4.5461 litre/h
	1 gallon per minute	= 0.07577 litre/s
	1 gallon per second	= 4.5461 litre/s
Fuel consumption	1 gallon per mile	= 2.825 litre/km
	1 mile per gallon	= 0.354 km/litre
	x miles per gallon	$= \dfrac{1}{x} \times 282.5$ litre 100 km
Velocity	1 mile per hour	= 1.609 km/h = **0.44704** m/s
	1 foot per minute	= **0.3048** m/min = 0.0051 m/s
	1 foot per second	= **0.3048** m/s
	1 inch per second	= **25.4** mm/s
	1 UK knot	= 0.5148 m/s = 1.853 km/h
		= 1.00064 international knot
Acceleration	1 foot per sec per sec	= **0.3048** m/s^2
	1 mile per hr per sec	= **0.44704** m/s^2
	1 g (standard gravity)	= **9.806 65** m/s^2
Heating		
Temperature	x° Fahrenheit	$= \frac{5}{9} \times (x - 32)$ ° Celsius
Temperature interval	1° F	= 0.5556 K = 0.5556° C
Energy (heat)	1 British thermal unit	= 1055 J = 1.055 kJ
	1 Therm	= 105.5 MJ
	1 calorie	= **4.1868** J
	1 kilowatt-hour	= 3.6 MJ
	1 foot pound-force	= 1.356 J
	1 kilogram force-metre	= **9.806 65** J
Power (also heat flow rate)	1 J/s	= **1** W
	1 Btu per hour	= 0.293 07 W
	1 horsepower	= 745.70 W
	1 ft-lbf per second	= 1.356 W
	1 kgf-metre per second	= **9.806 65** W
	1 calorie per second	= **4.1868** W
	1 kilocalorie per hour	= **1.163** W
	1 metric horsepower	= 735.5 W
Density of heat flow rate	1 Btu per square foot hour	= 3.155 W/m^2

*a (for annum) is the symbol for year.

Table 1 *Continued*

Quantity	Conversion factors	
Thermal conductivity k **value**	1 Btu inch per square foot hour degree Fahrenheit	= 0.1442 W/(m.K)
Thermal transmittance or coefficient of heat transfer or thermal conductance or U **value**	1 Btu per square foot hour degree Fahrenheit	= 5.678 W/(m²K)
Thermal resistivity $\frac{1}{k}$ **value**	1 sq ft hr °F per Btu inch	= 6.933 m.K/W
Thermal or specific heat capacity	1 Btu per lb °F 1 Btu per cu ft °F	= 4.187 kJ/(kg.K) = 67.07 kJ/(m³.K)
Calorific value	1 Btu per pound 1 Btu per cubic foot 1 Btu per gallon	= 2.326 kJ/kg = 37.26 kJ/m³ = 37.26 J/litre = 232.1 J/litre
Refrigeration	1 ton	= 3517 W
Lighting Illumination	1 foot-candle 1 lumen per sq ft	= 10.76 lx = 10.76 lx
Luminance	1 candela per square inch 1 candela per square foot 1 apostilb	= 1550 cd/m² = 10.76 cd/m² = $\frac{1}{\pi}$ cd/m² = 0.3183 cd/m²

Table 1 *Continued*

Quantity	Conversion factors	
Structural design (All tons are UK tons)		
Force	1 pound-force 1 kip-force 1 ton-force 1 kilogram-force 1 kilopond	= 4.448 N = 4.448 kN = 9.964 kN = 9.807 N = 9.807 N
Force per unit length	1 pound-force per foot 1 pound-force per inch 1 ton-force per foot 1 kilogram-force per metre 1 kilogram-force per centimetre	= 14.59 N/m = 175.1 kN/m = 175.1 N/mm = 32.69 kN/m = 9.807 N/m = 0.9807 kN/m
Force per unit area or Stress or Pressure	1 lbf per square foot 1 lbf per square inch 1 tonf per square foot 1 tonf per square inch 1 kgf per square metre 1 kgf per sq centimetre 1 bar 1 millibar 1 standard atmosphere 1 inch of mercury 1 foot of water	= 47.88 N/m² = 47.88 Pa = 0.04788 kN/m² = 6.895 kN/m² = 6.895 kPa = 107.3 kN/m² = 107.3 kPa = 15.44 MN/m² = 15.44 N/mm² = 15.44 MPa = 9.807 N/m² = 9.807 Pa = 98.07 kN/m² = 98.07 kPa = **100 kN/m² = 100 kPa** = **100 N/m² = 100 Pa** = **101.325 kPa** = 3.386 kPa = 2.989 kPa = 300 mbar approx
Bending moment of torque	1 pound-force foot 1 pound-force inch 1 kip-force foot 1 kip-force inch 1 ton-force foot 1 ton-force inch 1 kilogram-force metre	= 1.356 Nm = 0.1130 Nm = 113.0 Nmm = 1.356 kNm = 0.1130 kNm = 113.0 Nm = 3.037 kNm = 0.2531 kNm = 253.1 Nm = 9.807 Nm

Table II Inches and fractions of an inch to millimetres ($\frac{1}{16}$ in increments up to $11\frac{15}{16}$ in)

Inches	$\frac{1}{16}$	$\frac{1}{8}$	$\frac{3}{16}$	$\frac{1}{4}$	$\frac{5}{16}$	$\frac{3}{8}$	$\frac{7}{16}$	$\frac{1}{2}$	$\frac{9}{16}$	$\frac{5}{8}$	$\frac{11}{16}$	$\frac{3}{4}$	$\frac{13}{16}$	$\frac{7}{8}$	$\frac{15}{16}$
	millimetres														
0	–	1.6	3.2	4.8	6.4	7.9	9.5	11.1	12.7	14.3	15.9	17.5	19.1	20.6	22.2	23.8
1	25.4	27.0	28.6	30.2	31.8	33.3	34.9	36.5	38.1	39.7	41.3	42.9	44.5	46.0	47.6	49.2
2	50.8	52.4	54.0	55.6	57.2	58.7	60.3	61.9	63.5	65.1	66.7	68.3	69.9	71.4	73.0	74.6
3	76.2	77.8	79.4	81.0	82.6	84.1	85.7	87.3	88.9	90.5	92.1	93.7	95.3	96.8	98.4	100.0
4	101.6	103.2	104.8	106.4	108.0	109.5	111.1	112.7	114.3	115.9	117.5	119.1	120.7	122.2	123.8	125.4
5	127.0	128.6	130.2	131.8	133.4	134.9	136.5	138.1	139.7	141.3	142.9	144.5	146.1	147.6	149.2	150.8
6	152.4	154.0	155.6	157.2	158.8	160.3	161.9	163.5	165.1	166.7	168.3	169.9	171.5	173.0	174.6	176.2
7	177.8	179.4	181.0	182.6	184.2	185.7	187.3	188.9	190.5	192.1	193.7	195.3	196.9	198.4	200.0	201.6
8	203.2	204.8	206.4	208.0	209.6	211.1	212.7	214.3	215.9	217.5	219.1	220.7	222.3	223.8	225.4	227.0
9	228.6	230.2	231.8	233.4	235.0	236.5	238.1	239.7	241.3	242.9	244.5	246.1	247.7	249.2	250.8	252.4
10	254.0	255.6	257.2	258.8	260.4	261.9	263.5	265.1	266.7	268.3	269.9	271.5	273.1	274.6	276.2	277.8
11	279.4	281.0	282.6	284.2	285.8	287.3	288.9	290.5	292.1	293.7	295.3	296.9	298.5	300.0	301.6	303.2

Table III Feet to millimetres (up to 200 ft)

feet	0	1	2	3	4	5	6	7	8	9
	Millimetres									
0	–	304.8	609.6	914.4	1219.2	1524.0	1828.8	2133.6	2438.4	2743.2
10	3048.0	3352.8	3657.6	3962.4	4267.2	4572.0	4876.8	5181.6	5486.4	5791.2
20	6096.0	6400.8	6705.6	7010.4	7315.2	7620.0	7924.8	8229.6	8534.4	8839.2
30	9144.0	9448.8	9753.6	10058.4	10363.2	10668.0	10972.8	11277.6	11582.4	11887.2
40	12192.0	12496.8	12801.6	13106.4	13411.2	13716.0	14020.8	14325.6	14630.4	14935.2
50	15240.0	15544.8	15849.6	16154.4	16459.2	16764.0	17068.8	17373.6	17678.4	17983.2
60	18288.0	18592.8	18897.6	19202.4	19507.2	19812.0	20116.8	20421.6	20726.4	21031.2
70	21336.0	21640.8	21945.6	22250.4	22555.2	22860.0	23164.8	23469.6	23774.4	24079.2
80	24384.0	24688.8	24993.6	25298.4	25603.2	25908.0	26212.8	26517.6	26822.4	27127.2
90	27432.0	27736.8	28041.6	28346.4	28651.2	28956.0	29260.8	29565.6	29870.4	30175.2
100	30480.0	30784.8	31089.6	31394.4	31699.2	32004.0	32308.8	32613.6	32918.4	33223.2
110	33528.0	33832.8	34137.6	34442.4	34747.2	35052.0	35356.8	35661.6	35966.4	36271.2
120	36576.0	36880.8	37185.6	37490.4	37785.2	38100.0	38404.8	38709.6	39014.4	39319.2
130	39624.0	39928.8	40233.6	40538.4	40843.2	41148.0	41452.8	41757.6	42062.4	42367.2
140	42672.0	42976.8	43281.6	43586.4	43891.2	44196.0	44500.8	44805.6	45110.4	45415.2
150	45720.0	46024.8	46329.6	46634.4	46939.2	47244.0	47548.8	47853.6	48158.4	48463.2
160	48768.0	49072.8	49377.6	49682.4	49987.2	50292.0	50596.8	50901.6	51206.4	51511.2
170	51816.0	52120.8	52425.6	52730.4	53035.2	53340.0	53644.8	53949.6	54254.4	54559.2
180	54864.0	55168.8	55473.6	55778.4	56083.2	56388.0	56692.8	56997.6	57302.4	57607.2
190	57912.0	58216.8	58521.6	58826.4	59131.2	59436.0	59740.8	60045.6	60350.4	60655.2
200	60960.0	–	–	–	–	–	–	–	–	–

Note: use Tables II and III together to obtain the metric equivalent of any dimension up to 200 ft. For example

56 ft 3¾ in: 56 ft = 17068.8
$\qquad$ 3¾ in = $\underline{\quad 95.3}$
$\qquad$ TOTAL = 17164.1 mm = 17.164 m

Table IV Miles (up to 100 miles) to kilometres (to two places of decimals) may also be used to convert mph to kph

Miles	0	1	2	3	4	5	6	7	8	9
	Kilometres									
0	–	1.61	3.22	4.83	6.44	8.05	9.66	11.27	12.87	14.48
10	16.09	17.70	19.31	20.92	22.53	24.14	25.75	27.36	28.97	30.58
20	32.19	33.80	35.41	37.01	38.62	40.23	41.84	43.45	45.06	46.67
30	48.28	49.89	51.50	53.11	54.72	56.33	57.94	59.55	61.16	62.76
40	64.37	65.98	67.59	69.20	70.81	72.42	74.03	75.64	77.25	78.86
50	80.47	82.08	83.69	85.30	86.90	88.51	90.12	91.73	93.34	94.95
60	96.56	98.17	99.78	101.39	103.00	104.61	106.22	107.83	109.44	111.05
70	112.65	114.26	115.87	117.48	119.09	120.70	122.31	123.92	125.53	127.14
80	128.75	130.36	131.97	133.58	135.19	136.79	138.40	140.01	141.62	143.23
90	144.84	146.45	148.06	149.67	151.28	152.89	154.50	156.11	57.72	159.33
100	160.93	–	–	–	–	–	–	–	–	–

Table V Square inches (up to 100 sq in) to square millimetres (to one place of decimals)

Square inches	0	1	2	3	4	5	6	7	8	9
	Square millimetres (mm²)									
0	–	645.2	1290.3	1935.5	2580.6	3225.8	3871.0	4516.1	5161.3	5806.4
10	6451.6	7096.8	7741.9	8387.1	9032.2	9677.4	10322.6	10967.7	11612.9	12258.0
20	12903.2	13548.4	14193.5	14838.7	15483.8	16129.0	16774.2	17419.3	18064.5	18709.6
30	19354.8	20000.0	20645.1	21290.3	21935.4	22580.6	23225.8	23870.9	24516.1	25161.2
40	25806.4	26451.6	27096.7	27741.9	28387.0	29032.2	29677.4	30322.5	30967.7	31612.8
50	32258.0	32903.2	33548.3	34193.5	34838.6	35483.8	36129.0	36774.1	37419.3	38064.4
60	38709.6	39354.8	39999.9	40645.1	41290.2	41935.4	42580.6	43225.7	43870.9	44516.0
70	45161.2	45806.4	46451.5	47096.7	47741.8	48387.0	49032.2	49677.3	50322.5	50967.6
80	51612.8	52258.0	52903.1	53548.3	54193.4	54838.6	55483.8	56128.9	56774.1	57419.2
90	58064.4	58709.6	59354.7	59999.9	60645.0	61290.2	61935.4	62580.5	63225.7	63870.8
100	64516.0	–	–	–	–	–	–	–	–	–

Table VI Square feet (up to 500 ft²) to square metres (to two places of decimals)

Square feet	0	1	2	3	4	5	6	7	8	9
	Square metres (m²)									
0	–	0.09	0.19	0.28	0.37	0.46	0.56	0.65	0.74	0.84
10	0.93	1.02	1.11	1.21	1.30	1.39	1.49	1.58	1.67	1.77
20	1.86	1.95	2.04	2.14	2.23	2.32	2.42	2.51	2.60	2.69
30	2.79	2.88	2.97	3.07	3.16	3.25	3.34	3.44	3.53	3.62
40	3.72	3.81	3.90	3.99	4.09	4.18	4.27	4.37	4.46	4.55
50	4.65	4.74	4.83	4.92	5.02	5.11	5.20	5.30	5.39	5.48
60	5.57	5.67	5.76	5.85	5.95	6.04	6.13	6.22	6.32	6.41
70	6.50	6.60	6.69	6.78	6.87	6.97	7.06	7.15	7.25	7.34
80	7.43	7.53	7.62	7.71	7.80	7.90	7.99	8.08	8.18	8.27
90	8.36	8.45	8.55	8.64	8.73	8.83	8.92	9.01	9.10	9.20
100	9.29	9.38	9.48	9.57	9.66	9.75	9.85	9.94	10.03	10.13
110	10.22	10.31	10.41	10.50	10.59	10.68	10.78	10.87	10.96	11.06
120	11.15	11.24	11.33	11.43	11.52	11.61	11.71	11.80	11.89	11.98
130	12.08	12.17	12.26	12.36	12.45	12.54	12.63	12.73	12.82	12.91
140	13.01	13.10	13.19	13.29	13.38	13.47	13.56	13.66	13.75	13.84
150	13.94	14.03	14.12	14.21	14.31	14.40	14.49	14.59	14.68	14.77
160	14.86	14.96	15.05	15.14	15.24	15.33	15.42	15.51	15.61	15.70
170	15.79	15.89	15.98	16.07	16.17	16.26	16.35	16.44	16.54	16.63
180	16.72	16.82	16.91	17.00	17.09	17.19	17.28	17.37	17.47	17.56
190	17.65	17.74	17.84	17.93	18.02	18.12	18.21	18.30	18.39	18.49
200	18.58	18.67	18.77	18.86	18.95	19.05	19.14	19.23	19.32	19.42
210	19.51	19.60	19.70	19.79	19.88	19.97	20.07	20.16	20.25	20.35
220	20.44	20.53	20.62	20.72	20.81	20.90	21.00	21.09	21.18	21.27
230	21.37	21.46	21.55	21.65	21.74	21.83	21.93	22.02	22.11	22.20
240	22.30	22.39	22.48	22.58	22.67	22.76	22.85	22.95	23.04	23.13
250	23.23	23.32	23.41	23.50	23.60	23.69	23.78	23.88	23.97	24.06
260	24.15	24.25	24.34	24.43	24.53	24.62	24.71	24.81	24.90	24.99
270	25.08	25.18	25.27	25.36	25.46	25.55	25.64	25.73	25.83	25.92
280	26.01	26.11	26.20	26.29	26.38	26.48	26.57	26.66	26.76	26.85
290	26.94	27.03	27.13	27.22	27.31	27.41	27.50	27.59	27.69	27.78
300	27.87	27.96	28.06	28.15	28.24	28.34	28.43	28.52	28.61	28.71
310	28.80	28.89	28.99	29.08	29.17	29.26	29.36	29.45	29.54	29.64
320	29.73	29.82	29.91	30.01	30.10	30.19	30.29	30.38	30.47	30.57
330	30.66	30.75	30.84	30.94	31.03	31.12	31.22	31.31	31.40	31.49
340	31.59	31.68	31.77	31.87	31.96	32.05	32.14	32.24	32.33	32.42
350	32.52	32.61	32.70	32.79	32.89	32.98	33.07	33.17	33.26	33.35
360	33.45	33.54	33.63	33.72	33.82	33.91	34.00	34.10	34.19	34.28
370	34.37	34.47	34.56	34.65	34.75	34.84	34.93	35.02	35.12	35.21
380	35.30	35.40	35.49	35.58	35.67	35.77	35.86	35.95	36.05	36.14
390	36.23	36.33	36.42	36.51	36.60	36.70	36.79	36.88	36.98	37.07
400	37.16	37.25	37.35	37.44	37.53	37.63	37.72	37.81	37.90	38.00
410	38.09	38.18	38.28	38.37	38.46	38.55	38.65	38.74	38.83	38.93
420	39.02	39.11	39.21	39.30	39.39	39.48	39.58	39.67	39.76	39.86
430	39.95	40.04	40.13	40.23	40.32	40.41	40.51	40.60	40.69	40.78
440	40.88	40.97	41.06	41.16	41.25	41.34	41.43	41.53	41.62	41.71
450	41.81	41.90	41.99	42.09	42.18	42.27	42.36	42.46	42.55	42.64
460	42.74	42.83	42.92	43.01	43.11	43.20	43.29	43.39	43.48	43.57
470	43.66	43.76	43.85	43.94	44.04	44.13	44.22	44.31	44.41	44.50
480	44.59	44.69	44.78	44.87	44.97	45.06	45.15	45.24	45.34	45.43
490	45.52	45.62	45.71	45.80	45.89	45.99	46.08	46.17	46.27	46.36
500	46.45	–	–	–	–	–	–	–	–	–

Table VII Cubic feet (up to 100 ft³) to cubic metres (to two places of decimals)

Cubic feet	0	1	2	3	4	5	6	7	8	9
	Cubic metres (m³)									
0	–	0.03	0.06	0.08	0.11	0.14	0.17	0.20	0.23	0.25
10	0.28	0.31	0.34	0.37	0.40	0.42	0.45	0.48	0.51	0.54
20	0.57	0.59	0.62	0.65	0.68	0.71	0.73	0.76	0.79	0.82
30	0.85	0.88	0.91	0.93	0.96	0.99	1.02	1.05	1.08	1.10
40	1.13	1.16	1.19	1.22	1.25	1.27	1.30	1.33	1.36	1.39
50	1.42	1.44	1.47	1.50	1.53	1.56	1.59	1.61	1.64	1.67
60	1.70	1.73	1.76	1.78	1.81	1.84	1.87	1.90	1.93	1.95
70	1.98	2.01	2.04	2.07	2.10	2.12	2.15	2.18	2.21	2.24
80	2.27	2.29	2.32	2.35	2.38	2.41	2.44	2.46	2.49	2.52
90	2.55	2.58	2.61	2.63	2.66	2.69	2.72	2.75	2.78	2.80
100	2.83	–	–	–	–	–	–	–	–	–

Table VIII Pounds (up to 500 lb) to kilograms (to two places of decimals)

Pounds	0	1	2	3	4	5	6	7	8	9
	Kilogrammes (kg)									
0	–	0.45	0.91	1.36	1.81	2.27	2.72	3.18	3.63	4.08
10	4.54	4.99	5.44	5.90	6.35	6.80	7.26	7.71	8.16	8.62
20	9.07	9.53	9.98	10.43	10.89	11.34	11.79	12.25	12.70	13.15
30	13.61	14.06	14.52	14.97	15.42	15.88	16.33	16.78	17.24	17.69
40	18.14	18.60	19.05	19.50	19.96	20.41	20.87	21.32	21.77	22.23
50	22.68	23.13	23.59	24.04	24.49	24.95	25.40	25.85	26.31	26.76
60	27.22	27.67	28.12	28.58	29.03	29.48	29.94	30.39	30.84	31.30
70	31.75	32.21	32.66	33.11	33.57	34.02	34.47	34.93	35.38	35.83
80	36.29	36.74	37.19	37.65	38.10	38.56	39.01	39.46	39.92	40.37
90	40.82	41.28	41.73	42.18	42.64	43.09	43.54	44.00	44.45	44.91
100	45.36	45.81	46.27	46.72	47.17	47.63	48.08	48.53	48.99	49.44
110	49.90	50.35	50.80	51.26	51.71	52.16	52.62	53.07	53.52	53.98
120	54.43	54.88	55.34	55.79	56.25	56.70	57.15	57.61	58.06	58.51
130	58.97	59.42	59.87	60.33	60.78	61.24	61.69	62.14	62.60	63.05
140	63.50	63.96	64.41	64.86	65.32	65.77	66.22	66.68	67.13	67.59
150	68.04	68.49	68.95	69.40	69.85	70.31	70.76	71.21	71.67	72.12
160	72.57	73.03	73.48	73.94	74.39	74.84	75.30	75.75	76.20	76.66
170	77.11	77.56	78.02	78.47	78.93	79.38	79.83	80.29	80.74	81.19
180	81.65	82.10	82.55	83.01	83.46	83.91	84.37	84.82	85.28	85.73
190	86.18	86.64	87.09	87.54	88.00	88.45	88.90	89.36	89.81	90.26
200	90.72	91.17	91.63	92.08	92.53	92.99	93.44	93.89	94.35	94.80
210	95.25	95.71	96.16	96.62	97.07	97.52	97.98	98.43	98.88	99.34
220	99.79	100.24	100.70	101.15	101.61	102.06	102.51	102.97	103.42	103.87
230	104.33	104.78	105.23	105.69	106.14	106.59	107.05	107.50	107.96	108.41
240	108.86	109.32	109.77	110.22	110.68	111.13	111.58	112.04	112.49	112.95
250	113.40	113.85	114.31	114.76	115.21	115.67	116.12	116.57	117.03	117.48
260	117.93	118.39	118.84	119.30	119.75	120.20	120.66	121.11	121.56	122.02
270	122.47	122.92	123.38	123.83	124.28	124.74	125.19	125.65	126.10	126.55
280	127.01	127.46	127.91	128.37	128.82	129.27	129.73	130.18	130.64	131.09
290	131.54	132.00	132.45	132.90	133.36	133.81	134.26	134.72	135.17	135.62
300	136.08	136.53	136.99	137.44	137.89	138.35	138.80	139.25	139.71	140.16
310	140.61	141.07	141.52	141.97	142.43	142.88	143.34	143.79	144.24	144.70
320	145.15	145.60	146.06	146.51	146.96	147.42	147.87	148.33	148.78	149.23
330	149.69	150.14	150.59	151.05	151.50	151.95	152.41	152.86	153.31	153.77
340	154.22	154.68	155.13	155.58	156.04	156.49	156.94	157.40	157.85	158.30
350	158.76	159.21	159.67	160.12	160.57	161.03	161.48	161.93	162.39	162.84
360	163.29	163.75	164.20	164.65	165.11	165.56	166.02	166.47	166.92	167.38
370	167.83	168.28	168.74	169.10	169.64	170.10	170.55	171.00	171.46	171.91
380	172.37	172.82	173.27	173.73	174.18	174.63	175.09	175.54	175.99	176.45
390	176.90	177.36	177.81	178.26	178.72	179.17	179.62	180.08	180.53	180.98
400	181.44	181.89	183.34	182.80	183.25	183.71	184.16	184.61	185.07	185.52
410	185.97	186.43	186.88	187.33	187.79	188.24	188.69	189.15	189.60	190.06
420	190.51	190.96	191.42	191.87	192.32	192.78	193.23	193.68	194.14	194.59
430	195.05	195.50	195.95	196.41	196.86	197.31	197.77	198.22	198.67	199.13
440	199.58	200.03	200.49	200.94	201.40	201.85	202.30	202.76	203.21	203.66
450	204.12	204.57	205.02	205.48	205.93	206.39	206.84	207.29	207.75	208.20
460	208.65	209.11	209.56	210.01	210.47	210.92	211.37	211.83	212.28	212.74
470	213.19	213.64	214.10	214.55	215.00	215.46	215.91	216.36	216.82	217.27
480	217.72	218.18	218.63	219.09	219.54	219.99	220.45	220.90	221.35	221.81
490	222.26	222.71	223.17	223.62	224.08	224.53	224.98	225.44	225.89	226.34
500	226.80	–	–	–	–	–	–	–	–	–

Table IX Pounds per cubic foot to kilogrammes per cubic metre (to one place of decimals)

Pounds per cubic foot	0	1	2	3	4	5	6	7	8	9
	Kilogrammes per cubic metre (kg/m³)									
0	–	16.0	32.0	48.1	64.1	80.1	96.1	112.1	128.1	144.2
10	160.2	176.2	192.2	208.2	224.3	240.3	256.3	272.3	288.3	304.4
20	320.4	336.4	352.4	368.4	384.4	400.5	416.5	432.5	448.5	464.5
30	480.6	496.6	512.6	528.6	544.6	560.6	576.7	592.7	608.7	624.7
40	640.7	656.8	672.8	688.8	704.8	720.8	736.8	752.9	768.9	784.9
50	800.9	816.9	833.0	849.0	865.0	881.0	897.0	913.1	929.1	945.1
60	961.1	977.1	993.1	1009.2	1025.2	1041.2	1057.2	1073.2	1089.3	1105.3
70	1121.3	1137.3	1153.3	1169.4	1185.4	1201.4	1217.4	1233.4	1249.4	1265.5
80	1281.5	1297.5	1313.5	1329.5	1345.6	1361.6	1377.6	1393.6	1409.6	1425.6
90	1441.7	1457.7	1473.7	1489.7	1505.7	1521.8	1537.8	1553.8	1569.8	1585.8
100	1601.9	–	–	–	–	–	–	–	–	–

Table X UK gallons (up to 100 galls) to litres (to two places of decimals)

UK gallons	0	1	2	3	4	5	6	7	8	9
	Litres									
0	–	4.55	9.09	13.64	18.18	22.73	27.28	31.82	36.37	40.91
10	45.46	50.01	54.55	59.10	63.64	68.19	72.74	77.28	81.83	86.37
20	90.92	95.47	100.01	104.56	109.10	113.65	118.20	122.74	127.29	131.83
30	136.38	140.93	145.47	150.02	154.56	159.11	163.66	168.20	172.75	177.29
40	181.84	186.38	190.93	195.48	200.02	204.57	209.11	213.66	218.21	222.75
50	227.30	231.84	236.39	240.94	245.48	250.03	254.57	259.12	263.67	268.21
60	272.76	277.30	281.85	286.40	290.94	295.49	300.03	304.58	309.13	313.67
70	318.22	322.76	327.31	331.86	336.40	340.95	345.49	350.04	354.59	359.13
80	363.68	368.22	372.77	377.32	381.86	386.41	390.95	395.50	400.04	404.59
90	409.14	413.68	418.23	422.77	427.32	431.87	436.41	440.96	445.50	450.05
100	454.60	–	–	–	–	–	–	–	–	–

Table XI Acres (up to 1000 acres) to hectares (to two places of decimals)

Acres	0	1	2	3	4	5	6	7	8	9
	Hectares									
	–	0.40	0.81	1.21	1.62	2.02	2.43	2.83	3.24	3.64

Acres	0	10	20	30	40	50	60	70	80	90
	Hectares									
0	–	4.05	8.09	12.14	16.19	20.23	24.28	28.33	32.37	36.42
100	40.47	44.52	48.56	52.61	56.66	60.70	64.75	68.80	72.84	76.89
200	80.94	84.98	89.03	93.08	97.12	101.17	105.22	109.27	113.31	117.36
300	121.41	125.45	129.50	133.55	137.59	141.64	145.69	149.73	153.78	157.83
400	161.87	165.92	169.97	174.02	178.06	182.11	186.16	190.20	194.25	198.30
500	202.34	206.39	210.44	214.48	218.53	222.58	226.62	230.67	234.72	238.77
600	242.81	246.86	250.91	254.95	259.00	263.05	267.09	271.14	275.19	279.23
700	283.28	287.33	291.37	295.42	299.47	303.51	307.56	311.61	315.66	319.70
800	323.75	327.80	331.84	335.89	339.94	343.98	348.03	352.08	356.12	360.17
900	364.22	368.26	372.31	376.36	380.41	384.45	388.50	392.55	396.59	400.64
1000	404.69	–	–	–	–	–	–	–	–	–

Table XII Miles per hour (up to 100 mph) to metres per second (to two places of decimals)

Miles per hour	0	1	2	3	4	5	6	7	8	9
	Metres per second									
0	–	0.45	0.89	1.34	1.79	2.24	2.68	3.13	3.58	4.02
10	4.47	4.92	5.36	5.81	6.26	6.71	7.15	7.60	8.05	8.49
20	8.94	9.39	9.83	10.28	10.73	11.18	11.62	12.07	12.52	12.96
30	13.41	13.86	14.31	14.75	15.20	15.65	16.09	16.54	16.99	17.43
40	17.88	18.33	18.78	19.22	19.67	20.12	20.56	21.01	21.46	21.91
50	22.35	22.80	23.25	23.69	24.14	24.59	25.03	25.48	25.93	26.38
60	26.82	27.27	27.72	28.16	28.61	29.06	29.50	29.95	30.40	30.85
70	31.29	31.74	32.19	32.63	33.08	33.53	33.98	34.42	34.87	35.32
80	35.76	36.21	36.66	37.10	37.55	38.00	38.45	38.89	39.34	39.79
90	40.23	40.68	41.13	41.57	42.02	42.47	42.92	43.36	43.81	44.26
100	44.70	–	–	–	–	–	–	–	–	–

Table XIII Pressure and stress. Pounds-force per square inch to kilonewtons per square metre (to two places of decimals)

lbf per sq in	0	1	2	3	4	5	6	7	8	9
	kN/m² or kPa									
0	–	6.90	13.79	20.68	27.58	34.48	41.37	48.26	55.16	62.06
10	68.95	75.84	82.74	89.64	96.53	103.42	110.32	117.22	124.11	131.00
20	137.90	144.80	151.69	158.58	165.48	172.38	179.27	186.16	193.06	199.96
30	206.85	213.74	220.64	227.54	234.43	241.32	248.22	255.12	262.01	268.90
40	275.80	282.70	289.59	296.48	303.38	310.28	317.17	324.06	330.96	337.86
50	344.75	351.64	358.54	365.44	372.33	379.22	386.12	393.02	399.91	406.80
60	413.70	420.60	427.49	434.38	441.28	448.18	455.07	461.96	468.86	475.76
70	482.65	489.54	496.44	503.34	510.23	517.12	524.02	530.92	537.81	544.70
80	551.60	558.50	565.39	572.28	579.18	586.08	592.97	599.86	606.76	613.66
90	620.55	627.44	634.34	641.24	648.13	655.02	661.92	668.82	675.71	682.60
100	689.50	–	–	–	–	–	–	–	–	–

Note: the same table will convert kipf per.sq in to MN/m² or MPa

Table XIV British thermal units per hour to watts

Btu per hr	0	1	2	3	4	5	6	7	8	9
	W									
0	–	0.29	0.59	0.88	1.17	1.47	1.76	2.05	2.34	2.64
10	2.93	3.22	3.52	3.81	4.10	4.40	4.69	4.98	5.28	5.57
20	5.86	6.16	6.45	6.74	7.03	7.33	7.62	7.91	8.21	8.50
30	8.79	9.09	9.38	9.67	9.97	10.26	10.55	10.84	11.14	11.43
40	11.72	12.02	12.31	12.60	12.90	13.19	13.48	13.78	14.07	14.36
50	14.66	14.95	15.24	15.53	15.83	16.12	16.41	16.71	17.00	17.29
60	17.59	17.88	18.17	18.47	18.76	19.05	19.34	19.64	19.93	20.22
70	20.52	20.81	21.10	21.40	21.69	21.98	22.28	22.57	22.86	23.15
80	23.45	23.74	24.03	24.33	24.62	24.91	25.21	25.50	25.79	26.09
90	26.38	26.67	26.97	27.26	27.55	27.84	28.14	28.43	28.72	29.02
100	29.31	–	–	–	–	–	–	–	–	–

Table XV *U* value: British thermal units per square foot per hour per degree Fahrenheit to watts per square metre per kelvin

Btu per sq ft hr °F	0	0.01	0.02	0.03	0.04	0.05	0.06	0.07	0.08	0.09
	W/(m²K)									
0	–	0.057	0.114	0.170	0.227	0.284	0.341	0.397	0.454	0.511
0.1	0.568	0.624	0.681	0.738	0.795	0.852	0.908	0.965	1.022	1.079
0.2	1.136	1.192	1.249	1.306	1.363	1.420	1.476	1.533	1.590	1.647
0.3	1.703	1.760	1.817	1.874	1.931	1.987	2.044	2.101	2.158	2.214
0.4	2.271	2.328	2.385	2.442	2.498	2.555	2.612	2.669	2.725	2.782
0.5	2.839	2.896	2.953	3.009	3.066	3.123	3.180	3.236	3.293	3.350
0.6	3.407	3.464	3.520	3.577	3.634	3.691	3.747	3.804	3.861	3.918
0.7	3.975	4.031	4.088	4.145	4.202	4.258	4.315	4.372	4.429	4.486
0.8	4.542	4.599	4.656	4.713	4.770	4.826	4.883	4.940	4.997	5.053
0.9	5.110	5.167	5.224	5.281	5.337	5.394	5.451	5.508	5.564	5.621
1.0	5.678	–	–	–	–	–	–	–	–	–

Table XVI Feet and inches (up to 100 ft) to metres and millimetres (to nearest millimetre)

Feet	Inches											
	0	1	2	3	4	5	6	7	8	9	10	11
	Metres and millimetres											
0	–	0.025	0.051	0.076	0.102	0.127	0.152	0.178	0.203	0.229	0.254	0.279
1	0.305	0.330	0.356	0.381	0.406	0.432	0.457	0.483	0.508	0.533	0.559	0.584
2	0.610	0.635	0.660	0.686	0.711	0.737	0.762	0.787	0.813	0.838	0.864	0.889
3	0.914	0.940	0.965	0.991	1.016	1.041	1.067	1.092	1.118	1.143	1.168	1.194
4	1.219	1.245	1.270	1.295	1.321	1.346	1.372	1.397	1.422	1.448	1.473	1.499
5	1.524	1.549	1.575	1.600	1.626	1.651	1.676	1.702	1.727	1.753	1.778	1.803
6	1.829	1.854	1.880	1.905	1.930	1.956	1.981	2.007	2.032	2.057	2.083	2.108
7	2.134	2.159	2.184	2.210	2.235	2.261	2.286	2.311	2.337	2.362	2.388	2.413
8	2.438	2.464	2.489	2.515	2.540	2.565	2.591	2.616	2.642	2.667	2.692	2.718
9	2.743	2.769	2.794	2.819	2.845	2.870	2.896	2.921	2.946	2.972	2.997	3.023
10	3.048	3.073	3.099	3.124	3.150	3.175	3.200	3.226	3.251	3.277	3.302	3.327
11	3.353	3.378	3.404	3.429	3.454	3.480	3.505	3.531	3.556	3.581	3.607	3.632
12	3.658	3.683	3.708	3.734	3.759	3.785	3.810	3.835	3.861	3.886	3.912	3.937
13	3.962	3.988	4.013	4.039	4.064	4.089	4.115	4.140	4.166	4.191	4.216	4.242
14	4.267	4.293	4.318	4.343	4.369	4.394	4.420	4.445	4.470	4.496	4.521	4.547
15	4.572	4.597	4.623	4.648	4.674	4.699	4.724	4.750	4.775	4.801	4.826	4.851
16	4.877	4.902	4.928	4.953	4.978	5.004	5.029	5.055	5.080	5.105	5.131	5.156
17	5.182	5.207	5.232	5.258	5.283	5.309	5.334	5.359	5.385	5.410	5.436	5.461
18	5.486	5.512	5.537	5.563	5.588	5.613	5.639	5.664	5.690	5.715	5.740	5.766
19	5.791	5.817	5.842	5.867	5.893	5.918	5.944	5.969	5.994	6.020	6.045	6.071
20	6.096	6.121	6.147	6.172	6.198	6.223	6.248	6.274	6.299	6.325	6.350	6.375
21	6.401	6.426	6.452	6.477	6.502	6.528	6.553	6.579	6.604	6.629	6.655	6.680
22	6.706	6.731	6.756	6.782	6.807	6.833	6.858	6.883	6.909	6.934	6.960	6.985
23	7.010	7.036	7.061	7.087	7.112	7.137	7.163	7.188	7.214	7.239	7.264	7.290
24	7.315	7.341	7.366	7.391	7.417	7.442	7.468	7.493	7.518	7.544	7.569	7.595
25	7.620	7.645	7.671	7.696	7.722	7.747	7.772	7.798	7.823	7.849	7.874	7.899
26	7.925	7.950	7.976	8.001	8.026	8.052	8.077	8.103	8.128	8.153	8.179	8.204
27	8.230	8.255	8.280	8.306	8.331	8.357	8.382	8.407	8.433	8.458	8.484	8.509
28	8.534	8.560	8.585	8.611	8.636	8.661	8.687	8.712	8.738	8.763	8.788	8.814
29	8.839	8.865	8.890	8.915	8.941	8.966	8.992	9.017	9.042	9.068	9.093	9.119
30	9.144	9.169	9.195	9.220	9.246	9.271	9.296	9.322	9.347	9.373	9.398	9.423
31	9.449	9.474	9.500	9.525	9.550	9.576	9.601	9.627	9.652	9.677	9.703	9.728
32	9.754	9.779	9.804	9.830	9.855	9.881	9.906	9.931	9.957	9.982	10.008	10.033
33	10.058	10.084	10.109	10.135	10.160	10.185	10.211	10.236	10.262	10.287	10.312	10.338
34	10.363	10.389	10.414	10.439	10.465	10.490	10.516	10.541	10.566	10.592	10.617	10.643
35	10.668	10.693	10.719	10.744	10.770	10.795	10.820	10.846	10.871	10.897	10.922	10.947
36	10.973	10.998	11.024	11.049	11.074	11.100	11.125	11.151	11.176	11.201	11.227	11.252
37	11.278	11.303	11.328	11.354	11.379	11.405	11.430	11.455	11.481	11.506	11.532	11.557
38	11.582	11.608	11.633	11.659	11.684	11.709	11.735	11.760	11.786	11.811	11.836	11.862
39	11.887	11.913	11.938	11.963	11.989	12.014	12.040	12.065	12.090	12.116	12.141	12.167
40	12.192	12.217	12.243	12.268	12.294	12.319	12.344	12.370	12.395	12.421	12.446	12.471
41	12.497	12.522	12.548	12.573	12.598	12.624	12.649	12.675	12.700	12.725	12.751	12.776
42	12.802	12.827	12.852	12.878	12.903	12.929	12.954	12.979	13.005	13.030	13.056	13.081
43	13.106	13.132	13.157	13.183	13.208	13.233	13.259	13.284	13.310	13.335	13.360	13.386
44	13.411	13.437	13.462	13.487	13.513	13.538	13.564	13.589	13.614	13.640	13.665	13.691
45	13.716	13.741	13.767	13.792	13.818	13.843	13.868	13.894	13.919	13.945	13.970	13.995
46	14.021	14.046	14.072	14.097	14.122	14.148	14.173	14.199	14.224	14.249	14.275	14.300
47	14.326	14.351	14.376	14.402	14.427	14.453	14.478	14.503	14.529	14.554	14.580	14.605
48	14.630	14.656	14.681	14.707	14.732	14.757	14.783	14.808	14.834	14.859	14.884	14.910
49	14.935	14.961	14.986	15.011	15.037	15.062	15.088	15.113	15.138	15.164	15.189	15.215
50	15.240	15.265	15.291	15.316	15.342	15.367	15.392	15.418	18.443	15.469	15.494	15.519
51	15.545	15.570	15.596	15.621	15.646	15.672	15.697	15.723	15.748	15.773	15.799	15.824
52	15.850	15.875	15.900	15.926	15.951	15.977	16.002	16.027	16.053	16.078	16.104	16.129
53	16.154	16.180	16.205	16.231	16.256	16.281	16.307	16.332	16.358	16.383	16.408	16.434
54	16.459	16.485	16.510	16.535	16.561	16.586	16.612	16.637	16.662	16.688	16.713	16.739
55	16.764	16.789	16.815	16.840	16.866	16.891	16.916	16.942	16.967	16.993	17.018	17.043
56	17.069	17.094	17.120	17.145	17.170	17.196	17.221	17.247	17.272	17.297	17.323	17.348
57	17.374	17.399	17.424	17.450	17.475	17.501	17.526	17.551	17.577	17.602	17.628	17.653
58	17.678	17.704	17.729	17.755	17.780	17.805	17.830	17.856	17.882	17.907	17.932	17.958
59	17.983	18.009	18.034	18.059	18.085	18.110	18.136	18.161	18.186	18.212	18.237	18.263
60	18.288	18.313	18.339	18.364	18.390	18.415	18.440	18.466	18.491	18.517	18.542	18.567
61	18.593	18.618	18.644	18.669	18.694	18.720	18.745	18.771	18.796	18.821	18.847	18.872
62	18.898	18.923	18.948	18.974	18.999	19.025	19.050	19.075	19.101	19.126	19.152	19.177
63	19.202	19.228	19.253	19.279	19.304	19.329	19.355	19.380	19.406	19.431	19.456	19.482
64	19.507	19.533	19.558	19.583	19.609	19.634	19.660	19.685	19.710	19.736	19.761	19.787
65	19.812	19.837	19.863	19.888	19.914	19.939	19.964	19.990	20.015	20.041	20.066	20.091
66	20.117	20.142	20.168	20.193	20.218	20.244	20.269	20.295	20.320	20.345	20.371	20.396
67	20.422	20.447	20.472	20.498	20.523	20.549	20.574	20.599	20.625	20.650	20.676	20.701
68	20.726	20.752	20.777	20.803	20.828	20.853	20.879	20.904	20.930	20.955	20.980	21.006
69	21.031	21.057	21.082	21.107	21.133	21.158	21.184	21.209	21.234	21.260	21.285	21.311

Appendix C
Contributors

Chapter 3, Sanitary installations

Alan Tye Design specialise in product design, including architectural components and environments, office work stations, call centres and so on.

Over the last eight years ATD have developed a unique design process: Healthy Industrial Design HID™ as it became clear that conventional design and ergonomics have missing factors. Work includes architectural hardware of all kinds (the Modric Range), sanitary ware (Ideal Standard), toilet cubicles (Bushboard), home office and call centre furniture. Over 30 design awards for products sold worldwide.

ATD gladly work with architectural firms who wish to develop products which result in added revenue (royalties). They may be contacted at:

Alan Tye Design
Great West Plantation
Tring
Herts HP23 6DA

Tel: 01442 825 353
Fax: 01442 827 723
E-mail: atd@alantyedesign.ndirect.co.uk

Chapter 6, External and landscape

Michael Littlewood FLI FSDG can be contacted at:

Troutwells
Higher Hayne, Roadwater
Watchet
Somerset TA23 0RN

Tel and fax: 01984 641 330

Chapter 7, Terminal and transport interchanges

Chris Blow is a director of Scott Brownrigg & Turner Ltd with reponsibility for airport design and quality systems. He is author of *Airport Terminal* published by Butterworth-Heinemann 1996, and writes and lectures extensively on airports.

His projects include the design management of Heathrow Terminal 4, Bahrein International Airport redevelopment (1985–95), Birmingham Eurohub for British Airways (1988), Manchester Airport Terminal 2 (opened 1993), facilities for Cathay Pacific Airways at Hong Kong's new airport and the development of Terminal 2 at Lyon Satolas Airport (1992–97), as well as many airport consultancies and design competitions.

Chapter 8, Factories and Chapter 9, Industrial storage

Jolyon Drury RIBA, consultant architect on the design of production, distribution and storage systems and facilities, can be contacted at:

Jolyon Drury Consultancy
Regent House
190A Three Bridges Road
Crawley
West Sussex RH10 1LN

Tel: 01293 510 515
Fax: 01293 541 525
E-mail: jolyon@j-d-c.co.uk

Chapter 11, Offices

DEGW International Consultants and Architects specialise in the field of office planning and design. They are part of the Twynstra Management Consultancy, and can be contacted at:

Porters North
8 Crinan Street
London N1 9SQ

Tel: 0171 239 7777
Fax: 0171 278 3613

Chapter 12, Law courts

Napper Architects can be contacted at:

17 Carliol Square
Newcastle Upon Tyne NE1 6UQ

Tel: 0191 261 0491
Fax: 0191 261 4830
E-mail: nappers@compuserve.com

Chapter 13, Retail trading, Chapter 18, Eating and Chapter 36, Hotels

EurIng Dr F R Lawson is Visiting Professor of Service Industries, University of Bournemouth, and an international consultant and author of several books on planning and design. He is also Series Editor of the current Planning and Design Series from Architectural Press. He can be contacted at:

1 Firs Lane
Shamley Green
Guildford
Surrey GU5 0UT

Tel: 01483 898 259
Fax: 01484 894 817

Chapter 14, Payment offices and Chapter 15, Public service buildings

Derek Montefiore AADipl RIBA FArb can be contacted at:

MHM Architects Ltd
Marlborough House
Tower Street
Covent Garden
London WC2H 9LN

Tel: 0171 240 3506
Fax: 0171 240 3498

Chapter 16, Primary health care

Ann Noble can be contacted at:

Health facility planning and architecture
105 Euston Street
London NW1 2EW

Tel: 0171 387 7811
Fax: 0171 387 2320
E-mail: 106537.3212@compuserve.com

Chapter 17, Hospitals

MARU (Medical Architecture Research Unit) is now accommodated at:

South Bank University
Erlang House
128 Blackfriars Road
London SE1 8EQ

Tel: 0171 815 8395

Chapter 18, Drinking and Chapter 26, Equestrian design

Frank Bradbeer RIBA is now semi-retired. He is still prepared to give advice but is reluctant to undertake further full projects, despite the success of recent ones. He can be contacted at:

Ivy Cottage
High Street
Hunstanton
Norfolk PE36 6LY

Tel: 01485 26235

Chapter 19, Studios and Chapter 40, Sound

David Binns AADipl RIBA has now retired. Neil Spring BSc ARCS MInstP CEng MIEE FIOA can be contacted at:

Sandy Brown Associates
1 Coleridge Gardens
London NW6 3QH

Tel: 0171 624 6033
Fax: 0171 625 6688

Chapter 20, Auditoria

Dr Ian Appleton PhD DArch DipCD RIBA FRIA is an architect and partner in the Edinburgh-based firm of the Appleton Partnership. He was the architect for the West Yorkshire Playhouse in Leeds, among other theatres and building types. He has had experience of demand studies, feasibility and other aspects of the design and develpment of buildings for the performing arts, as well as wider involvement in urban, building and interior designs. He is also involved in teaching, research and writing on architecture.

The Appleton Partnership: Architects
Forth Gallery
Forth Street
Edinburgh EH1 3JX

Tel: 0131 557 8151
Fax: 0131 557 8145

Joe Aveline is a theatre consultant and lectures widely on the development of theatre and theatre equipment. He can be contacted at:

Tel: 0171 328 6174 & +356 561 269 (Malta)
Fax: 0171 328 5035
E-mail: aveline@sumack.freeserve.co.uk

Chapter 18, Eating and Chapter 23, Boating

John Rawson RIBA is an architect and journalist, and can be found at:

3 Downshire Hill
London NW3 1NR

Tel: 0171 794 4002
Fax: 0171 431 3017

Chapter 21, Community centres

Jim Tanner DipArch RIBA FRAIA can be contacted at:

Tanner and Partners
107 Camberwell Grove
London SE5 8JH

Tel: 0171 278 6884
Fax: 0171 278 6387

Chapter 22, Swimming

Gerald Perrin RIBA DipTP MRTPI can be contacted at:

Perrin Consult Ltd
38 Churchgate Street
Old Harlow
Essex CM17 0JT

Tel: 01279 429 222
Fax: 01279 835 029

Chapter 26, Equestrian design

Rod Sheard DipArch RIBA ARIA can be contacted at:

Hok + Lobb
Blades Court
Deodar Road
London SW15 2NU

Tel: 0181 874 7666
Fax: 0181 874 7470

Chapter 27, Buildings for religion

Leslie Fairweather RIBA was for many years the editor of the *Architects' Journal*. He is an international expert in the architectural design of both churches and prisons. He can be contacted at:

Honeywood House
Deanland Road
Haywards Heath
West Sussex RH17 6PJ
Tel: 01444 811 532

Atba Al-Samarraie BEng(Hons) MIStructE MIHT MIEI can be contacted at Bullen Consultant's Bradford office or at:

6 Coppice View
Idle
Bradford BD10 8UF

Tel (home): 01274 619 519
Tel (office): 01274 370 410
E-mail: alsam@globalnet.co.uk

Chapter 28, Schools

Guy Hawkins MA(Arch)(Lond) RIBA is an architect and a school building consultant. He worked previously in the the Architects and Building Branch of the then Department of Education and Science (now the DfEE), and in the Property Services Department of Essex County Council. He can be contacted at:

13 South Primrose Hill
Chelmsford
Essex CM1 2RF

Tel: 01245 260 867

Chapter 30, Laboratories

The Laboratories Investigation Unit (LIU) was previously part of the UK Government's Department of Education and Science. With that department's agreement, it was re-established in 1994 as a private company by leading members of the Unit. Auditing, planning and design services for buildings and facilities used for teaching, research and routine analytical applications of science and technology are availabe from the Unit. It can be contacted through Tony Branton DiplArch RIBA who is a co-director of the LIU whose address is:

Laboratories Investigation Unit Ltd
Micheldever Road
London SE12 8LX

Tel & fax: 0181 852 0337

Chapter 31, Museums, art galleries and small exhibition spaces

Dr Geoffrey Matthews BA PhD FRSA is an independent museum and exhibition consultant. He is a researcher and author on museums, their organisation and design, and also a senior lecturer in the Hull School of Architecture, University of Lincolnshire and Humberside. Contact him at:

115 Westcott Street
Holderness Road
Hull HU8 8LZ

Tel & fax: 01482 703 275
E-mail: gmatthews@humber.ac.uk

Chapter 33, Houses and flats

Ian Chown MA DiplArch RIBA was trained at Cambridge University School of Architecture, and has had twenty-five year's experience of designing housing in Greater London. His completed projects include the comprehensive refurbishment of Lea View House with the full participation of the tenants. He also designed the Mothers' Square (winner of an RIBA Architecture Award) and Schonfeld Square; all three projects with Hunt Thompson Associates in Hackney.

In 1994 he joined PRP Architects, one of the largest multi-disciplinary firms involved in housing. PRP's work encompasses all sectors of social and private housing, including all types of Special Needs, refurbishment and new-build projects. At PRP, Ian Chown has designed large projects for Waltham Forest Housing Action Trust in Leytonstone, for Fortunegate Community Housing at Church End, Brent, and for Stepney Housing and Development Agency in Central Stepney. He can be contacted at:

PRP Architects
1 Lindsey Street
London
EC1A 9HP

Tel: 0171 251 5101
Fax: 0171 251 5102
E-mail: cc.prp@dial.pipex.com

Chapter 34, Student housing

Liz Pride RIBA is an associate of MacCormac–Jamieson–Prichard who can be contacted at:

9 Heneage Street
Spitalsfields
London E1 5LJ

Tel: 0171 377 9262
Fax: 0171 247 7854
E-mail: mjp@mjparchitects.co.uk

Chapter 35, Homes with care

Ian Smith RIBA has designed a number of old people's homes, mainly for Methodist Homes for the Aged. He is now retired, but might give advice if requested. He can be contacted at:

Y Wern
Dyffryn Crawnon
Llangynidr
Powys NP8 1NU

Tel & fax: 01874 730 946

Chapter 38, Thermal environment

Professor Phil Jones can be contacted at:

Welsh School of Architecture
Bute Building
King Edward VII Avenue
Cardiff CF1 3AP

Tel: 01222 874 078
Fax: 01222 874 623
E-mail: jonesp@cardiff.ac.uk

Chapter 39, Lighting

Joe Lynes can be contacted at:

4 Aigburth Avenue
St Georges Road
Hull HU3 3QA

Tel & fax: 01482 216 792

Chapter 42, Fire

Beryl Menzies MBEng MIBC can be contacted at:

The Menzies Partnership
10 Brockwell Lane
Kelvedon
Essex CO5 9BB

Tel & fax: 01376 571 534
E-mail: menzies.pts@virgin.net

The Editor

EurIng David Adler BSc DIC CEng MICE took his first degree at the then Queen Mary College, University of London. His postgraduate qualification in Concrete Technology came from City and Guilds College. After National Service in the Royal Engineers he worked for such prestigious firms as F J Samuely, Trollope and Colls, Building Design Partnership and Robert Matthew, Johnson-Marshall and Partners. For some years he was Chief Structural Engineer for the London Borough of Hammersmith and Fulham. Now retired from salaried employment, he divides his time between the *Metric Handbook* and the British Standards Institution, where he chairs a technical committee.

David Adler would be grateful to receive comments about the *Handbook* (and its associated CD-rom). He can be contacted at:

38 Church Crescent
Muswell Hill
London N10 3NE

Tel & fax: 0181 444 6000
E-mail: David_Adler@compuserve.com

Index